# ACCOUNTING PRINCIPLES

Fifth
Edition

# ACCOUNTING PRINCIPLES

Fifth Edition

**Jack L. Smith**
School of Accountancy
University of South Florida

**Robert M. Keith**
School of Accountancy
University of South Florida

**William L. Stephens**
School of Accountancy
University of South Florida

McGraw-Hill, Inc.

New York   St. Louis   San Francisco   Auckland   Bogotá
Caracas   Lisbon   London   Madrid   Mexico   Milan   Montreal
New Delhi   Paris   San Juan   Singapore   Sydney   Tokyo   Toronto

# ACCOUNTING PRINCIPLES

1 2 3 4 5 6 7 8 9 0  VNH VNH  9 0 9 8 7 6 5

ISBN 0-07-059238-1

This book was set in Century Oldstyle by Progressive Information Technologies.
The editor was Constance Ditzel.
The cover designer was Pat Koch.
Cover photo was reprinted with permission. Copyright ©  Charly Franklin/FPG International.
Von Hoffmann Press, Inc. was printer and binder.

**Library of Congress Cataloging-in-Publication Data**

Smith, Jack L.
    Accounting principles / Jack L. Smith, Robert M. Keith, William L. Stephens.—5th ed.
       p.   cm.
    Includes index.
    ISBN 0-07-059238-1
    I. Accounting.       I. Keith, Robert M.      II Stephens, William L.      III. Title.  .
    HF5635.S644        1996                                     95-75394
    657-dc21

# About the Authors

**Jack L. Smith** is a professor and former Associate Director of the School of Accountancy at the University of South Florida. He received a Ph.D. in accounting at the University of Mississippi and is a CPA. Professor Smith is a member of the American Accounting Association, the American Institute of Certified Public Accountants, the Florida Institute of Certified Public Accountants, the Institute of Management Accountants (IMA), and the Florida Association of Accounting Educators, and has been active in a number of state and local organizations. Dr. Smith has served as a National Vice-President of the IMA and as president of the Florida Association of Accounting Educators. Professor Smith was the charter faculty advisor of the Delta Gamma Chapter of Beta Alpha Psi. He is also active in various local and national professional development programs and has received awards as an outstanding discussion leader. In addition to *Accounting for Financial Statement Presentation,* an MBA level introductory financial text coauthored with Robert M. Keith, *Accounting Principles 4e, Financial Accounting,* and *Managerial Accounting* coauthored with Robert M. Keith and William L. Stephens, Professor Smith is the author of numerous articles in the *Journal of Accountancy, The Financial Executive, The Journal of Taxation, The Journal of Accounting Education,* and *The Accounting Educators Journal,* as well as two award winning articles appearing in *Management Accounting.* In addition to his writing activities, Jack Smith is also an experienced teacher. His 30 years of working closely with students make this textbook one that actively involves students in the learning process.

**Robert M. Keith** is Professor of Accounting and Interim Director of the School of Accountancy at the University of South Florida. He received his Ph.D. from the University of Alabama, a Master of Accountancy from Florida State University, and a B.S. from Stetson University. He is also a CPA in the State of Florida. While his research interests center on financial accounting, Professor Keith has a strong interest in accounting education at both the college and professional levels. He has received an Outstanding Accounting Faculty Award and a University Undergraduate Teaching Excellence Award at USF. The Florida Institute of CPAs has named him Outstanding Seminar Leader for five consecutive years for his work in teaching continuing professional education programs. Professor Keith chaired the Post University Education Committee of the Federation of Schools of Accountancy and served on the American Institute of CPAs Curriculum and Instruction Subcommittee. Dr. Keith has presented several papers at regional and national meetings of the American Accounting Association and has published his research in professional journals. He coauthored *Accounting for Financial Statement Presentation,* published in 1979, with Jack L. Smith and joined Drs. Smith and Stephens in coauthoring *Financial Accounting* and *Managerial Accounting,* both published in 1988. Professor Keith is a member of the American Institute of CPAs, the Florida Institute of CPAs, and the American Accounting Association.

**William L. Stephens** is a professor at the School of Accountancy at the University of South Florida. He has a DBA from Florida State University and is a CPA. His primary research and teaching interests are in the area of managerial and cost accounting. Active in continuing professional education projects, Professor Stephens is also a member of the American Accounting Association, the Institute of Management Accountants, and the Florida Institute of Certified Public Accountants. For 22 of the last 23 years, he has been the faculty advisor to the Delta Gamma Chapter of Beta Alpha Psi, which has been recognized as a

Superior Chapter for 20 straight years. Dr. Stephens has been recognized for his distinguished service to Beta Alpha Psi, both at the local and national levels. Author of numerous articles in *The Journal of Accountancy* and *The Accounting Review,* Professor Stephens has also coauthored *Financial Accounting* and *Managerial Accounting.*

Dr. Stephens has been actively involved in the Institute of Management Accountants for many years, and recently served as the local chapter president. In addition, he has been the recipient of numerous teaching awards during his tenure at the University of South Florida.

*To Diane, Kristie, and Scott*

*To Phyllis, for her special love and support,
and to Rob and Kevin*

*To Brenda and Cindy, for giving my life meaning*

*To the Good Lord, for his eternal love*

# Contents

Following is a complete, detailed Table of Contents. If you are using a custom version, some chapters may not be included in your book.

## CHAPTER 4

### The Adjusting Process 4-1

## CHAPTER 5

### Preparing Worksheets, Closing Entries, and Reversing Entries 5-1

## CHAPTER 6

### Accounting for Merchandise 6-1

## CHAPTER 7

### Internal Control and Accounting Systems Design    7-1

## CHAPTER 8

### Cash    8-1

## CHAPTER 9

### Receivables    9-1

# Preface

The fifth edition of *Accounting Principles* is designed to be a comprehensive, balanced and flexible approach to the college student's first exposure to accounting. The text is intended for use in a two-semester or three-quarter sequence by those students who plan a business career, those who have an interest in broadening their business background, and those who plan to enter the accounting profession. The text can be used in the traditional two-thirds, one-third financial managerial split or as a one semester financial, one semester managerial split. Our assumption in writing this edition is that the student's exposure to business has been very limited. Consequently we have carefully explained and illustrated, where appropriate, all business terms and practices as they are first discussed.

The fifth edition offers the instructor the ability to pick and choose from 32 complete chapters to tailor a course specifically for his/her needs. An instructor can select only those chapters relevant to the course and the student pays only for the chapters selected.

The fifth edition is a blend of accounting concepts and procedures. Students are informed why information is accounted for in a certain manner. The *why* is reinforced by illustrating *how* the accounting is accomplished. Students cannot grasp concepts without adequate attention to the procedures.

## IMPORTANT FEATURES OF THE FIFTH EDITION

The authors are indebted to the users of the previous four editions for their many kind and helpful suggestions. We have considered each of these suggestions carefully and adopted those that we feel contribute to the effectiveness of the text. Numerous pedagogical devices and techniques have been incorporated in this edition. These are classified in the preface as *general* or *specific*. In the general category we include those items that are presented in all chapters of the text, while in the second category we highlight those features that are found only in specific chapters.

## GENERAL FEATURES

The following features are included in every chapter:

- *Learning Objectives.* Formal learning objectives are located at the beginning of each chapter to indicate for the student the direction the chapter will take. The objectives also appear within the chapter where each topic is located. All exercises, problems, and test bank materials are keyed to the learning objectives.
- *Chapter Outline.* A continued successful feature of the fourth edition is a brief outline of the chapter contents, with page references, which follows the learning objectives at the beginning of each chapter. This outline is most helpful in providing students with a guide to the topics covered in the chapter and serves as a quick review of the chapter.

- *Ask Yourself.* A set of review questions appear after each section of the chapter providing students with a focus on the important points of the section.
- *Real World Examples.* The examples have been selected to provide the student with illustrations of actual situations where an accounting topic under study has been applied or misused. Factual data are presented where appropriate to broaden the student's awareness of the business world.
- *Demonstration Problems.* Located at the end of each chapter, these problems and accompanying solutions are designed for the student to review the concepts discussed in the chapter and see how these concepts are applied.
- *Chapter Summaries.* Concise, well-organized chapter summaries provide an excellent review of each chapter.
- *Key Terms.* A listing of the key terms presented in each chapter, together with their definitions, appears after the chapter summaries. The chapter summary and key terms allow the student to review the chapter efficiently in preparation for examinations.
- *Objective Assignments.* These true-false and multiple-choice assignments provide a review of the chapter and help prepare students for the achievement tests or examinations generated from the test bank where true-false or multiple-choice items are selected. Answers to the objective assignments are located at the end of the chapter.
- *Exercises and Problems.* The exercise and problem numbers are followed by brief descriptions and are keyed to the learning objectives, allowing the student and instructor to quickly see the general thrust of the exercise or problem. These descriptions are particularly helpful to the instructor in making end-of-chapter assignments. Check figures are provided with the exercises and problems as a convenience for the student.
- *Decision Problems.* These problems place the student in a position where he or she must develop information from data provided and analyze the information to make a business decision.
- *Ethics Cases.* These outstanding cases are designed to increase the student's ability to identify ethical issues and to develop a logical, well-reasoned approach to solving ethical problems, giving cognizance to the various stakeholder groups.

## SPECIFIC FEATURES

- "The Accounting Environment," an Introduction in the fourth edition, has been moved to an opening chapter.
- The introduction of the income statement accounts in Chapter 2 provides the student with a complete set of financial statements at an early stage in the book rather than several chapters later.
- For the Chapters 3–7, all journal entry elements are identified as asset, liability, owner's equity, revenue or expense accounts in the entry so that the basic accounts are reinforced for the student.
- Chapters 2–6 illustrate the basic concepts using the same example (The Mary Abrems Dance Studio) making it easier for the student to follow.
- In Chapters 4 to 7, each step of the accounting cycle is reviewed after it is explained. This reinforces the student's understanding of the accounting process as it is developed.
- When explaining the closing process in Chapter 5, expense accounts are closed first. This makes it easier for the students to grasp the closing process for a merchandising concern in Chapter 6, where nominal accounts with debit balances are closed first, followed by nominal accounts with credit balances. Further, it allows the student to use the worksheet when preparing the closing entries.

- The topic of accounting policies for recording deferrals and the related reversing entries is in an appendix to Chapter 5.
- A graphic in Chapter 9 clearly and concisely summarizes accounting for uncollectible accounts receivable.
- The strong description and illustration of the periodic and perpetual inventory methods in Chapter 10 is reinforced by a common example demonstrating all of the inventory cost flow methods.
- For investments in and withdrawals from a partnership, the bonus method replaces the goodwill method for situations where the amount paid (received) by the investing (withdrawing) partner is different from the amount of equity in the partnership.
- A side-by-side comparison of proprietorships, partnerships, and corporations in Chapter 15 clearly illustrates the characteristics and owners' equity reporting for each type of business structure.
- Accounting for bonds payable (Chapter 17) and accounting for investments in bonds (Chapter 18) are tied together with a common example used in both chapters. This "mirror-image" approach enhances students' understanding of both topics.
- Temporary and long-term investments are now included in Chapter 18. This approach has been found to be more efficient to teach and easier for students to learn.
- The Statement of Cash Flows, Chapter 19, has been rewritten to emphasize the user's approach, rather than the preparer's approach.
- In Chapter 21, The Institute of Managements Code of Professional Ethics is introduced. The discussion of management accounting and its relationship to financial accounting has been expanded.
- In Chapter 21, a step-by-step approach employing T-accounts is used to explain the flow of product costs through a manufacturer's inventory accounts.
- Chapter 22 provides an expanded discussion of activity based costing (ABC).
- Detailed explanations in Chapter 24 accompany an easy-to-follow approach to process costing. The flow of production costs for a two-stage production process is examined with journal entries and T-accounts.
- In the 5th edition, the characteristics of and potential benefits from just in-time (JIT) inventory philosophy are examined for manufacturers who use either job order or process costing.
- Chapter 25 offers a detailed discussion of variable and fixed costs, with a greatly expanded analysis of mixed costs.
- In Chapter 26, a logical, step-by-step approach is used to develop the formulas needed in cost-volume-profit analysis. Direct Costing and Absorption Costing are compared as part of the discussion of the assumptions underlying cost-volume-profit analysis.
- The detailed example of a master budget and supporting schedules in Chapter 27 utilizes the retail form of organization as a far simpler alternative to that of a manufacturer. The student is led through the maze of calculations with easy-to-follow directions.
- In Chapter 28 and 29, a three-column approach to variance analysis is introduced that emphasizes the relationship of actual results to the appropriate flexible budgets.
- The chapter on Standard Costs and Variance Analysis has been broken into two parts. Chapter 28 covers direct materials and direct labor, while Chapter 29 covers factory overhead.
- A tight package of topics discusses in Chapter 30 how performance of cost centers, profit centers, and investments centers should be evaluated.

- Chapter 32 presents the internal rate of return method of capital budgeting in addition to the net present value method. A simplified discussion of the effects of income taxes on each of the capital budgeting methods is also included.

## ADDITIONAL FEATURES

- *Communication Skills.* In response to the suggestions made by the Accounting Education Change Commission (AECC), an increased emphasis has been made in the fifth edition to include additional assignments that require communication skills. These assignments have been indicated by the logo ⧉ .
- *Critical Thinking.* Integrated throughout the exercises and problems is material that will require students to exercise their critical thinking skills. This material has been added in response to the suggestions of the AECC.

## SUPPLEMENTARY MATERIALS FOR THE INSTRUCTOR

- *Solutions Manual.* Answers to all questions, exercises, and problems are contained in this comprehensive manual. The type is extra large so that any transparencies made from the manual will be clearly visible to the students in the last row of the classroom. The questions, exercises, and problems follow closely the textual material. Time estimates, difficulty levels, and descriptions of all exercises and problems are provided as an aid to the instructor in selecting material appropriate for the level of the course being taught.
- *Test Bank.* A computerized test bank containing over 4,500 items arranged by chapter and identified by learning objective is available. The test bank is available also in printed form.
- *Overhead Transparencies.* The publisher has prepared for the instructor a complete set of problem solution transparencies for classroom use. Adopters of the text can obtain transparencies upon request.
- *Instructor's Guide.*

## FOR THE STUDENT

- *Worksheets.* Set A and Set B worksheets can be bound with the softcover custom textbook versions, or separately, to complement required chapters. The instructor also has the advantage of assigning a Set A or Set B problem within the same term.
- *Study Guide.* A comprehensive study guide contains chapter-by-chapter reviews together with an abundance of multiple-choice, fill-in, and true or false questions. The study guide, like the worksheets, can be bound in with softcover custom versions of the textbook.

## ACKNOWLEDGEMENTS

To our colleagues at the University of South Florida we express appreciation for their encouragement and suggestions.

To our students who spent many hours proofing and problem checking we are most grateful. These students are Lora Jacobs, Laura Salazar and Maria Sonkin.

We also thank Mary Pat Rodenhouse for further proofreading, and Josh Pincus for editing the supplements.

We wish to express our sincere appreciation to the many individuals who contributed their efforts to this project. Comments and suggestions were received from: Ellen Platt, *Angelina College;* Debra Davis, *Blackfeet Community College;* Robert Maccini, Burdett School, Stan Ayres and Charles Savana, *Burlington County College;* David Mona and Edith K. Templin, *Champlain College;* Carl J. Fisher, *Foothill College;* John Atella, George O. Ritchey and Gary Schwartz, *Harrisburg Area Community College;* Phillip D. McBrayer, *High Point University;* John Delile, *Kennebec Valley Technical College,* Janet E. Mercincavage and Anita Singer, *King's College;* Peter L. Vico, *Lincoln University;* Bruce England, Robert H. Landry and Lynda Thompson, *Massasoit County College;* Irene P. Barr and Charles C. Dean, *New River Community College;* John Sedensky, *Newburg College;* Peter Doran, Terry Gemmel, Neal Keefe-Feldman, Paul Lospennato, Jeffrey Slater, John Sullivan and Joseph Tabet, *Northshore Community College;* Ed K. Bassey, *Oxnard College;* Betty Corbin, *Randolph Macon Women's College,* Gene Pibal, *Spoon River College;* Ray S. Wilson and Audrey Yancy, *St. Petersburg Junior College,* Rodney Kutcher, John Pace, Edward Rayfield and Robert Weinstein, *Suffolk Community College-Brentwood, NY;* Vincent Dicalogero, Anne Forrer, Chuck Heck, Henri Leclerc, Thomas Lohmann, Thomas McCartney, Charles Reilly, Dominic Riemma, Robert Rovegno, Al Ruggiero and Gunter Samuelsen, *Suffolk Community College-Selden, NY;* Richard Calvasina, *University of West Florida;* and Jim Poythress, *Virginia Western Community College.*

JACK L. SMITH
ROBERT M. KEITH
WILLIAM L. STEPHENS

FIFTH EDITION

# ACCOUNTING PRINCIPLES

# The Accounting Environment

**Exhibit 1** Decision Makers and Examples of the Decisions They Make

| Decision Maker | Sample Decision |
| --- | --- |
| Taxpayer | Should we support our city's proposed bond issue? |
| Club member | Should we support the proposed operating budget? |
| Corporate president | Should we open a new plant in Germany? |
| Insurance company portfolio manager | Should the company invest in stocks or bonds? |
| Labor union representative | Should the union demand a 6% or an 8% pay increase? |
| Bank loan officer | Should credit be granted for an auto loan? |
| Corporate purchasing agent | Should the corporation purchase computer chips from a Japanese firm? |
| Corporate board director | Should the corporation increase dividends? |
| Governmental agency director | Should additional funding be requested? |
| Spouse | Should I invest in a tax-deferred annuity offered by a particular insurance company? |
| Head of household | Should we continue to rent a house, or should we buy? |

All of us make economic decisions throughout our lives. As members of families, of groups, and of our society as a whole, as employees and employers, and even as club members, we face economic decisions constantly. The types of decisions we make will reflect our attitudes, our interests, our jobs, and our family concerns. Depending on our role at a particular time, we will have to make decisions such as those illustrated in Exhibit 1.

Not one of these decisions can be made without financial information. Sound economic decisions must be based on appropriate financial facts communicated in some meaningful form. **Accounting** is a service that provides the facts needed to make informed economic decisions. This information is typically provided in the form of financial reports.

Many people confuse accounting with bookkeeping, but bookkeeping is only a small subpart of accounting. While bookkeeping is important, it is only the beginning of the accounting service. Bookkeeping simply means the recording of financial transactions; accountants use this information in preparing financial reports on which decisions are based.

This introduction will focus on financial reports, exploring the various users and preparers of accounting information, the three basic financial statements, the ground rules for preparing financial information, and the institutions responsible for developing these ground rules.

## RELYING ON FINANCIAL REPORTS

Accounting, like any other discipline, has its own terms and concepts. Financial reports are based on these concepts, and the information in the reports is expressed in accounting terms. Before you can use financial reports to make economic decisions, you need to know how accounting information is generated, processed, and presented. You also need a basic understanding of accounting principles and of the terms used by accountants. With this knowledge, you can evaluate the information and be aware of its limitations.

The usefulness of financial reports rests on their reliability and comparability. Many of your economic decisions will be based on this information, and you may often need to compare different reports to make economic and management decisions. Over the years, certain ground rules, called *generally accepted accounting principles,* have been developed. These ground rules assure us that financial reports are prepared in specific ways so that they are reliable and comparable.

You may be surprised to learn that financial reports are not always precise measures. Values shown on financial reports might reflect either prices paid several years ago or current prices. Accounting is also based on estimates and consequently cannot provide the exact amount of customer accounts that will not be paid, warranty obligations that will have to be honored, and similar future events.

If you pursue a career in accounting, you will become a preparer of financial information; but whatever career you pursue, you will inevitably become a user of accounting information. You will make estimates and decisions on the basis of financial reports submitted to you. The better you understand how these reports are generated and how reliable they are, the better you will be able to make your estimates in order to reach the best decisions.

## USERS OF ACCOUNTING INFORMATION

**Learning Objective 1**

Identify the users and preparers of accounting information

Financial reports are used by managers, investors, potential investors, creditors, potential creditors, taxpayers, union representatives, regulatory agencies, and many others. But the principles underlying the gathering and presenting of accounting information are basically similar for all economic entities. An **economic entity** is an organization that provides products or services. Banks, retail stores, government agencies, automobile companies, student organizations, and charitable organizations are all economic entities.

Economic entities such as IBM, Toyota, Sears, and Pizza Hut were created and exist today with the objective of making profits. These *profit-motivated* economic entities are referred to as **business entities.** In contrast, entities such as the City of Houston, Bucks County Community College, Mount Sinai Hospital, and East Atlanta Pipefitters Union are not concerned with making a profit. We call the entities in this second group **not-for-profit entities.** The term *economic entity* refers to both groups.

This text focuses on accounting for business entities. Once you understand the principles of accounting as applied to business entities, it will be easy for you to apply the same principles to not-for-profit entities.

### Business Entities and User Groups

A business entity has three distinct groups that use accounting information related to the entity: a management group, a financing group, and a public group (see Figure 1 below).

**Figure 1** Users of Accounting Information

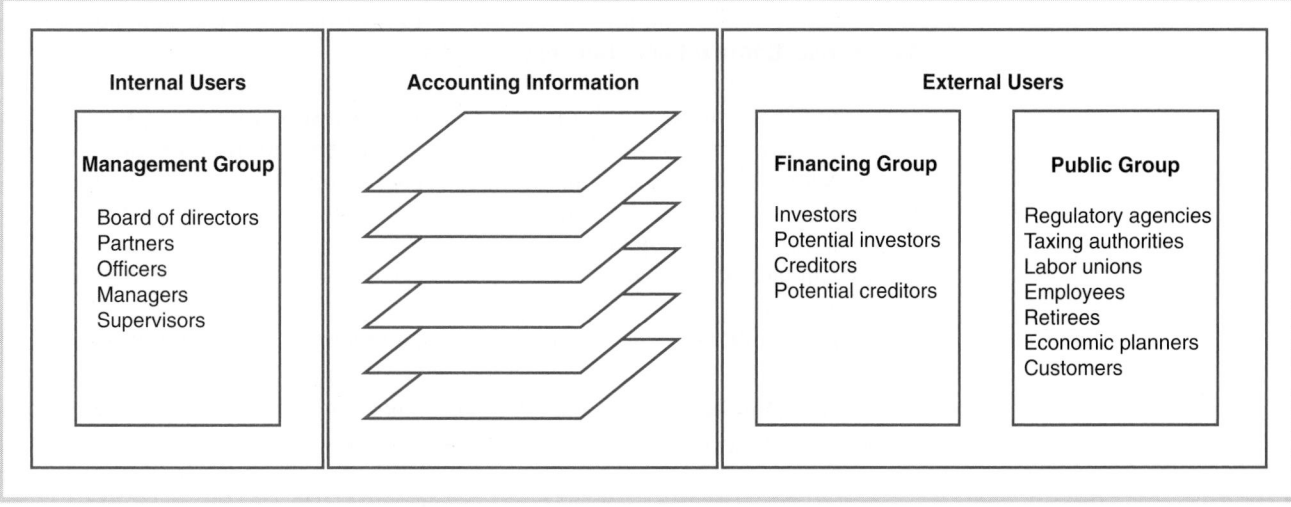

The *management group* includes the individuals who own and/or manage and control the business entity. The board of directors of Chrysler Corporation, the vice president of Bethlehem Steel, the director of marketing of Control Data, the partners of Price Waterhouse, and the supervisor of production of Ford's Atlanta Taurus plant are all members of their respective firms' management group.

The *financing group* consists of investors and potential investors as well as creditors and potential creditors. A company's financial group might include its owners or stockholders, stock brokerage firms, banks holding shares of stock in the business or lending money to it, insurance companies looking for investments, other companies selling on credit to the business, and members of the general public who are considering investing in the business entity. The financial group supplies or can supply the money the management group needs in order to run the business successfully.

The *public group* includes all parties that have an interest in a business entity but neither manage it nor provide it with financing. Examples are regulatory and taxing authorities such as the federal government's Internal Revenue Service (IRS) and Securities and Exchange Commission (SEC), and each state's Public Utility Commission. It also includes numerous other groups within our society such as labor unions, employees, retirees, economic planners, and the business's customers.

### Types of Financial Reports

**External financial reports** are prepared for those users of financial information who do not have direct access to the business entity's records. Some users in the public group have the power to generate and enforce laws about the kinds and amounts of information the entity must make available to them. As you may have guessed, these users are the IRS, the SEC, and the other governmental taxing and regulatory authorities. These agencies prescribe the exact manner in which the financial information is to be reported, what type of information is to be reported, and when and where it is to be submitted.

Users in the financing group and users in the public group other than taxing or regulatory authorities do not have the legislative power to require a business entity to report accounting information to them. Therefore, it is up to the management group to see that the information needs of the financing group and the public group are met. Management fulfills this responsibility by preparing **general-purpose financial statements** and making them available to nongovernmental users. These statements describe the results of business activities for a specified period of time and list the economic resources and obligations of the entity. The area of accounting concerned with the preparation and presentation of general-purpose financial statements is referred to as **financial accounting.**

**To operate and control the business effectively and efficiently, the management group needs much more detailed accounting information in addition to its general-purpose financial statements. Internal financial reports** are prepared exclusively for the use of the management group. These reports provide management with information to help them make operating decisions directed toward meeting the business's goals.

Examples of internal reports include:

- Reports contrasting the cost of leasing new service trucks with the costs of buying them
- Reports showing the savings that can be expected from eliminating a department
- Reports showing the cost of producing a certain item

The area of accounting that is concerned with internal reporting is referred to as **management accounting**.

**ASK YOURSELF** ▶

1. **Give examples of various decision makers and the decisions they must make.**
2. **What are generally accepted accounting principles?**
3. **Distinguish among economic, business, and not-for-profit entities.**
4. **What are the three groups that use accounting information?**
5. **Distinguish between external and internal financial reports.**

## PREPARERS OF ACCOUNTING INFORMATION

Two groups, management and certified public accountants, provide financial information about an economic entity. Management prepares and is responsible for the financial information. Certified public accountants assure the users that the financial information supplied to them by management represents fairly the business activity over a period of time and states fairly the resources and obligations of the entity at the end of that period of time.

### Management

Financial reports are prepared by accountants engaged or employed by the economic entity issuing the report, but the responsibility for the accounting information contained in the financial reports of business and not-for-profit entities ultimately rests with the entity's chief executive officer. The *chief executive officer* is the president or chairman of the board of directors of a business entity, or the director, head, mayor, president, or some other designee of a not-for-profit entity.

The executive officer in charge of the accounting function of a business entity is called the **controller.** The controller may supervise a staff of several hundred accounting and finance employees, as in the case of a large international corporation such as Mobil Oil Company, or a relatively small staff, as in the case of a local retail store. In some large companies the controller's functions are performed by the *chief accountant* or the *vice president of finance.*

Some small companies operate with only one or two executive officers, who, in addition to their other responsibilities, perform the function of a controller. They may employ a full-time or part-time accountant to prepare financial reports.

### Certified Public Accountants

**Certified public accountants (CPAs)** are individuals who have met the educational and experience requirements prescribed by state law and have passed the Uniform CPA Examination. CPAs are independent professional accountants, licensed by the state, who provide accounting services to clients for a fee, just as other professionals (such as physicians and lawyers) provide their services to the public. The major function of the CPA is to serve as a link between the management that prepares financial statements and the people who use the statements.

Since external users of financial statements—the financing and public groups —do not have access to the financial records of the economic entity in which they are interested, they have no way of ascertaining that the financial statements represent fairly and honestly the results of operating activities and the firm's resources and obligations. These external users must rely on assurance from someone else, and the

CPA provides that assurance by performing an independent **audit**, which is a financial examination of the firm's records. The CPA issues a formal audit report that is an integral part of the financial statements prepared and issued by the economic entity.

To obtain a license to practice public accounting, a person must fulfill educational requirements and pass certain tests. This assures the public of a high degree of competence in the practice of accounting. CPAs, like other professionals, are highly regarded by their clients for two basic qualities: the rigorous training they undergo to become a member of the profession and the high ethical standards they maintain.

The test that candidates are required to pass is the Uniform CPA Examination, prepared and graded by the American Institute of Certified Public Accountants (AICPA). The examination consists of four parts, administered over a two-day period every May and November on the same dates in all states. The four parts are: Business Law and Professional Responsibilities; Auditing; Accounting and Reporting—Taxation, Managerial, and Government and Not-for-Profit Organizations; and Financial Accounting and Reporting.

Although all applicants must pass the same national test, each state imposes a number of additional requirements. A candidate must fulfill the requirements of a specific state to be granted a CPA license to practice in that state. The most common requirements are that an individual must be of legal age as defined by the state, must be a college graduate with the equivalent of an accounting major, and must have obtained a passing grade (75%) or better on all parts of the CPA exam. Some states require a certain amount of work experience under the direction of a CPA before granting the license. Many states now require 150 total semester-hours of college work, which is in essence a fifth year. Most states will move to the 150-hour requirement by the year 2000.

## ACCOUNTING ACTIVITIES AND CAREERS

Learning Objective **2**

List the various types of accounting activities

What do accountants do? In this section we will answer that question with regard to accountants employed by business entities, not-for-profit entities, and CPA firms. In addition to being a prerequisite for most decision-making positions in business, accounting offers many career opportunities, as you will see.

Accounting activities and careers fall into two basic categories. People are said to be in *private accounting* when they work for a single enterprise, whether it is the corner store or the U.S. government. Accountants who offer their professional services to customers for a fee, like doctors or lawyers, are said to be in *public accounting*. Figure 2 shows the principal career areas in private and public accounting.

### Private Accounting Careers in Business

Large corporations divide their accounting staffs into departments according to specialized accounting functions. A smaller organization may employ a small staff of salaried accountants to perform all of its accounting activities or may hire a CPA on a fee basis to provide whatever accounting services management deems necessary.

#### General Financial Accounting

Each day, business entities conduct numerous business transactions, such as the purchase and sale of goods and services. Accountants involved in general financial accounting monitor these business transactions and prepare financial reports, to be used internally by management and externally by the financing and public groups. Accountants doing general financial accounting also prepare the financial reports required by most governmental agencies. These reports must be prepared according to, or in compliance with, the particular governmental agency's regulations, which are referred to as *compliance requirements*.

**Figure 2** Accounting Career Areas

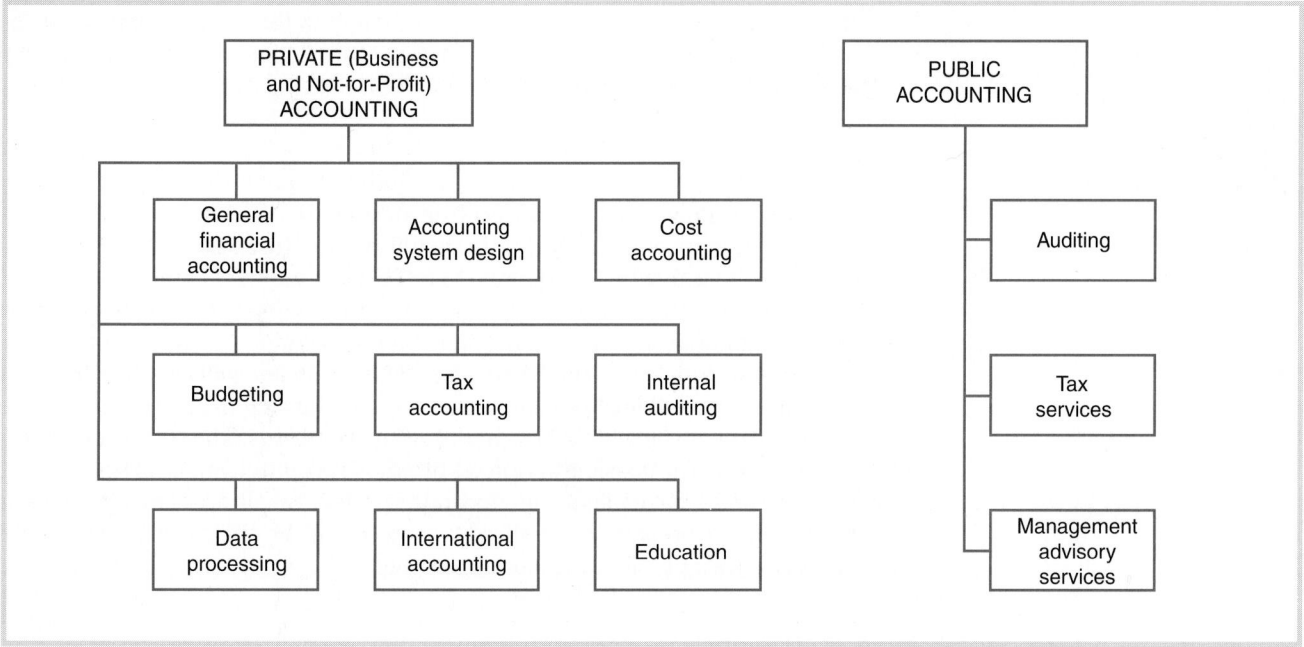

### Accounting Systems Design

The numerous business transactions processed and recorded by the general financial accounting staff must be summarized in a meaningful manner before financial reports can be issued. This involves grouping together and classifying, or labeling, related financial transactions. For example, all sales transactions must be grouped together and classified as sales. Likewise, all transactions involving the purchase of inventory must be grouped together and classified as purchases.

In simplest terms, the classification process is this: Sales are recorded on a sales form, purchases are recorded on a purchase form, and each of the many other types of business transactions are recorded on forms designed to convey its nature and purpose. One of the activities of accountants involved in **accounting systems design** is to design the forms used to record business activities, thus enabling the classification process to work smoothly and efficiently. The result is that the mass of accounting data can be summarized in a meaningful manner in the financial reports.

Systems design accountants are also charged with specifying the procedures by which an accounting system should be operated, for implementing these procedures, and for investigating new means of processing the mass of accounting data.

### Cost Accounting

**Cost accounting** involves gathering financial information for the purpose of planning and controlling the entity's activities and determining the cost of a product or service. While it is essential for management to know the cost of a product or service, it is even more important to control such costs. It is the responsibility of the cost accountant to provide the relevant information to help management do so.

### Budgeting

Business entities can be managed efficiently only if they first determine what their objectives are. Expressing these objectives in monetary terms is what **budgeting** is all about. A budget covers a specific period of time and attempts to predict what will happen financially during that time. Periodically, what actually happened is compared to what was expected to happen—the budget. Any differences are analyzed carefully by management to determine why they occurred and how they can be controlled. The purpose of this analysis is to improve the accuracy of projections and to narrow the gap between budgeted and actual performance in future periods.

### Tax Accounting

Corporations, like individuals, are subject to income taxes. Corporations must comply with the requirements of not only the IRS but also state, local, and foreign tax laws. The various tax laws to which corporations are subject are very complex.

Large corporations may have separate departments devoted to **tax accounting** —the preparation of various tax returns and also the planning necessary to minimize the impact of taxes on the firm. Tax accountants are thus specialists in both tax compliance and tax planning. *Tax compliance* means following the many detailed and specific rules of the taxing authorities in preparing tax returns. The term *tax planning* refers to the study of the possible tax effects of various proposed financial transactions in order to minimize taxes and thus maximize profits. Small firms may have their general accountants prepare the required tax returns, or they may use the services of a CPA for tax return preparation and tax planning.

### Internal Auditing

Some private accountants are involved in **internal auditing,** to ensure that transactions are recorded, classified, and summarized properly. A company's accountants must regularly review the records for each of these accounting activities, in a process known as *financial internal auditing. Operational internal auditing* seeks to ensure that accounting and operating policies and procedures are being properly and consistently followed.

Internal auditors do not report to an accounting or financial officer, because that arrangement would destroy the independence critical to their work. Instead, they report directly to an audit committee of the corporation's board of directors.

### Data Processing

Although general financial accountants are responsible for the recording of business transactions, they seldom do the actual **data processing**—recording the mass of accounting data—themselves. Accounting clerks and data processors use computers to record most of the thousands upon thousands of business transactions a business entity enters into during the year. Even the smallest firms today use computers to process financial data, thanks to the powerful personal computers (PCs) and the sophisticated bookkeeping software now available.

### International Accounting

Many companies now do business on an international basis. These companies need **international accounting** specialists with a background in the laws and tax requirements of all the countries in which the company does business.

### Education

Accountants in the field of **education** pursue teaching, research, and consulting careers. At the community college level, a typical professor will possess a master's degree and a CPA or CMA (certified management accountant) certificate plus some business experience. Many of these professors also bring into the classroom valuable background from their consulting activities. At the university level, the typical professor will have a Ph.D. and a CPA or CMA, and will be involved in research as well as teaching.

### Accounting Careers in Not-for-Profit Entities

Although they don't seek to make a profit, not-for-profit entities buy and sell goods and services and carry out many of the same kinds of transactions as business entities. Thus, the operating activities, the economic resources (things the entity owns), and the obligations of not-for-profit entities must be described and summarized in financial reports in much the same way that they are described and summarized in the financial reports of business entities. Executive officers of hospitals, directors of government agencies, taxpayers, elected school board officials, county commissioners, and investors in municipal bonds all need reliable accounting information on which to base decisions.

As we mentioned at the beginning of this section and illustrated in Figure 2, accounting careers in the not-for-profit area, including government, closely parallel those in the business sector.

### Careers in Public Accounting

Learning
Objective **3**

Describe how the CPA provides
credibility to the financial statements

CPAs are involved in auditing, tax services, and management advisory services. (For many Americans a CPA is the professional who helps them with their income tax returns.)

#### *Auditing*

As we mentioned earlier, the major function of the CPA is to serve as a link between the preparers of financial statements and the people who use them. Like most people, officers of business entities and directors of not-for-profit entities are generally ethical and honest people. The financial reports they present to users are prepared with the highest degree of integrity. However, two different officers or directors, given exactly the same financial data, may not produce identical reports. Differences of this type result because in accounting there are alternative ways, all of them quite legal, to treat many kinds of business transactions. Of course, even the most ethical people can make mistakes and, unfortunately, there always will be cheaters who prepare dishonest reports. But usually both honest errors and dishonest reports are eventually discovered.

To assure users that the financial statements are presented fairly and honestly, the CPA performs an **independent audit,** a review of the accounting records of an economic entity by a CPA who is neither employed by the entity nor related to any officer of the entity. An audit does not cover 100% of the accounting records. Instead the CPA reviews a statistically selected sample of the records, then issues an audit report. An audit report is an integral, required part of the financial statements issued by the entity. It declares that the financial reports issued by the economic entity are stated fairly and are prepared in accordance with generally accepted accounting principles (GAAP).

#### *Tax Services*

Tax services provided to a client by a CPA include preparing and filing tax returns and, perhaps of greater importance, tax planning. Tax planning directly affects the prime objective of business entities, which is to make profits. Any business decision about how to make those profits requires an awareness of the tax implications. With proper tax planning, decisions can be made that will reduce taxes and thus increase profits. CPAs are qualified to render service in this area because of their knowledge of tax laws, tax regulations, and various court decisions regarding taxes.

### Management Advisory Services

In addition to providing auditing and tax services, CPAs offer management advisory services. A CPA, in the course of auditing dozens of clients, observes many different accounting systems. This experience enables the CPA to analyze any particular client's strengths and weaknesses. Thus, as a CPA audits a business entity, a natural by-product of the audit is suggestions for improving the profitability of the business. Management may often want further specific services, such as engaging the CPA to establish an accounting system for determining costs, handling the payroll, or estimating future performance. It is not at all uncommon to find mathematicians, statisticians, and engineers on the management services staff of many large CPA firms.

**ASK YOURSELF ▶**

1. Who is responsible for the accounting information contained in financial reports?
2. What are the requirements for becoming a CPA?
3. List the nine areas of activity that offer career opportunities in private and not-for-profit accounting.
4. What are the three services provided by CPAs?
5. What purpose does an audit serve?

## TYPES OF BUSINESS ENTITIES

Learning Objective **4**

Distinguish the three types of business entities

There are three main types of business entities: proprietorships, partnerships, and corporations. All of them use basically the same kinds of financial statements, although there are minor differences in the way each type of business entity reports financial information.

### Proprietorship

A business entity that is owned by one person is called a **proprietorship.** Many attorneys, accountants, and physicians do their professional work as individual practitioners, and thus are proprietorships. The proprietorship form of business is also common for small retail enterprises. The main advantage of a proprietorship is the ease with which it can be formed. You simply decide to start a business, obtain an operating license, and register the name of your business (if legally necessary), and there it is—you've met the basic requirements for setting up a proprietorship.

Legally, the owner of a business entity (the proprietor) and the business entity (the proprietorship) are considered to be one and the same. If a proprietor dies, the proprietorship ceases to exist. However, for accounting purposes a distinction is made between the two, as explained by the following example:

Lew Coverhaus is a lawyer who owns a professional football team. That is, he owns both the law proprietorship, Lew Coverhaus, Attorney-at-Law, and the football proprietorship, the Tampa Bay Bulldogs. Coverhaus needs financial information on three separate entities: his law practice, his professional football team, and his personal affairs. But there is no legal distinction among these three entities. Income taxes are imposed on him only as an individual, and he is personally responsible for any liabilities incurred by any of the entities.

Figure 3 illustrates the legal and accounting concepts of a proprietorship.

**Figure 3** Legal and Accounting Concepts of a Proprietorship

Legal Concept

Accounting Concept

## Partnership

A non-incorporated business entity that is owned by two or more persons is called a **partnership.** Many small businesses and most professional service groups are partnerships. For example, several CPA firms have more than 1,000 partners and one CPA firm has more than 4,000. But most partnerships have just two or three partners. Like a proprietorship, a partnership is easy to form. The various partners simply agree (preferably in writing) to conduct a business entity as co-owners. The partnership agreement typically specifies how the profits will be shared among the partners and provides arrangements for settlements to be made to withdrawing partners or upon the death of a partner.

Legally, the owners of a partnership and the partnership itself are not considered to be separate. But as you may have guessed, for accounting purposes they are separate. Financial statements are prepared for the business entity and for the partnership, and may also be prepared for each of the individual partners. As with a proprietorship, partners are personally legally responsible for the partnership's liabilities. That is, if creditors cannot be satisfied from the partnership assets, then the creditors can demand and receive payment of their claims from the individual partners' personal assets.

An illustration of this dangerous feature of partnerships occurred in the fall of 1990, when Laventhol & Horwath, the seventh largest international CPA firm, filed for bankruptcy due to numerous past litigation losses and pending litigation. The 318 partners closed all 50 offices and terminated 3,500 employees. One lawsuit for $184 million alleges that Laventhol & Horwath helped Jim Bakker defraud members of his evangelical PTL ministry. Not only is the partnership bankrupt, but many of the partners may be forced into personal bankruptcy.

Due to the tremendous increase in litigation, such as the Laventhol & Horwath case, it is anticipated that within the next 5 years all CPA firms will operate under the shield of the corporate form of business organization.

## Corporation

A **corporation** is a business entity chartered under state laws and considered distinct from its owners. In fact, the U.S. Supreme Court has ruled that a corporation is an *artificial person,* which means that the corporation itself has many of the rights and

**Figure 4** Income Tax Returns and Business Receipts for the Three Types of Business Entities *(Source: Statistical Abstract of the United States.)*

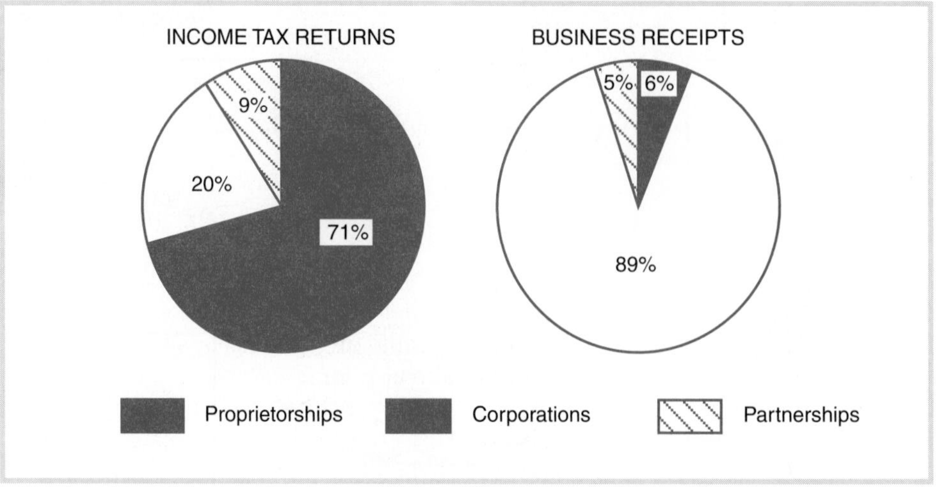

obligations that a person does. It can be sued and can sue, it can borrow money, it can enter into contracts, and it must pay income taxes. Proprietorships and partnerships as such can do none of these things; only the owner or partners can.

Persons wishing to form a corporation must present state officials with an application for a corporate charter, which provides legal evidence that the corporation has been created. The new corporation then issues shares of stock to its owners, who are referred to as *shareholders* or *stockholders.* The shareholders receive stock certificates as evidence of their ownership interests. Most large corporations have many thousands of shareholders.

Figure 4 indicates the relative sizes of the three types of business organization. It shows the number of tax returns filed with the Internal Revenue Service and the gross receipts reported by each type of entity.

The basic concepts and procedures of accounting apply to all three forms of business entities (as well as to not-for-profit entities).

## GENERALLY ACCEPTED ACCOUNTING PRINCIPLES

### Why Users Need GAAP

**Learning Objective 5**

Explain the meaning of the term *generally accepted accounting principles*

Consider the following situation: Atlanta Company, Boston Company, and Cleveland Company are competitors in the data processing industry. Several years ago, each of the three companies acquired identical Peach computers for $100,000 each. As a result of inflation, the $100,000 paid for the Peach would be equivalent to $120,000 today. However, thanks to rapid technological advances, a new Peach computer—equivalent in capacity to the old Peach—can be purchased today for $75,000. At the end of the current year, when the balance sheets are published, the value of the Peach computer is listed among the assets of Atlanta Company as $100,000, the acquisition price; Boston Company reports its Peach as an asset valued at its inflated price of $120,000; and Cleveland Company values its Peach at $75,000, the market price for an equivalent computer today. While each company has a valid explanation for its valuation, a potential investor would not have an accurate picture to use comparing the assets of these firms. Obviously, there is a need for some ground rules that all companies will follow when publishing financial statements. For this reason, accountants have agreed to use the acquisition price to value equipment in financial statements (so each company's Peach computer would be valued at $100,000).

The ground rules used by business entities in presenting financial information are called **generally accepted accounting principles (GAAP).** These principles have been developed by the accounting profession over the years to provide a consistent system of financial reporting in a constantly changing business environment. Unlike the natural laws of the physical sciences, which are universally and eternally true, accounting principles often change to meet the needs of emerging and changing financial situations. Reports that provided adequate financial information several years ago may not be adequate today.

Accounting principles develop as members of the accounting profession think about and seek solutions for various issues in accounting. A theoretically sound solution to a particular accounting problem may have certain practical limitations. The experience of the members of the accounting profession will determine when a practical rather than a conceptual solution to a problem is required. Thus, generally accepted accounting principles are a blend of theoretical principles and practical considerations.

Generally accepted accounting principles encompass not only principles, but also various procedures for their application. For example, one accounting principle holds that the price paid for a machine must be spread over a period of time, the expected life of the machine. There are several accepted procedures for applying this principle. We could spread the cost over the machine's life in equal amounts per year; we could spread the cost over the number of hours the machine was used each year; or we could spread the cost over the number of units the machine produced each year. But once we select a procedure, we must apply it consistently over the years.

### Major Developers of GAAP

**Learning Objective 6**

Identify the institutions that influence the development of accounting principles

Several groups have been influential in developing generally accepted accounting principles for the entire accounting profession: the Financial Accounting Standards Board, the American Institute of Certified Public Accountants, the Securities and Exchange Commission, the American Accounting Association, and the Institute of Management Accountants.

#### *Financial Accounting Standards Board*

The group responsible for originating generally accepted accounting principles today is the **Financial Accounting Standards Board,** commonly referred to as the **FASB** (pronounced "Fazbee"). These generally accepted accounting principles, called *Statements* of the Financial Accounting Standards Board, must be followed by all business entities that issue financial statements to investors or creditors.

The FASB consists of seven full-time members, who spend a considerable amount of time and effort in developing a new statement. *Discussion memorandums,* which are pamphlets explaining the basic issues of the topic under consideration, are prepared; *public hearings,* at which accountants and others can express their views orally and in writing, are held; and *exposure drafts,* which are the FASB's planned solutions to the problem, are written. After all this the FASB members vote, and if five of the seven approve, a new statement is issued.

#### *Securities and Exchange Commission*

The Securities and Exchange Act of 1934 created the **Securities and Exchange Commission (SEC),** an independent, quasi-judicial agency of the federal government, to administer the various laws concerning the distribution and sale of publicly held securities. Legal authority is vested in the SEC to require whatever specific accounting practices it deems necessary to protect the public. However, the SEC has taken the position that accounting principles are best set in the private sector rather than the public sector. As a consequence, the SEC has looked to the FASB to establish generally accepted accounting principles, and thus far most of the FASB standards have been accepted by the SEC as its own requirements for the reporting of financial and accounting data. On occasion the SEC differs with the FASB over certain accounting principles. When that happens, the SEC may issue its own ruling, describing the additional accounting information that must be reported to the SEC and perhaps also must be presented in the annual reports to stockholders.

### American Institute of Certified Public Accountants

The **American Institute of Certified Public Accountants (AICPA)** is the professional organization representing certified public accountants on a national basis. The AICPA is to the accounting profession what the American Bar Association is to the legal profession and the American Medical Association is to the medical profession.

Here are some of the ways the AICPA contributes to or affects generally accepted accounting principles:

- The AICPA collects reactions of its members to accounting issues and furnishes them to the FASB, which considers them in developing new statements.
- The AICPA represents the views of the profession in cases of congressional investigations.
- The AICPA publishes a monthly magazine called the *Journal of Accountancy,* which contains articles on accounting issues that are of interest to professional accountants.
- The AICPA provides courses and materials for the continuing professional education that is required of almost all CPAs.

Prior to the establishment of the FASB in 1973, the AICPA was involved directly in the development of generally accepted accounting principles. The predecessor to the FASB, the Accounting Principles Board (APB), was a committee within the AICPA responsible for issuing statements on accounting principles. These statements were called APB *Opinions* and, unless superseded by a later *Opinion* or by a *Statement* of the FASB, are still in effect today.

### American Accounting Association

The **American Accounting Association (AAA)** is an organization of professional accounting educators. As such, its influence on established accounting principles is indirect and long-range. The research done by AAA members leans toward the theoretical rather than the practical. The AAA is in continual search of solutions to accounting issues. The theoretical solution offered by the AAA today often finds its way into GAAP a number of years later. For example, the present concept of the financial report called the income statement was first expressed 30 years ago by the AAA. Today's articles in the *Accounting Review,* the AAA's quarterly publication, and AAA committee reports are likely to help establish tomorrow's accounting principles.

### Institute of Management Accountants

The **Institute of Management Accountants (IMA),** is an organization of private accountants whose primary concern is the continuing education of its members. In addition, the IMA provides research on current managerial accounting topics, service to communities by local IMA chapters, input to the FASB on proposed statements, and strong links with the academic community. Their publication, *Management Accounting,* is issued monthly.

The IMA sponsors the Certified Management Accountant examination, which is given in June and December of each year. The two-day examination consists of four parts: economics, finance and management; financial accounting and reporting; management reporting, analysis and behavioral issues; and decision analysis and information systems. A person who has passed this examination, and who has completed 2 years of professional experience in managerial accounting, may be certified as a **certified management accountant (CMA).**

## BUSINESS ETHICS

- At a recent meeting of a company's division managers, the vice president announced that a certain report was due the following Monday. One division manager was absent and the other managers did not inform him of the due date for the report. Are the other division managers legally responsible to the absent manager for this failure to communicate vital information to him? Are they morally responsible?
- A large company makes a product that has a 90-day warranty. Testing in the company's laboratory reveals that 35% of the products break within 6 months after normal use, yet the company makes no correction in manufacturing the product. Is the company legally responsible? Is it morally responsible?

Ethics is concerned with the moral duties and obligations of individuals or groups. The two examples above are ethical situations. They involve, not legal, but moral questions.

The topic of business ethics is much in the news as a result of the numerous financial scandals that have occurred over the past decade. These scandals have damaged the image of U.S. business and have resulted in losses of millions of dollars to investors, creditors, and taxpayers. A good case in point is the far-reaching debacle in the savings and loan industry, in which many thrift institutions failed in the late 1980s because of bad loans or managerial chicanery or both. The resulting "bailout" by the federal government will be a burden on taxpayers for years to come.

It is relatively easy to say what others should have done in an ethical situation. When you are yourself involved, however, deciding on the right thing to do is very difficult and requires a great deal of soul searching.

In order to provide ethical guidance to accountants, both the IMA and the AICPA have formulated codes of conduct for their members. The IMA's standards of ethical conduct are contained in its by-laws. As for the AICPA, the preamble to its Principles of Professional Conduct states that membership is voluntary, but by accepting membership a CPA assumes an obligation of self-discipline above and beyond the requirements of laws and regulations. The AICPA's code of conduct calls for an unswerving commitment to honorable behavior, even at the sacrifice of personal advantage.

The code consists of two sections: principles and rules. The principles provide the framework for the rules, which govern the performance of professional services.

The six principles of professional conduct are:

1. In carrying out their responsibilities as professionals, members should exercise sensitive professional and moral judgments in all their activities.
2. Members should accept the obligation to act in a way that will serve the public interest, honor the public trust, and demonstrate commitment to professionalism.
3. To maintain and broaden public confidence, members should perform all professional responsibilities with the highest sense of integrity.
4. A member should maintain objectivity and be free of conflicts of interest in discharging professional responsibilities. A member in public practice should be independent in fact and appearance when providing auditing and other attestation services.

5. A member should observe the profession's technical and ethical standards, strive continually to improve competence and the quality of services, and discharge professional responsibility to the best of the member's ability.

6. A member in public practice should observe the Principles of Professional Conduct in determining the scope and nature of the services to be provided.

Many businesses have their own written code stipulating the ethical conduct expected of their employees. Most of these codes also include instructions on when and how employees are expected to report the unethical conduct of others.

**ASK YOURSELF** ▶

1. Name and describe the types of business entities.
2. What is meant by the term *artificial person*?
3. Why are generally accepted accounting principles necessary?
4. Who are the major developers of accounting principles?
5. What is ethics?

## SUMMARY

• **Accounting** is a service that provides financial reports on which informed economic decisions are based.

• Financial reports are prepared for three user groups, a *management group*, a *financing group*, and a *public group*.

• Some users within the public group do not have direct access to a business entity's records, so external financial reports are prepared for them. These reports are called **general-purpose financial statements**.

• There are many different kinds of accounting activities, which provide numerous professional career opportunities. Principal among them are:

General **financial accounting**, concerned with recording business transactions

**Accounting systems design**, concerned with the development of business forms and records, with writing and implementing operating procedures, and with investigating new means of processing accounting data

**Cost accounting**, the gathering of accounting information to determine the cost of a product or service

**Budgeting**, the expression of business plans in monetary terms and the comparison of these plans to actual achievements in order to identify areas that need closer management control

**Tax accounting**, concerned with the preparation of various tax returns in compliance with the taxing authority's requirements and with tax planning to minimize the impact of taxes on the business entity

**Internal auditing**, a continual review of the business entity's accounting records, reports, policies, and procedures

**Data processing**, the recording of the mass of business transactions generated by a business entity

**International accounting**, concerned with accounting for activities of multinational companies, which requires a knowledge of the law and tax requirements of specific countries

**Education**, including teaching, research, and consulting at the community college and university levels.

- Users of external financial statements need assurance that the financial statements have been prepared in a manner that represents fairly the results of activities for the period. Such assurance is provided by the **certified public accountant (CPA)**.
- The CPA issues an audit report based on an independent review of the business transactions underlying the financial report.
- CPAs are professionals licensed by the various states only after passing the CPA exam and meeting any other specific requirements. Generally, a CPA candidate must have a college degree with a major in accounting to be eligible to take the CPA exam.
- There are three main types of business entities: a **proprietorship** is a business entity owned by one person; a **partnership** is a business entity owned by two or more persons; and a **corporation** is a business entity incorporated under the laws of one of the states.
- **Generally accepted accounting principles (GAAP)** have been developed to provide a rational system of financial reporting. These principles may be thought of as the ground rules of financial accounting.
- The most influential groups in the development of generally accepted accounting principles are the **Financial Accounting Standards Board (FASB)** and the **Securities and Exchange Commission (SEC).**
- The **American Institute of Certified Public Accountants (AICPA)**, the **American Accounting Association (AAA)**, and the **Institute of Management Accountants (IMA)** also provide input into the development of GAAP.

## 7   KEY TERMS

| | |
|---|---|
| **Accounting** | A service that provides the facts needed to make informed economic decisions. |
| **Accounting systems design** | The accounting career involved with designing the forms used to record business activities, specifying and implementing accounting operating procedures, and investigating new means of processing accounting data. |
| **American Accounting Association (AAA)** | The organization of professional accounting educators. |
| **American Institute of Certified Public Accountants (AICPA)** | The professional organization of CPAs. |
| **Audit** | A financial examination of a company's records. |
| **Budgeting** | The accounting activity concerned with expressing business plans in monetary terms and comparing those plans to actual achievements to isolate areas where management control needs to be exercised. |
| **Business entities** | Economic entities that provide a product or a service to customers at a price that includes a profit. |
| **Certified management accountant (CMA)** | An individual who has met the educational and experience requirements of the Institute of Management Accounting (IMA) and has passed the Uniform CMA Examination. |
| **Certified public accountant (CPA)** | An individual who has met the educational and experience requirements prescribed by state law and has passed the Uniform CPA Examination. A CPA is licensed to perform independent reviews (audits) of business entities' financial transactions and give a professional opinion on the fairness of these financial statements. |

| | |
|---|---|
| Controller | The executive officer of a business entity in charge of its accounting function. |
| Corporation | A business entity that is incorporated under state laws and considered distinct from its owners. |
| Cost accounting | The accounting activity concerned with determining the cost of producing a product or service, and with controlling such costs. |
| Data processing | The accounting activity concerned with the physical act of recording the mass of accounting data. |
| Economic entity | An organization that provides products or services. |
| Education | The field of accounting concerned with teaching, research, and consulting. |
| External financial reports | Reports, particularly the income statement and the balance sheet, prepared to meet the informational needs of those who do not have direct access to the business entity's records. |
| Financial accounting | The area of accounting concerned with the preparation and presentation of general-purpose financial statements. |
| Financial Accounting Standards Board (FASB) | The independent public board, comprising seven full-time members, which is responsible for the development of generally accepted accounting principles. |
| Generally accepted accounting principles | The ground rules used by economic entities in presenting financial information. |
| General-purpose financial statements | Financial statements prepared by a business entity to describe the results of business activities for a specified period of time and to list the economic resources and obligations of the entity. |
| Independent audit | A review of an economic entity's accounting records by a CPA who is neither employed by the entity nor related to an officer of it. |
| Institute of Management Accountants (IMA) | An organization of private accountants whose primary concern is the continuing education of its members. |
| Internal auditing | The area of accounting concerned with checking and reviewing the entity's records, reporting policies, and procedures. |
| Internal financial reports | Reports prepared exclusively for the use of management, which provide information to help the management group make operating decisions directed toward meeting the business's goals. |
| International accounting | The accounting career specializing in the laws and tax requirements of foreign countries. |
| Management accounting | The area of accounting that is concerned with internal reporting. |
| Not-for-profit entities | Economic entities such as hospitals, universities, and county water districts that provide a product or a service to customers at a cost that does not include a profit. |
| Partnership | A non-incorporated business entity that is owned by two or more persons. |
| Proprietorship | A business entity that is owned by one person. |
| Securities and Exchange Commission (SEC) | An independent, quasi-judicial agency of the federal government responsible for administrating the various acts concerning the distribution and sale of publicly held securities. |
| Tax accounting | The area of accounting concerned with preparation of various tax returns and with tax planning to minimize the impact of taxes on the business entity. |

## QUESTIONS FOR REVIEW AND FURTHER THOUGHT

### REVIEW QUESTIONS

1. Accountants and business persons often use the terms *economic entities, business entities,* and *not-for-profit entities*. What do these terms mean?

2. Three different groups use the accounting information of a business entity. Name and describe these groups.

3. Accounting careers can focus on several different areas of activity. List and describe six of these areas in the private sector.

4. A corporation's accounting reports are prepared by its accountants. Who in the corporation is responsible for providing the information contained in these reports?

5. What are the requirements to become a certified public accountant?

6. List and describe the three forms of business entities.

7. What does the term *generally accepted accounting principles* mean?

8. What does the Securities and Exchange Commission do?

9. How does the Securities and Exchange Commission relate to the Financial Accounting Standards Board?

10. What has the accounting profession done for its members in terms of ethical guidance?

### QUESTIONS FOR FURTHER THOUGHT

1. Are the accounting needs of economic, business and not-for-profit entities different? Explain.

2. What purpose does the independent certified public accountant serve in connection with a corporation's financial statements?

3. Why are the *Statements* of the Financial Accounting Standards Board and the *Opinions* of the old Accounting Principles Board important?

4. Why are generally accepted accounting principles important?

## OBJECTIVE ASSIGNMENT

*True/False*  Indicate whether each statement below is *true* or *false* by placing a *T* or an *F* in the space provided.

_____ 1. The term *economic entity* would not be applicable to the City of Atlanta.

_____ 2. The three distinct groups that use accounting information are known as the management group, the public group, and the financing group.

_____ 3. One major advantage of a proprietorship form of business is that it can be easily formed.

_____ 4. The term *artificial person* refers to a corporation's stockholders.

_____ 5. Generally accepted accounting principles are theoretical in nature and do not include procedures for applying the principles.

*Multiple Choice*  Select the best choice to complete each statement or answer each question below. Write the letter corresponding to your choice in the space provided.

_____ 1. IBM, Seven-Eleven, Delta Airlines, and Bethlehem Steel are examples of:
   a. Profit-motivated entities
   b. Not-for-profit entities
   c. Economic entities
   d. Both (a) and (c), but not (b)
   e. both (b) and (c), but not (a)

_____ 2. The financing group of a business entity includes each of the following except:
   a. Investors
   b. Internal Revenue Service
   c. Potential creditors
   d. Creditors
   e. All of the above

_____ 3. The responsibility for the accounting information contained in the financial reports of a business entity ultimately rests with the entity's:
   a. Accountant
   b. Controller
   c. Chief executive officer
   d. Treasurer
   e. None of the above

_____ 4. An area of responsibility to ensure that accounting and operating policies and procedures are being properly and consistently followed is called:

   a. Independent auditing
   b. Operational auditing
   c. Financial internal auditing
   d. All of the above
   e. None of the above

_____ 5. The major function of a CPA is to provide independent:
   a. Auditing services
   b. Corporate tax services
   c. Individual tax services
   d. Management advisory services
   e. None of the above

_____ 6. A financial examination of the firm's records is a:
   a. Peer review
   b. CMA examination
   c. Corporate examination
   d. CPA examination
   e. None of the above

_____ 7. The type of entity that is legally considered to be an artificial person is the
   a. Proprietorship
   b. Partnership
   c. Corporation
   d. Joint venture
   e. Estate

_____ 8. All of the following are directly associated with the FASB except:
   a. The _Journal of Accountancy_
   b. Statements of the Financial Accounting Standards Board
   c. Exposure drafts
   d. Discussion memorandums
   e. Seven full-time members

_____ 9. Accounting principles:
   a. Are universally and eternally true
   b. Often change to meet the needs of emerging and changing financial conditions
   c. Are passed by Congress
   d. Are part of the tax code
   e. None of the above

_____ 10. The Securities and Exchange Commission is the:
   a. Predecessor to the FASB
   b. Group that awards the CMA certificate
   c. Legal authority that requires whatever specific accounting practices are necessary to protect the public
   d. Largest organization representing certified public accountants on a national basis
   e. None of the above

## ETHICS CASE

A number of states now require 150 semester-hours of study for candidates to be eligible to take the CPA exam. Most colleges and universities require 120 semester-hours for a baccalaureate; so, in effect, the 150-hour rule requires a 5-year program of study.

In one state with a 150-hour rule, a CPA firm hired Jim Jameson, a 4-year graduate from a local university. The firm promised that Jim would have time to complete the fifth year of study by taking evening classes.

However, the demands of a very heavy tax season and a number of new clients forced the CPA firm to require Jameson to work extensive overtime. He had no extra time to pursue the fifth year of study. Thus he was ineligible to take the CPA examination.

In Jameson's second year with the firm, the managing partner called him in and told him that the firm had to let him go. Shortly after he was fired, Jameson discovered that the firm had hired a new staff member who had completed the 5 years of study required in the state.

**Required:**

Discuss the following two issues.

1. What should Jameson do?
2. Has letting Jameson go and hiring the fifth-year student helped the CPA firm?

## OBJECTIVE ASSIGNMENT ANSWERS

**True/False**

1. F    2. T    3. T    4. F    5. F

**Multiple Choice**

1. d    2. b    3. c    4. b    5. a
6. e    7. c    8. a    9. b    10. c

# Basic Concepts and the Accounting Model

We will start our study of the principles of financial accounting by examining the basic tools of financial accounting—the principal financial statements.

## THE PRINCIPAL FINANCIAL STATEMENTS

Learning
Objective

Identify and explain the basic purpose of the principal financial statements and the type of information contained in each

**1** The main objective of general financial accounting is to describe the financial condition and operations of a business entity, and that is done by preparing and publishing financial statements. The financial statements, the last step in the accounting process, are the starting point in the study of accounting. We start at the end because an understanding of the ultimate goal makes it easier to understand the concepts and procedures that are designed to achieve it.

The principal financial statements are the *income statement,* the *statement of owner's equity,* the *balance sheet,* and the *statement of cash flows.*

### The Income Statement

The financial statement that reports the profitability of a business entity is the **income statement.** Many business people consider the income statement more important than the statement of owner's equity, the balance sheet, or the statement of cash flows because it answers the first question asked by most users: Did the business earn a profit? The income statement reports on profitability by comparing the *revenue* earned during a specified period with the *expenses* incurred during that same period, as seen in the income statement for a proprietorship shown in Exhibit 1.

#### Revenue

The amount charged for goods sold or services rendered is called revenue. **Revenue** represents the inflow of economic resources to a business entity. Examples of revenues are sales, commissions earned, rental fees, and fees for professional services performed. Total revenue earned by Oceania Rehabilitation Services for the year is $226,800. This revenue resulted from the performance of rehabilitation services, shown as Rehabilitation Fees of $226,800. These fees are counted as revenue when the rehabilitation services are performed (as opposed to when payment for the services is actually received)

#### Expenses

A business's **expenses** represent the economic resources consumed in providing products or services to customers. Expenses include the cost of goods sold or services rendered to generate revenue—such as the cost of the supplies Oceania Rehabilitation Services uses and the technicians it hires to do the rehabilitation. Expenses also include the cost of goods or services the company buys to operate the business—such as salaries of employees, delivery costs, repairs, laboratory supplies, advertising costs, rent, cleaning services, travel expenses, and so on. Oceania Rehabilitation Services incurred $155,300 of expenses in generating revenue during the year. Just as revenue is counted as earned when services are rendered, expenses are incurred when the entity acquires or receives goods or services (as opposed to when it actually pays for them).

The financial statements for Oceania Rehabilitation Services are prepared using the **accrual basis of accounting.** This refers to the facts noted above: that revenue is considered to be earned when services are performed, not when payment is received, and that expenses are considered to be incurred when services are received,

**Exhibit 1** An Income Statement

### OCEANIA REHABILITATION SERVICES
### Income Statement
### Year Ended December 31, 1998

| | | |
|---|---|---|
| Revenues: | | |
| Rehabilitation Fees . . . . . . . . . . . . . . . . . . . . . . . . . . . . . . . . . . . . . . . . . . . | | $226,800 |
| Expenses: | | |
| Salaries Expense . . . . . . . . . . . . . . . . . . . . . . . . . . . . . . . . | $97,400 | |
| Rent Expense . . . . . . . . . . . . . . . . . . . . . . . . . . . . . . . . . . . | 25,300 | |
| Supplies Expense . . . . . . . . . . . . . . . . . . . . . . . . . . . . . . . . | 21,900 | |
| Utilities Expense . . . . . . . . . . . . . . . . . . . . . . . . . . . . . . . . . | 10,700 | |
| Total Expenses. . . . . . . . . . . . . . . . . . . . . . . . . . . . . . . . . . . . | | 155,300 |
| Net Income. . . . . . . . . . . . . . . . . . . . . . . . . . . . . . . . . . . . . . . . . . . . | | $ 71,500 |

not when cash is paid. The opposite approach, recording revenues only when cash is received and recording expenses only when cash is paid, is called the **cash basis of accounting.**

Many small businesses use the cash basis of accounting because it is much easier to use than the accrual basis. However, when a business has significant transactions that involve extending credit to customers, receiving credit from vendors, or acquiring goods for resale, generally accepted accounting principles require the use of the accrual method.

When a business has more revenue than expenses, the difference is its **profit,** also called **net income.** Oceania Rehabilitation Services' revenue for the year ended Dec. 31, 1998 exceeds its expenses by $71,500, which is its net income for the year. When expenses exceed revenue, the difference is called **net loss** and the business has been unprofitable.

### The Heading

Notice that the income statement is identified by a heading and that the heading consists of three lines:

> *Line 1.* The name of the company

> *Line 2.* The type of financial statement

> *Line 3.* The period of time covered by the financial statement

The last item is very important. Revenue and expenses are *time concepts.* Revenue is earned and expenses are incurred over a period of time. Common sense tells us that a net income of $71,500 *for the year* is quite different from a net income of $71,500 *for the month.* If we say that Oceania Rehabilitation Services had revenue of $18,800 in January, you will know that we mean Oceania Rehabilitation Services has sold goods or services amounting to $18,800 from Jan. 1 to Jan. 31. If we say that Oceania incurred $13,000 of expenses in the second quarter, you will know that this amount was incurred from Apr. 1 to June 30. And if we say that Oceania had revenue of $226,800 for the year, you will know that is the amount of revenue earned from Jan. 1 to Dec. 31. If they do not know what period of time the statement covers, users cannot interpret the financial data reported, nor can they compare them with previous financial statements or financial statements of other firms.

**Exhibit 2** The Statement of Owner's Equity

### OCEANIA REHABILITATION SERVICES
### Statement of Owner's Equity
### Year Ended December 31, 1998

| | |
|---|---:|
| O'Brien, Capital, Jan. 1, 1998 | $ 93,400 |
| Add: Net Income | 71,500 |
| Total | $164,900 |
| Less: Withdrawals | (62,500) |
| O'Brien, Capital, Dec. 31, 1998 | $102,400 |

## The Statement of Owner's Equity

The statement of owner's equity shows how the owner's investment has changed from the start of a period to the end of a period. It serves as a link between the income statement and the balance sheet, because the net income from the income statement is recorded on the statement of owner's equity and the ending balance of the owner's equity is shown on the balance sheet. The statement of owner's equity for Oceania Rehabilitation Services is shown in Exhibit 2.

Again, as with the income statement, the heading is important. It has three parts:

*Line 1.* The name of the company

*Line 2.* The name of the statement

*Line 3.* The period of time covered

This statement is like the income statement in that it too covers a period of time, from Jan. 1, 1998, to Dec. 31, 1998. The statement tells us that O'Brien (the owner of Oceania Rehabilitation Services) started the year with $93,400 of equity, or capital invested in his firm. O'Brien's investment is shown as O'Brien, Capital. During the year he increased his capital by $71,500, the net income we saw on the income statement. However, we see from the withdrawals line that O'Brien took $62,500 from the business for his personal use (the parentheses represent a subtraction). O'Brien ended the year with capital, or owner's equity, of $102,400.

## The Balance Sheet

The financial statement designed to show a business entity's financial position—what it owns and what it owes—on a particular date is called the **balance sheet.**

Study the balance sheet for Oceania Rehabilitation Services in Exhibit 3. Notice that the balance sheet consists of two sides. The left side represents what the firm owns, its *assets;* the right side represents what the firm owes, its *liabilities,* and the amount of the owner's investment in the business, the *owner's equity.* In a sense, the business owes the amount shown under owner's equity to the owner. That is, if the business were to be sold or dissolved and all the liabilities paid, the remaining money would be paid to the owner in compensation for the capital he or she had invested in the business.

The total of the assets ($139,300) on the left side of Oceania Rehabilitation Services' balance sheet must equal, or *balance* with, the sum of the liabilities ($36,900), and the owner's equity ($102,400) on the right side—hence the term *balance sheet.* This formula, *assets = liabilities + owner's equity,* is known as the balance sheet equation; it is fundamental in accounting, as we shall see.

**Exhibit 3** A Balance Sheet

### OCEANIA REHABILITATION SERVICES
### Balance Sheet
### December 31, 1998

| Assets | | Liabilities | |
|---|---|---|---|
| Cash . . . . . . . . . . . . . . . . . . . . | $  2,500 | | |
| Accounts Receivable . . . . . . . | 27,200 | Notes Payable . . . . . . . . . . . . | $ 25,000 |
| Supplies on Hand. . . . . . . . . . | 4,700 | Accounts Payable . . . . . . . . . | 11,900 |
| Land . . . . . . . . . . . . . . . . . . . . | 19,000 | Total Liabilities . . . . . . . . | $ 36,900 |
| Building. . . . . . . . . . . . . . . . . | 62,300 | | |
| Equipment . . . . . . . . . . . . . . | 23,600 | **Owner's Equity** | |
| | | O'Brien, Capital . . . . . . . . . . | $102,400 |
| | | Total Liabilities and | |
| Total Assets . . . . . . . . . . . . . | $139,300 | Owner's Equity . . . . . . . . . . | $139,300 |

Like the income statement and the statement of owner's equity, the balance sheet has a heading with three important parts, as follows:

*Line 1.* The name of the company

*Line 2.* The type of financial statement

*Line 3.* The date of the balance sheet

Unlike the income statement and statement of owner's equity, which cover a specified *period of time,* the balance sheet is a listing of assets, liabilities, and owner's equity at a *specific point in time.* That point in time for Oceania Rehabilitation Services is the close of business on Dec. 31, 1998.

### Assets

The **assets** of an economic entity are the economic resources—the things of measurable value—that are owned by the entity and are expected to provide future benefits. Assets may be either physical or nonphysical in nature. *Physical assets* include cash, merchandise, supplies, equipment, trucks, machines, buildings, and land. *Nonphysical assets* include legal claims, such as amounts due from customers (called accounts receivable), and legal rights, such as patents or copyrights. For example, when we sell a product for $10 to one of our customers, the customer may not pay the amount due today. He or she may charge it, and pay at the end of the month. We have sold our product *on account,* earning revenue of $10, and we have a nonphysical asset—an account receivable of $10—which we anticipate will be collected shortly. The future benefit of this asset is the cash we will receive at the end of the month.

To be included on the balance sheet as an asset, an economic resource must, by definition, be measurable; if it is not measurable, it cannot be an asset. For example, the managerial ability of the company's president is an economic resource that will provide future benefit, but it cannot be measured in dollars, so it does not appear on the balance sheet.

### Liabilities

The **liabilities** of an economic entity are its debts. The debts may be represented as *formal* claims or *informal* claims. A formal claim is a written contract, such as a written promise to repay a borrowed sum of money plus interest at a specified future date; this

**Exhibit 4** Owner's Equity on the Balance Sheet

YOUR NEW BUSINESS
Balance Sheet
April 30, 1998

| Assets | | Liabilities and Owner's Equity | |
|---|---|---|---|
| Cash | $ 10,000 | Liabilities | $ 60,000 |
| Land | 10,000 | Owner's Equity | 40,000 |
| Building | 30,000 | | |
| Machines | 50,000 | | |
| | | Total Liabilities and Owner's | |
| Total Assets | $100,000 | Equity | $100,000 |

is called a **note payable.** Or a debt may be represented as an informal claim such as an amount due to a creditor for goods and services acquired but not yet paid for; this is called an **account payable.**

### Owner's Equity

To convey to you the meaning of owner's equity, an example is needed. Assume that you decide to go into business. You invest $40,000 of your own money, buying an empty factory building for $30,000 and the land on which it is located for $10,000. Next, you borrow $60,000 from a bank; with it you buy machines for $50,000 to put in the factory, and you keep $10,000 on hand for expenses. That's all you need: you are ready to operate your business. At this point you could prepare a balance sheet. If you did, it would look like the one shown in Exhibit 4.

You have just one liability, the bank's claim on your assets amounting to $60,000. The difference between your assets and your liability represents your financial interest in the business as its owner. Thus your $40,000 interest in the business is your **owner's equity,** or **capital.** Since your creditors' claim on your assets takes precedence over yours, your owner's equity represents the difference between your assets and your liabilities.

### The Statement of Cash Flows

The fourth principal financial statement, the *statement of cash flows,* is illustrated in Exhibit 5. This statement provides information about cash receipts and cash payments in connection with the operating, investing, and financing activities of a business. Notice that the heading is the same as for the income statement and the statement of owner's equity. However, at this stage of your study of accounting the statement of cash flows is too complex to review in detail.

**ASK YOURSELF** ▶

1. Why are the financial statements presented early in the study of accounting?
2. What are the principal financial statements?
3. What are revenues? expenses?
4. What is the difference between the accrual basis and the cash basis of accounting?
5. What information must be included in the headings of financial statements?
6. Define the terms assets, liabilities, and owner's equity.

**Exhibit 5** The Statement of Cash Flows

**OCEANIA REHABILITATION SERVICES**
**Statement of Cash Flows**
**Year Ended December 31, 1998**

| | | |
|---|---:|---:|
| Cash Flows from Operating Activities: | | |
| Net Income. . . . . . . . . . . . . . . . . . . . . . . . . . . . . . . . . . . . . . . . . . . . . . . . . . . | | $71,500 |
| Adjustments to Reconcile Net Income to Net Cash Provided by | | |
| Operating Activities: | | |
| Increases: | | |
| Increase in Accounts Payable . . . . . . . . . . . . . . . . . . . . . . . . . . . . . . . | | 7,300 |
| Decreases: | | |
| Increase in Accounts Receivable. . . . . . . . . . . . . . . . . . . . . | $4,200 | |
| Increase in Supplies on Hand . . . . . . . . . . . . . . . . . . . . . . . . | 1,500 | ( 5,700) |
| Net Cash Provided by Operating Activities. . . . . . . . . . . . . . . . . . . | | $ 73,100 |
| Cash Flows from Investing Activities: | | |
| Decrease: Payment for Purchase of Land. . . . . . . . . . . . . . . . . . . . . . . . | | (17,600) |
| Cash Flows from Financing Activities: | | |
| Decrease: Withdrawals. . . . . . . . . . . . . . . . . . . . . . . . . . . . . . . . . . . . . . . . . | | $(62,500) |
| Net Decrease in Cash and Cash Equivalents . . . . . . . . . . . . . . . . . . . . . . . . | | $( 7,000) |
| Cash and Cash Equivalents at Beginning of Year . . . . . . . . . . . . . . . . . . . . | | 9,500 |
| Cash and Cash Equivalents at End of Year . . . . . . . . . . . . . . . . . . . . . . . . . | | $ 2,500 |

## FIVE BASIC GENERALLY ACCEPTED ACCOUNTING PRINCIPLES

**Learning Objective 2**

List the basic accounting concepts and principles and explain what they are

Accounting standards are needed to make the financial statements—the income statement, the statement of owner's equity, the balance sheet, and the statement of cash flows—useful to investors and creditors. Generally accepted accounting principles have been developed in response to this need, and they are continually revised by the FASB to keep up with changes in the practice of accounting. At this point, we'll explore just five basic and very important accounting principles that govern the preparation of financial statements:

**1.** The cost principle
**2.** The objectivity principle
**3.** The business entity concept
**4.** The going concern concept
**5.** The stable dollar concept

### The Cost Principle

The **cost principle** specifies that assets acquired by a business entity are to be recorded at the exchange price paid for them. The price the buyer pays in exchange for an asset is known as the *historical cost*. It is called a historical cost because, once recorded, it remains unchanged.

It is important to realize that *the assets listed on the balance sheet are measured in dollar amounts that represent the historical cost of those assets, not what could presently be obtained from their sale.*

Applying the cost principle to the situation of three companies that bought the same computer would require that these identical computers purchased by each company all be recorded at their historical cost. Neither the current market value nor the cost adjusted for inflation is acceptable, because neither is in accordance with this generally accepted accounting principle. The reason for the cost principle is rooted in the objectivity principle.

## The Objectivity Principle

The cost of an asset is established by an exchange transaction between an informed buyer and an informed seller. The **objectivity principle** requires that any independent party can confirm the asset's exchange price—its historical cost—by simply reviewing the information in the sale documents, such as purchase invoices, sales invoices, property deeds, and transfers of title. (An *independent party* is an unrelated person who does not have a financial interest in the business affairs of either the buyer or the seller.)

The objectivity principle establishes the reason for the cost principle—that is, for recording assets at cost. Any value other than cost could not be agreed upon by independent parties because estimated market values are subjective (that is, they depend entirely on the opinion of the one making the estimate).

## The Business Entity Concept

For accounting purposes, a business entity is considered to be separate and distinct from its owner or owners. This basic generally accepted accounting principle is called the **business entity concept.** For instance, when a travel agency and a dry cleaning store are owned by the same person but operated as two separate proprietorships, the business transactions of each must be recorded, summarized, and reported separately, resulting in financial statements for each enterprise. The purchase of a personal automobile by the owner of these two establishments would not be considered as relating to either business entity. Thus, accounting treats each business entity as generating its own revenue, incurring its own expenses, owning its own assets, and owing its own debts. (The law ignores these distinctions for a proprietorship or a partnership.)

## The Going Concern Concept

Business entities are established with the basic assumption that they will continue to exist indefinitely—at least as long as the owner can reasonably expect future earnings that will yield profits. This assumption is the basis for an accounting principle called the **going concern concept.**

This concept is the reason that assets are considered to have future economic benefits. Without it, we would be forced to record all assets as expenses on the income statement. We would not be able to anticipate that the asset would yield any future benefit, since we would be assuming that the business entity might not be in operation next year. For example, a building typically has an estimated useful life of 40 years for accounting purposes, but its full cost is not recorded as an expense when it is acquired. Instead, because the business entity expects to be in existence 40 years hence, part of the cost of the building will be allocated to each of 40 successive annual income statements as an expense. The market value of the building today is not considered relevant to users of the financial statements, since the entity does not plan to sell the building; it is an asset needed in order for the business to operate.

### The Stable Dollar Concept

The mile and the kilometer are standard units that enable us to measure distances. If we know the distance between two cities, we can use that information to estimate how much time is needed to travel between them or how much gasoline is needed to make the trip.

Money is the unit of measure employed in recording financial transactions. Knowing the money values assigned to financial transactions enables the users of financial statements to estimate the profitability or solvency of a business enterprise. Unlike the mile and the kilometer, however, the dollar is not a precise and unchanging unit of measure. A dollar of 1988 is not the same as a dollar of today, because of the effects of inflation.

Accountants know that the value of the dollar changes over time, but they cannot build useful statements with unstable units of measurement. Therefore, they prepare financial statements on the basis of the **stable dollar concept:** the value of a dollar does not change over time. Thus, they consider the dollar of a past year to be equal in value to a current dollar. When we compare revenues of 1988 to revenues of 1997, the same dollar is used to measure the revenues from each year. The accounting dollar is thus assumed to be "stable"—not changing in value over time. If only this were true! As we know, the dollar does indeed change in value over time. We could buy 1 gallon of gasoline for $0.34 in 1972. How much does a gallon of gasoline cost today? The measure of a gallon stayed the same, but the measure of a dollar certainly didn't.

**ASK YOURSELF ▶**

1. **Why are generally accepted accounting principles necessary?**
2. **List and describe five basic generally accepted accounting principles.**

## THE BASIC ACCOUNTING MODEL

The goal of the accounting activity for a business entity is to prepare financial statements that describe the entity. Before these statements can be prepared, the financial transactions of the business entity must be recorded, classified, and summarized. This process of analysis relies on a simple relationship called the **basic accounting model,** which is expressed by what is known as the balance sheet equation:

*Learning Objective* **3**

State and explain the basic accounting model

$$\text{Assets} = \text{Liabilities} + \text{Owner's Equity}$$
$$\text{A} = \text{L} + \text{OE}$$

This fundamental equality is *always true,* because the left side of the equation is simply another view of the right side. Assets represent resources owned by the business entity; liabilities and owner's equity represent the claims of those who supplied the assets. Since owner's equity represents the difference between assets and liabilities, the equation is always in balance. *Assets always equal the sum of liabilities and owner's equity.*

**Financial transactions** are events in which goods and services are exchanged between economic entities. Each financial transaction affects the balance sheet equation. Consider, for example, the acquisition of an asset. Assets may be acquired in three ways:

1. By paying cash—*giving up an asset already owned.* Buying an office desk for cash would be an example.
2. By promising to pay the amount due at some future date—*incurring a liability.* Buying an office desk, but not paying for it until next month, would illustrate incurring a liability.
3. By accepting a receipt from the owner of the business entity—*increasing the owner's equity* in the business. If the owner of a business used his or her own personal desk in the business, the business would have acquired the desk from the owner.

Can you see that each of these financial transactions has two parts? Assume that the desk costs $700 and the equation is as follows:

$$A \quad = \quad L \quad + \quad OE$$
$$\$12{,}000 = \$5{,}000 + \$7{,}000$$

On the one hand, acquiring the office desk by paying cash would increase the total assets of the business entity by the cost of the desk. On the other hand, the asset cash would be reduced by a like amount, so the equation would stay in balance:

$$A \quad = \quad L \quad + \quad OE$$
$$\begin{array}{rcl}
\$12{,}000 &=& \$5{,}000 + \$7{,}000 \\
+\ 700 && \\
-\ 700 && \\
\hline
\$12{,}000 &=& \$5{,}000 + \$7{,}000
\end{array}$$

Acquiring the desk by incurring a liability would increase the total assets, but also the liabilities:

$$A \quad = \quad L \quad + \quad OE$$
$$\begin{array}{rcl}
\$12{,}000 &=& \$5{,}000 + \$7{,}000 \\
+\ 700 &=& +\ 700 \\
\hline
\$12{,}700 &=& \$5{,}700 + \$7{,}000
\end{array}$$

Acquiring the desk from the owner would increase the total assets, but also the owner's equity:

$$A \quad = \quad L \quad + \quad OE$$
$$\begin{array}{rcl}
\$12{,}000 &=& \$5{,}000 + \$7{,}000 \\
+\ 700 &=& +\ \ \ 700 \\
\hline
\$12{,}700 &=& \$5{,}000 + \$7{,}700
\end{array}$$

Since every transaction has two parts, the term **double-entry accounting** is used to refer to the recording of financial transactions by balancing two elements within the basic accounting model.

Remember: The ultimate result of the accounting activity for an entity is its financial statements. The first step required to produce financial statements is to record the financial transactions within the framework of the basic accounting model.

### Effects of Financial Transactions on the Accounting Model

Learning
Objective   **5**

Record business transactions on a
financial transaction worksheet

Every financial transaction, whether very simple or extremely complex, can be analyzed or expressed in terms of its effect on the balance sheet equation. Every business entity, whether it's General Meat Market or General Motors, analyzes and expresses financial transactions in this way.

It is essential for you to understand the basic accounting model in order to understand the basis of financial statements. The following extended example explains the basic accounting model by illustrating how different types of transactions affect it.

# THE MARY ABREMS DANCE STUDIO

Mary Abrems decides to establish a business to be called The Mary Abrems Dance Studio. The dance studio will be operated as a proprietorship and as such all business decisions will be made solely by the owner, Mary Abrems. The assets of the dance studio will belong to Abrems and all obligations of the business will be her responsibility. Any income that the studio earns will belong solely to Abrems.

During November 1998, the first month of operations, various financial transactions take place. These transactions are described and analyzed below.

NOVEMBER 1   Abrems invests $11,000 from her personal savings in the new business, depositing the money at the First National Bank into an account titled The Mary Abrems Dance Studio.

In this chapter we will analyze financial transactions like these by means of a *financial transaction worksheet,* which is a form used to analyze increases and decreases in the assets, liabilities, or owner's equity of a business entity. (As we develop a financial transaction worksheet, you may notice its similarity to the spreadsheet that is available for use on personal computers.)

When a specific asset, liability, or owner's equity item is created by a financial transaction, it is listed on the financial transaction worksheet under the appropriate heading. These items, called **accounts,** are used to register money accounts. For example, when Abrems contributes her $11,000, it is listed under the asset account Cash.

The worksheet below shows the first transaction of The Mary Abrems Dance Studio. The amounts of assets, liabilities, and owner's equity are all zero before this transaction on Nov. 1, since the business entity did not exist prior to this date.

**THE MARY ABREMS DANCE STUDIO**
Financial Transaction Worksheet
Month of November 1998

| | | Assets | = Liabilities + | | Owner's Equity | |
| --- | --- | --- | --- | --- | --- | --- |
| Date | Cash | | = | + | Abrems, Capital | Owner's Equity Explanation |
| Nov. 1 | + $11,000 | | = | + | $11,000 | Initial investment |

Let's look at what Abrems has done by making this financial transaction.

- A business entity separate and distinct from Abrems' personal financial affairs has been created.

- An economic resource—the $11,000, which is the asset Cash—has been invested in the business entity. The source of this resource is the contribution made by the owner, which represents owner's equity. The owner's equity account heading is Abrems, Capital.

- The dual nature of the transaction is that cash has been invested and owner's equity created. The effect of this transaction on the basic accounting model—the balance sheet equation—is to increase an asset (Cash) from zero to $11,000 and to increase owner's equity from zero to $11,000. At this point, there are no liabilities.

NOVEMBER 5   Office equipment costing $7,800 is acquired by writing a check in that amount to the vendor.

**THE MARY ABREMS DANCE STUDIO**
**Financial Transaction Worksheet**
**Month of November 1998**

| | | Assets | = | Liabilities | + | Owner's Equity | |
|---|---|---|---|---|---|---|---|
| Date | Cash | + Office Equipment = | | + | Abrems, Capital | Owner's Equity Explanation |
| Nov.  1 | + $11,000 | = | | + | $11,000 | Initial investment |
| 5 | − 7,800 | + $ 7,800 | | | | |
| Totals | $ 3,200 | + $ 7,800 = | | + | $11,000 | |
| | | $11,000 = | $11,000 | | | |

This exchange transaction results in a decrease in one asset—Cash—but a corresponding increase in another asset—Office Equipment. Notice that while the value of total assets is unchanged after this transaction, the composition of the assets has changed.

NOVEMBER 9   Office supplies in the amount of $450 are acquired on account.

**THE MARY ABREMS DANCE STUDIO**
**Financial Transaction Worksheet**
**Month of November 1998**

| | | Assets | | = | Liabilities | + | Owner's Equity | |
|---|---|---|---|---|---|---|---|---|
| Date | Cash | Office Supplies + on Hand | + Office Equipment = | Accounts Payable | + | Abrems, Capital | Owner's Equity Explanation |
| Nov.  1 | + $11,000 | | = | | + | $11,000 | Initial investment |
| 5 | − 7,800 | | + $ 7,800 | | | | |
| 9 | | + $450 | | + $  450 | | | |
| Totals | $ 3,200 | + $450 | + $ 7,800 = | $  450 | + | $11,000 | |
| | | | $11,450 = | $11,450 | | | |

Acquiring the office supplies with a promise to pay the amount due at a later date is called buying **on account.** Buying *on credit* or *for credit* means the same thing. When we buy something in this manner, we call the amount we owe the creditor an *account payable.*

As a result of this transaction, a new asset account called Office Supplies on Hand is created. Whenever the business entity engages in activities that result in the need to establish a new account, accountants simply create a new account, giving it a name that describes that account in as few words as possible. The account Office Supplies on Hand is so called to distinguish it as an asset. The term *office supplies* might cause confusion, since it would not be clear whether the office supplies were "on hand" (an asset to be shown on the balance sheet) or an "expense" (office supplies used during the period to be shown on the income statement).

This transaction results in an increase in assets—Office Supplies on Hand— and an increase in the liability Accounts Payable.

**NOVEMBER 11**   The Mary Abrems Dance Studio collects $2,100 in cash for dance lessons.

**THE MARY ABREMS DANCE STUDIO**
**Financial Transaction Worksheet**
**Month of November 1998**

| | | Assets | | = | Liabilities | + | Owner's Equity | |
|---|---|---|---|---|---|---|---|---|
| Date | Cash | Office Supplies + on Hand | + Office Equipment = | | Accounts Payable | + | Abrems, Capital | Owner's Equity Explanation |
| Nov. 1 | + $11,000 | | | = | | + | $11,000 | Initial investment |
| 5 | − 7,800 | | + $ 7,800 | | | | | |
| 9 | | + $450 | | | + $ 450 | | | |
| 11 | + 2,100 | | | | | + | 2,100 | Dance lesson revenues |
| Totals | $ 5,300 | + $450 | + $ 7,800 | = | $ 450 | + | $13,100 | |
| | | | $13,550 | = | $13,550 | | | |

Receiving fees for services was the reason Abrems established the business entity. She expects to receive more revenue from dance lessons than she has to spend in providing the lessons. The excess is her *profit,* or *net income.* The $2,100 cash collected for dance lessons represents revenue and as such reflects an increase in the ownership interest in the business entity as well as an increase in cash. Remember, *revenue* is an inflow of cash or other properties in exchange for goods sold or services rendered. When the inflow of cash or other properties is recorded, another asset is not reduced, nor is a liability incurred. The owner is better off than she was before; this is why owner's equity—specifically, the account Abrems, Capital—is increased. The effect of this transaction—$2,100 cash revenue—on the basic accounting equation is to increase the asset Cash and to increase Abrems, Capital, by $2,100 each.

**NOVEMBER 15**   Abrems pays County Services Company $1,100 for the month of November for utilities.

## THE MARY ABREMS DANCE STUDIO
### Financial Transaction Worksheet
### Month of November 1998

| | | Assets | | = Liabilities + | Owner's Equity | |
|---|---|---|---|---|---|---|
| Date | Cash | + Office Supplies on Hand | + Office Equipment = | Accounts Payable + | Abrems, Capital | Owner's Equity Explanation |
| Nov. 1 | + $11,000 | | | = | + $11,000 | Initial investment |
| 5 | − 7,800 | | + $ 7,800 | | | |
| 9 | | + $450 | | + $ 450 | | |
| 11 | + 2,100 | | | | + 2,100 | Dance lesson revenues |
| 15 | − 1,100 | | | | − 1,100 | Utilities expense |
| Totals | $ 4,200 | + $450 + | $ 7,800 = | $ 450 + | $12,000 | |
| | | | $12,450 = | $12,450 | | |

The $1,100 for utilities is an expense for the month of November. It represents an outflow of resources and a reduction of owner's equity. Thus, the asset Cash is decreased by $1,100, and Abrems, Capital, is also decreased by $1,100.

NOVEMBER 17   The dance studio has an arrangement with several dance clubs whereby group lessons will be given to club members on various week nights. Abrems bills these clubs $6,300 for the month.

## THE MARY ABREMS DANCE STUDIO
### Financial Transaction Worksheet
### Month of November 1998

| | | | Assets | | = Liabilities + | Owner's Equity | |
|---|---|---|---|---|---|---|---|
| Date | Cash | + Accounts Receivable | + Office Supplies on Hand | + Office Equipment = | Accounts Payable + | Abrems, Capital | Owner's Equity Explanation |
| Nov. 1 | + $11,000 | | | | = | + $11,000 | Initial investment |
| 5 | − 7,800 | | | + $ 7,800 | | | |
| 9 | | | + $450 | | + $ 450 | | |
| 11 | + 2,100 | | | | | + 2,100 | Dance lesson revenues |
| 15 | − 1,100 | | | | | − 1,100 | Utilities expense |
| 17 | | + $6,300 | | | | + 6,300 | Dance lesson revenues |
| Totals | $ 4,200 + | $6,300 + | $450 + | $ 7,800 = | $ 450 + | $18,300 | |
| | | | | $18,750 = | $18,750 | | |

Even though she has not received cash, Abrems has earned revenue. She has performed her services and is entitled to payment for them. Performing the services creates an economic resource, namely, the amount owed to The Mary Abrems Dance Studio. This amount is called **accounts receivable.** As seen in the transaction on Nov. 11, revenue is an increase in owner's equity. Thus, this revenue transaction results in an increase in an asset—Accounts Receivable—and a like increase in owner's equity—Abrems, Capital—in the amount of $6,300.

NOVEMBER 19   Abrems pays $200 of the $450 bill for the Nov. 9 purchase of office supplies.

**THE MARY ABREMS DANCE STUDIO**
Financial Transaction Worksheet
Month of November 1998

| | | | Assets | | | = Liabilities + | Owner's Equity | |
| --- | --- | --- | --- | --- | --- | --- | --- | --- |
| Date | Cash | + Accounts Receivable + | Office Supplies on Hand + | Office Equipment = | Accounts Payable + | Abrems, Capital | Owner's Equity Explanation |
| Nov.  1 | + $11,000 | | | | = | + | $11,000 | Initial investment |
| 5 | − 7,800 | | | + $ 7,800 | | | | |
| 9 | | | + $450 | | + $ 450 | | | |
| 11 | + 2,100 | | | | | + 2,100 | Dance lesson revenues |
| 15 | − 1,100 | | | | | − 1,100 | Utilities expense |
| 17 | | + $6,300 | | | | + 6,300 | Dance lesson revenues |
| 19 | − 200 | | | | − 200 | | |
| Totals | $ 4,000 + | $6,300 + | $450 + | $ 7,800 = | $ 250 + | $18,300 | |
| | | | | $18,550 | = | $18,550 | |

The payment of the $200 is an outflow of resources, as evidenced by the cash expenditure and the reduction of a liability—Accounts Payable. This payment transaction reduces both Cash and Accounts Payable by $200.

NOVEMBER 20   A check in the amount of $3,350 is received from a large dance club for their monthly lessons, billed on Nov. 17.

**THE MARY ABREMS DANCE STUDIO**
Financial Transaction Worksheet
Month of November 1998

| | | | Assets | | | = Liabilities + | Owner's Equity | |
| --- | --- | --- | --- | --- | --- | --- | --- | --- |
| Date | Cash | + Accounts Receivable + | Office Supplies on Hand + | Office Equipment = | Accounts Payable + | Abrems, Capital | Owner's Equity Explanation |
| Nov.  1 | + $11,000 | | | | = | + | $11,000 | Initial investment |
| 5 | − 7,800 | | | + $ 7,800 | | | | |
| 9 | | | + $450 | | + $ 450 | | | |
| 11 | + 2,100 | | | | | + 2,100 | Dance lesson revenues |
| 15 | − 1,100 | | | | | − 1,100 | Utilities expense |
| 17 | | + $6,300 | | | | + 6,300 | Dance lesson revenues |
| 19 | − 200 | | | | − 200 | | |
| 20 | + 3,350 | − 3,350 | | | | | |
| Totals | $ 7,350 + | $2,950 + | $450 + | $ 7,800 = | $ 250 + | $18,300 | |
| | | | | $18,550 | = | $18,550 | |

While the total assets do not change, their composition does. The asset Cash is increased by $3,350 and the asset Accounts Receivable is decreased by a like amount. The collection of receivables and the payment of accounts payable are two of the most common business transactions.

NOVEMBER 21   Abrems withdraws $500 from the business for her personal use.

## THE MARY ABREMS DANCE STUDIO
### Financial Transaction Worksheet
### Month of November 1998

| | | Assets | | | = | Liabilities | + | Owner's Equity | |
|---|---|---|---|---|---|---|---|---|---|
| Date | Cash | + Accounts Receivable | + Office Supplies on Hand | + Office Equipment | = | Accounts Payable | + | Abrems, Capital | Owner's Equity Explanation |
| Nov. 1 | + $11,000 | | | | = | | + | $11,000 | Initial investment |
| 5 | − 7,800 | | | + $ 7,800 | | | | | |
| 9 | | | + $450 | | | + $ 450 | | | |
| 11 | + 2,100 | | | | | | | + 2,100 | Dance lesson revenues |
| 15 | − 1,100 | | | | | | | − 1,100 | Utilities expense |
| 17 | | + $6,300 | | | | | | + 6,300 | Dance lesson revenues |
| 19 | − 200 | | | | | − 200 | | | |
| 20 | + 3,350 | − 3,350 | | | | | | | |
| 21 | − 500 | | | | | | | − 500 | Withdrawals |
| Totals | $ 6,850 + | $2,950 + | $450 + | $ 7,800 | = | $ 250 | + | $17,800 | |
| | | | | $18,050 | = | $18,050 | | | |

A **withdrawal** of cash or other assets for personal use is the means by which owners of business entities receive a distribution of the profits. Remember the transaction of Nov. 1, in which Abrems invested $11,000. At that time we increased cash by $11,000 and also increased Abrems, Capital, by a like amount. This was an investment by the owner. It was *not* revenue. Abrems simply transferred funds from her personal account to the checking account of the business. A cash withdrawal, such as we have in this transaction of Nov. 21, is exactly the opposite. The $500 cash withdrawal transaction results in a reduction of both Cash and Abrems, Capital.

NOVEMBER 24 Abrems pays her dance instructors salaries in the amount of $2,500 on the last Friday of the month.

## THE MARY ABREMS DANCE STUDIO
### Financial Transaction Worksheet
### Month of November 1998

| | | Assets | | | = | Liabilities | + | Owner's Equity | |
|---|---|---|---|---|---|---|---|---|---|
| Date | Cash | + Accounts Receivable | + Office Supplies on Hand | + Office Equipment | = | Accounts Payable | + | Abrems, Capital | Owner's Equity Explanation |
| Nov. 1 | + $11,000 | | | | = | | + | $11,000 | Initial investment |
| 5 | − 7,800 | | | + $ 7,800 | | | | | |
| 9 | | | + $450 | | | + $ 450 | | | |
| 11 | + 2,100 | | | | | | | + 2,100 | Dance lesson revenues |
| 15 | − 1,100 | | | | | | | − 1,100 | Utilities expense |
| 17 | | + $6,300 | | | | | | + 6,300 | Dance lesson revenues |
| 19 | − 200 | | | | | − 200 | | | |
| 20 | + 3,350 | − 3,350 | | | | | | | |
| 21 | − 500 | | | | | | | − 500 | Withdrawal |
| 24 | − 2,500 | | | | | | | − 2,500 | Salary expense |
| Totals | $ 4,350 + | $2,950 + | $450 + | $ 7,800 | = | $ 250 | + | $15,300 | |
| | | | | $15,550 | = | $15,550 | | | |

The payment of employees' salaries is called Salary Expense. It reflects a reduction in owner's equity as well as a reduction in cash. By providing their labor to Abrems for the month, the employees have created an expense of the business.

**NOVEMBER 27**  The Summit Advertising Agency submitted a bill to Abrems for $400 worth of advertising for this first month of operations. Abrems will pay this bill next month.

### THE MARY ABREMS DANCE STUDIO
### Financial Transaction Worksheet
### Month of November 1998

| | Assets | | | | = Liabilities + | Owner's Equity | |
|---|---|---|---|---|---|---|---|
| Date | Cash | + Accounts Receivable + | Office Supplies on Hand + | Office Equipment = | Accounts Payable + | Abrems, Capital | Owner's Equity Explanation |
| Nov. 1 | + $11,000 | | | | = | + $11,000 | Initial investment |
| 5 | – 7,800 | | | + $ 7,800 | | | |
| 9 | | | + $450 | | + $ 450 | | |
| 11 | + 2,100 | | | | | + 2,100 | Dance lesson revenues |
| 15 | – 1,100 | | | | | – 1,100 | Utilities expense |
| 17 | | + $6,300 | | | | + 6,300 | Dance lesson revenues |
| 19 | – 200 | | | | – 200 | | |
| 20 | + 3,350 | – 3,350 | | | | | |
| 21 | – 500 | | | | | – 500 | Withdrawal |
| 24 | – 2,500 | | | | | – 2,500 | Salary expense |
| 27 | | | | | + 400 | – 400 | Advertising expense |
| Totals | $ 4,350 + | $2,950 + | $450 + | $ 7,800 = | $ 650 + | $14,900 | |
| | | | | $15,550 = | $15,550 | | |

Even though cash has not been paid, The Mary Abrems Dance Studio has incurred an expense in the amount of $400 by accepting Summit's advertising services. This expense results in a decrease in owner's equity and a corresponding increase in the liability Accounts Payable. The liability will be paid next month.

**ASK YOURSELF ▶**

1. **What is the basic accounting model?**
2. **What is a financial transaction worksheet?**
3. **Assets may be acquired in three ways. What are they?**

## PREPARING THE FINANCIAL STATEMENTS FROM THE TRANSACTION WORKSHEET

Learning Objective **6**

Explain how the basic financial statements relate to one another and prepare these statements

At the end of the month, after the last transaction has been recorded on the financial transaction worksheet and the various columns have been totaled, it is a relatively simple matter to prepare the financial statements—the income statement, the statement of owner's equity, and the balance sheet. We will not prepare a statement of cash flows here.

## The Income Statement

The income statement is prepared first. All the data for the income statement shown in Exhibit 6 are taken from the account Abrems, Capital, since revenues are increases in capital and expenses represent decreases in capital equity. Only revenues and expenses are shown on the income statement. The investments and withdrawals are not shown on the income statement, since they are neither revenues nor expenses.

**Exhibit 6** The Principal Financial Statements

### THE MARY ABREMS DANCE STUDIO
### Income Statement
### Month Ended November 30, 1998

| | | |
|---|---:|---:|
| Revenue: | | |
| Dance Lesson Revenues | | $8,400 |
| Expenses: | | |
| Salary Expense | $2,500 | |
| Utilities Expense | 1,100 | |
| Advertising Expense | 400 | |
| Total Expenses | | 4,000 |
| Net Income | | $4,400 |

### THE MARY ABREMS DANCE STUDIO
### Statement of Owner's Equity
### Month Ended November 30, 1998

| | |
|---|---:|
| Abrems, Capital, Nov. 1 | $ −0− |
| Add:  Investments | 11,000 |
| Net Income | 4,400 |
| Total | $15,400 |
| Less:  Withdrawals | 500 |
| Abrems, Capital, Nov. 30 | $14,900 |

### THE MARY ABREMS DANCE STUDIO
### Balance Sheet
### November 30, 1998

| Assets | | Liabilities and Owner's Equity | |
|---|---:|---|---:|
| | | **Liabilities** | |
| Cash | $ 4,350 | Accounts Payable | $ 650 |
| Accounts Receivable | 2,950 | **Owner's Equity** | |
| Office Supplies on Hand | 450 | | |
| Office Equipment | 7,800 | Abrems, Capital | 14,900 |
| | | Total Liabilities and | |
| Total Assets | $15,550 | Owner's Equity | $15,550 |

## The Statement of Owner's Equity

Once you have prepared the income statement, you have the net income (or net loss) figure you need to prepare the **statement of owner's equity,** which is done next. This statement, which shows how the investment of a business's owner changes over time, reflects the increases in capital due to net income—the excess of revenues over expenses—and investments by the owner, and the decreases due to withdrawals. The statement of owner's equity shown in Exhibit 6 explains how Abrems, Capital, increased from a $0 balance on Nov. 1 to a $14,900 balance on Nov. 30. The investment and withdrawal data for this statement are taken from the financial transaction worksheet, and the net income from the income statement.

## The Balance Sheet

After completing the statement of owner's equity, you have the balance of the capital account, which you need to prepare the balance sheet. The balance sheet is simply the totals of the left side of the financial transaction worksheet—the asset accounts—and the right side—the liability and owner's equity accounts. You could prepare the balance sheet directly from a financial transaction worksheet, but that is not done in business, as we will see in the next few chapters.

**ASK YOURSELF ▶**

1. **How is the income statement prepared from a financial transaction worksheet?**
2. **Why is the income statement prepared before the statement of owner's equity?**
3. **Why is the statement of owner's equity prepared before the balance sheet?**

## SUMMARY

- The **income statement,** the **statement of owner's equity,** the **balance sheet,** and the **statement of cash flows** are the principal financial statements generated by a business entity's accounting activity.
- The **income statement** compares **revenues** (the inflow of cash or other properties) earned during a specified period of time with **expenses,** the cost of goods sold or services rendered during the same period of time.
- The **statement of owner's equity** shows how the capital account has changed over a period of time. The capital account is increased by investments from the owner and net income. It is decreased by withdrawals and net losses.
- The **balance sheet** shows the financial position of a business entity at a specific date. It lists assets, liabilities, and owner's equity. **Assets** are the economic resources owned by the entity that are expected to provide future benefits. **Liabilities** are a business's debts. **Owner's equity** is the owner's interest or investment in the business entity.
- On the balance sheet, the total of the assets must equal the sum of the liabilities and the owner's equity. This is called the **balance sheet equation.**
- Generally accepted accounting principles (GAAP) have been developed over the years to provide a rational system of financial reporting so that the financial statements will be useful to investors and creditors.

  The **cost principle** states that assets acquired by a business entity are to be recorded at the exchange price paid for them and that this cost, once recorded, will remain unchanged.

The **objectivity principle** requires that the exchange price of transactions be independently verifiable through the evidence of invoices, deeds, transfers of title, or other business documents.

The **business entity concept** considers a business to be separate and distinct from its owners for accounting purposes.

The **going concern concept** assumes that the entity will continue to exist indefinitely.

The **stable dollar concept** assumes that the basic unit of measure employed in recording financial transactions—the dollar—does not change in value over time.

- Before the financial statements of economic entities can be prepared, the business transactions must be recorded, classified, and summarized within the framework of the **basic accounting model,** which is expressed by the balance sheet equation:

$$\text{Assets} = \text{Liabilities} + \text{Owner's Equity}$$

- Each transaction requires two elements to be considered, which will result in increases or decreases in assets, liabilities, or owner's equity. This dual nature of business transactions gives rise to the term **double-entry accounting.**
- After all business transactions have been recorded, classified, and summarized, the financial statements can be prepared.
- The income statement is prepared first because it yields the net income for the period. The net income is used on the statement of owner's equity to compute the ending capital account, which in turn will appear on the balance sheet.

## 7 KEY TERMS

**Account**
A specific asset, liability, owner's equity, revenue, or expense item used to accumulate money amounts.

**Accounts payable**
Amounts due to creditors for goods and services acquired but not yet paid for.

**Accounts receivable**
Amounts due from customers for goods and services acquired but not yet paid for.

**Accrual basis of accounting**
The system of accounting where revenues are recorded when they are earned and expenses are recorded when they are incurred.

**Assets**
Economic resources owned by an economic entity that are expected to provide future benefits.

**Balance sheet**
The financial statement that lists the assets owned, liabilities owed, and owner's equity at a specific point in time.

**Basic accounting model**
The algebraic expression depicting the balance sheet relationship between assets and the sum of liabilities plus owner's equity:

$$\text{Assets} = \text{Liabilities} + \text{Owner's Equity}$$

**Business entity concept**
The basic generally accepted accounting principle which states that a business entity is considered to be separate and distinct from its owners for accounting purposes.

**Capital**
A term often used in accounting to mean owner's equity. Abrems, Capital, for example, is an owner's equity account.

**Cash basis of accounting**
The accounting system that records revenue only when cash is received and records expenses only when cash is paid.

**Cost principle**
The principle whereby assets acquired by a business entity are to be recorded at the price paid in exchange for such assets and continue to be reported at that price.

| | |
|---|---|
| **Double-entry accounting** | The process of recording each business transaction by balancing two elements within the basic accounting model. |
| **Expenses** | The outflow of economic resources (usually in the form of cash, accounts payable, or cost of products sold) consumed in providing products or services to customers. |
| **Financial transactions** | Events in which goods and services are exchanged between economic entities. |
| **Going concern concept** | The assumption that a business entity will be in existence for as long as the owner can reasonably expect future profits. |
| **Income statement** | The external financial statement designed to report the profitability of a business entity by contrasting revenue earned with expenses incurred to determine net income or loss. |
| **Liabilities** | Debts of economic entities. |
| **Net income** | The excess of revenue over expenses; also called profit. |
| **Net loss** | The excess of expenses over revenue. |
| **Objectivity principle** | The principle requiring that objective verifiable evidence must underlie the recording of business transactions. |
| **On account** | A promise to pay later for an asset acquired now. |
| **Owner's equity** | The amount of the owner's investment in a business. |
| **Note payable** | A written promise to repay a borrowed sum of money plus interest at a specified future date. |
| **Profit** | The excess of revenue over expenses; also called net income. |
| **Revenue** | The inflow of economic resources (usually cash or accounts receivable) for goods sold or services rendered. |
| **Stable dollar concept** | The assumption in accounting that the unit of measure—the dollar—does not change in value over time. |
| **Statement of owner's equity** | A statement showing how the investment of the owner of a business entity has changed over a given time period. |
| **Withdrawal** | Cash or other assets removed from a business entity by the owner. |

## DEMONSTRATION PROBLEM

Jim Syme began operating his consulting business on Jan. 1, 1998. At that time he invested $2,500 of his personal funds in the business, which he called Syme Consulting Service. Listed below are the transactions for the month of January.

Jan. 2 Acquired $1,400 of equipment on account.

4 Acquired $700 of supplies, paying cash.

10 Paid rent for the month, $470.

13 Received $1,600 cash for consulting services completed this date.

16 Completed three consulting assignments and billed clients a total of $2,700.

17 Paid $350 on the equipment acquired on Jan. 2.

20 Collected $1,500 from the consulting completed on Jan. 13.

24 Withdrew $600 from the business.

30 Paid $250 for advertising that appeared in the local newspaper.

**Required:**

1. Record the transactions listed above in a financial transaction worksheet.
2. Prepare an income statement, a statement of owner's equity, and a balance sheet.

### ■ Solution to Demonstration Problem

1.

### SYME CONSULTING SERVICE
### Financial Transaction Worksheet
### Month of January 1998

| | Assets | | | | = Liabilities + | Owner's Equity | |
|---|---|---|---|---|---|---|---|
| Date | Cash | + Accounts Receivable + | Supplies on Hand + | Equipment = | Accounts Payable + | Syme, Capital | Owner's Equity Explanation |
| Jan. 1 | + $2,500 | | | | | + $2,500 | Investment |
| 2 | | | | + $1,400 | + $1,400 | | |
| 4 | − 700 | | + $700 | | | | |
| 10 | − 470 | | | | | − 470 | Rent expense |
| 13 | + 1,600 | | | | | + 1,600 | Consulting revenue |
| 16 | | + $2,700 | | | | + 2,700 | Consulting revenue |
| 17 | − 350 | | | | − 350 | | |
| 20 | + 1,500 | − 1,500 | | | | | |
| 24 | − 600 | | | | | − 600 | Withdrawal |
| 30 | − 250 | | | | | − 250 | Advertising expense |
| Totals | $3,230 + | $1,200 + | $700 + | $1,400 = | $1,050 + | $5,480 | |
| | | | | $6,530 = | $6,530 | | |

2.

### SYME CONSULTING SERVICE
### Income Statement
### Month Ended January 31, 1998

| | | |
|---|---|---|
| Revenue: | | |
| Consulting Revenue | | $4,300 |
| Expenses: | | |
| Rent Expense | $470 | |
| Advertising Expense | 250 | |
| Total Expenses | | 720 |
| Net Income | | $3,580 |

### SYME CONSULTING SERVICE
### Statement of Owner's Equity
### Month Ended January 31, 1998

| | |
|---|---|
| Syme, Capital, Jan. 1 | $ –0– |
| Add: Investment | 2,500 |
| Net Income | 3,580 |
| Total | $6,080 |
| Less: Withdrawals | 600 |
| Syme, Capital, Jan. 31 | $5,480 |

### SYME CONSULTING SERVICE
### Balance Sheet
### January 31, 1998

| Assets | | Liabilities | |
|---|---|---|---|
| Cash | $3,230 | Accounts Payable | $1,050 |
| Accounts Receivable | 1,200 | **Owner's Equity** | |
| Supplies on Hand | 700 | | |
| Equipment | 1,400 | Syme, Capital | 5,480 |
| | | Total Liabilities and | |
| Total Assets | $6,530 | Owner's Equity | $6,530 |

---

## QUESTIONS FOR REVIEW AND FURTHER THOUGHT

### REVIEW QUESTIONS

1. What are the four principal financial statements of business entities? What financial information is contained on each statement?

2. What information is contained in the heading of a financial statement?

3. Explain the meaning of the terms *revenue* and *expense*.

4. The following items appear on a balance sheet: *assets, liabilities,* and *owner's equity.* Explain each of these terms.

5. What does the term *withdrawals* mean?

6. List and explain the five generally accepted accounting principles discussed in the chapter.

7. What is the basic accounting model?

8. When financial statements are prepared, the balance sheet is prepared last, after both the income statement and the statement of owner's equity. Why?

### QUESTIONS FOR FURTHER THOUGHT

1. Why is the basic accounting model important?

2. Why does each business transaction have two elements?

3. Describe a business transaction that would:
   a. Decrease an asset and increase a second asset.
   b. Increase an asset and increase owner's equity.
   c. Increase an asset and increase a liability.

4. In December the Julia Company reported cash sales of $60,000 and sales on account of $85,000; expenses incurred during December were $42,000, of which $23,000 was paid in cash. Determine the amount of revenue, expenses, and net income for the month.

5. The capital account of Austin Company amounted to $6,000 on Jan. 1 of the current year. By year-end the capital account amounted to $24,000. If Austin withdrew $15,000 during the year, what was the net income for the year?

### OBJECTIVE ASSIGNMENT

*True/False*   Indicate whether each statement below is *true* or *false* by placing a *T* or an *F* in the space provided.

_____ 1. Expenses represent the cash paid for goods sold or services rendered in the process of generating revenue.

_____ 2. According to the balance sheet equation, the assets of a business entity must always equal the liabilities.

_____ 3. The cost principle specifies that assets acquired by a business entity are to be recorded at the exchange price paid for them.

_____ 4. All financial transactions can be analyzed in terms of the basic accounting model.

_____ 5. The balance sheet generally is prepared before the statement of owner's equity.

*Multiple Choice*   Select the best choice to complete each statement or answer each question below. Write the letter corresponding to your choice in the space below.

_____ 1. On an income statement you would expect to find all of the following except:
   a. Assets            d. Net loss
   b. Revenues          e. All of the above
   c. Net income

_____ 2. Expenses can be defined as:
   a. Increases in owner's equity
   b. Decreases in owner's equity
   c. Outflows or using up of assets or incurrences of liabilities from delivering or producing goods or rendering services
   d. Inflows of assets from delivering or producing goods or rendering services
   e. None of the above

_____ 3. The objectivity principle states that:
   a. The cost of an asset must be determined by the objectives of the business entity.
   b. All business transactions must be recorded in accord with the objectives of the FASB.
   c. The value of costs and expenses must be determined by the objectives of the SEC.
   d. The cost of an asset must be established at values that can be confirmed by independently verifiable evidence.
   e. None of the above.

_____ 4. Accountants do not recognize that the value of the dollar changes over time. This concept is called the:
   a. Objectivity principle       d. Business entity concept
   b. Going concern concept       e. None of the above
   c. Cost principle

_____ 5. The components of the balance sheet equation are:
   a. Assets, revenues, and owner's equity
   b. Assets, liabilities, and owner's equity
   c. Investments, withdrawals, and net income
   d. Revenues, expenses, and net income
   e. None of the above

_____ 6. When an entity acquires office equipment for cash:
   a. Assets and owner's equity are increased.
   b. An asset is increased and a liability is decreased.
   c. One asset is increased while another is decreased.
   d. One asset is increased and another is also increased.
   e. None of the above.

_____ 7. When an entity receives cash for services performed:
   a. An asset is decreased.
   b. The owner's equity is increased.
   c. The owner's equity is decreased.
   d. Total assets remain unchanged.
   e. None of the above.

_____ 8. When an entity pays employees for their work, the effect is an increase in:
   a. Owner's equity       d. Liabilities
   b. Assets               e. None of the above
   c. Revenues

_____ 9. The basic financial statement, which is generally prepared first, is the:
   a. Income statement
   b. Statement of owner's equity
   c. Balance sheet
   d. Statement of cash flows
   e. None of the above

_____ 10. The statement of owner's equity provides:
   a. The net income to be entered on the income statement
   b. The withdrawals to be entered on the balance sheet
   c. The beginning capital balance to be entered on the balance sheet
   d. The amount of additional investments to be entered on the balance sheet
   e. None of the above

## EXERCISES

3  4† **Exercise 1:** The Three Elements of the Basic Accounting Model

In each of the following five situations, the dollar amount of one of the elements in the balance sheet is missing. Determine the missing amount.

a. A department store has assets of $60,000 and owner's equity of $45,000.
b. A real estate agency has liabilities of $73,000 and owner's equity of $41,000.
c. A plumbing contractor has assets of $27,300 and liabilities of $15,370.
d. A sporting goods store has liabilities of $14,700 and owner's equity of $3,650.
e. A movie theater has assets of $62,400 and liabilities of $23,700.

4  **Exercise 2:** Revenue and Expense Amounts

In each of the following five situations, the dollar amount of one of the elements in the income statement is missing. Determine the missing amount.

a. A pet store has revenues of $32,500 and expenses of $23,700.
b. An advertising agency has expenses of $16,300 and net income of $2,200.
c. A computer equipment store has expenses of $15,300 and a net loss of $2,750.
d. A retail store has revenues of $73,700 and net income of $16,800.
e. A convenience store has revenues of $36,200 and a net loss of $2,600.

4  **Exercise 3:** Transactions That Change the Basic Accounting Model

For each of the following five situations, describe a transaction that will result in the indicated change in the elements of the basic accounting model.

a. Increase an asset and increase owner's equity.
b. Increase one asset and decrease another asset.
c. Increase an asset and increase a liability.
d. Decrease an asset and decrease a liability.
e. Decrease an asset and decrease owner's equity.

4  **Exercise 4:** Transaction Effects on the Basic Accounting Model

The transactions listed below were completed by the Dennison Company during the month of August of the current year. For each of the transactions, indicate the effect on the basic elements of the balance sheet equation, using (+) for an increase, (−) for a decrease, and (0) for no change. Use the headings shown at the right to record your answers.

† The numbers in the margin refer to the Learning Objectives.

| Date | | | Assets | Liabilities | Owner's Equity |
|------|---|--|--------|-------------|----------------|
| Aug. | 1 | Purchased supplies for cash. | ___ | ___ | ___ |
| | 3 | Purchased equipment on account. | ___ | ___ | ___ |
| | 7 | Paid a liability. | ___ | ___ | ___ |
| | 9 | Collected an accounts receivable. | ___ | ___ | ___ |
| | 14 | Received cash for services rendered. | ___ | ___ | ___ |
| | 17 | Invested additional cash in the business. | ___ | ___ | ___ |
| | 21 | Incurred expenses to be paid next month. | ___ | ___ | ___ |
| | 24 | Withdrew cash from the business. | ___ | ___ | ___ |
| | 25 | Billed a customer for services rendered. | ___ | ___ | ___ |
| | 28 | Received a bill for utilities expense used this month. | ___ | ___ | ___ |
| | 30 | Acquired equipment by issuing a note payable. | ___ | ___ | ___ |

2  **Exercise 5:** GAAP Violations

For each of the following independent situations, indicate which of the five generally accepted accounting principles you studied in this chapter has been violated.

a. Included on the balance sheet of Reeves Real Estate Agency was the cash from Mr. Reeves's personal checking account.
b. On the date that $15,000 of equipment was acquired, an expense was recorded for that amount.
c. Deltonics Company received equipment from the owner for use in the conduct of the business. Since no money was involved, the owner placed a value of $15,000 on the equipment.
d. Due to the effect of inflation, the value of land reflected on the company's balance sheet is increased. (List three principles.)

5  **Exercise 6:** Transactions in a Completed Worksheet

Nine transactions are reflected in the October transaction worksheet of the Justin Company presented below.

**THE JUSTIN COMPANY**
**Financial Transaction Worksheet**
**Month of October 1998**

| Transaction Date | Assets | | | | = Liabilities + | Owner's Equity |
|------------------|--------|---|---|---|-----------------|----------------|
| | Cash | + Accounts Receivable | + Supplies on Hand | + Office Equipment | Accounts Payable + | Justin, Capital |
| Beginning Bal. | $1,500 | + $1,750 | + $ 450 | + $15,300 | $6,000 | $13,000 |
| Oct. 1 | + 700 | − 700 | | | | |
| 4 | − 500 | | + 500 | | | |
| 5 | | | | + 2,500 | + 2,500 | |
| 11 | | + 2,450 | | | | + 2,450 |
| 12 | | | | | + 1,600 | − 1,600 |
| 23 | − 650 | | | | − 650 | |
| 25 | | | + 370 | | + 370 | |
| 30 | − 250 | | | | | − 250 |
| 31 | − 500 | | | | | − 500 |
| Totals | $ 300 + | $3,500 + | $1,320 + | $17,800 = | $9,820 + | $13,100 |

a. Describe each of these transactions. The transaction on Oct. 31 is the only transaction affecting the capital account that does not affect net income.
b. What was the change in the Cash account for the month? In Justin, Capital?
c. Determine the amount of net income for the month.

▶ *(Check Figure: Net income = $600)*

6 **Exercise 7:** Preparing a Balance Sheet from Account Data

Eight balance sheet items are listed below. Use this information to prepare a balance sheet for the Akins Company dated May 31, 1998.

| | | | |
|---|---|---|---|
| Office Supplies on Hand | $ 750 | Land | $ 9,000 |
| Cash | 1,500 | Equipment | 20,000 |
| Accounts Payable | 21,500 | Building | 15,000 |
| Accounts Receivable | 6,100 | Akins, Capital | 30,850 |

▶ *(Check Figure: Total assets = $52,350)*

6 **Exercise 8:** Preparing an Income Statement from Account Data

The information presented below is taken from the records of the Biltmore Company. Using this information, prepare an income statement for the year ended Dec. 31, 1998.

| | | | |
|---|---|---|---|
| Salaries Expense | $17,300 | Consulting Revenues | $26,700 |
| Rent Expense | 4,800 | Utilities Expense | 1,800 |
| Advertising Expense | 2,600 | | |

▶ *(Check Figure: Net income = $200)*

6 **Exercise 9:** Preparing a Statement of Owner's Equity

On Oct. 1, 1997, the balance in Amy Kelly's capital account in her Fashion Jewelry Company mounted to $2,800. One year later the account had increased to $4,650. Kelly had made additional capital investments totaling $1,500 during the year and had withdrawn $750 from the business. Using this information, prepare a statement of owner's equity for the year ended Sept. 30, 1998.

## PROBLEMS: SET A

6† **Problem A1:** Preparing an Income Statement and a Statement of Owner's Equity

The revenue and expense accounts of Reedner Real Estate Agency, which are listed below, represent the activity for the month of June 1998.

| | | | |
|---|---|---|---|
| Advertising Expense | $ 16,300 | Rent Expense | $ 4,800 |
| Commissions Expense | 47,500 | Salaries Expense | 26,400 |
| Office Supplies Expense | 2,700 | Utilities Expense | 4,200 |
| Real Estate Fees Earned | 125,000 | | |

**Required:**

1. Prepare an income statement for the month ended June 30, 1998.
2. On June 1, 1998, Reedner had a $12,300 balance in her capital account. During the month Reedner invested an additional $1,600 in the business and withdrew $25,000. Prepare a statement of owner's equity for the month ended June 30, 1998.

▶ *(Check Figure: Reedner, Capital, June 30, 1998 = $12,000)*

† The numbers in the margin refer to the Learning Objectives.

6  **Problem A2:** Preparing a Balance Sheet

The balance sheet accounts as of July 31, 1998, for the Altoona Company are as follows:

| | | | |
|---|---|---|---|
| Altoona, Capital | $35,630 | Cash | $7,820 |
| Office Equipment | 16,730 | Accounts Payable | 6,750 |
| Delivery Truck | 15,900 | Salaries Payable | 2,170 |
| Accounts Receivable | 14,180 | Delivery Supplies on Hand | 1,050 |
| Notes Payable | 12,000 | Office Supplies on Hand | 870 |

**Required:**

Prepare a balance sheet as of July 31, 1998.

▶ *(Check Figure: Total assets = $56,550)*

5  **Problem A3:** Recording Transactions

On May 1, 1998, Janice Walters opened a videotape rental store by investing $2,500 cash from her personal savings account. The name of the store is Walters Video. During the month of May the following activities took place:

May  1  Acquired office supplies on account, $670.

4  Acquired videotapes costing $2,350, on account.

5  Paid $850 to creditors.

8  Received $780 cash from video rental fees.

11  Billed Langley Corporation for video rentals, $1,050.

16  Paid salaries, $650.

17  Collected $770 from Langley Corporation.

23  Walters withdrew $470 from the business.

24  Paid rent for the month, $415.

30  Paid the telephone bill for the month, $175.

**Required:**

1. Record the transactions for the month of May 1998, using a financial transaction worksheet. Use the following accounts: Cash; Accounts Receivable; Supplies on Hand; Videotapes; Accounts Payable; Walters, Capital.

   ▶ *(Check Figure: Total assets = $4,790)*
2. Determine the amount of net income for the month.

   ▶ *(Check Figure: Net income = $590)*

**5 6 Problem A4:** Recording Transactions and Preparing Financial Statements

On Nov. 1, 1998, William Jennings purchased a pest-control company from its previous owner. Jennings paid $5,200 cash from his personal savings account for assets consisting of pesticide supplies, $1,750, and spraying equipment, $3,450. The company is to be operated under the name of Jennings Pest Control. The following transactions occurred during the month of November:

Nov.  1   Jennings invested an additional $2,300 in the business.

      2   Pest control service for customers was done on account, $420.

      3   Pesticide supplies were acquired on account, $395.

      6   Spraying equipment costing $670 was acquired on account.

      8   Pest control service for customers was rendered for cash in the amount of $870.

     10   Repairs were made to the equipment; $285 was paid in cash.

     14   Paid $170 cash on account due for pesticide supplies acquired on Nov. 3.

     15   Rendered pest control service for customers on account, $630.

     17   Paid for utilities, $95.

     24   Paid $515 in wages.

     27   Withdrew $600 for personal use.

     29   Collected $120 for pest control done on Nov. 2.

**Required:**

1. Record the transactions in a financial transaction worksheet. The following accounts will be needed: Cash; Accounts Receivable; Pesticide Supplies on Hand; Spraying Equipment; Accounts Payable; and Jennings, Capital.
2. Prepare the following statements:
   a. An income statement for the month ended Nov. 30, 1998
   b. A statement of owner's equity for the month ended Nov. 30, 1998
   c. A balance sheet as of Nov. 30, 1998

   ▶ *(Check Figure: Total assets = $8,820)*

**5 6 Problem A5:** Entering Initial Balances in a Transaction Worksheet, Recording Transactions, and Preparing Financial Statements

The Dec. 31, 1997, balance sheet for Stewart Sprinkler Service is presented below:

| STEWART SPRINKLER SERVICE | |
|---|---|
| Balance Sheet | |
| December 31, 1997 | |

| **Assets** | | **Liabilities** | |
|---|---|---|---|
| Cash. . . . . . . . . . . . . . . . . . . . . . | $ 1,570 | Notes Payable. . . . . . . . . . . . . . | $ 5,000 |
| Accounts Receivable. . . . . . . . | 3,960 | Accounts Payable . . . . . . . . . . | 2,230 |
| Sprinkler Supplies on Hand . . . | 1,970 | Total Liabilities . . . . . . . . | $ 7,230 |
| Sprinkler Equipment . . . . . . . . | 5,700 | | |
| Truck . . . . . . . . . . . . . . . . . . . . | 7,100 | **Owner's Equity** | |
| | | Stewart, Capital. . . . . . . . . . . . | 13,070 |
| | | Total Liabilities and | |
| Total Assets. . . . . . . . . . . . . . . | $20,300 | Owner's Equity. . . . . . . . . . . | $20,300 |

During the month of January 1998, the following transactions took place:

Jan. 2 Billed Hunter's Green Country Club for sprinkler services rendered, $920.

4 Collected $1,950 from accounts receivable due.

5 Acquired sprinkler supplies on account, $760.

9 Acquired sprinkler equipment for $4,200 by issuing a note payable for that amount.

12 Billed Greenleaf Apartments $960 for sprinkler services rendered.

16 Received a $560 bill for advertising for the month of January.

18 Received $870 cash from the Plaza Exchange Center for sprinkler services rendered this date.

19 Stewart withdrew $1,500 from the business for personal use.

24 Paid $1,000 due on the note payable.

25 In connection with the note payable above, paid $100 interest expense.

30 Paid $210 for utilities.

31 Paid salaries of $860.

**Required:**

1. Record the amounts from the Dec. 31, 1997, balance sheet in a financial transaction worksheet
2. Record the transactions for the month of January 1998.
3. Prepare the following statements:
   a. An income statement for the month ended Jan. 31, 1998.
   b. A statement of changes in owner's equity for the month ended Jan. 31, 1998.
   c. A balance sheet as of Jan. 31, 1998.

   ▶ *(Check Figure: Total assets = $24,340)*

6 **Problem A6:** Preparing the Financial Statements from an Alphabetical Listing of Accounts

The accounts from the balance sheet, statement of owner's equity, and income statement of Alfred Freeman, CPA, are as follows:

| | | | |
|---|---|---|---|
| Accounts Payable | $ 6,350 | Office Supplies Expense | $ 9,600 |
| Accounts Receivable | 19,800 | Office Supplies on Hand | 2,800 |
| Auditing Fees Earned | 136,150 | Professional Development | |
| Building | 75,000 | Expense | 8,650 |
| Cash | 11,850 | Rent Expense | 5,250 |
| Freeman, Capital, | | Salary Expense | 73,500 |
| Jan. 1, 1998 | 130,850 | Salaries Payable | 3,050 |
| Land | 7,500 | Travel Expense | 4,100 |
| Notes Receivable | 6,000 | Utilities Expense | 1,800 |
| Office Equipment | 36,250 | Withdrawals | 16,500 |

During the year just ended (Dec. 31, 1998), Freeman invested an additional $2,200 in the business.

**Required:**

Use these data to prepare the three principal financial statements for the year ended Dec. 31, 1998.

▶ *(Check Figure: Total assets = $159,200)*

## PROBLEMS: SET B

6† **Problem B1:** Preparing an Income Statement and a Statement of Owner's Equity

Listed below are the revenue and expense accounts of Braxton Body and Paint Shop for the month ended Mar. 31, 1998:

| | | | |
|---|---|---|---|
| Auto Repair Fees Earned | $37,300 | Paint Expense | $6,300 |
| Salaries Expense | 11,500 | Insurance Expense | 4,700 |
| Repair Parts Expense | 7,400 | Utilities Expense | 1,570 |

**Required:**

1. Prepare an income statement for the month ended Mar. 31, 1998.
2. Assume that on Mar. 1, 1998, Braxton had a balance of $6,250 in his Capital account, and that on Mar. 10 he invested another $1,500 into the business. Further assume that on Mar. 25, Braxton withdrew $500 from the business. Prepare a statement of owner's equity.

▶ *(Check Figure: Braxton, Capital, Mar. 31, 1998 = $13,080)*

6 **Problem B2:** Preparing a Balance Sheet

Listed below in alphabetical order are 10 accounts that are to appear on the balance sheet of the Dalton Company as of Apr. 30, 1998.

| | | | |
|---|---|---|---|
| Accounts Payable | $ 3,540 | Equipment | $21,300 |
| Accounts Receivable | 12,120 | Land | 7,500 |
| Cash | 5,920 | Notes Payable | 25,700 |
| Building | 19,000 | Salaries Payable | 950 |
| Dalton, Capital | 36,700 | Supplies on Hand | $1,050 |

**Required:**

Prepare a balance sheet as of Apr. 30, 1998.

▶ *(Check Figure: Total assets = $66,890)*

5 **Problem B3:** Recording Transactions

Terry Getz formed the Gainesville Sign Company on Oct. 1, 1998. He deposited $2,500 into the Gator National Bank in the name of the new business entity. During the month of October 1998, the following transactions occurred:

Oct. 2 Acquired a used truck in the amount of $1,950 on account.

3 Acquired supplies for cash, $570.

9 Received $875 cash for signs painted this date.

10 Paid the month's rent, $250.

11 Painted signs for Nexto Corporation on account, $1,700.

12 Paid $550 on account from Oct. 2.

16 Withdrew $250 for personal use.

23 Collected $350 from Nexto Corporation.

27 Paid salaries of $570 for the month.

30 Paid the local telephone company $75 for service for the month of October.

31 Paid a bill from the local radio station for $55 of advertising for the month of October.

† The numbers in the margin refer to the Learning Objectives.

**Required:**

1. Establish the following accounts in a financial transaction worksheet: Cash, Accounts Receivable, Supplies on Hand, Truck, Accounts Payable, and Getz, Capital. Record in the worksheet the transactions listed above.

   ▶ *(Check Figure: Total assets = $5,275)*

2. By analyzing the changes in Waldman's capital account, determine the amount of net income for the month.

   ▶ *(Check Figure: Net income = $1,625)*

**5 6   Problem B4:** Recording Transactions and Preparing Financial Statements

Tom Anderson withdrew $2,500 from his personal savings account on June 1, 1998, and deposited the cash in a new account for his newly established company, Anderson Carpet Cleaning Service. During the month of June, the following transactions occurred:

June  1   Paid rent for office space for the month, $250.

      2   Acquired office supplies on account, $450.

      5   Acquired a used truck for $5,000 by issuing a note payable in that amount, which will be due on May 31, 1999.

      6   Received cash in the amount of $1,200 for carpet cleaning services rendered to the First National Bank building.

      9   Paid $150 on account for supplies acquired on June 2.

     13   Billed clients $3,250 for carpet cleaning services rendered.

     15   Paid telephone bill of $120.

     16   Paid salaries of $640.

     20   Received $2,150 cash from clients billed on June 13.

     23   Anderson withdrew $750 from the business.

     28   Received a $560 invoice for repairs expense for the truck.

**Required:**

1. Using a financial transaction worksheet, record the transactions listed above. Use the following accounts: Cash, Accounts Receivable, Office Supplies on Hand, Truck, Notes Payable, Accounts Payable, and Anderson, Capital.
2. Prepare the following three financial statements:
   a. An income statement for the month ended June 30, 1998
   b. A statement of equity for the month of June 30, 1998
   c. A balance sheet as of June 30, 1998

   ▶ *(Check Figure: Total assets = $10,490)*

**5 6** **Problem B5:** Entering Initial Balances in a Transaction Worksheet, Recording Transactions, and Preparing Financial Statements

Presented below is the Dec. 31, 1997, balance sheet for the Beaufort Nursing Home:

### BEAUFORT NURSING HOME
### Balance Sheet
### December 31, 1997

| Assets | | Liabilities | |
|---|---|---|---|
| Cash. | $ 1,600 | Notes Payable | $35,000 |
| Accounts Receivable | 16,500 | Accounts Payable | 4,700 |
| Supplies on Hand | 2,100 | Total Liabilities | $39,700 |
| Land. | 9,000 | **Owner's Equity** | |
| Nursing Home | 35,000 | | |
| Nursing Equipment | 16,000 | Beaufort, Capital | 40,500 |
| | | Total Liabilities and | |
| Total Assets | $80,200 | Owner's Equity | $80,200 |

During the month of January 1998, the following transactions took place:

Jan. 2 Acquired supplies on account, $1,750.

6 Collected $8,200 from patients for services provided in 1997.

10 Acquired nursing equipment on account, $3,500.

11 Billed patients $16,700 for nursing fees.

12 Paid $3,100 on accounts payable.

17 Paid nursing salaries, $2,400.

20 Paid utilities expense, $900.

25 Beaufort withdrew $1,000 from the business.

27 Received a bill from the Victor Company for $1,250, representing the amount of advertising expense incurred by the company for the month.

31 Paid $1,500 of the note payable.

**Required:**

1. Record the amounts from the Dec. 31, 1997, balance sheet in a financial transaction worksheet.
2. Record the transactions for the month of January 1998.
3. Prepare the following statements:
   a. An income statement for the month of January
   b. A statement of owner's equity for the month of January
   c. A balance sheet for Jan. 31, 1998

▶ *(Check Figure: Total assets = $93,250)*

6 **Problem B6:** Preparing the Financial Statements from an Alphabetical Listing of Accounts

A number of account balances are listed below. These accounts relate to Keenan Real Estate Company. During the year just ended, Keenan invested an additional $7,500 in the business.

| | | | |
|---|---|---|---|
| Accounts Payable | $12,250 | Land | $ 12,000 |
| Accounts Receivable | 21,900 | Miscellaneous Expense | 2,460 |
| Advertising Expense | 10,500 | Mortgage Payable | 39,500 |
| Building | 45,000 | Notes Payable | 21,300 |
| Cash | 3,620 | Office Supplies on Hand | 1,720 |
| Entertainment Expense | 16,400 | Real Estate Commissions | |
| Equipment | 21,700 | Earned | 143,750 |
| Interest Expense | 3,700 | Salaries Payable | 1,730 |
| Keenan, Capital, Dec. 31, | | Salary Expense | 67,320 |
| 1998 | x | Travel Expense | 15,900 |
| Keenan, Capital, Jan. 1, 1998 | 11,050 | Withdrawals | 14,860 |

**Required:**

Prepare the three principal financial statements from the data for the year ended Dec. 31, 1998.

▶ *(Check Figure: Total assets = $105,940)*

## DECISION PROBLEM

Manuel Martinez worked seventeen years for Apex Electronics as a guidance systems analyst. On Jan. 1, 1998, Manuel left Apex to form his own small company, specializing in consulting with defense contractors on guidance systems. The company was called Martinez Guidance Systems and was established with an initial investment of $80,000.

The following financial statements for the first year of business were prepared by Manuel's wife Rosa on Dec. 31, 1998.

### MARTINEZ GUIDANCE SYSTEMS
### Balance Sheet
### December 31, 1998

| Assets | | Liabilities | |
|---|---|---|---|
| Cash. . . . . . . . . . . . . . . . . . . . | $ 85,000 | Notes Payable . . . . . . . . . . . . | $ 40,000 |
| Accounts Receivable . . . . . . . | 14,000 | Accounts Payable . . . . . . . . . | 7,000 |
| Supplies on Hand . . . . . . . . . | 1,000 | Salaries Payable . . . . . . . . . . | 2,000 |
| Equipment . . . . . . . . . . . . . . . | 50,000 | Total Liabilities . . . . . . . . | $ 49,000 |
| | | **Owner's Equity** | |
| | | Martinez, Capital . . . . . . . . . . | 101,000 |
| | | Total Liabilities | |
| Total Assets . . . . . . . . . . . . . . | $150,000 | and Owner's Equity . . . . . . . . | $150,000 |

### MARTINEZ GUIDANCE SYSTEMS
### Income Statement and a List of Cash Receipts and Cash Payments
### For the Year Ended December 31, 1998

| Income Statement | | Cash Receipts and Payments | |
|---|---|---|---|
| Revenues: | | Cash received for consulting. . . | $56,000 |
| Consulting Fees Earned . . . . | $70,000 | | |
| | | Cash paid for salaries . . . . . . . . | $25,000 |
| Expenses: | | Cash paid for rent . . . . . . . . . . | 3,000 |
| Salaries Expense. . . . . . . . . . | $30,000 | Cash paid for supplies. . . . . . . . | 2,000 |
| Rent Expense . . . . . . . . . . . | 5,000 | Cash paid for equipment. . . . . . | 10,000 |
| Supplies Used . . . . . . . . . . . | 3,000 | Cash paid to owner . . . . . . . . . | 11,000 |
| Equipment Purchased . . . . . . | –0– | Total payments. . . . . . . . . | $51,000 |
| Withdrawals . . . . . . . . . . . . . | –0– | | |
| Total Expenses . . . . . . . . | $38,000 | | |
| Net Income . . . . . . . . . . . . . . . | $32,000 | Increase in cash for the year. . . | $ 5,000 |

### Required:

If Martinez had remained with Apex Electronics for the year 1998, he would have earned a salary of $35,000. Do you think that he has made a good decision in leaving Apex to start his own business? Provide reasons to support your answer.

## ETHICS CASE

At the Lexington Corporation's annual company picnic, Sally Overton, the corporate comptroller, and Bob Keller, the company's east coast regional marketing manager, were discussing Bob's recent vacation trip to Europe. Bob informed Sally that the trip had cost him less than $500, since he had used his airline frequent-flier plan to pay for the airfare and hotel accommodations. Bob said that he and his wife had taken a similar trip to South America just 2 months before.

Upon returning to the office, Sally began thinking about Bob's two vacations, and wondering how he could have accumulated so many frequent-flier miles in such a short time. She reviewed Bob's most recent business trip, from the corporate headquarters in Montvale, New Jersey, to Atlanta. She found that Bob's ticket had routed him from Newark Airport to St. Louis, to New Orleans, and then to Atlanta. The return trip was Atlanta to Houston to Pittsburgh to Newark. She knew that numerous direct flights had been available from Newark to Atlanta and back on the dates of Bob's trip.

Concerned, Sally then reviewed Bob's previous business trip, when he had taken his wife along to Detroit. The airline had charged $599 for one round-trip business-class ticket direct to Detroit and $25 for the companion ticket, for which Bob had paid. Normally, a round-trip coach-class ticket to Detroit costs $399.

**Required:**

Discuss the following questions:

1. Who should receive the benefit of the frequent-flier mileage, Lexington Corporation or Bob Keller?
2. What is the cost to Lexington of its employees' personal use of the frequent-flier benefit?
3. What cost does the consumer of Lexington's products bear for the employees' use of frequent-flier programs?
4. Should Lexington require its employees to enroll in frequent-flier programs and turn in their accumulated mileage to Lexington for use on subsequent business trips?
5. What ethical issues do you see arising from Bob's two business trips?
6. Is there an ethical issue on the part of the airlines in offering the frequent-flier program?
7. What should Sally Overton do?

## OBJECTIVE ASSIGNMENT ANSWERS

### True/False

1. F  2. F  3. T  4. T  5. F

### Multiple Choice

1. a  2. c  3. d  4. e  5. b
6. c  7. b  8. e  9. a  10. e

# Analyzing and Recording Business Transactions

**LEARNING OBJECTIVES**

After studying this chapter, you should be able to do the following:

1 Explain the meaning of the term *account*

2 Prepare a chart of accounts

3 List the rules for debits and credits

4 Describe how business transactions are recorded using the double-entry accounting system

5 Distinguish between a ledger and a journal

6 Prepare a trial balance and financial statements

7 Describe how errors are found

8 Define the key terms listed at the end of the chapter

**CHAPTER OUTLINE**

**THE ACCOUNT** • **THE GENERAL LEDGER** • How Accounts Are Classified in the General Ledger • The Chart of Accounts • **DEBIT AND CREDIT** • **REVENUES AND EXPENSES** • **NORMAL BALANCES** • **RECORDING TRANSACTIONS: AN ILLUSTRATION** • **STANDARD LEDGER ACCOUNT FORMAT** • **THE JOURNAL** • Journalizing • Posting • **THE TRIAL BALANCE** • **ERRORS** • Common Types of Errors • Finding Errors • **SOME MINOR PROCEDURAL POINTS** • **REVIEW OF THE STEPS IN THE ACCOUNTING PROCESS**

The balance sheet, the income statement, the statement of owner's equity, and the statement of cash flows may all be prepared from the information generated by recording business transactions on financial transaction worksheets. But preparing financial statements from transaction worksheets, for any but the simplest of business entities, would be extremely cumbersome and impractical. Consequently, a simpler, more efficient method was developed long ago. This procedure is the basis for all accounting systems, from the small retail store employing a part-time bookkeeper to the giant multinational corporation using the latest computer technology.

The procedure, called the *double-entry accounting system,* is the subject of this chapter. The **double-entry accounting system** is a method of recording business transactions so that each transaction has two parts, debits and credits. The sum of the debit parts must always equal the sum of the credit parts. The double-entry system was invented several hundred years ago, in the days of quill pens and ledger books. Of course, anything that can be done with a pen-and-ink system can be done by a computer faster and more accurately. Today's accounting systems use computers to record, compile, classify, summarize, and prepare financial statements. But the programmed instructions for the computers are based on the concepts of the double-entry system, so a thorough understanding of double-entry principles is essential in order to understand today's sophisticated computerized accounting systems.

Learning Objective 1

Explain the meaning of the term *account*

# 1 THE ACCOUNT

The account is the basic building block of any accounting system. An *account* is a separate record that is established for each of the individual items that appear on the financial statements. An account exists, therefore, for each asset, liability, owner's equity, revenue, and expense item. The account is used to record increases and decreases resulting from business transactions. For example, when cash is received, the transaction is reflected in the Cash account as an increase. When cash is paid, the Cash account is decreased. Thus, a record is available on a day-by-day basis that will provide management with information concerning a particular item. Questions such as

What is the amount of accounts payable?

Is the inventory level sufficient to meet this week's demand?

Is there adequate cash on hand to pay wages due today?

can each be answered by information contained in one of the accounts.

In its most elementary form, an account has three parts:

1. *The account title,* which is the name of a particular accounting element, such as Cash
2. *A place to record increases* in the monetary amounts in the account and the date of the increase
3. *A place to record decreases* in the monetary amounts in the account and the date of the decrease

The elementary form of the account is shown below. The title of the account in this example is Cash. On the left side of the account are three accounting entries representing increases to this account. On the right side are two accounting entries representing decreases to this account.

|  | Cash |  |
|---|---|---|
| **Increases in Cash** | | **Decreases in Cash** |

Oct.   1   Owner's Investment . . . . . .   4,350       Oct. 15   Salaries Paid . . . . . . . . . . .   1,400
      12   Cash Received                                    30   Rent Paid . . . . . . . . . . . . .     700
             for Services . . . . . . . . . . .   2,670
      25   Accounts Receivable
             Collected  . . . . . . . . . . . . .   1,360

*These figures are footings: the total of a column of figures*

*8,380*                                                                            *2,100*

Balance                                                 6,280

The total of the three left side entries amounts to $8,380, which is indicated by the *footing*. The term **footing** refers to the addition of a column of figures. The total of the entries on the right side of the account is $2,100, also indicated by the footing. Footings are shown in this text in *italic* type. In a manual system, footings are written in pencil so that they will not be confused with entries, which are written in ink.

Notice that plus and minus signs are not needed in this account. This is because only increases are entered on one side of the account and only decreases are entered on the other side. All increases are added together to obtain the $8,380, and all decreases are added together to obtain the $2,100. Notice also that dollar signs are not used in the account. Dollar signs are used only on the financial statements, to indicate either the start of a column of numbers or a total.

The net difference between increases and decreases in the Cash account is an increase, and that's why the balance of $6,280 is recorded on the Increases in Cash side. Of course, total decreases in cash cannot exceed total increases; as much as we might like to, we cannot spend more cash than we have!

Notice that the elementary form of the account looks like the letter *T*. For this reason it is referred to as a **T-account.** The T-account is used by accountants to analyze accounting problems and by instructors to teach accounting. It is not used by economic entities to record business transactions. In the classroom we can easily write a dozen T-accounts on the chalkboard to demonstrate an accounting problem. The same can be done on the back of an envelope by a practicing accountant.

## THE GENERAL LEDGER

A **ledger** is simply a group of related accounts, contained in a book or in a computer-readable format. A **general ledger** is a ledger book containing all the accounts of an economic entity that appear on the financial statements. In a double-entry accounting system, each account has a separate page in the general ledger. Accounts that have substantial activity, such as the Cash account, may have more than one page. The pages are typically looseleaf and of heavy construction so that they may be inserted and removed from the ledger as the need arises. In a computer system the accounts are on floppy disks, hard drives, or tapes.

### How Accounts Are Classified in the General Ledger

The accounts in the general ledger are arranged in the same order in which they will appear in the financial statements. Balance sheet accounts are placed first, followed by the income statement accounts.

**The Chart of Accounts**

Prepare a chart of accounts

The accounts used in the general ledger differ from one business entity to the next, depending on the nature of the business and the way it operates; on the size of the business; and on the amount of detail that management needs to make decisions.

To facilitate the recordkeeping process, the accounts in the general ledger are numbered as well as titled. The numbers are used to identify accounts in business documents, which is much easier than using account titles. The coding on an invoice for consulting services might have space to indicate in which account the revenue earned should be recorded. It is much easier to type account number 410 in that space than to write the account title "Revenue from Consulting Services."

Each business entity normally devises its own numbering system. Numbering existing accounts consecutively will present a problem when new accounts have to be added, as often happens with most business entities. What is needed is a successive numbering system that allows new numbers to be inserted within the sequence. For example, a typical numbering system will use a series of multidigit numbers, with the first digit in each number indicating the major classification of the general ledger. Asset accounts may begin with *100*, liabilities with *200*, owner's equity accounts *300*, revenues *400*, and expenses *500*.

The second digit will be used to represent subclassifications of each major account. For example, within the assets, *110* to *150* may be used to indicate a group of like assets, *160* to *190* to indicate another group.

With this type of successive numbering system, it is easy to add new accounts as the need arises. For example, if the asset account Notes Receivable from Officers is added, it might be assigned the account number 123—1 for asset, 2 for receivables, and 3 for the specific type of receivable. The use of account numbers is especially important when using computerized accounting systems. An economic entity's system of numbered general ledger accounts is called its **chart of accounts.** Exhibit 1 illustrates the chart of accounts for The Mary Abrems Dance Studio.

**Exhibit 1** The Mary Abrems Dance Studio Chart of Accounts

| Assets (110–190) | Liabilities (210–290) |
|---|---|
| 110 Cash | 210 Notes Payable |
| 120 Accounts Receivable | 220 Accounts Payable |
| 130 Office Supplies on Hand | 230 Unearned Dance Lesson Revenues |
| 140 Prepaid Rent | **Owner's Equity (310–390)** |
| 150 Office Equipment | 310 Abrems, Capital |
| | 320 Abrems, Withdrawals |
| | **Revenue (410–490)** |
| | 410 Dance Lesson Revenue |
| | **Expenses (510–590)** |
| | 510 Salary Expense |
| | 520 Utilities Expense |
| | 530 Advertising Expense |

1. What are accounts used for?
2. What are the three parts of an account?
3. Describe the term footing as applied to accounting.
4. What is a ledger? A general ledger?
5. Why would a business entity want a chart of accounts?

Learning Objective **3**

List the rules for debits and credits

## DEBIT AND CREDIT

Many students come to this part of their study of accounting with a preconceived notion about debits and credits. Some think that credits are good things to have, while debits should be avoided. Others think just the reverse. For the moment, put aside your previous ideas about these two basic terms, and start from the beginning with us.

Long ago, during the Renaissance, accountants decided that entries recorded on the *left side* of any account should be called *debits* and entries recorded on the *right side* of any account should be called *credits*. And that's the way it's been ever since—debits on the left and credits on the right.

Every account must be capable of reflecting increases and decreases in monetary amounts resulting from business transactions. But which side of the account should be used to show increases? Which side should show decreases?

We have to start somewhere, so why not start with the first accounts—assets. It would seem logical to record increases first, for we cannot decrease something we do not yet have. And it would also seem logical to start with the left side rather than the right, because that is the way we read—from left to right. This is the logic the early accountants followed, and it still applies today.

The *left* side, or **debit** side, of an *asset* account is used to record *increases*. The *right* side, or **credit** side, of an *asset* account is used to record *decreases*.

| ASSET ACCOUNTS | |
| --- | --- |
| **Debit Side** | **Credit Side** |
| Shows increases | Shows decreases |

Now, each financial transaction has two parts. When an asset is increased, something else must happen if the basic model is to remain in balance. Each transaction entry must be balanced by another entry—hence the term *double entry* system. To keep the accounting equation in balance when we *increase* an asset,

1. Another *asset* must *decrease,* or
2. A *liability* must *increase,* or
3. *Owner's equity* must *increase.*

When a transaction is recorded on the debit side of an asset account to show an increase and another asset decreases, we enter the decrease on the credit side. The equation is in balance when one asset is increased—*debited*—and a second asset is decreased—*credited*—by a like amount. An example would be the acquisition of equipment for $500 cash. The asset Equipment *increases* with a $500 *debit,* and the asset Cash *decreases* with a $500 *credit.* The debit equals the credit; the basic equation remains in balance.

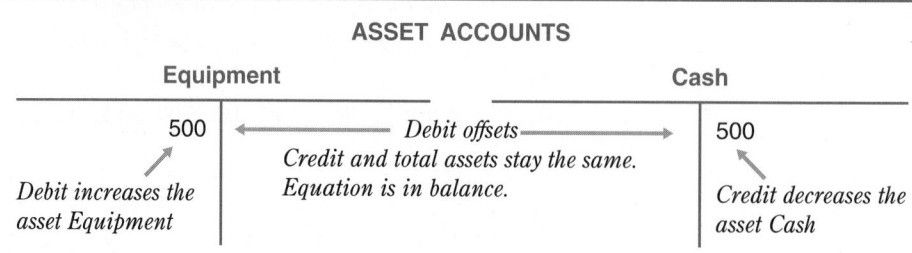

**ASSET ACCOUNTS**

Equipment | Cash

| 500 | ◄───── *Debit offsets* ─────► | 500 |
| *Debit increases the asset Equipment* | *Credit and total assets stay the same. Equation is in balance.* | *Credit decreases the asset Cash* |

If an increase in an asset account results from an increase in a liability account or an owner's equity account, we must use the *credit* side of that account to record increases. Why? Because the basic equation must balance. Liabilities and owner's equity accounts are on the *opposite* side of the basic equation from assets. If *debits* are used to *increase assets,* then the opposite, *credits,* must be used to *increase liabilities and owner's equity* on the opposite side of the equation to maintain equality.

For example, assume now that the equipment was acquired for $500 *on account.* The asset Equipment is still increased (debited), but Cash is no longer decreased. Instead, the liability Accounts Payable is increased—we owe $500 more. Our double entry is a debit to Equipment and a credit to Accounts Payable.

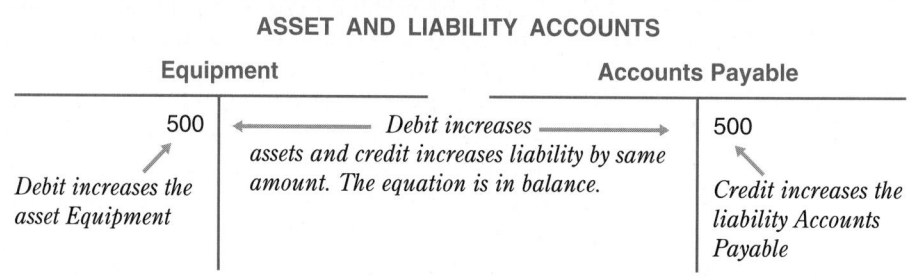

**ASSET AND LIABILITY ACCOUNTS**

Equipment | Accounts Payable

| 500 | ◄───── *Debit increases* ─────► | 500 |
| *Debit increases the asset Equipment* | *assets and credit increases liability by same amount. The equation is in balance.* | *Credit increases the liability Accounts Payable* |

Finally, assume that the equipment was acquired by the owner, Mr. Jenkins, who then contributes the asset to the business as part of his investment in the business. The asset Equipment is still increased (debited), and the owner's equity account Jenkins, Capital, is also increased to reflect his investment of the equipment. Our double entry is a debit to Equipment and a credit to Jenkins, Capital.

**ASSET AND OWNER'S EQUITY ACCOUNTS**

Equipment | Jenkins, Capital

| 500 | ◄───── *Debit increases* ─────► | 500 |
| *Debit increases the asset Equipment* | *assets and credit increases owner's equity by the same amount. The equation is in balance.* | *Credit increases the owner's equity, Jenkins, Capital* |

What we have just illustrated is referred to as the *rules of debit and credit.* It all flowed from the initial procedure of using debits to record increases in asset accounts.

Now let's summarize and expand on what we have developed. An account is debited (sometimes the word *charged* is used) when an amount is entered on the left side. An account is credited when an amount is entered on the right side. The word

**Exhibit 2** Double-Entry Requirement

| Assets | | | Liabilities | | | Owner's Equity | |
|---|---|---|---|---|---|---|---|
| **Debit** (increase) | **Credit** (decrease) | = | **Debit** (decrease) | **Credit** (increase) | + | **Debit** (decrease) | **Credit** (increase) |

*debit* is abbreviated *Dr.,* and the word *credit* is abbreviated *Cr.* The difference between the sum of the debits in an account and the sum of its credits is called the *account balance.* A *debit balance* results when the sum of the debits exceeds the sum of the credits. If the sum of the credits exceeds the sum of the debits, a *credit balance* results.

Debits and credits by themselves do *not* indicate increases or decreases. You must refer to a specific account to determine if a debit or credit represents an increase or decrease. This is illustrated in Exhibit 2.

*Every* financial transaction affects at least two accounts in the general ledger—an account in which a debit is recorded and an account in which the corresponding credit is recorded. The amount recorded in an account as a debit must equal the amount recorded in an account as a credit. If the amount recorded in an account as a debit requires more than one account to be credited, the *sum* of the dollar amount of the credits must equal the debited amount. Conversely, if the amount recorded in an account as a credit requires more than one account to be debited, the *sum* of the dollar amount of the debits must equal the credited amount. Transactions that involve more than one account to be debited or more than one account to be credited are called *compound entries.* (See Exhibit 3.)

Learning Objective **4**

Describe how business transactions are recorded using the double-entry accounting system

**Exhibit 3** Effects of Financial Transactions on Accounts

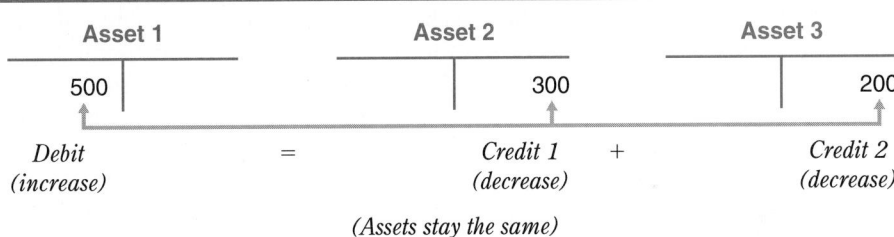

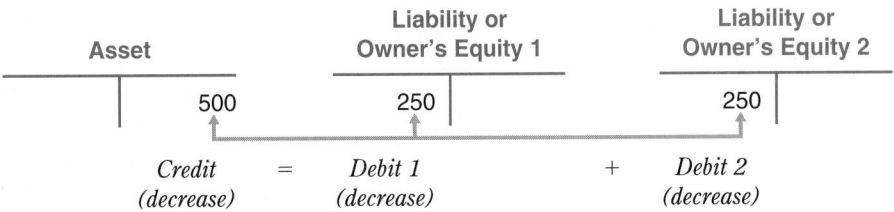

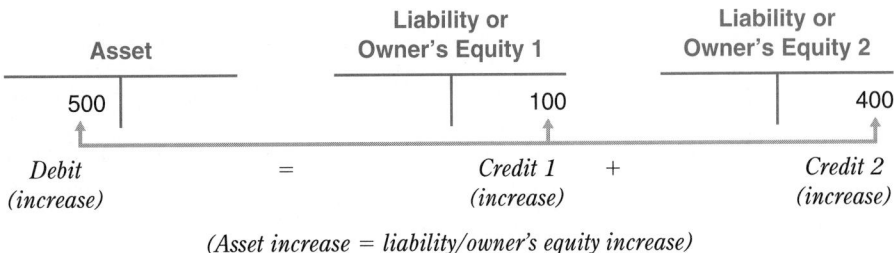

This **law of accounting**—that for every transaction, the sum of the debits must always equal the sum of the credits—is as basic to accounting as Newton's law of motion—that for every action there is an equal and opposite reaction—is to physics.

## REVENUES AND EXPENSES

For a small business, it is possible to prepare the income statement using a financial transaction worksheet in which all revenue and expense accounts are listed as plus (+) or minus (−) in the capital account. In such a situation you have to explain the nature of all changes in the capital account because some are reported on the income statement and some on the statement of owner's equity.

Rather than using a single capital account, it would be much easier if we were to list each revenue and expense account separately, and that is what is done in practice. But keep in mind that *revenue, expense, and withdrawals accounts are still part of the owner's equity account* and as such are part of the basic balance sheet equation, Assets = Liabilities + Owner's Equity.

Increases and decreases in asset and liability accounts are recorded directly into the asset or liability account, but other than additional investments made by the owner, *increases and decreases in the owner's equity account are recorded in the revenue, expense, and withdrawals accounts* that are subclassifications of the owner's equity account.

Since revenue, expenses, and the withdrawals account are part of the owner's equity account, the rules of debit and credit as applied to the owner's equity account also apply to these three component accounts *within* the owner's equity account.

*Revenues increase owner's equity.* If we wish *to increase a revenue account,* which in turn will increase the owner's equity account, *the revenue account must be credited.* This is so because owner's equity accounts are increased by credits. Notice in Exhibit 4A that the revenue account is represented as part of the owner's equity account. Specifically, it is represented as part of the credit side. Can you see why? Revenues will always have credit balances. We either earn some revenue or we earn zero revenue. We do not earn "negative" revenue.

*Expenses and withdrawals decrease owner's equity.* If we wish to record a decrease to the owner's equity account, we must debit the account. To increase expenses and

---

**Exhibit 4A** Owner's Equity Increases

| Owner's Equity | | |
|---|---|---|
| Debit (decrease) | Credit (increase) | *An* increase *in revenues* increases *owner's equity* |
| | **Revenue** | |
| | Debit (decrease)    Credit (increase) | |

**Exhibit 4B** Owner's Equity Decreases

|  | Owner's Equity | |
| --- | --- | --- |
| *An increase in expenses or withdrawals* decreases *owner's equity* | **Debit** (decreases) | **Credit** (increases) |

Expenses

| Debit (increases) | Credit (decreases) |
| --- | --- |

Withdrawals

| Debit (increases) | Credit (decreases) |
| --- | --- |

withdrawals is to decrease *owner's equity;* consequently, *expenses and withdrawals are increased by debits.* Like revenues, expenses and withdrawals either exist or they do not. And if they exist, they must have debit balances, which explains why they are shown on the debit side of Exhibit 4B.

## NORMAL BALANCES

For any account, the normal situation is for the sum of the increases to the account to exceed the sum of the decreases to the account—that is, for the resulting balance to be positive rather than negative. Accordingly, the positive balance of an account is referred to as its **normal balance.**

Asset accounts typically have total debits in excess of total credits and consequently have a normal debit balance. For example, consider the asset account Accounts Receivable. When receivables are acquired by providing services on account, the Accounts Receivable is debited; a debit represents the normal balance. When collections are received, the Accounts Receivable account must be decreased, and this is done by crediting the account. We cannot collect more receivables than we are owed. We can credit the Accounts Receivable account only to the extent of previous debits; once we have done so, the result is a zero balance. All receivables have been collected. The Accounts Receivable account cannot have a credit balance. It must have a debit balance, which is said to be its normal balance.

Likewise, we can credit the liability Accounts Payable to show increases. We would only debit (decrease) this account to a maximum of what we owe (total credits). Thus the balance in a liability account can be either *zero* or a credit balance (money still owed). The normal balance is a credit balance.

Like liabilities, owner's equity can be a positive balance from investments by the owner and revenues (credits) or a zero balance. Expenses or withdrawals will reduce the owner's equity account (debits), but only to the extent of existing credits. The normal balance is a credit balance. The normal balance of each type of account is always the "increase" side of the account.

We have now determined how to record increases and decreases for each of the six basic accounts and the normal balance of each of these accounts. These rules of increases and decreases and normal balances are summarized in Exhibit 5.

**Exhibit 5** Normal Balances and Rules of Account Increases and Decreases

| Account | To Increase Normal Balance | To Decrease Normal Balance |
|---|---|---|
| Asset Accounts | Debit | Credit |
| Liability Accounts | Credit | Debit |
| Owner's Equity Accounts: | | |
| Capital Account | Credit | Debit |
| Withdrawal Account | Debit | Credit |
| Revenue Accounts | Credit | Debit |
| Expense Accounts | Debit | Credit |

*Credits* decrease withdrawals and expenses *but* increase owner's equity

*Debits* increase withdrawals and expenses *but* decrease owner's equity

**ASK YOURSELF ▶**

1. What do the terms *debit* and *credit* mean?
2. How are asset accounts increased? How are they decreased?
3. How can debits be used to both increase and decrease accounts?
4. What is the law of accounting?
5. What are normal balances?

## RECORDING TRANSACTIONS: AN ILLUSTRATION

To illustrate the application of the rules of debit and credit and show how transactions are recorded in the accounts, we will take you through the transactions made by The Mary Abrems Dance Studio and analyze the transactions as we apply the rules and record them in the accounts. Three additional transactions will be added to the example.

Before being recorded, a transaction must be analyzed to determine which accounts must be increased or decreased. After this has been determined, the rules of debit and credit are applied to effect the appropriate increases and decreases to the accounts.

NOVEMBER 1   Abrems invests $11,000 from her personal savings in the new business, depositing the money at the First National Bank into an account titled The Mary Abrems Dance Studio. This initial investment of $11,000 is recorded as follows:

| ASSET (INCREASE) | | = | OWNER'S EQUITY (INCREASE) | |
|---|---|---|---|---|
| Cash | | | Abrems, Capital | |
| **Debit** | **Credit** | | **Debit** | **Credit** |
| Nov. 1    11,000 | | | | Nov. 1    11,000 |

This transaction increases the economic resource, the asset Cash, and also the owner's equity account, Abrems, Capital. According to the rules of debit and credit, debits will increase assets and credits will increase owner's equity accounts. Thus the transaction is debit Cash to increase it and credit Abrems, Capital, to increase it. Notice that the date of the transaction is placed next to both the $11,000 debit and the

$11,000 credit. The date is used to identify the source of the debit or credit in the account and serves as a cross-reference between the account debited and the account credited.

NOVEMBER 2  Office equipment in the amount of $3,000 is acquired by issuing a 12% note payable for that amount to the Deluxe Office Supply Company. The note is due in 6 months.

| ASSET (INCREASE) | | = | LIABILITY (INCREASE) | |
|---|---|---|---|---|
| Office Equipment | | | Note Payable | |
| **Debit** | **Credit** | | **Debit** | **Credit** |
| Nov. 2    3,000 | | | | Nov. 2    3,000 |

An asset (Office Equipment) is increased by this transaction, and a liability (Note Payable) is also increased, both in the amount of $3,000. Office Equipment must be debited to increase the asset and Note Payable must be credited to increase the liability. The accounting equation is in balance: debits = credits.

NOVEMBER 3  Abrems pays $900 to the Eastern Realty Company for rent on the dance studio for the months of November, December, and January.

| ASSET (DECREASE) | | = | ASSET (INCREASE) | |
|---|---|---|---|---|
| Cash | | | Prepaid Rent | |
| **Debit** | **Credit** | | **Debit** | **Credit** |
| Nov. 1    11,000 | Nov. 3    900 | | Nov. 3    900 | |

Prepaid Rent, a resource having future economic benefit, has been acquired for the cash payment of $900. The future economic benefit is the right to occupy the rented property for the next 3 months. (As each month goes by, $300 of Prepaid Rent will be transferred to the Rent Expense account.) Increases in assets are recorded by debits and decreases in assets are recorded by credits. The transaction is recorded by debiting (increasing) Prepaid Rent for $900 and crediting (decreasing) Cash for $900.

NOVEMBER 4  Cash in the amount of $1,800 is received from the Golden Years Dance Club for dance lessons for its club members for the next 9 months.

| ASSET (INCREASE) | | = | LIABILITY (INCREASE) | |
|---|---|---|---|---|
| | | | Unearned Dance | |
| Cash | | | Lesson Revenues | |
| **Debit** | **Credit** | | **Debit** | **Credit** |
| Nov. 1    11,000 | Nov. 3    900 | | | Nov. 4    1,800 |
| 4    1,800 | | | | |

The Mary Abrems Dance Studio now has an obligation to provide the Golden Years Dance Club with dance lessons for the next 9 months. This is a liability called Unearned Dance Lesson Revenue. Such unearned revenue is the reverse of an asset increase like prepaid rent. As it gives the lessons, the studio discharges its obligation at a rate of $200 per month for the next 9 months. Meanwhile, cash has been received and the asset Cash must be increased by a debit of $1,800. The liability Unearned Dance Lesson Revenue must also be increased, which requires a credit of $1,800.

NOVEMBER 5   Office equipment costing $7,800 is acquired by writing a check in that amount to the vendor.

| ASSET (DECREASE) | | | | = | ASSET (INCREASE) | | | |
|---|---|---|---|---|---|---|---|---|
| Cash | | | | | Office Equipment | | | |
| **Debit** | | **Credit** | | | **Debit** | | **Credit** | |
| Nov. 1 | 11,000 | Nov. 3 | 900 | | Nov. 2 | 3,000 | | |
| 4 | 1,800 | 5 | 7,800 | | 5 | 7,800 | | |

This transaction increases the asset Office Equipment and decreases the asset Cash. Assets are increased by debits and decreased by credits. A debit (increase) of $7,800 to Office Equipment and a credit (decrease) of $7,800 to the cash account record the transaction.

NOVEMBER 9   Office supplies in the amount of $450 are acquired on account.

| ASSETS (INCREASE) | | | | = | LIABILITY (INCREASE) | | | |
|---|---|---|---|---|---|---|---|---|
| Office Supplies on Hand | | | | | Accounts Payable | | | |
| **Debit** | | **Credit** | | | **Debit** | | **Credit** | |
| Nov. 9 | 450 | | | | | | Nov. 9 | 450 |

The asset account Office Supplies on Hand is increased by a debit of $450, while the liability account Accounts Payable is increased by a credit in a like amount.

NOVEMBER 11   The Mary Abrems Dance Studio collects $2,100 in cash for dance lessons.

| ASSETS (INCREASE) | | | | = | OWNER'S EQUITY (INCREASE) | | | |
|---|---|---|---|---|---|---|---|---|
| Cash | | | | | Dance Lesson Revenues | | | |
| **Debit** | | **Credit** | | | **Debit** | | **Credit** | |
| Nov. 1 | 11,000 | Nov. 3 | 900 | | | | Nov. 11 | 2,100 |
| 4 | 1,800 | 5 | 7,800 | | | | | |
| 11 | 2,100 | | | | | | | |

This transaction increases the asset Cash and increases the revenue account (Dance Lesson Revenues), which effects an increase in owner's equity by the amount that is received as payment for the lessons. Assets are increased by debits, revenues are increased by credits, and increases in revenues increase owner's equity. A debit of $2,100 to Cash and a credit of $2,100 to Dance Lesson Revenues record the transaction.

**NOVEMBER 15** Abrems pays County Services Company $1,100 for the month of November for utilities.

| ASSETS (DECREASE) | | | = | OWNER'S EQUITY (DECREASE) | |
|---|---|---|---|---|---|
| Cash | | | | Utilities Expense | |
| **Debit** | | **Credit** | | **Debit** | **Credit** |
| Nov. 1 | 11,000 | Nov. 3 | 900 | Nov. 15 | 1,100 |
| 4 | 1,800 | 5 | 7,800 | | |
| 11 | 2,100 | 15 | 1,100 | | |

As in the revenue transactions on Nov. 11, a separate expense account must be established for each expense item. This transaction increases the expense Utilities and reduces the asset Cash by $1,100. Assets are decreased by credits, and expenses are increased by debits (and owner's equity is thereby *decreased*).

**NOVEMBER 17** The dance studio has an arrangement with several dance clubs whereby group lessons will be given to club members on various week nights. Abrems bills these clubs $6,300 for lessons given to date.

| ASSETS (INCREASE) | | | = | OWNER'S EQUITY (INCREASE) | |
|---|---|---|---|---|---|
| Accounts Receivable | | | | Dance Lesson Revenues | |
| **Debit** | | **Credit** | | **Debit** | **Credit** |
| Nov. 17 | 6,300 | | | | Nov. 11 | 2,100 |
| | | | | | 17 | 6,300 |

Services have been performed entitling Abrems to receive a $6,300 payment in the near future. The dance lessons have already been given, so the $6,300 in revenue is earned. A future economic benefit has been received, the asset Accounts Receivable, in exchange for the service rendered. Assets are increased by debits, revenues are increased by credits, and increases in revenue increase owner's equity. A debit (increase) of $6,300 to Accounts Receivable and a credit (increase) of $6,300 to the revenue account Dance Lesson Revenues record the transaction.

**NOVEMBER 19** Abrems pays $200 of the $450 bill for the purchase of office supplies on Nov. 9.

| ASSETS (DECREASE) | | | = | LIABILITIES (DECREASE) | |
|---|---|---|---|---|---|
| Cash | | | | Accounts Payable | |
| **Debit** | | **Credit** | | **Debit** | **Credit** |
| Nov. 1 | 11,000 | Nov. 3 | 900 | Nov. 19 | 200 | Nov. 9 | 450 |
| 4 | 1,800 | 5 | 7,800 | | |
| 11 | 2,100 | 15 | 1,100 | | |
| | | 19 | 200 | | |

The asset Cash and the liability Accounts Payable each decrease $200 by this transaction. Assets are decreased by credits; liabilities are decreased by debits. The transaction is recorded by debiting (decreasing) Accounts Payable and crediting (decreasing) Cash.

**NOVEMBER 20**  A check in the amount of $3,350 is received from a large dance club for their lessons, billed on Nov. 17.

| ASSETS (INCREASE) | | | | = | ASSETS (DECREASE) | | | |
| --- | --- | --- | --- | --- | --- | --- | --- | --- |
| Cash | | | | | Accounts Receivable | | | |
| **Debit** | | **Credit** | | | **Debit** | | **Credit** | |
| Nov. 1 | 11,000 | Nov. 3 | 900 | | Nov. 17 | 6,300 | Nov. 20 | 3,350 |
| 4 | 1,800 | 5 | 7,800 | | | | | |
| 11 | 2,100 | 15 | 1,100 | | | | | |
| 20 | 3,350 | 19 | 200 | | | | | |

Payments on account reduce the asset Accounts Receivable and increase the asset Cash. Assets are increased by debits and decreased by credits. Debit (increase) Cash for $3,350 and credit (decrease) Accounts Receivable for $3,350.

**NOVEMBER 21**  Abrems withdraws $500 from the business for her personal use.

| ASSETS (DECREASE) | | | | = | OWNER'S EQUITY (DECREASE) | | | |
| --- | --- | --- | --- | --- | --- | --- | --- | --- |
| Cash | | | | | Abrems, Withdrawals | | | |
| **Debit** | | **Credit** | | | **Debit** | | **Credit** | |
| Nov. 1 | 11,000 | Nov. 3 | 900 | | Nov. 21 | 500 | | |
| 4 | 1,800 | 5 | 7,800 | | | | | |
| 11 | 2,100 | 15 | 1,100 | | | | | |
| 20 | 3,350 | 19 | 200 | | | | | |
| | | 21 | 500 | | | | | |

Withdrawals are a reduction of owner's equity but are not an expense of the business entity. A withdrawal is a personal transaction of the owner that is exactly the opposite of an investment by the owner. The investment increases the owner's equity account, owner's capital, and the withdrawal reduces owner's equity by increasing the owner's withdrawals account. Withdrawals are recorded separately from the owner's capital account in a special "withdrawals" account. This transaction *increases* the Abrems, Withdrawals, account (reducing owner's equity) and reduces cash. Debits record increases in the withdrawals account, and credits record decreases in asset accounts. The transaction is recorded by a debit in the amount of $500 to the Abrems, Withdrawals, account and a credit of $500 to Cash.

**NOVEMBER 24**  Abrems pays her dance instructors salaries in the amount of $2,500 on the last Friday of the month.

| ASSETS (DECREASE) | | | | = | OWNER'S EQUITY (DECREASE) | | | |
|---|---|---|---|---|---|---|---|---|
| **Cash** | | | | | **Salary Expense** | | | |
| **Debit** | | **Credit** | | | **Debit** | | **Credit** | |
| Nov. 1 | 11,000 | Nov. 3 | 900 | | Nov. 24 | 2,500 | | |
| 4 | 1,800 | 5 | 7,800 | | | | | |
| 11 | 2,100 | 15 | 1,100 | | | | | |
| 20 | 3,350 | 19 | 200 | | | | | |
| | | 21 | 500 | | | | | |
| | | 24 | 2,500 | | | | | |

The salaries expense transaction is recorded by *increasing an expense* and *decreasing an asset*. To record the transaction, a new account, Salary Expense, is debited (increased) in the amount of $2,500, and Cash is credited (decreased) in the amount of $2,500. The increase in Salaries Expense decreases owner's equity.

NOVEMBER 27   The Summit Advertising Agency submitted a bill to Abrems for $400 worth of advertising for this first month of operations. The bill will be paid next month.

| LIABILITY (INCREASE) | | | | = | OWNER'S EQUITY (DECREASE) | | | |
|---|---|---|---|---|---|---|---|---|
| **Accounts Payable** | | | | | **Advertising Expense** | | | |
| **Debit** | | **Credit** | | | **Debit** | | **Credit** | |
| Nov. 19 | 250 | Nov. 9 | 450 | | Nov. 27 | 400 | | |
| | | 27 | 400 | | | | | |

A separate expense account must be established for each expense item. This transaction increases the expense Advertising Expense and increases the liability Accounts Payable by $400. Expenses are increased by debits (and owner's equity is thereby *decreased*). Liabilities are increased by credits. Debit Advertising Expense in the amount of $400 and credit Accounts Payable in the amount of $400.

After all the transactions have been recorded, the accounts are footed, ruled, and totaled. If debits exceed credits, the balance is shown on the debit side of the account. If credits exceed debits, the balance is shown on the credit side of the account. The Cash account balancing is shown below:

| **Cash** | | | | | |
|---|---|---|---|---|---|
| | **Debit** | | **Credit** | | |
| Nov. 1 | 11,000 | Nov. 3 | 900 | | |
| 4 | 1,800 | 5 | 7,800 | | |
| 11 | 2,100 | 15 | 1,100 | | |
| 20 | 3,350 | 19 | 200 | | |
| | | 21 | 500 | | |
| | | 24 | 2,500 | | ← *Rule* |
| *Footing* → | 18,250 | | 13,000 | | |
| *Balance on greater side* → Bal. | 5,250 | | | | |

**Exhibit 6** The General Ledger

### THE MARY ABREMS DANCE STUDIO
### General Ledger

| Assets | = | Liabilities | + | Owner's Equity |

**Cash**

| Nov. | 1 | 11,000 | Nov. | 3 | 900 |
|------|---|--------|------|---|-----|
|      | 4 | 1,800  |      | 5 | 7,800 |
|      | 11 | 2,100 |      | 15 | 1,100 |
|      | 20 | 3,350 |      | 19 | 200 |
|      |   |        |      | 21 | 500 |
|      |   |        |      | 24 | 2,500 |
|      |   | 18,250 |      |   | 13,000 |
| Bal. |   | 5,250  |      |   |     |

**Notes Payable**

|  |  |  | Nov. | 2 | 3,000 |

**Abrems, Capital**

|  |  |  | Nov. | 1 | 11,000 |

**Accounts Receivable**

| Nov. | 17 | 6,300 | Nov. | 20 | 3,350 |
|------|----|-------|------|----|-------|
| Bal. |    | 2,950 |      |    |       |

**Accounts Payable**

| Nov. | 19 | 200 | Nov. | 9 | 450 |
|------|----|-----|------|---|-----|
|      |    |     |      | 27 | 400 |
|      |    | 200 |      |   | 850 |
|      |    |     | Bal. |   | 650 |

**Abrems, Withdrawals**

| Nov. | 21 | 500 |  |

**Unearned Dance Lesson Revenues**

|  |  |  | Nov. | 4 | 1,800 |

**Dance Lesson Revenues**

|  |  |  | Nov. | 11 | 2,100 |
|--|--|--|------|----|-------|
|  |  |  |      | 17 | 6,300 |
|  |  |  | Bal. |    | 8,400 |

**Office Supplies on Hand**

| Nov. | 9 | 450 |  |

**Salary Expense**

| Nov. | 24 | 2,500 |  |

**Prepaid Rent**

| Nov. | 3 | 900 |  |

**Utilities Expense**

| Nov. | 15 | 1,100 |  |

**Office Equipment**

| Nov. | 2 | 3,000 |  |
|------|---|-------|--|
|      | 5 | 7,800 |  |
| Bal. |   | 10,800 |  |

**Advertising Expense**

| Nov. | 27 | 400 |  |

The transactions that we have discussed in this extended illustration are summarized in the general ledger accounts in Exhibit 6. Notice that the accounts are organized under headings reflecting the basic elements of the accounting statements: assets, liabilities, owner's equity, revenues, and expenses.

## STANDARD LEDGER ACCOUNT FORMAT

T-accounts are simplified representations of actual general ledger accounts. Two standard formats of a ledger account are widely used. Some businesses use a two-money-column ledger account similar to the T-account, as shown in Exhibit 7. Other businesses prefer, as we do, a three-money-column or a *balance-column ledger account* (see Exhibit 8). Notice that both Exhibits 7 and 8 illustrate the Cash account related to The Mary Abrems Dance Studio example.

Learning Objective 5

Distinguish between a ledger and a journal

## THE JOURNAL

The accounting system does not start with the recording of a transaction in the general ledger accounts. Accountants need a record of each transaction, listed in chronological order—day by day, day after day.

**Exhibit 7** Two-Money-Column Ledger Account

**Account** Cash          **Account No.** 110

| Date | Explanation | Post. Ref. | Debit | Date | Explanation | Post. Ref. | Credit |
|------|-------------|-----------|-------|------|-------------|-----------|--------|
| 1998 |  |  |  | 1998 |  |  |  |
| Nov. 1 |  |  | 11,000 | Nov. 3 |  |  | 900 |
| 4 |  |  | 1,800 | 5 |  |  | 7,800 |
| 11 |  |  | 2,100 | 15 |  |  | 1,100 |
| 20 |  |  | 3,350 | 19 |  |  | 200 |
|  |  |  |  | 21 |  |  | 500 |
|  | Balance |  |  | 24 |  |  | 2,500 |
|  | 5,250 |  | 18,250 |  |  |  | 13,000 |

**Exhibit 8** Three-Money-Column Ledger Account

**Account** Cash          **Account No.** 110

| Date | Explanation | Post. Ref. | Debit | Credit | Balance |
|------|-------------|-----------|-------|--------|---------|
| 1998 |  |  |  |  |  |
| Nov. 1 |  |  | 11,000 |  | 11,000 |
| 3 |  |  |  | 900 | 10,100 |
| 4 |  |  | 1,800 |  | 11,900 |
| 5 |  |  |  | 7,800 | 4,100 |
| 11 |  |  | 2,100 |  | 6,200 |
| 15 |  |  |  | 1,100 | 5,100 |
| 19 |  |  |  | 200 | 4,900 |
| 20 |  |  | 3,350 |  | 8,250 |
| 21 |  |  |  | 500 | 7,750 |
| 24 |  |  |  | 2,500 | 5,250 |

The need for such a record can be seen if you look at the Cash account in the general ledger in Exhibit 6. A debit of $1,800 was made on Nov. 4. Someday Abrems might like to know why this debit was made. This information is not available in the Cash account. But if a chronological listing of transactions were available, Abrems could look for the Nov. 4 date and see that the transaction giving rise to $1,800 cash was the receipt of cash for dance lessons to be given over the next 9 months.

Such a chronological listing of transactions is called a **journal.** Transactions are recorded first in the journal; later they are transferred to the general ledger, a process referred to by accountants as **posting.** The journal provides a complete record of each transaction.

Because transactions are initially, or "originally," recorded in the journal, it is referred to as a **book of original entry.** A business will design journals to suit its own particular needs. Some entities may use only four or five different types of journals; others may use more. Common to most entities, however, is the *general journal.* The general journal is the simplest of the journals, and it provides the most flexibility.

## Journalizing

Recording transactions in the journal is called **journalizing.** In the general journal, information such as the date, the account to be debited, the amount to be debited, the account to be credited, the amount to be credited, and an explanation of the business

**Exhibit 9** A General Journal

THE MARY ABREMS DANCE STUDIO
General Journal

PAGE 1

| Date | Account Titles and Explanation | Post. Ref. | Debit | Credit |
|---|---|---|---|---|
| 1998<br>Nov. 1 | Cash **(A)**<br> Abrems, Capital **(OE)**<br>To record initial investment by Mary Abrems. | | 11,000 | 11,000 |
| 2 | Office Equipment **(A)**<br> Note Payable **(L)**<br>To record the acquisition of office equipment by issuing a 6 month, 12% note payable. | | 3,000 | 3,000 |

transaction are all recorded in appropriate places. A typical general journal page for the first two transactions of The Mary Abrems Dance Studio illustration is shown in Exhibit 9.

### 1. The Date

The year is recorded at the top of the date column of each journal page. The month is written on the first line of the date column. Neither the month nor the year is given again until it changes or a new page is begun. The date of each transaction is recorded in the journal.

### 2. Account Titles and Explanation

The title of the account to be debited is listed at the left of the description column next to the date column.

The title of the account to be credited is indented from the date column and listed on the line below the account debited.

The explanation of the transaction is recorded below the account credited but is not indented. The explanation should be as brief as possible while adequately explaining the transaction.

### 3. Amounts Debited and Credited

The debit amount is recorded in the debit money column opposite the title of the account debited. The credit amount is recorded in the credit money column opposite the title of the account credited.

The **posting reference** column (Post. Ref.) is not used at the time transactions are recorded in the general journal. It is used when the debits and credits are posted to the general ledger accounts to identify the source of the debit or credit. The accountant indicates that the posting has been done by placing the *account number* of the account to which the entry was posted in the posting reference column of the general journal. Only account titles used in general ledgers can be used to record entries in the general journal. If new accounts are needed, they must be added to the general ledger before entries to them can be recorded under their titles in the general journal.

To help you understand the nature of the affected accounts, we have inserted the letters **A, L,** or **OE** after each entry for asset, liability, or owner's equity. Similarly, we have used **OE : R** or **OE : E** to designate owner's equity: revenue or owner's equity: expense.

### Posting

As we noted before, transferring the journal entry debits and credits to their appropriate ledger accounts is called *posting.* In many accounting systems this process is done mechanically or electronically; in some systems it is still done manually. Periodically, at the end of each day or each week, the transactions recorded in the general journal since the last posting date are posted to the general ledger. Posting is done because the general journal shows transactions entered chronologically as they occur, but does not classify the entries by categories. The ledger does provide a classified record, while the journal provides a chronological listing with explanations and clear references to corresponding debits and credits. Both types of records are needed for smooth business operations. For example, a question such as "What was the cash expenditure on Nov. 19 for?" can be answered by reference to the general journal, but a question such as "What is our cash balance?" requires a look at the general ledger.

The steps in the posting process are described in Exhibit 10. As we describe

**Exhibit 10** Steps in the Posting Process

| Step | Description |
|---|---|
| ① | Locate in the general ledger the account debited in the journal entry. |
| ② | Record the date of the transaction in the general ledger account. |
| ③ | Record the general journal reference (GJ) and page number in the posting reference column of the account debited in the general ledger. |
| ④ | Enter the dollar amount of the debit from the journal into the debit column of that particular account in the ledger. |
| ⑤ | Determine the balance in the account. |
| ⑥ | Enter the account number of the ledger account debited in the posting reference column of the journal on the line of the debit portion of the transaction. |
| ⑦ | Repeat the steps above for the credit portion of the journal entry. |

**THE MARY ABREMS DANCE STUDIO**
General Journal

PAGE ___1___

| Date | Account Titles and Explanation | Post. Ref. | Debit | Credit |
|---|---|---|---|---|
| 1998 Nov. 1 | Cash **(A)** | ⑥ 110 | 11,000 | |
| |     Abrems, Capital **(OE)** | ⑥ 310 | | 11,000 |
| | To record initial investment by Mary Abrems. | | | |

**THE MARY ABREMS DANCE STUDIO**
General Ledger

**Account** Cash ①                          **Account No.** 110

| Date | Explanation | Post. Ref. | Debit | Credit | Balance |
|---|---|---|---|---|---|
| 1998 ② Nov. 1 | | ③ GJ 1 | ④ 11,000 | | ⑤ 11,000 |

**Account** Abrems, Capital ①                 **Account No.** 310

| Date | Explanation | Post. Ref. | Debit | Credit | Balance |
|---|---|---|---|---|---|
| 1998 ② Nov. 1 | | ③ GJ 1 | | ④ 11,000 | ⑤ 11,000 |

them, refer to the corresponding circled numbers in the journal and ledger entries. Notice that the numbers 1–6 appear twice in the entries. That is because step 7 requires that the posting process be repeated for the credit entry in the general journal.

The posting reference columns in both the journal and the ledger serve two purposes. First, they constitute a valuable cross-reference. If a question arises concerning an amount in a particular ledger account, the posting reference steers the questioner to the journal page where the transaction, the amount, the account titles, and the explanation can be found.

Second, an entry in the posting reference column provides evidence that the account has in fact been posted.

**ASK YOURSELF** ▶

1. **Why are T-accounts used in the classroom rather than standard two-money-column or three-money-column ledger accounts?**
2. **Why do business entities need journals?**
3. **How are transactions recorded in a general journal?**
4. **Describe the posting process.**

Learning Objective 6

Prepare a trial balance and financial statements

## THE TRIAL BALANCE

Our objective in using an accounting system is to prepare financial statements more efficiently than we could by use of a financial transaction worksheet. In our example, we have reached a stage where all the transactions for a period of time have been journalized and posted. What happens next?

Before the financial statements can be prepared, the balance in each account must be determined. Once this is done (and it was done in the general ledger shown in Exhibit 6), we may wish to prove the equality of the debits and credits. We know that every transaction is recorded by equal debits and credits, and that the total of the debits must equal the total of the credits in the general ledger. At this point, we need a list of all the account balances to see if the total of the debit balances accounts will equal, or *balance,* the total of the credit balances accounts. This is called preparing a *trial balance.*

The first step in preparing a **trial balance,** or schedule reflecting the balances of the individual ledger accounts, is, as stated above, to compute the balance of each account in the general ledger. Next, the balance from each account of the general ledger is listed on a two-column workpaper in the same order in which the accounts appear in the general ledger, as determined by the chart of accounts. The accounts in the general ledger having a debit balance are entered in the first column. The accounts having credit balances are entered in the second column. The debit column is added up and the credit column is added up. The sums of the two columns should be equal.

The trial balance for The Mary Abrems Dance Studio is presented in Exhibit 11. The total of the debit column equals $24,850, which is equal to the total of $24,850 for the credit column. The trial balance does in fact balance, thereby providing proof that the general ledger is in balance.

Once the trial balance has been prepared and reviewed for accuracy, it can easily be used to prepare the financial statements. Just copy—carefully!—the income statement accounts onto an income statement, the statement of owner's equity accounts onto a statement of owner's equity, and the balance sheet accounts onto a balance sheet. (See Exhibit 12.)

**Exhibit 11** Trial Balance

### THE MARY ABREMS DANCE STUDIO
### Trial Balance
### November 30, 1998

| | | |
|---|---:|---:|
| *These accounts, together with the ending capital account, will be used to prepare the balance sheet* | | |
| Cash | $ 5,250 | |
| Accounts Receivable | 2,950 | |
| Office Supplies on Hand | 450 | |
| Prepaid Rent | 900 | |
| Office Equipment | 10,800 | |
| Notes Payable | | $ 3,000 |
| Accounts Payable | | 650 |
| Unearned Dance Lesson Revenues | | 1,800 |
| *These accounts, together with the net income, will be used to prepare the statement of owner's equity* | | |
| Abrems, Capital | | 11,000 |
| Abrems, Withdrawals | 500 | |
| *And these accounts will be used to prepare the income statement* | | |
| Dance Lesson Revenues | | 8,400 |
| Salary Expense | 2,500 | |
| Utilities Expense | 1,100 | |
| Advertising Expense | 400 | |
| Totals | $24,850 | $24,850 |

**Exhibit 12** Financial Statements Prepared from the Trial Balance

### THE MARY ABREMS DANCE STUDIO
### Income Statement
### Month Ended November 30, 1998

| | |
|---|---:|
| Revenue: | |
| Dance Lesson Revenues | $8,400 |
| Expenses: | |
| Salary Expense | $2,500 |
| Utilities Expense | 1,100 |
| Advertising Expense | 400 |
| Total Expenses | $4,000 |
| Net Income | $4,400 |

### THE MARY ABREMS DANCE STUDIO
### Statement of Owner's Equity
### Month Ended November 30, 1998

| | | |
|---|---|---:|
| Abrems, Capital, Nov. 1, 1998 | | $ –0– |
| Add: | Investment | 11,000 |
| | Net Income | 4,400 |
| | Total | $15,400 |
| Less: | Withdrawals | 500 |
| Abrems, Capital, Nov. 30, 1998 | | $14,900 |

*(Continued)*

**Exhibit 12** (Continued)

THE MARY ABREMS DANCE STUDIO
Balance Sheet
November 30, 1998

| Assets | | Liabilities and Owner's Equity | |
| --- | --- | --- | --- |
| | | **Liabilities** | |
| Cash. | $ 5,250 | Notes Payable | $ 3,000 |
| Accounts Receivable | 2,950 | Accounts Payable | 650 |
| Office Supplies on Hand | 450 | Unearned Dance Lesson | |
| Prepaid Rent | 900 | Revenue | 1,800 |
| Office Equipment | 10,800 | Total Liabilities | $ 5,450 |
| | | **Owner's Equity** | |
| | | Abrems, Capital | 14,900 |
| | | Total Liabilities and | |
| Total Assets | $20,350 | Owner's Equity | $20,350 |

Learning Objective 7

## ERRORS

Describe how errors are found

If the trial balance does *not* balance, the accountant knows that one or more errors exist.

### Common Types of Errors

Errors are usually of the three following types:

#### 1. Transaction Errors

When a transaction is recorded, an incorrect amount may be entered in the general ledger account. One of the most typical errors is to record a debit entry incorrectly as a credit, or a credit as a debit. Another common transaction error is to record only one portion of the transaction, say, the debit, and forget to record the other portion of the transaction, the credit (or vice versa).

#### 2. Account Balance Errors

Errors can occur in calculating the balance of a specific account. Another account balance error is simply to misplace a debit balance in the credit column of the account or a credit balance in the debit column of the account.

#### 3. Trial Balance Errors

A trial balance error can occur when the amount of an account is incorrectly transferred to the trial balance. Another error involves incorrectly recording a debit account balance as a credit on the trial balance, or a credit as a debit. The simplest trial balance error is the incorrect totaling of the debit or credit columns.

*Caution:* You cannot automatically assume that because the trial balance balances, the accounts are correct. It is possible to have errors in the accounts and still have all the debits equal all the credits. Some ways this can happen are as follows:

- If an incorrect amount has been recorded as both a debit and a credit to the proper accounts, the trial balance will balance even though the totals are not correct.

- If either an entire transaction has been omitted or a transaction has been recorded twice, the trial balance will be incorrect even though it balances.
- If correct amounts have been recorded to incorrect accounts of the same type — for example, if a debit to Cash (asset) has mistakenly been recorded as a debit to Accounts Receivable (asset) — the trial balance will balance but it will still be in error.

It is important to review the trial balance to ensure its correctness and balancing.

### Finding Errors

Fra Luca Pacioli (1445–1520), the founder of modern accounting, once wrote:

> Who does nothing
> makes no mistakes;
>
> Who makes no mistakes
> Learns nothing.

As you will shortly realize, it is very easy to make errors in working accounting problems. You will also learn, alas, that it is not so easy to find your errors. You may discover an error by chance, but you are more likely to learn of an error when your trial balance does not balance.

If an error is discovered because the trial balance does not balance, the difference between the total debit balance and total credit balance should be determined. Often this difference will reveal the nature or location of the error. For example, assume that the debits of a trial balance amount to $13,384 and the credits total $13,700. The difference of $316 might have resulted from the omission of a debit posting of that amount or from the posting of a debit of $158 as a credit. This would cause the credits to be $158 larger than they should be and the debits to be $158 less than they should be, a difference of $316. Thus, it is often helpful to divide the difference between the debit total and credit total by 2 and look for the resulting amount in the trial balance.

A difference of 10, 100, 1,000, or 10,000 often indicates that the addition of the trial balance columns is in error.

If the error is divisible evenly by 9, a *slide* or a *transposition* or both may have occurred. Moving an entire number either to the right or left is a *slide* — for example, recording $36 as $360 or $3.60. Reversing the digits in a number is referred to as a *transposition.* Writing $36 as $63 is an example of a transposition. Notice that in both examples the differences are divisible evenly by 9.

| | | |
|---|---|---|
| *Slide:* | $36 as $360 = $324 difference ÷ 9 | = $36 |
| | $36 as $3.60 = $32.40 difference ÷ 9 | = $3.60 |
| *Transposition:* | $36 as $63 = $27 difference ÷ 9 | = $3 |

# The $10 Million Transposition

In the Congressional investigations of the Iran-contra affair held in May of 1987 it was discovered that Lieut. Col. Oliver L. North had mistakenly deposited 10 million dollars to the wrong Swiss bank account. The correct account number was 386; however, Col. North deposited the funds into account number 368. The owner of account number 368 at the Credit Suisse bank is a Swiss businessman who was expecting a deposit to be made to his account and thought this was it. 10 million dollars? In the period of time from the erroneous deposit to its discovery the funds earned $253,000 interest.

*Source: The New York Times,* May 13, 1987. Copyright © 1987 by The New York Times Company. Reprinted by permission.

Reversing the digits 386 to 368 is an illustration of a transposition error.

---

**Exhibit 13** Step-By-Step Procedure for Locating Errors

---

- Check the addition of the trial balance.
- Determine the difference between the balances and check omissions or duplications in that amount.
- If the difference is 10, 100, 1,000, or 10,000, check addition of the trial balance.
- If the error is evenly divisible by 9, check for a transposition or slide.
- Divide the difference by 2 and look for an error in the resulting amount as a debit or credit.
- Check the transfer of amounts from the general ledger to the trial balance.
- Recompute the account balances.
- Check the posting from the general journal to the general ledger.
- Examine the original transaction to determine if the entry was journalized correctly.

---

If determining the difference in the trial balance totals does not reveal the error, then each step in the recording process must be checked. The procedure for locating errors is summarized in Exhibit 13.

As you proceed through this sequence of steps, you will discover the error that causes the trial balance not to balance. Remember, if an error was made but the trial balance still balances, you will not know the error exists. Discovery then depends on chance—often on which accounts happen to be affected. For example, if an entry is made to Accounts Receivable and Revenues for $540 rather than the correct amount of $450, the trial balance will balance. However, when the customer is billed at the end of the month for $540, he or she will most certainly complain and the error will be discovered.

## SOME MINOR PROCEDURAL POINTS

- Dollar signs are not used when entries are recorded in the journals or posted to the ledgers.
- Commas to indicate thousands of dollars and decimal points to indicate cents are omitted, because the rule lines printed on the paper used for journals and ledgers serve the same purpose as these indicators. However, commas and decimal points are required on financial statements, which are prepared on unruled paper.
- For even dollar amounts, the cents column may be left blank, or zeroes or dashes may be used.
- Dollar signs are always used when financial reports are prepared. They are placed before the first amount at the top of each column of figures and also before amounts representing subtotals and totals.

## REVIEW OF THE STEPS IN THE ACCOUNTING PROCESS

At this point, let's review the steps involved in the accounting process.

1. First, the business entity enters into a transaction with a second party. A business document, such as a sales invoice, is prepared. This business document provides evidence that a transaction has in fact taken place. The transaction is analyzed and journalized—recorded in the general journal.
2. At frequent intervals the entries in the general journal are posted to the accounts in the general ledger.
3. Typically at the end of each month, the balances of the general ledger accounts are determined and a trial balance is prepared.

**4.** The financial statements are then prepared from the information contained in the trial balance—first the income statement, followed by the statement of owner's equity, and finally the balance sheet.

Always remember that the ultimate objective of the accounting system is to prepare the financial statements. Some students become so captivated by the logic of the accounting system that the system itself dominates their attention and activity. Do not fall into this trap. The chairman of the board of directors of General Motors does not care if the system is on the back of an envelope, or in a mainframe computer system, or if two-money-column or three-money-column ledgers are used, or if accounts are balanced daily or weekly. What does concern him is that *the system provides a timely, efficient method of preparing financial statements that will reflect fairly the results of operations and the financial position* (the income statement and balance sheet, respectively) of General Motors *for the period of time specified.*

**ASK YOURSELF** ▶

1. **What purpose does a trial balance serve?**
2. **If a trial balance is in balance, that does not necessarily mean that the accounts are free of errors. Explain.**
3. **What are transaction errors? Account balance errors? Trial balance errors?**
4. **What is a transposition? A slide?**
5. **List the steps to be followed for locating errors.**

## SUMMARY

- All financial accounting systems, from pen-and-ink through mainframe computerized systems, are based on the **double-entry accounting system.**
- The basic building block of any accounting system is the account. Each individual asset, liability, owner's equity, revenue, and expense is a separate account.
- An account consists of three elements: the account title, a location to record increases in the account, and a location to record decreases in the account.
- All the accounts that appear in the financial statements of a business entity are contained in a book called the **general ledger.**
- Accounts are arranged in the general ledger in the order in which they appear in the financial statements—balance sheet accounts first, followed by income statement accounts.
- As for the income statement accounts, the revenue accounts are listed first in the general ledger, followed by the expense accounts.
- The system of numbered accounts for any business entity is called its **chart of accounts.** The system of numbering allows for additional accounts to be added and existing accounts to be deleted.
- Financial transactions increase or decrease specific general ledger accounts. These increases or decreases in the accounts are recorded according to the *rules of debits and credits.*
- **Debits** refer to the left side of any account and **credits** refer to the right side. Since in the double-entry accounting system each financial transaction consists of two parts (debits and credits), for every account debited another account (or accounts) is credited. Debits must always equal credits.
- Debits increase asset, withdrawal, and expense accounts. Credits increase liability, owner's equity, and revenue accounts.
- The difference between total debits and total credits in an account is called the *account balance.* If the sum of the debits exceeds the sum of the credits, the account is said to have a *debit balance.* Conversely, when credits exceed debits, the account is said to have a *credit balance.*

- The typical balance of an account is called its **normal balance** and is determined by whatever causes the account balance to increase, whether a debit or a credit. Thus, assets, expenses, and withdrawals accounts have normal debit balances, whereas liabilities, owner's equity, and revenue accounts have normal credit balances.
- The recordkeeping process begins with the recording of business transactions in a book of original entry called a **journal.** Transactions are listed in the journal in chronological order.
- Periodically the journal entry debits and credits are transferred to the appropriate general ledger accounts. This process is referred to as **posting.**
- After the last entries are journalized and posted, a **trial balance** is prepared, typically at the end of every month. The trial balance simply lists all the balances of the general ledger accounts and totals all accounts having debit balances and all accounts having credit balances. The sum of the debits in the trial balance must equal the sum of the credits.
- In the event that a trial balance does not balance, a number of steps can and should be taken to locate the error.
- The financial statements are prepared from the trial balance.

## 8   KEY TERMS

**Book of original entry**    See **journal.**

**Chart of accounts**    An economic entity's system of numbered general ledger accounts.

**Credit**    The right side of an account, which reflects increases to liability, owner's equity, and revenue accounts and decreases to asset, expense, and withdrawals accounts.

**Debit**    The left side of an account, which reflects increases to asset, expense, and withdrawals accounts and decreases to liability, owner's equity, and revenue accounts.

**Double-entry accounting system**    A method of recording business transactions such that each transaction has two parts, debits and credits. The sum of the debit parts must always equal the sum of the credit parts.

**Footing**    The addition of a column of figures.

**General ledger**    A ledger containing all the accounts of an economic entity that appear on the financial statements.

**Journal**    A book of original entry listing in chronological order financial transactions that affect general ledger accounts.

**Journalizing**    The process of recording financial transactions in a journal.

**Law of accounting**    The rule that for every transaction, the sum of the debits must equal the sum of the credits.

**Ledger**    A group of related accounts of a business entity, collected in a book or a computer-readable format.

**Normal balance**    The positive balance of an account.

**Posting**    The process of transferring the debit and credit entries in a journal to the appropriate ledger accounts.

**Posting reference**    A transaction number used to identify the source of a debit or credit in an account.

**T-account**    The elementary form of an account, used by accountants and teachers to analyze accounting problems.

**Trial balance**    A schedule reflecting the balances of the individual general ledger accounts.

## DEMONSTRATION PROBLEM

After completing law school, Benjamin Rockney opened his legal practice on June 1, 1998, by investing $4,700 of his personal funds into the business. During the month of June, the following transactions occurred:

Jun. 3 Acquired $5,200 of office equipment on account.

7 Acquired $1,500 of office supplies paying cash.

10 Paid the rent for the month, $750.

11 Received $2,430 cash from clients for legal fees earned.

15 Completed legal work for several corporations and billed them a total of $3,600.

17 Paid $1,300 on the equipment acquired on June 3.

20 Collected $1,800 from the corporations billed on June 15.

24 Withdrew $2,000 from the business.

30 Paid $900 for utilities.

### Required:

1. Record the transactions listed above in a general journal. Use page number 1 as a posting reference.

2. Post the transactions to the general ledger. Use the following account numbers and titles:

| | | | |
|---|---|---|---|
| Cash | 10 | Rockney, Capital | 60 |
| Accounts Receivable | 20 | Rockney, Withdrawals | 70 |
| Office Supplies on Hand | 30 | Legal Fees Earned | 80 |
| Office Equipment | 40 | Rent Expense | 90 |
| Accounts Payable | 50 | Utilities Expense | 100 |

3. Prepare a trial balance for the month.

4. Prepare an income statement, a statement of owner's equity, and a balance sheet.

### ■ Solution to Demonstration Problem

1.

**BENJAMIN ROCKNEY, ATTORNEY AT LAW**
General Journal

PAGE __1__

| Date | Account Titles and Explanation | Post Ref. | Debit | Credit |
|---|---|---|---|---|
| 1998<br>June 1 | Cash **(A)**<br>  Rockney, Capital **(OE)**<br>To record initial investment by Mr. Rockney. | 10<br>60 | 4,700 | <br>4,700 |
| 3 | Office Equipment **(A)**<br>  Accounts Payable **(L)**<br>To record the acquisition of office equipment on account. | 40<br>50 | 5,200 | <br>5,200 |
| 7 | Office Supplies on Hand **(A)**<br>  Cash **(A)**<br>To record acquisition of office supplies for cash. | 30<br>10 | 1,500 | <br>1,500 |
| 10 | Rent Expense **(OE:E)**<br>  Cash **(A)**<br>To record payment of rent. | 90<br>10 | 750 | <br>750 |
| 11 | Cash **(A)**<br>  Legal Fees Earned **(OE:R)**<br>To record the receipt of cash for legal services rendered. | 10<br>80 | 2,430 | <br>2,430 |
| 15 | Accounts Receivable **(A)**<br>  Legal Fees Earned **(OE:R)**<br>To record legal services performed on account. | 20<br>80 | 3,600 | <br>3,600 |
| 17 | Accounts Payable **(L)**<br>  Cash **(A)**<br>To record partial payment of account. | 50<br>10 | 1,300 | <br>1,300 |
| 20 | Cash **(A)**<br>  Accounts Receivable **(A)**<br>To record collections on account. | 10<br>20 | 1,800 | <br>1,800 |
| 24 | Rockney, Withdrawals **(OE)**<br>  Cash **(A)**<br>To record cash withdrawals. | 70<br>10 | 2,000 | <br>2,000 |
| 30 | Utilities Expense **(OE:E)**<br>  Cash **(A)**<br>To record payment of utilities. | 100<br>10 | 900 | <br>900 |

2.

## BENJAMIN ROCKNEY, ATTORNEY AT LAW
### General Ledger

**Account** Cash                **Account No.**   10

| Date | Explanation | Post. Ref. | Debit | Credit | Balance |
|------|-------------|------------|-------|--------|---------|
| 1998 | | | | | |
| June 1 | | GJ 1 | 4,700 | | 4,700 |
| 7 | | GJ 1 | | 1,500 | 3,200 |
| 10 | | GJ 1 | | 750 | 2,450 |
| 11 | | GJ 1 | 2,430 | | 4,880 |
| 17 | | GJ 1 | | 1,300 | 3,580 |
| 20 | | GJ 1 | 1,800 | | 5,380 |
| 24 | | GJ 1 | | 2,000 | 3,380 |
| 30 | | GJ 1 | | 900 | 2,480 |

**Account** Accounts Receivable        **Account No.**   20

| Date | Explanation | Post. Ref. | Debit | Credit | Balance |
|------|-------------|------------|-------|--------|---------|
| 1998 | | | | | |
| June 15 | | GJ 1 | 3,600 | | 3,600 |
| 20 | | GJ 1 | | 1,800 | 1,800 |

**Account** Office Supplies on Hand       **Account No.**   30

| Date | Explanation | Post. Ref. | Debit | Credit | Balance |
|------|-------------|------------|-------|--------|---------|
| 1998 | | | | | |
| June 7 | | GJ 1 | 1,500 | | 1,500 |

**Account** Office Equipment            **Account No.**   40

| Date | Explanation | Post. Ref. | Debit | Credit | Balance |
|------|-------------|------------|-------|--------|---------|
| 1998 | | | | | |
| June 3 | | GJ 1 | 5,200 | | 5,200 |

**Account** Accounts Payable           **Account No.**   50

| Date | Explanation | Post. Ref. | Debit | Credit | Balance |
|------|-------------|------------|-------|--------|---------|
| 1998 | | | | | |
| June 3 | | GJ 1 | | 5,200 | 5,200 |
| 17 | | GJ 1 | 1,300 | | 3,900 |

**Account** Rockney, Capital          **Account No.** 60

| Date | Explanation | Post. Ref. | Debit | Credit | Balance |
|------|-------------|------------|-------|--------|---------|
| 1998 June 1 | | GJ 1 | | 4,700 | 4,700 |

**Account** Rockney, Withdrawals          **Account No.** 70

| Date | Explanation | Post. Ref. | Debit | Credit | Balance |
|------|-------------|------------|-------|--------|---------|
| 1998 June 24 | | GJ 1 | 2,000 | | 2,000 |

**Account** Legal Fees Earned          **Account No.** 80

| Date | Explanation | Post. Ref. | Debit | Credit | Balance |
|------|-------------|------------|-------|--------|---------|
| 1998 June 11 | | GJ 1 | | 2,430 | 2,430 |
| 15 | | GJ 1 | | 3,600 | 6,030 |

**Account** Rent Expense          **Account No.** 90

| Date | Explanation | Post. Ref. | Debit | Credit | Balance |
|------|-------------|------------|-------|--------|---------|
| 1998 June 10 | | GJ 1 | 750 | | 750 |

**Account** Utilities Expense          **Account No.** 100

| Date | Explanation | Post. Ref. | Debit | Credit | Balance |
|------|-------------|------------|-------|--------|---------|
| 1998 June 30 | | GJ 1 | 900 | | 900 |

3.

BENJAMIN ROCKNEY, ATTORNEY AT LAW
Trial Balance
June 30, 1998

| | | |
|---|---:|---:|
| Cash | $ 2,480 | |
| Accounts Receivable | 1,800 | |
| Office Supplies on Hand | 1,500 | |
| Office Equipment | 5,200 | |
| Accounts Payable | | $ 3,900 |
| Rockney, Capital | | 4,700 |
| Rockney, Withdrawals | 2,000 | |
| Legal Fees Earned | | 6,030 |
| Rent Expense | 750 | |
| Utilities Expense | 900 | |
| Totals | $14,630 | $14,630 |

4.

### BENJAMIN ROCKNEY, ATTORNEY AT LAW
### Income Statement
### Month Ended June 30, 1998

| | | |
|---|---|---:|
| Revenue: | | |
| Legal Fees Earned............................................. | | $6,030 |
| Expenses: | | |
| Rent Expense........................................ | $750 | |
| Utilities Expense....................................... | 900 | |
| Total Expenses............................................ | | $1,650 |
| Net Income.................................................. | | $4,380 |

### BENJAMIN ROCKNEY, ATTORNEY AT LAW
### Statement of Owner's Equity
### Month Ended June 30, 1998

| | |
|---|---:|
| Rockney, Capital, June 1, 1998 ...................................... | $ –0– |
| Add: Investment ..................................................... | 4,700 |
| Net Income ............................................... | 4,380 |
| Total ....................................................... | $9,080 |
| Less: Withdrawals.................................................. | 2,000 |
| Rockney, Capital, June 30, 1998 ..................................... | $7,080 |

### BENJAMIN ROCKNEY, ATTORNEY AT LAW
### Balance Sheet
### June 30, 1998

| Assets | | Liabilities and Owner's Equity | |
|---|---:|---|---:|
| | | **Liabilities** | |
| Cash..................... | $ 2,480 | Accounts Payable ........... | $ 3,900 |
| Accounts Receivable......... | 1,800 | **Owner's Equity** | |
| Office Supplies on Hand ...... | 1,500 | | |
| Office Equipment............ | 5,200 | Rockney, Capital ............ | 7,080 |
| | | Total Liabilities and | |
| Total Assets................ | $10,980 | Owner's Equity............. | $10,980 |

## QUESTIONS FOR REVIEW AND FURTHER THOUGHT

### REVIEW QUESTIONS

1. Explain the difference between an *account* and a *ledger*.

2. What is the purpose of an account?

3. Explain the meaning of the terms *debit* and *credit*.

4. What are *normal balances?* How are they determined?

5. What is a *T-account?*

6. What purpose does the *chart of accounts* serve?

7. What is the purpose of *journals?* How do they relate to *ledgers?*

8. What is meant by the term *posting?*

9. What is a *trial balance?* What purpose does it serve?

10. How are business transactions entered in the general journal?

11. Indicate whether each of the following accounts will have a normal debit or credit balance:

|  | **Normal Balance** |
|---|---|
| a. Cash | _____ |
| b. Rent Expense | _____ |
| c. Revenue Earned | _____ |
| d. Accounts Receivable | _____ |
| e. Johnson, Capital | _____ |
| f. Office Supplies on Hand | _____ |
| g. Accounts Payable | _____ |
| h. Unearned Revenue | _____ |

12. Ten events common to the accounting function of a business entity are listed below, out of chronological order. In the numbered spaces provided, place the letters of the events in the sequence in which they would logically occur.

| | | | |
|---|---|---|---|
| a. Determining ledger account balances | 1. _____ |
| b. Analyzing the transaction | 2. _____ |
| c. Preparing the balance sheet | 3. _____ |
| d. Preparing the trial balance | 4. _____ |
| e. Occurrence of a business transaction | 5. _____ |
| f. Posting from the journal to the ledger | 6. _____ |
| g. Preparing a business document | 7. _____ |
| h. Preparing an income statement | 8. _____ |
| i. Journalizing the transactions | 9. _____ |
| j. Preparing the statement of owner's equity | 10. _____ |

### QUESTIONS FOR FURTHER THOUGHT

1. One of the most important things about an accounting system is that the system itself is not the most important thing. Explain this statement.

2. Debits and credits are used to increase accounts. How is it possible for one of these items—say, debits—to be able to both increase and decrease accounts?

3. When cash is increased, the Cash account is debited. Why, then, does your bank say that it has "credited" your account when you deposit cash?

4. What types of errors could cause a trial balance not to balance?

5. A trial balance may be in balance but the accounts may still be incorrect. How is this possible?

6. In reviewing the accounts listed in a trial balance, you observe that Accounts Receivable has a credit balance of $250 and yet the trial balance is in balance. Explain.

7. Listed below are the total debits and credits from three trial balances that do not balance. For each case, indicate the type of error you would initially attempt to locate.

|    | Debit Total | Credit Total |
|----|-------------|--------------|
| a. | $18,700     | $18,600      |
| b. | 13,470      | 13,230       |
| c. | 87,614      | 87,974       |

8. A business entity performed services in the amount of $375 for a customer. The entry was recorded in the general journal as a debit to Accounts Receivable and a credit to Revenue in the amount of $735. How will this error probably be discovered?

9. Listed below are several errors. For each one, determine whether the trial balance totals would be equal or unequal.
   a. The Allentown Company paid $1,400 for office supplies. The transaction was recorded as a debit to Office Equipment and a credit to Cash for $1,400.
   b. The Bethlehem Company collected $275 from an account receivable. The entry was recorded as a debit to Cash for $275 and a credit to Accounts Receivable for $257.
   c. Carbondale Company purchased office supplies on account in the amount of $400. The entry was not recorded.
   d. Dunmore Company entered a $50 debit balance from the Accounts Receivable account in the general ledger as $50 in the credit column of the trial balance.
   e. Easton Company recorded rent expense of $150 as a debit to Office Equipment and a credit to Cash.

## OBJECTIVE ASSIGNMENT

*True/False*  Indicate whether each statement below is *true* or *false* by placing a *T* or an *F* in the space provided.

_____ 1. The double-entry accounting system is appropriate only for small businesses.

_____ 2. The chart of accounts is a system of organizing and numbering the accounts in the general ledger.

_____ 3. Debit entries increase accounts.

_____ 4. A trial balance may balance but not be correct.

_____ 5. The ledger is sometimes called the book of original entry.

*Multiple Choice*  Select the best choice to complete each statement or answer each question below. Write the letter corresponding to your choice in the space provided.

_____ 1. All of the following are assets *except:*
   a. Cash
   b. Equipment
   c. Inventory
   d. Unearned revenue
   e. All of the above

_____ 2. The term footing refers to:
   a. The addition of a column of figures
   b. The process of obtaining the top number in an account
   c. The process of obtaining the bottom number in an account
   d. The process of posting
   e. None of the above

_____ 3. Most companies use a chart of accounts prepared by:
    a. The Financial Accounting Standards Board
    b. The company's accounting department
    c. The Securities and Exchange Commission
    d. The Internal Revenue Service
    e. None of the above

_____ 4. Entries recorded on the right side of any account are called:
    a. Increases
    b. Decreases
    c. Debits
    d. Credits
    e. None of the above

_____ 5. Credits are used to record:
    a. Decreases in liabilities
    b. Decreases in owner's equity
    c. Increases in revenues
    d. Increases in expenses
    e. None of the above

_____ 6. When an asset increases, one of the following must occur:
    a. Another asset increases.
    b. A liability decreases.
    c. Owner's equity decreases.
    d. An expense increases.
    e. None of the above.

_____ 7. When owner's equity decreases, one of the following must occur:
    a. An asset increases.
    b. A liability increases.
    c. A revenue increases.
    d. Withdrawals decreases.
    e. None of the above.

_____ 8. When cash is debited, a typical credit is to:
    a. Accounts payable
    b. Expenses
    c. Withdrawals
    d. Accounts receivable
    e. None of the above

_____ 9. The first financial statement that is prepared from the trial balance is the
    a. Balance sheet
    b. Statement of cash flows
    c. Statement of owner's equity
    d. Income statement
    e. None of the above

_____ 10. Transactions are recorded chronologically, as they occur, in the:
    a. Journal
    b. Daybook
    c. Ledger
    d. T-account
    e. None of the above

## EXERCISES

4† **Exercise 1 :** Identifying and Journalizing Transactions
Found in T-Accounts

Joseph Illick established his TV repair service in February 1998. Listed in the following T-accounts are the first eight transactions of the new business, Illick TV Repair Service. Prepare the general journal entries corresponding to these eight transactions.

| Cash | | | | Accounts Payable | | | |
|---|---|---|---|---|---|---|---|
| (1) | 1,500 | (2) | 450 | (6) | 175 | (3) | 375 |
| (8) | 240 | (4) | 500 | | | (4) | 1,300 |
| | | (6) | 175 | | | | |
| | | (7) | 150 | | | | |

| Accounts Receivable | | | | Illick, Capital | | | |
|---|---|---|---|---|---|---|---|
| (5) | 740 | (8) | 240 | | | (1) | 1,500 |

| Repair Supplies on Hand | | | Repair Fees Earned | | |
|---|---|---|---|---|---|
| (3) | 375 | | | (5) | 740 |

| Office Equipment | | | Salary Expense | | |
|---|---|---|---|---|---|
| (2) | 450 | | (7) | 150 | |

| Repair Equipment | | |
|---|---|---|
| (4) | 1,800 | |

4 5 **Exercise 2:** Journalizing Transactions

Greth Company entered into the following transactions during the month of July 1998:

July  2  Acquired office supplies on account, $360.

3  Paid rent for the month, $250.

5  Paid telephone bill for the month, $45.

9  Received cash for services performed on this date, $560.

10  Paid for advertising in the local newspaper, $75.

14  Withdrew cash from the business, $250.

17  Billed customers for services rendered, $525.

19  Made a payment to the creditor for the supplies acquired in the July 2 transaction, $160.

23  Paid salary to employee, $85.

27  Received payment from customers, $255.

30  Paid electric bill for the month, $60.

Record the transactions in a general journal using the following accounts: Cash; Accounts Receivable; Office Supplies on Hand; Accounts Payable; Greth, Withdrawals; Fees Earned; Salary Expense; Advertising Expense; Rent Expense; Telephone Expense; Electricity Expense.

† The numbers in the margin refer to the Learning Objectives.

**2  Exercise 3:** Developing a Chart of Accounts

Amy Peterson recently opened a new business called Peterson Consulting Services. Listed below are the accounts that she will need in her general ledger:

| | |
|---|---|
| Accounts Payable | Notes Payable |
| Accounts Receivable | Office Supplies on Hand |
| Building | Office Supplies Expense |
| Cash | Peterson, Capital |
| Consulting Revenues | Peterson, Withdrawals |
| Equipment | Prepaid Rent |
| Land | Rent Expense |
| Miscellaneous Expense | Salary Expense |

Arrange these accounts in the order in which they would appear in the general ledger. Assign each account a number, using a three-digit numbering scheme: the 100 series for assets, the 200 series for liabilities, etc. Use the second digit to indicate specific accounts within a major category; for example, Cash would be account number 110.

**6  Exercise 4:** Preparing a Trial Balance

Kim Dalton has operated a travel agency for a number of years. Listed below are the accounts of Dalton Travel Agency, reflecting activity for the first quarter of 1998. The accounts are arranged in alphabetical order. Prepare a trial balance as of Mar. 31, 1998, listing the accounts in the proper order.

| | | | |
|---|---|---|---|
| Accounts Payable | $ 5,900 | Office Supplies Expense | $ 1,600 |
| Accounts Receivable | 27,400 | Office Supplies on Hand | 4,200 |
| Advertising Expense | 1,300 | Prepaid Rent | 2,400 |
| Cash | 6,800 | Rent Expense | 800 |
| Dalton, Capital | 34,000 | Salaries Payable | 3,220 |
| Dalton, Withdrawals | 9,400 | Salary Expense | 11,200 |
| Miscellaneous Expense | 480 | Travel Fees Earned | 40,400 |
| Notes Payable | 12,000 | Utilities Expense | 940 |
| Office Equipment | 29,000 | | |

▶ *(Check Figure: Trial balance total = $95,520)*

**6  7  Exercise 5:** Preparing a Corrected Trial Balance

The following trial balance has been prepared by the accountant for Ledbetter Office Cleaning Service:

---

**LEDBETTER OFFICE CLEANING SERVICE**
**Trial Balance**
**October 31, 1998**

| | | |
|---|---|---|
| Cash | $ 7,815 | |
| Accounts Receivable | 17,100 | |
| Prepaid Rent | 2,700 | |
| Supplies on Hand | | $ 4,200 |
| Equipment | 33,600 | |
| Notes Payable | | 12,000 |
| Accounts Payable | | 11,520 |
| Ledbetter, Capital | | 21,765 |
| Ledbetter, Withdrawals | | 4,500 |
| Office Cleaning Fees Earned | | 32,160 |
| Salary Expense | 6,720 | |
| Rent Expense | 900 | |
| Utilities Expense | 1,410 | |
| Totals | $69,245 | $86,145 |

As you can see, the trial balance does not balance. An investigation of the general journal entries and the general ledger accounts reveals the following information:

a. When the balance in the Cash account was transferred from the general ledger to the trial balance, the first two digits were transposed.
b. The total debits in the Accounts Receivable ledger account were $43,050. The credits total $28,950.
c. An entry found in the general journal for a $1,500 debit to Accounts Receivable and for a credit to Office Cleaning Fees Earned for the same amount was not posted to the general ledger.
d. A debit of $600 to Accounts Payable was not posted to the general ledger. The corresponding credit of $600 was posted to the Cash account.
e. All accounts had normal balances.

Prepare a corrected trial balance.

▶ *(Check Figure: Corrected trial balance total = $78,345)*

6 **Exercise 6:** Describing the Effects of Errors on the Trial Balance

Several errors were found in the accounting records of the Ness Company during the month of August 1998:

a. The debits in the general ledger account Accounts Receivable were correctly added to a total of $13,200. The credits were correctly added to $12,100. The balance of the Accounts Receivable account on the trial balance was $1,000.
b. Office Supplies were acquired for $6,700. The entry was recorded as a debit to Office Supplies on Hand for $6,700 and a credit to Accounts Payable for $7,600.
c. Repair Equipment was acquired for $7,875 Cash and recorded as a debit to Prepaid Insurance and a credit to cash for $7,875.
d. Repair services were rendered on account amounting to $2,475. The entry was recorded as a debit to Accounts Receivable for $2,675 and a credit to Repair Fees Earned for $2,675.

For each of these errors:

1. Indicate whether or not the trial balance will balance.
2. If the trial balance will not balance, decide whether the debit or the credit column will show the larger total.
3. Tell the most likely reason for the error's discovery.

4 **Exercise 7:** Account Analysis

Selected accounts from the Carlson Company appear below:

| | Balance as of | |
| --- | --- | --- |
| | **Oct. 1, 1998** | **Oct. 31, 1998** |
| Cash . . . . . . . . . . . . . . . . . . . . . . . . . . . . . . . . . . . . | $  900 | $ 2,400 |
| Accounts Receivable . . . . . . . . . . . . . . . . . . . . . . . . | 1,700 | 5,000 |
| Repair Supplies on Hand . . . . . . . . . . . . . . . . . . . . . | 700 | 2,000 |
| Accounts Payable . . . . . . . . . . . . . . . . . . . . . . . . . . . | 1,600 | 800 |
| Carlson, Capital. . . . . . . . . . . . . . . . . . . . . . . . . . . . . | 6,000 | 18,000 |

During the month of October the company earned revenues (all on account) in the amount of $9,100 and acquired repair supplies on account in the amount of $2,600. The only cash receipts were from the collection of accounts receivable. The only payments made were accounts payable and withdrawals. From this information, determine the following:

a. The amount of cash payments
b. The amount of payments made on accounts payable
c. The amount of withdrawals paid
d. The net income for the month

4   **Exercise 8:** Account Analysis

On Jan. 1, 1998, Dave Dallas invested $5,000 cash into a new business called the Dallas Company. During the year the Dallas Company provided service to its customers and recorded revenue, all on account, in the amount of $70,000. Operating expenses, all incurred on account, amounted to $50,000. Collections from customers for the year amounted to $30,000. Payments for operating expenses were $35,000.

a. What is the net income of the Dallas Company for the year?
b. What is the cash balance at year end?
c. What is the point of obtaining the information requested in parts (a) and (b)?

## PROBLEMS: SET A

4 6†   **Problem A1:** Recording Transactions in T-Accounts and Preparing a Trial Balance

Rob Atwell opened a plumbing service to be known as Atwell Plumbing. Operations began on Apr. 1, 1998, and the following transactions were completed during the month:

Apr.  1   Withdrew $6,700 from a personal savings account and used it to open a new account in the name of Atwell Plumbing.

     2   Acquired a new truck costing $8,100. A payment of $1,750 in cash was made and a note payable given for the $6,350 remainder.

     3   Paid rent for the month, $715.

     6   Acquired supplies on account $1,570.

     7   Paid for 3 months of advertising and recorded Prepaid Advertising in the amount of $600.

     8   Cash in the amount of $1,835 was received for plumbing services rendered.

     9   Acquired additional supplies for cash, $805.

   11   Paid salaries, $1,160.

   15   Rendered plumbing services to a large local business and billed the customer $4,220.

   16   Paid $570 of the amount owed from the transaction of Apr. 6.

   19   Paid miscellaneous expenses, $430.

   20   Collected $2,100 from the customer in the transaction of Apr. 15.

   21   Withdrew $1,450 from the business.

   22   Paid salaries, $1,410.

   24   Paid the first installment of the note payable, $385.

   25   Paid telephone expense, $125.

   27   Billed the Brenton Company for plumbing services rendered, $1,415.

**Required:**

1. Establish the following T-accounts: Cash; Accounts Receivable; Plumbing Supplies on Hand; Prepaid Advertising; Truck; Notes Payable; Accounts Payable; Atwell, Capital; Atwell, Withdrawals; Plumbing Fees Earned; Salary Expense; Rent Expense; Telephone Expense; Miscellaneous Expense.
2. Record the transactions directly into T-accounts using the dates of the transactions to identify each transaction.
3. Prepare a trial balance.

▶ *(Check Figure: Trial balance = $21,135)*

---

† The numbers in the margin refer to the Learning Objectives.

4  5  6    **Problem A2:** Journalizing and Posting; Preparing a Trial Balance

After several years with a large accounting firm, Anton Garrison decided to establish his own accounting practice. The following transactions of Anton Garrison, CPA, were completed during May 1998.

May  1   Transferred $9,250 cash from a personal savings account to a new checking account, Anton Garrison, CPA.

3   Acquired office equipment on account from Bender Furniture Company, $3,680.

4   Acquired office supplies on account from Merth Office Supply Company, $1,710.

6   Performed accounting services for Ajax Computer Company and submitted a bill of $2,920 for those services.

7   Paid for accounting and tax books for use in the practice, $1,950.

8   Paid Merth Office Supply Company, $410 on account.

10   Acquired land ($5,800) and a building ($20,700) for the accounting practice. A down payment of $3,800 was made and the remaining $22,700 was financed by issuing a mortgage payable.

12   Paid salaries to employees, $1,420.

13   Received $975 from Ajax Computer Company, billed on May 6.

16   Paid telephone expense, $65.

19   Received cash in the amount of $1,460 from Fenton Book Company for accounting services rendered this date.

22   Acquired office supplies on account from Merth Office Supply Company, $465.

23   Withdrew $815 for personal use.

25   Paid salaries to employees, $1,030.

26   Billed Yeaton Exporters $3,160 for accounting services rendered.

27   Paid New York Institute of Certified Public Accountants $550 for professional dues.

28   Paid $325 rent on an office copying machine.

**Required:**

1. Prepare general journal entries for the transactions listed above.
2. Post the entries to the ledger accounts, using account numbers for cross-reference and using general journal page number 1. The following accounts will be needed:

| Account Number | Account | Account Number | Account |
|---|---|---|---|
| 110 | Cash | 210 | Accounts Payable |
| 120 | Accounts Receivable | 220 | Mortgage Payable |
| 130 | Office Supplies on Hand | 310 | Garrison, Capital |
| 140 | Land | 320 | Garrison, Withdrawals |
| 150 | Building | 410 | Accounting Fees Earned |
| 160 | Office Equipment | 510 | Salary Expense |
| 170 | Accounting Library | 520 | Rent Expense |
| | | 530 | Telephone Expense |
| | | 540 | Professional Dues Expense |

3. Prepare a trial balance.

▶ (Check Figure: Trial balance = $44,935)

**Problem A3:** Preparing Journal Entries from Two Balance Sheets

Presented below are the comparative balance sheets for Jan. 1 and Jan. 31, 1998, together with an income statement for the month of January for Keenan's Repair Shoppe.

## KEENAN'S REPAIR SHOPPE
### Comparative Balance Sheets

| | January 1998 | | | January 1998 | |
| --- | --- | --- | --- | --- | --- |
| | 1 | 31 | | 1 | 31 |
| **Assets** | | | **Liabilities and Owner's Equity** | | |
| | | | **Liabilities** | | |
| Cash | $ 1,948 | $ 5,488 | | | |
| Accounts Receivable | 6,584 | 3,320 | | | |
| Repair Parts on Hand | 1,504 | 1,892 | Accounts Payable | $ 7,836 | $ 1,800 |
| Repair Equipment | 1,120 | 1,120 | **Owner's Equity** | | |
| Repair Truck | 4,680 | 4,680 | Keenan, Capital | 8,000 | 14,700 |
| | | | Total Liabilities and | | |
| Total Assets | $15,836 | $16,500 | Owner's Equity | $15,836 | $16,500 |

## KEENAN'S REPAIR SHOPPE
### Income Statement
### For the Month Ended January 31, 1998

| | | |
| --- | --- | --- |
| Repair Fees Earned | | $9,600 |
| Expenses: | | |
| Salaries Expense | $2,200 | |
| Insurance Expense | 268 | |
| Utilities Expense | 152 | |
| Advertising Expense | 280 | |
| Total Expenses | | 2,900 |
| Net Income | | $6,700 |

Keenan's Repair Shoppe acquires all goods and services on account except for salaries, which are paid in cash on paydays. Repair fees are made 80% on account, 20% for cash. Keenan made no withdrawals during the month.

**Required:**

Using the financial statements and the additional information, prepare the general journal entries (omitting explanations) that best reflect the transactions that transpired during the month.

4 6   **Problem A4:** Journalizing and Posting; Preparing a Trial Balance and Financial Statements

Nancy Anderson recently established a business that will operate as Anderson Home Cleaning Service. The transactions for February 1998, her first month of business, are presented below.

Feb.  1   Deposited $3,100 cash in a bank account in the name of the new company.

3   Acquired home cleaning supplies on account, $1,070.

5   Acquired home cleaning equipment on account, $780.

6   Acquired a used car costing $2,350 for the business, paying $500 cash and financing the remaining $1,850 by issuing a note payable.

7   Paid rent on office space for the month, $365.

9   Received $1,590 cash for home cleaning services rendered.

10   Paid for local newspaper advertising, $85.

12   Paid for insurance for the next 6 months by recording prepaid insurance, $240.

13   Paid creditors on account, $450.

14   Paid miscellaneous expenses, $110.

15   Billed customers $930 for home cleaning services rendered.

16   Paid salaries to employees, $420.

20   Received $490 from customers billed on Feb. 15.

22   Paid amount due on the note payable, $120.

25   Paid telephone expense, $45.

28   Paid salaries to employees, $395.

28   Billed customers for home cleaning services rendered, $1,125.

28   Withdrew $500 from the business.

**Required:**

1. Prepare general journal entries for the transactions listed above.
2. Post the entries to the ledger accounts using account numbers for cross-reference and using general journal page number 1. The following accounts will be needed:

| Account Number | Account | Account Number | Account |
|---|---|---|---|
| 110 | Cash | 310 | Anderson, Capital |
| 120 | Accounts Receivable | 320 | Anderson, Withdrawals |
| 130 | Prepaid Insurance | 410 | Home Cleaning Fees Earned |
| 140 | Cleaning Supplies on Hand | 510 | Salary Expense |
| 150 | Cleaning Equipment | 520 | Rent Expense |
| 160 | Car | 530 | Advertising Expense |
| 210 | Notes Payable | 540 | Telephone Expense |
| 220 | Accounts Payable | 550 | Miscellaneous Expense |

3. Prepare a trial balance.

   ▶ *(Check Figure: Trial balance = $9,875)*

4. Prepare an income statement, a statement of changes in owner's equity, and a balance sheet.

4 6   **Problem A5:** Journalizing and Posting; Preparing a Trial Balance and Financial Statements

Jorge Ortiz owns the Bethlehem Bulldogs, a professional football team in the National Football League. Presented below is the Nov. 30, 1998, trial balance representing activity from Jan. 1, 1998, to Nov. 30, 1998, together with the account numbers and titles.

## BETHLEHEM BULLDOGS
### Trial Balance
### November 30, 1998

**Acct. No.**

| | | | |
|---|---|---|---|
| 110 | Cash | $ 112,980 | |
| 120 | Accounts Receivable | 371,250 | |
| 130 | Uniform Supplies on Hand | 3,105 | |
| 140 | Prepaid Insurance | −0− | |
| 150 | Land | 202,500 | |
| 160 | Training Facilities | 1,275,000 | |
| 170 | Training Equipment | 262,500 | |
| 180 | Player Contracts | 1,125,000 | |
| 210 | Notes Payable | | $ 180,000 |
| 220 | Accounts Payable | | 472,500 |
| 230 | Mortgage Payable | | 1,050,000 |
| 310 | Ortiz, Capital | | 1,764,375 |
| 320 | Ortiz, Withdrawals | 187,500 | |
| 410 | Game Attendance Fees Earned | | 1,012,500 |
| 510 | Player Salaries | 487,500 | |
| 520 | Advertising Expense | 40,095 | |
| 530 | Travel Expense | 153,240 | |
| 540 | Laundry Expense | 52,800 | |
| 550 | Medical Expense | 19,455 | |
| 560 | Utilities Expense | 173,400 | |
| 570 | Miscellaneous Expense | 13,050 | |
| | Totals | $4,479,375 | $4,479,375 |

During the month of December 1998, the Bulldogs were participating in the 1998 playoffs and the following transactions took place.

Dec. 1 Acquired the contract of Larry Handyson from the Detroit Panthers for $187,500, paying $22,500 in cash and the remaining $165,000 by issuing a note payable.

2 Collected $280,950 on accounts receivable from season-ticket holders.

3 Paid accounts payable, $165,750.

4 Paid for TV advertising, $7,860.

5 Acquired on account additional uniforms for the upcoming series with the San Antonio Padres, $3,075.

9 Billed season-ticket holders for the last five games, $32,025.

10 Paid the amount due on this date for a note payable, $60,000.

11 Acquired insurance for the months of December to June by paying cash, $21,525. (Record as prepaid insurance)

12 Acquired additional training equipment on account, $31,950.

15 Paid players' salaries, $113,625.

17 Received $331,605 cash for tickets to playoff games.

19 Paid travel expenses to San Antonio, $55,800.

20 Paid laundry expenses, $1,260.

23 Paid creditors $94,185.

25 Paid miscellaneous expenses, $2,685.

26 Paid medical expenses, $1,890.

27 Paid utilities expenses, $21,045.

28 Paid player salaries, $124,065.

30 Jorge Ortiz withdrew $25,000.

**Required:**

1. Enter the amounts from the November 1998 trial balance into the appropriate general ledger accounts.
2. Prepare general journal entries for the December transactions.
3. Post the entries to the general ledger using page 12 as the general journal page reference.
4. Prepare a trial balance as of Dec. 31, 1998.

   ▶ *(Check Figure: Trial balance = $4,723,095)*
5. Prepare an income statement and a statement of owner's equity for the year ended Dec. 31, 1998, and a balance sheet as of Dec. 31, 1998.

6 7 **Problem A6:** Correcting a Trial Balance

The June 1998 trial balance for Uptown Store is presented below. The regular bookkeeper is on vacation, so Julie Johnson, the owner, attempted to prepare the trial balance herself, but could not make it balance. She has asked you to help.

| DOWNTOWN STORE Trial Balance June 30, 1998 | | |
|---|---|---|
| Cash | $ 4,480 | |
| Accounts Receivable | 18,960 | |
| Office Supplies on Hand | 7,080 | |
| Display Equipment | 21,000 | |
| Delivery Truck | 35,000 | |
| Accounts Payable | | $ 7,260 |
| Johnson, Capital | | 51,300 |
| Johnson, Withdrawals | | 5,000 |
| Revenue Earned | | 37,160 |
| Salaries Expense | 3,500 | |
| Rent Expense | | 1,000 |
| Telephone Expense | 640 | |
| Totals | $91,660 | $101,720 |

Upon reviewing the trial balance and the process whereby the amounts in the ledger accounts were transferred to the trial balance, you discover two errors:

a. The debit column in the trial balance was footed incorrectly.
b. The balance in the accounts payable general ledger account of $6,270 was transferred as $7,260.

When you recompute the balances of the general ledger accounts, you discover two more errors:

c. The Telephone Expense account balance was overstated by $180.
d. The total debits in the Cash account amounted to $18,460 and the credits totaled $14,980.

You discover four errors when you retrace the postings from the general journal to the general ledger:

e. A debit posting to Accounts Receivable in the amount of $5,200 should have been $520.
f. A debit posting to Accounts Payable for $4,600 was missing.
g. A credit posting to Revenues in the amount of $760 was missing.
h. A credit of $3,100 was posted to Accounts Payable rather than the correct amount of $3,010.

**Required:**

Prepare a corrected trial balance.

▶ *(Check Figure: Corrected trial balance = $90,800)*

## PROBLEMS: SET B

4 6† **Problem B1:** Recording Transactions in T-Accounts and Preparing a Trial Balance

Robert Dryfess recently established his own business, which he called Dryfess Delivery Service. During the first month of business, October 1998, the following transactions were completed.

Oct. 1 Deposited $1,950 of personal savings in an account at the First National Bank in the name of Dryfess Delivery Service.

2 Acquired a used delivery truck costing $6,300, paying $700 in cash and financing the remaining $5,600 by issuing a note payable.

4 Paid rent for the month, $295.

5 Acquired office supplies on account, $820.

6 Paid for 3 months' insurance and recorded prepaid insurance in the amount of $450.

8 Received $1,390 cash for delivery work done for the Lenton Corporation.

10 Acquired additional office supplies for cash, $205.

13 Paid salaries, $390.

16 Completed an assignment for Monroe Company and billed the company $1,525.

17 Paid $230 of the amount owed from the transaction of Oct. 5.

19 Paid miscellaneous expenses, $170.

21 Withdrew cash from the business, $615.

22 Collected $950 on account from Monroe Company.

24 Paid salaries, $420.

25 Paid utilities expense, $80.

27 Billed the Stanton Company for delivery services rendered, $1,340.

**Required:**

1. Establish the following T-accounts: Cash; Accounts Receivable; Office Supplies on Hand; Prepaid Insurance; Delivery Truck; Notes Payable; Accounts Payable; Dryfess, Capital; Dryfess, Withdrawals; Delivery Fees Earned; Salary Expense; Rent Expense; Utilities Expense; Miscellaneous Expense.
2. Record the transactions directly into T-accounts, using the dates of the transactions to identify each transaction.
3. Prepare a trial balance.

▶ *(Check Figure: Trial balance = $12,395)*

4 5 6 **Problem B2:** Journalizing and Posting; Preparing a Trial Balance

Marcy Montana, a recent medical school graduate, opened her new medical practice on Mar. 1, 1998. During the month of March, the following transactions were completed.

Mar. 1 Montana invested $4,250 of personal funds in a new bank account in the name of Marcy Montana, M.D.

2 Acquired medical equipment costing $9,500 from Silver Medical Equipment Company, paying $1,500 in cash and financing the remainder by issuing an $8,000 note payable.

3 Paid rent for the month of March, $750.

5 Acquired medical supplies from Cooney Medical Supply Company on account, $1,525.

7 Received $1,845 in cash from patients for medical services rendered this week.

† The numbers in the margin refer to the Learning Objectives.

Mar. 9 Paid Kline Labs for preparing laboratory work on a patient, $180.

12 Paid salaries to medical technician and receptionist, $960.

15 Billed patients $5,170 for services rendered.

17 Paid Cooney Medical Supply Company $375 on account.

20 Paid telephone expense, $85.

21 Paid miscellaneous expense, $115.

22 Received $2,750 from patients billed on Mar. 15.

23 Acquired additional medical supplies from Cooney Medical Supply Company on account, $910.

25 Paid salaries to employees, $1,120.

26 Billed patients $4,015 for services rendered.

27 Paid Cooney Medical Supply Company, $615 on account.

28 Withdrew $1,500 from the medical practice.

**Required:**

1. Prepare general journal entries for the transactions listed above.
2. Post the entries to the ledger accounts, using account numbers for cross-reference and using general journal page number 1. The following accounts will be needed:

| Account Number | Account | Account Number | Account |
|---|---|---|---|
| 110 | Cash | 320 | Montana, Withdrawals |
| 120 | Accounts Receivable | 410 | Medical Fees Earned |
| 130 | Medical Supplies on Hand | 510 | Salary Expense |
| 140 | Medical Equipment | 520 | Rent Expense |
| 210 | Notes Payable | 530 | Laboratory Expense |
| 220 | Accounts Payable | 540 | Telephone Expense |
| 310 | Montana, Capital | 550 | Miscellaneous Expense |

3. Prepare a trial balance.

▶ *(Check Figure: Trial balance = $24,725)*

4 6 **Problem B3:** Preparing Journal Entries from Two Trial Balances

The Salter Company follows the policy of acquiring all its goods and services, except salaries and withdrawals, on account. Payment is made only after appropriate billings are received and accounts payable established. Cash received for services rendered amounts to 20% of the total revenues earned. The remainder of revenues earned are recorded as accounts receivable.

Presented below are the trial balances for the months ended Oct. 31, 1998, and Nov. 30, 1998.

| | October 1998 | | November 1998 | |
|---|---|---|---|---|
| Cash. | $ 240 | | $2,340 | |
| Accounts Receivable. | 510 | | 300 | |
| Office Supplies on Hand | 120 | | 210 | |
| Office Equipment. | 1,230 | | 1,350 | |
| Accounts Payable | | $ 180 | | $ 90 |
| Salter, Capital | | 600 | | 600 |
| Salter, Withdrawals | 390 | | 420 | |
| Revenues Earned | | 2,400 | | 4,800 |
| Salary Expense | 630 | | 720 | |
| Utilities Expense | 60 | | 150 | |
| Totals. | $3,180 | $3,180 | $5,490 | $5,490 |

**Required:**

Prepare general journal entries (omitting explanations) that reflect the transactions that occurred during the month of November. You will need to establish T-accounts for Accounts Receivable, Accounts Payable, and Cash to determine the payment of accounts payable and the collection of accounts receivable.

2 4 6 **Problem B4:** Journalizing and Posting; Preparing a Trial Balance and Financial Statements

During the month of June 1998, the following transactions were completed by Jim Lance, the owner of the newly established Lance Language School.

June  1   Deposited $10,700 cash in a bank account in the name of the new company.

      2   Acquired land ($9,300) and a building ($27,700) by paying $7,000 cash and issuing a mortgage payable for $30,000.

      3   Acquired equipment for $3,750, paying $1,250 in cash and the remaining $2,500 on account.

      4   Acquired office supplies on account, $1,015.

      6   Paid insurance expense for the month, $430.

      8   Paid for newspaper advertising, $395.

    10   Received $3,100 cash from clients for language lessons.

    11   Paid salaries to employees, $940.

    12   Paid miscellaneous expenses, $305.

    15   Billed clients $5,300 for language lessons.

    18   Paid $650 on accounts payable.

    20   Received an invoice for $375 in repairs to the equipment.

    21   Received $2,345 from clients billed on June 15.

    22   Paid utilities, $370.

    25   Paid employees, $1,120.

    30   Billed clients $6,130 for language lessons.

    30   Withdrew $1,200 from the business.

**Required:**

1. Prepare general journal entries for the transactions listed above.
2. Post the entries to the ledger accounts, using account numbers for cross-reference and using general journal page number 1. The following accounts will be needed:

| Account Number | Account | Account Number | Account |
|---|---|---|---|
| 110 | Cash | 320 | Lance, Withdrawals |
| 120 | Accounts Receivable | 410 | Lesson Fees Earned |
| 130 | Supplies on Hand | 510 | Salary Expense |
| 140 | Land | 520 | Insurance Expense |
| 150 | Building | 530 | Advertising Expense |
| 160 | Equipment | 540 | Repairs Expense |
| 210 | Accounts Payable | 550 | Utilities Expense |
| 220 | Mortgage Payable | 560 | Miscellaneous Expense |
| 310 | Lance, Capital | | |

3. Prepare a trial balance.

▶ *(Check Figure: Trial balance = $58,470)*

4. Prepare an income statement, a statement of changes in owner's equity, and a balance sheet.

2 4 6   **Problem B5:** Journalizing and Posting; Preparing a Trial Balance and Financial Statements

Presented below is the Aug. 1, 1998, balance sheet of Jensen Consulting Company.

**JENSEN CONSULTING COMPANY**
**Balance Sheet**
**August 1, 1998**

| Assets | | Liabilities and Owner's Equity | |
|---|---|---|---|
| | | **Liabilities** | |
| Cash.................... | $ 2,515 | | |
| Accounts Receivable........ | 6,085 | Note Payable.............. | $12,500 |
| Prepaid Insurance........... | 1,200 | Accounts Payable........... | 2,380 |
| Office Supplies on Hand...... | 3,115 | Total Liabilities.......... | $14,880 |
| Land..................... | 3,000 | | |
| Building.................. | 4,295 | **Owner's Equity** | |
| Equipment................ | 41,050 | Jensen, Capital............. | 46,380 |
| | | Total Liabilities and | |
| Total Assets............... | $61,260 | Owner's Equity............ | $61,260 |

| Aug. | 1 | Billed clients for consulting service rendered, $635. |
|---|---|---|
| | 2 | Paid creditors $1,100. |
| | 3 | Paid for advertising, $90. |
| | 5 | Acquired office supplies on account, $505. |
| | 7 | Collected $3,270 from customers. (Credit accounts receivable) |
| | 8 | Paid $3,000 of the balance due on the note payable. |
| | 10 | Received $1,750 cash for consulting services rendered this date. |
| | 12 | Acquired equipment on account, $700. |
| | 15 | Paid salaries due this date, $225. |
| | 17 | Billed clients $685 for consulting services rendered. |
| | 19 | Received and paid an invoice for $470 for repairs. |
| | 20 | Collected accounts receivable, $2,020. |
| | 23 | Paid creditors $2,100. |
| | 25 | Paid miscellaneous expenses, $140. |
| | 30 | Jensen withdrew $500 for personal use. |
| | 30 | Paid salaries, $980. |

**Required:**

1. Enter the amounts from the Aug. 1, 1998, balance sheet into the appropriate general ledger accounts, using the following account numbers:

| 110 | Cash | 210 | Notes Payable |
|---|---|---|---|
| 120 | Accounts Receivable | 220 | Accounts Payable |
| 130 | Prepaid Insurance | 310 | Jensen, Capital |
| 140 | Office Supplies on Hand | | |
| 150 | Land | | |
| 160 | Building | | |
| 170 | Equipment | | |

2. Prepare general journal entries for the August transactions.
3. Post the entries to the general ledger, using page 15 as the general journal page reference and the following additional account numbers:

320  Jensen, Withdrawals
410  Consulting Revenues Earned
510  Salary Expense
520  Advertising Expense
530  Repairs Expense
540  Miscellaneous Expense

4. Prepare a trial balance as of Aug. 31, 1998.

▶ *(Check Figure: Trial balance = $59,335)*

5. Prepare an income statement, a statement of owner's equity, and a balance sheet.

6 7  **Problem B6:** Correcting a Trial Balance

Presented below is Bethel Repair Service's trial balance, which does not balance:

**BETHEL REPAIR SERVICE**
**Trial Balance**
**January 31, 1998**

| | | |
|---|---|---|
| Cash. | $1,104 | |
| Accounts Receivable | 2,846 | |
| Office Supplies on Hand | 664 | |
| Prepaid Insurance | 400 | |
| Office Equipment | 5,268 | |
| Notes Payable | | $ 1,300 |
| Accounts Payable | | 1,954 |
| Bethel, Capital | | 2,972 |
| Bethel, Withdrawals | | 1,000 |
| Repair Revenue Earned | | 8,214 |
| Salary Expense | 3,487 | |
| Advertising Expense | 122 | |
| Totals | $13,891 | $15,440 |

The following information is obtained from a review of the recordkeeping process.

a. An account receivable for $196 was incorrectly added as $169 when computing the balance of the Accounts Receivable account.
b. A debit posting from the general journal for $52 is missing from the Advertising Expense account.
c. A credit posting of $150 to Notes Payable should have been made to Accounts Payable.
d. A debit posting of $340 to Office Supplies on Hand was incorrectly posted as $34.
e. Credits to the general ledger Accounts Payable account were underfooted by $600.
f. Bethel's revenues are overstated in the ledger account by $400.
g. A credit posting for Repair Revenue from the general journal in the amount of $636 is missing.
h. Office supplies acquired in the amount of $174 have been incorrectly posted to the Office Equipment account.

**Required:**

Prepare a corrected trial balance.

▶ *(Check Figure: Corrected trial balance = $15,276)*

## DECISION PROBLEM

On Apr. 1, 1998, the National Football League granted a franchise to Art Davidson to establish a professional football team to be called the Bristol Badboys. Art invested $25,000 and received the franchise charter. Additional cash was obtained by means of a $40,000, 5-year note payable issued to a Bristol bank.

The newly established company acquired used training equipment on May 15 from the Denver Bucks for $18,600, paying $3,600 and financing the remainder by issuing an additional note payable to the Bucks, the 1994 Superbowl champs, due in October 2005.

During the 1998 season, Art Davidson worked diligently to establish a team. He hired a coaching staff, purchased player contracts for 43 professional athletes, rented a stadium and training facilities, and performed myriad other activities associated with professional sports. But no accounting records were kept. At the close of the season (the Badboys finished with a 6–10 record), Davidson wants to know how well the franchise did financially, and he comes to you for help.

From the checkbook you are able to determine that deposits of $325,000 were made from Apr. 1 to Dec. 31. These consisted of the $25,000 initial investment and the $40,000 note payable mentioned above, plus $60,000 admission fees and $200,000 TV revenues from NBS for television rights. The total of the checks written amounts to $251,300, consisting of $51,250 for training camp expenses, $124,720 for salaries, $10,800 for cleaning expenses, $11,000 for rent expense, $9,500 for player equipment, the $3,600 to the Denver Bucks, $18,210 for advertising, and $22,220 for withdrawals.

In addition to the above, you find that the last payment from NBS for $12,500 for televising the Dec. 28 game with the San Francisco Fifties has not yet been received. And the Badboys have unpaid items totaling $3,700, representing $1,920 in salaries and $1,780 in cleaning expenses.

**Required:**

1. Summarize for Art Davidson how well the team is doing financially. Is it profitable?
2. At the end of the year, what was Davidson's interest in the business?
3. At the end of the year, what were Davidson's assets and liabilities?

## ETHICS CASE

Atwater Company manufactures clothing for the collegiate market: T-shirts, sweatshirts and pants, and various other items with college logos. The company started operations several years ago and currently employs 45 people. While management thinks the company has great potential, the company is having difficulty paying its current obligations. Several suppliers are threatening to discontinue service unless they are paid within the month.

The owner, James Atwater, has asked Janice Eller, the company's comptroller, to prepare a set of financial statements that he can use to request additional financing from the bank. This financing will be used to pay current obligations and acquire additional supplies. It is hoped that this financing will enable the company not only to survive, but to become profitable within 2 years.

After Janice prepares the statements, she gives them to James for review. Upon arriving at work the following day, Janice is summoned into James's office. James is very upset. He points to the balance sheet and asks Janice why a note payable in the amount of $160,000 is reflected among the liabilities. He contends that the $160,000 should not be a liability, but part of his capital account. He tells Janice that she must redo the statements with this correction within the hour so that he can keep his appointment with the bank.

Janice returns to her office. She retrieves from her files the document that gave rise to the note payable. The document is handwritten on a yellow legal piece of paper. It states that $160,000 is given to the Atwater Company by three local investors (one of whom is James's sister-in-law). At the end of each year James is to pay the investors $16,000, which is reflected on the income statement as interest expense, and the $160,000 may be returned within 2 to 5 years. The note is signed by James and the three investors.

With the note in hand, Janice returns to James's office and informs him that she thinks this $160,000 should be classified as a liability. James responds that it is clearly his investment of funds obtained by him from the investors. He further states that if the note is classified as a liability, the bank will not extend any new financing. Without the financing, the company will not survive and not only Janice, but all the other employees, will be unemployed.

Janice tells James that she still does not agree. James answers that he understands and respects her position but he must think not only of himself but of the employees. Consequently, James has his secretary retype the statements showing the $160,000 as part of his capital account. He plans to give the revised statements to the bank.

### Required:

1. What are the different ways one could view the note?
2. What are the ethical issues?
3. What should Janice do?

## OBJECTIVE ASSIGNMENT ANSWERS

**True/False**

1. F    2. T    3. F    4. T    5. F

**Multiple Choice**

1. d    2. a    3. b    4. d    5. c
6. e    7. b    8. d    9. d    10. a

# The Adjusting Process

Explain why certain accounts require adjustments at the end of an accounting period

The ultimate objective of financial accounting is to prepare financial statements that represent meaningfully and fairly the results of operations of a business entity over a period of time and its financial position at a point in time.

The basic elements of the accounting model are never measured precisely on the financial statements of a business enterprise. Only after completing all the business transactions over the *entire life* of a business entity can the exact amount of assets, revenue, expenses, and net income be determined. In reality, that's utterly impractical.

To see what we mean, consider a company that owns a building acquired at a cost of $400,000 on Jan. 1, 1973, when the company began operations. At that time the company estimated that the building would have a useful life of 40 years and would be replaced by a new building on Jan. 1, 2013. But 25 years later, on Jan. 1, 1998, a new building is acquired because the original building no longer serves its intended purpose.

As you have probably guessed already, the cost of the original building must be assigned to the expense of doing business over the period of time that the building was in use. Therefore, on Jan. 1, 1973, the yearly building expense for the next 40 years was *estimated* at $10,000 per year ($400,000/40 years). But when the building was replaced in 1998, the *actual* yearly expense turned out to be $16,000 per year ($400,000/25 years) (see Figure 1). The precise amount of the yearly building expense can be determined only after the useful life of the building is over.

Of course, anyone who is interested in the affairs of a business entity cannot wait until the entity completes all the business transactions over its entire life before receiving financial reports on its financial position and results of operations. Though some business entities do cease operations after a few years, most remain in business decade after decade and will continue to remain in business as far into the future as can reasonably be projected. This is the basis of the *going concern* concept.

To provide timely information in financial statements, accountants break the life of business entities into time frames. At the end of each time frame, accountants prepare financial statements. These time frames are referred to as **accounting periods** and are typically a year, a quarter (3 months), or a month in length.

The annual report offers complete financial information to investors, creditors, and other outside users. Although financial statements cannot be regarded as precise,

**Figure 1** A Comparison of the Estimated Useful Life of a Building vs. the Actual Useful Life

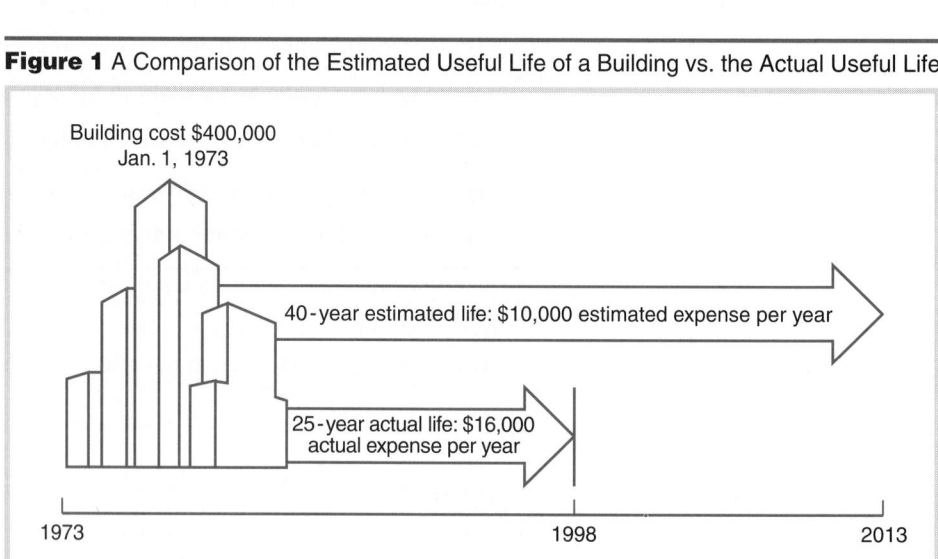

**Figure 2** Prepaid Insurance Becomes Insurance Expense as Insurance Coverage Is Consumed

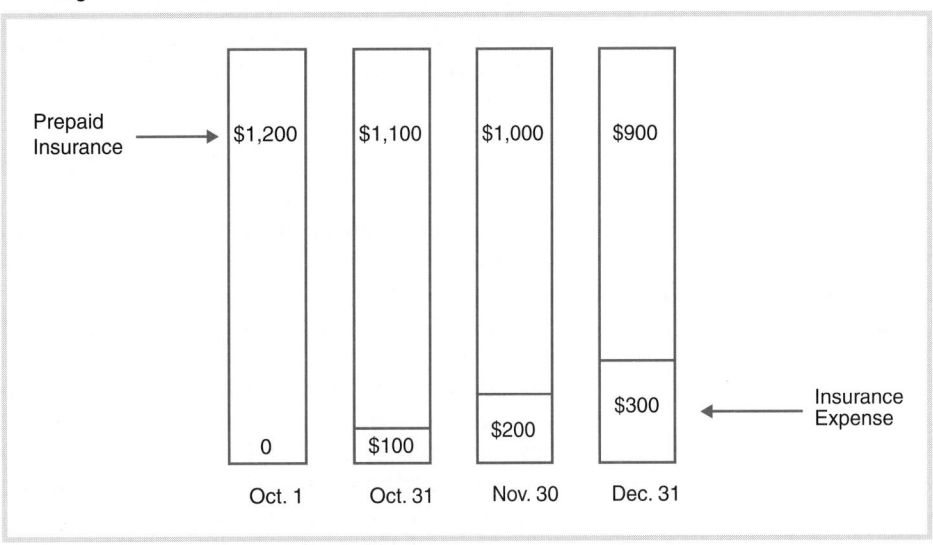

they do reflect fairly the financial position and results of operations for the accounting periods indicated. Business decisions are made with reliance on the belief that financial statements represent fairly what they are supposed to represent. The term *fairly* means that the financial statements reflect the underlying economic events and transactions within an acceptable range of accuracy; much of the study of accounting has to do with what the term *fairly* means.

One major advantage of recording the life of a business entity as a series of regular, successive accounting periods is *comparability*. The ability to compare the business activities of the current period with those of similar past periods makes it possible to judge how well the business has performed. Has revenue increased? Have expenses decreased? Has net income improved? Has the entity's financial position been strengthened? These are typical questions that can be answered by comparing the financial statements for successive accounting periods.

However, preparing financial statements at the end of accounting periods presents some problems as well. The types of entries you have already learned to make in the accounting records represent exchange transactions between a business entity and *second parties*—parties external to the entity. These we refer to as **external transactions.** Consider, for example, an external transaction made on Oct. 1 of the current year for a $1,200, 12-month insurance policy. On that date we would record prepaid insurance as an asset measured at $1,200. But 3 months later, on Dec. 31, only 9 months of insurance coverage remain, while 3 months of insurance expense has been incurred. In order to be fair reflections of the entity's financial situation, the financial statements prepared at the end of the accounting period *must* reflect these shifts in asset and expense values. The statements must show the following:

**1.** All assets owned    **3.** All revenue earned
**2.** All liabilities owed    **4.** All expenses incurred

To meet this objective, some of the accounts must be *adjusted*. The adjustment is accomplished by means of a general journal entry called an **adjusting entry.** Adjusting entries represent **internal transactions,** which do not involve second parties.

Figure 2 shows the values that should be reflected on the financial statements for prepaid insurance and insurance expense on Oct. 1 and Dec. 31. Insurance for 12 months was paid for in advance. A portion of this insurance was "consumed" over 3 months, while 9 months of insurance coverage have not yet been consumed and still represent a future economic benefit. At $100 per month, this would mean that $900 should be the amount of prepaid insurance reported on the balance sheet. Further, because 3 months of economic benefits have been received, at $100 per month, $300 of insurance *expense* should be reported on the income statement. Thus, on Dec. 31, an *adjusting entry* is needed that will reduce Prepaid Insurance by $300 and increase Insurance Expense by this amount.

## CASH VERSUS ACCRUAL ACCOUNTING

Learning Objective **2**

Distinguish between cash-basis and accrual-basis accounting

At this point the distinction between accounting on a cash basis and accounting using an accrual basis becomes important. We have seen in the first few chapters that revenue is considered to be earned when services are rendered, *not* when cash is received. Similarly, expenses are considered to be incurred when services are received, not when cash is paid. This approach is known as **accrual-basis accounting** as required by generally accepted accounting principles.

In **cash-basis accounting** (often used by small businesses and in certain cases for tax purposes), revenue is reported only if that revenue was in fact received in the form of cash. The same goes for expenses: An expense is reported only if it was indeed disbursed in cash.

Thus, net income under the cash basis represents simply the difference between cash receipts and cash disbursements. If the cash basis of accounting were used, this chapter on adjustments would not be necessary.

The accounting profession has determined that *financial statements prepared under the cash basis of accounting do not represent fairly the results of operations or the financial position of a business entity*. A company using the cash basis could easily increase its net income by encouraging its customers to pay their bills early. Net income could also be increased significantly if the company delayed payment of its own bills. Such practices are referred to as *profit manipulation*. The cash basis of accounting is therefore not part of generally accepted accounting principles.

*Accrual-basis accounting* relies on the *revenue-recognition principle* and the *matching concept*. According to the **revenue-recognition principle,** revenue is reported in the financial statements in the accounting period in which it is earned, not in the accounting period when the cash representing that revenue is received. For example, suppose a department store sells a shirt to a credit account customer on Dec. 28. The revenue representing the sale of that shirt is recognized on that date—not when the customer pays for the shirt, which may be in January or February.

Learning Objective **3**

Explain the revenue-recognition principle and the matching concept

According to the **matching concept,** expenses should be assigned to those periods in which they helped generate revenues. This may be easy in concept, as in the case of the sale of the shirt in the example above. The amount that the shirt cost the store would be matched against the revenue that the store earned from selling the shirt, and the salaries of the salespeople would be matched against revenues during the period in which the shirt was sold. Depreciation on the display counters is more difficult, as we saw earlier in the case of the $400,000 building. The point is that all expenses associated with the sale of the shirt must be reported when the shirt is sold, whether those expenses were paid for by then or not.

The following example will help explain the difference between the cash basis and the accrual basis of accounting, as well as clarify what we mean by the revenue-recognition principle and the matching concept.

Assume that Reston Pest Control Service enters into a contract on Jan. 18, 1998, with John Holland. Specifically, Reston agrees to treat Holland's home on Mar. 15, 1998, for termite infestation. The agreed price for the treatment is $900.

Feb. 21  Reston acquires the necessary pest control supplies on account for $350.

Mar. 15  Reston performs his service in a satisfactory manner as agreed on the specified date.

Apr. 2    Reston pays the $350 on account for the pest control supplies acquired on Feb. 21.

May 7    Reston receives payment in full, $900, from John Holland for the service rendered on Mar. 15.

Presented below is a summary of Reston Pest Control Service's activity from Jan. 18 to May 7, 1998.

Reston Pest Control: Summary of Events

| Jan. 18 | Feb. 21 | Mar. 15 | Apr. 2 | May 7 |
|---------|---------|---------|--------|-------|
| Agreed to treat home | Acquired supplies on account | Service rendered on account | Paid for supplies | Received payment |
| $900 | $350 | | $350 | $900 |

Under the cash basis of accounting, Reston's net income for each of the 5 months would be determined as follows:

| | Jan. | Feb. | Mar. | Apr. | May | Totals |
|---|------|------|------|------|-----|--------|
| Revenue | $ 0 | $ 0 | $ 0 | $ 0 | $900 | $900 |
| Expense | 0 | 0 | 0 | 350 | 0 | 350 |
| Net income | $ 0 | $ 0 | $ 0 | $(350) | $900 | $550 |

The accrual basis of accounting would report net income for each of the 5 months according to the following table:

| | Jan. | Feb. | Mar. | Apr. | May | Totals |
|---|------|------|------|------|-----|--------|
| Revenue | $ 0 | $ 0 | $900 | $ 0 | $ 0 | $900 |
| Expense | 0 | 0 | 350 | 0 | 0 | 350 |
| Net income | $ 0 | $ 0 | $550 | $ 0 | $ 0 | $550 |

It is the accrual basis that best provides the statement user with information that represents fairly the results of operations:

- In January an *agreement to provide services* was made between the two parties. This agreement does not constitute revenue for Reston, since the service has yet to be performed.
- The purchase of the pest control supplies for $350 in February represents the acquisition of an asset, Pest Control Supplies on Hand. At this point the supplies are not an expense, since they have not yet been used.
- Income is earned in March because:
  1. Revenue is recognized now that services have been rendered: The house has been treated for termite infestation.
  2. An expense is incurred: The pest control supplies have been used. Pest Control Supplies Used Expense will be matched against Pest Control Fees Earned to measure the net income.
- The collection of the $900 account receivable in May represents the increase in one asset, Cash, and the reduction of a second, Accounts Receivable.
- The payment of $350 in April represents the reduction of the asset Cash and the reduction of a current liability, Accounts Payable.

Under the cash basis, revenue of $900 is not recognized until actually received in May, and expenses of $350 are not recorded until actually paid in April. Clearly, the evidence exists in March that can provide the basis for reporting the economic substance of the transaction to those interested in such information. Service has in fact been provided. The subsequent receipt from the customer and payment to the supplier follow as a normal consequence that *can be predicted at the point of sale.*

Profit manipulation is difficult under the accrual basis, where there are established criteria for recognizing both revenue and expenses. These criteria specify the time when revenue and expenses are to be recognized; it cannot be manipulated.

With this understanding of revenue-recognition and matching, we are now ready to consider adjusting entries.

---

**ASK YOURSELF** ▶

1. **Distinguish between external and internal transactions.**
2. **Why is it necessary to adjust some accounts?**
3. **Distinguish between the cash-basis and the accrual-basis accounting systems.**
4. **What is meant by the term *revenue recognition?***
5. **Explain the matching concept.**

## TYPES OF ADJUSTING ENTRIES

There are two broad classifications of adjusting entries: *deferrals* and *accruals.*

Learning Objective **4**

Distinguish between deferral and accrual adjusting entries

1. **Deferrals** are adjustments for goods and services collected or paid for in advance of benefits given or received. In other words, the benefits are postponed, or *deferred,* until some time after payment. Deferrals require adjustments of external transactions previously entered in the general journal and posted to the ledger accounts. Deferral adjusting entries record the portion of the benefits that have been used.

2. **Accruals** are adjustments for revenue already earned and expenses already incurred for which no transaction has yet been recorded. That is, the revenue or expense has *accrued* to (or affected the balance of) an account and now must be recorded by means of an adjusting entry.

*Every adjusting entry affects both the income statement accounts (revenues and expenses) and the balance sheet accounts (assets, liabilities, and owner's equity).*

### Deferrals

Learning Objective **5**

List the various types of deferrals and prepare appropriate adjusting entries

The broad classification of deferrals encompasses three types of adjusting entries: *prepaid expenses, unearned revenue,* and *depreciation.*

#### Prepaid Expenses

Items that are paid for before they are used are called **prepaid expenses.** A cost is incurred at the time such items are acquired. Before the item is consumed, this cost is called an **unexpired cost** and represents an asset that will yield a future economic benefit. As time passes this asset is consumed in part or in total, and the consumed amount becomes an **expired cost,** which is an *expense* of doing business. Typical prepaid expenses include prepaid insurance, prepaid rent, office supplies on hand, repair parts on hand, and, in the broadest sense, buildings and office equipment.

**Exhibit 1** Unadjusted Trial Balance

## THE MARY ABREMS DANCE STUDIO
### Unadjusted Trial Balance
### November 30, 1998

**Line**

| | | | |
|---|---|---:|---:|
| | Cash | $ 5,250 | |
| | Accounts Receivable | 2,950 | |
| (b) | Office Supplies on Hand | 450 | |
| (a) | Prepaid Rent | 900 | |
| (d) | Office Equipment | 10,800 | |
| (f) | Note Payable, 12% due Apr. 30 | | $ 3,000 |
| | Accounts Payable | | 650 |
| (c) | Unearned Dance Lesson Revenues | | 1,800 |
| | Abrems, Capital | | 11,000 |
| | Abrems, Withdrawals | 500 | |
| | Dance Lesson Revenues | | 8,400 |
| (e) | Salary Expense | 2,500 | |
| | Utilities Expense | 1,100 | |
| | Advertising Expense | 400 | |
| | Totals | $24,850 | $24,850 |

To see how to adjust a prepaid expense, as well as how to make the other adjustments we will introduce in the following pages, consider the trial balance of The Mary Abrems Dance Studio shown in Exhibit 1.

Notice that the schedule is called the *unadjusted trial balance,* because we have not yet made the adjustments. Once the adjustments are made, we prepare another trial balance called the *adjusted trial balance.* More on this procedure later.

**Adjustment A: Prepaid Rent/Rent Expense**   On Nov. 3, rent at $300 per month for 3 months was paid in advance by the dance studio and recorded in the general journal by the following entry.*

| | | | |
|---|---|---:|---:|
| Nov. 3 | Prepaid Rent **(A)** | 900 | |
| | Cash **(A)** | | 900 |
| | To record payment of rent in advance for November, December, and January at $300 per month. | | |

At the end of November the dance studio has received the benefit of occupying space for 1 month and has the right to occupancy for 2 additional months. The accounting record—that is, the Prepaid Rent as seen in the Nov. 30 unadjusted trial balance [the line designated (a)]—does not reflect this situation. An adjusting entry is required. One month's expired cost, $300, must be recorded as rent expense, and 2 months' unexpired costs must remain as prepaid rent of $600. The adjusting entry would be recorded in the general journal as follows:

ADJUSTMENT A: Prepaid Rent/Rent Expense

| | | | |
|---|---|---:|---:|
| Nov. 30 | Rent Expense **(OE:E)** | 300 | |
| | Prepaid Rent **(A)** | | 300 |
| | To record rent expense. | | |

* The letters in parentheses in journal entries refer to the following accounts: **A** = Assets; **L** = Liabilities; **OE** = Owner's Equity; **OE:R** = Owner's Equity:Revenue; **OE:E** = Owner's Equity:Expense.

In essence, $300 has been transferred from the Prepaid Rent account to the Rent Expense account, as can be seen by the posted T-accounts:

| ASSET | | | EXPENSE | |
|---|---|---|---|---|
| **Prepaid Rent** | | | **Rent Expense** | |
| Nov. 3 | 900 | Nov. 30  (a)  300  →  Nov. 30  (a)  300 | |
| Bal. | 600 | | | |

Notice that the balance in the Prepaid Rent account after the posting of the adjusting entry is $600.

**Adjustment B: Supplies on Hand/Supplies Expense**  Office Supplies on Hand represents another type of prepaid expense. Line (b) of the unadjusted trial balance indicates that, as of Nov. 30, there is $450 of office supplies on hand. These supplies were acquired on Nov. 9 and recorded in the general journal by the following entry:

| Nov. 9 | Office Supplies on Hand **(A)** . . . . . . . . . . . . . . . . . . . . . . | 450 | |
|---|---|---|---|
| | Cash **(A)** . . . . . . . . . . . . . . . . . . . . . . . . . . . . . . . . . . | | 450 |
| | To record acquisition of office supplies. | | |

These supplies represent an asset worth $450 to the dance studio on Nov. 9. But as the studio uses office supplies during the month, the asset is reduced and an expense, Office Supplies Expense, is incurred. As you can imagine, no purpose would be served by recording Office Supplies Expense as an expense each time supplies are consumed. To do so would require extensive bookkeeping efforts with no benefit, since the financial statements are not needed until the end of the month. But at the end of the month, before the financial statements are prepared, an adjusting entry is required to properly reflect the total amount of supplies consumed—*the expense incurred*—and the amount of supplies remaining—*the value of supplies on hand.* The amount of supplies used is determined by counting (taking an inventory of) the office supplies remaining on hand at the end of the month, and then subtracting the supplies on hand at the end of the month from the total of supplies acquired during the month plus supplies on hand at the beginning of the month.

For example, if the dance studio has $140 of supplies on hand at the end of the month, the amount of supplies used is calculated as follows:

| Office Supplies | |
|---|---|
| On hand, Nov. 1 . . . . . . . . . . . . . . . . . . . . . . . . . . . . . . . . . . . . . . . . . . . . . . . . . . | $   0 |
| Acquired, Nov. 9 . . . . . . . . . . . . . . . . . . . . . . . . . . . . . . . . . . . . . . . . . . . . . . . . . . | 450 |
| Available . . . . . . . . . . . . . . . . . . . . . . . . . . . . . . . . . . . . . . . . . . . . . . . . . . . . . . . . | $450 |
| On hand, Nov. 30 . . . . . . . . . . . . . . . . . . . . . . . . . . . . . . . . . . . . . . . . . . . . . . . . . . | 140 |
| Used . . . . . . . . . . . . . . . . . . . . . . . . . . . . . . . . . . . . . . . . . . . . . . . . . . . . . . . . . . . | $310 |

From this information the appropriate adjusting entry would be recorded in the general journal as follows:

ADJUSTMENT B: Supplies on Hand/Supplies Expense

| Nov. 30 | Office Supplies Expense **(OE : E)** . . . . . . . . . . . . . . . . . . . | 310 | |
|---|---|---|---|
| | Office Supplies on Hand **(A)** . . . . . . . . . . . . . . . . . . | | 310 |
| | To record office supplies used. | | |

In the ledger accounts, a debit to Office Supplies Expense establishes the fact that a $310 expense has been incurred. A credit to Office Supplies on Hand reduces this asset from $450 to $140, the value of the asset at the end of the month. The adjusting entry is posted to the ledger accounts as follows:

| ASSET | | | EXPENSE | |
|---|---|---|---|---|
| **Office Supplies on Hand** | | | **Office Supplies Expense** | |
| Nov. 9      450 | Nov. 30  (b)  310 ⟶ | Nov. 30  (b)  310 | | |
| Bal.          140 | | | | |

### Unearned Revenue

**Unearned revenue** is the liability incurred when cash is received before goods or services are rendered. Unearned revenue is adjusted in the same way as prepaid expenses, except that liability and revenue accounts rather than asset and expense accounts are involved.

**Adjustment C: Unearned Revenue/Revenue**   The $1,800 account balance for Unearned Dance Lesson Revenues on The Mary Abrems Dance Studio unadjusted trial balance [Exhibit 1, line (c)] represents an $1,800 receipt by the studio from a client in advance of the dance lessons to be rendered in the future. The cash was received on Nov. 4 for 9 months of lessons. As of Nov. 4, the studio has received an asset, cash, of $1,800. It has also incurred an obligation, which accountants refer to as a liability, to perform a service in the amount of $1,800 for the client. On Nov. 4, the studio has not yet earned the revenue it received. This liability is called Unearned Dance Lesson Revenues.

As the weeks go by, the lessons are given, the obligation is reduced, and revenue is earned. Since financial statements are needed as of Nov. 30, an adjusting entry is required on that date to properly reflect all revenue earned during the month and all liabilities still owed at month-end. The appropriate adjusting entry reducing the liability Unearned Dance Lesson Revenues by $200 ($1,800/9 months) and recording the amount earned, Dance Lesson Revenues of $200, is as follows:

ADJUSTMENT C: Unearned Revenue/Revenue

| | | |
|---|---|---|
| Nov. 30 | Unearned Dance Lesson Revenues **(L)** . . . . . . . . . . . . | 200 |
| | Dance Lesson Revenues **(OE:R)** . . . . . . . . . . . . . | 200 |
| | To record dance lesson revenue earned. | |

Posting the adjusting entry to the ledger accounts is illustrated in the following T-accounts:

| LIABILITY | | | REVENUE | |
|---|---|---|---|---|
| **Unearned Dance Lesson Revenues** | | | **Dance Lesson Revenues** | |
| Nov. 30      200 | Nov. 4      1,800 | | | Nov. 30      8,400 |
| | | | | Nov. 30        200 |
| | Bal.         1,600 | | | Bal.         8,600 |

## Depreciation

The cost of such fixed assets as buildings, equipment, and vehicles must be allocated as an expense over the length of their estimated useful lives. This systematic expense allocation is called **depreciation.**

**Adjustment D: Depreciation/Accumulated Depreciation**   To illustrate the adjustment necessary to reflect the depreciation of fixed assets, refer again to Exhibit 1, The Mary Abrems Dance Studio unadjusted trial balance. Office Equipment totaling $10,800 was acquired on Nov. 2 and Nov. 5 [see line (d)]. The equipment is estimated by the company to have a 5-year life, after which it will be considered worthless. Depreciation expense is determined by assigning equal portions of the $10,800 to each of the 5 years, or allocating $2,160 per year. One month's depreciation expense would then be $180 ($2,160/12). Before financial statements are prepared, an adjusting entry to show monthly depreciation is required. When this entry is recorded, the asset account Office Equipment is not directly reduced. Rather, the amount of depreciation is recorded and accumulated in a separate, special account called *Accumulated Depreciation: Office Equipment.* (This is different from the adjustments made for prepaid assets, in which the asset account *is* directly reduced as the benefits of the asset are received; look again at adjustment A, above.)

ADJUSTMENT D: Depreciation/Accumulated Depreciation

| | | |
|---|---|---|
| Nov. 30 | Depreciation Expense: Office Equipment (**OE : E**) . . . . . | 180 |
| | Accumulated Depreciation: Office Equipment (**A**) . . | 180 |
| | To record one month's depreciation. | |

The ledger accounts would reflect the following:

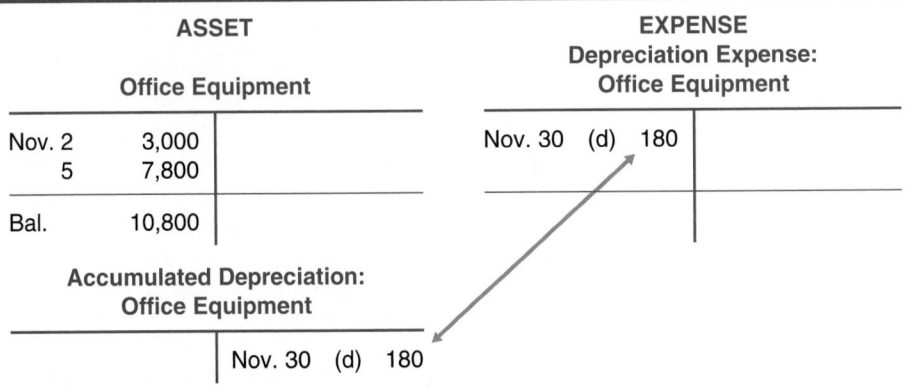

The Accumulated Depreciation account is a *contra account,* specifically a *contra-asset account.* The term **contra account** means an account that has a balance opposite, or contra, to the normal balance of the particular account to which it relates. We would expect an asset account to have a debit balance, but a contra-asset account has a credit balance and thus reduces assets. A *contra-liability account* has a debit balance and thus reduces the liability account to which it relates.

Both the Office Equipment account and the Accumulated Depreciation: Office Equipment account would appear on the balance sheet. The difference between the balances of these two accounts, $10,620 ($10,800 − $180), is called the **book value** of the asset, sometimes also called the **carrying value.** It is the value that is recorded in the firm's books, and it would appear on the balance sheet like this:

| | | |
|---|---|---|
| Office Equipment . . . . . . . . . . . . . . . . . . . . . . . . . . . . . . . . . . . . . . . | $10,800 | |
| Less: Accumulated Depreciation: Office Equipment . . . . . . . . . . . . | 180 | $10,620 |

**Figure 3** Book Value of Office Equipment as a Percentage of Original Cost after 4 out of 5 Years of Useful Life

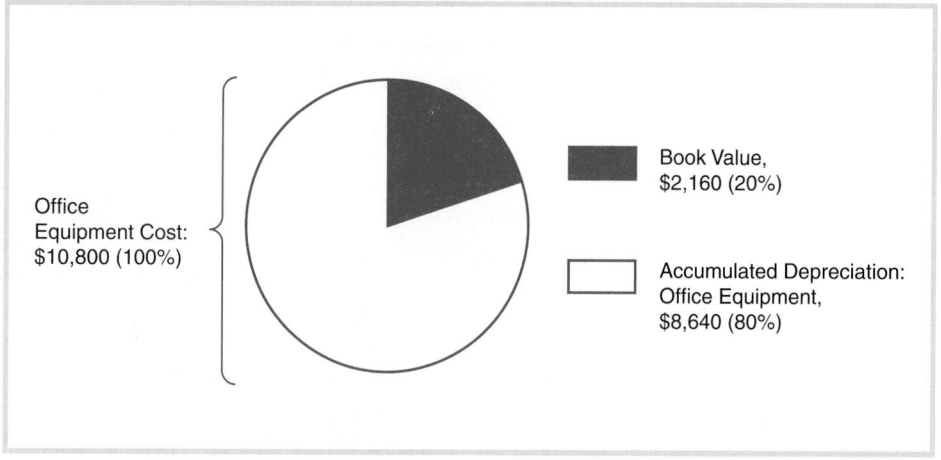

The reason we use a contra-asset account is to preserve a record of the original cost of the asset. Users of the financial statements can then compare the depreciation recorded to date—that is, the accumulated depreciation—with the original cost found in the asset account. This comparison provides the user with information as to the relative age of the assets. For example, on the balance sheet prepared 4 years from the date The Mary Abrems Dance Studio started business, the Accumulated Depreciation: Office Equipment account would have a balance of $8,640 ($2,160 per year × 4 years) and would appear as follows:

| | | |
|---|---|---|
| Office Equipment . . . . . . . . . . . . . . . . . . . . . . . . . . . . . . . . . . . . . . . | $10,800 | |
| Less: Accumulated Depreciation: Office Equipment . . . . . . . . . . . . . | 8,640 | $2,160 |

The book value of $2,160, when compared to the original cost of $10,800, would inform investors that the office equipment is nearing the end of its useful life and that the company may need to expend funds to replace these assets in the near future (see Figure 3).

The general ledger account Accumulated Depreciation: Office Equipment would have accumulated depreciation of $180 per month for 48 months (4 years × 12 months), as seen below:

**Accumulated Depreciation: Office Equipment**

| | | |
|---|---|---|
| | Nov. 30, 1998 | 180 |
| | Dec. 31, 1998 | 180 |
| | Jan. 31, 1999 | 180 |
| | Sept. 30, 2002 | 180 |
| | Oct. 31, 2002 | 180 |
| | Bal. Oct. 31, 2002 | 8,640 |

## Accruals

Learning
Objective **6**

List the various types of accruals and prepare appropriate adjusting entries

Adjustments for revenue already earned and expenses already incurred but for which no transaction has yet been recorded are called *accruals*. Examples of accruals are salaries and interest.

*Salaries*

Expenses are paid in one of three ways:

1. In advance of the benefits they provide, like the deferrals discussed earlier
2. During the accounting period when the benefits are received
3. After their benefits have already been received

The most common business expenses that are not paid for until after their benefits have been received are salaries and wages. Most of us are not paid until we have provided our services to our employers. Then we are paid at the end of each week, every 2 weeks, twice a month, or at the end of the month, but only *after* we have performed our services.

When salaries are paid before the end of the accounting period, the expense is recorded by a journal entry debiting Salary Expense and crediting Cash. A problem occurs when the last day of the accounting period is not a payday. In this case the employees have performed a service that represents an expense to the company, and the company in turn has a liability for these services. The financial statements must reflect both the *expense incurred* and the *liability owed.* An adjusting entry is required.

**Adjustment E: Salary Expense/Salaries Payable**  Referring again to The Mary Abrems Dance Studio's unadjusted trial balance (Exhibit 1), notice that Salary Expense amounts to $2,500 [line (e)]. Assume that rather than being paid on Nov. 24, the last Friday in the month, the salaries are paid biweekly, as shown in Figure 4.

During the last week of November there are four additional workdays, but the next scheduled payday is not until Friday, Dec. 8. Mary Abrems has two employees and pays each of them $62.50 per day for a 5-day work week. This amounts to $1,250 for both employees every 2 weeks ($62.50 × 2 × 10). Thus, $500 ($62.50 per day × 2 employees × 4 days) of additional Salary Expense must be recorded in the general

**Figure 4** Abrems Dance Studio Payday Calendar

| November | | | | | | |
|---|---|---|---|---|---|---|
| Working Days | | | | | Weekend | |
| Mon. | Tues. | Wed. | Thurs. | Fri. | Sat. | Sun. |
|  |  | 1 | 2 | 3 | 4 | 5 |
| 6 | 7 | 8 | 9 | Payday 10 $1,250 | 11 | 12 |
| 13 | 14 | 15 | 16 | 17 | 18 | 19 |
| 20 | 21 | 22 | 23 | Payday 24 $1,250 | 25 | 26 |
| 27 | 28 | 29 | 30 | December 1 | 2 | 3 |
| 4 | 5 | 6 | 7 | Payday 8 $1,250 | 9 | 10 |

journal on Nov. 30 to reflect properly all the expenses incurred during the month of November. The salary expense of $500 for the last week in November is not only an expense of doing business, it is also a liability. It represents salaries that have been earned but not paid and are therefore an obligation of the dance studio. Thus, the adjusting entry to accrue the $500 expense and liability would be recorded as follows:

ADJUSTMENT E: Salary Expense/Salaries Payable

| | | |
|---|---|---|
| Nov. 30 | Salary Expense **(OE:E)** . . . . . . . . . . . . . . . . . . . . . . . . | 500 |
| | Salaries Payable **(L)** . . . . . . . . . . . . . . . . . . . . . . . . | 500 |
| | To record accrual of salaries. | |

After the adjusting entry is recorded, Salary Expense will total $3,000, representing the proper expense for the month—salaries already paid, $2,500 ($1,250 × 2), plus salaries to be paid, $500. Salaries Payable will be $500, which is the liability as of Nov. 30. The effect of the adjusting entry is illustrated in T-accounts as follows:

| **EXPENSE** | **LIABILITY** |
|---|---|
| **Salary Expense** | **Salaries Payable** |
| Nov. 10    1,250 | Nov. 30   (e)    500 |
| Nov. 24    1,250 | |
| Nov. 30  (e)    500 | |
| Bal. Nov. 30  3,000 | |

Care must be taken when the Dec. 8 payroll is recorded. If the entry is made in the usual manner—that is, a debit to Salary Expense and a credit to Cash—then Salary Expense for December will be overstated by the $500 accrual already debited to Salary Expense. The appropriate entry for Dec. 8 should be recorded as follows:

| | | | |
|---|---|---|---|
| Dec. 8 | Salaries Payable **(L)** . . . . . . . . . . . . . . . . . . . . . . . . . . . . | 500 | |
| | Salary Expense **(OE:E)** . . . . . . . . . . . . . . . . . . . . . . . . | 750 | |
| | Cash **(A)** . . . . . . . . . . . . . . . . . . . . . . . . . . . . . . . . . . | | 1,250 |
| | To record payment of salaries. | | |

When the Dec. 8 entry is made, Salaries Payable must be debited because that liability was paid with the Dec. 8 payroll. Salary Expense is debited for $750, representing the expense incurred for the 6 working days in December. This amount is the difference between the total payroll for the 2-week period, $1,250, and the amount accrued for the last 4 days of November, $500, as the calendar illustrates.

### *Interest*

Like salaries, interest is earned day by day. However, accountants do not record interest until after it is paid—either by the company or to the company. Thus, if the accounting period ends before the interest is paid or received, an adjusting entry is required. This adjusting entry will record the amount of the interest expense (or interest income in the case of money lent to another company or individual) incurred during the period and the corresponding liability for the interest payable (or asset for the interest receivable).

**Adjustment F: Interest Expense/Interest Payable** To see how this works, consider the 12% note payable due on Apr. 30 [see line (f) in Exhibit 1]. The note was issued on Nov. 2, 1995, for office equipment, and will be repaid 6 months later, on April 30, 1996. Interest rates are expressed as annual rates, so if interest is being calculated for less than a year, the calculation must express time as a portion of a year. Thus, the interest expense incurred on this note during the month of November is determined by the following formula:

$$\text{Interest} = \text{principal} \times \text{rate} \times \text{time}$$

$$= \$3,000 \times 12\% \text{ per year} \times 1/12 \text{ year}$$
$$= \$3,000 \times .12 \times 1/12$$
$$= \$30$$

The adjusting entry to record the interest expense incurred in November is as follows:

ADJUSTMENT F: Interest Expense/Interest Payable

| | | |
|---|---|---|
| Nov. 30 | Interest Expense **(OE : E)**........................ | 30 |
| | Interest Payable **(L)**......................... | 30 |
| | To record accrual of interest. | |

| EXPENSE | | LIABILITY | |
|---|---|---|---|
| Interest Expense | | Interest Payable | |
| Nov. 30 (f) 30 | | Nov. 30 (f) 30 | |

**Adjustment for: Interest Receivable/Interest Income** While The Mary Abrems Dance Studio did not have a transaction in November that would give rise to the accrual of revenue, the Deluxe Office Supply Company did. Deluxe was the company that sold Abrems the office equipment on Nov. 2 for the $3,000, 12%, 6-month note.

For Deluxe, interest must be accrued for the month of November in the amount of $30, just as with The Mary Abrems Dance Studio. However, to Deluxe this is interest income, not interest expense, and the adjusting entry to record the $30 interest income would be as follows:

ADJUSTMENT: Interest Receivable/Interest Income

| | | |
|---|---|---|
| Nov. 30 | Interest Receivable **(A)**......................... | 30 |
| | Interest Income **(OE : R)** ..................... | 30 |
| | To record accrual of interest. | |

| ASSET | | REVENUE | |
|---|---|---|---|
| Interest Receivable | | Interest Income | |
| Nov. 30 30 | | Nov. 30 30 | |

**ASK YOURSELF ▶**

1. What are deferrals?
2. Prepaid expenses and unearned revenues are very similar. Explain.
3. What is a contra account?
4. Explain the term *book value.*
5. What are accruals?

## THE ADJUSTED TRIAL BALANCE

Learning Objective **7**

Explain the purpose of an adjusted trial balance and prepare one

After the adjusting entries are recorded and posted, a second trial balance is prepared. This second trial balance is the **adjusted trial balance.** In Exhibit 2 the unadjusted trial balance of The Mary Abrems Dance Studio is repeated from Exhibit 1. A pair of columns for debits and credits follows to show how the unadjusted trial balance accounts are increased or decreased by the adjusting process. And a final pair of columns shows the adjusted trial balance.

**Exhibit 2** Adjusting Entry Summary

THE MARY ABREMS DANCE STUDIO

| | Unadjusted Trial Balance November 30, 1998 | | Adjustments Debits | | Credits | | Adjusted Trial Balance November 30, 1998 | |
|---|---|---|---|---|---|---|---|---|
| Cash | $ 5,250 | | | | | | $ 5,250 | |
| Accounts Receivable | 2,950 | | | | | | 2,950 | |
| Office Supplies on Hand | 450 | | | | (b) | 310 | 140 | |
| Prepaid Rent | 900 | | | | (a) | 300 | 600 | |
| Office Equipment | 10,800 | | | | | | 10,800 | |
| Accumulated Depreciation: Office Equipment | | | | | (d) | 180 | | $ 180 |
| Note Payable, 12% due Apr. 30 | | $ 3,000 | | | | | | 3,000 |
| Interest Payable | | | | | (f) | 30 | | 30 |
| Accounts Payable | | 650 | | | | | | 650 |
| Salaries Payable | | | | | (e) | 500 | | 500 |
| Unearned Dance Lesson Revenues | | 1,800 | (c) | 200 | | | | 1,600 |
| Abrems, Capital | | 11,000 | | | | | | 11,000 |
| Abrems, Withdrawals | 500 | | | | | | 500 | |
| Dance Lesson Revenues | | 8,400 | | | (c) | 200 | | 8,600 |
| Salary Expense | 2,500 | | (e) | 500 | | | 3,000 | |
| Rent Expense | | | (a) | 300 | | | 300 | |
| Office Supplies Expense | | | (b) | 310 | | | 310 | |
| Depreciation Expense: Office Equipment | | | (d) | 180 | | | 180 | |
| Interest Expense | | | (f) | 30 | | | 30 | |
| Utilities Expense | 1,100 | | | | | | 1,100 | |
| Advertising Expense | 400 | | | | | | 400 | |
| Totals | $24,850 | $24,850 | | | | | $25,560 | $25,560 |

# Improper Adjusting Entry

The Securities and Exchange Commission reported on April 5, 1984, that as a result of

their investigation of Alpex Computer Corporation's financial statements for the year ended December 31, 1981, they found that the statements were materially false and misleading. Among other improprieties the SEC discovered that Alpex had improperly recorded as income $81,314 of accrued interest on worthless notes receivable. As a

result of the improper recording of the item, Alpex's revenues were overstated by 40%; operating losses were understated by 85%; and net income was overstated by 13%.

*Source:* Securities and Exchange Commission, *Accounting and Auditing Enforcement Release No. 27,* Apr. 5, 1984.

The purpose of the interest income accrual adjusting entry is to properly match revenue earned to the appropriate accounting period. Apparently Alpex Computer Corporation used this simple adjusting entry to significantly increase revenues on its 1981 income statement.

The financial statements are prepared directly from the adjusted trial balance. We prepare the income statement first because the net income figure is needed when we prepare the statement of owner's equity. The statement of owner's equity then provides the ending capital balance, which we need for the balance sheet. The income statement is relatively easy to prepare once the adjusted trial balance is prepared, as you can see in Exhibit 3.

For the statement of owner's equity we simply add to the initial investment of $11,000 the net income of $3,280, and subtract the withdrawals of $500 to arrive at the ending capital balance. The statement of owner's equity would appear as shown in Exhibit 4.

Finally, we prepare the balance sheet prepared for The Mary Abrems Dance Studio, again using the adjusted trial balance (see Exhibit 5).

**Exhibit 3** Income Statement

### THE MARY ABREMS DANCE STUDIO
### Income Statement
### Month Ended November 30, 1998

| | | |
|---|---|---|
| Revenues: | | |
| Dance Lesson Revenues | | $8,600 |
| Operating Expenses: | | |
| Salary Expense | $3,000 | |
| Rent Expense | 300 | |
| Office Supplies Expense | 310 | |
| Depreciation Expense: Office Equipment | 180 | |
| Interest Expense | 30 | |
| Utilities Expense | 1,100 | |
| Advertising Expense | 400 | |
| Total Operating Expenses | | 5,320 |
| Net Income | | $3,280 |

**Exhibit 4** Statement of Owner's Equity

## THE MARY ABREMS DANCE STUDIO
### Statement of Owner's Equity
### Month Ended November 30, 1998

| | | |
|---|---|---:|
| Abrems, Capital, Nov. 1, 1998 | | $ –0– |
| Add: Investment | | 11,000 |
| Net Income | | 3,280 |
| Total | | 14,280 |
| Less: Withdrawals | | 500 |
| Abrems, Capital, Nov. 30, 1998 | | $13,780 |

**Exhibit 5** Balance Sheet

## THE MARY ABREMS DANCE STUDIO
### Balance Sheet
### November 30, 1998

#### Assets

| | | |
|---|---:|---:|
| Cash | | $ 5,250 |
| Accounts Receivable | | 2,950 |
| Office Supplies on Hand | | 140 |
| Prepaid Rent | | 600 |
| Office Equipment | $10,800 | |
| Less: Accumulated Depreciation: Office Equipment | 180 | 10,620 |
| Total Assets | | $19,560 |

#### Liabilities

| | |
|---|---:|
| Notes Payable, 12% due Apr. 30 | $ 3,000 |
| Interest Payable | 30 |
| Accounts Payable | 650 |
| Salaries Payable | 500 |
| Unearned Dance Lesson Revenues | 1,600 |
| Total Liabilities | $ 5,780 |

#### Owner's Equity

| | |
|---|---:|
| Abrems, Capital | 13,780 |
| Total Liabilities and Owner's Equity | $19,560 |

## THE ACCOUNTING PROCESS REVIEWED

*Learning Objective* **8**

List the various steps involved in the accounting process

The ultimate objective of financial accounting is to prepare financial statements that represent meaningfully and fairly the results of operations of a business entity over a period of time and its financial position at a point in time. The process we have

**Figure 5** The Accounting Process

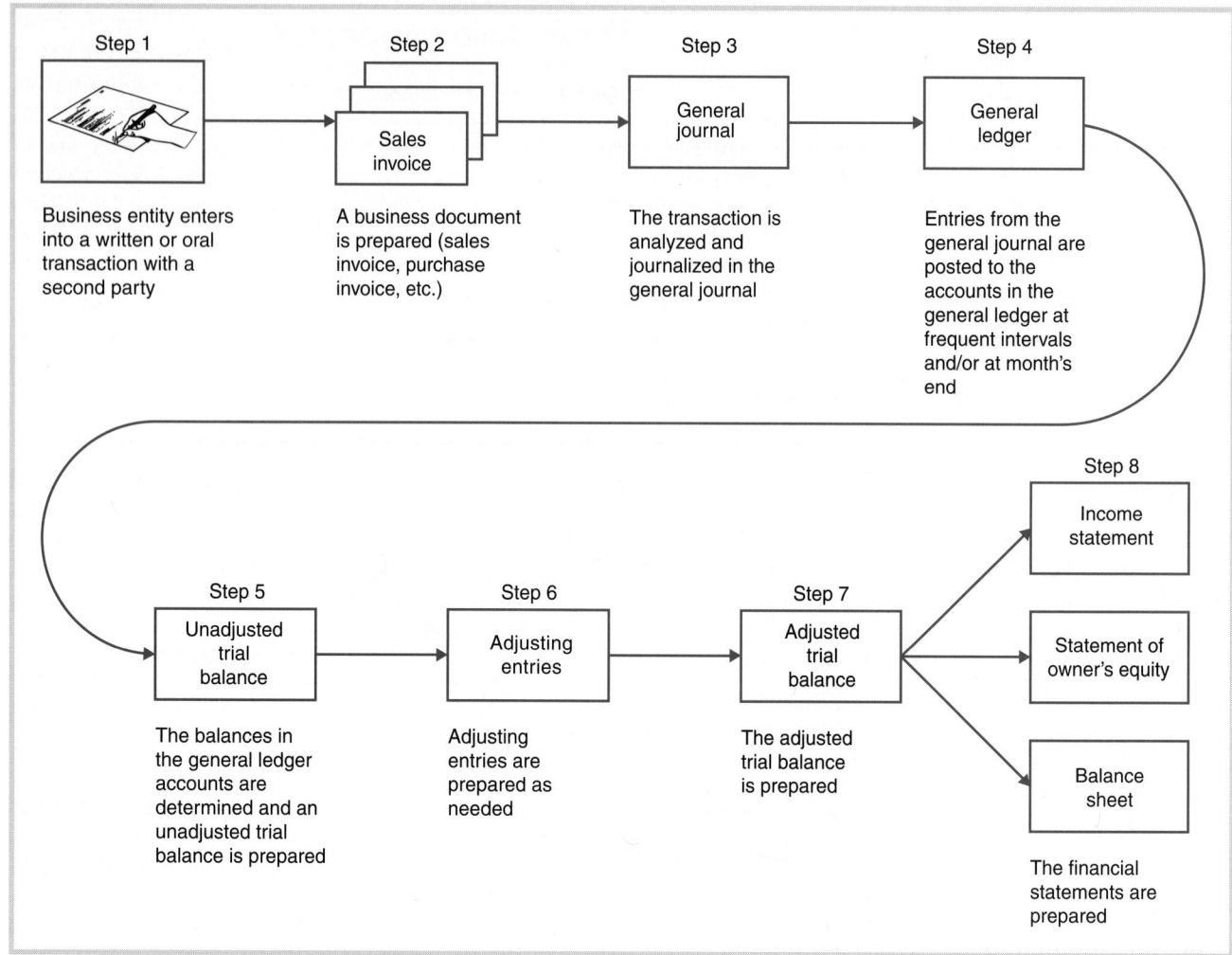

described is a practical means of achieving that objective. The steps involved in the financial accounting process are summarized in Figure 5.

ASK YOURSELF ▶

1. Explain how an adjusted trial balance is prepared.
2. Describe the steps involved in the financial accounting process.

## THE FORM AND CONTENT OF CLASSIFIED FINANCIAL STATEMENTS

Learning Objective **9**

Describe the form and content of classified financial statements

Financial statements become more useful when their basic elements—the individual asset accounts, liability accounts, revenue accounts, and expense accounts—are arranged in meaningful groups. Until now, we have presented only simple financial statements containing relatively few items. With so few items, we did not need to present **classified statements,** which are financial statements in which similar accounts are grouped together. However, people who use actual financial statements find classification very helpful when they are analyzing and comparing financial statements in order to make lending and investment decisions.

Users of classified financial statements can readily determine the profitability and solvency of a business entity by studying the relationship between significant asset and liability groupings on the balance sheet as well as the relationships between revenue and expense groupings on the income statement. Moreover, the use of standardized classifications makes it easier for users to compare the financial statements of different companies. Can you imagine the problems that statement users would have if each company used its own system of classification?

The form and content of financial statements evolved over time and continues to evolve in response to changing business practices. What was acceptable presentation in the early 1960s may not be acceptable today. Within the broad framework of standardized financial statement classification, individual business entities will attempt to give a clear, meaningful, and fair presentation of their results of operations and financial position.

## Classifying the Balance Sheet

Typically, assets on the balance sheet are classified into five major groupings: (1) current assets; (2) investments; (3) property, plant, and equipment; (4) intangibles; and (5) other assets.

Liabilities generally are classified into two groups: (1) current liabilities and (2) long-term liabilities. The classification of the components of owner's equity is dependent on the form of the entity. For a proprietorship, for example, the owner's equity section consists of the Capital and Withdrawals accounts.

The balance sheet of the Benson Retail Store (Exhibit 6) illustrates these classifications, each of which is discussed in the sections that follow.

### Assets

**Current Assets**  **Current assets** are assets that are expected to be converted into cash within a year or within the normal operating cycle, whichever is longer. Current assets include cash, marketable securities, notes receivable, accounts receivable, merchandise inventory, and prepaid expenses. The **operating cycle** is the average length of time between the purchase of merchandise inventory and the realization of cash from the sale of the merchandise inventory. It consists of three phases, shown graphically in Figure 6:

**1.** The purchase of merchandise inventory
**2.** The sale of the merchandise inventory on account, or for cash
**3.** The collection of cash from the accounts receivable.

**Figure 6** The Operating Cycle

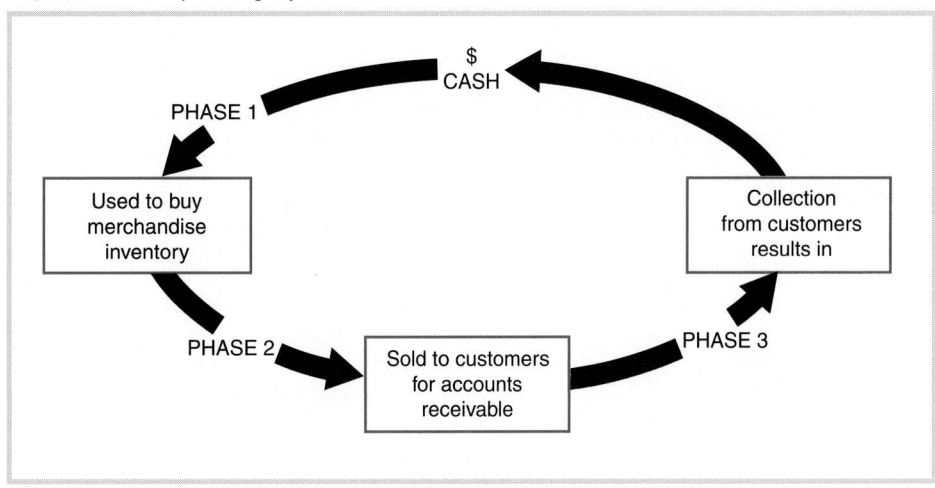

**Exhibit 6** Balance Sheet

**BENSON RETAIL STORE**
**Balance Sheet**
**December 31, 1998**

**Assets**

Current Assets:

| | | |
|---|---:|---:|
| Cash | $ 14,300 | |
| Marketable Securities | 17,200 | |
| Notes Receivable | 10,000 | |
| Accounts Receivable | 56,700 | |
| Merchandise Inventory | 85,600 | |
| Prepaid Expenses | 11,900 | |
| Total Current Assets | | $195,700 |

Investments:

| | | |
|---|---:|---:|
| Bonds | $ 33,100 | |
| Stocks | 15,300 | |
| Total Investments | | 48,400 |

Property, Plant, and Equipment:

| | | | |
|---|---:|---:|---:|
| Land | | $ 65,000 | |
| Buildings | $127,400 | | |
| Less: Accumulated Depreciation | 36,500 | 90,900 | |
| Equipment | $263,800 | | |
| Less: Accumulated Depreciation | 105,200 | 158,600 | |
| Total Property, Plant, and Equipment | | | 314,500 |

Intangibles:

| | | |
|---|---:|---:|
| Goodwill | $ 25,000 | |
| Patents | 17,000 | |
| Total Intangibles | | 42,000 |

Other Assets:

| | |
|---|---:|
| Land Held for Future Plant Site | 73,000 |
| Total Assets | $673,600 |

**Liabilities**

Currents Liabilities:

| | | |
|---|---:|---:|
| Notes Payable | $ 25,000 | |
| Accounts Payable | 51,700 | |
| Salaries Payable | 14,300 | |
| Unearned Revenue | 6,200 | |
| Total Current Liabilities | | $ 97,200 |

Long-Term Liabilities:

| | | |
|---|---:|---:|
| Mortgage Payable, $10\frac{1}{4}$% | $151,600 | |
| Notes Payable, $11\frac{5}{8}$% due May 1, 2003 | 105,000 | |
| Total Long-Term Liabilities | | 256,600 |

| | |
|---|---:|
| Total Liabilities | $353,800 |

**Owner's Equity**

| | | |
|---|---:|---:|
| Benson, Capital, Jan. 1, 1998 | $295,400 | |
| Net Income for the Year | 62,500 | |
| Total | $357,900 | |
| Less: Withdrawals | 38,100 | |
| Benson, Capital, Dec. 31, 1998 | | 319,800 |

| | |
|---|---:|
| Total Long-Term Liabilities and Owner's Equity | $673,600 |

For some entities, such as a grocery store, the operating cycle is only a few weeks. For others, it may extend over a number of years; an example is the lumber industry (many years must pass between the planting of seedlings and the harvesting of timber). Most businesses find, however, that their operating cycles are several months in duration, and if not, then commonly less than a year.

Current assets are listed on the balance sheet in order of their liquidity. The term **liquidity** refers to an asset's nearness to cash. The most liquid asset is cash. Assets become more liquid as they move through the operating cycle from merchandise inventory to accounts receivable to cash.

*Marketable securities* are classified as current assets because management intends to dispose of them within the year. U.S. Treasury bills, certificates of deposit, and common stocks and bonds of other business entities are typical examples. Companies will invest in temporary investments because they have excess cash available for short periods of time—30, 60, or 90 days. These financial instruments provide a rate of return that is not available when cash is held in checking accounts.

*Notes receivable* that the entity expects to collect within the year are current assets. Notes receivable commonly originate when a customer cannot pay his or her account receivable when it becomes due. The note, which bears interest, is a more formal agreement than the account receivable. It is a written promise to pay a certain amount on a specific future date.

*Merchandise inventory* is the product or products that the entity acquires from various suppliers and plans to resell to its customers.

*Prepaid expenses* consist of prepaid rent, prepaid insurance, and supplies on hand. These items are not typically shown separately but are included under the heading Prepaid Expenses since, even in total, they are not generally large in amount. Prepaid expenses represent current assets because, if they were not already owned, the business entity would be required to expend current assets to obtain them. They will be consumed during the operating cycle and become expenses.

**Investments** **Investments** are distinguished from marketable securities in that management does not intend to convert investments into cash within the year. Bonds, stocks, and real estate held for resale are typical assets classified as investments.

**Property, Plant, and Equipment** Tangible, long-lived assets that are used in the production or sale of inventory or in the providing of services are classified as *property, plant, and equipment.* Land, Buildings, and Equipment are the most common property, plant, and equipment accounts.

Land does not wear out; consequently, no depreciation is recorded for land. Buildings and equipment, however, have limited lives and do wear out, and their cost must be allocated over the period of time during which they provide usefulness. This, as you already know, is called *depreciation.* **Accumulated Depreciation** (a contra asset) is reflected under the plant and equipment classification as a subtraction from the related Building or Equipment account.

**Intangibles** Intangible assets, or **intangibles,** represent legal rights or certain economic relationships that provide their owners with future economic benefits. Goodwill, patents, franchises, and copyrights are common examples. Intangible assets do not have physical substance.

**Other Assets** Occasionally, a business entity has an asset that cannot be placed within any of these four asset classifications. In this situation the classification Other Assets is used. For example, land held for a future plant site would be classified under Other Assets.

### Liabilities

**Current Liabilities** Obligations that require the use of current assets for their payment are classified as **current liabilities.** Thus, they represent liabilities that will be paid within an operating cycle or a year, whichever is longer. Common current liability classifications are Notes Payable, Accounts Payable, Salaries Payable, Taxes Payable, and Unearned Revenue. Unearned Revenue represents advance payments received from customers. These payments oblige the company to provide future goods or services, so they are also classified as current liabilities. They may be listed as Advances from Customers, Unearned Revenue (as in the Benson Retail Store illustration), or Prepaid Income. Rent received in advance by property owners and payments received by publishers for magazine subscriptions are two examples of unearned revenue.

**Long-Term Liabilities**  Simply stated, liabilities that are not current are long-term. **Long-term liabilities** represent obligations that will be paid more than one year after the date on the balance sheet. Mortgages Payable and Bonds Payable are the two most common examples.

### Owner's Equity

*Owner's equity* represents the owner's interest in the business entity. The way this section is classified depends on whether the business is organized as a proprietorship, a partnership, or a corporation. For a proprietorship or a partnership, owner's equity will consist of the Beginning Capital account (a separate capital account is maintained for each partner in a partnership), plus additional investments made during the year, plus or minus any net income or loss for the year, minus withdrawals during the year, and the resulting Ending Capital account. All this is, of course, a summary of the activity in the Capital account (or accounts).

Rather than presenting this information on the balance sheet, a *statement of owner's equity* is typically prepared. In this case only the ending capital is listed on the balance sheet. While a separate Capital account is maintained for each partner in a partnership, only one account—called *Partners' Capital*—will typically appear on the balance sheet. Imagine a balance sheet listing all 4,000 partners of the largest CPA firm in the owners' equity section!

The owners' equity section of a corporation's financial statements will have at least three accounts: Capital Stock, Paid-In Capital, and Retained Earnings. These accounts will be explained when we discuss corporations.

### Classifying the Income Statement

A classified income statement for the Benson Retail Store appears in Exhibit 7. It shows three major classifications: sales, cost of merchandise sold, and operating expenses.

Operating expenses include both selling and general administrative expenses. Expenses that are incurred to support the marketing function—that is, the selling of merchandise or services—are properly classified as selling expenses. Examples are commissions to the sales force, sales salaries, and depreciation on store equipment (since store equipment is used in the marketing function).

Expenses related to the general operation of the business are classified as general and administrative expenses. Examples include executives' salaries, the salaries of the office staff, and depreciation on the office building and equipment (since these depreciable assets are used for the general operation of the business).

**ASK YOURSELF** ▶

1. Why are the accounts on a balance sheet arranged in meaningful groupings?
2. What is meant by an operating cycle?
3. What are the major classifications of a balance sheet?
4. How is an income statement organized?

**Exhibit 7** Income Statement

## BENSON RETAIL STORE
### Income Statement
### For the Year Ended December 31, 1998

| | | | |
|---|---:|---:|---:|
| Sales. . . . . . . . . . . . . . . . . . . . . . . . . . . . . . . . . . . . . . . . . . . . . . . . . . . . . . . . . . . . . . . | | $551,900 | |
| Cost of Merchandise Sold . . . . . . . . . . . . . . . . . . . . . . . . . . . . . . . . . . . . . . . . . . . | | 273,900 | |
|     Gross Profit on Sales . . . . . . . . . . . . . . . . . . . . . . . . . . . . . . . . . . . . . . . . . . . . | | | $278,000 |
| Operating Expenses: | | | |
|   Selling Expenses: | | | |
|     Sales Commissions . . . . . . . . . . . . . . . . . . . . . . . . . . . . . . . . . . . . | $27,100 | | |
|     Sales Salaries. . . . . . . . . . . . . . . . . . . . . . . . . . . . . . . . . . . . . . . . | 11,700 | | |
|     Depreciation Expense . . . . . . . . . . . . . . . . . . . . . . . . . . . . . . . . . | 10,300 | | |
|     Advertising Expense. . . . . . . . . . . . . . . . . . . . . . . . . . . . . . . . . . | 6,200 | | |
|     Insurance Expense. . . . . . . . . . . . . . . . . . . . . . . . . . . . . . . . . . . | 1,500 | | |
|       Total Selling Expenses . . . . . . . . . . . . . . . . . . . . . . . . . . . . . . . . | | $ 56,800 | |
| General and Administrative Expenses: | | | |
|     Executive Salaries . . . . . . . . . . . . . . . . . . . . . . . . . . . . . . . . . . . | $58,000 | | |
|     Clerical Salaries . . . . . . . . . . . . . . . . . . . . . . . . . . . . . . . . . . . . | 41,700 | | |
|     Interest Expense. . . . . . . . . . . . . . . . . . . . . . . . . . . . . . . . . . . . | 28,300 | | |
|     Insurance Expense. . . . . . . . . . . . . . . . . . . . . . . . . . . . . . . . . . . | 10,900 | | |
|     Depreciation Expense . . . . . . . . . . . . . . . . . . . . . . . . . . . . . . . . . | 9,700 | | |
|     Income Tax Expense . . . . . . . . . . . . . . . . . . . . . . . . . . . . . . . . . | 6,900 | | |
|     Office Supplies Expense . . . . . . . . . . . . . . . . . . . . . . . . . . . . . . | 3,200 | | |
|       Total General Administrative Expenses: . . . . . . . . . . . . . . . . . . . . . | | $158,700 | |
| Total Operating Expenses . . . . . . . . . . . . . . . . . . . . . . . . . . . . . . . . . . . . . . . . . . . . . | | | 215,500 |
| Net Income . . . . . . . . . . . . . . . . . . . . . . . . . . . . . . . . . . . . . . . . . . . . . . . . . . . . . . . . . | | | $ 62,500 |

## FINANCIAL STATEMENT ANALYSIS

*Learning Objective* **10**

Describe the use of working capital and the current ratio in financial statement analysis

Should we lend money to this company? Can we expect it to pay its obligations on time? Does it appear that the company is earning a fair rate of return? These and many more questions are of major concern to investors and creditors. Classified financial statements help in providing answers to these important questions. By analyzing the statement data investors and creditors can gain more insight into a company's financial health. And by comparing today's financial data with that of prior years investors and creditors can determine if the company is improving its financial strength. Comparing a company's financial data with other companies in the same industry can reveal a company's strengths and weaknesses.

Financial statement analysis is much like a medical doctor reviewing the results of various tests to determine if a patient is healthy or not. While 20-20 indicates good vision 20-15 would indicate better vision and 20-200 would indicate very poor vision. If we wanted to invest money in an individual that could see well we would select the one with 20-15 vision. But perhaps vision is only one of several things to consider, if the individual with 20-15 vision also has a cholesterol level of 330 he or she might not be a good investment. And the individual with 20-20 vision may have had 20-15 vision two years ago.

We can develop a number of tests of financial statements. These tests are called financial ratios and can be used by financial statement analysts to determine what companies appear to be good investments. At this early stage in your study of accounting we can introduce you to the concept of working capital and the current ratio. As we expand our knowledge of accounting in later chapters we will introduce additional ratios.

### Working Capital

**Working capital** is current assets less current liabilities; it is a measure of the liquid resources that management will control in the short term. A strong working capital position can be an advantage to a company attempting to obtain short-term credit at favorable interest rates. Long-term creditors view a strong working capital position as an indication that a firm will be able to make its interest payments in a timely manner. The balance sheet of Benson Retail Store in Exhibit 6 shows total current assets amounting to $195,700 and total current liabilities $97,200. The calculation of working capital for 1998 is as follows:

$$\text{Working Capital} = \text{Current Assets} - \text{Current Liabilities}$$

$$\text{Working Capital} = \$195,700 - \$97,200$$
$$= \underline{\$\ 98,500}$$

### Current Ratio

The **current ratio** is the current assets divided by current liabilities. This statistic is often assigned greater importance by lenders in making credit-granting decisions. The calculation of Benson Retail Store's current ratios is as follows:

$$\text{Current Ratio} = \frac{\text{Current Assets}}{\text{Current Liabilities}}$$

$$\text{Current Ratio} = \frac{\$195,700}{\$97,200}$$

$$= 2.01$$

This is often expressed as 2.01 to 1, meaning that there are $2.01 of current assets for every $1.00 of current liabilities. A general rule of thumb is that a current ratio should be about 2 to 1. But this is like saying that the average weight of an adult male is 170 pounds. Is that good or bad? Well it depends on individuals height, build, etc. Is 2.01 to 1 good or bad, well it depends on the industry, past history, etc.

### SUMMARY

- Creditors, potential owners, and other parties outside a business entity do not have direct access to its accounting records, but they are concerned about its financial resources, its obligations, and the results of its activities. These parties need to be informed in a timely and regular manner of the economic activity of the business entity.
- The life of a business entity is divided into time frames—months, quarters, and years—called **accounting periods.** Accountants prepare financial statements at the end of each period.
- The *balance sheet* reports the status as of the close of business *on the last day of the accounting period specified.* The *income statement* reports the activity *during the accounting period specified.*
- Generally accepted accounting principles require that financial statements be prepared using **accrual-basis accounting** rather than the **cash-basis accounting.** The underlying concept of the accrual basis of accounting is the **revenue-recognition principle:** Revenue must be reflected on the financial statements in the accounting period in which it is earned.
- Expenses must also be reflected on the financial statements in the accounting period in which they are incurred, and they must be matched against revenue earned. This is called the **matching concept.**

• A business entity buys assets such as buildings and equipment that are used during many years, including many accounting periods. Only after an asset is no longer useful would a business entity know exactly how long it had served and how to allocate its cost precisely over each of the accounting periods during its useful life. But it is impractical to wait for the end of an asset's useful life to account precisely for its cost during each accounting period. The practical solution is to estimate how long it will be useful, and to allocate its total cost over each of the accounting periods of its estimated life—a process called **depreciation.**

• Depreciation allocation results in an expense called *depreciation expense.* Because the calculation of depreciation expense depends on an estimate, it is only an approximation of the actual expense. And because depreciation expense is not precise, neither is the net income calculated and reported during an accounting period.

• A business entity makes exchanges with second parties (buyers, sellers, lenders). These exchanges are called **external transactions.** The economic result of an external transaction is recorded during the accounting period in which it was made, even though the actual result may not occur until a later period.

• The accounts debited or credited by some external transactions may not reflect the actual situation at the end of the accounting period. For example, some assets acquired during a period may have been consumed before the end of that period; interest income may have been earned but not yet received on money loaned; or salary expense may have been incurred for salaries earned by employees but not yet paid.

• Financial statements prepared at the end of the accounting period must reflect the following:

**1.** All assets owned      **3.** All revenue earned
**2.** All liabilities owed   **4.** All expenses incurred

Consequently, certain amounts must be increased or decreased by means of adjusting entries in the general journal—an **internal transaction**—as of the last day of the accounting period.

• There are two basic types of adjusting entries: **deferrals,** which require adjustment because the goods and/or services already paid for in full may not have been completely consumed at period-end; and **accruals,** which represent revenue earned and expenses incurred for which no transaction has been recorded during the period.

• Prepaid expenses, unearned revenue, and depreciation are examples of *deferrals.*

• At the moment an asset is acquired, it is represented as a **prepaid expense**—an **unexpired cost.** A prepaid expense becomes an **expired cost**—representing an expense—as the asset is consumed over time.

• When **unearned revenue** is received, it is represented as a liability. As services are performed or goods are delivered in fulfillment of the unearned revenue, the liability is reduced and revenue is represented as earned.

• The expenses for buildings and equipment are similar to prepaid expenses. Over time, as they are used, they become expired costs—represented as *depreciation expenses.* But, unlike Prepaid Expenses, the Building and Equipment accounts are not reduced directly as the expense is recorded. Rather, a *contra-asset* account called **Accumulated Depreciation** is increased. The use of the contra-asset account maintains the building or equipment account at its original cost, which provides useful information to statement users.

• Salary expense, interest expense, interest revenue, and the counterparts of these items—salaries payable, interest payable, and interest receivable—are examples of *accruals.* These accounts are accrued over time even though payment is made or received on specific dates.

• When financial statements are prepared on dates other than the date of a payment or a receipt, the accruals must be measured and recorded by adjusting entries to present fairly the results of operations and the financial position.

- After the adjusting entries are recorded in the general journal and posted to the general ledger accounts, an **adjusted trial balance** is prepared. The adjusted trial balance is used to prepare the financial statements.
- When accounts—asset accounts, liability accounts, revenue accounts, and expense accounts—are grouped in some meaningful way on financial statements, the statements are called **classified statements.**
- The asset section of the balance sheet is classified into five major groupings:

1. Current assets
2. Long-term investments
3. Property, plant, and equipment
4. Intangibles
5. Other assets

- The liabilities section of the balance sheet is classified into current liabilities and long-term liabilities.
- The income statement is classified as follows:

1. Revenue
2. Cost of merchandise sold
3. Operating expenses
   a. Selling expenses
   b. General and administrative expenses

- Financial statement analysis provides investors and creditors with insight into a company's financial health. *Working Capital* is a measure of the liquid resources of a company, it is the difference between current assets and current liabilities. The *current ratio* is current assets divided by current liabilities.

## 10  KEY TERMS

| | |
|---|---|
| **Accounting period** | The length of time for which financial activities are reported on the income statement. An accounting period is typically 1 year, though some entities prepare income statements quarterly or monthly. |
| **Accrual-basis accounting** | The generally accepted accounting principle requiring that revenue be recorded when earned and that expenses be recorded when incurred. |
| **Accruals** | Adjustments for expenses that are incurred and whose benefits have been consumed, but that have not yet been paid for; also, revenue that has been earned and whose benefits have been received but for which payment has not been recorded. |
| **Accumulated Depreciation** | A balance sheet account that is shown as a deduction from the related Building or Equipment account. It is a contra asset and accumulates the depreciation taken on the asset over its useful life. |
| **Adjusted trial balance** | A trial balance prepared after all adjusting entries have been made. |
| **Adjusting entries** | The entries made in the general journal at the end of an accounting period to reflect internal transactions during the period. |
| **Book value** | The difference between the amount shown in a specific fixed asset account and its accumulated depreciation |
| **Carrying value** | See **book value.** |
| **Cash-basis accounting** | The accounting system that records revenue only upon the receipt of cash and records expenses only upon payment (does not follow generally accepted accounting principles). |
| **Classified statements** | Financial statements in which similar accounts are grouped together to simplify analysis of the statements. |

| | |
|---|---|
| **Contra account** | An account with a balance opposite the normal balance of the particular account to which it relates. A contra-asset account, for example, has a credit balance, whereas a contra-liability account has a debit balance. |
| **Current assets** | Assets that are expected to be converted into cash within a year or within the normal operating cycle, whichever is longer. |
| **Current liabilities** | Obligations requiring the use of current assets for their liquidation or payment. |
| **Current ratio** | Current assets divided by current liabilities. |
| **Deferrals** | Adjustments for goods and services collected or paid for in advance of benefits given or received. |
| **Depreciation** | The cost of a noncurrent asset (such as buildings, equipment, and vehicles) that is allocated as an expense over the length of the asset's estimated useful life. |
| **Expired cost** | An expense representing the amount of an asset that is considered to have been used up over a period of time. |
| **External transactions** | Exchange transactions between the business entity and parties outside the entity. |
| **Intangibles** | Legal rights or certain economic relationships that provide their owners with future economic benefits. |
| **Internal transactions** | Adjusting entries made by a business entity to reflect more accurately the status of the accounts at the end of a period. Internal transactions do not involve second parties. |
| **Investments** | Bonds, stocks, and real estate that a business entity owns and does not intend to sell for cash within the year. |
| **Liquidity** | A term referring to an asset's nearness to cash. |
| **Long-term liabilities** | Obligations that will be paid at some future time beyond 1 year from the balance sheet date. |
| **Matching concept** | The generally accepted accounting principle that requires expenses incurred in providing a product or service during an accounting period to be matched against revenues earned by that product or service during the same accounting period. |
| **Operating cycle** | The average length of time between the purchase of merchandise inventory and the realization of cash from the sale of that merchandise inventory. |
| **Prepaid expenses** | Expenses that are paid for before they are used; classified as current assets. |
| **Revenue-recognition principle** | The generally accepted accounting principle that requires revenue to be reflected on the income statement in the period in which it is earned. |
| **Unearned revenue** | The liability incurred for cash received in advance of goods or services rendered. |
| **Unexpired cost** | That part of the cost of an asset representing the economic benefit it has not yet provided or services not yet consumed. |
| **Working capital** | Current assets minus current liabilities. |

## DEMONSTRATION PROBLEM

Presented below is the unadjusted trial balance of the Shaw Company as of Dec. 31, 1998:

### THE SHAW COMPANY
#### Unadjusted Trial Balance
#### December 31, 1998

| | | |
|---|---:|---:|
| Cash . . . . . . . . . . . . . . . . . . . . . . . . . . . . . . . . . . . . . . . . . . . . . . . . . . | $13,200 | |
| Accounts Receivable . . . . . . . . . . . . . . . . . . . . . . . . . . . . . . . . | 8,100 | |
| Advertising Supplies on Hand . . . . . . . . . . . . . . . . . . . . . . . . | 2,400 | |
| Office Equipment . . . . . . . . . . . . . . . . . . . . . . . . . . . . . . . . . . . | 35,000 | |
| Accounts Payable. . . . . . . . . . . . . . . . . . . . . . . . . . . . . . . . . . . | | $ 5,900 |
| Unearned Advertising Revenue. . . . . . . . . . . . . . . . . . . . . . . . | | 4,800 |
| Note Payable, due Mar. 31, 2001 . . . . . . . . . . . . . . . . . . . . . | | 20,000 |
| Shaw, Capital . . . . . . . . . . . . . . . . . . . . . . . . . . . . . . . . . . . . . . | | 14,600 |
| Shaw, Withdrawals. . . . . . . . . . . . . . . . . . . . . . . . . . . . . . . . . . | 1,400 | |
| Advertising Revenue . . . . . . . . . . . . . . . . . . . . . . . . . . . . . . . . | | 64,200 |
| Salary Expense . . . . . . . . . . . . . . . . . . . . . . . . . . . . . . . . . . . . | 37,300 | |
| Rent Expense. . . . . . . . . . . . . . . . . . . . . . . . . . . . . . . . . . . . . . | 9,000 | |
| Miscellaneous Expense . . . . . . . . . . . . . . . . . . . . . . . . . . . . . | 3,100 | |
| Totals . . . . . . . . . . . . . . . . . . . . . . . . . . . . . . . . . . . . . . . . . . . . | $109,500 | $109,500 |

On Dec. 31, 1998, Shaw Company had the following items that needed adjustment:

**a.** Office Equipment acquired on July 1, 1998, for $35,000 has an estimated life of 7 years.

**b.** Advertising supplies in the amount of $2,400 were acquired on Mar. 15, 1998. At year-end only $600 of supplies remained.

**c.** Shaw Company received $4,800 on Oct. 1, 1998, for advertising that Shaw will perform commencing Oct. 1 and ending Sept. 30, 1999.

**d.** At year-end, salaries earned in the amount of $2,000 have not been paid.

**e.** On Oct. 1, 1998, Shaw Company borrowed $20,000 at 12% interest per year to be repaid on Mar. 31, 2001. Interest will be paid annually on Oct. 1.

The Shaw Company has a policy of recording adjusting entries only at year-end.

**Required:**

1. Prepare the appropriate Dec. 31, 1998, adjusting entries.
2. Establish a general ledger account for each account found in the unadjusted trial balance.
3. Post the adjusting entries, establishing new accounts as needed.
4. Compute the adjusted balances.
5. Prepare an adjusted trial balance.
6. Prepare classified financial statements.
7. Compute working capital and the current ratio.

## ■ Solution to Demonstration Problem

1.

<table>
<tr><td colspan="5">THE SHAW COMPANY<br>General Journal</td><td>PAGE _____</td></tr>
<tr><th>Date</th><th>Account Titles and Explanation</th><th>Post.<br>Ref.</th><th>Debit</th><th>Credit</th></tr>
<tr><td>1998<br>Dec. 31</td><td>Depreciation Expense (OE:E)<br>    Accumulated Depreciation (A)<br>To record depreciation on office equipment.<br>($35,000/7)(1/2)</td><td></td><td>2,500</td><td><br>2,500</td></tr>
<tr><td>31</td><td>Advertising Supplies Expense (OE:E)<br>    Advertising Supplies on Hand (A)<br>To record advertising supplies expense.<br>($2,400 − $600)</td><td></td><td>1,800</td><td><br>1,800</td></tr>
<tr><td>31</td><td>Unearned Advertising Revenue (L)<br>    Advertising Revenue (OE:R)<br>To record advertising revenue earned.<br>($4,800/12)(3)</td><td></td><td>1,200</td><td><br>1,200</td></tr>
<tr><td>31</td><td>Salary Expense (OE:E)<br>    Salaries Payable (L)<br>To record accrued salaries.</td><td></td><td>2,000</td><td><br>2,000</td></tr>
<tr><td>31</td><td>Interest Expense (OE:E)<br>    Interest Payable (L)<br>To record accrued interest expense.<br>($20,000)(12%)(3/12)</td><td></td><td>600</td><td><br>600</td></tr>
</table>

2, 3, 4.

### General Ledger

**Account** Cash         **Account No.**

| Date | Explanation | Post<br>Ref. | Debit | Credit | Balance |
|------|-------------|-------------|-------|--------|---------|
| 1998<br>Dec. 31 | Balance | | 13,200 | | 13,200 |

**Account** Accounts Receivable         **Account No.**

| Date | Explanation | Post<br>Ref. | Debit | Credit | Balance |
|------|-------------|-------------|-------|--------|---------|
| 1998<br>Dec. 31 | Balance | | 8,100 | | 8,100 |

**Account** Advertising Supplies on Hand        **Account No.**

| Date | Explanation | Post Ref. | Debit | Credit | Balance |
|------|-------------|-----------|-------|--------|---------|
| 1998 Dec. 31 | | | 2,400 | | 2,400 |
| | Adjusting entry | | | 1,800 | 600 |

**Account** Office Equipment        **Account No.**

| Date | Explanation | Post Ref. | Debit | Credit | Balance |
|------|-------------|-----------|-------|--------|---------|
| 1998 Dec. 31 | Balance | | 35,000 | | 35,000 |

**Account** Accumulated Depreciation        **Account No.**

| Date | Explanation | Post Ref. | Debit | Credit | Balance |
|------|-------------|-----------|-------|--------|---------|
| 1998 Dec. 31 | Adjusting entry | | | 2,500 | 2,500 |

**Account** Accounts Payable        **Account No.**

| Date | Explanation | Post Ref. | Debit | Credit | Balance |
|------|-------------|-----------|-------|--------|---------|
| 1998 Dec. 31 | | | | 5,900 | 5,900 |

**Account** Salaries Payable        **Account No.**

| Date | Explanation | Post Ref. | Debit | Credit | Balance |
|------|-------------|-----------|-------|--------|---------|
| 1998 Dec. 31 | Adjusting entry | | | 2,000 | 2,000 |

**Account** Interest Payable        **Account No.**

| Date | Explanation | Post Ref. | Debit | Credit | Balance |
|------|-------------|-----------|-------|--------|---------|
| 1998 Dec. 31 | Adjusting entry | | | 600 | 600 |

**Account** Unearned Advertising Revenue        **Account No.**

| Date | Explanation | Post Ref. | Debit | Credit | Balance |
|------|-------------|-----------|-------|--------|---------|
| 1998 Dec. 31 | | GJ 1 | | 4,800 | 4,800 |
| 31 | Adjusting entry | | 1,200 | | 3,600 |

**Account** Note Payable                                        **Account No.**

| Date | Explanation | Post Ref. | Debit | Credit | Balance |
|------|-------------|-----------|-------|--------|---------|
| 1998 Dec. 31 | Balance | | | 20,000 | 20,000 |

**Account** Shaw, Capital                                       **Account No.**

| Date | Explanation | Post Ref. | Debit | Credit | Balance |
|------|-------------|-----------|-------|--------|---------|
| 1998 Dec. 31 | Balance | | | 14,600 | 14,600 |

**Account** Shaw, Withdrawals                                   **Account No.**

| Date | Explanation | Post Ref. | Debit | Credit | Balance |
|------|-------------|-----------|-------|--------|---------|
| 1998 Dec. 31 | Balance | | 1,400 | | 1,400 |

**Account** Advertising Revenue                                 **Account No.**

| Date | Explanation | Post Ref. | Debit | Credit | Balance |
|------|-------------|-----------|-------|--------|---------|
| 1998 Dec. 31 | Balance | | | 64,200 | 64,200 |
| 31 | Adjusting entry | | | 1,200 | 65,400 |

**Account** Salary Expense                                      **Account No.**

| Date | Explanation | Post Ref. | Debit | Credit | Balance |
|------|-------------|-----------|-------|--------|---------|
| 1998 Dec. 31 | Balance | | 37,300 | | 37,300 |
| 31 | Adjusting entry | | 2,000 | | 39,300 |

**Account** Rent Expense                                        **Account No.**

| Date | Explanation | Post Ref. | Debit | Credit | Balance |
|------|-------------|-----------|-------|--------|---------|
| 1998 Dec. 31 | Balance | | 9,000 | | 9,000 |

**Account** Advertising Supplies Expense                        **Account No.**

| Date | Explanation | Post Ref. | Debit | Credit | Balance |
|------|-------------|-----------|-------|--------|---------|
| 1998 Dec. 31 | Adjusting entry | | 1,800 | | 1,800 |

**Account** Depreciation Expense      **Account No.**

| Date | Explanation | Post Ref. | Debit | Credit | Balance |
|------|-------------|-----------|-------|--------|---------|
| 1998<br>Dec. 31 | Adjusting entry | | 2,500 | | 2,500 |

**Account** Interest Expense      **Account No.**

| Date | Explanation | Post Ref. | Debit | Credit | Balance |
|------|-------------|-----------|-------|--------|---------|
| 1998<br>Dec. 31 | Adjusting entry | | 600 | | 600 |

**Account** Miscellaneous Expense      **Account No.**

| Date | Explanation | Post Ref. | Debit | Credit | Balance |
|------|-------------|-----------|-------|--------|---------|
| 1998<br>Dec. 31 | Balance | | 3,100 | | 3,100 |

5.

**THE SHAW COMPANY**
**Adjusted Trial Balance**
**December 31, 1998**

| | | |
|---|---|---|
| Cash | $ 13,200 | |
| Accounts Receivable | 8,100 | |
| Advertising Supplies on Hand | 600 | |
| Office Equipment | 35,000 | |
| Accumulated Depreciation | | $ 2,500 |
| Accounts Payable | | 5,900 |
| Salaries Payable | | 2,000 |
| Interest Payable | | 600 |
| Unearned Advertising Revenue | | 3,600 |
| Note Payable | | 20,000 |
| Shaw, Capital | | 14,600 |
| Shaw, Withdrawals | 1,400 | |
| Advertising Revenue | | 65,400 |
| Salary Expense | 39,300 | |
| Rent Expense | 9,000 | |
| Advertising Supplies Expense | 1,800 | |
| Depreciation Expense | 2,500 | |
| Interest Expense | 600 | |
| Miscellaneous Expense | 3,100 | |
| Totals | $114,600 | $114,600 |

6.

### THE SHAW COMPANY
### Income Statement
### Year Ended December 31, 1998

| | | |
|---|---:|---:|
| Revenue: | | |
| Advertising Revenue | | $65,400 |
| Operating Expenses: | | |
| Salary Expense | $39,300 | |
| Rent Expense | 9,000 | |
| Advertising Supplies Expense | 1,800 | |
| Depreciation Expense | 2,500 | |
| Interest Expense | 600 | |
| Miscellaneous Expense | 3,100 | |
| Total Expenses | | $56,300 |
| Net Income | | $ 9,100 |

### THE SHAW COMPANY
### Statement of Owner's Equity
### Year Ended December 31, 1998

| | |
|---|---:|
| Shaw, Capital, Jan. 1, 1998 | $14,600 |
| Add: Net Income | 9,100 |
| Total | $23,700 |
| Less: Withdrawals | 1,400 |
| Shaw, Capital, Dec. 31, 1998 | $22,300 |

### THE SHAW COMPANY
### Balance Sheet
### December 31, 1998

| Assets | | | Liabilities | | |
|---|---:|---:|---|---:|---:|
| Current Assets: | | | Current Liabilities: | | |
| Cash | | $13,200 | Accounts Payable | | $ 5,900 |
| Accounts Receivable | | 8,100 | Salaries Payable | | 2,000 |
| Advertising Supplies on Hand | | 600 | Interest Payable | | 600 |
| Total Current Assets | | $21,900 | Unearned Advertising Revenue | | 3,600 |
| | | | Total Current Liabilities | | $12,100 |
| Property, Plant, and Equipment: | | | | | |
| Office Equipment | $35,000 | | Long-Term Liabilities: | | |
| Less: Accumulated Depreciation | 2,500 | 32,500 | Note Payable | | 20,000 |
| | | | Total Liabilities | | $32,100 |
| | | | **Owner's Equity** | | |
| | | | Shaw, Capital | | 22,300 |
| Total Assets | | $54,400 | Total Liabilities and Owner's Equity | | $54,400 |

7. Working capital = $21,900 − $12,100 = $9,800

$$\text{Current ratio} = \frac{\$21,900}{\$12,100} = 1.81 \text{ or } 1.81 \text{ to } 1$$

## QUESTIONS FOR REVIEW AND FURTHER THOUGHT

### REVIEW QUESTIONS

1. Business transactions can be referred to as *external* or *internal.* How do these two types of transactions differ?

2. Distinguish between unexpired and expired costs.

3. *Deferrals* and *accruals* are the two classifications of adjusting entries. Explain the meaning of each of these terms.

4. What is the nature of the Accumulated Depreciation account?

5. Name three unexpired costs and three related expired costs.

6. Explain the difference between the Office Supplies on Hand and Office Supplies Expense accounts.

7. Give examples of three different accrual adjusting entries.

8. What is the second trial balance called? What purpose does it serve?

9. What are the major balance sheet classifications of assets and liabilities?

10. What are *current assets?* What are *current liabilities?*

11. What is an *operating cycle?*

12. What is the difference between the terms *marketable securities* and *investments?*

13. What is working capital? What is a current ratio?

### QUESTIONS FOR FURTHER THOUGHT

1. Why must certain accounts be adjusted at the end of an accounting period?

2. Many people believe that net income is a precise measurement. Explain why this is not so.

3. Explain why the *cash basis* of accounting is not considered to be part of generally accepted accounting principles.

4. Explain the meaning of the generally accepted accounting principles **(a)** the *matching concept* and **(b)** the *revenue-recognition principle.*

5. Consider a new account that has not been discussed, Prepaid Income. What is the nature of this account, and how should it be classified?

6. Expenses are paid in one of three ways. What are these three ways?

7. At the end of an accounting period a company fails to record the salaries accrual adjusting entry. What effect will this have on the financial statements?

8. What is the ultimate objective of financial accounting?

9. What are the steps involved in the financial accounting process?

10. Why are classified financial statements prepared?

11. With a current ratio of 3 to 1 the Johnson Company is viewed as being in sound financial health. Evaluate this statement.

## OBJECTIVE ASSIGNMENT

*True/False*   Indicate whether each statement below is *true* or *false* by placing a *T* or an *F* in the space provided.

_____ 1. Accountants use the term "fairly" to mean that the financial statements reflect the underlying economic events and transactions within an acceptable range of accuracy.

_____ 2. Accruals include goods and services collected or paid for in advance of benefits given or received.

_____ 3. After all the external transactions have been recorded, an adjusted trial balance is prepared.

_____ 4. The operating cycle is the length of time it takes to pay the current liabilities.

_____ 5. Under the cash basis of accounting, it is easy to manipulate profits.

*Multiple Choice*   Select the best choice to complete each statement or answer each question below. Write the letter corresponding to your choice in the space provided.

_____ 1. An adjusting entry:
   a. Involves parties external to the entity
   b. Is an external transaction
   c. Is not recorded in any journal
   d. Is an internal transaction
   e. None of the above

_____ 2. The broad classifications of adjusting entries are:
   a. Accruals and closing
   b. Accruals and deferrals
   c. Trials and deferrals
   d. Closing and trials
   e. None of the above

_____ 3. A prepaid expense is not an:
   a. Asset
   b. Unexpired cost
   c. Expired cost
   d. Economic resource
   e. None of the above

_____ 4. The following account will have a normal debit balance:
   a. Accumulated Depreciation
   b. Depreciation Expense
   c. Unearned Revenue
   d. Accounts Payable
   e. All of the above

_____ 5. The following account will most likely require an accrual type of adjusting entry:
   a. Prepaid Insurance
   b. Unearned Revenue
   c. Office Supplies on Hand
   d. Equipment
   e. None of the above

_____ 6. Financial statements can be prepared directly from the
   a. Income statement
   b. General ledger
   c. Adjusted trial balance
   d. General journal
   e. Trial balance

_____ 7. The last group of accounts listed on the adjusted trial balance will be used to prepare the
   a. Income statement
   b. Statement of cash flows
   c. Balance sheet
   d. Statement of owner's equity
   e. None of the above

_____ 8. Which of the steps in the accounting process is performed first?
   a. Prepare statements
   b. Post
   c. Journalize
   d. Adjust
   e. Prepare adjusted trial balance

_____ 9. Classified financial statements are prepared because:
   a. They are required by the IRS
   b. They are helpful when analyzing and comparing financial statements
   c. They are helpful when submitting information to the FASB
   d. They are required by the AAA
   e. All of the above

_____ 10. The accrual basis of accounting is:
   a. A requirement of the IRS
   b. The same as the cash basis
   c. An option available to management
   d. Used only on the income statement
   e. A generally accepted accounting principle

## EXERCISES

6† **Exercise 1:** Adjusting Salaries

Lance Company pays its employees a total of $22,500 every Friday for a 5-day work week. Prepare the appropriate adjusting entry assuming first that the accounting year ends on May 31, 1998, which is a Wednesday. Then assume that the accounting year ends on Feb. 28, 1998, which is a Tuesday.

5 **Exercise 2:** Adjusting Entries

The Daniels Company's year ends on Dec. 31, 1998. Prepare in general journal entry form the year-end adjusting entry indicated by each of the following four items.

a. Prepaid Rent in the amount of $2,400 was paid on Oct. 1, 1998, for a 12-month period ending Sept. 30, 1999.
b. Office supplies were acquired on Mar. 12 in the amount of $4,320. On Dec. 31, 1998, the amount of office supplies remaining amounted to $1,060.
c. Daniels Company received $5,760 on May 1, 1998, for advertising that it will do for a client over the next 24 months.
d. New office equipment costing $8,640 was acquired on Nov. 1, 1998. The machine has an estimated life of 12 years, after which it will be worthless.

† The numbers in the margin refer to the Learning Objectives.

5 **Exercise 3:** Determining Supplies Expense and Supplies on Hand

For each of the four independent cases listed below, determine the amount indicated.

a. Supplies in the amount of $1,630 were acquired during the year. Supplies on hand at the beginning of the year amounted to $5,410. The ending balance was $2,040. What was the amount of supplies expense during the year?

b. The supplies on hand at the end of the year were $950. Supplies acquired during the year amounted to $3,270. Supplies used were $3,920. What was the amount of supplies on hand at the beginning of the year?

c. Supplies of $2,510 were consumed during the year. Supplies on hand at the beginning of the year amounted to $1,200. The ending balance was $1,470. What was the amount of supplies acquired?

d. Supplies acquired during the year amounted to $5,780. The beginning balance of supplies was $2,020. The supplies consumed during the year amounted to $4,310. What was the ending balance?

4 5 6 **Exercise 4:** Determining the Effects of Omissions

An error of omission occurs when one forgets to do something. If an accountant forgets to record the year-end adjusting entries, that is an error of omission and it will, of course, affect the financial statements.

   Using the following chart, indicate the effect of the five errors of omission on the financial statement classifications listed. If as a result of the omission a classification is overstated, place a (+) in the appropriate space. An understatement is to be indicated by a (−). If the omission has no effect on the classification, place a (0) in the appropriate space.

| | Effect of Omission | | | | |
| Classification | a | b | c | d | e |
|---|---|---|---|---|---|
| Revenue | | | | | |
| Expenses | | | | | |
| Net Income | | | | | |
| Current Assets | | | | | |
| Noncurrent Assets | | | | | |
| Current Liabilities | | | | | |
| Long-Term Liabilities | | | | | |
| Owner's Equity | | | | | |

a. Accrued salaries were not recorded.
b. Office Supplies on Hand was not adjusted at year-end.
c. Depreciation was not recorded.
d. Interest income on notes receivable was not recorded.
e. Unearned revenue was not adjusted at year-end.

4 5 6 **Exercise 5:** Preparing Adjusting Entries

The following four accounts were taken from the Jenkins Company's Dec. 31, 1998, unadjusted trial balance:

| | Debit | Credit |
|---|---|---|
| Prepaid Rent | $1,800 | |
| Office Supplies on Hand | 3,650 | |
| Accumulated Depreciation | | $10,800 |
| Unearned Service Revenue | | 7,200 |

Using the following additional information, prepare the appropriate year-end adjusting entries.

a. The prepaid rent represents the cash paid for 3 months' rent from Dec. 1, 1998, to Feb. 28, 1999.

b. A count of the office supplies on hand at Dec. 31, 1998, amounts to $1,080.
c. The accumulated depreciation relates to equipment acquired on Jan. 1, 1995.
d. A check in the amount of $7,200 was received on Nov. 1, 1998, for services to be performed over the next 6 months.

4 5 6 **Exercise 6:** Preparing Adjusting Entries

Listed below are the income statement accounts from the Dec. 31, 1998, unadjusted and adjusted trial balances of the Gibbons Company. Review the trial balances and prepare the adjusting entries that were made on Dec. 31, 1998.

| | Dec. 31, 1998 | |
|---|---|---|
| | Unadjusted Trial Balance | Adjusted Trial Balance |
| Service Fees Earned ......................... | $65,000 | $65,000 |
| Advertising Fees Earned...................... | 14,700 | 16,300 |
| Salary Expense............................... | 7,300 | 8,100 |
| Office Supplies Expense....................... | 1,750 | 2,070 |
| Insurance Expense ............................ | 350 | 410 |
| Interest Expense .............................. | 600 | 660 |
| Depreciation Expense......................... | 1,800 | 2,400 |

9 **Exercise 7:** Preparing a Classified Balance Sheet

Listed below in alphabetical order are the accounts of the Carlson Company. The General Motors stock will be held by Carlson until mid-2001. The Note Payable is due on Apr. 1, 2002. Using this information, prepare a classified balance sheet as of Dec. 31, 1998.

| | | | | |
|---|---|---|---|---|
| Accounts Payable .......... | $ 4,210 | General Motors Stock ........ | $11,000 |
| Accounts Receivable......... | 3,600 | Goodwill.................. | 2,750 |
| Accumulated Depreciation: | | Note Payable............... | 22,000 |
| Office Equipment........... | 3,750 | Office Equipment............ | 25,000 |
| Cash..................... | 1,250 | Office Supplies on Hand...... | 1,720 |
| Carlson, Capital, Dec. 31, 1998 | 13,730 | Salaries Payable ............ | 1,630 |

▶ *(Check Figure: Total Assets = $41,570)*
Compute the working capital and current ratio.

10 **Exercise 8:** Determining current assets

The Ellis Company has a current ratio of 3 to 1 and working capital amounts to $20,000. What is the total amount of current assets?

## PROBLEMS: SET A

4 5 6† **Problem A1:** Preparing Adjusting Entries at Year-End

The following information relating to the accounts of the Edwards Car Service Center is available prior to the Jan. 31, 1998, year-end.

a. Edwards paid $2,490 to the Olson Insurance Company on December 1, 1997, for insurance to cover the months of December 1997 to May 1998 inclusive.
b. The general ledger account Store Supplies on Hand shows a $4,350 debit balance. A count of the store supplies on Jan. 31 amounts to $980.

† The numbers in the margin refer to the Learning Objectives.

c. Edwards received a $2,700 payment from the City of Trenton for servicing police vehicles for a 9-month period commencing on Nov. 1, 1997. The payment is reflected in the Unearned Revenue account.

d. The Car Service Facility account shows a $25,200 balance at year-end, representing the acquisition of the facility on Aug. 1, 1997. The facility is estimated to have a 30-year life.

e. The last day of January 1998 falls on a Tuesday. Edwards' employees are paid $900 every Friday.

**Required:**

1. For each of the five items above, prepare the appropriate adjusting entry.
2. Record the payment of the $900 salaries on Friday, Feb. 3, 1998.

4 5 6 **Problem A2:** Preparing Adjusting Entries at Year-End

Vance Company's accounting year ends on Aug. 31, 1998. Information presented below relates to the year-end adjustments necessary for Vance to present its financial statements in accordance with generally accepted accounting principles.

a. The Prepaid Insurance account had a balance of $9,600 as of Aug. 31, 1998. The balance represents amounts paid for two 1-year insurance policies. Policy A was obtained on Feb. 1, 1998, for $5,100. Policy B was acquired on June 1, 1998, for $4,500.

b. Office supplies acquired during the year amounted to $17,600. The office supplies on hand at last year's end were worth $4,500. On Aug. 31, 1998, the amount was $6,700.

c. Yeaton Company paid Vance $5,400 in advance for services to be rendered over several months until the work was complete. As of year-end, 60% of the work had been completed.

d. New equipment was installed on Apr. 1, 1998, at a cost of $84,600. The equipment is estimated to have a 15-year life and will be of no value at the end of that time.

e. Vance employees are paid every Friday. In 1998, Aug. 31 falls on a Thursday. Vance is bound to the following union pay scale for its employees:

| Employee Category | Number in Category | Daily Rate per Employee |
|---|---|---|
| Foreman | 2 | $80 |
| Operator | 7 | 60 |
| Material handler | 3 | 30 |

f. On Jan. 1, 1998, Vance borrowed $68,400 from the Trenton Exchange Bank by issuing a 10%, 1-year note payable. (Interest is expressed at the annual rate.)

**Required:**

1. For each of the six items listed above, prepare the appropriate adjusting entry.
2. Record the entry to pay the salaries due on Sept. 1, 1998.

**4 5 6 7 Problem A3:** Preparing Adjusting Entries, Postings, and an Adjusted Trial Balance

Presented below, together with account numbers, is the unadjusted trial balance of Jackson Travel Agency for the year ended Dec. 31, 1998:

---

**JACKSON TRAVEL AGENCY**
**Unadjusted Trial Balance**
**December 31, 1998**

| | | | |
|---|---|---:|---:|
| 110 | Cash | $ 12,600 | |
| 120 | Accounts Receivable | 64,500 | |
| 130 | Prepaid Rent | 36,000 | |
| 140 | Office Supplies on Hand | 6,300 | |
| 150 | Furniture | 217,500 | |
| 155 | Accumulated Depreciation: Furniture | | $ 43,500 |
| 210 | Notes Payable | | 90,000 |
| 220 | Interest Payable | | –0– |
| 230 | Accounts Payable | | 28,500 |
| 240 | Salaries Payable | | –0– |
| 310 | Jackson, Capital | | 168,000 |
| 320 | Jackson, Withdrawals | 120,000 | |
| 410 | Travel Fees Earned | | 513,300 |
| 510 | Salary Expense | 377,100 | |
| 520 | Rent Expense | –0– | |
| 530 | Office Supplies Expense | –0– | |
| 540 | Depreciation Expense: Furniture | –0– | |
| 550 | Interest Expense | –0– | |
| 560 | Miscellaneous Expense | 9,300 | |
| | Totals | $843,300 | $843,300 |

---

Information pertaining to Jackson's accounts is as follows:

a. On Nov. 1, 1998, Jackson paid Reading Rental Agency $36,000 for 6 months' rent on the office building commencing that date.
b. Office supplies on hand at Dec. 31, 1998, amounted to $2,700.
c. Depreciation expense for the furniture amounts to $7,500 for the year 1998.
d. At Dec. 31, 1998, $10,500 of accrued salaries remain unpaid.
e. The $90,000 note payable was issued on Oct. 1, 1998. It will be repaid in 12 months together with interest at an annual rate of 12%.

**Required:**

1. Prepare the adjusting entries.
2. Establish a general ledger account for each account found on the unadjusted trial balance. Enter the amount found in the unadjusted trial balance into the general ledger accounts. Post the adjusting entries. Compute the adjusted balances. Use page number 11 for the general journal.
3. Prepare an adjusted trial balance.

▶ *(Check Figure: Adjusted trial balance = $864,000)*

4 5 6 7  **Problem A4:** Preparing Adjusting Entries from Unadjusted and Adjusted Trial Balances

The unadjusted and adjusted Dec. 31, 1998, trial balances for the Welker Company are presented below:

## THE WELKER COMPANY
### Trial Balances
### December 31, 1998

| | Unadjusted | | Adjusted | |
|---|---|---|---|---|
| Cash............................. | $   7,200 | | $   7,200 | |
| Accounts Receivable.............. | 33,100 | | 33,100 | |
| Prepaid Insurance ................ | 4,800 | | 3,600 | |
| Office Supplies on Hand ........... | 12,500 | | 7,200 | |
| Land............................ | 17,000 | | 17,000 | |
| Office Building ................... | 85,000 | | 85,000 | |
| Accumulated Depreciation: Office Building........................ | | $  23,000 | | $  24,500 |
| Office Equipment................. | 62,000 | | 62,000 | |
| Accumulated Depreciation: Office Equipment ...................... | | 10,600 | | 12,400 |
| Notes Payable ................... | | 55,000 | | 55,000 |
| Interest Payable.................. | | –0– | | 7,700 |
| Accounts Payable ................ | | 14,300 | | 14,300 |
| Salaries Payable ................. | | –0– | | 3,400 |
| Mortgage Payable ................ | | 47,000 | | 47,000 |
| Welker, Capital................... | | 31,000 | | 31,000 |
| Welker, Withdrawals .............. | 25,000 | | 25,000 | |
| Fees Earned..................... | | 147,000 | | 147,000 |
| Salary Expense .................. | 81,300 | | 84,700 | |
| Insurance Expense ............... | –0– | | 1,200 | |
| Office Supplies Expense ........... | –0– | | 5,300 | |
| Depreciation Expense: Office Building........................ | –0– | | 1,500 | |
| Depreciation Expense: Office Equipment ...................... | –0– | | 1,800 | |
| Interest Expense ................. | –0– | | 7,700 | |
| Totals......................... | $327,900 | $327,900 | $342,300 | $342,300 |

**Required:**

By comparing the two trial balances, determine the adjustments that were made and prepare the adjusting entries.

9 **Problem A5:** Preparing a Classified Balance Sheet

Listed below are the balance sheet accounts of the Charlton Company as of Dec. 31, 1998:

| | | | |
|---|---|---|---|
| Accumulated Depreciation: Shop Building | $ 60,000 | Long-term Investment in Stock | 12,000 |
| Accumulated Depreciation: Shop Equipment | 120,000 | Marketable Securities | 19,500 |
| Accounts Payable | 25,500 | Merchandise Inventory | 126,000 |
| Accounts Receivable | 24,000 | Mortgage Payable | 300,000 |
| Cash | 7,500 | Note Payable due 2001 | 87,000 |
| Charlton, Capital, Dec. 31, 1998 | 390,000 | Note Receivable due 1999 | 64,500 |
| Copyrights | 3,000 | Patents | 9,000 |
| Goodwill | 22,500 | Prepaid Advertising | 4,500 |
| Interest Receivable | 3,000 | Salaries Payable | 10,500 |
| Interest Payable | 12,000 | Shop Building | 375,000 |
| Land | 90,000 | Shop Equipment | 225,000 |
| Long-term Investment in Bonds | 31,500 | Shop Supplies on Hand | 3,000 |
| | | Unearned Revenue | 15,000 |

**Required:**

Prepare a classified balance sheet. Calculate working capital and the current ratio.

▶ *(Check Figure: Total assets = $840,000)*

4 5 6 **Problem A6:** Analyzing Accounts

Presented below are 10 accounts selected from the general ledger of the Elton Company after the adjusting entries have been made for the year ended Dec. 31, 1998, the first year of business. Notice that the total debits and total credits to the accounts, rather than the account balances, are given.

| | Debit | Credit |
|---|---|---|
| Cash | $19,500 | $18,600 |
| Prepaid Insurance | 4,800 | 3,600 |
| Office Supplies on Hand | 3,500 | 1,700 |
| Accounts Payable | 4,200 | 6,300 |
| Salaries Payable | | 700 |
| Unearned Revenue | | 1,300 |
| Salaries Expense | 8,500 | |
| Revenue | 1,300 | 16,300 |
| Insurance Expense | 4,000 | |
| Office Supplies Expense | 1,700 | |

**Required:**

Answer the following questions.

1. How much cash was paid for insurance for the year? Explain.
2. How much cash was paid to the employees in the form of salaries during the year?
3. What adjusting entry was made for office supplies?
4. What was the adjusting entry made for revenues? Explain.
5. Cash is expended for salaries, payments of accounts payable, insurance, and other items. How much cash was paid for items other than salaries, accounts payable, and insurance during the year?

## PROBLEMS: SET B

4 5 6† **Problem B1:** Preparing Adjusting Entries at Year-End

The Larkin Company presents the following information pertaining to accounts that will need adjusting for its Nov. 30, 1998, year-end financial statements.

a. On Oct. 1, 1998, Larkin Company paid $1,080 for 6 months' rent in advance.
b. The balance in the general ledger account Office Supplies on Hand amounts to $3,200. A count of the office supplies on Nov. 30, 1998, totals $1,280.
c. Larkin Company received $2,280 on Nov. 1, 1998, from a customer for services to be rendered during the months of November, December, January, and February.
d. Larkin acquired Office Equipment costing $35,280 on Apr. 1, 1998. The equipment is expected to last 7 years, after which it will be worthless.
e. Nov. 30, 1998, is a Thursday. Larkin pays its employees, on Fridays, a total of $8,750 per week.

**Required:**

1. Prepare the appropriate adjusting entry for each of the five items listed above.
2. Prepare the Dec. 1, 1998, entry to record the payment of the salaries.

4 5 6 **Problem B2:** Preparing Adjusting Entries at Year-End

Listed below is information pertaining to activities of the Nelson Company that require adjustments for the May 31, 1998, year-end financial statements.

a. Nelson Company entered into a lease agreement with Parker Corporation on Nov. 1, 1997, for rental of office space for the next 24 months for $15,600. A second lease was signed on Feb. 1, 1998, for storage space for 6 months, with $5,640 paid in advance.
b. On June 1, 1997, the Office Supplies on Hand account in the general ledger had a debit balance of $4,260. Office supplies in the amount of $16,520 had been acquired during the year. A physical count of the office supplies on May 31, 1998, totaled $3,170.
c. Nelson Company sells magazines by subscription for $1.50 per copy. During the course of the year, 47,200 two-year subscriptions were sold. As of June 1, 1997, the Unearned Magazine Revenue account had a balance of $31,500. At year-end it is determined that the liability to provide subscribers' future magazines amounts to $61,300.
d. On Dec. 1, 1997, Nelson Company acquired a new computer for $131,400. It is anticipated that the computer will be used for 15 years and will then be useless.
e. Nelson Company pays its employees every other Friday. The last payday was May 19, 1998, and May 31 is a Wednesday, so 8 days of salaries have accrued. The pay scale at Nelson is as follows:

| Employee Category | Number in Category | Daily Rate per Employee |
|---|---|---|
| Executives | 3 | $300 |
| Directors | 8 | 240 |
| Managers | 14 | 170 |
| Staff | 72 | 120 |

f. Nelson Company borrowed $100,000 from the First National Bank on Mar. 1, 1998, issuing a 14%, 1-year note payable for that amount. (Interest is expressed at the annual rate.)

**Required:**

1. Prepare adjusting entries for each of the six items listed above.
2. Refer to item (e) and record the entry to pay the salaries due on June 2, 1998.

† The numbers in the margin refer to the Learning Objectives.

4 5 6 7 **Problem B3:** Preparing Adjusting Entries, Postings, and an Adjusted Trial Balance

The unadjusted trial balance of Sunflower State Company for the year ended Dec. 31, 1998, is presented below together with account numbers:

---

**SUNFLOWER STATE COMPANY**
**Unadjusted Trial Balance**
**December 31, 1998**

| | | | |
|---|---|---|---|
| 110 | Cash | $ 4,200 | |
| 120 | Notes Receivable | 12,000 | |
| 130 | Interest Receivable | –0– | |
| 140 | Accounts Receivable | 18,300 | |
| 150 | Prepaid Advertising | 2,100 | |
| 160 | Office Supplies on Hand | 5,300 | |
| 170 | Land | 21,000 | |
| 180 | Building | 160,000 | |
| 185 | Accumulated Depreciation: Building | | $ 40,000 |
| 190 | Office Furniture | 25,000 | |
| 195 | Accumulated Depreciation: Office Furniture | | 10,000 |
| 210 | Accounts Payable | | 7,100 |
| 220 | Salaries Payable | | –0– |
| 310 | Landon, Capital | | 120,500 |
| 320 | Landon, Withdrawals | 12,000 | |
| 410 | Revenues | | 212,600 |
| 420 | Interest Income | | –0– |
| 510 | Salary Expense | 126,700 | |
| 520 | Advertising Expense | –0– | |
| 530 | Office Supplies Expense | –0– | |
| 540 | Depreciation Expense: Buildings | –0– | |
| 550 | Depreciation Expense: Office Furniture | –0– | |
| 560 | Utilities Expense | 3,600 | |
| | Totals | $390,200 | $390,200 |

---

Information pertaining to Sunflower State's accounts that need to be adjusted follows.

a. Sunshine paid $2,100 on Sept. 1, 1998, for 6 months of advertisements in the Kansas *Daily News*.
b. The amount of office supplies on hand at Dec. 31, 1998, is $1,700.
c. The company has computed the depreciation expense for 1998 to be $4,000 on the building and $2,500 on the office furniture.
d. Accrued salaries at Dec. 31, 1998, amount to $1,900.
e. The note receivable was accepted on Aug. 1, 1998 and is a 1-year note with annual interest of 14%.

**Required:**

1. Prepare the adjusting entries.
2. Establish a general ledger account for each account found in the unadjusted trial balance. Enter the amount found in the unadjusted trial balance into the general ledger accounts. Post the adjusting entries. Compute the adjusted balances. Use page number 25 for the general journal posting reference.
3. Prepare an adjusted trial balance.

▶ *(Check Figure: Adjusted trial balance = $399,300)*

4 5 6 7 **Problem B4:** Preparing Adjusting Entries from Unadjusted and Adjusted Trial Balances

Both the Dec. 31, 1998, unadjusted and adjusted trial balances from the Rider Plumbing Company are presented below:

**RIDER PLUMBING COMPANY**
**Trial Balances**
**December 31, 1998**

|  | Unadjusted | | Adjusted | |
| --- | ---: | ---: | ---: | ---: |
| Cash . . . . . . . . . . . . . . . . . . . . . . . . . | $ 4,700 | | $ 4,700 | |
| Notes Receivable. . . . . . . . . . . . . . . . | 16,000 | | 16,000 | |
| Interest Receivable . . . . . . . . . . . . . . | −0− | | 2,400 | |
| Accounts Receivable . . . . . . . . . . . . . | 26,700 | | 26,700 | |
| Prepaid Advertising . . . . . . . . . . . . . . | 3,500 | | 1,100 | |
| Office Supplies on Hand . . . . . . . . . . | 4,700 | | 2,900 | |
| Land . . . . . . . . . . . . . . . . . . . . . . . . . | 14,000 | | 14,000 | |
| Building. . . . . . . . . . . . . . . . . . . . . . . | 62,000 | | 62,000 | |
| Accumulated Depreciation: Building . . | | $ 16,000 | | $ 17,500 |
| Equipment . . . . . . . . . . . . . . . . . . . . | 53,000 | | 53,000 | |
| Accumulated Depreciation: | | | | |
| Equipment . . . . . . . . . . . . . . . . . . . . | | 20,400 | | 23,800 |
| Interest Payable. . . . . . . . . . . . . . . . . | | −0− | | 400 |
| Accounts Payable. . . . . . . . . . . . . . . | | 12,700 | | 12,700 |
| Salaries Payable . . . . . . . . . . . . . . . . | | −0− | | 2,200 |
| Mortgage Payable . . . . . . . . . . . . . . . | | 30,000 | | 30,000 |
| Rider, Capital . . . . . . . . . . . . . . . . . . . | | 46,000 | | 46,000 |
| Rider, Withdrawals. . . . . . . . . . . . . . . | 15,800 | | 15,800 | |
| Plumbing Fees Earned. . . . . . . . . . . . | | 165,700 | | 165,700 |
| Interest Income. . . . . . . . . . . . . . . . . . | | −0− | | 2,400 |
| Salary Expense . . . . . . . . . . . . . . . . . | 85,400 | | 87,600 | |
| Advertising Expense . . . . . . . . . . . . . | −0− | | 2,400 | |
| Office Supplies Expense . . . . . . . . . . | −0− | | 1,800 | |
| Depreciation Expense: Building. . . . . . | −0− | | 1,500 | |
| Depreciation Expense: Equipment . . . | −0− | | 3,400 | |
| Interest Expense . . . . . . . . . . . . . . . . | 5,000 | | 5,400 | |
| Totals . . . . . . . . . . . . . . . . . . . . . . . . | $290,800 | $290,800 | $300,700 | $300,700 |

**Required:**

By comparing the two trial balances, determine the adjustments that were made and prepare the adjusting entries.

9 **Problem B5:** Classified Balance Sheet

The balance sheet accounts of the Gerald Company are listed below.

| | | | |
|---|---|---|---|
| Gerald, Capital, | | Accounts Payable . . . . . . . . . | 13,700 |
| Dec. 31, 1998 . . . . . . . . . . . . | $349,400 | Notes Receivable . . . . . . . . . | 12,000 |
| Office Equipment . . . . . . . . . . | 310,000 | Unearned Revenue . . . . . . . . . | 9,200 |
| Office Building . . . . . . . . . . . . | 260,000 | Long-Term Investment | |
| Accumulated Depreciation: | | in Stocks . . . . . . . . . . . . . . . | 8,300 |
| Office Equipment . . . . . . . . . . | 130,000 | Marketable Securities . . . . . . . | 7,500 |
| Mortgage Payable . . . . . . . . . | 125,000 | Patents . . . . . . . . . . . . . . . . . | 6,600 |
| Merchandise Inventory . . . . . . | 73,400 | Long-Term Investment | |
| Note Payable due 2001 . . . . . . | 54,000 | in Bonds . . . . . . . . . . . . . . . | 6,100 |
| Accumulated Depreciation: | | Salaries Payable . . . . . . . . . . . | 3,900 |
| Office Building . . . . . . . . . . . . | 40,000 | Cash . . . . . . . . . . . . . . . . . . . | 5,300 |
| Note Payable due 1999 . . . . . . | 32,000 | Copyrights . . . . . . . . . . . . . . . | 2,700 |
| Land . . . . . . . . . . . . . . . . . . . | 27,000 | Prepaid Insurance . . . . . . . . . . | 2,300 |
| Goodwill . . . . . . . . . . . . . . . . | 18,600 | Office Supplies on Hand . . . . . | 1,200 |
| Accounts Receivable . . . . . . . . | 16,200 | | |

**Required:**

Prepare a classified balance sheet. Calculate working capital and the current ratio.

▶ *(Check Figure: Total assets = $587,200)*

2 4 5 6 **Problem B6:** Analyzing Accounts

Presented below are several accounts selected from the general ledger of the Ellen Company after the adjusting entries have been made for the year ended Dec. 31, 1998, the first year of business. Notice that the total debits and total credits to the accounts, rather than the account balances, are given.

| | Debit | Credit |
|---|---|---|
| Cash . . . . . . . . . . . . . . . . . . . . . . . . . . . . . . . . . . . . . . . . . . . | 28,300 | 23,500 |
| Accounts Receivable . . . . . . . . . . . . . . . . . . . . . . . . . . . . . . . . | 18,400 | 14,300 |
| Prepaid Insurance . . . . . . . . . . . . . . . . . . . . . . . . . . . . . . . . . | 1,700 | |
| Office Supplies on Hand . . . . . . . . . . . . . . . . . . . . . . . . . . . . . | 2,600 | 1,400 |
| Salaries Payable . . . . . . . . . . . . . . . . . . . . . . . . . . . . . . . . . . . | | 1,200 |
| Unearned Revenue . . . . . . . . . . . . . . . . . . . . . . . . . . . . . . . . . | 2,600 | 4,700 |
| Salaries Expense . . . . . . . . . . . . . . . . . . . . . . . . . . . . . . . . . . | 9,300 | |
| Revenue . . . . . . . . . . . . . . . . . . . . . . . . . . . . . . . . . . . . . . . . . | | 30,300 |
| Insurance Expense . . . . . . . . . . . . . . . . . . . . . . . . . . . . . . . . . | 5,300 | 1,700 |
| Office Supplies Expense . . . . . . . . . . . . . . . . . . . . . . . . . . . . . | 2,100 | |

**Required:**

Answer the following questions.

1. How much cash was paid for office supplies for the year? Explain.
2. How much cash was paid to the employees in the form of salaries during the year?
3. What adjusting entry was made for unearned revenues?
4. What was the adjusting entry made for insurance? Explain.
5. Cash receipts consist of collections from receivables, unearned revenues, and other sources. How much cash was received from other sources?

## DECISION PROBLEM

On Jan. 1, 1997, John Hodgson realized a life-long dream: He opened the Hodgson Fitness Center by investing $101,000 of his personal funds and $404,000 borrowed on an 11¾% mortgage with the Lutz National Savings and Loan. With these funds John acquired land, a building, and workout equipment. He concentrated on developing his business by making presentations to local groups on the value of exercise and nutrition and by paying close attention to his clients' exercise programs while they were in his facility.

John did not have a background in business, having graduated from Penn State with a degree in sports fitness. He hired Sally Nogood to handle the fitness center's business affairs.

Sally and John worked well together, and he was very disappointed when she resigned early in January 1998. Before Sally left, she prepared the following income statement for John:

### HODGSON FITNESS CENTER
### Income Statement
### For the Year Ended December 31, 1997

| | | |
|---|---:|---:|
| Revenues.............................................. | | $563,400 |
| Expenses: | | |
| Salaries Expense ................................... | $318,100 | |
| Supplies Expense................................... | 128,500 | |
| Rent Expense ...................................... | 30,000 | |
| Advertising Expense................................ | 19,000 | |
| Depreciation Expense............................... | 18,000 | |
| Miscellaneous Expense ............................. | 16,500 | |
| Total Expenses......................................... | | 530,100 |
| Net Income............................................. | | $ 33,300 |

John was somewhat surprised that his business had not done much better than $33,300. However, when he checked the bank statement, $33,300 was indeed the balance in his account.

John has asked you to handle his books while he is looking for a replacement for Sally. You find the following information relating to last year's activity:

- Revenues consist of contracts with customers for use of the fitness center for periods of from 3 months to 2 years. You determine that the contracts total $689,000, with $8,000 applicable to 1998. Collections amount to $597,400. Further, you find an adjusting entry in the general journal debiting Revenues and crediting Cash for $34,000.

- A review of the payroll records reveals that the employees earned $326,300 during the year but were paid $305,100. An adjusting entry made at year-end accrued $13,000 of salaries by a debit to Salary Expense and a credit to Cash.

- You determine that $28,100 of supplies are on hand at year-end. No supplies have been used since Dec. 31, 1997. Invoices for supply acquisitions amount to $152,300, and a call to the vendor reveals that payments in the amount of $117,500 have been made. Sally's adjusting entry was a debit to Supplies Expense and a credit to Cash for $11,000.

- Payments were made during the year for rent of certain exercise equipment, $30,000, and for advertising, $19,000. The rent and advertising will carry over to 1998: $6,000 as prepaid rent and $4,000 as prepaid advertising.

- Depreciation was recorded as a debit to Depreciation Expense and a credit to Cash of $18,000. You determine that $18,000 is the appropriate amount of depreciation.

- Miscellaneous expenses were incurred and paid in the amount of $7,500. An adjusting entry debits Miscellaneous Expense and credits Cash for $9,000.

**Required:**

1. Prepare the following, in four adjacent columns:
    a. A correct income statement for the year ended Dec. 31, 1997.
    b. A statement of cash receipts and cash payments for the same period of time as income statement.
    c. Sally Nogood's income statement.
    d. A list indicating the amount that Sally apparently stole from each income statement item.
2. Comment on the situation described here.

---

## ETHICS CASE

As comptroller for international operations of the Bender Company, you are responsible for selecting the chief accountants of the company's various plants. The chief accountant of the largest plant, in the country of Arnique, has just retired. He was a native of St. Louis and had lived in Arnique for the past 5 years.

You are considering two individuals for the position, both of whom already work at the Arnique plant. One candidate is a native of Arnique and has worked for the company for 23 years. The other is a U.S. national from Los Angeles who has been in Arnique for 3 years, speaks the language fluently, and has been with the company 12 years.

For a number of reasons, you consider the second individual to be clearly more qualified than the first. However, the custom in Arnique is to base promotions on seniority.

**Required:**

What factors should you consider in selecting the new chief accountant?

---

## COMPREHENSIVE PROBLEMS

### Comprehensive Problem 1

Presented below is the unadjusted trial balance of the Siebel Information Systems Company for the year ended Dec. 31, 1998:

| SIEBEL INFORMATION SYSTEMS COMPANY<br>Unadjusted Trial Balance<br>December 31, 1998 | | |
|---|---|---|
| Cash | $ 4,500 | |
| Notes Receivable | 36,000 | |
| Accounts Receivable | 15,600 | |
| Office Supplies on Hand | 6,300 | |
| Land | 30,000 | |
| Building | 159,000 | |
| Accumulated Depreciation: Building | | $ 25,400 |
| Equipment | 215,000 | |
| Accumulated Depreciation: Equipment | | 61,200 |
| Accounts Payable | | 21,300 |
| Unearned Revenue | | 45,000 |
| Siebel, Capital, Jan. 1, 1998 | | 265,500 |
| Siebel, Withdrawals | 60,000 | |
| Revenues Earned | | 210,800 |
| Salary Expense | 87,500 | |
| Repairs Expense | 11,600 | |
| Miscellaneous Expense | 3,700 | |
| Totals | $629,200 | $629,200 |

**Required:**

1. Establish a general ledger account, for each item found in the unadjusted trial balance.
2. Additional information is presented below. From this information, prepare the necessary adjusting entries and post the adjusting entries to the general ledger, establishing accounts as needed.
   a. The amount of Office Supplies on Hand on Dec. 31, 1998, is $2,100.
   b. One-third of the unearned revenue had been earned as of Dec. 31, 1998.
   c. Depreciation for the year amounts to $3,800 for the building and $12,300 for the equipment.
   d. Salaries in the amount of $1,400 have been earned but not paid as of the last day of the year.
   e. The notes receivable were accepted from several customers. The notes were issued on Sept. 1, 1998, and will be paid, together with 10% interest, on May 30, 2001. Interest is expressed as an annual rate.
3. Prepare an adjusted trial balance.

   ▶ *(Check Figure: Adjusted trial balance = $647,900)*
4. Prepare an income statement, a statement of owner's equity, and a classified balance sheet.

## Comprehensive Problem 2

The unadjusted trial balance of the Troutman Company for the year ended June 30, 1998, appears below:

**TROUTMAN COMPANY**
**Unadjusted Trial Balance**
**June 30, 1998**

| | | |
|---|---:|---:|
| Cash | $ 1,200 | |
| Accounts Receivable | 5,300 | |
| Office Supplies on Hand | 2,700 | |
| Land | 14,000 | |
| Office Building | 80,000 | |
| Accumulated Depreciation: Office Building | | $ 12,000 |
| Office Equipment | 45,000 | |
| Accumulated Depreciation: Office Equipment | | 25,200 |
| Accounts Payable | | 3,100 |
| Unearned Revenue | | 21,200 |
| Note Payable due Dec. 31, 2002 | | 36,000 |
| Troutman, Capital, July 1, 1997 | | 19,900 |
| Troutman, Withdrawals | 26,000 | |
| Revenue | | 154,600 |
| Salary Expense | 89,700 | |
| Utilities Expense | 4,200 | |
| Miscellaneous Expense | 3,900 | |
| Totals | $272,000 | $272,000 |

**Required:**

1. Establish a general ledger account for each item found in the unadjusted trial balance.
2. Use the following additional information to prepare the necessary adjusting entries, and post the adjusting entries to the general ledger, establishing accounts as needed.
   a. Office Supplies on Hand on June 30, 1998, is determined to be $1,100.
   b. By the end of June, one-fourth of Unearned Revenue had been earned.
   c. Depreciation for the year amounts to $2,000 for the office building and $4,200 for the office equipment.

    d. As of June 30, 1998, $3,700 in salaries has accrued and remains unpaid.

    e. The interest rate on the note payable is 12% per year. The note was issued to the Liberty National Bank on Sept. 1, 1997, and will be repaid on Aug. 31, 2002. The interest is to be paid on Dec. 31 of each year.

3. Prepare an adjusted trial balance.

    ▶ *(Check Figure: Adjusted trial balance = $285,500)*

4. Prepare an income statement, a statement of owner's equity, and a classified balance sheet.

## OBJECTIVE ASSIGNMENT ANSWERS

### True/False

1. T    2. F    3. F    4. F    5. T

### Multiple Choice

1. d    2. b    3. c    4. b    5. e

6. c    7. a    8. c    9. b    10. e

# Preparing Worksheets, Closing Entries, and Reversing Entries

**LEARNING OBJECTIVES**

After studying this chapter, you should be able to do the following:

1 **Prepare a worksheet**

2 **Use a worksheet to prepare interim financial statements**

3 **Prepare closing entries**

4 **Prepare a post-closing trial balance**

5 **Explain why reversing entries are used**

6 **List the steps in the accounting process**

*7 **Record transactions initially in expense and revenue accounts and make the appropriate adjusting entry**

*8 **Determine which adjusting entries require reversing entries**

9 **Define the key terms listed at the end of the chapter**

**CHAPTER OUTLINE**

**THE WORKSHEET** • Unadjusted Trial Balance Columns • Adjustments Columns • Adjusted Trial Balance Columns • Income Statement and Balance Sheet Columns • Preparing the Financial Statements • Interim Financial Statements • **THE CLOSING PROCESS** • Closing the Expense Accounts • Closing the Revenue Accounts • Closing the Income Summary Account • Closing the Withdrawals Account • Journalizing the Adjusting and Closing Entries • The Post-Closing Trial Balance • **REVERSING ENTRIES** • **THE ACCOUNTING PROCESS REVIEWED** • **APPENDIX: THE EFFECT OF ACCOUNTING POLICY ON ADJUSTING ENTRIES** • Recording a Deferral as an Asset or as an Expense • Recording a Deferral as a Liability or as Revenue • Reversal of Adjusting Entries: Deferrals • Reversal of Adjusting Entries: Accruals

* Learning Objectives marked with an asterisk relate to material contained in the appendix to this chapter.

For small businesses, we could prepare financial statements directly from the adjusted trial balance at the end of each accounting period—monthly, quarterly, and annually. Because small businesses have relatively few accounts, no additional end-of-period accounting procedures would be required.

But the more transactions a company makes, the greater is the risk of error, because a mistake can occur at any point where data is recorded—in recording the journal entries, posting from the journals to the ledger, or adjusting the accounts. Not only does a large number of transactions increase the risk of error, but so does the frequency with which the accounts are used. Larger companies must prepare financial statements more frequently, usually on a monthly basis, than smaller companies. And a company that prepares financial statements more frequently suffers a greater risk of error in its reporting.

To help deal with the possibility of error, accountants use a tool called a *worksheet*. The worksheet helps in four ways:

1. It organizes the process of preparing the financial statements.
2. It reduces the possibility of introducing errors in that process.
3. It aids in discovering errors that do occur.
4. It provides monthly statements without the formal adjusting and closing process.

## THE WORKSHEET

A **worksheet** is a multicolumn form used by accountants as a temporary record to organize a business entity's end-of-period accounting procedures. The worksheet is extremely important and helpful, but it is not part of the permanent accounting records of an entity.

Records such as the general journal, the general ledger, and the financial statements are permanent, so they are maintained in a durable state—written in ink in a manual system or stored on magnetic tape in a computerized system. Worksheets, in contrast, are prepared in pencil so that any errors detected can be easily erased and corrected prior to preparing the permanent period-end financial statements.

After the worksheet has been prepared, it is examined for errors and corrected. It is then an easy matter to prepare the formal—and permanent—financial statements from the corrected, error-free worksheet. Also, the worksheet's organization simplifies the adjusting and closing processes (which we shall study in the second half of this chapter).

The worksheet has five column headings, each embracing a pair of debit-credit columns, as follows:

Learning Objective 1

Prepare a worksheet

Worksheet Column Headings

| Unadjusted Trial Balance | | Adjustments | | Adjusted Trial Balance | | Income Statement | | Balance Sheet | |
|---|---|---|---|---|---|---|---|---|---|
| Debit | Credit | Debit | Credit | Debit | Credit | Debit | Credit | Debit | Credit |
| | | | | | | | | | |
| | | | | | | | | | |
| | | | | | | | | | |

Those of you who are familiar with electronic spreadsheets such as Lotus 1-2-3 will immediately notice the similarity between the worksheet and the spreadsheet. As you study the worksheet, you will see that it could easily be prepared on an electronic spreadsheet. The computer program completes the worksheet and prepares the financial statements once the initial data have been entered in the "blanks" on the spreadsheet format.

### Unadjusted Trial Balance Columns

After all external transactions during the accounting period have been recorded in the general journal and posted to the general ledger, the **unadjusted trial balance** is prepared and entered in the first pair of columns on the worksheet.

To demonstrate how to use the worksheet, we'll begin with the Nov. 30, 1998, unadjusted trial balance of The Mary Abrems Dance Studio, shown in Exhibit 1.

Mary Abrems opened her dance studio on Nov. 1, 1998. At the end of November 1998, in addition to what we see in the unadjusted trial balance, we also know the following facts:

a. The Prepaid Rent account represents 3 months rent paid in advance on Nov. 3, 1998.

b. The value of office supplies on hand as of Nov. 30, 1998, is $140.

c. Cash in the amount of $1,800 has been received on Nov. 4 for 9 months of dance lessons.

d. The office equipment has a 5-year life, and depreciation is $180 per month.

e. Salaries in the amount of $500 are owed to Abrems' employees.

f. Interest in the amount of $30 has accrued on the note payable.

**Exhibit 1** Unadjusted Trial Balance on a Worksheet

**THE MARY ABREMS DANCE STUDIO**
Worksheet
Month Ended November 30, 1998

| | Unadjusted Trial Balance | | Adjustments | | Adjusted Trial Balance | | Income Statement | | Balance Sheet | |
|---|---|---|---|---|---|---|---|---|---|---|
| | **Debit** | **Credit** | **Debit** | **Credit** | **Debit** | **Credit** | **Debit** | **Credit** | **Debit** | **Credit** |
| Cash | 5,250 | | | | | | | | | |
| Accounts Receivable | 2,950 | | | | | | | | | |
| Office Supplies on Hand | 450 | | | | | | | | | |
| Prepaid Rent | 900 | | | | | | | | | |
| Office Equipment | 10,800 | | | | | | | | | |
| Notes Payable | | 3,000 | | | | | | | | |
| Accounts Payable | | 650 | | | | | | | | |
| Unearned Dance Lesson Revenues | | 1,800 | | | | | | | | |
| Abrems, Capital | | 11,000 | | | | | | | | |
| Abrems, Withdrawals | 500 | | | | | | | | | |
| Dance Lesson Revenues | | 8,400 | | | | | | | | |
| Salary Expense | 2,500 | | | | | | | | | |
| Utilities Expense | 1,100 | | | | | | | | | |
| Advertising Expense | 400 | | | | | | | | | |
| Totals | 24,850 | 24,850 | | | | | | | | |

## Adjustments Columns

As you may have realized already, adjustments are not entered directly into the general journal. They are first entered on the worksheet in the second pair of columns, labeled Adjustments. Let's see how adjustments are handled on the worksheet by making adjustments for the six items listed above.

**Adjustment A: Prepaid Rent/Rent Expense**  The $900 in the Prepaid Rent account on the unadjusted trial balance represents rent for the next 3 months—that is, $300 a month for 3 months. Since 1 month has expired, we must recognize 1 month's rent expense and reduce the Prepaid Rent account by $300.

The first step in making this adjustment is to enter $300 in the credit column under Adjustments on the worksheet opposite the Prepaid Rent account.

The debit portion of the adjustment is to recognize $300 of rent expense. But no Rent Expense account appears on the unadjusted trial balance, so we need to *add* Rent Expense to the worksheet and the $300 debit under Adjustments, as shown in Exhibit 2 below.

One purpose of the worksheet is to help us analyze, review, and convert all the adjustments for the period. We need a way of quickly and easily identifying the corresponding pairs of debits and credits that constitute each adjustment. Thus, we *key* with a reference letter the debit and credit entries that make up an adjustment, as in Exhibit 2 for the rent adjustment. To identify the adjustments originating with unadjusted Prepaid Rent, we use the letter *(a)* to designate both the $300 credit adjustment to Prepaid Rent and the corresponding $300 debit adjustment to Rent Expense.

**Exhibit 2**  Rent Adjustment on a Worksheet

**THE MARY ABREMS DANCE STUDIO**
**Worksheet**
**Month Ended November 30, 1998**

| | Unadjusted Trial Balance | | Adjustments | | Adjusted Trial Balance | | Income Statement | | Balance Sheet | |
|---|---|---|---|---|---|---|---|---|---|---|
| | Debit | Credit | Debit | Credit | Debit | Credit | Debit | Credit | Debit | Credit |
| Cash | 5,250 | | | | | | | | | |
| Accounts Receivable | 2,950 | | | | | | | | | |
| Office Supplies on Hand | 450 | | | | | | | | | |
| Prepaid Rent | 900 | | | (a) 300 | | | | | | |
| Office Equipment | 10,800 | | | | | | | | | |
| Notes Payable | | 3,000 | | | | | | | | |
| Accounts Payable | | 650 | | | | | | | | |
| Unearned Dance Lesson Revenues | | 1,800 | | | | | | | | |
| Abrems, Capital | | 11,000 | | | | | | | | |
| Abrems, Withdrawals | 500 | | | | | | | | | |
| Dance Lesson Revenues | | 8,400 | | | | | | | | |
| Salary Expense | 2,500 | | | | | | | | | |
| Utilities Expense | 1,100 | | | | | | | | | |
| Advertising Expense | 400 | | | | | | | | | |
| Totals | 24,850 | 24,850 | | | | | | | | |
| Rent Expense | | | (a) 300 | | | | | | | |

*Prepaid Rent is reduced*

*While Rent Expense is recorded*

**Exhibit 3** Adjustments on a Worksheet

### THE MARY ABREMS DANCE STUDIO
### Worksheet
### Month Ended November 30, 1998

| | Unadjusted Trial Balance | | Adjustments | | Adjusted Trial Balance | | Income Statement | | Balance Sheet | |
|---|---|---|---|---|---|---|---|---|---|---|
| | Debit | Credit | Debit | Credit | Debit | Credit | Debit | Credit | Debit | Credit |
| Cash | 5,250 | | | | | | | | | |
| Accounts Receivable | 2,950 | | | | | | | | | |
| Office Supplies on Hand | 450 | | | (b) 310 | | | | | | |
| Prepaid Rent | 900 | | | (a) 300 | | | | | | |
| Office Equipment | 10,800 | | | | | | | | | |
| Notes Payable | | 3,000 | | | | | | | | |
| Accounts Payable | | 650 | | | | | | | | |
| Unearned Dance Lesson Revenues | | 1,800 | (c) 200 | | | | | | | |
| Abrems, Capital | | 11,000 | | | | | | | | |
| Abrems, Withdrawals | 500 | | | | | | | | | |
| Dance Lesson Revenues | | 8,400 | | (c) 200 | | | | | | |
| Salary Expense | 2,500 | | (e) 500 | | | | | | | |
| Utilities Expense | 1,100 | | | | | | | | | |
| Advertising Expense | 400 | | | | | | | | | |
| Totals | 24,850 | 24,850 | | | | | | | | |
| Rent Expense | | | (a) 300 | | | | | | | |
| Office Supplies Expense | | | (b) 310 | | | | | | | |
| Depreciation Expense | | | (d) 180 | | | | | | | |
| Accumulated Depreciation | | | | (d) 180 | | | | | | |
| Salaries Payable | | | | (e) 500 | | | | | | |
| Interest Expense | | | (f) 30 | | | | | | | |
| Interest Payable | | | | (f) 30 | | | | | | |
| Totals | | | 1,520 | 1,520 | | | | | | |

*Office Supplies on Hand is reduced while Office Supplies Expense is recorded*

*Unearned Dance Lesson Revenues is reduced while Dance Lesson Revenues is increased*

*Salary Expense is increased and Salaries Payable is recorded*

*Interest Expense and Interest Payable are recorded*

*Depreciation Expense and Accumulated Depreciation are recorded*

**Adjustment B: Office Supplies on Hand/Office Supplies Expense** A count of the office supplies on hand on the last day of the month reveals that their value is $140. Since the Office Supplies on Hand account had a $450 debit balance, we will need an adjustment for the difference, $310 ($450 − $140). Under the Adjustments heading of the worksheet, a $310 credit is entered for the Office Supplies on Hand account. This $310 credit adjustment will result in a $140 debit balance when the adjusted trial balance column is completed at the end of the period.

Since office supplies were used during the year but no Office Supplies Expense account was listed in the unadjusted trial balance, we must introduce that account. The $310 expense is then recognized on the worksheet by entering a $310 debit adjustment. The credit and debit are both keyed with the letter *(b)* to identify this adjustment. (See Exhibit 3.)

**Adjustment C: Unearned Dance Lesson Revenues/Dance Lesson Revenues Earned** Unearned dance lesson revenues in the amount of $1,800 were previously recorded during the month. Of that amount, $200 was earned by the end of the month. The adjustment for this is a $200 debit to reduce the Unearned Dance Lesson Revenues account and a $200 credit to increase the Dance Lesson Revenues account. Each of these entries is keyed with the letter *(c)*.

**Adjustment D: Depreciation Expense/Accumulated Depreciation** Depreciation for the month amounts to $180. Notice, however, that neither Depreciation Expense (an expense account) nor Accumulated Depreciation (a contra-asset account) appears on the unadjusted trial balance. Because both accounts are needed in order to account for—that is, *adjust*—the $180 depreciation, we simply introduce them on the worksheet. Under the Adjustments heading, opposite the newly introduced Depreciation Expense account, we enter a $180 debit; corresponding to that, we enter a $180 credit under the Adjustments heading opposite the newly introduced Accumulated Depreciation account. The letter *(d)* identifies the debit and the credit corresponding to the depreciation adjustment. (Note: Because this is the first year of operations, there are no activities for prior years. Specifically, no depreciation is reflected in an Accumulated Depreciation account. In subsequent periods, the account Accumulated Depreciation will, of course, have a balance.)

**Adjustment E: Salary Expense/Salaries Payable** Accrued salaries on Nov. 30, 1998, amount to $500. By now you should be able to make this adjustment quickly and easily: Increase the Salary Expense account with a $500 debit adjustment and introduce the Salaries Payable account with a $500 credit, which increases the liability. Key both adjustments with the letter *(e)*.

**Adjustment F: Interest Expense/Interest Payable** The last adjustment is for the accrued interest of $30 on the note payable. It is entered by introducing both the Interest Expense and Interest Payable accounts at the bottom of the worksheet. The Interest Expense account is debited for $30 and the Interest Payable account is credited for $30, both adjustments being keyed with the letter *(f)*.

After we have entered the last adjustment, we should check our work before proceeding to the next set of columns. We total the debit column and the credit column to make sure that the sum of the debits equals the sum of the credits. If not, then the adjustments columns have an error somewhere, which must be corrected.

### Adjusted Trial Balance Columns

The next step in using a worksheet is to prepare an adjusted trial balance. For each account, the unadjusted trial balance debits and the adjustments debits are *added* and the sum is recorded in the debit column under the *adjusted* trial balance heading. For example, Salary Expense has a $2,500 debit in the unadjusted trial balance. This debit is added to the $500 debit adjustment, so the result is the $3,000 debit in the adjusted trial balance shown in Exhibit 4. And Dance Lesson Revenues, which has a credit balance of $8,400, is adjusted by adding $200, resulting in the $8,600 credit balance.

When an account has a debit balance and a credit adjustment *or* a credit balance and a debit adjustment, *subtract* the smaller amount from the larger amount and record the *difference* in the debit or credit column (depending on which amount was larger) of the adjusted trial balance.

Note how the $310 credit adjustment is subtracted from the larger $450 debit balance of Office Supplies on Hand and the difference, $140, is entered in the debit column of the adjusted trial balance.

Likewise, the $200 debit adjustment to Unearned Dance Lesson Revenues is subtracted from the larger $1,800 credit balance on the unadjusted trial balance to arrive at the $1,600 credit balance on the adjusted trial balance.

Unadjusted balances *with no adjustments* are simply carried over to the adjusted trial balance columns. Accounts that are newly introduced at the bottom of the

**Exhibit 4**  The Adjusted Trial Balance on a Worksheet

THE MARY ABREMS DANCE STUDIO
Worksheet
Month Ended November 30, 1998

| | Unadjusted Trial Balance | | Adjustments | | Adjusted Trial Balance | | Income Statement | | Balance Sheet | |
|---|---|---|---|---|---|---|---|---|---|---|
| | Debit | Credit | Debit | Credit | Debit | Credit | Debit | Credit | Debit | Credit |
| Cash | 5,250 | | | | 5,250 | | | | | |
| Accounts Receivable | 2,950 | | | | 2,950 | | | | | |
| Office Supplies on Hand | 450 | | | (b) 310 | 140 | | | | | |
| Prepaid Rent | 900 | | | (a) 300 | 600 | | | | | |
| Office Equipment | 10,800 | | | | 10,800 | | | | | |
| Notes Payable | | 3,000 | | | | 3,000 | | | | |
| Accounts Payable | | 650 | | | | 650 | | | | |
| Unearned Dance Lesson Revenues | | 1,800 | (c) 200 | | | 1,600 | | | | |
| Abrems, Capital | | 11,000 | | | | 11,000 | | | | |
| Abrems, Withdrawals | 500 | | | | 500 | | | | | |
| Dance Lesson Revenues | | 8,400 | | (c) 200 | | 8,600 | | | | |
| Salary Expense | 2,500 | | (e) 500 | | 3,000 | | | | | |
| Utilities Expense | 1,100 | | | | 1,100 | | | | | |
| Advertising Expense | 400 | | | | 400 | | | | | |
| Totals | 24,850 | 24,850 | | | | | | | | |
| Rent Expense | | | (a) 300 | | 300 | | | | | |
| Office Supplies Expense | | | (b) 310 | | 310 | | | | | |
| Depreciation Expense | | | (d) 180 | | 180 | | | | | |
| Accumulated Depreciation | | | | (d) 180 | | 180 | | | | |
| Salaries Payable | | | | (e) 500 | | 500 | | | | |
| Interest Expense | | | (f) 30 | | 30 | | | | | |
| Interest Payable | | | | (f) 30 | | 30 | | | | |
| Totals | | | 1,520 | 1,520 | 25,560 | 25,560 | | | | |

Subtract *when the type of adjustment (debit or credit) is different from the unadjusted balance*

Add *when the type of adjustment (debit or credit) is the same as the unadjusted balance*

worksheet—the adjustment debits and credits—are also simply carried over into the adjusted trial balance columns.

When the adjusted trial balance columns are complete, we do the same thing we just did with the adjustments columns: We add up all the debits and add up all the credits. If the sum of the debits equals the sum of the credits, then we can be assured that we have not made any arithmetic errors in the amounts in the adjusted trial balance columns. If the sums don't balance, we must look for the error and correct it.

**Income Statement and Balance Sheet Columns**

Once the adjusted debits and credits are equal, the adjusted trial balance is ready for us to use in preparing the income statement and balance sheet columns of the worksheet. The procedure is simple. First, transfer from the adjusted trial balance columns the debit or credit balance for each income statement account to its proper place in the income statement columns. Then transfer the debit or credit balance for each balance sheet account to its proper place in the balance sheet columns. To do that, of course, you must know which are income statement accounts and which are

**Exhibit 5** The Income Statement and Balance Sheet Columns on a Worksheet

### THE MARY ABREMS DANCE STUDIO
### Worksheet
### Month Ended November 30, 1998

| | Unadjusted Trial Balance | | Adjustments | | Adjusted Trial Balance | | Income Statement | | Balance Sheet | |
|---|---|---|---|---|---|---|---|---|---|---|
| | Debit | Credit | Debit | Credit | Debit | Credit | Debit | Credit | Debit | Credit |
| Cash | 5,250 | | | | 5,250 | | | | 5,250 | |
| Accounts Receivable | 2,950 | | | | 2,950 | | | | 2,950 | |
| Office Supplies on Hand | 450 | | | (b) 310 | 140 | | | | 140 | |
| Prepaid Rent | 900 | | | (a) 300 | 600 | | | | 600 | |
| Office Equipment | 10,800 | | | | 10,800 | | | | 10,800 | |
| Notes Payable | | 3,000 | | | | 3,000 | | | | 3,000 |
| Accounts Payable | | 650 | | | | 650 | | | | 650 |
| Unearned Dance Lesson Revenues | | 1,800 | (c) 200 | | | 1,600 | | | | 1,600 |
| Abrems, Capital | | 11,000 | | | | 11,000 | | | | 11,000 |
| Abrems, Withdrawals | 500 | | | | 500 | | | | 500 | |
| Dance Lesson Revenues | | 8,400 | | (c) 200 | | 8,600 | | 8,600 | | |
| Salary Expense | 2,500 | | (e) 500 | | 3,000 | | 3,000 | | | |
| Utilities Expense | 1,100 | | | | 1,100 | | 1,100 | | | |
| Advertising Expense | 400 | | | | 400 | | 400 | | | |
| Totals | 24,850 | 24,850 | | | | | | | | |
| Rent Expense | | | (a) 300 | | 300 | | 300 | | | |
| Office Supplies Expense | | | (b) 310 | | 310 | | 310 | | | |
| Depreciation Expense | | | (d) 180 | | 180 | | 180 | | | |
| Accumulated Depreciation | | | | (d) 180 | | 180 | | | | 180 |
| Salaries Payable | | | | (e) 500 | | 500 | | | | 500 |
| Interest Expense | | | (f) 30 | | 30 | | 30 | | | |
| Interest Payable | | | | (f) 30 | | 30 | | | | 30 |
| Totals | | | 1,520 | 1,520 | 25,560 | 25,560 | 5,320 | 8,600 | 20,240 | 16,960 |
| Net Income | | | | | | | 3,280 | | | 3,280 |
| | | | | | | | 8,600 | 8,600 | 20,240 | 20,240 |

balance sheet accounts. (Refer to Exhibit 5 as you proceed through the following discussion.)

Remember that assets, liabilities, and capital (owner's equity) are balance sheet accounts, as is the contra-asset account Accumulated Depreciation. The withdrawals account is listed on the balance sheet debit column because it is a part of the Capital account but is not a revenue or expense account. Revenues and expenses are income statement accounts.

Our first example, Cash, is an asset and a balance sheet account. Therefore, we carry forward the $5,250 debit from the adjusted trial balance to the balance sheet debit column. Accounts Receivable is also an asset and a balance sheet account, so we carry forward the $2,950 debit balance to the balance sheet debit column. Dance Lesson Revenues is a revenue account and Salary Expense is an expense account, so both are income statement accounts. Thus, the $8,600 adjusted Dance Lesson Revenues credit is carried forward as an income statement credit, and the $3,000 Salary Expense debit is carried forward as a debit on the income statement.

As always, attention to detail is very important. Carrying an account balance forward to the wrong column is a common error, as you will soon discover. Carrying the Salaries Payable balance to the income statement credit column is perhaps the most common error. This happens because Salaries Payable does not appear near the other balance sheet accounts. When added to the bottom of the worksheet by the salaries adjusting entry *(e)*, Salaries Payable is grouped with several income statement accounts. This creates a tendency to *incorrectly* carry its balance to the income statement credit column along with most of the other accounts in this worksheet section. Remember, Salaries Payable is a *liability* (the word *Payable* is a good reminder of this) and therefore a *balance sheet account.*

After all items from the adjusted trial balance have been carried forward to their proper places, each income statement column is totaled and each balance sheet column is totaled. The total of the income statement credit column is $8,600. The total of the income statement debits is $5,320. The income statement credits exceed the income statement debits by $3,280, which represents the *net income* for the month. If the debit column had exceeded the credit column, a *net loss* would have been the result.

The balance sheet debits add up to $20,240, and the balance sheet credits add up to $16,960. Balance sheet debits exceed balance sheet credits by $3,280, which represents the net income. The balance sheet cannot balance until net income is added to the Capital account. Remember, the Capital account amount ($11,000) shown in the worksheet reflects the *beginning* rather than the *ending* balance. Net income must be added (and withdrawals subtracted) to arrive at the ending Capital balance; this is done when the statement of owner's equity is prepared. Withdrawals are already included in the balance sheet columns. Add the net income to the balance sheet section to reflect the *increase* in owner's equity. *Remember:* Owner's equity is increased by a *credit,* so *net income* is added to the credit column of the balance sheet section. (A loss would be *debited.*) Once net income is added, the debit and credit columns of the balance sheet should be equal.

If the net income (or loss) determined from the totals of the income statement column debits and credits turns out to be different from the net income (or loss) shown by the totals of the balance sheet column debits and credits, then you can be sure the worksheet contains one or more errors.

But if the net income (or loss) determined from the income statement columns turns out to be the same as the net income (or loss) shown on the balance sheet columns, can you be sure that there are no errors in the worksheet? The answer is *no.* For example, if Interest Payable had been entered incorrectly as an income statement credit item rather than a balance sheet credit item, the affected parts of the worksheet would appear as shown below.

Effect of Error in Classifying Interest Payable Account

| | Unadjusted Trial Balance | | Adjustments | | Adjusted Trial Balance | | Income Statement | | Balance Sheet | |
|---|---|---|---|---|---|---|---|---|---|---|
| | Debit | Credit | Debit | Credit | Debit | Credit | Debit | Credit | Debit | Credit |
| Cash | 5,250 | | | | 5,250 | | | | 5,250 | |
| Interest Payable | | | | *(f)* 30 | | 30 | | 30 | | |
| Totals | | | 1,520 | 1,520 | 25,560 | 25,560 | 5,320 3,310 | 8,630 | 20,240 | 16,930 3,310 |
| | | | | | | | 8,630 | 8,630 | 20,240 | 20,240 |

Although Interest Payable was entered in the wrong place, net income is $3,310 as determined by both the income statement columns and the balance columns arithmetic. But the $3,310 is not the correct income, because the total credits on both the income statement column and the balance sheet column are wrong. We would most likely discover the error when we prepared the income statement, because we would recognize that interest payable should not be classified as a revenue item.

**Exhibit 6** Income Statement

### THE MARY ABREMS DANCE STUDIO
### Income Statement
### Month Ended November 30, 1998

| | | |
|---|---:|---:|
| Revenues: | | |
| Dance Lesson Revenues............................................. | | $8,600 |
| Operating Expenses: | | |
| Salary Expense.......................................... | $3,000 | |
| Rent Expense ............................................ | 300 | |
| Office Supplies Expense................................. | 310 | |
| Depreciation Expense: Office Equipment.................... | 180 | |
| Interest Expense ......................................... | 30 | |
| Utilities Expense ......................................... | 1,100 | |
| Advertising Expense ...................................... | 400 | |
| Total Operating Expenses................................ | | 5,320 |
| Net Income ............................................... | | $3,280 |

## Preparing the Financial Statements

Keep in mind that the sole purpose of preparing the worksheet is to help you prepare the financial statements. Once a worksheet has been completed and checked, it is easy to prepare the financial statements. The income statement is prepared from the information contained on the worksheet in the income statement columns. For The Mary Abrems Dance Studio, it looks like Exhibit 6.

The statement of owner's equity is prepared next (Exhibit 7). The beginning balance was zero, since the dance studio just commenced operations. The $11,000 in the Capital account in the credit column of the worksheet's balance sheet section represents the initial investment. The net income is obtained from the bottom of the worksheet and the withdrawals from the debit column of the balance sheet section.

The balance sheet (Exhibit 8) is prepared in a similar manner to the income statement. Remember, however, that the worksheet's Capital account contains the initial investment, $11,000, not the ending capital of $13,780 as seen on the statement of owner's equity.

## Interim Financial Statements

A principal advantage of the worksheet is that we can prepare financial statements from it directly, without having to formally adjust the general ledger accounts. We will often wish to do this for interim periods. By the term *interim periods* we mean the

Learning
Objective  **2**

Use a worksheet to prepare interim financial statements

**Exhibit 7** Statement of Owner's Equity

### THE MARY ABREMS DANCE STUDIO
### Statement of Owner's Equity
### Month Ended November 30, 1998

| | | |
|---|---:|---:|
| Abrems, Capital, Nov. 1, 1998 ..................................... | | $ –0– |
| Add: Investment ............................................ | | 11,000 |
| Net Income................................................ | | 3,280 |
| Total ..................................................... | | $14,280 |
| Less: Withdrawals ............................................ | | 500 |
| Abrems, Capital, Nov. 30, 1998 .................................... | | $13,780 |

**Exhibit 8** Balance Sheet

## THE MARY ABREMS DANCE STUDIO
### Balance Sheet
### November 30, 1998

### Assets

| | | |
|---|---|---|
| Cash | | $ 5,250 |
| Accounts Receivable | | 2,950 |
| Office Supplies on Hand | | 140 |
| Prepaid Rent | | 600 |
| Office Equipment | $10,800 | |
| Less: Accum. Depr.: Office Equipment | 180 | 10,620 |
| Total Assets | | $19,560 |

### Liabilities

| | |
|---|---|
| Notes Payable | $ 3,000 |
| Interest Payable | 30 |
| Accounts Payable | 650 |
| Salaries Payable | 500 |
| Unearned Dance Lesson Revenues | 1,600 |
| Total Liabilities | $ 5,780 |

### Owner's Equity

| | |
|---|---|
| Abrems, Capital | 13,780 |
| Total Liabilities and Owner's Equity | $19,560 |

monthly and quarterly accounting periods contained within the company's **fiscal year,** which is the annual accounting period adopted by an economic entity. Note that The Mary Abrems Dance Studio's fiscal year starts on Nov. 1; it will end the following Oct. 31. Many companies adopt a fiscal year that matches their annual cycle of activities rather than the calendar year. A survey by the AICPA of 600 companies various months of closing revealed the following:

| Month of Fiscal Year-End | Percent of Companies |
|---|---|
| January | 4 |
| February | 3 |
| March | 2 |
| April | 1 |
| May | 3 |
| June | 7 |
| July | 2 |
| August | 3 |
| September | 3 |
| October | 4 |
| November | 3 |
| December | 63 |

Some companies have fiscal year-ends on days other than the last day of the month. For example, Capital Cities–ABC's year ends on the Sunday closest to Dec. 31, and West Point–Pepperell's year ends on the last Sunday in September.

Financial statements often are prepared informally from the worksheet on a monthly or quarterly basis. Such statements are called **interim statements.**

For the first month of the fiscal year, the monthly interim financial statements are prepared directly from the worksheet, just as described in the previous sections. But the adjusting and closing entries are generally *not journalized*. At the end of the second month, another worksheet is prepared. The adjustments on this second worksheet must be recorded *cumulatively* for the 2 months. Thus, since The Mary Abrems Dance Studio started operations on Nov. 1, 1998, the adjustments on the worksheet as of Nov. 30, 1998, represent *only 1 month's activity*. For the second worksheet, which would be dated Dec. 31, 1998, *2 months'* activity would be reflected by the worksheet adjustments. For example, the Prepaid Rent adjustment for Dec. 31, 1998, would appear as follows:

### THE MARY ABREMS DANCE STUDIO
### Worksheet
### Two-Month Period Ended December 31, 1998

| | Unadjusted Trial Balance | | Adjustments | | Adjusted Trial Balance | | Income Statement | | Balance Sheet | |
|---|---|---|---|---|---|---|---|---|---|---|
| | Debit | Credit | Debit | Credit | Debit | Credit | Debit | Credit | Debit | Credit |
| Prepaid Rent | 900 | | | (a) 600 | 300 | | | | 300 | |
| Rent Expense | | | (a) 600 | | 600 | | 600 | | | |

Rent Expense is recorded as a $600 ($900 $\times \frac{2}{3}$) debit representing *2 months'* expense.

When the income statement is prepared at the end of December, it will represent financial activity for the 2-month period. In order to prepare an income statement solely for the month of December, we must subtract the income statement items for the month of November from the income statement items for the 2-month period ended Dec. 31, 1998, as illustrated in Exhibit 9.

Unlike the income statement, the balance sheet can be prepared directly from the Dec. 31, 1998, worksheet, since balance sheet accounts, by their nature, are cumulative anyway.

**Exhibit 9** Preparing an Interim Income Statement

| | From the Dec. 31 Worksheet Representing 2 Months | From the Nov. 30 Worksheet Representing 1 Month | Income Statement For the Month of December |
|---|---|---|---|
| Revenue: | | | |
| Dance Lesson Revenues . . . . . . . . . . . . . . . . . . | $17,700 | $8,600 | $9,100 |
| Expenses: | | | |
| Salary Expense . . . . . . . . . . . . . . . . . | $6,200 | $3,000 | $3,200 |
| Rent Expense. . . . . . . . . . . . . . . . . . . | 600 | 300 | 300 |
| Office Supplies Expense . . . . . . . . . . | 530 | 310 | 220 |
| Depreciation Expense . . . . . . . . . . . . . | 360 | 180 | 180 |
| Interest Expense. . . . . . . . . . . . . . . . . | 60 | 30 | 30 |
| Utilities Expense. . . . . . . . . . . . . . . . . | 2,450 | 1,100 | 1,350 |
| Advertising Expense. . . . . . . . . . . . . . | 750 | 400 | 350 |
| Total Expense. . . . . . . . . . . . . . . . . . . . . . . . | 10,950 | 5,320 | 5,630 |
| Net Income . . . . . . . . . . . . . . . . . . . . . . . . . . | $ 6,750 | $3,280 | $3,470 |

**ASK YOURSELF** ▶

1. **Why do accountants use worksheets?**
2. **What are the various sets of column headings on a worksheet?**
3. **How are adjusting entries entered on a worksheet?**
4. **What happens if an adjusting entry requires a certain account, but that account does not appear on the worksheet?**
5. **Explain how a worksheet can balance and still be incorrect.**
6. **What is meant by the term** *interim periods?*
7. **Explain how worksheets are used to prepare an interim income statement.**
8. **Explain how worksheets are used to prepare a balance sheet at the end of an interim period.**

## THE CLOSING PROCESS

Learning
Objective **3**

Prepare closing entries

The closing process represents another periodic procedure that most business entities find necessary. As the number of accounts increases, it becomes more difficult to prepare the financial statements and commence a new accounting period. Closing entries make this process easier. Consider for a moment the problem of a company that recorded salaries expense in the general ledger totaling $87,000 for the entire year 1997. During the month of January 1998, salaries of $8,000 are incurred. In preparing financial statements for January 1998, we can see that salaries *should be* reported at $8,000. But without some way of identifying the end of the 1997 accounting period and the start of the 1998 period, the journalization of the 1998 salaries would result in an $8,000 posting to the Salary Expense account in the general ledger:

| Salary Expense | | |
|---|---|---|
| Jan. to Dec. 1997 | 87,000 | |
| Jan. 1998 | 8,000 | |

The result is that in the general ledger, salaries would be reflected at $95,000, representing the total from 1997 plus the first month of 1998.

We must find a way to identify clearly the 1997 salaries and distinguish them from the 1998 salaries. What we need to show is that:

| Salary Expense | | |
|---|---|---|
| Jan. to Dec. 1997 | 87,000 | |

| Salary Expense | | |
|---|---|---|
| Jan. 1998 | 8,000 | |

The *closing process* enables us to do this.

To prepare you for the discussion of the closing process, we will briefly review and expand on two accounts: the balance sheet and income statement accounts.

**Balance sheet accounts** represent the *balance* of an asset, liability, or owner's equity (capital) account *at a particular point in time.* For example, business transactions cause increases and decreases in the Cash account regularly throughout the accounting period. But the balance in a Cash account represents the amount of cash on hand at the time the balance is calculated. Balance sheet accounts are sometimes called *permanent accounts* or *real accounts* because, once established, they generally remain on the books for many years.

**Income statement accounts,** which comprise *revenue accounts* and *expense accounts,* represent *accumulations* of revenue and expenses *during a particular period of time.* For example, a Salary Expense account represents the total salary expense incurred between the start of the accounting period and the date of the income statement. When we discuss salary expense, we must specify not only the amount of the expense but also the time period during which those salaries were incurred. Are the salaries for the month? The quarter? Last year? The current year? Because revenue accounts and expense accounts reflect activity only for the period of time they cover, both of these income statement accounts are sometimes referred to as *temporary accounts,* or *nominal accounts. Temporary* describes the nature of these accounts: They exist for only one accounting period. For example, Salary Expense exists only for the year 1997. Next year a new Salary Expense account will gather the salary information for 1998. Conceptually, income statement accounts will show increases over time; they cannot show decreases.

If we were to rely solely on what we have learned thus far to prepare financial statements, our work would be more difficult than it has to be. We would have two problems:

1. At the end of a period the capital account will not reflect the period-end balance. That's because we record only investments in the capital account during the period. Revenues, expenses and withdrawals are all recorded in their separate accounts. What we must do is get the capital account to show an end-of-period balance, just like all other balance sheet accounts.

2. The balances in the revenue, expense, and withdrawals accounts would not be for the latest accounting period (for example, the year 1997), but rather would be cumulative balances, starting from the date the company began operations. That is, revenue, expense, and withdrawals account balances, as we now know them, are not period-end balances, but cumulative balances. We have to find some way of getting the accounts to show totals for only a single period.

The closing process solves both these problems. It uses **closing entries** to transfer the revenue, expense, and withdrawals accounts—that is, all the income statement and withdrawals accounts—to the capital account and makes it simpler to end one accounting period and start another.

Each revenue, expense, and withdrawals account is "closed out" at the end of an accounting period. By *closed out* we simply mean that at period-end the account is reduced to a zero balance. If we do that for each of the revenue and expense accounts, and the withdrawals account, then the amount we close out will be a total for the period, not a cumulative total. A zero balance at the end of one accounting period means, of course, that the account starts with a zero balance at the beginning of the next period.

What do we do with the closed-out balances from each of the revenue and expense accounts? The answer is: We transfer them to the capital account. In doing that, we accomplish our other objective: transferring the period-end balances from each of the revenue and expense accounts to the capital account gives us a capital account that reflects period-end balances.

That's the basic idea behind the **closing process.** It consists of four steps:

1. Close the expense accounts to a temporary account called the Income Summary account.

**2.** Close the revenue accounts to the temporary Income Summary account.

**3.** Close the Income Summary account to the Capital account.

**4.** Close the Withdrawals account.

We'll now show you how this four-step sequence works, using The Mary Abrems Dance Studio worksheet (Exhibit 5).

### Closing the Expense Accounts

The worksheet for The Mary Abrems Dance Studio contains seven expense accounts: Salary Expense, Utilities Expense, Advertising Expense, Rent Expense, Office Supplies Expense, Depreciation Expense, and Interest Expense. An expense account accumulates a debit balance. It is closed by "crediting" it for an amount equal to the debit balance. This results in a zero balance or, to be more consistent and precise, a zero debit balance. Remember: *A zero balance is our objective in closing an expense account at the end of a period.*

But what do we do with the debit balance that was in the expense account before we credited it? For the closing process, we must establish a temporary **Income Summary,** or *Profit and Loss Summary,* account. It is so called because it contains a record of the expenses, or debit balances, for the period and, as we shall see, the revenue or credit balances for the period. The sum of the debit balances for the expense accounts is recorded as a debit to this newly established Income Summary account.

The closing entry recorded in the general journal for The Mary Abrems Dance Studio to close the expense accounts would appear as follows:

| | | | | | |
|---|---|---|---|---|---|
| | **THE MARY ABREMS DANCE STUDIO** | | PAGE <u>13</u> | | |
| | **General Journal** | | | | |

| Date | Account Titles and Explanation | Post. Ref. | Debit | Credit |
|---|---|---|---|---|
| 1998<br>Nov. 30 | Income Summary **(OE : IS)***<br>   Salary Expense **(OE : E)**<br>   Utilities Expense **(OE : E)**<br>   Advertising Expense **(OE : E)**<br>   Rent Expense **(OE : E)**<br>   Office Supplies Expense **(OE : E)**<br>   Depreciation Expense **(OE : E)**<br>   Interest Expense **(OE : E)**<br>To close the expense accounts. | | 5,320 | 3,000<br>1,100<br>400<br>300<br>310<br>180<br>30 |

Notice that these accounts can be copied directly from the income statement debit column on the worksheet and that the total is also available for the debit to the Income Summary account. It is the total of the income statement debit column on the worksheet.

After the closing entry is posted as credits to the individual expense accounts in the general ledger, each expense account will have a zero balance. The sum of the debit balances of the expense accounts is transferred to the Income Summary account as a debit. The Effect of the closing process on the expense accounts is illustrated in the following T-accounts:

---

\* The letters in parentheses in journal entries refer to the following accounts: **A** = Assets; **L** = Liabilities; **OE** = Owner's Equity; **R** = Revenue; **E** = Expense; **IS** = Income Summary; **W** = Withdrawals.

T-Accounts Illustrating Closing of Expense Accounts

| Salary Expense | | | |
|---|---|---|---|
| Bal. | 3,000 | Nov. 30 | 3,000 |
| Bal. | –0– | | |

| Utilities Expense | | | |
|---|---|---|---|
| Bal. | 1,100 | Nov. 30 | 1,100 |
| Bal. | –0– | | |

| Advertising Expense | | | |
|---|---|---|---|
| Bal. | 400 | Nov. 30 | 400 |
| Bal. | –0– | | |

| Rent Expense | | | |
|---|---|---|---|
| Bal. | 300 | Nov. 30 | 300 |
| Bal. | –0– | | |

| Office Supplies Expense | | | |
|---|---|---|---|
| Bal. | 310 | Nov. 30 | 310 |
| Bal. | –0– | | |

| Depreciation Expense | | | |
|---|---|---|---|
| Bal. | 180 | Nov. 30 | 180 |
| Bal. | –0– | | |

| Interest Expense | | | |
|---|---|---|---|
| Bal. | 30 | Nov. 30 | 30 |

| Income Summary | | | |
|---|---|---|---|
| Nov. 30 | 5,320 | | |

## Closing the Revenue Accounts

The Mary Abrems Dance Studio has one revenue account (Dance Lesson Revenues), which, of course, has a credit balance. A revenue account is closed by debiting it by an amount equal to its credit balance. The result is a zero balance or, more correctly, a zero credit balance. A corresponding credit to Income Summary completes the closing.

The credit balance to be closed is recorded in the general journal as follows:

### THE MARY ABREMS DANCE STUDIO
### General Journal

PAGE 13

| Date | Account Titles and Explanation | Post. Ref. | Debit | Credit |
|---|---|---|---|---|
| 1998 Nov. 30 | Dance Lesson Revenues (OE : R) | | 8,600 | |
| | Income Summary (OE : IS) | | | 8,600 |
| | To close the revenue accounts. | | | |

The credit balance of $8,600 from the Dance Lesson Revenues account is transferred as a credit entry to the Income Summary account:

T-Accounts Illustrating Closing of Revenue Accounts

| Dance Lesson Revenue | | | |
|---|---|---|---|
| Nov. 30 | 8,600 | Bal. | 8,600 |
| Bal. | –0– | | |

| Income Summary | | | |
|---|---|---|---|
| Nov. 30 | 5,320 | Nov. 30 | 8,600 |

After all the debit and credit balances have been transferred to Income Summary, each expense and revenue account is left with a zero balance, ready to accumulate the next accounting period's debits and credits.

## Closing the Income Summary Account

Income Summary is now just that—a summary. The *summary balance* is the difference between the sum of the transferred debits—the expenses—and the sum of the transferred credits—the revenue—which is the net income for the period. In this case, the credit balance is $3,280, or the net income for the period as seen on the worksheet. If the debits had exceeded the credits, a net loss would have resulted (expenses would have been larger than revenue).

The balance in the Income Summary account—the $3,280 net income—is now transferred to the Capital account by a closing entry. This will increase the Capital account by the amount of the net income and reduce Income Summary to a zero balance. After this is done, our objectives have been accomplished:

**1.** The Capital account reflects the effects of its component revenue and expense accounts.
**2.** All revenue and expense accounts from this accounting period have zero balances.

The general journal entry closing the Income Summary account and the effect of posting this entry to the general ledger Capital account for The Mary Abrems Dance Studio are shown below:

### THE MARY ABREMS DANCE STUDIO
#### General Journal

PAGE _13_

| Date | Account Titles and Explanation | Post. Ref. | Debit | Credit |
|------|-------------------------------|-----------|-------|--------|
| 1998 Nov. 30 | Income Summary **(OE : IS)** | | 3,280 | |
| | Abrems, Capital **(OE)** | | | 3,280 |
| | To close the Income Summary account. | | | |

| Income Summary | | | | Abrems, Capital | | | |
|------|------|------|------|------|------|------|------|
| Nov. 30 | 5,320 | Nov. 30 | 8,600 | | | Bal. | 11,000 |
| Nov. 30 | 3,280 | Bal. | 3,280 | | | Nov. 30 | 3,280 |

## Closing the Withdrawals Account

One more step is needed to complete the closing process: We need to close out the Withdrawals account. Recall that the Withdrawals account is used whenever the owner of a business entity removes funds from the business for personal use. Accordingly, withdrawals are not expenses, so we are not closing the Withdrawals account by closing the expense accounts to the Income Summary account. Instead, withdrawals are reductions in the capital of the business, just as are expenses. Also, withdrawals accumulate over time just as expenses do.

Thus for the same two reasons we closed the expense and revenue accounts—to reflect the ending Capital balance and to obtain a zero balance in the temporary accounts—we also close the Withdrawals account. This is accomplished by the following general journal entry:

THE MARY ABREMS DANCE STUDIO    PAGE __13__
General Journal

| Date | Account Titles and Explanation | Post. Ref. | Debit | Credit |
|------|-------------------------------|-----------|-------|--------|
| 1998 Nov. 30 | Abrems, Capital (OE)<br>   Abrems, Withdrawals (OE:W)<br>To close the withdrawals account. | | 500 | 500 |

| Abrems, Withdrawals | | | | Abrems, Capital | | |
|------|------|------|------|------|------|------|
| Bal. | 500 | Nov. 30 | 500 | | Bal. | 11,000 |
| Bal. | −0− | | | Nov. 30   500 | Nov. 30 | 3,280 |
| | | | | | Bal. | 13,780 |

With the closing of the Withdrawals account, the closing process is completed: All expense and revenue accounts and the Withdrawals account have a zero balance, and the Capital account reflects the period-end balance.

Exhibit 10 provides a visual summary of the closing process for your review.

## Journalizing the Adjusting and Closing Entries

Adjusting and closing entries may be recorded in the general journal and posted to the general ledger at the end of each month, each quarter, or each year, depending on the company's policy. The formal adjustment and closing of the accounts is most often

**Exhibit 10** A Review of the Closing Process

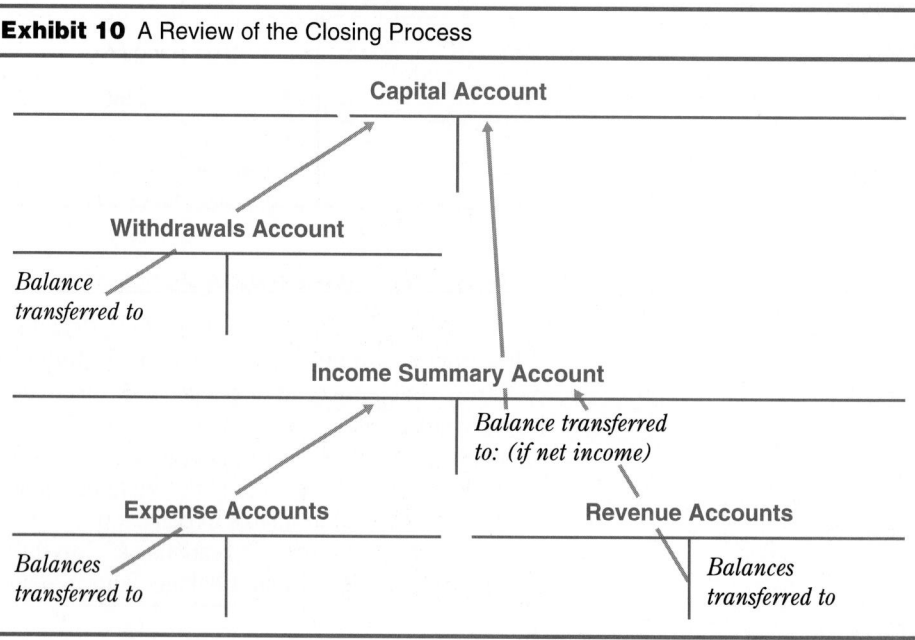

done annually. If a company's policy is to formally adjust and close at the end of each fiscal year, then after an interim worksheet is completed and interim financial statements are prepared at the end of each period, no further periodic procedures are needed. The adjusting and closing entries are not journalized and consequently not posted.

The Mary Abrems Dance Studio's policy is to formally adjust and close the accounts each month. Therefore, at month-end, after the worksheet is completed and the financial statements are prepared, the adjustment columns of the worksheet are used as a guide for the adjusting entries, and the income statement columns of the worksheet are used as a guide for the closing entries. Exhibit 11 shows the adjusting and closing entries for The Mary Abrems Dance Studio. Notice again that the income statement debit column total of $5,320 on the worksheet in Exhibit 5 is the debit for the expense closing entry to Income Summary in Exhibit 11. The income statement credit column total of $8,600 in Exhibit 5 is the credit for the Dance Lesson Revenues entry to Income Summary in Exhibit 11. The $3,280 net income figure on the worksheet (Exhibit 5) is the amount that will close out the Income Summary account. And the Withdrawals account is closed by the $500 amount in the balance sheet debit column of Exhibit 5.

**Exhibit 11** Adjusting and Closing Entries

### THE MARY ABREMS DANCE STUDIO
#### General Journal

PAGE __12__

| Date | Account Titles and Explanation | Post. Ref. | Debit | Credit |
|---|---|---|---|---|
| | **Adjusting Entries** | | | |
| 1998 Nov. 30 | Rent Expense **(OE:E)** | | 300 | |
| |     Prepaid Rent **(A)** | | | 300 |
| | To record rent expense for the month. | | | |
| 30 | Office Supplies Expense **(OE:E)** | | 310 | |
| |     Office Supplies on Hand **(A)** | | | 310 |
| | To record office supplies used during the month. | | | |
| 30 | Unearned Dance Lesson Revenues **(OE:L)** | | 200 | |
| |     Dance Lesson Revenue **(OE:R)** | | | 200 |
| | To record dance lesson revenue earned for the month. | | | |
| 30 | Depreciation Expense **(OE:E)** | | 180 | |
| |     Accumulated Depreciation **(OE:A)** | | | 180 |
| | To record depreciation expense. | | | |
| 30 | Salary Expense **(OE:E)** | | 500 | |
| |     Salaries Payable **(OE:L)** | | | 500 |
| | To record accrued salaries. | | | |
| 30 | Interest Expense **(OE:E)** | | 30 | |
| |     Interest Payable **(OE:L)** | | | 30 |
| | To record accrued interest. | | | |

*(Continued)*

## THE MARY ABREMS DANCE STUDIO
### General Journal

| Date | Account Titles and Explanation | Post. Ref. | Debit | Credit |
|---|---|---|---|---|
| | **Closing Entries** | | | |
| 1998 Nov. 30 | Income Summary **(OE:IS)** | | 5,320 | |
| | Salary Expense **(OE:E)** | | | 3,000 |
| | Utilities Expense **(OE:E)** | | | 1,100 |
| | Advertising Expense **(OE:E)** | | | 400 |
| | Rent Expense **(OE:E)** | | | 300 |
| | Office Supplies Expense **(OE:E)** | | | 310 |
| | Depreciation Expense **(OE:E)** | | | 180 |
| | Interest Expense **(OE:E)** | | | 30 |
| | To close the expense accounts. | | | |
| 30 | Dance Lesson Revenues **(OE:R)** | | 8,600 | |
| | Income Summary **(OE:IS)** | | | 8,600 |
| | To close the revenue accounts. | | | |
| 30 | Income Summary **(OE:IS)** | | 3,280 | |
| | Abrems, Capital **(OE)** | | | 3,280 |
| | To close the income summary account. | | | |
| 30 | Abrems, Capital **(OE)** | | 500 | |
| | Abrems, Withdrawals **(OE:W)** | | | 500 |
| | To close the withdrawals account. | | | |

## The Post-Closing Trial Balance

We need a final check on the adjusting and closing process. This check is called a **post-closing trial balance,** which, as the name implies, is prepared from the general ledger after the adjusting and closing entries have been posted. A post-closing trial balance contains only asset, liability, and capital accounts because all revenue, expense, and withdrawals accounts *have been closed,* their balances having been trans-

**Exhibit 12** Post-Closing Trial Balance

### THE MARY ABREMS DANCE STUDIO
### Post-Closing Trial Balance
### November 30, 1998

| | | |
|---|---|---|
| Cash | $ 5,250 | |
| Accounts Receivable | 2,950 | |
| Office Supplies on Hand | 140 | |
| Prepaid Rent | 600 | |
| Office Equipment | 10,800 | |
| Accumulated Depreciation | | $ 180 |
| Note Payable | | 3,000 |
| Accounts Payable | | 650 |
| Salaries Payable | | 500 |
| Interest Payable | | 30 |
| Unearned Dance Lesson Revenues | | 1,600 |
| Abrems, Capital | | 13,780 |
| Totals | $19,740 | $19,740 |

**Exhibit 13** General Ledger T-Accounts

| Cash | |
|---|---|
| Bal.    5,250 | |

| Notes Payable | |
|---|---|
| | Bal.    3,000 |

| Dance Lesson Revenues | |
|---|---|
| | Bal.          8,400 |
| | GJ 12 A       200 |
| GJ 13 C    8,600 | Bal.          8,600 |

| Accounts Receivable | |
|---|---|
| Bal.    2,950 | |

| Accounts Payable | |
|---|---|
| | Bal.    650 |

| Salary Expense | |
|---|---|
| Bal.       2,500 | |
| GJ 12 A      500 | |
| Bal.       3,000 | GJ 13 C    3,000 |

| Office Supplies on Hand | |
|---|---|
| Bal.    450 | GJ 12 A    310 |
| Bal.    140 | |

| Salaries Payable | |
|---|---|
| | GJ 12 A    500 |

| Utilities Expense | |
|---|---|
| Bal.    1,100 | GJ 13 C    1,100 |

| Prepaid Rent | |
|---|---|
| Bal.    900 | GJ 12 A    300 |
| Bal.    600 | |

| Interest Payable | |
|---|---|
| | GJ 12 A    30 |

| Advertising Expense | |
|---|---|
| Bal.    400 | GJ 13 C    400 |

| Office Equipment | |
|---|---|
| Bal.    10,800 | |

| Unearned Dance Lesson Revenues | |
|---|---|
| GJ 12 A    200 | Bal.    1,800 |
| | Bal.    1,600 |

| Rent Expense | |
|---|---|
| GJ 12 A    300 | GJ 13 C    300 |

| Accumulated Depreciation | |
|---|---|
| | GJ 12 A    180 |

| Abrems, Capital | |
|---|---|
| | Bal.       11,000 |
| GJ 13 C    500 | GJ 13 C     3,280 |
| | Bal.       13,780 |

| Office Supplies Expense | |
|---|---|
| GJ 12 A    310 | GJ 13 C    310 |

| Income Summary | |
|---|---|
| GJ 13 C    5,320 | GJ 13 C    8,600 |
| GJ 13 C    3,280 | |

| Abrems, Withdrawals | |
|---|---|
| Bal.    500 | GJ 13 C    500 |

| Depreciation Expense | |
|---|---|
| GJ 12 A    180 | GJ 13 C    180 |

| Interest Expense | |
|---|---|
| GJ 12 A    30 | GJ 13 C    30 |

ferred to the Capital account. Exhibit 12 shows the Nov. 30, 1998, post-closing trial balance of The Mary Abrems Dance Studio; the general ledger from which it has been prepared is illustrated in T-account form in Exhibit 13. In the general ledger, we have indicated the adjusting entries as having come from general journal page 12, and we have placed the letter A next to the page reference so that you can quickly identify the posting as an adjusting entry. The closing entries are identified by page 13 and the letter C.

Notice the double lines drawn under all the income statement accounts as well as the Abrems, Withdrawals and the Income Summary accounts. These double lines in the ledger indicate that these accounts have been closed and are ready to receive postings for the new year.

1. **Why are the accounts closed?**
2. **What accounts are closed?**
3. **What purpose does the Income Summary Account serve?**
4. **Explain the closing process.**
5. **What accounts appear on the post-closing trial balance?**

## REVERSING ENTRIES

Learning Objective 5

Explain why reversing entries are used

Preparing the post-closing trial balance may not be the last step in the accounting process. Some companies may elect to reverse certain period-end adjusting entries on the first day of the new period to simplify the recordkeeping process. A **reversing entry** is the opposite of an adjusting entry, debiting an account that an adjusting entry has credited for the same amount, and vice versa. We can illustrate the use of reversing entries by considering the salary accrual adjusting entry for The Mary Abrems Dance Studio.

Abrems' employees currently earn a total of $125 per day. The month ends on Thursday, Nov. 30, 1998, and payday is on Friday, Dec. 8, 1998. This means that on Nov. 30, $500 ($125 × 4 days) in salaries has been earned but not yet paid. Thus, the adjusting entry for this accrual is $500:

### THE MARY ABREMS DANCE STUDIO
#### General Journal

| Date | Account Titles and Explanation | Post. Ref. | Debit | Credit |
|------|-------------------------------|-----------|-------|--------|
| 1998 Nov. 30 | Salary Expense (OE : E) | | 500 | |
| |     Salaries Payable (L) | | | 500 |
| | To record accrual of salaries. | | | |

Prior to this accrual, from Nov. 1, 1998, to Nov. 24, 1998, salary expense amounted to $2,500. The general ledger accounts Salary Expense and Salaries Payable would appear as follows after the adjusting entry was posted:

General Ledger Accounts

| Salary Expense | | | | Salaries Payable | | |
|----------------|------|--|--|------------------|--|--|
| 11/1/98–11/24/98 | 2,500 | | | | | |
| 11/30/98 Adj. | 500 | | | 11/30/98 Adj. | 500 | |
| 11/30/98 Bal. | 3,000 | | | | | |

Salary Expense for the entire month would then be closed by the following entry:

**THE MARY ABREMS DANCE STUDIO**
General Journal

| Date | Account Titles and Explanation | Post. Ref. | Debit | Credit |
|---|---|---|---|---|
| 1998 Nov. 30 | Income Summary **(OE : IS)**<br>    Salary Expense **(OE : E)**<br>To close the salary expense account. | | 3,000 | 3,000 |

Posting the closing entry as a credit to the Salary Expense account in the general ledger would result in a zero balance in that account:

General Ledger Accounts

**Salary Expense**

| | | | |
|---|---|---|---|
| 11/1/98–11/24/98 | 2,500 | | |
| 11/30/98 Adj. | 500 | | |
| 11/30/98 Bal. | 3,000 | 11/30/98 Clo. | 3,000 |

Thus far there are no problems in the way things were handled in 1998. Now we come to the problem of having to reverse the adjusting entry to start the new year.

On Friday, Dec. 8, 1998, $1,250 ($125 × 10) is paid to the employees for their biweekly service. For each biweekly period during the preceding month the payroll entry has been recorded in the following manner:

**THE MARY ABREMS DANCE STUDIO**
General Journal

| Date | Account Titles and Explanation | Post. Ref. | Debit | Credit |
|---|---|---|---|---|
| 1998 Nov. Paydays | Salary Expense **(OE : E)**<br>    Cash **(A)**<br>To record payment of salaries. | | 1,250 | 1,250 |

Unfortunately, if the same entry is recorded on Dec. 8, 1998, it will be incorrect. Only $750 of the $1,250 represents salary expense for the first week of the new month commencing Dec. 1, 1998; the other $500 is salary expense from the last 4 days of the month ending Nov. 30, 1998 as you can see in the following diagram:

| November 1998 | | | | | December 1998 | | | | |
|---|---|---|---|---|---|---|---|---|---|
| **M** | **T** | **W** | **T** | **F** | **M** | **T** | **W** | **T** | **F** |
| 27 | 28 | 29 | 30 | 1 | 4 | 5 | 6 | 7 | 8 |
| $125 | $125 | $125 | *$500*<br>$125 | $125 | $125 | $125 | $125 | $125 | *$750*<br>$125 |

There are two ways to solve this accounting problem. In one method, the Dec. 8, 1998, entry could be recorded as:

### THE MARY ABREMS DANCE STUDIO
#### General Journal

| Date | Account Titles and Explanation | Post. Ref. | Debit | Credit |
|------|-------------------------------|-----------|-------|--------|
| 1998<br>Dec. 8 | Salaries Payable **(L)**<br>Salary Expense **(OE:E)**<br>　　Cash **(A)**<br>To record payment of salaries. | | 500<br>750 | <br><br>1250 |

The general ledger accounts, after this entry is posted, would appear as follows:

**General Ledger Accounts**

**Salary Expense**

| | | | |
|---|---|---|---|
| 11/1/98–11/24/98 | 2,500 | | |
| 11/30/98 Adj. | 500 | | |
| 11/30/98 Bal. | 3,000 | 11/30/98 Clo. | 3,000 |
| 12/8/98 | 750 | | |

**Salaries Payable**

| | | | |
|---|---|---|---|
| 12/1/98 | 500 | 11/30/98 Adj. | 500 |
| | | 12/1/98 Bal. | –0– |

A problem with this method is that the accountant must remember that the first biweekly salary entry of the new month is different from that of the other biweekly entries. Many of us would forget this and record the Dec. 8, 1998, salary payment in the same way we did all the others—debiting Salary Expense and crediting Cash for $1,250—which would be incorrect.

An alternative procedure would be to use a reversing entry, which would be made as of Dec. 1, 1998. The accrued salaries adjusting entry of Nov. 30, 1998, would be reversed as follows:

### THE MARY ABREMS DANCE STUDIO
#### General Journal

| Date | Account Titles and Explanation | Post. Ref. | Debit | Credit |
|------|-------------------------------|-----------|-------|--------|
| 1998<br>Dec. 1 | Salaries Payable **(L)**<br>　　Salary Expense **(OE:E)**<br>To reverse the salary adjusting entry. | | 500 | <br>500 |

The ledger accounts, after the reversing entries are posted, would look like this:

General Ledger Accounts

| Salary Expense | | | | | Salaries Payable | | | |
|---|---|---|---|---|---|---|---|---|
| 11/1/98–11/24/98 | 2,500 | | | | | | | |
| 11/30/98 Adj. | 500 | | | | 12/1/98 Rev. | 500 | 11/30/98 Adj. | 500 |
| 11/30/98 Bal. | 3,000 | 11/30/98 Clo. | 3,000 | | | | 12/1/98 Bal. | –0– |
| | | 12/1/98 Rev. | 500 | | | | | |

Notice that the liability account—Salaries Payable—now has a zero balance and that the expense account—Salary Expense—has a $500 *credit* balance. The credit in the Salary Expense account is in *anticipation* of the $1,250 debit to be received when the payroll entry of Dec. 8 is made. Now the Dec. 8 payroll entry can be made in exactly the same way as the entry for each of the other weeks of the month:

**THE MARY ABREMS DANCE STUDIO**
General Journal

| Date | Account Titles and Explanation | Post. Ref. | Debit | Credit |
|---|---|---|---|---|
| 1998 Dec. 8 | Salary Expense (OE : E)<br>    Cash (A)<br>To record the payment of salaries. | | 1,250 | 1,250 |

Posting this entry to the Salary Expense account—which has been adjusted and closed on Nov. 30, 1998, and reversed for $500 on Dec. 1, 1998, results in a $750 debit balance for the first biweekly pay period of the month starting on Dec. 1, 1998:

General Ledger Accounts

| Salary Expense | | | |
|---|---|---|---|
| 11/1/98–11/30/98 | 2,500 | | |
| 11/30/98 Adj. | 500 | | |
| 11/30/98 Bal. | 3,000 | 11/30/98 Clo. | 3,000 |
| 12/8/98 | 1,250 | 12/1/98 Rev. | 500 |
| 12/8/98 Bal. | 750 | | |

Which of these two methods is better? There is no "right" answer. The selection of one method over the other depends on the decision maker's background, the system utilized by the company, and tradition ("that's the way we've always done it"). Either method will provide the identical information, so it isn't important to the user of the financial statement which method is selected.

From this salary accrual example we can generalize: If a company elects to use reversing entries, then *all accrual adjusting entries should be reversed.* In addition to

# The Case of an Accountant's Blind Trust

Several years ago a stock loan company called MESCO Broker Services, Inc., was organized in New York City. The company was 70% to 80% owned by Mesirow & Company, which was located in Chicago. The president of MESCO engaged the services of an accountant on a part-time basis to prepare the books of original entry, post to the general ledger, make adjusting entries, and prepare the financial statements that were sent to Mesirow & Company.

From the inception of MESCO the company president began taking salary advances. When the salary advances became excessive, Mesirow officials in Chicago insisted that the practice be stopped and that the advances be treated as a loan to be repaid promptly. Shortly thereafter the accoun-

tant discovered that the president had again taken an advance. The president assured the accountant that the advance would be repaid. Consequently, the accountant recorded the advance as a prepaid expense which was covered by not issuing a paycheck to the president the next pay period.

Several months later the accountant discovered that the president was again taking advances. The president again assured the accountant that they would be repaid. As the accountant discovered the advances in the checkbook, he would record them as advances in the cash payments journal but cancel them out by a month-end adjusting entry showing the advances as deposits in transit. On the first business day of the following month a *reversing entry* was made to reestablish the advance account. By this means the advances were not disclosed on the financial statements that were sent to Mesirow in Chicago.

After 6 months, just prior to the company's year-end, the advances had accumulated to $22,400. Since the year-end audit would uncover the missing funds, the cash

shortage had to be covered. The president accomplished this by borrowing $2,400 from the accountant and $20,000 from two individuals in the stock loan business. The $20,000 was repaid by 12 installments from MESCO by charging the payments to "Stock Loan Fees," a regular expense account. The president repaid the accountant $1,000. (The remaining $1,400 was never repaid.)

Commencing in November for the following year, the president began writing checks for fictitious disbursements, entering a fictitious payee on the check stub. The accountant covered these checks by reflecting a transfer of funds between various bank accounts, thus overstating MESCO's cash balance.

Just before the next year-end, the president showed the accountant a deposit slip for $55,000 to cover the missing funds. The deposit slip was a forgery, but by the time this was discovered the president was missing.

*Source:* Securities Exchange Act of 1934, Release No. 21135, July 12, 1984.

---

The MESCO case illustrates the use of reversing entries to hide improper cash advances. The case also illustrates the need for healthy skepticism when accountants deal with unusual requests from corporate executives.

---

the Salary Expense/Salaries Payable accrual adjusting entry, we have encountered two other common accruals: the Interest Expense/Interest Payable and the Interest Income/Interest Receivable adjustments. *Accrual adjusting entries are reversed to simplify the record-keeping process.*

As with most accounting procedures, reversing entries can be used improperly. They can unintentionally be used incorrectly, or deliberately used to cover fraud, as the accompanying box demonstrates.

**ASK YOURSELF ▶**

1. **What is a reversing entry?**
2. **Why are reversing entries used?**
3. **Does a company have to use reversing entries?**

## THE ACCOUNTING PROCESS REVIEWED

Learning Objective **6**

List the steps in the accounting process

You must not forget the ultimate objective of financial accounting: to prepare financial statements that represent meaningfully and fairly the results of operations of a business entity over a period of time and its financial position at a point in time. The financial accounting process, which we have described, is a practical means of achieving that objective. The steps involved in financial accounting are summarized in Figure 1.

**Figure 1** A Review of the Steps in the Accounting Process

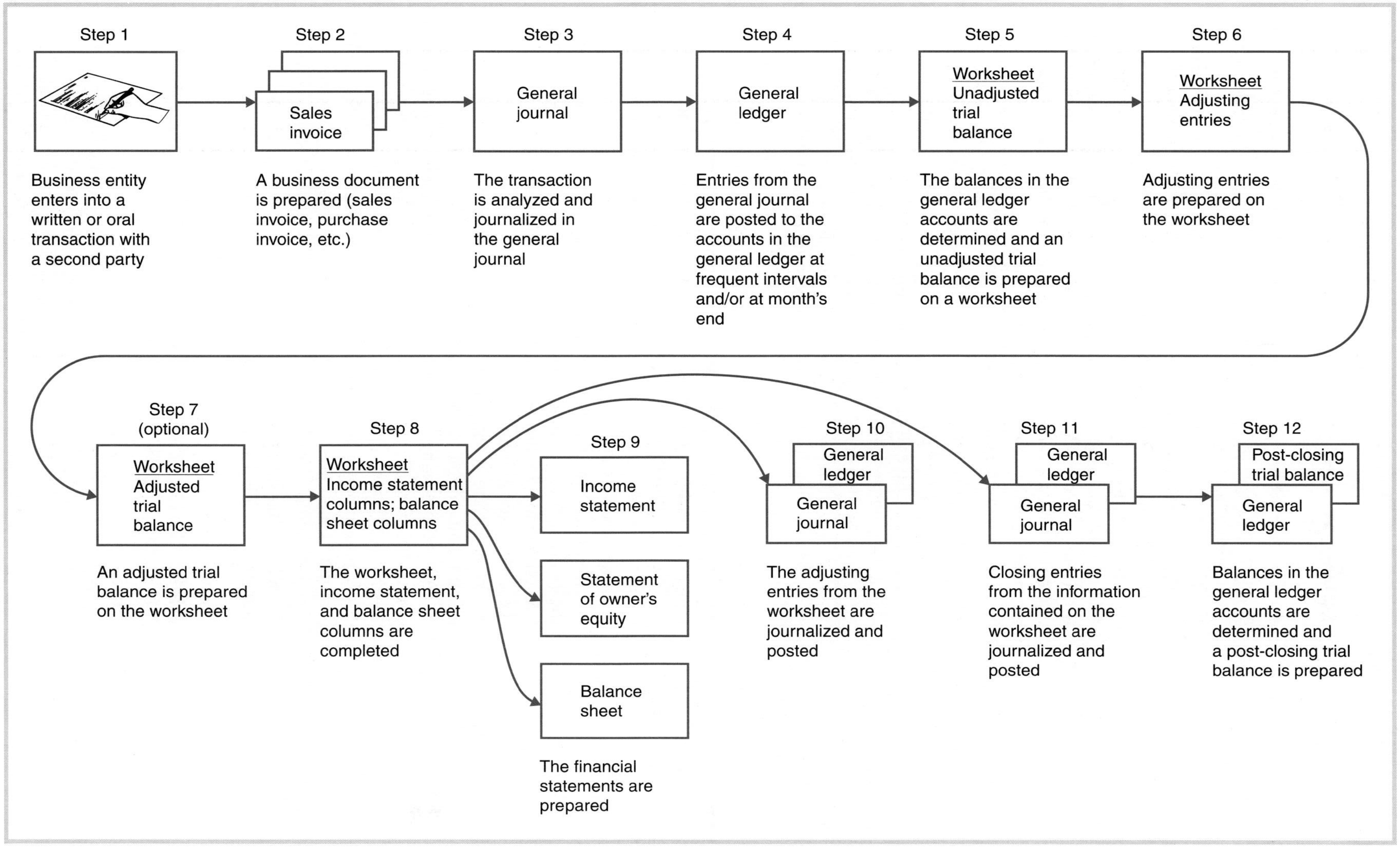

**Step 1**

Business entity enters into a written or oral transaction with a second party

**Step 2**

Sales invoice

A business document is prepared (sales invoice, purchase invoice, etc.)

**Step 3**

General journal

The transaction is analyzed and journalized in the general journal

**Step 4**

General ledger

Entries from the general journal are posted to the accounts in the general ledger at frequent intervals and/or at month's end

**Step 5**

Worksheet
Unadjusted trial balance

The balances in the general ledger accounts are determined and an unadjusted trial balance is prepared on a worksheet

**Step 6**

Worksheet
Adjusting entries

Adjusting entries are prepared on the worksheet

**Step 7** (optional)

Worksheet
Adjusted trial balance

An adjusted trial balance is prepared on the worksheet

**Step 8**

Worksheet
Income statement columns; balance sheet columns

The worksheet, income statement, and balance sheet columns are completed

**Step 9**

Income statement

Statement of owner's equity

Balance sheet

The financial statements are prepared

**Step 10**

General ledger

General journal

The adjusting entries from the worksheet are journalized and posted

**Step 11**

General ledger

General journal

Closing entries from the information contained on the worksheet are journalized and posted

**Step 12**

Post-closing trial balance

General ledger

Balances in the general ledger accounts are determined and a post-closing trial balance is prepared

## SUMMARY

• The **worksheet** is a tool used by accountants to organize the adjustments to the accounts and to simplify the process of preparing the monthly, quarterly, and yearly financial statements.

• The worksheet is used to make adjustments in the trial balance.

• From the resulting adjusted trial balance on the worksheet, the interim and annual income statement and balance sheet can be prepared.

• Monthly income statements are obtained from the worksheet by subtracting the accumulated amounts in the most recent worksheet income statement columns from the accumulated amounts up through the prior month. The difference represents the current month's income statement because the adjustments made on the worksheet are cumulative from the beginning of the year.

• The use of **closing entries** solves two problems:

1. Closing entries transfer the revenue, expense, and withdrawals accounts back to the Capital account. This enables us to determine the balance of the Capital account at the end of the accounting period.

2. Closing entries reduce to a zero balance all revenue, expense, and withdrawals accounts. This enables us to accumulate data in these temporary accounts for the next accounting period. These new accumulations will reflect data *just for the new period.* No data from previous periods will be included, since the accounts will now start with a zero balance.

• Expense accounts are closed by crediting each expense account for an amount equal to the balance in the account. We make the corresponding debit, which will be equal to the sum of the expenses, to an account called **Income Summary.**

• We close the revenue accounts by debiting each revenue account for an amount equal to the balance in the account. The corresponding credit for the sum of the revenue accounts is made to the Income Summary account.

• We transfer the balance in Income Summary, which is the *net income* or *net loss* for the period, to the Capital account by debiting Income Summary and crediting the Capital account. In the case of a net loss the Income Summary account is credited and the Capital account debited.

• We close the Withdrawals account by a credit to that account for the Withdrawals amount and a debit to the Capital account.

• After the closing entries are posted, the Capital account correctly reflects the ending balance. The beginning Capital balance has been increased by the net income (or decreased by a net loss) and decreased by withdrawals.

• A **post-closing trial balance** is prepared after the closing entries have been journalized and posted. The post-closing trial balance contains only balance sheet accounts and is a final check on the adjusting and closing process.

• **Reversing entries** are used to simplify the recordkeeping process. Reversing entries are made by simply reversing the adjusting entry.

## APPENDIX: THE EFFECT OF ACCOUNTING POLICY ON ADJUSTING ENTRIES

The text discussion on Preparing Worksheets, Closing Entries, and reversing entries has provided you with an understanding of why adjusting entries are necessary and how to make these entries. You should also be aware that all the transactions that required adjustments in the text discussion were initially recorded in balance sheet accounts. For example, when The Mary Abrems Dance Studio paid for 3 months rent in advance, the account Prepaid Rent was debited. This transaction is an external transaction that will provide future economic benefits, and we recorded it in the asset account.

The mirror image of this transaction is the payment received from Abrems by the owner of the dance studio, who rents the space to Abrems. The owner has incurred an obligation that must be fulfilled over the next 3 months. If we were accounting for the owner, we would record this obligation in a liability account called Unearned Rental Revenue.

We have used balance sheet accounts to record both sides of the transaction (Prepaid Rent and Unearned Rental Revenue). These accounts must be adjusted as each month passes and monthly financial statements are prepared. Abrems' Prepaid Rent account will be reduced and the Rent Expense account increased as service is received. On the opposite side, the studio owner's Unearned Rental Revenue account will be reduced and its Rental Revenue account will be increased as it "delivers" the monthly rental service. The financial statements will reflect the expense incurred or revenue earned, and the remaining future economic benefit or future obligation.

But what would happen if Abrems had elected to record the $900 advance rental payment for 3 months' rent in the Rent Expense account rather than the Prepaid Rent account? Would the FASB expel Abrems from the business community? Of course not. No one cares how Abrems elects to record her transactions, *so long as her financial statements reflect the economic substance of the transactions.* That is why adjusting entries are made: to adjust the accounts so that the financial statements prepared from the accounts—or, as we know from the text, from the worksheet—truly reflect the economic substance of the multitude of transactions the business entered into during the accounting period.

*A business entity may elect to record a transaction in an expense account rather than an asset account. And the mirror image of the transaction may be recorded in a revenue account rather than a liability account.* This is an *accounting policy decision.* Once the decision is made, the accountant must always follow it when recording the transaction and making the appropriate adjusting entries. A decision can be made always to record rent in the expense account and always to record office supplies acquired in an asset account rather than an expense account. The point is that a company may be *inconsistent* in its overall policy, but must be *consistent* when dealing with the individual accounts.

In the following two sections, we will show through examples how the accounting policy selected determines the way accounts are adjusted.

## RECORDING A DEFERRAL AS AN ASSET OR AS AN EXPENSE

Learning Objective **7**

Record transactions initially in revenue and expense accounts and make the appropriate adjusting entries

On Nov. 3, 1998, when Abrems rented the dance studio for $900 paid in advance, the company could have recorded this transaction in either of two ways, depending on which of two possible accounting policies the company follows. The $900 payment could have initially been recorded either as an asset or as an expense; both possibilities are illustrated here:

| Initial Entry Recorded as | | | |
|---|---|---|---|
| An Asset | | An Expense | |
| 1998 | | | |
| Nov. 3  Prepaid Rent **(A)** . . . . . . . . . . . . .  900 | | Rent Expense **(OE : E)** . . . . . . . .  900 | |
| Cash **(A)** . . . . . . . . . . . . . . .  | 900 | Cash **(A)** . . . . . . . . . . . . . . .  | 900 |

Financial statements are prepared at month-end, Nov. 30, 1998. The amount of actual rent expense for the month is only $300 ($900/3). Thus, at month-end, $300 of the potential service, prepaid rent, has been consumed, leaving $600 unconsumed (which represents 2 more months of future service).

Prepaid Rent must reflect a $600 debit balance, and Rent Expense must be stated at $300. To arrive at these debit balances, an adjusting entry is required. The appropriate adjustment depends on how the initial transaction was recorded. In general journal entry form, the required adjusting entries look like this:

| | Adjusting Entry Required If Initial Entry Recorded as | | | |
| | An Asset | | An Expense | |
| --- | --- | --- | --- | --- |
| **1998** | | | | |
| Nov. 30 | Rent Expense **(OE:E)** . . . . . . . . | 300 | Prepaid Rent **(A)** . . . . . . . . . . . . . | 600 |
| | Prepaid Rent **(A)** . . . . . . . . . | 300 | Rent Expense **(OE:E)** . . . . . | 600 |

The effect of the adjusting entries on the general ledger accounts for both accounting policies is as follows:

**GENERAL LEDGER ACCOUNTS AFTER ADJUSTING ENTRY IF INITIAL ENTRY RECORDED AS**

| AN ASSET | | | | AN EXPENSE | | | |
| --- | --- | --- | --- | --- | --- | --- | --- |

**Prepaid Rent** (AN ASSET)

| 11/3/98 | 900 | 11/30/98 Adj. | 300 |
| --- | --- | --- | --- |
| 11/30/98 | 600 | | |

**Rent Expense** (AN ASSET)

| 11/30/98 Adj. | 300 | |
| --- | --- | --- |

**Prepaid Rent** (AN EXPENSE)

| 11/30/98 Adj. | 600 | |
| --- | --- | --- |

**Rent Expense** (AN EXPENSE)

| 11/3/98 | 900 | 11/30/98 Adj. | 600 |
| --- | --- | --- | --- |
| 11/30/98 | 300 | | |

Notice that under both methods, the balance in Prepaid Rent ($600) and in Rent Expense ($300) is identical.

## RECORDING A DEFERRAL AS A LIABILITY OR AS REVENUE

The Mary Abrems Dance Studio received a check on Nov. 4, 1998, for $1,800, representing 9 months' dance lessons paid in advance. At this date, Abrems may record a credit in that amount for either Unearned Dance Lesson Revenues or Dance Lesson Revenues, depending on its accounting policy:

| | Initial Entry Recorded as | | | |
| | A Liability | | A Revenue | |
| --- | --- | --- | --- | --- |
| **1998** | | | | |
| Nov. 4 | Cash **(A)** . . . . . . . . . . . . . . . . . . | 1,800 | Cash **(A)** . . . . . . . . . . . . . . . . . . | 1,800 |
| | Unearned Dance Lesson | | Dance Lesson Revenues | |
| | Revenues **(L)** . . . . . . . . . . . | 1,800 | **(OE:R)** . . . . . . . . . . . . . . . . | 1,800 |

On Nov. 30, 1998, financial statements are required. At $1,800 for 9 months the revenue from dance lessons (assuming that they will be earned evenly over the 9-month period) will be $200 per month. On Nov. 30, 1 month's revenue has been earned, or $200, leaving 8 months' unearned dance lesson revenues, amounting to $1,600.

On Nov. 30, Unearned Dance Lesson Revenues must reflect a $1,600 credit balance and Dance Lesson Revenues must be stated at $200. The adjusting entries required to achieve these balances are as follows:

| Adjusting Entry Required If Initial Entry Recorded as | | | |
|---|---|---|---|
| A Liability | | A Revenue | |
| 1998 | | | |
| Nov. 30  Unearned Dance Lesson<br>            Revenues **(L)**. . . . . . . . . . . . . . .  200 | | Dance Lesson Revenues<br>   **(OE:R)** . . . . . . . . . . . . . . . . . . .  1,600 | |
|            Dance Lesson Revenues<br>            **(OE:R)**. . . . . . . . . . . . . . . .  200 | | Unearned Dance Lesson<br>   Revenues **(L)**. . . . . . . . . . .  1,600 | |

Illustrated below are the general ledger accounts after the appropriate adjusting entries have been made.

**GENERAL LEDGER ACCOUNTS AFTER ADJUSTING ENTRY IF INITIAL ENTRY RECORDED AS**

| A LIABILITY | | A REVENUE | |
|---|---|---|---|
| **Unearned Dance Lesson Revenues** | | **Unearned Dance Lesson Revenues** | |
| 11/30/98          200 | 11/4/98          1,800 | | 11/30/98 Adj.          1,600 |
| | 11/30/98 Bal.          1,600 | | |
| **Dance Lesson Revenues** | | **Dance Lesson Revenues** | |
| | 11/30/98 Adj.          200 | 11/30/98 Adj.          1,600 | 11/4/98          1,800 |
| | | | 11/30/98 Bal.          200 |

## REVERSAL OF ADJUSTING ENTRIES: DEFERRALS

Learning
Objective        8

Determine which adjusting entries
require reversing entries

In the preceding section we have seen how the choice of an accounting policy affects the way adjusting entries are recorded. Recording the advance payment for rent in the Rent Expense account requires an adjusting entry at month-end that establishes the Prepaid Rent account and reduces the Rent Expense account to the amount actually consumed. Likewise, when payments are received in advance and recorded in Dance Lesson Revenues, the appropriate adjustment at month-end is to establish the Unearned Dance Lesson Revenues account and reduce the Dance Lesson Revenues account to the amount actually earned.

These procedures reflect a policy of recording entries in income statement accounts (Rent Expense and Dance Lesson Revenues, for example). These accounts require month-end adjustments, a fact that presents a bookkeeping problem in subsequent accounting periods.

Recall the $900 that Abrems paid for rent on her dance studio on Nov. 4, 1998. Now look ahead to December 1998 and assume that Abrems rents additional studio space for $4,800. It's a 1-year lease. How will this be recorded? Let's assume that the accounting policy is to use income statement accounts; thus the entry will be as follows:

### THE MARY ABREMS DANCE STUDIO
General Journal

| Date | Account Titles and Explanation | Post. Ref. | Debit | Credit |
|------|-------------------------------|------------|-------|--------|
| 1998 Dec. 1 | Rent Expense **(OE : E)**<br>    Cash **(A)**<br>To record payment of rent for 1 year. | | 4,800 | 4,800 |

But wait a minute: Where is the unconsumed rent from the first year—the Prepaid Rent? It's in the Prepaid Rent account, having been transferred there by the Nov. 30 adjusting entry. Further, the Rent Expense account for November has been closed out by the Nov. 30 closing entry. Accordingly, the ledger accounts on Dec. 1, 1998, would appear like this:

### GENERAL LEDGER ACCOUNTS

| Prepaid Rent | | | |
|---|---|---|---|
| 11/30/98 Adj | 600 | | |

| Rent Expense | | | |
|---|---|---|---|
| 11/3/98 | 900 | 11/30/98 Adj. | 600 |
| 11/30/98 Bal. | 300 | 11/30/98 Closing | 300 |
| 12/1/98 Bal. | –0– | | |
| 12/1/98 | 4,800 | | |

We now have our eggs in two baskets when they should be in one. We have $600 in Prepaid Rent and $4,800 in Rent Expense. What we need to do is to *transfer* the $600 from the Prepaid Rent account to the Rent Expense account, because it is the studio's accounting policy to record rent in the Rent Expense account. The general journal entry required to accomplish this is as follows:

### THE MARY ABREMS DANCE STUDIO
General Journal

| Date | Account Titles and Explanation | Post. Ref. | Debit | Credit |
|------|-------------------------------|------------|-------|--------|
| 1998 Dec. 1 | Rent Expense **(OE : E)**<br>    Prepaid Rent **(A)**<br>To reverse prepaid rent adjusting entry. | | 600 | 600 |

Compare this entry to the adjusting entry recorded on Nov. 30, 1998, where the rent was recorded as an expense. This entry is exactly the opposite, or the reverse, which is why it is called a *reversing entry.*

Reversing entries are prepared as of the first day of a new accounting period. To reverse the dance studio's Nov. 30, 1998, adjusting entry for dance lesson revenues (assuming that the Dance Lesson Revenues account was used to record the initial receipt of the $1,800 commissions paid in advance) requires the following reversing entry:

### THE MARY ABREMS DANCE STUDIO
General Journal

| Date | Account Titles and Explanation | Post. Ref. | Debit | Credit |
|---|---|---|---|---|
| 1998 Dec. 1 | Unearned Dance Lesson Revenues **(L)** | | 1,600 | |
| | Dance Lesson Revenues **(OE : E)** | | | 1,600 |
| | To reverse unearned dance lesson revenues adjusting entry. | | | |

We can draw a general conclusion from these two examples. Whenever a company elects to record a transaction initially in an income statement account, and that transaction must later be adjusted, then the adjusting entry must be reversed at the beginning of the next period. This is done to *achieve internal accounting consistency.*

## REVERSAL OF ADJUSTING ENTRIES: ACCRUALS

Remember that accrual adjusting entries are also reversed. If a company elects to use reversing entries, then *all accrual adjusting entries should be reversed.* Accrual adjusting entries are reversed to simplify the record-keeping process.

A simple way to determine when a reversing entry must be made is this: *If the adjusting entry increases a balance sheet account, then that adjusting entry must be reversed.* Look at the first adjusting entry we discussed in the preceding section: When rent was recorded as an expense, the adjusting entry increased the Prepaid Rent account. And so it was with the second adjusting entry: When dance lesson revenues were recorded in a revenue account, the adjusting entry increased the Unearned Dance Lesson Revenues account. And when we discussed payroll, the adjusting entry increased the Salaries Payable account. All of these accounts—Prepaid Rent, Unearned Dance Lesson Revenues, and Salaries Payable—are balance sheet accounts that were increased, so all need reversing entries.

**9 KEY TERMS**

**Balance sheet accounts**  Asset, liability, and capital accounts representing the amount of the particular account at a point in time. They are also called *permanent accounts* or *real accounts.*

**Closing entries**  Internal transactions recorded by business entities to clear all income statement accounts to a zero balance at the end of an accounting period and to transfer these balances to the Capital account.

**Closing process**  The accounting procedure used to clear all income statement accounts to a zero balance at the end of an accounting period and to transfer these balances to the Capital account.

**Fiscal year**  The annual accounting period adopted by an economic entity; fiscal years generally begin on the first day of a month and end on the last day of the twelfth month thereafter.

| | |
|---|---|
| **Income statement accounts** | Revenue and expense accounts. These accounts are extensions of the capital account and accumulate data for a month, a quarter, or a year, but no longer. They are also called *nominal accounts,* or *temporary accounts.* |
| **Income Summary** | An account used to simplify the closing process. Income statement accounts are first closed to the Income Summary account, which in turn is closed to the Capital account. This account is also called the *Profit and Loss Summary.* |
| **Interim statements** | Financial statements prepared on a monthly or quarterly basis directly from worksheets. |
| **Post-closing trial balance** | A list of the general ledger accounts after the adjusting and closing entries have been journalized and posted. Only balance sheet accounts will contain balances in a post-closing trial balance. |
| **Reversing entry** | A journal entry that is exactly the opposite of an adjusting entry. When an adjusting entry debits an account, the reversing entry will credit that account for the same amount, and vice versa. Reversing entries are used to simplify the recordkeeping process. |
| **Unadjusted trial balance** | A list of the general ledger accounts after all external transactions have been recorded and posted but prior to any needed adjustments. |
| **Worksheet** | A multicolumn form used by accountants as a temporary record to organize a business entity's end-of-accounting procedures. |

## DEMONSTRATION PROBLEM

Several years ago Martha Gilbertson opened a law firm under the name of Gilbertson, Attorney at Law. At year-end, Dec. 31, 1998, an unadjusted trial balance was prepared, as shown on the worksheet below.

The four year-end adjustments (lettered *a* to *d* on the worksheet) reflect these changes:

**a.** One-fourth of the prepaid insurance expired during the year.

**b.** Office supplies remaining on hand on Dec. 31, 1998, amount to $1,100.

**c.** Depreciation on the office equipment for the year amounts to $1,000.

**d.** Salaries in the amount of $1,900 are accrued at year-end.

**Required:**

1. Complete the worksheet.
2. Prepare the financial statements from the worksheet, with a separate statement of owner's equity.
3. Journalize the adjusting and closing entries.
4. Prepare the Jan. 1, 1999, reversing entry necessary for the salaries.

■ **Solution to Demonstration Problem**

1.

### GILBERTSON, ATTORNEY AT LAW
#### Worksheet
#### Year Ended December 31, 1998

| | Unadjusted Trial Balance | | Adjustments | | Adjusted Trial Balance | | Income Statement | | Balance Sheet | |
|---|---|---|---|---|---|---|---|---|---|---|
| | **Debit** | **Credit** | **Debit** | **Credit** | **Debit** | **Credit** | **Debit** | **Credit** | **Debit** | **Credit** |
| Cash | 4,200 | | | | 4,200 | | | | 4,200 | |
| Accounts Receivable | 8,700 | | | | 8,700 | | | | 8,700 | |
| Prepaid Insurance | 3,600 | | | (a) 900 | 2,700 | | | | 2,700 | |
| Office Supplies on Hand | 2,800 | | | (b) 1,700 | 1,100 | | | | 1,100 | |
| Office Equipment | 23,000 | | | | 23,000 | | | | 23,000 | |
| Accumulated Depreciation | | 4,000 | | (c) 1,000 | | 5,000 | | | | 5,000 |
| Accounts Payable | | 6,100 | | | | 6,100 | | | | 6,100 |
| Gilbertson, Capital | | 21,600 | | | | 21,600 | | | | 21,600 |
| Gilbertson, Withdrawals | 26,000 | | | | 26,000 | | | | 26,000 | |
| Legal Fees Earned | | 125,000 | | | | 125,000 | | 125,000 | | |
| Salary Expense | 56,400 | | (d) 1,900 | | 58,300 | | 58,300 | | | |
| Rent Expense | 18,000 | | | | 18,000 | | 18,000 | | | |
| Legal Research Expense | 12,500 | | | | 12,500 | | 12,500 | | | |
| Telephone Expense | 1,500 | | | | 1,500 | | 1,500 | | | |
| Totals | 156,700 | 156,700 | | | | | | | | |
| Insurance Expense | | | (a) 900 | | 900 | | 900 | | | |
| Office Supplies Expense | | | (b) 1,700 | | 1,700 | | 1,700 | | | |
| Depreciation Expense | | | (c) 1,000 | | 1,000 | | 1,000 | | | |
| Salaries Payable | | | | (d) 1,900 | | 1,900 | | | | 1,900 |
| Totals | | | 5,500 | 5,500 | 159,600 | 159,600 | 93,900 | 125,000 | 65,700 | 34,600 |
| Net Income | | | | | | | 31,100 | | | 31,100 |
| | | | | | | | 125,000 | 125,000 | 65,700 | 65,700 |

2.

## GILBERTSON, ATTORNEY AT LAW
### Income Statement
### Year Ended December 31, 1998

| | | |
|---|---:|---:|
| Revenue: | | |
| Legal Fees Earned............................................. | | $125,000 |
| Expenses: | | |
| Salary Expense ..................................... | $58,300 | |
| Rent Expense ....................................... | 18,000 | |
| Legal Research Expense ............................. | 12,500 | |
| Telephone Expense.................................. | 1,500 | |
| Insurance Expense .................................. | 900 | |
| Office Supplies Expense ............................. | 1,700 | |
| Depreciation Expense ............................... | 1,000 | |
| Total Expense ..................................... | | 93,900 |
| Net Income................................................. | | $ 31,100 |

## GILBERTSON, ATTORNEY AT LAW
### Statement of Owner's Equity
### Year Ended December 31, 1998

| | |
|---|---:|
| Gilbertson, Capital, Jan. 1, 1998................................... | $21,600 |
| Add: Net Income .................................................. | 31,100 |
| Total ......................................................... | $52,700 |
| Less: Withdrawals ................................................ | 26,000 |
| Gilbertson, Capital, Dec. 31, 1998 ................................. | $26,700 |

## GILBERTSON, ATTORNEY AT LAW
### Balance Sheet
### December 31, 1998

| Assets | | | Liabilities | | |
|---|---:|---:|---|---:|---:|
| Current Assets: | | | Current Liabilities: | | |
| Cash........................ | $ 4,200 | | Accounts Payable ............... | $6,100 | |
| Accounts Receivable............ | 8,700 | | Salaries Payable ................ | 1,900 | |
| Prepaid Insurance .............. | 2,700 | | Total Current Liabilities ................. | | $ 8,000 |
| Office Supplies on Hand ......... | 1,100 | | | | |
| Total Current Assets .................. | | $16,700 | **Owner's Equity** | | |
| Plant and Equipment: | | | Gilbertson, Capital....................... | | 26,700 |
| Office Equipment............... | $23,000 | | | | |
| Less: Accumulated Depreciation... | 5,000 | | | | |
| Total Plant and Equipment .............. | | 18,000 | | | |
| Total Assets............................. | | $34,700 | Total Liabilities and Owner's Equity .......... | | $34,700 |

*(Continued)*

3, 4.

## GILBERTSON, ATTORNEY AT LAW
### General Journal

| Date | Account Titles and Explanation | Post. Ref. | Debit | Credit |
|------|-------------------------------|-----------|-------|--------|
| | **Adjusting Entries** | | | |
| 1998 Dec. 31 | Insurance Expense **(OE:E)** | | 900 | |
| | Prepaid Insurance **(A)** | | | 900 |
| | To record expired insurance. | | | |
| 31 | Office Supplies Expense **(OE:E)** | | 1,700 | |
| | Office Supplies on Hand **(A)** | | | 1,700 |
| | To record office supplies used. | | | |
| 31 | Depreciation Expense **(OE:E)** | | 1,000 | |
| | Accumulated Depreciation **(A)** | | | 1,000 |
| | To record depreciation expense. | | | |
| 31 | Salary Expense **(OE:E)** | | 1,900 | |
| | Salaries Payable **(L)** | | | 1,900 |
| | To record accrued salaries. | | | |
| | **Closing Entries** | | | |
| 31 | Income Summary **(OE:IS)** | | 93,900 | |
| | Salary Expense **(OE:E)** | | | 58,300 |
| | Rent Expense **(OE:E)** | | | 18,000 |
| | Legal Research Expense **(OE:E)** | | | 12,500 |
| | Telephone Expense **(OE:E)** | | | 1,500 |
| | Insurance Expense **(OE:E)** | | | 900 |
| | Office Supplies Expense **(OE:E)** | | | 1,700 |
| | Depreciation Expense **(OE:E)** | | | 1,000 |
| | To close the expense accounts. | | | |
| 31 | Legal Fees Earned **(OE:R)** | | 125,000 | |
| | Income Summary **(OE:IS)** | | | 125,000 |
| | To close the revenue accounts. | | | |
| 31 | Income Summary **(OE:IS)** | | 31,100 | |
| | Gilbertson, Capital **(OE)** | | | 31,100 |
| | To close the income summary account. | | | |
| 31 | Gilbertson, Capital **(OE)** | | 26,000 | |
| | Gilbertson, Withdrawals **(OE:W)** | | | 26,000 |
| | To close the withdrawals account. | | | |
| | **Reversing Entry** | | | |
| 1999 Jan. 1 | Salaries Payable **(L)** | | 1,900 | |
| | Salary Expense **(OE:E)** | | | 1,900 |
| | To reverse salary accrual adjusting entry. | | | |

## QUESTIONS FOR REVIEW AND FURTHER THOUGHT

### REVIEW QUESTIONS

*Note:* Questions marked with an asterisk relate to material contained in the appendix.

1. What purpose does the worksheet serve?

2. It is not necessary to prepare an adjusted trial balance on a worksheet. Comment.

3. Explain why some companies may not journalize the general journal adjustments entered on a worksheet.

4. A balance sheet cannot be prepared directly from the information contained in the balance sheet columns of a worksheet. Why not?

5. What advantage does the worksheet offer an accountant when preparing interim financial statements?

6. What is the difference between *closing the books* and *adjusting the accounts?*

7. Why is a *post-closing trial balance* prepared?

8. Explain why the revenue, expense, and withdrawals accounts are called *temporary* or *nominal* accounts.

9. Why are closing entries necessary?

10. What is the difference between the *Expense and Revenue Summary* account and the *Income Summary* account? How are these accounts used?

11. Are reversing entries required? Why or why not?

12. Summarize the steps in the accounting process.

*13. When a company pays in advance for 6 months of advertising, the transaction must be recorded in the Prepaid Advertising account, since an asset has been acquired. Comment on this statement.

### QUESTIONS FOR FURTHER THOUGHT

1. Comment on this statement: If the total debits from the unadjusted trial balance are added to the total debits from the adjustments column on a worksheet, the result will be the total debits for the adjusted trial balance.

2. Depreciation Expense does not appear on an unadjusted trial balance on a worksheet, yet an adjustment requires that depreciation be recorded. How is this situation handled?

3. Comment on this statement: By using a worksheet, accountants are assured that all errors will be found, since a worksheet must balance.

4. The initial totals of the income statement debit column on a worksheet will not equal the credit column totals. Nor will the initial totals of the balance sheet debit column equal the credit column totals. Why not?

5. What are reversing entries? Why are they necessary?

*6. If a company uses reversing entries, how does it determine which adjusting entries to reverse?

## OBJECTIVE ASSIGNMENT

*True/False*   Indicate whether each statement below is *true* or *false* by placing a *T* or an *F* in the space provided.

_____ 1. Worksheets are not part of the permanent accounting records of a business entity.

_____ 2. Interim statements are prepared informally from the worksheet on a monthly or quarterly basis.

_____ 3. Unearned Rental Revenue is an example of a temporary, or nominal, account.

_____ 4. The post-closing trial balance is prepared directly from the adjusted trial balance.

_____ 5. The adjusting and closing entries are typically journalized after the worksheet is completed.

*Multiple Choice*   Select the best choice to complete each statement or answer each question below. Write the letter corresponding to your choice in the space provided.

_____ 1. Worksheets are prepared because:
   a. They are required by generally accepted accounting principles.
   b. They aid in the preparation of the financial statements, adjusting entries, and closing entries.
   c. They constitute a permanent record of all adjusting entries made for the period.
   d. They are necessary for the preparation of the financial statements.
   e. None of the above.

_____ 2. If the initial sum of the balance sheet credit column on a worksheet is greater than the initial sum of the balance sheet debit column, then:
   a. The sum of the income statement credit column must exceed the sum of the income statement debit column.
   b. A loss occurred during the period.
   c. An error was made on the worksheet.
   d. All of the above.
   e. None of the above.

_____ 3. Some firms adjust their accounts and close their books only on an annual basis. For these firms:
   a. Worksheets may be prepared on an interim basis.
   b. Worksheets are not needed.
   c. Worksheets are prepared only on an annual basis.
   d. Worksheets are not prepared.
   e. None of the above.

_____ 4. On an adjusted trial balance, the Capital account reflects
   a. the results of adjusting entries
   b. the increase to revenue and expense
   c. the period end balance
   d. the beginning-of-the-period balance
   e. none of the above

_____ 5. Closing entries reduce the following type of accounts to a zero balance at period end:
   a. revenues
   b. expenses
   c. income summary
   d. withdrawals
   e. all of the above

_____ 6. A final check on the adjusting and closing process is provided by
   a. the worksheet
   b. the financial statements
   c. the post-closing trial balance
   d. the adjusting trial balance
   e. none of the above

_____ 7. If the last item on a trial balance reads "Abrems, Capital," this must be
   a. the post-closing trial balance
   b. the unadjusted trial balance
   c. the adjusted trial balance
   d. the reversed trial balance
   e. none of the above

_____ 8. If a trial balance were to be prepared on the first day of the new year, and the account Salaries Expense had a credit balance, you would know that:
   a. The trial balance is a post-closing trial balance.
   b. The adjusting entries have been recorded.
   c. A reversing entry has been made.
   d. The trial balance is an adjusted trial balance.
   e. None of the above.

_____ 9. Reversing entries are
   a. optional
   b. made to record a change in corporate objectives
   c. required by generally accepted accounting principles
   d. made prior to preparing a post-closing trial balance
   e. none of the above

_____ 10. Which of the following comes first in the accounting process?
   a. preparation of an unadjusted trial balance
   b. worksheet preparation
   c. journalizing external transactions
   d. preparation of an adjusted trial balance
   e. none of the above

## EXERCISES

_Note:_ Exercises marked with an asterisk relate to material contained in the appendix.

1† **Exercise 1:** Preparing a Worksheet

Presented below are the accounts of Post Consulting Service prior to the Dec. 31, 1998, year-end adjustments.

| | | | |
|---|---|---|---|
| Revenues Earned.............. | $175 | Unearned Revenue ............. | $40 |
| Office Equipment .............. | 100 | Accounts Payable.............. | 35 |
| Post, Capital................. | 70 | Accounts Receivable ........... | 30 |
| Salary Expense ............... | 65 | Post, Withdrawals.............. | 25 |
| Office Supplies on Hand........ | 60 | Cash ........................ | 20 |
| Accumulated Depreciation ...... | 50 | Rent Expense................. | 15 |
| Prepaid Insurance ............. | 45 | Miscellaneous Expense......... | 10 |

The following data are available for the Dec. 31, 1998, year-end adjustments:

| | |
|---|---|
| Accrued salaries ............................. | $25 |
| Depreciation................................. | 20 |
| Expired insurance ........................... | 15 |
| Unearned revenue earned during the year.......... | 10 |
| Office supplies on hand....................... | 5 |

Prepare and complete a worksheet.

▶ _(Check Figure: Total adjusted trial balance = $415)_

† The numbers in the margin refer to the Learning Objectives.

1   **Exercise 2:** Completing a Worksheet

Presented below is a worksheet from which a number of figures are missing. However, sufficient information is given for you to determine the missing figures and complete the worksheet.

**HANDLEY COMPANY**
**Worksheet**
**Year Ended December 31, 1998**

| | Unadjusted Trial Balance | | Adjustments | | Adjusted Trial Balance | | Income Statement | | Balance Sheet | |
|---|---|---|---|---|---|---|---|---|---|---|
| | Debit | Credit | Debit | Credit | Debit | Credit | Debit | Credit | Debit | Credit |
| Cash | | | | | | | | | 4 | |
| Accounts Receivable | 24 | | | | | | | | | |
| Prepaid Advertising | 12 | | | 4 | 8 | | | | | |
| Office Supplies on Hand | | | | 2 | 4 | | | | 4 | |
| Office Equipment | | | | | | | | | 30 | |
| Accumulated Depreciation | | 10 | | | | | | | | |
| Accounts Payable | | | | | | 14 | | | | |
| Salaries Payable | | | | 8 | | 8 | | | | 8 |
| Unearned Revenue | | 8 | | | | | | | | 6 |
| Handley, Capital | | 28 | | | | | | | | |
| Handley, Withdrawals | | | | | | | | | 16 | |
| Fees Earned | | 60 | | 2 | | | | | | |
| Salary Expense | | | | | 36 | | | | | |
| Advertising Expense | | | | | | | 4 | | | |
| Office Supplies Expense | | | | | | | | | | |
| Depreciation Expense | | | | | 6 | | | | | |
| Totals | 120 | | | 22 | 134 | | 48 | | 86 | |
| Net Income | | | | | | | | 62 | | |

▶ *(Check Figure: Net income = $14)*

2   **Exercise 3:** Preparing an Interim Income Statement

Presented below are the income statement columns of the October and November 1998 worksheets for Lennarz Biomedical Company. Use this information to prepare the November 1998 income statement.

**LENNARZ BIOMEDICAL COMPANY**
**Worksheet Income Statement Columns**

| | October 1998 | | November 1998 | |
|---|---|---|---|---|
| Biomedical Research Revenue . . . . . . . | | $56,100 | | $75,300 |
| Salary Expense. . . . . . . . . . . . . . . . . . . | $22,400 | | $31,200 | |
| Rent Expense . . . . . . . . . . . . . . . . . . . . | 1,800 | | 2,400 | |
| Depreciation Expense. . . . . . . . . . . . . . | 7,200 | | 9,000 | |
| Office Supplies Expense. . . . . . . . . . . . | 1,300 | | 2,400 | |
| Utilities Expense . . . . . . . . . . . . . . . . . . | 700 | | 1,200 | |
| Totals . . . . . . . . . . . . . . . . . . . . . . | $33,400 | $56,100 | $46,200 | $75,300 |
| Net Income . . . . . . . . . . . . . . . . . . . . . . | 22,700 | | 29,100 | |
| | $56,100 | $56,100 | $75,300 | $75,300 |

▶ *(Check Figure: Net income = $6,400)*

3 **Exercise 4:** Preparing Closing Entries

The T-accounts listed below are representations of the general ledger accounts of Jim Gonering, CPA, after the closing entries for the year ended Dec. 31, 1998, have been made:

| Gonering, Capital | | | | | Gonering, Withdrawals | | | |
|---|---|---|---|---|---|---|---|---|
| | | Bal. | 35,000 | | Bal. 9,000 | | GJ 3 | 9,000 |
| GJ 3 | 9,000 | GJ 3 | 23,000 | | | | | |
| | | Bal. | 49,000 | | | | | |

| Income Summary | | | |
|---|---|---|---|
| GJ 3 | 39,000 | GJ 3 | 62,000 |
| GJ 3 | 23,000 | | |

Prepare the four closing entries that were made on Dec. 31, 1998, in the general journal. The expenses consist of salary expense, $27,400, and rent expense, $11,600. Accounting fees earned amounts to $62,000.

4 **Exercise 5:** Preparing Closing Entries and a Post-Closing Trial Balance

Here is the adjusted trial balance of the Benton Company:

**THE BENTON COMPANY**
**Adjusted Trial Balance**
**January 31, 1998**

| | | |
|---|---|---|
| Cash | $ 1,400 | |
| Accounts Receivable | 2,300 | |
| Prepaid Rent | 900 | |
| Office Supplies on Hand | 1,500 | |
| Office Equipment | 7,800 | |
| Accumulated Depreciation | | $ 3,200 |
| Accounts Payable | | 1,200 |
| Salaries Payable | | 700 |
| Benton, Capital | | 7,500 |
| Benton, Withdrawals | 1,700 | |
| Service Fees Earned | | 8,300 |
| Miscellaneous Income | | 1,100 |
| Salary Expense | 3,200 | |
| Office Supplies Expense | 2,100 | |
| Depreciation Expense | 600 | |
| Rent Expense | 500 | |
| Total | $22,000 | $22,000 |

a. Prepare the closing entries for Jan. 31, 1998.
b. Prepare a post-closing trial balance for Jan. 31, 1998.

▶ *(Check Figure: Total post-closing trial balance = $13,900)*

7  8   **Exercise 6:** Adjusting the Supplies Account

At the start of the current year, American, Continental, and National Companies each had $7,500 of supplies on hand. The three companies use different accounting procedures for recording supplies. American and National show this beginning balance in the Supplies on Hand account, but Continental reflects the beginning balance in the Supplies Expense account. American debits the account Supplies on Hand when supplies are acquired, while Continental and National follow the policy of debiting Supplies Expense upon acquisition.

Each of the three companies acquired $45,200 of supplies at various times throughout the year, and each has $9,600 of supplies on hand at year-end.

Prepare the appropriate adjusting entry for each company.

7  8   **Exercise 7:** Analyzing Accounts

The following selected accounts from the Time Company's general ledger appear below:

| | | |
|---|---:|---:|
| Supplies on Hand | $1,500 | |
| Unearned Revenue | 1,200 | $ 7,200 |
| Salaries Payable | 5,500 | 5,500 |
| Revenues | | 71,000 |
| Salary Expense | | 5,500 |
| Supplies Expense | 6,200 | 1,500 |

Notice that both debits and credits appear.

a. Assume that Time Company were to acquire $2,000 of supplies. How would Time record this entry?

b. Assume that Time Company were to receive $1,000 for services to be performed next year. How would Time record this entry?

c. Expense accounts have a normal debit balance. Why, then, does the Salary Expense account have a credit of $5,500?

7  8   **\*Exercise 8:** Adjusting Entries and Accounting Policy

Presented below are three transactions made by Jensen Cleaners during the year 1998.

Apr. 1   Acquired cleaning supplies in the amount of $2,600. On Dec. 31, 1998, a count of the supplies remaining on hand is $1,100.

Aug. 1   Received $3,600 from GTO Corporation for cleaning janitorial uniforms over the next 3 years.

Nov. 1   Paid $2,400 for rent for the next 12 months.

a. Assume that Jensen records these three transactions in the following three accounts, and record the appropriate adjusting entries for Dec. 31, 1998:

Office Supplies on Hand
Prepaid Rent
Unearned Cleaning Revenues

b. Now, assume that Jensen records these three transactions in the following three accounts, and record the appropriate adjusting entries for Dec. 31, 1998:

Office Supplies Expense
Rent Expense
Cleaning Revenues

c. If Jensen were to use reversing entries, which set of entries, (a) or (b), would have to be reversed? Why?

7  8  **\*Exercise 9:** Reversing Entries

Presented below are a number of adjusting entries.

| | 1998 | | | |
|---|---|---|---|---|
| a. | Dec. 31 | Office Supplies on Hand...................... | 6,100 | |
| | | Office Supplies Expense ................... | | 6,100 |
| | | To record office supplies on hand at year end. | | |
| b. | 31 | Unearned Subscription Revenue ................ | 1,900 | |
| | | Subscription Revenue ..................... | | 1,900 |
| | | To record subscription revenue earned at year end. | | |
| c. | 31 | Rent Expense ............................... | 600 | |
| | | Prepaid Rent ............................ | | 600 |
| | | To record rent expense for the year. | | |
| d. | 31 | Salary Expense............................. | 1,600 | |
| | | Salaries Payable ........................ | | 1,600 |
| | | To record accrued salaries. | | |
| e. | 31 | Interest Receivable .......................... | 700 | |
| | | Interest Income ......................... | | 700 |
| | | To record accrued interest. | | |

Indicate which of these adjusting entries will require reversing entries when the new accounting year starts on Jan. 1, 1999. Identify these adjusting entries by letter.

## PROBLEMS: SET A

*Note:* Problems marked with an asterisk relate to material contained in the appendix.

1†  **Problem A1:** Preparing a Worksheet

The unadjusted trial balance of Dan Dillon Real Estate Agency for the year ended Dec. 31, 1998, is presented below:

| | | |
|---|---|---|
| Cash ............................................... | $  800 | |
| Commissions Receivable................................ | 1,400 | |
| Prepaid Insurance ...................................... | 500 | |
| Office Supplies on Hand ................................ | 600 | |
| Office Equipment ...................................... | 3,200 | |
| Accumulated Depreciation: Office Equipment................. | | $  1,000 |
| Accounts Payable...................................... | | 700 |
| Dillon, Capital ........................................ | | 4,200 |
| Dillon, Withdrawals..................................... | 8,000 | |
| Commissions Earned.................................... | | 20,000 |
| Office Salaries Expense................................. | 9,500 | |
| Rent Expense......................................... | 1,200 | |
| Advertising Expense.................................... | 400 | |
| Telephone Expense .................................... | 300 | |
| Totals ............................................... | $25,900 | $25,900 |

† The numbers in the margin refer to the Learning Objectives.

The following information pertaining to the year-end adjustments is available:

a. A physical count of the office supplies on hand on Dec. 31, 1998, amounts to $200.
b. Insurance in the amount of $100 has expired.
c. Depreciation of the office equipment for the year is $500.
d. Office salaries accrued on Dec. 31, 1998, amount to $300.

**Required:**

Enter the unadjusted trial balance on a worksheet, record the required adjustments, and complete the worksheet.

▶ *(Check Figure: Net income = $7,300)*

1 3 **Problem A2:** Preparing a Worksheet, Adjusting, and Closing Entries

The May 31, 1998, trial balance for West Coast Surveyors is presented at the top of the facing page. The following information pertaining to the year-end adjustments is available:

a. The $3,600 prepaid advertising represents an expenditure made on Nov. 1, 1997, for monthly advertising over the next 18 months.
b. A count of the engineering supplies on hand at May 31, 1998, amounts to $900.
c. Depreciation on the surveying equipment amounts to $1,600.
d. One-third of the unearned survey revenue has been earned at year-end.
e. At year-end salaries in the amount of $1,400 have accrued.
f. Interest on the note payable in the amount of $600 has accrued at year-end.

| | | |
|---|---:|---:|
| Cash | $ 2,100 | |
| Accounts Receivable | 9,300 | |
| Prepaid Advertising | 3,600 | |
| Engineering Supplies on Hand | 2,700 | |
| Survey Equipment | 18,900 | |
| Accumulated Depreciation: Survey Equipment | | $ 6,400 |
| Accounts Payable | | 1,900 |
| Unearned Survey Revenues | | 1,200 |
| Note Payable | | 5,000 |
| Stevenson, Capital | | 11,200 |
| Stevenson, Withdrawals | 7,000 | |
| Survey Revenues Earned | | 65,100 |
| Salary Expense | 32,700 | |
| Rent Expense | 9,600 | |
| Insurance Expense | 2,500 | |
| Utilities Expense | 1,600 | |
| Miscellaneous Expense | 800 | |
| Totals | $90,800 | $90,800 |

**Required:**

1. Record the unadjusted trial balance on the appropriate columns of a worksheet.
2. Prepare the appropriate adjustments on the worksheet and complete the worksheet.

   ▶ *(Check Figure: Total adjusted trial balance = $94,400)*
3. Prepare the general journal adjusting and closing entries.

**3**  **Problem A3:** Preparing Closing Entries

Listed below are the accounts taken from the Dec. 31, 1998, adjusted trial balance of Charlton Company:

| | | | |
|---|---|---|---|
| Accounts Receivable......... | $ 2,600 | Interest Payable............. | $   400 |
| Supplies Expense ........... | 7,100 | Cash...................... | 1,400 |
| Salary Expense............. | 22,700 | Repairs Expense........... | 300 |
| Fees Earned ............... | 81,300 | Accounts Payable .......... | 1,900 |
| Prepaid Insurance........... | 3,200 | Telephone Expense ......... | 800 |
| Depreciation Expense........ | 2,500 | Utilities Expense ............ | 200 |
| Supplies on Hand ........... | 1,600 | Unearned Fees ............. | 2,100 |
| Salaries Payable............. | 3,100 | Interest Expense ............ | 3,000 |
| Office Equipment............ | 55,200 | Charlton, Capital ............ | 3,400 |
| Prepaid Advertising......... | 700 | Note Payable............... | 25,000 |
| Charlton, Withdrawals........ | 15,000 | Miscellaneous Expense....... | 900 |

**Required:**

Prepare the appropriate year-end closing entries.

▶ *(Check Figure: Charlton, ending capital = $32,200)*

**1  3  4  6**  **Problem A4:** Preparing a Worksheet and Completing the Year-End Procedures

Presented below is the unadjusted trial balance of the Melton Company for Dec. 31, 1998, followed by data pertaining to the year-end adjustments.

| | | |
|---|---|---|
| Cash ............................................. | $  7,600 | |
| Accounts Receivable ................................. | 28,900 | |
| Prepaid Rent....................................... | 7,200 | |
| Office Supplies on Hand.............................. | 5,700 | |
| Land ............................................. | 47,000 | |
| Office Building...................................... | 125,000 | |
| Accumulated Depreciation: Office Building ................ | | $ 41,300 |
| Office Equipment ................................... | 87,000 | |
| Accumulated Depreciation: Office Equipment............... | | 21,200 |
| Accounts Payable.................................... | | 11,700 |
| Note Payable ...................................... | | 140,000 |
| Melton, Capital ..................................... | | 143,500 |
| Melton, Withdrawals.................................. | 24,000 | |
| Professional Fees Earned ............................. | | 225,600 |
| Salary Expense...................................... | 161,900 | |
| Travel Expense...................................... | 42,700 | |
| Advertising Expense.................................. | 21,500 | |
| Insurance Expense................................... | 14,000 | |
| Utilities Expense .................................... | 6,200 | |
| Miscellaneous Expense ............................... | 4,600 | |
| Totals ........................................... | $583,300 | $583,300 |

**Additional Data:**

a. One-half of the prepaid rent has expired.
b. Office supplies remaining on hand at year-end amount to $2,500.
c. Depreciation on the office building and the office equipment amount to $2,800 and $5,200, respectively.
d. Accrued salaries at year-end amount to $2,700.
e. Interest amounting to $16,800 has accrued on the note payable. Interest on the note payable will be paid annually every Jan. 15 until the note matures on Jan. 15, 1999.

**Required:**

1. Record the unadjusted trial balance in the appropriate columns of a worksheet.
2. Prepare the appropriate adjustments on the worksheet and complete the worksheet.

   ▶ *(Check Figure: Total adjusted trial balance = $610,800)*

3. Prepare an income statement, a statement of owner's equity, and a balance sheet.
4. Prepare the general journal adjusting and closing entries.
5. Enter the unadjusted account balances into general ledger accounts. Post the adjusting and closing entries.
6. Prepare a post-closing trial balance.

**\*Problem A5:** Adjusting Reversing Entries

Listed below are three transactions made by the Orlando Company during 1998:

July 1    Received a check from Mrs. Tanzey in the amount of $2,700 for professional services to be rendered over the next 18 months.

Oct. 1    Paid $1,350 for advertising to be provided for the next 9 months.

Dec. 31   As of Dec. 31, 1998, $2,900 of salaries had accrued. Payday is on Friday, Jan. 5, 1999, and $6,200 in salaries were paid on that date.

**Required:**

1. Assume that these transactions were initially recorded in balance sheet accounts, and record the three adjusting entries required. Then record the Jan. 5, 1999, payment of salaries.
2. Now assume that these transactions were initially recorded in income statement accounts, and record the three adjusting entries required. Then record the Jan. 1, 1999, reversing entries and the Jan. 5, 1999, payment of salaries.

7 8   **\*Problem A6:** Preparing Adjusting Entries

Presented below is the Jan. 1, 1999, trial balance of the Oldtimer Retirement Home. It was prepared after the reversing entries were made but before any of the 1998 transactions were recorded. (Companies do not prepare this type of trial balance; we are using it here to develop your understanding of adjusting and reversing entries.)

The retirement home was acquired on July 1, 1996, and has an estimated useful life of 40 years. An insurance policy was acquired on the same date, covering the building and the contents. At that time the entire 3-year premium was paid in advance.

No office supplies were acquired during 1998. The balance in the Office Supplies on Hand account on Jan. 1, 1999, represents one-third of the amount on hand at the same date 1 year previously.

**OLDTIMER RETIREMENT HOME**
**Trial Balance**
**January 1, 1999**

| | | |
|---|---:|---:|
| Cash | $ 12,800 | |
| Accounts Receivable | 10,600 | |
| Prepaid Insurance | 1,500 | |
| Office Supplies on Hand | 900 | |
| Land | 10,000 | |
| Retirement Home | 230,000 | |
| Accumulated Depreciation: Retirement Home | | $ 15,000 |
| Accounts Payable | | 3,700 |
| Mortgage Payable | | 195,000 |
| Oldtimer, Capital | | 51,400 |
| Retirement Fees Earned | | 2,600 |
| Salary Expense | | 2,200 |
| Linen Supplies Expense | 4,600 | |
| Interest Expense | | 500 |
| Totals | $270,400 | $270,400 |

**Required:**

Oldtimer Retirement Home made seven adjusting entries on Dec. 31, 1998. From the information presented, record these entries in general journal form without explanations.

## PROBLEMS: SET B

1† **Problem B1:** Preparing a Worksheet

Blacker Janitorial Service Company has just completed its first year of operations and presents its unadjusted Dec. 31, 1998, trial balance below:

| | | |
|---|---:|---:|
| Cash | $ 800 | |
| Accounts Receivable | 1,100 | |
| Prepaid Advertising | 600 | |
| Janitorial Supplies on Hand | 1,300 | |
| Janitorial Equipment | 2,500 | |
| Notes Payable | | $ 1,500 |
| Blacker, Capital | | 2,400 |
| Blacker, Withdrawals | 5,000 | |
| Janitorial Service Revenue | | 22,300 |
| Salary Expense | 13,500 | |
| Rent Expense | 700 | |
| Insurance Expense | 500 | |
| Repairs Expense | 200 | |
| Totals | $26,200 | $26,200 |

Information pertaining to the year-end adjustments follows:

a. Janitorial supplies remaining at the end of the year amounted to $600 as determined by a physical count.
b. As of Dec. 31, 1998, $400 of salaries has accrued.
c. Depreciation on the janitorial equipment amounts to $200.
d. One-third of the prepaid advertising has expired.

† The numbers in the margin refer to the Learning Objectives.

**Required:**

Enter the unadjusted trial balance on a worksheet, record the required adjustments, and complete the worksheet.

▶ *(Check Figure: Net income = $5,900)*

1 3 **Problem B2:** Preparing a Worksheet, Adjusting Entries, and Closing Entries

The unadjusted trial balance for the Greentown Service Company as of Feb. 28, 1998, is presented below. The following information pertaining to the year-end adjustments is available:

a. One-fourth of the prepaid rent has expired.
b. Office supplies in the amount of $1,100 remain on hand at year-end.
c. Depreciation on the building amounts to $2,700 for the year. Depreciation on office equipment amounts to $5,300 for the year.
d. Unearned service revenues of $1,400 have been earned by year-end.
e. Salaries in the amount of $1,600 are accrued at year-end.
f. Interest amounting to $6,600 has accrued on the note payable.

| | | |
|---|---:|---:|
| Cash | $ 1,700 | |
| Accounts Receivable | 5,200 | |
| Prepaid Rent | 2,400 | |
| Office Supplies on Hand | 1,900 | |
| Land | 31,000 | |
| Building | 45,100 | |
| Accumulated Depreciation: Building | | $ 23,400 |
| Office Equipment | 74,700 | |
| Accumulated Depreciation: Office Equipment | | 21,900 |
| Accounts Payable | | 14,600 |
| Unearned Service Revenue | | 9,300 |
| Note Payable | | 55,000 |
| Newton, Capital | | 22,900 |
| Newton, Withdrawals | 27,000 | |
| Service Revenue Earned | | 226,800 |
| Salary Expense | 142,300 | |
| Advertising Expense | 21,200 | |
| Insurance Expense | 8,300 | |
| Travel Expense | 6,100 | |
| Utilities Expense | 3,500 | |
| Telephone Expense | 2,200 | |
| Miscellaneous Expense | 1,300 | |
| Totals | $373,900 | $373,900 |

**Required:**

1. Record the unadjusted trial balance on the appropriate columns of a worksheet.
2. Prepare the appropriate adjustments on the worksheet and complete the worksheet.

   ▶ *(Check Figure: Total adjusted trial balance = $390,100)*
3. Prepare the general journal adjusting and closing entries.

## 3  Problem B3: Preparing Closing Entries

The following accounts were obtained from the adjusted trial balance of Golden State Advertising Agency as of Dec. 31, 1998:

| | | | |
|---|---:|---|---:|
| Accounts Payable | $ 4,700 | Accounts Receivable | $ 5,300 |
| Miscellaneous Expense | 1,200 | Hamilton, Withdrawals | 6,500 |
| Rent Expense | 7,200 | Building | 130,000 |
| Accumulated Depreciation | 16,100 | Salaries Payable | 1,700 |
| Notes Payable | 85,000 | Depreciation Expense | 5,900 |
| Office Supplies on Hand | 3,700 | Telephone Expense | 1,400 |
| Interest Payable | 1,200 | Equipment | 60,000 |
| Office Supplies Expense | 2,300 | Utilities Expense | 3,300 |
| Fees Earned | 81,200 | Interest Expense | 10,200 |
| Salary Expense | 44,300 | Cash | 2,900 |
| Prepaid Rent | 2,100 | Land | 35,000 |
| Hamilton, Capital | 134,400 | | |

**Required:**

Prepare the appropriate year-end closing entries.

▶ *(Check Figure: Hamilton ending capital = $133,300)*

## 1 3 4 6  Problem B4: Preparing a Worksheet and Completing the Year-End Procedures

The Boston Company prepared the following trial balance and provided the additional adjustment data for the year ended Dec. 31, 1998:

| | | |
|---|---:|---:|
| Cash | $ 3,700 | |
| Accounts Receivable | 23,500 | |
| Prepaid Insurance | 4,800 | |
| Store Supplies on Hand | 6,200 | |
| Land | 50,000 | |
| Store Building | 250,000 | |
| Accumulated Depreciation: Store Building | | $ 47,500 |
| Store Equipment | 210,000 | |
| Accumulated Depreciation: Store Equipment | | 65,300 |
| Accounts Payable | | 12,800 |
| Note Payable | | 150,000 |
| Boston, Capital | | 250,000 |
| Boston, Withdrawals | 60,000 | |
| Service Revenues Earned | | 372,600 |
| Salary Expense | 165,700 | |
| Professional Training Expense | 78,200 | |
| Storage Rental Expense | 19,000 | |
| Repairs Expense | 12,100 | |
| Utilities Expense | 8,600 | |
| Telephone Expense | 6,400 | |
| Totals | $898,200 | $898,200 |

**Additional Data:**

a. Insurance in the amount of $1,200 has expired.
b. During the year $2,100 of the store supplies have been used.
c. Depreciation on the store building and the store equipment amount to $7,100 and $15,400, respectively.
d. At year-end, salaries in the amount of $4,500 have accrued.
e. Interest on the long-term note payable amounts to $15,000 for the year.

**Required:**

1. Record the unadjusted trial balance in the appropriate columns of a worksheet.
2. Prepare the appropriate adjustments on the worksheet and complete the worksheet.

   ▶ *(Check Figure: Total adjusted trial balance = $940,200)*
3. Prepare an income statement, a statement of owner's equity, and a balance sheet.
4. Prepare the general journal adjusting and closing entries.
5. Enter the unadjusted account balances into general ledger accounts. Post the adjusting and closing entries.
6. Prepare a post-closing trial balance.

7  8   **\*Problem B5:** Adjusting and Reversing Entries

Three 1998 transactions of the Bently Company are described below:

Apr. 1   Bently paid the Martin Leasing Agency $3,600 in advance to rent certain equipment over the next 12 months.

July 1   A check in the amount of $7,200 was received from Constant Consultants for professional services to be rendered over the next 24 months.

Dec. 31   Salaries in the amount of $2,700 were accrued. On Friday, Jan. 5, 1999, salaries in the amount of $7,100 were paid.

**Required:**

1. Record the three adjusting entries required from the preceding facts, assuming that the transactions were initially recorded in balance sheet accounts. Then record the Jan. 5, 1999, payment of salaries.
2. Record the three adjusting entries required from the preceding facts, assuming that the transactions were initially recorded in income statement accounts. Then record the Jan. 1, 1999, reversing entries and the Jan. 5, 1999, payment of salaries.

7  8   **\*Problem B6:** Preparing Adjusting Entries

The Jan. 1, 1999, trial balance of the Brandon Cleaning Company is presented below. The Jan. 1 reversing entries have been recorded in the accounts, but no external entries have yet been made. (Companies do not actually prepare this type of trial balance; we are using it here to reinforce the concepts of adjusting and reversing entries.)

Brandon Cleaning began operations on July 1, 1998. At that time a 2-year contract was signed with Tampa Advertising Agency to provide monthly advertising in the local newspapers, radio, and television stations. The 2-year fee was paid in advance.

**BRANDON CLEANING COMPANY**
Trial Balance
January 1, 1999

| | | |
|---|---:|---:|
| Cash | $ 700 | |
| Notes Receivable | 3,000 | |
| Accounts Receivable | 1,000 | |
| Prepaid Advertising | 1,800 | |
| Cleaning Equipment | 3,100 | |
| Accumulated Depreciation: Cleaning Equipment | | $ 500 |
| Accounts Payable | | 1,600 |
| Brandon Capital | | 6,900 |
| Cleaning Revenue | | 1,500 |
| Salary Expense | | 1,000 |
| Cleaning Supplies Expense | 1,200 | |
| Rent Expense | 500 | |
| Interest Income | 200 | |
| Totals | $11,500 | $11,500 |

**Required:**

Brandon Cleaning Company made seven adjusting entries on Dec. 31, 1998. From the information presented, record these entries in general journal form without explanations.

## DECISION PROBLEM

You are a loan officer of the First National Bank. Your first appointment on Jan. 5, 1999, is with a research scientist, Dr. Lennarz. For the past 5 years, Dr. Lennarz has owned and operated a research laboratory and wishes to obtain a $50,000 loan from your bank to expand his research program.

Preliminary investigations appear favorable for the loan. All that remains is to examine the laboratory's financial data; if those are satisfactory, the loan will be approved. Aware of its responsibility to invest its resources prudently, your bank has established the following tests that must be satisfied before any loan can be granted:

1. The current assets must be twice the current liabilities.
2. Long-term debt may never exceed 60% of year-end total assets.
3. Net income must be greater than 15% of revenues.
4. Net income must exceed 10% of the year-end total assets.

Promptly at 9:00 a.m. and after brief pleasantries, Dr. Lennarz provides you with a neatly typed financial statement derived from his checkbook. In addition to the information on the financial statement, you determine that the research laboratory owes $1,000 for laboratory supplies as of Dec. 31, 1998, and has receivables from various hospitals amounting to $5,000 as of the same date.

---

### DR. LENNARZ RESEARCH LABORATORY
#### Financial Statement
#### December 31, 1998

Cash Receipts:

| | |
|---|---:|
| Cash at start of business Jan. 1, 1994 | $      0 |
| Initial investment by Dr. Lennarz, Jan. 1, 1994 | 5,000 |
| Cash received from research fees 1/1/94 – 12/31/98 | 750,000 |
| Note payable received July 1, 1994, due June 30, 1999 | 10,000 |
| Mortgage payable received Jan. 1, 1994 | 100,000 |
| Total cash taken into the business | $865,000 |

Cash Expenditures:

| | |
|---|---:|
| For Salaries | $550,000 |
| Land | 40,000 |
| Building | 120,000 |
| Office Equipment | 30,000 |
| Withdrawals | 50,000 |
| Reduction of Mortgage | 3,000 |
| Interest on Mortgage | 9,000 |
| Interest on Note, $100 due on Jan. 1, 1999 | 500 |
| Advertising, of which $1,000 applies to 1999 | 16,000 |
| Supplies, of which $250 are on hand on Dec. 31, 1998 | 7,750 |
| Insurance | 9,000 |
| Utilities | 6,000 |
| Total cash spent by the business | $841,250 |

| | |
|---|---:|
| Cash at end of business Dec. 31, 1998 | $ 23,750 |

---

You inform Dr. Lennarz that you will call him tomorrow with your decision, after you have reviewed the financial information he has provided.

You find that Dr. Lennarz has not maintained adequate accounting records. What you must do is to convert his records into a proper set of financial statements before you can apply your bank's four tests. You can assume that revenues and expenses are earned and incurred evenly over the 5-year time period. You also can assume that depreciation on the building would be $3,000 per year and on the equipment, $2,000 per year.

### Required:

1. Prepare an income statement for the 5-year period and an income statement for 1998.
2. Prepare a statement of owner's equity.
3. Prepare a balance sheet.
4. Compute values for the four tests and determine if the loan should be granted.

## ETHICS CASE

Tracy Hamilton is the assistant comptroller for Napa Valley Technology, Inc., a large California computer software company. Several weeks ago Kevin Nanceworth, vice president of production, approached Tracy with a request that she complete an accounting assignment for the executive MBA course that Kevin was taking at Cal State University.

Tracy suggested several resource materials that Kevin might use to help him with the assignment, but did not complete the assignment for him.

Several weeks later Tracy overheard a phone conversation between Kevin and a classmate in which several members of the class were going to complete segments of a large accounting assignment and share their solutions by exchanging computer disks. The following week Tracy noticed that two company secretaries were busy for one full day working on Kevin's MBA accounting assignment.

Napa Valley pays Kevin's tuition to the Cal State University's Executive MBA program at a cost of $14,000 per year for the two-year program, and allows Kevin to attend classes all day, every other Friday. Classes are also held on alternate Saturdays.

**Required:**

What, if anything, should Tracy do?

---

## COMPREHENSIVE PROBLEMS

1 3 4 6† **Comprehensive Problem 1:** Completing the Accounting Cycle

Joan Adams, after two decades of service to Software Incorporated, retired on July 1, 1998, to establish the Adams Computer Advisory Service. The following transactions occurred during the first month of operations:

July 1 Adams established an account for the new company by removing $9,500 from her personal account and depositing it in the name of the Adams Computer Advisory Service.

1 Obtained office space by paying $4,200 to the Big Time Rental Agency for a 6-month lease.

2 Acquired office equipment costing $17,500 and office supplies amounting to $3,100 by paying $2,600 cash and issuing a note payable for $18,000 due June 30, 2002.

3 Paid $800 for advertising for the next 4 months.

5 Was advanced $9,000 by BMI Corporation for consulting services over the next 6 months.

8 Acquired office supplies in the amount of $4,200 on account.

10 Billed clients $15,000 for services rendered.

14 Paid for repairs to office equipment, $700.

15 Paid salaries to employees, $6,200.

21 Received $2,400 cash from Arther Wateryoung & Company for services rendered this date.

23 Paid $1,500 on account for office supplies acquired on July 8.

25 Collected $8,100 from clients billed on July 10.

25 Withdrew $5,000 from the agency for personal use.

27 Paid telephone bill, $200.

28 Billed clients $11,000 for computer consulting services completed.

30 Paid $2,700 for travel expenses.

† The numbers in the margin refer to the Learning Objectives.

**Required:**

1. Establish the following accounts in a general ledger using the account numbers given.

| Account | No. | Account | No. |
|---------|-----|---------|-----|
| Cash | 110 | Adams, Capital | 310 |
| Accounts Receivable | 120 | Adams, Withdrawals | 320 |
| Office Supplies on Hand | 130 | Income Summary | 330 |
| Prepaid Rent | 140 | Consulting Fees Earned | 410 |
| Prepaid Advertising | 150 | Salary Expense | 510 |
| Office Equipment | 160 | Office Supplies Expense | 520 |
| Accumulated Depreciation: | | Rent Expense | 530 |
|   Office Equipment | 165 | Advertising Expense | 540 |
| Accounts Payable | 210 | Depreciation Expense | 550 |
| Salaries Payable | 220 | Repairs Expense | 560 |
| Unearned Consulting Fees | 230 | Telephone Expense | 570 |
| Interest Payable | 240 | Travel Expense | 580 |
| Note Payable | 250 | Interest Expense | 590 |

2. Record the transactions for the month of July in a general journal (page 1) and post the entries to the general ledger. (Use balance sheet accounts to record those transactions that will later require adjustments.)
3. Prepare a trial balance on a worksheet and record the following adjustments on the worksheet.
   a. One-sixth of the rent has expired.
   b. One-fourth of the prepaid advertising has expired.
   c. Office supplies used during the month amount to $2,900.
   d. Depreciation on the office equipment amounts to $300.
   e. Unearned consulting fees in the amount of $1,500 have been earned.
   f. Salaries of $5,300 have accrued.
   g. Interest in the amount of $100 has accrued and will be paid on Jan. 2, 1999.
4. Complete the worksheet and prepare an income statement, a statement of owner's equity, and a balance sheet.

   ▶ *(Check Figure: Adjusted trial balance total = $73,300)*
5. Record the adjusting and closing entries in the general journal (page 2) and post the entries to the general ledger.
6. Prepare a post-closing trial balance.
7. Prepare the salaries and interest reversing entries in the general journal (page 3) and post them to the general ledger.

1 3 4 6 **Comprehensive Problem 2:** Completing the Accounting Cycle

Dr. Martha Knotts, upon completing a residency program at Jefferson Hospital in Philadelphia, established a medical practice in Jenkintown, Pennsylvania. During October 1998, the first month of operations, the following transactions occurred:

Oct. 1 Dr. Knotts transferred $25,000 from her personal checking account to a new bank account titled Dr. Knotts, M.D.

     1 A medical building ($100,000) and land ($25,000) were acquired by paying $5,000 in cash and issuing a 5-year, 10% note payable (interest is payable every 6 months) for the $120,000 balance.

     1 Acquired medical equipment costing $42,000 and medical supplies amounting to $3,900 by paying $5,900 cash and issuing a 12% note payable, maturing in 6 months, for the $40,000 balance.

Oct. 2 Acquired malpractice insurance for the next 6 months at a cost of $12,000.

4 Received cash from patients amounting to $11,700.

7 Acquired additional medical supplies on account from Doyletown Medical Supply Company, $1,700.

10 Paid salaries of nurses and office staff, $7,300.

12 Received $9,000 from the Newark Experimental Drug Center for research to be conducted by Dr. Knotts over the next 3 months.

18 Billed patients $31,700 for services rendered.

21 Paid $2,300 for repairs to the medical equipment.

23 Paid the telephone bill, $300.

24 Acquired medical equipment costing $4,500 on account from Dr. Henry.

25 Collected $11,300 from patients billed on the 18th.

27 Paid $1,300 on account to Doyletown Medical Supply Company.

30 Withdrew $20,000 in cash from the medical practice.

30 Paid $1,500 dues to the Pennsylvania Medical Association.

**Required:**

1. Establish the following accounts and account numbers in a general ledger:

| Account | No. | Account | No. |
|---------|-----|---------|-----|
| Cash | 110 | Knotts, Capital | 310 |
| Accounts Receivable | 120 | Knotts, Withdrawals | 320 |
| Medical Supplies on Hand | 130 | Income Summary | 330 |
| Prepaid Insurance | 140 | Medical Fees Earned | 410 |
| Land | 150 | Research Fees Earned | 420 |
| Medical Building | 160 | Salary Expense | 510 |
| Accumulated Depreciation: | | Insurance Expense | 520 |
|   Medical Building | 165 | Repairs Expense | 530 |
| Medical Equipment | 170 | Medical Supplies Expense | 540 |
| Accumulated Depreciation: | | Medical Association | |
|   Medical Equipment | 175 |   Dues Expense | 550 |
| 12% Note Payable | 210 | Depreciation Expense: | |
| Interest Payable | 220 |   Medical Building | 560 |
| Accounts Payable | 230 | Depreciation Expense: | |
| Salaries Payable | 240 |   Medical Equipment | 570 |
| Unearned Research Fees | 250 | Interest Expense | 580 |
| 10% Note Payable | 260 | Telephone Expense | 590 |

2. Record the transactions for the month of October in a general journal (page 1) and post the entries to the general ledger. (Use balance sheet accounts to record those transactions that will later require adjustments.)

3. Prepare a trial balance on a worksheet and record the following adjustments on the worksheet.

a. Insurance for 1 month has expired.

b. Medical supplies on hand on Oct. 31 amount to $2,100.

c. Depreciation on the medical building and the medical equipment is $500 and $900, respectively.

d. Unearned research fees in the amount of $3,000 have been earned.

e. Salaries of $5,100 have accrued.

f. Interest on the 10% and 12% notes are $1,000 and $400, respectively. Make one entry for the combined amounts.

4. Complete the worksheet and prepare an income statement, a statement of owner's equity, and a balance sheet.

▶ *(Check Figure: Adjusted total trial balance = $250,200)*

5. Record the adjusting and closing entries in the general journal (page 2) and post the entries to the general ledger.
6. Prepare a post-closing trial balance.
7. Prepare the salaries and interest reversing entries in the general journal (page 3) and post them to the general ledger.

## OBJECTIVE ASSIGNMENT ANSWERS

### True/False

**1.** T     **2.** T     **3.** F     **4.** F     **5.** T

### Multiple Choice

**1.** b     **2.** b     **3.** a     **4.** d     **5.** e
**6.** c     **7.** a     **8.** c     **9.** a     **10.** c

# Accounting for Merchandise

**Exhibit 1** An Income Statement for a Service Firm

### GREENWATER MOTEL

| | | |
|---|---:|---:|
| Revenue: | | |
| Room Rentals......................... | | $52,300 |
| Expenses: | | |
| Salary Expense............... | $28,200 | |
| Advertising Expense ........... | 7,100 | |
| Repairs Expense.............. | 3,400 | |
| Depreciation Expense.......... | 1,500 | |
| Insurance Expense ............ | 900 | |
| Linen Supplies Expense ........ | 2,600 | |
| Total Expenses..................... | | 43,700 |
| Net Income........................... | | $ 8,600 |

**Exhibit 2** An Income Statement for a Merchandising Concern

### COMPTON'S STORE

| | | |
|---|---:|---:|
| Sales..................................... | | $177,200 |
| Cost of Goods Sold ..................... | | 124,900 |
| Gross Profit ............................ | | $ 52,300 |
| Operating Expenses: | | |
| Salary Expense............... | $28,200 | |
| Advertising Expense ........... | 7,100 | |
| Repairs Expense.............. | 3,400 | |
| Depreciation Expense.......... | 1,500 | |
| Insurance Expense ............ | 900 | |
| Store Supplies Used ........... | 2,600 | |
| Total Operating Expenses ............. | | 43,700 |
| Net Income........................... | | $ 8,600 |

The accounting process begins with an economic entity's business transactions (sometimes referred to as external transactions) and ends with the financial statements that depict the entity's financial activity during a period and its financial status at the end of that period. The financial statements prepared by an economic entity can be either formal or informal. *Informal* financial statements covering monthly and quarterly accounting periods are prepared for internal use to help management determine if it is achieving its objectives. *Formal* financial statements are prepared annually; external users can examine them to see how well the entity is performing.

Now let us examine the way the accounting process works for *merchandising firms* (also called *trading firms*), whose business activity is to buy and sell products, either at the *retail* level (the shop from which you, the consumer, buy the product) or at the *wholesale* level (the firm from which the retail shop buys what it sells).

Let's compare and contrast the income statements of a service firm, the Greenwater Motel, and a merchandising concern, Compton's Store (Exhibits 1 and 2).

The net income for the service company, Greenwater Motel, is simply the difference between revenue earned and total expenses incurred. A merchandising concern like Compton's Store, in contrast, has two types of expenses that must be considered: the cost of goods sold and operating expenses. The cost of goods sold is the expense of the merchandise sold for the period; the operating expenses are all the other expenses necessary to run the business.

To determine the net income for a merchandising concern, the cost of goods sold is subtracted from the revenue represented by the sale of that merchandise; the difference is **gross profit,** also called *gross margin.* (A service concern does not have gross profit because it does not sell merchandise.) Operating expenses are then deducted from gross profit to determine net income. As you can see, the merchandising concern's operating expenses are similar to the service concern's expenses; cost of goods sold represents the crucial difference between the two types of income statements.

This chapter deals with accounting for a merchandising concern, particularly how to measure the cost of goods sold.

## THE INCOME STATEMENT OF A MERCHANDISING CONCERN

Exhibit 3 illustrates how a merchandising firm's income statement is organized. Refer to the exhibit, which is keyed to the text by letter, as we examine some of the basic details within it.

Notice that the Compton's Store income statement, like every merchandising firm's income statement, comprises three distinct sections: *sales, cost of goods sold,* and *operating expenses.*

### The Operating Expenses Section

While every merchandising firm's income statement includes an operating expenses section, some merchandising firms break it down into two subsections—selling expenses and general expenses. *Selling expenses* are those expenses related to the marketing function, such as sales salaries or commissions, delivery expenses, and

Learning Objective 1

Prepare an income statement for a merchandising concern

**Exhibit 3** Detailed Income Statement

### COMPTON'S STORE
### Income Statement
### Year Ended December 31, 1998

| | | | | |
|---|---|---|---|---|
| *(a)* Gross Sales | | | | $182,200 |
| *(b)* Less: Sales Returns and Allowances | | $ 2,300 | | |
| *(c)* Sales Discounts | | 2,700 | | (5,000) |
| Net Sales | | | | $177,200 |
| Cost of Goods Sold: | | | | |
| *(d)* Merchandise Inventory, Jan. 1, 1998 | | | $ 19,100 | |
| *(e)* Purchases | $127,900 | | | |
| *(f)* Less: Purchases Returns and Allowances | $ 800 | | | |
| *(g)* Purchases Discounts | 2,000 | (2,800) | | |
| Net Purchases | | $125,100 | | |
| *(h)* Plus: Freight-In | | 3,100 | | |
| *(i)* Cost of Goods Purchased | | | 128,200 | |
| *(j)* Cost of Goods Available for Sale | | | $147,300 | |
| *(k)* Less: Merchandise Inventory, Dec. 31, 1998 | | | 22,400 | |
| *(l)* Cost of Goods Sold | | | | 124,900 |
| *(m)* Gross Profit | | | | $ 52,300 |
| Operating Expenses: | | | | |
| Salary Expense | | $ 28,200 | | |
| Advertising Expense | | 7,100 | | |
| Repairs Expense | | 3,400 | | |
| Depreciation Expense | | 1,500 | | |
| Insurance Expense | | 900 | | |
| Store Supplies Expense | | 2,600 | | |
| Total Operating Expenses | | | | 43,700 |
| Net Income | | | | $ 8,600 |

**Exhibit 4** Operating Expenses Broken Down into Selling Expenses and General Expenses

| | | |
|---|---:|---:|
| Operating Expenses: | | |
| Selling Expenses: | | |
| Salary Expense | $18,300 | |
| Advertising Expense | 7,100 | |
| Depreciation Expense: Store Equipment. | 800 | |
| Store Supplies Expense. | 2,600 | |
| Total Selling Expenses | | $28,800 |
| General Expenses: | | |
| Salary Expense | $ 9,900 | |
| Repairs Expense | 3,400 | |
| Depreciation Expense: Office Equipment | 700 | |
| Insurance Expense | 900 | |
| Total General Expenses | | 14,900 |
| Total Operating Expenses: | | $43,700 |

depreciation on store equipment. *General expenses* include all other expenses, such as executive and office salaries and depreciation on office equipment. For example, Compton's operating expenses might appear as in Exhibit 4.

1. How do the income statements of service and merchandising companies differ?
2. What is the meaning of the term *gross profit?*
3. What are the two parts of the operating expenses section of an income statement?

### The Sales Section

*Learning Objective 2*

Journalize sales and sales returns and allowances transactions

The primary objective of a merchandising concern is the same as for any business entity: to earn a profit. For a merchandising firm to earn a profit, the amount of its sales revenue must exceed the sum of its cost of goods sold and its operating expenses.

Merchandise, like services, can be paid for with cash at the time of the purchase. This is commonly referred to as a *cash sale.* The seller may instead agree to accept payment at some time after delivery of the merchandise. This is referred to as a *sale on account.*

Cash registers are used by a merchandising concern to record cash sales. The daily cash sales are then entered in the general journal as a debit to Cash and a credit to Sales. The following entry reflects the cash sales made by Compton's Store for Jan. 2, 1998:

| | | |
|---|---:|---:|
| Cash **(A)**\* | 200 | |
| Sales **(OE:R)** | | 200 |
| To record cash sales for the day. | | |

Likewise, sales made on account would be recorded daily in the general journal as a debit to Accounts Receivable and a credit to sales:

| | | |
|---|---:|---:|
| Accounts Receivable **(A)** | 700 | |
| Sales **(OE:R)** | | 700 |
| To record sales on account to the Jones Company. | | |

\* The letters in parentheses in journal entries refer to the following accounts: **A** = Assets; **L** = Liabilities; **OE** = Owner's Equity; **R** = Revenue; **E** = Expenses.

At the end of the year the total dollar amount of all the daily cash sales and sales on account for Compton's Store comes to $182,200, as shown on line *(a)* of the income statement in Exhibit 3. This cumulative revenue amount becomes the **Sales** account in the general ledger.

### Sales Returns and Allowances

After purchasing an item, a customer may find that it is defective in some way and return it to the merchandising firm, which acknowledges receipt of the returned item—a transaction that essentially negates the original sale.

Perhaps the defective item is not totally useless (it's merely the wrong color, let's say). As an alternative to returning it, the customer may be allowed to keep it and receive a refund of part of the purchase price. This allowance on price (also called a *price concession*) helps to avoid the costs of freight, and sometimes storage, which the merchandising firm incurs in accepting returned items.

In either case, the amount of the return or the allowance can be recorded as an entry in the general journal by simply debiting Sales and crediting Cash or Accounts Receivable. But that's not the way it is generally done. First we'll explain why not; then we'll show how returns and allowances are usually accounted for.

The owners of a merchandising firm need to know how much merchandise is being returned and why. Some merchandise is inevitably returned because it is defective, but such returns should not represent a significant percentage of sales. If they do, management should act to identify and correct the problem. Returns that exceed expected levels are a signal that management action is needed.

How efficiently that signal reaches management depends on the way in which returns and allowances are accounted for. Representing returns and allowances in the general journal by debiting Sales is seldom done because it gives no helpful warnings about the level of returns. A separate account in the general ledger, **Sales Returns and Allowances,** can be established in order to provide timely information on returns and allowances. This is a *contra account,* like Accumulated Depreciation. Accumulated Depreciation is a contra-asset account having a balance (credit) opposite that of its related asset account (debit). Similarly, Sales Returns and Allowances, which is a contra-*revenue* account, has a debit balance opposite that of the related Sales account, which has a credit balance.

When merchandise is returned, the transaction is recorded in the contra account by a debit to Sales Returns and Allowances and a credit to Cash or Accounts Receivable:

| | | |
|---|---|---|
| Sales Returns and Allowances **(OE : R)**..................... | 100 | |
| Cash (or Accounts Receivable) **(A)** .................... | | 100 |
| To record returned merchandise. | | |

Compton's general ledger account for Sales Returns and Allowances shows that entries during the year totaled $2,300, as you can see on line *(b)* of Compton's income statement in Exhibit 3.

### Sales Discounts

In a sales transaction, the seller and the buyer agree to an exchange. The seller agrees to exchange merchandise in return for a specified payment. The exchange agreement—that is, the terms of the sale—requires payment, generally in the form of cash, either immediately at the point of sale or at some future date.

The arrangement between the seller and the buyer of merchandise concerning the method of payment is usually expressed on the *sales invoice*—the bill. This arrangement is referred to as the *credit terms* of the sale. One common arrangement is

Learning Objective **3**

Calculate and journalize sales discounts transactions

to require that the bill be paid 10 days after the end of the month in which the sale was made. This is expressed on the sales invoice as *n/10, EOM:*

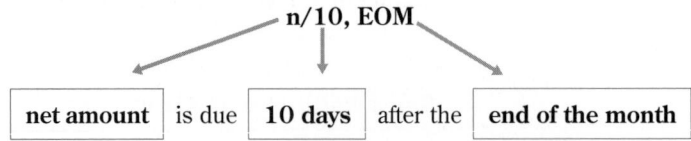

The *net amount* is the price of the merchandise less any discounts or other price reductions allowed by the seller. It is the amount that the buyer must pay.

Another common credit term is to require payment 30 days after the sale, as evidenced by the date on the sales invoice. The term *n/30* is used to express this arrangement:

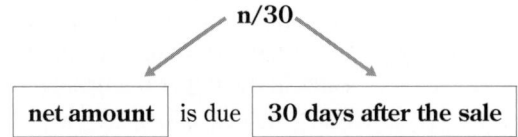

Selling merchandise on account has an obvious disadvantage: The seller has already delivered the merchandise but must wait a period of time before cash is received in payment. While waiting for payment, the seller has salaries to pay, new merchandise to acquire, and other obligations to pay for. Clearly, it is in the seller's interest to encourage the buyer to pay promptly.

Many sellers offer a **sales discount** (also called a *cash discount*) if the bill is paid within a specified period of time. For example, it is common practice to offer a 2% discount off the price of the merchandise if the bill is paid in full within 10 days of the sale. And, of course, if it isn't paid within 10 days, then it must be paid within the period specified. Assuming that the terms are n/30, with a 2% discount if paid within 10 days, terms would be represented on the sales invoice as *2/10, n/30:*

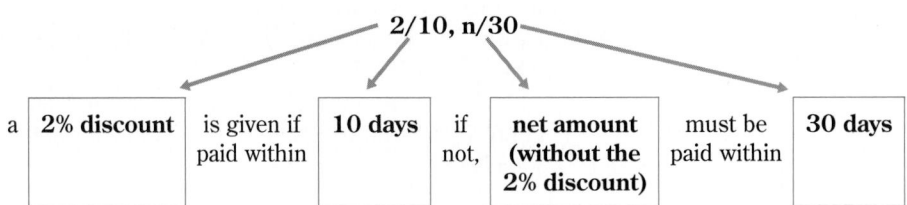

The discount and the time period are established by the seller. A seller might offer terms of 3/10, n/30, meaning that a 3% discount if paid within 10 days of the invoice date, or payable in full within 30 days.

To illustrate the accounting for sales discounts, assume that Compton's credit sales are subject to the credit terms 2/10, n/30, and that a customer with a $400 sale on account pays within the 10-day discount period. The amount of the sales discount would be $400 × 2% = $8, which means that the customer would have to pay Compton's only $400 − $8 = $392. The general journal entry to record the payment would increase (debit) Cash by $392, the amount received, and decrease (credit) Accounts Receivable by $400, the full amount of the sale previously recorded. The difference between these amounts is debited to **Sales Discounts,** maintaining the equality of the debits and credits. The entry is:

| | | |
|---|---|---|
| Cash **(A)** . . . . . . . . . . . . . . . . . . . . . . . . . . . . . . . . . . . . . . . . . . . . . . | 392 | |
| Sales Discounts **(OE : R)** . . . . . . . . . . . . . . . . . . . . . . . . . . . . . . . | 8 | |
|     Accounts Receivable **(A)**. . . . . . . . . . . . . . . . . . . . . . . . . . . . . | | 400 |
| To record collection of accounts receivable subject to 2/10, n/30 credit terms. | | |

The total of all the sales discounts for the year for Compton's Store amounts to $2,700 and is reflected on line *(c)* in Exhibit 3.

Sales Discounts, like Sales Returns and Allowances, is a *contra-revenue account,* and as such it also has a *debit balance.* Both Sales Discounts and Sales Returns and Allowances are subtracted from gross sales to arrive at net sales because these two accounts represent concessions on the sales price given to the buyer, and as such reduce the seller's revenue.

### Sales Tax

Another important item to consider is the tax imposed by many states on the sales of merchandise. This liability is incurred when the sale takes place (whether for cash or on account). Amounts not yet paid to the state government are reported on the company's balance sheet as a liability, Sales Tax Payable.

The seller collects the tax from the buyer at the time it receives cash from the sale or the payment of the account receivable. A cash sale of $80 in a state having a 5% sales tax would be recorded as follows:

| | | |
|---|---|---|
| Cash **(A)** | 84 | |
|     Sales **(OE:R)** | | 80 |
|     Sales Tax Payable **(L)** | | 4 |
| To record cash sales of merchandise and related sales tax payable. | | |

If the $80 sale were made on account, the entry would be:

| | | |
|---|---|---|
| Accounts Receivable **(A)** | 84 | |
|     Sales **(OE:R)** | | 80 |
|     Sales Tax Payable **(L)** | | 4 |
| To record sale of merchandise on account and related sales tax payable. | | |

Assuming that the state requires the payment of the sales tax on a quarterly basis and that the amount of the sales tax collected for the quarter was $3,200, the entry to pay the sales tax to the state would be:

| | | |
|---|---|---|
| Sales Tax Payable **(L)** | 3,200 | |
|     Cash **(A)** | | 3,200 |
| To record the payment of sales taxes. | | |

**ASK YOURSELF** ▶

1. **Describe the components of the sales section of an income statement.**
2. **Why doesn't a company simply debit Sales when merchandise is returned?**
3. **Why are sales discounts given?**

## The Cost of Goods Sold Section

To determine the net income for any business entity, whether a service business or a merchandising business, you must utilize the familiar *matching concept.* According to this principle, the costs incurred in providing goods and services for sale must be matched against the revenue generated by these goods or services in the accounting period when they are sold. For example, in the case of a service business—say, Mullin Home Cleaning Service—the cost of providing cleaning service to Mrs. Jor-

**Figure 1** A How Cost of Goods Sold is Determined

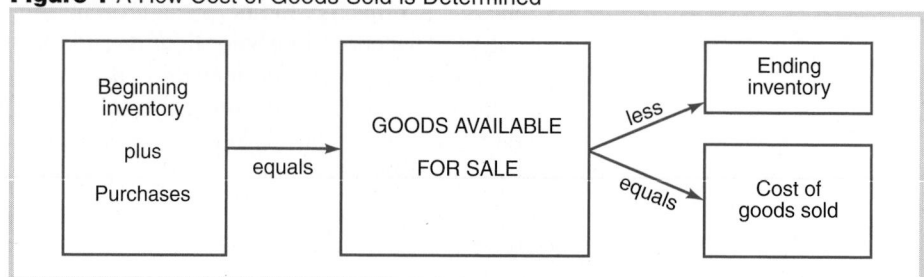

dan may be the $50 wages paid by Mullin to its two employees. These wages would be *matched* against the $75 revenue—the fee charged Mrs. Jordan—that the expenditure of the labor was able to generate. The idea of matching for a merchandising business proceeds along the same lines. If Pipperidge Donuts sells you a dozen cream-filled donuts for $1.00, the price that Pipperidge paid for the donuts—say, $0.60—must be matched against the $1.00 revenue generated.

For a merchandising firm the cost of the products that the firm offers for sale constitutes a major expenditure. The matching concept requires that only those products sold during an accounting period be matched against the revenue earned. This significant expense is called the **cost of goods sold.** The amount of product purchased but not yet sold is called the **merchandise inventory,** so the product on hand at the end of an accounting period is called the *ending merchandise inventory.* Of course, the merchandise inventory at the end of one accounting period is still on hand at the beginning of the next accounting period. At that time it is called *beginning merchandise inventory.*

Because cost of goods sold represents the largest expense on the income statement, it deserves special attention. As Exhibit 3, lines *(d)* to *(l)*, show, it appears on the income statement immediately following the sales section—so that it can be matched directly with the revenue shown there. The cost of goods sold section represents, or accounts for, all the costs that were incurred to provide the products that were sold during the accounting period. Thus, the cost of goods sold is determined by first adding together beginning merchandise inventory and purchases. This gives us the cost of all goods available for sale during the period. Next, the cost of goods still available for sale at the end of the period—the ending inventory—is subtracted from the cost of goods available during the period. The result is the cost of goods sold (see Figure 1).

The system we will describe here for inventories is called the **periodic inventory system.** It is used by many merchandising concerns to determine the cost of goods sold at the end of an accounting period. Another system, called the *perpetual inventory system,* is used by companies that wish to keep a running total of the amount of inventory on hand at any point in time.

### Beginning Merchandise Inventory

To calculate the cost of goods sold, we begin with the merchandise inventory on hand at the start of the accounting period. This year's beginning merchandise inventory is simply last year's ending merchandise inventory, which was determined by a physical count of the items composing the merchandise inventory at the close of the last business day of the year. The beginning merchandise inventory of Compton's Store amounts to $19,100 [line *(d)* on the income statement, Exhibit 3].

### Purchases

Learning
Objective **4**

Journalize purchases, purchases
returns and allowances, and
purchases discount transactions

The second item we need to calculate for cost of goods sold is the cost of the purchases. We use the term *purchases* in accounting to refer to merchandise that is bought for one purpose—to be resold. We have exercised great care to avoid the use of the word *purchases* elsewhere for this reason. Office supplies, prepaid insurance, buildings, repair parts, automobiles, etc., are all said to be *acquired*. Only merchandise held for resale is said to be *purchased*. Thus, the general ledger account **Purchases** records only the merchandise inventory obtained during the year for resale.

Like sales, purchases may be for cash or on account. Cash purchases are recorded as a debit to Purchases and a credit to Cash, as shown by this Jan. 5 entry for Compton's Store:

| | | |
|---|---|---|
| Purchases **(OE:E)** . . . . . . . . . . . . . . . . . . . . . . . . . . . . . . . . . . . | 600 | |
|     Cash **(A)** . . . . . . . . . . . . . . . . . . . . . . . . . . . . . . . . . . . . . . . | | 600 |
| To record cash purchases. | | |

Purchases on account are recorded as a debit to Purchases and a credit to Accounts Payable, like this Jan. 29 entry made by Compton's Store:

| | | |
|---|---|---|
| Purchases **(OE:E)** . . . . . . . . . . . . . . . . . . . . . . . . . . . . . . . . . . . | 550 | |
|     Accounts Payable **(L)** . . . . . . . . . . . . . . . . . . . . . . . . . . . . . | | 550 |
| To record purchases on account from the Whaller Company. | | |

The sum of all the purchases for cash and on account is $127,900—the total purchases [line *(e)*] made by Compton's Store for the year 1995.

### Purchases Returns and Allowances

As a purchaser, a merchandising firm may have to return some of its purchases because of some kind of defect, just as its customers (purchasers) had returns to the firm as a seller. *Sales returns and allowances* to a seller are equivalent to *purchases returns and allowances* to a buyer. Merchandising firms that purchase goods for resale need a place in their accounting systems to record and account for purchase returns and allowances.

A general ledger account, **Purchases Returns and Allowances,** is established to accumulate this information for a merchandising firm's management to review. It provides the same kind of signal to management as does the information on Sales Returns and Allowances. Management should expect a certain amount of Purchase Returns and Allowances, but a sudden increase in the amount indicates that management needs to evaluate its purchasing system and the quality of its merchandise.

Purchases Returns and Allowances are recorded in the same manner as Sales Returns and Allowances. The entry is made by debiting either Cash or Accounts Payable and crediting the contra-expense account Purchases Returns and Allowances. An illustration would be a return on Feb. 4 to the Whaller Company of $50 out of the $550 worth of merchandise bought on account by Compton's Store on Jan. 29:

| | | |
|---|---|---|
| Accounts Payable **(L)** . . . . . . . . . . . . . . . . . . . . . . . . . . . . . . . . | 50 | |
|     Purchases Returns and Allowances **(OE:E)** . . . . . . . . . . . . | | 50 |
| To record merchandise returned to the seller. | | |

Purchases Returns and Allowances represents a transaction in which merchandise is "returned" to the seller and the amount of the price of that merchandise is "returned" to the buyer. Therefore, the amount of Purchases Returns and Allowances appears on the income statement as a subtraction from Purchases. The sum of all the purchases returns for our example is shown as $800 subtracted from Purchases in Compton's income statement on line *(f)* of Exhibit 3.

### Purchases Discounts

A seller's sales discounts are at the same time the buyer's purchases discounts. To see how a buyer accounts for and reports purchases discounts on an income statement, consider the Jan. 29 $550 purchase on account from the Whaller Company and the subsequent $50 Feb. 4 return.

Whaller allows terms of 2/10, n/30. By now we know this means that the seller will accept, as payment in full, 2% less than the amount payable if payment is made within 10 days from the invoice date; otherwise the full amount is payable within 30 days. Compton pays Whaller $490 on Feb. 7, which is within the 10-day period. Compton is thus entitled to a 2% purchase discount on the balance of $500 ($550 − $50), which amounts to $500 × 0.02 = $10.

Compton records the reduction in its obligation by debiting Accounts Payable for the full $500, crediting the contra-expense account **Purchases Discounts** $10, and crediting the Cash account $490:

| | | |
|---|---|---|
| Accounts Payable **(L)** . . . . . . . . . . . . . . . . . . . . . . . . . . . . . . . . . . . . . . . | 500 | |
| Purchases Discounts **(OE : E)** . . . . . . . . . . . . . . . . . . . . . . . . . . | | 10 |
| Cash **(A)** . . . . . . . . . . . . . . . . . . . . . . . . . . . . . . . . . . . . . . . . . . . | | 490 |
| To record payment to Whaller Company less the Feb. 4 return and a 2% discount. | | |

Since purchases discounts represent a part of the total purchases amount that does not have to be paid, they are subtracted from total purchases, as shown in line *(g)* of Compton's income statement.

Purchasers of merchandise should take advantage of any purchase discount offered. Failure to do so can be very expensive. For instance, merchandise costing $1,000 and subject to credit terms of 2/10, n/30 requires a payment of $980 within the 10-day period. Later than 10 days but within the 30-day period, the full $1,000 must be paid. In effect, $20 interest is charged on $1,000 for 20 days, which is an interest rate of 36% [($1,000) (36%) (20/360) = $20].

### Trade Discounts

In the jewelry, auto parts, and certain other industries, manufacturers and suppliers provide catalogs of their merchandise, listing suggested prices for retailers to charge their customers. These prices are referred to as *suggested retail prices* or *manufacturer's suggested list prices*. Retailers receive a discount, commonly referred to as the **trade discount**—the amount the retailers deduct from the catalog price to determine their cost (the price they pay to the manufacturer or supplier).

Learning Objective **5**

Calculate trade discounts

Because catalogs are expensive to produce, manufacturers and suppliers do not publish new ones every time they change their prices. Instead, they keep the manufacturer's suggested list prices, but change the trade discount by mailing the retailers a list of changes in the discount terms.

Manufacturers and suppliers may also offer discounts when a retailer orders large quantities of merchandise. This type of discount is called a **quantity discount.**

To distinguish among the three types of discounts we have discussed in this chapter—sales, trade, and quantity discounts—consider the credit purchase made by Compton's Store on Feb. 12. The merchandise purchased was listed by the manufacturer at $700 and subject to a 30% trade discount and a 10% quantity discount for all orders over $300. If the invoice is paid within 10 days, a 2% sales discount with also apply.

| | |
|---|---:|
| Suggested list price. . . . . . . . . . . . . . . . . . . . . . . . . . . . . . . . . . . . . . . . . . . . . . | $700.00 |
| Less: 30% *trade discount*. . . . . . . . . . . . . . . . . . . . . . . . . . . . . . . . . . . . . . . . | 210.00 |
| Total. . . . . . . . . . . . . . . . . . . . . . . . . . . . . . . . . . . . . . . . . . . . . . . . . . . | $490.00 |
| Less: 10% *quantity discount*. . . . . . . . . . . . . . . . . . . . . . . . . . . . . . . . . . . . . . | 49.00 |
| Total. . . . . . . . . . . . . . . . . . . . . . . . . . . . . . . . . . . . . . . . . . . . . . . . . . . | $441.00 |
| Less: 2% *sales discount*. . . . . . . . . . . . . . . . . . . . . . . . . . . . . . . . . . . . . . . . | 8.82 |
| Price Compton pays manufacturer. . . . . . . . . . . . . . . . . . . . . . . . . . . . . . . . | $432.18 |

Thus, Compton will pay $432.18, which represents a total discount of $267.82 off the manufacturer's suggested list price. Compton will record the acquisition of the merchandise at $441.00 in the Purchases account and the cash discount of $8.82 in the Purchases Discount account, assuming that payment is made within the discount period. Compton will in turn sell the merchandise to its customers for $700, or for more or less if it so desires.

The entries by Compton's store to record the acquisition of the merchandise and subsequent payment within the discount period are presented below:

| | | |
|---|---:|---:|
| Purchases **(OE:E)** . . . . . . . . . . . . . . . . . . . . . . . . . . . . . . . . . . . . . . | 441.00 | |
| Accounts Payable **(L)** . . . . . . . . . . . . . . . . . . . . . . . . . . . . . . . | | 441.00 |
| To record the acquisition of merchandise on account, terms 2/10, n/30. | | |
| | | |
| Accounts Payable **(L)** . . . . . . . . . . . . . . . . . . . . . . . . . . . . . . . . . . . . | 441.00 | |
| Purchases Discounts **(OE:E)** . . . . . . . . . . . . . . . . . . . . . . . | | 8.82 |
| Cash **(A)** . . . . . . . . . . . . . . . . . . . . . . . . . . . . . . . . . . . . . . . . . . | | 432.18 |
| To record payment within discount period. | | |

### *Freight-In*

Learning Objective **6**

Distinguish between the terms *FOB shipping point* and *FOB destination*

Thus far, we have explored several basic elements of an economic transaction between a seller (manufacturer, wholesaler, supplier) and a buyer (retailer or wholesaler) of merchandise. But we haven't yet discussed two very important questions: how will the merchandise be transported from seller to buyer; and who will pay the cost of transportation?

Generally, the terms of the sale specify who pays the cost of transportation, commonly referred to as the *freight charges.* The term **FOB shipping point** means that the seller agrees to place the merchandise on trucks, railroad cars, or other transportation *free on board*—at the shipping point. The cost of transportation from the shipping point to wherever the buyer wants the merchandise delivered is paid for by the buyer. As a convenience, the seller may prepay the freight and simply add the cost to the amount of the invoice for the merchandise purchased by the buyer.

When the seller agrees to pay the cost of transportation, that agreement is referred to as **FOB destination.** The seller places the merchandise *free on board* the transportation vehicle from the shipping point to its destination. There is no freight cost to the buyer.

When a seller pays transportation costs, they are recorded as Delivery Expenses—one of the selling expenses included in the operating expenses section of the seller's income statement. For example, if a seller shipped merchandise FOB destination and the freight charges were $150, the general journal entry to record these charges would be:

| | | |
|---|---:|---:|
| Delivery Expenses **(OE:E)** . . . . . . . . . . . . . . . . . . . . . . . . . . . . . . . | 150 | |
| Cash **(A)** . . . . . . . . . . . . . . . . . . . . . . . . . . . . . . . . . . . . . . . . . . . . | | 150 |
| To record freight charges under FOB destination terms. | | |

**Figure 2** Freight-In and Delivery Expense

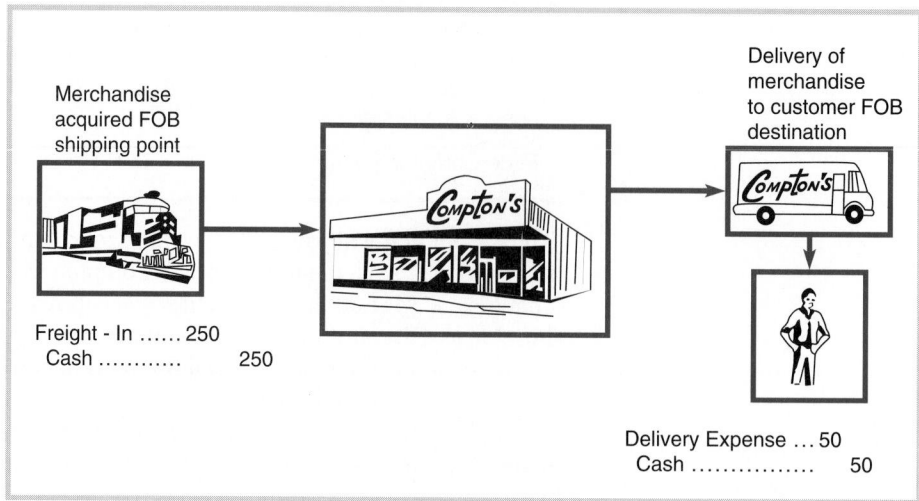

Any transportation costs, or freight charges, paid by the buyer are usually referred to as *freight-in.* A separate account, **Freight-In,** is established in the buyer's general ledger to accumulate these costs.

Although the freight charges must be incurred along with the purchase cost, they are segregated from the Purchases account for one specific reason. The Freight-In account gives management the information it needs to determine what its transportation needs are, whether its transportation expenses are reasonable, and whether or not it should buy or lease its own transportation equipment.

The general journal entry for the FOB shipping point freight charges paid by Compton's Store on a Mar. 14 purchase was recorded as follows:

| | | |
|---|---|---|
| Freight-In (**OE:E**) . . . . . . . . . . . . . . . . . . . . . . . . . . . . . . . . . . . . . . . . . . . . | 250 | |
|     Cash (**A**) . . . . . . . . . . . . . . . . . . . . . . . . . . . . . . . . . . . . . . . . . . . . . . . . | | 250 |
| To record freight charges on merchandise purchased. | | |

Freight-in is a cost that must be incurred in buying merchandise and is shown as $3,100 in line *(h)* of Compton's Store's income statement (see Exhibit 3). The difference between freight-in and delivery expense is further illustrated by Figure 2.

Clearly, the amount paid for merchandise—Purchases—does not fully account for the value of that merchandise—that is, the cost of goods purchased. To determine the *cost of goods purchased:*

- Subtract the total of Purchases Returns and Allowances and Purchases Discounts from the amount of Purchases to get Net Purchases.
- Add to the Net Purchases the Freight-In costs to get the Cost of Goods Purchased.

The Cost of Goods Purchased for Compton's Store [line *(i)* of Exhibit 3] is determined as follows:

| | | |
|---|---|---|
| Purchases. . . . . . . . . . . . . . . . . . . . . . . . . . . . . . . . . . . . . . . . . . . . . . . . . . . | | $127,900 |
| Less: Purchases Returns and Allowances. . . . . . . . . . . . . . . . . | $ 800 | |
|        Purchases Discounts . . . . . . . . . . . . . . . . . . . . . . . . . . . . | 2,000 | (2,800) |
| Net Purchases . . . . . . . . . . . . . . . . . . . . . . . . . . . . . . . . . . . . . . . . . . . . . . | | $125,100 |
| Plus: Freight-In . . . . . . . . . . . . . . . . . . . . . . . . . . . . . . . . . . . . . . . . . . . . . . | | 3,100 |
| Cost of Goods Purchased . . . . . . . . . . . . . . . . . . . . . . . . . . . . . . . . . . . . | | $128,200 |

## Cost of Goods Available for Sale

All the merchandise purchased during the accounting period, plus all the merchandise in inventory at the beginning of the period, represents the total amount of merchandise that could possibly be sold during the period. The *cost of goods available for sale* is the sum of the cost of the beginning inventory, plus the cost of goods purchased during the period (which includes the freight-in costs). Cost of goods available for sale for Compton's Store amounts to $147,300 [line *(j)* of Exhibit 3], determined as follows:

| | |
|---|---:|
| Merchandise Inventory, Jan. 1, 1998 . . . . . . . . . . . . . . . . . . . . . . . . . . . . . . . | $ 19,100 |
| Cost of Goods Purchased . . . . . . . . . . . . . . . . . . . . . . . . . . . . . . . . . . . . . | 128,200 |
| Cost of Goods Available for Sale . . . . . . . . . . . . . . . . . . . . . . . . . . . . . . . . | $147,300 |

## Ending Merchandise Inventory

No firm sells all its purchases and merchandise inventory during an accounting period. A merchandising business must always have some stock immediately available for sale. After the close of business on the last business day of the year, the amount of merchandise on hand is determined by a physical count of the various items of merchandise in stock at the time. The cost of this ending merchandise inventory is then determined by multiplying the unit price of each item by the item quantities and accumulating the total. For example, assume that the count of boxes of $8\frac{1}{2}'' \times 11''$ paper was 27 and the count of So Simple word processing software totaled 9. Also assume that the unit price paid for each item was $39.25 and $179.85, respectively. The total cost of these items would be determined as follows:

| Item | Quantity | Unit Price | Cost |
|---|:---:|:---:|---:|
| Boxes of $8\frac{1}{2}'' \times 11''$ paper | 27 | $ 39.25 | $1,059.75 |
| So Simple software | 9 | 179.85 | 1,618.65 |
| Total cost | | | $2,678.40 |

The cost of all the other items in merchandise inventory is calculated in exactly the same manner. A typical merchandising firm could have several thousand items in stock at year-end, so the process of taking inventory is no small task.

The cost of the ending merchandise inventory for Compton's Store was calculated as $22,400 [line *(k)* of Exhibit 3]. The ending merchandise inventory represents the cost of the merchandise that has *not* been sold during the period.

## Cost of Goods Sold

Learning
Objective **7**
Calculate the cost of goods sold

We now have all the information we need to calculate the cost of goods sold during a period. As we saw earlier, the cost of goods sold is determined by subtracting from the cost of the goods available for sale the cost of the goods that were *not* sold by the end of the period. That is, cost of goods sold is the cost of goods available for sale less the ending merchandise inventory. The $124,900 cost of goods sold [line *(l)* of Exhibit 3] for Compton's Store is calculated as follows:

| | |
|---|---:|
| Cost of Goods Available for Sale . . . . . . . . . . . . . . . . . . . . . . . . . . . . . . . . | $147,300 |
| Less: Merchandise Inventory, Dec. 31, 1998 . . . . . . . . . . . . . . . . . . . . . . . | 22,400 |
| Cost of Goods Sold . . . . . . . . . . . . . . . . . . . . . . . . . . . . . . . . . . . . . . . . | $124,900 |

## Gross Profit

Once we know the cost of goods sold, we can determine the gross profit. This figure is one of the most important bits of information reported on the income statement of a merchandising concern. People who work with financial statements use gross profit to study the relationship between sales and merchandise sold over time. To determine gross profit, the cost of goods sold for the period is deducted from net sales for the same period. Gross profit for Compton's Store is $52,300 [line *(m)* in Exhibit 3], calculated as follows:

| | | |
|---|---|---|
| Net Sales | $177,200 | |
| Less: Cost of Goods Sold | 124,900 | [line l] |
| Gross Profit | $ 52,300 | [line m] |

**ASK YOURSELF** ▶

1. What are the components of cost of goods sold?
2. Distinguish among trade, quantity, and sales discounts.
3. How do businesses determine who will pay for the freight charges when merchandise is acquired?
4. What is the difference between freight-in and delivery expense?
5. How is gross profit measured.

## PERIODIC PROCEDURES OF A MERCHANDISING CONCERN

### The Closing-Entry Approach

A merchandising firm follows the same sequence of period-end procedures as does a service company:

Learning Objective 8

Prepare closing entries for a merchandising concern

1. Record external transactions in the general journal daily.
2. Post the amounts in the general journal to the appropriate general ledger accounts weekly or monthly.
3. Prepare the unadjusted trial balance on the worksheet.
4. Enter adjustments on the worksheet.
5. Complete the worksheet.
6. Prepare the financial statements.

Closing, adjusting, and reversing entries are all procedures that a merchandising firm must do periodically, just like a service firm. The types of accounts that are common to both a merchandising business and a service business are recorded and treated in exactly the same way. The accounts that are unique to a merchandising business, such as the Merchandise Inventory account, are boxed on Compton's worksheet in Exhibit 5.

Note that this worksheet does not have adjusted trial balance columns. Accountants, like other people, don't want to do any more work than necessary, so they typically proceed directly from the adjustments to the income statement and balance sheet columns.

**Exhibit 5** A Worksheet for a Merchandising Concern—Closing-Entry Approach

### COMPTON'S STORE
### Worksheet
### Year Ended December 31, 1998

| | Unadjusted Trial Balance | | Adjustments | | Income Statement | | Balance Sheet | |
|---|---|---|---|---|---|---|---|---|
| | **Debit** | **Credit** | **Debit** | **Credit** | **Debit** | **Credit** | **Debit** | **Credit** |
| Cash | 6,200 | | | | | | 6,200 | |
| Accounts Receivable | 11,300 | | | | | | 11,300 | |
| Merchandise Inventory* | 19,100 | | | | 19,100 | 22,400 | 22,400 | |
| Store Supplies on Hand | 3,500 | | | (b) 2,600 | | | 900 | |
| Store Equipment | 11,400 | | | | | | 11,400 | |
| Accum. Depr.: Store Equipment | | 3,000 | | (a) 1,500 | | | | 4,500 |
| Accounts Payable | | 5,100 | | | | | | 5,100 |
| Compton, Capital* | | 37,200 | | | | | | 37,200 |
| Compton, Withdrawals | 4,000 | | | | | | 4,000 | |
| Sales | | 182,200 | | | | 182,200 | | |
| Sales Returns and Allowances | 2,300 | | | | 2,300 | | | |
| Sales Discounts | 2,700 | | | | 2,700 | | | |
| Purchases | 127,900 | | | | 127,900 | | | |
| Purchases Returns and Allow. | | 800 | | | | 800 | | |
| Purchases Discounts | | 2,000 | | | | 2,000 | | |
| Freight-In | 3,100 | | | | 3,100 | | | |
| Salary Expense | 27,400 | | (c) 800 | | 28,200 | | | |
| Advertising Expense | 7,100 | | | | 7,100 | | | |
| Repairs Expense | 3,400 | | | | 3,400 | | | |
| Insurance Expense | 900 | | | | 900 | | | |
| Totals | 230,300 | 230,300 | | | | | | |
| Depr. Expense: Store Equip. | | | (a) 1,500 | | 1,500 | | | |
| Store Supplies Expense | | | (b) 2,600 | | 2,600 | | | |
| Salaries Payable | | | | (c) 800 | | | | 800 |
| Totals | | | 4,900 | 4,900 | 198,800 | 207,400 | 56,200 | 47,600 |
| | | | | | 8,600 | | | 8,600 |
| Net Income | | | | | 207,400 | 207,400 | 56,200 | 56,200 |

\* All accounts on the unadjusted trial balance, except that Compton, Capital, and Merchandise Inventory reflect end-of-period balances.

Compton's made three adjustments as of Dec. 31, 1998:

**a.** Depreciation Expense: Store Equipment of $1,500 was recorded.

**b.** Store Supplies on Hand was adjusted to reflect $2,600 Store Supplies Expense.

**c.** Salaries Accrued, $800.

The trial balance columns and the adjustments columns are treated in exactly the same way for both service businesses and merchandising businesses. The two worksheets differ only in the way the balances in the accounts that distinguish merchandising firms are carried over to the income statement and the balance sheet columns.

The accounts dealing with sales and purchases, which are income statement accounts, are carried over to the income statement columns just like any other revenue or expense accounts. The accounts that pertain to sales and purchases are illustrated in the larger of the dark green areas on the worksheet.

### The Merchandise Inventory Account on the Worksheet

There is a parallel between the way the Capital and Merchandise Inventory accounts are handled. All accounts shown on the adjusted trial balance reflect their end-of-period balances, except the Capital and Merchandise Inventory accounts. These two accounts represent beginning balances.

Remember, the revenue accounts, the expense accounts, and the Withdrawals account are all *part of* the Capital account. As revenue is earned, the Capital account is increased. As expenses are incurred and withdrawals are made, the Capital account is decreased. The revenue, expense, and withdrawals accounts, although part of the Capital account, are kept separate from the Capital account until the end of the accounting period. The reason for keeping these accounts separate is to provide information for the preparation of the income statement and the statement of owner's equity.

At the end of the accounting period, after the adjusting entries are recorded in the general journal and posted to the ledger account, the balances in the revenue, expense, and withdrawals accounts are transferred to the Capital account by means of the closing entries. This procedure serves two purposes. First, the revenue, expense, and withdrawals account balances are reduced to zero—ready to receive transactions for the new accounting period. Second, the Capital account is brought up to date; it now has a balance that reflects the *end-of-period* position.

Like the Capital account, the Merchandise Inventory account represents a beginning balance in the period-end trial balance. That means that although many transactions cause changes in merchandise inventory during an accounting period, those changes are not recorded in the Merchandise Inventory account.

Yet, of course, the company purchases merchandise during the period. Where is that merchandise accounted for, if not in the Merchandise Inventory account? It is accounted for in the Purchases account, which does change as a result of these transactions during the accounting period.

Keep in mind these two basic ideas as you proceed through this section:

**1.** The Merchandise Inventory account does *not* change during an accounting period.
**2.** Merchandise purchased during the period is recorded in the Purchases account, which, in effect, represents changes in Merchandise Inventory.

Like the ending Capital balance, the ending Merchandise Inventory balance is obtained in the accounting records via the closing process. To provide the information required for the closing entries, as well as for preparing the income statement and balance sheet, both the beginning and ending Merchandise Inventory balances are reflected on the worksheet. (As we have noted, the amount of ending merchandise inventory is determined by physically counting all the merchandise on hand.)

Compton's Jan. 1, 1998, beginning merchandise inventory of $19,100 is carried over as a debit balance to the income statement columns of the worksheet. This procedure is similar to carrying Purchases or Salary Expense to the income statement debit column. In other words, the beginning merchandise inventory is similar to an expense allocated to this period. This period's beginning merchandise inventory was last period's ending merchandise inventory—that is, the merchandise inventory that remains on hand to be sold *this period.* Once sold, it must be considered as part of the total cost of goods sold—an expense to be matched against this period's revenue.

The ending merchandise inventory, $22,400 (determined by a physical count), is entered in *both* the income statement credit column and the balance sheet debit column. The ending merchandise inventory represents those items acquired during the year that have not been sold. The ending merchandise inventory will be sold next year and, therefore, should not be considered as an expense to be matched against revenue of the current period. The ending merchandise inventory must be subtracted from the total merchandise available for sale to determine the proper expense for the current period—the cost of goods sold. That is why the ending merchandise inventory is entered as a credit on the worksheet income statement columns: It reflects a reduction of the expenses to be matched against revenues.

The ending Merchandise Inventory debit balance of $22,400 on the worksheet balance sheet represents an *asset* until it is sold, like any other prepaid expense. It will become an *expense* next year as it is sold and matched against revenues.

Look back at Compton's income statement in Exhibit 3, specifically the cost of goods sold section. Line *(k)*—the ending merchandise inventory—is subtracted from line *(j)*—the cost of goods available for sale—to determine line *(l)*, the cost of goods sold. This income statement was prepared from the information contained in the income statement columns on the worksheet in Exhibit 5.

### Closing Entries for a Merchandising Concern

When we used the worksheet as an aid in preparing the closing entries for a service business, we first closed all the expense accounts, but we did not have any contra-revenue accounts (Sales Returns and Allowances and Sales Discounts) or contra-expense accounts (Purchases Returns and Allowances and Purchases Discounts). A merchandiser does have contra accounts, which makes it easier to first close all income statement accounts with debit balances. On Compton's worksheet the total of the income statement debit column is $198,800. This amount must be debited to the Income Summary account. In the first closing entry, below, notice that in addition to the Purchases account, both Sales Returns and Allowances and Sales Discounts have debit balances, as does the Beginning Merchandise Inventory.

Learning Objective **9**

Prepare closing entries for a merchandising concern

| | | | |
|---|---|---|---|
| 1998 | | | |
| Dec. 31 | Income Summary **(OE)**. . . . . . . . . . . . . . . . . . . . . . . . . . . | 198,800 | |
| | Merchandise Inventory **(A)**. . . . . . . . . . . . . . . . . . . . | | 19,100 |
| | Sales Returns and Allowances **(OE:R)**. . . . . . . . . | | 2,300 |
| | Sales Discounts **(OE:R)**. . . . . . . . . . . . . . . . . . . . . | | 2,700 |
| | Purchases **(OE:E)**. . . . . . . . . . . . . . . . . . . . . . . . . . | | 127,900 |
| | Freight-In **(OE:E)**. . . . . . . . . . . . . . . . . . . . . . . . . . . | | 3,100 |
| | Salary Expense **(OE:E)**. . . . . . . . . . . . . . . . . . . . . . | | 28,200 |
| | Advertising Expense **(OE:E)**. . . . . . . . . . . . . . . . . . | | 7,100 |
| | Repairs Expense **(OE:E)**. . . . . . . . . . . . . . . . . . . . . | | 3,400 |
| | Insurance Expense **(OE:E)**. . . . . . . . . . . . . . . . . . . | | 900 |
| | Depreciation Expense: Store Equipment **(OE:E)** . . | | 1,500 |
| | Store Supplies Expense **(OE:E)**. . . . . . . . . . . . . . . | | 2,600 |
| | To close income statement accounts having debit balances including beginning inventory. | | |

What has this closing entry accomplished? For one thing, the Purchases, Sales Returns and Allowances, Sales Discounts, and Freight-In accounts are all "zeroed out." For another, the cost of the beginning merchandise inventory is eliminated from the Merchandise Inventory general ledger account, which now looks like this:

**Merchandise Inventory (A)**

| 1998 | | | |
|---|---|---|---|
| Bal. 1/1 | 19,100 | Closing 12/31 | 19,100 |

The second closing entry, below, is to close all income statement accounts having a credit balance.

| 1998 | | | |
|---|---|---|---|
| Dec. 31 | Merchandise Inventory **(A)**.................... | 22,400 | |
| | Sales **(OE:R)**................................ | 182,200 | |
| | Purchases Returns and Allowances **(OE:E)**......... | 800 | |
| | Purchases Discounts **(OE:E)** .................... | 2,000 | |
| | Income Summary **(OE)**...................... | | 207,400 |
| | To close income statement accounts having credit balances and to establish ending inventory. | | |

The $207,400 credit to the Income Summary account is the total of the credit income statement column on the worksheet. This entry closes all the remaining income statement accounts and establishes the ending merchandise inventory. The Merchandise Inventory account now appears as follows:

**Merchandise Inventory (A)**

| 1998 | | | |
|---|---|---|---|
| Bal. 1/1 | 19,100 | Closing 12/31 | 19,100 |
| Closing 12/31 | 22,400 | | |

In the third closing entry we close the Income Summary account to the Capital account, as follows:

| Dec. 31 | Income Summary **(OE)**......................... | 8,600 | |
|---|---|---|---|
| | Compton, Capital **(OE)**...................... | | 8,600 |
| | To close the Income Summary account and to transfer the net income to the Capital account. | | |

Finally, we close the Withdrawals account:

| Dec. 31 | Compton, Capital **(OE)**.......................... | 4,000 | |
|---|---|---|---|
| | Compton, Withdrawals **(OE:W)**............... | | 4,000 |
| | To close the Withdrawals account. | | |

## The Adjusting-Entry Approach

While many accounting instructors favor the closing-entry approach for merchandise inventory and we will use that approach in this text, a large number of instructors would rather use a second method: the *adjusting-entry approach*. The two alternatives

**Exhibit 6** A Worksheet for a Merchandising Concern—Adjusting-Entry Approach

COMPTON'S STORE
Worksheet
Year Ended December 31, 1998

| | Unadjusted Trial Balance | | Adjustments | | Income Statement | | Balance Sheet | |
|---|---|---|---|---|---|---|---|---|
| | **Debit** | **Credit** | **Debit** | **Credit** | **Debit** | **Credit** | **Debit** | **Credit** |
| Cash | 6,200 | | | | | | 6,200 | |
| Accounts Receivable | 11,300 | | | | | | 11,300 | |
| Merchandise Inventory* | 19,100 | | (e) 22,400 | (d) 19,100 | | | 22,400 | |
| Store Supplies on Hand | 3,500 | | | (b) 2,600 | | | 900 | |
| Store Equipment | 11,400 | | | | | | 11,400 | |
| Accum. Depr.: Store Equipment | | 3,000 | | (a) 1,500 | | | | 4,500 |
| Accounts Payable | | 5,100 | | | | | | 5,100 |
| Compton, Capital* | | 37,200 | | | | | | 37,200 |
| Compton, Withdrawals | 4,000 | | | | | | 4,000 | |
| Sales | | 182,200 | | | | 182,200 | | |
| Sales Returns and Allowances | 2,300 | | | | 2,300 | | | |
| Sales Discounts | 2,700 | | | | 2,700 | | | |
| Purchases | 127,900 | | | (d) 127,900 | | | | |
| Purchases Returns and Allow. | | 800 | (d) 800 | | | | | |
| Purchases Discounts | | 2,000 | (d) 2,000 | | | | | |
| Freight-In | 3,100 | | | (d) 3,100 | | | | |
| Salary Expense | 27,400 | | (c) 800 | | 28,200 | | | |
| Advertising Expense | 7,100 | | | | 7,100 | | | |
| Repairs Expense | 3,400 | | | | 3,400 | | | |
| Insurance Expense | 900 | | | | 900 | | | |
| Totals | 230,300 | 230,300 | | | | | | |
| | | | | | | | | |
| Depr. Expense: Store Equip. | | | (a) 1,500 | | 1,500 | | | |
| Store Supplies Expense | | | (b) 2,600 | | 2,600 | | | |
| Salaries Payable | | | | (c) 800 | | | | 800 |
| Cost of Goods Sold | | | (d) 147,300 | (e) 22,400 | 124,900 | | | |
| Totals | | | 177,400 | 177,400 | 173,600 | 182,200 | 56,200 | 47,600 |
| | | | | | 8,600 | | | 8,600 |
| Net Income | | | | | 182,200 | 182,200 | 56,200 | 56,200 |

* All accounts on the unadjusted trial balance, except that Compton, Capital, and Merchandise Inventory reflect end-of-period balances.

result in identical financial statements, so it does not really matter which one is selected.

Exhibit 6 illustrates the adjusting-entry approach. An adjusting entry is made that eliminates the beginning inventory from the unadjusted trial balance and transfers it—together with the balances in the Purchases, Purchases Discount, Purchases Returns and Allowances, and Freight-In accounts—to the Cost of Goods Sold account. At this point the Cost of Goods Sold account measures the goods available for sale.

A second adjusting entry establishes the ending inventory and removes from the Cost of Goods Sold account those goods that were not sold. These two entries are keyed *(d)* and *(e)* on the adjustment columns of the worksheet.

The adjusting and closing entries used under the adjusting-entry approach are presented below:

ADJUSTING ENTRIES

| | | | |
|---|---|---|---|
| 1998 | | | |
| Dec. 31 | Cost of Goods Sold **(OE:E)**........................ | 147,300 | |
| | Purchases Returns and Allowances **(OE:E)**.......... | 800 | |
| | Purchases Discounts **(OE:E)**...................... | 2,000 | |
| |     Merchandise Inventory **(A)**..................... | | 19,100 |
| |     Purchases **(OE:E)**........................... | | 127,900 |
| |     Freight-In **(OE:E)**.......................... | | 3,100 |
| | To transfer to the Cost of Goods Sold account the goods available for sale. | | |
| | | | |
| 31 | Merchandise Inventory **(A)**....................... | 22,400 | |
| |     Cost of Goods Sold **(OE:E)**................... | | 22,400 |
| | To remove from the Cost of Goods Sold account the cost of goods not sold. | | |

CLOSING ENTRIES

| | | | |
|---|---|---|---|
| Dec. 31 | Income Summary **(OE)**........................... | 173,600 | |
| |     Sales Returns and Allowances **(OE:R)**.......... | | 2,300 |
| |     Sales Discounts **(OE:R)**...................... | | 2,700 |
| |     Salary Expense **(OE:E)**...................... | | 28,200 |
| |     Advertising Expense **(OE:E)**.................. | | 7,100 |
| |     Repairs Expense **(OE:E)**..................... | | 3,400 |
| |     Insurance Expense **(OE:E)**................... | | 900 |
| |     Depreciation Expense: Store Equipment **(OE:E)** .. | | 1,500 |
| |     Store Supplies Expense **(OE:E)** .............. | | 2,600 |
| |     Cost of Goods Sold.......................... | | 124,900 |
| | To close income statement accounts having debit balances. | | |
| | | | |
| 31 | Sales **(OE:R)**................................. | 182,200 | |
| |     Income Summary **(OE)**...................... | | 182,200 |
| | To close income statement accounts having credit balances. | | |
| | | | |
| 31 | Income Summary **(OE)**........................... | 8,600 | |
| |     Compton, Capital **(OE)** ...................... | | 8,600 |
| | To close the Expense and Revenue Summary account and to transfer the net income to the Capital account. | | |
| | | | |
| 31 | Compton, Capital **(OE)**........................... | 4,000 | |
| |     Compton, Withdrawals **(OE:W)** ............... | | 4,000 |
| | To close the Withdrawals account. | | |

ASK YOURSELF ▶

1. What are the period-end accounting procedures for a merchandising firm?
2. Under the closing-entry approach, how is merchandise inventory handled on the worksheet?
3. Under the adjusting-entry approach, how is merchandise inventory handled on the worksheet?

# Mattel, Inc., Sales

Several years ago, Mattel, Inc., had recorded half a decade of record sales and earnings, and the company had projected another record year to follow. The company's fiscal year-end was Jan. 31, by which time management was aware that the projections would not be met; they had miscalculated the market for its products. In order to reflect a sixth straight year of record sales, Mattel's management, among other things, recorded falsely $14.7 million of sales, which resulted in overstating the year's pretax earnings by $7.8 million.

Sales are recognized under generally accepted accounting principles when the seller has completed all the obligations to the buyer and risk of ownership has transferred to the buyer.

Mattel recorded sales to 35 customers using 156 invoices under a procedure referred to by Mattel as the "bill and hold" program. This program was a practice whereby the customer agreed to buy goods but the seller held the goods until the buyer requested them. In the past Mattel had a limited number of these transactions, all evidenced by written agreement and the physical segregation of the inventory items. Under the January "bill and hold" program, the merchandise was not shipped by Jan. 31, nor was it physically segregated from Mattel's inventory; the customer did not have to pay for the merchandise until the goods were received and could cancel the order at any time prior to receipt; the risks of ownership remained with Mattel; and in many cases the invoices were prepared without consultation with or participation of the customer.

All the "bill and hold" invoices were recorded in the last 11 days of January.

Since Mattel had adjusted its inventory records to account for the "bill and hold" sales of January, even though the merchandise was not shipped, problems developed in inventory control. The inventory records were unreliable; employees could not tell how much inventory was on hand or whether an order was a next-year sale or a current-year "bill and hold" item.

To compensate for these difficulties, Mattel reversed the "bill and hold" sales on its books in May for $6.3 million of "bill and hold" sales of January and $6.6 million of fiscal sales. When this reversing entry was recorded in the Accounts Receivable control account, the subsidiary accounts receivable accounts, and the Sales account, another problem was created. The general ledger sales account reflected negative sales for the month of May. To cover the negative sales figure, Mattel recorded $11.1 million of fictitious sales, which were posted to its Accounts Receivable account and the Sales account but not to the subsidiary ledgers. Of course, that resulted in a difference of $11.1 million between the control account and the subsidiary ledgers. The schedule of accounts receivable for the months May to August all showed a reconciling item of $11.1 million called "May Shipping." By September normal sales were sufficient to absorb the cancellation of the $11.1 million in fictitious sales and the remaining "bill and hold" sales.

*Source:* Securities Exchange Act of 1934, Release No. 17878, *Accounting Series Release No. 292,* June 22, 1981.

---

The Mattel case illustrates the chain of problems that can develop when a company attempts to "adjust" sales figures to reflect higher earnings.

## SUMMARY

- A merchandising firm sells a product, and the cost of that product is referred to as the **cost of goods sold.**
- The cost of goods sold is matched against the net sales to determine the **gross profit,** and operating expenses are subtracted from gross profit to determine net income.
- To account for the revenue of a merchandising firm, we have to consider several things that do not exist for the revenue of a service business. The revenue section of an income statement for a merchandising firm contains a revenue account, **Sales,** and also two contra-revenue accounts, **Sales Returns and Allowances** and **Sales Discounts.**
- To calculate cost of goods sold we have to consider the accounts for **Beginning Merchandise Inventory** and **Ending Merchandise Inventory; Purchases,** the two contra accounts **Purchases Returns and Allowances** and **Purchases Discounts,** and **Freight-In.**
- The sum of the beginning merchandise inventory and net purchases during the period is equivalent to goods available for sale. Ending merchandise inventory is subtracted from goods available for sale to determine the cost of goods sold.
- A **sales discount** (or *cash discount*) is used to encourage a buyer to pay a sale on account promptly. This cash discount is available only if the bill is paid within a specified period.
- A **trade discount** is a reduction off the *list price* of an item to determine the price a buyer pays.

- A **quantity discount** is a reduction for buyers who place orders for multiple items over a certain specified quantity.
- Many states levy a sales tax on goods and services. The tax is recorded when the goods or services are sold by crediting the account Sales Taxes Payable.
- A merchandising firm's periodic accounting procedures are not significantly different from those of a service entity. The revenue and expense accounts particular to a merchandising firm are represented in the trial balance on a worksheet just as are any other business entity's expense or revenue accounts.
- Only the Merchandise Inventory account is handled differently on a merchandiser's worksheet. The beginning merchandise inventory is carried over to the income statement debit column like an expense item. The ending merchandise inventory is placed in both the income statement credit column (because it is not sold) and the balance sheet debit column because it is also an asset.
- The Beginning Merchandise Inventory is eliminated by the closing entry that credits that account. At the same time, the Sales Returns and Allowances, Sales Discounts, Purchases, and Freight-In accounts are closed out with all other expense accounts by credits. The corresponding debit is to the Income Summary.
- The ending merchandise inventory is established in the closing entry that debits Ending Merchandise Inventory, Sales, Purchases Returns and Allowances, and Purchases Discounts. The corresponding credit is to the Income Summary.

## 10  KEY TERMS

| | |
|---|---|
| **Cost of goods sold** | A calculation that determines the amount sold during a period. It is reflected as a separate section of a merchandising firm's income statement. |
| **FOB destination** | Terms in a sales contract specifying that the seller of merchandise is obligated to pay for the freight cost to the buyer's location. |
| **FOB shipping point** | Terms in a sales contract specifying that the buyer is obligated to pay for the freight cost of shipping merchandise from the seller's location. |
| **Freight-In** | A general ledger account used to accumulate the buyer's cost of transporting merchandise. *Transportation-In* is another commonly used title for this account. |
| **Gross profit** | The difference between net sales and cost of goods sold; also called *gross margin*. |
| **Merchandise Inventory** | Merchandise purchased by a merchandising firm for resale but not yet sold. |
| **Periodic inventory system** | A system of determining the ending inventory and the cost of goods sold at the end of an accounting period by counting the units on hand. |
| **Purchases Discounts** | A general ledger contra-expense account used to record the reduction from the purchase price that is allowed if payment is made within a specified period of time. |
| **Purchases Returns and Allowances** | A general ledger account used to accumulate the cost of merchandise returned to the seller as well as the amount of a concession granted by the seller for unsatisfactory goods. |
| **Purchases** | A general ledger account used to accumulate the cost of merchandise purchased during the period for resale. |
| **Quantity discount** | A reduction allowed on the sale price of merchandise when a specified minimum amount is purchased. |
| **Sales** | A general ledger account used to accumulate the revenue earned from the sale of merchandise. |

| | |
|---|---|
| Sales Discounts | A general ledger account used to accumulate the amount allowed as a reduction from the sales price when the invoice is paid within a specified period. It is sometimes called a *cash discount*. |
| Sales Returns and Allowances | A general ledger account used to accumulate the cost of merchandise returned by buyers as well as the amount of a concession granted to buyers for unsatisfactory goods. |
| Trade discount | A deduction allowed to wholesalers and retailers from the price of merchandise listed in catalogs. |

## DEMONSTRATION PROBLEM

Presented below is the adjusted trial balance for Ned's Flower Shop as of Dec. 31, 1998.

**NED'S FLOWER SHOP**
**Adjusted Trial Balance**
**December 31, 1998**

| | Adjusted Trial Balance | |
|---|---|---|
| | Debit | Credit |
| Cash . . . . . . . . . . . . . . . . . . . . . . . . . . . . . . . . . . . . . . . . . . . . . | $  2,300 | |
| Accounts Receivable . . . . . . . . . . . . . . . . . . . . . . . . . . . . . . . . . | 12,500 | |
| Merchandise Inventory. . . . . . . . . . . . . . . . . . . . . . . . . . . . . . . . . | 23,700 | |
| Store Supplies on Hand. . . . . . . . . . . . . . . . . . . . . . . . . . . . . . . | 3,100 | |
| Store Equipment. . . . . . . . . . . . . . . . . . . . . . . . . . . . . . . . . . . . . | 7,500 | |
| Accum. Depr.: Store Equipment . . . . . . . . . . . . . . . . . . . . . . . | | $  4,000 |
| Accounts Payable. . . . . . . . . . . . . . . . . . . . . . . . . . . . . . . . . . . . | | 3,500 |
| Salaries Payable . . . . . . . . . . . . . . . . . . . . . . . . . . . . . . . . . . . . | | 900 |
| Ned, Capital . . . . . . . . . . . . . . . . . . . . . . . . . . . . . . . . . . . . . . . | | 25,600 |
| Ned, Withdrawals. . . . . . . . . . . . . . . . . . . . . . . . . . . . . . . . . . . . | 3,000 | |
| Sales. . . . . . . . . . . . . . . . . . . . . . . . . . . . . . . . . . . . . . . . . . . . . | | 110,200 |
| Sales Returns and Allowances . . . . . . . . . . . . . . . . . . . . . . . | 3,100 | |
| Sales Discounts . . . . . . . . . . . . . . . . . . . . . . . . . . . . . . . . . . . . | 2,300 | |
| Purchases. . . . . . . . . . . . . . . . . . . . . . . . . . . . . . . . . . . . . . . . . | 67,800 | |
| Purchases Returns and Allowances . . . . . . . . . . . . . . . . . . . . . | | 1,200 |
| Purchases Discounts . . . . . . . . . . . . . . . . . . . . . . . . . . . . . . . . | | 1,300 |
| Freight-In . . . . . . . . . . . . . . . . . . . . . . . . . . . . . . . . . . . . . . . . . | 3,900 | |
| Salary Expense . . . . . . . . . . . . . . . . . . . . . . . . . . . . . . . . . . . . | 12,300 | |
| Insurance Expense . . . . . . . . . . . . . . . . . . . . . . . . . . . . . . . . . | 1,400 | |
| Repairs Expense . . . . . . . . . . . . . . . . . . . . . . . . . . . . . . . . . . . | 700 | |
| Depreciation Expense . . . . . . . . . . . . . . . . . . . . . . . . . . . . . . . | 500 | |
| Store Supplies Used Expense. . . . . . . . . . . . . . . . . . . . . . . . . . | 2,600 | |
| Totals . . . . . . . . . . . . . . . . . . . . . . . . . . . . . . . . . . . . . . . . . . . | $146,700 | $146,700 |

**Required:**

1. Record the closing entries for the year ended Dec. 31, 1998. The ending merchandise inventory amounts to $18,500.

2. Prepare an income statement and a statement of owner's equity for the year ended Dec. 31, 1998.

3. Prepare a balance sheet dated Dec. 31, 1998.

## ■ Solution to Demonstration Problem

1.

### NED'S FLOWER SHOP
### General Journal

| Date | Account Titles and Explanation | Post. Ref. | Debit | Credit |
|------|-------------------------------|-----------|-------|--------|
| 1998 Dec. 31 | Income Summary | | 118,300 | |
| | Merchandise Inventory | | | 23,700 |
| | Sales Returns and Allowances | | | 3,100 |
| | Sales Discounts | | | 2,300 |
| | Purchases | | | 67,800 |
| | Freight-In | | | 3,900 |
| | Salary Expense | | | 12,300 |
| | Insurance Expense | | | 1,400 |
| | Repairs Expense | | | 700 |
| | Depreciation Expense | | | 500 |
| | Store Supplies Used Expense | | | 2,600 |
| | To close income statement accounts having debit balances including beginning inventory. | | | |
| 31 | Merchandise Inventory | | 18,500 | |
| | Sales | | 110,200 | |
| | Purchases Returns and Allowances | | 1,200 | |
| | Purchases Discounts | | 1,300 | |
| | Income Summary | | | 131,200 |
| | To close income statement accounts having credit balances and to establish ending inventories. | | | |
| 31 | Income Summary | | 12,900 | |
| | Ned, Capital | | | 12,900 |
| | To close the Income Summary account. | | | |
| 31 | Ned, Capital | | 3,000 | |
| | Ned, Withdrawals | | | 3,000 |
| | To close the withdrawals account. | | | |

2.

### NED'S FLOWER SHOP
### Income Statement
### Year Ended December 31, 1998

| | | |
|---|---|---|
| Gross Sales .............................................. | | $110,200 |
| Less: Sales Returns and Allowances..................... | $ 3,100 | |
| Sales Discounts ................................ | 2,300 | (5,400) |
| Net Sales............................................... | | $104,800 |

*(Continued)*

Cost of Goods Sold:

| | | | | |
|---|---|---|---|---|
| Merchandise Inventory, Jan. 1, 1998 . . . . . . . . . . . . . . . . . . | | | $23,700 | |
| Purchases. . . . . . . . . . . . . . . . . . . . . . . . . . . . . . | | $67,800 | | |
| Less:  Purchases Returns | | | | |
| and Allowances . . . . . . . . . . . | $1,200 | | | |
| Purchases Discounts. . . . . . . . | 1,300 | (2,500) | | |
| Net Purchases. . . . . . . . . . . . . . . . . . . . . . | | $65,300 | | |
| Plus: Freight-In. . . . . . . . . . . . . . . . . . . . . . . . . | | 3,900 | | |
| Cost of Goods Purchased . . . . . . . . . . . . . . . . . . . . . . . . | | | 69,200 | |
| Cost of Goods Available for Sale . . . . . . . . . . . . . . . . . . . . . | | | $92,900 | |
| Less:  Merchandise Inventory, Dec. 31, 1998. . . . . . . . . . . . | | | 18,500 | |
| Cost of Goods Sold. . . . . . . . . . . . . . . . . . . . . . . . . . . . . . . | | | | 74,400 |
| Gross Profit. . . . . . . . . . . . . . . . . . . . . . . . . . . . . . . . . . . . . | | | | $ 30,400 |

Operating Expenses:

| | | |
|---|---|---|
| Salary Expense . . . . . . . . . . . . . . . . . . . . . . . . . . . . . . . . | $12,300 | |
| Insurance Expense . . . . . . . . . . . . . . . . . . . . . . . . . . . . . | 1,400 | |
| Repairs Expense . . . . . . . . . . . . . . . . . . . . . . . . . . . . . . . | 700 | |
| Depreciation Expense . . . . . . . . . . . . . . . . . . . . . . . . . . . | 500 | |
| Store Supplies Used Expense. . . . . . . . . . . . . . . . . . . . . | 2,600 | |
| Total Operating Expenses . . . . . . . . . . . . . . . . . . . . . . . . . . . | | 17,500 |
| Net Income . . . . . . . . . . . . . . . . . . . . . . . . . . . . . . . . . . . . . . . . . | | $ 12,900 |

## NED'S FLOWER SHOP
### Statement of Changes in Owner's Equity
### Year Ended December 31, 1998

| | |
|---|---|
| Ned, Capital, Jan. 1, 1998 . . . . . . . . . . . . . . . . . . . . . . . . . . . . . . . . . . . | $25,600 |
| Add: Net Income . . . . . . . . . . . . . . . . . . . . . . . . . . . . . . . . . . . . . . . . . . | 12,900 |
| Total . . . . . . . . . . . . . . . . . . . . . . . . . . . . . . . . . . . . . . . . . . . . . | $38,500 |
| Less: Withdrawals. . . . . . . . . . . . . . . . . . . . . . . . . . . . . . . . . . . . . . . | 3,000 |
| Ned, Capital, Dec. 31, 1998 . . . . . . . . . . . . . . . . . . . . . . . . . . . . . . . . . . | $35,500 |

3.

## NED'S FLOWER SHOP
### Balance Sheet
### December 31, 1998

| Assets | | | Liabilities | | |
|---|---|---|---|---|---|
| Current Assets: | | | Current Liabilities: | | |
| Cash. . . . . . . . . . . . . . . . . . . . . . | $ 2,300 | | Accounts Payable . . . . . . . . . . . . . | $3,500 | |
| Accounts Receivable . . . . . . . . . | 12,500 | | Salaries Payable . . . . . . . . . . . . . . | 900 | |
| Merchandise Inventory. . . . . . . . | 18,500 | | Total Current Liabilities . . . . . . . . . . . . . . | | $ 4,400 |
| Store Supplies on Hand. . . . . . . . | 3,100 | | | | |
| Total Current Assets . . . . . . . . . . . . . . . . | | $36,400 | **Owner's Equity** | | |
| | | | | | |
| Plant and Equipment: | | | Ned, Capital . . . . . . . . . . . . . . . . . . . . . . . . | | 35,500 |
| Store Equipment . . . . . . . . . . . . . | $ 7,500 | | | | |
| Less: Accumulated Depreciation . | 4,000 | | | | |
| Total Plant and Equipment . . . . . . . . . . . | | 3,500 | | | |
| | | | | | |
| Total Assets. . . . . . . . . . . . . . . . . . . . . . . | | $39,900 | Total Liabilities and Owner's Equity . . . . . . . . | | $39,900 |

## QUESTIONS FOR REVIEW AND FURTHER THOUGHT

 **REVIEW QUESTIONS**

1. Will an income statement of a service company look just like an income statement of a merchandising concern? Explain your answer.

2. The term *gross profit* appears on the income statement of a merchandising concern. What does this term mean?

3. If a merchandising concern reports gross profit, does that mean that the concern is assured of having net income for the period? Why or why not?

4. Describe the operating expenses section of an income statement.

5. Sales agreements often contain terms such as *2/10, n/30*. What does this term mean?

6. How does a business entity account for sales taxes?

7. What are the differences among a *trade discount*, a *quantity discount*, and a *sales (cash) discount?*

8. Why is *freight-in* considered part of the cost of goods sold?

9. What do the terms *FOB shipping point* and *FOB destination* mean?

10. When a trial balance is prepared for a merchandising concern, it includes the beginning inventory, not the ending inventory. How is the worksheet used to provide the appropriate inventories for the income statement?

11. How do the closing entries of a merchandising concern differ from the closing entries of a service company?

 **QUESTIONS FOR FURTHER THOUGHT**

1. What is the purpose of the Sales Returns and Allowances account?

2. Often, when merchandise is sold on account, the buyer is given a *sales* (or *cash*) *discount* when the bill is paid. Why?

3. An important figure on an income statement is the *cost of goods sold.* How is this figure determined?

4. Why is the Purchases Returns and Allowances account like the Purchases Discounts, Sales Returns and Allowances, Sales Discounts, and Accumulated Depreciation accounts?

5. Snow Company acquired merchandise costing $4,500. The sales agreement called for a 20% trade discount and a cash discount of 3/10, n/30. If the invoice is paid within 10 days, how much will the merchandise cost?

## OBJECTIVE ASSIGNMENT

*True/False*   Indicate whether each statement below is *true* or *false* by placing a *T* or an *F* in the space provided.

_____ 1. The accounting for operating expenses of a trading concern is different from that of a service company.

_____ 2. Sales Returns and Allowances has a normal credit balance.

_____ 3. Cash discounts are used to encourage customers to pay their bills early.

_____ 4. Cost of Goods Sold is an expense account.

_____ 5. *Purchases* refers to the acquisition of goods and services.

*Multiple Choice*   Select the best choice to complete each statement or answer each question below. Write the letter corresponding to your choice in the space provided.

_____ 1. The following account would *not* appear on the income statement of a service-type company:
   a. Purchases Discounts
   b. Office Supplies Expense
   c. Rent Income
   d. Revenue from Fees Earned
   e. None of the above

_____ 2. When merchandise is returned to the seller, the entry made on the seller's books:
   a. Credits Sales
   b. Debits Accounts Receivable
   c. Debits Sales
   d. Debits Cash
   e. None of the above

_____ 3. Sales discounts are recorded:
   a. At the time of the sale
   b. When the receivable is collected prior to the end of the discount period
   c. When the receivable is collected after the discount period
   d. At the time of the month-end closing entry
   e. None of the above

_____ 4. The following is *not* a contra account:
   a. Purchases Discounts
   b. Sales Returns and Allowances
   c. Cost of Goods Sold
   d. Accumulated Depreciation
   e. None of the above

_____ 5. Trade discounts are offered:
   a. To encourage buyers to pay promptly
   b. To encourage buyers to purchase large quantities
   c. To achieve a consistent pricing policy
   d. All of the above
   e. None of the above

____ 6. To the seller, transportation charges will be part of:
   a. Current assets
   b. Cost of goods sold
   c. Current liabilities
   d. Operating expenses
   e. None of the above

____ 7. The determination of cost of goods sold includes all of the following *except:*
   a. An addition for purchases
   b. A deduction for purchases discounts
   c. A deduction for freight-in
   d. An addition for beginning inventory
   e. All of the above

____ 8. On a trading concern's worksheet, the ending inventory would appear as a
   a. Debit in the trial balance
   b. Credit in the trial balance
   c. Debit in the income statement column
   d. Credit in the income statement column
   e. None of the above

____ 9. The following step would *not* be appropriate when closing the accounts:
   a. Close all accounts with a debit balance.
   b. Close the revenue accounts.
   c. Close the expense accounts.
   d. Close the Withdrawals account.
   e. None of the above.

____ 10. The following account is closed at year-end:
   a. Cash
   b. Purchases Discounts
   c. Johnson, Capital
   d. Accumulated Depreciation
   e. None of the above

## EXERCISES

2† **Exercise 1:** Journalizing Sales Transactions

Presented below are several transactions relating to the sales activities of the Everlast Company (whose credit terms are 2/10, n/30):

Apr. 1 Cash sales, $18,000.

   4 Sales on account, $65,000.

   7 Merchandise in the amount of $9,000 relating to the credit sales of the 4th are returned.

   10 Collected the amount due from the credit sales.

Record the transactions in general journal entry form.

† The numbers in the margin refer to the Learning Objectives.

**2**  **Exercise 2:** Journalizing Sales and Sales Tax Transactions

The following transactions relate to the sales activity of the Newkirk Company for the month of October 1998 (credit terms are 2/10, n/30):

Oct.  3   Sales on account $8,000, subject to a $6\frac{1}{2}$% sales tax.

  9   Cash sales amount to $6,000, subject to a $6\frac{1}{2}$% sales tax.

  11   Received payment for the sales made on account on Oct. 3.

Record the transactions in general journal entry form.

**4 6**  **Exercise 3:** Journalizing Purchase Transactions

Several transactions relating to the purchasing activity of the Jenkins Company are presented below (credit terms are 3/10, n/30):

Sept.  6   Purchased merchandise for cash, $20,000.

  12   Purchased on account merchandise costing $70,000.

  15   Returned merchandise costing $5,000 from the transaction of the 12th to the supplier.

  17   Paid the supplier the amount due.

  19   Paid freight charges of $1,400 on merchandise acquired on the 6th. Terms were FOB shipping point.

Record the transactions in general journal entry form.

**4 5**  **Exercise 4:** Computing Trade, Quantity, and Cash Discounts

The Moody Auto Parts Company acquired for resale auto parts on account for a total cost of $54,000 on Apr. 15, 1998. The supplier, Nelson Mfg., allows a 30% trade discount and a 15% quantity discount as well as credit terms of 3/10, n/30. Moody pays the invoice in full on Apr. 20, 1998. Record in general journal entry form the transactions of Apr. 15 and 20 for Moody Auto Parts. Round to the nearest whole dollar.

**4 5 6**  **Exercise 5:** Calculating Purchases Amounts

Using the chart below, calculate the amount to be paid to settle each purchase. All returns are made one day after the goods are received, and all purchases are paid within the discount period.

| Suggested List Price | FOB Terms | Freight Charges | Purchase Returns and Allowances | Credit Terms | Trade Discount | Quantity Discount |
|---|---|---|---|---|---|---|
| $22,400 | Shipping Point | $  400 | $2,100 | 2/10, n/30 | 30% | 10% |
| 12,600 | Destination | 900 | — | 1/10, n/30 | 20% | — |
| 9,000 | Shipping Point | 200 | 700 | 2/10, n/30 | — | 5% |
| 4,100 | Shipping Point | 100 | 900 | n/30 | 25% | 10% |
| 35,700 | Destination | 1,400 | 2,400 | 3/10, n/30 | 20% | 5% |

**7** **Exercise 6:** Determining Missing Elements of an Income Statement

Several items are missing (as indicated by blanks) in each of the following five income statement tabulations. Compute the missing items and fill in the blanks.

| | 1 | 2 | 3 | 4 | 5 |
|---|---|---|---|---|---|
| Net Sales | ____ | ____ | 2,500 | 2,900 | 4,000 |
| Merchandise Inventory, Jan. 1, 1998 | ____ | 500 | 700 | ____ | 1,200 |
| Net Purchases | 800 | ____ | ____ | 1,600 | 3,900 |
| Goods Available for Sale | 1,100 | 1,600 | ____ | ____ | ____ |
| Merchandise Inventory, Dec. 31, 1998 | 400 | ____ | 300 | 700 | ____ |
| Cost of Goods Sold . . . . . . . . . . . . . . | ____ | 1,400 | 2,300 | ____ | 3,800 |
| Gross Profit | 500 | 400 | ____ | 1,600 | ____ |

**7** **Exercise 7:** Determining the Beginning Merchandise Inventory

Using the data presented below for the Elton Company, compute the beginning merchandise inventory as of Jan. 1, 1998.

| | | | |
|---|---|---|---|
| Cost of Goods Sold . . . . . . . . . | $83,600 | Purchases Discounts . . . . . . . . | $ 1,600 |
| Freight-In . . . . . . . . . . . . . . . . . | 2,000 | Purchases Returns | |
| Merchandise Inventory, | | and Allowances . . . . . . . . . . . | 800 |
| Jan. 31, 1998 . . . . . . . . . . . . . | 18,000 | Purchases . . . . . . . . . . . . . . . . | 90,000 |

▶ *(Check Figure: $12,000)*

**7** **Exercise 8:** Determining Ending Merchandise Inventory

A fire destroyed the ending merchandise inventory of the Williams Company on Feb. 18, 1998. The following information was available at the company's accounting office:

| | | | |
|---|---|---|---|
| Beginning Merchandise | | Purchases Discounts . . . . . . . . | $ 2,000 |
| Inventory, Jan. 1, 1998 . . . . . | $ 30,000 | Purchases Returns | |
| Cost of Goods Sold . . . . . . . . | 126,000 | and Allowances . . . . . . . . . . | 3,000 |
| Freight-In . . . . . . . . . . . . . . . | 6,000 | Purchases . . . . . . . . . . . . . . . | 132,000 |

Compute the value of the lost ending merchandise inventory.

▶ *(Check Figure: Ending merchandise inventory = $37,000)*

8   **Exercise 9:** Preparing a Worksheet for a Merchandising Concern

The unadjusted trial balance of the Out West Company on Dec. 31, 1998, appears below:

---

**OUT WEST COMPANY**
**Unadjusted Trial Balance**
**December 31, 1998**

| | | |
|---|---:|---:|
| Cash | $ 100 | |
| Accounts Receivable | 500 | |
| Merchandise Inventory | 700 | |
| Prepaid Rent | 300 | |
| Shop Equipment | 1,600 | |
| Accumulated Depreciation | | $ 200 |
| Accounts Payable | | 400 |
| Williams, Capital | | 1,300 |
| Williams, Withdrawals | 100 | |
| Sales | | 2,900 |
| Sales Discounts | 100 | |
| Purchases | 800 | |
| Purchases Returns and Allowances | | 200 |
| Freight-In | 100 | |
| Salary Expense | 400 | |
| Advertising Expense | 300 | |
| Totals | $5,000 | $5,000 |

---

**Additional Information:**

a. Accrued salaries at year-end amount to $300.
b. Rent in the amount of $100 has expired during the year.
c. Depreciation on shop equipment is $200.
d. The Dec. 31 merchandise inventory amounts to $500.

Prepare a worksheet dated Dec. 31, 1998.

▶ *(Check Figure: Net income = $600)*

9   **Exercise 10:** Preparing Closing Entries

The following accounts appeared in the general ledger of the Telton Company at the end of 1998:

| | | | | |
|---|---:|---|---|---:|
| Accounts Payable | $ 30 | | Purchases Discounts | $ 20 |
| Accounts Receivable | 50 | | Purchases | 400 |
| Cash | 20 | | Salaries Payable | 10 |
| Freight-In | 10 | | Salary Expense | 110 |
| Insurance Expense | 40 | | Sales Returns and Allowances | 20 |
| Merchandise Inventory, Dec. 31, 1998 | 100 | | Sales | 680 |
| | | | Telton, Capital, Jan. 1, 1998 | 120 |
| Merchandise Inventory, Jan. 1, 1998 | 80 | | Telton, Withdrawals | 30 |

Using this information, prepare the year-end closing entries dated Dec. 31, 1998.

1  **Exercise 11:** Preparing an Income Statement

Using the information presented below, prepare an income statement for the Fellows Company for the year ended Dec. 31, 1998.

| | | | |
|---|---|---|---|
| Freight-In. . . . . . . . . . . . . . . . . . . . . . . | $ 3 | Purchases Returns and Allowances | $ 3 |
| Merchandise Inventory, | | Purchases Discounts . . . . . . . . . . . . | 2 |
| Jan. 1, 1998 . . . . . . . . . . . . . . . . . | 12 | Rent Expense . . . . . . . . . . . . . . . . . . | 4 |
| Merchandise Inventory, | | Salary Expense. . . . . . . . . . . . . . . . . | 6 |
| Dec. 31, 1998 . . . . . . . . . . . . . . . . | 19 | Sales. . . . . . . . . . . . . . . . . . . . . . . . . | 60 |
| Miscellaneous Expenses . . . . . . . . . | 5 | Sales Returns and Allowances . . . . | 2 |
| Purchases. . . . . . . . . . . . . . . . . . . . . | 43 | Sales Discounts . . . . . . . . . . . . . . . . | 4 |

▶ *(Check Figure: Net income = $5)*

## PROBLEMS: SET A

1†  **Problem A1:** Preparing an Income Statement for a Merchandising Concern

Accounts selected from the Dec. 31, 1998, trial balance of the Queensland Company are listed below:

| | | | |
|---|---|---|---|
| Sales . . . . . . . . . . . . . . . . . . . . . | $96,300 | Insurance Expense . . . . . . . . . . | $ 2,600 |
| Purchases . . . . . . . . . . . . . . . . | 47,200 | Sales Discounts. . . . . . . . . . . . . | 2,100 |
| Merchandise Inventory, | | Delivery Expense. . . . . . . . . . . . | 1,700 |
| Jan. 1, 1998. . . . . . . . . . . . . . | 21,700 | Depreciation Expense: | |
| Merchandise Inventory, | | Store Equipment . . . . . . . . . . | 1,600 |
| Dec. 31, 1998 . . . . . . . . . . . . | 14,300 | Purchases Returns and | |
| Salary Expense: Selling . . . . . . | 11,400 | Allowances. . . . . . . . . . . . . . . | 1,100 |
| Salary Expense: General . . . . . | 9,200 | Selling Supplies Expense . . . . . . | 800 |
| Office Supplies Expense. . . . . . | 4,600 | Purchases Discounts. . . . . . . . . | 700 |
| Depreciation Expense: | | Freight-In . . . . . . . . . . . . . . . . . | 500 |
| Office Equipment. . . . . . . . . . | 3,200 | Miscellaneous Expenses. . . . . . | 300 |
| Sales Returns and | | | |
| Allowances. . . . . . . . . . . . . . . | 2,800 | | |

**Required:**

Prepare an income statement dividing the statement into three distinct sections: sales, cost of goods sold, and operating expenses. Subdivide the operating expenses section into selling expenses and general expenses.

▶ *(Check Figure: Net income = $2,700)*

2 3 4 5 6  **Problem A2:** Journalizing Sales and Purchase-Related Transactions

The Outback Sales Company and the DownUnder Supply Company entered into the following transactions during the month of November 1998:

Nov.  4  Outback sold merchandise on account to DownUnder, $16,200, credit terms FOB destination 2/10, n/30. Freight charges amount to $200.

  5  Outback sold merchandise on account to DownUnder, $71,000, credit terms FOB shipping point 2/10, n/30. Freight charges amount to $800.

† The numbers in the margin refer to the Learning Objectives.

Nov.  6  DownUnder paid freight charges on the purchase of Nov. 5.

7  Outback received returned merchandise from DownUnder in the amount of $3,100 from the Nov. 4 sale.

9  Outback received payment from DownUnder for the Nov. 4 transaction less the return of Nov. 7 and the appropriate discount.

10  Outback paid the transportation charges of the Nov. 4 shipment.

12  Outback received payment from DownUnder for the Nov. 5 transaction.

18  Outback sold merchandise amounting to $25,000 on account to DownUnder, credit terms FOB shipping point, 2/10, n/30, plus a 40% trade discount.

21  Freight charges on the Nov. 18 transaction were paid, $600.

23  Outback received payment from DownUnder of the amount due from the transaction of Nov. 18.

### Required:

1. Record in a general journal the transactions for the Outback Company.
2. Record in a general journal the transactions for the DownUnder Company.

8  9  **Problem A3:** Preparing a Worksheet and Closing Entries

The unadjusted trial balance of the Shelton Company as of the end of its current business year, Dec. 31, 1998, is presented below:

| SHELTON COMPANY | | |
|---|---|---|
| Unadjusted Trial Balance | | |
| December 31, 1998 | | |
| Cash | $ 3,100 | |
| Accounts Receivable | 8,300 | |
| Merchandise Inventory | 62,700 | |
| Prepaid Insurance | 5,400 | |
| Office Supplies on Hand | 6,800 | |
| Office Equipment | 37,000 | |
| Accumulated Depreciation | | $ 5,000 |
| Accounts Payable | | 5,800 |
| Shelton, Capital | | 51,700 |
| Shelton, Withdrawals | 8,700 | |
| Sales | | 267,500 |
| Sales Returns and Allowances | 2,600 | |
| Sales Discounts | 2,300 | |
| Purchases | 151,200 | |
| Purchases Returns and Allowances | | 1,400 |
| Purchases Discounts | | 1,900 |
| Freight-In | 3,800 | |
| Salary Expense | 32,700 | |
| Advertising Expense | 6,100 | |
| Rent Expense | 2,600 | |
| Totals | $333,300 | $333,300 |

A count of the merchandise inventory on hand as of Dec. 31, 1998, amounted to $53,200.

**Additional Information:**

a. Insurance in the amount of $1,800 has expired during the year.
b. Depreciation for the year amounts of $2,500.
c. Office supplies remaining on hand at year-end amount to $1,500.
d. Salaries in the amount of $900 have accrued as of Dec. 31, 1998.

**Required:**

1. Prepare a complete worksheet for the year ended Dec. 31, 1998.

   ▶ *(Check Figure: Net income = $49,500)*
2. Record the appropriate general journal entries to close the accounts.

**1 8 9  Problem A4:** Preparing a Worksheet, Journalizing Adjusting and Closing Entries, and Preparing Financial Statements

Listed below are the general ledger accounts of the Green Company for the year ended Dec. 31, 1998:

| | | | |
|---|--:|---|--:|
| Accum. Depr.: Office Building. | $ 10,000 | Notes Payable due 2001 . . . . . | $ 20,000 |
| Accum. Depr.: Office Equip. . . | 15,000 | Office Equipment . . . . . . . . . . | 57,000 |
| Accounts Receivable . . . . . . . | 13,600 | Office Building . . . . . . . . . . . . | 160,000 |
| Accounts Payable . . . . . . . . . | 7,400 | Office Supplies on Hand . . . . . | 4,200 |
| Cash. . . . . . . . . . . . . . . . . . . | 7,200 | Prepaid Advertising . . . . . . . . | 7,500 |
| Freight-In . . . . . . . . . . . . . . . | 4,700 | Purchases Discounts. . . . . . . . | 17,200 |
| Insurance Expense . . . . . . . . | 11,000 | Purchases Returns and All. . . | 13,300 |
| Interest Expense . . . . . . . . . . | 15,600 | Purchases . . . . . . . . . . . . . . . | 264,300 |
| Green, Capital . . . . . . . . . . . . | 151,000 | Salary Expense . . . . . . . . . . . | 86,200 |
| Green, Withdrawals . . . . . . . . | 20,000 | Sales Discounts. . . . . . . . . . . | 16,100 |
| Land . . . . . . . . . . . . . . . . . . . | 40,000 | Sales Returns and All. . . . . . . | 18,700 |
| Merchandise Inventory . . . . . . | 59,800 | Sales . . . . . . . . . . . . . . . . . . . | 460,000 |
| Mortgage Payable . . . . . . . . . | 110,000 | Travel Expense . . . . . . . . . . . | 18,000 |

**Additional Information:**

a. Office supplies consumed during the year amount to $1,700.
b. Advertising expense in the amount of $2,500 has expired during the year.
c. Salaries of $2,100 have accrued as of Dec. 31, 1998.
d. Depreciation on the office building and the office equipment amount to $1,500 and $2,000, respectively.
e. The Dec. 31, 1998, ending inventory is $72,300.

**Required:**

1. Prepare and complete a worksheet for the year.

   ▶ *(Check Figure: Net income = $58,600)*
2. Prepare the financial statements.
3. Journalize the appropriate adjusting and closing entries.

1-9 **Problem A5:** Analyzing Various Accounts

Presented below is the adjusted trial balance of the Norton Company as of Jan. 31, 1998. The company's fiscal year ends on Dec. 31. Notice that the trial balance contains the *total* debits and credits for each account, rather than the usual account balances. All adjustments for the month of January have been made.

| Account | Debit | Credit |
|---|---|---|
| Cash . . . . . . . . . . . . . . . . . . . . . . . . . . . . . . . . . . . . . . . . . . . . . . . | $ 96,800 | $ 84,500 |
| Accounts Receivable . . . . . . . . . . . . . . . . . . . . . . . . . . . . . . . . | 100,000 | 65,000 |
| Merchandise Inventory . . . . . . . . . . . . . . . . . . . . . . . . . . . . . . | 32,500 | |
| Prepaid Rent . . . . . . . . . . . . . . . . . . . . . . . . . . . . . . . . . . . . . . | 7,500 | 2,500 |
| Supplies on Hand . . . . . . . . . . . . . . . . . . . . . . . . . . . . . . . . . . | 2,800 | |
| Equipment . . . . . . . . . . . . . . . . . . . . . . . . . . . . . . . . . . . . . . . . | 60,000 | |
| Accumulated Depreciation . . . . . . . . . . . . . . . . . . . . . . . . . . . | | 7,000 |
| Accounts Payable . . . . . . . . . . . . . . . . . . . . . . . . . . . . . . . . . . | 38,000 | 50,000 |
| Salaries Payable . . . . . . . . . . . . . . . . . . . . . . . . . . . . . . . . . . . | | 1,400 |
| Interest Payable . . . . . . . . . . . . . . . . . . . . . . . . . . . . . . . . . . . | | 100 |
| Note Payable . . . . . . . . . . . . . . . . . . . . . . . . . . . . . . . . . . . . . | | 40,000 |
| Norton, Capital . . . . . . . . . . . . . . . . . . . . . . . . . . . . . . . . . . . | | 72,700 |
| Norton, Withdrawals . . . . . . . . . . . . . . . . . . . . . . . . . . . . . . . | 5,200 | |
| Sales . . . . . . . . . . . . . . . . . . . . . . . . . . . . . . . . . . . . . . . . . . . . | | 110,000 |
| Sales Discounts . . . . . . . . . . . . . . . . . . . . . . . . . . . . . . . . . . . | 1,200 | |
| Sales Returns and Allowances . . . . . . . . . . . . . . . . . . . . . . . . | 5,000 | |
| Purchases . . . . . . . . . . . . . . . . . . . . . . . . . . . . . . . . . . . . . . . | 60,000 | |
| Purchases Discounts . . . . . . . . . . . . . . . . . . . . . . . . . . . . . . . | | 600 |
| Purchases Returns and Allowances . . . . . . . . . . . . . . . . . . . . | | 3,000 |
| Freight-In . . . . . . . . . . . . . . . . . . . . . . . . . . . . . . . . . . . . . . . | 1,600 | |
| Salary Expense . . . . . . . . . . . . . . . . . . . . . . . . . . . . . . . . . . . | 21,400 | |
| Rent Expense . . . . . . . . . . . . . . . . . . . . . . . . . . . . . . . . . . . . . | 2,500 | |
| Supplies Expense . . . . . . . . . . . . . . . . . . . . . . . . . . . . . . . . . | 3,700 | 2,800 |
| Depreciation Expense . . . . . . . . . . . . . . . . . . . . . . . . . . . . . . | 1,000 | |
| Interest Expense . . . . . . . . . . . . . . . . . . . . . . . . . . . . . . . . . . | 400 | |
| Totals . . . . . . . . . . . . . . . . . . . . . . . . . . . . . . . . . . . . . . . . . . . | $439,600 | $439,600 |

**Required:**

Using the amounts of debits and credits in the adjusted trial balance of the Norton Company and the additional information given below, answer the following questions.

1. Assuming that no interest was payable as of Dec. 31, 1997, what was the amount of cash paid for interest for the month of January?
2. If the cash balance was $8,000 on Jan. 1, and the accounts receivable balance was $20,000, what was the amount from sales?
3. On what date was the equipment acquired?
4. How much cash was paid for salaries for the month?
5. What was the balance of the merchandise inventory account on Jan. 1?
6. No purchases were made during the last 10 days of January, and all vendors sell to Norton on terms of 2/10, n/30. What is the total amount of discounts that were allowed to lapse?
7. If the balance in the Prepaid Rent account was –0– on Jan. 1, what is the term of the lease?
8. What journal entry does Norton make to record the acquisition of supplies?
9. The note payable has neither increased nor decreased during the month. What interest rate is applicable on the note payable?
10. If the amount of supplies on hand on Jan. 1 was $1,200, what was the amount of supplies acquired during the month?
11. What was the balance of the Norton, Capital, account on Jan. 1?
12. If only the acquisition of merchandise on account is recorded in the accounts payable account and all other expense and asset acquisitions are paid for in cash, what was the amount of purchases acquired directly for cash? The beginning balance of accounts payable was $5,000.

13. How much cash was paid on accounts payable during the month?
14. If the Norton Company uses reversing entries, what accounts were most likely reversed on Jan. 1?

## PROBLEMS: SET B

1† **Problem B1:** Preparing an Income Statement for a Merchandising Concern

Listed below are the accounts of Bartow Company selected from the July 31, 1998, year-end trial balance:

| | | | |
|---|---|---|---|
| Advertising Expense | $ 1,500 | Purchases | $67,100 |
| Delivery Expense | 2,600 | Purchases Returns | |
| Depr. Expense: Office Equip. | 1,100 | and Allowances | 2,500 |
| Depr. Expense: Store Equip. | 1,400 | Purchases Discounts | 1,800 |
| Freight-In | 1,000 | Salary Expense: Selling | 9,600 |
| Merchandise Inventory, | | Salary Expense: General | 11,300 |
| Aug. 1, 1997 | 11,600 | Sales | 98,100 |
| Merchandise Inventory, | | Sales Returns and Allowances | 2,600 |
| July 31, 1998 | 10,400 | Sales Discounts | 1,400 |
| Miscellaneous Expenses | 900 | Selling Supplies Expense | 700 |
| Office Supplies Expense | 4,300 | | |

**Required:**

Prepare an income statement, dividing the statement into three distinct sections: sales, cost of goods sold, and operating expenses. Subdivide the operating expenses section into selling expenses and general expenses.

▶ *(Check Figure: Net loss = $4,300)*

2 3 4 5 6 **Problem B2:** Journalizing Sales and Purchase Related Transactions

During the month of August 1998, the Lexington Company and the Park Supply Company entered into the following transactions.

Aug. 5 Lexington purchased merchandise on account from Park, $24,300, credit terms FOB shipping point 3/10, n/30. Freight charges amount to $400 and were paid this date.

7 Lexington purchased merchandise on account from Park, $47,000, credit terms FOB destination 3/10, n/30. Freight charges amount to $700.

8 Lexington returned $1,800 of merchandise to Park from the Aug. 5 purchase.

10 Lexington paid Park the amount due on the Aug. 5 transaction, less the return of Aug. 8 and the appropriate discount.

11 Park paid the transportation charges of the Aug. 7 shipment.

14 Lexington paid Park the amount due from the Aug. 7 transaction.

21 Lexington purchased $27,000 of merchandise from Park on account, credit terms 3/10, n/30, FOB shipping point, less a 20% quantity discount.

25 Freight charges on the Aug. 21 transaction amounted to $500 and were paid this date.

26 Lexington paid Park the amount due on the Aug. 21 transaction.

**Required:**

1. Record in a general journal the transactions for the Lexington Company.
2. Record in a general journal the transactions for the Park Company.

† The numbers in the margin refer to the Learning Objectives.

8 9 **Problem B3:** Preparing a Worksheet and Closing Entries

Presented below is the unadjusted trial balance of the Nolan Company as of the end of its current business year, Dec. 31, 1998:

---

**NOLAN COMPANY**
**Unadjusted Trial Balance**
**December 31, 1998**

| | | |
|---|---:|---:|
| Cash . . . . . . . . . . . . . . . . . . . . . . . . . . . . . . . . . . . . . . . . . . . . . . | $ 2,100 | |
| Accounts Receivable . . . . . . . . . . . . . . . . . . . . . . . . . . . . . . . | 9,600 | |
| Merchandise Inventory . . . . . . . . . . . . . . . . . . . . . . . . . . . . . . . | 39,300 | |
| Prepaid Advertising . . . . . . . . . . . . . . . . . . . . . . . . . . . . . . . . | 2,400 | |
| Store Supplies on Hand . . . . . . . . . . . . . . . . . . . . . . . . . . . . . | 5,300 | |
| Store Equipment . . . . . . . . . . . . . . . . . . . . . . . . . . . . . . . . . . . | 21,000 | |
| Accumulated Depreciation: Store Equipment . . . . . . . . . . . . . . | | $ 2,500 |
| Accounts Payable . . . . . . . . . . . . . . . . . . . . . . . . . . . . . . . . . . . | | 7,200 |
| Nolan, Capital . . . . . . . . . . . . . . . . . . . . . . . . . . . . . . . . . . . . . | | 64,200 |
| Nolan, Withdrawals . . . . . . . . . . . . . . . . . . . . . . . . . . . . . . . . . | 14,500 | |
| Sales . . . . . . . . . . . . . . . . . . . . . . . . . . . . . . . . . . . . . . . . . . . . | | 236,200 |
| Sales Returns and Allowances . . . . . . . . . . . . . . . . . . . . . . . . | 2,700 | |
| Sales Discounts . . . . . . . . . . . . . . . . . . . . . . . . . . . . . . . . . . . | 3,300 | |
| Purchases . . . . . . . . . . . . . . . . . . . . . . . . . . . . . . . . . . . . . . . . | 147,500 | |
| Purchases Returns and Allowances . . . . . . . . . . . . . . . . . . . . . | | 1,600 |
| Purchases Discounts . . . . . . . . . . . . . . . . . . . . . . . . . . . . . . . | | 2,300 |
| Freight-In . . . . . . . . . . . . . . . . . . . . . . . . . . . . . . . . . . . . . . . . . | 4,200 | |
| Salary Expense . . . . . . . . . . . . . . . . . . . . . . . . . . . . . . . . . . . . | 51,700 | |
| Rent Expense . . . . . . . . . . . . . . . . . . . . . . . . . . . . . . . . . . . . . | 6,600 | |
| Insurance Expense . . . . . . . . . . . . . . . . . . . . . . . . . . . . . . . . . | 3,800 | |
| Totals . . . . . . . . . . . . . . . . . . . . . . . . . . . . . . . . . . . . . . . . . . . | $314,000 | $314,000 |

---

A count of the merchandise inventory on hand as of Dec. 31, 1998, amounted to $36,700.

**Additional Information:**

a. Salaries in the amount of $1,900 are accrued at year-end.
b. Prepaid advertising in the amount of $600 expired during the year.
c. Depreciation on the store equipment amounts to $2,500 for the year.
d. Store supplies on hand at year-end are valued at $2,100.

**Required:**

1. Prepare a complete worksheet for the year ended Dec. 31, 1998.

   ▶ *(Check Figure: Net income = $9,500)*
2. Record the appropriate general journal entries to close the accounts.

1 8 9 **Problem B4:** Preparing a Worksheet, Journalizing Adjusting and Closing Entries, and Preparing Financial Statements

The following accounts reflect the business activity of Crawely Sales Company as of Dec. 31, 1998.

| | | | |
|---|---|---|---|
| Sales .................... | $420,000 | Note Payable due 2001....... | $12,000 |
| Purchases ............... | 237,100 | Sales Ret. and All............ | 11,300 |
| Store Building ............ | 170,000 | Accum. Depr.: Store Building .. | 10,000 |
| Mortgage Payable.......... | 140,000 | Accounts Receivable......... | 9,200 |
| Crawely, Capital ........... | 137,500 | Store Supplies on Hand ...... | 8,900 |
| Salary Expense............ | 94,200 | Sales Discounts............. | 8,400 |
| Store Equipment ........... | 60,000 | Purchases Discounts........ | 7,100 |
| Merchandise Inventory ...... | 57,100 | Freight-In.................. | 6,500 |
| Land..................... | 51,000 | Prepaid Insurance........... | 6,000 |
| Crawely, Withdrawals ....... | 25,000 | Accounts Payable ........... | 5,700 |
| Accum. Depr.: Store Equip. ... | 24,000 | Cash..................... | 5,600 |
| Purch. Ret. and All.......... | 19,700 | Advertising Expense ......... | 4,300 |
| Interest Expense ........... | 18,200 | Entertainment Expense....... | 3,200 |

**Additional Information:**

a. Depreciation for the year on the store equipment and on the building amounts to $2,500 and $3,000, respectively.
b. A count of the store supplies on hand amounts to $3,100.
c. Insurance in the amount of $2,000 has expired.
d. Salaries of $2,700 have accrued as of the last day of the year.
e. A count of the ending merchandise inventory amounted to $62,700.

**Required:**

1. Prepare and complete a worksheet for the year.

   ▶ (Check Figure: Net income = $53,200)
2. Prepare the financial statements.
3. Journalize the appropriate adjusting and closing entries.

1–9 **Problem B5:** Analyzing Various Accounts

The trial balance that appears on page 6-39 for the Dillard Company, whose fiscal year ends on Dec. 31, is an adjusted trial balance as of Jan. 31, 1998. Notice that the trial balance contains the total debits and credits for each account, rather than the usual account balances. All adjustments for the month of January have been made.

**Required:**

Using the amounts of debits and credits in the adjusted trial balance of the Dillard Company and the following additional information, answer these questions.

1. Assuming that no interest was payable as of Dec. 31, 1997, what was the amount of cash paid for interest for the month of January?

(Continued)

| Account | Debit | Credit |
|---|---|---|
| Cash | $179,500 | $163,600 |
| Accounts Receivable | 148,000 | 135,000 |
| Merchandise Inventory | 26,300 | |
| Prepaid Rent | 10,500 | |
| Supplies on Hand | 5,300 | 2,600 |
| Equipment | 90,000 | |
| Accumulated Depreciation | | 6,000 |
| Accounts Payable | 95,200 | 106,500 |
| Salaries Payable | | 1,700 |
| Interest Payable | | 200 |
| Unearned Sales Revenue | | 3,000 |
| Note Payable | | 60,000 |
| Dillard, Capital | | 81,300 |
| Dillard, Withdrawals | 6,100 | |
| Sales | 3,000 | 160,000 |
| Sales Discounts | 2,500 | |
| Sales Returns and Allowances | 8,000 | |
| Purchases | 120,000 | |
| Purchases Discounts | | 2,100 |
| Purchases Returns and Allowances | | 1,500 |
| Freight-In | 2,700 | |
| Salary Expense | 19,700 | |
| Rent Expense | 12,600 | 10,500 |
| Supplies Expense | 2,600 | |
| Depreciation Expense | 1,500 | |
| Interest Expense | 500 | |
| Totals | $734,000 | $734,000 |

2. If the cash balance was $15,000 on Jan. 1, and the accounts receivable balance was $28,000, what was the amount of cash received from cash sales including the amount in the Unearned Sales Revenue Account?
3. On what date was the equipment acquired?
4. How much cash was paid for salaries for the month?
5. What was the balance of the Merchandise Inventory account on Jan. 1?
6. No purchases were made during the last 10 days of January, and all vendors sell to Dillard on terms of 2/10, n/30. What is the total amount of discounts that were allowed to lapse?
7. If the balance in the Rent Expense account was –0– on Jan. 1, what is the term of the lease?
8. What journal entry does Dillard make to record the acquisition of supplies?
9. The note payable has neither increased nor decreased during the month. What interest rate is applicable on the note payable?
10. If the amount of supplies on hand on Jan. 1 was $1,900, what was the amount of supplies acquired during the month?
11. What was the balance of the Dillard, Capital, account on Jan. 1?
12. If only the acquisition of merchandise on account is recorded in the Accounts Payable account and all other expense and asset acquisitions are paid for in cash, what was the amount of purchases acquired directly for cash? The beginning balance of Accounts Payable was $16,500.
13. How much cash was paid on accounts payable during the month?
14. Why is there a debit to the Sales account?
15. If the Dillard Company uses reversing entries, what accounts were most likely reversed on Jan. 1?

## DECISION PROBLEM

The general manager of the Austin Division of Texas Supplies and Materials has just received the financial statements for the division for the year ended Dec. 31, 1998. He is very concerned because he had anticipated the division's net income to be about $130,000, but the actual figure is just over $90,000. The general manager assigns you the task of determining the cause of the difference and provides you with a 118-page computer printout of the division's activity.

You find on the first summary page the following:

```
TEXAS SUPPLIES AND MATERIALS      DATE: 1/17/99      PAGE 1 OF 118
DIVISION 012 (AUSTIN)             TIME: 14:30:17
SUMMARY INCOME STATEMENT          PERIOD: 1/1/98 TO 12/31/98

NET SALES                                  $2,496,986
COST OF GOODS SOLD                          1,977,654
GROSS PROFIT                               $  519,332
OPERATING EXPENSES                            427,018
NET INCOME                                 $   92,314
```

From past experience, you know that the net income should be about $5\frac{1}{4}$% of sales.

Included on page 17 of the report is the following:

```
TEXAS SUPPLIES AND MATERIALS      DATE: 1/17/99      PAGE 17 OF 118
DIVISION 012 (AUSTIN)             TIME: 14:30:53
COST OF GOODS SOLD                PERIOD: 1/1/98 TO 12/31/98

MERCHANDISE INVENTORY 1/1/98                            $  547,026
PURCHASES                                  $1,978,315
PURCHASES RETURNS             $79,133
PURCHASES DISCOUNTS            18,719          97,852
  NET PURCHASES                            $1,880,463
FREIGHT-IN                                     42,117
COST OF GOODS PURCHASED                                  1,922,580
COST OF GOODS AVAILABLE FOR SALE                        $2,469,606
MERCHANDISE INVENTORY 12/31/98                             491,952
COST OF GOODS SOLD                                      $1,977,654
```

A review of the past year's activity reveals that purchase returns usually average about 3.8% to 4.2% of purchases and that purchases discounts from vendors are a constant 3%. Moreover, the division never buys materials from Dec. 15 to the following Jan. 15 due to the holiday season.

**Required:**

1. What can you identify as the problem with the Austin Division?
2. How much should net income be? Show supporting computations.
3. How would you suggest the problem be solved?

## ETHICS CASE

American Products compensates its regional sales managers by means of annual salary plus a year-end bonus. Each manager's bonus is determined on Dec. 31 and is based on the region's net sales for the year according to the following schedule:

| Net Sales | Percent Bonus |
|---|---|
| $1,000,000–$5,000,000 | $\frac{1}{4}$% |
| $5,000,001–$10,000,000 | $\frac{1}{2}$% |
| $10,000,001–$20,000,000 | 1% |
| Over $20,000,000 | 3% |

John Appleworth is the sales manager for the northeastern region. In late October 1998 he negotiated a large contract, amounting to $655,300, with Newark Wholesale Company. The merchandise was shipped from American's Philadelphia plant in early December. With this order John will finish the year with total sales of $23,175,200 and will receive a bonus of $232,756.

On Dec. 19, Appleworth received a call at home from the office manager of the Philadelphia plant, informing him that Newark Wholesale is facing financial difficulties and will be returning the merchandise within the week. Early the next morning, Appleworth called Newark Wholesale and told them to hold the merchandise until Jan. 10, 1999, because the Philadelphia warehouse would not be able to receive the returned merchandise due to the holiday season.

**Required:**

Discuss the implications of Appleworth's phone call to Newark Wholesale.

## COMPREHENSIVE PROBLEMS

1–9† **Comprehensive Problem 1:** Completing the Accounting Cycle for a Merchandising Concern

The account balances of the Bridgeport Company as of Dec. 1, 1998, are listed below:

| | | | |
|---|---|---|---|
| 110 | Cash | $21,400 | |
| 120 | Accounts Receivable | 33,800 | |
| 130 | Merchandise Inventory | 42,600 | |
| 140 | Office Supplies on Hand | 3,100 | |
| 150 | Prepaid Insurance | 4,800 | |
| 160 | Land | 37,000 | |
| 170 | Building | 90,000 | |
| 175 | Accumulated Depreciation: Building | | $ 25,000 |
| 180 | Office Equipment | 80,000 | |
| 185 | Accumulated Depreciation: Office Equipment | | 20,000 |
| 210 | Accounts Payable | | 17,200 |
| 220 | Salaries Payable | | –0– |
| 230 | Mortgage Payable | | 120,000 |
| 310 | Bridgeport, Capital | | 130,500 |
| 320 | Bridgeport, Withdrawals | –0– | |
| 330 | Income Summary | | –0– |
| 420 | Sales Returns and Allowances | –0– | |
| 430 | Sales Discounts | –0– | |
| 510 | Purchases | –0– | |
| 520 | Purchases Returns and Allowances | | –0– |
| 530 | Purchases Discounts | | –0– |
| 540 | Freight-In | –0– | |
| 610 | Salary Expense | –0– | |
| 610 | Salary Expense | –0– | |
| 620 | Office Supplies Expense | –0– | |

*(Continued)*

† The numbers in the margin refer to the Learning Objectives.

| 630 | Insurance Expense | –0– |
| 640 | Depreciation Expense: Building | –0– |
| 650 | Depreciation Expense: Office Equipment | –0– |
| 660 | Delivery Expense | –0– |
| 670 | Entertainment Expense | –0– |
| 680 | Repairs Expense | –0– |
| 690 | Interest Expense | –0– |

The following transactions occurred during the month of December 1998:

Dec. 1 Accounts payable in the amount of $11,500 were paid, less a 2% discount.

3 Received payment from customers on accounts receivable of $18,000 less a 3% discount.

4 Sold merchandise on account to Dillon Supply Company in the amount of $21,000 under credit terms of 3/10, n/30, FOB destination.

5 Received from the Dillon Supply Company returned merchandise in the amount of $2,500.

7 Purchased merchandise from Newton Mfg. under credit terms of 2/10, n/30, FOB shipping point, $23,200.

9 Returned to Newton Mfg. $1,200 of merchandise acquired on December 7.

10 Paid interest for the month on the mortgage payable, $800.

11 Received payment from Dillon Supply for amount due, less the return of Dec. 5 and the appropriate discount.

12 Paid freight charges on the Dec. 4 shipment, $1,300.

13 Paid Newton Mfg. for merchandise purchased on Dec. 7, less the return of Dec. 9 and the appropriate discount.

14 Sold merchandise to Bristol Retail Outlet under credit terms of 3/10, n/30, FOB shipping point, $33,000.

14 Paid freight charges of $600 for the merchandise acquired from Newton Mfg. on Dec. 7.

15 Paid salaries, $7,400.

18 Purchased merchandise on account from Greely Supply Company under credit terms of 2/10, n/30, FOB shipping point, $11,300.

18 Acquired office supplies for cash, $900.

19 Received payment from Bristol Retail for the Dec. 14 transaction, less the appropriate discount.

20 Returned $800 of the merchandise purchased on Dec. 18 from Greely Supply Company.

21 Paid entertainment expense, $300.

23 Sold merchandise to Hamilton Shop, $24,200, under credit terms of 3/10, n/30, FOB shipping point.

24 Paid Greely Supply Company for merchandise purchased on Dec. 18 less return of Dec. 20 and appropriate discount.

26 Paid $900 for entertainment expense.

28 Paid freight charges on the merchandise purchased from Greely Supply Company on Dec. 18, $400.

29 Purchased merchandise on account from Whily Wholesale Company, $54,000 under credit terms of 3/10, n/30, F.O.B. destination. A 30% trade discount is allowed.

29 Received from Hamilton returned merchandise in the amount of $1,800 from the sale of Dec. 23.

30 Paid $1,900 for repairs to the office equipment.

31 Mr. Bridgeport withdrew $17,000 from the business.

**Required:**

1. Post the Dec. 1, 1998, account balances to the general ledger accounts.
2. Record the transactions for the month of December in a general journal (journal page 9) and post the transactions to the general ledger.
3. Prepare on a worksheet the Dec. 31, 1998, trial balance and complete the worksheet using the following information:
   a. Salaries in the amount of $7,300 were accrued on Dec. 31.
   b. Insurance in the amount of $200 has expired at month's end.
   c. Depreciation on the building and on office equipment for the month amounts to $300 and $450, respectively.
   d. Office supplies on hand at month's end amount to $700.
   e. A count of the ending inventory amounts to $65,300 on Dec. 31, 1998.

   ▶ *(Check Figure: Net loss = $55)*
4. Prepare an income statement and a statement of owner's equity for the month ended Dec. 31, 1998, and a balance sheet dated Dec. 31, 1998.
5. Record in the general journal the adjusting entries (journal page 10) and the closing entries (journal page 11) for the month.
6. Post the adjusting and closing entries to the ledger accounts.

1–9 **Comprehensive Problem 2:** Completing the Accounting Cycle for a Merchandising Concern

Listed below are the Feb. 1, 1998, account balances of the Redford Company:

| | | | |
|---|---|---:|---:|
| 110 | Cash | $ 3,300 | |
| 120 | Accounts Receivable | 19,200 | |
| 130 | Merchandise Inventory | 41,300 | |
| 140 | Supplies on Hand | 5,100 | |
| 150 | Prepaid Insurance | 4,800 | |
| 160 | Land | 46,000 | |
| 170 | Building | 175,000 | |
| 175 | Accumulated Depreciation: Building | | $ 35,000 |
| 180 | Equipment | 231,000 | |
| 185 | Accumulated Depreciation: Equipment | | 63,000 |
| 210 | Accounts Payable | | 10,800 |
| 220 | Salaries Payable | | –0– |
| 230 | Mortgage Payable | | 260,000 |
| 310 | Redford, Capital | | 156,900 |
| 320 | Redford, Withdrawals | –0– | |
| 330 | Income Summary | –0– | |
| 410 | Sales | | –0– |
| 420 | Sales Returns and Allowances | –0– | |
| 430 | Sales Discounts | –0– | |
| 510 | Purchases | –0– | |
| 520 | Purchases Returns and Allowances | | –0– |
| 530 | Purchases Discounts | | –0– |
| 540 | Freight-In | –0– | |
| 610 | Salary Expense | –0– | |
| 620 | Supplies Expense | –0– | |
| 630 | Insurance Expense | –0– | |
| 640 | Depreciation Expense: Building | –0– | |
| 650 | Depreciation Expense: Cannery Equipment | –0– | |
| 660 | Delivery Expense | –0– | |
| 670 | Advertising Expense | –0– | |
| 680 | Interest Expense | –0– | |
| 690 | Miscellaneous Expense | –0– | |

During the month of February 1998, the following transactions occurred:

Feb. 1   Collected $11,300 from customers on past-due accounts.

2   Paid $6,400 of accounts due this date, less purchase discount of 3%.

4   Purchased merchandise in the amount of $17,000 under credit terms of 3/10, n/30, FOB shipping point.

5   Sold merchandise on account to Engle Company in the amount of $27,000 under credit terms of 2/10, n/30, FOB shipping point.

7   Paid for local advertising for the month of February, $600.

7   Sold merchandise, $25,000, for cash.

8   Paid the amount due from the Feb. 4 transaction.

9   Paid Penn Freight $400 for delivering merchandise on the Feb. 4 transaction.

10  Received from the Engle Company $7,000 of returned merchandise from the Feb. 5 sale.

12  Received payment from the Engle Company, less return of Feb. 10, and less the discount.

14  Paid $2,600 interest on the mortgage payable.

15  Paid salaries, $5,100.

16  Sold merchandise on account $39,200 to Better Company, terms 2/10, n/30, FOB destination.

18  Paid $400 freight charges on the sale of Feb. 16.

19  Acquired supplies for cash, $2,100.

20  Purchased $12,500 of merchandise from Potter Company on account, terms 3/10, n/30, FOB destination.

22  Paid $700 miscellaneous expenses.

23  Received payment due from Better Company less appropriate discount.

24  Purchased $37,300 of merchandise on account from Jenkins Company, terms 3/10, n/30, FOB shipping point.

24  Paid PineTown Express $900 freight for delivering merchandise acquired from Jenkins.

25  Sold to Better Company on account $42,000 of merchandise, credit terms of 2/10, n/30, FOB shipping point.

26  Received from Better Company returned merchandise in the amount of $7,100.

28  Mr. Redford withdrew $40,000 from the business.

28  Returned $2,500 of merchandise purchased from Jenkins on June 24.

**Required:**

1. Post the Feb. 1, 1998, account balances to the general ledger accounts.
2. Record the transactions for the month of February in a general journal (journal page 6) and post the transactions to the general ledger.
3. Prepare on a worksheet the Feb. 28, 1998, trial balance and complete the worksheet using the following information:
   a. Salaries in the amount of $5,100 were accrued on Feb. 28.
   b. Insurance in the amount of $200 has expired at month-end.
   c. Depreciation on the building and on equipment for the month amounts to $900 and $1,200, respectively.
   d. Supplies on hand at month-end amount to $1,400.
   e. A count of the ending merchandise inventory amounts to $39,700 on Feb. 28, 1998.

▶ (Check Figure: Net income = $28,818)

4. Prepare an income statement and a statement of owner's equity for the month ended Feb. 28, 1998, and a balance sheet dated Feb. 28, 1998.
5. Record in the general journal the adjusting (journal page 7) and closing (page 8) entries for the month.
6. Post the adjusting and closing entries to the ledger accounts.

## OBJECTIVE ASSIGNMENT ANSWERS

### True/False

**1.** T    **2.** F    **3.** T    **4.** T    **5.** F

### Multiple Choice

**1.** a    **2.** e    **3.** b    **4.** c    **5.** e

**6.** d    **7.** c    **8.** d    **9.** a    **10.** b

# Internal Control and Accounting Systems Design

# Handy Food Store Plays the Lottery

Handy Food Store officials discovered $70,000 missing during an internal audit of a local convenience store. The funds were taken between May 1989 and August 1990 by the store manager, who had responsibility for cash receipts and the accounting records.

The theft was discovered when the records received from the convenience store did not agree with vouchers kept by the Florida Lottery Department . The store manager had changed the records to indicate that the store was paying lottery winners much larger amounts than was the case.

*Source:* Ken Wright, Tampa (Fla.) *Tribune-Times,* Aug. 24, 1990, p. 3, Brandon Section.

"But Mr. Potter was our most trusted employee," lamented the office manager after the embezzlement was discovered. "For 15 years he's been the most diligent worker in the funds transfers section. Mr. Potter never even took a day's vacation. How could he do this to me?"

That is an all too familiar scene to those of us in accounting. Read your local newspaper for the next few months and you will find at least one story about a similar situation (as in the accompanying box). The hardest-working employee is not necessarily the most trustworthy one. And it is not surprising that Mr. Potter never took a vacation. If he had, someone else would have had to handle his duties and would have discovered his "unique" methods of transferring company funds. The problem here is that the company evidently did not have a system of checks and balances built into its operations to prevent this particular fraud. In short, there was no internal control.

## OBJECTIVES OF INTERNAL CONTROL AND ACCOUNTING SYSTEMS DESIGN

**Learning Objective 1**

State the objectives of internal control and accounting systems design

**Internal control** includes all the procedures, techniques, and practices designed to provide a dependable and efficient accounting system that will help management plan and control the company's business activities as well as safeguard the company's resources. Internal control and system design are inseparable, because system design develops the forms, records, reports, procedures, and other controls that make internal control work for a company.

The first thing we need to realize about any internal control and accounting system design, no matter how tightly structured, is that it cannot be made 100% foolproof. That's why casualty insurance is carried on company assets, and why fidelity bonds are carried on employees who handle company funds. But an internal control system can be designed so that it is almost impossible for one person to perpetrate a fraud. A good internal control system ensures that several dishonest employees would have to conspire to defraud the company. The necessity for such collusion makes embezzlement less likely.

## SYSTEM INSTALLATION

**Learning Objective 2**

Describe the stages of accounting system installation

Accountants specializing in management information systems identify three distinct stages in the installation of an internal control and accounting system:

1. System analysis
2. System design
3. System implementation

### System Analysis

In the first stage of system installation, **system analysis,** the accountant (or, more likely, an accounting systems team) prepares a complete study of management's information needs and reporting requirements, and an analysis of where that information is available (or could be made available). Also essential is a review of the way the firm is organized, including job descriptions for all personnel and a study of the various forms, records, reports, procedures, and controls already used by the firm.

### System Design

Using the information gathered in the system analysis stage, the systems team develops new forms, records, reports, procedures, and controls. This process of **system design** will be tailored to the specific needs of the firm and the firm's personnel. The systems team must have a knowledge of the various types of computer and mechanical data processing equipment, as well as a knowledge of internal control.

### System Implementation

In the last stage, **system implementation,** the team installs the newly designed system. Personnel are trained by the team in the use of new forms, procedures, and perhaps equipment. Often the old and new systems coexist for a time. Dual records are maintained to assure that the new system is doing what it was designed to do and to minimize the possible loss of data. This overlap is especially useful when an organization is converting from a manual system to a computerized system. As experience develops, some modification of the system usually occurs.

**ASK YOURSELF** ▶

1. **List the three stages of system installation.**
2. **What do these terms mean?**
   a. **System analysis**
   b. **System design**
   c. **System implementation**

## INTERNAL CONTROL

Internal controls may be either administrative or accounting. We will describe both types, although our primary concern is with accounting controls.

### Administrative Controls

Learning
Objective **3**

Distinguish between accounting and administrative controls

**Administrative controls** are the procedures and methods that govern the operational efficiency of the organization and compliance with the organization's policies. They include time-and-motion studies, performance reports, statistical analyses, and various policy directives, such as a requirement that company executives have annual medical examinations.

### Accounting Controls

**Accounting controls** are the internal procedures, techniques, and practices designed to protect the company's resources and provide for reliable financial statements. Internal accounting controls are of three types: personnel controls, records

**Exhibit 1** Types of Accounting Controls and Their Components

| | Accounting Controls | | |
| --- | --- | --- | --- |
| | **Personnel Controls** | **Records Controls** | **Checks and Balances** |
| **Components** | Employee competence<br>Assignment of duties<br>Division of Work<br>Rotation of duties | Custodianship<br>Adequacy<br>Documentation | Reconciliations<br>Internal audits<br>External audits |

Learning Objective 4

List the elements of accounting controls

controls, and checks and balances. Each of these types has several components, which are listed in Exhibit 6-1 and discussed below.

### Personnel Controls

Four basic considerations govern the development of a strong system of internal **personnel controls.** These considerations are: employee competence, assignment of responsibility, division of work, and rotation of duties.

**Employee Competence**  The organization must be sure that employees are carefully selected and that they have the necessary talents, intelligence, and training for the duties assigned to them. It is equally important that employees be properly supervised as they perform their duties. Talent and intelligence are wasted if employees have not been adequately trained to perform their tasks. A supervisor's most important assignment is to train people so that they can reach their highest potential within the organization.

**Clear Assignment of Responsibility**  Picture 10 employees assigned to the accounts receivable section of a large department store. An irate customer calls, complaining about an error in her account. As manager of this section, you need to discuss the error with the individual who made it. Now, errors are an unavoidable fact of life. But you can attempt to prevent the individual from repeating the error by helping him or her to learn from it. As Fra Pacioli wrote:

> Who does nothing
> makes no mistakes;
>
> Who makes no mistakes
> Learns nothing.

FRA LUCA PACIOLI (1445–1520)

First, however, you must be able to identify the source of the error. Clearly, the system must be designed so that you can pinpoint the responsibility. The accounts receivable section should be organized so that each employee is responsible for a specific series of customer account numbers.

**Division of Work**  In the case of Mr. Potter, the embezzler, good personnel controls could have kept him honest by making someone else responsible for some of the duties he performed—either for depositing customer checks or for maintaining the accounts receivable records. In general, employee assignments should be divided so that related operations are not performed by the same individual. Such division of responsibilities is what makes it necessary for several employees to collude in order to defraud the company.

**Rotation of Duties**  Rotating individual assignments within the work unit serves several purposes. It familiarizes employees with all areas of the unit, thus providing them with a clearer picture of the unit's role in the organization and enabling them to fill in for absent employees. Such broad experience enhances the value of employees. Rotation also strengthens the system, since any departure from standard operating procedures will be discovered when another employee performs the assignment. Lastly, the experience provided by rotation gives employees a basis for future promotion to management responsibility over several functions.

The organization should have a policy requiring all employees to take annual vacation. Clearly, such a policy benefits not only employees but also the firm. Mr. Potter's company would have been much better off if he had been forced to take vacations.

### Records Controls

**Records controls** involve monitoring a firm's recordkeeping procedures in order to maintain proper custodianship, adequacy, and documentation.

**Custodianship**  Someone within the firm must be responsible for the company's small tools and replacement parts. If that individual is also made responsible for maintaining the inventory records for this equipment, then the company is inviting that individual to supply himself and his friends with all the tools and parts they need at company expense. Similarly, the individual assigned the responsibility for maintaining the accounts receivable records must not have any access to cash. Those who prepare the payroll records must not be authorized to draw checks from the payroll cash account. The point is that the person assigned the custodianship of any of the firm's resources must not have access to the records pertaining to those resources, and vice versa.

**Adequacy**  To provide control over the firm's resources as well as to provide management with timely, accurate, and reliable information, adequate records must be maintained. In fact, all publicly held corporations in the United States are required by the Foreign Corrupt Practices Act to maintain adequate records to assure that the corporation's resources are what and where the corporation says they are. The law requires that a system of internal control must be adequate to ensure that the management of the corporation has knowledge of all the entity's business transactions and has approved of them. Adequate records include a chart of accounts, control accounts and the related subsidiary records, and prenumbered sequential paper forms such as sales orders and checks.

All the company's recordkeeping equipment—cash registers, check protectors, bookkeeping machines, and computer hardware and software—must provide the safeguards necessary to meet this standard of adequacy.

**Documentation**  Each function within the organization must have thorough **documentation** of its activity so that each transaction can be traced and verified. Consider a firm's sales function, for example. Proper documentation of each sale would include the purchase order from a company wishing to buy the product, the credit approval from the firm's credit department, the sales invoice, the shipping invoice marked "shipped," the accounts receivable subsidiary ledger account for the customer, and whatever other documents, properly authorized with appropriate signatures, are necessary to verify that an order was authorized, filled, sent, received, and paid for. In accounting lingo this documentation sequence is called an "adequate audit trail."

### Checks and Balances

The last aspect of internal accounting control that we will consider is the checks and balances provided by any good system. **Checks and balances** provide for a continual review of the recordkeeping functions and for the verification of resources by means of reconciliations, internal auditing, and external auditing.

**Reconciliations**  Every month the company receives a statement of the amount of cash the company has on deposit at its bank. The company must compare the amount shown on the bank statement with the amount in the general ledger Cash account, and explain any differences. This comparison is called a **reconciliation.** Similarly, the Accounts Receivable Control account must be reconciled with the accounts receivable subsidiary ledger (that is, the individual accounts receivable accounts). We will see how to do this in the next section of this chapter. The Inventory account (in a perpetual inventory system) must be reconciled with the physical count of the inventory. And so it goes for all the company's resources. The records and the actual resources are compared, and any discrepancy is tracked down and corrected.

**Internal Audits**  Internal auditing is usually associated with large corporations, but many of the functions of corporate internal auditing departments can be carried out by the owners of small companies. In an **internal audit,** the organization reviews its own activities to discover errors or irregularities, to determine whether the established procedures and policies are being followed, and to uncover inefficiency or fraud.

**External Audits**  Before providing an opinion on a company's financial statements, a CPA must review the company's system of internal control. This outside review, or **external audit,** offers the company an impartial check of the company's system and often results in many suggestions for improvement in controls and operations.

**ASK YOURSELF** ▶

1. **What is the difference between administrative and accounting controls?**
2. **What are the four components of personnel controls?**
3. **What are the three parts of records controls?**
4. **List and describe the three components of checks and balances.**

## SPECIAL JOURNALS

Learning Objective **5**

Describe and make entries in the following special journals: sales journal, cash receipts journal, purchases journal, and cash payments journal

We have just emphasized that a good internal control and accounting system design requires adequate records. To handle a large mass of business activities and to divide the work among more employees, we need to have a recordkeeping system that uses special journals.

The use of a single journal, the general journal, permits any transaction, no matter how simple or complex, to be handled. *Any number* of transactions can also be handled via the general journal, *given an unlimited amount of time.* However, time is limited and expensive, and most business entities have many transactions.

**Figure 1** The Accounting System with Special Journals

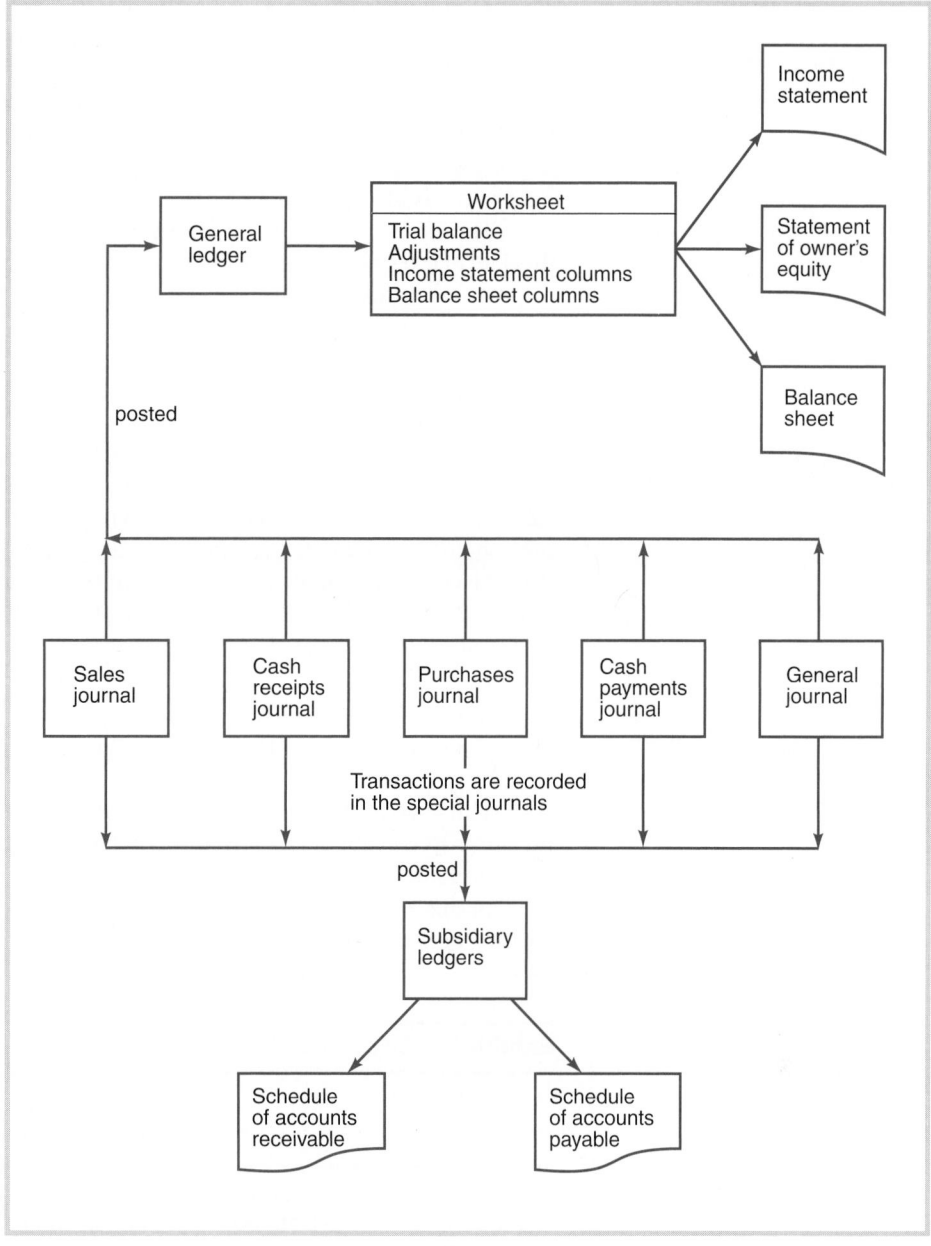

## Four Major Groups of Transactions

Although an entity engages in many transactions in the normal course of doing business, almost all of them can be classified into one of four major groups. For example, a merchandising firm sells merchandise on account, purchases merchandise for resale on account, receives cash, and pays cash. For each of these distinct activities, a special journal is designed. A **special journal** is a book of original entry (a book in which transactions are first recorded) that is designed to record only one class of business transactions. The four most common special journals are the *sales journal,* the *cash receipts journal,* the *purchases journal,* and the *cash payments journal.* In a system that uses special journals, the general journal is used only to record transactions that cannot be recorded in one of the special journals. Figure 1 illustrates how the accounting system works when special journals are used. The following discussion will explain the use of special journals.

## The Sales Journal

The **sales journal** is a book of original entry designed to record only sales of merchandise on credit. This transaction requires a debit to Accounts Receivable and a credit to Sales. No other type of transaction should be recorded in the sales journal. A cash sale, for example, should be recorded not in the sales journal, but in the cash receipts journal. The sales journal is a single-column journal, as you can see in Exhibit 2, because only one money column is needed. The amount debited to Accounts Receivable is also the amount credited to Sales.

The evidence, or **source document,** of each sale is a **sales invoice,** which lists the date of the sale, the customer's name, the credit terms, the amount of the sale, and the invoice number. The sales invoice representing The Finn Company's sale of merchandise on account to Susan Harper is shown in Exhibit 3.

A copy of the sales invoice provides the authority and the information needed to record the transaction in the sales journal. Notice that a description or explanation of the transaction is not required in the sales journal. It is obvious that the transaction is a sale of merchandise on account, because only that type of transaction is recorded in this special journal. The invoice number provides a reference to the sales invoice, in case any additional information or a review of the original information is needed. At the end of each month the *total* sales on account from the sales journal is posted to the general ledger as a single debit to Accounts Receivable and a single credit to Sales. In Exhibit 2, this posting is represented by putting the account numbers below the total as a posting reference:

| | |
|---|---|
| $1,205 | Total sales for August |
| (120/410) | Posting reference |

The left/right order of the account numbers indicates that $1,205 is debited to Accounts Receivable (account number 120) and $1,205 is credited to Sales (account number 410).

In this simple illustration, eight sales transactions were recorded but only one posting was required. A real business might record hundreds or thousands of sales

---

**Exhibit 2** A Sales Journal

THE FINN COMPANY
Sales Journal                                                    PAGE 16

| Date | Account Debited | Invoice Number | Post. Ref. | Amount |
|---|---|---|---|---|
| 1998 | | | | |
| Aug. 4 | Grace Miller | 418 | ✔ | $ 100 |
| 6 | Ben Rogers | 419 | ✔ | 85 |
| 7 | James Hollis | 420 | ✔ | 20 |
| 15 | Susan Harper | 421 | ✔ | 90 |
| 18 | Sally Rogers | 422 | ✔ | 200 |
| 21 | Robert Tanner | 423 | ✔ | 450 |
| 27 | William Fisher | 424 | ✔ | 80 |
| 30 | Becky Thatcher | 425 | ✔ | 180 |
| Total | | | | $1,205 |
| | | | | (120/410) |

---

**Exhibit 3** Sales Invoice

---

**THE FINN COMPANY**
1531 Hannibal Ave.
St. Petersburg, Mo.

Invoice no. _____ 421

Invoice date _____ Aug. 15, 1998

Sold to: _____ Susan Harper _____

Terms _____ 2/10, n/30

_____ 3116 Second Street _____

Shipped via _____ Customer pickup

_____ St. Louis, Mo. _____

Date shipped _____ Aug. 15, 1998

| Quantity | Description | | Unit Price | Amount |
|----------|-------------|------|------------|--------|
| 8 | 13EL7 | Fans | $7.50 | $60.00 |
| 24 | 20AQ1 | Belts | 1.25 | 30.00 |
| | | | | $90.00 |

---

transactions during a month's time. The advantage of the sales journal is that no matter how many transactions are recorded, only one posting is required.

Let's look at the debit side of this entry—Accounts Receivable. There is a disadvantage in relying solely on the sales journal. The Accounts Receivable account informs management of the total amount of credit outstanding to its customers, but provides no information on the status of individual customers' credit. Management must know on a daily basis the credit status of each of its customers. Has anyone exceeded his or her credit limit? If so, can additional credit be granted? How overdue is the account? Answers to these and other credit-related questions are vital to a well-managed company.

### The Subsidiary Ledger and the Control Account

Learning
Objective 6

Describe the relationship between subsidiary and control accounts

Information on the credit of individual customers is recorded in a *subsidiary ledger,* separate from the general ledger. A separate account for each customer is maintained in the subsidiary ledger, which is alphabetized by customer name. Subsidiary ledgers are most commonly used for accounts receivable, accounts payable, and equipment.

The subsidiary ledger of the general ledger's Accounts Receivable account is called the **accounts receivable ledger.** Accounts Receivable is called the **control account** when it is supported by a subsidiary ledger.

A subsidiary ledger should be established for any general ledger account that comprises many individual accounts. For example, if a business entity had 20 different cash accounts, a subsidiary ledger would be established in which each of the individual cash accounts could be found, and the general ledger account Cash would be a control account.

A subsidiary ledger may contain 10 accounts or 10,000 accounts. (With a large number of accounts, it is common to assign customers account numbers rather than listing them alphabetically). When a subsidiary ledger contains many individual accounts, it becomes impossible to list each one on a trial balance. However, we don't have to deal with this impossibility because only the control account, reflecting the total of the balances of all the individual subsidiary accounts, is given in the trial balance.

### Posting from the Sales Journal to the Subsidiary and General Ledgers

Let's return to The Finn Company's sales journal to explore more fully the relationship between the subsidiary ledger and the control account. Exhibit 4 illustrates the process of posting from the sales journal to the subsidiary ledger and the general ledger. The subsidiary ledger is posted every day that credit sales are made; the general ledger is posted only on the last day of the month. When The Finn Company makes a sale, such as the $100 credit sale to Grace Miller on Aug. 4, two things happen: (1) The sale is recorded in the sales journal; and (2) the sale is posted as a debit in the Accounts Receivable account kept for Miller in Finn's subsidiary ledger.

In this subsidiary ledger account, the S16 refers to page 16 of the sales journal, thus identifying the source of the information recorded. The check mark (✔) in the sales journal's posting reference column indicates that the information given in the entry has been posted to the subsidiary ledger.

---

**Exhibit 4** Posting from the Sales Journal to the Subsidiary and General Ledgers

**THE FINN COMPANY**
**Sales Journal**   PAGE 16

| Date | Account Debited | Invoice No. | Post. Ref. | Amount |
|------|-----------------|-------------|------------|--------|
| 1998 | | | | |
| Aug. 4 | Grace Miller | 418 | ✔ | $ 100 |
| 6 | Ben Rogers | 419 | ✔ | 85 |
| 7 | James Hollis | 420 | ✔ | 20 |
| 15 | Susan Harper | 421 | ✔ | 90 |
| 18 | Sally Rogers | 422 | ✔ | 200 |
| 21 | Robert Tanner | 423 | ✔ | 450 |
| 27 | William Fisher | 424 | ✔ | 80 |
| 30 | Becky Thatcher | 425 | ✔ | 180 |
| | | | | $1,205 |
| | | | | (120/410) |

**THE FINN COMPANY**
**General Ledger**

| Accounts Receivable | | 120 |
|---------------------|------|-----|
| Aug. 31 S16 | 1,205 | |

| Sales | | 410 |
|-------|------|-----|
| | Aug. 31 S16 | 1,205 |

**THE FINN COMPANY**
**Accounts Receivable Subsidiary Ledger**

| Fisher, William | | | Rogers, Ben | | |
|-----------------|----|---|-------------|----|---|
| Aug. 27 S16 | 80 | | Aug. 6 S16 | 85 | |

| Harper, Susan | | | Rogers, Sally | | |
|---------------|----|---|---------------|-----|---|
| Aug. 15 S16 | 90 | | Aug. 18 S16 | 200 | |

| Hollis, James | | | Tanner, Robert | | |
|---------------|----|---|----------------|-----|---|
| Aug. 7 S16 | 20 | | Aug. 21 S16 | 450 | |

| Miller, Grace | | | Thatcher, Becky | | |
|---------------|-----|---|-----------------|-----|---|
| Aug. 4 S16 | 100 | | Aug. 30 S16 | 180 | |

**Exhibit 5** Three-Column Ledger Card Postings

### General Ledger

| | Accounts Receivable | | | | Account No. 120 |
|---|---|---|---|---|---|
| **Date** | **Explanation** | **Post. Ref.** | **Debit** | **Credit** | **Balance** |
| 1998 Aug. 31 | | SJ16 | 1,205 | | 1,205 |

| | Sales | | | | Account No. 410 |
|---|---|---|---|---|---|
| **Date** | **Explanation** | **Post. Ref.** | **Debit** | **Credit** | **Balance** |
| 1998 Aug. 31 | | SJ16 | | 1,205 | 1,205 |

### ACCOUNTS RECEIVABLE SUBSIDIARY LEDGER

| | Miller, Grace | | | | Account No. ___ |
|---|---|---|---|---|---|
| **Date** | **Explanation** | **Post. Ref.** | **Debit** | **Credit** | **Balance** |
| 1998 Aug. 4 | | SJ16 | 100 | | 100 |

At the end of the month the total amount of the sales on account, $1,205, is posted to the general ledger Accounts Receivable control account. Note that a posting reference, S16, is placed in the control account to identify the source of the information posted.

At the end of the month, all the debit balances in the accounts receivable subsidiary ledger also are totaled, to see if the total agrees with the debit balance in the Accounts Receivable control account in the general ledger. If no errors have been made, the two balances will be identical.

Exhibit 5 shows the postings from the sales journal to the three-column general ledger accounts, Accounts Receivable and Sales, and to the first subsidiary ledger account, Grace Miller.

### The Cash Receipts Journal

The special journal used to record transactions in which cash is received is called the **cash receipts journal.** Unlike the single-column sales journal, the cash receipts journal may contain many money columns. There is only one source for data recorded in the sales journal—sales on account—so one money column is sufficient. But cash may be received from many different sources, so the cash receipts journal needs a column to record each source of cash. Note, however, that only one column is needed to record the *receipt* of cash.

In designing a cash receipts journal, each business entity must consider all its sources of cash. The two most common regular sources of cash are the collection of

**Exhibit 6** Cash Receipts Journal

THE FINN COMPANY
Cash Receipts Journal

PAGE __9__

| Date | Account Credited | Post. Ref. | Cash Dr. | Sales Discounts Dr. | Accounts Receivable Cr. | Sales Cr. | Sundry Accounts Cr. |
|------|-----------------|-----------|---------|---------------------|------------------------|-----------|---------------------|
| 1998 | | | | | | | |
| Aug. 3 | | — | 500 | | | 500 | |
| 5 | Finn, Capital | 310 | 1,000 | | | | 1,000 |
| 11 | Miller, Grace | ✓ | 98 | 2 | 100 | | |
| 15 | | — | 300 | | | 300 | |
| 17 | Rogers, Ben | ✓ | 45 | | 45 | | |
| 20 | Notes Payable | 210 | 600 | | | | 600 |
| 21 | | — | 400 | | | 400 | |
| 22 | Rogers, Sally | ✓ | 196 | 4 | 200 | | |
| 30 | Hollis, James | ✓ | 20 | | 20 | | |
| | | | 3,159 | 6 | 365 | 1,200 | 1,600 |
| | | | (110) | (430) | (120) | (410) | (—) |

accounts receivable and cash sales. Thus, the cash receipts journal of The Finn Company in Exhibit 6 shows a credit column for each of these accounts: Accounts Receivable and Sales. Because The Finn Company's other sources of cash do not occur regularly, they are lumped together in one column labeled Sundry Accounts Credit. If any source begins to produce more than a few cash transactions each month, a new column should be established for it.

Cash sales are recorded in the cash receipts journal by entering the amount of the cash received in the cash debit and the sales credit columns. The amount entered typically represents the total of each day's cash sales as indicated by cash register tapes. Exhibit 6 shows three cash sales entries—on Aug. 3 for $500, on Aug. 15 for $300, and on Aug. 21 for $400, for a total of $1,200. Each of these daily totals sums up numerous cash sales transactions.

Collection of customer accounts is recorded in the cash debit and the accounts receivable credit columns. If the account is paid within the discount period, the sales discounts debit column must also be used. Exhibit 6 shows four transactions involving the collection of receivables.

The first transaction is the $98 payment received from Grace Miller on Aug. 11, recorded on the third line of Exhibit 6. When credit terms are granted and the customer pays the bill within the discount period, a sales discount is given. The general journal entry to record the collection of Grace Miller's $100 purchase on account would be:

General Journal

| Date | Account Titles and Explanation | Post. Ref. | Debit | Credit |
|------|-------------------------------|-----------|-------|--------|
| 1998 | | | | |
| Aug. 11 | Cash (**A**)* | 110 | 98 | |
| | Sales Discounts (**OE:R**) | 430 | 2 | |
| |     Accounts Receivable (**A**)—Miller, G. | 120 ✓ | | 100 |
| | To record collection of accounts receivable subject to 2/10, n/30 credit terms. | | | |

* The letters in parentheses in journal entries refer to the following accounts: **A** = Assets; **L** = Liabilities; **OE** = Owner's Equity; **R** = Revenue; **E** = Expense; **IS** = Income Statement; **W** = Withdrawals.

**Exhibit 7** Crossfooting the Cash Receipts Journal

| Cash Dr. | | Sales Discounts Dr. | | Total | | Accounts Receivable Cr. | | Sales Cr. | | Sundry Accounts Cr. |
|---|---|---|---|---|---|---|---|---|---|---|
| $3,159 | + | $6 | = | $3,165 | = | $365 | + | $1,200 | + | $1,600 |

To record this transaction in the cash receipts journal, three money columns are needed: two debit columns, one for cash and one for sales discounts, and a credit column for accounts receivable.

The Finn Company made a sale on account in the amount of $100 to Grace Miller on Aug. 4, as reported in the sales journal back in Exhibit 2. Miller paid in full on Aug. 11. Therefore, $98 is recorded in the cash debit column. Because she paid her bill within 10 days (assuming credit terms of 2/10, n/30), she gets a discount of 2% (of $100), or $2, which is entered as a debit in the sales discounts column. Finally, a $100 credit is entered for Grace Miller in the accounts receivable column of the cash receipts journal.

Notice the check mark (✔) in the posting reference column after the account of Grace Miller. This indicates that the $100 credit was posted to her accounts receivable account in the subsidiary ledger. As with the sales journal, the subsidiary ledger accounts are posted each day.

The three other collections in the cash receipts journal (Exhibit 6) are as follows: On Aug. 17, Ben Rogers paid $45 in settlement of a past-due account receivable; on Aug. 22, Sally Rogers paid $196 in settlement of a $200 account receivable, taking a $4 sales discount; and on Aug. 30, James Hollis paid a $20 past-due account.

Sources of cash other than cash sales or collections of accounts receivable are entered in the sundry accounts credit column. Two examples are shown in Exhibit 6: On Aug. 5 the owner invested an additional $1,000 in the business, and on Aug. 20 the company borrowed $600 from the bank by issuing a note payable. In each case the general ledger account title must be entered in the account credited column. At the end of the month the amounts found in the sundry accounts column are posted to their respective general ledger accounts. The account numbers of these accounts are entered in the posting reference column to show that the amounts have been posted to the general ledger.

The amounts within each column of the cash receipts journal are added up—or *footed,* as accountants say—at the end of the month. The totals of the debit columns are then added together, or *crossfooted.* The credit columns are also crossfooted. The purpose of crossfooting is to prove the equality of the debits and credits. The cross-footing of the column totals from The Finn Company's cash receipts journal is shown in Exhibit 7.

Once the equality of the debits and credits in the cash receipts journal is proved, the totals of each of the columns are posted to their respective accounts in the general ledger. As evidence that this posting has been done, the number that identifies each account in the general ledger is inserted in parentheses below the column total in the cash receipts journal. Thus, the column totals from Exhibit 6 are posted as follows:

- The $3,159 total of the cash debit column is posted as a single sum to the general ledger's cash account, number 110. This posting is evidenced by the (110) under the $3,159 in the cash debit column.

- The $6 total of the sales discounts debit column is posted to the general ledger account 430, Sales Discounts, and is evidenced by the (430) directly below the $6 total.

- The $365 total of the accounts receivable credit column is posted as a credit to the accounts receivable control account in the general ledger at the end of the month. To indicate that this posting has been done, the accounts receivable control account number (120) is placed at the bottom of the accounts receivable credit column.

- The $1,200 total of the sales credit column is posted to the sales account (410) in the general ledger. Note that all the company's sales transactions for the month are recorded in the general ledger account with only two postings, one from the sales journal and the other from the cash receipts journal.

- Two entries appear in the sundry accounts credit column. These entries must be posted individually to the general ledger accounts Finn, Capital, and Notes Payable, and the identifying account numbers for each must be entered in the posting reference column.

  The total of the sundry accounts credit column is used only in crossfooting to prove equality of the debits and credits. Because that column is a combination of several accounts, no account number is placed under its total. Instead, a dash (—) is placed under the column to show that it has been considered in the crossfooting. The items in this column are then posted individually.

Notice that the source of each posting is referenced in the ledgers (Exhibit 8) by its journal page number. The postings from page 16 of the sales journal are referenced as S16, while the postings from page 9 of the cash receipts journal are referenced as CR9.

**Exhibit 8** General Ledger and Accounts Receivable Subsidiary Ledger

### THE FINN COMPANY
### General Ledger

**Cash**  110

| | | | |
|---|---|---|---|
| Aug. 31 CR9 | 3,159 | | |

**Accounts Receivable**  120

| | | | |
|---|---|---|---|
| Aug. 31 S16 | 1,205 | Aug. 31, CR9 | 365 |

**Notes Payable**  210

| | | | |
|---|---|---|---|
| | | Aug. 20 CR9 | 600 |

**Finn, Capital**  310

| | | | |
|---|---|---|---|
| | | Aug. 5 CR9 | 1,000 |

**Sales**  410

| | | | |
|---|---|---|---|
| | | Aug. 31 SI6 | 1,205 |
| | | 31 CR9 | 1,200 |

**Sales Discounts**  430

| | | | |
|---|---|---|---|
| Aug. 31 CR9 | 6 | | |

### THE FINN COMPANY
### Accounts Receivable Subsidiary Ledger

**Fisher, William**

| | | | |
|---|---|---|---|
| Aug. 27 S16 | 80 | | |

**Harper, Susan**

| | | | |
|---|---|---|---|
| Aug. 15 S16 | 90 | | |

**Hollis, James**

| | | | |
|---|---|---|---|
| Aug. 7 S16 | 20 | Aug. 30 CR9 | 20 |

**Miller, Grace**

| | | | |
|---|---|---|---|
| Aug. 4 S16 | 100 | Aug. 11 CR9 | 100 |

**Rogers, Ben**

| | | | |
|---|---|---|---|
| Aug. 6 S16 | 85 | Aug. 17 CR9 | 45 |

**Rogers, Sally**

| | | | |
|---|---|---|---|
| Aug. 18 S16 | 200 | Aug. 22 CR9 | 200 |

**Tanner, Robert**

| | | | |
|---|---|---|---|
| Aug. 21 S16 | 450 | | |

**Thatcher, Becky**

| | | | |
|---|---|---|---|
| Aug. 30 S16 | 180 | | |

**Exhibit 9** Purchases Journal, General Ledger, and Accounts Payable Subsidiary Ledger Accounts

THE FINN COMPANY
Purchases Journal                    PAGE __11__

| Date | Account Credited | Invoice Date | Post. Ref. | Amount |
|------|-----------------|--------------|-----------|--------|
| 1998 | | | | |
| Aug.  2 | Temple Print Company | 8/2 | ✓ | $  275 |
|  9 | Jackson Island Company | 8/6 | ✓ | 150 |
| 14 | St. Louis Lumber | 8/10 | ✓ | 100 |
| 19 | Aunt Polly Supply, Inc. | 8/19 | ✓ | 320 |
| 22 | Jackson Island Company | 8/21 | ✓ | 15 |
| 24 | McDougal Dry Goods | 8/20 | ✓ | 255 |
| | | | | $1,115 |
| | | | | (510/220) |

THE FINN COMPANY
General Ledger

**Accounts Payable**                    220

| | | |
|---|---|---|
| | Aug. 31 P11 | 1,115 |

**Purchases**                    510

| | | |
|---|---|---|
| Aug. 31 P11 | 1,115 | |

THE FINN COMPANY
Accounts Payable Subsidiary Ledger

**Aunt Polly Supply, Inc.**

| | | |
|---|---|---|
| | Aug. 19 P11 | 320 |

**Jackson Island Company**

| | | |
|---|---|---|
| | Aug.  9 P11 | 150 |
| | 22 P11 | 15 |

**McDougal Dry Goods**

| | | |
|---|---|---|
| | Aug. 24 P11 | 255 |

**St. Louis Lumber**

| | | |
|---|---|---|
| | Aug. 14 P11 | 100 |

**Temple Print Company**

| | | |
|---|---|---|
| | Aug.  2 P11 | 275 |

### The Purchases Journal

Like the sales journal, the **purchases journal** is a book of original entry designed to record just one type of business transaction: the company's purchase of merchandise on account for resale. (A firm's purchases for cash are recorded in the cash payments journal, discussed below.) The purchases journal is a one-column journal in which each entry is a debit to Purchases and a credit to Accounts Payable.

The **accounts payable ledger** is a subsidiary ledger containing the individual creditor accounts.

The Finn Company's purchases journal for August is illustrated in Exhibit 9, along with the relevant general ledger and accounts payable subsidiary ledger accounts.

Each transaction is recorded in the purchases journal by entering the date of the transaction, the vendor's (creditor's) name, the date of the invoice, and the amount of the purchase. The various vendors' accounts are posted each day to their accounts payable in the subsidiary ledger. For example, see the posting of the Temple Print Company account of Aug. 2 in Exhibit 9. The procedure is much like posting from the sales journal to the subsidiary and general ledgers. The purchases journal page number, P11, is recorded as a posting reference in the subsidiary ledger account of the Temple Print Company as the source of authority for the posting.

At the end of the month, the purchases journal is footed and the total is posted as a debit to Purchases and also as a credit to Accounts Payable in the general ledger. The numbers of these two accounts—510 and 220, respectively—are noted under the total of the amount column to indicate that the total has been posted to both accounts. The journal page number is recorded as a posting reference in the general ledger account as evidence of the posting.

### The Cash Payments Journal

The payment of cash is recorded in the **cash payments journal.** The format of the cash payments journal is similar to that of a cash receipts journal. Because cash is paid out for various purposes, a cash payments journal usually has several columns. Cash and Purchases Discounts are the typical column headings for recording the credits, while Accounts Payable, Purchases, and Sundry Accounts are column headings for the debits recorded in the cash payments journal. The cash payments journal of The Finn Company is illustrated in Exhibit 10.

Business entities typically make cash payments by check rather than in currency, because checks provide security and control by furnishing a record of the amount, the date, the payee's name, and the reason for the payment. Thus, the format of a cash payments journal differs from that of a cash receipts journal in one respect: It has a column for recording the number of the check used for the cash payment. If anyone needs to know the nature of the payment, that information can be found in the checkbook records.

There is one exception to the rule that cash payments must be made by check: Petty cash payments are made in currency.

Each cash payment is posted from the cash payments journal to the appropriate general and subsidiary ledger accounts, just as each cash receipt was posted from the cash receipts journal.

Transactions with vendors are posted each day to appropriate accounts in the accounts payable subsidiary ledger. When a transaction is posted from the journal to the subsidiary ledger, a check mark (✔) is entered in the posting reference column. In Exhibit 10, the check marks for the entries on Aug. 11 to Jackson Island Company for $150, on Aug. 17 to Temple Print Company for $175, and on Aug. 24 to St. Louis Lumber for $100 indicate that these accounts have been posted to the subsidiary ledger accounts.

Notice that Jackson Island and St. Louis Lumber were both paid within the discount period by check no. 318 for $147 and no. 322 for $98, respectively. But Finn did not pay Temple Print in time to receive a purchase discount; consequently, check no. 320 was for $175, the total amount of that account payable.

Cash purchases are recorded in the Purchases debit column, as illustrated by the purchases of Aug. 9 for $135 (check no. 317) and Aug. 22 for $400 (check no. 321). Notice the dash (—) in the posting reference column for these two items: This indicates that no individual posting is required for them.

At the end of the month, each entry in the sundry accounts debit column is posted to its appropriate account in the general ledger. Instead of a check mark, the account number of the general ledger account is entered in the posting reference column of the cash payments journal to indicate that the transaction has been posted.

**Exhibit 10** Cash Payments Journal, General Ledger, and Accounts Payable Subsidiary Ledger Accounts

## THE FINN COMPANY
## Cash Payments Journal
PAGE __24__

| Date | Check No. | Account Debited | Post. Ref. | Cash Cr. | Purchases Discounts Cr. | Accounts Payable Dr. | Purchases Dr. | Sundry Accounts Dr. |
|------|-----------|-----------------|------------|----------|------------------------|----------------------|---------------|---------------------|
| 1998 | | | | | | | | |
| Aug. 3 | 316 | Rent Expense | 660 | 175 | | | | 175 |
| 9 | 317 | Purchases | — | 135 | | | 135 | |
| 11 | 318 | Jackson Island Company | ✔ | 147 | 3 | 150 | | |
| 16 | 319 | Salary Expense | 610 | 200 | | | | 200 |
| 17 | 320 | Temple Print Company | ✔ | 175 | | 175 | | |
| 22 | 321 | Purchases | — | 400 | | | 400 | |
| 24 | 322 | St. Louis Lumber | ✔ | 98 | 2 | 100 | | |
| 26 | 323 | Freight-In | 540 | 10 | | | | 10 |
| | | | | 1,340 | 5 | 425 | 535 | 385 |
| | | | | (110) | (530) | (220) | (510) | (—) |

### THE FINN COMPANY
### General Ledger

**Cash**     110

| | | | |
|---|---|---|---|
| Aug. 31 CR9 | 3,159 | Aug. 31 CP24 | 1,340 |

**Notes Payable**     210

| | | | |
|---|---|---|---|
| | | Aug. 20 CR9 | 600 |

**Accounts Payable**     220

| | | | |
|---|---|---|---|
| Aug. 31 CP24 | 425 | | |
| | | Aug. 31 P11 | 1,115 |

**Purchases**     510

| | | | |
|---|---|---|---|
| Aug. 31 P11 | 1,115 | | |
| 31 CP24 | 535 | | |

**Purchases Discounts**     530

| | | | |
|---|---|---|---|
| | | Aug. 31 CP24 | 5 |

**Freight-In**     540

| | | | |
|---|---|---|---|
| Aug. 26 CP24 | 10 | | |

**Salary Expense**     610

| | | | |
|---|---|---|---|
| Aug. 16 CP24 | 200 | | |

**Rent Expense**     660

| | | | |
|---|---|---|---|
| Aug. 3 CP24 | 175 | | |

### THE FINN COMPANY
### Accounts Payable Subsidiary Ledger

**Aunt Polly Supply, Inc.**

| | | | |
|---|---|---|---|
| | | Aug. 19 P11 | 320 |

**Jackson Island Company**

| | | | |
|---|---|---|---|
| Aug. 11 CP24 | 150 | Aug. 9 P11 | 150 |
| | | 22 P11 | 15 |

**McDougal Dry Goods**

| | | | |
|---|---|---|---|
| | | Aug. 24 P11 | 255 |

**St. Louis Lumber**

| | | | |
|---|---|---|---|
| Aug. 24 CP24 | 100 | Aug. 14 P11 | 100 |

**Temple Print Company**

| | | | |
|---|---|---|---|
| Aug. 17 CP24 | 175 | Aug. 2 P11 | 275 |

**Exhibit 11** Crossfooting the Cash Payments Journal

| Cash Cr. | | Purchases Discounts Cr. | | Total | | Accounts Payable Dr. | | Purchases Dr. | | Sundry Accounts Dr. |
|---|---|---|---|---|---|---|---|---|---|---|
| $1,340 | + | $5 | = | $1,345 | = | $425 | + | $535 | + | $385 |

Examples of these cash payments are the Aug. 3 payment of $175 for rent expense (account no. 660, check no. 316), the Aug. 16 payment of $200 for salary expense (account no. 610, check no. 319), and the Aug. 26 payment of $10 for freight-in (account no. 540, check no. 323), as shown in the sundry accounts debit column in Exhibit 10.

The cash payments journal is footed and crossfooted to prove the equality of the debits and credits (see Exhibit 11), as was done for the cash receipts journal. Finally, the totals of the columns are posted in their respective accounts in the general ledger; to indicate that this has been done, the account numbers are entered below the column totals of the cash payments journal.

## THE GENERAL JOURNAL

When the four special journals we have just discussed are used, relatively few transactions remain to be recorded in the general journal. Only transactions that do not involve cash receipts, cash payments, or the purchase or sale of merchandise on credit, are entered as original entries in the general journal. *Adjusting, closing,* and *reversing* entries are examples of such entries.

Two transactions that must be recorded in the general journal are illustrated in Exhibit 12. The first, dated Aug. 20, is the acquisition of office equipment on account. This entry cannot be recorded in the purchases journal because that journal records only *purchases of merchandise on account for resale.*

The second transaction is the return on Aug. 23 of some items previously sold to a customer. Because this entry does not involve cash, a purchase, or a sale, the only place for this entry is in the general journal.

**Exhibit 12** General Journal Entries

| General Journal | | | | PAGE ___3___ |
|---|---|---|---|---|

| Date | Account Titles and Explanation | Post. Ref. | Debit | Credit |
|---|---|---|---|---|
| 1998 Aug. 20 | Office Equipment **(A)** | 140 | 575 | |
| |     Accounts Payable **(L)**—Walters Office Supply | 220/✔ | | 575 |
| | To record the acquisition of office equipment, terms 3/10, n/30. | | | |
| 23 | Sales Returns and Allowances **(OE:R)** | 420 | 50 | |
| |     Accounts Receivable **(A)**—Susan Harper | 120/✔ | | 50 |
| | To record the return of merchandise sold on Aug. 15, 1998. | | | |

The general journal entries for these two transactions are posted to the appropriate general ledger accounts just as usual. The account numbers in the posting reference column indicate that the entries have been posted to the general ledger, while the check marks indicate that postings have been made to individual accounts in the accounts payable (Walters Office Supply) and accounts receivable (Susan Harper) ledgers.

## PROVING THE CONTROL ACCOUNTS

Exhibit 13 shows the general ledger and subsidiary ledgers for The Finn Company after all the journals have been posted at the end of the month. A trial balance (see

---

**Exhibit 13** General and Subsidiary Ledgers after Posting

THE FINN COMPANY
General Ledger

| Cash | | | 110 |
|---|---|---|---|
| Aug. 31 CR9 | 3,159 | Aug. 31 CP24 | 1,340 |
| Bal. | 1,819 | | |

| Sales Returns and Allowances | | 420 |
|---|---|---|
| Aug. 23 G3 | 50 | |

| Accounts Receivable | | | 120 |
|---|---|---|---|
| Aug. 31 S16 | 1,205 | Aug. 23 G3 | 50 |
| | | 31 CR9 | 365 |
| Bal. | 790 | | |

| Sales Discounts | | 430 |
|---|---|---|
| Aug. 31 CR9 | 6 | |

| Office Equipment | | 140 |
|---|---|---|
| Aug. 20 G3 | 575 | |

| Purchases | | | 510 |
|---|---|---|---|
| Aug. 31 P11 | 1,115 | | |
| 31 CP24 | 535 | | |
| Bal. | 1,650 | | |

| Notes Payable | | | 210 |
|---|---|---|---|
| | | Aug. 20 CR9 | 600 |

| Purchases Discounts | | | 530 |
|---|---|---|---|
| | | Aug. 31 CP24 | 5 |

| Accounts Payable | | | 220 |
|---|---|---|---|
| Aug. 31 CP24 | 425 | Aug. 20 G3 | 575 |
| | | 31 P11 | 1,115 |
| | | Bal. | 1,265 |

| Freight-In | | 540 |
|---|---|---|
| Aug. 26 CP24 | 10 | |

| Finn, Capital | | | 310 |
|---|---|---|---|
| | | Aug. 5 CR | 1,000 |

| Salary Expense | | 610 |
|---|---|---|
| Aug. 16 CP24 | 200 | |

| Sales | | | 410 |
|---|---|---|---|
| | | Aug. 31 S16 | 1,205 |
| | | 31 CR9 | 1,200 |
| | | Bal. | 2,405 |

| Rent Expense | | 660 |
|---|---|---|
| Aug. 3 CP24 | 175 | |

*(Continued)*

## THE FINN COMPANY
### Subsidiary Ledgers

### Accounts Receivable Ledger

#### Fisher, Williams

| | | | |
|---|---|---|---|
| Aug. 27 S16 | 80 | | |

#### Rogers, Ben

| | | | |
|---|---|---|---|
| Aug. 6 S16 | 85 | Aug. 17 CR9 | 45 |
| Bal. | 40 | | |

#### Harper, Susan

| | | | |
|---|---|---|---|
| Aug. 15 S16 | 90 | Aug. 23 G3 | 50 |
| Bal. | 40 | | |

#### Rogers, Sally

| | | | |
|---|---|---|---|
| Aug. 18 S16 | 200 | Aug. 22 CR9 | 200 |
| Bal. | 0 | | |

#### Hollis, James

| | | | |
|---|---|---|---|
| Aug. 7 S16 | 20 | Aug. 30 CR9 | 20 |
| Bal. | 0 | | |

#### Tanner, Robert

| | | | |
|---|---|---|---|
| Aug. 31 S16 | 450 | | |
| Bal. | 450 | | |

#### Miller, Grace

| | | | |
|---|---|---|---|
| Aug. 4 S16 | 100 | Aug. 11 CR9 | 100 |
| Bal. | 0 | | |

#### Thatcher, Becky

| | | | |
|---|---|---|---|
| Aug. 30 S16 | 180 | | |

## THE FINN COMPANY
### Schedule of Accounts Receivable
### August 31, 1998

| | |
|---|---|
| Fisher, William............................ | $ 80 |
| Harper, Susan............................. | 40 |
| Rogers, Ben ............................. | 40 |
| Tanner, Robert ........................... | 450 |
| Thatcher, Becky .......................... | 180 |
| Total................................... | $790 |

### Accounts Payable Ledger

#### Aunt Polly Supply, Inc.

| | | | |
|---|---|---|---|
| | | Aug. 19 P11 | 320 |

#### St. Louis Lumber

| | | | |
|---|---|---|---|
| Aug. 24 CP24 | 100 | Aug. 14 P11 | 100 |
| | | Bal. | 0 |

#### Jackson Island Company

| | | | |
|---|---|---|---|
| Aug. 11 CP24 | 150 | Aug. 9 P11 | 150 |
| | | 22 P11 | 15 |
| | | Bal. | 15 |

#### Temple Print Shop

| | | | |
|---|---|---|---|
| Aug. 17 CP24 | 175 | Aug. 2 G3 | 275 |
| | | Bal. | 100 |

#### McDougal Dry Goods

| | | | |
|---|---|---|---|
| | | Aug. 24 P11 | 255 |

#### Walters Office Supply

| | | | |
|---|---|---|---|
| | | Aug. 20 G3 | 575 |

*(Continued)*

**THE FINN COMPANY**
Schedule of Accounts Payable
August 31, 1998

| | |
|---|---:|
| Aunt Polly Supply, Inc.................... | $ 320 |
| Jackson Island Company.................. | 15 |
| McDougal Dry Goods .................... | 255 |
| Temple Print Company ................... | 100 |
| Walters Office Supply .................... | 575 |
| Total ................................. | $1,265 |

Exhibit 14) is prepared from the general ledger to test that the sum of its debits equals the sum of its credits. In Exhibit 14 the sum of the debits, $5,275, does equal the sum of the credits, $5,275.

Before continuing with the period-end procedures—preparing the adjusting entries, the closing entries, and the financial statements—we prepare a *schedule* (list) of the subsidiary ledgers and their balances. We do this to prove that the total balance of the subsidiary ledger accounts equals the balance of the corresponding control account in the general ledger. Schedules of accounts receivable and accounts payable appear at the end of Exhibit 13, and their totals ($790 and $1,265, respectively) do equal the balances shown in the general ledger accounts.

Note that the schedule of accounts receivable does not include the accounts of James Hollis, Grace Miller, or Sally Rogers. These customers all have zero balances, and consequently do not owe The Finn Company anything on the last day of the month. Likewise, the schedule of accounts payable does not list the St. Louis Lumber account, because this vendor has a zero balance.

With the proving of the control accounts, we have described the last of the new procedures in our expanded manual accounting system. Our system now includes five journals, subsidiary ledgers, and the worksheet, and is illustrated in Fig. 1.

**Exhibit 14**

**THE FINN COMPANY**
Trial Balance
August 31, 1998

| | Debit | Credit |
|---|---:|---:|
| Cash ........................................................ | $1,819 | |
| Accounts Receivable ..................................... | 790 | |
| Office Equipment ........................................ | 575 | |
| Notes Payable ........................................... | | $ 600 |
| Accounts Payable........................................ | | 1,265 |
| Finn, Capital ............................................. | | 1,000 |
| Sales...................................................... | | 2,405 |
| Sales Returns and Allowances ........................... | 50 | |
| Sales Discounts ......................................... | 6 | |
| Purchases................................................. | 1,650 | |
| Purchases Discounts ..................................... | | 5 |
| Freight-In ................................................ | 10 | |
| Salary Expense .......................................... | 200 | |
| Rent Expense............................................. | 175 | |
| Totals .................................................... | $5,275 | $5,275 |

1. What is the difference between special journals and the general journal?
2. Why is only one column used in the sales and purchases journals?
3. What is the relationship between subsidiary and control accounts?
4. How is the posting reference column used in the cash receipts and cash payments journals?
5. Why is the general journal still needed when a company has special journals?

## MANUAL VERSUS ELECTRONIC ACCOUNTING SYSTEMS

The accounting process you have learned about so far is the basic manual accounting system. Electronic accounting systems are computer-based, often using the latest and most powerful computers and peripheral equipment. They are much more sophisticated and complex than manual systems. Which type of system a business entity needs depends on how easily its various types of business transactions can be classified into groups. For example, a manual system may group together all sales on account for recording. An electronic system may batch all daily customer billings together to update customer files, update inventory stocks, send bills to customers, and compute the Accounts Receivable balance. An electronic accounting system is based on the same principles as a manual accounting system, and it performs the same functions as a manual system. The difference, of course, is that the electronic system can handle far more transactions than a manual system and can do it much faster.

Accounting textbooks describe the basic manual accounting system as a means of explaining how transactions are analyzed, classified, and summarized to produce the final accounting product—the financial statements. Even the smallest firms today use some electronic equipment, generally personal computers (PCs), but even the most sophisticated electronic system is based on the same principles and procedures as the simplest double-entry manual system.

## SUMMARY

- A system of **internal control** contains procedures, techniques, and practices to provide a dependable, efficient accounting system that will help management plan and control the company's business activities as well as safeguard its resources.
- Installation of an accounting system takes place in three stages: **system analysis, system design,** and **system implementation.**
- There are two types of internal controls: **administrative controls** and **accounting controls.**
- **Administrative controls** govern the operational efficiency of the organization and compliance with its policies.
- **Accounting controls** protect the company's resources and provide for reliable financial statements. Accounting controls include three major elements: *personnel controls, records controls,* and *checks and balances.*
- **Personnel controls** involve monitoring of employee competence, assignment of responsibilities, division of work, and rotation of duties. The organization should select and train employees who have the necessary talents and intelligence for the duties assigned. The employees should be assigned duties that are clearly identifiable, so that responsibility can be pinpointed. Employee assignments should be divided so that related operations are not performed by the same person. Employees should be rotated within the work unit, to broaden employee experience, increase the unit's flexibility, and expose departures from standard operating procedures.

- **Records controls** consist of *custodianship, adequacy,* and *documentation.*
- The employee assigned the responsibility of **custodianship** of certain resources should never be allowed access to the records pertaining to those resources.
- Records and the recordkeeping equipment should be **adequate** to provide timely, accurate, and reliable information.
- Each function within the organization must **document** its actions with adequate records, so that management can trace the activity and verify that it has been approved at all stages of the transaction.
- **Checks and balances** consist of *reconciliations, internal auditing,* and *external auditing.*
- **Reconciliations** are required periodically to compare the actual resources to company records, to verify that the resources do exist and that their proper value is reflected on the company books.
- The **internal audit** function reviews the organization's activities to discover errors or irregularities, to determine if company procedures and policies are being followed, and to uncover inefficiencies.
- The **external audit,** which is performed by a certified public accountant, provides an impartial review of the company records and may result in suggestions for improvement.
- Each transaction can be represented in a **special journal** which is part of a system of internal control and which also saves time in recording many business transactions of the same type.
- There are four types of special journals: (1) the **sales journal,** to record all sales of merchandise on account; (2) the **purchases journal,** used to record merchandise bought on account; (3) the **cash receipts journal,** used to record all transactions involving cash receipts; and (4) the **cash payments journal,** used to record all transactions involving cash payments.
- Sales journals and purchases journals are typically one-column journals. The amount of the Accounts Receivable debit is identical to the amount of the Sales credit; similarly, the Purchases debit is identical to the Accounts Payable credit.
- The cash receipts and the cash payments journals are multicolumn journals that are typically tailor-made for the business entity using them.
- Transactions that cannot be handled in one of the special journals must be recorded in the general journal.
- Posting the special journals to the general ledger accounts involves posting only the special journal's column totals to the appropriate account. However, postings from the special journals must also be made to the individual subsidiary ledger accounts in the case of accounts receivable and accounts payable.

## 7 KEY TERMS

| | |
|---|---|
| **Accounting controls** | The procedures, techniques, and practices designed to protect the company's resources and provide for reliable financial statements. |
| **Accounts payable ledger** | A subsidiary ledger containing the individual creditor accounts. |
| **Accounts receivable ledger** | A subsidiary ledger containing the individual customer accounts. |
| **Administrative controls** | The procedures and methods that govern the operational efficiency of the organization and compliance with its policies. |
| **Cash payments journal** | A book of original entry designed for recording those transactions involving expenditures of cash. |
| **Cash receipts journal** | A book of original entry designed for recording business transactions involving receipts of cash. |

| | |
|---|---|
| **Checks and balances** | Accounting controls that provide for a continual review of a firm's recordkeeping functions and for the verification of its resources by means of reconciliations, internal auditing, and external auditing. |
| **Control account** | A general ledger account, such as Accounts Receivable, which is supported by a subsidiary ledger containing the details of the control account. |
| **Documentation** | The providing of adequate records to trace and verify each transaction from its beginning to its end. |
| **External audit** | A CPA's review of a company's financial statements as well as the company's system of internal controls. |
| **Internal audit** | An organization's review of its own activities to discover errors or irregularities, to determine whether the established procedures and policies are being followed, and to uncover inefficiency or fraud. |
| **Internal control** | The procedures, techniques, and practices designed to provide a dependable and efficient accounting system that will help management plan and control the company's business activities as well as safeguard the company's resources. |
| **Personnel controls** | Accounting controls that monitor employee competence, assignment of responsibilities, division of work, and rotation of duties. |
| **Purchases journal** | A book of original entry used to record purchases of merchandise on account. |
| **Reconciliation** | A company's comparison of the amount shown on its bank statement with the amount in the general ledger Cash account. |
| **Records controls** | Accounting controls that monitor a firm's recordkeeping procedures in order to maintain proper custodianship, adequacy, and documentation. |
| **Sales invoice** | The evidence of a sale, listing the amount and the date of the sale, the customer's name, the credit terms, and the invoice number. |
| **Sales journal** | A book of original entry used only to record sales of merchandise on account. |
| **Source document** | A document, such as a sales invoice, that provides evidence of a transaction and the amount involved. |
| **Special journal** | A book of original entry that is designed to record only one class of business transactions. |
| **System analysis** | A study of a company's information needs, reporting requirements, job descriptions, and existing forms, records, reports, procedures, and controls. |
| **System design** | Development of new forms, records, reports, procedures, and controls for a company. |
| **System implementation** | Installation of a newly designed accounting and internal control system in a company. |

## DEMONSTRATION PROBLEM

The seven transactions below were selected from the activities of the Clemens Company for the month of July 1998:

July 2 Sold merchandise on account to Twain Company, 2/10, n/30, $1,200. Invoice no. 127.

3 Sold merchandise for cash, $950.

6 Purchased merchandise on account from Samuel Langhorne, Inc., 3/10, n/30, $600.

7 Received from the Twain Company, $400 of returned merchandise from the sale of July 2.

8 Purchased merchandise for cash, $350. Issued check no. 53.

9 Paid Samuel Langhorne, Inc., the amount due less appropriate discount. Issued check no. 54.

10 Received from Twain Company the amount due from the July 2 sale less the return of July 7 and appropriate discount.

**Required:**

Record the seven transactions in the appropriate special or general journal.

### ■ Solution to Demonstration Problem

**CLEMENS COMPANY**
Sales Journal

| Date | Account Debited | Invoice Number | Post. Ref. | Amount |
|---|---|---|---|---|
| 1998 July 2 | Twain Company | 127 | | $1,200 |

**CLEMENS COMPANY**
Purchases Journal

| Date | Account Credited | Invoice Date | Post. Ref. | Amount |
|---|---|---|---|---|
| 1998 July 6 | Samuel Langhorne, Inc. | 7/6 | | $ 600 |

**CLEMENS COMPANY**
Cash Receipts Journal

| Date | Account Credited | Post. Ref. | Cash Dr. | Sales Discounts Dr. | Accounts Receivable Cr. | Sales Cr. | Sundry Accounts Cr. |
|---|---|---|---|---|---|---|---|
| 1998 July 3 | Sales | | 950 | | | 950 | |
| 10 | Twain Company | | 784 | 16 | 800 | | |

### CLEMENS COMPANY
Cash Payments Journal

| Date | Check No. | Account Debited | Post. Ref. | Cash Cr. | Purchases Discounts Cr. | Accounts Payable Dr. | Purchases Dr. | Sundry Accounts Dr. |
|---|---|---|---|---|---|---|---|---|
| 1998 | | | | | | | | |
| July 8 | 53 | Purchases | | 350 | | | 350 | |
| 9 | 54 | Samuel Langhorne, Inc. | | 582 | 18 | 600 | | |

### General Journal

| Date | Account Titles and Explanation | Post. Ref. | Debit | Credit |
|---|---|---|---|---|
| 1998 July 7 | Sales Returns and Allowances **(OE : R)** | | 400 | |
| | Accounts Receivable **(A)**—Twain Co. | | | 400 |
| | To record receipt of returned merchandise from sale of July 2, 1990. | | | |

# QUESTIONS FOR REVIEW AND FURTHER THOUGHT

## REVIEW QUESTIONS

1. What are the three distinct stages of systems installation?

2. What do the terms *system analysis, system design,* and *system implementation* mean?

3. What are two types of internal controls? Explain each.

4. What is internal control?

5. What factors must an internal control system consider regarding personnel?

6. How are custodianship, adequacy, and documentation all part of records control? Describe each of these functions.

7. In any good system of internal control, checks and balances exist. Name and describe three such checks and balances.

8. Does internal auditing have the same objectives as external auditing? Explain.

9. What is the relationship between a *control account* and its *subsidiary ledger?*

10. Does a company that uses special journals also need a general journal? Explain.

11. What purpose do the posting references serve in the journals and ledgers?

12. What do the terms *foot* and *crossfoot* mean? Why is it necessary to crossfoot the cash payments journal?

## QUESTIONS FOR FURTHER THOUGHT

1. A company with a strong system of internal control will never have to worry about fraud. How true is this statement?

2. The Ward Company bills its customers monthly and receives payments the following month by check. The receptionist opens the daily mail, makes a list of the checks, and gives this list to the bookkeeper. The receptionist then deposits the checks in the bank. At the end of each month the bank sends a statement to the office manager, who reconciles the balance shown on the bank statement with the balance shown in the bookkeeper's general ledger Cash account. Does Ward's system have good control?

3. Why should a firm establish special journals when it can enter any transaction, no matter how complex, in the general journal?

4. The sales journal and the cash receipts journal are posted once a month to the general ledger, yet all the individual entries contained in those journals that affect accounts receivable are posted daily to the subsidiary ledger. Why?

5. The sales journal of the Riverson Company has 326 entries for the month of October. Assuming that no cash sales were made, how many posting entries must be made to the Sales account for the month? Under the same assumption, how many postings from the sales journal must be made to the accounts receivable subsidiary ledger?

## OBJECTIVE ASSIGNMENT

*True/False*   Indicate whether each statement below is *true* or *false* by placing a *T* or an *F* in the space provided.

____ 1. A good system of internal control can prevent fraud even if several dishonest employees act in collusion.

____ 2. The three stages of system installation are analysis, design, and implementation.

____ 3. Administrative controls and general controls are the two types of internal controls.

____ 4. The total of the sales journal is posted as a debit to Sales and a credit to Accounts Receivable.

____ 5. A general ledger account made up of many individual accounts is called a Control account.

*Multiple Choice*   Select the best choice to complete each statement or answer each question below. Write the letter corresponding to your choice in the space provided.

____ 1. The purpose of internal control and system design is to:
   a. Help management plan the company's business activities
   b. Help management control the company's activities
   c. Safeguard the company's resources
   d. Provide an efficient accounting system
   e. All of the above

____ 2. The study of a company's information needs and reporting requirements, and of where that information is available, is the function of:
   a. System design
   b. System analysis
   c. System implementation
   d. All of the above
   e. None of the above

____ 3. Administrative controls include:
   a. Time-and-motion studies
   b. Performance reports
   c. Statistical analysis
   d. Directives for executives to have medical exams
   e. All of the above

____ 4. Procedures, techniques, and practices intended to protect a company's resources and provide for reliable financial statements are referred to as:
   a. Internal auditing controls
   b. Administrative controls
   c. Accounting controls
   d. External auditing controls
   e. None of the above

____ 5. The following item is *not* an example of a personnel control within a system of internal control:
   a. Employee competence
   b. Custodianship
   c. Assignment of responsibilities
   d. Rotation of duties
   e. Division of work

____ 6. Which of the following is necessary for adequate documentation of the sales function?
   a. Shipping invoice
   b. Sales invoices
   c. Credit approval
   d. Accounts receivable subsidiary ledger accounts
   e. All of the above

____ 7. The following types of transactions would be recorded in the sales journal:
   a. Office equipment sold on account
   b. All sales transactions
   c. Merchandise returned which has not yet been paid for
   d. Merchandise sold on account
   e. All of the above

____ 8. The largest dollar-amount total in a cash receipts journal is found in the
   a. Sundry accounts column
   b. Accounts receivable column
   c. Cash column
   d. Sales column
   e. None of the above

____ 9. The following types of transactions would be recorded in the general journal:
   a. Sales on account
   b. Purchase of equipment for cash
   c. Payment of rent
   d. Return of merchandise not yet paid for
   e. None of the above

____ 10. A purchase recorded correctly in the purchases journal as $815 is posted as $185 in the accounts payable ledger. This error will most likely be discovered when
   a. The trial balance is prepared
   b. The payment is made to the vendor
   c. The schedule of accounts payable is prepared
   d. The financial statements are prepared
   e. None of the above

## EXERCISES

4† **Exercise 1:** Analyzing Internal Controls

Jenkingtown Dog Track has 10 windows at which fans can place bets on the dog races. All employees operate out of a central cash fund, from which each window is allocated $5,000 at the start of the day. As each employee takes a break, another employee takes over at his or her wagering window. Once an employee comes off break, he or she is assigned to the next window where an employee is scheduled for a break. Comment on this practice.

4 **Exercise 2:** Analyzing Internal Controls

A number of customers of the Atlas Supply Store have written to the manager complaining that they are being billed again for accounts that have been paid in full. Atlas makes work assignments according to function: sales, purchases, payroll, inventory control, and miscellaneous. The person in charge of the sales function is responsible for the following activities: recording sales, maintaining the subsidiary ledgers, billing customers, collecting the accounts, and making cash deposits. Comment on this assignment of tasks to the sales function.

† The numbers in the margin refer to the Learning Objectives.

**4**  **Exercise 3:** Analyzing Internal Controls

The University of Southern Pennsylvania recently networked all personal computers (PCs) on campus to the mainframe computer in the administration building. Now all a user need do is turn on a PC anywhere on campus to obtain access to the mainframe. Powerful statistical programs are available for the students and faculty. Class schedules are available for students. Registration for courses can be done by PCs. At each PC station a complete list of the items on the mainframe is available, along with directions on how to log onto the system of interest to the user. Comment on this situation.

**5**  **Exercise 4:** Identifying Appropriate Journals

For each of the 10 transactions listed below, indicate in the space provided which of the five basic journals should be used to record each transaction. Use the following symbols for the basic journals:

| Journal | Symbol |
|---|---|
| Cash Receipts | CR |
| Cash Payments | CP |
| General | G |
| Purchases | P |
| Sales | S |

\_\_\_\_\_ **a.** Purchase of merchandise for cash

\_\_\_\_\_ **b.** Purchase of office equipment by issuing a 6-month note payable

\_\_\_\_\_ **c.** Payment for merchandise previously acquired on account

\_\_\_\_\_ **d.** Adjusting entry for accrued salaries

\_\_\_\_\_ **e.** Collection of accounts receivable

\_\_\_\_\_ **f.** Return of merchandise previously purchased on account but not yet paid for

\_\_\_\_\_ **g.** Sale of merchandise on account

\_\_\_\_\_ **h.** The owner's provision of four personal computers for the business

\_\_\_\_\_ **i.** Purchase of merchandise on account

\_\_\_\_\_ **j.** Sale of merchandise for cash

**Exercise 5:** Posting the Purchases Journal and Cash Payments Journals

The purchases and cash payments journals of the Elkton Company for its first month of operations are presented below.

| | ELKTON COMPANY | | | |
|---|---|---|---|---|
| | **Purchases Journal** | | | PAGE __1__ |
| **Date** | **Account Credited** | **Invoice Date** | **Post. Ref.** | **Amount** |
| 1998 | | | | |
| Jan. 4 | General Supply Company | 1/4 | | 600 |
| 9 | Johnson Office Equipment | 1/7 | | 800 |
| 14 | Dustin Windows | 1/12 | | 1,500 |
| 19 | Atlanta Brake | 1/19 | | 700 |
| 25 | Central Storage Company | 1/22 | | 400 |

### ELKTON COMPANY
### Cash Payments Journal

PAGE ___1___

| Date | Check No. | Account Debited | Post. Ref. | Cash Cr. | Purchases Discounts Cr. | Accounts Payable Dr. | Purchases Dr. | Sundry Accounts Dr. |
|------|-----------|-----------------|------------|----------|-------------------------|----------------------|---------------|---------------------|
| 1998 | | | | | | | | |
| Jan. 2 | 01 | Purchases | | 800 | | | 800 | |
| 9 | 02 | General Supply Company | | 588 | 12 | 600 | | |
| 12 | 03 | Office Equipment | | 700 | | | | 700 |
| 14 | 04 | Johnson Office Equip. | | 786 | 14 | 800 | | |
| 17 | 05 | Note Payable | | 500 | | | | 500 |

Foot the journals (add the amounts in the columns) and indicate in the journals the posting to the general and subsidiary ledger accounts using the following account numbers:

| Account | Number |
|---------|--------|
| Cash . . . . . . . . . . . . . . . . . . . . . . . . . . . . . . . . . . . . . | 110 |
| Office Equipment . . . . . . . . . . . . . . . . . . . . . . . . . . . | 140 |
| Notes Payable . . . . . . . . . . . . . . . . . . . . . . . . . . . . | 210 |
| Accounts Payable. . . . . . . . . . . . . . . . . . . . . . . . . . | 220 |
| Purchases. . . . . . . . . . . . . . . . . . . . . . . . . . . . . . . . | 510 |
| Purchases Discounts . . . . . . . . . . . . . . . . . . . . . . . | 530 |

5  **Exercise 6:** Identifying Journal Sources of Debits

For each of the accounts listed below, identify the journal that provides the most common source of the debit to that account.

| Account | Journal |
|---------|---------|
| Cash | _____ |
| Accounts Receivable | _____ |
| Prepaid Rent | _____ |
| Accounts Payable | _____ |
| Sales Returns and Allowances | _____ |
| Sales Discounts | _____ |
| Purchases | _____ |
| Salary Expense | _____ |

5  **Exercise 7:** Identifying Journal Sources of Credits

For each of the accounts listed below, identify the journal that provides the most common source of the credit to that account.

| Account | Journal |
|---------|---------|
| Cash | _____ |
| Accounts Receivable | _____ |
| Accounts Payable | _____ |
| Sales | _____ |
| Purchases Returns and Allowances | _____ |
| Purchases Discounts | _____ |

**5  6  Exercise 8:** Discovering Errors

During the past month, Lancer Company made the following four errors:

a. The total of the sales journal amounts to $4,620. It is posted as a debit to Accounts Receivable and a credit to Sales of $4,120.

b. The accounts receivable column of the cash receipts journal is incorrectly totaled to $7,450. The total should be $7,540.

c. A purchase invoice of $360 is entered in the purchases journal as $630.

d. A posting of $235 appears in the general ledger's Accounts Payable account. However, the total of the accounts payable column in the cash payments journal is correctly footed (added) to $325.

Explain whether and how the system will eventually uncover these errors.

## PROBLEMS: SET A

**4†  Problem A1:** Analyzing Internal Control

Mike Linebacker, a professional football player for the St. Louis Blues, owns a tavern in State College, Pennsylvania, called the Nittany Lion Drinking Establishment. Mike is an absentee owner, visiting State College only once or twice a month. The bar caters to the Penn State student body and sells mostly Blue & White beer on tap. In the past Mike has had problems with some dishonest employees. Some would sell glasses of beer and pocket the money instead of ringing up the sales. One employee even brought in his own cash register so that the customers could see him ring up his sales. Mike never saw any of the money that went into that cash register.

**Required:**

Provide some suggestions to develop a system of internal control for Mike's bar.

**4  Problem A2:** Describing a System of Internal Controls

Southeast Homes, Inc., is a large regional builder of medium-priced homes. The company's project managers supervise the construction of subdivisions of homes in many major metropolitan areas in Georgia and Florida. Each project manager engages all the subcontractors and hires numerous local people to perform the necessary tasks. When hiring new employees, the project manager completes all the necessary paperwork and forwards it to the main office in Atlanta. If employees prove satisfactory, the project manager initiates the paperwork for pay raises. If employees are not satisfactory, the project manager terminates their employment.

The project manager prepares the payroll weekly for all the individuals who report to him or her, sending the appropriate paperwork to Atlanta, and pays the employees from a special fund established for that purpose by the main office. The monies in the fund are deposited weekly from Atlanta after the project manager determines the total payroll and calls the amount in to the disbursing department of the home office.

**Required:**

Describe the abuses that could arise under Southeast's system.

† The numbers in the margin refer to the Learning Objectives.

5  6    **Problem A3:** Recording Transactions in Sales, Purchases, and General Journals and Posting to the Ledgers

The sales- and purchases-related transactions listed below represent activities of the Mellon Company during its first month of operations, March 1998. All sales and purchases are made on account.

Mar.  2   Purchased merchandise from Taft Company, $3,600; invoice dated Mar. 1.

3   Purchased merchandise from Leftwich Company, $8,500; invoice dated Mar. 3.

6   Returned $300 of the merchandise purchased from Leftwich Company on Mar. 3.

9   Sold merchandise to West Company, invoice no. 1001, $4,200.

11   Sold merchandise to Courtney Company, invoice no. 1002, $2,400.

12   Purchased merchandise from Wilkey Corp., $6,400; invoice dated Mar. 11.

14   Sold merchandise to Trump, Inc., invoice no. 1003, $3,900; invoice dated Mar. 14.

16   Purchased merchandise from Erickson Company, $2,500; invoice dated Mar. 15.

22   Sold merchandise to Tucker Company, invoice no. 1004, $4,400.

25   Received from Trump, Inc., $400 of merchandise returned from the sale of Mar. 14.

### Required:

1. Record the transactions listed above in a sales journal, a purchases journal, or a general journal, as appropriate.
2. Post these transactions to the general and subsidiary ledger accounts, creating accounts as needed. Use the following general ledger account numbers:

| | | | |
|---|---|---|---|
| Accounts Receivable | 120 | Purchases | 510 |
| Accounts Payable | 210 | Purchases Returns | |
| Sales | 410 | and Allowances | 520 |
| Sales Returns and Allowances | 420 | | |

Use page number 1 for the sales journal, page number 2 for the purchases journal, and page number 3 for the general journal.

▶ *(Check Figures: Sales journal total = $14,900; purchases journal total = $21,000)*

5  6    **Problem A4:** Recording Transactions in the Cash Receipts and Cash Payments Journals

The following cash transactions of the Dallas Company occurred during the month of June 1998. The company uses both a cash receipts journal and a cash payments journal.

June  1   Borrowed $6,000 from the First Cowboy Bank by issuing a 12%, 60-day note payable.

2   Purchased merchandise, $4,700. Check no. 271.

4   Sold merchandise, $6,200.

6   Paid an invoice amounting to $2,800 to Douglas Company, less 2% discount. Check no. 272.

7   Collected amount due less 3% discount on an invoice of $2,900 from Backwater Company.

10   Collected amount due less 3% discount on an invoice of $2,200 from San Antonio Supplies.

12   Paid freight charges, $100. Check no. 273.

14   Paid for advertising, $300. Check no. 274.

15   Paid salaries, $1,200. Check no. 275.

18   Sold merchandise, $3,300.

June 19 Paid an invoice amounting to $2,900 to the Tallgrass company less 2% discount. Check no. 276.

20 Collected $2,600 past due on an invoice from J. Harper.

23 Purchased merchandise, $900. Check no. 277.

26 Paid a past due invoice to Lincoln, Inc., $3,200. No discount is allowed. Check no. 278.

28 Mr. Wallace, the owner of the Dallas Company, withdrew $3,000 of personal funds from the business. Check no. 279.

**Required:**

Record the transactions in the cash receipts and cash payments journals. Foot and crossfoot the journals.

▶ *(Check Figures: Cash receipts journal total = $23,047; cash payments journal total = $18,986)*

5 6 **Problem A5:** Recording and Posting Sales Transactions Using Special Journals

The following sales and sales-related transactions were completed during the month of April 1998 by the Nelson Company. All credit sales have terms of 3/10, n/30, and all invoices are dated as of the transaction date.

Apr. 1 Mr. Nelson invested $5,200 of his personal funds in the business.

1 Sold merchandise on account to C. Baldwin, $3,200. Invoice no. 377.

3 Sold merchandise on account to J. Larson, $5,400. Invoice no. 378.

4 Sold $4,600 of merchandise for cash.

7 Received payment from C. Baldwin less appropriate discount.

9 Received payment from J. Larson less appropriate discount.

13 Sold merchandise to D. Salty on account, $6,200. Invoice no. 379.

15 Borrowed $3,000 from the First Exchange Bank by issuing a 10% note payable due 3 months hence.

15 D. Salty returned $1,100 of merchandise from the Apr. 13 sale.

16 Sold merchandise to E. Wisner on account, $1,700. Invoice no. 380.

21 Collected amount due from D. Salty less return of Apr. 15 and appropriate discount.

29 Received $600 from E. Wisner. No discount allowed.

30 Sold merchandise on account to G. Conrad, $3,400. Invoice no. 381.

**Required:**

1. Record the transactions in the appropriate journals.
2. Total the sales and cash receipts journals.
3. Using the following account numbers and journal page numbers, post to the general and accounts receivable ledgers.

| Account | Number | Journal | Page No. |
|---|---|---|---|
| Cash | 110 | Sales | 23 |
| Accounts Receivable | 120 | Cash Receipts | 35 |
| Notes Payable | 210 | General | 12 |
| Nelson, Capital | 310 | | |
| Sales | 410 | | |
| Sales Returns and Allowances | 420 | | |
| Sales Discounts | 430 | | |

4. Prepare a schedule of accounts receivable.

▶ *(Check Figure: Accounts receivable balance = $4,500)*

5  6    **Problem A6:** Recording and Posting Purchasing Transactions
Using Special Journals

Listed below are the purchase-related transactions for the Trenton Company for the month of
October 1998. All merchandise purchased on account has 2/10, n/30, credit terms.

Oct.  1    Purchased merchandise on account from New Jersey Supply Company, $5,400;
invoice dated Oct. 1.

4    Paid New Jersey Supply Company amount due less appropriate discount. Issued
check no. 279.

6    Purchased merchandise on account from Camden Company, $9,200; invoice
dated Oct. 6.

7    Paid freight charges on the merchandise purchased from Camden Company, $300.
Issued check no. 280.

9    Returned $500 of merchandise purchased from Camden Company on Oct. 6.

10    Paid Camden Company amount due less return of Oct. 9 and appropriate discount.
Issued check no. 281.

15    Paid salaries, $1,200. Issued check no. 282.

16    Purchased merchandise for cash, $1,900. Issued check no. 283.

17    Purchased merchandise on account from Garden State Company, $3,900. Invoice
dated Oct. 16.

19    Purchased merchandise on account from Washington Company, $4,100. Invoice
dated Oct. 19.

21    Paid insurance expense, $200. Check no. 284.

24    Ms. Trenton withdrew $1,500 from the business. Issued check no. 285.

25    Purchased merchandise from Clifton Company, $5,800. Invoice dated Oct. 24.

30    Paid Washington Company $1,100 on account from the Oct. 19 purchase. No
discount is allowed. Issued check no. 286.

31    Returned $800 of merchandise purchased on Oct. 25 from Clifton Company.

**Required:**

1. Record the transactions in the appropriate journals.
2. Total the purchases and cash payments journals.
3. Using the following account and journal page numbers, post to the general and accounts
payable ledgers.

| Account | Number |  | Journal | Page No. |
|---|---|---|---|---|
| Cash | 110 |  | Purchases | 22 |
| Accounts Payable | 210 |  | Cash Payments | 37 |
| Trenton, Capital | 310 |  | General | 16 |
| Trenton, Withdrawals | 320 |  |  |  |
| Purchases | 510 |  |  |  |
| Purchases Returns and Allowances | 520 |  |  |  |
| Purchase Discounts | 530 |  |  |  |
| Freight-In | 540 |  |  |  |
| Salary Expense | 610 |  |  |  |
| Insurance Expense | 620 |  |  |  |

4. Prepare a schedule of accounts payable.

▶ *(Check Figure: Accounts payable balance = $11,900)*

## PROBLEMS: SET B

4† **Problem B1:** Analyzing Internal Control

Sally Dunford's responsibilities at the Brittany Company are to maintain the general and subsidiary ledgers as well as all cash receipts. Cash disbursements are made by the company treasurer, Mrs. Tillman. On the morning of Dec. 12, 1998, Sally does not appear for work, and you are assigned her duties until she returns.

Early that afternoon Sam Holt appears at your desk with a check for $1,276.43, the amount of his last invoice. When you access his subsidiary ledger via the microcomputer, you see that the invoice for $1,276.43 is indeed unpaid, and the previous invoice for $941.53 shows an unpaid balance of $600.00. Sam states that he paid his invoice in full last week.

A review of the several other accounts receivable also shows partial payments.

**Required:**

Explain the possible reason for the partial payments being posted to the accounts.

4 **Problem B2:** Designing a System of Internal Controls

You have been appointed the athletic director of Great Western University. Western has just completed a new facility for its basketball program. The new arena has a capacity of 25,578 seats. Since the Western Golden Lilies have always been a national powerhouse in basketball, near-capacity crowds can be expected in the new facility.

Your responsibility is to design a system of internal control to assure the university that all monies for the basketball games are collected and accounted for. Season tickets for this year's 12 home games are sold at $40 to students (about 7,500 are expected to be sold), at $90 to faculty (about 500), at $140 to Gold Jacket Club members (about 9,300), and at $180 to White Jacket Club members (about 1,500). The remaining tickets are sold for $6 each on a game-by-game basis at local retail stores, at the box office, and at the four gates on game nights.

**Required:**

Design a system for distributing, accounting for, and controlling the tickets and controlling cash receipts.

5  6  **Problem B3:** Recording Transactions in Sales, Purchases, and General Journals and Posting to the Ledgers

During its first month of operations in September 1998, the Clarkson Company had the following transactions. (All purchases and sales are on account.)

Sept.  1   Purchased merchandise from Denton, Inc., $4,800; invoice dated Sept. 1.

3   Purchased merchandise from Zalk Company, $5,900; invoice dated Sept. 2.

5   Sold merchandise to Alton Company, invoice no. 101, $6,200.

8   Sold merchandise to Smother Company, invoice no. 102, $5,100.

9   Returned $400 of the merchandise purchased from Denton, Inc., on Sept. 1.

12   Purchased merchandise from Fenster Company, $7,300; invoice dated Sept. 10.

14   Sold merchandise to Wendle Company, invoice no. 103, $6,700.

19   Received from Smother Company, $300 of merchandise returned from the sale of Sept. 8.

22   Purchased merchandise from Cantz, Inc., $7,100, invoice dated Sept. 22.

29   Sold merchandise to Mincher Company, invoice no. 104, $9,300.

† The numbers in the margin refer to the Learning Objectives.

**Required:**

1. Record the transactions listed above in a sales, purchases, or general journal, as appropriate.
2. Post these transactions to the general and subsidiary ledger accounts, creating accounts as needed. Use the following general ledger account numbers:

| | | | |
|---|---|---|---|
| Accounts Receivable | 120 | Purchases | 510 |
| Accounts Payable | 210 | Purchases Returns | |
| Sales | 410 | and Allowances | 520 |
| Sales Returns and Allowances | 420 | | |

Use page number 1 for the sales journal, page number 2 for the purchases journal, and page number 3 for the general journal.

▶ *(Check Figures: Sales journal total = $27,300; purchases journal total = $25,100)*

5 6 **Problem B4:** Cash Receipts and Cash Payments Journal

The Bolton Company uses both a cash receipts journal and a cash payments journal. The following cash transactions occurred during the month of November 1998.

Nov. 1 Sold merchandise, $5,100.

3 Collected amount due less 2% discount on an invoice of $900 from Easy Company dated Oct. 28, 1995.

5 Paid an invoice amounting to $2,100 to Levitt Company, less 3% discount. Check no. 417.

6 Purchased merchandise, $3,500. Check no. 418.

8 Paid freight charges, $100. Check no. 419.

10 Mr. Bolton invested $3,500 of personal funds in the business.

11 Collected amount due less 2% discount on an invoice of $3,300 from Vener, Inc., dated Nov. 7, 1995.

12 Paid rent on the office building, $600. Check no. 420.

15 Paid salaries, $7,500. Check no. 421.

17 Paid an invoice amounting to $1,100 to Scannen Company, less 3% discount. Check no. 422.

18 Sold merchandise, $2,400.

20 Collected $4,700 past due on an invoice from Molt, Inc. The invoice was dated Oct. 2, 1995.

25 Purchased Merchandise, $2,000. Check no. 423.

27 Paid a past-due invoice to Getz Company, $1,900. No discount is allowed. Check no. 424.

28 Borrowed $1,500 from the First National Bank by issuing a 10%, 90-day note payable.

**Required:**

Record the transactions in the cash receipts and cash payments journals. Foot and crossfoot the journals.

▶ *(Check Figures: Cash receipts journal total = $21,316; cash payments journal total = $18,704)*

**5 6** **Problem B5:** Recording and Posting Sales Transactions
Using Special Journals

The Reeves Company completed the following sales and sales-related transactions during the month of August 1998. All credit sales have terms of 2/10, n/30, and all invoices are dated as of the transaction date.

Aug. 1 Borrowed $2,500 from the Union Bank by issuing a 12%, 6-month note payable.

3 Sold merchandise on account to D. Dozier, $3,300. Invoice no. 1210.

4 Sold merchandise on account to T. Dorsey, $4,600. Invoice no. 1211.

8 Received payment from D. Dozier less appropriate discount.

10 Sold $3,600 of merchandise for cash.

11 Received payment from T. Dorsey less appropriate discount.

16 Sold merchandise to S. Kenton on account, $4,100. Invoice no. 1212.

18 Sold merchandise to N. Getty on account, $1,900. Invoice no. 1213.

19 Mr. Reeves invested $900 in the business.

21 S. Kenton returned $500 of merchandise from the Aug. 16 sale.

25 Collected amount due from S. Kenton less return of Aug. 21 and appropriate discount.

27 Sold merchandise on account to T. Dorsey, $2,900. Invoice no. 1214.

30 Received $1,000 from N. Getty. No discount allowed.

31 Sold merchandise on account to D. Dozier, $700. Invoice no. 1215.

**Required:**

1. Record the transactions in the appropriate journals.
2. Total the sales and cash receipts journals.

3. Using the following account and journal page numbers, post to the general and accounts receivable ledgers.

| Account | Number |
|---|---|
| Cash | 110 |
| Accounts Receivable | 120 |
| Notes Payable | 210 |
| Reeves, Capital | 310 |
| Sales | 410 |
| Sales Returns and Allowances | 420 |
| Sales Discounts | 430 |

| Journal | Page No. |
|---|---|
| Sales | 32 |
| Cash Receipts | 29 |
| General | 18 |

4. Prepare a schedule of accounts receivable

▶ *(Check Figure: Accounts receivable balance = $4,500)*

5 6   **Problem B6:** Recording and Posting Purchasing Transactions
Using Special Journals

The purchase-related transactions for the Weston Company for the month of May 1998 are
listed below. All merchandise purchases on account have 3/10, n/30, credit terms.

May 1   Purchased merchandise on account from Lanton, Inc., $4,200. Invoice dated
May 1.

2   Purchased merchandise on account from Freedman Company, $2,900. Invoice
dated May 2.

3   Returned $300 of merchandise purchased from Freedman Company on May 2.

6   Paid Lanton, Inc., amount due less appropriate discount. Issued check no. 526.

8   Paid freight charges on the merchandise purchased from Lanton, $100. Issued
check no. 527.

10   Paid Freedman Company amount due less return of May 3 and appropriate discount. Issued check no. 528.

15   Paid salaries, $2,500. Issued check no. 529.

18   Purchased merchandise on account from Plant Company, $2,100. Invoice dated
May 16.

20   Purchased merchandise on account from Freedman Company, $3,700. Invoice
dated May 20.

22   Purchased merchandise for cash, $800. Issued check no. 530.

24   Mr. Weston withdrew $1,500 from the business. Issued check no. 531.

25   Purchased merchandise from Williams Company, $900. Invoice dated May 24.

29   Paid Plant Company $700 on account from the May 18 purchase. No discount is
allowed. Issued check no. 532.

30   Returned $200 of merchandise purchased on May 25 from Williams Company.

**Required:**

1. Record the transactions in the appropriate journals.
2. Total the purchases and cash payments journals.
3. Using the following account and journal page numbers, post to the general and accounts
   payable ledgers.

| Account | Number | | Journal | Page No. |
|---|---|---|---|---|
| Cash . . . . . . . . . . . . . . . . . . . . . . | 110 | | Purchases . . . . . . . . . . . . . . . . . . | 17 |
| Accounts Payable . . . . . . . . . . . . | 210 | | Cash Payments . . . . . . . . . . . . . . | 15 |
| Weston, Withdrawals . . . . . . . . . . | 320 | | General . . . . . . . . . . . . . . . . . . . . . | 11 |
| Purchases . . . . . . . . . . . . . . . . . . | 510 | | | |
| Purchases Returns | | | | |
| and Allowances . . . . . . . . . . . . . | 520 | | | |
| Purchases Discounts . . . . . . . . . . | 530 | | | |
| Freight-In . . . . . . . . . . . . . . . . . . . | 540 | | | |
| Salary Expense . . . . . . . . . . . . . . | 610 | | | |
| Sales Discounts . . . . . . . . . . . . . . | 430 | | | |

4. Prepare a schedule of accounts payable.

▶ *(Check Figure: Accounts payable balance = $5,800)*

## DECISION PROBLEM

You have been assigned by the Special Projects Manager of Mississippi Transport Company to visit the St. Petersburg, Missouri, divisional offices and evaluate their system of internal controls.

The St. Petersburg division transports freight up and down the Mississippi River, billing its customers monthly. Jessie Clemens, the assistant office manager, records the transportation fees daily in the transportation revenue journal on a microcomputer. The computer is programmed to record automatically the charges in the client's account when the entry is made in the transportation revenue journal.

Jessie goes to the post office daily to deposit and pick up the division's mail. Upon returning from the post office, she gives the mail to Mr. Twain, the office manager, with the exception of the payments from the clients. Jessie records the payments in the record of cash receipts journal on the microcomputer. The computer is programmed to post these receipts to the accounts receivable ledger.

After she has finished entering the receipts into the microcomputer, Jessie gives the checks to Mrs. Mark, the Division Manager. Mrs. Mark then prepares the deposit slip and deposits the checks in the division's account with the First National Bank of St. Petersburg.

Each month Jessie uses a program she developed to generate bills for all customers based on the balances in their accounts receivable. The computer generates the bills and addresses envelopes. Joe Finn, the division's receptionist, inserts the bills in the envelopes and drops them off at the post office on his way home.

As a convenience to Mrs. Mark, Jessie reconciles the bank statement monthly.

**Required:**

Evaluate the system of internal control, providing suggestions for its improvement.

### ETHICS CASE*

Wolfe Ruston, a well-known mystery writer, has just finished reading an article in the *Hollywood Movie Weekly Journal* concerning a film by Global Pictures Corporation made from his best-selling book, *The Paris-New York Connection*. The article stated that the film generated over $242 million in revenues. Wolfe has a "net profit" deal with Global, which is common for writers, producers, and actors. The arrangement is for Wolfe to receive 12% of the net profit on the project.

Excited, Wolfe calls Global to determine what he is due. To his utter amazement, Global informs him that while the project generated record-setting revenues, it has unfortunately recorded a $25 million loss. Wolfe immediately calls his agent, lawyer, and accountant, and the group schedules an appointment with Global officials to review the accounting records for the project.

At the meeting, Global reveals that $8.3 million was paid to Susan Meloday and Tug Powerhouse, the film's stars. In addition, $1.7 million was paid to the two stars' valets, bodyguards, and a personal trainer for Mr. Powerhouse. Furthermore, interest costs of $12.3 million were charged on the film's $63.2 million budget. Global states that this is the industry practice; the $12.3 million represents the interest the studio would have earned if it had invested the $63.2 million instead of spending it on the film.

Other costs include overhead charges of 25% of the film's production budget and 15% of the advertising budget. Global contends that these charges are normal in the movie-making business and are necessary to protect the studio against the failure of some of its other projects. Global further contends that it is taking all the risk; if *The Paris-New York Connection* flopped, it would not cost Wolfe a dime.

A last item that Wolfe's group finds in the accounting records is a bill for $976 from Winged Delights, a local fried chicken franchise. Wolfe's group believes that this bill is for Susan Meloday's birthday party. Global says it is for dinner for the film's extras.

**Required:**

Comment on Global's accounting practices.

* (Ronald Grover, "Curtains for Tinseltown Accounting?" Reprinted from the January 14, 1991, issue of *Business Week* by special permission, copyright © 1991 by McGraw-Hill, Inc.)

## COMPREHENSIVE PROBLEMS

5  6† **Comprehensive Problem 1:** Recording Transactions and Completing the Accounting Cycle

At the close of business on June 30, 1998, the Thompson Retail Store had the following post-closing trial balance (with account numbers):

---

**THOMPSON RETAIL STORE**
**Post-Closing Trial Balance**
**June 30, 1998**

| | | | |
|---|---|---:|---:|
| 110 | Cash | $ 1,800 | |
| 120 | Accounts Receivable | 1,200 | |
| 130 | Merchandise Inventory | 5,100 | |
| 140 | Prepaid Insurance | 900 | |
| 150 | Office Supplies on Hand | 600 | |
| 160 | Office Equipment | 6,000 | |
| 165 | Accumulated Depreciation | | $ 1,500 |
| 210 | Notes Payable | | 2,000 |
| 220 | Accounts Payable | | 500 |
| 230 | Salaries Payable | | –0– |
| 310 | Thompson, Capital | | 11,600 |
| 320 | Thompson, Withdrawals | –0– | |
| 330 | Income Summary | | –0– |
| 410 | Sales | | –0– |
| 420 | Sales Returns and Allowances | –0– | |
| 430 | Sales Discounts | –0– | |
| 510 | Purchases | –0– | |
| 520 | Purchases Returns and Allowances | | –0– |
| 530 | Purchases Discounts | | –0– |
| 540 | Freight-In | –0– | |
| 610 | Salary Expense | –0– | |
| 620 | Insurance Expense | –0– | |
| 630 | Office Supplies Expense | –0– | |
| 640 | Depreciation Expense | –0– | |
| 650 | Interest Expense | –0– | |
| | | $15,600 | $15,600 |

---

Thompson completed the transactions listed below during the month of July 1998. All credit sales are 4/10, n/30, and all credit purchases are 2/10, n/30. The account receivable represents a sale made to N. Anderson on June 29. The account payable represents a purchase from Tinker, Inc., on June 30.

July  1  Purchased merchandise on account from Able, Inc., $2,100. Invoice dated July 1.

2  Sold merchandise on account to T. Trent, $4,400; invoice no. 126.

3  Paid Tinker, Inc., amount due less appropriate discount. Issued check no. 173.

4  Collected amount due from N. Anderson less appropriate discount.

5  Mr. Thompson withdrew $300 from the business. Issued check no. 174.

6  Paid freight charges on the merchandise purchased from Able, Inc., on July 1, $100. Issued check no. 175.

7  Paid amount due to Able, Inc., for the purchase of July 1 less appropriate discount. Issued check no. 176.

8  Sold merchandise for cash, $6,500.

† The numbers in the margin refer to the Learning Objectives.

July 9 Sold merchandise on account to G. Ord, $3,700; invoice no. 127.

9 Purchased merchandise on account from Asbury Company, $4,600; invoice dated July 9.

10 Received returned merchandise from G. Ord, $700.

11 Collected amount due from G. Ord less return of July 10 and appropriate discounts.

11 Sold merchandise on account to C. Childs, $4,500. Invoice no. 128.

13 Paid Asbury amount due from purchase of July 9 less appropriate discount. Issued check no. 177.

13 Sold merchandise on account to T. Trent, $5,200; invoice no. 129.

15 Paid salaries, $1,500. Issued check no. 178.

16 Sold merchandise on account to G. Ord, $2,700; invoice no. 130.

17 Purchased merchandise on account from Newton Company, $3,100; invoice dated July 17.

19 Acquired office supplies for cash, $700. Issued check no. 179.

20 Returned merchandise purchased from Newton Company, $900.

21 Collected amount due from C. Childs from sale of July 11 less appropriate discount.

25 Paid interest expense on the note payable, $20. Issued check no. 180.

26 Purchased merchandise on account from Tinker, Inc., $1,900. Invoice date July 24.

27 Received $900 investment from Mr. Thompson.

28 Purchased merchandise for cash, $600. Issued check no. 181.

28 Sold merchandise on account to N. Anderson, $1,900. Invoice no. 131.

30 Purchased merchandise on account from Able, Inc., $600. Invoice dated July 29.

30 Paid Newton Company $300 in partial settlement of account. Issued check no. 182.

**Required:**

1. Record the June 30, 1998, post-closing trial balance amounts in the general and subsidiary ledgers.
2. Using the five special journals, record the transactions listed above.
3. Total the journals and post to the general and subsidiary ledger accounts. Use the following journal page numbers:

| | | | |
|---|---|---|---|
| Sales Journal . . . . . . . . . . . . . . . . . . | 8 | Cash Payments Journal . . . . . . . . . . | 17 |
| Purchases Journal . . . . . . . . . . . . . . | 9 | General Journal . . . . . . . . . . . . . . . . | 11 |
| Cash Receipts Journal . . . . . . . . . . . | 15 | | |

4. Determine the balance in each account and prepare an unadjusted trial balance on a worksheet.
5. Record the following adjusting entries on the worksheet.
   a. Insurance expense expired, $200
   b. Office supplies on hand, $100
   c. Depreciation, $300
   d. Accrued salaries, $1,200
6. Complete the worksheet. The ending inventory amounts to $3,600.

   ▶ *(Check Figure: Net income = $9,976)*
7. Prepare the financial statements.
8. Record the adjusting and closing entries in the general journal. Post entries to the general ledger.
9. Prepare schedules of accounts receivable and payable.

5 6 **Comprehensive Problem 2:** Recording Transactions and Completing the Accounting Cycle

The Dec. 31, 1997, post-closing trial balance (with account numbers) for the Troutman Company follows:

**TROUTMAN COMPANY**
**Post-Closing Trial Balance**
**December 31, 1997**

| | | | |
|---|---|---|---|
| 110 | Cash | $ 2,400 | |
| 120 | Accounts Receivable | 2,100 | |
| 130 | Merchandise Inventory | 7,300 | |
| 140 | Prepaid Rent | 900 | |
| 150 | Office Supplies on Hand | 1,600 | |
| 160 | Office Equipment | 10,000 | |
| 165 | Accumulated Depreciation | | $ 2,500 |
| 210 | Notes Payable | | 4,000 |
| 220 | Accounts Payable | | 1,300 |
| 230 | Salaries Payable | | –0– |
| 310 | Troutman, Capital | | 16,500 |
| 320 | Troutman, Withdrawals | –0– | |
| 330 | Income Summary | | –0– |
| 410 | Sales | | –0– |
| 420 | Sales Returns and Allowances | –0– | |
| 430 | Sales Discounts | –0– | |
| 510 | Purchases | –0– | |
| 520 | Purchases Returns and Allowances | | –0– |
| 530 | Purchases Discounts | | –0– |
| 540 | Freight-In | –0– | |
| 610 | Salary Expense | –0– | |
| 620 | Rent Expense | –0– | |
| 630 | Office Supplies Expense | –0– | |
| 640 | Depreciation Expense | –0– | |
| 650 | Interest Expense | –0– | |
| | | $24,300 | $24,300 |

The account receivable of $2,100 represents a sale on Dec. 28, 1997, to A. Adams. All credit sales are 2/10, n/30. The account payable of $1,300 represents a purchase on Dec. 29, 1997, from Nance, Inc. All credit purchases are 3/10, n/30.

During the month of January 1998 the following transactions were completed:

Jan. 2 Sold merchandise on account to B. Baker, $2,400. Invoice no. 316.

3 Purchased merchandise on account from Olson, Inc., $900. Invoice dated Jan. 2.

4 Collected amount due from Dec. 28 sale to A. Adams less appropriate discount.

5 Sold merchandise for cash, $4,300.

7 Paid amount due to Nance, Inc., for the purchase of Dec. 29, 1994, less appropriate discount. Issued check number 683.

8 Sold merchandise on account to C. Charlton, $3,100. Invoice no. 317.

9 Returned merchandise purchased from Olson, Inc., $100.

10 Collected amount due from B. Baker less appropriate discount.

11 Purchased merchandise on account from Petersen Company, $1,200. Invoice dated Jan. 10.

11 Paid Olson, Inc., amount due less return of Jan. 9 and appropriate discount. Issued check no. 684.

Jan. 12   Purchased merchandise for cash, $700. Issued check no. 685.

13   Sold merchandise on account to D. Denton, $1,300. Invoice no. 318.

14   Paid interest expense on the note payable, $100. Issued check no. 686.

15   Paid salaries, $800. Issued check no. 687.

17   Purchased merchandise on account from Nance, Inc., $1,900. Invoice dated Jan. 14.

18   Sold merchandise on account to A. Adams, $4,600. Invoice no. 319.

19   Mr. Troutman withdrew $10,000 from the business. Issued check no. 688.

21   Acquired office supplies for cash, $400. Issued check no. 689.

22   Paid freight charges on the merchandise purchased from Nance, Inc., on Jan. 17, $200. Issued check no. 690.

22   Collected amount due from D. Denton less appropriate discount.

23   Sold merchandise on account to B. Baker, $1,100. Invoice no. 320.

24   Received returned merchandise from C. Charlton, $300.

25   Received amount due from C. Charlton on sale of Jan. 8 less return of Jan. 24. Account is past due.

25   Purchased merchandise on account from Queen Company, $3,400. Invoice date Jan. 24.

26   Paid $900 to Nance, Inc., in partial payment of account. Issued check no. 691. Account is past due.

27   Received $1,700 from the First Union Bank by increasing the note payable.

28   Purchased merchandise on account from Petersen Company, $2,700. Invoice dated Jan. 27.

29   Sold merchandise on account to D. Denton, $1,700. Invoice no. 321.

30   Purchased merchandise on account from Olson, Inc., $3,600. Invoice dated Jan. 29.

30   Sold merchandise for cash, $13,100.

### Required:

1. Record the Dec. 31, 1997, post-closing trial balance amounts in the general and subsidiary ledgers.
2. Using the five special journals, record the transactions listed above.
3. Total the journals and post to the general and subsidiary ledger accounts. Use the following journal page numbers:

Sales Journal . . . . . . . . . . . . . . . . . . . 15      Cash Payments Journal . . . . . . . . . . . 42
Purchases Journal . . . . . . . . . . . . . . . 22      General Journal . . . . . . . . . . . . . . . . . 13
Cash Receipts Journal . . . . . . . . . . . . 31

4. Determine the balance in each account and prepare an unadjusted trial balance on a worksheet
5. Record the following adjusting entries on the worksheet:
   a. Rent expired, $300
   b. Office supplies on hand, $700
   c. Depreciation, $100
   d. Accrued salaries, $900
6. Complete the worksheet. The ending inventory amounts to $4,700.

   ▶ *(Check Figure: Net income = $10,647)*
7. Prepare the financial statements.
8. Record the adjusting and closing entries in the general journal. Post entries to the general ledger.
9. Prepare schedules of accounts receivable and payable.

## OBJECTIVE ASSIGNMENT ANSWERS

**True/False**

1. F     2. T     3. F     4. F     5. T

**Multiple Choice**

1. e     2. b     3. e     4. c     5. b
6. e     7. d     8. c     9. d     10. c

# Cash

## THE NATURE OF CASH

For accounting purposes, "cash" represents more than the paper currency and coins that we use in everyday financial transactions. To an accountant, "cash" on the balance sheet includes money in other forms as well, although not all other forms. For example, many people consider savings accounts, travelers' checks, checking accounts, money orders, U.S. government savings bonds, and postage stamps to be money. Not all of these, however, are cash. **Cash,** as the term is used by accountants, means either:

*Learning Objective 1*

*Define cash in accounting terminology*

1. A current asset on deposit in a bank that can be withdrawn immediately and used for any business purpose; *or*
2. A current asset that a bank will readily accept for deposit.

According to the accountant's definition, cash includes paper currency and coins, the money in a checking account, a check written on a checking account (also called a *demand deposit account*), the money in certain savings accounts (withdrawals from some types of savings accounts are penalized), money orders (a form of check usually issued at a bank, post office, or convenience store), and travelers' checks (a form of check requiring the user to sign at the time the check is issued and again at the time it is used to pay for something).

Cash does *not* include postage stamps, U.S. government savings bonds, or promissory notes (which are simply formal IOUs), whether from individuals or companies. None of these forms of money is considered cash, because they cannot be deposited directly into a bank account. Money held in a special bank account that can be used for only one purpose, such as to retire long-term debt or pay retirement benefits, would not be represented as cash on the balance sheet because its use is restricted. Management could not legally use it to pay employees for their services or to purchase merchandise. Items not included as cash do appear elsewhere on the balance sheet, under such headings as "Temporary Investments," "Prepaid Postage," and "Long-Term Investments."

## INTERNAL CONTROL OVER CASH

Cash is an asset that can be used to acquire almost any other good or service, and every business and individual will accept cash as payment. A great deal of value can be contained in a small package of cash. In short, cash is an asset that everyone would like to have. Such a desirable asset must be carefully protected. If it is not protected and controlled, small amounts of cash may be lost to pilfering and enormous sums may be lost to clever schemes of theft. Of course, cash is also lost through honest mistakes. For these reasons, cash flowing through a business must be protected and controlled.

*Learning Objective 2*

*Explain how the system of internal control is used to safeguard cash receipts and cash payments*

In this chapter we will focus on how the system of internal control can be used to protect the company's cash.

### Control over Cash Receipts

Businesses receive cash directly from customers, either at the time of purchase in the store or by payments mailed to the company. While both currency and checks are received over the counter, currency is not typically sent through the mail. Control systems are needed to safeguard cash received over the counter and cash mailed to the company.

### *Controlling Cash Received over the Counter*

When customers pay salesclerks for purchases made in the store, the cash is commonly stored in a cash register until it is collected or turned in to the company cashier. If a large amount of cash is received, as in a department store during the Christmas season, cash may be removed from the register several times a day. At less busy times all the cash received is turned in at the end of the business day. The control system over cash flowing through cash registers includes the following:

- The cash register itself is a physical control used to keep the cash secure until it can be taken to the company safe.
- The cash register displays the amount rung up so that the customer can see what the salesclerk has entered. Many times the customer will point out errors in register entries.
- The cash register automatically makes a record of each transaction directly into the company's computerized accounting system, or on a paper or magnetic tape locked in the register. The salesclerk responsible for handling the cash does not have access to these records. Later, another designated individual, typically from the accounting department, compares a form showing the amount taken from the cash register drawer with the amount shown on the register record. This comparison will reveal discrepancies that may be due to employee errors or theft.
- The cashier to whom the cash is given verifies the salesclerk's count and issues a written receipt. The cashier then sees that the cash is deposited in the bank as soon as possible. Good internal control procedures require that all cash be deposited each day. Cash is more easily stolen from a company safe than from a bank vault!

### *Controlling Cash Received through the Mail*

For companies that receive cash through the mail, internal control begins with the people who open the mail. The internal control procedures over cash flowing into a company through the mail include the following:

- Two employees open the mail together, to reduce the likelihood of a single dishonest employee stealing cash undetected.
- The two employees prepare three copies of a schedule showing the name of the customer sending money, the purpose for which the money was sent, and the amount received. One copy is sent to the cashier with the cash; the second copy is sent to the accounting department for recording purposes; the third copy is filed.
- The cashier deposits the cash in the bank as soon as possible.
- The accounting department credits customers' accounts and makes other appropriate entries.
- Later, another individual compares the amount deposited by the cashier with the total amount credited to various accounts. Theft or error will be revealed whenever these two amounts are not the same.

Notice that in both types of cash transactions, two people are present when cash is initially received by the company: the customer and the salesclerk or two mailroom clerks. Records for the asset cash are never controlled by the same person who has responsibility for the cash itself. Finally, in each case someone compares the records of the amount of cash received with the amount of cash deposited. These three basic internal control principles should be maintained in every situation where cash is received by a business.

### Control over Cash Payments

We want to be sure that the business pays no more than it owes, that it pays only valid bills, and that the proper payee receives the company's payment. Large thefts have been accomplished by employees who have paid fictitious invoices to phantom companies they have created or who have paid invoices for goods and services never received. Internal controls over cash payments are designed to ensure that this form of fraud doesn't happen. In the remaining sections of this chapter we will discuss bank reconciliations, petty cash funds, another system for recording purchase discounts, and the voucher system. Bank reconciliations help control both cash receipts and cash payments; the other systems serve primarily to control cash payments.

**ASK YOURSELF** ▶

1. **How do accountants define cash?**
2. **What three basic internal control principles should be maintained in every situation in which cash is received by a business?**

## BANK RECONCILIATION

Checks written to employees, vendors, and others are presented by these payees' banks to the business's bank for payment. The bank sends the business a bank statement, usually once each month, which summarizes the checks that have been presented for payment as well as the deposits and service charges for the period. Exhibit 1 shows a typical monthly bank statement. Notice that the check numbers and amounts of all checks processed by the bank during the month are shown. Deposits and service charges are identified by the date they were added to or deducted from the account.

Learning Objective **3**

Describe what a bank reconciliation is and why it is necessary

The ending balance in the monthly statement compiled by the bank often does not agree with the ending balance that appears in the checkbook. When this happens, someone in the business must determine the reasons for the difference between the two ending balances. A complete and satisfactory explanation of the differences between the bank's records and the company's is called a **bank reconciliation.**

Some differences may be expected routinely every month. For example, the amount of checks written by the business but not received by the bank before it prepares the monthly bank statement will appear as a deduction in the checkbook but not in the bank's records. Similarly, deposits mailed but not yet received by the bank will appear in the business's records but not on the bank's monthly statement. Bank service charges will appear on the bank statement but not in the checkbook.

Other differences may result from errors or embezzlement by an employee. The bank may have incorrectly deducted the amount of a check, or the business may have entered an amount incorrectly in its checkbook. An employee may have stolen a blank check, forged it, and cashed it. Since the check was never entered in the checkbook, a difference will exist between the bank balance and the checkbook balance.

Bank reconciliations are an important part of the internal control system. They help locate errors in the recordkeeping system and assist in discovering employee schemes to defraud the company. The bank reconciliation should always be prepared by an individual who is not involved with preparing and approving payments. Only an *independent* party can verify that the work of the other employees was accurate and proper.

**Exhibit 1** Bank Statement

## MERCHANTS NATIONAL BANK

| Direct Inquiries to: | Statement Date |
|---|---|
| Merchants National Bank of Texas | 11/30/98 |

Direct Inquiries to:
Merchants National Bank of Texas
PO Box 35907
Temple, Texas 76501
(817)555-4444

Statement Date
11/30/98

Account Number
1098674399

### KIM'S APPLIANCES
478 Hill Street
Temple, Texas 76501

| Balance Last Statement | Deposits and Credits | | Checks and Debits | | Balance This Statement |
|---|---|---|---|---|---|
| | No. | Total Amount | No. | Total Amount | |
| 32,917.79 | 7 | 4,925.54 | 16 | 3,669.53 | 34,173.80 |

| Date | Amount Credited | Description |
|---|---|---|
| 11/2 | 1,385.56 | Deposit |
| 11/7 | 347.78 | Deposit |
| 11/9 | 1,244.56 | Deposit |
| 11/13 | 527.91 | Deposit |
| 11/18 | 876.30 | Deposit |
| 11/24 | 462.87 | Deposit |
| 11/29 | 80.56 | Deposit |

**Checks:**

| Date | Check No. | Amount | Date | Check No. | Amount |
|---|---|---|---|---|---|
| 11/2 | 1862 | 188.95 | 11/2 | 1875 | 222.77 |
| 11/4 | 1876 | 160.73 | 11/5 | 1884 | 88.33 |
| 11/7 | 1896 | 346.00 | 11/9 | 1899 | 275.75 |
| 11/10 | 1900 | 25.79 | 11/10 | 1901 | 120.00 |
| 11/14 | 1902 | 890.50 | 11/17 | 1903 | 84.19 |
| 11/19 | 1905 | 308.61 | 11/22 | 1906 | 170.87 |
| 11/26 | 1907 | 400.80 | 11/30 | 1909 | 178.64 |

**Other Debits:**

| Date | Amount | Description |
|---|---|---|
| 11/30 | 25.00 | Service charge |
| 11/30 | 182.60 | NSF check |

MEMBER FDIC

Most businesses use the bank-and-books-to-correct-cash reconciliation to trace the differences between the bank statement and the checking account. This method allows the firm to show corrections needed in the checkbook (and accounting records) and still derive a correct ending balance. Using Kim's Appliances as an example, we will illustrate how to reconcile both the ending balance on the bank statement and the ending balance in the checkbook to the same correct cash balance.

Learning Objective **4**

Prepare a bank reconciliation

# KIM'S APPLIANCES

Ron Dollar, an accountant employed by Kim's Appliances, is responsible for preparing the monthly bank reconciliation. The bank statement shows an ending balance for Nov. 30, 1998, of $34,173.80, whereas the balance in the company's checkbook is $30,388.60. Ron's task is to adjust each of the balances to reflect the correct end-of-month balance and, in doing so, to reconcile the two. Adjusting the bank balance begins with the ending balance from the bank statement; adjusting the checkbook balance begins with the ending balance in the checkbook. Each is adjusted independently; the resulting corrected balances should be identical.

Ron uses the November bank statement shown in Exhibit 1 and the company's checkbook and cash accounts to prepare the reconciliation. Exhibit 2 shows how each of the following items would appear on the reconciliation.

1. Cash in the amount of $1,970 was placed in the night depository on Thursday, Nov. 30. This deposit does not appear on the bank statement because the bank processed it on Friday, Dec. 1. This $1,970 **deposit in transit** must be added to the ending balance, since it is cash that was at Kim's disposal on Nov. 30. A correct Nov. 30 cash balance must include this amount.

2. In comparing the checkbook stubs with the canceled checks, Ron discovers that 15 checks totaling $5,854.80 have not yet been processed by the bank. Checks written but not yet presented to the bank or processed by the bank are called **outstanding checks.** The $5,854.80 of outstanding checks must be deducted from the $34,173.80 balance reported by the bank, since Kim's Appliances no longer has control over this amount of cash. From Kim's point of view the cash has been spent; only the mechanical process of presenting the checks to Kim's bank remains.

3. Ron finds a bank error when he compares canceled checks with check stubs. The bank had deducted check no. 1896 from Kim's account as $346. The actual amount of the check was $364. The bank should be notified at once so that its records can be corrected. For the correct cash balance to be derived on the bank reconciliation, the $18 error ($364 − $346) must be deducted from the balance reported by the bank.

4. Ron also discovers an error in the checkbook. In comparing the canceled checks with the check stubs, Ron notices that check no. 1901, written for $120, was deducted from the checkbook as $210. Thus the checkbook balance is too low by $90 ($210 − $120). This error must be corrected by adding $90 to the Nov. 30 checkbook balance.

5. A **not sufficient funds (NSF) check** (a check stamped "NSF") was returned with the bank statement. J. Hays, a customer, had given Kim's the check to pay for merchandise. Kim thought that Hays's check was cash at the time it was received. The bank clearing process revealed that it was in fact nothing more than a written promise to pay cash (an IOU). Hays's bank account did not have enough money to "cash his check" and transfer funds to Kim's account. Thus, Kim's had less cash than the checkbook balance represents. Hays's check for $182.60 must be deducted from the balance shown in Kim's checkbook to reflect the correct cash balance. Until Kim's collects from Hays, the check represents not cash but a receivable.

6. The November bank statement shows a $25.00 service charge. Bank service charges are fees levied by the bank for printing and processing the company's checks, returning NSF checks, and providing other banking services. These service charges have not been deducted from Kim's checkbook because the amount was unknown until the bank statement was received. This amount must be deducted from the checkbook balance on the reconciliation.

**Exhibit 2** Bank Reconciliation

KIM'S APPLIANCES
Bank Reconciliation
November 30, 1998

| | | | | |
|---|---|---|---|---|
| Balance per bank statement,<br>    Nov. 30, 1998 . . . . . . . . . . . . . . . . . . . . . . | | $34,173.80 | Balance per checkbook, Nov. 30, 1998 . . . . . | $30,388.60 |
| Add: (1)  Deposits in transit on | | | Add: (4)  Check no. 1901 for $120 | |
| | Nov. 30, 1998 . . . . . . . . . . . . . . . . | 1,970.00 |             deducted from checkbook | |
| | Total . . . . . . . . . . . . . . . . . . . . . . . . . | $36,143.80 |             as $210 . . . . . . . . . . . . . . . . . . . . . . | 90.00 |
| Deduct: | | | Total . . . . . . . . . . . . . . . . . . . . . . . . . . . . . | $30,478.60 |
| (2)  Checks outstanding on | | | Deduct: | |
| | Nov. 30, 1998    . . . . . . . . . .$5,854.80 | | (5) NSF check of J. Hays . . . . . $182.60 | |
| (3)  Check no. 1896 for | | | (6) Bank service fees. . . . . . . . .    25.00 | (207.60) |
| |     $364 deducted from | | | |
| |     account as $346. . . . . . . .    18.00 | (5,872.80) | | |
| Correct ending balance, Nov. 30, 1998. . . . . | | $30,271.00 | Correct ending balance, Nov. 30, 1998. . . . . | $30,271.00 |

*When the reconciliation is complete,*
*these amounts should be the same.*

Since no other errors or differences can be detected, the Nov. 30 balances and adjustments are totaled, each total producing a correct ending cash balance of $30,271. This amount should appear as Cash in Bank on Kim's balance sheet on Nov. 30, 1998, despite the fact that it appears neither in Kim's checkbook nor on the Nov. 30 bank statement. Exhibit 2 shows how the completed reconciliation would appear; the numbers in parentheses correspond to the items listed above.

### Recording Unrecorded Transactions and Correcting Errors

As you have just seen, the reconciliation process often uncovers transactions that by their nature haven't been recorded in the checkbook records, as well as errors in some of the transactions that have been recorded. All unrecorded transactions and errors detected—whether uncovered in the bank balance reconciliation or the firm's checkbook balance reconciliation—must be accounted for and recorded in the bank's records or in the firm's accounting records. The firm is responsible for correcting errors and recording corrections and unrecorded transactions in its records; the bank is responsible for doing the same in its records.

The company must analyze each adjustment in the checkbook section of the reconciliation and determine which accounts are in error. There are few general rules for deciding how unrecorded transactions and errors should be recorded in the accounting records; each adjustment must be considered independently. Let's analyze the adjustments, which are typical, shown for Kim's Appliances in the preceding illustration and shown as items 4, 5, and 6 in the list above. (The bank is responsible for correcting items 1, 2, and 3.)

*Correcting an Error in Recording a Check* (Item 4)

Adjustment

| | |
|---|---|
| Check no. 1901 in the amount of $120 erroneously deducted from the<br>checkbook as $210. . . . . . . . . . . . . . . . . . . . . . . . . . . . . . . . . . . . . . . . . | $90 |

**Analysis**   When this transaction was originally recorded in a journal, some account was debited for $210 and Cash was credited for $210. We must discover which account was debited so that we can correct it. Inspection of the book of original entry (the cash disbursements journal or the general journal) will reveal which account was debited for a larger amount than it should have been. Assume that the account was Advertising Expense. We have determined by inspecting the original journal entry, then, that too much advertising expense was recorded and too much was deducted from Cash.

Entry

| | | |
|---|---|---|
| Cash . . . . . . . . . . . . . . . . . . . . . . . . . . . . . . . . . . . . . . . . . . . . . . . . . . . | 90 | |
|     Advertising Expense . . . . . . . . . . . . . . . . . . . . . . . . . . . . . . . . | | 90 |
| To correct an error in recording check no. 1901 | | |
| ($210 − $120 = $90). | | |

### *Recording an NSF Check* (Item 5)

Adjustment

| | |
|---|---|
| NSF check of J. Hays . . . . . . . . . . . . . . . . . . . . . . . . . . . . . . . . . . . . . . . . . . | $182.60 |

**Analysis**   When the check was received from Hays, Kim's debited Cash and credited another account, let's say Sales. The book of original entry (the cash receipts journal or the general journal) will show the credit to the Sales account. The only account in error in the original entry is Cash, since a sale was made and recorded in the correct amount. The problem is that cash was not received from the customer; the check represents not cash but an IOU. Proper recording of this transaction will involve debiting Accounts Receivable to record the IOU from the customer and crediting Cash to reduce it by the amount of Hays's check, which turned out not to represent cash after all.

Entry

| | | |
|---|---|---|
| Accounts Receivable: J. Hays . . . . . . . . . . . . . . . . . . . . . . . . . . . | 182.60 | |
|     Cash. . . . . . . . . . . . . . . . . . . . . . . . . . . . . . . . . . . . . . . . . . . . . . | | 182.60 |
| To record an NSF check received with the November bank statement. | | |

### *Recording Bank Service Fees* (Item 6)

Adjustment

| | |
|---|---|
| Bank service fees . . . . . . . . . . . . . . . . . . . . . . . . . . . . . . . . . . . . . . . . . . . | $25.00 |

**Analysis**   Since the amount of bank service charges may vary with the number of checks processed and the number and types of other services a firm uses, Kim's first learned the amount of the bank service charges for November by seeing it on the bank statement. Kim's must record the fees by debiting an expense account and reducing Cash.

Entry

| | | |
|---|---|---|
| Bank Service Charge Expense . . . . . . . . . . . . . . . . . . . . . . . . . . . . | 25.00 | |
|     Cash. . . . . . . . . . . . . . . . . . . . . . . . . . . . . . . . . . . . . . . . . . . . . . | | 25.00 |
| To record November bank service charge. | | |

Note that when a correction or unrecorded transaction requires that an amount be *added* to the checkbook balance on the reconciliation, there is a corresponding entry that includes a *debit (increase) to Cash* in the same amount. Similarly, for adjustments requiring a *deduction* from the checkbook balance on the reconciliation, there is a corresponding journal entry requiring a *credit (decrease) to Cash.*

**ASK YOURSELF** ▶

1. **What is the purpose of a bank reconciliation?**
2. **What are deposits in transit?**
3. **Why are outstanding checks subtracted from the bank balance in preparing a bank reconciliation?**
4. **Are NSF checks considered cash? If not, what are they?**
5. **Why is it usually necessary to make journal entries as a result of preparing a bank reconciliation?**

## PETTY CASH

Most cash payments made by businesses are in the form of checks. The fact that each check must be individually prepared and signed gives a company good control over the outflow of cash. The canceled checks provide proof that payment was made.

Learning Objective **5**

Explain how a petty cash fund works

In spite of these advantages, payment by check is sometimes impractical. In these instances, payment is made in the form of currency and coin. A small amount of currency and coin set aside for this purpose is called a **petty cash fund.** Examples of proper uses of petty cash include payment of taxi fare for an employee to deliver urgently needed business documents across town, payment for delivery charges on a machine part that was shipped collect, and purchase of a small number of postage stamps. Petty cash should not be used for loans to employees or to pay for large quantities of merchandise purchased from established suppliers.

### Setting up a Petty Cash Fund

The petty cash fund is established by transferring a small amount of cash from the checking account, say, $50, in the form of currency, to a person who is designated to be responsible for it—the *petty cashier.* This person may be a receptionist, a secretary, a bookkeeper, or any responsible and reliable employee in a position to disburse it effectively. The petty cash fund is set up by a check made payable to Petty Cash. The petty cashier cashes this check and keeps the money in a container that he or she is responsible for safeguarding.

The accounting entry to establish the petty cash fund is as follows:

Learning Objective **6**

Prepare entries to establish and replenish a petty cash fund

| | | |
|---|---|---|
| Petty Cash. . . . . . . . . . . . . . . . . . . . . . . . . . . . . . . . . . . . . . . . . . . | 50 | |
|     Cash. . . . . . . . . . . . . . . . . . . . . . . . . . . . . . . . . . . . . . . . . . . . . | | 50 |
| To establish a petty cash fund. | | |

This entry merely transfers cash from a cash-in-bank (checking) account to a cash-on-hand account. The total cash of the business at this point remains unchanged.

Payments from the petty cash fund can be made only with authorization in writing. This written authorization to disburse petty cash is called a **petty cash voucher,** and looks something like the one shown in Exhibit 3 on the next page.

**Exhibit 3** Petty Cash Voucher

## RIVERBEND CORP.
### Petty Cash Disbursement Voucher

Date _December 28, 1998_      Voucher No. _____104_____

Amount of Payment $ _14.35_

Reason for Payment _To pay for office machine part received_

_on C.O.D. shipment_

Signature of Person Receiving Payment _J.P. Hall_

Approved by _Andrea Johnson_

Usually the petty cashier fills out the voucher and has the person requesting the cash sign it. The petty cashier then files the voucher in the petty cash container and disburses money from the container in the amount of the voucher. The total of the money and the amounts represented by the vouchers must at all times equal the original total of the petty cash fund. That is, the petty cashier must have either the money or approved vouchers showing what the money was used for.

### Replenishing the Petty Cash Fund

Whenever the money in the petty cash fund runs low, the petty cashier presents the vouchers to the manager who has the authority to replenish it.

Assume that the following vouchers are presented for reimbursement:

| Petty Cash Voucher No. | Reason for Disbursement | Amount |
|---|---|---|
| 101 | Paid messenger to deliver package | $ 5.25 |
| 102 | Purchased postage stamps | 1.50 |
| 103 | Purchased office supplies | 6.40 |
| 104 | Paid for office machine part that was shipped COD | 14.35 |
| 105 | Purchased office supplies | 4.40 |
| | Total | $31.90 |

A check would be made out to Petty Cash for $31.90 and the various expenses represented by each of the vouchers would be recorded. The following entry would be made:

| | | |
|---|---|---|
| Delivery Expense . . . . . . . . . . . . . . . . . . . . . . . . . . . . . . . . . . . . | 5.25 | |
| Office Supplies Expense . . . . . . . . . . . . . . . . . . . . . . . . . . . . . | 10.80 | |
| Postage Expense . . . . . . . . . . . . . . . . . . . . . . . . . . . . . . . . . . . | 1.50 | |
| Repairs Expense. . . . . . . . . . . . . . . . . . . . . . . . . . . . . . . . . . . . | 14.35 | |
|    Cash. . . . . . . . . . . . . . . . . . . . . . . . . . . . . . . . . . . . . . . . . . . | | 31.90 |
| To replenish petty cash fund and record expenses. | | |

The replenishment entry makes no debit to Petty Cash, since we are not increasing the petty cash fund. The petty cash fund asset shows a total of $50 before and after the reimbursement. Before reimbursement the asset Petty Cash was, of course, overstated by $31.90 because some of the money had been spent. The replenishment entry formally records the disbursements of money for expenses that have already taken place. The petty cashier now has $50 in money in the cash box and no paid vouchers. The process of petty cash outlays and fund reimbursement can begin again.

The asset Petty Cash is credited only when the fund is decreased or terminated. It is debited only when the fund is originally established or increased. Whenever the fund is replenished, expense accounts are debited. The fund is also replenished at the end of the accounting cycle, to record all previously unrecorded expenses in accordance with the matching principle.

Management should review the petty cash fund activity periodically. If the fund is being replenished too often, it may mean that the amount of the fund is too small, or possibly that fraudulent vouchers are being submitted by the petty cashier. But if long periods pass between reimbursements, the amount of the fund may be too large and management should consider reducing the size of the fund.

### Cash Short and Over

In spite of safeguards designed to control the inflows and outflows of money, small mistakes do occur. For example, assume that in the previous example the petty cash vouchers total $31.90 and the currency and coins in the petty cash box total $16.70. The petty cash fund, which should total $50, now totals only $48.60 ($31.90 + $16.70). The $1.40 shortage in the petty cash fund was due to a petty cashier mistake —probably paying out more than a petty cash voucher authorized.

The entry to replenish the petty cash fund must also record the cash shortage:

| | | |
|---|---|---|
| Delivery Expense | 5.25 | |
| Office Supplies Expense | 10.80 | |
| Postage Expense | 1.50 | |
| Repairs Expense | 14.35 | |
| Cash Short and Over | 1.40 | |
|     Cash | | 33.30 |
| To replenish a petty cash fund, record expenses and a $1.40 cash shortage. | | |

The Cash Short and Over account is debited for $1.40 to record the shortage. If there had been an overage, the same account would be credited for the amount of the overage. If Cash Short and Over has a debit balance at the end of the accounting period, it is reported as a miscellaneous expense on the income statement. A credit balance in the account would be reported as miscellaneous income.

The Cash Short and Over account is also used when the money in a cash register drawer (say, $530) does not total to the same amount that is recorded on the cash register tape (say, $528). In this case the entry to record the cash sales must also record the cash shortage or overage:

| | | |
|---|---|---|
| Cash | 530 | |
|     Sales | | 528 |
|     Cash Short and Over | | 2 |
| To record cash sales for the day and a cash overage of $2. | | |

Management should monitor the amount and frequency of cash shortages and overages from a particular petty cash fund or cash register. Frequent shortages and overages indicate that employees are being careless. Repeated shortages may mean that employees are stealing.

**ASK YOURSELF ▶**

1. **Why do companies use petty cash funds?**
2. **What is the purpose of a petty cash voucher?**
3. **When is the Cash Short and Over account used?**

## CASH DISCOUNTS

The purpose of cash discounts is to encourage buyers to pay for their purchases quickly. Discounts are expressed by abbreviations such as *2/10, n/30.* This means that the buyer may deduct 2% from the invoice price if payment is made within 10 days of the invoice date; otherwise the full invoice price is due within 30 days. A buyer who does not take the cash discount is, in effect, borrowing money from the seller for the last 20 days at 2%. This 2% for 20 days translates into an annual interest rate of 36%. (There are 18 twenty-day periods in 1 year; 2% × 18 periods = 36%.) We want to avoid paying 36%; if we needed a loan, we could borrow from a bank at a much lower rate. Therefore, our internal control system should produce accounting information promptly, to ensure that all invoices are paid within the discount period.

Say that Lumin Lamps, Inc., purchased lighting fixtures at an invoice price of $456 and terms of 2/10, n/30. If Lumin pays within 10 days, a discount of $456 × 2% = $9.12 may be deducted from the amount sent to the supplier. Lumin will owe $456 − $9.12 = $446.88. Let's look at two ways of recording this purchase and see which is better at ensuring payment of invoices within the discount period.

### The Gross Method

The method of recording purchases on credit at the gross invoice price is the **gross method.** When cash discounts are taken, Purchases Discounts is credited for the amount of the discount. If Lumin elects to use this method, the following entry will be made on the date of purchase:

| | | |
|---|---|---|
| Purchases . . . . . . . . . . . . . . . . . . . . . . . . . . . . . . . . . . . . . . . . . . . . . | 456.00 | |
|     Accounts Payable . . . . . . . . . . . . . . . . . . . . . . . . . . . . . . . . . . | | 456.00 |
| To record the purchase of merchandise. | | |

If Lumin pays within 10 days, it receives the $9.12 discount and records the payment like this:

| | | |
|---|---|---|
| Accounts Payable . . . . . . . . . . . . . . . . . . . . . . . . . . . . . . . . . . . . . . | 456.00 | |
|     Purchases Discounts . . . . . . . . . . . . . . . . . . . . . . . . . . . . . . . | | 9.12 |
|     Cash . . . . . . . . . . . . . . . . . . . . . . . . . . . . . . . . . . . . . . . . . . . . . | | 446.88 |
| To record the purchase of merchandise. | | |

If Lumin fails to pay within the 10-day period, no discount is recorded. Accounts Payable is debited and Cash credited for the full $456.

The Purchases Discounts account is deducted from Purchases when we prepare the cost of goods sold section of the income statement.

The gross method tells Lumin's management the amount of discounts that have been taken but not the amount of discounts that were lost due to failure to pay invoices on time. Lumin wants a system that assumes that all discounts will be taken—one that will tell management when a discount is *not* taken. The net method helps accomplish this objective.

*Learning Objective 7*

Describe the advantage of the net method of recording purchases

### The Net Method

*Learning Objective 8*

Prepare entries to record purchases using the net method

If Lumin followed the **net method** rather than the gross method, the purchase would be recorded at the invoice price less cash discounts—$446.88. The anticipated cash discount is deducted; remember, Lumin is planning to take all cash discounts.

Here are the purchase and payment entries assuming that Lumin takes advantage of the cash discount:

On the date of purchase:

| | |
|---|---|
| Purchases.......................................... | 446.88 |
|     Accounts Payable..................................... | 446.88 |
| To record purchase of merchandise at the net amount. | |

On the date of payment 9 days later:

| | |
|---|---|
| Accounts Payable...................................... | 446.88 |
|     Cash.......................................... | 446.88 |
| To record payment within the discount period. | |

If Lumin fails to pay within the 10-day discount period, the full $456 must be paid. Cash is credited for the amount of the payment, $456, and the account payable is eliminated with a debit equal to the amount recorded at the time of the purchase, $446.88. This leaves the $9.12 difference ($456 − $446.88), which is recorded in a new account called Purchases Discounts Lost. Here is Lumin's entry if payment is *not* made within the discount period:

| | |
|---|---|
| Accounts Payable...................................... | 446.88 |
| Purchases Discounts Lost ............................... | 9.12 |
|     Cash.......................................... | 456.00 |
| To record payment of account after the discount period has expired. | |

This new account, Purchases Discounts Lost, is a red flag to management, indicating a failure in the company's operating procedure for taking all discounts allowed. Purchases discounts lost is not used in the calculation of cost of goods sold. Since it is really an interest charge for postponing payment for the merchandise, purchases discounts lost is shown on the income statement as a nonoperating expense, just as interest expense would be.

The partial income statements in Exhibit 4 illustrate the location of purchases

**Exhibit 4** Partial Income Statements Showing Disclosure of Purchases Discounts and Purchases Discounts Lost Accounts

**GROSS PRICE METHOD COMPANY**
**Partial Income Statement**

| | | |
|---|---:|---:|
| Sales ........................................ | | $10,000 |
| Cost of Goods Sold: | | |
|   Merchandise Inventory (beginning) ...... | $ 4,000 | |
|   Add: Purchases ............. | $3,200 | |
|   Deduct: **Purchases Discounts** .. | (64) | |
|   Net Purchases....................... | 3,136 | |
|   Goods Available for Sale ............... | $7,136 | |
|   Less: Merchandise Inventory (ending)..... | (2,500) | |
|     Cost of Goods Sold...................... | | (4,636) |
|     Gross Profit on Sales...................... | | $ 5,364 |
| Operating Expenses: | | |
|   Selling Expenses ..................... | $  850 | |
|   General and Administrative Expenses..... | 614 | |
|     Total Operating Expenses................... | | (1,464) |
| Income from Primary Operations................... | | $ 3,900 |
| Other Income and Expenses: | | |
|   Interest Expense............................ | | (1,380) |
| Net Income ...................................... | | $ 2,520 |

**NET PRICE METHOD COMPANY**
**Partial Income Statement**

| | | |
|---|---:|---:|
| Sales ........................................ | | $26,000 |
| Cost of Goods Sold: | | |
|   Merchandise Inventory (beginning) ...... | $ 9,000 | |
|   Add: Purchases...................... | 6,800 | |
|   Goods Available for Sale .............. | $15,800 | |
|   Less: Merchandise Inventory (ending).... | (8,300) | |
|     Cost of Goods Sold ........................ | | (7,500) |
| Gross Profit on Sales ........................... | | $18,500 |
| Operating Expenses: | | |
|   Selling Expenses .................... | $ 2,200 | |
|   General and Administrative Expenses.... | 1,400 | |
|     Total Operating Expenses.................... | | (3,600) |
| Income from Primary Operations................... | | $14,900 |
| Other Income and Expenses: | | |
|   Interest Expense..................... | $ 1,380 | |
|   **Purchases Discounts Lost** .......... | 510 | |
|     Total Other Expenses ..................... | | (1,890) |
| Net Income ...................................... | | $13,010 |

discounts and purchases discounts lost. These statements are for two different companies—a single company will use either the gross or the net method but not both.

ASK YOURSELF ▶

1. **Which method of accounting for cash discounts tells management the amount of discounts taken during a period?**
2. **How is the Purchases Discounts Lost account shown on the income statement?**

## THE VOUCHER SYSTEM

Learning
Objective **9**

Explain what a voucher system is

A petty cash fund helps a business control disbursements that cannot be made by check. The *voucher system,* in contrast, is designed to control the majority of the company's expenditures—those that are in the form of checks. The **voucher system** is used by businesses to ensure that:

1. All expenditures are authorized.
2. The goods or services are received.
3. Only the goods and services received are paid for.
4. Payment takes place in time to take advantage of cash discounts.

The **voucher** is a document that provides the authorization to pay, contains written evidence that each of four verifications have been performed, and specifies the accounts to be debited and credited.

The main purpose of the voucher system is to control the outflow of cash by ensuring that only valid bills are paid, that they are correct in amount, and that they are paid in a timely manner. In accomplishing this purpose, the company also must control the process of ordering and receiving goods and services. In a small business the owner is usually involved directly in each activity relating to ordering, receiving, and paying for goods and services. Thus, in safeguarding his or her interests, the owner effects an informal system of internal control.

However, owners of large businesses cannot be closely involved in all the activities of the business. The activities are organized into many separate functions, and different groups of employees are delegated the authority to perform each function. For example, one group of employees orders goods and services, another group receives and inspects them, a third group decides the proper amount and timing of payment, and still another group actually writes and mails the checks. In large firms it is necessary to have a formal system of internal control to assure that the activity of incurring obligations (acquiring goods and services) is separated from the activity of paying for them. Of course, the purpose of separating these activities is to have different individuals performing them. The voucher system provides a written form of communication (what to pay, how much, when, etc.) linking the various activities of the employees, to allow management to control and monitor what goes on.

To understand more about how the voucher system works, we will begin at the earliest point in the process of acquiring goods or services. As we review this process, we will describe the written communication that documents each step and ultimately concludes with the preparation of a voucher and a check.

### Steps in Documenting the Acquisition of Goods and Services

A large firm is typically organized into different departments, each performing a particular function. To perform their functions, the departments need goods and services that must be bought from other firms. These goods and services may be used up in operating the business—for instance, computer paper and paper bags—or may be sold to customers—typically, from merchandise inventory. Rather than give each

**Figure 1** The Voucher System

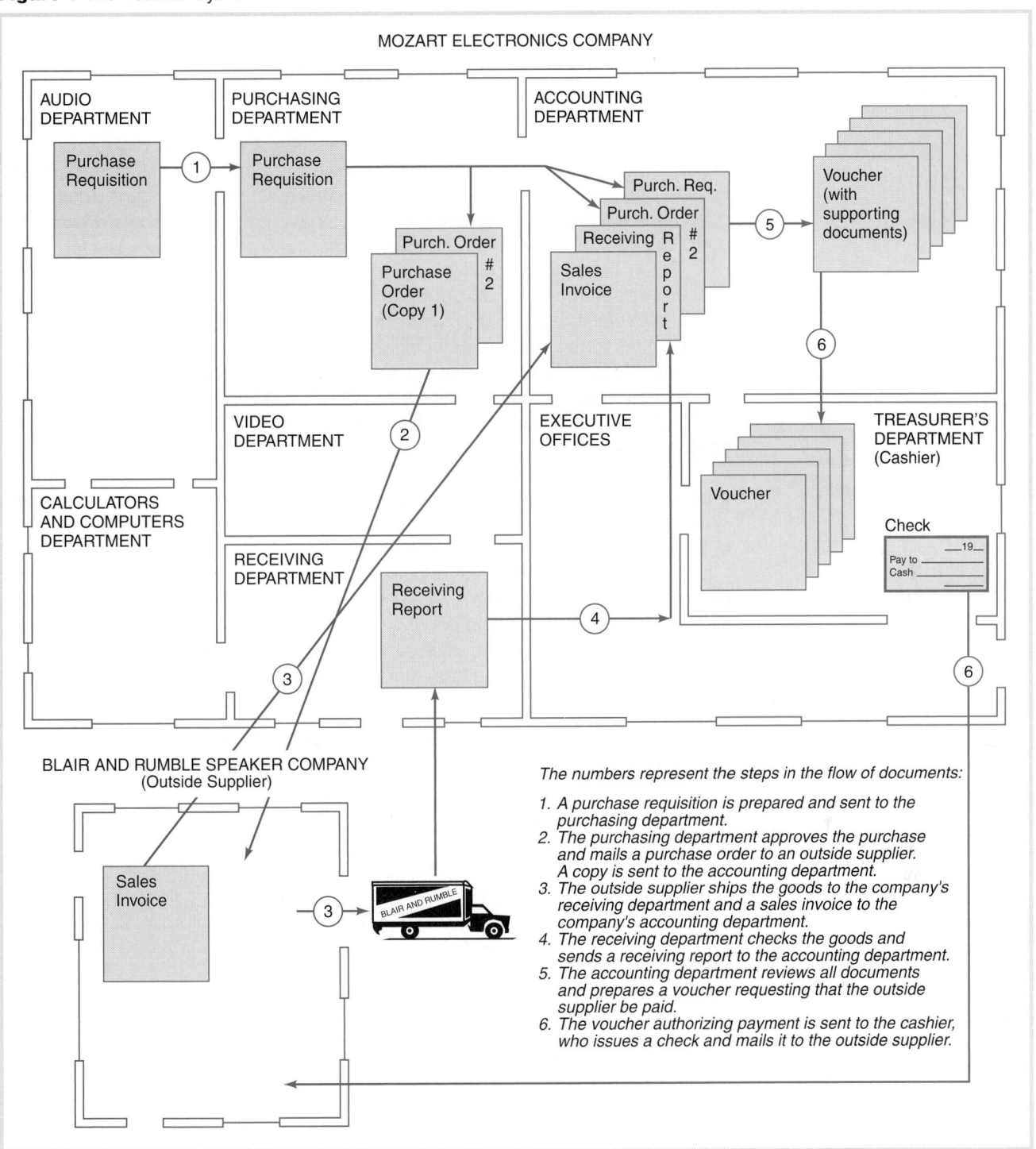

MOZART ELECTRONICS COMPANY

The numbers represent the steps in the flow of documents:

1. A purchase requisition is prepared and sent to the purchasing department.
2. The purchasing department approves the purchase and mails a purchase order to an outside supplier. A copy is sent to the accounting department.
3. The outside supplier ships the goods to the company's receiving department and a sales invoice to the company's accounting department.
4. The receiving department checks the goods and sends a receiving report to the accounting department.
5. The accounting department reviews all documents and prepares a voucher requesting that the outside supplier be paid.
6. The voucher authorizing payment is sent to the cashier, who issues a check and mails it to the outside supplier.

department the authority to buy its goods and services, a large firm will often give that authority to a single person or department—the *purchasing agent* or *purchasing department*—which does the buying for all departments. A central purchasing department not only offers a means of internal control, it also offers the opportunity to combine acquisitions of identical goods required by different departments, and thus obtains discounts that might not be available for acquisitions in smaller quantities.

Let's follow a purchase of merchandise through a typical voucher system from beginning to end. The steps in this system are diagrammed in Figure 1, which provides a good overview of the process discussed below.

# MOZART ELECTRONICS COMPANY

The audio department of Mozart Electronics Company needs more stereo speakers to sell. The manager of this department has been authorized to spend a certain amount on merchandise during the year. Now the need to spend some of these budgeted funds on speakers must be communicated to the central purchasing department in writing, using a standard form called a **purchase requisition.** This document is used only to communicate needs to the central purchasing department; it never goes outside the firm. Its internal control function is to limit the purchase of goods and services to those managers who have authority to acquire them. The audio department's requisition for speakers is shown in Exhibit 5.

When the purchasing department receives the purchase requisition, it will check to be sure that the audio department hasn't already spent its total authorization for the year. The purchasing department will then approve the request and order the speakers from a manufacturer or wholesaler by sending it a purchase order. A **purchase order** is a written request for an outside **vendor,** or supplier, to provide goods or services. This document implies a promise to pay for the goods or services under conditions agreed upon by the buyer and seller. The purchase order for the speakers is shown in Exhibit 6.

Blair and Rumble Speaker Co. will fill the order and ship the speakers to Mozart Electronics Company. At the same time they will mail Mozart a bill, called a *sales invoice,* for the goods shipped. The sales invoice gives the quantity and description of the goods shipped and terms of payment (see Exhibit 7).

When the speakers reach Mozart Electronics, someone must inspect them to be sure that the merchandise received was in fact ordered, that the correct quantity was received, and that it is in good condition. Large businesses have a *receiving department* to perform these internal control tasks. (The receiving department is separate from the purchasing department so that no one in purchasing can place an

---

**Exhibit 5** Purchase Requisition Sent by the Requesting Department to the Purchasing Department

---

PURCHASE REQUISITION

### MOZART ELECTRONICS COMPANY

From ———————————— Audio    Date ———— May 15, 1998 ————

Suggested Vendor ——— Blair and Rumble Speaker Company ————

St. Louis, MO ————

**Purchase the Following:**

| Quantity | Number | Description |
|----------|--------|-------------|
| 100 | SE-21406 | stereo speakers |

Reason for Request ——— Resupply ————

inventory of speakers.

*To be completed by purchasing department:*

Date Ordered ——— 5-18-98 ————

Authorized by ——— J.L. Johnson ————    Purchase Order No. ——— G-134 ————

**Exhibit 6** Purchase Order Prepared by the Purchasing Department

PURCHASE ORDER

No. _____ *G-134* _____

MOZART ELECTRONICS COMPANY
1691 Lanier Drive
Columbus, WV 22305

To ___ Blair and Rumble Speaker Co. ___   Date ___ May 18, 1998 ___

___ 2530 Jefferson Ave ___

___ St. Louis, MO 44620 ___

**Shipping Instructions** ___ Ship to Mozart Electronics Company at above address ___

___ FOB destination ___

Ship via ___ Truck ___   **Date Needed** ___ 6/20/98 ___

**Terms Requested** ___ 2/10, n/30 ___

**Please Accept Our Order for the Following:**

| Quantity | ✓ | Number | Description | Price Each | Amount |
|---|---|---|---|---|---|
| 100 | | SE-21406 | stereo speakers | $240 | $24,000 |

*Purchase order number must appear on all invoices.*

Ordered by ___ *R. J. Wood* ___

---

**Exhibit 7** A Sales Invoice Received from an Outside Supplier

SALES INVOICE

**BLAIR AND RUMBLE SPEAKER COMPANY**
2530 Jefferson Ave
St. Louis, MO 44620

No. ___ B10-1173 ___

Date ___ June 15, 1998 ___

Your Order No. ___ G-134 ___

Sold to ___ Mozart Electronics Company ___

___ 1691 Lanier Drive ___

___ Columbus, WV 22305 ___

Shipping Instructions ___
Ship to same

| Quantity | Description | Price Each | Amount |
|---|---|---|---|
| 100 | SE-21406 stereo speakers | $240 | $24,000 |

Shipped via ___   Date Shipped ___ 6/15/98 ___   Terms ___ 2/10, n/30 ___
___ Ajax Express ___   FOB ___ delivered ___

**Exhibit 8** A Receiving Report Prepared by the Receiving Department

RECEIVING REPORT

## MOZART ELECTRONICS COMPANY

Date _____June 18, 1998_____

Purchase Order No. _____G-134_____

Vendor _____Blair and Rumble Speaker Co._____

Carrier _____Ajax Express_____

**The Following Was Received:**

| Quantity | Description | Condition |
|----------|-------------|-----------|
| 100 | SE-21406 Speakers | Good |

**Received and Checked by** _____Herman Carlisle_____

unauthorized order and steal the goods as soon as they arrive.) The receiving department prepares an internal document called a **receiving report** to verify that these tasks have been accomplished. Mozart Electronics' receiving report is shown in Exhibit 8.

Smaller firms usually combine many of the functions that large businesses keep separate. Thus, the department that needs the goods might also place the order and might even receive and inspect the goods. Internal control in smaller businesses is weakened by this lack of separation, although the disadvantage is overcome to some degree by the owner's active involvement in all phases of the operation.

Copies of all four of the documents we have described—the purchase requisition, the purchase order, the sales invoice, and the receiving report—are sent to the *accounting department,* which is responsible for the following functions:

1. Comparing the purchase requisition and purchase order with the sales invoice to verify the quantities, prices, and terms of the goods or services ordered
2. Comparing the sales invoice with the receiving report to verify that the goods or services have been received
3. Verifying that an authorized person has signed the purchase requisition, the purchase order, and the receiving report
4. Verifying the arithmetic accuracy of the sales invoice to ensure that the company is not paying too much

We have now reached the point at which the voucher—the written authorization for payment—is used. A voucher is usually a preprinted standard form on which the details characterizing a liability are inserted. The accounting department will prepare a voucher to verify that it has performed the comparisons and verifications described above. The accounting department prepares a voucher for each check that is to be written, no matter what the check is to pay for: purchases of goods, employee salaries, loan repayment, advertising, or any other business acquisitions.

A typical voucher (front and back) is shown in Exhibit 9. The front of the voucher simply repeats the information from the sales invoice. This information is

**Exhibit 9** A Typical Voucher
(a) Front

Voucher No. 317

**MOZART ELECTRONICS COMPANY**
1691 Lanier Drive
Columbus, WV 22305

Payee Blair and Rumble Speaker Co.          Date          June 20, 1998

2530 Jefferson Ave.

St. Louis, MO 44620

*Attach supporting documents*

| Invoice Date | Terms | Details | Amount |
|---|---|---|---|
| June 15, 1998 | 2/10, n/30 | Invoice no. B10-1173 | |
| | | FOB Columbus | $24,000 |
| | | Less: Cash discount | 480 |
| | | Net amount due | $23,520 |

Approved for Payment _____ *R. G. Adams* _____

(Accounting Department)

(b) Back

| Invoice Approval | | | Accounting Distribution | |
|---|---|---|---|---|
| | **Date** | **By** | **Debit** | **Amount** |
| Credit terms | 6/20 | CR | Purchases | $24,000 |
| Amount | 6/20 | CR | Freight-In | |
| Arithmetic | 6/20 | CR | Office Supplies | |
| Quantities | 6/20 | CR | Office Salaries | |
| Authorizations | 6/20 | CR | Advertising Expense | |

| | **Credit** | **Amount** |
|---|---|---|
| | Vouchers Payable | $24,000 |

*Payment:*

Check No. _____ 4304 _____

Check Date _____ June 24, 1998 _____

Check Amount _____ $23,520 _____      Distribution Approved _____ *J.L. Battle* _____

(Accounting Department)

used in preparing and mailing the check to pay the liability. The back of the voucher shows that the comparisons and verifications have been completed. As each task of verification is accomplished, the clerk responsible for it indicates this with his or her initials. (See the upper left corner of the voucher back.) Also on the back of the voucher is a section called "Accounting Distribution." This section contains (1) the name of the account or accounts debited; (2) the amount credited to **Vouchers Payable,** the liability account that is used for all obligations in the voucher system;

and (3) the signature of the accounting department person responsible for deciding which accounts should be debited. The information in the accounting distribution section is recorded as an entry in a journal called a *voucher register,* which is discussed below.

The accounting department representative "vouches for"—accepts responsibility for the truthfulness and accuracy of—the information on the voucher and attests that the voucher represents a liability properly incurred. The signature at the lower right-hand corner of the back of the voucher indicates that all is well with the information on the voucher and that approval is given to issue a check in payment. The purchase requisition, purchase order, sales invoice, and receiving report are stapled to the voucher. Now the authorization of payment (the voucher) and all of the supporting documents are together in one neat package. This package is sent to the cashier, who issues a check to pay the liability.

When payment is made, the check number, date, and amount are entered on the voucher in the spaces provided. This information is needed to resolve any questions that might arise concerning settlement of the liability.

## The Voucher Register

Learning Objective **10**

Prepare entries used in the operation of a voucher system

In a voucher system a voucher is prepared for each expenditure, so each voucher represents a specific liability. Payment of the liabilities is made only by check and only after the supporting documents indicating authorizations are attached. Information from the voucher is recorded in the **voucher register,** a journal of original entry that combines features of the purchases journal and the cash payments journal. A typical voucher register is shown in Exhibit 10.

The voucher register is similar to the purchases journal in that it records purchases made on account. For example, the purchase of stereo speakers from Blair

**Exhibit 10** The Voucher Register

### MOZART ELECTRONIC COMPANY
### Voucher Register

PAGE 43

| Date | Voucher Number | Payee | Payment Date | Check Number | Vou. Payable Credit | Purchases Debit | Freight-In Debit | Salary Expense Debit | Other Accounts Debited Title | Post. Ref. | Amount |
|------|---------|-------|---------|--------|------|------|------|------|------|------|------|
| 1998 | | | | | | | | | | | |
| June 5 | 315 | ABC Warehouse | 6/7 | 4297 | 600 | 600 | | | | | |
| 13 | 316 | Payroll | 6/15 | 4298 | 5,200 | | | 5,200 | | | |
| 20 | 317 | Blair and Rumble Co. | 6/24 | 4304 | 24,000 | 24,000 | | | | | |
| 21 | 318 | Jones Transport | 6/25 | 4307 | 50 | | 50 | | | | |
| 30 | 335 | Lutz Bank | 6/30 | 4346 | 100 | | | | Interest Expense | 710 | 100 |
| 30 | 336 | Brown Co. | | | 3,400 | 3,400 | | | | | |
| 30 | 337 | Payroll | 6/30 | 4347 | 4,800 | | | 4,800 | | | |
| 30 | 338 | Don's Furniture | | | 3,850 | | | | Office Furniture | 250 | 3,850 |
| | | | | | 53,020 | 33,500 | 1,220 | 10,000 | | | 8,300 |
| | | | | | (220) | (510) | (604) | (610) | | | (—) |

# Miami Firm Accused of Sending Fake Bills

Officials say a company sent out more than 4,000 bills for advertising in non-existent telephone yellow pages, complete with "let your fingers do the walking" picture on the invoice —except one finger was missing.

U.S. Attorney Jonathan Goodman on Friday persuaded a federal judge to seal a post office box used by the business, Yellow Pages Inc. More than 100 companies had paid the bills, Goodman said, even though no ads were published.

"You may well ask, 'Why did they pay the bills?'" Goodman said. "That's a good question."

Goodman told U.S. District Judge William Hoeveler that Paul Goldberg, 24, of Lauderdale Lakes, ran the phony-invoice scheme by himself. He claimed that Goldberg sent 4,075 bills for yellow pages advertising to companies across the nation.

No charges have been filed against Goldberg. Hoeveler ordered the sealing of a post office box so that no checks could be collected from it.

*Source: Tampa Tribune-Times,* Monday, Apr. 8, 1985, p. 5-B. Copyright © 1985 The Tampa Tribune.

---

Companies with an effective voucher system would not have paid these fake bills. Someone would have had to request the purchase of the yellow pages advertisement through a purchase requisition. A valid purchase order would have had to be issued. And someone would have been responsible for checking to be sure the proper advertisement appeared before payment was made. None of these verifications would have been possible since the yellow pages didn't exist.

and Rumble Co. that we have been discussing is the third item on the Mozart voucher register in Exhibit 10. The voucher register is similar to the cash payments journal in that it has many columns—one for each particular expenditure that occurs frequently and one to handle all other types of expenditures. Mozart Electronics has special columns for Purchases, Freight-In, and Salary Expense.

The information from every voucher is entered in the voucher register. The vouchers are entered in numerical order as illustrated in column 2 of the register shown in Exhibit 10. The date of the voucher, the voucher number, the payee, the Vouchers Payable credit, and the account(s) to be debited are all entered when the voucher is recorded in the register. When the voucher is paid, the payment date (fourth column) and number of the check (fifth column) issued in payment of the voucher are entered. Notice in the exhibit that the payment dates and check numbers have not been entered for vouchers no. 336 and 338, which simply means that they have not yet been paid.

The amounts from the voucher register are transferred (posted) to the accounts in the same manner as the amounts from the special journals. Before posting, the arithmetic accuracy is verified by footing (adding down the columns) and crossfooting (adding across the rows). Postings are indicated by placing the account number in parentheses at the bottom of an account column; for example, (220) indicates that the $53,020 credit has been posted to Vouchers Payable in the general ledger. A special posting reference column is used in the other accounts debited section of the register, as illustrated with voucher no. 335, indicating that $100 has been posted as a debit to Interest Expense (account no. 710) in the general ledger.

Also note that since Mozart has elected to use the gross method of recording purchases, both Purchases and Vouchers Payable are recorded at the gross amount. Thus, the full invoice price, $24,000, of the speakers bought from Blair and Rumble is recorded. If the net method were used, both accounts would be recorded at the net amount—$23,520 in the case of Blair and Rumble (the check amount noted on the voucher shown in Exhibit 9). Purchases Discounts (gross method) and Purchases Discounts Lost (net method) would be entered in the check register when the payment is made.

## The Check Register

After the voucher has been approved in the accounting department and entered in the voucher register, it is sent to the cashier for payment. The accounting department representative's signature on a voucher represents the authority to the cashier to issue a check in payment. As the cashier receives each voucher, he or she inspects it to see if immediate payment is required. If a check is not required immediately, the unpaid voucher is filed according to the date on which payment is to be made. This filing system serves an internal control purpose by assuring that payment will be made in time to take advantage of purchases discounts—the deduction from the sales price the company gets for paying within a specified time. (Remember the terms—2/10, n/30—on Mozart's purchase from Blair and Rumble.)

When the day for payment arrives, the cashier writes a check. The disbursement of cash is recorded in the **check register,** a special journal consisting of three columns. Since Mozart uses the gross method to record purchases, the check register will have columns for Vouchers Payable Debit, Purchases Discounts Credit, and Cash Credit. Mozart's check register is illustrated in Exhibit 11. A company using the net method would have columns for Vouchers Payable Debit, Purchases Discounts Lost Debit, and Cash Credit.

In addition to the debit and credit columns, the check register has columns for the date the check was issued, the check number, and the payee, as well as the voucher number paid by the check. Payment of vouchers is indicated by recording the voucher number in the voucher number column. Voucher no. 317 is paid by issuing check no. 4304 to Blair and Rumble. Exhibit 11 shows how this payment is entered in the check register.

The process of posting the check register is similar to that of posting any special journal. For example, posting the debit to Vouchers Payable in Mozart's check register is indicated by the account number (220) placed at the bottom of the Vouchers Payable Debit column.

**Exhibit 11** The Check Register

### MOZART ELECTRONICS COMPANY
### Check Register

| Date | Check No. | Payee | Voucher No. | Vouchers Payable Debit | Purchases Discounts Credit | Cash Credit |
|------|-----------|-------|-------------|------------------------|----------------------------|-------------|
| 1998 June 7 | 4297 | ABC Warehouse | 315 | 600 | | 600 |
| 24 | 4304 | Blair and Rumble Co. | 317 | 24,000 | 480 | 23,520 |
| 24 | 4305 | B & R Supply Co. | 310 | 250 | | 250 |
| 24 | 4306 | Quality Plumbing Co. | 305 | 150 | | 150 |
| 25 | 4307 | Jones Transport | 318 | 50 | | 50 |
| 30 | 4347 | Payroll | 337 | 4,800 | — | 4,800 |
| | | | | 42,550 | 1,250 | 41,300 |
| | | | | (220) | (512) | (110) |

A company that uses a voucher register and a check register will not need a purchases journal or a cash payments journal. Everything the company acquires, including merchandise, is recorded in the voucher register, and every payment by check is entered in the check register. Some companies even do away with the use of a subsidiary ledger for vouchers payable. Since every payable is represented by a voucher, the subsidiary ledger merely becomes a stack of unpaid vouchers. When a voucher is paid it is canceled, usually by punching holes in it that spell "PAID." The total of the amounts from the unpaid vouchers should agree with the total in the Vouchers Payable general ledger account.

**ASK YOURSELF** ▶

1. **How does the function of a purchase requisition differ from that of a purchase order?**
2. **Why is a receiving report necessary?**
3. **Who prepares a sales invoice, and what purpose does it serve?**
4. **What supporting documentation is attached to a voucher before it is approved for payment?**
5. **Which special journals do the voucher register and check register replace?**

Learning Objective **11**

Calculate and explain the quick ratio

## FINANCIAL STATEMENT ANALYSIS: THE QUICK RATIO

The **quick ratio** is used by investors and creditors to help evaluate a company's liquid position—its ability to pay for current operations and retire short-term debts.

The **quick ratio,** also known as the **acid-test ratio,** shows the relationship between highly liquid (quick) assets and current liabilities. Quick assets are those that may be converted directly into cash within a short period of time. These include cash, temporary investments, and receivables. Merchandise inventory is omitted because merchandise is normally sold on credit (converted into a receivable) and then the receivable must be collected before cash is realized. Thus inventory is two steps away from cash rather than just one. Prepaid expenses are also omitted because they are usually relatively small in amount and because they are used up in operations rather than converted into cash.

The quick ratio is calculated by the following formula:

$$\text{Quick ratio} = \frac{\text{quick assets}}{\text{current liabilities}}$$

Baxter, Inc. has the following current assets and current liabilities:

| | |
|---|---:|
| Cash . . . . . . . . . . . . . . . . . . . . . . . . . . . . . . . . . . . . . | $ 18,400 |
| Temporary Investments . . . . . . . . . . . . . . . . . . . . . | 6,800 |
| Accounts Receivable (Net). . . . . . . . . . . . . . . . . . | 33,600 |
| Merchandise Inventory . . . . . . . . . . . . . . . . . . . . . . | 86,400 |
| Total Current Assets . . . . . . . . . . . . . . . . . . | $145,200 |
| | |
| Accounts Payable. . . . . . . . . . . . . . . . . . . . . . . . . | $ 56,000 |
| Income Taxes Payable. . . . . . . . . . . . . . . . . . . . . | 7,200 |
| Total Current Liabilities . . . . . . . . . . . . . . . . | $ 63,200 |

Baxter's quick ratio would be:

$$\text{Quick ratio} = \frac{\$18,\!400 + 6,\!800 + 33,\!600}{\$56,\!000 + 7,\!200} = \frac{\$58,\!800}{\$63,\!200} = \underline{\underline{.93:1}}$$

Baxter has about $.93 of highly liquid assets to pay each dollar of current liabilities. Investors and creditors generally look for a quick ratio of about 1:1.

## SUMMARY

- **Cash** is all money on deposit in banks that can be obtained immediately and used at the discretion of company management, and all items on hand that a bank will accept immediately for deposit.
- Because cash is the asset most readily acceptable for purchasing all goods and services, it is universally desirable. For that reason, special internal controls must be established to protect it from theft.
- Controls over the receipt of cash include having two employees present when cash is received to ensure that the proper amount is recorded, having the records for the cash controlled by someone other than the person responsible for the cash itself, and having someone verify that the amount of cash received agrees with the amount of cash recorded in the financial records.
- Controls over cash payments include use of a petty cash fund, recording purchases at their net amount, and use of a voucher system.
- **Bank reconciliations** are an important part of the system of internal control. Reconciliations are prepared to explain the differences between the cash balance shown on the bank statement and the cash amount in the company's checkbook.
- Bank reconciliations help locate errors made by the company and by the bank. Since a bank reconciliation verifies both deposits and checks written, it may be viewed as an internal control over both cash receipts and cash payments. The bank reconciliation is used by most companies to reveal unrecorded transactions that need to be recorded in the journals, and errors that need to be corrected by making an entry in the general journal.
- A **petty cash fund** is used where small payments are made in currency and coin because issuing a check is impractical. Petty cash payments are controlled by using petty cash vouchers, which are reviewed each time the fund is replenished.
- Purchases may be recorded using the **gross method** or the **net method.** By failing to take a cash discount, a company is, in effect, borrowing from a supplier at a high interest rate. Management wants to avoid this high interest by being sure that all available discounts are taken.
- The net method of recording purchases is better at ensuring that cash discounts will be taken because it alerts management to the accounts payable department's failure to take a cash discount.
- A **voucher** is an internal document on which is recorded the verifications that authorized goods and services were acquired as well as authorizations for payment.
- Under a voucher system, (1) all expenditures must be authorized; (2) the goods or services must be received, inspected, and reported; and (3) the proper amounts must be paid in a timely fashion.
- Information from vouchers is recorded in a special journal called a **voucher register.**
- When a check is written to pay a liability represented by a voucher, it is entered in the **check register** and the check number is entered in the voucher register.
- The **quick ratio** is an indication of a company's ability to pay for current operations and retire its current debts as they come due. The quick ratio is calculated by dividing quick assets (cash, temporary investments and receivables) by current liabilities.

## 12  KEY TERMS

**Bank reconciliation**  An explanation of the differences between the ending cash balance as reported by the bank and the ending cash balance as recorded in the company's records.

**Cash**  All money on deposit in banks that can be obtained immediately and used at the discretion of management, and all assets on hand that will be accepted by a bank for deposit.

**Check register** A three-column journal of original entry used to record the disbursement of cash by check. It has a minimum of two columns to record a debit to Vouchers Payable and a credit to Cash. A third column is usually added to record Purchases Discounts or Purchases Discounts Lost.

**Deposit in transit** Cash sent to the bank—sent through the mail or placed in a night depository—for deposit but not received in time to be included in the ending balance on the bank statement.

**Gross method** A method of recording purchases on credit at the gross invoice price. When cash discounts are taken, Purchases Discounts is credited for the amount of the discount.

**Net method** A method of recording purchases on credit at the net invoice price, anticipating that cash discounts will be taken. If the cash discount is not taken, Purchases Discounts Lost is debited at the time of the payment.

**NSF check** A "not sufficient funds check" presented for payment to the bank and rejected because the depositor's account does not contain sufficient cash to process the check.

**Outstanding checks** Checks written but not yet presented to the bank or processed by the bank.

**Petty cash fund** A small amount of cash used for payments when a check is impractical. The contents of the fund must always total the same amount. The fund may contain cash or cash and paid vouchers.

**Petty cash voucher** A written authorization to disburse petty cash.

**Purchase order** A business document that serves as an order for goods or services from an outside supplier or vendor. This document implies a promise to pay for the goods or services under conditions agreed upon by the buyer and seller.

**Purchase requisition** An internal business document that originates and remains within the firm, specifying goods or services needed and requesting the firm to acquire them.

**Quick ratio** Highly liquid (quick assets) divided by current liabilities; also called the **acid-test ratio.**

**Receiving report** An internal business document to indicate the quantity and condition of goods or services that have been received.

**Vendor** An outside supplier of goods or services.

**Voucher** A written authorization to pay. Vouchers usually show the name of the individual or company to be paid, the amount of the payment, the reason for the payment, a signature authorizing payment, and the accounts to be debited or credited as a result of the payment.

**Voucher register** A multicolumn journal of original entry used to record transactions authorized by vouchers. It has one credit column to record vouchers payable and debit columns for purchases, freight-in, salary expense, and any other expense that must be recorded often. It also has a section called "Other Accounts Debited" for recording debits to accounts that occur less frequently.

**Voucher system** The system used by a business to ensure that all expenditures are authorized; that the goods or services are received; and that only the goods or services received are paid for, and within a time period that allows the firm to take advantage of cash discounts.

**Vouchers Payable** A general ledger account used in a voucher system to represent all liabilities created by the purchase of goods or services.

## DEMONSTRATION PROBLEM

The following information has been assembled for the purpose of preparing the Apr. 30, 1998, bank reconciliation of Hanson, Inc.:

**a.** The balance on the Apr. 30 bank statement is $18,862; the Cash account shows a $17,250 balance on the same date.

**b.** A bank service charge of $25 appears on the bank statement; this charge has not been recorded in the books.

**c.** Checks written by Hanson which have not yet cleared the bank total $1,220.

**d.** A deposit of $887 appears on the bank statement. Hanson did not make such a deposit. This is a bank error.

**e.** A deposit for $645 made late on Apr. 30 does not appear on the bank statement.

**f.** A customer's check for $140 was returned with the bank statement marked NSF.

**g.** The bank collected $315 on a customer's note that Hanson left for collection. The $315 includes $15 interest in addition to the face value of $300. The bank has collected cash from an individual who owes Hanson. The amount collected was added to the checking account, but it has not been recorded in Hanson's financial records.

### Required:

1. Prepare the Apr. 30 bank reconciliation for Hanson, Inc.
2. Prepare any journal entries that will be necessary as a result of this reconciliation. Hanson does not use the voucher system.

### ■ Solution to Demonstration Problem

1.

**HANSON, INC.**
**Bank Reconciliation**
**April 30, 1998**

| | | |
|---|---:|---:|
| Balance per bank statement, Apr. 30 . . . . . . . . . . . . . . . . . . . . . . . . . . . . . | | $18,862 |
| Add: Deposits in transit on Apr. 30 . . . . . . . . . . . . . . . . . . . . . . . . . . . . . . | | 645 |
| Total. . . . . . . . . . . . . . . . . . . . . . . . . . . . . . . . . . . . . . . . . . . . . . | | $19,507 |
| Deduct: Outstanding checks . . . . . . . . . . . . . . . . . . . . . . . . . . . . . | $1,220 | |
| Bank error—Deposit credited in error. . . . . . . . . . . . . . . . . | 887 | (2,107) |
| Correct cash balance, Apr. 30 . . . . . . . . . . . . . . . . . . . . . . . . . . . . . . . . | | $17,400 |
| Balance per books, Apr. 30 . . . . . . . . . . . . . . . . . . . . . . . . . . . . . . . . . | | $17,250 |
| Add: Principal of note collected by bank. . . . . . . . . . . . . . . . . . . . . . | $ 300 | |
| Interest on note collected by bank . . . . . . . . . . . . . . . . . . . . . | 15 | 315 |
| Total . . . . . . . . . . . . . . . . . . . . . . . . . . . . . . . . . . . . . . . . . . . . . | | $17,565 |
| Deduct: Bank service fees. . . . . . . . . . . . . . . . . . . . . . . . . . . . . . . . | $ 25 | |
| NSF check received from customer . . . . . . . . . . . . . . . . . . | 140 | (165) |
| Correct cash balance, Apr. 30 . . . . . . . . . . . . . . . . . . . . . . . . . . . . . . . . | | $17,400 |

2.

| | | | |
|---|---|---|---|
| Apr. 30 | Cash .......................................... | 315 | |
| | Note Receivable............................. | | 300 |
| | Interest Income ............................. | | 15 |
| | To record collection of note and interest by bank. | | |
| Apr. 30 | Bank Service Fee Expense...................... | 25 | |
| | Cash...................................... | | 25 |
| | To record bank service charge for April. | | |
| Apr. 30 | Accounts Receivable........................... | 140 | |
| | Cash...................................... | | 140 |
| | To record NSF check returned with April bank statement. | | |

## QUESTIONS FOR REVIEW AND FURTHER THOUGHT

### REVIEW QUESTIONS

1. What is the accountant's definition of cash?

2. List four controls over cash received over the counter from customers.

3. What are three basic internal control principles that a business should follow in every situation in which it receives cash?

4. What is the purpose of a bank reconciliation?

5. What are outstanding checks? Why are they subtracted from the bank statement cash balance on bank reconciliations?

6. What is an NSF check? How will it appear on a bank reconciliation?

7. What are petty cash funds? Why are they used?

8. What is a petty cash voucher? What is the purpose of petty cash vouchers?

9. Where does Cash Short and Over appear on an income statement? Explain.

10. Conner Co. has an account called Purchases Discounts on its books. Is Conner using the gross or the net method of recording cash discounts? Explain.

11. Where do Purchases Discounts and Purchases Discounts Lost appear on an income statement? Would you expect to find both accounts on a single company's income statement? Explain.

12. What internal control system assures that appropriate planned acquisitions are made, received in good condition, billed at correct amounts, and paid for on time?

13. Describe the purpose of each of the following business documents:
    a. Purchase requisition  c. Sales invoice
    b. Purchase order  d. Receiving report

14. A voucher is prepared for each check that a company writes. Describe the information appearing on the front and back of a voucher.

15. Two special journals are replaced by the voucher register and the check register when a voucher system is used. Name these special journals and explain why they are replaced.

16. What supporting documents should be attached to a voucher authorizing payment for a new desk-top computer? Explain the purpose of each of the documents you list.

17. When a voucher system is used what form may the subsidiary ledger for Vouchers Payable take?

### QUESTIONS FOR FURTHER THOUGHT

1. Explain why a traveler's check for $1,000 is cash according to the accountant's definition, while a U.S. government savings bond is not cash.

2. A salesclerk is stealing money from the cash register. Explain how the system of internal control will reveal this theft.

3. Which of the following items on a bank reconciliation require the company to make a journal entry:
   Outstanding checks  Deposits in transit
   Bank service fees  NSF checks
   Checkbook errors  Bank errors

4. "The contents of a $50 petty cash fund must always equal $50, even if $38 has been paid from it." Explain what is meant by this statement.

5. Codall Co. buys from most of its suppliers on terms of 2/10, n/30. Since the discount (2%) is only a small percentage of the price, it is not important enough to be concerned about. Do you agree? Explain.

6. Explain which method of recording cash discounts provides management with the best information for ensuring that all discounts are taken?

7. Separation of duties related to accounting for cash is an internal control technique that may not be possible in a small business with only a few employees. Explain how a small business may attempt to compensate for its inability to divide cash-related duties among employees.

## OBJECTIVE ASSIGNMENT

*True/False* Indicate whether each statement below is *true* or *false* by placing a *T* or an *F* in the space provided.

_____ 1. A good internal control over cash is to be sure that the individual controlling the cash asset always controls the records for the cash.

_____ 2. A voucher system is used to prevent a company from paying fictitious invoices for goods and services never received.

_____ 3. When a bank reconciliation is prepared, the company will need to make an entry for each item added to or deducted from the balance in the checkbook but not for the items added to or deducted from the bank statement balance.

_____ 4. Cash Short and Over will have a credit balance when accumulated shortages exceed accumulated overages.

_____ 5. When a voucher system is used, a purchases journal is unnecessary.

*Multiple Choice* Select the best choice to complete each statement or answer each question below. Write the letter corresponding to your choice in the space provided.

_____ 1. Which of the following does *not* meet the accountant's definition of cash?
   a. A passbook savings account at a savings and loan
   b. A traveler's check
   c. An NSF check
   d. A money order

_____ 2. Which of the following primarily helps control cash receipts?
   a. Bank reconciliations
   b. Petty cash funds
   c. Voucher system
   d. Cash registers

_____ 3. In a bank reconciliation, which of the following would be added to the balance on the company's books?
   a. Outstanding checks
   b. A check that was written for $45 but was entered in the checkbook as $54
   c. A bank service fee of $37 which appeared on the bank statement
   d. Deposits in transit

_____ 4. After completing a bank reconciliation, Pam Fogarty prepared a correcting entry debiting Utilities Expense and crediting Cash. From this entry we know that there was an item in the reconciliation that was:
   a. Deducted from the balance on the bank statement
   b. Deducted from the balance on the company's books
   c. Added to the balance on the bank statement
   d. Added to the balance on the company's books

_____ 5. A $75 petty cash fund contains vouchers totaling $69.50 and $4.25 in cash. The entry to replenish the fund will include:
   a. A debit to Petty Cash for $75
   b. A credit to Cash for $75
   c. A debit to Cash Short and Over for $1.25
   d. A credit to Cash Short and Over for $1.25

_____ 6. Tucan, Inc., uses the net method to record purchases. Goods with an invoice price of $400 and terms of 3/15, n/45 were purchased. Tucan's entry to record the payment 12 days later will include:
   a. A debit to Accounts Payable for $388
   b. A debit to Purchases Discounts Lost for $12
   c. A credit to Cash for $400
   d. A credit to Purchases Discounts for $12

_____ 7. The document that serves as an order for goods or services from an outside supplier is called:
   a. A purchase requisition
   b. A purchase order
   c. A receiving report
   d. A voucher

_____ 8. The document that is prepared to authorize payment for all acquisitions of goods or services by a company is called:
   a. A purchase requisition
   b. A purchase order
   c. A receiving report
   d. A voucher

_____ 9. By looking at the voucher register, you know that a voucher has been paid if:
   a. The bookkeeper's initials appear in the proper column
   b. The voucher number has been entered
   c. The check number has been entered
   d. The dollar amount has been entered in the proper column

_____ 10. When a voucher system is used, this journal is unnecessary:
   a. Cash receipts
   b. Cash payments
   c. Sales
   d. General

## EXERCISES

1†  **Exercise 1:** Calculating Correct Balance Sheet Cash

Crown Linen Supply's bookkeeper calculates the balance of cash for the Dec. 31, 1997, balance sheet to be $8,501.78. He included the following items in his calculation:

| | |
|---|---:|
| A petty cash fund......................... | $ 50.00 |
| A U.S. government savings bond ........... | 100.00 |
| Currency and coin ....................... | 107.40 |
| A check received from a customer and returned by the bank marked NSF.................. | 45.78 |
| Postage stamps.......................... | 18.60 |
| Checking account balance ................ | 7,680.00 |
| Passbook savings account at Carter Savings .. | 450.00 |
| Travelers' checks received from customers .... | 20.00 |
| A promissory note from Abe Rosen, a customer | 30.00 |

What is the correct amount of cash that Crown Linen Supply should report on its balance sheet?

▶ *(Check Figure: Correct cash = $8,307.40)*

† The numbers in the margin refer to the Learning Objectives.

**2**  **Exercise 2:** Evaluating Internal Control over Cash

At Lynn Johnson's Kash and Karry Market, each department is headed by a salesclerk who prepares a handwritten receipt for each sale. At the end of the day the salesclerk removes the cash from a locked drawer in the sales table, counts it, and prepares a deposit slip. Ms. Johnson deposits the receipts in the bank each evening. She uses copies of the deposit slip and the handwritten sales tickets to prepare the daily entry to record sales. At the end of each month she reconciles the company bank statement. What internal control weaknesses do you see in this system? How can it be improved?

**4**  **Exercise 3:** Preparing a Bank Reconciliation

Ellen Simpson compiled the following information for use in preparing Ruleco's bank reconciliation on Sept. 30, 1998:

a. The Sept. 30 balance in Ruleco's checkbook is $5,612.80.
b. The Sept. 30 balance on Ruleco's bank statement is $4,890.25.
c. A comparison of the check stubs with the canceled checks revealed that checks in the amount of $316.40 have not yet cleared the bank.
d. Ruleco's bank statement shows a $20 charge for a safe deposit box. Ruleco does not have a safe deposit box.
e. Other bank service fees for the month of September are $24. These appear on the bank statement; they have not been recorded in Ruleco's books.
f. Ruleco entered check no. 4202 as $95 in the financial records. Examination of this canceled check used to pay an account payable reveals that the correct amount of the check is $59.
g. Ruleco made a deposit of $1,015.25 in the night depository on Sept. 30. This deposit does not appear on the bank statement.
h. A customer's check for $15.70 was returned with the bank statement, marked NSF.

Prepare Ruleco's Sept. 30, 1998, bank reconciliation.

▶ *(Check Figure: Correct ending balance on Sept. 30 = $5,609.10)*

**4**  **Exercise 4:** Preparing Entries Indicated by a Bank Reconciliation

Using the information given in Exercise 3, prepare all the entries that Ruleco should make. Your entries should be in general journal form.

▶ *(Check Figure: Three entries will be necessary.)*

**6**  **Exercise 5:** Establishing and Replenishing a Petty Cash Fund

On June 1, 1997, Delta, Inc., established a $150 petty cash fund. On June 30, the petty cash box contained the following:

a. Petty cash disbursement vouchers:

| Voucher No. | Purpose of Disbursement | Amount of Disbursement |
|---|---|---|
| 101 | Two reams of copying paper | $14.00 |
| 102 | Postage stamps | 29.00 |
| 103 | Freight charges on merchandise shipment | 42.00 |
| 104 | Payment to Hoppy Delivery Service to deliver merchandise to customer | 18.00 |
| 105 | Payment for temporary help to unload truck | 35.00 |

b. $11.00 in currency and coins

Prepare the appropriate entries to establish the petty cash fund on June 1 and to replenish the fund on June 30.

▶ *(Check Figure: The June 30 entry includes a $139.00 credit to Cash)*

**8**   **Exercise 6:** Preparing Entries Using the Net Method of Recording Purchases

On Oct. 1, 1998, Electro Sales purchased 20 digital audio tape players from DAT Electronics for $250 each on terms of 2/10, n/30. Electro uses the net method of accounting for purchases.

a.  Assuming that Electro paid on Oct. 9, prepare entries for Oct. 1 and Oct. 9.
b.  Assuming that Electro paid on Oct. 30, prepare entries for Oct. 1 and Oct. 30.

▶ *(Check Figure: Purchases Discounts Lost recorded on Oct. 30 = $100)*

**10**   **Exercise 7:** Indicating Which Journal Is Used to Record a Transaction

Boulevard Bakery uses an accounting system that includes the following journals and other books of original entry:

Sales journal                    Check register
Cash receipts journal            General journal
Voucher register

Which journal or register would be used to record each of the transactions listed below? You may need to list more than one journal or register to completely record a transaction.

a.  An invoice for $2,470 was received from Baker's Supply Co. All supporting documentation (purchase requisition, purchase order, and receiving report) are on file.
b.  $645.90 was collected from Mary Jennus, a customer.
c.  A cash sale of $450 was made to Silver Sandwich Shop.
d.  A sale of $3,980 was made to Sandra's Catering. Terms of the sale were 2/10, n/30.
e.  Check no. 2490 was written to pay the Baker's Supply invoice.
f.  An invoice for $4,775 was received from Valley Box & Packaging. All supporting documentation is on file.
g.  The month's telephone bill for $135.75 was received from Metro Communications Company.
h.  The week's payroll was paid by cashing check no. 2512 and placing cash in the employees' pay envelopes.
i.  A bill for $1,250 was received from Michelle's Painting for work completed earlier in the month.
j.  An adjusting entry was made to record the amount of prepaid insurance used up during the month.

**11**   **Exercise 8:** Calculating and Explaining the Quick Ratio

Jackson Corp. has calculated the following quick ratios for each of the past three years:

| | |
|---|---|
| 1995 | 1.00 : 1.0 |
| 1996 | .98 : 1.0 |
| 1997 | 1.05 : 1.0 |

The following information was taken from the 1998 balance sheet of Jackson Corp.:

| | |
|---|---|
| Cash | $13,250 |
| Temporary Investments | 6,000 |
| Accounts Receivable (net) | 27,000 |
| Merchandise Inventory | 40,000 |
| Prepaid Expenses | 9,950 |
| Accounts Payable | 16,770 |
| Accrued Payables | 3,800 |
| Notes Payable (due in 6 months) | 20,000 |
| Mortgage Payable (due in 2005) | 80,000 |

Calculate Jackson's 1998 quick ratio. What does the 1998 ratio mean? Is Jackson's liquid position improving? Explain.

▶ *(Check Figure: Jackson's 1998 quick ratio = 1.14 : 1.0)*

## PROBLEMS: SET A

4† **Problem A1:** Preparing a Bank Reconciliation

Simpson Co. has engaged you to reconcile its bank statement as of Sept. 30, 1998. You have gathered the following information:

a. The Sept. 30 balance in the cash account is $931.20; the bank statement for the same date shows a balance of $2,520.80.
b. Checks written by Simpson but not yet cleared by the bank total $1,807.
c. A customer's check for $70 was returned with the bank statement, marked NSF.
d. Check no. 472 was written for $40.80 and entered in the checkbook as $408.00. The check was payable to Gotham Cellular to pay the monthly cellular phone bill.
e. A deposit of $1,000.20 placed in the night depository on Sept. 30 does not appear on the bank statement.
f. Simpson had left a customer's note at the bank for collection. When the customer paid the $400 note and $100 interest, the bank added $500 to the checking account. Simpson has not entered this collection in its financial records.
g. A bank service charge of $14.40 appears on the bank statement. Simpson has not entered this charge in the financial records.

**Required:**

1. Prepare the Sept. 30 bank reconciliation for Simpson.
2. Prepare any journal entries that Simpson should make as a result of this reconciliation. Simpson does not use a voucher system.

▶ *(Check Figure: Correct cash balance on Sept. 30 = $1,714.00)*

4 **Problem A2:** Preparing a Bank Reconciliation

Dianne King owns and operates an answering service. You have been hired to prepare a reconciliation of the business's cash balance on the bank statement with the amount that appears in her company's books. You are also to determine the correct cash amount. Dianne provides you with the following information:

### MOUNTAIN NATIONAL BANK
### Evergreen, Virginia

King Answers, Inc.
2145 Broad Street
Evergreen, VA

**Account Number:** 1027-867-230
**Statement Date:** May 31, 1998

| Balance Last Statement | Deposits and Credits | | Checks and Debits | | Balance This Statement |
|---|---|---|---|---|---|
| | No. | Total Amount | No. | Total Amount | |
| 1,936.60 | 4 | 11,673.58 | 12 | 8,689.62 | 4,920.56 |

**Deposits and Other Credits:**

| Date | Amount Credited | Description |
|---|---|---|
| 5/3 | 2,355.98 | Deposit |
| 5/15 | 4,461.28 | Deposit |
| 5/22 | 2,856.32 | Deposit |
| 5/25 | 2,000.00 | Deposit |

*(Continued)*

† The numbers in the margin refer to the Learning Objectives.

**Checks and Other Debits:**

**Checks:**

| Date | Check No. | Amount | Date | Check No. | Amount |
|------|-----------|--------|------|-----------|--------|
| 5/4 | 2376 | 286.80 | 5/19 | 2489 | 511.64 |
| 5/7 | 2484 | 123.00 | 5/21 | 2490 | 957.75 |
| 5/8 | 2486 | 1,388.55 | 5/25 | 2491 | 848.32 |
| 5/10 | 2487 | 2,477.00 | 5/29 | 2492 | 1,821.64 |
| 5/17 | 2488 | 109.22 | | | |

**Other Debits:**

| Date | Amount | Description |
|------|--------|-------------|
| 5/31 | 40.00 | Safe deposit box rental (1 year) |
| 5/31 | 75.70 | NSF check (J. Armas) |
| 5/31 | 50.00 | Monthly service charge |

**From May Cash Receipts Journal**
(All cash receipts are deposited):

| Date | Cash (Dr.) |
|------|------------|
| 5/5 | 2,355.98 |
| 5/15 | 4,461.28 |
| 5.22 | 2,856.32 |
| 5/25 | 2,000.00 |
| 5/31 | 859.12 |
| Total | 12,532.70 |

**From May Cash Payments Journal**
(All cash payments are made by check):

| Date | Check No. | Cash (Cr.) |
|------|-----------|------------|
| 5/5 | 2484 | 213.00 |
| 5/6 | 2485 | 616.20 |
| 5/7 | 2486 | 1,388.55 |
| 5/7 | 2487 | 2,477.00 |
| 5/12 | 2488 | 109.22 |
| 5/15 | 2489 | 511.64 |
| 5/18 | 2490 | 957.75 |
| 5/21 | 2491 | 848.32 |
| 5/23 | 2492 | 1,821.64 |
| 5/25 | 2493 | 11.76 |
| 5/28 | 2494 | 556.24 |
| 5/31 | 2495 | 47.80 |
| Total | | 9,559.12 |

**From the General Ledger Cash Account:**

| Date | Explanation | Post. Ref. | Dr. | Cr. | Balance |
|------|-------------|-----------|-----|-----|---------|
| Apr. 30 | Balance | ✔ | | | 1,601.30 |
| May 31 | | C/R-2 | 12,532.70 | | 14,134.00 |
| May 31 | | C/P-5 | | 9,559.12 | 4,574.88 |

a. In reviewing the April bank statement, you discover that checks no. 2370 ($48.50) and no. 2376 ($286.80) were outstanding on Apr. 30.

b. The $40 charge for safe deposit box rental was incorrect. Dianne had canceled the box rental on Apr. 30.

c. Check no. 2484 was written to pay for an advertisement in the local newspaper. An incorrect amount was entered in the checkbook and the cash payments journal. The correct amount, $123.00, appears on the check.

d. The bank returned a customer's check marked NSF. Dianne believes that she will collect from J. Armas, the customer.

**Required:**

1. Prepare a bank reconciliation that reconciles Dianne's bank statement balance and her cash book balance to a correct cash amount.
2. Prepare any journal entries that the reconciliation indicates are needed on Dianne's books.

▶ *(Check Figure: Correct cash balance = $4,539.18)*

**4** **Problem A3:** Reconstructing a Bank Reconciliation

Bernard's Book Bindery prepared the following entries, that the April 1998 bank reconciliation indicated were necessary:

| | | | |
|---|---|---|---|
| Apr. 30 | Cash ......................................... | 18 | |
| | Advertising Expense ......................... | | 18 |
| | To correct error in recording check no. 1329. | | |
| | | | |
| Apr. 30 | Bank Service Charge Expense..................... | 45 | |
| | Cash....................................... | | 45 |
| | To record bank service charges for April. | | |
| | | | |
| Apr. 30 | Accounts Receivable: AAA Bookstore .............. | 135 | |
| | Cash....................................... | | 135 |
| | To record NSF check received with the April bank statement. | | |
| | | | |
| Apr. 30 | Rent Expense ................................. | 467 | |
| | Cash....................................... | | 467 |
| | To record check no. 1354, which was not entered in the financial records. | | |

**Additional Facts:**

a. Bernard's financial records show an Apr. 30 cash balance of $5,974; the balance on the Apr. 30 bank statement is $6,785.
b. Outstanding checks on Apr. 30 amount to $2,390.
c. Deposits in transit on Apr. 30 total $950.

**Required:**

Using all the information given above, reconstruct the Apr. 30 bank reconciliation.

**6 8** **Problem A4:** Preparing Entries for a Petty Cash Fund and for Recording Purchases Using the Net Method

A listing of Arena Co.'s accounts payable on Mar. 31, 1998, follows:

| Name of Supplier | Invoice Date | Terms | Gross Invoice Amount |
|---|---|---|---|
| Stein, Inc. | Mar. 17 | 3/15, n/45 | $2,400 |
| O'Grady Co. | Mar. 25 | 2/20, n/60 | 2,040 |
| Gilbert Co. | Mar. 29 | 3/5, n/60 | 1,050 |

The following financial information relates to the month of April:

Apr. 1 Established a $100 petty cash fund. A check for that amount was written and cashed, and the money was given to the petty cashier.

5 Paid Stein, Inc., the amount due.

10 Purchased merchandise from McNeal Co., invoice price $1,500, terms 2/10, n/30, invoice date Apr. 10.

11 Paid O'Grady Co. the amount due.

Apr. 15 Replenished the petty cash fund and increased it to $150. The following vouchers were presented by the petty cashier:

No. 1001 For paper for copying machine . . . . . . . $21.00
No. 1002 For postage stamps . . . . . . . . . . . . . . . . 29.00
No. 1003 For freight on merchandise
purchased . . . . . . . . . . . . . . . . . . . . . . . 17.00
No. 1004 For blank videotapes . . . . . . . . . . . . . . 23.25

At the time of replenishment, $10.75 remains in the petty cash box.

19 Paid McNeal Co. the amount due.

22 Purchased merchandise from Carson Co., invoice price $1,800, terms 2/20, n/60, invoice date Apr. 23.

27 Received merchandise from Hernandez Inc., invoice price $400, terms 3/5, n/20, invoice date Apr. 26.

28 Paid Gilbert Co. the amount due.

30 Replenished the petty cash fund. The following vouchers were presented for payment:

No. 1005 For emergency plumbing repair . . . . . . . $50.00
No. 1006 For freight on merchandise received
from Hernandez Co. . . . . . . . . . . . . . . . . 31.25
No. 1007 For computer diskettes . . . . . . . . . . . . . . 22.55
No. 1008 For postage due on package . . . . . . . . . 1.30
No. 1009 For contribution to local charity drive . . . 25.00

At the time of replenishment, $19.80 remains in the petty cash box.

**Required:**

Assuming that Arena uses the net method of recording purchases, prepare general journal entries to record the transactions described above.

▶ *(Check Figure: Purchases Discounts Lost on Apr. 5 = $72.00)*

8 **Problem A5:** Recording Purchases Using the Gross and Net Methods

During September 1998, Dive-Free Co. entered into the following transactions relating to the purchase of merchandise:

Sept. 1 Acquired fins on account from Flipper Fins. The gross invoice price of the merchandise was $12,000; terms 2/10, n/30.

Sept. 3 Purchased air tanks and wet suits for $2,600 from Water Wear Co.; terms 3/5, n/60.

6 Paid freight on merchandise received from Flipper Fins, $330.

7 Paid Water Wear the amount due.

14 Purchased $5,400 of goggles and snorkels from Wet Ones Ltd.; terms 2/10, n/30.

16 Purchased miscellaneous diving accessories from Going Under, Inc.; invoice price $6,200; terms 2/15, n/45.

18 Paid freight on the Wet Ones shipment, $68.

22 Paid Flipper Fins the amount due.

24 Purchased T-shirts and shorts from Cayman Fashions for $3,560 cash.

27 Paid Wet Ones the amount due.

29 Paid Going Under the amount due.

Dive-Free's September sales totaled $58,600; inventory on hand on Sept. 1 had a cost of $11,000; Sept. 30 inventory amounted to $7,900. During the month, Dive-Free had $14,800 of operating expenses and paid $1,290 interest on a bank loan.

**Required:**

Assuming that the invoice date for each purchase is the same as the transaction date:

1. Prepare general journal entries to record the September transactions using the gross method to record purchases.
2. Prepare an income statement for the month of September reflecting use of the gross method to record purchases.
3. Prepare general journal entries to record the September transactions using the net method to record purchases.
4. Prepare an income statement for the month of September reflecting use of the net method to record purchases.

▶ *(Check Figure: Purchases Discounts Lost total = $348)*

10 **Problem A6:** Recording Transactions Using a Voucher System

To help control expenditures, Tracy Security Co. uses a voucher system. During January 1998, the following transactions occurred:

Jan. 1 Inventory in the amount of $5,000 was purchased on account from Key Alarms Co. with credit terms of 2/10, n/30. Recorded voucher no. 606.

4 Purchased inventory on account in the amount of $4,000 from Star Locks, Inc. Credit terms 3/15, n/45. Recorded voucher no. 607.

8 Paid voucher no. 606 by issuing check no. 2367.

15 Recorded voucher no. 608 payable to Payroll in the amount of $9,000. Issued check no. 2368 in payment of the voucher.

16 Issued check no. 2369 in payment of voucher no. 607.

21 Issued voucher no. 609 payable to Hunter Equipment in the amount of $28,500 for a new truck. Issued check no. 2370 in payment of this voucher.

24 Purchased inventory on account from Silent Sentry $6,000, terms 2/10, n/30. Recorded voucher no. 610.

26 Returned $1,000 of inventory to Silent Sentry. The systems were defective.

27 Recorded voucher no. 611 payable to Pecos Freight in the amount of $200 for freight on inventory purchased from Silent Sentry.

28 Recorded voucher no. 612 for $432 payable to Progress Electric Co. for the monthly electric bill. Issued check no. 2371 in payment of this voucher.

31 Recorded voucher no. 613 payable to Payroll in the amount of $7,500. Issued check no. 2372 in payment of the voucher.

**Required:**

Using a voucher register, a check register, and a general journal, record the Tracy Security Co. transactions listed above. Assume that Tracy uses the gross method of recording purchases.

▶ *(Check Figure: Total of vouchers payable from voucher register = $60,632)*

## PROBLEMS: SET B

4† **Problem B1:** Preparing a Bank Reconciliation

You have been assigned the task of preparing the May 1998 bank reconciliation for Kingery, Inc. You have assembled the following information:

a. The balance on the May 31 bank statement is $16,870; the Cash account shows a $13,540 balance on the same date.
b. A bank service charge of $90 appears on the bank statement; this charge has not been recorded in the books.
c. Checks written by Kingery that have not yet cleared the bank total $3,160.
d. An error was made in recording check no. 9872. The $28 check to pay for freight on merchandise purchased was recorded on the books as $82.
e. A deposit for $1,496 made late on May 31 does not appear on the bank statement.
f. A customer's check for $58 was returned with the bank statement marked NSF.
g. The bank collected for Kingery $1,760 on a note left for collection. The $1,760 includes $160 interest that was collected in addition to the face value of $1,600.

**Required:**

1. Prepare the May 31 bank reconciliation.
2. Prepare any journal entries that will be necessary as a result of this reconciliation. Kingery does not use a voucher system.

▶ *(Check Figure: Correct cash balance on May 31 = $15,206)*

4 **Problem B2:** Preparing a Bank Reconciliation

Brian Power owns and operates a pool supply store. Each month when the bank statement arrives in the mail, Brian compares the balance the bank says he has with the balance in his books; they are never the same. Brian has asked you to review his records and prepare a schedule that reconciles the balance on the bank statement for the month of February with the balance in the company's books.

Mr. Power provides you with the following information:

### CREEKSIDE NATIONAL BANK
### Blaine, North Carolina

Power Pool Supply
1067 Moore Road
Blaine, NC

Account Number: 987-043-224
Statement Date:   February 28, 1998

| Balance Last Statement | Deposits and Credits | | Checks and Debits | | Balance This Statement |
|---|---|---|---|---|---|
| | No. | Total Amount | No. | Total Amount | |
| 968.30 | 4 | 5,836.79 | 12 | 4,344.81 | 2,460.28 |

**Deposits and Other Credits:**

| Date | Amount Credited | Description |
|---|---|---|
| 2/6 | 1,177.99 | Deposit |
| 2/23 | 2,230.64 | Deposit |
| 2/20 | 1,428.16 | Deposit |
| 2/27 | 1,000.00 | Loan Proceeds |

*(Continued)*

† The numbers in the margin refer to the Learning Objectives.

**Checks and Other Debits:**

**Checks:**

| Date | Check No. | Amount | Date | Check No. | Amount |
|------|-----------|--------|------|-----------|--------|
| 2/2  | 676 | 143.30 | 2/19 | 689 | 255.82 |
| 2/5  | 684 | 61.50 | 2/21 | 690 | 478.85 |
| 2/8  | 686 | 694.25 | 2/24 | 691 | 424.16 |
| 2/10 | 687 | 1,238.50 | 2/24 | 692 | 910.82 |
| 2/17 | 688 | 54.61 | | | |

**Other Debits:**

| Date | Amount | Description |
|------|--------|-------------|
| 2/28 | 40.00 | Safe deposit box rental (1 year) |
| 2/28 | 15.00 | Check printing charge |
| 2/28 | 28.00 | Monthly service charge |

**From February Cash Receipts Journal**
(All cash receipts are deposited):

| Date | Cash (Dr.) |
|------|------------|
| 2/6  | 1,177.99 |
| 2/12 | 2,230.64 |
| 2/20 | 1,428.16 |
| 2/28 | 492.56 |
| Total | 5,329.35 |

**From February Cash Payments Journal**
(All cash payments are made by check):

| Date | Check No. | Cash (Cr.) |
|------|-----------|------------|
| 2/3  | 684 | 61.50 |
| 2/4  | 685 | 308.10 |
| 2/4  | 686 | 694.25 |
| 2/9  | 687 | 1,238.50 |
| 2/17 | 688 | 45.61 |
| 2/18 | 689 | 255.82 |
| 2/19 | 690 | 478.85 |
| 2/20 | 691 | 424.16 |
| 2/22 | 692 | 910.82 |
| 2/26 | 693 | 5.88 |
| 2/27 | 694 | 278.12 |
| 2/27 | 695 | 23.90 |
| Total | | 4,725.51 |

**From the General Ledger Cash Account:**

| Date | Explanation | P/R | Dr. | Cr. | Balance |
|------|-------------|-----|-----|-----|---------|
| Jan. 31 | Balance | ✔ | | | 730.70 |
| Feb. 28 | | C/R-4 | 5,329.35 | | 6,060.05 |
| Feb. 28 | | C/P-6 | | 4,725.51 | 1,334.54 |

a. In reviewing the January bank statement, you discover that checks no. 619 ($94.30) and no. 676 ($143.30) were outstanding as of Jan. 31.

b. Brian did not order or receive any new checks this month. The check printing charge is an error.

c. In paying the $54.61 monthly phone bill, Brian wrote the correct amount on check no. 688, but entered $45.61 in the checkbook and cash payments journal.

d. Brian had applied for a $1,000, 6-month loan from the bank. The loan was approved on Feb. 27 and the amount added to the bank account. Brian made no entry to record the loan.

**Required:**

1. Prepare a bank reconciliation that reconciles Brian's bank statement balance and his cash book balance to a correct cash amount.

2. Prepare any journal entries that the reconciliation indicates are needed on Brian's books.

▶ *(Check Figure: Correct cash balance = $2,257.54)*

**4** **Problem B3:** Reconstructing a Bank Reconciliation

Rainbow Cleaners prepared the following entries, that the January 1998 bank reconciliation indicated were necessary:

| | | | |
|---|---|---|---|
| Jan. 31 | Cash .......................................... | 184.50 | |
| | Maintenance Expense......................... | | 184.50 |
| | To correct error in recording check no. 619. | | |
| | | | |
| Jan. 31 | Bank Service Charge Expense..................... | 20.00 | |
| | Cash....................................... | | 20.00 |
| | To record bank service charges for January. | | |
| | | | |
| Jan. 31 | Accounts Receivable: John Davit................... | 8.65 | |
| | Cash....................................... | | 8.65 |
| | To record NSF check received with the January bank statement. | | |
| | | | |
| Jan. 31 | Cleaning Supplies............................. | 361.35 | |
| | Cash....................................... | | 361.35 |
| | To correct error in recording check no. 640. | | |

**Additional Facts:**

a. Rainbow's financial records show a Jan. 31 cash balance of $4,378.50; the Jan. 31 bank statement shows a balance of $4,607.50.
b. Deposits in transit on Jan. 31 amount to $240.
c. Outstanding checks on Jan. 31 total $674.50.

**Required:**

Using all the information given above, reconstruct the Jan. 31 bank reconciliation.

**6 8** **Problem B4:** Preparing Entries for a Petty Cash Fund and for Recording Purchases Using the Net Method

A listing of Arrow Co.'s accounts payable on July 31, 1998, follows:

| Name of Supplier | Invoice Date | Terms | Gross Invoice Amount |
|---|---|---|---|
| Dial, Inc. | July 15 | 1/15, n/30 | $  900 |
| Howell Co. | July 28 | 2/10, n/30 | 480 |
| Butler Co. | July 30 | 3/5, n/30 | 1,350 |

The following financial information relates to the month of August:

Aug.  1   Established a $225 petty cash fund. A check for that amount was written and cashed, and the money was given to the petty cashier.

2   Paid the Butler Co. the amount due.

8   Purchased merchandise from Posey, Inc., invoice price $840, terms 2/10, n/30, invoice date Aug. 8.

11   Paid Howell Co. the amount due.

14   Paid Dial, Inc., the amount due.

Aug. 15 Replenished the petty cash fund. The following petty cash vouchers were presented by the petty cashier:

No. 101   For purchase of postage stamps. . . . . . .   $66.00
No. 102   For freight on merchandise received. . . .   37.20
No. 103   For repair of fax machine. . . . . . . . . . . .   90.00
No. 104   For box of manila envelopes . . . . . . . . . .   14.25

At the time of replenishment, $13.95 remains in the petty cash box.

17   Purchased merchandise from Datek Co., invoice price $1,440, terms 2/20, n/60, invoice date Aug. 18.

20   Paid Posey, Inc., the amount due.

25   Received merchandise from Ziffle Supply Co., invoice price $1,080, terms 3/15, n/45, invoice date Aug. 24.

30   Replenished the petty cash fund and increased it to $300. The following vouchers were presented for payment:

No. 105   For $100 travel advance to
          salesperson . . . . . . . . . . . . . . . . . . . . . . .   $100.00
No. 106   For freight on merchandise received
          from Datek Co. . . . . . . . . . . . . . . . . . . . .   48.75
No. 107   For a laser printer cartridge . . . . . . . . . .   69.25

At the time of replenishment, $6.50 remains in the petty cash box.

### Required:

Assuming that Arrow uses the net method of recording purchases, prepare general journal entries to record the transactions described above.

▶ *(Check Figure: Purchases Discounts Lost on Aug. 11 = $9.60)*

8   **Problem B5:** Recording Purchases Using the Gross and Net Methods

During December 1998, Lanier Fabrics entered into the following transactions relating to the purchase of merchandise:

Dec.  1   Acquired on account from Breman Mills merchandise with a gross invoice price of $3,000; terms 2/10, n/30.

    4   Purchased sewing patterns from Tropical Designs for $1,800; terms 3/15, n/60.

    8   Paid freight on merchandise received from Breman Mills, $84.

   10   Paid Breman Mills the amount due.

   12   Purchased $4,500 of merchandise from Pizzaz Notions; terms 1/15, n/20.

   14   Purchased drapery fabric from Regal Textiles, Inc.; gross invoice price $1,350; terms 2/10, n/30.

   17   Paid freight on the Tropical Designs shipment, $126.

   21   Paid Tropical Designs the amount due.

   23   Paid Regal Textiles the amount due.

   27   Acquired a selection of buttons, zippers, and other fasteners from Garment Accessories for $7,200 cash.

   30   Paid Pizzaz the amount due.

Lanier's December sales totaled $38,160; inventory on hand on Dec. 1 had a cost of $12,000; Dec. 31 inventory amounted to $8,640. During the month, Lanier had $12,000 of operating expenses and paid $3,600 interest on a bank loan.

**Required:**

Assuming that the invoice date for each purchase is the same as the transaction date:

1. Prepare general journal entries to record the December transactions using the gross method to record purchases.
2. Prepare an income statement for the month of December reflecting use of the gross method to record purchases.
3. Prepare general journal entries to record the December transactions using the net method to record purchases.
4. Prepare an income statement for the month of December reflecting use of the net method to record purchases.

▶ *(Check Figure: Purchases Discounts Lost total = $99)*

**10**   **Problem B6:** Recording Transactions Using a Voucher System

To help control expenditures, Classic Chemicals uses a voucher system. During May 1998, the following transactions occurred:

May  1   Purchased merchandise from Assary Wholesale Co., $3,600, terms 2/10, n/30. Recorded voucher no. 806 payable to Assary.

3   Recorded voucher no. 807 payable to Redi Freight in the amount of $240 for shipping charges on the merchandise acquired from Assary.

8   Issued check no. 1490 in payment of voucher no. 806.

9   Recorded voucher no. 808 payable to Payroll, $6,200. Issued check no. 1491 in payment of the voucher.

11   Recorded voucher no. 809 payable to Lee's Garage in the amount of $2,400 for routine maintenance on Classic's fleet of company vehicles. The work had been completed on Apr. 5.

12   Purchased merchandise from Inert Chemicals, Inc., in the amount of $4,800, terms 3/20, n/45. Recorded voucher no. 810 payable to Inert.

18   Issued check no. 1492 in payment of voucher no. 809.

21   Purchased a laptop computer from Acme World Electronics Company in the amount of $6,380. Recorded voucher no. 811 payable to Acme.

21   Returned defective merchandise to Inert. List price $500.

22   Issued check no. 1493 in payment of voucher no. 811.

27   Recorded voucher no. 812 payable to Payroll, $6,880. Issued check no. 1494 in payment of the voucher.

**Required:**

Using a voucher register, a check register, and a general journal, record the Classic Chemicals transactions that are listed above. Assume that Classic uses the gross method of recording purchases.

▶ *(Check Figure: Total of vouchers payable from voucher register = $30,500)*

## DECISION PROBLEM

 Global Imports has a $300 petty cash fund, which is kept by Walter Amscot. When Walter fails to report for work for several days, the company investigates. Walter's landlady reports that he has vacated his apartment and left no forwarding address. Sharon Mitchell, Global's controller, notices that the petty cash fund has not been replenished or audited in several months. She assigns you the task of auditing the petty cash box. When you open the small metal box, you find the following items:

a. A receipt for new printer ribbons purchased from Central Computer Supplies for $40.50.

b. Invoices showing cash purchases of merchandise from Asian Exports Co. Walter Amscot's signature is on the invoices as the recipient of the goods. The invoices total $2,700.

c. Sales invoices totaling $29,916. W. Amscot is listed as the salesperson on each invoice. All of these were cash sales.

d. Several receipts for postage stamps totaling $120.

e. Currency and coin in the amount of $7.50.

**Required:**

1. Write a memorandum to Sharon Mitchell explaining the ways in which Walter misused the petty cash fund. Your memo should also contain recommendations for new procedures to ensure that the next petty cashier does not steal from the petty cash fund.

2. Prepare a schedule to be attached to your memo which shows a calculation of the amount of cash that should be in the petty cash fund and the amount stolen by Walter Amscot.

3. Prepare the general journal entry that would be required to record all of the items in the petty cash box and to replenish the fund on May 16, 1998.

## ETHICS CASE

Hickory Construction is owned and managed by Rod Cochran. Since the company is located in Placid Corners, a very small town, it must be involved in all phases of commercial and residential construction in order to survive. Hickory has eight permanent full-time employees, including Kevin Simmons, who is the company's controller. Kevin and Rod have lived in Placid Corners all their lives, and their families are involved in every aspect of community life.

As owner of the company, Rod maintains the checkbook and writes checks to pay all invoices that Kevin approves as valid. Kevin is responsible for being sure that proper documentation is on file to support each invoice he approves. Kevin also does the company's bookkeeping and prepares the monthly bank reconciliation. While reconciling the May bank statement, Kevin discovers a $20,000 deposit credited to the company's account, apparently in error. When Kevin informs Rod, he is assured that Rod will take care of notifying the bank when he goes in to make the daily deposit.

Kevin gives the error no further thought until he reconciles the June bank statement. His analysis reveals that Rod not only has apparently failed to notify the bank but also has withdrawn the $20,000 by writing several checks payable to "Cash" during the month. Kevin suspects that Rod has used the cash to pay selected subcontractors, because the usual invoices have not been received for several jobs that have been completed.

Kevin knows that the $20,000 has probably saved Rod from having to file for bankruptcy and dismiss the employees who depend on the company for a living. However, Kevin's father is the vice president of the bank, and the family owns stock in that institution. Kevin knows that the small-town bank works on an extremely narrow profit margin, especially in the recessionary economy that the community has faced for the past few months. The bank can ill afford a $20,000 loss.

**Required:**

What action, if any, do you believe Kevin should take?

## OBJECTIVE ASSIGNMENT ANSWERS

### True/False

1. F     2. T     3. T     4. F     5. T

### Multiple Choice

1. c     2. d     3. b     4. b     5. c
6. a     7. b     8. d     9. c     10. b

# Receivables

**LEARNING OBJECTIVES**

After studying this chapter, you should be able to do the following:

1 Record uncollectible accounts using the direct write-off method

2 Write off and reinstate accounts receivable

3 Account for uncollectible accounts using the percentage of credit sales estimation method

4 Account for uncollectible accounts using the aging of receivables method

5 Calculate and explain the use of accounts receivable turnover and average age of receivables in financial statement analysis

6 Explain what notes receivable are

7 Account for notes receivable

8 Calculate the proceeds when discounting a note receivable

9 Prepare entries needed to record discounted notes

10 Prepare entries used by a retailer to account for sales when the customer uses a credit card

11 Define the key terms listed at the end of this chapter

**CHAPTER OUTLINE** ACCOUNTS RECEIVABLE • METHODS OF ACCOUNTING FOR UNCOLLECTIBLE ACCOUNTS RECEIVABLE • The Direct Write-Off Method • Estimation Methods • FINANCIAL STATEMENT ANALYSIS • Accounts Receivable Turnover • Average Age of Receivables • NOTES RECEIVABLE • Notes Receivable versus Accounts Receivable • Determining the Due Date of Notes • Determining Interest on Notes • Recording Notes and Interest • Dishonored Notes • Discounting Notes Receivable • RECEIVABLES FROM OFFICERS AND OWNERS • EXTERNAL CREDIT CARD SALES

Now we will examine several problems related to receivables: how to account for customer accounts that prove uncollectible, and how to account for notes—including recording interest earned and the sale or discounting of a note.

We will also discuss the receivables created when a business lends cash to officers and owners, and receivables resulting from sales made with national credit cards such as American Express.

## ACCOUNTS RECEIVABLE

When an entity makes a sale on credit, an **account receivable,** also called an **open account** or a **trade receivable,** is created. In a credit sale, the seller and buyer enter into a contract, written or oral, in which the buyer agrees to pay the seller within a specified time for all goods and services purchased. The buyer typically has 30, 60, or 90 days after he or she is billed in which to pay the seller. From the time the seller records the sale until the time cash is collected, the seller has a claim against the buyer for the value of the goods or services delivered. This claim is carried in the seller's records as an account receivable.

Sales on account are recorded in the sales journal and then posted to the general ledger account receivable and the subsidiary ledger account receivable for each individual customer. The column total of the sales journal is posted to the general ledger and each individual sale is posted to the subsidiary ledger. Thus, when you look at the balance sheet for any account period, you will see one line listing accounts receivable, which might be in the amount of, say, $57,385. That amount is the sum of perhaps thousands of individual accounts receivable, all recorded in individual ledger accounts. These ledger accounts might be recorded in the form of hand-printed notations on ledger sheets, or in the modern medium of a computer memory device. The total of all the accounts receivable ledger accounts in the subsidiary ledger must always equal the Accounts Receivable account total in the general ledger.

As an example, assume that the Quartz Company made a sale of $1,000 to G. Prince on account. The entry to record this sale in general journal form[1] is as follows:

| | | | |
|---|---|---|---|
| Dec. 28 | Accounts Receivable: G. Prince . . . . . . . . . . . . . . . . . . | 1,000 | |
| | Sales . . . . . . . . . . . . . . . . . . . . . . . . . . . . . . . . . . . . . . | | 1,000 |
| | To record sale on account. | | |

All of Quartz's accounts receivable on Dec. 31, 1998, are listed in the reconciliation in Exhibit 1. This schedule proves that the total of the accounts receivable in the subsidiary ledger equals the balance of the Accounts Receivable control account in the general ledger.

## METHODS OF ACCOUNTING FOR UNCOLLECTIBLE ACCOUNTS RECEIVABLE

Any business entity should carefully evaluate a customer's current financial condition and credit history before selling to that customer on account. Nevertheless, every company will occasionally grant credit to customers who turn out to be unable or unwilling to pay their accounts. Accounts receivable that will never be collected become the company's **uncollectible accounts expense,** or **bad debts expense.**

---

[1] All our journal entries in the examples are in general journal form, even though the entry may actually be made in a special journal. This will make illustrations much easier because we won't have to construct special journals each time we make an entry.

---

**Exhibit 1** Reconciliation of General and Subsidiary Accounts Receivable Ledgers

---

**QUARTZ COMPANY**
**Reconciliation of General and Subsidiary Accounts Receivable Ledgers**
**December 31, 1998**

| | | |
|---|---:|---:|
| Accounts Receivable general ledger account balance . . . . . . . . . . . . . . . . . . . | | $5,660 |
| Subsidiary ledger accounts receivable: | | |
| B. Connolly . . . . . . . . . . . . . . . . . . . . . . . . . . . . . . . . . . . . . . . . . . . . . | $ 840 | |
| M. Gilbert . . . . . . . . . . . . . . . . . . . . . . . . . . . . . . . . . . . . . . . . . . . . . | 300 | |
| K. Hajek . . . . . . . . . . . . . . . . . . . . . . . . . . . . . . . . . . . . . . . . . . . . . . | 1,620 | |
| T. Ireland. . . . . . . . . . . . . . . . . . . . . . . . . . . . . . . . . . . . . . . . . . . . . . | 240 | |
| T. McNeal . . . . . . . . . . . . . . . . . . . . . . . . . . . . . . . . . . . . . . . . . . . . . | 810 | |
| N. Olson . . . . . . . . . . . . . . . . . . . . . . . . . . . . . . . . . . . . . . . . . . . . . . | 350 | |
| G. Prince. . . . . . . . . . . . . . . . . . . . . . . . . . . . . . . . . . . . . . . . . . . . . . | 1,000 | |
| O. Stone . . . . . . . . . . . . . . . . . . . . . . . . . . . . . . . . . . . . . . . . . . . . . . | 500 | |
| Total. . . . . . . . . . . . . . . . . . . . . . . . . . . . . . . . . . . . . . . . . . . . . . . . . | | $5,660 |

---

The two most common ways of accounting for uncollectible accounts are:

1. Recognize the uncollectible accounts expense only when the company knows which specific customers' accounts are uncollectible. This technique is called the **direct write-off method.**
2. Estimate and recognize the uncollectible accounts expense *before* the company knows which specific customers' accounts are uncollectible. Two common estimating techniques are the *percentage of credit sales method* and the *aging of receivables method.*

## The Direct Write-Off Method

As an example of the direct write-off method, assume that during 1997, Retail, Inc., made sales on account to several thousand customers. One of them, Q. Carr, later declared bankruptcy, having no cash available to satisfy creditors' demands. Upon learning of Carr's bankruptcy in February 1998, Retail determined that Carr's account was uncollectible and at the same time recognized it as an uncollectible accounts expense. Retail, Inc., made the following entry to write off Carr's account:

*Learning* 1
*Objective*

Record uncollectible accounts using the direct write-off method

---

| | | |
|---|---:|---:|
| 1998 | | |
| Feb. 23   Uncollectible Accounts Expense . . . . . . . . . . . . . . . . . . | 290 | |
|           Accounts Receivable: Q. Carr. . . . . . . . . . . . . . . . . | | 290 |
|          To write off account of Q. Carr that is uncollectible. | | |

---

Uncollectible accounts expense will appear as an operating expense on Retail's income statement. The credit will be posted to Retail's accounts receivable general ledger account and to the Accounts Receivable: Q. Carr subsidiary ledger account. The write-off removes Carr's account receivable from Retail's books; that account now has a zero balance.

Generally accepted accounting principles (GAAP) limit the use of the direct write-off method because of two major objections to it: it violates the matching principle, and it distorts the amount of accounts receivable on the balance sheet. The violation of the matching principle distorts what is reported on the income statement. Remember: According to the matching principle, the expenses incurred in earning revenue during a period of time should be matched with the revenue earned during that period.

For example, Retail's sale on account to Q. Carr is made in 1997. This sale is recorded as an account receivable and a 1997 revenue. This revenue appears on the 1997 income statement. Now 1998 has arrived, but Q. Carr's payment has not. It is a year later, and Retail has just learned that Q. Carr's payment will never be received. The account is declared uncollectible and becomes uncollectible accounts expense. The sales revenue appeared on the 1997 income statement, but some of the expenses that contributed to 1997 income—namely, uncollectible accounts expense—appear on the income statement for 1998, not 1997. The result of this mismatching is that both 1997 and 1998 incomes are distorted.

The other major objection to the direct write-off method is that it distorts accounts receivable on the balance sheet. If, in 1997, the company reasonably expects to collect all the accounts, there is no distortion. However, the company knows that some accounts will later prove uncollectible. Failure to recognize this fact and to estimate these uncollectibles implies that every cent of every sale on account will be received in payment. Thus, the direct write-off method will result in an accounts receivable amount on the 1997 balance sheet that is greater than the amount that the company realistically expects to collect.

The direct write-off method offers two advantages: It is simple, and it is accurate. It is simple because the company does not have to develop a means of estimating uncollectibles—no estimate is needed. It is accurate because no estimation errors are made—there are no estimates.

*Publicly held companies must abide by GAAP, so they cannot use the direct write-off method.* Owners of small businesses often ignore the major objections to the direct write-off method and use it because it is so simple to apply. The Internal Revenue Service also requires its use on income tax returns.

**ASK YOURSELF ▶**

1. **When is uncollectible accounts expense recognized under the direct write-off method?**
2. **What are the two major objections to the direct write-off method?**

### Estimation Methods

Unlike the direct write-off method, the estimation methods record uncollectible accounts expense before the company knows which specific customers' accounts will be uncollectible. The two objections to the direct write-off method are thus answered. When we estimate uncollectible accounts expense we improve matching, because now the expense can be recorded in the same year that the sales revenue is recognized. Also, we reduce the net amount of accounts receivable on the balance sheet, thus showing the user of the statement the approximate net amount we expect to collect—a more conservative and more accurate measure of the accounts receivable asset.

Management estimates uncollectibles by examining the past experience of its own collections, as well as the collection experience of similar companies having comparable credit-granting policies. Before discussing techniques for calculating the amount of this estimate, we will illustrate the typical entries related to recording estimated uncollectibles.

*Recording Uncollectible Accounts Expense*

Meadow Co. estimates uncollectible accounts at $14,800 for 1997, so at the end of the year the firm makes this adjusting entry to record its estimated uncollectible accounts:

---

1997
Dec. 31  Uncollectible Accounts Expense . . . . . . . . . . . . . . . . . .  14,800
            Allowance for Uncollectible Accounts. . . . . . . . . . . .            14,800
         To record an estimate of the current year's uncollectible
         accounts.

---

Uncollectible accounts expense, or bad debts expense, is classified on the income statement as an operating expense—it is a cost of doing business. Allowance for Uncollectible Accounts, sometimes called Allowance for Bad Debts, is a contra account to the current asset Accounts Receivable. Remember: A *contra asset* is subtracted from an asset account—in this case Accounts Receivable.

In the direct write-off method our debit was to Uncollectible Accounts Expense and our credit was to Accounts Receivable. Why do we credit a contra account when we're estimating? One reason is that the use of this account allows the balance sheet to show both the total accounts receivable and the portion of this total that the company expects not to collect. A second and more practical reason is that unless we use a contra asset, it is impossible to properly post the credit to Accounts Receivable. Remember, whenever Accounts Receivable is debited or credited, we must post the amount to the general ledger account and to the subsidiary ledger account(s). When we estimate our bad debts, we have a good idea of the total amount of our uncollectibles, but we don't know which specific customers will fail to pay. We can't post to subsidiary ledger accounts because we don't know whose account to post. We use Allowance for Uncollectible Accounts until we can determine which customers' accounts are bad.

Assuming that Meadow Co. has $346,000 of accounts receivable on Dec. 31, 1997, the balance sheet presentation of accounts receivable would look like this:

---

Accounts Receivable . . . . . . . . . . . . . . . . . . . . . . . . . . . . . . . . . .  $346,000
Less: Allowance for Uncollectible Accounts . . . . . . . . . . . . . . .    14,800    $331,200

---

*Writing off Specific Accounts*

On Jan. 14, 1998, Meadow learns that one of its customers, K. Wood, has gone bankrupt. Wood's account is removed from Meadow's records by the following entry:

---

1998
Jan. 14  Allowance for Uncollectible Accounts. . . . . . . . . . . . . . .  240
            Accounts Receivable: K. Wood. . . . . . . . . . . . . . . . .            240
         To write off account of K. Wood that is determined to be
         uncollectible.

---

Meadow can now post the credit to the accounts receivable general ledger account and to K. Wood's accounts receivable subsidiary ledger account. Notice that no expense is recorded when the account is written off. The expense was estimated in advance as part of the $14,800 uncollectible accounts expense recorded at the end of 1997. If K. Wood never pays, and Meadow doesn't expect him to at this point, no further action is necessary.

### Reinstating an Account

Sometimes a particular account is identified and written off as uncollectible, and then later the customer pays either all or part of the amount owed. The following entries would be used in this situation:

**1.** On Feb. 5, when Meadow wrote off H. Fawn's $375 account as uncollectible,

| | | | |
|---|---|---|---|
| Feb. 5 | Allowance for Uncollectible Accounts . . . . . . . . . . . . . | 375 | |
| | Accounts Receivable: H. Fawn. . . . . . . . . . . . . . | | 375 |
| | To write off account of H. Fawn. | | |

**2.** On Mar. 1, when Meadow received a check for $375 in settlement of Fawn's account,

| | | | |
|---|---|---|---|
| Mar. 1 | Accounts Receivable: H. Fawn . . . . . . . . . . . . . . . . . | 375 | |
| | Allowance for Uncollectible Accounts . . . . . . . . . | | 375 |
| | To reinstate H. Fawn's account, previously written off. | | |

| | | | |
|---|---|---|---|
| | Cash . . . . . . . . . . . . . . . . . . . . . . . . . . . . . . . . . . . . . . . | 375 | |
| | Accounts Receivable: H. Fawn. . . . . . . . . . . . . . | | 375 |
| | To record payment of account in full. | | |

The entry on Mar. 1 to reinstate Fawn's account does just that—it restores the account to where it was before the Feb. 5 write-off entry. Fawn's account is reinstated in Meadow's general and subsidiary ledgers, showing that it is no longer considered a write-off; rather, it is a paid-up account. The subsidiary ledger accounts give a credit history for each customer. Reinstating Fawn's account puts the customer's credit history in a favorable position for possible future sales on credit.

What if Fawn had paid only $300? If Meadow expected to receive the remaining $75, it could reinstate the full $375, record the $300 payment, and wait until the final payment is received. If Meadow had good reason to believe that no further payment would be received, however, only the $300 reinstatement and the $300 payment would be recorded.

Let's return for a moment to the Allowance for Uncollectible Accounts. Remember: Last year Meadow estimated that $14,800 of accounts receivable would not be paid. If Fawn pays the $375 due, what does that do to the estimate of uncollectibles? Nothing, because the estimate did not target specific accounts. If the estimate is accurate, a total of $14,800 will prove uncollectible. Instead of Fawn, someone else, not yet identified, will turn out to be the nonpaying culprit.

Now that we've seen the typical entries used to record the estimate of uncollectible accounts expense, let's discuss the two commonly used estimation methods.

### Percentage of Credit Sales Estimation Method

Learning Objective **3**

Account for uncollectible accounts using the percentage of credit sales estimation method

The **percentage of credit sales method** of estimating is sometimes called the *income statement approach* because it directly calculates uncollectible accounts expense for the year. This method calculates uncollectible accounts by multiplying the current year's credit sales by a percentage which reflects management's estimate of the portion of the current year's credit sales that will ultimately prove uncollectible. For example, Sylvan, Inc., had total sales of $2,800,000 during 1997, of which $300,000 were cash sales and $2,500,000 were on credit. On the basis of its previous collection experience and industry standards, Sylvan's management determines that approximately $1\frac{1}{2}\%$ of total credit sales will eventually prove uncollectible. That is, at the end of

1997, management estimates that $1\frac{1}{2}$% of all the credit sales made during 1997 will never be collected.

Using this percentage, the 1997 uncollectible accounts expense to be shown on the income statement would be determined as follows:

| | |
|---|---:|
| Total Sales............................................. | $2,800,000 |
| Less: Cash Sales....................................... | 300,000 |
| Credit Sales ........................................... | $2,500,000 |
| Uncollectible Accounts Percentage, $1\frac{1}{2}$%, or ...................... | × .015 |
| 1997 Uncollectible Accounts Expense ........................... | $   37,500 |

The adjusting entry to record this estimate is:

| | | |
|---|---|---:|
| 1997 | | |
| Dec. 31 | Uncollectible Accounts Expense ................... | 37,500 |
| | Allowance for Uncollectible Accounts............ | 37,500 |
| | To record an estimate of the 1997 uncollectible credit sales. | |

The percentage of credit sales method directly calculates uncollectible accounts expense for the period. Since this method is an income statement approach, it ignores the existing balance in Allowance for Uncollectible Accounts. This is not true of the aging of receivables method discussed in the next section.

### Aging of Receivables Estimation Method

Learning **4**<br>Objective<br><br>Account for uncollectible accounts<br>using the aging of receivables method

The **aging of receivables method** is sometimes called the *balance sheet approach* because it focuses on the balance sheet account Allowance for Uncollectible Accounts instead of the uncollectible accounts expense in the income statement. Our objective is still to calculate uncollectible accounts expense, but with this method we will calculate the amount needed in Allowance for Uncollectible Accounts first, then derive the expense amount.

Instead of looking at the total credit sales made during a period, this method looks at how old an account receivable is at the end of a period. Collection experience shows that the older a particular account receivable is, the less likely it is ever to be collected.

The aging of receivables method entails performing three steps at the end of each period:

1. Receivables are grouped by age. For example, a 2-months-past-due $10,000 account receivable and a 2-month-old $50 receivable are grouped together, while a 1-year-past-due, $1,000 receivable and a $100 1-year-old receivable are grouped together.

2. A percentage reflecting management's estimate of how much will never be collected is applied to the total amount of receivables in each age group. Perhaps 5% of the current (2-month-old) receivables is estimated to be uncollectible. This means that of the $10,000 + $50 = $10,050 total, .05 × $10,050 = $502.50 is expected not to be collected. For the year-old receivables, let's say that 90% is estimated to be uncollectible. Of the $1,000 + $100 = $1,100 of receivables in this group, .90 × $1,100 = $990 are expected to be bad.

3. Finally, the amounts of the uncollectibles for each age group are added to obtain the total amount of uncollectibles estimated for the period. In our simple example, $502.50 + $990.00 = $1,492.50 total uncollectibles.

The estimates for the percentages to apply in each age group are determined from past experience, in much the same way as the estimates for the percentage of credit sales method. Note that the estimate is based only on those accounts that are *unpaid at the end of the period*. Sales on credit that were made and collected during the period are *not* part of this estimate, as they were with the percentage of credit sales method. Thus, percentages used in the aging method are likely to be significantly higher, since many paying accounts are not included.

The following example illustrates the aging of receivables technique.

Murphy Company began operations on Jan. 1, 1997. On Dec. 31, 1997, the following aging schedule for accounts receivable is prepared:

**MURPHY COMPANY**
**Accounts Receivable Aging Schedule**
**December 31, 1997**

| Customer's Name | Not Yet Due | 1–30 Days Past Due | 31–60 Days Past Due | 61–90 Days Past Due | Over 90 Days Past Due |
|---|---|---|---|---|---|
| C. Abel | $    250 | | | | |
| B. Barker | 348 | | | | |
| A. Carwile | | | $   615 | | |
| K. Dennis | | | | | $  100 |
| T. Eagleton | | | | $   78 | |
| F. Farmer | | $   198 | | | |
| H. Whitley | | 491 | | | |
| R. Zifer | 90 | | | | |
| Totals | $160,000 | $45,000 | $14,000 | $2,500 | $1,000 |

After carefully considering this schedule and the collection experience of similar companies in the industry, Murphy's management prepares the estimate of uncollectible accounts shown in Exhibit 2.

**Exhibit 2** Estimate of Uncollectible Accounts Using the Aging of Receivables Method

**MURPHY COMPANY**
**Estimate of Uncollectible Accounts**
**December 31, 1997**

| Age Category | Amount in the Age Category | Percentage Expected to Be Uncollectible | Amount Expected to Be Uncollectible |
|---|---|---|---|
| Not yet due | $160,000 | 2% | $3,200 |
| 1–30 days past due | 45,000 | 5 | 2,250 |
| 31–60 days past due | 14,000 | 15 | 2,100 |
| 61–90 days past due | 2,500 | 40 | 1,000 |
| Over 90 days past due | 1,000 | 80 | 800 |
| Totals | $222,500 | | $9,350 |

The aging of receivables method calculates the amount needed in Allowance for Uncollectible Accounts. Since this is Murphy's first year of operation, the $9,350 will also be the Uncollectible Accounts Expense for 1997:

---

1997
Dec. 31   Uncollectible Accounts Expense . . . . . . . . . . . . . . . . . .          9,350
                    Allowance for Uncollectible Accounts. . . . . . . . . . . .                      9,350
            To record uncollectible accounts expense estimate for
            1997.

---

During 1998, Murphy wrote off $7,150 of accounts that it specifically identified as uncollectible. Before the estimate for its second year, 1998, is made, Murphy's Allowance for Uncollectible Accounts will have a $2,200 credit balance ($9,350 − $7,150). Murphy still expects $2,200 of its 1997 accounts to be written off, but the individuals haven't yet been identified.

Assume that Murphy applies the same aging technique at the end of 1998 and determines that the allowance account should have a $16,710 balance. Murphy's uncollectible accounts expense for 1998 would be calculated as follows:

---

Total accounts estimated to be uncollectible on Dec. 31, 1998
   (from aging schedule) . . . . . . . . . . . . . . . . . . . . . . . . . . . . . . . . . . . . . . . . . .   $16,710
Less: Credit balance in Allowance for Uncollectible Accounts before 1998
   uncollectible accounts expense is recorded . . . . . . . . . . . . . . . . . . . . . .    (2,200)

1998 Uncollectible accounts expense. . . . . . . . . . . . . . . . . . . . . . . . . . . . . .   $14,510

---

Murphy's 1998 uncollectible accounts adjusting entry would be:

---

1998
Dec. 31   Uncollectible Accounts Expense . . . . . . . . . . . . . . . . . .         14,510
                    Allowance for Uncollectible Accounts. . . . . . . . . . . .                     14,510
            To record uncollectible accounts expense estimate for
            1998.

---

During 1999, Murphy wrote off $17,410 as uncollectible. An aging schedule prepared on Dec. 31, 1999, indicates that Murphy needs an $18,200 balance in the allowance account. How much is bad debts expense for 1999? Before we answer this, let's look at the Allowance for Uncollectible Accounts:

---

| **Allowance for Uncollectible Accounts** | | | |
|---|---|---|---|
| | | 1997 Uncollectible accounts expense estimate | 9,350 |
| 1998 Total accounts written off | 7,150 | | |
| | | Balance, Dec. 31, 1998, before adjustment | 2,200 |
| | | 1998 Uncollectible accounts expense estimate | 14,510 |
| | | Balance, Jan. 1, 1999 | 16,710 |
| 1999 Total accounts written off | 17,410 | | |
| Balance, Dec. 31, 1999, before adjustment | 700 | | |

---

The allowance account now has a *debit* balance of $700. If Murphy's aging schedule tells him that he needs a $18,200 *credit* balance in the allowance, the uncollectible accounts adjustment will need to be for $18,200 + $700 = $18,900. Murphy would make the following entry:

| | | | |
|---|---|---|---|
| 1999 | | | |
| Dec. 31 | Uncollectible Accounts Expense . . . . . . . . . . . . . . . . . . | 18,900 | |
| | Allowance for Uncollectible Accounts. . . . . . . . . . . | | 18,900 |
| | To record uncollectible accounts expense estimate for 1999. | | |

After this entry is posted to Allowance for Uncollectible Accounts, that account will have an $18,200 credit balance—exactly what the aging schedule indicated was needed:

**Allowance for Uncollectible Accounts**

| | | | |
|---|---|---|---|
| | | 1997 uncollectible accounts expense estimate | 9,350 |
| 1998 Total accounts written off | 7,150 | | |
| | | Balance, Dec. 31, 1998, before adjustment | 2,200 |
| | | 1998 uncollectible accounts expense estimate | 14,510 |
| | | Balance, Jan. 1, 1999 | 16,710 |
| 1999 Total accounts written off | 17,410 | | |
| Balance, Dec. 31, 1999, before adjustment | 700 | | |
| | | 1999 uncollectible accounts expense estimate | 18,900 |
| | | Balance, Dec. 31, 1999 | 18,200 |

Remember, the aging schedule calculates the balance needed in the allowance account. If the allowance has a *credit* balance at the time the uncollectible amount is being calculated, deduct the credit balance from the aging schedule amount to derive uncollectible accounts expense. If the allowance has a *debit* balance, add the debit balance to the aging schedule amount to calculate uncollectible accounts expense.

### Correcting Inaccurate Estimates

The objectives of accounting for uncollectibles are to determine as accurately as possible the amount of accounts that will indeed be collected, and to match the uncollectible accounts expense with the revenue it helped to generate.

The direct write-off method accomplishes the first objective but ignores the second. The percentage of credit sales and aging of receivables methods attempt to fulfill both objectives by using estimates of future uncollectibles. Like most predictions, these estimates can be inaccurate. Inaccurate estimates must be adjusted for—corrected—periodically (say, every 2 years or every 5 years). The accounting department of the company will be asked to analyze the company's collections and write-offs to determine the amount that should be in Allowance for Uncollectible Accounts. While we won't focus on how the analysis is made, we will discuss how the adjustment is recorded. Let's look at an example.

Salkward Co. has used the percentage of credit sales method to estimate bad debts for the past 5 years. On Dec. 31, 1997, *after* uncollectible accounts expense has been recorded for 1997, the receivables, allowance, and expense accounts have the following balances:

| | |
|---|---|
| Accounts Receivable . . . . . . . . . . . . . . . . . . . . . . | $612,300 |
| Allowance for Uncollectible Accounts . . . . . . . . . | 12,200 |
| Uncollectible Accounts Expense (1997) . . . . . . . | 5,000 |

Salkward's accounting department conducts an analysis which shows that a total of $14,800 is expected to be uncollectible. Salkward has accumulated an inaccuracy—an error—in its estimated uncollectible accounts over the last 5 years of $14,800 − $12,200 = $2,600. This inaccuracy means that uncollectible accounts expense has been too low by a total of $2,600 over the past 5 years:

| | |
|---|---|
| Amount needed in Allowance for Uncollectible Accounts on Dec. 31, 1997. . . . . . . . . . . . . . . . . . . . . . . . . . . . . . . . . . . . . . . . . . . . . . . . . | $14,800 |
| Less: Amount actually in Allowance for Uncollectible Accounts on Dec. 31, 1997. . . . . . . . . . . . . . . . . . . . . . . . . . . . . . . . . . . . . . . . . . . . | (12,200) |
| Amount by which allowance must be increased. . . . . . . . . . . . . . . . . . . . . . . | $ 2,600 |

Inaccurate estimates are corrected by adjusting the current year's Uncollectible Accounts Expense and the Allowance for Uncollectible Accounts balance. Salkward needs to increase both accounts by making the following journal entry:

| | | | |
|---|---|---|---|
| 1997 | | | |
| Dec. 31 | Uncollectible Accounts Expense (1997) . . . . . . . . . . . . . | 2,600 | |
| | Allowance for Uncollectible Accounts. . . . . . . . . . . | | 2,600 |
| | To correct for inaccurate estimates in uncollectible accounts over the past 5 years. | | |

If Salkward's estimated uncollectible accounts had been too high instead of too low, the expense account would have been credited and the allowance account debited.

Account balances before and after the correcting entry are:

| | Balance Before Correction | Balance After Correction |
|---|---|---|
| Accounts Receivable . . . . . . . . . . . . . . . . . . . . . . . | $612,300 | $612,300 |
| Allowance for Uncollectible Accounts . . . . . . . . . . . | 12,200 | 14,800 |
| Uncollectible Accounts Expense (1997). . . . . . . . . . | 5,000 | 7,600 |

After the correction, Uncollectible Accounts Expense for 1997 has a balance of $7,600: $5,000 that applies directly to 1997 credit sales and $2,600 that is a correction of inaccurate estimates over the past 5 years. Generally accepted accounting principles require that errors in estimates be corrected in this way even though some mismatching is introduced—the $7,600 is shown as a 1997 expense even though it applies to 1993–1996 as well as 1997.

When the percentage of credit sales method is used to estimate bad debts, management will adjust the percentage applied to each year's credit sales in the future to calculate a more accurate estimate of uncollectibles. Instead of, say, $1\frac{1}{4}$% of credit sales, $1\frac{1}{2}$% may be a better estimate. If the aging of receivables method is used, the "percentage expected to be uncollectible" in one or more of the age categories of accounts (see Exhibit 2) may need to be modified.

### Interim Estimates

The concepts and methods learned from any accounting textbook often are modified to meet the needs of actual operating companies. In our examples we have shown uncollectible accounts estimated on Dec. 31, the last day of the accounting period. In practice, a company may prepare an income statement each month. Monthly state-

**Exhibit 3** Methods of Accounting for Uncollectible Accounts Receivable

| | Direct Write-Off Method | Estimation Techniques | |
|---|---|---|---|
| | | **Percentage of Credit Sales Method (Income Statement Approach)** | **Aging of Receivables Method (Balance Sheet Approach)** |
| *Uncollectible Accounts Expense equals* | Total of accounts written off during the period | % × total credit sales for the period | Amount from aging schedules − previous credit balance in allowance or + previous debit balance in allowance |
| *Entry to record uncollectible accounts expense* | Uncollectible Accts. Expense . . . . . . . . . Accts. Receivable: Cust. Name. . . . | Uncollectible Accts. Expense. . . . Allow. for Uncoll. Accts . . . . . | Uncollectible Accts. Expense . . . . . . . . Allow. for Uncoll. Accts . . . . . . . . . |
| *Ending balance in Allowance for Uncollectibles equals* | −0− (This method does not use an allowance account) | Previous balance + amount credited in uncollectible accounts entry | Amount indicated in the aging schedule |
| *Comments* | • *Is not GAAP* <br> • *Can result in mismatching of expense and revenues* <br> • *Distorts amount of accounts receivable on balance sheet* <br> • *Sometimes used by small businesses because it is simple and requires no estimates* | • *Is GAAP* <br> • *Better matching than direct write-off method* <br> • *Better measure of amount of accounts receivable than direct write-off method* <br> • *Requires estimation of credit sales expected to be uncollectible* | • *Is GAAP* <br> • *Better matching than direct write-off method* <br> • *Better measure of amount of accounts receivable than direct write-off method* <br> • *Requires estimation of percent of accounts receivable amounts expected to be uncollectible* |

ments require monthly estimates of uncollectible accounts expense. The procedures you have learned for the year-end also can be used at the end of a month, a quarter, or a semiannual period. To simplify the process of estimating, a company may choose to use the percentage of credit sales method at the end of each month and the more accurate aging of receivables method at year-end.

Exhibit 3 summarizes the three methods that we have discussed for determining uncollectible accounts expense.

## FINANCIAL STATEMENT ANALYSIS

*Learning Objective 5*

Calculate and explain accounts receivable turnover and average age of receivables

Users of financial statements may evaluate how well a company is managing its receivables by looking at the Accounts Receivable Turnover and Average Age of Receivables ratios. To illustrate these ratios we will use the following information extracted from Underhill, Inc.'s 1998 and 1999 financial statements:

| | 12/31/98 | 12/31/99 |
|---|---|---|
| Accounts Receivable (net) . . . . | $135,374 | $152,304 |
| Credit Sales . . . . . . . . . . . . . . | | $1,625,380 |

### Accounts Receivable Turnover

**Accounts receivable turnover** indicates the number of times per year that the average balance of Accounts Receivable is collected. This ratio of sales on credit to average accounts receivable is calculated as follows:

$$\text{Accounts receivable turnover} = \frac{\text{credit sales}}{\text{average accounts receivable}}$$

Since all of Underhill, Inc.'s, sales are on credit, the firm's 1999 receivables turnover is as follows:

$$= \frac{\$1,625,380}{(\$135,374 + \$152,304) \div 2}$$

$$= \frac{\$1,625,000}{\$143,839} = 11.3 \text{ times}$$

This ratio takes on more meaning when used in the calculation of the statistic discussed next.

### Average Age of Receivables

**Average age of receivables** provides a rough approximation of the average time that it takes to collect receivables. Average age of receivables is determined as follows:

$$\text{Average age of receivables} = \frac{365 \text{ days}}{\text{accounts receivable turnover}}$$

1999 average age of Underhill's receivables:

$$= \frac{365 \text{ days}}{11.3 \text{ times}} = 32.3 \text{ days}$$

Underhill, Inc., takes an average of 32 days to collect its receivables. If Underhill's credit terms are net 15 days, its collection efforts could be improved. If the credit terms are 30 or 45 days, Underhill's collection efforts appear to be good.

Creditors are interested in receivables turnover and the average age of receivables as indicators of how quickly the company's receivables are converted into the cash required for operations and debt repayment. Investors and creditors use receivables turnover as one more index of management efficiency.

**ASK YOURSELF** ▶

1. Where is the allowance for uncollectible accounts shown on the financial statements?
2. When is it necessary to reinstate an account receivable?
3. Why is the percentage of credit sales method sometimes called the income statement approach? How is uncollectible accounts expense calculated using this approach?
4. If the accounting department concludes that the balance in Allowance for Uncollectible Accounts is too high, what correcting entry would be made?
5. Why is the aging of receivables method sometimes called the balance sheet approach?
6. If the amount expected to be uncollectible equals $5,000, how much is uncollectible accounts expense if the Allowance for Uncollectible Accounts has: a $1,000 credit balance; a $1,000 debit balance?

# Separating the Sheep from the Goats

If necessity is the mother of invention, the banking industry may finally be ready to tell the outside world about the quality of its loan portfolios. That's a substantial change on the part of executives who have traditionally viewed their loans and lending practices as closely guarded secrets.

The necessity for change is undeniable. Failures are near a record high among the nation's 13,000 commercial banks. So are loan losses. In the last four years banks charged off $75 billion of bad loans, compared with only $28 billion between 1948 and 1981, according to a study by management consultants McKinsey & Co. And that's without a recession.

To survive, let alone prosper, most banks will need to tap Wall Street for new equity capital. But Wall Street puts little faith in what the banks say publicly about the loans on their books; most banks trade substantially below book value these days.

\* \* \*

The data clearly shows that in recent years bank earnings have varied almost en-tirely as a result of loan losses and loss provisions. So it's not unreasonable for investors to want to know whether their banks' portfolios contain risky loans that are likely to translate into future losses. But that isn't what the banks tell them.

The banks disclose lots of historical information—how much they set aside last quarter as a provision for loan losses; how much they have classified as "nonperforming loans," how much they were left with in the way of reserves; and so on. But, as investors have painfully learned, the historical information doesn't prevent surprise write-offs. Witness Bank of New England's unexpected $1.4 billion provision for loan losses in December 1989, or Valley National's $348 million provision for loan losses during 1989. Nor does it help investors assess the probability of further charge-offs this year or next.

\* \* \*

Viewing the sorry state of affairs, a growing group of banking industry leaders, among them Thomas Theobald, chairman of Continental Bank, support improving the banks' disclosure of their loan portfolios' quality. Christopher Snyder, president of New York's Loan Pricing Corp., a research firm specializing in banking, would do just that.

Snyder plans to ask the country's largest banks to rank the loans they have out-standing along a standardized nine-point scale of riskiness. Snyder will then compare the way the banks rank identical loans—to see if what is considered "minimal risk" by Bank A is considered to be "substandard" by Bank B. He will adjust the rankings of banks that tend to be consistently more optimistic or pessimistic than average, in order to make the rankings comparable.

In addition, the banks will be asked to report the rate of return they receive in each of the risk categories. All this information will be collected and published, bank by bank, once a quarter.

While no panacea for all that ails the American banking system, Snyder's proposal should go a long way toward helping the credit and equity markets more accurately assess an individual bank's financial standing. Suppose, for example, a bank has a pipeline of problem loans. That will become evident from a comparison of the bank's internal credit assessment scores for a few quarters. Investors could reasonably expect the bank's future loan losses to rise. Conversely, loan portfolio improvements could be detected earlier.

\* \* \*

*Source:* Dana Wechsler Linden, *Forbes,* Oct. 1, 1990, pp. 48, 50. Reprinted by permission of *Forbes* magazine. Copyright © 1990 by Forbes, Inc.

A bank's loans are the primary receivable on its balance sheet. As this article indicates, many banks have not adequately estimated their uncollectible loans and thus have understated loan "reserves" (allowance for uncollectible loans). The proposal described here would have banks not only disclose their expense and allowance amounts, but also provide information about how they rank loans according to risk and what interest rate they expect for each category of risk. This new information is expected to help investors better evaluate banks' future profitability.

## NOTES RECEIVABLE

Learning Objective **6**

Explain what notes receivable are

A **promissory note** is a written promise to a person or organization to pay a specific sum of money either on demand or at a specified future date. The person or organization that will receive payment calls this note a **note receivable.** The person who signs the note—the **maker**—calls it a *note payable.* The note is usually payable to the **payee** or an agent (such as a bank) designated by the payee. The *maturity value* of a note is the total amount that must be paid by the maker on the date when the note becomes due.

**Exhibit 4** An Interest-Bearing Note

| $10,000 | Lincoln, Nebraska | June 19, 1997 |
|---|---|---|

sixty days      after date      I      **promise to pay to**

**the order of**      Morgan Office Equipment Company

Ten Thousand and 00/100- - - - - - - - - - - - - - - - - - - - - - - - - - - - - - - - - - - - - - - - - dollars

**for value received with interest at**      9%

**payable at**    Creekside National Bank.

*Leigh Page,* Page Export Company

Notes may be *interest-bearing* or *non-interest-bearing.* An **interest-bearing note,** like the one shown in Exhibit 4, requires the maker to pay the face amount of the note *plus* interest. This interest, specified at an annual rate, is usually paid along with the principal on the maturity date of the note.

A **non-interest-bearing note** includes interest in the face amount specified as the note's value at maturity. For example, if you borrow $10,000 and give a non-interest-bearing note, the maker may require that the face value of the note be specified as $10,600. When the note is paid at maturity, you will pay the $10,600 face value of the note—$10,000 to repay what you borrowed and $600 for interest.

## Notes Receivable versus Accounts Receivable

Some companies prefer to sell on credit by accepting a customer's promissory note rather than maintaining an open account receivable for the customer. Let's examine the differences between notes receivable and accounts receivable and see why one might be preferred over the other.

Remember: An account receivable comes from an open credit arrangement in which the seller and the buyer have a contract providing that the buyer will pay the seller for any goods and services purchased within a specified time—typically 30, 60, or 90 days. The buyer hasn't agreed to pay any specific amount, but rather to pay for whatever is purchased. The buyer may later refuse to pay, claiming that no goods or services were received, that the quantity received was not that billed by the seller, that some goods were returned but his or her account was not credited, or that the quality was so poor that some adjustment should be made to the sales price. In short, there are many grounds for argument about the amount due to the seller.

A note receivable, however, has the advantage of being a written instrument defining specific terms of payment, signed by the buyer. The buyer must pay the amount shown on the face of the note—there can be no argument about conditions existing outside of what appears on the note itself. Of course, a buyer who has been wronged by the seller may sue the seller for relief. Such a lawsuit, however, is separate from the question of the payment of the note.

Another advantage of a note receivable is that it is a *negotiable instrument,* which means that the holder of the promised payment can sell that promise to someone else who is willing to buy it. Selling a note is called *discounting a note,* a process we will examine later in this chapter. In contrast, accounts receivable are not negotiable instruments; although they may be sold, the process is cumbersome and is usually done only for very large amounts.

Finally, notes are usually for a longer period and they bear interest. Accounts receivable are normally used where the credit period is short and no interest charge is made.

Notes, then, are preferable to accounts receivable because they represent a stronger claim, are negotiable instruments, are for longer terms, and bear interest. For these reasons many companies will accept a note receivable in payment of a past-due account receivable.

ASK YOURSELF ▶

1. What is a promissory note?
2. What is the difference between an interest-bearing note and a non-interest-bearing note?
3. What advantages does a note receivable have over an account receivable?

### Determining the Due Date of Notes

The note payable shown in Exhibit 4 does not list a specific due date; it merely states that the note is due 60 days after June 19. The due date, or maturity date, of such notes can be found by remembering one simple rule: *Don't count the first day* (June 19, the day the note was signed), *but do count the last day.* Count the number of days in each month until you reach 60 days; the sixtieth day is the due date:

| | |
|---|---:|
| June 20–June 30 . . . . . . . . . . . . . . . . . . . . . . . . . . . . . . . . . . . . . . . . . . . . | 11 days |
| July 1–July 31 . . . . . . . . . . . . . . . . . . . . . . . . . . . . . . . . . . . . . . . . . . . . . . | 31 days |
| Aug. 1–Aug. 18 . . . . . . . . . . . . . . . . . . . . . . . . . . . . . . . . . . . . . . . . . . . . . . | 18 days |
| Total . . . . . . . . . . . . . . . . . . . . . . . . . . . . . . . . . . . . . . . . . . . . . . . . . . . . . . | 60 days |

The due date of the Morgan Company's note receivable (Exhibit 4) is Aug. 18, 1997.

When a note's life is stated in terms of months, do not count days, even though the months have different numbers of days; just count the months from the day the note was signed. For example, a note signed on Feb. 1 and due in 4 months would mature on June 1; a note signed on Oct. 3 and due in 3 months would mature on Jan. 3.

### Determining Interest on Notes

Interest earned on notes receivable can be calculated by the simple interest formula:

$$\text{Interest} = \text{principal} \times \text{rate} \times \text{time}$$
$$I \quad = \quad P \quad \times R \times T$$

**where** principal = the face value of the note (excluding interest)

          rate = the interest rate specified on the face of the note (Interest rates are always stated as annual rates.)

          time = (1) the number of *days* for which interest is calculated divided by 360 (we're using 360 days for simplicity; most financial institutions use 365 days) *or*

                 (2) the number of *months* for which interest is calculated divided by 12

The interest due for the interest-bearing note payable to Morgan (Exhibit 4) is calculated as follows:

$$\textbf{Interest} = \textbf{principal} \times \textbf{rate} \times \textbf{time}$$

$$= \$10,000 \times .09 \times \frac{60}{360}$$

$$= \$900 \times \frac{60}{360}$$

$$= \$150$$

If Morgan's accounting year ended on July 31, an adjusting entry would be needed to record interest earned through that date:

$$\text{Interest} = \$10,000 \times .09 \times \text{time}$$

$$\text{Time} = 11 \text{ days in June (June 20–June 30)} + 31 \text{ days in July (July 1–July 31)}$$

$$= 42 \text{ days} \quad \text{(June 20–July 31)}$$

In calculating interest, don't count the first day (June 19), but do count the last day (July 31):

$$\text{Interest} = \$10,000 \times .09 \times \frac{42}{360}$$

$$= \$900 \times \frac{42}{360}$$

$$= \$105$$

Learning Objective  **7**  **Recording Notes and Interest**

Account for notes receivable

The Morgan Office Equipment Company example that follows will illustrate the recording of notes and interest.

# MORGAN OFFICE EQUIPMENT COMPANY

Morgan Office Equipment Company would record a note received from Page Export Company as follows:

JUNE 19  Morgan receives Page's $10,000 note in a sale transaction. If the note had been received in payment of an account receivable, the credit in the entry would have been to Accounts Receivable: Page. No interest is recorded on the note until it is earned (until the note has been held for a period of time).

| | | | |
|---|---|---|---|
| June 19 | Notes Receivable............................. | 10,000 | |
| | Sales...................................... | | 10,000 |
| | To record sale, 60-day, 9% note received. | | |

JULY 31  Since Morgan's fiscal year ends July 31, interest earned through that day, $105, is accrued. Interest receivable, $105, appears along with the notes receivable,

$10,000, under current assets on the July 31 balance sheet. The Interest Receivable account is carried forward into the next accounting year, when it will be collected. Interest income, $105, is shown as other income and expenses on the income statement for the year ended July 31, 1997. Interest Income is closed to Income Summary on July 31.

| | | | |
|---|---|---|---|
| July 31 | Interest Receivable . . . . . . . . . . . . . . . . . . . . . . . . . . . . | 105 | |
| | Interest Income. . . . . . . . . . . . . . . . . . . . . . . . . . . . . | | 105 |
| | To record interest earned on Page note. | | |

AUGUST 18  The full amount of the principal and interest are collected. The remaining $10,000 $\times$ .09 $\times$ $\frac{18}{360}$ = $45 interest earned is recorded. Note that Morgan has earned 42 days of interest, $105, before July 31; and 18 days of interest, $45, after July 31.

| | | | |
|---|---|---|---|
| Aug. 18 | Cash . . . . . . . . . . . . . . . . . . . . . . . . . . . . . . . . . . . . . . . | 10,150 | |
| | Notes Receivable . . . . . . . . . . . . . . . . . . . . . . . . . . | | 10,000 |
| | Interest Receivable . . . . . . . . . . . . . . . . . . . . . . . . . | | 105 |
| | Interest Income . . . . . . . . . . . . . . . . . . . . . . . . . . . . | | 45 |
| | To record receipt of principal and interest on Page note at maturity. | | |

## Dishonored Notes

A note that is not paid at maturity is a **dishonored note receivable.** When a note becomes dishonored, the holder transfers the record of it from Notes Receivable to Accounts Receivable. For example, assume that the Selmon Co. received a $2,000, 6% note due in 90 days from Helms, Inc., in payment of a past-due account receivable. At maturity Helms failed to pay the $2,000 plus $30 interest due.

| | | | |
|---|---|---|---|
| Day 1 | Notes Receivable . . . . . . . . . . . . . . . . . . . . . . . . . . . . | 2,000 | |
| | Accounts Receivable: Helms . . . . . . . . . . . . . . . . . . | | 2,000 |
| | To record receipt of $2,000, 6%, 90-day note in settlement of an account receivable. | | |
| | | | |
| Day 90 | Accounts Receivable: Helms . . . . . . . . . . . . . . . . . . . . | 2,030 | |
| | Interest Income. . . . . . . . . . . . . . . . . . . . . . . . . . . . . | | 30 |
| | Notes Receivable . . . . . . . . . . . . . . . . . . . . . . . . . . . | | 2,000 |
| | To record interest earned ($2,000 $\times$ .06 $\times$ 90/360) and dishonoring of note by Helms. | | |

Selmon records the $30 interest earned even though Helms did not pay. Selmon has allowed Helms the use of the $2,000 for 90 days and is entitled to the $30 interest charge for the 90 days of credit extended to Helms. Selmon's claim on day 90 is $2,030, not just the $2,000 face value of the note. Interest will continue to accrue on the past-due receivable. Some state laws allow the rate to increase to the maximum legal limit. The longer the maker of the note delays paying, the more he or she will owe the payee of the note.

The probability of collecting Helms' account receivable may be very low. This fact should be considered by Selmon's management in estimating uncollectible accounts expense at the end of the current year.

**ASK YOURSELF** ▶

1. **What is the simple rule for finding the specific due date of a note?**
2. **What is the formula for calculating the interest on a note?**
3. **What end-of-period adjusting entry is made to accrue interest earned on a note?**
4. **What is a dishonored note?**

## Discounting Notes Receivable

A holder of a note who needs cash before the note matures may take the note to a bank or other financial institution, which *discounts* it. **Discounting a note receivable** means simply that the bank "buys" the note from the holder, paying the holder an amount of cash that is normally less than the maturity value of the note, and then collects the maturity value from the maker at the maturity date. The difference between the amount that the payee receives from the bank and the maturity value of the note is the bank's fee for discounting the note. In effect, this difference is the interest the bank will earn instead of the payee.

The bank calculates its fee for accepting the note from the holder, the *discount,* by applying a discount rate to the maturity value of the note. This *discount rate* is really an interest rate charged by the bank for holding the note for the remainder of its life. The bank will determine its discount rate on the basis of such factors as the current market rate, the credit rating of the maker of the note, the term of the note, and whether the bank can collect from anyone else should the maker fail to pay at maturity.

What happens if the maker of the note fails to pay the bank at maturity? If the note was discounted **with recourse,** the bank will demand payment from the original payee. Discounting with recourse means that the bank requires the payee to agree to pay the amount of the note if the maker doesn't pay at maturity. If the note was discounted **without recourse,** the bank is stuck with the loss — so you can be sure that very few notes are ever discounted without recourse.

### Calculating the Proceeds upon Discounting a Note

Learning Objective **8**

Calculate the proceeds when discounting a note receivable

The cash received from a financial institution that discounts a note for the payee is called the **proceeds.** Proceeds are calculated by means of the following formulas:

1. **Maturity value = face value + interest for life of note**
2. **Discount = maturity value × discount rate × discount period**
3. **Proceeds = maturity value − discount**

Suppose that on Jan. 1, 1997, Evans Co. received a $5,000, 6-month, 6% note from Melrose, Inc. On May 1, 1997, the Village National Bank discounted the note for Evans with recourse and charged a 7% discount rate. The amount that Evans would receive from Village Bank is calculated as follows:

1. *Calculate the maturity value.* The maturity value is the face value of the note plus interest for its entire life. It's the amount Evans would receive if it held the note for its full 6-month life.

| | |
|---|---|
| Face value................................................ | $5,000 |
| Add: Interest for full life of note ($5,000 × .06 × $\frac{6}{12}$) .................... | 150 |
| Maturity value .......................................... | $5,150 |

**2.** *Calculate the discount.* The discount is the amount the financial institution deducts *from the maturity value.* It's the amount the bank charges for holding the note from the day it is discounted until the day it matures. To calculate the discount, multiply the *maturity value* by the discount rate.

| | |
|---|---:|
| Maturity value. . . . . . . . . . . . . . . . . . . . . . . . . . . . . . . . . . . . . . . . . . . | $5,150.00 |
| × Discount rate . . . . . . . . . . . . . . . . . . . . . . . . . . . . . . . . . . . . . . . . . . | × .07 |
| × Discount period = May 1–July 1 = 2 months . . . . . . . . . . . . . . . . . . . | × $\frac{2}{12}$ |
| Discount. . . . . . . . . . . . . . . . . . . . . . . . . . . . . . . . . . . . . . . . . . . . . . . . . | $ 60.08 |

**3.** *Calculate the proceeds* by subtracting the discount from the maturity value.

| | |
|---|---:|
| Maturity value . . . . . . . . . . . . . . . . . . . . . . . . . . . . . . . . . . . . . . . . . . . . | $5,150.00 |
| Less: Discount . . . . . . . . . . . . . . . . . . . . . . . . . . . . . . . . . . . . . . . . . . . | (60.08) |
| Proceeds. . . . . . . . . . . . . . . . . . . . . . . . . . . . . . . . . . . . . . . . . . . . . . . . | $5,089.92 |

Notes whose maturity is stated in days rather than months require a slight modification in the calculations of interest and discount. If the Melrose note were a "180-day" rather than a "6-month" note, for example, the interest and discount calculations would be as follows:

Interest for full life of note: $5,000 \times .06 \times \frac{180}{360} = \$150$

Discount: $5,150 \times .07 \times \frac{60}{360} = \$60.08$

### Entries Related to Discounting a Note

Learning Objective **9**

Prepare entries needed to record discounted notes

Evans's entries related to the Melrose note would be as follows:

| | | | |
|---|---|---:|---:|
| Jan. 1 | Notes Receivable . . . . . . . . . . . . . . . . . . . . . . . . . . . . | 5,000.00 | |
| | Sales . . . . . . . . . . . . . . . . . . . . . . . . . . . . . . . . | | 5,000.00 |
| | To record sale to Melrose, and receipt of a 6-month, 6% note. | | |
| | | | |
| May 1 | Cash . . . . . . . . . . . . . . . . . . . . . . . . . . . . . . . . . . . . | 5,089.92 | |
| | Notes Receivable. . . . . . . . . . . . . . . . . . . . . . . . . | | 5,000.00 |
| | Interest Income . . . . . . . . . . . . . . . . . . . . . . . . . . . | | 89.92 |
| | To record discounting the Melrose note at the Village National Bank. | | |

The $89.92 is the net amount of interest earned by Evans after the bank has deducted its fee for discounting the note. Sometimes the bank will pay less than the face value of a note when it is discounted. A financing expense may occur, for example, when the bank's discount rate is higher than the interest rate on the note and the discount period is relatively long in relation to the life of the note. When this happens, it is necessary to debit Financing Expense instead of crediting Interest Income.

The fact that the Village Bank discounted the note with recourse means that Evans has a *contingent liability,* a potential obligation to pay the maturity value of the note if Melrose, Inc., fails to do so. Contingent liabilities should be shown on the balance sheet or in the accompanying notes.

If Melrose dishonors the note, Evans's contingent liability will become a real obligation. Evans will have to pay the full maturity value, $5,150, and possibly a service charge as well. Assuming that Melrose dishonors the note and Evans pays the $5,150 plus a $25 service charge, Evans would make the following entry:

| | | | |
|---|---|---|---|
| July 2 | Accounts Receivable: Melrose . . . . . . . . . . . . . . . . . . . . | 5,175 | |
| | Cash . . . . . . . . . . . . . . . . . . . . . . . . . . . . . . . . . . . | | 5,175 |
| | To record payment to bank on note discounted at the bank and dishonored by Melrose. | | |

Evans still has a claim against Melrose for the maturity value of the note, the service fee, and additional interest that will continue to accrue. Notice that Evans recorded no interest income on July 2. This is because Evans has earned no interest since May 1, the date the note was discounted; it was the bank that earned the May and June interest. Evans also did not record the $25 bank charge as a service fee expense. This fee is ultimately the responsibility of Melrose, and Melrose will record the expense.

**ASK YOURSELF ▶**

1. **What does it mean to discount a note?**
2. **How does discounting a note with recourse differ from discounting without recourse?**
3. **What are the three steps involved in calculating the proceeds of a discounted note?**

## RECEIVABLES FROM OFFICERS AND OWNERS

Occasionally a business firm will lend available cash to its owners or to its managers for their personal use. After all, if a firm has surplus cash and is expected to put it to use earning income, it can accomplish this by making interest-earning loans to its owners and managers. In some cases these loans are represented by formal instruments, such as promissory notes; in other cases they exist only in the form of verbal agreements. Most accountants believe that while these agreements may be entirely proper, it is best to identify such receivables separately on the balance sheet—specifying them as loans to owners, managers, or officers of the company. This disclosure will highlight the fact that the business has entered into a transaction with a party who is closely related to it. Readers of the balance sheet will then be fully informed of the loan and may investigate the circumstances surrounding the transaction if they so desire.

## EXTERNAL CREDIT CARD SALES

Learning Objective **10**

Prepare entries used by a retailer to account for sales when the customer uses a credit card

Most retailers today make sales to customers by accepting credit cards such as VISA, MasterCard, Discover, American Express, and Diners' Club. Each of these credit cards represents credit provided by an organization—a credit card company or bank—external to both the customer and the retailer. Thus, this form of credit is sometimes referred to as **external credit.**

A customer making a purchase with a credit card signs a standard form agreeing to pay to the credit card company or bank the amount of the sale. The retailer sends this form to the credit card company or bank, which in turn sends the amount of the credit sale (less a fee) to the retailer.

The credit card company or bank charges the retailer a fee for providing credit to the customer. The fee is commonly a percentage of the amount of credit—the sales price of the product or service—provided. For this fee, the credit card company not only provides the credit but also assumes the costs of doing so, including credit investigation, recordkeeping, billing, and uncollectible account losses.

Accounting for credit card sales takes two basic forms, depending on whether the credit card is issued by a bank (VISA or MasterCard) or by a credit card company (American Express or Diners' Club). When the credit card is issued by a bank, the retailer will have an account with the bank. As soon as the credit card sales forms are received by the bank, the appropriate amount of cash is added to the retailer's account. The credit card sales forms are treated almost like checks. Accounting for bank credit cards is demonstrated in the following example.

Buckeye Stores has an agreement with Riverside National Bank, which issues Global Credit cards. When Buckeye remits credit card sales forms to Riverside National Bank's Global Credit division, a 4% fee is deducted from the gross sale amount and the balance is added to Buckeye's checking account at the Riverside National Bank. Since Buckeye receives the cash almost instantly, the retailer debits cash as soon as the sale is made. On Aug. 1, Buckeye has charge sales of $10,000 and makes the following journal entry:

| 1997 | | | |
|---|---|---|---|
| Aug. 1 | Cash ....................................... | 9,600 | |
| | Financing Expense............................. | 400 | |
| | Sales ..................................... | | 10,000 |
| | To record sales less a financing expense of $400 ($10,000 × 4%). The credit card sales forms have been remitted to the Riverside National Bank. | | |

No receivable is created for credit cards issued by banks. The credit card sales forms are sent in each day; the bank processes these immediately and adds the appropriate amount to the retailer's checking account.

Let's look at the same illustration assuming that the Global Credit card is issued by a separate company, *not* a bank. Buckeye will still send the credit card sales forms to Global Credit Card Company, Global will still charge a fee (we'll assume 4%), but Buckeye will have to wait several days for the company to send a check for the appropriate amount. During this waiting period a receivable account is created. In this case, Buckeye would make the following entries:

| 1997 | | | |
|---|---|---|---|
| Aug. 1 | Receivable from Global Credit..................... | 9,600 | |
| | Financing Expense............................. | 400 | |
| | Sales ..................................... | | 10,000 |
| | To record sales less a financing expense of $400 ($10,000 × 4%). The credit card sales forms have been remitted to Global Credit for reimbursement. | | |
| 5 | Cash ....................................... | 9,600 | |
| | Receivable from Global Credit ................. | | 9,600 |
| | To record cash received from credit card company. | | |

**ASK YOURSELF** ▶

1. Why are receivables from officers and owners shown separately on the balance sheet?
2. How does accounting for credit card sales differ when the card is issued by a bank rather than by a credit card company?

## SUMMARY

- When customers buy on credit, the seller's accounting records show this transaction as an **account receivable,** also referred to as an *open account* or *trade receivable.*
- All credit sales are posted to the Accounts Receivable control account in the general ledger and the individual customers' accounts in a subsidiary ledger. The total of all the subsidiary ledger accounts must agree with the balance in the control account.
- When customers fail to pay, the seller has uncollectible accounts expense. The **direct write-off method** recognizes uncollectible accounts expense only when a specific customer's account is deemed to be uncollectible. This method is not in accordance with GAAP because it does not properly match expenses and revenues and because it distorts the measurement of the amount of accounts receivable.
- Estimates of uncollectible accounts may be made using the **percentage of credit sales method** or the **aging of receivables method.** These methods recognize uncollectible accounts expense before a specific customer's account is identified as being uncollectible.
- The percentage of credit sales method is sometimes called the *income statement approach* because it yields the amount of uncollectible accounts expense that will be shown on the income statement. This method calculates the portion of the current year's credit sales that is expected to be uncollectible.
- The aging of receivables method is sometimes called the *balance sheet approach* because it yields the amount of allowance for uncollectibles that is needed on the balance sheet. This method calculates the portion of the receivables balance that is expected to be uncollectible.
- The Accounts Receivable Turnover and Average Age of Receivables ratios are indicators of how quickly a company's receivables are converted into the cash required for operations and debt repayment.
- Promissory notes are recorded as notes receivable. They are often used as a way of offering credit when a sale is made or as a way of formally extending the length of the credit period when an account receivable is past due.
- **Promissory notes** are written promises to pay. The promise may specify either a face amount (the principal) and interest separately, or only a face amount that includes principal and interest.
- When the **maker** of a note fails to pay at maturity, the note is *dishonored.* The **payee** changes the account from a note receivable to an account receivable and, of course, continues to try to collect.
- Promissory notes may be either held until maturity or discounted at a bank prior to maturity. When a note is discounted **with recourse,** the payee is responsible for paying the bank at maturity if the maker dishonors the note. A note that is discounted **without recourse** carries no such obligation.
- Receivables from officers and owners—a firm's loans to its officers and owners—are identified on the balance sheet separately from other receivables. This is done to inform readers that transactions have occurred between the business and individuals who are closely related to it.
- Many retailers rely on **external credit**—credit card plans—to provide credit for their customers. Credit card companies normally charge a fee that is a percentage of the sales price for assuming all the risks and costs of providing credit.

## 11 KEY TERMS

| | |
|---|---|
| **Accounts receivable** | Claims against customers for goods or services sold on credit. These claims are not supported by formal written promises to pay specific amounts, but rather are based on agreement by the buyer to pay for goods or services purchased. Also called an **open account** or a **trade receivable.** |
| **Accounts receivable turnover** | Credit sales divided by average accounts receivable. |
| **Aging of receivables method** | A method of calculating the amount of uncollectible accounts and uncollectible accounts expense on the basis of the age of uncollected accounts; also called the **balance sheet approach.** |
| **Average age of receivables** | 365 days divided by accounts receivable turnover. |
| **Bad debts expense** | See **uncollectible accounts expense.** |
| **Direct write-off method** | A method of accounting for uncollectible receivables in which the uncollectible accounts expense is recognized only when the company knows which specific customer's accounts are uncollectible. This method requires no estimate of uncollectible accounts expense and is not generally accepted accounting practice because it fails to match expenses and revenues and to properly measure the amount of receivables. |
| **Discounting a note receivable** | The process of "selling" a note receivable before its maturity date for a cash value less than its maturity value. |
| **Dishonored note receivable** | A promissory note that the maker fails to pay on the maturity date. |
| **External credit** | Credit advanced by a third party, such as a credit card company or a bank, to enable a customer to make a credit purchase from a retailer. |
| **Interest-bearing note** | A promissory note requiring repayment of principal plus interest at a specified annual rate. |
| **Maker** | An individual who signs a promissory note, agreeing to pay a specified amount at maturity. |
| **Non-interest-bearing note** | A promissory note that includes interest in the face amount specified as the note's maturity value. |
| **Note receivable** | A promissory note held by the person or business entity that will receive payment under the terms of the note. |
| **Payee** | The individual or company specified to receive payment at the maturity date of a promissory note. |
| **Percentage of credit sales method** | A method of calculating uncollectible accounts expense, based on the total credit sales made during a period; also called the **income statement approach.** |
| **Proceeds** | The amount of cash received for a discounted promissory note. The proceeds are less than the maturity value, and the difference is the discount amount. |
| **Promissory note** | A written promise to pay a specific sum of money on demand or at a specified future time. |
| **Uncollectible accounts expense** | The amount of accounts receivable that will never be collected. Also called **bad debts expense.** |
| **With recourse** | A stipulation in discounting a note receivable which provides that the individual discounting the note will be responsible for paying the maturity value should the maker fail to pay. |
| **Without recourse** | A stipulation in discounting a note receivable which provides that only the maker is responsible for paying the maturity value of the note. |

## DEMONSTRATION PROBLEM

The Razor Corp. balance sheet on Dec. 31, 1997, shows the following receivables:

| | | |
|---|---:|---:|
| Notes Receivable . . . . . . . . . . . . . . . . . . . . . . . . . . . . . . . . . . . | | $ 25,000 |
| Accounts Receivable . . . . . . . . . . . . . . . . . . . . . . . . . . . . . . . | $350,000 | |
| Less: Allowance for Uncollectible Accounts . . . . . . . . . . . . . . | 6,500 | 343,500 |

During January 1998, the following events and transactions occurred:

a. During January, credit sales totaled $50,000.

b. During January, $150,000 was collected on account.

c. During January, $7,200 of accounts receivable were written off as uncollectible.

d. On Jan. 31, one account for $200 which had been written off earlier in the month was collected from the customer.

e. On Jan. 31, a $10,000, 12% note was discounted with recourse at the Merchant's Bank. The 3-month note had been received on Dec. 31, 1997, and matures on Mar. 31, 1998. The bank charged a 15% discount rate.

f. On Jan. 31, interest was accrued on a $15,000, 10% note. The note had been received on Dec. 31.

g. On Jan. 31, an aging schedule was prepared. This schedule estimates that $5,900 of accounts receivable will be uncollectible.

**Required:**

1. Prepare entries to record the events and transactions listed.
2. Prepare the balance sheet disclosure of receivables on Jan. 31, 1998.

### ■ Solution to Demonstration Problem

1. *Entries*

| | | | | |
|---|---|---|---:|---:|
| Jan. 1–31 | Accounts Receivable . . . . . . . . . . . . . . . . . . . . . . | | 50,000 | |
| | | Sales . . . . . . . . . . . . . . . . . . . . . . . . . . . . . . . . | | 50,000 |
| | To record credit sales for January. | | | |
| 1–31 | Cash . . . . . . . . . . . . . . . . . . . . . . . . . . . . . . . . . . | | 150,000 | |
| | | Accounts Receivable . . . . . . . . . . . . . . . . . | | 150,000 |
| | To record collections on account for January. | | | |
| 1–31 | Allowance for Uncollectible Accounts . . . . . . . . . . | | 7,200 | |
| | | Accounts Receivable . . . . . . . . . . . . . . . . . | | 7,200 |
| | To record accounts written off as uncollectible in January. | | | |
| Jan. 31 | Accounts Receivable . . . . . . . . . . . . . . . . . . . . . . | | 200 | |
| | | Allowance for Uncollectible Accounts . . . . . . | | 200 |
| | To reinstate an account previously written off. | | | |
| 31 | Cash . . . . . . . . . . . . . . . . . . . . . . . . . . . . . . . . . . | | 200 | |
| | | Accounts Receivable . . . . . . . . . . . . . . . . . | | 200 |
| | To record collection from customer. | | | |

*(Continued)*

Jan. 31 Cash................................... 10,042.50
     Interest Income....................... 42.50
     Notes Receivable ..................... 10,000.00
  To record discounting of note with recourse.

*Calculations:*

| | |
|---|---|
| Face value.................. | $10,000.00 |
| Interest ($10,000 $\times$ 12% $\times \frac{3}{12}$).. | 300.00 |
| Maturity value ............... | $10,300.00 |
| Discount ($10,300 $\times$ 15% $\times \frac{2}{12}$). | (257.50) |
| Proceeds................... | $10,042.50 |

31 Interest Receivable ...................... 125
     Interest Income....................... 125
  To accrue interest on $15,000 note.
  ($15,000 $\times$ 10% $\times \frac{1}{12}$ = $125)

31 Uncollectible Accounts Expense.............. 6,400
     Allowance for Uncollectible Accounts ...... 6,400
  To record uncollectible accounts expense for
  January. ($6,500 − $7,200 + $200 = $500 debit
  balance; $500 debit balance + $5,900 = $6,400
  expense)

2. *Balance sheet disclosure:*

| | | |
|---|---|---|
| Notes Receivable ............................................. | | $ 15,000 |
| Accounts Receivable................................. | $242,800 | |
| Less: Allowance for Uncollectible Accounts ................. | 5,900 | 236,900 |
| Interest Receivable........................................... | | 125 |

## QUESTIONS FOR REVIEW AND FURTHER THOUGHT

### REVIEW QUESTIONS

1. What is an account receivable? How does an account receivable differ from a trade receivable or an open account?

2. What is the purpose of reconciling general and subsidiary accounts receivable ledgers?

3. What are the two major objections to the use of the direct write-off method of accounting for uncollectible accounts?

4. Under what circumstances is it necessary to reinstate a customer's account?

5. Does the percentage of credit sales method of estimating uncollectible accounts violate the matching principle? Explain.

6. Why is the percentage of credit sales method sometimes called the income statement approach? Why is the aging of receivables method sometimes called the balance sheet approach?

7. What is the purpose of aging receivables?

8. Lewis Co.'s accounting department has determined that over the past 5 years uncollectible accounts expense has been too high by $4,200. What will Lewis do to correct this error in estimating?

9. What is the difference between an account receivable and a note receivable?

10. What is a dishonored note receivable?

11. Tribco, Inc., can discount a customer's note at the bank "with recourse" or "without recourse." What is the difference? Which will Tribco prefer?

12. What special treatment is given receivables from officers and owners of a company? Why is this special treatment necessary?

13. What is external credit?

### QUESTIONS FOR FURTHER THOUGHT

1. When uncollectible accounts expense is estimated, a contra asset, Allowance for Uncollectible Accounts, is credited. Why isn't Accounts Receivable credited instead?

2. A customer pays an account after it has been written off as uncollectible. Why is it necessary to reinstate the account (debit Accounts Receivable) and then record the payment (credit Accounts Receivable) instead of just debiting Cash and crediting Allowance for Uncollectible Accounts for the amount received?

3. When the aging of receivables method is used, why is it necessary to consider the balance in Allowance for Uncollectible Accounts in determining the current Uncollectible Accounts Expense?

4. On Dec. 31, 1998, before Uncollectible Accounts Expense is recorded, Allowance for Uncollectible Accounts has a $2,200 *debit* balance. Explain how it is possible for the allowance account to have a debit balance.

5. Is it true that no interest is earned when a non-interest-bearing note is held?

6. Why might a company prefer to hold a note receivable from a customer rather than an account receivable?

7. If notes are preferable to accounts receivable, why do companies use accounts receivable at all?

8. Jones discounts Zack's note with recourse at a bank. Zack dishonors the note. The maturity value of the note is $6,360, but Jones is required to pay the bank $6,385. Explain.

9. Clyde Co.'s average age of receivables is 35 days. What additional information is necessary before this average can be evaluated as relatively good or bad?

## OBJECTIVE ASSIGNMENT

*True/False*   Indicate whether each statement below is *true* or *false* by placing a *T* or an *F* in the space provided.

_____ 1. The direct write-off method is not used by most large companies because it does not match expenses with revenues very well and because it produces a distorted measure of the amount of accounts receivable on the balance sheet.

_____ 2. The percentage of credit sales method is sometimes referred to as the balance sheet approach because it calculates the amount of Allowance for Uncollectible Accounts needed on the balance sheet.

_____ 3. The aging of receivables method ignores the balance in Allowance for Uncollectible Accounts when calculating uncollectible accounts expense for the period.

_____ 4. A dishonored note is one that the maker has failed to pay at maturity.

_____ 5. No contingent liability exists when a note receivable is discounted without recourse.

*Multiple Choice*   Select the best choice to complete each statement or answer each question below. Write the letter corresponding to your choice in the space provided.

_____ 1. The following journal entry was prepared by Duraco:

| | | |
|---|---|---|
| Allowance for Uncollectible Accounts . . . . . . . . . . . . . . . | 400 | |
|     Accounts Receivable: H. Weinstein . . . . . . . . . . . . . | | 400 |

The purpose of this entry was to:
a. Reinstate an account receivable
b. Recognize uncollectible accounts expense for a period
c. Write off an account as uncollectible
d. Record payment of an account

_____ 2. On Dec. 31, 1998, Valiant Co.'s Allowance for Uncollectible Accounts has a debit balance of $4,000. The aging of receivables schedule for 1998 states that $7,500 of accounts are expected to be uncollectible. Valiant's uncollectible accounts expense for 1998 is:
a. $11,500    c. $4,000
b. $7,500    d. $3,500

_____ 3. Thorpe Co. began operations in November 1998. On Dec. 31, 1998, $4,600 of uncollectible accounts expense was recorded using the percentage of credit sales method. During 1999, $3,900 of accounts were written off, $100 of accounts were reinstated, and $6,200 of uncollectible accounts expense was recorded. On Dec. 31, 1999, Allowance for Uncollectible Accounts should have a credit balance of:
a. $2,200    c. $7,000
b. $6,800    d. $14,600

_____ 4. Which of the following entries would require a posting to the accounts receivable subsidiary ledger?
a. Entry to record a sale on account
b. Entry to write off an uncollectible account
c. Entry to reinstate an account receivable
d. All of the above

_____ 5. One feature that makes a promissory note preferable to an open account is that:
   a. The amount of a note can change as the customer buys additional merchandise.
   b. A note is a negotiable instrument, so it can be sold more easily than an account receivable.
   c. Complicated interest calculations can be avoided, because notes do not usually bear interest.
   d. The term of a note is limited to a maximum of 90 days.

_____ 6. On Nov. 12, Apex, Inc., receives a note that matures in 45 days. The maturity date will be:
   a. Dec. 17       c. Dec. 27
   b. Dec. 26       d. Dec. 31

_____ 7. Site Co. receives a $10,000, 8% note, due in 90 days. The maturity value of this note is:
   a. $10,000       c. $10,400
   b. $10,200       d. $10,800

_____ 8. Valley, Inc., has a note with a maturity value of $12,500. Valley discounts the note at a bank. The bank charges a 12% discount rate and will hold the note for 3 months. What is the amount of the discount charged by the bank?
   a. $375          c. $750
   b. $500          d. $1,500

_____ 9. Keystone received a $1,000, 6%, 120-day note. After holding the note for 30 days, Keystone discounted the note with recourse. If the maker of the note fails to pay the bank at maturity, Keystone must pay the bank:
   a. $0            c. $1,015
   b. $1,000        d. $1,020

_____ 10. Mulberry accepts a note from Ferndale, Inc. Mulberry has a contingent liability when:
   a. The note is accepted from Ferndale.
   b. Ferndale's note matures.
   c. The note is discounted without recourse.
   d. The note is discounted with recourse.

## EXERCISES

2† **Exercise 1:** Preparing Entries to Write off and Reinstate an Account

Duragreen Sod Co. sold $56,500 of turf to Best Athletic Fields Co. during 1998. When Best had not paid by Aug. 5, 1998, Duragreen decided to write off the account as uncollectible. On Nov. 2, 1998, a check arrived from Best paying the account in full. Prepare the entries to write off the account, to reinstate the account, and to record the receipt of the $56,500. Duragreen estimates its uncollectible accounts expense; it does not use the direct write-off method.

**Exercise 2:** Calculating Uncollectible Accounts Expense
Using Three Methods

Calculate Dask Co.'s uncollectible accounts expense for 1998 under each of the three methods discussed in this chapter. The following information is available:

Total sales during the year. . . . . . . . . . . . . . . . . . $800,000
Total credit sales during the year. . . . . . . . . . . . .    720,000
Total accounts written off during the year . . . . . .     12,000

a. What is Dask's uncollectible accounts expense under the direct write-off method?
b. What is Dask's uncollectible accounts expense under the percentage of credit sales method? Dask estimates that 2.5% of credit sales will prove uncollectible.
c. What is Dask's uncollectible accounts expense under the aging of receivables method? The aging schedule estimates that $35,400 of accounts receivable will prove uncollectible; before the entry to record uncollectible accounts is prepared, Allowance for Uncollectible Accounts has a credit balance of $4,000.

▶ *(Check Figure: Uncollectible accounts expense under aging of receivables method = $31,400)*

4 **Exercise 3:** Calculating Uncollectible Accounts Expense Using the Aging
of Receivables Method

Reck, Inc., uses the aging of receivables method to calculate uncollectible accounts expense. The 1998 aging schedule indicates that $90,000 of accounts will be uncollectible. Immediately before Reck prepares the uncollectible accounts expense entry, Accounts Receivable has a debit balance of $1,068,000 and Allowance for Uncollectible Accounts has a debit balance of $5,000. How much is Reck's uncollectible accounts expense for 1998?

▶ *(Check Figure: Uncollectible accounts expense = $95,000)*

5 **Exercise 4:** Calculating Receivables Ratios

You have been assigned the task of evaluating Jesup, Inc.'s, management of receivables. You decide that accounts receivable turnover, and average age of receivables statistics will prove valuable in your analysis.
      The following data are available from Jesup's annual report:

Accounts Receivable:
      Jan. 1. . . . . . . . . . . . . . . . . . . . . . . . . . . . .    250,000
      Dec. 31 . . . . . . . . . . . . . . . . . . . . . . . . . .     297,000
Cash Sales . . . . . . . . . . . . . . . . . . . . . . . . . . .   1,000,000
Total Sales . . . . . . . . . . . . . . . . . . . . . . . . . . .   5,100,000
Jesup's Credit Terms . . . . . . . . . . . . . . . . . . .   Net 30 days

a. Calculate accounts receivable turnover, and average age of receivables.
b. In your opinion, is Jesup doing a good job of managing receivables? Explain.

      ▶ *(Check Figure: Accounts receivable turnover = 15 times)*

† The numbers in the margin refer to the Learning Objectives.

7  **Exercise 5:** Calculating Due Dates and Interest on Notes Receivable

Tweed Co. has the following notes receivable:

| Maker's Name | Date of Note | Face Amount | Term of Note | Interest Rate |
|---|---|---|---|---|
| W. Buhl | Apr. 1 | $4,000 | 60 days | 9% |
| O. DeWitt | July 17 | $9,000 | 45 days | 12% |
| L. Maltry | Sept. 4 | $2,500 | 120 days | 10% |

a. Calculate the due date of each note.
b. Calculate the total interest for the life of each note.

▶ *(Check Figure: Maltry note matures on Jan. 2)*

7  **Exercise 6:** Preparing Entries for a Note Receivable

During 1998, Carnes Kitchen Cabinets entered into the following transactions with Solomon Homebuilders:

June 15   Carnes received a $12,000, 10%, 90-day note from Solomon for a set of country-style cabinets.

30   Carnes's accounting year ends.

Sept. 13   Carnes received payment in full from Solomon.

Prepare the proper journal entry for Carnes on each of the three dates. Show supporting calculations.

▶ *(Check Figure: Interest income recorded on June 30 = $50)*

7  **Exercise 7:** Preparing Entries for a Note Receivable Dishonored

On Mar. 1, 1998, Society Fabrics accepted a $8,400, 11%, 120-day note from Sun Designs Co. in settlement of Sun's past-due account receivable. When the note matured on June 29, Sun failed to pay. Society hopes to collect from Sun in the near future. Prepare the proper entries to record the receipt of the note on Mar. 1 and the dishonoring of the note on June 29.

▶ *(Check Figure: Interest income recorded on June 29 = $308)*

8  **Exercise 8:** Calculating the Proceeds from Discounting Notes

Solar Products, Inc., accepted two notes from customers in settlement of past-due accounts receivable. Needing cash desperately, Solar took the notes to Lakewood Bank and discounted them with recourse. The bank charged a 12% discount rate. Information about each note follows:

| Face Value | Interest Rate | Term of Note | Time Solar Held Note |
|---|---|---|---|
| $24,000 | 10% | 120 days | 30 days |
| $10,000 | 9% | 90 days | 60 days |

Calculate the proceeds that Solar will receive from each discounted note.

▶ *(Check Figure: Proceeds from discounting $24,000 note = $24,056)*

10  **Exercise 9:** Preparing Entries for Credit Card Sales

Lyn's Fashions accepts credit cards issued by World Credit Card Company. Lyn's agreement with World is that World will withhold 5% of gross sales charged on World cards and remit the balance to Lyn within 10 days. On Feb. 1, Lyn sold $3,000 of goods on the World Card and remitted the credit card sales forms to World. On Feb. 11, Lyn received a check from World. World cards are not issued by a bank. Prepare entries needed by Lyn's Fashions on Feb. 1 and Feb. 11.

▶ *(Check Figure: Financing expense recorded on Feb. 1 = $150)*

## PROBLEMS: SET A

2† **Problem A1:** Preparing Entries for Accounts Receivable
and Uncollectible Accounts

Century Office Supply opened for business on Nov. 1, 1998. The information below describes
selected transactions that occurred during 1998 and 1999:

**1998**

| | |
|---|---|
| Nov. 1–Dec. 31 | Century's cash sales amounted to $40,000; credit sales totaled $120,000. (Prepare one entry to record the entire year's sales.) |
| Nov. 1–Dec. 31 | Century collected 60% of the total sales on account. (Prepare one entry to record the entire year's collections.) |
| Dec. 31 | Century estimated that uncollectible accounts for the year would amount to about $2,400. Century does not use the direct write-off method. |

**1999**

| | |
|---|---|
| Jan. 5 | Century wrote off the $156 account of Dee Ceased as uncollectible. |
| Apr. 22 | The $75 account of B. Hank Rupp was written off as uncollectible. |
| June 10 | A check was received from Rupp in full settlement of his account. |
| Jan.–Dec | Various other individual accounts amounting to $1,268 were written off. (Prepare one entry to record all these write-offs.) |
| Jan.–Dec. | Total sales were $480,000: 88% on account, the remainder for cash. |
| Jan.–Dec. | Total other cash collections on account were $320,000. |
| Dec. 31 | Century estimated uncollectible accounts expense for 1999 to be $8,448. |

**Required:**

1. Prepare general journal entries to record the transactions described above.
2. Calculate the balance of Accounts Receivable and Allowance for Uncollectible Accounts on
   Dec. 31, 1999.

   ▶ *(Check Figure: Balance of Allowance for Uncollectible Accounts, Dec. 31, 1999 = $9,424)*

1 3 4 5 **Problem A2:** Calculating Uncollectible Accounts Expense
Using Three Methods

An examination of the financial records of Tanner Marine Accessories reveals the following
facts:

a. Sales for 1998 were $650,000; 98% of sales were on credit.
b. Allowance for Uncollectible Accounts had a credit balance of $9,990 on Jan. 1, 1998.
c. During 1998, Tanner wrote off $8,800 of customer accounts as uncollectible.

**Required:**

1. Calculate uncollectible accounts expense for 1998 under the direct write-off method.
2. Calculate uncollectible accounts expense for 1998 under the percentage of credit sales
   method. Management estimates that 1.75% of credit sales will prove uncollectible.
3. Calculate uncollectible accounts expense for 1998 under the aging of receivables method.
   An aging schedule prepared on Dec. 31 indicates that accounts totaling $11,750 will be
   uncollectible.
4. Assuming the aging of receivables method is used, and that Accounts Receivable (gross)
   has a balance of $56,990 on January 1, 1998 and $68,750 on December 31, 1998, calculate
   Tanner Marine's accounts receivable turnover and average age of receivables.

   ▶ *(Check Figure: Uncollectible accounts expense under the percentage of credit sales method =
   $11,148)*

---

† The numbers in the margin refer to the Learning Objectives.

4   **Problem A3:** Calculating and Recording Uncollectible Accounts Expense Using an Aging Schedule

Plesser Gourmet Catering has the following uncollected accounts receivable on Dec. 31, 1998:

| Customer Name | Amount | Collection Status |
|---|---|---|
| Mosley Advertising | $2,775 | 15 days past due |
| Buckner Public Relations | 5,600 | Not yet due |
| Stevens Developments | 4,462 | Not yet due |
| Spivey Legal Service | 600 | 130 days past due |
| Murphy Wedding Chapel | 5,013 | 45 days past due |
| Waters Gallery | 162 | 98 days past due |
| Ezelle Sports Promotions | 1,938 | Not yet due |
| Jacob Bookkeeping Service | 762 | 103 days past due |
| Geiger & Geiger, Inc. | 4,300 | 75 days past due |
| Bidwell Clinic | 5,263 | Not yet due |
| Van Zant Jewelry | 3,625 | 105 days past due |
| Hutson Automotive | 1,812 | 8 days past due |
| Eller Stereo, Inc. | 1,276 | 240 days past due |
| Cooke Boutique | 3,100 | Not yet due |
| Parsons Mortgage Brokers | 1,050 | 90 days past due |
| Moore Party Planners | 312 | 80 days past due |
| Knipe Trucking Co. | 625 | Not yet due |
| Pricher Bakery | 2,500 | 40 days past due |

Plesser uses an aging schedule to prepare an estimate of uncollectible accounts for the year. Estimates of the percentage uncollectible in each category of the schedule are as follows:

| | |
|---|---|
| Not yet due . . . . . . . . . . . . . . . . . . . . . . . . . . . . . . . . . . . | 2% |
| 1–60 days past due . . . . . . . . . . . . . . . . . . . . . . . . . . | 5% |
| 61–90 days past due . . . . . . . . . . . . . . . . . . . . . . . . . | 10% |
| 91–120 days past due . . . . . . . . . . . . . . . . . . . . . . . . | 40% |
| Over 120 days past due . . . . . . . . . . . . . . . . . . . . . . | 85% |

**Required:**

1. Prepare an aging schedule and an estimate of the total amount expected to be uncollectible. Round the total estimate to the nearest dollar.
2. Prepare an adjusting entry to record uncollectible accounts expense on Dec. 31, 1998. Allowance for Uncollectible Accounts has a credit balance before adjustment of $1,188.
3. Prepare an adjusting entry to record uncollectible accounts expense on Dec. 31, 1998, assuming that Allowance for Uncollectible Accounts has a debit balance before adjustment of $83.

   ▶ *(Check Figure: Balance needed in Allowance for Uncollectible Accounts = $5,005)*

7   **Problem A4:** Preparing Basic Notes Receivable Entries

Fabian Engines, Inc., has an account receivable from Turtle Mowers in the amount of $40,000. Being temporarily short of cash, Turtle proposes to give Fabian a 120-day note to settle the account. Fabian agrees, and the 12% note is signed on Aug. 31, 1998. Fabian's accounting year ends on Sept. 30.

**Required:**

1. Prepare Fabian's journal entries on Aug. 31, Sept. 30, and Dec. 29, assuming that Turtle pays the note when due. Show supporting calculations.
2. Prepare Fabian's journal entries on Aug. 31, Sept. 30, and Dec. 29, assuming that Turtle dishonors the note.

   ▶ *(Check Figure: Interest income recorded on Dec. 29 = $1,200)*

8 9 **Problem A5:** Calculating Proceeds and Recording Notes Receivable Discounted

On Nov. 1, 1999, Empire Roofing discounted the three notes described below at the Valrico Fidelity Bank. The bank charged a 15% discount rate on each note.

> Note 1: An $8,000, 12%, 120-day note received on Sept. 2, 1999
> Note 2: A $30,000, 18%, 60-day note received on Oct. 2, 1999
> Note 3: An $18,000, 9%, 90-day note received on Nov. 1, 1999

**Required:**

1. Calculate the amount of cash that Empire would receive from discounting each of the three notes. Label your calculations. Round calculations to the nearest cent.
2. Prepare Empire's journal entries to record discounting each of the three notes.

▶ *(Check Figure: Proceeds from discounting Note 2 = $30,513.75)*

7 8 **Problem A6:** Preparing Entries to Record Notes Receivable Transactions

Powell Security sells electronic security systems to businesses, government agencies, and large estates. Normally, these sales are on 30-day open accounts, but occasionally Powell will accept a longer-term note. The transactions below relate to four such notes that were received in 1999:

Sept.  1   Powell received an $8,000, 9%, 6-month note from Dexter School when Dexter purchased a security system.

2   Powell sold Carlos Lopez a large system with a total sales price of $100,000. Lopez gave Powell a 12%, 120-day note for $80,000 and $20,000 in cash.

Oct.  2   Powell received a $10,000, 12%, 90-day note from Ingram Foods in settlement of a past-due receivable.

Nov.  1   Powell discounted the Dexter School note at the Fortune National Bank with recourse. The bank charged a discount rate of 12%.

1   Powell sold Lamb Imports a system for $60,000. Lamb gave Powell a 10%, 3-month note.

Dec.  1   Powell discounted the Ingram note at the Fortune Bank with recourse. The bank charged a 15% discount rate.

30   Ingram failed to pay the note at the bank. Powell paid the maturity value of the note plus a $20 fee. Powell still expects to collect from Ingram.

31   Lopez failed to pay his note when due. Powell has engaged an attorney to begin legal proceedings against Lopez. Powell expects to collect the full amount due.

31   Powell's accounting year ends.

**Required:**

1. Prepare the appropriate journal entries to record each of the transactions above. Show supporting calculations as part of your journal entry explanations.
2. What is the total interest earned during 1999 by Powell on these four notes?

▶ *(Check Figure: Proceeds from discounting Dexter note = $8,025.60)*

10 **Problem A7:** Preparing Entries to Record External Credit Card Sales

Wyatt Music & Stereo sells cassettes, compact disks, stereo equipment, and accessories. Wyatt accepts cash, a 30-day Wyatt charge account, or either of two credit cards: National Express and Bank-Kard. Bank-Kard is issued by the Mideast National Bank; National Express is a national credit card company. Wyatt remits credit card sales forms to National Express weekly. National Express assesses a fee of 5% of gross sales for its credit card services, while Bank-Kard charges

6% of gross sales. National Express remits cash to Wyatt within 10 days, while Bank-Kard adds cash to Wyatt's checking account immediately upon receipt of the credit card sales forms. Wyatt has the following sales and collections during December 1999:

| | Dec. 1-7 | Dec. 8-14 | Dec. 15-21 | Dec. 22-31 |
|---|---|---|---|---|
| Cash sales | $1,000 | $1,600 | $2,240 | $ 600 |
| Wyatt's charge sales | 400 | 1,240 | 1,750 | 300 |
| National Express sales | 2,400 | 4,800 | 6,000 | 1,800 |
| Bank-Kard sales | 1,600 | 2,800 | 3,600 | 1,400 |
| Collected on Wyatt's accounts | | 160 | 600 | 870 |
| Collected from National Express | | 2,280 | 4,560 | 5,700 |

On Dec. 31, Wyatt provided for estimated uncollectible accounts using the percentage of credit sales method. Wyatt estimates that 3% of credit sales will prove uncollectible.

**Required:**

1. For each of the four weeks of December, prepare an entry to record sales; for each of the last three weeks, prepare a second entry to record collections from credit customers and credit card companies.
2. Prepare the entry to record uncollectible accounts expense on Dec. 31.
3. Calculate the receivable amounts that will appear on the Dec. 31, 1999, balance sheet.

▶ *(Check Figure: Uncollectible accounts expense = $110.70)*

3 4 7 **Problem A8:** Identifying and Correcting Errors in Receivables Transactions

Consider the following independent situations.

a. At the end of Ute Co.'s first year of operations, the bookkeeper recorded a 1999 uncollectible accounts expense of $1,800 using the direct write-off method. The company's controller observed that Ute had not concluded that any specific customer's account was uncollectible. She also recommended that the percentage of credit sales method be used. It was decided that $1\frac{1}{4}$% of credit sales would be appropriate. Ute's 1999 credit sales totaled $200,000.
b. Crowne Co.'s Allowance for Uncollectible Accounts has a $4,500 debit balance. The company's aging schedule indicates that a $6,800 balance is needed. Crown makes the following entry:

| | | |
|---|---|---|
| Uncollectible Accounts Expense. . . . . . . . . . . . . . . . . . . . . . . | 2,300 | |
| Allowance for Uncollectible Accounts . . . . . . . . . . . . . . . . | | 2,300 |

c. On Sept. 1, 1999, Victory, Inc., received a $100,000, 12%, 6-month note. Victory made the following entry when the note was received:

| | | |
|---|---|---|
| Notes Receivable . . . . . . . . . . . . . . . . . . . . . . . . . . . . . . . . . | 100,000 | |
| Interest Receivable . . . . . . . . . . . . . . . . . . . . . . . . . . . . . . . . | 6,000 | |
| Sales. . . . . . . . . . . . . . . . . . . . . . . . . . . . . . . . . . . . . . . . | | 100,000 |
| Interest Income . . . . . . . . . . . . . . . . . . . . . . . . . . . . . . . . | | 6,000 |

No Dec. 31 accrual entry has been made for this note.

**Required:**

1. Examine each of the three independent situations described above and describe any error that was committed. If no error was committed, explain why the accounting was correct.
2. Prepare an entry to correct each of the errors that you have identified. Assume that each company's books have not been closed.

▶ *(Check Figure: Victory, Inc., debit to interest income = $2,000)*

## PROBLEMS: SET B

2† **Problem B1:** Preparing Entries for Accounts Receivable
and Uncollectible Accounts

Selected transactions of Hoven Electric Supply for the years 1998 and 1999 are shown below:

**1998**

Jan.–Dec.  Total cash sales were $150,000; total credit sales were $600,000. (Prepare one entry to record the entire year's sales.)

Jan.–Dec.  Collections on accounts amounted to $465,000. (Prepare one entry to record the entire year's collections.)

Dec. 31  Hoven estimated that uncollectible accounts would amount to about $9,000. Hoven estimates uncollectibles instead of using the direct write-off method.

**1999**

Mar. 15  Hoven wrote off the $435 account of Samantha Shiftless as uncollectible.

Apr. 12  The $2,330 account of D. Ed Beat was written off as uncollectible.

June 21  A check was received from Samantha Shiftless in full settlement of her account, $435.

Jan.–Dec.  Various other individual accounts amounting to $14,275 were written off. (Prepare one entry to record all these write-offs.)

Jan.–Dec.  Total sales were $900,000: 8% for cash, the remainder on account.

Jan.–Dec.  Total other cash collections on account were $682,000.

Dec. 31  Hoven estimated uncollectible accounts expense for 1999 to be $12,420.

**Required:**

1. Prepare general journal entries to record the transactions described above.
2. Calculate the balance of Accounts Receivable and Allowance for Uncollectible Accounts on Dec. 31, 1999.

▶ *(Check Figure: Balance of Allowance for Uncollectible Accounts = $4,815)*

1 3 4 5  **Problem B2:** Calculating Uncollectible Accounts Expense
Using Three Methods

The following facts relate to Maggio Exercise Equipment:

a. Jan. 1, 1999, balance of Allowance for Uncollectible Accounts = $22,600 (credit).
b. Total of customer accounts written off during 1999 = $16,920.
c. Total sales during 1999 = $1,620,000; 90% of sales are on credit.

**Required:**

1. Calculate uncollectible accounts expense under the direct write-off method.
2. Calculate uncollectible accounts expense under the percentage of credit sales method. Maggio uses $3\frac{1}{4}$% to estimate.
3. Calculate uncollectible accounts expense under the aging of receivables method. An aging schedule shows that accounts totaling $38,480 are estimated to be uncollectible.
4. Assuming the aging of receivables method is used, and that Accounts Receivable (gross) has a balance of $202,600 on January 1, 1999 and $359,500 on December 31, 1999, calculate Maggio's accounts receivable turnover and average age of receivables.

▶ *(Check Figure: Uncollectible accounts expense under the percentage of credit sales method = $47,385)*

† The numbers in the margin refer to the Learning Objectives.

4 **Problem B3:** Calculating and Recording Uncollectible Accounts Expense
Using an Aging Schedule

Doan Florist has the following uncollected accounts receivable on June 30, 1998:

| Customer Name | Amount | Collection Status |
|---|---|---|
| N. Julian | $3,720 | Not yet due |
| J. Cleland | 1,500 | 20 days past due |
| R. Hennessy | 2,700 | 51 days past due |
| O. Juarez | 1,320 | Not yet due |
| T. Barnard | 4,380 | 63 days past due |
| T. Fay | 1,200 | 105 days past due |
| J. Upchurch | 3,960 | Not yet due |
| J. Earnhardt | 2,460 | Not yet due |
| R. Henry | 2,100 | 35 days past due |
| D. Clayton | 3,360 | 30 days past due |
| J. Durham | 600 | Not yet due |
| H. Perry | 540 | 45 days past due |
| R. Rasco | 7,200 | Not yet due |
| F. Connell | 1,680 | 74 days past due |
| H. Kinnan | 2,940 | Not yet due |
| B. Humphries | 1,020 | 95 days past due |
| J. Davis | 5,040 | 29 days past due |

Doan uses an aging schedule to prepare an estimate of uncollectible accounts for the year.
Estimates of the percentage uncollectible in each category of the schedule are as follows:

Not yet due . . . . . . . . . . . . . . . . . . . . . . . . . . . . . . . . . . 1%
1–30 days past due . . . . . . . . . . . . . . . . . . . . . . . . . . 4%
31–60 days past due . . . . . . . . . . . . . . . . . . . . . . . . . 10%
61–90 days past due . . . . . . . . . . . . . . . . . . . . . . . . . 50%
Over 90 days past due . . . . . . . . . . . . . . . . . . . . . . . 75%

**Required:**

1. Prepare an aging schedule and an estimate of the total amount expected to be uncollectible.
2. Prepare an adjusting entry to record uncollectible accounts expense on June 30, 1998, assuming that Allowance for Uncollectible Accounts has a credit balance before adjustment of $2,190.
3. Prepare an adjusting entry to record uncollectible accounts expense on June 30, 1998, assuming that Allowance for Uncollectible Accounts has a debit balance before adjustment of $1,050.

   ▶ *(Check Figure: Balance needed in Allowance for Uncollectible Accounts = $5,847)*

7 **Problem B4:** Preparing Basic Notes Receivable Entries

D&S Jewelry Imports has an account receivable from Severance Stores in the amount of $28,000. Being temporarily short of cash, Severance proposes to give D&S a 90-day note to settle the account. D&S agrees, and the 15% note is signed on Mar. 31, 1998. D&S's accounting year ends on Apr. 30.

**Required:**

1. Prepare D&S's journal entries on Mar. 31, Apr. 30, and June 29, assuming that Severance pays the note when due. Show supporting calculations.
2. Prepare D&S's journal entries on Mar. 31, Apr. 30, and June 29, assuming that Severance dishonors the note.

   ▶ *(Check Figure: Interest income recorded on June 29 = $700)*

**8 9**   **Problem B5:** Calculating Proceeds and Recording Notes
Receivable Discounted

On June 1, 1998, McCoy Windows discounted the three notes described below at the Lake
Ridge Bank. The bank charged an 18% discount rate on each note.

> Note 1: A $2,000, 12%, 60-day note received on May 2, 1998
> Note 2: A $15,000, 15%, 6-month note received on Apr. 1, 1998
> Note 3: A $5,000, 14%, 1-year note received on June 1, 1998

**Required:**

1. Calculate the amount of cash that McCoy would receive from discounting each of the three
   notes. Label your calculations. Round calculations to the nearest cent.
2. Prepare general journal entries to record discounting each of the three notes.

▶ *(Check Figure: Proceeds from Note 2 = $15,157.50)*

**7 8**   **Problem B6:** Preparing Entries to Record Notes Receivable Transactions

Instate Equipment Company sells machinery to wholesalers, retailers, and manufacturers. The
machines are normally sold on 60-day open accounts, but occasionally Instate will accept a
longer-term note. The transactions below relate to four such notes that were received in 1998.

Feb.   1   Instate received a $12,000, 18%, 12-month note from Ponte Cleaners in exchange
           for a machine with a retail price of $12,000.

May    1   Instate discounted the Ponte note at the Liberty Bank with recourse. The bank
           charged a discount rate of 20%.

Aug.   1   Instate sold Glenn Refining Company equipment for $24,000. Glenn gave Instate a
           $24,000, 18%, 6-month note for the full $24,000.

       1   Instate accepted a $35,000, 12%, 90-day note from Eckel Photo in settlement of a
           past-due account receivable.

Sept.  1   Instate discounted the Eckel note at the Liberty Bank with recourse. The bank
           charged a 20% discount rate.

Oct.   2   Instate sold Euclid Textiles two machines with a total sales price of $60,000. Euclid
           gave Instate a 12%, 90-day note for $50,000 and $10,000 in cash.

       30  Liberty Bank informed Instate that Eckel had dishonored the $35,000 note. Instate
           paid the bank the maturity value of the note plus a $30 fee. Instate believes that it
           will be able to collect from Eckel.

Dec. 31    Euclid failed to pay the $50,000 note when due. Euclid is having temporary cash-
           flow problems; Instate expects to collect from Euclid within a few weeks.

       31  Instate's accounting year ends.

**Required:**

1. Prepare the appropriate journal entries to record each of the transactions above. Show
   supporting calculations as part of your journal entry explanations.
2. What is the net interest earned during 1998 by Instate on these four notes?

▶ *(Check Figure: Proceeds from discounting Eckel note = $34,848)*

**10**   **Problem B7:** Preparing Entries to Record External Credit Card Sales

Surety Lawn Equipment sells a full line of equipment for lawn and landscape maintenance.
Surety sells to customers for cash, on a 30-day Surety charge account, or through two national
credit cards: Adventure, which is issued by a national credit card company, and Charge-All,
which is issued by the Progress National Bank. Surety remits credit card sales forms to
Adventure weekly. Adventure assesses a fee of 6% of gross sales, while Charge-All charges 3% of

gross sales. Charge-All adds cash to Surety's checking account immediately upon receipt of the credit card sales forms, while Adventure remits cash to Surety within 10 days. Surety has the following sales and collections during January 1998:

| | Jan. 1–7 | Jan. 8–14 | Jan. 15–21 | Jan. 22–31 |
|---|---|---|---|---|
| Cash sales | $2,000 | $ 3,360 | $ 4,200 | $2,480 |
| Surety's charge sales | 3,200 | 5,040 | 12,320 | 9,840 |
| Adventure sales | 8,000 | 11,600 | 10,400 | 4,000 |
| Charge-All sales | 5,200 | 8,800 | 6,400 | 9,600 |
| Collected on Surety accounts | | 2,760 | 5,920 | 7,320 |
| Collected from Adventure | | 7,520 | 10,904 | 9,776 |

On Jan. 31, Surety provided for estimated uncollectible accounts using the percentage of credit sales method. Surety estimates that 2% of credit sales will prove uncollectible.

**Required:**

1. For each of the four weeks of January, prepare an entry to record sales; for each of the last three weeks, prepare a second entry to record collections from credit customers and Charge-All.
2. Prepare the entry to record Uncollectible Accounts Expense on Jan. 31.
3. Calculate the receivable amounts that will appear on the Jan. 31, 1998, balance sheet.

▶ (Check Figure: Uncollectible Accounts Expense = $608)

2 3 8 **Problem B8:** Identifying and Correcting Errors in Receivables Transactions

Consider the following independent situations.

a. Kansas Co. has the following accounts on the books before 1998 adjusting entries are prepared (all accounts have normal balances):

Accounts Receivable........ $250,000     Sales (all on credit)......... $800,000
Allowance for Uncollectible
  Accounts ..............     1,500

Kansas estimates uncollectible accounts expense to be 2% of credit sales. Taking into account the balance in the Allowance account, Kansas records $14,500 of uncollectible accounts expense.

b. On Jan. 1, 1998, Luther, Inc., has the following on its balance sheet:

| | |
|---|---|
| Accounts Receivable ......................................... | $650,000 |
| Allowance for Uncollectible Accounts ............................ | 12,000 |
| Net Accounts Receivable....................................... | 638,000 |

During 1998, Luther wrote off $8,500 of accounts receivable by debiting Uncollectible Accounts Expense and crediting Accounts Receivable.

c. Varney received a $10,000, 12%, 90-day note on Nov. 1. Varney discounted the note on Dec. 2 with recourse. The bank charged an 18% discount rate. Varney recorded the discounting transaction correctly. On Dec. 31, Varney accrued $100 of interest income on the note.

**Required:**

1. Examine each of the three independent situations described below and describe any error that was committed. If no error was committed, explain why the accounting was correct.
2. Prepare an entry to correct each of the errors that you have identified. Assume that each company's books have not been closed.

▶ (Check Figure: Varney debit to interest income = $100)

## DECISION PROBLEM

Lorello Restaurant Supply sells cooking utensils, china, and other restaurant-related supplies to retail and institutional food preparation firms. All sales are either for cash or on 30-day accounts. Data regarding Lorello's operations during the past three years are shown below:

|  | 1996 | 1997 | 1998 |
|---|---|---|---|
| Cash sales ................................. | $ 75,000 | $105,000 | $142,500 |
| Credit sales................................. | 300,000 | 400,000 | 600,000 |
| Uncollectible accounts expense................ | 4,500 | 6,000 | 9,000 |
| Accounts written off as uncollectible ............ | 1,000 | 6,500 | 10,000 |
| Dec. 31 balance of Allowance for Uncollectible Accounts ................................... | 3,500 | 3,000 | 2,000 |

Early in 1999, Lorello's accounting department did an analysis of the accounts written off to determine the year the account originated. A summary of this analysis follows:

|  | Written Off | | | Total Accounts |
|---|---|---|---|---|
|  | In 1996 | In 1997 | In 1998 | Written off |
| From 1996 credit sales | $1,000 | $5,000 | — | $6,000 |
| From 1997 credit sales |  | 1,500 | $6,500 | $8,000 |
| From 1998 credit sales |  |  | 3,500 | $3,500* |

\* Some 1998 accounts remain. These accounts will be collected or written off in 1999.

Lorello uses the percentage of credit sales method to estimate uncollectible accounts. All of Lorello's 1996 and 1997 accounts have been either collected or written off as uncollectible.

**Required:**

1. Calculate the percentage that Lorello has been using to estimate its uncollectible accounts expense.
2. Determine if this percentage appears to be adequate. If not, what percentage do you believe would be more realistic? Support your recommendation with calculations.
3. Determine what adjustment should be made in 1999 to correct for the errors in the 1996, 1997, and 1998 estimates. Prepare a suggested journal entry to record the correction.

## ETHICS CASE

Gadsby's department stores have operated since 1953 in several mid-Atlantic states. Gadsby's is owned by approximately 5,000 stockholders, most of whom live in Maryland, the company's home state.

After 40 years of growing profits, Gadsby's income has slowly declined over the past few years. This deterioration is having a negative effect on the company's stock price. Alvin Tully, Gadsby's president for the past 20 years, has come under increasing pressure to improve the firm's profitability. The local financial press has written several articles questioning Tully's ability and willingness to keep up with the latest retailing innovations.

Tully has several ideas that he believes will return Gadsby's to the forefront of retailing. It will take about 3 years to implement these plans and for their effect to be seen in net income. In order to "buy time," Tully instructs his credit manager and controller to implement the following "temporary" profit-enhancing measures:

1. Lower the threshold family income required for granting credit, thus making it easier for young singles and families to acquire major appliances and furniture.
2. Modify the aging schedule categories and percentages used in calculating uncollectible accounts expense. Tully says that this change will bring Gadsby's policy "into line with others in the retailing industry." The following schedules show the current year's first-quarter results before and after Tully's plan is implemented:

### Original Estimate of Uncollectible Accounts
### First Quarter, Current Year

| Age Category | Amount in the Age Category | Percentage Expected to Be Uncollectible | Amount Expected to Be Uncollectible |
|---|---|---|---|
| Not yet due | $12,000,000 | 2% | $   240,000 |
| 1–30 days past due | 4,300,000 | 6 | 258,000 |
| 31–60 days past due | 2,500,000 | 20 | 500,000 |
| 61–90 days past due | 1,100,000 | 35 | 385,000 |
| Over 90 days past due | 800,000 | 80 | 640,000 |
| Totals | $20,700,000 | | $2,023,000 |

### Revised Estimate of Uncollectible Accounts
### First Quarter, Current Year

| Age Category | Amount in the Age Category | Percentage Expected to Be Uncollectible | Amount Expected to Be Uncollectible |
|---|---|---|---|
| Not yet due | $12,000,000 | 1% | $   120,000 |
| 1–30 days past due | 4,300,000 | 5 | 215,000 |
| 31–60 days past due | 2,500,000 | 15 | 375,000 |
| 61–90 days past due | 1,100,000 | 28 | 308,000 |
| 91–120 days past due | 700,000 | 60 | 420,000 |
| Over 120 days past due | 100,000 | 80 | 80,000 |
| Totals | $20,700,000 | | $1,518,000 |

Tully estimates that these two measures alone will improve profits by almost $1,000,000 in the next quarter alone.

**Required:**

1. Explain how Tully's actions will improve net income.

2. Do you believe that there is an ethical issue here, or is Tully just exercising good business judgment?
3. What are the potential effects of Tully's changes on Gadsby's management, employees, stockholders, and customers?

## OBJECTIVE ASSIGNMENT ANSWERS

**True/False**

1. T    2. F    3. F    4. T    5. T

**Multiple Choice**

1. c    2. a    3. c    4. d    5. b
6. c    7. b    8. a    9. d    10. d

# Merchandise Inventory

**LEARNING OBJECTIVES**

After studying this chapter, you should be able to do the following:

1 Define *merchandise inventory*

2 Calculate the cost of inventory purchased

3 Calculate the number of physical units that should be included in ending merchandise inventory

4 Calculate ending inventory and cost of goods sold using each of the periodic cost methods: first-in, first-out; last-in, first-out; weighted average; and specific identification

5 Calculate ending inventory value using the lower-of-cost-or-market method

6 Estimate ending inventory using the gross profit and retail inventory methods

7 Explain and demonstrate how an error in inventory accounting affects income

8 Describe a perpetual inventory system

9 Record acquisitions and sales under a perpetual inventory system

10 Calculate ending inventory and cost of goods sold using perpetual FIFO and LIFO

11 Calculate and explain the use of the inventory turnover ratio

12 Define the key terms listed at the end of this chapter

**CHAPTER OUTLINE**

**DETERMINING THE COST OF MERCHANDISE PURCHASED** • **DETERMINING PHYSICAL UNITS IN ENDING INVENTORY** • The Physical Count • Goods in Transit • Goods on Consignment • **PERIODIC COST METHODS OF DETERMINING ENDING INVENTORY** • The First-in, First-out (FIFO) Method • The Last-in, First-out (LIFO) Method • The Weighted Average Method • The Specific Identification Method • Advantages and Disadvantages of the Four Inventory Cost Methods • Consistency of Inventory Method • **VALUING INVENTORY AT LOWER-OF-COST-OR-MARKET** • **METHODS OF ESTIMATING ENDING INVENTORY** • The Gross Profit Method • The Retail Inventory Method • **INVENTORY ERRORS** • **THE PERPETUAL INVENTORY SYSTEM** • Recording Inventory Acquisitions and Sales • Perpetual FIFO • Perpetual LIFO • Perpetual Weighted Average • Computerized Perpetual Inventory Records • **FINANCIAL STATEMENT ANALYSIS: INVENTORY TURNOVER** • Current Assets on the Balance Sheet: A Review

Learning
Objective 1

Define merchandise inventory

**Merchandise inventory** is finished goods held for sale by retailers and wholesalers. Completed goods held for sale by manufacturers is usually called **finished goods inventory.** Since accounting is the same for merchandise inventory and for finished goods inventory, we will use the term *merchandise inventory* to refer to both in this chapter.

Some goods are purchased in finished condition, ready to sell. For example, retail firms such as hardware stores purchase hammers, nails, wrenches, and bolts, all of which are immediately ready for resale. Another example is the shirts and blouses that a clothing shop buys and places on racks for immediate resale.

Other goods are purchased that require some minor finishing or assembly before they are ready for sale. Thus, bicycles are shipped unassembled and put together by the bicycle shop, and some furniture must be assembled before it is sold. Since such finishing activities are minor, goods such as these are included in merchandise inventory.

In contrast to merchandisers, manufacturing firms purchase raw materials that they must convert into finished products. For example, a furniture manufacturer buys wood, plastic, glue, nails, and other raw materials and converts them into tables, desks, and bookcases. The wood, plastic, glue, and nails are the manufacturer's *raw materials inventory.* The completed tables, desks, and bookcases are merchandise inventory, or finished goods inventory, even if they still require minor assembly.

To be included in merchandise inventory, the finished goods must be held for sale. Thus, the same assets represented by one firm as merchandise inventory may be considered differently by another firm. Suppose, for instance, that Byron Office Supply Company has desks and file cabinets in its warehouses ready for sale; these are assets that Byron represents as merchandise inventory. The Culbreath Plumbing Supply Company buys some of these desks and file cabinets; these assets are represented by Culbreath's accountants as office equipment, because that's what they are. Culbreath "consumes" desks and file cabinets; it doesn't sell them. Culbreath sells pipes, valves, bathtubs, and sinks—these items are Culbreath's merchandise inventory.

Any good, whether it is iron ore or sheet steel or toy trains, if it is a finished good and ready for sale, is the merchandise inventory of the firm that owns it. In this chapter, we will be concerned only with merchandise that is completely finished or that requires only minor assembly. That will keep manufacturing costs out of our discussion of accounting for merchandise inventory.

Accounting for merchandise inventory involves two steps:

1. Determining the total cost of inventory acquired
2. Allocating those costs between the goods that have been sold (cost of goods sold) and those that remain (ending inventory)

## DETERMINING THE COST OF MERCHANDISE PURCHASED

Learning
Objective 2

Calculate the cost of inventory
purchased

The following is a general rule for determining the cost of merchandise:

*The cost of merchandise includes the invoice price and all reasonable and necessary costs incurred in getting the merchandise to a condition and place where it is ready for sale.*

This rule means that the merchandise inventory's cost includes not only its invoice price but also the costs of freight, insurance during shipment, handling, and storage —all reasonable costs incurred in getting the asset to the point where it becomes

---

**Exhibit 1** Partial Income Statement Emphasizing Cost of Goods Sold

---

**NORTH CORP.**
**Partial Income Statement**
**Cost of Goods Sold Section**
**Month Ended June 30, 1998**

---

| | | |
|---|---:|---:|
| Merchandise Inventory, June 1 . . . . . . . . . . . . . . . . . . . . . . . . . . . . . . . . . . . . | | $ 37,100 |
| Add: Merchandise purchased during June: | | |
|     Purchases . . . . . . . . . . . . . . . . . . . . . . . . . . . . . . . . . . . | $92,250 | |
|     Less: Purchases Returns and Allowances . . . . . . . . . . . | (3,800) | |
|         Purchases Discounts . . . . . . . . . . . . . . . . . . . . . . | (1,750) | |
|     Net Purchases . . . . . . . . . . . . . . . . . . . . . . . . . . . . . . . | $86,700 | |
|     Add: Freight-In . . . . . . . . . . . . . . . . . . . . . . . . . . . . . . | 2,550 | |
|     Net Cost of Merchandise Acquired . . . . . . . . . . . . . . . . . . . . . . . . | | 89,250 |
| Goods Available for Sale during June . . . . . . . . . . . . . . . . . . . . . . . . . . . . . | | $126,350 |
| Less: Merchandise Inventory, June 30 . . . . . . . . . . . . . . . . . . . . . . . . . . . | | (43,550) |
| Cost of Goods Sold . . . . . . . . . . . . . . . . . . . . . . . . . . . . . . . . . . . . . . . . . . | | $ 82,800 |

---

merchandise inventory on the shelf, ready for the consumer to purchase. Most firms have many different products on their shelves for sale. Yet some of the costs, such as fire insurance, handling, and storage, represent costs that cover all merchandise. In reality, a firm's accounting system does not trace each of these costs to each item in inventory. To do so would prove unnecessarily expensive in comparison to the value of the information obtained. For example, applying the cost rule literally would mean dividing the salary of a receiving clerk in a department store among all the various items of inventory in proportion to the time spent unloading each one. Allocating the clerk's salary, typically around $20,000 per year, among $5,000,000 of inventory would cost more than it could possibly contribute to the profitability of the department store. Nor would it provide relevant information on the income statement.

The first thing to consider in determining the cost of inventory is the price paid to the seller for it. The amount paid is often less than the price listed in the seller's catalog, because the seller has discounted the catalog (or list) price. Sellers offer three types of discounts: trade discounts, quantity discounts, and cash discounts (purchases discounts). *Trade discounts* are deductions allowed to wholesalers and retailers from the price of merchandise listed in catalogs. *Quantity discounts* are offered to customers buying a large quantity of the same item. Quantity discounts are generally offered in addition to the trade discount. *Cash discounts,* called *purchases discounts* by buyers, are offered to encourage customers to pay for their purchases promptly. Wise managers will always take advantage of cash discounts rather than pay the cost of waiting—the difference between the discount price and the amount that must be paid at the end of the credit period.

In addition to the price paid to the seller, the buyer of merchandise may be required to pay the cost of transporting that merchandise; the transportation cost becomes a part of the total inventory cost. Remember that the cost of transportation on merchandise purchased is debited to Freight-In.

The total cost of inventory available for sale is calculated in the cost of goods sold section of the income statement, as shown in Exhibit 1.

Now that we have reviewed how to determine the cost of inventory purchased and how this information appears in the cost of goods sold section of the income statement, we are ready to focus on the determination of the number of units and the cost of ending inventory.

1. What is merchandise inventory as defined by accountants?
2. What is the general rule for determining the cost of merchandise?
3. What are trade, quantity, and cash discounts?
4. Where on the financial statements do you find the total cost of inventory available for sale?

## DETERMINING PHYSICAL UNITS IN ENDING INVENTORY

Learning
Objective **3**

Calculate the number of physical units that should be included in ending merchandise inventory

To determine the cost of ending inventory, you must measure, or count, the number of physical units of merchandise owned by the firm—that is, the units available for sale but not yet sold—and then determine the total cost represented by those unsold units.

### The Physical Count

A reliable ending inventory cost depends on an accurate count of all the merchandise in inventory. This means a visual inspection and a physical count of all the merchandise not sold at the end of the period. Teams of employees are assigned to count all units on the shelves, in the stockrooms, and in other storage areas. Their count totals are entered on tally sheets like the one shown in Exhibit 2. Note that no costs are entered on the tally sheet at the time of the physical count. The costs are supplied later by the accounting department. To ensure the accuracy of the total inventory, the original counter's totals are checked and verified on a random basis by another counter.

All businesses that own inventory should count it at least once a year. Even firms with sophisticated computer systems or complex hand-kept records of each item entering and leaving the firm need to count the inventory. These counts are made to ensure that no recordkeeping errors were made and to discover the amount of any inventory stolen or spoiled.

The number of units to be physically counted in inventory includes:

1. Units *on the premises*—the units in the firm's warehouses, stockrooms, shelves, and even in the windows and showcases for display
2. Units *in transit*—the units ordered and owned by the firm but not yet received, and the units on their way to a customer or sales agent but still owned by the firm
3. Units *out on consignment*—the units in the hands of a sales agent but still owned by the firm

Some of the units on the firm's premises should *not* be included in ending inventory. These units may be *in on consignment,* meaning that the firm has them but doesn't own them—it's keeping them to sell for someone else. The important thing to realize is that goods owned by the firm, whatever their physical location, are the ones to be included in ending inventory.

### Goods in Transit

When goods are purchased from a supplier, the terms of the shipment are either FOB (free on board) shipping point or FOB destination. These terms specify who pays the freight and the point at which legal title to the goods passes from buyer to seller.

**Exhibit 2** Inventory Tally Sheet

## INVENTORY TALLY SHEET

Department _____Air Conditioners_____     Date _____December 31, 1998_____

Location _____Stockroom_____

Counter's Signature _____I. M. Accurate_____

Verified by _____

| Stock No. | Description | Number of Units | Unit Cost | Total Cost |
|---|---|---|---|---|
| 85-1291 | 4,000 BTU portable | 4 | | |
| 85-1292 | 5,000 BTU portable | 2 | | |
| 85-0796 | 12,800 BTU window unit | 6 | | |
| 85-0798 | 11,700 BTU window unit | 10 | | |

*FOB shipping point* means that the seller pays freight only to the shipping point, usually the seller's plant or warehouse, and title passes to the buyer at the shipping point. The buyer owns the goods while in shipment and is responsible for all freight charges. A company purchasing goods FOB shipping point must include these units in its ending Merchandise Inventory account and in its Purchases account even though the goods have not been physically received.

*FOB destination* means that the seller pays the freight to the destination, usually the buyer's place of business, and title to the goods passes when they arrive. A company purchasing goods FOB destination does not own the goods in transit, is not responsible for freight charges, and does not include these goods in ending Merchandise Inventory or Purchases until they have been physically received.

### Goods on Consignment

A firm may choose to market its goods through an agent, using a system called **consignment.** The agent doesn't own the goods even though they may be in his or her possession; the firm owns the goods until the agent sells them. The owner of the merchandise is called the *consignor;* the agent is called the *consignee.* Although the consignee never actually owns the merchandise, he or she agrees to exercise due care over it until it is sold. After the sale, the consignee deducts from the proceeds of the sale a selling commission and expenses incurred in carrying out the sale, and sends the balance to the consignor.

The consignor—a company that has goods *out* to an agent on consignment—must include these goods in its ending inventory because it still owns the goods.

The consignee—an agent that has goods *in* on consignment—must exclude these goods from its ending inventory count because the goods are still the property of the consignor.

**ASK YOURSELF** ▶

1. What is the function of an inventory tally sheet?
2. Under what shipping terms would merchandise be included in ending inventory before it is received?
3. How are goods in on consignment and goods out on consignment treated in calculating ending inventory?

## PERIODIC COST METHODS OF DETERMINING ENDING INVENTORY

To begin to understand what is involved in determining the cost represented in ending inventory, consider the following situation.

It is Jan. 31, and the Ready Company has determined by physical count that it has 220 units of inventory in stock. Ready started the month with 50 units that had cost $1 each. During January, Ready purchased 100 units for $1.50 each, 200 units for $2 each, 100 units for $2.50 each, and 50 units for $4 each. So Ready purchased four batches during the month to add to those on hand, and the cost per unit was different for each batch. What, then, should Ready use as the unit cost for its 220 unsold units to calculate the total cost represented in ending inventory on Jan. 31; and what amount should be assigned to the goods that were sold during the month?

The following simple diagram summarizes this quandary:

There are several ways to assign a unit cost to the units in ending inventory: the *first-in, first-out method,* called *FIFO;* the *last-in, first-out method,* or *LIFO;* the *weighted average method;* and the *specific identification method.* Each of these four methods may be used to determine the cost of inventory and cost of goods sold only at the end of a period of time, in a **periodic inventory system;** or each may be used to keep an up-to-date record of the cost of inventory on hand and cost of goods sold at all times, in a **perpetual inventory system.** The periodic inventory system will be discussed first; the perpetual method is explained at the end of this chapter.

Figure 1 provides an overview of the cost flow calculations for all four of the methods in a periodic inventory system. In this section we will explain how to use each method to determine the costs assigned to ending inventory and cost of goods sold. The data shown in Exhibit 3 for Ready Company will be used to demonstrate the calculations involved under each method.

A word of caution: You must keep in mind that all these methods are based on the *flow of costs,* not the *flow of physical units,* into and out of the firm. To be sure you realize the difference between the two flows, consider the following:

1. *Physical flow* may be understood by visualizing the merchandise moving through the firm's departments, from the receiving dock to the stockroom to the display counter to the customer's vehicle. The goods have no cost amount indelibly printed on them—and every box or bag is exactly alike.

2. *Cost flow* is the movement of costs through the firm's accounts, from the Purchases account to either ending Merchandise Inventory or Cost of Goods Sold. Whereas physical flows are determined by actual movement of goods, cost flows are controlled by the accountant's pencil (or computer).

*Learning Objective 4*

Calculate ending inventory and cost of goods sold using each of the periodic cost methods: first-in, first-out; last-in, first-out; weighted average; and specific identification

### The First-in, First-out (FIFO) Method

Under the **first-in, first-out (FIFO) method,** the earliest costs (the first costs) are assigned to cost of goods sold and the remaining costs (the more recent costs) are assigned to ending inventory. Using the data in Exhibit 3, let's explore how FIFO works.

**Exhibit 3** Data for Illustrating Calculation of Ending Inventory and Cost of Goods Sold under FIFO, LIFO, Weighted Average, and Specific Identification Methods

### READY COMPANY
### Inventory Data
### Month Ended January 31, 1998

| | Units | × | Cost Each | = | Total |
|---|---|---|---|---|---|
| Goods available for sale: | | | | | |
| Beginning inventory.................... | 50 | × | $1.00 | = | $    50.00 |
| Jan. 12 purchase...................... | 100 | × | 1.50 | = | 150.00 |
| Jan. 18 purchase...................... | 200 | × | 2.00 | = | 400.00 |
| Jan. 20 purchase...................... | 100 | × | 2.50 | = | 250.00 |
| Jan. 27 purchase...................... | 50 | × | 4.00 | = | 200.00 |
| Total available ..................... | 500 units | | | | $1,050.00 |
| Units remaining at end of month, by physical count ........................ | | | 220 units remaining | | |
| Units sold during the month: | | | | | |
| Total units available ..................... | 500 | | | | |
| Less: Total units remaining................. | − 220 | | | | |
| | 280 units sold | | | | |

If Ready Company sold only one unit during the month, the cost of goods sold would be recorded as $1.00; that is, it would assume that the cost comes from its beginning inventory. The remaining costs (the cost of the 49 units remaining in beginning inventory and all cost of the January purchases) would be assigned to ending inventory.

Now let's assume that Ready sold 51 units. The unit cost of these 51 units sold would be the cost of the first 51 units purchased—50 units from the beginning inventory and 1 unit from the batch purchased on Jan. 12. The cost of ending inventory would include the remaining 99 units from the Jan. 12 purchase and the costs of all other units purchased during the month.

Using the data in Exhibit 3, Ready Company calculates its ending merchandise inventory and its cost of goods sold under the FIFO method as follows:

### FIFO Ending Inventory, January 31, 1998

| | Units Unsold | × | Unit Cost | = | Total Cost |
|---|---|---|---|---|---|
| From Jan. 18 purchase ....................... | 70 | × | $2.00 | = | $140.00 |
| From Jan. 20 purchase ....................... | 100 | × | 2.50 | = | 250.00 |
| From Jan. 27 purchase ....................... | 50 | × | 4.00 | = | 200.00 |
| FIFO ending inventory cost.................... | 220 total units unsold | | | | $590.00 |

### FIFO Cost of Goods Sold during January 1998

| | Units Sold | × | Unit Cost | = | Total Cost |
|---|---|---|---|---|---|
| From beginning inventory.................... | 50 | × | $1.00 | = | $ 50.00 |
| From Jan. 12 purchase...................... | 100 | × | 1.50 | = | 150.00 |
| From Jan. 18 purchase...................... | 130 | × | 2.00 | = | 260.00 |
| FIFO cost of goods sold .................... | 280 total units sold | | | | $460.00 |

**Figure 1** Four Inventory Cost Flow Methods

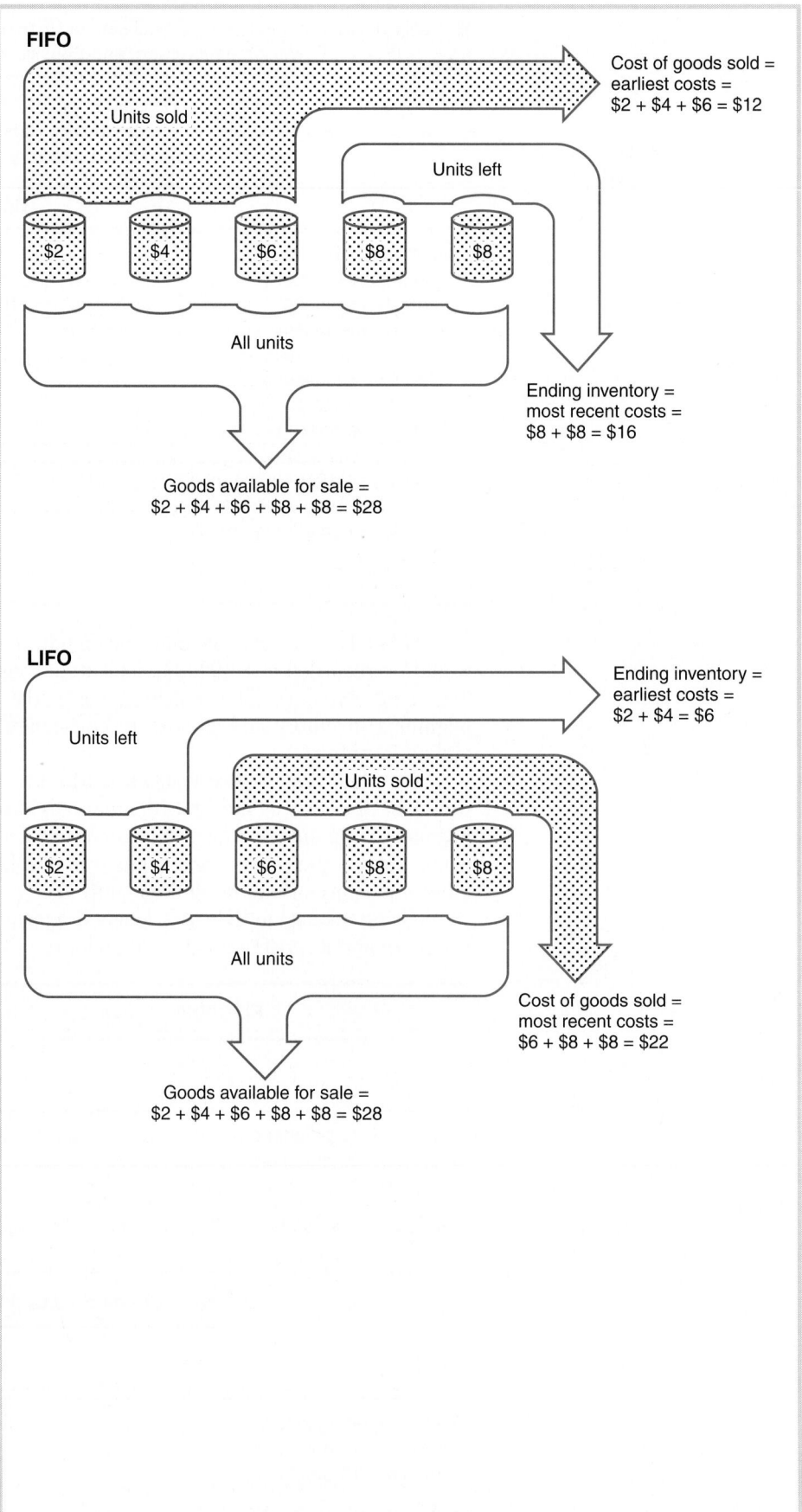

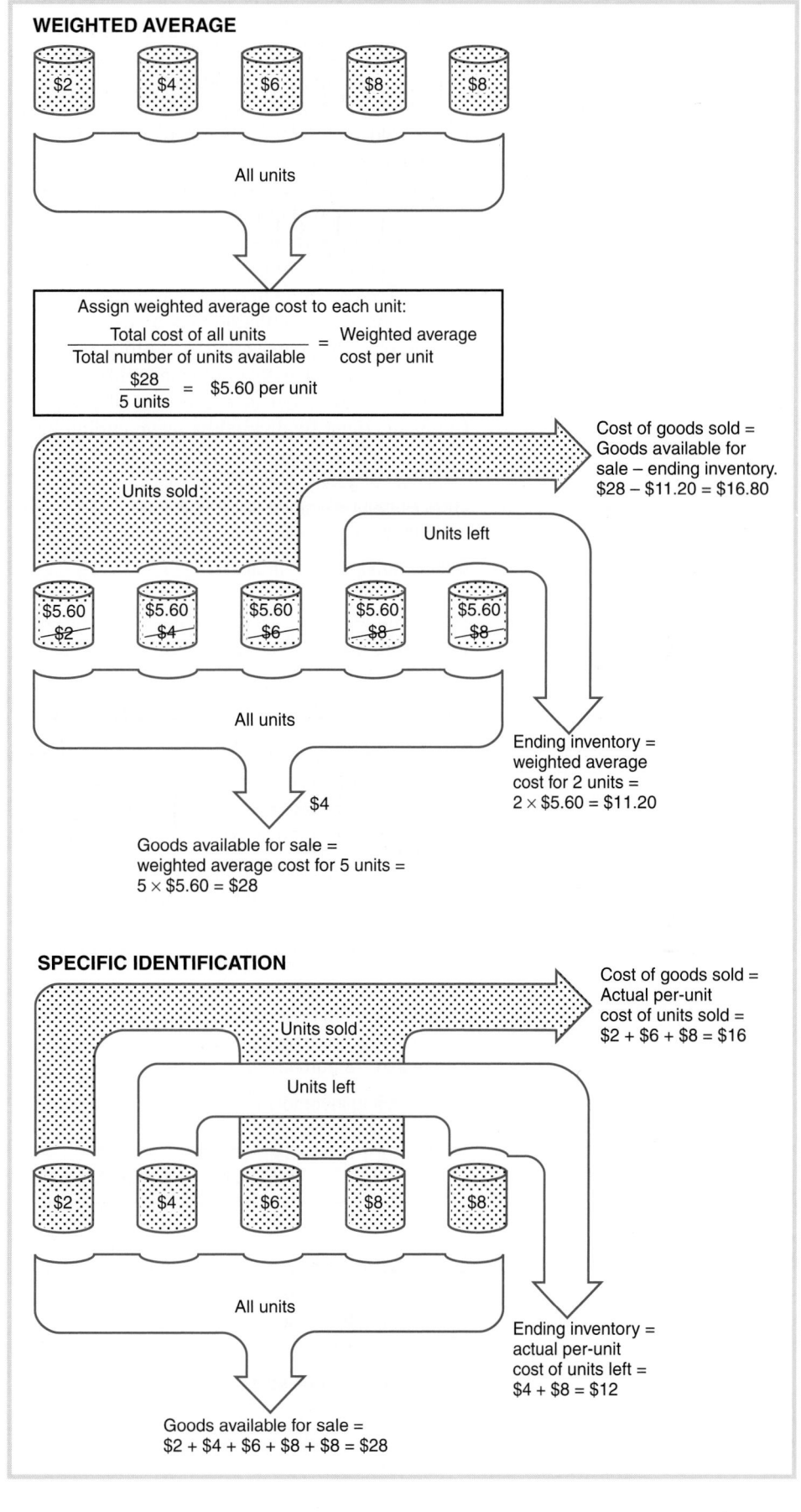

**WEIGHTED AVERAGE**

All units

Assign weighted average cost to each unit:

$$\frac{\text{Total cost of all units}}{\text{Total number of units available}} = \frac{\text{Weighted average}}{\text{cost per unit}}$$

$$\frac{\$28}{5 \text{ units}} = \$5.60 \text{ per unit}$$

Cost of goods sold =
Goods available for
sale − ending inventory.
$28 − $11.20 = $16.80

Units sold

Units left

All units

$4

Ending inventory =
weighted average
cost for 2 units =
2 × $5.60 = $11.20

Goods available for sale =
weighted average cost for 5 units =
5 × $5.60 = $28

**SPECIFIC IDENTIFICATION**

Cost of goods sold =
Actual per-unit
cost of units sold =
$2 + $6 + $8 = $16

Units sold

Units left

All units

Ending inventory =
actual per-unit
cost of units left =
$4 + $8 = $12

Goods available for sale =
$2 + $4 + $6 + $8 + $8 = $28

These calculations show that the total number of units purchased during the month, plus beginning inventory, equaled 500 units; the total number sold was 280. This means that 280 units ÷ 500 units, or 56% of all units on hand, physically "flowed" through the firm's departments.

Now let's turn to cost flow. The total cost for all the units was $1,050; the cost of goods sold was $460. This means that $460 ÷ $1,050, or 44% of the total cost of all goods purchased, flowed through the firm's accounts.

Clearly, the flow of physical units and the flow of costs are not the same in this case. The reason should also be clear: The lower unit costs from purchases made at the beginning of the month were charged to the cost of the units sold. That left the higher unit costs from the purchases made toward the end of the month to be assigned to the units in the ending inventory.

A shortcut calculation may be used with each of the four methods we discuss. Instead of calculating ending inventory and cost of goods sold separately as we did above, we may calculate ending inventory and simply subtract to derive cost of goods sold. This works because the cost of goods available for sale, $1,050 for Ready Company, must be divided between ending inventory and cost of goods sold.

| | |
|---|---:|
| Total cost of goods available for sale . . . . . . . . . . . | $1,050 |
| Less: Amount assigned to FIFO ending inventory. . . . . . . . . . . . . . . . . . . . . . . . . . . . . . . . . . | (590) |
| Cost of goods sold (FIFO). . . . . . . . . . . . . . . . . . . . | $ 460 |

Be careful in using this shortcut. If an error is made in calculating ending inventory, the cost of goods sold will also be incorrect.

### The Last-in, First-out (LIFO) Method

The **last-in, first-out (LIFO) method** is the reverse of the FIFO method. Under LIFO, the earliest costs are assigned to ending merchandise inventory and the costs of the most recent purchases are assigned to cost of goods sold.

Ready Company's cost calculations under LIFO are shown below:

**LIFO Ending Inventory, January 31, 1998**

| | Units Unsold | × | Unit Cost | = | Total Cost |
|---|---:|:-:|---:|:-:|---:|
| From beginning inventory . . . . . . . . . . . . . . . . . . . . . | 50 | × | $1.00 | = | $ 50.00 |
| From Jan. 12 purchase . . . . . . . . . . . . . . . . . . . . . . | 100 | × | 1.50 | = | 150.00 |
| From Jan. 18 purchase . . . . . . . . . . . . . . . . . . . . . . | 70 | × | 2.00 | = | 140.00 |
| LIFO ending inventory cost . . . . . . . . . . . . . . . . . . . | 220 total units unsold | | | | $340.00 |

**LIFO Cost of Goods Sold during January 1998**

| | Units Sold | × | Unit Cost | = | Total Cost |
|---|---:|:-:|---:|:-:|---:|
| From Jan. 18 purchase . . . . . . . . . . . . . . . . . . . . . . | 130 | × | $2.00 | = | $260.00 |
| From Jan. 20 purchase . . . . . . . . . . . . . . . . . . . . . . | 100 | × | 2.50 | = | 250.00 |
| From Jan. 27 purchase . . . . . . . . . . . . . . . . . . . . . . | 50 | × | 4.00 | = | 200.00 |
| LIFO cost of goods sold. . . . . . . . . . . . . . . . . . . . . | 280 total units sold | | | | $710.00 |

The shortcut LIFO calculation of cost of goods sold is:

| | |
|---|---|
| Total cost of goods available for sale............................... | $1,050 |
| Less: Amount assigned to LIFO ending inventory...................... | (340) |
| Cost of goods sold (LIFO)......................................... | $ 710 |

## The Weighted Average Method

The **weighted average method** considers that each unit of inventory of a particular type is identical and can be sold for the same price, and therefore has equal economic significance to the firm. Units having equal economic significance are assigned equal costs. Unlike the FIFO or LIFO method, the weighted average method assigns an equal cost to each unit, sold or unsold. Under this method, the cost of each unit is considered to be the weighted average of all goods available for sale during the period. This weighted average cost per unit is used to calculate ending inventory, as well as the cost of goods sold.

Ready Company's weighted average ending inventory and cost of goods sold would be determined as follows:

---

**Weighted Average Cost per Unit, January 1998**

Weighted average cost per unit of goods available $=$ $\dfrac{\text{Total cost of all units available for sale}}{\text{Total units available for sale}}$

Weighted average cost $= \dfrac{\$1,050}{500 \text{ units}}$

$= \underline{\$\ 2.10}$ per unit

**Weighted Average Ending Inventory, January 31, 1998**

$2.10 per unit $\times$ 220 units left $= \underline{\$462}$ ending inventory

**Weighted Average Cost of Goods Sold for January 1998**

| | |
|---|---|
| $1,050 | Cost of goods available for sale |
| − 462 | Cost of ending inventory |
| $ 588 | Weighted average cost of goods sold |

---

We always use the subtraction shortcut to calculate cost of goods sold for the weighted average method. To see why, consider the following example:

Sweeney, Inc., had 100,000 units available that cost $53,250. Sweeney's ending inventory count revealed 20,000 units on hand; 80,000 units had been sold. The weighted average cost per unit is $.5325 ($53,250 ÷ 100,000 units), which most companies would round to $.53 per unit. If we don't use the shortcut, here's what can happen:

Ending inventory ($.53 × 20,000 units) . . . . . . . .  $10,600
Cost of goods sold ($.53 × 80,000 units) . . . . . . .   42,400

Total costs assigned. . . . . . . . . . . . . . . . . . . . . . . $53,000

Because of rounding, $250 of the $53,250 ends up "lost"—not assigned to either ending inventory or cost of goods sold. The shortcut prevents such losses by automatically assigning rounding errors to cost of goods sold:

Ending inventory ($.53 × 20,000 units) . . . . . . . .  $10,600
Cost of goods sold ($53,250 − $10,600). . . . . . . .   42,650

Total costs assigned. . . . . . . . . . . . . . . . . . . . . . . $53,250

## The Specific Identification Method

The **specific identification method** is based on the assumption that each unit purchased, sold, or in inventory is separate and distinguishable from any other unit. Since each unit sold or remaining in inventory is identified, its specific unit cost can be used in calculating cost of goods sold or ending inventory cost.

The specific identification method is appropriate only for companies that handle a relatively low volume of physical units, each having a relatively high cost. Each unit must be easily distinguishable from the others, as would be the case with original oil paintings, antiques, diamonds, or custom-built houses.

The specific identification method is *not* appropriate for large volumes of identical, low-cost items or where each unit is the same in appearance but is differentiated from other units by serial numbers, such as the same model of washers, refrigerators, or televisions.

It is highly unlikely that Ready Company's merchandise would be suitable for the specific identification method. Nevertheless, let's assume that it *is* suitable so that we can demonstrate how it is used to calculate cost of goods sold and ending inventory.

To illustrate specific identification, the units remaining at the end of January were selected arbitrarily. Management in a real-world situation would be required to trace each unit to the purchase invoice to determine its cost. Unlike the other three methods, the specific identification method has no regular cost flow pattern.

### Specific Identification Ending Inventory, January 31, 1998

|  | Units Unsold | × | Unit Cost | = | Total Cost |
|---|---|---|---|---|---|
| From beginning inventory . . . . . . . . . . . . . . . . . . . . | 50 | × | $1.00 | = | $ 50.00 |
| From Jan. 12 purchase. . . . . . . . . . . . . . . . . . . . . . | 50 | × | 1.50 | = | 75.00 |
| From Jan. 18 purchase. . . . . . . . . . . . . . . . . . . . . . | 50 | × | 2.00 | = | 100.00 |
| From Jan. 20 purchase. . . . . . . . . . . . . . . . . . . . . . | 20 | × | 2.50 | = | 50.00 |
| From Jan. 27 purchase. . . . . . . . . . . . . . . . . . . . . . | 50 | × | 4.00 | = | 200.00 |
| Specific identification ending inventory cost. . . . . . . | 220 | total units unsold | | | $475.00 |

**Specific Identification Cost of Goods Sold during January 1998**

|  | Units Sold | × | Unit Cost | = | Total Cost |
|---|---|---|---|---|---|
| From Jan. 12 purchase . . . . . . . . . . . . . . . . . . . . . . . . | 50 | × | $1.50 | = | $ 75.00 |
| From Jan. 18 purchase . . . . . . . . . . . . . . . . . . . . . . . . | 150 | × | 2.00 | = | 300.00 |
| From Jan. 20 purchase . . . . . . . . . . . . . . . . . . . . . . . . | 80 | × | 2.50 | = | 200.00 |
| Specific identification cost of goods sold . . . . . . . . | 280 | total units sold |  |  | $575.00 |

The shortcut calculation for the specific identification method is as follows:

| | |
|---|---|
| $1,050 | Cost of goods available for sale |
| − 475 | Ending inventory—Specific identification |
| $ 575 | Cost of goods sold—Specific identification |

### Advantages and Disadvantages of the Four Inventory Cost Methods

Each of the four methods explained thus far yields a different ending inventory and cost of goods sold, even though the selling price per unit is the same and the same number of units were sold. That means that each method yields a different profit. Exhibit 4 compares gross profits under the four different methods. In each case, we assume that the selling price is $6 per unit for each of the 280 units sold during January.

Depending on which inventory cost method Ready uses, the company can show a profit for the month ranging from $970 to $1,220. Yet in each case sales and purchases are exactly the same. The only difference lies in the method used to calculate ending inventory costs.

Why are so many different methods available? How is it possible that different methods, applied to the same data, can produce such different results? These questions are difficult, perhaps impossible, to answer satisfactorily. Nevertheless, let's try to gain some insight by examining some of the advantages and disadvantages of each method.

**Exhibit 4** Comparing Gross Profit under Four Inventory Methods

**READY COMPANY**
**Gross Profits under Four Inventory Methods**
**For Month Ended January 31, 1998**

|  | FIFO | LIFO | Weighted Average | Specific Identification |
|---|---|---|---|---|
| Sales (280 × $6) . . . . . . . . . . . . . . . . . | $1,680 | $1,680 | $1,680 | $1,680 |
| Cost of Goods Sold: |  |  |  |  |
|    Jan. 1, 1995, inventory. . . . . . . . . . . | $ 50 | $ 50 | $ 50 | $ 50 |
|    Purchases . . . . . . . . . . . . . . . . . . . | 1,000 | 1,000 | 1,000 | 1,000 |
|    Goods available . . . . . . . . . . . . . . . | $1,050 | $1,050 | $1,050 | $1,050 |
|    Jan. 31, 1995, inventory. . . . . . . . . | 590 | 340 | 462 | 475 |
|    Cost of goods sold . . . . . . . . . . . . . | $ 460 | $ 710 | $ 588 | $ 575 |
| Gross Profit . . . . . . . . . . . . . . . . . . . . | $1,220 | $ 970 | $1,092 | $1,105 |

**Exhibit 5** Characteristics of Four Inventory Costing Methods

| | FIFO | LIFO | Weighted Average | Specific Identification |
|---|---|---|---|---|
| Ending inventory costs | The more recent unit costs are assigned to the units not sold—those in ending inventory. | The earliest unit costs are assigned to the units not sold—those in ending inventory. | The same unit costs—the weighted average cost per unit—are assigned to units not sold and to units sold. | The actual per-unit cost of each unit unsold is assigned to ending inventory. |
| Cost of goods sold | Earliest unit costs are assigned to units sold—those in cost of goods sold expense. | The more recent unit costs are assigned to the units sold—those in cost of goods sold expense. | The same unit costs—the weighted average cost per unit—are assigned to units sold and unsold. | The actual per-unit cost of each unit sold is assigned to cost of goods sold expense. |
| Advantages | 1. Simple to use. <br> 2. Yields ending inventory amount on the balance sheet comprising more current costs than if weighted average or LIFO is used. <br> 3. Usually produces cost flow that approximates physical flow better than does weighted average or LIFO. | 1. Matches more recent costs with current revenue better than FIFO or weighted average. <br> 2. Yields the lowest income, thus the lowest income tax obligation during periods of rising prices. | 1. Assigns equal unit cost to each unit of inventory. <br> 2. Does not produce widely fluctuating profits when inventory costs are fluctuating, as FIFO and LIFO do. | 1. Simple to use. <br> 2. Cost flows and physical flows are the same. <br> 3. Matches each unit's cost with the revenue the unit helped produce. |
| Disadvantages | 1. Does not match recent costs with current revenue as well as LIFO does. <br> 2. Yields a higher taxable income than LIFO or weighted average during periods of rising prices. | 1. Does not produce an ending inventory amount that contains costs as recent as those included under FIFO or weighted average. <br> 2. Complicated to use by a firm with many different products. | 1. Does not match recent costs with current revenue as well as LIFO does. <br> 2. Does not produce an ending inventory amount that contains costs as recent as those included under FIFO. | 1. Use is limited to those firms dealing in a small quantity of high-cost, unique goods. |

Exhibit 5 lists the underlying characteristics of each method and summarizes the advantages and disadvantages that we are about to discuss. An assumption underlying our conclusions is that inventory costs are rising; that is, a period of inflation exists.

### FIFO

Ending inventory calculated using the FIFO method contains the more recent, highest costs. That implies that the units sold were assigned the older, lower costs. Thus FIFO calculates the highest ending inventory costs and a cost of goods sold lower than the weighted average or LIFO inventory method.

Ending inventory is reported as a current asset on the balance sheet. If you believe that the balance sheet should report the most recent costs possible, you would use the FIFO method for inventory costs.

The main advantage of FIFO is that it is a simple method to use. Also, for most merchandising businesses, the flow of costs approximates the flow of physical units. Even though accounting theory does not emphasize the relationship between cost and physical flow, some businesspeople prefer FIFO because of this logical relationship.

A disadvantage of FIFO is that it does not match current costs with current revenue, certainly not as well as does LIFO. (Remember: Using FIFO, the cost of goods sold is based on older, hence lower, unit costs.) Another disadvantage is that in periods of rapidly rising prices, this mismatch will produce an artificially high income, causing the firm to pay higher income taxes than if the LIFO method were used.

### LIFO

One advantage of LIFO is that it matches the most recent costs with the most current revenue, because under LIFO the costs of the units purchased most recently are assigned to cost of goods sold. Because of this better matching, LIFO provides a better measure of income than either FIFO or weighted average.

Furthermore, in periods of rising costs, LIFO produces a lower income than does either FIFO or weighted average. Exhibit 4 shows this clearly. Why would a company want to show a lower income? The lower a firm's taxable income, the lower the income taxes the firm has to pay. The Internal Revenue Service requires that if a company adopts LIFO, it must use LIFO for both income statement reporting and on its income tax return. In the highly inflationary 1970s, many corporations switched to the LIFO method of calculating ending inventory and cost of goods sold in order to gain this income tax advantage.

The disadvantages of LIFO are: (1) It may be rather complicated to implement in companies having a large number of different types of inventory; and (2) it may result in very old and currently unrealistic ending inventory costs, and thus an unrealistic measure of current assets on the balance sheet.

### Weighted Average

An advantage of the weighted average method is that it produces costs of goods sold, and thus profits, that fluctuate less sharply than they do under FIFO and LIFO. A substantial increase or decrease in inventory cost will cause FIFO and LIFO incomes suddenly to increase or decrease. Weighted average will combine these new costs with old costs in calculating the average cost per unit. Charging these average unit costs to cost of goods sold will result in a less dramatic change in income.

Disadvantages of the weighted average method are: (1) It fails to match current costs with current revenue as well as LIFO does; and (2) it does not produce an ending inventory cost that approximates current inventory costs as well as FIFO does.

### Specific Identification

The specific identification cost method is impractical for companies with extremely large numbers of units of inventory and is undesirable for companies dealing in units that are not clearly different from one another. Because specific identification is not based on orderly patterns of costs flowing through the accounts, there is no basis for comparison between it and the other cost flow methods.

### Consistency of Inventory Method

The **consistency principle** of accounting requires that the same accounting method be applied from period to period. This means that when a company selects an inventory method, such as FIFO or LIFO, it must use that method each year. The method used is disclosed in the footnotes to the financial statements or as a parenthetical note alongside the merchandise inventory on the balance sheet. This consistency enables readers of the income statement and the balance sheet to follow trends in cost of goods sold and ending inventory costs over a period of time, because they will know that any change in income or asset valuation will be caused by a change in actual costs, not by a change in the method of determining inventory costs.

The consistency principle does not prohibit a firm from ever changing accounting methods. A firm can change methods if it has a good reason to do so. The effects of the change on income and asset measurement are disclosed in the financial statement footnotes.

**ASK YOURSELF** ▶

1. **The cost of all goods available for sale must be divided into two parts at the end of the period. What are these two parts?**
2. **Which method assigns the earliest costs to ending inventory—FIFO or LIFO?**
3. **How does the shortcut calculation of cost of goods sold work?**
4. **Why is the shortcut always used when the weighted average method is applied?**
5. **Under what circumstances is the specific identification method appropriate?**
6. **Does the consistency principle mean that a company must choose one inventory method and use it forever?**

## VALUING INVENTORY AT LOWER-OF-COST-OR-MARKET

Learning Objective **5**

Calculate ending inventory value using the lower-of-cost-or-market methods

Sometimes there is plenty of an item in inventory when the demand for it suddenly falls off. Two things will then happen:

1. At the wholesale or supplier level, the replacement cost of those items will decline. This replacement cost is what we will call the *market price of inventory.*
2. At the level of the merchandising firm, the selling price will have to be lowered to get rid of—that is, to be competitive in selling—what remains in inventory.

# FIFO Contributes to Amerada Hess Loss

Amerada Hess Corp., hurt by a continuing drop in oil prices, omitted its quarterly dividend of 27.5 cents a share, which would have been paid March 31.

The oil company also forecast a "substantial" first-quarter loss and said it will cut costs by lowering capital spending, shrinking its work force and reducing its refining activity.

Hess has incurred losses in its refining and marketing operations for two years while earning money on exploration and production, a spokesman said. He didn't specify the company's cost-saving goal.

Much of the expected loss in the first quarter, one analyst said, will stem from Hess's use of the first-in, first-out, or FIFO, method of inventory accounting. Under the method, Hess bases its cost of goods sold on the cost of its oldest crude oil inventories, which were more expensive than the current market level. Most oil companies use a last-in, first-out, or LIFO, method. The Hess spokesman conceded that the company's method of accounting makes its financial results appear weaker than those of competitors when prices for crude are declining.

In the year-earlier first quarter, Hess's net income was $37.2 million, or 44 cents a share, after a special gain of $2.3 million from the sale of stock. Revenue was $2.1 billion.

*Source:* John D. Williams, *The Wall Street Journal,* Mar. 6, 1986, p. 30. Reprinted by permission of The Wall Street Journal, copyright © 1986 Dow Jones & Company, Inc. All rights reserved.

When one company in an industry uses one accounting method and others use another, it may be difficult to compare their operating results. During periods of rising prices, Amerada Hess's use of FIFO would result in older, lower prices being matched with current high revenues. Hess's income would thus tend to be higher than that of companies using LIFO. Falling oils prices produce an opposite effect. Hess now must match older, higher costs with current lower revenues. As this article reports, the income disadvantage produced by using FIFO can cause negative results at a time when the other parts of a company's operations are profitable.

Thus the firm is caught in a squeeze between lower selling prices and higher inventory costs (the amount the firm paid *before* replacement cost declined). The firm's inventory isn't valued at the lower replacement cost, because none has been bought at that price. Indeed, the firm is loaded with inventory purchased at the older, higher price, which is the cost of that inventory.

Further, since the firm must sell its inventory at a lower selling price, the company's ability to generate the normal gross profit on sales is impaired. That is, its cost of goods sold will be at the old, higher costs while its sales will be at the new, lower selling price. Such a loss in profit is measurable. The loss—and the reduction in the inventory's value—should be recognized in the period when the drop in replacement costs occurs, not in a later period when the items are sold.

The loss in value that results from a reduction in the replacement cost of inventory is calculated by the **lower-of-cost-or-market** technique, often simply called **LCM.** LCM is calculated by comparing inventory cost, as determined by one of the methods discussed earlier in the chapter, with market, which is the current replacement cost of the goods. LCM can be applied to each item of inventory, to various subgroupings of inventory, or to the inventory as a whole, as shown below.

| Inventory Item No. | Description | Quantity | Cost (FIFO) | Market (Replacement Cost) | LCM Item by Item |
|---|---|---|---|---|---|
| 101 | Hose | 10 | $ 20 | $ 18 | $ 18 |
| 102 | Bracket | 40 | 40 | 42 | 40 |
| 103 | Clamp | 5 | 20 | 15 | 15 |
| 206 | Motor | 2 | 125 | 100 | 100 |
| 208 | Mount | 60 | 180 | 165 | 165 |
| 210 | Generator | 4 | 188 | 208 | 188 |
| Totals | | | $573 | $548 | $526 |

The LCM item-by-item column amounts are determined by comparing the cost and market for each item and choosing the lower of the two in each case. The cost is lower for items no. 102 and no. 210; market is lower for all the others. These LCM item-by-item amounts are totaled and this amount, $526, is used to calculate the loss, as follows:

Cost (FIFO) ................................. $573
LCM (item by item) .......................... 526

Loss ....................................... $ 47

The loss in value can also be estimated by comparing the total cost of all the inventory with the total market of all the inventory:

Cost (FIFO) ................................. $573
Market (total inventory) ....................... 548

Loss ....................................... $ 25

A firm will choose whichever method—item-by-item or total inventory—is easier for it to use. Either method of estimating the loss is acceptable, provided that it is used consistently from period to period. The loss will then be reported on the income statement either as a separate item or under cost of goods sold.

The principle of conservatism is the justification for the LCM rule. *Conservatism* in accounting means that we should choose accounting methods that are least likely to overstate assets and income. Valuing inventory at cost when its replacement cost is lower overstates the asset merchandise inventory. Thus, we apply the conservatism principle and use LCM to reduce inventory to a more realistic value and, at the same time, recognize the loss in value that has occurred.

We have only demonstrated the basic idea behind LCM here. The more complex refinements of this technique are explored in more advanced accounting courses.

## METHODS OF ESTIMATING ENDING INVENTORY

Learning 6
Objective

Estimate ending inventory using the gross profit and retail inventory methods

When the periodic inventory system is used, it is necessary to count inventory to prepare an income statement; but sometimes counting is inconvenient or even impossible. For most firms, the time and expense involved in counting inventory each month would make it too costly to prepare monthly income statements. Also, a catastrophe, such as a fire, could destroy inventory, making it impossible to count. Thus, it would be impossible to prepare a meaningful income statement—we wouldn't know how much of the inventory purchased had been sold before the fire and how much had been destroyed. To overcome these problems, two methods have been devised for estimating ending inventory without taking a physical count: the gross profit method and the retail inventory method.

### The Gross Profit Method

The **gross profit method** relies on the relationships among sales, cost of goods sold, and gross profit to derive an estimate of ending inventory cost. The following illustration demonstrates how this method works.

A partial income statement (we have left out operating expenses and income taxes) for the year 1997 for the Billings Company follows.

**BILLINGS COMPANY**
**Partial Income Statement**
**Year Ended December 31, 1997**

| | | | |
|---|---|---|---|
| Sales . . . . . . . . . . . . . . . . . . . . . . . . . . . . . . . . . . . . . . . . . . . . . . . . . . . . | | $100,000 | 100% |
| Cost of Goods Sold: | | | |
| Beginning Inventory . . . . . . . . . . . . . . . . . . . . . . . . . . . . | $16,000 | | |
| Purchases . . . . . . . . . . . . . . . . . . . . . . . . . . . . . . . . . . . . . | 74,000 | | |
| Goods Available for Sale . . . . . . . . . . . . . . . . . . . . . . . | $90,000 | | |
| Ending Inventory . . . . . . . . . . . . . . . . . . . . . . . . . . . . . . . | 10,000 | 80,000 | 80% |
| Gross Profit on Sales . . . . . . . . . . . . . . . . . . . . . . . . . . . . . . . . . . . . . . | | $ 20,000 | 20% |

On Apr. 4, 1998, the Billings Company warehouse was destroyed by fire. The accounting records were stored in a fireproof vault, so the information about sales revenue, beginning inventory cost, and purchases for the period Jan. 1–Apr. 4, 1998, were still available.

Percentages have been added to the 1997 Billings income statement so that the relationships among sales, cost of goods sold, and gross profit can be seen. Cost of goods sold is 80% of sales ($80,000 ÷ $100,000), and gross profit is 20% of sales ($20,000 ÷ $100,000). There were no changes in inventory costs or selling prices during the first part of 1998. The assumption is, then, that the same percentage relationships existed until the date of the fire. The salvaged 1998 accounting records provide these data:

Sales (Jan. 1–Apr. 4, 1998) . . . . . . . . . . . . . . . .    $24,000
Purchases (Jan. 1–Apr. 4, 1998) . . . . . . . . . . . .    16,200
Beginning inventory (Jan. 1, 1998) . . . . . . . . . . .    10,000

Ending inventory can be calculated as follows:

Goods available for sale:
   Beginning inventory (known) (Jan. 1) . . . . . . . .    $10,000
   Purchases (known) (Jan. 1–Apr. 4) . . . . . . . . .    16,200
     Goods available for sale . . . . . . . . . . . . . . .    $26,200
Less: Cost of goods sold:
   Sales (known) (Jan. 1–Apr. 4) . . .    $24,000
   × Cost of goods sold % (assumed)    80%    19,200

Estimated ending inventory, Apr. 4, 1998 . . . . . . .    $ 7,000

You should be aware of two things when you consider using the gross profit method:

1. Accounting records are normally protected against fire and theft, so it is not unrealistic to expect that the necessary figures would be available. To use the gross profit method we must know sales, a gross profit percentage, beginning inventory, and purchases.
2. Percentages expressing the relationship between past gross profit and sales, and cost of goods sold and sales, should not be used blindly. Always ask yourself whether you need to modify these percentages to reflect any recent changes in costs or selling prices.

## The Retail Inventory Method

The **retail inventory method** is based on the percentage relationship between the cost of inventory and its retail price. As its name implies, this method was developed for use by retail establishments, particularly department stores. The retailer accumulates the cost of inventory acquired in the way that we discussed in the early part of this chapter: The store records purchases, purchases returns and allowances, purchases discounts, and freight-in just as any other business does. A supplementary system accumulates and keeps up with the retail price of the merchandise offered for sale. Retail prices of inventory are not recorded in the formal accounting journals and ledgers.

The following illustration explains how the retail inventory method works.

CAREFREE CASUALS
Calculation of Ending Inventory
Using Retail Inventory Method
September 30, 1998

|  | Cost | Retail |
|---|---|---|
| Beginning inventory . . . . . . . . . . . . . . . . . . . . . . . . . . . . . . . | $ 76,000 | $102,000 |
| Purchases (net) . . . . . . . . . . . . . . . . . . . . . . . . . . . . . . . . . | 185,000 | 246,000 |
| Total cost and retail price of goods available . . . . . . . . . . . . | $261,000 | $348,000 |
| Less: Sales (net) . . . . . . . . . . . . . . . . . . . . . . . . . . . . . . . . |  | (228,000) |
| Ending inventory at retail price . . . . . . . . . . . . . . . . . . . . . . . |  | $120,000 |
| × Cost-to-retail ratio ($261,000/$348,000) . . . . . . . . . . . . . . |  | 75% |
| Ending inventory at cost . . . . . . . . . . . . . . . . . . . . . . . . . . . |  | $ 90,000 |

For all goods available for sale during the period, Carefree first accumulated the total cost, $261,000, and the total retail price, $348,000. These amounts were used to compute a **cost-to-retail ratio:** the ratio of the cost of goods available to the retail price of those same goods ($261,000 ÷ $348,000 = 75%). This ratio means that the cost of goods on hand was, on the average, 75% of their selling price.

Next, actual sales *at the retail price* are deducted from the total retail price of all goods available for sale. This reveals the ending inventory at its retail price, $120,000.

Ending inventory at retail price is then converted to ending inventory at cost by multiplying by the cost-to-retail ratio ($120,000 × 75% = $90,000).

Care must be used in applying the retail inventory method. A retailer should not include goods having a cost-to-retail ratio of 50%, such as furniture, in the same calculation with goods having a cost-to-retail ratio of 75%, such as shoes. To do so would distort the cost-to-retail ratio and yield an incorrect estimate of ending inventory. Many retailers prepare a separate calculation for each retail department and then add up the resulting inventory cost amounts to determine total ending inventory cost.

A simplified version of the retail inventory method was used here to estimate the cost of ending inventory. In actual practice this method may be used to estimate ending inventory at lower-of-cost-or-market or at replacement cost. The calculations must be modified if an estimate of LIFO cost is desired. The complexities of these applications are covered in advanced accounting courses.

## INVENTORY ERRORS

Learning Objective **7**

Explain and demonstrate how an error in inventory accounting affects income

Errors can happen in the process of calculating ending inventory costs under the periodic inventory system. After all, it is a complex process that includes counting inventory, determining which units to include or exclude on the basis of FOB and consignment terms, and applying one of the four cost flow methods.

To understand how an error in the calculation of ending inventory cost affects the income statement, consider Exhibit 6. Note that an error in ending inventory for year 1 also affects the next year because the ending inventory cost in year 1 becomes the beginning inventory cost for year 2. If the ending inventory cost of year 2 is correct, there will be no additional effect on year 3 because the beginning inventory for year 3 will be correct. Thus the impact of the error is confined to a 2-year period, and the error is said to *self-correct* or *counterbalance* over the 2 years. In this illustration the understatement of ending inventory in year 1 causes an understatement of year 1 gross profit. This is counterbalanced in year 2 by the understatement of beginning inventory, which causes an overstatement of year 2 gross profit.

There is a quick way to determine the effects of errors in inventory cost without constructing a cost of goods sold section. Simply visualize the Income Summary account after all revenue, expenses, and inventory items have been closed. It would look like this:

| Income Summary | |
|---|---|
| Expenses | Revenue |
| Beginning inventory | Ending inventory |
| Purchases | |

Note the following:

Revenue appears on the credit side of the Income Summary (the closing entry is to debit the Revenue account and credit Income Summary).

**Exhibit 6** Illustration of the Effects of Inventory Errors

## MARK COMPANY
### *Correct* Gross Profit Computation
### Years 1 and 2

|  | Year 1 | | Year 2 | |
|---|---|---|---|---|
| Sales . . . . . . . . . . . . . . . . . . . . . . . . . . . . . . . . . . . . . . . . | | $100 | | $160 |
| Cost of goods sold: | | | | |
| Beginning inventory. . . . . . . . . . . . . . . . . . . . . . . . . . | $ 20 | | $ 50 | |
| Purchases . . . . . . . . . . . . . . . . . . . . . . . . . . . . . . . . | 90 | | 120 | |
| Goods available for sale . . . . . . . . . . . . . . . . . . . . . | $110 | | $170 | |
| Ending inventory . . . . . . . . . . . . . . . . . . . . . . . . . . . . | 50 | 60 | 70 | 100 |
| Gross profit (correct). . . . . . . . . . . . . . . . . . . . . . . . . . | | $ 40 | | $ 60 |

## MARK COMPANY
### *Inventory Error* in Gross Profit Computation
### Years 1 and 2

|  | Year 1 | | Year 2 | |
|---|---|---|---|---|
| Sales . . . . . . . . . . . . . . . . . . . . . . . . . . . . . . . . . . . . . . . . | | $100 | | $160 |
| Cost of goods sold: | | | | |
| Beginning inventory (erroneous in year 2) . . . . . . . . . . | $ 20 | | $ 30 | |
| Purchases . . . . . . . . . . . . . . . . . . . . . . . . . . . . . . . . | 90 | | 120 | |
| Goods available for sale (erroneous in year 2) . . . . . . | $110 | | $150 | |
| Ending inventory (erroneous in year 1) . . . . . . . . . . . . | 30 | 80 | 70 | 80 |
| Gross profit (erroneous) . . . . . . . . . . . . . . . . . . . . . . . . | | $ 20 | | $ 80 |

## MARK COMPANY
### Effect of Inventory Error

|  | Year 1 | Year 2 | Total |
|---|---|---|---|
| Correct gross profit. . . . . . . . . . . . . . . . . . . | $40 | $60 | $ 100 |
| Erroneous gross profit . . . . . . . . . . . . . . . . | 20 | 80 | 100 |
| Effect of error . . . . . . . . . . . . . . . . . . . . . . . | $20 | ($20) | $–0– |
|  | *Gross profit understated by $20* | *Gross profit overstated by $20* | *No effect for 2-year period* |

Expenses appear on the debit side (the closing entry is to debit Income Summary and credit the Expense account).

Since Beginning Inventory and Purchases have debit balances, the closing entry will be to debit Income Summary and credit these two accounts.

Ending inventory is then established by debiting Merchandise Inventory and crediting Income Summary.

Now observe that an error in either beginning inventory or purchases will have the *same effect* as an error in an expense account. For example, an understatement of beginning inventory will have the same effect as understating an expense—to overstate income. An error in ending inventory will have the *same effect* as an error in a revenue account. For example, an understatement of ending inventory will have the same effect as understating revenue—to understate income.

Use this mental shortcut to review the Mark Company illustration presented in Exhibit 6.

---

**ASK YOURSELF ▶**

1. **When lower-of-cost-or-market is used for valuing inventory, how is "market" defined?**
2. **What is the principle of conservatism as used in accounting?**
3. **What circumstances may cause a firm to estimate inventory amounts?**
4. **What information must be known in order to apply the gross profit method of estimating inventory?**
5. **How is the cost-to-retail ratio derived? What is it used for?**
6. **How are inventory errors "self-correcting"?**

## THE PERPETUAL INVENTORY SYSTEM

Under the *periodic inventory system,* ending inventory units, ending inventory cost, and cost of goods sold are determined only at the end of each time period.

Learning Objective **8**

Describe a perpetual inventory system

Under the *perpetual inventory system,* the business constantly updates its record of merchandise inventory on hand. This means that each time inventory is acquired, the Merchandise Inventory account is increased, and whenever sales are made, the Merchandise Inventory account is decreased. When management wants to know the cost of merchandise on hand, it needs only to consult the Merchandise Inventory account. To find out the amount of inventory on hand under the periodic system, it is necessary to make a physical count or rely on an estimate.

In the discussion that follows, we'll illustrate recording inventory acquisitions and sales under the perpetual method, we'll demonstrate how perpetual FIFO and LIFO work, and then we'll consider the impact of the computer on perpetual inventory records.

### Recording Inventory Acquisitions and Sales

Learning Objective **9**

Record acquisitions and sales under a perpetual inventory system

The following illustration reviews inventory acquisitions and sales using the periodic system and shows the same transactions under the perpetual method.

Lever Co. acquires merchandise on account—list price $10,000, credit terms 2/10, n/30. Lever uses the net method of recording purchases.

| Perpetual Inventory System | | |
|---|---|---|
| Merchandise Inventory .......... | 9,800 | |
|     Accounts Payable.......... | | 9,800 |

| Periodic Inventory System | | |
|---|---|---|
| Purchases .................... | 9,800 | |
|     Accounts Payable.......... | | 9,800 |

Lever returns goods with a net price of $1,225 to the seller.

| Perpetual Inventory System | | | Periodic Inventory System | | |
|---|---|---|---|---|---|
| Accounts Payable . . . . . . . . . . . . . . | 1,225 | | Accounts Payable . . . . . . . . . . . . . . | 1,225 | |
| Merchandise Inventory . . . . . . . | | 1,225 | Purchases Returns & | | |
| | | | Allowances . . . . . . . . . . . . . . | | 1,225 |

Lever pays for the remaining goods within the discount period. Amount = $8,575 ($9,800 − $1,225).

| Perpetual Inventory System | | | Periodic Inventory System | | |
|---|---|---|---|---|---|
| Accounts Payable . . . . . . . . . . . . . | 8,575 | | Accounts Payable . . . . . . . . . . . . . | 8,575 | |
| Cash . . . . . . . . . . . . . . . . . . . . | | 8,575 | Cash . . . . . . . . . . . . . . . . . . . . | | 8,575 |

Lever pays $150 freight on the merchandise purchased.

| Perpetual Inventory System | | | Periodic Inventory System | | |
|---|---|---|---|---|---|
| Merchandise Inventory . . . . . . . . . . | 150 | | Freight-In . . . . . . . . . . . . . . . . . . . . | 150 | |
| Cash . . . . . . . . . . . . . . . . . . . . | | 150 | Cash . . . . . . . . . . . . . . . . . . . . | | 150 |

Lever sells inventory which cost $1,090 for $2,200 on account.

| Perpetual Inventory System | | | Periodic Inventory System | | |
|---|---|---|---|---|---|
| Accounts Receivable . . . . . . . . . . . | 2,200 | | Accounts Receivable . . . . . . . . . . . | 2,200 | |
| Sales . . . . . . . . . . . . . . . . . . . | | 2,200 | Sales . . . . . . . . . . . . . . . . . . . | | 2,200 |
| Cost of Goods Sold . . . . . . . . . . . . | 1,090 | | No entry for cost of goods sold under | | |
| Merchandise Inventory . . . . . . . | | 1,090 | periodic system. | | |

A customer returns merchandise which cost $350 and sold for $702.

| Perpetual Inventory System | | | Periodic Inventory System | | |
|---|---|---|---|---|---|
| Sales Returns and Allowances . . . . | 702 | | Sales Returns and Allowances . . . . | 702 | |
| Accounts Receivable . . . . . . . . | | 702 | Accounts Receivable . . . . . . . . | | 702 |
| Merchandise Inventory . . . . . . . . . . | 350 | | No entry for the cost of the inventory | | |
| Cost of Goods Sold . . . . . . . . . | | 350 | returned under the periodic system. | | |

A customer pays for merchandise which had been bought on account. The sales price is $1,200, terms 2/10, n/30. The customer pays within the discount period.

| Perpetual Inventory System | | | Periodic Inventory System | | |
|---|---|---|---|---|---|
| Cash . . . . . . . . . . . . . . . . . . . . . . | 1,176 | | Cash . . . . . . . . . . . . . . . . . . . . . . | 1,176 | |
| Sales Discounts . . . . . . . . . . . . . . . | 24 | | Sales Discounts . . . . . . . . . . . . . . . | 24 | |
| Accounts Receivable . . . . . . . . | | 1,200 | Accounts Receivable . . . . . . . . | | 1,200 |

In contrasting the two inventory systems, notice the following:

1. The perpetual system uses no Purchases account. It records all purchases directly in the Merchandise Inventory account. The periodic system uses a Purchases account.
2. The perpetual system records merchandise returned to suppliers by directly reducing the Merchandise Inventory account. The periodic system uses a Purchases Returns and Allowances account.
3. The perpetual system records cost of goods sold and reduces Merchandise Inventory when merchandise is sold. The periodic system calculates cost of goods sold on the basis of the inventory remaining on hand at the end of the period and records cost of goods sold through the closing process.
4. The perpetual system records customer returns by reducing Cost of Goods Sold and increasing Merchandise Inventory. The periodic system makes no entry; the merchandise is returned to stock.
5. The cost of goods sold and inventory amounts are readily available at any time under the perpetual system. Cost of goods sold and inventory amounts are usually not available until they are calculated at year-end under the periodic system.

### Perpetual FIFO

The same methods may be employed under the perpetual inventory system as under the periodic system: FIFO, LIFO, weighted average, and specific identification. When we use the periodic system, we wait until the end of the period to decide which costs to assign to Merchandise Inventory and which to Cost of Goods Sold. With the perpetual system, in contrast, we must decide which costs to assign to Cost of Goods Sold at the time each sale is made. So each time we make a sale, we record the sale in one entry and the cost of goods sold in another.

The same Ready Company data used to illustrate the periodic inventory methods will be used here to demonstrate calculation of cost of goods sold and ending inventory under perpetual FIFO and LIFO. Assume that the inventory item is a filter (stock no. 105). Sales information has been added to the recap of beginning inventory and purchases shown below:

Learning Objective **10**

Calculate ending inventory and cost of goods sold using perpetual FIFO and LIFO

---

**READY COMPANY**
**Inventory and Sales Data**
**Month Ended January 31, 1998**

| Date | Description | Units | Cost Each | Total |
|---|---|---|---|---|
| Jan.  1 | Beginning Inventory . . . . . . . . . . . . . . . . . | 50 | $1.00 | $    50.00 |
| Jan. 12 | Purchase . . . . . . . . . . . . . . . . . . . . . . . . . | 100 | 1.50 | 150.00 |
| Jan. 15 | Sale . . . . . . . . . . . . . . . . . . . . . . . . . . . . . | 50 | | |
| Jan. 18 | Purchase . . . . . . . . . . . . . . . . . . . . . . . . . | 200 | 2.00 | 400.00 |
| Jan. 20 | Purchase . . . . . . . . . . . . . . . . . . . . . . . . . | 100 | 2.50 | 250.00 |
| Jan. 22 | Sale . . . . . . . . . . . . . . . . . . . . . . . . . . . . . | 150 | | |
| Jan. 27 | Purchase . . . . . . . . . . . . . . . . . . . . . . . . . | 50 | 4.00 | 200.00 |
| Jan. 30 | Sale . . . . . . . . . . . . . . . . . . . . . . . . . . . . . | 80 | | |
| | | | Total cost of goods available | $1,050.00 |

**Exhibit 7** Perpetual FIFO Inventory Ledger Card

Item: Filter no. 105

| Date | Purchases No. of Units | Unit Cost | Total Cost | Cost of Goods Sold No. of Units | Unit Cost | Total Cost | Inventory on Hand No. of Units | Unit Cost | Total Cost |
|---|---|---|---|---|---|---|---|---|---|
| Jan. 1 | 50 | $1.00 | $ 50 | | | | 50 | $1.00 | $ 50 |
| 12 | 100 | 1.50 | 150 | | | | 50<br>100 | 1.00<br>1.50 | 50<br>150 |
| 15 | | | | 50 | $1.00 | $50 | 100 | 1.50 | 150 |
| 18 | 200 | 2.00 | 400 | | | | 100<br>200 | 1.50<br>2.00 | 150<br>400 |
| 20 | 100 | 2.50 | 250 | | | | 100<br>200<br>100 | 1.50<br>2.00<br>2.50 | 150<br>400<br>250 |
| 22 | | | | 100<br>50 | 1.50<br>2.00 | 150<br>100 | 150<br>100 | 2.00<br>2.50 | 300<br>250 |
| 27 | 50 | 4.00 | 200 | | | | 150<br>100<br>50 | 2.00<br>2.50<br>4.00 | 300<br>250<br>200 |
| 30 | | | | 80 | 2.00 | 160 | 70<br>100<br>50 | 2.00<br>2.50<br>4.00 | 140<br>250<br>200 |

*Perpetual FIFO*
*Cost of goods sold = $460*

*Perpetual FIFO*
*Ending inventory = $590*

Perpetual FIFO assigns the earliest cost to cost of goods sold each time a sale is made and assigns the most recent costs to ending inventory. The subsidiary inventory ledger card for Ready Company's filter no. 105 is illustrated in Exhibit 7. It can be used to calculate the cost of filters sold for January, $460 ($50 + $150 + $100 + $160), and the FIFO perpetual ending inventory for January, $590 ($140 + $250 + $200). Indeed, the cost of goods sold and inventory on hand at any time can be calculated simply by looking at the inventory ledger card.

### Perpetual LIFO

Perpetual LIFO assigns the most recent costs to cost of goods sold each time a sale is made and assigns the earliest costs to inventory on hand. Exhibit 8 illustrates the subsidiary inventory ledger card for filter no. 105 assuming the perpetual LIFO method.

Again, the subsidiary inventory ledger card can be used to calculate the cost of filters sold for January, $685 ($75 + $250 + $100 + $200 + $60), and the LIFO perpetual ending inventory for January, $365 ($50 + $75 + $240).

**Exhibit 8** Perpetual LIFO Inventory Ledger Card

Item: Filter no. 105

| Date | Purchases No. of Units | Unit Cost | Total Cost | Cost of Goods Sold Units | Unit Cost | Total Cost | Inventory on Hand No. of Units | Unit Cost | Total Cost |
|---|---|---|---|---|---|---|---|---|---|
| Jan. 1 | 50 | $1.00 | $ 50 | | | | 50 | $1.00 | $ 50 |
| 12 | 100 | 1.50 | 150 | | | | 50 100 | 1.00 1.50 | 50 150 |
| 15 | | | | 50 | $1.50 | $75 | 50 50 | 1.00 1.50 | 50 75 |
| 18 | 200 | 2.00 | 400 | | | | 50 50 200 | 1.00 1.50 2.00 | 50 75 400 |
| 20 | 100 | 2.50 | 250 | | | | 50 50 200 100 | 1.00 1.50 2.00 2.50 | 50 75 400 250 |
| 22 | | | | 100 50 | 2.50 2.00 | 250 100 | 50 50 150 | 1.00 1.50 2.00 | 50 75 300 |
| 27 | 50 | 4.00 | 200 | | | | 50 50 150 50 | 1.00 1.50 2.00 4.00 | 50 75 300 200 |
| 30 | | | | 50 30 | 4.00 2.00 | 200 60 | 50 50 120 | 1.00 1.50 2.00 | 50 75 240 |

*Perpetual LIFO*
*Cost of goods sold = $685*

*Perpetual LIFO*
*Ending inventory = $365*

## Perpetual Weighted Average

When the periodic weighted average method was used, the weighted average cost of the units was calculated at the end of the period, and this average was used to calculate ending inventory and cost of goods sold. In contrast, the perpetual weighted average method requires that we calculate an average each time a purchase is made. Each time a sale is made, the most recent average is used to determine cost of goods sold. This *moving average method* can require a large number of calculations each period. These calculations are complex, so they are best left for a more advanced course.

## Computerized Perpetual Inventory Records

Today's high-speed, relatively low-cost computer systems enable many businesses to keep their inventory records on a perpetual basis. You have probably been through the checkout line of a discount department store and watched the clerk key in a long number from the tag of each item, or use a light-pencil or computerized checkout device to read a code on each product you are buying. These codes record the stock number and possibly the size, color, and other information about each item. These data are fed by the cash register into a computer which instantly updates the store's merchandise inventory records.

Some businesses use the computerized perpetual inventory system to keep track of only the number of units of items sold and on hand. This information tells the manager how quickly a particular item is selling and how low the stock on hand may be. The manager can then use this information to order additional goods to avoid running out of a profitable product. Or the computer may be programmed to order an optimum quantity of goods automatically whenever a certain stock level is reached.

Other companies track not only the number of units but also the cost of all units on hand and sold. These businesses are keeping records similar to the perpetual subsidiary inventory ledger cards illustrated earlier. These "cards" are now in the form of information stored on a computer memory device, such as a tape or disk, and may contain additional information such as color and size.

No matter how sophisticated the perpetual inventory record system is, a physical inventory count must be made at least once each year. This count, when compared with the perpetual inventory records, will reveal errors in the perpetual records and possibly shortages caused by theft. Differences between the amounts determined by physical count and those in the perpetual inventory records are recorded by debiting a loss account and crediting Merchandise Inventory. The loss account should appear on the income statement among operating expenses.

## FINANCIAL STATEMENT ANALYSIS: INVENTORY TURNOVER

Learning Objective 11

Calculate and explain the use of the inventory turnover ratio

**Inventory turnover** shows how many times the average dollars invested in merchandise inventory were sold (turned over) during the year. This statistic, when compared with the year-end merchandise inventory, provides a basis for judging whether the company has an excessive investment in merchandise at the end of the year. A too-large ending inventory may indicate that sales volume was not as high as expected near year-end, or possibly that management was inefficient in allowing too many unsold goods to accumulate. However, a large inventory may be present because of an unusually high sales volume expected near the beginning of the next period.

Inventory turnover is calculated by dividing cost of goods sold by average merchandise inventory (beginning inventory plus ending inventory divided by 2). Cost of goods sold is used instead of sales because sales includes gross profit, while cost of goods sold, like merchandise inventory, does not. The general formula is:

$$\text{Inventory turnover} = \frac{\text{cost of goods sold}}{\text{average merchandise inventory}}$$

Using data from the Ready Company perpetual LIFO example above:

$$\text{Inventory turnover} = \frac{\$685}{(\$50 + \$365) \div 2}$$

$$= \frac{\$685}{\$207.50} = 3.30 \text{ times}$$

Since Ready's inventory turns over about 3 times per year, the year-end inventory should be about one-third of cost of goods sold. Ready's inventory of $365 is above this amount ($1/3 \times \$685 = \$228$). This excess is probably explained by Ready's increasing sales volume.

## CURRENT ASSETS ON THE BALANCE SHEET: A REVIEW

Since we have reached the end of our detailed discussion of the current asset accounts, it is a good time to review what you know about current assets and illustrate how the current assets section of a balance sheet looks with all of the accounts that you have learned about.

*Current assets* include all those assets that will be converted into cash or used up in the operations of the business within the next year. The current asset accounts are arranged in order of liquidity — first is the asset most readily converted into cash and last is the asset least readily converted into cash.

The following current assets section of a balance sheet shows the accounts in their proper order:

| Current Assets: | | |
|---|---:|---:|
| Cash | | $ 120,000 |
| Notes Receivable | | 10,300 |
| Accounts Receivable | $364,000 | |
| Less: Allowance for Uncollectible Accounts | (18,000) | 346,000 |
| Receivable from Credit Card Companies | | 45,000 |
| Interest Receivable | | 6,100 |
| Receivable from Company Officers | | 10,000 |
| Merchandise Inventory at Lower of FIFO Cost or Market | | 579,000 |
| Supplies on Hand | | 19,400 |
| Prepaid Rent | | 3,600 |
| Prepaid Insurance | | 4,400 |
| Total Current Assets | | $1,143,800 |

**ASK YOURSELF** ▶

1. What is the difference between a periodic and a perpetual inventory system?
2. How do the entries to record a purchase and a sale of inventory differ under the periodic and perpetual systems?
3. Under the perpetual inventory system, how do you decide how much cost to charge to cost of goods sold when a unit is sold?
4. Is a physical inventory count necessary when the perpetual inventory system is used? Why or why not?
5. What assets are included among current assets?

### SUMMARY

• **Merchandise inventory**—the goods held for sale—is a major part of the total assets of retailers and wholesalers. Merchandise inventory for a manufacturer is usually called **finished goods inventory.**
• Accounting for merchandise inventory involves three tasks: (1) calculating the cost of units purchased; (2) determining the number of physical units on hand; and (3) allocating cost between those units on hand and those that were sold.
• The cost of units purchased is calculated as follows: Purchases − purchases discounts − purchases returns and allowances + freight-in. The amount recorded as purchases is the list price of the goods less trade and quantity discounts.
• For the number of physical units on hand to be determined, they must be physi-

cally counted and consideration must be given to goods in transit and consignment arrangements. Units purchased *FOB shipping point* must be included in ending inventory even though not yet received. Goods purchased *FOB destination* are not included; they are owned by the business only after they have been received. Goods sold FOB destination are included; goods sold FOB shipping point are excluded. *Goods in on consignment* are excluded from ending inventory because they are the legal property of another company, the *consignor. Goods out on consignment* must be included in ending inventory because they belong to the firm even though they are not physically present.

- There are four methods of assigning cost to the units in ending inventory: (1) **first-in, first-out (FIFO),** (2) **last-in, first-out (LIFO),** (3) **weighted average,** and (4) **specific identification.** Under identical starting, operating, and ending conditions, each method will produce a different gross profit. The inventory method chosen must be used consistently year after year unless a change in method can be justified. When there is a change in inventory method, it must be disclosed on the financial statements.

- If the demand for an item falls off at the retail level, the value of the inventory of those items will similarly decline. And at the wholesale level, their replacement cost will also decline. When this happens, the problem is what to use as inventory "cost" —the actual cost already paid, or the current replacement cost (also referred to as *market cost).* A solution to this problem is **lower-of-cost-** (actual cost paid) **or-market** (current replacement cost), or **LCM.** LCM recognizes a loss in the period during which the value of the inventory declined, not in the period during which the inventory is sold.

- When a physical count of inventory is inconvenient, impractical, or impossible, the cost of ending inventory may be estimated by the **gross profit method** or the **retail inventory method.**

- An error in the ending inventory of one year will automatically cause an error in the beginning inventory of the next period. Errors in ending inventory amounts are said to be *self-correcting,* or *counterbalancing,* over a 2-year period.

- Any of the four methods of determining ending inventory cost may be applied in a perpetual or a periodic inventory system. Under a complete **perpetual inventory system,** both the cost and the number of units on hand are known at all times. In a **periodic inventory system,** the ending inventory is determined by physical count and costs are assigned on the basis of this count. The periodic system determines ending inventory only at the end of a period.

- When the perpetual inventory method is used, purchases of merchandise are entered directly into the Merchandise Inventory account—no Purchases account is used. Sales of inventory under the perpetual system require two entries. One entry records the revenue at the retail price; the other entry records cost of goods sold and reduces merchandise inventory for the inventory's cost.

- High-speed, relatively low-cost computer systems enable many businesses to keep their inventory records on a perpetual basis. Perpetual inventory systems may be used to keep track of only the number of physical units on hand or both the cost and the number for physical units on hand.

- **Inventory turnover** indicates how many times the average amount invested in inventory has been sold during a period. This statistic provides a measure of how efficient management has been in managing inventory.

- The current assets section of the balance sheet includes all assets that will be converted into cash or used up within the next year. Current assets are listed in order of liquidity—the asset most easily converted into cash is listed first and the one least readily converted is listed last.

## 12 KEY TERMS

**Consignment**
An arrangement in which one business, the *consignee,* sells goods owned by another business, the *consignor.* The consignee receives a commission for selling the consignor's goods and is responsible for them while they are in his or her possession.

**Consistency principle**
The principle requiring that the accounting methods used in a current period have been used in past periods and will continue to be used in future periods.

**Cost-to-retail ratio**
The cost of merchandise available for sale divided by its retail price. The retail inventory method uses this ratio in estimating ending inventory.

**Finished goods inventory**
The name that manufacturers use for merchandise inventory.

**First-in, first-out (FIFO) method**
A method of accounting for inventory costs that assumes that the first, or earliest, costs incurred are the first costs that will be charged to cost of goods sold expense and the most recent costs will be assigned to ending inventory.

**Gross profit method**
A method of estimating the cost of inventory based on past records of sales, cost of goods sold, and gross profit and on the relationships among these amounts.

**Last-in, first-out (LIFO) method**
A method of accounting for inventory costs that assumes that the most recent costs incurred are the costs that will be charged to cost of goods sold, and the first costs, the oldest costs, will be assigned to ending inventory.

**Lower-of-cost-or-market (LCM)**
A comparison of the cost of inventory with the replacement cost of that inventory to determine if there has been a loss in the value of inventory which should be recorded. When replacement cost is lower than cost, a loss is recorded.

**Merchandise inventory**
Goods held for sale. In manufacturing concerns, merchandise inventory is usually called finished goods inventory.

**Periodic inventory system**
A system for determining the ending inventory units, ending inventory cost, and cost of goods sold only at the end of a period of time.

**Perpetual inventory system**
A system for keeping an up-to-date record of the cost of inventory on hand and the cost of goods sold.

**Retail inventory method**
A system for estimating the cost of ending inventory that is based on the relationship between the retail price and the cost of goods available for sale.

**Specific identification method**
A method of accounting for inventory costs that identifies each specific unit of inventory and its costs. When the inventory is sold, its cost is assigned to cost of goods sold; otherwise the cost remains in ending inventory. This method can be used only when each item is clearly different from the others.

**Inventory turnover**
Cost of goods sold divided by average merchandise inventory.

**Weighted average method**
A method of accounting for inventory costs that assigns the same cost to each unit sold and each unit remaining in inventory. The weighted average cost for each unit equals the total cost of goods available for sale divided by the total number of units available for sale.

### DEMONSTRATION PROBLEM

Midwest Microchips buys microchips from Huchu Electronics and sells them to computer manufacturers. The following information relates to microchip stock no. 8099 for the month of December:

|  |  | Units Sold | Units Purchased | Cost Each | Total Cost |
|---|---|---|---|---|---|
| Dec. 1 | Beginning Inventory |  | 8 | $200 | $1,600 |
| 10 | Purchase |  | 9 | 225 | 2,025 |
| 18 | Sale | 7 |  |  |  |
| 20 | Purchase |  | 7 | 240 | 1,680 |
| 29 | Sale | 6 | — |  | —— |
| Totals |  | 13 | 24 |  | $5,305 |

**Required:**

1. Calculate the cost of ending inventory and cost of goods sold under periodic FIFO, LIFO, and weighted average.
2. Prepare a perpetual subsidiary ledger card to calculate ending inventory and cost of goods sold using perpetual LIFO.
3. Calculate inventory turnover when periodic FIFO is used.

### ■ Solution to Demonstration Problem

**1.**

FIFO ending inventory:
7 units × $240 = $1,680
4 units × $225 = 900

Total. . . . . . . . . . . . . . . . . . . $2,580

FIFO cost of goods sold:
8 units × $200 = $1,600
5 units × $225 = 1,125

Total. . . . . . . . . . . . . . . . . . . $2,725

LIFO ending inventory:
8 units × $200 = $1,600
3 units × $225 = 675

Total. . . . . . . . . . . . . . . . . . . $2,275

LIFO cost of goods sold:
7 units × $240 = $1,680
6 units × $225 = 1,350

Total. . . . . . . . . . . . . . . . . . . $3,030

Weighted average cost per unit:

$$\frac{\$5,305}{24 \text{ units}} = \$221.0417 = \$221.04 \text{ per unit}$$

Weighted average ending inventory:

$$\$221.04 \times 11 \text{ units} = \underline{\$2,431.44}$$

Weighted average cost of goods sold:

$$\$5,305 - \$2,431.44 = \underline{\$2,873.56}$$

2.

Item: Microchip no. 8099

| Date | Purchases | | | Cost of Goods Sold | | | Inventory on Hand | | |
|---|---|---|---|---|---|---|---|---|---|
| | Quantity | Unit Cost | Total Cost | Quantity | Unit Cost | Total Cost | Quantity | Unit Cost | Total Cost |
| Dec. 1 | 8 | $200 | $1,600 | | | | 8 | $200 | $1,600 |
| 10 | 9 | 225 | 2,025 | | | | 8<br>9 | 200<br>225 | 1,600<br>2,025 |
| 18 | | | | 7 | $225 | $1,575 | 8<br>2 | 200<br>225 | 1,600<br>450 |
| 20 | 7 | 240 | 1,680 | | | | 8<br>2<br>7 | 200<br>225<br>240 | 1,600<br>450<br>1,680 |
| 29 | | | | 6 | 240 | 1,440 | 8<br>2<br>1 | 200<br>225<br>240 | 1,600<br>450<br>240 |

Perpetual LIFO ending inventory = $1,600 + $450 + $240 = $2,290

Perpetual LIFO cost of goods sold = $1,575 + $1,440 = $3,015

3. Inventory Turnover (Periodic FIFO):

$$\frac{\$2,725}{(\$1,600 + \$2,580) \div 2} = \frac{\$2725}{\$2090} = \underline{\underline{1.3 \text{ times}}}$$

## QUESTIONS FOR REVIEW AND FURTHER THOUGHT

### REVIEW QUESTIONS

1. How is raw materials inventory different from merchandise inventory?

2. A shortcut calculation may be used to determine cost of goods sold. How does that shortcut work?

3. What are the advantages of the FIFO inventory method?

4. What are the advantages of the LIFO inventory method?

5. Which inventory method usually has the same cost flow and physical flow? Why?

6. How are cost and market determined in the lower-of-cost-or-market technique?

7. What are two methods of determining an estimated ending inventory amount? Under what circumstances might a company want to estimate ending inventory?

8. When the gross profit method is used, what two assumptions are made?

9. What estimation method makes use of a cost-to-retail ratio? How is this ratio calculated?

10. What is the primary difference between a periodic inventory system and a perpetual inventory system?

11. What rule is used to determine the order in which current assets are listed on the balance sheet?

### QUESTIONS FOR FURTHER THOUGHT

1. Are dump trucks merchandise inventory? Explain.

2. Explain why each of the following is omitted from the ending physical inventory: goods in on consignment, goods in transit purchased FOB destination, goods in transit sold FOB shipping point.

3. FIFO, LIFO, and weighted average are said to be inventory cost flow assumptions. Does cost flow differ from physical flow? Explain.

4. Merchandise inventory may be purchased at several different prices during a period, yet the weighted average method assigns the same amount to each unit in ending inventory. What is the justification for this weighted average procedure?

5. The consistency principle means that the same accounting principles (or methods) used this period were also used last period. Does this mean that once a company decides to use FIFO, it can never switch to LIFO or weighted average?

6. How does the principle of conservatism serve to justify the use of lower-of-cost-or-market for valuing inventory?

7. Why does an error in the ending inventory of year 1 also cause an error in year 2 income?

8. Errors in ending inventory are said to be self-correcting. What does this mean?

9. Even when the perpetual inventory method is used, physical inventory should be taken at least once each year. Why is this necessary?

10. Ending inventory will be the same under both periodic FIFO and perpetual FIFO. Why?

## OBJECTIVE ASSIGNMENT

*True/False*  Indicate whether each statement below is *true* or *false* by placing a *T* or an *F* in the space provided.

_____ 1. Goods available for sale = beginning merchandise inventory + purchases + freight-in − purchases returns and allowances.

_____ 2. No goods in transit are included in the number of physical units in merchandise inventory.

_____ 3. The FIFO method assigns the earliest costs to cost of goods sold.

_____ 4. In a period of rising prices and increasing inventory quantities FIFO yields the lowest taxable income.

_____ 5. When the periodic inventory method is used, physical inventory is seldom, if ever, taken.

*Multiple Choice*  Select the best choice to complete each statement or answer each question below. Write the letter corresponding to your choice in the space provided.

_____ 1. Which of the following would *not* be included in ending inventory?
  a. Goods in transit purchased FOB shipping point
  b. Goods in on consignment
  c. Goods in transit sold FOB destination
  d. Goods out on consignment

_____ 2. Which of the following inventory methods consistently assigns the earliest (oldest) costs to ending merchandise inventory?
  a. FIFO
  b. Weighted average
  c. LIFO
  d. Gross profit

_____ 3. Under which method are cost flow and physical flow the same?
  a. FIFO
  b. Weighted average
  c. LIFO
  d. Specific identification

_____ 4. When prices and inventory quantities are rising, which method will yield the highest gross profit?
  a. FIFO
  b. LIFO
  c. Weighted average
  d. All methods will yield the same gross profit.

_____ 5. The lower-of-cost-or-market technique for valuing merchandise inventory is justified by this accounting principle:
  a. Consistency
  b. Conservatism
  c. Matching
  d. Revenue realization

_____ 6. Which of the following inventory methods is used to estimate the amount of inventory on hand?
  a. FIFO
  b. Weighted average
  c. LIFO
  d. Gross profit

_____ 7. Which of the following calculates the cost-to-retail ratio used in the retail inventory method?
   a. Net sales ÷ goods available at retail
   b. Goods available at cost ÷ goods available at retail
   c. Goods available at retail ÷ goods available at cost
   d. Purchases at cost ÷ purchases at retail

_____ 8. Belle, Inc., failed to include 100 units costing $5,000 in ending merchandise inventory. The effect of this understatement of 1997 inventory will be to:
   a. Understate 1997 income, overstate 1998 income
   b. Overstate 1997 income, understate 1998 income
   c. Understate 1997 income, understate 1998 income
   d. Overstate 1997 income, overstate 1998 income

_____ 9. Which of the following transactions requires two entries when the perpetual inventory method is used?
   a. Purchase of merchandise from supplier
   b. Return of merchandise to supplier
   c. Payment of freight on merchandise purchased
   d. Sale of merchandise to customer

_____ 10. Rodgers Co. uses the perpetual LIFO method of accounting for merchandise inventory. On June 12 Rodgers Co. has the following inventory on hand:

   3 units acquired on June 1 which cost $6.00 each = $18
   2 units acquired on June 4 which cost $6.50 each = $13
   3 units acquired on June 9 which cost $7.00 each = $21

The cost of goods sold for 5 units sold on June 13 would be:
   a. $21
   b. $31
   c. $34
   d. $40

## EXERCISES

2† **Exercise 1:** Calculating the Cost of Merchandise Inventory

Bend, Inc., purchased 300 sinks from Dalles Plumbing Supply on Mar. 1. The sinks have a list price in Dalles's catalog of $60 each. Dalles allows a 30% trade discount and a quantity discount of 5% on orders of 100 or more sinks. The credit terms of the purchase are 2/15, n/45. Bend paid for the order on Mar. 12. What was the cost of the sinks to Bend?

▶ _(Check Figure: Cost of sinks = $11,730.60)_

† The numbers in the margin refer to the Learning Objectives.

**3   Exercise 2:** Calculating the Number of Units in Ending Inventory

Using the information below, calculate the total number of physical units that should be in Salem Wholesale Products' ending inventory. Give a reason for omitting any item that you believe should *not* be included in ending inventory.

| Disposition | Number of Units |
|---|---|
| In stockroom ..................... | 60,000 |
| In shipment from suppliers (purchased FOB shipping point).............. | 4,500 |
| In shipment from suppliers (purchased FOB destination) ................. | 18,400 |
| Out on consignment .............. | 13,600 |
| On loading platform awaiting shipment to customers (legal title has not yet passed to customers) ............. | 2,800 |
| In on consignment (not in stockroom)... | 1,800 |
| In shipment to customers (merchandise was sold FOB shipping point) ........ | 4,400 |

▶ *(Check Figure: Total units in ending inventory = 80,900)*

**4   Exercise 3:** Calculating Ending Inventory and Cost of Goods Sold Using Periodic FIFO, LIFO, and Weighted Average

Rose Burch, President of Burch Packaging Co., wants you to prepare a comparison of ending inventory and cost of goods sold using three different periodic inventory methods. Data from the company's records follow:

| | Units | Purchase Price per Unit |
|---|---|---|
| Beginning merchandise inventory..................... | 40 | $2.00 |
| Apr. 3 purchase.................................. | 60 | 3.00 |
| Apr. 12 purchase................................. | 120 | 3.25 |
| Apr. 28 purchase................................. | 100 | 3.50 |

At the end of April 140 units were on hand.

Calculate the amount of ending merchandise inventory, cost of goods sold, and inventory turnover using periodic FIFO, LIFO, and weighted average. (Round weighted average per-unit cost to the nearest cent.)

▶ *(Check Figure: Ending inventory under LIFO = $390)*

**4   Exercise 4:** Calculating Ending Inventory and Cost of Goods Sold Using Periodic FIFO, LIFO, and Weighted Average

The following inventory data is available for Albany Camera:

| | Units | Purchase Price per Unit | Total Amount of Purchase |
|---|---|---|---|
| Merchandise inventory, Mar. 1 .......... | 80 | $130 | $10,400 |
| Mar. 9 purchase .................... | 50 | 125 | 6,250 |
| Mar. 20 purchase ................... | 90 | 120 | 10,800 |
| Mar. 30 purchase ................... | 10 | 100 | 1,000 |
| Total available...................... | 230 | | $28,450 |

A physical inventory on Mar. 31 revealed that 100 units were on hand.

Calculate the amount of ending merchandise inventory and cost of goods sold using periodic FIFO, LIFO, and weighted average. (Round weighted average per-unit cost to the nearest cent.)

▶ *(Check Figure: Cost of goods sold under weighted average = $16,080)*

5    **Exercise 5:** Calculating Ending Inventory Using LCM

The cost and replacement cost of Gold's merchandise inventory on Dec. 31 are as follows:

| Inventory Stock No. | Quantity | Cost (FIFO) | Replacement Cost |
|---|---|---|---|
| RB431 | 110 | $  880 | $  905 |
| JA247 | 200 | 4,500 | 4,310 |
| RK039 | 50 | 235 | 246 |
| RG384 | 600 | 9,350 | 9,150 |

Calculate the amount of ending merchandise inventory and any loss that should be recognized using the lower-of-cost-or-market method applied on both (a) an item-by-item basis and (b) a total-inventory basis.

▶ *(Check Figure: Loss on total-inventory basis = $354)*

6    **Exercise 6:** Estimating Inventory Using the Gross Profit Method

Palette Art lost all of its inventory in a recent earthquake. Since the company uses the periodic inventory method, there is no record of exactly how much inventory was on hand at the time of the disaster. The controller asks you to provide an estimate of the amount that was on hand. The following information was available:

Purchases (net) . . . . . . . . . . . . . . . . . . . . . . . .    $540,000
Sales . . . . . . . . . . . . . . . . . . . . . . . . . . . . . . . .    $400,000
Beginning Inventory. . . . . . . . . . . . . . . . . . . . .    $ 80,000
Gross profit percentage for the prior period . . .    30%
Cost of goods sold percentage
  for the prior period . . . . . . . . . . . . . . . . . . . . .    70%

Use the gross profit method to calculate the inventory lost in the tremor.

▶ *(Check Figure: Cost of inventory lost = $340,000)*

6    **Exercise 7:** Estimating Inventory Using the Retail Inventory Method

Brian's Hardware wants to determine its approximate quarterly income without going to the expense and bother of counting ending inventory. The following information has been gathered for the quarter:

| | Cost | Retail |
|---|---|---|
| Sales. . . . . . . . . . . . . . . . . . . . . . . . . . . . . . . . . . . . . . . . . | — | $300,000 |
| Beginning Inventory . . . . . . . . . . . . . . . . . . . . . . . . . . . . . . | $ 62,000 | 88,000 |
| Purchases (net) . . . . . . . . . . . . . . . . . . . . . . . . . . . . . . . . . | 221,500 | 290,000 |

Calculate the cost of Brian's ending merchandise inventory using the retail inventory method.

▶ *(Check Figure: Cost-to-retail ratio = 75%)*

7 **Exercise 8:** Determining the Effect of an Inventory Error

Elgin's Heating sells central heating units. At the end of 1997, the bookkeeper omitted from ending inventory some units that were out on consignment. The cost of the omitted units was $24,000. The error was discovered on Dec. 31, 1998. Before the error was discovered, the following income statements had been prepared:

| ELGIN'S HEATING<br>Income Statements<br>Years Ended December 31 | | | |
| --- | --- | --- | --- |
| | | **1997** | **1998** |
| Sales | | $97,500 | $127,500 |
| Cost of goods sold: | | | |
| Beginning inventory | $24,500 | | $ 36,000 |
| Purchases | 69,500 | | 75,000 |
| Goods available for sale | 94,000 | | 111,000 |
| Ending inventory | 36,000 | | 44,500 |
| Cost of goods sold | | 58,000 | 66,500 |
| Gross profit | | 39,500 | 61,000 |
| Operating expenses | | 17,000 | 23,500 |
| Net income | | $22,500 | $ 37,500 |

Ending inventory on Dec. 31, 1998, was correct. What effect will the bookkeeper's error have on 1997 and 1998 income? Prepare corrected income statements to prove your answer.

▶ *(Check Figure: Correct 1998 income = $13,500)*

9 **Exercise 9:** Recording Inventory Transactions Using the Perpetual and Periodic Methods

Amherst Machinery opened for business on June 1, 1998. During the month of June, the following transactions occurred:

June 3 Purchased merchandise on account from the Reliable Motors Co., $89,300.

8 Sold merchandise to Jan Construction on account, $96,250. The merchandise cost $41,300.

14 Returned merchandise costing $18,550 to Reliable Motors.

22 Merchandise costing $2,050 was returned by Jan Construction. The merchandise had been sold for $4,800.

Prepare journal entries for these transactions, using first the perpetual inventory system and then the periodic inventory system.

10    **Exercise 10:** Calculating Cost of Goods Sold and Ending Inventory Using Perpetual FIFO and LIFO

Blake, Inc., provides you with the following data concerning purchases and sales:

| Date | Description | Units | Cost Each | Total Cost |
|------|-------------|-------|-----------|------------|
| Nov. 1 | Purchase | 26 | $10 | $260 |
| 8 | Purchase | 34 | 11 | 374 |
| 14 | Sale | 22 | | |
| 22 | Purchase | 30 | 12 | 360 |
| 30 | Sale | 34 | | |
| | | | Total cost of goods available | $994 |

Calculate ending inventory and cost of goods sold using perpetual FIFO and perpetual LIFO.

▶ *(Check Figure: Perpetual LIFO ending inventory = $348)*

## PROBLEMS: SET A

4†    **Problem A1:** Calculating Ending Inventory and Cost of Goods Sold Using Periodic FIFO, LIFO, and Weighted Average

Webster Co. has the following inventory record for the month of November:

| | Units | Cost per Unit | Total Cost |
|-----|-------|---------------|------------|
| Inventory Nov. 1 | 20 | $20 | $400 |
| Purchase Nov. 5 | 8 | 22 | 176 |
| Purchase Nov. 12 | 18 | 25 | 450 |
| Purchase Nov. 20 | 20 | 26 | 520 |
| Purchase Nov. 28 | 14 | 28 | 392 |

A count of the inventory on hand on Nov. 30 revealed that 21 units remained.

**Required:**

Calculate ending inventory and cost of goods sold under the periodic FIFO, LIFO, and weighted average methods. Round the weighted average cost per unit to the nearest cent. Do not use the shortcut except for weighted average.

▶ *(Check Figure: Weighted average ending inventory = $508.83)*

† The numbers in the margin refer to the Learning Objectives.

4   **Problem A2:** Calculating Ending Inventory and Goods Sold in Units
and in Dollars Using Periodic FIFO, LIFO, and Weighted Average

The manager of Dunbar Medical Supplies has prepared the following schedules of inventory
and sales activity:

### DUNBAR MEDICAL SUPPLIES
### Summary of Purchasing Activity
### Quarter Ended March 31, 1998

| Date | Description | Units | Cost per Unit |
|------|-------------|-------|---------------|
| Jan. 1 | Inventory on hand | 4,500 | $3.20 |
| Jan. 16 | Purchase | 1,000 | 3.30 |
| Jan. 20 | Return of defective units | 200 | 3.30 |
| Feb. 4 | Purchase | 2,000 | 3.40 |
| Feb. 13 | Purchase | 4,000 | 3.50 |
| Feb. 27 | Purchase | 1,000 | 3.48 |
| Mar. 17 | Purchase | 3,000 | 3.60 |
| Mar. 28 | Return of defective units | 500 | 3.60 |

### DUNBAR MEDICAL SUPPLIES
### Summary of Sales
### Quarter Ended March 31, 1998

| Period Covered | Description | Units | Sales Price per Unit |
|----------------|-------------|-------|----------------------|
| Jan. 1–15 | Sales | 1,500 | $8.00 |
| Jan. 16–31 | Sales | 2,845 | 8.20 |
| Jan. 16–31 | Customer returns | 45 | 8.20 |
| Feb. 1–15 | Sales | 1,400 | 8.50 |
| Feb. 16–28 | Sales | 925 | 8.55 |
| Feb. 16–28 | Customer returns | 25 | 8.55 |
| Mar. 1–31 | Sales | 2,630 | 8.60 |
| Mar. 1–31 | Customer returns | 30 | 8.60 |

1. Use these summaries of purchasing activity and sales to calculate the goods available for
sale in units and dollars, the number of units sold, and the number of units that should be on
hand on Mar. 31.
2. Calculate Dunbar's ending merchandise inventory and cost of goods sold for the first
quarter of 1998 under the periodic FIFO, LIFO, and weighted average methods. Use the
shortcut. If necessary, round the weighted average cost per unit to the nearest cent.

▶ (Check Figure: FIFO ending inventory = $19,830)

4 **Problem A3:** Calculating Ending Inventory for 2 Years Using LIFO, FIFO, and Weighted Average

Covington Co. began operations on Jan. 1, 1997. The following purchases were made during 1997 and 1998:

| Date of Purchase | Units | Unit Cost | Total Cost |
|---|---|---|---|
| Jan. 5, 1997 | 25 | $4,000 | $100,000 |
| Mar. 27, 1997 | 18 | 4,300 | 77,400 |
| July 6, 1997 | 15 | 4,400 | 66,000 |
| Sept. 14, 1997 | 20 | 4,500 | 90,000 |
| Feb. 9, 1998 | 12 | 4,600 | 55,200 |
| June 12, 1998 | 26 | 4,800 | 124,800 |
| Oct. 14, 1998 | 27 | 5,000 | 135,000 |
| Dec. 20, 1998 | 34 | 5,100 | 173,400 |

Sales totaled 46 units in 1997 and 75 units in 1998.

**Required:**

1. Calculate ending inventory on Dec. 31, 1997, and Dec. 31, 1998, using periodic FIFO, LIFO, and weighted average. Round weighted average per-unit cost to the nearest dollar.
2. Calculate inventory turnover for 1998 for each of the inventory methods.

▶ *(Check Figure: 1997 weighted average inventory = $136,768)*

5 **Problem A4:** Calculating Ending Inventory on an LCM Basis

Jan's Restaurant Supply is preparing financial statements for the year ended June 30, 1998. Jan wants to use lower-of-cost-or-market to value ending inventory. The following inventory summary has been prepared:

| Inventory Group | Inventory Item No. | Quantity | Cost (FIFO) | Market (Replacement Cost) |
|---|---|---|---|---|
| Crockery | 1001 | 11 cases | $ 1,280 | $ 1,290 |
| | 1002 | 33 cases | 3,700 | 3,520 |
| | 1003 | 21 cases | 1,920 | 1,840 |
| | 1004 | 50 cases | 6,200 | 6,240 |
| Cooking utensils | 2021 | 15 units | 392 | 400 |
| | 2022 | 23 units | 2,340 | 2,240 |
| | 2023 | 14 units | 1,278 | 1,260 |
| Silverware | 3041 | 510 settings | 2,500 | 2,484 |
| | 3042 | 2,450 settings | 7,792 | 7,840 |
| | 3043 | 6,560 settings | 26,736 | 26,720 |

**Required:**

Calculate the amount of inventory that Jan's will show on the June 30, 1998, balance sheet, and the loss that should be recognized assuming that lower-of-cost-or-market is applied:

1. On an item-by-item basis
2. To the inventory as a whole

▶ *(Check Figure: Loss when LCM is applied to inventory as a whole = $304)*

**6**    **Problem A5:** Using the Gross Profit Method to Estimate Inventory

On Aug. 4, 1998, a hurricane destroyed much of the inventory of Norfolk Dive Shop. Some merchandise was salvaged, amounting to $8,000. Norfolk's owner has asked you to help prepare an estimate of the loss so that he can file a claim with the insurance company. You are handed the following schedule of available data:

---

**NORFOLK DIVE SHOP**
**Income Statement**
**Year Ended June 30, 1998**

|  |  |  |
|---|---:|---:|
| Sales (Net) | | $250,000 |
| Cost of Goods Sold: | | |
|    Merchandise Inventory, July 1, 1997 | $ 34,000 | |
|    Purchases (Net) | 152,000 | |
|    Goods Available for Sale | 186,000 | |
|    Merchandise Inventory, June 30, 1998 | 36,000 | 150,000 |
| Gross Profit on Sales | | 100,000 |
| Operating Expenses | | 27,000 |
| Net Income | | $ 73,000 |

---

| | |
|---|---|
| Sales (July 1–Aug. 4, 1998) | $64,000 |
| Purchases (July 1–Aug. 4, 1998) | 32,000 |

**Required:**

Calculate the cost of the inventory that should have been on hand on Aug. 4 and the cost of the inventory that was lost in the hurricane.

▶ *(Check Figure: Inventory that should have been on hand = $29,600)*

**6**    **Problem A6:** Calculating Ending Inventory Using the Retail Inventory Method

Vienna Linens sells linens for the bedroom and bath. Craig Hubbard, the owner, wants to prepare an income statement on May 31, 1998, without counting his inventory. He supplies you with the following information:

| | |
|---|---|
| Sales (May 1–May 31) | $260,000 |
| Sales returns (May 1–May 31) | 10,000 |
| Purchases (cost) (May 1–May 31) | 174,600 |
| Purchases (retail price) (May 1–May 31) | 242,900 |
| Merchandise inventory (cost) (May 1) | 72,216 |
| Merchandise inventory (retail price) (May 1) | 99,900 |

**Required:**

Use the retail inventory method to calculate the cost of ending inventory so that Craig can prepare an income statement for the month of May.

▶ *(Check Figure: Cost-to-retail ratio = 72%)*

6 **Problem A7:** Estimating Ending Inventory and Preparing an Income Statement and Balance Sheet

Computer Systems Co. is applying for a loan at the Union National Bank. The bank has asked to see up-to-date financial statements. Mark Hawke, owner of the store, explains to you that he isn't due to count his inventory for another 2 months—the end of the fiscal year. You volunteer to help Mark in the preparation of his financial statements. You suggest that the retail inventory method be used to estimate ending inventory. Mark provides you with the following trial balance and additional information:

---

**COMPUTER SYSTEMS CO.**
**Adjusted Trial Balance**
**June 30, 1998**

| | Debit | Credit |
|---|---|---|
| Cash . . . . . . . . . . . . . . . . . . . . . . . . . . . . . . . . . . . . . . . . . . | $ 124,500 | |
| Merchandise Inventory, Sept. 1, 1997 . . . . . . . . . . . . . . . . | 81,000 | |
| Supplies on Hand . . . . . . . . . . . . . . . . . . . . . . . . . . . . . . . | 4,500 | |
| Equipment . . . . . . . . . . . . . . . . . . . . . . . . . . . . . . . . . . . . | 470,000 | |
| Accumulated Depreciation: Equipment . . . . . . . . . . . . . . . . | | $ 144,000 |
| Accounts Payable . . . . . . . . . . . . . . . . . . . . . . . . . . . . . . . | | 251,000 |
| Hawke, Capital . . . . . . . . . . . . . . . . . . . . . . . . . . . . . . . . . | | 102,000 |
| Sales . . . . . . . . . . . . . . . . . . . . . . . . . . . . . . . . . . . . . . . . | | 630,000 |
| Sales Returns . . . . . . . . . . . . . . . . . . . . . . . . . . . . . . . . . . | 30,000 | |
| Purchases . . . . . . . . . . . . . . . . . . . . . . . . . . . . . . . . . . . . | 180,000 | |
| Purchases Discounts . . . . . . . . . . . . . . . . . . . . . . . . . . . . . | | 6,000 |
| Freight-In . . . . . . . . . . . . . . . . . . . . . . . . . . . . . . . . . . . . . | 21,000 | |
| Depreciation Expense . . . . . . . . . . . . . . . . . . . . . . . . . . . | 72,000 | |
| Other Operating Expenses . . . . . . . . . . . . . . . . . . . . . . . . | 150,000 | |
| Total . . . . . . . . . . . . . . . . . . . . . . . . . . . . . . . . . . . . . . . . | $1,133,000 | $1,133,000 |

---

**Other Information:**

> Merchandise on hand on Sept. 1, 1997, had a retail price of $162,000.
> Net purchases were marked to sell for $528,000.

**Required:**

1. Prepare a schedule calculating your estimate of ending inventory.
2. Prepare an income statement for the period Sept. 1, 1997–June 30, 1998.
3. Prepare a balance sheet for Mark as of June 30, 1998.

▶ *(Check Figure: Net income = $138,000)*

7 **Problem A8:** Calculating the Effects of Inventory Errors

You have been reviewing the past 4 years of inventory records of Weston Co. Your investigation has revealed the following errors:

a. Ending inventory for 1996 was overstated by $25,200 because goods purchased FOB destination were included.
b. Sales for 1997 were overstated by $20,000 because sales shipped to customers FOB destination were included. (These goods had not been included in cost of goods sold for 1997.) The sales should have been recorded in 1998. (The goods were included in cost of goods sold for 1998.)
c. Ending inventory for 1997 was overstated by $6,000. The cost of goods in on consignment was inadvertently included in ending inventory.

d. Ending inventory for 1998 was understated by $9,000. Employees had failed to count one bin of merchandise.

e. Purchases for 1998 were overstated by $10,400. A clerk recorded one purchase invoice twice.

f. Ending inventory for 1999 was understated by $4,000. Goods out on consignment were not included.

**Required:**

Set up a schedule similar to the one below to show the calculation of the correct net income for each of the 4 years. The reported net income for each year is shown on the first line. Note additions to and subtractions (in parentheses) from the reported net income to correct the effects of each error. Be sure to put your adjustment amounts in the proper columns. The first correction is done for you. When you have analyzed and corrected all the errors, total each column to find corrected net income.

| Description | 1996 | 1997 | 1998 | 1999 |
|---|---|---|---|---|
| Net income (loss) reported | $90,000 | $64,200 | $42,000 | ($6,000) |
| (a) 1996 Ending inventory overstated | (25,200) | 25,200 | | |

▶ *(Check Figure: Correct net loss for 1999 = $11,000)*

9  **Problem A9:** Recording Inventory Transactions Using the Perpetual and Periodic Inventory Systems

During the month of October, the Smoot Company had the following transactions:

Oct. 2  Purchased merchandise on account from the Bristol Products Company, $105,000, credit terms 2/10, n/30.

4  Purchased merchandise from Fairmont, Inc., $30,000 cash.

5  Paid $345 freight on the Fairmont, Inc., merchandise received.

7  Sold merchandise to Dunbar, Inc., on account, credit terms 3/10, n/30, $27,000. The net inventory cost was $11,700.

10  Returned defective merchandise with a gross price of $8,250 to Bristol Products.

11  Paid Bristol Products the amount due.

11  Received payment from Dunbar.

15  Sold merchandise to Elkins Manufacturing, credit terms 3/10, n/30, $22,500. The net inventory cost was $7,350.

17  Elkins returned goods it had bought for $3,800 (net cost $1,242).

24  Elkins paid the amount due.

**Required:**

Prepare general journal entries to record these transactions, assuming first that the perpetual inventory system is used and then that the periodic inventory system is used. Smoot records acquisitions of merchandise inventory net of cash discounts.

10  **Problem A10:** Calculating Ending Inventory and Cost of Goods Sold Using Perpetual FIFO and LIFO

Virginia Supply provides you with the following data about its purchases and sales of roofing cement (stock no. RA119) for the month of June 1998, its first month of operations:

| Purchases | | | |
| --- | --- | --- | --- |
| Date | Units | Cost per Unit | Total Cost |
| June  1 | 75 | $8.00 | $  600 |
| 5 | 30 | 8.20 | 246 |
| 15 | 90 | 8.50 | 765 |
| 24 | 30 | 8.70 | 261 |
| 30 | 15 | 8.80 | 132 |
| Totals | 240 | | $2,004 |

| Sales | |
| --- | --- |
| Date | Units |
| June  8 | 38 |
| 17 | 60 |
| 29 | 15 |

**Required:**

1. Calculate ending inventory and cost of goods sold using perpetual FIFO and perpetual LIFO.
2. Prepare perpetual inventory subsidiary ledger cards like those shown in Exhibits 7 and 8 to support your calculations.

▶ *(Check Figure: Cost of goods sold under perpetual FIFO = $914)*

## PROBLEMS: SET B

4†  **Problem B1:** Calculating Ending Inventory and Cost of Goods Sold Using Periodic FIFO, LIFO, and Weighted Average

Princeton Company began business in July. The following purchases were made during the month:

| Date | Units | Cost per Unit | Total Cost |
| --- | --- | --- | --- |
| July  2 | 140 | $12.00 | $1,680 |
| 12 | 120 | 12.40 | 1,488 |
| 18 | 210 | 13.20 | 2,772 |
| 26 | 150 | 13.60 | 2,040 |
| 30 | 110 | 14.00 | 1,540 |

Princeton's stock clerk reported that 280 units were on hand at the end of the month.

**Required:**

Calculate the ending inventory and cost of goods sold under the periodic FIFO, LIFO, and weighted average methods. Do not use the shortcut except for the weighted average method. (Round the weighted average cost per unit to the nearest cent.)

▶ *(Check Figure: LIFO ending inventory = $3,432)*

† The numbers in the margin refer to the Learning Objectives.

4 **Problem B2:** Calculating Ending Inventory and Goods Sold in Units and in Dollars Using Periodic FIFO, LIFO, and Weighted Average

Lynchburg Electronics received the following schedules from the purchasing department manager and the marketing director:

**LYNCHBURG ELECTRONICS**
**Summary of Purchasing Activity**
**Quarter Ended March 31, 1998**

| Date | Description | Units | Cost per Unit |
|------|-------------|-------|---------------|
| Jan. 1 | Inventory on hand | 1,980 | $ 9.60 |
| Jan. 10 | Purchase | 2,000 | 9.90 |
| Jan. 12 | Return of defective units | 125 | 9.90 |
| Feb. 18 | Purchase | 750 | 10.20 |
| Feb. 21 | Purchase | 1,500 | 10.50 |
| Feb. 28 | Purchase | 375 | 10.40 |
| Mar. 14 | Purchase | 1,125 | 10.80 |
| Mar. 28 | Return of defective units | 200 | 10.80 |

**LYNCHBURG ELECTRONICS**
**Summary of Sales**
**Quarter Ended March 31, 1998**

| Period Covered | Description | Units | Sales Price per Unit |
|----------------|-------------|-------|----------------------|
| Jan. 1–15 | Sales | 575 | $24.00 |
| Jan. 1–15 | Customer returns | 15 | 24.00 |
| Jan. 16–31 | Sales | 1,050 | 24.60 |
| Jan. 16–31 | Customer returns | 5 | 24.60 |
| Feb. 1–15 | Sales | 850 | 25.00 |
| Feb. 16–28 | Sales | 300 | 25.50 |
| Feb. 16–28 | Customer returns | 10 | 25.50 |
| Mar. 1–31 | Sales | 1,000 | 25.60 |

**Required:**

1. Using these summaries of purchasing activity and sales, calculate goods available for sale in units and dollars, the number of units sold, and the number of units that should be on hand on Mar. 31.
2. Calculate Lynchburg's ending merchandise inventory and cost of goods sold for the first quarter of 1998 under the periodic FIFO, LIFO, and weighted average methods. Use the shortcut. Round the weighted average cost per unit to the nearest cent.

▶ *(Check Figure: LIFO ending inventory = $35,640)*

4 **Problem B3:** Calculating Ending Inventory for 2 Years Using LIFO, FIFO, and Weighted Average

Charleston, Inc., began operations on Jan. 1, 1997. The following purchases were made during 1997 and 1998:

| Date of Purchase | Units | Unit Cost | Total Cost |
|---|---|---|---|
| Jan. 13, 1997 | 12 | $6,000 | $ 72,000 |
| Apr. 21, 1997 | 10 | 6,450 | 64,500 |
| Aug. 11, 1997 | 8 | 6,600 | 52,800 |
| Oct. 16, 1997 | 11 | 6,750 | 74,250 |
| Mar. 8, 1998 | 6 | 6,900 | 41,400 |
| May 31, 1998 | 13 | 7,200 | 93,600 |
| Sept. 24, 1998 | 14 | 7,500 | 105,000 |
| Nov. 29, 1998 | 16 | 7,650 | 122,400 |

Sales totaled 21 units in 1997 and 40 units in 1998.

**Required:**

1. Calculate ending inventory on Dec. 31, 1997, and Dec. 31, 1998, using periodic FIFO, LIFO, and weighted average. Round weighted average per-unit cost to the nearest dollar.
2. Calculate inventory turnover for 1998 for each of the inventory methods.

▶ *(Check Figure: 1997 weighted average inventory = $128,560)*

5 **Problem B4:** Calculating Ending Inventory on a LCM Basis

Roanoke Paint Store uses lower-of-cost-or-market to value ending inventory. The following inventory summary was prepared on Oct. 31, 1998, Roanoke's year-end:

| Inventory Group | Inventory Stock No. | Quantity | Cost (FIFO) | Market (Replacement Cost) |
|---|---|---|---|---|
| Paint | P401 | 100 cases | $2,800 | $2,650 |
| | P415 | 40 cases | 1,800 | 1,700 |
| | P420 | 50 cases | 1,350 | 1,470 |
| Brushes | B101 | 30 cases | 380 | 400 |
| | B115 | 80 cases | 1,900 | 1,936 |
| | B117 | 10 cases | 188 | 210 |
| | B119 | 5 cases | 78 | 38 |
| Ladders | L940 | 40 each | 892 | 800 |
| | L945 | 200 each | 5,120 | 4,600 |
| | L948 | 6 each | 180 | 198 |

**Required:**

Calculate the amount of inventory that Roanoke should disclose on the Oct. 31, 1998, balance sheet and the amount of loss that should be recognized assuming lower-of-cost-or-market is applied:

1. On an item-by-item basis
2. To the inventory as a whole

▶ *(Check Figure: Loss when LCM is applied to inventory as a whole = $686)*

6 **Problem B5:** Using the Gross Profit Method to Estimate Inventory

On Apr. 26, 1998, an ice storm destroyed much of the inventory of Woolsey's Plants. Lionel Woolsey, the owner, managed to salvage only merchandise costing $1,000. The insurance adjuster needs to have an estimate of the total inventory on hand at the time of the storm in order to pay Lionel for his losses. Lionel has assembled the following information:

**WOOLSEY'S PLANTS**
**Income Statement**
**Year Ended December 31, 1997**

| | | |
|---|---:|---:|
| Sales (Net) | | $210,000 |
| Cost of Goods Sold: | | |
| Merchandise Inventory, Jan. 1, 1997 | $ 12,250 | |
| Purchases (Net) | 156,000 | |
| Goods Available for Sale | 168,250 | |
| Merchandise Inventory, Dec. 31, 1997 | 21,250 | 147,000 |
| Gross Profit on Sales | | 63,000 |
| Operating Expenses | | 40,000 |
| Net Income | | $ 23,000 |

| | |
|---|---:|
| Sales (Jan. 1–Apr. 26, 1998) | $89,500 |
| Purchases (Jan. 1–Apr. 26, 1998) | 64,400 |

**Required:**

Calculate the amount of inventory that Woolsey had at the time of the storm and the amount he lost in the storm.

▶ *(Check Figure: Inventory on hand at the time of the storm = $23,000)*

6 **Problem B6 :** Calculating Ending Inventory Using the Retail Inventory Method

Hit the Trail specializes in hiking clothing and supplies. Emma Cobb, the owner, wants to prepare an income statement on Jan. 31, 1998, without counting her inventory. She supplies you with the following information:

| | |
|---|---:|
| Sales (Jan. 1–Jan. 31) | $152,000 |
| Sales returns (Jan. 1–Jan. 31) | 950 |
| Purchases (cost) (Jan. 1–Jan. 31) | 93,262 |
| Purchases (retail price) (Jan. 1–Jan. 31) | 145,450 |
| Merchandise inventory (cost) (Jan. 1) | 32,210 |
| Merchandise inventory (retail price) (Jan. 1) | 50,600 |

**Required:**

Use the retail inventory method to calculate the cost of ending inventory so that Emma can prepare an income statement for the month of January.

▶ *(Check Figure: Cost-to-retail ratio = 64%)*

6 **Problem B7:** Estimating Ending Inventory and Preparing an Income Statement and Balance Sheet

Laura Wiley, owner of Music Expo, is considering selling a part of the business to Brad Goode. Brad has asked to see an up-to-date set of financial statements. Laura is upset because her fiscal year doesn't end for another 2 months and she believes it will be expensive and time-consuming to count inventory. You volunteer to help Laura in the preparation of her financial statements. You suggest that the retail inventory method be used to estimate ending inventory. Laura provides the following information:

**MUSIC EXPO**
**Adjusted Trial Balance**
**April 30, 1998**

| | Debit | Credit |
|---|---|---|
| Cash. . . . . . . . . . . . . . . . . . . . . . . . . . . . . . . . . . . . . . . . . . . . . . . . | $ 32,000 | |
| Merchandise Inventory, July 1, 1997 . . . . . . . . . . . . . . . . . . . | 17,000 | |
| Supplies on Hand . . . . . . . . . . . . . . . . . . . . . . . . . . . . . . . . . . | 1,600 | |
| Store Fixtures . . . . . . . . . . . . . . . . . . . . . . . . . . . . . . . . . . . . . | 64,000 | |
| Accumulated Depreciation: Store Fixtures . . . . . . . . . . . . . . . . | | $ 16,800 |
| Accounts Payable . . . . . . . . . . . . . . . . . . . . . . . . . . . . . . . . . . | | 23,000 |
| Wiley, Capital. . . . . . . . . . . . . . . . . . . . . . . . . . . . . . . . . . . . . . | | 67,200 |
| Sales . . . . . . . . . . . . . . . . . . . . . . . . . . . . . . . . . . . . . . . . . . . | | 290,000 |
| Sales Returns . . . . . . . . . . . . . . . . . . . . . . . . . . . . . . . . . . . . . | 7,000 | |
| Purchases . . . . . . . . . . . . . . . . . . . . . . . . . . . . . . . . . . . . . . . | 252,800 | |
| Purchases Returns and Allowances. . . . . . . . . . . . . . . . . . . . . | | 8,000 |
| Freight-In . . . . . . . . . . . . . . . . . . . . . . . . . . . . . . . . . . . . . . . . | 5,000 | |
| Depreciation Expense . . . . . . . . . . . . . . . . . . . . . . . . . . . . . . . | 5,600 | |
| Other Operating Expenses . . . . . . . . . . . . . . . . . . . . . . . . . . . | 20,000 | |
| Total. . . . . . . . . . . . . . . . . . . . . . . . . . . . . . . . . . . . . . . . . . . . | $405,000 | $405,000 |

**Other Information:**

Merchandise on hand July 1, 1997, had a retail price of $21,200.
Net purchases were marked to sell for $312,300.

**Required:**

1. Prepare a schedule calculating your estimate of the cost of ending inventory.
2. Prepare an income statement for the period July 1, 1997, through Apr. 30, 1998.
3. Prepare a balance sheet for Laura as of Apr. 30, 1998.

▶ *(Check Figure: Net income = $31,000)*

7 **Problem B8:** Calculating the Effects of Inventory Errors

You have been hired as the inventory accounting clerk for Mingo, Inc. Your first task is to review the inventory records for the past 4 years and determine if there were any mistakes. You discover the following errors:

a. Ending inventory for 1996 was understated because goods shipped to customers FOB destination were not included. The understatement amounted to $2,100.
b. Sales for 1996 were overstated by $5,000 because sales of goods described in (a), above, were also included. These sales were erroneously omitted in 1997.
c. Ending inventory for 1997 was overstated by $3,300 because goods in on consignment were included.
d. Ending inventory for 1998 was understated by $7,500. Employees neglected to count the inventory in a basement room.

e. Purchases for 1999 totaling $1,500 were not recorded. The bookkeeper had overlooked the invoice. The goods were included in ending inventory.

f. Ending inventory for 1999 was understated due to a transposition error. The correct amount, $9,787, was incorrectly written as $7,987.

**Required:**

Set up a schedule similar to the one below to show the calculation of the correct net income for each of the 4 years. The reported net income for each year is shown on the first line. Note additions to and subtractions (in parentheses) from the reported net income to correct the effects of each error. Be sure to put your adjustment amounts in the proper columns. The first correction is done for you. When you have analyzed and corrected all the errors, total each column to find corrected net income.

| Description | 1996 | 1997 | 1998 | 1999 |
|---|---|---|---|---|
| Net income (loss) reported | $14,200 | $11,600 | ($1,000) | $9,900 |
| a. 1996 Ending inventory understated | 2,100 | (2,100) | | |

▶ *(Check Figure: Correct net income for 1998 = $9,800)*

9 **Problem B9:** Recording Inventory Transactions Using the Perpetual and Periodic Inventory Systems

During the month of February, the Blair Company had the following transactions:

Feb. 1 Purchased merchandise on account from Bluefield Mills, Inc., $39,000, credit terms 2/10, n/30.

3 Purchased merchandise from Linwood Garments, $45,000 cash.

4 Paid $75 freight on the Linwood Garments merchandise received.

6 Sold merchandise to Radford Co. on account, credit terms 3/10, n/30, $19,500. The net inventory cost was $9,600.

9 Returned defective merchandise with a gross price of $4,500 to Bluefield Mills.

10 Paid Bluefield Mills the amount due.

10 Received payment from Radford.

14 Sold merchandise to Pulaski, Inc., credit terms 3/10, n/45, $15,000. The net inventory cost was $6,000.

16 Pulaski returned goods that it had bought for $4,000 (net cost $1,600).

23 Pulaski paid the amount due.

**Required:**

Prepare general journal entries to record these transactions, assuming first that the perpetual inventory system is used and then that the periodic inventory system is used. Blair records acquisitions of merchandise inventory net of cash discounts.

10   **Problem B10:** Calculating Ending Inventory and Cost of Goods Sold Using Perpetual FIFO and LIFO

Fairfax Co. has the following record of purchases and sales of electric motors (stock no. EM557) for the first month of its operations, May 1999:

| Purchases | | | |
|---|---|---|---|
| **Date** | **Units** | **Cost per Unit** | **Total Cost** |
| May  2 | 300 | $4.10 | $1,230 |
| 10 | 120 | 4.60 | 552 |
| 17 | 360 | 5.10 | 1,836 |
| 23 | 120 | 5.60 | 672 |
| 30 | 60 | 6.10 | 366 |
| Totals | 960 | | $4,656 |

| Sales | |
|---|---|
| **Date** | **Units** |
| May 13 | 100 |
| 20 | 240 |
| 27 | 60 |

**Required:**

1. Calculate ending inventory and cost of goods sold using perpetual FIFO and perpetual LIFO.
2. Prepare perpetual inventory subsidiary ledger cards like those shown on the next two pages* to support your calculations.

* These Exhibits also appear in the chapter "Merchandise Inventory."

**Perpetual FIFO Inventory Ledger Card**

**Item:** Filter no. 105

| Date | Purchases | | | Cost of Goods Sold | | | Inventory on Hand | | |
|---|---|---|---|---|---|---|---|---|---|
| | No. of Units | Unit Cost | Total Cost | No. of Units | Unit Cost | Total Cost | No. of Units | Unit Cost | Total Cost |
| Jan. 1 | 50 | $1.00 | $ 50 | | | | 50 | $1.00 | $ 50 |
| 12 | 100 | 1.50 | 150 | | | | 50<br>100 | 1.00<br>1.50 | 50<br>150 |
| 15 | | | | 50 | $1.00 | $50 | 100 | 1.50 | 150 |
| 18 | 200 | 2.00 | 400 | | | | 100<br>200 | 1.50<br>2.00 | 150<br>400 |
| 20 | 100 | 2.50 | 250 | | | | 100<br>200<br>100 | 1.50<br>2.00<br>2.50 | 150<br>400<br>250 |
| 22 | | | | 100<br>50 | 1.50<br>2.00 | 150<br>100 | 150<br>100 | 2.00<br>2.50 | 300<br>250 |
| 27 | 50 | 4.00 | 200 | | | | 150<br>100<br>50 | 2.00<br>2.50<br>4.00 | 300<br>250<br>200 |
| 30 | | | | 80 | 2.00 | 160 | 70<br>100<br>50 | 2.00<br>2.50<br>4.00 | 140<br>250<br>200 |

*Perpetual FIFO*
*Cost of goods sold = $460*

*Perpetual FIFO*
*Ending inventory = $590*

Perpetual FIFO Inventory Ledger Card

Item: Filter no. 105

| Date | Purchases | | | Cost of Goods Sold | | | Inventory on Hand | | |
|---|---|---|---|---|---|---|---|---|---|
| | No. of Units | Unit Cost | Total Cost | Units | Unit Cost | Total Cost | No. of Units | Unit Cost | Total Cost |
| Jan. 1 | 50 | $1.00 | $ 50 | | | | 50 | $1.00 | $ 50 |
| 12 | 100 | 1.50 | 150 | | | | 50 | 1.00 | 50 |
| | | | | | | | 100 | 1.50 | 150 |
| 15 | | | | 50 | $1.50 | $75 | 50 | 1.00 | 50 |
| | | | | | | | 50 | 1.50 | 75 |
| 18 | 200 | 2.00 | 400 | | | | 50 | 1.00 | 50 |
| | | | | | | | 50 | 1.50 | 75 |
| | | | | | | | 200 | 2.00 | 400 |
| 20 | 100 | 2.50 | 250 | | | | 50 | 1.00 | 50 |
| | | | | | | | 50 | 1.50 | 75 |
| | | | | | | | 200 | 2.00 | 400 |
| | | | | | | | 100 | 2.50 | 250 |
| 22 | | | | 100 | 2.50 | 250 | 50 | 1.00 | 50 |
| | | | | 50 | 2.00 | 100 | 50 | 1.50 | 75 |
| | | | | | | | 150 | 2.00 | 300 |
| 27 | 50 | 4.00 | 200 | | | | 50 | 1.00 | 50 |
| | | | | | | | 50 | 1.50 | 75 |
| | | | | | | | 150 | 2.00 | 300 |
| | | | | | | | 50 | 4.00 | 200 |
| 30 | | | | 50 | 4.00 | 200 | | 1.00 | 50 |
| | | | | 30 | 2.00 | 60 | 50 | 1.50 | 75 |
| | | | | | | | 120 | 2.00 | 240 |

*Perpetual LIFO*
*Cost of goods sold = $685*

*Perpetual LIFO*
*Ending inventory = $365*

▶ *(Check Figure: Ending inventory under perpetual FIFO = $2,966)*

## DECISION PROBLEM

Arrowhead Optics has hired you as a consultant. Your assistance is needed in preparing an income statement to submit to the Kansas National Bank for a $1,000,000 loan.

Arrowhead sells fiber optic telephone systems to large businesses. Arrowhead buys the systems from Santa Fe Communications Electronics. Purchases during the first year of operations were as follows:

| Month of Purchase | Units Purchased | Cost per Unit | Total Cost |
|---|---|---|---|
| November | 1,000 | $1,500 | $1,500,000 |
| February | 5,000 | 1,400 | 7,000,000 |
| April | 4,000 | 1,200 | 4,800,000 |
| May | 2,000 | 1,100 | 2,200,000 |

Arrowhead has 3,500 units on hand on May 31, the company's fiscal year-end. Since this is its first year of operations, Arrowhead has not formally chosen an inventory method. Sales for the year totaled $14,800,000; operating expenses amounted to $1,700,000.

**Required:**

1. Prepare income statements for Arrowhead using the periodic FIFO, LIFO, and weighted average methods. (Round weighted average cost per unit to the nearest dollar.)
2. Which inventory cost method do you recommend that Arrowhead use for the income statement submitted to the bank for the loan? Why?
3. Assuming that Arrowhead's income tax rate is 40%, which inventory cost method would you recommend that Arrowhead use for income tax purposes? Why?

## ETHICS CASE

Virginia Airmont is president and general manager of Active Electronics, a retail business that sells portable CD players, tape players, calculators, and other consumer electronics merchandise. On Dec. 8, 1998, Active's controller gives Virginia an income statement for the first 11 months of the year (Jan. 1–Nov. 30). Virginia is concerned that by Dec. 31 the firm's profit projections will not meet the goals that Active's board of directors has set. Gwen Kimball, chairwoman of the board, has often emphasized the importance of meeting the profit goal for the year. Virginia knows that Gwen has two primary concerns: (1) that Active has not performed up to expectations for the past 2 years and the stockholders are becoming restless with the leadership of the board of directors and the president; and (2) Active will need to obtain additional loans early in 1999 to refinance (pay off) some existing debt that is coming due. Continued weak income performance could result in higher interest rates or even a rejection of the loan request.

Virginia knows that it is too late in the year to make much of an impact on income by increasing sales or decreasing operating expenses. She does conceive a plan to achieve higher profits that hinges on two facts: (1) Active uses the periodic LIFO inventory method, so the most recent costs of inventory are charged to cost of goods sold; and (2) the costs of many of the products that Active sells have gone down substantially during the past year. Virginia reasons that if Active buys a significant quantity of inventory at the lower prices, these lower (very recent) costs will immediately find their way to the cost of goods sold section of the income statement. The lower cost of goods sold will result in a higher income for the company. Virginia can help Active meet its profit projections simply by buying a large quantity of inventory before the end of the year.

**Required:**

1. Will Virginia's contemplated action increase the company's income for 1998?
2. What are the potential positive and negative consequences of Virginia's contemplated action for the company, and the stockholders?
3. Is Virginia's contemplated action ethical?

## OBJECTIVE ASSIGNMENT ANSWERS

**True/False**

1. T   2. F   3. T   4. F   5. F

**Multiple Choice**

1. b   2. c   3. d   4. a   5. b
6. d   7. b   8. a   9. d   10. c

# Property, Plant, and Equipment, and Intangible Assets

All of a firm's assets can be classified as either current assets or long-lived assets. Assets that will be used up in a firm's operations or are soon to be converted into cash (within 1 year or one operating cycle, whichever is longer) are current assets. All other assets are long-lived assets. **Long-lived assets** provide benefits for more than 1 year or one operating cycle. The typical balance sheet classifications of long-lived assets are: investments; property, plant, and equipment; and intangibles. In this chapter we will cover two of these long-lived assets—property, plant, and equipment, and intangibles.

## PROPERTY, PLANT, AND EQUIPMENT COST DETERMINATION

Learning Objective 1

Identify the assets normally classified as property, plant, and equipment

Typical assets included in **property, plant, and equipment** are land, buildings, machinery, office equipment, delivery equipment, and natural resources—all tangible long-lived assets owned by a business and used in its operations.

Examples of assets *not* considered as property, plant, and equipment are investments in stocks and bonds of other companies, patents (not tangible), land held for investment purposes (not used in the firm's operations), and buildings under construction (not yet used in the operations of the business).

### Acquisition Cost

Learning Objective 2

Determine the cost of property, plant, and equipment assets

As you might imagine, the cost of a long-lived asset that fits into the category of property, plant, and equipment is more than the price tag on the asset itself. Many other costs must be either necessarily or reasonably incurred to acquire the asset. Some costs associated with the acquisition may seem necessary or reasonable, but upon close examination will be determined to be chargeable elsewhere. It's the accountant's job to determine which costs are to become part of the total cost of the asset and which costs are not.

The general rule for determining the cost of inventory also applies to the cost of property, plant, and equipment assets:

*All reasonable and necessary costs to get an asset in position and condition ready for use may be included as part of the cost of the asset.*

### Machinery and Equipment

We'll use an example involving the acquisition of machinery to illustrate how to determine which costs are part of the asset cost and which are not. Print-It Company incurred the following costs when it acquired a printing press:

| | |
|---|---|
| Catalog list price ........................................ | $30,000 |
| Trade discount ........................................ | 20% |
| Cash discount terms .................................... | 4/20, n/60 |
| Freight cost (terms FOB shipping point) ................... | $900 |
| Insurance while in shipment ............................. | $150 |
| Repair cost (Forklift operator dropped machine while clowning around during unloading. Repair was necessary before the machine could be placed in service. Because the damage occurred after receipt, the shipment insurance does not cover it and Print-It must pay for repairs.) ................................... | $2,500 |

Rewiring cost (Accessible power was inadequate to supply the requirements of the new machine.) ........................ $250

Concrete slab cost (It was necessary to pour a slab to which the machine could be bolted to prevent excessive vibration.) ...... $100

Consulting engineer's fee (A consulting engineer was called in to thoroughly test the machine and demonstrate its operation.) ... $500

Materials used in testing (Cost of materials used by consulting engineer to test machine and demonstrate its operation) ...... $80

Maintenance cost (Cost of materials needed during first month of operations) ......................................... $25

Operator's salary (Salary during the first month of operations) . $800

Print-It Company would calculate the cost of the printing press as follows:

| | |
|---|---:|
| List price ............................................... | $30,000 |
| Less:  Trade discount (.20 × $30,000) ............................ | (6,000) |
| Net price .............................................. | $24,000 |
| Less:  Cash discount (.04 × $24,000) ............................ | (960) |
| Add:  Freight cost ...................................... | 900 |
| Add:  Insurance while in shipment ................................ | 150 |
| Add:  Rewiring cost ...................................... | 250 |
| Add:  Cost of concrete slab ................................. | 100 |
| Add:  Consulting engineer's fee ................................. | 500 |
| Add:  Materials used in testing ................................. | 80 |
| Total cost of printing press ...................................... | $25,020 |

All of these costs are considered reasonable and necessary to get the machine ready for use. The repair cost was excluded because it could have been avoided if the employee had been careful. The machine operator's salary and the maintenance costs were incurred after the machine became operational; they are operating costs, not acquisition costs.

Learning Objective **3**

Record acquisition of property, plant, and equipment assets

The following entry[1] records all of Print-It's costs. Note that it summarizes the total costs of acquiring the machine and identifies each of the other costs associated with but not part of the total machine cost.

| | | | |
|---|---|---:|---:|
| Dec. 1–31 | Machinery ................................. | 25,020 | |
| | Repair Expense............................ | 2,500 | |
| | Maintenance Expense ...................... | 25 | |
| | Salary Expense............................ | 800 | |
| | Cash.................................. | | 28,345 |
| | To record the cost of the printing press, costs incidental to its acquisition, a repair caused by employee negligence, and costs of operating it during December. | | |

Now let's briefly discuss some of the common acquisition costs for other types of property, plant, and equipment assets.

---

[1] All our journal entries in the examples are in general journal form, even though the entry may actually be made in a special journal. This will make illustrations much easier because we won't have to construct special journals each time we make an entry.

### Land

Land is an asset that is considered to have an unlimited useful life. Costs of surveying to determine the boundaries of the land, title insurance and legal fees, costs incurred in removing old buildings, and the costs of making permanent changes, such as draining swampy land or filling to level land, are all considered part of the cost of the land.

### Land Improvements

The costs of driveways, sidewalks, shrubbery, sprinkler systems, and parking lots are all recorded in one account called Land Improvements. These items differ from land in that each has a limited useful life.

### Buildings

The cost of a building includes construction costs, architectural fees, insurance (for fire, theft of materials, and natural disasters) while under construction, building permit fees, the cost of surveying for the purpose of locating the building on the land, and the cost of grading associated with the construction of a basement or providing adequate drainage of surface water.

### Natural Resources

Mineral deposits, oil wells, and timberland are natural resources—that is, material resources that exist in a natural state. The cost of a natural resource includes not only the costs associated with acquiring land (including the natural resource borne by the land) but also, for example, the cost of building access roads, sinking mine shafts, laying rail tracks into the mine, and other costs incurred in getting ready to extract the resource.

### Leased Assets

Businesses often sign contracts to rent assets for a long period of time (5, 10, 25, or more years). These contracts are called *leases*. Certain lease contracts are considered to be equivalent to buying the asset. If a firm leased an automobile for 5 years, and if the expected useful life of the car is 5 years, the company is said to have obtained all the benefits of owning the asset. These kinds of leased assets are recorded just as if the company actually owned them.

Thus far, to keep the discussion simple, we haven't indicated how property, plant, and equipment assets are paid for. We have implied that they were acquired either with cash or on short-term credit. In the real world, however, long-lived assets are often acquired in exchange for other assets, on long-term credit, in exchange for an ownership interest in the business, or through a combination of all these means of payment.

## Lump-Sum Acquisitions

Occasionally, a business may acquire several assets for one price. In such cases it is necessary to allocate the one lump-sum cost among several assets. Normally, this is done by a **relative-value allocation,** that is, the total cost is allocated among the various assets on the basis of each asset's value relative to the value of the whole group of assets.

For example, Delta, Inc., acquired land, a building, and machinery from Calamity Company for $1,000,000. A professional appraiser valued each of the assets at the following amounts: land, $800,000; building, $560,000; and machinery, $240,000. The $1,000,000 is allocated among the assets as follows:

| Asset | Appraised Value | Percent of Total Appraised Value × Total Cost = | | Cost Allocated to Asset |
|---|---|---|---|---|
| Land......... | $ 800,000 | $800,000 ÷ $1,600,000 = 50% | × $1,000,000 = | $ 500,000 |
| Building....... | 560,000 | $560,000 ÷ $1,600,000 = 35% | × $1,000,000 = | 350,000 |
| Machinery..... | 240,000 | $240,000 ÷ $1,600,000 = 15% | × $1,000,000 = | 150,000 |
| Totals | $1,600,000 | 100% | | $1,000,000 |

The following entry would be made to record the acquisition:

| | | | |
|---|---|---|---|
| Mar. 15 | Land..................................... | 500,000 | |
| | Building.................................. | 350,000 | |
| | Machinery................................ | 150,000 | |
| | Cash.................................. | | 1,000,000 |
| | To record acquisition of land, building, and machinery. | | |

Observe that the appraised value is $600,000 over actual cost. Nevertheless, the assets are recorded at cost, not at the value someone says they have, because recording them at cost is objective and verifiable.

## Capital Expenditures and Revenue Expenditures

Costs incurred for, or associated with, assets that will provide economic benefits over several accounting periods are called **capital expenditures.** All capital expenditures associated with a particular asset are added to the cost of that asset.

Learning Objective 4

Explain what capital expenditures and revenue expenditures are

At the time an asset is acquired, all costs that meet the requirements of the general acquisition cost rule are considered capital expenditures. As we saw for the Print-It Company's new printing press, the invoice price less discounts, plus the costs of freight, insurance during shipment, rewiring, concrete slab, consulting engineer's fee, and materials used in testing are all proper acquisition costs; therefore they are all capital expenditures.

Some expenditures incurred after the asset is acquired and placed in service are considered capital expenditures if they increase the life of the asset or improve the quantity or quality of the asset's output. Examples are the cost of replacing a truck engine with a more fuel-efficient one, the cost of adding a solar-powered heating unit to a building, the cost of overhauling a machine's motor, and the cost of resurfacing a parking lot.

In contrast, costs incurred that will provide economic benefits only during the current accounting period are called **revenue expenditures.** Revenue expenditures are recorded in expense accounts and consist primarily of the costs of regular maintenance, cleaning, and minor repairs. Examples of revenue expenditures include the costs of oil, grease, and other lubricants; lightbulbs; window panes; oil filters; tires; and the salaries of custodians and mechanics who perform regular maintenance functions.

It is important to distinguish between capital expenditures and revenue expenditures, because they affect the measurement of income differently. A capital expenditure is allocated to income over all the years during which it provides benefits. If a capital expenditure is erroneously treated as a revenue expenditure and entirely expensed during the current period, current expenses will be too high and therefore income will be too low. In subsequent years, when part of the capital expenditure should have been expensed, expenses will be too low and income will be too high. There will be a mismatching between expenses and revenues.

Revenue expenditures incorrectly charged to an asset account will also mismatch expenses and revenues, in this case causing the opposite effect: Expenses on the current income statement will be understated and thus current income will be overstated.

**ASK YOURSELF** ▶

1. What is the rule for deciding whether an asset should be classified under property, plant, and equipment on the balance sheet?
2. What is the general rule for determining the cost of a property, plant, and equipment asset?
3. When several assets are acquired for a lump-sum amount, how is this cost allocated among the assets?
4. What is the basic difference between a capital expenditure and a revenue expenditure?

## DEPRECIATION OF PLANT AND EQUIPMENT

When someone complains, "My new car is just 1 year old and it has already depreciated $4,000," they are talking about a decrease in the market value of their asset. This is *not* what accountants mean by depreciation. In accounting, **depreciation** means the allocation of the cost of a plant and equipment asset over its useful economic life.

When a company purchases a long-lived plant and equipment asset, it is really buying a large bundle of service benefits that will be provided by that asset over time in the future. These future service benefits enable the asset's owner to earn revenue by providing a place (buildings) in which to manufacture, store, and sell its products; by furnishing a means (machines) of fashioning and packaging the products; or by providing a way (trucks) to deliver goods. As an asset is used over time, the bundle of future service benefits available from it becomes smaller and smaller. The part of the original cost of the asset that is assigned to the bundle of service benefits that have been used up is called depreciation.

The following entry shows how depreciation is recorded:

| | | | |
|---|---|---|---|
| Dec. 31 | Depreciation Expense . . . . . . . . . . . . . . . . . . . . . . . . . | 10,000 | |
| | Accumulated Depreciation . . . . . . . . . . . . . . . . . . . | | 10,000 |
| | To record depreciation for the year. | | |

### Causes of Depreciation

The common causes of depreciation are physical wear and tear and obsolescence. In today's rapidly developing technological economy, obsolescence is a more important consideration than physical deterioration. For example, in evaluating how to depreciate the $800,000 cost of its new computer, Pitch Company first has to decide how many years the machine will last. Management concludes that, with proper maintenance, the machine will continue processing information for a period of 20 years. But management also knows that within 5 years the computer industry will probably develop a more efficient machine that will handle Pitch's increased information needs more efficiently. The current computer's useful life to Pitch will be 5, *not* 20, years. At the end of the 5 years, Pitch will probably be able to sell its computer to a smaller company whose information needs match the machine's capability. The asset will not have deteriorated much at all, but it will be obsolete for Pitch's purposes—though not necessarily for other businesses.

Management's estimate of an asset's useful economic life is an essential ingredient in calculating depreciation.

### Methods of Calculating Depreciation

Learning Objective **5**

Calculate depreciation using the Straight line, units-of-output, sum-of-the-years'-digits, and double declining-balance methods for full and partial years

There are several methods of determining how to depreciate the cost of an asset over its useful economic lifetime. That is, there are different ways of determining the cost that should be allocated to each year of its life. We will use the same basic information to demonstrate how to use each of these methods:

| | |
|---|---|
| Acme Company purchases a new precision drill press on Jan. 1, year 1. | |
| Acquisition cost of drill press . . . . . . . . . . . . . . . . . . . . . . . . . . . . . . . . . . . . | $125,000 |
| Estimated **salvage value** (what Acme estimates it can sell the asset for at the end of its useful life). . . . . . . . . . . . . . . . . . . . . . . . . . . . . . . . . . . . | 15,000 |
| **Depreciable cost** (the amount of cost that will be allocated to depreciation expense during the asset's life) . . . . . . . . . . . . . . . . . . . . . . . . . . . | $110,000 |
| Estimated useful life in years. . . . . . . . . . . . . . . . . . . . . . . . . . . . . . . . . . . . | 10 years |
| Estimated useful life in units of output (the total units Acme can expect the machine to produce during its useful life) . . . . . . . . . . . . . . . . . . . . . | 220,000 units |

#### The Straight-Line Depreciation Method

The **straight-line depreciation method** assumes that we receive equal benefits from an asset each day of the asset's life. The method, then, allocates an equal part of the total cost to each day of an asset's useful life. We usually record depreciation on a monthly or annual basis rather than daily. The basic idea is that depreciation recognizes the same amount of depreciation per unit of time—whatever that unit of time is. Here is the depreciation formula and the yearly depreciation for Acme's $125,000 asset:

$$\text{Straight-line depreciation per year} = \frac{\textbf{acquisition cost} - \textbf{estimated salvage value}}{\textbf{estimated useful life in years}}$$

$$= \frac{\$125,000 - \$15,000}{10 \text{ years}}$$

$$= \frac{\$110,000}{10 \text{ years}}$$

$$= \$11,000 \text{ per year}$$

The straight-line method assumes that an equal amount of the asset's total service benefits is used up each year. Thus, if the machine is acquired on Jan. 1, the depreciation for the first year would be the full $11,000.

**Straight-Line Depreciation: Partial Years**  If the machine were acquired at some point other than at the beginning of the year—say, on Oct. 1—depreciation would be recorded only for 3 months ($\frac{1}{4}$ of a year) on Dec. 31. Acme's depreciation on the drill press for years 1 and 2 would then be:

Year 1:      $11,000 \times \frac{3}{12} = \$2,750$      (3 months' depreciation)

Year 2:                   $= \$11,000$      (full year's depreciation)

**Figure 1** Straight-Line Depreciation

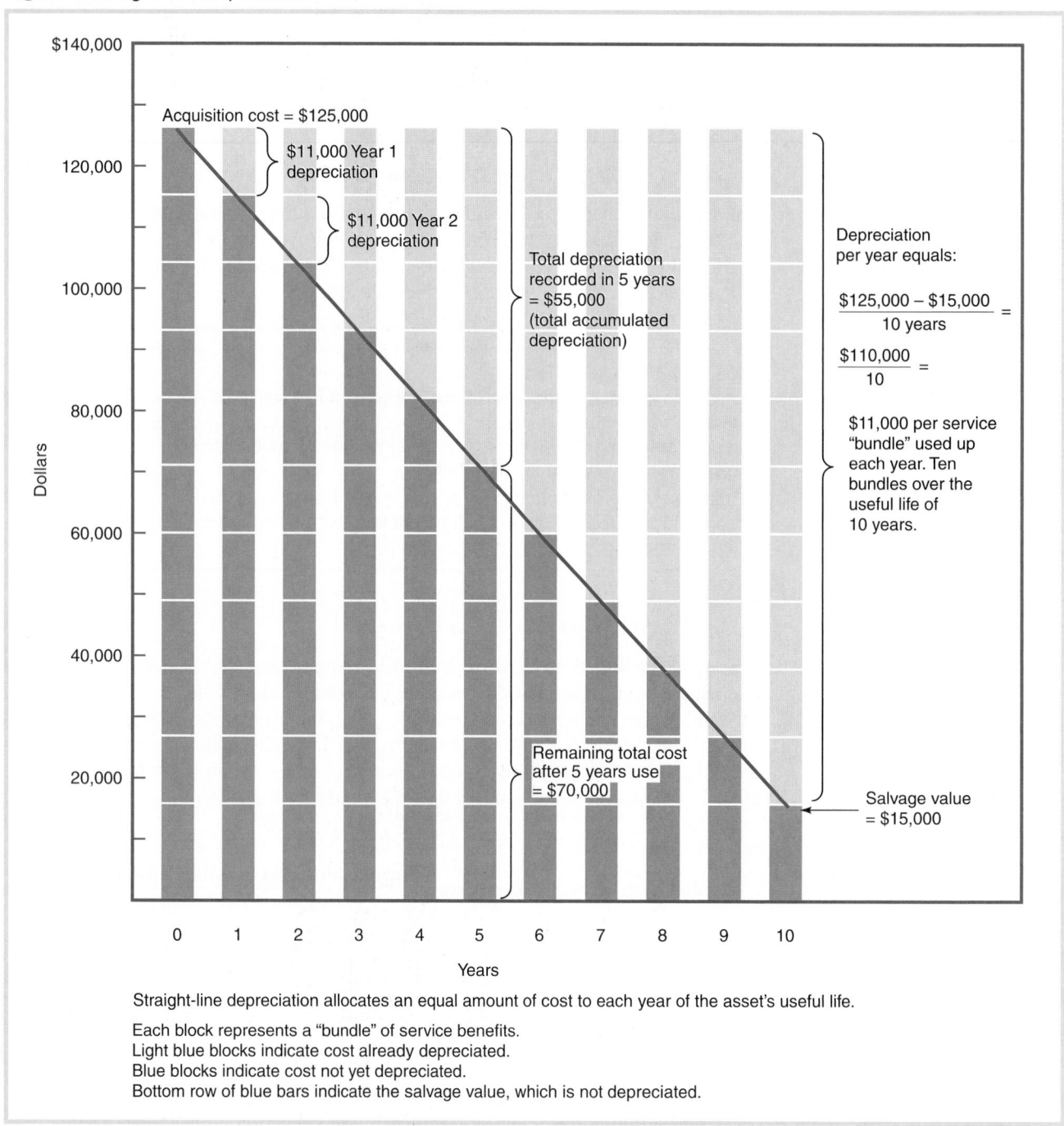

Acquisition cost = $125,000

$11,000 Year 1 depreciation

$11,000 Year 2 depreciation

Total depreciation recorded in 5 years = $55,000 (total accumulated depreciation)

Remaining total cost after 5 years use = $70,000

Depreciation per year equals:

$$\frac{\$125,000 - \$15,000}{10 \text{ years}} =$$

$$\frac{\$110,000}{10} =$$

$11,000 per service "bundle" used up each year. Ten bundles over the useful life of 10 years.

Salvage value = $15,000

Dollars

Years

Straight-line depreciation allocates an equal amount of cost to each year of the asset's useful life.

Each block represents a "bundle" of service benefits.
Light blue blocks indicate cost already depreciated.
Blue blocks indicate cost not yet depreciated.
Bottom row of blue bars indicate the salvage value, which is not depreciated.

Figure 1 shows graphically how the straight-line method works.

### The Units-of-Output Depreciation Method

The **units-of-output depreciation method** is used for assets whose useful life is limited by physical wear and tear rather than obsolescence. According to the units-of-output method, as an asset produces a unit of output, it also uses up some of the service benefits available from the asset. Each unit produced uses up the same amount of the asset's service benefits. The more units the asset produces in a period, the more service benefits it uses up in that period. What all this means is simply that the part of the asset's total cost to be depreciated in a period depends directly on the number of units the asset produces in that period.

To use the units-of-output method, we need to know the acquisition cost of the asset, its estimated salvage value, and the total estimated units the asset is expected to produce. Determination of cost was discussed earlier in this chapter. We rely on professional purchasing agents or other experts to provide an estimate of salvage value. Professional engineers and information furnished by manufacturers often can provide an estimate of the total number of units an asset can be expected to produce.

The units-of-output method would be appropriate for a delivery truck. The truck will not become obsolete; it will deliver products year after year until it is worn out. The more it is used, the more quickly it will wear out, and the greater will be the depreciation. The service benefits used would be measured in miles driven per period.

The units-of-output depreciation method requires some way of measuring the asset's output during a particular period of time. For the delivery truck, an odometer measures the miles driven. Automatic counters are used on production-line machinery, and devices measuring flying hours are used for company airplanes.

Returning to Acme's drill press, let's assume that 10,000 units are produced in year 1 and 24,000 units in year 2. The depreciation for each of these years is calculated as follows:

$$\text{Units-of-output depreciation per unit} = \frac{\text{acquisition cost} - \text{estimated salvage value}}{\text{estimated total lifetime units of production}}$$

$$= \frac{\$125,000 - \$15,000}{220,000 \text{ units}}$$

$$= \frac{\$110,000}{220,000 \text{ units}}$$

$$= \$0.50 \text{ per unit}$$

Year 1 depreciation: 10,000 units $\times$ \$0.50 per unit = \$ 5,000

Year 2 depreciation: 24,000 units $\times$ \$0.50 per unit = \$12,000

**Units-of-Output Depreciation: Partial Years**  Units-of-output depreciation for a machine acquired late in the year is easy to calculate. If a machine is used less, it will produce fewer units. Fewer units multiplied by the per-unit depreciation cost will result in a lower depreciation expense.

### The Sum-of-the-Years'-Digits Depreciation Method

The basic idea behind the **sum-of-the-years'-digits depreciation method** is that more service benefits are received in the early years of an asset's life when it is new, and fewer benefits are received each year as the asset grows older. Many assets are efficient when first purchased but become less efficient as time passes. This decrease in utility may be caused by technological obsolescence or by the accumulated effects of physical wear and tear, which cause increased maintenance costs.

The sum-of-the-years'-digits (SYD) method is a method of *accelerated depreciation* because it assigns more depreciation expense to the early years of the asset's life and less to later ones. Copying machines and computers are typically depreciated by an accelerated depreciation method such as sum-of-the-years'-digits.

The procedure for calculating SYD depreciation for Acme's drill press is as follows:

**STEP 1:** Determine the sum of the digits of the number of years of the asset's useful life, in this case 10 years.

$$1 + 2 + 3 + 4 + 5 + 6 + 7 + 8 + 9 + 10 = 55$$

**Figure 2** Sum-of-the-Years'-Digits Depreciation

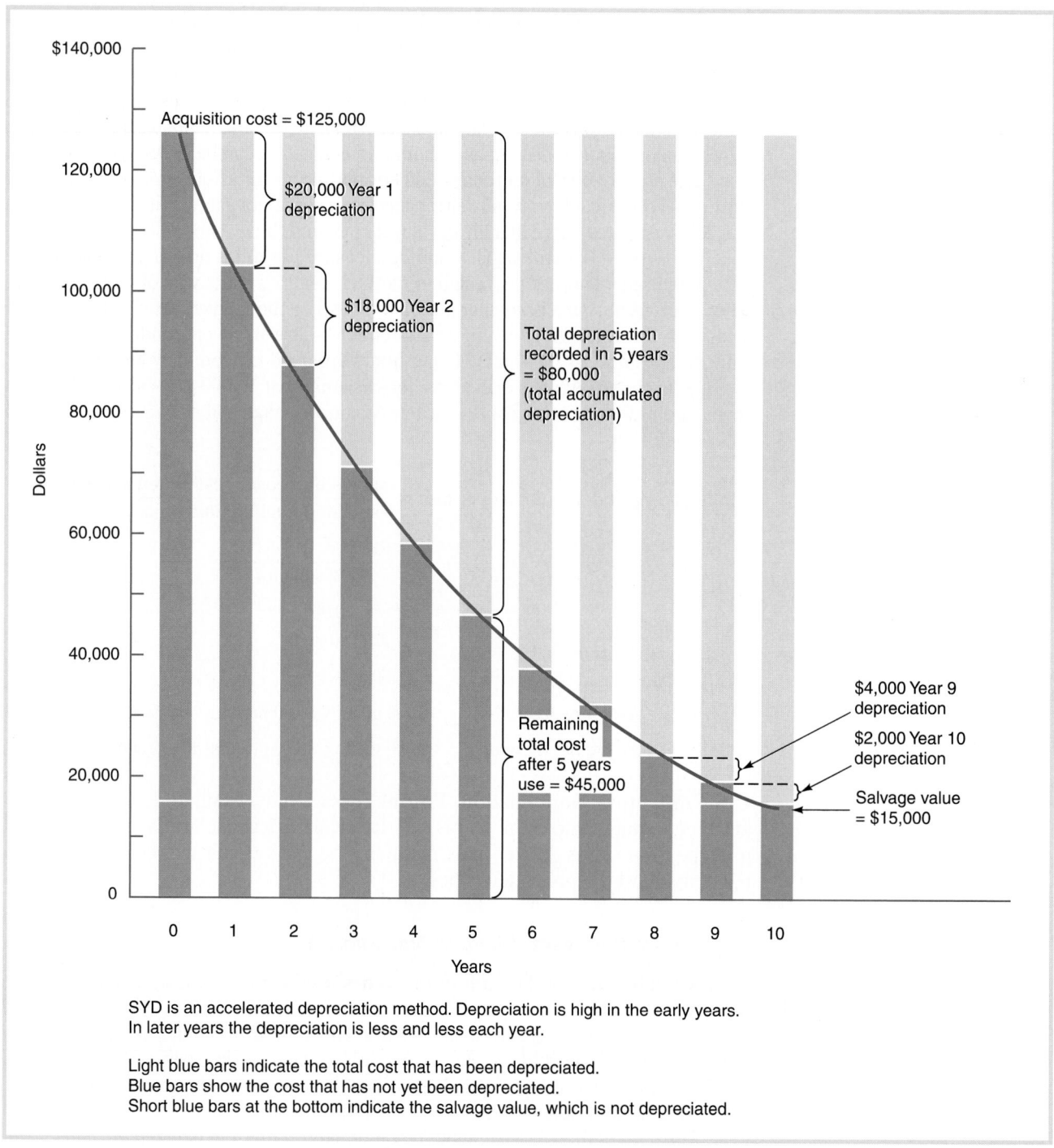

SYD is an accelerated depreciation method. Depreciation is high in the early years.
In later years the depreciation is less and less each year.

Light blue bars indicate the total cost that has been depreciated.
Blue bars show the cost that has not yet been depreciated.
Short blue bars at the bottom indicate the salvage value, which is not depreciated.

Of course, you can see how cumbersome this process would be for an asset with, say, a 15-, 20-, or 25-year life. A shortcut formula that yields the same results as the more tedious addition process is:

$$\text{Sum of the years' digits} = n\left(\frac{n+1}{2}\right)$$

where $n$ = number of years in the asset's life. So, for our example,

$$\text{10-year sum of the digits} = 10\left(\frac{10+1}{2}\right) = 10(5.5) = 55$$

**STEP 2:** Determine the difference between the asset's cost and its estimated salvage value, to find the amount to be depreciated. In Acme's case these are given as $125,000 and $15,000, respectively, and the difference is $110,000, the total amount to be depreciated.

**STEP 3:** Multiply the total amount to be depreciated by a fraction whose numerator represents the number of years of life remaining at the beginning of the current year and whose denominator represents the sum of the digits determined in step 1. The largest fraction represents the largest proportion of the cost; it will be depreciated in year 1. The fractions that will be used for Acme's drill press are as follows:

| Year of Asset's Life | Years Remaining in Asset's Life | Fraction = | Years Remaining / Sum of the Years' Digits |
|:---:|:---:|:---:|:---:|
| 1 | 10 | *Highest proportion depreciated* | 10/55 |
| 2 | 9 | | 9/55 |
| 3 | 8 | | 8/55 |
| 4 | 7 | | 7/55 |
| 5 | 6 | | 6/55 |
| 6 | 5 | | 5/55 |
| 7 | 4 | | 4/55 |
| 8 | 3 | *Lowest proportion depreciated* | 3/55 |
| 9 | 2 | | 2/55 |
| 10 | 1 | | 1/55 |
| 55 sum of the years' digits | | | 55/55 = 100% |

The three SYD depreciation steps are summarized in the following formula, which may be used to calculate SYD depreciation for each full year of an asset's life:

$$\text{SYD depreciation per year} = \left(\frac{\text{years remaining}}{\text{sum of the years' digits}}\right)(\text{cost} - \text{salvage value})$$

Using this formula, we can calculate depreciation expense for Acme's drill press as follows:

| Year | Years Remaining ÷ Sum of the Years' Digits = Fraction | × | Total Amount to Be Depreciated: Cost − Salvage ($125,000 − $15,000) | = | Depreciation Expense |
|:---:|:---:|:---:|:---:|:---:|:---:|
| 1 | 10/55 | | $110,000 | | $20,000 |
| 2 | 9/55 | | 110,000 | | 18,000 |
| 3 | 8/55 | | 110,000 | | 16,000 |
| 4 | 7/55 | | 110,000 | | 14,000 |
| 5 | 6/55 | | 110,000 | | 12,000 |
| 6 | 5/55 | | 110,000 | | 10,000 |
| 7 | 4/55 | | 110,000 | | 8,000 |
| 8 | 3/55 | | 110,000 | | 6,000 |
| 9 | 2/55 | | 110,000 | | 4,000 |
| 10 | 1/55 | | 110,000 | | 2,000 |
| | | | | Total depreciated | $110,000 |

Figure 2 is a graphic illustration of how the sum-of-the-years'-digits method works.

**Sum-of-the-Years'-Digits Depreciation: Partial Years**  If Acme had acquired its drill press on Oct. 1 rather than Jan. 1, depreciation for years 1 and 2 would be calculated as follows:

Year 1:  $\frac{10}{55} \times \$110,000 = \$20,000 \times \frac{3}{12} = \underline{\$\ 5,000}$  (depreciation for 3 months)

Year 2:  $\frac{10}{55} \times \$110,000 = \$20,000 \times \frac{9}{12} = \$15,000$

$+ \frac{9}{55} \times \$110,000 = \$18,000 \times \frac{3}{12} = \underline{\ \ \ 4,500}$

$=$ total depreciation for year 2   $\underline{\$19,500}$

During year 1, Acme depreciates the asset for the 3 months that it was used; $\frac{3}{12}$ of the $\frac{10}{55}$ fraction was used. In year 2, the remaining $\frac{9}{12}$ of the $\frac{10}{55}$ fraction must be used before switching to the $\frac{9}{55}$ fraction. This same pattern would be followed for the remainder of the asset's life. During the last year of the asset's life, the last $\frac{9}{12}$ of the $\frac{1}{55}$ fraction would be used to complete the depreciation process.

### The Double Declining-Balance Depreciation Method

Another method, which accelerates depreciation even more during the early years than the sum-of-the-years'-digits method, is declining-balance depreciation, or a simplified version commonly referred to as the **double declining-balance method (or DDB).** This method is based on the same idea as the sum-of-the-years'-digits method and is used for assets that provide even more consumable service benefits in the early years, and therefore require more depreciation in those years.

Declining-balance depreciation, like the other depreciation methods, looks at (1) the acquisition cost, (2) an estimate of the life of the asset, and (3) its estimated salvage value. Plugging that information into a complex formula and solving it yields a percentage. Starting with the acquisition cost, this percentage is applied to that cost to determine the depreciation expense for the first year. The same percentage is applied to the **book value** (the asset's total cost less its accumulated depreciation, i.e., the remaining cost) of the asset after the first year to determine the depreciation expense for the second year. And so on. Applying the same percentage to the book value of the asset in each subsequent year—the declining balance—allocates the depreciation expense each year in such a way that the balance of the cost of the asset declines precisely to the salvage value at the end of the estimated lifetime. Hence the name "declining-balance depreciation."

This precise but complex declining-balance method can be replaced with the double declining-balance method, a very simple and reasonably close approximation. Calculate the percentage that would result if you used the straight-line method, then double that percentage and apply it to the remaining balance (book value) each year. The DDB method can be summarized as follows:

$$\text{DDB depreciation per year}^* = \frac{2}{\text{useful life}} \times \text{book value at beginning of the year}$$

\* **Caution: DDB stops depreciating when salvage value is reached.**

To understand the components of this formula better, let's see how it is used to calculate depreciation for Acme's drill press:

**STEP 1:** Determine, for the straight-line method, the percentage used to calculate the depreciation expense in each year of the asset's useful life. The percentage is the reciprocal of the number of years of useful life, that is,

$$\frac{1}{\text{Number of years of useful life}}$$

For example, an asset with a 10-year life, such as the drill press, has a straight-line depreciation rate of $\frac{1}{10}$, or a percentage of 10% each year.

**STEP 2:** Double the percentage rate calculated in step 1

$$2 \times \tfrac{1}{10} = \tfrac{2}{10} \text{ or } 20\%$$

*Hint:* Whenever the rate contains a repeating decimal, use the fraction rather than the decimal equivalent. For example, $\frac{1}{3} = .333$ (use $\frac{1}{3}$), $\frac{1}{12} = .0833$ (use $\frac{1}{12}$). Using the fraction will make your calculation easier and more accurate.

**STEP 3:** Apply this percentage rate to the acquisition cost of the asset (*do not* deduct salvage). This will yield year 1 depreciation expense.

$$\text{Year 1 depreciation expense} = 20\% \times \$125,000$$

$$= \$25,000$$

**STEP 4:** For each succeeding year, multiply the percentage calculated in step 2 by the book value at the beginning of that year. (Remember, book value is cost minus all prior depreciation.)

**a.** Year 2 depreciation expense:

$$20\% \times (\$125,000 - \$25,000) = \$20,000$$

**b.** Year 3 depreciation expense:

$$20\% \times (\$125,000 - \$25,000 - \$20,000) = \$16,000$$

**c.** And so on

The depreciation for each of the 10 years is shown in the schedule below and graphically in Figure 3 at top of the next page. Note that the double declining-balance method will not usually depreciate the cost down to exactly salvage value over the useful life. (Remember, the double declining-balance rate is just an approximation of the precise declining-balance rate.) It may be necessary, then, to adjust the amount of depreciation in the final year so as to avoid depreciating below the salvage value. Sometimes it may be necessary to record no depreciation in the final year or years of the asset's useful life. *When using the double declining-balance method, depreciate down to salvage value and then stop depreciating.*

| Year | Asset Cost | − | Accum. Depr. Jan. 1 | = | Book Value Jan. 1 | × | Depreciation Rate | = | Double Declining-Balance Depreciation Expense |
|------|-----------|---|--------------------|---|------------------|---|-------------------|---|----------------------------------------------|
| 1 | $125,000 | | $      0 | | $125,000 | | .20 | | $ 25,000 |
| 2 | $125,000 | | 25,000 | | 100,000 | | .20 | | 20,000 |
| 3 | $125,000 | | 45,000 | | 80,000 | | .20 | | 16,000 |
| 4 | $125,000 | | 61,000 | | 64,000 | | .20 | | 12,800 |
| 5 | $125,000 | | 73,800 | | 51,200 | | .20 | | 10,240 |
| 6 | $125,000 | | 84,040 | | 40,960 | | .20 | | 8,192 |
| 7 | $125,000 | | 92,232 | | 32,768 | | .20 | | 6,554 |
| 8 | $125,000 | | 98,786 | | 26,214 | | .20 | | 5,243 |
| 9 | $125,000 | | 104,029 | | 20,971 | | .20 | | 4,194 |
| 10 | $125,000 | | 108,223 | | 16,777 | | * | | 1,777 |
| | | | | | | | Total amount depreciated | | $110,000 |

* Since salvage is $15,000, the final-year depreciation is limited to $1,777 ($16,777 − $15,000), not .20 × $16,777 = $3,355. At the end of year 10, accumulated depreciation will total $110,000 ($108,223 + $1,777), leaving a book value of $15,000 ($125,000 − $110,000), which is exactly equal to the salvage value.

**Figure 3** Double Declining-Balance Depreciation

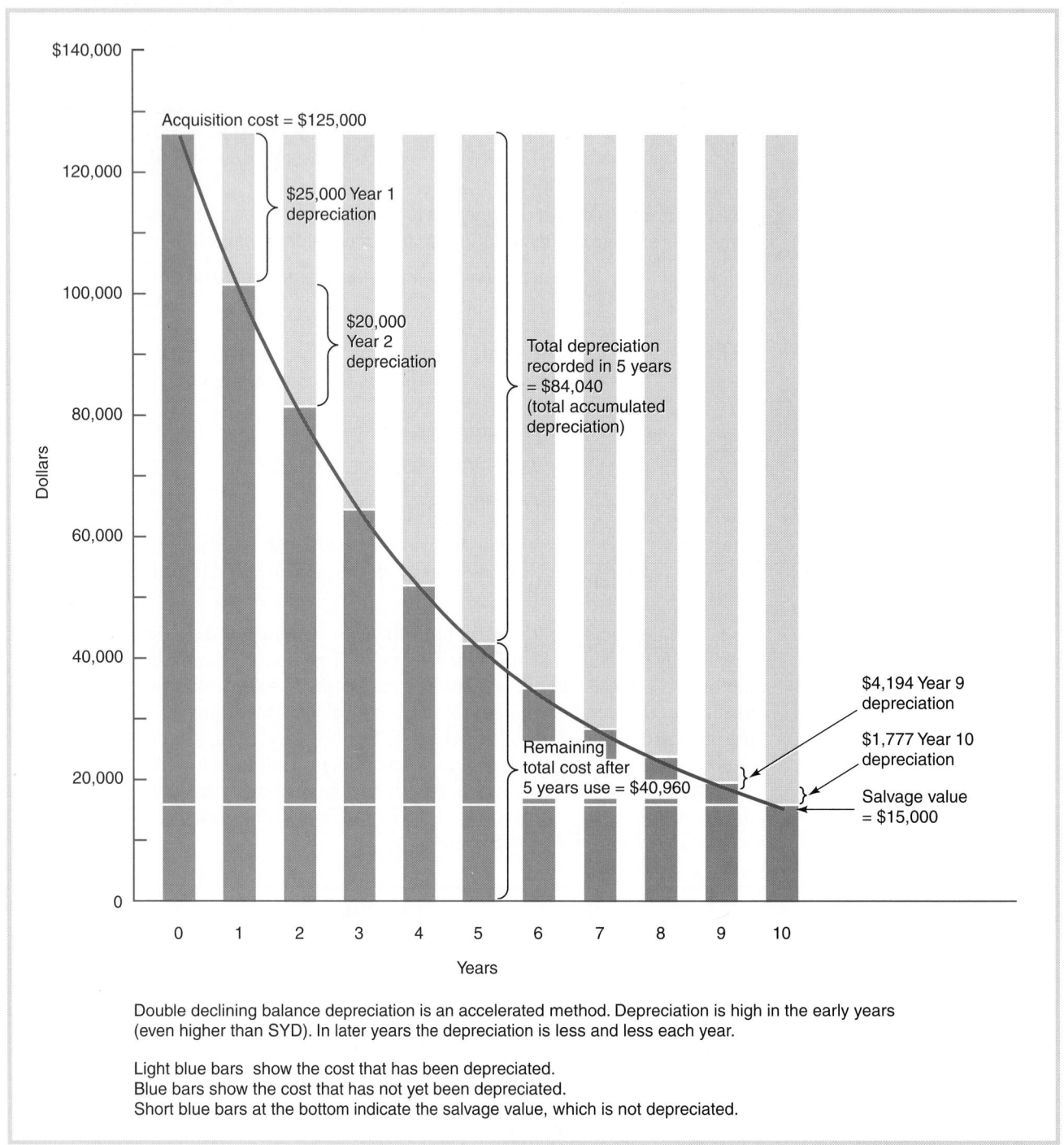

Double declining balance depreciation is an accelerated method. Depreciation is high in the early years (even higher than SYD). In later years the depreciation is less and less each year.

Light blue bars show the cost that has been depreciated.
Blue bars show the cost that has not yet been depreciated.
Short blue bars at the bottom indicate the salvage value, which is not depreciated.

**Double Declining-Balance Depreciation: Partial Years** Double declining-balance depreciation for the first 2 years, assuming the asset had been acquired on Oct. 1, would be calculated as follows:

Year 1: $125,000 − $0 = $125,000 × .20 = $25,000 × $\frac{3}{12}$ = $6,250 (3 months' depreciation)

Year 2: $125,000 − $6,250 = $118,750 × .20 = $23,750 (full year's depreciation)

In each subsequent year, the book value at the beginning of the year would be multiplied by the 20% rate to yield the depreciation for the year.

**Exhibit 1**  Comparison of Three Depreciation Methods

| Year | Straight-Line Method | | | Sum-of-the-Years'-Digits Method | | | Double Declining-Balance Method | | |
| --- | --- | --- | --- | --- | --- | --- | --- | --- | --- |
| | Depreciation Expense | Accumulated Depreciation | Book Value | Depreciation Expense | Accumulated Depreciation | Book Value | Depreciation Expense | Accumulated Depreciation | Book Value |
| 1 | $ 11,000 | $ 11,000 | $114,000 | $ 20,000 | $ 20,000 | $105,000 | $ 25,000 | $ 25,000 | $100,000 |
| 2 | 11,000 | 22,000 | 103,000 | 18,000 | 38,000 | 87,000 | 20,000 | 45,000 | 80,000 |
| 3 | 11,000 | 33,000 | 92,000 | 16,000 | 54,000 | 71,000 | 16,000 | 61,000 | 64,000 |
| 4 | 11,000 | 44,000 | 81,000 | 14,000 | 68,000 | 57,000 | 12,800 | 73,800 | 51,200 |
| 5 | 11,000 | 55,000 | 70,000 | 12,000 | 80,000 | 45,000 | 10,240 | 84,040 | 40,960 |
| 6 | 11,000 | 66,000 | 59,000 | 10,000 | 90,000 | 35,000 | 8,192 | 92,232 | 32,768 |
| 7 | 11,000 | 77,000 | 48,000 | 8,000 | 98,000 | 27,000 | 6,554 | 98,786 | 26,214 |
| 8 | 11,000 | 88,000 | 37,000 | 6,000 | 104,000 | 21,000 | 5,243 | 104,029 | 20,971 |
| 9 | 11,000 | 99,000 | 26,000 | 4,000 | 108,000 | 17,000 | 4,194 | 108,223 | 16,777 |
| 10 | 11,000 | 110,000 | 15,000 | 2,000 | 110,000 | 15,000 | 1,777 | 110,000 | 15,000 |
| Total depreciation | $110,000 | | | $110,000 | | | $110,000 | | |

### Comparison of the Depreciation Methods

The straight-line, sum-of-the-years'-digits, and double declining-balance methods produce depreciation expense amounts that follow a pattern. The units-of-output depreciation method depends on the asset's use, so it yields no predictable pattern of depreciation expense. As a review, let's look at the three methods that do generate a pattern of depreciation expense side by side, first in the table in Exhibit 1 and then graphically in Figure 4.

**Total amount to be depreciated = acquisition cost less salvage value**

$$= \$125,000 - \$15,000 = \$110,000$$

**Figure 4** A Comparison of the Straight-Line, Sum-of-the-Years'-Digits, and Double Declining-Balance Methods of Determining Depreciation.

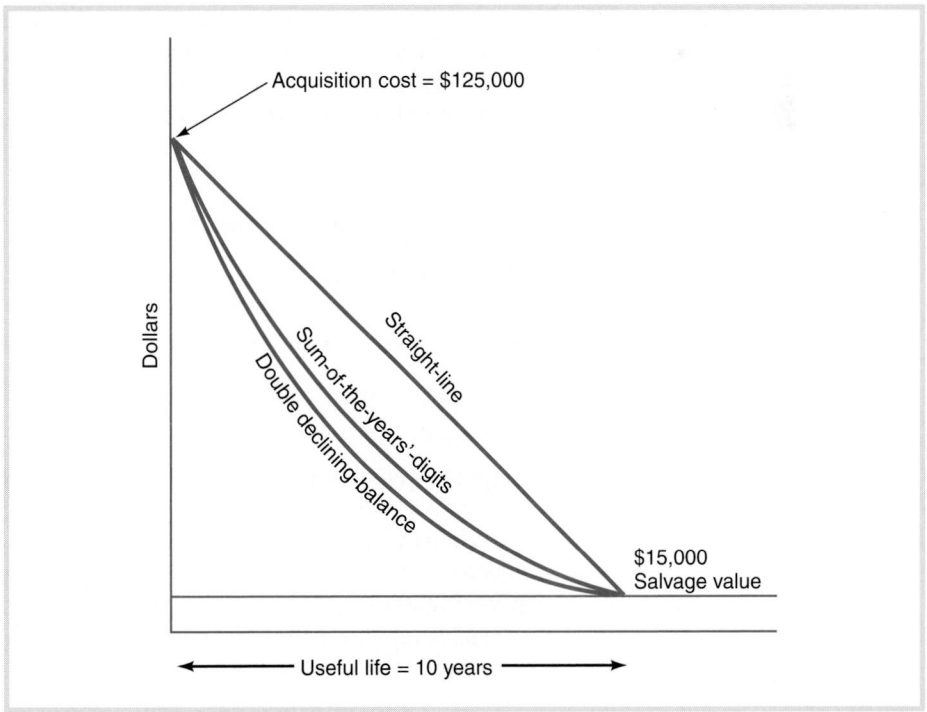

*Each depreciation line shows the decline in book value from acquisition cost to salvage value.*

**Exhibit 2** Depreciation on the Balance Sheet

## FLETCHER COMPANY
### Partial Balance Sheet
### December 31, 1998

### Assets

Current Assets:

Property, Plant, and Equipment:

| | | |
|---|---|---|
| Land . . . . . . . . . . . . . . . . . . . . . . . . . . . . . . . . . . | | $ 5,000,000 |
| Building . . . . . . . . . . . . . . . . . . . . . . . . | $12,000,000 | |
| Less: Accumulated Depreciation . . . . . | 1,500,000 | 10,500,000 |
| Machinery . . . . . . . . . . . . . . . . . . . . . . | $ 2,300,000 | |
| Less: Accumulated Depreciation . . . . . | 1,800,000 | 500,000 |
| Office Equipment . . . . . . . . . . . . . . . . . | $   250,000 | |
| Less: Accumulated Depreciation . . . . . | 45,000 | 205,000 |
| Total Property, Plant, and Equipment . . . . . . . . . . . . . . . . . . . . . . . . . . . . . . . . . . . . . . . . | | $16,205,000 |

### Disclosure of Depreciation on the Balance Sheet

Earlier, we showed that depreciation expense is recorded by debiting Depreciation Expense and crediting Accumulated Depreciation. **Accumulated Depreciation**, a contra-asset account, keeps a running total of the amount of service benefits that have been used up. By deducting this amount from the asset's cost, financial statement readers get the information they need to estimate the portion of the asset used up and to get some idea of when the company will have to make a large capital outlay to replace it. In addition to this information shown on the balance sheet, the notes to the financial statements will show the depreciation method used for each type of asset and its estimated life. An illustration of the property, plant, and equipment section of a balance sheet is shown in Exhibit 2.

### Changes in Depreciation Estimates

**Learning Objective 6**

Explain how changes in estimated useful life or salvage value are handled

The process of depreciation involves estimating an asset's useful life and its salvage value. As time passes, management may discover that these original estimates were incorrect for any number of reasons, including the following:

1. Technology advances at a faster or slower rate than originally predicted.
2. The asset physically wears out more quickly or lasts longer than expected.
3. The market value for used equipment is stronger or weaker than anticipated.

When the useful life or salvage value changes for whatever reason, depreciation is affected and must also change. Generally accepted accounting principles require that we implement changes in depreciation estimates by allocating the remaining depreciable cost over the remaining life of the asset without changing the depreciation method.

To illustrate how this change would work, let's return to the Acme Company's purchase of a drill press for $125,000. Assume that, early in year 6, a management analysis revealed that the asset will last 8 more years (that is, the total useful life will be 13 years rather than 10) and that salvage value will still be $15,000 at the end of that time. We now need to take the remaining book value at the beginning of year 6, subtract the salvage value, and spread this remaining depreciable cost over the remaining 8 years. By referring to Exhibit 1 and assuming the straight-line method, we can determine the remaining depreciable cost at the beginning of year 6 as follows:

$$\text{Cost} - \frac{\text{accumulated}}{\text{depreciation}} - \text{salvage} = \frac{\text{remaining}}{\text{depreciable cost}}$$

$$\$125,000 - \quad \$55,000 \quad - \$15,000 = \$55,000$$

Depreciation for year 6 and each of the remaining years would be:

$$\frac{\text{Revised annual}}{\text{depreciation}} = \frac{\text{remaining depreciable cost}}{\text{remaining useful life}} = \frac{\$55,000}{8 \text{ years}} = \$6,875$$

By recording $6,875 depreciation expense in years 6 through 13, we will depreciate the asset to its $15,000 salvage value.

The procedure for revising estimates is similar under the other methods. We start out as if we had just purchased the asset, treating the book value just like the acquisition cost and the revised remaining useful life just like the original life. We then calculate depreciation for each remaining year just as we would if the asset were new.

## Depreciation Does Not Affect Cash

An accountant depreciates an asset—that is, spreads its cost over its useful life—by debiting an expense account and crediting a contra-asset account at the end of each period. Cash is *never* a part of a depreciation transaction. Any depreciation expense entry clearly shows that Cash is neither debited nor credited.

Remember, an Accumulated Depreciation account shows the total portion of an asset's cost that has been charged to expense through the end of a current period—that is, it represents the part of the asset's total available bundle of services which has been used up. Accumulated depreciation dos not represent accumulated cash. Sometimes students get the idea that Accumulated Depreciation is an account that sets aside cash for replacing the asset. Not so. The replacement of an asset may be financed by borrowing, leasing, or using cash that has been set aside for this purpose. None of these transactions has anything to do with depreciation.

## Depreciation Theory and Income Tax Laws

The depreciation methods discussed thus far have traditionally been used to measure depreciation expense for the purpose of preparing income statements and balance sheets. These methods attempt to allocate an asset's cost over its useful life in proportion to the benefits received in each year.

In preparing financial statements, we are bound by the rules of good accounting theory. In preparing income tax returns, we are required to use the rules specified in the tax laws. Sometimes tax rules and good accounting theory agree, but often they do not. Depreciation is one area in which we are likely to use calculations for financial accounting purposes that are different from those used for tax purposes.

Tax laws are complex and constantly changing, so the calculation of depreciation expense for tax purposes can become rather involved. A company that has been in business for the past 20 years, for example, may be required to use one set of rules to calculate tax depreciation for assets acquired before 1980, another set to calculate depreciation for assets acquired between 1981 and the end of 1986, and still a third set for assets acquired after 1986. And none of these rules may be the same as the ones used in calculating depreciation for the financial statements.

For most assets, current tax laws require the use of a method similar to the double declining-balance method. The tax laws have some special provisions spelling out how the useful life must be determined, how the first-year depreciation must be calculated, and how the depreciation amounts must be modified later in the asset's useful life.

### Low-Cost Assets Not Depreciated

The depreciation methods you have learned about are normally applied to assets having a relatively high cost (buildings, machinery, delivery equipment, computers, office furniture, etc.). Many companies use items that have a relatively low cost and may last longer than 1 year, such as hammers and wrenches, patterns, and dies. Rather than going to the expense of keeping depreciation records for each of these assets, a company may charge their cost to an expense account when they are acquired. This procedure is acceptable as long as expensing these assets will not materially distort the company's net income.

ASK YOURSELF ▶

1. What is the accounting definition of depreciation?
2. What are the two most common causes of depreciation?
3. Which depreciation techniques are straight-line methods? Which are accelerated methods?
4. Which depreciation method would be most appropriate for assets whose depreciation is caused primarily by wear and tear?
5. Which depreciation method yields the most depreciation the first year of an asset's life?
6. What would cause management to revise the depreciation amount during an asset's useful life?

### SUBSIDIARY LEDGER FOR PROPERTY, PLANT, AND EQUIPMENT ASSETS

Companies that own a large number of relatively high-cost assets need a system for keeping track of each one. Such a recordkeeping system should clearly identify each asset, tell where it is, who is responsible for it, and what it cost, and provide a history of the depreciation that has been recorded on it. A subsidiary property, plant, and equipment ledger can accomplish this objective.

Subsidiary ledgers are used for accounts receivable; the same idea is used here for property, plant, and equipment assets. For example, Precision Company may have a general ledger account called Delivery Equipment. The supporting subsidiary ledger will contain a record for each item of delivery equipment that Precision owns. The amounts on the subsidiary ledger records should be reconciled with the amount in the general ledger account at least annually—the same procedure you used for accounts receivable.

Subsidiary ledgers may take a number of different forms and contain a variety of information. Some subsidiary ledgers are pen-and-ink records; most are found on

**Exhibit 3** Subsidiary Ledger Record for a Delivery Equipment Asset

## PROPERTY, PLANT, AND EQUIPMENT SUBSIDIARY LEDGER RECORD

Asset: _____ Delivery Van _____          General Ledger Account: _____ No. 301 Delivery Equipment _____

Identification No. _____ 301-7557 _____          Mfg. Serial No. _____ 21GNA69D6H1229366 _____

Location: _____ Atlanta Motor Pool _____

Acquired from: _____ Commercial Truck Co. _____          Brand: _____ Chevrolet _____

Responsible Person: _____ Atlanta Motor Pool Supervisor _____

Est. Life: _____ 4 years _____          Salvage Value: _____ $1,000 _____          Depr. Method: _____ St. Line _____

Depr. per Year: _____ $5,040 _____          Depr. per Month: _____ $420 _____

| Date | P/R | Asset | | | Accumulated Depreciation | | | Book Value |
|------|-----|-------|-----|------|--------------------------|-----|------|------------|
|      |     | Dr. | Cr. | Bal. | Dr. | Cr. | Bal. |  |
| May 1, 1997 | CPJ8 | 21,160 |  | 21,160 |  |  |  | 21,160 |
| Dec. 31, 1997 | GJ12 |  |  |  |  | 3,360 | 3,360 | 17,800 |
| Dec. 31, 1998 | GJ34 |  |  |  |  | 5,040 | 8,400 | 12,760 |
| Dec. 31, 1999 | GJ56 |  |  |  |  | 5,040 | 13,440 | 7,720 |
|  |  |  |  |  |  |  |  |  |
|  |  |  |  |  |  |  |  |  |

computer tapes or disks. The subsidiary ledger record for Precision Company's delivery van is illustrated in Exhibit 3.

Each plant and equipment asset has an identification number given it by the company. Note the delivery van's number, 301-7557, on the subsidiary ledger record in Exhibit 3. At least once each year, the company's internal audit staff, or other designated individual, should use the identification number to check the physical existence and condition of each asset. This will verify that the asset hasn't been stolen or damaged so badly that it is no longer operational.

**ASK YOURSELF** ▶

1. **What is the purpose of a property, plant, and equipment subsidiary ledger?**
2. **At least once each year the internal audit staff checks the subsidiary ledger record against each physical property, plant or equipment asset. What is the purpose of this check?**

## DISPOSAL OF PROPERTY, PLANT, AND EQUIPMENT ASSETS

Learning Objective **7**

Record disposal of property, plant, and equipment assets

As assets wear out, become obsolete, or are no longer needed, the business may decide to dispose of them by writing them off, selling them, or trading them in on new ones. The disposal of property, plant, and equipment assets is considered to be incidental or peripheral to the business' main activity—selling products or services. Such a disposal, then, does not generate revenue, but rather results in a gain or a loss. *Gains* occur from incidental disposals of assets for more than their book value; incidental disposals for less than book value result in *losses*.

### Write-off of Assets

Flax Company owns a machine that cost $20,000. Accumulated depreciation through Dec. 31, 1997, is $20,000. The machine is fully depreciated; its salvage value is zero. (It would cost more to sell than it would be worth.) Flax takes it to the city dump and writes it off by the following entry:

| | | | |
|---|---|---|---|
| Dec. 31 | Accumulated Depreciation: Machine . . . . . . . . . . . . . . . | 20,000 | |
| | Machine . . . . . . . . . . . . . . . . . . . . . . . . . . . . . . . . . . | | 20,000 |
| | To write off a fully depreciated machine removed from service and disposed of. | | |

### Sale of Assets

Hawke Company owns equipment that originally cost $189,000 and has an estimated useful life of 10 years and a $9,000 salvage value. The equipment was purchased on Jan. 1, 1992, and was used continuously until it was sold on Oct. 1, 1998, for $70,000.

The equipment was shown on the Dec. 31, 1997, balance sheet as follows:

| | | |
|---|---|---|
| Equipment . . . . . . . . . . . . . . . . . . . . . . . . . . . . . . . . . . . . . . . . . . . . | $189,000 | |
| Less: Accumulated Depreciation . . . . . . . . . . . . . . . . . . . . . . . . | 108,000* | $81,000 |

* Calculation of accumulated depreciation, using straight-line depreciation: [($189,000 − $9000) ÷ 10 years] × 6 years (1992–1997) = $18,000 per year × 6 years = $108,000.

For the year in which the equipment is sold, the depreciation must be recorded for the part of the year in which the asset was used. In this case, the equipment was used for 9 months, up through Sept. 30, the day before the sale. This adjustment will bring total lifetime accumulated depreciation right up to date prior to the recording of the sale.

| | | | |
|---|---|---|---|
| 1998 | | | |
| Oct. 1 | Depreciation Expense . . . . . . . . . . . . . . . . . . . . . . . . . . . . | 13,500 | |
| | Accumulated Depreciation: Equipment . . . . . . . . . . . | | 13,500 |
| | To record 9 months' depreciation. | | |
| | [($189,000 − $9,000) ÷ 10 years = $18,000 per year × $\frac{9}{12}$ = $13,500] | | |

The gain or loss on the sale is calculated as follows:

| | | |
|---|---|---|
| Selling price of equipment . . . . . . . . . . . . . . . . . . . . . . . . . . . . . . . . . . . . | | $70,000 |
| Less book value of equipment: | | |
| Cost . . . . . . . . . . . . . . . . . . . . . . . . . . . . . . . . . . . . . . . . . | $189,000 | |
| Less: Total accumulated depreciation since acquisition ($108,000 + $13,500) . . . . . . . . . . . . . . . . . . . . . . . . . | 121,500 | 67,500 |
| Gain on sale of equipment . . . . . . . . . . . . . . . . . . . . . . . . . . . . . . . . . . . | | $ 2,500 |

The entry to record the sale is:

---

1998
Oct. 1  Cash ........................................ 70,000
         Accumulated Depreciation: Equipment .............. 121,500
            Gain on Sale of Equipment ..................... 2,500
            Equipment ................................. 189,000
         To record sale of equipment.

---

If the asset had been sold for $60,000, a loss would have resulted, calculated as follows:

---

| | | |
|---|---:|---:|
| Selling price of equipment....................................... | | $60,000 |
| Less book value of equipment: | | |
|   Cost........................................... | $189,000 | |
|   Less: Total accumulated depreciation since acquisition | | |
|     ($108,000 + $13,500)........................... | 121,500 | 67,500 |
| Loss on sale of equipment ....................................... | | $ (7,500) |

---

In this case, the entry to record the sale is:

---

1998
Oct. 1  Cash ........................................ 60,000
         Accumulated Depreciation: Equipment .............. 121,500
         Loss on Sale of Equipment........................ 7,500
            Equipment ................................. 189,000
         To record sale of equipment.

---

When recording sales of long-lived assets, remember:

1. Be sure depreciation has been recorded from the date acquired up to the day of sale.
2. Recognize the gain or loss on the sale. A gain is indicated when the seller receives more for an asset than its book value. A loss is indicated when the seller receives less for an asset than its book value.

## Exchange of Dissimilar Assets

An exchange of dissimilar assets occurs when a business exchanges one asset for another that performs a different function, as when a machine is exchanged for a delivery van or land is exchanged for a computer system. Dissimilar exchanges may involve either a straight exchange of one asset for another or an exchange of assets plus cash given or received.

Dissimilar exchanges are treated just like sales of assets. The company is really selling an asset but receiving another asset instead of getting cash. The selling price of the old asset is the value of the new asset(s) received. Gains and losses are recognized just as they are for cash sales of assets.

On Feb. 1, Latrobe Company exchanged a piece of land with a cost of $6,000 for a machine with a fair market value (FMV) of $12,000. In addition to the land, Latrobe agreed to give $4,000 cash. The gain or loss calculation is as follows:

| Selling price of the land (FMV of machine received)................... | | $ 12,000 |
|---|---|---|
| Less: Book value given: | | |
| Land........................................... | $6,000 | |
| Cash........................................... | 4,000 | (10,000) |
| Gain (or loss) on the exchange ..................................... | | $  2,000 |

The following entry is made to record the exchange:

| Feb. 1 | Machine....................................... | 12,000 | |
|---|---|---|---|
| | Land....................................... | | 6,000 |
| | Cash....................................... | | 4,000 |
| | Gain on Exchange of Assets.................... | | 2,000 |
| | To record exchange of assets. | | |

The cost of the new asset will be the fair market value of the asset received.

## Exchange of Similar Assets

Businesses often trade an old asset plus some cash for a new one that performs the same function as the old one, as when an old dump truck is traded for a new one. This is called an *exchange of similar assets*. The procedures governing similar exchanges are very much like those used for dissimilar exchanges, except that we are not allowed to recognize gains when cash is given. Let's look at some specific illustrations of similar exchanges.

### Loss Indicated and Recorded

Grand, Inc., traded a computer that originally cost $12,500 and has an accumulated depreciation of $8,500 for a new computer having a fair market value (FMV) of $19,000. Grand agreed to give the old computer and $18,000 in exchange for the new one. The gain or loss in this transaction would be:

| Sales price of old computer (FMV of new computer) ................... | | $ 19,000 |
|---|---|---|
| Less book value of all assets given: | | |
| Book value of old computer: | | |
| Cost .......................................... | $12,500 | |
| Less: Accumulated depreciation ....................... | 8,500 | (4,000) |
| Book value of cash given ...................................... | | (18,000) |
| Loss indicated (and recorded) ..................................... | | $ (3,000) |

The calculation reveals that Grand has a loss in this exchange; generally accepted accounting principles require that this loss be recorded in the following entry:

| Computer (new) ......................................... | 19,000 | |
|---|---|---|
| Accumulated Depreciation (old computer).................... | 8,500 | |
| Loss on Exchange of Assets ............................. | 3,000 | |
| Computer (old)....................................... | | 12,500 |
| Cash............................................. | | 18,000 |
| To record exchange of assets. | | |

Normally the cost of a new asset is measured by the value of what is given up to get it. In this case, though, the book value of the assets given up in exchange is apparently more than their market value: Grand had to give up $22,000 of book value to get $19,000 in new asset value. The actual value of the old assets and the fair market value of the new asset, then, must be $19,000. The cost of the new computer is $19,000. *Generally accepted accounting principles limit the cost of an asset to its fair market value.*

### Gain Indicated but Not Recorded

Assume the same facts as in the previous example except that Grand acquires a new computer in exchange for the old computer and $10,000 cash. The gain or loss calculation reveals that a gain is indicated:

| | | |
|---|---:|---:|
| Sales price of old computer (FMV of new computer) | | $ 19,000 |
| Less: Book value of all assets given: | | |
|   Book value of old computer: | | |
|     Cost | $12,500 | |
|     Accumulated depreciation | (8,500) | (4,000) |
|   Book value of cash given | | (10,000) |
| Gain indicated (not recorded) | | $ 5,000 |

The following entry would be made to record the exchange:

| | | |
|---|---:|---:|
| Computer (new) | 14,000 | |
| Accumulated Depreciation (old computer) | 8,500 | |
|     Computer (old) | | 12,500 |
|     Cash | | 10,000 |
| To record exchange of assets. | | |

Good accounting theory says that Grand cannot record the indicated gain because it didn't receive cash or another current asset when it "sold" the old computer. This is said to be an *unrealized gain,* because Grand didn't receive a liquid asset such as cash. Since this gain can't be recognized, the cost of the new computer, $14,000, is considered to be equal to the book value of what Grand gave up—cash ($10,000) and the old computer ($4,000).

### No Gain or Loss Indicated

If Grand had traded the old computer and $15,000 cash for the new one, no gain or loss would have been indicated or recorded. The cost of the new computer, $19,000, would again be equal to the book value of the assets given. This amount also would be the same as the market value of the new computer:

| | | |
|---|---:|---:|
| Sales price of old computer (FMV of new computer) | | $ 19,000 |
| Less: Book value of all assets given: | | |
|   Book value of old computer: | | |
|     Cost | $12,500 | |
|     Accumulated depreciation | 8,500 | (4,000) |
|   Book value of cash given | | (15,000) |
| Gain or (loss) indicated | | –0– |

| | | |
|---|---:|---:|
| Computer (new) | 19,000 | |
| Accumulated Depreciation (old computer) | 8,500 | |
|     Computer (old) | | 12,500 |
|     Cash | | 15,000 |
| To record exchange of assets. | | |

**Figure 5** Recording Exchanges of Similar Assets

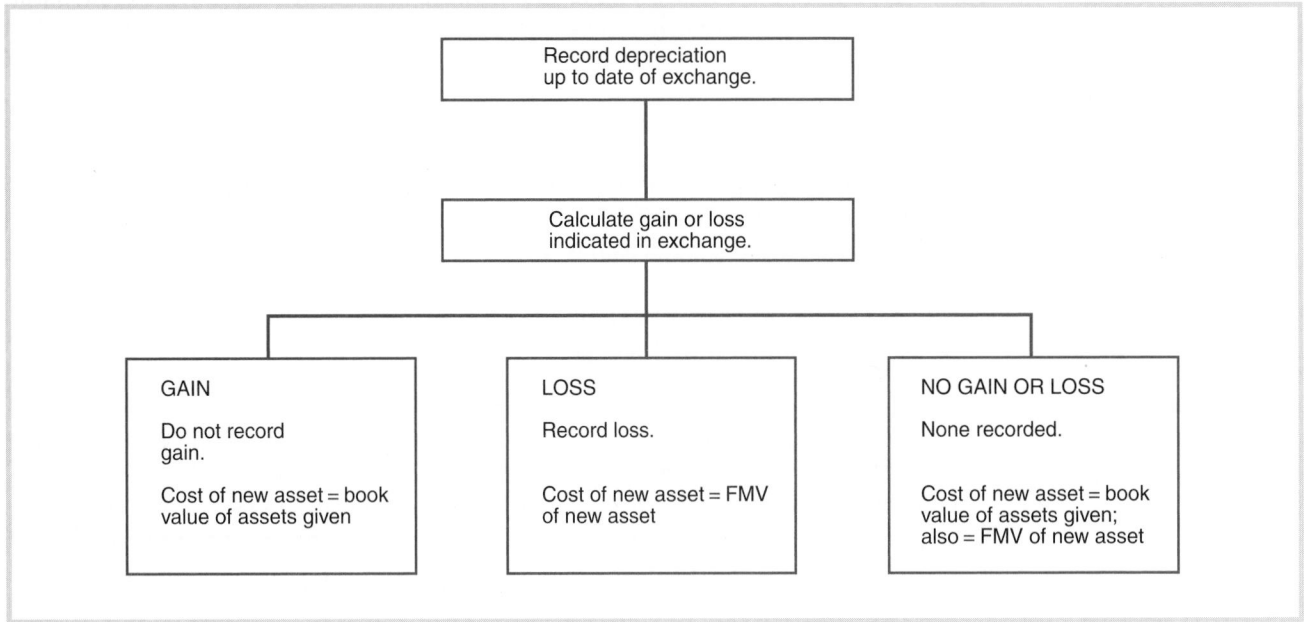

Figure 5 summarizes the procedure for recording exchanges of similar assets.

**Exchanges and Income Taxes**

The income tax laws forbid the recognition of either gains or losses in the exchange situations described above. In an exchange of similar assets when no cash is received, the cost, or tax basis, of the new asset is equal to the book value of the old asset plus the cash given. Since the cost basis is different for tax purposes, the amount of depreciation will be different and any gain or loss on later sales will also be different. As you can see, keeping records for financial reporting and for tax purposes can become quite complex.

**ASK YOURSELF ▶**

1. What is the difference between an exchange of similar assets and an exchange of dissimilar assets?
2. Are gains recognized when:
   a. Assets are sold?
   b. Assets are exchanged for dissimilar ones?
   c. Assets are exchanged for similar ones?
3. In an exchange of similar assets, what is the cost of the new asset if a loss is recorded?

**NATURAL RESOURCES AND DEPLETION**

Learning
Objective  **8**

Calculate and record depletion

When the concept of depreciating an asset was explained, we suggested that you think of an asset as a bundle of services that are used up during its lifetime. Depletion is like depreciation, but it is more tangible. With depletion, you can *see* the service bundles being used up, because depletion measures the consumption of a *natural resource*. Natural resources—such as trees, coal, oil, iron ore, and phosphate—are typically used as raw materials in the production of other goods.

A quantity of a natural resource can be thought of as a bundle of materials—the number of tons of coal in a mine or barrels of oil in an oil field. As these materials are removed, a part of the natural resource is used up, or depleted. The amount of the materials used up can be measured with fair accuracy. **Depletion** is the allocation of the cost of the part of a natural resource that is estimated to be used up during an accounting period. Depletion is calculated in exactly the same way as depreciation is calculated under the units-of-output method. This is the only acceptable way to calculate depletion (there are no accelerated depletion methods).

The cost and salvage value of the natural resource are determined, along with an estimate of the total number of units (tons, barrels, etc.) that it is capable of producing. The cost less salvage value is divided by the estimated total units. The result is depletion per unit produced.

Eureka Mining Co. paid $3,800,000 for a piece of land, including mining rights. Geologists estimated that 15 million tons of iron ore could be mined from this plot. Appraisers estimated that the land could be sold for $800,000 after mining is completed. Eureka mined 1 million tons of iron ore in year 1 and 3 million tons in year 2.

The calculation of depletion per unit, and the journal entries to record the depletion in each year, are as follows:

$$\text{Depletion per ton} = \frac{\text{cost of property} - \text{salvage value of property}}{\text{total number of tons of iron ore}}$$

$$= \frac{\$3,800,000 - \$800,000}{15,000,000 \text{ tons}}$$

$$= \frac{\$3,000,000}{15,000,000 \text{ tons}}$$

$$= \$0.20 \text{ per ton}$$

---

Year 1
Dec. 31  Depletion Expense............................  200,000
           Accumulated Depletion......................          200,000
           To record depletion for year 1.
           [($0.20 per ton) × (1,000,000 tons) = $200,000]

Year 2
Dec. 31  Depletion Expense............................  600,000
           Accumulated Depletion......................          600,000
           To record depletion for year 2.
           [($0.20 per ton) × (3,000,000 tons) = $600,000]

---

In debiting Depletion Expense for the amount of the natural resource mined, we are assuming that all of the ore was sold during the current period. If some ore remains at the end of the period, however, a proportionate part of this depletion amount would be transferred to an inventory account.

**ASK YOURSELF** ▶

1. How does depletion differ from depreciation?
2. What method is always used for calculating depletion?

## INTANGIBLE ASSETS

Learning
Objective 9

Identify assets which are normally
classified as intangible

Long-lived assets that (1) lack physical substance and (2) are not held for investment are classified as **intangible assets.** Examples include patents, copyrights, goodwill, franchises, and trademarks.

Short-lived assets such as accounts receivable and prepaid expenses lack physical substance and are not investments, but they are not classified as intangible assets; rather, they are classified as current assets.

Similarly, long-term investments in stocks and bonds are not classified as intangibles; rather, they are classified according to their purpose—they are investments.

### Cost of Intangible Assets

The acquisition cost of intangible assets is determined according to the same general rule we noted at the beginning of the chapter for property, plant, and equipment:

*All reasonable and necessary costs to get an asset in a position and condition ready for use may be included as part of the cost of the asset.*

An intangible asset can be acquired, like a patent bought from an inventor; or it can be created internally, like a copyright for an advertising jingle created by an employee of the company's advertising department. In either case, the cost of acquisition or the cost of development is included as part of an intangible's cost. Legal fees, costs of filing documents with government agencies, and costs of defending ownership are other costs commonly associated with intangibles.

Because it is sometimes difficult to establish the existence of an asset that lacks physical substance, great care must be taken in classifying internally created intangibles. When a company spends money, it may be buying future benefits (an asset) or it may be deriving all benefits now (an expense). If an asset account is charged when an expense should have been used, expenses on the income statement will be understated and net income will be overstated.

### *Research and Development Costs*

**Research and Development (R&D) costs** are an example of expenditures whose future benefit may be open to question. These costs are incurred to support experimentation and research that it is hoped will lead to new products or services that can be sold. For many years some businesses treated R&D costs as an expense when incurred; other companies did the opposite and recorded R&D costs in an intangible asset account. To promote uniform reporting, the Financial Accounting Standards Board ruled in 1974 that expenditures on R&D should be expensed when incurred.

Generally accepted accounting principles *do* permit recording costs as intangible assets in the case of patents, copyrights, goodwill, franchises, trademarks, and organization costs.

### *Patents*

**Patents** are exclusive rights granted by the U.S. government to one person or firm to manufacture, use, and sell a certain product, or to use a certain manufacturing process. Products or processes are patented when they are different from anything else that has been previously patented. Polaroid film is a good example of a breakthrough product that is completely different from any other on the market or previously patented. The owner of a patent may allow others to make and sell the product, usually charging a fee for this right. A patent is granted for a period of 17 years. The product a

# Polaroid's Patent-Case Award, Smaller than Anticipated, Is a Relief for Kodak

Eastman Kodak Co. was ordered to pay $909.5 million for infringing on Polaroid Corp.'s instant photography patents, a record patent award that nonetheless disappointed Polaroid and heartened Kodak.

For Polaroid, which had been seeking $12 billion in damages and was widely expected to receive at least $1.5 billion or $2 billion, the lower award could mean less money for its efforts to revive its sluggish instant-camera business. And its stockholders, who had been promised a share of any large award with a special payout, probably will receive little or nothing.

Kodak, on the other hand, which has been operating under the shadow of a potentially crippling multibillion-dollar award, will emerge from the bitter 14-year-old case chastened but financially sound. "Obviously, writing a billion-dollar check is not an enjoyable task, but for Kodak it certainly beats the alternative," said David Nelson, an analyst at Shearson Lehman Brothers.

\* \* \*

Federal Judge A. David Mazzone ordered Kodak to pay Polaroid $454.2 million in lost profit and royalties for bringing out instant cameras in 1976 that infringed on seven Polaroid patents, plus $455.3 million in interest.

Kodak's instant cameras were removed from the market in 1986 after an earlier ruling in the case. In calculating the damages, the judge said that Polaroid could have sold most of the cameras sold by Kodak during the 10-year period. Kodak had losses totaling $675 million on sales of $3.3 billion of cameras and film during its 10 years in the business.

But Judge Mazzone ruled against Polaroid on a couple of key points. He rejected Polaroid's contention that it could have sold its cameras and film at much higher prices if Kodak hadn't entered the market. "Even in Kodak's absence, Polaroid would have lowered camera prices," Judge Mazzone's 194-page opinion said.

In addition, the judge determined that Kodak's infringement was not "willful" and turned down Polaroid's request that the damages be tripled. "That dog will not hunt," Judge Mazzone said. "Polaroid has failed to produce a single shred of evidence that supports this claim [of deliberate infringement]."

\* \* \*

Analysts said the settlement relieves Kodak of a major uncertainty that has depressed its share price and handcuffed management. What's more, the penalty will not force Kodak, which already is highly leveraged, to sell major assets, take on substantial new debt or restructure the company, as many analysts felt would have been necessary had the award surpassed $2 billion.

"It's very positive" for Kodak, said Eugene Glazer, an analyst at Dean Witter. "It gets out of the way a major overhanging liability and allows management to conduct itself looking at underlying businesses. . . . This is a manageable award."

Still, it is the largest patent-infringement award by far, topping the $205 million that Smith International, Inc., was ordered to pay Baker Hughes, Inc., for infringing on a patent on an oil drilling bit seal; the two companies later agreed to settle for $95 million. The largest payment in a patent case was $125 million paid to Procter & Gamble by several defendants that infringed on soft-cookie recipes.

The case also will go down as one of the most celebrated patent battles ever because it pitted two of the country's best-known companies against one another. Polaroid filed its suit April 26, 1976, just six days after Kodak introduced its instant cameras. In 1985, Polaroid won a ruling that Kodak had infringed on its patents, leaving the award decision to a second trial eventually heard by Judge Mazzone.

*Source:* Lawrence Ingrassia and James S. Hirsch, *The Wall Street Journal,* Oct. 15, 1990, pp. 3, 18. Reprinted by permission of *The Wall Street Journal,* copyright © 1990 Dow Jones & Company, Inc. All rights reserved.

---

patent protects may become obsolete in a much shorter time, so a patent's useful life may be less than its 17-year legal life.

The costs of bringing successful suits against those who seek to infringe a patent by copying a product are considered a part of the cost of the patent. Unsuccessful patent infringement suits mean that the court ruled that the defendants didn't copy the product or, if they did, that they had a right to do so. The result of an unsuccessful suit may be that a patent no longer exists. The reading above describes a patent infringement suit brought by Polaroid against Kodak.

Patents can be purchased from their owners. Patents purchased from others are good only until the originally granted 17-year life expires. For example, a 16-year-old patent will provide rights to a purchaser for only 1 more year.

### Copyrights

**Copyrights** are rights granted by the U.S. government for the exclusive use of a literary or artistic work for the creator's life plus 50 years. The copyright gives the creator, heirs, or persons to whom the right has been sold the exclusive right to publish or reproduce the work for this period of time.

The cost of obtaining a copyright is very small—just the cost of completing a form and paying a small fee to the U.S. Copyright Office. The cost of purchasing a copyright from someone else, however, may be very high. Can you imagine how much it might cost to purchase the copyright to the *Jurassic Park* movies?

### Goodwill

**Goodwill** represents a number of intangible advantages such as superior operating efficiency, an unusually well-trained sales force, excellent client relations or public relations, an outstanding reputation or image in the marketplace, and an advantageous location. A firm that has all or many of these advantages has goodwill and will earn a higher return on its income-producing assets than will a firm having the same assets except for goodwill.

Goodwill is one of those internally created assets that is almost impossible to value with any objectivity. Nevertheless, goodwill can be acquired—but not by itself. It comes along with all the other tangible and intangible assets that make up a business acquired. Goodwill can be valued objectively only at acquisition, and that's when it is recorded. The value of goodwill is the part of the total acquisition cost that cannot be assigned to the other assets acquired. Consider the following example.

Roof Company agreed to purchase all the assets of Branch, Inc., for $530,000. The net assets (total assets minus total liabilities) on Branch's balance sheet were $385,000; their fair market value, the amount for which they could be sold, at the time totaled $505,000. The negotiated price of Branch was higher than the total market value of the individual assets because Branch had consistently been able to earn a much higher rate of return on its assets than other firms in the industry. Roof Company therefore recorded goodwill of $25,000 (acquisition price of total asset package, $530,000, less the total market value of the assets acquired, $505,000 = $25,000).

### Franchises

**Franchises** are exclusive rights to sell a specific brand of products or services in a certain geographic area. Franchise agreements to operate a fast-food restaurant such as McDonald's or Burger King probably come to mind immediately. Many municipalities grant franchises to private firms to provide such services as garbage removal, cable television, and electric power. The cost of the franchise includes payments made in advance of operating the franchised business, and legal fees for preparing contracts specifying the terms of the franchise agreement.

### Trademarks

**Trademarks** are exclusive rights to use a certain name or symbol for an unlimited future period. For a new trademark, the initial cost of these assets may be quite small, consisting of the artist's fee to develop a symbol and a nominal filing fee to register the trademark with a government agency. The cost of acquiring an established and well-known trademark may involve substantial sums. Imagine what it would cost to purchase the name Coke or Pepsi, if this were even possible.

### Organization Costs

**Organization costs** are expenditures made in establishing a business. Organization costs include attorneys' fees for drawing up a partnership agreement or articles of incorporation (the legal document creating a corporation), and fees paid to state and local governments to register as a business organization. The costs of organizing a business provide benefits for the life of the business and are considered to be an intangible asset.

### Amortization of Intangibles

Learning Objective **10**

Calculate and record amortization of intangible assets

The process of allocating the cost of an intangible asset over all the periods during which it provides benefits is called **amortization.** Intangibles are normally amortized on a straight-line basis unless some other system can be shown to be clearly preferable. Straight-line amortization is identical to straight-line depreciation:

$$\text{Amortization per year} = \frac{\text{cost of intangible asset} - \text{salvage value}}{\text{number of years of useful life}}$$

The *cost* of specific intangibles is determined by applying the general acquisition cost rule.

Generally, an intangible asset has no *salvage value.* At the end of an intangible's life, there is nothing of value left.

The *useful life* of an intangible may be much less than its legal life; as noted above, a patent may provide benefits for 5 years instead of the legal maximum of 17 years. In any case, *authoritative accounting rules establish an arbitrary maximum of 40 years for the amortization of any intangible.* A copyright with a possible 90-year life usually loses substantially all of its economic usefulness over a period of 40 years or less. Goodwill has such an indeterminate life that some maximum was needed.

For example, Lee Company purchased a patent from Grant, Inc., for $17,500. The remaining legal life of the patent is 12 years, but Lee believes that it will be useful for only 7 years. The calculation of the amortization and the annual journal entry to record amortization are as follows:

$$\text{Amortization per year} = \frac{\$17,500 - 0}{7 \text{ years}} = \$2,500 \text{ per year}$$

| | | | |
|---|---|---|---|
| Dec. 31 | Patent Amortization Expense.................... | 2,500 | |
| | Patents ................................ | | 2,500 |
| | To record patent amortization for the year. | | |

Accumulated amortization accounts are not customarily used for intangibles, since these assets are difficult if not impossible to replace at the end of their useful lives. Appropriate footnotes disclose the estimated useful lives of intangibles.

**ASK YOURSELF** ▶

1. **Accounts receivable and investments in stock of other companies are not tangible. Why aren't they classified as intangible assets?**
2. **What method is used to amortize intangible assets?**
3. **A trademark may provide benefits to a company for 100 years or more. Over what maximum period must it be amortized?**

## SUMMARY

- **Property, plant, and equipment** is a balance sheet classification that includes all tangible long-lived assets owned by a business and used in its operations.
- The acquisition cost of a property, plant, and equipment asset includes all reasonable and necessary costs to get it in position and condition ready for use. Common property, plant, and equipment assets include land, buildings, machinery, equipment, and natural resources.
- Expenditures made after the acquisition may be added to the cost of the asset — **capital expenditures** — or charged to expense — **revenue expenditures.** The asset account is increased whenever the expenditure benefits several future accounting periods. An expense account is debited when only the current accounting period is benefitted.
- **Depreciation** is the process of allocating the cost of a property, plant, and equipment asset (except a natural resource) over its useful life. Depreciation results from physical wear and tear as well as from technical obsolescence.
- **Straight-line depreciation** allocates an equal cost to each time period; **units-of-output depreciation** allocates an equal cost to each unit produced. The **sum-of-the-years'-digits** and **double declining-balance** methods recognize higher depreciation amounts in the early years of an asset's life when it is more productive and requires less maintenance; as a result, lower depreciation is recognized in later years, when the asset is less efficient.
- Property, plant, and equipment assets are disclosed on the balance sheet at original cost. For assets other than property and natural resources, an accumulated depreciation account is also shown subtracted from the cost amount. A comparison between cost and accumulated depreciation gives the statement reader an idea of how long it will be before the asset must be replaced.
- During the life of an asset, new facts may come to light that cause management to change its estimate of the asset's useful life or salvage value. A change in estimate causes the company to recalculate the depreciation for the remainder of the asset's useful life. The remaining depreciable cost is spread over the remainder of the asset's life using the same method that was employed before the change in estimate.
- The process of recording depreciation provides no cash fund for the replacement of the asset, or for any other purpose.
- Depreciation calculated for income tax purposes must conform to the income tax laws. These depreciation amounts are usually different from those used for accounting purposes. Thus, the amount of depreciation on a company's income tax return will usually be different from the amount on the company's income statement.
- When a property, plant, and equipment asset is disposed of, depreciation must be recorded up to the date of the disposal. When assets are discarded or sold, gains or losses may be recorded. When assets are traded in for similar assets, losses may be recorded, but not gains.
- **Depletion** is the process of recording as an expense the portion of a natural resource that has been consumed. Depletion calculations are similar to units-of-output depreciation calculations.
- **Intangible assets** is a balance sheet classification for a firm's long-lived assets that lack physical substance but that are used in its operations. The acquisition cost of an intangible asset is amortized over its useful life, usually on a straight-line basis. A maximum life of 40 years is allowed. Expenditures for research and development must be expensed as incurred; they are not intangible assets. Common intangible assets are patents, copyrights, goodwill, franchises, trademarks, and organization costs.

## 11   KEY TERMS

| | |
|---|---|
| **Accumulated depreciation** | The part of the cost of a property, plant, and equipment asset that is considered to be "consumed" and that has been charged to Depreciation Expense. |
| **Amortization** | Allocation of the cost of an intangible asset over its useful life. |
| **Book value** | An asset's total cost less its accumulated depreciation. |
| **Capital expenditures** | Costs incurred for assets that will provide benefits over several accounting periods. |
| **Copyright** | A right granted by the U.S. government for the exclusive use of a literary or artistic work for the creator's life plus 50 years; an intangible asset. |
| **Depletion** | Allocation of the cost of the part of a natural resource that is estimated to be used up during an accounting period. An equal cost is assigned to each unit of natural resource extracted. |
| **Depreciable cost** | The amount of a property, plant, and equipment asset's cost that will be allocated to depreciation expense during the asset's useful life; cost minus salvage value. |
| **Depreciation** | Allocation of the total cost of a tangible long-lived asset over its useful life. |
| **Double declining-balance depreciation method** | A system of allocating an asset's cost over its useful life in decreasing amounts each year. Depreciation per year is calculated by multiplying a fixed percentage (twice the straight-line rate) by the asset's declining book value. |
| **Franchise** | The exclusive right to sell a specific brand of products or services in a certain geographic area; an intangible asset. |
| **Goodwill** | Intangible advantages, such as high efficiency and an outstanding reputation, that allow a firm to earn a higher return on its income-producing assets than it otherwise would. This intangible asset is recorded only when purchased. |
| **Intangible assets** | A balance sheet classification for assets that lack physical substance and are not held for investment, but are an important part of a business's operations. |
| **Long-lived assets** | Assets that provide benefits for more than 1 year or one operating cycle. Typical long-lived assets include property, plant, and equipment; intangibles; and investments. |
| **Organization costs** | Costs, such as attorneys' fees and registration fees, incurred to establish a business; an intangible asset. |
| **Patent** | A right granted by the U.S. government for the exclusive manufacture, use, and sale of a certain product, or to use a certain manufacturing process for a 17-year period; an intangible asset. |
| **Property, plant, and equipment** | A balance sheet classification for tangible long-lived assets owned by a business and used in its operations. |
| **Relative-value allocation** | The allocation of the total cost of a group of assets among the various assets on the basis of each asset's value relative to the value of the whole group. |
| **Research and development (R&D) costs** | The cost of experimentation and research that it is hoped will lead to new products or services that can be sold; an expense, not an intangible asset. |
| **Revenue expenditures** | Costs incurred that will provide benefits only during the current accounting period. |
| **Salvage value** | An estimate of the amount for which an asset can be sold at the end of its useful life. |

| | |
|---|---|
| **Straight-line depreciation method** | A system of depreciating an asset's cost that allocates an equal amount of cost in each time period of the asset's useful life. Depreciation per period = (cost − salvage value) ÷ estimated useful life. |
| **Sum-of-the-years'-digits depreciation method** | A system of depreciation that allocates a decreasing cost to each successive period in an asset's life. Depreciation for a period = number of years left in the asset's life (as of the beginning of the year) ÷ the sum of the digits of the asset's useful life × (cost − salvage value). |
| **Trademark** | Exclusive right to use a certain name or symbol for an unlimited future period; an intangible asset. |
| **Units-of-output depreciation method** | A system of depreciation that allocates an equal cost to each unit produced. Depreciation per period = number of units produced this period × [(cost − salvage value) ÷ useful life stated in units]. |

## DEMONSTRATION PROBLEM

Sarasota Sodas distributes soft drinks manufactured by other companies. On Dec. 31, 1997, Sarasota had the following long-lived assets:

| | | |
|---|---:|---:|
| Land .......................................... | | $300,000 |
| Building ....................................... | $250,000 | |
| Less: Accumulated Depreciation: Building ............... | 22,500 | 227,500 |
| | | |
| Delivery Equipment ................................. | $ 60,000 | |
| Less: Accumulated Depreciation: Delivery Equipment ...... | 22,000 | 38,000 |

The following transactions and events affecting long-lived assets occurred during 1998:

Jan. 1  Sold a delivery truck for $23,000. The truck had cost $35,000 and has accumulated depreciation on Dec. 31, 1997, of $15,000.

Feb. 1  Acquired a patent for Guava-Fizz, a new soft drink, for $30,000. The patent is expected to have an economic life of 5 years and no salvage value.

Apr. 1  Purchased a canning machine for $320,000 and a packaging machine for $150,000 to use in canning and packaging Guava-Fizz. The canning machine is expected to have a useful life of 8 years and a salvage value of $40,000; the packaging machine is expected to last 6 years and have a $3,000 salvage. The double declining-balance method will be used to depreciate the canning machine; the sum-of-the-years'-digits depreciation method will be used for the packaging machine.

Nov. 1  Exchanged an old delivery truck for a new one. The old truck had cost $25,000, had an estimated salvage value of $1,000, and had an estimated useful life of 5 years. The straight-line method of depreciation was used. Accumulated depreciation on the old truck on Dec. 31, 1997, was $7,000. The new truck has a fair market value of $40,000. Sarasota gave the old truck and $28,000 cash in the exchange.

Dec. 31  The accounting year ended. Recorded all depreciation and amortization. The building has a useful life of 10 years and a $25,000 salvage value; straight-line depreciation is used. Straight-line is used also for the new delivery truck, which has a useful life of 5 years and a salvage value of $4,000.

**Required:**

Prepare entries to record each of the transactions and events listed above.

### ■ Solution to Demonstration Problem

| | | | |
|---|---|---:|---:|
| Jan. 1 | Cash ....................................... | 23,000 | |
| | Accumulated Depreciation: Delivery Equipment ....... | 15,000 | |
| | Delivery Equipment ......................... | | 35,000 |
| | Gain on Sale of Delivery Equipment ............ | | 3,000 |
| | To record sale of delivery truck. | | |
| | | | |
| Feb. 1 | Patent ...................................... | 30,000 | |
| | Cash ................................... | | 30,000 |
| | To record purchase of patent. | | |
| | | | |
| Apr. 1 | Machinery ................................... | 470,000 | |
| | Cash ................................... | | 470,000 |
| | To record purchase of canning and packaging machines. | | |

*(Continued)*

| | | | | |
|---|---|---|---|---|
| Nov. 1 | Depreciation Expense ........................... | | 4,000 | |
| |     Accumulated Depreciation: Delivery Equipment ... | | | 4,000 |

To record depreciation for 10 months on delivery equipment traded.

$[(\$25,000 - \$1,000) \div 5 \text{ years} = \$4,800/\text{year};$
$\$4,800 \times 10/12 = \$4,000]$

| | | | | |
|---|---|---|---|---|
| 1 | Delivery Equipment ............................ | | 40,000 | |
| | Accumulated Depreciation: Delivery Equipment ....... | | 11,000 | |
| | Loss on Trade of Equipment ..................... | | 2,000 | |
| |     Delivery Equipment.......................... | | | 25,000 |
| |     Cash ..................................... | | | 28,000 |

To record exchange of old delivery truck for a new one.

Calculations:

| | | |
|---|---|---|
| Fair market value of new truck ........... | | $ 40,000 |
| Less: Book value of all assets given: | | |
|     Book value of old truck | | |
|     ($25,000 − $11,000)............. | (14,000) | |
|     Book value of cash given ........ | (28,000) | |
| Loss indicated ........................ | | $ (2,000) |

| | | | | |
|---|---|---|---|---|
| Dec. 31 | Depreciation Expense ........................... | | 22,500 | |
| |     Accumulated Depreciation: Building............. | | | 22,500 |

To record depreciation on building.

$[(\$250,000 - \$25,000) \div 10 \text{ years} = \$22,500]$

| | | | | |
|---|---|---|---|---|
| 31 | Patent Amortization Expense...................... | | 5,500 | |
| |     Patent ..................................... | | | 5,500 |

To record 11 months' amortization on patent.

$(\$30,000 \div 5 \text{ years} = \$6,000; \$6,000 \times \frac{11}{12} = \$5,500)$

| | | | | |
|---|---|---|---|---|
| 31 | Depreciation Expense ........................... | | 60,000 | |
| |     Accumulated Depreciation: Machine ............ | | | 60,000 |

To record 9 months' depreciation on canning machine.

$(\$320,000 \times \frac{2}{8} = \$80,000 \times \frac{9}{12} = \$60,000)$

| | | | | |
|---|---|---|---|---|
| 31 | Depreciation Expense ........................... | | 31,500 | |
| |     Accumulated Depreciation: Machine ............ | | | 31,500 |

To record 9 months' depreciation on packaging machine.

$[(\$150,000 - \$3,000) \times \frac{6}{21} = \$42,000 \times \frac{9}{12} = \$31,500]$

| | | | | |
|---|---|---|---|---|
| 31 | Depreciation Expense ........................... | | 1,200 | |
| |     Accumulated Depreciation: Delivery Equipment ... | | | 1,200 |

To record 2 months' depreciation on new truck.

$[(\$40,000 - \$4,000) \div 5 \text{ years} = \$7,200 \times \frac{2}{12} = \$1,200]$

## QUESTIONS FOR REVIEW AND FURTHER THOUGHT

### REVIEW QUESTIONS

1. What is the general rule for determining the cost of a long-lived asset? Give examples of at least four costs that would be included in the cost of a building.

2. What are the two most common causes of depreciation? Which cause is more crucial in determining the useful life of an asset in the contemporary U.S. economy? Explain.

3. What is meant by the term *accelerated depreciation?* List two accelerated depreciation methods.

4. What may happen to cause management to change estimates used in calculating depreciation?

5. Winger Co.'s balance sheet shows a truck with a cost of $23,000 and an accumulated depreciation of $8,700. How much cash has been set aside for the replacement of the truck through the depreciation process? Explain.

6. Management may elect not to record depreciation on low-cost assets such as hand tools even though they are expected to last longer than 1 year. How are these low-cost assets accounted for? Explain why.

7. What information is usually found in a subsidiary ledger for a property, plant, and equipment asset?

8. What is the difference between depreciation and depletion? Is accelerated depletion allowed under GAAP?

9. Accounts receivable, investment in City of Charleston bonds, and copyrights are examples of assets which lack physical substance. Which of these will *not* appear under the intangible assets heading on the balance sheet? Explain why.

10. How does amortization differ from depreciation? What method of amortization is most widely used?

11. Over what time period is an intangible asset amortized?

### QUESTIONS FOR FURTHER THOUGHT

1. Charter Co. added an underground sprinkler system to the front lawn of the company's home office. Should the cost be debited to Land? Explain.

2. The cost of freight on a machine acquired on Dec. 31, 1998, was debited to Miscellaneous Expense rather than Machinery. What effect will this error have on 1998 income? On 1999 income?

3. Which depreciation method would be best for an asset whose life is limited by physical wear and tear? Explain.

4. At times the amount of depreciation indicated by the double declining-balance formula will not be the amount of depreciation recorded. Under what conditions does this happen?

5. Curlew Co. shows the following on its Dec. 31, 1997, balance sheet:

| | | |
|---|---|---|
| Building . . . . . . . . . . . . . . . . . . . . . . . . . . . . . . . . . . . . . . . . | $250,000 | |
| Less: Accumulated Depreciation . . . . . . . . . . . . . . . . . . . . . . | 75,000 | $175,000 |

Does this tell the statement reader that Curlew's building is worth $250,000? $175,000? Explain.

6. When an asset's cost and its accumulated depreciation are equal in amount, the asset is said to be fully depreciated. Are the asset and the accumulated depreciation accounts removed from the financial records when this happens? Explain.

7. Under what conditions will a company record a loss on an asset that is traded or sold?

8. Auden, Inc., has been manufacturing computer furniture for 10 years. Auden has consistently earned a much higher rate of return on its assets than its competitors and is widely recognized as the most successful firm in the industry. Would you expect Auden to have goodwill and to include goodwill on its financial statements? Explain.

## OBJECTIVE ASSIGNMENT

*True/False*   Indicate whether each statement below is *true* or *false* by placing a *T* or an *F* in the space provided.

_____ 1. All capital expenditures associated with a particular asset are added to the cost of the asset.

_____ 2. An asset's depreciable cost is the amount for which we can sell the asset at the end of its useful life.

_____ 3. The double declining-balance method will record the same depreciation over an asset's useful life as the straight-line method.

_____ 4. The depreciation process sets aside cash equal to the amount of accumulated depreciation for the replacement of the asset.

_____ 5. Gains may be recognized when a property, plant, and equipment asset is sold, but not when it is exchanged for a dissimilar asset.

*Multiple Choice*   Select the best choice to complete each statement or answer each question below. Write the letter corresponding to your choice in the space provided.

_____ 1. Which of the following would *not* be added to the cost of land?
   a. Cost of title insurance
   b. Cost incurred in demolishing an old building
   c. Amount paid to surveyors to determine the best placement of a new building on the land
   d. Cost of fill brought in to level the land

_____ 2. Query Co. bought three assets for a total of $500. The three assets were appraised at the following amounts: asset A, $300; asset B, $500; asset C, $200. In recording the acquisition, Query should debit asset C for:
   a. $1,000
   b. $500
   c. $200
   d. $100

_____ 3. GAD Co. uses the sum-of-the-years'-digits method of depreciation. On Jan. 1, 1998, GAD acquired an asset for $45,000. The asset has a useful life of 15 years and a salvage value of $1,000. Which of the following calculations will yield the correct depreciation for 1998?
   a. $(15/120) \times \$45,000$
   b. $(15/120) \times \$44,000$
   c. $(1/120) \times \$45,000$
   d. $(1/120) \times \$44,000$

_____ 4. On Jan. 1, 1998, Corry, Inc., purchased a machine for $200,000. The machine has a useful life of 20 years and a salvage value of $50,000. Depreciation for 1999, the second year of the asset's life, using the double declining-balance method would be:
   a. $13,500
   b. $18,000
   c. 20,000
   d. $48,000

_____ 5. On Jan. 1, 1997, Echo, Inc., acquired a machine for $110,000. The machine has a useful life of 5 years and a salvage value of $10,000. Echo properly applied the straight-line method of depreciation for 1997 and 1998; early in 1999, Echo management decided the machine would last 5 more years and still have a salvage value of $10,000. How much depreciation should Echo record in 1999?
   a. $12,000
   b. $13,200
   c. $20,000
   d. $22,000

_____ 6. Burke Co. sold an asset for $56,000. The asset cost $100,000 and had an accumulated depreciation of $50,000 at the time of the sale. In recording this transaction, Burke should recognize:
   a. No gain or loss
   b. A loss of $6,000
   c. A gain of $6,000
   d. A loss of $44,000

_____ 7. Which of the following would be correct for recording gains and losses when disposing of assets?

|  |  | Gains Recorded | Losses Recorded |
|---|---|---|---|
| a. | Sale of an asset............................ | No | Yes |
| b. | Exchange of dissimilar assets ................ | No | No |
| c. | Exchange of dissimilar assets ................ | No | Yes |
| d. | Exchange of similar assets................... | No | Yes |

_____ 8. Discovery Corp. paid $1,200,000 for a piece of land which is estimated to contain 5,000,000 tons of iron ore. The land is estimated to have a $200,000 salvage value when all of the ore has been removed. If Discovery mines 400,000 tons in 1999, which of the following amounts of depletion should be recorded?
   a. $80,000
   b. $96,000
   c. $100,000
   d. $112,000

_____ 9. Which of the following would be shown under the classification of intangible assets on the balance sheet of Sands Co.?
   a. Land improvements
   b. Notes receivable due in 5 years
   c. Delta Airlines stock owned by Sands Co.
   d. Franchise purchased by Sands Co. to provide cable TV service to Putnam County

_____ 10. McBooks, Inc., has just acquired a copyright that is expected to provide royalties for the company for at least 25 years. The copyright has a legal life of 60 years. Royalties will be highest early in the 25 years and then will decline as sales of the work taper off. Which method should McBooks use to amortize the copyright?
   a. Straight-line over 25 years
   b. Straight-line over 40 years
   c. Straight-line over 60 years
   d. Double declining-balance over 25 years

## EXERCISES

2† **Exercise 1:** Calculating the Cost of a Machine

Grange Co. acquired a new electronic machine from Howe, Inc. The following costs were incurred:

| | |
|---|---|
| List price of the machine .................. | $300,000 |
| Trade discount allowed to Grange............ | 20% |
| Cash discount allowed for payment within 30 days............................ | 3% |
| Cost of air-conditioning equipment for the room where the new machine is to be used. The machine requires a certain temperature and humidity to operate properly ............ | $ 3,750 |
| Insurance on the machine (3-year premium). The policy covers damage from vandalism, fire, flood, and certain other natural disasters ......................... | $ 1,080 |
| Cost of 1-year maintenance contract. The machine will be serviced weekly by Howe technicians...................... | $ 4,800 |
| Cost of rewiring needed to provide proper electric power ..................... | $ 1,260 |

Calculate the cost of the new machine to Grange Co. Explain how any amounts you omitted from the machine's cost would be accounted for by Grange.

▶ *(Check Figure: Cost of machine = $237,810)*

2  3  **Exercise 2:** Using Relative-Value Allocation to Assign Cost to Assets Acquired

Johnstown Co. bought some assets from Reel Auto Sales, which was disposing of one of its sales and service locations. The assets purchased and their appraised values were as follows:

| Asset | Appraised Value |
|---|---|
| Courtesy vans | $ 50,000 |
| Furniture | 125,000 |
| Shop equipment | 187,500 |
| Mechanics' tools | 262,500 |
| Total | $625,000 |

Assuming that Johnstown paid $500,000 for all the assets listed, calculate the portion of the cost which would be assigned to each one. Prepare the general journal entry to record the acquisition.

▶ *(Check Figure: Amount allocated to furniture = $100,000)*

† The numbers in the margin refer to the Learning Objectives.

5   **Exercise 3:** Calculating Depreciation Using Four Methods

Merrick's Derricks acquired a large piece of equipment on Jan. 1, 1998, for $1,920,000. The equipment is estimated to have a useful life of 5 years and a salvage value of $120,000. Merrick expects to be able to use the equipment for 10,000 hours before it is worn out. It was used for 4,000 hours in 1998 and 2,350 hours in 1999. Calculate depreciation for 1998 and 1999 using each of the following methods: (a) straight-line; (b) units-of-output; (c) sum-of-the-years'-digits; (d) double declining-balance.

▶ *(Check Figure: 1998 SYD depreciation = $600,000)*

5   **Exercise 4:** Calculating Partial and Full-Year Depreciation Using Three Methods

Perkins Lumber acquired a computerized cutting machine on Apr. 1, 1998, for $270,000. The machine is expected to last 10 years and to have a salvage value of $22,500 at that time. Calculate depreciation on this machine for the 9 months in 1998 and for the full year 1999 using each of the following methods: (a) straight-line; (b) sum-of-the-years'-digits; and (c) double declining-balance.

▶ *(Check Figure: 1999 SYD depreciation = $41,625)*

6   **Exercise 5:** Revising Depreciation for a Change in an Estimate

Emporium, Inc., acquired an automatic wrapping machine on Jan. 1, 1996. The $240,000 machine has an estimated useful life of 10 years and a salvage value of $15,000. Early in 1999, Emporium management, taking into consideration rapid technological advances in the field, revised the estimated life and salvage value of the machine. The useful life of the machine is expected to extend only through 2002; salvage value at that time is estimated to be $10,000. Assuming that Emporium uses the straight-line method, calculate the revised depreciation for 1999.

▶ *(Check Figure: 1999 depreciation = $40,625)*

7   **Exercise 6:** Recording the Sale of Long-Lived Assets

During 1998, Glasgow Co. disposed of two assets, as follows:

a.  A trailer that had cost $22,300 was hauled to the county dump. The trailer was fully depreciated, had no salvage value, and was no longer of any use to the company.
b.  A lathe was sold for $3,780. The lathe had cost $13,000 and had an accumulated depreciation on the sale date of $8,900.

Prepare general journal entries to record Glasgow's asset disposals.

▶ *(Check Figure: Loss on sale of lathe = $320)*

7   **Exercise 7:** Recording Exchanges of Dissimilar Long-Lived Assets

Millwood Co. exchanged a building for a piece of land. The building cost $84,000 and had an accumulated depreciation of $60,000 on the date of the exchange. Prepare journal entries to record the exchange assuming the land has a fair market value of (a) $26,000; and (b) $21,500.

▶ *(Check Figure: Gain on exchange assuming land has FMV of $26,000 = $2,000)*

7 **Exercise 8:** Recording an Exchange of Similar Long-Lived Assets

Clairton Music exchanged a used sound system for a new one. The old system had cost $22,950 and had an accumulated depreciation on the date of the trade of $16,150. Clairton gave the old system and $15,300 cash for the new one, which had a fair market value of $20,700. Calculate the gain or loss indicated in this trade and prepare a general journal entry to record the exchange.

▶ *(Check Figure: Loss on exchange = $1,400)*

7 **Exercise 9:** Recording an Exchange of Similar Long-Lived Assets

Portlan, Inc., exchanged a used concrete-mixing machine for a new one. The old machine had cost $249,000 and had an accumulated depreciation on the date of the exchange of $217,400. Portlan gave the old machine and $273,700 for a new concrete-mixing machine with a fair market value of $310,000. Calculate the gain or loss indicated in this trade and prepare a general journal entry to record the exchange.

▶ *(Check Figure: Cost of new machine = $305,300)*

8 **Exercise 10:** Calculating and Recording Depletion

Rockwood Mining purchased a tract of land containing coal. The tract cost $8,280,000 and is expected to be worth $912,000 when all the ore has been removed. Geologists estimate that 18,420,000 tons of coal can be mined from the tract. During 1999, 2,560,000 tons of coal were mined and sold. Calculate the depletion per ton of ore and prepare the general journal entry to record the 1999 depletion.

▶ *(Check Figure: 1999 depletion = $1,024,000)*

10 **Exercise 11:** Calculating and Recording Amortization of Intangible Assets

On Jan. 1, 1998, Milton Co. purchased two intangible assets as part of its acquisition of Sunbury, Inc.: a franchise for $87,000 to provide waste removal for the City of Pottstown for 3 years; and goodwill for $96,000, which is expected to last for an indefinite time. Prepare the amortization entries for the franchise and for goodwill on Dec. 31, 1998, assuming that goodwill is to be amortized over the maximum period allowed. Support your entries with clearly labeled calculations.

▶ *(Check Figure: Goodwill amortization expense = $2,400)*

## PROBLEMS: SET A

1 2† **Problem A1:** Deciding Which Long-Lived Asset Account Should Be Debited

Instead of recording long-lived assets in separate accounts, Gartz, Inc., incorrectly debits a single account called Long-Lived Assets for the purchase of any asset which is expected to last longer than 1 year. During its first year of operations, Gartz debited Long-Lived Assets for the following transactions:

a. $300,000 was paid for a parcel of land.
b. $8,750 was paid for title insurance and legal fees related to the purchase of the land.
c. $34,000 was paid to have the land cleared, filled, and leveled so that it would be suitable for use.
d. $12,800 was paid to erect a permanent fence around the property.
e. $500 was paid for a building permit.
f. $210,000 was paid to an architect to design the building and supervise construction.
g. $5,200 was paid for a survey to determine the exact placement of a building on the land.
h. $1,900,000 was paid to a contractor to erect the building.
i. $4,500 was paid for a full-page ad in the local newspaper to announce the construction of the company's new facility.

† The numbers in the margin refer to the Learning Objectives.

j. $162,000 was paid for paving parking lots and driveways.
k. $153,500 was paid for landscaping.
l. $6,500 was paid to a lawn service to maintain the lawns and shrubbery for the next year.
m. $4,800 was paid for entertainment and refreshments at an "open house" to allow the public to tour the new building.

**Required:**

Set up a solutions paper with the following headings:

| | | | | Other Accounts | |
|---|---|---|---|---|---|
| Description | Land | Buildings | Land Improvements | Title | Amount |

For each of the transactions listed above, place the amount under the correct account heading. If an amount should not be debited to any of the accounts listed, decide which account would be proper and place that account title and the amount under the "Other Accounts" heading.

▶ *(Check Figure: Cost of building = $2,115,700)*

5   **Problem A2:** Calculating Depreciation Using Four Different Methods

Zerbe Industries purchased a machine for $192,000 on Jan. 1, 1997. Zerbe expects to use the machine for 6 years, at which time its estimated salvage value will be $21,900. Production from the machine over the 6 years is budgeted at a total of 150,000 units, allocated to each year as follows: 1997, 25,000 units; 1998, 30,000 units; 1999, 35,000 units; 2000, 30,000 units; 2001, 20,000 units; 2002, 10,000 units.

**Required:**

Calculate the amount of depreciation in each of the 6 years using each of the following methods. Round all calculations (except depreciation per unit) to the nearest whole dollar.

1. The straight-line method
2. The units-of-output method
3. The sum-of-the-years'-digits method
4. The double declining-balance method

▶ *(Check Figure: 1997 SYD depreciation = $48,600)*

5   **Problem A3:** Calculating Partial-Year and Full-Year Depreciation Using Three Different Methods

Hazleton, Inc., acquired the following new assets during 1998:

| Asset | Cost | Salvage Value | Date Acquired | Estimated Useful Life (Years) | Depreciation Method |
|---|---|---|---|---|---|
| Laser Printers | $ 75,000 | $7,000 | 3/1/98 | 5 | Double declining-balance |
| Furniture | 98,000 | 3,000 | 8/1/98 | 10 | Straight-line |
| Computers | 172,000 | 4,000 | 9/1/98 | 6 | Sum-of-the-years'-digits |

**Required:**

Calculate the depreciation that should be recorded on Dec. 31, 1998, 1999, and 2000, for each of the three assets listed. Round your answers to the nearest dollar.

▶ *(Check Figure: 1999 SYD depreciation = $45,333)*

6   **Problem A4:** Calculating Depreciation when Estimated Life Is Revised

Darby Dairy purchased automated milking and feeding equipment on Jan. 1, 1998, for $937,500. The equipment was estimated to have a 10-year useful life and a salvage value of $37,500. On

Jan. 1, 2001, Darby's management revised the useful-life estimate to a total of 15 years (through Dec. 31, 2012). This was necessary because equipment innovations had not occurred as rapidly as originally expected. Salvage is expected to remain at $37,500.

**Required:**

1. Calculate the depreciation that should be recorded on Dec. 31, 1998, 1999, and 2000. Assume that Darby uses the straight-line method of depreciation.
2. Calculate the depreciation that should be recorded on Dec. 31, 2001, based on the revised useful life and straight-line depreciation.
3. Calculate the depreciation that should be recorded on Dec. 31, 1998, 1999, and 2000. Assume that Darby uses the double declining-balance method of depreciation.
4. Calculate the depreciation that should be recorded on Dec. 31, 2001, based on the revised useful life and double declining-balance depreciation.

▶ *(Check Figure: 2001 double declining-balance depreciation = $80,000)*

3 5 7 **Problem A5:** Recording Acquisition, Depreciation, and Disposal of an Asset and Preparing a Subsidiary Ledger Record

People Movers Co. uses a system of subsidiary ledger records for each of its major property, plant, and equipment assets. The transactions described below relate to one of those assets:

Nov. 1, 1997     Purchased a tram (serial no. 22K3345RT) for $201,600 from Norris Equipment, Inc. The tram is assigned to the Trenton, New Jersey, branch and is the responsibility of the branch manager. The chief property accountant assigned the tram an identification number, 437-7450, and specified that it be depreciated on the straight-line method. The tram's expected useful life is 8 years and its salvage value is estimated to be $17,280.

Dec. 31, 1997     Recorded depreciation for the year.

Dec. 31, 1998     Recorded depreciation for the year.

Apr. 30, 1999     Sold the tram for $172,000 cash. Recorded depreciation for the first 4 months of the year and recorded the sale.

**Required:**

1. Prepare general journal entries to record each of the transactions and events above. Trams are recorded in general ledger account no. 437, Light Equipment. Show calculations to support each entry.
2. The head bookkeeper will post the transactions to the general ledger accounts. Establish a subsidiary ledger record similar to the one shown below and post the transactions to it.

Subsidiary Ledger Record for a Delivery Equipment Asset

## PROPERTY, PLANT, AND EQUIPMENT SUBSIDIARY LEDGER RECORD

Asset: _____ Delivery Van _____    General Ledger Account: _____ No. 301 Delivery Equipment _____

Identification No. _____ 301-7557 _____    Mfg. Serial No. _____ 21GNA69D6H1229366 _____

Location: _____ Atlanta Motor Pool _____

Acquired from: _____ Commercial Truck Co. _____    Brand: _____ Chevrolet _____

Responsible Person: _____ Atlanta Motor Pool Supervisor _____

Est. Life: _____ 4 years _____    Salvage Value: _____ $1,000 _____    Depr. Method: _____ St. Line _____

Depr. per Year: _____ $5,040 _____    Depr. per Month: _____ $420 _____

| Date | P/R | Asset | | | Accumulated Depreciation | | | Book Value |
|---|---|---|---|---|---|---|---|---|
| | | Dr. | Cr. | Bal. | Dr. | Cr. | Bal. | |
| May 1, 1997 | CPJ8 | 21,160 | | 21,160 | | | | 21,160 |
| Dec. 31, 1997 | GJ12 | | | | | 3,360 | 3,360 | 17,800 |
| Dec. 31, 1998 | GJ34 | | | | | 5,040 | 8,400 | 12,760 |
| Dec. 31, 1999 | GJ56 | | | | | 5,040 | 13,440 | 7,720 |
| | | | | | | | | |
| | | | | | | | | |

▶ *(Check Figure: Gain on sale of tram = $4,960)*

---

7  **Problem A6:** Recording Sales and Exchanges of Long-Lived Assets

Topton, Inc.'s, Dec. 31, 1998, balance sheet includes the following property, plant, and equipment assets:

| | | |
|---|---|---|
| Land . . . . . . . . . . . . . . . . . . . . . . . . . . . . . . . . . . . . . . . . . . . . . . . . . . . . . . . | | $750,000 |
| Building . . . . . . . . . . . . . . . . . . . . . . . . . . . . . . . . . . . . . . . . . | $1,800,000 | |
| Less: Accumulated Depreciation . . . . . . . . . . . . . . . . . . . . . . | 1,600,000 | 200,000 |
| Refrigeration Equipment. . . . . . . . . . . . . . . . . . . . . . . . . . . . . . | $ 460,000 | |
| Less: Accumulated Depreciation . . . . . . . . . . . . . . . . . . . . . . | 220,000 | 240,000 |
| Delivery Trucks. . . . . . . . . . . . . . . . . . . . . . . . . . . . . . . . . . . . . | $ 125,000 | |
| Less: Accumulated Depreciation . . . . . . . . . . . . . . . . . . . . . . | 99,200 | 25,800 |

The following transactions affecting property, plant, and equipment assets took place during 1999:

a. On Jan. 1, the land and building were sold for $1,175,000. Topton has decided to lease space as soon as an acceptable facility can be located.

b. On June 1, the old refrigeration equipment was traded in for similar units with a larger capacity. The fair market value of the new assets was $650,000. Topton was required to pay $450,000 cash in addition to giving the old equipment. Straight-line depreciation on the old equipment is $1,000 per month.

c. On Oct. 1, the old delivery trucks were traded for new ones. Topton was required to pay $158,000 in addition to trading the old trucks. The new trucks have a fair market value of $182,000. Straight-line depreciation on the old trucks is $1,600 per month.

**Required:**

Prepare journal entries to record each of the 1999 transactions. Support each entry with clearly labeled calculations.

▶ *(Check Figure: Cost of new delivery trucks = $169,400)*

3 5 7   **Problem A7:** Recording Sales and Exchanges of Long-Lived Assets

During 1998, Glyde Air Freight engaged in the following transactions relating to property, plant, and equipment assets:

Jan. 1   Traded a computer which had a cost of $200,000 and accumulated depreciation of $70,000 for a new airplane having a fair market value of $1,900,000. Glyde was required to pay $1,700,000 in addition to giving the old computer.

Apr. 1   Sold a building for $375,000. The building cost $450,000 and has an accumulated depreciation of $150,000 on Jan. 1, 1998. Glyde uses the straight-line method of depreciation. The building was estimated to have a useful life of 30 years and a salvage value of $30,000.

June 30   Sold old forklifts for $500 as scrap. This equipment had been purchased on July 1, 1993, for $12,000; they were estimated to have a useful life of 5 years and a salvage value of $800. Accumulated depreciation on Jan. 1, 1998, was $10,080. The straight-line method is used.

Sept. 30   Traded an old airplane for a new one having a fair market price of $5,000,000. The old airplane had been purchased on Feb. 1, 1989, for $2,000,000, had no salvage value, and was fully depreciated as of Jan. 1, 1998. Glyde was required to pay $4,950,000 in addition to giving the old airplane.

**Required:**

Prepare the entry to record each of the transactions listed above. You may also need an entry to record depreciation for part of the year. Assume that Glyde has not recorded any depreciation since Dec. 31, 1997. Support your entries with clearly labeled calculations.

▶ *(Check Figure: Loss on sale of forklifts = $300)*

2 3 5 7   **Problem A8:** Recording Acquisition, Depreciation, and Disposal of a Truck

Bucks Co. was established to move hazardous waste to federally approved disposal stations. Debra Dublin, owner of the company, entered into the following transactions related to a truck during the first 2 years of operation:

1998
Mar. 2   Purchased a truck chassis for $30,000 cash.

3   Paid $7,050 to have the truck fitted with special shock absorbers, double-walled tanks, and heavy-duty bumpers.

15   Paid $1,350 to have the truck painted with the company's colors and logo.

Apr. 1   Placed the truck in service and began to operate.

Oct. 14   Paid $235 to Willow Garage for a tune-up and oil change.

Dec. 31   Recorded straight-line depreciation on the truck beginning with the day it was placed in service. Estimated life is 3 years; estimated salvage value is $4,380.

1999
Aug. 31   Traded the truck for a new one. The new truck has a fair cash price of $105,000. Debra gave the old truck and $81,465 cash. The new truck was placed in service the next day. (Record depreciation on the old truck for 8 months.)

Oct. 5   Paid Willow Garage $1,200 to perform routine maintenance on the new truck for the next 12 months. Bucks Co.'s first service was Oct. 5.

Dec. 31   Recorded straight-line depreciation on the new truck. Estimated life is 4 years; estimated salvage value is $10,200.

31   Recorded the appropriate adjusting entry for maintenance contract.

**Required:**

Prepare entries in general journal form to record each of the transactions and events listed. Where appropriate, show calculations to support your entries.

▶ *(Check Figure: Depreciation expense, Dec. 31, 1999 = $7,800)*

10   **Problem A9:** Recording Acquisition and Amortization of Intangible Assets

Burbank Discoveries is a diversified company involved in many agriculture-oriented business ventures. Selected Burbank transactions for 1998 are as follows:

Jan.   1   Acquired a patent for a new pesticide that is made from orange pulp and is completely safe for the environment. The patent cost $496,000 and is expected to have an economic life of 16 years.

Apr.   1   Purchased from Green Thumb Depot a 5-year franchise to sell garden products. The franchise price was $118,000; one-fourth of the price was paid in 1998; the remainder is due within 1 year.

June 30   Purchased an operating plant nursery. Goodwill purchased as a part of the transaction totaled $50,000.

Oct.   1   Purchased a copyright for a series of instructional gardening videos for $218,000. The copyright is expected to have a useful life of 10 years.

**Required:**

1. Analyze each of these transactions and events. Prepare all necessary journal entries. If no entry is required, write "no entry" and give the reason none is needed.
2. Prepare the amortization entries needed on Dec. 31, 1998. Assume that goodwill is to be amortized over the maximum number of years.

▶ *(Check Figure: Goodwill amortization = $625)*

## PROBLEMS: SET B

1  2†   **Problem B1:** Calculating the Cost of Several Assets

The management of Lynde Corp. has asked for your assistance in determining the cost of their property, plant, and equipment assets. Lynde began operations on Jan. 3, 1998. During the year, the following transactions took place which management believes may relate to long-lived assets:

a. Paid $850,000 for land, building, and machinery. The land was appraised at $195,000, the building at $487,500, and the machinery at $292,500. Lynde was able to acquire the assets at less than their appraised value because the seller was badly in need of cash.
b. $7,500 was paid for title insurance on the land.
c. $4,000 was paid to drain a portion of the land and to haul in fill dirt so that the land could be used for a parking lot.
d. $1,800 was paid for a survey to determine the exact location of the driveways and parking lots to be constructed.
e. $32,000 was paid for grading and paving driveways and parking lots.
f. $4,800 was paid to a cleaning service to sweep the driveways and parking lots for the remainder of 1998.
g. $96,000 was paid to have a new roof put on the building. The roof is expected to last 20 years, which is also the remaining life of the building.
h. $36,500 was paid to have the motors in several of the machines overhauled.
i. $120 was paid to replace several window panes which were broken after Lynde moved into the building.
j. $750 was paid for a supply of oil, grease, and cleaning compounds which would be needed to assure efficient operation of the machines.
k. $6,200 was paid for a sprinkler system for the lawn.

† The numbers in the margin refer to the Learning Objectives.

**Required:**

Set up a solutions paper with the following column headings:

| Description | Land | Buildings | Machinery | Land Improvements | Other Accounts Title | Other Accounts Amount |
|---|---|---|---|---|---|---|

For each of the items listed above, place the amount under the correct account heading. If the amount should not be debited to any of the accounts listed, decide which account would be proper and place that account title and the amount under the "Other Accounts" heading.

▶ *(Check Figure: Cost of buildings = $521,000)*

5 **Problem B2:** Calculating Depreciation Using Four Different Methods

On Jan. 1, 1997, Rocke Hauling Co. purchased a large crane. Rocke estimates the $472,500 crane will last for 8 years, at which time its salvage value will be $60,000. Rocke believes the crane can be used for a total of 12,000 hours, distributed over the 8 years as follows: 1997, 1,200; 1998, 1,500; 1999, 2,000; 2000, 2,000; 2001, 1,800; 2002, 1,700; 2003, 1,000; 2004, 800.

**Required:**

Calculate the amount of depreciation in each of the 8 years using each of the following methods. Round all calculations (except depreciation per hour) to the nearest whole dollar.

1. The straight-line method
2. The units-of-output-method
3. The sum-of-the-years'-digits method
4. The double declining-balance method

▶ *(Check Figure: 1997 SYD depreciation = $91,667)*

5 **Problem B3:** Calculating Partial-Year and Full-Year Depreciation Using Three Different Methods

Natrona Corp. purchased the following new assets during 1998:

| Asset | Cost | Salvage Value | Date Acquired | Estimated Useful Life (Years) | Depreciation Method |
|---|---|---|---|---|---|
| Dishwashers | $21,000 | $3,500 | 2/1/98 | 5 | Straight-line |
| Deep Fryers | 38,500 | 2,500 | 5/1/98 | 4 | Sum-of-the-years'-digits |
| Grills | 18,500 | 300 | 9/1/98 | 8 | Double declining-balance |

**Required:**

Calculate the depreciation that should be recorded on Dec. 31, 1998, 1999, and 2000 for each of the three assets listed. Round all calculations to the nearest dollar.

▶ *(Check Figure: 1999 double declining-balance depreciation = $4,240)*

6 **Problem B4:** Calculating Depreciation when Estimated Life Is Revised

Yeadon Foods purchased automated bottle washing and filling equipment on Jan. 1, 1998, for $1,700,000. The equipment was estimated to have a 10-year useful life and a salvage value of $50,000. On Jan. 1, 2000, Yeadon's management revised the useful-life estimate to a total of 7 years (5 years remain as of Jan. 1, 2000). This was necessary because equipment innovations have occurred more rapidly than originally expected. Salvage is expected to remain at $50,000.

**Required:**

1. Calculate the depreciation that should be recorded on Dec. 31, 1998 and 1999. Assume that Yeadon uses the straight-line method of depreciation.
2. Calculate the depreciation that should be recorded on Dec. 31, 2000, based on the revised useful life and straight-line depreciation.
3. Calculate the depreciation that should be recorded on Dec. 31, 1998 and 1999. Assume that Yeadon uses the sum-of-the-years'-digits method of depreciation.
4. Calculate the depreciation that should be recorded on Dec. 31, 2000, based on the revised useful life and sum-of-the-years'-digits depreciation.

▶ *(Check Figure: Book value on Jan. 1, 2000, when SYD is used = $1,130,000; 2000 SYD depreciation = $360,000)*

3 5 7 **Problem B5:** Recording Acquisition, Depreciation, and Disposal of a Machine and Preparing a Subsidiary Ledger Record

Lion Excavation uses a system of subsidiary ledger records for each of its major property, plant, and equipment assets. The transactions described below relate to one of those assets:

| | |
|---|---|
| Mar. 1, 1997 | Purchased a drag line (serial no. 34J4241B) for $900,000 from Chester Heavy Equipment. The drag line is assigned to the Reading, Pennsylvania, branch and is the responsibility of the chief engineer. The chief property accountant assigned the machine an identification number, 390-2141, and specified that it be depreciated on the straight-line method. The machine's expected useful life is 6 years, and its salvage value is estimated to be $29,880. |
| Dec. 31, 1997 | Recorded depreciation for the year. |
| Dec. 31, 1998 | Recorded depreciation for the year. |
| Aug. 31, 1999 | Sold the machine for $500,000 cash. Recorded depreciation for the first 8 months of the year and recorded the sale. |

**Required:**

1. Prepare general journal entries to record each of the transactions and events above. Drag lines are recorded in general ledger account no. 390, Mining Equipment. Show calculations to support each entry.
2. The head bookkeeper will post the transactions to the general ledger accounts. Establish a subsidiary ledger record similar to the one shown below and post the transactions to it.

Subsidiary Ledger Record for a Delivery Equipment Asset

## PROPERTY, PLANT, AND EQUIPMENT SUBSIDIARY LEDGER RECORD

Asset: _____Delivery Van_____  General Ledger Account: _____No. 301 Delivery Equipment_____

Identification No. _____301-7557_____  Mfg. Serial No. _____21GNA69D6H1229366_____

Location: _____Atlanta Motor Pool_____

Acquired from: _____Commercial Truck Co._____  Brand: _____Chevrolet_____

Responsible Person: _____Atlanta Motor Pool Supervisor_____

Est. Life: _____4 years_____  Salvage Value: _____$1,000_____  Depr. Method: _____St. Line_____

Depr. per Year: _____$5,040_____  Depr. per Month: _____$420_____

| Date | P/R | Asset | | | Accumulated Depreciation | | | Book Value |
|------|-----|-------|-----|------|------|-----|------|------|
| | | Dr. | Cr. | Bal. | Dr. | Cr. | Bal. | |
| May 1, 1997 | CPJ8 | 21,160 | | 21,160 | | | | 21,160 |
| Dec. 31, 1997 | GJ12 | | | | | 3,360 | 3,360 | 17,800 |
| Dec. 31, 1998 | GJ34 | | | | | 5,040 | 8,400 | 12,760 |
| Dec. 31, 1999 | GJ56 | | | | | 5,040 | 13,440 | 7,720 |
| | | | | | | | | |
| | | | | | | | | |

▶ *(Check Figure: Loss on sale of equipment = $37,450)*

7 **Problem B6:** Recording Sales and Exchanges of Long-Lived Assets

On Jan. 1, 1998, Penn Amusement Corp.'s balance sheet lists the following equipment:

| | | |
|---|---|---|
| Carousel . . . . . . . . . . . . . . . . . . . . . . . . . . . . . . . . . . . . . . . | $138,000 | |
| Less: Accumulated Depreciation . . . . . . . . . . . . . . . . . . . . . . | 29,200 | $108,800 |
| Ferris Wheel . . . . . . . . . . . . . . . . . . . . . . . . . . . . . . . . . . . . . | $530,000 | |
| Less: Accumulated Depreciation . . . . . . . . . . . . . . . . . . . . . . | 211,200 | 318,800 |
| Food Service Trailer . . . . . . . . . . . . . . . . . . . . . . . . . . . . . . . | $148,000 | |
| Less: Accumulated Depreciation . . . . . . . . . . . . . . . . . . . . . . | 136,000 | 12,000 |

The following transactions affecting equipment took place during 1998:

a. On Jan. 2, the carousel was sold for $106,400.
b. On Mar. 31, the Ferris wheel was traded in on a larger one that operated more safely and efficiently. The fair market value of the new Ferris wheel was $638,000. In addition to giving the old ride, Penn was required to pay $345,000 cash. Straight-line depreciation on the old Ferris wheel was $4,400 per month.
c. On July 1, the food service trailer was traded for a new one having a fair market value of $130,000. Penn was required to pay $125,000 in addition to the trailer. Straight-line depreciation on the old trailer was $1,500 per month.

**Required:**

Prepare journal entries to record each of the transactions described above. Support each entry with clearly labeled calculations.

▶ *(Check Figure: Cost of the new trailer = $128,000)*

3 5 7   **Problem B7:** Recording Sales and Exchanges of Long-Lived Assets

During 1998, Lansdale's Tree Service disposed of several long-lived assets and acquired several others. Information relating to these transactions follows:

Jan. 1    Traded an old truck having a cost of $54,000 and an accumulated depreciation of $18,000 for a new one having a fair market value of $81,600. Lansdale was required to pay $48,000 in addition to giving the old truck.

May 1    Sold an old stump-grinding machine for $2,000. The machine cost $13,000 and had an accumulated depreciation on Jan. 1, 1998, of $8,400. Lansdale uses the straight-line method of depreciation. The machine has an estimated useful life of 5 years and a $1,000 salvage value.

Oct. 1    Sold old chain saws for $750. The saws had been purchased on Sept. 30, 1993, for $4,500; they were estimated to have a useful life of 5 years and a salvage value of $720. Depreciation had been correctly recorded through Dec. 31, 1997.

Nov. 1    Traded a chipping-and-shredding machine for a new log-loading machine having a fair market value of $7,500. The old machine had been purchased on Jan. 1, 1991, for $4,500. The estimated useful life of the old machine was 12 years; the estimated salvage value was $180. Accumulated depreciation on Jan. 1, 1998, was $2,520. Lansdale was required to pay $5,500 in addition to giving the old machine.

**Required:**

Prepare the entry to record each of the transactions listed above. You may also need an entry to record depreciation for part of the year. Assume that Lansdale has not recorded any depreciation since Dec. 31, 1997. Support your entries with clearly labeled calculations.

▶ *(Check Figure: Loss on trade of truck = $2,400)*


2 3 5 7   **Problem B8:** Recording Acquisition, Depreciation, and Disposal of a Truck

Dauphin Delivery specializes in delivering live animals to pet stores and zoos. The following transactions related to a truck took place during the first 2 years of operation:

1998
Jan.   2    Purchased a used truck for $4,250 cash.

        3    Paid $125 to have the truck towed to the city that serves as the base of operations.

Feb. 15    Paid $1,125 to have the engine, brakes, and transmission overhauled.

       21    Paid $2,000 to have cushioned, air-conditioned compartments installed in the bed of the truck.

Mar.   1    Placed the truck in service and began to operate.

July 27    Paid $65 to Pete's Garage for a tune-up and oil change.

Dec. 31    Recorded straight-line depreciation on the truck beginning with the day it was placed in service. Estimated life is 3 years, and estimated salvage value is $750.

1999
Nov. 30    Traded the truck for a new one. The new truck has a fair cash price of $21,000. Dauphin gave the old truck and $16,938 cash. The new truck was placed in service the next day. (Record depreciation on the old truck for 11 months.)

Dec. 31    Recorded straight-line depreciation on the truck. Estimated life is 4 years, and estimated salvage value is $660.

**Required:**

Prepare entries in general journal form to record each of the transactions and events listed. Round all calculations to the nearest dollar.

▶ *(Check Figure: Depreciation expense, Dec. 31, 1998 = $1,875)*

10 **Problem B9:** Recording Acquisition and Amortization of Intangible Assets

Jamison Corp. began business in 1999. The controller has made the following list of transactions and events, all of which she believes relate to long-lived assets:

Jan. 1 Paid attorney $3,500 to draw up articles of incorporation and file them with the state government.

May 1 Purchased a franchise to sell Borge Pianos. Paid $12,000 cash; the balance of $18,000 is due within 1 year.

July 1 Paid $16,000 to a music consultant to create a series of video music lessons for the company. The fee included a copyright on the video presentation that was developed.

Oct. 1 Paid $1,500 to an artist to design a logo as a trademark for the company. This logo was registered at an additional cost of $100.

Dec. 31 Jamison has had such a successful first year that the managers feel that some goodwill has been created. They estimate the value of this goodwill to be at least $9,000.

**Required:**

1. Analyze each of these transactions and events. Prepare all necessary journal entries. If no entry is required, write "no entry" and give the reason none is needed.
2. Prepare the entries needed on Dec. 31 to amortize the intangible assets. Assume that all the intangibles are to be amortized over a 10-year period.

▶ (Check Figure: Trademark amortization = $40)

## DECISION PROBLEM

Jason Garcia and his sister, Angela, each plan to open a donut shop in different sections of the same town. They each plan to purchase a small used building, counters and fixtures, and cooking equipment. The cost, salvage value, and useful lives of these assets are the same for each one:

|  | Cost of Each | Salvage of Each | Useful Life of Each |
|---|---|---|---|
| Building | $168,000 | $8,000 | 20 years |
| Fixtures | 32,000 | 4,000 | 5 years |
| Equipment | 54,000 | 6,000 | 10 years |

In addition, they estimate that each building will require painting and a new roof before it can be occupied. The cost of this renovation will be $24,000 on each building.

The projected first-year income statements for each donut shop are as follows:

| JASON'S DONUTS<br>Projected Income Statement<br>For Year Ended December 31, 1999 | | | ANGELA'S DONUTS<br>Projected Income Statement<br>For Year Ended December 31, 1999 | | |
|---|---|---|---|---|---|
| Sales | | $180,000 | Sales | | $180,000 |
| Cost of Goods Sold | | 73,000 | Cost of Goods Sold | | 73,000 |
| Gross Profit on Sales | | $107,000 | Gross Profit on Sales | | 107,000 |
| Operating Expenses: | | | Operating Expenses: | | |
| Salaries Expense | $19,200 | | Salaries Expense | $19,200 | |
| Depreciation Expense: | | | Depreciation Expense: | | |
| Building | 16,800 | | Building | 9,200 | |
| Fixtures | 12,800 | | Fixtures | 5,600 | |
| Equipment | 10,800 | | Equipment | 4,800 | |
| Building Repair Expense | 24,000 | | Other Expenses | 10,400 | |
| Other Expenses | 10,400 | | | | |
| Total Expenses | | 94,000 | Total Expenses | | 49,200 |
| Net Income | | $ 13,000 | Net Income | | $ 57,800 |

Jason doesn't understand how his sister's projected profits can be so much higher than his when they are both projected to make the same sales, employ the same number of people, and spend about the same amount for other necessary operating items.

**Required:**

Analyze the projected income statements to answer the following questions regarding profitability.

1. Which depreciation method has Jason elected to use for his property, plant, and equipment assets? Show the calculation of depreciation for each of his assets.
2. What error did Jason make in accounting for the cost of his building? What effect did this error have on his projected 1999 income?
3. Which depreciation method did Angela use for her property, plant, and equipment assets? Show the calculation of depreciation for each of her assets.
4. Did Angela commit the same error as Jason in accounting for the cost of her building?
5. Assuming that Jason corrects his accounting error and continues to use the same depreciation method, do you feel that this method best reflects the planned first-year performance? Why or why not?

## ETHICS CASE

Mammoth Industries has decided to build a new manufacturing facility to enable the company to compete more effectively with foreign firms in their industry. Roger Anderson is in charge of Mammoth's task force responsible for examining alternative ways of setting up the new production line. Anderson's team has been careful to consider the cost of acquiring and installing each piece of machinery and equipment, the cost of maintenance, the cost and availability of spare parts, the amount of labor required for operation, the cost of utilities, potential hazards to machinery operators, and the difficulty of training workers to operate the equipment.

In addition to charts, graphs, and pictorial aids, Roger's team has prepared a detailed written analysis outlining all the strong and weak points of each alternative, including a total cost estimate for the project and estimated per-unit cost of output at several production levels. Roger presents a detailed analysis of the three best proposals to Lou Diamond, his supervisor, who will study the report and make a recommendation to top-level management.

Alternative A is the lowest-cost one but includes a higher probability of employee injury and a greater risk of environmental damage from the venting of toxic gases. Alternative B has a higher cost but, while reducing the risk of employee injury, still has a potential for environmental damage. Alternative C is the highest-cost alternative but is the safest for employees and poses the lowest environmental risk.

Lou congratulates the task force for a job well done and promises that their good work will be remembered in the next performance evaluation. Later in the week, Roger comes across a copy of the report that Lou has prepared for presentation to top-level management. A quick review causes Roger a great deal of concern. Lou has deleted all references to many of the weaknesses associated with each alternative and has left the analysis as basically a cost comparison among the three. His recommendation is to be alternative A.

Roger is faced with a dilemma: Should he pretend that he never saw Lou's version of the analysis and leave well enough alone? Should he discuss the situation with Lou and risk losing his favorable performance evaluation (and possibly his job)? Should he bypass Lou and take his concerns to someone at a higher level? Is this really Roger's problem? After all, he isn't the one making the decisions. He has done his job; isn't his responsibility at an end? Will Roger ultimately be blamed if an accident or environmental disaster occurs? Even if he isn't, how will he feel if something terrible happens and he has taken no action?

**Required:**

What should Roger do? Are there courses of action he might take, other than those mentioned here?

## OBJECTIVE ASSIGNMENT ANSWERS

**True/False**

1. T    2. F    3. T    4. F    5. F

**Multiple Choice**

| 1. c | 2. d | 3. b | 4. b | 5. a |
| 6. c | 7. d | 8. a | 9. d | 10. a |

# Payroll

The ability to borrow money enables us to enjoy many of the advantages our society offers. Very few people would own their own homes if they could not borrow money. Nor would many of us have cars, furniture, or a multitude of goods and services (including college educations) if we could not borrow money from stores, banks, and other sources. Our national and international economies also depend on the availability of credit. Practically all businesses purchase inventories and acquire plant and equipment by incurring liabilities. If credit is not available, or if its cost is too high, goods and services cannot be paid for; as a result, plants close and thousands of people lose their jobs.

When one party extends credit, the other party incurs a liability. For instance, we extend credit to our employer for the service we render, and our employer satisfies this liability on payday. When a company extends credit for goods sold, it records an account receivable, which is a current asset; the buyer records an account payable, which is a current liability.

This chapter is devoted to a discussion of current liabilities other than accounts payable: payrolls, notes payable, and product warranties.

## PAYROLL ACCOUNTING

Learning Objective 1

List and describe the various payroll-related taxes for employees

Payroll accounting involves lots of activity. Many types of part-time and full-time jobs are involved. Some people are paid weekly—typically those who work in factories, small retail stores, and some offices. Some are paid biweekly (every 2 weeks)—usually clerical workers for larger retail stores and larger businesses, including work-study programs at most universities. A few, including most middle managers, are paid semimonthly. Executives are typically paid monthly. Some companies pay all employees at the same interval, while others pay different employee groups at different times.

Payroll constitutes a significant cost to an employer. For many companies, the cost of labor exceeds 40% to 50% of total operating costs. When we consider the size and frequency of payrolls, it's no wonder that payroll accounting is a major activity for most companies.

### Overview of the Payroll System

Figure 1 provides an overview of a large company's payroll system. Study this flow chart carefully, but don't worry about the details. The payroll register, the employee individual earnings records, W-4's, and all the other elements will be explained in this chapter. For now, we just want you to have a general idea of what is involved in paying employees.

Observe from the figure that many different departments are involved. This is a key to achieving strong internal control over payrolls. Of course, a small company whose owner prepares the payroll does not need such an elaborate system. The owner knows all the employees and who did or did not work during the pay period. But for larger companies, separation of duties is essential for providing the checks and balances needed to ensure proper control.

Notice that employee attendance is recorded by *time cards* or *attendance reports.* Department heads must also prepare an absentee report to compare with the time cards. This redundancy deters an employee from punching in an absent co-worker's time card so that the co-worker will be paid for time not worked.

When an employee is hired, a *personnel record* is established. The employee's address, Social Security number, birthdate, next of kin, work experience, education, and military experience are all recorded on this document. Over time, additional information is recorded: positions held within the company, salary changes, leaves of

**Figure 1** Payroll Flow Chart

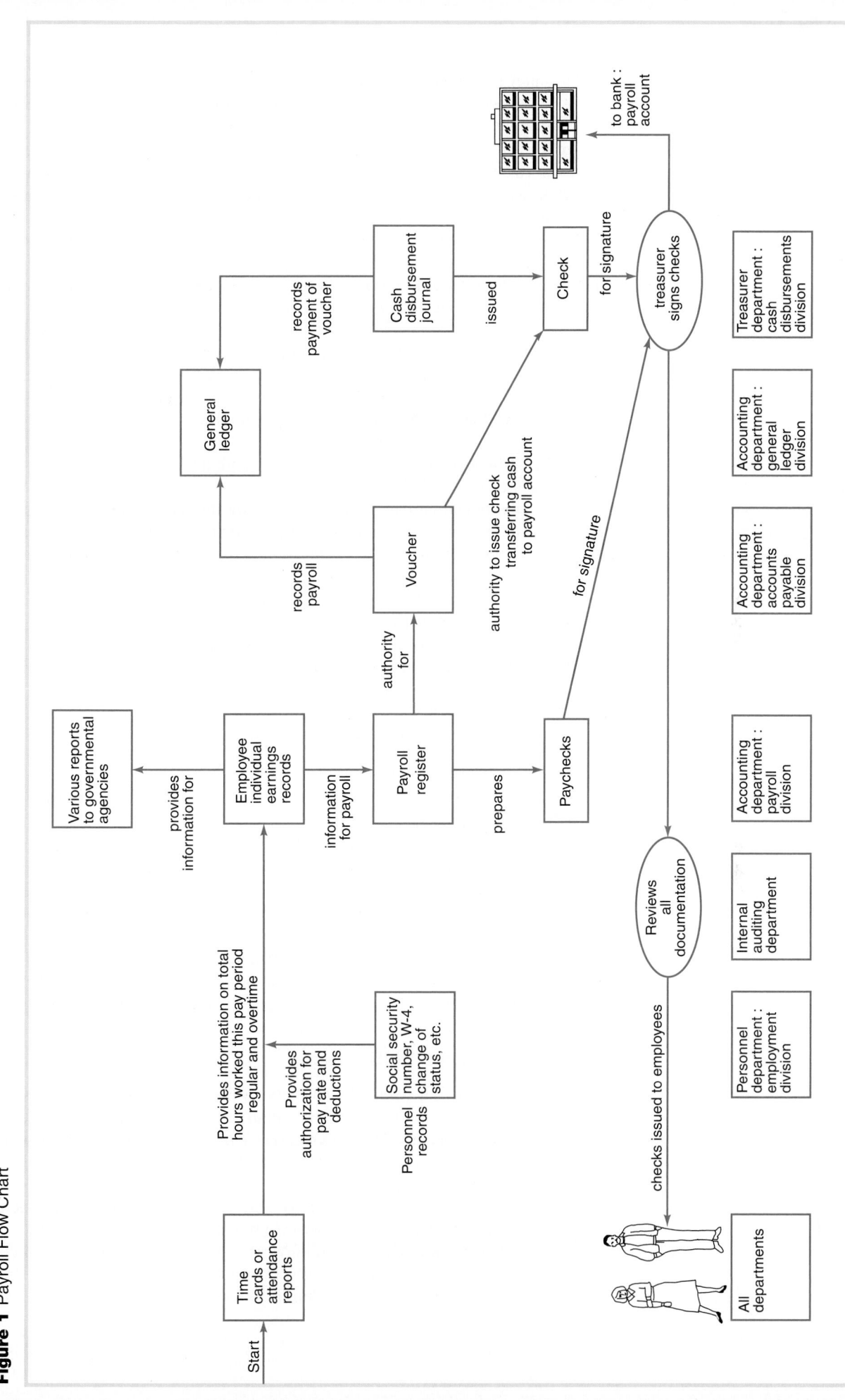

absence, performance evaluations, accidents, insurance plans, and termination date.

In large companies personnel records are maintained by a personnel department. Usually each piece of new information to be added to a personnel file must be authorized by a written change-of-status report. A personnel record will also contain authorization from the employee directing the company to withhold certain amounts from paychecks for deductions such as medical insurance premiums, union dues, and savings bonds.

The time cards, together with information from the personnel records, enable the payroll division of the accounting department to update the *employee earnings record.* These records are used to prepare the *payroll register,* the paychecks, and the many reports required by governmental agencies.

The payroll register totals are used by the accounts payable division to prepare a voucher authorizing the cash disbursements division of the treasurer's department to issue a check for the total payroll. This check transfers cash from the company's general funds to a special payroll account at its bank.

The voucher also authorizes the general ledger division to record the payroll. When the cash disbursements division issues the check, it records it in the cash disbursements journal, which in turn is recorded by the general ledger division in the general ledger.

The individual paychecks prepared by the payroll division are signed by the treasurer and then reviewed and co-signed by another executive. The signed checks are distributed to the various departments to be given to the employees.

The internal auditor must be constantly on guard against both unintentional errors and outright dishonesty. Payrolls have often tempted unscrupulous employees to defraud the company through such schemes as:

- Listing fictitious employees
- Maintaining former employees on the payroll
- Increasing certain employees' pay rates without authorization
- Listing incorrect totals on the payroll register
- Not deducting employees' absent time
- Preparing a payroll cash account deposit greater than the payroll
- Making duplicate paychecks

The separation of duties shown by the payroll flow chart makes it very difficult, *but not impossible,* for dishonest employees to commit a payroll fraud. The people in the personnel department have no authority to prepare payrolls or write checks. Those in accounting cannot increase or decrease payroll deductions for individual employees, nor can they sign the paychecks. The treasurer can sign only those checks which he or she is authorized to sign, and he or she cannot record entries in the general ledger.

### Some Important Distinctions

Before we begin our detailed discussion of the payroll system, we must make a few important distinctions. First, the term **salary** refers to the cash compensation given to professional, administrative, managerial, and clerical employees, usually at a flat weekly, monthly, or yearly rate; in contrast, **wages** are normally based on the number of hours worked.

Second, the salary or wages may be determined by mutual agreement between employee and employer or by union contract.

Finally, we must distinguish between employees and independent contractors. An **employee** is a person who is subject to the control and direction of the company for which he or she works. An **independent contractor** also performs services for a company, but is not subject to the company's control and direction. We can illustrate this important difference by comparing the director of accounting and finance of a large company with the certified public accountant who audits the company's accounting records. The director of accounting and finance may have considerable freedom in the exercise of his or her authority, but is still an employee responsible to, controlled by, and directed by the vice president, president, and board of directors of the company. The CPA is obligated to perform in accordance with professional standards but is independent of the client company. Similarly, a construction company may employ workers to frame houses, or it may engage the services of an independent framing contractor.

This distinction has important implications for payroll accounting, because the wages or salary paid to an employee is subject to the employee withholding tax and the related payroll tax requirements imposed by governmental agencies. When a company pays a *fee* to an independent contractor, that amount is not subject to these requirements.

With this overview of the payroll system and with an awareness of the distinctions between salaries and wages and between independent contractors and employees, we are ready to discuss the details of payroll preparation and the related payroll accounting considerations.

### Computing Gross Pay

**Gross pay** is the amount that an employee has earned during a pay period before any required or authorized deductions are subtracted. The amount of gross pay depends on the type of position held and the number of hours worked. Most business entities are subject to the provisions of the federal Fair Labor Standards Act, referred to as the Wages and Hours Law. The law requires the employer to pay a minimum hourly wage ($4.25 since Apr. 1, 1991, though some states set their own minimum wage at a higher level). Employers must also pay overtime—at least one and one-half times the regular hourly rate—for all hours worked in excess of a stated number. For many years this number has been 40 hours per week. Administrative, executive, and supervisory employees generally are exempt from the time-and-a-half requirement.

In addition to the provisions of the Wages and Hours Law, premium pay rates are common for employees who work nights or weekends. Of course, union contracts may provide for pay scales well in excess of the minimum wage and time-and-a-half for overtime.

Consider the following example. Carl Neely is employed by the Page Export Company at an annual salary of $43,680. His position is covered by the Wages and Hours Law, so all hours he works in excess of 40 hours per week are compensated at one and a half times his regular hourly rate. The number of working hours in a year is considered to be 2,080 (40 × 52 weeks per year). During the current biweekly pay period Neely has worked 86 hours, which includes 6 hours of overtime. His regular biweekly pay is $1,680 ($43,680 ÷ 26 biweekly periods per year). He will be paid that amount even if he works less than 80 hours, since he is a salaried employee and the Page Export Company has provided him with this benefit. On an hourly basis, Neely is paid at a rate of $21.00 ($43,680 ÷ 2,080 working hours per year). Therefore, he is paid for overtime at a rate of $31.50 per hour ($21.00 × $1\frac{1}{2}$). Neely's gross earnings are computed as follows:

| | |
|---|---|
| Base biweekly salary . . . . . . . . . . . . . . . . . . . . . . | $1,680.00 |
| Overtime earnings (6 hr × $31.50) . . . . . . . . . . . | 189.00 |
| Total gross earnings . . . . . . . . . . . . . . . . . . . . . | $1,869.00 |

Determining the total hours an employee worked during the week is a function of the payroll system. Each company establishes its own method for compiling such information. In a small office the office manager may simply note the hours worked in a log book. A large office or factory will use a more formal timekeeping system; typically, each direct supervisor fills in a weekly form, accounting for every hour of each employee's work time. Many large companies use a time clock, placed at the entrance to a work area with a rack for holding employee time cards. A new card is provided for each employee at the beginning of each pay period. To sign in, employees remove the card from the rack, insert it in the time clock to have the time of arrival stamped onto it, and then replace the card in the rack. The process is repeated at the end of the workday to record the time of departure. At the end of the pay period the time card provides a record of the hours each person worked and serves as the basis for computing gross pay.

In high-security areas of a workplace, computerized time clocks may also serve as security devices to control admittance. A time card that looks like a plastic credit card is issued to each employee. Inserting the card in a slot not only opens the door but also records the employee's name and time of arrival. Time clocks can be combined with computers to automate the process of recording the payroll, accumulating the necessary payroll information for governmental agencies, and computing the amount of net pay for each employee.

## Deductions from Gross Pay

Learning Objective 1

List and describe the various payroll-related taxes for employees

What most workers take home from the job is much less than their gross pay. That is because several deductions are subtracted from gross pay in arriving at **net pay** (also called **take-home pay**). Deductions required by law include federal income taxes, Social Security and Medicare taxes, state and city income taxes where applicable, and union dues and a state unemployment compensation tax on employees where applicable. Employees may also authorize deductions for such items as medical and health insurance, life insurance, U.S. savings bonds, and stock purchase plans.

### Federal Income Taxes

The federal government requires employers to act as tax-collecting agents for their employees' income taxes. Employers are required to compute the amount of income taxes to be withheld from each employee and to collect and deposit that amount to the account of the federal government. This *pay-as-you-go system* assures the government that most taxes due on employee earnings will be collected in a timely manner.

The amount deducted from an employee's gross earnings for federal income taxes depends on the amount of gross pay for the pay period and the number of allowances the individual claims. Every new employee must prepare an **Employee's Withholding Allowance Certificate (Form W-4,** illustrated in Exhibit 1), which authorizes the employer to compute the amount of taxes to be withheld.

For an employee like Carl Neely, whose wife does not have a job and who has one child, the number of allowances would be 4, determined according to Form W-4 as follows:

1. Employee
2. Married, spouse not working
3. Spouse
4. One dependent other than spouse

Employees can claim additional allowances if they qualify according to the rules set forth on Form W-4. Note that the number of allowances is not necessarily the same as the number of dependents.

The amount withheld from an employee's salary or wages is calculated according to pay rate and allowances, so the total withheld during the year should match the

**Exhibit 1**

| Form **W-4** Department of the Treasury Internal Revenue Service | Employee's Withholding Allowance Certificate ▶ **For Privacy Act and Paperwork Reduction Act Notice, see reverse.** | OMB No. 1545-0010 19**94** |
|---|---|---|

| 1 Type or print your first name and middle initial | Last name | 2 Your social security number |
|---|---|---|
| Carl    W. | Neely | 172-31-1681 |

| Home address (number and street or rural route) 1506 Nicaragua St. | 3 ☐ Single ☒ Married ☐ Married, but withhold at higher Single rate. **Note:** *If married, but legally separated, or spouse is a nonresident alien, check the Single box.* |
|---|---|
| City or town, state, and ZIP code Ruston, Virginia, 23471 | 4 If your last name differs from that on your social security card, check here and call 1-800-772-1213 for more information ▶ ☐ |

| 5 | Total number of allowances you are claiming (from line G or from the Worksheets on back if they apply) | 5 | 4 |
|---|---|---|---|
| 6 | Additional amount, if any, you want deducted from each paycheck . . . . . . . . . . . . . . . | 6 | $ |
| 7 | I claim exemption from withholding and I certify that I meet **BOTH** of the following conditions for exemption: | | |

- Last year I had a right to a refund of **ALL** Federal income tax withheld because I had **NO** tax liability; **AND**
- This year I expect a refund of **ALL** Federal income tax withheld because I expect to have **NO** tax liability.

If you meet all of the above conditions, enter the year effective and "EXEMPT" here . . . . . . ▶ | 7 |

Under penalties of perjury, I certify that I am entitled to the number of withholding allowances claimed on this certificate or entitled to claim exempt status.

| Employee's signature ▶ *Carl W. Neely* | Date ▶ *January 4* *94* |
|---|---|

| 9 Employer's name and address (Employer: Complete 8 and 10 only if sending to the IRS) PAGE EXPORT COMPANY 216 Central American Drive Washington, D.C. 20000 | 9 Office code (optional) | 10 Employer identification number 171 ⁞ 21648 |
|---|---|---|

Cat. No. 10220Q

individual's tax liability at the end of the year. The United States uses a graduated income tax system: The more a person earns, the higher the tax rate used in determining the amount of taxes that he or she must pay. Thus, people who earn larger salaries and wages have proportionately larger amounts withheld.

The amount of federal income taxes to be withheld from gross earnings is determined with a **wage-bracket withholding table** similar to the one shown in Exhibit 2, found in the federal government tax publication entitled *Circular E Employer's Tax Guide.* These tables are prepared for weekly, biweekly, semimonthly, and monthly pay periods and for single, married, and head-of-household taxpayers.

**Exhibit 2** Married Persons—Biweekly Payroll Period

| And the wages are— | | And the number of withholding allowances claimed is— | | | | | | | | | | |
|---|---|---|---|---|---|---|---|---|---|---|---|---|
| At least | But less than | 0 | 1 | 2 | 3 | 4 | 5 | 6 | 7 | 8 | 9 | 10 |
| | | The amount of income tax to be withheld shall be— | | | | | | | | | | |
| 560 | 580 | 64 | 51 | 38 | 24 | 11 | 0 | 0 | 0 | 0 | 0 | 0 |
| 580 | 600 | 67 | 54 | 41 | 27 | 14 | 1 | 0 | 0 | 0 | 0 | 0 |
| 600 | 620 | 70 | 57 | 44 | 30 | 17 | 4 | 0 | 0 | 0 | 0 | 0 |
| 620 | 640 | 73 | 60 | 47 | 33 | 20 | 7 | 0 | 0 | 0 | 0 | 0 |
| 640 | 660 | 76 | 63 | 50 | 36 | 23 | 10 | 0 | 0 | 0 | 0 | 0 |
| 660 | 680 | 79 | 66 | 53 | 39 | 26 | 13 | 0 | 0 | 0 | 0 | 0 |
| 1,740 | 1,760 | 271 | 246 | 222 | 201 | 188 | 175 | 162 | 148 | 135 | 122 | 108 |
| 1,760 | 1,780 | 277 | 252 | 227 | 204 | 191 | 178 | 165 | 151 | 138 | 125 | 111 |
| 1,780 | 1,800 | 282 | 258 | 233 | 208 | 194 | 181 | 168 | 154 | 141 | 128 | 114 |
| 1,800 | 1,820 | 288 | 263 | 238 | 214 | 197 | 184 | 171 | 157 | 144 | 131 | 117 |
| 1,820 | 1,840 | 294 | 269 | 244 | 219 | 200 | 187 | 174 | 160 | 147 | 134 | 120 |
| 1,840 | 1,860 | 299 | 274 | 250 | 225 | 203 | 190 | 177 | 163 | 150 | 137 | 123 |
| 1,860 | 1,880 | 305 | 280 | 255 | 230 | 206 | 193 | 180 | 166 | 153 | 140 | 126 |
| 1,880 | 1,900 | 310 | 286 | 261 | 236 | 211 | 196 | 183 | 169 | 156 | 143 | 129 |
| 1,900 | 1,920 | 316 | 291 | 266 | 242 | 217 | 199 | 186 | 172 | 159 | 146 | 132 |
| 1,920 | 1,940 | 322 | 297 | 272 | 247 | 222 | 202 | 189 | 175 | 162 | 149 | 135 |

The wage-bracket withholding table for married persons paid biweekly works like this for Carl Neely. He earned $1,869 for the current biweekly pay period, and he has claimed four withholding allowances. To find the amount of his income taxes to be withheld, locate the line on the table that includes $1,869, which is the $1,860–$1,880 bracket. Next, locate the column for four withholding allowances. Where the $1,860–$1,880 line intersects the four allowances column, you will find $206, which is the amount of income taxes to be withheld from Neely's biweekly paycheck.

### FICA Taxes

The funds for retirement, disability, survivors', and medical benefits for qualified workers come from payroll deductions authorized by the Federal Insurance Contributions Act (FICA). These deductions are called **FICA taxes.** The benefits are provided under the terms of the Social Security Act.

Employers are required to withhold FICA taxes from each employee's gross earnings. In 1994 FICA tax rates were 6.2% on the first $60,600 of earned wages for retirement, disability, and survivors' benefits, and 1.45% of earned wages for medical benefits. In addition to collecting the employee's contribution, the employer must contribute a matching amount. But once the limit of $60,600 has been reached, no further deductions or contributions are required for the first group of benefits.

Since both the dollar limit and the percentage increase frequently, we will use a rate of 7% on $60,000 for retirement, disability, and survivors' benefits and 1.5% for medical benefits in all problems. This is a total of 8.5% on the first $60,000, and 1.5% on amounts greater than $60,000. Consequently, the amount of FICA taxes to be withheld from Neely's $1,869 gross pay for the current pay period would be $158.87 ($1,869 × .085), assuming that he has not yet exceeded the $60,000 lower limit for the year.

### Other Payroll Deductions

All states have unemployment insurance programs in which the federal government participates. Most states finance this program by taxes imposed only on the employer. A few states impose the tax on employees as well, and these states require employers to withhold such taxes from employees' earnings.

In addition to federal income taxes, FICA taxes, and some state unemployment compensation taxes, a large number of states require employers to withhold state income taxes. In some cities, a city wage tax withholding is also required. These withholdings are typically found in wage-bracket tables like the federal one in Exhibit 2. Other deductions from employees' gross earnings may include union dues (which may or may not be voluntary), health and life insurance premiums, amounts authorized by the employee for savings bonds, stock purchase plans, and repayments of loans from the employer.

Assuming that Carl Neely has authorized a deduction of $64.86 for hospitalization insurance, the amount of net pay he would receive for the current biweekly pay period would be determined as follows:

Learning Objective **2**

Compute take-home pay for an individual

| | | |
|---|---|---|
| Gross earnings | | $1,869.00 |
| Deductions: | | |
| Federal income taxes withheld | $206.00 | |
| FICA tax withheld | 158.87 | |
| Hospitalization insurance premium | 64.86 | |
| Total deductions | | 429.73 |
| Net earnings | | $1,439.27 |

## Payment of Taxes Withheld

The Federal income tax laws and the Federal Insurance Contribution Act require that employers maintain adequate records for each employee. These records must be kept for 4 years, and must show the amount of federal income taxes withheld and the amount of wages subject to FICA taxes.

The amounts withheld from employees' gross earnings, together with the employer's portion of the FICA taxes, must be remitted to the Internal Revenue Service. The combined withheld taxes and employer-employee Social Security taxes are deposited in a bank authorized by the U.S. Treasury Department to accept these deposits.

An **Employer's Quarterly Federal Tax Return (Form 941)** and any payments due must be filed with the IRS by the last day of the month after the end of each calendar quarter. The form shows the total income tax withheld, the amount of wages subject to FICA taxes, the amount of FICA taxes paid (both employee and employer portions), the deposits made during previous periods of the quarter, and the amount due with the return.

**ASK YOURSELF** ▶

1. What is the difference between an employee and an independent contractor? Why is this distinction important?
2. How is gross pay determined?
3. List several common deductions from gross pay.
4. What is an Employee's Withholding Allowance Certificate? How is it used?
5. How is the amount of federal income taxes to be withheld from an employee determined?

## Employer Payroll Taxes

Learning Objective **3**

List and describe the various payroll-related taxes for employers

Employers, too, are subject to **payroll taxes.** These taxes are based on the amount of gross earnings (up to the prescribed limits) earned by the company's employees. Just as real estate taxes or occupational licenses are an operating expense of doing business, so are payroll taxes. They are recorded as debits to expense accounts, just like any other expense.

### FICA Taxes

The amount that an employee contributes to the Social Security program is matched by the employer. An employer's FICA tax expense and corresponding liability is determined by multiplying the total amount of wages subject to FICA tax by the appropriate tax rate. As with the employee portion, we will use a rate of 7% on the first $60,000 and 1.5% on amounts greater than $60,000.

### Federal and State Unemployment Compensation Tax

**Unemployment compensation taxes** are levied by the federal and state governments on an economic entity's payroll in order to provide funds for the payment of unemployment benefits. These funds are provided under a joint federal–state program. The funds are administered by the state governments for the relief of qualified persons who are temporarily unemployed. The federal unemployment compensation (FUTA) tax and the state unemployment compensation (SUTA) tax are levied only on employers and are not typically deducted from an

**Exhibit 3** Employee Earnings Record

Name _____ Neely, Carl W. _____   Telephone _____ (813) 974 4186 _____   Social Security Number _____ 172-31-1681

Address _____ 1506 Nicaragua St. _____   Date Employed _____ April 1, 1987 _____   Date of Birth _____ September 15, 1943

_____ Ruston, Virginia, 23471 _____

Date Terminated _____   Reason _____

Married         (xx)         _____

Single          (  )         Pay Rate _____ $43,680 _____

Head of Household (  )        Hourly Pay _____ $21.00 _____

Department _____ Administration _____

| 1995 Period Ending | Earnings | | | | | Deductions | | | | | | Net Pay | Check No. |
| | Total Hours | Regular Hours | Overtime Hours | Total | Cumulative | Federal Income Tax | SS and Medicare | Union Dues | Health Ins. | U.S. Bonds | Total | | |
| --- | --- | --- | --- | --- | --- | --- | --- | --- | --- | --- | --- | --- | --- |
| Jan. 13 | 80 | 1,680.00 | | 1,680.00 | 1,680.00 | 179.00 | 142.80 | | 51.86 | | 373.66 | 1,306.34 | 526 |
| Jan. 27 | 84 | 1,680.00 | 126.00 | 1,806.00 | 3,486.00 | 202.00 | 153.51 | | 51.86 | | 407.37 | 1,398.63 | 731 |
| June 30 | 80 | 1,680.00 | | 1,680.00 | 21,966.00 | 179.00 | 142.80 | | 51.86 | | 373.66 | 1,306.34 | 993 |
| 2d Qtr. | 560 | 11,760.00 | 0.00 | 11,760.00 | 21,966.00 | 1,729.00 | 882.00 | | 335.02 | | 2,946.02 | 8,813.98 | |
| July 14 | 80 | 1,680.00 | | 1,680.00 | 23,646.00 | 179.00 | 142.80 | | 51.86 | | 373.66 | 1,306.34 | 1230 |
| July 28 | 82 | 1,680.00 | 63.00 | 1,743.00 | 25,389.00 | 188.00 | 148.16 | | 51.86 | | 388.02 | 1,354.98 | 1417 |
| Aug. 11 | 86 | 1,680.00 | 189.00 | 1,869.00 | 27,258.00 | 206.00 | 158.87 | | 64.86 | | 429.73 | 1,439.27 | 1561 |
| 3d Qtr. | | | | | | | | | | | | | |
| 4th Qtr. | | | | | | | | | | | | | |
| Total | | | | | | | | | | | | | |

employee's gross earnings. (Some states do require an employee contribution to be withheld by the employer.)

Currently the FUTA tax is 6.2% on the first $7,000 of wages paid to each employee. The federal government allows a credit against the FUTA of up to 5.4% for amounts contributed to SUTA, so most states set their rate at this 5.4%. Thus, a total tax of 6.2% is levied, with .8% going to the federal government for approving the state programs and for paying a portion of the state's administrative expenses. The state's 5.4% is used to pay unemployment compensation.

To encourage employers to maintain a stable work force and thus reduce unemployment, a merit-rating plan is used by many states. For employers within the state whose employees have applied for little or no unemployment compensation, the total unemployment tax rate is reduced from the 6.2% to the basic FUTA tax of .8% in some cases.

An example will show how an employer's payroll taxes are calculated. The Page Export Company has a total biweekly payroll for the current period of $65,430. Of this amount, $58,730 is subject to the combined FICA and Medicare taxes at the 8.5% rate, $65,430 is subject to the Medicare 1.5% rate, and $12,390 is subject to unemployment compensation taxes of .8% FUTA and 4.5% SUTA. The full payroll of $65,430 is used only for calculating Medicare taxes, since some employees have exceeded the $60,000 cap for FICA and many employees have exceeded the $7,000 FUTA/SUTA cap. The total amount of Page's payroll taxes expense for this biweekly period is computed like this:

| | |
|---|---|
| FICA taxes [($58,730 × .085) + ($65,430 − $58,730) × .015]. . . . . . . . . . | $5,092.55 |
| FUTA taxes ($12,390 × .008). . . . . . . . . . . . . . . . . . . . . . . . . . . . . . . . . . | 99.12 |
| SUTA taxes ($12,390 × .045). . . . . . . . . . . . . . . . . . . . . . . . . . . . . . . . . . | 557.55 |
| Total payroll taxes . . . . . . . . . . . . . . . . . . . . . . . . . . . . . . . . . . . . . . . . . . | $5,749.22 |

## The Employee Earnings Record

The cumulative amount of the employee earnings and other payroll data are recorded on the **employee earnings record.** This form shows when the employee has reached the earnings limit of $7,000 for the employer unemployment taxes and when the employee has reached the Social Security tax limit. Thus, the employee's earnings record provides the basis for recording the amount of taxable Social Security, and unemployment compensation earnings in the payroll register (discussed in the next section). It also provides the basis for preparing the federal and state payroll tax returns. An employee earnings record for Carl Neely is shown in Exhibit 3.

The information in the employee earnings record is cumulated by quarter and totaled at year-end. The year-end totals provide the necessary data for the **Form W-2 Wage and Tax Statement** (Exhibit 4), which employers must give to each employee by Jan. 31 of the year following the tax year. Copies of Form W-2 go to the Internal Revenue Service and the Social Security Administration. Entries 1 and 2 of Form W-2 show the IRS the total wages paid to the employee and the amount of income taxes withheld. Entries 11 and 13 tell the Social Security Administration the amount of FICA employee taxes withheld and the total wages that were subject to FICA taxes. This information is credited to the individual's account with the Social Security Administration.

Learning Objective **4**

Describe the function of an employee earnings record, and record payroll data therein

### Exhibit 4

| a  Control number | 22222 | Void ☐ | For official Use only ▶ | | |
|---|---|---|---|---|---|
| b  Employer's identification number | | | | 1  Wages, tips, other compensation | 2  Federal income tax withheld |
| c  Employer's name, address, and ZIP code | | | | 3  Social security wages | 4  Social security tax withheld |
| | | | | 5  Medicare wages and tips | 6  Medicare tax withheld |
| | | | | 7  Social security tips | 8  Allocated tips |
| d  Employee's social security number | | | | 9  Advance EIC payment | 10  Dependent care benefits |
| e  Employee's name (first, middle initial, last) | | | | 11  Nonqualified plans | 12  Benefits included in Box 1 |
| | | | | 13  See Instrs. for Box 13 | 14  Other |
| f  Employee's address and ZIP code | | | | 15 Statuary employee ☐  Deceased ☐  Pension plan ☐  Legal rep. ☐  942 emp. ☐  Subtotal ☐  Deferred compensation | |
| 16  State     Employer's state I.D. No. | 17  State wages, tips, etc. | 18 State income tax | 19  Locality name | 20 Local wages, tips, etc. | 21  Local income tax |

Cat. No. 10134D          Department of the Treasury—Internal Revenue Service

Form **W-2** **Wage and Tax Statement** **1993**

For paperwork Reduction Act Notice, see separate instructions.

Copy A for Social Security Administration

PMB no. 1545-0008

**Exhibit 11-5** Page Export Company Biweekly Payroll Period Ending August 11, 1998

| Employee | Total Hours | Earnings | | | Taxable Earnings | |
|---|---|---|---|---|---|---|
| | | Regular | Overtime | Total | Social Security | Unemployment Compensation |
| Carpenter, Roberta | 80 | $ 1,800.00 | | $ 1,800.00 | $ 1,800.00 | |
| Christian, Dave | 80 | 1,250.00 | | 1,250.00 | 1,250.00 | |
| Hawgood, Gene | 87 | 800.00 | $ 105.00 | 905.00 | 905.00 | $ 905.00 |
| Moog, Alan | 80 | 600.00 | | 600.00 | 600.00 | 600.00 |
| Neely, Carl | 86 | 1,680.00 | 189.00 | 1,869.00 | 1,869.00 | |
| Wesley, Galvin | 80 | 3,200.00 | | 3,200.00 | | |
| | | $61,720.00 | $3,710.00 | $65,430.00 | $58,730.00 | $12,390.00 |

## The Payroll Register

Employers use **payroll registers** to assemble the necessary data for preparing the payroll for the period and for recording their payroll taxes. A payroll register is usually designed to suit the needs of the company using it.

Learning Objective 5

Prepare a payroll register

The biweekly payroll register of the Page Export Company is shown in Exhibit 5. Note that columns are provided for listing the total hours worked during the biweekly period and the regular, overtime, and total earnings. The hours worked are determined by time cards or attendance records kept at the work stations. The earnings are determined by multiplying the individual's hourly rate times the regular hours (or, for overtime hours, one and one-half times the hourly rate). The two taxable earnings columns provide information for determining the payroll taxes. Data for these columns are obtained from the employee earnings record. Notice that no amount is listed under the taxable earnings—Social Security column for the employee named Galvin Wesly. That's because he has earned more than $60,000 (the FICA limit we will use in this text) for the year and thus is no longer subject to FICA taxes. For the same reason, no amounts are listed in the taxable earnings—unemployment compensation column for Roberta Carpenter, Dave Christian, Carl Neely, and Galvin Wesley. All these employees have exceeded the $7,000 limit for the year.

Once all additional deductions from total earnings are recorded in the appropriate columns, total deductions and net pay are determined and checked for accuracy, the paycheck is cut, and the check number is recorded in the payroll register. The last two columns are used to indicate the distribution of the salaries to the proper expense account. For the Page Export Company these accounts are Shipping Department Salary Expense and Administration Department Salary Expense. Other typical distributions are to Sales Salary Expense, Office Salary Expense, and Shop Salary Expense.

After the register is complete and has been verified for arithmetic accuracy, the checks are issued and the payroll is entered in the books of account. Verification of the arithmetic involves comparing earnings, deductions, net pay, and distribution, as follows:

| | Deductions | | | | | Payment | | Distribution | |
|---|---|---|---|---|---|---|---|---|---|
| Federal Income Taxes | Social Security and Medicare | Union Dues | Health Ins. | U.S. Savings Bonds | Total Deductions | Net Pay | Check No. | Shipping Dept. Salaries | Admin. Dept. Salaries |
| $240.00 | $ 153.00 | | $ 47.86 | $ 100.00 | $ 540.86 | $ 1,259.14 | 1536 | $ 1,250.00 | $1,800.00 |
| 165.00 | 106.25 | $ 35.00 | 23.93 | | 330.18 | 919.82 | 1537 | | |
| 99.00 | 76.93 | 25.00 | 23.93 | | 224.86 | 680.14 | 1559 | 905.00 | |
| 76.00 | 51.00 | 20.00 | 23.93 | | 170.93 | 429.07 | 1560 | 600.00 | |
| 206.00 | 158.87 | | 64.86 | | 429.73 | 1,439.27 | 1561 | | 1,869.00 |
| 829.00 | 48.00 | | 47.86 | 50.00 | 974.86 | 2,225.14 | 1562 | | 3,200.00 |
| $9,932.00 | $5,092.55 | $525.00 | $1,783.12 | $1,250.00 | $18,582.67 | $46,847.33 | | $16,820.00 | $48,610.00 |

Earnings:
Regular.............. $61,720.00
Overtime............ 3,710.00

Total................. $65,430.00

Deductions:
Federal income taxes... $ 9,932.00
FICA taxes .......... 5,092.55
Union dues.......... 525.00
Health insurance ...... 1,783.12
U.S. savings bonds .... 1,250.00
    Total ........... $18,582.67
Net pay............... 46,847.33

Total................. $65,430.00

Distribution:
Shipping department
  salary expense....... $16,820.00
Administration depart-
  ment salary expense .. 48,610.00

Total.................. $65,430.00

When the payroll register has been completed and checked, the general journal entries relating to payroll can be made. The Page Export Company's first entry for employees' salaries, various payroll deductions, and net pay is as follows:

| | | | |
|---|---|---|---|
| 1998 | | | |
| Aug. 10 | Shipping Department Salary Expense............ | 16,820.00 | |
| | Administration Department Salary Expense ....... | 48,610.00 | |
| |     Federal Income Taxes Payable ............. | | 9,932.00 |
| |     FICA Taxes Payable..................... | | 5,092.55 |
| |     Union Dues Payable..................... | | 525.00 |
| |     Health Insurance Premiums Payable......... | | 1,783.12 |
| |     U.S. Savings Bonds Deductions Payable ..... | | 1,250.00 |
| |     Salaries Payable........................ | | 46,847.33 |
| | To record biweekly payroll from the payroll register. | | |

A second payroll-related general journal entry is required, to record the payroll taxes imposed on the employer: (see calculation on page 501)

| | | |
|---|---|---|
| Aug. 10 | Payroll Taxes Expense ......................... 5,749.22 | |
| | FICA Taxes Payable....................... | 5,092.55 |
| | FUTA Taxes Payable ...................... | 99.12 |
| | SUTA Taxes Payable ...................... | 557.55 |
| | To record payroll taxes. | |

The withholdings from the employees and the payroll taxes imposed on the employer are paid not on the dates that the employees are paid, but on dates specified by the federal government and the various state governments. Similarly, the unions, health insurance companies, and other entities that receive funds withheld from employees all make agreements with employers as to when funds are to be remitted.

### The Payroll Bank Account

Typically, payroll checks are written against a special payroll bank account maintained by the company. Once the payroll register is complete and the general journal entries relating to the payroll are recorded, a check drawn against the company's regular bank account in the amount of the total net pay ($46,847.33 in the example) is deposited in the payroll bank account. Then individual paychecks are prepared and issued to the employees. When all the employees have cashed their checks, the payroll bank account's balance will be reduced to zero.

Having a separate payroll account simplifies the reconciliation of the regular bank account and serves as a control over payrolls. Since only one check is written for the entire payroll, no outstanding payroll checks need to be considered when the regular cash account is being reconciled. Moreover, only paychecks are involved when the payroll bank account is reconciled.

A paycheck usually presents the details of the net pay computation, printed either on a detachable stub or on a separate form. Information about the current-period and the year-to-date earnings and deductions is also generally provided.

**ASK YOURSELF** ▶

1. What are payroll taxes?
2. Describe the relationship between Federal and State Unemployment Compensation (FUTA and SUTA) taxes.
3. What information does an employee earnings record provide?
4. Why do companies use payroll registers, and how are they prepared?
5. What is the purpose of a payroll bank account?

## OTHER CURRENT LIABILITIES

### Notes Payable

A written promise to a person or organization to pay a specific sum of money either on demand or at a specified future date is called a **promissory note.** To the maker of the note it is a **note payable.** (To the payee of the note it is a *note receivable.*)

Notes payable are issued for various reasons. Perhaps a company is unable to pay an account payable when due and wishes an extension of the deadline. Or perhaps a firm wants to take advantage of a cash discount, paying the invoice early with funds borrowed from another source. A note may be issued for the acquisition of inventory or other assets. The need for cash to pay other maturing obligations also may prompt the incurrence of a note payable.

Objective
Record transactions relating to notes payable

To demonstrate the accounting for a note payable, we'll use as an example Page Export Company's acquisition of certain office equipment from the Morgan Office Equipment Company on Monday, June 19, 1998, by issuing a 60-day, 9% note payable in the amount of $10,000. Page Export Company will record[1] the note as follows:

| | | | |
|---|---|---|---|
| June 19 | Office Equipment . . . . . . . . . . . . . . . . . . . . . . . . . . . . | 10,000 | |
| | Notes Payable. . . . . . . . . . . . . . . . . . . . . . . . . . . | | 10,000 |
| | To record the issuance of a 60-day, 9% note due Aug. 18, 1995, for office equipment. | | |

Should legal proceedings later become necessary to obtain payment from Page Export Company, the note payable places Morgan Office Equipment Company in a stronger position than does an account payable. The note payable is a formal written promise to pay a certain sum at a definite time, whereas an account payable may have been simply an oral agreement.

Page Export Company's accounting year ends on July 31. On that date Page must make an accrual adjusting entry. The entry records the amount of interest owed to Morgan Office Equipment Company so that the interest expense can be reported on Page's income statement and so that the current liability, interest payable, can be reported on its balance sheet. The amount of accrued interest for the 42 days from June 19 to July 31 is $105 ($10,000 \times 9\% \times \frac{42}{360}$), and the adjusting entry is recorded as follows:

| | | | |
|---|---|---|---|
| July 31 | Interest Expense . . . . . . . . . . . . . . . . . . . . . . . . . . . . | 105 | |
| | Interest Payable . . . . . . . . . . . . . . . . . . . . . . . . . . | | 105 |
| | To record accrual of interest expense on note payable to Morgan. | | |

On Friday, Aug. 18, 1998, the due date of the note payable, Page Export Company will pay Morgan Office Equipment Company $10,150. To the $10,000 principal is added $105 of interest for the 42 days from June 19 to July 31, and $45 of interest for the 18 days in August ($10,000 \times 9\% \times \frac{18}{360}$). To record the payment to Morgan, Page Export will make the following entry:

| | | | |
|---|---|---|---|
| Aug. 18 | Notes Payable . . . . . . . . . . . . . . . . . . . . . . . . . . . . | 10,000 | |
| | Interest Payable . . . . . . . . . . . . . . . . . . . . . . . . . . . | 105 | |
| | Interest Expense. . . . . . . . . . . . . . . . . . . . . . . . . . . | 45 | |
| | Cash . . . . . . . . . . . . . . . . . . . . . . . . . . . . . . . . | | 10,150 |
| | To record payment of amount due to Morgan on note issued June 19, 1998. | | |

Notice that the entry has a debit to Notes Payable, to eliminate the liability; a debit to Interest Payable, to eliminate the liability for the accrued interest; and a debit

---

[1] All our journal entries in the examples are in general journal form, even though the entry may actually be made in a special journal. This will make illustrations much easier because we won't have to construct special journals each time we make an entry.

to Interest Expense, to record the new accounting year's interest expense for the period from July 31, 1998, to Aug. 18, 1998.

Money may be lent in either of two ways. First, a note may be issued, which must be repaid on the maturity date together with interest. The example above was such a note.

The second way in which money is lent is called **discounting.** Under this procedure the lender deducts the interest on the date the note is issued. Thus, the interest charge is included in the *face amount* of the note. In this case the note would read: *Sixty days after June 19, 1998, the undersigned promises to pay the sum of $10,000.*

In the first case a lender (Morgan Office Equipment Company) will give the borrower (Page Export Company) $10,000—called the **proceeds**—on the date the note is signed. But in the second case the proceeds will be only $9,850, assuming a 9% **discount rate.** The discount of $150 ($10,000 $\times$ .09 $\times \frac{60}{360}$) is subtracted from the face of the note in determining the proceeds.

Page Company's entries to record its $10,000 note payable to Morgan, assuming the note was discounted, would be:

| | | | |
|---|---|---|---|
| June 19 | Purchases ................................... | 9,850 | |
| | Discount on Notes Payable .................... | 150 | |
| | Notes Payable............................ | | 10,000 |
| | To record the issuance of a 60-day, $10,000 note to Morgan, discount rate 9%. | | |

It is important to realize that issuing a discounted note means that Page will receive $150 less than the full $10,000 of merchandise.

The July 31 year-end adjusting entry would be:

| | | | |
|---|---|---|---|
| July 31 | Interest Expense ............................... | 105 | |
| | Discount on Notes Payable ................... | | 105 |
| | To record interest expense on the note payable to Morgan ($150 $\times \frac{42}{60}$). | | |

Upon payment the following entries would be made:

| | | | |
|---|---|---|---|
| Aug. 18 | Interest Expense............................... | 45 | |
| | Discount on Notes Payable ................... | | 45 |
| | To record interest expense on the note payable to Morgan ($150 $\times \frac{18}{60}$). | | |
| 18 | Notes Payable ................................ | 10,000 | |
| | Cash ...................................... | | 10,000 |
| | To record payment of amount due to Morgan on note issued June 19, 1998. | | |

Under the discounting procedure, the contra-liability account **Discount on Notes Payable** is established on the date funds are borrowed, June 19. If a balance sheet were prepared at this time, the note payable would be presented as follows:

| | | |
|---|---|---|
| Current Liabilities: | | |
| Notes Payable........................................ | $10,000 | |
| Less: Discounts on Notes Payable ....................... | 150 | $9,850 |

This presentation shows that the liability as of June 19 amounts to only $9,850. The $150 discount on notes payable represents the amount of interest cost that will be incurred over the life of the note. For this reason an adjusting entry was required on July 31, to record the interest expense incurred and to reduce the discount on notes payable by $105. In addition, a second entry is required on the payment date, Aug. 18, to record the interest expense for 18 days and to eliminate the remaining $45 of the discount on notes payable.

## Product Warranties

Sometimes liabilities exist at the time financial statements are prepared, but their exact amount is not known. An example of this type of liability is the obligation incurred when products are sold with warranties. Most household appliances are sold with the guarantee that if they malfunction within a certain period of time after acquisition, the seller will repair them at no cost to the buyers. This type of guarantee is called a *product warranty.*

Learning Objective **8**

Record transactions relating to product warranties

The accountant's job is to estimate the amount of the liability and show this on the balance sheet. The related expense that will be reflected on the income statement also must be estimated. In accordance with the matching principle, the expense is incurred in the period when the appliance is sold, not in a subsequent period when the repairs are performed. The liability is eliminated when the repairs are made.

Consider the following example. BestBuy Appliance Company sold 400 appliances during the year 1998. From past experience, the firm can estimate that 10% of these appliances will need repairs and that repairs will cost them an average of $20. During 1998, 15 appliances require service calls at a total cost of $315. In 1999, 27 additional appliances sold in 1998 require service calls at a total cost of $490. BestBuy would make these entries in 1998:

| | | | |
|---|---|---|---|
| 1998 Various dates | Warranty Expense . . . . . . . . . . . . . . . . . . . . . . . . . . . . . | 315 | |
| | Cash, Parts, Labor . . . . . . . . . . . . . . . . . . . . . . . . | | 315 |
| | To record expenditures amounting to $315 for repair service on 15 appliances that were sold in 1998. | | |
| Dec. 31 | Warranty Expense . . . . . . . . . . . . . . . . . . . . . . . . . . . . . | 500 | |
| | Warranty Payable . . . . . . . . . . . . . . . . . . . . . . . . | | 500 |
| | To record estimated liability under warranty for repair services to be performed on appliances sold in 1998. | | |

| | |
|---|---|
| Appliances estimated to require repairs: | (400 × 10%) = 40 |
| 1998 appliances to be repaired in 1999: | (40 − 15) = 25 |
| Estimated liability: | (25 × $20) = $500 |

The income statement prepared for the year ended Dec. 31, 1998, would reflect estimated warranty expenses of $815 matched against appliance sale revenues. BestBuy's expenditures in 1998 amounted to $315 on 15 actual repairs, which are recorded as 1998 expenses. In addition, the company estimates that 25 more repairs must be made [(400)(10%) − 15 = 25], at an estimated cost of $500 (25 × $20), and this amount is also expensed in 1998. The result is the total warranty expense of $815.

## Circuit City and Extended Warranties

Circuit City will reduce its 1991 profit by 16% due to a new accounting rule concerning the accounting for its very lucrative extended warranty sales. In the past Circuit City and many other consumer-electronics retailers recorded revenue from extended warranties when they received payment. This very liberal accounting approach enabled many consumer electronics stores to boost earnings substantially.

The new accounting rule will require extended warranty sellers to record revenue not at the time of sale, but rather over the life of the warranty contract. The new rule applies not only to consumer-electronics dealers, but to auto makers, television and other home appliances manufacturers. These companies have followed the more conservative approach for years and will not be affected by the new rule.

*Source:* Lois Therrien, "Electronics Stores Get a Cruel Shock." Reprinted from the Jan. 14, 1991, issue of *Business Week,* by special permission, copyright © 1991 by McGraw-Hill, Inc.

---

The Dec. 31, 1998, balance sheet would show the estimated liability of $500. This amount represents the company's estimate of its obligation for future repair services that relate to 1998 sales.

In 1999 the following entry would be made to record the actual expenditure of $490 relating to the 27 service calls for appliances sold in 1998:

| 1999 Various dates | | | |
|---|---|---|---|
| | Warranty Payable............................. | 490 | |
| |     Cash, Parts, Labor ......................... | | 490 |
| | To record expenditures amounting to $490 relating to 1998 sales. | | |

At this point the balance in the liability account is a $10 credit ($500 estimated liability − $490 actual liability). No one can see into the future, so the actual liability will almost always differ from the estimate, at least a little. No adjustment of the liability account is required unless a trend develops that makes it obvious that the estimate is either too high or too low. In that case, a revision of the estimating process is in order.

**ASK YOURSELF** ▶

1. Describe two ways in which money can be lent.
2. What is the nature of the account Discount on Notes Payable?
3. How would a discounted note be presented on a balance sheet?
4. Describe the accounting for product warranties.

---

## Secret Warranties

Goodwill adjustments, that's what the auto industry calls secret warranties. These warranties are made to auto dealers authorizing them to repair known defects to only those customers who complain. The car owners are not notified of the defects and, as a consequence, are charged for the repairs.

The auto industry saves billions of dollars per year on repairs covered by secret warranties. While these defects do not constitute a safety threat, they can represent a significant cost to the consumer. A 1987 study by the Center for Auto Safety found defects ranging in cost from $50 to $3,000.

New York and other states are proposing goodwill-adjustment laws requiring direct disclosure to car owners.

*Source: Modern Maturity,* Apr.–May 1991, p. 10. Reprinted with permission from *Modern Maturity.* Copyright © 1991, American Association of Retired Persons.

## SUMMARY

- Accounting for the cost of labor begins with the establishment of a *payroll system* designed to process the basic payroll information, generate employee paychecks in a timely manner, generate appropriate reports and remittances as required by various governmental agencies, and safeguard the entity against improper payments.
- The computation of each individual's gross pay begins the process that culminates with the issuance of a paycheck to the employee.
- In computing **gross pay,** consideration is given to the employee's rate of pay, regular hours worked, and overtime hours worked if the employee is subject to the Wages and Hours Law.
- Deductions are subtracted from an employee's gross pay in arriving at his or her **net take-home pay.** The deductions are of two types: those required by law or contract and those that are voluntary.
- *Deductions required by law* are federal income taxes withheld, Federal Insurance Contributions Act (FICA) withholdings, state and city income taxes where appropriate, and union dues where appropriate.
- *Voluntary deductions* are those the employee authorizes the employer to withhold from his or her gross earnings, such as health insurance premiums and U.S. savings bonds payments.
- In addition to withholding income tax and FICA taxes on behalf of employees, employers themselves are required to pay certain taxes based on employee earnings. Employers must pay FICA, federal unemployment compensation (FUTA), and state unemployment compensation (SUTA) taxes.
- The **employee earnings record** provides basic data for determining appropriate payroll deductions and recording the individual employee's gross earnings, deductions, and net earnings in the payroll register.
- The **payroll register** is useful for summarizing individual payroll information needed for the preparation of the general journal entries relating to payroll.
- Accounting for **notes payable** reveals two methods of obtaining funds from a lender: by discounting a note or by issuing a note at its face value.
- If a note is issued at face value, the interest is paid at the maturity date of the note.
- If a note is discounted, the interest is deducted in advance from the proceeds of the note.
- *Product warranties* are an example of an estimated liability. The accountant must estimate the amount of liability associated with products sold under warranty that are likely to need repair and must record the appropriate expense and related liability.

## 9  KEY TERMS

| | |
|---|---|
| Discount on Notes Payable | A contra-liability account reflecting the amount of interest expense that has been paid, but not yet recorded, until the maturity of a discounted note payable. |
| Discount rate | The rate used to calculate the amount of interest that must be deducted from the face of a note to determine the proceeds of a discounted note. |
| Discounting | A loan in which the lender deducts interest from the amount borrowed before the money is advanced to the borrower. |
| Employee | An individual who is subject to the control and direction of the business entity for which he or she works. |
| Employee earnings record | A form maintained by an employer for each employee to provide a record of the employee's cumulative earnings, deductions, net pay, and other payroll data. |

| | |
|---|---|
| **Employee's Withholding Allowance Certificate (Form W-4)** | A form used by the employer to determine the amount of federal income tax to withhold from an employee. The employee prepares the form stating his or her marital status and the number of withholding allowances claimed. |
| **Employer's Quarterly Federal Tax Return (Form 941)** | A form required by the last day of the month after the end of each calendar quarter showing the total income tax withheld from employees, the amount of wages subject to FICA taxes, the amount of FICA taxes paid (both employee and employer portions), the deposits made during previous periods of the quarter, and the amount due with the tax return. |
| **FICA taxes** | Taxes imposed by the Federal Insurance Contributions Act to finance the Social Security program. Equal FICA tax amounts are paid by the employer and the employee. |
| **Gross pay** | The total amount of an employee's earnings before deductions. |
| **Independent contractor** | An individual who performs services for an economic entity but is not subject to the entity's control and direction. |
| **Net pay** | The amount of pay left after deducting such items as FICA taxes, federal income taxes, and union dues. Net pay is also called **take-home pay.** |
| **Note payable** | A term used by the maker of a promissory note to record the note in its accounts. |
| **Payroll register** | A record maintained by an employer showing the amount of gross pay, deductions, and net pay for each employee and the total for all employees. |
| **Payroll taxes** | Taxes levied on employers based on the gross wages (subject to certain limits) of their employees. |
| **Proceeds** | The amount of money a borrower receives from a lender upon discounting a note. |
| **Promissory note** | A written promise to repay a specified sum of money on demand or at a definite future date. Called a *note payable* by the maker and a *note receivable* by the payee. |
| **Salary** | Cash compensation paid to professional, administrative, management, or clerical employees, usually at a flat weekly, monthly, or yearly rate. |
| **Take-home pay** | See **net pay.** |
| **Unemployment compensation taxes** | Federal and state taxes levied on an economic entity's payroll that provide funds for the payment of unemployment benefits. |
| **Wage and Tax Statement (Form W-2)** | A form used by an employer to report to the federal government the amount of wages paid to an employee, the amount of federal income taxes withheld, the amount of wages subject to Social Security taxes, and the amount of Social Security taxes withheld. |
| **Wage-bracket withholding table** | A table provided by the government for employers' use in determining the amount of income tax to withhold from employees. |
| **Wages** | Cash compensation paid to employees, normally on the basis of number of hours worked. |

## DEMONSTRATION PROBLEM

The following selected transactions were completed by the Active Company during the year 1998:

Jan. 15   Recorded the payroll from the payroll register, which contained the following information:

| | |
|---|---:|
| Gross pay | $16,000 |
| Federal income tax withheld | 3,500 |
| FICA taxes | 1,200 |
| Union dues | 730 |
| Health insurance | 520 |
| Net pay | 10,050 |

    15   Issued a check in payment of the salaries payable.

    15   Recorded the following employer payroll taxes:

| | |
|---|---:|
| FICA taxes | 1,200 |
| FUTA taxes | 96 |
| SUTA taxes | 800 |

May   1   Issued a $6,000, 90-day note which was discounted by the First National Bank at 10%.

July 30   Paid the First National Bank the amount due on the discounted noted of May 1, 1995.

Nov.  1   Issued a 12%, 180-day note for $10,000 to D.C. Distributors.

Dec. 31   Recorded the accrued interest expense on the note of Nov. 1, 1998.

    31   Recorded an estimated liability in the amount of $1,475 for product warranties.

**Required:**

Record the above transactions in a general journal.

### ■ Solution to Demonstration Problem

ACTIVE COMPANY
General Journal

PAGE _____

| Date | Account Titles and Explanation | Post. Ref. | Debit | Credit |
|---|---|---|---:|---:|
| 1998 | | | | |
| Jan. 15 | Salary Expense | | 16,000 | |
| |    Federal Income Tax Payable | | | 3,500 |
| |    FICA Tax Payable | | | 1,200 |
| |    Union Dues Payable | | | 730 |
| |    Health Insurance Premiums Payable | | | 520 |
| |    Salaries Payable | | | 10,050 |
| |    To record payroll from the payroll register. | | | |
| | | | | |
| 15 | Salaries Payable | | 10,050 | |
| |    Cash | | | 10,050 |
| |    To record payment of salaries. | | | |

*(Continued)*

| | | | | |
|---|---|---|---|---|
| Jan. 15 | Payroll Taxes Expense | | 2,096 | |
| |     FICA Taxes Payable | | | 1,200 |
| |     FUTA Taxes Payable | | | 96 |
| |     SUTA Taxes Payable | | | 800 |
| | To record payroll taxes | | | |
| | | | | |
| May 1 | Cash | | 5,850 | |
| | Discount on Notes Payable | | 150 | |
| |     Notes Payable | | | 6,000 |
| | To record 90-day promissory note to First National Bank in the amount of $6,000, discount rate 10%. | | | |
| | | | | |
| July 30 | Notes Payable | | 6,000 | |
| |     Cash | | | 6,000 |
| | To record payment to First National Bank of Note Payable issued May 1. | | | |
| | | | | |
| 30 | Interest Expense | | 150 | |
| |     Discount on Notes Payable | | | 150 |
| | To record interest expense incurred and to eliminate Discount on Notes Payable. | | | |
| | | | | |
| Nov. 1 | Cash | | 10,000 | |
| |     Notes Payable | | | 10,000 |
| | To record 180-day promissory note in the amount of $10,000, interest rate 12%, issued to D.C. Distributors. | | | |
| | | | | |
| Dec.31 | Interest Expense | | 200 | |
| |     Interest Payable | | | 200 |
| | To record accrual of interest expense on note payable issued on Nov. 1, 1998, to D.C. Distributors. $(\$10,000)(12\%)(\frac{60}{360})$ | | | |
| | | | | |
| 31 | Warranty Expense | | 1,475 | |
| |     Warranty Payable | | | 1,475 |
| | To record estimated liability under warranty for repair services. | | | |

## QUESTIONS FOR REVIEW AND FURTHER THOUGHT

### REVIEW QUESTIONS

1. What is the difference between the terms *wages* and *salaries?*

2. What are the most common deductions from gross earnings in computing net pay?

3. How does an employer determine the amount of federal income taxes to withhold from an employee?

4. How does an employer determine the amount of FICA taxes to withhold from an employee?

5. Describe the various employer payroll taxes.

6. What is the purpose of a payroll register?

7. What purpose does the employee earnings record serve?

8. What type of information is maintained in an employee's personnel file?

9. What source documents are required in order to prepare paychecks for a company's employees?

10. Distinguish between a note issued at face value and a discounted note.

### QUESTIONS FOR FURTHER THOUGHT

1. Why is it important for a company clearly to establish whether an individual rendering services is an employee or an independent contractor?

2. How is the amount of an employee's gross pay determined?

3. Generally a company will establish a special checking account for the purpose of writing payroll checks. Why?

4. Time cards are a common means of recording employee attendance, but many companies require department or section heads to prepare an absentee report as well. Why?

5. What is to prevent a dishonest employee in the accounting department from inserting a fictitious or former employee's name into the payroll register, making the paycheck, and then cashing it?

6. How can a dishonest accounting department employee benefit from overstating the total amount of the net pay column on the payroll register?

7. A 10% interest rate and a 10% discount rate are not the same. Explain.

8. When a note is discounted, a liability is recorded for the face value of the note and cash is increased by the proceeds. How is the difference between the proceeds and the face value of the note accounted for?

9. If a promissory note were issued in one accounting period and repaid in a second accounting period, an adjusting entry would be required at the end of the first accounting period. Explain.

10. Explain why year-end adjusting entries are needed for estimated liabilities such as product warranties.

## OBJECTIVE ASSIGNMENT

*True/False*   Indicate whether each statement below is *true* or *false* by placing a *T* or an *F* in the space provided.

_____ 1. The Federal Insurance Contribution Act (FICA) requires that employers pay retirement benefits to their employees.

_____ 2. Take-home pay and gross pay are different terms for the same thing.

_____ 3. FICA taxes are contributed by employers but not employees.

_____ 4. The payroll register is a multicolumn form used to assemble the necessary data for preparing the payroll.

_____ 5. An 11% discount rate is higher than an 11% interest rate.

*Multiple Choice*   Select the best choice to complete each statement or answer each question below. Write the letter corresponding to your choice in the space below.

_____ 1. The term *salary* would most likely refer to remuneration given to
    a. A CPA preparing a client's tax return
    b. A material handler
    c. A production supervisor
    d. A salesclerk
    e. None of the above

_____ 2. Assuming that Ellen Graf works 44 hours during her first pay period and earns $10 per hour, the amount of FICA taxes to be withheld from her pay would be (FICA tax rate = 8%):
    a. $32.00        d. $52.50
    b. $35.20        e. None of the above
    c. $36.80

_____ 3. Albert Johnson is paid at a rate of $8 per hour. Last week Albert worked 50 hours. His wages are subject to the Fair Labor Standards Act; federal income tax withheld amounts to 20% of gross wages; FICA and Medicare taxes are 8% of gross wages (the limit has not been reached for FICA); and union dues are $15. Johnson's take-home pay is:
    a. $316.80        d. $215.40
    b. $301.80        e. None of the above
    c. $273.00

_____ 4. Which of the following is considered to be a payroll tax?
    a. FICA taxes
    b. Federal income taxes
    c. New Jersey real estate taxes
    d. New Jersey sales taxes
    e. None of the above

_____ 5. Data for recording the amount of taxable FICA earnings is found in:
    a. The payroll register
    b. The federal and state wage-bracket table
    c. The employer's cumulative payroll tax report
    d. The employee earnings record
    e. None of the above

_____ 6. A payroll register is:
   a. A standard form provided by the federal government
   b. A standard form provided by the various state governments
   c. A standard form provided by the FASB
   d. A form designed to suit the needs of the company using it
   e. None of the above

_____ 7. A special payroll bank account is established by most companies:
   a. To achieve control over the payroll
   b. To satisfy the requirements of generally accepted accounting principles
   c. To avoid payroll taxes
   d. To lower payroll taxes
   e. None of the above

_____ 8. In the payroll entry, the difference between the debit to Salary Expense and the credit to Salaries Payable is:
   a. Not usually material
   b. The net pay for the period
   c. FICA taxes payable
   d. The total payroll deductions for the period
   e. None of the above

_____ 9. On June 1 of the current year, Control Corporation issued a $30,000, 12%, 60-day note payable. On the maturity date of the note, Control will settle the obligation by issuing a check for:
   a. $33,600          d. $30,000
   b. $33,000          e. None of the above
   c. $30,600

_____ 10. When a product is sold under warranty:
   a. A liability is created
   b. An expense is incurred
   c. The expense must be estimated
   d. All of the above
   e. None of the above

## EXERCISES

1† **Exercise 1:** Selecting Employee-Related Payroll Taxes

Listed below are several types of taxes. Select those taxes that would be withheld from an employee's paycheck.

| | |
|---|---|
| City income tax | Estimated tax |
| Excise tax | Federal income tax |
| Federal unemployment tax | FICA tax |
| Import tax | Marginal tax |
| State sales tax | State unemployment tax |

1 2 **Exercise 2:** Computing Take-Home Pay for an Individual

Janice Atwell works for Tom's Dry Cleaning and is paid at the rate of $7 per hour. Last week she worked 52 hours. Determine Janice's take-home pay assuming the following: Tom's Dry Cleaning is subject to the Federal Fair Labor Standards Act; Janice's federal income taxes withheld amounts to $45 for the week; and FICA taxes are 8.5% on the first $60,000 of earned wages (Janice has not exceeded this limit).

In addition to the above, Janice has $6.75 withheld weekly for her union dues and $4.50 withheld weekly for hospitalization insurance.

Calculate Janice's net pay.

▶ *(Check Figure: Net pay = $315.24)*

3 **Exercise 3:** Selecting Employer-Related Payroll Taxes

Listed below are several types of taxes. Select those taxes that are imposed on an employer's payroll.

| | |
|---|---|
| City income tax | Estimated tax |
| Excise tax | Federal income tax |
| Federal unemployment tax | FICA tax |
| Import tax | Marginal tax |
| State sales tax | State unemployment tax |

5 **Exercise 4:** Preparing a Payroll Register

Cox's Bakery employs three people. Last week these three worked 52, 40, and 48 hours, respectively. The pay rate for all three employees is $6.50 per hour. The first two employees had earned over $7,000 prior to last week's pay period. The third employee was hired only 2 weeks ago and will not exceed $7,000 total earnings for the entire year. All employees have a weekly medical insurance deduction of $7.75. Federal income taxes to be withheld are $37, $21, and $31, respectively.

Assume that FICA taxes are determined by using an 8.5% rate on all earnings up to a maximum of $60,000 (which no employee has exceeded), and that federal and state unemployment compensation taxes are imposed on employee earnings up to a maximum of $7,000.

Prepare a payroll register for the week.

▶ *(Check Figure: Total net pay = $779.88)*

† The numbers in the margin refer to the Learning Objectives.

5 6 **Exercise 5:** Preparing a Payroll Journal Entry

The following data, selected from the payroll register of Ashburn Corporation, represent the column totals for the current weekly pay period:

| | | | |
|---|---|---|---|
| Regular earnings | $85,000 | Federal income taxes | |
| Department A expense | 62,000 | withheld | $18,400 |
| Department B expense | 30,000 | Overtime earnings | 7,000 |
| FICA tax withheld | 7,800 | Union dues withheld | 1,400 |

From this information prepare, without explanation, the general journal entry to record the weekly payroll.

6 **Exercise 6:** Recording Payroll-Related Journal Entries

The cumulative earnings of the five employees of Constant Connie's Consulting Company are presented below. These sums do *not* include the current pay period, which is shown in a separate column. All data reflect gross pay. Using this information, prepare, without explanation, the general journal entries to record the payroll and the payroll taxes for the current period.

Assume that the total federal income tax withheld for the current period is 22% of current pay; FICA taxes are imposed at the rate of 7% on the first $60,000 of earned income for Social Security and 1.5% for Medicare; the federal unemployment tax rate is .6% on the first $7,000 of earned income; and the state unemployment tax rate is 4% on the first $7,000 of earned income. No other deductions are made from the employees' pay.

| Employee | Earnings to Date (Prior to Current Period) | Earnings (Current Period) |
|---|---|---|
| Blocker, Don | $ 58,300 | $3,100 |
| Elton, Susan | 37,000 | 1,950 |
| Hillary, Nathan | 23,900 | 1,260 |
| Smith, Jane | 6,650 | 780 |
| Wilson, Ann | 133,500 | 6,500 |

▶ *(Check Figure: Payroll tax expense = $543.25)*

7 **Exercise 7:** Journalizing Notes Payable

On Nov. 1, 1998, Dancer Products, Inc., issued a 6-month promissory note to the Denver National Bank in the amount of $650,000. Prepare general journal entries for the issuance of the note; for the Dec. 31, 1998, adjustment; and for the Apr. 30, 1999, payment in *each* of the following situations:

a. The bank pays Dancer Products $650,000 on Nov. 1, 1998, and collects the face amount of the note plus 12% interest on Apr. 30, 1999.
b. The bank discounts the note at 12% on Nov. 1, 1998, subtracting the total 6 months of interest from the face amount of the note, and collects the $650,000 borrowed funds on Apr. 30, 1999.

8 **Exercise 8:** Journalizing Product Warranty Expense

From Jan. 1, 1998, to Dec. 31, 1998, the National Appliance Company sold 2,600 washers and dryers. The appliances are sold under a 1-year warranty plan whereby the company will repair any appliance it sells at no cost to the customer for the first year of service. The company estimates that repair costs will be $60 per unit and that 7% of the units will require repairs.

During 1998, 86 units were repaired at a cost of $5,400. An additional 114 units sold in 1995 were repaired in 1999 at a cost of $7,100 before the warranties expired.

Record a single entry to summarize the repairs made in 1998; record the Dec. 31, 1998, adjusting entry to recognize the remaining liability at that date; and record a single entry to summarize the repairs made in 1999.

## PROBLEMS: SET A

2 6† **Problem A1:** Computing Net Pay and Preparing the Payroll Entry

Presented below is the payroll information data pertaining to the three employees of PaceSetters Telemarketing Company for the week ended May 12, 1998:

| Employee | Total Hours Worked | Hourly Pay Rate | Income Tax Rate | FICA Tax Rate | Union Dues |
|---|---|---|---|---|---|
| Hanson, Ben | 52 | $14.50 | 25% | 8.5% | $9 |
| Stewart, Charles | 42 | 7.75 | 15 | 8.5 | 9 |
| Underwood, Patty | 48 | 10.50 | 20 | 8.5 | 9 |

**Required:**

1. Compute the net pay for each employee. No employee has exceeded the FICA limit.

   ▶ *(Check Figure: Total net pay = $1,177.58)*
2. Prepare the payroll entry for May 12, 1998.

2 5 6 **Problem A2:** Recording Payroll and Payroll Tax Entries

The totals of the Nov. 10, 1998, payroll register of the Daytona Company are as follows:

Earnings:
Regular............. $62,300
Overtime............ 3,600
Total ............. $65,900

Taxable Earnings:
FICA............... $54,000
Unemployment....... 25,000

Deductions:
Federal income tax ... $13,200
FICA tax............. 4,590
Union dues.......... 640
Health insurance ..... 1,375
U.S. Savings Bonds... 800

Net Pay:
Total ............. $45,295

Distribution:
Department A........ $41,700
Department B........ 24,200

The following tax rates apply:

FICA: 8.5%     SUTA: 4.5%     FUTA: 0.8%

**Required:**

1. Prepare the entry to record the payroll.
2. Prepare the entry to record the employer's payroll taxes.

   ▶ *(Check Figure: Payroll tax expense = $5,915)*

2 6 **Problem A3:** Recording Payroll Entries in a Voucher Register, Check Register, and General Journal

The five employees of California Window Company are paid semimonthly, on the 15th and on the 30th of each month. The following general ledger accounts relating to payroll are from the Oct. 31, 1998, trial balance.

Federal Income Taxes
Withheld.................. $3,480
FICA Taxes Payable ........ 1,130

FUTA Taxes Payable ......... $ 160
SUTA Taxes Payable........... 470
Union Dues Withheld ........... 250

† The numbers in the margin refer to the Learning Objectives.

The following transactions relating to payroll were completed during the month of November 1998.

Nov. 8    Voucher no. 216 payable to the United Window Workers of America was prepared for the union dues withheld to date.

      8    Check no. 178 was issued in payment of voucher no. 216.

     15    The first semimonthly payroll is prepared and recorded in the general journal. Gross earnings amount to $36,500, and the following deductions were taken:

| | |
|---|---:|
| Federal income taxes........................ | $7,300 |
| FICA taxes ............................... | 3,150 |
| Union dues ............................... | 125 |

     15    Voucher no. 234 made payable to Payroll Account was prepared for the net amount of the payroll.

     15    Check no. 196 was issued in payment of voucher no. 234.

     17    Prepared voucher no. 251, payable to the State of California, for the SUTA taxes payable.

     17    Check no. 211 was issued in payment of voucher no. 251.

     19    Prepared voucher no. 265, payable to the Bank of California, for federal income taxes withheld and FICA taxes payable as of Oct. 31, 1995.

     19    Issued check no. 231 in payment of voucher no. 265.

     30    Recorded in the general journal the payroll due this date. The gross earnings amounted to $39,300, and the following deductions were taken:

| | |
|---|---:|
| Federal income taxes........................ | $7,920 |
| FICA taxes ............................... | 3,340 |
| Union dues ............................... | 125 |

     30    Recorded in the general journal the employer's payroll taxes for the month of November. The employer's FICA taxes amount to $6,490, the SUTA tax is $2,250, and the FUTA tax is $450.

     30    Prepared voucher no. 287 for the net amount of the payroll.

     30    Issued check no. 241 in payment of voucher no. 287.

**Required:**

Record these transactions in a voucher register, check register, or general journal, as appropriate.

**Problem A4:** Preparing a Payroll Register and Payroll Entries

Presented below is information pertaining to the Nov. 17, 1998, weekly payroll of New York Marketing Specialists:

| Employee | Regular Hours | Over-time Hours | Pay Rate | Federal Income Taxes | Medical Insurance Premiums | Earnings to End of Previous Period |
|---|---|---|---|---|---|---|
| Benton, Connie | 40 | | Salary | $713.00 | $15.00 | $134,300.00 |
| Dennis, David | 40 | 8 | 14.50 | 113.00 | 7.00 | 23,750.00 |
| Fenton, Jim | 40 | | Salary | 330.00 | 15.00 | 59,150.00 |
| Harris, Jane | 40 | 12 | 8.50 | 74.00 | 15.00 | 14,950.00 |
| Ickles, Nancy | 40 | 6 | 6.00 | 44.00 | 7.00 | 6,920.00 |
| Kelly, Tom | 40 | | 10.25 | 62.00 | 7.00 | 18,100.00 |

The two salaried employees, Benton and Fenton, receive weekly salaries of $2,850 and $1,350, respectively. Both of these individuals work in the executive office; the other four, hourly employees, work in the staff room.

The company is subject to these payroll taxes: 7% Social Security taxes on earnings up to $60,000; Medicare taxes of 1.5%; .8% federal unemployment compensation taxes; and 4.5% state unemployment compensation taxes. The federal and state unemployment taxes are imposed on the first $7,000 of salaries and wages.

**Required:**

1. Prepare a payroll register for the current pay period; the payroll checks to the employees start with check no. 156.

   ▶ *(Check Figure: Total net pay = $4,460.66)*
2. Prepare, without explanations, the general journal entries to record the payroll and the employer's payroll taxes.

4   **Problem A5:** Entering Data in an Employee Earnings Record

The biweekly employee earnings record of Joan Kessler just prior to the Mar. 24, 1998, payroll is presented below:

Name: Kessler, Joan  Telephone: (404) 432 1376  Social Security Number: 242-21-5788

Address: 2731 Roswell Road  Date Employed: Oct. 18, 1975  Date of Birth: May 15, 1955

Roswell, Georgia 30067

Date Terminated _____  Reason _____

Married (xx)

Single ( )  Pay Rate: $33,800

Head of Household ( )  Hourly Pay: $16.25

Department: Production

| 1998 Period Ending | Total Hours | Regular Hours | Overtime Hours | Total | Cumulative | Federal Income Tax | FICA | Union Dues | Health Ins. | U.S. Bonds | Total | Net Pay | Check No. |
|---|---|---|---|---|---|---|---|---|---|---|---|---|---|
| Jan. 13 | 80 | 1,300.00 | | 1,300.00 | 1,300.00 | 139.00 | 110.50 | 12.00 | 14.25 | | 275.75 | 1,024.25 | 116 |
| 27 | 86 | 1,300.00 | 146.25 | 1,446.25 | 2,746.25 | 160.00 | 122.93 | 12.00 | 14.25 | | 309.18 | 1,137.07 | 193 |
| Feb. 10 | 80 | 1,300.00 | | 1,300.00 | 4,046.25 | 139.00 | 110.50 | 12.00 | 14.25 | | 275.75 | 1,024.25 | 243 |
| 24 | 80 | 1,300.00 | | 1,300.00 | 5,346.25 | 139.00 | 110.50 | 12.00 | 14.25 | | 275.75 | 1,024.25 | 298 |
| Mar. 10 | 88 | 1,300.00 | 195.00 | 1,495.00 | 6,841.25 | 166.00 | 127.08 | 12.00 | 14.25 | | 319.33 | 1,175.67 | 341 |
| 24 | | | | | | | | | | | | | |
| 1st Qtr. | | | | | | | | | | | | | |

During the biweekly period ending Mar. 24, 1998, Kessler had worked 92 hours and had the following payroll deductions:

Federal income tax withheld. . . . . . . . . . . . . . . . . $184.00
FICA tax . . . . . . . . . . . . . . . . . . . . . . . . . . . . . . . . 135.36
Union dues . . . . . . . . . . . . . . . . . . . . . . . . . . . . . . 12.00
Health insurance. . . . . . . . . . . . . . . . . . . . . . . . . . 14.25

**Required:**

1. Enter the data for the Mar. 24, 1998, payroll in the employee earnings record, calculating overtime pay, total pay, total deductions, and net pay. Use check no. 443 for the payment.
2. Complete the employee earnings record for the first quarter of 1998 by adding up the various columns.

▶ *(Check Figure: Total net pay = $6,632.38)*

7 **Problem A6:** Recording Notes Payable Entries

Several transactions relating to notes payable for 1998–1999 for the Mellon Company are listed below:

Jan. 16  Purchased office equipment on account from the Best Eastern Office Equipment Company, terms 2/10, n/30, $48,000.

Feb. 14  Mellon issued a 10%, 60-day note payable to Best Eastern in the amount of $48,000 in full settlement of the account payable. (The note is due on Apr. 15, 1998, which is a Saturday.)

Apr. 17  Mellon paid Fairchild the amount due on the $48,000 note issued on Feb. 14, 1998.

May  1  Borrowed funds from the Nashville National Exchange Bank by discounting a 12%, 90-day note with a face amount of $24,000.

July  31  The $24,000 discounted note of May 1 is paid to the Nashville National Exchange Bank.

Nov.  1  Issued a 12%, 90-day note payable to the New York State Bank in the amount of $225,000.

Dec. 31  Accrued the interest on the note issued to New York State Bank.

Jan. 30  Paid New York State Bank the amount due.

**Required:**

Record each of these transactions in a general journal.

8 **Problem A7:** Recording Product Warranty Entries

The Dunwoody Company provides a 1-year warranty with each appliance that it sells. During the years 1998 and 1999, Dunwoody had the following experiences relating to the 1998 sales of appliances.

1998
Jan. 1–June 30  Sold 6,300 units. Repaired 198 units, incurring $7,620 in cash, labor, and parts.

July 1–Dec. 31  Sold 7,100 units. Repaired 476 units, incurring $17,960 in cash, labor, and parts.

Dec. 31  Estimated that 7% of the total units sold for the year 1995 would require repairs at an estimated cost of $37 per unit.

1999
Jan. 1–June 30  Repaired 233 units, incurring $9,150 in cash, labor, and parts.

**Required:**

Prepare the appropriate general journal entries to record these transactions.

7 8 **Problem A8:** Reflecting Current Liabilities on a Balance Sheet

At the end of its accounting year, Dec. 31, 1998, Asbury Park Products, Inc., gathered the following information pertaining to its liabilities:

a. Accrued salaries and wages amounted to $4,700.

b. Certain products are sold under a 36-month warranty; 45,000 units of these products were sold in 1998. Estimates from previous years indicate that 10% of the units sold will require maintenance and repairs at an average cost of $15 per unit. During 1998, 2,750 of the units sold in 1998 were repaired under the terms of the warranty.

c. Customers advanced Asbury Park Products $10,000 for the delivery of specific products to be sold during the first quarter of 1999.

d. Asbury Park Products issued two notes which were discounted by the Freehold Bank. These notes are summarized below:

| Face Amount | Discount Rate | Date Issued | Maturity Date |
|---|---|---|---|
| $25,000 | 10% | 4/1/98 | 3/30/99 |
| 10,000 | 12 | 10/1/98 | 3/30/99 |

e. Three promissory notes issued by Asbury Park Products are outstanding at year-end. These notes are summarized below. (Interest will be paid at maturity.)

| Face Amount | Interest Rate | Date Issued | Maturity Date |
|---|---|---|---|
| $30,000 | 8% | 7/1/98 | 6/30/00 |
| 5,000 | 12 | 10/1/98 | 6/30/99 |
| 20,000 | 12 | 4/1/97 | 3/30/99 |

f. Accounts payable amounted to $110,000.

**Required:**

Prepare the current liability section of Asbury Park Products, Inc., as of Dec. 31, 1998.

▶ *(Check Figure: Total current liabilities = $214,375)*

## PROBLEMS: SET B

2 6† **Problem B1:** Computing Net Pay and Preparing the Payroll Entry

Data pertaining to the three employees of Jenkins Company are presented below for the week ending Jan. 13, 1998:

| Employee | Total Hours Worked | Hourly Pay Rate | Income Tax Rate | FICA Tax Rate | Union Dues |
|---|---|---|---|---|---|
| Molton, Terry | 46 | 12.25 | 25% | 8.5% | $15.00 |
| Nance, Alice | 54 | 8.50 | 15% | 8.5% | 15.00 |
| Olson, Robert | 42 | 9.75 | 20% | 8.5% | 15.00 |

**Required:**

1. Compute the net pay for each employee. No employee has exceeded the FICA limit.

▶ *(Check Figure: Total net pay = $1,050.58)*

2. Prepare the payroll entry for Jan. 13, 1998.

2 5 6 **Problem B2:** Recording Payroll and Payroll Tax Entries

Presented below are the totals taken from the Sept. 8, 1998, payroll register of the Pennsylvania Corporation:

Earnings:
- Regular.............. $75,400
- Overtime............ 6,200
- Total ............. $81,600

Taxable Earnings:
- FICA............... $57,295
- Unemployment....... 21,250

Deductions:
- Federal Income Tax... $16,300
- FICA Tax ........... 4,870
- Union Dues ......... 1,600
- Health Insurance ..... 1,330
- U.S. Savings Bonds... 300

Net Pay:
- Total ............. $57,200

Distribution:
- Sales Dept........... $48,900
- Administration Dept.... 32,700

The following tax rates apply:

FICA: 8.5%
SUTA: 4.0%
FUTA: .8%

**Required:**

1. Prepare the entry to record the payroll.
2. Prepare the entry to record the employer's payroll taxes.

▶ *(Check Figure: Total payroll tax expense = $5,890)*

† The numbers in the margin refer to the Learning Objectives.

**2 6** **Problem B3:** Recording Payroll Entries in a Voucher Register, Check Register, and General Journal

On Sept. 30, 1998, the trial balance of Fellows Real Estate Agency contained the following selected accounts relating to payrolls:

| | | | |
|---|---|---|---|
| Federal Income | | SUTA Taxes Payable . . . . . . . . . | 900 |
| Taxes Withheld . . . . . . . . . . . . | $5,100 | Medical Insurance | |
| FICA Taxes Payable . . . . . . . . . . | 1,900 | Premiums Withheld . . . . . . . . . | 2,100 |
| FUTA Taxes Payable . . . . . . . . . | 300 | | |

During the month of October, the following transactions relating to payrolls occurred:

Oct. 4 Voucher no. 231 in the amount of $7,000 was prepared, payable to First National Bank, a federal depository. This voucher authorizes payment of the federal income taxes withheld and the FICA taxes payable.

4 Check no. 275 was issued in payment of voucher no. 231.

15 The semimonthly pay period ends this date. Recorded the payroll in the general journal, using the following data:

| | |
|---|---|
| Gross earnings . . . . . . . . . . . . . . . . . . . . . . . . . . . | $19,500 |
| Federal income taxes withheld . . . . . . . . . . . . . . . | 3,900 |
| FICA taxes payable. . . . . . . . . . . . . . . . . . . . . . . . | 1,600 |
| Medical insurance premiums withheld . . . . . . . . . . | 600 |

15 Prepared voucher no. 263, payable to Payroll Account, for the net amount of the payroll.

16 Issued check no. 281 in payment of voucher no. 263. The check was deposited in the payroll account.

20 Voucher no. 297 was prepared payable to Chicago Insurance Company for the amount of medical insurance premiums due as of Sept. 30, 1998.

Oct. 20 Issued check no. 314 in payment of voucher no. 297.

24 Voucher no. 304 was prepared payable to the State of Illinois for the amount of state unemployment tax payable.

24 Issued check no. 326 in payment of voucher no. 304.

30 The semimonthly pay period ended this date. The payroll is recorded in the general journal, using the following data:

| | |
|---|---|
| Gross earnings . . . . . . . . . . . . . . . . . . . . . . . . . . . | $21,400 |
| Federal income taxes withheld . . . . . . . . . . . . . . . | 4,200 |
| FICA taxes payable. . . . . . . . . . . . . . . . . . . . . . . . | 1,800 |
| Medical insurance premiums withheld . . . . . . . . . . | 600 |

30 Prepared voucher no. 317 for the net amount of the payroll.

30 Check no. 341 was issued in payment of voucher no. 317.

30 A general journal entry was prepared to record the employer's payroll taxes due for the month of July. The following taxes apply:

| | |
|---|---|
| FICA taxes. . . . . . . . . . . . . . . . . . . . . . . . . . . . . . . . | $3,400 |
| State unemployment tax . . . . . . . . . . . . . . . . . . . . . | 650 |
| Federal unemployment tax . . . . . . . . . . . . . . . . . . . | 200 |

**Required:**

Record these transactions in a voucher register, check register, or general journal, as appropriate.

5  6  **Problem B4:** Preparing a Payroll Register and Payroll Entries

The Athens Manufacturing Company pays its employees every Friday. The payroll data for the week ending Nov. 10, 1998 are presented below:

| Employee | Regular Hours | Over-time Hours | Pay Rate | Federal Income Taxes | Medical Insurance Premiums | Earnings to End of Previous Period |
|---|---|---|---|---|---|---|
| Belcher, Tom | 40 | 4 | $ 9.50 | $ 87.00 | $ 6.00 | $ 19,200.00 |
| Dunmore, Betty | 40 | | Salary | 325.00 | 24.00 | 59,200.00 |
| Fisher, Fran | 40 | 10 | 8.00 | 81.00 | 12.00 | 18,600.00 |
| Ireland, James | 40 | 6 | 7.00 | 31.00 | 12.00 | 6,800.00 |
| Kirkland, Clyde | 40 | | Salary | 675.00 | 24.00 | 133,600.00 |
| Lawton, Kim | 40 | | 12.75 | 102.00 | 6.00 | 21,900.00 |

The two salaried employees, Dunmore and Kirkland, receive weekly salaries of $1,300 and $2,700, respectively. Both of these individuals work in the office; the other four, hourly employees, work in the factory.

Athens Manufacturing is subject to these payroll taxes: 7% Social Security taxes on earnings up to $60,000; Medicare taxes of 1.5%; .8% federal unemployment compensation taxes; and 5.4% state unemployment compensation taxes. The federal and state unemployment taxes are imposed on the first $7,000 of salaries and wages.

**Required:**

1. Prepare a payroll register for the current pay period; the payroll checks to the employees start with check no. 127.

   ▶ *(Check Figure: Total net pay = $4,081.94)*
2. Prepare, without explanations, the general journal entries to record the payroll and the employer's payroll taxes.

4  **Problem B5:** Entering Data in an Employee Earnings Record

The employee earnings record for Robert Zimmerman presented below represents accumulation of biweekly payroll data prior to the Mar. 24, 1998, payroll.

| | | |
|---|---|---|
| Name ___Zimmerman, Robert___ | Telephone ___(212) 512 3045___ | Social Security Number ___196-16-3142___ |
| Address ___1220 Avenue of the Americas___ | Date Employed ___May 12, 1983___ | Date of Birth ___October 22, 1949___ |
| ___New York, New York 10020___ | | |
| Date Terminated _____ | Reason _____ |
| Married         (xx) | _____ |
| Single            (  ) | Pay Rate ___$39,000___ |
| Head of Household (  ) | Hourly Pay ___$18.75___ |
| Department ___Advertising___ | |

*(Continued)*

| 1998 Period Ending | Total Hours | Regular Hours | Overtime Hours | Total | Cumulative | Federal Income Taxes | FICA | Union Dues | Health Ins. | U.S. Bonds | Total | Net Pay | Check No. |
|---|---|---|---|---|---|---|---|---|---|---|---|---|---|
| | | | Earnings | | | | | Deductions | | | | | |
| Jan. 13 | 80 | 1,500.00 | | 1,500.00 | 1,500.00 | 156.00 | 127.50 | 10.00 | 21.50 | | 315.00 | 1,185.00 | 175 |
| 27 | 80 | 1,500.00 | | 1,500.00 | 3,000.00 | 156.00 | 127.50 | 10.00 | 21.50 | | 315.00 | 1,185.00 | 315 |
| Feb. 10 | 80 | 1,500.00 | | 1,500.00 | 4,500.00 | 156.00 | 127.50 | 10.00 | 21.50 | | 315.00 | 1,185.00 | 396 |
| 24 | 86 | 1,500.00 | 168.75 | 1,668.75 | 6,168.75 | 180.00 | 141.84 | 10.00 | 21.50 | | 353.34 | 1,315.41 | 423 |
| Mar. 10 | 80 | 1,500.00 | | 1,500.00 | 7,668.75 | 156.00 | 127.50 | 10.00 | 21.50 | | 315.00 | 1,185.00 | 472 |
| 24 | | | | | | | | | | | | | |
| 1st Qtr. | | | | | | | | | | | | | |

Zimmerman worked 94 hours during the biweekly period ending Mar. 24, 1998, and had the following payroll deductions:

Federal Income Tax Withheld . . . . . . . . . . . . . . . $228.00
FICA . . . . . . . . . . . . . . . . . . . . . . . . . . . . . . . . . . . 160.97
Union Dues . . . . . . . . . . . . . . . . . . . . . . . . . . . . . . 10.00
Health Insurance. . . . . . . . . . . . . . . . . . . . . . . . . . 21.50

**Required:**

1. Enter the data for the Mar. 24, 1998, payroll in the employee earnings record, calculating overtime pay, total pay, total deductions, and net pay. Use check no. 527 for the payment.
2. Complete the employee earnings record for the first quarter of 1998 by adding up the various columns.

▶ *(Check Figure: Net pay = $7,528.69)*

7 **Problem B6:** Recording Notes Payable Entries

Listed below are several transactions of the Dallas Corporation relating to notes payable for 1998–1999:

Feb.   1   Acquired office equipment on account from Waco Office Equipment Company, terms 2/10, n/30, $22,000.

Mar.   1   Waco agreed to accept a 12%, 90-day note for $22,000 as payment of the account payable.

May  30   Paid Waco the amount due on the note issued on Mar. 1, 1998.

Aug.   1   Discounted at the Southwest National Bank a 9%, 60-day note payable issued this date for $225,000.

Sept. 30   Paid Southwest the amount due on the discounted note of Aug. 1, 1998.

Dec.   1   Issued a 12%, 180-day note payable to Denton Loan Company in the amount of $65,000.

Dec. 31   Accrued the interest on the note issued to Denton.

May  30   Paid Denton the amount due.

**Required:**

Record each of these transactions in a general journal.

8    **Problem B7:** Recording Product Warranty Entries

WashWell Appliance Company sells appliances for $450 per unit. The appliances carry a 1-year warranty. During the years 1998 and 1999 WashWell had the following experiences relating to the 1998 sales of appliances.

1998
Jan. 1–June 30    Sold 2,100 units. Repaired 127 units, incurring $4,650 in cash, labor, and parts.

July 1–Dec. 31    Sold 2,800 units. Repaired 352 units, incurring $13,510 in cash, labor, and parts.

Dec. 31    Estimated that 14% of the total units sold for the year 1995 would require repairs at an estimated cost of $35 per unit.

1999
Jan. 1–June 30    Repaired 216 units, incurring $8,340 in cash, labor, and parts.

**Required:**

Prepare the appropriate general journal entries to record these transactions.

7  8    **Problem B8:** Reflecting Current Liabilities on the Balance Sheet

Thomas Company obtains the following information relating to its liabilities for the year ended Dec. 31, 1998.

a. The company has five notes outstanding, as summarized below:

| Face Amount | Interest or Discount Rate | Date Issued | Maturity Date | Type of Note |
|---|---|---|---|---|
| $ 2,000 | 10% | 10/1/98 | 3/31/99 | Face value |
| 5,000 | 12 | 10/1/98 | 1/31/99 | Discount |
| 10,000 | 12 | 1/1/98 | 6/30/99 | Discount |
| 8,000 | 18 | 9/1/98 | 2/28/99 | Face value |
| 25,000 | 8 | 7/1/98 | 6/30/01 | Face value |

Interest is paid at maturity on all notes.
b. Salaries accrued at year-end amount to $2,350.
c. Included in rent revenue are $1,745 of rents collected for the first quarter of 1999.
d. The company, in addition to its rental activities, sells a product that carries a 24-month warranty. During 1998, 20,000 units were sold. Repairs were made on 480 units in 1998. It is estimated that 8% of the units sold in 1998 will require repairs at an average cost of $11.25 each.
e. Accounts payable at year-end amounted to $20,000.

**Required:**

Prepare the current liabilities section of Thomas Company's balance sheet as of Dec. 31, 1998.

▶ *(Check Figure: Total liabilities = $61,575)*

## DECISION PROBLEM

Continental Motors Company employs several hundred people as inventory counters. These individuals visit the various plant sites and count inventories of parts and supplies on a continual basis.

The company is considering engaging We-Count Inventories, Inc., instead of continuing to use its own counters. We-Count has submitted a proposal to do a sample inventory for Continental's Studepacker Division. The proposal estimates that the work will take 102,000 person-hours, to be billed at the following rates:

| Person-Hours | Classification | Hourly Billing Rate |
|---|---|---|
| 90,000 | Counters | $ 7.75 |
| 8,000 | Reviewers | 12.00 |
| 4,000 | Supervisors | 20.00 |

Continental currently employs 50 counters in the Studepacker Division, whose inventory takes 1 year to count. The counters earn an average wage of $22,500 per year, which is subject to normal payroll taxes (FICA taxes of 8.5%; federal unemployment compensation tax of .8%; and state unemployment compensation tax of 5.4% up to $7,000). In addition, benefits to the employees amount to 6.5% of the total payroll, and its costs $1.10 per employee per week to process the various payroll and personnel records.

**Required:**

Develop for Continental Motors Company an analysis of the cost of taking inventory in the Studepacker Division by the present method and by We-Count under the proposed sample inventory. How much will Continental save by engaging We-Count?

## ETHICS CASE

Thomas Madison, assistant comptroller for the Newcastle Corporation, has just received a copy of the company's published 1998 annual report and is greatly disturbed by it.

Several weeks earlier, as part of his responsibilities, Thomas had prepared the financial statements for the company and had made his annual presentation on the financial condition of the company to the comptroller, the president, and the board of directors of the company. In his presentation he had pointed out to the group that net income had decreased by 6.3% compared to last year.

Now, however, upon reading the published annual report, Thomas sees that the president's letter to the stockholders states that the company can take great pride in achieving a 4.3% increase in net income in the face of difficult economic times. The income statement printed in the report does in fact show net income as 4.3% higher than last year. But missing from the balance sheet is $14,500,000 of unearned revenue that represents advance payments made in 1998 by various customers for work to be performed in the first quarter of 1999. As a result of these omissions, revenues are $14,500,000 higher than Thomas's figures.

Thomas confronts his boss, who tells him that the board had decided to consider these advance cash payments as revenue. They had instructed the comptroller to change the financial statements before they were published. The board did not want to upset the stockholders needlessly, since it appears that 1996 will be a banner year for the company. The comptroller tells Thomas not to worry about the discrepancy, because next year's anticipated sales will more than make up for it and the stockholders will lose nothing.

**Required:**

What should Thomas do?

## OBJECTIVE ASSIGNMENT ANSWERS

### True/False

**1.** T    **2.** F    **3.** F    **4.** T    **5.** F

### Multiple Choice

**1.** b    **2.** a    **3.** b    **4.** d    **5.** c
**6.** c    **7.** d    **8.** d    **9.** c    **10.** d

# Generally Accepted Accounting Principles and International Accounting

**LEARNING OBJECTIVES**

After studying this chapter, you should be able to do the following:

1 Explain the need for generally accepted accounting principles (GAAP)

2 Explain what is meant by authoritative support for GAAP

3 List and discuss the three objectives of financial statements

4 List and explain the qualitative characteristics of accounting

5 List and explain the four basic assumptions or concepts of GAAP

6 List and explain the six basic principles of GAAP

7 List and explain the three basic modifiers of GAAP

8 Describe the three major accounting problems in accounting for multinational companies

9 Prepare general journal entries for international transactions involving purchases, payments, sales, and receipts

10 Prepare general journal entries recording unrealized exchange gains and losses

11 Define the key terms listed at the end of the chapter

**CHAPTER OUTLINE** THE NEED FOR GAAP • AUTHORITATIVE SUPPORT FOR GAAP • OBJECTIVES OF FINANCIAL STATEMENTS • QUALITATIVE CHARACTERISTICS OF ACCOUNTING INFORMATION • THE BASIC ASSUMPTIONS OF GAAP • The Business Entity Concept • The Accounting Period Concept • The Going Concern Concept • The Stable Dollar Concept • THE BASIC PRINCIPLES OF GAAP • The Cost Principle • The Matching Principle • The Revenue-Recognition Principle • The Expense-Recognition Principle • The Full Disclosure Principle • The Consistency Principle • THE BASIC MODIFIERS OF GAAP • Materiality • Conservatism • Industry Practices • INTERNATIONAL ACCOUNTING • International Accounting Standards • Foreign Currency Transactions • Unrealized Exchange Gains and Losses

This chapter will provide you with an appreciation of the need for generally accepted accounting principles—GAAP, the authoritative support for GAAP, the meaning and development of GAAP, the objectives of financial statements, the qualitative characteristics of accounting information, and the structure of GAAP.

GAAP applies to financial statements prepared in the United States. While accounting standards in the United States and other industrial countries are the most sophisticated and complex, each global community has its own set of accounting principles. Differences in cultures and economies result in differences in the general objectives of financial statements. As we approach the twenty-first century, the need for international standards is increasing. They would make it possible for the international community to analyze financial statements of companies from different countries on a comparable basis. The International Accounting Standards Committee, a worldwide organization, is in the process of developing basic standards. The process will be lengthy, but these standards will be of significant benefit to global capital markets. The last half of this chapter will introduce this important topic and will illustrate some of the basic accounting problems that arise when exchange rates fluctuate between countries.

## THE NEED FOR GAAP

Generally accepted accounting principles (GAAP) can be considered the ground rules of accounting. Actually, **generally accepted accounting principles** is a technical accounting term referring to the conventions, concepts, standards, rules, principles, and procedures that are necessary to define accepted accounting at a particular time. Their purpose is to ensure that similar economic events will be reported in the same manner by everyone. When several acceptable alternatives exist for recording an economic event—say, inventory cost flows or depreciation—these ground rules require us to disclose which alternative was used in the financial statements. Since everyone in the United States must follow GAAP, the result is a consistent system of financial reporting that provides users of financial statements with information that is reliable, understandable, and comparable to prior years and among companies. Without these ground rules there would be chaos in financial reporting. General Motors might use the FIFO inventory method, Ford might use LIFO, and neither would have to tell us which it used. We couldn't meaningfully compare the two companies, and that's the point—that's why we need GAAP.

Learning
Objective    1

Explain the need for generally
accepted accounting principles
(GAAP)

## AUTHORITATIVE SUPPORT FOR GAAP

Who decides what GAAP are? Even more important, who tells us that we must follow GAAP? What happens if we don't?

The authority of GAAP rests on their acceptance by the accounting profession. And that's true, but it's not quite the whole story. Actually, GAAP have what is known as **authoritative support,** meaning the pronouncements of the Financial Accounting Standards Board (FASB), the Securities and Exchange Commission (SEC), and other accounting bodies that follow a due-process procedure in establishing accounting principles. Furthermore, some accounting bodies provide generally accepted accounting principles with what is known as *substantial authoritative support*. In addition

Learning
Objective    2

Explain what is meant by
authoritative support for GAAP

to APB *Opinions* and FASB *Standards,* these other sources lend substantial authoritative support:

- APB and FASB interpretations of *Opinions* and *Standards*
- Industry audit guides
- Industry accounting practices
- APB *Statements*
- AICPA Statements of Position
- Pronouncements of the SEC
- Accounting textbooks and articles

The independent auditor—the CPA—provides statement users with assurance that the statements represent fairly the results of operations and the financial condition of a company. The auditor gives this objective opinion after examining the accounting records. And the auditor's opinion of the statements' fairness is an integral part of the statements themselves.

In his or her opinion, the auditor must state whether or not the financial statements are presented fairly and prepared in accordance with GAAP. Why? Because the auditor must follow the pronouncements of the accounting profession in order to remain and practice in it. Failure to follow the pronouncements is cause for expulsion—the state board of accountancy could remove the CPA's license to practice public accounting.

One of the pronouncements is found in the American Institute of Certified Public Accountants (AICPA) *Statements on Auditing Standards.* It says that the auditor's report must state whether the financial statements are presented in accordance with GAAP. Another pronouncement, found in the AICPA Code of Professional Ethics, states that the CPA must not express an opinion that financial statements are in conformity with GAAP if they contain any departure from an accounting principle issued by the FASB or the old APB.

Moreover, many companies fall under the regulations of the SEC. The SEC has direct legal power to force these companies to follow its accounting rules; failure to comply could mean a prison sentence. Most of the SEC's accounting rules are the same as those of the FASB and APB, because the SEC normally looks to the FASB to establish accepted accounting principles.

Thus, authoritative support for GAAP comes from two main sources:

1. Indirectly, from the CPAs who must follow professional accounting pronouncements
2. From the SEC, which has legal authority to enforce compliance with these pronouncements

## OBJECTIVES OF FINANCIAL STATEMENTS

As you know, financial reporting should provide information that is useful to present and potential investors and creditors. That's the first objective of a financial statement. The FASB considers only present and potential investors and creditors as users, because only they do not have any direct access to an entity's financial records. In contrast, other user groups—the IRS, the SEC, and management, to name a few—are able to obtain whatever financial information they need concerning the company. The IRS and the SEC have legal authority to obtain any information they want, and management need only ask employees for it. The financial statements, as the end product of the accounting activity, represent the classification and summarization of

Learning **3**
Objective

List and discuss the three objectives
of financial statements

many financial transactions, some of which are very complex. These activities simply cannot be presented in the financial statements in such a way that everyone—from a skilled financial analyst to an unskilled small investor—can understand what they mean. The FASB assumes that readers of financial statements have a basic background in business and economics and will take the time and effort to study the statements and related notes.

The second objective of financial statements is to provide information that is useful in assessing the amounts, timing, and uncertainty of the net cash inflow to the company. People invest to increase their cash, so for investors the final test is whether or not they received more cash from an investment than they spent on it. They want information that will help them choose between receiving cash now and selling their stock at some future date.

The third objective of financial statements is to provide information about the economic resources (assets); the claims on those resources (liabilities and owners' equity); and the effects of transactions, events, and circumstances that change resources and claims on those resources. Investors want this information to help them assess the company's strengths and weaknesses; to assess the company's liquidity (ability to convert assets to cash) and solvency (ability to pay its bills); and to evaluate information about the company's performance during the period.

**ASK YOURSELF** ▶

1. **Why do we need GAAP?**
2. **What authority does GAAP have?**
3. **What is the meaning of the term** *generally accepted accounting principles?*

## QUALITATIVE CHARACTERISTICS OF ACCOUNTING INFORMATION

The FASB has identified nine qualitative characteristics of accounting information, many of which are interdependent.

1. **Usefulness.** Usefulness, of course, is the most important characteristic of any reported information. People want accounting information that's *useful*—but what's useful to one user may not be useful to another. Accounting standards require that:

   Learning Objective **4**

   List and explain the qualitative characteristics of accounting

   a. The information be useful to most of the people who want to use it; and
   b. Preparation of the information not be so expensive, time-consuming, or complex a task that it becomes burdensome.

2. **Understandability.** If you can't understand the accounting information given to you, it isn't useful, even though it may be relevant to whatever decision you want to make. To expand on an example used by the FASB, suppose you're a vegetarian on a summer trip to Paris. Ordering a meal in a restaurant will present you with a problem. The information you need for ordering a meatless meal is on the menu, but it's useless if you don't understand French.

   To have the characteristic of *understandability,* therefore, accounting information must be presented in a manner that investors and creditors understand. As we said before, however, it is assumed that investors and creditors have a basic knowledge of business and economics and that they will spend some time and effort in studying the financial statements.

3. **Relevance.** For information to be *relevant,* it must have some bearing on the decision being made. Back in the French restaurant, assume that you ask the waiter for a menu printed in English. He returns with an English-language menu of meat dishes. Now you have information that is understandable, but not useful or relevant. Finally, the waiter brings an English-language menu of vegetarian dishes; that is both relevant and useful for your decision about what to order.

   Consider an accounting example: When accounts receivable are reported on the financial statements, the dollar amount is the relevant information, not the number of accounts.

4. **Reliability.** Accounting information should be *reliable,* or free from errors. It should also be free from any bias on the part of those who are providing it. This freedom from error and bias must be independently verifiable. That is, if two accountants working independently but using the same accounting methods arrive at the same results, the information has been verified and proved to be reliable.

   Be careful what conclusions you draw from the reliability characteristic. You can be sure that the amounts reported on a set of financial statements are reliable, just as you can be sure that the tablets in a bottle of aspirin conform to the formula written on the side of the bottle. But when you take the aspirin, it's because of the relevant information that two tablets will cure your headache, not because of the reliability of the formula. Similarly, accounting information does not claim to cure any financial headaches; it just claims to conform to the accounting measurement formulas.

5. **Timeliness.** Accounting information must become available before it loses its capacity to influence decisions. How fast information loses its *timeliness* and becomes irrelevant and useless depends on the decision to be made. Accounting information needed for a corporate takeover bid may have value for only a few days or even hours. In contrast, information needed for an annual report would have value over a much longer period of time.

   Sometimes we have to sacrifice precision for timeliness because approximate information now is more useful than precise information later. For example, under a pension plan a company agrees to pay its employees retirement benefits in the future for their current service. The employees' current service is an expense of this year's operations, but that expense cannot be measured precisely until the employees retire. But by then the information would no longer be useful. Consequently, we have to estimate the pension expense to prepare timely and useful financial statements.

6. **Verifiability.** When other accountants review independently the information in purchase invoices, sales invoices, property deeds, transfers of title, and other similar documents and arrive at the same values reported in the financial statements, the information is said to be *verifiable.* The verifiability characteristic is concerned with the ability to review the underlying documents, not with the results of the review. If the underlying documents are not available, the information reported on the financial statements can't be verified and is thus unreliable.

7. **Neutrality.** Accounting information should not favor one group of users or preparers over another group. By *neutrality,* we mean that accounting information should be free from bias. Both in making and in using accounting standards, the accountant's major concern should be the relevance and reliability of the information, not its effect on one group or another.

   For example, if the recording of purchases made in the last week of December were postponed until January, the income statement would show higher reported earnings for the current year. The higher reported earnings would reflect favorably on management this year, thus favoring that group over the stockholders and other users of the statement. However, neutrality requires that purchases be recorded when acquired, regardless of the effect on management's reported performance.

8. **Comparability.** Usefulness is enhanced if accounting information can be compared with similar information for the same company at different times, and for different companies at the same time. The principal reason for developing accounting standards is to reduce the use of different accounting methods, which is what makes comparisons difficult. *Comparability* thus enables users to detect and explain similarities and differences among companies and to evaluate the performance of each over time.

9. **Completeness.** For accounting information to be reliable, it must be complete. *Completeness* implies that nothing material is left out that would be essential to investors or creditors in assessing the condition of the business. The materiality and the cost of additional information are limiting factors on completeness. Relevance is the determining factor. A map for buried treasure may be complete except for two details: the name of the person who drew the map and the approximate value of the treasure. The first item is irrelevant and not worth the cost of getting. But the second item is certainly relevant, and some effort should be made to obtain it before substantial time and money are invested in recovering the treasure.

**ASK YOURSELF** ▶

1. **Identify the nine qualitative characteristics of accounting information.**

## THE BASIC ASSUMPTIONS OF GAAP

Thirteen generally accepted accounting principles form a structure from which all the others are derived. We can organize these 13 GAAP into three basic areas: assumptions, principles, and modifiers. Let's consider each of these groups in turn.

To begin with, GAAP rest on four basic assumptions or concepts:

Learning
Objective **5**

List and explain the four basic assumptions or concepts of GAAP

1. The business entity concept
2. The accounting period concept
3. The going concern concept
4. The stable dollar concept

### The Business Entity Concept

The **business entity concept** means that for accounting purposes a business entity is considered to be separate and distinct from its owners—generating its own revenue, incurring its own expenses, owning its own assets, and owing its own liabilities. Now that's not *legally* true if the entity is a proprietorship or a partnership. Accountants report on the economic substance of activities, and that may not always reflect the legal form of the entity.

To understand what we mean by the business concept, look at Exhibit 1, which lists the business entities of John Jay, a very ambitious young man. John operates a law practice. It's a proprietorship, which means that it doesn't legally have a separate existence from John. Its assets are John's assets as far as the law is concerned. The law practice's assets are available to John's personal creditors if they can't be satisfied from his individual assets, and vice versa. If John can't pay his personal creditors, they can sue to be paid out of the law practice's assets. The same goes for the law

**Exhibit 1**  John Jay's Business Entities

| Year | 1995 | | | | 1996 | | | | 1997 | | | | 1998 | | | |
|---|---|---|---|---|---|---|---|---|---|---|---|---|---|---|---|---|
| **Quarter** | 1 | 2 | 3 | 4 | 1 | 2 | 3 | 4 | 1 | 2 | 3 | 4 | 1 | 2 | 3 | 4 |
| Individual:<br>    John Jay Himself<br>Proprietorship:<br>    John Jay, Attorney-at-Law<br>Partnership:<br>    Jay and Wilson, Legal Forms Supply<br>Corporations:<br>    Jay Finance Corporation<br>    DownHome First National Bank<br>    Classic Title Insurance Company<br>    High Finance Mortgage Corporation | | | | | | | | | | | | | | | | |

practice's creditors: If they aren't paid, they can sue to be paid out of John's personal assets. For accounting purposes, however, we ignore the legal form and, as John's accountants, prepare separate sets of financial statements for John the individual and for John Jay, Attorney-at-Law.

John Jay and Susan Wilson are partners in a legal forms supply business. That's a business entity and we would prepare a separate set of financial statements for it. Legally, of course, the assets of the partnership are available to *both* John's and Susan's personal creditors, just as John's assets are available for the proprietorship.

Several years ago John established a local bank, which he organized as a corporation. What he actually did was first to organize the Jay Finance Company, whose objective was to provide financial and marketing activities for the bank, title insurance, and mortgage companies. John became the principal stockholder but sold 40% of the stock to 1,000 interested investors. Then he set up three other corporations: Down-Home First National Bank, Classic Title Insurance Company, and High Finance Mortgage Corporation. All the stock of these companies is owned by Jay Finance Company. Each of the four corporations is a legal entity. Each owns its own assets and owes its own debts. Each generates its own revenue and incurs its own expenses. Each prepares its own set of financial statements.

But Jay Finance Company owns 100% of the other three. Investors and creditors are interested in the financial activities of the group as a whole. So the four sets of statements for the investors and creditors are combined, or *consolidated,* and only one set of statements is issued. The business entity is the whole group, even though there are four corporations. Thus, the business entity concept emphasizes economic substance over legal form.

### The Accounting Period Concept

We would know exactly how well all of John Jay's business ventures did from the time he started them if we could wait until he received his last payment on a mortgage or consulted with his last client. We could then measure precisely the revenue and expenses, the assets and liabilities. But of course we can't wait. John wants to know how he is doing *now* and at *frequent intervals* as long as he is in business, and so do his creditors and the investors in Jay Finance Corporation.

Because John's business ventures don't stop operating when John wants financial statements, his accountant has to "stop" the business artificially to prepare the financial statements at frequent intervals—yearly and quarterly for John's creditors and investors, and monthly for John. These periods, although artificial, are timely and provide a consistent frame of reference for measuring John's activities and for comparing those measurements with accounting information from previous periods and other companies. (John can also compare his actual performance with his goals from one accounting period to another.)

When we divide the life of a business entity into short segments, we lose exactness; but it is the qualitative characteristic of timeliness that makes accounting information useful, even if we have to approximate some of the information.

These practices reflect the **accounting period concept.** This is the assumption that it is necessary to measure accounting income for periods of time less than the life of a company and that the measurement will not be precise but will be timely and therefore useful.

A complete set of financial statements with related footnotes is prepared annually for investors and creditors. However, only the major items of the income statement are reported to investors and creditors on quarterly *interim statements*. (Investors and creditors do not receive monthly interim statements.)

Look at the column headings 1995, 1996, 1997, and 1998 in Exhibit 1. These year-ends represent the periods of time for which we will issue complete financial statements for each of John's business entities. Notice that each year is divided into four quarters, which represent the periods of time for which we will issue interim statements for the businesses. We probably won't issue a fourth-quarter report, because at the end of that quarter it's time to make the annual report.

## The Going Concern Concept

John established his various business ventures assuming that they would have a long life. He fully expects that each of them will continue as far into the future as he can see—through good times and bad, profits and losses—and that over their continued existence, there will be mostly good times and profits.

Accountants similarly assume that a business entity will continue in existence for a long time. They call this assumption the **going concern concept.** It is the rationale for recording probable future economic benefits as assets rather than as expenses. For example, we record a building or a patent as an asset because we assume that we will be in business long enough to allocate the cost of the item to the periods of time in which we use it. If we did not make this assumption, we would charge off the building and patent as expenses in the year we bought them. That would really mess up the income statement, because we would be matching this year's revenue with this year's expenditures (as opposed to expenses); the resulting figure would be virtually meaningless.

## The Stable Dollar Concept

Money is a common unit of measure that we can use to record economic transactions and prepare financial statements. Everybody understands money—it's universally available, it's certainly relevant to financial transactions, and it's easy to use. Imagine trying to see how well Xerox did this year if the unit of measure were chickens or automobiles or wheat. These last three items have value, and as such can certainly be used to measure the value of other goods. But they are not *common* economic denominators—only money is.

But money—the dollar—as a measure of economic activity does not have a constant value over time. Actually, the value of a dollar has decreased over time, especially in recent years. It is not time in itself that causes the change in the value of money, but economic events, such as a shortage of oil, a Democratic or Republican majority in the House, or a military crisis in the Middle East.

The **stable dollar concept** assumes that the monetary unit of measure does not change in value over time, even if in fact it does. The assumption is made in order to ensure objectivity in reporting data on the financial statements.

Several ways have been proposed to deal with changes in the value of the dollar so that financial reports today can be meaningfully related to financial reports of the past. The dollar values on the financial statements might be adjusted to reflect replacement values or price-level changes or both. But there are problems with these approaches. If we adjusted for replacement values, we would be leaving the comfortable area of objective, verifiable evidence to support the values shown on the financial statements. Adjusting for price-level changes would mean that we were using just one index to measure many different factors that can cause changes in prices.

**ASK YOURSELF** ▶

1. **Into what three basic areas can GAAP be organized?**
2. **What are the four assumptions on which GAAP rest?**

## THE BASIC PRINCIPLES OF GAAP

Learning Objective **6**

List and explain the six basic principles of GAAP

Six principles form the framework for the practice of accounting. They rest on the four basic assumptions we just discussed. These six principles are:

1. The cost principle
2. The matching principle
3. The revenue-recognition principle
4. The expense-recognition principle
5. The full disclosure principle
6. The consistency principle

### The Cost Principle

Exchange prices offer us objective, verifiable evidence of the value of the goods and services we exchange with others. On the day that exchanges are made we record the exchange prices in the accounting records. These prices are thus the *historical costs,* and in recording them we are adhering to the cost principle. The **cost principle** requires that we record assets at their historical costs so that their values can be verified through comparison with the source documents.

As time goes on, the values for the items we acquired may increase or decrease. But we will not record these changes in values. One major reason is that if we did so, we would have no objective, verifiable evidence as to the item's new value. Yes, we would know it was worth more (or less) now, and some expert could tell us what he or she thought it was worth. But so could another expert, whose valuations would not be the same as the first expert's. Expert opinions are subjective, not objective, so the change in value cannot be verified by independent parties. And that's very important, because the values on the financial statements must be capable of being verified so that investors and creditors can rely on the financial statements. Independent auditors will insist on verifying the values given in the accounting records before they issue their opinion. In verifying values, the auditors will look to various source documents for the objective evidence—purchase invoices, titles of ownership, property deeds, brokers' advice, and other such items.

A second reason we use historical costs is that we have acquired goods and services for use in our operations; and once they are acquired, only the price we paid for them is relevant—not what they're worth today. We will assign the *costs* we paid to those periods of time that have received the benefit of the goods or services we acquired. There is substantial disagreement over this point. Some say that today's values *are* relevant and should be measured and disclosed.

### The Matching Principle

How well did we do? That's a question often asked by management, investors, and creditors. (The answer is on the income statement.) It's asked more often than the question, What resources do we have? (The answer is on the balance sheet.) For this reason, the income statement is considered even more important than the balance sheet. The income statement measures a company's earnings by comparing revenue with expenses. The **matching principle** requires that expenses incurred in a particular time period be compared — matched — with the revenues earned during the same time period. Expenses are incurred because they are directly or indirectly responsible for generating revenue. By matching expenses against revenues, we can measure net income for the period.

### The Revenue-Recognition Principle

Revenue is the inflow of assets that results from producing goods or rendering services. Revenue is not earned all at one point in time. Instead, the *earning process* extends over a considerable length of time. So when should revenue be recorded?

As a concrete example of this dilemma, let's look at John Jay, Attorney-at-Law. John has to do a number of things to earn revenue. He has to hire and pay administrative staff, he has to rent an office, he has to obtain clients who wish legal services, he has to provide legal services, the staff has to bill the clients for services, and revenue must be collected. In the midst of all these activities aimed at *earning* revenue, when should John *recognize* revenue?

Accountants answer this question with the **revenue-recognition principle,** which states that revenue should be recognized when *both* of the following conditions are met:

**1.** The earning process is essentially complete; and
**2.** An exchange has taken place.

#### The Point-of-Sale Method

For most companies these two conditions are met at the time the goods are sold or services are rendered. This is called the **point-of-sale method** of recognizing revenue. For John Jay, Attorney-at-Law, revenue is recognized at the point in time when the legal services are rendered.

There are some exceptions to the general rule, and good reasons for using them.

#### The Installment Sales Method

Consider first the **installment sales method** of recognizing revenue. Many goods and services are sold on an installment basis. We sell a $600 appliance to a customer today and receive a down payment of $100. The appliance is delivered and the $500 balance (plus interest, of course) will be paid in installments over the next 36 months. Since the sale was made today, we should recognize $600 of revenue. We should also recognize the expenses of selling the appliance, and that would include an estimate of the bad debts expense (based on all the appliances we sold this year).

But what if we can't estimate the bad debts expense — the amount of accounts that will not be paid? Then, instead of recognizing revenue when the sale is made, we will recognize revenue a little bit at a time as the cash payments are received. This is a very conservative approach, and we use it when we are not sure that the receivables we booked when the sale was made are ever going to be collected.

For example, assume that a parcel of land is sold on an installment basis for $1,000 on Jan. 1, 1998. A down payment of $250 is made on Jan. 1, 1998, and three additional payments of $250 are made each year thereafter until Jan. 1, 2001. The land cost $800.

The gross profit on the land is $200 ($1,000 − $800). Under the installment sales basis of revenue recognition, the $200 will be recognized as revenue not in 1998, but as the payments are received. Specifically, a *gross margin percentage* is calculated, and this percentage is used to determine the amount of revenue to be recognized when payments are made. In the example this gross margin percentage is 20% ($200 gross margin ÷ $1,000 sale).

Each payment made is considered to consist of an element of cost (100% − 20% gross profit = 80%) and an element of gross profit (20%). Thus, the $250 down payment consists of $200 cost ($250 × 80%) and $50 gross profit ($250 × 20%). The following table summarizes how revenue would be recognized for the $1,000 land sale:

| | 1998 | 1999 | 2000 | 2001 | Total |
|---|---|---|---|---|---|
| Cash received | $250 | $250 | $250 | $250 | $1,000 |
| Cost of land (80%) | 200 | 200 | 200 | 200 | 800 |
| Gross profit (20%) | $ 50 | $ 50 | $ 50 | $ 50 | $ 200 |

### The Percentage-of-Completion Method

Another exception to the point-of-sale method involves contract projects, which are very common in the construction industry. Consider a new construction company that has a contract to build a nuclear aircraft carrier for the U.S. government for $4 billion. It will take about 6 years to build the carrier. Now, if we follow the point-of-sale method, the construction company will show no profits for the first 5 years. But in year 6, when the sale takes place, the company will show a profit—and what a profit! Don't you think the economic facts are badly distorted here? Was the construction company doing poorly for the first 5 years? Certainly not with the contract it had. Do you think the company will have any problem selling the aircraft carrier? Of course not—the U.S. government must buy it for the agreed price when it's completed according to the specifications. It's all spelled out in the contract the company and Uncle Sam signed before the work started.

What the construction company will do is recognize revenue over the 6-year life of the project. How? Based on reasonable estimates of the project's progress. The amount of revenue to be recognized in any year is determined by comparing the costs incurred that year to the total estimated costs for the entire project. The resulting percentage is applied against the total revenue for the project, and that tells us how much revenue to recognize. This is called the **percentage-of-completion method** of recognizing revenue.

As another example, assume that the BigTime Construction Company contracts with the State of Pennsylvania for a bridge across the Susquehanna River. The contract price for the bridge is $60 million, and the estimated cost to build the bridge is $45 million. During 1998, $15 million of costs are incurred, representing one-third of the total estimated costs ($15 ÷ $45 = $\frac{1}{3}$). For 1998, one-third of the total revenue would be recognized, or $20 million ($60 × $\frac{1}{3}$).

For 1999, total costs are now estimated to be $50 million, of which a total of $40 million has now been incurred. The project is now four-fifths complete ($40 ÷ $50), and *total* revenue for the 2 years should be $48 million ($60 × $\frac{4}{5}$). Revenue for 1999 is then $48 million − $20 million, or $28 million.

The bridge is completed in 2000 and total costs amount to $49 million. The revenue recognized in 2000 would be $60 million − $20 million − $28 million, or $12 million.

The following table summarizes the recognition of revenue for the BigTime Construction Company on the Susquehanna bridge project:

|  | 1998 | 1999 | 2000 | Total |
|---|---|---|---|---|
| Revenue recognized | $20 | $28 | $12 | $60 |
| Cost incurred | 15 | 25 | 9 | 49 |
| Gross profit | $ 5 | $ 3 | $ 3 | $11 |

### *The Production Method*

One more exception to recognizing revenue at the point of sale is called the **production method** of recognizing revenue. Here revenue is recognized when production is complete even though a sale hasn't been made. We can use this method only when we are dealing with businesses whose products we are sure will be sold — businesses that produce things like precious metals (gold, silver, uranium) or certain government-supported farm products (corn, wheat, soybeans).

## The Expense-Recognition Principle

The **expense-recognition principle** concerns the point in time when a cost becomes an expense. Everything we acquire is a cost before it becomes an expense. We show costs on the balance sheet as assets; they are *unexpired costs,* meaning that we have paid them but we haven't yet received any economic benefits from them. We show expenses on the income statement; they are *expired costs,* meaning that we have paid them and have received the economic benefits from them. But when do we move costs from the balance sheet to show them as expenses on the income statement?

We recognize expenses in three ways.

**1.** Certain costs become expenses through *direct association* with revenue. For example, at the time a retail store sells merchandise, the costs of the merchandise — which are reflected as inventory on the company's balance sheet — become expenses recorded under cost of goods sold on the income statement.

**2.** Certain costs become expenses by *systematic and rational allocation.* If we can't associate costs directly with revenue, the next best approach is to assign the costs to expenses over time periods in some reasonable manner. That's basically the idea behind the depreciation of buildings and equipment and the amortization of intangibles.

**3.** Some costs don't fit the first method and are too elusive for the second to be applied. These costs receive *immediate recognition* as expenses, as soon as they are incurred. A good example is a corporation president's salary, which should be allocated to those periods of time that receive the benefits of the president's efforts. Now, if the president is really concerned about his ongoing business, he spends some time on this year's activities, but is likely to spend more time planning future years' activities. It would be impossible to trace the president's current salary and activity to results that are to come in future years.

## The Full Disclosure Principle

Investors and creditors have every right to expect that the financial statements they are using contain all the significant economic and financial information that is relevant to their understanding of the entity's financial status. This is known as the **full disclosure principle.**

Full disclosure does not mean that everything must be disclosed. That would be too costly. A balance must be maintained between the cost of gathering and disclosing information and its relevance to users. Basically, if the information will make a difference in investor or creditor decisions, it should be disclosed.

### The Consistency Principle

Accounting information is useful if it can be compared with similar information for the same company through time and with similar information between companies at the same time. But you have seen in this text that there are alternative generally accepted accounting principles for a number of areas—inventories, depreciation, and uncollectibles, for example. For accountants, the **consistency principle** requires that the same accounting method be applied to accounting events from period to period. If we choose the LIFO method of accounting for inventories, we would expect to continue using LIFO year after year. We can't use LIFO in year 2 and switch to the average cost method in year 3.

The consistency principle does not prohibit a company from switching to another accounting method. Companies can and do change accounting methods—but only if they can demonstrate that the new method is preferable to the old one. In addition, if a change is made, the full disclosure principle would require that the nature and effect of the accounting change, and the reason for making it, be disclosed in the financial statements at the time of the change.

**ASK YOURSELF** ▶

1. **What are the six basic principles of GAAP?**
2. **Identify the various methods of revenue recognition.**
3. **Identify the various methods of expense recognition.**

## THE BASIC MODIFIERS OF GAAP

Learning Objective 7

List and explain the three basic modifiers of GAAP

We can't always follow these six basic principles blindly. Sometimes practical considerations force us to modify them. The following are three basic modifiers:

1. Materiality
2. Conservatism
3. Industry practices

### Materiality

Let's look at a couple of examples to develop the idea of materiality. First, consider an automobile company whose engineering department has decided to install an additional part on one of the engine assembly machines. This is not a repair; it's a new part. The cost is $14.11. Now, the cost principle requires us to record the part as an asset and allocate its cost over the 12-year remaining life of the machine. But do you think it's worth the effort to record as an asset the $14.11 and then depreciate it? Of course not. Capitalizing the part would probably cost more in accounting effort than the part is worth.

A second example. At year-end a company's equipment subsidiary ledger has a balance that is $15,000 greater than the general ledger equipment control account. That's a pretty big difference—or is it? We can't tell until we know the total of all the equipment. Let's say that the control account has a balance of $150,000. The $15,000 is 10% of that amount, and that difference is material. But let's say the control account balance is $150,000,000. The $15,000 is only .1% of the total, and that difference is not material.

As these examples indicate, materiality is a relative thing. The way accountants apply the **materiality modifier** is to determine whether or not they think the item in question will affect decisions made by users of the financial statements. If it will, then it's material and must be reported in accordance with generally accepted accounting principles.

We may sometimes find that while an individual transaction is immaterial, a series of related transactions—even though they are individually immaterial—are material in the aggregate.

### Conservatism

In recording business transactions, we often find that GAAP permit us to record a given transaction in a number of ways. We simply select the alternative that we feel most fairly represents the economic substance of the transaction. But sometimes the choice is not clear-cut. When this happens, we apply the **conservative modifier**— that is, we select the alternative that is least likely to overstate net assets and net income. Whenever we are uncertain, it's better to err by understating rather than overstating net assets and net income.

### Industry Practices

Almost every major industry has some peculiarity that we must carefully consider when we are deciding how to report the economic affairs of a company in that industry in accordance with GAAP. Most often we can reconcile the industry practice with generally accepted accounting principles. But when we cannot, we have to rely on the **industry practices modifier**—that is, we use those practices that are common within the industry, and those practices become modifiers to GAAP.

Perhaps the best example of an industry practice is found in the meat-packing industry, where market values are used to measure inventories of the various cuts of meat. This practice is an acceptable modification of GAAP because it's just impossible to allocate the costs of a steer to the various by-products in any meaningful way, as GAAP would require.

**ASK YOURSELF** ▶

**1. What are the three basic modifiers of GAAP?**

## INTERNATIONAL ACCOUNTING

As mentioned in the introduction to this chapter, generally accepted accounting standards in the United States and other industrial nations are significantly more developed than in most other countries. In today's business environment, it is essential that managers of Exxon, Mitsubishi, Volkswagenwerk, British Petroleum, and other **multinational corporations,** which conduct business in many different countries, understand that accounting standards are different from country to country. Accounting for foreign operations presents a number of problems. First, companies that trade overseas must consider the risk that the relative values of currencies of the trading partners will change between the time of sale and the time of payment. Accordingly, one company will reflect a foreign currency gain while another will reflect a foreign currency exchange loss.

Learning
Objective **8**

Describe the three major accounting problems in accounting for multinational companies

Second, each country in which a multinational company has a subsidiary has its own financial accounting standards. For example, LIFO inventory is not allowed in Germany; the equity method of reporting investments is not allowed in Japan.

Third, a multinational corporation that has subsidiaries overseas must prepare consolidated statements. Income statements and balance sheets of German subsidiaries are expressed in German marks, French subsidiaries' financial statements are expressed in French francs, and so on. But only one set of financial statements is prepared for the consolidated group, and those statements must be expressed in the currency of the parent company.

Only the problems of international accounting standards and of recording exchange gains and losses will be considered in this section. Problems dealing with consolidation of domestic and foreign companies are beyond the scope of an accounting principles text.

## International Accounting Standards

Consider the following example: On January 1, 1998 a company acquired all the assets and liabilities of a second company in a transaction that indicates the existence of $160 million goodwill. If the company were a United States company an intangible asset of $160 would be recorded on January 1 and a minimum expense of $4 million would be reflected on each year's income statement for the next 40 years. If the company were a Japanese company the entire $160 would be written off in the first year or it could be amortized over a period of time not to exceed 5 years, $32 million per year. Dozens of other examples could be cited but the question is, what difference does it make that different countries have different accounting rules?

There are three significant reasons why there is a problem with companies doing international business using their own countries accounting rules.

First, companies in the same industry can not be compared. General Motors balance sheet, income statement, and statement of cash flows are not prepared on the same basis as are Toyota's or BMW. Not only are many measurement standards different but Germany does not even require a statement of cash flows.

Second, companies doing business in other countries have to incur additional costs in order to comply with statutory reporting requirements.

Third, companies wishing to raise capital in foreign markets have difficulties listing their securities on the exchanges. A case in point is the enormous cost Damilar Benz incurred in order to be listed on the New York Stock Exchange so that they could reach the United State's capital market.

Clearly comparable financial information is needed for companies doing international business and competing for world-wide capital and investors can look to the International Accounting Standards Committee (IASC) to play a major role in the haronization of accounting standards.

## Foreign Currency Transactions

International sales (and consequently purchases) may be billed in the currency of either the domestic company or the foreign country, depending on the arrangement the two companies have agreed on. If the transaction is billed in U.S. currency (that is, dollars) and paid in U.S. currency, no problem exists for the U.S. company (the seller). But the foreign company (the purchaser) is at risk of losing money as a result of changes in the relative values of the dollar and the local currency. If the transaction is billed and paid in the foreign company's currency, the U.S. company is exposed to the risk.

**Learning Objective 9**

Prepare general journal entries for international transactions involving purchases, payments, sales, and receipts

To illustrate the problem, assume that on Dec. 1, 1998, United Motors acquires on account $700,000 worth (100,000,000 yen; the symbol for the Japanese yen is ¥) of engines from Nipponese Mfg. of Japan. The account is paid on Dec. 10, 1998. Also assume that United Motors sells $400,000 (¥57,142,880) of automobiles to Sanson Imports on Dec. 1, 1998, receiving payment on Dec. 10, 1998. The **foreign exchange** rate (the value of a foreign currency in terms of U.S. currency) between the U.S. dollar and the Japanese yen on the dates crucial to our example were as follows:

| Date | Dollar/Yen | Yen/Dollar |
|---|---|---|
| Dec. 1, 1998 | .0070 | 142.8572 |
| Dec. 10, 1998 | .0080 | 125.0000 |
| Dec. 31, 1998 | .0075 | 133.3333 |
| Jan. 10, 1999 | .0085 | 117.6471 |

The transactions between these companies and the journal entries to record the transactions are shown in Exhibits 2 to 5.

In the transactions for the $700,000 of engines (Exhibit 2), Nipponese Mfg. incurs an exchange *loss* of ¥12,500,000 when the transactions are billed and paid in U.S. dollars. This is because the contractual agreement put Nipponese Mfg. at risk and the exchange rate between the United States and Japan dropped from ¥142.8572 per dollar to ¥125.0000 per dollar. Thus, it cost United Motors ¥12,500,000 fewer yen to pay its $700,000 debt [($700,000) $\times$ (142.8572 − 125.000)], and Nipponese Mfg. received fewer yen than it would have if United Motors had paid cash at the time of purchase.

If the terms of the transaction were to bill and pay in yen, as in Exhibit 3, the risk would shift to United Motors. Since the conversion rate went from $.007 per yen to $.008, United Motors would incur a loss of $100,000 [(¥100,000,000) $\times$ (.007 − .008)] because more dollars would be required to settle the account.

**Exhibit 2** Purchase of and Payment for $700,000 of Engines Recorded in U.S. Dollars: Collection Date, December 10, 1998

### UNITED MOTORS

| Date | Explanation | Debit (Dollars) | Credit (Dollars) |
|---|---|---|---|
| Dec. 1 | Purchase | 700,000 | |
| | Accounts Payable | | 700,000 |
| 10 | Accounts Payable | 700,000 | |
| | Cash | | 700,000 |

### NIPPONESE MFG.

| Date | Explanation | Debit (Yen) | Credit (Yen) |
|---|---|---|---|
| Dec. 1 | Accounts Receivable | 100,000,000 | |
| | Sales | | 100,000,000 |
| | $700,000 \times$ ¥142.8572. | | |
| 10 | Cash | 87,500,000 | |
| | Exchange Loss | 12,500,000 | |
| | Accounts Receivable | | 100,000,000 |
| | $700,000 \times$ ¥125.000. | | |

**Exhibit 3** Purchase of and Payment for $700,000 of Engines Recorded in Japanese Yen (¥): Collection Date, December 10, 1998

### UNITED MOTORS

| Date | Explanation | Debit (Dollars) | Credit (Dollars) |
|---|---|---|---|
| Dec. 1 | Purchase | 700,000 | |
| | Accounts Payable | | 700,000 |
| | ¥100,000,000 × $.007. | | |
| 10 | Accounts Payable | 700,000 | |
| | Exchange Loss | 100,000 | |
| | Cash | | 800,000 |
| | ¥100,000,000 × $.008. | | |

### NIPPONESE MFG.

| Date | Explanation | Debit (Yen) | Credit (Yen) |
|---|---|---|---|
| Dec. 1 | Accounts Receivable | 100,000,000 | |
| | Sales | | 100,000,000 |
| 10 | Cash | 100,000,000 | |
| | Accounts Receivable | | 100,000,000 |

**Exhibit 4** Sale and Collection of $400,000 of Automobiles Recorded in U.S. Dollars: Collection Date, December 10, 1998

### UNITED MOTORS

| Date | Explanation | Debit (Dollars) | Credit (Dollars) |
|---|---|---|---|
| Dec. 1 | Accounts Receivable | 400,000 | |
| | Sales | | 400,000 |
| 10 | Cash | 400,000 | |
| | Accounts Receivable | | 400,000 |

### SANSON IMPORTS

| Date | Explanation | Debit (Yen) | Credit (Yen) |
|---|---|---|---|
| Dec. 1 | Purchases | 57,142,880 | |
| | Accounts Payable | | 57,142,880 |
| | $400,000 × ¥142.8572. | | |
| 10 | Accounts Payable | 57,142,880 | |
| | Exchange Gain | | 7,142,880 |
| | Cash | | 50,000,000 |
| | $400,000 × ¥125.000. | | |

**Exhibit 5** Sale and Collection of $400,000 of Automobiles Recorded in Japanese Yen (¥): Collection Date, December 10, 1998

### UNITED MOTORS

| Date | Explanation | Debit (Dollars) | Credit (Dollars) |
|---|---|---|---|
| Dec. 1 | Accounts Receivable | 400,000 | |
| | Sales | | 400,000 |
| | ¥57,142,880 × $.007. | | |
| 10 | Cash | 457,143 | |
| | Exchange Gain | | 57,143 |
| | Accounts Receivable | | 400,000 |
| | ¥57,142,880 × $.008. | | |

### SANSON IMPORTS

| Date | Explanation | Debit (Yen) | Credit (Yen) |
|---|---|---|---|
| Dec. 1 | Purchases | 57,142,880 | |
| | Accounts Payable | | 57,142,880 |
| 10 | Accounts Payable | 57,142,880 | |
| | Cash | | 57,142,880 |

With the transactions for the $400,000 of automobiles (Exhibits 4 and 5), an exchange *gain* occurs when payment is made. Sanson Imports receives a gain of ¥7,142,880 [($400,000) × (142.8572 − 125.000)] if the transactions are billed and paid in U.S. dollars, because the yen fell from ¥142.8572 per dollar to ¥125.0000 per dollar (see Exhibit 4). Thus, ¥7,142,880 fewer yen would be required to pay off the debt of $400,000. United Motors would have received the gain if the transactions had been billed and collected in yen, since the rate expressed in dollars went from .0070 to .0080 dollars per yen (see Exhibit 5). That is, United Motors would have received $57,143 more dollars [(¥57,142,880) × (.0080 − .0070)] than the $400,000 due when it exchanged the yen for dollars.

### Unrealized Exchange Gains and Losses

In the illustrations above, the gains and losses are called **realized exchange gains and losses,** because the transactions were completed within the accounting year. Often, however, the transactions are not completed within the year, so exchange gains and losses must be measured at year-end in order to be reported on the financial statements. Adjusting entries record these gains and losses, which are called **unrealized exchange gains and losses.**

Learning Objective **10**

Prepare general journal entries recording unrealized exchange gains and losses

To illustrate the adjusting entries and subsequent collection transactions, we will change the example for United Motors, Nipponese Mfg., and Sanson Imports simply by changing the collection date from Dec. 10, 1998, to Jan. 10, 1999. The same transactions are again shown in Exhibits 6 to 9.

As shown in Exhibit 6, Nipponese Mfg. would record an unrealized exchange loss of ¥6,666,730 due to the drop in the exchange rate from ¥142.8572 per dollar on Dec. 1 (our original date of sale) to ¥133.3333 per dollar on Dec. 31. This loss must be reported on the Nipponese Mfg. financial statements at year-end, since it was Nipponese that bore the risk of the change in the exchange rates. An additional loss of ¥10,980,300 would be recorded on Jan. 10, our new payment date, because there has been a further drop in the value of the yen relative to the dollar [(¥133.3333 − ¥117.6471) × $700,000].

As shown in Exhibit 7, U.S. Motors is at risk, since the exchange is to be paid in yen. Thus, if the number of dollars needed to buy yen increases, as it has in the example, U.S. Motors will incur a loss. An unrealized loss must be recorded at Dec. 31 when the rate increases from .0070 dollar per yen to .0075 dollar per yen. And an additional exchange loss must be recorded on the Jan. 10 payment date because the rate increased again, from .0075 to .0085 dollar per yen.

**Exhibit 6** Purchase of and Payment for $700,000 of Engines Recorded in U.S. Dollars: Collection Date, January 10, 1999

### UNITED MOTORS

| Date | Explanation | Debit (Dollars) | Credit (Dollars) |
|---|---|---|---|
| 1998 Dec. 1 | Purchase          Accounts Payable | 700,000 | 700,000 |
| 31 | No entry | | |
| 1999 Jan. 10 | Accounts Payable          Cash | 700,000 | 700,000 |

### NIPPONESE MFG.

| Date | Explanation | Debit (Yen) | Credit (Yen) |
|---|---|---|---|
| 1998 Dec. 1 | Accounts Receivable          Sales       $700,000 × ¥142.8572. | 100,000,000 | 100,000,000 |
| 31 | Exchange Loss          Accounts Receivable       $700,000 × (142.8572 − 133.3333). | 6,666,730 | 6,666,730 |
| 1999 Jan. 10 | Cash       Exchange Loss          Accounts Receivable       $700,000 × ¥117.6471. | 82,352,970 10,980,300 | 93,333,270 |

**Exhibit 7** Purchase of and Payment for $700,000 of Engines Recorded in Japanese Yen (¥): Collection Date, January 10, 1999

### UNITED MOTORS

| Date | Explanation | Debit (Dollars) | Credit (Dollars) |
|------|-------------|-----------------|------------------|
| 1998 Dec. 1 | Purchase<br>    Accounts Payable<br>¥100,000,000 × $.0070. | 700,000 | 700,000 |
| 31 | Exchange Loss<br>    Accounts Payable<br>¥100,000,000 − (.0070 − .0075). | 50,000 | 50,000 |
| 1999 Jan. 10 | Accounts Payable<br>Exchange Loss<br>    Cash<br>¥100,000,000 × $.0085. | 750,000<br>100,000 | 850,000 |

### NIPPONESE MFG.

| Date | Explanation | Debit (Yen) | Credit (Yen) |
|------|-------------|-------------|--------------|
| 1998 Dec. 1 | Accounts Receivable<br>    Sales | 100,000,000 | 100,000,000 |
| 31 | No entry | | |
| 1999 Jan. 10 | Cash<br>    Accounts Receivable | 100,000,000 | 100,000,000 |

In Exhibit 8, Sanson Imports is at risk, since the exchange is to be in U.S. dollars. But as a purchaser, Sanson will gain on the exchange rates if the number of yen needed to buy dollars decreases, as is the case in the illustrations. Specifically, on Dec. 31 an unrealized gain of ¥3,809,560 must be recorded. And on Jan. 10, the payment date, Sanson needs to use only ¥47,058,840 to "buy" $400,000, gaining an additional ¥6,274,480.

When United Motors enters into a sales transaction to be paid in Japanese yen (see Exhibit 9) and the exchange rate favors the yen, United Motors will gain, since at the time payment is made, the same number of yen can "buy" more dollars. Thus,

United Motors will record a $28,571 unrealized gain on Dec. 31 and an additional $57,143 gain on the Jan. 10 payment date.

**ASK YOURSELF** ▶

1. **What kinds of problems exist in accounting for multinational companies?**
2. **What are realized exchange gains and losses?**
3. **What are unrealized exchange gains and losses?**

**Exhibit 8** Sale and Collection of $400,000 of Automobiles Recorded in U.S. Dollars: Collection Date, January 10, 1999

### UNITED MOTORS

| Date | Explanation | Debit (Dollars) | Credit (Dollars) |
|------|-------------|-----------------|------------------|
| 1998 Dec. 1 | Accounts Receivable | 400,000 | |
| | Sales | | 400,000 |
| 31 | No entry | | |
| 1999 Jan. 10 | Cash | 400,000 | |
| | Accounts Receivable | | 400,000 |

### SANSON IMPORTS

| Date | Explanation | Debit (Yen) | Credit (Yen) |
|------|-------------|-------------|--------------|
| 1998 Dec. 1 | Purchases | 57,142,880 | |
| | Accounts Payable | | 57,142,880 |
| | $400,000 \times ¥142.8572.$ | | |
| 31 | Accounts Payable | 3,809,560 | |
| | Exchange Gain | | 3,809,560 |
| | $400,000 \times (142.8572 - 133.3333).$ | | |
| 1999 Jan. 10 | Accounts Payable | 53,333,320 | |
| | Exchange Gain | | 6,274,480 |
| | Cash | | 47,058,840 |
| | $400,000 \times ¥117.6471.$ | | |

**Exhibit 9** Sale and Collection of $400,000 of Automobiles Recorded in Japanese Yen: Collection Date, January 10, 1999

## UNITED MOTORS

| Date | Explanation | Debit (Dollars) | Credit (Dollars) |
|---|---|---|---|
| 1998 Dec. 1 | Accounts Receivable<br>    Sales<br>¥57,142,880 × .0070. | 400,000 | 400,000 |
| 31 | Accounts Receivable<br>    Exchange Gain<br>¥57,142,880 × (.0075 − .0080). | 28,571 | 28,571 |
| 1999 Jan. 10 | Cash<br>    Exchange Gain<br>    Accounts Receivable<br>¥57,142,880 × .0085. | 485,714 | 57,143<br>428,571 |

## SANSON IMPORTS

| Date | Explanation | Debit (Yen) | Credit (Yen) |
|---|---|---|---|
| 1998 Dec. 1 | Purchases<br>    Accounts Payable | 57,142,880 | 57,142,880 |
| 31 | No entry | | |
| 1999 Jan. 10 | Accounts Payable<br>    Cash | 57,142,880 | 57,142,880 |

## SUMMARY

- **Generally accepted accounting principles** are the ground rules of accounting. They ensure a consistent system of financial reporting that provides users with information that is reliable, understandable, and comparable.
- **Authoritative support** for GAAP comes from two main sources: CPAs, who must follow professional pronouncements; and the SEC, which has the legal authority to enforce compliance.
- Generally accepted accounting principles have substantial authoritative support, consisting of:

  - FASB *Standards* and APB *Opinions*
  - FASB and FASB Interpretations
  - Industry audit guides
  - Industry accounting practices
  - APB *Statements*
  - AICPA Statements of Position
  - Pronouncements of the SEC
  - Accounting textbooks and articles

- The objectives of financial statements are to provide information that:

  - Is useful to present and potential investors and creditors
  - Is useful in assessing net cash flows
  - Reveals the economic resources (assets); the claims on those resources (liabilities and owner's equity); and the effects of transactions, events, and circumstances that change resources and claims on those resources

- The FASB has identified nine qualitative characteristics of accounting information:

  - **Usefulness**
  - **Reliability**
  - **Neutrality**
  - **Understandability**
  - **Timeliness**
  - **Comparability**
  - **Relevance**
  - **Verifiability**
  - **Completeness**

- The conventions, concepts, standards, rules, principles, and procedures of generally accepted accounting principles can be organized into three basic areas:

  - Assumptions
  - Principles
  - Modifiers

- GAAP rest on four basic assumptions:

  - The **business entity concept**
  - The **accounting period concept**
  - The **going concern concept**
  - the **stable dollar concept**

- The six principles that form the framework for the practice of accounting are:

  - The **cost principle**
  - The **matching principle**
  - The **revenue-recognition principle**
  - The **expense-recognition principle**
  - The **full disclosure principle**
  - The **consistency principle**

- Practical considerations give rise to the three basic modifiers:

  - **Materiality**
  - **Conservatism**
  - **Industry practices**

- International accounting poses three major accounting problems:

  - Most international transactions involve a foreign currency whose value must be translated into the currency of the home country.
  - **Multinational corporations** must prepare consolidated financial statements reflecting the different currencies used by the countries in which it has foreign subsidiaries.
  - Each country in which a multinational company does business has its own financial accounting standards.

- International transactions can be billed in the currency of the domestic or foreign country. Depending on how the transaction is billed, one of the parties to the transaction will be at risk for changes in the relative value of the two countries' currencies.

When settlement of the transaction is made, a **realized exchange gain** or **loss** must be recorded by the country at risk.

- If transactions between two international companies are not complete at year-end, the company at risk must record an **unrealized exchange gain** or **loss.**

## 11 KEY TERMS

| | |
|---|---|
| **Accounting period concept** | The assumption that it is necessary to measure accounting income for periods of time less than the life of a company and that the measurements will not be precise but will be timely and therefore useful. |
| **Authoritative support** | The pronouncements of the Financial Accounting Standards Board, the Securities and Exchange Commission, and other accounting bodies that follow a due-process procedure in establishing accounting principles. |
| **Business entity concept** | The concept that considers a business entity for accounting purposes to be separate and distinct from its owners. |
| **Comparability** | The characteristic of accounting that usefulness is enhanced if accounting information can be compared with similar information for the same company through time, and similar information among companies at the same time. |
| **Completeness** | The accounting characteristic implying that nothing material is left out that would be vital to investors or creditors in assessing the underlying events and conditions of the business. |
| **Conservative modifier** | The modifier used to select the alternative least likely to overstate net assets and net income. |
| **Consistency principle** | The accounting principle that requires the same accounting method to be applied to accounting events from period to period. |
| **Cost principle** | The principle that assets must be recorded at their historical costs (their exchange prices on the day of acquisition) so that their values can be verified through comparison with the source documents. |
| **Expense-recognition principle** | The principle that determines the point in time when a cost becomes an expense. |
| **Full disclosure principle** | The accounting principle that investors and creditors have every right to expect that the financial statements they are using contain all the significant economic and financial information that is relevant to their understanding of the entity's financial status. |
| **Foreign exchange rate** | The value of a foreign currency in terms of U.S. currency. |
| **Generally accepted accounting principles (GAAP)** | A technical term referring to the conventions, concepts, standards, rules, principles, and procedures that define accepted accounting at a particular time. |
| **Going concern concept** | The concept that allows accountants to assume that a business entity will continue in existence for a long time. |
| **Industry practices modifier** | The modifier of GAAP that allows accountants to use the conventions, concepts, standards, rules, principles, and procedures that are applicable only to a certain industry. |
| **Installment sales method** | Recognizing revenue as cash payments on installment sales are received. |
| **Matching principle** | The principle requiring that expenses incurred in a particular time period be compared—matched—with the revenue earned during the same time period. |

| | |
|---|---|
| **Materiality modifier** | The modifier used to determine whether or not accountants think the item in question will affect decisions of users of the financial statements. If it will, then it's material and must be reported in accordance with generally accepted accounting principles. |
| **Multinational corporations** | Companies that conduct business in many different countries. |
| **Neutrality** | The accounting characteristic that accounting information should be free from bias. |
| **Percentage-of-completion method** | Recognizing revenue as a percent of completion corresponding to the percentage of total expenses/costs incurred. |
| **Point-of-sale method** | Recognizing revenue at the time a sale is made or services are rendered. |
| **Production method** | Recognizing revenue when production is completed even when the sale hasn't been made. |
| **Realized exchange gains and losses** | Gains or losses resulting from fluctuations in exchange rates for transactions completed within the accounting year. |
| **Relevance** | The accounting characteristic that requires information to have a bearing on a decision to be made—it must make a difference in that decision. |
| **Reliability** | The accounting characteristic that accounting information is free from errors. |
| **Revenue-recognition principle** | The accounting principle which states that revenue should be recognized when both of the following conditions are met: (1) The earning process is essentially complete; and (2) an exchange has taken place. |
| **Stable dollar concept** | The accounting concept that assumes the monetary unit of measure does not change in value over time, even if in fact it does. |
| **Timeliness** | The accounting characteristic that accounting information must be available to users before it loses its capacity to influence decisions. |
| **Understandability** | The accounting characteristic that requires accounting information to be presented in a manner that investors and creditors understand. |
| **Unrealized exchange gains and losses** | Gains or losses resulting from fluctuations in exchange rates for transactions that have not been completed at the end of the accounting year and require adjusting entries to recognize the gains or losses. |
| **Usefulness** | The accounting characteristic that (1) accounting information must be useful to most of the people who want to use it, and (2) preparing that useful information will not be a burdensome (costly, time-consuming, complex) task for those who have to prepare it. |
| **Verifiability** | The accounting characteristic that the underlying documents used to develop accounting information should be capable of being reviewed. |

## QUESTIONS FOR REVIEW AND FURTHER THOUGHT

### REVIEW QUESTIONS

1. Why do we need generally accepted accounting principles?

2. How are generally accepted accounting principles enforced?

3. What does "accounting principles" in the term *generally accepted accounting principles* mean?

4. What are the basic objectives of financial statements?

5. What are the nine qualitative characteristics of accounting information?

6. The most important characteristic of accounting information is usefulness. How do the other characteristics relate to usefulness?

7. How are generally accepted accounting principles organized into a structure?

8. How does the stable dollar concept prohibit companies from providing investors and creditors with important relevant information?

9. The matching principle requires that revenue earned in a particular time period be compared with those expenses incurred during the same time period that were directly or indirectly responsible for generating the revenue. Specifically, how are expenses recognized?

10. What does the full disclosure principle mean to investors and creditors?

11. Sometimes practical considerations cause the basic principles to be modified. Is this statement true? Explain.

12. What are the three major types of problems involved in accounting for multinational companies?

13. If a U.S. company sells goods to a Japanese company and the number of yen needed to buy dollars increases between the date of sale and the date of payment, what effect will this have on the U.S. company?

14. What is the difference between realized and unrealized exchange gains and losses?

### QUESTIONS FOR FURTHER THOUGHT

1. "General-purpose financial statements are prepared in such a way that the general public should be able to understand them." Is this statement true? Explain.

2. The Buick is a popular domestic automobile, and its manufacture is financed by numerous investors and creditors. But these investors and creditors never see Buick's balance sheet and income statement? Why not?

3. Do financial statements precisely measure revenue, expenses, assets, and liabilities? Explain.

4. Certain accounting principles rest on the basic assumptions of accounting. How does the cost principle rest on the going concern concept?

5. Revenue is recognized when the earning process is essentially complete and an exchange has taken place. Generally, this is at the point of sale, but there are three exceptions to this general rule. What are these other methods of recognizing revenues, and when is each used?

6. Atlas Company adopted the FIFO method of inventory costing in 1954 when it first started business. The company wishes to switch to the LIFO method this year. Would this switch violate the consistency principle? Explain.

## OBJECTIVE ASSIGNMENT

*True/False*  Indicate whether each statement below is *true* or *false* by placing a *T* or an *F* in the space provided.

_____ 1. Generally accepted accounting principles assure that similar economic events will be reported in the same manner by everyone.

_____ 2. The authority of GAAP rests on the pronouncements of the Internal Revenue Service.

_____ 3. The most important qualitative characteristic of accounting information is reliability.

_____ 4. Consolidated financial statements are a good illustration of the business entity concept.

_____ 5. When an international sale is billed in foreign currency, the foreign company is at risk of losing money.

*Multiple Choice*  Select the best choice to complete each statement or answer each question below. Write the letter corresponding to your choice in the space provided.

_____ 1. The first objective of a financial statement is to:
   a. Measure net income
   b. Provide useful information
   c. Report a corporation's financial position
   d. All of the above
   e. None of the above

_____ 2. The following is *not* a qualitative characteristic of accounting information:
   a. Consistency
   b. Comparability
   c. Completeness
   d. Verifiability
   e. None of the above

_____ 3. Accounting information that is free from bias reflects the qualitative characteristic of:
   a. Equality
   b. Neutrality
   c. Freedom
   d. Verifiability
   e. None of the above

_____ 4. At year-end 1995, the Big Corporation presents five sets of financial statements to its stockholders—one set for itself and one for each of its four subsidiaries. This is a violation of:
   a. The going concern concept
   b. The comparability concept
   c. The consistency concept
   d. The business entity concept
   e. None of the above

_____ 5. When financial statements are prepared, it is assumed that the user group:
   a. Are all college graduates
   b. Do not have a financial background
   c. Will take the time and effort to study the financial statements
   d. Are financial analysts
   e. None of the above

_____ 6. The most important qualitative characteristic of accounting information is:
   a. Understandability
   b. Relevance

   c. Usefulness
   d. Reliability
   e. None of the above

_____ 7. Revenue can be recognized:
   a. When a sale is made
   b. When production is complete
   c. When cash is received
   d. All of the above
   e. None of the above

_____ 8. An accounting problem exists for multinational companies because:
   a. Most international transactions involve a foreign currency.
   b. Consolidated statements involving subsidiaries using different currencies must be prepared.
   c. Foreign subsidiaries must use the accounting procedures of the country in which they are incorporated.
   d. All of the above.
   e. None of the above.

_____ 9. The Alpha Company of the United States acquired D300,000 ($2,000) of merchandise from the Beta Company of Donkaland on Dec. 1, 1998. The account is paid in donkas on Dec. 10, when the exchange rate is $.008/donka. Consequently:
   a. Alpha will record an exchange gain of $400.
   b. Beta will record an exchange loss of D7,500.
   c. Alpha will record an exchange loss of $400.
   d. Beta will record an exchange gain of D7,500.
   e. None of the above.

_____ 10. The Alpha Company of the United States sold $2,000 (D300,000) of merchandise to the Beta Company of Donkaland on Dec. 1, 1998. The account is paid in dollars on Dec. 10, when the exchange rate is D125/dollar. Consequently:
   a. Alpha will record an exchange gain of $500.
   b. Beta will record an exchange loss of D50,000.
   c. Alpha will record an exchange loss of $500.
   d. Beta will record an exchange gain of D50,000.
   e. None of the above.

## EXERCISES

4† **Exercise 1:** Identifying Qualitative Characteristics

The nine qualitative characteristics of accounting information are as follows:

| | | |
|---|---|---|
| Comparability | Relevance | Understandability |
| Completeness | Reliability | Usefulness |
| Neutrality | Timeliness | Verifiability |

Identify the qualitative characteristics that each of the following five situations violates.

a. The accounting year for Aston Enterprises ends on Dec. 31, 1998. The financial statements are issued on Oct. 14, 1999.

b. The Bartle Corporation switched its method of accounting for inventory from the LIFO to the FIFO method.

c. The president of Charlton Company donated certain equipment to the company. The president insists that the value of the equipment be recorded on the balance sheet at $45,000.

d. The financial statements of the Dalton Company are all expressed in 1962 dollars in order to achieve comparability.

e. The Ellenton Corporation financial statements issued for the year ended Dec. 31, 1998, consist of a balance sheet and an income statement.

5 **Exercise 2:** Identifying Basic Assumption Violations

The four basic assumptions of accounting are:

| | |
|---|---|
| The business entity concept | The going concern concept |
| The accounting period concept | The stable dollar concept |

Identify the assumption that each of the following four situations violates.

a. In order to achieve comparability, Florida Electronics Corporation issues financial statements whenever gross sales equals $20,000,000.

b. At the end of each business day, Gaston, Inc., records in its accounts the total dollar amount of the transactions of its stock listed on the New York Stock Exchange.

c. The Halifax Company, in an attempt to be conservative, expenses all property, plant, and equipment items.

d. Information Systems Corporation adjusts all its accounts on the financial statements using the current consumer price index.

6 **Exercise 3:** Identifying Basic Principle Violations

The six basic principles of accounting are:

The cost principle
The matching principle
The revenue-recognition principle
The expense-recognition principle
The full disclosure principle
The consistency principle

Identify the principle(s) that each of the following five situations violates.

a. Jacksonville Company records depreciation only when operations are profitable.

b. Kate Company records revenue from the salespersons' daily estimates of potential customers for its product.

c. Lumpton, Inc., recently increased the value of its land by 50% to reflect market value.

d. Molton Company does not provide its stockholders with any footnotes to the financial statements, because they are too difficult to understand.

e. Depreciation at the Nixon Company is recorded in odd years using the straight-line method, but in even years the sum-of-the-years'-digits method is used.

† The numbers in the margin refer to the Learning Objectives.

**7** **Exercise 4:** Identifying Basic Modifiers

The three basic modifiers of accounting are:

Materiality
Conservatism
Industry practices

Identify the modifier involved in each of the following five situations.

a. In its plant accounts, Ocean Atlantic Power and Light Company records a value for interest equivalents on stock it issued to construct the plant.
b. Pacific Fabricating Company writes off all inventory items in stock if those items have a shelf life of more than 9 months.
c. Queenstown Semiconductors expenses all equipment items less than $750.
d. Ralston Railways records revenues on the cash basis.
e. Scranton Airways never reconciles the equipment control accounts with their respective subsidiary ledgers if the balances differ by less than $3,000.

**6** **Exercise 5:** Installment Sales Revenue Recognition

The Wilkins Company sold a parcel of land to the Malone Company for $60,000 on Jan. 1, 1998. The land had cost Wilkins $36,000 some years earlier. The terms of the sales agreement are that Malone will pay $5,000 on Jan. 1, 1998, and $7,000 on Dec. 31, 1998, followed by $16,000 payments on Dec. 31 of 1999, 2000, and 2001.

Prepare a table showing the amount of revenue that will be recognized by Wilkins in each of the years from 1998 to 2001; assume the installment sales method of revenue recognition.

**6** **Exercise 6:** Percentage-of-Completion Revenue Recognition

In early 1998 Rivers Construction Company agrees to construct a tunnel under the Delaware River at a contract price of $192 million. The cost of the project incurred each year is summarized as follows:

| | **1998** | **1999** | **2000** | **2001** | **Total** |
|---|---|---|---|---|---|
| Estimated costs (in millions) | $20 | $60 | $50 | $30 | $160 |

Prepare a table showing the amount of revenue that will be recognized by Rivers over the life of the contract; assume that the percentage-of-completion method is used.

▶ *(Check Figure: Gross profit, 2001 = $6 million)*

**9** **Exercise 7:** Calculating Exchange Gains and Losses

On Dec. 10, 1998, Shore Oil Company of the United States sold ¥50,000,000 of oil on account to Nippon Import Corporation of Japan. The payment for the oil was made on Jan. 10, 1999, in Japanese yen. Pertinent exchange rates are as follows:

| **Date** | **Dollar/Yen** |
|---|---|
| Dec. 10, 1998 | .0060 |
| Dec. 31, 1998 | .0050 |
| Jan. 10, 1999 | .0055 |

Record the transactions for the sale and receipt of the payment for the oil and the Dec. 31, 1995, adjusting entry for Shore Oil Company.

▶ *(Check Figure: Exchange gain on Jan. 10, 1999 = $25,000)*

9  **Exercise 8:** Calculating Exchange Gains and Losses

On Dec. 10, 1998, Shore Oil Company of the United States sold $300,000 of oil on account to Nippon Import Corporation of Japan. The payment for the oil was made on Jan. 10, 1999, in U.S. dollars. Pertinent exchange rates are as follows:

| Date | Yen/Dollar |
| --- | --- |
| Dec. 10, 1998 | 166.6667 |
| Dec. 31, 1998 | 200.0000 |
| Jan. 10, 1999 | 181.8182 |

Record the transactions for the purchase and payment of the oil and the Dec. 31, 1998, adjusting entry for Nippon Import Corporation.

▶ *(Check Figure: Exchange gain on Jan. 10, 1999 = ¥5,454,540)*

## PROBLEMS: SET A

4† **Problem A:** Identifying the Qualifying Characteristics
of Accounting Information

The FASB has identified nine qualitative characteristics of accounting information. These characteristics are listed below, followed by nine statements.

A. Comparability     D. Reliability     G. Understandability
B. Completeness     E. Relevance     H. Usefulness
C. Neutrality     F. Timeliness     I. Verifiability

_____ 1. Accounting information must be available to users before it loses its capacity to influence decisions.

_____ 2. Accounting information must leave out nothing material that would be vital to investors or creditors in assessing the underlying events and conditions of the business.

_____ 3. Accounting information must have a bearing on a decision to be made.

_____ 4. Accounting information must be presented in a manner that investors and creditors comprehend.

_____ 5. Accounting information must be free from bias.

_____ 6. The underlying documents of accounting information must be capable of being reviewed.

_____ 7. Accounting information must be helpful to most of the people who want to use that information.

_____ 8. Usefulness is enhanced if accounting information can be compared with similar information for the same company through time, and for different companies at the same time.

_____ 9. Accounting information must be free from errors.

**Required:**

In the space provided, place the letter of the qualitative characteristic that corresponds to the statement.

5 6 7 **Problem A2:** Identifying Accounting Assumptions, Principles, and Modifiers

Thirteen assumptions, principles, and modifiers have been identified and discussed in the chapter. These items are listed below, followed by thirteen statements.

A. Accounting period concept     H. Going concern concept
B. Business entity concept     I. Industry practices
C. Conservatism     J. Matching principle
D. Consistency principle     K. Materiality
E. Cost principle     L. Revenue-recognition principle
F. Expense-recognition principle     M. Stable dollar concept
G. Full disclosure principle

_____ 1. The concept that assumes the monetary unit of measure does not change in value over time

_____ 2. The modifier used to determine whether or not accountants think the item in question will affect decisions of users of the financial statements

_____ 3. The concept that considers a company separate and distinct from its owners

† The numbers in the margin refer to the Learning Objectives.

_____ 4. The principle that requires assets to be recorded at the exchange price on the day of acquisition and not to be revalued due to external factors

_____ 5. The principle that requires that expenses incurred in a particular time period be compared with the revenue earned during that same time period

_____ 6. The modifier that allows accountants to use procedures that are generally accepted within that group of businesses

_____ 7. The accounting principle that investors and creditors have every right to expect the financial statements they are using to contain all the significant economic and financial information that is relevant to their understanding of the entity's financial status

_____ 8. The concept that assumes it is necessary to measure accounting income for periods of time shorter than the life of a company

_____ 9. The modifier used to select the alternative that is least likely to overstate net assets and net income

_____ 10. The accounting principle that applies when the earning process is essentially complete and an exchange has taken place

_____ 11. The concept that allows accountants to assume a business entity will continue in existence for a long time

_____ 12. The accounting principle that the same accounting method will be applied to accounting events from period to period

_____ 13. The principle that determines the point in time at which a cost becomes an expense

**Required:**

In the space provided, place the appropriate letter of the assumption, principle, or modifier that matches the statement.

6  **Problem A3:** Determining Revenue Recognized Using the Installment Sales Method

The Willis Company reported installment sales for the years 1998, 1999, and 2000 in the amounts of $120,000, $150,000, and $200,000, respectively. The costs of the merchandise sold under installment sales contracts for those 3 years were $72,000, $97,500, and $136,000, respectively. Cash is collected for each year's sales as follows: 20% in the first year; 50% in the second year; and 30% in the third year.

**Required:**

1. Determine the gross profit percentage for each year.
2. Prepare a schedule that will reflect the gross profit earned by the Willis Company for each of the 3 years.

▶ *(Check Figure: Gross profit, 2000 = $53,450)*

6  **Problem A4:** Determining the Amount of Gross Profit Using the Percentage-of-Completion Method

The Webb Construction Company contracted with the State of Georgia to build a dam across the Chattahoochee River for $8,000,000. The project was begun in 1998 and completed in 2001. Data relating to the project is presented in the table below:

| | 1998 | 1999 | 2000 | 2001 |
|---|---|---|---|---|
| Construction costs incurred to date.................. | $ 720,000 | $1,984,000 | $4,225,000 | $6,700,000 |
| Estimated costs to complete .. | 5,280,000 | 4,216,000 | 2,275,000 | –0– |

**Required:**

Prepare a schedule that will reflect Webb's gross profit earned in each of the 4 years for the Chattahoochee River Dam.

▶ *(Check Figure: Gross profit, 1998 = $325,000)*

9  **Problem A5:** Calculating Exchange Gains and Losses

Wagner Sales Company of Germany sold $50,000 of industrial cleaning fluids on account to New York Iron Works of the United States on June 15, 1998. Payment was received on July 20, 1998, in U.S. dollars. Pertinent exchange rates are as follows:

| Date | Mark/Dollar |
|---|---|
| June 15, 1998 | 1.7000 |
| June 30, 1998 | 1.8500 |
| July 20, 1998 | 2.0000 |

**Required:**

Record the transactions for the sale and receipt of the payment for cleaning fluids and the June 30, 1998, adjusting entry for Wagner Sales Company.

▶ *(Check Figure: Exchange gain July 20, 1998 = DM7,500)*

9  **Problem A6:** Calculating Exchange Gains and Losses

Hans Guber Company of Germany sold DM85,000 of materials on account to Adler Mfg. Company of the United States on June 15, 1998. Payment was received on July 20, 1998, in U.S. dollars. Exchange rates for June 15, June 30, and July 20, 1998, are as follows:

| Date | Dollar/Mark |
|---|---|
| June 15, 1998 | 0.5882 |
| June 30, 1998 | 0.5405 |
| July 20, 1998 | 0.5000 |

**Required:**

Record the transactions for the purchase of and payment for cleaning fluids and the June 30, 1995, adjusting entry for Adler Mfg. Company.

▶ *(Check Figure: Exchange gain July 20, 1998 = $3,445)*

## PROBLEMS: SET B

4† **Problem B1:** Identifying the Qualifying Characteristics
of Accounting Information

The FASB has identified nine qualitative characteristics of accounting information. These characteristics are listed below, followed by nine statements.

A. Usefulness          D. Reliability          G. Neutrality
B. Understandability    E. Timeliness           H. Comparability
C. Relevance            F. Verifiability         I. Completeness

_____ 1. Accounting information must be available to users before it loses its capacity to influence decisions.

_____ 2. Accounting information must leave out nothing material that would be vital to investors or creditors in assessing the underlying events and conditions of the business.

_____ 3. Accounting information must have a bearing on a decision to be made.

_____ 4. Accounting information must be presented in a manner that investors and creditors comprehend.

_____ 5. Accounting information must be free from bias.

_____ 6. The underlying documents of accounting information must be capable of being reviewed.

_____ 7. Accounting information must be helpful to most of the people who want to use that information.

_____ 8. Usefulness is enhanced if accounting information can be compared with similar information for the same company through time, and for different companies at the same time.

_____ 9. Accounting information must be free from errors.

**Required:**

In the space provided, place the letter of the qualitative characteristic that corresponds to the statement.

5 6 7 **Problem B2:** Identifying Accounting Assumptions, Principles, and Modifiers

Thirteen assumptions, principles, and modifiers have been identified and discussed in the chapter. These items are listed on the next page, followed by thirteen statements.

A. Business entity concept          H. Expense-recognition principle
B. Accounting period concept        I. Full disclosure principle
C. Going concern concept            J. Consistency principle
D. Stable dollar concept            K. Materiality
E. Cost principle                   L. Conservatism
F. Matching Principle               M. Industry practices
G. Revenue-recognition principle

_____ 1. The concept that assumes the monetary unit of measure does not change in value over time

_____ 2. The modifier used to determine whether or not accountants think the item in question will affect decisions of users of the financial statements

_____ 3. The concept that considers a company separate and distinct from its owners

† The numbers in the margin refer to the Learning Objectives.

_____ 4. The principle that requires assets to be recorded at the exchange price on the day of acquisition and not to be revalued due to external factors

_____ 5. The principle that requires that expenses incurred in a particular time period be compared with the revenue earned during that same time period

_____ 6. The modifier that allows accountants to use procedures that are generally accepted within that group of businesses

_____ 7. The accounting principle that investors and creditors have every right to expect the financial statements they are using to contain all the significant economic and financial information that is relevant to their understanding of the entity's financial status

_____ 8. The concept that assumes it is necessary to measure accounting income for periods of time shorter than the life of a company

_____ 9. The modifier used to select the alternative that is least likely to overstate net assets and net income

_____ 10. The accounting principle that applies when the earning process is essentially complete and an exchange has taken place

_____ 11. The concept that allows accountants to assume a business entity will continue in existence for a long time

_____ 12. The accounting principle that the same accounting method will be applied to accounting events from period to period

_____ 13. The principle that determines the point in time at which a cost becomes an expense

**Required:**

In the space provided, place the letter of the assumption, principle, or modifier that corresponds to the statement.

6  **Problem B3:** Determining Revenue Recognized Using the Installment Sales Method

In addition to its regular sales, the Battle Company reported installment sales for the years 1998, 1999, and 2000 in the amounts of $220,000, $275,000, and $310,000, respectively. The costs of goods sold associated with these installment sales amounted to $154,000 in 1998, $198,000 in 1999, and $248,000 in 2000. Cash is collected for each year's sales as follows: 30% in the first year; 60% in the second year; and 10% in the third year.

**Required:**

1. Determine the gross profit percentage for each year.
2. Prepare a schedule that will reflect the gross profit earned by the Battle Company for each of the 3 years.

▶ *(Check Figure: Gross profit earned, 2000 = $71,400)*

6  **Problem B4:** Determining the Amount of Gross Profit Using the Percentage-of-Completion Method

In early 1995, the Long Construction Company contracted with the State of Georgia to build an addition to the Atlanta airport for $5,000,000. The project was begun in 1998 and completed in 1998. Data relating to the project are as follows:

|  | 1998 | 1999 | 2000 | 2001 |
|---|---|---|---|---|
| Construction costs incurred to date............... | $ 400,000 | $1,470,000 | $3,680,000 | $4,700,000 |
| Estimated costs to complete .. | 3,600,000 | 2,730,000 | 920,000 | –0– |

**Required:**

Prepare a schedule that will reflect Long's gross profit earned in each of the 4 years for the Atlanta airport addition.

▶ *(Check Figure: Gross profit, 2000 = $40,000)*

9   **Problem B5:** Calculating Exchange Gains and Losses

Muchen Motor Works of Germany sold $300,000 of automobiles on account to MMW Dealership of the United States on Dec. 15, 1998. Payment was received on Jan. 20, 1999, in U.S. dollars. Pertinent exchange rates are as follows:

| Date | Mark/Dollar |
|------|-------------|
| Dec. 15, 1998 | 1.6000 |
| Dec. 31, 1998 | 1.7500 |
| Jan. 20, 1999 | 1.9500 |

**Required:**

Record the transactions for the sale and receipt of the payment for automobiles and the Dec. 31, 1998, adjusting entry for Muchen Motor Works.

▶ *(Check Figure: Exchange gain, Jan. 20, 1999 = DM60,000)*

9   **Problem B6:** Calculating Exchange Gains and Losses

Muchen Motor Works of Germany sold DM480,000 of automobiles on account to MMW Dealership of the United States on Dec. 15, 1998. Payment was received on Jan. 20, 1999, in U.S. dollars. Exchange rates on Dec. 15, 1998, Dec. 31, 1998, and Jan. 20, 1999, were as follows:

| Date | Dollar/Mark |
|------|-------------|
| Dec. 15, 1998 | 0.6250 |
| Dec. 31, 1998 | 0.5714 |
| Jan. 20, 1999 | 0.5263 |

**Required:**

Record the transactions for the purchase and payment of automobiles and the Dec. 31, 1998, adjusting entry for MMW Dealership.

▶ *(Check Figure: Exchange gain, Jan. 20, 1999 = $21,648)*

## ETHICS CASE

You are the comptroller of the Bender Company. It has just been reported to you that a salesperson of the company's Kattoo Division has an opportunity to gain access to Prince Alphonse, the director of procurement for the government of Kattoo. If an audience with Prince Alphonse can be obtained, Bender may win a contract worth $800 million. If the contract is granted, a plant will be built in Kattoo and 1,750 local people will be employed. Kattoo is a very poor nation with a high unemployment rate. You are aware that the Fontenet Society, a large French company, is also interested in the contract.

The new plant in Kattoo would mean the creation of 500 jobs in Bender's Tulsa, Oklahoma, plant. Tulsa has a large unemployment problem.

In order to be received by Prince Alphonse, the salesperson must pay $6,300 to the prince's appointment secretary. This is a normal business practice in Kattoo. The salesperson is requesting an advance of $6,300 for the payment.

### Required:

Should you authorize the payment? What are the issues in this case?

## OBJECTIVE ASSIGNMENT ANSWERS

### True/False

1. T    2. F    3. F    4. T    5. F

### Multiple Choice

1. b    2. a    3. b    4. d    5. c
6. c    7. d    8. d    9. c    10. d

# Partnerships

Although the accounting for assets and liabilities is basically the same for all types of business entities, in this chapter we will study the partnership.

1  **PARTNERSHIP CHARACTERISTICS**

If three members of your class decide to form a group to help elderly citizens with their tax returns, then that's a partnership. It's a partnership because the Uniform Partnership Act—which more than 90% of the states have adopted—says it is. The act defines a **partnership** as "an association of two or more persons to carry on, as co-owners, a business for profit."

Since nearly 10% of all businesses are partnerships, you've most likely dealt with one at some time, even though you might not have realized it. If your doctor or dentist does not work alone (as a proprietorship), then he or she probably conducts business in partnership with one or more other doctors or dentists. The partnership form of business is common to the professions; many public accounting and law firms, as well as medical and dental practices, operate as partnerships. So do many small manufacturing, assembling, wholesale, retail, and service companies.

People join together as a partnership for a number of reasons. Some people have more organizational and managerial skill than others; while others have more knowledge and experience and still others have more money to invest. A partnership utilizes the combined abilities, experiences, and capital of the partners to make the business much stronger than it would be if only one individual owned it.

A partnership is like a proprietorship in that, although it is a separate *accounting* entity, it is not considered to be a separate *legal* entity. The partners are the individual legal entities. And the characteristics of partnerships all relate to this fact.

## Ease of Formation

The fact that you and one or more other people can create a partnership by agreeing to start a business with the object of earning a profit means that you don't need permission from the county commissioners, the IRS, the SEC, the state attorney general, or anyone else. In fact, you don't even need a written contract between the partners. An oral agreement is sufficient.

## Voluntary Association

A partnership is a voluntary alliance of individuals, each of whom has the right to select the people with whom he or she associates. As a partner, you are legally responsible for the acts of all the other partners, and that legal responsibility extends beyond the funds you have invested in the partnership to your personal assets. Therefore it wouldn't be reasonable or fair to force you into a partnership with people you don't like or trust. Forming a partnership is a voluntary decision that you and each other partner must make.

## Articles of Partnership

Even though an oral agreement is all that is needed to form a partnership, it is common—and wise—to formalize a partnership relationship with a written agreement, called the **articles of partnership** (or **partnership agreement**). Some of the typical elements of this document are as follows:

- The name, location, and purpose of the partnership
- The duties of each partner
- The manner in which each partner shares profits and losses

- The amount each partner is to invest
- How new partners are to be admitted
- How partners are to be allowed to withdraw
- The procedures for ending the partnership (through dissolution or liquidation) if the need arises

## Mutual Agency

If you do business with a partnership, you have the right to assume that the partner you are talking to has the authority to bind the partnership to any legal business transaction that is part of the normal operations of the partnership's business. This is because all partners within a partnership are agents for the partnership. Because of this **mutual agency** characteristic, the city of Bethlehem, Pennsylvania, can enter into an agreement with Mr. Garcia of Weinstein, Garcia, and Trovanivich, for an audit of the city's general fund, knowing that Mr. Garcia has the full authority to bind the CPA firm to a contract for accounting services. But if the city signs an agreement with Mr. Garcia for the sale of sewer pipes to the city, it should be obvious that Mr. Garcia is acting on his own and does not legally represent the accounting firm. The city should not expect this contract to be binding on the CPA firm, because selling sewer pipe is not within the normal scope of an accounting firm's business.

As you can see, it is very important to select your partners carefully. Mutual agency, coupled with unlimited liability (see the discussion below), could cause you a good deal of grief and large financial losses if you select an irresponsible or unethical partner.

## Unlimited Liability

Suppose things don't go well for your partnership and you can't pay your bills. What then? Well, your creditors can look to the partnership assets for the settlement of their claims. And if the partnership assets aren't enough, creditors can lay claim to the personal assets of you and your partners. This is the **unlimited liability** characteristic of a partnership. When all partners have unlimited liability, meaning that all partners are equally liable to the creditors for the debts incurred by the partnership, the partnership is referred to as a **general partnership.** We will assume throughout this chapter that the partnership is a general partnership.

There is another type of partnership, called a **limited partnership,** in which one or more partners have unlimited liability, while the liability of the remaining partners is limited to their investment in the partnership. Within a limited partnership, the partners who risk not only their investment in the partnership but also their personal assets are the **general partners.** Those partners who risk only their investment in the partnership are **limited partners.**

Why, you may ask, would some partners be willing to accept unlimited risks, but allow other partners to risk no more than their investment in the partnership? Offering a limited partnership may be the only way to attract new capital from potential investors, who may be unwilling to risk all their personal possessions.

Until recently, many states required members of the professions (doctors, accountants, and the like) to use the partnership form of organization, and did not allow them to operate as corporations. Since the liability of corporate owners is limited to the money they have invested in the corporation, so that their personal assets are not subject to attack by lawsuits, it was felt that the corporate form might be used to gain protection against lawsuits for poor-quality work. Many states have recently enacted legislation allowing professional organizations to become corporations. Even so, the largest of the partnerships, the international certified public accounting firms (most of which have in excess of 1,500 partners) have not elected to become corporations.

### Limited Life

The life of a partnership is limited. A partnership dissolves when a new partner is admitted or when one of the partners withdraws, dies, is forced into personal bankruptcy, or becomes incapacitated. A partnership is also dissolved when the specific objective for which the partnership was formed is achieved. If the articles of partnership specify the life of the partnership to be for a certain period, then when the time has expired the partnership is dissolved.

The **dissolution of a partnership** does not necessarily mean that its business operations are halted or even interrupted. Large partnerships, such as regional and national CPA firms and certain law firms, specify in the partnership agreement how the admission of new partners and the retirement of old partners are to be handled without interruption of the conduct of business.

### Co-ownership of Property

When a partnership is formed, some partners may invest cash, some may invest office equipment or other assets, some may simply invest their talents. But whatever assets are invested become the property of all the partners. The partner contributing an asset no longer retains any personal right to it. If the partnership is terminated, the individual partners may not receive back the same assets they contributed. Of course, if it is agreeable to all the partners, the assets may be given back to those who contributed them. But partners usually settle their claims against the partnership by the distribution of cash.

### Income Participation

All partners have the right to share in the income of the partnership. How they share this income is usually arranged by mutual consent and is specified in the articles of partnership. If an agreement is not specified in written or oral form, then profits and losses are shared equally.

Learning Objective

## 2 ADVANTAGES AND DISADVANTAGES OF THE PARTNERSHIP FORM

Evaluate the advantages and disadvantages of the partnership form of organization

The partnership form of organization offers certain advantages over the proprietorship and the corporation. It also has a number of disadvantages. We will discuss each briefly in turn.

### Advantages

#### Capitalization

The amount of money invested by the owners of the business is called its *capitalization*. The more owners, the more capital. This is one of the main reasons to have a partner (rather than being a single proprietor) — for his or her money, to help finance business activities.

#### Talent

The more partners you have, the more talent you have available. Each partner can specialize in the aspect of the business that can best use his or her talents.

#### Ease of Formation

It is easy to form a partnership. You and the other partners just say you are a partnership, and you are. That is not the case if you want to operate as a corporation.

### Cost of Organization

The only cost of becoming a partnership is the legal fees to have the articles of partnership drawn up. If the partners choose not to do this, then there are no costs at all. By contrast, becoming a corporation requires cash outlays for the application to the state in which you wish to be incorporated plus legal fees to file the application and to prepare the corporate charter and by-laws.

### Tax Advantages

A partnership, like a proprietorship, is not a legal entity, which means it doesn't have to pay income taxes (although each partner pays income taxes on personal income, including his or her share of the partnership income). Corporations, however, must pay an income tax based on the amount of income it has earned. Then, when the income is distributed to the corporation's owners (that is, the stockholders) in the form of dividends, owners must pay a second tax on the dividend income received, based on the amount of their personal income.

### Informality

Corporations require formal legal procedures to do many of the things that you can do as a partnership without such rigidity. For example, in a corporation, the distribution of income requires a board of directors' meeting to declare a dividend before payment can be made to the stockholders. In a partnership, partners may withdraw funds without such legal action.

### Less Government Supervision

Generally, partnerships receive less government supervision than corporations.

## Disadvantages

### Loss of Freedom

You can't run a partnership as you would a proprietorship. As a sole owner of a business, you answer to no one. But with a partnership, you must answer to your partners, and they to you. You have mutual agency and unlimited liability. Mutual agreement on the affairs of the partnership is necessary.

### Limited Life

If one partner dies or withdraws, a new partner is admitted, or the specified life of a partnership expires, the partnership is dissolved. This does not necessarily mean that the business is over, however. Partners usually provide for this situation in the articles of partnership.

### Unlimited Liability

Because partnerships are not legal entities, each partner is legally responsible for the other partners' actions. As you know, once the partnership assets are used to settle creditors' claims, the personal assets of the partners may be required to settle any unsettled creditors' claims. In contrast, corporations are legal entities and as a result are responsible for their actions, but only to the extent of their capitalization; the personal assets of a corporation's stockholders are never in jeopardy.

### Mutual Agency

As we've seen, mutual agency means that any partner can bind the partnership to any business contract he or she enters into that is within the apparent scope of the partnership's business activities. Thus, one partner's bad judgment can cost all the other partners large losses, even to the extent of the partners' personal assets, even if the partner was not authorized by the other partners to make the agreement.

### Capitalization

If you need large sums of money to operate the business, the partnership may not be the best form of organization. Instead, the corporate form of organization is a much better vehicle for raising what you need. That's because you can sell shares of stock to a large number of people who are interested in a good investment for their money but who don't want to become involved in the operations of the business.

**ASK YOURSELF ▶**

1. **What is a partnership? What are the characteristics of all partnerships?**
2. **What advantages does the partnership have over the proprietorship and the corporation? What are its disadvantages?**

## PARTNERSHIP ACCOUNTING

Accounting for business transactions with external parties is the same for partnerships as it is for proprietorships. Assets, liabilities, revenues, and expenses are all recorded according to the generally accepted accounting principles. It is the owners' equity section that differs.

Whereas proprietorships use a single capital account and a single withdrawals account, partnership accounting requires that we establish a separate capital and a separate withdrawals account for each partner. The manner in which we divide the net income or loss among the partners is unique for partnerships and differentiates a partnership from a corporation.

Learning Objective 3

### Partnership Formation

Explain how to account for the formation of a partnership

When a partnership is formed, a journal entry[1] is made to record the assets contributed by each partner and the liabilities of each partner that are assumed by the partnership. If only cash is contributed and no liabilities are assumed, valuation is simple. The entry to record the formation of the partnership in this situation is simply to debit Cash and credit the two partners' capital accounts, like this:

| | | |
|---|---|---|
| Cash . . . . . . . . . . . . . . . . . . . . . . . . . . . . . . . . . . . . . . . . . . . . . . . . . . | 25,000 | |
| Jones, Capital . . . . . . . . . . . . . . . . . . . . . . . . . . . . . . . . . . . . | | 10,000 |
| Smith, Capital . . . . . . . . . . . . . . . . . . . . . . . . . . . . . . . . . . . . | | 15,000 |
| To record cash investment by Smith and Jones. | | |

But if other assets are contributed in addition to cash, we have a valuation problem. At what value should we record the noncash assets? The original cost? The book value of the assets on the individual partners' books? The fair value today? Some other value?

Generally accepted accounting principles require that noncash assets contributed by individual partners be valued at their fair value on the date they are transferred

---

[1] All our journal entries in the examples are in general journal form, even though the entry may actually be made in a special journal. This will make illustrations much easier because we won't have to construct special journals each time we make an entry.

to the partnership. What constitutes fair value is subject to the mutual agreement of the partners.

Let's look at the firm of Abbott and Kingery to see how we would account for the formation of a new partnership when cash and other assets are contributed.

# ABBOTT AND KINGERY

On July 1 of the current year, Debbie Abbott and Mark Kingery agree to combine their competing sporting goods stores and form a partnership. The partners are to contribute the assets of their previous stores. It is agreed that the liabilities of the proprietorships will be assumed by the partnership. A capital account is established for each partner, with a credit balance equal to the total assets less the total liabilities contributed by that partner. These are the journal entries to open the accounts of the partnership:

| | | | |
|---|---|---:|---:|
| July 1 | Cash............................................. | 3,500 | |
| | Accounts Receivable............................. | 6,200 | |
| | Merchandise Inventory ........................... | 12,700 | |
| | Store Supplies on Hand .......................... | 900 | |
| |     Accounts Payable............................. | | 2,400 |
| |     Abbott, Capital .............................. | | 20,900 |
| | To record the investment of Abbott. | | |
| | | | |
| 1 | Cash............................................. | 1,700 | |
| | Accounts Receivable............................. | 7,300 | |
| | Merchandise Inventory ........................... | 9,100 | |
| | Store Equipment ................................. | 6,500 | |
| | Building ......................................... | 65,200 | |
| | Land............................................. | 10,000 | |
| |     Accounts Payable............................. | | 4,500 |
| |     Mortgage Payable ........................... | | 26,200 |
| |     Kingery, Capital ............................. | | 69,100 |
| | To record the investment of Kingery. | | |

The assets, other than cash, are valued at the amounts that Debbie and Mark agree upon. The amounts represent the fair value as of July 1 of the store supplies, inventories, equipment, building, and land. The Accounts Receivable balance represents the face amount of only those receivables from the partnership that can reasonably be expected to be collected. Accounts that have only a small chance of collectibility are not transferred to the partnership.

The values of the assets other than cash normally do not agree with the amounts recorded in the books of the two proprietorships. That's because the values have increased (or decreased) since they were first acquired by Debbie and Mark. That's what happened with the land Mark contributed. He paid $8,000 for it 5 years ago. And the building cost him $47,000 to build, shortly after he purchased the land. Those were the values recorded on the books of Mark Kingery's Sporting Goods Store. The building also had $34,200 of accumulated depreciation recorded, but its fair value today is $65,200. The $65,200 is the amount the partnership would have to pay to buy the building if it were not being contributed by an organizing partner. The $65,200 is the amount recorded on the partnership books (without any related accumulated depreciation account) — not the original cost of $47,000, nor the book value of $12,800 ($47,000 − $34,200). Since the building has increased in value over the last 5 years, and since Mark could sell the building for $65,200 if he were not contributing it to the new partnership, Mark is the one who should receive the credit for the increase. And he does this by recording the building at $65,200 and crediting his capital account for a similar amount. (The $65,200 credit is merely one of several debits and credits which net to the $69,100 credit in Mark's capital account in the entry above.)

## Partnership Income Division

Learning Objective 4

Describe the various methods of determining how partnership profits and losses are divided, and how the profits or losses earned by each partner are recorded.

**Income division** is the manner in which profits and losses are allocated to individual partners. Partners can agree to divide partnership income any way they want. What they will most likely consider are the services performed by each partner, the talent and capital contributed, and perhaps the length of time in the partnership.

You can adjust for differences in time devoted to the business and in managerial and technical ability by providing *allowances* for salaries. Partnership salaries are merely a means of dividing partnership profits in an equitable manner; they are not salaries in the legal sense of the word, because the partners are owners of the business entity, not employees.

You can adjust for differences in capital contributions by *allowing* interest on the capital balances. Interest allowed in this manner is not interest expense on borrowed funds; it is again a *means to achieve an equitable division* of profits.

Most often you will find that partners share earnings (or losses) in one of these three general ways:

**1.** An established ratio
**2.** The capital investment relationship
**3.** Salary and interest allowances, with the excess shared in an established ratio

### Established Ratio

Remember that if the articles of partnership do not spell out the manner of profit sharing, profits and losses are divided equally. Any other ratio must be established by the partnership agreement. Whatever ratio the partners agree on is an attempt to adjust for their service and capital contributions.

For example, when Debbie Abbott and Mark Kingery formed their sporting goods partnership, they agreed that Debbie would work full time and Mark part time. Therefore they felt that it would be fair to share profits in the ratio of 75% for Debbie and 25% for Mark ($\frac{3}{4}$ and $\frac{1}{4}$, or a 3 : 1 ratio). The income for the first half-year of operation was $28,000. Here is how it was divided:

Debbie Abbott ($28,000 × .75) . . . . . . . . . . . . . . . $21,000
Mark Kingery ($28,000 × .25) . . . . . . . . . . . . . . .   7,000
                                              $28,000

The net income of $28,000 appeared as a credit balance in the Income Summary account after the normal closing entries were made. Then the Income Summary account was closed like this:

| Dec. 31 | Income Summary . . . . . . . . . . . . . . . . . . . . . . . . . . . . . | 28,000 | |
|---|---|---|---|
| | Abbott, Capital. . . . . . . . . . . . . . . . . . . . . . . . . . . . | | 21,000 |
| | Kingery, Capital. . . . . . . . . . . . . . . . . . . . . . . . . . . | | 7,000 |
| | To close the Income Summary account and divide the partnership profits. | | |

If Debbie or Mark had made any withdrawals during the year, entries would have been made at the time of the withdrawal, just as in proprietorship accounting. For example, if Debbie had a withdrawal of $3,000 on July 7 and Mark had one of $10,000 on Nov. 4, the entries would have been as follows:

| July 7 | Abbott, Withdrawals .............................. | 3,000 | |
| | Cash ...................................... | | 3,000 |
| | To record a withdrawal by Abbott. | | |

| Nov. 4 | Kingery, Withdrawals ............................ | 10,000 | |
| | Cash ...................................... | | 10,000 |
| | To record a withdrawal by Kingery. | | |

If these had been the only withdrawals during the year, the entry required at year-end to record the closing of the withdrawals accounts to the capital accounts would be:

| Dec. 31 | Abbott, Capital ................................ | 3,000 | |
| | Kingery, Capital ............................... | 10,000 | |
| | Abbott, Withdrawals ......................... | | 3,000 |
| | Kingery, Withdrawals ........................ | | 10,000 |
| | To close the withdrawals accounts to the respective capital accounts. | | |

### Capital Investment Relationship

Sometimes a partnership's profitability is closely related to the amount of capital invested by the partners. In such cases, you should consider sharing the profits in proportion to the partners' capital balances, especially if neither partner is actively involved in running the business.

Various capital balances can be used in dividing partnership income—the balances at the time of the investment, the balances at the beginning of the year, the average balances throughout the year. Using average capital balances is considered the most equitable approach, since it includes all investments and withdrawals during the current year in addition to the cumulative capital balances for the previous years. Since the calculation of the average capital balance is more involved than it may appear at first glance, it will be provided in all this chapter's examples and assignments.

Let's see how it works when Debbie Abbott and Mark Kingery share profits based on average capital balances. The partnership earned $28,000 in its first 6 months of operation, and the two partners' capital balances averaged $18,000 and $66,000, respectively. The income is distributed as follows:

| Partner | Average Capital Account Balances | Fraction of Total | × | Total Profits | = | Amount Allocated to Each Partner |
|---|---|---|---|---|---|---|
| Abbott | $18,000 | $\frac{18}{84}$ | × | $28,000 | = | $ 6,000 |
| Kingery | 66,000 | $\frac{66}{84}$ | × | $28,000 | = | 22,000 |
| | $84,000 | | | | | $28,000 |

Debbie gets eighteen eighty-fourths ($18,000/$84,000 = 18/84) of the profits because her average capital balance ($18,000) is that fraction of the total capital ($18,000 + $66,000 = $84,000). Mark would then receive sixty-six eighty-fourths ($66,000/$84,000 = 66/84).

### Allowance for Salaries and Interest

Suppose that you and your two partners, Corrigan and Gomez, make different types of contributions to a partnership. Corrigan provides all the money you need to start up;

you—Craven—contribute the most management time to running the organization; and Gomez has special talents or skills the partnership needs. How can each of you be compensated fairly for your unique contributions? The three of you could make an arrangement that rewards you and Gomez with a salary for your time and her talents. Then the arrangement could allow for Corrigan to receive interest on the money he invested. Any profits that are left over after allowing for the salaries and interest could then be shared among the three of you equally, since you have already adjusted for the differences in the amounts of time, talent, and capital invested.

These profit shares are not literally salaries and interest. Rather, they are a way of approaching the division of profits among the three of you in an equitable manner —an approach that recognizes the different contributions that each of you makes to the partnership. No salaries expense or interest expense will appear on the income statement, because these are not expenses that are subtracted in determining net income; the profits have already been determined.

Assume that the partnership of Craven, Gomez, and Corrigan earns $100,000, during its first year of operation; let's see how the arrangement might work. Since Craven devotes full time to the partnership's affairs, he is allowed a salary of $30,000 for his managerial ability. Gomez spends less time in the business, but it's her technical know-how that makes the partnership go. So she is given credit for a salary of $31,000. Each partner will be allowed interest at 8% of his or her average capital balance. Since Corrigan was the only partner who made an investment, he is the only one who has a balance in his capital account (averaging $150,000) during the first year of operation. Any remaining profits will be split equally among the three partners. Here is how the $100,000 partnership net income would be divided:

**CRAVEN, GOMEZ, AND CORRIGAN**
**Division of Income Schedule**
**Year Ended December 31, 1998**

| Allowance | Craven | Gomez | Corrigan | Totals |
|---|---|---|---|---|
| Salary | $30,000 | $31,000 | $ −0− | $ 61,000 |
| Interest | −0− | −0− | 12,000 | 12,000 |
| Totals | $30,000 | $31,000 | $12,000 | $ 73,000 |
| Remainder | 9,000 | 9,000 | 9,000 | 27,000 |
| Net Income | $39,000 | $40,000 | $21,000 | $100,000 |

After the credit of $61,000 for salaries and the $12,000 for interest, a balance of $27,000 ($100,000 − $61,000 − $12,000) remains to be shared equally by the three partners ($9,000 each).

The general journal entry to record the division of profits would look like this:

| Dec. 31 | Income Summary | 100,000 | |
| | Craven, Capital | | 39,000 |
| | Gomez, Capital | | 40,000 |
| | Corrigan, Capital | | 21,000 |
| | To close the Income Summary account and divide partnership profits. | | |

Remember that interest and salaries *have not* actually been paid to the partners, even though the partners may have been making withdrawals throughout the year. The allowances for interest and salaries are only a means of determining how the net income for the period should be distributed.

What happens if the salary and interest allowances exceed net income? It doesn't matter: The division of income is done the same way. Let's say that in 1998, Craven, Gomez, and Corrigan had a partnership income of only $46,000, which is shared as follows:

---

**CRAVEN, GOMEZ, AND CORRIGAN**
Division of Income Schedule
Year Ended December 31, 1998

| Allowance | Craven | Gomez | Corrigan | Totals |
|---|---|---|---|---|
| Salary.......................... | $30,000 | $31,000 | $ –0– | $ 61,000 |
| Interest......................... | –0– | –0– | 12,000 | 12,000 |
| Totals.......................... | $30,000 | $31,000 | $12,000 | $ 73,000 |
| Remainder...................... | (9,000) | (9,000) | (9,000) | (27,000) |
| Net Income ..................... | $21,000 | $22,000 | $ 3,000 | $ 46,000 |

---

Notice that the total allowance for salaries and interest exceeds net income by $27,000 ($46,000 − $61,000 − $12,000) and that this negative excess is shared equally by the individual partners in the same manner as the positive excess was shared in the previous example. The result is a reduction of $9,000 for each partner after allowing for salary and interest. The journal entry to record this division of profits would be:

---

| | | | |
|---|---|---|---|
| Dec. 31 | Income Summary.............................. | 46,000 | |
| | Craven, Capital............................ | | 21,000 |
| | Gomez, Capital............................ | | 22,000 |
| | Corrigan, Capital........................... | | 3,000 |
| | To close the Income Summary account and divide partnership profits. | | |

---

Learning Objective 5

Prepare the basic financial statements for a partnership

## Partnership Financial Statements

The financial statements of a partnership and a proprietorship are similar. The income statements are identical in format except that the partnership income statement may present the division of income on the bottom portion of the statement. For the Craven, Gomez, and Corrigan partnership, the income statement for 1998 would look like this:

---

**CRAVEN, GOMEZ, AND CORRIGAN**
Income Statement
Year Ended December 31, 1998

| | | |
|---|---|---|
| Sales................................................... | | $787,000 |
| Less: Sales Discounts................................... | $11,400 | |
| ~~~~~~~~~~~~~~~~~~~~~~~~~~~~~~~~~~~~~~~~~ | | |
| ~~~~~~~~~~~~~~~~~~~~~~~~~~~~~~~~~~~~~~~~~ | | |
| Net Income ........................................... | | $100,000 |
| | | |
| Income Division: | | |
| Craven .......................................... | $39,000 | |
| Gomez .......................................... | 40,000 | |
| Corrigan ......................................... | 21,000 | $100,000 |

---

Next we need to prepare a statement of owners' equity, which for a partnership is called a **statement of partners' capital accounts.** This statement provides the partners with a summary of the increases and decreases in their respective capital accounts during the year as well as the beginning and ending balances. It looks like this:

### CRAVEN, GOMEZ, AND CORRIGAN
#### Statement of Partners' Capital Accounts
#### Year Ended December 31, 1998

|  | Craven | Gomez | Corrigan | Totals |
|---|---|---|---|---|
| Capital, Jan. 1, 1998 | $ –0– | $ –0– | $140,000 | $140,000 |
| Add: Investments |  |  | 20,000 | 60,000 |
| Net Income | 39,000 | 40,000 | 21,000 | 100,000 |
|  | $39,000 | $40,000 | $181,000 | $260,000 |
| Less: Withdrawals | 22,000 | 18,000 | 27,000 | 67,000 |
| Capital, Dec. 31, 1998 | $17,000 | $22,000 | $154,000 | $193,000 |

Naturally, if the partnership experienced a loss, each partner's share of the loss would reduce his or her capital account in the statement of partners' capital accounts.

The balances in the partners' capital accounts are then placed in the owners' equity section of the balance sheet. The balance sheet of a partnership differs from that of a proprietorship only in the capital section. Whereas the proprietorship has only one capital account, the typical partnership has a different capital account for each partner. A partnership that has many partners will show only one account, Partners' Capital, which is the total of all the individual partners' accounts.

The balance sheet for Craven, Gomez, and Corrigan might appear as follows:

### CRAVEN, GOMEZ, AND CORRIGAN
#### Balance Sheet
#### December 31, 1998

| Assets | | Liabilities | |
|---|---|---|---|
| Cash | $ 15,000 | Accounts Payable | $ 50,000 |
| Accounts Receivable | 65,000 | Salaries Payable | 2,000 |
| Merchandise Inventory | 50,000 | Total Liabilities | $ 52,000 |
| Land | 40,000 | | |
| Building | 175,000 | **Owners' Equity** | |
| Accumulated Depreciation | (100,000) | Craven, Capital | $ 17,000 |
| | | Gomez, Capital | 22,000 |
| | | Corrigan, Capital | 154,000 |
| | | Total Owners' Equity | $193,000 |
| | | | |
| | | Total Liabilities and | |
| Total Assets | $ 245,000 | Owners' Equity | $245,000 |

---

**ASK YOURSELF ▶**

1. The accounting for proprietorships, partnerships, and corporations differs in only one section of the balance sheet. What is that section, and how is it different?

2. When a partnership is being formed and assets other than cash are being invested by the partners, what value is assigned to these assets?

3. What are the three ways in which partnerships may provide for the sharing of profits among partners?

4. How do the financial statements (income statement, statement of owners' equity, and balance sheet) for a partnership differ from those for a proprietorship?

### Partnership Dissolution

We mentioned earlier that a partnership is dissolved whenever a new partner is admitted or an old partner withdraws. Either way, the *business* can continue, but the *partnership* is dissolved. It is the legal arrangement between the partners that ceases to exist, not the business. When the partnership is dissolved, new articles of partnership should be prepared, or the original articles of partnership should contain provisions for the admission of new partners or the withdrawal of old partners. Both of these possibilities require special accounting treatment, as we will see next.

Learning Objective **6**

Distinguish between the admission of a new partner by the purchase of an interest and the admission of a new partner by an investment, and demonstrate the accounting treatment under each method

### *Admission of a New Partner*

You can admit a new partner to your partnership in one of two ways. The new partner can either *purchase an interest* from one or more of the old partners, or *invest in the partnership*. Of course, the admission of a new partner requires the consent of the other partners.

**Purchase of an Interest**   If one partner sells his or her interest in the partnership to someone, and that person is accepted by all the remaining partners, the transaction is a private one between the departing partner and the new partner. It is called a **purchase of an interest.** The amount paid to the departing partner does not affect the capital account of the other partners. The transaction is shown on the partnership books by transferring the departing partner's capital account to the new partner. Let's see how this works.

Assume that the partnership of Dunes, Field, and Howe is dissolved when Dunes sells his interest in the partnership to Sands. Both Field and Howe agree to accept Sands as a partner. Just before the dissolution, the partners had these capital balances:

| Capital Balances Prior to Purchase of an Interest | | | |
|---|---|---|---|
| **Dunes** | **Field** | **Howe** | **Total** |
| $10,000 | $30,000 | $20,000 | $60,000 |

The partnership has been very successful, and all indications are that it will continue to be so. Sands has evaluated the partnership very carefully and considers Dunes's asking price of $14,000 for his interest in the partnership to be reasonable. Sands pays Dunes $14,000 and is admitted to the partnership of Field, Howe, and Sands. Here is how we record Sands' admission to the partnership by the purchase of an interest:

| | | |
|---|---|---|
| Dunes, Capital . . . . . . . . . . . . . . . . . . . . . . . . . . . . . . . . . . . . . . | 10,000 | |
|     Sands, Capital . . . . . . . . . . . . . . . . . . . . . . . . . . . . . . . . . . . . | | 10,000 |
| To record the admission of Sands by a transfer of Dunes's capital. | | |

An important point is that the $14,000 paid by Sands to Dunes, representing the price paid for Dunes's interest in the partnership, is not recorded in the partnership's records. Since Sands is purchasing the interest that Dunes had in the partnership—represented by Dunes's balance in his capital account of $10,000—only $10,000 can now be transferred from Dunes's capital account to Sands's capital account. Since the purchase of Dunes's interest is a private transaction between Sands and Dunes, Field and Howe may never know the amount Dunes received.

Whenever a new partner is admitted by the purchase of an interest, the total assets, total liabilities, and total owners' equity of the partnership do not change. Only the composition of the capital accounts changes. In this case Dunes's capital account of $10,000 is replaced by Sands's capital account of $10,000.

Now let's assume that, rather than buying an interest only from Dunes, Sands gains admission by paying $2,800 to Dunes, $8,400 to Field, and $5,600 to Howe for a 20% interest in the partnership. His admission would be recorded like this:

| | | |
|---|---|---|
| Dunes, Capital ($10,000 × 20%) | 2,000 | |
| Field, Capital ($30,000 × 20%) | 6,000 | |
| Howe, Capital ($20,000 × 20%) | 4,000 | |
|     Sands, Capital | | 12,000 |
| To record the admission of Sands by a transfer of a 20% interest of each partner. | | |

Once again, the price Sands paid to the individual partners is not recorded in the partnership books. What is recorded is a reduction of each continuing partner's capital account by 20%, and the establishment of Sands's capital account for the sum of the three debits.

Notice again that when the new partner is admitted by purchasing an interest, the total owners' equity of the partnership—the combined capital accounts—does not change. It is $60,000 before and after the purchase, divided as follows:

| Partner | Balance in Capital Account |
|---|---|
| Dunes ($10,000 − $2,000) | $ 8,000 |
| Field ($30,000 − $6,000) | 24,000 |
| Howe ($20,000 − $4,000) | 16,000 |
| Sands ($2,000 + $6,000 + $4,000) | 12,000 |
| | $60,000 |

**Investment in a Partnership** Instead of purchasing an interest in the partnership from the current or retiring partners, a new partner may gain admittance by an **investment of assets** in the partnership. This time assets are invested directly into the partnership and not given to the individual partners. The investment will increase the partnership's total assets and as a result the total partners' equity. Let's look again at the partnership of Dunes, Field, and Howe. They agree to admit Sands to a 20% interest in the partnership with an investment of $15,000 cash. After the investment, assets will have increased by $15,000, as will partners' equity. Specifically, the partners' equity will equal $75,000, consisting of the following:

| | |
|---|---|
| Dunes, Capital | $10,000 |
| Field, Capital | 30,000 |
| Howe, Capital | 20,000 |
| Investment by Sands | 15,000 |
| | $75,000 |

Since Sands is to receive a 20% interest of the $75,000, his capital account will be established for $15,000 ($75,000 × 20%), the amount of his investment. His admission would be recorded in the general journal as follows:

| | | |
|---|---|---|
| Cash | 15,000 | |
|     Sands, Capital | | 15,000 |
| To record admission of Sands to a 20% interest in the firm. | | |

Once Sands is admitted, new articles of partnership will be prepared specifying how profits and losses are to be shared. While Sands has a 20% interest in the net assets of the partnership, it does not necessarily follow that he will receive 20% of all profits and losses. His share of profits and losses will be established by the new articles of partnership.

*Investment with Bonus to Old Partners*   In the example above, when Sands purchased a 20% interest in the Dunes, Field, and Howe partnership for $15,000, he got credit in his capital account for exactly what he paid (20% of the total capital of $75,000 equals $15,000). Sometimes, however, a new partner has to invest more in the partnership than is credited in his or her capital account. This can occur whenever a partnership is so successful that the old partners can charge the new one a premium for the privilege of participating. We call this premium a **bonus,** and it's shared by the old partners — according to their agreed-upon profit-and-loss ratio — because they are the ones who made the partnership successful.

To demonstrate this situation, let's assume that Sands's $15,000 bought him only a 15% interest in the partnership, instead of a 20% interest. Let's also assume that the old partners share profits and losses according to the following formula: 25% to Dunes, 25% to Field, and 50% to Howe. Sands will receive credit in his capital account for 15% of the total net assets ($75,000) of the new partnership, which amounts to $11,250:

| | |
|---|---:|
| Net assets prior to admission of Sands (equal to the sum of the capital accounts of Dunes, $10,000; Field, $30,000; and Howe, $20,000) . . . . . . . . | $60,000 |
| Cash invested by Sands. . . . . . . . . . . . . . . . . . . . . . . . . . . . . . . . . . . . . . . . | 15,000 |
| Net assets after admission of Sands . . . . . . . . . . . . . . . . . . . . . . . . . . . . . . | $75,000 |
| Sands' equity of 15% ($75,000 × .15). . . . . . . . . . . . . . . . . . . . . . . . . . . . . | $11,250 |

The bonus paid by Sands to the old partners is $3,750, the difference between the cash he invested ($15,000) and the credit he is given in his capital account ($11,250). This bonus amount is divided among the old partners according to their profit-and-loss ratio, as follows:

| | |
|---|---:|
| Dunes ($3,750 × .25). . . . . . . . . . . . . . . . . . . . . . . | $   937 |
| Field ($3,750 × .25) . . . . . . . . . . . . . . . . . . . . . . . . | 938 |
| Howe ($3,750 × .50) . . . . . . . . . . . . . . . . . . . . . . . | 1,875 |
| Total . . . . . . . . . . . . . . . . . . . . . . . . . . . . . . . . . . | $3,750 |

We record Sands's admission with the following general journal entry:

| | | |
|---|---:|---:|
| Cash . . . . . . . . . . . . . . . . . . . . . . . . . . . . . . . . . . . . . . . . . . . . . . . | 15,000 | |
| Dunes, Capital. . . . . . . . . . . . . . . . . . . . . . . . . . . . . . . . . . . . . | | 937 |
| Field, Capital . . . . . . . . . . . . . . . . . . . . . . . . . . . . . . . . . . . . . . | | 938 |
| Howe, Capital . . . . . . . . . . . . . . . . . . . . . . . . . . . . . . . . . . . . . | | 1,875 |
| Sands, Capital. . . . . . . . . . . . . . . . . . . . . . . . . . . . . . . . . . . . . | | 11,250 |
| To record admission of Sands to a 15% interest in the firm. | | |

*Investment with Bonus to New Partner*   Now suppose that the old partnership hasn't been very successful and the old partners desperately need Sands's managerial ability or capital. The tables have turned and Dunes, Field, and Howe may be willing to give Sands the premium — the bonus — to join the firm. If Sands is to receive the bonus, then his investment will be less than the credit he'll receive in his capital account. And the bonus (again divided according to their profit-and-loss ratio) will have to come out of the old partners' capital accounts.

Let's assume that Sands is admitted to the partnership by investing $15,000 in cash, for which he receives a 25% interest. We can determine the amount to be credited to Sands's capital account with the following calculations:

| | |
|---|---|
| Net assets prior to admission of Sands (equal to the sum of the capital accounts of Dunes, $10,000; Field, $30,000; and Howe, $20,000) . . . . . . . . | $60,000 |
| Cash invested by Sands. . . . . . . . . . . . . . . . . . . . . . . . . . . . . . . . . . . . . . . . . . . | 15,000 |
| Net assets after admission of Sands . . . . . . . . . . . . . . . . . . . . . . . . . . . . . . . | $75,000 |
| Sands' equity of 25% ($75,000 × .25). . . . . . . . . . . . . . . . . . . . . . . . . . . . . . | $18,750 |

The bonus paid to Sands by the old partners is the difference between the cash Sands invested ($15,000) and the credit he is given in his capital account ($18,750), which is $3,750. The amount of Sands's bonus is allocated to the old partners according to the old partnership's profit-and-loss ratio of 1:1:2 (25%, 25%, and 50%). So Dunes's and Field's capital accounts are reduced by $937.50 ($3,750 × .25) and Howe's by $1,875 ($3,750 × .50). Here's the entry to record Sands's admission to the partnership:

| | | |
|---|---|---|
| Cash . . . . . . . . . . . . . . . . . . . . . . . . . . . . . . . . . . . . . . . . . . . . . . . . . . | 15,000 | |
| Dunes, Capital . . . . . . . . . . . . . . . . . . . . . . . . . . . . . . . . . . . . . . . . . . | 937 | |
| Field, Capital. . . . . . . . . . . . . . . . . . . . . . . . . . . . . . . . . . . . . . . . . . . . | 938 | |
| Howe, Capital . . . . . . . . . . . . . . . . . . . . . . . . . . . . . . . . . . . . . . . . . . . | 1,875 | |
| Sands, Capital . . . . . . . . . . . . . . . . . . . . . . . . . . . . . . . . . . . . . . . . . | | 18,750 |
| To record admission of Sands to a 25% interest in the firm. | | |

Learning Objective **7**

## *Withdrawal of a Partner*

Demonstrate the accounting treatment for the withdrawal of a partner and for the death of a partner

A partner may withdraw from a partnership for a variety of reasons. A partner may decide to leave voluntarily because he or she has found a better opportunity, wants to retire, or even finds the remaining partners incompatible. Common reasons for involuntary withdrawal include death and mandatory retirement (the age for which is typically written into the partnership agreement). Whatever the reason, a withdrawal from a partnership can be accomplished in one of two ways: the withdrawing partner's interest can be sold to another partner, or it can be sold back to the partnership itself.

**Sale of an Interest to Another Partner**   When a partner's interest is sold to another, continuing partner or partners, the withdrawing partner is paid from the personal assets of the purchasing partner(s). The assets of the partnership are not affected. Such a withdrawal, by **sale of an interest to another partner,** is exactly the opposite of the admission of a new partner by the purchase of an interest (which we discussed earlier). Instead of a new partner buying an interest from a continuing partner to get into the partnership, an old partner is now selling his or her interest to a continuing partner to get out of the partnership.

The accounting is quite simple. First you close the partnership books at the date of the withdrawal and allocate the income earned since the end of the previous year among the capital accounts of the withdrawing and continuing partners. Then you debit the capital account of the withdrawing partner to take his or her account completely off the partnership books. Finally, you credit the capital account(s) of the purchasing partner(s) for the exact same total. The amount credited to each continuing partner's capital account depends on what percentage of the withdrawing partner's interest each partner is purchasing.

To show you how this works, consider the partnership of Bash, Quigley and Bicker, who share profits in a ratio of 2:2:1 (40%, 40%, and 20%), respectively. The partners have the following balances in their capital accounts: $25,000, $20,000, and $30,000. On Jan. 1, Bash plans to withdraw from the firm. (Since the withdrawal takes place on the first day of the year, there is no income that needs to be allocated among the capital accounts.) Quigley and Bicker are so pleased to take over Bash's share of the business that they each agree to buy one-half of Bash's interest in the business for a total of $15,000. The general journal entry for Bash's withdrawal is the following:

| | | |
|---|---|---|
| Bash, Capital. . . . . . . . . . . . . . . . . . . . . . . . . . . . . . . . . . . . . . . . . . . . . | 25,000 | |
| Quigley, Capital (25,000 $\times \frac{1}{2}$) . . . . . . . . . . . . . . . . . . . . . . . . . | | 12,500 |
| Bicker, Capital (25,000 $\times \frac{1}{2}$) . . . . . . . . . . . . . . . . . . . . . . . . . | | 12,500 |
| To record withdrawal of Bash from partnership. | | |

Just like the admission of a partner by the purchase of an interest, this transaction is a private one between the withdrawing partner and whoever is purchasing the interest. It does not involve any partnership assets. Quigley and Bicker are simply purchasing Bash's $25,000 interest in the firm, which is why their capital accounts increase by the exact same amount that Bash's decreases. The amount paid to Bash, $15,000, is in no way reflected on the partnership's books. Quigley and Bicker could have paid Bash $100,000 for his interest and the entry above would still have been the same.

**Sale of an Interest Back to the Partnership** When a partner withdraws through **sale of an interest back to the partnership,** the withdrawing partner is paid from the assets of the partnership, instead of from the personal assets of the continuing partners. This type of withdrawal—which reduces the assets of the partnership—is the reverse of the admission of a new partner by an investment in the partnership (which we discussed earlier). Instead of a new partner entering the partnership by investing cash or other assets in the partnership, an old partner is now leaving the partnership and the partnership is distributing cash or other assets to the departing partner.

Accounting for this type of withdrawal requires that the income earned since the start of the year be divided among the partners' capital accounts. It also requires that the current value of the partnership's assets at the date of withdrawal be agreed upon in order to help determine the withdrawing partner's interest in the partnership. Next we debit the capital account of the withdrawing partner to take it completely off the partnership books. And then we credit the assets that are paid by the partnership to the withdrawing partner.

In some situations the value of the assets paid to the withdrawing partner is *exactly the same as* the balance in his or her capital account. This is the easiest possibility for the accountant, since the debits to the withdrawing partner's capital account are exactly the same as the credits to the partnership assets.

In other situations the value of the withdrawing partner's interest—represented by the amount paid to the withdrawing partner by the partnership—may be *more than* the balance in his or her capital account. In this case the partnership needs to pay the retiring partner an amount in excess of the balance in his or her capital account. The excess, which represents a bonus paid to the withdrawing partner, is allocated among the remaining partners on the basis of their profit-and-loss ratio and thereby reduces their capital accounts.

As a third possibility, the partnership may compensate the withdrawing partner with an amount *less than* the balance in his or her capital account. In this situation a bonus is being paid to the partnership. The bonus is allocated among the continuing partners on the basis of their profit-and-loss ratio and thereby increases their capital accounts.

To illustrate these last two possibilities, let's go back to the partnership of Bash, Quigley, and Bicker and assume that, on Jan. 1, Quigley and Bicker decide to use partnership assets to buy out Bash's interest. The partnership pays $30,000 in cash for Bash's interest (which, remember, is on the books for only $25,000). The entry to record this withdrawal would be:

| | | |
|---|---|---|
| Bash, Capital. . . . . . . . . . . . . . . . . . . . . . . . . . . . . . . . . . . . . . . | 25,000 | |
| Quigley, Capital ($5,000 × $\frac{2}{3}$). . . . . . . . . . . . . . . . . . . . . . . . . | 3,333 | |
| Bicker, Capital ($5,000 × $\frac{1}{3}$). . . . . . . . . . . . . . . . . . . . . . . . . | 1,667 | |
| Cash. . . . . . . . . . . . . . . . . . . . . . . . . . . . . . . . . . . . . . . . . . . | | 30,000 |
| To record the withdrawal of Bash from the partnership. | | |

The extra $5,000 paid to Bash constitutes a bonus, which is allocated between the remaining partners on the basis of their profit-and-loss ratio. When Bash was in the partnership, Quigley's share of the profits was 40% and Bicker's was 20%. This means that, with or without Bash, Quigley gets twice as big a share of the profits or losses as does Bicker. So with Bash gone, Quigley gets $\frac{2}{3}$ [40%/(40% + 20%)] of the profits and losses and Bicker gets the remaining $\frac{1}{3}$ [20%/(40% + 20%)]. Therefore two-thirds of the $5,000 bonus, or $3,333, is allocated to Quigley, and the remaining one-third, or $1,667, is allocated to Bicker.

If the partnership had paid only $20,000 to Bash for his interest, then Bash would have to pay the $5,000 bonus to the partnership. In this situation, the journal entry would be:

| | | |
|---|---|---|
| Bash, Capital. . . . . . . . . . . . . . . . . . . . . . . . . . . . . . . . . . . . . . . | 25,000 | |
| Quigley, Capital ($5,000 × $\frac{2}{3}$) . . . . . . . . . . . . . . . . . . . . . . . . | | 3,333 |
| Bicker, Capital ($5,000 × $\frac{1}{3}$) . . . . . . . . . . . . . . . . . . . . . . . . | | 1,667 |
| Cash. . . . . . . . . . . . . . . . . . . . . . . . . . . . . . . . . . . . . . . . . . . | | 20,000 |
| To record the withdrawal of Bash from the partnership. | | |

### Death of a Partner

Upon the death of a partner, the partnership is automatically dissolved. However, because of provisions written into most partnership agreements, the partnership will probably continue to operate exactly as it did before the partner's death. In order to compensate the deceased partner's estate for his or her share of the partnership, the accountant must take basically the same steps as with the withdrawal of a partner. The partnership books need to be closed, and the income earned since the end of the previous year must be allocated among the capital accounts of the deceased and the surviving partners. (The partnership agreement may also require that an audit be performed by a licensed CPA.) The current value of the partnership assets at the date of death is determined. The deceased partner's capital account is then removed from the partnership's books.

Finally, the deceased partner's share of the partnership assets are distributed to his or her estate, in one of two ways: the surviving partners can purchase (with their personal assets) the deceased partner's interest from the estate, or the partnership can distribute partnership assets directly to the estate. The entries for the distribution of assets are the same as the entries for the withdrawal of a partner. They are completely consistent with those we discussed for the sale of an interest to other partners and the sale of an interest back to the partnership.

Many partnerships carry life insurance on each partner, in order to pay the estate if a partner dies. In this way the deceased partner's estate will be compensated for the partner's interest without sapping the partnership's resources so severely that it cannot continue to operate.

**ASK YOURSELF** ▶

1. What are the different ways in which a partnership can be dissolved?
2. What are the two ways in which a new partner can be admitted to a partnership?
3. How does a bonus arise when a new partner is being admitted to a partnership? How do we account for such a bonus on the books of the partnership?
4. What are the two ways to account for the withdrawal of a partner from a partnership? How do they compare to the two ways to account for the admission of a new partner?

Learning
Objective 8 **Partnership Liquidation**

Identify the accounting problems
associated with the liquidation of a
partnership and demonstrate how
liquidations are recorded

Remember that the dissolution of a partnership—whether by the death of a partner, the addition of a partner, or the withdrawal of a partner—does *not* mean that the *business* is terminated. The termination of a business is called a **liquidation,** and when that happens all the partnership assets are distributed to creditors and the individual partners. A liquidation may be a voluntary agreement by the partners, or it may be the result of legal action initiated by the partnership's creditors.

Whether voluntary or involuntary, a liquidation typically has three phases. First you must sell the assets of the partnership and divide any gain or loss among the partners' capital accounts. Next you pay the creditors. And finally you distribute the remaining cash to the partners. Since you typically cannot sell all the assets at once, liquidations often take place in installments. This usually involves selling the assets over an extended period of time. Then, as cash becomes available, creditors can be paid and final distributions can be made to the partners. For simplicity, however, we will consider liquidations as being accomplished in a single step rather than in installments.

Let's start with the partnership of Able, Baker, and Charlie. Their partnership agreement calls for profits and losses to be shared in a 2:2:1 ratio. On the date of the liquidation the partnership balance sheet looks as follows:

---

**ABLE, BAKER, AND CHARLIE**
**Balance Sheet**
**July 15, 1998**

| Assets | | Liabilities and Owners' Equity | |
|---|---|---|---|
| Cash..................... | $10,000 | Accounts Payable .......... | $20,000 |
| Other Assets .............. | 60,000 | Able, Capital .............. | 5,000 |
| | | Baker, Capital ............. | 20,000 |
| | | Charlie, Capital ............ | 25,000 |
| | | Total Liabilities and | |
| Total Assets............... | $70,000 | Owners' Equity............. | $70,000 |

---

### Gain on Sale of Partnership Assets

If the partnership sells its other assets for $75,000, it will have a gain of $15,000 ($75,000 − $60,000), which we will record in an account called Gain on Liquidation. Each gain or loss is then divided among the partners' capital accounts at the time of sale, in the agreed-upon profit-and-loss ratio. For Able, Baker, and Charlie the ratio is 2:2:1, so the amounts divided are $6,000 to Able and Baker, and $3,000 to Charlie. The general journal entries for the sale of assets and the division of the gain are as follows:

---

| | | |
|---|---|---|
| Cash ............................................... | 75,000 | |
|     Other Assets ...................................... | | 60,000 |
|     Gain on Liquidation ................................. | | 15,000 |
| To record the sale of other assets. | | |
| | | |
| Gain on Liquidation................................... | 15,000 | |
|     Able, Capital ...................................... | | 6,000 |
|     Baker, Capital ..................................... | | 6,000 |
|     Charlie, Capital ................................... | | 3,000 |
| To divide the gain among the partners' capital accounts. | | |

---

Next we pay the creditors the $20,000 owed to them:

| | | |
|---|---|---|
| Accounts Payable........................................ | 20,000 | |
| Cash.......................................... | | 20,000 |
| To record the payment of accounts payable. | | |

The partnership now has a $65,000 cash balance ($10,000 + $75,000 − $20,000), no other assets, and no liabilities. We now distribute the cash to the partners in accordance with their *respective capital balances.* So Able will get $11,000 ($5,000 + $6,000); Baker, $26,000 ($20,000 + $6,000); and Charlie, $28,000 (25,000 + $3,000). The final distribution is determined not by the profit-and-loss ratio, but by the balances in the respective capital accounts at that time. We record the distribution of the $65,000 cash to the individual partners this way:

| | | |
|---|---|---|
| Able, Capital ......................................... | 11,000 | |
| Baker, Capital........................................ | 26,000 | |
| Charlie, Capital ...................................... | 28,000 | |
| Cash.......................................... | | 65,000 |
| To record the distribution of cash to the individual partners. | | |

A partnership liquidation schedule helps to summarize the liquidation process. The worksheet works like the transaction analysis worksheet. Each transaction is recorded on a single line and the appropriate accounts are either increased or decreased. This way we always know the balance in each account. Like the transaction analysis worksheet, the liquidation schedule should balance after each transaction. Since we have a running record of each account, we will know how much is in each capital account after the assets are sold and the creditors are paid. And the total of the capital accounts must equal the cash balance, because that's all that's left. When the cash is distributed to the partners according to their capital balances, all accounts will have a zero balance. The partnership liquidation schedule for Able, Baker, and Charlie, when the assets are sold for a gain, is shown in Exhibit 2.

### Loss on Sale of Partnership Assets: Capital Accounts Sufficient to Absorb Loss

Partners sometimes have to sell the partnership assets at a loss. If the individual partners' capital accounts are sufficient to absorb the loss, we go through the same procedures that we followed in the last example. To show you this, let us assume that the assets of the Able, Baker, and Charlie partnership are sold for $50,000 rather than $75,000. We would recognize a loss of $10,000 ($50,000 − $60,000) and allocate it $4,000 ($10,000 × .40) to Able, $4,000 ($10,000 × .40) to Baker, and $2,000 ($10,000 × .20) to Charlie. The $20,000 of accounts payable would be paid and the remaining $40,000 cash ($10,000 + $50,000 − $20,000) distributed in accordance with the balances in the capital accounts: $1,000 for Able ($5,000 − $4,000), $16,000 for Baker ($20,000 − $4,000), and $23,000 for Charlie ($25,000 − $2,000). Exhibit 3 shows the partnership liquidation schedule summarizing the sale of the partnership's assets at a loss (when capital balances are sufficient to absorb the loss) and the final distribution.

Within the partnership liquidation schedule, phase one of the liquidation (the sale of assets and division of gain or loss to the capital accounts) is shown in a single step. As in the previous example, however, we typically use two general journal entries to record this first phase:

**Exhibit 2** Partnership Liquidation Schedule: Sale of Assets at a Gain

A partnership liquidation schedule summarizes the liquidation process

**ABLE, BAKER, AND CHARLIE**
**Partnership Liquidation Schedule**
**July 15, 1998**

|  | Cash | + | Other Assets | = | Accounts Payable | + | Able, Capital | + | Baker, Capital | + | Charlie, Capital |
|---|---|---|---|---|---|---|---|---|---|---|---|
|  | $ 10,000 |  | $ 60,000 |  | $ 20,000 |  | $ 5,000 |  | $ 20,000 |  | $ 25,000 |
| Sale of assets for gain | 75,000 |  | (60,000) |  |  |  | 6,000 |  | 6,000 |  | 3,000 |
|  | $ 85,000 |  | –0– |  | $ 20,000 |  | $ 11,000 |  | $ 26,000 |  | $ 28,000 |
| Payment of liabilities | (20,000) |  |  |  | (20,000) |  |  |  |  |  |  |
|  | $ 65,000 |  | –0– |  | –0– |  | $ 11,000 |  | $ 26,000 |  | $ 28,000 |
| Cash distribution | (65,000) |  |  |  |  |  | (11,000) |  | (26,000) |  | (28,000) |
|  | –0– |  | –0– |  | –0– |  | –0– |  | –0– |  | –0– |

| | | |
|---|---|---|
| Cash . . . . . . . . . . . . . . . . . . . . . . . . . . . . . . . . . . . . . . . . . . . . . . . . . . | 50,000 | |
| Loss on Liquidation. . . . . . . . . . . . . . . . . . . . . . . . . . . . . . . . . . . . . . | 10,000 | |
|     Other Assets . . . . . . . . . . . . . . . . . . . . . . . . . . . . . . . . . . . . . . . | | 60,000 |
| To record the sale of other assets. | | |

| | | |
|---|---|---|
| Able, Capital . . . . . . . . . . . . . . . . . . . . . . . . . . . . . . . . . . . . . . . . . . | 4,000 | |
| Baker, Capital . . . . . . . . . . . . . . . . . . . . . . . . . . . . . . . . . . . . . . . . . | 4,000 | |
| Charlie, Capital . . . . . . . . . . . . . . . . . . . . . . . . . . . . . . . . . . . . . . . . | 2,000 | |
|     Loss on Liquidation . . . . . . . . . . . . . . . . . . . . . . . . . . . . . . . . . . . | | 10,000 |
| To divide the loss among the partners' capital accounts. | | |

The entry to record the payment of liabilities is:

| | | |
|---|---|---|
| Accounts Payable. . . . . . . . . . . . . . . . . . . . . . . . . . . . . . . . . . . . . . . | 20,000 | |
|     Cash. . . . . . . . . . . . . . . . . . . . . . . . . . . . . . . . . . . . . . . . . . . . . . . | | 20,000 |
| To record the payment of accounts payable. | | |

**Exhibit 3** Partnership Liquidation Schedule: Sale of Assets at a Loss

(Capital accounts sufficient to absorb loss)

**ABLE, BAKER, AND CHARLIE**
**Partnership Liquidation Schedule**
**July 15, 1998**

|  | Cash | + | Other Assets | = | Accounts Payable | + | Able, Capital | + | Baker, Capital | + | Charlie, Capital |
|---|---|---|---|---|---|---|---|---|---|---|---|
|  | $ 10,000 |  | $ 60,000 |  | $ 20,000 |  | $ 5,000 |  | $ 20,000 |  | $ 25,000 |
| Sale of assets for loss | 50,000 |  | (60,000) |  |  |  | (4,000) |  | (4,000) |  | (2,000) |
|  | $ 60,000 |  | –0– |  | $ 20,000 |  | $ 1,000 |  | $ 16,000 |  | $ 23,000 |
| Payment of liabilities | (20,000) |  |  |  | (20,000) |  |  |  |  |  |  |
|  | $ 40,000 |  | –0– |  | –0– |  | $ 1,000 |  | $ 16,000 |  | $ 23,000 |
| Cash distribution | (40,000) |  |  |  |  |  | (1,000) |  | (16,000) |  | (23,000) |
|  | –0– |  | –0– |  | –0– |  | –0– |  | –0– |  | –0– |

And the entry to record the distribution of cash to the partners is:

| | | |
|---|---|---|
| Able, Capital | 1,000 | |
| Baker, Capital | 16,000 | |
| Charlie, Capital | 23,000 | |
|     Cash | | 40,000 |
| To record the distribution of cash to individual partners. | | |

### Loss on Sale of Partnership Assets: At Least One Capital Account Insufficient to Absorb Loss

When the partnership assets are sold for a loss, one or more of the partners' capital accounts may end up with a debit balance. If that happens, the partner(s) with the debit balance must, if possible, contribute personal assets to the partnership to cover the deficit. When the partner(s) don't have enough personal assets to contribute to eliminate the deficit, the remaining partners must absorb the deficit between them in their *remaining profit-and-loss ratio.*

Let us look at three possibilities. First, we assume that the partner with a debit balance has no personal assets to contribute to the partnership. Then we assume that the partner with a deficit is able to contribute only enough personal assets to partially eliminate his or her deficit. And finally we assume that the partner with a deficit contributes enough personal assets to completely eliminate the deficit.

**No Assets Provided to Cover Deficit** Let's go back to our example and this time sell the assets for only $40,000. Now a $20,000 loss ($40,000 − $60,000) must be absorbed − $8,000 by Able ($20,000 × .40), $8,000 by Baker ($20,000 × .40), and $4,000 by Charlie ($20,000 × .20). Able ends up with a $3,000 deficit ($5,000 − $8,000). Able must make up this deficit from her personal assets. However, if she cannot, the $3,000 deficit must be absorbed by Baker and Charlie in their remaining profit-and-loss ratio: 40% for Baker and 20% for Charlie, or two-thirds (40%/60%) for Baker and one-third (20%/60%) for Charlie. So Baker will pick up another $2,000 loss ($3,000 × $\frac{2}{3}$), and Charlie will absorb $1,000 ($3,000 × $\frac{1}{3}$). That leaves Baker with a $10,000 credit in his capital account ($20,000 − $8,000 − $2,000) and Charlie with a $20,000 credit ($25,000 − $4,000 − $1,000), all of which is summarized in the partnership liquidation schedule in Exhibit 4.

Here are the general journal entries to record this liquidation:

| | | |
|---|---|---|
| Cash | 40,000 | |
| Loss on Liquidation | 20,000 | |
|     Other Assets | | 60,000 |
| To record the sale of other assets. | | |

| | | |
|---|---|---|
| Able, Capital | 8,000 | |
| Baker, Capital | 8,000 | |
| Charlie, Capital | 4,000 | |
|     Loss on Liquidation | | 20,000 |
| To divide the loss among the partners' capital accounts. | | |

*(Continued)*

| | |
|---|---:|
| Accounts Payable................................... | 20,000 |
|     Cash....................................... | 20,000 |
| To record the payment of accounts payable. | |

| | |
|---|---:|
| Baker, Capital...................................... | 2,000 |
| Charlie, Capital..................................... | 1,000 |
|     Able, Capital .................................... | 3,000 |
| To record absorption of deficit in Able's capital account by Baker and Charlie. | |

| | |
|---|---:|
| Baker, Capital...................................... | 10,000 |
| Charlie, Capital..................................... | 20,000 |
|     Cash....................................... | 30,000 |
| To record the distribution of cash to Baker and Charlie. | |

**Assets Provided That Partially Cover the Deficit**  In the example above, the partner having a deficit in her capital account could not provide any personal assets to the partnership to eliminate the deficit. The remaining partners had to absorb the entire $3,000 deficit on the basis of their remaining profit-and-loss ratio. Sometimes the partner having the deficit can contribute assets to the partnership to partially or completely cover the deficit. In either of these situations, the liquidation schedule is a little different from the one we just looked at.

Assume, for example, that Able is able to provide $1,800 cash to the partnership. Able's final deficit of $1,200 ($3,000 − $1,800) must be absorbed by Baker and Charlie in their remaining profit-and-loss ratio. That is, Baker must absorb $800 of Able's remaining deficit ($1,200 × $\frac{2}{3}$) and Charlie must absorb $400 ($1,200 × $\frac{1}{3}$). This is summarized in the partnership liquidation schedule shown in Exhibit 5, which picks up on line 5 of the schedule in Exhibit 4, just following the payment of liabilities.

**Exhibit 4**  Partnership Liquidation Schedule: Sale of Assets at a Loss
(Capital accounts not sufficient to absorb loss; no assets provided to cover deficit)

**ABLE, BAKER, AND CHARLIE**
**Partnership Liquidation Schedule**
**July 15, 1998**

| | Cash | + Other Assets | = Accounts Payable | + Able, Capital | + Baker, Capital | + Charlie, Capital |
|---|---:|---:|---:|---:|---:|---:|
| | $ 10,000 | $ 60,000 | $ 20,000 | $ 5,000 | $ 20,000 | $ 25,000 |
| Sale of assets for loss | 40,000 | (60,000) | | (8,000) | (8,000) | (4,000) |
| | $ 50,000 | −0− | $ 20,000 | $(3,000) | $ 12,000 | $ 21,000 |
| Payment of liabilities | (20,000) | | (20,000) | | | |
| | $ 30,000 | −0− | −0− | $(3,000) | $ 12,000 | $ 21,000 |
| Deficit absorbed | | | | 3,000 | (2,000) | (1,000) |
| | $ 30,000 | −0− | −0− | −0− | $ 10,000 | $ 20,000 |
| Cash distribution | (30,000) | | | | (10,000) | (20,000) |
| | −0− | −0− | −0− | −0− | −0− | −0− |

**Exhibit 5** Partnership Liquidation Schedule: Sale of Assets at a Loss
(Capital accounts not sufficient to absorb loss; assets provided to partially cover deficit)

### ABLE, BAKER, AND CHARLIE
### Partnership Liquidation Schedule
### July 15, 1998

| | Cash | + Other Assets | = Accounts Payable | + Able, Capital | + Baker, Capital | + Charlie, Capital |
|---|---|---|---|---|---|---|
| Balances prior to payment by Able | $ 30,000 | –0– | –0– | $(3,000) | $ 12,000 | $ 21,000 |
| Partial receipt of deficit | 1,800 | | | 1,800 | | |
| | $ 31,800 | –0– | –0– | $(1,200) | $ 12,000 | $ 21,000 |
| Deficit absorbed | | | | 1,200 | (800) | (400) |
| | $ 31,800 | –0– | –0– | –0– | $ 11,200 | $ 20,600 |
| Cash distribution | (31,800) | | | | (11,200) | (20,600) |
| | –0– | –0– | –0– | –0– | –0– | –0– |

Here are the journal entries to account for the liquidation. They begin with the $1,800 payment by Able.

| | | |
|---|---|---|
| Cash .......................................................... | 1,800 | |
| Able, Capital ...................................... | | 1,800 |
| To record the payment by Able to cover part of her deficit. | | |
| | | |
| Baker, Capital ...................................... | 800 | |
| Charlie, Capital .................................... | 400 | |
| Able, Capital .................................... | | 1,200 |
| To record absorption of deficit in Able's capital account by Baker and Charlie. | | |
| | | |
| Baker, Capital ...................................... | 11,200 | |
| Charlie, Capital .................................... | 20,600 | |
| Cash............................................ | | 31,800 |
| To record the distribution of cash to Baker and Charlie. | | |

**Assets Provided That Completely Cover the Deficit** Assume finally that Able is able to provide $3,000 of cash to the partnership, exactly enough to cover her deficit. In this case Able ends up with a final deficit of zero, so no additional deficit has to be absorbed by Baker and Charlie. The liquidation steps, liquidation schedule, and general journal entries are similar to those for Able's partial elimination of her deficit, explained above.

**ASK YOURSELF ▶**

1. What is a partnership liquidation? How does it differ from a partnership dissolution?
2. When a partnership is liquidated, how do you account for a gain or loss on the sale of assets?
3. How should a partnership account for a deficit in the capital account of one or more partners?

## SUMMARY

- A **partnership** is defined by the Uniform Partnership Act as "an association of two or more persons to carry on, as co-owners, a business for profit." Partnerships are a common form of business organization for the professions—law, medicine, and accounting. Small business entities in the wholesale and retail trades and in manufacturing also use the partnership form of organization.
- A major reason for a business person to seek a partner is to obtain additional capital. Individuals also find it advantageous to combine their experience, knowledge, organizational, and managerial abilities.
- When choosing the appropriate form of business organization, whether to incorporate or to be a partnership, individuals must consider the characteristics of each form and the advantages and disadvantages resulting from these characteristics.
- The characteristics of all partnerships are ease of formation, voluntary association, articles of partnership, mutual agency, unlimited liability, limited life, co-ownership of property, and income participation.
- Advantages of the partnership form are the ability to generate more capital than a proprietorship, combination of talents, ease of formation, low cost of organizing, certain tax advantages, informality, and relatively less government regulation than corporations.
- The disadvantages of the partnership form are loss of freedom of action, limited life, unlimited liability to the general partners, partners' mutual agency, and limited amount of capital that can be raised (compared to a corporation).
- The problems related to partnership accounting fall into four categories: formation, income division, dissolution, and liquidation.
- When a partnership is formed, a separate capital account must be established for each partner. Assets contributed by each partner must be valued at their fair value on the date the partnership is formed.
- Profits and losses for a partnership are divided among the individual partners in accordance with the provisions of the articles of partnership. If no such provisions exist, profits and losses are divided equally. Provisions generally attempt to consider differences in the services and capital contributed by the partners.
- Profits and losses can be divided on the basis of certain fixed ratios, by capital balance relationships, or by considering salary and interest allowances.
- The financial statements of a partnership and a proprietorship are similar. The income statements are identical in format, except that an income division may also be presented at the bottom of the partnership income statement. The **statement of partners' capital accounts** (the partnership equivalent of a statement of owners' equity) summarizes the changes in the capital accounts during the year as well as showing the beginning and ending balances. The balance sheet for a partnership usually includes a separate capital account for each partner.
- Partnership dissolution occurs whenever a new partner is admitted or an old partner withdraws. The business entity does not necessarily terminate, but the legal relationship does. The types of partnership dissolutions include the admission of a new partner, the withdrawal of a partner, and the death of a partner.
- Admitting a new partner usually requires mutual consent of the old partners. The admission may be accomplished by the **purchase of an interest** of an old partner or partners for a mutually agreeable consideration. The amount of consideration is not reflected on the partnership books. Only the transfer of the ownership interest is recorded.
- Admission may also be gained by an **investment of assets.** In this case a new partner contributes assets directly to the partnership, receiving credit in a newly established capital account with a balance that is less than, equal to, or greater than the fair value of the contributed assets. The difference between the fair value of the assets and the capital account credit is reflected on the partnership books as a **bonus.**

- When a bonus is paid by the new partner to the continuing partners, the capital accounts of the continuing partners are increased. The bonus is allocated among the continuing partners' capital accounts on the basis of their agreed-upon profit-and-loss ratio.
- When a bonus is paid by the continuing partners to the new partner, just the reverse is true. The capital accounts of the continuing partners are decreased, and the amount of the bonus is allocated to them on the basis of their profit-and-loss ratio.
- The withdrawal of a partner typically calls for the partnership's books to be closed and for the income earned since the end of the previous year to be allocated among the partners' capital accounts. It also requires a valuation of the partnership's assets so that the value of the withdrawing partner's interest in the partnership can be determined.
- A partner can withdraw either by selling his or her interest to another, continuing partner or by selling it back to the partnership itself.
- Accounting for the **sale of an interest to another partner** is the opposite of accounting for the admission of a new partner by the purchase of an interest. And accounting for the **sale of an interest back to the partnership** is the reverse of accounting for the admission of a new partner by an investment of assets in the partnership.
- When a partner dies, the partnership is automatically dissolved, though most partnership agreements provide for business operations to continue. The accounting for the death of a partner is nearly identical to that for the withdrawal of a partner.
- In a partnership **liquidation,** the business activities are terminated. The gains or losses from the sale of partnership assets are divided among the individual partners in accordance with their profit-and-loss ratio. After the liabilities are paid, all remaining cash (or other assets) is distributed to the individual partners in accordance with the balances remaining in their respective capital accounts.
- If a deficit appears in a capital account as a result of a loss on the sale of partnership assets, that partner must contribute cash (or other assets) to the partnership equal to the amount of the deficit. If he or she is unable to do so, the remaining partners must absorb the deficit according to their profit-and-loss ratio.

## 9  KEY TERMS

**Articles of partnership**  A written agreement between the partners in a partnership that establishes responsibilities, commitments, and the manner in which profits and losses are to be divided. (Also called **partnership agreement.**)

**Bonus**  The difference between (1) the amount paid to a partnership by a partner newly admitted by the investment of assets and (2) the amount of interest received (the amount credited to the capital account). A bonus also arises with the withdrawal of a partner by the sale of his or her interest to the partnership, when the amount paid to the departing partner is different from the amount in his or her capital account.

**Dissolution of a partnership**  The termination of a partnership as a result of the admission of a new partner or the withdrawal of an old partner. The relationship terminates, but business operations do not necessarily end.

**General partners**  Partners in a limited partnership who have unlimited liability.

**General partnership**  A partnership in which all partners have unlimited liability.

**Income division**  The manner in which profits and losses are allocated to individual partners.

**Investment of assets**  A new partner's admission to a partnership by investing assets directly into the partnership.

| | |
|---|---|
| **Limited partners** | Those partners in a limited partnership who have limited liability and who usually do not participate in day-to-day decision making. |
| **Limited partnership** | A type of partnership in which at least one partner has unlimited liability, while the liability of the remaining partners is limited to their investment in the partnership. |
| **Liquidation** | The termination of a business entity by the sale of its assets and the distribution of the resulting cash to the creditors and owners. |
| **Mutual agency** | The authority of each partner in a partnership to legally bind all other partners to contracts. |
| **Partnership** | According to the Uniform Partnership Act, "an association of two or more persons to carry on, as co-owners, a business for profit." |
| **Purchase of an interest** | A business transaction involving the transfer of an ownership interest between a departing partner or partners and a new partner. |
| **Sale of an interest to another partner** | A partner's withdrawal from a partnership by selling his or her interest to another, continuing partner in exchange for payment from the personal assets of the purchasing partner. |
| **Sale of an interest back to the partnership** | A partner's withdrawal from a partnership by selling his or her interest back to the partnership in exchange for payment from the assets of the partnership. |
| **Statement of partners' capital accounts** | A statement of owners' equity for a partnership; it shows the increases and decreases in each partner's capital account, as well as the beginning and ending balances. |
| **Unlimited liability** | The legal obligation by which some (limited partnerships) or all (general partnerships) partners are personally responsible for the partnership's obligations. |

## DEMONSTRATION PROBLEM

The CPA firm of Vance, Carols, and Lee has experienced several unsuccessful years, and the partners have decided to liquidate the partnership. On Jan. 1, 1998, the date of the liquidation, their condensed balance sheet looked like this:

| Assets | | Liabilities and Owners' Equity | |
|---|---|---|---|
| Cash | $ 16,000 | Liabilities | $ 50,000 |
| Other Assets | 160,000 | Capital, Vance | 103,000 |
| | | Capital, Carols | 9,000 |
| | | Capital, Lee | 14,000 |
| | | Total Liabilities and | |
| Total Assets | $176,000 | Owners' Equity | $176,000 |

Profits and losses are shared in the following manner: Vance 40%, Carols 40%, and Lee 20%.

The other assets are sold for $100,000 on Jan. 1, 1998. Final cash distributions are based on the remaining capital balances prior to distribution. If any deficits are experienced, the contributions that each partner can make to cover his or her deficit are as follows:

| | |
|---|---|
| Vance | 100% of deficit |
| Carols | None |
| Lee | 50% of deficit |

**Required:**

1. Prepare a partnership liquidation schedule.
2. Prepare the general journal entries to record the partnership liquidation.

## ■ Solution to Demonstration Problem

**1.**

| | Cash | + Other Assets | = Liabilities | + Vance, Capital | + Carols, Capital | + Lee, Capital |
|---|---|---|---|---|---|---|
| | $ 16,000 | $ 160,000 | $ 50,000 | $103,000 | $ 9,000 | $ 14,000 |
| Sale of assets for loss* | 100,000 | (160,000) | | (24,000) | (24,000) | (12,000) |
| | $116,000 | –0– | $ 50,000 | $ 79,000 | $(15,000) | $ 2,000 |
| Payment of liabilities | (50,000) | | (50,000) | | | |
| | $ 66,000 | –0– | –0– | $ 79,000 | $(15,000) | 2,000 |
| Deficit absorbed† | | | | (10,000) | 15,000 | (5,000) |
| | $ 66,000 | –0– | –0– | $ 69,000 | –0– | $ (3,000) |
| Cash contribution | 1,500 | | | | | 1,500 |
| | $ 67,500 | –0– | –0– | $ 69,000 | –0– | $ (1,500) |
| Deficit absorbed | | | | (1,500) | | 1,500 |
| | $ 67,500 | –0– | –0– | $ 67,500 | –0– | –0– |
| Cash distribution | (67,500) | | | (67,500) | | |
| | –0– | –0– | –0– | –0– | –0– | –0– |

\* Division of loss:
Vance.....................$60,000 × 40% = $24,000
Carols....................$60,000 × 40% = $24,000
Lee.......................$60,000 × 20% = $12,000

† Distribution of deficit:
Vance .......................$15,000 × ⅔ = $10,000
Lee..........................$15,000 × ⅓ = $ 5,000

**2.**

| | | |
|---|---|---|
| Cash ................................................. | 100,000 | |
| Loss on Liquidation...................................... | 60,000 | |
|     Other Assets ..................................... | | 160,000 |
| To record sale of partnership assets. | | |

| | | |
|---|---|---|
| Capital, Vance........................................ | 24,000 | |
| Capital, Carols ...................................... | 24,000 | |
| Capital, Lee.......................................... | 12,000 | |
|     Loss on Liquidation ................................ | | 60,000 |
| To record division of loss among partners' capital accounts. | | |

| | | |
|---|---|---|
| Liabilities ............................................ | 50,000 | |
|     Cash......................................... | | 50,000 |
| To record payment of partnership liabilities. | | |

| | | |
|---|---|---|
| Capital, Vance........................................ | 10,000 | |
| Capital, Lee.......................................... | 5,000 | |
|     Capital, Carols.................................... | | 15,000 |
| To record the absorption of Carols' deficit by Vance and Lee. | | |

| | | |
|---|---|---|
| Cash ................................................. | 1,500 | |
|     Capital, Lee ...................................... | | 1,500 |
| To record partial recovery of Lee's deficit. | | |

| | | |
|---|---|---|
| Capital, Vance........................................ | 1,500 | |
|     Capital, Lee ...................................... | | 1,500 |
| To record the absorption of Lee's deficit by Vance. | | |

| | | |
|---|---|---|
| Capital, Vance........................................ | 67,500 | |
|     Cash............................................ | | 67,500 |
| To record the distribution of remaining cash to Vance. | | |

## QUESTIONS FOR REVIEW AND FURTHER THOUGHT

### REVIEW QUESTIONS

1. To what does the term *articles of partnership* refer? Why is it considered necessary?

2. What is a partnership?

3. What is meant by the term *unlimited liability?* Which partners have unlimited liability in a general partnership? In a limited partnership?

4. Define the term *mutual agency.*

5. Indicate whether each of the following characteristics of a partnership is an advantage or a disadvantage:
   a. Unlimited liability
   b. 1Informality
   c. Limited life
   d. Ease of formation
   e. Mutual agency
   f. Government supervision
   g. Capitalization

6. How can a partnership agreement provide for an equitable division of profits and losses when the individual partners have different amounts of capital invested in the partnership?

7. When a new partner is admitted to a partnership, he or she may be admitted by a purchase of an interest or by an investment of assets. Distinguish between the two approaches.

8. Brown has a 25% interest in the partnership of Brown and Clark. His capital account has a credit balance of $25,000 and Clark has a credit balance of $75,000. With Clark's consent, Brown sells his 25% to Ellenton for $33,000. Comment on the appropriate accounting treatment for this transaction.

9. Moon, Night, Owl, and Peters share profits according to a ratio of $4:3:2:2$. If profits for the current year are $88,000, how much will Owl's share be?

10. Explain how each of the financial statements below differ for a proprietorship and a partnership:
    a. Income statement
    b. Statement of owners' equity
    c. Balance sheet

11. Name the three different types of partnership dissolutions.

12. What is a bonus? How does it arise when a new partner is being admitted to a partnership? When a partner is withdrawing?

13. How should a deficit in a partner's capital account be accounted for in a partnership liquidation?

### QUESTIONS FOR FURTHER THOUGHT

1. Over the past several years, Martha Jones and Raphael Garcia have operated a profitable flower shop. They are currently thinking of admitting Bill Darryl into their partnership. Explain why they might consider this action.

2. When forming a partnership, why is it necessary to value assets contributed by the partners at their fair value on the date of formation?

3. When partners are allowed a salary, or interest on their invested capital, this allowance is considered a division of profits rather than an expense of doing business. Explain.

4. If a partner is allowed a monthly salary of $1,000 for the time she spends in the business, what account is debited when the salary is paid to the partner? Explain.

5. The partnership of E, F, and G is liquidated on Oct. 31 of the current year. After the assets are sold for cash and the creditors paid, F has a deficit in his capital account. Must he contribute cash to the partnership equal to the deficit in the capital account? Why? Assume that he cannot contribute cash; what must be done next? If he cannot contribute cash now but at a later date acquires cash equal to the deficit, must he then contribute cash to F and G?

6. Atlas is an audit partner of Foote and Tie Company, CPAs. He contracts with Johnson Supply Company for five, 15-horsepower tractors to be delivered in a few weeks. The CPA firm refuses to accept delivery at that time. Does Johnson Supply Company have an enforceable claim against the CPA firm?

7. In a partnership liquidation, gains and losses are divided according to the profit-and-loss ratio, but the final cash settlement is made to the partners in accordance with the balances in their capital accounts. Explain.

## OBJECTIVE ASSIGNMENT

*True/False*   Indicate whether each statement below is *true* or *false* by placing a *T* or an *F* in the space provided.

_____ 1. The manner in which profits are to be shared should be specified in the articles of partnership.

_____ 2. One advantage of a partnership over a corporate form of organization is the unlimited liability for partners.

_____ 3. The withdrawal of a partner from a partnership is a type of dissolution.

_____ 4. A partnership dissolution is basically the same as a partnership liquidation.

_____ 5. When a partner withdraws from a partnership and the value of assets paid to the partner by the partnership is greater than the balance in his or her capital account, the partnership is, in effect, paying the withdrawing partner a bonus.

*Multiple Choice*   Select the best choice to complete each statement or answer each question below. Write the letter corresponding to your choice in the space provided.

_____ 1. The Piper and Pickle partnership had a $45,000 profit during 1998. Piper gets credit for a salary of $12,000 and Piper and Pickle share profits in a 60:40 ratio. How much of the profit is credited to Piper's capital account?
   a. $27,000
   b. $12,000
   c. $19,800
   d. $31,800

_____ 2. In which situation below are the business operations of a partnership being terminated?
   a. Admission of a partner
   b. Withdrawal of a partner
   c. Death of a partner
   d. Liquidation

_____ 3. Which of the following is *not* considered a legitimate expense of a partnership?
   a. Interest paid to partners based on the amount of their invested capital
   b. Depreciation on assets contributed to the partnership by the partners
   c. Salaries for management hired to run the business
   d. Supplies used in the partners' offices

___ **4.** At the beginning of 1998, the balance sheet for LUV Company showed the following balances in the partners' capital accounts:

Cupid .................................... $24,000
Valentino ............................... 56,000

Cupid and Valentino share profits and losses in a 30:70 ratio. During 1998, LUV Company experienced a $40,000 loss. Cupid withdrew $10,000 from the partnership during the year, and Valentino withdrew $18,000. What will be the balance in Cupid's capital account on Dec. 31, 1998?
a. $2,000
b. $3,600
c. $12,000
d. $26,000

___ **5.** Finnegan and Quinn start a partnership. Finnegan contributes a building that she purchased 10 years ago for $100,000. The accumulated depreciation on the building on the date of formation of the partnership is $25,000, and the fair value is $110,000. For what amount will Finnegan's capital account be credited on the books of the partnership?
a. $100,000
b. $75,000
c. $25,000
d. $110,000

___ **6.** The following condensed balance sheet is provided for Washington and Adams Company, immediately prior to the admission of Jefferson to the partnership:

| | | | |
|---|---|---|---|
| Assets ............. | $145,000 | Liabilities ........... | $ 25,000 |
| | | Capital, Washington ... | 40,000 |
| | | Capital, Adams ....... | 80,000 |
| | | | $145,000 |

Assume that Jefferson purchases 50% of Washington's and Adams' interests by giving $25,000 to Washington and $50,000 to Adams. Washington and Adams share profits and losses equally. What amount would be credited to the capital account of Jefferson?
a. $120,000
b. $60,000
c. $37,500
d. $75,000

___ **7.** Refer to the facts in question 6, above. This time assume that Jefferson acquired a 50% interest in the partnership by paying $100,000 to the partnership. What will be the bonus (if any) in this transaction?
a. None
b. $10,000 paid to the partnership, shared evenly between Washington and Adams
c. $10,000 paid to Jefferson
d. $5,000 paid to Jefferson, $2,500 paid to Washington and $2,500 paid to Adams

___ **8.** The following condensed balance sheet is provided for Torello and Furillo Company, immediately prior to Furillo's withdrawal from the partnership:

| | | | |
|---|---|---|---|
| Cash ................ | $49,000 | Liabilities ............. | $25,000 |
| Inventory ............. | 30,000 | Capital, Torello ........ | 40,000 |
| Fixed assets .......... | 16,000 | Capital, Furillo......... | 30,000 |
| | $95,000 | | $95,000 |

Torello purchases Furillo's interest in the partnership for $25,000. Torello and Furillo share profits and losses in a ratio of 50:50. What bonus will result from this transaction?

a. None
b. $5,000 paid to Furillo
c. $5,000 paid to Torello
d. $2,500 paid to each of the two partners

_____ 9. The XYZ Company decides to liquidate its operations on Jan. 1. The capital accounts and profit-and-loss percentages on that date for the three partners are as follows:

| Partner | Balance in Capital Accounts | Profit- and-Loss Percentages |
|---------|----------------------------|------------------------------|
| X | $10,000 | 20% |
| Y | 12,000 | 30% |
| Z | (4,000) | 50% |

Partner Z is unable to contribute any assets to the partnership to cover its deficit. How much would be distributed to partner X from the liquidation?

a. $10,000
b. $8,400
c. $6,000
d. $9,200

_____ 10. The following condensed balance sheet is provided for Malone and Chambers Company, immediately prior to its liquidation:

| | | | |
|---|---|---|---|
| Cash . . . . . . . . . . . . . . | $100,000 | Liabilities . . . . . . . . . . . | $ 10,000 |
| Other assets . . . . . . . . | 50,000 | Capital, Malone . . . . . . . | 50,000 |
| | | Capital, Chambers . . . . | 90,000 |
| | $150,000 | | $150,000 |

If the other assets are sold for $90,000 and Malone and Chambers share profits and losses equally, what will be the final cash distribution to Malone?

a. $65,000
b. $50,000
c. $70,000
d. $95,000

## EXERCISES

3† **Exercise 1:** Forming a Partnership

Effective Aug. 1, 1998, Blanche and Rose agree to form a partnership from their respective proprietorships. The balance sheets presented below reflect the financial position of each proprietorship on July 31, 1998.

† The numbers in the margin refer to the Learning Objectives.

**BLANCHE AND ROSE**
Balance Sheets
July 31, 1998

| | Blanche | Rose |
|---|---|---|
| **Assets** | | |
| Cash | $ 2,400 | $ 4,000 |
| Accounts Receivable | 14,400 | 5,600 |
| Merchandise Inventory | 39,600 | 33,600 |
| Prepaid Rent | — | 3,200 |
| Store Equipment | 48,000 | 24,000 |
| Accumulated Depreciation | (18,000) | (14,400) |
| Building | 150,000 | — |
| Accumulated Depreciation | (30,000) | — |
| Land | 72,000 | — |
| Total Assets | $278,400 | $ 56,000 |
| **Liabilities and Owners' Equity** | | |
| Accounts Payable | $ 9,000 | $ 2,400 |
| Notes Payable | 72,000 | — |
| Blanche, Capital | 197,400 | — |
| Rose, Capital | — | 53,600 |
| Total Liabilities and Owners' Equity | $278,400 | $ 56,000 |

As of Aug. 1, 1998, the fair value of Blanche's and Rose's assets were as follows:

| | Blanche | Rose |
|---|---|---|
| Merchandise Inventory | $ 32,400 | $36,000 |
| Prepaid Rent | — | –0– |
| Store Equipment | 18,000 | 5,200 |
| Building | 300,000 | — |
| Land | 120,000 | — |

All other items on the two balance sheets are stated at their fair values.

From this information, present journal entries to record the opening of the partnership accounts.

▶ *(Check Figure: Credit to Blanche's Capital account: $406,200)*

4 **Exercise 2:** Dividing Partnership Profits between Partners

Grant and Lee are partners in a card shop that reported a $225,000 profit this year. Determine each partner's share of the profits under each of the following assumptions:
a. Nothing is mentioned in the partnership agreement concerning the sharing of partnership profits and losses.
b. Two-fifths of the profits or losses are Grant's, and three-fifths are Lee's.
c. Profits are to be shared by Grant and Lee in a 3:1 ratio.

▶ *(Check Figure: c. Grant's share: $168,750)*

4 **Exercise 3:** Dividing Partnership Profits among Partners

The partnership agreement among Larry, Balki, and Jennifer provides that profits and losses shall be divided in the following manner:

1. Each partner will receive an interest allowance of 10% on his or her average capital balance during the year.
2. Salary allowances will be provided for each partner: $20,000 each to Larry and Balki and $25,000 to Jennifer.
3. The remainder will be shared equally among the three partners.

During the year, Larry, Balki, and Jennifer maintained average capital balances of $100,000, $140,000, and $200,000, respectively.

a. Prepare a schedule that shows how the income for the partnership will be divided among the three partners, assuming that the income for the year was $124,000.
b. Prepare a schedule that shows how the income for the partnership will be divided among the three partners, assuming that the income for the year was $85,000.

▶ (Check Figure: **b.** Larry's share: $22,000)

## 4 Exercise 4: Making Journal Entries Affecting the Capital Accounts of a Partnership

The capital accounts for the Sugarbaker partnership are given below:

| Anthony, Capital | | Julia, Capital | |
|---|---|---|---|
| Balance, Jan. 1 | $60,000 | Balance Jan. 1 | $10,000 |
| Withdrawal, June 12 | 22,000 | Investment, July 4 | 35,000 |
| Investment, Oct. 1 | 16,000 | | |

Sugarbaker had a $55,000 loss during the year. Anthony and Julia share profits and losses in a 60:40 ratio.

From the information presented above, make all the journal entries for the year that affect each partner's capital account.

## 5 Exercise 5: Preparing Financial Statements for a Partnership

The Newhart Company's trial balance on Dec. 31, 1998, showed the following accounts:

| | Debits | Credits |
|---|---|---|
| Cash | $ 4,000 | |
| Inventory | 24,000 | |
| Other Assets | 22,000 | |
| Accounts Payable | | $ 3,000 |
| Michael, Capital | | 30,000 |
| Stephanie, Capital | | 17,000 |
| Michael, Withdrawals | 11,000 | |
| Stephanie, Withdrawals | 9,000 | |
| Sales | | 60,000 |
| Cost of Goods Sold | 20,000 | |
| Depreciation Expense | 1,000 | |
| Insurance Expense | 1,200 | |
| Other Expenses | 17,800 | |
| Totals | $110,000 | $110,000 |

Profits and losses are allocated 75% to Stephanie and 25% to Michael.

Prepare in good form the income statement, statement of partners' capital accounts, and balance sheet for the Newhart Company on Dec. 31, 1998.

▶ (Check Figure: Ending Capital balance for Stephanie: $23,000)

6 **Exercise 6:** Recording the Admission of a New Partner
by the Purchase of an Interest

The Mayberry Deli is owned and operated as a partnership by Andy, Barney, and Opie. On Nov. 1, the partners decide to admit a new partner, Floyd. On this date the capital accounts for the three original partners are as follows:

Andy . . . . . . . . . . . . . . . . . . . . . . . . . . . . . . . . . . . . . $90,000
Barney. . . . . . . . . . . . . . . . . . . . . . . . . . . . . . . . . . . . 52,500
Opie. . . . . . . . . . . . . . . . . . . . . . . . . . . . . . . . . . . . . . 22,500

Floyd is going to purchase Andy's interest in the partnership (with Barney's and Opie's approval) by paying Andy $115,000 in cash.

a. Record the admission of Floyd on Nov. 1 in general journal form on the books of the partnership.
b. Assume instead that Floyd paid the following amounts to each of the three partners for a percentage of each partner's interest:

| Partner | Amount Paid to Partner | Percentage of Partner's Interest |
|---------|------------------------|----------------------------------|
| Andy | $20,000 | 20% |
| Barney | 12,000 | 20% |
| Opie | 19,000 | 80% |

Record Floyd's admission on Nov. 1 on the partnership's books.

▶ *(Check Figure:* **a.** *Credit to Floyd, Capital: $90,000;* **b.** *Credit to Floyd, Capital: $46,500)*

6 **Exercise 7:** Recording the Admission of a New Partner
by an Investment of Assets

Larue has been admitted into the partnership of Belker, Grace, and Bates with a 20% interest by an investment of cash. The old partners share profits in a 3:1:1 ratio and, prior to Larue's admission, had capital accounts of $80,000, $100,000 and $60,000, respectively.

a. Record the general journal entry or entries to admit Larue, assuming that the investment by Larue is $60,000. Identify the amount of bonus (if any) associated with Larue's admission.
b. Record the general journal entry or entries to admit Larue, assuming that the investment by Larue is $50,000. Identify the amount of bonus (if any) associated with Larue's admission.
c. Record the general journal entry or entries to admit Larue, assuming that the investment by Larue is $70,000. Identify the amount of bonus (if any) associated with Larue's admission.

▶ *(Check Figure:* **b.** *Debit to Belker, Capital: $4,800;* **c.** *Credit to Bates, Capital: $1,600)*

7 **Exercise 8:** Accounting for the Withdrawal of a Partner by the Sale
of an Interest to Another Partner

Kevin is planning to withdraw from the partnership of Kevin, Winnie, and Paul on Jan. 1, 1998. At that time the balances in the partners' capital accounts are as follows:

Kevin. . . . . . . . . . . . . . . . . . . . . . . . . . . . . . . . . . . . . $60,000
Winnie . . . . . . . . . . . . . . . . . . . . . . . . . . . . . . . . . . . . 10,000
Paul . . . . . . . . . . . . . . . . . . . . . . . . . . . . . . . . . . . . . . 20,000

Prior to Kevin's withdrawal, the three partners shared profits and losses equally. Kevin plans to sell his interest in the partnership to Paul for $70,000.

a. Prepare the general journal entry on the partnership books to record Kevin's withdrawal.
b. Suppose instead that Kevin sold half his interest to Winnie for $35,000 and half his interest to Paul for $35,000. Make the general journal entry on the partnership books to record the withdrawal of Kevin.

▶ *(Check Figure:* **b.** *Credit to Winnie, Capital: $30,000)*

**7**   **Exercise 9:** Accounting for the Withdrawal of a Partner by the Sale of an Interest Back to the Partnership

The following condensed balance sheet is for the partnership of Harry, Christine, and Dan (who shared profits evenly) immediately prior to Dan's withdrawal from the partnership:

| | | | | |
|---|---|---|---|---|
| Cash | $ 40,000 | Liabilities | $ 10,000 |
| Other Assets | 90,000 | Capital, Harry | 40,000 |
| | | Capital, Christine | 30,000 |
| | | Capital, Dan | 50,000 |
| | $130,000 | | $130,000 |

a. Assume that the partnership purchases Dan's interest for $50,000 cash. Prepare the general journal entry to record Dan's withdrawal from the partnership.

b. Assume now that the partnership purchases Dan's interest for $55,000 cash. Prepare the general journal entry to record Dan's withdrawal from the partnership.

c. Assume now that the partnership purchases Dan's interest for $45,000 cash. Prepare the general journal entry to record Dan's withdrawal from the partnership.

▶ *(Check Figure: **b.** Debit to Harry, Capital: $2,500; **c.** Credit to Christine, Capital, $2,500)*

**8**   **Exercise 10:** Determining the Amount to Distribute to Each Partner in a Partnership Liquidation

The partnership of Rudy, Vanessa, and Cleo is about to be liquidated. All the assets have been sold for cash, and the creditors have been fully paid. The capital accounts of the partners have the following balances at the date of liquidation:

| | |
|---|---|
| Rudy | $60,000 credit |
| Vanessa | $24,000 debit |
| Cleo | $36,000 credit |

Profits and losses are shared equally by the three partners.

a. Assuming that Vanessa has no personal assets, determine how the remaining $72,000 cash balance is to be distributed.

b. Assume instead that Vanessa has enough personal assets to fully repay the partnership for the deficit in her capital account. Determine how the remaining cash balance is to be distributed if $72,000 is available before Vanessa's repayment.

c. Assume now that Vanessa has only enough personal assets to repay the partnership for 60% of the deficit in her capital account. Determine how the remaining cash balance is to be distributed if $72,000 is available before Vanessa's repayment.

▶ *(Check Figure: **b.** Distribution to Cleo: $36,000; **c.** Distribution to Cleo: $31,200)*

**8**   **Exercise 11:** Calculating the Distribution to Each Partner in a Partnership Liquidation

On Jan. 1, 1998, the partnership of Hickory, Dickory, and Doc decides to liquidate. At that time the condensed balance sheet looks like this:

| | | | |
|---|---|---|---|
| Cash | $25,000 | Liabilities | $40,000 |
| Fixed Assets | 47,000 | Capital, Hickory | 20,000 |
| | | Capital, Dickory | 10,000 |
| | | Capital, Doc | 2,000 |
| | $72,000 | | $72,000 |

Profits and losses are shared in the following manner: 40% to Hickory, 20% to Dickory, and 40% to Doc. During January 1998, the fixed assets were sold, and the creditors were fully paid. The remaining cash was distributed to the partners on Jan. 31.

a. Assuming that the fixed assets were sold for $60,000, determine the amount of cash distributed to each partner.
b. Assuming that the fixed assets were sold for $20,000 and that none of the partners was able to repay the partnership for any deficits in his or her capital account, determine the amount of cash distributed to each partner.

▶ (Check Figure: **b.** Distribution to Dickory: $1,667)

## PROBLEMS: SET A

3 5† **Problem A1:** Accounting for Partnership Formation

Jim Jaynes, the owner of a successful fertilizer business, feels that it is time to expand operations. Jim offers to form a partnership with Wayne Barthles, the owner of a nearby warehouse. The partnership would be called Barthles and Jaynes Storage and Sales. Barthles accepts Jaynes's offer, and the partnership is formed on July 1, 1998.

Presented below is the trial balance for Jaynes Fertilizer Supply on June 30, 1998:

| | | |
|---|---:|---:|
| Cash | $ 22,950 | |
| Accounts Receivable | 210,300 | |
| Allowance for Uncollectible Accounts | | $ 11,700 |
| Merchandise Inventory | 101,250 | |
| Prepaid Rent | 2,925 | |
| Store Equipment | 39,000 | |
| Accumulated Depreciation | | 9,750 |
| Notes Payable | | 33,000 |
| Accounts Payable | | 50,550 |
| Jaynes, Capital | | 271,425 |
| Totals | $376,425 | $376,425 |

The partners agree to share profits and losses equally and decide to invest an equal amount in the partnership. Barthles and Jaynes agree that Barthles' land is worth $45,000 and his building $150,000. Barthles is to contribute cash in an amount sufficient to make his capital account balance equal to Jaynes's.

Agreement is reached by the two partners on the following items concerning the transfer of Jaynes Fertilizer Supply to the partnership.

a. The accounts receivable are to be valued at $179,900, and the allowance for uncollectible accounts will be eliminated.
b. Merchandise inventory is to be decreased by $13,200.
c. The prepaid rent is for the warehouse used by Jaynes. All merchandise will be transferred to Barthles's building. No refund will be received on the unused rent paid in advance.
d. The store equipment has a fair value of $30,000.
e. All other items, assets and liabilities, are to be transferred at their book values.

**Required:**

1. Prepare the general journal entries to record the formation of the new partnership.
2. At the end of the year, Dec. 31, 1998, a profit of $89,000 is shown. Each partner has made withdrawals of $24,500. Prepare a statement of partners' capital accounts.

▶ (Check Figure: **a.** Credit to Jaynes, Capital: $237,350)

4 **Problem A2:** Determining the Division of Profits for Different Partnership Agreements

During the first year of operations, the law firm of Downey, Slocum, and Heard earned $136,350. Summarized below are the individual partners' capital accounts.

† The numbers in the margin refer to the Learning Objectives.

| | Downey | Slocum | Heard |
|---|---|---|---|
| Capital .................................... | $30,000 | $45,000 | $ 60,000 |
| Mar. 31, Investment......................... | 30,000 | | |
| May 31, Withdrawal .......................... | | (7,500) | |
| June 30, Investment.......................... | | | 7,500 |
| July 31, Withdrawal .......................... | | (7,500) | |
| Oct. 31, Investment .......................... | | 9,000 | |
| Nov. 30, Withdrawal.......................... | | | (22,500) |
| Capital, Dec. 31 ............................. | $60,000 | $39,000 | $ 45,000 |
| Average capital balance...................... | $52,500 | $39,000 | $61,875 |

**Required:**

Determine each partner's share of the partnership profits under each of the following assumptions:

1. Profits are shared equally.
2. Profits are shared in a 5:2:2 ratio.
3. Profits are shared in the ratio of the average capital balances for the year.
4. Profits are shared equally after allowing for 10% interest on the average capital balances and for salaries of $19,300, $15,200, and $16,300, respectively.

▶ *(Check Figure: 3. Downey's share: $46,672; 4. Downey's share: $47,954)*

4   **Problem A3:** Calculating the Profit Division for Different Levels of Profit

The partnership agreement of Othello, Hamlet, and Macbeth provides for the following: Profits and losses shall be divided equally after allowing for 10% interest on the average capital balances; salaries of $37,500, $67,500 and $22,500, respectively; and a bonus of 5% of reported profits (if any) to Macbeth before distribution of salaries. Average capital balances for 1998 are: Othello, $300,000; Hamlet, $225,000; and Macbeth, $450,000.

**Required:**

Prepare a division of income schedule for each of the following levels of profits and losses:

1. $270,000 profit
2. $225,000 profit
3. $45,000 loss

▶ *[Check Figure: 3. Othello's share: $(22,500)]*

6   **Problem A4:** Recording the Admission of a New Partner

Kirby and Stickney have a successful hot dog concession business in Manhattan and are seeking to expand. They decide to admit a new partner and have interested Drossner in joining the firm. They are able to convince Drossner to invest $5,000 in exchange for a 25% interest. Prior to admitting Drossner to the partnership, Kirby received 60% of the profits and Stickney received 40%. In addition, Kirby's capital account was $5,000 and Stickney's was $10,000 on the date of the admission.

**Required:**

1. Record the journal entries that are needed to admit Drossner to the partnership.
2. Assuming that Drossner's $5,000 investment gives him a 30% interest in the partnership, record the journal entry that is needed to admit Drossner to the partnership.

3. Assuming that Drossner's $5,000 investment gives him a 15% interest in the partnership, record the journal entry that is needed to admit Drossner to the partnership.

▶ *(Check Figure:* **2.** *Credit to Drossner, Capital: $6,000;* **3.** *Credit to Drossner, Capital: $3,000)*

5 **Problem A5:** Preparing Financial Statements for a Partnership

Hewey, Dewey, and Lewey who are partners in the Dizzy Video Store, share profits in a ratio of 25:25:50. The trial balance for Dizzy Video on Dec. 31, 1998, after all the adjusting entries have been made, is as follows:

|  | Debits | Credits |
|---|---|---|
| Cash . . . . . . . . . . . . . . . . . . . . . . . . . . . . . . . . . . . . . . . . . . . . | $ 6,000 | |
| Accounts Receivable . . . . . . . . . . . . . . . . . . . . . . . . . . . . . . | 8,000 | |
| Inventory. . . . . . . . . . . . . . . . . . . . . . . . . . . . . . . . . . . . . . . | 80,000 | |
| Prepaid Rent. . . . . . . . . . . . . . . . . . . . . . . . . . . . . . . . . . . . | 2,000 | |
| Prepaid Insurance . . . . . . . . . . . . . . . . . . . . . . . . . . . . . . . | 1,500 | |
| Accounts Payable. . . . . . . . . . . . . . . . . . . . . . . . . . . . . . . . | | $ 5,000 |
| Notes Payable . . . . . . . . . . . . . . . . . . . . . . . . . . . . . . . . . . | | 11,500 |
| Capital, Hewey . . . . . . . . . . . . . . . . . . . . . . . . . . . . . . . . . . | | 12,500 |
| Capital, Dewey . . . . . . . . . . . . . . . . . . . . . . . . . . . . . . . . . . | | 27,500 |
| Capital, Lewey . . . . . . . . . . . . . . . . . . . . . . . . . . . . . . . . . . | | 11,000 |
| Sales. . . . . . . . . . . . . . . . . . . . . . . . . . . . . . . . . . . . . . . . . . | | 220,000 |
| Cost of Goods Sold . . . . . . . . . . . . . . . . . . . . . . . . . . . . . . | 120,000 | |
| Salaries Expense . . . . . . . . . . . . . . . . . . . . . . . . . . . . . . . . | 45,000 | |
| Rent Expense. . . . . . . . . . . . . . . . . . . . . . . . . . . . . . . . . . . | 20,000 | |
| Insurance Expense . . . . . . . . . . . . . . . . . . . . . . . . . . . . . . | 3,000 | |
| Utilities Expense. . . . . . . . . . . . . . . . . . . . . . . . . . . . . . . . | 2,000 | |
| Totals. . . . . . . . . . . . . . . . . . . . . . . . . . . . . . . . . . . . . . . . | $287,500 | $287,500 |

**Required:**

1. Prepare an income statement for 1998 for Dizzy Video. Show the division of net income at the bottom of the income statement.
2. Prepare a statement of partners' capital accounts for 1998. Assume the following additional information:

|  | Capital Accounts Jan. 1, 1998 | Investments during Year | Withdrawals during Year |
|---|---|---|---|
| Hewey | $ 7,500 | $5,000 | $ –0– |
| Dewey | 30,000 | 2,500 | 5,000 |
| Lewey | 15,000 | –0– | 4,000 |

3. Prepare the balance sheet on Dec. 31, 1998.

▶ *(Check Figure:* **2.** *Balance in Capital, Dewey, on Dec. 31, 1998: $35,000;* **3.** *Total Assets: $97,500)*

6 7 **Problem A6:** Accounting for a Withdrawal from a Partnership

Mahon, Severs, and Cordoba are partners who share profits in a 3:2:1 ratio. On Dec. 31, 1998, Severs decides to withdraw from the partnership due to a disagreement with the other two partners. The partners' trial balance on Dec. 31, after all adjusting entries have been made, is presented below (all accounts except Income Summary have been closed for the year):

---

### MAHON, SEVERS, AND CORDOBA
### Trial Balance
### December 31, 1998

| | | |
|---|---:|---:|
| Cash .......................................... | $ 58,200 | |
| Accounts Receivable ................................. | 38,760 | |
| Allowance for Uncollectible Accounts ..................... | | $ 2,040 |
| Merchandise Inventory ................................ | 78,600 | |
| Machinery ....................................... | 32,400 | |
| Accumulated Depreciation ............................ | | 12,600 |
| Accounts Payable.................................. | | 49,620 |
| Income Summary ................................. | | 12,000 |
| Mahon, Capital .................................. | | 65,940 |
| Severs, Capital .................................. | | 43,956 |
| Cordoba, Capital.................................. | | 21,804 |
| Totals ........................................ | $207,960 | $207,960 |

---

**Required:**

1. Determine the balances in each of the partners' capital accounts on the day of Severs's withdrawal.
2. For each of the following independent situations, prepare the general journal entries necessary to record Severs's withdrawal.
   a. Severs sells one-fourth of his interest to Mahon for $12,000; one-fourth to Cordoba for $12,000; and the remaining one-half to Carr for $24,000. Both Mahon and Cordoba agree to accept Carr into the partnership.
   b. Severs is paid cash by the partnership equal to the balance in his capital account.
   c. Severs is paid cash by the partnership in the amount of $54,516.
   d. Severs is paid cash by the partnership in the amount of $36,012.

▶ *(Check Figure: **1.** Severs: $47,956; **2. a.** Credit to Mahon, Capital: $11,989; **c.** Debit to Mahon, Capital: $4,920)*

---

8   **Problem A7:** Preparing Journal Entries for a Partnership Liquidation

The partnership of Jackson, Cipriano, and Ackerman had the following trial balance on Feb. 1, 1998:

---

### JACKSON, CIPRIANO, AND ACKERMAN
### Trial Balance
### February 1, 1998

| | | |
|---|---:|---:|
| Cash.......................................... | $ 120,000 | |
| Accounts Receivable .............................. | 657,600 | |
| Allowance for Uncollectible Accounts .................. | | $ 36,000 |
| Land ......................................... | 144,000 | |
| Building....................................... | 1,488,000 | |
| Accumulated Depreciation.......................... | | 780,000 |
| Office Equipment ................................ | 336,000 | |
| Accumulated Depreciation.......................... | | 72,000 |
| Accounts Payable ................................ | | 408,000 |
| Mortgage Payable ................................ | | 480,000 |
| Jackson, Capital.................................. | | 489,600 |
| Cipriano, Capital.................................. | | 120,000 |
| Ackerman, Capital ................................ | | 360,000 |
| Totals ........................................ | $2,745,600 | $2,745,600 |

---

Jackson, Cipriano, and Ackerman share profits and losses in a 2:2:1 ratio. During the month of February 1998, the partnership is liquidated.

**Required:**

Given the following additional information, prepare the general journal entries to record the February transactions to liquidate the partnership. Allocate any gain or loss to the appropriate partners' accounts at the time of the transaction.

Feb. 2 Accounts receivable in the amount of $556,800 are collected. The remaining accounts and the Allowance for Uncollectible Accounts are written off.

4 The office equipment is sold to the Atlanta Company for $156,000.

9 The land and building are sold to Such Crust Bakery for $64,800 cash. The mortgage payable is transferred to the bakery in this transaction.

14 The accounts payable are paid.

15 Cipriano contributes cash necessary to remove the deficit in her capital account.

15 Cash is distributed to Jackson and Ackerman equal to their credit balances in their respective capital accounts.

▶ *(Check Figure: Cash distributed to Jackson, Feb. 15: $297,600)*

8 **Problem A8:** Preparing a Partnership Liquidation Schedule

On Dec. 1, 1998, Larry, Darryl, and Bob decide to liquidate their partnership. On the date of the liquidation, partnership assets total $630,000, of which $150,000 is cash. The partnership has liabilities of $270,000, and the partners' capital accounts (prior to closing Income Summary for the year-to-date income) reflect balances of $170,000 for Larry, $54,000 for Darryl, and $118,000 for Bob. Income Summary has a credit balance (after all adjusting and closing entries) of $18,000.

The partners share profits and losses in a 5:3:1 ratio. No partner has personal assets that can be contributed to the partnership.

**Required:**

1. Divide among the three partners the income earned by the partnership up to Dec. 1, 1995, and determine the balances in each capital account as of that date.
2. Prepare partnership liquidation schedules assuming that the other assets were sold during December for:
   a. $300,000
   b. $210,000
   c. $147,000

▶ *(Check Figure:* **1.** *Balance for Larry: $180,000;* **2. c.** *Distribution to Bob: $27,000)*

8 **Problem A9:** Preparing a Partnership Liquidation Schedule

Assume the same facts as in Problem A-8, above, except that each partner has personal assets that can be contributed to cover 75% of any deficit in his capital account.

**Required:**

Prepare partnership liquidation schedules assuming that the other assets were sold for:

a. $300,000
b. $210,000
c. $147,000

▶ *(Check Figure:* **c.** *Distribution to Bob: $69,000)*

## PROBLEMS: SET B

3 5† **Problem B1:** Accounting for Partnership Formation

Hatfield and McCoy are fierce competitors who sell hunting equipment. They finally decide to join forces in order to increase their business and reduce their costs. An agreement is reached

† The numbers in the margin refer to the Learning Objectives.

between the two men to begin operations as a partnership on Mar. 1, 1998. Since Hatfield will work full time in the business but McCoy will work only half time, they decide that an equitable way to share profits and losses is for McCoy to receive two-thirds and McCoy to receive the remaining one-third.

The balance sheets for Hatfield's and McCoy's businesses on Mar. 1 are presented below:

| Balance Sheets March 1, 1998 | | |
|---|---|---|
| | **Hatfield** | **McCoy** |
| **Assets** | | |
| Cash | $ 42,000 | $ 30,000 |
| Accounts Receivable | 389,200 | 169,200 |
| Allowance for Uncollectible Accounts | (22,400) | (14,400) |
| Merchandise Inventory | 461,600 | 300,800 |
| Prepaid Rent | — | 6,000 |
| Office Supplies on Hand | 30,400 | 4,000 |
| Land | 40,000 | — |
| Building | 128,000 | — |
| Accumulated Depreciation | (32,000) | — |
| Office Equipment | 24,000 | 62,000 |
| Accumulated Depreciation | (6,000) | (13,200) |
| Repair Equipment | 172,000 | — |
| Accumulated Depreciation | (68,000) | — |
| Total Assets | $1,158,800 | $544,400 |
| **Liabilities and Owner's Equity** | | |
| Notes Payable | $ 120,000 | — |
| Accounts Payable | 170,000 | $111,600 |
| Mortgage Payable | 200,000 | — |
| Hatfield, Capital | 668,800 | — |
| McCoy, Capital | — | 432,800 |
| Total Liabilities and Owner's Equity | $1,158,800 | $544,400 |

The partners agree that the name of the partnership will be Hatfield and McCoy Hunting Outfitters. They also agree to the following:

a. Concerning the transfer of Hatfield's assets and liabilities to the partnership:
   1. The accounts receivable are to be valued at $302,400, and Allowance for Uncollectible Accounts will have a zero balance when operations commence.
   2. Merchandise Inventory is to be reduced by $105,200.
   3. Office Supplies on Hand will remain as stated.
   4. Land will be established at its fair value of $108,000.
   5. Fixed assets will be recorded as follows:

   | | |
   |---|---|
   | Office Equipment | $ 16,000 |
   | Building | 192,000 |
   | Repair Equipment | 124,000 |

   6. Accumulated Depreciation will have a zero balance to commence operations.
   7. One-half of the notes payable are personal notes of Hatfield. All other liabilities are accepted by the partnership.
b. Concerning the transfer of McCoy's assets and liabilities to the partnership:
   1. The accounts receivable are to be valued at $136,800, and Allowance for Uncollectible Accounts will have a zero balance.
   2. Merchandise Inventory is to be increased by $7,200.

3. The prepaid rent is for a building that McCoy occupies. The partnership will continue to rent, occupying two locations, until its planned new building is completed.
4. Office Supplies on Hand will remain as stated.
5. Office equipment will be valued at $40,000, but accumulated depreciation will be zero.
6. Accounts payable will be accepted as stated.

**Required:**

1. Prepare the general journal entries to record the formation of the new partnership.
2. For the 10 months ending Dec. 31, the partnership reports a profit of $600,000. During this period, Hatfield has withdrawn $150,000 for personal use and McCoy has withdrawn $75,000. Prepare a statement of partners' capital accounts.

▶ *(Check Figure: 1. Credit to Hatfield, Capital: $741,200)*

4 5 **Problem B2:** Calculating the Profit Division for Different Profit Arrangements

The partnership of Ivey, Adam, and Hughes had a profit of $832,500 in 1998. During the year the partners had the following transactions in their capital accounts:

|  | Ivey | Adam | Hughes |
|---|---|---|---|
| Balance, Jan. 1, 1998 . . . . . . . . . . . . . . . . . . . . . | $150,000 | $ 180,000 | $120,000 |
| Investments . . . . . . . . . . . . . . . . . . . . . . . . . . . . . | 75,000 | 90,000 | 120,000 |
| Withdrawals . . . . . . . . . . . . . . . . . . . . . . . . . . . . . | (60,000) | (108,000) | (60,000) |
| Balance, Dec. 31, 1998 . . . . . . . . . . . . . . . . . . . | 165,000 | 162,000 | 180,000 |
| Average Balance . . . . . . . . . . . . . . . . . . . . . . . . . | 165,000 | 210,000 | 180,000 |

**Required:**

Determine the division of profits for each of the four different assumptions below:

1. Profits are shared equally.
2. Profits are shared in a ratio of 6:4:2.
3. Profits are shared in the ratio of the average capital balances for the year.
4. Profits are shared equally after allowing for 14% interest on the average capital balances and for salaries of $156,000, $108,000, and $132,000, respectively.

▶ *(Check Figure: 3. Ivey's share: $247,500; 4. Ivey's share: $298,700)*

4 **Problem B3:** Calculating the Profit Division for Different Levels of Profit

Kennedy, King, and Roberts enter into a partnership that provides for the division of profits and losses among the partners according to the following provisions:

a. Salary allowances as follows:

| Kennedy . . . . . . . . . . . . . . . . . . . . . . . . . . . . . . . . . | $10,500 |
|---|---|
| King . . . . . . . . . . . . . . . . . . . . . . . . . . . . . . . . . . . . . | 9,000 |
| Roberts . . . . . . . . . . . . . . . . . . . . . . . . . . . . . . . . . | 12,000 |

b. Interest allowance of 15% on the average capital balances for the year.
c. A bonus to Kennedy of 10% of any profits after allowing for salaries and interest.
d. The remainder shared equally.

The average capital balances for the three partners during the year were:

| Kennedy . . . . . . . . . . . . . . . . . . . . . . . . . . . . . . . . . | $24,000 |
|---|---|
| King . . . . . . . . . . . . . . . . . . . . . . . . . . . . . . . . . . . . . | 30,000 |
| Roberts . . . . . . . . . . . . . . . . . . . . . . . . . . . . . . . . . | 18,000 |

**Required:**

Prepare a division of income schedule for each of the following levels of profits and losses:

1. $60,000 profit
2. $45,000 profit
3. $9,000 loss

▶ *[Check Figure: **3.** King's share: $(3,600)]*

6 **Problem B4:** Recording the Admission of a New Partner

Field and Tyson have agreed to let Armor join their partnership by investing $100,000. At the time of Armor's admission, Field and Tyson share profits and losses at 60% and 40%, respectively; and the capital balances are $54,000 for Field and $46,000 for Tyson.

**Required:**

Prepare general journal entries to admit Armor to the partnership, under each of the following assumptions:

1. Armor's $100,000 investment gives him a 50% interest in the partnership.
2. Armor's $100,000 investment gives him a 45% interest in the partnership.
3. Armor's $100,000 investment gives him a 55% interest in the partnership.

▶ *(Check Figure: **2.** Credit to Armor, Capital: $90,000; **3.** Credit to Armor, Capital: $110,000)*

5 **Problem B5:** Preparing Financial Statements for a Partnership

Tinker, Evers, and Chance operate a sporting-goods store as a partnership and share profits and losses in a ratio of 50% to Tinker, 30% to Evers, and 20% to Chance. The trial balance for their store on December 31, 1998, is presented below:

| | Debits | Credits |
|---|---|---|
| Cash | $ 5,000 | |
| Accounts Receivable | 10,000 | |
| Inventory | 8,000 | |
| Building | 20,000 | |
| Accumulated Depreciation: Building | | $ 4,000 |
| Machinery and Equipment | 16,000 | |
| Accumulated Depreciation: Machinery and Equipment | | 3,000 |
| Land | 4,000 | |
| Accounts Payable | | 2,400 |
| Salaries Payable | | 300 |
| Capital, Tinker | | 13,200 |
| Capital, Evers | | 10,900 |
| Capital, Chance | | 12,200 |
| Sales | | 60,000 |
| Cost of Goods Sold | 24,300 | |
| Salaries Expense | 16,000 | |
| Depreciation Expense: Building | 600 | |
| Depreciation Expense: Machinery and Equipment | 800 | |
| Property Tax Expense | 500 | |
| Utilities Expense | 800 | |
| Totals | $106,000 | $106,000 |

**Required:**

1. Prepare an income statement for 1998 for the sporting-goods store. Show the division of net income at the bottom of the income statement.
2. Prepare a statement of partners' capital accounts for 1998. Assume the following additional information:

|  | Tinker | Evers | Chance |
|---|---|---|---|
| Capital, Jan. 1, 1998 | $10,000 | $12,000 | $10,800 |
| Investments | 3,200 | –0– | 2,400 |
| Withdrawals | –0– | 1,100 | 1,000 |

3. Prepare the balance sheet on Dec. 31, 1998.

▶ *(Check Figure: 2. Balance in Capital, Evers, on Dec. 31, 1998: $16,000; 3. Total Assets: $56,000)*

6  7  **Problem B6:** Accounting for the Death of a Partner

McKenzie, Shayes, and Fuentes, who are partners in a Los Angeles law firm, share profits in the following ratio:

| McKenzie | 50% |
|---|---|
| Shayes | 40% |
| Fuentes | 10% |

After the firm's New Year's Eve party at the end of 1998, Shayes falls to her death down an open elevator shaft. This accident was extremely unfortunate for the remaining partners, since 1998 was the firm's best year ever, with profits of $400,000.

The partners' trial balance on Dec. 31 is presented below (all accounts except Income Summary have been closed for the year):

**McKENZIE, SHAYES, AND FUENTES**
**Trial Balance**
**December 31, 1998**

| | | |
|---|---|---|
| Cash | $  189,000 | |
| Accounts Receivable | 387,600 | |
| Allowance for Uncollectible Accounts | | $     40,500 |
| Office Supplies | 43,500 | |
| Prepaid Rent | 9,000 | |
| Office Equipment | 800,000 | |
| Accumulated Depreciation | | 92,600 |
| Notes Payable | | 150,900 |
| Accounts Payable | | 284,100 |
| Income Summary | | 400,000 |
| McKenzie, Capital | | 200,000 |
| Shayes, Capital | | 100,000 |
| Fuentes, Capital | | 161,000 |
| Totals | $1,429,100 | $1,429,100 |

**Required:**

1. Determine the balances in each of the partners' capital accounts on the day of Shayes's death.
2. For each of the following independent situations, prepare the general journal entries necessary to record the remaining partners' settlement with Shayes's estate.
   a. Shayes's estate sells one-half of her interest to McKenzie for $200,000, and one-half to Fuentes for $200,000.
   b. Shayes's estate is paid cash by the partnership equal to the balance in her capital account.
   c. Shayes's estate is paid cash by the partnership in the amount of $300,000.
   d. Shayes's estate is paid cash by the partnership in the amount of $200,000.

▶ *(Check Figure: 1. Shayes: $260,000; 2. a. Credit to Fuentes, Capital: $130,000; c. Debit to Fuentes, Capital: $6,667)*

8  **Problem B7:** Preparing Journal Entries for a Partnership Liquidation

Hale, McBird, and Pairsh are all famous athletes who have been operating a sports memorabilia store for many years. The partnership has decided to liquidate its operation rather than sell the business because they are each about to retire and want to go their separate ways. They have been sharing profits in the ratio of 40% to Hale, 40% to McBird, and 20% to Pairsh. The trial balance for their business on Jan. 1, 1998, is given below:

| Trial Balance January 1, 1998 | | |
|---|---:|---:|
| Cash | $   42,000 | |
| Accounts Receivable | 189,600 | |
| Allowance for Uncollectible Accounts | | $   11,100 |
| Merchandise Inventory | 293,100 | |
| Prepaid Insurance | 9,000 | |
| Office equipment | 31,500 | |
| Accumulated Depreciation: Office Equipment | | 10,500 |
| Machinery | 81,600 | |
| Accumulated Depreciation: Machinery | | 32,100 |
| Building | 375,000 | |
| Accumulated Depreciation: Building | | 112,500 |
| Land | 120,000 | |
| Notes Payable | | 120,000 |
| Accounts Payable | | 220,500 |
| Mortgage Payable | | 240,000 |
| Hale, Capital | | 135,000 |
| McBird, Capital | | 60,000 |
| Pairsh, Capital | | 200,100 |
| Totals | $1,141,800 | $1,141,800 |

**Required:**

The following transactions all took place in January 1998, during the process of liquidating the partnership. Prepare general journal entries to record each transaction. Allocate any gains or losses to the appropriate partners' capital accounts at the time of the transaction. Remember that if any partner's capital account shows a deficit, he will not be able to contribute any personal assets to cover it.

Jan.  6   $151,500 of the accounts receivable are collected, and the allowance for uncollectible accounts is written off the books.

   9   The merchandise inventory is sold for $160,500.

   11   A refund on the prepaid insurance is expected, totaling $3,000.

   14   The fixed assets were sold to Pinckney Company for the lump sum of $111,000. The mortgage on the building was also transferred to Pinckney.

   20   The remaining creditors were paid in full.

   20   The deficit in McBird's capital account was absorbed by Hale and Pairsh.

   20   The deficit in Hale's capital account was absorbed by Pairsh.

   24   The remaining partnership cash is distributed to Pairsh.

▶ *(Check Figure: Cash distributed to Pairsh on Jan. 20: $127,500)*

8  **Problem B8:** Preparing a Partnership Liquidation Schedule

On June 1, 1998, Christopher, Steffs, and Jenner decide to liquidate their tennis camp operation. On the date of the liquidation the partnership has cash of $30,000 and other assets on the books for $420,000. In addition, the partnership has debts totaling $180,000.

During the first 5 months of 1998, up to the date of liquidation, the tennis camp experienced a $75,000 loss, which is shared in the following manner:

Christopher ............................. one-half
Steffs .................................... one-third
Jenner ................................... one-sixth

On June 1, the balances in the partners' capital accounts (prior to closing Income Summary for the first 5 months of 1998) are $96,000 for Christopher, $205,000 for Steffs, and $44,000 for Jenner. No partner has personal assets that can be contributed to the partnership, in case her capital account develops a deficit.

**Required:**

1. Divide among the three partners the loss that was sustained by the partnership up to June 1, 1998, and determine the balances in each capital account as of that date.
2. Prepare partnership liquidation schedules assuming that the other assets were sold during December for:
   a. $330,000
   b. $285,000
   c. $258,000

▶ *(Check Figure:* **1.** *Balance for Steffs: $180,000;* **2. c.** *Distribution to Steffs: $108,000)*

8   **Problem B9:** Preparing a Partnership Liquidation Schedule

Assume the same facts as in Problem B8, above, except that each partner has personal assets that can cover 60% of any deficit in her capital account.

**Required:**

Prepare partnership liquidation schedules assuming that the other assets were sold for:

a. $330,000
b. $285,000
c. $258,000

▶ *(Check Figure:* **c.** *Distribution to Steffs: $120,000)*

## DECISION PROBLEM

Ten years after graduation, three ex-fraternity brothers decide to start their own business manufacturing robots. Bill, who worked with a major toy manufacturer, will be in charge of production; Jack, who was in advertising with a New York agency, will handle sales and promotion; and Bob, who was a stockbroker, will handle all financial affairs. Their initial investments are as follows:

Bill...................................... $150,000
Jack..................................... 100,000
Bob ..................................... 50,000
                                          —————
                                          $300,000

The major problem they have is deciding on the way to divide profits among the three partners. They have asked a fourth ex-fraternity brother, Jim, who is a CPA, to recommend an equitable system of distribution. Jim comes up with the following three possible ways of dividing profits:

a. Base the profit ratio on each member's relative value to the firm. The relative value would be based roughly on the typical salary that each partner would be making if he were an employee in a comparable company. Under this approach, profits would be distributed in the following manner:

Bill ...................................... 25%
Jack...................................... 30%
Bob ...................................... 45%

b. Allow each partner a salary equal to the amount earned at his last job. This would be $50,000 for Bill, $60,000 for Jack, and $80,000 for Bob. All remaining profits would be allocated according to the ratio of the partners' original capital balances.

c. Allow each partner interest of 10% on his original invested capital. Share all remaining profits equally.

**Required:**

Evaluate each of these suggested ways of dividing profits, and decide which plan would be preferred by each partner. In coming to your conclusion, consider the following three possible levels of income for the partnership:

1. $40,000
2. $100,000
3. $500,000

▶ *(Check Figure: For profit sharing recommendation No. 2, share to Bill at the $40,000 level, $(25,000); at the $100,000 level, $5,000; at the $500,000 level, $205,000)*

---

## ETHICS CASE

Matty Lucas has a reasonably successful accounting practice that performs bookkeeping work for a large number of individuals and small businesses. Matty would like to expand his practice into tax preparation, but he doesn't feel he has the necessary expertise to perform the tax work by himself. He'd like to find a qualified tax person to become his partner.

Matty's new next-door neighbor, Vance Carrols, has recently retired from the IRS, where he was a regional supervisor. Vance is currently looking for a position with a small accounting firm for at least the next 2 or 3 years, and has talked extensively with Matty about becoming his partner. Matty sees this opportunity as a match made in heaven.

Unfortunately, Vance has very little to bring to the partnership other than his expertise. He can invest only $10,000, whereas Matty has invested $90,000. Since Matty is so impressed by Vance's credentials and potential for building a thriving tax practice, he is willing to let Vance enter the partnership with this small investment.

The only issue left to iron out is the manner in which the partners will share profits. Since Vance has become very familiar with partnership agreements while auditing the tax returns of numerous individuals, he volunteers to work out an equitable arrangement that compensates each partner for the relative value of his contribution to the firm.

Vance evaluates the income stream for Matty's practice over the last 5 years, and he factors in the potential for expansion in the next few years. He is not encouraged, because his most optimistic projections for the firm are profits (before allowances for salaries) of $60,000 per year during each of the next 3 years. Vance is about to call off the deal when he thinks of a way to share profits that he thinks will be acceptable. The next day he makes the following proposals to Matty:

1. Since Vance's major contribution to the firm is his tax experience, which would bring a salary of $100,000 with a large CPA firm, he should be compensated with a comparable salary allowance. The partnership would be a lot smaller than a CPA firm, however, so Vance would be willing to receive only $80,000 per year. Since Matty's work is primarily that of a bookkeeper, he should receive the going rate for a good bookkeeper, about $20,000 per year.
2. Since Matty's investment in the firm is much larger than Vance's, Vance feels that it would only be fair that Matty receive a much larger share of the partnership profits (after salary allowances) as compensation for the difference in resources that each partner has committed to the partnership. Therefore profits (after salary allowances) should be allocated to the partners in a ratio based on the initial balances in their capital accounts.

Although Matty feels that a good bookkeeper is worth a lot more than $20,000, he feels that the provision about sharing profits on the basis of the balances in the begining capital accounts is a fair way to offset the difference in salaries. Matty agrees to the terms, and Matty and Vance sign the agreement and shake hands.

**Required**

1. If Vance's most optimistic projections are correct, how would the profits be divided between Vance and Matty?
2. How would the profits be divided between Vance and Matty if the partnership profits (before salary allowances) were: (a) $77,778 and (b) $175,000?
3. Do these different possible results lead you to conclude that Vance's recommendations for sharing profits are unethical? Or do they just represent good negotiation skills?

---

## OBJECTIVE ASSIGNMENT ANSWERS

**True/False**

1. T    2. F    3. T    4. F    5. T

**Multiple Choice**

1. d    2. d    3. a    4. a    5. d
6. b    7. c    8. a    9. b    10. c

# Corporations: Formation and Operations

**LEARNING OBJECTIVES**

After studying this chapter, you should be able to do the following:

1 Describe what a corporation is and how corporate management is structured

2 List the advantages and disadvantages of being organized as a corporation

3 Describe the rights possessed by common stockholders

4 List and explain the steps followed in organizing a new corporation

5 Prepare journal entries to record an issuance of common stock on a subscription basis, for cash, and for assets other than cash

6 Define treasury stock and prepare journal entries to record the acquisition and sale of treasury stock

7 Describe the characteristics of preferred stock

8 Allocate dividends between preferred and common stockholders

9 Prepare a journal entry to issue preferred stock

10 Define and prepare journal entries to record donated capital

11 Prepare the stockholders' equity section of the balance sheet

12 Calculate and discuss the stockholders' equity to total assets and debt to total assets ratios.

13 Define par value, stated value, market value, liquidation value, and equity per share of stock

14 Define the key terms listed at the end of the chapter

**CHAPTER OUTLINE**

**THE CORPORATION DESCRIBED** • Articles of Incorporation • Advantages of Corporations • Disadvantages of Corporations • Corporate Organization Structure • Corporations versus Proprietorships and Partnerships • **CORPORATE OWNERS' EQUITY: AN OVERVIEW** • Paid-In Capital: Capital Stock • Earned Capital: Retained Earnings • Owners' Equity versus Stockholders' Equity • **ORGANIZING A CORPORATION AND ISSUING COMMON STOCK** • Par versus No-Par Stock • Issuing Stock for Cash • Issuing Stock by Subscription • Issuing Stock in Exchange for Noncash Consideration • **TREASURY STOCK** • Purchase of Treasury Stock • Sale of Treasury Stock above Cost • Sale of Treasury Stock below Cost • **PREFERRED STOCK** • Characteristics of Preferred Stock • Accounting for Preferred Stock • **DONATED CAPITAL** • **STOCKHOLDERS' EQUITY ON THE BALANCE SHEET** • **FINANCIAL STATEMENT ANALYSIS** • Stockholders' Equity to Total Assets Ratio • Debt to Total Assets Ratio • **STOCK VALUE: A REVIEW** • Par Value and Stated Value • Market Value • Equity per Share • Liquidation Value

## THE CORPORATION DESCRIBED

Learning
Objective 1

Describe what a corporation is and
how corporate management is
structured

A **corporation** is an artificial legal being created by a government charter that endows it with certain powers. A corporation exists in the eyes of the law as though it were a person separate and distinct from the people who own it. It has many of the rights that a natural person possesses. It may own property, borrow money, sue and be sued, and in a sense it may even "marry" another corporation through a merger.

Corporations are the dominant form of business organization in the United States. While proprietorships and partnerships are far more numerous, corporations own the largest amount of resources, produce and sell the most products, and employ the greatest number of individuals.

Some corporations are established by the federal government to operate in the public interest. An example is the Federal Deposit Insurance Corporation (FDIC), which insures the safety of many deposits in banks. The corporations you are most familiar with, those in business to make and sell products and services, are created under the laws of the various states. A corporation must meet the requirements set forth by the state in which it is incorporated. A company may incorporate in one state, have its main office in another state, and operate in many states. The Coca-Cola Company, for instance, is incorporated in Delaware, has its primary executive offices in Georgia, and operates in all 50 states (and in many foreign countries).

### Articles of Incorporation

When we decide we want to do business as a corporation, we must apply to a state government for permission to be a corporation—to *incorporate*.

We begin the incorporation process by filing proposed articles of incorporation, plus the required fee, with the appropriate state office. A lawyer should be consulted when writing the proposed articles, so that they will be in the proper form and will include all information required by state law. When these **articles of incorporation** are approved, they become a part of the charter creating the corporation. The **charter** is the document issued by a state government giving a business the legal right to begin operating as a corporation.

Since each state has its own laws governing what should be included in the articles of incorporation, their contents will vary from state to state. Here are some of the frequently required articles:

*Name and purpose of the corporation.* We can choose almost any name for our corporation, as long as no other group is already using it. We may state our purpose narrowly; for example, we could say that we are establishing a corporation to sell peanuts at high school football games in Michigan. Or we may state our purpose broadly, so that we can diversify into many types of businesses without having to form a new corporation each time. In some states, for example, we can say that our purpose is to enter into any lawful business activity permitted by the state.

*Capital stock.* Ownership of a corporation is represented by shares of stock. Every corporation must have one type of stock, called *common stock*. In addition, other types, or classes, of stock may be issued. The charter must identify our *authorized stock*—that is, classes of stock that our corporation has permission to issue, the number of shares of each type that we are permitted to issue, what rights or special preferences are granted to each type of stock, and what restrictions are imposed upon each class. The amount of assets contributed by owners at the beginning of the new business must also be specified. We will discuss the various classes of stock and their rights and restrictions later in this chapter.

*Place of business.* We must specify the location of our principal office or place of business, so that an official address will be registered with the state. Our tax bills, lawsuits filed against us, and other legal correspondence will be sent to this legal address.

*Duration.* The life of our corporation must be defined. Although we may select a short life, such as 10 years, most corporations elect a perpetual—unending—life.

*Directors and officers.* We must list the names and addresses of the first governing body of our corporation, the board of directors, and its operating managers, the officers. After the corporation begins operations, the stockholders (owners) will meet and elect new members to the board of directors.

*Incorporators.* The names and addresses of the individuals filing the articles of incorporation, the *incorporators,* must be listed. We must also disclose the number of shares of stock that each incorporator has agreed to buy, and how the shares are to be paid for. Cash or some other asset—building, land, equipment—may be used to pay for shares.

If all the required information is properly presented, the state will issue a certificate of incorporation, or charter. Once we receive the charter, we may begin issuing stock and operating our business.

Before we explain how to account for the issuance of stock, let's examine the advantages and disadvantages of the corporate form of business, see what the management structure of a corporation looks like, and contrast the characteristics of corporations with those of proprietorships and partnerships.

## Advantages of Corporations

Learning Objective **2**

List the advantages and disadvantages of being organized as a corporation

Corporations have several advantages that may make this form of organization more desirable than either a partnership or a proprietorship.

*Larger amounts of capital can be raised.* Large numbers of individuals and institutions can more easily and efficiently acquire and dispose of ownership interests in a corporation than in a partnership. Many corporations have several million stockholders who have cumulatively invested more than $100 million.

*Owners' liability is limited.* Liability of the owners is limited to the amount invested in the corporation—the amount that each stockholder paid for his or her stock. Creditors having a claim against the corporation must be paid only from the assets of the corporation; personal assets of the stockholders are not available to the corporation's creditors. In contrast, in a partnership one or more partners must have unlimited liability, thus risking personal as well as business assets.

*Ownership shares are easily transferred.* After the initial issuance of stock, shares may be transferred in private sale transactions, traded (sold) on established securities markets such as the New York Stock Exchange, or given away. The only involvement of the corporation in these transactions is in keeping an up-to-date list of the names and addresses of the stockholders.

The billions of dollars that change hands daily through sales of stock on the New York Stock Exchange and the American Stock Exchange do not flow into the coffers of the corporations whose stock is being traded. Corporations acquire capital, cash, and other assets only upon a new issuance of stock or the sale of stock previously reacquired. Of course, corporations may also borrow money by issuing bonds or by getting a loan from a bank or other financial institution.

Sale of a partnership interest is usually a much more complex affair. Remember, each new partner must be acceptable to all of the old partners.

*A corporation has continuity of existence. Continuity of existence* refers to the unlimited life of a corporation. The transfer of ownership shares does not affect the corporation's ability to operate routinely over decades. In contrast, a partnership's life ends each time a new partner enters or an old one retires. Continuity of existence makes long-term borrowing easier for a corporation than for partnerships and proprietorships.

*Professional managers run the business.* In all but the smallest corporations, a team of professionals is hired to manage the day-to-day operations of the business. Corporations are more likely to have managers trained specifically in accounting, finance, marketing, and production than are proprietorships or partnerships.

*Corporations lack mutual agency.* Any partner can sign a contract on behalf of the partnership and thereby commit all the other partners to honor the contract. Stockholders do not have this mutual agency. In a corporation, only designated individuals have the authority to sign contracts. Thus, owners are protected from impulsive and possibly unwise decisions of other owners.

## Disadvantages of Corporations

If the corporate form were preferable in every way, there would be little reason for proprietorships and partnerships to exist. In fact, however, corporations have some disadvantages, which anyone thinking of forming a corporation should consider.

*The income of a corporation is taxed twice.* Corporate income is taxed for the first time when it is earned by the entity. As an artificial person, the corporation enjoys the natural person's obligation to pay income taxes. Corporate income is taxed at a maximum rate of approximately 34%.

Corporate income is taxed a second time when it is distributed to shareholders as dividends. While the amount of tax the individual pays will depend on many factors, the maximum tax rate is 31%. Only after this double tax is paid is the remaining corporate income available for the individual owner to spend. Some small corporations may avoid double taxation by electing to be taxed as partnerships. For tax purposes these entities are called *Subchapter S corporations.*

Income is taxed only once in a partnership or individual proprietorship. Individual partners and proprietors pay taxes at personal income tax rates when the income is earned. The partnership or proprietorship entity is not required to pay income taxes.

To illustrate the impact of double taxation, assume that you own one-fourth of the stock of a corporation with income before income tax of $100,000, and a one-fourth interest in a partnership with income before income tax of $100,000. If the corporation distributed all its after-tax income to the stockholders, it would have $66,000 to distribute after paying $100,000 × 34% = $34,000 in corporate income taxes. You would receive $\frac{1}{4}$ × $66,000 = $16,500. Out of this $16,500, you would have to pay $16,500 × 31% = $5,115 in personal income tax. You would then have $11,385 of the corporate income to spend.

Assuming that the partnership also distributed all its income to the owners, you would receive $\frac{1}{4}$ × $100,000 = $25,000. Out of this $25,000 you would pay 31% × $25,000 = $7,750 in personal income tax, leaving you $17,250 to spend.

We have made some simplifying assumptions in this example, but the point is still valid: Corporate income is taxed twice and ultimately provides less spendable cash for its owners than if the business were operated as a partnership or proprietorship.

*Corporations are subject to more government regulations than either proprietorships or partnerships.* One federal agency that regulates all publicly owned corporations is the Securities and Exchange Commission (SEC). It has influence over the activities of only a very few partnerships.

The SEC has the responsibility for seeing that truthful information is presented to potential investors in corporate stocks. Subject to certain minimum size limitations, a corporation planning to sell stock to the public must file extensive information about its business activities, directors, operating performance (income), and financial position (balance sheet). After careful review by SEC staff members, this factual information can be made public by the corporation. The public can then study the data and decide whether to purchase stock from the corporation. The corporation must also file quarterly financial reports (called *10Q's*) and annual financial reports (called *10K's*) with the SEC. These reports are also available to stockholders and other interested parties.

Compliance with the regulations of the SEC and the various other federal, state, and local agencies is an expensive and time-consuming activity.

*Ownership is separated from control of operations.* Proprietors and partners normally are closely involved with and interested in the day-to-day operation of the business. Their personal financial well-being may rest on the success or failure of the company. Stockholders rely on professional managers to run the corporation, so they have little continuous contact with ongoing operations. This lack of contact is fine if the business is operating smoothly and profitably; but if things are not going well, the stockholders may wish they had more direct control. Since control is exercised through the election of the board of directors and through other actions at the annual stockholders' meeting, the corporate owner can have little immediate effect on corporate management or operations.

## Corporate Organization Structure

The organization structure of most large corporations follows the same basic pattern. You will find that this pattern is modified somewhat to fit the needs of specific organizations. But if you understand the basic structure, you will have a good grasp of the various parts of the corporate structure.

Figure 1 shows the basic corporate organization structure and the function of each group in the structure.

**Figure 1** Basic Corporate Organization Structure

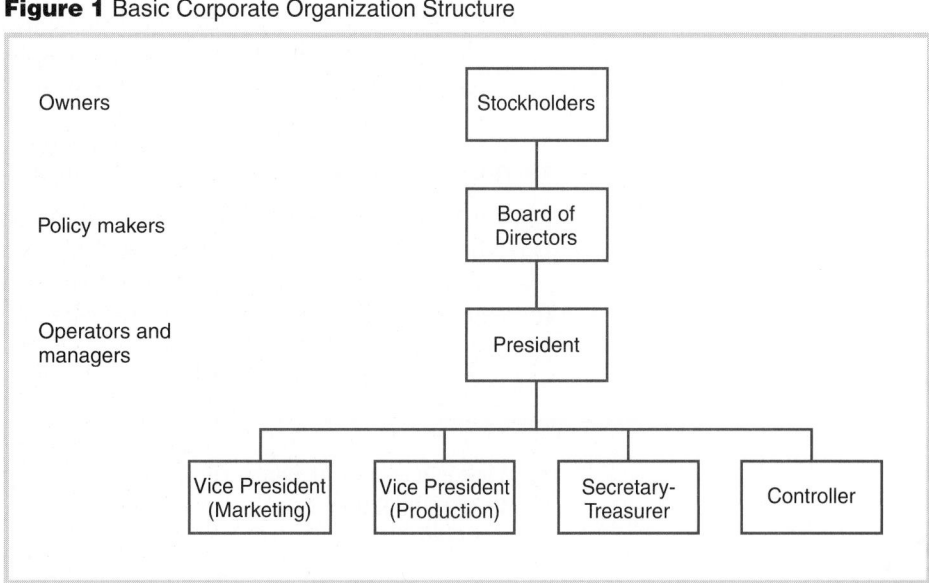

## Stockholders

The stockholders are the owners of the corporation: A **stockholder** (or **share-holder**) is an entity owning one or more shares of stock. Most state corporation laws give stockholders certain rights, which usually include the following:

1.  The right to receive a certificate as evidence of ownership interest, and to transfer such shares as they choose through either sale or gift.
2.  The right to vote at stockholders' meetings on the election of directors and on other such matters as may be brought before them for action.
3.  The right to purchase a portion of any new shares issued such that they will own the same percentage of the total shares after the new issuance of stock as before. This **preemptive right** may be given up in some cases by a vote of the stockholders. One such case may exist when a special stock purchase plan (stock option plan) is initiated to reward top-level executives.
4.  The right to receive dividends declared by the board of directors. This distribution of profits usually takes the form of cash, but other assets may be distributed as well.
5.  The right to receive assets upon dissolution of the corporation if any remain after the creditors have been paid.

### Board of Directors

The **board of directors,** elected by the stockholders, is responsible for the management of the corporation. The board usually delegates the power to make operating decisions and to run the day-to-day activities of the business to a professional management team.

The board normally confines its attention to (1) making policy, (2) reviewing management performance, and (3) acting on matters that only it can legally decide. Decisions to expand the business by introducing a new product or by opening operations in a new geographic area are examples of major policy decisions. Declaring that dividends will be paid to stockholders is an action that can be taken legally only by the board.

### President and Other Operating Officers

The president, various vice presidents, the secretary-treasurer, and the controller are responsible for carrying out the policies set by the board. They operate the corporation by supervising the purchase (or manufacture) of the product, and by selling and distributing the product. They hire employees, prepare budgets, arrange short-term borrowing, and attend to all the other details necessary to run a business.

### Corporations versus Proprietorships and Partnerships

Exhibit 1 contrasts the major characteristics of corporations with those of the other two types of organizations that we have discussed previously—proprietorships and partnerships. Keep in mind that the statements in the exhibit are generalizations; there are exceptions to many of them.

**ASK YOURSELF** ▶

1.  **What is a corporate charter?**
2.  **What is the life of a corporation?**

**Exhibit 1** Proprietorship, Partnership, and Corporation Compared

| Characteristic | Proprietorship | Partnership | Corporation |
|---|---|---|---|
| Ownership | Single owner. | Few owners. (Large partnerships may have more than 1,000 partners.) | Many stockholders. (Small corporations may have only two or three stockholders.) |
| Owner's liability (risk) | Proprietor personally liable for all obligations of the business. | Partners personally liable for all obligations of the business. (Some partners may have limited liability.) | Stockholders' liability is limited to the amount of their initial investment—the amount each paid for his or her stock. |
| Management | Proprietor usually manages the business. | Some partners usually actively involved in managing the business. (Some partners may not be involved in management.) | Board of directors sets policy; professional management team operates the business. Owners of large corporations are not involved in management. |
| Life span | Limited. Life of the business is limited to the life of the proprietor. | Limited. Technically, a new partnership is formed each time a partner leaves and a new one is admitted. | Unlimited. New owners do not affect the continuity of the business. |
| Transferability of ownership | Not transferable. When proprietor sells the proprietorship, a new business is formed. | May be difficult. Each time a partner sells his interest, all the old partners must agree to admit the new one. | Generally easy. Stockholders may sell shares privately or through an established exchange. |
| Ease of raising capital | Difficult. Capital is usually limited to owner's personal resources and the amount he or she can personally borrow. | May be difficult. The amount of capital is limited to the personal resources of the individual partners and the amount they can personally borrow. Additional partners may be admitted in order to raise more capital. | Usually easier than for a proprietorship or partnership. Corporation may borrow money or issue more shares of stock. Registration and reporting to federal and state agencies is usually required. |
| Income taxes | Proprietor is taxed as an individual on profits of the business as they are earned. | Partners are taxed as individuals on profits of partnership when profits are earned, not when they are distributed to the partners. | Corporation is taxed on profits when they are earned. Stockholders are taxed when profits are distributed as dividends. |
| Division of profits | All profits and losses go to proprietor. | Profits and losses are divided according to the partnership agreement. | Common stockholders receive an equal amount per share, but only when a dividend is declared by the board of directors. |

3. **How does a corporate owner's personal liability differ from a partner's personal liability?**

4. **How are corporate earnings taxed twice?**

5. **What is the preemptive right of stockholders?**

6. **What is the primary function of a corporate board of directors?**

## CORPORATE OWNERS' EQUITY: AN OVERVIEW

Before we discuss in detail the transactions that affect corporate owners' equity, or stockholders' equity, let's look briefly at its major components and contrast it with owner's equity in a proprietorship and a partnership.

**Stockholders' equity** has two major components, paid-in capital and earned capital. **Paid-In capital** reflects the amount of resources received by a corporation as a result of investment by stockholders, donation, or other capital stock transactions that we will discuss later in the chapter. The law mandates that a corporation keep the amount of resources contributed by owners and others separate from **earned capital,** the resources generated through the operations of the corporation. Now let's look briefly at capital stock and retained earnings, the two basic subcomponents of paid-in capital and earned capital, respectively.

### Paid-In Capital: Capital Stock

We noted earlier that **capital stock** refers to all types of ownership shares in a corporation. Stockholders normally acquire one of two basic types of capital stock as evidence of their ownership interest: common or preferred.

**Common stock** represents the primary ownership of the corporation. Common stockholders possess all the stockholder rights listed earlier. More than any other security holders, they reap the rewards or suffer the consequences of a volatile stock market. If only one class of stock is issued, it is common stock.

When stock is sold and paid for in full, the owner is sent a stock certificate showing how many shares he or she owns. At this point the stock is said to be *issued.*

**Preferred stock** is issued by many corporations to appeal to investors who are unwilling to take all the risks involved in common stock ownership. The rights of the common stockholder are modified to provide the preferred stockholder with certain advantages, or preferences. For example, dividends are paid to preferred stockholders before any are paid to common stockholders. At the same time, preferred stockholders give up some of the privileges accorded to common stockholders, such as the right to vote for members of the board of directors. We will take a closer look at preferred stock later in this chapter.

As we discuss stock transactions, keep in mind that **authorized stock** is the total number of shares of each type of stock that the corporate charter allows the corporation to sell. **Issued stock** is the amount of capital stock that has been sold at some point in the corporation's history. **Outstanding stock** is the amount of capital stock that is in the hands of the shareholders.

### Earned Capital: Retained Earnings

Retained Earnings is a stockholders' equity account that shows the income accumulated since the corporation's creation and still retained in the business in some form. It's the accumulated income that the corporation still has in the form of assets.

Retained Earnings emerges from the final step in closing all corporate income accounts. The Income Summary balance is closed to Owner's Capital in a proprietorship or into the partners' capital accounts in a partnership. Since the corporate capital accounts, shown under paid-in capital, must be kept separate from the earnings account, Income Summary is closed to Retained Earnings.

### Owners' Equity versus Stockholders' Equity

Condensed balance sheets of a proprietorship, a partnership, and a corporation will help clarify the major difference among the three statements:

| A. KEE, PROPRIETOR<br>Balance Sheet<br>December 31, 1998 | | BECK & COX, PARTNERS<br>Balance Sheet<br>December 31, 1998 | | OXFORD, CORPORATION<br>Balance Sheet<br>December 31, 1998 | |
|---|---|---|---|---|---|
| **Assets** | | **Assets** | | **Assets** | |
| Current Assets | $ 20,000 | Current Assets | $ 30,000 | Current Assets | $ 80,000 |
| Property, Plant, and Equipment | 95,000 | Property, Plant, and Equipment | 240,000 | Property, Plant, and Equipment | 580,000 |
| Intangible Assets | 1,000 | Intangible Assets | 5,000 | Intangible Assets | 20,000 |
| Total Assets | $116,000 | Total Assets | $275,000 | Total Assets | $680,000 |
| **Liabilities and Owner's Equity** | | **Liabilities and Owner's Equity** | | **Liabilities and Stockholders' Equity** | |
| Liabilities: | | Liabilities: | | Liabilities: | |
| Current Liabilities | $ 16,000 | Current Liabilities | $ 15,000 | Current Liabilities | $ 35,000 |
| Noncurrent Liabilities | 5,000 | Noncurrent Liabilities | 32,000 | Noncurrent Liabilities | 200,000 |
| Total Liabilities | $ 21,000 | Total Liabilities | $ 47,000 | Total Liabilities | $235,000 |
| Owner's Equity: | | Owner's Equity: | | Stockholders' Equity: | |
| A. Kee, Capital | $ 95,000 | R. Beck, Capital | $178,000 | Paid-in Capital: | |
| | | O. Cox, Capital | 50,000 | Common Stock | $300,000 |
| | | Total Owner's Equity | $228,000 | Earned Capital: | |
| | | | | Retained Earnings | $145,000 |
| | | | | Total Stockholders' Equity | $445,000 |
| Total Liabilities and Owner's Equity | $116,000 | Total Liabilities and Owners' Equity | $275,000 | Total Liabilities and Stockholders' Equity | $680,000 |

The asset and liability sections of the balance sheet are not affected by the type of business organization chosen, whether proprietorship, partnership, or corporation. The only difference among the three balance sheets is in the owners' equity sections. As we have noted, proprietorships and partnerships use capital accounts and combine owners' contributions and accumulated earnings. Corporate stockholders' equity keeps contributed capital separate from accumulated earnings.

**ASK YOURSELF ▶**

1. What are the two major subsections shown in the stockholders' equity section of the balance sheet?
2. How does preferred stock differ from common stock?
3. What is authorized, issued, and outstanding capital stock?

## ORGANIZING A CORPORATION AND ISSUING COMMON STOCK

**Learning Objective 4**
List and explain the steps followed in organizing a new corporation

Let's turn now to the accounting process involved in organizing a corporation and issuing common stock. In doing so, we'll follow the experiences of John and Karen Hood in establishing a ski shop.

# SKI WORLD, INC.

John and Karen Hood and two of their friends decide to go into the business of selling skis, boots, ski clothing, and accessories. After discussing the merits of the various types of business organizations, they elect to incorporate as Ski World, Inc. ("Inc." is an abbreviation for "incorporated." It denotes that the owners established this business as a corporation rather than as a proprietorship or partnership.) They hire an attorney and a CPA to prepare the necessary articles of incorporation, to set up the accounting system, and to advise them regarding the various tax forms they will need to file. Before long, the articles of incorporation are approved and the charter is received. The corporation is ready to sell stock.

The charter of incorporation authorizes Ski World to issue 100,000 shares of $10-par common stock and 10,000 shares of $10-par, 8% preferred stock.

## Par versus No-Par Stock

Many state laws require that stock have a par value. **Par value** is determined arbitrarily and bears no relation to the actual market value of the stock. In some states par value defines an amount of **legal capital** that must be retained in the business. The amount represented as legal capital cannot be distributed to stockholders except when the corporation is liquidated. (A corporation is liquidated when it goes out of business, pays all its debts, and gives any remaining assets to the stockholders.)

Because many investors are confused about the meaning of par value, many states now permit the issuance of *no-par* stock. Some of these states allow the board of directors to arbitrarily select a **stated value.** If this is done, the stock is said to be *no-par with a stated value.* A stated value serves the same purpose as par value but is not printed on the stock certificates, so there is less risk of confusing investors.

Remember, par and stated values are legal concepts, not actual prices; do not confuse them with a stock's market value. **Market value per share** is the amount that a share of stock sells for. Market value almost always will be higher than the nominal par or stated value of the stock.

In accounting for the issuance of stock, the par or stated value, if any, is recorded in the Common Stock account. This method preserves the legal capital in a separate account and makes balance sheet disclosure easier. Any amount received over and above par or stated value is credited to Paid-In Capital in Excess of Par (or Stated Value). Since par or stated value is usually set at a nominal amount , common stock is rarely sold for less than that value. No-par stock without a stated value is accounted for simply by crediting Common Stock for its sale price.

Throughout our Ski World illustration we will assume that common stock is issued for more than its par or stated value. This is also called issuing stock at a *premium.* In those rare instances when common stock is issued for less than par value, at a *discount,* the entry to record the sale includes a debit to Discount on Common Stock and a credit to Common Stock.

## Issuing Stock for Cash

Learning
Objective 5

Prepare journal entries to record an
issuance of common stock on a
subscription basis, for cash, and for
assets other than cash

Each of the four Ski World incorporators agrees to purchase 5,000 shares themselves for $15 per share. The entry to record[1] this sale on Jan. 5, 1998—20,000 shares (4 × 5,000)—of stock is:

| | | | |
|---|---|---:|---:|
| Jan. 5 | Cash ....................................... | 300,000 | |
| | Common Stock ............................. | | 200,000 |
| | Paid-In Capital in Excess of Par: Common ........ | | 100,000 |
| | To record the sale of 20,000 shares of $10-par stock for $15 per share to the incorporators. (20,000 shares × $15 = $300,000.) | | |

If the Ski World, Inc., stock had been no-par with no stated value, the sale would have been recorded by debiting Cash and crediting Common Stock for $300,000.

## Issuing Stock by Subscription

Corporations that wish to sell stock to the public may choose to sell the shares on subscription. In a **subscription sale,** a subscriber agrees to purchase a specified number of shares at an agreed price. The subscriber usually makes a down payment when he or she signs the subscription contract; the balance is paid in installments. The subscriber receives no shares until he or she pays the contract price in full.

On Jan. 30, 1998, Ski World, Inc., sells subscriptions to 5,000 shares of stock at $18 per share. A 20% down payment is received at the time the subscription contract is signed. The remainder is due in two equal installments on Mar. 1 and Apr. 1, 1998. The journal entry is:

| | | | |
|---|---|---:|---:|
| Jan. 30 | Subscriptions Receivable: Common ............... | 72,000 | |
| | Cash ....................................... | 18,000 | |
| | Common Stock Subscribed .................. | | 50,000 |
| | Paid-In Capital in Excess of Par: Common ....... | | 40,000 |
| | To record the sale of subscriptions to 5,000 shares of $10-par common stock and the receipt of a 20% down payment. [(5,000 × $18) = $90,000 × 20% = $18,000.] | | |

A current asset, Subscriptions Receivable: Common, is debited for the unpaid balance of the subscription contract. A temporary stockholders' equity account, Common Stock Subscribed, is credited for the par or stated value of the shares subscribed. This account will remain only until the shares are paid in full and certificates are issued. Common Stock Subscribed is shown in the stockholders' equity section immediately below the Common Stock account. Paid-In Capital in Excess of Par: Common is credited for the difference between the subscription price and the par value.

---

[1] All our journal entries in the examples are in general journal form, even though the entry may actually be made in a special journal. This will make illustrations much easier because we won't have to construct special journals each time we make an entry.

Ski World, Inc., receives the two subscription installments. The entries are:

| | | | |
|---|---|---:|---:|
| Mar. 1 | Cash ..................................................... | 36,000 | |
| | Subscriptions Receivable: Common ............. | | 36,000 |
| | To record receipt of first installment. | | |
| | | | |
| Apr. 1 | Cash ..................................................... | 36,000 | |
| | Subscriptions Receivable: Common ............. | | 36,000 |
| | To record receipt of second installment. | | |

When subscribers pay the installments due, the entry is similar to that which is made when customers pay on account: Cash is debited, and the receivable is credited.

Ski World, Inc., issues the shares for the fully paid subscriptions. The entry is:

| | | | |
|---|---|---:|---:|
| Apr. 1 | Common Stock Subscribed ....................... | 50,000 | |
| | Common Stock ............................... | | 50,000 |
| | To record the issuance of 5,000 shares of $10-par common stock. | | |

When subscriptions have been paid in full, we remove the temporary account, Common Stock Subscribed, and credit Common Stock. Remember that Common Stock Subscribed was originally for the *par value* of the subscribed shares. Par value, then, is the amount we transfer to the Common Stock account.

### Issuing Stock in Exchange for Noncash Consideration

Occasionally stock is issued in exchange for services or assets. Transactions of this type are especially common in small corporations.

The issue price of the stock in this type of transaction is considered to be either the fair market value of the stock or the fair market value of the service or asset, whichever can be determined more objectively.

The fair market value of the stock being sold is usually more objective when the stock is actively traded on a stock exchange. To find the market value, simply call a stockbroker or check *The Wall Street Journal* for a stock price quotation. This quotation will provide an objective measure of the values exchanged in the noncash transaction.

Appraisal values of the services or assets received for the stock are more reliable when stocks are not actively traded. Stock in small, closely held corporations (that is, those with only a few shareholders) may change hands rarely, if at all. No current, bargained market value will be available for these shares.

The par or stated value of the stock should never be used to determine selling price. Remember, these amounts are nominal and are arbitrarily determined when the corporation is formed. Par or stated value rarely reflects the current value of either the stock issued or the asset received.

### *Issuing Stock for Services*

A corporation may issue shares in exchange for legal, accounting, architectural, or other services. When stock is issued for services involved in organizing a corporation, **Organization Cost** is debited. This intangible asset account is charged for legal costs, fees paid to the chartering state, the expense of printing stock certificates, and other amounts expended in organizing a new corporation.

Organization cost, like all other intangible assets, must be amortized over its useful life, subject to a maximum of 40 years. Many corporations amortize organization cost over 5 years because this is the life they use to amortize this asset on their income tax returns. Since the amount of amortization per year is relatively small (not material), no serious mismatching problems are created by using this short life.

Ski World, Inc., issues 100 shares of stock to J. Barrister in exchange for legal services rendered in drawing up the articles of incorporation. The journal entry is:

| | | | |
|---|---|---|---|
| Apr. 2 | Organization Cost ............................... | 1,800 | |
| | Common Stock ............................... | | 1,000 |
| | Paid-In Capital in Excess of Par: Common ........ | | 800 |
| | To record issuance of 100 shares of stock in exchange | | |
| | for legal services. ($18 × 100 = $1,800.) | | |

The amount we used in the preceding entry could have been determined in two ways:

1. The current market price of the stock issued could be used as a measure of the value of the services received. However, since Ski World stock is not actively traded on a stock exchange, and since no sale of the stock has been negotiated since January, another measure of value may be more appropriate.

2. The normal fee for performing this type of legal service could be used if this fee is well known. We will assume for this example that lawyers have a fairly standard fee of $1,800 for preparing simple articles of incorporation like Ski World's. We will also want to check this value against earlier selling prices of the stock to make sure it seems reasonable. The stock sold in January for $18 per share, and this stock is also being valued at $18 per share; this amount is clearly reasonable. If the value in this transaction came to $50 per share, however, we would have to reconsider the method of choosing the stock value.

### Issuing Stock for Assets

Often in smaller corporations a prospective stockholder will contribute assets that the corporation needs in its operations in exchange for stock.

Ski World issues 500 shares of stock to Rods and Plots for 1 acre of land. The journal entry is:

| | | | |
|---|---|---|---|
| Sept. 1 | Land ........................................ | 12,000 | |
| | Common Stock ............................ | | 5,000 |
| | Paid-In Capital in Excess of Par: Common ....... | | 7,000 |
| | To record issuance of 500 shares of stock in exchange | | |
| | for 1 acre of land. (Land appraised at $12,000.) | | |

Approximately 5 months have elapsed since Ski World last issued stock, on Apr. 2, 1998. Since the stock is not actively traded, the old market value may not accurately reflect the current worth of the stock. In most cases no standard price is available for land, because each piece is unique. In such instances one or more independent appraisals are used to establish an estimate of the asset's market value. This appraised value is used as the selling price of the stock and the acquisition price of the land.

**ASK YOURSELF ▶**

1. **What is the difference between the par value, stated value, and market value of stock?**
2. **In a cash sale of common stock, what amount is credited to Common Stock?**
3. **When stock is issued for noncash consideration, how is the issue price of the stock determined?**

## TREASURY STOCK

Learning
Objective  **6**

Define treasury stock and prepare
journal entries to record the
acquisition and sale of treasury stock.

A corporation may reacquire its own stock by purchasing it on a stock exchange (through a stockbroker) or by making a private transaction with an individual stockholder. This reacquired stock is called **treasury stock.**

Treasury stock may be purchased for later issuance to executives or employees under a stock option or stock purchase plan, for the purpose of buying out a disgruntled shareholder, or for a variety of other reasons.

While shares are held in the treasury, they do not possess the rights of outstanding shares: They cannot vote or receive dividends.

### Purchase of Treasury Stock

Ski World, Inc., repurchases 50 shares of its own stock at $25 per share. The journal entry is:

| | | | |
|---|---|---|---|
| Sept. 15 | Treasury Stock ............................... | 1,250 | |
| | Cash .................................... | | 1,250 |
| | To record acquisition of 50 shares of stock at $25 per share. | | |

Treasury Stock is debited for the cost of the reacquired shares. Since these shares are to be held for only a short time and not retired, the transaction reflects a temporary reduction in total stockholders' equity. This reduction is shown by reporting Treasury Stock on the balance sheet as a contra-stockholders' equity account. Even though Treasury Stock has a debit balance, it is not an asset. Remember, the par value and any amounts originally received in excess of par still appear in the Common Stock and Paid-In Capital in Excess of Par accounts.

Treasury Stock is subtracted from total paid-in and earned capital on the balance sheet. This disclosure is illustrated in the section entitled "Stockholders' Equity on the Balance Sheet" at the end of this chapter.

### Sale of Treasury Stock above Cost

Ski World sells 20 shares of treasury stock for $30 per share. The treasury stock had been purchased for $25 per share. The journal entry is:

| | | | |
|---|---|---|---|
| Sept. 30 | Cash ...................................... | 600 | |
| | Treasury Stock ........................... | | 500 |
| | Paid-In Capital from Treasury Stock ........... | | 100 |
| | To record sale for $30 each of 20 shares of treasury stock that originally cost $25. | | |

A corporation may decide to sell treasury stock to an employee or to another person who wants to invest in the business. If the treasury stock is sold for more than the corporation originally paid, the following procedure is used:

1. Debit Cash to record the asset.
2. Credit Treasury Stock to decrease this account.
3. Credit Paid-In Capital from Treasury Stock to record the amount received over and above what was originally paid for the treasury stock. Paid-In Capital from Treasury Stock specifically identifies the source of the new paid-in capital.

When an asset is sold for more than its cost, a gain is recorded—but treasury stock is not an asset. *Corporations are not allowed to recognize gains or losses as a result of buying and selling their own stock.* Corporate income results from carrying on the business of the company, not from speculating in or attempting to manipulate the price of its own stock.

### Sale of Treasury Stock below Cost

Ski World sells 20 shares of treasury stock for $22 per share, $3 less than each share had originally cost. The entry is:

| | | | |
|---|---|---|---|
| Oct. 31 | Cash ......................................... | 440 | |
| | Paid-In Capital from Treasury Stock ................ | 60 | |
| | Treasury Stock ............................. | | 500 |
| | To record sale for $22 each of 20 shares of treasury stock that originally cost $25. | | |

1. Paid-In Capital from Treasury Stock, until that account's balance reaches zero; then to
2. Retained Earnings.

Such decreases are never reported on the income statement as a loss.

In the Ski World illustration, Paid-In Capital from Treasury Stock was created when treasury stock was sold on Sept. 30. That account is debited for the $60 excess of the cost of the treasury stock over the amount for which Ski World sold it on Oct. 31. If the Sept. 30 transaction had not occurred, Ski World would not have had a Paid-In Capital from Treasury Stock account. In that case Retained Earnings would have been debited for the $60.

Notice that in all cases Treasury Stock is debited for the cost of shares acquired and credited for their cost when the shares are resold. When all treasury shares have been disposed of, Treasury Stock will have a zero balance.

Accounting for treasury stock is summarized in Exhibit 2.

**Exhibit 2** Accounting for Treasury Stock

| | |
|---|---|
| **When Buying Treasury Stock:** | |
| For cash | Record treasury stock at the amount of cash given. |
| **When Selling Treasury Stock:** | |
| For more than it cost | Remove the cost of treasury stock from the accounts. |
| | Record the extra amount received as paid-in capital from treasury stock. |
| For less than it cost | Remove the cost of treasury stock from the accounts. |
| | Decrease stockholders' equity for the excess of the cost over the selling price of the treasury stock by: |
| | 1. Debiting Paid-In Capital from Treasury Stock, until the balance of this account is reduced to zero; then |
| | 2. Debiting Retained Earnings. |

# Losses? What Losses?

Last September, Hospital Corp. of America, flush with cash from the sale of 103 acute-care facilities, decided to invest a portion of the proceeds in some of its own stock. Its board authorized a buyback of 12 million shares at $47 a share. HCA has spent $564 million to repurchase about 12 million shares, but after Black Monday the stock plunged. By year's end the shares stood at only $31\frac{1}{8}$. So is HCA now out $190.5 million on its own investment?

Common sense would answer with a resounding yes. But beyond common sense lurks the logic of accounting, and according to current accounting principles, HCA didn't lose a penny on the buyback. Moreover, that's exactly what the company's annual report will reflect.

Call it the no-risk investment, a key reason buybacks have become the with-it new way to deploy shareholder money. In this era of stock market volatility, no other use of money offers firms the same opportunity to tell shareholders that they have made a terrific investment—without ever having to own up to the bad news if it turns sour. Says John Tighe, partner at the accounting firm of Deloitte Haskins & Sells, "You'd have to be a pretty sophisticated investor to figure out that a company lost money on its own stock."

Many of the 1,500 corporations that authorized buybacks in 1987 have since seen their stock prices drop below the purchase price. But investors won't see those losses in the financial statements. Why not? Because a 1938 securities rule, which effectively prevents firms from speculating in their own corporate stock, requires repurchased shares to be held as treasury stock or retired.

To account for a buyback, either the company's assets get reduced or its debt load gets raised by an amount equivalent to the cash used (or borrowed) to pay for the deal. Doing so reduces corporate equity. But the shares that are acquired in the process also disappear. "You're simply closing out a transaction that began when you issued the securities," says Peter Knutson, associate professor of accounting at the Wharton School. "There are no further losses to write down."

It's a different story when a company buys stock in another firm. Then, the corporation usually counts its equity holdings as long-term assets. If the stock goes down, those assets must be marked to market at the end of each reporting period. Moreover, if there are significant losses in that item, the firm must disclose the loss, often in a footnote. In 1986 the Williams Cos. lost $239.7 million, mainly because of a writedown of its long-term investments.

As a practical matter, the only real advantage arising from a buyback is to reduce the number of shares outstanding in the market. One reason for wanting to do so might be to help guard against a hostile takeover. That's what GenCorp., an aerospace concern, had in mind last spring when it paid $1.6 billion to acquire 12.5 million shares from the public at $130 a share, only to see the stock

price eventually decline to $22\frac{1}{2}$ by year's end anyway.

Alternatively, the purpose of a buyback might be simply to ginger up the stock. This could occur if a company's business generates more net income than the yield available on T bills, for example, or perhaps short-term certificates of deposit. In that case, earnings per share would go up and (presumably) the stock's price would subsequently rise.

Though buybacks, practically speaking, amount to little more than zero-sum games, such companies as ITT, Kraft and IBM now routinely refer to them instead as "investment opportunities" and "good buys." Says a spokesman for Burlington Industries, "We feel that our stock repurchases are an attractive investment and an excellent opportunity to build shareholder value." Burlington authorized the buyback of up to 5 million shares after the market crash.

And small wonder it did so, since current accounting rules offer so few useful clues that buybacks can just as easily be a waste of money as a clever use of it. Says Jerry Castellini, vice president at Kemper Financial Services: "Anytime you make an investment with corporate assets and lose money, it's a loss to shareholders and poor use of corporate capital." Shouldn't accounting rules reveal this important truth, rather than help obscure it?

*Source:* Penelope Wang, *Forbes,* Feb. 8, 1988, p. 118. Reprinted by permission of FORBES Magazine. Copyright © 1988 by Forbes, Inc.

---

Many companies say they buy their own common stock because they feel it is a "good investment." This article points out that accounting for treasury stock is quite a bit different from accounting for investments. Generally accepted accounting principles allow no income statement gains or losses in accounting for treasury stock. Gains and losses are recognized in accounting for long-term investments.

**ASK YOURSELF** ▶

1. **What is treasury stock?**
2. **At what amount is treasury stock recorded?**
3. **When is the Paid-In Capital from Treasury Stock account created?**
4. **Where is treasury stock disclosed on the balance sheet?**

## PREFERRED STOCK

Ski World's charter of incorporation authorized the issuance of both common and preferred stock. Our discussion up until now has concentrated on common stock; now we will focus on preferred stock.

## Characteristics of Preferred Stock

Learning
Objective 7

**Describe the characteristics of preferred stock**

The authorization to issue preferred stock usually specifies:

1. The par value or the stipulation that the stock is to be no-par
2. The total number of shares authorized
3. The annual dividend rate or amount
4. The other characteristics that the stock is to possess—dividend privileges, voting rights, conversion privileges, callability, and liquidation preference

Assume that Ski World's charter authorizes the issuance of 10,000 shares of $10-par, 8% cumulative, nonparticipating preferred stock, callable after the year 2009 at $25 per share. Ski World's preferred will not have voting rights. Let's look at these characteristics of preferred stock to clarify their meaning.

### Dividend Privileges

Dividends on preferred stock are normally stated as a percentage of par value or, if the stock has no par value, as a specified number of dollars per year. Ski World's $10-par, 8% stock would pay an $.80-per-share dividend per year—if the board of directors votes to pay it. A $1.00 preferred stock would refer to no-par stock paying a dividend of $1.00 each year.

Dividends on preferred, like dividends on common, must be *declared* by the board of directors before they can be paid. If the board votes to pay any dividends during a year, however, preferred shareholders will receive their dividends before common stockholders do.

What happens if the board chooses not to declare a preferred dividend in a given year? If the preferred stock is **cumulative stock,** the dividends must be paid in a later year before any distributions can be made to common stockholders. Past dividends "owed" to preferred stockholders are called **dividends in arrears.** These obligations are not liabilities until declared by the board of directors. The existence of this obligation is disclosed in the notes to the financial statements. Holders of *noncumulative* preferred stock would lose the right to receive dividends not declared in the current year.

Preferred stockholders are normally limited to receiving the amount of dividends specified—8% of $10-par in Ski World's case. When this limitation applies, the preferred is said to be *nonparticipating.*

A corporation may also be authorized to issue participating preferred stock. **Participating preferred stock** gives the stockholder the right to receive the specified dividend and to receive more after a matching percentage of dividends is paid to common stockholders.

Learning
Objective 8

**Allocate dividends between preferred and common stockholders**

Let's leave the Ski World example briefly to illustrate how a corporation would allocate a dividend between the common and preferred stock outstanding.

Elfin Company has the following stock outstanding on Dec. 31, 1999:

| | |
|---|---|
| 8% cumulative, participating preferred stock, $100-par, 500 shares authorized, issued, and outstanding ........................ | $ 50,000 |
| Common stock, $1-par, 150,000 shares authorized, issued, and outstanding ......... | 150,000 |
| Total preferred and common stock ........... | $200,000 |

Elfin did not declare or pay any dividends during 1998; therefore, there are $4,000 (8% × $50,000) in preferred dividends in arrears. Elfin would follow this procedure in allocating the 1999 dividend:

1. Give cumulative preferred all dividends in arrears. (Noncumulative preferred does not receive dividends in arrears.)
2. Give preferred its current year's dividend amount.
3. Give common a matching percentage for the current dividend. (Do not match dividends in arrears.)
4. If preferred stock is participating, allocate any remaining dollars such that common and preferred each receive an equal percentage. The percentage to give each is determined as follows:

$$\frac{\text{Number of dollars remaining to be distributed}}{\text{Total par value of common and preferred stock}} = \frac{\text{additional percent of par}}{\text{to give to each}}$$

Elfin declared a 1999 dividend of $30,000, which would be allocated to preferred and common as follows:

| | Preferred | Common | Total |
|---|---|---|---|
| Total outstanding stock (par)................ | $50,000 | $150,000 | $200,000 |
| Total dividend declared..................... | | | $ 30,000 |
| First, preferred dividend in arrears ........... | $ 4,000 | | (4,000) |
| Amount remaining .................... | | | $ 26,000 |
| Second, regular current preferred dividend (8% × $50,000 par)...................... | 4,000 | | (4,000) |
| Amount remaining .................... | | | $ 22,000 |
| Third, matching common dividend (8% × $150,000)........................ | | $ 12,000 | (12,000) |
| Amount remaining .................... | | | $ 10,000 |
| Fourth, remainder allocated to give each the same percentage ($10,000 ÷ $200,000 = 5%): | | | |
| (5% × $50,000) ...................... | 2,500 | | (2,500) |
| (5% × $150,000) .................... | | 7,500 | (7,500) |
| Amount remaining .................... | | | –0– |
| Total distribution ......................... | $10,500 + | $ 19,500 = | $ 30,000 |

Notice that the matching common dividend matches only the percentage received by preferred shareholders for the current year. Dividends in arrears are not matched.

In this illustration, preferred shareholders received a 21% total distribution (8% for 1998 arrears and 13% for 1999). Common stockholders received a 13% total distribution. The current dividend of 13% is the same for both classes of stock.

### Voting Rights

The right to vote for members of the corporate board of directors and other matters requiring stockholder approval is not ordinarily given to preferred stockholders. Some states allow corporations to issue voting preferred stock. Voting, then, while not an automatic right of preferred stockholders, sometimes may be conferred as a special privilege.

### Conversion Privilege

Owners of *convertible preferred stock* have the right to turn in their preferred shares to the corporation and receive common shares in their place. The number of common shares to be received is specified on the preferred stock certificate.

For example, F. Hemmer owns 100 shares of 6% noncumulative preferred stock which is convertible into common at the rate of one share of preferred for three shares of common. At any time Hemmer may submit his 100 preferred shares and receive 300 shares of common. The corporation can't force Hemmer to convert; the decision is his.

Preferred stock is nonconvertible unless the corporate charter specifically adds this **conversion privilege.** We assume, then, that Ski World's preferred stock is nonconvertible.

### Callability

Some preferred stock has a **callability** provision. A corporation may retire *callable preferred stock* by paying the stockholder a predetermined amount—the *call price.* Ski World's preferred stock, for example, is callable after the year 2009 at a call price of $25 per share. Ski World has the option to retire preferred stock in 2010 and beyond by notifying shareholders that the stock is being called. The shareholders cannot force Ski World to call the stock, nor can they refuse to let the corporation purchase it at the call price.

### Liquidation Preference

All preferred stock includes a **liquidation preference.** This feature means that if the corporation decides to cease operations and distribute its assets to creditors and owners, the preferred stockholders are entitled to receive assets in settlement of their claims before the common stockholders do. The amount of the liquidation claim of preferred stockholders will usually be specified when the stock is authorized by the charter. We will assume that Ski World's liquidation claim is the same as the call price—$25 per share.

To succeed in raising capital by issuing preferred stock, management must put together a "package" of preferences. Their objective will be to offer sufficient appeal to investors without placing an undesirable burden on the corporation or the common stockholders. All preferred stock has dividend and liquidation preferences. Management must decide whether to add cumulative, participitating, convertibility, and voting privileges—or possibly impose a callable restriction.

## Accounting for Preferred Stock

Learning
Objective **9**

Prepare a journal entry to issue preferred stock

Accounting for preferred stock is almost identical to accounting for common stock. The only difference is in the account titles used. Substitute the accounts Preferred Stock, Paid-In Capital in Excess of Par: Preferred, Preferred Stock Subscribed, and Subscriptions Receivable: Preferred for the corresponding accounts applicable to common stock.

Ski World would use the following entry to record the issuance of 100 shares of its $10 preferred stock for $1,200:

| | | | |
|---|---|---|---|
| Nov. 2 | Cash . . . . . . . . . . . . . . . . . . . . . . . . . . . . . . . . . . . . . . . . . | 1,200 | |
| | Preferred Stock . . . . . . . . . . . . . . . . . . . . . . . . . . . . . . | | 1,000 |
| | Paid-In Capital in Excess of Par: Preferred . . . . . . . . | | 200 |
| | To record the sale of 100 shares of $10-par preferred stock. | | |

It is unusual to purchase preferred stock as treasury stock. When preferred treasury stock is acquired, we use the same procedures as we used for common treasury stock.

## DONATED CAPITAL

Learning Objective **10**

Define and prepare journal entries to record donated capital

Profit-making corporations may receive donations of assets or donations of shares of the corporation's own stock. The value of these assets or shares is **donated capital.** Stockholders may donate shares in order for the corporation to have stock available to sell to raise additional capital or to use in stock option plans designed to keep or attract outstanding management talent. The cost of these treasury shares is zero; therefore we make no formal journal entry to record the acquisition. A memorandum entry is often made in the general journal to officially note the fact that shares were received. This stock is treasury stock with no cost.

Ski World receives 50 shares of common stock as a donation.

| | | |
|---|---|---|
| Nov. 5 | Memorandum: Received 50 shares of donated common stock. | |

When donated treasury stock is later sold, Donated Capital is credited for the sales price.

Ski World sells the donated shares for $650 ($13 per share).

| | | | |
|---|---|---|---|
| Nov. 24 | Cash . . . . . . . . . . . . . . . . . . . . . . . . . . . . . . . . . . . . . . . | 650 | |
| | Donated Capital . . . . . . . . . . . . . . . . . . . . . . . . . . . | | 650 |
| | To record the sale of 50 donated shares of treasury stock. | | |

Cities and counties often donate land and occasionally other assets to attract new industry to their locality. When a company moves in, the area benefits through the creation of jobs and the taxes that the company pays. The company benefits by having the use of an asset at no cost.

Ski World receives the donation of a run-down old building from the City of Parrish, which will move the building from its present site to Ski World's land. Ski World will refurbish the structure and maintain it as a historic landmark while also using it as a retail store. The fair market value of the building in its present condition is $15,000.

| | | | |
|---|---|---|---|
| Dec. 15 | Building . . . . . . . . . . . . . . . . . . . . . . . . . . . . . . . . . . . | 15,000 | |
| | Donated Capital . . . . . . . . . . . . . . . . . . . . . . . . . . . | | 15,000 |
| | To record the donation of a building by the City of Parrish. | | |

Assets donated to the company are recorded at their fair value when they are received. Donated Capital, a stockholders' equity account, is credited to record the source of the asset that is entering the pool of resources available for management's use. In the unusual event that assets are donated to a business by someone other than a governmental entity or owner, a revenue account would be credited.

**ASK YOURSELF** ▶

1. What are dividends in arrears on cumulative preferred stock?
2. What is participating preferred stock?
3. Can preferred stock be converted into common stock? Explain.
4. Preferred stock is said to have a liquidation preference; what does this mean?
5. When an asset is donated to a corporation, for what amount is Donated Capital credited?

## STOCKHOLDERS' EQUITY ON THE BALANCE SHEET

Learning
Objective **11**

Prepare the stockholders' equity section of the balance sheet

The general ledger T-accounts and the Dec. 31, 1998, stockholders' equity section of Ski World's balance sheet are shown in Exhibits 3 and 4. First, trace each of the transactions discussed in this chapter to the general ledger, Exhibit 3. Then see how each general ledger account is disclosed on the balance sheet, Exhibit 4. Be sure to notice the following points:

1. The stockholders' equity section of the balance sheet (Exhibit 4) is designed to report the capital of the corporation according to its sources—that is, according to where the assets came from. For this reason we divide stockholders' equity into two basic subsections: paid-in capital and earned capital.

2. In the paid-in capital section, preferred stock is listed first, followed by common stock. We include a listing of the characteristics of preferred stock, as well as the par value and the number of shares authorized, issued, and outstanding for both preferred and common. The Common Stock Subscribed account immediately follows common stock in this portion of the stockholders' equity section. Common Stock Subscribed is omitted in the Ski World stockholders' equity section because it has a zero balance.

3. The additional paid-in capital section lists the accounts that arose either as a result of stockholders' paying more than par or stated value for their shares or from other contributed capital transactions, such as donated capital and paid-in capital from treasury stock. Generally accepted accounting principles also allow donated capital to be shown in a separate stockholders' equity section.

4. The earned capital section follows the paid-in capital accounts.

5. The temporary contra-stockholders' equity account, Treasury Stock, is subtracted from the total of paid-in capital and earned capital.

6. Several of the accounts in Ski World's stockholders' equity section are minor in amount; for instance, Paid-In Capital from Treasury Stock is only $40. In actual companies these immaterial amounts would not be disclosed separately, but we want to demonstrate the proper location of each item on the balance sheet.

## FINANCIAL STATEMENT ANALYSIS

Learning
Objective **12**

Calculate and discuss the stockholders' equity to total assets and debt to total assets ratios.

Creditors and investors use balance sheet information to analyze the capital structure of a business. The stockholders' equity to total assets ratio and the debt to total assets ratio provide an understanding of how much of the resources of the company were provided by owners, and how much by creditors.

### The Stockholders' Equity to Total Assets Ratio

The **stockholders' equity to total assets ratio,** sometimes called the **equity ratio,** shows the percentage of a firm's assets financed by stockholders. The higher this ratio, the smaller the risk that the company will be unable to meet its obligations when due. This ratio may be calculated by the following formula:

$$\text{Stockholders' equity to total assets ratio} = \frac{\text{total stockholders' equity}}{\text{total assets}}$$

**Exhibit 3** Ski World's General Ledger Accounts

### SKI WORLD, INC.
### General Ledger: Stockholders' Equity Accounts
### December 31, 1998

#### Preferred Stock

| | | | | | |
|---|---|---|---|---|---|
| | | Nov. | 2 | (100 shares) | 1,000 |
| | | Dec. | 31 | Bal. (100 shares) | 1,000 |

#### Common Stock

| | | | | | |
|---|---|---|---|---|---|
| | | Jan. | 5 | (20,000 shares) | 200,000 |
| | | Apr. | 1 | (5,000 shares) | 50,000 |
| | | | 2 | (100 shares) | 1,000 |
| | | Sept. | 1 | (500 shares) | 5,000 |
| | | Dec. | 31 | Bal. (25,600 shares) | 256,000 |

#### Paid-In Capital in Excess of Par: Preferred

| | | | |
|---|---|---|---|
| | Nov. | 2 | 200 |
| | Dec. | 31 | Bal. | 200 |

#### Paid-In Capital in Excess of Par: Common

| | | | |
|---|---|---|---|
| | Jan. | 5 | 100,000 |
| | | 30 | 40,000 |
| | Apr. | 2 | 800 |
| | Sept. | 1 | 7,000 |
| | Dec. | 31 | Bal. | 147,800 |

#### Common Stock Subscribed

| | | | | | | |
|---|---|---|---|---|---|---|
| Apr. 1 | (5,000 shares) | 50,000 | Jan. 30 | (5,000 shares) | 50,000 |
| | | | Dec. 31 | Bal. | –0– |

#### Paid-In Capital from Treasury Stock

| | | | | |
|---|---|---|---|---|
| Oct. 31 | | 60 | Sept. 30 | 100 |
| | | | Dec. 31 | Bal. | 40 |

#### Donated Capital

| | | | |
|---|---|---|---|
| | Nov. 24 | 650 |
| | Dec. 15 | 15,000 |
| | Dec. 31 | Bal. | 15,650 |

#### Treasury Stock

| | | | | |
|---|---|---|---|---|
| Sept. 15 | (50 shares) | 1,250 | Sept. 30 | (20 shares) | 500 |
| | | | Oct. 31 | (20 shares) | 500 |
| Total | (50 shares) | 1,250 | Total | (40 shares) | 1,000 |
| Dec. 31 | Bal. (10 shares) | 250 | | |

---

**Exhibit 4** Stockholders' Equity Section of Ski World's Balance Sheet

---

**SKI WORLD, INC.**
**Stockholders' Equity**
**December 31, 1998**

---

Paid-In Capital:

| | | |
|---|---:|---:|
| 8% Preferred Stock ($10-par, cumulative, nonparticipating, callable, 10,000 shares authorized, 100 shares issued and outstanding) . . . . . . . | | $ 1,000 |
| Common Stock [$10-par, 100,000 shares authorized, 25,600 shares issued, 25,590 shares outstanding (10 shares are in the treasury)] . . . . . . . . . . . . . . . . . . . . . . . . . . . . . . . . . . | | 256,000 |
| Additional Paid-In Capital: | | |
|   Paid-In Capital in Excess of Par: Preferred . . . . . . . . . . . . | $ 200 | |
|   Paid-In Capital in Excess of Par: Common . . . . . . . . . . . . | 147,800 | |
|   Paid-In Capital from Treasury Stock. . . . . . . . . . . . . . . . . | 40 | |
|   Donated Capital. . . . . . . . . . . . . . . . . . . . . . . . . . . . . . . | 15,650 | |
|     Total Additional Paid-In Capital . . . . . . . . . . . . . . . . . . . . . . . . . . . | | 163,690 |
|     Total Paid-In Capital . . . . . . . . . . . . . . . . . . . . . . . . . . . . . . . . . . . | | $420,690 |
| Earned Capital: | | |
|   Retained Earnings (amount assumed for this example). . . . . . . . . . . . . | | 12,600 |
|     Total. . . . . . . . . . . . . . . . . . . . . . . . . . . . . . . . . . . . . . . . . . . . . | | $433,290 |
| Less: Treasury Stock (10 shares) at Cost . . . . . . . . . . . . . . . . . . . . . . . . | | (250) |
| Total Stockholders' Equity. . . . . . . . . . . . . . . . . . . . . . . . . . . . . . . . . . . . | | $433,040 |

---

Ski World, Inc.'s total stockholders' equity is $433,040 (Exhibit 4). We have looked at the transactions affecting stockholders' equity in this chapter, but not those related to liabilities. Assume for purposes of this illustration that each side of the balance sheet totals $721,733. With this information we can calculate Ski World's stockholders' equity to total assets ratio.

$$\text{1998 Ski World, Inc., stockholders'} \atop \text{equity to total assets ratio} = \frac{\$433,040}{\$721,733} = .60, \text{ or } 60\%$$

Thus, 60% of Ski World's assets come from stockholders (including reinvested earnings).

### The Debt to Total Assets Ratio

The **debt to total assets ratio** shows the percentage of the firm's assets financed by debt. The higher this percentage, the greater the risk that the company will be unable to meet its obligations when due. Assuming Ski World's total liabilities are obligations when due. Assuming Ski World's total liabilities are $288,693, the formula for calculating the debt to total assets ratio and the 1998 calculation for Ski World, Inc., are:

$$\textbf{Debt to total assets ratio} = \frac{\textbf{total liabilities}}{\textbf{total assets}}$$

$$\text{Ski World, Inc., 1998 debt} \atop \text{to total assets ratio} = \frac{\$288,693}{\$721,733} = .399 \text{ or } .40, \text{ or } 40\%$$

Thus, 40% of Ski World's total assets were financed by debt. After a moment's reflection, you should see that the debt to total assets ratio and the stockholders' equity to total assets ratio are complementary; that is, the two percentages should always add to 100%. This is true because all assets are financed by either debt or equity funds. Either of these two ratios may be found by subtracting the other one from 100%:

$$\text{Debt to total assets ratio} = \frac{100\% - \text{stockholders' equity to}}{\text{total assets ratio}}$$

$$= 100\% - 60\% = 40\%$$

$$\text{Stockholders' equity to total} = 100\% - \text{debt to total assets ratio}$$
$$\text{assets ratio}$$

$$= 100\% - 40\% = 60\%$$

Thus, 60% of Ski World's assets come from stockholders (including reinvested earnings) and 40% from creditors. This ratio should be satisfactory to long-term creditors, although of course, statistics that one analyst considers satisfactory may cause concern to another.

## STOCK VALUE: A REVIEW

Learning Objective 13

Define par value, stated value, market value, liquidation value, and equity per share of stock

The word *value* is used in several different ways when applied to stock. The purpose of this final section of the chapter is to review the concepts of par value, stated value, and market value and to introduce two new terms: *equity per share* and *liquidation value*.

### Par Value and Stated Value

Par value is an arbitrary amount per share set by the charter of incorporation. Par value is usually a nominal amount and does not reflect the actual value of a share of stock. Many states require that all stock have a par value. Some states use par value to set the minimum amount of capital (known as legal capital) that must be retained in the business. Legal capital cannot be distributed to the stockholders except when the corporation is liquidated.

In some corporations whose stock does not have a par value, a stated value may be designated. Stated value is also an arbitrary amount per share, but it is set by the board of directors instead of the charter of incorporation. Unlike par value, stated value is not printed on the stock certificate, so investors are less likely to believe mistakenly that stated value is the stock's worth. Some states use stated value like par value, to establish the legal capital of the corporation.

### Market Value

A stock's market value per share is the amount for which a share of stock is selling. Market value is determined by investor expectations about the future of the company and future general economic conditions. Such factors as expected company earnings, expected dividend payments, the general financial condition of the company, expected future interest rates, and expected changes in tax rates may influence an investor's decision about the worth of a share of stock.

### Equity per Share

The **equity per share,** sometimes called **book value per share,** of common stock is the claim against a company's assets represented by one share of common stock. Equity per share is calculated by determining total common stockholders' equity and then dividing common stockholders' equity by the total number of shares of common stock *outstanding,* or in the hands of shareholders, plus any shares subscribed but not yet issued. Treasury shares are not outstanding, so they are omitted.

Assuming that Ski World's charter specifies a preferred stock liquidation value equal to the call price of $25 per share, the Ski World common stockholders' equity is:

Total stockholders' equity . . . . . . . . . . . . . . . . . $433,040
Less: Call price of preferred stock:
$25 × 100 shares. . . . . . . . . . . . . . . . . . . . . . .    (2,500)
Common stockholders' equity . . . . . . . . . . . . .   430,540

Dividends in arrears on cumulative preferred stock would be subtracted in a similar manner. Preferred stockholders would have the right to collect arrears in addition to the liquidation value.

The equity per share of Ski World's common stock (rounded to the nearest cent) would be calculated as follows:

$$\frac{\text{Total common stockholders' equity}}{\text{Total common shares outstanding}} = \frac{\$430,540}{25,590 \text{ shs}} = \$16.82 \text{ per share}$$

Ski World has no subscribed but unissued common shares. If it did, the number of these shares would be added to the shares outstanding.

### Liquidation Value

The **liquidation value** of a share of stock is the amount that a stockholder will receive if the corporation ceases operations, sells all its assets, pays off all its liabilities, and distributes the remaining cash to the stockholders.

The liquidation value for preferred stock is often stated in advance. We have assumed in Ski World's case that the liquidation value will be the call price of $25 per share. If any cumulative preferred dividends are in arrears, these would normally be paid as well. Preferred stockholders would be entitled to these assets only after the creditors have been paid. If the company lacks sufficient assets to pay creditors, the preferred stockholders may receive nothing.

After all creditors and preferred stockholders have been paid, the common stockholders will share any remaining assets. When a financially troubled corporation liquidates, the common stockholders normally receive few, if any, assets.

**ASK YOURSELF** ▶

1. **Why is market value per share of more interest to a stockholder than par value or stated value per share?**
2. **Why are treasury shares omitted from the calculation of equity per common share?**
3. **What does liquidation value mean when applied to preferred stock?**

### SUMMARY

- **Corporations** are legal beings established by state charter after the incorporators file acceptable articles of incorporation and pay the proper fee.
- The **articles of incorporation** spell out the corporation's name and purpose for existence; the types of stock that it can issue, including the number of shares and par value; the location of the principal corporate office; and the corporation's permitted legal life. In addition, the names and addresses of the first board of directors and incorporators are listed.
- Corporations have certain advantages over proprietorships and partnerships: (1) Corporations can raise greater amounts of capital, (2) their owners have limited liability, (3) their owners can easily transfer ownership shares, (4) corporations have almost unlimited lives, (5) they lack mutual agency, and (6) they usually employ professional managers to run the company. The primary disadvantages of corpora-

tions are double taxation, extensive government regulation, and separation of ownership from control of the business.

• The corporate organization structure consists of stockholders, who own the corporation; a board of directors, who are responsible for making corporate policy; and a president and other officers, who are responsible for the day-to-day operation of the corporation.

• As owners of a corporation, common stockholders have legal rights to: (1) receive a certificate of ownership (stock certificate), (2) vote in corporate elections, (3) maintain their percentage ownership share (the preemptive right), (4) receive dividends, and (5) receive residual assets in liquidation.

• **Capital stock** refers to the ownership shares that a corporation sells to acquire assets. **Common stock** represents the primary ownership shares of a corporation. **Preferred stock** is sometimes used to attract investors who desire a security that is less risky than common stock.

• Both common and preferred stock may be sold for cash, on subscription, or exchanged for services or noncash assets. The par value of the stock is recorded in the stock account, and any excess amount is recorded in a paid-in capital in excess of par account.

• When a corporation purchases its own stock, these shares are called **treasury stock.** Since treasury stock may be acquired for a number of purposes, it is recorded in a temporary contra-stockholders' equity account until it is needed. Reissuance of treasury stock above its cost creates additional paid-in capital. Reissuance below cost decreases paid-in capital and, in some cases, earned capital.

• The corporate charter specifies the privileges granted to preferred stockholders. Among these may be the right to: (1) receive dividends before common stockholders do, (2) vote in corporate elections, (3) convert preferred shares into common shares, (4) receive assets in liquidation before common stockholders do. The corporation may reserve the right to purchase, or call, preferred stock at a predetermined price.

• **Donated capital** may take the form of cash or other assets. Donations of stock are recorded by a memorandum entry. When assets are received as a donation or from the sale of donated stock, Donated Capital is credited for the fair market value of the cash or other assets received.

• The primary purpose of the stockholders' equity section of the balance sheet is to report a corporation's capital according to its source. The stockholders' equity section is divided into two basic subcategories: paid-in capital and earned capital.

• Creditors and investors use the stockholders' equity to total assets and the debt to total assets ratios to indicate the portion of the company financed by owners and the portion provided by borrowing. In general the higher the amount financed by debt, the higher the risk that the company will be unable to meet its debt obligations.

• The word "value" may be used in several ways when applied to stock. **Par** or **stated value** is an arbitrary amount set when the corporation is formed. **Market value per share** is what a share of stock is selling for. **Equity per share,** or **book value per share,** is the claim against a company's assets represented by one share of common stock. **Liquidation value** is the amount that stockholders will receive for each share of stock if the company ceases operations, sells all its assets, pays off all its liabilities, and distributes the remaining cash to stockholders.

## 14  KEY TERMS

| | |
|---|---|
| Articles of incorporation | The written documents filed with a state government outlining basic information about the corporation, including its name, purpose, capital structure, and the names of individuals involved in its creation. |
| Authorized stock | The total capital stock that may be issued by the corporation as stipulated in the articles of incorporation. The classes of stock, par value, and total number of shares are specified. |

| | |
|---|---|
| Board of directors | The group of individuals elected by the stockholders and entrusted with the responsibility for managing the corporation, establishing corporate policy, and acting on matters only they can legally decide. Day-to-day operation of the business is usually delegated to a professional management team. |
| Book value per share | See **equity per share.** |
| Callability | A provision in some preferred stock that allows the corporation to purchase, or call, the stock at a predetermined call price. |
| Capital stock | Ownership shares issued by a corporation. *Capital stock* may refer to common stock or preferred stock or both. |
| Charter | The document issued by a state government that gives a business the legal right to begin operating as a corporation. |
| Common stock | A class of capital stock that represents the basic ownership of a corporation. Common stock carries the right to vote, share in earnings, maintain percentage ownership share, and receive residual assets in liquidation. |
| Conversion privilege | The right to submit shares of preferred stock and receive a predetermined number of shares of common stock. Preferred stockholders possess this right only when it is specified by the corporate charter. |
| Corporation | An artificial legal being created by government charter and possessing many of the rights of a natural person. |
| Cumulative stock | If a stock is cumulative, preferred stockholders have the right to receive dividends for past years and the current year before any can be paid to common stockholders. This right must be specifically granted by corporate charter. |
| Debt to total assets ratio | Total liabilities divided by total assets. |
| Dividends in arrears | Past years' dividends "owed" to holders of cumulative preferred stock. |
| Donated capital | The value of assets or shares of stock given to a corporation. |
| Earned capital | The amount of resources generated through the operations of a corporation, minus dividends paid to stockholders. |
| Equity per share | The claim against a company's assets represented by one share of common stock. Also called **book value per share.** |
| Issued stock | Shares of capital stock that have been sold at some point in the corporation's history. |
| Legal capital | An amount of paid-in capital that must be retained in the corporation. Minimum legal capital, defined by state law, usually consists of the par value or stated value of the issued stock. |
| Liquidation preference | The right of preferred stockholders to receive assets when the corporation dissolves before any assets are distributed to common stockholders. |
| Liquidation value | The amount that will be received in liquidation by stockholders for each share of stock owned. The liquidation value of preferred shares may be specified in advance. The liquidation value per common share can be known only after all assets have been sold and all liabilities have been paid. |
| Market value per share | The amount that a share of stock is selling for on the open market. |
| Organization Cost | An intangible asset account consisting of legal fees, state charter fees, and other costs incurred in creating a corporation. |
| Outstanding stock | Shares of capital stock in the hands of stockholders. |
| Paid-In capital | The amount of resources received by a corporation as a result of investment by stockholders, donation, or certain treasury stock transactions. |

| | |
|---|---|
| Par value | An arbitrary per-share amount specified in the articles of incorporation (and printed on the face of each stock certificate); in some states, it defines the legal capital of the corporation. |
| Participating preferred stock | Preferred stock having the privilege of sharing in dividends with common stockholders after both groups have been paid a specified percentage of par. Preferred stock not having this privilege is *nonparticipating*. |
| Preemptive right | The right of a common stockholder to maintain his or her percentage ownership share of a corporation by purchasing a proportionate share of all new common shares issued. |
| Preferred stock | A class of capital stock carrying certain rights that have priority over those of common stock. Priority rights to dividends and to distributions of assets in liquidation are typical. |
| Shareholder | See **stockholder.** |
| Stated value | An arbitrary per-share amount specified by official action of the board of directors for no-par stock. The legal capital of the corporation may be defined by stated value. |
| Stockholder | An entity (a person or another corporation) owning one or more shares of stock. |
| Stockholders' equity | The owners' equity section of a corporate balance sheet. Stockholders' equity has two major components: paid-in capital and earned capital. |
| Stockholders' equity to total assets ratio | Total stockholders' equity divided by total assets; also called the **equity ratio.** |
| Subscription sale | A method of selling capital stock in which a purchaser signs a contract agreeing to buy a specified number of shares at a negotiated price. The stock is often paid for in installments. |
| Treasury stock | Shares of capital stock reacquired and held by the issuing corporation. |

## DEMONSTRATION PROBLEM

Woodview, Inc., was authorized by its charter to issue 500,000 shares of $5-par common stock and 10,000 shares of $100-par, 8% preferred stock. The preferred stock is noncumulative and nonparticipating. During 1998, its first year of existence, Woodview completed the following transactions affecting the stockholders' equity:

**a.** Sold 50,000 shares of common stock for $400,000.

**b.** Sold subscriptions to 10,000 shares of common stock. One-fourth of the subscription price of $10 per share was received as a down payment.

**c.** Acquired 1,000 shares of common stock. The treasury stock cost $9,750.

**d.** Sold 500 shares of preferred stock for $130 per share.

**e.** Sold 500 treasury shares for $11 per share.

**f.** Received a plot of land as a donation from Grant County. The land has a fair market value of $16,000.

**g.** Sold 200 treasury shares for $9 per share.

**Required:**

**1.** Prepare general journal entries to record the transactions listed.
**2.** Prepare the stockholders' equity section of the Dec. 31, 1998, balance sheet. Assume that the Dec. 31, 1998, balance of Retained Earnings is $82,000.

### ■ Solution to Demonstration Problem

**1.**

| | | | |
|---|---|---:|---:|
| a. | Cash | 400,000 | |
| | Common Stock | | 250,000 |
| | Paid-In Capital in Excess of Par: Common | | 150,000 |
| | | | |
| b. | Subscriptions Receivable: Common | 75,000 | |
| | Cash | 25,000 | |
| | Common Stock Subscribed | | 50,000 |
| | Paid-In Capital in Excess of Par: Common | | 50,000 |
| | | | |
| c. | Treasury Stock | 9,750 | |
| | Cash | | 9,750 |
| | | | |
| d. | Cash | 65,000 | |
| | Preferred Stock | | 50,000 |
| | Paid-In Capital in Excess of Par: Preferred | | 15,000 |
| | | | |
| e. | Cash | 5,500 | |
| | Treasury Stock | | 4,875 |
| | Paid-In Capital from Treasury Stock | | 625 |
| | | | |
| f. | Land | 16,000 | |
| | Donated Capital | | 16,000 |
| | | | |
| g. | Cash | 1,800 | |
| | Paid-In Capital from Treasury Stock | 150 | |
| | Treasury Stock | | 1,950 |

2.

---

**WOODVIEW INC.**
**Stockholders' Equity**
**December 31, 1998**

---

Paid-In Capital:

8% Preferred Stock ($100-par, noncumulative,
nonparticipating, 10,000 shares authorized,
500 shares issued and outstanding) . . . . . . . . . . . . . . . . . . . . . . . . . . . . $ 50,000

Common Stock [$5-par, 500,000 shares authorized,
50,000 shares issued, 49,700 shares outstanding
(300 shares are in the treasury)] . . . . . . . . . . . . . . . . . . . . . . . . . . . . . . 250,000

Common Stock Subscribed (10,000 shares) . . . . . . . . . . . . . . . . . . . . . . 50,000

Additional Paid-In Capital:

| | | |
|---|---:|---:|
| Paid-In Capital in Excess of Par: Preferred . . . . . . . . . . . . . | $ 15,000 | |
| Paid-In Capital in Excess of Par: Common . . . . . . . . . . . . . | 200,000 | |
| Paid-In Capital from Treasury Stock . . . . . . . . . . . . . . . . . . | 475 | |
| Donated Capital . . . . . . . . . . . . . . . . . . . . . . . . . . . . . . . . . . | 16,000 | |
|     Total Additional Paid-In Capital . . . . . . . . . . . . . . . . . . . . . . . . . . | | 231,475 |
|       Total Paid-In Capital . . . . . . . . . . . . . . . . . . . . . . . . . . . . . . . . | | $581,475 |

Earned Capital:

Retained Earnings (amount given) . . . . . . . . . . . . . . . . . . . . . . . . . . . . . . 82,000

Total . . . . . . . . . . . . . . . . . . . . . . . . . . . . . . . . . . . . . . . . . . . . . . . . . . . $663,475

Less: Treasury Stock (300 shares) at Cost . . . . . . . . . . . . . . . . . . . . . . . (2,925)

Total Stockholders' Equity . . . . . . . . . . . . . . . . . . . . . . . . . . . . . . . . . . . $660,550

## QUESTIONS FOR REVIEW AND FURTHER THOUGHT

### REVIEW QUESTIONS

1. Explain briefly what a corporation is and how it is created.

2. List the advantages and disadvantages of organizing a business as a corporation.

3. Describe the function of each of the following groups in the corporate organization structure: stockholders, board of directors, president and other operating officers.

4. Describe the rights possessed by a common stockholder.

5. The One Corporation's stock has a par value of $1 per share; the Two Corporation's stock has a stated value of $1; the Three Corporation's stock has no par or stated value. Explain how each of these corporations would account for the sale of one share of stock for $5.

6. How does a sale of stock on a subscription basis differ from a sale of stock for immediate cash?

7. How is the account Stock Subscriptions Receivable shown on a corporation's balance sheet? How is Common Stock Subscribed shown?

8. What are organization costs? How are they shown on the balance sheet?

9. What is treasury stock? How is it shown on a corporation's balance sheet?

10. List and describe briefly the characteristics of preferred stock.

11. Preferred stock may be cumulative or noncumulative and participating or nonparticipating. Explain what each of these terms means.

12. Assuming that preferred stock is cumulative and participating, list the steps that would be followed in allocating a dividend between the preferred and common stockholders.

13. Is accounting for preferred stock similar to accounting for common stock? Explain.

14. Explain the difference between paid-in capital and earned capital.

### QUESTIONS FOR FURTHER THOUGHT

1. Recently, 100,000 shares of a large corporation's stock traded on the New York Stock Exchange for $50 per share. How much will the corporation receive as a result of this transaction? Explain.

2. Corporation A's stock has a par value of $1. Corporation B's stock has a par value of $10. Which stock is worth more? Explain.

3. The Oz Corp. exchanged 100 shares of its $10-par common stock for some office furniture. Explain how Oz should determine the proper amount for furniture and common stock in this transaction.

4. The Kermit Corp. purchased treasury stock for $100 and later sold it for $125. How will this $25 "gain" be reported on the financial statements?

5. Daly, Inc., acquired treasury stock to use for executive compensation. Why didn't Daly just issue new shares to the executives?

6. Are owners of preferred stock assured of receiving dividends on their stock? Would your answer be different if the preferred stock were cumulative?

7. The Squires Corp. received a pickup truck and 100 shares of its own stock as a donation from a stockholder. Explain the amount that would be assigned to Donated Capital for each of these items.

8. Herix stock has an equity per share of $38.20. Does this mean that, if the corporation liquidates, each stockholder will receive $38.20 for each share of stock owned? Describe the difference, if any, between equity per share and liquidation value per share.

## OBJECTIVE ASSIGNMENT

*True/False*   Indicate whether each statement below is *true* or *false* by placing a *T* or an *F* in the space provided.

_____ 1.  When the articles of incorporation are approved, they become a part of the charter that creates a corporation.

_____ 2.  The preemptive right is the right of corporate officers to acquire common stock through a stock option plan.

_____ 3.  The board of directors has a legal obligation to declare dividends each year on preferred stock.

_____ 4.  Par value and stated value are not intended to reflect the amount that a share of stock is worth.

_____ 5.  Treasury stock is a corporation's own stock that has been reacquired by purchasing it on a stock exchange or by acquiring it in a private transaction with an individual shareholder.

*Multiple Choice*   Select the best choice to complete each statement or answer each question below. Write the letter corresponding to your choice in the space provided.

_____ 1.  Which of the following is a disadvantage of the corporate form of business?
a.  Corporations lack mutual agency.
b.  Ownership shares can be easily transferred.
c.  Ownership is separated from control of operations.
d.  Owners' liability is limited.

_____ 2.  The amount of stock that a corporation has sold at some point in time is called
a.  Authorized stock
b.  Capital stock
c.  Outstanding stock
d.  Issued stock

_____ 3.  The Income Summary account of a proprietorship is closed into the owner's capital account; for a corporation, Income Summary is closed into
a.  Common Stock
b.  Paid-In Capital in Excess of Par
c.  Retained Earnings
d.  Donated Capital

_____ 4.  Filko, Inc., sold 100 shares of $2-par common stock for $1,400. In recording this transaction, Filko would include:
a.  A credit to Common Stock for $1,400
b.  A credit to Paid-In Capital in Excess of Par: Common for $1,400
c.  A credit to Paid-In Capital in Excess of Par: Common for $1,200
d.  A credit to Paid-In Capital in Excess of Par: Common for $200

_____ 5.  When common stock is sold on subscription:
a.  The Common Stock account is credited when the subscription price has been fully paid and the stock is issued.
b.  The Common Stock account is credited when the subscription contract is signed and a down payment is received.
c.  The Common Stock account is not used. Shares issued on subscription are credited to Common Stock Subscribed, a permanent stockholders' equity account.
d.  A stockholders' equity account called Subscriptions Receivable: Common is used to record the par value of the shares issued.

_____ 6. When common stock is exchanged for an asset, such as land or a building, the issue price of the stock is considered to be:
   a. The appraisal value of the asset
   b. The value of the asset
   c. The value of the stock
   d. The fair market value of the stock or the fair market value of the asset, whichever can be determined more objectively

_____ 7. The Hilo Corp. pays an attorney $2,500 to prepare articles of incorporation. In recording this transaction, Hilo will debit:
   a. Common Stock
   b. Organization Cost
   c. Donated Capital
   d. Treasury Stock

_____ 8. A share of treasury stock that was acquired for $40 was sold to a new stockholder for $60. In recording this transaction:
   a. Treasury Stock would be credited for $60.
   b. Common Stock would be credited for $40.
   c. Paid-In Capital from Treasury Stock would be credited for $60.
   d. Paid-In Capital from Treasury Stock would be credited for $20.

_____ 9. When preferred stockholders have the right to receive a specified dividend and to receive more after a matching dividend percentage is given to common stockholders, the preferred shares are said to be:
   a. Cumulative
   b. Participating
   c. Convertible
   d. Callable

_____ 10. Equity per share is:
   a. The claim against a company's assets represented by one share of common stock
   b. The claim against a company's income represented by one share of common stock
   c. The amount that each share of common stock will receive if the corporation liquidates
   d. The par or stated value of each share of common stock outstanding

## EXERCISES

5† **Exercise 1:** Recording the Issuance of Common Stock for Cash

Freeman Corp.'s charter authorizes the issuance of 100,000 shares of common stock. Freeman sold the following common stock during 1998:

Feb. 12   Sold 1,000 shares for $10,000.

July 10   Sold 5,000 shares for $63,000.

Nov. 5   Sold 7,500 shares for $105,000.

Prepare general journal entries to record each of these issuances, assuming that:

a. Common stock has a $10-par value.
b. Common stock has a $1 stated value.
c. Common stock has no par or stated value.

▶ *(Check Figure: When common stock has no par or stated value, the Nov. 5 credit to Common Stock = $105,000)*

5 **Exercise 2:** Recording the Issuance of Common Stock on Subscription

Prepare the proper journal entries to record each of the following 1998 transactions:

Feb. 3   Hernandez, Inc., sold subscriptions for 600 shares of $2-par common stock. The subscription price of $12 per share is to be paid in three installments: $4 down at the time of the subscription, $4 on Mar. 1, and $4 on Apr. 1.

Mar. 1   Hernandez collected the first installment.

Apr. 1   Hernandez collected the second installment and issued the stock.

▶ *(Check Figure: Apr. 1 credit to Common Stock = $1,200)*

5 **Exercise 3:** Determining the Effect of Stock Issuances on Categories of Stockholders' Equity

Union, Inc., is authorized by its charter to issue 100,000 shares of no-par stock. During its first year of operations, 60,000 shares were sold for $15 per share.

States Corp. is authorized by its charter to issue 500,000 shares of $5-par stock. During its first year of operations, States sold 10,000 shares for $20 per share and 40,000 shares for $17.50 per share.

Bay, Inc., is authorized by its charter to issue 1 million shares of no-par stock. Bay's board of directors adopted a stated value of $1 per share. During Bay's first year of operations, 100,000 shares were sold for $500,000 and 80,000 shares were sold for $400,000.

Calculate the amount of common stock, additional paid-in capital, and total paid-in capital for Union, States, and Bay, respectively.

▶ *(Check Figure: Total paid-in capital for States Corp. = $900,000)*

**Exercise 4:** Recording Issuance of Stock for Cash, Noncash Assets, and Services

Lawnscope, Inc., was authorized by its charter of incorporation to issue 100,000 shares of $5-par common stock. Prepare journal entries to record each of the following 1998 transactions.

† The numbers in the margin refer to the Learning Objectives.

Explain why you chose the amount that you did for the account debited.

Aug. 1 Lawnscope sold 40,000 shares of stock for $15 per share.

     2 Lawnscope issued 300 shares to Ajax Machinery in exchange for a mower. The advertised price of the mower was $4,995.

   16 Lawnscope issued 200 shares to A. Longstreet, attorney, for services rendered in the process of applying for a charter of incorportion.

Dec. 31 Lawnscope issued 12,000 shares for a plot of land to be used as a plant nursery. The land was appraised by two independent appraisers at $140,000 and $160,000.

▶ *(Check Figure: Dec. 31 debit to Land = $150,000)*

6 **Exercise 5:** Recording Treasury Stock Transactions

Perkins, Inc., has the following stock outstanding on Dec. 31, 1998:

Common stock, $100-par, 100,000 shares
  authorized, 45,000 shares issued and
  outstanding. . . . . . . . . . . . . . . . . . . . . . . . . . .   $4,500,000
Paid-in capital in excess of par value . . . . . . . .    3,600,000

Prepare journal entries to record the following transactions that took place in 1999:

Mar. 10 Perkins repurchased 1,000 shares for $195 per share.

June 19 Perkins sold 600 of the shares purchased on Mar. 10 for $210 per share.

Oct. 2 Perkins sold the remaining 400 shares purchased on Mar. 10 for $190 per share.

▶ *(Check Figure: June 19 credit to Paid-In Capital from Treasury Stock = $9,000)*

8 **Exercise 6:** Allocating Dividends between Common and Preferred Stockholders

Erwin Corp. has the following stock outstanding:

6% preferred stock, $5-par, cumulative and par-
  ticipating, 50,000 shares authorized, 40,000
  shares issued and outstanding. . . . . . . . . . . . . .   $200,000
Common stock, $1-par, 1,000,000 shares
  authorized, 800,000 shares issued and
  outstanding . . . . . . . . . . . . . . . . . . . . . . . . . . .    800,000

On Dec. 31, 1999, Erwin's board declared a $100,000 cash dividend. No dividends were paid on preferred stock during 1997 and 1998.

     Calculate the portion of the $100,000 that will be paid to preferred stockholders and the portion that will be paid to common stockholders.

▶ *(Check Figure: Allocation to common stockholders = $60,800)*

5 9 **Exercise 7:** Recording Issuance of Common and Preferred Stock

On Jan. 3, 1998, Hope, Inc., received its charter of incorporation authorizing the issuance of the following stock:

     5% preferred stock, $10-par, 100,000 shares
     Common stock, $5-par, 10,000,000 shares

The following stock transactions took place during 1998:

Jan. 15 Hope sold 10,000 shares of common stock for $64,000 cash.

Feb. 5 Hope exchanged 8,000 shares of common stock for a small building with a fair market value of $51,200.

Mar. 24 Hope issued 10,000 shares of preferred stock for $18 per share.

June 30 Hope sold 19,000 shares of common stock for $7.20 per share.

Oct. 25 Hope sold 7,500 shares of preferred stock for $165,000.

Prepare general journal entries to record each of the transactions listed. Calculate the total paid-in capital for Hope on Dec. 31, 1998.

▶ (Check Figure: Total paid-in capital = $597,000)

10 **Exercise 8:** Recording Donations of Assets and Stock

Lea Corp. received the following items as donations during 1999:

Mar. 21 Mulberry County gave the corporation 15 acres of land valued at $60,000. Lea agreed to build a distribution warehouse on the property and to employ at least 50 local residents.

Apr. 30 A stockholder donated 10,000 shares of Lea $2-par common stock. The stock was selling for $4.25 per share on Apr. 30.

June 25 Mulberry County Aviation Authority donated a surplus portable building, which was moved to the donated land and used as a temporary office. An independent appraisal established the value of the building at $6,750.

July 15 4,000 of the common shares received as a donation on Apr. 30 were sold for $18,200.

Prepare general journal entries to record the transactions related to the donations described above. Calculate the amount of donated capital that Lea would show on the Dec. 31, 1999, balance sheet as a result of these transactions.

▶ (Check Figure: Total donated capital = $84,950)

11 12 **Exercise 9:** Preparing the Stockholders' Equity Section of the Balance Sheet and Calculating Ratios

The Embassy Corp. was authorized by its charter to issue 500,000 shares of $10-par common stock and 50,000 shares of $100-par, 8% preferred stock. Embassy issued 200,000 shares of common stock; it is currently holding 4,000 shares as treasury stock. The company issued 2,000 shares of preferred stock, which are still outstanding. The following stockholders' equity accounts were taken from Embassy's general ledger on Dec. 31, 1998:

| | | | |
|---|---|---|---|
| Preferred Stock | $ 200,000 | Paid-In Capital from Treasury | |
| Common Stock | 2,000,000 | Stock | 14,600 |
| Paid-In Capital in Excess | | Donated Capital | 29,500 |
| of Par: Preferred | 65,000 | Retained Earnings | 116,000 |
| Paid-In Capital in Excess | | Treasury Stock | 62,500 |
| of Par: Common | 1,250,000 | | |

Prepare the stockholders' equity section for Embassy Corp. Include all disclosures discussed in this chapter. Assuming total assets are $12,042,000, calculate the stockholders' equity to total asset ratio and the debt to total asset ratio.

▶ (Check Figure: Total stockholders' equity = $3,612,600)

13 **Exercise 10:** Calculating Equity per Share of Common Stock

Tudor Corporation's stockholders' equity totals $856,250. Tudor has 4,000 shares of preferred stock issued and outstanding; the preferred shares have a liquidation price of $15 per share. Tudor has issued 50,000 shares of common stock, 2,000 of which are currently held as treasury stock. Calculate the equity per share of common stock. Round your answer to the nearest cent.

▶ (Check Figure: Equity per share = $16.59)

## PROBLEMS: SET A

5  10† **Problem A1:** Recording Issuance of Common Stock and Donations

Danvers Corp. is chartered by the state of Delaware. Transactions for 1998 related to the issuance of common stock are as follows:

Jan. 22  Danvers Corp. received its charter of incorporation from the state of Delaware. Danvers was authorized to issue 200,000 shares of no-par common stock. The board of directors established a stated value of $25 per share.

26  Danvers sold 30,000 shares for $810,000.

30  Danvers issued 2,000 shares to Barnes, Lopez and Stein, Attorneys at Law, as payment for legal services rendered in preparing the articles of incorporation.

Feb. 12  Danvers issued 1,000 shares to Robert Cawthon for a piece of land. The land had been appraised by several independent appraisers at an average of $27,500.

Mar. 5  Danvers sold 8,000 shares for $28 per share.

8  Danvers issued 1,000 shares to Olive Griffin in exchange for a portable modular building. The building will be used for office space until a more permanent structure can be built.

Apr. 1  The City of Malden donated 50 acres of land appraised at $2,250 per acre to Danvers Corp. The land is to be used as the site for Danvers' primary manufacturing facility.

**Required:**

Prepare journal entries to record each of the transactions described above. If no entry is necessary, write "No entry." Include calculations in your journal entry explanations where appropriate.

▶ *(Check Figure: Jan. 30 debit to Organization Cost = $54,000)*

5  **Problem A2:** Recording the Issuance of Stock on Subscription

Warren, Inc., has been authorized to issue 125,000 shares of $10-par common stock. The following 1998 transactions relate to the initial issuance of Warren stock:

Feb. 1  Warren sold subscriptions for 25,000 shares of stock. The shares have a subscription price of $15 per share. One-third of the subscription price was received as a down payment.

15  Warren sold 10,000 shares for $180,000.

Mar. 1  An installment amounting to one-third of the subscription price was received.

19  Warren exchanged 200 shares of stock for a new two-way radio system having a fair market value of $3,800.

Apr. 1  The final one-third of the subscription price was received and the stock issued.

**Required:**

Prepare journal entries to record the transactions described above. Include calculations in your journal entry explanations where appropriate.

▶ *(Check Figure: Feb. 1  Common Stock Subscribed = $250,000)*

**Problem A3:** Recording Treasury Stock Transactions

Dedham Manufacturing Co. has the following stockholders' equity on the Dec. 31, 1998, balance sheet:

† The numbers in the margin refer to the Learning Objectives.

---

**DEDHAM MANUFACTURING CO.**
Partial Balance Sheet
December 31, 1998

**Stockholders' Equity Section**

Paid-In Capital:

| | |
|---|---|
| Common Stock ($5-par, 100,000 shares authorized, 50,000 shares issued and outstanding)...................................... | $ 250,000 |
| Paid-In Capital in Excess of Par ............................... | 700,000 |
| Total Paid-In Capital....................................... | $ 950,000 |
| Earned Capital: | |
| Retained Earnings .......................................... | 300,000 |
| Total Stockholders' Equity...................................... | $1,250,000 |

---

**Required:**

Prepare Dedham Manufacturing's journal entries to record the following transactions that took place during January 1999:

Jan.  3  Purchased 2,500 shares of its own Dedham stock for $20 per share.

  6  Sold 750 shares of the treasury stock for $22 per share.

  10  Sold 1,250 shares of the treasury stock for $18 per share.

  20  Sold the remaining 500 shares of the treasury stock for $20 per share.

▶ *(Check Figure: Jan. 10 debit to Retained Earnings = $1,000)*

8  **Problem A4:** Allocating Dividends between Preferred and Common Stockholders

Norwood, Inc., has the following preferred and common stock outstanding on Dec. 31, 1999:

| | |
|---|---|
| 6% Preferred Stock ($20 par, cumulative, participating, 100,000 shares authorized, 6,000 shares issued and outstanding) ............. | $120,000 |
| Common Stock ($10 par, 1,000,000 shares authorized, 84,000 shares issued and outstanding) ............................ | 840,000 |
| Total Preferred and Common Stock........... | $960,000 |

**Required:**

Calculate the amount of dividends received by preferred and common stockholders, respectively, under each of the following assumptions:

1. Preferred dividends for 1998 are in arrears. On Dec. 31, 1999, Norwood declared a total dividend of $64,800.
2. No dividends are in arrears. On Dec. 31, 1999, Norwood declared a total dividend of $76,800.
3. Preferred dividends for 1997 and 1998 are in arrears. On Dec. 31, 1999, Norwood declared a total dividend of $110,400.

▶ *[Check Figure: In assumption (3), preferred stockholder allocation = $26,400]*

5 6 9 10 11  **Problem A5:** Recording Effects of Stockholders' Equity Transactions in Ledger Accounts and Preparing Stockholders' Equity Section of Balance Sheet

The following events and transactions relate to the stockholders' equity accounts of the Heath Corporation for 1998:

Jan. 3 The charter of incorporation was received, authorizing Heath to issue 100,000 shares of $5-par common stock and 30,000 shares of $50-par preferred stock.

5 8,000 common shares were sold to the incorporators of the business for $100,000.

9 1,000 shares of preferred stock were sold for $56 per share.

15 Subscriptions to 12,000 common shares were sold. The subscription price was $15 per share; one-third of the total was received as a down payment.

31 200 preferred shares were issued to the firm's attorneys in payment for legal services rendered in drawing up the articles of incorporation. A value of $56 per share was deemed appropriate.

Feb. 1 One-third of the subscription price of the subscribed shares was received.

15 Heath Corporation purchased 2,000 common shares from one of the incorporators for $14 per share.

Mar. 1 The final balance due was received on the subscribed shares. The shares were issued.

20 Heath Corporation sold 500 shares of treasury stock for $17.50 per share.

May 30 Heath received 10 acres of land as a donation from Gardner City. The land has a market value of $75,000.

Sept. 15 Heath sold, for $13.50 per share, 500 shares of the treasury stock purchased on Feb. 15.

The balance of the Retained Earnings account after all 1998 entries is $36,400. (Establish a Retained Earnings account with a $36,400 credit balance.)

**Required:**

1. Prepare T-account entries for each of these events and transactions. Do not make entries in general journal form, but instead set up the T-accounts you need and post your entries directly to the T-accounts.

2. Prepare the stockholders' equity section of Heath Corporation's balance sheet for Dec. 31, 1998. Include all appropriate disclosures discussed in this chapter.

▶ (Check Figure: Total stockholders' equity = $446,100)

11 12 **Problem A6:** Preparing the Stockholders' Equity Section of the Balance Sheet

The following accounts were selected from the Dec. 31, 1998, trial balance of Chelsea, Inc.:

| | Debit | Credit |
|---|---|---|
| Retained Earnings | | $155,000 |
| Common Stock Subscribed (2,000 shares) | | 10,000 |
| Notes Payable (due 12/31/02) | | 60,000 |
| 5% Preferred Stock, $10-par | | 150,000 |
| Paid-In Capital in Excess of Par: Common | | 135,000 |
| Subscriptions Receivable | $12,000 | |
| Paid-In Capital from Treasury Stock | | 28,000 |
| Organization Cost | 20,000 | |
| Paid-In Capital in Excess of Par: Preferred | | 85,000 |
| Common Stock, $5-par | | 250,000 |
| Donated Capital | | 59,000 |
| Treasury Stock (450 shares) at Cost | 4,000 | |

Chelsea was authorized by its charter of incorporation to issue 500,000 shares of $5-par-common stock and 25,000 shares of $10-par cumulative, nonparticipating preferred stock.

**Required:**

Choose the appropriate stockholders' equity accounts from those listed above and prepare in good form the stockholders' equity section of Chelsea, Inc.'s, Dec. 31, 1998, balance sheet. Assume that Chelsea's total assets are $2,630,303, calculate the stockholders' equity to total assets ratio and the debt to total assets ratio.

▶ *(Check Figure: Total stockholders' equity = $868,000)*

5 6 9 10 **Problem A7:** Calculating Correct Balances for Stockholders' Equity Accounts

Lowell Corp. received its charter of incorporation on June 15, 1998, and began operations on that day. An inexperienced bookkeeper has been recording all of Lowell Corp.'s stockholders' equity transactions in one account called Paid-In Capital. On Sept. 30, 1998, this account had a $462,545 credit balance. The following selected transactions relate to Lowell's stockholders' equity:

June 16 Lowell received its charter of incorporation, authorizing the issuance of 400,000 shares of $2.50-par common stock and 10,000 shares of $10-par, noncumulative, nonparticipating 5% preferred stock.

18 Sold 80,000 shares of common stock to the incorporators for $4.25 per share.

30 Sold subscriptions to 20,000 shares of common stock. The subscription price is $6.00 per share; half of the subscription price was received on June 30, and the remainder is due on Oct. 1.

July 5 Issued 1,000 shares of preferred stock for a plot of land. The appraised value of the land is $12,000.

31 Acquired 600 shares of treasury stock for $5.75 per share.

Aug. 10 Issued 100 shares of treasury stock to Beacon Printing as payment for printing stock certificates. The agreed-upon amount for this service was $620.

22 Received 500 shares of treasury stock as a donation. The quoted market price of the stock on this day is $6.50 per share.

Sept. 15 Sold the 500 treasury shares received on Aug. 22 for $3,125.

30 Income Summary has a debit balance, before closing, of $9,750. The bookkeeper closed this account into Paid-In Capital.

**Required:**

Assist in correcting the stockholders' equity accounts. (Assume that all asset and liability accounts are correct.) Set up working papers with the following column headings:

| Date | Preferred Stock | Common Stock | Common Stock Subscribed | Paid-In Capital in Excess of Par: Preferred | Paid-In Capital in Excess of Par: Common | Paid-In Capital from Treasury Stock | Donated Capital | Retained Earnings | Treasury Stock |
|---|---|---|---|---|---|---|---|---|---|

1. Enter the correct amounts in each column for each of the transactions listed. Total the columns to determine the correct balance for each account. If you do not need a column, leave it blank. Put parentheses around amounts debited to any account.
2. Using the working paper totals, prepare a correcting entry. (*Hint:* One of your debits should be to Paid-In Capital for $462,545.)

▶ *(Check Figure: Paid-In Capital from Treasury Stock = $45)*

## PROBLEMS: SET B

5  10†  **Problem B1:** Recording Issuance of Common Stock and Donations

Barre, Inc., was recently chartered by the state of Massachusetts. Transactions relating to the issuance of common stock during 1998 are as follows:

July  8  Barre, Inc., received its charter of incorporation from the Commonwealth of Massachusetts. Barre was authorized to issue 2,000,000 shares of no-par common stock. The board of directors voted to establish a stated value of $10 per share.

12  Barre issued 60,000 shares for $1,080,000 cash.

July  18  Barre issued 1,000 shares to Steinburg and O'Leary, Attorneys at Law, in payment for legal services rendered in preparing the articles of incorporation.

Aug.  6  Barre issued 2,000 shares to Harriett Whitley in exchange for a plot of land. The land's value has been established by independent appraisers at $32,800.

22  Barre sold 10,000 shares of stock for $22 per share.

25  Barre issued 1,500 shares of stock to Vernon Pope in exchange for some office equipment.

Sept. 13  Monson Township donated a building valued at $350,000 to Barre. Barre has agreed to move the building and preserve its basic architectural style. The moving is expected to be completed by Sept. 28, 1998.

**Required:**

Prepare journal entries to record each of the transactions described above. If no entry is necessary, write "No entry." Include calculations in your journal entry explanations where appropriate.

▶ *(Check Figure: Aug. 25 debit to Office Equipment = $33,000)*

5  **Problem B2:** Recording Issuance of Common Stock on Subscription

Holyoke Corp. has been authorized to issue 250,000 shares of $4-par common stock. Holyoke's 1999 stock issuance transactions are described below:

Oct.  14  Holyoke sold subscriptions for 75,000 shares of stock. The shares have a subscription price of $10 each. Twenty percent of the subscription price was received as a down payment.

Nov.  8  100,000 shares were sold for $1,200,000.

15  Subscribers paid an installment amounting to 40% of the subscription price.

Dec.  12  2,500 shares were exchanged for a full-page advertisement in a national magazine. The ad appeared in the Dec. 27 edition. The rate charged for such an advertisement is $37,500.

15  The final 40% of the subscription price was received and the stock was issued.

**Required:**

Prepare journal entries to record the transactions described above.

▶ *(Check Figure: Oct. 14  Common Stock Subscribed = $300,000)*

† The numbers in the margin refer to the Learning Objectives.

**6** **Problem B3:** Recording Treasury Stock Transactions

The Dec. 31, 1997, stockholders' equity section of Adams Corp.'s balance sheet is as follows:

**ADAMS CORP.**
**Partial Balance Sheet**
**December 31, 1997**

**Stockholders' Equity Section**

Paid-In Capital:
Common Stock ($4-par, 200,000 shares authorized, 150,000 shares
  issued and outstanding ...................................... $ 600,000
  Paid-In Capital in Excess of Par .............................. 375,000
    Total Paid-In Capital...................................... $ 975,000
Earned Capital:
  Retained Earnings ......................................... 365,000

Total Stockholder's Equity...................................... $1,340,000

**Required:**

Prepare Adams Corp.'s journal entries to record the following transactions that took place during Jan. 1998:

Jan.  4  Purchased 24,000 shares of its own Adams stock for $168,000.

     10  Sold 4,000 shares of the treasury stock for $9 per share.

     29  Sold 14,000 shares of the treasury stock for $6 per share.

     31  Sold the remaining 6,000 shares of treasury stock for $7 per share.

▶ *(Check Figure: Jan. 29 debit to Retained Earnings = $6,000)*

**8** **Problem B4:** Allocating Dividends between Preferred and Common Stockholders

Needham, Inc., has the following preferred and common stock outstanding on Dec. 31, 1999:

8% Preferred Stock ($10-par, cumulative,
  participating, 40,000 shares authorized, 10,000
  shares issued and outstanding) ............ $100,000
Common Stock ($2-par, 10,000,000 shares
  authorized, 250,000 shares issued and
  outstanding) ........................... 500,000

Total Preferred and Common Stock.......... $600,000

**Required:**

Calculate the amount of dividends received by preferred and common stockholders, respectively, under each of the following assumptions:

1. Preferred dividends for 1998 are in arrears. On Dec. 31, 1999, Needham declared a total dividend of $56,000.
2. No dividends are in arrears. On Dec. 31, 1999, Needham declared a total dividend of $66,000.
3. Preferred dividends for 1997 and 1998 are in arrears. On Dec. 31, 1999, Needham declared a total dividend of $88,000.

▶ *[Check Figure: In assumption (3), allocation to common stockholders = $60,000]*

5 6 9 10 11 **Problem B5:** Recording Effects of Stockholders' Equity Transactions in Ledger Accounts and Preparing Stockholders' Equity Section of Balance Sheet

Becket Pools, Inc., was incorporated in 1998. The following events and transactions relate to the company's stockholders' equity accounts during the first year of its existence:

Jan. 6 The charter of incorporation was received, authorizing Becket to issue 250,000 shares of $20-par common stock and 20,000 shares of $10-par preferred stock.

7 25,000 shares of common stock were issued to the incorporators for $562,500.

9 2,000 shares of preferred stock were sold for $16 per share.

21 Subscriptions to 25,000 common shares were sold. The subscription price of $24 per share is to be received as follows: one-third on Jan. 21, one-third on Feb. 15, and one-third on Mar. 15. The one-third down payment was received.

Feb. 5 400 shares of preferred stock were issued to Rubin and Perot, Attorneys at Law, in payment for legal services received in establishing the corporation. A value of $6,400 was deemed appropriate.

15 The one-third installment due on the subscribed shares was received.

Mar. 1 Becket purchased 2,500 common shares from one of the incorporators for $25 per share.

15 The final installment due on the subscribed shares was received. The shares were issued.

31 Becket sold 1,000 shares of treasury stock for $28 per share.

Apr. 15 Becket received 2 acres of land adjoining the city dump as a chlorine storage area. The land, which had a fair market value of $20,000, was donated by Chester Township.

May 27 Becket sold, for $24 per share, 500 shares of the treasury stock purchased on Mar. 1.

The balance of the Retained Earnings account after all 1998 entries is $48,000. (Establish a Retained Earnings account with a $48,000 credit balance.)

**Required:**

1. Prepare T-account entries for each of these events and transactions. Do not make entries in general journal form, but instead set up T-accounts and post your entries directly to the T-accounts.
2. Prepare the stockholders' equity section of Becket's balance sheet for Dec. 31, 1998. You should include all appropriate disclosures discussed in this chapter.

▶ *(Check Figure: Total stockholders' equity = $1,246,400)*

11 12 **Problem B6:** Preparing the Stockholders' Equity Section of the Balance Sheet

The following accounts were selected from the Dec. 31, 1998, trial balance of Pfame, Inc.:

|  | Debit | Credit |
| --- | --- | --- |
| 7% Preferred Stock. . . . . . . . . . . . . . . . . . . . . . . . . . . . . . . . . . . . |  | $ 50,000 |
| Organization Cost . . . . . . . . . . . . . . . . . . . . . . . . . . . . . . . . . . . . | $15,700 |  |
| Paid-In Capital from Treasury Stock . . . . . . . . . . . . . . . . . . . . . . |  | 35,000 |
| Subscriptions Receivable . . . . . . . . . . . . . . . . . . . . . . . . . . . . . . | 9,000 |  |
| Retained Earnings . . . . . . . . . . . . . . . . . . . . . . . . . . . . . . . . . . . . |  | 112,000 |
| Paid-In Capital in Excess of Par: Common . . . . . . . . . . . . . . . . . . |  | 900,000 |
| Treasury Stock (2,000 shares) at Cost . . . . . . . . . . . . . . . . . . . . . | 24,000 |  |
| Common Stock . . . . . . . . . . . . . . . . . . . . . . . . . . . . . . . . . . . . . . . |  | 300,000 |
| Bonds Payable (due 1/1/2010). . . . . . . . . . . . . . . . . . . . . . . . . . . . |  | 50,000 |
| Donated Capital . . . . . . . . . . . . . . . . . . . . . . . . . . . . . . . . . . . . . . |  | 44,000 |
| Common Stock Subscribed (1,500 shares) . . . . . . . . . . . . . . . . . . |  | 7,500 |
| Paid-In Capital in Excess of Par: Preferred . . . . . . . . . . . . . . . . . . |  | 67,500 |

Pfame was authorized by its charter of incorporation to issue 400,000 shares of $5-par common stock and 10,000 shares of $100-par cumulative, participating preferred stock.

**Required:**

Choose the appropriate stockholders' equity accounts from those listed above and prepare in good form the stockholders' equity section of Pfame Inc.'s Dec. 31, 1998, balance sheet. Assume that Pfame's total assets are $2,043,836, calculate the stockholders' equity to total assets ratio and the debt to total assets ratio.

▶ *(Check Figure: Total stockholders' equity = $1,492,000)*

5 6 9 10 **Problem B7:** Calculating Correct Balances for Stockholders' Equity Accounts

In reviewing the financial records of Amherst, Inc., you discover that the asset and liability accounts are correct but the stockholders' equity transactions have been recorded in one account, Corporate Capital. On Dec. 31, 1998, this account has a $772,650 credit balance. The following 1998 transactions and events relate to stockholders' equity:

Feb. 14  Amherst, Inc., received its charter of incorporation, authorizing the issuance of 500,000 shares of $5-par common stock and 20,000 shares of $100-par, noncumulative, nonparticipating preferred stock.

25  Sold 40,000 common shares to the incorporators for $7.25 per share.

Mar. 31  Received a donation of land and building from the City of Brookfield. The fair market value of these assets was $109,000.

Apr. 1  Sold subscriptions to 20,000 shares of common stock. Of the subscription price of $8 per share, one-fourth will be received now, one-fourth on Oct. 1, 1998, and the remainder on Jan. 1, 1999.

June 30  Sold 2,000 shares of preferred stock for $105 per share.

Sept. 1  Acquired 1,000 shares of treasury stock for $7.90 per share.

Oct. 1  Received installment payment on common stock subscription.

15  Sold 200 shares of treasury stock for $8.25 per share.

Dec. 12  Sold 500 shares of treasury stock for $7.80 per share.

31  Income Summary had a credit balance of $6,000. In the records, you find this account closed into Corporate Capital.

**Required:**

Assist in correcting the stockholders' equity accounts. (Assume that all asset and liability accounts are correct.) Set up working papers with the following column headings:

| Date | Preferred Stock | Common Stock | Common Stock Subscribed | Paid-In Capital in Excess of Par: Preferred | Paid-In Capital in Excess of Par: Common | Paid-In Capital from Treasury Stock | Donated Capital | Retained Earnings | Treasury Stock |
|------|------|------|------|------|------|------|------|------|------|

1. Enter the correct amounts in each column for each of the transactions listed. Total the columns to determine the correct balance for each account. If you do not need a column, leave it blank. Put parentheses around amounts debited to any account.
2. Using the working paper totals, prepare a correcting entry. (*Hint:* One of your debits should be to Corporate Capital for $772,650.)

▶ *(Check Figure: Treasury Stock = $2,370 − debit balance)*

## DECISION PROBLEM

 The following stockholders' equity section was prepared by Quincy Corp.'s accounting department:

---

### QUINCY CORP.
### Partial Balance Sheet
### December 31, 1998

#### Stockholders' Equity Section

| | |
|---|---:|
| 8% Preferred Stock ($2-par, cumulative, participating) ................ | $ 10,000 |
| Common Stock (no par, 20,000 shares issued) ...................... | 50,000 |
| Common Stock Subscribed ...................................... | 5,000 |
| Paid-In Capital in Excess of Stated Value: Common .................. | 47,000 |
| Paid-In Capital in Excess of Par Value: Preferred ................... | 4,600 |
| Donated Capital ............................................. | 8,000 |
| Retained Earnings ........................................... | 38,000 |
| Total ................................................. | $162,600 |
| Less: Treasury Stock (300 shares) ............................... | (1,305) |
| Total Stockholders' Equity ..................................... | $161,295 |

---

You are responsible for reviewing the stockholder's equity section of the balance sheet before it goes to the printer. You notice that several pieces of important information are omitted. These missing items may be calculated by using the information given above.

**Required:**

Answer each of the following questions using the data given in the stockholders' equity section above. Show calculations where appropriate.

1. What is the stated value per share of common stock?
2. How many shares of preferred stock are issued and outstanding?
3. What is total paid-in capital?
4. How many shares of common stock have been subscribed but not issued?
5. How many shares of common stock are outstanding?
6. How much was paid for each share of treasury stock?
7. What was the average amount paid for the common shares issued and subscribed? (Round your answer to the nearest cent.)
8. What is the equity per share of common stock? (Assume that the liquidation value of preferred stock is $5 per share.)

## ETHICS CASE

When John and Mary Lewis passed away in 1952, they left all of the common stock of the family-owned corporation, Lewis Broadcasting, to their three children, Lynn, Tom, and June. Since Lynn had the most business talent and had always helped run the company, she inherited 60% of the stock, the controlling interest. The Lewis family had owned KNAP, a small radio station, since 1936. While the station never made them rich, it provided a steady income. The station's quality of programming and community involvement were always a source of family pride.

Lynn's origination of the town's first television station in 1954 and the addition of a profitable FM radio station in 1960 were evidence of her astute business insight. The continued growth in profitability of Lewis Broadcasting was testimony to her excellent management skills. Lynn continued to keep the interests of the community at the forefront of the company's philosophy. Tom and June, never active in the business, moved away, and pursued other interests in New York and Los Angeles.

When June and Tom passed away in the early 1980s, their stock was divided among their five children, none of whom was actively involved with Lewis Broadcasting. In light of Lynn's advancing age and the fact that she had no immediate family, her nieces and nephews pressed her to sell her stock to Federal Broadcasting, a large conglomerate with stations in many major cities. Federal's offer was to buy all the common stock at a very attractive price. Federal was not interested in buying less than a controlling interest; hence, Lynn would have to sell her stock if the nieces and nephews were to be able to sell theirs. Lynn was concerned that, with ownership in a distant city, the accent on local community affairs and causes would give way to an emphasis on maximizing income. Accordingly, Federal's offer was rejected.

In 1985 Lynn had Lewis Broadcasting's corporate charter modified to allow the issuance of 10,000 shares of $1,000-par,

10% cumulative, participating preferred stock. As soon as the stock was authorized, Lynn used most of her personal fortune to purchase all of it at par, for $10,000,000. Lewis Broadcasting used the proceeds to finance some much-needed modernization at the television station.

Lynn subsequently transferred ownership of all her common and preferred stock to a nonprofit foundation that operated a children's hospital in the town. The trustees of the foundation had gained the power to elect the majority of Lewis Broadcasting's board of directors and effectively control the company. Lynn's bequest was made with the stipulation that the Lewis Broadcasting stock never be sold, thus ensuring local control over the radio and television stations after she died. The $1,000,000 per year in dividends on the preferred stock were to be used to support the work of the children's hospital. Without this source of income, the hospital could not have survived.

In the years since the preferred stock was issued, dividends on common stock have been minimal. The board of directors, controlled by the foundation, has faithfully paid the preferred dividends and plowed most of the remaining profits back into the business. Lynn's nieces and nephews feel that they have been cheated out of their rights in the business. Their stock's value has been eroded because the company is effectively controlled in perpetuity by a foundation, which pays small dividends. The foundation has offered to buy them out, but at a price far below what they believe the stock of such a successful, profitable corporation is worth.

**Required:**

Was Lynn's plan to keep Lewis Broadcasting under local control a fair and ethical thing to do? In framing your answer, consider the rights of the other stockholders as well as Lynn's objective.

## OBJECTIVE ASSIGNMENT ANSWERS

**True/False**

1. T    2. F    3. F    4. T    5. T

**Multiple Choice**

1. c    2. d    3. c    4. c    5. a
6. d    7. b    8. d    9. b    10. a

# Corporations: Retained Earnings and Corporate Income

**LEARNING OBJECTIVES**

After studying this chapter, you should be able to do the following:

1 Explain what a Retained Earnings account is

2 Describe and prepare entries to record Retained Earnings: Appropriated

3 Describe and record prior period adjustments

4 Prepare a statement of retained earnings

5 Prepare appropriate entries to record cash dividends, property dividends, and large and small stock dividends

6 Explain the effect of stock dividends and stock splits on the stockholders' equity section of the balance sheet

7 Prepare the stockholders' equity section for a comprehensive balance sheet, including all information needed for fair disclosure

8 Explain how corporations estimate and pay federal income taxes and prepare related entries

9 Explain how the provision for income taxes is calculated when permanent differences exist

10 Explain what temporary differences are, and prepare entries to record income taxes when temporary differences exist

11 Explain what discontinued operations, extraordinary items, and cumulative effects of changes in accounting principles are and how they are shown on a corporate income statement

12 Explain historical earnings per share, primary earnings per share, and fully diluted earnings per share

13 Calculate and explain rate of return on total assets, rate of return on common stockholders' equity, and dividend yield rate

14 Prepare a corporate income statement that includes income taxes, unusual items, and earnings per share

15 Define the key terms listed at the end of the chapter

**CHAPTER OUTLINE**

**RETAINED EARNINGS** • Retained Earnings: Appropriated and Unappropriated • Prior Period Adjustments • Retained Earnings: A Recap • Statement of Retained Earnings • **DIVIDENDS** • Cash Dividends • Property Dividends • Stock Dividends • Liquidating Dividends • Dividends and Treasury Stock • Stock Splits • Recording Dividends on Preferred Stock • **STOCKHOLDERS' EQUITY— A COMPREHENSIVE ILLUSTRATION** • **ACCOUNTING FOR CORPORATE INCOME TAXES** • Estimating and Paying Income Taxes • Permanent Differences • Temporary Differences • Income Taxes on the Corporate Income Statement • **UNUSUAL INCOME STATEMENT ITEMS** • Discontinued Operations • Extraordinary Items • Changes in Accounting Principles • **EARNINGS PER SHARE** • Historical Earnings per Share • Primary and Fully Diluted Earnings per Share • **FINANCIAL STATEMENT ANALYSIS** • Rate of Return on Total Assets • Rate of Return on Common Stockholders' Equity • Dividend Yield Rate • **THE CORPORATE INCOME STATEMENT**

**Exhibit 1** Balance Sheet Illustrating the Concept of Retained Earnings

DUNLAP CORP.
Balance Sheet
December 31, 1998

| Assets | | Liabilities and Stockholders' Equity | |
|---|---|---|---|
| Assets are the **resources** (cash, inventory, land, buildings, patents) that a corporation has to use in earning income . . . . . . . . . . . . . . | $587,000 | Liabilities: | |
| | | Liabilities show the **source** of some of the assets—those acquired by borrowing money to purchase them . . . . . . . . . . . . . . . | $200,000 |
| | | Stockholders' Equity: | |
| | | Paid-In Capital shows a **source** of some assets—those acquired through investment by stockholders . . . . . . . . . . . . . . . . . | 300,000 |
| | | Retained Earnings shows a **source** of assets—those acquired through the income earned by the corporation. . . . . . . . . . . . . . | 87,000 |
| Total Assets . . . . . . . . . . . . . . . . . . . . . . . . . . . | $587,000 | Total Liabilities and Stockholders' Equity . . . | $587,000 |

## RETAINED EARNINGS

**Learning Objective 1**
Explain what a Retained Earnings account is

**Retained Earnings** is a stockholders' equity account that shows the income that has accumulated since the corporation's beginning and is still retained in the business in some form. It's the accumulated income that the corporation still has in the form of assets.

When you think of $58 million of retained earnings, visions of large stacks of cash may flash through your mind. To understand what retained earnings is, forget that vision. Retained earnings is not cash; it is not any *specific* asset. It merely shows where a certain dollar amount of assets originally came from.

Exhibit 1, a sample corporation's balance sheet, helps illustrate this concept. You should see by studying this balance sheet that:

**Assets           are           resources**
**Liabilities and stockholders' equity are sources of resources**

The amount shown as retained earnings doesn't mean that we have that amount of cash on hand. It shows where an amount of assets originally came from—the income earned by the corporation. Retained Earnings identifies a source of the corporation's assets, but is not an asset itself. In fact, it represents a counter balance for assets in the accounting equation.

### Retained Earnings: Appropriated and Unappropriated

**Learning Objective 2**
Describe and prepare entries to record Retained Earnings: Appropriated

When a company earns large profits for several years, the Retained Earnings balance will grow rapidly. Stockholders may become restless and begin to ask why these earnings are not being used as a source for dividend distribution. Some of the reasons that management may be accumulating retained earnings are:

- To expand productive capacity by constructing a new factory building
- To purchase the assets of another corporation in order to expand into new markets
- To take care of unforeseen contingencies such as a loss from a natural disaster or a lawsuit

Remember, when retained earnings are accumulating on one side of the balance sheet, total assets will be growing on the other side of the balance sheet. If the assets that happen to be growing are liquid assets, stockholders may become especially impatient. Management can and should communicate the reason for not paying larger dividends to stockholders, either by adding a note to the financial statements or by appropriating retained earnings.

An appropriation is accomplished by transferring an amount from the unrestricted retained earnings account (called **Retained Earnings: Unappropriated**) into a restricted retained earnings account called **Retained Earnings: Appropriated.** (When the term *Retained Earnings* is used, it refers to Retained Earnings: Unappropriated.) Let's look at an example of this process.

# MASON CORPORATION

Mason Corporation plans to build a new warehouse 5 years from now. The board of directors decides to appropriate $70,000 of retained earnings on Dec. 31, 1998, and each succeeding Dec. 31 through 2002. Construction of the new building is to take place in 2000. The appropriation entry for each Dec. 31 is:

| 1998–2002 | | | |
|---|---|---|---|
| Dec. 31 | Retained Earnings: Unappropriated . . . . . . . . . | 70,000 | |
| | Retained Earnings Appropriated for Plant Expansion . . . . . . . . . . . . . . . . . . . . . . . . . . . | | 70,000 |
| | To record a restriction placed upon retained earnings. | | |

An appropriation of retained earnings has no effect on assets, and no effect on total retained earnings. Note that the entry in the above illustration involves two retained earnings accounts—no asset account is debited or credited.

Since no specific fund of assets is set aside by appropriating retained earnings, Mason Corporation will have $70,000 × 5 years = $350,000 of appropriated retained earnings on Dec. 31, 2002, but it may still lack sufficient cash to construct a new building. *Remember, appropriating retained earnings communicates a restriction on retained earnings; it does not set aside a fund of assets.*

Exhibit 2 shows an appropriation of retained earnings in the stockholders' equity section of Mason's balance sheet.

**Exhibit 2** Partial Balance Sheet Showing Appropriation of Retained Earnings

**MASON CORPORATION**
**Partial Balance Sheet**
**December 31, 1998**

**Stockholders' Equity**

| | | |
|---|---|---|
| Paid-In Capital: | | |
| Common Stock ($10-par, 100,000 shares authorized, issued, and outstanding) . . . . . . . . . . . . . . . . . . . . . . . . . . . . . . . . . . . | | $1,000,000 |
| Earned Capital: | | |
| Retained Earnings: Unappropriated . . . . . . . . . . . . . . . . . . | $540,000 | |
| Retained Earnings: Appropriated for Plant Expansion. . . . . . | 70,000 | |
| Total Earned Capital. . . . . . . . . . . . . . . . . . . . . . . . . . . . . . . . . . . | | 610,000 |
| Total Stockholders' Equity. . . . . . . . . . . . . . . . . . . . . . . . . . . . . . . . . . . | | $1,610,000 |

When the restriction on retained earnings is no longer needed, the appropriation is removed by debiting the Retained Earnings: Appropriated account and crediting Retained Earnings: Unappropriated. When the plant expansion is completed in 2003, Mason Corporation removes the restriction by the following entry:

| | | | |
|---|---|---|---|
| 2003 | | | |
| Dec. 31 | Retained Earnings: Appropriated for Plant Expansion................................... | 350,000 | |
| | Retained Earnings: Unappropriated.......... | | 350,000 |
| | To remove restriction placed upon retained earnings. | | |

When Mason finishes the new warehouse building, an entry is made debiting Building and crediting either (1) Cash, if the building was financed by using accumulated cash; (2) a liability account, if the expansion was financed by borrowing; (3) or possibly Common Stock if additional shares were issued to finance the building. In any case, no Retained Earnings account is involved in the entry to record the construction of the building.

Many corporations believe that the disclosure of appropriated retained earnings does more to confuse stockholders than to inform them. These firms disclose retained earnings restrictions by explaining them in a footnote.

Financial statement footnotes often contain important supplemental information not found on the financial statements. Investors should study these notes carefully. Exhibit 3 shows how the stockholders' equity section and related footnote would look if Mason chose this method.

## Prior Period Adjustments

Learning Objective 3
Describe and record prior period adjustments

Sometimes prior period adjustments are needed to correct errors made in the past. To understand why, let's examine how errors affect the accounts.

Assume that an error was made in an income statement account 3 years ago. Utilities Expense was understated by $33,000.

The income statement account Utilities Expense was closed—and the error was transferred—to Income Summary at the end of the year.

**Exhibit 3** Footnote Disclosure of Appropriated Retained Earnings

**MASON CORPORATION**
**Partial Balance Sheet**
**December 31, 1998**

### Stockholders' Equity

| | |
|---|---|
| Paid-In Capital: | |
| Common Stock ($10-par, 100,000 shares authorized, issued, and outstanding) ..................................... | $1,000,000 |
| Earned Capital: | |
| Retained Earnings (see Note 3) ............................... | 610,000 |
| Total Stockholders' Equity....................................... | $1,610,000 |

*Note 3.  Retained earnings restrictions*
The corporation has been limiting the payment of dividends because of a planned plant expansion. Retained earnings restricted for this purpose amount to $70,000.

Income Summary was then closed to Retained Earnings. The effect of the error is now in Retained Earnings. Retained Earnings is a permanent balance sheet account that is carried forward from year to year—it is not closed.

The effect of the error, then, must still be in Retained Earnings 3 years later. More specifically, the current beginning balance of Retained Earnings is wrong if the prior year's error was not corrected. The process of correcting this beginning balance of Retained Earnings is called making a **prior period adjustment.**

In 1997, Mason Corporation's bookkeeper debited Advertising Expense and credited Cash instead of debiting Land and crediting Cash. The effect of this $25,000 error was to overstate 1997 advertising expense and therefore understate 1997 income by $25,000. The asset land is also understated by $25,000.

The error was discovered in 1998 by an astute auditor. The following entry is made to correct the error:

| 1998 | | | |
|---|---|---|---|
| Dec. 31 | Land .................................... | 25,000 | |
| | Retained Earnings: Unappropriated.......... | | 25,000 |
| | To correct an error on the 1994 income statement. | | |

Mason's entry involved a debit to Land to increase this asset and a credit to Retained Earnings to increase this stockholders' equity account because these are the two accounts that were still wrong in 1998. Remember that the 1997 Advertising Expense was closed to Retained Earnings in 1997, so it is retained earnings that is wrong in 1998—not advertising expense.

A prior period adjustment increased Retained Earnings in the Mason example, but it may also decrease Retained Earnings. For instance, if the bookkeeper failed to record depreciation expense last year, a prior period adjustment entry would be made this year to debit Retained Earnings and credit Accumulated Depreciation. The effects of each error must be analyzed to determine whether the Retained Earnings balance is too high or too low. Once this decision is made, we know whether the prior period adjustment requires a debit or a credit to Retained Earnings.

## Retained Earnings: A Recap

There are only a few types of transactions that affect the Retained Earnings: Unappropriated account. We have explained all of them except one: dividends.

When assets are distributed to stockholders as dividends, Retained Earnings: Unappropriated is debited and an asset account is credited. After we finish looking at retained earnings, we will examine dividends in detail. The only thing you need to know now is that Retained Earnings is debited when dividends are declared.

Now you have seen all the reasons for debiting and crediting Retained Earnings: Unappropriated. These reasons are summarized in the following T-account:

**Retained Earnings: Unappropriated**

| DECREASES | INCREASES |
|---|---|
| Net loss for the period | Net income for the period |
| Negative prior period adjustments | Positive prior period adjustments |
| Dividends declared (cash, property, and stock) | Cancellation of appropriations of retained earnings |
| Negative effects of certain treasury stock sales | |
| Additional appropriations of retained earnings | |

**Exhibit 4** Statement of Retained Earnings

### MASON CORPORATION
### Statement of Retained Earnings
### For the Year Ended December 31, 1998

| | | |
|---|---:|---:|
| Retained Earnings: Unappropriated: | | |
| Balance, Jan. 1, 1998 . . . . . . . . . . . . . . . . . . . . . . . . . . . . . . . . . . . . . . . | | $ 447,000 |
| Prior Period Adjustment: Correction of 1997 Error . . . . . . . . . . . . . . . . . . | | 25,000 |
| Balance, Jan. 1, 1998, Corrected . . . . . . . . . . . . . . . . . . . . . . . . . . . . . . . | | $ 472,000 |
| Add: Net Income for the Year . . . . . . . . . . . . . . . . . . . . . . . . . . . . . . . . . | | 188,000 |
| Total . . . . . . . . . . . . . . . . . . . . . . . . . . . . . . . . . . . . . . . . . . . . . | | $ 660,000 |
| Deduct: Dividends Declared . . . . . . . . . . . . . . . . . . . . . . . . . . | $50,000 | |
| Appropriation for Plant Expansion . . . . . . . . . . . . . . . . | 70,000 | (120,000) |
| Balance, Dec. 31, 1998 . . . . . . . . . . . . . . . . . . . . . . . . . . . . . . . . . . . . . | | $ 540,000 |
| Retained Earnings: Appropriated for Plant Expansion: | | |
| Balance, Jan. 1, 1998 . . . . . . . . . . . . . . . . . . . . . . . . . . . . . . . . . . . . . . . | | –0– |
| Add: Appropriation during the Year . . . . . . . . . . . . . . . . . . . . . . . . . . . . . | | $ 70,000 |
| Deduct: (none) . . . . . . . . . . . . . . . . . . . . . . . . . . . . . . . . . . . . . . . . . . . | | –0– |
| Balance, Dec. 31, 1998 . . . . . . . . . . . . . . . . . . . . . . . . . . . . . . . . . . . . . | | $ 70,000 |

## Statement of Retained Earnings

*Learning Objective* **4**

Prepare a statement of retained earnings

The statement of retained earnings is one of the four financial statements published by corporations in annual reports to their stockholders. We have already discussed two of these statements: the balance sheet and the income statement. The third is the statement of cash flows. Here we will look at the statement of retained earnings.

The statement of retained earnings shows what has happened to the retained earnings accounts during the time period covered by the statement. The 1998 statement of retained earnings for Mason Corporation in Exhibit 4 shows the disclosure of dividends as well as income, the appropriation of retained earnings, and the prior period adjustment that we have discussed.

Look back at Exhibit 2 to refresh your memory on how retained earnings is shown in the stockholders' equity section of the balance sheet.

**ASK YOURSELF** ▶

1. **What is Retained Earnings?**
2. **In what two ways may restrictions on retained earnings be communicated to stockholders?**
3. **When is it necessary to make a prior period adjustment?**
4. **After the beginning balance, what is the first item shown on the statement of retained earnings?**

## DIVIDENDS

*Learning Objective* **5**

Prepare appropriate entries to record cash dividends, property dividends, and large and small stock dividends

**Dividends** are distributions of the earned capital of a corporation to its stockholders. Dividends may take the form of cash, property (assets other than cash), or additional shares of the corporation's stock.

The declaration and payment of dividends is at the discretion of the board of directors. Some corporations have a policy of paying regular, consistent amounts as dividends. Generally, owners of these corporations purchase the stock because they count on the regular receipt of dividends. They use these regular cash inflows from dividends to pay their living expenses. Banks and utilities are examples of industries that pay regular dividends. Bank of Boston Corp. has paid a dividend every year since 1784. Several other banks have paid dividends for more than 150 consecutive years.

At the other extreme, some corporations seldom, if ever, pay dividends to stockholders. These corporations use all the assets generated by earnings to expand the business. Stockholders purchase shares in these growth industries primarily to benefit from the increasing market value of the corporations' stock. Shares sold at the increased market value yield large cash profits to the investor. The electronics industry is an example of a rapidly growing field in which few corporations pay dividends.

Three points in time are important in the distribution of any dividend: (1) the declaration date, (2) the record date, and (3) the payment date.

The **declaration date** is the day that the board of directors meets and votes to distribute a dividend. The form of the dividend (cash, other assets, or stock), the amount of the dividend, and the record and payment dates are specified at this meeting. At this point the board has legally committed the corporation to pay the dividend. An accounting entry is required on this date to record the obligation.

The **record date** is the day that the list of the names and addresses of the stockholders is compiled. These are the owners who will receive the dividend when paid. This date is normally 2 or 3 weeks later than the declaration date. No accounting entry is necessary on the record date, because no further financial transaction or commitment has taken place.

The **payment date** is the day on which the dividends are sent to the shareholders. An accounting entry is necessary on this date to record the payment of cash, or the distribution of noncash assets or stock.

## Cash Dividends

The majority of dividends paid are cash dividends. These distributions may be made at any time, but they typically occur at the end of a quarter or a year. Two items are needed before the board of directors should consider declaring a cash dividend: earned capital and cash.

Most state laws require that corporations declare dividends out of accumulated earnings. Since paid-in capital may be considered to be the minimum legal capital that must be maintained in the corporation, it would be illegal in those states to declare dividends out of paid-in capital. Paid-in capital and earned capital are accounted for separately and are clearly distinguished on the balance sheet. The board should have little trouble determining whether adequate earned capital exists for a legal dividend to be declared.

The existence of earned capital does not guarantee that cash exists. The company may have reinvested the assets realized through earnings in inventory or in property, plant, and equipment assets. It may have used some of these assets to repay debt.

If the board sees that extra cash will be available after operating needs are met and that earned capital exists as represented by the balance in Retained Earnings, it may declare a cash dividend.

The following illustration shows what we do on the declaration, record, and payment dates.

## CLARK, INC.

On May 1, 1998—the declaration date—the board of directors of Clark, Inc., meet and declare a cash dividend. The $1.50 per share is to be paid on May 31—the payment date—to stockholders of record as of May 15, the record date. Clark has 100,000 shares of common stock outstanding.[1]

| | | | |
|---|---|---|---|
| May 1 | Retained Earnings............................ | 150,000 | |
| | Dividends Payable........................ | | 150,000 |
| | To record declaration of cash dividend of $1.50 per share on 100,000 shares of outstanding stock. | | |
| 15 | No entry is required on the record date. | | |
| 31 | Dividends Payable ........................... | 150,000 | |
| | Cash.................................... | | 150,000 |
| | To record payment of the dividend declared on May 1. | | |

Instead of debiting Retained Earnings on the declaration date, some companies debit a temporary account called Dividends. This account is closed into Retained Earnings: Unappropriated at the end of the year.

The Dividends Payable account is a current liability because the dividend is paid in a short period of time.

The declaration and payment of a cash dividend reduces the total assets and the total equities of the corporation. The decrease in Cash reduces total assets; the decrease in Retained Earnings (either directly, or by closing the Dividends account) reduces stockholders' equity.

### Property Dividends

Occasionally, assets other than cash are distributed as dividends. Inventory, land, and equipment have all been used for this purpose. The three basic requirements of cash dividends also apply to such **property dividends:** The corporation must have adequate earned capital, it must have assets that it can distribute, and the dividend must be declared by the board of directors.

With property dividends a question must be answered that didn't arise with cash dividends: At what amount should the dividend be recorded? Generally accepted accounting principles tell us that the proper amount is the *fair market value* of the assets that will be distributed.

The fact that assets are carried in the accounting records at cost, or cost less accumulated depreciation, means that assets may require revaluation. When assets are revalued, a gain or loss is recognized to increase or decrease the asset to its fair value. Price quotations, known selling prices, or appraisals are used to determine fair value.

The effect of revaluing the asset is the same as if we had sold the asset and then distributed the proceeds as a cash dividend.

Let's look at an example of accounting for a property dividend.

[1] All our journal entries in the examples are in general journal form, even though the entry may actually be made in a special journal. This will make illustrations much easier because we won't have to construct special journals each time we make an entry.

# AZTEC COMPANY

The board of directors of the Aztec Company decides to declare a property dividend consisting of 1,000 shares of IBM Corp. stock costing $90,000. Since Aztec Company has 10 stockholders, each of whom owns an equal number of Aztec shares, the IBM Corp. shares will be divided evenly among them. The dividend is declared on Sept. 15, payable on Oct. 15 to stockholders of record on Oct. 1. On Sept. 15, the IBM Corp. stock is selling on the New York Stock Exchange for $112,000.

| | | | |
|---|---|---|---|
| Sept. 15 | Investment in IBM Stock . . . . . . . . . . . . . . . . . . . . . | 22,000 | |
| | Gain to Increase Investment to Fair Market Value . . . . . . . . . . . . . . . . . . . . . . . . . . . . . . . | | 22,000 |
| | To increase investment from cost, $90,000, to market value of $112,000. | | |
| 15 | Retained Earnings: Unappropriated . . . . . . . . . . . . | 112,000 | |
| | Property Dividend Payable . . . . . . . . . . . . . . . | | 112,000 |
| | To record *declaration* of a property dividend consisting of 1,000 shares of IBM stock with a current market value of $112,000. | | |
| Oct. 1 | Record date—no entry required. | | |
| 15 | Property Dividend Payable . . . . . . . . . . . . . . . . . . . | 112,000 | |
| | Investment in IBM Stock . . . . . . . . . . . . . . . . . | | 112,000 |
| | To record distribution of the property dividend. | | |

Aztec does not realize a gain as a result of declaring the dividend but as a result of revaluing the asset. The Gain to Increase Investment to Fair Market Value is shown on the income statement under Other Gains and Losses.

Property dividends have the same effect on the balance sheet as cash dividends. Total assets decrease, because some asset—Investment in IBM Stock, for example—is distributed. Total stockholders' equity is lower because Retained Earnings is decreased.

## Stock Dividends

Learning Objective **6**

Explain the effect of stock dividends and stock splits on the stockholders' equity section of the balance sheet

Remember that three things are necessary for a cash or property dividend: an asset to distribute, earned capital, and a declaration by the board of directors. What happens when a corporation has plenty of earned capital and a board willing to declare a dividend but no assets to distribute? The board may declare a stock dividend.

A **stock dividend** consists of additional shares of a corporation's own stock issued to its stockholders on a pro rata basis. Usually, shares previously unissued are used for stock dividend distributions.

For example, Irving Akard owns 10 shares of Tribune Company stock. When the Tribune Company declares and issues a 20% stock dividend, Irving receives two additional shares. Since each other stockholder also receives a 20% dividend, the total number of shares outstanding increases by 20%. Each shareholder has the same proportionate ownership after the dividend was declared as before:

Total shares outstanding before dividend . . . . .   100 shares
Total shares issued in 20% stock dividend . . . .    20 shares

Total shares outstanding after dividend . . . . . .   120 shares

**Exhibit 5** Partial Balance Sheet before Stock Dividend

**HASTINGS COMPANY**
**Partial Balance Sheet**
**Before Stock Dividend**
**June 30, 1999**

**Stockholders' Equity**

Paid-In Capital:
  Common Stock ($10-par, 200,000 shares authorized,
    120,000 shares issued and outstanding)........................ $1,200,000
  Paid-In Capital in Excess of Par ................................  300,000
    Total Paid-In Capital........................................ $1,500,000
Earned Capital:
  Retained Earnings .........................................  940,000

Total Stockholders' Equity..................................... $2,440,000

Irving owned 10% of the Tribune Company before the dividend was declared (10% × 100 shares = 10 shares), and he owns 10% after the dividend is distributed (10% × 120 shares = 12 shares). So what did Irving gain as a result of the stock dividend? Nothing, except that he now has more "pieces of paper" to represent the same ownership. If he desires to realize cash out of the stock dividend, he must sell some of his shares and thus reduce his percentage of ownership in the corporation—which he could have done even before the dividend.

Caution: Don't confuse this stock dividend with the property dividend explained above. A stock dividend involves distributing additional shares of a corporation's *own* stock. A property dividend *may* involve the distribution of another corporation's stock held as an investment.

Why do corporations issue stock dividends? The two most commonly given reasons are:

1. To reduce the market price of the stock. When a large number of new shares is issued (over 25% more), the total number of shares of the corporation's stock available in the marketplace is increased to such an extent that the market price of each share drops. The lower market price per share makes the stock more affordable for individuals with small amounts to invest.

2. To distribute something to the shareholders when all cash and noncash assets are needed in the business. In a growing corporation the distribution of a stock dividend is a way of notifying stockholders that these retained earnings have been distributed in the form of additional shares of stock and that they will never be distributed in the form of cash or other assets.

In spite of the questionable merit of stock dividends, many corporations issue them and thus it is necessary to understand the proper accounting procedures for them. The effect of a stock dividend on the balance sheet is to reduce earned capital and to increase paid-in capital. The amount we record depends on the size of the dividend.

We will use the Hastings Co. information shown in Exhibit 5 to illustrate the correct recording of a small stock dividend and a large stock dividend.

*Small Stock Dividends*

Small stock dividends involve the issuance of new shares amounting to less than 20% to 25% of the shares previously outstanding. In the case of a small stock dividend, we assume that too few new shares are issued to affect the market value of the stock. Each new share, then, has a value equal to the market value of each of the shares previously outstanding. This market value is considered by GAAP to be the proper amount to use to account for a small stock dividend.

# HASTINGS COMPANY

On July 1, 1999, the Hastings Company board of directors declared a 5% stock dividend to be distributed on Aug. 15 to stockholders of record on July 20. Hastings' stock was trading for $18 per share on July 1.

| | | | |
|---|---|---:|---:|
| July 1 | Retained Earnings: Unappropriated | | |
| | (6,000 shares × $18) . . . . . . . . . . . . . . . . . . . . . . . | 108,000 | |
| | Stock Dividend Distributable | | |
| | (6,000 shares × $10). . . . . . . . . . . . . . . . . . . . . | | 60,000 |
| | Paid-In Capital in Excess of Par | | |
| | (6,000 shares × $8). . . . . . . . . . . . . . . . . . . . . . | | 48,000 |
| | To record *declaration* of a 5% stock dividend (5% × 120,000 shares = 6,000 new shares). | | |

In the declaration entry we debit Retained Earnings just as we did for property dividends. The amount of the debit is the value of the shares we will issue—the number of new shares that will be issued multiplied by the market value (on the declaration date) of each share.

Stock Dividend Distributable is credited for the par value (or stated value) of the new shares issued. Paid-In Capital in Excess of Par is credited for the amount by which market value of the stock exceeds par (or stated) value. Stock Dividend Distributable is a temporary stockholders' equity account that we use until the stock is issued (see Aug. 15 entry below).

We do not credit a liability account in this case because no true liability exists. A liability is an obligation that requires the disbursement of assets or the performance of a service for its satisfaction. We have no such obligation. The board of directors has committed the corporation to issue additional shares of common stock, not to pay out assets or perform services; this commitment, therefore, fails to meet the definition of a liability.

| | | | |
|---|---|---:|---:|
| July 20 | No journal entry is required on the *record* date. | | |
| | | | |
| Aug. 15 | Stock Dividend Distributable . . . . . . . . . . . . . . . . . . | 60,000 | |
| | Common Stock . . . . . . . . . . . . . . . . . . . . . . . . . . | | 60,000 |
| | To record distribution of 6,000 shares of stock as a dividend. | | |

When we issue the dividend, we remove the temporary stockholders' equity account Stock Dividend Distributable and increase Common Stock. We have now replaced the temporary stockholders' equity account with a permanent one.

The effect of this stock dividend was to move $108,000 out of earned capital into paid-in capital. Total assets, total liabilities, and total stockholders' equity remain unchanged. Hastings does have 6,000 more shares of common stock outstanding after the dividend.

Exhibit 6 shows Hastings' stockholders' equity section before and after the small stock dividend.

**Exhibit 6** Effect of *Small* Stock Dividend on Stockholders' Equity

|  | Before Small Stock Dividend | After Small Stock Dividend |
|---|---|---|
| Common Stock | $1,200,000 | $1,260,000 |
| Paid-In Capital in Excess of Par | 300,000 | 348,000 |
| Total Paid-In Capital | $1,500,000 | $1,608,000 |
| Total Earned Capital (Retained Earnings) | 940,000 | 832,000 |
| Total Stockholders' Equity | $2,440,000 | $2,440,000 |

*Total paid-in capital increased $108,000* → Total Paid-In Capital

*Total earned capital decreased $108,000* → Total Earned Capital (Retained Earnings)

*Total stockholders' equity is unchanged* → Total Stockholders' Equity

### Large Stock Dividends

A large stock dividend is a pro rata distribution of newly issued shares amounting to more than 20% to 25% of the stock previously outstanding. When a large stock dividend is distributed, so many additional shares are placed into the marketplace that the market price of the stock will probably drop. Since we don't know how large this drop will be, GAAP require that we use the par value of the shares issued as the amount for recording the new shares.

Let's assume that, instead of issuing a 5% stock dividend, Hastings' board declared a 40% stock dividend.

On July 1, 1999, the Hastings Company board of directors declared a 40% stock dividend (*instead of* the 5% dividend in the previous illustration). The shares will be distributed on Aug. 31 to stockholders of record on Aug. 1. Hastings' stock was trading for $18 per share on July 1.

| | | | | |
|---|---|---|---|---|
| July | 1 | Retained Earnings: Unappropriated (48,000 shares × $10-par) | 480,000 | |
| | |     Stock Dividends Distributable | | 480,000 |
| | | To record the *declaration* of a 40% stock dividend (40% × 120,000 shares = 48,000 new shares). | | |
| Aug. | 1 | No journal entry is required on the *record* date. | | |
| | 31 | Stock Dividend Distributable | 480,000 | |
| | |     Common Stock | | 480,000 |
| | | To record the *distribution* of a large stock dividend. | | |

The entries to record a large stock dividend are exactly the same ones we use for a small stock dividend—with one exception. We won't need to credit Paid-In Capital in Excess of Par, because there is no excess—the large stock dividend is recorded at par.

The effect of this large stock dividend is to move $480,000 out of earned capital into paid-in capital. Total assets and total stockholders' equity are unchanged. Hastings now has 48,000 more shares outstanding but the same total stockholders' equity, total assets, and total liabilities.

Exhibit 7 shows Hastings' stockholders' equity section before and after the large stock dividend.

### Liquidating Dividends

Liquidating dividends are not dividends as we have been using the term. We have been using *dividends* to mean distributions out of earned capital—giving the stockholders some of the accumulated income of the corporation.

**Liquidating dividends** are pro rata distributions of *paid-in capital* (not earned capital) to the stockholders. We are giving the owners back some of the assets they invested in the company. Liquidating dividends are paid only when a corporation is either permanently reducing its size or going out of business.

The board of directors must exercise care to declare liquidating dividends only when they are allowed by state statutes. Many of these laws require that liquidating dividends be approved by the stockholders or a court of law. In some states the directors are personally liable for any illegally declared liquidating dividends.

### Dividends and Treasury Stock

No dividends of any kind—cash, property, stock, or liquidating—are paid on treasury stock. When a corporation owns treasury stock, it is holding shares of its own stock. To pay dividends on treasury stock would amount to the corporation paying itself a dividend—a useless exercise.

### Stock Splits

A **stock split** occurs when the board of directors, acting with the permission of the state, reduces the par or stated value of all the corporation's common stock. It accomplishes this reduction by issuing additional new shares for each old share held by a stockholder. Like large stock dividends, the purpose of a stock split is to put many new shares into the marketplace and thus reduce the market price per share.

Corporations used to require stockholders to send in their old shares in exchange for the new stock certificates. In the case of a 4-for-1 split, you sent in 1 old share and the corporation sent you 4 new ones. But the modern practice is to consider the old shares as part of the new distribution. For example, if you have 100 shares of a stock that is split 4 for 1, the corporation sends you 300 new shares. You now have a total of 400 shares—4 for 1.

---

**Exhibit 7** Effect of *Large* Stock Dividend on Stockholders' Equity

| | Before Large Stock Dividend | After Large Stock Dividend |
|---|---|---|
| *Common stock and total paid-in capital increased by $480,000* → Common Stock . . . . . . . . . . . . . . . . . . . . . . . . . . . . . . . . . . . . . . . . . . | $1,200,000 | $1,680,000 |
| Paid-In Capital in Excess of Par . . . . . . . . . . . . . . . . . . . . . . . . . . . . | 300,000 | 300,000 |
| Total Paid-In Capital . . . . . . . . . . . . . . . . . . . . . . . . . . . . . . . . . . . . . | $1,500,000 | $1,980,000 |
| *Earned capital decreased by $480,000* → Total Earned Capital (Retained Earnings) . . . . . . . . . . . . . . . . . . | 940,000 | 460,000 |
| *Total stockholders' equity is unchanged* → Total Stockholders' Equity . . . . . . . . . . . . . . . . . . . . . . . . . . . . . | $2,440,000 | $2,440,000 |

When a corporation distributes a stock split, the *only* amounts that change on the balance sheet are the number of shares authorized, issued, and outstanding, and the par or stated value per share. The dollars assigned to Common Stock, Paid-In Capital in Excess of Par, Retained Earnings, and the other stockholders' equity accounts remain the same. Because no monetary amounts are involved, only a memorandum entry is needed to record a stock split.

The following example demonstrates the effects of a stock split.

# FIREBRAND CORPORATION

Firebrand Corporation's stockholders' equity section shows the common stock authorized, issued and outstanding on Sept. 30, 1998:

**FIREBRAND CORPORATION**
**Partial Balance Sheet**
**September 30, 1998**
**(Before Stock Split)**

**Stockholders' Equity**

| | |
|---|---|
| Paid-In Capital: | |
| Common Stock ($1-par, 100,000 shares authorized, 60,000 shares issued and outstanding) | $ 60,000 |
| Paid-In Capital in Excess of par | 170,000 |
| Total Paid-In Capital | $230,000 |
| Earned Capital: | |
| Retained Earnings | 315,000 |
| Total Stockholders' Equity | $545,000 |

On Oct. 1, 1998, Firebrand receives permission to make a 4-for-1 stock split. Three additional new shares of $.25-par-value stock are issued for each old share of $1-par stock. Stockholders retain their original shares, which are now treated as $.25-par-value shares too. Thus 400,000 shares are now authorized (100,000 × 4); 240,000 shares are now issued and outstanding (60,000 × 4); 160,000 shares are still unissued (400,000 − 240,000).

Firebrand would make the following memorandum entry:

Oct. 1   Memorandum. $1-par common stock is split 4 for 1.
        New par value $.25 per share for 400,000 authorized shares.

A stockholder who previously owned 100 shares of Firebrand stock would now own 400 shares. Stock can be split 10 for 1, 2 for 1, $1\frac{1}{2}$ for 1, or in any other way the corporation desires.

The steps for calculating the new par or stated value and the new number of shares are:

1. Divide the par value by the number of new shares issued plus old shares outstanding. In the Firebrand example we divided $1.00 by 4 shares (3 new + 1 old) = $.25 per share.

2. Multiply the number of shares authorized, issued, and outstanding, and in the

treasury by the number of new shares replacing 1 old share. In the Firebrand example we multiplied 100,000 shares authorized by 4 = 400,000 new authorized shares, and 60,000 shares issued and outstanding by 4 = 240,000 new shares issued and outstanding.

After the stock split, the stockholders' equity section of the balance sheet reflects the fact that more shares of a lower-par-value stock are outstanding, but the dollar amount of all stockholders' equity accounts remains unchanged.

---

**FIREBRAND CORPORATION**
**Partial Balance Sheet**
**October 2, 1998**
**(After Stock Split)**

**Stockholders' Equity**

| | |
|---|---:|
| Paid-In Capital: | |
| Common Stock ($.25-par, 400,000 shares authorized, 240,000 shares issued and outstanding) | $ 60,000 |
| Paid-In Capital in Excess of Par | 170,000 |
| Total Paid-In Capital | $230,000 |
| Earned Capital: | |
| Retained Earnings | 315,000 |
| Total Stockholders' Equity | $545,000 |

---

If a corporation owns treasury stock at the time of the split, the treasury stock must be split as well. If Firebrand had owned 500 shares of treasury stock before the split, it would have 2,000 shares (4 × 500) after the split. The par value of this stock is also adjusted to $.25 per share.

## Recording Dividends on Preferred Stock

Dividends on preferred stock are recorded in exactly the same way as dividends on common stock. Once the amounts have been determined, the declaration and payment entries are identical to those illustrated in the previous sections of this chapter. For example, the following entries would record the declaration and payment of a $56,000 dividend, $16,000 to preferred and $40,000 to common stockholders:

---

| | | |
|---|---:|---:|
| Retained Earnings | 56,000 | |
| Dividend Payable, Preferred | | 16,000 |
| Dividend Payable, Common | | 40,000 |
| To record declaration of dividend on preferred and common stock. | | |
| | | |
| Dividend Payable, Preferred | 16,000 | |
| Dividend Payable, Common | 40,000 | |
| Cash | | 56,000 |
| To record payment of dividend. | | |

---

It would be very unusual for the board of directors to declare property or stock dividends, or stock splits, on preferred stock. Preferred dividends are almost exclusively paid in cash.

1. What three dates are important in the distribution of any dividend?
2. At what amount is a property dividend recorded?
3. For what amount is Retained Earnings debited when a small stock dividend is declared?
4. Which stockholders' equity accounts change when a large stock dividend is declared and distributed?
5. What is a stock split?

## STOCKHOLDERS' EQUITY—A COMPREHENSIVE ILLUSTRATION

**Learning Objective 7**

Prepare the stockholders' equity section for a comprehensive balance sheet, including all information needed for fair disclosure

We have completed our discussion of the various accounts that may appear in the stockholders' equity section of the balance sheet. Exhibit 8 shows how each of the accounts would appear on a balance sheet. We have added the descriptive information (shares authorized, issued, and outstanding, par value, etc.) needed for fair disclosure.

## ACCOUNTING FOR CORPORATE INCOME TAXES

Corporations must pay income taxes to the federal government and, in some cases, to municipalities and states. These taxes are costs of doing business just as much as salaries, rent, and utilities are. Income taxes, then, will appear as a deduction on the corporate income statement. We will focus on the problems of calculating and disclosing federal income taxes. State and local income taxes are accounted for in a similar manner.

### Estimating and Paying Income Taxes

**Learning Objective 8**

Explain how corporations estimate and pay federal income taxes and prepare related entries

Corporations are required to estimate the amount of income taxes for a year and to pay those taxes in four quarterly installments. Corporations that use a calendar year for tax purposes must send these estimated payments by Apr. 15, June 15, Sept. 15, and Dec. 15. Knox, Inc., for example, estimates that it will pay $132,000 of income tax on $400,000 of taxable income for the year. Knox will send $33,000 (one-fourth of the estimated amount) to the Internal Revenue Service (IRS) on Apr. 15 for the first quarter and make the following entry:

| | | | |
|---|---|---|---|
| Apr. 15 | Provision for Income Taxes .................... | 33,000 | |
| | Cash................................. | | 33,000 |
| | To pay estimated income taxes for the first quarter. | | |

Knox will revise its estimated income and income taxes each quarter in an attempt to pay neither too much nor too little. If Knox's estimate requires no revision, the entry above will be made on each of the payment dates. Let's assume that Knox's estimate appears to be accurate until the Dec. 15 payment is due. Knox has paid $33,000 on each of the first three payment dates but, since fourth-quarter earnings are better than expected, the total tax for the year is estimated to be $136,000. The December installment will need to be $37,000 ($136,000 − $33,000 − $33,000 − $33,000). Knox will make the following entry:

| | | | |
|---|---|---|---|
| Dec. 15 | Provision for Income Taxes .................... | 37,000 | |
| | Cash ................................. | | 37,000 |
| | To pay estimated income taxes for the fourth quarter. | | |

**Exhibit 8** Stockholders' Equity Illustrated

## MODEL CORPORATION
### Partial Balance Sheet
### September 30, 1998

~~~~~~~~~~~~~~~~~~~~~~~~~~~~~~~~~~~~~~~~~~~~~~~~~~~~

### Stockholders' Equity

Paid-In Capital:

| | | |
|---|---:|---:|
| 6% Preferred Stock ($100-par, noncumulative, nonvoting, participating, 10,000 shares authorized, 4,000 shares issued and outstanding) . . . . . . . . . . . . . . | $ 400,000 | |
| 6% Preferred Stock Subscribed ($100-par, 500 shares). . | 50,000 | |
| Total Preferred Stock . . . . . . . . . . . . . . . . . . . . . . . . . . . . . . . . | | $ 450,000 |
| Common Stock [no-par, stated value $25, 100,000 shares authorized, 60,000 shares issued, 58,500 shares outstanding (1,500 shares in the treasury)] . . . . . | $1,500,000 | |
| Common Stock Subscribed (no-par, stated value $25, 1,000 shares) . . . . . . . . . . . . . . . . . . . . . . . . . . . . | 25,000 | |
| Common Stock Dividend Distributable (5,950 shares, no-par, $25 stated value per share) . . . . . . . . . . . . . . . . | 148,750 | |
| Total Common Stock. . . . . . . . . . . . . . . . . . . . . . . . . . . . . . . | | 1,673,750 |
| Additional Paid-In Capital: | | |
| Paid-In Capital in Excess of Par: Preferred . . . . . . . . . . | $ 45,000 | |
| Paid-In Capital in Excess of Stated Value: Common. . . | 750,000 | |
| Paid-In Capital from Treasury Stock. . . . . . . . . . . . . . . | 25,000 | |
| Donated Capital. . . . . . . . . . . . . . . . . . . . . . . . . . . . . . | 135,000 | |
| Total Additional Paid-In Capital. . . . . . . . . . . . . . . . . . . . . . . . . | | 955,000 |
| Total Paid-In Capital . . . . . . . . . . . . . . . . . . . . . . . . . . . . . . . | | $3,078,750 |
| Earned Capital: | | |
| Retained Earnings: Unappropriated. . . . . . . . . . . . . . . . . | $ 875,000 | |
| Retained Earnings: Appropriated: | | |

|  | | | |
|---|---:|---:|---:|
| For Plant Expansion. . . . . . . . . . . . . . . . . . | $250,000 | | |
| For Contingencies . . . . . . . . . . . . . . . . . . . | 125,000 | | |
| Total Appropriated. . . . . . . . . . . . . . . . . . . . . . . . . . | | 375,000 | |
| Total Earned Capital . . . . . . . . . . . . . . . . . . . . . . . . . . . . . . . . | | | 1,250,000 |
| Total Paid-In and Earned Capital . . . . . . . . . . . . . . . . . . . . . . . | | | $4,328,750 |
| Less: Treasury Stock: Common (1,500 shares at cost) . . . . . . . . . . . . . . | | | (67,500) |
| Total Stockholders' Equity . . . . . . . . . . . . . . . . . . . . . . . . . . . . . . . . . . . | | | $4,261,250 |

The exact amount of taxes due will not be known until all of the income and expenses have been determined for the year. At this time the provision for income taxes will be adjusted up or down to reflect the actual taxes for the year. If too much has been recorded and paid, Receivable from IRS will be debited and Provision for Income Taxes will be credited for the overpayment. More commonly, additional taxes will be due. Assuming that Knox determines the actual tax for the year to be $138,000 ($2,000 more than the $136,000 estimated), the following adjusting entry would be made on Dec. 31:

| | | | |
|---|---|---:|---:|
| Dec. 31 | Provision for Income Taxes . . . . . . . . . . . . . . . . . . . . | 2,000 | |
| | Income Tax Payable . . . . . . . . . . . . . . . . . . . . . . | | 2,000 |
| | To revise estimated income taxes to reflect actual taxes due for the year. | | |

This final $2,000 will be remitted with the corporate tax return due by Mar. 15 of the following year. Corporations must estimate income taxes carefully. A significant error in the estimated payments could result in a financial penalty.

The provision for income taxes appears on the income statement as illustrated in Exhibit 9 at the end of this chapter.

## Permanent Differences

Selected revenue and expense items on the income statement may never appear on the corporate tax return or may appear in one year on the income statement and in a different year on the tax return. These situations occur when the rules for measuring income for tax purposes, governed by the tax laws, differ from the rules for measuring income for financial reporting purposes, governed by generally accepted accounting principles.

**Permanent differences** occur when a revenue or expense appears on the income statement but will never appear on the income tax return. Interest earned on investments in municipal bonds and goodwill amortization expense are examples of permanent differences.

For example, let us assume a taxable income (from the tax return) of $50,000. Income taxes due to the IRS would be:

| | |
|---|---:|
| Taxable income . . . . . . . . . . . . . . . . . . . . . . . . . . . . . . . . . . . . . . . . . . . | $50,000 |
| × Current tax rate (assumed) . . . . . . . . . . . . . . . . . . . . . . . . . . . . . . . . . . | × 15% |
| Tax due to IRS. . . . . . . . . . . . . . . . . . . . . . . . . . . . . . . . . . . . . . . . . . . . . | $ 7,500 |

Of course, some of this will have already been paid in quarterly installments.

The income before taxes on the income statement shown below is $56,000. The $6,000 difference is due to the $8,000 interest income on municipal bonds and the $2,000 goodwill amortization expense, neither of which will appear on the tax return. The provision for income taxes is still $7,500, because no taxes will ever be paid on the $6,000 of extra income—it is a permanent difference.

| Abbreviated Income Statement | | |
|---|---:|---:|
| Revenues: | | |
| Sales . . . . . . . . . . . . . . . . . . . . . . . . . . . . . . . . . . . . . . . . . . . . . . | | $110,000 |
| Interest on Municipal Bonds . . . . . . . . . . . . . . . . . . . . . . . . . . . . . . | | 8,000 |
| Total Revenues . . . . . . . . . . . . . . . . . . . . . . . . . . . . . . . . . . . . | | $118,000 |
| Expenses: | | |
| Operating Expenses (excluding goodwill amortization). . . | $60,000 | |
| Goodwill Amortization Expense . . . . . . . . . . . . . . . . . . . . . | 2,000 | |
| Total Expenses . . . . . . . . . . . . . . . . . . . . . . . . . . . . . . . . . . | | 62,000 |
| Income before Income Taxes . . . . . . . . . . . . . . . . . . . . . . . . . . . . . | | $ 56,000 |
| Provision for Income Taxes . . . . . . . . . . . . . . . . . . . . . . . . . . . . . . . | | 7,500 |
| Net Income . . . . . . . . . . . . . . . . . . . . . . . . . . . . . . . . . . . . . . . . . . . . . | | $ 48,500 |

When only permanent differences exist, the amount of income tax due the IRS calculated on the tax return will be used as the provision for income taxes on the income statement.

## Temporary Differences

**Temporary differences** exist when revenue or expense items appear on the income statement in one year and on the income tax return in a different year. For example, an asset may be depreciated for accounting income statement purposes over a 5-year life using the straight-line method. The income tax laws may require that this asset be depreciated over a 3-year life using the double declining-balance method. During the early part of the asset's life, depreciation expense on the income statement will be much lower than the depreciation deduction on the income tax return, because the income statement is depreciating the asset more slowly and over a longer life than the tax return.

During the later years of the asset's life, the income statement depreciation will be much higher than the amount on the tax return, because the tax method depreciates the asset over 3 years, so no depreciation will appear on the tax return in the last 2 years of the asset's life. The *total* depreciation during the asset's life may be the same amount for income statement and for tax purposes, but the timing of the depreciation deductions may be different.

We must allow for all these temporary timing differences in the accounts. For example, revenues and expenses on the Lowry Corp. income statement and income tax return for year 1 are identical except for the amount of depreciation expense:

| | Income Statement | Income Tax Return |
|---|---|---|
| Income before depreciation expense................ | $400,000 | $400,000 |
| Depreciation expense............................ | 9,000 | 30,000 |
| Income before income taxes ..................... | $391,000 | $370,000 |
| × Income tax rate (assumed)...................... | × 34% | × 34% |
| Provision for income taxes....................... | $132,940 | |
| Income taxes due to the IRS ..................... | | $125,800 |

Lowry has deferred $7,140 ($132,940 − $125,800) of income taxes to a future year. Lowry would make the following entry to record income taxes in year 1:

| | | |
|---|---|---|
| Provision for Income Taxes ......................... | 132,940 | |
|    Income Taxes Payable............................ | | 125,800 |
|    Deferred Income Taxes ........................... | | 7,140 |
| To record income taxes for year 1. | | |

The $132,940 provision for income taxes is shown on the year 1 income statement even though that amount will not be paid in year 1. We are applying the matching principle again—matching the cost of earning revenue with the revenues earned. The $7,140 in the Deferred Income Taxes account will be shown on the balance sheet among liabilities. Any part of this amount expected to be paid within the next year is a current liability; the remainder is a long-term liability.

During the last few years of the asset's life, the income tax payable will be higher than the provision for income taxes. During this time Lowry will be "paying off" the taxes that had been deferred during the early years of the asset's life. The following shows how this paying off would be calculated and recorded in the accounts during the last year of the asset's life:

| | Income Statement | Income Tax Return |
|---|---|---|
| Income before depreciation expense................ | $500,000 | $500,000 |
| Depreciation expense............................ | 9,000 | −0− |
| Income before income taxes ..................... | $491,000 | $500,000 |
| × Income tax rate................................. | × 34% | × 34% |
| Provision for income taxes....................... | $166,940 | |
| Income taxes due to the IRS ..................... | | $170,000 |

Lowry would make the following entry in the last year of the asset's life:

| | | |
|---|---:|---:|
| Provision for Income Taxes . . . . . . . . . . . . . . . . . . . . . . . . . . . | 166,940 | |
| Deferred Income Taxes . . . . . . . . . . . . . . . . . . . . . . . . . . . . . | 3,060 | |
|    Income Taxes Payable . . . . . . . . . . . . . . . . . . . . . . . . . . . | | 170,000 |
| To record income taxes for last year of asset's life. | | |

Deferred Income Taxes has been debited in each of the last few years of the asset's life as this liability was paid off. Deferred Income Taxes should have a zero balance following this entry.

This simplified illustration is intended to demonstrate only the fundamentals of accounting for income taxes. Actual companies may have several different situations that cause permanent and temporary differences. Tax laws and tax rates are constantly changing. Even generally accepted accounting principles are modified from time to time. All of these factors contribute to making taxes an extremely complex accounting issue.

## Income Taxes on the Corporate Income Statement

To illustrate how income taxes are shown on a corporate income statement, assume that Executive Corporation has income before taxes of $1,847,000. Executive has paid $545,000 estimated taxes on this income during the year and, because of timing differences, has $83,000 of deferred taxes. Exhibit 9 at the end of this chapter shows how the provision for income taxes would appear on Executive's income statement.

**ASK YOURSELF** ▶

1. **When do corporations normally pay their income taxes?**
2. **What is a permanent difference?**
3. **Deferred income tax accounts are created by temporary differences; what are temporary differences?**

## UNUSUAL INCOME STATEMENT ITEMS

### Discontinued Operations

Learning **11**
Objective

Explain what discontinued operations, extraordinary items, and cumulative effects of changes in accounting principles are, and how they are shown on a corporate income statement

When a corporation sells or abandons a segment of the business, the gain or loss from this **discontinued operation** must be shown separately on the income statement. A portion of a business is considered a **segment** if it involves either a line of business separate from the others of the company or a major class of customers that is different from others served by the firm. If a company that owns a chain of retail ice cream stores and a truck rental business sells the ice cream stores at a gain, the gain would be shown as a gain from a discontinued operation because the ice cream stores are a different line of business from truck rentals. Other examples of discontinued operations involving a different line of business would include a communications corporation that sells its radio stations but keeps its television station and publishing company; a meat packing company that sells its interest in a professional football team; or a restaurant chain that sells a subsidiary that operates a dog kennel. If an international mining company sells its South American mining operations, however, the sale would *not* be a discontinued operation because the company has not disposed of a different line of business; it still has mining operations in other countries.

A company that owns a wholesale meat business and a chain of fast-food restaurants would eliminate a major class of customers (that is, wholesale buyers) if it sold the wholesale meat division. Other examples of discontinued operations involving elimination of a major class of customers are a book publisher that sells its chain of retail bookstores but still sells wholesale to bookstores; and a transportation company that sells a division that operates cargo ships but keeps its cruise ship business. The sale of a chain of pizza restaurants by a company that also owns hamburger stands and Oriental-food take-out shops would *not* be a discontinued operation because the company is still serving retail food consumers.

A gain or loss on the sale of a segment is shown separately on the income statement net of any income tax effects. (A gain would require payment of additional taxes; a loss would save taxes that would otherwise have been paid on other income earned.)

Executive Corp. sells its mattress manufacturing division for $550,000 while keeping the retail furniture division. Since the assets of the mattress division have a book value of $467,000, Executive has an $83,000 gain. After it pays $28,000 of this gain in federal income taxes, the net gain is $55,000. Exhibit 9 at the end of the chapter shows how Executive would disclose the gain on this discontinued operation in its income statement.

The following additional information would be shown in the notes to the financial statements:

The identity of the discontinued segment

The date of disposal

The manner of disposal

A description of any segment assets and liabilities that the company may still own

## Extraordinary Items

Separate income statement disclosure is required for gains and losses resulting from transactions or events so unusual that they are considered extraordinary. In order to be considered an **extraordinary item,** a transaction or event must meet two tests:

1. It must be *unusual in nature.* Considering the environment in which the business operates, the event or transaction should be abnormal and unrelated to the typical activities of the business.
2. It must *occur infrequently.* Considering the environment in which the business operates, the event or transaction should be of a type that is not expected to occur again in the foreseeable future.

Sometimes an extraordinary event is obvious: If a meteor destroyed some company property that was not covered by appropriate insurance, the loss would be extraordinary. Sometimes, however, judgment may be required in deciding whether an extraordinary loss has occurred. For example, a loss from damage caused by a blizzard would be considered extraordinary for a company in Miami, but a company operating in Montana may not consider the loss unusual or infrequent.

Generally accepted accounting principles identify certain situations as extraordinary—condemnation of property by a governmental entity or a major disaster such as an earthquake. Other items are specifically identified as *not* extraordinary. Examples include losses due to writing off receivables and gains or losses from the sale of property, plant, or equipment assets.

Extraordinary items are shown on the income statement immediately following discontinued operations. Like discontinued operations, they are shown net of their income tax effects.

Executive Corp.'s Cincinnati outlet experienced a flash flood. Losses not covered by insurance totaled $150,000. Since floods are considered unusual and infrequent in this community, GAAP require that the loss be disclosed as an extraordinary item. Executive will be able to offset this loss against other income for income tax purposes, thus saving $51,000 in taxes that would otherwise have been paid. The net effect of the extraordinary event, then, is a $99,000 loss. Look at Executive's disclosure on the income statement in Exhibit 9.

### Changes in Accounting Principles

A company may change from one generally accepted accounting principle or method to another. For example, a company may decide to change from the straight-line method of depreciation to the double declining-balance method. The consistency principle normally assumes that the same methods will be used from year to year, but it does not prohibit a company from changing. Any such **change in accounting principle** must be justifiable, and the effect of the change must be disclosed on the income statement and in the notes to the financial statements. The following illustration will demonstrate how the effects of a change in depreciation method would be calculated and recorded.

Executive Corp. has a $500,000 asset that it has been depreciating over a 10-year life using the straight-line method of depreciation. Salvage value is estimated to be $50,000. Straight-line depreciation during the first 3 years (1996–1998) of the asset's life was calculated as follows:

Depreciation per year: ($500,000–$50,000) ÷ 10 years = $45,000

Straight-line depreciation for 3 years: $45,000 × 3 years = $135,000

Early in 1999, the fourth year, Executive decided to switch to the double declining-balance method. Executive must decide how much depreciation would have been recorded if double declining-balance had been used ever since the asset was acquired:

| | | |
|---|---|---:|
| 1993 | $500,000 × 20% | $100,000 |
| 1994 | ($500,000 − $100,000) × 20% = $400,000 × 20% | 80,000 |
| 1995 | ($400,000 − $80,000) × 20% = $320,000 × 20% | 64,000 |
| | Total depreciation under double declining-balance | $244,000 |

Executive would adjust the accounts to reflect amounts that would have been recorded if the new method had been used ever since 1996. Executive would make an entry to increase the Jan. 1, 1999, balance of Accumulated Depreciation by $109,000 ($244,000–$135,000). After this entry is made, Accumulated Depreciation will have a balance of $244,000, just as it would have had if the double declining-balance method had been used since 1996.

An income statement account called Cumulative Adjustment due to Change in Accounting Principle would be debited for $109,000 to "make up" for the fact that a lower amount of depreciation had been recorded under the straight-line method:

| | | |
|---|---|---:|
| Cumulative Adjustment due to Change in Accounting Principle | 109,000 | |
| Accumulated Depreciation | | 109,000 |
| To record effect of changing from straight-line to double declining-balance depreciation. | | |

Assuming that this change in accounting principle would result in a tax saving of $37,000, the following entry could be made to adjust Income Tax Payable downward and reduce the Cumulative Adjustment account to reflect the net effect of the change:

| | | |
|---|---|---|
| Income Taxes Payable............................... | 37,000 | |
|     Cumulative Adjustment due to Change in Accounting | | |
|     Principle....................................... | | 37,000 |
| To record the tax effect of the adjustment due to change in | | |
| accounting principle. | | |

The cumulative adjustment would be shown after extraordinary items on the income statement. Study the disclosure of this adjustment in Exhibit 9. The notes to the financial statements would describe the change, the justification for it, and the effect it will have on the current year's income.

Special rules govern changes involving the LIFO method of inventory and some other special cases. These complex procedures are discussed in more advanced accounting courses.

## EARNINGS PER SHARE

Learning
Objective **12**

Explain historical earnings per share, primary earnings per share, and fully diluted earnings per share

Owners of stock in a larger corporation are naturally interested in how well the corporation is doing. One measure of a corporation's success is the amount of income it earns as reported on the income statement.

Suppose a stockholder looking at the corporation's income statement finds a net income of $127,000. Should that make the stockholder happy? It certainly looks better than if the corporation had a $127,000 loss. But in order to see just how successful the company was, the stockholder needs to evaluate the income in several different ways. We will discuss one such evaluation, earnings per share, here.

**Earnings per share (EPS),** in its simplest form, is the net income earned by a corporation divided by the number of common shares outstanding. If Wise, Inc., earns $127,000 and has 10,000 shares outstanding during the year, the EPS is $127,000 ÷ 10,000 = $12.70. If there are 100,000 shares outstanding, the EPS is $127,000 ÷ 100,000 = $1.27.

Clearly, just knowing total net income is not enough. A stockholder also needs to know how much net income is when it is spread over all the shares of stock. The more stock there is outstanding, the less beneficial the income is to each shareholder.

Authoritative financial accounting standards require disclosure of earnings per share on the face of the income statements of all corporations whose stock is traded publicly (sold on a stock exchange or over-the-counter). A **closely held corporation,** such as one whose stock is owned by the members of a family and not traded publicly, is not required to disclose earnings per share. (Proprietorships and partnerships do not disclose earnings per share—remember, they do not issue stock, so they have no shares.)

### Historical Earnings per Share

Corporations with simple capital structures report only historical earnings-per-share amounts. A **simple capital structure** means that the corporation has no convertible preferred stock, convertible bonds, or stock options outstanding that could cause the corporation to issue additional shares of stock.

**Convertible securities**—convertible preferred stock and convertible bonds —are securities that can be turned in to the corporation by their owners. In return, the

# Extraordinary?, Special?, Unusual?, Nonrecurring?

You don't have to be a philologist to be an accountant. But an appreciation of words can be a real asset, especially for those interested in minimizing the impact of unexpected events on operating earnings.

Consider Primerica Corp., the big financial services supplier and owner of the brokerage firm Smith Barney. In the Oct. 19, 1987, Wall Street crash, Smith Barney got creamed. But you'd never know that from the unaudited income that Primerica released. Net income was down, but only slightly, to $199 million—and the year-to-year comparison is owed to big gains on discontinued operations the year before. Primerica's 1987 income on continuing operations, by contrast, was up 43%, to $183 million.

But what of that well-publicized $61 million bath Smith Barney took on its arbitrage business during the October stock market crash? Primerica buried that little embarrassment in a footnote on "nonrecurring items." [Arbitrage is the acquisition of securities in one market to resell in another in order to profit from the price discrepancy between the markets.]

Confused? Think of it this way: Had the $61 million arb loss not been filtered through the nonrecurring items account, earnings from continuing operations would have been $61 million ($43 million aftertax) lower than reported for last year.

Still confused? You're in good company. "The rules governing the use of terms like nonrecurring are not that clear," warns Robert Wilkins, project manager at the Financial Accounting Standards Board. "It all comes down to a judgment."

Ted O'Glove, publisher of *Quality of Earnings Report,* isn't confused. He's outraged. "Arbitrage losses are part and parcel of the brokerage business," he blasts. "It is no more nonrecurring than previous periods' gains were nonrecurring. Who are they trying to kid?"

Primerica might well have wanted to report the arbitrage loss as an "extraordinary" loss. Extraordinary items are reported separately—after income from continuing operations. Both Standard & Poor's and Value Line, in reporting earnings from continuing operations, relegate extraordinary items to a footnote.

There was one problem. Back in 1973 the Accounting Principles Board decreed that to be "extraordinary," an item must be both unusual in nature and infrequent in occurrence. A loss from a lawsuit, for example, would be an extraordinary item. But a securities firm's loss on arbitrage would not necessarily satisfy the definition.

"An arbitrage loss by a brokerage firm may be infrequent but is usual in nature in that kind of business," explains Leopold A. Bernstein, professor of accounting at Baruch College. "Primerica calls the loss 'nonrecurring' because it knows the loss is usual and does not fit the definition of extraordinary."

"Nonrecurring" is not the only fudge word accountants have come up with to get around the definition of "extraordinary." Other choices are "one-time" and "special." Many of these words—"nonrecurring" among them—don't have a technical meaning in the accounting glossary. But the clients use them anyway.

Why did Primerica judge its arb losses to be "nonrecurring"? The real advantage to Primerica, notes Baruch's Bernstein, is the effect of aggregating the different "nonrecurring" items in a footnote, more than canceling out losses with gains. Besides the arb loss, the footnote includes a handsome gain from the sale of Primerica's Looart Press. Net nonrecurring items: $16 million, aftertax. Again it seems that Black Monday never happened—unless, of course, you peruse the footnote.

Why didn't Primerica report the arb disaster as a "loss from discontinued operations"? That's what computer lessor Comdisco did when it closed its arbitrage operation and booked an $80 million (aftertax) loss in its most recent quarter. Like "extraordinary items," "discontinued operations" receive aftertax, below-the-line exposure. But they are defined as the sale or disposal of a division or subsidiary that can be clearly distinguished from other assets. Smith Barney was not likely to convince anyone that arbitrage is a separate business segment.

Primerica declined to discuss its accounting of the $61 million arb loss with *Forbes.* But in a statement the company insisted that treating the loss as "nonrecurring" was "an informative disclosure to the public and is entirely consistent with our practice of highlighting significant events."

The next day, a company spokesman called to assure us that when Primerica releases its audited figures this spring, the "nonrecurring" loss will indeed be included as an element of income from continuing operations. The investing public may grumble about such obfuscation, but accounting's philologists will have a field day.

*Source:* Adapted from Penelope Wang, "Dictionary Please," *Forbes,* Mar. 17, 1988, pp. 88–90. Reprinted by permission of FORBES magazine. Copyright © 1988 by Forbes, Inc.

---

Since investors and creditors focus on the "income from continuing operations" amount, many corporate managers will go to great lengths to make this figure look as attractive as possible. As we discuss in this chapter, GAAP assign very specific conditions to reporting gains or losses that are not included in the total for income from continuing operations. Extraordinary items and discontinued operations are carefully scrutinized to ensure that the items reported qualify under the GAAP definitions. This reading emphasizes how important the understanding of GAAP terminology can be.

corporation must give the owners a predetermined number of shares of common stock. Thus, these securities can cause the corporation to issue more shares of common stock.

**Stock options** are arrangements that allow an individual, usually an executive of the company, to purchase stock at a discount from its market price. This stock option discount is a reward for the executive's efforts in making the company successful. Stock option plans may also cause the corporation to issue stock. When the executive elects to exercise this option and pay for the stock, the corporation must issue the shares.

Historical earnings-per-share calculations ignore any potential new shares that the corporation may be required to issue. By definition, in a simple capital structure, the corporation has no convertible securities or stock option plans.

**Historical earnings per share** is calculated by the following formula:

$$\text{Historical EPS} = \frac{\text{net income} - \text{preferred dividends}}{\text{average common shares outstanding}}$$

Earnings per share is really per *common* share. Preferred dividends must be subtracted from reported net income to derive that portion of the income available to common stockholders. (Remember, preferred dividends must be paid before any distributions may be made to common stockholders.)

When corporations have complex income statements that include discontinued operations, extraordinary items, and adjustments due to changes in accounting principles, they must show earnings per share for income from continuing operations, for each of the unusual items, and for net income. For example, Executive Corporation has 200,000 shares of common stock issued and outstanding. Assuming that Executive has a simple capital structure (no preferred stock, options, or convertible securities), we would calculate historical EPS as follows:

$$\text{EPS on income from continuing operations} = \frac{\$1,219,000}{200,000 \text{ shs}} = \$6.10$$

$$\text{EPS on gain from discontinued operation} = \frac{\$55,000}{200,000 \text{ shs}} = \$.28$$

$$\text{EPS on loss from extraordinary item} = \frac{\$99,000}{200,000 \text{ shs}} = \$.50$$

$$\text{EPS on cumulative adjustment due to change in accounting principle} = \frac{\$72,000}{200,000 \text{ shs}} = \$.36$$

$$\text{EPS on net income} = \frac{\$1,103,000}{200,000 \text{ shs}} = \$5.52$$

Exhibit 9 at the end of the chapter illustrates how each of these amounts would appear on Executive's income statement.

## Primary and Fully Diluted Earnings per Share

Corporations with complex capital structures are required to report two prospective earnings per share amounts: primary earnings per share and fully diluted earnings per share. A corporation with a **complex capital structure** has securities outstanding that may cause the issuance of additional shares of common stock.

Holders of convertible bonds or convertible preferred stock can submit their securities at any time and receive common shares. Holders of stock options are also free to pay an exercise price and receive common stock. Earnings per share calculated without considering these potential issuances may present a misleading picture to investors.

For example, suppose that you are evaluating Apex Corporation. Earnings per share is $4.15 without considering potential issuances. If new shares are issued and the exercise of stock options is included, earnings per share would be $2.95. Would you make the same investment decision knowing the $2.95 amount that you would make if only the $4.15 figure were available?

To alert investors to the potential effects of convertible securities and options, GAAP require that certain assumptions be made about these possible stock issuances. We must calculate earnings per share *as if* the potential issuance of common stock actually did occur.

**Primary earnings per share** is calculated including the effects of securities that are *most likely* to cause issuances of new stock. **Fully diluted earnings per share** considers *all* potential new issuances. Fully diluted EPS thus yields the lowest possible earnings-per-share amount.

The rules for determining whether potential shares should be included in primary or fully diluted EPS (or both) are complex. Intermediate accounting courses consider these detailed requirements. The following illustration will give you a general idea of the procedures followed in calculating primary and fully diluted EPS.

The information below pertains to Valentine, Inc.:

Net income for 1998 . . . . . . . . . . . . . . . . . . $284,800
Average common stock outstanding . . . . . . . 80,000 shs
Preferred dividends paid in 1998 . . . . . . . . . $ 8,800
New shares that may be issued if
convertible preferred is converted . . . . . . . . 9,000 shs
New shares that may be issued if stock
options are exercised . . . . . . . . . . . . . . . . . . . 12,000 shs

Assume that the effects of stock options are included in calculating both primary and fully diluted EPS and that the effect of convertible preferred is included in calculating fully diluted EPS only. The stock options are included in both primary and fully diluted because they are likely to cause issuance of common stock in the future.

The convertible preferred stock is not as likely to be converted; but since the possibility exists, the potential for new shares must be included in calculating fully diluted earnings per share.

$$\textbf{1998 primary EPS} = \frac{\textbf{net income} - \textbf{preferred dividends}}{\textbf{average common shares}}$$
$$\textbf{outstanding} + \textbf{likely new issuances}$$

$$= \frac{\$284{,}800 - \$8{,}800}{80{,}000 \text{ shs} + 12{,}000 \text{ shs}}$$

$$= \frac{\$276{,}000}{92{,}000 \text{ shs}}$$

$$= \$3.00 \text{ per share}$$

$$\textbf{1998 fully diluted EPS} = \frac{\textbf{net income (see note below)}}{\textbf{average common shares outstanding}}$$
$$+ \textbf{all possible new issuances}$$

$$= \frac{\$284{,}800}{80{,}000 \text{ shs} + 12{,}000 \text{ shs} + 9{,}000 \text{ shs}}$$

$$= \frac{\$284{,}800}{101{,}000 \text{ shs}}$$

$$= \$2.82 \text{ per share}$$

*Note:* Preferred dividends are not deducted because this calculation is being made *as if* the preferred stock were converted. If conversion had taken place, no dividends would have been paid on the preferred stock.

The following information would be disclosed at the bottom of the Valentine income statement:

| | |
|---|---|
| Net Income.......................................... | $284,800 |
| Primary Earnings per Common Share ............................ | $ 3.00 |
| Fully Diluted Earnings per Common Share ......................... | $ 2.82 |

The calculation of Valentine's primary EPS assumes that:

- Since the convertible preferred stock is *unlikely* to be converted, we ignore the potential effects of conversion—issuing more shares and not paying preferred dividends.
- Since the options are *likely* to be exercised, we include the potential effect of issuing 12,000 more shares to the individuals who could exercise these options at any time.

The assumptions change a little when Valentine's fully diluted EPS is calculated:

- Since the convertible preferred stock may be converted, we include the potential effects of this conversion.
- If the preferred stock were converted at the beginning of 1998, no preferred dividends would have been paid, so none are deducted.
- If the preferred stock were converted, more common shares (9,000) would be outstanding; so these potential new shares are added to the shares that were outstanding.
- Since the options are still likely to be exercised, we include the effect of issuing 12,000 more common shares.

## FINANCIAL STATEMENT ANALYSIS

Earnings per share is one reflection of how well a company is doing. Several other ratios may be calculated also to indicate how well management is using the company's resources.

### Rate of Return on Total Assets

Learning Objective **13**

Calculate and explain rate of return on total assets, rate of return on common stockholders' equity, and dividend yield rate

**Rate of return (ROR) on total assets** is a measure of management's efficiency in using all resources at its disposal. The formula for computing this ratio is:

$$\text{Rate of return (ROR) on total assets} = \frac{\text{income before interest expense}}{\text{average total assets}}$$

Income before interest is used so that earnings will not be influenced by the manner in which the assets are financed. Interest is a cost of financing the business, not a cost of operating it. Average total assets reflect resources employed throughout the year, not those on hand at the beginning or at the end. This average could be computed by weighting the dollars of assets used by the number of days they are employed and dividing by 365. An approximation of this average may be obtained by adding the beginning and ending assets amounts and dividing by 2.

Using Executive Corporation (Exhibit 9) to illustrate and assuming the company had $6,420,000 of assets on January 1 and $8,360,000 on December 31, the rate of return on total assets for 1998 is calculated as follows:

$$\text{ROR on total assets} = \frac{\text{net income} + \text{interest expense}}{(\text{total assets, beg. of year} + \text{total assets, end of year}) \div 2}$$

$$= \frac{\$1,103,000 + \$35,000}{(\$6,420,000 + \$8,360,000) \div 2}$$

$$= \frac{\$1,138,000}{\$7,390,000} = .154, \text{ or } 15.4\%$$

Executive's management earned an average of 15.4% on each dollar of assets invested in the company.

## RATE OF RETURN ON COMMON STOCKHOLDERS' EQUITY

**Rate of return (ROR) on common stockholders' equity** is a measure of management's effectiveness in using the resources invested by the common stockholders. This rate may be higher or lower than the return on total assets, depending on how judiciously management has combined debt and preferred stock with common stock in financing the company's resources. The formula for computing this ratio is:

$$\text{Rate of return (ROR) on common stockholders' equity} = \frac{\text{net income} - \text{preferred dividends}}{\text{average common stockholders's equity}}$$

The earnings amount in the numerator excludes both payments to holders of debt (interest expense) and payments to holders of preferred stock (preferred dividends). Thus the net income less preferred dividends is the net amount earned on the equity of the common stockholders. Average common stockholders' equity is an approximation of the amount invested by this group of owners throughout the year.

Executive Corp. had no preferred stock outstanding during 1998. Common stockholders' equity was $6,140,000 on January 1 and $8,080,000 on December 31. The rate of return on Executive's common stockholders' equity for 1998 is:

$$\text{ROR on common stockholders' equity} = \frac{\$1,103,000 - \$0}{(\$6,140,000 + \$8,080,000) \div 2}$$

$$= \frac{\$1,103,000}{\$7,110,000}$$

$$= .155 \text{ or } 15.5\%$$

Since the 15.5% return on common stockholders' equity exceeds the 15.4% return on total assets, management has made effective use of **leverage, or trading on the equity.** Leverage, or trading on the equity, involves using the assets invested by common stockholders as collateral for debt financing (borrowing on notes or bonds) and limited-return equity financing (selling preferred stock) in an attempt to earn a higher return for the common stockholder.

## DIVIDEND YIELD RATE

**Dividend yield rate** shows the current year's dividends as a percentage of the current market price of the stock. This indication of the cash payout rate on an investment allows stockholders and potential stockholders to compare interest rates on certificates of deposit, corporate bonds, and other securities with this measure of return on common stock. The investor should be aware that dividend yield rates ignore the potential increase in the market value of common stock. For this reason the dividend yield rate should be combined with other statistics in making investment decisions.

Holders of Executive Corporation's 200,000 shares of common stock received a total of $5,000,000 in dividends. On December 31, the Executive stock was selling for $110 per share. The formula for calculating dividend yield rates and the 1998 dividend yield rate for Executive Corp. is:

$$\text{Dividend yield rate} = \frac{\textbf{dividends per share of common stock}}{\textbf{current market price per share of common stock}}$$

$$\begin{array}{l}\text{1998 dividend yield rate} \\ \text{for Executive Corp.}\end{array} = \frac{\$5,000,000 \div 200,000 \text{ shs}}{\$110} = \frac{\$2.50}{\$110} = .0227, \text{ or } 2.27\%$$

This relatively low dividend yield rate of about 2% on Executive Corp., common stock would not attract investors who count on cash flow from dividends to pay their living expenses. A potential Executive Corp. stockholder would probably be more interested in speculating on the growth in the market value of the stock. This type of investor would rely more heavily on growth in earnings per share and recent trends in the market price of the stock than on the dividend yield rate.

---

**ASK YOURSELF** ▶

1. To be disclosed as a discontinued operation, the portion of the business being sold must qualify as a segment. What is a segment?
2. What two tests must be met for a gain or loss to qualify as an extraordinary item?
3. Where is a cumulative adjustment due to change in accounting principle shown on the income statement?
4. When would a corporation report only historical earnings per share?
5. What makes a corporate capital structure complex?
6. Why do stockholders' want the rate of return on common stockholders' equity to be higher than the rate of return on total assets?

## THE CORPORATE INCOME STATEMENT

Learning Objective **14**

Prepare a corporate income statement that includes income taxes, unusual items, and earnings per share

The corporate income statement shown in Exhibit 9 highlights the disclosure of income taxes, discontinued operations, extraordinary items, adjustments due to changes in accounting principles, and earnings per share. Notes to the financial statements, omitted for purposes of this illustration, would provide additional information about each of these items.

The single set of earnings-per-share amounts tells the reader that the corporation has a simple capital structure. A complex capital structure would require primary earnings per share and fully diluted earnings per share.

**Exhibit 9** Model Income Statement Highlighting Income Taxes and Unusual Items

## EXECUTIVE CORPORATION
### Income Statement
### For Year Ended December 31, 1999
### (000s Omitted)

| | | |
|---|---|---|
| Operating Revenue: | | |
| Sales | | $4,450 |
| Less: Sales Discounts | $ 34 | |
| Sales Returns | 12 | 46 |
| Net Sales | | $4,404 |
| Cost of Goods Sold: | | |
| ~~~~~~~~~~~~~~~~~~~~~~~~~~~~~~~~~~~~~~~~~~~~~~~~~~~~~ | | |
| ~~~~~~~~~~~~~~~~~~~~~~~~~~~~~~~~~~~~~~~~~~~~~~~~~~~~~ | | |
| Cost of Goods Sold | | 2,118 |
| Gross Profit on Sales | | $2,286 |
| Operating Expenses: | | |
| ~~~~~~~~~~~~~~~~~~~~~~~~~~~~~~~~~~~~~~~~~~~~~~~~~~~~~ | | |
| ~~~~~~~~~~~~~~~~~~~~~~~~~~~~~~~~~~~~~~~~~~~~~~~~~~~~~ | | |
| Total Operating Expenses | | 472 |
| Income from Primary Operations | | $1,814 |
| Other Income and Gains: | | |
| Gain on Sale of Delivery Equipment | $ 4 | |
| Interest Income | 12 | |
| Income from Investment in Quartile Inc. | 63 | |
| Total Other Income | | $ 79 |
| Other Expenses and Losses: | | |
| Interest Expense | $ 35 | |
| Loss on Sale of Building | 11 | |
| Total Other Expenses | | $ 46 |
| Income from Continuing Operations before Income Tax | | $1,847 |
| Provision for Income Taxes: | | |
| Current | $545 | |
| Deferred | 83 | |
| Total Provision for Income Taxes | | 628 |
| Income from Continuing Operations | | $1,219 |
| Discontinued Operations: | | |
| Gain from Discontinued Operations (net of applicable income tax of $28,000) | | 55 |
| Income before Extraordinary Items and Cumulative Adjustment due to Change in Accounting Principle | | $1,274 |
| Extraordinary Item: | | |
| Loss from Flood Damage (net of income tax savings of $51,000) | | 99 |
| Income before Cumulative Adjustment due to Change in Accounting Principle | | $1,175 |
| Cumulative Adjustment due to Change in Accounting Principle: | | |
| Cumulative Effect of Changing from Straight-Line to Double Declining-Balance Depreciation (net of income tax savings of $37,000) | | 72 |
| Net Income | | $1,103 |
| Earnings per Common Share: | | |
| Income from Continuing Operations | $6.10 | |
| Discontinued Operations | 0.28 | |
| Extraordinary Item | (0.50) | |
| Cumulative Adjustment due to Change in Accounting Principle | (0.36) | |
| Net Income | $5.52 | |

## SUMMARY

- **Retained Earnings** accumulates the net income of the corporation from its inception. The Retained Earnings account is created when Income Summary is closed.
- Net income increases the balance of Retained Earnings. Corrections of prior years' errors may cause an increase or decrease in the Retained Earnings balance. Other decreases in Retained Earnings are caused by net losses, dividend declarations, and the negative effects of certain treasury stock transactions.
- The corporate board of directors may appropriate, or restrict, an amount of retained earnings.
- All changes in retained earnings are shown in the statement of retained earnings.
- Corporations may distribute earned capital in the form of cash, noncash assets, or additional shares of stock. On the declaration date the board of directors declares a dividend, on the record date a list of stockholders who are to receive the dividend is prepared, and on the payment date the assets or stock is distributed.
- Small and large stock dividends involve reducing earned capital and increasing paid-in capital for the par value (large dividend) or market value (small dividend) of the stock distributed.
- A stock split has no effect on earned capital or paid-in capital. Stock splits decrease the par or stated value of the shares and increase the number of shares authorized, issued, outstanding, and in the treasury.
- Corporations must pay federal income taxes. These taxes must be estimated and paid to the Internal Revenue Service in four installments each year.
- A **permanent difference** occurs when a revenue or expense appears on the income statement but will never appear on the income tax return. When a permanent difference exists, the Provision for Income Taxes equals the tax due to the IRS.
- A **temporary difference** exists when a revenue or expense appears on the income statement in one year and on the income tax return in a different year. When a temporary difference exists, a deferred tax liability may be created. This liability is paid off when the taxes come due in later years.
- When a corporation disposes of a separate line of business or major class of customers, it has discontinued a segment of its operations. Gains and losses from discontinued operations are disclosed separately on the income statement after income from continuing operations.
- Extraordinary gains and losses occur from transactions that are unusual in nature and infrequent in occurrence. In determining whether an item is extraordinary the corporation must take into consideration the environment in which it operates. Extraordinary gains and losses are shown separately on the income statement after discontinued operations.
- When a corporation changes from one generally accepted accounting principle to another generally accepted accounting principle, it may be required to calculate the effect of the change on income. These cumulative adjustments due to changes in accounting principles are shown separately net of income taxes on the income statement as the last item before net income.
- Earnings-per-share amounts must be published in the income statements of corporations whose stock is traded publicly. Corporations with **simple capital structures** report only historical earnings per share.
- Corporations that have convertible securities and stock options outstanding may be required to issue additional shares of common stock upon demand of these securities holders. Such corporations have **complex capital structures** and are required to disclose primary earnings per share reflecting the effects of the most likely new share issuances and fully diluted earnings per share, taking into account all potential common stock issuances.
- Investors and creditors employ several ratios to evaluate a corporation's earnings performance. In addition to earnings per share rate of return on total assets, rate of return on common stockholders' equity, and dividend yield rate are among the most widely used.

### 15 KEY TERMS

| | |
|---|---|
| **Change in accounting principle** | The process of switching from one generally accepted accounting method or procedure to another generally accepted accounting method or procedure. |
| **Closely held corporation** | A corporation whose stock is not traded publicly. All stock in a closely held corporation is owned by a few individuals, often members of a family. |
| **Complex capital structure** | A corporate financial structure that includes securities that may cause the company to issue common stock. Publicly owned corporations with complex capital structures must report primary and fully diluted earnings-per-share amounts on their income statement. |
| **Convertible securities** | Preferred stock or bonds that carry the privilege, at the option of the holder, of being submitted to the corporation in exchange for a specified number of common shares. Preferred stocks and bonds without this privilege are nonconvertible. |
| **Declaration date** | The date on which the corporate board of directors votes to distribute a dividend. |
| **Discontinued operation** | The sale or abandonment of a separate line of business or major class of customers. |
| **Dividends** | Distributions of corporate earned capital to stockholders. These distributions may be in the form of cash, noncash assets, or shares of the corporation's own stock. |
| **Dividend yield rate** | Dividends per share of common stock divided by the current market price of common stock. |
| **Earnings per share (EPS)** | Net income to which the common stockholder has a claim, divided by the average number of common shares outstanding. |
| **Extraordinary item** | An event or transaction that is unusual in nature and infrequent in occurrence considering the environment in which the business operates. |
| **Fully diluted earnings per share** | Net income to which the common stockholder has a claim, divided by the average number of common shares actually outstanding plus *all* potential new issuances of common shares. Fully diluted earnings per share is the lowest possible earnings-per-share amount. |
| **Historical earnings per share** | Net income to which the common stockholder has a claim, divided by the average number of common shares outstanding. Historical earnings per share ignores potential new issuances of common stock. |
| **Liquidating dividends** | Distributions of corporate paid-in capital. These distributions are not dividends in the true sense of the word because they do not distribute earnings. |
| **Payment date** | The date on which previously declared dividends are distributed to stockholders. |
| **Permanent differences** | Differences between the income statement and the income tax return caused by revenues or expenses that appear on the income statement but will never appear on the income tax return. |
| **Primary earnings per share** | Net income to which the common stockholders have a claim, divided by the number of common shares actually outstanding, plus the most likely issuances of new shares. |
| **Prior period adjustment** | An adjustment of the beginning balance of Retained Earnings as a result of correcting an accounting error committed in an earlier period. |
| **Property dividends** | The distribution of earned capital to stockholders in the form of assets other than cash. |
| **Rate of return (ROR) on common stockholders' equity** | Net income minus preferred dividends divided by average common stockholders' equity. |
| **Rate of return (ROR) on total assets** | Income before interest expense divided by average total assets. |

**Record date**  The date on which owners of stock are identified as those eligible to receive a previously declared dividend.

**Retained Earnings**  A stockholders' equity account representing the accumulated income of a corporation since its beginning. Prior period adjustments, all dividends declared, and certain other adjustments must be deducted in calculating the current balance of this account.

**Retained Earnings: Appropriated**  A stockholders' equity account that reflects a restriction imposed on retained earnings by the board of directors. Appropriated retained earnings are not available for dividend distributions.

**Retained Earnings: Unappropriated**  See **Retained Earnings.**

**Segment**  A portion of a business involving a separate line of business or a different major class of customers.

**Simple capital structure**  A corporate financial structure that contains no securities that may cause the company to issue additional shares of common stock. Public corporations with simple capital structures must report historical earnings per share.

**Stock dividend**  Distribution of earned capital to stockholders in the form of additional shares of the company's own common stock.

**Stock options**  Arrangements that allow an individual, usually an executive of the company, to purchase the corporation's stock at a discount from its market price. This stock option discount is a reward for the executive's efforts in making the company successful.

**Stock split**  A reduction of the par or stated value of the authorized stock and a simultaneous increase in the number of shares authorized, issued, outstanding, and in the treasury.

**Temporary differences**  Differences between the income on the income statement and the income on the income tax return caused by revenues or expenses that appear on the income statement in one year and on the income tax return in a different year.

## DEMONSTRATION PROBLEM

On Jan. 1, 1998, Virgil Corporation has a balance in Retained Earnings: Unappropriated of $3,400,000. No appropriations exist. The following transactions and events took place during 1998:

1. On Jan. 15, 1998, an error committed in 1996 was discovered. The bookkeeper had debited Advertising Expense and credited Cash for $75,000. The debit should have been to Accounts Payable.

2. On Mar. 1, a $.50 per share cash dividend was declared. 200,000 shares of common stock have been issued; 190,000 shares are outstanding. The dividend is payable Mar. 31 to stockholders of record on Mar. 15.

3. On June 1, a property dividend was declared. Virgil Corp. will distribute 2 shares of Telephone, Inc., stock for each share of Virgil stock owned. 190,000 shares of Virgil Corp. are outstanding. The Telephone, Inc., stock cost Virgil $2.50 per share; it is currently worth $3.25 per share. The dividend is payable June 30 to stockholders of record on June 15.

4. On Sept. 1, Virgil Corp. declared a 10% stock dividend distributable on Sept. 30 to stockholders of record on Sept. 15. The 190,000 outstanding shares of Virgil stock have a par value of $10 and a current market value of $14.

5. On Dec. 30, the Virgil Corp. board of directors voted to appropriate $20,000 of retained earnings for contingencies.

6. After all adjusting and closing entries, Income Summary has a credit balance of $425,000.

**Required:**

1. Prepare entries to record the events and transactions listed.
2. Prepare a statement of retained earnings in good form.

### ■ Solution to Demonstration Problem

1.

| | | | | |
|---|---|---|---|---|
| Jan. | 15 | Accounts Payable . . . . . . . . . . . . . . . . . . . . . . . . . . | 75,000 | |
| | |      Retained Earnings: Unappropriated . . . . . . . . . | | 75,000 |
| | | To correct 1993 error. | | |
| Mar. | 1 | Retained Earnings: Unappropriated . . . . . . . . . . . . . | 95,000 | |
| | |      Dividends Payable . . . . . . . . . . . . . . . . . . . . . . | | 95,000 |
| | | To record dividend declaration<br>($.50 × 190,000 shs = $95,000). | | |
| | 15 | No entry required on record date. | | |
| | 31 | Dividends Payable. . . . . . . . . . . . . . . . . . . . . . . . . . | 95,000 | |
| | |      Cash . . . . . . . . . . . . . . . . . . . . . . . . . . . . . . . . . | | 95,000 |
| | | To record dividend payment. | | |
| June | 1 | Investment in Telephone, Inc. . . . . . . . . . . . . . . . . . | 285,000 | |
| | |      Gain to Increase Investment to Fair Market<br>     Value . . . . . . . . . . . . . . . . . . . . . . . . . . . . . . . . | | 285,000 |
| | | To increase investment to current value<br>($.75 × 380,000 shs = $285,000). | | |

*(Continued)*

| | | | | |
|---|---|---|---|---|
| June | 1 | Retained Earnings: Unappropriated . . . . . . . . . . . . . | 1,235,000 | |
| | |     Property Dividend Payable . . . . . . . . . . . . . . . | | 1,235,000 |
| | | To record declaration of property dividend | | |
| | | ($3.25 × 380,000 shs = $1,235,000). | | |
| | | | | |
| | 15 | No entry required on record date. | | |
| | | | | |
| | 30 | Property Dividend Payable . . . . . . . . . . . . . . . . . . | 1,235,000 | |
| | |     Investment in Telephone, Inc. . . . . . . . . . . . . . . | | 1,235,000 |
| | | To record payment of property dividend. | | |
| | | | | |
| Sept. | 1 | Retained Earnings: Unappropriated . . . . . . . . . . . . | 266,000 | |
| | |     Common Stock Dividend Distributable . . . . . . . | | 190,000 |
| | |     Paid-In Capital in Excess of Par . . . . . . . . . . . | | 76,000 |
| | | To record declaration of stock dividend. | | |
| | | (.10 × 190,000 shs = 19,000 shs × $14 | | |
| | | = $266,000.) | | |
| | | | | |
| | 15 | No entry required on record date. | | |
| | | | | |
| | 30 | Common Stock Dividend Distributable . . . . . . . . . . | 190,000 | |
| | |     Common Stock. . . . . . . . . . . . . . . . . . . . . . . | | 190,000 |
| | | To record distribution of stock dividend. | | |
| | | | | |
| Dec. | 30 | Retained Earnings: Unappropriated . . . . . . . . . . . . | 20,000 | |
| | |     Retained Earnings Appropriated for Contin- | | |
| | |     gencies . . . . . . . . . . . . . . . . . . . . . . . . . . . . . | | 20,000 |
| | | To record appropriation of retained earnings. | | |
| | | | | |
| | 31 | Income Summary . . . . . . . . . . . . . . . . . . . . . . . . . | 425,000 | |
| | |     Retained Earnings: Unappropriated . . . . . . . . . | | 425,000 |
| | | To close income summary for the year. | | |

**2.**

## VIRGIL CORPORATION
## Statement of Retained Earnings
## For the Year Ended December 31, 1998

| | | |
|---|---:|---:|
| Retained Earnings: Unappropriated: | | |
| Balance, Jan. 1, 1998 . . . . . . . . . . . . . . . . . . . . . . . . . . . . . . . . . . . . . | | $3,400,000 |
| Prior Period Adjustment: | | |
|    Correction of 1996 Error . . . . . . . . . . . . . . . . . . . . . . . . . . . . . . . . | | 75,000 |
| Balance, Jan. 1, 1998, Corrected . . . . . . . . . . . . . . . . . . . . . . . . . . . . | | $3,475,000 |
| Add: Net Income for the Year . . . . . . . . . . . . . . . . . . . . . . . . . . . . . . | | 425,000 |
|    Total . . . . . . . . . . . . . . . . . . . . . . . . . . . . . . . . . . . . . . . . . . . . . . | | $3,900,000 |
| Deduct: Cash Dividend . . . . . . . . . . . . . . . . . . . . . . . . . . | $   95,000 | |
|        Property Dividend. . . . . . . . . . . . . . . . . . . . . . . | 1,235,000 | |
|        Stock Dividend. . . . . . . . . . . . . . . . . . . . . . . . . | 266,000 | |
|        Appropriation for Contingencies . . . . . . . . . . . . | 20,000 | (1,616,000) |
| Balance, Dec. 31, 1998. . . . . . . . . . . . . . . . . . . . . . . . . . . . . . . . . . . . | | $2,284,000 |
| Retained Earnings: Appropriated for Contingencies: | | |
| Balance, Jan. 1, 1998 . . . . . . . . . . . . . . . . . . . . . . . . . . . . . . . . . . . . . | | -0- |
|    Add: Appropriation during the Year. . . . . . . . . . . . . . . . . . . . . . . . . | | 20,000 |
|    Deduct: (none) . . . . . . . . . . . . . . . . . . . . . . . . . . . . . . . . . . . . . . . | | -0- |
| Balance, Dec. 31, 1998. . . . . . . . . . . . . . . . . . . . . . . . . . . . . . . . . . . . | | $   20,000 |

## QUESTIONS FOR REVIEW AND FURTHER THOUGHT

### REVIEW QUESTIONS

1. The Zeta Corp. board of directors wishes to place restrictions on retained earnings in order to limit the amount that can be used for dividends. In what two ways may these restrictions be shown in the corporation's annual report?

2. What are prior period adjustments? How are they disclosed in the financial statements?

3. Explain what takes place on the dividend declaration date, record date, and payment date. On which of these dates is an accounting entry necessary?

4. The board of directors must declare a dividend before it may be distributed. What two additional conditions must be met before a dividend is distributed?

5. Cheever, Inc., estimates that it will earn a pretax income of $560,000 during 1998. Can Cheever wait until the end of 1998 to pay the $190,400 of income taxes that will be due? Explain.

6. Goodwill Amortization Expense is a permanent income statement–tax return difference. Explain what a permanent difference is and how the Provision for Income Taxes is determined when permanent differences exist.

7. Due to a temporary income statement–tax return difference, Amory, Inc., has a Provision for Income Taxes of $272,000 while the amount due to the IRS is only $200,000. What is a temporary difference? Explain how the $72,000 difference will appear on the balance sheet.

8. A company must sell or abandon a segment of the business in order to classify it as a discontinued operation. What is a business segment?

9. Lima, Inc., decides to change from one generally accepted accounting method to another. How would the company disclose this change in its financial statements?

10. What are the three unusual income statement items discussed in this chapter? Where and in what order will they be shown on the income statement?

11. Perry Corp. has a complex capital structure. Which earnings-per-share amounts must Perry report? On which financial statement are earnings-per-share amounts shown?

### QUESTIONS FOR FURTHER THOUGHT

1. Cupid Corp. has a $6,423,000 balance in Retained Earnings: Unappropriated, yet there is not sufficient cash to build a new building costing $275,000. Explain what retained earnings is. What is a possible explanation for the small amount of cash Cupid has on hand in relation to the large amount of retained earnings?

2. What effect does appropriating retained earnings have on total assets and total stockholders' equity?

3. Mullins Corp. appropriates $25,000 of retained earnings each year to build a new warehouse. How much cash will Mullins have accumulated after 5 years? Explain.

4. Lamb, Inc., has total retained earnings of $594,600, of which $480,600 is appropriated for contingencies. What is the maximum dividend that the board of directors can declare? Explain.

5. How can a corporation recognize a gain by giving assets to its stockholders?

6. What is the effect on assets, liabilities, and stockholders' equity of declaring and issuing each of the following types of dividends?
   a. Cash dividend
   b. Property dividend
   c. Stock dividend

7. What is the basic difference in accounting for small and large stock dividends?

8. A large stock dividend and a stock split can be used to accomplish the same purpose. Explain.

9. A citrus grower in Florida experiences a large loss due to freeze damage. Damaging freezes occur every 5 years or so in that part of the state. Can the grower disclose the loss as an extraordinary item? Why or why not?

10. The accountant for King, Inc., has calculated historical, primary, and fully diluted earnings per share. Which of these amounts would you expect to be the highest? The lowest? Explain.

## OBJECTIVE ASSIGNMENT

*True/False*   Indicate whether each statement below is *true* or *false* by placing a *T* or an *F* in the space provided.

_____ 1. The Retained Earnings account shows income accumulated only in the most current year.

_____ 2. Prior period adjustments may decrease Retained Earnings but they may not increase Retained Earnings.

_____ 3. Corporations are required to pay dividends of some type at least once each year.

_____ 4. Liquidating dividends are paid when a corporation is permanently reducing its size or going out of business.

_____ 5. A gain from the sale of a corporation's factory building would *not* be shown on the income statement as an extraordinary item.

*Multiple Choice*   Select the best choice to complete each statement or answer each question below. Write the letter corresponding to your choice in the space provided.

_____ 1. One acceptable way to communicate a restriction on retained earnings is:
a. To set aside a fund of assets
b. To establish a special paid-in capital account
c. To explain the restriction in a financial statement note
d. To establish a deferred retained earnings account as a liability

_____ 2. Which of the following would result in an increase in the Retained Earnings: Unappropriated account?
a. Net loss for the period
b. Positive prior period adjustments
c. Cash dividends declared
d. Stock dividends declared

_____ 3. Which of the following combinations of dates accurately describes when journal entries are required to record dividends?

|     | Declaration Date | Record Date | Payment Date |
|-----|------------------|-------------|--------------|
| a.  | Yes              | Yes         | Yes          |
| b.  | Yes              | No          | No           |
| c.  | No               | No          | Yes          |
| d.  | Yes              | No          | Yes          |

_____ 4. When a small stock dividend is declared, Retained Earnings: Unappropriated is debited for:
a. The par value of the shares to be distributed
b. The liquidation value of the shares to be distributed
c. The market value of the shares to be distributed
d. –0–; Retained Earnings: Unappropriated is unaffected by the declaration of a small stock dividend

_____ 5. The journal entry to record the declaration of a large stock dividend includes:
   a. A debit to Retained Earnings for the market value of the shares to be distributed
   b. A debit to Retained Earnings for the par value of the shares to be distributed
   c. A credit to Stock Dividend Distributable for the market value of the shares to be distributed
   d. A credit to Paid-In Capital in Excess of Par for the difference between the market value and the par value of the shares to be distributed

_____ 6. In accounting for income taxes, a permanent difference means that:
   a. An item of revenue or expense appears on the income statement but will never appear on the tax return
   b. An item of revenue or expense appears on the income statement in one time period and on the tax return in a different time period
   c. The corporation and the IRS have a difference of opinion over the deductibility of a certain expense
   d. The corporation has changed accounting principles and therefore will never pay tax on any resulting adjustment to income

_____ 7. Which of the following events could be disclosed as a discontinued operation on the income statement?
   a. Sidney Corp. sold its silver mine in Brazil at a gain. Sidney operates other silver mines in the United States.
   b. Troy Company sold its chain of battery and muffler shops at a loss. Troy still sells batteries and mufflers to auto manufacturers.
   c. Findlay, Inc., sold its Italian children's clothing manufacturing facility. Findlay manufacturers adult clothing in Germany.
   d. Kenton Co. sold its retail drugstores in Indiana. Kenton has other retail drugstores in Ohio and Michigan.

_____ 8. A meteor destroyed a building owned by Morris, Inc. This uninsured loss would be shown on the corporate income statement under the caption:
   a. Other Expenses and Losses
   b. Discontinued Operations
   c. Operating Expenses
   d. Extraordinary Items

_____ 9. Changes in accounting principles:
   a. Are not allowed because of the consistency principle
   b. Are allowed as long as the effects are disclosed on the income statement and described in the financial statement notes
   c. Are allowed only for changes in depreciation methods
   d. Are allowed but may _not_ be shown net of tax on the income statement

_____ 10. Coast-to-Coast, Inc., is a large, publicly owned corporation with a complex financial capital structure. On its income statement, Coast-to-Coast must show:
   a. Historical earnings per share
   b. Historical and primary earnings per share
   c. Historical and fully diluted earnings per share
   d. Primary and fully diluted earnings per share

## EXERCISES

**1  2  3†**    **Exercise 1:** Preparing Entries Affecting Retained Earnings

Record the following 1998 and 1999 transactions and events for Grant, Inc.:

a. After all adjusting entries, Grant's 1998 Income Summary account has a credit balance of $345,000. Grant's first year of operations is 1998.
b. On Mar. 15, 1999, an error committed in 1998 was discovered. The bookkeeper had debited Interest Expense and credited Cash for $6,500. The correct 1998 entry was to debit Interest Payable and credit Cash.
c. On Sept. 30, 1999, Grant sold 100 shares of treasury stock for $8 per share. Grant had bought the treasury stock in 1998 for $12 per share. No Paid-In Capital from Treasury Stock account exists.
d. On Dec. 30, 1999, Grant's board of directors voted to appropriate $25,000 of retained earnings for factory expansion.

▶ *(Check Figure: On Sept. 30, debit Retained Earnings for $400)*


**5**    **Exercise 2:** Recording a Cash Dividend

Anna Corp.'s board of directors declared a $75,000 cash dividend on Sept. 1, 1998, payable on Oct. 1, to stockholders of record on Sept. 15. Prepare all appropriate entries needed on the declaration, record, and payment dates.


**5**    **Exercise 3:** Recording a Property Dividend

Lorain Marine, Inc.'s, board of directors voted to distribute some surplus inventory to its 10 stockholders as a dividend. Each stockholder will receive one ski boat and outboard motor. Each boat-and-motor combination has a fair market value of $15,900. The boat/motor combinations cost $12,500 each. The property dividend was declared on Aug. 1, 1999, distributable on Sept. 1, to stockholders of record as of Aug. 15. Prepare all appropriate entries needed on the declaration, record, and distribution dates. Lorain uses a perpetual inventory system; the boats and motors are carried in a Merchandise Inventory account.

▶ *(Check Figure: Gain recorded on Aug. 1 = $34,000)*


**5**    **Exercise 4:** Recording a Small Stock Dividend

The Alliance, Inc., board of directors voted on June 1, 1998, to declare a 10% stock dividend, distributable on July 1, to stockholders of record as of June 15. On June 1, Alliance had 500,000 shares of $1-par common stock authorized. 55,000 shares were issued and 50,000 shares were outstanding (5,000 shares were held as treasury stock). Alliance stock was selling for $4.50 per share on June 1. Prepare the appropriate journal entries needed on June 1, June 15, and July 1.

▶ *(Check Figure: June 1 debit to Retained Earnings = $22,500)*


† The numbers in the margin refer to the Learning Objectives.

**Exercise 5:** Recording a Large Stock Dividend

The Ravenna Corp. board of directors voted on Nov. 1, 1998, to declare a 45% stock dividend, distributable on Dec. 31, to stockholders of record as of Dec. 1. Ravenna's charter authorizes the issuance of 200,000 shares of $4-par common stock. As of Nov. 1, 1998, 50,000 shares of common stock are issued and outstanding. The market price of Ravenna stock on Nov. 1, is $8.50 per share. Prepare any entries needed on the declaration, record, and payment dates.

▶ *(Check Figure: Nov. 1 debit to Retained Earnings = $90,000)*

4   **Exercise 6:** Preparing a Statement of Retained Earnings

The following events and transactions affecting Lyons Corp.'s retained earnings occurred during 1998:

a. A $95,000 cash dividend was declared and paid.
b. Retained Earnings: Unappropriated was debited for $8,100 to correct a mistake made in 1996.
c. Net income for the year was $239,000.
d. Lyons appropriated $40,000 for possible litigation loss.

Retained Earnings: Unappropriated had a credit balance of $355,400 on Jan. 1, 1998. Prepare a statement of retained earnings for 1998 in good form.

▶ *(Check Figure: Retained Earnings: Unappropriated balance on Dec. 31, 1998 = $451,300)*

8  9  10   **Exercise 7:** Recording Corporate Income Taxes

a. Rice, Inc., estimates and pays federal income taxes quarterly. For each of the first three quarters, the estimated amount was $34,000; the last quarter estimate was $38,200. Prepare entries to record the income tax estimates for the first and last quarters.
b. Lena Corp. calculates federal income taxes due in the amount of $91,300. Lena's income statement shows a pretax income of $273,500. Included on the income statement is $5,000 interest income on municipal bonds. This interest will never be shown on the income tax return. How much will Lena show as Provision for Income Taxes on the income statement?
c. Rimer Corp. correctly calculates income taxes due in the amount of $124,400 and a provision for income taxes in the amount of $151,000. Prepare the entry to record Rimer's income taxes for the year.

▶ *(Check Figure: Rimer credit to Deferred Income Taxes = $26,600)*

11   **Exercise 8:** Identifying Unusual Income Statement Items

Identify each of the following as a discontinued operation, an extraordinary item, a change in accounting principle, or none of the above.

a. Loss due to damage caused by an iceberg in Galveston, Texas.
b. Gain due to selling a professional soccer team. The remaining operations of the corporation involve operating a wholesale bakery and selling auto parts.
c. Loss due to selling a downtown department store. The remaining department stores owed by the company are located in suburban shopping malls.
d. Loss due to writing off uncollectible accounts receivable.
e. "Gain" due to changing from double declining-balance to straight-line depreciation.
f. Gain from selling land to the City of Toledo. The land was condemned by the city for use as a city park.
g. Loss due to sale of a copying machine.

12  **Exercise 9:** Calculating Earnings per Share

Bremen Enterprises, Inc., reported 1998 income of $868,900. The accountant calculated a weighted average of 728,000 common shares outstanding during the year. The following additional facts are known about Bremen:

a. Paid $32,000 of dividends on convertible preferred stock. If the stock is converted, 88,224 new common shares will be issued. It is not likely that this stock will be converted, but it is possible.
b. Paid $20,000 of dividends on nonconvertible preferred stock.
c. Executives of the corporation have the right to acquire 100,000 shares of common stock by exercising stock options. It is considered likely that these options will be exercised.

Calculate Bremen's primary and fully diluted earnings per share for 1998. (Round to the nearest cent.)

▶ *(Check Figure: Fully diluted EPS = $.93)*

13  **Exercise 10:** Calculating Earnings Performance Ratios

The following data are from the financial statements of Home, Inc.:

|  | Dec. 31, 1998 | Jan. 1, 1998 |
|---|---|---|
| Total Assets. . . . . . . . . . . . . . . . . . . . . . . . . . . . . . . . | $180,000 | $140,000 |
| Total Stockholders' Equity . . . . . . . . . . . . . . . . . . . . | 144,000 | 112,000 |
| Total Preferred Stockholders' Equity . . . . . . . . . . . . . | 30,000 | 30,000 |
| Total Common Stockholders' Equity . . . . . . . . . . . . . | 114,000 | 82,000 |
| Preferred Dividends Declared. . . . . . . . . . . . . . . . . . | 2,400 | — |
| Common Dividends Declared. . . . . . . . . . . . . . . . . . | 14,850 | — |
| Market Price of Common Stock (per share). . . . . . . . | 50 | — |
| Net Income . . . . . . . . . . . . . . . . . . . . . . . . . . . . . . . | 20,000 | — |
| Interest Expense. . . . . . . . . . . . . . . . . . . . . . . . . . . | 5,750 | — |

Assuming that 5,400 shares of common stock are outstanding, calculate the following ratios:

a. Rate of return on total assets
b. Rate of return on common stockholders' equity
c. Dividend yield rate

▶ *(Check figure: Rate of return on common stockholders' equity = 17.96%)*

## PROBLEMS: SET A

1 2 3 4† **Problem A1:** Preparing Retained Earnings Entries and the Statement of Retained Earnings

Columbus Ventures, Inc., began 1999 with a Retained Earnings: Unappropriated account having a credit balance of $250,000 and Retained Earnings Appropriated for Plant Expansion of $60,000. The following occurred during 1999:

Mar. 11   A review of the Patents account reveals that a patent acquired on May 1, 1998, for $150,000 was not amortized. The patent should be written off over a 10-year useful life.

Apr. 16   The board of directors voted to remove $10,000 of Appropriated Retained Earnings and return this amount to the Unappropriated account.

May 30   The board of directors voted to pay a cash dividend totaling $90,000 on June 30 to stockholders of record on June 15.

June 30   The dividend declared on May 30 was paid.

Sept. 18   Columbus sold 500 shares of common stock which had been held in the treasury for $9,000. The treasury stock had cost $10,000. (Columbus originally issued all common stock at par, and no Paid-In Capital from Treasury Stock account exists.)

Dec. 31   After all revenue and expense accounts for the year are closed, Income Summary has a debit balance of $68,000.

**Required:**

1.  Prepare general journal entries to record each of the 1999 events and transactions outlined above.
2.  Prepare a statement of retained earnings in good form for the year ended Dec. 31, 1999.

▶ *(Check Figure: Sept. 18 debit to Retained Earnings = $1,000)*

2 3 5   **Problem A2:** Preparing Retained Earnings Entries

**LEVIN CORPORATION**
**Statement of Retained Earnings**
**For Year Ended December 31, 1998**

| | | |
|---|---:|---:|
| Retained Earnings Unappropriated: | | |
| Balance, Jan. 1, 1998 . . . . . . . . . . . . . . . . . . . . . . . . . . . . . . . . . . . . . | | $342,000 |
| Prior Period Adjustment (To correct a 1997 error in recording | | |
| sales. Accounts Payable was credited on a cash sale rather | | |
| than the Sales Revenue account) . . . . . . . . . . . . . . . . . . . . . . . . . . . | | 2,500 |
| Balance, Jan. 1, 1998, as Adjusted. . . . . . . . . . . . . . . . . . . . . . . . . . | | $344,500 |
| Add: Net Income for the Year . . . . . . . . . . . . . . . . . . . . . . . . . . . . . . . | | 67,000 |
| Total . . . . . . . . . . . . . . . . . . . . . . . . . . . . . . . . . . . . . . . . . . . . . . . . . | | $411,500 |
| Deduct: Dividend declared and paid on preferred stock . . . . . | $ 28,000 | |
| Dividend declared and distributed (stock | | |
| dividend on $10-par common stock, 10,000 | | |
| shares distributed). . . . . . . . . . . . . . . . . . . . . . . . . . | 240,000 | |
| Appropriated for Self-Insurance . . . . . . . . . . . . . . . . | 15,000 | (283,000) |
| Balance Dec. 31, 1998 . . . . . . . . . . . . . . . . . . . . . . . . . . . . . . . . . . . | | $128,500 |
| Retained Earnings Appropriated for Self-Insurance: | | |
| Balance, Jan. 1, 1998 . . . . . . . . . . . . . . . . . . . . . . . . . . . . . . . . . . . . | | $ 60,000 |
| Add: Appropriation during 1998. . . . . . . . . . . . . . . . . . . . . . . . . . . . . | | 15,000 |
| Deduct: (none) . . . . . . . . . . . . . . . . . . . . . . . . . . . . . . . . . . . . . . . . . . | | –0– |
| Balance, Dec. 31, 1998 . . . . . . . . . . . . . . . . . . . . . . . . . . . . . . . . . . . | | $ 75,000 |

† The numbers in the margin refer to the Learning Objectives.

**Required:**

Examine the Levin Corp. statement of retained earnings for 1998 and prepare in general journal form all the entries that affected the Retained Earnings account for the year. Dates may be omitted from your entries. (Prepare both declaration and distribution entries for any dividends.)

▶ *(Check Figure: Seven journal entries are required.)*

5 **Problem A3:** Recording Cash and Stock Dividends

During 1998, Findlay, Inc.'s, board of directors took the following actions affecting stockholders' equity:

Jan.  1  The board of directors declared the annual cash dividend on the 5,000 shares of 8% noncumulative, nonparticipating, $100-par, preferred stock outstanding.

1  The board declared a quarterly cash dividend of $1 per share to common stockholders. There were 400,000 shares of $10-par common stock outstanding.

15  Common stockholders of record on this day will receive the cash dividend.

31  Preferred stockholders of record on this day will receive the cash dividend.

Feb. 15  The cash dividend is distributed to common stockholders.

Apr. 13  Findlay acquired 20,000 common shares as treasury stock, paying $13.50 for each share.

May  1  The cash dividend is distributed to preferred stockholders.

Oct.  1  Since Findlay's cash position was unfavorable, no dividends on common stock were declared during the second and third quarters of the year. The board of directors voted to declare a 15% stock dividend in lieu of the fourth-quarter cash dividend. The market price per share was $14 on Oct. 1.

Nov.  1  Common stockholders of record on this day will receive the stock dividend.

Dec. 15  The common stock dividend was distributed. The market price per share of common stock was $15 on December 15.

**Required:**

Prepare the general journal entries to record the tansactions and events listed above. If no entry is needed on a particular date, write, "No entry."

▶ *(Check Figure: Oct. 1 debit to Retained Earnings = $798,000)*

5 6 7  **Problem A4:** Recording Dividends and Stock Splits and Preparing Stockholders' Equity Section

The Dec. 31, 1998, stockholders' equity section for Dayton, Inc., appears on the next page.

**DAYTON, INC.**
**Partial Balance Sheet**
**December 31, 1998**

### Stockholders' Equity

Paid-In Capital:
  Common stock [$2-par, 500,000 shares authorized, 100,000
    shares issued, 95,000 shares outstanding (5,000 shares

| | | |
|---|---:|---:|
| in treasury)] . . . . . . . . . . . . . . . . . . . . . . . . . . . . . . . . . . . . . . . . . . . . . | | $  200,000 |
| Additional Paid-In Capital: | | |
|   Paid-In Capital in Excess of Par . . . . . . . . . . . . . . . . . . . | $180,000 | |
|   Donated Capital . . . . . . . . . . . . . . . . . . . . . . . . . . . . . . . . . | 25,000 | 205,000 |
|     Total Paid-In Capital . . . . . . . . . . . . . . . . . . . . . . . . . . . . . | | 405,000 |
| Earned Capital: | | |
|   Retained Earnings: Unappropriated. . . . . . . . . . . . . . . . . . . . . . . . . | | 750,000 |
|     Total. . . . . . . . . . . . . . . . . . . . . . . . . . . . . . . . . . . . . . . . . . . . | | $1,155,000 |
| Less: Treasury Stock (5,000 shares) at Cost . . . . . . . . . . . . . . . . . . . . . | | (21,000) |
| Total Stockholders' Equity . . . . . . . . . . . . . . . . . . . . . . . . . . . . . . . . . . | | $1,134,000 |

The following events took place during 1999:

a. During January, a property dividend was declared and distributed. Home Chemical, Inc., stock that Dayton had owned as an investment, was distributed to the Dayton stockholders. The per-share book value and fair market values of the Home Chemical stock on the date of declaration were $2.50 and $2.90, respectively. Two shares of Home Chemical stock will be distributed for each share of Dayton a stockholder owns.
b. During April, a 2-for-1 stock split was implemented.
c. During December, the Dayton board of directors voted to appropriate $30,000 of retained earnings for plant expansion.
d. Income for the year, including all effects of the transactions listed above, was $187,600.

**Required:**

Prepare Dayton's stockholders' equity section on Dec. 31, 1999, incorporating the information in (a) through (d) above. Support your solution with calculations showing how each amount was derived.

▶ *(Check Figure: Total stockholders' equity = $770,600)*

7  **Problem A5:** Preparing a Comprehensive Stockholders' Equity Section

The accounts listed below were taken from the general ledger of the Atlas Corp. on June 30, 1998. Each account has a normal balance.

| | | | |
|---|---:|---|---:|
| Common Stock. . . . . . . . . . | $1,300,000 | Paid-In Capital in Excess | |
| Common Stock | |   of Par: Preferred. . . . . . . . . | $  325,000 |
|   Subscribed . . . . . . . . . . . . | 100,000 | Paid-In Capital from Treasury | |
| Common Stock Dividend | |   Stock. . . . . . . . . . . . . . . . . | 17,500 |
|   Distributable . . . . . . . . . . . | 70,000 | Donated Capital . . . . . . . . . . | 62,500 |
| Treasury Stock: Common | | Retained Earnings: | |
|   (3,000 shares) . . . . . . . . . | 117,500 |   Unappropriated. . . . . . . . . | 1,870,000 |
| Paid-In Capital in Excess | | Retained Earnings | |
|   of Par: Common . . . . . . . . . | 2,075,000 |   Appropriated for Plant | |
| 7% Preferred Stock . . . . . . . | 250,000 |   Expansion. . . . . . . . . . . . . | 125,000 |
| 7% Preferred Stock | | | |
|   Subscribed . . . . . . . . . . . . | 25,000 | | |

**Additional Information:**

a. Preferred stock has a par value of $50 per share. Atlas was authorized to issue 10,000 shares. The preferred stock is cumulative and participating.

b. Common stock has a par value of $5 per share. Atlas was authorized to issue 500,000 shares.

**Required:**

Prepare the stockholders' equity section of Atlas Corp.'s June 30, 1998, balance sheet. Include all disclosures needed for fair presentation. (*Hint:* Use the par values of preferred and common stock to calculate the number of shares issued and outstanding.)

▶ (*Check Figure: Total stockholders' equity = $6,102,500*)

2 5 **Problem A6:** Recording Entries in T-Accounts and Preparing a Stockholders' Equity Section

Marietta Manufacturing Co. has the following stockholders' equity on Oct. 31, 1998:

| | |
|---|---:|
| 6% Preferred Stock ($100-par, 5,000 shares authorized, 500 shares issued and outstanding) | $ 50,000 |
| Common Stock ($5-par, 200,000 shares authorized, 50,000 shares issued and outstanding) | 250,000 |
| Paid-In Capital in Excess of Par: Preferred | 10,000 |
| Paid-In Capital in Excess of Par: Common | 275,000 |
| Retained Earnings: Unappropriated | 350,000 |
| Total Stockholders' Equity | $935,000 |

The following transactions occurred during the following fiscal year:

Nov. 5 Purchased 1,000 shares of common stock for the treasury, $10,000.

Dec. 1 Declared a 6% cash dividend on the preferred stock payable on Dec. 31 to stockholders of record on Dec. 15.

31 Paid the dividend to preferred stockholders.

Jan. 15 Declared a cash dividend of $.50 per share on common stock payable Mar. 1 to stockholders of record Feb. 1.

Mar. 1 Paid the cash dividend declared on Jan. 15.

25 Sold 5,000 shares of common stock on subscription. The subscription price was $8 per share. A 20% down payment was received.

Apr. 4 Sold the treasury stock bought on Nov. 5 for $12 per share.

June 1 Collected half of the remaining balance on the common stock subscriptions.

July 31 Appropriated $100,000 of retained earnings for a possible lawsuit loss.

Sept. 1 Collected the balance due on the stock subscription and issued the shares.

Sept.15 Issued 5,000 shares of common stock in exchange for a custom made machine. The stock has a market value of $11 per share. No market price was available for the equipment.

30 Declared a 15% common stock dividend distributable on Nov. 1 to stockholders of record on Oct. 15. The market price of the stock on Sept. 30 was $12 per share.

Oct. 20 Received a donation of 10 acres of land valued at $25,000.

31 Calculated net income for the year at $106,000. (Close Income Summary account.)

**Required:**

1. Set up the following stockholders' equity T-accounts:

> 6% Preferred Stock
> Common Stock
> Paid-In Capital in Excess of Par: Preferred
> Paid-In Capital in Excess of Par: Common
> Common Stock Subscribed
> Common Stock Dividend Distributable
> Donated Capital
> Paid-In Capital from Treasury Stock
> Retained Earnings: Unappropriated
> Retained Earnings: Appropriated for Lawsuit Loss
> Treasury Stock

2. Enter the beginning balances in 6% Preferred Stock, Common Stock, Paid-In Capital in Excess of Par: Preferred, Paid-In Capital in Excess of Par: Preferred, and Retained Earnings: Unappropriated.

3. Enter the transactions for the year in the appropriate T-accounts. (You may wish to set up the asset and liability accounts in addition to the stockholders' equity accounts listed above.) Identify each debit and credit by placing the date of the transaction next to the amount.

4. Prepare the stockholders' equity section of Marietta's balance sheet on Oct. 31, 1999, in good form.

▶ *(Check Figure: Total stockholders' equity, Oct. 31, 1999 = $1,135,500)*

14 **Problem A7:** Preparing a Complex Income Statement

After preparing all adjusting entries, Stryker, Inc., has the following temporary accounts in its general ledger on Nov. 30, 1998:

| | |
|---|---:|
| Accounts with credit balances: | |
| Sales. . . . . . . . . . . . . . . . . . . . . . . . . . . . . . . . . . . . . . . . . . . . | $3,996,000 |
| Interest Income. . . . . . . . . . . . . . . . . . . . . . . . . . . . . . . . . . . . | 50,000 |
| Gain on Sale of Building . . . . . . . . . . . . . . . . . . . . . . . . . . . . | 12,800 |
| Gain from Discontinued Operations (net of income taxes of $83,042) . . | 161,200 |
| Extraordinary Gain from Condemnation of Company Property by City (net of income taxes of $136,000). . . . . . . . . . . . . . . . . . . . . . . . | 264,000 |
| Accounts with debit balances: | |
| Sales Returns and Allowances . . . . . . . . . . . . . . . . . . . . . . . . . | 56,000 |
| Cost of Goods Sold Expense. . . . . . . . . . . . . . . . . . . . . . . . . . . | 1,798,000 |
| Salaries Expense. . . . . . . . . . . . . . . . . . . . . . . . . . . . . . . . . . . . | 388,000 |
| Utilities Expense. . . . . . . . . . . . . . . . . . . . . . . . . . . . . . . . . . . . | 39,800 |
| Depreciation Expense . . . . . . . . . . . . . . . . . . . . . . . . . . . . . . . | 213,000 |
| Loss from Sale of Equipment. . . . . . . . . . . . . . . . . . . . . . . . . . | 46,600 |
| Advertising Expense . . . . . . . . . . . . . . . . . . . . . . . . . . . . . . . . | 577,200 |
| Interest Expense . . . . . . . . . . . . . . . . . . . . . . . . . . . . . . . . . . . | 340,800 |
| Provision for Income Taxes ($162,000 are currently payable). . . . . . . . | 204,000 |
| Cumulative Adjustment due to Change in Accounting Principles (net of tax savings of $38,000) . . . . . . . . . . . . . . . . . . . . . . . . . . . . | 73,800 |

**Required:**

Prepare a comprehensive income statement in good form for the year ended Nov. 30, 1998, including appropriate earnings per share disclosures. Stryker had 50,000 shares of common stock outstanding (weighted average). Stryker has a simple capital structure.

▶ *(Check Figure: Net income = $746,800)*

8 **Problem A8:** Recording Estimated Income Taxes

Kirby, Inc., is a calendar-year taxpayer. Kirby estimates that the applicable income tax rate for 1998 will be 34%. The following income estimates were prepared during the year:

| Date | Estimated Total Income for the Year |
|------|------|
| Apr. 15 | $400,000 |
| June 15 | 480,000 |
| Sept. 15 | 480,000 |
| Dec. 15 | 490,000 |
| Dec. 31 | 506,000 |

**Required:**

Prepare general journal entries to record Kirby's estimated income tax payments on Apr. 15, June 15, Sept. 15, and Dec. 15, and the entry to record the tax adjustment on Dec. 31.

▶ *(Check Figure: Dec. 31 debit to Provision for Income Taxes = $5,440)*

13 **Problem A9:** Calculating Earnings Performance Ratios

The following financial data have been assembled for Thistle, Inc., on Dec. 31, 1998:

| | |
|---|---|
| Average total assets for 1998. . . . . . . . . . . . . . . . . . . . . . . . . . . . . . . . . . . | $550,000 |
| Total stockholders' equity (average for 1998) . . . . . . . . . . . . . . . . . . . . . . . | 440,000 |
| Common stock, $.25 par . . . . . . . . . . . . . . . . . . . . . . . . . . . . . . . . . . . . . . . | 220,000 |
| 8% preferred stock, $5 par. . . . . . . . . . . . . . . . . . . . . . . . . . . . . . . . . . . . . . | 110,000 |
| Net income . . . . . . . . . . . . . . . . . . . . . . . . . . . . . . . . . . . . . . . . . . . . . . . . . | 33,000 |
| Interest expense . . . . . . . . . . . . . . . . . . . . . . . . . . . . . . . . . . . . . . . . . . . . . | 2,200 |
| Provision for income taxes (40% of income before income taxes) | |
| Market price of common stock, Dec. 31, 1998 . . . . . . . . . . . . . . . . . . . . . . | 2.50 |
| Market price of preferred stock, Dec. 31, 1998 . . . . . . . . . . . . . . . . . . . . . . | 16.50 |
| Common dividends were paid at the rate of $.05 per share per quarter. | |
| Preferred dividends were declared and paid. | |
| No preferred stock or common stock was issued or reacquired during 1998. | |

**Required:**

Using whatever data you need from the above list, calculate:

1. Rate of return on total assets
2. Rate of return on common stockholders' equity
3. Earnings per common share
4. Dividend yield rate

▶ *(Check figure: Earnings per common share = $.0275)*

## PROBLEMS: SET B

1 2 3 4† **Problem B1:** Preparing Retained Earnings Entries and the Statement of Retained Earnings

On Jan. 1, 1998, McComb Supply Co. had a Retained Earnings: Unappropriated account with a credit balance of $240,000, and Retained Earnings Appropriated for Contingencies with a credit balance of $40,000. The following events occurred during 1998:

Apr. 15 Since the possibility of a strike has passed, the board of directors voted to remove $20,000 of appropriated retained earnings and to return this amount to the unappropriated account.

July 12 The board of directors voted to pay a cash dividend totaling $62,500 on Sept. 1 to stockholders of record on Aug. 1.

Aug. 9 A review of the Land account reveals that $9,000 which was debited to Land in 1997 should have been debited to Property Tax Expense.

Sept. 1 The dividend declared on July 12 was paid.

Oct. 15 The board of directors voted to appropriate retained earnings for plant expansion in the amount of $25,000.

Dec. 31 After all revenue and expense accounts for the year are closed, Income Summary has a debit balance of $14,250.

### Required:

1. Prepare general journal entries to record each of the 1998 events and transactions outlined above.
2. Prepare a statement of retained earnings for the year ended Dec. 31, 1998.

▶ *(Check Figure: Retained Earnings: Unappropriated, Dec. 31, 1998 = $149,250)*

2 3 5 **Problem B2:** Preparing Retained Earnings Entries

**KINGERY CORPORATION**
**Statement of Retained Earnings**
**For Year Ended December 31, 1998**

| | | |
|---|---:|---:|
| Retained Earnings Unappropriated: | | |
| Balance, Jan. 1, 1998 . . . . . . . . . . . . . . . . . . . . . . . . . . . . . . . . . . . . . | | $740,000 |
| Prior Period Adjustment (To correct a 1996 error in recording insurance expense. Insurance Expense was debited when a cash payment was made; Notes Payable should have been debited): . . . . . . . . . . . . . . . . . . | | 18,500 |
| Balance, Jan. 1, 1998, as Adjusted . . . . . . . . . . . . . . . . . . . . . . . . . . . | | $758,500 |
| Add: Net Income for the Year . . . . . . . . . . . . . . . . . . . . . . . . . | $120,000 | |
| Reduction of Appropriation for Contingencies . . . . . . . . | 100,000 | 220,000 |
| Total . . . . . . . . . . . . . . . . . . . . . . . . . . . . . . . . . . . . . . . . . . . | | $978,500 |
| Deduct: Dividend declared and paid on preferred stock . . . . . | $ 60,000 | |
| Dividend declared and distributed (stock dividend on $5-par common stock, 5,000 shares distributed) . . . . . . . . . . . . . . . . . . . . . . . . . . . . . . . | 95,000 | (155,000) |
| Balance, Dec. 31, 1998 . . . . . . . . . . . . . . . . . . . . . . . . . . . . . . . . . . . . | | $823,500 |

*(Continued)*

† The numbers in the margin refer to the Learning Objectives.

| Retained Earnings Appropriated for Contingencies: | |
|---|---|
| Balance, Jan. 1, 1998 | $250,000 |
| Add: (none) | –0– |
| Deduct: Appropriation Removed during 1998 | (100,000) |
| Balance, Dec. 31, 1998 | $150,000 |

**Required:**

Examine Kingery's statement of retained earnings for 1998 and prepare in general journal form all the entries that affected the Retained Earnings account during the year. Dates may be omitted from your entries. (Prepare both declaration and distribution entries for any dividends.)

▶ *(Check Figure: Seven journal entries are required.)*

5 **Problem B3:** Recording Cash and Stock Dividends

Stow Corp. had the following stock outstanding on Dec. 31, 1998:

| | |
|---|---|
| 10% Preferred Stock ($40-par, 10,000 shares authorized, issued, and outstanding) | $ 400,000 |
| Common Stock ($10-par, 500,000 shares authorized, 100,000 shares issued and outstanding) | 1,000,000 |

Stow has traditionally paid the preferred dividend in equal quarterly installments. Common dividends have followed an irregular pattern.

Stow's board of directors took the following dividend actions during 1998:

Mar. 1  The board declared the quarterly preferred dividend of $1 per share (10% × $40 × $\frac{1}{4}$).

15  Those owning preferred stock on this date will receive the preferred dividend.

28  Stow acquired 10,000 shares of treasury stock (common) at $18 per share.

31  The quarterly cash dividend is distributed to preferred shareholders.

Aug. 15  Stow purchased an additional 5,000 shares of common stock for the treasury. Stow paid $17 per share.

Dec. 1  Since Stow has been having cash flow problems, the board declared no dividends in the second and third quarters. The board voted on Dec. 1 to declare the remaining preferred dividends for the second, third, and fourth quarters of the year.

Dec. 2  The board declared a 16% stock dividend on common stock. The market price per common share was $15 on Dec. 2.

15  Preferred and common stockholders of record on this day will receive dividends.

30  The common stock dividend was distributed. The market price of common stock was $18 per share on Dec. 30.

31  The cash was distributed to preferred stockholders.

**Required:**

Prepare general journal entries to record the transactions and events listed above. If no entry is needed on a particular date, write, "No entry."

▶ *(Check Figure: Dec. 2 debit to Retained Earnings = $204,000)*

**5 6 7**    **Problem B4:** Recording Dividends and Stock Splits and Preparing a Stockholders' Equity Section

The stockholders' equity section of Hamilton, Inc.'s, balance sheet on Dec. 31, 1997, appears below:

---

### HAMILTON, INC.
### Partial Balance Sheet
### December 31, 1997

#### Stockholders' Equity

Paid-In Capital:
Common Stock [$15-par, 500,000 shares authorized, 250,000 shares
   issued, 245,000 shares outstanding (5,000 shares in treasury)]. . . . . .  $3,750,000
Additional Paid-In Capital:
  Paid-In Capital in Excess of Par. . . . . . . . . . . . . . . . . . $1,875,000
  Paid-In Capital from Treasury Stock. . . . . . . . . . . . . . . _____50,000_    1,925,000
    Total Paid-In Capital . . . . . . . . . . . . . . . . . . . . . . . . . . . . . . . .    $5,675,000
Earned Capital:
Retained Earnings Unappropriated . . . . . . . . . . . . . . . . . . . . . . . . . . .    _3,550,000_
    Total. . . . . . . . . . . . . . . . . . . . . . . . . . . . . . . . . . . . . . . . . . . . . . .    $9,225,000
Less: Treasury Stock (5,000 shares), at Cost . . . . . . . . . . . . . . . . . . . .    (150,000)

Total Stockholders' Equity . . . . . . . . . . . . . . . . . . . . . . . . . . . . . . . . . .    $9,075,000

---

The following events took place during 1998:

a. During March, the Hamilton board of directors voted to appropriate $100,000 for future plant expansion.
b. During June, a property dividend was declared and distributed. Xenia Corp. stock, which Hamilton had owned as an investment, was distributed to the Hamilton stockholders. The per-share book value and market value of the Xenia stock on the date of declaration were $4 and $4.50, respectively. Two shares of Xenia stock will be distributed for each share of Hamilton stock owned.
c. During August, a 3-for-1 stock split was implemented.
d. Income for the year, including all effects of the transactions and events listed above, was $460,000.

**Required:**

Prepare Hamilton's stockholders' equity section on Dec. 31, 1998, after incorporating the information in (a) through (d) above. Support your solution by showing the calculations indicating how each amount was derived.

▶ *(Check Figure: Total stockholders' equity = $7,330,000)*

**7**    **Problem B5:** Preparing a Comprehensive Stockholders' Equity Section

The accounts listed below were taken from the general ledger of the Ripley, Inc., on Sept. 30, 1998. Each account has a normal balance.

| | | | |
|---|---|---|---|
| 5% Preferred Stock . . . . . . . | $ 400,000 | Paid-In Capital in Excess | |
| 5% Preferred Stock | | of Par: Common . . . . . . . . . | $6,120,000 |
|   Subscribed . . . . . . . . . . . . . | 20,000 | Paid-In Capital from Treasury | |
| Paid-In Capital in Excess | |   Stock. . . . . . . . . . . . . . . . . . | 100,000 |
|   of Par: Preferred. . . . . . . . | 650,000 | Donated Capital . . . . . . . . . . | 150,000 |
| Common Stock. . . . . . . . . . | 2,500,000 | Retained Earnings: | |
| Common Stock Subscribed. | 160,000 |   Unappropriated. . . . . . . . . | 8,840,000 |
| Common Stock Dividend | | Retained Earnings | |
|   Distributable . . . . . . . . . . . | 133,000 |   Appropriated for | |
| Treasury Stock: Preferred | |   Contingencies. . . . . . . . . . | 300,000 |
|   (500 shares) . . . . . . . . . . . | 190,000 | | |

**Additional Information:**

a. Preferred stock has a par value of $100 per share. Ripley was authorized to issue 10,000 shares. The preferred stock is cumulative and nonparticipating.

b. Common stock has a par value of $5 per share. Ripley was authorized to issue 2,000,000 shares.

**Required:**

Prepare the stockholders' equity section of Ripley, Inc.'s, Sept. 30, 1998, balance sheet. Include all disclosures needed for fair presentation. (*Hint:* Use the par values of preferred and common stock to calculate the number of shares issued and outstanding.)

▶ *(Check Figure: Total stockholders' equity = $19,183,000)*

2 5 **Problem B6:** Recording Entries in T-Accounts and Preparing Stockholders' Equity Section

Oakwood Enterprises, Inc., has the following stockholders' equity on Apr. 30, 1997:

| | |
|---|---:|
| 5% Preferred Stock ($50-par, 5,000 shares authorized, 2,000 shares issued and outstanding) | $ 100,000 |
| Common Stock ($10-par, 100,000 shares authorized, 30,000 shares issued and outstanding) | 300,000 |
| Paid-In Capital in Excess of Par: Preferred | 40,000 |
| Paid-In Capital in Excess of Par: Common | 305,000 |
| Retained Earnings: Unappropriated | 355,000 |
| Total Stockholders' Equity | $1,100,000 |

The following transactions occurred during the following fiscal year:

| | | |
|---|---|---|
| July | 8 | Purchased 500 shares of common stock for the treasury, $11,500. |
| Sept. | 21 | Declared a cash dividend of $1 per share to common stockholders of record on Oct. 15. |
| Nov. | 1 | Paid the cash dividend. |
| | 26 | Sold 10,000 shares of common stock on subscription. The subscription price was $25 per share. A 30% down payment was received. |
| Dec. | 15 | Declared a 5% cash dividend on preferred stock. |
| | 21 | Sold the treasury stock for $28 per share. (The stock was originally issued for $17 per share.) |
| | 31 | Paid the preferred cash dividend. |
| Jan. | 26 | Collected half of the remaining balance on the stock subscriptions. |
| Feb. | 4 | Appropriated $150,000 of retained earnings for plant expansion. |
| Feb. | 26 | Collected the balance due on the stock subscriptions and issued the shares. |
| Mar. | 3 | Issued 10,000 shares of common stock with a market value of $31 per share in exchange for a piece of land. No objective market price is available for the land. |
| | 14 | Declared a 10% common stock dividend distributable on July 1 to stockholders of record on June 15. The market price of the common stock on Mar. 14 was $32 per share. |
| Apr. | 15 | Received a donation of a building which will be moved to the land acquired on Mar. 3. The building was valued at $42,000. |
| | 30 | Net income for the year was calculated to be $168,500. |

**Required:**

1. Set up the following stockholders' equity T-accounts:

   > 5% Preferred Stock
   > Common Stock
   > Paid-In Capital in Excess of Par: Common
   > Paid-In Capital in Excess of Par: Preferred
   > Common Stock Subscribed
   > Common Stock Dividend Distributable
   > Donated Capital
   > Paid-In Capital from Treasury Stock
   > Retained Earnings: Unappropriated
   > Retained Earnings: Appropriated for Plant Expansion
   > Treasury Stock

2. Enter the beginning balance in 5% Preferred Stock, Common Stock, Paid-In Capital in Excess of Par: Common, Paid-In Capital in Excess of Par: Preferred, and Retained Earnings: Unappropriated.

3. Enter the transactions for the year in the appropriate T-accounts. (You may wish to set up the asset and liability accounts in addition to the stockholders' equity accounts listed above.) Identify each debit and credit by placing the date of the transaction next to the amount.

4. Prepare the stockholders' equity section of Oakwood's balance sheet on Apr. 30, 1998.

▶ *(Check Figure: Total stockholders' equity, Apr. 30, 1998 = $1,838,500)*

---

14  **Problem B7:** Preparing a Complex Income Statement

After preparing all adjusting entries, Wadsworth Corp. has the following temporary accounts in its general ledger on Aug. 31, 1998:

| | |
|---|---:|
| Accounts with credit balances: | |
| Sales . . . . . . . . . . . . . . . . . . . . . . . . . . . . . . . . . . . . . . . . . . . . . . . . . . | $894,000 |
| Interest Income . . . . . . . . . . . . . . . . . . . . . . . . . . . . . . . . . . . . . . . . . | 25,000 |
| Gain on Sale of Machinery . . . . . . . . . . . . . . . . . . . . . . . . . . . . . . . . | 6,400 |
| Cumulative Adjustment due to Change in Accounting Principle | |
|   (net of income taxes of $42,000) . . . . . . . . . . . . . . . . . . . . . . . . . | 81,600 |
| Accounts with debit balances: | |
| Cost of Goods Sold Expense . . . . . . . . . . . . . . . . . . . . . . . . . . . . . . . | $256,000 |
| Salaries Expense . . . . . . . . . . . . . . . . . . . . . . . . . . . . . . . . . . . . . . . . | 76,000 |
| Utilities Expense . . . . . . . . . . . . . . . . . . . . . . . . . . . . . . . . . . . . . . . . | 11,200 |
| Depreciation Expense. . . . . . . . . . . . . . . . . . . . . . . . . . . . . . . . . . . . . | 46,900 |
| Loss from Sale of Land. . . . . . . . . . . . . . . . . . . . . . . . . . . . . . . . . . . . | 17,900 |
| Advertising Expense . . . . . . . . . . . . . . . . . . . . . . . . . . . . . . . . . . . . . | 88,300 |
| Interest Expense . . . . . . . . . . . . . . . . . . . . . . . . . . . . . . . . . . . . . . . . | 67,600 |
| Provision for Income Taxes ($98,500 are currently payable) . . . . . . . . . . | 122,900 |
| Loss from Discontinued Operations (net of applicable tax savings | |
|   of $22,700) . . . . . . . . . . . . . . . . . . . . . . . . . . . . . . . . . . . . . . . . . . | 44,000 |
| Loss from Extraordinary Casualty (net of applicable tax savings | |
|   of $2,800). . . . . . . . . . . . . . . . . . . . . . . . . . . . . . . . . . . . . . . . . . . . | 5,400 |
| Sales Discounts. . . . . . . . . . . . . . . . . . . . . . . . . . . . . . . . . . . . . . . . . | 7,800 |

**Required:**

Prepare a comprehensive income statement in good form for the year ended Aug. 31, 1998, including appropriate earnings-per-share disclosures. Wadsworth Corp. had 200,000 shares of common stock outstanding (weighted average). Wadsworth has a simple capital structure.

▶ *(Check Figure: Net income = $263,000)*

**8**   **Problem B8:** Recording Estimated Income Taxes

Elgin, Inc., is a calendar-year taxpayer. Elgin estimates that the applicable income tax rate for 1998 will be 34%. The following income estimates were prepared during the year:

| Date | Estimated Total Income for the Year |
|------|-------------------------------------|
| Apr.  15 | $340,000 |
| June 15 | 360,000 |
| Sept. 15 | 360,000 |
| Dec.  15 | 400,000 |
| Dec.  31 | 409,000 |

**Required:**

Prepare general journal entries to record Elgin's estimated income tax payments on Apr. 15, June 15, Sept. 15, and Dec. 15, and the entry to record the tax adjustment on Dec. 31.

▶ *(Check Figure: Dec. 31 debit to Provision for Income Taxes = $3,060)*

**13**   **Problem B9:** Calculating Earnings Performance Ratios

The following financial data have been assembled for Thorne, Inc., on Dec. 31, 1998:

| | |
|---|---|
| Average total assets for 1998. . . . . . . . . . . . . . . . . . . . . . . . . . . . . . . . . . | $400,000 |
| Total stockholders' equity (average for 1998) . . . . . . . . . . . . . . . . . . . . . . | 300,000 |
| Common stock, $2 par . . . . . . . . . . . . . . . . . . . . . . . . . . . . . . . . . . . . . . . | 175,000 |
| 8% preferred stock, $50 par . . . . . . . . . . . . . . . . . . . . . . . . . . . . . . . . . . . | 75,000 |
| Net income . . . . . . . . . . . . . . . . . . . . . . . . . . . . . . . . . . . . . . . . . . . . . . . | 31,000 |
| Interest expense . . . . . . . . . . . . . . . . . . . . . . . . . . . . . . . . . . . . . . . . . . . | 3,000 |
| Provision for income taxes (40% of income before income taxes) | |
| Market price of common stock, Dec. 31, 1998 . . . . . . . . . . . . . . . . . . . . . . | 2.75 |
| Market price of preferred stock, Dec. 31, 1998 . . . . . . . . . . . . . . . . . . . . . | 60.00 |
| Common dividends were paid at the rate of $.10 per share per quarter. | |
| Preferred dividends were declared and paid. | |
| No preferred stock or common stock was issued or reacquired during 1998. | |

**Required:**

Using whatever data you need from the above list, calculate:

1. Rate of return on total assets
2. Rate of return on common stockholders' equity
3. Earnings per common share
4. Dividend yield rate

▶ *(Check figure: Dividend yield rate = 14.5%)*

## DECISION PROBLEM

 The chairman of the board of directors of Lakewood Corp. is concerned about the possible effects of some upcoming board decisions on the corporation's balance sheet. The chairman has asked you to prepare an analysis of a number of proposed transactions to determine how each will affect the major balance sheet categories.

**Required:**

1. For each of the possible independent (unrelated) board decisions listed below, enter the dollar effect in each column of your analysis sheet. Show increases by placing a plus (+) in front of the amount, decreases by placing a minus (−) in front of the amount, and no effect by placing a zero (0) in the column. Suggested headings for your analysis sheet are as follows:

| Description | Total Assets | Total Liabilities | Total Common Stock | Total Additional Paid-In Capital | Total Retained Earnings | Total Stockholders' Equity |
|---|---|---|---|---|---|---|
| *Example:* Declare a cash dividend of $20,000 | −0− | + $20,000 | −0− | −0− | − $20,000 | − $20,000 |

   a. Sell 5,000 shares of $5-par common stock for $8 per share.
   b. Sell 500 shares of $5-par common stock on subscription for $12 per share. A one-third down payment would be received.
   c. Declare a 10% stock dividend. 100,000 shares of $5-par common stock are outstanding. The market price of the stock is $11 per share.
   d. Pay a $10,000 cash dividend that was declared last year.
   e. Collect $500 due on a common stock subscription and issue common stock with a par value of $2,500.
   f. Distribute 30,000 shares of $5-par common stock in payment of a stock dividend. (The 30% dividend had been declared in the previous year, when the market value of the stock was $12.50 per share.)
   g. Implement a 2-for-1 stock split. Before the split, 115,500 shares of $5-par common stock were outstanding.
   h. Acquire 5,000 shares of Lakewood's own $5-par common stock for $11.50 per share.
   i. Appropriate $50,000 of retained earnings for plant expansion.
   j. Correct a $68,000 error which was made in a prior year. An entry to record sales had erroneously credited Donated Capital. (Cash was correctly debited.)

2. The board of directors wants to increase the amount of paid-in capital without diluting the individual stockholders' claim against the business. Which of the possible decisions listed above would you recommend to accomplish this objective?

## ETHICS CASE

Gertrude Rogers and Ernest Flood each own 5,000 shares of common stock in Gulf Cable, Inc., a company that has the franchise to provide cable television service to several Ohio counties. Gulf's remaining stock is divided among approximately 50 other individuals, none of whom owns more than 1,500 shares. Since Gulf is owned by so few individuals, the closely held company's stock is not traded on the stock exchanges or over-the-counter.

Gert and Ernie formed Gulf Cable 20 years ago, and they continue to control the board of directors. Gert is president and CEO, while Ernie is the chief financial officer. The company has been profitable over the years, partially because it is in a growth industry but largely due to the efforts and management skills of Gert and Ernie.

On Dec. 31, 1997, the common stock has a book value of $25 per share. No market value is available, since the stock is not traded. Industry analysts agree that triple the book value would be a conservative estimate of the actual market value.

On Jan. 3, 1998, Gert and Ernie propose to consolidate their control over the company by having the board of directors declare a 2,500-for-1 reverse stock split; that is, for every 2,500 shares of Gulf stock owned, a stockholder would receive 1 new Gulf share. Shareholders who owned less than 2,500 shares would receive $25 per share for their old stock and would, in effect, be bought out by the corporation. The corporation's attorney assures the board that the action is perfectly legal in every respect.

By June 30, 1998, the reverse split has been completed. Gert and Ernie each now own 2 shares of the corporation; these four shares represent 100% of the common stock.

**Required:**

1. In your opinion, did Gert and Ernie act in an ethical manner in acquiring all the stock in Gulf? Give reasons for your opinion.
2. What arguments would you expect the stockholders to make against the reverse split?
3. How would you expect Gert and Ernie to defend their actions?

## OBJECTIVE ASSIGNMENT ANSWERS

**True/False**

1. F  2. F  3. F  4. T  5. T

**Multiple Choice**

1. c  2. b  3. d  4. c  5. b
6. a  7. b  8. d  9. b  10. d

# Corporations: Long-Term Liabilities

**LEARNING OBJECTIVES**

After studying this chapter, you should be able to do the following:

1 Evaluate the alternatives for financing on a long-term basis

2 Describe the differences between the various types of bonds

3 Record the entries associated with a bond issued at face value

4 Record the entries associated with a bond issue sold between interest payment dates

5 Use the straight-line amortization method to record the entries for a bond issue sold at a discount or at a premium

6 Determine the selling price of a bond

7 Use the effective-interest amortization method to record the entries for a bond issue sold at a discount or at a premium

8 Prepare bond amortization schedules

9 Understand the accounting for contingent liabilities

10 Record the entries associated with the capitalization of a lease

11 Describe the use of the times interest earned ratio in financial statement analysis

12 Define the key terms listed at the end of the chapter

**CHAPTER OUTLINE**  SELECTING A METHOD OF LONG-TERM FINANCING • BONDS PAYABLE • Bonds Issued at Face Value • Bonds Sold between Interest Payment Dates • Bonds Issued at a Discount • Bonds Issued at a Premium • THE PRESENT VALUE OF LONG-TERM LIABILITIES • The Effective-Interest Method of Amortizing Bond Discounts and Premiums • Financial Statement Disclosure of Bonds Payable • CONTINGENT LIABILITIES • LONG-TERM LEASES • FINANCIAL STATEMENT ANALYSIS • Times Interest Earned

Business entities usually finance their normal, recurring operations by incurring current liabilities. Purchases of inventory are made on account; wages and salaries are paid weekly, biweekly, or semimonthly; temporary drains on cash are eased by issuing short-term notes. However, some situations that require substantial cash outlays, such as the acquisition of heavy equipment or the construction of a new building, cannot be financed with current liabilities. Funds for such projects can be generated either by issuing stock or by incurring long-term liabilities.

Suppose that Scraps Pet Food Corporation wants to expand its operations by constructing a new plant that will cost $1 million. Scraps could obtain the funds by retaining cash in the business. But to accumulate $1 million, the corporation would have to severely limit the amount of dividends paid to its stockholders. An advantage of this plan is that no additional stockholders or creditors would be needed. But like many other small corporations, Scraps may not have accumulated $1 million at the time they wish to expand.

One alternative is to issue additional stock. But unless profits increase proportionately with the increase in the number of shares, the present stockholders' shares of the corporation's earnings will be less than they were before the new stock was issued.

A third possibility is to borrow the $1 million from creditors on a long-term basis. There are several forms of long-term financing. Businesses of any type—proprietorship, partnership, or corporation—may issue long-term notes or enter into long-term lease arrangements. Corporations have the additional option of issuing bonds. **Bonds** are securities issued by corporations as a way of borrowing large sums of money. More funds can usually be obtained from creditors through bonds than through long-term notes or leases. The reason for this is that long-term notes and leases are typically issued to a single investor or relatively few investors, such as a bank, a leasing company, or an insurance company. Bonds, in contrast, are sold to many investors.

If Scraps obtains the $1 million from creditors, the corporation incurs the disadvantage of having to make interest and principal repayments when due. However, it also obtains two significant advantages: Ownership of the corporation will not be spread thinner among a larger number of stockholders; and the corporation can deduct the interest on the borrowed money on the corporate tax return.

## SELECTING A METHOD OF LONG-TERM FINANCING

No single rule can be applied to determine which method of financing would be best in each situation. Many factors must be considered before one means of long-term financing is selected over the others. However, an analysis of the alternatives will help management choose the best available method for each situation.

**Learning Objective 1**

Evaluate the alternatives for financing on a long-term basis

Assume that Scraps Pet Food has 100,000 shares of common stock outstanding. We can summarize its three alternatives for obtaining the $1 million it needs as follows:

1. Use cash the company has accumulated
2. Find new investors and issue 50,000 additional shares of common stock worth $1 million
3. Obtain the money from a long-term note, lease, or bond issue requiring a 12% interest expense each year

Let's analyze these alternatives at two arbitrary levels of net income: $800,000 and $120,000, both before the interest expense and income taxes (assumed to be 34% of earnings before income taxes) have been deducted. (See Exhibit 1.)

**Exhibit 1** Alternatives for Financing Construction of a New Plant

|  | From Cash Accumulation (100,000 shares outstanding) | | From Additional Stockholders (150,000 shares outstanding) | | From Long-Term Creditors (100,000 shares outstanding) | |
|---|---|---|---|---|---|---|
| Earnings before interest and income taxes<br>Interest ($1,000,000 × 12%) | $800,000 | $120,000 | $800,000 | $120,000 | $800,000<br> | $120,000<br>120,000 |
|  |  |  |  |  | 120,000 |  |
| Earnings before income taxes<br>Income taxes at 34% | $800,000<br>272,000 | $120,000<br>40,800 | $800,000<br>272,000 | $120,000<br>40,800 | $680,000<br>231,200 | –0–<br>–0– |
| Net income | $528,000 | $ 79,200 | $528,000 | $ 79,200 | $448,800 | –0– |
| Earnings per share | $    5.28 | $    0.79 | $    3.52 | $    0.53 | $    4.49 | 0.00 |

If you were a stockholder, *and if Scraps Pet Food had $1 million in the corporate treasury,* the first alternative would be the most attractive. Why? Because using accumulated cash provides the highest projected earnings per share (EPS). Remember that earnings per share is the net income divided by the average number of common shares outstanding. At the $800,000 earnings level, EPS is $5.28, which exceeds both the $3.52 EPS projected if the $1 million is obtained from 50,000 new shares and the $4.49 EPS projected if the $1 million is obtained from long-term creditors. Also, the $0.79 EPS at the $120,000 earnings level under the first alternative exceeds the $0.53 and the zero EPS under each of the alternatives.

If, however, Scraps does not have the $1 million in cash, issuing bonds would be more attractive to the stockholders at the $800,000 earnings level (EPS $4.49) than issuing stock (EPS 3.52). But if the earnings level falls to $120,000, issuing stock would be more attractive ($.53 EPS for stock vs. zero EPS for bonds).

Even assuming that the company has the $1 million cash, which is not always the case, financing a construction from internally generated funds is not always the best alternative. In that event, corporations must instead issue stock or bonds or lease the needed building or equipment. Here we will turn our attention first to bonds and then to leases.

## BONDS PAYABLE

Once they decide to obtain financing by issuing bonds, the corporate managers must decide what *type* of bonds to issue. Most corporations do not have the expertise to market their own securities. They usually work with an **investment banker,** or **underwriter,** who helps the corporation develop the bonds into a marketable product as it decides on the type of bonds to issue, the interest rate the bonds should carry, the maturity date of the bonds, and other important matters. The corporation usually sells the bonds to the underwriter or to several underwriters, who in turn sell the bonds to the public at a somewhat higher price. Rather than buying the bonds for resale, the underwriter may contract to sell the bonds on a commission basis. The corporation may also sell the bonds directly to a large institution such as an insurance company.

The corporation enters into a contract with an agent, called the **trustee,** who represents the bondholders. The trustee is responsible to the bondholders for seeing that the corporation meets the various requirements of the bond contract. The contract is referred to as a **bond indenture** (also called a **deed of trust** or **trust indenture**). The trustee is typically a large bank.

Learning Objective **2**

Describe the differences between the various types of bonds

In order to make its bond issue widely affordable so that it can generate large sums of money, a corporation commonly issues bond certificates in units valued at $1,000 each. The amount of each bond, $1,000, is called its **face value** or **par value.** The bond indenture provides for the payment of periodic interest on the face value of the bond. Most bonds pay interest on a semiannual basis. For trading purposes, prices of bonds are expressed per $1,000 of face value. *Priced at 98* means that a $1,000 bond will sell for 98% of $1,000, or $980. Bonds that sell for less than face value are said to be sold at a **discount.** If a $1,000 bond is quoted at $102\frac{1}{4}$, it will sell for $102\frac{1}{4}$% of $1,000, or $1,022.50. Bonds that sell for more than face value are said to be sold at a **premium.** (Discounts and premiums will be covered shortly.) If a bond is quoted at 100, it will sell at par or face value.

Bonds may be either *secured* or *unsecured.* **Secured bonds** provide the bondholder with a claim on a specified asset, typically equipment or buildings owned by the corporation, in the event that the corporation does not fulfill its responsibilities under the terms of the bond indenture. **Unsecured bonds** are issued on the general credit rating of the issuing corporation and are known as **debenture bonds.** Only the financially strongest corporations can successfully issue bonds on the basis of their name alone.

Bonds may also be either *term* or *serial.* **Term bonds** are those in which the entire bond issue matures and the face value must be paid to the bondholders on a specified date in the future, known as the *maturity date.* **Serial bonds** mature at various dates over the length of the bond contract. For example, a $50 million serial bond issue dated 1998 might provide for $10 million of bonds to mature commencing in 2008 and each year thereafter through 2012.

Finally, bonds may be either *callable* or *convertible.* **Callable bonds** provide the corporation with the right to redeem the bonds prior to their maturity date. The bond indenture usually provides that the issuing corporation pay a penalty when the bonds are called. This penalty is in the form of a **call price,** which is slightly higher than the face value. **Convertible bonds** give the bondholders the right to exchange their bonds for an ownership interest (stock) in the corporation.

### Bonds Issued at Face Value

Learning Objective 3

Record the entries associated with a bond issued at face value

After a corporation has decided on the type of bond to issue, the amount, the interest rate, the interest payment dates, and the maturity date, then the stockholders of the corporation must approve the issue. Next, the trust indenture is prepared and the bonds are printed and issued.

Assume that the Aztec Motor Corporation issues $7 million of 12%, 5-year bonds on May 1, 1998, at face value with interest payable semiannually on Nov. 1 and May 1. The bonds are said to be dated and issued on May 1, 1998. The entry[1] to record the issuance of the bonds would be:

| 1998 | | | |
|------|------|-----------|-----------|
| May 1 | Cash ..................................... | 7,000,000 | |
| | Bonds Payable.......................... | | 7,000,000 |
| | To record the sale of $7,000,000 of 12%, 5-year bonds at face value. | | |

On Nov. 1, the first semiannual interest payment is due. This will amount to $420,000 computed as follows: $7,000,000 \times 12\% \times \frac{6}{12} = \$420,000$. The entry to record the interest payment is:

[1] All our journal entries in the examples are in general journal form, even though the entry may actually be made in a special journal. This will make illustrations much easier because we won't have to construct special journals each time we make an entry.

| 1998 | | | |
|---|---|---|---|
| Nov. 1 | Bond Interest Expense........................ | 420,000 | |
| | Cash .................................... | | 420,000 |
| | To record payment of semiannual interest on bonds payable. | | |

At the end of the accounting period, Dec. 31, the interest expense applicable between Nov. 2 and Dec. 31, 1998, must be accrued and the liability for interest payable must be recorded. This entry would be recorded as follows:

| 1998 | | | |
|---|---|---|---|
| Dec. 31 | Bond Interest Expense........................ | 140,000 | |
| | Bond Interest Payable.................... | | 140,000 |
| | To record accrued interest on bonds payable. Interest expense computed as follows: $7,000,000 \times 12\% \times \frac{2}{12}$. | | |

Assuming that the business entity does not use reversing entries, the journal entry to record the May 1, 1999, interest payment would be:

| 1999 | | | |
|---|---|---|---|
| May 1 | Bond Interest Payable........................ | 140,000 | |
| | Bond Interest Expense ........................ | 280,000 | |
| | Cash.................................... | | 420,000 |
| | To record payment of semiannual interest on bonds payable. Interest expense computed as follows: $7,000,000 \times 12\% \times \frac{4}{12}$. | | |

Throughout the life of the bonds, the entries made on Nov. 1, Dec. 31, and May 1 will be repeated year after year until May 1, 2003, when the bonds are finally retired by the following entry:

| 2003 | | | |
|---|---|---|---|
| May 1 | Bonds Payable ............................. | 7,000,000 | |
| | Cash.................................... | | 7,000,000 |
| | To record payment of bonds at maturity. | | |

## Bonds Sold between Interest Payment Dates

Learning Objective 4

Record the entries associated with a bond issue sold between interest payment dates

The bond indenture requires that bond interest payments be paid on specified dates that are printed on the bond certificates. Bonds may be sold, however, on any date. Thus, it is highly likely that bonds will be sold on a date other than a bond interest payment date. When this occurs, it is necessary to add to the selling price of the bond the interest that has accrued on it. The reason for doing so is that when the first interest payment is made, the bondholders will receive 6 months' interest. The bond contract requires that interest be paid on a specified date every 6 months.

If the new bond purchasers pay the corporation a price that, in effect, includes 2 months' accrued interest when the bonds are issued, and receive 6 months' interest 4 months later, they would, in effect, have received interest for only 4 months.

To illustrate, assume that the Aztec Motor Corporation bonds were issued on July 1, 1998, rather than on May 1, when the bonds were dated. The investors must pay, in addition to the $7 million for the bonds, $140,000 for the 2 months' accrued interest ($7,000,000 \times .12 \times \frac{2}{12}$) which then will be returned on the next interest payment date. The entry to record the sale of the bonds on July 1 would be:

```
1998
July 1  Cash ....................................... 7,140,000
            Bond Interest Payable.....................          140,000
            Bonds Payable............................        7,000,000
        To record the sale of $7,000,000 of 12%, 5-year
        bonds at par plus 2 months' accrued interest.
```

Aztec is obligated, by the terms of the bond indenture (which specifies a 12% interest rate), to make a semiannual interest payment on Nov. 1 in the amount of $420,000—no more and no less. When the $420,000 interest payment is received by the bondholders, they will be receiving 6 months' interest. However, the bondholders who bought bonds in July will actually receive the equivalent of only 4 months' interest because they paid Aztec for 2 months' interest when they purchased the bonds on July 1. Aztec's entry to record the interest payment on Nov. 1 is presented below. Notice that the entry eliminates the Bond Interest Payable established from the July 1 entry and records interest expense for only 4 months.

```
1998
Nov. 1  Bond Interest Payable .......................  140,000
        Bond Interest Expense........................  280,000
            Cash ....................................            420,000
        To record payment of semiannual interest on bonds
        payable.
```

Aztec could have recorded the entry made on July 1 in a slightly different manner. Rather than crediting the Bond Interest Payable account for the accrued interest, the company could have credited the Bond Interest Expense account *in anticipation* of the Nov. 1 debit from the semiannual interest payment. The July 1 entry would then appear as follows:

```
1998
July 1  Cash ....................................... 7,140,000
            Bond Interest Expense ...................          140,000
            Bonds Payable............................        7,000,000
        To record the sale of $7,000,000 of 12%, 5-year
        bonds at par plus 2 months' accrued interest.
```

The Nov. 1 entry is then recorded simply as follows:

```
1998
Nov. 1  Bond Interest Expense........................  420,000
            Cash ....................................            420,000
        To record payment of semiannual interest on bonds
        payable.
```

The result is that after the Nov. 1 entry is made, the balance in Bond Interest Expense is $280,000, reflecting 4 months' interest expense, as can be seen in the following account. This procedure has the same effect as using a reversing entry.

### BOND INTEREST EXPENSE

| 1998 | | 1998 | |
|------|------|------|------|
| Nov. 1 | $420,000 | July 1 | $140,000 |
| Bal. | $280,000 | | |

**ASK YOURSELF** ▶

1. Describe several different ways for a corporation to obtain funds to finance major expenditures.
2. Discuss the roles of investment bankers and trustees in the issuing of corporate bonds.
3. List and describe several different types of bonds.
4. Explain the accounting for bonds issued at face value.
5. Explain the accounting for bonds sold between interest payment dates.

### Bonds Issued at a Discount

Learning Objective 5

Use the straight-line amortization method to record the entries for a bond issue sold at a discount or at a premium

More often than not, bonds are sold at a price that differs from their face value. As stated earlier, bonds sold at a price greater than their face value are said to be sold at a *premium,* and bonds sold at a price lower than their face value are said to be sold at a *discount.*

You may ask why bonds are sold at a price that is less—or more—than their face value. When bonds are sold, an interest rate is stated in the bond indenture and on the face of the bond certificates; this is called the **nominal interest rate.** Aztec Motor Corporation *must* pay 12% interest on the bonds. But suppose that, at the time Aztec tries to sell its bonds, other companies are willing to pay 14% on their bonds. Nobody would want to buy Aztec's bonds. So Aztec must do something to make its bonds attractive to investors. It can't change the 12% interest rate specified by the bond indenture, but it can change the *price* of the bonds. Aztec will sell the bonds at a price that will allow investors to earn a 14% return on their investment. By selling the Aztec bonds at $6,508,349 and paying 12% interest a year on the full $7 million for 5 years, Aztec will give the investor a 14% return. (The section on present value later in this chapter will discuss how these calculations are done.) In short, the reason bonds are sold at a discount is to adjust the nominal interest rate—which is too low—to the *market interest rate*—the rate investors are willing to accept.

Assume that the $7 million Aztec bonds issued on and dated May 1, 1998, were sold for $6,508,349. This $491,651 difference between the face value and the selling price is called the *discount.* Generally accepted accounting principles require that the liability account Bonds Payable be recorded at the face value, $7 million. A contra-liability account, Discount on Bonds Payable, must then be established to adjust the face value of the bonds to the amount of cash received from selling the bonds. We would record the general journal entry on May 1, 1998, when the bonds are issued, as follows:

| | | | |
|---|---|---|---|
| 1998 | | | |
| May 1 | Cash ...................................... | 6,508,349 | |
| | Discount on Bonds Payable .................... | 491,651 | |
| | Bonds Payable........................... | | 7,000,000 |
| | To record the sale of $7,000,000 of 12%, 5-year bonds, maturing May 1, 2000. | | |

If a balance sheet were prepared on this date, the information pertaining to the bonds would be presented in the long-term liabilities section like this:

| | | |
|---|---|---|
| Long-Term Liabilities: | | |
| 12% Bonds Payable Due May 1, 2000 .............. | $7,000,000 | |
| Less: Discount on Bonds Payable .................. | 491,651 | $6,508,349 |

The $6,508,349, which represents the difference between the $7 million face value and the $491,651 discount, is called the **carrying value** of the bonds. Aztec owes the bondholders $7 million, not today, but on May 1, 2003. That is why the liability is valued at $6,508,349—an approximation of what the liability is worth today. In the section on present value and long-term liabilities you will see how to determine the value of the liability today.

Now, move ahead to the maturity date, May 1, 2003, when the bonds are retired—the face value of the bonds is paid to the creditors and the bonds are canceled. On that date Aztec Corporation will issue a check in the amount of $7 million and record this entry:

```
2003
May 1  Bonds Payable ............................. 7,000,000
           Cash...................................              7,000,000
       To record the retirement of $7,000,000 of 12%,
       5-year bonds due this date.
```

What about the Discount on Bonds Payable account? If the bonds no longer exist, neither should the discount! The Discount on Bonds Payable account must be credited to eliminate its debit balance. But when the credit is made, what account is debited? Three possibilities exist.

First, on May 1, 2003, Aztec could record a loss on the retirement of the bonds, because it has to pay $7 million to retire the bonds but received only $6,508,349 on May 1, 1998, when the money was borrowed. The loss might also be called a fee paid for the use of money, or interest expense. But was this fee incurred all on one date—May 1, 2003?

Second, on the date the bonds were issued—May 1, 1998—Aztec could make a credit to Discount on Bonds Payable and a debit to Loss on the Retirement of Bonds for the $491,651. Again, what the corporation is doing is paying for the use of money, and that's interest expense. But was the entire $491,651 expense incurred on May 1, 1998?

Logically, the $491,651 would have been incurred, not all at once, but over the period of time Aztec Motor Corporation used the money—5 years, or 60 months. And that's the third alternative: Allocate the discount over the life of the bonds—in this case, $8,194 per month ($491,651 ÷ 60). This process is called **amortization.**

The bond discount doesn't have to be amortized every month; it can be amortized on bond interest payment dates and on the year-end closing dates. That's what Aztec will do. On the first bond interest payment date—Nov. 1, 1998—Aztec will record the interest expense as:

The sum of the cash paid
($7,000,000 × 12% × $\frac{6}{12}$) ................. $420,000
Plus 6 months' amortization of the discount
($491,651 × $\frac{6}{60}$) ......................... 49,165

Equals a total interest expense for the
6 months............................... $469,165

The general journal entry would be:

```
1998
Nov. 1  Bond Interest Expense........................ 469,165
            Discount on Bonds Payable ................          49,165
            Cash .....................................          420,000
        To record payment of semiannual interest on bonds
        and amortization of bond discount.
```

The Dec. 31 adjusting entry required to accrue the bond interest payable and the entry to amortize the discount would be recorded like this:

| 1998 | | | |
|---|---|---|---|
| Dec. 31 | Bond Interest Expense...................... | 140,000 | |
| |     Bond Interest Payable.................... | | 140,000 |
| | To record accrual of bond interest payable ($7,000,000 $\times$ 12% $\times \frac{2}{12}$). | | |
| 31 | Bond Interest Expense...................... | 16,388 | |
| |     Discount on Bonds Payable .............. | | 16,388 |
| | To record the amortization of the bond discount ($491,651 $\times \frac{2}{60}$). | | |

These two entries are usually combined, as seen below:

| 1998 | | | |
|---|---|---|---|
| Dec. 31 | Bond Interest Expense...................... | 156,388 | |
| |     Discount on Bonds Payable .............. | | 16,388 |
| |     Bond Interest Payable.................... | | 140,000 |
| | To record accrual of bond interest payable and amortization of bond discount. | | |

The Dec. 31, 1998, balance sheet would show the carrying value of the bond as follows:

| Long-Term Liabilities: | | |
|---|---|---|
| 12% Bonds Payable Due May 1, 2003 ............... | $7,000,000 | |
| Less: Discount on Bonds Payable .................. | 426,098 | $6,573,902 |

The balance in the discount account has been reduced to $426,098 ($491,651—$49,165—$16,388) by the amortization process.

On May 1, 1999, Aztec will make the semiannual interest payment of $420,000 and amortize 4 months' discount, Jan. 1 to Apr. 30. The following entry will be used to record this payment:

| 1999 | | | |
|---|---|---|---|
| May 1 | Bond Interest Payable....................... | 140,000 | |
| | Bond Interest Expense ...................... | 312,777 | |
| |     Discount on Bonds Payable ................ | | 32,777 |
| |     Cash.................................... | | 420,000 |
| | To record payment of semiannual interest on bonds and amortization of bond discount ($491,651 $\times \frac{4}{60}$). | | |

Notice that Bond Interest Payable has been debited for $140,000, thus eliminating the liability that was accrued on Dec. 31, 1998.

Over the remaining life of the bonds, entries will be made on May 1 and Nov. 1 identical to the ones illustrated for May 1 and Nov. 1, 1998. And on Dec. 31 of each year an accrual entry will be made identical to the one made on Dec. 31, 1998.

## Bonds Issued at a Premium

Bonds may be sold at a *premium*—a price that exceeds face value—when the market interest rate is less than the nominal interest rate specified in the bond contract.

Assume that the Aztec bonds, with a face value of $7 million, sell at a premium for $7,540,522 on May 1, 1998, the date of issue. A premium of $540,522 results, because the market rate of interest was less than the nominal rate of 12%. We would record the following entry:

| 1998 | | | |
|---|---|---|---|
| May 1 | Cash ...................................... | 7,540,522 | |
| | Premium on Bonds Payable ................. | | 540,522 |
| | Bonds Payable............................. | | 7,000,000 |
| | To record the sale of $7,000,000 of 12%, 5-year bonds, maturing May 1, 2000. | | |

On this date the information relating to the bonds would be presented in the long-term liabilities section of the balance sheet as follows:

| Long-Term Liabilities: | | |
|---|---|---|
| 12% Bonds Payable Due May 1, 2000 .............. | $7,000,000 | |
| Plus: Premium on Bonds Payable .................. | 540,522 | $7,540,522 |

The carrying value of the bond, $7,540,522, is the sum of the $7,000,000 face value and the $540,522 premium.

The premium will have to be amortized over the period of time the bonds are outstanding, just as was done with the discount. Thus, the Nov. 1, 1998, entries for bond interest payment and premium amortization would be recorded as follows:

| 1998 | | | |
|---|---|---|---|
| Nov. 1 | Bond Interest Expense........................ | 420,000 | |
| | Cash .................................... | | 420,000 |
| | To record payment of semiannual interest on bonds ($7,000,000 × 12% × $\frac{6}{12}$). | | |
| 1 | Premium on Bonds Payable ................... | 54,052 | |
| | Bond Interest Expense .................... | | 54,052 |
| | To record the amortization of bond premium ($540,522 × $\frac{6}{60}$). | | |

More commonly, one entry would be made, as seen below:

| 1998 | | | |
|---|---|---|---|
| Nov. 1 | Bond Interest Expense........................ | 365,948 | |
| | Premium on Bonds Payable ................... | 54,052 | |
| | Cash .................................... | | 420,000 |
| | To record payment of semiannual interest on bonds ($7,000,000 × 12% × $\frac{6}{12}$) and amortization of bond premium ($540,522 × $\frac{6}{60}$). | | |

This time the interest expense is the difference between the cash paid, $420,000, and the $54,052 amortization of the premium ($540,522 × $\frac{6}{60}$). With the discount, the interest expense was the sum of the cash and the amortization of the discount. The premium amortization *decreases* the interest expense, while the discount amortization *increases* the interest expense.

On Dec. 31, 1998, the bond interest payable must be accrued and the premium must be amortized. The two entries to accomplish this would be recorded as follows:

| 1998 | | | |
|---|---|---|---|
| Dec. 31 | Bond Interest Expense...................... | 140,000 | |
| |     Bond Interest Payable.................... | | 140,000 |
| | To record accrual of bond interest payable ($7,000,000 $\times$ 12% $\times \frac{2}{12}$). | | |
| 31 | Premium on Bonds Payable ................. | 18,017 | |
| |     Bond Interest Expense ................... | | 18,017 |
| | To record amortization of bond premium ($540,522 $\times \frac{2}{60}$). | | |

The combined entry would be:

| 1998 | | | |
|---|---|---|---|
| Dec. 31 | Bond Interest Expense...................... | 121,983 | |
| | Premium on Bonds Payable ................. | 18,017 | |
| |     Bond Interest Payable.................... | | 140,000 |
| | To record accrual of bond interest payable and amortization of bond premium ($540,522 $\times \frac{2}{60}$). | | |

The balance sheet on Dec. 31, 1998, would reflect the value of the bond as follows:

Long-Term Liabilities:
  12% Bonds Payable Due May 1, 2003 .............. $7,000,000
  Plus: Premium on Bonds Payable .................. 468,453  $7,468,453

The Premium account balance of $540,522 on May 1, 1998, has been reduced by the amortization of $54,052 on Nov. 1, 1998, and $18,017 on Dec. 31, 1998.

The interest payment on May 1, 1999, of $420,000 and the 4-month amortization of the premium is recorded as follows:

| 1999 | | | |
|---|---|---|---|
| May 1 | Bond Interest Payable........................ | 140,000 | |
| | Bond Interest Expense ....................... | 243,965 | |
| | Premium on Bonds Payable.................... | 36,035 | |
| |     Cash.................................... | | 420,000 |
| | To record the payment of semiannual interest on bonds and amortization of bond premium ($540,522 $\times \frac{4}{60}$). | | |

The bond interest payments on each Nov. 1 and May 1 over the remaining life of the bonds will be identical to the ones made on May 1, 1999, and Nov. 1, 1998. Each year's Dec. 31 accrual entry will be identical to the one made on Dec. 31, 1998.

**ASK YOURSELF ▶**

1. Why are bonds sold at a discount or a premium?
2. What is meant by the carrying value of a bond?
3. Explain the process of bond discount amortization.
4. How are bonds presented in the long-term liabilities section of the balance sheet?

## THE PRESENT VALUE OF LONG-TERM LIABILITIES

So far in our discussion of bonds payable we have ignored a very significant factor: *Money has a time value.* That is, the passage of time affects the value of a given sum of money. The time value of money may be expressed in terms of either the present or the future. *Present value* is the amount that must be invested today, at a specific rate of interest, in order to accumulate a specified amount by a certain date in the future. *Future value* is the sum to which a given amount will grow if invested at a specific rate of interest for a stated number of periods. We will concentrate on **present value techniques**—procedures for finding the value of money today under assumed rates of interest—because present value represents the value of long-term liabilities on the current balance sheet.

A $100,000 bank deposit made today at 12% interest is worth more than a $100,000 deposit made 1 year from today. That is because the deposit made today will earn interest during that year, and the interest plus the initial deposit will exceed the $100,000 deposited 1 year from now.

A $100,000 deposit made today, to be collected 2 years hence, would accumulate interest at a rate that is effectively higher than the 12% nominal rate, thanks to *compound interest.* When interest is compounded, it is calculated on the entire amount accrued in previous periods, not just on the principal, or the original amount. To continue our example:

Year 1:  $100,000 + (12\% \times \$100,000) = \$112,000$

Year 2:  $112,000 + (12\% \times \$112,000) = \$125,440$

In contrast, if the amount at the end of the 2-year period were to be calculated at *simple interest,* it would be:

Year 1:  $100,000 + (12\% \times \$100,000) = \$112,000$

Year 2:  $112,000 + (12\% \times \$100,000) = \$124,000$

All our present-value calculations are based on the concept of compound, not simple, interest.

The present value of any amount, for any period of time, at any interest rate, can be found by multiplying the amount by the factor $1/(1 + i)^n$. The value $i$ represents the interest rate *per period.* The value $n$ is the number of periods.

In practice, accountants calculate present values by using personal computers or hand-held calculators. Present values can also be obtained from tables such as Tables 1 and 2. We can find the value of the factor $1/(1 + i)^n$ for one period at 12% by looking in Table 1 at the intersection of the $n = 1$ row and the $i = 12\%$ column. The factor is 0.892. To seven decimal places, the factor would be 0.8928751. Tables 1 and 2 have been trimmed to three decimal places to simplify your homework computations. Multiplying the seven-decimal factor 0.8928571 times $112,000 results in the present value $100,000. If we had used the 0.892 figure, we would have computed the present value as $99,904. The larger the dollar amount, the larger will be the difference between the true value and the approximate value when the three-place tables are used.

As an aid in notation for solving present value problems, we will use the lower-case letter $p$ to mean the present value of a single sum of money. The present value factor is represented by the symbol $p_{\overline{n}|i}$, which we read as *the present value of a single sum of money for* n *periods at* i *percent.*

To express the present value of $100,000 at 12% for one period, we would write:

$$p = \$100,000 p_{\overline{1}|12\%}$$

Unless you are told otherwise, you should express interest at an annual rate. Thus, when using the present value tables, you must *adjust the interest and the periods*

**Table 1** Present Value of $1

$$p_{\overline{n}|1} = \frac{1}{(1 + i)^n}$$

| $n$ \ $i$ | 1% | 2% | 3% | 4% | 5% | 6% | 7% | 8% | 9% | 10% | 12% | 14% | 15% |
|---|---|---|---|---|---|---|---|---|---|---|---|---|---|
| 1 | 0.990 | 0.980 | 0.970 | 0.961 | 0.952 | 0.943 | 0.934 | 0.925 | 0.917 | 0.909 | 0.892 | 0.877 | 0.869 |
| 2 | 0.980 | 0.961 | 0.942 | 0.924 | 0.907 | 0.889 | 0.873 | 0.857 | 0.841 | 0.826 | 0.797 | 0.769 | 0.756 |
| 3 | 0.970 | 0.942 | 0.915 | 0.888 | 0.863 | 0.839 | 0.816 | 0.793 | 0.772 | 0.751 | 0.711 | 0.675 | 0.657 |
| 4 | 0.960 | 0.923 | 0.888 | 0.854 | 0.822 | 0.792 | 0.762 | 0.735 | 0.708 | 0.683 | 0.635 | 0.592 | 0.571 |
| 5 | 0.951 | 0.905 | 0.862 | 0.821 | 0.783 | 0.747 | 0.712 | 0.680 | 0.649 | 0.620 | 0.567 | 0.519 | 0.497 |
| 6 | 0.942 | 0.887 | 0.837 | 0.790 | 0.746 | 0.704 | 0.666 | 0.630 | 0.596 | 0.564 | 0.506 | 0.455 | 0.432 |
| 7 | 0.932 | 0.870 | 0.813 | 0.759 | 0.710 | 0.665 | 0.622 | 0.583 | 0.547 | 0.513 | 0.452 | 0.399 | 0.375 |
| 8 | 0.923 | 0.853 | 0.789 | 0.730 | 0.676 | 0.627 | 0.582 | 0.540 | 0.501 | 0.466 | 0.403 | 0.350 | 0.326 |
| 9 | 0.914 | 0.836 | 0.766 | 0.702 | 0.644 | 0.591 | 0.543 | 0.500 | 0.460 | 0.424 | 0.360 | 0.307 | 0.284 |
| 10 | 0.905 | 0.820 | 0.744 | 0.675 | 0.613 | 0.558 | 0.508 | 0.463 | 0.422 | 0.385 | 0.321 | 0.269 | 0.247 |
| 11 | 0.896 | 0.804 | 0.722 | 0.649 | 0.584 | 0.526 | 0.475 | 0.428 | 0.387 | 0.350 | 0.287 | 0.236 | 0.214 |
| 12 | 0.887 | 0.788 | 0.701 | 0.624 | 0.556 | 0.496 | 0.444 | 0.397 | 0.355 | 0.318 | 0.256 | 0.207 | 0.186 |
| 13 | 0.878 | 0.773 | 0.680 | 0.600 | 0.530 | 0.468 | 0.414 | 0.367 | 0.326 | 0.289 | 0.229 | 0.182 | 0.162 |
| 14 | 0.869 | 0.757 | 0.661 | 0.577 | 0.505 | 0.442 | 0.387 | 0.340 | 0.299 | 0.263 | 0.204 | 0.159 | 0.141 |
| 15 | 0.861 | 0.743 | 0.641 | 0.555 | 0.481 | 0.417 | 0.362 | 0.315 | 0.274 | 0.239 | 0.182 | 0.140 | 0.122 |
| 16 | 0.852 | 0.728 | 0.623 | 0.533 | 0.458 | 0.393 | 0.338 | 0.291 | 0.251 | 0.217 | 0.163 | 0.122 | 0.106 |
| 17 | 0.844 | 0.714 | 0.605 | 0.513 | 0.436 | 0.371 | 0.316 | 0.270 | 0.231 | 0.197 | 0.145 | 0.107 | 0.092 |
| 18 | 0.836 | 0.700 | 0.587 | 0.493 | 0.415 | 0.350 | 0.295 | 0.250 | 0.211 | 0.179 | 0.130 | 0.094 | 0.080 |
| 19 | 0.827 | 0.686 | 0.570 | 0.474 | 0.395 | 0.330 | 0.276 | 0.231 | 0.194 | 0.163 | 0.116 | 0.082 | 0.070 |
| 20 | 0.819 | 0.672 | 0.553 | 0.456 | 0.376 | 0.311 | 0.258 | 0.214 | 0.178 | 0.148 | 0.103 | 0.072 | 0.061 |
| 21 | 0.811 | 0.659 | 0.537 | 0.438 | 0.358 | 0.294 | 0.241 | 0.198 | 0.163 | 0.135 | 0.092 | 0.063 | 0.053 |
| 22 | 0.803 | 0.646 | 0.521 | 0.421 | 0.341 | 0.277 | 0.225 | 0.183 | 0.150 | 0.122 | 0.082 | 0.055 | 0.046 |
| 23 | 0.795 | 0.634 | 0.506 | 0.405 | 0.325 | 0.261 | 0.210 | 0.170 | 0.137 | 0.111 | 0.073 | 0.049 | 0.040 |
| 24 | 0.787 | 0.621 | 0.491 | 0.390 | 0.310 | 0.246 | 0.197 | 0.157 | 0.126 | 0.101 | 0.065 | 0.043 | 0.034 |
| 25 | 0.779 | 0.609 | 0.477 | 0.375 | 0.295 | 0.232 | 0.184 | 0.146 | 0.115 | 0.092 | 0.058 | 0.037 | 0.030 |
| 26 | 0.772 | 0.597 | 0.463 | 0.360 | 0.281 | 0.219 | 0.172 | 0.135 | 0.106 | 0.083 | 0.052 | 0.033 | 0.026 |
| 27 | 0.764 | 0.585 | 0.450 | 0.346 | 0.267 | 0.207 | 0.160 | 0.125 | 0.097 | 0.076 | 0.046 | 0.029 | 0.022 |
| 28 | 0.756 | 0.574 | 0.437 | 0.333 | 0.255 | 0.195 | 0.150 | 0.115 | 0.089 | 0.069 | 0.041 | 0.025 | 0.019 |
| 29 | 0.749 | 0.563 | 0.424 | 0.320 | 0.242 | 0.184 | 0.140 | 0.107 | 0.082 | 0.063 | 0.037 | 0.022 | 0.017 |
| 30 | 0.741 | 0.552 | 0.411 | 0.308 | 0.231 | 0.174 | 0.131 | 0.099 | 0.075 | 0.057 | 0.033 | 0.019 | 0.015 |
| 31 | 0.734 | 0.541 | 0.399 | 0.296 | 0.220 | 0.164 | 0.122 | 0.092 | 0.069 | 0.052 | 0.029 | 0.017 | 0.013 |
| 32 | 0.727 | 0.530 | 0.388 | 0.285 | 0.209 | 0.154 | 0.114 | 0.085 | 0.063 | 0.047 | 0.026 | 0.015 | 0.011 |
| 33 | 0.720 | 0.520 | 0.377 | 0.274 | 0.199 | 0.146 | 0.107 | 0.078 | 0.058 | 0.043 | 0.023 | 0.013 | 0.009 |
| 34 | 0.712 | 0.510 | 0.366 | 0.263 | 0.190 | 0.137 | 0.100 | 0.073 | 0.053 | 0.039 | 0.021 | 0.011 | 0.008 |
| 35 | 0.705 | 0.500 | 0.355 | 0.253 | 0.181 | 0.130 | 0.093 | 0.067 | 0.048 | 0.035 | 0.018 | 0.010 | 0.007 |
| 36 | 0.698 | 0.490 | 0.345 | 0.243 | 0.172 | 0.122 | 0.087 | 0.062 | 0.044 | 0.032 | 0.016 | 0.008 | 0.006 |
| 37 | 0.692 | 0.480 | 0.334 | 0.234 | 0.164 | 0.115 | 0.081 | 0.057 | 0.041 | 0.029 | 0.015 | 0.007 | 0.005 |
| 38 | 0.685 | 0.471 | 0.325 | 0.225 | 0.156 | 0.109 | 0.076 | 0.053 | 0.037 | 0.026 | 0.013 | 0.006 | 0.004 |
| 39 | 0.678 | 0.461 | 0.315 | 0.216 | 0.149 | 0.103 | 0.071 | 0.049 | 0.034 | 0.024 | 0.012 | 0.006 | 0.004 |
| 40 | 0.671 | 0.452 | 0.306 | 0.208 | 0.142 | 0.097 | 0.066 | 0.046 | 0.031 | 0.022 | 0.010 | 0.005 | 0.003 |
| 41 | 0.665 | 0.444 | 0.297 | 0.200 | 0.135 | 0.091 | 0.062 | 0.042 | 0.029 | 0.020 | 0.009 | 0.004 | 0.003 |
| 42 | 0.658 | 0.435 | 0.288 | 0.192 | 0.128 | 0.086 | 0.058 | 0.039 | 0.026 | 0.018 | 0.008 | 0.004 | 0.002 |
| 43 | 0.651 | 0.426 | 0.280 | 0.185 | 0.122 | 0.081 | 0.054 | 0.036 | 0.024 | 0.016 | 0.007 | 0.003 | 0.002 |
| 44 | 0.645 | 0.418 | 0.272 | 0.178 | 0.116 | 0.077 | 0.050 | 0.033 | 0.022 | 0.015 | 0.006 | 0.003 | 0.002 |
| 45 | 0.639 | 0.410 | 0.264 | 0.171 | 0.111 | 0.072 | 0.047 | 0.031 | 0.020 | 0.013 | 0.006 | 0.002 | 0.001 |
| 46 | 0.632 | 0.402 | 0.256 | 0.164 | 0.105 | 0.068 | 0.044 | 0.029 | 0.018 | 0.012 | 0.005 | 0.002 | 0.001 |
| 47 | 0.626 | 0.394 | 0.249 | 0.158 | 0.100 | 0.064 | 0.041 | 0.026 | 0.017 | 0.011 | 0.004 | 0.002 | 0.001 |
| 48 | 0.620 | 0.386 | 0.241 | 0.152 | 0.096 | 0.060 | 0.038 | 0.024 | 0.015 | 0.010 | 0.004 | 0.001 | 0.001 |
| 49 | 0.614 | 0.378 | 0.234 | 0.146 | 0.091 | 0.057 | 0.036 | 0.023 | 0.014 | 0.009 | 0.003 | 0.001 | 0.001 |
| 50 | 0.608 | 0.371 | 0.228 | 0.140 | 0.087 | 0.054 | 0.033 | 0.021 | 0.013 | 0.008 | 0.003 | 0.001 | 0.000 |

**Table 2** Present Value of an Ordinary Annuity of $1

$$P_{\overline{n}|i} = \frac{1 - \dfrac{1}{(1 + i)n}}{i}$$

| n \ i | 1% | 2% | 3% | 4% | 5% | 6% | 7% | 8% | 9% | 10% | 12% | 14% | 15% |
|---|---|---|---|---|---|---|---|---|---|---|---|---|---|
| 1 | 0.990 | 0.980 | 0.970 | 0.961 | 0.952 | 0.943 | 0.934 | 0.925 | 0.917 | 0.909 | 0.892 | 0.877 | 0.869 |
| 2 | 1.970 | 1.941 | 1.913 | 1.886 | 1.850 | 1.833 | 1.808 | 1.783 | 1.759 | 1.735 | 1.690 | 1.646 | 1.625 |
| 3 | 2.940 | 2.883 | 2.828 | 2.775 | 2.723 | 2.673 | 2.624 | 2.577 | 2.531 | 2.486 | 2.401 | 2.321 | 2.283 |
| 4 | 3.901 | 3.807 | 3.717 | 3.629 | 3.545 | 3.465 | 3.387 | 3.312 | 3.239 | 3.169 | 3.037 | 2.913 | 2.834 |
| 5 | 4.853 | 4.713 | 4.579 | 4.451 | 4.329 | 4.212 | 4.100 | 3.992 | 3.889 | 3.790 | 3.604 | 3.433 | 3.352 |
| 6 | 5.795 | 5.601 | 5.417 | 5.242 | 5.075 | 4.917 | 4.766 | 4.622 | 4.485 | 4.355 | 4.111 | 3.888 | 3.784 |
| 7 | 6.728 | 6.471 | 6.230 | 6.002 | 5.786 | 5.582 | 5.389 | 5.206 | 5.032 | 4.868 | 4.563 | 4.288 | 4.160 |
| 8 | 7.651 | 7.325 | 7.019 | 6.732 | 6.463 | 6.209 | 5.971 | 5.746 | 5.534 | 5.334 | 4.967 | 4.638 | 4.487 |
| 9 | 8.566 | 8.162 | 7.786 | 7.435 | 7.107 | 6.801 | 6.515 | 6.246 | 5.995 | 5.759 | 5.328 | 4.946 | 4.771 |
| 10 | 9.471 | 8.982 | 8.530 | 8.110 | 7.721 | 7.360 | 7.023 | 6.710 | 6.417 | 6.144 | 5.650 | 5.216 | 5.018 |
| 11 | 10.367 | 9.786 | 9.252 | 8.760 | 8.306 | 7.886 | 7.498 | 7.138 | 6.805 | 6.495 | 5.937 | 5.452 | 5.233 |
| 12 | 11.255 | 10.575 | 9.954 | 9.385 | 8.863 | 8.383 | 7.942 | 7.536 | 7.160 | 6.813 | 6.194 | 5.660 | 5.420 |
| 13 | 12.133 | 11.348 | 10.634 | 9.985 | 9.393 | 8.852 | 8.357 | 7.903 | 7.486 | 7.103 | 6.423 | 5.842 | 5.583 |
| 14 | 13.003 | 12.106 | 11.296 | 10.563 | 9.898 | 9.294 | 8.745 | 8.244 | 7.786 | 7.366 | 6.628 | 6.002 | 5.724 |
| 15 | 13.865 | 12.849 | 11.937 | 11.118 | 10.379 | 9.712 | 9.107 | 8.559 | 8.060 | 7.606 | 6.810 | 6.142 | 5.847 |
| 16 | 14.717 | 13.577 | 12.561 | 11.652 | 10.837 | 10.105 | 9.446 | 8.851 | 8.312 | 7.823 | 6.973 | 6.265 | 5.954 |
| 17 | 15.562 | 14.291 | 13.166 | 12.165 | 11.274 | 10.477 | 9.763 | 9.121 | 8.543 | 8.021 | 7.119 | 6.372 | 6.047 |
| 18 | 16.398 | 14.992 | 13.753 | 12.659 | 11.689 | 10.827 | 10.059 | 9.371 | 8.755 | 8.201 | 7.249 | 6.467 | 6.127 |
| 19 | 17.226 | 15.678 | 14.323 | 13.133 | 12.058 | 11.158 | 10.335 | 9.603 | 8.950 | 8.364 | 7.365 | 6.530 | 6.198 |
| 20 | 18.045 | 16.351 | 14.877 | 13.590 | 12.462 | 11.469 | 10.594 | 9.818 | 9.128 | 8.513 | 7.469 | 6.623 | 6.259 |
| 21 | 18.856 | 17.011 | 15.415 | 14.029 | 12.821 | 11.764 | 10.835 | 10.016 | 9.292 | 8.648 | 7.562 | 6.686 | 6.312 |
| 22 | 19.660 | 17.658 | 15.936 | 14.451 | 13.163 | 12.041 | 11.061 | 10.200 | 9.442 | 8.771 | 7.644 | 6.742 | 6.358 |
| 23 | 20.455 | 18.292 | 16.443 | 14.856 | 13.488 | 12.303 | 11.272 | 10.371 | 9.580 | 8.883 | 7.718 | 6.749 | 6.398 |
| 24 | 21.243 | 18.913 | 16.935 | 15.246 | 13.798 | 12.550 | 11.469 | 10.528 | 9.706 | 8.984 | 7.784 | 6.835 | 6.433 |
| 25 | 22.023 | 19.523 | 17.413 | 15.622 | 14.093 | 12.783 | 11.653 | 10.674 | 9.822 | 9.077 | 7.843 | 6.872 | 6.464 |
| 26 | 22.795 | 20.121 | 17.876 | 15.982 | 14.375 | 13.003 | 11.825 | 10.809 | 9.928 | 9.160 | 7.895 | 6.906 | 6.490 |
| 27 | 23.559 | 20.706 | 18.327 | 16.329 | 14.643 | 13.210 | 11.986 | 10.935 | 10.026 | 9.237 | 7.942 | 6.935 | 6.513 |
| 28 | 24.316 | 21.281 | 18.764 | 16.663 | 14.898 | 13.406 | 12.137 | 11.051 | 10.116 | 9.306 | 7.984 | 6.960 | 6.533 |
| 29 | 25.065 | 21.844 | 19.188 | 16.983 | 15.141 | 13.590 | 12.277 | 11.158 | 10.198 | 9.369 | 8.021 | 6.983 | 6.550 |
| 30 | 25.807 | 22.396 | 19.600 | 17.292 | 15.372 | 13.764 | 12.409 | 11.257 | 10.273 | 9.426 | 8.055 | 7.002 | 6.563 |
| 31 | 26.542 | 22.937 | 20.000 | 17.589 | 15.592 | 13.929 | 12.531 | 11.349 | 10.342 | 9.479 | 8.084 | 7.019 | 6.579 |
| 32 | 27.269 | 23.468 | 20.388 | 17.873 | 15.802 | 14.084 | 12.646 | 11.434 | 10.406 | 9.526 | 8.111 | 7.034 | 6.590 |
| 33 | 27.989 | 23.988 | 20.765 | 18.147 | 16.002 | 14.230 | 12.753 | 11.513 | 10.464 | 9.569 | 8.135 | 7.048 | 6.600 |
| 34 | 28.702 | 24.498 | 21.131 | 18.411 | 16.192 | 14.368 | 12.854 | 11.586 | 10.517 | 9.608 | 8.156 | 7.059 | 6.609 |
| 35 | 29.408 | 24.998 | 21.487 | 18.664 | 16.374 | 14.498 | 12.947 | 11.654 | 10.566 | 9.644 | 8.175 | 7.070 | 6.616 |
| 36 | 30.107 | 25.488 | 21.832 | 18.908 | 16.546 | 14.620 | 13.035 | 11.717 | 10.611 | 9.676 | 8.192 | 7.078 | 6.623 |
| 37 | 30.799 | 25.969 | 22.167 | 19.142 | 16.711 | 14.736 | 13.117 | 11.775 | 10.652 | 9.705 | 8.207 | 7.086 | 6.628 |
| 38 | 31.484 | 26.440 | 22.492 | 19.367 | 16.867 | 14.846 | 13.193 | 11.828 | 10.690 | 9.732 | 8.220 | 7.093 | 6.633 |
| 39 | 32.163 | 26.902 | 22.808 | 19.584 | 17.071 | 14.949 | 13.264 | 11.878 | 10.725 | 9.756 | 8.233 | 7.099 | 6.638 |
| 40 | 32.834 | 27.355 | 23.114 | 19.792 | 17.159 | 15.046 | 13.331 | 11.924 | 10.757 | 9.779 | 8.243 | 7.105 | 6.641 |
| 41 | 33.499 | 27.799 | 23.412 | 19.993 | 17.294 | 15.138 | 13.394 | 11.967 | 10.786 | 9.799 | 8.253 | 7.109 | 6.645 |
| 42 | 34.158 | 28.234 | 23.701 | 20.185 | 17.423 | 15.224 | 13.452 | 12.006 | 10.813 | 9.817 | 8.261 | 7.113 | 6.647 |
| 43 | 34.810 | 28.661 | 23.981 | 20.370 | 17.545 | 15.306 | 13.506 | 12.043 | 10.837 | 9.833 | 8.269 | 7.117 | 6.650 |
| 44 | 35.455 | 29.079 | 24.254 | 20.548 | 17.662 | 15.383 | 13.557 | 12.077 | 10.860 | 9.849 | 8.276 | 7.120 | 6.652 |
| 45 | 36.094 | 29.490 | 24.518 | 20.720 | 17.774 | 15.455 | 13.605 | 12.108 | 10.881 | 9.862 | 8.282 | 7.123 | 6.654 |
| 46 | 36.727 | 29.892 | 24.775 | 20.884 | 17.880 | 15.524 | 13.650 | 12.137 | 10.900 | 9.875 | 8.287 | 7.125 | 6.655 |
| 47 | 37.353 | 30.286 | 25.024 | 21.042 | 17.981 | 15.589 | 13.691 | 12.164 | 10.917 | 9.886 | 8.292 | 7.127 | 6.657 |
| 48 | 37.973 | 30.673 | 25.266 | 21.195 | 18.077 | 15.650 | 13.730 | 12.189 | 10.933 | 9.896 | 8.297 | 7.129 | 6.658 |
| 49 | 38.588 | 31.052 | 25.601 | 21.341 | 18.168 | 15.707 | 13.766 | 12.212 | 10.948 | 9.906 | 8.301 | 7.131 | 6.659 |
| 50 | 39.196 | 31.423 | 25.729 | 21.482 | 18.255 | 15.761 | 13.800 | 12.233 | 10.961 | 9.914 | 8.304 | 7.132 | 6.660 |

when interest is compounded more frequently than annually. For example, assume that you wish to know the present value of $179,211 payable 5 years from now if interest is 12% compounded semiannually. Since interest is compounded twice a year for 5 years, the number of periods involved is 10. And the interest rate per period is 6%, the annual rate of 12% divided by the number of periods in a year. The present value is expressed as:

$$p = \$179,211 \, p_{\overline{10}|6\%}$$

$$= \$179,211 \, (0.558)$$

$$= \$100,000$$

With this background in present value calculations, we can return to the Aztec Company example to see how the present value of its $7 million bond issue will be computed. Aztec incurred two separate obligations when it issued the $7,000,000, 12% 5-year bonds on May 1, 1998. First, it promised to pay the face amount of the bonds, $7,000,000, 5 years hence. Second, it promised to pay interest of $420,000 ($7,000,000 × 12% × $\frac{1}{2}$) every 6 months—on Nov. 1 and May 1—for the 5-year life of the bonds. These two promises can be expressed on a time line like this:

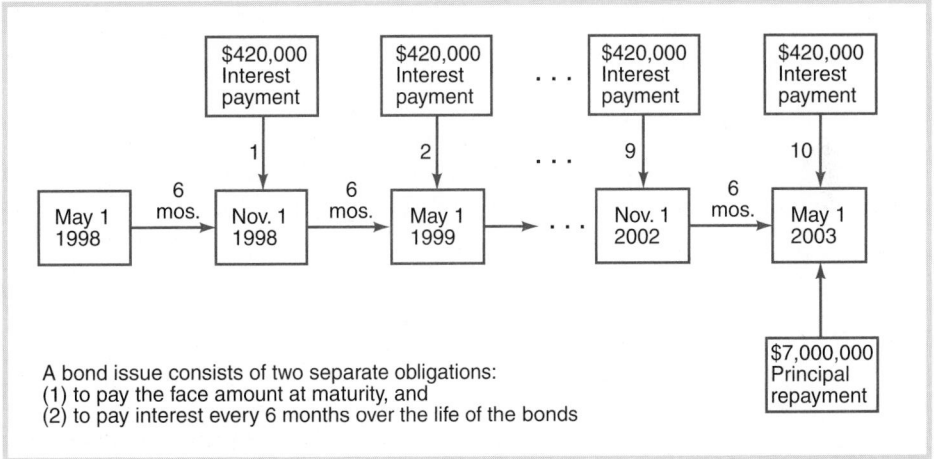

A bond issue consists of two separate obligations:
(1) to pay the face amount at maturity, and
(2) to pay interest every 6 months over the life of the bonds

The second promise represents a series of payments (10 in all) to be made at the *end of each period.* This is called an **ordinary annuity.** Table 2 is a present value table of ordinary annuity factors; it works in the same way as Table 1. We use the capital letter *P* to represent the present value of an ordinary annuity, so the factor is summarized by the expression $P_{\overline{n}|i}$.

The present value of the $420,000 ordinary annuity of 10 payments at 12% per year (6% per period) would be calculated like this:

$$P = \$ \; 420,000 \, P_{\overline{10}|6\%}$$

$$= \$ \; 420,000 \times (7.360)$$

$$= \$3,091,200$$

Now we can determine the present value of Aztec's $7,000,000, 12%, 5-year bond issue. It is the sum of the present values of the two separate obligations—the promise to pay $7,000,000, 5 years hence, and the promise to pay $420,000, twice a year for those 5 years. The present value of the bonds, then, is:

$$\$7,000,000 \, p_{\overline{10}|6\%} = \$7,000,000(0.558) \; = \$3,906,000$$

$$420,000 \, P_{\overline{10}|6\%} = \quad 420,000(7.360) \; = \underline{\quad 3,091,200}$$

$$\text{Present value of the bonds} = \underline{\$6,997,200}$$

If we had used seven-place factors, the computation would have been:

$$\$7,000,000\ p\,\overline{_{10}}_{6\%} = \$7,000,000(0.5583948) = \$3,908,764$$

$$420,000\ P\,\overline{_{10}}_{6\%} = 420,000(7.3600871) = \underline{3,091,237}$$

$$\text{Present value of the bonds} = \underline{\$7,000,001}$$

If the present value of the bonds is $7,000,000, the same as the face value, why do we need to bother with all these present value calculations? This is a good question. We have used the 12% interest rate to determine the present value of the bonds. Remember that 12% was the *nominal rate*—the rate specified in the bond indenture. Using the nominal rate to determine the present value of the bonds when the nominal rate equals the market rate will always result in a present value that equals the face value. It means simply that the bonds will sell at face value.

But remember that bonds seldom do sell at face value. They sell at a *discount* if the market rate of interest exceeds the nominal rate. And they sell at a *premium* if the market rate of interest is less than the nominal rate.

If the 12% Aztec bonds are issued at a time when the market rate of interest is 14%, the present value of the bonds will be:

$$\$7,000,000\ p\,\overline{_{10}}_{7\%} = \$7,000,000(0.5083493) = \$3,558,445$$

$$420,000\ P\,\overline{_{10}}_{7\%} = 420,000(7.0235815) = \underline{2,949,904}$$

$$\text{Present value of the bonds} = \underline{\$6,508,349}$$

If all other economic factors remain constant, this is the price the bonds will sell for. They will sell for a discount of $7,000,000 − $6,508,349 = $491,651.

If the 12% Aztec bonds are issued at a time when the market rate of interest is 10%, the present value of the bonds will be:

$$\$7,000,000\ p\,\overline{_{10}}_{5\%} = \$7,000,000(0.6139133) = \$4,297,393$$

$$420,000\ P\,\overline{_{10}}_{5\%} = 420,000(7.7217349) = \underline{3,243,129}$$

$$\text{Present value of the bonds} = \underline{\$7,540,522}$$

A premium of $540,522 results, which will be added to the face value in selling the bonds.

In these discount and premium examples, the market rate of interest is used to compute the present value. The market rate is called the **effective interest rate.** The $7,000,000 face value of the bonds and the $420,000 semiannual interest payment cannot be changed, since they are fixed by the terms of the bond indenture. The only way to change the price the bonds sell for is to use the effective rate of interest.

## The Effective-Interest Method of Amortizing Bond Discounts and Premiums

In the previous discussion of accounting for bonds issued at discounts or premiums, we amortized the discount or premium *equally* over the 10 periods. This is called the **straight-line method** of amortization because the amortization is the same for each 6-month period. While this method is easy, it does not reflect the true rate of interest on the bond.

Learning Objective 7

Use the effective interest amortization method to record the entries for a bond issue sold at a discount or at a premium.

For example, when the Aztec Motor Corporation's $7,000,000, 12%, 5-year bond sold at a price ($6,508,349) that would provide investors with a 7% yield, interest expense for every period was the sum of the interest payment, $420,000, and the amortization of the discount, $49,165 per period, which comes to $469,165. The interest rate for the first period would be determined by the following calculation:

$$\frac{\text{Interest expense}}{\text{Carrying value of the bond}} = \frac{\$469,165}{\$6,508,349} = 7.21\%$$

# Present Value Inconsistency

Time has a value. That's the basis of the present value calculations discussed in this section. Liabilities such as bonds payable must be reported on the balance sheet at their present value. Other liabilities are also measured by using present value; notes payable, pensions, and health-care benefits are some examples. But many liabilities ignore the time value of money: product and manufacturers' warranties, loss reserves for property-casualty insurers (like the allowance for uncollectibles), and deferred tax liabilities.

If these liabilities were accounted for using present value accounting, the liability side of the balance sheet would be reduced significantly. Consider, for example, General Electric's $3.1 *billion* deferred tax liability. That's a liability that extends over many years, but it is on the books at its face value, not its discounted value. The discounted value is hundreds of millions of dollars less than book value, according to Bernard Doyle, GE's manager of corporate accounting services.

*Source:* Penelope Wang, "Time is Money," *Forbes,* Jan. 9, 1989, p. 300. Reprinted by permission of FORBES magazine. Copyright © Forbes Inc., 1989.

The interest rate for the second period would be determined as follows:

$$\frac{\$469,165}{\$6,508,349 + 49,165} = 7.15\%$$

And the interest rate for the tenth and last period would be:

$$\frac{\$469,165}{\$6,508,349 + (9)(49,165)} = 6.75\%$$

You can see that using the straight-line method of amortizing the discount results in an interest rate that decreases over the life of the bond, not a constant 7% as it should be. A method of amortization that does show the true interest rate, the **effective-interest method,** is preferred; in fact, this method is required by generally accepted accounting principles unless the difference in interest expense between the two methods is not material.

Here's how the effective-interest method works. The interest expense for each period is determined by multiplying the carrying value—the face value plus the unamortized premium or minus the unamortized discount—of the bond at the beginning of the period by the effective rate of interest. The amount of discount to be amortized is the difference between the interest expense and the interest payment for the period.

### Amortizing Bond Discounts by the Effective-Interest Method

Let's look again at the example in which the Aztec bonds were sold at a discount. We would calculate the interest expense for the first interest period, ending on Nov. 1, 1998, like this:

$$\left(\underset{\substack{\text{face value} \quad \text{discount}}}{\$7,000,000 - \$491,651}\right) \times \underset{\substack{\text{interest rate}}}{7\% \text{ per period effective}} = \underset{\substack{\text{interest expense}}}{\$455,584}$$

The discount amortization is calculated as follows:

| | |
|---|---|
| Interest expense | = $455,584 |
| Interest payment | = 420,000 |
| Discount amortization | = $ 35,584 |

We now need to determine the amount of discount remaining after the amortization of the $35,584. This unamortized discount is $491,651 − $35,584 = $456,067 and is subtracted from the $7,000,000 face value of the bonds to arrive at the Nov. 1, 1998, carrying value of $6,543,933.

**Table 3** Aztec Motor Corporation Bond Discount Amortization Schedule under the Effective-Interest Method

| Interest Period | A<br>Interest Payment<br>(face value × 6%) | B<br>Interest Expense<br>(col. E × 7%) | C<br>Discount Amortization<br>(B − A) | D<br>Unamortized Discount<br>(D − C) | E<br>Carrying Value of Bonds (face value − D) |
|---|---|---|---|---|---|
| May 1, 1998 | | | | $491,651 | $6,508,349 |
| Nov. 1, 1998 | $420,000 | $455,584 | $35,584 | 456,067 | 6,543,933 |
| May 1, 1999 | 420,000 | 458,075 | 38,075 | 417,992 | 6,582,008 |
| Nov. 1, 1999 | 420,000 | 460,741 | 40,741 | 377,251 | 6,622,749 |
| May 1, 2000 | 420,000 | 463,592 | 43,592 | 333,659 | 6,666,341 |
| Nov. 1, 2000 | 420,000 | 466,644 | 46,644 | 287,015 | 6,712,985 |
| May 1, 2001 | 420,000 | 469,909 | 49,909 | 237,106 | 6,762,894 |
| Nov. 1, 2001 | 420,000 | 473,403 | 53,403 | 183,703 | 6,816,297 |
| May 1, 2002 | 420,000 | 477,141 | 57,141 | 126,562 | 6,873,438 |
| Nov. 1, 2002 | 420,000 | 481,141 | 61,141 | 65,421 | 6,934,579 |
| May 1, 2003 | 420,000 | 485,421 | 65,421 | −0− | 7,000,000 |

For the next interest period, May 1, 1999, the process is repeated. We multiply the bonds' Nov. 1 carrying value, $6,543,933, by the 7% per-period effective interest rate to arrive at $458,075 interest expense. The difference between the $420,000 interest payment and this $458,075 interest expense determines the amount of discount amortization, $38,075, for the second interest period.

Learning Objective **8**

Prepare bond amortization schedules

A bond discount amortization schedule, such as Table 3, is usually prepared for the life of the bonds when the bonds are issued. These tables are easily prepared by using a personal computer and a software spreadsheet package such as Lotus 123.

We can clarify this concept of amortization using the effective-interest method by presenting it in a diagram, as shown in Figure 1.

**Figure 1** Aztec Motor Corporation: Bond Discount Amortization Diagram under the Effective-Interest Method

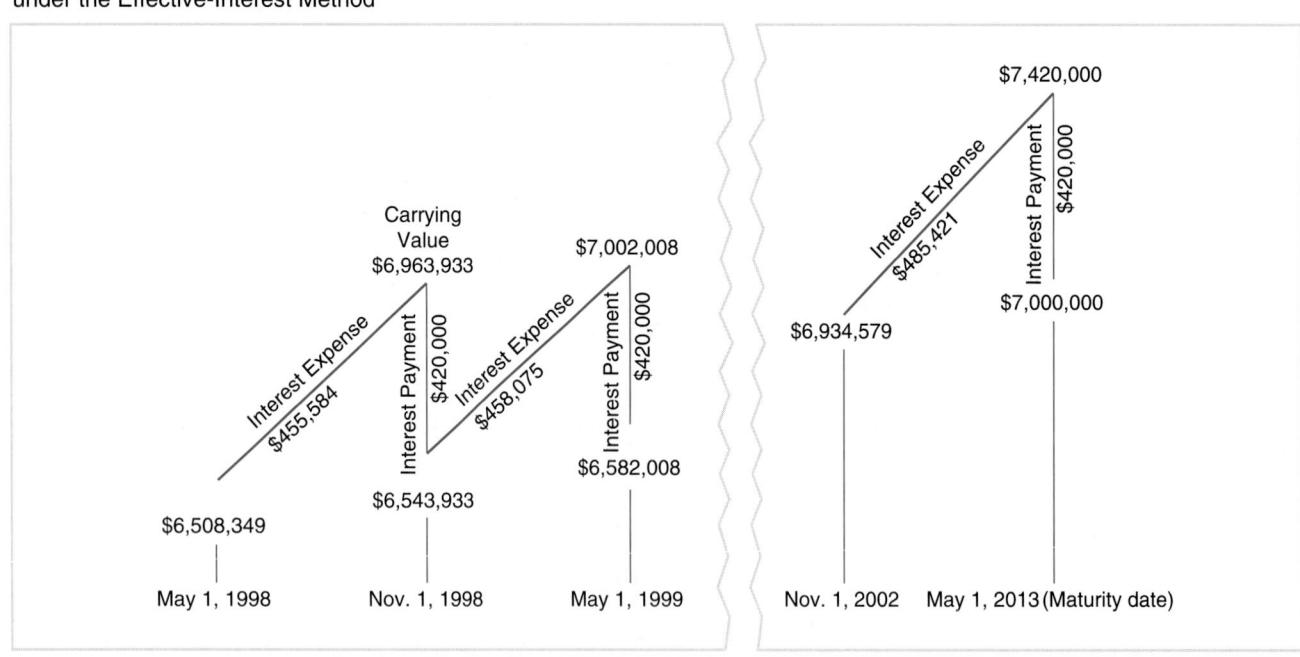

What is happening is that the carrying value of the bond is increasing as it earns interest. And it earns interest *every day;* we just record the interest once every 6 months when a cash payment is made. Figure 1 shows that the initial carrying value of the bond increases to $6,963,933 ($6,508,349 + interest of $455,584 for the first 6 months) and then is reduced by the cash payment of $420,000. The cash interest payment is made all at one time, so the reduction is shown as a straight drop to the new carrying value of $6,543,933. Each successive 6-month period first increases the carrying value by the amount of the interest, then reduces the carrying value by the amount of the cash payment. But each successive carrying value is a little greater than the previous one—until 5 years pass and the carrying value reaches $7,000,000, the maturity value of the bond.

Using the bond discount amortization schedule, let's compare the general journal entries required under the effective-interest and straight-line methods for three successive events: the Nov. 1, 1998, interest payment; the Dec. 31, 1998, accrual; and the May 1, 1999, interest payment. First, the Nov. 1, 1998, entry:

| | | Method Used | | | |
| | | Effective-Interest | | Straight-Line | |
| Entry | | Debit | Credit | Debit | Credit |
|---|---|---|---|---|---|
| 1998 | | | | | |
| Nov. 1 | Bond Interest Expense.............................. | 455,584 | | 469,165 | |
| | Discount on Bonds Payable ....................... | | 35,584 | | 49,165 |
| | Cash ......................................... | | 420,000 | | 420,000 |
| | To record payment of semiannual interest on bonds and amortization of bond discount. | | | | |

Compare Bond Interest Expense under both procedures. A significant difference, $13,581 ($469,165 − $455,584), exists. When there is such a material difference between the two methods, the effective-interest method is required because it reflects the true interest cost, while the straight-line method provides only an approximate cost, for convenience.

Second, the Dec. 31, 1998, adjusting entry for accrued interest is recorded like this:

| | | Method Used | | | |
| | | Effective-Interest | | Straight-Line | |
| Entry | | Debit | Credit | Debit | Credit |
|---|---|---|---|---|---|
| 1998 | | | | | |
| Dec. 31 | Bond Interest Expense............................. | 152,692 | | 156,388 | |
| | Discount on Bonds Payable ....................... | | 12,692 | | 16,388 |
| | Bond Interest Payable ........................... | | 140,000 | | 140,000 |
| | To record accrual of bond interest payable and amortization of bond discount. | | | | |

Can you determine how we arrived at the $12,692 discount amortization under the effective-interest method? Remember that the $16,388 straight-line amortization was calculated by taking $\frac{2}{60}$ of the initial $491,651 discount. This would be the same as taking $\frac{2}{6}$ of the $49,165 semiannual amortization. That's what we did for the effective-interest method, $\frac{2}{6}$ of the $38,075 second-period discount amortization (see Table 2). Amortization between interest payment dates under the effective-interest method is done on a straight-line basis.

Third, on May 1, 1999, the semiannual interest payment is recorded like this:

| | Method Used | | | |
| | Effective-Interest | | Straight-Line | |
| Entry | Debit | Credit | Debit | Credit |
|---|---|---|---|---|
| **1999** | | | | |
| May 1  Bond Interest Payable............................ | 140,000 | | 140,000 | |
| Bond Interest Expense ............................. | 305,383 | | 312,777 | |
| Discount on Bonds Payable........................ | | 25,383 | | 32,777 |
| Cash .......................................... | | 420,000 | | 420,000 |
| To record payment of semiannual interest on bonds and amortization of bond discount. | | | | |

### Amortizing Bond Premiums by the Effective Interest Method

If the Aztec Motor Corporation bonds were issued on May 1, 1998, at a premium of $540,522, representing a 10% effective interest rate, a bond premium amortization schedule such as the one illustrated in Table 4 would be prepared. This schedule is prepared in exactly the same manner as the bond discount amortization schedule.

Using this amortization schedule, we would record the entries for Nov. 1, 1998, Dec. 31, 1998, and May 1, 1999, as follows:

| | Method Used | | | |
| | Effective-Interest | | Straight-Line | |
| Entry | Debit | Credit | Debit | Credit |
|---|---|---|---|---|
| **1998** | | | | |
| Nov. 1  Bond Interest Expense............................. | 377,026 | | 365,948 | |
| Premium on Bonds Payable ......................... | 42,974 | | 54,052 | |
| Cash .......................................... | | 420,000 | | 420,000 |
| To record payment of semiannual interest on bonds and amortization of bond premium. | | | | |
| Dec. 31  Bond Interest Expense............................. | 124,959 | | 121,983 | |
| Premium on Bonds Payable ......................... | 15,041 | | 18,017 | |
| Bond Interest Payable ........................... | | 140,000 | | 140,000 |
| To record payment of semiannual interest on bonds and amortization of bond discount. | | | | |
| **1999** | | | | |
| May 1  Bond Interest Payable ............................. | 140,000 | | 140,000 | |
| Bond Interest Expense............................. | 249,918 | | 243,965 | |
| Premium on Bonds Payable ......................... | 30,082 | | 36,035 | |
| Cash .......................................... | | 420,000 | | 420,000 |
| To record payment of semiannual interest on bonds and amortization of bond premium. | | | | |

**Table 4** Aztec Motor Corporation Bond Premium Amortization Schedule under the Effective-Interest Method

| | A | B | C | D | E |
|---|---|---|---|---|---|
| Interest Period | Interest Payment (face value × 6%) | Interest Expense (col. E × 5%) | Premium Amortization (B − A) | Unamortized Premium (D − C) | Carrying Value of Bonds (face value + D) |
| May 1, 1998 | | | | $540,522 | $7,540,522 |
| Nov. 1, 1998 | $420,000 | $377,026 | $42,974 | 497,548 | 7,497,548 |
| May 1, 1999 | 420,000 | 374,877 | 45,123 | 452,425 | 7,452,425 |
| Nov. 1, 1999 | 420,000 | 372,621 | 47,379 | 405,046 | 7,405,046 |
| May 1, 2000 | 420,000 | 370,252 | 49,748 | 355,298 | 7,355,298 |
| Nov. 1, 2000 | 420,000 | 367,765 | 52,235 | 303,063 | 7,303,063 |
| May 1, 2001 | 420,000 | 365,153 | 54,847 | 248,216 | 7,248,216 |
| Nov. 1, 2001 | 420,000 | 362,411 | 57,589 | 190,627 | 7,190,627 |
| May 1, 2002 | 420,000 | 359,531 | 60,469 | 130,158 | 7,130,158 |
| Nov. 1, 2002 | 420,000 | 356,508 | 63,492 | 66,666 | 7,066,666 |
| May 1, 2003 | 420,000 | 353,333 | 66,666* | −0− | 7,000,000 |

* $1 error due to rounding.

### Financial Statement Disclosure of Bonds Payable

Generally accepted accounting principles require that bonds payable be classified on the balance sheet as long-term liabilities. As we have previously illustrated, bonds payable are reported at their face value plus or minus their unamortized discount or premium. In addition, information as to their interest rate, maturity date, interest payment dates, and collateral must be shown either parenthetically next to the account titles on the balance sheet or in a footnote to the financial statements.

If the business entity has several bonds outstanding, they may be reflected on the balance sheet as one total, but a supporting schedule providing detailed information on each bond must accompany the financial statements.

Current maturities of bonds payable are transferred to the current liabilities section of the balance sheet *if* they are to be settled by the expenditure of a current asset or creation of a new current liability. However, if settlement is to be made by expending a noncurrent asset or by issuing a new long-term obligation, the current maturity should remain in the long-term liabilities section. A footnote would be required explaining the method of settlement.

**ASK YOURSELF** ▶

1. **What is the difference between the nominal rate of interest and the market rate of interest?**
2. **How is the value of a bond determined?**
3. **Explain how a bond discount amortization schedule is prepared.**
4. **Why is the effective-interest method of discount and premium amortization favored over the straight-line method?**

### CONTINGENT LIABILITIES

Learning Objective **9**

Understand the accounting for contingent liabilities

The existence and amount of certain corporate long-term liabilities are indefinite. Some future event must take place (or not take place) that determines if the liability must be paid and the amount of the payment. Examples of such **contingent liabilities** are litigation, expropriation, and accommodation endorsements. *Litigation* refers to lawsuits in progress. *Expropriation* is the act of a country taking control of businesses operating within its jurisdiction. In an *accommodation endorsement,* a corporation co-signs a note in order to provide the creditor with additional security; if the maker of the note fails to pay the note, the co-signer must do so.

Accounting for contingent liabilities requires a decision to be made regarding the degree of likelihood that the specific event will take place: *probable, reasonably possible,* or *remote.* Only in the case of a contingency classified as probable do we record a liability and the corresponding loss. Even if a liability is classified as probable, the amount of the loss must be capable of reasonable estimation before the entry can be recorded.

To illustrate, assume the Exmo Oil Company operates a fleet of oil tankers. Two of the tankers collide off the coast of Florida, spilling large amounts of oil into the sea. The oil is washed ashore, killing wildlife and severely damaging the beaches. The company considers it *probable* that it will be liable for the damages and estimates that such damages will amount to $100 million over the next 4 years. The entry to record the contingent liability is:

| | | |
|---|---|---|
| Loss due to Oil Spill . . . . . . . . . . . . . . . . . . . . . . . . . . . . . | 100,000,000 | |
| Contingent Liability for Oil Spill . . . . . . . . . . . . . . . . . | | 100,000,000 |

If the contingent liability is classified as reasonably possible or if it is probable but the amount cannot be estimated, a footnote to the financial statements is prepared describing the contingency. If the contingent liability is classified as remote, in most cases no accounting is necessary. Remember that only *material* contingent items would be reported on the financial statements or disclosed in the footnotes.

## LONG-TERM LEASES

**Learning Objective 10**

Record the entries associated with the capitalization of a lease

Sometimes business entities find it advantageous to lease buildings and equipment —that is, to rent them on a long-term basis—rather than to purchase them. Many lease arrangements are fairly simple, requiring the **lessee** (the party receiving the right to use the asset) to record rent expense when the periodic lease payment is made. Upon the completion of the lease term, the lessee may choose between entering into a new lease and vacating the building or returning the equipment to the **lessor** (the party that owns the asset).

In recent years, however, leases have become much more flexible and consequently much more complex. Accounting for these new leases has given the accounting profession a very interesting challenge. While legal title to the leased property may remain with the lessor, the terms of the lease may indicate that the transaction is in essence the same as an installment purchase. For instance, generally accepted accounting principles require the accountant to treat a lease as if it were a purchase transaction if any one of these conditions exist:

* The asset may be transferred to the lessee at the end of the lease term.
* The lease may allow the lessee to purchase the asset for a bargain price at the end of the lease term.
* The lease term covers 75% or more of the economic life of the leased asset.
* The present value of the lease payments equals 90% or more of the fair market value of the leased asset.

Under these circumstances the appropriate accounting treatment goes beyond simply debiting Rent Expense and crediting Cash. Where the terms of the lease transaction indicate that the lessee has the rights and benefits of ownership, we must account for the transaction by recognizing the future economic benefits of the asset and by recognizing the obligation of the liability. This recording of the present value of lease payments is called **lease capitalization.**

Let's see how lease capitalization works. PanSouthern Company enters into a lease arrangement on Jan. 1. 1998, with the Nationwide Leasing Company to lease equipment for 3 years. The terms of the lease require PanSouthern to make payments of $10,000 to Nationwide on June 30 and Dec. 31 in 1998, 1999, and 2000. Interest is 14%. The useful life of the equipment is estimated to be 3 years. We will assume that the terms of this lease arrangement require capitalization of the lease.

On June 1, 1998, we will record the following entry for PanSouthern Company:

| 1998 | | | |
|---|---|---|---|
| Jan. 1 | Leased Equipment . . . . . . . . . . . . . . . . . . . . . . . . . . . | 47,660 | |
| | Obligation under Capitalized Lease . . . . . . . . . . . | | 47,660 |
| | To record a capitalized lease for equipment. Lease terms require semi-annual payments of $10,000 every 6 months. | | |

In leasing equipment on this date, PanSouthern receives an asset, which must be recorded on the books at its fair value. This value is determined by computing the present value of an annuity of 6 payments at 14% per annum, or 7% per period. Using the annuity Table 2, we determine the value as follows:

$$P = \$10,000 \ P_{\overline{6}|7\%}$$

$$= \$10,000 \ (4.766)$$

$$= \$47,660$$

As of Jan. 1, 1998, the $47,660 also represents PanSouthern's long-term liability to Nationwide Leasing.

The first lease payment is to be made on June 30, 1998, at which date the following entry is made:

| 1998 | | | |
|---|---|---|---|
| June 30 | Obligation under Capitalized Lease . . . . . . . . . . . . | 6,664 | |
| | Interest Expense. . . . . . . . . . . . . . . . . . . . . . . | 3,336 | |
| | Cash . . . . . . . . . . . . . . . . . . . . . . . . . . . . . . . . | | 10,000 |
| | To record lease payment due this date. Interest is $3,336 (.07 × $47,660). | | |

We record interest expense in the amount of $3,336, which we can think of as interest for the use of the $47,660 "borrowed" funds for the 6-month period. We then reduce the long-term liability by $10,000 − $3,336 = $6,664, representing a repayment of the "principal." The obligation is reduced by $6,664 and is now $47,660 − $6,664 = $40,996.

In a similar manner we record the Dec. 31 payment for the year:

| 1998 | | | |
|---|---|---|---|
| Dec. 31 | Obligation under Capitalized Lease. . . . . . . . . . . . . | 7,130 | |
| | Interest Expense. . . . . . . . . . . . . . . . . . . . . . . | 2,870 | |
| | Cash . . . . . . . . . . . . . . . . . . . . . . . . . . . . . . . . | | 10,000 |
| | To record lease payment due this date. Interest is equal to $2,870 (.07 × $40,996). | | |

**Table 5** Pansouthern Company Lease Obligation Amortization Schedule

| Lease Period | A Lease Payment | B Interest Expense (col. D × 7%) | C Reduction of Obligation (A − B) | D Obligation Under Capitalized Lease (face value − C) |
|---|---|---|---|---|
| Jan.   1, 1998 | | | | $47,660 |
| June 30, 1998 | $10,000 | $3,336 | 6,664 | 40,996 |
| Dec. 31, 1998 | 10,000 | 2,870 | 7,130 | 33,866 |
| June 30, 1999 | 10,000 | 2,371 | 7,629 | 26,237 |
| Dec. 31, 1999 | 10,000 | 1,837 | 8,163 | 18,074 |
| June 30, 2000 | 10,000 | 1,265 | 8,735 | 9,339 |
| Dec. 31, 2000 | 10,000 | 661* | 9,339* | −0− |

* Error due to rounding.

The amount of the interest expense and the reduction of the obligation for each period over the entire life of the lease can be seen in Table 5.

The lease is considered in essence the same type of transaction as if PanSouthern had purchased the equipment; so at the end of the year, PanSouthern must record depreciation on this leased equipment just as it does for equipment that it owns. The depreciation adjusting entry, assuming straight-line depreciation, would be recorded as follows:

| | | | |
|---|---|---|---|
| 1998 | | | |
| Dec. 31 | Depreciation Expense on Leased Equipment . . . . . . | 15,887 | |
| | Accumulated Depreciation on Leased Equipment. . . . . . . . . . . . . . . . . . . . . . . . . . . . . . . . . . | | 15,887 |
| | To record depreciation on leased equipment of $15,887 ($47,660/3). | | |

On the Dec. 31, 1998, balance sheet, PanSouthern would show the capitalized lease and the obligation as follows:

| | | |
|---|---|---|
| Plant, Property, and Equipment: | | |
| Leased Asset. . . . . . . . . . . . . . . . . . . . . . . . . . . . . . . . . . . . . . . | $47,660 | |
| Less: Accumulated Depreciation on Leased Asset . . . . . . . . . . . | 15,887 | $31,773 |

and the obligation (as obtained from Table 5) would be presented like this:

| | |
|---|---|
| Long-Term Liabilities: | |
| Obligations under Capitalized Lease. . . . . . . . . . . . . . . . . . . . . . . . . . . . . . | $33,866 |

**ASK YOURSELF** ▶

1. Describe the accounting for contingent liabilities.
2. What are the conditions that would require a lease to be considered as a purchase transaction?
3. How is accounting for leases similar to accounting for bonds?
4. Describe how a lease would be reflected on a balance sheet.

## FINANCIAL STATEMENT ANALYSIS

Three statistics that provide information about a company's long-term debt-paying ability are the times interest earned ratio, the debt to total assets ratio, and the equity to total assets ratio. These ratios allow creditors and potential creditors to evaluate a company's ability to meet long-term debt responsibilities. The latter two ratios were discussed in previous chapters.

### The Times Interest Earned Ratio

*Learning Objective*

Describe the use of the times interest earned ratio in financial statement analysis

The **times interest earned ratio** indicates the margin of safety provided by current earnings in meeting the company's interest responsibilities. The formula for calculating this ratio is:

$$\text{Times interest earned} = \frac{\text{income before interest expense and income taxes}}{\text{annual interest expense}}$$

The ratio uses income before interest expense and income taxes because this is the amount that could be used to pay interest—provided it was available in the form of cash. Income taxes are excluded because interest is deductible in calculating income tax.

For example, if the Atlas Company reported 1998 net income equal to $30,000; interest expense of $7,000; and income taxes of $10,000; times interest earned would be calculated as follows:

$$\text{Times interest earned} = \frac{\$30,000 + \$7,000 + \$10,000}{\$7,000} = 6.7 \text{ times}$$

Thus, Atlas' income available to meet its interest responsibilities was about 7 times the amount of its interest expense. Usually, if interest is covered several times, long-term creditors consider this an acceptable margin of safety.

# ComputerLand's Valuable Note Payable

ComputerLand is owned by the William H. Millard family. The Oakland, California company operates nearly 800 franchised outlets all over the world. Prior to building the ComputerLand empire, Mr. Millard founded and operated another company called Information Management Science Associates, Inc. (IMS). That company created a manufacturing subsidiary that went bankrupt in 1979. Included among the $1.9 million of liabilities of the subsidiary was a $250,000 promissory note payable due in May of 1981. The note was issued to the Mariner & Co. venture capital group in 1976 to help keep IMS going. The promissory note was originally convertible into shares of IMS but an agreement signed by Mr. Millard granted Mariner the right to convert the note into any other company Millard might establish.

Mr. Millard paid all the scheduled interest payments on the note until May 1981 when he attempted to pay off the principal amount of the note to Mariner & Co. Meanwhile the note was sold to Micro/Vest (for $300,000 plus another $100,000 payable if the note were eventually converted into stock) and this company informed Mr. Millard in March of 1981 that it intended to exercise the conversion provision and convert the note into 20% of ComputerLand's stock. Mr. Millard contended that the note could only be converted into shares of IMS. The dispute went to court.

Micro/Vest sold shares in the note to dozens of outsiders including William Agee and Mary Cunningham, formerly of the Bendix Corporation. Mr. Millard contended that these individuals had no interest in the case other than to buy shares in the outcome of the lawsuit. Micro/Vest contended that selling the shares in the note was necessary to finance the $1.3 million legal fees.

In early 1985 a jury in Oakland awarded Micro/Vest a 20% interest in ComputerLand plus $115 million in punitive damages.

*Source:* Michael Brody, "ComputerLand's Suddenly Poorer Boss." *Fortune*, Apr. 15, 1985. Copyright 1985 by Time, Inc. All rights reserved.

In addition to bonds and leases, notes payable are often issued on a long-term basis. One such note issued by ComputerLand caused a considerable amount of controversy.

## SUMMARY

- Various types of bonds can be issued by a corporation seeking outside financing. The bonds can be *secured* or *unsecured, term* or *serial, callable* or *convertible.*
- A **secured bond** provides the bondholder with a claim on a specified asset in the event that a corporation does not fulfill its responsibilities, while an **unsecured bond** is issued on the general credit rating of the corporation.
- A **term bond** matures in total at the maturity date specified in the bond contract, while a **serial bond** matures at various successive dates over the life of the bond contract.
- A **callable bond** may be redeemed by the issuing corporation prior to maturity, while a **convertible bond** may be exchanged at the bondholders' option for an ownership interest in the corporation.
- Market conditions, the relative strength of the business entity at the time the bonds are to be issued, and the purpose for which the requested financing is to be used are all determining factors in the type of bonds to be issued.
- When bonds are issued, a contract between the issuing entity and a **trustee,** called a **bond indenture,** is prepared. The trustee, usually a large bank, acts as a agent for the bondholders.
- Bonds may be issued at face value, at a discount, or at a premium. Bonds issued at **face value** (or **par value**) are sold for the same amount that will be paid back to the bondholders at maturity. Bonds sold at a **discount** are sold for an amount that is lower than the amount that will be paid back at maturity. Bonds sold at a **premium** are sold for an amount greater than the amount that will be paid back at maturity.
- The price of bonds is dependent on the *market rate of interest* at the time the bonds are issued. When the market rate of interest is *lower* than that stated on the bond indenture, the bond will be sold at premium. When the market rate of interest is *higher* than that stated on the bond, the bond will sell at a discount.
- Given the market rate of interest, the selling price of bonds can be determined by the use of **present value techniques.** The price will be the sum of the present value of the face of the bond (present value of a single sum—Table 1) and the present value of the stream of contractual interest payments (present value of an ordinary annuity —Table 2), both discounted at the market rate of interest.
- The amount of discount or premium involved in the issuance of a bond must be amortized to record periodic interest expense over the life of the bond. Two accounting alternatives accomplish this amortization: the **effective-interest method,** which uses the true interest rate and results in unequal interest expense each interest period; and the **straight-line method,** which allocates the premium or discount equally each period and results in equal interest expense per interest period.
- Leasing is an alternative to long-term financing through bonds. Under certain conditions, **lease capitalization** is required: that is, the lease must be treated in the same manner as a purchase, with interest expense and depreciation expense being recorded each year.

## 11  KEY TERMS

**Amortization**  The allocation process of writing off bond premiums or discounts to Interest Expense over the life of the bond issue.

**Bond indenture**  A contract between the business entity issuing bonds and the bondholders. Also called **deed of trust** or **trust indenture.**

**Bonds**  Securities issued by corporations as a means of borrowing large sums of money.

**Call price**  The price that callable bonds are redeemed at prior to maturity.

**Callable bonds**  Bonds that may be redeemed by the issuing corporation prior to maturity.

| | |
|---|---|
| Carrying value | The value of a long-term liability reflected on the balance sheet. For a bond it is the face amount less the discount or plus the premium. |
| Contingent liabilities | Liabilities that are indefinite as to their existence and their amount. |
| Convertible bonds | Bonds that may be exchanged at the bondholders' option for an ownership interest in a corporation. |
| Debenture bonds | Bonds that are unsecured; they are issued on the general credit rating of a corporation. |
| Deed of trust | See **bond indenture.** |
| Discount | The difference between lower selling price and face value of a bond. |
| Effective-interest method | The method used to amortize bond discounts and premiums over the life of the bond issue, by use of the interest rate in effect at the time the bonds were issued. |
| Effective interest rate | The interest rate found in the marketplace at the time bonds are issued. It is this rate that is used to determine the present value of a bond and to amortize bond discounts and premiums. |
| Face value | The amount that will be paid to bondholders at the maturity date of the bonds. Also called **par value** or 100. |
| Investment banker | An individual or firm that helps a corporation market its bond issue. Often known as an **underwriter.** |
| Lease capitalization | The recording of the present value of future lease payments as an asset and liability on the balance sheet. |
| Lessee | The corporation or party leasing an asset and receiving the right to use it. |
| Lessor | The party that owns the asset being leased. |
| Nominal interest rate | The rate of interest specified in a bond indenture. |
| Ordinary annuity | A series of payments beginning one period from now and ending at the end of the last period. |
| Par value | See **face value.** |
| Present value techniques | The procedures for finding the value of money today under assumed rates of interest. |
| Premium | The excess paid above face value of a bond. |
| Secured bonds | Bonds that provide the bondholder with a claim on a specified asset in the event the business entity does not fulfill its responsibilities under the terms of the bond indenture. |
| Serial bonds | Bonds that mature at various successive dates over the life of the bond contract. |
| Straight-line method | A method used to amortize bond discounts or premiums evenly over the life of the bond issue. |
| Term bonds | Bonds that mature in total at the maturity dates specified in the bond contract. |
| Times interest earned ratio | Income before interest expense and income taxes divided by annual interest expense. |
| Trust indenture | See **bond indenture.** |
| Trustee | Typically, a bank acting as an agent for the bondholders which has entered into a contract with the business entity issuing bonds. |
| Underwriter | See **investment banker.** |
| Unsecured bonds | See **debenture bonds.** |

## DEMONSTRATION PROBLEM

On Oct. 1, 1998, Jackson Company issued $2,000,000 of 12%, 20-year debenture bonds for $2,084,000. The bonds pay interest semiannually on Oct. 1 and Apr. 1.

**Required:**

Record general journal entries related to the bond issue for the years 1998 and 1999, assuming that the straight-line method of amortizing premiums is used.

### ■ Solution to Demonstration Problem

| 1998 | | | | |
|---|---|---|---|---|
| Oct. 1 | Cash | | 2,084,000 | |
| |     Premium on Bonds Payable | | | 84,000 |
| |     Bonds Payable | | | 2,000,000 |
| | To record the issuance of 12%, 20-year debenture bonds. | | | |
| | | | | |
| Dec. 31 | Premium on Bonds Payable | | 1,050 | |
| | Interest Expense | | 58,950 | |
| |     Interest Payable | | | 60,000 |
| | To record accrual of interest payable ($2,000,000 × .12 × $\frac{3}{12}$), amortization of premium ($84,000 × $\frac{3}{240}$), and interest expense. | | | |
| | | | | |
| 1999 | | | | |
| Apr. 1 | Premium on Bonds Payable | | 1,050 | |
| | Interest Payable | | 60,000 | |
| | Interest Expense | | 58,950 | |
| |     Cash | | | 120,000 |
| | To record payment of semiannual interest ($2,000,000 × .12 × $\frac{6}{12}$). | | | |
| | | | | |
| Oct. 1 | Premium on Bonds Payable | | 2,100 | |
| | Interest Expense | | 117,900 | |
| |     Cash | | | 120,000 |
| | To record payment of semiannual interest. | | | |
| | | | | |
| Dec. 31 | Premium on Bonds Payable | | 1,050 | |
| | Interest Expense | | 58,950 | |
| |     Interest Payable | | | 60,000 |
| | To record accrual of interest payable ($2,000,000 × .12 × $\frac{3}{12}$), amortization of premium ($84,000 × $\frac{3}{240}$), and interest expense. | | | |

## QUESTIONS FOR REVIEW AND FURTHER THOUGHT

### REVIEW QUESTIONS

1. What advantages and disadvantages do a corporation's owners incur when they obtain additional financing by issuing bonds?

2. Distinguish between term and serial bonds and between convertible and callable bonds.

3. Describe the accounting for bonds issued at face value.

4. What problem is encountered when bonds are sold between interest payment dates? How is this problem solved?

5. What is the carrying value of a bond? How is it reflected on the balance sheet?

6. What is an ordinary annuity?

7. Describe the effective-interest method of amortizing bond discounts.

8. Why is the effective-interest method required by generally accepted accounting principles?

9. Describe how a bond discount amortization schedule is prepared.

10. What is a contingent liability? How are contingent liabilities accounted for?

11. What does the term *capitalization* mean in the context of a lease contract?

12. What are the conditions necessary to capitalize a lease?

13. How are capitalized leases accounted for?

14. What is the times interest earned for a company with net income of $60,000, interest expense of $45,000, and income taxes of $30,000?

### QUESTIONS FOR FURTHER THOUGHT

1. When a business entity issues bonds, it incurs two separate liabilities. Explain.

2. How are bond prices determined?

3. What is the difference between the effective-interest method and the straight-line method of accounting for bond premiums and discounts?

4. Why must bond discounts or premiums be amortized?

5. On June 1 the Dickens Company issued a $1,500,000, 10%, 20-year bond in a 12% market. The bond is dated Apr. 1 and interest is payable semiannually.
   a. What is the face value of the bonds?
   b. Does the bond sell for a premium or a discount?
   c. How much is the accrued interest on June 1, the date of issue?
   d. How much interest is paid on the first interest payment date?
   e. What is the nominal interest rate?
   f. What is the effective interest rate?
   g. What is the maturity value of the bond?
   h. Independently of any previous answer, assume that the bond sells for a discount of $70,000. What is the carrying value on the date of issue?

6. Several years ago the Irving Company issued a $100,000 bond. Interest is payable semiannually. The carrying value of the bond on Jan. 1 of the current year was $98,612. The amount of interest expense recorded for the bond this year was $3,945, while the cash payment of interest was $3,500.
   a. Did the bonds initially sell for a premium or a discount?
   b. What is the carrying value of the bonds at the end of the current year?

7. Assume that a lease contract requires capitalization of the asset at $100,000 and that an 8% interest factor was used to determine the present value of the lease payment. If the lease requires annual payments of $12,000 and the asset has a 10-year life, determine the amounts that will appear on the financial statements at the end of the first year of the lease.

## OBJECTIVE ASSIGNMENT

*True/False*   Indicate whether each statement below is *true* or *false* by placing a *T* or an *F* in the space provided.

_____ 1. An advantage of issuing bonds to finance new construction is that dividends legally do not have to be paid.

_____ 2. The face value of a bond is the sum of the principal and the interest payments.

_____ 3. If bonds are sold between interest payment dates, the first interest payment will be less than all the others.

_____ 4. If a bond's stated rate of interest is greater than the market rate, the bond will sell for a premium.

_____ 5. Capitalizing a lease means that the future economic benefits under the lease contract are recorded as an asset on the balance sheet.

*Multiple Choice*   Select the best choice to complete each statement or answer each question below. Write the letter corresponding to your choice in the space provided.

_____ 1. Issuing bonds provides the following advantages:
  a. Interest must be paid when due.
  b. Interest is tax deductible.
  c. Interest is paid only when authorized by the board of directors.
  d. Interest can replace dividends.
  e. None of the above.

_____ 2. The individual who helps a corporation determine the type of bonds to issue, the bond interest rate, the maturity date, and other bond-related matters is the
  a. Attorney
  b. CPA
  c. Trustee
  d. Underwriter
  e. None of the above

_____ 3. A $100,000, 18%, 20-year bond with interest payable every 6 months will have periodic interest payments of
  a. $1,800
  b. $900
  c. $18,000
  d. $9,000
  e. None of the above.

_____ 4. When bonds are sold between interest payment dates, the amount of accrued interest for the first interest payment must be paid by the buyer:
  a. When the bonds are sold
  b. Over the life of the bond contract
  c. When the bonds mature
  d. To the trustees
  e. None of the above

_____ 5. To determine interest expense on a bond, we adjust the interest paid by
  a. Adding the periodic amortization of the bond discount
  b. Deducting the periodic amortization of the bond discount
  c. Adding the unamortized bond discount
  d. Deducting the unamortized bond discount
  e. None of the above

____ 6. The generally accepted accounting principle that requires bond discounts and premiums to be amortized is
    a. Historical cost
    b. Going concern
    c. Economic entity
    d. Revenue recognition
    e. None of the above

____ 7. To find the present value of a $2 million, 12%, 20-year bond sold in a 14% market, the factors used from the present value tables would be found in the 40-period row and the
    a. 6% column
    b. 7% column
    c. 12% column
    d. 14% column
    e. None of the above

____ 8. The method by which a discount or a premium is allocated to interest expense over the life of a bond in such a way that the amount of interest expense each period reflects the market rate of interest at the time the bond was issued is called the
    a. Straight-line method
    b. Declining-balance method
    c. Bonds-outstanding method
    d. Effective-interest method
    e. None of the above

____ 9. A contingent liability that is classified as remote
    a. Must be recorded as an expense on the income statement
    b. Must be described in footnote to the financial statements
    c. Must be reflected in the liabilities section of the balance sheet
    d. Does not require measurement nor disclosure
    e. None of the above

____ 10. The amount of the reduction in the account Obligation under Capitalized Lease
    a. Is constant over the life of the lease
    b. Decreases each period
    c. Increases each period
    d. Cannot be determined in this question
    e. None of the above

## EXERCISES

1† **Exercise 1:** Determining EPS with Different Capital Structures

Winter Park Corporation and Keystone Company each have bonds payable and stockholders' equity that total $8 million, but their capital structures (the sum of stockholders' equity and bonds payable) are different. Winter Park has $2 million of bonds payable and Keystone has $2 million of stockholders' equity. Winter Park has 400,000 shares outstanding and Keystone has 250,000. Assuming that both companies' bonds were issued at face value and have a 14% interest rate, and that income taxes are 30% of taxable income, determine the amount of earnings per share if income before bond interest expense is first $900,000, then $4,500,000.

▶ *(Check Figure: Keystone's EPS = $.17 on $900,000 and $10.25 on $4,500,000)*

3 **Exercise 2:** Recording Entries for Bonds Issued at Face Value

On May 1, 1998, the Vail Corporation issued bonds at a face value of $1,250,000, payable in 20 years at 8% interest. Interest is paid semiannually on May 1 and Nov. 1. Prepare the general journal entries relating to the bonds for the years 1998 and 1999.

▶ *(Check Figure: Accrued interest, Dec. 31, 1998 and 1999 = $16,667)*

4 **Exercise 3:** Recording Entries for Bonds Sold between Interest Payment Dates

On Dec. 1, 1998, the Breckinridge Company issued $600,000 of 10%, 10-year bonds at par. The bonds were dated Nov. 1 and will pay interest semiannually. Prepare the entry to record the issuance of the bonds, the Dec. 31, 1998, adjusting entry, and the Apr. 30, 1999, interest payment.

5 **Exercise 4:** Recording Entries for Bonds Issued at a Premium

On Apr. 1, 1998, the Copper Mountain Corporation issued $900,000 of 14%, 20-year bonds, for which it received $928,800 cash. Interest is paid on Apr. 1 and Oct. 1 of each year. Prepare the general journal entries relating to the bonds for the year 1998, using the straight-line method to amortize the premium.

▶ *(Check Figure: Premium amortization, Dec. 31, 1998 = $360)*

6 **Exercise 5:** Determining Bond Selling Prices

On Oct. 1, 1998, Dillon Corporation issued $9,000,000 of 10%, 20-year bonds. Interest is paid on Oct. 1 and Apr. 1. Compute the price the bonds will sell for if the market rate is 12%.

▶ *(Check Figure: $7,643,700)*

6 **Exercise 6:** Determining Bond Selling Prices

On Oct. 1, 1998, Dillon Corporation issued $9,000,000 of 10%, 20-year bonds. Interest is paid on Oct. 1 and Apr. 1. Compute the price the bonds will sell for if the market rate is 8%.

▶ *(Check Figure: $10,778,400)*

† The numbers in the margin refer to the Learning Objectives.

**7 8** **Exercise 7:** Preparing a Bond Discount Amortization Schedule and Recording Bonds Sold at Discount

The Avon Company issued $4,000,000 of 11%, 3-year bonds on Jan. 1, 1998, at a time when the market interest rate was 13%. The bonds sold for $3,806,359. Interest is payable semiannually on July 1 and Dec. 31. Prepare a bond discount amortization schedule (rounding the data to the nearest whole dollar) for the 3 years and the general journal entry to record the July 1, 1998, interest payment and discount amortization, using the effective-interest method.

▶ *(Check Figure: Interest expense, July 1, 1998 = $247,413)*

**9** **Exercise 8:** Accounting for Contingent Liabilities

Aspen Electric Company operates a nuclear power plant. In April 1998, a series of errors caused the cooling system to malfunction and the nuclear fuel core to overheat. As a result of the accident, several people have died and more than 300 others have been exposed to excessive levels of radiation. The company estimates that the ensuing lawsuits will total $300 million.

a. Assuming that it is *probable* that the courts will order the company to pay the damages and that company accountants determine that the eventual settlements will total $200 million, what accounting treatment will be required for the Dec. 31, 1998, financial statements?
b. Assuming that it is *reasonably possible* that the courts will require Aspen to pay $200 million damages, what accounting treatment is required?

**10** **Exercise 9:** Recording Entries for a Capitalized Lease

Boulder Corporation leases certain equipment from Denver Equipment Company. The terms of the lease contract specify that the lease must be capitalized. The lease payments of $1,500 are to be paid to Denver Equipment at the end of every month for the next 3 years, commencing 30 days from today's date, Oct. 1, 1998. Money is considered to be worth 12%, and the equipment has an estimated useful life of 5 years. Prepare the entry to record the lease, to record the first payment (Oct. 31, 1998), and to record the depreciation of the leased asset on Dec. 31, 1998. Round your answers to the nearest whole dollar.

▶ *(Check Figure: Interest expense, Oct. 31, 1998 = $452)*

## PROBLEMS: SET A

1† **Problem A1:** Determining EPS with Different Capital Structures

The stockholders of Silvercreek Steel Company are considering expanding their business. They have decided to issue both additional stock and bonds such that the firm's capital structure (the sum of stockholders' equity and bonds payable) will total $45 million. The bonds will be issued at face value.

The company president feels that the best arrangement would be to issue $24 million of 10% secured bonds, $12 million of 12% debenture bonds, and the remainder in stock. The financial vice president thinks that it would be better to issue only $12 million of 10% secured bonds and $9 million of 12% debenture bonds, and to have $24 million in common stock. The president's plan would mean 300,000 shares of stock outstanding, while the vice president thinks that there should be 550,000. A 30% tax rate would apply to Silvercreek Steel under either plan.

### Required:

Determine the amount of earnings per share under each plan for earnings before interest and taxes of $4 million and $9 million.

▶ *(Check Figures: EPS under vice president's plan = $2.19 for $4 million earnings and $8.55 for $9 million earnings)*

3 4 **Problem A2:** Recording Journal Entries for a Bond Issued at Face Value between Interest Payment Dates

Steamboat Springs Company was authorized to issue, at face value, $12 million of 10%, 20-year bonds dated Nov. 1, 1998. However, the bonds were not issued until Dec. 1, 1998. Interest payment dates are Nov. 1 and May 1.

### Required:

Prepare the general journal entries relating to the bond issue for 1998 and 1999, including the year-end adjusting and closing entries for the interest expense.

5 **Problem A3:** Recording Journal Entries for a Bond Issued at a Premium

On June 1, 1998, the Colorado Company issued $6 million of 12%, 20-year bonds. Interest is payable semiannually on June 1 and Dec. 1. The bonds sold for $6,297,600. The Colorado Company amortizes bond premiums and discounts on the straight-line basis and does so on bond interest payment dates.

### Required:

1. Prepare the general journal entries for 1998 and 1999 relating to the bond issue.
2. How will the bonds be presented on the Dec. 31, 1999, balance sheet?
3. If net income and income tax expense for 1999 were $794,880 and $510,000 respectively, what was the times interest earned?

   ▶ *(Check Figure: Unamortized premium, Dec. 31, 1999 = $274,040)*

† The numbers in the margin refer to the Learning Objectives.

5 **Problem A4:** Recording Journal Entries for a Bond Issued at a Discount

On May 1, 1998, the Mountain States Corporation issued $800,000 of 12%, 10-year bonds and received $764,000 cash proceeds on that date. Interest is payable semiannually on May 1 and Nov. 1. The bonds mature on May 1, 2008. Mountain States uses the straight-line method of amortizing bond discounts and does so on bond interest payment dates.

**Required:**

1. Prepare (without explanations) the general journal entries for the years 1998 and 1999 relating to the bond transactions.
2. How will the bonds be presented on the Dec. 31, 1999, balance sheet?

▶ *(Check Figure: Bond carrying value, Dec. 31, 1999 = $770,000)*

6 **Problem A5:** Determining Bond Selling Prices

Compute the bond selling prices for each of the following:

1. $2 million of 10%, 20-year bonds priced to yield 12% interest paid semiannually.
2. $4 million of 8%, 5-year bonds priced to yield 12% interest paid quarterly.
3. $6 million of 11%, 30-year bonds priced to yield 8% interest paid annually.

▶ *(Check Figures: $1,698,600; $3,402,160; $8,023,620)*

7 8 **Problem A6:** Using the Effective-Interest Method to Record Bonds Issued at a Discount

The Rocky Mountain Company received $2,626,134 on Apr. 1, 1998, for the issuance of $3 million of 8%, 10-year bonds dated Apr. 1, 1998. The bonds were sold in a 10% market and pay interest every 6 months. Rocky Mountain uses the effective-interest method of amortizing bond discounts.

**Required:**

1. Prepare a bond discount amortization schedule for 1998, 1999, and 2000.

▶ *(Check Figure: Bond carrying value, Oct. 1, 2000 = $2,688,611)*
2. Prepare the general journal entries relating to the bond issue for 1998 and 1999. Round your answers to the nearest whole dollar.

7 8 **Problem A7:** Using the Effective-Interest Method to Record Journal Entries for a Bond Issued at a Premium

Golden Buffalo Company issued $6 million in 9%, 20-year bonds to yield 8% on Mar. 1, 1998, and received $6,593,783 cash on that date. The bonds pay interest semiannually on Mar. 1 and Sept. 1. Golden Buffalo uses the effective-interest method to amortize bond premiums.

**Required:**

1. Prepare a bond premium amortization schedule for 1998, 1999, and 2000.
2. Prepare the general journal entries for 1998 and 1999 relating to the bond transactions. Round your answers to the nearest whole dollar.
3. How will the bonds be presented on the Dec. 31, 1999, balance sheet?

▶ *(Check Figure: Bond carrying value, Dec. 31, 1999 = $6,569,590)*

10 **Problem A8 (A16-8):** Recording Journal Entries for a Capitalized Lease

On Sept. 1, 1998, Ski Heaven Data Service leased from Route 70 Computers a model 720 computer under a lease that requires capitalization. Payments of $625 must be made at the end of every month for 3 years. The asset has an estimated economic life of 4 years and will be depreciated over that period of time. Interest of 12% is to be used for the capitalization.

**Required:**

1. Prepare the general journal entries for 1998 pertaining to the lease for Ski Heaven Data Service. Round your answers to the nearest whole dollar.
2. What information pertaining to the lease will appear on the Dec. 31, 1998, financial statements?

▶ *(Check Figure: Lease obligation, Dec. 31, 1998 = $17,043)*

## PROBLEMS: SET B

1† **Problem B1:** Determining EPS with Different Capital Structures

Due to a large increase in the demand for its product line, Salt Lake Business Machines, Inc., is considering expanding its plant capacity by raising additional funds. The funds will come from several sources: a 12%, 10-year, secured bond issue; a 14%, 20-year, debenture bond issue; and a common stock issue. The amount of each issue is the subject of the Nov. 15, 1998, board of directors meeting.

The chairperson of the board feels that $10 million of financing is needed and that $1.5 million should come from the 12% bonds, $4 million from the 14% bonds, and the remaining $4.5 million from the stock issue. This plan would result in a total of 650,000 (old plus new) shares of stock outstanding.

The president of the company feels that the total capitalization is fine but the mix is wrong. The president would like to see the 12% bonds increased to $3.5 million, the 14% bonds increased to $5 million, and the common stock reduced to $1.5 million. This plan would result in a total of 500,000 (old plus new) shares of stock outstanding.

Under either plan, the bonds would be issued at face value, and the company's tax rate would be 30%.

**Required:**

Compute the amount of earnings per share of common stock under each of the two plans.

1. Assume that earnings before interest and taxes under each plan are $2 million.
2. Assume that earnings before interest and taxes under each plan are $8 million.

▶ *(Check Figure: EPS under president's plan = $1.23 for $2 million earnings and $9.63 for $8 million earnings)*

3 4 **Problem B2:** Recording Journal Entries for a Bond Issued at Face Value between Interest Payment Dates

On Mar. 1, 1998, the Park City Company was authorized to issue at face value $6 million of 13%, 20-year bonds dated Mar. 1, 1998. However, the bonds were not issued until May 1, 1998. Interest payment dates are Mar. 1 and Sept. 1.

**Required:**

Prepare the general journal entries relating to the bond issue for 1998 and 1999, including the year-end adjusting and closing entries for the interest expense.

5 **Problem B3:** Recording Journal Entries for a Bond Issued at a Premium

On Feb. 1, 1998, the Ogden Company issued $4 million of 15%, 20-year bonds, and received $4,240,000 on that date. Interest is payable semiannually on Feb. 1 and Aug. 1.

**Required:**

1. Prepare the general journal entries for 1998 and 1999 relating to the bond issue. Assume that the straight-line method of amortizing bond premiums is used and that the premiums are amortized on interest payment dates.
2. How will the bonds be presented on the Dec. 31, 1999, balance sheet?
3. If net income and income tax expense for 1999 were $2,412,000 and $900,000 respectively, what was the times interest earned?

▶ *(Check Figure: Bond carrying value, Dec. 31, 1999 = $4,217,000)*

† The numbers in the margin refer to the Learning Objectives.

**5**   **Problem B4:** Preparing Journal Entries for a Bond Issued at a Discount

On Apr. 1, 1998, the Garden City Corporation issued $9 million of 11%, 20-year bonds and received $8,935,200 cash proceeds on that date. Interest is payable semiannually on Apr. 1 and Oct. 1. Garden City amortizes bond premiums and discounts on the straight-line basis and does so on bond interest payment dates.

**Required:**

1. Prepare (without explanations) the general entries for 1998 and 1999 relating to the bond transactions.
2. How will the bonds be presented on the Dec. 31, 1999, balance sheet?

   ▶ *(Check Figure: Bond carrying value, Dec. 31, 1999 = $8,940,870)*

**6**   **Problem B5:** Determining Bond Selling Prices

Compute the bond selling prices for each of the following:

1. $300,000 of 10%, $12\frac{1}{2}$-year bonds priced to yield 12% interest paid quarterly.
2. $600,000, of 9%, 15-year bonds priced to yield 8% interest paid semiannually.
3. $900,000 of 10%, 10-year bonds priced to yield 10% interest paid annually.

   ▶ *(Check Figures: $261,368; $651,684; $899,460)*

**7 8**   **Problem B6:** Using the Effective-Interest Method to Record Bonds Issued at a Discount

Henefer Company received $1,920,058 on May 1, 1998, for the issuance of $2,400,000 of 11%, 20-year bonds dated May 1, 1998. The bonds were sold in a 14% market and pay interest semiannually. The company uses the effective-interest method of amortizing bond discounts.

**Required:**

1. Prepare a bond discount amortization schedule for 1998, 1999, and 2000.

   ▶ *(Check Figure: Bond carrying value, Nov. 1, 2000 = $1,933,882)*
2. Prepare the general journal entries relating to the bond issue for 1998 and 1999. Round your answers to the nearest whole dollar.

**7 8**   **Problem B7:** Using the Effective-Interest Method to Record Journal Entries for a Bond Issued at a Premium

The *Snowbird Times* issued $7 million of 13%, 10-year bonds on Apr. 1, 1998, and received $8,308,532 on that date. The bonds pay interest on Apr. 1 and Oct. 1, and have an effective interest rate of 10%.

**Required:**

1. Prepare a bond premium amortization schedule for 1998, 1999, and 2000.
2. Prepare the general journal entries for 1998 and 1999 relating to the bond transactions. Round your answers to the nearest whole dollar.
3. How will the bonds be presented on the Dec. 31, 1999, balance sheet?

   ▶ *(Check Figure: Bond carrying value, Dec. 31, 1999 = $8,160,871)*

10    **Problem B8:** Recording Journal Entries for a Capitalized Lease

Denver Airways entered into a contract with Western Leasing Company on Oct. 1, 1998, for the lease of several aircraft. According to the terms of the contract, the lease must be capitalized. On the last day of every month for the next 4 years, Denver Airways is required to pay Western Leasing $450,000. The aircraft have an estimated economic life of 10 years and will be depreciated over that period of time. Interest of 12% is to be used for the capitalization.

**Required:**

1. Prepare the 1998 general journal entries pertaining to the lease for Denver Airways. Round your answers to the nearest whole dollar.
2. What information pertaining to the lease will appear on the Dec. 31, 1998, financial statements?

▶ *(Check Figure: Lease obligation, Dec. 31, 1998 = $16,242,084)*

## DECISION PROBLEM

The Red River Petrochemical Company is considering acquiring an existing plant from the DinoSor Oil Company. Red River could acquire the facility for $12 million by issuing that amount of common stock or corporate bonds, or by leasing the facility from DinoSor.

**Required:**

What must the board of directors of Red River Petrochemical consider before deciding on a method of financing the purchase?

## ETHICS CASE

Bill Jenkins, chief accountant in the actuarial division of Big Sky Motor Company, has just finished a crucial project for the president of the company. When he assigned this project to Bill, the president said that it had to be kept completely confidential.

The project consisted of two parts. The first part required the aid of three people from the engineering department. The problem facing the group was a result of several fatal accidents with the company's 1996 Seminole sedan. It seems that under certain conditions the Seminole's power brakes fail. The engineering division had been aware of the problem in the development stage of the Seminole, but was told to ignore it. The problem was corrected in the design for the 1997 model. The engineering group was asked to estimate the cost of recalling and repairing all 250,000 units of the Seminole made in the 1996 model year. After several days of intense work, it was determined that the nationwide recall would cost $125 million.

The second part of the project required two actuaries. This team was asked to estimate the number of accidents that might occur as a result of the faulty power brakes, to estimate the number of lawsuits that would result, and to estimate the cost of the eventual settlements. The actuarial group eventually determined that the lawsuits would cost the company $90 million over the next 10 years.

Now, having given the information to the president, Bill asks if the comptroller should be brought into the discussion, since a liability for the cost of the recall will have to be reflected on the financial statements. The president informs him that that will not be necessary, because the executive committee of the board has decided not to recall the 1996 Seminoles.

**Required:**

What, if anything, should Bill do about this situation?

## OBJECTIVE ASSIGNMENT ANSWERS

**True/False**

**1.** F    **2.** F    **3.** F    **4.** T    **5.** T

**Multiple Choice**

**1.** b    **2.** d    **3.** d    **4.** a    **5.** a
**6.** e    **7.** b    **8.** d    **9.** d    **10.** c

# Corporations: Investments and Consolidations

**LEARNING OBJECTIVES**

After studying this chapter, you should be able to do the following:

1 Explain the difference between a temporary and a long-term investment

2 Account for temporary and long-term investments in bonds:
   a At acquisition
   b While the corporation owns them
   c At the time of sale

3 Account for trading securities and available-for-sale securities

4 Explain when the equity method should be implemented and use it to account for appropriate long-term investments in stock

5 Explain the reasons for issuing consolidated financial statements

6 Use the purchase method of accounting for the acquisition of a subsidiary

7 Prepare consolidated balance sheets under the purchase method on the date of acquisition

8 Explain what minority interest is and how it is reported on consolidated balance sheets

9 Define the key terms listed at the end of this chapter

**CHAPTER OUTLINE**

**INVESTMENTS IN BONDS** • Temporary Investments in Bonds • Long-Term Investments in Bonds • **INVESTMENTS IN STOCK** • Reasons for Investing in Stock • Accounting for Investments in Stock—An Overview • Accounting for Investments in Stock—Trading Securities • Accounting for Investments in Stock—Available-for-Sale Securities • Accounting for Investments in Stock—Significant Influence Securities • **CONSOLIDATED FINANCIAL STATEMENTS** • The Parent and Subsidiary Relationship • Consolidation on the Date of Acquisition—100% Ownership • Consolidation on the Date of Acquisition—Less Than 100% Ownership

Anyone can buy stocks and bonds traded on the securities exchanges, and that includes corporations. Securities owned by corporations are shown on the balance sheet as assets, just like merchandise inventory, land, or patents.

The investment decision—whether a corporation should buy stocks or bonds, and which particular stocks or bonds it should buy—is a complex one. Generally, the objective is to earn a desirable rate of return for the firm at an acceptable level of risk. Highly rated bonds may be safer than many stocks, since interest on bonds must be paid to investors each year. In contrast, stockholders must rely on the board of directors to declare dividends before any are paid. In the event of liquidation, claims of the bondholders must be satisfied before those of the stockholders. Even with these advantages, some lower-rated bonds may be more risky than highly rated stocks in blue-chip companies. The investment decision is discussed extensively in finance courses. Here we will discuss the accounting for these assets once the investment decision has been made.

A corporation's investment in securities may be either temporary or long-term. **Temporary investments** (also known as **marketable securities** or **trading securities**) are stocks or bonds purchased with seasonally idle cash that will be invested only for a short time until it is needed in operations. An investment qualifies as temporary if it meets these two tests:

**Learning Objective 1**

Explain the difference between a temporary and a long-term investment

1. Management intends to hold the investment for a short time, usually less than one year.
2. The investment is readily marketable; management must be able to sell quickly.

Temporary investments are shown on the balance sheet as a current asset immediately following cash.

**Long-term investments** are acquired with resources that will not be needed in the operations of the business in the foreseeable future. Investments that do not meet the temporary investment criteria listed above are automatically classified as long-term investments. For example, a company accumulating funds to build a new building or to acquire another company may invest in stocks or bonds for an extended period of time. Long-term investments are shown as a separate major category on the balance sheet following current assets.

Whether stocks or bonds are purchased from the previous owners or from the issuing corporation, the investment is accounted for in exactly the same way. The type of security purchased—stocks or bonds—does affect the accounting procedures, however, as we will see in the next two sections.

## INVESTMENTS IN BONDS

Here we will look at bonds from the point of view of the investor. In the examples below we will assume that Thermal Heaters, Inc., is buying Aztec Motor Corporation bonds with a $7,000,000 face value.

### Temporary Investments in Bonds

Bonds acquired as a temporary investment are simply recorded at cost. If cost is above par, the bonds are said to be purchased at a premium; bonds acquired below par are said to be purchased at a discount. Since the bonds will be held for such a short period of time, premiums and discounts are not amortized. Interest income must be recorded[1]

---

[1] All our journal entries in the examples are in general journal form, even though the entry may actually be made in a special journal. This will make illustrations much easier because we won't have to construct special journals each time we make an entry.

when received and accrued at the company's year-end. Temporary investments in bonds must be reported on the year-end balance sheet at their market value. Gains and losses are recognized when bonds are adjusted to their year-end market value and when these temporary investments are sold.

**Learning Objective 2**

Account for temporary and long-term investments in bonds at acquisition

On May 1, 1998, Thermal Heaters, Inc., using $6,508,349 of surplus cash that will be needed in the fall, acquires Aztec Motor Corp. bonds paying interest at an annual rate of 12% and having a face value of $7,000,000. The Aztec bonds pay interest semiannually on May 1 and Nov. 1. Thermal purchases the Aztec bonds at a discount but does not record this fact in a separate account, as it would for bonds payable.

| 1998 | | | |
|---|---|---|---|
| May 1 | Trading Securities: Debt............................ | 6,508,349 | |
| | Cash........................................ | | 6,508,349 |
| | To record purchase of Aztec bonds having a face value of $7,000,000 and paying 12% annual interest on May 1 and Nov. 1. | | |

On Nov. 1, 1998, Thermal receives the semiannual interest on the Aztec bonds:

**Learning Objective 2**

Account for temporary and long-term investments in bonds while the corporation owns them

| Nov. 1 | Cash.......................................... | 420,000 | |
|---|---|---|---|
| | Interest Income............................. | | 420,000 |
| | To record receipt of 6 months' interest on investment in Aztec bonds. ($7,000,000 $\times$ 12% $\times \frac{6}{12}$ = $420,000) | | |

On Dec. 31, Thermal's accounting year ends. Two months' interest has been earned and must be accrued:

| Dec. 31 | Interest Receivable............................ | 140,000 | |
|---|---|---|---|
| | Interest Income............................. | | 140,000 |
| | To accrue 2 months' interest earned on investment in Aztec bonds. ($7,000,000 $\times$ 12% $\times \frac{2}{12}$ = $140,000) | | |

On Dec. 31, the Aztec bonds are trading on the market for $6,540,000. Thermal must adjust the bonds to this market value and recognize a $31,651 ($6,540,000 − $6,508,349) unrealized gain. Gains and losses are said to be unrealized when no liquid asset such as cash is received when the gain or loss is recognized. Thermal would prepare the following entry:

| Trading Securities: Debt................................ | 31,651 | |
|---|---|---|
| Unrealized Gain.................................... | | 31,651 |
| To adjust temporary investment in Aztec bonds to market value. | | |

Unrealized gains and losses on trading securities are reported on the income statement as other income or other losses.

**Learning Objective 2**

Account for temporary and long-term investments in bonds at the time of sale

On Jan. 2, 1999, because Thermal needs cash for acquisition of inventory, salaries, and other operating purposes, the Aztec bonds are sold for $6,545,000 plus $140,000 accrued interest, or a total of $6,685,000.

| 1999 | | | |
|---|---|---|---|
| Jan. 2 | Cash.......................................... | 6,685,000 | |
| | Trading Securities: Debt..................... | | 6,540,000 |
| | Interest Receivable.......................... | | 140,000 |
| | Gain on Sale of Trading Security ............. | | 5,000 |
| | To record sale of Aztec Corp. bonds. | | |

Note that Thermal's management used $6,508,349 of seasonally surplus cash to earn $596,651—$560,000 interest plus a $36,651 ($31,651 + $5,000) increase in the value of the bonds—during the 8-month period. Had the cash been left in a checking account, it would have produced little or no income for the company.

## Long-Term Investments in Bonds

The accounting events for long-term investments in bonds are similar to the ones described for temporary investments: recording interest received, accruing interest at the end of the year, and recognizing gains or losses upon sale of the investment. In addition, any discounts or premiums on long-term investments must be amortized, using either the straight-line or the effective-interest method. If management intends to hold these long-term investments in bonds until they mature, there is no need to adjust for changes in their market value at the end of each year.

### Bonds Purchased at Face Value

**Learning Objective 2**

Account for temporary and long-term investments in bonds at acquisition

When bonds are purchased at their face (or par) value, the interest earned will be at the rate printed on the face of the bond. The interest earned will also equal the amount of cash interest received.

On Nov. 1, 1999, Thermal Heaters, Inc., purchased at face value $7 million, 12% bonds of Aztec Motor Corp., maturing in 5 years. Thermal intends to hold these bonds until they mature. The bonds pay interest on May 1 and Nov. 1 each year. Thermal's entries for the first year it owns the bonds are as follows:

| 1999 | | | |
|---|---|---|---|
| Nov. 1 | Investment in Bonds.......................... | 7,000,000 | |
| | Cash .................................... | | 7,000,000 |
| | To record purchase of Aztec bonds as a long-term investment. | | |
| | | | |
| Dec. 31 | Interest Receivable.......................... | 140,000 | |
| | Interest Income .......................... | | 140,000 |
| | To accrue interest at the end of the accounting year ($7,000,000 × 12% × $\frac{2}{12}$ = $140,000). | | |
| | | | |
| 2000 | | | |
| May 1 | Cash...................................... | 420,000 | |
| | Interest Receivable ....................... | | 140,000 |
| | Interest Income .......................... | | 280,000 |
| | To record semiannual interest received on Aztec bonds. | | |
| | | | |
| Nov. 1 | Cash...................................... | 420,000 | |
| | Interest Income .......................... | | 420,000 |
| | To record semiannual interest received on Aztec bonds. ($7,000,000 × 12% × $\frac{6}{12}$ = $420,000) | | |

The interest entries on May 1, Nov. 1, and Dec. 31 will be repeated each year that Thermal holds the bonds.

Note that Thermal bought the bonds on the day the interest had been paid to the previous owner of the bonds. This assumption simplified the illustration. Let's make the example a little more complex by assuming that Thermal buys these same bonds on Apr. 1, 2000.

Since the bonds are acquired between interest dates, the former owner must be paid the interest he or she has earned since the last interest payment date. As the new owner of the bonds, Thermal will receive cash for a full 6 months' interest. Thermal must be careful to recognize as income only the amount earned — interest for the time it has held the bonds. Here are Thermal's entries for bonds purchased between interest dates:

| | | | |
|---|---|---|---|
| **2000** | | | |
| Apr. 1 | Investment in Bonds . . . . . . . . . . . . . . . . . . . . . . . . . . | 7,000,000 | |
| | Interest Receivable . . . . . . . . . . . . . . . . . . . . . . . . . . | 350,000 | |
| | Cash. . . . . . . . . . . . . . . . . . . . . . . . . . . . . . . . . | | 7,350,000 |
| | To record purchase of Aztec bonds as a long-term investment. ($7,000,000 $\times$ 12% $\times \frac{5}{12}$ = $350,000) | | |
| | | | |
| May 1 | Cash . . . . . . . . . . . . . . . . . . . . . . . . . . . . . . . . . . | 420,000 | |
| | Interest Receivable . . . . . . . . . . . . . . . . . . . . . . . | | 350,000 |
| | Interest Income . . . . . . . . . . . . . . . . . . . . . . . . . . | | 70,000 |
| | To record semiannual interest received on Aztec bonds. ($7,000,000 $\times$ 12% $\times \frac{6}{12}$ = $420,000) | | |

On April 1, Thermal bought two things: (1) $7,000,000 of Aztec bonds and (2) the right to receive $350,000 earned by the former owner. Thermal didn't earn the $350,000 and therefore must be careful not to record it as income. Thermal debited Interest Receivable for the $350,000 because Thermal actually purchased this asset and will receive this amount along with another $70,000 on May 1. The $70,000 represents the interest income Thermal earned by holding the bonds for one month.

### Bonds Purchased at a Discount or Premium

Bonds are often issued at amounts below or above their face, or par, value. Let's review the reasons for the existence of discounts and premiums.

Bonds sell for less than face value when the interest rate in the market — the rate paid by competing bonds — is higher than the rate printed on the bonds. Thermal would be foolish to pay the same price for Aztec bonds paying 12% as for Tallow Corp. bonds paying 14%. To compensate and remain competitive, the Aztec bonds will sell at a discount, that is, for less than face value. Thermal and other buyers of Aztec bonds will still receive the face value when the bonds mature. The difference between face and the selling price is the extra interest income earned by the investor over the life of the bonds.

Bonds sell for more than face value when the market rate of interest is lower than the rate printed on the bonds. Naturally, Aztec, the issuing company, doesn't want to pay any higher rate on its bonds than it has to. If the competing interest rate in the market is 10% at the current time, Aztec will be willing to pay no more than that. Even though the rate printed on the bonds is 12%, Aztec will simply charge Thermal and other investors more for the bonds. Remember, the investor will still receive only the face value at maturity. The premium — that is, the extra amount paid by the investor — serves to decrease the 12% interest paid on the bond to the equivalent of 10%, the market interest rate. Thus the premium decreases the interest expense for Aztec and decreases the interest income earned by Thermal.

We also increase or decrease the interest each period by amortizing the discount or premium, respectively. The same two methods of amortization — straight-line and effective-interest — may be used for investments in bonds as well as for bonds payable.

Learning Objective **2**

Account for temporary and long-term investments in bonds while the corporation holds them

**Straight-Line Amortization of Discounts and Premiums**  The entries in parallel columns in Exhibit 1 show how Thermal uses straight-line amortization to account for the Aztec bonds if they are purchased at a discount or at a premium. Studying these entries reveals some very important information.

**Exhibit 1** Straight-Line Amortization

| Transaction | $7,000,000 Bonds Purchased at a Discount ($6,508,349) (Effective-interest rate = 14%) | | |
|---|---|---|---|

**May 1, 1998**
Thermal purchases Aztec bonds ($7,000,000 face) for cash.

Investment in Bonds ..................... 6,508,349
   Cash ...............................    6,508,349
To record purchase of Aztec bonds, face = $7,000,000.

**Nov. 1, 1998**
Thermal receives $420,000 semiannual interest ($7,000,000 × 12% × $\frac{6}{12}$ = $420,000) and amortizes the discount or premium.

Cash................................... 420,000
Investment in Bonds ..................... 49,165
   Interest Income......................    469,165
To record receipt of semiannual interest and amortization of discount:
   Discount = $7,000,000 − $6,508,349 = $491,651.
   Divide by number of periods (5 years × 2 periods per year) = 10
   Amortization per period (rounded to the nearest dollar)
   ($491,651/10 periods = $49,165)

**Dec. 31, 1998**
Thermal accrues the interest earned since Nov. 1 and amortizes 2 months of discount or premium.

Interest Receivable ..................... 140,000
Investment in Bonds ..................... 16,388
   Interest Income......................    156,388
To accrue interest and amortize discount at the year-end.
($7,000,000 × 12% × $\frac{2}{12}$ = $140,000) ($49,165 × $\frac{2}{6}$ = $16,388)

**May 1, 1999**
Thermal receives $420,000 semiannual interest and amortizes the discount or premium.

Cash................................... 420,000
Investment in Bonds ..................... 32,777
   Interest Receivable..................    140,000
   Interest Income......................    312,777
To record receipt of semiannual interest and amortize 4 months of discount. ($49,165 × $\frac{4}{6}$ = $32,777)

*Date of purchase.* Thermal records its investment in Aztec bonds at the amount paid. No separate discount or premium account is established. Separate accounts are used for discounts or premiums on bonds payable. There is no theoretical reason for not using separate discount or premium accounts to record bond purchases; it's just customary to use only one account for investments.

*Cash interest received.* Thermal receives $420,000 in cash because this amount is specified in the bond contract. The fact that the bonds were purchased at an amount other than face value makes no difference.

*Discount or premium amortization.* Thermal determines how much of the discount or premium to amortize by dividing the total discount or premium by the number of 6-month periods remaining in the bonds' life. The **straight-line method** amortizes the same amount each period until the bonds mature or are sold. Thermal records the amortization of the discount by debiting Investment

---

#### $7,000,000 Bonds Purchased at a Premium ($7,540,522)
#### (Effective-interest rate = 10%)

---

| | | |
|---|---|---|
| Investment in Bonds. . . . . . . . . . . . . . . . . . . . . . . . . . . . . . . . . . . . . . . . . | 7,540,522 | |
|    Cash . . . . . . . . . . . . . . . . . . . . . . . . . . . . . . . . . . . . . . . . . . . . . . . . . | | 7,540,522 |
| To record purchase of Aztec bonds, face = $7,000,000. | | |

| | | |
|---|---|---|
| Cash . . . . . . . . . . . . . . . . . . . . . . . . . . . . . . . . . . . . . . . . . . . . . . . . . . . . . . | 420,000 | |
|    Investment in Bonds . . . . . . . . . . . . . . . . . . . . . . . . . . . . . . . . . . . . | | 54,052 |
|    Interest Income . . . . . . . . . . . . . . . . . . . . . . . . . . . . . . . . . . . . . . . | | 365,948 |

To record receipt of semiannual interest and amortization of premium:
Premium = $7,540,522 − $7,000,000 = $540,522.
Divide by number of periods
(5 years × 2 periods per year) = 10
Amortization per period (rounded to the nearest dollar)
($540,522/10 = $54,052)

| | | |
|---|---|---|
| Interest Receivable. . . . . . . . . . . . . . . . . . . . . . . . . . . . . . . . . . . . . . . . | 140,000 | |
|    Investment in Bonds . . . . . . . . . . . . . . . . . . . . . . . . . . . . . . . . . . . | | 18,017 |
|    Interest Income . . . . . . . . . . . . . . . . . . . . . . . . . . . . . . . . . . . . . . | | 121,983 |

To accrue interest and amortize premium at the year-end.
($7,000,000 × 12% × $\frac{2}{12}$ = $140,000)
($54,052 × $\frac{2}{6}$ = $18,017)

| | | |
|---|---|---|
| Cash . . . . . . . . . . . . . . . . . . . . . . . . . . . . . . . . . . . . . . . . . . . . . . . . . . . . . . | 420,000 | |
|    Investment in Bonds . . . . . . . . . . . . . . . . . . . . . . . . . . . . . . . . . . . | | 36,035 |
|    Interest Receivable . . . . . . . . . . . . . . . . . . . . . . . . . . . . . . . . . . . | | 140,000 |
|    Interest Income . . . . . . . . . . . . . . . . . . . . . . . . . . . . . . . . . . . . . . | | 243,965 |

To record receipt of semiannual interest and amortize 4 months of
premium. ($54,052 × $\frac{4}{6}$ = $36,035)

---

in Bonds for $49,165 each period; premium amortization requires crediting Investment in Bonds for $54,052 each period. If Thermal keeps the bonds until maturity, the Investment in Bonds account will be increased or decreased to $7,000,000.

Interest income when bonds are purchased at a discount is more than the $420,000 cash received. This is logical: remember, when bonds are purchased at a discount, Thermal earns a higher rate of interest (14%) than the printed rate (12%). Interest income when bonds are acquired at a premium is less than the $420,000 cash received. This also makes sense: when Thermal buys at a premium, interest earned (10%) is less than the printed rate (12%).

**Effective-Interest Amortization of Discounts and Premiums**  Unlike the straight-line method, which amortizes an equal number of dollars each period and recognizes an equal amount of interest income each period, the effective-interest method recognizes interest income at the same rate each period but yields a different number of dollars each period.

Under the **effective-interest method** the interest expense is calculated by multiplying the book value of the bonds at the beginning of an interest period by the effective-interest rate. In this chapter interest income is calculated in a similar manner: multiply the balance in the investment account at the beginning of an interest period by the effective-interest rate. The discount or premium to be amortized is the difference between interest income and the cash interest received. Thermal's interest income and the amortization for each 6-month period is calculated in Exhibits 2 and 3.

**Exhibit 2** Schedule of Interest Earned and Bond Discount to be Amortized—Effective-Interest Method
12% Bonds Purchased to Yield 14%
(All amounts rounded to the nearest dollar)

| Date | Cash Received | Interest Earned | Discount Amortized | Carrying Amount of Bonds |
|---|---|---|---|---|
| May 1, 1998 | | | | $6,508,349 |
| Nov. 1, 1998 | $420,000 | $455,584 | $35,584 | 6,543,933 |
| May 1, 1999 | 420,000 | 458,075 | 38,075 | 6,582,008 |
| Nov. 1, 1999 | 420,000 | 460,741 | 40,741 | 6,622,749 |
| May 1, 2000 | 420,000 | 463,592 | 43,592 | 6,666,341 |
| Nov. 1, 2000 | 420,000 | 466,644 | 46,644 | 6,712,985 |
| May 1, 2001 | 420,000 | 469,909 | 49,909 | 6,762,894 |
| Nov. 1, 2001 | 420,000 | 473,403 | 53,403 | 6,816,297 |
| May 1, 2002 | 420,000 | 477,141 | 57,141 | 6,873,438 |
| Nov. 1, 2002 | 420,000 | 481,141 | 61,141 | 6,934,579 |
| May 1, 2003 | 420,000 | 485,421 | 65,421 | 7,000,000 |

$7,000,000 \times .12 \times \frac{1}{2}$ yr. = $420,000
$6,508,349 \times .14 \times \frac{1}{2}$ yr. = $455,584
$455,584 - $420,000 = $35,584
$6,508,349 + $35,584 = $6,543,933

**Exhibit 3** Schedule of Interest Earned and Bond Premium to be Amortized—Effective-Interest Method
12% Bonds Purchased to Yield 10%
(All amounts rounded to the nearest dollar)

| Date | Cash Received | Interest Earned | Premium Amortized | Carrying Amount of Bonds |
|---|---|---|---|---|
| May 1, 1998 | | | | $7,540,522 |
| Nov. 1, 1998 | $420,000 | $377,026 | $42,974 | 7,497,548 |
| May 1, 1999 | 420,000 | 374,877 | 45,123 | 7,452,425 |
| Nov. 1, 1999 | 420,000 | 372,621 | 47,379 | 7,405,046 |
| May 1, 2000 | 420,000 | 370,252 | 49,748 | 7,355,298 |
| Nov. 1, 2000 | 420,000 | 367,765 | 52,235 | 7,303,063 |
| May 1, 2001 | 420,000 | 365,153 | 54,847 | 7,248,216 |
| Nov. 1, 2001 | 420,000 | 362,411 | 57,589 | 7,190,627 |
| May 1, 2002 | 420,000 | 359,531 | 60,469 | 7,130,158 |
| Nov. 1, 2002 | 420,000 | 356,508 | 63,492 | 7,066,666 |
| May 1, 2003 | 420,000 | 353,333 | 66,666* | 7,000,000 |

$7,000,000 \times .12 \times \frac{1}{2}$ yr. = $420,000
$7,540,522 \times .10 \times \frac{1}{2}$ yr. = $377,026
$420,000 - $377,026 = $42,974
$7,540,522 - $42,974 = $7,497,548
* $1 rounding error

Entries recording Thermal's investment in Aztec's bonds are shown in Exhibit 4. Note that at the end of the accounting year Thermal must recognize a portion of the interest earned since the last interest payment date and amortization for the same period. This is accomplished by looking in the appropriate amortization schedule (Exhibit 2 or Exhibit 3) to determine the interest income and amortization planned for the *next* interest payment date. These amounts are then split between the months prior to the year-end and those between the year-end and the next interest date. In Thermal's case 2 months' interest income and amortization are shown at the year-end (Dec. 31) and 4 months' are recorded at the next interest payment date (May 1).

Thermal's amortization of the discount or premium will bring the balance in the Investment in Bonds account to $7 million at the end of 5 years. The straight-line and effective-interest methods end up at the same place (a $7 million balance); they just get there in different ways. The effective-interest method is required by generally accepted accounting principles unless the difference in interest income between the two methods is not material.

If Thermal holds the bonds until they mature in 5 years, the firm will receive $7 million from Aztec. The following entry records this transaction:

| | | | | |
|---|---|---|---:|---:|
| **2003** | | | | |
| May 1 | Cash | | 7,000,000 | |
| | | Investment in Bonds | | 7,000,000 |
| | | To record receipt of maturity value of Aztec Corp. bonds. [We are assuming that Thermal has already recorded the May 1, 2003, interest income and amortization.] | | |

### Sale of Long-Term Bond Investment

Learning Objective **2**

Account for temporary and long-term investments in bonds at the time of sale

The sale of a long-term bond investment is recorded in the same way as the sale of a temporary bond investment. The difference between the amount received and the carrying value of the investment is recorded as a gain or loss. With temporary investments, the carrying value and cost are the same because the discount or premium is not amortized. In contrast, the carrying value of a long-term investment changes as amortization takes place. To illustrate, assume that Thermal bought the Aztec bonds on May 1, 1998, for $7,540,522 and sold them for $7,500,000 on Nov. 1, 1999. The entry to record the sale is as follows:

| | | | | |
|---|---|---|---:|---:|
| **1999** | | | | |
| Nov. 1 | Cash | | 7,500,000 | |
| | | Investment in Bonds | | 7,405,046 |
| | | Gain on Sale of Investment | | 94,954 |
| | | To record sale of Aztec bonds. | | |
| | | Balance of Investment account 11/1/99: | | |
| | | Cost 5/1/98 . . . . . . . . . . . . . . . . . $7,540,522 | | |
| | | Premium amortized 11/1/98 . . . . . (42,974) | | |
| | | Premium amortized 5/1/99 . . . . . (45,123) | | |
| | | Premium amortized 11/1/99 . . . . . (47,379) | | |
| | | Balance 11/1/99 . . . . . . . . . . . . . . $7,405,046 | | |

Gains and losses on sales of bonds are shown on the income statement under Other Gains and Losses. Losses and gains from the sale of other assets (buildings, machinery, land, copyrights) also are disclosed in this section of the income statement.

**Exhibit 4** Effective-Interest Amortization

| Transaction | $7,000,000 Bonds Purchased at a Discount ($6,508,349) (Effective-interest rate = 14%) | | |
|---|---|---|---|

*May 1, 1998*
Thermal purchases Aztec bonds ($7,000,000 face) for cash.

| | | | |
|---|---|---|---|
| Investment in Bonds | | 6,508,349 | |
| Cash | | | 6,508,349 |

To record purchase of Aztec bonds, face = $7,000,000.

*Nov. 1, 1998*
Thermal receives $420,000 semiannual interest ($7,000,000 × 12% × $\frac{6}{12}$) and amortizes the discount or premium.

| | | | |
|---|---|---|---|
| Cash | | 420,000 | |
| Investment in Bonds | | 35,584 | |
| Interest Income | | | 455,584 |

To record receipt of semiannual interest and amortization of discount:
($6,508,349 × 14% × $\frac{6}{12}$ = $455,584)
($455,584 − $420,000 = $35,584) (See Exhibit 2)

*Dec. 31, 1998*
Thermal accrues the interest earned since Nov. 1 and amortizes 2 months of discount or premium. ($7,000,000 × 12% × $\frac{2}{12}$ = $140,000)

| | | | |
|---|---|---|---|
| Interest Receivable | | 140,000 | |
| Investment in Bonds | | 12,692 | |
| Interest Income | | | 152,692 |

To accrue interest and amortize discount at the year-end:

| | | |
|---|---|---|
| Interest income next 6 months (see Exhibit 2) | $458,075 | |
| | × $\frac{2}{6}$ | |
| Interest income for 2 months | $152,692 | |
| Discount amortized (6 months) (see Exhibit 2) | $ 38,075 | |
| | × $\frac{2}{6}$ | |
| Discount amortized (2 months) | $ 12,692 | |

*May 1, 1999*
Thermal receives $420,000 semiannual interest and amortizes the discount or premium for 4 months

| | | | |
|---|---|---|---|
| Cash | | 420,000 | |
| Investment in Bonds | | 25,383 | |
| Interest Receivable | | | 140,000 |
| Interest Income | | | 305,383 |

To record receipt of semiannual interest and amortization of discount:

| | | |
|---|---|---|
| Interest income for 6 months (see Exhibit 2) | $458,075 | |
| | × $\frac{4}{6}$ | |
| Interest income for 4 months | $305,383 | |
| Amortization for 6 months (see Exhibit 2) | $ 38,075 | |
| | × $\frac{4}{6}$ | |
| Amortization for 4 months | $ 25,383 | |

### $7,000,000 Bonds Purchased at a Premium ($7,540,522)
### (Effective-interest rate = 10%)

| | | |
|---|---:|---:|
| Investment in Bonds . . . . . . . . . . . . . . . . . . . . . . . . . . . . . . . . . . | 7,540,522 | |
|     Cash . . . . . . . . . . . . . . . . . . . . . . . . . . . . . . . . . . . . . . . . . | | 7,540,522 |

To record purchase of Aztec bonds, face = $7,000,000.

| | | |
|---|---:|---:|
| Cash . . . . . . . . . . . . . . . . . . . . . . . . . . . . . . . . . . . . . . . . . . . . . | 420,000 | |
|     Investment in Bonds . . . . . . . . . . . . . . . . . . . . . . . . . . . | | 42,974 |
|     Interest Income . . . . . . . . . . . . . . . . . . . . . . . . . . . . . . . | | 377,026 |

To record receipt of semiannual interest and amortization of premium:

$(\$7,540,522 \times 10\% \times \frac{6}{12} = \$377,026)$
$(\$377,026 - \$420,000 = \$42,974)$
(See Exhibit 3)

| | | |
|---|---:|---:|
| Interest Receivable . . . . . . . . . . . . . . . . . . . . . . . . . . . . . . . . . . | 140,000 | |
|     Investment in Bonds . . . . . . . . . . . . . . . . . . . . . . . . . . . | | 15,041 |
|     Interest Income . . . . . . . . . . . . . . . . . . . . . . . . . . . . . . . | | 124,959 |

To accrue interest and amortize premium at the year-end:

| | |
|---|---:|
| Interest income next 6 months (see Exhibit 3) . . . . | $374,877 |
| | $\times \frac{2}{6}$ |
| Interest income for 2 months . . . . . . . . . . . . . . . . | $124,959 |
| Amortization for 6 months (see Exhibit 3) . . . . . . . . | $ 45,123 |
| | $\times \frac{2}{6}$ |
| Premium amortized (2 months) . . . . . . . . . . . . . . . | $ 15,041 |

| | | |
|---|---:|---:|
| Cash . . . . . . . . . . . . . . . . . . . . . . . . . . . . . . . . . . . . . . . . . . . . . | 420,000 | |
|     Investment in Bonds . . . . . . . . . . . . . . . . . . . . . . . . . . . | | 30,082 |
|     Interest Receivable . . . . . . . . . . . . . . . . . . . . . . . . . . . . | | 140,000 |
|     Interest Income . . . . . . . . . . . . . . . . . . . . . . . . . . . . . . . | | 249,918 |

To record receipt of semiannual interest and amortization of discount:

| | |
|---|---:|
| Interest income for 6 months (see Exhibit 3) . . . . . . | $374,877 |
| | $\times \frac{4}{6}$ |
| Interest income for 4 months . . . . . . . . . . . . . . . . . | $249,918 |
| Amortization for 6 months (see Exhibit 3) . . . . . . . . | $ 45,123 |
| | $\times \frac{4}{6}$ |
| Amortization for 4 months . . . . . . . . . . . . . . . . . . . | $ 30,082 |

1. What criteria must be satisfied in order for an investment to be classified as temporary?
2. When bonds are purchased at a discount, how does the treatment of the discount differ if the investment is temporary rather than long-term?
3. What two things are purchased when bonds are acquired between interest dates?
4. Does a 10% bond purchased at a premium earn more or less than 10% interest?
5. What is the difference between the straight-line and effective-interest methods of amortization? Which is normally required by generally accepted accounting principles?

## INVESTMENTS IN STOCK

### Reasons for Investing in Stock

A corporation will probably invest any cash it's accumulating for capital expansion or other reasons. Further, it may want to earn a higher rate of return than savings accounts, government securities, or even corporate bonds may offer. The corporation may be willing to take a little more risk in exchange for higher earnings on its investment.

Common stocks are sometimes selected as corporate investments because their dividend payout rates are high or because their market values are expected to increase. The dividends received plus the increase in market value may be projected to be greater than the interest that could be earned by investing in interest-bearing securities such as bonds.

Another reason for stock investment is that a corporation may want to acquire another corporation by purchasing its stock. Any one individual or entity that acquires enough voting stock of a corporation may elect enough directors to significantly influence or even control the actions of the company. The ability to influence another corporation's actions may be especially important if that corporation, for example, is a supplier of critical raw materials and supplies, or if it provides a crucial distribution system. If the ownership percentage is high enough, the financial statements of the two corporations may be combined and treated as one entity for reporting purposes, as we will discuss later.

### Accounting for Investments in Stock—An Overview

Investments in stock may be divided into four groups, or portfolios, depending on management's intent for each investment:

**Trading Securities: Equity**  Stock that is bought principally for the purpose of holding it for only a short time then selling it.

**Available-for-Sale Securities**  Stock that management intends to hold for a longer period. Management does not intend to acquire enough stock to significantly influence or acquire these investee companies.

**Significant Influence Securities**  Stock investments that are significantly large enough for management to influence the operations of the investee company. These long-term investments are accounted for by the equity method.

**Acquired Company Securities**  Stock investments that are so large that they give management control over the investee company. Since management has acquired the investee through purchase of their stock, the financial statements of the investee are combined, or consolidated, with those of the investor company.

## Accounting for Investments in Stock—Trading Securities

Learning
Objective 3

Account for trading securities and
available-for-sale securities

When an investor buys stock with the intent of holding it for a short period of time, the stock is placed in a trading securities portfolio. These temporary investments are shown on the balance sheet at their fair market value. Accounting for trading securities is relatively simple and straight forward: When acquired, these securities are recorded at cost, including any brokerage fees paid to acquire them. Dividends declared by the investee are recognized as income. The securities are adjusted to their fair value at the end of the year and an unrealized gain or loss is recognized. When sold, the difference between the selling price and carrying value is recorded as realized gain or loss. A simple example will illustrate the entries for each of these events:

On June 15, 1998, Slate, Inc.'s financial managers decide to invest in common stock of Utica Environmental Systems Corp. that is selling for $9.25 per share. Slate buys 5,000 shares, which constitute 1% of Utica's 500,000 shares of outstanding common stock. The entry to record the acquisition of these shares and the payment of a $250 brokerage fee is as follows:

| | | | |
|---|---|---|---|
| June 15 | Trading Securities: Stock. . . . . . . . . . . . . . . . . . . . | 46,500 | |
| | Cash . . . . . . . . . . . . . . . . . . . . . . . . . . . . . . . . | | 46,500 |
| | To record acquisition of 5,000 shares at $9.25 per share plus a broker's commission of $250. | | |

Slate is purchasing stock on the open market (e.g., the New York or American Stock Exchange). The stock is being acquired not from Utica Corp. but from another investor. Slate records the investment *at cost,* without regard to the stock's par value, original issue price, or any other value. Short-term investments in stock may be debited to a general account called Trading Securities, Temporary Investments, or Marketable Securities.

On Oct. 1, the Utica board of directors declares a $0.25 per share quarterly dividend to stockholders of record on Oct. 15, payable Oct. 31. Slate's entries to record the dividend declaration and the receipt of the cash look like this:

| | | | |
|---|---|---|---|
| Oct. 1 | Dividends Receivable . . . . . . . . . . . . . . . . . . . . . . | 1,250 | |
| | Dividend Income . . . . . . . . . . . . . . . . . . . . . . . . | | 1,250 |
| | To record Utica's declaration of a $0.25 per share dividend. ($0.25 × 5,000 shares = $1,250) | | |
| 31 | Cash . . . . . . . . . . . . . . . . . . . . . . . . . . . . . . . . . | 1,250 | |
| | Dividends Receivable . . . . . . . . . . . . . . . . . . . . | | 1,250 |
| | To record receipt of Utica Corp. dividend. | | |

Dividend income is recorded when the dividend is declared. It is on this date that the Utica board incurred a liability to pay the dividend and thus Slate is assured of receiving it.

On Nov. 5, Utica declares and issues a 20% stock dividend. Slate prepares a memorandum entry noting that additional shares are received. No income is recognized because no assets are distributed: Slate just has more "pieces of paper" to represent the same 1% ownership interest. Slate now owns 6,000 of the 600,000 shares of Utica stock—still 1%. Slate prepares the following memorandum entry:

| | |
|---|---|
| Nov. 5 | Received 1,000 shares of Utica Environmental Systems Corp. stock as the company's share of a 20% stock dividend. |

Slate's total cost of $46,500, or $9.30 per share ($46,500 ÷ 5,000 shares) should now be distributed over 6,000 shares. The average cost of the Utica stock is now $7.75 per share ($46,500 ÷ 6,000 shares).

On Dec. 31, 1998, Slate must value its Utica stock at fair market value. Since Utica is widely traded, reference to closing stock market quotations on December 31, provide a quick way to determine fair value. Assuming that Utica is quoted at $7.50 per share, Slate would need to recognize a $.25 ($7.75 − $7.50) per share loss:

| | | | |
|---|---|---|---|
| Dec. 31 | Unrealized Loss | 1,500 | |
| | Trading Securities: Stock | | 1,500 |
| | To adjust temporary investment in Utica Stock to market value. ($.25 × 6,000 shs. = $1,500) | | |

Quoted market prices provide an objective measure of the value of investments at the end of each period. Since trading securities are expected to be sold in a very short time, GAAP requires that gains and losses be reported as soon as they can be objectively measured—at the end of each accounting period. This $1,500 loss, then, is reported on Slate's 1998 income statement under the caption, "Other Losses."

On Mar. 1, 1999, Slate sells the 6,000 shares of Utica stock at $8 per share less brokerage fees of $700. This disposal is recorded by the following entry:

| | | | |
|---|---|---|---|
| Mar. 1 | Cash [($8 × 6,000 shares)—$700] | 47,300 | |
| | Trading Securities: Stock | | |
| | ($7.50 × 6,000 shares) | | 45,000 |
| | Realized Gain on Sale of Stock | | 2,300 |
| | To record the sale of 6,000 shares of Utica stock having a carrying value of $7.50 per share. | | |

Remember that following the stock dividend, each share of Utica had a carrying value of $7.75 which was reduced to $7.50 fair value at the end of the year. The difference between the carrying value ($45,000) and the net proceeds received ($47,300) is recorded as either a gain or a loss. This realized gain is reported on Slate's 1999 income statement under the caption, "Other Gains."

### Accounting for Investments in Stock—Available-for-Sale Securities

Available-for-Sale Securities are those that management does not intend to sell in the short term, nor does management intend to keep buying shares until it acquires significant influence or control over the investee company. In short, these are usually long-term investments made primarily for dividends and/or growth in the value of the investee's stock.

Except for changes in a few account titles and classifications, accounting for these securities is almost identical to the accounting for trading securities discussed in the previous section. Acquisitions are recorded at cost, cash dividends are recorded as income when declared by the investee, the stock is adjusted to fair value at the end of the year, and disposals require removing the investment and recording gains or losses. The one major difference in accounting lies in how the adjustment to fair value is recorded at the year-end. A repeat of the Slate's accounting for the Utica stock investment will quickly highlight the similarities and differences:

Recording the purchase of 5,000 shares is identical except for the change in the name of the investment account.

| | | | |
|---|---|---|---|
| June 15 | Investment in Utica Corp. Stock | 46,500 | |
| | Cash | | 46,500 |
| | To record acquisition of 5,000 shares at $9.25 per share plus a broker's commission of $250. | | |

The declaration and payment of a cash dividend and receipt of the stock by Utica are identical.

| | | | |
|---|---|---|---|
| Oct. 1 | Dividends Receivable . . . . . . . . . . . . . . . . . . . . . . . . | 1,250 | |
| |     Dividend Income . . . . . . . . . . . . . . . . . . . . . . . . | | 1,250 |
| | To record Utica's declaration of a $0.25 per share dividend. ($0.25 × 5,000 shares = $1,250) | | |
| | | | |
| 31 | Cash . . . . . . . . . . . . . . . . . . . . . . . . . . . . . . . . . . . | 1,250 | |
| |     Dividends Receivable . . . . . . . . . . . . . . . . . . . . | | 1,250 |
| | To record receipt of Utica Corp. dividend. | | |
| | | | |
| Nov. 5 | Received 1,000 shares of Utica Environmental Systems Corp. stock as the company's share of a 20% stock dividend. | | |

Slate's entry to reduce the Utica investment to fair value:

| | | | |
|---|---|---|---|
| Dec. 31 | Unrealized Loss . . . . . . . . . . . . . . . . . . . . . . . . . . . . | 1,500 | |
| |     Investment in Utica Corp. Stock . . . . . . . . . . . . | | 1,500 |
| | To adjust investment in Utica Stock to market value. ($.25 × 6,000 shs. = $1,500) | | |

This $1,500 loss is reported on Slate's 1998 balance sheet as a stockholders' equity account. Since this account has a debit balance, it will be a negative stockholders' equity item. Unrealized gains will be positive stockholders' equity accounts. GAAP requires that management wait until available-for-sale securities are actually sold to recognize losses and gains on the company's income statement.

The sale of the Utica stock involves removing the Unrealized Loss account from stockholders' equity and recording the realized gain:

| | | | |
|---|---|---|---|
| Mar. 1 | Cash [($8 × 6,000 shares) − $700] . . . . . . . . . . . . . . | 47,300 | |
| |     Unrealized Loss. . . . . . . . . . . . . . . . . . . . . . . . . | | 1,500 |
| |     Investment in Utica Corp. Stock | | |
| |       ($7.50 × 6,000 shares) . . . . . . . . . . . . . . . . . . . | | 45,000 |
| |     Realized Gain on Sale of Stock . . . . . . . . . . . . . . . . | | 800 |
| | To record the sale of 6,000 shares of Utica stock having a carrying value of $7.50 per share. | | |

The expectation is that available-for-sale securities will not be sold in as short a time as will trading securities. GAAP requires a company to disclose increases or decreases in the value of these investments by using a stockholders' equity account. Since sale of the available-for-sale security is not likely to happen in the near future, a company must wait to disclose these gains and losses on its income statement until the actual sale takes place.

The ultimate effect on Slate's income statement is the same whether securities are classified as trading or available-for-sale. Gains and losses on trading securities just appear on the income statement sooner. The following analysis illustrates this fact for the Utica transactions described above:

| | Trading | Available-for-Sale |
|---|---|---|
| Unrealized loss on 1998 income statement | $(1,500) | $ 0 |
| Realized gain on 1999 income statement | 2,300 | 800 |
| Net realized gain reported | $ 800 | $ 800 |

## Accounting for Investments in Stock—Significant Influence Securities

Learning Objective 4

Explain when the equity method should be implemented and use it to account for appropriate long-term investments in stock

When an investor corporation exerts significant influence over the investee corporation, the **equity method** of accounting is used. We presume that an investor that has acquired 20% or more of the investee's stock exerts significant influence. If the investor elects members to the investee's board of directors, exchanges management personnel with the investee, or enters into substantial transactions with the investee, these are further indications of significant influence.

The equity method accounts for the acquisition of stock at cost; recognizes income (or loss) as it is earned by the investee; reduces the Investment account when dividends are received; and records a gain or loss upon disposal of the stock. The following example illustrates the equity method.

### Purchase of Stock Investment—Equity Method

On Jan. 1, 1998, Bodie Corporation purchases 40,000 of the 100,000 outstanding shares of Dawn, Inc., for $816,000, including all brokerage fees. The entry to record the acquisition is:

| | | | |
|---|---|---|---|
| Jan. 1 | Investment in Dawn, Inc., Stock............... | 816,000 | |
| | Cash.................................. | | 816,000 |
| | To record purchase of 40,000 shares (40%) of Dawn, Inc., stock. | | |

### Income on Stock Investment—Equity Method

On Dec. 31, 1998, Dawn reports a net income of $240,000. Under the equity method Bodie recognizes 40% of these earnings at the time reported by Dawn, not at the time Dawn distributes them as dividends. Since the investor may exert significant influence over the investee, the investor may be able to control the timing and amount of dividends. If income was recognized by the investor company at the time dividends were declared, the investor would be able to manipulate its net income by regulating the dividend declarations of the investee. *The equity method eliminates the possibility of manipulation by requiring the investor to recognize income (or loss) when it is earned by the investee.* Bodie records its share of Dawn's 1998 income as follows:

| | | | |
|---|---|---|---|
| Dec. 31 | Investment in Dawn, Inc., Stock ............... | 96,000 | |
| | Income from Investment in Dawn, Inc......... | | 96,000 |
| | To record 40% equity in the $240,000 net income of Dawn, Inc. | | |

Since Dawn earned a $240,000 net income during 1998, its net assets (total assets minus total liabilities) increased by $240,000 and stockholders' equity (retained earnings) increased by $240,000. If Bodie's Investment account is to continue to reflect a 40% equity in Dawn's net assets, Bodie's Investment account must be increased by $96,000 (40% of $240,000).

If a net loss is reported by the investee, the decrease in net assets is recorded by the investor by debiting a loss account and crediting (reducing) the Investment account.

### Dividends from Investee—Equity Method

On Jan. 2, 1999, Dawn, Inc., declares a $0.50 per share dividend. The dividend will be paid on Jan. 15 to stockholders of record as of Jan. 7. Declaration of a cash or property dividend reduces the net assets of the investee. Under the equity method, the investor reduces the Investment account to record this fact. Also, since Bodie records income when it is earned by Dawn, any further income recognition when dividends are distributed would constitute double counting. Bodie prepares the following entries to record the declaration and receipt of the dividend:

| | | | |
|---|---|---|---|
| Jan. 2 | Dividends Receivable........................ | 20,000 | |
| | Investment in Dawn, Inc., Stock............. | | 20,000 |
| | To record declaration of a $0.50 per share dividend by investee. ($0.50 × 40,000 shares = $20,000) | | |
| Jan. 15 | Cash....................................... | 20,000 | |
| | Dividends Receivable ..................... | | 20,000 |
| | To record receipt of cash dividend from Dawn, Inc. | | |

Stock dividends are handled under the equity method by preparing a memorandum entry to note the fact that additional shares of stock have been received. The ownership percentage and the equity in the net assets of the investee remain unchanged.

### Sale of Stock Investment—Equity Method

An investor may sell some shares of the investee but still have a high enough ownership percentage to exercise significant influence. In such cases the investor determines the carrying value per share of the investment and records the difference between this carrying value and the selling price of the stock as a gain or loss.

On Jan. 17, 1999, Bodie disposes of 10,000 shares of Dawn at $23 per share. This transaction is recorded as follows:

| | | | |
|---|---|---|---|
| Jan. 17 | Cash ($23 × 10,000 shares) ................... | 230,000 | |
| | Investment in Dawn, Inc., Stock............. | | 223,000 |
| | Gain on Sale of Investment................. | | 7,000 |
| | To record the sale of 10,000 shares of Dawn, Inc. | | |

The carrying value per share of investment is calculated as follows:

| | |
|---|---|
| Acquisition cost......................................... | $816,000 |
| Portion of 1998 income.................................... | 96,000 |
| Less: Dividends received ................................. | (20,000) |
| Balance of Investment account............................. | $892,000 |
| Divide by number of shares owned ........................ | ÷ 40,000 shs |
| Carrying value per share owned............................ | $ 22.30 |
| Number of shares sold .................................... | × 10,000 shs |
| Carrying value of shares sold.............................. | $223,000 |

If the ownership drops below 20% or if significant influence ceases to exist for some other reason, the investor converts to the cost method of accounting for future periods.

The authoritative financial accounting standard covering marketable equity securities states that lower-of-cost-or-market is not appropriate when the investment is accounted for by the equity method. This makes sense, because the investor is not carrying the investment at cost.

1. What determines whether an investment will be accounted for as a trading security or as an available-for-sale security?
2. How does accounting for unrealized gains and losses differ for trading and available-for-sale securities?
3. When is the equity method required for investments in stock?
4. What event is recorded under the equity method but not under the cost method?

## CONSOLIDATED FINANCIAL STATEMENTS

### The Parent and Subsidiary Relationship

If corporation P owns a large enough percentage of the stock of corporation S, it may do more than exert significant influence over corporation S: it may effectively control the activities of corporation S. When this situation exists, the controlling corporation is referred to as the **parent** and the corporation being controlled is called the **subsidiary.** A parent and subsidiary relationship is generally assumed when one corporation owns more than 50% of the outstanding common stock of another.

How does corporation P (Parent) control corporation S (Subsidiary)? Remember that each share of common stock gives its owner a vote in electing the members of the board of directors. If P owns more than 50% of S, P can elect all the people it wants to S's board. The S board members elected by P (and loyal to P) can then set operating policies and hire the managers to run S. Thus P controls S.

The parent and subsidiary companies are separate legal entities. They may be in different industries, and they may seem to have no relationship at all to each other. But an investor that purchases shares in the parent company is really acquiring indirect ownership interest in its subsidiary companies as well. The investor must rely on the financial statements published by the parent to disclose the financial position and operating results of all corporations under the parent's control.

Because the parent owns more than 20% of the stock in a subsidiary corporation, the equity method of accounting is used to account for the investment in the parent company records. The equity method will yield a single amount on P's balance sheet, Investment in Subsidiary Corporation, and a single amount on P's income statement, Income from Investment in Subsidiary Corporation. But these two individual amounts provide no information about the subsidiary's various assets, liabilities, revenues, and expenses.

Investors' decisions may be influenced by the amount of the parent's and the subsidiary's combined assets and liabilities. Some of the questions investors might ask include: Are the assets composed primarily of cash, receivables, and inventories, or do plant and equipment assets predominate? Are liabilities primarily current or long-term? What assets are pledged as collateral for liabilities?

Investors may also be curious about the subsidiary's and the parent's combined revenues and expenses. Are revenues primarily from merchandise sales, or do disposals of nonoperating assets and miscellaneous income items play a major role? How significant is cost of goods sold expense in relation to administrative and selling costs?

Learning Objective **5**

Explain the reasons for issuing consolidated financial statements

**Consolidated financial statements** are designed to inform investors about the combined total assets, liabilities, revenues, and expenses of the subsidiary and the parent. In other words, consolidated financial statements portray the parent and subsidiary companies as a *single economic entity.* The entity concept provides the underlying theoretical support for the preparation of consolidated financial statements. A single consolidated balance sheet shows all the assets and liabilities of the parent and all subsidiary companies. A single consolidated income statement similarly discloses the revenues and expenses of the parent and all its subsidiary companies.

The consolidation process may be accomplished by using the purchase or the pooling-of-interests method. The **purchase method** is used when a parent acquires the subsidiary's stock by using cash, other assets, or debt securities. The purchase method is also used if the subsidiary is acquired by exchanging the parent's stock for the subsidiary's stock *and* less than 90% of the subsidiary's stock is acquired. The **pooling-of-interests method** is used when 90% or more of a subsidiary is acquired by an exchange of parent company stock for subsidiary stock *and* when a number of other conditions are satisfied. In the business world, the vast majority of consolidations are accomplished using the purchase method.

We will demonstrate the basics of the purchase method in the remainder of this chapter. The pooling method and complex applications of the purchase method are covered in an advanced accounting course.

**Learning Objective 6**

Use the purchase method of accounting for the acquisition of a subsidiary

## Consolidation on the Date of Acquisition—100% Ownership

Two important things must be understood about combining financial statements when one company *purchases* another:

1. The subsidiary's assets are placed on the consolidated balance sheet at their cost to the parent corporation. When the parent company buys the assets of the subsidiary, it must pay the fair market value for these assets. This fair market value is the parent's cost.

    If the parent pays more for the subsidiary's assets than the total of their individual fair market values, the difference is known as **goodwill.** Goodwill must also appear on the consolidated balance sheet.

    The parent's cost will probably be different from the carrying value on the books of the subsidiary company. Remember that the subsidiary's asset carrying value is its original cost (or its original cost minus accumulated depreciation). The market value of these assets may have changed substantially since the subsidiary acquired them.

2. The subsidiary's postacquisition income is combined with the parent's income on the consolidated income statement. Revenues and expenses incurred by the subsidiary *before* the acquisition date are *not* included in determining the combined net income.

These two points are very logical if you remember that the purchase method assumes that one company is *buying* another at a point in time. The accounting, then, is similar to what is done when any asset is bought: record it at acquisition cost, and recognize profit that it earns only after it is purchased.

The following illustration shows how to prepare a consolidated balance sheet on the day the subsidiary is acquired. We don't have to be concerned with a consolidated income statement on the day of acquisition because that would include only the parent company's revenues and expenses and would not include the subsidiary's earnings up to the day of acquisition.

Company P acquired all the outstanding stock of Company S on Jan. 1, 1998, for $200,000. The individual condensed balance sheets of Company P and Company S immediately after the acquisition are shown in Exhibit 5.

What did Company P get for its $200,000? An examination of Company S's balance sheet reveals that the *net assets* (assets minus liabilities) purchased have a carrying value of $170,000 ($250,000 − $80,000). Company P paid $30,000 in excess of the carrying value. This $30,000 may be attributed to the fact that S's carrying value of certain assets may be less than their market value. Or P may have purchased goodwill, an asset possessed by Company S but not listed on its balance sheet. In most cases both undervalued assets and goodwill exist.

**Exhibit 5** Separate Company P and Company S Balance Sheets

## COMPANY P AND COMPANY S
### Condensed Balance Sheets
### January 1, 1998

| Company P | | Company S | |
|---|---|---|---|
| Assets: | | Assets: | |
| Current Assets (total)..... | $1,000,000 | Current Assets (total)..... | $100,000 |
| Investment in S......... | 200,000 | Property, Plant, and Equip- | |
| Property, Plant, and Equip- | | ment Assets (net)....... | 150,000 |
| ment Assets (net).... | 2,000,000 | Total Assets............. | $250,000 |
| Total Assets............. | $3,200,000 | | |
| | | Equities: | |
| Equities: | | Current Liabilities........ | $ 10,000 |
| Current Liabilities........ | $ 360,000 | Long-Term Liabilities..... | 70,000 |
| Long-Term Liabilities..... | 1,040,000 | Common Stock.......... | 120,000 |
| Common Stock.......... | 1,400,000 | Retained Earnings....... | 50,000 |
| Retained Earnings....... | 400,000 | | |
| Total Equities............. | $3,200,000 | Total Equities............. | $250,000 |

Assume that an appraisal of Company S's assets shows land with a market value that is $10,000 higher than its carrying value. All other assets' market and carrying values are the same. We assume that the remaining $20,000 excess payment ($30,000 − $10,000) is for goodwill, because no other purchased asset can be identified.

Learning Objective 7

Prepare consolidated balance sheets under the purchase method on the date of acquisition

Now that the market value of the various assets and the amount of goodwill have been determined, the balance sheets can be combined. This combination is accomplished by the following three steps:

**STEP 1:** Eliminating the Investment account found on the parent company's balance sheet and the stockholders' equity accounts on the subsidiary's balance sheet. Any difference between these two amounts will be taken care of by steps 2 and 3 below.

**STEP 2:** Adding (or deducting) appropriate amounts to adjust all subsidiary assets and liabilities to their fair values.

**STEP 3:** Entering goodwill to account for any difference not explained by market value adjustments in step 2.

The worksheet in Exhibit 6 illustrates this procedure.

**Intercompany accounts** may exist between a parent and a subsidiary. These accounts must be eliminated (offset against each other) in the consolidation process. For example, if Company P had loaned Company S $10,000 during 1997, Company P would have a $10,000 receivable on its balance sheet and Company S would have a $10,000 payable on its balance sheet. This transaction gives the consolidated entity no right to receive cash from an outside party, nor does it create an obligation to pay an outside party. The consolidated entity owes itself $10,000. This illogical situation is taken care of by removing both the receivable and the payable in preparing the consolidated balance sheet.

**Exhibit 6**

**COMPANIES P AND S**
Consolidated Balance Sheet—Purchase Method Worksheet
Time of Acquisition—100% Ownership
January 1, 1998

| Accounts | Individual Company Balance Sheets | | Adjustments and Eliminations | | Consolidated Balance Sheet |
|---|---|---|---|---|---|
| | Company P | Company S | Debit | Credit | |
| Assets: | | | | | |
| Current Assets | $1,000,000 | $100,000 | | | $1,100,000 |
| Investment in S | 200,000 | | | (a) $200,000 | |
| Goodwill | | | (b) $ 20,000 | | 20,000 |
| Property, Plant & Equip. | 2,000,000 | 150,000 | (c)     10,000 | | 2,160,000 |
| Total Assets | $3,200,000 | $250,000 | | | $3,280,000 |
| Equities: | | | | | |
| Current Liabilities | $  360,000 | $  10,000 | | | $  370,000 |
| Long-Term Liabilities | 1,040,000 | 70,000 | | | 1,110,000 |
| Common Stock | 1,400,000 | 120,000 | (d)   120,000 | | 1,400,000 |
| Retained Earnings | 400,000 | 50,000 | (d)     50,000 | | 400,000 |
| Total Equities | $3,200,000 | $250,000 | (e) $200,000 | (e) $200,000 | $3,280,000 |

(a) The Investment account is eliminated. It is being replaced by S's various assets and liabilities.
(b) Goodwill is added because Company P paid $20,000 more for Company S's assets than their fair market value.
(c) $10,000 must be added because S's land was undervalued. Company P paid fair market value for the land.
(d) Company S's Common Stock and Retained Earnings accounts are eliminated. The stockholders' equity accounts of Company P reflect the ownership of the consolidated entity.
(e) Note that the totals of the debit and credit eliminations are equal.

## Consolidation on the Date of Acquisition—Less Than 100% Ownership

As we discussed earlier, the existence of a parent–subsidiary relationship is generally assumed when one corporation owns more than 50% of the outstanding common stock of another. What if Company P purchased 90% of Company S's stock? The other 10% is owned by individuals and corporations (other than Company P) and is referred to as a **minority interest.** Those holding a minority interest still have a claim against the subsidiary's assets that will be shown in the stockholders' equity or liabilities section of the consolidated balance sheet. A part of all future consolidated income also belongs to the minority shareholders.

Let's repeat the Company P and Company S illustration, this time assuming that Company P purchased only 90% of Company S's stock for $200,000. All other facts of the example are the same. The new worksheet is shown in Exhibit 7.

Now assume that Company P is paying $200,000 for 90% of the $170,000 net assets of Company S. Since the same price is paid for less equity in Company S,

Learning Objective **8**

Explain what minority interest is and how it is reported on consolidated balance sheets

**Exhibit 7**

### COMPANIES P AND S
#### Consolidated Balance Sheet—Purchase Method Worksheet
#### Time of Acquisition—90% Ownership
#### January 1, 1998

| | Individual Company Balance Sheets | | | Adjustments and Eliminations | | Consolidated Balance Sheet |
|---|---|---|---|---|---|---|
| **Accounts** | **Company P** | **Company S** | **Debit** | **Credit** | |
| Assets: | | | | | |
| Current Assets | $1,000,000 | $100,000 | | | $1,100,000 |
| Investment in S | 200,000 | | | $200,000 | |
| Goodwill | | | (a) $ 38,000 | | 38,000 |
| Property, Plant & Equip. | 2,000,000 | 150,000 | 9,000 | | 2,159,000 |
| Total Assets | $3,200,000 | $250,000 | | | $3,297,000 |
| Equities: | | | | | |
| Current Liabilities | $ 360,000 | $ 10,000 | | | $ 370,000 |
| Long-Term Liabilities | 1,040,000 | 70,000 | | | 1,110,000 |
| Common Stock | 1,400,000 | 120,000 | (b) 120,000 | | 1,400,000 |
| Retained Earnings | 400,000 | 50,000 | (b) 50,000 | | 400,000 |
| Minority Interest: | | | | | |
| Common Stock | | | | (b) 12,000 | 12,000 |
| Retained Earnings | | | | (b) 5,000 | 5,000 |
| Total Equities | $3,200,000 | $250,000 | $217,000 | $217,000 | $3,297,000 |

(a) Goodwill is greater than in Exhibit 6 because Company P is paying the same amount for a smaller portion of Company S's net assets.

(b) 10% of Company S's Common Stock and Retained Earnings is transferred to minority interest. Minority Interest appears on the published statement as one amount, $17,000.

Company P must be purchasing more goodwill. The revised calculation of goodwill is as follows:

| | |
|---|---|
| Purchase price of 90% of Company S................................. | $ 200,000 |
| Deduct carrying value of 90% of the net assets of Company S (90% × $170,000) .............................................. | (153,000) |
| Difference ........................................................ | $ 47,000 |
| Deduct portion of difference attributable to undervalued Company S land purchased by Company P (90% × $10,000)......................... | (9,000) |
| Portion of difference attributable to goodwill ......................... | $ 38,000 |

The minority interest on the consolidated balance sheet amounts to 10% of the stockholders' equity of Company S. In the consolidation process 90% of Company S's Common Stock and Retained Earnings is eliminated, leaving the 10% still owned by outside parties. The following consolidated balance sheet shows that the minority interest is disclosed as a single amount in the stockholders' equity section.

---

**P AND S COMPANIES**
**Consolidated Balance Sheet**
**January 1, 1998**

---

### Assets

| | |
|---|---|
| Current Assets . . . . . . . . . . . . . . . . . . . . . . . . . . . . . . . . . . . . . . . . . . . . . . . . . . . | $1,100,000 |
| Property, Plant, and Equipment. . . . . . . . . . . . . . . . . . . . . . . . . . . . . . . . . . . . | 2,159,000 |
| Intangible Asset: Goodwill . . . . . . . . . . . . . . . . . . . . . . . . . . . . . . . . . . . . . . . . | 38,000 |
| Total Assets . . . . . . . . . . . . . . . . . . . . . . . . . . . . . . . . . . . . . . . . . . . . . . . . . . | $3,297,000 |

### Liabilities & Stockholders' Equity

| | |
|---|---|
| Liabilities: | |
| Current Liabilities . . . . . . . . . . . . . . . . . . . . . . . . . . . . . . . . . . . . . . . . . . . . . | $ 370,000 |
| Long-Term Liabilities . . . . . . . . . . . . . . . . . . . . . . . . . . . . . . . . . . . . . . . . . | 1,110,000 |
| Total Liabilities . . . . . . . . . . . . . . . . . . . . . . . . . . . . . . . . . . . . . . . . . . . . . | $1,480,000 |
| Stockholders' Equity: | |
| Common Stock. . . . . . . . . . . . . . . . . . . . . . . . . . . . . . . . . . . . . . . . . . . . . . . | $1,400,000 |
| Retained Earnings . . . . . . . . . . . . . . . . . . . . . . . . . . . . . . . . . . . . . . . . . . . . | 400,000 |
| Minority Interest in Company S . . . . . . . . . . . . . . . . . . . . . . . . . . . . . . . . . . | 17,000 |
| Total Stockholders' Equity . . . . . . . . . . . . . . . . . . . . . . . . . . . . . . . . . . . . . | $1,817,000 |
| Total Liabilities & Stockholders' Equity . . . . . . . . . . . . . . . . . . . . . . . . . . . . | $3,297,000 |

---

When a consolidated income statement is prepared in years subsequent to acquisition, the minority claim against the earnings of the consolidated entity will be deducted as the last item on the income statement.

---

**ASK YOURSELF** ▶

1. **When does a parent–subsidiary relationship exist?**
2. **What are consolidated financial statements?**
3. **At what amount will a subsidiary's assets appear on a consolidated balance sheet?**
4. **What are intercompany accounts?**
5. **When does minority interest exist?**

---

# Invisible Debt

Picture this: It's early 1988, and you've just received your General Motors 1987 annual report. You sit down with a cup of coffee while you skim the statement. This shouldn't take long—but wait a minute. What's this? It seems that in the space of a single year GM's short-term debt has gone from next to nothing to nearly $53 billion. What's happened? Has GM secretly acquired Belgium? Nope. It's just more magic from the accounting profession.

If the Financial Accounting Standards Board has its way, investors in hundreds of companies like General Motors will suddenly discover that the companies are deeper in debt than they previously thought. The list of firms affected includes Deere & Co., Textron, Gulf & Western, Xerox, IBM, and many, many more.

The change will come in the way companies consolidate their subsidiaries. In years past, companies with subsidiaries in finance, real estate, insurance, and leasing have not been forced to combine the financial subsidiaries' liabilities and their own. Yet at the same time they have added the net income and equity of the subs to their own. The parent company gets a boost from the subsidiary without having to reflect its debt, in short, a free ride.

But now, if the Board's ruling passes, the ride will come to a skidding halt, as all that debt, buried in the balance sheets of subsid-iaries, gets unearthed on the balance sheets of the parent corporation.

The old nonconsolidation rule was based on the idea that finance, real estate, and insurance subsidiaries use capital so differently from their parents that a combined balance sheet would be meaningless. But the logic behind the change is that a corporation is an economic entity and shouldn't have arbitrary distinctions between its components. "If you consolidate one subsidiary, you ought to consolidate all," says Paul Rosenfeld, director of accounting standards at the American Institute of CPAs.

Unconsolidated balance sheets can conceal plenty when most of a sub's business comes from a parent. The three auto manu-facturers alone have over $125 billion of liabilities in their finance subs that don't show up on their balance sheets.

Take General Motors. By last fall the company had unloaded 5 million cars and trucks from its bloated inventory by offering buyers incentives, including 2.9% financing. The resulting $78 billion in short- and long-term debt it had to take on to offer such give-away finance rates got squirrled away on the unconsolidated balance sheet of General Motors Finance Corp., the company's captive finance subsidiary. That left GM itself with a seemingly gilt-edged third-quarter debt-to-equity ratio of 0.2 to 1, instead of a much more leveraged—and more accurate—ratio of $2.80 of debt to each dollar of equity.

Do consolidated numbers really present a fairer picture of the complete company? Says John Vivian, comptroller at Sears, "It would be very difficult to perform any analyses on our consolidated statements if one were not able to see the pieces."

Take a firm like ITT. More than half its assets presently aren't shown on its balance sheet, because they belong to ITT's insurance company, Hartford Fire Insurance. But say that the two statements were consolidated. Would ITT bondholders or shareholders be right to conclude that their company suddenly acquired a huge new source of assets they could reach for in the event of a liquidation? No way. In reality, first claim goes to Hartford Fire policyholders.

It seems as if there's no winning. If you don't consolidate, firms can shuffle away their problems into subsidiaries. If you do consolidate, the problems can often disappear into huge, unrevealing numbers.

One sensible solution comes from Arthur Andersen partner Benjamin Neuhausen, who argues that the accounting profession should consider a "tiered" balance sheet. "If major categories, such as debt or fixed assets, were dissected by major lines of business, the balance sheet would show exactly what corporate assets and liabilities really do exist at the subsidiary level and how much they contribute to the parent company itself."

*Source:* Laura Jereski, "Invisible Debt," *Forbes,* Feb. 9, 1987, p. 68. Reprinted by permission of FORBES magazine. Copyright © 1987 by Forbes, Inc.

---

For years generally accepted accounting principles allowed companies to exclude the assets and liabilities of certain subsidiaries from consolidated balance sheets. An automobile manufacturer, for example, could exclude a banking or finance subsidiary because its assets are so unlike those of a manufacturer. This article discusses a change, recently passed by the Financial Accounting Standards Board, that requires *all* majority-owned subsidiaries to be consolidated.

## SUMMARY

- A corporation purchases shares of stock or bonds issued by other corporations to earn a return on cash that it does not immediately need for current operations.
- Investments in stocks or bonds are considered to be **trading securities** or **temporary investments** if they are readily marketable and if management intends to hold them for less than one year.
- Bond investments purchased at face value earn interest at the printed rate. Bonds purchased at a discount earn interest at higher than the printed rate; those purchased at a premium earn interest at less than the printed rate. Investment bond discounts and premiums are not recorded in separate accounts.
- Premiums and discounts on bonds classified as trading securities are not amortized because they are held for such a short period of time. Trading securities must be adjusted to their market value at the end of each accounting period. Long-term bond investment premiums and discounts must be amortized over the remaining life of the bonds. Generally accepted accounting principles usually require that the effective-interest method of amortization be employed. The straight-line method may be used if it produces results that are not materially different from those produced by the effective-interest method.
- Bond investments may be either held until maturity or sold at any time. If a bond investment is sold, a gain or loss is recognized if the selling price is above or below the carrying value of the investment.
- Stock that one corporation purchases in other corporations may be classified in four basic groups. **Trading securities** and **available-for-sale securities** are acquired to earn dividends and reap the growth in the stock's market value. Trading securities are those that management intends to hold for a short time; available-for-sale securities are usually held for longer periods. **Significant influence and acquired company securities** are purchased to gain some degree of influence or control over the actions of another corporation.
- Trading securities and available-for-sale securities are shown at fair market value on the investor's balance sheet. Unrealized gains and losses for trading securities are shown on the income statement. Unrealized gains and losses on available-for-sale securities must be disclosed in a stockholders' equity account.

- Significant influence securities must be accounted for by the **equity method.** Significant influence is presumed to exist in cases where more than 20% of an investee's stock is owned.
- Acquired company securities exist when an investor corporation controls an investee corporation, usually through ownership of more than 50% of the investee's common stock, **consolidated financial statements** are prepared. Consolidated financial statements report the financial position and operating results of the parent corporation and all subsidiaries as if they were one entity.
- The **purchase method** is used when a parent acquires controlling interest in a subsidiary by using assets, or stock (if less than 90% of the subsidiary's stock is acquired in exchange for the parent's stock).
- Consolidation under the purchase method involves:

1. Recording the subsidiary's assets on the combined balance sheet at their fair market value.
2. Recognizing any goodwill purchased.
3. Combining revenues and expenses of the parent and subsidiary beginning with the date of acquisition.

- When less than 100% of a subsidiary's stock is acquired, **minority interest** claims against the assets and income of the subsidiary must be disclosed on the consolidated balance sheet and income statement, respectively.

## 9  KEY TERMS

| | |
|---|---|
| **Available-for-sale securities** | Investment in stock that management intends to hold for a long period of time. These investments are made to earn dividends and gain the benefit of increases in a stock's value, not to influence or control the investee. |
| **Acquired company securities** | Stock investments that are so large that they give management control over the investee company. |
| **Consolidated financial statements** | Financial statements that portray a parent and one or more subsidiary companies as a single economic entity. Consolidated statements are prepared when the parent owns more than 50% of the subsidiary's stock. |
| **Effective-interest method** | The method used to amortize discounts and premiums on bond investments over the remaining life of the bond by using the interest rate in effect at the time the bonds were purchased. |
| **Equity method** | A system of accounting used by investors to account for investments in other companies over which the investor exerts significant influence. |
| **Goodwill** | The excess of the purchase price of a business over the total fair market value of the net assets of that business. |
| **Intercompany accounts** | Accounts arising from transactions between a parent and a subsidiary corporation. Intercompany accounts are eliminated in the process of preparing consolidated financial statements. |
| **Long-term investments** | Investments in bonds or stock acquired with resources that will not be needed in the operations of the business in the foreseeable future. |

| Marketable securities | See **Temporary investments.** |
|---|---|
| Minority interest | The claim of the minority shareholders against the assets and income of a consolidated entity. |
| Parent corporation | An investor corporation that owns more than 50% of the common stock of an investee corporation. |
| Pooling-of-interests method | A system of preparing consolidated financial statements. This method must be used when the parent corporation exchanges its stock for 90% or more of the subsidiary's common stock and when other defined criteria are satisfied. |
| Purchase method | A system of preparing consolidated financial statements. This method must be used when the parent corporation acquires stock in a subsidiary by giving cash or other assets, or by exchanging stock (if less than 90% of the subsidiary's stock is acquired in exchange for the parent's stock). |
| Significant influence securities | Stock investments that are significantly large enough for management to influence the operations of the investee company. Significant influence is presumed to exist when the investor owns 20% or more of the investee's stock. |
| Straight-line method | A method used to amortize discounts or premiums on bond investments. This method amortizes an equal amount of discount or premium each year for the remainder of the bond's life. |
| Subsidiary corporation | A corporation that has more than 50% of its common stock owned by another corporation. |
| Temporary investments | Investments in bonds or stock that can be readily sold and that management intends to keep for less than one year. Also known as **marketable securities** or **trading securities.** |
| Trading Securities | Stocks or bonds that are bought principally for the purpose of holding them for a short time and then selling them. |

## DEMONSTRATION PROBLEM

Anvil Corp. has the following 1998 transactions related to investments. (Assume that all investments are long-term unless they are specifically identified as temporary.)

July 2  Anvil purchased Gant Corp. bonds for $384,880 as a long-term investment. The 8% bonds have a par value of $500,000 and pay interest on June 30 and Dec. 31 each year. The Gant bonds will yield 12% interest and mature in 10 years.

10  Anvil purchased 30,000 shares of Tanner Co. stock for $18 per share plus $27,000 broker's commission. These shares represent 30% of Tanner's stock.

28  Anvil purchased 15,000 shares of Bene, Inc., stock for $94,500 including broker's commission. The shares are 5% of Bene's outstanding stock. Anvil considers the Bene stock an available-for-sale security.

Aug. 1  Tanner declared a $1 per share dividend payable Sept. 30 to stockholders of record as of Aug. 31.

Aug. 12  Anvil's management invested seasonally idle cash in 1,000 shares of Peak Publishing Co. common stock. Anvil paid $22.50 per share plus a brokerage fee of $1,100 for the temporary investment. This investment represents less than 1% of Peak's outstanding stock and is considered a trading security.

Sept. 15  Bene, Inc., declared a $0.50 per share cash dividend payable on Oct. 31 to stockholders of record as of Oct. 1.

Dec. 31   Anvil received the interest from Gant Corp. and amortized the discount on the bonds using the effective-interest method.

  31   The following information is available about the Anvil stock investments:

| Company | Quoted Market Price per Share | Reported Net Income for 1998 |
|---------|---------------------|---------------------|
| Tanner | $15.00 | $340,000 |
| Bene | 5.75 | 125,000 |
| Peak | 22.25 | 690,000 |

**Required:**

Prepare entries to record each of the 1998 transactions and events related to Anvil Corp.'s investments. What amounts will Anvil disclose on its income statement under the captions "other income and gains" or "other expenses and losses?"

### ■ Solution to Demonstration Problem

| | | | | | |
|---|---|---|---|---|---|
| 1998 | | | | | |
| July | 2 | Investment in Gant Bonds.................... | | 384,880 | |
| | | Cash.................................. | | | 384,880 |
| | | To record purchase of bonds. | | | |
| | 10 | Investment in Tanner Co. Stock................ | | 567,000 | |
| | | Cash.................................. | | | 567,000 |
| | | To record purchase of stock as an investment. (30,000 shs × $18 = $540,000 + $27,000 = $567,000) | | | |
| | 28 | Investment in Bene, Inc., Stock ............... | | 94,500 | |
| | | Cash.................................. | | | 94,500 |
| | | To record purchase of 15,000 shares of stock as an investment. | | | |
| Aug. | 1 | Dividends Receivable ........................ | | 30,000 | |
| | | Investment in Tanner Co. Stock ............. | | | 30,000 |
| | | To record dividend declared by Tanner. ($1 × 30,000 shs = $30,000) | | | |
| | 12 | Trading Securities: Stock .................... | | 23,600 | |
| | | Cash.................................. | | | 23,600 |
| | | To record investment in Peak stock. ($22.50 × 1,000 = $22,500 + $1,100 = $23,600) | | | |
| Sept. | 15 | Dividends Receivable ........................ | | 7,500 | |
| | | Dividend Income ........................ | | | 7,500 |
| | | To record dividend declared by Bene. ($0.50 × 15,000 shs = $7,500) | | | |
| | 30 | Cash...................................... | | 30,000 | |
| | | Dividends Receivable ................... | | | 30,000 |
| | | To record receipt of dividend from Tanner. | | | |
| Oct. | 31 | Cash...................................... | | 7,500 | |
| | | Dividends Receivable ................... | | | 7,500 |
| | | To record receipt of dividend from Bene. | | | |

*(Continued)*

| Dec. 31 | Cash...................................... | 20,000 | |
| | Investment in Gant Co. Bonds ................. | 3,093 | |
| | Interest Income ......................... | | 23,093 |
| | To record receipt of interest and amortization of | | |
| | discount on Gant Co. bonds. | | |
| | ($500,000 × 8% × ½ = $20,000) | | |
| | ($384,880 × 12% × ½ = $23,093) | | |
| | ($23,093 − $20,000 = $3,093) | | |
| | | | |
| 31 | Investment in Tanner Co. Stock ................ | 102,000 | |
| | Investment Income...................... | | 102,000 |
| | To record 30% interest in income of Tanner Co. | | |
| | (30% × $340,000 = $102,000) | | |
| | | | |
| 31 | Unrealized Loss............................ | 8,250 | |
| | Investment in Bene, Inc., Stock............. | | 8,250 |
| | To record the fact that the market value of the | | |
| | Bene stock is less than its cost. | | |
| | Cost............................. $94,500 | | |
| | Market (15,000 shs × $5.75)......... 86,250 | | |
| | Unrealized Loss ................... $ 8,250 | | |
| | | | |
| 31 | Unrealized Loss............................ | 1,350 | |
| | Trading Securities: Stock................. | | 1,350 |
| | To record the fact that the market value of the | | |
| | Peak stock is less than its cost. | | |
| | Cost............................. $23,600 | | |
| | Market (1,000 shs × $22.25)......... 22,250 | | |
| | Unrealized Loss ................... $ 1,350 | | |

Anvil's income statement will include the following:

| Other Income and Gains: | | |
| Dividend income........................ | $ 7,500 | |
| Interest income........................ | 23,093 | |
| Investment income...................... | 102,000 | $132,593 |
| Other Expenses and Losses: | | |
| Unrealized loss......................... | | 1,350 |

*Note:* The unrealized loss on the Bene investment is shown on the balance sheet as a negative stock-holders' equity account.

---

## QUESTIONS FOR REVIEW AND FURTHER THOUGHT

### REVIEW QUESTIONS

*Note:* Questions preceded by an asterisk relate to consolidations.

1. Pierce Corp. purchases some 9% bonds of Rose Corp. and pays face value for them. Will Pierce's investment yield 9%, more than 9%, or less than 9%? Explain.

2. Harris, Inc., owns 8% bonds of Lader Corp. The $200,000 face value bonds pay semiannual interest and were purchased to yield 10%. Assuming that the carrying value of the bonds is $188,428 at the beginning of an interest period, how much interest will be earned during the period if the effective-interest method is used?

3. What percentage ownership of common stock must investors hold before they are presumed to have significant influence over an investee? Why is the determination of significant influence important?

4. Tower Corp. acquires 40,000 shares of Texas, Inc., common stock for $5.83 per share plus an $11,600 brokerage fee. Assuming that this purchase represents 10% of the outstanding Texas stock, for how much will Tower debit Investment in Stock? Would your answer be the same if Tower's purchase represented 40% of the Texas stock? Explain.

5. How does a corporation decide whether to classify an investment security as trading or available-for-sale?

6. What is the major difference in accounting for trading securities and available-for-sale securities?

7. Petcorp receives notice of a dividend declaration by Fulford, Inc., an investee. Petcorp makes the following entry:

| | | |
|---|---|---|
| Dividends Receivable. . . . . . . . . . . . . . . . . . . . . . . . . . . . | 7,500 | |
|     Investment in Fulford Stock. . . . . . . . . . . . . . . . . . . . | | 7,500 |
| To record dividend declaration by Fulford Inc. | | |

Which method is Petcorp using to account for the investment in Fulford? Explain.

*8. Explain how a parent–subsidiary relationship comes into existence.

*9. What basic accounting concept provides the underlying support for the preparation of consolidated financial statements?

*10. What are intercompany accounts? Why are they eliminated in the consolidation process?

*11. Phar Corp. owns 95% of the common stock of Jelko, Inc. How is the claim of the owners of the other 5% of Jelko's stock reported on the consolidated financial statements? What is this claim called?

 ## QUESTIONS FOR FURTHER THOUGHT

*Note:* Questions preceded by an asterisk relate to consolidations.

1. Commercial Corp. paid $102,000 for a bond with a face value of $100,000. Why would Commercial be willing to pay more than face value for this bond investment?

2. Allday, Inc., purchased a $10,000 face value bond for $9,750. Allday did not create a discount account when the investment was recorded. Must Allday still amortize a discount? Explain.

3. On Jan. 1, 1997, Kelly Corp. acquired a long-term investment in bonds with a face value of $400,000, maturing on Jan. 1, 2002. Assuming that Kelly paid $347,000 for the bonds, what will be the balance of the Investment in Bonds account on Jan. 1, 1997, immediately after the purchase? And on Dec. 31, 2001, immediately before they are redeemed by the issuer? Explain each of your answers.

4. Under what circumstances must the purchaser of a bond investment pay interest to the previous owner of the bond?

5. Why do corporations invest in stock of other corporations?

6. Since discounts and premiums on short-term investments are not amortized, isn't interest income misstated?

7. Apex Corp. owns 40% of Quad, Inc., and can exert significant influence over Quad. If Apex were allowed to account for the investment as an available-for-sale security, how could Apex management manipulate its own income?

*8. Why are consolidated financial statements more useful to investors than parent-only financial statements?

## OBJECTIVE ASSIGNMENT

*True/False*   Indicate whether each statement below is *true* or *false* by placing a *T* or an *F* in the space provided.

_____ 1. When bonds are purchased at face value, the interest rate earned will be greater than if the bonds had been purchased at a premium.

_____ 2. The effective-interest method amortizes the same amount of discount or premium each time amortization is recorded.

_____ 3. A bond maturing in 25 years is purchased as an investment. Considering the maturity date, this must be a long-term investment.

_____ 4. When an investor corporation is unable to exert significant influence over the investee corporation, the investor should account for the investment using the equity method.

_____ 5. If company P owns 90% of company S, the minority interest in company S will appear on the consolidated balance sheet in the Investments section.

*Multiple Choice*   Select the best choice to complete each statement or answer each question below. Write the letter corresponding to your choice in the space provided.

_____ 1. A $1,000 bond was purchased for $1,075. The additional $75 cost of making this investment is referred to as a:
a. Loss     b. Discount     c. Premium     d. Bonus

_____ 2. Which of the following statements is true about a temporary bond investment?
a. Discounts and premiums must be amortized using the straight-line method.
b. Discounts and premiums are amortized over the period that management intends to hold the investment.
c. Bonds acquired as temporary investments must mature within one year.
d. Interest income on a temporary bond investment will be the same amount each full month that the bond is held.

_____ 3. Artesia, Inc., purchases a long-term bond investment at a premium. The effective-interest method of amortization is used. Artesia's interest income will:
a. Be the same amount each period throughout the bond's life.
b. Decrease in amount each period throughout the bond's life.
c. Increase in amount each period throughout the bond's life.
d. Fluctuate in amount each period as the interest rate in the market changes.

_____ 4. An investor is presumed to have significant influence over an investee once its ownership interest is at least:
a. 10%
b. 20%
c. 30%
d. 50%

_____ 5. An investor should report an unrealized loss on available-for-sale security in:
a. The stockholders' equity section of the balance sheet.
b. The long-term investments section of the balance sheet.
c. The current assets section of the balance sheet.
d. The other expenses and losses section of the income statement.

_____ 6. Trading securities should be valued on an investor's balance sheet at:
a. cost
b. the amount of equity acquired in the investee
c. lower-of-cost-or-market
d. market value

____ 7. Which of the following describes proper accounting when the equity method of accounting for long-term investments is employed?
   a. The investor records income when it is earned by the investee.
   b. The investor records income when a cash dividend is declared by the investee.
   c. The investor records income when a stock dividend is declared by the investee.
   d. The investor must use LCM to evaluate the investment at the end of each period.

____ 8. Which of the following accounting concepts or principles provides the basic theoretical support for the preparation of consolidated financial statements?
   a. The monetary unit concept
   b. The principle of conservatism
   c. The entity concept
   d. The materiality principle

____ 9. In which of the following situations would a parent company record goodwill in acquiring a new subsidiary?
   a. The purchase price is greater than the fair market value of the subsidiary's net assets.
   b. The purchase price is less than the fair market value of the subsidiary's net assets.
   c. The purchase price is equal to the fair market value of the subsidiary's net assets.
   d. The purchase price is less than the book value of the subsidiary's net assets.

____ 10. Consolidated financial statements are prepared only when:
   a. The parent and subsidiary companies are in the same industry.
   b. The parent and subsidiary companies are operating as totally separate entities.
   c. The parent owns at least 95% of the subsidiary company.
   d. The parent owns more than 50% of the subsidiary company.

## EXERCISES

*Note:* Exercises preceded by two asterisks relate to consolidations.

2† **Exercise 1:** Accounting for Bonds as Trading Securities

On July 1, 1998, Lean Corp. purchased bonds of Ligant Co. for $107,722 as a temporary investment. The 12% bonds have a face value of $100,000 and are purchased to yield 14%. The bonds pay interest on June 30 and Dec. 31 each year. The Ligant bonds had a market value of $107,200 on Dec. 31, 1998. Lean holds the bonds until Feb. 1, 1999, when they are sold for $108,000 plus $1,000 accrued interest. Prepare entries on July 1 and Dec. 31, 1998, and Feb. 1, 1999.

▶ *(Check Figure: Gain on sale of trading security = $800)*

2 **Exercise 2:** Purchasing Bonds with Accrued Interest

On Aug. 1, 1998, Thomas Co. purchased Oster Corp. bonds having a $200,000 face value and paying 12% annual interest. Interest is paid semiannually on June 30 and Dec. 31 each year.

Assuming that Thomas purchased the bonds as a long-term investment for face value plus accrued interest, prepare the entries Thomas would make on Aug. 1 and Dec. 31, 1998.

▶ *(Check Figure: Credit to Cash on Aug. 1 = $202,000)*

† The numbers in the margin refer to the Learning Objectives.

**2** **Exercise 3:** Amortizing Bond Premium Using the Straight-Line and Effective-Interest Methods

On Mar. 2, 1999, Young, Inc., purchased Green Co. 7% bonds having a face value of $500,000. The bonds pay interest on Mar. 1 and Sept. 1 each year and mature in 5 years. Young purchased the bonds for $521,324. At this price the bonds yield an effective interest rate of 6%.

Prepare Young's entries for the purchase on Mar. 2, 1999, and the first interest receipt on Sept. 1, 1999. Use (a) the straight-line method and (b) the effective-interest method. Round to the nearest dollar.

▶ *(Check Figure: On Sept. 1, 1999, Investment in Bonds is credited for $1,860 using the effective-interest method.)*

**2** **Exercise 4:** Preparing an Effective-Interest Bond Amortization Schedule and Year-End Accrual Entry

On Jan. 1, 1998, Pennywitt, Inc., acquired bonds as a long-term investment for $93,537. The bonds have a face value of $100,000, pay 8% annual interest, and were purchased to yield 10% annually. The bonds pay interest on June 30 and Dec. 31 each year and will mature on Dec. 31, 2001.

a. Prepare a schedule of interest earned and bond discount to be amortized for the life of the bond.
b. Prepare the Oct. 31, 1998, accrual entry, assuming that Pennywitt's accounting year ends on Oct. 31. Use the effective-interest method.

Round all calculations to the nearest dollar.

▶ *(Check Figure: Interest earned Oct. 31, 1998 = $3,141)*

**3** **Exercise 5:** Recording Trading and Available-for-Sale Securities

On October 15, 1998, Blomster, Inc., purchased 10,000 shares of Hitech Corp. for $14.25 per share. On Nov. 30, a $.15 per share dividend was received from Hitech. The per-share market price on Dec. 31 was $14.50.

Prepare entries to record the transactions and events described, assuming that the investment is treated as (a) an available-for-sale security, and (b) a trading security. (c) Under which alternative will Blomster's income be higher? Explain.

▶ *(Check Figure: Unrealized gain to be recorded on Dec. 31, 1998 = $2,500)*

**3 4** **Exercise 6:** Recording Available-for-Sale and Equity Method Investments

On Feb. 1, 1998, Kiwi, Inc., purchased 20,000 shares of White Corp. common stock as a long-term investment for $13.50 per share plus a brokerage commission of $4,000. On June 1, 1998, White declared a $0.50 per share dividend to be paid on July 1, to stockholders of record as of June 15.

Prepare any journal entries needed on Feb. 1, June 1, June 15, and July 1 to record these events, assuming these securities are accounted for as (a) available-for-sale securities and (b) an equity method investment. If no entry is required on a given date, write, "No Entry."

▶ *(Check Figure: Dividend income recognized as available-for-sale securities = $10,000)*

**3 4** **Exercise 7:** Calculating Investment Income for Available-for-Sale and Equity Method Securities

Castle Corp. owns 10,000 common shares (20%) of Bishop Corp. During 1998 Bishop reported income of $500,000 and declared dividends as follows:

| | | |
|---|---|---|
| Jan. | 1 | $0.55 per share payable Feb. 1. |
| Apr. | 1 | $0.65 per share payable May 1. |
| July | 1 | A 5,000-share (total) stock dividend distributable Aug. 1. |
| Sept. | 1 | $0.75 per share dividend payable Oct. 1. |

How much income from the long-term investment will Castle report if (a) the security is treated as available-for-sale or (b) the equity method is used?

▶ *(Check Figure: Income reported using the equity method = $100,000)*

4 **Exercise 8:** Recording Investment in Stock Using the Equity Method

Owl Oil Co. owns 20,000 shares of Flo-tru Pumps Inc. The stock, representing 40% ownership of Flo-tru, was purchased for $178,200 on Oct. 1, 1998. Prepare journal entries for each of the following dates, assuming that Owl exerts significant influence over Flo-tru:

1998
Nov. 1 Flo-tru declares a $0.15 per share cash dividend.

Dec. 1 Flo-tru pays the dividend previously declared.

31 Flo-tru reports a $9,000 net income for the year. Flo-tru stock is selling for $8.25 per share on the stock exchange.

1999
Jan. 15 Owl sells 5,000 shares of Flo-tru for $8.25 per share less a broker's commission of $250. Owl still exerts significant influence.

Dec. 31 Flo-tru reports a $14,000 net income for the year. Flo-tru stock is selling for $8.00 per share on the stock exchange. Owl now owns 30% of Flo-tru.

▶ *(Check Figure: Loss on sale of stock = $3,700)*

6 **\*\*Exercise 9:** Calculating Purchased Goodwill

Determine the amount of goodwill, if any, in each of the following acquisitions treated as purchases:

a. Chris Co. purchased 100% of the stock of Harp, Inc., for $300,000. Harp's net assets had a book value of $180,000. Harp's copyrights were undervalued by $8,000, and its land was undervalued by $110,000.

b. Star, Inc., purchased 100% of the stock of Angelo Corp. for $750,000. Angelo's net assets have a carrying value of $815,000. Angelo's accounts receivable were overvalued by $32,000, merchandise inventory was overvalued by $38,000, and buildings were undervalued by $2,000.

c. Stanco purchased 100% of the stock of Clifton Corp. for $1,680,000. Clifton's assets have a carrying value of $2,200,000; its liabilities totaled $800,000. The following Clifton assets were undervalued: land by $90,000, buildings by $126,000, and equipment by $64,000.

▶ *(Check Figure: Goodwill in purchase b = $3,000)*

8 **\*\*Exercise 10:** Calculating Goodwill and Minority Interest

a. Castro Corp. acquired 70% of Riggs, Inc., for $320,000. At the time of the acquisition Riggs' net assets had a carrying value of $400,000 and a market value of $440,000. Compute the goodwill and the minority interest at the date of acquisition.

b. Chemicals, Inc., acquired 75% of the assets of Plastics Corp. for $240,000. Plastics' net assets had a carrying value of $150,000. Plastics' patents were undervalued by $80,000; land was undervalued by $100,000; merchandise inventory was overvalued by $18,000. Compute the goodwill and minority interest on the date of acquisition.

▶ *(Check Figure: Minority interest purchase in b = $37,500)*

## PROBLEMS: SET A

*Note:* Problems preceded by two asterisks relate to consolidations.

2†  **Problem A1:** Calculating Interest Income and Recording Entries
for Investments in Bonds

Quincy Corp. follows a policy of investing seasonally surplus cash as well as the funds it is accumulating to build new retail outlets. The following bond investment transactions took place in 1998:

Jan.  1   Quincy purchased $20,000 of 16% Burr Corp. bonds as a trading security. The bonds pay interest each year on Mar. 1 and Oct. 1. The bonds were purchased for $19,400 plus accrued interest.

Mar.  1   Quincy received the semiannual interest on the Burr bonds.

June  1   Quincy purchased $100,000 of 18% Hamilton, Inc., bonds as a long-term investment. The bonds pay interest each year on Feb. 1 and Aug. 1. The bonds were purchased for $100,000 plus accrued interest. Quincy intends to hold the bonds until they mature.

Aug.  1   Quincy received the semiannual interest on the Hamilton bonds.

Oct.  1   Quincy received the semiannual interest on the Burr bonds.

      2   Quincy sold the Burr bonds for face value.

Dec. 31   Quincy accrued interest on the Hamilton bonds.

**Required:**

1. Prepare general journal entries to record each of these transactions and events. Round calculations to the nearest dollar.
2. How much interest income did Quincy earn during 1998? Support your answer with clearly labeled calculations.

▶ *(Check Figure: Interest income for 1998 = $12,900)*

2  **Problem A2:** Recording an Investment in Bonds on an Interest Date and
Amortizing a Premium Using Both the Straight-Line and Effective-Interest Methods

On July 1, 1998, Carthage Corp. purchased Hannibal, Inc., bonds having a face value of $400,000 and paying 14% annual interest. The bonds mature in 10 years and pay interest on June 30 and Dec. 31 each year. Carthage paid $445,878 for the bonds. This purchase price means that Carthage will earn 12% annual effective interest. Carthage intends to hold the bonds until they mature.

**Required:**

1. Assuming that the straight-line amortization method is used, prepare Carthage's entries on July 1 and Dec. 31, 1998, and June 30, 1999. Round to the nearest dollar.
2. Assuming that the effective-interest amortization method is used, prepare Carthage's entries on July 1 and Dec. 31, 1998, and June 30, 1999. Round to the nearest dollar.

▶ *(Check Figure: Interest income on June 30, 1999, under the effective-interest method = $26,678)*

† The numbers in the margin refer to the Learning Objectives.

2 **Problem A3:** Recording Investment in Bonds, Preparing a Schedule
of Interest Earned and Discount Amortized, Preparing Entries

On May 1, 1998, Fairdale Co. purchased Langston Corp. bonds as a long-term investment. The
following data relate to these bonds:

| | |
|---|---|
| Face value . . . . . . . . . . . . . . . . . . . . . . | $200,000 |
| Stated interest rate. . . . . . . . . . . . . . . | 14% annual rate |
| Interest payment dates . . . . . . . . . . . . | Apr. 30 and Oct. 31 |
| Remaining life of bonds . . . . . . . . . . . . | 3 years |
| Purchase price . . . . . . . . . . . . . . . . . . | $190,754 |
| Effective-interest rate earned. . . . . . . . | 16% annual rate |

**Required:**

1. Prepare a schedule of interest earned and bond discount to be amortized for Fairdale's
   investment in the Langston Corp. bonds, assuming that Fairdale plans to hold the bonds
   until they mature. Use the effective-interest method of amortization and round to the
   nearest dollar.
2. Prepare Fairdale's entries on May 1 and Oct. 31, 1998, and Apr. 30 and Oct. 31, 1999,
   assuming that the effective-interest method of amortization is used. Fairdale's accounting
   year ends on Oct. 31.
3. Prepare the entry that would be required on Dec. 31, 1998, assuming that Fairdale's accounting year ends on that date.

▶ *(Check Figure: Discount amortized on Apr. 30, 1999 = $1,361)*


3 4 **Problem A4:** Preparing Entries and Balance Sheet Disclosures
for Long Term Investment in Stock

Holley, Inc., makes long-term investments in common stock of other corporations. During 1998
and 1999 the following transactions took place:

1998
Jan. 1 Holley purchased 30,000 shares of Palmetto Co. for $2.50 per share plus $1,500
brokerage commission.

Dec. 1 Palmetto declared a $0.10 per share cash dividend payable on Jan. 15, 1999, to
stockholders of record as of Jan. 1, 1999.

31 Palmetto reported a net income of $96,000 for the year. Palmetto's stock was
trading for $2.75 at the close of the year.

1999
Jan. 15 Holley received the cash dividend from Palmetto.

Apr. 20 Holley sold 6,000 shares of Palmetto for $4 per share less a brokerage commission
of $1,200.

Sept. 1 Palmetto declared a 20% stock dividend distributable on Oct. 1 to stockholders of
record as of Sept. 15.

Oct. 1 Holley received the new shares from Palmetto.

Dec. 31 Palmetto reported a net loss of $20,000 for the year. Palmetto stock was trading for
$2 per share at the close of the year.

**Required:**

1. Prepare general journal entries for Holley assuming that the long-term investment is accounted for as an available-for-sale security.
2. Assuming an available-for-sale security, show what will appear under Investments on the
   balance sheet related to the investment in Palmetto on Dec. 31, 1998 and 1999. How much
   dividend income and other gains or losses will Holley report for 1998 and 1999?

3. Prepare general journal entries for Holley assuming that the equity method is used to account for the long-term investment. (*Note:* On Dec. 31, 1998, Holley owned 25% of Palmetto; on Dec. 31, 1999 Holley owned 20% of Palmetto.)

4. Assuming the equity method, show what will appear under Investments on the balance sheet related to the Investment in Palmetto account on Dec. 31, 1998 and 1999. How much investment income and other gains and losses will Holley report for 1998 and 1999?

▶ (*Check Figure: Balance of Investment in Palmetto on Dec. 31, 1999, under the equity method = $74,000*)

**4  Problem A5:** Calculating Beginning Balance of Stock Investment Using the Equity Method When Ending Balance and Transactions for the Year Are Known

On Dec. 31, 1998, Network International has on its balance sheet as a long-term investment "Investment in Optics, Inc., $700,250." The following additional information is available:

a. Network exerted significant influence over Optics during the entire year.
b. On Dec. 31, 1998, Network owned 35% (175,000 shares) of Optics' common stock.
c. Optics reported a net income of $620,000 for the year.
d. During August Optics declared and paid a $0.05 per share dividend.
e. During July Network purchased 25,000 shares of Optics for $81,250 plus a $1,250 brokerage fee. This transaction increased Network's ownership interest from 30 to 35% of Optics.
f. During February Optics declared and paid a $0.05 dividend.
g. During January Network sold 10,000 shares of Optics, receiving a net of $31,500 after brokerage fees. Network recognized a gain of $3,700 on the sale. This transaction reduced Network's ownership from 32 to 30%.

**Required:**

Prepare a schedule calculating the balance of Investment in Optics, Inc., on Jan. 1, 1998. (*Note:* In this problem you must work backward to calculate the amount at the beginning of the year.)

▶ (*Check Figure: Balance of Investment on Jan. 1, 1998 = $444,800*)

**6  7  \*\*Problem A6:** Preparing a Consolidation Worksheet on the Day of Acquisition

Winston Co. purchased 100% of the stock of Bradey Corp. on Jan. 1, 1999. Immediately following the cash purchase separate balance sheets of the two companies appeared as follows:

### WINSTON AND BRADEY
### Balance Sheets
### January 1, 1999
### (000's omitted)

|  | Winston | Bradey |
|---|---|---|
| Assets: | | |
| Current Assets | $ 430 | $ 25 |
| Investment in Bradey | 180 | |
| Other Assets | 1,250 | 85 |
| Total Assets | $1,860 | $110 |
| Equities: | | |
| Liabilities | $ 290 | $ 35 |
| Common Stock | 500 | 50 |
| Retained Earnings | 1,070 | 25 |
| Total Equities | $1,860 | $110 |

**Required:**

Prepare a consolidated balance sheet worksheet on the day of the acquisition. Assume that the fair market value of Bradey's current assets was $25,000 and of other assets was $145,000.

▶ (*Check Figure: Total Consolidated Assets = $1,895*)

7 8 **\*\*Problem A7:** Preparing a Consolidation Worksheet with Minority Interest

Buckeye, Inc., acquired 75% of Keystone Corp. for $600,000 cash. On Jan. 1, 1998, the date of acquisition, Keystone's inventory was undervalued by $100,000; the carrying values of all other assets were approximately the same as their market values. Individual company balance sheets on the acquisition date are shown below:

## BUCKEYE, INC., AND KEYSTONE CORP.
### Balance Sheets
### January 1, 1998

| | Buckeye | Keystone |
|---|---|---|
| **Assets:** | | |
| Current Assets | $2,160,000 | $212,500 |
| Investment in Keystone | 600,000 | |
| Other Assets | 5,080,000 | 642,500 |
| Total Assets | $7,840,000 | $855,000 |
| **Equities:** | | |
| Current Liabilities | $ 990,000 | $ 40,000 |
| Long-Term Liabilities | 1,250,000 | 125,000 |
| Common Stock | 4,000,000 | 375,000 |
| Retained Earnings | 1,600,000 | 315,000 |
| Total Equities | $7,840,000 | $855,000 |

**Required:**

Prepare a worksheet to develop a consolidated balance sheet for Buckeye and Keystone on Jan. 1, 1998.

▶ *(Check Figure: Minority Interest = $172,500)*

## PROBLEMS: SET B

*Note:* Problems preceded by two asterisks relate to consolidations.

2† **Problem B1:** Calculating Interest Income and Recording Entries for Investments in Bonds

The board of directors of Electro Corp. decided to invest in corporate bonds. The following transactions took place in 1998:

Mar. 1 Electro purchased $10,000 of 14% Bull Implements Co. bonds as a temporary investment. The bonds pay interest each year on June 30 and Dec. 31. The bonds were purchased for $10,250 plus accrued interest.

Apr. 1 Electro purchased $100,000 of 12% Team Machine, Inc., bonds as a long-term investment. The bonds pay interest each year on Jan. 31 and July 31. The bonds were purchased for $100,000 plus accrued interest. Electro intends to hold the bonds until they mature.

June 30 Electro received the semiannual interest on the Bull bonds.

July 1 Electro sold the Bull bonds for $10,400.

31 Electro received the semiannual interest on the Team bonds.

Dec. 31 Electro accrued interest on the Team, Inc., bonds.

† The numbers in the margin refer to the Learning Objectives.

**Required:**

1. Prepare general journal entries to record each of these transactions and events. Round all calculations to the nearest dollar.
2. How much interest income did Electro earn during 1998? Support your answer with clearly labeled calculations.

▶ *(Check Figure: Interest Income for 1998 = $9,467)*

2   **Problem B2:** Recording an Investment in Bonds on an Interest Date and Amortizing a Premium Using Both the Straight-Line and Effective-Interest Methods

On July 1, 1998, Bennett Enterprises purchased Olson Co. bonds having a face value of $300,000 and paying 12% annual interest. The bonds mature in 5 years and pay interest on June 30 and Dec. 31 each year. Bennett paid $323,164 for the bonds. This purchase price means that Bennett will earn 10% annual effective interest. Bennett intends to hold the bonds until they mature.

**Required:**

1. Assuming that the straight-line amortization method is used, prepare Bennett's entries on July 1 and Dec. 31, 1998, and June 30, 1999. Round to the nearest dollar.
2. Assuming that the effective-interest amortization method is used, prepare Bennett's entries on July 1 and Dec. 31, 1998 and June 30, 1999. Round to the nearest dollar.

▶ *(Check Figure: Interest income on June 30, 1999, under the effective-interest method = $16,066)*

2   **Problem B3:** Recording Investment in Bonds, Preparing a Schedule of Interest Earned and Discount Amortized, Preparing Entries

On June 1, 1998, Reece Construction purchased Coast Corp. bonds as a long-term investment. The following data relate to these bonds:

| | |
|---|---|
| Face value....................... | $500,000 |
| Stated interest rate ............... | 8% annual rate |
| Interest payment dates ............ | May 31 and Nov. 30 |
| Remaining life of bonds .......... | 3 years |
| Purchase price .................. | $474,623 |
| Effective interest rate earned ....... | 10% annual rate |

**Required:**

1. Prepare a schedule of interest earned and bond discount to be amortized for Reece's investment in the Coast Corp. bonds, assuming that Reece plans to hold the bonds until they mature. Use the effective-interest method of amortization and round to the nearest dollar.
2. Prepare Reece's entries on June 1 and Nov. 30, 1998, and May 31 and Nov. 30, 1999, assuming that the effective-interest method of amortization is used. Reece's accounting year ends on Nov. 30.
3. Prepare the Dec. 31, 1998, accrual entry, assuming that Reece's accounting year ends on that date.

▶ *(Check Figure: Discount Amortized on May 31, 1999 = $3,918)*

3 4 **Problem B4:** Preparing Entries and Balance Sheet Disclosures
for Investment in Stock

Terrace Industries makes long-term investments in common stock of other corporations. The
following transactions took place during 1998 and 1999:

1998
Jan. 15 Terrace purchased 6,000 shares of Circle E Corp. for $21.50 per share plus $4,500
brokerage fee.

Dec. 31 Circle E declared a $1.30 per share cash dividend payable on Feb. 1, 1999, to
stockholders of record as of Jan. 15, 1999.

31 Circle E reported a net income of $164,000 for the year. Circle E's stock was
trading for $22.50 per share at the close of the year.

1999
Feb. 1 Terrace received the cash dividend from Circle E.

May 15 Terrace sold 1,000 shares of Circle E for $28 per share less a brokerage commis-
sion of $1,500.

June 30 Circle E declared a 10% stock dividend distributable on Aug. 1 to stockholders of
record as of July 15.

Aug. 1 Terrace received the new shares from Circle E.

Dec. 31 Circle E reported a net income of $150,000 for the year. Circle E stock was trading
for $19 per share at the close of the year.

**Required:**

1. Prepare general journal entries for Terrace assuming that the long-term investment is
   accounted for as an available-for-sale security. (Round any per-share calculations to the
   nearest cent.)
2. Assuming an available-for-sale security, show what will appear under Investments on the
   balance sheet related to the investment in Circle E on Dec. 31, 1998 and 1999. How much
   dividend income and other gains and losses will Terrace report for 1998 and 1999? (Round
   any per-share calculations to the nearest cent.)
3. Prepare general journal entries for Terrace assuming that the equity method is used to
   account for the investment. (*Note:* On Dec. 31, 1998, Terrace owned 30% of Circle E; on Dec.
   31, 1999, Terrace owned 25% of Circle E.)
4. Assuming the equity method, show what will appear under Investments on the balance
   sheet related to the investment in Circle E on Dec. 31, 1998 and 1999. How much investment
   income and other gains or losses will Terrace report for 1998 and 1999?

▶ *(Check Figure: Balance of Investment in Circle E on Dec. 31, 1999, under the equity method = $183,250)*

**Problem B5:** Calculating Beginning Balance of Stock Investment Using the
Equity Method When Ending Balance and Transactions for the Year Are Known

On Dec. 31, 1998, Tiffany Equipment Co. has as a long-term investment on its balance sheet,
"Investment in Crystal Corp., $1,013,500." The following additional information is available:

a. Tiffany exerted significant influence over Crystal during the entire year.
b. On Dec. 31, 1998, Tiffany owned 45% (225,000 shares) of the Crystal stock.
c. Crystal reported a net income of $850,000 for the year.
d. During November Crystal declared and paid a $0.15 per share cash dividend.
e. During October Tiffany sold 15,000 shares of Crystal, receiving a net of $51,000 after
   brokerage fees. Tiffany recognized a $6,750 gain on the sale. This transaction reduced
   Tiffany's ownership interest from 48 to 45% of Crystal.
f. During May Crystal declared and paid a $0.15 per share cash dividend.
g. During February Tiffany purchased 5,000 shares of Crystal for a total of $16,500. This
   purchase increased Tiffany's ownership percentage from 47 to 48% of Crystal.

**Required:**

Prepare a schedule calculating the balance of Investment in Crystal on Jan. 1, 1998. (*Note:* In this problem you must work backward to compute the amount at the beginning of the year.)

▶ *(Check Figure: Balance of Investment on Jan. 1, 1998 = $728,500)*

6 7 **\*\*Problem B6:** Preparing a Consolidation Worksheet on the Day of Acquisition

Britt Co. purchased 100% of the stock of Kory Corp. on Jan. 1, 1997. Immediately after the cash purchase, separate balance sheets of the two companies appeared as follows:

| BRITT AND KORY COMPANIES<br>Balance Sheets<br>January 1, 1997<br>(000's omitted) | | |
| --- | --- | --- |
| | **Britt** | **Kory** |
| Assets: | | |
| Current Assets . . . . . . . . . . . . . . . . . . . . . . . . . . . . . . . . . . . . . . . . . . | $ 700 | $ 80 |
| Investment in Kory . . . . . . . . . . . . . . . . . . . . . . . . . . . . . . . . . . . . . | 400 | |
| Other Assets . . . . . . . . . . . . . . . . . . . . . . . . . . . . . . . . . . . . . . . . . . | 1,640 | 300 |
| Total Assets . . . . . . . . . . . . . . . . . . . . . . . . . . . . . . . . . . . . . . . . . . . | $2,740 | $380 |
| Equities: | | |
| Liabilities. . . . . . . . . . . . . . . . . . . . . . . . . . . . . . . . . . . . . . . . . . . . . | $ 600 | $120 |
| Common Stock. . . . . . . . . . . . . . . . . . . . . . . . . . . . . . . . . . . . . . . . . | 1,600 | 200 |
| Retained Earnings . . . . . . . . . . . . . . . . . . . . . . . . . . . . . . . . . . . . . | 540 | 60 |
| Total Equities . . . . . . . . . . . . . . . . . . . . . . . . . . . . . . . . . . . . . . . . . | $2,740 | $380 |

**Required:**

Assuming that the fair market value of Kory's current assets was $80,000 and of other assets was $360,000 on Jan. 1, 1997, prepare a consolidated balance sheet worksheet on the day of acquisition.

▶ *(Check Figure: Total Consolidated Assets = $2,860)*

7 8 **\*\*Problem B7:** Preparing a Consolidation Worksheet with Minority Interest

Ellis Manufacturing acquired 80% of Pebble Stone Corp. for $475,000 cash. On Jan. 1, 1999, the date of the acquisition, Pebble's inventory was undervalued by $50,000; the book values of all other assets were approximately the same as their market values. Individual company balance sheets on the acquisition date are shown below:

---

**ELLIS CORP. AND PEBBLE CORP.**
Balance Sheets
January 1, 1999
(000's omitted)

|  | Ellis | Pebble |
|---|---|---|
| Assets: | | |
| Current Assets | $ 350 | $200 |
| Investment in Pebble | 475 | |
| Other Assets | 1,225 | 500 |
| Total Assets | $2,050 | $700 |
| Equities: | | |
| Current Liabilities | $ 175 | $ 50 |
| Long-Term Liabilities | 500 | 150 |
| Common Stock | 1,000 | 425 |
| Retained Earnings | 375 | 75 |
| Total Equities | $2,050 | $700 |

**Required:**

Prepare a worksheet to develop a consolidated balance sheet for Ellis and Pebble on Jan. 1, 1999.

▶ *(Check Figure: Minority Interest = $100,000)*

---

## DECISION PROBLEM

A friend of yours who is a music major recently received a large gift of money from a wealthy aunt. Knowing that you are taking an accounting course, this friend seeks your help in trying to understand the financial statements of some companies in which she is considering investing her aunt's gift. Her questions are stated below. Answer each as fully as possible.

1. One of the companies I am interested in has issued both bonds and common stock. Would the same degree of risk be associated with an investment in stock as with an investment in bonds?

2. What obligation does the company have to pay periodic interest or dividends to the owners of these securities?

3. The company's financial statements indicate that the bonds have a face value of $1,000 each, but in today's *Wall Street Journal* the price of one of their bonds was given as $940. Why did it go down in value?

4. The financial statements of another company I am looking at have the word "consolidated" in the financial statement title. What does that mean?

5. This company's balance sheet has a category on it called "intangible assets," and under that category I saw something called "goodwill," which I guess means that people think highly of this company. Is that what "goodwill" means? If so, is this company a better one than those that do not show "goodwill" on their balance sheets?

6. The footnotes to the financial statements of a third company I am looking at say that this company invests in the common stock of other companies. The note also says that this company accounts for some of these investments using something called the equity method and it accounts for others using the cost method. How can they use two different methods to account for the same kind of thing?

## ETHICS CASE

Trout Group, Inc., recently sold substantial real estate holdings in Hawaii to a Japanese corporation. Trout's management is looking for ways to invest the large amount of cash the company received in this transaction. Pete Roberts, an administrative assistant to Trout's CEO, has been charged with recommending ways to invest the funds. During his analysis of potential investments, Pete discovered Cinema Cyclops, Inc., a large company that produces and distributes films and television series. The book value of Cyclops' assets is significantly less than market value for the following reasons:

1. Cyclops owns a number of classic movies and television series whose cost was written off the first time they were released. These films and TV shows can be leased to cable television stations and released in home video form at very little cost, thus producing enormous profits.
2. The Cyclops production facility is located on several hundred acres of prime real estate in Los Angeles. This property was acquired in the late 1920s and 1930s, so its carrying value is negligible. The development potential for this property is outstanding, as is the profit potential if it is sold.

Cyclops' management has been conservative and manages the company's profits by only occasionally releasing a classic movie or television series when current profits are lower than desired.

Pete notices that Cyclops' market price per share is only about $1\frac{1}{2}$ times the book value per share. On the basis of the projected value of the company's assets, he believes that the stock is grossly undervalued and that a change in management policy is all that would be necessary for Cyclops to become much more profitable. Pete makes the following proposal:

Trout should buy as many shares as possible of Cinema Cyclops, Inc. Shares would be acquired initially through the stock exchange and then directly from existing shareholders for up to $10 per share in excess of the market price. This strategy would accomplish one of two objectives, either of which would be profitable for Trout:

1. If Trout succeeded in buying enough shares to control Cyclops, the company's real estate could be sold off at a considerable gain. Trout would more than recoup the investment in Cyclops stock, and the remaining Cyclops stock could then be sold at the prevailing market price.
2. Cyclops management might be willing to purchase the Cyclops stock investment from Trout at an amount materially exceeding what Trout paid. Cyclops management would need to borrow money to buy out Trout's holdings and thwart its takeover bid. Trout would be required to sign an agreement not to attempt another such takeover within a defined period of time, say 10 years.

Pete is convinced that his suggested strategy is a "no-lose" proposition for Trout and urges the CEO to give authorization to begin acquiring Cyclops stock as soon as possible.

**Required:**

1. Who are the stakeholders that will be affected by Trout's decision?
2. What are the potential ramifications for Cinema Cyclops if either the takeover or the buyback occurs?
3. Are there possible outcomes other than the two Pete suggests?

## OBJECTIVE ASSIGNMENT ANSWERS

**True/False**

1. T    2. F    3. F    4. F    5. F

**Multiple Choice**

1. c    2. d    3. b    4. b    5. a
6. d    7. a    8. c    9. a    10. d

# The Statement of Cash Flows

**LEARNING OBJECTIVES**

After studying this chapter, you should be able to do the following:

1 Explain how the statement of cash flows may be used by investors and creditors

2 Explain the meaning of the terms *cash* and *cash equivalents*

3 Describe the basic content of the statement of cash flows

4 Prepare a statement of cash flows using the T-account method

5 Explain the logic underlying the conversion of an accrual income statement to cash provided by operations

6 Analyze a complex statement of cash flows

7 Define the key terms at the end of this chapter

**CHAPTER OUTLINE**

WHY ANOTHER FINANCIAL STATEMENT? • PURPOSE AND CONTENT OF THE STATEMENT OF CASH FLOWS • Operating Activities • Investing Activities • Financing Activities • Cash Reconciliation • Investing and Financing Activities Not Affecting Cash • PREPARING THE STATEMENT OF CASH FLOWS • CONVERTING ACCRUAL INCOME TO CASH FROM OPERATIONS • Revenue Earned to Cash Received • Cost of Goods Sold to Cash Paid for Merchandise • Operating Expenses to Cash Paid for Expenses • ANALYZING A COMPLEX STATEMENT OF CASH FLOWS • Analysis of Operating Activities • Analysis of Investing Activities • Analysis of Financing Activities • Other Observations

## WHY ANOTHER FINANCIAL STATEMENT?

Learning
Objective    1

Explain how the statement of cash
flows may be used by investors and
creditors

Imagine that you have just inherited some money and you're attempting to decide whether to invest in Interface Marketing, Inc., a local company that has been growing rapidly over the past few years. An inspection of the company's income statement for the most recent year shows a profit of $600,000 on sales of $7,000,000. The balance sheet reveals that cash increased last year, accounts receivable and inventory are both up, and property, plant, and equipment grew substantially. All of these facts seem very positive. A friend warns you that she invested in a company with a similar glowing financial report only to find that the company was bankrupt within three years. Since you want to avoid a similar experience, you contact another friend who works for a local CPA firm. He tells you to ask the company for a statement of cash flows, then come to see him.

The company provides the following statement:

**INTERFACE MARKETING, INC.**
Statement of Cash Flows
For the Year Ended December 31, 1998
(000'S Omitted)

| | |
|---|---:|
| Cash Flows from Operating Activities: | |
| Net Income | $ 600 |
| Adjustments to Reconcile Net Income to Net | |
| Cash Provided by Operating Activities: | |
| Increase in Accounts Receivable | (1,200) |
| Increase in Inventory | (1,000) |
| Depreciation Expense | 1,100 |
| Net Cash Used by Operating Activities | $ (500) |
| Cash Flows from Investing Activities: | |
| Purchase of Equipment | $(2,000) |
| Cash Flows from Financing Activities: | |
| Proceeds from Borrowing on Long-term Debt | $ 2,800 |
| Net Increase in Cash and Cash Equivalents | $ 300 |
| Cash and Cash Equivalents at Beginning of Year | 150 |
| Cash and Cash Equivalents at End of Year | $ 450 |

Your CPA friend points out some things that you can learn from this report that the other statements don't tell you. He emphasizes that the first section of the report translates the accrual income into the amount of cash generated by operations. Interface's net income of $600,000 became a negative cash flow of $500,000. The profit-directed operations of the company used up $500,000 more cash than they produced!

Is this bad? Well, you'd certainly prefer to see a positive cash flow from operations, but negative operating cash flow may be understandable for a rapidly growing company. Collections on accounts receivable always come later than the revenue recognized on the income statement. In expanding companies this lag in collections is compounded by the fact that accounts receivable are increasing quickly. Interface, then, subtracted the increase in accounts receivable from net income in calculating cash from operations to account for revenues that have been reported, but not collected.

Growing companies also must acquire larger and larger quantities of inventory so that goods will be on hand to meet demands caused by increasing sales. When suppliers are paid for these goods before they are sold, cash outflow for inventory exceeds cost of goods sold. Interface deducts an additional amount from income representing goods paid for, but not yet sold.

Why is depreciation added back? This expense on the income statement does not use any cash. Since this expense was deducted in deriving net income, the deduction must be "canceled out" by adding it back to calculate cash from operations.

So, the cash used by operations can be explained and justified. What else does the statement tell us? The second section, investing activities, indicates that Interface spent $2,000,000 to purchase new equipment. This is also expected in a growing expanding company. Now we know that the company used $500,000 for operations and $2,000,000 for new equipment; where did this cash come from?

The third section reveals how the company was financed. Interface borrowed $2,800,000 on a long-term debt arrangement. This should wave a red flag of caution to the potential investor. Interface will need to pay the interest on this loan each year and eventually repay the principal. If the company continues its dynamic growth pattern without a source of cash that does not have to be repaid, financial trouble could be close. Interface will need to decide whether expansion should be slowed until operations begin producing a positive cash flow, or whether equity financing can be obtained to ensure that the company is not placing itself in a position where it will be unable to meet its obligations. Many "successful" companies have been doomed by trying to grow too fast with too little capital.

As you can see by this simple illustration, the statement of cash flows provides some vital information that is not included on the income statement or balance sheet. For this reason, generally accepted accounting principles require a statement of cash flows as a part of every complete set of financial statements.

## PURPOSE AND CONTENT OF THE STATEMENT OF CASH FLOWS

The purpose of the statement of cash flows is to provide information about inflows and outflows from an entity's pool of cash. These disclosures provide information that is not shown in any other financial statement.

Learning
Objective 2
Explain the meaning of the terms
*cash* and *cash equivalents*

Technically, the entity's cash pool is not limited to cash alone—it includes cash equivalents as well. **Cash equivalents** are short-term, highly liquid investments that are both readily convertible to known amounts of cash and so near their maturity that there is little risk of loss of value because of interest rate changes. Practically speaking, only investments with original maturities of three months or less are considered cash equivalents. For example, a U.S. Treasury bill issued and purchased on Nov. 15, 1998, and maturing on Jan. 12, 1999, would be considered a cash equivalent on the Dec. 31, 1998, financial statements. In our discussion of the statement of cash flows, references to cash flows should be interpreted as cash and cash equivalent flows.

When you think for a moment about the many instances when cash flows into and out of a business you may come up with many examples:

> An owner invests in the business
> A customer buys a product or service for cash
> The business pays a dividend to stockholders
> The business buys buildings and equipment
> The business borrows money
> The business pays its employees
> The business buys advertisements in a local newspaper
> The business buys goods to sell

With a little thought you can probably come up with a list at least three times this long.

In order for the statement of cash flows to be meaningful, these inflows and outflows are grouped into the three major categories that we mentioned earlier:

- Operating Activities
- Investing Activities
- Financing Activities

Now we will take a closer look at each of these three to discover what is included in each.

Learning Objective 3

Describe the basic content of the statement of cash flows

## 3 Operating Activities

**Cash flows from operating activities** includes all inflows and outflows relating to the income-producing endeavors of a business. In general if an item appears on the income statement, its cash flow equivalent will appear in the operating activities section of the statement of cash flows.

The operating activities section may be structured in two ways: the direct method and the indirect method. These two methods merely refer to different ways of displaying the same information. The net cash inflow or outflow from operations will be exactly the same no matter which is used. Compare the statements in Exhibits 1 and 2 to get a general idea of how each will look:

**Exhibit 1** Operations Section Using the Direct Method

### MILLENNIUM, INC.
### Statement of Cash Flows—Operating Activities Section
### For the Year Ended December 31, 1998

Cash Flows from Operating Activities:

| | |
|---|---|
| Cash Collected from Customers | $255,000 |
| Cash Paid for Merchandise | (165,000) |
| Cash Paid for Salaries and Wages | (36,000) |
| Cash Paid for Administrative and Selling | (30,000) |
| Cash Paid for Interest | (8,000) |
| Cash Paid for Income Taxes | (3,000) |
| Net Cash provided by Operating Activities | $ 13,000 |

**Exhibit 2** Operations Section Using the Indirect Method

### MILLENNIUM, INC.
### Statement of Cash Flows—Operating Activities Section
### For the Year Ended December 31, 1998

Cash Flows from Operating Activities:

| | |
|---|---|
| Net Income | $10,000 |
| Adjustments to Reconcile Net Income to Net Cash Provided by Operating Activities: | |
| Decrease in Accounts Receivable | 5,000 |
| Depreciation on Building | 4,000 |
| Depreciation on Equipment | 1,000 |
| Increase in Salaries Payable | 3,000 |
| Increase in Merchandise Inventory | (10,000) |
| Net Cash provided by Operating Activities | $13,000 |

## The Direct Method

As its name implies, the **direct method** shows cash inflows and outflows for each of the major items on the income statement. Revenues are adjusted to reflect the amount of cash that was actually collected from customers; and each expense item is likewise translated from the accrual basis expense to the amount of cash paid. In published statements, expenses usually are grouped into major categories similar to those shown in Exhibit 1 for presentation on the statement of cash flows. The direct method offers the advantage of being easy to understand. On the other hand, the direct method is more difficult to prepare and it does not provide an amount that ties directly to anything on the income statement. In actual practice less than 5% of companies use the direct method.

## The Indirect Method

The **indirect method** of presentation begins with net income from the income statement and adjusts this amount to derive cash from operations. Since 95% or more of cash flow statements are prepared using this method, we will discuss it more extensively.

An examination of the indirect method presentation in Exhibit 2 will help illustrate how this method works. Note that we begin with net income, an amount that you can trace to the income statement to tie the two statements together. We may say that our initial assumption is that the amount of net income is the cash from operations. We know, of course, that this amount will need to be adjusted for revenues and expenses whose cash inflows and outflows differ from the amounts reported on the income statement.

We must adjust for revenues recognized on the accrual basis that may have provided a different amount of cash inflow. In Millennium's case, accounts receivable decreased indicating that more cash was collected this period than the amount of accrual basis revenues recognized. Cash flow from operations, then, is greater than the accrual basis net income reported, so we add back the amount of decrease in accounts receivable, $5,000. An increase in accounts receivable would indicate that revenues on the accrual basis are greater than the cash collections. In that case the increase in accounts receivable would have been deducted.

An increase in inventory means that the company paid for more goods than were expensed as cost of goods sold on the income statement. Not enough, then, has been deducted on the income statement to reflect the actual amount of cash outflow. Millennium deducts an additional $10,000 to adjust for this fact. A decrease in inventory would indicate that some inventory purchased and paid for last period was sold this period. In this case cost of goods sold would be more than the cash paid for inventory and an addition to net income would be required.

Millennium's salaries payable increased during the year indicating that salaries expense on the income statement is higher than the amount of salaries actually paid. In a sense "too much" was deducted on the income statement requiring us to add back $3,000 to derive cash from operations. A decrease in salaries payable would signal that more salaries were paid than expensed. This situation requires a subtraction to calculate cash from operations.

In each of the three adjustments that we have discussed the revenue or expense item was tied directly to a current asset (Accounts Receivable, Merchandise Inventory) or current liability account (Salaries Payable) on the balance sheet. Remember these balance sheet relationships, you will be using them later when you learn how to prepare a statement of cash flows.

Two final observations about the operations section. First, the amount of cash from operations is $13,000 no matter which method of display is used. The direct and indirect methods will always yield the same results. Secondly, from a user's point of view, the fact that cash flow from operations is positive means that Millennium's operations have generated funds that can be used to buy productive assets, retire debt or pay dividends to stockholders.

## Investing Activities

When you think of investing usually you think of buying and selling stocks and bonds of other companies as investments. Investing activities on the statement of cash flows includes these transactions as well as a company's investment in long-lived assets that are used in the business such as land, buildings, equipment, and patents. **Investing activities** include loans made to and collected from other entities, acquisitions and sales of stocks and bonds of other companies, and purchase and disposal of property, plant and equipment assets, and intangibles.

A look at Millennium's investing activities, Exhibit 3, shows that the company did not use the cash generated by operations to invest in long-lived assets. Indeed, some of the cash received from the sale of equipment is still available after buying some new equipment and investing in bonds. We might wonder if Millennium is reducing the size of its operations by failing to replace all of the equipment, or if, perhaps, they have decided to lease equipment instead of buying it. An examination of the financial statement notes will provide additional information about these matters.

**Exhibit 3** Investing Activities Section

MILLENNIUM, INC.
Statement of Cash Flows—Investing Activities
For the Year Ended December 31, 1998

Cash Flows from Investing Activities:

| | |
|---|---:|
| Proceeds from Disposal of Equipment | $ 8,000 |
| Purchase of Equipment | (4,000) |
| Purchase of Investment Bonds | (2,000) |
| Net Cash Provided by Investing Activities | 2,000 |

Each of these acquisitions and disposals also is reflected in a balance sheet account. The purchase and sale of equipment is, of course, reflected as an increase or decrease in the Equipment account. The purchase of bonds causes an increase in the Investment in Bonds account.

## Financing Activities

The **financing activities** section reports a company's transactions that involve obtaining resources from owners and major creditors and repaying owners and creditors. This is the place to look to find out where a company acquired the pool of resources that were used to buy the productive assets it needed, and perhaps even to finance its income producing operations. Financing activities include inflows of cash from the sale of stock or from borrowing and outflows of cash from paying dividends to stockholders, buying treasury stock, or repaying loans. Interest payments on loans are included in operating activities.

Millennium's financing activities section, Exhibit 4, tells the reader that $7,000 of the $15,000 cash generated from operating and investing activities was used by financing activities. Specifically, Millennium raised $10,000 through the issuance of some common stock and then used $17,000 to pay dividends and retire long-term debt.

**Exhibit 4** Financing Activities Section

### MILLENNIUM, INC.
### Statement of Cash Flows—Financing Activities
### For the Year Ended December 31, 1998

| | |
|---|---|
| Cash Flows from Financing Activities: | |
| Proceeds from Issuing Common Stock . . . . . . . . . . . . . . . . . . . . | $10,000 |
| Dividends Paid . . . . . . . . . . . . . . . . . . . . . . . . . . . . . . . . . . . . | (3,000) |
| Retirement of Bonds Payable. . . . . . . . . . . . . . . . . . . . . . . . . . | (14,000) |
| Net Cash Used by Financing Activities . . . . . . . . . . . . . . . . . . . . . . . . | (7,000) |

## Cash Reconciliation

We have seen how the statement of cash flows ties to the income statement by including net income in the calculation of cash flows from operations. Exhibit 5 shows another part of Millennium's statement of cash flows illustrating a link with the balance sheet.

**Exhibit 5** Cash Reconciliation Section

### MILLENNIUM, INC.
### Statement of Cash Flows—Cash Reconciliation Section
### For the Year Ended December 31, 1998

| | |
|---|---|
| Net Increase in Cash and Cash Equivalents . . . . . . . . . . . . . . . . . . . . . . . . . . | $ 8,000 |
| Cash and Cash Equivalents at Beginning of Year. . . . . . . . . . . . . . . . . . . . . . | 9,000 |
| Cash and Cash Equivalents at End of Year. . . . . . . . . . . . . . . . . . . . . . . . . . | $17,000 |

This portion of the statement merely adds the net amounts from the operating, investing, and financing sections ($13,000 + $2,000 − $7,000) to determine the change in cash for the year (+ $8,000). When this change is added to the beginning cash balance, the ending cash amount should be derived. We can see that Millennium's statement shows the cash flows that caused its cash to increase from a beginning amount of $9,000 to an ending balance of $17,000.

## Investing and Financing Activities Not Affecting Cash

As its name implies, the primary objective of the statement of cash flows is to show an entity's inflows and outflows of cash. What happens if Millennium issues shares of its own common stock in exchange for land? Since no cash changed hands, this transaction would not be reported in any of the statement sections that we have discussed. As a reader you would probably like to know about significant transactions like this because they result in major changes in the company's assets, debt, or equity without using any of its liquid cash resources. Since this information is not disclosed elsewhere in the financial statements, GAAP requires that it be shown as supplemental information on the statement of cash flows.

Exhibit 6 shows how Millennium would report an exchange of common stock for land. Other examples of investing and financing activities not affecting cash include acquiring assets solely in exchange for debt, retiring debt by giving assets or issuing stock and converting debt into common stock.

**Exhibit 6** Investing and Financing Activities Not Affecting Cash

MILLENNIUM, INC.
Statement of Cash Flows
Investing and Financing Activities Not Affecting Cash
For the Year Ended December 31, 1998

Significant Investing and Financing Activities not
affecting Cash:
Common stock was issued in exchange for land. . . . . . . . . . . . . . . . . . . . . . . $40,000

Now that we have discussed the pieces of Millennium's statement, look at Exhibit 7 to see them assembled into a complete statement.

**Exhibit 7** Millennium's Completed Statement of Cash Flows

MILLENNIUM, INC.
Statement of Cash Flows
For the Year Ended December 31, 1998

Cash Flows from Operating Activities:
Net Income. . . . . . . . . . . . . . . . . . . . . . . . . . . . . . . . . . . . . . . . . . . . . . . . . $10,000
Adjustments to Reconcile Net Income to Net
Cash Provided by Operating Activities:
Decrease in Accounts Receivable. . . . . . . . . . . . . . . . . . . . . . . . . . . . . . 5,000
Depreciation on Building . . . . . . . . . . . . . . . . . . . . . . . . . . . . . . . . . . . . 4,000
Depreciation on Equipment . . . . . . . . . . . . . . . . . . . . . . . . . . . . . . . . . . 1,000
Increase in Salaries Payable . . . . . . . . . . . . . . . . . . . . . . . . . . . . . . . . . 3,000
Increase in Merchandise Inventory . . . . . . . . . . . . . . . . . . . . . . . . . . . . . (10,000)
Net Cash Provided by Operating Activities . . . . . . . . . . . . . . . . . . . . $13,000

Cash Flows from Investing Activities:
Proceeds from Disposal of Equipment . . . . . . . . . . . . . . . . . . . $ 8,000
Purchase of Equipment . . . . . . . . . . . . . . . . . . . . . . . . . . . . . . . (4,000)
Purchase of Investment Bonds . . . . . . . . . . . . . . . . . . . . . . . . . (2,000)
Net Cash Provided by Investing Activities . . . . . . . . . . . . . . . . . . . . . 2,000

Cash Flows from Financing Activities:
Proceeds from Issuing Common Stock. . . . . . . . . . . . . . . . . . . $10,000
Dividends Paid. . . . . . . . . . . . . . . . . . . . . . . . . . . . . . . . . . . . . . (3,000)
Retirement of Bonds Payable . . . . . . . . . . . . . . . . . . . . . . . . . . (14,000)
Net Cash Used by Financing Activities . . . . . . . . . . . . . . . . . . . . . . . (7,000)

Net Increase in Cash and Cash Equivalents . . . . . . . . . . . . . . . . . . . . . . . . $ 8,000
Cash and Cash Equivalents at Beginning of Year . . . . . . . . . . . . . . . . . . . . . 9,000
Cash and Cash Equivalents at End of Year . . . . . . . . . . . . . . . . . . . . . . . . . $17,000

Significant Investing and Financing Activities not
affecting Cash:
Common stock was issued in exchange for land . . . . . . . . . . . . . . . . . . . $40,000

**ASK YOURSELF** ▶

1. What are at least two things that can be learned from the statement of cash flows that are not shown on the other financial statements?
2. What are the three major sections of the statement of cash flows?
3. What is a cash equivalent?
4. What are two ways of presenting cash flows from operating activities?
5. When the indirect method is used for operating activities, why is depreciation added to net income?
6. What are at least two types of cash inflow from investing activities? From financing activities?

## PREPARING THE STATEMENT OF CASH FLOWS

Learning
Objective **4**

Prepare a statement of cash flows using the T-account method

Now you should understand why we have a statement of cash flows, how this information is used to better appreciate a company's financial condition, and what information GAAP requires on every statement of cash flows. In this section you will learn how to construct the working papers necessary to prepare a simple statement of cash flows. Since you are already familiar with Millennium's statement, we will go back to the beginning and see what was necessary to produce the statement.

To prepare Millennium's statement of cash flows we must assemble the company's income statement, statement of retained earnings, and comparative balance sheet. These items appear in Exhibits 8, 9, and 10.

**Exhibit 8** Millennium, Inc. Income Statement

### MILLENNIUM, INC.
#### Condensed Income Statement
#### Year Ended December 31, 1998

| | | |
|---|---:|---:|
| Sales | | $250,000 |
| Cost of Goods Sold | | (155,000) |
| Gross Profit on Sales | | $ 95,000 |
| Operating Expenses: | | |
|   Administrative Expenses | $(12,000) | |
|   Selling Expenses | (18,000) | |
|   Depreciation Expense: Buildings | ( 4,000) | |
|   Depreciation Expense: Equipment | ( 1,000) | |
|   Salaries Expense | (39,000) | (74,000) |
| Other Income and Expenses: | | |
|   Interest Expense | | (8,000) |
| Income before Income Taxes | | $ 13,000 |
| Provision for Income Taxes | | (3,000) |
| Net Income | | $ 10,000 |

**Exhibit 9** Millennium, Inc. Statement of Retained Earnings

### MILLENNIUM, INC.
#### Statement of Retained Earnings
#### Year Ended December 31, 1998

| | |
|---|---:|
| Balance, Jan. 1, 1998 | $62,000 |
| Add: Net Income for the Year | 10,000 |
| Deduct: Dividends Declared and Paid during 1998 | (3,000) |
| Balance, Dec. 31, 1998 | $69,000 |

**Exhibit 10** Millennium, Inc. Comparative Balance Sheets

## MILLENNIUM, INC.
### Comparative Balance Sheets
### December 31

| | 1998 | 1997 | Increase (Decrease) |
|---|---|---|---|
| **Assets** | | | |
| Current Assets: | | | |
| Cash | $ 17,000 | $ 9,000 | $ 8,000 |
| Accounts Receivable (Net) | 25,000 | 30,000 | (5,000) |
| Merchandise Inventory | 23,000 | 13,000 | 10,000 |
| Total Current Assets | $ 65,000 | $ 52,000 | |
| Investments: | | | |
| Investment in Bonds | $ 27,000 | $ 25,000 | 2,000 |
| Property, Plant, and Equipment: | | | |
| Land | $107,000 | $ 67,000 | 40,000 |
| Buildings | 190,000 | 190,000 | 0 |
| Less: Accum. Depr.: Building | (10,000) | (6,000) | (4,000) |
| Equipment | 45,000 | 55,000 | (10,000) |
| Less: Accum. Depr.: Equipment | (12,000) | (17,000) | 5,000 |
| Total Property, Plant, and Equipment | $320,000 | $289,000 | |
| Total Assets | $412,000 | $366,000 | |
| **Liabilities and Stockholders' Equity** | | | |
| Current Liabilities: | | | |
| Accounts Payable | $ 5,000 | $ 5,000 | $ 0 |
| Salaries Payable | 23,000 | 20,000 | 3,000 |
| Total Current Liabilities | $ 28,000 | $ 25,000 | |
| Long-Term Liabilities: | | | |
| Bonds Payable | $120,000 | $134,000 | (14,000) |
| Total Liabilities | 148,000 | 159,000 | |
| **Stockholders' Equity** | | | |
| Common Stock, $10 par | $140,000 | $100,000 | 40,000 |
| Paid-in Capital in Excess of Par | 55,000 | 45,000 | 10,000 |
| Retained Earnings | 69,000 | 62,000 | 7,000 |
| Total Stockholders' Equity | $264,000 | $207,000 | |
| Total Liabilities and Stockholders' Equity | $412,000 | $366,000 | |

The following additional information was assembled from examining Millennium's general ledger:

1. Cash dividends of $3,000 were paid to Millennium's stockholders.
2. Equipment costing $14,000 was sold for $8,000. The equipment has a book value of $8,000.
3. Land valued at $40,000 was acquired in exchange for 3,200 shares of common stock.

In our earlier discussion we observed that each time there was a transaction that affected cash some other balance sheet account was ultimately affected as well. Several short examples will help your understanding of this concept:

- When cash is received upon the issuance of stock, the Common Stock account, and possibly the Paid-in Capital in Excess of Par account, increases.
- A loan from a bank increases cash and a liability account, Bank Loan Payable.
- When a customer buys merchandise, cash is increased and a revenue account is credited. This revenue account, along with all of the expenses, is ultimately closed to Retained Earnings, a balance sheet account.
- When an invoice for advertising is paid, an expense account is charged and Cash is credited. The expense account is ultimately closed to Retained Earnings.

Even items that do not directly affect cash cause changes in balance sheet accounts; examples include sales on credit, or recording depreciation expense.

Once we realize that all of a company's transactions ultimately affect the balance sheet, we also know that we can explain the change in cash by examining the changes in the balance sheet accounts. While investigating these changes we isolate those that affect cash. Once we have explained the change in each balance sheet account, we will have gathered all of the information we need to prepare the statement of cash flows. Our investigation is made relatively simple by using T-accounts for analysis.

First, set up a cash account, providing space for information pertaining to the company's operating, investing and financing activities. When we're finished this account will contain virtually all of the information we will need for the statement of cash flows. Exhibit 11 shows you what this analysis account looks like for Millennium.

Notice that we have entered the beginning balance of the account (BB) and the ending balance (EB) leaving space to summarize entries that the company prepared during the year. Once we have reproduced these entries, we should be able to add the debits (cash inflows) and subtract the credits (cash outflows) and derive the ending balance.

We repeat this process for each account on Millennium's balance sheet. We need the operating, investing, and financing captions only for the cash account. An extra account is added to capture the investing and financing activities not affecting cash. The complete set of accounts used for Millennium is shown in Exhibit 12.

---

**Exhibit 11** Millennium, Inc. Cash Account Before Analysis

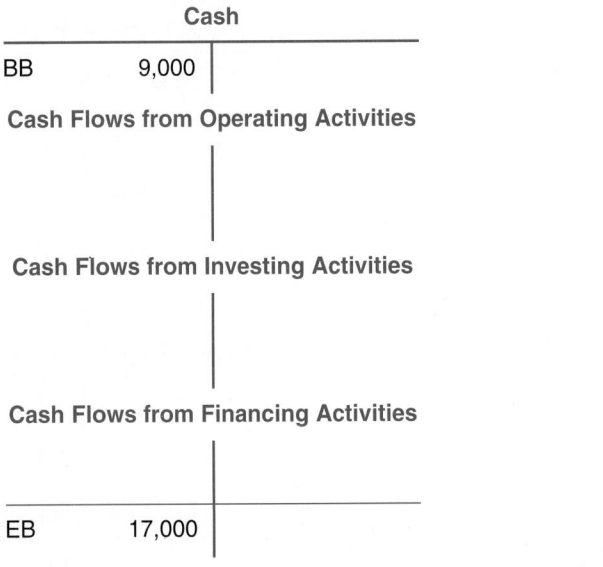

Cash

| | |
|---|---|
| BB | 9,000 |

**Cash Flows from Operating Activities**

**Cash Flows from Investing Activities**

**Cash Flows from Financing Activities**

| | |
|---|---|
| EB | 17,000 |

**Exhibit 12** Millennium, Inc., T-Accounts before Analysis Entries

**MILLENNIUM, INC.**
**Statement of Cash Flows**
**T-Account Approach**
**(Before Analysis)**

| Cash | | | | Merchandise Inventory | | |
|---|---|---|---|---|---|---|
| BB | 9,000 | | | BB | 30,000 | |
| | | | | EB | 25,000 | |

| Cash Flows from Operating Activities | | | | Investment in Bonds | | |
|---|---|---|---|---|---|---|
| | | | | BB | 13,000 | |
| | | | | EB | 23,000 | |

| Cash Flows from Investing Activities | | | | Land | | |
|---|---|---|---|---|---|---|
| | | | | BB | 25,000 | |
| | | | | EB | 27,000 | |

| Cash Flows from Financing Activities | | | | Building | | |
|---|---|---|---|---|---|---|
| | | | | BB | 67,000 | |
| EB | 17,000 | | | EB | 107,000 | |

| Noncash Investing and Financing | | | | Accum. Depr.: Building | | |
|---|---|---|---|---|---|---|
| | | | | | | BB | 6,000 |
| | | | | | | EB | 10,000 |

| Equipment | | | | Accum. Depr.: Equipment | | |
|---|---|---|---|---|---|---|
| BB | 190,000 | | | | | BB | 17,000 |
| EB | 190,000 | | | | | EB | 12,000 |

| Accounts Payable | | | | Salaries Payable | | |
|---|---|---|---|---|---|---|
| BB | 55,000 | | | | | BB | 20,000 |
| EB | 45,000 | | | | | EB | 23,000 |

| Bonds Payable | | | | Common Stock | | |
|---|---|---|---|---|---|---|
| | | BB | 5,000 | | | BB | 100,000 |
| | | EB | 5,000 | | | EB | 140,000 |

| Paid-in Capital in Excess of Par | | | | | | |
|---|---|---|---|---|---|---|
| | | BB | 134,000 | | | | |
| | | EB | 120,000 | | | | |

| Accounts Receivable | | | | Retained Earnings | | |
|---|---|---|---|---|---|---|
| | | BB | 45,000 | | | BB | 62,000 |
| | | EB | 55,000 | | | EB | 69,000 |

The next step is to analyze the transactions made by Millennium, Inc., in terms of their effects on cash flows. Here we will discuss the transactions, and illustrate how they are entered in the T-accounts affected. The complete T-accounts are shown in Exhibit 13, with all the explanations coded by letter to the transaction analyses in the text. Examine this exhibit carefully to see what the completed analysis looks like.

*In our analysis we will be explaining how the accounts changed from the beginning to the ending balances. We are not actually recording the transactions in the ledger accounts of the Millennium, Inc. That has already been done during the course of the year. These T-accounts are used just for analytical purposes.*

### Transaction A: Net Income for the Year

Reported income for the year was $10,000, as seen on the income statement. Since all of the revenue and expense accounts have been closed, this amount now resides on the balance sheet in the Retained Earnings account. Our initial assumption is that all revenue involved an inflow of cash and all expenses involved an outflow of cash. We will make adjustments later to determine the actual cash flows. Since a positive net income figure is reported, an inflow is the initial assumption. The entry then is to debit Cash, or, more precisely, the Cash Flows from Operating Activities section of Cash, to reflect the assumed increase in cash and to credit Retained Earnings.

| Cash | | | Retained Earnings | | |
|---|---|---|---|---|---|
| BB | 9,000 | | | BB | 62,000 |
| | | | | **A** | **10,000** |
| | **Cash Flows from Operating Activities** | | | | |
| **A Net Income** | **10,000** | | | | |

Note that whenever an entry is made in the Cash account, a brief description is entered, to act as a reminder of what the amount reflects when we are ready to prepare the statement of cash flows. For example, without the description we would have no way of knowing what the $10,000 represents in our Cash Flows from Operations subsection.

As a next step, we suggest that you enter the transactions that are known from the additional information gathered from Millennium's general ledger.

### Transaction B: Dividends Paid

The additional information reports that a $3,000 dividend was paid to holders of common stock. This information may be seen on the Statement of Retained Earnings as well. The dividend payment represents an outflow of cash from financing activities. Remember that, with the exception of interest, inflows and outflows to creditors and owners are shown under the financing activities caption. Retained Earnings is debited and this, together with the net income entry A, will explain how Retained Earnings went from a beginning balance of $62,000 to an ending balance of $69,000.

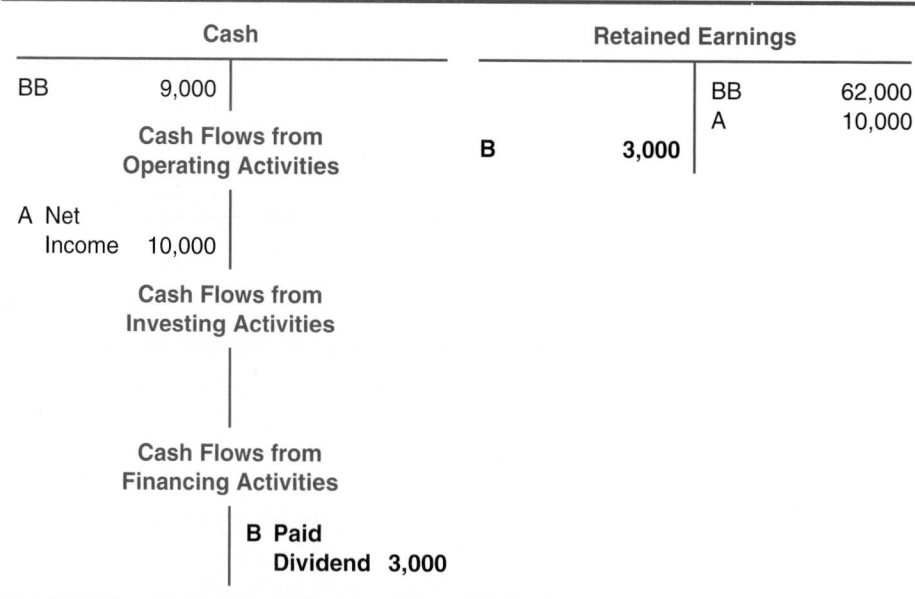

| Cash | | | | Retained Earnings | | |
|---|---|---|---|---|---|---|
| BB | 9,000 | | | | | BB | 62,000 |
| | Cash Flows from Operating Activities | | B | 3,000 | A | 10,000 |
| A Net Income | 10,000 | | | | | |
| | Cash Flows from Investing Activities | | | | | |
| | Cash Flows from Financing Activities | | | | | |
| | B Paid Dividend 3,000 | | | | | |

## Transaction C: Equipment Sold

Millennium sold equipment for $8,000. The equipment cost $14,000 and had a book value of $8,000; this means that there must have been $6,000 in accumulated depreciation. You already know how this transaction would be recorded:

| | | |
|---|---|---|
| Cash .......................................................... | 8,000 | |
| Accumulated Depreciation: Equipment ......................... | 6,000 | |
| Equipment .......................................... | | 14,000 |

All that remains is to make this entry in the analysis T-accounts. The debit to cash will be shown under Cash Flows from Investing Activities since it involves the sale of productive equipment that the company had invested in.

| Cash | | | Equipment | | |
|---|---|---|---|---|---|
| BB | 9,000 | | BB | 55,000 | |
| | Cash Flows from Operating Activities | | | | C 14,000 |
| A Net Income | 10,000 | | **Accum. Depr.: Equipment** | | |
| | Cash Flows from Investing Activities | | | | BB 17,000 |
| C Sold Equipment | 8,000 | | C | 6,000 | |
| | Cash Flows from Financing Activities | | | | |
| | B Paid Dividend 3,000 | | | | |

## Transactions D1 and D2: Land Acquired for Stock

A parcel of land valued at $40,000 was acquired in exchange for 3,200 shares of common stock. Cash is unaffected by this transaction, but since it is a significant financing activity it must be shown on the statement of cash flows. This is accomplished by showing the transaction as a noncash investing and financing activity. Reproducing the entry in the T-accounts would involve merely debiting Land and crediting Common Stock and Paid-in Capital in Excess of Par. But this procedure would bury the entry among the non-cash accounts, it would fail to highlight the data needed for preparation of the statement of cash flows.

The dilemma is solved by arbitrarily splitting the transaction into two parts: (1) issuing the stock and (2) acquiring the land. The two analysis entries below make use of a Noncash Investing and Financing Activities account to show the inflow of non-cash resources from issuing common stock (entry D-1) and the outflow of non-cash resources in acquiring the land (entry D-2). This procedure keeps all information needed to prepare the statement of cash flows in the analysis account.

| Noncash Investing and Financing Activities | | | | Land | |
|---|---|---|---|---|---|
| D-1 Noncash Resource from Issuing Common Stock  40,000 | D-2 Noncash Resource Used to Acquire Land  40,000 | | BB<br>D-2 | 67,000<br>40,000 | |

| | Common Stock | |
|---|---|---|
| | BB<br>D-1 | 100,000<br>32,000 |

| | Paid-in Capital<br>in Excess of Par | |
|---|---|---|
| | BB<br>D-1 | 45,000<br>8,000 |

Remember that our procedure is to explain the changes in each of Millennium's balance sheet accounts. Now that we have prepared entries to explain each of the pieces of additional information provided for Millennium, we go back and examine each account in turn to see if we have completely explained its change.

## Transaction E: Adjustment for Accounts Receivable

We have recorded no explanation for the $5,000 decrease in the Accounts Receivable account. What is the most reasonable explanation for this change? The answer is that we collected $5,000 more on account than the revenues reported on the income statement this year. Since we began our analysis by assuming that net income reflected the cash from operations, we must now adjust this assumption by adding $5,000 to the net income amount. Cash flows from operations are at least $5,000 greater than net income.

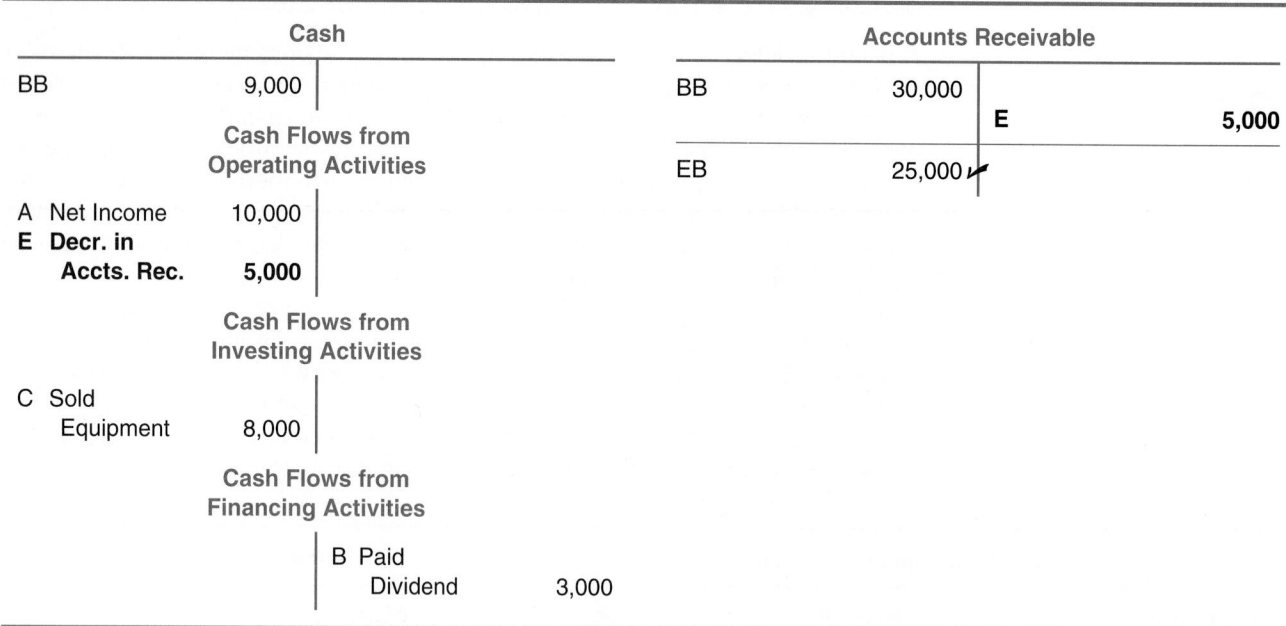

| | Cash | | | Accounts Receivable | |
|---|---|---|---|---|---|
| BB | 9,000 | | BB | 30,000 | |
| | | | | | E 5,000 |
| | *Cash Flows from Operating Activities* | | EB | 25,000 ✔ | |
| A Net Income | 10,000 | | | | |
| **E Decr. in Accts. Rec.** | **5,000** | | | | |
| | *Cash Flows from Investing Activities* | | | | |
| C Sold Equipment | 8,000 | | | | |
| | *Cash Flows from Financing Activities* | | | | |
| | | B Paid Dividend | 3,000 | | |

Since the full amount of the change in Accounts Receivable has been explained, we add a check mark (✔) to note this fact.

### Transaction F: Adjustment for Merchandise Inventory

Merchandise inventory increased by $10,000. There has been no explanation for this change. The most logical explanation is that the company bought and paid for $10,000 more inventory than has been expensed as cost of goods sold. This additional $10,000 cash outflow must be shown as a deduction from net income. Cash flow from operations was at least $10,000 less than reported net income.

| | Cash | | | Merchandise Inventory | |
|---|---|---|---|---|---|
| BB | 9,000 | | BB | 13,000 | |
| | | | **F** | **10,000** | |
| | *Cash Flows from Operating Activities* | | EB | 23,000 ✔ | |
| A Net Income | 10,000 | **F Incr. in** | | | |
| E Decr. in Accts. Rec. | 5,000 | **Mdse. Inty.** **10,000** | | | |
| | *Cash Flows from Investing Activities* | | | | |
| C Sold Equipment | 8,000 | | | | |
| | *Cash Flows from Financing Activities* | | | | |
| | | B Paid Dividend | 3,000 | | |

## Transaction G: Purchase Investment in Bonds

The next account for analysis, Investment in Bonds, increased by $2,000. The most logical explanation is that Millennium bought bonds issued by another company as an investment. This type of venture is appropriately disclosed as an outflow of cash under investing activities.

| Cash | | | | |
|---|---|---|---|---|
| BB | 9,000 | | | |
| | | **Cash Flows from Operating Activities** | | |
| A  Net Income | 10,000 | F  Incr. in | | |
| E  Decr. in | | Mdse. Inty. | 10,000 | |
| Accts. Rec. | 5,000 | | | |
| | | **Cash Flows from Investing Activities** | | |
| C  Sold | | **G Acquired** | | |
| Equipment | 8,000 | **Bond Invest.** | **2,000** | |
| | | **Cash Flows from Financing Activities** | | |
| | | B  Paid | | |
| | | Dividend | 3,000 | |

| Investment in Bonds | | |
|---|---|---|
| BB | 25,000 | |
| **G** | **2,000** | |
| EB | 27,000 | |

## Transaction H: Adjustment for Depreciation on Buildings

The next T-accounts we encounter are Land and Buildings. We have already explained the change in land by a previous entry; buildings did not change. We may conclude, then, that we are finished with these accounts. They are shown on the next page with the appropriate check marks.

Accumulated Depreciation: Buildings increased by $4,000. Since no other entries have been made to this account, we conclude that this increase must have been due to depreciation expense. A glance at the income statement confirms this. This expense does not use cash; therefore net income must be increased to eliminate this noncash expense and reflect the cash from operations.

| Cash | | | | Land | | |
|---|---|---|---|---|---|---|
| BB | 9,000 | | | BB | 67,000 | |
| | | | | D-2 | 40,000 | |
| | **Cash Flows from** | | | EB | 107,000 | |
| | **Operating Activities** | | | | | |

**Building**

| | | |
|---|---|---|
| BB | 190,000 | |
| EB | 190,000 | |

| A Net Income | 10,000 | F Incr. in | |
|---|---|---|---|
| E Decr. in | | Mdse. Inty. | 10,000 |
| Accts. Rec. | 5,000 | | |
| **H Depr. Bldg.** | **4,000** | | |

**Accum Depr.: Building**

| | | | |
|---|---|---|---|
| **Cash Flows from** | | BB | 6,000 |
| **Investing Activities** | | **H** | **4,000** |
| | | EB | 10,000 |

| C Sold | | G Acquired | |
|---|---|---|---|
| Equipment | 8,000 | Bond Invest. | 2,000 |

**Cash Flows from**
**Financing Activities**

| | | B Paid | |
|---|---|---|---|
| | | Dividend | 3,000 |

## Transaction I: Acquisition of Equipment

We explained a $14,000 decrease in equipment reflecting the cost of equipment sold in Transaction C. The balance sheet indicates that this account decreased by only $10,000. To explain the $10,000 decrease, we must conclude that $4,000 of equipment was purchased. Acquisition of a long-lived asset is shown under investing activities.

| Cash | | | | Equipment | | |
|---|---|---|---|---|---|---|
| BB | 9,000 | | | BB | 55,000 | |
| | | | | I | **4,000** | C 14,000 |
| | **Cash Flows from** | | | EB | 45,000 | |
| | **Operating Activities** | | | | | |

| A Net Income | 10,000 | F Incr. in | |
|---|---|---|---|
| E Decr. in | | Mdse, Inty. | 10,000 |
| Accts. Rec. | 5,000 | | |
| H Depr. Bldg. | 4,000 | | |

**Cash Flows from**
**Investing Activities**

| C Sold | | G Acquired | |
|---|---|---|---|
| Equipment | 8,000 | Bond Invest. | 2,000 |
| | | **I Bought** | |
| | | **Equipment** | **4,000** |

**Cash Flows from**
**Financing Activities**

| | | B Paid | |
|---|---|---|---|
| | | Dividend | 3,000 |

### Transaction J: Adjustment for Depreciation on Equipment

Accumulated Depreciation: Equipment reflects a $6,000 decrease thus far. We know from looking at the balance sheet that only a $5,000 decrease occurred. Our suspicion that a $1,000 depreciation expense must have been recorded is confirmed by checking Millennium's income statement. This noncash expense is added back under operations exactly as we did depreciation on buildings.

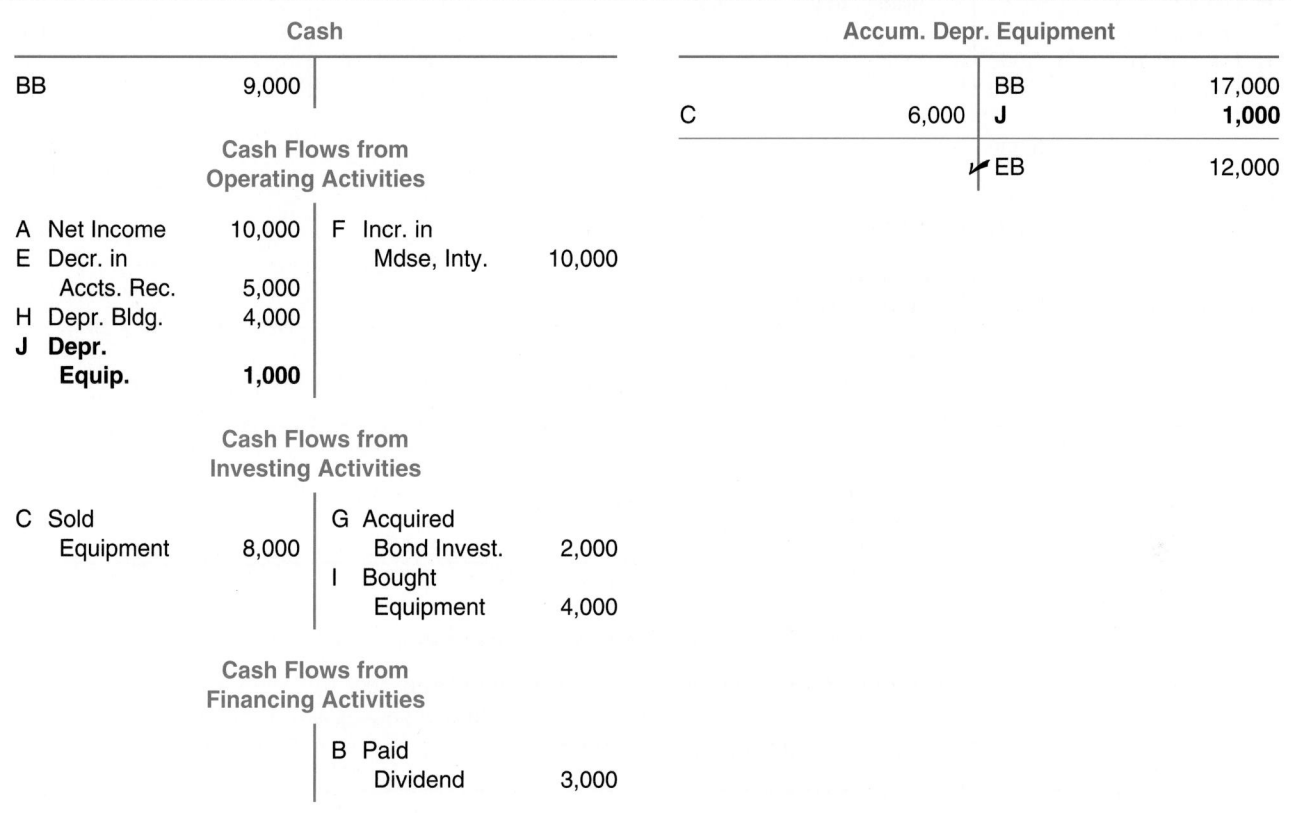

### Transaction K: Adjustment for Salaries Payable

Accounts Payable, the next account on our worksheet, did not change so we merely check it off. Salaries Payable increased by $3,000 indicating that salaries expense on the income statement is higher that the amount of salaries actually paid. We must add $3,000 back to income to reflect the portion of the expense not paid in cash. Cash flow from operations is $3,000 higher than net income due to this noncash expense amount.

### Cash

| | | | |
|---|---|---|---|
| BB | 9,000 | | |

**Cash Flows from Operating Activities**

| | | | | |
|---|---|---|---|---|
| A | Net Income | 10,000 | F Incr. in | |
| E | Decr. in | | Mdse. Inty. | 10,000 |
| | Accts. Rec. | 5,000 | | |
| H | Depr. Bldg. | 4,000 | | |
| J | Depr. Equip. | 1,000 | | |
| **K** | **Incr. in** | | | |
| | **Sal. Pay.** | **3,000** | | |

**Cash Flows from Investing Activities**

| | | | | |
|---|---|---|---|---|
| C | Sold | | G Acquired | |
| | Equipment | 8,000 | Bond Invest. | 2,000 |
| | | | I Bought | |
| | | | Equipment | 4,000 |

**Cash Flows from Financing Activities**

| | | | |
|---|---|---|---|
| | | B Paid | |
| | | Dividend | 3,000 |

### Accounts Payable

| | | | |
|---|---|---|---|
| | | BB | 5,000 |
| | | ✔ EB | 5,000 |

### Salaries Payable

| | | | |
|---|---|---|---|
| | | BB | 20,000 |
| | | **K** | **3,000** |
| | | ✔ EB | 23,000 |

## Transaction L: Retire Bonds Payable

Bonds Payable decreased by $14,000 indicating that Millennium paid off some long-term bonds. Transactions involving debt are shown as inflows and outflows under cash flows from financing activities.

### Cash

| | | | |
|---|---|---|---|
| BB | 9,000 | | |

**Cash Flows from Operating Activities**

| | | | | |
|---|---|---|---|---|
| A | Net Income | 10,000 | F Incr. in | |
| E | Decr. in | | Mdse. Inty. | 10,000 |
| | Accts. Rec. | 5,000 | | |
| H | Depr. Bldg. | 4,000 | | |
| J | Depr. Equip. | 1,000 | | |
| K | Incr. in | | | |
| | Sal. Pay. | 3,000 | | |

**Cash Flows from Investing Activities**

| | | | | |
|---|---|---|---|---|
| C | Sold | | G Acquired | |
| | Equipment | 8,000 | Bond Invest. | 2,000 |
| | | | I Bought | |
| | | | Equipment | 4,000 |

**Cash Flows from Financing Activities**

| | | | |
|---|---|---|---|
| | | B Paid Dividend | 3,000 |
| | | **L Retired Bonds** | **14,000** |

### Bonds Payable

| | | | |
|---|---|---|---|
| | | BB | 134,000 |
| **L** | **14,000** | | |
| | | ✔ EB | 120,000 |

## Transaction M: Issued Common Stock

Common Stock increased from $100,000 to $140,000. This increase has been explained in part by Transaction D, issuing stock for land. The remaining $8,000 of the change must have been due to a cash sale of stock. Since there is still $2,000 of paid-in capital in excess of par to be explained, the $8,000 par value stock must have been sold for $10,000. The cash inflow from issuance of equity securities is reported as a financing activity.

The change in retained earnings has been explained by two previous transactions. This last account can now be checked off indicating that our analysis should be finished. To be sure, the cash account should be audited to verify that the beginning balance plus the debits minus the credits equals the ending balance.

| Cash | | | | |
|---|---|---|---|---|
| BB | 9,000 | | | |
| | | **Cash Flows from** | | |
| | | **Operating Activities** | | |
| A Net Income | 10,000 | F Incr. in | | |
| E Decr. in | | Mdse. Inty. | 10,000 | |
| Accts. Rec. | 5,000 | | | |
| H Depr. Bldg. | 4,000 | | | |
| J Depr. Equip. | 1,000 | | | |
| K Incr. in | | | | |
| Sal. Pay. | 3,000 | | | |
| | | **Cash Flows from** | | |
| | | **Investing Activities** | | |
| C Sold | | G Acquired | | |
| Equipment | 8,000 | Bond Invest. | 2,000 | |
| | | I Bought | | |
| | | Equipment | 4,000 | |
| | | **Cash Flows from** | | |
| | | **Financing Activities** | | |
| **M Issued** | | B Paid | | |
| **Stock** | **10,000** | Dividend | 3,000 | |
| | | L Retired | | |
| | | Bonds | 14,000 | |
| Total Drs. | 50,000 | Total Crs. | 33,000 | |
| EB | 17,000 ✔ | | | |

| Common Stock | | |
|---|---|---|
| | BB | 100,000 |
| | D-1 | 32,000 |
| | **M** | **8,000** |
| | ✔ EB | 140,000 |

| Paid-in Capital in Excess of Par | | |
|---|---|---|
| | BB | 45,000 |
| | D-1 | 8,000 |
| | **M** | **2,000** |
| | ✔ EB | 55,000 |

| Retained Earnings | | | |
|---|---|---|---|
| | | BB | 62,000 |
| B | 3,000 | A | 10,000 |
| | | ✔ EB | 69,000 |

Now that you have seen the analysis one transaction at a time, let's take a look at all of the completed T-accounts in Exhibit 13.

Once the T-account analysis is complete, preparation of the formal statement of cash flows is just a matter of extracting the information from the Cash and the Noncash Investing and Financing Activities T-accounts and placing it in the proper sequence on the statement. Look back at Exhibit 7 and trace the items in the completed T-accounts to the formal statement.

In the Millennium, Inc., case we encountered only a small sample of the types of transactions that may appear on the statement of cash flows. Exhibit 14 provides a more complete listing.

**Exhibit 13** Millennium, Inc., Completed T-Accounts

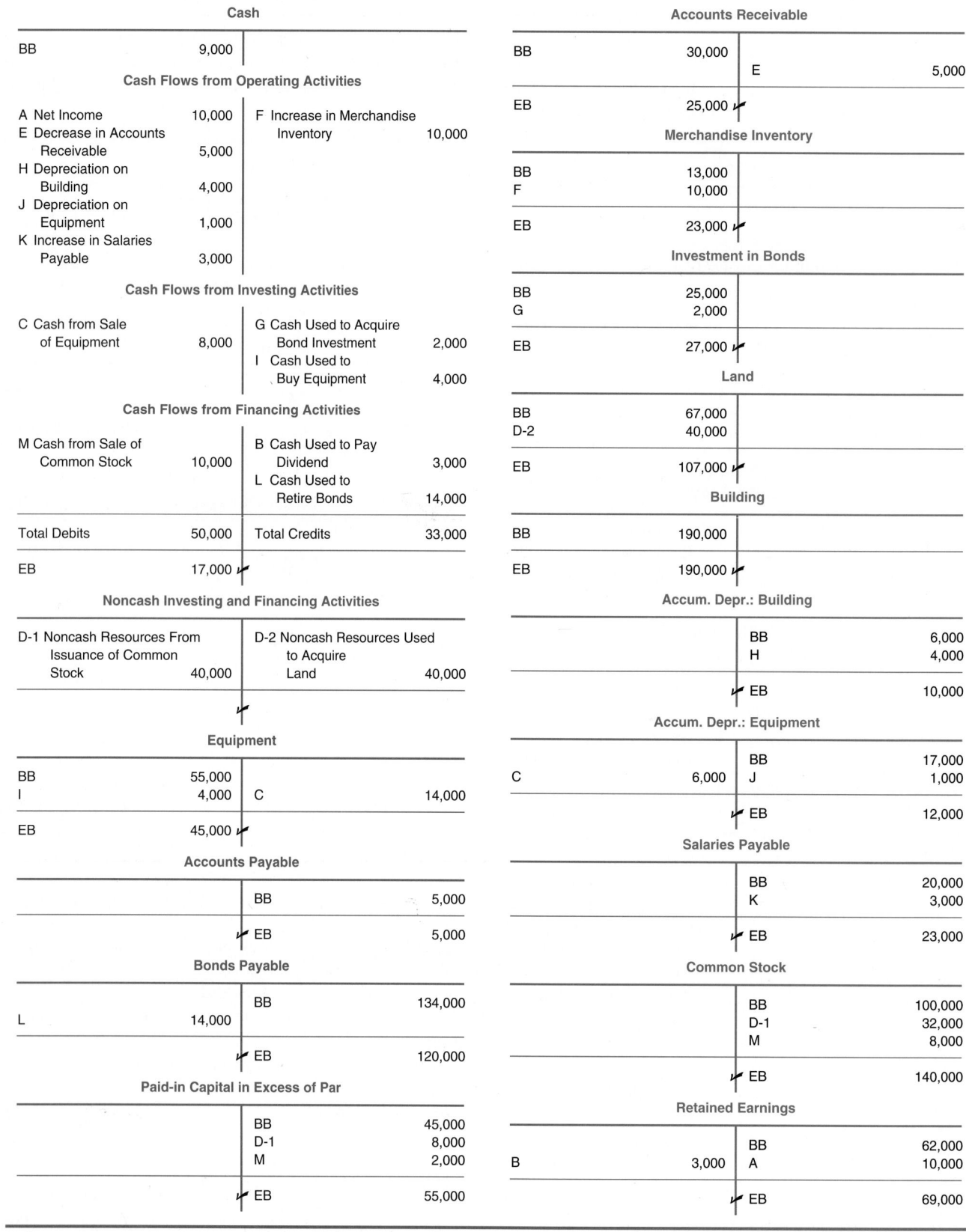

MILLENNIUM, INC.
Statement of Cash Flows
T-Account Approach
(After Analysis)

**Exhibit 14** Typical Cash Flows for Operating, Investing, and Financing Activities

| | CASH INFLOWS | CASH OUTFLOWS |
|---|---|---|
| OPERATING ACTIVITIES | Collections from customers from sales of goods or services<br>Interest received<br>Dividends received from investees | Payments to suppliers for goods<br>Payments to employees for services<br>Payments for other expenses<br>Payments for interest<br>Payments for taxes |
| INVESTING ACTIVITIES | Sale of property, plant, and equipment assets<br>Sale of intangible assets<br>Sale of long-term investments in stocks, bonds and other property<br>Collection of loans made to other entities | Purchase of property, plant, and equipment assets<br>Purchase of intangible assets<br>Purchase of long-term investments in stocks and bonds<br>Lending funds to other entities<br>Purchase of land to hold as an investment |
| FINANCING ACTIVITIES | Sale of common or preferred stock<br>Borrowing by issuing notes or bonds | Payment of cash dividends<br>Purchase of treasury stock<br>Payment of debt principal |

**ASK YOURSELF** ▶

1. When the T-account approach is used, what are the three major subsections of the Cash account?
2. Why is it necessary to set up a Noncash Investing and Financing Activities account?
3. When the T-account working papers are completed, where is the information that will be needed to prepare the statement of cash flows?
4. In which section would each of the following appear on the statement of cash flows: Interest paid to creditors? Dividends received from investees? Dividends paid to shareholders? Interest received from debtors?

## CONVERTING ACCRUAL INCOME TO CASH FROM OPERATIONS

Learning
Objective **5**

Explain the logic underlying the conversion of an accrual income statement to cash provided by operations

Since cash generated by operations is often the life blood of a company, managers and financial analysts often want to know this amount at times other than when a complete statement of cash flows is published. At these times cash from operations may be derived by converting a company's accrual basis income to a cash basis. When you calculated cash from operations using the T-account method, you were actually making this conversion. We may also compute a cash income amount by using logic in analyzing a company's accrual income statement and balance sheet.

*Accrual income* recognizes revenue when it is earned and matches expenses with the revenues they helped to generate. *Cash flows from operations* recognizes "revenue" when cash is collected from customers and expenses when cash is paid out. The following diagram shows how the conversion from accrual to cash is accomplished. Take a few minutes to study it and then we'll discuss the logic of each conversion.

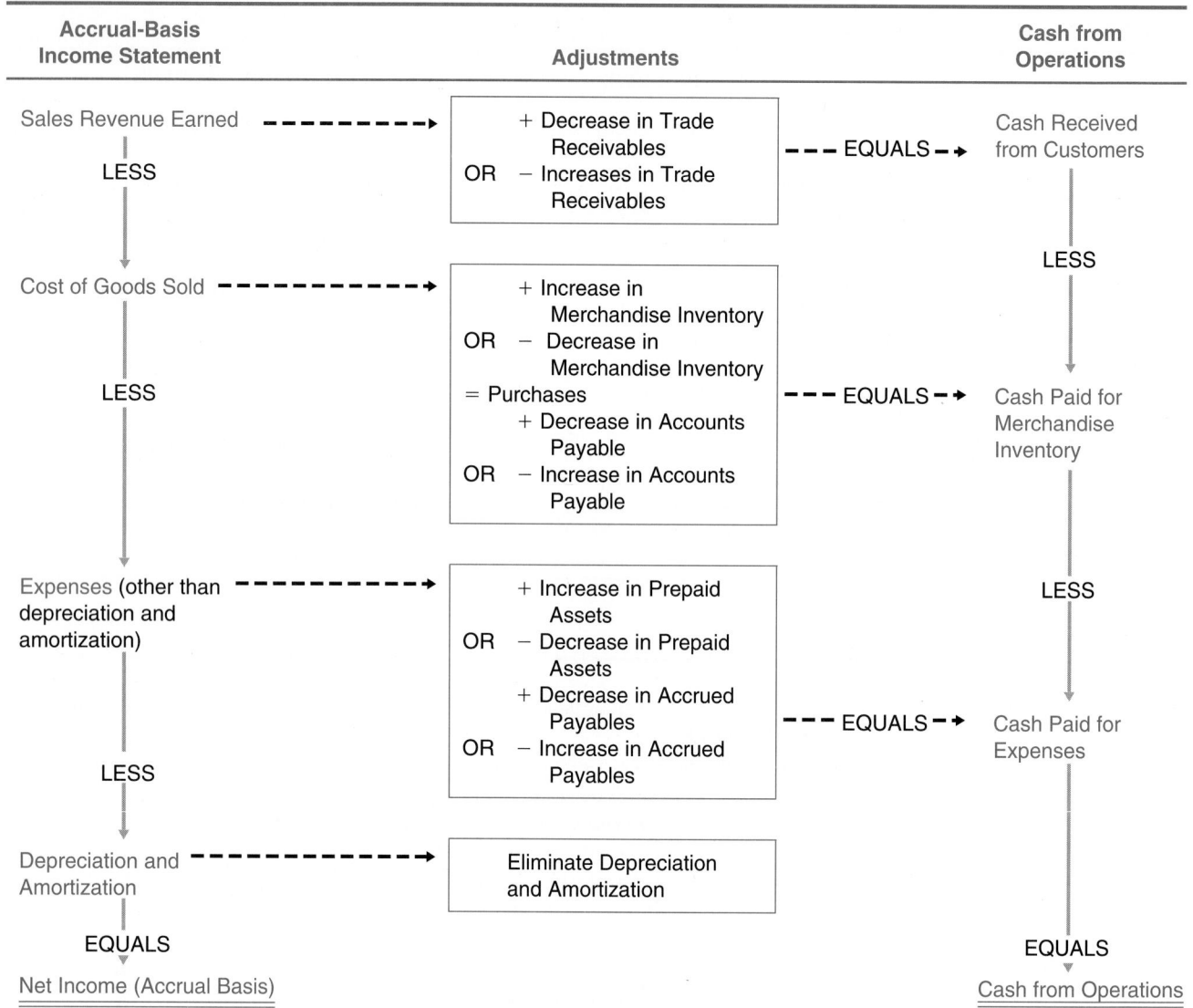

| Accrual-Basis Income Statement | Adjustments | Cash from Operations |
|---|---|---|

Sales Revenue Earned ------> 
```
+ Decrease in Trade
  Receivables
OR - Increases in Trade
  Receivables
```
--- EQUALS --> Cash Received from Customers

LESS

Cost of Goods Sold ------>
```
    + Increase in
      Merchandise Inventory
OR  - Decrease in
      Merchandise Inventory
= Purchases
    + Decrease in Accounts
      Payable
OR  - Increase in Accounts
      Payable
```
--- EQUALS --> Cash Paid for Merchandise Inventory

LESS

LESS

Expenses (other than depreciation and amortization) ------>
```
    + Increase in Prepaid
      Assets
OR  - Decrease in Prepaid
      Assets
    + Decrease in Accrued
      Payables
OR  - Increase in Accrued
      Payables
```
--- EQUALS --> Cash Paid for Expenses

LESS

LESS

Depreciation and Amortization ------>
```
Eliminate Depreciation
and Amortization
```

EQUALS

Net Income (Accrual Basis)

EQUALS

Cash from Operations

## Revenue Earned to Cash Received

Revenue is recognized on the accrual basis when it is earned. A decrease in trade receivables, usually accounts receivable, indicates that the accounts collected exceed the revenues recognized for the period. In this case revenues are lower than cash collections and the decrease in receivables must be added to revenues. Millennium, Inc., had a decrease in receivables that we added back when we completed the T-account analysis.

An increase in trade receivables indicates that more revenue was recognized than cash collected. The increase, then, must be deducted to find the amount of cash collected from customers.

## Cost of Goods Sold to Cash Paid For Merchandise

A two step process is necessary to find cash paid for merchandise. First we calculate purchases, then we determine how much was paid this period for these purchases. Cost of goods sold plus an increase (or minus a decrease) in merchandise inventory yields the amount of purchases. This is logical if you remember that if we sell only what we purchased this period, cost of goods sold would equal purchases. If we sell less than we purchased, inventory must be larger at the end of the period than it was at the beginning. This increase must be added to determine purchases for the period.

A decrease in inventory would indicate that we sold more than we purchased. The decrease would need to be subtracted from cost of goods sold to derive purchases.

Now that we have determined how much the company bought, we are ready to calculate the amount that was paid. When a business acquires inventory, it almost always acquires the goods on credit. For purposes of this analysis we will assume that all purchases are on credit. If the Accounts Payable account decreases during the period, we know that the company paid for all of this period's purchases plus some that were made in a prior period. The decrease in Accounts Payable must be added to purchases to derive the amount of cash paid for merchandise.

If the company does not pay for all of this period's purchases, Accounts Payable will increase. This increase is subtracted from purchases to calculate the cash paid for merchandise.

### Operating Expenses to Cash Paid for Expenses

We need to examine prepaid assets, accrued payables, depreciation and amortization to determine how much cash was paid for expenses this period.

### Prepaid Assets

For some expenses, such as rent or advertising, a company may pay in advance and record a prepaid asset. An increase in one of these prepaid items indicates that the company has paid more than it has expensed this period. We will need to add this increase to operating expenses to reflect the amount of cash paid.

A decrease in a prepaid asset would, of course, signal that the company paid less this period that it had expensed. This decrease would be subtracted from the operating expense to determine the amount of cash paid.

### Accrued Payables

In your study of accounting you have encountered a number of situations that have required accrual of an expense and a payable at the end of the period. Examples include accrual of interest expense and payable on borrowed funds, accrual of utilities expense and payable for phone and electric usage, and salaries expense and payable for wages earned by employees but not yet paid.

A decrease in these accruals signifies that more cash has been paid than the corresponding expense on the income statement. The company has paid an amount equivalent to the expense on the income statement plus some of the debt that existed at the beginning of the period. This decrease, then, must be added to the expense to derive the total cash paid.

An increase would signal just the opposite, that less cash was paid than the amount expensed. This increase in the liability is subtracted from the expense to calculate the amount of cash paid.

### Depreciation and Amortization

Neither depreciation of long-lived tangible assets nor amortization of intangible assets involves cash. In converting from accrual income to cash from operations, we may ignore, or eliminate, these amounts from consideration.

Now that you understand the logic of each of the conversions, let's reinforce your understanding with a calculation for Millennium, Inc. Exhibit 15 shows the conversion of Millennium's 1998 accrual income to cash from operations. Note that we grouped all of the expenses except cost of goods sold and depreciation into one amount. Millennium had no prepaid assets, and accounts payable did not change but we included these adjustments at a $0 amount to remind you that they should be made.

**Exhibit 15** Millennium, Inc. Conversion of 1998 Accrual Income to Cash from Operations

| Accrual Basis Income | | Adjustment | | Cash from Operations | |
|---|---|---|---|---|---|
| Sales Revenue | $250,000 | + Decrease in Accts. Receivable | +$ 5,000 | Cash collected = from customers | $255,000 |
| Cost of Goods Sold | (155,000) | + Increase in Mdse. Inventory | +$10,000 | | |
| | | ± Change in Accts. Payable | $ 0 | = Cash paid for merchandise | (165,000) |
| Administrative, Selling, Interest, Inc. Tax, Salaries | (80,000) | ± Change in Prepaid Assets<br>− Increase in Salaries Payable | $ 0<br>− $ 3,000 | = Cash paid for Operating Exp. | (77,000) |
| Depreciation | (5,000) | Eliminate: No cash paid. | | | |
| Net income | $ 10,000 | | | Cash Provided by Operations | $ 13,000 |

## ANALYZING A COMPLEX STATEMENT OF CASH FLOWS

**Learning Objective 6**

Analyze a complex statement of cash flows

Now we have looked at most of the basics related to the statement of cash flows. Next we'll examine a more complex statement as a way of sharpening your analytical skills and introducing you to some additional concepts. The Cartridge Company statement of cash flows shown in Exhibit 16 will be used as the basis for our discussion.

**Exhibit 16** Cartridge Company Statement of Cash Flows

**CARTRIDGE COMPANY**
**Statement of Cash Flows**
**For the Year Ended December 31, 1998**

| | | |
|---|---|---|
| Cash Flows from Operating Activities: | | |
| Net Income. . . . . . . . . . . . . . . . . . . . . . . . . . . . . . . . . . . . . . . | | $ 14,500 |
| Adjustments to Reconcile Net Income to Net Cash Provided by Operating Activities: | | |
| Add: | | |
| Decrease in Prepaid Expenses . . . . . . . . . . . . . . . . . . . | $ 1,500 | |
| Increase in Accrued Liabilities . . . . . . . . . . . . . . . . . . . . | 4,500 | |
| Amortization of Discount on Bonds Payable . . . . . . . . . . | 600 | |
| Depreciation Expense. . . . . . . . . . . . . . . . . . . . . . . . . . | 12,000 | |
| Patent Amortization . . . . . . . . . . . . . . . . . . . . . . . . . . . | 1,000 | 19,600 |
| Deduct: | | |
| Increase in Accounts Receivable. . . . . . . . . . . . . . . . . . | $(19,000) | |
| Increase in Merchandise Inventory . . . . . . . . . . . . . . . . | (22,000) | |
| Decrease in Accounts Payable . . . . . . . . . . . . . . . . . . . | (6,000) | |
| Gain on Sale of Land . . . . . . . . . . . . . . . . . . . . . . . . . . | (3,700) | (50,700) |
| Net Cash Used in Operating Activities . . . . . . . . . . . . | | $(16,600) |
| | | |
| Cash Flows from Investing Activities: | | |
| Proceeds from Sale of Land. . . . . . . . . . . . . . . . . . . . . . . | $ 30,000 | |
| Payment for Purchase of Land . . . . . . . . . . . . . . . . . . . . . | (48,400) | |
| Net Cash Used in Investing Activities. . . . . . . . . . . . . | | $(18,400) |

**Exhibit 16** *(Continued)*

| Cash Flows from Financing Activities: | | |
|---|---|---|
|     Proceeds from Issuance of Common Stock . . . . . . . . . . . . | $ 40,000 | |
|     Dividends Paid . . . . . . . . . . . . . . . . . . . . . . . . . . . . . . . . | (10,000) | |
|         Net Cash Provided by Financing Activities . . . . . . . . . | | 30,000 |
| Net Decrease in Cash and Cash Equivalents. . . . . . . . . . . . . . | | $( 5,000) |
| Cash and Cash Equivalents at Beginning of Year . . . . . . . . . . . | | 55,000 |
| Cash and Cash Equivalents at End of Year . . . . . . . . . . . . . . . | | $ 50,000 |

Supplemental Disclosures of Cash Flow Information:
    Cash paid during 1998 for interest        $16,000
    Cash paid during 1998 for income taxes    $ 9,700

Noncash Investing and Financing Activities:
    The company acquired a building in exchange for common
      stock valued at $50,000.

## Analysis of Operating Activities

Cartridge has a positive net income and yet their operations used cash during the year. Their increase in accounts receivable may indicate either that sales are growing and the lag in collections is causing an increase in this account; or Cartridge is doing a poor job of collecting its accounts. We would look to comparative income statements to track sales growth, and use accounts receivable turnover and average age of receivables to test our hypothesis about collection of accounts.

    The decline in prepaid expenses simply means that more of these assets were expensed this period than were paid in cash. We can guess that either the company is delaying payments to those who normally expect prepayments, or Cartridge is dealing with fewer suppliers who demand prepayments. Payment delays along with the other facts we are discovering may cause us some concern as investors or creditors.

    Accounts payable decreased while accrued payables increased. From this information we may guess that Cartridge's suppliers of merchandise are insisting on shorter credit terms and Cartridge is making up for this by postponing payments to others, where possible. The decrease in accounts payable coupled with the increase in merchandise inventory raises questions that may be answered by management's discussion and analysis in the annual report. Otherwise, we may be left wondering and somewhat concerned about this one as well.

    You should have noticed two items in Cartridge's operating section that we have not encountered before: amortization of discount on bonds payable, and gain on sale of land. Let's look at each of these and see why they are reported as they are.

    When you learned to account for bonds that had been issued at a discount, you amortized some of the discount each time an interest payment was made. The journal entry looked something like this:

| | | |
|---|---|---|
| Interest Expense. . . . . . . . . . . . . . . . . . . . . . . . . . . . . . . . . . . . | 16,600 | |
|     Discount on Bonds Payable . . . . . . . . . . . . . . . . . . . . . . . . . . | | 600 |
|     Cash. . . . . . . . . . . . . . . . . . . . . . . . . . . . . . . . . . . . . . . . . . | | 16,000 |

You can see that the amount of interest expense is greater than the amount of cash that was paid by the amount of discount that has been amortized. Net income is lower than the cash from operations, then, because more expense was deducted than cash paid. Our calculation of cash flows from operations requires adding back the amount of discount amortization. Premium amortization would be subtracted because the amount of cash paid out is larger than the interest expense amount.

In preparing T-account working papers remember you are adjusting only for the noncash part of the interest expense. The cash portion has already been deducted, as it should have been, in deriving net income. The T-accounts for the amortization of bond discount would look like this:

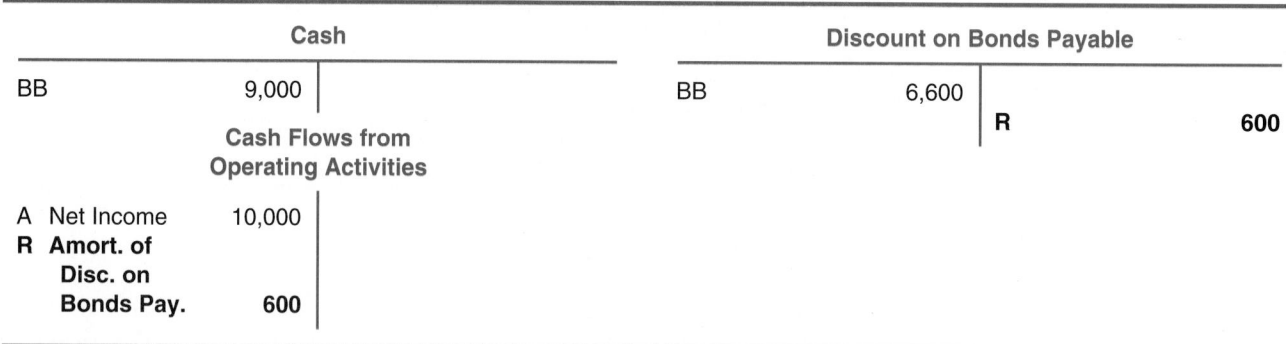

When a company sells assets other than inventory, a gain or loss is recognized when the sales price is above or below book value. Cartridge sold some land at a $3,700 gain; the entry may have looked like this:

| | | |
|---|---|---|
| Cash .......................................... | 30,000 | |
| Gain on Sale of Land................................. | | 3,700 |
| Land......................................... | | 26,300 |

This transaction provided $30,000 cash to Cartridge which must be reported as cash flows from investing activities according to GAAP. The $3,700 is shown as a positive item on Cartridge's income statement, but it provided no additional cash. We must eliminate this noncash gain by deducting it. Losses on sales of assets would likewise be eliminated by adding them. Your analysis T-accounts will appear as shown below:

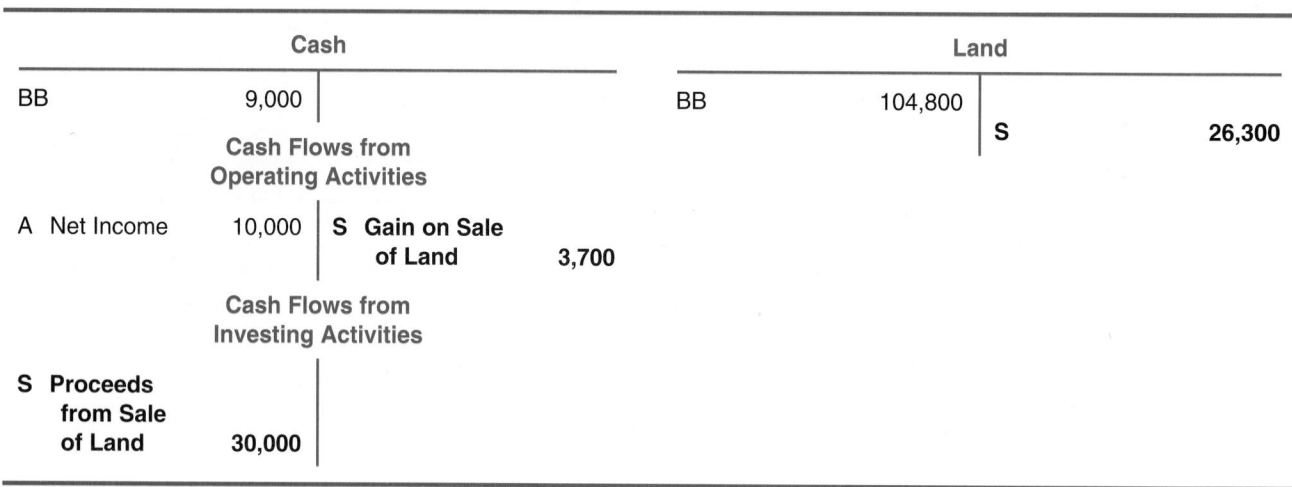

Neither the adjustment for discount amortization nor for the gain on sale of land provides additional information about the company's cash flows that is not found elsewhere in the financial statements. The same may be said for the add back of depreciation and amortization. All of these adjustments are necessary because some or all of each item did not provide or use cash.

### Analysis of Investing Activities

Cartridge has only two transactions reported under investing activities. The company sold one parcel of land and purchased another one. A careful reading of the statement also reveals that a building was acquired by issuing common stock. Perhaps Cartridge sold a piece of land that it had been planning to use for a new building in order to acquire another, more desirable, one. At any rate we know that Cartridge is expanding its operations because no buildings were sold. The company has acquired a new office, store, warehouse, or factory. The management discussion and analysis or footnotes in the annual report may provide more insight into this matter.

### Analysis of Financing Activities

Cartridge is financing its expansion and its operations by issuing common stock. The financing activities section indicates that $40,000 cash was received through a stock issuance. The supplementary information reveals that a building was acquired by issuing common stock valued at $50,000. The fact that Cartridge can raise this relatively large amount of capital through the issuance of equity securities may be viewed as a positive sign. We would want to examine the balance sheet and calculate a debt-to-equity ratio to get a better idea about the relationship between debt and equity financing.

We may raise also the question of why debt financing was rejected. Perhaps interest rates are too high, perhaps management believes that additional debt would be imprudent given the company's capital structure. Insight into these questions may be found in the management's discussion and analysis in the annual report or in articles in the financial press discussing the company's issuance of common stock.

Management's decision to pay a $10,000 cash dividend at a time when operations are using cash is a cause for concern. Management may believe that payment of dividends is necessary to keep stockholders happy regardless of the cash flows from operations. Financing a dividend through borrowing, issuing stock, or selling assets is not normally considered wise management. An informed stockholder should be knowledgeable enough to see this as a possible sign of weak financial management.

### Other Observations

The amounts of cash paid for interest and income taxes are shown among the supplementary information at the bottom of the statement of cash flows. The amount of interest expense and income tax expense on the income statement often are different from the amounts actually paid. Since many financial statement analysts are interested in this information, GAAP requires this disclosure.

As you can see, analysis of the statement of cash flows provides some information and raises many questions. This statement should be studied in conjunction with the other financial statements, the notes to the financial statements, the auditor's opinion, management's discussion and analysis, and the other information from the company's annual report. The serious student of a company will want to calculate financial ratios and read articles about the firm in the financial press. The statement of cash flows provides no magic key to a company's financial condition; but it does furnish some very important information.

## SUMMARY

• The statement of cash flows is the fourth major financial statement that must be published for external users. The purpose of this statement is to provide information about the cash receipts and cash payments and about the investing and financing activities of a business.

• The information provided by the statement of cash flows together with the information contained in the three other financial statements, helps financial statement users assess:

1. An entity's ability to generate positive future cash flows
2. An entity's ability to meet its obligations, its need for external financing, and its ability to pay dividends
3. The reasons for differences between income and associated cash receipts and payments
4. Both the cash and noncash aspects of an entity's investing and financing transactions

• The statement is divided into three major sections:

1. Cash flows from operating activities
2. Cash flows from investing activities
3. Cash flows from financing activities

• Information about significant noncash investing and financing activities, cash used for interest and income taxes, and a reconciliation of net income to cash from operations must be shown in the body of the statement or in supplemental disclosures.

• Cash flows from operating activities are generally the cash effects of transactions that enter into the determination of income.

• The operating activities can be disclosed by using either the indirect or the direct method.

• Cash flows from investing activities involve lending money, collecting loans, and acquiring or selling securities and productive assets.

• Cash flows from financing activities involve obtaining resources from owners and creditors, providing owners a return on and a return of their investment, and repaying creditors.

• Working papers for preparing the statement of cash flows can be constructed using T-accounts.

• In the T-account approach, a T-account is established for each balance sheet item. The beginning and ending balances are entered in each T-account. Analysis T-accounts are prepared for Cash and for Noncash Investing and Financing Activities. After the analysis is completed these two accounts will contain all the information necessary to prepare the statement. Entries are recorded in the T-accounts to reproduce, in summary form, the transactions that took place during the period. Whenever cash is involved, it is placed in the appropriate operating, investing, or financing section of the Cash T-account. The corresponding debit or credit is entered into the appropriate balance sheet account.

• When analyzing a company's financial condition, the statement of cash flows should be used in conjunction with other information in its annual report, financial ratios, and information about the company from the financial press.

7 **KEY TERMS**

| | |
|---|---|
| Cash equivalent | Short-term, highly liquid investments that are readily convertible to known amounts of cash and have original maturities of three months or less; thus, there is insignificant risk of loss of value caused by changes in interest rates. |
| Direct method | The method of preparing the operating activities section of the statement of cash flows that reports major classes of gross cash receipts and gross cash payments. |
| Financing activities | Transactions entered into by a business entity that include obtaining resources from owners and providing them with a return on, and a return of, their investment; borrowing money; and repaying amounts borrowed. |
| Indirect method | The method of preparing the operating activities section of the statement of cash flows that reconciles net income to cash flows from operating activities. |
| Investing activities | Transactions entered into by a business entity that include making and collecting loans and acquiring and disposing of debt or equity instruments and property, plant, and equipment. |
| Operating activities | Transactions entered into by a business entity that include delivering or producing goods for sale and providing services. |
| Statement of cash flows | A financial statement that provides information about the inflows and outflows of cash and cash equivalents from a firm's operating, investing, and financing activities. |

---

## DEMONSTRATION PROBLEM

The 1998 financial statements of Nantucket Products, Inc., are shown below:

**NANTUCKET PRODUCTS, INC.**
**Income Statement**
**Year Ended December 31, 1998**
**(000's omitted)**

| | | |
|---|---:|---:|
| Sales. | | $16,400 |
| Cost of Goods Sold | | (8,600) |
| Gross Profit on Sales. | | $ 7,800 |
| Operating Expenses: | | |
|   Depreciation | $(400) | |
|   Other. | (300) | |
| Total Operating Expenses | | ( 700) |
| Other Expenses and Losses: | | |
|   Interest | $(700) | |
|   Loss on Sale of Building | (100) | |
| Total Other Expenses and Losses | | ( 800) |
| Income Before Income Taxes | | 6,300 |
| Provision for Income Taxes | | (1,200) |
| Net Income. | | $ 5,100 |

---

**NANTUCKET PRODUCTS, INC.**
Comparative Balance Sheets
(000's omitted)

|  | Dec. 31 | |
| --- | --- | --- |
|  | **1998** | **1997** |
| **Assets** | | |
| Current Assets: | | |
| Cash.......................................... | $ 2,200 | $ 1,500 |
| Accounts Receivable (net) ........................... | 3,200 | 800 |
| Merchandise Inventory .............................. | 5,600 | 6,100 |
| Current Assets (total)............................. | $11,000 | $ 8,400 |
| Property, Plant, and Equipment: | | |
| Land......................................... | $ 2,800 | $ 1,800 |
| Building ...................................... | 14,400 | 15,000 |
| Accumulated Depreciation: Building..................... | (300) | (800) |
| Total Property, Plant, and Equipment.................. | $16,900 | $16,000 |
| Total Assets...................................... | $27,900 | $24,400 |
| **Equities** | | |
| Current Liabilities: | | |
| Accounts Payable ................................... | $ 1,600 | $ 1,900 |
| Salaries Payable .................................... | 2,000 | 1,100 |
| Total Current Liabilities ............................ | $ 3,600 | $3,000 |
| Noncurrent Liabilities.................................. | 800 | 4,000 |
| Common Stock ...................................... | 15,400 | 14,400 |
| Retained Earnings.................................... | 8,100 | 3,000 |
| Total Equities....................................... | $27,900 | $24,400 |

The following additional information is from the financial records of Nantucket Products, Inc.:

1. A building costing $1,400,000 was acquired for cash.
2. Cash was used to pay off noncurrent liabilities amounting to $3,200,000.
3. A building costing $2,000,000 and having a book value of $1,100,000 was sold for $1,000,000 cash.
4. Common stock was issued in exchange for a land with a fair market value of $1,000,000.

**Required:**

Prepare in good form a statement of cash flows (using the T-account approach and the indirect method) for the year ended Dec. 31, 1998.

## ■ Solution to Demonstration Problem

Nantucket Products, Inc., T-Accounts

### Cash

| BB | 1,500 | | |
|----|-------|---|---|

#### Cash Flows from Operating Activities

| A | Net Income | 5,100 | F | Increase in Accounts Receivable | 2,400 |
| D | Loss on Sale of Building | 100 | H | Decrease in Accounts Payable | 300 |
| G | Decrease in Inventories | 500 | | | |
| I | Increase in Salaries Payable | 900 | | | |
| J | Depreciation Expense | 400 | | | |

#### Cash Flows from Investing Activities

| D | Proceeds from Sale of Building | 1,000 | B | Cash for Purchase of Building | 1,400 |

#### Cash Flows from Financing Activities

| | | | C | Cash Used to Pay Noncurrent Liabilities | 3,200 |

| Total Debits | 9,500 | Total Credits | 7,300 |
|--------------|-------|---------------|-------|
| EB | 2,200 | | |

#### Noncash Investing and Financing Activities

| E-1 | Noncash Resources From Issuance of Common Stock | 1,000 | E-2 | Noncash Resources Used to Acquire Land | 1,000 |

### Building

| BB | 15,000 | | |
| B | 1,400 | D | 2,000 |
| EB | 14,400 | | |

### Common Stock

| | | BB | 14,400 |
| | | E-1 | 1,000 |
| | | EB | 15,400 |

### Accounts Receivable

| BB | 800 | | |
| F | 2,400 | | |
| EB | 3,200 | | |

### Merchandise Inventory

| BB | 6,100 | | |
| | | G | 500 |
| EB | 5,600 | | |

### Accounts Payable

| | | BB | 1,900 |
| H | 300 | | |
| | | EB | 1,600 |

### Salaries Payable

| | | BB | 1,100 |
| | | I | 900 |
| | | EB | 2,000 |

### Land

| BB | 1,800 | | |
| E-2 | 1,000 | | |
| EB | 2,800 | | |

### Accumulated Depreciation

| | | BB | 800 |
| D | 900 | J | 400 |
| | | EB | 300 |

### Noncurrent Liabilities

| | | BB | 4,000 |
| C | 3,200 | | |
| | | EB | 800 |

### Retained Earnings

| | | BB | 3,000 |
| | | A | 5,100 |
| | | EB | 8,100 |

**NANTUCKET PRODUCTS, INC.**
**Statement of Cash Flows**
**For the Year Ended December 31, 1998**
**(000's omitted)**

Cash Flows from Operating Activities:

| | | |
|---|---|---|
| Net Income | | $ 5,100 |

Adjustments to Reconcile Net Income to Net Cash
Provided by Operating Activities:

Add:

| | | |
|---|---|---|
| Loss on Sale of Building | $  100 | |
| Decrease in Inventories | $  500 | |
| Increase in Salaries Payable | 900 | |
| Depreciation Expense | 400 | 1,900 |

Deduct:

| | | |
|---|---|---|
| Increase in Accounts Receivable | $(2,400) | |
| Decrease in Accounts Payable | (300) | (2,700) |
| Net Cash Flow from Operating Activities | | $ 4,300 |

Cash Used for Investing Activities:

| | | |
|---|---|---|
| Proceeds from Sale of Building | $ 1,000 | |
| Payment for Purchase of Building | (1,400) | |
| Net Cash Used by Investing Activities | | (400) |

Cash Used for Financing Activities:

| | | |
|---|---|---|
| Payment of Noncurrent Liabilities | | (3,200) |

| | | |
|---|---|---|
| Net Increase in Cash and Cash Equivalents | | $  700 |
| Cash and Cash Equivalents at Beginning of Year | | 1,500 |
| Cash and Cash Equivalents at End of Year | | $ 2,200 |

Supplemental Schedule of Cash Flow Information:
Cash paid during the year for interest and taxes was $700
and $1,200, respectively.

Supplemental Schedule of Noncash Investing and Financing
Activities:
The company acquired land in exchange for common stock
valued at $1,000.

---

# QUESTIONS FOR REVIEW AND FURTHER THOUGHT

## REVIEW QUESTIONS

1. The statement of cash flows contains three major sections. What are these sections, and what information is contained in each?

2. How is a "cash equivalent" defined?

3. Explain the difference between determining cash flows from operations by the *direct* method and by the *indirect* method.

4. Information about operating, investing, and financing activities is shown in the main body of the statement of cash flows. What supplemental information must be disclosed with the statement?

5. List four examples of transactions that would be reported in the investing activities section of the statement of cash flows.

6. List four examples of transactions that would be reported in the financing activities section of the statement of cash flows.

7. In calculating cash flows from operations, we add depreciation expense back to net income and deduct amortization of premium on bonds payable from net income. Where is each of these pieces of information found in the T-accounts—that is, in which T-account, and on which side?

8. Why is it necessary in the T-account analysis to split an investing and financing activity not affecting cash flows into two parts and analyze it as if it were two transactions?

9. A company recently acquired a desk-top computer, giving a 60-day note for the full price. How is this transaction reflected on the statement of cash flows?

 **QUESTIONS FOR FURTHER THOUGHT**

1. Why is the statement of cash flows needed when a company already issues a balance sheet, income statement, and statement of retained earnings?

2. When a statement of cash flows is prepared, net income must be adjusted to derive cash flows from operations. Why is this adjustment necessary?

3. Why is it logical to analyze balance sheet accounts when preparing to construct a statement of cash flows?

4. By inspecting a statement of cash flows, could you learn the amount of cash collected from customers? Explain.

5. Recently in the financial press it was stated that a company had a source of cash flows of $150,000 from depreciation. Comment on this statement. Is depreciation really a source of cash?

6. Why is an increase in Accounts Receivable subtracted from net income when the indirect method of determining cash flows from operations is used?

7. How does the calculation of cash flow from operating activities differ from the calculation of accrual-basis income?

8. A gain on the disposal of equipment would be reported as a deduction from net income on the statement of cash flows. Why?

---

**OBJECTIVE ASSIGNMENT**

*True/False*  Indicate whether each statement below is *true* or *false* by placing a *T* or an *F* in the space provided.

____ 1. Under the indirect method, depreciation is added to net income to determine the amount of cash flows from investing activities.

____ 2. A 3-year U.S. Treasury note purchased on Feb. 1, 1996, and maturing on Feb. 1, 1999, would be classified as a cash equivalent on the Dec. 31, 1998, statement of cash flows, because the note will mature within 3 months.

____ 3. The statement of cash flows has three major sections: cash flows from operating activities, cash flows from investing activities, and cash flows from financing activities.

____ 4. Dividends paid must be reported under the Cash Flows from Investing Activities heading on the statement of cash flows.

____ 5. The FASB encourages the use of the direct method when the operating activities section of a statement of cash flows is prepared, but the indirect method is more commonly used in practice.

*Multiple Choice*  Select the best choice to complete each statement or answer each question below. Write the letter corresponding to your choice in the space provided.

_____ 1. Glacier Co. borrowed $400,000 from a bank. The loan is secured by a mortgage on the factory building. This transaction would be shown on the statement of cash flows as:
   a. Cash from operating activities
   b. Cash from investing activities
   c. Cash from financing activities
   d. Noncash investing and financing activities

_____ 2. Which of the following describes how depreciation expense would be shown on the statement of cash flows?

| Direct Method | Indirect Method |
|---|---|
| a. Add to net income | Not shown |
| b. Not shown | Add to net income |
| c. Not shown | Not shown |
| d. Not shown | Deduct from net income |

_____ 3. Noncash financing and investing activities are disclosed in the statement of cash flows as:
   a. Operating activities
   b. Financing activities
   c. Investing activities
   d. None of the above

_____ 4. Sales on account for a company for the year ended Dec. 31, 1998, amounted to $50,000. If the beginning balance of Accounts Receivable was $10,000 and the ending balance was $20,000, the cash received from customers must have been:
   a. $40,000
   b. $50,000
   c. $60,000
   d. $70,000

_____ 5. The statement of cash flows will help the user of financial statements to
   a. Predict future sales
   b. Assess the reasons for differences between accrual and cash income
   c. Determine the market value of the company's stock
   d. Assess the ability of the company to safeguard cash and cash equivalents

_____ 6. When preparing the statement of cash flows, a company would *not* need any information from
   a. Last year's balance sheet
   b. Last year's income statement
   c. This year's balance sheet
   d. This year's income statement

_____ 7. Cash flows from operating activities is a negative amount. From this fact you know that:
   a. The company's cash balance decreased during the period.
   b. The company's cash flows from operations are less than its net income.
   c. The company's operations used more cash resources than they generated.
   d. The company's accounts receivable balance is increasing quickly.

_____ 8. A company receives a dividend from an investee and pays a dividend to its own shareholders. Which of the following combinations describes how these two transactions would be shown on the statement of cash flows?

| Dividend Received | Dividend Paid |
|---|---|
| a. Cash Flows from Operating Activities | Cash Flows from Financing Activities |
| b. Cash Flows from Financing Activities | Cash Flows from Financing Activities |
| c. Cash Flows from Operating Activities | Cash Flows from Operating Activities |
| d. Cash Flows from Investing Activities | Cash Flows from Financing Activities |

___ 9. In converting from accrual income to cash flows from operations, a decrease in Prepaid Advertising would be subtracted from Advertising Expense indicating that:
   a. An error was made in calculating Advertising Expense
   b. The amount of cash paid out was higher than the amount expensed this period.
   c. The amount of cash paid out was lower than the amount expensed this period.
   d. The company's accounts receivable is increasing quickly.

___ 10. Chance Co. sold for $50,000 land that had a carrying value of $40,000. Which of the following describes how this transaction would be disclosed on the statement of cash flows when the indirect method is used?

|    | Cash Flows from Operating Activities | Cash Flows from Investing Activities | Cash Flows from Financing Activities |
|----|---|---|---|
| a. | $ –0– | + $50,000 | $ –0– |
| b. | – $10,000 | + $40,000 | $ –0– |
| c. | – $10,000 | $ –0– | + $50,000 |
| d. | – $10,000 | + $50,000 | $ –0– |

## EXERCISES

1 3 6 † **Exercise 1:** Analyzing a Statement of Cash Flows

Quill, Inc.'s, statement of cash flows for the year ended December 31, 1998 appears below:

---

### QUILL, INC.
### Statement of Cash Flows
### For the Year Ended December 31, 1998

Cash Flows from Operating Activities:
| | |
|---|---|
| Net Income | $ 250,000 |

Adjustments to Reconcile Net Income to Net
Cash Provided by Operating Activities:

| | |
|---|---|
| Decrease in Accounts Receivable | 47,000 |
| Depreciation on Buildings and Equipment | 81,000 |
| Decrease in Merchandise Inventory | 22,000 |
| Decrease in Accounts Payable | (20,000) |
| Net Cash provided by Operating Activities | $ 380,000 |

Cash Flows from Investing Activities:

| | | |
|---|---|---|
| Proceeds from Disposal of Equipment | $ 144,000 | |
| Proceeds from Sale of Land and Buildings | 1,248,000 | |
| Purchase of Equipment | (74,000) | |
| Net Cash Provided by Investing Activities | | $1,318,000 |

Cash Flows from Financing Activities:

| | | |
|---|---|---|
| Retirement of Long-term Debt | ($1,000,000) | |
| Dividends Paid | (56,000) | |
| Acquire Treasury Stock | (473,000) | |
| Net Cash Used by Financing Activities | | ($1,529,000) |

| | |
|---|---|
| Net Increase in Cash and Cash Equivalents | $ 169,000 |
| Cash and Cash Equivalents at Beginning of Year | 200,000 |
| Cash and Cash Equivalents at End of Year | $ 369,000 |

---

† The numbers in the margin refer to the Learning Objectives.

Write an analysis of Quill, Inc.'s, statement of cash flows. Your discussion should include observations and/or questions about the following:

1. The relationship between net income and cash flows from operations.
2. The implications of significant items added to or deducted from net income.
3. The amount and components of cash flows from investing activities.
4. The amount and components of cash flows from financing activities.
5. Any overall observations that you believe are relevant.

3† **Exercise 2:** Determining the Effect on Cash Flows from Operations of Changes in Account Balances

Listed below are seven independent items. For each one, explain what effect the change in the account balance would have on net income when cash flow from operations is determined by the indirect method.
**Example:** Accounts Payable increases by $23,200.
**Effect:** Net income is adjusted by adding $23,200.

a. Merchandise Inventory decreases by $16,200.
b. Prepaid Insurance increases by $4,500.
c. Supplies on Hand decreases by $7,300.
d. Accounts Receivable decreases by $3,670.
e. Income Taxes Payable decreases by $25,700.
f. Allowance for Uncollectibles increases by $890.
g. Accrued Liabilities decreases by $12,560.

3 **Exercise 3:** Determining Cash Flows from Operations

At the conclusion of the 1998 fiscal year, Dec. 31, 1998, Canaan Company reported net income in the amount of $52,000. Using the following information obtained from Canaan's comparative balance sheets, determine the cash flows from operating activities by the indirect method.

a. Depreciation amounted to $7,500.
b. Merchandise Inventory decreased by 4,300.
c. Accounts Receivable increased by $6,700.
d. Accounts Payable increased by $8,100.
e. Goodwill amortization totaled $3,400.

▶ (Check Figure: Cash flows from operating activities = $68,600)

4 **Exercise 4:** Re-creating Entries and Determining Effect on Cash Flows

Several transactions entered into by Stamford Corporation during 1998 are presented below. Re-create each entry that Stamford should have made, determine the effect of the entry on cash flows, and state where the transaction would be reported on the statement of cash flows.
**Example:** Stamford borrowed $15,000 from the bank on a long-term note.
**Entry:**   Cash............................................... 15,000
                    Notes Payable...................................          15,000
**Effect:** Cash flows from financing activities increased by $15,000.

a. Patent amortization for the year amounted to $4,000.
b. A parcel of land having an original cost of $14,000 was sold for $19,000.
c. A parcel of land was exchanged for equipment having a fair value of $38,000.
d. Stamford issued 3,000 shares of $4-par common stock for $15,600.
e. The principal of a long-term note receivable in the amount of $3,600 was collected.
f. Stamford purchased 150 shares of Swiss Chocolate U.S.A., Inc., as a long-term investment for $6,000.

▶ (Check Figure: Transaction c would be disclosed as supplemental information on the statement of cash flows.)

3  **Exercise 5:** Calculating Cash Flows from Operations

The 1998 income statement of Danbury Co. appears below:

| DANBURY CO.<br>Income Statement<br>Year Ended December 31, 1998 | | | |
|---|---:|---:|---:|
| Sales | | | $450,000 |
| Cost of Goods Sold | | | (215,000) |
| Gross Profit on Sales | | | $235,000 |
| Operating Expenses: | | | |
| Advertising Expense | | $26,000 | |
| Depreciation Expense | | 37,000 | |
| Patent Amortization Expense | | 10,000 | |
| Salary Expense | | 83,000 | (156,000) |
| Net Income | | | $ 79,000 |

Calculate the cash flows from operations for 1998 using the indirect method. The following current asset and liability accounts changed during the year:

Accounts Receivable decreased . . . . . . . . . . . . . . $45,000
Prepaid Advertising increased . . . . . . . . . . . . . . . $ 7,500
Accrued Salaries Payable decreased . . . . . . . . . $ 5,700

▶ *(Check Figure: Cash flows from operations = $157,800)*

3  **Exercise 6:** Analyzing Transactions to Determine Their Effects
on the Statement of Cash Flows

Each of the transactions listed below will affect one of the four categories on the statement of cash flows: cash flows from operating activities, cash flows from investing activities, cash flows from financing activities, or noncash investing and financing activities. Analyze each transaction and state which category will be affected.

a.  Interest was paid in the amount of $2,500.
b.  Equipment in the amount of $73,000 was acquired for cash.
c.  A patent was sold for $18,500 that had a book value of $15,000.
d.  Bonds maturing in 20 years were issued in the amount of $350,000.
e.  Office supplies on hand valued at $1,600 were exchanged for a used computer.
f.  Dividends in the amount of $4,500 were paid.
g.  Used machinery having a book value of $16,500 was traded for 250 shares of stock in another corporation. The stock acquired is to be held for an extended period.
h.  Long-term notes payable in the amount of $25,000 were paid.

▶ *(Check Figure: Entry (g) is shown as a noncash investing and financing activity.)*

4  **Exercise 7:** Preparing Cash Flows from the Operating Activities Section
of the Statement of Cash Flows

The following T-account was used by the Newington Company to gather information about its cash flows from operations for the 1998 calendar year:

| Cash | | | | |
|---|---|---:|---|---:|
| (3) | Depreciation Expense | 37,500 | (1) Net Loss for the Year | 12,900 |
| (4) | Patent Amortization | | (2) Gain on Sale of Land | 4,200 |
| | Expense | 4,500 | (5) Amortization of Premium | |
| (6) | Loss on Sale of Equipment | 8,300 | on Bond Payable | 7,000 |

Using the information in this T-account, prepare the Cash Flows from Operating Activities section of the statement of cash flows.

▶ *(Check Figure: Cash flows from operations = $26,200)*

5 **Exercise 8:** Converting Accrual Income to Cash Provided by Operations

The Haven Company income statement for 1998 appears below:

| HAVEN COMPANY |
|---|
| Income Statement |
| Year Ended December 31, 1998 |
| (000's omitted) |

| | | |
|---|---|---|
| Sales. . . . . . . . . . . . . . . . . . . . . . . . . . . . . . . . . . . . . . . . . . . . . . . . . . . . . . . . . | | $85,000 |
| Cost of Goods Sold . . . . . . . . . . . . . . . . . . . . . . . . . . . . . . . . . . . . . . . . . . . . . | | (32,000) |
| Gross Profit on Sales . . . . . . . . . . . . . . . . . . . . . . . . . . . . . . . . . . . . . . . . . . . . | | $53,000 |
| Operating Expenses: | | |
|    Rent Expense. . . . . . . . . . . . . . . . . . . . . . . . . . . . . . . . . . . | $15,000 | |
|    Depreciation Expense . . . . . . . . . . . . . . . . . . . . . . . . . . . | 10,000 | |
|    Other Operating Expenses. . . . . . . . . . . . . . . . . . . . . . . . | 20,000 | |
| Total Operating Expenses . . . . . . . . . . . . . . . . . . . . . . . . . . . . . . . . . . . . . . . | | (45,000) |
| Net Income . . . . . . . . . . . . . . . . . . . . . . . . . . . . . . . . . . . . . . . . . . . . . . . . . . . . | | $ 8,000 |

The following data was selected from Haven's balance sheet:

| Account Title | Balance Jan. 1 | Balance Dec. 31 |
|---|---|---|
| Accounts Receivable | $14,000 | $ 9,000 |
| Merchandise Inventory | 3,000 | 10,000 |
| Prepaid Rent | 1,000 | 3,000 |
| Accounts Payable | 16,000 | 18,000 |

Convert Haven's income statement from an accrual basis to a calculation of cash flows from operations.

▶ *(Check Figure: Cash flow operations = $16,000)*

## PROBLEMS: SET A

3† **Problem A1:** Determining Cash Flows from Operating Activities

In each of the three columns below are income statement data for the year ended Dec. 31, 1998:

| | Company X | Company Y | Company Z |
|---|---|---|---|
| Sales Revenue. . . . . . . . . . . . . . . . . . . . . . | $ 80,000 | $150,000 | $200,000 |
| Cost of Goods Sold . . . . . . . . . . . . . . . . . | 30,000 | 90,000 | 100,000 |
| Advertising Expense . . . . . . . . . . . . . . . . | 6,000 | 8,000 | 20,000 |
| Sales Commission Expense . . . . . . . . . . | 3,000 | 15,000 | 30,000 |
| Goodwill Amortization Expense. . . . . . . . | 1,000 | –0– | –0– |
| Depreciation Expense: Building. . . . . . . . | 1,500 | 4,000 | 36,000 |
| Depreciation Expense: Equipment . . . . . . | 500 | 16,000 | 12,000 |
| Patent Amortization Expense . . . . . . . . . . | 1,800 | 20,000 | –0– |
| Provision for Income Taxes. . . . . . . . . . . . | 14,100 | –0– | 4,800 |
| Loss on Sale of Machinery . . . . . . . . . . . . | 800 | –0– | –0– |
| Gain on Sale of Land. . . . . . . . . . . . . . . . . | –0– | –0– | 10,000 |

† The numbers in the margin refer to the Learning Objectives.

**Required:**

Prepare the Cash Flows from Operating Activities sections (using the indirect method) of the statements of cash flows for Companies X, Y, and Z. The current asset and current liability accounts did not change during the period. (*Hint:* First calculate net income for each company.)

▶ *(Check Figure: Company X's cash flows from operations = $26,900)*

3   4    **Problem A2:** Preparing a Statement of Cash Flows

The 1998 income statement and comparative balance sheets of Fairfield, Inc., are shown below:

---

**FAIRFIELD, INC.**
**Income Statement**
**Year Ended December 31, 1998**
**(000's omitted)**

| | |
|---|---:|
| Sales | $6,400 |
| Cost of Goods Sold | (3,280) |
| Gross Profit on Sales | 3,120 |
| Operating Expenses: | |
| Depreciation | (160) |
| Other | (880) |
| Net Income | $2,080 |

---

**FAIRFIELD, INC.**
**Comparative Balance Sheets**
**(000's omitted)**

| | December 31 | |
|---|---:|---:|
| | **1998** | **1997** |
| **Assets** | | |
| Current Assets: | | |
| Cash | $ 480 | $ 600 |
| Accounts Receivable (net) | 1,280 | 320 |
| Merchandise Inventory | 2,240 | 2,440 |
| Current Assets (total) | $ 4,000 | $3,360 |
| Property, Plant, and Equipment: | | |
| Land | $ 1,120 | $ 720 |
| Building | 6,560 | 6,000 |
| Accumulated Depreciation: Building | (480) | (320) |
| Total Property, Plant, and Equipment | $ 7,200 | $6,400 |
| Total Assets | $11,200 | $9,760 |
| **Equities** | | |
| Current Liabilities: | | |
| Accounts Payable | $ 640 | $ 320 |
| Salaries Payable | 800 | 880 |
| Total Current Liabilities | $ 1,440 | $1,200 |
| Noncurrent Liabilities | 320 | 1,600 |
| Common Stock | 6,160 | 5,760 |
| Retained Earnings | 3,280 | 1,200 |
| Total Equities | $11,200 | $9,760 |

The following additional information is taken from the financial records of Fairfield, Inc.:

a. A building costing $560,000 was acquired for cash.
b. Cash was used to pay off noncurrent liabilities amounting to $1,280,000.
c. Common stock was issued in exchange for land with a fair market value of $400,000.

**Required:**

Prepare a statement of cash flows (using the indirect method) in good form for the year ended Dec. 31, 1998. T-account working papers are optional. All the information needed to prepare this simple statement of cash flows is given in the income statement, balance sheets, and additional information above.

▶ *(Check Figure: Cash from operating activities = $1,720,000)*

**3 4 6 Problem A3:** Preparing and Analyzing a Statement of Cash Flows

Financial statements for Trumbull Company are shown below:

**TRUMBULL COMPANY**
**Income Statement**
**Year Ended Dec. 31, 1998**
**(000's omitted)**

| | | |
|---|---|---|
| Sales | | $2,400 |
| Cost of Goods Sold | | (1,350) |
| Gross Profit on Sales | | $1,050 |
| Operating Expenses: | | |
| Depreciation | $195 | |
| Other (including taxes) | 555 | (750) |
| Net Income | | $ 300 |

**TRUMBULL COMPANY**
**Comparative Balance Sheets**
**(000's omitted)**

| | December 31 1998 | December 31 1997 | Increase (Decrease) in Account Balance |
|---|---|---|---|
| **Assets** | | | |
| Cash | $ 531 | $ 114 | $417 |
| Accounts Receivable | 651 | 348 | 303 |
| Merchandise Inventory | 735 | 528 | 207 |
| Prepaid Expenses | 27 | 33 | (6) |
| Land | 600 | 420 | 180 |
| Building | 3,000 | 2,400 | 600 |
| Accumulated Depreciation | (615) | (420) | 195 |
| Total Assets | $4,929 | $3,423 | |
| **Equities** | | | |
| Accounts Payable | $ 258 | $ 291 | $ (33) |
| Accrued Payables | 99 | –0– | 99 |
| Bonds Payable (due 2005) | 600 | –0– | 600 |
| Common Stock | 3,300 | 2,700 | 600 |
| Retained Earnings | 672 | 432 | 240 |
| Total Equities | $4,929 | $3,423 | |

Other relevant data:

a. Land was purchased for $180,000 cash.
b. Bonds payable in the amount of $600,000 were issued for a new building.
c. A $60,000 cash dividend was declared and paid.
d. Common stock was issued for $600,000 cash.

**Required:**

1. Prepare a statement of cash flows (indirect method) using the T-account approach.
2. Write an analysis of Trumbull's statement of cash flows. Your discussion should include observations and/or questions about the following:
   a. The relationship between net income and cash flows from operations.
   b. The implications of significant items added to or deducted from net income.
   c. The amount and components of cash flows from investing activities.
   d. The amount and components of cash flows from financing activities.
   e. Any overall observations that you believe are relevant.

▶ *(Check Figure: Cash from operating activities = $57,000)*

6   **Problem A4:** Analyzing A Statement of Cash Flows

Stratford Company's statement of cash flows is shown below:

**STRATFORD COMPANY**
**Statement of Cash Flows**
**Year Ended December 31, 1998**

| | | |
|---|---:|---:|
| Cash Flows from Operating Activities: | | |
| Net Income . . . . . . . . . . . . . . . . . . . . . . . . . . . . . . . . . . . . . . . | | $ 50,250 |
| Adjustments to reconcile net income to net cash provided by operating activities: | | |
| Add: | | |
| Depreciation Expense: Building . . . . . . . . . . . . . . . . . . | $ 18,750 | |
| Depreciation Expense: Machinery . . . . . . . . . . . . . . . . | 5,625 | |
| Patent Amortization. . . . . . . . . . . . . . . . . . . . . . . . . . . | 900 | |
| Decrease in Accounts Receivable . . . . . . . . . . . . . . . . | 7,650 | |
| Increase in Salaries Payable . . . . . . . . . . . . . . . . . . . . | 4,125 | 37,050 |
| Deduct: | | |
| Increase in Inventory. . . . . . . . . . . . . . . . . . . . . . . . . . . | $(20,250) | |
| Decrease in Accounts Payable. . . . . . . . . . . . . . . . . . . | (9,375) | (29,625) |
| Net cash provided by Operating Activities:. . . . . . . . . . . . . . . . . | | $ 57,675 |
| | | |
| Cash flows from Investing Activities: | | |
| Decrease: Payment for purchase of land. . . . . . . . . . . . . | $(45,000) | |
| Payment for purchase of building. . . . . . . . . . | (90,000) | |
| Net cash used in Investing Activities: . . . . . . . . . . . . . . . . . . . . . | | (135,000) |
| | | |
| Cash flows from Financing Activities: | | |
| Increase: Proceeds from issuance of | | |
| Common Stock . . . . . . . . . . . . . . . . . . . . . . . . . . . . . . . | $135,000 | |
| Decrease: Retirement of Bonds Payable. . . . . . . . . . . . . | (37,500) | |
| Net cash provided by Financing Activities . . . . . . . . . . . . . . . . . | | 97,500 |
| | | |
| Net increase in cash and cash equivalents. . . . . . . . . . . . . . . . . . . . . | | $ 20,175 |
| Cash and cash equivalents at beginning of year . . . . . . . . . . . . . . . . | | 3,975 |
| | | |
| Cash and cash equivalents at end of year . . . . . . . . . . . . . . . . . . . . . | | $ 24,150 |

**Required:**

Write an analysis of Stratford's statement of cash flows. Your discussion should include observations and/or questions about the following:

a. The relationship between net income and cash flows from operations.
b. The implictions of significant items added to or deducted from net income.
c. The amount and components of cash flows from investing activities.
d. The amount and components of cash flows from financing activities.
e. Any overall observations that you believe are relevant.

3   4   **Problem A5:** Preparing a Statement of Cash Flows

Easton Gaskets, Inc.'s condensed balance sheets for 1997 and 1998 and income statement for 1998 are shown below:

**EASTON GASKETS, INC.**
**Comparative Balance Sheets (Condensed)**
**(000's omitted)**

| | December 31 | |
| --- | --- | --- |
| | **1998** | **1997** |
| **Assets** | | |
| Current Assets: | | |
| Cash | $    60 | $    35 |
| Accounts Receivable (net) | 285 | 255 |
| Merchandise Inventory | 675 | 505 |
| Prepaid Expenses | 40 | 55 |
| Total Current Assets | $ 1,060 | $   850 |
| Property, Plant, and Equipment: | | |
| Land | 3,020 | 2,140 |
| Building | 7,800 | 7,000 |
| Less: Accumulated Depreciation | (840) | (440) |
| Equipment | 3,100 | 3,300 |
| Less: Accumulated Depreciation | (1,080) | (1,000) |
| Total Property, Plant, and Equipment | $12,000 | $11,000 |
| Total Assets | $13,060 | $11,850 |
| **Liabilities and Stockholders' Equity** | | |
| Current Liabilities: | | |
| Accounts Payable | $    550 | $   300 |
| Accrued Liabilities | 130 | 100 |
| Total Current Liabilities | $    680 | $   400 |
| Noncurrent Liabilities: | | |
| Bonds Payable (issued at par) | $    900 | $   100 |
| Total Liabilities | $ 1,580 | $   500 |
| Common Stock (no par) | $10,000 | $10,000 |
| Retained Earnings | 1,480 | 1,350 |
| Total Stockholders' Equity | $11,480 | $11,350 |
| Total Liabilities and Stockholders' Equity | $13,060 | $11,850 |

### Liabilities and Stockholders' Equity

Current Liabilities:

| | | | |
|---|---|---|---|
| Accounts Payable | $ 1,845 | $ 2,160 | $ (315) |
| Bank Loan Payable | –0– | 1,350 | (1,350) |
| Accrued Payables | 270 | 387 | (117) |
| Total Current Liabilities | $ 2,115 | $ 3,897 | |

Noncurrent Liabilities:

| | | | |
|---|---|---|---|
| Notes Payable (due 9/30/05) | $ 2,070 | $ –0– | 2,070 |
| Bonds Payable (due 12/31/10) | 9,000 | 9,000 | –0– |
| Premium on Bonds Payable | 1,800 | 1,980 | (180) |
| Total Noncurrent Liabilities | $12,870 | $10,980 | |
| Total Liabilities | $14,985 | $14,877 | |

Stockholders' Equity:

| | | | |
|---|---|---|---|
| Preferred Stock | $ 900 | $ –0– | 900 |
| Common Stock (no par) | 14,850 | 14,850 | –0– |
| Retained Earnings | 3,285 | 1,980 | 1,305 |
| Total Stockholders' Equity | $19,035 | $16,830 | |
| Total Liabilities and Stockholders' Equity | $34,020 | $31,707 | |

**Required:**

1. Prepare a statement of cash flows (indirect method), using the T-account approach.
2. Write an analysis of Waterbury Product's statement of cash flows. Your discussion should include observations and/or questions about the following:
   a. The relationship between net income and cash flows from operations.
   b. The implications of significant items added to or deducted from net income.
   c. The amount and components of cash flows from investing activities.
   d. The amount and components of cash flows from financing activities.
   e. Any overall observations that you believe are relevant.

▶ *(Check Figure: Cash used in operations = $288,000)*

 5  **Problem A7:** Converting Accrual Basis Income to Cash from Operations

Manchester Company's 1998 income statement and comparative balance sheets for 1997 and 1998 are shown below:

**MANCHESTER COMPANY**
**Income Statement**
**Year Ended September 30, 1998**

| | | |
|---|---|---|
| Sales | | $720,000 |
| Cost of Goods Sold | | (300,000) |
| Gross Profit on Sales | | $420,000 |
| Operating Expenses: | | |
| Depreciation Expense | $140,000 | |
| Salaries Expense | 70,000 | |
| Advertising Expense | 30,000 | |
| Other Operating Expenses | 80,000 | (320,000) |
| Net Income | | $100,000 |

**MANCHESTER COMPANY**
Comparative Balance Sheets

| | September 30 | |
| --- | --- | --- |
| | **1998** | **1997** |
| Assets: | | |
| Cash.......................................... | $ 120,000 | $ 80,000 |
| Accounts Receivable (net) ........................... | 240,000 | 320,000 |
| Merchandise Inventory ............................ | 320,000 | 140,000 |
| Prepaid Advertising ................................ | 50,000 | 0 |
| Noncurrent Assets (net) ...................... | 450,000 | 220,000 |
| Total Assets...................................... | $1,180,000 | $760,000 |
| Equities: | | |
| Accounts Payable ................................... | $ 160,000 | $100,000 |
| Accrued Salaries Payable............................ | 40,000 | 160,000 |
| Noncurrent Liabilities............................... | 420,000 | 40,000 |
| Total Liabilities .................................... | $ 620,000 | $300,000 |
| Paid-In Capital..................................... | $ 400,000 | $400,000 |
| Retained Earnings................................... | 160,000 | 60,000 |
| Total Stockholders' Equity.......................... | $ 560,000 | $460,000 |
| Total Equities...................................... | $1,180,000 | $760,000 |

**Required:**

Convert Manchester's accrual income statement into a schedule calculating cash from operations. .

▶ *(Check Figure: Cash provided by operations = $30,000)*

## PROBLEMS: SET B

3† **Problem B1:** Determining Cash Flows from Operating Activities

In each of the three columns below are income statement data for the year ended Dec. 31, 1998:

| | Company A | Company B | Company C |
| --- | --- | --- | --- |
| Sales Revenue ..................... | $150,000 | $95,000 | $260,000 |
| Cost of Goods Sold.................. | 90,000 | 67,000 | 140,000 |
| Patent Amortization Expense .......... | 4,000 | 2,000 | –0– |
| Depreciation Expense: Machinery ...... | 12,000 | 8,000 | 21,750 |
| Organization Cost Amortization Expense. | 1,250 | –0– | 1,750 |
| Depreciation Expense: Building ........ | 11,400 | 6,500 | 14,700 |
| Provision for Income Taxes ........... | 740 | –0– | 16,640 |
| Salary Expense..................... | 19,000 | 13,500 | 37,500 |
| Utilities Expense .................... | 10,500 | 2,700 | 14,200 |
| Gain on Sale of Machine ............. | –0– | –0– | 11,500 |
| Loss on Sale of Land ................ | –0– | 4,300 | –0– |

† The numbers in the margin refer to the Learning Objectives.

**Required:**

Using the indirect method, prepare the Cash Flows from Operating Activities sections of the statement of cash flows for Companies A, B, and C. The current asset and current liability accounts did not change during the period. (*Hint:* First calculate net income for each company.)

▶ *(Check Figure: Company A's cash flows from operations = $29,760)*

3 4 **Problem B2:** Preparing a Statement of Cash Flows

Presented below are the income statement and the comparative balance sheets for Westport Company for the year ended Dec. 31, 1998:

---

**WESTPORT COMPANY**
**Income Statement**
**Year Ended December 31, 1998**
**(000's omitted)**

| | |
|---|---:|
| Sales. | $ 6,000 |
| Cost of Goods Sold | (2,880) |
| Gross Profit on Sales | 3,120 |
| Operating Expenses: | |
| Depreciation | (360) |
| Other | (1,320) |
| Net Income | $ 1,440 |

---

**WESTPORT COMPANY**
**Comparative Balance Sheets**
**December 31,**
**(000's omitted)**

| | December 31 1998 | 1997 |
|---|---:|---:|
| **Assets** | | |
| Cash | $ 180 | $ 240 |
| Accounts Receivable (net) | 2,250 | 1,500 |
| Merchandise Inventory | 1,950 | 2,100 |
| Land. | 1,320 | 1,248 |
| Building | 5,040 | 4,800 |
| Accumulated Depreciation: Building. | (1,020) | (660) |
| Total Assets. | $ 9,720 | $9,228 |
| **Equities** | | |
| Accounts Payable | $ 1,152 | $1,200 |
| Noncurrent Liabilities. | 120 | 1,260 |
| Common Stock | 5,040 | 4,800 |
| Retained Earnings. | 3,408 | 1,968 |
| Total Equities. | $ 9,720 | $9,228 |

---

The following additional information is taken from the financial records of the Westport Company:

a. Land costing $72,000 was acquired for cash.
b. $1,140,000 of noncurrent liabilities were paid off with cash.
c. Common stock was issued in exchange for a building with a fair market value of $240,000.

**Required:**

Prepare a statement of cash flows (using the indirect method) in good form for the year ended Dec. 31, 1998. T-account working papers are optional. All the information needed to prepare this statement is given in the income statement, balance sheets, and additional information above.

▶ *(Check Figure: Cash from operating activities = $1,152,000)*

3 4 6 **Problem B3:** Preparing and Analyzing a Statement of Cash Flows

Financial statements for Wallingford Enterprises are presented below:

---

**WALLINGFORD ENTERPRISES**
**Income Statement**
**Year Ended December 31, 1998**
**(000's omitted)**

| | | |
|---|---:|---:|
| Sales. . . . . . . . . . . . . . . . . . . . . . . . . . . . . . . . . . . . . . . . . . . . | | $2,000 |
| Cost of Goods Sold . . . . . . . . . . . . . . . . . . . . . . . . . . . . . . . . | | (1,125) |
| Gross Profit on Sales . . . . . . . . . . . . . . . . . . . . . . . . . . . . . . . | | $ 875 |
| Operating Expenses: | | |
| Depreciation . . . . . . . . . . . . . . . . . . . . . . . . . . . . . . . . . . . . | $165 | |
| Other (including taxes) . . . . . . . . . . . . . . . . . . . . . . . . . . . . | 460 | (625) |
| Net Income . . . . . . . . . . . . . . . . . . . . . . . . . . . . . . . . . . . . . . | | $ 250 |

---

**WALLINGFORD ENTERPRISES**
**Comparative Balance Sheets**
**(000's omitted)**

| | December 31 1998 | December 31 1997 | Increase (Decrease) in Account Balance |
|---|---:|---:|---:|
| **Assets** | | | |
| Cash . . . . . . . . . . . . . . . . . . . . . . . . . . . . . . . . . . . . | $ 445 | $ 95 | $350 |
| Accounts Receivable . . . . . . . . . . . . . . . . . . . . . . | 540 | 290 | 250 |
| Merchandise Inventory. . . . . . . . . . . . . . . . . . . . . | 615 | 440 | 175 |
| Prepaid Expenses . . . . . . . . . . . . . . . . . . . . . . . . | 20 | 25 | (5) |
| Land . . . . . . . . . . . . . . . . . . . . . . . . . . . . . . . . . . . | 500 | 350 | 150 |
| Building. . . . . . . . . . . . . . . . . . . . . . . . . . . . . . . . . | 2,500 | 2,000 | 500 |
| Accumulated Depreciation. . . . . . . . . . . . . . . . . . . | (515) | (350) | (165) |
| Total Assets . . . . . . . . . . . . . . . . . . . . . . . . . . . | $4,105 | $2,850 | |
| **Equities** | | | |
| Accounts Payable. . . . . . . . . . . . . . . . . . . . . . . . . | $ 215 | $ 245 | ($ 30) |
| Accrued Payables. . . . . . . . . . . . . . . . . . . . . . . . . | 80 | –0– | 80 |
| Bonds Payable (due 2005). . . . . . . . . . . . . . . . . . | 500 | –0– | 500 |
| Common Stock. . . . . . . . . . . . . . . . . . . . . . . . . . . | 2,750 | 2,250 | 500 |
| Retained Earnings . . . . . . . . . . . . . . . . . . . . . . . . | 560 | 355 | 205 |
| Total Equities . . . . . . . . . . . . . . . . . . . . . . . . . . | $4,105 | $2,850 | |

---

Other relevant data:

a. Land was purchased for $150,000.
b. Bonds payable in the amount of $500,000 were issued for a new building.
c. A $45,000 cash dividend was declared and paid.
d. Common stock was sold for $500,000 cash.

**Required:**

1. Prepare a statement of cash flows (indirect method) using the T-account approach.
2. Write an analysis of Wallingford's statement of cash flows. Your discussion should include observations and/or questions about the following:
   a. The relationship between net income and cash flows from operations.
   b. The implications of significant items added to or deducted from net income.
   c. The amount and components of cash flows from investing activities.
   d. The amount and components of cash flows from financing activities.
   e. Any overall observations that you believe are relevant.

▶ (Check Figure: Cash from operations = $45,000)

6 **Problem B4:** Analyzing A Statement of Cash Flows

Salem Company's statement of cash flows is shown below:

---

**SALEM COMPANY**
**Statement of Cash Flows**
**Year Ended December 31, 1998**

| | | |
|---|---:|---:|
| Cash Flows from Operating Activities: | | |
| Net Income . . . . . . . . . . . . . . . . . . . . . . . . . . . . . . . . . . . . . | | $ 22,700 |
| Adjustments to reconcile net income to net | | |
| cash provided by operating activities: | | |
| Increases: | | |
| Depreciation Expense: Building . . . . . . . . . . . . . . . . . . | $ 6,000 | |
| Depreciation Expense: Equipment. . . . . . . . . . . . . . . . | 5,600 | |
| Copyright Amortization . . . . . . . . . . . . . . . . . . . . . . . . | 1,400 | |
| Decrease in Accounts Receivable . . . . . . . . . . . . . . . . | 2,490 | |
| Increase in Salaries Payable . . . . . . . . . . . . . . . . . . . . | 300 | 15,790 |
| Decreases: | | |
| Increase in Inventory . . . . . . . . . . . . . . . . . . . . . . . . . . | (2,500) | |
| Decrease in Accounts Payable . . . . . . . . . . . . . . . . . . | (4,200) | (6,700) |
| Net Cash provided by Operating Activities . . . . . . . . . . . . . . . . . | | $ 31,790 |
| | | |
| Cash Flows from Investing Activities: | | |
| Decrease: Payment for purchase of land . . . . . . . . . . . . | $ (8,800) | |
| Payment for purchase of building . . . . . . . . . | (12,500) | |
| Net cash used in Investing Activities . . . . . . . . . . . . . . . . . . . . . | | (21,300) |
| | | |
| Cash flows from Financing Activities: | | |
| Increase: Proceeds from issuance of | | |
| Common Stock. . . . . . . . . . . . . . . . . . . . . . . . . . . . . | $ 10,000 | |
| Decrease: Retirement of Bonds Payable . . . . . . . . . . . . | (20,000) | |
| Net cash used by Financing Activities . . . . . . . . . . . . . . . . . . . . | | (10,000) |
| | | |
| Net Increase in cash and cash equivalents. . . . . . . . . . . . . . . . . . . | | $ 490 |
| | | |
| Cash and cash equivalents at beginning of year . . . . . . . . . . . . . . . . | | 730 |
| | | |
| Cash and cash equivalents at end of year . . . . . . . . . . . . . . . . . . . . | | $ 1,220 |

**Required:**

Write an analysis of Salem's statement of cash flows. Your discussion should include observations and/or questions about the following:

a. The relationship between net income and cash flows from operations.
b. The implications of significant items added to or deducted from net income.
c. The amount and components of cash flows from investing activities.
d. The amount and components of cash flows from financing activities.
e. Any overall observations that you believe are relevant.

3  4  **Problem B5:** Preparing a Statement of Cash Flows

Hamden Hardware, Inc.'s condensed balance sheets for 1997 and 1998 and income statement for 1998 are shown below.

**HAMDEN HARDWARE, INC.**
**Comparative Balance Sheets (Condensed)**
**(000's omitted)**

| | December 31 | |
|---|---|---|
| | **1998** | **1997** |
| **Assets** | | |
| Current Assets: | | |
| Cash ......................................... | $ 460 | $ 80 |
| Accounts Receivable (net) ............................ | 860 | 740 |
| Merchandise Inventory................................ | 1,800 | 2,340 |
| Prepaid Expenses ................................... | 360 | 200 |
| Current Assets (total) ............................. | $3,480 | $3,360 |
| Property, Plant, and Equipment: | | |
| Land ......................................... | 1,024 | 624 |
| Building....................................... | 968 | 1,064 |
| Less: Accumulated Depreciation ..................... | (336) | (416) |
| Machinery..................................... | 1,200 | 560 |
| Less: Accumulated Depreciation ..................... | (240) | (200) |
| Total Property, Plant, and Equipment ................. | $2,616 | $1,632 |
| Total Assets ...................................... | $6,096 | $4,992 |
| **Liabilities and Stockholders' Equity** | | |
| Current Liabilities: | | |
| Accounts Payable................................... | $1,040 | $ 840 |
| Accrued Liabilities................................. | 344 | 280 |
| Current Liabilities (total) .......................... | $1,384 | $1,120 |
| Noncurrent Liabilities: | | |
| Bonds Payable (issued at par)........................ | 800 | 800 |
| Total Liabilities ................................. | $2,184 | $1,920 |
| Preferred Stock ................................... | $ 640 | $ −0− |
| Common Stock (no par)............................... | 2,400 | 2,400 |
| Retained Earnings .................................. | 872 | 672 |
| Total Stockholders' Equity ......................... | $3,912 | $3,072 |
| Total Liabilities and Stockholders' Equity ................. | $6,096 | $4,992 |

---

**HAMDEN HARDWARE, INC.**
**Income Statement (Condensed)**
**Year Ended December 31, 1998**
**(000's omitted)**

| | | |
|---|---:|---:|
| Sales . . . . . . . . . . . . . . . . . . . . . . . . . . . . . . . . . . . . . . . . . . . . . . . . . . . . . . . | | $3,360 |
| Cost of Goods Sold . . . . . . . . . . . . . . . . . . . . . . . . . . . . . . . . . . . . . . . . . . . | | 2,192 |
| Gross Profit on Sales. . . . . . . . . . . . . . . . . . . . . . . . . . . . . . . . . . . . . . . . . . | | $1,168 |
| Operating Expenses: | | |
|    Selling Expenses . . . . . . . . . . . . . . . . . . . . . . . . . . . . . . . . . . . . . | $608 | |
|    Administrative Expenses . . . . . . . . . . . . . . . . . . . . . . . . . . . . . . . | 256 | |
|    Depreciation Expense: Building. . . . . . . . . . . . . . . . . . . . . . . . . . | 64 | |
|    Depreciation Expense: Machinery. . . . . . . . . . . . . . . . . . . . . . . . | 40 | 968 |
| Net Income. . . . . . . . . . . . . . . . . . . . . . . . . . . . . . . . . . . . . . . . . . . . . . . . . . . | | $ 200 |

---

In addition, the following information was compiled from the company's records:

a. A building was purchased for $160,000 cash.
b. Machinery for a new assembly line was "purchased" by giving the manufacturer preferred stock. The machinery acquired has a fair market value of $640,000.
c. A building was sold for $112,000. The building originally cost $256,000 and had accumulated depreciation of $144,000.
d. Land was purchased for $400,000.

**Required:**

Prepare a statement of cash flows (indirect method) using the T-account approach.

▶ *(Check Figure: Cash from operating activities = $828,000)*

3 4 6   **Problem B6:** Preparing and Analyzing a Statement of Cash Flows

Bristol Company's financial statements for 1998 appear on the next two pages. An analysis of Bristol's financial records reveals the following information:

a. A building costing $1,240,000 and having accumulated depreciation of $760,000 was sold for $640,000. The $160,000 gain appears on the income statement.
b. Short-term notes are regularly used to acquire billboard advertising.
c. Common stock was issued in exchange for 10 acres of land. The common stock and the land were fairly valued at $1,250,000.
d. The entry to record interest expense on the bonds was as follows:

| | | |
|---|---:|---:|
| Interest Expense. . . . . . . . . . . . . . . . . . . . . . . . . . . . . . . . . . . . . . . | 290,000 | |
|    Cash. . . . . . . . . . . . . . . . . . . . . . . . . . . . . . . . . . . . . . . . . . . . . . | | 250,000 |
|    Discount on Bonds Payable . . . . . . . . . . . . . . . . . . . . . . . . . . | | 40,000 |

(Less cash was used than is reflected in the Interest Expense account.)
e. $1,400,000 was borrowed from the bank; a note due in 2005 was signed.
f. An addition to the building costing $1,500,000 was constructed for cash.
g. $970,000 in dividends were declared and paid.

## BRISTOL COMPANY
### Income Statement
### Year Ended September 30, 1998
### (000's omitted)

| | | |
|---|---:|---:|
| Sales.......................................................... | | $ 59,460 |
| Cost of Goods Sold ....................................... | | (42,330) |
| Gross Profit on Sales..................................... | | $ 17,130 |
| Operating Expenses: | | |
| Depreciation Expense: Building ........................ | $ 650 | |
| Depreciation Expense: Equipment...................... | 230 | |
| Other Operating Expenses............................. | 12,400 | (13,280) |
| Income from Primary Operations..................... | | $ 3,850 |
| Other Income and Expense: | | |
| Interest Expense ................................... | $ (290) | |
| Gain on Sale of Building ............................ | 160 | (130) |
| Income before Tax...................................... | | $ 3,720 |
| Provision for Income Taxes............................. | | (1,150) |
| Net Income............................................. | | $ 2,570 |

## BRISTOL COMPANY
### Statement of Retained Earnings
### For Year Ended September 30, 1998
### (000's omitted)

| | |
|---|---:|
| Retained Earnings Balance, Oct. 1, 1997 ............................ | $5,120 |
| Add: Net Income for the Year...................................... | 2,570 |
| Total..................................................... | $7,690 |
| Deduct: Dividends Declared and Paid............................... | (970) |
| Retained Earnings Sept. 30, 1998................................. | $6,720 |

## BRISTOL COMPANY
### Comparative Balance Sheets
### (000's omitted)

| | September 30 1998 | September 30 1997 | Increase (Decrease) in Account Balance |
|---|---:|---:|---:|
| **Assets** | | | |
| Current Assets: | | | |
| Cash ................................. | $ 3,380 | $ 3,040 | $ 340 |
| Accounts Receivable (net) ............... | 6,400 | 4,270 | 2,130 |
| Merchandise Inventory................... | 4,440 | 5,170 | (730) |
| Total Current Assets................... | $14,220 | $12,480 | |
| Property, Plant and Equipment: | | | |
| Land ................................ | $ 5,550 | $ 4,300 | 1,250 |
| Buildings............................. | 10,510 | 10,250 | 260 |
| Less: Accumulated Depreciation ........... | (5,050) | (5,160) | (110) |
| Equipment............................ | 7,300 | 7,300 | –0– |
| Less: Accumulated Depreciation ........... | (3,180) | (2,950) | 230 |
| Total Property Plant and Equipment ...... | $15,130 | $13,740 | |
| Total Assets ............................ | $29,350 | $26,220 | |

### Liabilities and Stockholders' Equity

| | | | |
|---|---|---|---|
| **Current Liabilities:** | | | |
| Accounts Payable . . . . . . . . . . . . . . . . . . . . . . | $ 3,680 | $ 4,500 | (820) |
| Notes Payable . . . . . . . . . . . . . . . . . . . . . . . . | 1,000 | 1,400 | (400) |
| Accrued Payable . . . . . . . . . . . . . . . . . . . . . . | 660 | 600 | 60 |
| Total Current Liabilities . . . . . . . . . . . . . . . . | 5,340 | 6,500 | |
| | | | |
| **Noncurrent Liabilities:** | | | |
| Notes Payable (due 6/30/05) . . . . . . . . . . . . . | $ 1,400 | $ –0– | 1,400 |
| Bonds Payable (due 12/31/10) . . . . . . . . . . . . | 3,000 | 3,000 | –0– |
| Discount on Bonds Payable . . . . . . . . . . . . . . . | (360) | (400) | (40) |
| Total Noncurrent Liabilities . . . . . . . . . . . . . | $ 4,040 | $ 2,600 | |
| Total Liabilities . . . . . . . . . . . . . . . . . . . . . . . . | $ 9,380 | $ 9,100 | |
| | | | |
| **Stockholders' Equity:** | | | |
| Common Stock (no par) . . . . . . . . . . . . . . . . . | $13,250 | $12,000 | 1,250 |
| Retained Earnings . . . . . . . . . . . . . . . . . . . . . | 6,720 | 5,120 | 1,600 |
| Total Stockholders' Equity . . . . . . . . . . . . . . . | $19,970 | $17,120 | |
| | | | |
| Total Liabilities and Stockholders' Equity . . . . . . | $29,350 | $26,220 | |

**Required:**

1. Prepare a statement of cash flows (indirect method) using the T-account approach.
2. Write an analysis of Bristol's statement of cash flows. Your discussion should include observations and/or questions about the following:
   a. The relationship between net income and cash flows from operations.
   b. The implications of significant items added to or deducted from net income.
   c. The amount and components of cash flows from investing activities.
   d. The amount and components of cash flows from financing activities.
   e. Any overall observations that you believe are relevant.

▶ *(Check Figure: Cash from operating activities = $770,000)*

5   **Problem B7:** Converting Accrual Basis Income to Cash from Operations

Wethersfield, Inc.'s, 1998 income statement and comparative balance sheets for 1997 and 1998 are shown below:

### WETHERSFIELD, INC.
### Income Statement
### Year Ended June 30, 1998

| | | |
|---|---|---|
| Sales . . . . . . . . . . . . . . . . . . . . . . . . . . . . . . . . . . . . . . . . . . . . . . . . | | $180,000 |
| Cost of Goods Sold . . . . . . . . . . . . . . . . . . . . . . . . . . . . . . . . . . . . . | | (75,000) |
| Gross Profit on Sales . . . . . . . . . . . . . . . . . . . . . . . . . . . . . . . . . . . . | | $105,000 |
| Operating Expenses: | | |
| Depreciation Expense . . . . . . . . . . . . . . . . . . . . . . . . . . . . . . . | $15,000 | |
| Salaries Expense . . . . . . . . . . . . . . . . . . . . . . . . . . . . . . . . . . . . | 50,000 | |
| Rent Expense . . . . . . . . . . . . . . . . . . . . . . . . . . . . . . . . . . . . . . . | 12,000 | |
| Other Operating Expenses . . . . . . . . . . . . . . . . . . . . . . . . . . . | 8,000 | (85,000) |
| Net Income . . . . . . . . . . . . . . . . . . . . . . . . . . . . . . . . . . . . . . . . . . . . . | | $ 20,000 |

## WETHERSFIELD, INC.
### Comparative Balance Sheets

| | June 30 | |
| --- | --- | --- |
| | **1998** | **1997** |
| **Assets:** | | |
| Cash | $ 30,000 | $ 20,000 |
| Accounts Receivable (net) | 60,000 | 80,000 |
| Merchandise Inventory | 80,000 | 35,000 |
| Prepaid Rent | 14,000 | 20,000 |
| Noncurrent Assets (net) | 136,000 | 55,000 |
| Total Assets | $320,000 | $210,000 |
| **Equities:** | | |
| Accounts Payable | $ 40,000 | $ 25,000 |
| Accrued Salaries Payable | 10,000 | 40,000 |
| Noncurrent Liabilities | 135,000 | 30,000 |
| Total Liabilities | $185,000 | $ 95,000 |
| Paid-In Capital | $100,000 | $100,000 |
| Retained Earnings | 35,000 | 15,000 |
| Total Stockholders' Equity | $135,000 | $115,000 |
| Total Equities | $320,000 | $210,000 |

**Required:**

Convert Wethersfield's accrual income statement into a schedule calculating cash from operations.

▶ *(Check Figure: Cash provided by operations = $1,000)*

## DECISION PROBLEM

The president of Torrington Company has recently received from the accounting department a complete set of financial statements for the year ended Dec. 31, 1998. Included with these statements was the following Statement of Cash Flows:

---

**TORRINGTON COMPANY**
**Statement of Cash Flows**
**For the Year Ended December 31, 1998**

---

| | | |
|---|---:|---:|
| Cash Flows from Operating Activities: | | |
| Net Income | | $ 48,450 |
| Adjustments to Reconcile Net Income to Net | | |
| Cash Provided by Operating Activities | | |
| Add: | | |
| Decrease in Prepaid Expenses | $ 3,500 | |
| Increase in Accrued Liabilities | 1,900 | |
| Depreciation Expense | 8,100 | 13,500 |
| Deduct: | | |
| Increase in Accounts Receivable | $ 9,500 | |
| Increase in Merchandise Inventory | 22,000 | |
| Decrease in Accounts Payable | 2,800 | |
| Amortization of Bond Premium | 250 | |
| Gain on Sale of Land | 3,600 | (38,150) |
| Net Cash Flows from Operating Activities | | $ 23,800 |
| | | |
| Cash Flows from Investing Activities: | | |
| Increase: Proceeds from Sale of Land | $25,000 | |
| Decrease: Payment for Purchase of Equipment | (9,200) | |
| Net Cash Flows from Investing Activities | | 15,800 |
| | | |
| Cash Flows from Financing Activities: | | |
| Increase: Proceeds from Issuance of Common Stock | $15,000 | |
| Decrease: Dividends Paid | (3,000) | |
| Net Cash Provided by Financing Activities | | 12,000 |
| | | |
| Net Decrease in Cash and Cash Equivalents | | $ 51,600 |
| Cash and Cash Equivalents at Beginning of Year | | 27,200 |
| | | |
| Cash and Cash Equivalents at End of Year | | $ 78,800 |

Supplemental schedule of noncash investing and financing activities:
  The company acquired a building in exchange for common stock valued at $125,000.

After reviewing all the statements, the president asks the following questions:

1. I understand from discussions with my financial advisors that depreciation is a source of cash. If that's so, why isn't our ending cash balance $56,550, the net income figure of $48,450 plus the depreciation of $8,100? Where did the other $22,250 ($78,800 − $56,550) come from?

2. This statement tells me that $23,800 cash came from operating activities, but I'm having difficulty understanding the disclosures in this section. Why can't I tell how much we received from customers, paid for merchandise, or paid for expenses? Is there an easy way for me to determine these cash inflows and outflows?

3. And what's this about the building we acquired? We didn't use any cash at all. Why is this on a statement called "cash flows"? That doesn't make any sense!

**Required:**

Respond to each of the questions raised by the president.

## ETHICS CASE

Will and Trisha Grant own English Country Gardens, a landscaping and plant nursery business. Even though sales and income have grown in each of the five years since the business began, it has absorbed virtually all the cash that Will and Trisha have been able to raise from their personal resources.

Will and Trisha hope to expand their operations by doing a great deal of work for developers who are about to start building single-family homes in the area. In anticipation, the Grants have expanded their plant inventory and would like to add a new greenhouse and purchase additional property to use as a tree nursery.

Trisha's preliminary discussions with the company's bank about a loan to finance the new additions have been encouraging, but the bank has just notified her that it wants to examine a set of financial statements for each of the last three years before making a final decision. Since English Country Gardens is a small business organized as a partnership, no audited financial statements are required, so the Grants never prepared any. The bank has merely asked for statements "in good form," and does not require an audit.

Will and Trisha majored in horticulture in college and have very little knowledge of accounting. Their accounting system consists of a checkbook and listings of inventory, receivables, and payables. Will asks Jim Jensen, a graduate student in accounting at the local college, to help him put together a set of financial statements to show to the bank's loan officers. Jim reconstructs income statements, balance sheets, and statements of cash flows for each of the five years that the business has been in existence. The income statements show just what

Will and Trisha expected, a steady rise in profits. The statements of cash flows, however, reveal that cash from operations has been negative in each year of the business's life. Jim counsels Will and Trisha that this situation should be taken seriously, especially since inventory, accounts receivable, and accounts payable have continuously increased during the five-year period. Jim states that in some larger businesses he has read about, negative cash flows from operating activities signaled declining income and eventual bankruptcy.

Will and Trisha plan to use some of the cash from the bank loan for operating purposes until the housing construction begins and they can get some hoped-for business from developers. They decide that the best thing for the business and their employees is to give the bank only balance sheets and income statements. Will's philosophy is, "If we're going to continue to pay our employees and get new business, we need that loan. We should put our best foot forward. If the loan officers want cash flow information, let them ask for it or figure it out themselves."

**Required:**

1. Who are the stakeholders in this situation?
2. Does the Grant's decision to withhold cash flow information from the bank represent merely a business decision, or is an ethical dilemma involved?
3. Do you believe that Will and Trisha acted properly? Why or why not?

## OBJECTIVE ASSIGNMENT ANSWERS

### True/False

1. F   2. F   3. T   4. F   5. T

### Multiple Choice

1. c   2. b   3. d   4. a   5. b
6. b   7. c   8. a   9. c   10. d

# Financial Statement Analysis

**LEARNING OBJECTIVES**

After studying this chapter, you should be able to do the following:

1 Prepare comparative financial statements

2 Calculate trend percentages

3 Prepare common-size financial statements

4 Calculate ratios that analyze a company's short-term debt-paying ability:
  a. Working capital    d. Inventory turnover
  b. Current ratio    e. Accounts receivable turnover
  c. Quick ratio    f. Average age of accounts receivable

5 Calculate ratios that analyze a company's long-term debt-paying ability:
  a. Times interest earned    c. Stockholders' equity to total assets ratio
  b. Debt to total assets ratio

6 Calculate ratios that analyze a company's earnings performance:
  a. Rate of return on total assets    c. Earnings per share
  b. Rate of return on common stockholders' equity    d. Price–earnings ratio
   e. Dividend yield rate

7 Describe the types of information found in financial statement footnotes that assist in evaluating a company's performance and financial strength

8 Describe the purpose and structure of the independent auditor's report

9 Describe sources of financial and nonfinancial information that may be used to supplement published financial statements

10 Define the key terms listed at the end of the chapter

**CHAPTER OUTLINE**

**HORIZONTAL ANALYSIS: COMPARISON OF 2 OR MORE YEARS** • Comparative Financial Statements • Trend Analysis • **VERTICAL ANALYSIS: COMPARISON OF ITEMS WITHIN A SINGLE TIME PERIOD** • Common-Size Financial Statements • Ratios • **ANALYSIS OF LIQUID POSITION** • Working Capital • The Current Ratio • The Quick Ratio • Inventory Turnover • Accounts Receivable Turnover • Average Age of Receivables • **ANALYSIS OF DEBT-PAYING ABILITY** • The Times Interest Earned Ratio • The Debt to Total Assets Ratio • The Stockholders' Equity to Total Assets Ratio • **ANALYSIS OF EARNINGS PERFORMANCE** • Rate of Return on Total Assets • Rate of Return on Common Stockholders' Equity • Earnings per Share of Common Stock • The Price–Earnings Ratio • Dividend Yield Rate • **INTERPRETATION OF FINANCIAL RATIOS** • Company History • External Standards • **ANALYSIS OF NOTES TO THE FINANCIAL STATEMENTS** • Accounting Policies Note • Contingencies Note • Other Descriptive Notes • **ANALYSIS OF THE INDEPENDENT AUDITOR'S REPORT** • **OTHER SOURCES OF INFORMATION**

The four major financial statements provide a great deal of information about a company's resources, earnings, and ability to generate cash, and users of these statements can gain more insight into a company's financial health and operating efficiency by analyzing the statement data. Investors and creditors can compare the company's current results with those from prior years to see whether and how the company's performance is improving; they can compare the company's data to those of other companies in the same industry to discover its relative strengths and weaknesses. Examining relationships among data in the company's financial statements can provide knowledge that can't be gained from just looking at individual items in the statements. In this chapter we will examine some ways of using financial statements to discover some of the information that they can reveal about the efficiency of the company's management, the company's short- and long-term debt-paying ability, its earnings performance, and its financial structure.

## HORIZONTAL ANALYSIS: COMPARISON OF 2 OR MORE YEARS

One approach to financial statement analysis is to compare the financial data of a single company for 2 or more years. This **horizontal analysis** makes it possible to focus attention on items that have changed significantly during the period being reviewed. Comparison of an item over several periods with a base year may show a trend developing. A *base year* is any year chosen as a beginning point.

### Comparative Financial Statements

**Learning Objective 1**

Prepare comparative financial statements

**Comparative financial statements** usually show financial statement data for 2 or more years, the increase or decrease in each item on the statement, and the percentage change as compared with the earliest year reported. Exhibits 1 and 2 show comparative balance sheets and income statements for Kelly-Miller, Inc.

On comparative statements the most current year's information is normally presented in the first column. Successive columns show amounts for progressively earlier years. The Kelly-Miller, Inc., 2-year comparative statements show the dollar amount of the change in each statement item. These increases and decreases are calculated simply by subtracting 1997 amounts from 1998 amounts, such as for cash: $5,368 − $6,574 = − $1,206. The percentage increase or decrease in each statement amount is also disclosed in the final column. These percentages are calculated by dividing the amount of change by the earliest-year amount, such as for cash: − $1,206 ÷ $6,574 = − 18.3%. The analyst will give most attention to material comparative statement items that show a significant percentage change during the year. Merchandise inventory is a material item showing a significant percentage change (24.1%). The analyst must be careful not to look at these percentage changes without considering the relative importance (that is, the *materiality*) of the item. For example, Kelly-Miller's temporary investments had a very large percentage increase (96.8%), but this item would be viewed as much less important than, say, merchandise inventory, because of its relatively small dollar amount.

Generally speaking, there were no dramatic shifts in the assets, liabilities, or stockholders' equity structure of Kelly-Miller between 1997 and 1998. The most important observations are as follows:

1. The decrease in cash is accompanied by an increase in temporary investments, indicating that Kelly-Miller may be managing its idle cash better in 1998 by investing a larger part of it.

**Exhibit 1** Comparative Balance Sheets

### KELLY-MILLER, INC.
### Comparative Balance Sheets
### (000's Omitted)

| | December 31 1998 | December 31 1997 | Amount Increase (Decrease) | Percent Increase (Decrease) |
|---|---|---|---|---|
| **Assets** | | | | |
| Current Assets: | | | | |
| Cash | $ 5,368 | $ 6,574 | $ (1,206) | (18.3)% |
| Temporary Investments | 3,090 | 1,570 | 1,520 | 96.8 |
| Accounts Receivable (Less Allowance for Uncollectibles of $710 in 1998 and $814 in 1997) | 35,382 | 32,936 | 2,446 | 7.4 |
| Merchandise Inventory | 62,582 | 50,434 | 12,148 | 24.1 |
| Prepaid Expenses | 2,870 | 2,590 | 280 | 10.8 |
| Total Current Assets | $109,292 | $ 94,104 | $15,188 | 16.1 |
| Investments: | | | | |
| Investment in Common Stock | $ 6,000 | $ 6,000 | –0– | –0– |
| Property, Plant, and Equipment: | | | | |
| Land | $ 4,520 | $ 4,300 | $ 220 | 5.1 |
| Building | 72,540 | 72,540 | –0– | –0– |
| Less: Accumulated Depreciation | (30,696) | (29,196) | (1,500)* | 5.1 |
| Equipment | 18,907 | 16,717 | 2,190 | 13.1 |
| Less: Accumulated Depreciation | (7,980) | (7,840) | (140)* | 1.8 |
| Total Property, Plant, and Equipment | $ 57,291 | $ 56,521 | $ 770 | 1.4 |
| Total Assets | $172,583 | $156,625 | $15,958 | 10.2 % |
| **Liabilities and Stockholders' Equity** | | | | |
| Current Liabilities: | | | | |
| Accounts Payable | $ 24,235 | $ 30,353 | $ (6,118) | (20.2)% |
| Accrued Payables | 9,758 | 6,137 | 3,621 | 59.0 |
| Income Tax Payable | 2,040 | 1,425 | 615 | 43.2 |
| Current Portion of Long-Term Debt | 3,000 | 3,000 | –0– | –0– |
| Total Current Liabilities | $ 39,033 | $ 40,915 | $ (1,882) | (4.6) |
| Long-Term Liabilities: | | | | |
| 8% Mortgage Bonds Payable | $ 25,000 | $ 28,000 | $ (3,000) | (10.7) |
| 10% Unsecured Note Payable | 5,000 | 0 | 5,000 | ∞ † |
| Total Long-Term Liabilities | $ 30,000 | $ 28,000 | $ 2,000 | 7.1 |
| Total Liabilities | $ 69,033 | $ 68,915 | $ 118 | .2 |
| Stockholders' Equity: | | | | |
| 5% Preferred Stock ($10-par) | $ 500 | $ 500 | –0– | –0– |
| Common Stock ($1-par) | 10,000 | 9,500 | $ 500 | 5.3 |
| Paid-In Capital in Excess of Par: Common Stock | 35,843 | 30,053 | 5,790 | 19.3 |
| Retained Earnings | 57,207 | 47,657 | 9,550 | 20.0 |
| Total Stockholders' Equity | $103,550 | $ 87,710 | $15,840 | 18.1 |
| Total Liabilities and Stockholders' Equity | $172,583 | $156,625 | $15,958 | 10.2 % |

* The amounts of accumulated depreciation increased. The effect of these increases is to decrease assets. Remember, accumulated depreciation is a contra asset.

† When an amount increases or decreases from zero to another number, the percentage change is infinitely large and therefore meaningless (5,000/0 = ∞).

**Exhibit 2** Comparative Income Statements

### KELLY-MILLER, INC.
### Comparative Income Statements
### (000's Omitted)

| | For the Year Ended December 31 | | Amount Increase (Decrease) | Percent Increase (Decrease) |
|---|---|---|---|---|
| | **1998** | **1997** | | |
| Net Sales.................................... | $ 862,915 | $ 673,488 | $189,427 | 28.1% |
| Cost of Goods Sold........................ | (564,346) | (454,335) | 110,011 | 24.2 |
| Gross Profit on Sales ..................... | $ 298,569 | $ 219,153 | $ 79,416 | 36.2 |
| Operating Expenses: | | | | |
|   Selling Expenses........................ | $(212,062) | $(162,571) | $ 49,491 | 30.4 |
|   General and Administrative Expenses ..... | (58,771) | (35,928) | 22,843 | 63.6 |
|     Total Operating Expenses............. | $(270,833) | $(198,499) | $ 72,334 | 36.4 |
| Other Income and Expenses: | | | | |
|   Dividend Income ....................... | $ 516 | $ 430 | $ 86 | 20.0 |
|   Interest Expense ....................... | (3,120) | (3,016) | 104 | 3.4 |
|     Net Other Income (Expense).......... | $ (2,604) | $ (2,586) | $ 18 | .7 |
| Income before Income Taxes ............. | $ 25,132 | $ 18,068 | $ 7,064 | 39.1 |
| Income Tax Expense ..................... | (7,557) | (5,693) | 1,864 | 32.7 |
| Net Income ............................. | $ 17,575 | $ 12,375 | $ 5,200 | 42.0% |
| Earnings per Common Share............. | $ 1.80 | $ 1.30 | | |

2. While merchandise inventory has increased significantly (24.1%), there appears to be no cause for alarm because sales have also experienced a large boost (28.1%). It is necessary to have more inventory on hand to meet growing customer demand.

3. There seems to be a slight shift from using debt to using equity to finance the company. Total liabilities increased only .2%, while total stockholders' equity increased 18.1%. These changes occurred while total liabilities and stockholders' equity increased by 10.2%.

Comparative statements provide a means for alerting the analyst to significant shifts in financial statement items that require further attention. He or she will then employ the various techniques we will discuss later in this chapter to analyze those shifts.

## Trend Analysis

Learning Objective 2

Calculate trend percentages

**Trend analysis** is another type of horizontal examination that compares proportionate changes in selected financial statement information over time. Trend analysis usually covers at least 5 years and may extend to 10 or 20 years.

Trend percentages are calculated by selecting a base year and calculating amounts of selected items in following years as percentages of the base year amount. (All amounts in the base year are set equal to 100%.) To illustrate, selected income statement amounts for Kelly-Miller, Inc., for the years 1994 through 1998 are given here:

KELLY-MILLER, INC.
Selected Income Statement Amounts
for the Years Ended December 31
(000's Omitted)

| | 1998 | 1997 | 1996 | 1995 | 1994 |
|---|---|---|---|---|---|
| Net Sales............. | $862,915 | $673,488 | $562,104 | $401,982 | $388,500 |
| Gross Profit........... | 298,569 | 219,153 | 218,181 | 213,986 | 209,790 |
| Net Income ........... | 17,575 | 12,375 | 11,088 | 10,666 | 10,560 |

These amounts are converted into trend percentages by dividing the amount in a given year by the 1994 base-year amount. For instance, 1995 sales = $401,982 ÷ $388,500 = 103%; 1996 sales = $562,104 ÷ $388,500 = 145%, and so on. The Kelly-Miller, Inc., trend percentages are tabulated below.

KELLY-MILLER, INC.
Selected Income Statement Data
Shown as Percentages of 1994 Base Year
Years Ended December 31

| | 1998 | 1997 | 1996 | 1995 | 1994 |
|---|---|---|---|---|---|
| Net Sales .......................... | 222% | 173% | 145% | 103% | 100% |
| Gross Profit........................ | 142 | 104 | 104 | 102 | 100 |
| Net Income ........................ | 166 | 117 | 105 | 101 | 100 |

Comparisons of dollar amounts over the years indicate that sales, gross profit, and net income are increasing. Comparisons of the trend percentages reveal that gross profit has not increased nearly as rapidly as sales—an indication that the cost of inventory may have been increasing more quickly than the sales price. The percentage increase in net income is not nearly as great as the percentage increase in sales, but it generally exceeds the percentage increase in gross profit. One possible explanation for these trend relationships is that management is doing a good job of controlling either selling or general and administrative expenses, or both.

Trend percentages, like comparative financial statements, are used to obtain an overview of an entity's performance. This overview will highlight particular areas where further, more detailed analysis is needed. The analyst of Kelly-Miller, Inc.'s, trend percentages, for example, would probably want to look closely at other ratios and comparisons relating to cost of goods sold and operating expenses.

## VERTICAL ANALYSIS: COMPARISON OF ITEMS WITHIN A SINGLE TIME PERIOD

Relating financial statement items to each other within a single time period is called **vertical analysis.** Common-size financial statements and financial ratios are two tools employed in vertical analysis.

### Common-Size Financial Statements

*Learning Objective* **3**

Prepare common-size financial statements

A **common-size financial statement** shows each item on a statement as a percentage of one key item on that statement. No dollar amounts appear. On a common-size income statement, each item is usually stated as a percentage of net sales. Common-size balance sheets often state each amount as a percentage of total assets or total equities (liabilities plus stockholders' equity).

Common-size income statements for Kelly-Miller are shown in Exhibit 3. The computational technique is to take each item and divide by sales of that year. For example, cost of goods sold for 1998 = $564,346 ÷ $862,915 = 65.40%; for 1997 = $454,335 ÷ $673,488 = 67.46%.

Common-size statements are useful for seeing how significant the components of a statement are. Dividend income and interest expense have a very minor effect on Kelly-Miller's net income (they are only .06% and .36% of 1998 sales respectively), while cost of goods sold and selling expenses are of great significance (they are 65.4% and 24.58% of 1998 sales).

The vertical analysis of a single period's statements—common-size statements—may be combined with horizontal analysis—comparative statements—to detect significant changes in financial statement components from year to year. Exhibit 3 shows such comparative common-size statements. Perhaps the most notable changes occurred in cost of goods sold (which went down from 67.46% to 65.40% of sales) and in operating expenses (which increased from 29.47% to 31.39% of sales). While these changes are not substantial, they bear watching in future periods to see if they represent trends.

Common-size statements are especially helpful in comparing two companies that differ in size. Try comparing Kelly-Miller, Inc.'s, 1998 income statement (Exhibit 2) with that of the Carson-Barnes Company, shown below.

---

**CARSON-BARNES COMPANY**
**Income Statement**
**Year Ended December 31, 1998**
**(000's Omitted)**

| | |
|---|---|
| Net Sales | $ 4,535,600 |
| Cost of Goods Sold | (2,585,292) |
| Gross Profit on Sales | $ 1,950,308 |
| Operating Expenses: | |
| Selling | $ (689,411) |
| General and Administrative | (317,492) |
| Total Operating Expenses | $(1,006,903) |
| Income before Income Tax | $ 943,405 |
| Income Tax Expense | (452,834) |
| Net Income | $ 490,571 |

---

Carson-Barnes is so much larger that comparison of any numbers on the two income statements seems meaningless. When Carson-Barnes's statement is converted to a common size, however, comparisons with Kelly-Miller are possible.

---

**CARSON-BARNES COMPANY**
**Common-Size Income Statement**
**Year Ended December 31, 1998**

| | |
|---|---|
| Sales | 100.0% |
| Cost of Goods Sold | (57.0) |
| Gross Profit on Sales | 43.0 |
| Operating Expenses: | |
| Selling | (15.2) |
| General and Administrative | (7.0) |
| Total Operating Expenses | (22.2) |
| Income before Income Tax | 20.8 |
| Income Tax Expense | (10.0) |
| Net Income | 10.8% |

**Exhibit 3** Common-Size Income Statements

### KELLY-MILLER, INC.
### Common-Size Income Statements
### Year Ended December 31

|  | 1998 | 1997 |
|---|---|---|
| Net Sales | 100.00%* | 100.00% |
| Cost of Goods Sold | (65.40) | (67.46) |
| Gross Profit on Sales | 34.60 | 32.54 |
| Operating Expenses: |  |  |
|   Selling Expenses | (24.58) | (24.14) |
|   General and Administrative Expenses | (6.81) | (5.33) |
|     Total Operating Expenses | (31.39) | (29.47) |
| Other Income and Expense: |  |  |
|   Dividend Income | .06 | .06 |
|   Interest Expense | (.36) | (.45) |
|     Net Other Income (Expense) | (.30) | (.39)† |
| Income before Income Taxes | 2.91 | 2.68 |
| Income Tax Expense | (.88) | (.85) |
| Net Income | 2.03%† | 1.83%† |

* Percentages have been rounded.
† Rounding error = .01.

Kelly-Miller, Inc.'s, cost of goods sold (see Exhibit 3) is a much higher percentage of sales (65.4%) than is Carson-Barnes's (57.0%). If the companies are in the same industry, we may question whether the difference is due to volume buying, better inventory management, or possibly just a difference in the inventory costing method (Kelly-Miller may be using LIFO and Carson-Barnes FIFO). In addition, Carson-Barnes's selling expenses are a much lower percentage (15.2%) than Kelly-Miller's (24.58%). The analyst may wonder what efficiencies Carson-Barnes may have discovered that have eluded Kelly-Miller. Differences in advertising policies, policies on commissions paid to sales representatives, or economies of scale could account for the differences in selling expenses. As you can see, common-size statements make it possible to compare companies of different sizes. Comparisons of companies of different sizes raise some questions in the analyst's mind about differences in operating policies that a large firm can implement that a small firm cannot. Comparison of companies of similar size is usually more meaningful.

Many industry trade associations gather statistics from member firms and produce common-size financial statements based on averages for businesses of similar size. For example, sporting goods stores with annual retail sales under $3 million might submit their income statements in a standardized format to a trade association, which would then compute average cost of goods sold and the other percentages for stores in this size range. Size categories are used because we would expect all these companies to be able to implement the same operating policies, such as discounts for buying certain quantities, and amounts spent on advertising. These common-size statistics would provide one standard basis for comparisons that could be used to evaluate the relative performance of a company, in much the same way that we evaluated Kelly-Miller in comparison with Carson-Barnes, but without the problems introduced by comparing companies of vastly differing size.

## Ratios

A **ratio** is an expression of the relationship between two amounts; it results from dividing one amount by the other. For example, the ratio of 1,000 to 500 would be 2 (1,000 ÷ 500), sometimes expressed as 2 : 1. This means that the first number is twice as large as the second. The ratio of 25 to 50 would be expressed as .5 (25 ÷ 50) or .5 : 1, signifying that the first number is half as large as the second. Ratio analysis can provide additional insights into the operating performance and financial position of a firm.

ASK YOURSELF ▶

1. **What is the difference between horizontal and vertical analysis?**
2. **What is trend analysis used for?**
3. **What device is used to compare companies that differ in size?**
4. **What is a ratio?**

## ANALYSIS OF LIQUID POSITION

Creditors and potential creditors are interested in continuously monitoring a company's ability to pay interest as it comes due and to repay the principal of the debt at maturity. An analysis of a firm's liquid position provides indicators of its short-term debt-paying ability. Measures of liquid position also are used to evaluate management's current operating efficiency. Thus both investors and creditors are particularly interested in these liquid position statistics.

In this section we will discuss several ratios and other measures of liquid position: working capital, the current ratio, the quick ratio, inventory turnover, accounts receivable turnover, and average age of receivables. (In the next section we will discuss several measures of a firm's ability to meet its long-term debt-paying responsibilities.)

### Working Capital

Learning Objective **4**

Calculate ratios that analyze a company's short-term debt-paying ability: working capital

**Working capital** is current assets minus current liabilities; it is a measure of the liquid resources that management will control in the short term. A strong working capital position can be an advantage to a company attempting to obtain short-term credit at favorable interest rates. Investors and long-term creditors view a strong working capital position as an indication that a firm will be able to make its expected dividend and interest payments in a timely manner. Kelly-Miller's working capital for 1998 is computed as follows:

| | | |
|---|---:|---:|
| Current Assets: | | |
| Cash | | $ 5,368,000 |
| Temporary Investments | | 3,090,000 |
| Accounts Receivable | | 35,382,000 |
| Merchandise Inventory | | 62,582,000 |
| Prepaid Expenses | | 2,870,000 |
| Total Current Assets | | $109,292,000 |
| Less: Current Liabilities: | | |
| Accounts Payable | $24,235,000 | |
| Accrued Payables | 9,758,000 | |
| Income Tax Payable | 2,040,000 | |
| Current Portion of Long-Term Debt | 3,000,000 | |
| Total Current Liabilities | | 39,033,000 |
| Working Capital | | $ 70,259,000 |

The general formula and the calculation of Kelly-Miller's working capital for 1998 are as follows:

$$\textbf{Working capital = current assets − current liabilities}$$

1998 Kelly-Miller, Inc., working capital = $109,292,000 − $39,033,000
= $70,259,000

Kelly-Miller's working capital for 1997 was $53,189,000 (current assets of $94,104,000 minus current liabilities of $40,915,000). During 1998, Kelly-Miller's working capital increased by $17,070,000 ($70,259,000 − $53,189,000). This increase indicates that more liquid resources were created than were used during the year. A decrease in working capital would have indicated that the company was using more liquid resources than it was creating.

## The Current Ratio

Learning Objective **4**

Calculate ratios that analyze a company's short-term debt-paying ability: current ratio

The **current ratio** is current assets divided by current liabilities. This statistic is often assigned great importance by lenders in making credit-granting decisions. The general formula and the 1998 current ratio for Kelly-Miller, Inc., are as follows:

$$\text{Current ratio} = \frac{\textbf{current assets}}{\textbf{current liabilities}}$$

1998 Kelly-Miller, Inc., current ratio $= \dfrac{\$109,292,000}{\$39,033,000} = 2.80$, or 2.8 : 1

This means that for every dollar of current liabilities, Kelly-Miller has $2.80 of current assets. Many creditors feel that a current ratio of 2.0 or higher is satisfactory.

Relying too heavily on the current ratio may not be advisable, as the following illustration demonstrates.

The current ratios for company A and company B are calculated as follows:

|  | Company A | Company B |
|---|---|---|
| Current Assets: |  |  |
| Cash.................................... | $ 40,000 | $175,000 |
| Accounts Receivable........................ | 60,000 | 125,000 |
| Merchandise Inventory ..................... | 180,000 | 95,000 |
| Prepaid Expenses ........................... | 20,000 | 5,000 |
| Total Current Assets ........................ | $300,000 | $400,000 |
| Current Liabilities........................... | $100,000 | $200,000 |
| Current Ratio................................ | $\dfrac{\$300,000}{\$100,000} = 3$ | $\dfrac{\$400,000}{\$200,000} = 2$ |

Company A's current ratio of 3 : 1 is much better than company B's 2 : 1. If we inspect the composition of the current assets, however, we see that A's cash and accounts receivable are only one-third of total current assets, whereas three-fourths of B's current assets are composed of these two particular liquid resources. So in reality, B may be in a better position to meet its current obligations than A is.

Company A could further improve its current ratio by paying off $40,000 of current liabilities with the $40,000 cash on hand. If this were done, the new current ratio would be:

$$\text{Company A current ratio (revised)} = \frac{\$300,000 - \$40,000}{\$100,000 - \$40,000} = \frac{\$260,000}{\$60,000} = 4.33$$

Such manipulation of current assets near the end of an accounting period can produce a ratio that may satisfy creditors while actually weakening the immediate liquid position of the company. Accountants sometimes call this practice *window dressing.* It demonstrates that limiting an analysis to too few statistics, relying on arbitrary rules of thumb, and not understanding the limitations behind the calculation of a ratio are pitfalls that should be carefully avoided.

## The Quick Ratio

Learning Objective 4

Calculate ratios that analyze a company's short-term debt-paying ability: quick ratio

The **quick ratio,** also known as the **acid-test ratio,** shows the relationship between highly liquid (quick) assets and current liabilities. Quick assets are those that may be converted directly into cash within a short period of time. These include cash, temporary investments, and receivables. Merchandise inventory is omitted because merchandise is normally sold on credit (converted into a receivable) and then the receivable must be collected before cash is realized. Thus inventory is two steps away from cash rather than just one. Prepaid expenses are also omitted because they are usually relatively small in amount and because they are used up in operations rather than converted into cash.

$$\text{Quick ratio} = \frac{\text{quick assets}}{\text{current liabilities}}$$

Kelly-Miller, Inc.'s, quick ratio on Dec. 31, 1998, is calculated as follows:

| | |
|---|---:|
| Cash . . . . . . . . . . . . . . . . . . . . . . . . . . . . . . . . . . . . . . . . . . . . . . . . | $ 5,368,000 |
| Temporary Investments . . . . . . . . . . . . . . . . . . . . . . . . . . . . . . . . . . . | 3,090,000 |
| Accounts Receivable (Net). . . . . . . . . . . . . . . . . . . . . . . . . . . . . . . . . . | 35,382,000 |
| Total Quick Assets . . . . . . . . . . . . . . . . . . . . . . . . . . . . . . . . . . . . . . . . | $43,840,000 |

$$1998 \text{ Kelly-Miller, Inc., quick ratio} = \frac{\$43,840,000}{\$39,033,000} = 1.12, \text{ or } 1.12:1$$

Creditors generally use the rule of thumb that a quick ratio of at least 1:1 is satisfactory. Kelly-Miller's quick ratio appears to be acceptable.

The quick ratio, when considered with the current ratio, gives an idea of the influence of merchandise inventory and prepaid expenses. Looking at the company A–company B illustration again, we can see that the quick ratio is a tipoff that company A's current ratio may be misleading as a sole indicator of short-term debt-paying ability.

| | Company A | Company B |
|---|---|---|
| Quick Assets: | | |
| Cash . . . . . . . . . . . . . . . . . . . . . . . . . . . . | $ 40,000 | $175,000 |
| Accounts Receivable . . . . . . . . . . . . . . . . . . | 60,000 | 125,000 |
| Total Quick Assets . . . . . . . . . . . . . . . . . . . . . | $100,000 | $300,000 |
| Quick Ratio. . . . . . . . . . . . . . . . . . . . . . . . . | $\frac{\$100,000}{\$100,000} = 1$ | $\frac{\$300,000}{\$200,000} = 1.5$ |

Company B has the stronger quick ratio and the weaker current ratio, indicating that merchandise inventory and prepaid expenses play a less important role in its current position than these assets do in company A's.

### Inventory Turnover

**Inventory turnover** shows how many times the average dollars invested in merchandise inventory were sold (turned over) during the year. This statistic, when compared with the year-end merchandise inventory, gives analysts a basis for judging whether the company has an excessive investment in merchandise at the end of the year. A too-large ending inventory may indicate that sales volume was not as high as expected near year-end, or possibly that management was inefficient in allowing too many unsold goods to accumulate. However, a large inventory may be present because of an unusually high sales volume expected near the beginning of the next period. In any case, the analyst will be wise to attempt to discover the reasons for low turnover and excessive ending inventory.

Inventory turnover is calculated by dividing cost of goods sold by average merchandise inventory (beginning inventory plus ending inventory divided by 2). Cost of goods sold is used instead of sales because sales includes gross profit, while cost of goods sold, like merchandise inventory, does not. The general formula and the 1998 Kelly-Miller, Inc., inventory turnover are as follows:

$$\text{Inventory turnover} = \frac{\text{cost of goods sold}}{\text{average merchandise inventory}}$$

$$\text{1998 Kelly-Miller, Inc., inventory turnover} = \frac{\$564,346,000}{(\$50,434,000 + \$62,582,000)/2}$$

$$= \frac{\$564,346,000}{\$56,508,000} = 9.99 \text{ times}$$

Since Kelly-Miller's inventory turns over about 10 times per year, the year-end inventory should be about 10% of cost of goods sold. Kelly-Miller's inventory of $62,582,000 is a little above this amount (10% × $564,346,000 = $56,434,600). This excess is probably explained by Kelly-Miller's increasing sales volume.

### Accounts Receivable Turnover

**Accounts receivable turnover** indicates the number of times per year that the average balance of Accounts Receivable is collected. This ratio of sales on credit to average accounts receivable is calculated as follows:

$$\text{Accounts receivable turnover} = \frac{\text{credit sales}}{\text{average accounts receivable}}$$

Assuming that substantially all of Kelly-Miller, Inc.'s, sales are on credit, the firm's 1998 receivables turnover is as follows:

$$\text{1998 Kelly-Miller, Inc., accounts receivable turnover} = \frac{\$862,915,000}{(\$32,936,000 + \$35,382,000)/2}$$

$$= \frac{\$862,915,000}{\$34,159,000} = 25.3 \text{ times}$$

This ratio takes on more meaning when used in the calculation of the statistic discussed next.

### Average Age of Receivables

**Average age of receivables** provides a rough approximation of the average time that it takes to collect receivables. Average age of receivables is determined as follows:

$$\text{Average age of receivables} = \frac{365 \text{ days}}{\text{accounts receivable turnover}}$$

$$1998 \text{ average age of Kelly-Miller receivables} = \frac{365 \text{ days}}{25.3 \text{ times}} = 14.4 \text{ days}$$

Kelly-Miller, Inc., takes an average of 14 days to collect its receivables. If Kelly-Miller's credit terms are net 10 days, its collection efforts could be improved. If the credit terms are 15 or 30 days, Kelly-Miller's collection efforts appear to be excellent.

Creditors are interested in receivables turnover and the average age of receivables as indicators of how quickly the company's receivables are converted into the cash required for operations and debt repayment. Investors and creditors use receivables turnover as one more index of management efficiency.

**ASK YOURSELF** ▶

1. What is the difference between the current ratio and the quick ratio?
2. How is inventory turnover calculated?
3. What does the average age of receivables tell the statement analyst?

## ANALYSIS OF DEBT-PAYING ABILITY

Three statistics that provide information about a company's long-term debt-paying ability are the times interest earned ratio, the debt to total assets ratio, and the equity to total assets ratio. These ratios, along with the liquid position indicators just discussed, allow creditors and potential creditors to evaluate a company's ability to meet both long- and short-term debt responsibilities.

### The Times Interest Earned Ratio

The **times interest earned ratio** indicates the margin of safety provided by current earnings in meeting the company's interest responsibilities. The formula for calculating this ratio is:

$$\text{Times interest earned} = \frac{\text{income before interest expense and income taxes}}{\text{annual interest expense}}$$

The ratio uses income before interest expense and income taxes because this is the amount that could be used to pay interest—provided it was available in the form of cash. Income taxes are excluded because interest is deductible in calculating income tax.

Times interest earned for Kelly-Miller, Inc., in 1998 is:

$$\text{Times interest earned} = \frac{\$17{,}575{,}000 + \$3{,}120{,}000 + \$7{,}557{,}000}{\$3{,}120{,}000}$$

$$= \frac{\$28{,}252{,}000}{\$3{,}120{,}000} = 9.1 \text{ times}$$

Thus, Kelly-Miller's income available to meet its interest responsibilities was about 9 times the amount of its interest expense. Usually, if interest is covered several times, long-term creditors consider this an acceptable margin of safety. Kelly-Miller's times interest earned ratio should be quite satisfactory to its creditors.

### The Debt To Total Assets Ratio

Learning Objective 5

Calculate ratios that analyze a company's long-term debt-paying ability: debt to total assets ratio

The **debt to total assets ratio** shows the percentage of the firm's assets financed by debt. The higher this percentage, the greater the risk that the company will be unable to meet its obligations when due. The formula for calculating the debt to total assets ratio and the 1998 calculation for Kelly-Miller, Inc., is:

$$\text{Debt to total assets ratio} = \frac{\text{total liabilities}}{\text{total assets}}$$

$$\text{Kelly-Miller, Inc., 1998 debt to total assets ratio} = \frac{\$69{,}033{,}000}{\$172{,}583{,}000} = .399 \text{ or } .40, \text{ or } 40\%$$

Thus, 40% of Kelly-Miller's total assets were financed by debt.

### The Stockholders' Equity to Total Assets Ratio

Learning Objective 5

Calculate ratios that analyze a company's long-term debt-paying ability: stockholders' equity to total assets ratio

The **stockholders' equity to total assets ratio,** sometimes called the **equity ratio,** shows the percentage of the firm's assets financed by stockholders. The higher this ratio, the smaller the risk that the company will be unable to meet its obligations when due. After a moment's reflection, you should see that the debt to total assets ratio and the stockholders' equity to total assets ratio are complementary; that is, the two percentages should always add to 100%. This is true because all assets are financed by either debt or equity funds. The stockholders' equity to total assets ratio may be found by subtracting the debt to total assets ratio from 100%:

$$\text{Stockholders' equity to total assets ratio} = 100\% - \text{debt to total assets ratio}$$

$$\text{1998 Kelly-Miller, Inc., stockholders' equity to total assets ratio} = 100\% - 40\% = 60\%$$

This ratio may also be calculated by the following formula:

$$\text{Stockholders' equity to total assets ratio} = \frac{\text{total stockholders' equity}}{\text{total assets}}$$

$$\text{1998 Kelly-Miller, Inc., stockholders' equity to total assets ratio} = \frac{\$103{,}550{,}000}{\$172{,}583{,}000} = .60, \text{ or } 60\%$$

Thus, 60% of Kelly-Miller's assets come from stockholders (including reinvested earnings) and 40% from creditors. This ratio should be satisfactory to long-term creditors, although, of course statistics that one analyst considers satisfactory may cause concern to another.

1. Why is income before interest and income taxes used to calculate times interest earned?
2. The debt to total assets ratio and the stockholders' equity to total assets ratio are complementary. What does this mean?
3. Why would a potential creditor normally prefer a high stockholders' equity to total assets ratio?

## ANALYSIS OF EARNINGS PERFORMANCE

Stockholders and potential stockholders employ several ratios to help them evaluate management performance in using the resources of the entity to earn profits. Rate of return on total assets and rate of return on stockholders' equity are two such ratios.

### Rate of Return on Total Assets

**Learning Objective 6**

Calculate ratios that analyze a company's earnings performance: rate of return on total assets

**Rate of return (ROR) on total assets** is a measure of management's efficiency in using all resources at its disposal. The formula for computing this ratio is:

$$\text{Rate of return (ROR) on total assets} = \frac{\text{income before interest expense}}{\text{average total assets}}$$

Income before interest is used so that earnings will not be influenced by the manner in which the assets are financed. Interest is a cost of financing the business, not a cost of operating it. Average total assets reflect resources employed throughout the year, not those on hand at the beginning or at the end. This average could be computed by weighting the dollars of assets used by the number of days they are employed and dividing by 365. An approximation of this average may be obtained by adding the beginning and ending asset amounts and dividing by 2.

Kelly-Miller, Inc.'s, return on total assets for 1998 is calculated as follows:

$$\text{ROR on total assets} = \frac{\text{net income} + \text{interest expense}}{(\text{total assets, beg. of year} + \text{total assets, end of year})/2}$$

$$= \frac{\$17,575,000 + \$3,120,000}{(\$156,625,000 + \$172,583,000)/2}$$

$$= \frac{\$20,695,000}{\$164,604,000} = .1257, \text{ or } 12.57\%$$

Kelly-Miller's management earned an average of 12.57% on each dollar of assets invested in the company.

### Rate of Return on Common Stockholders' Equity

**Learning Objective 6**

Calculate ratios that analyze a company's earnings performance: rate of return on common stockholders' equity

**Rate of return (ROR) on common stockholders' equity** is a measure of management's effectiveness in using the resources invested by the common stockholders. This rate may be higher or lower than the return on total assets, depending on how judiciously management has combined debt and preferred stock with common stock in financing the company's resources. The formula for computing this ratio is:

$$\frac{\text{Rate of return (ROR) on}}{\text{common stockholders' equity}} = \frac{\text{net income} - \text{preferred dividends}}{\text{average common stockholders' equity}}$$

The earnings amount in the numerator excludes both payments to holders of debt (interest expense) and payments to holders of preferred stock (preferred dividends). Thus the net income less preferred dividends is the net amount earned on the equity of the common stockholders. Average common stockholders' equity is an approximation of the amount invested by this group of owners throughout the year.

| Preferred Dividends: | |
|---|---|
| Par Value of Preferred Stock (at the time dividends are declared) . . . . . . . | $500,000 |
| Dividend Rate Paid . . . . . . . . . . . . . . . . . . . . . . . . . . . . . . . . . . . . . . | 5% |
| Amount of Preferred Dividends . . . . . . . . . . . . . . . . . . . . . . . . . . . . . . . . | $ 25,000 |

Average common stockholders' equity:

| | Total stockholders' equity | − | preferred stockholders' equity | = | common stockholders' equity |
|---|---|---|---|---|---|
| Jan. 1, 1998 | $ 87,710,000 | − | $500,000 | = | $ 87,210,000 |
| + Dec. 31, 1998 | 103,550,000 | − | 500,000 | = | 103,050,000 |
| | | | | Total = | $190,260,000 |
| | | | | | ÷ 2 |
| | Average common stockholders' equity for 1998 | | | = | $ 95,130,000 |

The rate of return on Kelly-Miller's common stockholders' equity for 1998 is:

$$\text{ROR on common stockholders' equity} = \frac{\$17,575,000 - \$25,000}{\$95,130,000} = .1845, \text{ or } 18.45\%$$

Since the 18.45% return on common stockholders' equity exceeds the 12.57% return on total assets, management has made effective use of **leverage, or trading on the equity.** Leverage, or trading on the equity, involves using the assets invested by common stockholders as collateral for debt financing (borrowing on notes or bonds) and limited-return equity financing (selling preferred stock) in an attempt to earn a higher return for the common stockholder. A simple example will help clarify this concept.

# SUE AND JOHN'S LAWN-CARE SERVICE

Sue and John operate a lawn-care service. They have $100 of their own money invested and earn a $5 profit (or 5% return). An additional $100 is borrowed from a friend at 6% interest. In order for Sue and John to come out ahead on this loan, they must use the borrowed money to earn more than the $6 interest they will have to pay. Assuming that the net income on the $200 of assets is $7, Sue and John have used someone else's money to increase their rate of return. Remember, the $7 net income is *after* the interest expense deduction, so the rate of return on Sue and John's total assets is:

$$\frac{\text{Net income} + \text{interest expense}}{\text{Average total assets}} = \frac{\$7 + \$6}{(\$200 + \$200)/2} = \frac{\$13}{\$200}$$

Return of return on total assets = .065, or 6.5%

The rate of return on Sue and John's stockholders' equity is:

$$\frac{\text{Net income} - \text{preferred dividends}}{\text{Average common stockholders' equity}} = \frac{\$7 - \$0}{(\$100 + \$100)/2}$$

$$\text{Rate of return on stockholders' equity} = \frac{\$7}{\$100} = .07, \text{ or } 7\%$$

Leverage, then, is simply an *attempt* to use funds supplied by nonowners to increase the return to owners. Any time the rate of return on common stockholders' equity exceeds the rate of return on total assets, leverage has been used to the stockholders' advantage.

Leverage may also work to the detriment of common stockholders. If the return on the borrowed and preferred stock capital is not sufficient to pay the interest and preferred dividends on that capital, some of the earnings that would normally be available to common stockholders are absorbed in making up the difference. Any time the rate of return on total assets is more than the rate of return on common stockholders' equity, leverage has been used to the detriment of the stockholders.

### Earnings per Share of Common Stock

Learning
Objective **6**

Calculate ratios that analyze a company's earnings performance: earnings per share

**Earnings per share (EPS) of common stock** is a measure of the income earned on each share of common stock. The formula for a simple capital structure and the calculation of 1998 EPS for Kelly-Miller, Inc., are as follows:

$$\text{EPS (simple capital structure)} = \frac{\text{net income} - \text{preferred dividends}}{\text{average number of common shares outstanding}}$$

$$\text{EPS} = \frac{\$17,575,000 - \$25,000}{(9,500,000 \text{ shs} + 10,000,000 \text{ shs})/2}$$

$$= \frac{\$17,550,000}{9,750,000 \text{ shs}} = \$1.80$$

Earnings per share amounts must appear on the income statements of public companies. Nonpublic (closely held, or nonpublicly traded) companies are not required to disclose earnings per share amounts. If you review Kelly-Miller, Inc.'s, income statement in Exhibit 2, you will see that EPS is properly shown for 1998 and 1997.

### The Price–Earnings Ratio

Learning
Objective **6**

Calculate ratios that analyze a company's earnings performance: price–earnings ratio

The **price–earnings ratio** is one more indicator of the earnings performance of common stock. The formula for calculating the price–earnings ratio is:

$$\text{Price–earnings ratio} = \frac{\text{market price per share of common stock}}{\text{earnings per share of common stock}}$$

Assuming a current market price of $27 for Kelly-Miller, Inc.'s, stock, the price–earnings ratio for 1998 would be calculated as follows:

$$\text{Price–earnings ratio} = \frac{\$27}{\$1.80} = 15, \text{ or } 15:1$$

This simply means that Kelly-Miller's stock is currently selling for 15 times the amount that each share earned. Price–earnings ratios of 15 are not uncommon. They may range as high as 20 or even more. The price–earnings ratio reflects the stock market's assessment of the future earnings of the company. Investors are generally willing to buy a share of stock for as many as 15 to 20 times the current per-share earnings because they feel that the future income growth of the firm will be sufficient to provide an adequate return on this investment. This return is normally received through a combination of dividends and an increased market value of the stock.

### Dividend Yield Rate

Learning Objective 6

Calculate ratios that analyze a company's earnings performance: dividend yield rate

**Dividend yield rate** shows the current year's dividends as a percentage of the current market price of the stock. This indication of the cash payout rate on an investment allows stockholders and potential stockholders to compare interest rates on certificates of deposit, corporate bonds, and other securities with this measure of return on common stock. The investor should be aware that dividend yield rates ignore the potential increase in the market value of common stock. For this reason the dividend yield rate should be combined with other statistics in making investment decisions.

The formula for calculating dividend yield rates and the 1998 dividend yield rate for Kelly-Miller, Inc., assuming that $8,000,000 dividends were paid to common stockholders, is:

$$\text{Dividend yield rate} = \frac{\text{dividends per share of common stock}}{\text{current market price per share of common stock}}$$

$$\text{1998 dividend yield rate for Kelly-Miller, Inc.} = \frac{\$8,000,000 \div 10,000,000 \text{ shs}}{\$27} = \frac{\$.80}{\$27} = \begin{array}{l} .0296, \\ \text{or } 2.96\% \end{array}$$

This relatively low dividend yield rate of about 3% on Kelly-Miller, Inc., common stock would not attract investors who count on cash flow from dividends to pay their living expenses. A potential Kelly-Miller, Inc., stockholder would probably be more interested in speculating on the growth in the market value of the stock. This type of investor would rely more heavily on growth in earnings per share and recent trends in the market price of the stock than on the dividend yield rate.

**ASK YOURSELF** ▶

1. **Is favorable leverage present when ROR on total assets is higher than ROR on common stockholders' equity?**
2. **How is the price–earnings ratio calculated?**
3. **Why would someone who depends on dividends for living expenses be more interested in the dividend yield rate than in earnings per share?**

## INTERPRETATION OF FINANCIAL RATIOS

A quick ratio of 1.12, an inventory turnover of 9.99, or a price–earnings ratio of 15 means very little when considered in a vacuum. A financial ratio becomes relevant for decision making only when compared with some standard. Each analyst must decide on a standard for each ratio that he or she relies on to gauge the performance of the company being analyzed. Some common bases for establishing standards are considered next.

### Company History

We have seen that horizontal analysis involves the comparison of financial data for a single company for 2 or more years. In addition, we have looked at comparative financial statements and trend analysis as applications of horizontal analysis. An analyst may compute each of the financial ratios for a number of years and then use the results in a horizontal analysis, comparing the various years' ratios to form an opinion about whether the company's performance is getting better or worse. If Kelly-Miller's inventory turnover has been 10, 12, and 16 during 1998, 1997, and 1996, respectively, the analyst should be concerned enough to attempt to discover the reason for the deterioration in this ratio. If management inefficiency seems to be the only plausible explanation, the analyst may expect continued problems and will probably decide to reject a credit application or not to invest in stock of the corporation.

A major limitation of comparing amounts and ratios for a single company is that there is no basis for drawing a conclusion about the significance of these statistics. Some external standard is needed against which to measure the company's ratios. For example, if the average inventory turnover in Kelly-Miller's industry is 4, a turnover of 10 may appear excellent. If the industry average is 12, however, the turnover of 10 may be a cause for concern.

### External Standards

Ratio information about other companies is often used as a yardstick against which to compare the statistics of the firm being analyzed. These external data may be obtained by analyzing the financial statements of the other firms; by obtaining copies of industry averages from the publications of trade associations; by examining data on industry norms, average ratios, and credit ratings from credit agencies such as Dun & Bradstreet; or by consulting statistics available in investment service publications such as *Annual Statement Studies,* published by Robert Morris Associates.

Care must be taken in deciding which ratios are to be used as standards of comparison. Many companies are so diversified that it is difficult to identify one particular industry in which they operate. A current ratio or inventory turnover ratio for such a conglomerate would be meaningless for comparing with those statistics of another firm operating in only one industry.

In most industries, comparability will be affected by size. Large firms will be able to make use of economies of scale and sophisticated quantitative management techniques that may not be practical for smaller ones. Smaller companies may be able to maintain closer client relations and better customer relations than larger ones. These differences in operating techniques may influence different ratios in different ways. The larger firm, for example, may be expected to have a higher gross profit percentage and inventory turnover, while the smaller one may have a quicker receivables turnover and a lower percentage spent on advertising. Comparisons of similar-size entities in the same industry are desirable whenever possible.

The differences in accounting methods used to generate financial information may also influence the comparability of ratios and other statistics. Firms may employ different inventory techniques, depreciation methods, estimates of useful lives, methods of accounting for income taxes, and revenue recognition procedures. It is fairly easy to discover which methods a particular company is using, but adjusting the financial information to compensate for differences in accounting methods may be difficult, if not impossible.

Learning Objective **7**

Describe the types of information found in financial statement footnotes that assist in evaluating a company's performance and financial strength

## ANALYSIS OF NOTES TO THE FINANCIAL STATEMENTS

Notes to the financial statements, commonly called *footnotes,* provide additional information that may greatly influence an analyst's overall judgment about the potential of the company. Some of the more important types of footnotes are discussed in this section.

## Accounting Policies Note

Generally accepted accounting principles require that all financial statements contain a note outlining the various accounting methods that the company has elected to use. The **accounting policies note** explains which accounting method was selected from among several acceptable ones: for example, FIFO or LIFO inventory methods, straight-line or double declining-balance depreciation. The accounting policies note, usually the first note to the financial statements, is helpful in deciding how comparable the financial statistics for two different companies are. The following accounting policies note is typical.

### SUMMARY OF ACCOUNTING POLICIES

**Inventories**   Inventories are stated generally at cost, which is not in excess of market. The cost of substantially all inventories is determined by the last-in, first-out (LIFO) method.

**Depreciation and Depletion**   The cost of most manufacturing plant and equipment is depreciated using an accelerated method based primarily on a sum-of-the-years'-digits formula. The cost of mining properties is depreciated or depleted mainly by the units-of-production method.

Methods of accounting for research and development costs, recognition of warranty expenses, and translating foreign subsidiary statements into U.S. currency are not appropriate accounting policy disclosures, because only one method is acceptable for each of these.

## Contingencies Note

A *contingency* is an event whose occurrence is possible, but not certain. The **contingencies note** must include descriptions of all future losses that are probable, reasonably possible, and in some cases even remote. Where an estimate or a range of estimates of the amount of loss can be made, these must also be disclosed. Thus, a large potential lawsuit loss could significantly change an analyst's forecast about the future of the company. This vital information can be obtained by reading the contingencies note.

The following contingencies note is typical of the disclosures that may be made:

### NOTE 7 CONTINGENCIES

Early in fiscal 1997, the Federal Trade Commission filed a formal complaint against the company and two other manufacturers of steel casings, charging them with sharing an unlawful monopoly in violation of the Federal Trade Commission Act. The commission seeks, among other things, divestiture of certain assets and royalty-free licensing of certain trademarks. The company denies that it has violated the act and is vigorously defending its position. Trial is continuing before an administrative law judge of the Federal Trade Commission, and it is expected that the litigation will continue for some time at considerable expense.

A lawsuit has been filed against the company claiming damages from alleged environmental contamination by our Riverview plant. The suit, filed on Mar. 30, 1998, in the federal court in Florida, alleges damages of $1,000,000. The State of Florida has moved to intervene as plaintiff in this case, seeking $25,000,000 in compensatory and $1,000,000 in punitive damages. The company will vigorously defend against this lawsuit.

Contingencies that are probable in nature and subject to reasonable estimation must be recognized as current period losses. The loss (or expense) must be shown on the income statement, and the corresponding liability (or allowance account) must appear on the balance sheet. Bad debts and warranty expenses are examples of contingencies considered probable and subject to estimation.

### Other Descriptive Notes

Some information vital to the understanding of the financial statements is simply too long and detailed to be shown on the statements themselves. Such information is usually shown in descriptive notes referenced to particular items on the income statement or balance sheet. Typical notes and the supplementary information they provide are as follows:

| Subject of Note | Information Included |
|---|---|
| Property, plant, and equipment | The types of assets included in this category, their estimated useful lives, and whether they are pledged as collateral for loans |
| Long-term liabilities | The effective interest rate, maturity dates, repayment terms, collateral for the debt, any restriction imposed by the creditor (such as limitation on the amount of dividends the company can pay) |

Other common descriptive notes relate to pension plans, income taxes, earnings per share calculations, and stock option plans.

## ANALYSIS OF THE INDEPENDENT AUDITOR'S REPORT

**Learning Objective 8**

Describe the purpose and structure of the independent auditor's report

All publicly owned companies must publish an annual report for their shareholders. The financial statements contained in annual reports must include an auditor's opinion about the fairness of the financial statements. The auditor, an independent outside party, gives an opinion on the financial statements only after carefully reviewing and analyzing the statements and supporting financial records.

The standard wording recommended for the **auditor's report** consists of three paragraphs describing which financial statements are covered by the audit, summarizing what the auditor did, and giving the auditor's opinion about the fairness of the financial statements.

In the first paragraph the auditor lists the financial statements audited—usually the balance sheets, income statements, statements of retained earnings, and statements of cash flows for the current year and the previous year. (Remember that the content of the financial statements is the responsibility of management, not the auditor.)

The second paragraph tells the reader that standard auditing practices were used in conducting the audit and that the supporting documentation was examined on a sample basis (not every journal entry and invoice is investigated). The auditor also states that the procedures used provide "reasonable assurance" that there is no "material misstatement" in the financial statements. This usually means that the auditor is accepting responsibility for discovering fraud or errors that would result in *major* financial statement inaccuracies. The auditor does not say that every small error, petty theft, or minor fraud will be detected.

The final paragraph gives the auditor's opinion of the financial statements. If the auditor is satisfied, he or she states that the financial information is presented *fairly,* in conformity with generally accepted accounting principles. The auditor does *not* say that the statements are completely accurate, true, or free of all minor errors.

The recommended standard wording of the auditor's report is as follows:

We have audited the accompanying balance sheets of X Company as of Dec. 31, 19X2 and 19X1, and the related statements of income, retained earnings, and cash flows for the years then ended. These financial statements are the responsibility of the company's management. Our responsibility is to express an opinion on these financial statements based on our audits.

We conducted our audits in accordance with generally accepted auditing standards. Those standards require that we plan and perform the audit to obtain reasonable assurance about whether the financial statements are free of material misstatement. An audit includes examining, on a test basis, evidence supporting the amounts and disclosures in the financial statements. An audit also includes assessing the accounting principles used and significant estimates made by management, as well as evaluating the overall financial statement presentation. We believe that our audits provide a reasonable basis for our opinion.

In our opinion, the financial statements referred to above present fairly, in all material respects, the financial position of X Company as of (at) Dec. 31, 19X2 and 19X1, and the results of its operations and its cash flows for the years then ended in conformity with generally accepted accounting principles.

# Still Pussyfooting

It used to be that when auditors caught their corporate clients lying, Form 8-K protected both parties from an embarrassing public row. Form 8-K? That's the document that management must file with the Securities & Exchange Commission explaining why it has changed auditors. Generally the departing auditor must also comment on management's explanation.

These filings used to be as dull and unrevealing as minutes from a Rumanian agricultural committee meeting. But they're getting a lot less so. A rule implemented by the SEC last year, but only now showing up in filings, requires outside auditors to be much more specific on why they resign from an account. And if you miss the 8-K, don't worry: The substance of the auditor/client disagreements must now also be reported in a company's annual proxy statement.

This makes for some spicy reading. Consider this passage from the 8-K filed in May, 1989 by New York's Bombay Palace Restaurants, Inc.:

"On Apr. 18, 1988, Peat Marwick advised the company that it could no longer rely on the representations of management and thus resigned as the company's auditors." And in an extraordinarily blunt follow-up letter to the SEC, the auditors said they had discovered "invoice documentation prepared by the company to be false and inaccurate."

In sum, Peat Marwick Main & Co. was saying, they dropped Bombay Palace because management lied. The SEC's enforcement division began an investigation of Bombay Palace in January.

"We're not making a legal judgment," says Peat Marwick's Associate General Counsel John Shutkin. "We came to a conclusion about the integrity of management." In other words, we don't trust the rascals.

Are the accountants finally becoming what many people have long thought them to be: corporate policemen, responsible for digging out managerial wrongdoing? The answer here is definitely no. Independent auditors don't—can't—check every transaction and every invoice. The cost of doing so would be prohibitive.

What that means, of course, is that the auditor's letter certifying a company's books merely signifies that the auditors came across no specific instances of wrongdoing and found no reasons for distrusting management's words. It doesn't guarantee that everything is kosher; only that the auditor found nothing that wasn't kosher. "What the reader [of financial statements] infers is that the opinion letter is a Good Housekeeping Seal of Approval (of the accuracy of the financial statements)" says John Shank, Noble Professor of management accounting at the Tuck School of Business at Dartmouth. "But what the opinion really says is vacuous and innocuous: 'We did what auditors do, and nothing came to our attention that would suggest that things are not okay.'"

For an example of how pussyfooting the auditor's opinion can sometimes be, look at Convenient Food Mart, Inc., a Rosemont, Ill.-based chain of retail convenience stores. In an 8-K filed in February, management reported that the company's auditors, Laventhol & Horwath, had conducted a study of the company's internal controls back in the spring of 1988. That study concluded that the Convenient Food Mart's internal accounting system was such a mess that Laventhol couldn't be sure of the accuracy of the company's financial statements. Nevertheless, Laventhol issued an unqualified opinion on the company's 1987 results. Then, three months later, after management began an investigation of its books, Laventhol withdrew that opinion. The company later restated its results to reflect numerous accounting errors. In January 1989 Laventhol quit the account altogether. In other words, Laventhol's certification was meaningless. Both Laventhol and the company are being sued.

Should the accountants take responsibility for rooting out managerial messes and evildoings? Peat Marwick's Shutkin says this is not practical, given current auditing standards. "You can perform an audit entirely consistent with Generally Accepted Auditing Standards and not detect a fraud that exists," says Shutkin. "That's simply the way life is."

*Source:* Subrata N. Chakravarty, in *Forbes,* Aug. 21, 1989, p. 51. Reprinted by permission of FORBES magazine. Copyright © 1989 by Forbes Inc.

This reading stresses the fact that auditors aren't responsible for detecting all fraud and errors. Auditors rely on the company's system of internal control and test a statistical sample of the company's transactions in formulating their opinion.

## OTHER SOURCES OF INFORMATION

Learning
Objective 9

Describe sources of financial and nonfinancial information that may be of use to supplement published financial statements

The serious student of financial statement analysis will supplement all of the techniques described thus far with several other sources of financial and nonfinancial information. Magazines such as *Business Week, Fortune,* and *Forbes* and financial newspapers such as *The Wall Street Journal, Barron's,* and the *Commercial and Financial Chronicle* provide data on prospects for the economy as a whole and for various industries. In addition, articles on management personnel, company strategy, and significant legislation affecting the business community expand the analyst's background knowledge. Up-to-date quarterly operating results and current stock prices also appear in many of these publications.

Several research firms publish financial services that are available on a subscription basis. These are also found in most university and large public libraries. As already mentioned, industry trade associations and credit-reporting bureaus are additional sources of information.

Many large corporations provide interview sessions for professional analysts working for large stock brokerage firms, trust departments of banks, and other institutions that invest vast sums of money. While these sessions do provide an opportunity for analysts to ask questions that may interest them and to hear management's hopes for the future of the company, they may not be used as a means of communicating secret inside information to a chosen few money managers. Such activities would be illegal.

**ASK YOURSELF** ▶

1. What information is contained in the accounting policies note?
2. Where would a potential lawsuit loss be disclosed?
3. What is contained in each paragraph of the standard auditor's report?
4. What are some sources of general financial and economic information that may be used to supplement ratio statistics in the analysis of financial statements?

## SUMMARY

• Financial statements may be analyzed both **horizontally** and **vertically.** One horizontal approach compares balance sheets of several years expressed in dollars and percentages. A similar comparison is made of income statements of several years.

• **Trend analysis** compares proportionate changes in selected financial information over time. These proportionate changes are expressed as percentages of designated base year amounts.

• A third horizontal approach involves comparing financial ratios for several years in order to detect significant changes in them over time.

• Vertical financial statement analysis involves comparing items on financial statements of a single period. **Common-size financial statements** state each component of the statements in terms of one other component.

• A common-size income statement usually states each component as a percentage of sales. A common-size balance sheet typically presents each item as a percentage of total assets.

• *Ratio analysis,* another form of the vertical approach, may be used to examine earnings performance, debt-paying ability, and liquid position.

• The following ratios were discussed in this chapter:

| Ratio | Formula for Calculation | Use |
|---|---|---|
| **Liquid position ratios:** | | |
| Working capital | Current assets minus current liabilities | Measures the liquid resources that can be controlled by management in the short term |
| Current ratio | $\dfrac{\text{Current assets}}{\text{Current liabilities}}$ | Shows the number of dollars of current assets for each dollar of current liabilities |
| Quick ratio | $\dfrac{\text{Quick assets}}{\text{Current liabilities}}$ | Shows the number of dollars of highly liquid assets for each dollar of current liabilities |
| Inventory turnover | $\dfrac{\text{Cost of goods sold}}{\text{Average merchandise inventory}}$ | Shows how many times the average dollars invested in inventory were sold during the year |
| Accounts receivable turnover | $\dfrac{\text{Credit sales}}{\text{Average accounts receivable}}$ | Indicates the number of times per year that the average balance of accounts receivable is collected |
| Average age of receivables | $\dfrac{\text{365 days}}{\text{Accounts receivable turnover}}$ | Provides an approximation of the average time that it takes to collect receivables |
| **Debt-paying-ability ratios:** | | |
| Times interest earned ratio | $\dfrac{\text{Income before interest expense and income taxes}}{\text{Annual interest expense}}$ | Indicates a margin of safety provided by current earnings in meeting the company's interest responsibilities |
| Debt to total assets ratio | $\dfrac{\text{Total liabilities}}{\text{Total assets}}$ | Shows the percentage of the company's assets financed by debt |
| Stockholders' equity to total assets ratio | $\dfrac{\text{Total stockholders' equity}}{\text{Total assets}}$ | Shows the percentage of the company's assets financed by stockholders |
| **Earnings performance ratios:** | | |
| Rate of return on total assets | $\dfrac{\text{Income before interest expense}}{\text{Average total assets}}$ | Indicates management's efficiency in using all resources at its disposal |
| Rate of return on common stockholders' equity | $\dfrac{\text{Net income} - \text{preferred dividends}}{\text{Average common stockholders' equity}}$ | Indicates management's efficiency in using resources invested by common stockholders |
| Earnings per share | $\dfrac{\text{Net income} - \text{preferred dividends}}{\text{Average number of common shares outstanding}}$ | Measures the income earned on each share of common stock |

*(Continued)*

| Ratio | Formula for Calculation | Use |
|---|---|---|
| Price–earnings ratio | $$\frac{\text{Market price per share of common stock}}{\text{Earnings per share of common stock}}$$ | Shows the relationship of the market price per share to the income per share of common stock |
| Dividend yield rate | $$\frac{\text{Dividends per share of common stock}}{\text{Current market price per share of common stock}}$$ | Measures the return to the common stockholder |

- Ratios take on much more meaning when they can be compared to measures of what they "should be." Standards of comparison are usually obtained by analyzing financial statements of other companies in the same industry and averaging the ratios thus determined. Industry averages may also be acquired from trade associations and financial research firms.
- Ratio comparisons are most useful when the companies studied are in the same industry, are of approximately the same size, and use similar accounting methods.
- *Notes to the financial statements,* commonly called footnotes, are an integral part of the statements. Financial analysis is not complete until the notes have been carefully examined.
- Each company must disclose choices made from among different accounting methods in an **accounting policies note.**
- Events that may have a significant effect on future financial statements are disclosed in a **contingencies note.** Common contingencies include pending lawsuits and administrative complaints filed by regulatory agencies.
- Other descriptive notes provide detailed information about certain financial statement items such as property, plant, and equipment and long-term debt.
- The **auditor's report** contains the independent auditor's opinion about whether the financial statements are presented fairly in conformity with generally accepted accounting principles. A careful study of this report may alert the reader to weaknesses in financial measurement or disclosure.
- Background information about the firm, its industry, and the economy as a whole may be obtained from business magazines and newspapers, publications of financial research firms, industry trade associations, credit-rating bureaus, and interviews with management.

## 10   KEY TERMS

| | |
|---|---|
| **Accounting policies note** | A description of the various accounting methods that the company has elected to use in preparing its financial statements. |
| **Accounts receivable turnover** | Credit sales divided by average accounts receivable. |
| **Acid test ratio** | See **quick ratio.** |
| **Auditor's report** | An independent auditor's opinion regarding the fairness of presentation of the financial statements. |
| **Average age of receivables** | 365 days divided by accounts receivable turnover. |
| **Common-size financial statement** | A financial statement in which each component is stated as a percentage of one other component. A common-size income statement usually states each component as a percentage of sales. A common-size balance sheet typically presents each item as a percentage of total assets. |

| | |
|---|---|
| **Comparative financial statements** | Presentation of financial statements of more than one period in columnar form. Changes between periods expressed in dollars and/or percentages may also be included. |
| **Contingencies note** | A description of future losses that are probable, reasonably possible, or in some cases remote. The contingencies note explains the nature of the loss situation and, where possible, an estimate or range of estimates of the amount of the loss. |
| **Current ratio** | Current assets divided by current liabilities. |
| **Debt to total assets ratio** | Total liabilities divided by total assets. |
| **Dividend yield rate** | Dividends per share of common stock divided by the current market price of common stock. |
| **Earnings per share (EPS)** | Net income minus preferred dividends divided by the average number of common shares outstanding. |
| **Equity ratio** | See **stockholders' equity to total assets ratio.** |
| **Horizontal analysis** | The comparison of the financial data of a single company for 2 or more years. |
| **Inventory turnover** | Cost of goods sold divided by average merchandise inventory. |
| **Leverage** | The use of debt or preferred stock financing in an attempt to earn a higher rate of return on common stockholders' equity than would have been possible without this financing; also called **trading on the equity.** |
| **Price–earnings ratio** | Market price per share of common stock divided by the earnings per share of common stock. |
| **Quick ratio** | Highly liquid (quick) assets divided by current liabilities; also called the **acid-test ratio.** |
| **Rate of return (ROR) on common stockholders' equity** | Net income minus preferred dividends divided by average common stockholders' equity. |
| **Rate of return (ROR) on total assets** | Income before interest expense divided by average total assets. |
| **Ratio** | An expression of the relationship of two amounts; it results from dividing one amount by the other. |
| **Stockholders' equity to total assets ratio** | Total stockholders' equity divided by total assets; also called the **equity ratio.** |
| **Times interest earned ratio** | Income before interest expense and income taxes divided by annual interest expense. |
| **Trading on the equity** | See **leverage.** |
| **Trend analysis** | The comparison of proportionate changes in selected financial information over time. These proportionate changes are expressed as percentages of amounts in a designated base year. |
| **Vertical analysis** | The comparison of items on financial statements of a single period. |
| **Working capital** | Current assets minus current liabilities. |

## DEMONSTRATION PROBLEM

The comparative balance sheets for 1997 and 1998 and the 1998 income statement for Morris's Costume Shop are as follows:

### MORRIS'S COSTUME SHOP
### Balance Sheet

| | December 31 | |
| --- | ---: | ---: |
| | **1998** | **1997** |
| **Assets:** | | |
| Cash ......................................... | $ 110,000 | $ 36,000 |
| Accounts Receivable ............................ | 220,000 | 360,000 |
| Merchandise Inventory ........................... | 660,000 | 480,000 |
| Property, Plant, and Equipment...................... | 1,540,000 | 1,644,000 |
| Total Assets ................................... | $2,530,000 | $2,520,000 |
| **Liabilities and Shareholders' Equity:** | | |
| Current Liabilities .................................. | $ 495,000 | $ 600,000 |
| Mortgage Payable ................................ | 940,000 | 996,000 |
| Common Stock (150,000 shs outstanding) .............. | 600,000 | 600,000 |
| Retained Earnings ................................ | 495,000 | 324,000 |
| Total Equities ................................... | $2,530,000 | $2,520,000 |

### MORRIS'S COSTUME SHOP
### Income Statement
### For Year Ended December 31, 1998

| | | |
| --- | ---: | ---: |
| Sales ......................................... | | $1,703,000 |
| Less: Cost of Goods Sold ......................... | | 950,000 |
| Gross Profit on Sales............................. | | $ 753,000 |
| Less: Operating Expenses: | | |
| Administrative Expenses....................... | $215,000 | |
| Selling Expenses............................. | 231,000 | |
| Total Operating Expenses ............................ | | 446,000 |
| Operating Income ......................................... | | $ 307,000 |
| Other Expenses: | | |
| Interest Expense .......................................... | | 44,000 |
| Income before Taxes........................................ | | $ 263,000 |
| Income Tax Expense........................................ | | 92,000 |
| Net Income....................................... | | $ 171,000 |

**Additional Information:**

1. Morris's common stock is currently selling for $20.50 per share.

2. Morris's paid a dividend of $1.00 per share during 1998.

**Required:**

Calculate the following ratios and financial statistics:

a. Working capital

b. Current ratio

c. Quick ratio

d. Inventory turnover

e. Accounts receivable turnover (assume that all sales are on credit)

f. Average age of receivables

g. Times interest earned

h. Debt to total assets ratio

i. Stockholders' equity to total assets ratio

j. Rate of return on total assets

k. Rate of return on common stockholders' equity

l. Earnings per share

m. Price–earnings ratio

n. Dividend yield rate

## ■ Solution to Demonstration Problem

a. **Working capital = current assets − current liabilities**

$$= \$110,000 + \$220,000 + \$660,000 - \$495,000$$

$$= \$495,000$$

b. **Current ratio** $= \dfrac{\textbf{current assets}}{\textbf{current liabilities}}$

$$= \frac{\$110,000 + \$220,000 + \$660,000}{\$495,000}$$

$$= 2.0 : 1$$

c. **Quick ratio** $= \dfrac{\textbf{quick assets}}{\textbf{current liabilities}}$

$$= \frac{\$110,000 + \$220,000}{\$495,000}$$

$$= .667 \text{ or } .67 : 1$$

d. **Inventory turnover** $= \dfrac{\textbf{cost of goods sold}}{\textbf{average merchandise inventory}}$

$$= \frac{\$950,000}{(\$660,000 + \$480,000)\,/2}$$

$$= \frac{\$950,000}{\$570,000}$$

$$= 1.67 \text{ times}$$

e. **Accounts receivable turnover** $= \dfrac{\textbf{credit sales}}{\textbf{average accounts receivable}}$

$$= \frac{\$1,703,000}{(\$220,000 + \$360,000)\,/2}$$

$$= \frac{\$1,703,000}{\$290,000}$$

$$= 5.87 \text{ times}$$

f. $\text{Average age of receivables} = \dfrac{365 \text{ days}}{\text{accounts receivable turnover}}$

$$= \dfrac{365 \text{ days}}{5.87 \text{ times}}$$

$$= 62.2 \text{ days}$$

g. $\text{Times interest earned} = \dfrac{\text{income before interest expense and income taxes}}{\text{annual interest expense}}$

$$= \dfrac{\$171,000 + \$44,000 + \$92,000}{\$44,000}$$

$$= \dfrac{\$307,000}{\$44,000}$$

$$= 6.98 \text{ times}$$

h. $\text{Debt to total assets} = \dfrac{\text{total liabilities}}{\text{total assets}}$

$$= \dfrac{\$1,435,000}{\$2,530,000}$$

$$= .567 \text{ or } 56.7\%$$

i. $\text{Stockholders' equity to total assets} = \dfrac{\text{total stockholders' equity}}{\text{total assets}}$

$$= \dfrac{\$1,095,000}{\$2,530,000}$$

$$= .433 \text{ or } 43.3\%$$

j. $\text{Rate of return on total assets} = \dfrac{\text{income before interest expense}}{\text{average total assets}}$

$$= \dfrac{\$171,000 + \$44,000}{(\$2,530,000 + \$2,520,000)\,/2}$$

$$= \dfrac{\$215,000}{\$2,525,000}$$

$$= .085 \text{ or } 8.5\%$$

k. $\text{Rate of return on common stockholders' equity} = \dfrac{\text{net income} - \text{preferred dividends}}{\text{average common stockholders' equity}}$

$$= \dfrac{\$171,000}{(\$1,095,000 + \$924,000)\,/2}$$

$$= \dfrac{\$171,000}{\$1,009,500}$$

$$= .169 \text{ or } 16.9\%$$

l. $\text{Earnings per share} = \dfrac{\text{net income} - \text{preferred dividends}}{\text{average number of common shares outstanding}}$

$$= \dfrac{\$171,000}{150,000}$$

$$= \$1.14$$

m. Price–earnings ratio $= \dfrac{\text{market price per share of common stock}}{\text{earnings per share of common stock}}$

$$= \dfrac{\$20.50}{\$1.14}$$

$$= 17.98 \text{ or } 17.98:1$$

n. Dividend yield rate $= \dfrac{\text{dividends per share of common stock}}{\text{current market price per share of common stock}}$

$$= \dfrac{\$1.00}{\$20.50}$$

$$= 4.88\%$$

---

## QUESTIONS FOR REVIEW AND FURTHER THOUGHT

### REVIEW QUESTIONS

1. Can a horizontal analysis be made of a single year's financial statements? Explain.

2. Jan Investor is calculating trend percentages for sales and net income of Toco, Inc. If Jan selects 1998 as his base year, what will the trend percentages be for 1998? How will he calculate the trend percentages for 1999?

3. Explain how vertical analysis differs from horizontal analysis.

4. Which tool of financial statement analysis is most useful in comparing two companies that are vastly different in size? Explain how this tool makes the comparison possible.

5. Explain how a company's working capital is calculated.

6. What is meant by favorable leverage? Is favorable leverage present in a company that has a rate of return on total assets of 12% and a rate of return on common stockholders' equity of 10%? Explain.

7. How is the dividend yield rate calculated? Would an investor interested primarily in speculating in the growth in the market value of the stock find a high dividend yield rate desirable? Explain.

8. List some external standards against which the performance of a company may be compared.

9. Describe briefly the type of information that you will find in an accounting policies note.

10. What information is contained in each of the three paragraphs of a standard audit report?

11. A serious financial analyst will want to learn more about a company, its industry, and the economy as a whole. What are some sources of this type of background information?

### QUESTIONS FOR FURTHER THOUGHT

1. What is the analyst attempting to learn by studying comparative financial statements?

2. Why is the quick ratio often a better measure of a company's very short-term liquid position than is the current ratio?

3. How is inventory turnover used to evaluate the amount of inventory on hand at the end of a time period?

4. Clyde Co.'s average age of receivables is 35 days. What additional information is necessary before this average can be evaluated as relatively good or bad?

5. What does a times interest earned ratio of .95 mean? How would this statistic be evaluated by a long-term creditor? Explain.

6. Why might an investor prefer a company's common stock as an investment over the company's bonds even though the dividend yield rate on the stock is lower than the interest rate on the bonds?

7. Willco's rate of return on total assets is 11%; what does this rate tell the analyst?

8. "The notes to the financial statements merely amplify the information contained in the statements themselves." Do you agree with this statement? Why or why not?

9. What does the auditor's report say about the truthfulness and accuracy of the company's financial statements?

---

## OBJECTIVE ASSIGNMENT

*True/False*   Indicate whether each statement below is *true* or *false* by placing a *T* or an *F* in the space provided.

_____ 1. Trend analysis is a type of horizontal analysis that compares financial data for several years.

_____ 2. The rate of return on total assets is a measure of management's effectiveness in using the resources invested by common stockholders.

_____ 3. When a company's return on common stockholders' equity exceeds the company's return on total assets, the company has made favorable use of leverage, or trading on the equity.

_____ 4. When a company's working capital increases during the year, the company has created more liquid resources than were used during the year.

_____ 5. The auditor's opinion assures the public that the company's financial statements are error-free.

*Multiple Choice*   Select the best choice to complete each statement or answer each question below. Write the letter corresponding to your choice in the space provided.

_____ 1. The vertical analysis technique that shows each item on a financial statement as a percentage of one key item on that statement is known as:
   a. Trend analysis
   b. Comparative financial statements
   c. Common-size financial statements
   d. Working capital schedule

_____ 2. FPB, Inc., reported the following amounts in its 1998 financial statements:

| | |
|---|---|
| Current assets . . . . . . . . . . . . . . . . . . . . . . . . . . . . | $180,000 |
| Current liabilities. . . . . . . . . . . . . . . . . . . . . . . . . | 90,000 |
| Stockholders' equity. . . . . . . . . . . . . . . . . . . . . . | 210,000 |
| Total assets . . . . . . . . . . . . . . . . . . . . . . . . . . . . . | 600,000 |
| Total liabilities. . . . . . . . . . . . . . . . . . . . . . . . . . | 390,000 |

What is the company's stockholders' equity to total assets ratio?
   a. .35
   b. .462
   c. .538
   d. .65

_____ 3. Given the information for FPB, Inc., in question (2), determine the company's working capital.
   a. $180,000
   b. $210,000
   c. $90,000
   d. $600,000

_____ 4. Which of the following assets would be used in computing the current ratio but not in computing the quick ratio?
   a. Accounts receivable
   b. Cash
   c. Temporary investments
   d. Merchandise inventory

_____ 5. PMK Corp. reported the following amounts in its 1998 financial statements:

| | |
|---|---:|
| Beginning inventory | $200,000 |
| Cost of goods sold | 600,000 |
| Ending inventory | 280,000 |
| Sales | 900,000 |

What is the company's inventory turnover?
a. 2.5    c. 3.75
b. 3.0    d. 4.5

_____ 6. Watmax Co. reported the following amounts in its 1998 financial statements:

| | |
|---|---:|
| Beginning accounts receivable | $ 250,000 |
| Cost of goods sold | 1,200,000 |
| Credit sales | 1,800,000 |
| Ending accounts receivable | 150,000 |

What is the average age of the company's accounts receivable?
a. 30.4 days    c. 50.7 days
b. 40.6 days    d. 60.8 days

_____ 7. Which of the following is considered an earnings performance ratio?
a. Accounts receivable turnover    c. Working capital
b. Rate of return on total assets    d. Inventory turnover

_____ 8. The ratio that shows the percentage of the company's assets financed by debt is the:
a. Rate of return on common stockholders' equity
b. Acid test ratio
c. Debt to total assets ratio
d. Stockholders' equity to total assets ratio

_____ 9. The two ratios that are compared in evaluating a company's use of leverage are:
a. Current ratio and debt to total assets ratio
b. Accounts receivable turnover and average age of receivables
c. Price–earnings ratio and dividend yield rate
d. Rate of return on total assets and rate of return on common stockholders' equity

_____ 10. To learn which inventory method a company has chosen to use, one could look in the:
a. Contingencies note
b. Accounting policies note
c. Auditor's report
d. _Wall Street Journal_

## EXERCISES

2† **Exercise 1:** Calculating Trend Percentages

Pro Foods, Inc., is concerned about the level of its advertising and office salaries expense. Selected income statement data for the past 3 years appear below:

| | 1998 | 1997 | 1996 |
|---|---:|---:|---:|
| Sales | $140,000 | $60,000 | $37,500 |
| Gross Profit | 89,600 | 37,200 | 22,500 |
| Advertising Expense | 7,000 | 3,300 | 2,250 |
| Office Salaries Expense | 22,400 | 9,000 | 4,500 |
| Net Income | 30,800 | 13,800 | 9,000 |

Calculate trend percentages for sales, advertising expense, and office salaries expense. Use 1996 as a base year. Round to the nearest percent.

▶ _(Check Figure: 1998 advertising expense = 311%)_

† The numbers in the margin refer to the Learning Objectives.

3  **Exercise 2:** Preparing a Common-Size Income Statement

Convert the following income statement into a common-size statement that uses sales as 100%.

| TUCKER, INC.<br>Income Statement<br>Year Ended September 30, 1998 | | |
|---|---|---|
| Sales . . . . . . . . . . . . . . . . . . . . . . . . . . . . . . . . . . . . . . . . . . . . . . . . . . | | $180,000 |
| Cost of Goods Sold. . . . . . . . . . . . . . . . . . . . . . . . . . . . . . . . . . . . . . | | 99,000 |
| Gross Profit on Sales . . . . . . . . . . . . . . . . . . . . . . . . . . . . . . . . . . . . . | | $ 81,000 |
| Operating Expenses: | | |
|    Selling Expenses . . . . . . . . . . . . . . . . . . . . . . . . . . . . . . . . . . | $43,200 | |
|    General and Administrative Expenses . . . . . . . . . . . . . . . . . . . . | 16,200 | 59,400 |
| Income before Income Taxes. . . . . . . . . . . . . . . . . . . . . . . . . . . . . . . . . | | $ 21,600 |
| Provision for Income Taxes . . . . . . . . . . . . . . . . . . . . . . . . . . . . . . . . . | | 9,720 |
| Net Income . . . . . . . . . . . . . . . . . . . . . . . . . . . . . . . . . . . . . . . . . . . . . | | $ 11,880 |

▶ *(Check Figure: Selling expenses = 24%)*

4  **Exercise 3:** Calculating Three Liquid Position Ratios

The following information was taken from the balance sheet of Ready Corp.:

| | |
|---|---|
| Cash . . . . . . . . . . . . . . . . . . . . . . . . . . . . . . . . | $13,250 |
| Accounts Receivable (net) . . . . . . . . . . . . . . . . . . | 33,000 |
| Merchandise Inventory . . . . . . . . . . . . . . . . . . . . . | 40,000 |
| Prepaid Expenses. . . . . . . . . . . . . . . . . . . . . . . . . | 9,950 |
| Accounts Payable. . . . . . . . . . . . . . . . . . . . . . . . . | 25,200 |
| Accrued Payables. . . . . . . . . . . . . . . . . . . . . . . . . | 1,800 |
| Notes Payable (due in 6 months). . . . . . . . . . . . . . | 10,000 |

Calculate:

a. Working capital    b. Current ratio    c. Quick ratio

▶ *(Check Figure: Current ratio = 2.6 : 1)*

4  **Exercise 4:** Calculating Inventory and Receivables Ratios

You have been assigned the task of evaluating Jesup, Inc.'s, management of merchandise and receivables. You decide that inventory turnover, accounts receivable turnover, and average age of receivables statistics will prove valuable in your analysis. The following data are available from Jesup's annual report:

| | |
|---|---|
| Merchandise Inventory: | |
|    Jan. 1. . . . . . . . . . . . . . . . . . . . . . . . . . . . . . . . . . . . . . . . . . . . . . . . . . | $ 245,000 |
|    Dec. 31 . . . . . . . . . . . . . . . . . . . . . . . . . . . . . . . . . . . . . . . . . . . . . . . . | 375,000 |
| Accounts Receivable: | |
|    Jan. 1. . . . . . . . . . . . . . . . . . . . . . . . . . . . . . . . . . . . . . . . . . . . . . . . . . | 250,000 |
|    Dec. 31 . . . . . . . . . . . . . . . . . . . . . . . . . . . . . . . . . . . . . . . . . . . . . . . . | 297,000 |
| Cost of Goods Sold . . . . . . . . . . . . . . . . . . . . . . . . . . . . . . . . . . . . . . . . | 2,480,000 |
| Cash Sales . . . . . . . . . . . . . . . . . . . . . . . . . . . . . . . . . . . . . . . . . . . . . . | 1,000,000 |
| Total Sales . . . . . . . . . . . . . . . . . . . . . . . . . . . . . . . . . . . . . . . . . . . . . . | 5,100,000 |
| Jesup's Credit Terms . . . . . . . . . . . . . . . . . . . . . . . . . . . . . . . . . . . . . . | Net 30 days |

a. Calculate inventory turnover, accounts receivable turnover, and average age of receivables.
b. In your opinion, is Jesup doing a good job of managing inventory and receivables? Explain.

▶ *(Check Figure: Accounts receivable turnover = 15 times)*

4   **Exercise 5:** Calculating Liquid Position Ratios

You have been asked to evaluate the liquid positon of Macon Fitness Center. The following data are from Macon's annual report:

| | |
|---|---:|
| Cash. . . . . . . . . . . . . . . . . . . . . . . . . . . . . . . . . . . . . . . . . . . . . . . . . . . . . . . . | $  130,000 |
| Temporary Investments. . . . . . . . . . . . . . . . . . . . . . . . . . . . . . . . . . . | 60,000 |
| Accounts Receivable: | |
| Jan. 1 . . . . . . . . . . . . . . . . . . . . . . . . . . . . . . . . . . . . . . . . . . . . . . | 156,000 |
| Dec. 31. . . . . . . . . . . . . . . . . . . . . . . . . . . . . . . . . . . . . . . . . . . . | 214,000 |
| Merchandise Inventory: | |
| Jan. 1 . . . . . . . . . . . . . . . . . . . . . . . . . . . . . . . . . . . . . . . . . . . . . . | 252,000 |
| Dec. 31. . . . . . . . . . . . . . . . . . . . . . . . . . . . . . . . . . . . . . . . . . . . | 186,000 |
| Current Liabilities. . . . . . . . . . . . . . . . . . . . . . . . . . . . . . . . . . . . . . | 240,000 |
| Cost of Goods Sold . . . . . . . . . . . . . . . . . . . . . . . . . . . . . . . . . . . . . | 3,000,000 |
| Credit Sales . . . . . . . . . . . . . . . . . . . . . . . . . . . . . . . . . . . . . . . . . . . | 5,000,000 |

Using these data, calculate Macon's:

a. Working capital    c. Quick ratio       e. Accounts receivable turnover
b. Current ratio      d. Inventory turnover f. Average age of receivables

▶ *(Check Figure: Inventory turnover = 13.7 times)*

5   **Exercise 6:** Calculating Three Debt-Paying Ability Ratios

The president of Tifton Togs, Inc., has asked you to gather some statistics about his company's debt-paying ability. You have compiled the following data:

| | |
|---|---:|
| Net income . . . . . . . . . . . . . . . . . . . . . . . . . . . . . | $900,000 |
| Income tax rate. . . . . . . . . . . . . . . . . . . . . . . . . . | 40% |
| Interest expense. . . . . . . . . . . . . . . . . . . . . . . . . | 100,000 |
| Total liabilities. . . . . . . . . . . . . . . . . . . . . . . . . . . | 2,048,000 |
| Total stockholders' equity. . . . . . . . . . . . . . . . . | 4,352,000 |

Using these data, calculate:

a. Times interest earned
b. Debt to total assets ratio
c. Stockholders' equity to total assets ratio

▶ *(Check Figure: Times interest earned = 16 times)*

6   **Exercise 7:** Calculating Earnings Performance Ratios

The following data are from the financial statements of Rome, Inc:

| | Dec. 31, 1998 | Jan. 1, 1998 |
|---|---:|---:|
| Total Assets. . . . . . . . . . . . . . . . . . . . . . . . . . . . . . . . . . . . . . | $180,000 | $140,000 |
| Total Stockholders' Equity. . . . . . . . . . . . . . . . . . . . . . . | 144,000 | 112,000 |
| Total Preferred Stockholders' Equity . . . . . . . . . . . . . . | 30,000 | 30,000 |
| Preferred Dividends Declared. . . . . . . . . . . . . . . . . . . . | 2,400 | — |
| Net Income . . . . . . . . . . . . . . . . . . . . . . . . . . . . . . . . . . . | 20,000 | — |
| Interest Expense . . . . . . . . . . . . . . . . . . . . . . . . . . . . . . | 5,750 | — |

Calculate the following ratios:

a. Rate of return on total assets
b. Rate of return on common stockholders' equity

▶ *(Check Figure: Rate of return on common stockholders' equity = 17.96%)*

6 **Exercise 8:** Calculating Three Earnings Performance Ratios

N. Vester is analyzing the earnings performance of the Bowden Transport Corp. She has gathered the following data from Bowden's financial statements and from a report of the closing market prices of stock:

Net income for 1998 . . . . . . . . . . . . . . . . . . $743,000
Preferred dividends declared
during 1998 . . . . . . . . . . . . . . . . . . . . . . . . . 60,000
Common dividends declared
Dec. 31, 1998 . . . . . . . . . . . . . . . . . . . . . . . 620,000
Number of shares of Bowden common
stock outstanding:
    Jan. 1, 1998 . . . . . . . . . . . . . . . . . . . . . . 1,100,000 shs
    Dec. 31, 1998 . . . . . . . . . . . . . . . . . . . . 1,300,000 shs
Market price per share of common
stock on Dec. 31, 1998 . . . . . . . . . . . . . . . . $15

Calculate the following ratios relating to the Bowden stock:

a. Earnings per share of common stock
b. The price–earnings ratio
c. The dividend yield rate on common stock

▶ *(Check Figure: Earnings per share of common stock = $.569)*

6 **Exercise 9:** Calculating Ratios to Evaluate the Use of Leverage

You have been asked to evaluate Marietta Hardware and Tate Building Supply to determine which one is doing the better job of using leverage to increase the return to common stockholders. The data for the two firms are presented below.

| Marietta Hardware | | Tate Building Supply | |
|---|---|---|---|
| Total Assets: | | Total Assets: | |
|   Jan. 1 . . . . . . . . . . . . . . . | $1,340,000 |   Jan. 1 . . . . . . . . . . . . . . . | $250,000 |
|   Dec. 31 . . . . . . . . . . . . . . | 1,500,000 |   Dec. 31 . . . . . . . . . . . . . . | 280,000 |
| Total Stockholders' Equity: | | Total Stockholders' Equity: | |
|   Jan. 1 . . . . . . . . . . . . . . . | 650,000 |   Jan. 1 . . . . . . . . . . . . . . . | 150,000 |
|   Dec. 31 . . . . . . . . . . . . . . | 830,000 |   Dec. 31 . . . . . . . . . . . . . . | 175,000 |
| Interest Expense . . . . . . . . | 64,000 | Interest Expense . . . . . . . . | 10,000 |
| Net Income. . . . . . . . . . . . | 156,000 | Net Income. . . . . . . . . . . . | 37,500 |

a. Calculate the rate of return on total assets and the rate of return on common stockholders' equity for both firms.
b. In your opinion, which firm is making the better use of leverage to increase the return to common stockholders?

▶ *(Check Figure: Marietta's ROR on common stockholders' equity = 21.08%)*

4 **Exercise 10:** Calculating Missing Balance Sheet Amounts

You are given the following ratios and amounts for the Elijay Corp. for 1998:

Current ratio . . . . . . . . . . . . . . . . . . . . . . . . . . . . 2.7
Quick ratio. . . . . . . . . . . . . . . . . . . . . . . . . . . . . 1.17
Inventory turnover. . . . . . . . . . . . . . . . . . . . . . . 3.4
Accounts receivable turnover . . . . . . . . . . . . . . . 6.5
Cost of goods sold for 1998 . . . . . . . . . . . . . . . $197,200
Credit sales for 1998 . . . . . . . . . . . . . . . . . . . . . 260,000
Accounts receivable, Jan. 1, 1998 . . . . . . . . . . . 38,200
Merchandise inventory, Jan. 1, 1998 . . . . . . . . . 62,000

**ELIJAY CORP.**
**Schedule of Current Assets**
**and Current Liabilities**
**December 31, 1998**

Current Assets:

| | | |
|---|---|---|
| Cash ......................................................... | | $ 5,000 |
| Accounts Receivable..................................... | (2) | ———— |
| Merchandise Inventory .................................. | (3) | ———— |
| Prepaid Insurance........................................ | | 7,200 |
|    Total Current Assets .................................... | (1) | $———— |
| Current Liabilities: | | |
| Accounts Payable ........................................ | (4) | $———— |
| Accrued Payables........................................ | | 5,000 |
|    Total Current Liabilities ................................. | | $40,000 |

Supply the missing amounts in this schedule. *Hint:* Do your calculations in the numerical order indicated in the schedule (total current assets first, etc.).

▶ *(Check Figure: Total current assets = $108,000)*

## PROBLEMS: SET A

1†    **Problem A1:** Completing and Analyzing Comparative Statements

The comparative balance sheets and income statements that follow are included in the 1998 annual report of Federal Company:

**FEDERAL COMPANY**
**Comparative Balance Sheets**
**(000's omitted)**

| | June 30 | |
|---|---|---|
| | **1998** | **1997** |
| **Assets** | | |
| Current Assets: | | |
| Cash ......................................... | $ 31,600 | $ 6,000 |
| Accounts Receivable (Net of Allowances for | | |
|   Uncollectibles of $560 in 1998 and $192 in 1997) ....... | 19,200 | 9,600 |
| Merchandise Inventory.............................. | 22,100 | 20,000 |
|    Total Current Assets............................ | $ 72,900 | $ 35,600 |
| Property, Plant, and Equipment: | | |
| Land ......................................... | $ 80,000 | $ 90,000 |
| Buildings...................................... | 20,000 | 20,000 |
| Less: Accumulated Depreciation ..................... | (2,700) | (2,500) |
| Equipment..................................... | 15,000 | 14,000 |
| Less: Accumulated Depreciation ..................... | (2,000) | (1,500) |
|    Total Property, Plant, and Equipment .............. | $110,300 | $120,000 |
| Intangibles: | | |
| Patents ....................................... | $ 1,500 | $ 1,600 |
| Total Assets ..................................... | $184,700 | $157,200 |

*(Continued)*

† The numbers in the margin refer to the Learning Objectives.

### Liabilities and Stockholders' Equity

| | | |
|---|---|---|
| **Current Liabilities:** | | |
| Accounts Payable.................................... | $ 20,000 | $ 16,600 |
| Accrued Payables.................................... | 3,500 | 3,000 |
| Total Current Liabilities............................ | $ 23,500 | $ 19,600 |
| | | |
| **Long-Term Liabilities:** | | |
| 8% Note Payable (Due in 2000) ..................... | $ 12,000 | — |
| 10% Bonds Payable (Due in 2005) ................... | 81,000 | 81,000 |
| Total Long-Term Liabilities......................... | $ 93,000 | $ 81,000 |
| Total Liabilities................................... | $116,500 | $100,600 |
| | | |
| **Stockholders' Equity:** | | |
| Common Stock, $1-par ............................. | $ 10,000 | $ 10,000 |
| Paid-In Capital in Excess of Par ..................... | 26,400 | 26,400 |
| Retained Earnings ................................. | 31,800 | 20,200 |
| Total Stockholders' Equity ......................... | $ 68,200 | $ 56,600 |
| | | |
| Total Liabilities and Stockholders' Equity ................ | $184,700 | $157,200 |

### FEDERAL COMPANY
### Comparative Income Statements
### Years Ended June 30 (000's omitted)

| | 1998 | 1997 |
|---|---|---|
| Net Sales ......................................... | $160,000 | $104,000 |
| Cost of Goods Sold ................................. | 59,200 | 37,500 |
| Gross Profit on Sales ................................ | $100,800 | $ 66,500 |
| | | |
| **Operating Expenses:** | | |
| Sales Salary Expense................................ | $ 25,800 | $ 21,600 |
| Utilities Expense ................................... | 14,000 | 11,800 |
| Advertising Expense................................. | 27,200 | 16,800 |
| Other Expenses .................................... | 5,000 | 4,200 |
| Total Operating Expenses ......................... | $ 72,000 | $ 54,400 |
| | | |
| **Other Income and Expenses:** | | |
| Interest Expense.................................... | $ 10,000 | $ 8,600 |
| Income before Income Taxes.......................... | $ 18,800 | $ 3,500 |
| Provision for Income Taxes ........................... | 7,200 | 1,200 |
| | | |
| Net Income ........................................ | $ 11,600 | $ 2,300 |

**Required:**

1. Comparative income statements and balance sheets for 1998 and 1997 are presented above. Prepare columns showing the amount and percentage increase or decrease for each item on the statements.

2. Use your solution for part (1) to answer the following questions:
   a. Which three balance sheet accounts experienced the greatest percentage change?
   b. Which three revenue or expense accounts on the income statement had the highest percentage change?
   c. Does the large increase in current assets appear to have been generated by profits for the year? Explain.
   d. Sales in 1998 increased over 1997. Did expenses seem to increase proportionately? Comment on any exceptions.

▶ (Check Figure: Income statement items with the highest percentage change = Provision for Income Taxes, Cost of Goods Sold, Advertising Expense)

3  **Problem A2:** Preparing and Analyzing Common-Size Income
Statements

Inman, Inc., and Reno Co. are in the same industry and have the same fiscal years, ending on
Aug. 31. Income statements for the two companies appear below.

| INMAN, INC. Income Statement Year Ended August 31, 1998 | | |
|---|---|---|
| Sales | | $150,000 |
| Cost of Goods Sold | | 105,000 |
| Gross Profit | | $ 45,000 |
| Operating Expenses: | | |
| Selling | $15,000 | |
| General and Administrative | 9,000 | |
| Total Operating Expenses | | 24,000 |
| Income from Operations | | $ 21,000 |
| Other Income and Expenses: | | |
| Interest Expense | | 7,000 |
| Income before Taxes | | $ 14,000 |
| Provision for Income Taxes | | 4,600 |
| Net Income | | $ 9,400 |

| RENO CO. Income Statement Year Ended August 31, 1998 | | |
|---|---|---|
| Sales | | $1,440,000 |
| Cost of Goods Sold | | 849,600 |
| Gross Profit | | $ 590,400 |
| Operating Expenses: | | |
| Selling | $216,000 | |
| General and Administrative | 144,000 | |
| Total Operating Expenses | | 360,000 |
| Income from Operations | | $ 230,400 |
| Other Income and Expenses: | | |
| Interest Expense | | 122,400 |
| Income before Taxes | | $108,000 |
| Provision for Income Taxes | | 36,000 |
| Net Income | | $ 72,000 |

**Required:**

1. Prepare common-size income statements for Inman, Inc., and Reno Co.
2. Compare percentages for cost of goods sold, selling expenses, general and administrative
   expenses, and interest expense. What factors may have caused differences in these percentages? Which company is earning more profit per dollar of sales?

4 **Problem A3:** Calculating Liquid Position Ratios

Rome, Inc., and Albany Company both sell irrigation equipment for agricultural use. Both companies have applied for a short-term loan. Data from the Dec. 31, 1998, balance sheets appear below:

| | Rome, Inc. | Albany Co. |
|---|---|---|
| Cash. | $ 27,200 | $ 75,000 |
| Temporary Investments. | 1,800 | 60,000 |
| Accounts Receivable (Net) | 31,000 | 44,000 |
| Merchandise Inventory | 180,000 | 120,000 |
| Property, Plant, and Equipment (Net). | 350,000 | 360,000 |
| Intangibles | 1,800 | — |
| Total Assets. | $591,800 | $659,000 |
| | | |
| Current Liabilities. | $ 60,000 | $100,000 |
| Long-Term Liabilities. | 100,000 | 100,000 |
| Common Stock, $10-par. | 400,000 | 400,000 |
| Retained Earnings. | 31,800 | 59,000 |
| Total Equities. | $591,800 | $659,000 |

**Other Information:**

| | Rome, Inc. | Albany Co. |
|---|---|---|
| Accounts Receivable, Jan. 1, 1998 | $ 39,000 | $ 35,000 |
| Merchandise Inventory, Jan. 1, 1998 | 160,000 | 130,000 |
| 1998 Sales: | | |
| Cash. | 258,000 | 120,000 |
| Credit | 342,000 | 480,000 |
| 1998 Cost of Goods Sold | 528,000 | 360,000 |

**Required:**

1. Calculate for each company the current ratio, quick ratio, inventory turnover, accounts receivable turnover, and average age of receivables.
2. Which company would you recommend to receive the short-term loan? Explain.
3. What additional ratios would you consider if the companies were requesting a long-term loan? Explain.

▶ *(Check Figure: Albany Co.'s quick ratio = 1.8:1)*

4  5  6  **Problem A4:** Calculating Ratios and Evaluating the Use of Leverage

Brunswick, Inc.'s, income statement and balance sheet for 1998 are presented below:

## BRUNSWICK, INC.
### Income Statement
### Year Ended October 31, 1998

| | | |
|---|---:|---:|
| Sales . . . . . . . . . . . . . . . . . . . . . . . . . . . . . . . . . . . . . . . . . . . . . | | $900,000 |
| Cost of Goods Sold: | | |
|   Merchandise Inventory, Nov. 1, 1997. . . . . . . . . . . . . . . . . . | $ 82,500 | |
|   Purchases (Net) . . . . . . . . . . . . . . . . . . . . . . . . . . . . . . . . . . | 375,000 | |
|   Goods Available for Sale . . . . . . . . . . . . . . . . . . . . . . . . . . . . | $457,500 | |
|   Merchandise Inventory, Oct. 31, 1998 . . . . . . . . . . . . . . . . . . | 97,500 | |
|   Cost of Goods Sold. . . . . . . . . . . . . . . . . . . . . . . . . . . . . . . . | | 360,000 |
| Gross Profit. . . . . . . . . . . . . . . . . . . . . . . . . . . . . . . . . . . . . . . . | | $540,000 |
| Operating Expenses. . . . . . . . . . . . . . . . . . . . . . . . . . . . . . . . . . | | 375,000 |
| Income from Operations. . . . . . . . . . . . . . . . . . . . . . . . . . . . . . . | | $165,000 |
| Other Income and Expenses: | | |
|   Interest Expense. . . . . . . . . . . . . . . . . . . . . . . . . . . . . . . . . . | | 6,000 |
| Income before Taxes . . . . . . . . . . . . . . . . . . . . . . . . . . . . . . . . . | | $159,000 |
| Provision for Income Taxes . . . . . . . . . . . . . . . . . . . . . . . . . . . . | | 72,000 |
| Net Income . . . . . . . . . . . . . . . . . . . . . . . . . . . . . . . . . . . . . . . . | | $ 87,000 |

## BRUNSWICK, INC.
### Balance Sheet
### October 31, 1998

### Assets

| | |
|---|---:|
| Cash . . . . . . . . . . . . . . . . . . . . . . . . . . . . . . . . . . . . . . . . . . . . . . . . . . . . . . . . . . | $ 11,250 |
| Temporary Investments . . . . . . . . . . . . . . . . . . . . . . . . . . . . . . . . . . . . . . . . . . . | 16,200 |
| Accounts Receivable (Net). . . . . . . . . . . . . . . . . . . . . . . . . . . . . . . . . . . . . . . . . | 28,950 |
| Merchandise Inventory . . . . . . . . . . . . . . . . . . . . . . . . . . . . . . . . . . . . . . . . . . . . | 97,500 |
| Property, Plant, and Equipment (Net) . . . . . . . . . . . . . . . . . . . . . . . . . . . . . . . | 240,000 |
| Patents . . . . . . . . . . . . . . . . . . . . . . . . . . . . . . . . . . . . . . . . . . . . . . . . . . . . . . . . | 8,100 |
| Total Assets . . . . . . . . . . . . . . . . . . . . . . . . . . . . . . . . . . . . . . . . . . . . . . . . . . . . | $402,000 |

### Liabilities and Owners' Equity

| | |
|---|---:|
| Accounts Payable. . . . . . . . . . . . . . . . . . . . . . . . . . . . . . . . . . . . . . . . . . . . . . . . . | $ 24,300 |
| Accrued Salaries Payable . . . . . . . . . . . . . . . . . . . . . . . . . . . . . . . . . . . . . . . . . . | 4,050 |
| Income Taxes Payable. . . . . . . . . . . . . . . . . . . . . . . . . . . . . . . . . . . . . . . . . . . . . | 14,400 |
| 8% Bonds Payable (Due in 2003) . . . . . . . . . . . . . . . . . . . . . . . . . . . . . . . . . . . | 75,000 |
| Common Stock ($10-Par). . . . . . . . . . . . . . . . . . . . . . . . . . . . . . . . . . . . . . . . . . | 150,000 |
| Retained Earnings . . . . . . . . . . . . . . . . . . . . . . . . . . . . . . . . . . . . . . . . . . . . . . . . | 134,250 |
| Total Liabilities and Stockholders' Equity. . . . . . . . . . . . . . . . . . . . . . . . . . . . . | $402,000 |

Of all sales, 60% were on credit. On Nov. 1, 1997, Brunswick had total assets of $348,000 (including accounts receivable of $31,050 and merchandise inventory of $82,500), total liabilities of $151,500, and total stockholders' equity of $196,500.

**Required:**

1. Calculate the following ratios:
   a. Rate of return on total assets
   b. Rate of return on common stockholders' equity
   c. Working capital
   d. Current ratio
   e. Quick ratio
   f. Inventory turnover
   g. Accounts receivable turnover
   h. Average age of receivables
   i. Times interest earned
   j. Debt to total assets ratio
   k. Stockholders' equity to total assets ratio
2. In your opinion, is the company using leverage to increase the return to common stockholders?
3. What does the company's current ratio and quick ratio tell you about the composition of current assets?
4. Given that the company's credit terms are net 10 days, do you think that the company is managing its accounts receivable effectively?

▶ *(Check Figure: Average age of receivables = 20.28 days)*

## 6 **Problem A5:** Calculating Earnings Performance Ratios

The following financial data have been assembled for Americus Coatings, Inc., on Dec. 31, 1998:

| | |
|---|---|
| Average total assets for 1998. . . . . . . . . . . . . . . | $400,000 |
| Total stockholders' equity (average for 1998) . . . . | 300,000 |
| Common stock, $2-par . . . . . . . . . . . . . . . . . . . . . | 175,000 |
| 8% preferred stock, $50-par . . . . . . . . . . . . . . . . . | 75,000 |
| Net income . . . . . . . . . . . . . . . . . . . . . . . . . . . . . | 31,000 |
| Interest expense . . . . . . . . . . . . . . . . . . . . . . . . . . | 3,000 |
| Provision for income taxes (40% of income before income taxes) | |
| Market price of common stock, Dec. 31, 1998 . . . . . . | 2.75 |
| Market price of preferred stock, Dec. 31, 1998 . . . . . | 60.00 |
| Common dividends were paid at the rate of $.10 per share per quarter. | |
| Preferred dividends were declared and paid. | |
| No preferred stock or common stock was issued or reacquired during 1998. | |

**Required:**

Using whatever data you need from the above list, calculate:

1. Rate of return on total assets
2. Rate of return on common stockholders' equity
3. Earnings per common share
4. Price–earnings ratio
5. Dividend yield rate

▶ *(Check Figure: Dividend yield rate = 14.5%)*

4 5 6 **Problem A6:** Calculating Liquid Position, Debt-Paying Ability, and Earnings Performance Ratios

Morrow, Inc.'s, income statement and balance sheet for 1998 are presented below:

### MORROW, INC.
### Income Statement
### Year Ended August 31, 1998

| | | |
|---|---:|---:|
| Sales . . . . . . . . . . . . . . . . . . . . . . . . . . . . . . . . . . . . . . . . . . . . | | $150,000 |
| Cost of Goods Sold: | | |
| Merchandise Inventory, Sept. 1, 1997 . . . . . . . . . . . . . . . . . . | $ 24,000 | |
| Purchases (Net) . . . . . . . . . . . . . . . . . . . . . . . . . . . . . . | 99,000 | |
| Goods Available for Sale . . . . . . . . . . . . . . . . . . . . . . . . . | $123,000 | |
| Merchandise Inventory, Aug. 31, 1998 . . . . . . . . . . . . . . . . | 18,000 | |
| Cost of Goods Sold . . . . . . . . . . . . . . . . . . . . . . . . . . . . . | | 105,000 |
| Gross Profit . . . . . . . . . . . . . . . . . . . . . . . . . . . . . . . . . . . . . | | $ 45,000 |
| Operating Expenses . . . . . . . . . . . . . . . . . . . . . . . . . . . . . . . | | 24,000 |
| Income from Operations . . . . . . . . . . . . . . . . . . . . . . . . . . . . | | $ 21,000 |
| Other Income and Expenses: | | |
| Interest Expense . . . . . . . . . . . . . . . . . . . . . . . . . . . . . . . . | | 7,000 |
| Income before Taxes . . . . . . . . . . . . . . . . . . . . . . . . . . . . . . | | $ 14,000 |
| Provision for Income Taxes . . . . . . . . . . . . . . . . . . . . . . . . . | | 4,900 |
| Net Income . . . . . . . . . . . . . . . . . . . . . . . . . . . . . . . . . . . . | | $ 9,100 |

### MORROW, INC.
### Balance Sheet
### August 31, 1998

#### Assets

| | |
|---|---:|
| Cash . . . . . . . . . . . . . . . . . . . . . . . . . . . . . . . . . . . . . . . . . . . | $ 6,000 |
| Temporary Investments . . . . . . . . . . . . . . . . . . . . . . . . . . . . . . . | 3,000 |
| Accounts Receivable (Net) . . . . . . . . . . . . . . . . . . . . . . . . . . . . . | 17,000 |
| Merchandise Inventory . . . . . . . . . . . . . . . . . . . . . . . . . . . . . . . | 18,000 |
| Property, Plant, and Equipment (Net) . . . . . . . . . . . . . . . . . . . . . . | 160,000 |
| Goodwill . . . . . . . . . . . . . . . . . . . . . . . . . . . . . . . . . . . . . . . . | 6,000 |
| Total Assets . . . . . . . . . . . . . . . . . . . . . . . . . . . . . . . . . . . . . . | $210,000 |

#### Liabilities and Owners' Equity

| | |
|---|---:|
| Accounts Payable . . . . . . . . . . . . . . . . . . . . . . . . . . . . . . . . . . . | $ 16,000 |
| Accrued Salaries Payable . . . . . . . . . . . . . . . . . . . . . . . . . . . . . | 2,000 |
| Income Taxes Payable . . . . . . . . . . . . . . . . . . . . . . . . . . . . . . . | 1,500 |
| Other Accrued Payables . . . . . . . . . . . . . . . . . . . . . . . . . . . . . . | 500 |
| 10% Note Payable (Due in 2008) . . . . . . . . . . . . . . . . . . . . . . . . | 60,000 |
| 6% Preferred Stock ($100-Par) . . . . . . . . . . . . . . . . . . . . . . . . . | 20,000 |
| Common Stock ($2.50-Par) . . . . . . . . . . . . . . . . . . . . . . . . . . . . | 70,000 |
| Retained Earnings . . . . . . . . . . . . . . . . . . . . . . . . . . . . . . . . . . | 40,000 |
| Total Liabilities and Stockholders' Equity . . . . . . . . . . . . . . . . . . . . | $210,000 |

**Other information:**

a. All sales were on credit.

b. On Sept. 1, 1997, Morrow had total assets of $240,000 (including accounts receivable of $13,000 and merchandise inventory of $24,000), total liabilities of $127,600, and total stockholders' equity of $112,400.

c. Morrow paid a $.25 per share dividend to common stockholders and the required dividend to preferred stockholders.
d. No preferred or common stock was issued during the year.
e. The market price of Morrow common stock was $8.00 on Aug. 31, 1998.

### Required:

1. Calculate the following liquid position ratios: current ratio, quick ratio, inventory turnover, and accounts receivable turnover.
2. Calculate the following ratios indicating debt-paying ability: times interest earned, debt to total assets ratio, and stockholders' equity to total assets ratio.
3. Calculate the following earnings performance statistics: rate of return on total assets, rate of return on common stockholders' equity, earnings per share, price–earnings ratio, and dividend yield rate.

▶ *(Check Figure: Debt to total assets ratio = 38.1%)*

4 5 6 **Problem A7:** Completing Financial Statements Given Selected Data

The following financial information is available for Dallas Machinery Corp.:

a. All sales were on credit.
b. The debt to total assets ratio is 52%.
c. Working capital is $828.
d. Net income is 14% of sales; gross profit is 65% of sales.
e. The only interest paid was on long-term debt.
f. Inventory turnover = 5. (Beginning inventory = $150.)
g. Accounts Receivable turnover = 10. (Beginning Accounts Receivable = $240.)
h. Of the total cost of the building, 46% has been depreciated.

### Required:

Complete the Dallas Machinery Corp. financial statements shown below. Round all calculations to the nearest dollar. (*Hint:* Do your calculations in the numerical order indicated in the statements.)

---

**DALLAS MACHINERY CORP.**
**Income Statement**
**Year Ended December 31, 1998**

| | | |
|---|---|---|
| Sales........................................... | (1) | $_____ |
| Cost of Goods Sold ....................................... | (3) | _____ |
| Gross Profit on Sales ....................................... | (2) | _____ |
| Operating Expenses....................................... | (15) | _____ |
| Interest Expense........................................... | (14) | _____ |
| Income before Income Taxes................................... | (4) | _____ |
| Provision for Income Taxes (34.67% of income before income taxes) ........................................ | (5) | _____ |
| Net Income ......................................... | | $ 392 |

### DALLAS MACHINERY CORP.
### Balance Sheet
### December 31, 1998

#### Assets

| | | |
|---|---|---|
| Cash . . . . . . . . . . . . . . . . . . . . . . . . . . . . . . . . . . . . . . . . . . . . . . . | | $ 418 |
| Accounts Receivable (Net) . . . . . . . . . . . . . . . . . . . . . . . . . . . . . . . . | (6) | _____ |
| Merchandise Inventory . . . . . . . . . . . . . . . . . . . . . . . . . . . . . . . . . . | (7) | _____ |
| Building . . . . . . . . . . . . . . . . . . . . . . . . . . . . . . . . . . . . . . . . . . . . . | (10) | _____ |
| Accumulated Depreciation . . . . . . . . . . . . . . . . . . . . . . . . . . . . . . . | (11) | (_____) |
| Total Assets. . . . . . . . . . . . . . . . . . . . . . . . . . . . . . . . . . . . . . . . . | (9) | $_____ |

#### Liabilities and Stockholders' Equity

| | | |
|---|---|---|
| Accounts Payable . . . . . . . . . . . . . . . . . . . . . . . . . . . . . . . . . . . . . . | (8) | $_____ |
| 10% Bonds Payable (Due in 2010) . . . . . . . . . . . . . . . . . . . . . . . . . | (12) | _____ |
| Common Stock . . . . . . . . . . . . . . . . . . . . . . . . . . . . . . . . . . . . . . . . | | 500 |
| Retained Earnings. . . . . . . . . . . . . . . . . . . . . . . . . . . . . . . . . . . . . . | (13) | _____ |
| Total Equities . . . . . . . . . . . . . . . . . . . . . . . . . . . . . . . . . . . . . . . | | $ 2,600 |

## PROBLEMS: SET B

1† **Problem B1:** Completing and Analyzing Comparative Statements

The following financial statements are included in the 1998 annual report of Rydal Company:

### RYDAL COMPANY
### Comparative Balance Sheets
### (000's omitted)

| | September 30 | |
|---|---|---|
| | **1998** | **1997** |
| **Assets** | | |
| Current Assets: | | |
| Cash . . . . . . . . . . . . . . . . . . . . . . . . . . . . . . . . . . . . . . . . . | $ 7,200 | $ 3,600 |
| Accounts Receivable (Net of Allowances for Uncollectibles | | |
| of $120 in 1998 and $40 in 1997) . . . . . . . . . . . . . . . . . . . | 5,600 | 3,800 |
| Merchandise Inventory. . . . . . . . . . . . . . . . . . . . . . . . . . . . | 15,400 | 11,000 |
| Total Current Assets. . . . . . . . . . . . . . . . . . . . . . . . . . . | $ 28,200 | $ 18,400 |
| Property, Plant, and Equipment: | | |
| Land . . . . . . . . . . . . . . . . . . . . . . . . . . . . . . . . . . . . . . . . . | $ 50,000 | $ 44,000 |
| Buildings . . . . . . . . . . . . . . . . . . . . . . . . . . . . . . . . . . . . . | 36,000 | 36,000 |
| Less: Accumulated Depreciation . . . . . . . . . . . . . . . . . . . | (600) | (500) |
| Equipment. . . . . . . . . . . . . . . . . . . . . . . . . . . . . . . . . . . . | 7,000 | 6,000 |
| Less: Accumulated Depreciation . . . . . . . . . . . . . . . . . . . | (200) | (100) |
| Total Property, Plant, and Equipment . . . . . . . . . . . . . . . | $ 92,200 | $ 85,400 |
| Intangibles: | | |
| Copyrights. . . . . . . . . . . . . . . . . . . . . . . . . . . . . . . . . . . . | $ 2,900 | $ 2,800 |
| Total Assets . . . . . . . . . . . . . . . . . . . . . . . . . . . . . . . . . . . | $123,300 | $106,600 |

*(Continued)*

† The numbers in the margin refer to the Learning Objectives.

### Liabilities and Stockholders' Equity

| | | |
|---|---:|---:|
| Current Liabilities: | | |
| Accounts Payable. . . . . . . . . . . . . . . . . . . . . . . . . . . . . . . . . . . . | $ 2,000 | $ 8,000 |
| Accrued Payables. . . . . . . . . . . . . . . . . . . . . . . . . . . . . . . . . . . . | 1,300 | 1,000 |
| Total Current Liabilities. . . . . . . . . . . . . . . . . . . . . . . . . . . | $ 3,300 | $ 9,000 |
| Long-Term Liabilities: | | |
| 6% Note Payable (Due in 2003) . . . . . . . . . . . . . . . . . . . . . | $ 20,000 | $20,000 |
| 12% Bonds Payable (Due in 2005) . . . . . . . . . . . . . . . . . . . | 20,000 | — |
| Total Long-Term Liabilities. . . . . . . . . . . . . . . . . . . . . . . . | $ 40,000 | $ 20,000 |
| Total Liabilities . . . . . . . . . . . . . . . . . . . . . . . . . . . . . . . . . . . . . . | $ 43,300 | $ 29,000 |
| Stockholders' Equity: | | |
| Common Stock, $10-Par . . . . . . . . . . . . . . . . . . . . . . . . . . . . . | $ 20,000 | $ 20,000 |
| Paid-In Capital in Excess of Par . . . . . . . . . . . . . . . . . . . . . | 8,000 | 8,000 |
| Retained Earnings . . . . . . . . . . . . . . . . . . . . . . . . . . . . . . . . . . | 52,000 | 49,600 |
| Total Stockholders' Equity . . . . . . . . . . . . . . . . . . . . . . . | $ 80,000 | $ 77,600 |
| Total Liabilities and Stockholders' Equity . . . . . . . . . . . . . . . | $123,300 | $106,600 |

### RYDAL COMPANY
### Comparative Income Statements
### Years Ended September 30
### (000's omitted)

| | 1998 | 1997 |
|---|---:|---:|
| Net Sales . . . . . . . . . . . . . . . . . . . . . . . . . . . . . . . . . . . . . . . . . . . . | $ 68,400 | $76,000 |
| Cost of Goods Sold . . . . . . . . . . . . . . . . . . . . . . . . . . . . . . . . . . | 24,472 | 26,600 |
| Gross Profit on Sales . . . . . . . . . . . . . . . . . . . . . . . . . . . . . . . . . | $ 43,928 | $ 49,400 |
| Operating Expenses: | | |
| Sales Salary Expense. . . . . . . . . . . . . . . . . . . . . . . . . . . . . . . | $ 10,944 | $12,160 |
| Utilities Expense . . . . . . . . . . . . . . . . . . . . . . . . . . . . . . . . . . | 12,312 | 9,120 |
| Other Selling Expenses . . . . . . . . . . . . . . . . . . . . . . . . . . . | 6,156 | 6,840 |
| Other General Expenses . . . . . . . . . . . . . . . . . . . . . . . . . . . | 2,052 | 2,280 |
| Total Operating Expenses . . . . . . . . . . . . . . . . . . . . . . . | $ 31,464 | $30,400 |
| Other Income and Expenses: | | |
| Interest Expense. . . . . . . . . . . . . . . . . . . . . . . . . . . . . . . . . . | $ 3,600 | $ 1,200 |
| Income before Income Taxes. . . . . . . . . . . . . . . . . . . . . . . . . . | $ 8,864 | $ 17,800 |
| Provision for Income Taxes . . . . . . . . . . . . . . . . . . . . . . . . . . . | 3,988 | 8,010 |
| Net Income . . . . . . . . . . . . . . . . . . . . . . . . . . . . . . . . . . . . . . . . . | $ 4,876 | $ 9,790 |

**Required:**

1. Comparative income statements and balance sheets for 1998 and 1997 are presented above. Prepare columns showing the amount and percentage increase or decrease for each item on the statements.
2. Use your solution for part one to answer the following questions:
   a. Which four balance sheet accounts experienced the greatest percentage change?
   b. Which three revenue or expense accounts on the income statement had the highest percentage change?
   c. Does the large increase in current assets appear to have been generated by profits for the year? Explain.
   d. Sales in 1998 decreased over 1997. Did expenses seem to decrease proportionately? Comment on any exceptions.

   ▶ *(Check Figure: Income statement items with the highest percentage change = Utilities Expense, Interest Expense, and Provision for Income Taxes)*

3  **Problem B2:** Preparing and Analyzing Common-Size Income Statements

Harbor Corp. and Coast, Inc., are in the same industry and have the same fiscal years, ending on Oct. 31. Income statements for the two companies appear below.

### HARBOR CORP.
### Income Statement
### Year Ended October 31, 1998

| | | |
|---|---:|---:|
| Sales | | $400,000 |
| Cost of Goods Sold | | 272,000 |
| Gross Profit | | $128,000 |
| Operating Expenses: | | |
| Selling | $60,000 | |
| General and Administrative | 12,000 | |
| Total Operating Expenses | | 72,000 |
| Income from Operations | | $ 56,000 |
| Other Income and Expenses: | | |
| Interest Expense | | 40,000 |
| Income before Taxes | | $ 16,000 |
| Provision for Income Taxes | | 4,000 |
| Net Income | | 12,000 |

### COAST, INC.
### Income Statement
### Year Ended October 31, 1998

| | | |
|---|---:|---:|
| Sales | | $3,600,000 |
| Cost of Goods Sold | | 1,908,000 |
| Gross Profit | | $1,692,000 |
| Operating Expenses: | | |
| Selling | $612,000 | |
| General and Administrative | 504,000 | |
| Total Operating Expenses | | 1,116,000 |
| Income from Operations | | $ 576,000 |
| Other Income and Expenses: | | |
| Interest Expense | | 108,000 |
| Income before Taxes | | $ 468,000 |
| Provision for Income Taxes | | 159,120 |
| Net Income | | $ 308,880 |

**Required:**

1. Prepare common-size income statements for Harbor Corp. and Coast, Inc.
2. Compare percentages for cost of goods sold, selling expenses, general and administrative expenses, and interest expense. What factors may have caused differences in these percentages? Which company is earning more profit per dollar of sales?

4 **Problem B3:** Calculating Liquid Position Ratios

Macon, Inc., and Cairo Company both sell machinery for washing large trucks. Both companies have applied for a short-term loan. Data from the Dec. 31, 1998, balance sheets appear below.

| | Macon, Inc. | Cairo Co. |
|---|---|---|
| **Assets** | | |
| Cash | $ 55,000 | $ 150,000 |
| Temporary Investments | 3,600 | 120,000 |
| Accounts Receivable (Net) | 61,400 | 90,000 |
| Merchandise Inventory | 360,000 | 240,000 |
| Property, Plant, and Equipment (Net) | 700,000 | 750,000 |
| Intangibles | 3,000 | — |
| Total Assets | $1,183,000 | $1,350,000 |
| **Liabilities and Owners' Equity** | | |
| Current Liabilities | $ 120,000 | $ 200,000 |
| Long-Term Liabilities | 200,000 | 200,000 |
| Common Stock, $10-Par | 800,000 | 800,000 |
| Retained Earnings | 63,000 | 150,000 |
| Total Equities | $1,183,000 | $1,350,000 |

**Other Information:**

| | Macon, Inc. | Cairo Co. |
|---|---|---|
| Accounts Receivable, Jan. 1, 1998 | $ 78,600 | $ 70,000 |
| Merchandise Inventory, Jan. 1, 1998 | 320,000 | 260,000 |
| 1998 Sales: | | |
| Cash | 516,000 | 240,000 |
| Credit | 684,000 | 960,000 |
| 1998 Cost of Goods Sold | 1,054,000 | 700,000 |

**Required:**

1. Calculate for each company the current ratio, quick ratio, inventory turnover, accounts receivable turnover, and average age of receivables.
2. Which company would you recommend to receive the short-term loan? Explain.
3. What additional ratios would you consider if the companies were requesting a long-term loan? Explain.

   ▶ *(Check Figure: Inventory turnover for Cairo Co. = 2.8)*

4 5 6 **Problem B4:** Calculating Ratios and Evaluating the Use of Leverage

Blakely, Inc.'s, income statement and balance sheet for 1998 follow.

## BLAKELY, INC.
### Income Statement
### Year Ended August 31, 1998

| | | |
|---|---:|---:|
| Sales.......................................... | | $420,000 |
| Cost of Goods Sold: | | |
|   Merchandise Inventory, Sept. 1, 1997................... | $ 67,200 | |
|   Purchases (Net)...................................... | 277,200 | |
|   Goods Available for Sale............................. | $344,400 | |
|   Merchandise Inventory, Aug. 31, 1998................ | 86,400 | |
|   Cost of Goods Sold................................. | | 258,000 |
| Gross Profit...................................... | | $162,000 |
| Operating Expenses............................... | | 76,800 |
| Income from Operations........................... | | $ 85,200 |
| Other Income and Expenses: | | |
|   Interest Expense.................................... | | 20,000 |
| Income before Taxes.............................. | | $ 65,200 |
| Provision for Income Taxes........................ | | 23,200 |
| Net Income...................................... | | $ 42,000 |

## BLAKELY, INC.
### Balance Sheet
### August 31, 1998

#### Assets

| | |
|---|---:|
| Cash............................................. | $ 14,400 |
| Temporary Investments............................ | 4,800 |
| Accounts Receivable (Net)......................... | 33,600 |
| Merchandise Inventory............................ | 86,400 |
| Property, Plant, and Equipment (Net).............. | 256,000 |
| Total Assets...................................... | $395,200 |

#### Liabilities and Owners' Equity

| | |
|---|---:|
| Accounts Payable................................. | $ 56,000 |
| Income Taxes Payable............................. | 7,200 |
| 10% Note Payable (Due in 2005)................... | 200,000 |
| Common Stock ($10-Par)........................... | 80,000 |
| Retained Earnings................................ | 52,000 |
| Total Liabilities and Stockholders' Equity.......... | $395,200 |

Of the $420,000 in sales, 80% were on credit and the remaining 20% were cash. On Sept. 1, 1997, Blakely had total assets of $376,000 (including accounts receivable of $28,000 and merchandise inventory of $67,200), total liabilities of $286,000, and total stockholders' equity of $90,000.

**Required:**

1. Calculate the following ratios:
   a. Rate of return on total assets
   b. Rate of return on common stockholders' equity
   c. Working capital
   d. Current ratio
   e. Quick ratio
   f. Inventory turnover

g. Accounts receivable turnover
h. Average age of receivables
i. Times interest earned
j. Debt to total assets ratio
k. Stockholders' equity to total assets ratio

2. In your opinion, is the company using leverage to increase the return to common stockholders?

3. What does the company's current ratio and quick ratio tell you about the composition of current assets?

4. Given that the company's credit terms are "net 30 days," do you think that the company is managing its accounts receivable effectively?

▶ *(Check Figure: Accounts receivable turnover = 10.9 times)*

6 **Problem B5:** Calculating Earnings Performance Ratios

The following financial data have been assembled for Statesboro Industries, Inc., on Dec. 31, 1998:

| | |
|---|---|
| Average total assets for 1998................ | $550,000 |
| Total stockholders' equity (average for 1998) ... | 440,000 |
| Common stock, $.25-par ................... | 220,000 |
| 8% preferred stock, $5-par................. | 110,000 |
| Net income ............................. | 33,000 |
| Interest expense......................... | 2,200 |
| Provision for income taxes (40% of income before income taxes) | |
| Market price of common stock, Dec. 31, 1998 .. | 2.50 |
| Market price of preferred stock, Dec. 31, 1998 .. | 16.50 |

Common dividends were paid at the rate of $.05 per share per quarter.
Preferred dividends were declared and paid.
No preferred stock or common stock was issued or reacquired during 1998.

**Required:**

Using whatever data you need from the above list, calculate:

1. Rate of return on total assets
2. Rate of return on common stockholders' equity
3. Earnings per common share
4. Price–earnings ratio
5. Dividend yield rate

▶ *(Check Figure: Earnings per common share = $.0275)*

4 5 6 **Problem B6:** Calculating Liquid Position, Debt-Paying Ability, and Earnings Performance Ratios

Dalton, Inc.'s, income statement and balance sheet for 1998 follow.

## DALTON, INC.
### Income Statement
### Year Ended April 30, 1998

| | | |
|---|---:|---:|
| Sales | | $360,000 |
| Cost of Goods Sold: | | |
|   Merchandise Inventory, May 1, 1997 | $ 33,000 | |
|   Purchases (Net) | 150,000 | |
|   Goods Available for Sale | $183,000 | |
|   Merchandise Inventory, Apr. 30, 1998 | 39,000 | |
|     Cost of Goods Sold | | 144,000 |
| Gross Profit | | $216,000 |
| Operating Expenses | | 150,000 |
| Income from Operations | | $ 66,000 |
| Other Income and Expenses: | | |
|   Interest Expense | | 2,400 |
| Income before Taxes | | $ 63,600 |
| Provision for Income Taxes | | 21,200 |
| Net Income | | $ 42,400 |

## DALTON, INC.
### Balance Sheet
### April 30, 1998

### Assets

| | |
|---|---:|
| Cash | $ 4,500 |
| Temporary Investments | 6,480 |
| Accounts Receivable (Net) | 11,580 |
| Merchandise Inventory | 39,000 |
| Property, Plant, and Equipment (Net) | 96,000 |
| Franchise | 3,240 |
| Total Assets | $160,800 |

### Liabilities and Stockhoders' Equity

| | |
|---|---:|
| Accounts Payable | $ 9,720 |
| Accrued Salaries Payable | 1,620 |
| Income Taxes Payable | 5,760 |
| 8% Bonds Payable (Due in 2010) | 20,000 |
| 5% Preferred Stock ($10-Par) | 25,000 |
| Common Stock ($4-Par) | 60,000 |
| Retained Earnings | 38,700 |
| Total Liabilities and Stockholders' Equity | $160,800 |

### Other Information:

a. All sales were on credit.
b. On May 1, 1997, Dalton had total assets of $139,200 (including accounts receivable of $12,420 and merchandise inventory of $33,000), total liabilities of $60,600, and total stockholders' equity of $78,600.

c. Dalton paid a $.50 per share cash dividend to common stockholders and the required dividend to preferred stockholders.

d. No common or preferred stock was issued during the year.

e. The market price of Dalton common stock was $5.75 on Apr. 30, 1998.

**Required:**

1. Calculate the following liquid position ratios: current ratio, quick ratio, inventory turnover, accounts receivable turnover, and average age of receivables.

2. Calculate the following ratios indicating debt-paying ability: times interest earned, debt to total assets ratio, and stockholders' equity to total assets ratio.

3. Calculate the following earnings performance statistics: rate of return on total assets, rate of return on common stockholders' equity, earnings per share, price–earnings ratio, and dividend yield rate.

▶ *(Check Figure: Times interest earned = 27.5 times)*

4 5 6 **Problem B7:** Completing Financial Statements When Given Selected Data

The following financial information is available for Waco Sales, Inc.:

a. All sales were on credit.

b. The debt to total assets ratio is 55%.

c. Working capital is $1,310.

d. Net income is 9.0% of sales; gross profit is 30% of sales.

e. The only interest paid was on long-term debt.

f. Inventory turnover = 6. (Beginning inventory = $500.)

g. Accounts Receivable turnover = 12. (Beginning Accounts Receivable = $300.)

h. Of the total cost of the building, 45% has been depreciated.

**Required:**

Complete the Waco Sales, Inc., financial statements shown below. Round all calculations to the nearest dollar. (*Hint:* Do your calculations in the numerical order indicated in the statements.)

**WACO SALES, INC.**
**Income Statement**
**Year Ended December 31, 1998**

| | | |
|---|---|---|
| Sales. . . . . . . . . . . . . . . . . . . . . . . . . . . . . . . . . . . . . . . . . . . . . . . . . . . . . . . . . . . . . . | (1) | $_____ |
| Cost of Goods Sold . . . . . . . . . . . . . . . . . . . . . . . . . . . . . . . . . . . . . . . . . . . . . . . | (3) | _____ |
| Gross Profit on Sales . . . . . . . . . . . . . . . . . . . . . . . . . . . . . . . . . . . . . . . . . . . . . | (2) | _____ |
| Operating Expenses. . . . . . . . . . . . . . . . . . . . . . . . . . . . . . . . . . . . . . . . . . . . . . . | (15) | _____ |
| Interest Expense . . . . . . . . . . . . . . . . . . . . . . . . . . . . . . . . . . . . . . . . . . . . . . . . . | (14) | _____ |
| Income before Income Taxes . . . . . . . . . . . . . . . . . . . . . . . . . . . . . . . . . . . . | (4) | _____ |
| Provision for Income Taxes (60% of income before income taxes) . . . | (5) | _____ |
| Net Income. . . . . . . . . . . . . . . . . . . . . . . . . . . . . . . . . . . . . . . . . . . . . . . . . . . . . . . | | $ 540 |

**WACO SALES, INC.**
Balance Sheet
December 31, 1998

### Assets

| | | |
|---|---|---|
| Cash . . . . . . . . . . . . . . . . . . . . . . . . . . . . . . . . . . . . . . . . . . . . . . . . . . . . . . | | $    310 |
| Accounts Receivable (Net) . . . . . . . . . . . . . . . . . . . . . . . . . . . . . | (6) | _____ |
| Merchandise Inventory . . . . . . . . . . . . . . . . . . . . . . . . . . . . . . . . . | (7) | _____ |
| Building . . . . . . . . . . . . . . . . . . . . . . . . . . . . . . . . . . . . . . . . . . . . . . | (10) | _____ |
| Accumulated Depreciation . . . . . . . . . . . . . . . . . . . . . . . . . . . . . | (11) | (_____) |
| Total Assets . . . . . . . . . . . . . . . . . . . . . . . . . . . . . . . . . . . . . . . . . | (9) | $_____ |

### Liabilities and Stockholders' Equity

| | | |
|---|---|---|
| Accounts Payable . . . . . . . . . . . . . . . . . . . . . . . . . . . . . . . . . . . . . | (8) | $_____ |
| 6% Bonds Payable (Due in 2005) . . . . . . . . . . . . . . . . . . . . . . . | (12) | _____ |
| Common Stock . . . . . . . . . . . . . . . . . . . . . . . . . . . . . . . . . . . . . . . . | | 800 |
| Retained Earnings . . . . . . . . . . . . . . . . . . . . . . . . . . . . . . . . . . . . | (13) | _____ |
| Total Equities . . . . . . . . . . . . . . . . . . . . . . . . . . . . . . . . . . . . . . . . | | $   4,000 |

## DECISION PROBLEM

Savannah, Inc., and Cordele Co. both sell custom-designed machinery and equipment. Data from the two companies' Dec. 31, 1998, balance sheets appear below.

| | Savannah | Cordele |
|---|---|---|
| **Assets** | | |
| Cash . . . . . . . . . . . . . . . . . . . . . . . . . . . . . . . . . . . . . . . . . . . . . | $    87,040 | $  240,000 |
| Temporary Investments . . . . . . . . . . . . . . . . . . . . . . . . . . . . . | 5,760 | 192,000 |
| Accounts Receivable (Net) . . . . . . . . . . . . . . . . . . . . . . . . . . | 99,200 | 140,800 |
| Merchandise Inventory . . . . . . . . . . . . . . . . . . . . . . . . . . . . . . | 576,000 | 384,000 |
| Property, Plant, and Equipment (Net) . . . . . . . . . . . . . . . . | 1,120,000 | 1,152,000 |
| Intangibles. . . . . . . . . . . . . . . . . . . . . . . . . . . . . . . . . . . . . . . . | 5,760 | — |
| Total Assets . . . . . . . . . . . . . . . . . . . . . . . . . . . . . . . . . . . . . | $1,893,760 | $2,108,800 |
| **Liabilities and Stockholders' Equity** | | |
| Current Liabilities . . . . . . . . . . . . . . . . . . . . . . . . . . . . . . . . . | $  192,000 | $  320,000 |
| Long-Term Liabilities . . . . . . . . . . . . . . . . . . . . . . . . . . . . . . | 320,000 | 320,000 |
| Common Stock ($10-Par). . . . . . . . . . . . . . . . . . . . . . . . . . . | 1,280,000 | 1,280,000 |
| Retained Earnings . . . . . . . . . . . . . . . . . . . . . . . . . . . . . . . . | 101,760 | 188,800 |
| Total Equities . . . . . . . . . . . . . . . . . . . . . . . . . . . . . . . . . . . . | $1,893,760 | $2,108,800 |

**Other Information:**

| | Savannah | Cordele |
|---|---|---|
| Accounts Receivable, Jan. 1, 1998 . . . . . . . . . . . . . . . . . . . | $ 124,800 | $ 112,000 |
| Merchandise Inventory, Jan. 1, 1998. . . . . . . . . . . . . . . . . . | 512,000 | 416,000 |
| 1998 Sales: | | |
|    Cash . . . . . . . . . . . . . . . . . . . . . . . . . . . . . . . . . . . . . . . | 825,600 | 384,000 |
|    Credit. . . . . . . . . . . . . . . . . . . . . . . . . . . . . . . . . . . . . . | 1,094,400 | 1,536,000 |
| 1998 Cost of Goods Sold. . . . . . . . . . . . . . . . . . . . . . . . . . | 1,689,600 | 1,152,000 |
| 1998 Net Income . . . . . . . . . . . . . . . . . . . . . . . . . . . . . . . . | 300,000 | 384,000 |
| 1998 Interest Expense . . . . . . . . . . . . . . . . . . . . . . . . . . . . | 64,000 | 32,000 |
| Total Stockholders' Equity, Jan. 1, 1998 . . . . . . . . . . . . . . | 1,321,240 | 1,167,200 |
| Total Assets, Jan. 1, 1998 . . . . . . . . . . . . . . . . . . . . . . . . . | 1,750,240 | 1,860,000 |

**Required:**

1. Calculate the following for each company: working capital, current ratio, quick ratio, inventory turnover, accounts receivable turnover, and average age of receivables.
2. Which company appears to have a better liquid position? Explain.
3. Calculate for each company the rate of return on total assets and the rate of return on common stockholders' equity.
4. Which company is doing the better job of using leverage to increase the rate of return to common stockholders? Explain.
5. What do accountants mean by "window dressing"? How could these companies use this technique to improve their liquid position ratios?

---

## ETHICS CASE

Jason Howell is president of Valdosta Windows, a company that manufactures custom wooden- and metal-frame windows for commercial installations. Valdosta Windows is owned by a group of approximately 100 stockholders, none of whom is actively engaged in the operation of the business. Stockholders' equity finances about 40% of the company's assets; the remaining 60% comes from short-term financing from suppliers (accounts payable) and borrowing on a long-term line of credit provided by the Lowndes Bank of Commerce. The stockholders and the bank rely on the company's annual report as their primary source of information about the firm.

Esther Moultrie, Valdosta's controller and chief financial officer, approached Jason in mid-December with a preliminary set of financial statements through Nov. 30. She has two major concerns: First, it looks like the current and quick ratios for the year will be about 1.2:1 and .75:1, respectively. Esther knows that the bank requires a minimum current ratio of 2:1 and a minimum quick ratio of 1:1 if Valdosta is to keep its current line of credit. If these ratios are not maintained, the loan agreement provides that Valdosta:

1. Will not be able to borrow additional funds on the line of credit;

2. Will be required to pay the current balance of the debt within 1 year; and
3. Will be subject to a 15% interest rate on the current debt, an automatic increase from 12%.

Esther's second concern is that, while she expects net income for the year to be a positive amount, she knows that this will be due largely to a $200,000 extraordinary gain from sale of land through a condemnation proceeding brought by the state transportation department. The land is to be used for expansion of an interstate highway. Without the extraordinary gain, the company would show a net loss of about $80,000. Esther knows that the board of directors, composed of five major stockholders, has been discussing the sale of Valdosta to a national building materials firm that has a reputation for firing existing management and bringing in its own people to run companies they acquire. She believes that the board will keep Valdosta only as long as it continues to meet their profit expectations. She fears that the year's loss from operations will convince the board to sell the company. If this happens, she and Jason will lose their jobs.

Jason proposes to answer Esther's concerns by taking two actions. First, he will use as much of the available cash as possible to pay off current liabilities. If this action does not bring Valdosta's quick and current ratios within the bank's requirements, he will borrow cash on the line of credit and pay off enough current liabilities to do so.

Second, in his President's Letter at the front of the annual report, Jason will discuss only the company's success in earning a net income of $120,000 and will emphasize the improvement in earnings performance over the prior year. He will not mention the extraordinary item or its one-time impact on net income. He believes that most of the stockholders are not sophisticated enough in reading financial statement disclosures to realize the implications of the extraordinary item.

**Required:**

1. Is Jason's strategy for improving Valdosta's current and quick ratios misleading to the bank, or is it just a good management strategy to protect his company?
2. Is Jason's emphasis on net income in his President's Letter appropriate? Do you believe it is his best alternative for dealing with the current situation?
3. Is either or both of the two actions Jason is contemplating unethical? If so, why?

## OBJECTIVE ASSIGNMENT ANSWERS

### True/False

**1.** T    **2.** F    **3.** T    **4.** T    **5.** F

### Multiple Choice

**1.** c    **2.** a    **3.** c    **4.** d    **5.** a
**6.** b    **7.** b    **8.** c    **9.** d    **10.** b

# FINANCIAL STATEMENTS
# PepsiCo, Inc.

On the following 16 pages are the financial statements of PepsiCo, Inc., a company listed on the New York Stock Exchange. KPMG Peat Marwick audited the statements, and their report is found on the last page. PepsiCo's statements were selected because the company is widely known and the statements illustrate many of the accounting and disclosure issues discussed in the text.

Included with the financial statements are *Management's Analysis* of the income statement, balance sheet, and statement of cash flows as well as *Notes to Consolidated Financial Statements.* These are an integral part of the statements.

# Consolidated Statement of Income

(in millions except per share amounts)
PepsiCo, Inc. and Subsidiaries
Fifty-two weeks ended December 25, 1993, December 26, 1992 and December 28, 1991

|  | 1993 | 1992 | 1991 |
|---|---|---|---|
| **Net Sales** | **$25,020.7** | $21,970.0 | $19,292.2 |
| **Costs and Expenses, net** | | | |
| Cost of sales | **11,946.1** | 10,611.7 | 9,366.2 |
| Selling, general and administrative expenses | **9,864.4** | 8,721.2 | 7,605.9 |
| Amortization of intangible assets | **303.7** | 265.9 | 208.3 |
| **Operating Profit** | **2,906.5** | 2,371.2 | 2,111.8 |
| Interest expense | **(572.7)** | (586.1) | (613.7) |
| Interest income | **88.7** | 113.7 | 161.6 |
| **Income Before Income Taxes and Cumulative Effect of Accounting Changes** | **2,422.5** | 1,898.8 | 1,659.7 |
| **Provision for Income Taxes** | **834.6** | 597.1 | 579.5 |
| **Income Before Cumulative Effect of Accounting Changes** | **1,587.9** | 1,301.7 | 1,080.2 |
| **Cumulative Effect of Change in Accounting for Postretirement Benefits Other Than Pensions** (net of income tax benefit of $218.6) | **—** | (356.7) | — |
| **Cumulative Effect of Change in Accounting for Income Taxes** | **—** | (570.7) | — |
| **Net Income** | **$ 1,587.9** | $ 374.3 | $ 1,080.2 |
| **Income (Charge) Per Share** | | | |
| Before cumulative effect of accounting changes | **$ 1.96** | $ 1.61 | $ 1.35 |
| Cumulative effect of change in accounting for postretirement benefits other than pensions | **—** | (0.44) | — |
| Cumulative effect of change in accounting for income taxes | **—** | (0.71) | — |
| **Net Income Per Share** | **$ 1.96** | $ 0.46 | $ 1.35 |
| Average shares outstanding used to calculate income (charge) per share | **810.1** | 806.7 | 802.5 |

See accompanying Notes to Consolidated Financial Statements.

**Allocation of 1993
Net Sales**

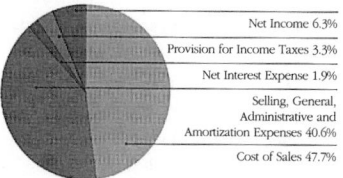

Net Income 6.3%
Provision for Income Taxes 3.3%
Net Interest Expense 1.9%
Selling, General, Administrative and Amortization Expenses 40.6%
Cost of Sales 47.7%

# Management's Analysis—Results of Operations

*(See "Management's Analysis—Overview" on page 24 for background information, "Business Segments" on page 27 for detail of segment results and Note 3 for details of unusual items.)*

To improve comparability, Management's Analysis includes, where significant, analytical data to indicate the impact of beverage and snack food acquisitions and the unfavorable currency translation impact of a stronger U.S. dollar. In comparing results, acquisition impacts represent the results of the acquired businesses for periods in the current year corresponding to the prior year periods that did not include the results of the businesses. Restaurant units acquired, principally from franchisees, and constructed units are treated the same for purposes of this analysis and are collectively referred to as "additional restaurant units." Also, the analysis indicates the impact of unusual charges and the effect on comparisons of 1992 to 1991 of adopting SFAS 106 and SFAS 109, collectively referred to as "the unusual items."

**Net Sales** rose $3.1 billion or 14% in 1993. Acquisitions contributed $1.1 billion or 5 points to sales growth. The balance of the increase reflected $913 million from additional restaurant units, volume gains that contributed about $850 million and higher pricing. Both the volume gains and higher pricing were led by worldwide snack foods. Sales grew $2.7 billion or 14% in 1992. Acquisitions contributed $965 million or 5 points to this advance. The balance of the increase reflected $937 million from additional restaurant units, about $375 million from volume gains, driven by domestic snack foods, and higher pricing led by worldwide beverages. International sales grew 24% in 1993. Acquisitions contributed 16 points to the increase, but the unfavorable currency translation impact depressed sales growth by 4 points. International sales rose 31% in 1992. Acquisitions contributed 19 points to this advance. International sales represented 27%, 25% and 21% of total sales in 1993, 1992 and 1991, respectively. The long-term trend of an increasing international component of sales is expected to continue.

**Cost of sales** as a percentage of Net Sales was 47.7%, 48.3% and 48.6% in 1993, 1992 and 1991, respectively. The 1993 gross margin improvement was driven by lower product costs (packaging and ingredients) in domestic beverages. The 1992 gross margin improvement was driven by beverages, reflecting higher worldwide net pricing and lower product costs.

**Selling, general and administrative expenses** rose 13% in 1993 and 15% in 1992. The increase in both years reflected base business growth and acquisitions. Excluding the unusual items, selling, general and administrative expenses rose 16% in 1993 and 14% in 1992, and as a percentage of Net Sales were 39.4%, 38.8% and 38.5% in 1993, 1992 and 1991, respectively. In 1993, selling and distribution expenses grew at a faster rate than sales, but marketing expenditures grew at a slower rate. These changes reflect the impact of worldwide bottling acquisitions and flat marketing expenditures in domestic beverages.

**Amortization of intangible assets** rose 14% in 1993 and 28% in 1992 due primarily to acquisition activity. The 1992 increase also reflected the impact of adopting SFAS 109. This significant, noncash expense reduced net income per share by $0.28, $0.24 and $0.22 in 1993, 1992 and 1991, respectively. The 1992 per share increase was mitigated by incremental tax benefits recognized on nondeductible amortization of identifiable intangibles, in accordance with SFAS 109.

**Operating Profit** increased 23% in 1993 and 12% in 1992. The following discussion excludes the impact of the unusual items. Operating profit increased $342 million or 13% in 1993 and $356 million or 16% in 1992, driven by combined segment operating profit growth of 14% in 1993 and 16% in 1992. Growth in 1993 reflected about $425 million from higher volumes and $89 million from additional restaurant units, partially offset by increased operating expenses that exceeded higher pricing. The 1992 increase reflected about $200 million from volume growth and $108 million from additional restaurant units, as well as higher prices that exceeded increased operating expenses. International segment profits grew 8% in 1993. The unfavorable translation impact depressed this growth by 6 points. The higher profits reflected double-digit increases in snack foods and beverages, partially offset by a decline in restaurants, particularly in Australia. International segment profits grew 32% in 1992. Acquisitions contributed 14 points to this advance. The balance of the increase reflected double-digit growth in all three segments. International profits represented 18%, 19% and 16% of combined segment operating profits in 1993, 1992 and 1991, respectively. The international component of profits is expected to increase in future years. Increased foreign exchange losses and lower equity in net income of affiliates, which are not included in segment profits, slowed 1993 total operating profit growth.

**Interest expense, net of Interest income,** increased 2% in 1993 and 4% in 1992. The change in 1993 reflected higher average borrowings, and lower average short-term investment balances held outside the U.S., which are managed as part of PepsiCo's overall financing strategy. In 1992, average borrowings were higher and the average short-term investment balances rose slightly. In both years, this financing activity was partially offset by a decline in interest rates, which is not expected to continue. Excluding the net impact of acquisitions, net interest expense declined 9% in 1993.

**Provision for Income Taxes** as a percentage of pretax income was 34.5%, 31.4% and 34.9% in 1993, 1992 and 1991, respectively. Excluding the impact of the 1993 U.S. tax legislation on deferred taxes, the effective tax rate in 1993 was 33.3%. The increase of 1.9 points over 1992 reflects higher U.S. and foreign effective rates, an increase in the proportion of income taxed at the higher U.S. tax rate and higher state taxes, partially offset by a favorable adjustment of certain prior year accruals. Excluding the impact of the adoption of SFAS 109 in 1992 and an unusual tax effect on a 1991 restructuring charge, the effective rates were 32.9% in 1992 and 34.2% in 1991. The decrease of 1.3 points in 1992 reflected lower effective rates on higher foreign income and resolutions of tax audits. The effective rate is expected to increase to about 35.5% in 1994, due primarily to lapping the 1993 accrual adjustments.

**Income and Income Per Share Before Cumulative Effect of Accounting Changes** ("income" and "income per share") in 1993 increased 22% to $1.6 billion and $1.96, respectively, and in 1992 increased 21% to $1.3 billion and 19% to $1.61, respectively. Excluding the unusual items, income and income per share rose 13% and 12% in 1993 and 21% and 20% in 1992, respectively. Growth in 1993 income per share was depressed by estimated dilution from acquisitions of $0.05 or 3 points, all related to international beverage and snack food acquisitions.

# Consolidated Balance Sheet

(in millions except per share amount)
PepsiCo, Inc. and Subsidiaries
December 25, 1993 and December 26, 1992

|  | 1993 | 1992 |
|---|---|---|
| **ASSETS** | | |
| **Current Assets** | | |
| Cash and cash equivalents | $ 226.9 | $ 169.9 |
| Short-term investments, at cost which approximates market | 1,629.3 | 1,888.5 |
|  | 1,856.2 | 2,058.4 |
| Accounts and notes receivable, less allowance: $128.3 in 1993 and $112.0 in 1992 | 1,883.4 | 1,588.5 |
| Inventories | 924.7 | 768.8 |
| Prepaid expenses, taxes and other current assets | 499.8 | 426.6 |
| **Total Current Assets** | 5,164.1 | 4,842.3 |
| **Investments in Affiliates and Other Assets** | 1,756.6 | 1,707.9 |
| **Property, Plant and Equipment, net** | 8,855.6 | 7,442.0 |
| **Intangible Assets, net** | 7,929.5 | 6,959.0 |
| **Total Assets** | $23,705.8 | $20,951.2 |
| **LIABILITIES AND SHAREHOLDERS' EQUITY** | | |
| **Current Liabilities** | | |
| Short-term borrowings | $ 2,191.2 | $ 706.8 |
| Accounts payable | 1,390.0 | 1,164.8 |
| Income taxes payable | 823.7 | 621.1 |
| Accrued compensation and benefits | 726.0 | 638.9 |
| Accrued marketing | 400.9 | 327.0 |
| Other current liabilities | 1,043.1 | 1,099.0 |
| **Total Current Liabilities** | 6,574.9 | 4,557.6 |
| **Long-term Debt** | 7,442.6 | 7,964.8 |
| **Other Liabilities** | 1,342.0 | 1,390.8 |
| **Deferred Income Taxes** | 2,007.6 | 1,682.3 |
| **Shareholders' Equity** | | |
| Capital stock, par value 1⅔¢ per share: authorized 1,800.0 shares, issued 863.1 shares | 14.4 | 14.4 |
| Capital in excess of par value | 879.5 | 667.6 |
| Retained earnings | 6,541.9 | 5,439.7 |
| Currency translation adjustment and other | (183.9) | (99.0) |
|  | 7,251.9 | 6,022.7 |
| Less: Treasury stock, at cost: 64.3 shares in 1993 and 1992 | (913.2) | (667.0) |
| **Total Shareholders' Equity** | 6,338.7 | 5,355.7 |
| **Total Liabilities and Shareholders' Equity** | $23,705.8 | $20,951.2 |

See accompanying Notes to Consolidated Financial Statements.

# Management's Analysis—Financial Condition

*(See "Management's Analysis—Overview" on page 24 for background information.)*

**Assets** increased $2.8 billion or 13% over 1992, reflecting purchases of property, plant and equipment (capital spending), acquisitions and base business growth.

Short-term investments largely represent high-grade marketable securities portfolios held outside the U.S. The portfolio in Puerto Rico, which totaled $1.3 billion at year-end 1993 and $1.5 billion at year-end 1992, arises from the operating cash flows of the centralized concentrate manufacturing facilities that operate there under a tax incentive grant. The grant provides that the portfolio funds may be remitted to the U.S. without any additional tax. PepsiCo remitted $564 million of the portfolio to the U.S. in 1993 and $360 million in 1992. PepsiCo continually reassesses its alternatives to redeploy this and other portfolios held outside the U.S., considering other investment opportunities and risks, tax consequences and overall financing strategies.

Accounts and notes receivable increased $295 million or 19% and inventories increased $156 million or 20%, led by acquisitions and base business growth in worldwide beverages.

Intangible assets increased $971 million or 14% over 1992, reflecting the allocation of purchase prices of acquisitions, partially offset by amortization.

**Liabilities** rose $1.8 billion or 11% over 1992, primarily reflecting an increase in total debt, accounts payable and income taxes payable. Accounts payable increased $225 million or 19% due to growth in the business and timing of a large year-end employee benefits prepayment. Income taxes payable increased $203 million or 33%, reflecting an anticipated prepayment of taxes in early 1994 related to a federal tax audit for the years 1985 through 1989.

The $962 million or 11% increase in total short-term and long-term debt partially funded investing and other financing activities. PepsiCo's unused credit facilities with lending institutions, which exist largely to support the issuances of short-term borrowings, were $3.5 billion at year-end 1993 and 1992. This amount of short-term borrowings was classified as long-term at year-end 1993 and 1992, reflecting PepsiCo's intent and ability, through the existence of the credit facilities, to refinance these borrowings. Deferred income taxes increased $325 million or 19%, led by deferred tax liabilities arising in the allocation of purchase prices of acquisitions.

**Financial Leverage** is measured by PepsiCo on both a market value and historical cost basis. PepsiCo believes that the most meaningful measure of debt is on a net basis, which takes into account its large short-term investment portfolios held outside the U.S. These portfolios are managed as part of PepsiCo's overall financing strategy and are not required to support day-to-day operations. Net debt reflects the pro forma remittance of the portfolios (net of related taxes) as a reduction of total debt. As of year-end 1993, total debt for the purpose of measuring leverage also includes the estimated present value of long-term operating lease commitments, and prior year leverage ratios have been restated for this change. Long-term operating lease commitments have characteristics similar to debt.

PepsiCo believes that market leverage (defined as net debt as a percentage of net debt plus the market value of equity, based on the year-end stock price) better measures PepsiCo's financial leverage from the perspective of the investors in its securities, as it reflects the portion of the current value of PepsiCo that is financed with debt. Unlike historical cost measures, the market value of equity is based primarily on the expected future cash flows that will both support debt and provide returns to shareholders. The market net debt ratio was 22% at year-end 1993 and 19% at year-end 1992. The increase was driven by an 18% increase in net debt. Inclusion of long-term operating lease commitments contributed 2 percentage points to both the 1993 and 1992 ratios. PepsiCo has established a target range for its market net debt ratio of 20-25% to optimize its cost of capital. PepsiCo believes that it can safely exceed this range on a short-term basis to take advantage of strategic acquisition opportunities.

As measured on a historical cost basis, the ratio of net debt to net capital employed (defined as net debt, other liabilities, deferred income taxes and shareholders' equity) was 50% at year-end 1993 and 49% at year-end 1992. The increase was due to the growth in net debt, partially offset by a 16% increase in net capital employed. Inclusion of long-term operating lease commitments contributed 4 percentage points to both the 1993 and 1992 ratios.

At year-end 1993, about half of PepsiCo's net debt portfolio was exposed to variable interest rates, up from about 40% in 1992. All net debt with maturities of less than one year is categorized as variable.

PepsiCo's negative operating working capital position, which principally reflects the cash sales nature of its restaurant operations, effectively provides additional capital for investment. Operating working capital, which excludes short-term investments and short-term borrowings, was a negative $849 million and $897 million at year-end 1993 and 1992, respectively. The $48 million decline reflected the impact of base business growth and acquisitions in the more working capital intensive bottling and snack food operations, as well as the changes in accounts payable and income taxes payable discussed above.

**Shareholders' Equity** increased $983 million or 18% from 1992. This change reflected a 20% increase in retained earnings due to $1.6 billion in net income less dividends declared of $486 million, and a $212 million or 32% increase in capital in excess of par value due to acquisitions for stock and exercises of stock options. This growth was offset by a $246 million or 37% increase in treasury stock that reflected share repurchases net of shares used for acquisitions and stock option exercises, and an $85 million or 86% decline in currency translation adjustment and other. This change reflected the impact of a stronger U.S. dollar on the translation of the net assets of operations in Canada and Spain, partially offset by the impact of a weaker U.S. dollar on the translation of net assets in Japan and the change in the functional currency of operations in Mexico from the U.S. dollar to local currency.

Based on income before cumulative effect of accounting changes, PepsiCo's return on average shareholders' equity (ROAE) was 27.2% in 1993 and 23.9% in 1992. The ROAE was 25.3% in 1993 and 24.0% in 1992, excluding from both income and shareholders' equity the impact of the 1993 and 1992 unusual items as well as the cumulative effect of the 1992 accounting changes.

# Consolidated Statement of Cash Flows

(in millions)
PepsiCo, Inc. and Subsidiaries
Fifty-two weeks ended December 25, 1993, December 26, 1992 and December 28, 1991

| | 1993 | 1992 | 1991 |
|---|---|---|---|
| **Cash Flows — Operating Activities:** | | | |
| Income before cumulative effect of accounting changes | $ 1,587.9 | $ 1,301.7 | $ 1,080.2 |
| Adjustments to reconcile income before cumulative effect of accounting changes to net cash provided by operating activities: | | | |
| Depreciation and amortization | 1,444.2 | 1,214.9 | 1,034.5 |
| Deferred income taxes | 83.3 | (52.0) | 98.0 |
| Other noncash charges and credits, net | 344.8 | 315.6 | 227.2 |
| Changes in operating working capital, excluding effect of acquisitions: | | | |
| Accounts and notes receivable | (161.0) | (45.7) | (55.9) |
| Inventories | (89.5) | (11.8) | (54.8) |
| Prepaid expenses, taxes and other current assets | 3.3 | (27.4) | (75.6) |
| Accounts payable | 143.2 | (102.0) | 57.8 |
| Income taxes payable | (125.1) | (16.9) | (3.4) |
| Other current liabilities | (96.7) | 135.2 | 122.3 |
| Net change in operating working capital | (325.8) | (68.6) | (9.6) |
| **Net Cash Provided by Operating Activities** | 3,134.4 | 2,711.6 | 2,430.3 |
| **Cash Flows — Investing Activities:** | | | |
| Acquisitions and investments in affiliates | (1,011.2) | (1,209.7) | (640.9) |
| Purchases of property, plant and equipment (Capital spending) | (1,981.6) | (1,549.6) | (1,457.8) |
| Proceeds from sales of property, plant and equipment | 72.5 | 89.0 | 69.6 |
| Short-term investments, by original maturity: | | | |
| More than three months–purchases | (578.7) | (1,174.8) | (1,849.2) |
| More than three months–maturities | 846.0 | 1,371.8 | 1,873.2 |
| Three months or less, net | (8.3) | (249.4) | (164.9) |
| Other, net | (109.4) | (30.8) | (105.8) |
| **Net Cash Used for Investing Activities** | (2,770.7) | (2,753.5) | (2,275.8) |
| **Cash Flows — Financing Activities:** | | | |
| Proceeds from issuances of long-term debt | 710.8 | 1,092.7 | 2,799.6 |
| Payments of long-term debt | (1,201.9) | (616.3) | (1,348.5) |
| Short-term borrowings, by original maturity: | | | |
| More than three months–proceeds | 3,033.6 | 911.2 | 2,551.9 |
| More than three months–payments | (2,791.6) | (2,062.6) | (3,097.4) |
| Three months or less, net | 839.0 | 1,075.3 | (467.1) |
| Cash dividends paid | (461.6) | (395.5) | (343.2) |
| Purchases of treasury stock | (463.5) | (32.0) | (195.2) |
| Proceeds from exercises of stock options | 68.6 | 82.8 | 15.8 |
| Other, net | (36.7) | (30.9) | (47.0) |
| **Net Cash Provided by (Used for) Financing Activities** | (303.3) | 24.7 | (131.1) |
| **Effect of Exchange Rate Changes on Cash and Cash Equivalents** | (3.4) | 0.4 | (7.5) |
| **Net Increase (Decrease) in Cash and Cash Equivalents** | 57.0 | (16.8) | 15.9 |
| **Cash and Cash Equivalents — Beginning of Year** | 169.9 | 186.7 | 170.8 |
| **Cash and Cash Equivalents — End of Year** | $ 226.9 | $ 169.9 | $ 186.7 |
| **Supplemental Cash Flow Information:** | | | |
| **Cash Flow Data** | | | |
| Interest paid | $ 549.5 | 574.7 | 490.1 |
| Income taxes paid | $ 675.6 | 519.7 | 385.9 |
| **Schedule of Noncash Investing and Financing Activities** | | | |
| Liabilities assumed in connection with acquisitions | $ 897.0 | 383.8 | 70.9 |
| Issuance of treasury stock and debt for acquisitions | $ 364.5 | 189.5 | 162.7 |
| Book value of net assets exchanged for investment in affiliates | $ 60.8 | 86.7 | — |

See accompanying Notes to Consolidated Financial Statements.

# Management's Analysis—Cash Flows

*(See "Management's Analysis—Overview" on page 24 for background information.)*

Cash flow activity in 1993 reflected strong cash flows from operations of $3.1 billion, net proceeds of $590 million from debt activities and $259 million in net proceeds from short-term investment activities. Major funding needs included capital spending of $2.0 billion, acquisition and affiliate investment activity of $1.0 billion, purchases of treasury stock totaling $464 million and dividend payments of $462 million.

One of PepsiCo's most significant financial strengths is its internal cash generation capability. In 1993, cash flows generated, after capital spending and acquisitions, in snack foods and beverages were partially offset by a cash use in restaurants that reflected funding of additional units, both constructed and acquired. Net cash flows from PepsiCo's domestic businesses were partially offset by international uses of cash, reflecting strategies to accelerate growth of international operations.

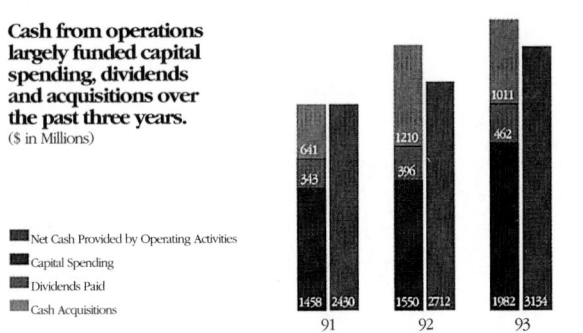

**Cash from operations largely funded capital spending, dividends and acquisitions over the past three years.**
($ in Millions)

■ Net Cash Provided by Operating Activities
■ Capital Spending
■ Dividends Paid
■ Cash Acquisitions

**Net Cash Provided by Operating Activities** in 1993 rose $423 million or 16% over 1992, and in 1992 grew $281 million or 12% over 1991. Income before noncash charges and credits rose 24% in 1993 and 14% in 1992. The increases in depreciation and amortization noncash charges of $229 million in 1993 and $180 million in 1992 reflected capital spending and acquisitions. The 1993 increase of $135 million in the deferred income tax provision was primarily due to the lapping of 1992 effects related to restructuring accruals and prefunded employee benefit expenses and the impact of new U.S. tax legislation. The 1992 decline of $150 million in the deferred income tax provision was primarily due to the impact of SFAS 106 and SFAS 109, higher restructuring accruals and lower prefunding of employee benefit expenses. The 1992 increase in other net noncash charges and credits reflected higher accruals of noncurrent liabilities. Funding in 1993 of operating working capital increased $257 million over 1992, reflecting slower collections of domestic accounts receivable, advance domestic purchases of product ingredients, higher payments of income taxes and the lapping of 1992 and 1991 effects related to restructuring accruals, partially offset by the impact on accounts payable of the timing of a large year-end payment to prefund employee benefits. The 1992 over 1991 net increase of $59 million in funding of operating working capital was driven by the timing of year-end payments of accounts payable, partially offset by lower prefunding of employee benefits, which is recorded as prepaid expense.

**Investing Activities** over the past three years reflected strategic spending in all three industry segments through capital spending, acquisitions and investments in affiliates. Acquisitive activity in all three years primarily reflected acquisitions of franchised bottling and restaurant operations and international snack food businesses. Noncash acquisition activity, consisting of treasury stock and debt issuances, totaled $365 million, $190 million and $163 million in 1993, 1992 and 1991, respectively. About 45% of the total acquisitive activity in 1993 represented international transactions, compared to 60% in 1992 and 25% in 1991. PepsiCo continues to seek opportunities to strengthen its position in its domestic and international industry segments through such strategic acquisitions. Capital spending increases have been driven by restaurants, which represented about half of the spending in all three years, led by new units. Capital spending is expected to increase to approximately $2.2 billion in 1994. About half of the 1994 amount is targeted for restaurants, led by new units, and the balance is evenly divided between beverages and snack foods, reflecting productive capacity expansion and equipment replacements. Approximately one-third of the planned 1994 capital spending relates to international businesses, about the same as the prior three years. Cash provided by operations is expected to be sufficient to fund expected capital spending. Short-term investment activity in PepsiCo's portfolios outside the U.S. provided $259 million in 1993, compared to net investments of $52 million in 1992 and $141 million in 1991.

**Financing Activities.** The 1993 over 1992 change in cash flows from net financing activities was a $328 million use, compared to a 1992 over 1991 source of $156 million, principally due to changes in treasury stock purchases. Financing activities reflected net issuances of short and long-term debt of $590 million in 1993, $400 million in 1992 and $439 million (which included the retirement of a $300 million nonrecourse obligation) in 1991.

During 1993, PepsiCo issued $1.1 billion of notes. Subsequent to year-end, PepsiCo issued $814 million of notes through February 1994. The proceeds were used to refinance short-term borrowings. These issuances utilized the remaining availability under a $3.3 billion shelf registration statement effective in December 1991 and $250 million of a $2.5 billion shelf registration statement effective in February 1994 for the principal purposes of financing growth activities and refinancing other borrowings.

Cash dividends declared were $486 million in 1993 and $405 million in 1992. PepsiCo targets a dividend payout of about one-third of the prior year's income, thus retaining sufficient earnings to provide financial resources for growth opportunities.

Share repurchase decisions are evaluated considering management's target capital structure and other investment opportunities. In 1993, PepsiCo repurchased 12.4 million shares at a cost of $464 million. Subsequent to year-end, PepsiCo repurchased 4.8 million shares through February 1994 at a cost of $186 million. Of the total 17.2 million shares, 12.0 million were purchased under the 45 million share repurchase authority granted by PepsiCo's Board of Directors (the Board) in 1987. The remaining 5.2 million shares were purchased under the new 50 million share repurchase authority, granted by the Board on July 22, 1993. This new authority replaced the 11.2 million shares remaining under the 1987 authority.

# Consolidated Statement of Shareholders' Equity

(shares in thousands, dollars in millions except per share amounts)
PepsiCo, Inc. and Subsidiaries
Fifty-two weeks ended December 25, 1993, December 26, 1992 and December 28, 1991

| | Capital Stock | | | | Capital in Excess of Par Value | Retained Earnings | Currency Translation Adjustment and Other | Total |
| | Issued | | Treasury | | | | | |
| | Shares | Amount | Shares | Amount | | | | |
|---|---|---|---|---|---|---|---|---|
| Shareholders' Equity, December 29, 1990..... | 863,083 | $ 14.4 | (74,694) | $ (611.4) | $ 365.0 | $ 4,753.0 | $ 383.2 | $ 4,904.2 |
| 1991 Net income......................... | — | — | — | — | — | 1,080.2 | — | 1,080.2 |
| Cash dividends declared (per share-$0.46).................... | — | — | — | — | — | (363.2) | — | (363.2) |
| Currency translation adjustment.......... | — | — | — | — | — | — | (52.9) | (52.9) |
| Purchases of treasury stock.............. | — | — | (6,392) | (195.2) | — | — | — | (195.2) |
| Shares issued in connection with acquisitions....................... | — | — | 5,613 | 46.7 | 95.0 | — | — | 141.7 |
| Stock option exercises, including tax benefits, and compensation awards..... | — | — | 1,446 | 13.6 | 16.4 | — | — | 30.0 |
| Other, principally conversion of debentures..................... | — | — | 45 | 0.4 | 0.2 | — | — | 0.6 |
| Shareholders' Equity, December 28, 1991.... | 863,083 | $ 14.4 | (73,982) | $ (745.9) | $ 476.6 | $ 5,470.0 | $ 330.3 | $ 5,545.4 |
| 1992 Net income........................ | — | — | — | — | — | 374.3 | — | 374.3 |
| Cash dividends declared (per share-$0.51).................... | — | — | — | — | — | (404.6) | — | (404.6) |
| Currency translation adjustment.......... | — | — | — | — | — | — | (429.3) | (429.3) |
| Shares issued in connection with acquisitions....................... | — | — | 4,265 | 44.2 | 115.3 | — | — | 159.5 |
| Stock option exercises, including tax benefits, and compensation awards..... | — | — | 6,333 | 65.5 | 75.5 | — | — | 141.0 |
| Purchases of treasury stock.............. | — | — | (1,000) | (32.0) | — | — | — | (32.0) |
| Other, principally conversion of debentures..................... | — | — | 107 | 1.2 | 0.2 | — | — | 1.4 |
| Shareholders' Equity, December 26, 1992.... | 863,083 | $ 14.4 | (64,277) | $ (667.0) | $ 667.6 | $ 5,439.7 | $ (99.0) | $ 5,355.7 |
| 1993 Net income........................ | — | — | — | — | — | 1,587.9 | — | 1,587.9 |
| Cash dividends declared (per share-$0.61).................... | — | — | — | — | — | (485.7) | — | (485.7) |
| Currency translation adjustment.......... | — | — | — | — | — | — | (77.0) | (77.0) |
| Purchases of treasury stock.............. | — | — | (12,371) | (463.5) | — | — | — | (463.5) |
| Shares issued in connection with acquisitions....................... | — | — | 8,896 | 170.2 | 164.6 | — | — | 334.8 |
| Stock option exercises, including tax benefits, and compensation awards..... | — | — | 3,415 | 46.6 | 47.1 | — | — | 93.7 |
| Pension liability adjustment, net of deferred taxes..................... | — | — | — | — | — | — | (7.9) | (7.9) |
| Other, principally conversion of debentures..................... | — | — | 35 | 0.5 | 0.2 | — | — | 0.7 |
| **Shareholders' Equity, December 25, 1993..** | **863,083** | **$14.4** | **(64,302)** | **$(913.2)** | **$879.5** | **$6,541.9** | **$(183.9)** | **$6,338.7** |

See accompanying Notes to Consolidated Financial Statements.

# Notes to Consolidated Financial Statements

*(tabular dollars in millions except per share amounts)*

## Note 1 – Summary of Significant Accounting Policies

Significant accounting policies are discussed below, and where applicable, in the Notes that follow.

**Principles of Consolidation.** The financial statements reflect the consolidated accounts of PepsiCo, Inc. and its controlled affiliates. Intercompany accounts and transactions have been eliminated. Investments in affiliates in which PepsiCo exercises significant influence but not control are accounted for by the equity method, and the equity in net income is included in Selling, general and administrative expenses in the Consolidated Statement of Income. Certain other reclassifications were made to prior year amounts to conform with the 1993 presentation.

**Marketing Costs.** Marketing costs are reported in Selling, general and administrative expenses and include costs of advertising, marketing and promotional programs. Promotional discounts are expensed as incurred, and other marketing costs not deferred are charged to expense ratably in relation to sales over the year in which incurred. Marketing costs deferred consist of media and personal service advertising prepayments, materials in inventory and production costs of future media advertising; these assets are expensed in the year used.

**Cash Equivalents.** Cash equivalents represent funds temporarily invested (with original maturities not exceeding three months) as part of PepsiCo's management of day-to-day operating cash receipts and disbursements. All other investment portfolios, primarily held outside the U.S., are classified as short-term investments.

**Net Income Per Share.** Net income per share is computed by dividing net income by the weighted average number of shares and share equivalents outstanding during each year.

**Research and Development Expenses.** Research and development expenses, which are expensed as incurred, were $113 million, $102 million and $99 million in 1993, 1992 and 1991, respectively.

## Note 2 – Business Segments

Information regarding industry segments and geographic areas of operations is provided on pages 27 through 29.

## Note 3 – Unusual Items

In 1993, PepsiCo recorded a charge of $29.9 million ($0.04 per share) to increase its net deferred tax liabilities, as required by Statement of Financial Accounting Standards No. 109 (SFAS 109), "Accounting for Income Taxes," for the 1% statutory rate increase under U.S. tax legislation enacted in 1993. (See Note 13.)

Unusual charges, principally for restructurings, totaled $193.5 million in 1992 ($128.5 million after-tax or $0.16 per share) and $170.0 million in 1991 ($119.8 million after-tax or $0.15 per share). In 1992, PepsiCo adopted the Statement of Financial Accounting Standards No. 106 (SFAS 106), "Employers' Accounting for Postretirement Benefits Other Than Pensions" and SFAS 109 effective December 29, 1991. (See Notes 10 and 13.) As compared to the previous accounting methods, the adoption of SFAS 106 and SFAS 109 reduced 1992 operating profit by $72.8 million ($19.3 million after-tax or $0.02 per share). Information regarding the effect of these actions on comparability of operating profits is provided on page 27.

## Note 4 – Acquisitions and Investments in Affiliates

During 1993, PepsiCo completed a number of acquisitions and affiliate investments in all three industry segments aggregating $1.4 billion, principally comprised of $1.0 billion in cash and $335 million in PepsiCo Capital Stock. Approximately $307 million of debt, including capital lease obligations, was assumed in these transactions, more than half of which was subsequently retired. This activity included acquisitions of domestic and international franchised restaurant operations, the buyout of PepsiCo's joint venture partners in a franchised bottling operation in Spain and the related acquisition of their fruit-flavored beverage operation, the acquisition of the remaining 85% interest in a large franchised bottling operation in the Northwestern U.S., the acquisition of a regional Mexican-style casual dining restaurant chain in the U.S. and equity investments in certain franchised bottling operations in Argentina and Mexico.

During 1992, acquisitions and affiliate investment activity aggregated $1.4 billion, principally for cash. This activity included acquisitions of international (primarily Canada) and domestic franchised bottling operations and a number of domestic and international franchised restaurant operations, the buyout of PepsiCo's joint venture partner in a Canadian snack food business and an equity investment in a domestic casual dining restaurant chain featuring gourmet pizza. In addition, PepsiCo exchanged certain previously consolidated snack food operations in Europe with a net book value of $87 million for a 60% equity interest in an international snack food joint venture with General Mills, Inc. PepsiCo secured a controlling interest in its Mexican cookie affiliate, Gamesa, through an exchange of certain non-cookie operations of Gamesa for its joint venture partner's interest.

During 1991, acquisition and affiliate investment activity aggregated $804 million, principally for cash, led by acquisitions of domestic franchised restaurant operations.

The acquisitions have been accounted for by the purchase method; accordingly, their results are included in the Consolidated Financial Statements from their respective dates of acquisition. The aggregate impact of acquisitions was not material to PepsiCo's net sales, net income or net income per share; accordingly, no related pro forma information is provided.

## Note 5 – Inventories

Inventories are valued at the lower of cost (computed on the average, first-in, first-out or last-in, first-out methods) or net realizable value. The cost of 41% of 1993 inventories and 44% of 1992 inventories was computed using the last-in, first-out (LIFO) method. Use of the LIFO method increased the 1993 total year-end inventory amount below by $8.9 million, but reduced the 1992 amount by $3.4 million.

| | 1993 | 1992 |
|---|---|---|
| Raw materials, supplies and in-process | **$463.9** | $388.1 |
| Finished goods . . . . . . . . . . . . . . . . . . . | **460.8** | 380.7 |
| | **$924.7** | $768.8 |

PepsiCo hedges certain raw material purchases through commodity futures contracts to reduce its exposure to market price fluctuations. Gains and losses on these contracts are included in the cost of the raw materials.

## Note 6 – Property, Plant and Equipment

Property, plant and equipment are stated at cost. Depreciation is calculated principally on a straight-line basis over the estimated useful lives of the assets. Depreciation expense in 1993, 1992 and 1991 was $1.1 billion, $923 million and $800 million, respectively.

| | 1993 | 1992 |
|---|---|---|
| Land | $ 1,186.4 | $ 1,010.0 |
| Buildings and improvements | 5,017.6 | 4,269.5 |
| Capital leases, primarily buildings | 402.6 | 330.5 |
| Machinery and equipment | 7,643.4 | 6,485.2 |
| | 14,250.0 | 12,095.2 |
| Accumulated depreciation | (5,394.4) | (4,653.2) |
| | $ 8,855.6 | $ 7,442.0 |

## Note 7 – Intangible Assets

Identifiable intangible assets arose from the allocation of purchase prices of businesses acquired, and consist principally of reacquired franchise rights and trademarks. Reacquired franchise rights relate to acquisitions of franchised bottling and restaurant operations, and the trademarks principally relate to acquisitions of international snack food operations and KFC. Values assigned to such identifiable intangibles were based on independent appraisals or internal estimates. Goodwill represents any residual purchase price after allocation to all identifiable net assets.

| | 1993 | 1992 |
|---|---|---|
| Reacquired franchise rights | $3,959.7 | $3,476.9 |
| Trademarks | 898.5 | 734.2 |
| Other identifiable intangibles | 154.7 | 159.6 |
| Goodwill | 2,916.6 | 2,588.3 |
| | $7,929.5 | $6,959.0 |

Intangible assets are amortized on a straight-line basis over appropriate periods generally ranging from 20 to 40 years. Accumulated amortization was $1.3 billion and $1.0 billion at year-end 1993 and 1992, respectively.

The recoverability of carrying values of intangible assets is evaluated on a recurring basis. The primary indicators of recoverability are current or forecasted profitability of the related acquired business, measured as profit before interest, but after amortization of the intangible assets. Consideration is also given to the estimated disposal values of certain identifiable intangible assets compared to their carrying values. For the three-year period ended December 25, 1993, there were no adjustments to the carrying values of intangible assets resulting from these evaluations.

## Note 8 – Short-term Borrowings and Long-term Debt

| | 1993 | 1992 |
|---|---|---|
| **Short-term Borrowings** | | |
| Commercial paper (3.3% and 3.5% weighted average interest rate at year-end 1993 and 1992, respectively) | $ 3,535.0 | $ 2,113.6 |
| Current maturities of long-term debt issuances | 1,183.1 | 1,052.6 |
| Notes (A) | 394.0 | 600.0 |
| Other borrowings | 529.1 | 440.6 |
| Amount reclassified to long-term debt (B) | (3,450.0) | (3,500.0) |
| | $ 2,191.2 | $ 706.8 |
| **Long-term Debt** | | |
| Short-term borrowings, reclassified (B) | $ 3,450.0 | $ 3,500.0 |
| Notes due 1994-2008 (6.5% and 6.6% weighted average interest rate at year-end 1993 and 1992, respectively) (A) | 3,873.8 | 4,209.1 |
| Zero coupon notes, $935 million due 1994-2012 (14.4% semi-annual weighted average yield to maturity at year-end 1993 and 1992) | 327.2 | 300.4 |
| Swiss franc perpetual Foreign Interest Payment bonds (C) | 212.2 | 211.4 |
| Pound sterling 9 1/8% notes (D) | – | 91.0 |
| Swiss franc 5 1/4% bearer bonds due 1995 (D) | 90.1 | 89.1 |
| Swiss franc 7 1/8% notes due 1994 (D) | 69.8 | 69.1 |
| Capital lease obligations (See Note 9) | 291.4 | 242.0 |
| Other, due 1994-2020 (6.6% and 6.8% weighted average interest rate at year-end 1993 and 1992, respectively) | 311.2 | 305.3 |
| | 8,625.7 | 9,017.4 |
| Less current maturities of long-term debt issuances | (1,183.1) | (1,052.6) |
| Total long-term debt | $ 7,442.6 | $ 7,964.8 |

Long-term debt is carried net of any related discount or premium and unamortized debt issuance costs. The debt agreements include various restrictions, none of which is presently significant to PepsiCo.

The annual maturities of long-term debt through 1998, excluding capital lease obligations and the reclassified short-term borrowings, are: 1994-$1.2 billion, 1995-$692 million, 1996-$1.1 billion, 1997-$278 million and 1998-$1.1 billion.

(A) PepsiCo has entered into interest rate swap agreements to effectively convert $193 million and $725 million of fixed rate debt issuances to variable rate debt with a weighted average interest rate of 3.3% and 3.4% at year-end 1993 and 1992, respectively, as well as effectively convert $214 million of variable rate debt to fixed rate debt with an interest rate of 7.0% at year-end 1993 and 1992. The differential to be paid or received on interest rate swaps is accrued as interest rates change and is charged or credited to interest expense over the life of the agreements.

**(B)** At year-end 1993 and 1992, $3.5 billion of short-term borrowings were classified as long-term, reflecting PepsiCo's intent and ability to refinance these borrowings on a long-term basis, through either long-term debt issuances or rollover of existing short-term borrowings. At year-end 1993 and 1992, PepsiCo had revolving credit agreements covering potential borrowings aggregating $3.5 billion, with the current agreements expiring in 1995 through 1999. These unused credit facilities provide the ability to refinance short-term borrowings.

**(C)** The coupon rate of the Swiss franc 400 million perpetual Foreign Interest Payment bonds issued in 1986 is 7 1/2% through 1996. The interest payments are made in U.S. dollars at a fixed contractual exchange rate. The bonds have no stated maturity date. At the end of each 10-year period after the issuance of the bonds, PepsiCo and the bondholders each have the right to cause redemption of the bonds. If not redeemed, the coupon rate will be adjusted based on the prevailing yield of 10-year U.S. Treasury Securities. The principal of the bonds is denominated in Swiss francs. PepsiCo can, and intends to, limit the ultimate redemption amount to the U.S. dollar proceeds at issuance, which is the basis of the carrying value.

**(D)** PepsiCo has entered into currency exchange agreements to hedge its foreign currency exposure on these issues of non-U.S. dollar denominated debt. At year-end 1993, the carrying value of this debt aggregated $160 million and the net receivable under related currency exchange agreements aggregated $41 million, resulting in a net effective U.S. dollar liability of $119 million with a weighted average fixed interest rate of 6.5%. At year-end 1992, the aggregate carrying values of the debt and the net receivable under related currency exchange agreements were $249 million and $20 million, respectively, resulting in a net effective U.S. dollar liability of $229 million with a weighted average fixed interest rate of 7.2%. The carrying values of the currency exchange agreements are reflected in the Consolidated Balance Sheet as gross receivables and payables under the appropriate current and noncurrent asset and liability captions. Changes in the carrying value of a currency exchange agreement resulting from exchange rate movements are offset by changes in the carrying value of the related non-U.S. dollar denominated debt, as both values are based on current exchange rates.

The maturity dates of interest rate swaps and currency exchange agreements correspond with those of the related debt instruments. The counterparties to PepsiCo's interest rate swaps and currency exchange agreements consist of a diversified group of financial institutions. PepsiCo is exposed to credit risk to the extent of nonperformance by these counterparties; however, PepsiCo regularly monitors its positions and the credit ratings of these counterparties and considers the risk of default to be minimal. Additionally, due to the frequency of interest payments and receipts, PepsiCo's credit risk related to interest rate swaps is not significant.

## Note 9 – Leases

PepsiCo has noncancelable commitments under both capital and long-term operating leases, primarily for restaurant units. Certain of these units have been subleased to restaurant franchisees. Commitments on capital and operating leases expire at various dates through 2088 and, in many cases, provide for rent escalations and renewal options. Most leases require payment of related occupancy costs which include property taxes, maintenance and insurance.

Future minimum commitments and sublease receivables under noncancelable leases are as follows:

|  | Commitments | | Sublease Receivables | |
|---|---|---|---|---|
|  | Capital | Operating | Direct Financing | Operating |
| 1994 ...... | $ 56.8 | $ 247.2 | $ 3.5 | $ 9.7 |
| 1995 ...... | 52.4 | 219.7 | 3.3 | 9.1 |
| 1996 ...... | 46.5 | 197.7 | 3.1 | 8.2 |
| 1997 ...... | 39.9 | 171.6 | 2.8 | 7.3 |
| 1998 ...... | 59.8 | 155.5 | 2.4 | 6.1 |
| Later years | 229.0 | 894.9 | 9.0 | 25.5 |
|  | $484.4 | $1,886.6 | $24.1 | $65.9 |

At year-end 1993, the present value of minimum payments under capital leases was $291 million, after deducting $1 million for estimated executory costs (taxes, maintenance and insurance) and $192 million representing imputed interest. The present value of minimum receivables under direct financing subleases was $15 million after deducting $9 million of unearned interest income.

Total rental expense and income and the contingent portions of these totals were as follows:

|  | **1993** | 1992 | 1991 |
|---|---|---|---|
| Total rental expense .............. | **$419.8** | 379.0 | 323.2 |
| Contingent portion of expense ..... | **$ 27.5** | 27.5 | 22.3 |
| Total rental income ............... | **$ 16.6** | 14.7 | 13.0 |
| Contingent portion of income ...... | **$ 4.4** | 4.5 | 4.8 |

Contingent rentals are based on sales by restaurants in excess of levels stipulated in the lease agreements.

## Note 14 – Franchise Arrangements

Franchise arrangements with restaurant franchisees generally provide for initial fees and continuing royalty payments to PepsiCo based upon a percentage of sales. The arrangements are intended to assist franchisees through, among other things, product development and marketing programs initiated by PepsiCo for both its company-owned and franchised operations. On a limited basis, franchisees have also entered into leases of restaurant properties leased or owned by PepsiCo. (See Note 9.) Royalty revenues, initial fees and rental payments from franchisees, which are included in Net Sales, aggregated $357 million, $344 million and $326 million in 1993, 1992 and 1991, respectively. Franchise royalty revenues, which represent the majority of these amounts, are recognized when earned. PepsiCo also has franchise arrangements with beverage bottlers, which do not provide for royalty payments.

## Note 15 – Employee Incentive Plans

PepsiCo has established certain employee incentive plans under which stock options are granted. A stock option allows an employee to purchase a share of PepsiCo Capital Stock (Stock) in the future at the fair market value on the date of the grant.

Under the PepsiCo SharePower Stock Option Plan (SharePower), approved by the Board of Directors and effective in 1989, essentially all employees other than executive officers, part-time and short-service employees may be granted stock options annually. The number of options granted is based on each employee's annual earnings. The options generally become exercisable ratably over five years from the grant date and must be exercised within 10 years of the grant date. SharePower options were granted to approximately 118,000 employees in 1993 and 114,000 employees in 1992.

The shareholder-approved 1987 Long-Term Incentive Plan (the Plan), which has provisions similar to plans in place in prior years, provides incentives to eligible senior and middle management employees. In addition to grants of stock options, which are generally exercisable between 1 and 15 years from the grant date, the Plan allows for grants of performance share units (PSUs) to eligible senior management employees. A PSU is equivalent in value to a share of Stock at the grant date and vests for payment four years from the grant date, contingent upon attainment of prescribed performance goals. PSUs are not directly granted, as certain stock options granted may be surrendered by employees for a specified number of PSUs within 60 days of the option grant date. During 1993, 96,165 stock options were surrendered for 32,055 PSUs. At year-end 1993 and 1992, there were 491,200 and 484,698 outstanding PSUs, respectively.

The Plan also provides for incentive stock units (ISUs), which were granted to eligible middle management employees. Since 1989 these employees have been granted stock options rather than ISUs. ISUs vest for payment at specified dates over a six-year period, and each ISU is equivalent in value to a share of Stock at those respective dates. At year-end 1993 and 1992, there were 5,700 and 127,565 outstanding ISUs, respectively.

Grants under the Plan are approved by the Compensation Committee of the Board of Directors (the Committee), which is composed of outside directors. Payment of awards other than stock options is made in cash and/or Stock as approved by the Committee, and amounts expensed for such awards were $5 million, $11 million and $15 million in 1993, 1992 and 1991, respectively. Under the Plan, a maximum of 54 million shares of Stock can be purchased or paid pursuant to grants. There were 20 million and 22 million shares available for future grants at year-end 1993 and 1992, respectively.

1993 and 1992 activity for the stock option plans included:

| (options in thousands) | SharePower | Long-Term Incentive |
| --- | --- | --- |
| Outstanding at December 28, 1991 | 23,801 | 27,834 |
| Granted | 8,477 | 12,653 |
| Exercised | (1,155) | (5,155) |
| Surrendered for PSUs | – | (503) |
| Canceled | (2,327) | (1,839) |
| Outstanding at December 26, 1992 | 28,796 | 32,990 |
| Granted | **9,121** | **2,834** |
| Exercised | **(1,958)** | **(1,412)** |
| Surrendered for PSUs | **–** | **(96)** |
| Canceled | **(2,524)** | **(966)** |
| Outstanding at December 25, 1993 | **33,435** | **33,350** |
| Exercisable at December 25, 1993 | **11,733** | **10,665** |
| Option prices per share: | | |
| Exercised during 1993 | $17.58 to $36.75 | $4.11 to $36.31 |
| Exercised during 1992 | $17.58 to $35.25 | $4.11 to $29.88 |
| Outstanding at year-end 1993 | $17.58 to $36.75 | $4.11 to $42.81 |

## Note 16 – Fair Value of Financial Instruments

PepsiCo's financial instruments include cash, cash equivalents, short-term investments, debt, interest rate swap agreements, currency exchange agreements and guarantees. Because of the short maturity of cash equivalents and investments which mature in less than one year, the carrying value approximates fair value. The fair value of investments which mature in more than one year is based upon market quotes. The fair value of debt issuances, interest rate swap agreements and currency exchange agreements is estimated using market quotes, valuation models and calculations based on market rates. At year-end 1993 and 1992, the carrying value of all financial instruments was not materially different from fair value.

## Note 17 – Contingencies

PepsiCo is subject to various claims and contingencies related to lawsuits, taxes, environmental and other matters arising out of the normal course of business. Management believes that the ultimate liability, if any, in excess of amounts already provided arising from such claims or contingencies is not likely to have a material adverse effect on PepsiCo's annual results of operations or financial condition. At year-end 1993 and 1992, PepsiCo was contingently liable under guarantees aggregating $276 million and $200 million, respectively. The guarantees are primarily issued to support financial arrangements of certain bottling and restaurant franchisees and PepsiCo joint ventures. PepsiCo manages the risk associated with these guarantees by performing appropriate credit reviews in addition to retaining certain rights as a franchisor or joint venture partner.

# Management's Responsibility for Financial Statements

To Our Shareholders:

Management is responsible for the reliability of the consolidated financial statements and related notes, which have been prepared in conformity with generally accepted accounting principles and include amounts based upon our estimates and judgments, as required. The financial statements have been audited and reported on by our independent auditors, KPMG Peat Marwick, who were given free access to all financial records and related data, including minutes of the meetings of the Board of Directors and Committees of the Board. We believe that the representations made to the independent auditors were valid and appropriate.

PepsiCo maintains a system of internal control over financial reporting designed to provide reasonable assurance as to the reliability of the financial statements. The system is supported by formal policies and procedures, including an active Code of Conduct program intended to ensure key employees adhere to the highest standards of personal and professional integrity. PepsiCo's internal audit function monitors and reports on the adequacy of and compliance with the internal control system, and appropriate actions are taken to address control deficiencies and other opportunities for improving the system as they are identified. The Audit Committee of the Board of Directors, which is composed solely of outside directors, provides oversight to the financial reporting process through periodic meetings with our independent auditors, internal auditors and management. Both our independent auditors and internal auditors have free access to the Audit Committee.

Although no cost effective internal control system will preclude all errors and irregularities, we believe our controls provide reasonable assurance that the financial statements are reliable.

*Wayne Calloway*

Wayne Calloway
Chairman of the Board and Chief Executive Officer

*Robert H. Dettmer*

Robert G. Dettmer
Executive Vice President and Chief Financial Officer

*Robert L. Carleton*

Robert L. Carleton
Senior Vice President and Controller

February 1, 1994

---

# Report of Independent Auditors

Board of Directors and Shareholders
PepsiCo, Inc.

We have audited the accompanying consolidated balance sheet of PepsiCo, Inc. and Subsidiaries as of December 25, 1993 and December 26, 1992, and the related consolidated statements of income, shareholders' equity, and cash flows for each of the years in the three-year period ended December 25, 1993, appearing on pages 27, 28, 29, 30, 32, 34 and 36 through 44. These consolidated financial statements are the responsibility of PepsiCo, Inc.'s management. Our responsibility is to express an opinion on these consolidated financial statements based on our audits.

We conducted our audits in accordance with generally accepted auditing standards. Those standards require that we plan and perform the audit to obtain reasonable assurance about whether the financial statements are free of material misstatement. An audit includes examining, on a test basis, evidence supporting the amounts and disclosures in the financial statements. An audit also includes assessing the accounting principles used and significant estimates made by management, as well as evaluating the overall financial statement presentation. We believe that our audits provide a reasonable basis for our opinion.

In our opinion, the consolidated financial statements referred to above present fairly, in all material respects, the financial position of PepsiCo, Inc. and Subsidiaries as of December 25, 1993 and December 26, 1992, and the results of its operations and its cash flows for each of the years in the three-year period ended December 25, 1993, in conformity with generally accepted accounting principles.

As discussed in Notes 10 and 13 to the consolidated financial statements, PepsiCo, Inc. adopted the provisions of the Financial Accounting Standards Board's Statements of Financial Accounting Standards No. 106, "Employers' Accounting for Postretirement Benefits Other Than Pensions" and No. 109, "Accounting for Income Taxes" in 1992.

*KPMG Peat Marwick*

KPMG Peat Marwick
New York, New York
February 1, 1994

# Introduction to Management Accounting

**LEARNING OBJECTIVES**
After studying this chapter, you should be able to do the following:

1 Explain how management accounting assists management in the decision-making process

2 Explain how financial accounting differs from management accounting

3 Describe how the management accountant assists management in planning, control, and inventory costing

4 Explain the role of accounting in an organization

5 Understand the ethical considerations facing management accountants

6 Define the key terms listed at the end of the chapter

**CHAPTER OUTLINE**
**THE DIFFERENCES BETWEEN MANAGEMENT ACCOUNTING AND FINANCIAL ACCOUNTING** • Two Basic Differences • Other Differences • **THE PRIMARY ROLES OF MANAGEMENT ACCOUNTANTS AND COST ACCOUNTANTS** • Planning • Control • Inventory Costing • **ROLE OF ACCOUNTING WITHIN AN ORGANIZATION** • **ETHICS AND MANAGEMENT ACCOUNTING** • Competence Standards • Confidentiality Standards • Integrity Standards • Objectivity Standards

So far this book has focused entirely on financial accounting issues, practices, and rules. You have learned how to account for a variety of transactions and how to prepare and evaluate the general-purpose financial statements that result from these transactions. However, the financial statements you have studied have been limited to service and merchandising organizations; manufacturers have been ignored—until now, that is.

This part of the book takes a major change in direction. First, it introduces a new and different discipline of accounting, called **management accounting.** Second, it discusses in great detail financial accounting issues that are unique to manufacturers. In addition, this part presents numerous accounting tools that management accountants in all types of organizations—service, merchandising, and manufacturing, can use to assist management in the decision-making process.

This chapter provides a general discussion of the nature of management accounting—what it is, why it is important to an organization, and how it compares to financial accounting and cost accounting. It also discusses the importance of ethics for management accountants and examines the code of ethics for the management accounting profession.

## THE DIFFERENCES BETWEEN MANAGEMENT ACCOUNTING AND FINANCIAL ACCOUNTING

The managers of any business entity use the best available quantitative information to make their organization function in the most effective and efficient manner possible. The accounting system provides this information to management, which uses it to accomplish three broad purposes:

1. To provide the financial statements to interested external users
2. To plan the operations of the organization in both the short run and the long run
3. To control the results of operations

### Two Basic Differences

Management accounting and financial accounting differ in two basic areas: the purposes and the users of the information gathered. *Financial accounting* accomplishes the first of these three purposes. That is, financial accountants record, classify, analyze, summarize, and report the results of the activities of the organization to creditors, stockholders and prospective investors, governmental bodies and labor unions, environmental organizations, and others. For corporations, the reports to external users consist of four general-purpose financial statements: the income statement, the balance sheet, the statement of retained earnings, and the statement of cash flows. They are used primarily by investors, creditors, and those who are trying to protect their investments in the organization, as well as by others who have a special interest in the organization.

**Learning Objective 1**

Explain how management accounting assists management in the decision-making process

Management accounting fulfills the second and third purposes listed above by performing two primary roles: helping managers to plan and helping them to control. To plan operations and control results efficiently, management needs more, and more detailed, information than is provided in the four financial statements. The accounting system that provides this special information for internal management is called **management accounting.**

Management accounting information is used in making decisions concerning the internal workings of the organization. There are many different types of decisions for which managers need accounting information. Here are some typical decision questions that regularly confront managers:

- Should the organization develop its own products internally, or purchase patents to new product lines from other organizations?
- Should internally developed products be designed to be as simple as possible or to accommodate all the features that customers may want to have?
- Is a particular product line generating sufficient profit? If not, should we discontinue making the product?
- What sales price should we set for units awaiting sale to customers? How will a change in a product's sales price affect the income generated by that product?
- What method of sales promotion would most effectively market our products?
- If we provide home delivery to our customers, what amount should they be charged?
- How can we improve the quality of our products in order to reduce subsequent costs of customer service?

For managers to make the best decisions to resolve questions such as these, the management accountant must focus on providing information that is timely, relevant, understandable, and most useful to management in the decision making process. As the list above suggests, the decision making process involves all areas of the business. Certainly the production and sale of a product are essential to the success of any organization, but equally important may also be research and development, product design, distribution, and customer service. As Figure 1 below indicates there are many business functions within an organization that are part of a value chain. Each of these sequential functions is important to the overall success of the organization, because each function adds value to the product.

Learning Objective   **2**

Explain how financial accounting differs from management accounting

## Other Differences

Exhibit 1 summarizes the distinctions between management accounting and financial accounting. The most basic differences are the two discussed above: the purposes and the users of each discipline. There are several other differences as well.

### *Time Orientation*

The information gathered by financial accountants relates significantly to the past; the information gathered by management accountants deals substantially with the future. Whereas financial accounting reports the results of past activities, management accounting typically looks to the potential effect of planned activities on the future.

**Figure 1** Value Chain: Business Functions That Add Value to a Product

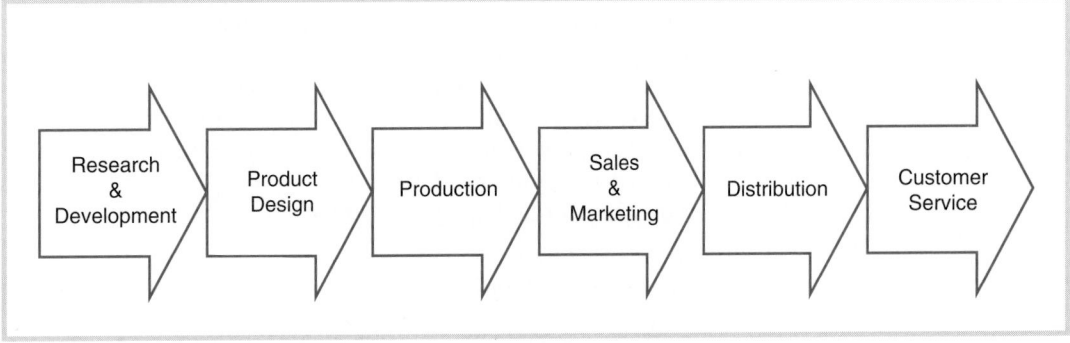

**Exhibit 1** Differences between Financial Accounting and Management Accounting

| Issue | Financial Accounting | Management Accounting |
|---|---|---|
| Purposes | Provide general-purpose financial statements | Provide information for planning and control |
| Users | External parties | Internal users—management |
| Time orientation | Primarily the past | Substantially the future |
| Mandatory nature of reports | Required by GAAP | Not required by GAAP, only by common sense |
| Restrictions on presentation of information | Must be consistent, conservative, objective, and historical to be GAAP | No restrictions—information presented in any way that is most useful to management |
| Flexibility of reports | Inflexible | Flexible |
| Perspective on the organization | Aggregate | Detailed |
| Timeliness of reports | Annual and possibly quarterly | As needed |

### Mandatory Nature of Reports

Publicly held organizations are required by generally accepted accounting principles (GAAP) to provide financial accounting information to external users. Management has no choice but to issue financial statements, and users have the right to see them. Since external users are by definition outside the organization, financial statements are their main source of information about how well management is performing. No one is going to invest in or lend to an organization that has no financial accounting system or is unwilling to distribute its financial statements to interested parties.

In contrast, the decision as to whether or not an organization's accounting system produces management accounting information and makes it available to its managers is completely up to management itself. If management feels that it can make its many decisions without the help of management accounting information, then it has the option of doing so. However, most managers consider it foolish to do without this valuable source of information.

### Restrictions on Presentation of Information

Much of the information that management accountants provide to managers is never made available to outside users, so the outsiders never have any idea how it is prepared or what it consists of. As a result, management accountants usually don't have to be concerned about the restrictions on the presentation of information that financial accountants must observe. Unlike financial accounting information, management accounting information needed only for internal use does not have to be (though it certainly may be) consistent, conservative, objective, or historical.

### Flexibility of Reports

Financial accountants have relatively little flexibility when deciding how much information to include in the financial statements, what the format of the statements will be, and when the financial statements will be prepared for the external users. These decisions are substantially dictated by GAAP.

In contrast, management accountants have a great deal of leeway. They can decide on the amount of detail to include in their reports to management, the format of their reports, and the timing of the reports.

### Perspective on the Organization

Whereas financial accounting takes an aggregate view of the organization as a whole, management accounting takes a detailed view of the different segments of the organization. The management accountant helps managers at any and all levels of responsibility within the organization. Therefore, his or her reports are geared to the appropriate level: a division, a business function, a department, a product line within a department, or one or more product-line foremen.

### Timeliness of Reports

Financial statements are usually provided to external users on an annual or sometimes quarterly basis. Some observers believe that annual or even quarterly reports become out of date too quickly to be helpful to users in making critical investing or lending decisions. In contrast, management accounting reports are prepared on an as-needed basis. They may be issued annually, quarterly, monthly, daily, or even hourly. Their frequency depends on the needs of management, the sophistication of the management accounting system, and the expense involved.

These differences between financial and management accounting certainly do not constitute an exhaustive list. These characteristics are simply the most basic to an understanding of how the two accounting disciplines differ.

## THE PRIMARY ROLES OF MANAGEMENT ACCOUNTANTS AND COST ACCOUNTANTS

We noted earlier that the role of management accountants is to assist management in the *planning* and *control* of a company's operations. Let's see now exactly what we mean by these two terms, and then look at another important area in which accountants are involved: inventory costing. You should understand how the work of cost accountants, who are heavily involved in inventory costing, is closely related to that of management accountants.

Learning
Objective  **3**

Describe how the management accountant assists management in planning, control, and inventory costing

## Planning

**Planning,** in its most basic form, involves two things: determining the goals for an organization and determining how to achieve them. Management needs to know not only what it hopes to accomplish in a future period, but also how it expects to do so. Planning takes place at all levels within an organization. Because an organization is typically composed of subunits such as divisions, and each division is itself composed of subunits such as departments, the planning of an organization is only as good as the planning within each subunit. Thus even the smallest subunit's plans must be coordinated with the plans of the organization as a whole.

The tool used by accountants to assist management in the planning process is the budget. A **budget** is a formal quantitative expression of the goals of management.

There are several types of budgets, each representing a different aspect of the planning process, as you will learn later in this book. The different types of budgets are interrelated, and all are designed to support the organization's short- and long-term objectives.

Exhibit 2 is a simple budget for a machine maintenance department for August, 1997. It shows, for example, that the maintenance department is expected to spend $43,000 for wages to repair machinery during August and $15,000 for a foreman to

**Exhibit 2** Machine Maintenance Department Budget
August, 1997

| | |
|---|---|
| Supplies. | $18,000 |
| Utilities. | 3,400 |
| Supervision | 15,000 |
| Rent. | 2,000 |
| Wages | 43,000 |
| Total. | $81,400 |

supervise the laborers. In total, the maintenance department is expected to spend $81,400 in August in order to efficiently maintain the machines of the production departments.

## Control

After an organization has determined its goals and planned the ways to achieve them, the plans are implemented. Management now needs to monitor operations to be sure that these goals are being achieved. In other words, management needs to control the operations they manage. **Control** involves four steps:

1. *Implementing* operating plans
2. *Monitoring* those plans at work and gathering information on how well they are progressing—often called **feedback**
3. *Deciding* what action is necessary if feedback shows that the implemented plans are not attaining the intended goals
4. *Acting* to remedy the problem, if any, and getting the plans back on track

As you can see, the control function picks up where the planning function leaves off.

The management accountant uses the accumulated feedback to prepare a **performance report,** the principal accounting tool for assisting management in controlling operations. A performance report compares a subunit's actual results with its budget. Any differences between actual and budget are listed.

Exhibit 3 portrays a simple version of a performance report for the maintenance department. The original budget for this department was shown in Exhibit 2.

This performance report offers feedback on how well the maintenance department met its plans—represented by the budget. And this feedback indicates that the department's cost of supplies ($2,700 over budget), utilities ($1,600 over budget), and wages ($50 over budget) were higher than expected; supervision costs ($200 under budget) were lower than expected; and rent was exactly as predicted.

**Exhibit 3** Machine Maintenance Department Performance Report
August, 1997

| | Budget | Actual | Differences |
|---|---|---|---|
| Supplies. | $18,000 | $20,700 | $2,700 over budget |
| Utilities. | 3,400 | 5,000 | 1,600 over budget |
| Supervision | 15,000 | 14,800 | 200 under budget |
| Rent. | 2,000 | 2,000 | — |
| Wages | 43,000 | 43,050 | 50 over budget |
| Totals. | $81,400 | $85,550 | $4,150 over budget |

Having received this report from an accountant, a manager can immediately see where the plans are working and where they aren't. It appears from the performance report in Exhibit 3 that the only item for which the plans are working is the rent. This does not mean, however, that management should devote considerable time and energy to analyzing the causes of the differences for the remaining four items. Usually, only large differences will warrant investigation.

### Management by Exception

Investigating differences can be time-consuming and costly, requiring careful attention and evaluation by the manager and workers most closely associated with the operation that did not meet the budget. Unless the benefits from knowing the cause of a difference exceed the costs of determining the cause, investigation is not warranted. The costs of investigating a difference are probably about the same regardless of the size of the difference—it shouldn't take any longer to determine the cause of a large difference than it does for a small difference. The potential benefits, however, from investigating a large difference should be much greater than for a small difference. Therefore, the net effect—benefits from investigation less costs of investigation—will probably be positive for large differences (those considered material in amount), but negative for small differences. Since the net effect is positive only for the differences that are large in relation to the amount budgeted—the **material differences**—these are the ones to receive the time and attention needed to determine their causes. The spotlighting of material differences for investigation is referred to as **management by exception.**

What is material to one person, however, may not be to another. Each manager must set his or her own guidelines for determining what is material or significant, and use this guide for spotlighting differences to investigate. For example, the manager of the maintenance department whose performance report is shown in Exhibit 3 may decide that any variance that exceeds 10% of the original budget is material and is to be investigated.

In Exhibit 3, the differences for supervision and wages would probably both be considered immaterial, since each one represents a very small variation from the budget. On the other hand, the differences for supplies and utilities each represent a substantial variation from the amounts budgeted. Since these differences are material, they would probably be spotlighted for investigation.

### Cost Benefit

We pointed out above that investigating material differences rather than immaterial differences is more likely to produce benefits that exceed the costs of investigation. We could express this another way by saying that the results of **cost-benefit analysis** indicate that it is **cost-effective** to investigate only material differences.

Cost-benefit analysis is an approach that should be considered in developing any good management accounting system. It is based on the premise that the costs of providing management with information cannot be justified unless the information pays for itself—the benefits must be greater than the costs of preparation. This concept is obviously applicable to the determination of which variances to investigate, but it is also applicable to every other topic in management accounting as well. For example, the only reason that master budgets or capital budgets are prepared in an organization is that management feels that the value of having the information exceeds the costs of getting it.

We feel that every management accounting tool that we introduce in this book is usually cost-effective for an organization to use. However, in a situation where the cost of providing information—or of providing more information or better information—

exceeds the benefits of having and using that information, then we feel just as strongly that the information is not needed and should not be prepared.

### Inventory Costing

One important way to measure the operations of a company is to keep track of all of the costs associated with the company's product. Keeping track of all of these related costs, called **inventory (or product) costs,** is the responsibility of both management accountants and cost accountants. Management accountants want to know the cost of the product in order to help management make a variety of decisions that depend on an accurate determination of costs—decisions such as whether to accept a special order at a reduced price, whether to drop one or more apparently unprofitable product lines, or where to set the price for a new product line.

Accountants also want to know the cost of the company's products in order to prepare accurate financial statements. For many organizations, the product (inventory) is a significant asset on the balance sheet, which results in a significant expense (cost of goods sold) on the income statement when it is sold. Therefore the costs of making or buying the product represented as inventory must be properly accounted for. The area of accounting that is involved in determining the cost of the inventory for financial statement purposes is **cost accounting**—which is actually part management accounting and part financial accounting. The management accounting aspect of cost accounting focuses on inventory costs in order to assist management in the planning and control of operations, while the financial accounting aspect focuses on inventory costs in order to prepare financial statements in accordance with GAAP.

The way a cost accountant determines the cost of the inventory for an organization is first to determine all the costs that went into making or buying the units during the period. Then all the costs are split up—or **allocated**—between the units sold and the units not yet sold, as follows:

1. Collect all the costs that went into making or buying all units.
2. Calculate the cost for each unit.
3. Determine how many units were sold during the period, and how many units were unsold at the end of the period.

Now we can determine the expense for the cost of goods sold and place that amount on the income statement. The units available for sale, but not yet sold, represent an asset—the ending inventory. Once this cost is determined, it is placed on the balance sheet. The process of determining the costs of the product and then allocating them between the income statement and the balance sheet is referred to as **inventory costing** or **product costing.**

As an example of inventory costing, assume that a company incurred $40,000 in costs to produce 10,000 units. Also assume that 9,000 of these units had been sold by the end of the year, and the remaining 1,000 remained unsold. First, the accumulated costs associated with the units produced are divided by the number of those units to obtain an average cost per unit produced during the period:

$$\text{Cost per unit} = \frac{\$40,000}{10,000} = \$4.00$$

Next, the cost of goods sold, which goes in the income statement, is found to be $36,000:

$$\text{Cost of goods sold} = 9,000 \text{ units sold} \times \$4.00/\text{unit} = \$36,000$$

Finally, the cost of the ending inventory, which is needed for the balance sheet, is determined to be $4,000:

$$\text{Cost of ending inventory} = 1,000 \text{ unsold units} \times \$4.00 = \$4,000.$$

Figure 2 distinguishes between financial accounting and management accounting and shows how cost accounting relates to the two. The figure shows that **cost accounting** includes all of management accounting plus that part of financial accounting known as inventory costing.

The terms *management accounting* and *cost accounting* have gradually come to mean different things to different people. For example, some people's definition of management accounting embraces the inventory costing purpose—that is, they include planning, control, and inventory costing in the definition of management accounting. We refer to this combination as cost accounting. On the other hand, where we include the inventory costing purpose as only one of three cost accounting purposes, some people associate cost accounting strictly with inventory costing.

In addition, the term *management accounting* has been used in an even broader sense. The National Association of Accountants, (now called the Institute of Management Accountants) included in the term "management accounting" *all* accounting functions performed in private organizations—that is, organizations that aren't CPA firms and aren't the government. In this broadest sense, management accounting includes financial accounting, management accounting as we define it, tax accounting, and internal auditing.

Obviously, the terminology is not consistent among all who teach and practice these areas of accounting. For our purposes, *when we refer to management accounting, we mean assisting managers in planning and control. When we refer to cost accounting, we mean assisting managers in planning, control, and inventory costing.*

**Figure 2** Relationship of Financial Accounting and Management Accounting to Cost Accounting

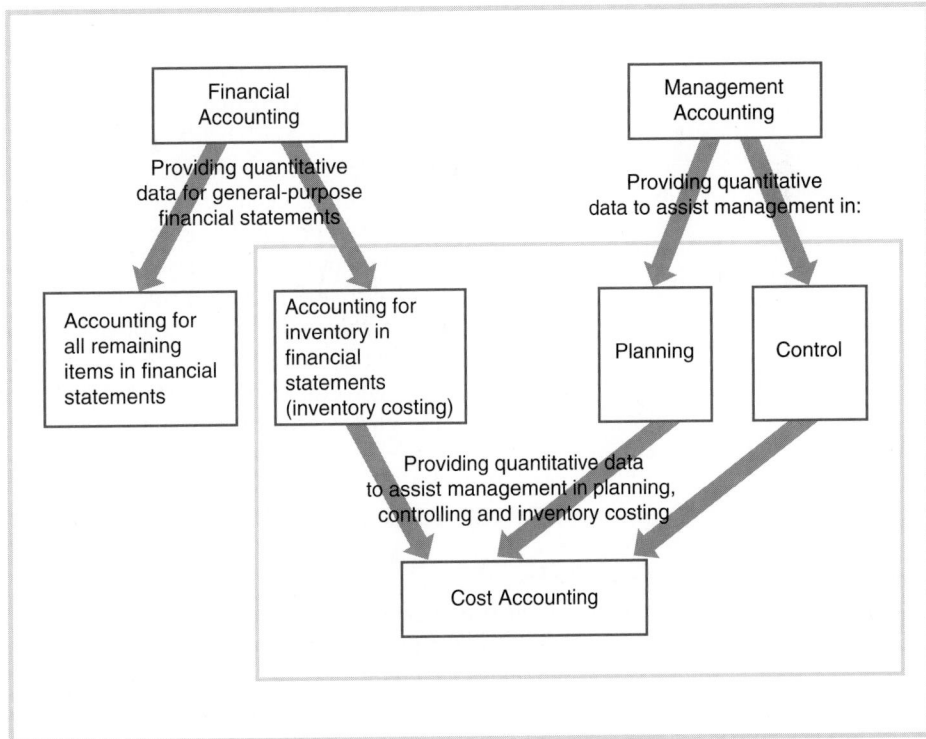

1. What are the three broad purposes of an accounting system?
2. Explain several ways that financial accounting differs from management accounting.
3. What are meant by the terms planning, control, and inventory costing?

Learning
Objective **4**

Explain the role of accounting in an organization

## ROLE OF ACCOUNTING WITHIN THE ORGANIZATION

The role of the accounting department, and the chief accounting executive, the **controller,** is to provide information that managers need in making decisions. The controller gives managers advice that helps them make decisions; he or she does not make the decisions for managers. The controller is in a position of staff responsibility rather than line responsibility. **Staff responsibility** is the responsibility of giving advice, counsel, or service to other departments; **line responsibility** is the responsibility of making decisions and giving directives that guide the activities toward the organization's goals.

The controller is responsible for more than the planning and control aspects of management accounting. The controller's responsibilities also include general accounting, internal audit, and taxes, among others. Although the controller is involved in much more than merely management accounting, we will focus primarily on the role of the controller as a management accountant.

The controller's relationship to department managers typically is a staff relationship. However, the controller has line responsibility over subordinate managers within the accounting department itself. The controller gives directives to the managers of general accounting, taxes, and internal audit departments, advising them how to run their respective departments.

The controller also exerts some line responsibility over the managers of nonaccounting departments. Once the controller has determined the accounting procedures and methods for each department to follow, and has recommended to top management that they be followed by the other departments, the president of the organization then delegates to the controller the authority to implement the accounting system. When the controller gives directives to line managers as to their role in generating quantitative information, the controller acts in a line rather than a staff capacity.

Because the accounting department provides much of the information management uses in reaching decisions, sometimes it appears that the controller is doing the actual planning and controlling. This is why managers of other departments sometimes resent the accountants and resist their advice. These managers might feel that the accountants are attempting to run their departments and make their decisions. The accountants' role in the organization must be understood and agreed upon by the managers of other departments and the accountants themselves. Only through good communication and cooperation can they together carry out their functions and strive to achieve the goals of the organization.

Learning
Objective **5**

Understand the ethical considerations facing management accountants

## ETHICS AND MANAGEMENT ACCOUNTING

Most of the major issues in business ethics that are widely publicized involve the role of the organization's top management. Usually there is little, if any, mention of the role of the management accountant inside the organization. Unfortunately, since many business scandals have financial causes, it is likely that accountants have some involvement or at least some knowledge of what is going on.

Accountants and other financial professionals face a variety of challenges that can test their resolve to make the ethically desirable decision. Consider these situations:

- A company controller is instructed to find ways to improve the company's chances of receiving a major loan from a bank. The bank has asked for a budget for the next year, and the controller has been told to make the projections as favorable as possible but sufficiently plausible to keep the bank's loan officers from seeing how unlikely the projections are.
- A company controller is asked to find ways to boost sales in the fourth quarter of the year so that the annual budget projections can be achieved and incentive bonuses will be assured. The controller has a friend who would like to make a major purchase from the company at year-end that would put sales over the top. The friend's credit history is quite weak, however, and she would not normally meet the company's criteria for an acceptable credit risk.
- The new vice president for sales is a good friend of the company president. Since joining the company, the vice president has been submitting expense reports that the internal auditor suspects have been padded. When the two meet to discuss the matter, the vice president makes it clear that the internal auditor will jeopardize his career if he makes an issue of the suspicious expense reports.

In each of these situations, and others like them, the accountant is naturally expected to do what is honest, moral, and ethical, regardless of how hard it may be to make the right choice and regardless of how it may affect the accountant personally. Unfortunately, in our highly complex and competitive world, the most ethical decision may not always be obvious to the accountant. For this reason, in 1983 the National Association of Accountants (NAA)—now called the Institute of Management Accountants (IMA)—published its Standards of Ethical Conduct for Management Accountants in the hope of emphasizing the critical importance of ethics for management accountants and providing a framework, or thought process, for accountants to use in making ethical decisions. These standards, which must be followed by the 100,000 members of the IMA, are divided into four categories: (1) competence standards, (2) confidentiality standards, (3) integrity standards, and (4) objectivity standards.[1]

## Competence Standards

Management accountants have the responsibility to be competent in the profession they serve. This means that they must:

1. Maintain an appropriate level of professional competence by ongoing development of their knowledge and skills
2. Perform their professional duties in accordance with relevant laws, regulations, and technical standards
3. Prepare complete and clear reports and recommendations after appropriate analysis of relevant and reliable information

---

[1] National Association of Accountants, *Statement No. 1C,* "Standards of Ethical Conduct for Management Accountants" (Montvale, N.J.: NAA, June 1, 1983).

### Confidentiality Standards

Management accountants have the responsibility to be confidential. This means that they must:

1. Refrain from disclosing confidential information acquired in the course of their work except when authorized, unless legally obligated to do so
2. Inform subordinates as appropriate regarding the confidentiality of information acquired in the course of their work and monitor their activities to assure the maintenance of that confidentiality
3. Refrain from using or appearing to use confidential information acquired in the course of their work for unethical or illegal advantage, either personally or through third parties

### Integrity Standards

Management accountants must always perform their duties with the highest level of integrity. This means that they must:

1. Avoid actual or apparent conflicts of interest and advise all appropriate parties of any potential conflict
2. Refrain from engaging in any activity that would prejudice their ability to carry out their duties ethically
3. Refuse any gift, favor, or hospitality that would influence or appear to influence their actions
4. Refrain from either actively or passively subverting the attainment of the organization's legitimate and ethical objectives
5. Recognize and communicate professional limitations and other constraints that would preclude responsible judgment or successful performance of an activity
6. Communicate favorable as well as unfavorable information and professional judgments and opinions
7. Refrain from engaging in or supporting any activity that would discredit the profession

### Objectivity Standards

Management accountants also have the responsibility to be objective in their actions. This means that they must:

1. Communicate information fairly and objectively
2. Disclose fully all relevant information that could reasonably be expected to influence an intended user's understanding of the reports, comments, and recommendations presented

ASK YOURSELF ▶

1. **What type of responsibility does an accountant have within an organization-line or staff?**
2. **What are the four categories of standards of ethical conduct for management accountants?**

## CHAPTER SUMMARY

- The purpose of **management accounting** is to provide quantitative information that managers need for planning and controlling the activities of an organization in order to reach the organization's goals.
- Management accounting differs from financial accounting in several ways, including its purposes, its users, the time orientation, the mandatory nature of reports, the restrictions on presentation of information, the flexibility of reports, the perspective on the organization, and the timeliness of the reports.
- **Planning** involves (1) determining the goals for an organization, and (2) determining how to achieve them.
- The tool used by accountants to assist management in the planning function is the **budget,** the quantitative expression of goals set by management.
- In **controlling,** management (1) puts the plans to work, (2) observes the plans at work and gathers **feedback** on performance, (3) determines if corrective actions are necessary, and (4) takes the necessary actions to remedy any problems and meet the organization's goals.
- The tool used by accountants to assist management in the control function is the **performance report,** which compares the actual results to the budget so that differences can be identified and investigated.
- **Inventory costing** (or **Product costing**) involves determining the costs of inventory and allocating those costs between the units sold and the units unsold in order to prepare financial statements for a firm. The term *product costing* also refers to the accumulation of all costs within a firm that relate to a product in order to help managers make a variety of decisions concerning that product.
- The **controller,** as the chief accounting officer within an organization, is in charge of the accounting department. The accounting department's relationship to other departments involves **staff** rather than **line** responsibilities. By providing information to managers, the accounting department gives advice, counsel, and service to the other departments. It does not make the decisions that affect the activities taken by these departments to reach their goals.
- The National Association of Accountants (now called the Institute of Management Accountants) has developed a code of ethics called the Standards of Ethical Conduct for Management Accountants. It sets forth guidelines for ethical behavior in the areas of competence, confidentiality, integrity, and objectivity.

## 6  KEY TERMS

Budget   The tool used by management accountants to assist management in the planning function. It is a quantitative representation of the goals set by management.

Control   A management activity directed toward achieving the organization's goals. It involves four steps: (1) *implementing* operating plans; (2) *monitoring* those plans at work and gathering information on how well they are progressing, often called **feedback;** (3) *deciding* what action is necessary if feedback shows plans are not attaining the intended goals; (4) *acting* to remedy the problem and get the plans back on track.

Controller   The chief accounting executive within an organization.

Cost accounting   An accounting system for providing managers with the quantitative information they need for planning and control (management accounting), and inventory costing (a part of financial accounting).

| | |
|---|---|
| Cost-benefit analysis | An approach to developing a good management accounting system that is based on the premise that the costs of providing management with information can be justified only if the benefits to the organization from having and using that information exceed the costs of its preparation. |
| Feedback | The information collected to assess the performance of the organization in reaching its goals. |
| Inventory costing | The process of determining the costs of all units produced by a manufacturer or purchased for resale by a merchandiser, and the allocation of those costs between the units that are sold and the units that are unsold. |
| Line responsibility | The responsibility of making decisions and giving commands that directly affect the attainment of an organization's goals. |
| Management accounting | The accounting system for providing managers with the quantitative information they need for planning and controlling. |
| Management by exception | Spotlighting the material differences in a performance report as the ones that warrant investigation. |
| Material differences | Those differences in a performance report that are large in relation to the amount budgeted. |
| Performance report | A principal accounting tool showing the budget, the actual results, and any differences between budget and actual results. Performance reports are used to assist management in the control function. |
| Planning | Setting an organization's goals and deciding how to attain them. |
| Staff responsibility | The responsibility of giving advice, counsel, or service to other departments. |

---

## QUESTIONS FOR REVIEW AND FURTHER THOUGHT

### REVIEW QUESTIONS

1. Discuss several differences in management accounting and financial accounting.

2. What is meant by the term *planning*, and what is the management accountant's role in this function?

3. The management accountant assists management in the decision-making process. List several types of management decisions that would require the accountant's assistance.

4. Discuss what is meant by the term *inventory costing*.

5. Explain how financial accounting and management accounting differ with regard to:
   a. The users of each discipline's information
   b. The timeliness of the reports
   c. The purpose of each discipline
   d. The time orientation
   e. The restrictions on the presentation of information
   f. The level of flexibility of reports
   g. The perspective on the organization
   h. The mandatory nature of reports

6. Explain what is meant by the term *management by exception*.

7. Explain what we mean by the term *cost-benefit analysis*.

8. The NAA (now called IMA) has published standards of ethical conduct for management accountants. What are the four categories into which these standards are divided?

## QUESTIONS FOR FURTHER THOUGHT

1. Since financial accounting is required for most organizations, it is a much more important accounting discipline than is management accounting, which is purely voluntary. Discuss.

2. "Management accounting is nothing more than a modern term to describe cost accounting." Comment.

3. "Planning is a much more vital management function than control." Comment on this statement.

4. When a manager is evaluating the differences between actual and budgeted results on a performance report, the term *management by exception* means that the manager is concerned with *all unfavorable* differences. Discuss.

5. It should be obvious how a performance report assists management in the control function. But how does it help in the planning function?

6. "Accountants assist management by doing the planning and controlling of management's routine decisions." Do you agree? Explain.

7. "The controller does plan in a special sense." Explain what is meant by this statement.

8. A college professor of management accounting was teaching class one night, explaining why a particular approach to making a certain decision was conceptually superior to all others, even though it was probably more complicated, more time-consuming, and more costly than other approaches. One of her students remarked that at his company the same type of decision is usually made with a much more simplistic approach and that the managers at his company feel that the approach must be pretty good because they've been quite successful for several years. The student wanted to know why the class was wasting its time learning something that probably wasn't being used in the real world. If you were the teacher, how might you respond to the student—after you had calmed down?

9. Does a controller within an organization have line responsibility or staff responsibility? Explain.

10. Generally accepted accounting principles provide guidelines for the preparation of general-purpose financial statements. Do the same principles serve as guidelines for the preparation of reports to management for internal decisions?

11. The controllers of Companies A and B are discussing how they help management control costs with the aid of performance reports. The controller of Company A says that he examines all variances larger than $500. The controller of Company B (which is much larger than Company A) responds that variances as small as $500 are ignored and only those variances greater than $2,500 are investigated. Which controller is correct in the variances he selects for investigation?

12. How would you react to a production manager's criticism to the controller that the accounting department was attempting to run her operation rather than merely keeping records? Instead of providing information for management's use, it sometimes appeared to the manager that the controller was attempting to do the planning and controlling himself.

13. The NAA issued a statement of objectives for management accounting which specifies that management accountants have a responsibility (1) to provide management with information to assist in the decision making process and (2) to participate actively with management in the decision-making process. How do these stated objectives differ from the objectives of management accounting discussed in this chapter?

## OBJECTIVE ASSIGNMENT

*True/False*   Indicate whether each statement below is *true* or *false* by placing a *T* or *F* in the space provided.

_____ 1. Management accountants assist management by providing information for planning, controlling, and inventory costing.

_____ 2. Cost accounting is synonymous with management accounting.

_____ 3. Management by exception means that all variances, big and small, are to be investigated.

_____ 4. It is usually cost-beneficial to investigate material variances.

_____ 5. Legality is one of the four standards of ethical conduct for management accountants.

*Multiple Choice*   Select the best choice to complete each statement or answer each question below. Write the letter corresponding to your choice in the space provided.

_____ 1. A performance report is the tool used by accountants to assist management in the:
   a. Control purpose      c. Inventory costing purpose
   b. Planning purpose      d. Financial statements purpose

_____ 2. Only one of the following is a user of management accounting information. Which one is it?
   a. Management      c. Government
   b. Creditors      d. Investors

_____ 3. Which of the following is not part of an organization's value chain?
   a. Product design      c. Distribution
   b. Customer      d. Marketing

_____ 4. Which of the following does not represent a difference between financial accounting and management accounting?
   a. Purposes      c. Timeliness of reports
   b. Users      d. Usefulness of information

_____ 5. The tool used by accountants to assist management in the planning of operations is:
   a. the financial statement      c. the performance report
   b. the budget      d. the planning tool

_____ 6. A company budgets a cost to be $10,000 for the period. Only one of the following variances in a subsequent performance report would be investigated. Which one would it be?
   a. $0      c. $1,500 under budget
   b. $100 more than budget      d. All of the above would be investigated.

_____ 7. Which of the cost accounting purposes relates to financial accounting?
   a. Planning      c. Inventory costing
   b. Control      d. All of the above

_____ 8. The accumulation of costs related to inventory and the allocation of those costs between the sold and the unsold units is:
   a. Planning      c. Inventory costing
   b. Control      d. Financial statement allocation

_____ 9. Which of the following categories of ethical standards is not part of the NAA's Standards of Ethical Conduct?
   a. Competence      c. Integrity
   b. Confidentiality      d. Subjectivity

_____ 10. Which ethical situation below represents a violation of the NAA's confidentiality standard?

  a. The accountant fails to stay up to date on recent FASB pronouncements that affect the company's financial statements.

  b. Plans for a new line of computers are leaked by the financial vice president to the company's major competitor.

  c. A cost accountant is arrested for theft of inventory from one of the company's plants.

  d. A division controller arbitrarily writes down division assets in a year of loss so that future years will appear to be more profitable.

## EXERCISES

2† **Exercise 1:** Determining Characteristics of Financial Accounting and Management Accounting

For each of the following descriptions of accounting reports, indicate whether the description relates to financial accounting (F), management accounting (M), both disciplines of accounting (B), or neither discipline of accounting (N).

_____ a. There is a great deal of flexibility in the form of the reports prepared for management.

_____ b. The reports are produced no more often than annually or quarterly.

_____ c. Reports can be as timely as management wants, regardless of the sophistication of the accounting system and the cost of providing the information.

_____ d. Reports must be prepared in accordance with generally accepted accounting principles.

_____ e. It is important that each report be useful to its user.

_____ f. Reports are used primarily by individuals outside the organization.

_____ g. The purpose of the reports is to assist management in planning and control.

_____ h. Reports must be precise in all respects in order to be useful.

_____ i. Reports are often prepared for the individual subunits of the organization.

_____ j. The emphasis in reports is primarily on the past.

5 **Exercise 2:** Classifying Actions of Ethical Conduct

The NAA's Standards of Conduct for Management Accountants is broken down into four categories: (1) competence standards, (2) confidentiality standards, (3) integrity standards, and (4) objectivity standards. For each specific standard described below, indicate in which of the four categories it belongs.

  a. Do not disclose information about the company to outsiders.

  b. Refrain from any and all illegal activities.

  c. Prepare complete and clear reports and recommendations.

  d. Refrain from activities that discredit the profession.

  e. Communicate information fairly.

  f. Do not use insider information for illegal advantage.

  g. Fully disclose relevant information to interested users.

5 **Exercise 3:** Classifying Violations of Ethical Conduct

For each of the ethical situations described below, indicate which of the four categories (competence, confidentiality, integrity, or objectivity) of the NAA's Standards of Conduct for Management Accountants is being violated.

  a. An accountant in the payroll department discloses the salaries of key personnel to a local newspaper.

† The numbers in the margin refer to the Learning Objectives.

b. The company tax accountant prepares the company's tax return without having first familiarized herself with the latest changes in the tax law.

c. The controller accepts a vacation trip from a computer company in exchange for the controller's recommendation of its computers to the board of directors.

d. The controller agrees with the company president that it would hurt the company if a major lawsuit against the company were to be disclosed in the footnotes to the financial statements. Therefore, to protect the company, the lawsuit is not disclosed in the financial statements.

e. The company controller is aware that the company is arranging a merger with a major competitor that should significantly increase the price of the company stock. He and his friends purchase as much stock as possible before the merger is announced to the public.

f. A new accounting clerk is having trouble making ends meet on his current salary, so he starts a small illegal bookmaking operation in order to supplement his income.

## ETHICS CASE

Steve Sperry and Bob Bowd have been best friends all their lives. Each has become a successful controller with a large company and has achieved a very comfortable lifestyle. Although Steve and Bob see little of each other during the year, they do make sure to get together at least once a year to go hunting in Wyoming. A week away from all responsibilities helps Steve and Bob relax from a hectic year and renew their friendship.

This year Steve and Bob left on their trip on the day after Christmas, during a severe snowstorm. Their plane experienced mechanical difficulties and was forced to make an emergency landing in the barren wilderness. The pilot was killed; Bob was seriously injured; and since the radio had malfunctioned, no one was aware of their crash or location.

Expecting that he was about to die, Bob made a special request of Steve. On their last hunting trip, Bob had seen some accounting information in Steve's briefcase about a new product line Steve's company was about to introduce. Bob felt so sure that the new product would greatly enhance the value of the company stock that he bought a large block of stock as soon as he returned from the vacation. The stock subsequently tripled in price and Bob made a huge profit from the deal. Now Bob felt guilty about the way he had obtained the information, and wanted Steve to make amends. He asked Steve to contribute the profits plus accrued interest to a local charity that was supported by Steve's company. Furthermore he asked Steve not to tell anyone about the source of the contribution.

Steve was willing to accommodate his dying friend since he wanted his friend to be able to die at peace. He agreed to honor both of Bob's requests.

Several days after Bob's death, Steve was rescued by some campers and was taken to a hospital, where he stayed several days recovering from frostbite. The more he thought about his promise to Bob, the less comfortable he felt. Since he had been negligent about letting Bob see the information in the first place, he felt that he should probably tell the president of his company about what had happened. He felt sure the president would understand and could be counted on not to disclose the source of the contribution to any other party.

After being released from the hospital, Steve made sure the money was sent to the charity that Bob had requested. In addition, he also informed the president about the whole matter. To Steve's great surprise the president reacted quite differently than he expected. Accusing Steve of using insider information for personal gain, Steve was fired, and the board of directors was immediately informed of what had taken place.

**Required:**

1. Did Steve's decision to tell the president about Bob's actions violate the NAA's Standards of Ethical Conduct for Management Accountants? If Steve had not told the president, would his silence have violated the code of ethics?

2. Do you feel it was ethical for Steve to tell the president? Discuss.

## OBJECTIVE ASSIGNMENT ANSWERS

**True/False**

1. F    2. F    3. F    4. T    5. F

**Multiple Choice**

1. a    2. a    3. b    4. d    5. b
6. c    7. c    8. c    9. d    10. b

# Introduction to Cost Accounting Systems

**LEARNING OBJECTIVES**

After studying this chapter, you should be able to do the following:

1 Describe what is meant by the phrase "different costs for different purposes"

2 Use the concept of activity to distinguish between total costs and average costs

3 Define and explain what inventoriable costs and period costs are and how they differ for manufacturers, merchandisers, and service organizations

4 Trace the flow of inventoriable costs through the inventory accounts—from initial purchase to final sale—for a merchandiser and a manufacturer using a perpetual iinventory system

5 Prepare an income statement and supporting schedules for a manufacturer

6 Define the key terms listed at the end of the chapter

7 Prepare an income statement and supporting schedules for a manufacturer

**CHAPTER OUTLINE**  DIFFERENT COSTS FOR DIFFERENT PURPOSES • CENTERS OF ACTIVITY • Total Costs and Average Costs • INVENTORIABLE COSTS AND PERIOD COSTS • Noninventoriable Unexpired Costs • Types of Organizations and Their Inventories • Categories of Inventoriable Costs and Period Costs for Manufacturers • The Flow of Costs Under a Perpetual Inventory System • FINANCIAL STATEMENTS FOR MERCHANDISERS AND MANUFACTURERS • The Income Statement • Schedules for Determining a Manufacturer's Cost of Goods Sold • The Balance Sheet • Beginning and Ending Inventories: A Simplifying Assumption THE JOB ORDER COSTING AND PROCESS COSTING METHODS

It is the job of the accountant to provide managers with quantitative information, who then use it to make a variety of decisions. A few examples of the many decisions regularly confronting managers include:

- What costs should we assign to the company's product in determining its cost of goods sold and ending inventory?
- What sales price should we set for units awaiting sale to customers?
- How many units should we sell in order to generate a profit for the organization?
- Should we accept a special order?
- Should we improve the warranty on our products as a way of better promoting the products to the public?

## DIFFERENT COSTS FOR DIFFERENT PURPOSES

Learning
Objective 1

Describe what is meant by the phrase "different costs for different purposes."

Each of the different decision situations above to some degree depends on costs. Management accountants often use the phrase "different costs for different purposes." This means that in each of these decisions, management has a specific purpose for needing cost information, which may differ from what management needs for other decisions. Depending on the situation to be evaluated, the accountant must first decide which type of costs are needed, and then supply the appropriate cost information to management to help make the decision.

Because we are going to be concerned with many types of costs in management accounting and cost accounting, let's begin with the most basic definition of cost:

Cost is a measurable sacrifice of resources exchanged for goods and services.

This definition is way too broad however to be of any practical use to an accountant, because there are so many different types of costs that the accountant is going to use. Without preceding the word "cost" with a descriptive adjective—such as total, average, variable, fixed, inventoriable, period, relevant, or irrelevant, to name a few—there is no way to know exactly which type of cost is being referred to.

Within this chapter, you will be introduced to four different types of costs—total costs, average costs, inventoriable costs, and period costs. A clear understanding of these basic terms is essential to an understanding of the many additional cost terms that come later.

## CENTERS OF ACTIVITY

Learning
Objective 2

Use the concept of activity to distinguish between total costs and average costs

Costs can be identified with any subunit of the organization in which some sort of activity is taking place. An **activity** represents something done to create a product or an output that can be measured. To a management accountant, activity can be measured whenever there is a clear indicator of (1) what was done, (2) in a particular place, (3) during a specific period of time, (4) to produce measurable results.

For example, a firm that manufactures interactive computer video games employs technicians who assemble components into a complete game. The number of games assembled during a month is a good indicator of the activity of the assembly shop. The number of square feet cleaned by janitors each night would be a good way to measure the activity of the janitorial maintenance department, but it would not help in measuring the activity of the assembly shop.

Management accountants would say that we are discussing two different **centers of activity,** subunits within an organization that perform a particular function or produce measurable results. A center of activity can actually be anything within an organization for which costs can be measured, accumulated, or assigned. For this reason centers of activity are also called **cost objects.** Centers of activity (or cost objects) might consist of different divisions, departments, products, services, or projects within a firm.

Thus, a typical manufacturing firm is made up of many different centers of activity. For example, the production department is a center of activity. Within production, each different product line might also be a center of activity; and each specific function performed within that department (such as material handling, assembly, inspection, or repair) might be a center of activity. In addition to the production department, a firm's centers of activity could include the research & development department, the product design department, sales department, the shipping department, and the customer service department, among others.

For a retailer, a center of activity could be a storeroom or the purchasing department; for a hospital, the intensive-care wing; for a university, the college of business or the school of accountancy; for a CPA firm, the tax department or an audit engagement.

Activity can be measured in many different ways, depending on the type of organization and the types of centers of activity within that organization. For the production department of a manufacturer, a good measure of activity is the number of units produced or the number of hours worked. For a storeroom, a good measure of activity could be the number of requisitions processed; for the intensive-care wing in a hospital, the number of patients treated; for a college of business administration, the number of semester hours enrolled by students.

### Total Costs and Average Costs

Within each center of activity (or cost object), cost information can be maintained in total or on the average. Total costs are the sum of all the costs related to a center of activity for a period of time. The level of total costs depends upon the amount of activity—also called the **cost driver,** because the level of activity tends to "drive" the total costs up or down. **Average costs** are the total costs for a center of activity divided by the amount of activity (the cost driver) for the period. A typical production department may calculate an average cost per unit produced or per hour worked. A hospital may compute an average cost per patient treated. And a college may compute an average cost per semester hour enrolled.

Clearly, no single measure of activity (or cost driver) applies to all centers of activity. A suitable measure of activity for a center is the one that most logically influences—or drives up and down—the total costs incurred for a period of time. For example, the number of units produced is a meaningful measure of activity for a production department—it has a significant influence on the total costs incurred. But the number of units produced is not a useful way to measure the activity of a hospital.

## INVENTORIABLE COSTS AND PERIOD COSTS

Learning
Objective 3

Define and explain what inventoriable costs and period costs are and how they differ for manufacturers, merchandisers, and service organizations

In the previous chapter we defined inventory costing as the process of determining the costs of inventory and then allocating these costs between the units that are sold during the year and the units that are unsold at the end of the year. In order for accountants to prepare financial statements in accordance with GAAP, it is vital that they distinguish inventoriable costs from period costs, so they can properly value cost of goods sold on the income statement and the ending inventory on the balance sheet.

**Inventoriable costs** (also called product costs) are costs associated directly with units that are produced by a manufacturer or purchased for sale by a retailer or wholesaler. Inventoriable costs are considered assets when incurred, because they are resources that are expected to provide future economic benefits to the firm. When the units are sold, the inventoriable costs become an expense—cost of goods sold. In short, inventoriable costs (product costs) are (1) assigned to inventory when incurred, and (2) expensed when the units to which they are assigned are sold.

In contrast, **period costs** are costs that are recognized as expenses as soon as they are incurred. They are never assigned to the inventory; instead they are assigned immediately to the income statement as an expense of that period.

Period costs are not assets because they are not expected to provide any future economic benefit to the firm. The benefits provided by period costs are received fully in the same period that the costs are incurred, so they are recognized as expenses in the current period.

### Noninventoriable Unexpired Costs

In addition to inventoriable costs and period costs, there is a third group into which costs can be classified when they occur: *noninventoriable unexpired costs.*

The term *noninventoriable unexpired costs* tells you exactly what these costs are. **Noninventoriable unexpired costs** *represent assets when they are incurred, but they are not costs that can be assigned to inventory*—at least not yet. Examples of noninventoriable unexpired costs include expenditures for prepaid insurance, prepaid rent, machinery, and buildings. Each of these costs is an asset (or unexpired cost) other than inventory. Many of these assets are used up or consumed as time passes. As they expire over time, the amount expired can then be classified as an inventoriable cost or a period cost.

For instance, assume that a 3-year insurance policy is acquired for $900. At the time of acquisition, the $900 is an asset, but it is not classified as an inventoriable cost—it is classified as prepaid insurance, not inventory. At this moment, the $900 of prepaid insurance is a noninventoriable unexpired cost. After the first year of coverage, $300 worth of insurance has been consumed. This $300 of coverage used up must now be classified as either an inventoriable cost or period cost. (The proper classification will depend on the type of organization to which the costs apply, i.e., manufacturer or retailer, as we shall see in the next section.) The remaining $600 is still unexpired after 1 year of the policy; it will continue to be classified as an asset (but not as inventory) on the balance sheet until it expires in the next 2 years. In short, the remaining $600 of insurance cost is still a noninventoriable unexpired cost.

In later sections of this chapter and in most homework problems, for simplicity's sake it will be assumed that all costs can be classified as inventoriable costs or period costs. Whenever we introduce noninventoriable unexpired costs, they will be specifically identified.

### Types of Organizations and Their Inventories

Whether a cost is an inventoriable cost or a period cost depends on the type of organization (and the type of department within the organization) in which the cost is incurred. For our purposes, we will classify all organizations as service organizations, merchandisers (retailers and wholesalers), or manufacturers. Exhibit 1 summarizes the following discussion of how these three types of organizations classify costs as either inventoriable costs or period costs.

Service organizations are in business to make a profit from the sale of a personal service. Since service organizations have no physical inventories, there are no inventoriable costs—all of their costs are period costs.

**Exhibit 1** Classification of Inventory Costs (Product Costs) and Period Costs for Various Types of Organizations

| Type of Organization | Classification of Costs |
|---|---|
| Service | All costs are period costs, since there are no inventories. Costs are expensed as incurred. |
| Merchandising | The invoice and freight-in costs are inventoriable costs. They are assigned to Merchandise Inventory when incurred, then transferred to Cost of Goods Sold when the units are sold. All other costs are period costs. |
| Manufacturing:<br>  Production departments<br>    Direct materials ⎫<br>            ⎬ Prime costs<br>    Direct labor ⎫<br>            ⎬ Conversion costs<br>    Factory overhead ⎭ | All costs are inventoriable costs when incurred. They are first assigned to Work-in-Process Inventory, then transferred to Finished Goods Inventory when the units are completed. When the units are sold, the costs are transferred to Cost of Goods Sold. |
|   Selling and administrative departments | All costs are period costs. |

Merchandisers and manufacturing organizations are both in business to make a profit from the sale of inventory. The difference between them is that the **merchandiser** sells the product in the same physical form in which it is purchased, while the **manufacturer** converts raw material into a finished product before selling it.

Merchandising organizations have only one inventory account: **Merchandise Inventory.** The costs assigned to this account—the inventoriable costs—consist of all the costs of getting the merchandise inventory from the supplier to the merchant and placing it in position and condition for sale, including the invoice price of the merchandise and any cost of transporting it to the merchant. The costs are assigned to Merchandise Inventory as incurred, and they are transferred to Cost of Goods Sold at the time of sale.

Theoretically, the costs of ordering, receiving, and storing merchandise could be treated as inventory costs. However, it can be extremely difficult to determine the amount of these costs to assign to the different orders purchased, so these costs are usually treated as period costs. All other costs for the merchandiser—such as salaries, expired insurance, expired rent, advertising, utilities, property taxes, depreciation, and the cost of shipping the units sold—are also considered to be related to the period, not the product, and are expensed when incurred.

Unlike merchandisers, manufacturers must maintain three different inventory accounts, one for each physical form as the product progresses from its raw to its finished state:

1. **Raw Materials Inventory**—For materials purchased from a supplier and awaiting use in production
2. **Work-in-Process Inventory**—For unfinished goods in production; the units that are being worked on
3. **Finished Goods Inventory**—For completed products awaiting sale

When materials are acquired, their costs are entered in the Raw Materials Inventory account. Once production begins, all inventoriable costs, including raw materials costs, are accumulated in the Work-in-Process Inventory account and remain there until the product is completed. Once production is completed, the cost of these units becomes Finished Goods Inventory. As the units are sold, these costs are transferred to Cost of Goods Sold.

A simple way to picture this progression of costs through the inventory accounts is shown in the T-accounts in Exhibit 2. We'll look at this progression of costs in more

**Exhibit 2** Basic Flow of Costs for a Manufacturer

| Raw Materials Inventory | | Work-in-Process Inventory | | Finished Goods Inventory | | Cost of Goods Sold | |
|---|---|---|---|---|---|---|---|
| Purchased | Used → | Units started | Units completed → | Units completed | Units sold → | Units sold | |

detail shortly; first let's discuss which costs flow through these inventory accounts and which ones don't.

The distinction between inventoriable costs and period costs is somewhat different for a manufacturer than it is for a merchandiser. For a manufacturer, the classification of costs depends on whether it is a cost of a department that is producing a product.

To see what we mean, assume that a manufacturing company can be divided into the six business functions of the value chain (research and development, product design, production, sales and marketing, distribution, and customer service) as well as administration. All costs of the production departments are inventoriable costs; all costs incurred within research and development, product design, sales and marketing, distribution, customer service, and administration are period costs.

**Inventoriable Costs versus Product Costs**  Remember, our reference to the costs of a product as inventoriable costs relates to the accounting issue of preparing financial statements in accordance with GAAP. Only production costs are inventoriable costs. Remember also the phrase at the beginning of this chapter, "different costs for different purposes." If we were accumulating product costs for the purpose of a special decision such as accepting a special order, adding or dropping a product line, or setting the price for a new product, then the product costs for this purpose would include all costs that relate to the product, no matter which business function they come from. Although the costs of the nonproduction departments are not inventoriable costs, they will, in addition to the inventoriable costs, be an integral part of the analysis of special decisions that comes later in the book.

Although it is quite common to use the terms inventoriable costs and product costs interchangeably, technically the two terms have slightly different meanings. Inventoriable costs are actually a subset of product costs.

### Categories of Inventoriable Costs and Period Costs for Manufacturers

The costs of the production department for a manufacturer—the inventoriable costs —fall into three main categories: direct materials, direct labor, and factory overhead.

**Direct Materials**  **Direct materials** are the raw materials that become an integral part of the completed product and whose purchase and delivery costs are significant enough to warrant being traced to the finished item. For example, if the production process involves making classroom desks, direct materials would include the wood, the laminated top, and the metal legs. Although each desk also includes glue, screws, and varnish, the cost of these raw materials is insignificant. We probably could determine the precise cost of these minor raw materials, but such accurate product costs would confer no benefit. The cost of obtaining such information is often higher than its value to management. It is not cost-beneficial. As with anything else, you should pay for only as much information as you need.

Nevertheless, cost accountants don't forget about the cost of minor raw materials. Such materials as glue, varnish, and screws are called **indirect materials.** In addition, those raw materials which do not go into the finished product, such as janitorial supplies, are also classified as indirect materials. The cost of indirect materials is one of the costs covered under *factory overhead,* which we will explain shortly.

**Direct Labor** **Direct labor** is the work that directly converts the raw materials into finished goods. Like direct materials, direct labor costs can be clearly traced to the product being worked on—from the raw to the finished state. For example, the salaries of laborers who combine the wood, top, glue, and other raw materials into finished desks are direct labor costs. But the salaries of workers who bring raw materials to the direct laborers, of managers who supervise laborers, and of machinery maintenance personnel are examples of **indirect labor** costs. Like indirect materials, indirect labor is a component of factory overhead.

**Factory Overhead** Factory overhead includes all the indirect costs of production. If we add up all the costs of the production department, then subtract from the total the direct materials costs and direct labor costs, what remains is the **factory overhead** costs, also called **manufacturing overhead** costs. Factory overhead costs represent all the costs that are needed to produce the product, that we cannot trace, or shouldn't bother to trace, directly to the product. Examples include indirect materials, indirect labor, expired insurance, expired rent, property taxes, maintenance, repairs, utilities, depreciation, payroll taxes, and the amortization of intangible assets.

Sometimes accountants find it helpful to combine the direct materials costs and the direct labor costs. They call this combination of direct costs **prime costs.** Prime costs represent the direct costs of manufacturing the product. Similarly, accountants sometimes find it helpful to combine direct labor costs and factory overhead costs, a cost combination referred to as **conversion costs.** Conversion costs represent the costs of converting raw materials into a finished product but do not include the cost of those raw materials. In some organizations, as direct labor costs are reduced to a small percentage of total manufacturing costs, direct labor is not even identified as an individual inventoriable cost category, but is simply treated as a conversion cost along with numerous factory overhead items.

Learning Objective 4
Trace the flow of inventoriable costs through the inventory accounts—from initial purchase to final sale—for a merchandiser and a manufacturer using a perpetual inventory system

### The Flow of Costs under a Perpetual Inventory System

We have discussed the types of inventory accounts and the types of inventoriable costs for both manufacturers and merchandisers. Now we are going to examine how the inventoriable costs flow through the inventory accounts from purchase to ultimate sale.

Analyzing a merchandiser's flow of costs is far simpler than analyzing a manufacturer's cost flow. Because the product sold by the merchandiser is in the same physical form as it was when purchased, there are very few inventoriable costs to keep track of. Manufacturers, by contrast, incur a large number of costs in converting the raw materials to a finished product.

Exhibit 3 uses T-accounts to show how simply inventoriable costs for a merchandiser flow from the initial purchase of merchandise inventory (assumed to be $200,000) to the cost of goods sold ($175,000). All other costs, such as expired insurance ($4,000), expired rent ($5,000), and salaries ($90,000), are expensed as incurred because they are period costs.

The cost flow analysis for a manufacturer is more complex. A manufacturer has many inventoriable costs, which flow among three inventory accounts (Raw Materials Inventory, Work-in-Process Inventory, and Finished Goods Inventory), instead of one (Merchandise Inventory). We will trace the flow of costs through the inventory accounts of a manufacturer using a perpetual inventory system.

In the example that follows, note that every time an inventory account is affected by a transaction, that account is immediately updated. This is done because we are using a *perpetual inventory system,* which matches the physical flow of goods from one account to another, and thus makes it easier to learn about a manufacturer's accounting system. In using a perpetual inventory system, each increase or decrease is

**Exhibit 3** T-Accounts for Cost Flow of a Merchandiser

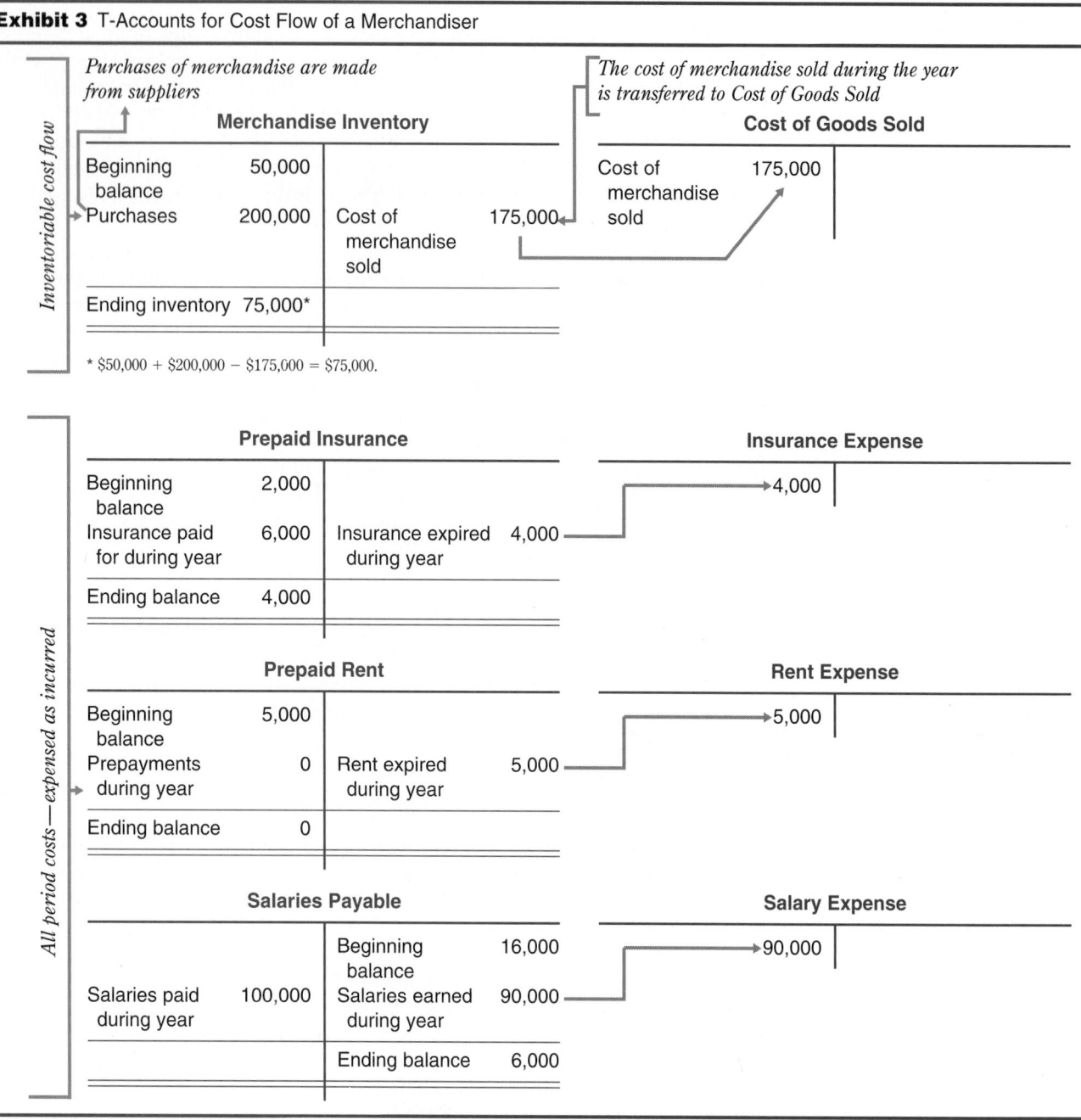

* $50,000 + $200,000 − $175,000 = $75,000.

recorded directly—immediately—in the appropriate inventory account. Thus, purchases are added to Raw Materials Inventory and usage of raw materials is subtracted from it. Direct materials, direct labor, and factory overhead are added to Work-in-Process Inventory and the cost of completed goods is subtracted. The cost of completed goods is added to Finished Goods Inventory and the cost of goods sold is subtracted. At any time during the year, the debit balance in each inventory account will be correct.

Some manufacturers use a *periodic inventory system* instead of a perpetual inventory system.

1. What is involved in inventory costing?
2. How do inventoriable costs differ from period costs?
3. What are the three types of inventories for a manufacturer? What are the three types of inventoriable costs?
4. Describe how the inventoriable costs for a manufacturer flow from one inventory account to another, when the manufacturer uses the perpetual inventory system.

Now let's turn to our example, in which we use a separate exhibit to show each of the six steps involved in the flow of costs through a manufacturer's inventory accounts:

1. Purchase and use of raw materials
2. Use of labor
3. Use of other factory overhead
4. Transfer of factory overhead costs to Work-in-Process Inventory
5. Completion of production
6. Sale of finished goods

**Step 1: Purchase and Use of Raw Materials** Exhibit 4 shows that purchases of raw materials are $200,000. This amount, added to the $50,000 on hand at the beginning of the year, makes a total of $250,000 of raw materials available to be used during

**Exhibit 4** Purchase and Use of Raw Materials

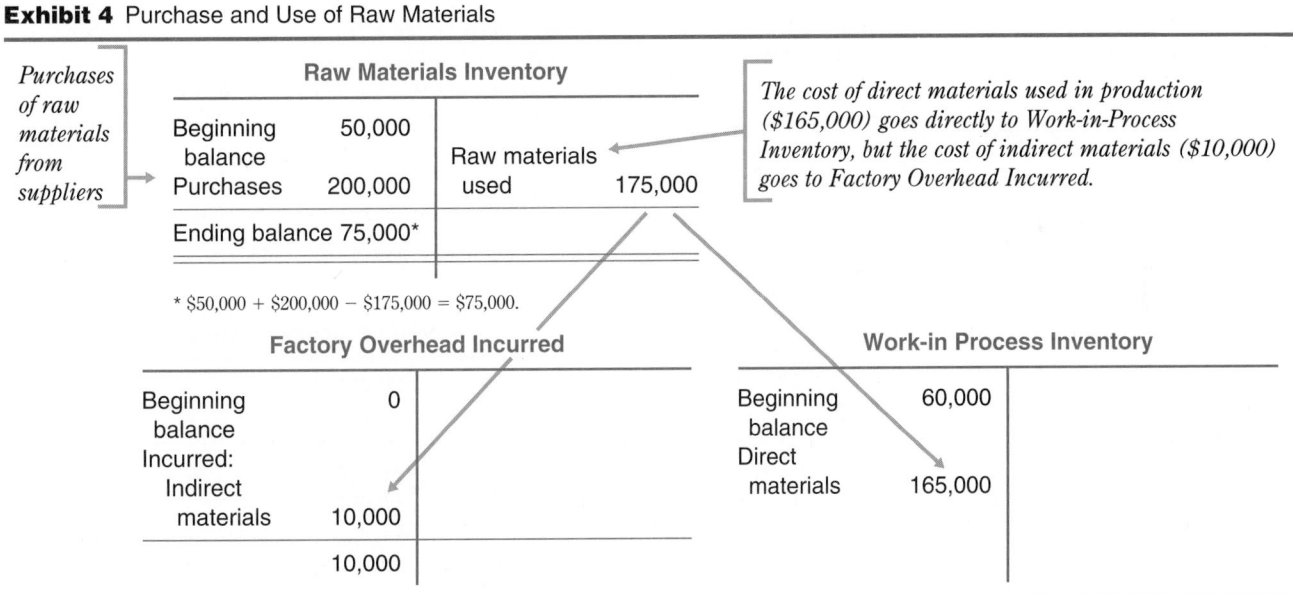

the year. If $175,000 of raw materials were used, then the amount on hand at the end of the year is represented as follows:

Total raw materials available for use . . . . . . . . . . $250,000
Raw materials used during the year. . . . . . . . . .   175,000

Ending inventory of raw materials . . . . . . . . . . .  $ 75,000

 Of the $175,000 of raw materials that was used, assume that $165,000 was for direct materials and that the remaining $10,000 was for indirect materials. Notice in Exhibit 4 that the direct materials cost goes directly to Work-in-Process Inventory, but that the indirect materials cost goes to an account called Factory Overhead Incurred.

 The **Factory Overhead Incurred** account accumulates all overhead costs that are incurred during a period; they are represented by debits in the account. Indirect materials is just the first of many debits. At the end of the period, when the total overhead costs are accounted for, the account is closed to a zero balance (which it will still have at the beginning of the next period) with a credit. This total is then transferred to Work-in-Process Inventory, with a debit to that account. In fact, there will be three debits to Work-in-Process Inventory each period: one for direct materials, which we have already seen in Exhibit 4; one for direct labor, which we will see in Exhibit 5; and one for factory overhead, which we will see in Exhibit 7. We can also see in Exhibit 4 that Work-in-Process Inventory has a beginning balance of $60,000. This represents the costs of direct materials, direct labor, and factory overhead that were incurred during the last year and have been assigned to those units that were started but not finished by the end of last year.

---

**Exhibit 5** Use of Labor

**Salaries Payable**

| Salaries paid during year | 90,000 | Beginning balance | 0 |
| | | Salaries earned during year | 90,000 |
| | | Ending balance | 0 |

*The cost of labor for the year is $90,000. The direct labor ($65,000) is debited to Work-in-Process Inventory, and the indirect labor ($5,000) is debited to Factory Overhead Incurred. The nonproduction labor ($20,000) is a period cost and is debited to Salary Expense.*

**Factory Overhead Incurred**

| Beginning balance | 0 |
| Incurred: | |
|  Indirect materials | 10,000 |
|  Indirect labor | 5,000 |
| | 15,000 |

**Work-in-Process Inventory**

| Beginning balance | 60,000 |
| Direct materials | 165,000 |
| Direct labor | 65,000 |

**Salary Expense**

| Nonproduction labor | 20,000 |

**Step 2: Use of Labor** During the period, the total wages earned by workers are $90,000. Of this amount, $70,000 relates to the production department, and $5,000 of these production wages are for indirect laborers. Exhibit 5 shows how the payroll is distributed. The direct labor ($65,000) goes to Work-in-Process Inventory, and indirect labor ($5,000) goes to Factory Overhead Incurred. Both direct and indirect labor costs are inventoriable costs, but only the direct labor goes directly to Work-in-Process Inventory. Remember that factory overhead costs will eventually get to Work-in-Process Inventory, but in a roundabout manner. The rest of the $90,000 ($20,000) goes to Salary Expense—it is a period cost.

**Step 3: Use of Other Factory Overhead** The amounts of insurance and rent determined to have expired during the year are as follows:

Costs of production department: $3,000 insurance, $4,000 rent

Costs of nonproduction department: $1,000 insurance, $1,000 rent

As shown in Exhibit 6, the insurance and rent related to the production department ($3,000 and $4,000) are classified as factory overhead costs and are debited to Factory Overhead Incurred. The remaining insurance and rent ($1,000 and $1,000) are expensed as incurred since they are period costs, being debited to Insurance Expense and Rent Expense, respectively.

Other types of factory overhead costs include depreciation, property taxes, utilities, maintenance, and janitorial costs. We are using just insurance and rent in order to keep our example as simple as possible.

**Step 4: Transfer of Factory Overhead to Work-in-Process Inventory** The Work-in-Process Inventory account in Exhibit 6 is still incomplete. It is supposed to accumulate all inventoriable costs for the period, but factory overhead, which is just as much an inventoriable cost as direct materials and direct labor, is missing. Remember that factory overhead costs have been stored temporarily in the Factory Overhead Incurred account, until they are completely accounted for. Since there are no additional factory overhead costs to account for in this period, it is time to transfer the cumulative factory overhead costs in Factory Overhead Incurred to Work-in-Process Inventory. To do this we simply credit Factory Overhead Incurred, thus closing the account, and debit Work-in-Process Inventory, as shown in Exhibit 7.

All the inventoriable costs have been recorded in Work-in-Process Inventory, shown by the debit balance of $312,000 in Exhibit 7. This balance is referred to as "total manufacturing costs to account for." Notice that this balance includes the total manufacturing costs incurred during the period ($252,000) plus the beginning balance of this account ($60,000).

Most of this total will be assigned to the units completed during the year (finished goods). The remainder will be assigned to the units that have been started but are not completed by the end of the year. The remainder becomes the beginning balance in the Work-in-Process Inventory account for the next period.

**Step 5: Completion of Production** Throughout the year, units in process are being completed, and the cost of these units is transferred from Work-in-Process Inventory to Finished Goods Inventory, as shown in Exhibit 8. Of the $312,000 total manufacturing costs to account for, the costs related to the units completed during the year are $280,000. The amount remaining ($32,000) is assigned to the unfinished units still in Work-in-Process Inventory at year-end.

Although there is no reason to suspect that either this $32,000 balance in

**Exhibit 6** Use of Factory Overhead

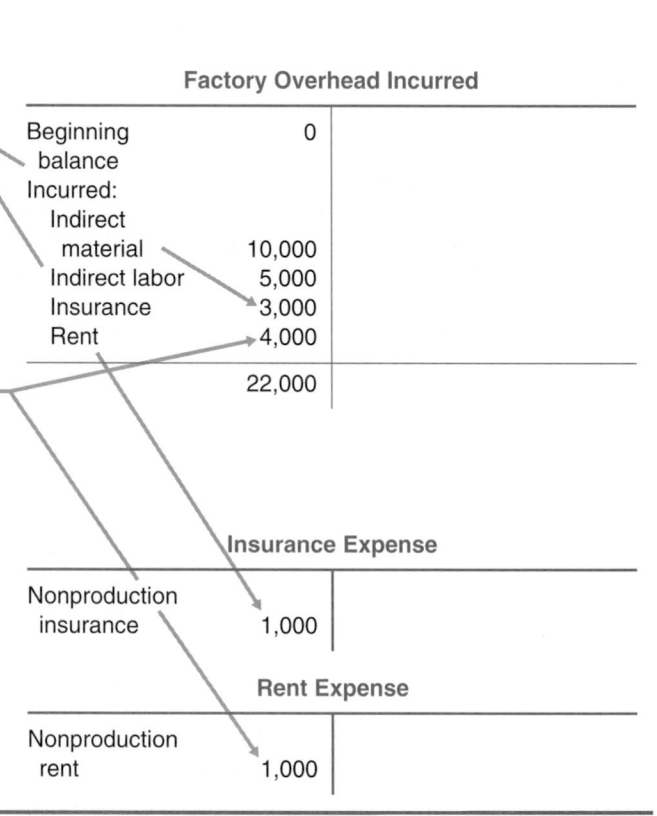

*Insurance and rent consumed during the year are determined. The amounts related to production are assigned to Factory Overhead Incurred ($3,000 and $4,000). The remainder is expensed during the period ($1,000 and $1,000).*

**Work-in-Process Inventory**

| | |
|---|---|
| Beginning balance | 60,000 |
| Direct materials | 165,000 |
| Direct labor | 65,000 |

**Prepaid Insurance**

| | | | |
|---|---|---|---|
| Beginning balance | 2,000 | | |
| Insurance purchased | 6,000 | Insurance expired | 4,000 |
| Ending balance | 4,000 | | |

**Prepaid Rent**

| | | | |
|---|---|---|---|
| Beginning balance | 5,000 | | |
| Rent prepaid during year | 0 | Rent expired | 5,000 |
| Ending balance | 0 | | |

**Factory Overhead Incurred**

| | |
|---|---|
| Beginning balance | 0 |
| Incurred: | |
| Indirect material | 10,000 |
| Indirect labor | 5,000 |
| Insurance | 3,000 |
| Rent | 4,000 |
| | 22,000 |

**Insurance Expense**

| | |
|---|---|
| Nonproduction insurance | 1,000 |

**Rent Expense**

| | |
|---|---|
| Nonproduction rent | 1,000 |

**Exhibit 7** Transfer of Factory Overhead to Work-in-Process Inventory

**Factory Overhead Incurred**

| | | | |
|---|---|---|---|
| Beginning balance | 0 | | |
| Incurred: | | | |
| Indirect material | 10,000 | | |
| Indirect labor | 5,000 | | |
| Insurance | 3,000 | | |
| Rent | 4,000 | | |
| | 22,000 | | 22,000 |

**Work-in-Process Inventory**

| | |
|---|---|
| Beginning balance | 60,000 |
| Direct materials | 165,000 |
| Direct labor | 65,000 |
| Factory overhead | 22,000 |
| Total manufacturing costs to account for | 312,000 |

$$\left.\begin{array}{l}\text{} \\ \text{} \\ \text{} \\ \text{}\end{array}\right\} \begin{array}{l}\textit{Total manufacturing} \\ \textit{costs incurred} \\ = \$252,000\end{array}$$

*The factory overhead that has been accumulated in the Factory Overhead Incurred account is now transferred to Work-in-Process Inventory—which now has debits for all three inventoriable costs.*

**Exhibit 8** Completion of Production

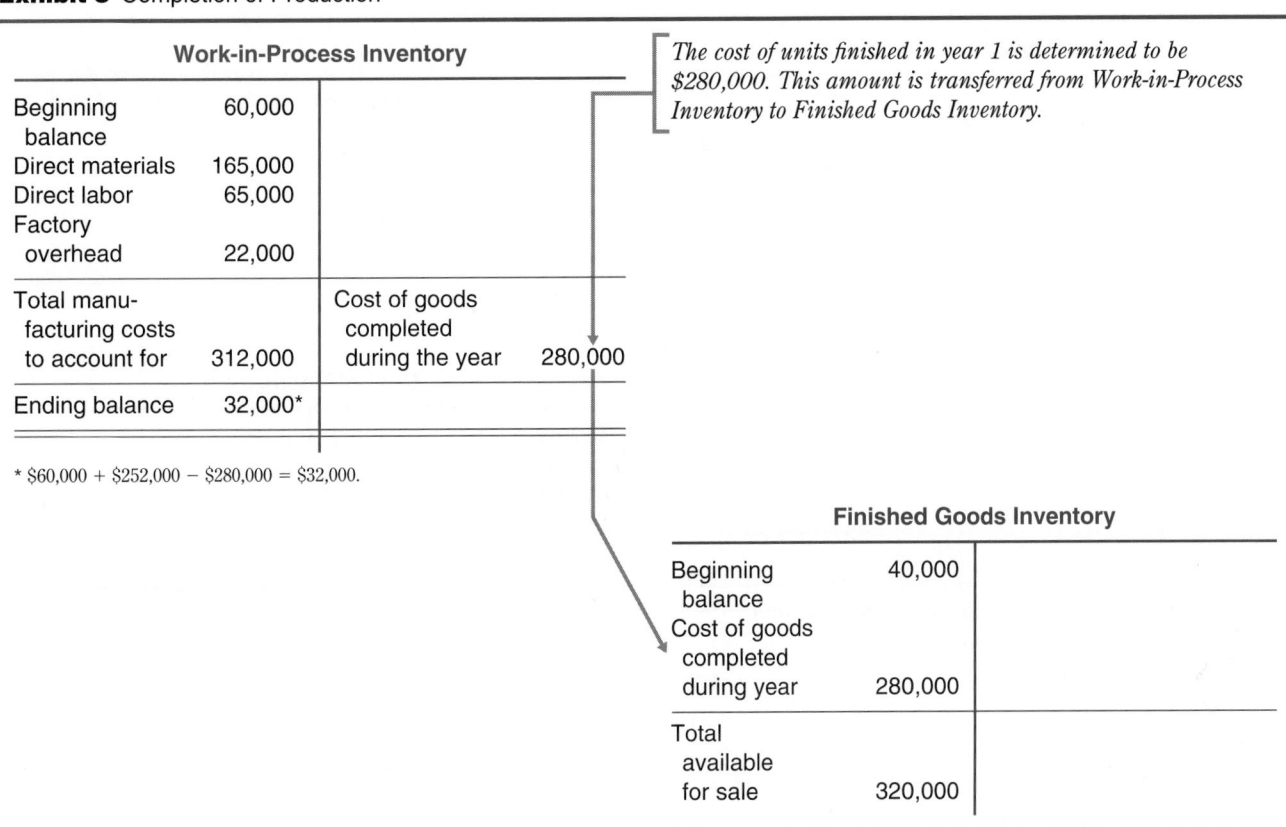

Work-in-Process Inventory

| | | | |
|---|---|---|---|
| Beginning balance | 60,000 | | |
| Direct materials | 165,000 | | |
| Direct labor | 65,000 | | |
| Factory overhead | 22,000 | | |
| Total manufacturing costs to account for | 312,000 | Cost of goods completed during the year | 280,000 |
| Ending balance | 32,000* | | |

\* $60,000 + $252,000 − $280,000 = $32,000.

*The cost of units finished in year 1 is determined to be $280,000. This amount is transferred from Work-in-Process Inventory to Finished Goods Inventory.*

**Finished Goods Inventory**

| | |
|---|---|
| Beginning balance | 40,000 |
| Cost of goods completed during year | 280,000 |
| Total available for sale | 320,000 |

Work-in-Process or the $75,000 ending balance in Raw Materials is incorrect, a physical count at year-end is required under a perpetual inventory system. This count is performed to verify that the balances shown in the accounting records do in fact match the quantities on hand.

We can see in Exhibit 8 that there is a $40,000 beginning balance in Finished Goods Inventory—the amount assigned to units completed but not yet sold by the end of last year. When we add this beginning balance ($40,000) to the cost of goods completed ($280,000), we get $320,000—the total goods that are available for sale. This means that during the year we had ready for sale finished goods having a cost of $320,000.

**Step 6: Sale of Finished Goods** The production costs we are tracing have traveled a long way—starting in Raw Materials Inventory, transferring to Work-in-Process Inventory when production began, and coming to Finished Goods Inventory when production was completed. The costs are still inventoriable costs, but they are now in the final stage before becoming expenses. All that is left is for the product to be sold.

The cost of the units sold during the year is $310,000, shown in Exhibit 9; this amount is debited to Cost of Goods Sold and credited to Finished Goods Inventory. Finally we have an expense—*now, and only now, do the inventoriable costs become expenses.*

The production costs associated with the unsold units in Finished Goods Inventory are $10,000. These costs are still part of an asset. They will not be expensed until the units to which they are assigned are sold—probably next year.

At year-end it is necessary to take a physical count of finished goods, as was done for raw materials and work-in-process in step 5. The reason is the same: to ensure that there is actually $10,000 of completed and unsold goods on hand, as the Finished Goods Inventory account indicates.

---

**Exhibit 9** Sale of Finished Goods

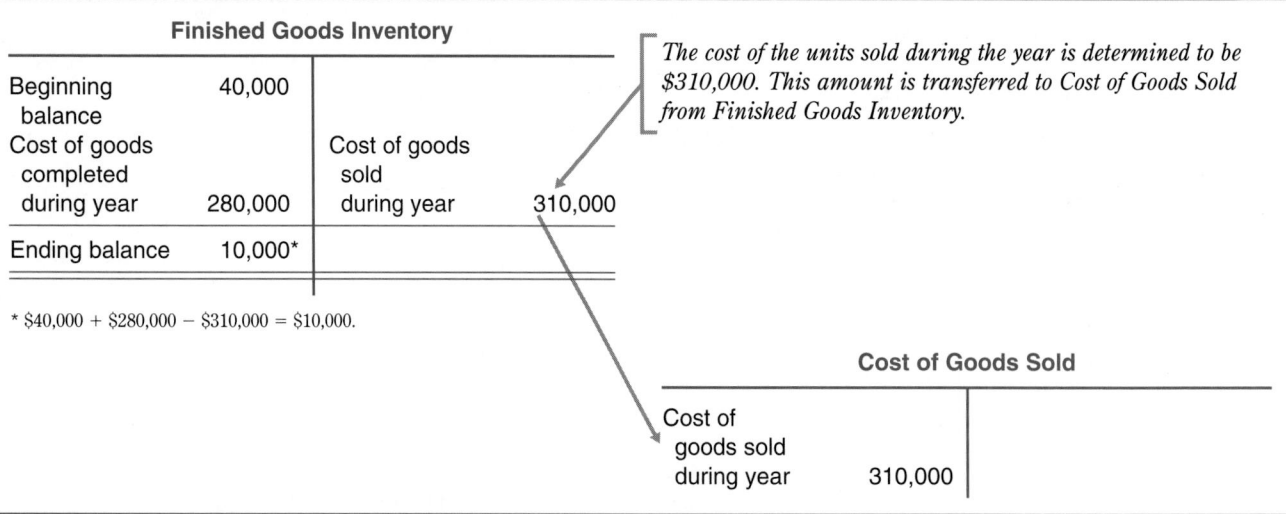

|  | Finished Goods Inventory | | |
|---|---|---|---|
| Beginning balance | 40,000 | | |
| Cost of goods completed during year | 280,000 | Cost of goods sold during year | 310,000 |
| Ending balance | 10,000* | | |

*$40,000 + $280,000 − $310,000 = $10,000.

*The cost of the units sold during the year is determined to be $310,000. This amount is transferred to Cost of Goods Sold from Finished Goods Inventory.*

|  | Cost of Goods Sold | |
|---|---|---|
| Cost of goods sold during year | 310,000 | |

---

**Figure 1** Overview of Cost Flow for a Manufacturer

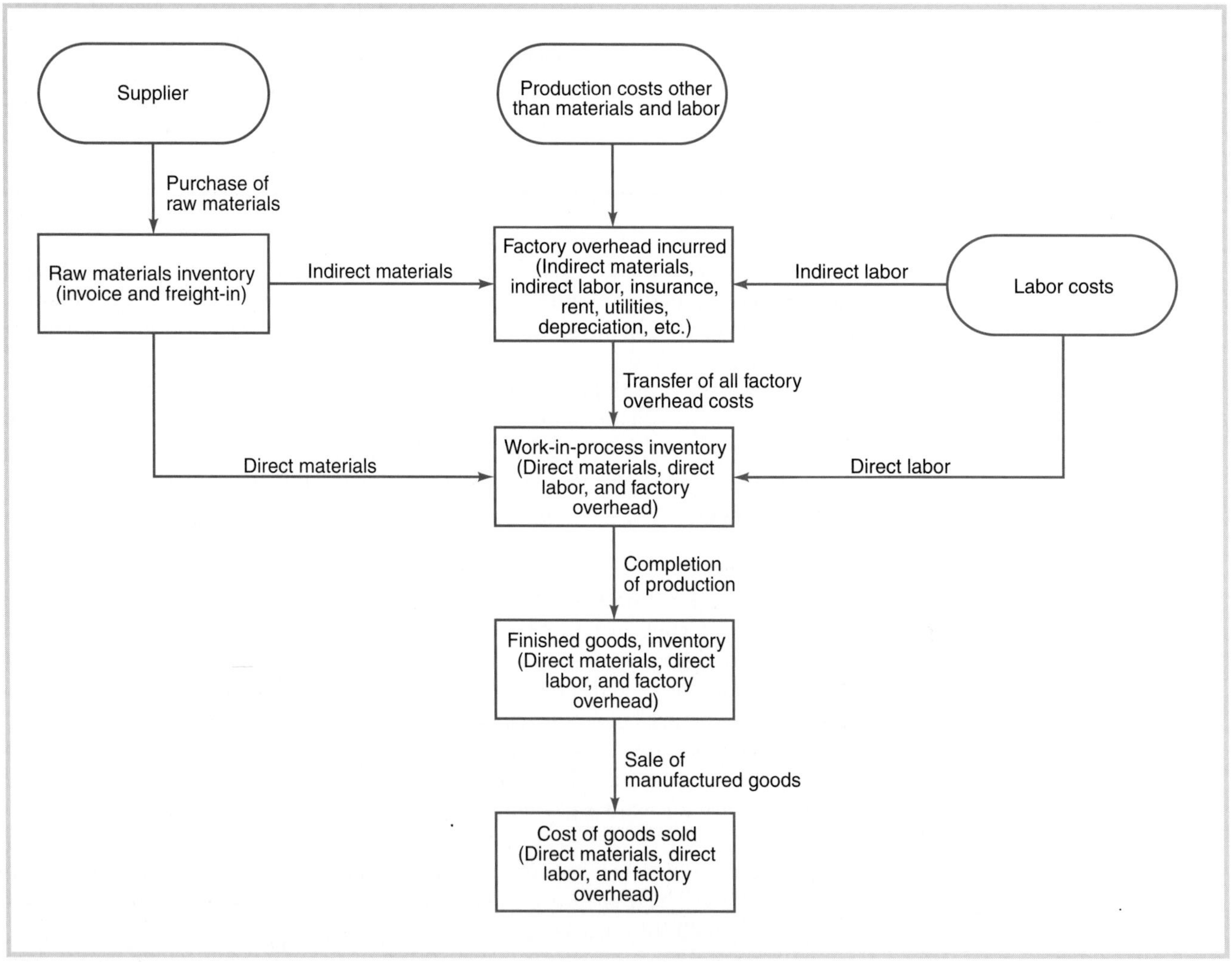

```
      Supplier                              Production costs other
                                            than materials and labor

         │ Purchase of
         │ raw materials
         ▼
   Raw materials inventory   Indirect materials   Factory overhead incurred   Indirect labor   Labor costs
   (invoice and freight-in) ──────────────────▶  (Indirect materials,        ◀──────────────
                                                  indirect labor, insurance,
                                                  rent, utilities,
                                                  depreciation, etc.)
         │                                             │ Transfer of all factory
         │                                             │ overhead costs
         │                                             ▼
         │       Direct materials          Work-in-process inventory       Direct labor
         └───────────────────────────────▶ (Direct materials, direct      ◀──────────────
                                             labor, and factory
                                             overhead)
                                                   │ Completion
                                                   │ of production
                                                   ▼
                                             Finished goods, inventory
                                             (Direct materials, direct
                                             labor, and factory
                                             overhead)
                                                   │ Sale of
                                                   │ manufactured goods
                                                   ▼
                                             Cost of goods sold
                                             (Direct materials, direct
                                             labor, and factory
                                             overhead)
```

Overview of the Flow of Costs for a Manufacturer   Figure 1 is a diagram of the same flow of costs through the accounts of a manufacturer described in the six steps just discussed. Look it over very closely before you go on, to be sure that you understand completely the relationship of a manufacturer's inventoriable costs to its three inventory accounts and cost of goods sold.

**ASK YOURSELF** ▶

1. **What term represents the addition of beginning inventory of raw materials plus purchases of raw materials?**
2. **What items are debited to the account Factory Overhead Incurred? When is this account credited? For what amount is it credited?**
3. **The cost of goods completed during the period is debited to what account? What account is credited?**
4. **The cost of units sold during the period are transferred to what account?**

Learning
Objective   5

Prepare an income statement and supporting schedules for a manufacturer

# FINANCIAL STATEMENTS FOR MERCHANDISERS AND MANUFACTURERS

Having traced the flow of inventoriable costs through the inventory accounts of both merchandising and manufacturing organizations, we come now to the final step in the accounting cycle: the preparation of financial statements. In other words, the effects of the flow of costs depicted in the T-accounts shown in Exhibits 3 through 9 are eventually represented in the income statement and balance sheet.

## The Income Statement

The basic format for the income statement is the same for both a merchandiser and a manufacturer. Using the same facts as were introduced earlier about the cost flows for a merchandiser (Exhibit 3) and a manufacturer (Exhibits 4 through 9), condensed income statements are shown in Exhibit 10.

**Exhibit 10**

Income Statements for a Merchandiser and a Manufacturer
Year Ended December 31, 1997

|  | Merchandiser | Manufacturer |
|---|---|---|
| Sales. | $400,000 | $400,000 |
| Less: Cost of Goods Sold | 175,000 | 310,000 |
| Gross Profit | $225,000 | $ 90,000 |
| Less: Operating Expenses. | 99,000 | 22,000 |
| Net Income. | $126,000 | $ 68,000 |

For the merchandiser, the determination of cost of goods sold, $175,000, is quite simple. The proper form is:

| | |
|---|---|
| Merchandise Inventory, Jan. 1, 1997. | $ 50,000 |
| Plus: Purchases | 200,000 |
| Goods Available for Sale | $250,000 |
| Less: Merchandise Inventory, Dec. 31, 1997. | 75,000 |
| Cost of Goods Sold. | $175,000 |

Now look back at Exhibit 3. Notice how the organization of the schedule of cost of goods sold is nothing more than a formal way to show the flow through the Merchandise Inventory T-account.

### Schedules for Determining a Manufacturer's Cost of Goods Sold

Determining the cost of goods sold for a manufacturer is much more detailed, since it involves the flow of inventoriable costs through three inventory accounts rather than one. Often two schedules are used by cost accountants to calculate the cost of goods sold; these are shown in Exhibit 11.

#### Schedule of Cost of Goods Completed

The first schedule in Exhibit 11 shows the calculation of cost of goods completed —that is, the cost assigned to all units finished during the year 1997. It's a formal way to show the flow of inventoriable costs from raw materials to finished goods. We showed the same flow in a less formal manner with T-accounts in Exhibits 4 through 8. As you read through Schedule 1, compare it to the appropriate T-accounts. You will find that the order within the T-accounts is nearly identical to the order in Schedule 1.

**Exhibit 11** Cost of Goods Completed and Sold for a Manufacturer

**Schedule 1**
**Cost of Goods Completed**
**Year Ended December 31, 1997**

| | | |
|---|---:|---:|
| Raw Materials Inventory, Jan. 1. 1997 | $ 50,000 | |
| Plus: Purchases | 200,000 | |
| Raw Materials Available for Use | $250,000 | |
| Less: Raw Materials Inventory, Dec. 31, 1997 | 75,000 | |
| Raw Materials Used | $175,000* | |
| Direct Materials Used | | $165,000 |
| Plus: Direct Labor | | 65,000 |
| Plus: Factory Overhead | | 22,000 |
| Total Manufacturing Costs Incurred during 1997 | | $252,000 |
| Plus: Work-in-Process Inventory, Jan. 1, 1997 | | 60,000 |
| Total Manufacturing Costs to Account for | | $312,000 |
| Less: Work-in-Process Inventory, Dec. 31, 1997 | | 32,000 |
| Cost of Goods Completed | | $280,000 |

\* Of the $175,000 of raw materials used, $165,000 is direct materials and $10,000 is indirect materials (part of the $22,000 of factory overhead.)

**Schedule 2**
**Cost of Goods Sold**
**Year Ended December 31, 1997**

| | |
|---|---:|
| Finished Goods Inventory, Jan. 1, 1997 | $ 40,000 |
| Plus: Cost of Goods Completed | 280,000 |
| Total Available for Sale | $320,000 |
| Less: Finished Goods Inventory, Dec. 31, 1997 | 10,000 |
| Cost of Goods Sold | $310,000 |

Keep in mind that there are four basic elements in the calculation of cost of goods completed. The first three elements represent the total manufacturing costs incurred during 1997:

direct materials ($165,000) + direct labor ($65,000) + factory overhead ($22,000)
= total manufacturing costs ($252,000)

The fourth element is the adjustment for the beginning and ending balances in Work-in-Process Inventory. With the addition of the beginning balance in Work-in-Process Inventory ($60,000) to the total manufacturing costs incurred, we now have the total manufacturing costs to account for ($312,000). And when we subtract the ending balance in Work-in-Process Inventory ($32,000), we see that the cost of goods completed is $280,000.

### Schedule of Cost of Goods Sold

The second schedule in Exhibit 11 shows how to calculate the cost of goods sold once you have determined the cost of goods completed. Schedule 2 traces the progression of costs through Finished Goods Inventory, in much the same order shown in T-account form in Exhibit 9.

By adding the beginning balance of Finished Goods Inventory to the cost of goods completed, we get the cost of goods available for sale, $320,000. Finally, we see that the ending balance in Finished Goods Inventory is $10,000; when we subtract this amount from the $320,000, the difference is the cost of goods sold, $310,000.

Rather than computing the cost of goods sold using two schedules, we can combine the two schedules into one. Once we determine the cost of goods completed, $280,000, as we did in the first schedule, we simply add the beginning and subtract the ending balances of Finished Goods Inventory, as shown in Exhibit 12.

---

**Exhibit 12**

---

**Combined Schedule of Cost of Goods Completed and Sold**
**Year Ended December 31, 1997**

---

| | |
|---|---:|
| Raw Materials Inventory, Jan. 1, 1997 .................... | $ 50,000 |
| Plus: Purchases....................................... | 200,000 |
| Raw Materials Available for Use .......................... | $250,000 |
| Less: Raw Materials Inventory, Dec. 31, 1997 .............. | 75,000 |
| Raw Materials Used.................................... | $175,000 |

| | |
|---|---:|
| Direct Materials Used ........................................... | $165,000 |
| Plus: Direct Labor ............................................. | 65,000 |
| Plus: Factory Overhead ......................................... | 22,000 |
| Total Manufacturing Costs Incurred during 1997...................... | $252,000 |
| Plus: Work-in-Process Inventory, Jan. 1, 1997 ...................... | 60,000 |
| Total Manufacturing Costs to Account for .......................... | $312,000 |
| Less: Work-in-Process Inventory, Dec. 31, 1997 .................... | 32,000 |
| Cost of Goods Completed ....................................... | $280,000 |
| Plus: Finished Goods Inventory, Jan. 1, 1997........................ | 40,000 |
| Total Available for Sale.......................................... | $320,000 |
| Less: Finished Goods Inventory, Dec. 31, 1997 ..................... | 10,000 |
| Cost of Goods Sold............................................. | $310,000 |

### The Balance Sheet

Although a merchandiser's income statement is considerably different from a manufacturer's, their balance sheets will differ in only one respect: the number of inventory accounts listed in the current assets section. As we have seen, a merchandiser has only one inventory account: Merchandise Inventory. A manufacturer has three inventory accounts: Raw Materials Inventory, Work-in-Process Inventory, and Finished Goods Inventory.

### Beginning and Ending Inventories: A Simplifying Assumption

Some examples, exercises, and homework problems assume that the cost of the ending work-in-process inventory is equal to the cost of the beginning work-in-process inventory and that the cost of the ending finished goods inventory is equal to the cost of the beginning finished goods inventory. These assumptions may not be realistic, but they are often made in order to simplify the computing of cost of goods sold. For example, let's say that in Schedule 1 of Exhibit 11, the beginning and ending work-in-process costs are both equal to $60,000, and in Schedule 2 that the beginning and ending finished goods costs are both equal to $40,000. In that case, Schedules 1 and 2 would look as follows:

#### Schedule 1
#### Cost of Goods Completed

| | |
|---|---:|
| Total Manufacturing Costs Incurred during 1997 . . . . . . . . . . . . . . . . . . | $252,000 |
| Plus: Work-in-Process Inventory, Jan. 1, 1997 . . . . . . . . . . . . . . . . . . . . | 60,000 |
| Total Manufacturing Cost to Account for . . . . . . . . . . . . . . . . . . . . . . . . . | $312,000 |
| Less: Work-in-Process Inventory, Dec. 31, 1997 . . . . . . . . . . . . . . . . . . | 60,000 |
| Cost of Goods Completed . . . . . . . . . . . . . . . . . . . . . . . . . . . . . . . . . . . . | $252,000 |

#### Schedule 2
#### Cost of Goods Sold

| | |
|---|---:|
| Finished Goods Inventory, Jan. 1, 1997 . . . . . . . . . . . . . . . . . . . . . . . . . | $ 40,000 |
| Cost of Goods Completed . . . . . . . . . . . . . . . . . . . . . . . . . . . . . . . . . . . . | 252,000 |
| Total Available for Sale . . . . . . . . . . . . . . . . . . . . . . . . . . . . . . . . . . . . . . | $292,000 |
| Less: Finished Goods Inventory, Dec. 31, 1997 . . . . . . . . . . . . . . . . . . | 40,000 |
| Cost of Goods Sold . . . . . . . . . . . . . . . . . . . . . . . . . . . . . . . . . . . . . . . . . | $252,000 |

You can see from these schedules that when the beginning and ending balances for Work-in-Process Inventory are equal, and the beginning and ending balances for Finished Goods Inventory are equal, the cost of goods sold turns out to be $252,000, which is equal to the cost of goods completed, which is also equal to the total manufacturing costs incurred (direct materials + direct labor + factory overhead).

## THE JOB ORDER COSTING AND PROCESS COSTING METHODS

In this chapter we defined the term *inventory costing,* and we discussed the different types of inventoriable costs as well as the flow of inventoriable costs through the inventory accounts of both the retailer and the manufacturer. What we failed to mention was exactly *how* the inventoriable costs for a manufacturer are assigned to

individual units or batches of units. In order to cover this topic, it is necessary to discuss the two extremes of inventory costing—job order costing and process costing.

Even though the topics of job order costing and process costing are covered in detail in the next two chapters, since some of you may not cover these chapters, we would like to give you now just a brief explanation of what each method is all about.

Sometimes a production process is making a rather small number of units (or batches of units)—which we call jobs. Each job is distinctly different from all the rest—probably because the jobs are being made to different customer specifications. Not only is it possible to determine the exact cost of each different job, but it is also usually mandatory that we do so, in order to properly value inventory on the balance sheet and cost of goods sold on the income statement. In this situation the production process would be accounted for with the **job order costing method** of inventory costing.

A construction company is a likely candidate to use the job order costing method to account for its different construction projects. In addition, companies in the aircraft and printing industries would also probably use job order costing.

**Process costing** is used in those production processes where units are produced continuously in large batches, and each unit is basically the same as every other unit. Not only is it probably impossible to determine the exact cost of each unit—one at a time—but it would also be completely impractical to do so. It would hardly be cost-effective. So instead we determine all the production costs for an entire period and spread them evenly among the "equivalent units" of production during that period. The key to understanding process costing is understanding the concept of equivalent units. In overly simplified terms, the concept of equivalent units represents a way of measuring activity which allows us to combine completed units and incomplete units as if they were all completed. Incomplete units are converted into an equivalent number of completed units.

Typically, industries that are involved in the production of cement, paints, chemicals, and gasoline, among many others, employ process costing.

---

**ASK YOURSELF** ▶

1. How do the calculations of cost of goods sold for a merchandiser differ from those for a manufacturer?
2. "Total available for sale" for a manufacturer, represents the addition of what two amounts?
3. When will total manufacturing costs incurred equal cost of goods completed and cost of goods sold?
4. How does job order costing differ from process costing?

## SUMMARY

* **Centers of activity** are subunits within an organization that perform a particular function or produce measurable results.

- **Activity** (or **cost driver**) is something done to produce a result or an output that can be measured. Activity can be measured in many different ways, depending on the type of organization and the types of centers of activity within the organization.
- **Total costs** are the sum of all costs incurred within a center of activity for a specific period of time.
- **Average costs** are the total of all costs for a center of activity for a specific period of time divided by the amount of activity (or cost driver) for that period.
- **Inventory costing** involves determining the costs of inventory and allocating those costs between the units sold and the units unsold in order to prepare financial statements for a firm.
- **Inventoriable costs** (or **product costs**) are closely related to a product. They are costs that are assigned to inventory when incurred and become expenses when the units they are assigned to are sold. The term *product costs* also refers to all costs within a firm that relate to a product in order to help managers make a variety of decisions concerning that product.
- **Period costs** are expensed as soon as they are incurred.
- A manufacturer has three classifications of inventory—*raw materials, work-in-process,* and *finished goods*—which represent different stages of completion in the production process.
- A manufacturer has three types of inventoriable costs: **direct materials, direct labor,** and **factory overhead.**
- The sum of direct materials and direct labor costs is called **prime costs;** the sum of direct labor and factory overhead costs is called **conversion costs.**
- The flow of inventoriable costs through the inventories is as follows: Raw materials are purchased and debited to the **Raw Materials Inventory** account. Direct materials are requisitioned for production and along with the direct labor are transferred directly to work-in-process by debiting **Work-in-Process Inventory** and crediting Raw Materials Inventory and Salaries Payable, respectively. The Factory Overhead costs are first debited to an account called **Factory Overhead Incurred.** At the end of each period, the account is closed out and the balance from that account is transferred to Work-in-Process Inventory. When units are completed, they are transferred to finished goods with a debit to **Finished Goods Inventory** and a credit to Work-in-Process Inventory. As completed units are sold, their costs are transferred from the Finished Goods Inventory account to the Cost of Goods Sold account.
- When a *perpetual inventory system* is used to account for a manufacturer, all additions or subtractions are recorded directly in the inventory accounts. At any time during the year, the debit balance in an inventory account represents the correct balance at that time.
- The basic format of the income statement is the same for a merchandiser and a manufacturer: Sales − cost of goods sold = gross profit; gross profit − operating expenses = net income.
- The calculation of cost of goods sold is much more detailed for a manufacturer than it is for a merchandiser. For a manufacturer, the cost of goods completed must be determined first. It is found by first adding together direct materials, direct labor, and factory overhead, then adding to this total the beginning balance of Work-in-Process Inventory and subtracting the ending balance in Work-in-Process Inventory. Cost of goods sold is then determined by adding the beginning balance in Finished Goods Inventory to the cost of goods completed and subtracting the ending balance in Finished Goods Inventory.

## 6  KEY TERMS

| | |
|---|---|
| **Activity** | A clear indicator of (1) what was accomplished, (2) in a particular center of activity, (3) during a specific period of time, (4) to produce measurable results. Also referred to as the cost driver. |
| **Average costs** | The total costs of a center of activity for a period divided by the activity (or cost driver) during the period. |
| **Center of activity** | A subunit within an organization that performs a particular function or produces measurable results. Also called a **cost object.** |
| **Conversion costs** | The sum of direct labor costs plus factory overhead costs. |
| **Cost object** | See **center of activity.** |
| **Direct labor** | Labor costs needed to convert raw materials into a finished product that are clearly and easily traceable to the units being produced. |
| **Direct materials** | The raw materials that become an integral part of the finished product and are significant enough to warrant tracing their purchase and delivery costs from Raw Materials to Finished Goods. |
| **Factory overhead** | The indirect costs of production—total production costs less direct materials and direct labor. Also referred to as **manufacturing overhead.** |
| **Factory Overhead Incurred** | An account that accumulates actual factory overhead costs incurred by production departments. At the end of each period the account is closed to a zero balance, and the total is transferred to Work-in-Process Inventory. |
| **Finished Goods Inventory** | The inventory account for units that are completed and awaiting sale. |
| **Indirect labor** | Labor costs needed to keep a manufacturing department running, but not related directly to converting raw materials into a finished product. Indirect labor costs are classified as part of factory overhead. |
| **Indirect materials** | Raw materials that either do not become a physical part of the finished product, or are not significant enough in amount to justify tracing the cost to the finished product. Indirect materials are classified as part of factory overhead. |
| **Inventoriable costs** | Costs that are assigned to inventory when incurred, and expensed (as cost of goods sold) when the units to which they are assigned are sold. |
| **Job order costing method** | The method of accounting for the production of identifiable products, often made to customer specifications. The costs of each job are carefully accumulated and kept separate from the costs of any other job. |
| **Manufacturer** | An organization that converts a raw material to a finished product prior to sale. |
| **Manufacturing overhead** | See **factory overhead.** |
| **Merchandise inventory** | The inventory that is sold by a merchandiser. |
| **Merchandiser** | An organization that sells a product in the same physical form in which it was purchased from the supplier. |
| **Noninventoriable Unexpired Costs** | Costs that are assets other than inventory when they are incurred (prepaid expenses, depreciable assets, intangible assets). As they expire over time, the expired cost is classified as either an inventoriable cost (if related to a production department) or a period cost (if related to a nonproduction department). |
| **Period costs** | Costs that are expensed when incurred. |
| **Prime costs** | The combined costs of direct materials and direct labor. |

| | Definition |
|---|---|
| Process costing method | The method of accounting for the production of a large volume of units in a continuous process. An average cost is determined by dividing the production costs by the equivalent whole units of production. |
| Product costs | Sometimes used interchangeably with the term inventoriable costs. However, it is also used to represent all costs relating to a product whether they come from a production department (inventoriable costs) or from nonproduction departments (marketing, customer service, distribution etc.). |
| Raw Materials Inventory | The inventory account for materials purchased by a manufacturer to be used in production. When used in production, raw materials will be classified as either direct materials or indirect materials. |
| Total costs | The sum of all costs incurred in a center of activity for a specific period of time. |
| Work-in-Process Inventory | The inventory account for unfinished goods in production. |

## DEMONSTRATION PROBLEM

During 1997, the Underhill Can Company had sales of $650,000. Its purchases of raw materials (all of which were direct materials) were $143,000. Other costs incurred during the year, and their allocation between the production department and the selling and administrative departments were as follows:

| | Production Department | Selling and Administrative Departments |
|---|---|---|
| Depreciation | $ 18,000 | $ 7,000 |
| Insurance expired | 6,000 | 3,000 |
| Salaries accrued and paid | 310,000 | 90,000 |
| Utilities | 12,000 | 3,000 |
| | $346,000 | $103,000 |

Of the production salaries, $250,000 was for direct labor and the remaining $60,000 was for indirect labor.

The balances in each of the inventory accounts at the beginning and end of 1997 were as follows:

| | Jan. 1, 1997 | Dec. 31, 1997 |
|---|---|---|
| Raw Materials | $57,000 | $40,000 |
| Work-in-Process | 34,000 | 10,000 |
| Finished Goods | 37,000 | 25,000 |

**Required:**

1. Prepare a schedule of cost of goods completed.
2. Prepare a schedule of cost of goods sold.
3. Prepare an income statement for the year ended Dec. 31, 1997.

■ **Solution to Demonstration Problem**

### Schedule of
### Cost of Goods Completed

| | | |
|---|---:|---:|
| Raw Materials Inventory, Jan. 1, 1997 ................. | $ 57,000 | |
| Purchases....................................... | 143,000 | |
| Total Available for Use............................. | $200,000 | |
| Raw Materials Inventory, Dec. 31, 1997 ............... | 40,000 | |
| Direct Materials Used ...................................... | | $160,000 |
| Direct Labor.............................................. | | 250,000 |
| Factory Overhead: | | |
| Indirect Labor .................................... | $ 60,000 | |
| Depreciation ..................................... | 18,000 | |
| Insurance ....................................... | 6,000 | |
| Utilities......................................... | 12,000 | 96,000 |
| Total Manufacturing Costs Incurred ........................... | | $506,000 |
| Work-in-Process Inventory, Jan. 1, 1997 ...................... | | 34,000 |
| Total Manufacturing Costs to Account for..................... | | $540,000 |
| Work-in-Process, Dec. 31, 1997................................ | | 10,000 |
| Cost of Goods Completed................................... | | $530,000 |

### Schedule of
### Cost of Goods Sold

| | |
|---|---:|
| Finished Goods Inventory, Jan. 1, 1997......................... | $ 37,000 |
| Cost of Goods Completed...................................... | 530,000 |
| Goods Available for Sale...................................... | $567,000 |
| Finished Goods Inventory, Dec. 31, 1997 ...................... | 25,000 |
| Cost of Goods Sold ......................................... | $542,000 |

### UNDERHILL CAN COMPANY
### Income Statement
### Year Ended December 31, 1997

| | | |
|---|---:|---:|
| Sales ................................................. | | $650,000 |
| Cost of Goods Sold......................................... | | 542,000 |
| Gross Profit .............................................. | | $108,000 |
| Selling and Administrative Expenses: | | |
| Salaries........................................ | $90,000 | |
| Insurance ...................................... | 3,000 | |
| Depreciation .................................... | 7,000 | |
| Utilities......................................... | 3,000 | 103,000 |
| Net Income ............................................ | | $   5,000 |

## QUESTIONS FOR REVIEW AND FURTHER THOUGHT

### REVIEW QUESTIONS

1. What do we mean by the expression, "different costs for different purposes"?

2. Define the term *activity* and list the appropriate measure(s) of activity for the following centers of activity of a manufacturer:
   a. Production department

    **b.** Janitorial department
    **c.** Sales department
    **d.** Purchasing department

3. What is the difference between an average cost and a unit cost?

4. For each center of activity listed below, give a possible measure of activity:
    **a.** A school library
    **b.** A computer center
    **c.** A restaurant
    **d.** A maintenance department
    **e.** An assembly department
    **f.** A hospital
    **g.** A telephone company's installation department
    **h.** A personnel department

5. Distinguish between inventoriable costs and period costs.

6. Explain what is meant by the term "noninventoriable unexpired costs".

7. Distinguish between the operations of a merchandiser and a manufacturer.

8. What are the three inventory accounts for a manufacturer?

9. What is the difference between raw materials and direct materials for a manufacturer?

10. Prime costs plus conversion costs equal total manufacturing costs incurred for a period of time. Do you agree? Explain.

11. List five examples of factory overhead.

12. Describe the flow of costs for a manufacturer. Use T-accounts to illustrate your description.

13. What is the difference between "Total Manufacturing Costs to Account for" and "Cost of Goods Sold"?

14. Explain how perpetual and periodic inventory systems would differ in the accounting for:
    **a.** The purchase of raw materials
    **b.** The use of direct labor

15. Distinguish the job order costing method from the process costing method.

## QUESTIONS FOR FURTHER THOUGHT

1. All costs that are treated as assets when incurred are classified as inventoriable costs. Do you agree? Explain.

2. All inventoriable costs are product costs, but all product costs are not inventoriable costs. Explain.

3. All costs of a manufacturer are treated alike. Do you agree? Explain.

4. Period costs can be defined as costs that are expensed in the current period. Do you agree? Why or why not?

5. Identify the following items as either inventoriable costs or period costs: depreciation, salaries, and utilities.

6. Why do you suppose the combination of direct labor costs and factory overhead costs are referred to as conversion costs?

## OBJECTIVE ASSIGNMENT

*True/False*    Indicate whether each statement below is *true* or *false* by placing a *T* or an *F* in the space provided.

_____ 1. Companies usually have different costs for different purposes.

_____ 2. Period costs are expensed as incurred for a retail organization, but not for a manufacturer.

_____ 3. Whether or not there are zero beginning and ending inventories, cost of goods sold always equals the sum of direct materials, direct labor, and factory overhead.

_____ 4. Insurance on a company's factory building is classified as part of factory overhead costs.

_____ 5. Indirect labor costs include the salary paid to a factory supervisor.

*Multiple Choice*    Select the best choice to complete each statement or answer each question below. Write the letter corresponding to your choice in the space provided.

_____ 1. Which of the following would probably be a noninventoriable unexpired cost when it is incurred?
   a. A prepayment for a one-year insurance policy
   b. salaries paid to administrative personnel
   c. materials purchased and used in production
   d. commissions paid to sales personnel

_____ 2. Which of the following is an inventoriable cost for a company that is not a manufacturer?
   a. Freight paid on merchandise purchased
   b. Freight paid on merchandise sold
   c. Depreciation on the president's car
   d. Fee paid to a certified public accountant

_____ 3. Which of the following costs is not a conversion cost?
   a. Salaries of material handlers in production
   b. Indirect materials
   c. Supplies used by the sales force
   d. Direct labor

_____ 4. The account debited when indirect materials are used in production is:
   a. Indirect Materials Used          c. Raw Materials Inventory
   b. Work-in-Process Inventory        d. Factory Overhead Incurred

_____ 5. Direct materials and direct labor for the month were $88,000 and $120,000, respectively. If the factory overhead costs totaled $60,000 (including $8,000 of indirect materials and $18,000 of indirect labor), what were the prime costs for the month?
   a. $208,000      c. $182,000
   b. $234,000      d. $88,000

_____ 6. A company is trying to decide whether or not it should drop one of its unsuccessful product lines. Which of the following costs might be considered a product cost but not an inventoriable cost?
   a. direct materials for the product
   b. commissions to sales personnel for the sale of the product
   c. salaries to laborers who assemble the product
   d. depreciation on production machinery

_____ 7. Vance Ski Makers purchases $500,000 of raw materials during 1997. The inventory balance for raw materials is $25,000 on Jan. 1, 1997, and $40,000 on Dec. 31, 1997. What is the cost of materials used?
   a. $500,000      c. $515,000
   b. $485,000      d. $15,000

_____ 8. Carol's Christmas Ornaments produces 100,000 boxes of ornaments during 1997, which cost $4.50 per box. Carol had a beginning balance in Finished Goods Inventory on Jan. 1 of $70,000 and an ending balance on Dec. 31 of $100,000. What is Carol's cost of goods sold for the year?

a. $480,000    c. $130,000
b. $70,000     d. $420,000

_____ 9. The production costs for Ace Archery Supplies were as follows for 1997:

| | |
|---|---|
| Direct materials . . . . . . . . . . . . . . . . . . . . . . . . . . | $160,000 |
| Direct labor . . . . . . . . . . . . . . . . . . . . . . . . . . . . | 240,000 |
| Factory overhead . . . . . . . . . . . . . . . . . . . . . . . . | 500,000 |

On Jan. 1, Work-in-Process Inventory had a balance of $60,000; on Dec. 31, the balance was $65,000. What are the "Total Costs to Account for"?

a. $900,000    c. $895,000
b. $905,000    d. $960,000

_____ 10. Factory overhead costs incurred during 1997 were $150,000. Ten thousand units were started and completed in 1997, of which 7,500 were sold. How much factory overhead was in the ending inventories for work-in-process and finished goods?

a. $150,000 in Work-in-Process Inventory; –0– in Finished Goods Inventory
b. –0– in Work-in-Process Inventory; $37,500 in Finished Goods Inventory
c. $37,500 in Work-in-Process Inventory; $37,500 in Finished Goods Inventory
d. $112,500 in Work-in-Process Inventory; $37,500 in Finished Goods Inventory

---

## EXERCISES

**2†**  **Exercise 1:** Calculating Total Costs and Average Costs

The Kingery Manufacturing Co. worked 30,000 hours in June of this year, and its operating costs averaged $6 per hour. The firm expects the total costs to increase by $20,000 in July, to accompany the 20% increase in hours worked. What will be the total and average costs for July?

▶ *(Check Figure: Average costs = $5.56/hr.)*

**2**  **Exercise 2:** Distinguishing Total Costs from Average Costs

Dan Kirby is preparing for a test and realizes that cutting all his classes has taken its toll. Dan is in dire need of a tutor. He hears that his friend was tutored the night before for $10. His friend needed only 2 hours of the tutor's time, but Dan expects to need the help continuously until test time (approximately 12 hours). If Dan is able to interest the tutor in an all-night tutoring session, how much should Dan plan to pay for it?

▶ *(Check Figure: $60)*

**3**  **Exercise 3:** Classifying Costs as Inventoriable Costs or Period Costs

Darby's Dollhouse Company produces dollhouses and needs some help in classifying its costs. It has gathered the following list of costs and asks your help in distinguishing between inventoriable costs and period costs. Place an ✕ in the appropriate column(s) for each cost listed on the next page.

† The numbers in the margin refer to the Learning Objectives.

| | Inventoriable Cost | | | |
| Cost | Direct Materials | Direct Labor | Factory Overhead | Period Cost |
| --- | --- | --- | --- | --- |
| Transportation costs on raw materials purchased | X | | | |
| Salaries of machine maintenance personnel | | | X | |
| Sales representatives' commissions | | | | X *outside of factory* |
| Transportation costs for units sold | | | | X |
| Screws connecting dollhouses | | | X | |
| Rent on factory building | | | X | |
| Fuel cost to heat administrative offices | | | | X |
| Insurance on factory building | | | X | |
| Property taxes on factory building | | | X | |
| Depreciation on sales representatives' cars | | | | ✓ |
| Salaries of dollhouse assemblers | | X | | |

3 **Exercise 4:** Classifying costs as inventoriable costs, period costs, or noninventoriable unexpired costs

The Underhill Company has just completed its first year of operation, 1997, and has gathered the following list of costs incurred during the year. Look over the list and additional facts carefully and then prepare three lists, classifying the costs as **(a)** inventoriable costs, **(b)** period costs, or **(c)** noninventoriable unexpired costs.

| | |
| --- | --- |
| Land ..................................... | $75,000 |
| Prepaid insurance (paid on Jan. 1 for 3 years) ... | 3,000 |
| Sales and wages: | |
|    Production ............................. | 35,000 |
|    Salespersons' commissions ................ | 27,000 |
|    President's salary ........................ | 40,000 |
| Machinery (10-year life) ..................... | 90,000 |
| Utilities: | |
|    Production ............................... | 6,000 |
|    Selling and administrative.................. | 1,200 |
| Purchases of materials and supplies ........... | 80,000 |

One-fourth of the materials and supplies purchased were used in production in 1997. Another one-fourth was used in the selling and administrative departments. All but $20,000 of the machinery was used in the production department; the remaining machinery was used in the selling and administrative departments.

Two-thirds of the insurance coverage is related to production and the remainder to selling and administration.

None of the units were finished by the end of 1997.

▶ *(Check figure: (a) $68,667)*

3    **Exercise 5:** Distinguishing Inventoriable Costs From Product Costs

The Rachelcindy Company manufactures several different types of dental devices for ortho-
dontists and other dental products for the general public. It has two production departments—
assembly and inspection, a sales and marketing department, a distribution center, and a customer service department. The president of Rachelcindy is considering dropping one of its less
profitable lines—teeth spacers; is interested in knowing exactly the product costs for that line;
and asks the controller for a report. The controller is unsure whether the president is referring
only to those product costs that are inventoriable or to all costs that relate to the product and
might be affected by the decision. She therefore provides the president with two reports—one
that itemizes just the inventoriable costs, and a second one that itemizes all product costs.

Below is a listing of several costs that the controller may have included in her two reports.
You are to identify which costs were included in each report, by placing an X in the appropriate
column(s).

|   | Report Itemizing Inventoriable Costs | Report Itemizing All Costs | Does Not Appear on Either Report |
|---|---|---|---|
| 1. Materials used to produce spacers. | _____ | _____ | _____ |
| 2. Labor costs to produce teeth bands (a different product) | _____ | _____ | _____ |
| 3. Depreciation of plant that produces several different product lines | _____ | _____ | _____ |
| 4. Commissions for sale of teeth spacers | _____ | _____ | _____ |
| 5. Costs to ship spacers to orthodontists' offices | _____ | _____ | _____ |
| 6. Costs of repairing and replacing defective spacers | _____ | _____ | _____ |
| 7. Costs of advertising product lines sold to general public | _____ | _____ | _____ |

5    **Exercise 6:** Determining the Cost of Goods Sold

Use the list of account balances below for Abra Debra Company for 1998 to prepare a schedule
of cost of goods sold. For simplicity, assume that all beginning and ending inventories are zero.

| | | | |
|---|---|---|---|
| Raw Materials Added to the Physical Units Produced . . . . | $200,000 | Labor Employed Directly for Production . . . . . . . . . . . . . | $80,000 |
| Supplies Used . . . . . . . . . . . . . | 8,000 | Indirect Labor. . . . . . . . . . . . . . | 12,000 |
| Insurance. . . . . . . . . . . . . . . . | 1,400 | Depreciation. . . . . . . . . . . . . . | 3,500 |
| Utilities . . . . . . . . . . . . . . . . . | 1,000 | Rent . . . . . . . . . . . . . . . . . . . . | 1,150 |
| Property Taxes . . . . . . . . . . . . | 3,000 | Idle Time . . . . . . . . . . . . . . . . | 200 |

▶ *(Check Figure: Cost of Goods Sold = $310,250)*

4 **Exercise 7:** Determining the Cost of Direct Materials Used

Compute the cost of direct materials used for the month of November 1998, on the basis of the following account balances:

| | | | |
|---|---|---|---|
| Raw Materials Inventory, Nov. 1, 1998 . . . . . . . . . . . . . | $ 5,400 | Invoice Cost of Units Purchased . . . . . . . . . . . . . . . | 84,000 |
| Transportation Costs of Purchases . . . . . . . . . . . . | 1,800 | Purchase Returns . . . . . . . . . . | 5,000 |
| Transportation Costs of Units Sold . . . . . . . . . . . . . | 2,500 | Raw Materials Inventory, Nov. 30, 1998 . . . . . . . . . . . . . | 4,000 |

The raw materials used that were classified as factory overhead amounted to $4,000.

▶ *(Check Figure: $78,200)*

5 **Exercise 8:** Calculating Cost of Goods Sold

Fill in the blanks of the following schedules of cost of goods sold for 1997 and 1998.

| | 1997 | 1998 |
|---|---|---|
| Raw Materials Inventory, Jan. 1. . . . . . . . . . . . . . . . . . . . . . . . . | $ 15,000 | $ |
| Purchases. . . . . . . . . . . . . . . . . . . . . . . . . . . . . . . . . . . . . . . | 200,000 | 160,000 |
| | $ | $ |
| Raw Materials Inventory, Dec. 31 . . . . . . . . . . . . . . . . . . . . . . | | 32,000 |
| Direct Materials Used. . . . . . . . . . . . . . . . . . . . . . . . . . . . . . . | $180,000 | $ |
| Direct Labor . . . . . . . . . . . . . . . . . . . . . . . . . . . . . . . . . . . . . | | 110,000 |
| Factory Overhead. . . . . . . . . . . . . . . . . . . . . . . . . . . . . . . . . . | 120,000 | 130,000 |
| | $400,000 | $ |
| Work-in-Process Inventory, Jan. 1. . . . . . . . . . . . . . . . . . . . . . | 20,000 | |
| | $ | $ |
| Work-in-Process Inventory, Dec. 31 . . . . . . . . . . . . . . . . . . . . | 10,000 | |
| Cost of Goods Completed . . . . . . . . . . . . . . . . . . . . . . . . . . . | $ | $400,000 |
| Finished Goods Inventory, Jan. 1 . . . . . . . . . . . . . . . . . . . . . . | | |
| | $460,000 | $ |
| Finished Goods Inventory, Dec. 31 . . . . . . . . . . . . . . . . . . . . . | 40,000 | 35,000 |
| Cost of Goods Sold . . . . . . . . . . . . . . . . . . . . . . . . . . . . . . . . | $ | $ |

▶ *(Check Figure: Cost of Goods Sold (1998) = $405,000)*

3 **Exercise 9:** Classifying Costs as Inventoriable, Period, Prime, and Conversion

During 1997, Rita Reader purchased $10,000 of raw materials on account, of which $9,000 was paid for at year-end; $6,000 was used, of which $1,000 was for indirect materials; and $500 was used in the selling department.

Rita accrued a total payroll for the year of $50,000, of which $5,000 was still unpaid on Dec. 31, 1997. Of the total payroll, $40,000 related to production ($30,000 direct and $10,000 indirect).

Rita prepaid a 3-year insurance policy on Jan. 1, 1997, for $2,400, which provided coverage on the company's assets (three-fourths of which related to production activities).

Determine the amounts of period costs and inventoriable costs, and calculate the prime costs and the conversion costs.

▶ *(Check Figure: Conversion costs = $41,600)*

5 **Exercise 10:** Preparing an Income Statement and Determining Cost of Goods Sold

Prepare an income statement for Rettig Ironworks, based on the following information:

Finished goods inventory:

| | |
|---|---|
| Jan. 1, 1997............................ | $ 67,000 |
| Dec. 31, 1997 .......................... | 22,000 |
| Costs of goods completed .................. | 226,000 |
| Sales revenue............................ | 560,000 |
| Selling expenses.......................... | 57,000 |
| Administrative expenses................... | 105,000 |

Determine the cost of goods sold within the income statement, rather than determining it in a separate schedule.

▶ *(Check Figure: Net income = $127,000)*

## PROBLEMS: SET A

4† **Problem A1:** Using T-accounts to Trace the Flow of Costs

Mr. Carlson began his company, WARP, Inc., on Jan. 1, 1997. During his second year, 1998, the following transactions related to production took place:

| | |
|---|---|
| Raw materials purchased.................... | $30,000 |
| Direct materials used ....................... | 27,500 |
| Indirect materials used ..................... | 2,500 |
| Direct labor accrued ....................... | 32,500 |
| Indirect labor accrued...................... | 12,500 |
| Depreciation ............................. | 1,500 |
| Utilities used ............................. | 1,000 |
| Property taxes accrued..................... | 900 |
| Cost of goods finished during 1998 ........... | 75,900 |
| Cost of items sold in 1998 .................. | 95,000 |

In addition, the controller found the following balances from the general ledger, on Jan. 1, 1998:

| | |
|---|---|
| Raw Materials Inventory..................... | $ 5,000 |
| Work-in-Process Inventory .................. | 12,500 |
| Finished Goods Inventory................... | 25,000 |

### Required:

1. Record the beginning inventory balances in T-accounts.
2. Record all transactions that took place in 1998 in T-account form, showing the progression of costs from Raw Materials Inventory to Cost of Goods Sold.
3. Indicate the ending balances in the three inventory accounts.

▶ *(Check Figure: 2. Cost of Goods Sold = $95,000; 3. Finished Goods Inventory = $5,900)*

† The numbers in the margin refer to the Learning Objectives.

5   **Problem A2:** Preparing a Schedule of Costs of Goods Sold

The controller for Dryeffis Company has gathered the following information about 1997:

| | |
|---|---:|
| Direct materials used . . . . . . . . . . . . . . . . . . . . . . | $280,000 |
| Indirect materials used . . . . . . . . . . . . . . . . . . . . | 16,000 |
| Direct labor . . . . . . . . . . . . . . . . . . . . . . . . . . . . . | 320,000 |
| Indirect labor . . . . . . . . . . . . . . . . . . . . . . . . . . . . | 120,000 |
| Sales labor . . . . . . . . . . . . . . . . . . . . . . . . . . . . . | 200,000 |
| Insurance on factory and machinery . . . . . . . . . . | 32,000 |
| Insurance on salespeople's cars . . . . . . . . . . . . . | 12,000 |
| Depreciation on production machinery. . . . . . . . . | 40,000 |
| Utilities of factory . . . . . . . . . . . . . . . . . . . . . . . . . | 49,600 |
| Freight costs for units sold . . . . . . . . . . . . . . . . . . | 19,200 |
| Inventories: | |
| Jan. 1, 1997: | |
| Work-in-Process . . . . . . . . . . . . . . . . . . . . . . | 60,000 |
| Finished Goods . . . . . . . . . . . . . . . . . . . . . . . | 100,000 |
| Dec. 31, 1997: | |
| Work-in-Process . . . . . . . . . . . . . . . . . . . . . . | 68,000 |
| Finished Goods . . . . . . . . . . . . . . . . . . . . . . . | 84,000 |

**Required:**

Prepare the schedule of cost of goods sold for 1997.

▶ *(Check Figure: Cost of Goods Sold = $865,600)*

5   **Problem A3:** Preparing an Income Statement and Schedule of Cost of Goods Sold

The Recycled Paper Company produces newsprint by the roll. Each roll sells for $250. The following information relates to the production and sales of paper by Recycled for 1997. There was no beginning or ending balance in Work-in-Process Inventory, and no beginning balance in Finished Goods Inventory.

| | |
|---|---:|
| Rolls produced. . . . . . . . . . . . . . . . . . . . . . . . . . . | 80,000 |
| Rolls sold . . . . . . . . . . . . . . . . . . . . . . . . . . . . . . . | 70,000 |
| Direct materials: | |
| Beginning balance . . . . . . . . . . . . . . . . . . . . . | $1,000,000 |
| Purchased . . . . . . . . . . . . . . . . . . . . . . . . . . . | 7,000,000 |
| Ending balance . . . . . . . . . . . . . . . . . . . . . . . | 500,000 |
| Labor costs: | |
| Direct labor. . . . . . . . . . . . . . . . . . . . . . . . . . . | 4,000,000 |
| Indirect labor . . . . . . . . . . . . . . . . . . . . . . . . . | 500,000 |
| Selling and administrative . . . . . . . . . . . . . . . | 1,000,000 |
| Other costs: | |
| Payroll taxes: Factory . . . . . . . . . . . . . . . . . . | 450,000 |
| Selling and administrative. . . . | 100,000 |
| Utilities: Factory . . . . . . . . . . . . . . . . . . . . . . . | 300,000 |
| Selling and administrative . . . . . . . . | 150,000 |
| Janitorial: Factory. . . . . . . . . . . . . . . . . . . . . . | 88,000 |
| Selling and administrative . . . . . . . | 44,000 |
| Miscellaneous nonmanufacturing . . . . . . . . . | 480,000 |

**Required:**

1. Prepare a detailed schedule for cost of goods sold.
2. Prepare an income statement for 1997.

▶ *(Check Figure: 1. Cost of Goods Sold = $11,233,250; 2. Net Income = $4,492,750)*

5 **Problem A4:** Preparing a Detailed Income Statement and Supporting Schedules

The Vickers Company has gathered the following information concerning the operations during 1997, and would like you to prepare a detailed income statement for the year.

*Revenues.* Sales for 1997 (of which $135,000 were returned) were $6,000,000. The costs of shipping the product were $90,000.

*Inventories.* The balances in Work-in-Process Inventory and Finished Goods Inventory were:

|  | Jan. 1 | Dec. 31 |
|---|---|---|
| Work-in-Process Inventory | $270,000 | $240,000 |
| Finished Goods Inventory | 330,000 | 292,500 |

*Materials and supplies.* Purchases of materials and supplies for the year were $1,500,000, which were added to a beginning inventory of $225,000. At year-end there was a $150,000 balance remaining in inventory. Of the materials and supplies used, three-fourths were used in production ($975,000 of which were direct materials) and the remaining one-fourth was used in the selling and administrative departments.

*Salaries and wages.* The payroll for the year was $3,000,000, broken down as follows:

| | |
|---|---|
| Direct labor. | $1,950,000 |
| Indirect labor | 600,000 |
| Selling and administrative personnel | 450,000 |

*Insurance.* A 3-year insurance policy was purchased on Jan. 1, 1997, for $45,000. The insurance was related to departments in the following manner:

| | |
|---|---|
| Production. | three-fifths |
| Selling and administrative. | two-fifths |

*Depreciation.* The cost of the depreciable assets used by the company was $3,450,000, and the balances in the Accumulated Depreciation account on Jan. 1 and Dec. 31 were $1,425,000 and $1,800,000, respectively. All but 20% of the depreciable assets are used in production.

*Other items.* Interest expense for 1997 was $40,500, and income taxes were 40% of income before tax.

**Required:**

Prepare, in good form, a detailed income statement for Vickers Company with a supporting schedule of costs of goods sold.

▶ *(Check Figure: Cost of Goods Sold = $4,107,750; Net Income = $421,200)*

5   **Problem A5:** Preparing a Revised Income Statement and a Schedule of Cost of Goods Sold

Alisha Chase has recently taken over the controller's position and has luckily had the chance to review the income statement before it was submitted to the president. Chase was quite confused to see the following:

---

### PETALUMA COMPANY
### Income Statement
### December 31, 1997

| | | | |
|---|--:|--:|--:|
| Sales . . . . . . . . . . . . . . . . . . . . . . . . . . . . . . . . . . . . . . . . . . . . . | | | $750,000 |
| Expenses: | | | |
| Purchases. . . . . . . . . . . . . . . . . . . . . . . . . . . . . . . . . . . . . . . | | $250,000 | |
| Freight-In . . . . . . . . . . . . . . . . . . . . . . . . . . . . . . . . . . . . | | 10,000 | |
| Freight-Out . . . . . . . . . . . . . . . . . . . . . . . . . . . . . . . . . . . . | | 20,000 | |
| Operating Expenses. . . . . . . . . . . . . . . . . . . . . . . . . . . . | | 100,000 | |
| Interest Expense . . . . . . . . . . . . . . . . . . . . . . . . . . . . . . | | 5,000 | |
| Factory Costs | | | |
| Labor ($170,000 direct labor) . . . . . . . . . . . . . . | $200,000 | | |
| Utilities . . . . . . . . . . . . . . . . . . . . . . . . . . . . . . . . | 25,000 | | |
| Depreciation. . . . . . . . . . . . . . . . . . . . . . . . . . . | 16,000 | | |
| Rent . . . . . . . . . . . . . . . . . . . . . . . . . . . . . . . . . . | 24,000 | 265,000 | |
| Total Costs Incurred . . . . . . . . . . . . . . . . . . . | | $650,000 | |
| Beginning Inventories: | | | |
| Raw Materials . . . . . . . . . . . . . . . . . . . . . . . . . . . . | $ 10,000 | | |
| Work-in-Process . . . . . . . . . . . . . . . . . . . . . . . . . . | 15,000 | | |
| Finished Goods . . . . . . . . . . . . . . . . . . . . . . . . . . | 17,000 | 42,000 | |
| Total Costs to Account for . . . . . . . . . . . . . . . | | $692,000 | |
| Ending Inventories: | | | |
| Raw Materials . . . . . . . . . . . . . . . . . . . . . . . . . . . . | $ 19,000 | | |
| Work-in-Process . . . . . . . . . . . . . . . . . . . . . . . . . . | 11,000 | | |
| Finished Goods . . . . . . . . . . . . . . . . . . . . . . . . . . | 21,000 | 51,000 | 641,000 |
| Net Income . . . . . . . . . . . . . . . . . . . . . . . . . . . . . . . . . . | | | $109,000 |

---

### Required:

Prepare the revised income statement that Chase would certainly make before sending it to the president. Prepare a separate schedule for cost of goods sold.

▶ *(Check Figure: Cost of Goods Sold = $516,000; Net Income = $109,000)*

## PROBLEMS: SET B

4†   **Problem B1:** Using T-Accounts to Trace the Flow of Inventoriable Costs

During 1997, the following transactions related to production took place for Ponderosa Company:

| | |
|---|--:|
| Raw materials purchased . . . . . . . . . . . . . . . . | $  112,000 *a* |
| Raw materials used . . . . . . . . . . . . . . . . . . . . . . | 178,000 *b* |
| Direct labor accrued . . . . . . . . . . . . . . . . . . . . . | 260,000 *c, d* |
| Indirect labor accrued . . . . . . . . . . . . . . . . . . . | 24,000 *e* |
| Utilities paid . . . . . . . . . . . . . . . . . . . . . . . . . . | 5,400 *f* |
| Accrued rent. . . . . . . . . . . . . . . . . . . . . . . . . . . | 8,600 *g* |
| Insurance used . . . . . . . . . . . . . . . . . . . . . . . . | 2,800 *h* |
| Cost of goods transferred to finished | |
| goods inventory . . . . . . . . . . . . . . . . . . . . . . . | 612,000 *j* |
| Cost of goods sold. . . . . . . . . . . . . . . . . . . . . . | 1,022,000 *k* |

Ponderosa began 1997 with the following balances in inventory:

Raw Materials............................ $ 80,000
Work-in-Process.......................... 260,000
Finished Goods........................... 570,000

**Required:**

1. Place the beginning inventory balances in T-accounts.
2. Record all transactions that took place in 1997 in T-account form, showing the progression of costs from Raw Materials Inventory to Cost of Goods Sold.
3. Indicate the ending balance in the three inventory accounts.

▶ *(Check Figure: 2. Cost of Goods Sold = $1,022,000; Finished Goods Inventory = $160,000)*

5  **Problem B2:** Preparing a Schedule of Cost of Goods Sold

The Caruso Company had the following balances in inventory for 1997:

Work-in-Process, Jan. 1, 1997............... $195,000
Work-in-Process, Dec. 31, 1997 ............. 243,000
Finished Goods, Jan. 1, 1997 ............... 297,000
Finished Goods, Dec. 31, 1997 .............. 276,000

In addition, there were the following balances in other general ledger accounts for 1997:

Materials Used:
   Direct................................. $570,000
   Indirect............................... 112,000
Labor:
   Direct................................. 435,000
   Indirect............................... 181,500
Insurance on Factory Building and Machinery... 15,000
Property Taxes on Factory Building........... 9,900
Rent on Production Equipment .............. 87,000
Utilities on Factory Building ............... 57,000
Transportation Costs Associated with Units Sold  55,500

*— Operating expenses section of Income Statement*

**Required:**

Prepare a schedule of cost of goods sold for 1997.

▶ *(Check Figure: Cost of Goods Sold = $1,440,400)*

5  **Problem B3:** Preparing an Income Statement and a Schedule of Cost of Goods Sold

The Fantasy Film Company produces a new type of film that can be used only for night photography. The sales price for the film is $6.50 per package. During 1997, 250,000 packages were started, completed, and sold, and the following information was gathered by the accountant concerning the year:

| | |
|---|---:|
| Cost per pound of direct materials. . . . . . . . . . . . . . . . . . . . . . . . . . . . . . . . . . . . | $5.50 |
| Direct materials purchased. . . . . . . . . . . . . . . . . . . . . . . . . . . . . . . . . . . . . | 20,000 lb |
| Direct materials used in production. . . . . . . . . . . . . . . . . . . . . . . . . . . . . . . | 18,000 lb |
| Cost per hour for labor: | |
|     Direct labor . . . . . . . . . . . . . . . . . . . . . . . . . . . . . . . . . . . . . . . . . . . . . . . | $12.00 |
|     Indirect labor . . . . . . . . . . . . . . . . . . . . . . . . . . . . . . . . . . . . . . . . . . . . . | 4.00 |
| Hours worked: | |
|     Direct labor . . . . . . . . . . . . . . . . . . . . . . . . . . . . . . . . . . . . . . . . . . . . . . . | 70,000 hr |
|     Indirect labor . . . . . . . . . . . . . . . . . . . . . . . . . . . . . . . . . . . . . . . . . . . . . | 50,000 hr |
| Other factory costs: | |
|     Payroll taxes . . . . . . . . . . . . . . . . . . . . . . . . . . . . . . . . . . . . . . . . . . . . . . | $ 45,000 |
|     Utilities. . . . . . . . . . . . . . . . . . . . . . . . . . . . . . . . . . . . . . . . . . . . . . . . . . . | 32,000 |
|     Janitorial . . . . . . . . . . . . . . . . . . . . . . . . . . . . . . . . . . . . . . . . . . . . . . . . . | 41,000 |
|     Property taxes. . . . . . . . . . . . . . . . . . . . . . . . . . . . . . . . . . . . . . . . . . . . | 25,000 |
|     Miscellaneous . . . . . . . . . . . . . . . . . . . . . . . . . . . . . . . . . . . . . . . . . . . . | 37,000 |
| Selling and administrative costs: | |
|     Payroll . . . . . . . . . . . . . . . . . . . . . . . . . . . . . . . . . . . . . . . . . . . . . . . . . . . | 150,000 |
|     Taxes. . . . . . . . . . . . . . . . . . . . . . . . . . . . . . . . . . . . . . . . . . . . . . . . . . . . . | 88,000 |
|     Supplies. . . . . . . . . . . . . . . . . . . . . . . . . . . . . . . . . . . . . . . . . . . . . . . . . . | 34,000 |
|     Rent. . . . . . . . . . . . . . . . . . . . . . . . . . . . . . . . . . . . . . . . . . . . . . . . . . . . . | 55,000 |
|     Utilities. . . . . . . . . . . . . . . . . . . . . . . . . . . . . . . . . . . . . . . . . . . . . . . . . . . | 12,000 |
|     Miscellaneous . . . . . . . . . . . . . . . . . . . . . . . . . . . . . . . . . . . . . . . . . . . . | 17,000 |

There were no beginning balances in any of the inventory accounts.

**Required:**

1. Prepare a detailed schedule for cost of goods sold.
2. Prepare an income statement for 1997.

▶ *(Check Figure: 1. Cost of Goods Sold = $1,319,000; 2. Net Loss = $50,000)*

5   **Problem B4:** Preparing a Detailed Income Statement and Supporting Schedules

The Ward Corporation's controller needs to prepare an income statement for the year 1997. She has her head bookkeeper gather the following information for the year:

*Revenues.* Revenue from the sale of Ward's product totaled $6,215,000, of which $350,000 was returned. Freight costs were $90,000.

*Materials and supplies.* Purchases of materials and supplies during 1997 were $1,650,000. Of the materials and supplies used, 80% were for raw materials needed for production and 20% were for administrative supplies. Seventy percent of the raw materials issued to production were direct and the remainder were indirect.

*Salaries and wages.* The total payroll was distributed as follows:

| | |
|---|---:|
| Production: | |
|     Direct . . . . . . . . . . . . . . . . . . . . . . . . . . . . . . | $1,950,000 |
|     Indirect . . . . . . . . . . . . . . . . . . . . . . . . . . . . . | 442,500 |
| Selling and administrative . . . . . . . . . . . . . . . . . | 607,500 |

*Rent.* The building was rented on Jan. 1, 1997, for 3 years. The rent, paid in advance for the 3 years, was $675,000. The building was used by the different departments in the following proportions:

| | |
|---|---|
| Production. . . . . . . . . . . . . . . . . . . . . . . . . . . . . . . . . | four-fifths |
| Selling and administrative. . . . . . . . . . . . . . . . . . | one-fifth |

*Depreciation.* Machinery having a 5-year life, costing $1,000,000, was purchased on Jan. 1, 1997. All of the machinery is used in production activities.

*Inventory balances.* At the beginning and end of 1997, Ward Corporation had the following inventory balances:

|  | Jan. 1 | Dec. 31 |
|---|---|---|
| Raw Materials and Supplies.......................... | $ 75,000 | $150,000 |
| Work-in-Process..................................... | 270,000 | 240,000 |
| Finished Goods..................................... | 230,000 | 192,500 |

**Required:**

Prepare a detailed income statement for Ward Corporation with a supporting schedule of cost of goods sold.

▶ *(Check Figure: Cost of Goods Sold = $4,100,000; Net Income = $707,500)*

5    **Problem B5:** Preparing a Revised Income Statement and a Schedule of Cost of Goods Sold

Shown below is a schedule of cost of goods sold for Clutz Company for 1997. Read it over carefully and make any corrections that are needed to make it more presentable.

**CLUTZ COMPANY**
**Schedule of Cost of Goods Sold**
**December 31, 1997**

|  |  |  |  |
|---|---|---|---|
| Direct Materials, Jan. 1, 1997 ................ |  | $ 15,000 |  |
| Purchases................................. | $100,000 |  |  |
| Freight-Out ............................... | 5,000 | 105,000 |  |
| Total Available for Sale ...................... |  | $120,000 |  |
| Direct Materials, Dec. 31, 1997 ............... |  | 12,000 |  |
| Direct Materials Used (including indirect) ........ |  |  | $108,000 |
| Labor: |  |  |  |
|    Direct.................................... |  | $ 65,000 |  |
|    Indirect ................................. |  | 15,000 | 80,000 |
| Factory Expense: |  |  |  |
|    Utilities................................... |  | $ 1,200 |  |
|    Payroll Taxes ............................ |  | 3,000 |  |
|    Rent..................................... |  | 8,000 |  |
|    Depreciation ............................. |  | 6,000 |  |
|    President's Salary......................... |  | 30,000 | 48,200 |
| Prime Costs Plus Conversion Costs ............ |  |  | $236,200 |
| Increase in Work-in-Process Inventory .......... |  |  | 20,000 |
| Cost of Production Finished during Year......... |  |  | $216,200 |
| Finished Goods Inventory, Jan. 1, 1997 ......... |  |  | 35,000 |
| Total Available for Sale ...................... |  |  | $251,200 |
| Finished Goods Inventory, Dec. 31, 1997........ |  |  | 31,000 |
| Cost of Goods Sold ......................... |  |  | $220,200 |

## DECISION PROBLEM

The Hiddenitems Manufacturing Co. was quite profitable in 1997, generating a $6,850,000 profit. Its income statement showed the following detail:

| | | |
|---|--:|--:|
| Sales | | $22,000,000 |
| Cost of Goods | | 12,000,000 |
| Gross Profit | | $10,000,000 |
| Selling and Administrative Expenses: | | |
| Salaries and Commissions | $2,000,000 | |
| Insurance | 250,000 | |
| Rent | 800,000 | |
| Utilities | 100,000 | 3,150,000 |
| Net Income | | $6,850,000 |

Hiddenitems' banker, Shomey Ware, is skeptical that the income statement includes all the expenses incurred by Hiddenitems during the year. Shomey points out that substantial costs of salaries, rents, insurance, and utilities were most likely incurred in production but were apparently deleted from the income statement. If you were Hiddenitems's accountant, how would you respond to Shomey's concern?

## ETHICS CASE

Home Square has a small chain of discount home improvement retail stores in a very competitive market. Its first year of operations hasn't been as successful as its founder Tim Valli was hoping for. Near the end of the year, Tim instructs his controller, Al Borely to do some accounting magic in order to improve Home Square's profits for the year. Al, who has been treated so far as no more than a glorified bookkeeper, appreciates the opportunity to be included in the decision making team for the company and looks upon this challenge with vigorous enthusiasm.

Al realizes that a more creative classification of costs can make a significant difference in the amount of expenses that Home Square must recognize this year. First of all, Al contends that many of the costs of operating the retail stores, such as the salaries of sales personnel, the costs of advertising, and the customer service department costs should all be assigned to inventory since they cannot provide any benefit to the company until the units are sold. In addition, Al feels that other operating costs that were originally prepaid during the year, such as insurance, property taxes and rent, should all be maintained in a single Prepaid Expense account. Only after all the items are fully expired, will the total be expensed.

By treating these costs as assets until they have been used, consumed, or sold, the timing of their expense will be more appropriately matched with the revenues that Home Square hopes to generate in the future.

**Required:**

1. How will Al's actions affect the reported profits for Home Square?
2. Whether or not Al is properly classifying the costs for Home Square, depends upon an understanding of which important issue discussed in the chapter?
3. Would you consider Al's actions to be an ethical way of improving Home Square's profit picture? Discuss.

## OBJECTIVE ASSIGNMENT ANSWERS

**True/False**

**1.** T   **2.** F   **3.** F   **4.** T   **5.** T

**Multiple Choice**

**1.** a   **2.** a   **3.** c   **4.** d   **5.** a
**6.** b   **7.** b   **8.** d   **9.** d   **10.** b

# APPENDIX
# The Periodic Method of Accounting for Manufacturing Costs

**LEARNING OBJECTIVES**

After studying this appendix, you should be able to do the following:

1 Explain the differences between the perpetual and the periodic inventory systems

2 Make the journal entries that trace the flow of costs through the accounts of a manufacturer that uses the periodic inventory system

3 Perform the year-end worksheet procedures for a manufacturer that uses the periodic inventory system

4 Prepare the financial statements and closing entries for a manufacturer that uses the periodic inventory system

5 Define the key terms listed at the end of the appendix

We have shown you how to account for the flow of production costs through the inventory accounts of a manufacturer that uses the perpetual inventory system. Now we will explain how to account for the flow of production costs when the periodic inventory system is used. We will show you how to record the journal entries throughout the year and how to prepare worksheets, financial statements, and closing entries at year-end.

**Learning Objective 1**

Explain the differences between the perpetual and the periodic inventory systems

## PERPETUAL VERSUS PERIODIC INVENTORY SYSTEMS

Under the perpetual inventory system, the inventory accounts are continuously updated as transactions take place. The process involves the following steps:

1. Purchases of raw materials are debited to Raw Materials Inventory and the raw materials used are credited to this account.
2. Direct materials, direct labor, and factory overhead are debited to Work-in-Process Inventory and the cost of goods completed is credited.
3. The cost of goods completed is debited to Finished Goods Inventory and the cost of goods sold is credited.
4. The cost of goods sold during the period is debited to Cost of Goods Sold.

With the perpetual inventory system, at the end of the year—assuming that no mistakes have been made during the year—the correct balances for each inventory account and for Cost of Goods Sold have already been entered in the general ledger accounts, so no year-end adjustments are needed to determine the correct amounts in preparing the financial statements.

The journal entries for a manufacturer that uses the periodic rather than the perpetual inventory system are quite different. Under the **periodic inventory system,** purchases, direct labor, and factory overhead are recorded in individual accounts, called Purchases, Direct Labor, and Factory Overhead Incurred. During the year, no entries are made in the inventory or Cost of Goods Sold accounts. As a result, the balances in the inventory accounts at the end of the year are exactly the same as their balances at the beginning of the year, and the balance in the Cost of Goods Sold account is zero. Only through the closing entry process will the correct balances in Raw Materials Inventory, Work-in-Process Inventory, Finished Goods Inventory, and Cost of Goods Sold be determined.

<table>
<tr><td>Learning Objective   **2**</td></tr>
<tr><td>Make the journal entries that trace the flow of costs through the accounts of a manufacturer that uses the periodic inventory system</td></tr>
</table>

## JOURNAL ENTRIES UNDER THE PERIODIC INVENTORY SYSTEMS

The transactions that we recorded with the perpetual inventory system will now be recorded with the periodic inventory system. The key facts are as follows:

| | |
|---|---:|
| Inventory balances, Jan. 1: | |
| Raw Materials | $ 50,000 |
| Work-in-Process | 60,000 |
| Finished Goods | 40,000 |
| Purchases of raw materials | 200,000 |
| Usage of raw materials: | |
| Direct | 165,000 |
| Indirect | 10,000 |
| Labor: | |
| Direct | 65,000 |
| Indirect | 5,000 |
| Selling and administrative | 20,000 |
| Rent expired: | |
| Production | 4,000 |
| Selling and administrative | 1,000 |
| Insurance expired: | |
| Production | 3,000 |
| Selling and administrative | 1,000 |
| Inventory balances, Dec. 31: | |
| Raw Materials | 75,000 |
| Work-in-Process | 32,000 |
| Finished Goods | 10,000 |

### Purchase and Usage of Raw Materials

When the periodic inventory system is employed, purchases of raw materials are recorded in an account called **Purchases,** with a corresponding credit to Cash or Accounts Payable:

| | | |
|---|---:|---:|
| Purchases | 200,000 | |
| Cash (or Accounts Payable) | | 200,000 |

Raw materials used during the year are not recorded at the time the materials are used. Instead, raw materials used for the entire year are recorded at year-end, when closing entries are made for the Raw Materials Inventory account.

### Use of Labor

Direct labor costs are debited to an account appropriately called **Direct Labor.** The indirect labor costs, which are factory overhead costs, are debited to Factory Overhead Incurred. The nonmanufacturing labor costs are period costs and are debited to

Salaries Expense as part of the selling and administrative expenses. The total of these debits is credited to Salaries Payable.

| | | |
|---|---|---|
| Direct Labor | 65,000 | |
| Factory Overhead Incurred | 5,000 | |
| Salaries Expense | 20,000 | |
| Salaries Payable | | 90,000 |

### Insurance and Rent

Part of the insurance and rent costs relates to production, so this portion is factory overhead cost and as such is debited to the Factory Overhead Incurred account. The remaining costs of insurance and rent are period costs and are recorded in expense accounts as shown below. They are part of the company's selling and administrative expenses.

| | | |
|---|---|---|
| Factory Overhead Incurred | 7,000 | |
| Rent Expense | 1,000 | |
| Insurance Expense | 1,000 | |
| Prepaid Rent | | 5,000 |
| Prepaid Insurance | | 4,000 |

### Simplifying Assumptions

We have simplified our analysis by reducing the number of accounts involved. There are certainly many more accounts related to production (for depreciation, property taxes, etc.) than we have shown. There are also numerous other accounts related to selling and administrative activities. The small number of accounts we have used simply illustrates the overall process for the manufacturer, and serves as a guideline for other typical transactions and accounts. In addition, although above we made only one set of entries for the entire year, we would actually make entries each month to reflect that month's activities. For simplicity, the sum of all 12 months has been totaled and shown as a single entry for each type of transaction.

## YEAR-END TRIAL BALANCE UNDER THE PERIODIC INVENTORY SYSTEM

Assume now that the year is over and that the company has the adjusted trial balance shown in Exhibit 1. Do not be concerned about where many of the numbers came from. Just direct your attention to those accounts related to the three inventories and to cost of goods sold (shown in the boxed areas of the exhibit).

Notice the following key aspects of the trial balance, each of which is typical of the periodic inventory system:

1. The balance in each inventory account is still the begining balance shown earlier. The ending balances are nowhere to be seen—at least not yet.
2. There is no cost of goods sold on the books—at least not yet.
3. The Factory Overhead Incurred account balance is only $12,000, rather than the $22,000 it would be if the perpetual inventory system were used. That is because the cost of the indirect materials used, $10,000, has not yet been recorded. The cost of the indirect materials used will be recorded at the same time as the direct materials, when the closing entries are made.

**Exhibit 1** Periodic Inventory System: Adjusted Trial Balance

## Adjusted Trial Balance
## Year Ended December 31, 1997

|  | Debits | Credits |
|---|---|---|
| Cash . . . . . . . . . . . . . . . . . . . . . . . . . . . . . . . . . . . . . . . . . . . . . . . . . . . . . . . . | $ 26,000 |  |
| Accounts Receivable . . . . . . . . . . . . . . . . . . . . . . . . . . . . . . . . . . . | 50,000 |  |
| Raw Materials Inventory. . . . . . . . . . . . . . . . . . . . . . . . . . . . . . . . . . | 50,000 |  |
| Work-in-Process Inventory. . . . . . . . . . . . . . . . . . . . . . . . . . . . . . . | 60,000 |  |
| Finished Goods Inventory . . . . . . . . . . . . . . . . . . . . . . . . . . . . . . . | 40,000 |  |
| Prepaid Insurance. . . . . . . . . . . . . . . . . . . . . . . . . . . . . . . . . . . . . . | 4,000 |  |
| Prepaid Rent. . . . . . . . . . . . . . . . . . . . . . . . . . . . . . . . . . . . . . . . . . | –0– |  |
| Accounts Payable. . . . . . . . . . . . . . . . . . . . . . . . . . . . . . . . . . . . . . |  | $ 40,000 |
| Salaries Payable. . . . . . . . . . . . . . . . . . . . . . . . . . . . . . . . . . . . . . . |  | 6,000 |
| Common Stock. . . . . . . . . . . . . . . . . . . . . . . . . . . . . . . . . . . . . . . . |  | 50,000 |
| Retained Earnings . . . . . . . . . . . . . . . . . . . . . . . . . . . . . . . . . . . . . |  | 33,000 |
| Purchases. . . . . . . . . . . . . . . . . . . . . . . . . . . . . . . . . . . . . . . . . . . . | 200,000 |  |
| Direct Labor . . . . . . . . . . . . . . . . . . . . . . . . . . . . . . . . . . . . . . . . . | 65,000 |  |
| Factory Overhead Incurred . . . . . . . . . . . . . . . . . . . . . . . . . . . . . | 12,000 |  |
| Insurance Expense. . . . . . . . . . . . . . . . . . . . . . . . . . . . . . . . . . . . . | 1,000 |  |
| Rent Expense . . . . . . . . . . . . . . . . . . . . . . . . . . . . . . . . . . . . . . . . . | 1,000 |  |
| Other Selling and Administrative Expenses. . . . . . . . . . . . . . . . . . | 20,000 |  |
| Sales Revenue . . . . . . . . . . . . . . . . . . . . . . . . . . . . . . . . . . . . . . . . |  | 400,000 |
| Totals . . . . . . . . . . . . . . . . . . . . . . . . . . . . . . . . . . . . . . . . . . . . . . . | $529,000 | $529,000 |

Since the trial balance includes the beginning balances in the inventory accounts rather than the ending balances, and since there is not yet a Cost of Goods Sold account on the books, we are not ready to prepare the year-end financial statements. For these reasons, accountants using the periodic system often use worksheets to place the proper balances in each of the inventory accounts as well as in Cost of Goods Sold. They also use worksheets to organize the accounts so that the items needed for each financial statement are easily found.

Learning
Objective  **3**

Perform the year-end worksheet procedures for a manufacturer that uses the periodic inventory system

## YEAR-END WORKSHEET PROCEDURES UNDER THE PERIODIC INVENTORY SYSTEM

Exhibit 2, the worksheet for a manufacturer, has four pairs of columns. The first pair is for the adjusted trial balance, the second pair is for calculating cost of goods sold, the third is for the income statement, and the fourth is for the balance sheet.

Many companies start with an unadjusted trial balance and then have a pair of columns for the year-end adjustments. We have assumed for simplicity that any year-end adjustments (except those involved in determining cost of goods sold) have already been made and that the trial balance is an adjusted trial balance. These assumptions allow us to emphasize only those adjustments that affect cost of goods sold—adjustments that are characteristic of the periodic inventory system.

Some manufacturers also use separate columns for cost of goods completed, and then determine the cost of goods sold in the income statement columns. Others even include a separate pair of columns to determine retained earnings.

**Exhibit 2** Periodic Inventory System: Worksheet for a Manufacturer

## Manufacturer's Worksheet
### Year Ended December 31, 1997

| Account Title | Adjusted Trial Balance Debit | Adjusted Trial Balance Credit | Cost of Goods Sold Debit | Cost of Goods Sold Credit | Income Statement Debit | Income Statement Credit | Balance Sheet Debit | Balance Sheet Credit |
|---|---|---|---|---|---|---|---|---|
| Cash | 26,000 | | | | | | 26,000 | |
| Accounts Receivable | 50,000 | | | | | | 50,000 | |
| Raw Materials Inventory | 50,000 | | 50,000 | 75,000 | | | 75,000 | |
| Work-in-Process Inventory | 60,000 | | 60,000 | 32,000 | | | 32,000 | |
| Finished Goods Inventory | 40,000 | | 40,000 | 10,000 | | | 10,000 | |
| Prepaid Insurance | 4,000 | | | | | | 4,000 | |
| Prepaid Rent | –0– | | | | | | –0– | |
| Accounts Payable | | 40,000 | | | | | | 40,000 |
| Salaries Payable | | 6,000 | | | | | | 6,000 |
| Common Stock | | 50,000 | | | | | | 50,000 |
| Retained Earnings | | 33,000 | | | | | | 33,000 |
| | | | | | | | | 68,000 |
| Purchases | 200,000 | | 200,000 | | | | | |
| Direct Labor | 65,000 | | 65,000 | | | | | |
| Factory Overhead Incurred | 12,000 | | 12,000 | | | | | |
| Insurance Expense | 1,000 | | | | 1,000 | | | |
| Rent Expense | 1,000 | | | | 1,000 | | | |
| Other Selling and Admin. Expenses | 20,000 | | | | 20,000 | | | |
| Sales Revenue | | 400,000 | | | | 400,000 | | |
| | 529,000 | 529,000 | | | | | | |
| | | | 427,000 | 117,000 | | | | |
| Cost of Goods Sold | | | | 310,000 | 310,000 | | | |
| | | | 427,000 | 427,000 | | | | |
| | | | | | 332,000 | 400,000 | | |
| Net Income | | | | | 68,000 | | | |
| | | | | | 400,000 | 400,000 | | |
| | | | | | | | 197,000 | 197,000 |

*Cost of goods sold is $310,000. It goes to the debit column of the income statement columns of the worksheet.*

*Net income is $68,000. It is added to the beginning balance in retained earnings in the balance sheet columns of the worksheet.*

Before you proceed, you may want to review the general procedures used with all worksheets. You will see many similarities in the worksheet techniques for merchandising and manufacturing concerns.

## Raw Materials

The first step in calculating cost of goods sold is to determine the raw materials used (see Schedule 1 of Exhibit 11 on page 22-16 and mark the page for you will be referring to it again). Its calculation is:

| | |
|---|---:|
| Raw Materials Inventory, beginning balance . . . . . . . . . . . . . . . . . . . . . . . | $ 50,000 |
| + Purchases . . . . . . . . . . . . . . . . . . . . . . . . . . . . . . . . . . . . . . . . . . . . . . . . . | 200,000 |
| = Raw Materials Available for Use . . . . . . . . . . . . . . . . . . . . . . . . . . . . . . | $250,000 |
| − Raw Materials Inventory, ending balance . . . . . . . . . . . . . . . . . . . . . . . | 75,000 |
| = Raw Materials Used . . . . . . . . . . . . . . . . . . . . . . . . . . . . . . . . . . . . . . . . . | $175,000 |

On the worksheet, this is determined as follows:

1. Transfer the Raw Materials Inventory beginning balance, $50,000, to the debit column of Cost of Goods Sold.
2. Transfer the purchases, $200,000, to the debit column of Cost of Goods Sold.
3. Place the ending balance of Raw Materials Inventory, $75,000, in the credit column of Cost of Goods Sold. At the same time the $75,000 is placed in in the debit column of the balance sheet. The ending balance will be an asset in the year-end balance sheet.
4. The net of the debits ($50,000 + $200,000) less the credit ($75,000) is the amount of raw materials used, $175,000. Although this amount is not shown in the complete worksheet, the partial worksheet below shows how it is derived.

**Partial Manufacturer's Worksheet**
**Year Ended December 31, 1997**

| Account Title | Adjusted Trial Balance | | Cost of Goods Sold | | Income Statement | | Balance Sheet | |
|---|---|---|---|---|---|---|---|---|
| | **Debit** | **Credit** | **Debit** | **Credit** | **Debit** | **Credit** | **Debit** | **Credit** |
| • • • | | | | | | | | |
| Raw Materials Inventory | 50,000 | | 50,000 | 75,000 | | | 75,000 | |
| • • • | | | | | | | | |
| Purchases | 200,000 | | 200,000 | | | | | |

*The net of these two debits and one credit is $175,000*

Looking again at Schedule 1 of Exhibit 3, you can see $175,000 as the first major subtotal. Notice in the schedule for cost of goods completed that this amount is split between direct materials ($165,000) and indirect materials ($10,000).

The statements for the manufacturer will be the same whether we are using the perpetual or the periodic inventory system.

### Direct Labor and Factory Overhead Costs

Next, the direct labor costs ($65,000) and the factory overhead costs other than indirect materials ($12,000) are transferred in the worksheet to the debit column of Cost of Goods Sold. These costs are added to the raw materials used ($165,000 + $10,000), and the $252,000 subtotal represents the "total manufacturing costs incurred" in Schedule 1 of Exhibit 11 on page 22-16. This amount is not shown in the formal worksheet, but you can see its components in the partial worksheet below.

**Partial Manufacturer's Worksheet**
**Year Ended December 31, 1997**

| Account Title | Adjusted Trial Balance Debit | Credit | Cost of Goods Sold Debit | Credit | Income Statement Debit | Credit | Balance Sheet Debit | Credit |
|---|---|---|---|---|---|---|---|---|
| ⋮ | | | | | | | | |
| Raw Materials Inventory | 50,000 | | 50,000 | 75,000 | | | 75,000 | |
| ⋮ | | | | | | | | |
| Purchases | 200,000 | | 200,000 | | | | | |
| Direct Labor | 65,000 | | 65,000 | | | | | |
| Factory Overhead Incurred | 12,000 | | 12,000 | | | | | |

*The net of these five items is $252,000—the total manufacturing costs incurred. (Remember, the $10,000 indirect materials are not in the Factory Overhead Incurred account.)*

### Work-in-Process Inventory

The $60,000 beginning balance in Work-in-Process Inventory is transferred to the debit column of Cost of Goods Sold. This is in addition to the $252,000 of costs of direct materials, direct labor, and factory overhead discussed above. The $312,000 subtotal for these four items is called the total manufacturing costs to account for in Schedule 1 of Exhibit 11 on page 22-16. The $32,000 ending balance in Work-in-Process Inventory is placed in the credit column of Cost of Goods Sold. This reduces the total manufacturing costs to account for, leaving the remaining $280,000 as cost of goods completed—which is shown in the schedule of cost of goods completed in Exhibit 11 on page 22-16. If you were to add the line for Work-in-Process Inventory—a debit of $60,000 and a credit of $32,000—in the partial worksheet below, the net of all these debits and credits is $280,000.

**Partial Manufacturer's Worksheet**
**Year Ended December 31, 1997**

| Account Title | Adjusted Trial Balance Debit | Credit | Cost of Goods Sold Debit | Credit | Income Statement Debit | Credit | Balance Sheet Debit | Credit |
|---|---|---|---|---|---|---|---|---|
| ⋮ | | | | | | | | |
| Raw Materials Inventory | 50,000 | | 50,000 | 75,000 | | | 75,000 | |
| Work-in-Process Inventory | 60,000 | | 60,000 | 32,000 | | | 32,000 | |
| ⋮ | | | | | | | | |
| Purchases | 200,000 | | 200,000 | | | | | |
| Direct Labor | 65,000 | | 65,000 | | | | | |
| Factory Overhead Incurred | 12,000 | | 12,000 | | | | | |

*The net of these seven items is $280,000—the cost of goods completed*

The ending balance in Work-in-Process Inventory is also placed in the debit column of the balance sheet columns, and it appears on the year-end balance sheet.

### Finished Goods Inventory

Next, the beginning balance in Finished Goods Inventory, $40,000, is transferred to the debit column of Cost of Goods Sold, and the ending balance, $10,000, is transferred to the credit column. This is the same as the addition of the beginning balance and the subtraction of the ending balance that we saw in Schedule 2 of Exhibit 11 on page 22-16. The final result is $310,000 for Cost of Goods Sold, shown at the bottom of the credit column for Cost of Goods Sold in the worksheet in Exhibit 2.

### Net Income

The cost of goods sold, $310,000, is transferred to the debit column of the income statement columns in the worksheet. The other income statement items (insurance expense, rent expense, other selling and administrative expenses, and sales revenue) are transferred from the adjusted trial balance to the appropriate income statement columns. The difference between the debits (expenses of $332,000) and the credits (revenues of $400,000) in the income statement columns represents net income, $68,000. The net income is then added to the debit column so that the two columns will balance at $400,000. Next, the net income is transferred to the credit column of the balance sheet. It is added to the $33,000 beginning balance of retained earnings. The sum of the two, $101,000, will be the ending balance in retained earnings on the year-end balance sheet. All other balance sheet items (cash, accounts receivable, prepaid insurance, accounts payable, salaries payable, and common stock) are transferred from the adjusted trial balance columns to the two balance sheet columns. The worksheet is completed when all the account balances in the two balance sheet columns are summed; they are both $197,000.

Learning Objective  **4**

Prepare the financial statements and closing entries for a manufacturer that uses the periodic inventory system

## FINANCIAL STATEMENTS UNDER THE PERIODIC INVENTORY SYSTEM

The financial statements can now be prepared. The items included within each major statement are taken from the appropriate columns of the worksheet.

The balance sheet is:

**Balance Sheet**
**December 31, 1997**

| Assets | | Liabilities and Stockholders' Equity | |
|---|---|---|---|
| Cash. . . . . . . . . . . . . . . . . . . . | $ 26,000 | Accounts Payable . . . . . . . . . . | $ 40,000 |
| Accounts Receivable. . . . . . . . | 50,000 | Salaries Payable . . . . . . . . . . . | 6,000 |
| Raw Materials Inventory . . . . . | 75,000 | | 46,000 |
| Work-in-Process Inventory . . . | 32,000 | Common Stock . . . . . . . . . . . . | 50,000 |
| Finished Goods Inventory . . . . | 10,000 | Retained Earnings. . . . . . . . . . | 101,000 |
| Prepaid Insurance . . . . . . . . . . | 4,000 | | $151,000 |
| | | Total Liabilities and | |
| Total Assets. . . . . . . . . . . . . . . | $197,000 | Stockholders' Equity . . . . . . . | $197,000 |

## YEAR-END CLOSING ENTRIES UNDER THE PERIODIC INVENTORY SYSTEM

The closing entries for a manufacturer that uses the periodic inventory system are similar to those for a retailer or a wholesaler. The key to understanding the closing entries for a manufacturer is to focus on the numerous entries that relate to the determination of cost of goods sold.

Preparing the closing entries for a manufacturer involves the following five steps:

1. Closing Purchases and the beginning and ending balances in Raw Materials Inventory to Cost of Goods Sold
2. Closing the Direct Labor and Factory Overhead Incurred accounts to Cost of Goods Sold
3. Closing the beginning and ending balances in Work-in-Process Inventory and Finished Goods Inventory to Cost of Goods Sold
4. Closing Sales Revenue, Cost of Goods Sold, and all remaining expenses to Income Summary
5. Closing Income Summary to Retained Earnings

Let's consider each of these steps in some detail.

### Step 1: Closing Entries for Raw Materials

The first step is to determine the cost of raw materials used during the year. This is accomplished by closing the Purchases account, and the beginning and ending balances in the Raw Materials Inventory account, to Cost to Goods Sold. The net of these three entries is a debit balance of $175,000 in Cost of Goods Sold, which represents the cost of raw materials (direct materials plus indirect materials) used in production.

| | | | |
|---|---|---:|---:|
| Dec. 31 | Cost of Goods Sold | 175,000 | |
| | Raw Materials Inventory (ending balance) | 75,000 | |
| | Purchases | | 200,000 |
| | Raw Materials Inventory (beginning balance) | | 50,000 |
| | Closing entry to record the cost of raw materials used in production. | | |

### Step 2: Closing Entry for Direct Labor Costs and Factory Overhead Costs

The second step is to close the Direct Labor and Factory Overhead Incurred accounts to Cost of Goods Sold.

| | | | |
|---|---|---:|---:|
| Dec. 31 | Cost of Goods Sold | 77,000 | |
| | Direct Labor | | 65,000 |
| | Factory Overhead Incurred | | 12,000 |
| | To close direct labor and factory overhead costs to Cost of Goods Sold. | | |

The sum of the two debits to Cost of Goods Sold, $252,000 ($175,000 + $77,000), represents the total manufacturing costs incurred.

## Step 3: Closing Entries for Work-in-Process Inventory and Finished Goods Inventory

The beginning balance in Work-in-Process Inventory is closed with a credit; the ending balance is recorded with a debit; the net of the two, $28,000, is debited to Cost of Goods Sold. The balance in Cost of Goods Sold of $280,000 ($252,000 + $28,000) now represents the cost of goods completed.

| | | | |
|---|---|---|---|
| Dec. 31 | Cost of Goods Sold | 28,000 | |
| | Work-in-Process Inventory (ending balance) | 32,000 | |
| |     Work-in-Process Inventory (beginning balance) | | 60,000 |
| | To close the beginning and ending balances in | | |
| | Work-in-Process Inventory to Cost of Goods Sold. | | |

Next, the beginning balance in Finished Goods Inventory is closed with a credit; the ending balance is recorded with a debit; and the net of the two, $30,000, is debited to Cost of Goods Sold. The balance in the Cost of Goods Sold account of $310,000 ($280,000 + $30,000) is finally the cost of goods sold for the year.

| | | | |
|---|---|---|---|
| Dec. 31 | Cost of Goods Sold | 30,000 | |
| | Finished Goods Inventory (ending balance) | 10,000 | |
| |     Finished Goods Inventory (beginning balance) | | 40,000 |
| | To close the beginning and ending balances in Fin- | | |
| | ished Goods Inventory to Cost of Goods Sold. | | |

## Step 4: Closing Sales, Cost of Goods Sold, and Other Expenses to Income Summary

The entry to close the sales for the year is as follows:

| | | | |
|---|---|---|---|
| Dec. 31 | Sales | 400,000 | |
| |     Income Summary | | 400,000 |
| | To close Sales to Income Summary. | | |

And the entry to close the Cost of Goods Sold and all remaining expenses to Income Summary is:

| | | | |
|---|---|---|---|
| Dec. 31 | Income Summary | 332,000 | |
| |     Cost of Goods Sold | | 310,000 |
| |     Insurance Expense | | 1,000 |
| |     Rent Expense | | 1,000 |
| |     Other Selling and Administrative Expenses | | 20,000 |
| | To close all expenses to Income Summary. | | |

The balance in Income Summary of $68,000 ($400,000 − $332,000) is the net income for the year. All that remains to be done in the closing process is to close this amount to Retained Earnings.

### Step 5: Closing Income Summary to Retained Earnings

The final entry closes Income Summary to Retained Earnings.

| | | | |
|---|---|---|---|
| Dec. 31 | Income Summary . . . . . . . . . . . . . . . . . . . . . . . . . . . . . | 68,000 | |
| | Retained Earnings. . . . . . . . . . . . . . . . . . . . . . . . . | | 68,000 |
| | To close Income Summary to Retained Earnings. | | |

When the net income for the year is added to the beginning balance of $33,000 in Retained Earnings, the sum of the two, $101,000, is the ending balance for the year.

## 5  KEY TERMS

**Direct Labor account**    The account used by a manufacturer to record direct labor costs under the periodic inventory system.

**Periodic inventory system**    A system of accounting for inventory in which no entries are recorded in the inventory accounts or Cost of Goods Sold during the year. Instead, during the year and at year-end (prior to closing entries), the balances in Raw Materials, Work-in-Process, and Finished Goods are the same as the beginning-of-year balances, and Cost of Goods Sold has a zero balance.

**Purchases account**    The account used by a manufacturer to record the cost of purchases under the periodic inventory system.

# Job Order Costing

*Inventory costing* is the accumulation of costs associated with inventory and the assignment of these costs to the units in inventory. Accountants must be able to determine accurate inventoriable costs so that they can assist management in the planning and control of a company's operations. Properly determining inventoriable costs is important in order to have correct amounts in cost of goods sold on the income statement and in the inventory accounts on the balance sheet. The three types of inventoriable costs for a manufacturer (direct materials, direct labor, and factory overhead) must be traced through the production accounts from Raw Materials Inventory, to Work-in-Process Inventory, to Finished Goods Inventory, to Cost of Goods Sold. In this chapter you will see how the inventoriable costs are assigned to individual units produced by a manufacturer.

Is the cost of an individual unit determined by spreading the total production costs for a period evenly over the many units being worked on? Should the cost of each unit be exactly the same, even when there are obvious differences in the physical appearance of, materials used for, and attention given to different units? Or do accountants painstakingly keep track of the exact amount of materials, labor, and overhead to produce each unit? Will each unit have a slightly different cost even when all units appear to be identical?

To answer these questions, you first need to know which cost accounting method—job order costing or process costing—is the more appropriate way to account for inventoriable costs.

## JOB ORDER COSTING VERSUS PROCESS COSTING

Learning Objective 1

Explain the characteristics of a job order costing system of accounting and distinguish job order costing from process costing

The type of manufacturing operation determines the type of inventory costing system used. When manufacturing operations show many of the following characteristics, the **job order costing method** is used to account for the costs of the finished product:

1. Each unit or batch of units is clearly identifiable and easily distinguished from others produced within the same production environment.
2. Each unit or batch is produced according to customer specifications.
3. A relatively small number of units or batches of units is produced.
4. Considerable costs are represented in each unit or batch produced.

The name of the method describes the process: The manufacturer produces a product, referred to as a *job,* according to a customer *order.* Each job is assigned a job number, in order to keep track of it and its *costs,* and to distinguish its costs from the costs of other jobs as they all progress toward completion. The key to accumulating inventoriable costs under job order costing is to make sure that the costs of a specific job are carefully separated from the costs of any other job. At year-end it is easy to identify the costs associated with the jobs that are sold and belong on the income statement, and the costs that relate to the jobs that are unsold and belong on the balance sheet.

Industries in manufacturing that typically employ job order costing include custom furniture, heavy machinery, construction, publishing, shipbuilding, and aircraft manufacturing. Although we direct most of our attention to job order costing for a manufacturer, many of the concepts we introduce apply to any type of organization that finds it necessary to distinguish among the costs of different projects being worked on. We will discuss the application of job order costing techniques to firms in service industries (for example, CPA firms, law firms, advertising agencies, and repair centers) at the end of this chapter.

**Process costing** is quite a bit different from job order costing. It is used in situations where:

1. Units are produced continuously in large batches; and
2. Units are all exactly the same.

In process costing the total costs of production for a period are divided by the number of units produced during that period to obtain a cost per unit that is exactly the same for all the units produced. Products for which process costing is likely to be used include bottled drinks, cement, paints, oil products, flour, and pharmaceuticals.

Some companies may use job order costing for some of its products and process costing for others. For example, a car manufacturer such as the Ford Motor Company may use process costing for the thousands of identical Escorts or Mustangs that are produced in a single large batch, but use job order costing for a limousine that is made to order for a Hollywood celebrity. In addition, Ford might use process costing for its Mustangs to account for the costs of those features that are identical in all models (such as body, paint job, and engine), but use job order costing for additional unique features (such as leather upholstery, deluxe stereo system, built-in television, and security system) that must be specially ordered.

## ACCOUNTING RECORDS IN JOB ORDER COSTING

The previous chapter used T-accounts (which are simplified versions of a company's general ledger accounts) to show the flow of inventoriable costs for a manufacturer from one inventory account to another, finally ending up in Cost of Goods Sold. The basic progression was from Raw Materials Inventory to Work-in-Process Inventory to Finished Goods Inventory to Cost of Goods Sold, as shown below:

| Raw Materials Inventory | Work-in-Process Inventory | Finished Goods Inventory | Cost of Goods Sold |
|---|---|---|---|
| | → | → | → |

We will now look at the journal entries needed for job order costing to record this progression of costs from one inventory account to the next. In addition, we will look at the subsidiary ledgers that provide the detailed support for each inventory account and at the source documents that provide the details of each transaction.

To illustrate how job order costing works, we will examine one month of operations for the Collier Safe Company, which manufactures safes exclusively to customer order. Collier Safe's first month of operation was January 1997. At the end of the first month its general ledger inventory accounts show the following balances:

| Raw Materials Inventory | Work-in-Process Inventory | Finished Goods Inventory |
|---|---|---|
| Bal. Jan. 31 8,000 | Bal. Jan. 31 37,000 (Job 2) | Bal. Jan. 31 24,000 (Job 1) |

On Jan. 31, Collier Safe still has one unfinished safe (Job 2) in work-in-process and one completed safe (Job 1) in finished goods awaiting delivery. The individual costs assigned to these jobs are as follows:

| Job 2 (Incomplete) Work-in-Process | | Job 1 (Completed) Finished Goods | |
|---|---|---|---|
| Direct materials | $10,000 | Direct materials | $ 6,000 |
| Direct labor | 18,000 | Direct labor | 12,000 |
| Factory overhead. | 9,000 | Factory overhead. | 6,000 |
| Totals | $37,000 | Totals | $24,000 |

**Learning Objective 2**

Explain the purpose of subsidiary ledgers and the types of subsidiary ledgers needed for job order costing

These lists of costs are actually summaries of the subsidiary ledgers for work-in-process and finished goods. **Subsidiary ledgers** provide detailed breakdowns of general ledger accounts. We will now introduce you to the subsidiary ledgers for the inventory accounts of a manufacturer that is using job order costing.

The most important subsidiary ledger in job order costing is the **job cost sheet** that is maintained for each job. All the inventoriable costs (direct materials, direct labor, and factory overhead) associated with that job are recorded on the job cost sheet. When the job cost sheets for all the *unfinished* jobs are combined, they make up the subsidiary ledger for work-in-process. At the end of each reporting period, the balance in the subsidiary ledger for work-in-process (that is, the sum of the balances in the job cost sheets for incomplete jobs) should be equal to the balance in the general ledger account.

As soon as a job is completed, the job cost sheet is removed from the subsidiary ledger for work-in-process and is transferred to the subsidiary ledger for finished goods.

A typical job cost sheet that makes up a subsidiary ledger is shown in Exhibit 1. This job cost sheet is for Job 2, which was in process on Jan. 31 and completed in February.

Notice that the total of the Jan. 31 balances ($37,000) agrees with the balance in the general ledger T-account for work-in-process shown on the previous page. On Jan. 31, the job cost sheet was in the subsidiary ledger for work-in-process. The transactions affecting Job 2 during February have been posted to the subsidiary ledger account, and you may want to refer back to Exhibit 1 when you read about the specific transactions that are discussed later.

In addition to the subsidiary ledgers for work-in-process and finished goods, there is a subsidiary ledger for raw materials inventory. For each different raw material there will be a **stores card.** Each stores card identifies the type of raw material, the quantity and costs of any purchases and usage, and the remaining balance after each transaction. On Jan. 31, the sum of all the balances for the stores cards for Collier Safe should equal $8,000—the balance shown in the general ledger T-account for raw materials.

Like other companies that employ job order costing, Collier Safe uses a perpetual inventory system. When a perpetual inventory system is used, the inventory accounts are continuously updated as transactions take place. At the end of each month, the balance in each inventory account represents the correct balance.

**ASK YOURSELF ▶**

1. What is the difference between job order costing and process costing?
2. What is the purpose of subsidiary ledgers for a company that uses the job order costing method?

**Exhibit 1** A Job Cost Sheet

## JOB COST SHEET—JOB 2

Job No. _____2_____

Customer ____Lake State Bank____    Date Completed _____2/10_____

Date Started ____1/28____    Date Delivered _____

| Direct Materials | | Direct Labor | | Factory Overhead | | |
|---|---|---|---|---|---|---|
| Requisition Number | Amount | Work Ticket No. | Amount | Rate | Amount | Totals |
| 0031 | $ 8,000 | 0081–0117 | $ 3,000 | | | |
| 0032 | 2,000 | 0188–0225 | 6,000 | | | |
| | | 0300–0341 | 4,000 | $10 per | | |
| | | 0352–0360 | 2,000 | direct | | |
| | | 0375–0402 | 3,000 | labor hour | $ 9,000 | |
| **Bal. 1/31** | $10,000 | | $18,000 | | $ 9,000 | $37,000 |
| 0033 | $12,000 | 0403–0419 | $ 4,500 | | | |
| | | 0440–0463 | 3,400 | | | |
| | | 0490–0545 | 10,200 | | | |
| | | 0557–0565 | 3,000 | $10 per | | |
| | | 0568–0572 | 2,900 | direct | | |
| | | 0575–0600 | 2,000 | labor hour | $13,000 | |
| **Bal. 2/28** | $22,000 | | $44,000 | | $22,000 | $88,000 |

Costs of Completed Job:
Direct Materials . . . . . . . . . . . . . . . . . . . . . . . . . . . . . . . . . . $22,000
Direct Labor . . . . . . . . . . . . . . . . . . . . . . . . . . . . . . . . . . . . . 44,000
Factory Overhead Applied . . . . . . . . . . . . . . . . . . . . . . . . . . . 22,000

Total Costs . . . . . . . . . . . . . . . . . . . . . . . . . . . . . . . . . . . . . . $88,000

## JOB ORDER COSTING PROCEDURES

Learning Objective **3**

Determine the flow of costs through the production accounts and integrate this flow into the accounting records with source documents, journal entries, and postings to general ledger accounts

We will now follow the procedures for job order costing using the Collier Safe Company's February activity. As we cover the facts for February, we will:

1. Examine the source documents that provide the evidence of each transaction
2. Examine the subsidiary ledgers affected by the transaction
3. Make the journal entry to record each transaction
4. Post the journal entry to the appropriate general ledger accounts

### Purchases of Raw Materials

During February, Collier Safe Company's purchasing agent purchases raw materials costing $30,200, which are placed in the storeroom under the storekeeper's control. As evidence of the purchases, Collier receives **invoices** from its suppliers. These

**Exhibit 2** An Invoice

## INVOICE

**THE WALLER BULK METALS YARD**
101 Gator Drive
Port Richey, FL. 32111

No. _____ 12144 _____

Date _____ 2/1/97 _____

**Sold to:** Collier Safe Company
1011 Lake Saxon Lane
Paradise Lakes, FL. 34639

| Terms | FOB | Date Shipped | |
|-------|-----|-------------|---|
| 2/10, net 30 | Shipping point | 2/1/97 | |

| Description | Quantity | Unit Price | Amount |
|-------------|----------|-----------|--------|
| Bulk metal | 2,500 lb | $4/lb | $10,000 |

invoices are the **source documents** that provide evidence for each purchase transaction. An invoice indicates (1) the date, (2) the name of the supplier, (3) the terms of the purchase, (4) the items purchased, (5) the quantity purchased, and (6) the total cost of the purchase. An invoice for the purchase of bulk metal is shown in Exhibit 2.

As soon as each purchase is received, the stores card for the raw materials purchased (the subsidiary ledger for raw materials) needs to be updated. The stores card listing the bulk metal received from Waller Bulk Metals is shown in Exhibit 3. Note that the receipt of these goods on Feb. 3 has been recorded and the balance updated.

As raw materials are issued to the production department, the issue is recorded and new balances are computed, since a perpetual inventory system is being used.

### Journalizing and Posting Purchases of Raw Materials

At the end of the month, a single journal entry is made that summarizes all the raw materials purchases made during the month, as shown in entry 1 on the next page.

**Exhibit 3** Subsidiary Ledger for Raw Materials: A Stores Card

## STORES CARD

Stock No. _____ 43 _____

Item _____ Bulk metal _____

| | Received | | | Issued | | | | Balance | | |
|---|---|---|---|---|---|---|---|---|---|---|
| Date | Pounds | Unit Cost | Total Cost | Requisition Number | Pounds | Unit Cost | Total Cost | Pounds | Unit Cost | Total Cost |
| Bal. 1/1 | | | | | | | | 1,000 | $4 | $ 4,000 |
| 2/3 | 2,500 | $4 | $10,000 | | | | | 3,500 | 4 | 14,000 |
| 2/4 | | | | 0033 | 3,000 | $4 | $12,000 | 500 | 4 | 2,000 |

**Exhibit 4** A Stores Requisition

### STORES REQUISITION

Date ____2/4/97____  No. 0033

Job. No. ____2____

Requested by ____P. Loche____

| Stock No. | Item | Quantity | Unit Cost | Amount |
|---|---|---|---|---|
| 43 | Bulk metal | 3,000 lb | $4/lb | $12,000 |

The $10,000 purchase of bulk metal shown on the stores card (Exhibit 3) is included in the $30,200 summary entry.

| | | | | |
|---|---|---|---|---|
| **1.** Feb. 28 | Raw Materials Inventory . . . . . . . . . . . . . . . . . . . . . . | 30,200 | |
| | Accounts Payable (or Cash) . . . . . . . . . . . . . . . | | 30,200 |
| | Purchased raw materials on account (or for cash). | | |

Also at the end of each month, the debits and credits for each journal entry are posted to the general ledger accounts for Raw Materials Inventory and Accounts Payable.

### Direct Materials Used

During February, $33,000 of direct materials are transferred from Raw Materials to Work-in-Process Inventory. These materials are needed (1) to continue the work on Job 2, which was begun in January, and (2) to start work on Job 3. The $33,000 is distributed to the two jobs in the following manner:

| Job Number | Amount |
|---|---|
| 2 | $12,000 |
| 3 | 21,000 |
| Total direct materials used | $33,000 |

To obtain the materials, a **stores requisition,** which is a source document requesting materials, is filled out by a supervisor or a designated individual in production and given to the storekeeper in exchange for the required materials. For example, the stores requisition for materials needed on Feb. 4 for Job 2 is illustrated in Exhibit 4.

Two subsidiary ledgers are affected by the requisition of raw materials for use as direct materials. The first is the stores cards, which are reduced by the direct materials issued to production. As you can see in Exhibit 3, the stores card for bulk metal in the raw materials subsidiary ledger was reduced by $12,000 on Feb. 4. The second ledger affected by the use of direct materials is the work-in-process subsidiary ledger. The amount of direct materials used must be recorded in the job cost sheets for Jobs 2 and 3. In Exhibit 1, the $12,000 issue of bulk metal is entered in the direct materials column of the job cost sheet for Job 2.

### Journalizing and Posting Direct Materials Used

At the end of February, a summarizing journal entry, entry 2, is made for the total of all direct materials used during the month:

| | | | |
|---|---|---|---|
| **2.** Feb. 28 | Work-in Process Inventory | 33,000 | |
| | Raw Materials Inventory | | 33,000 |

Direct materials used during February, distributed to jobs as follows:

| | |
|---|---|
| Job 2: | $12,000 |
| Job 3: | 21,000 |
| | $33,000 |

Following this journal entry, the debits and credits are posted to the general ledger accounts for Work-in-Process Inventory and Raw Materials Inventory.

### Direct Labor Costs

The labor that is easily traceable to the manufacture of a specific product is called *direct labor.* To determine the exact amount of direct labor cost incurred for a particular job, it is necessary for each employee to fill out a source document called a **work ticket** for each job worked on. A work ticket for a single laborer who is working on Job 2 on Feb. 6 is shown in Exhibit 5. The work ticket shows the time the worker spent on Job 2, the worker's hourly wage rate, and the total direct labor cost for the work performed.

The summary of all work tickets used during February shows that $36,000 was spent for direct labor, distributed as follows between the two jobs:

| Job | Hours | Rate | Amount |
|---|---|---|---|
| 2 | 1,300 | $20/hr | $26,000 |
| 3 | 500 | $20/hr | 10,000 |
| Totals | 1,800 | | $36,000 |

The direct labor costs are posted to the individual job cost sheets daily. As you can see in Exhibit 1, numerous work tickets accumulating to $4,500 are posted to Job 2 early in February. The total accumulation of Job 2 work tickets for the month of February equals $26,000 ($4,500 + $3,400 + $10,200 + $3,000 + $2,900 + $2,000), the amount shown above.

**Exhibit 5** A Work Ticket

**WORK TICKET** 0440

| | | | |
|---|---|---|---|
| Employee | O. B. Harris | | |
| Department | Casting | Hours Worked | 8 |
| Job No. | 2 | Rate | $20 |
| Date | 2/6 | Total | $160 |

### Journalizing and Posting Direct Labor

Entry 3, the summarized journal entry made on Feb. 28, records a debit to Work-in-Process Inventory and a credit to Salaries Payable:

| | | | |
|---|---|---|---|
| **3.** Feb. 28 | Work-in-Process Inventory . . . . . . . . . . . . . . . . . . . . | 36,000 | |
| | Salaries Payable. . . . . . . . . . . . . . . . . . . . . . . . | | 36,000 |
| | Direct labor earned by laborers during February, distributed as follows: | | |

|  | | |
|---|---|---|
| Job 2: | $26,000 | |
| Job 3: | 10,000 | |
| | $36,000 | |

The total debits and credits in the entry above would now be posted to the general ledger accounts for Work-in-Process and Salaries Payable.

### The Declining Emphasis on Direct Labor

Twenty years ago, direct labor costs were typically greater than 40% of the total production costs for most manufacturers. Since that time the manufacturing environment has become highly automated. Significant investments have been made in labor-saving equipment in order to increase productivity and product quality and thereby improve the competitive position of American companies in world markets. With this change in emphasis, direct labor costs as a percentage of total production costs have dropped below 10% for many companies. In some companies, direct labor is such a small component of total costs that it is no longer treated as a separate inventoriable cost, but has become just one of many conversion costs, along with indirect labor, insurance, depreciation, and other overhead items. Direct labor remains a significant inventoriable cost for many companies, however, so we will continue to assume that it receives individual attention from the manufacturers in our examples.

**ASK YOURSELF** ▶

1. **What are the source documents and subsidiary ledgers affected by the purchase and usage of direct materials and the usage of direct labor?**
2. **What are the journal entries needed to record direct materials and direct labor?**

### Factory Overhead Incurred

All manufacturing costs other than direct materials and direct labor are classified as factory overhead. During February, Collier Safe's total factory overhead incurred is as follows:

| | |
|---|---|
| Indirect materials . . . . . . . . . . . . . . . . . . . . . . . . . . | $   200 |
| Indirect labor . . . . . . . . . . . . . . . . . . . . . . . . . . . . . | 10,000 |
| Utilities. . . . . . . . . . . . . . . . . . . . . . . . . . . . . . . . . | 1,000 |
| Depreciation . . . . . . . . . . . . . . . . . . . . . . . . . . . . . | 2,800 |
| Total factory overhead incurred . . . . . . . . . . . . . . | $14,000 |

A factory overhead subsidiary ledger is kept for each production department. This ledger, called a **factory overhead cost sheet,** accumulates the *actual* factory overhead costs incurred in a department. Each cost sheet has a column for each

**Exhibit 6** A Factory Overhead Cost Sheet

## FACTORY OVERHEAD COST SHEET

Department _____ Inspection _____

| Date | Indirect Materials | Indirect Labor | Utilities | Depreciation | Total |
|------|------|------|------|------|------|
| Jan. | . . . | . . . | . . . | . . . | . . . |
| Feb. | $50 | $1,200 | $350 | $280 | $1,880 |
| Mar. | . . . | . . . | . . . | . . . | . . . |
| Apr. | . . . | . . . | . . . | . . . | . . . |

different type of factory overhead item. The cost sheet for Collier Safe's inspection department, showing February factory overhead, is shown in Exhibit 6.

Factory overhead cost sheets are similar to job cost sheets except that factory overhead cost sheets accumulate overhead costs by department, while job cost sheets accumulate inventoriable costs by job.

Examples of indirect materials include glue, screws, nails, varnish, maintenance supplies, and janitorial supplies. The cost of indirect materials is determined from stores requisitions. At the time of requisition, the stores cards are reduced by the amount and cost of the raw materials used.

Indirect laborers include supervisors, inspectors, maintenance people, material handlers, and janitors. The total cost of indirect labor, $10,000 for Collier Safe in February, comes from the work tickets filled out in each department. The utility charges, $1,000, reflect the monthly bill from the utility company. The depreciation, $2,800, is based on the depreciation schedules for the different assets used in each department.

### Journalizing and Posting Factory Overhead

The summarized journal entry for factory overhead incurred is made at the end of the month, as shown in entry 4. In addition, on Feb. 28, the debits and credits are posted to the appropriate general ledger accounts. Note that the debit for the factory overhead incurred is not to the account Factory Overhead Incurred but to **Factory Overhead Incurred and Applied.**

| | | | |
|---|---|---|---|
| 4. Feb. 28 | Factory Overhead Incurred and Applied. . . . . . . . . . . | 14,000 | |
| | Raw Materials Inventory. . . . . . . . . . . . . . . . . . . | | 200 |
| | Salaries Payable. . . . . . . . . . . . . . . . . . . . . . . | | 10,000 |
| | Accounts (or Utilities) Payable. . . . . . . . . . . . . . | | 1,000 |
| | Accumulated Depreciation. . . . . . . . . . . . . . . . . | | 2,800 |
| | To record overhead incurred in February. | | |

**Learning Objective 4**

Explain why the overhead that becomes part of the cost of the product is not the actual factory overhead incurred but rather the factory overhead applied

Remember that factory overhead is an inventoriable cost, just like direct materials and direct labor. As an inventoriable cost, factory overhead has to be debited to work-in-process. In a job order costing system, the factory overhead costs will be assigned to individual jobs—on individual job cost sheets—just like direct materials and direct labor. In the previous chapter we debited the account Factory Overhead Incurred for the actual overhead costs incurred. Then, after all the overhead had been accounted for, we closed out that account with a credit and transferred the total to Work-in-Process Inventory with a debit. In this way, the actual overhead costs incurred ended up as the inventoriable costs in Work-in-Process Inventory.

It would be extremely simple to accumulate the actual overhead costs in the Factory Overhead Incurred account for the entire year; close out the factory overhead account only at year-end; and debit Work-in-Process Inventory for the actual overhead costs incurred for the entire year. Then, the total overhead costs for the year could be distributed among the different jobs according to a reasonable proportion of work performed on each job during the year, with each job cost sheet being assigned its appropriate portion. Unfortunately, we can't wait until the end of the year to do this. If we did, then we wouldn't be able to prepare monthly financial statements for management. In order to prepare a monthly income statement and balance sheet, we need to know on a monthly basis what the total inventoriable costs are for each job. So we must still assign factory overhead to work-in-process on a monthly basis. But now, we are not going to assign *actual factory overhead costs* incurred during the month to work-in-process. Instead, we are going to assign factory overhead costs to work-in-process using a predetermined rate, for two very important reasons:

**1.** Some costs are incurred at erratic intervals during the year. For example, heating costs usually occur only in winter months; air conditioning costs are incurred only in the summer. Repair costs occur whenever machines break down or when there is idle time in production. Employees take vacations sporadically, although companies probably encourage them to do so during the least busy time of year. The occurrence of these and other overhead costs has nothing to do with any particular job—they just happen to occur in a particular month. They are costs that should probably be shared by all jobs worked on during the year. If actual overhead costs are assigned to jobs on a monthly basis, then the jobs that are assigned these costs are likely to be burdened with more than their fair share. And the jobs that are worked on in months when these costs do not occur are likely to receive less than their fair share.

**2.** Many overhead costs are considered to be fixed, which means that they are exactly the same each month, no matter how many jobs are worked on. Examples of fixed overhead costs include rent, depreciation, property taxes, and insurance. In a month of very little activity, these fixed costs are spread over few jobs, resulting in a very high cost per job. But in months of high activity, the same type of job is assigned very little overhead, since there are many jobs among which the fixed costs can be spread. Thus when there are significant fluctuations in activity during the year, the cost of nearly identical jobs may fluctuate widely and the resulting interim income statements can be quite misleading.

For these two reasons, many companies apply overhead to work-in-process using a predetermined factory overhead rate, rather than assigning the actual overhead costs incurred during the month. Let's see how that rate is determined and applied.

**Learning Objective 5**

Calculate the factory overhead rate and factory overhead applied

## Factory Overhead Applied

At the beginning of each year, each production department makes an estimate of its total overhead costs and expected level of the cost driver (or activity) for the year.

Then the estimated overhead costs are divided by the estimated cost driver to obtain an average annual predetermined overhead rate. Each month, the actual cost driver for that month is multiplied by the predetermined overhead rate to get the overhead costs to assign to work-in-process, called the **factory overhead applied.** On the basis of the amount of the cost driver related to each job, the total overhead applied is then distributed to the individual job cost sheets.

### Direct Labor Hours as a Measure of Activity

Management must make an important decision when calculating the predetermined overhead rate at the beginning of the year: How should it measure activity (the cost driver)? Although there are many alternative ways of measuring a cost driver (such as direct labor dollars, machine hours, units started, direct materials used, etc.), a typical measure is direct labor hours, as used by Collier Safe Company when it made the following estimates at the beginning of 1997:

Estimated total factory overhead
costs for 1997 . . . . . . . . . . . . . . . . . . . . . . . . . . . .$200,000
Estimated direct labor hours for 1997 . . . . . . . . . 20,000

The factory overhead rate for 1997 was determined as follows:

$$\text{Predetermined factory overhead rate} = \frac{\text{estimated factory overhead for 1997}}{\text{estimated cost driver for 1997}}$$

$$= \frac{\$200,000}{20,000 \text{ hr}} = \$10 \text{ per direct labor hour}$$

Every job worked on at any time during the year will be assigned—or *applied*—overhead costs at the same rate: $10 for every hour worked on a given job. If you look back at the discussion of entry 3 for direct labor, you can see that the total hours of direct labor in February were 1,800 (1,300 for Job 2 and 500 for Job 3). Under the $10-per-hour rate, the total factory overhead applied and its distribution to the two jobs are:

| Job | Activity for Month (direct labor hours) | | Factory Overhead Rate (per hour) | | Factory Overhead Costs Applied to Production |
|-----|------------------------------------------|---|----------------------------------|---|----------------------------------------------|
| 2 | 1,300 | × | $10 | = | $13,000 |
| 3 | 500 | × | $10 | = | 5,000 |
| | 1,800 | | | | $18,000 |

The $18,000 of overhead costs must be posted to appropriate job cost sheets. As you can see in Exhibit 1, Job 2 was correctly assigned $13,000 of the $18,000.

### Journalizing and Posting Factory Overhead Applied

To record factory overhead applied, journal entry 5 is needed on Feb. 28:

| 5. Feb. 28 | Work-in-Process Inventory ..................... | 18,000 | |
| | Factory Overhead Incurred and Applied ....... | | 18,000 |
| | Factory overhead applied to production, based on a $10 rate per direct labor hour for the 1,800 hours of direct labor. | | |

Note that the account being *credited*—Factory Overhead Incurred and Applied—is the same account we *debited* for the factory overhead incurred in entry 4. Now we are crediting it for the overhead applied.

The amounts shown in entry 5 are now posted to the general ledger accounts Work-in-Process Inventory and Factory Overhead Incurred and Applied.

Collier Safe's controller decided to measure the cost driver for the year in terms of *direct labor hours,* and then applied total overhead on the basis of the number of direct labor hours worked each month. The use of direct labor hours for applying overhead is typical of most manufacturers. Its use assumes that the amount of factory overhead costs incurred is closely related to the number of direct labor hours worked—the more direct labor, the more overhead costs. Therefore, any job that has a lot of direct labor hours must also create a lot of factory overhead costs.

In recent years the use of a single cost driver (whether it be direct labor hours, direct labor dollars, machine hours, or anything else) for applying total overhead costs to the product has been harshly criticized. A significant refinement of this approach, called Activity-Based Costing (ABC), is gaining a great deal of acceptance, and will be discussed at the end of this chapter. Despite the growing popularity of ABC however, since most companies do continue to use a single cost driver, and since the use of a single cost driver is a far easier approach for applying overhead costs, in this text we will typically emloy the easier (although admittedly less precise) approach to overhead application.

Learning Objective **6**

Explain the meaning of overapplied or underapplied overhead, why it comes about, and how it is accounted for at year-end

## Overapplied and Underapplied Overhead

Let's look again at Collier Safe's account for Factory Overhead Incurred and Applied for February. The debit of $14,000, from entry 4, was for the actual overhead costs for the month. The credit of $18,000, from entry 5, was for the factory overhead applied to Work-in-Process Inventory; it was one of three inventoriable costs for the jobs being worked on.

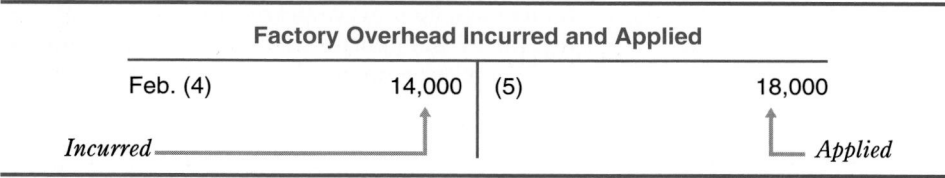

Factory Overhead Incurred and Applied

| Feb. (4) | 14,000 | (5) | 18,000 |

*Incurred*           *Applied*

As you can see, the credits exceed the debits by $4,000—the excess of what we applied during February over the amount that was actually incurred. When the applied exceeds the actual like this, we refer to the overhead as being *overapplied,* and the difference is called **overapplied overhead.** When the applied is less than the actual (the credits being less than the debits), we refer to the overhead as being *underapplied,* and the difference is called **underapplied overhead.**

The credit difference of $4,000 in Factory Overhead Incurred and Applied is for the month of February. Similar differences, which are either overapplied or underapplied, will occur each month. By the end of the year there will be 12 sets of debits and credits in this account, and at that time the cumulative difference in the account will need to be closed. We'll tell you more about this year-end closing entry after we discuss the remaining entries needed for the month of February.

ASK YOURSELF ▶

1. **What is the subsidiary ledger for Factory Overhead Incurred and Applied?**
2. **Why is it better to apply factory overhead to different jobs by using a predetermined factory overhead rate than to assign the actual overhead costs incurred each month?**
3. **When is the factory overhead rate determined? How is it calculated? How do we determine the amount of factory overhead applied each month?**
4. **What is underapplied (or overapplied) factory overhead?**

## Payment of Salaries

The direct labor costs accrued for the month of February were recorded in entry 3 (direct labor) and entry 4 (indirect labor—factory overhead). They totaled $46,000:

| | |
|---|---:|
| Direct labor | $36,000 |
| Indirect labor | 10,000 |
| | $46,000 |

Information concerning the payment of salaries comes from the clock cards (or time cards) that are filled out by each employee. The clock card, which is usually punched in a time clock at the beginning and end of each day, shows the number of hours each employee spends at work each pay period. The **clock card** is the source document that informs the accounting department of the number of hours for which each employee should be paid. The clock card does not specify which jobs were worked on; that's the purpose of the work ticket.

### Journalizing and Posting the Payment of Salaries

If we assume that the salaries are paid on the last day of each month and that the total labor cost from the clock cards of all employees is $46,000, then the entry to record the payment of salaries to laborers is:

| | | | | |
|---|---|---|---:|---:|
| **6.** | Feb. 28 | Salaries Payable | 46,000 | |
| | | Cash | | 46,000 |
| | | $36,000 was paid to direct laborers and $10,000 was paid to indirect laborers. | | |

The entry to record the payment of salaries is then posted to the appropriate general ledger accounts.

### Summary of Costs of Producing Jobs 2 and 3

Now that all the costs of producing Jobs 2 and 3 have been recorded for February, let's look at Exhibit 7, the general ledger account (in T-account form) for Work-in-Process Inventory and the related job cost sheets (the subsidiary ledger) for Jobs 2 and 3. The job cost sheet for Job 1 is also shown, although it is part of the finished goods subsidiary ledger rather than work-in-process.

As Exhibit 7 shows, the job cost sheet for Job 1 is the same as it was on Jan. 31 because Job 1 was completed in January. The heading of the job cost sheet shows that

**Exhibit 7** General Ledger for Work-in-Process Inventory and Related Job Cost Sheets

#### General Ledger

#### Work-in-Process Inventory

| | |
|---|---|
| Beginning Balance | 37,000 |
| Direct Materials | 33,000 |
| Direct Labor | 36,000 |
| Factory Overhead Applied | 18,000 |

#### Subsidiary Ledgers for Work-in-Process Inventory and Finished Goods

##### Job 3 (Incomplete)

| Month | Direct Materials | Direct Labor | Factory Overhead Applied | Total |
|---|---|---|---|---|
| Jan. | –0– | –0– | –0– | –0– |
| Feb. | 21,000 | 10,000 | 5,000 | 36,000 |

##### Job 2 (Completed but Not Sold)

| Month | Direct Materials | Direct Labor | Factory Overhead Applied | Total |
|---|---|---|---|---|
| Jan. | 10,000 | 18,000 | 9,000 | 37,000 |
| Feb. | 12,000 | 26,000 | 13,000 | 51,000 |
| | 22,000 | 44,000 | 22,000 | 88,000 |

##### Job 1 (Sold)

| Month | Direct Materials | Direct Labor | Factory Overhead Applied | Total |
|---|---|---|---|---|
| Jan. | 6,000 | 12,000 | 6,000 | 24,000 |
| | 6,000 | 12,000 | 6,000 | 24,000 |

Job 1 was sold in February. Therefore its total cost of $24,000 must be transferred from Finished Goods Inventory to Cost of Goods Sold.

Additional production costs for February were added to Job 2's beginning balance. According to the job cost sheet, Job 2 was completed during the month, so its total costs of $88,000 must be transferred from Work-in-Process Inventory to Finished Goods Inventory. But since the sale of this job was not yet finalized, its balance of $88,000 represents the balance in Finished Goods Inventory on Feb. 28.

Exhibit 7 also shows that Job 3, which was started in February, was still in process at the end of the month. Its total costs to date of $36,000 represent the ending balance in Work-in-Process Inventory on Feb. 28.

Let's look now at the journal entries needed to record the completion of Job 2 and the sale of Job 1.

### Completion of Job 2

When Job 2 is completed during the month, its job cost sheet is transferred from the subsidiary ledger for work-in-process to the subsidiary ledger for finished goods. The total costs of $88,000 are transferred to Finished Goods Inventory by journal entry 7:

| | | | | |
|---|---|---|---|---|
| **7.** Feb. 28 | Finished Goods Inventory . . . . . . . . . . . . . . . . . . . . . . | 88,000 | |
| | Work-in-Process Inventory. . . . . . . . . . . . . . . . . . | | 88,000 |
| | Completion in February of Job 2 and transfer of | | |
| | costs to finished goods. | | |

The debits and credits for the entry above are posted to the general ledger accounts for Finished Goods Inventory and Work-in-Process Inventory.

### Sale of Job 1

If Collier Safe prices its inventory to sell at a markup of 50% over cost, then the sales price for Job 1 will be $24,000 + .50($24,000) = $36,000. The entry to record the sale would be:

| | | | | |
|---|---|---|---|---|
| **8.** Feb. 28 | Accounts Receivable (or Cash). . . . . . . . . . . . . . . . . | 36,000 | |
| | Sales. . . . . . . . . . . . . . . . . . . . . . . . . . . . . . . . | | 36,000 |

And the entry to record the cost of goods sold would be:

| | | | | |
|---|---|---|---|---|
| **9.** Feb. 28 | Cost of Goods Sold . . . . . . . . . . . . . . . . . . . . . . . . . | 24,000 | |
| | Finished Goods Inventory . . . . . . . . . . . . . . . . . | | 24,000 |

These last two entries would be posted to the appropriate general ledger accounts, and the job cost sheet for Job 1 would be transferred from the subsidiary ledger for finished goods to the subsidiary ledger for cost of goods sold.

### OVERVIEW OF THE MONTHLY FLOW OF INVENTORIABLE COSTS

The flow of inventoriable costs through the production accounts of Collier Safe Company in February, which were journalized in entries 1–9, are summarized in T-accounts in Exhibit 8.

If financial statements are prepared for Collier for February, the $24,000 balance in Cost of Goods Sold goes on the income statement, and the $36,000 balance in

**Exhibit 8** Overview of the Flow of Product Costs

| Raw Materials Inventory | | |
| --- | --- | --- |
| Beg. Bal. | 8,000 | 33,000 |
| Purchases | 30,200 | 200 |
| End. Bal. | 5,000 | |

| Work-in-Process Inventory | | |
| --- | --- | --- |
| Beg. Bal. | 37,000 | |
| Dir. Mat. | 33,000 | |
| Dir. Labor | 36,000 | |
| Fact. Over. | | |
| Applied | 18,000 | 88,000 |
| End. Bal. | 36,000 | |

| Finished Goods Inventory | | |
| --- | --- | --- |
| Beg. Bal. | 24,000 | |
| Cost of Goods | | |
| Completed | 88,000 | 24,000 |
| End. Bal. | 88,000 | |

| Factory Overhead Incurred and Applied | | |
| --- | --- | --- |
| Ind. Mat. | 200 | |
| Ind. Labor | 10,000 | |
| Utilities | 1,000 | |
| Deprec. | 2,800 | 18,000 |
| | | 4,000 |

| Cost of Goods Sold | | |
| --- | --- | --- |
| Cost of Goods | | |
| Sold | 24,000 | |

Work-in-Process Inventory (Job 3) and the $88,000 balance in Finished Goods Inventory (Job 2) go on the balance sheet.

## YEAR-END HANDLING OF UNDER- OR OVERAPPLIED OVERHEAD

The actual and applied factory overhead probably differ for each month of the year. Therefore each month a difference is likely to occur between the debits and the credits to Factory Overhead Incurred and Applied. In some months there may be overapplied overhead, and in other months there may be underapplied overhead. Ideally, by the end of the year, the overapplied and underapplied amounts will balance out to zero. Realistically, however, there is usually at least a small balance remaining in the Factory Overhead Incurred and Applied account at year-end.

In fact, that balance may be significant, for a variety of reasons. The original estimates of overhead and the cost driver may have been way off the mark. The hours worked may have been much too great for the number of jobs worked on. The production process may have been extremely efficient or inefficient.

Regardless of the size of the balance remaining in Factory Overhead Incurred and Applied at year-end, we still need a closing entry to remove the balance from the books. Assuming that Factory Overhead Incurred and Applied has an immaterial debit balance of $500 at the end of the year, we simply make the following entry:

| | | | | |
| --- | --- | --- | --- | --- |
| **10.** | Dec. 31 | Cost of Goods Sold . . . . . . . . . . . . . . . . . . . . . . . . | 500 | |
| | | Factory Overhead Incurred and Applied . . . . . . | | 500 |

Cost of Goods Sold is increased by $500, and Factory Overhead Incurred and Applied is closed to a zero balance. If Factory Overhead Incurred and Applied had a $500 credit balance at the end of the year, the closing entry would be just the reverse of the one above.

If the balance remaining in the Factory Overhead Incurred and Applied account is considered material, then the over- or underapplied overhead must be allocated among Work-in-Process Inventory, Finished Goods Inventory, and Cost of Goods Sold, based on the ending balances in each of these three accounts. We use this second approach when the overhead is over- or underapplied, because all accounts with overhead assigned to them are misstated. When there are incomplete jobs and completed but unsold jobs, in addition to jobs that have been sold, then all three accounts—not just Cost of Goods Sold—are incorrect. And if the over- or underapplied amount is large, then each of these accounts might be materially misstated. That is why the over- or underapplied overhead must be allocated among all three accounts. This allocation increases each account when overhead is underapplied, and decreases each account when overhead is overapplied.

For example, assume that the underapplied overhead was $5,000 for the year, and the year-end balances in Work-in-Process Inventory, Finished Goods Inventory, and Cost of Goods Sold were as follows:

| Account | Year-End Balance |
|---|---|
| Work-in Process Inventory...... | $ 40,000 |
| Finished Goods Inventory ...... | 60,000 |
| Cost of Goods Sold ........... | 700,000 |
| | $800,000 |

In this case the amount of underapplied overhead allocated to each account would be determined as follows:

| Account | Percentage of Total Balances × | Underapplied Overhead | Amount Allocated to Each Account |
|---|---|---|---|
| Work-in-Process Inventory | 40/800 = 5.0% × | $5,000 | $ 250 |
| Finished Goods Inventory | 60/800 = 7.5% × | $5,000 | 375 |
| Cost of Goods Sold | 700/800 = 87.5% × | $5,000 | 4,375 |
| | | | $5,000 |

## APPLICATIONS OF JOB ORDER COSTING TO OTHER AREAS OF THE VALUE CHAIN

Our emphasis within this chapter has been on inventory costing—accumulating the costs of inventory in order to have the correct amounts in cost of goods sold on the income statement and in the inventories on the balance sheet. The only product costs we dealt with related to the production department of the value chain. If we were accumulating the costs of different jobs in order to make a special decision such as accepting a special order or adding a new product line, the product costs for this purpose would include any costs associated with the product, regardless of which business function they relate to. They might include research and development costs, product design costs, marketing costs, distribution costs, and customer service costs —in addition to the costs of production.

Learning
Objective 7

Explain how the job order costing method can be adapted to nonmanufacturing applications

## APPLICATIONS OF JOB ORDER COSTING TO SERVICE ORGANIZATIONS

So far all the applications of job order costing have related to manufacturers. A tangible physical product is being produced to customer specifications, and the costs associated with manufacturing that product are being carefully traced to each different order and maintained on an individual job cost sheet. Job order costing is not limited to manufacturers, however. It can also be adapted to other types of organizations as well—especially service organizations.

Service organizations have no tangible physical product—no inventory—but they do have products in the form of the services they perform. When a service organization is providing distinctly different services to different clients, each client represents a job. If the costs of performing a service for a particular client can be determined, then these costs are identified and accumulated in something equivalent to a job cost sheet. And a different job cost sheet is kept for each different client.

For example, each of the clients of the CPA firm of Deloitte & Touche represents a different job, having distinctly different costs. The costs of auditing General Motors, one of its many clients, can be estimated at the beginning of each year as a basis for quoting a fee for the engagement. As the audit progresses, Deloitte & Touche would keep track of the costs of the General Motors audit, separate from the costs of auditing any other client. At the end of the engagement, the total costs associated with the General Motors audit would be known and could be compared to the audit fee to determine the amount of profit.

Although the costs of the General Motors engagement would be considered product costs—where the audit is the product—they would not be considered inventoriable costs, since there are no physical inventories equivalent to Work-in-Process and Finished Goods for a manufacturer. Whereas the costs of an unfinished engagement for a CPA is quite similar to the idea of Work-in-Process, and is even conceptually appealing, generally accepted accounting principles do not treat it as an inventory that goes on the balance sheet. Instead, all the costs associated with the engagement would be expensed in the year they are incurred even if the job is still in process at year end.

Other examples of service organizations that could use job order costing include: Toyota Service Centers (each car repair); an advertising agency or law firm (each different client); and a hospital (each patient).

**ASK YOURSELF** ▶

1. **What two entries are needed to account for the sale of a job?**
2. **What is the proper treatment of over- or underapplied overhead at year-end?**
3. **Can job order costing techniques be adapted to companies that are not manufacturers? Explain.**

## A REVIEW OF JOB ORDER COSTING

Now that you have read extensively about job order costing, you may want to review what you have learned. To help you with your review, the basic elements of job order costing are summarized in matrix form in Exhibit 9. For each of the 10 transactions we have discussed in the chapter, you can see the journal entry, the subsidiary ledgers, and the source documents involved.

**Exhibit 9** Matrix Overview of Job Order Costing

| No. | Transaction | Journal Entry | Subsidiary Ledgers | Source Documents |
|---|---|---|---|---|
| 1. | Purchase of raw materials | Raw Materials Inventory<br>  Accounts Payable | Stores cards | Invoice |
| 2. | Use of direct materials | Work-in-Process Inventory<br>  Raw Materials<br>  Inventory | Job cost sheets<br><br>Stores cards | Stores requisition |
| 3. | Accrual of direct labor | Work-in-Process Inventory<br>  Salaries Payable | Job cost sheets | Work tickets |

*(Continued)*

**Exhibit 9** Matrix Overview of Job Order Costing *Continued*

| No. | Transaction | Journal Entry | Subsidiary Ledgers | Source Documents |
|---|---|---|---|---|
| **4.** | Actual factory overhead incurred | Factory Overhead Incurred and Applied<br>　　Miscellaneous credits | Factory overhead cost sheets<br>Stores cards | Stores requisition, work tickets, utility bills, depreciation schedules |
| **5.** | Factory overhead applied | Work-in-Process Inventory<br>　　Factory Overhead<br>　　Incurred and Applied | Job cost sheets | Schedule showing the determination of the pre-determined factory overhead rate |
| **6.** | Payment of salaries | Salaries Payable<br>　　Cash | | Clock cards |
| **7.** | Completion of jobs | Finished Goods Inventory<br>　　Work-in-Process<br>　　Inventory | Job cost sheets | Combined totals on job cost sheets for jobs completed and transferred to Finished Goods Inventory |
| **8.** | Sale of jobs: revenue | Accounts Receivable (Cash)<br>　　Sales | Accounts receivable subsidiary ledger | Invoice |
| **9.** | Sale of jobs: costs | Cost of Goods Sold<br>　　Finished Goods<br>　　Inventory | Job cost sheets | Combined totals on job cost sheets for jobs sold |
| **10.** | Closing of over- or underapplied overhead at year-end | Cost of Goods Sold<br>　　Factory Overhead<br>　　Incurred and Applied* | | |

*This is the entry for underapplied overhead. For overapplied overhead the entry would be reversed. If the over- or underapplied overhead is material, then the debit (or credit) to Cost of Goods Sold would be allocated among Finished Goods Inventory, Work-in-Process Inventory, and Cost of Goods Sold.

Learning Objective 8

Explain how Activity-Based Costing can enhance the accuracy of product costs with the job order costing method

## A COSTING ALTERNATIVE THAT'S AS SIMPLE AS ABC

In our example for Collier Safe Company, we assumed that there was only one production department, for which we combined all the overhead costs into a single group of costs—called *a cost pool*. We then assigned that department's overhead costs to jobs based upon a single overhead rate determined at the beginning of the year, using direct labor hours as the cost driver. It is typical for many companies to use a single departmental overhead rate, or even a single plant-wide rate when there are several departments. It is also typical for them to employ direct labor hours as the single cost driver for applying overhead costs to individual jobs. Unfortunately this reliance upon direct labor can often lead to inaccurate product costs, resulting in poor decisions.

The assignment of overhead costs to different jobs based upon direct labor hours, assumes that there is a cause and effect relationship between the amount of direct labor hours used on a job and the amount of resources consumed in order to make that job. It assumes that the occurrence of direct labor hours "drives" the amount of total overhead. Since factory overhead is made up of many different types of overhead costs, the use of direct labor hours as the only cost driver also assumes that each individual overhead cost is driven by this single cost driver. If these assumptions are correct, then the amount of overhead costs assigned to a particular job accurately reflects the amount of resources consumed by the company in producing that job.

Unfortunately, however, direct labor hours may not be the best cost driver for all types of overhead costs, for it may not be the appropriate measure of what truly causes the resources to be consumed. As a consequence, applying overhead to each job based only on the number of direct labor hours may result in inaccurate product costs.

Some jobs may be overcosted while others may be undercosted. When a product is **overcosted,** this means that the accounting system reports that a product costs a certain amount, when in reality the resources that are consumed to make that product are less than the reported amount. Conversely, when a product is **undercosted,** the accounting system reports that a product costs an amount that is actually less than the resources consumed to make that product. In either case, when the products are inaccurately costed, not only are the income statement and balance sheet incorrect, but any decisions regarding those products may lead to potentially disastrous conclusions.

To see what can happen when the wrong cost driver is employed, assume that a single overhead cost—wages of machine maintenance personnel—is applied to jobs at a rate of $10 per direct labor hour. The amount applied to jobs A and B below would be a total of $15,000, $10,000 to A and $5,000 to B.

|  | **Job A** | **Job B** |
|---|---|---|
| Number of Direct Labor Hours | 1,000 | 500 |
| Predetermined rate per direct labor hour | $ 10 | $ 10 |
| Amount applied to each job | $10,000 + | $5,000 = $15,000 |

If however, the wages of personnel doing maintenance on machinery are influenced more by the number of hours that machines are used, than by the number of direct labor hours used in production, then machine maintenance costs should be applied using machine hours instead of direct labor hours. If we assume the proper overhead rate is $20 per machine hour, notice below how the costs assigned to each individual job are quite a bit different from what they were above, even though the total costs assigned to the two jobs is still $15,000.

|  | **Job A** | **Job B** |
|---|---|---|
| Number of Machine Hours | 350 | 400 |
| Predetermined rate per machine hour | $ 20 | $ 20 |
| Amount applied to each job | $7,000 + | $8,000 = $15,000 |

If direct labor hours are inappropriately used instead of machine hours, then Product A will be overcosted by $3,000 ($10,000 − $7,000) and Product B will be undercosted by $3,000 ($5,000 − $8,000). This inaccurate costing of products A and B could then lead to such incorrect decisions as:

1. Overpricing Product A and underpricing Product B,
2. Dropping the wrong product line after doing product profitability analysis that reveals that Product A appears to be losing money for the company, while Product B is slightly profitable,
3. Misstating the ending balance in inventory and the cost of goods sold on the financial statements.

## Activity Based Costing (ABC)

Many organizations, especially multi-product manufacturers, are now refining their accounting systems to provide for a more accurate costing of their products. They see the need to have an accounting system where the reported product costs truly reflect the resources that are consumed in making the product. These companies are using a refinement called **Activity-Based Costing (ABC)** which aims to provide a more detailed tracking of costs to each product by focusing on the critical activities (such as purchasing, material handling, machine set-ups, assembly, machine maintenance, quality inspections, rework, etc.) that make up the manufacturing process, rather than the specific types of overhead costs (such as supplies, utilities, salaries, rent, property taxes, depreciation, etc.) that are incurred within a department. All overhead costs that are incurred within a department are assumed to be caused by the activities that take place within the department. The activities consume resources that result in overhead costs being incurred.

In order to implement an Activity-Based Costing system, it is first necessary to determine which costs are associated with each different activity, and then to assign the costs of each activity to each product based on the amount of activities needed to produce each different product.

### Steps in ABC

The total overhead cost of each product in an ABC system is the sum of all the overhead costs of all the activities that take place to manufacture the product. Determining this summation involves the following steps:

**STEP 1:** Identify the various activities that relate to the products

**STEP 2:** Estimate the annual overhead costs within a department that are associated with each of the different activities

**STEP 3:** Identify the cost drivers (and their estimated levels for the year) that have the best relationship between the costs of each activity and the products that are being manufactured

**STEP 4:** Calculate a predetermined overhead rate for the costs associated with each different activity

**STEP 5:** Multiply the overhead rate for each activity times the level of the cost driver required for the products' completion

**STEP 6:** Sum all the costs of all the activities

### An ABC Example

Layaway Custom Pools, a manufacturer of custom above-ground swimming pools, usually works closely with contractors for new home owners. Layaway is currently working on two projects for new home owners, Kinsey and Eulalia. The costs of direct materials and direct labor are easily identified with each different job:

|  | Costs of Each Job | |
| --- | --- | --- |
|  | **Kinsey** | **Eulalia** |
| Direct materials | $2,000 | $3,000 |
| Direct labor hours | 100 | 110 |
| Direct labor costs | $ 450 | $ 350 |

The overhead costs however, are not quite so obvious, so the controller decides to employ Activity-Based Costing in order to accurately determine the overhead costs associated with each job. She then proceeds through the following steps:

**STEP 1:** Identify the various activities that relate to the products. The controller identified the following activities associated with the production of pools for Kinsey and Eulalia: material handling, supervision, machine maintenance, and quality control.

**STEP 2:** Estimate the annual overhead costs within a department that are associated with each of the different activities. At the beginning of the year, the controller estimated the following overhead costs for each of the activities within the production department, that were expected for the year:

|  | Estimated Costs for the Year |
|---|---|
| Material handling | $ 500,000 |
| Supervision | 300,000 |
| Machine maintenance | 100,000 |
| Quality control | 400,000 |
|  | $1,300,000 |

**STEP 3:** Identify the cost drivers (and their estimated levels for the year) that have the best relationship between the costs of each activity and the products that are being manufactured. The controller identified the following cost drivers for each activity and estimated the amount of each cost driver for the year:

| Activity | Cost Driver and Related Estimated Level for the Year |
|---|---|
| Material handling | number of different material parts (12,500 parts) |
| Supervision | number of direct labor hours (12,000 DLH) |
| Machine maintenance | number of machine hours (10,000 MH) |
| Quality control | number of hours of inspection and rework (4,000 IH) |

**STEP 4:** Calculate a predetermined overhead rate for the costs associated with each different activity. Each individual rate is found at the beginning of the year by dividing the estimated costs for the year by the estimated amount of the cost driver for the year. They are:

| | Estimated Costs | ÷ Estimated Cost Driver = | Predetermined Overhead Rate |
|---|---|---|---|
| Material handling | $ 500,000 | 12,500 parts | $40/part |
| Supervision | 300,000 | 12,000 DLH | $25/DLH |
| Machine maintenance | 100,000 | 10,000 MH | $10/MH |
| Quality control | 400,000 | 4,000 IH | $100/IH |
| | $1,300,000 | | |

**STEP 5:** Multiply the overhead rate for each activity times the level of the cost driver required for the products' completion. For Kinsey the overhead costs would be as follows, based on the actual amounts for each cost driver given in the middle column:

| | Overhead Costs for Kinsey | | |
|---|---|---|---|
| Activity | Overhead Rate | Amount of × Cost Driver = | Overhead Applied |
| Material handling | $40 | 20 parts | $ 800 |
| Supervision | $25 | 30 DLH | 750 |
| Machine maintenance | $10 | 30 MH | 300 |
| Quality control | $100 | 4 IH | 400 |
| | | | $2,250 |

And for Eulalia, the overhead costs would be:

**Overhead Costs for Eulalia**

| Activity | Overhead Rate | Amount of × Cost Driver | Total = Applied |
|---|---|---|---|
| Material handling | $40 | 40 parts | $1,600 |
| Supervision | $25 | 25 DLH | 625 |
| Machine maintenance | $10 | 40 MH | 400 |
| Quality control | $100 | 6 IH | 600 |
| | | | $3,225 |

**STEP 6:** Sum all the costs of all the activities. For the two jobs, the total costs would be $4,700 for Kinsey and $6,575 for Eulalia:

| | Kinsey | Eulalia |
|---|---|---|
| Direct materials | $2,000 | $3,000 |
| Direct labor | 450 | 350 |
| Material handling | 800 | 1,600 |
| Supervision | 750 | 625 |
| Machine maintenance | 300 | 400 |
| Quality control | 400 | 600 |
| | $4,700 | $6,575 |

## Other Applications of ABC

The Layaway Custom Pools example of Activity-Based Costing was for a production department of a manufacturer that was using the job order costing method. Its use, however, is not limited to the job order costing method, to production departments, or to manufacturers. Any company can benefit from using Activity-Based Costing whenever the following conditions exist:

1. Factory overhead costs are significant,
2. There are a variety of different activities that influence the amount of overhead costs,
3. The company has widely diverse products, requiring different amounts of each type of activity.

The benefits of using Activity-Based Costing are not limited to job order costing situations, but can be useful in process costing environments as well. It is important to realize that ABC is not a method; it is a way to refine whatever method is being used, by helping the cost accounting system develop more accurate product costs. So, as long as the three conditions above exist, ABC can be a useful complement to either the job order or process costing method.

The benefits of Activity-Based Costing are not restricted to production activities for a manufacturer. ABC can also be employed in other areas within a company's value chain, such as research and development, product design, sales and marketing, distribution, and customer service. Although we limited the example for Layaway to production overhead costs, a company needs to have accurate product costs for all costs that are associated with the product, and not just for those that are assigned to the product for inventory costing purposes. It is just as important to accurately associate nonproduction costs with the product when management is making a decision relating to the company's profitability.

Finally, even though most of the companies that employ ABC are manufacturers, the benefits of ABC are not confined to this type of organization. Benefits from ABC can also be derived by service organizations, such as CPA firms, law firms, advertising agencies, etc.

1. **Should all overhead costs be applied to jobs using a single cost driver? Should the cost driver always be direct labor?**
2. **What is Activity-Based Costing?**
3. **What types of organizations, and areas of an organization, might benefit from ABC?**

## SUMMARY

• The **Job order costing method** is used in manufacturing processes that possess most of the following characteristics:

1. A relatively small number of units (or batches of units) is produced, each of which is different from any other unit (or batch) produced.
2. Each unit (or batch) is clearly identifiable and distinguishable from others produced within the same production environment.
3. Each unit (or batch) is produced according to customer specifications.
4. Considerable costs are represented in each unit (or batch) produced.

• The journal entries required for the job order costing method trace the flow of manufacturing costs from one production account to another:

Raw Materials Inventory ⟶ Work-in-Process Inventory ⟶ Finished Goods Inventory ⟶ Cost of Goods Sold

• The main subsidiary ledger account employed in job order costing is the **job cost sheet,** used to accumulate the inventoriable costs associated with a particular job.
• The total of all job cost sheets for unfinished jobs should be equal to the debit balance in Work-in-Process Inventory.
• The total of all job cost sheets for finished but unsold jobs should be equal to the debit balance in Finished Goods Inventory.
• The total of all job cost sheets for jobs that are finished and sold should be equal to the debit balance in Cost of Goods Sold.
• The costs of direct materials and direct labor are easily traceable and assignable to the specific units of production.
• Factory overhead costs are not related directly to specific units being produced and cannot be easily traced to individual jobs. The factory overhead debited to Work-in-Process Inventory and assigned to the individual job cost sheets is the amount of **factory overhead applied** rather than the amount of actual factory overhead incurred.
• The overhead applied is debited to Work-in-Process Inventory and is credited to **Factory Overhead Incurred and Applied.** The actual factory overhead costs incurred are debited to Factory Overhead Incurred and Applied and are credited to a wide variety of miscellaneous accounts.
• The difference between the applied overhead and the actual overhead is called overapplied and underapplied overhead.
• If the applied overhead exceeds the actual overhead it is called **overapplied overhead.** If the applied overhead is less than the actual overhead it is called **underapplied overhead.**
• Overapplied overhead is represented by a credit balance in the account Factory Overhead Incurred and Applied; underapplied overhead is represented by a debit balance.
• At the end of the year, any balance in the account Factory Overhead Incurred and Applied must be closed out, either entirely to Cost of Goods Sold, or allocated among Work-in-Process Inventory, Finished Goods Inventory, and Cost of Goods Sold.

- Job order costing is not only used by manufacturers. It can also be used by any service organization that finds it necessary to distinguish the costs of different projects that are being worked on.
- Many organizations are using a refined cost accounting system called Activity-Based Costing (ABC) which aims to provide a more detailed tracking of overhead costs to each product by focusing on the critical activities that make up the process. The total overhead cost of each product in an ABC system is the sum of all the overhead costs of all the activities that take place to make the product. An ABC system usually employs a different overhead cost pool for each activity, and a different cost driver for applying each overhead cost pool to the product.

## 8  KEY TERMS

| | |
|---|---|
| **Activity-Based Costing (ABC)** | A refinement of a company's cost accounting system which aims to provide a more detailed tracking of overhead costs to each product by focusing on the critical activities that make up the process. The total overhead cost of each product in an ABC system is the sum of all the overhead costs of all the activities that take place to make the product. |
| **Clock card** | A source document that shows the number of hours worked and the salary earned by an employee during a pay period. |
| **Cost pool** | A group of overhead costs that are assigned to a company's products based upon an appropriate cost driver. |
| **Factory overhead applied** | Overhead debited to Work-in-Process Inventory for inventory costing purposes. Applied overhead is determined by multiplying a predetermined factory overhead rate by the cost driver for the period. |
| **Factory overhead cost sheet** | The subsidiary ledger for factory overhead incurred and applied. The sheet itemizes for each department the types of factory overhead costs incurred. |
| **Factory Overhead Incurred and Applied** | An account that is debited for actual factory overhead costs incurred and credited for factory overhead applied. |
| **Invoice** | The source document for the purchase or sale of goods. It indicates the quantity and costs of what was bought or sold. |
| **Job cost sheet** | The basic document used in job order costing that accumulates the inventoriable costs associated with each job. The combination of all job cost sheets is the subsidiary ledger for Work-in-Process Inventory, Finished Goods Inventory, and Cost of Goods Sold. |
| **Job order costing method** | The method of accounting for the production of identifiable products, often to customer specifications. The costs of each job are carefully accumulated and kept separate from the costs of any other job. |
| **Overapplied overhead** | The difference between the higher factory overhead applied and the actual factory overhead costs incurred. |
| **Overcosting** | When the accounting system reports that a product costs a certain amount, when the resources that are actually consumed to make that product are less than the reported amount. |
| **Process costing** | The method of accounting for the production of identical units in a continuous process. The cost per unit is determined by dividing the total costs for all units produced by the number of units produced during the period. |
| **Source document** | A document giving evidence of a transaction and the amount involved. |

| | |
|---|---|
| Stores card | A card indicating the receipts, the withdrawals, and the balance for each different type of raw material. The combination of all stores cards is the subsidiary ledger for raw materials inventory. |
| Stores requisition | A written request presented to the storekeeper by the operating department to acquire raw materials needed in production. |
| Subsidiary ledger | A file of accounts that provides the detail of a general ledger account. The job cost sheets make up the subsidiary ledger for Work-in-Process Inventory, Finished Goods Inventory, and Cost of Goods Sold, and the stores cards comprise the subsidiary ledger for Raw Materials Inventory. |
| Underapplied overhead | The difference between the lower factory overhead applied and the actual factory overhead costs incurred. |
| Undercosting | When the accounting system reports that a product costs a certain amount, when the resources that are actually consumed to make that product are greater than the reported amount. |
| Work ticket | A source document that indicates the time and salary a direct laborer spends on a specific job and the time and salary an indirect laborer spends in a particular department. |

## DEMONSTRATION PROBLEM

The Gonzalez Company uses job order costing to account for its production of luxury spas. At the beginning of June 1997, one spa was partially finished, for a customer named Jillanne Shields. Its accumulated costs were as follows:

**Work-in-Process
Shields Spa**

| | |
|---|---:|
| Direct materials . . . . . . . . . . . . . . . . . . . . . . . . | $3,000 |
| Direct labor . . . . . . . . . . . . . . . . . . . . . . . . . . | 1,500 |
| Overhead (40% of direct labor costs) . . . . . . . | 600 |
| | $5,100 |

During June, the company purchased materials costing $12,000, for cash. These were needed to complete the Shields spa and start a new spa for Darrell Ferrigno. The cost of direct materials used and direct labor costs incurred during June were as follows:

| | Customer | |
|---|---|---|
| | **Shields** | **Ferrigno** |
| Direct materials . . . . . . . . . . . . | $1,500 | $10,000 |
| Direct labor . . . . . . . . . . . . . . . . | 2,000 | 9,000 |

In addition, the overhead costs incurred during the month were as follows:

| | |
|---|---:|
| Utilities. . . . . . . . . . . . . . . . . . . . . . . . . . . . . . . . . . | $  250 |
| Rentals . . . . . . . . . . . . . . . . . . . . . . . . . . . . . . . . . . | 650 |
| Depreciation . . . . . . . . . . . . . . . . . . . . . . . . . . . . . | 150 |
| Supervisory salaries . . . . . . . . . . . . . . . . . . . . . . . | 2,000 |
| | $3,050 |

The balance in Raw Materials Inventory on June 1 was $2,500. The overhead rate was determined at the beginning of the year and has been used to apply overhead throughout the year. The Shields spa was finished by the end of June, and Shields was billed for $18,000. The Ferrigno spa was partially finished on June 30.

**Required:**

1. Record the journal entries for June.
2. Determine the balance in the general ledger accounts for Raw Materials Inventory, Work-in-Process Inventory and Finished Goods Inventory on June 30.
3. Determine the amount of over- or underapplied overhead for June.
4. Prepare a combined schedule of cost of goods completed and sold.

## ■ Solution to Demonstration Problem

1. The journal entries for June are:

| | | |
|---|---|---|
| **1. Purchase of raw materials:** | | |
| Raw Materials Inventory | 12,000 | |
| Cash | | 12,000 |
| | | |
| **2. Usage of direct materials:** | | |
| Work-in-Process Inventory | 11,500 | |
| Raw Materials Inventory | | 11,500 |
| | | |
| **3. Direct labor:** | | |
| Work-in-Process Inventory | 11,000 | |
| Salaries Payable | | 11,000 |
| | | |
| **4. Actual factory overhead incurred:** | | |
| Factory Overhead Incurred and Applied | 3,050 | |
| Cash ($250 + $650) | | 900 |
| Accumulated Depreciation | | 150 |
| Salaries Payable | | 2,000 |
| | | |
| **5. Factory overhead applied:** | | |
| Work-in-Process Inventory | 4,400 | |
| Factory Overhead Incurred and Applied | | 4,400 |
| $11,000 × .40 = $4,400. | | |
| | | |
| **6. Payment of salaries:** | | |
| Salaries Payable | 13,000 | |
| Cash | | 13,000 |
| $11,000 + $2,000 = $13,000. | | |
| | | |
| **7. Completion of Shields spa:** | | |
| Finished Goods Inventory | 9,400 | |
| Work-in-Process Inventory | | 9,400 |
| $5,100 + $1,500 + $2,000 + $2,000(.40) = $9,400. | | |
| | | |
| **8. Sales revenue for Shields spa:** | | |
| Accounts Receivable | 18,000 | |
| Sales | | 18,000 |
| | | |
| **9. Cost of Shields spa:** | | |
| Cost of Goods Sold | 9,400 | |
| Finished Goods Inventory | | 9,400 |

2. The balances in each of the general ledger inventory accounts are determined as shown in the T-accounts on the next page.

| Raw Materials Inventory | | | |
|---|---|---|---|
| June 1 | 2,500 | | |
| (1) | 12,000 | (2) | 11,500 |
| June 30 | 3,000 | | |

| Work-in-Process Inventory | | | |
|---|---|---|---|
| June 1 | 5,100 | | |
| (2) | 11,500 | | |
| (3) | 11,000 | | |
| (5) | 4,400 | (7) | 9,400 |
| June 30 | 22,600 | | |

| Finished Goods Inventory | | | |
|---|---|---|---|
| June 1 | –0– | | |
| (7) | 9,400 | (8) | 9,400 |
| June 30 | –0– | | |

**3.** The overapplied overhead for June is $1,350:

Actual overhead incurred .................... $3,050
Overhead applied .......................... 4,400

Overapplied overhead ..................... $1,350

**4.**

### GONZALEZ COMPANY
### Combined Schedule of Cost of Goods Completed and Sold
### For the Month of June 1997

| | |
|---|---|
| Raw Materials Inventory, June 1, 1997 .............................. | $ 2,500 |
| Plus: Purchases ................................................ | 12,000 |
| Raw Materials Available for Use ................................. | $14,500 |
| Less: Raw Materials Inventory, June 30, 1997 ...................... | 3,000 |
| Direct Materials Used ........................................... | $11,500 |
| Plus: Direct Labor .............................................. | 11,000 |
| Plus: Factory Overhead .......................................... | 4,400 |
| Total Manufacturing Costs Incurred in June ....................... | $26,900 |
| Plus: Work-in-Process Inventory, June 1, 1997..................... | 5,100 |
| Total Manufacturing Costs to Account for ......................... | $32,000 |
| Less: Work-in-Process Inventory, June 30, 1997 ................... | 22,600 |
| Cost of Goods Completed ......................................... | $ 9,400 |
| Plus: Finished Goods Inventory, June 1, 1997 ..................... | –0– |
| Total Available for Sale......................................... | $ 9,400 |
| Less: Finished Goods Inventory, June 30, 1997 .................... | –0– |
| Cost of Goods Sold.............................................. | $ 9,400 |

## QUESTIONS FOR REVIEW AND FURTHER THOUGHT

### REVIEW QUESTIONS

1. Explain the characteristics of a manufacturing process that would typically use job order costing. Give several examples of industries that use job order costing.

2. Distinguish the accounting procedures under job order costing from those under process costing.

3. Name and describe the inventory subsidiary ledger accounts for a manufacturer.

4. What is the purpose of the job cost sheet? What types of costs are recorded in the job cost sheet? Give several examples.

5. Explain what we mean by the term *source document,* and describe at least three types of source documents.

6. Explain two reasons why it is preferable to apply factory overhead to jobs using a predetermined rate, rather than to assign the actual costs incurred each month to the jobs produced that month.

7. What is factory overhead applied? How is it determined?

8. What is overapplied overhead? Underapplied overhead?

9. What would be several different cost drivers (measures of activity) that could be used to calculate a predetermined factory overhead rate?

10. What is the required accounting treatment for over- or underapplied overhead at year-end?

11. What does it mean when a product is said to be overcosted? Undercosted?

## QUESTIONS FOR FURTHER THOUGHT

1. The job order costing method can only be employed for companies that are involved in manufacturing. Comment.

2. Describe the steps that must be taken in order for factory overhead to become the cost of different jobs being worked on.

3. The factory overhead rate for applying overhead to jobs must be based on the number of direct labor hours. Do you agree? Explain.

4. The only reason to use the job order costing method is for the inventory costing purpose. Do you agree? Why or why not?

5. Give some examples of how the job order costing method could be adapted to organizations that are not manufacturers.

6. If the Factory Overhead Incurred and Applied account has a debit balance at the end of the year, does this mean that the account received nothing but debits during the year? Is the overhead overapplied or underapplied for the year? What adjustment do we make for the overapplied or underapplied overhead balance at the end of each month? At the end of the year?

7. The three extremes of product costing are job order costing, process costing and Activity-Based Costing. Explain why you agree or disagree with this statement.

8. A company manufactures and sells two products that the accounting system has inaccurately costed. One product is overcosted, and the other is undercosted. As long as the two products are properly costed in total, what difference should it make to the company?

## OBJECTIVE ASSIGNMENT

*True/False* Indicate whether each statement below is *true* or *false* by placing a *T* or an *F* in the space provided.

_____ 1. An aircraft manufacturer is a good example of a company that would typically use the job order costing method.

_____ 2. Job order costing can be adapted to service companies as well as to those that are involved in manufacturing.

_____ 3. At the end of a month, the sum of all the job cost sheets for incomplete jobs should be equal to the ending balance in the general ledger Work-in-Process Inventory account.

_____ 4. In the journal entry for the factory overhead applied, the debit should be to Factory Overhead Incurred and Applied.

_____ 5. The ABC system focuses its attention on the activities that take place within a department or a company.

*Multiple Choice*   Select the best choice to complete each statement or answer each question below. Write the letter corresponding to your choice in the space provided.

_____ 1. Which of the following represents the subsidiary ledger for Factory Overhead Incurred and Applied?
   a. Job cost sheet
   b. Work ticket
   c. Factory overhead cost sheet
   d. Work-in-process

_____ 2. All but one of the characteristics listed below is typical of job order costing. Which one does not belong?
   a. Production to customer specifications
   b. Indistinguishable units
   c. Ability to determine the cost of each unit or batch
   d. Production of few units or batches

_____ 3. Which of the organizations listed below could use the job order costing method?
   a. A custom printing shop
   b. A lawyer's office
   c. A wedding catering service
   d. All of the above

_____ 4. Which account is credited for the factory overhead applied?
   a. Work-in-Process Inventory
   b. Factory Overhead Incurred
   c. Factory Overhead Applied
   d. Factory Overhead Incurred and Applied

_____ 5. At the beginning of 1997, a company expected to work 10,000 direct labor hours and to incur $40,000 of direct labor costs and $25,000 of factory overhead costs. The company's measure of activity for applying factory overhead is direct labor hours. What is the factory overhead rate for 1995?
   a. $4.00
   b. $2.50
   c. $1.60
   d. $.375

_____ 6. Which of the following might be used as a measure of activity (a cost driver) to determine a factory overhead rate?
   a. Direct labor hours
   b. Direct labor dollars
   c. Machine hours
   d. All of the above

_____ 7. If there are $45,000 of debits and $55,000 of credits in the Factory Overhead Incurred and Applied account at year-end, which statement below would be correct?
   a. The overapplied overhead is $55,000.
   b. The overapplied overhead is $10,000.
   c. the underapplied overhead is $45,000.
   d. The underapplied overhead is $10,000.

_____ 8. If the amount of overapplied overhead at year-end is material, the closing entry would *not* credit which account below?
   a. Raw Materials Inventory
   b. Work-in-Process Inventory
   c. Finished Goods Inventory
   d. Cost of Goods Sold

_____ 9. The factory overhead costs applied to Products A and B were $10 and $30 respectively, based upon direct labor hours as the cost driver. If the number of machine hours used is the more appropriate cost driver, and if an equal number of machine hours are used for both products, which of the following statements would be true?
   a. Both Product A and Product B are overcosted
   b. Both Product A and Product B are undercosted
   c. Product A is overcosted and Product B is undercosted
   d. Product B is overcosted and Product A is undercosted

_____ 10. In order for a company to benefit from using Activity-Based Costing, several conditions must be evident. Which of the following would be a necessary condition?
   a. Overhead costs should be immaterial
   b. There are only a few activities that influence the company's overhead costs
   c. The company has few products, all of which require equal proportions of the different activities
   d. All of the above are necessary conditions
   e. None of the above are necessary conditions

## EXERCISES

2   **Exercise 1:** Identifying subsidiary ledgers and source documents

For each of the following transactions, identify the subsidiary ledger(s) and source documents that would be involved.

1. Use of direct materials
2. Application of factory overhead
3. Completion of jobs
4. Purchase of raw materials
5. Use of direct labor
6. Use of indirect labor
7. Payment of wages and salaries

3†   **Exercise 2:** Recording the Purchase and Usage of Raw Materials

During January 1997, the Haden Coach Company purchased the following raw materials (direct and indirect materials):

Part 22. . . . . . . . . . . . . . . . . . . . . . . . . . . . . . . . . .    $43,000
Part 23. . . . . . . . . . . . . . . . . . . . . . . . . . . . . . . . . .     16,000
Supplies . . . . . . . . . . . . . . . . . . . . . . . . . . . . . . . .      2,900

The raw materials used during the month were:

|  | Part 22 | Part 23 | Supplies |
|---|---|---|---|
| Job 232. . . . . . . . . . . . . . . . . . . . . . . . . . . . . . . . . . | $22,000 | $11,000 | — |
| Job 233. . . . . . . . . . . . . . . . . . . . . . . . . . . . . . . . . . | 14,000 | 4,000 | — |
| Indirect costs. . . . . . . . . . . . . . . . . . . . . . . . . . . . . . | — | — | $2,200 |

Prepare journal entries to record the purchase and usage of raw materials.

▶ *(Check Figure: Debit to Work-in-Process Inventory $51,000)*

3   **Exercise 3:** Recording Direct and Indirect Labor Costs

The Majesty Company was working on three jobs during July: Jobs 111, 112, and 113. The labor costs that were accrued for the month were as follows:

† The numbers in the margin refer to the Learning Objectives.

| Work Tickets | Related to Job Number | Related Directly to Jobs | Related Indirectly to Jobs |
|---|---|---|---|
| 2201–2209 | 111 | $2,200 | — |
| 2210–2220 | 112 | 3,400 | — |
| 2221–2231 | — | — | 2,700 |
| 2232–2251 | 111 | 1,400 | — |
| 2252–2265 | 113 | 1,700 | — |
| 2266–2272 | 112 | 2,100 | — |
| 2273–2275 | — | — | 700 |
| 2276–2277 | 111 | 900 | — |

Record the labor costs for the month in general journal form.

▶ (Check Figure: Debit to Factory Overhead Incurred and Applied, $3,400)

**3 5 6**   **Exercise 4:** Recording Factory Overhead Incurred and Applied

The Callie Manufacturing Company applies overhead to its jobs using a rate of $9 per direct labor hour. During April 1998, Callie had the following results:

| | | |
|---|---|---|
| Direct labor hours . . . . . . . . . . . . . . . . . . . . . . . . . . . . . . . . . . . . . . . . . . . . . . . . . . . | | 20,000 |
| Direct labor costs . . . . . . . . . . . . . . . . . . . . . . . . . . . . . . . . . . . . . . . . . . . . . . . . . . | | $200,000 |
| Factory overhead incurred: | | |
| Salaries. . . . . . . . . . . . . . . . . . . . . . . . . . . . . . . . . . . . . . . . . . . . . . . | $120,000 | |
| Depreciation: Building . . . . . . . . . . . . . . . . . . . . . . . . . . . . . . . | 40,000 | |
| Property taxes . . . . . . . . . . . . . . . . . . . . . . . . . . . . . . . . . . . . . . | 14,000 | $174,000 |

a. Make the entries for April related to factory overhead.
b. How much overhead was over- or underapplied?

▶ (Check Figure: b. $6,000 overapplied)

**3**   **Exercise 5:** Making Journal Entries for Job Order Costing

Jackson's Video Games uses the job order costing method to account for the video games that it makes to individual customer specifications. During the month of July, Jackson's had the following transactions:

| | | |
|---|---|---|
| 1. Purchases of materials . . . . . . . . . . . . . . . . . . . . . . . . . . . . . . . . . . . . . . . | | $145,000 |
| 2. Usage of direct materials. . . . . . . . . . . . . . . . . . . . . . . . . . . . . . . . . . . . . . | | 123,000 |
| 3. Direct labor costs . . . . . . . . . . . . . . . . . . . . . . . . . . . . . . . . . . . . . . . . . . . | | 5,000 |
| 4. Factory overhead costs incurred: | | |
| Depreciation. . . . . . . . . . . . . . . . . . . . . . . . . . . . . . . . . . . . . . . . . . . . . | $3,000 | |
| Supervision . . . . . . . . . . . . . . . . . . . . . . . . . . . . . . . . . . . . . . . . . . . . | 6,000 | |
| Expiration of prepaid rentals . . . . . . . . . . . . . . . . . . . . . . . . . . . | 2,000 | |
| 5. Factory overhead applied . . . . . . . . . . . . . . . . . . . . . . . . . . . . . . . . . . . . . | | 10,000 |
| 6. Cost of jobs completed . . . . . . . . . . . . . . . . . . . . . . . . . . . . . . . . . . . . . . . | | 111,000 |
| 7. Cost of jobs sold . . . . . . . . . . . . . . . . . . . . . . . . . . . . . . . . . . . . . . . . . . . . | | 100,000 |
| 8. Revenue from jobs sold. . . . . . . . . . . . . . . . . . . . . . . . . . . . . . . . . . . . . . . | | 175,000 |

Record the transactions for the month in journal entry form.

▶ (Check Figure: Total debits to Work-in-Process, $138,000)

3 5 **Exercise 6:** Recording the Transfer of Costs for Three Jobs

At the beginning of November 1997, Willem Manufacturing was working on a single job. Its cost sheet on November 1 looked like this:

| Job 100 | | |
| --- | --- | --- |
| Direct materials.............................................. | $ 6,500 | |
| Direct labor ................................................. | 11,000 | |
| Factory overhead applied.................................... | 5,500 | $23,000 |

During November, another $4,000 of direct labor costs were incurred to complete Job 100, and factory overhead was applied to Job 100 at the same rate per direct labor dollar. No additional direct materials were required. Job 100 was shipped to a customer, who was billed $50,000.

Jobs 101 and 102 were started during November and Job 101 was completed. The job cost sheets for these two jobs looked like this at the end of November:

| Job 101 | | |
| --- | --- | --- |
| Direct materials.............................................. | $1,500 | |
| Direct labor ................................................. | 6,000 | |
| Factory overhead applied.................................... | 3,000 | $10,500 |

| Job 102 | | |
| --- | --- | --- |
| Direct materials.............................................. | $1,250 | |
| Direct labor ................................................. | 3,500 | |
| Factory overhead applied.................................... | 1,750 | $6,500 |

Make the journal entries to:

a. Finish Job 100, transfer Job 100 to Finished Goods, and sell Job 100.
b. Start Jobs 101 and 102, and finish Job 101.

▶ *(Check Figure: a. Debit to Cost of Goods Sold, $29,000)*

5 6 **Exercise 7:** Accounting for Factory Overhead

The Marante Manufacturing Company uses the job order costing method. On Apr. 1, there were no incomplete jobs on hand. During April, the following facts related to production:

| | |
| --- | --- |
| Direct materials............................ | $50,000 |
| Direct labor (1,000 hours)................... | 20,000 |
| Factory overhead incurred .................. | 7,000 |

Factory overhead is applied using a predetermined rate of 40% of direct labor cost. None of the jobs worked on during April were finished at month-end.

a. Determine the Apr. 30 balance in Work-in-Process Inventory.
b. Determine the over- or underapplied overhead.

▶ *(Check Figure: b. $1,000 overapplied)*

5 6 **Exercise 8:** Determining Factory Overhead Applied Using Different Cost Drivers

At the beginning of 1998, the controller of Fraser Laser Printers made the following projections:

| | |
| --- | --- |
| Factory overhead for the year .............. | $500,000 |
| Direct labor hours ......................... | 5,000 |
| Direct labor dollars ....................... | $100,000 |
| Machine hours ............................. | 250,000 |

During the month of January 1998, the following actual results took place:

| | |
|---|---|
| Factory overhead incurred . . . . . . . . . . . . . . . . . . . | $70,000 |
| Direct labor hours worked. . . . . . . . . . . . . . . . . . . | 500 |
| Direct labor costs incurred . . . . . . . . . . . . . . . . . . | $12,000 |
| Machine hours worked . . . . . . . . . . . . . . . . . . . . . | 21,000 |

a. Determine the factory overhead applied during January, assuming that direct labor hours is the cost driver for applying overhead. Also determine the amount of over- or underapplied overhead.

b. Determine the factory overhead applied during January, assuming that direct labor dollars is the cost driver for applying overhead. Also determine the amount of over- or underapplied overhead.

c. Determine the factory overhead applied during January, assuming that machine hours is the cost driver for applying overhead. Also determine the amount of over- or underapplied overhead.

▶ *(Check Figure: b. Factory overhead applied = $60,000; c. $28,000 underapplied)*

**8** **Exercise 9:** Determining Overcosted and Undercosted Products

At the beginning of 1997, the Mr. Jeffrey Perfume Company makes the following estimates for the year related to the application of factory overhead.

| | |
|---|---|
| Estimated factory overhead. . . . . . . . . . . . . . . . | $2,000,000 |
| Estimated direct labor hours . . . . . . . . . . . . . . . | 100,000 |
| Estimated machine hours . . . . . . . . . . . . . . . . . | 400,000 |

The controller decides to use direct labor hours as the cost driver for applying factory overhead costs to different jobs. During January, jobs for two customers, Channel and Fabber, had the following experiences:

| | |
|---|---|
| Actual direct labor hours | |
| Channel | 1,000 |
| Fabber | 2,000 |
| Actual machine hours | |
| Channel | 6,000 |
| Fabber | 6,000 |

a. Determine the overhead costs applied to each job based upon direct labor hours as the cost driver.

b. Determine the overhead costs that would have been applied to each job if machine hours had been the cost driver instead.

c. Assume that machine hours is the appropriate cost driver. Determine how much each job would be overcosted or undercosted if direct labor hours had been used to apply overhead costs to the jobs.

▶ *(Check Figure: b. Channel = $30,000)*

**5 6** **Exercise 10:** Making Annual and Year-End Entries for Factory Overhead for Two Departments

The Clothes Minded Company applies overhead on the basis of direct labor dollars in Department A and on the basis of machine hours in Department B. The budgeted and actual results for 1997 were as follows:

| Budgeted | Department A | Department B |
|---|---|---|
| Direct labor hours . . . . . . . . . . . . . . . . . . . . . . . . | 30,000 | 20,000 |
| Direct labor dollars . . . . . . . . . . . . . . . . . . . . . . . | $150,000 | $ 80,000 |
| Machine hours. . . . . . . . . . . . . . . . . . . . . . . . . . | 45,000 | 40,000 |
| Factory overhead . . . . . . . . . . . . . . . . . . . . . . . . | $120,000 | $ 80,000 |

| Actual | Department A | Department B |
|---|---|---|
| Direct labor hours . . . . . . . . . . . . . . . . . . . . . . . . | 32,000 | 24,000 |
| Direct labor dollars . . . . . . . . . . . . . . . . . . . . . . . | $156,000 | $100,000 |
| Machine hours. . . . . . . . . . . . . . . . . . . . . . . . . . | 47,000 | 43,000 |
| Factory overhead . . . . . . . . . . . . . . . . . . . . . . . . | $125,000 | $ 81,000 |

a. Make all entries required for factory overhead for 1997 for both departments.
b. Determine the over- or underapplied overhead for the year, both by department and in total.
c. Make the year-end entry to close the over- or underapplied overhead for each department to Cost of Goods Sold.

▶ *(Check Figure: c. Credit Cost of Goods Sold, $4,800)*

6   **Exercise 11:** Closing Entry for Overapplied Overhead

At the end of 1998, the X-Files Company had the following selected facts for the year:

| | |
|---|---|
| Factory overhead applied................... | $450,000 |
| Actual factory overhead incurred............. | 350,000 |
| Year-end balances: | |
|    Raw Materials Inventory................. | 75,000 |
|    Work-in-Process Inventory............... | 150,000 |
|    Finished Goods Inventory................ | 150,000 |
|    Cost of Goods Sold..................... | 700,000 |

Make the year-end closing entry for overhead. Allocate the over- or underapplied overhead among the appropriate accounts.

▶ *(Check Figure: Credit Cost of Goods Sold, $70,000)*

8   **Exercise 12:** Applications of Activity-Based Costing

For each of the situations below indicate whether Activity-Based Costing *might* be beneficial, by placing an X in the space provided.

_____ 1. A company using job order costing

_____ 2. A company using process costing

_____ 3. A company having many products

_____ 4. A company that has only one product

_____ 5. A company that is a manufacturer

_____ 6. A company that is a service entity

_____ 7. A company having an immaterial amount of overhead costs

_____ 8. A company having a material amount of overhead costs

_____ 9. A nonproduction department of a manufacturer

## PROBLEMS: SET A

3 5 6†   **Problem A1:** Determining the Inventory Costs for Different Jobs

During December 1997, Justice Company worked on two jobs, both of which were completed on Dec. 31. The costs incurred in December were as follows:

| | | |
|---|---|---|
| Direct labor: | | |
|   Job 1 (9,000 hours) ............................... | $75,000 | |
|   Job 2 (3,000 hours) ................................ | 25,000 | $100,000 |
| Factory overhead ............................................ | | 80,000 |
| Direct materials: | | |
|   Job 1......................................... | $45,000 | |
|   Job 2......................................... | 54,000 | 99,000 |

† The numbers in the margin refer to the Learning Objectives.

At the beginning of the year Justice had estimated its factory overhead for 1997 to be $1,000,000. It also estimated its direct labor hours and direct labor costs for the year to be 200,000 hours and $1,200,000, respectively.

**Required:**

1. Determine the factory overhead assigned to each job if overhead is applied using a predetermined overhead rate, with the activity measured in terms of direct labor hours.
2. Was the factory overhead overapplied or underapplied? By what amounts?
3. Determine the total costs assigned to each job in December.

▶ *(Check Figure: 1. Factory overhead applied to Job 1, $45,000; 3. Total costs assigned to Job 2, $94,000)*

3  5    **Problem A2:** Making Journal Entries

The Deluxe Mail Company produces brick mailboxes based on customer specifications. On Jan. 1, 1998, the accountant determines the following balances in the company's inventories:

Raw Materials Inventory . . . . . . . . . . . . . . . . . . . . . . .  $1,000
Work-in-Process Inventory . . . . . . . . . . . . . . . . . . . . .  1,500
Finished Goods Inventory . . . . . . . . . . . . . . . . . . . . . .  400

**Required:**

1. For each transaction below, make the required journal entry.
   a. Purchased materials in the amount of $800.
   b. Materials used in production were direct materials, $1,200; and indirect materials, $150.
   c. Labor used in production amounted to $450 for direct labor and $200 for indirect labor.
   d. Miscellaneous items included:

   Utilities . . . . . . . . . . . . . . . . . . . . . . . . . . . . . . . . . . . . . . .  $150
   Insurance . . . . . . . . . . . . . . . . . . . . . . . . . . . . . . . . . . . . .  75
   Depreciation . . . . . . . . . . . . . . . . . . . . . . . . . . . . . . . . . .  90

   e. Factory overhead is applied at a rate of 50% of direct labor cost.
   f. The jobs completed totaled $1,700.
   g. The sales revenue for January was $4,000 and the cost of jobs sold was $1,900.
2. Determine the Jan. 31 balance in each of the three inventory accounts.
3. Prepare a schedule of cost of goods sold for Deluxe Mail Company.

▶ *(Check Figure: 2. Finished Goods Inventory = $200)*

2 3 5 6    **Problem A3:** Making Journal Entries, Maintaining Subsidiary Ledgers, and Closing Overhead

The Exposé Custom Publishing Company used job order costing to account for its different projects. At the beginning of 1997, Exposé had the following balances in its subsidiary ledgers for its inventory accounts:

| Raw Materials | | Work-in-Process Inventory | | Finished Goods Inventory | |
|---|---|---|---|---|---|
| Paper | $30,000 | Devoe job | $11,000 | Lynch job | $67,000 |
| Ink | 2,000 | | | | |
| Other supplies | 14,000 | | | | |

During 1997, Exposé had the following transactions:

Purchases (on account):

Paper . . . . . . . . . . . . . . . . . . . . . . . . . . . . . . . . . . . . .  $83,000
Ink . . . . . . . . . . . . . . . . . . . . . . . . . . . . . . . . . . . . . . . . .  30,000
Other supplies . . . . . . . . . . . . . . . . . . . . . . . . . . . . . .  45,000

Material usage:

| | Devoe Job | Rehberger Job | Elia Job | Totals |
|---|---|---|---|---|
| Paper | $50,000 | $40,000 | $10,000 | $100,000 |
| Ink | 9,000 | 8,000 | 3,000 | 20,000 |
| Other supplies | | | | 50,000 |

Labor:

| | Devoe Job | Rehberger Job | Elia Job | Totals |
|---|---|---|---|---|
| Direct | $12,000 | $5,000 | $3,000 | $20,000 |
| Indirect | | | | 85,000 |

Machine hours worked:

| Devoe Job | Rehberger Job | Elia Job | Totals |
|---|---|---|---|
| 1,000 | 800 | 200 | 2,000 |

Other factory overhead:

| | |
|---|---|
| Insurance expired | $ 6,000 |
| Utilities paid | 12,000 |
| Depreciation | 16,000 |
| Rent | 18,000 |

Factory overhead is applied to jobs at $100 per machine hour.

During the year, the Devoe job was finished and the Lynch job was sold on account for $150,000. The Rehberger and Elia jobs were still in process at the end of the year.

**Required:**

1. Record the journal entries for 1997. Ignore for now the closing entry for factory overhead.
2. Determine the balances in the general ledger accounts for Raw Materials Inventory, Work-in-Process Inventory, and Finished Goods Inventory. Also show the subsidiary ledgers for each inventory account.
3. Prepare the closing entry for factory overhead. Assume that the amount of over- or underapplied overhead is material and must be allocated among the appropriate accounts.

▶ *(Check Figure: 2. Work-in-Process Inventory, $169,000; 3. Credit cost of goods sold, $2,084)*

3 5 6 **Problem A4:** Calculating Cost of Goods Sold and the Ending Balances in Inventories

LeBrone Harris is in the custom travel trailer business and is usually working on several custom jobs at one time. On Sept. 1, 1997, LeBrone was working on trailers for Audrey Limbaw and Ilsa Cordone. The costs assigned to these jobs on Sept. 1 were as follows:

| | Client | |
|---|---|---|
| | Limbaw | Cordone |
| Direct materials | $19,500 | $22,875 |
| Direct labor hours | 750 | 1,575 |
| Direct labor dollars | $ 6,000 | $12,993 |
| Factory overhead applied as a percent of direct labor costs | $ 1,260 | $ 2,730 |

During September, LeBrone completed and sold the Limbaw job, and started work on a new job for Sheri Shanks. The costs incurred during September were:

| | Client | | |
| --- | --- | --- | --- |
| | Limbaw | Cordone | Shanks |
| Direct materials. . . . . . . . . . . . . . . . . . . . . . . . . . . . . | $3,750 | $9,375 | $7,500 |
| Direct labor hours . . . . . . . . . . . . . . . . . . . . . . . . . . . | 750 | 375 | 720 |
| Direct labor dollars . . . . . . . . . . . . . . . . . . . . . . . . . . | $5,887 | $3,075 | $6,000 |

The factory overhead incurred during the month was $1,050.

**Required:**

1. Determine the balances in Work-in-Process Inventory, Finished Goods Inventory, and Cost of Goods Sold on Sept. 30.
2. Calculate the over- or underapplied overhead for September.

▶ *(Check Figure: 1. Work-in-Process Inventory, $66,454; 2. $2,092 overapplied)*

3 5 6 **Problem A5:** Answering Questions about a Job Order Costing System

Terry Price runs a small metalworking shop and is usually working on several jobs at any one time. She determines the price for each job by taking a 25% markup, in addition to the costs of materials, direct labor, and factory overhead applied. Terry applies overhead to jobs on the basis of direct labor hours.

On Jan. 1, 1997, Terry predicted that the factory overhead would be $22,750 for the year. She also figured that the direct labor costs would be $31,200.

On Dec. 1, 1997, Terry's firm had only one job (for D. Swain) in process, and the costs associated with that job were as follows:

| | **D. Swain** |
| --- | --- |
| Materials . . . . . . . . . . . . . . . . . . . . . . . . . . . . . . . . . | $ 250 |
| Direct Labor (160 hours) . . . . . . . . . . . . . . . . . . . . | 1,900 |
| Factory Overhead Applied . . . . . . . . . . . . . . . . . . | 1,400 |
| | $3,550 |

There were no completed jobs in finished goods inventory on Dec. 1, but there was a $1,500 balance in Raw Materials at that time.

During December, two new jobs were started, and the following costs were incurred for the three jobs worked on:

| | |
| --- | --- |
| Materials purchased . . . . . . . . . . . . . . . . . . . . . . . . . | $ 500 |

Materials used:

| | |
| --- | --- |
| On Swain job . . . . . . . . . . . . . . . . . . . . . . . . . . . . . | $ 50 |
| On Hamway job . . . . . . . . . . . . . . . . . . . . . . . . . . . | 150 |
| On Spurlin job . . . . . . . . . . . . . . . . . . . . . . . . . . . . | 95 |
| | $ 295 |

Labor:

| | |
| --- | --- |
| Supervisor (160 hours) . . . . . . . . . . . . . . . . . . . . . | $1,600 |
| Direct laborers: | |
| Used on Swain job (20 hours) . . . . . . . . . . . . . | 250 |
| Used on Hamway job (120 hours) . . . . . . . . . . | 1,450 |
| Used on Spurlin job (85 hours) . . . . . . . . . . . . | 1,000 |
| Clean-up crew (40 hours) . . . . . . . . . . . . . . . . . | 100 |
| | $4,400 |

Other Costs:

| | |
|---|---|
| Rent.................................. | $ 500 |
| Insurance............................. | 100 |
| Utilities.............................. | 150 |
| | $ 750 |

The Swain job was completed, shipped, and billed to the customer. The Hamway and Spurlin jobs were incomplete on Dec. 31.

The direct labor and actual factory overhead for the first 11 months of 1997 were $28,000 and $20,000, respectively. The factory overhead applied for this same period was $20,125.

**Required:**

1. What was the Dec. 31 balance in Raw Materials Inventory?
2. What was the overhead rate used during the year?
3. How much was debited to Work-in-Process Inventory during December?
4. What was the cost of goods sold for December? What was the sales revenue?
5. How many direct labor hours were worked in 1997?
6. What was the under- or overapplied overhead for December 1997? For the entire year?

▶ *(Check Figure: 2. $8.75/hr.; 5. 2,525 hours)*

3    **Problem A6:** Completing T-Accounts by Filling in the Unknowns

The Lanier Company, which employs the job order costing method of accounting for its inventories, had the following incomplete general ledger accounts at the end of 1998:

### Raw Materials Inventory

| | | | |
|---|---|---|---|
| 1998 | | | |
| Jan. 1 | 60,000 | Materials used | 201,000 |
| Purchases | 210,000 | | |
| Dec. 31 | _____ | | |

### Work-in-Process Inventory

| | | | |
|---|---|---|---|
| 1998 | | | |
| Jan. 1 | 96,000 | Completed and Transferred | _____ |
| Direct Materials | _____ | | |
| Direct Labor | 264,000 | | |
| Factory Overhead Applied | _____ | | |
| Dec. 31 | _____ | | |

### Finished Goods Inventory

| | | | |
|---|---|---|---|
| 1998 | | | |
| Jan. 1 | _____ | Sold | _____ |
| Completed | 600,000 | | |
| Dec. 31 | 75,000 | | |

### Cost of Goods Sold

| | | | |
|---|---|---|---|
| Sold | 645,000 | | |
| | _____ | | |

*(Continued)*

### Accounts Payable

| | | | |
|---|---|---|---|
| Paid | 216,000 | 1998 Jan. 1 | 6,000 |
| | | Purchases | 210,000 |
| | | Dec. 31 | ——— |

### Factory Overhead Incurred and Applied

| | | | |
|---|---|---|---|
| Indirect Labor | ——— | Applied | ——— |
| Insurance | 90,000 | | |
| Depreciation | 51,000 | | |
| Miscellaneous | 48,000 | | |
| | ——— | | ——— |

### Salaries Payable

| | | | |
|---|---|---|---|
| Paid | 363,000 | 1998 Jan. 1 | 3,000 |
| | | Direct Labor Accrued | ——— |
| | | Indirect Labor Accrued | 105,000 |
| | | Dec. 31 | ——— |

### Additional Information:

a. All purchases are made on account, and no returns were made to the supplier.
b. All raw materials are used directly in production.
c. Factory overhead was predicted to be $300,000 for 1998. The predetermined overhead rate was computed using direct labor hours for activity. The direct labor hours were estimated as 60,000 for the year. The actual direct labor hours for 1998 were 66,000.

### Required:

Complete the T-accounts above by filling in the blanks.

▶ *(Check Figure: Ending balance in Work-in-Process, $291,000; Total debits to Factory Overhead Incurred and Applied = $294,000)*

8  **Problem A7:** Using Activity-Based Costing for a Manufacturer

Swings n' More is a manufacturer of children's playground sets for elementary schools. Swings n' More is currently working on two projects for new schools in Florida, Temple Terrace Elementary and San Antonio Elementary. The costs of direct materials and direct labor for each job are as follows:

| | School | |
|---|---|---|
| | Temple Terrace | San Antonio |
| Direct materials | $1,000 | $1,500 |
| Direct labor costs | $ 400 | $ 900 |

Overhead costs are going to be applied to production using an Activity-Based Costing system. The controller for Swings n' More identifies the following activities and related cost drivers:

| Activity | Cost Driver |
|---|---|
| Welding | number of welds (W) |
| Supervision | number of direct labor hours (DLH) |
| Inspection | time to inspect (IH) |

At the beginning of the year, the controller estimated the annual overhead costs for each of the activities within the production department, as well as the amount of each related cost driver:

| | Estimated Costs for the Year | Estimated Cost Driver |
|---|---|---|
| Welding | $ 800,000 | 1,000,000 welds |
| Supervision | 1,500,000 | 100,000 DLH |
| Inspection | 200,000 | 10,000 IH |
| | $2,500,000 | |

During January, the actual amounts for each cost driver were as follows:

| | Temple Terrace | San Antonio |
|---|---|---|
| Number of welds | 1,000 | 1,500 |
| Direct labor hours | 40 | 90 |
| Hours of inspection | 5 | 7 |

Required: Determine the total costs of each job.

▶ *(Check Figure: Total costs of Temple Terrace job = $2,900)*

## PROBLEMS: SET B

3 5 6† **Problem B1:** Determining the Production Costs for Different Jobs

On Jan. 1, 1997, the Bullock Company estimates that the factory overhead for 1997 will be $500,000. It also estimates its direct labor hours and direct labor costs for the year to be 100,000 hours and $250,000, respectively.

During January 1997, Bullock worked on two jobs, neither of which was completed on Jan. 31. The direct labor hours worked in January were 7,000. The costs incurred in January were as follows:

| | | | |
|---|---|---|---|
| Direct labor: | | | |
| Job 1 (5,000 hours) | | $ 12,500 | |
| Job 2 (2,000 hours) | | 5,200 | $ 17,700 |
| Factory overhead | | | 50,000 |
| Direct materials: | | | |
| Job 1 | | $ 80,000 | |
| Job 2 | | 100,000 | 180,000 |

## Required:

1. Determine the factory overhead assigned to each job if overhead is applied using a predetermined overhead rate, with the activity measured in terms of direct labor hours.
2. Was the factory overhead overapplied or underapplied? By what amount?
3. Determine the total costs assigned to each job in January.

▶ *(Check Figure: 1. Factory overhead applied to Job 1, $25,000; 3. Total costs assigned to Job 2, $115,200)*

† The numbers in the margin refer to the Learning Objectives.

**3  5   Problem B2:** Journal Entries and Income Statement for Job Order Costing

The Lorahill Corporation is a manufacturer that uses the job order costing method of product costing. At the beginning of 1998, it had the following general ledger balances related to production:

| Raw Materials Inventory | |
|---|---|
| 1998 Jan. 1 | 100,000 |

| Work-in-Process Inventory | |
|---|---|
| 1998 Jan. 1 | 250,000 |

| Finished Goods Inventory | |
|---|---|
| 1998 Jan. 1 | 175,000 |

The transactions for January 1998 were as follows:

a. Raw materials purchased, $400,000
b. Indirect materials used in production, $12,500
c. Direct materials used in production, $375,000
d. Direct labor employed, $500,000 (100,000 hours)
e. Additional factory overhead incurred:

| | |
|---|---|
| Indirect labor........................... | $75,000 |
| Utilities .............................. | 10,000 |
| Property taxes .......................... | 5,000 |
| Prepaid insurance expired................. | 2,500 |

f. Factory overhead applied, $1.25 per direct labor hour
g. Cost of jobs completed, $1,050,000
h. Cost of jobs sold, $950,000
i. Sales revenue from jobs during January, $1,500,000

**Required:**

1. Prepare the proper journal entry for each transaction given above.
2. Determine the Jan. 31 balance in each of the three inventory accounts.
3. Prepare a schedule of cost of goods sold for Lorahill Corporation.

▶ *(Check Figure: 2. Finished Goods Inventory = $275,000)*

**2  3  5  6   Problem B3:** Making Journal Entries, Maintaining Subsidiary Ledgers, and Closing Overhead

The Bedingfield Company uses a job order costing system to account for its production process. At the beginning of 1998, it had the following balances in its inventory accounts:

| | |
|---|---|
| Raw Materials Inventory..................... | $36,000 |
| Work-in-Process Inventory................... | 33,000 |
| Finished Goods Inventory.................... | 57,000 |

The subsidiary ledgers for the general ledger accounts showed the following balances:

| Raw Materials Inventory | | Work-in-Process Inventory | | Finished Goods Inventory | |
|---|---|---|---|---|---|
| Part 23 . . . . . . | $11,000 | Job 99 . . . . . . | $33,000 | Job 98 . . . . . . | $23,000 |
| Part 45 . . . . . . | 25,000 | | | Job 97 . . . . . . | 34,000 |

During 1998, the following transactions took place:

Purchases (all on account):

| | |
|---|---|
| Part 23. . . . . . . . . . . . . . . . . . . . . . . . . . . . . . . . . . . . . | $25,000 |
| Part 45. . . . . . . . . . . . . . . . . . . . . . . . . . . . . . . . . . . . . | 34,000 |
| | $59,000 |

Usage of direct materials:

| | Part 23 | Part 45 | Totals |
|---|---|---|---|
| Job 99 . . . . . . . . . . . . . . . . . . . . . . . . . . . . . . . . . . | $ 1,100 | $ 900 | $ 2,000 |
| Job 100 . . . . . . . . . . . . . . . . . . . . . . . . . . . . . . . . . | 17,000 | 12,000 | 29,000 |
| Job 101 . . . . . . . . . . . . . . . . . . . . . . . . . . . . . . . . . | 6,000 | 8,000 | 14,000 |
| | $24,100 | $20,900 | $45,000 |

Direct labor (all paid for):

| | |
|---|---|
| Job 99 . . . . . . . . . . . . . . . . . . . . . . . . . . . . . . . . . . . | $23,000 |
| Job 100 . . . . . . . . . . . . . . . . . . . . . . . . . . . . . . . . . . | 27,000 |
| Job 101 . . . . . . . . . . . . . . . . . . . . . . . . . . . . . . . . . . | 19,000 |
| | $69,000 |

Factory overhead:

| | |
|---|---|
| Insurance expired . . . . . . . . . . . . . . . . . . . . . . . . . | $ 1,400 |
| Property taxes. . . . . . . . . . . . . . . . . . . . . . . . . . . . | 2,000 |
| Depreciation: machinery. . . . . . . . . . . . . . . . . . . . | 3,000 |
| Rent: building . . . . . . . . . . . . . . . . . . . . . . . . . . . . | 14,000 |
| Salaries (all paid for). . . . . . . . . . . . . . . . . . . . . . | 21,000 |
| | $41,400 |

Factory overhead is applied at 40% of direct labor cost. During the year 1998, Job 99 was completed and Jobs 97 and 98 were sold on account (at a 100% markup over cost). Jobs 100 and 101 were still in process at year-end.

**Required:**

1. Record the journal entries for 1998. Ignore for now the closing entry for Factory Overhead.
2. Determine the balances in the general ledger accounts for Raw Materials Inventory, Work-in-Process Inventory, and Finished Goods Inventory. Also show the subsidiary ledgers for each inventory account.
3. Prepare the closing entry for Factory Overhead. Assume that the amount of over- or under-applied overhead is material and must be allocated among the appropriate accounts.

▶ (Check Figure: 2. Work-in-Process Inventory, $107,400; 3. Debit Cost of Goods Sold, $3,396)

3 5 6   **Problem B4:** Determining the Ending Balances in Inventories

The Hurricane Proof Construction Company builds custom homes and uses the job order costing method to keep track of its different buyers. Hurricane Proof applies overhead to each home (using direct labor hours as its measure of activity) on the basis of an overhead rate determined at the beginning of the year. At the end of March 1997, Hurricane Proof is working on two homes. The cost information related to these two homes is as follows:

| | Vickers Home | Dryetis Home |
|---|---|---|
| Direct materials. . . . . . . . . . . . . . . . . . . . . . . . . . . . . . . . . . . . . . . . . . . | $24,000 | $31,000 |
| Direct labor (at $5/hour) . . . . . . . . . . . . . . . . . . . . . . . . . . . . . . . . . . . | 60,000 | 57,000 |
| Factory overhead applied. . . . . . . . . . . . . . . . . . . . . . . . . . . . . . . . . . | 42,000 | 39,900 |

During April, the following direct costs are incurred to continue work on the Vickers and Dryetis homes and to start building a house for Craven:

| | Vickers | Dryetis | Craven |
|---|---|---|---|
| Direct materials . . . . . . . . . . . . . . . . . . . . . . . . . . . . . . . . . | $18,000 | $24,000 | $18,000 |
| Direct labor (at $5/hour) . . . . . . . . . . . . . . . . . . . . . . . . . . | 15,750 | 25,200 | 37,800 |

The overhead incurred in April was $60,000. The Vickers and Dryetis homes were finished during April, and the Vickers home was sold for $210,000. There were no completed homes in finished goods on Apr. 1.

**Required:**

1. Determine the Apr. 30 balances in (a) Work-in-Process Inventory; (b) Finished Goods Inventory; and (c) Cost of Goods Sold.
2. Calculate the over- or underapplied overhead for April.

▶ *(Check Figure: 1. Work-in-Process Inventory, $82,260; 2. $4,875 underapplied)*

3 5 6 **Problem B5:** Answering Questions about a Job Order Costing System

The Roswell Company uses a job order costing system and had one incomplete job (Job 7) on December 31, 1997.

**Job 7**

| | |
|---|---|
| Direct materials. . . . . . . . . . . . . . . . . . . . . . . . . . . . | $ 60,000 |
| Direct labor (960 hours) . . . . . . . . . . . . . . . . . . . | 48,000 |
| Factory overhead (based on direct labor hours) . | 24,000 |
| | $132,000 |

The December 31, 1997, balances in Raw Materials Inventory and Finished Goods Inventory were $24,000 and $111,000, respectively. On Jan. 1, 1998, Roswell estimated its direct labor and factory overhead costs to be $3,570,000 and $1,890,000, respectively. Overhead is applied on the basis of direct labor hours.

During January, the following costs were incurred:

| | | |
|---|---|---|
| Purchases: | | |
|     Direct materials . . . . . . . . . . . . . . . . . . . . . . . . . . . . . . . . . . . . . | $84,000 | |
|     Indirect materials. . . . . . . . . . . . . . . . . . . . . . . . . . . . . . . . . . . . . | 15,000 | $99,000 |
| Requisitions: | | |
|     Direct materials: | | |
|         Job 7 . . . . . . . . . . . . . . . . . . . . . . . . . . . . . . . . . . . . . . . . . . . | $ 9,000 | |
|         Job 8 . . . . . . . . . . . . . . . . . . . . . . . . . . . . . . . . . . . . . . . . . . . | 48,000 | |
|     Indirect materials. . . . . . . . . . . . . . . . . . . . . . . . . . . . . . . . . . . . . | 21,000 | 78,000 |

*(Continued)*

| Production labor: | | |
|---|---:|---:|
| Used on Job 7 (200 hours) | $10,500 | |
| Used on Job 8 (800 hours) | 39,000 | |
| Foremen's salaries (120 hours) | 4,320 | |
| Maintenance (200 hours) | 4,500 | |
| Security (80 hours) | 2,400 | 60,720 |
| | | |
| Factory overhead applied: | | |
| Job 7 | $ 5,400 | |
| Job 8 | 21,600 | 27,000 |
| | | |
| Insurance | $ 2,400 | |
| Property taxes | 2,700 | |
| Utilities | 1,350 | 6,450 |

Job 7 was finished in January and sold for $225,000. Job 8 was unfinished on Jan. 31, 1998.

**Required:**

1. What was the Jan. 31 balance in Raw Materials Inventory?
2. How much was debited to Work-in-Process Inventory during January?
3. What was the factory overhead rate in 1997?
4. What was the factory overhead rate in 1998?
5. How many hours of direct labor were estimated for 1998?
6. What was the under- or overapplied overhead for January 1998?
7. If the Jan. 31 balance in Finished Goods Inventory was zero, what was the cost of goods sold for January?

▶ *(Check Figure: 2. $133,500; 5. 70,000 hours)*

3 **Problem B6:** Filling in the Blanks in T-Accounts

The Inez Publishing Co. publishes yearbooks for high schools and universities and uses a job order costing system to keep track of the orders from different schools. It keeps its records in T-accounts, which are shown in incomplete form for 1997.

| Raw Materials Inventory | | | |
|---|---:|---|---:|
| 1997 | | | |
| Jan. 1 | 20,000 | Direct Materials | 130,000 |
| Purchases | _____ | Indirect Materials | 10,000 |
| | | | |
| Dec. 31 | 60,000 | | |

| Work-in-Process Inventory | | | |
|---|---:|---|---:|
| 1997 | | | |
| Jan. 1 | 150,000 | | |
| Direct Materials | _____ | Cost of Goods Completed | _____ |
| Direct Labor | _____ | | |
| Factory Overhead Applied | _____ | | |
| | | | |
| Dec. 31 | 120,000 | | |

*(Continued)*

## Finished Goods Inventory

| | | | |
|---|---|---|---|
| 1997 | | | |
| Jan. 1 | 120,000 | Cost of Goods Sold | 360,000 |
| Cost of Goods Completed | ———— | | |
| | | | |
| Dec. 31 | ———— | | |

## Cost of Goods Sold

| | | |
|---|---|---|
| ———— | | |

## Factory Overhead Incurred and Applied

| | | | |
|---|---|---|---|
| Indirect Materials | ———— | | |
| Indirect Labor | 100,000 | Factory Overhead Applied | ———— |
| Insurance | ———— | | |
| Depreciation | ———— | | |
| Other | 30,000 | | |
| | ———— | | ———— |

## Salaries Payable

| | | | |
|---|---|---|---|
| | | 1997 | |
| Salaries Paid | 280,000 | Jan. 1 | 16,000 |
| | | Direct Labor | 200,000 |
| | | Indirect Labor | ———— |
| | | | |
| | | Dec. 31 | ———— |

## Prepaid Insurance

| | | | |
|---|---|---|---|
| 1997 | | | |
| Jan. 1 | 6,000 | Insurance Used | 2,000 |
| | | | |
| Dec. 31 | 4,000 | | |

## Accumulated Depreciation

| | | | |
|---|---|---|---|
| | | 1997 | |
| | | Jan. 1 | 30,000 |
| | | Depreciation | ———— |
| | | | |
| | | Dec. 31 | 34,000 |

**Additional Information:**

a. All purchases are for cash.
b. Factory overhead is applied at a rate of 70% of direct labor cost.

**Required:**

Complete the T-accounts above by inserting the missing information into the blanks.

▶ *(Check Figure: Ending balance in Work-in-Process, $120,000; Total debits to Factory Overhead Incurred and Applied = $146,000)*

**8  Problem B7:** Using Activity-Based Costing for a Manufacturer

Mr. Muscle, a manufacturer of custom weight-lifting equipment for body building gymnasiums, is working on jobs for two customers—Bodies R' Us and Bodies in Motion. Mr. Muscle's controller, Sam Swartzenager, decides to use Activity-Based Costing for determining the conversion costs of each job. Sam identifies the following activities and related cost drivers:

| Activity | Cost Driver |
|---|---|
| Assembly | number of machine hours (MH) |
| Material handling | number of parts (PT) |
| Testing | hours of testing time (HTT) |

At the beginning of 1997, Sam estimated the annual overhead costs for each of the activities within production, as well as the amount of each related cost driver:

|  | Estimated Costs for the Year | Estimated Cost Driver |
|---|---|---|
| Assembly | $125,000 | 5,000 MH |
| Material handling | 36,000 | 3,600 PT |
| Testing | 30,000 | 600 HTT |
|  | $191,000 | |

During the month, the actual direct materials and the amounts for each cost driver were as follows:

|  | Bodies R' Us | Bodies in Motion |
|---|---|---|
| Direct materials | $3,000 | $2,500 |
| Machine hours | 80 | 60 |
| Number of parts | 60 | 50 |
| Hours of testing time | 8 | 10 |

**Required:**

Determine the total costs of the jobs for Bodies R' Us and Bodies in Motion.

▶ *(Check Figure: Total costs of Bodies R' Us job = $6,000)*

**DECISION PROBLEM**

The Lutz Manufacturing Company uses job order costing to account for its production during the year. At the beginning of 1997, its accountant made the following estimates for the year:

|  | Estimated Factory Overhead | Estimated Direct Labor Hours |
|---|---|---|
| January | $ 30,000 | 2,000 |
| February | 40,000 | 4,000 |
| March | 60,000 | 8,000 |
| ⋮ | ⋮ | ⋮ |
| July | 170,000 | 30,000 |
| ⋮ | ⋮ | ⋮ |
| December | 50,000 | 6,000 |
| For the year | $750,000 | 100,000 |

During the months of February and July, Lutz's results were as follows:

|  | February | July |
|---|---|---|
| Actual factory overhead | $42,000 | $162,000 |
| Number of jobs worked on | 2 | 4 |
| Direct labor hours: | | |
| Job: . | . | . |
| . | | . |
| . | . | . |
| 6 | 2,400 | . |
| 7 | 1,200 | . |
| . | . | . |
| . | . | . |
| 21 | — | 12,000 |
| 22 | — | 8,000 |
| 23 | — | 10,000 |
| 24 | — | 2,000 |

Jobs 6 and 7 were the only ones worked on in February, and Jobs 21 through 24 were the only ones worked on during July.

**Required:**

1. Find the overhead that would probably be assigned to Job 6 in February and to Job 21 in July if Lutz was not using a predetermined factory overhead rate.
2. Determine the overhead to be assigned to the same jobs if Lutz employs a predetermined factory overhead rate, based on direct labor hours.
3. Using the results you obtained in part 2, determine the overapplied or underapplied factory overhead in February and in July.

## ETHICS CASE

The Blackstone Instruments Division of a large electronics company produces scientific instruments made to customer specifications. A significant portion of Blackstone's business is with the federal government on a "cost-plus" basis, which means that the profit on a contract is based on a negotiated percentage of the allowable costs assigned to the contract. Allowable costs are defined in the contract as the materials and labor that can be traced directly to the contract plus overhead based on a predetermined rate using an appropriate application base. The remainder of Blackstone's business is with nongovernment customers on a "fixed-price" basis. For these contracts the price to the customer is the same regardless of the costs incurred in completing the contract.

During 1998, Blackstone expects to spend most of its time working on two contracts, one for the Department of Defense and another for Drummond Aircraft. The contract with the Department of Defense involves a great deal of labor time (but relatively little machine time) for the manual insertion of a large number of parts into each unit of the instrument. Conversely, the contract with Drummond involves a highly automated process where a significant amount of machine time (but very little labor time) is needed to insert the instrument's many parts.

At the beginning of the year, Blackstone's controller decided to apply overhead on the basis of a single measure of activity, but was uncertain as to whether direct labor hours or machine hours was the more appropriate measure of activity. After a careful study of the relationship of overhead costs to the different measures of activity, the controller reported to the president that most of the overhead costs are much more closely related to the number of machine hours than to the number of direct labor hours. Therefore, she recommended that machine hours be employed as the company's overhead application base.

Nevertheless, the president decided to use direct labor hours as the application base, because the company's profits would be significantly higher than they would be if machine hours were used instead. His reasoning was as follows: "Our profit on government contracts is based on the amount of costs assigned to that project. So it makes sense to load up on the costs assigned to the government contracts and cut down on the costs assigned to the nongovernment contracts. Since the contract with the Department of Defense requires a lot of labor but very little machine time, the most effective way to assign a large amount of costs to the government contract is to use a factory overhead rate that is based on the number of direct labor hours. If we use a rate based on the number of machine hours, then the amount of costs assigned to the government contract will be much lower, and our profits will be less than they could have been. Besides, if we use direct labor hours as the application base, profits on the Drummond contract will also be higher than they would have been."

The controller has no quarrel with the president's logic, but has some doubts about the ethics of using that logic to choose an application base. However, she is reluctant to question the president on the matter, and agrees to use direct labor hours to apply factory overhead to all the jobs worked on in 1998.

**Required:**

1. How can the use of direct labor hours instead of machine hours increase Blackstone's profits on contracts with both the Department of Defense and with Drummond Aircraft?
2. What is your opinion about the ethics of using direct labor hours as the measure of activity for applying factory overhead to both governmental and private contracts?

## OBJECTIVE ASSIGNMENT ANSWERS

### True/False

1. T    2. T    3. T    4. F    5. T

### Multiple Choice

1. c    2. b    3. d    4. d    5. b
6. d    7. b    8. a    9. d    10. e

# Process Costing

**LEARNING OBJECTIVES**

After studying this chapter, you should be able to do the following:

1 Explain what process costing is and how it differs from job order costing

2 Explain what equivalent whole units are and how to calculate them for a process

3 Organize the solution to a process costing problem into its three steps

4 Determine the number of units completed in a process and the number still incomplete at the end of the period

5 Prepare a production report that determines the cost per equivalent whole unit

6 Allocate the production costs between the complete and the incomplete units in the summary of costs report

7 Record the journal entries to account for the flow of production costs from one inventory account to another

8 Explain how the just-in-time inventory philosophy can help an organization reduce its costs by preventing waste

9 Define the key terms listed at the end of the chapter

**CHAPTER OUTLINE**

**THE PROCESS COSTING METHOD** • Equivalent Whole Units • **BASIC STEPS IN ACCOUNTING FOR THE PROCESS COSTING METHOD** • **PROCESS COSTING ILLUSTRATED: PROCESSING DEPARTMENT 1** • Step 1 for Processing Department 1: Tracing the Physical Flow • Step 2 for Processing Department 1: Preparing a Production Report • Step 3 for Processing Department 1: Preparing a Summary of Costs Report • Journal Entries and T-Accounts for Processing Department 1 • **THE ILLUSTRATION CONTINUED: PROCESSING DEPARTMENT 2** • Step 1 for Processing Department 2: Tracing the Physical Flow • Step 2 for Processing Department 2: Preparing a Production Report • Step 3 for Processing Department 2: Preparing a Summary of Costs Report • Journal Entries and T-Accounts for Processing Department 2 • **THE ILLUSTRATION CONCLUDED: SOME FINAL COMMENTS** • Combining Direct Labor and Factory Overhead • Raw Materials Added at the End of Processing • Sale of Goods • The Flow of Costs from Beginning to End • **AN OVERVIEW OF PROCESS COSTING** • **JUST-IN-TIME (JIT) PHILOSOPHY** • "Just-in-Time" versus "Just-in-Case" • Major Concepts of the JIT Philosophy

There are two different methods of accounting for the production costs of a manufacturer: job order costing and process costing. Job order costing is used to account for the costs of a product whenever small numbers of identifiable units, or batches of units, are produced to customer specifications. Job order costing must accumulate costs by individual job and keep the costs of one job separate from the costs of any other job.

In this chapter we will look at process costing. **Process costing** is used to account for costs in manufacturing situations that have the following characteristics:

1. Units are produced continuously in large batches through one or more processing departments. Once units are started within a department, work on them continues until it is completed, after which they are transferred to another processing department or to finished goods.
2. Units are all exactly the same. They have all been processed in the same manner, each taking the same amount of materials, time, and attention. Each unit is assigned exactly the same cost as any other unit.

The manufacture of units with these characteristics takes place in a series of steps, or processes. For example, the manufacture of potato chips begins with the cleaning process, in which the potatoes are washed and peeled. Next, in the mixing process, the potatoes are cut and seasonings are added. Then the potatoes are cooked and allowed to dry until crisp. Finally, the potato chips are packaged in bags and boxed in cartons and sent to finished goods to await sale. Other manufacturing industries that use process costing include paper, plastics, glass, steel, paint, sugar, and textiles.

Process costing can also be adapted to organizations that are in the service industry. For any service that is repetitive in large numbers, with each repetition being virtually the same, the calculation of an average cost of providing that service to many customers might be appropriate. For example, when H&R Block prepares thousands of 1040 tax returns, the average cost of preparing those returns would involve process costing. The same would be true for calculating: the average cost of washing cars at a car wash; the average cost per customer waited on by a waiter/waitress at a restaurant; the average cost of reading X-rays or processing a blood test at a hospital; the average cost of installing security systems in homes; and the average cost of processing a deposit at a bank.

Figure 1 shows the typical flow of inventoriable costs through the accounts for a manufacturer that has two processing departments. The order in which the physical product, and its related costs, flow from one work-in-process account to another in Figure 1 is called a *sequential flow*. The units start out in process 1, go to process 2, and then to process 3 and 4 (if they exist) in numerical sequence, with one process following another.

The flow from one process to another can take many forms. For example, assume that a company manufactures swim goggles. In process 1 the rubber goggles themselves are produced, and in process 2 the plastic face mask is produced. Then in process 3 the two parts are assembled into a finished pair of goggles, and in process 4 the goggles are packaged. This flow would not take place in perfect sequence, because processes 1 and 2 would be simultaneous. Instead, the flow would look like Figure 2.

## THE PROCESS COSTING METHOD

Under the process costing method, we determine the cost of a unit produced as follows:

1. Determine the total costs of a processing department for an entire period.
2. Determine the number of units produced within that department during the period.

**Figure 1** Flow of Inventoriable Costs: Process Costing

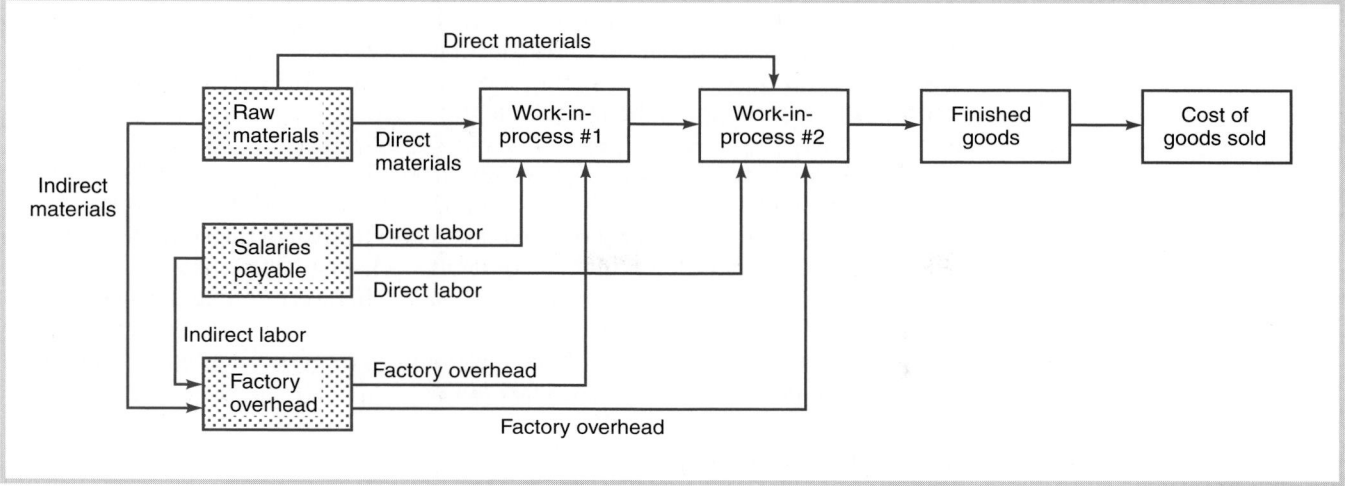

3. Divide the total costs by the number of units produced to get a cost per unit, which is the same for all the units produced.

Let's look at two simple examples of how we do this.

# DEON COMPANY

The Deon Company produces an item that is processed though only one manufacturing stage. At the end of that one process the units are complete and are transferred to finished goods. During August, 80,000 units were started and completed, and $80,000 of production costs were incurred. There were no beginning or ending inventories of work-in-process for the month. The cost per unit for Deon in August is simply:

$$\text{Cost per unit} = \frac{\$80,000}{80,000 \text{ units}} = \$1$$

What makes this example so simple is that there are no beginning or ending inventories of work-in-process. In other words, all the units that were started during the period were completed by the end of the period. Now, let's assume that there is an ending inventory of work-in-process.

**Figure 2** Flow of Inventoriable Costs: Nonsequential Order

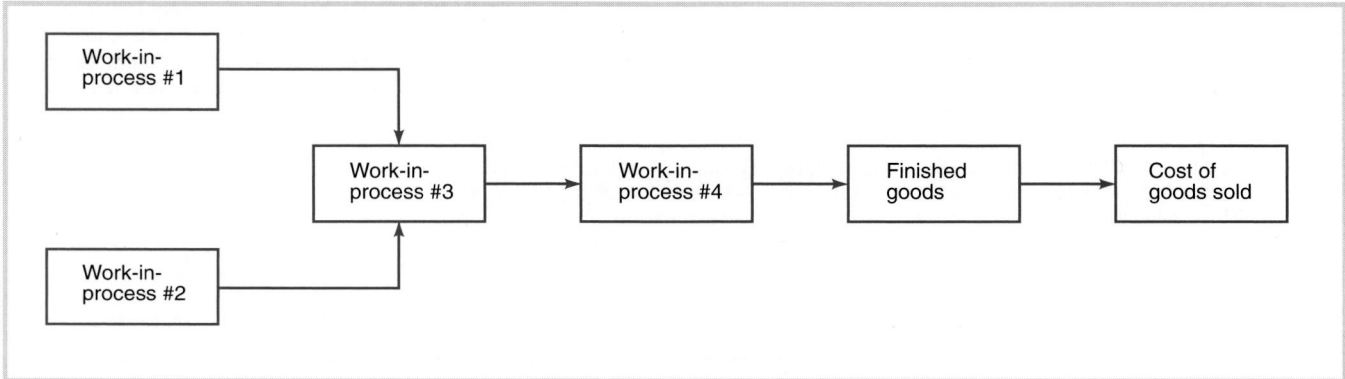

Assume for the Deon Company that: (1) there was no beginning inventory of work-in-process; (2) 80,000 units were started during August; (3) 76,000 units were completed by the end of the month; (4) the remaining 4,000 incomplete units were left one-half completed (that is, half of the total processing time had elapsed); and (5) the production costs incurred during the month were $78,000, and they were incurred evenly throughout the manufacturing process.

How do we calculate the cost per unit now?

Do we divide the production costs of $78,000 by the 80,000 units started? No, because this would assign the same amount of cost to each of the completed units as would be assigned to each of the units that are only one-half completed.

Do we divide the $78,000 by the 76,000 units that were completed, and thereby ignore the 4,000 incomplete units altogether? No, because the $78,000 of production costs also helped to process the 4,000 half-completed units. Therefore, some of the costs should be assigned to those 4,000 units.

Learning Objective 2

Explain what equivalent whole units are and how to calculate them for a process.

## Equivalent Whole Units

Clearly, we have to divide the $78,000 by the finished units plus some portion of the unfinished units. If the 4,000 units were exactly one-half finished at the end of the period, then the work—and the costs—that went into them are equivalent to the work and the costs that go into 2,000 finished units.

# Process Costing: For Hockey Fans the Puck Starts Here

We cherish some sporting gear: the baseball glove anointed with oil, golf clubs hooded under monogrammed cozies, the handmade, ebony-inlaid, two-piece pool cue caressed with expensive waxes.

But nobody loves the hockey puck. Even the name is cold and hard. Puck: breaker of teeth, blackener of eyes, an obsidian villain that at best evokes indifference from Moose Jaw to Minnetonka. It may sound friendly in French—la rondelle—but even in Quebec, hockey's gelid Garden of Eden, no one thinks much of, or much about, the game's object of contention. Is there nothing, then, to say for this neglected disk? On the contrary.

There is some debate over when the first hockey game was played, and the genesis of the modern puck is equally uncertain. But hockey lore holds that the first disk took shape in the 1880s when the owner of the Victoria Skating Rink in Montreal sliced off the top and bottom of a solid rubber ball, so it would slide rather than bounce across the ice.

Most of the pucks found in sporting goods stores are Czechoslovakian-made cheapies. But virtually all game pucks used in the National, American, Western, Ontario, and Quebec Hockey Leagues, and many of those in collegiate play, are made for In Glas Co Ltd. of Sherbrooke, Quebec, at the Baron Rubber Ltd. factory in St.-Jérôme, 20 miles north of Montreal.

Light and amber blocks of natural and synthetic rubber are the basic ingredients from which pucks spring. Following an industrial recipe, a technician loads the spongy slabs of raw rubber (at a 1.9 ratio of natural to synthetic material) into the bin of a machine called a Banbury. The operator also pours in an activator, a chemical agent such as sulfur, that affects how quickly the rubber will cure. Carbon black, which gives the mixture color and influences the chemical reaction, and oils, which also helps in the mixing process, are added to the conglomeration, which is then blended by two large rotor blades.

After being thoroughly mixed for about four minutes, the hot, 65-kilogram glob drops out of the bin onto motorized rollers, which squeeze out bubbles and flatten the wad. The resulting sheet is then cut off the rollers, rolled up and cooled in a bath. Samples are taken to ensure that the batch will produce a rubber of the desired hardness, resiliency and density. When the lab gives the go-ahead, the rolled sheets of rubber are loaded into another machine, called a Barwell, which produces the

blanks from which the pucks will be molded. The Barwell pushes the rubber through holes that admit the precise amount of material needed to form each one-inch thick, three-inch diameter, six-ounce puck. The blanks then move on a conveyor belt through a refrigerated compartment, which slows the curing process before the final molding.

Once they've been rolled, squeezed and cooked into existence, pucks are popped out of the molds and packed in wooden cases, 5,760 to a crate. Those destined for NHL action go to the In Glas Co facility in Sherbrooke, where the league logo is silk-screened on one side, team emblems the other. In Glas Co sells game pucks for about $1 apiece in boxes of 100; practice pucks cost about 65 cents each.

NHL clubs store game pucks in freezers to deaden their bounce. During games, two or three dozen are kept on hand at the scorer's table. Denis Drolet, In Glas Co's president, says each NHL team buys about 5,000 game and 10,000 practice pucks a year, which means that the league as a whole goes through more than 100,000 game pucks and 200,000 unadorned practice disks.

Thus, if we add together the finished units and an *equivalent number of finished units* that are still in process, we can spread the total costs over the appropriate number of units—that is, the *equivalent whole units*. Here's how:

76,000 completed units + (4,000 in process × 1/2 completed) = 78,000 equivalent whole units

$$\text{Cost per unit} = \frac{\$78,000}{78,000 \text{ equivalent whole units}} = \$1 \text{ per equivalent whole unit}$$

**Equivalent whole units** is thus a measure of activity in process costing that expresses the number of partially completed units in terms of an equivalent number of fully completed units. It indicates how many fully completed units could have been produced if the materials, time, effort, and energy that went into the partially completed units had been used instead to produce fully completed units. For example, the 80,000 units above, consisting of 76,000 fully completed units and 4,000 half-completed units, can be shown graphically:

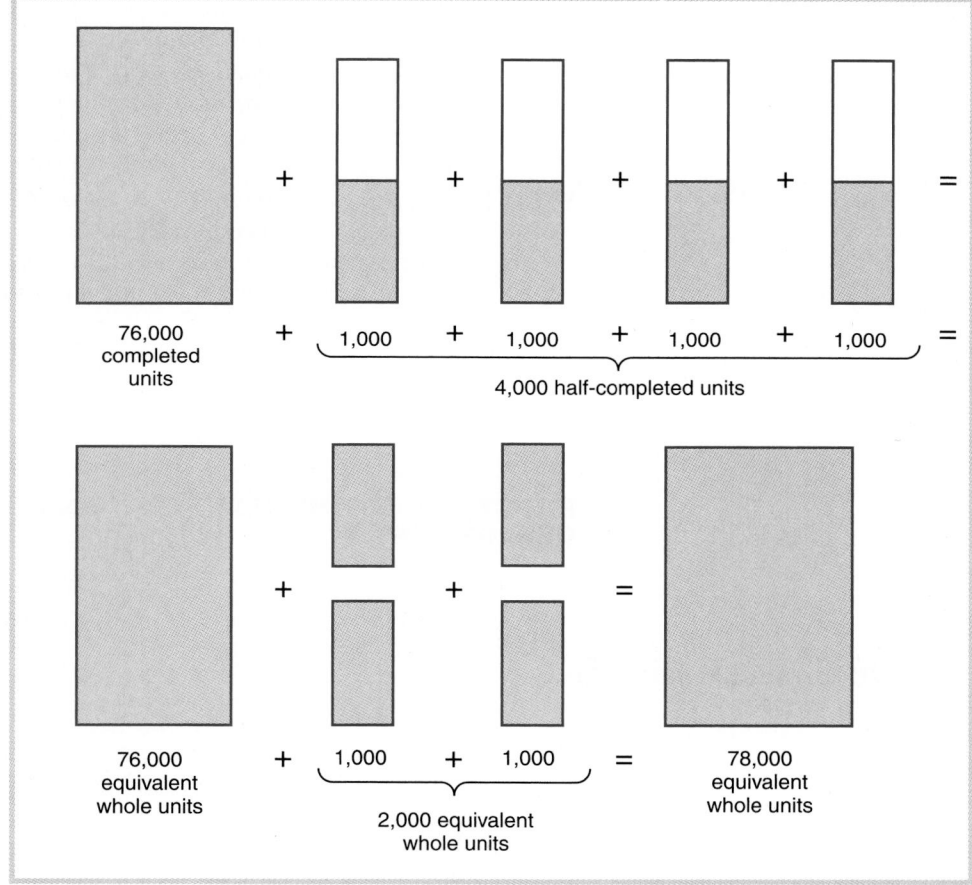

Naturally, the unfinished units can't be combined physically to form finished units, as this illustration seems to suggest. But the boxes illustrate graphically how the amount of materials, time, effort, and energy needed to make 4,000 half-completed units equals—or is the *equivalent* of—the amount needed to make 2,000 fully completed units. Since both complete and incomplete units are now expressed by a single common denominator—equivalent whole units—we are now adding together two similar items rather than two dissimilar items.

1. What are the characteristics of a production environment that uses process costing?
2. What are equivalent whole units? How do they differ from the number of units started? The number of units completed?

Learning Objective 3

Organize the solution to a process costing problem into its three steps

## BASIC STEPS IN ACCOUNTING FOR THE PROCESS COSTING METHOD

The Deon Company example illustrates some basic ideas about how to determine the cost of units produced. Now we will look in greater detail at the accounting procedures involved in process costing, using a company that has two distinct processing departments. The basic accounting steps for each processing department are as follows:

**STEP 1:** *Tracing the physical flow.* First, you determine two things: the number of units completed during the period and the number of incomplete units still in production at the end of the period (the ending inventory).

**STEP 2:** *Preparing a production report.* Next, using the completed units and the ending work-in-process determined in step 1, you calculate the equivalent whole units, the total costs to account for, and the cost per equivalent whole unit. These three calculations constitute a **production report.**

**STEP 3:** *Preparing a summary of costs report.* After the production report has been completed, you need to distribute the total costs to account for between: (1) the completed units and (2) the units in the ending work-in-process. This distribution is shown in a **summary of costs report.**

We will explain these three basic steps in the following discussion.

## PROCESS COSTING ILLUSTRATED: PROCESSING DEPARTMENT 1

# TROPICAL BLENDS

Tropical Blends produces citrus beverages, which are sold to customers, who distribute the products under their own private labels. To make one of its product lines, an orange drink called Orangeade, Tropical Blends processes orange juice into Orangeade in two distinct stages. In the first stage—which takes place in processing department 1— oranges are cut and squeezed, after which the juice is pasteurized for several hours. The juice is then transferred to the second stage— processing department 2—where a water solution containing preservatives and artificial sweetners is added evenly throughout this stage of the process. At the end of the second stage, Orangeade is pumped into large storage containers in the finished goods warehouse, where it awaits shipment by tanker trucks to customers who bottle the drink for sale to retail stores.

The steps in this production process are summarized in the following diagram:

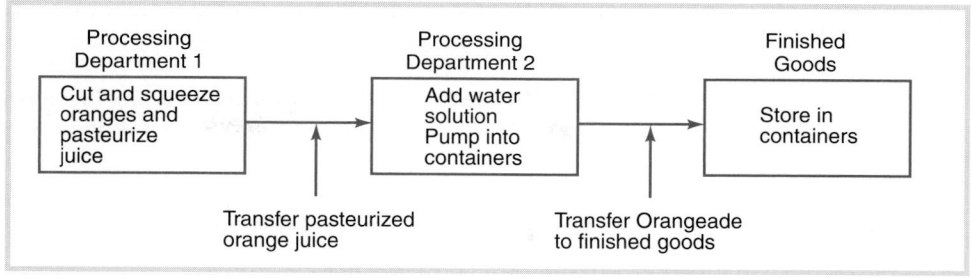

On Aug. 1, Tropical Blends had 10,000 gallons of orange juice in process, one-fifth complete (that is, one-fifth of the total processing time had elapsed). These gallons were started in the pasteurization process on the last day of July and will be completed in August. The costs of the 10,000 gallons incurred in July were as follows:

| | |
|---|---|
| Direct materials (orange juice) . . . . . . . . . . . . . . . | $30,000 |
| Direct labor . . . . . . . . . . . . . . . . . . . . . . . . . . . . . | 1,000 |
| Factory overhead . . . . . . . . . . . . . . . . . . . . . . . . | 7,570 |
| | $38,570 |

During August, 40,000 additional gallons were started in processing department 1. At the end of the day on Aug. 31, there were still 20,000 gallons in process, three-fourths complete. The pasteurization process for the 20,000 gallons will be completed at the beginning of September. All other gallons processed during August were completed during the month and transferred to processing department 2.

The costs incurred in the month of August by processing department 1 were as follows:

| | |
|---|---|
| Direct materials (orange juice) . . . . . . . . . . . . . . . | $120,000 |
| Direct labor . . . . . . . . . . . . . . . . . . . . . . . . . . . . . | 21,500 |
| Factory overhead . . . . . . . . . . . . . . . . . . . . . . . . | 172,430 |
| | $313,930 |

The direct labor and factory overhead costs (the conversion costs) are incurred evenly throughout the pasteurization process.

Information concerning Tropical Blends' processing department 2 will be provided after we complete the discussion of processing department 1.

Learning 4
Objective

Determine the number of units completed in a process and the number still incomplete at the end of the period

## Step 1 for Processing Department 1: Tracing the Physical Flow

The first of the three basic steps in process costing is to trace the physical flow. In this step, remember, we determine two things: (1) the number of units completed during the period; and (2) the number of units remaining in work-in-process at the end of the period. This information is necessary for the production report to be prepared in step 2. In many process costing problems, only one of these two quantities is known; the other must be determined. In most situations, we know the beginning inventory and we know the number of units that were started. The addition of these two represents the *total units to account for* in production.

$$\text{Beginning inventory in work-in-process} + \text{units started} = \text{total units to account for}$$

If we know the number of units in the ending work-in-process, we can calculate the number of units completed during the period, as follows:

$$\text{Total units to account for} - \text{ending inventory in work-in-process} = \text{units completed}$$

Conversely, if we know the number of units completed, we can determine the number of unfinished units in the ending work-in-process:

$$\text{Total units to account for} - \text{units completed} = \text{ending inventory in work-process}$$

In our Tropical Blends example, the ending inventory is given, but the number of units completed is not. Therefore we do the following calculation to determine the completed units for August:

|  | Gallons |
|---|---|
| Beginning inventory, processing department 1 | 10,000 |
| Add: Units started | 40,000 |
| Total units to account for | 50,000 |
| Less: Ending inventory, processing department 1 | 20,000 |
| Units completed and transferred to processing department 2 | 30,000 |

<table>
<tr><td>Learning Objective 5</td><td></td></tr>
</table>

Prepare a production report that determines the cost per equivalent whole unit

## Step 2 for Processing Department 1: Preparing a Production Report

Once the number of completed units (30,000) and the number of units in the ending inventory of work-in-process (20,000) are known, a production report is prepared. The purpose of a *production report* is to calculate a cost per equivalent whole unit for each different inventoriable cost: direct materials, direct labor, and factory overhead. A production report for processing department 1 is shown in Exhibit 1. It is essentially divided into three sections:

1. In columns 1–4, the equivalent whole units are calculated.
2. In column 5, all the costs associated with the production for the period—the **total costs to account for**—are accumulated. In most situations the total costs to account for will be found by adding together the costs of the beginning inventory and the costs incurred during the period.
3. In column 6, the appropriate costs are divided by the equivalent whole units to get the **cost per equivalent whole unit (CPEWU).**

Let's take a closer look at each column in this production report for processing department 1.

### Beginning Inventory and Units Started and Completed

In Exhibit 1, we assume that the 10,000 gallons in inventory on Aug. 1 are the first 10,000 gallons completed in August. When we traced the physical flow of gallons, we found that 30,000 gallons were completed in August. If 10,000 of this total came from the beginning inventory, then the remaining 20,000 gallons must have come from the gallons that were started during the month.

$$\text{Units started and completed} = \text{total units completed} - \text{beginning inventory}$$

$$20,000 = 30,000 - 10,000$$

**Exhibit 1** Production Report for Processing Department 1

| Inventoriable Cost | Units Completed (gal) | | | (2) Ending Inventory Work-in-Process | (3) Fraction Completed This Period | (4) Equivalent Whole Units | (5) Total Costs to Account for | (6) Cost per Equivalent Whole Unit |
|---|---|---|---|---|---|---|---|---|
| | (1a) Beginning Inventory Work-in-Process | (1b) Fraction Completed This Period | (1c) Started and Completed This Period | | | | | |
| Direct materials. . | 10,000 | 0 | 20,000 | 20,000 | 1 | 40,000 | $120,000 | $3.00 |
| Direct labor . . . . . | 10,000 | $\frac{4}{5}$ | 20,000 | 20,000 | $\frac{3}{4}$ | 43,000 | 21,500 | .50 |
| Factory overhead | 10,000 | $\frac{4}{5}$ | 20,000 | 20,000 | $\frac{3}{4}$ | 43,000 | 172,430 | 4.01 |

30,000
Completed

$313,930    $7.51

Costs of beginning inventory  →   30,000
1,000
7,570

$352,500   *Costs incurred during August*

We refer to these 20,000 gallons as the units that were *started and completed* during the month.

As you can see in the exhibit, the 30,000 gallons completed are split into these two components: Column 1a shows the beginning inventory of 10,000 gallons, and column 1c shows the 20,000 gallons started and completed. The sum of the two components is always the total completed, which for Tropical Blends is 30,000 gallons.

### Fraction Completed for Beginning Work-in-Process

Column 1b, "Fraction Completed This Period," represents the fraction of the total materials, labor, and overhead that were added in August to complete the beginning inventory. Some of the materials, labor, and overhead were incurred last period, and that portion was included in last period's production report. All we want to include in this month's production report is the portion needed to complete the gallons in August.

**Direct Materials**  Remember, the beginning inventory was one-fifth complete on Aug. 1 and the direct material—orange juice—is added at the start of the process. Since these 10,000 gallons of Orangeade were started in July, all the orange juice needed for this batch was added last month. No additional orange juice must be added to this particular batch to complete it in August, so the fraction in column 1b is a zero.

Whenever a material is added at the beginning of a process, the fraction of materials needed to complete the beginning inventory will always be a zero.

**Direct Labor and Factory Overhead**  The key thing to remember about direct labor and factory overhead is that we assume that the costs are incurred evenly throughout the production process. Because Tropical Blends' beginning inventory of 10,000 gallons was one-fifth complete on Aug. 1, we assume that one-fifth of the total labor and overhead needed to complete these 10,000 gallons was added in July. Only the remaining four-fifths of the total labor and overhead has to be added in August to complete the gallons. Therefore the fraction completed this period, column 1b, is four-fifths for both direct labor and factory overhead.

The fraction completed, for both direct labor and factory overhead, is almost always found by subtracting from 1 the fraction that represents the stage of completion for the beginning inventory. For the 10,000 gallons, the beginning inventory was one-fifth completed on Aug. 1; subtract this fraction from 1 ($\frac{5}{5} - \frac{1}{5}$), and you have $\frac{4}{5}$.

### Units Started and Completed

Column 1c represents the number of units that were both started and completed during the month of August. Since all the materials, labor, and overhead were added to these units during August, there is no reason to have a separate "fraction completed" column for them. The "fraction completed" will always be 1 for each of these costs.

### Fraction Completed for Ending Work-in-Process

The ending inventory of work-in-process on Aug. 31—20,000 gallons, three-fourths completed—is shown in column 2. Column 3, the fraction completed this period, shows the fraction of the total materials, direct labor, and factory overhead that has already been added by the end of August to get the units to the three-fourths stage in production.

**Direct Materials**  Remember, all the direct materials (namely, orange juice) in processing department 1 are added at the beginning of production. The ending inventory of 20,000 gallons is three-fourths complete, which means that all this juice must have passed the beginning stage in production (or it could not have gotten to the three-quarters stage). Therefore 100% of the materials associated with this batch of gallons has been added in August, and the correct fraction for direct materials in column 3 is a 1. Next month, in September, no materials will be needed to complete the 20,000 gallons, which will represent the beginning inventory for that month.

For any materials that are added in lump sum at the beginning of a process, the appropriate fraction completed for the ending inventory will always be 1.

**Direct Labor and Factory Overhead**  As long as we assume that direct labor and factory overhead costs are added evenly throughout production, then the fraction completed for these costs will be the same as the stage in production reached by the ending inventory. The 20,000 gallons are three-fourths completed on Aug. 31; therefore three-fourths of the direct labor and factory overhead has been incurred. The fractions in column 3 for these costs are both $\frac{3}{4}$.

### Equivalent Whole Units

The figures in column 4 of Exhibit 1—the equivalent whole units—are found by adding together the following three parts:

1. The beginning inventory (column 1a) multiplied by the fraction completed (column 1b)

   PLUS

2. The units started and completed (column 1c)

   PLUS

3. The ending inventory (column 2) multiplied by the fraction completed (column 3)

For processing department 1, the equivalent whole units for each inventoriable cost are determined as follows:

| | (1a)<br>(Beginning<br>Inventory | × | (1b)<br>Fraction) | + | (1c)<br>Started and<br>Completed | + | (2)<br>(Ending<br>Inventory | × | (3)<br>Fraction) | = | (4)<br>Equivalent<br>Whole Units |
|---|---|---|---|---|---|---|---|---|---|---|---|
| Direct materials . . . . . . . | (10,000 | × | 0) | + | 20,000 | + | (20,000 | × | 1) | = | 40,000 |
| Direct labor . . . . . . . . . . | (10,000 | × | $\frac{4}{5}$) | + | 20,000 | + | (20,000 | × | $\frac{3}{4}$) | = | 43,000 |
| Factory overhead. . . . . . | (10,000 | × | $\frac{4}{5}$) | + | 20,000 | + | (20,000 | × | $\frac{3}{4}$) | = | 43,000 |

### Total Costs to Account for

Look now at column 5 in Exhibit 1, the total costs to account for. Remember, these costs include both the beginning inventory costs and the costs incurred in the current period. The beginning inventory costs for Tropical Blends were $38,570 ($30,000 for direct materials plus $1,000 for direct labor plus $7,570 for factory overhead). This amount, shown in the lower portion of column 5, is added to the $313,930 ($120,000, $21,500, and $172,430) incurred during August. The total for column 5 is $352,500. We will account for these costs in step 3, when we prepare the summary of costs report.

### Cost per Equivalent Whole Unit

When we calculate the cost per equivalent whole unit (CPEWU), we use the following components:

$$\text{CPEWU} = \frac{\text{costs incurred in current period}}{\text{equivalent whole units}}$$

As you can see in Exhibit 1, the CPEWU for each inventoriable cost is determined as follows:

$$\text{CPEWU (direct materials)} = \frac{\$120,000}{40,000} = \$3.00$$

$$\text{CPEWU (direct labor)} = \frac{\$21,500}{43,000} = .50$$

$$\text{CPEWU (factory overhead)} = \frac{\$172,430}{43,000} = \underline{4.01}$$

$$\text{CPEWU (all three combined)} = \underline{\underline{\$7.51}}$$

Notice that the numerator of each CPEWU calculation includes only the costs incurred in the current period and excludes the costs of beginning inventory. This is because the equivalent units in the denominator of the CPEWU calculation include only the equivalent units of work performed in the current period. The equivalent units of work performed on the beginning inventory in the previous period have been excluded from the calculation because we want the CPEWU to represent the costs of the current period divided by the work of the current period. This doesn't mean that we ignore the costs of beginning inventory; they are still part of the total costs to account for in column 5 of the production report. They are shown at the bottom of the column, however, so they are not included in the CPEWU calculation.

Learning
Objective **6**

Allocate the production costs between the complete and the incomplete units in the summary of costs report

### Step 3 for Processing Department 1: Preparing a Summary of Costs Report

Remember that the total costs to account for in column 5 of the production report represent the total costs associated with all the units worked on (both completed and incomplete) during the month. Our last step is to allocate these costs—$352,500 for processing department 1—between the 30,000 completed gallons and the 20,000 gallons that are still in process on Aug. 31. We do this in the *summary of costs report,* shown for processing department 1 in Exhibit 2.

The costs we assign to the 30,000 completed gallons are made up of the following:

1. The total costs associated with the 10,000 gallons that were in beginning inventory on Aug. 1. These costs can be further broken down into: (a) the costs of the 10,000 gallons that were incurred last period, represented as the beginning inventory on Aug. 1, and (b) the costs incurred in the current period to complete the 10,000 gallons.

   PLUS

2. The costs assigned to the 20,000 gallons that were started and completed during the current period.

The total costs associated with the beginning inventory are calculated by adding:

1. The costs of beginning inventory, $38,570 ($30,000 + $1,000 + $7,570, shown at the bottom of column 5 in the production report)

   PLUS

2. The costs to complete the beginning inventory, $36,080 (0 + $4,000 + $32,080). The costs to complete the beginning inventory are determined by multiplying the beginning inventory for direct materials, direct labor, and factory overhead (column 1a) by the fraction completed for each cost (column 1b) and then by each inventoriable cost's CPEWU (column 6).

The total cost of the 10,000 gallons from beginning inventory is $74,650 ($38,570 + $36,080).

The cost of the gallons started and completed is 20,000 × $7.51 = $150,200. When this is added to the $74,650, the total of $224,850 represents the total costs of producing the 30,000 gallons that were completed in August. This amount will be transferred, along with the 30,000 gallons, to processing department 2.

The cost assigned to the ending work-in-process inventory is $60,000 + $7,500 + $60,150 = $127,650. Each cost is found by multiplying the ending inventory

---

**Exhibit 2** Summary of Costs Report for Processing Department 1

| | | | |
|---|---|---|---|
| Cost of completed units (30,000 gal): | | | |
| Costs of beginning inventory (10,000 gal) . . . . . . . . . . . . . . . . | | $38,570 | |
| Costs to complete beginning inventory (10,000 gal): | | | |
| Direct materials (10,000 × 0 × $3.00) . . . . . . . . . | −0− | | |
| Direct labor (10,000 × $\frac{4}{5}$ × $.50) . . . . . . . . . . . . . . | $ 4,000 | | |
| Factory overhead (10,000 × $\frac{4}{5}$ × $4.01) . . . . . . . . | 32,080 | 36,080 | |
| Total cost of 10,000 gal in beginning inventory . . . . . . . . | | | $ 74,650 |
| Units started and completed (20,000 gal × $7.51) . . . . . . . . . . | | | 150,200 |
| Total cost of 30,000 gal completed. . . . . . . . . . . . . . . . . . | | | $224,850 |
| Cost of ending work-in-process (20,000 gal) | | | |
| Direct materials (20,000 × 1 × $3.00). . . . . . . . . . . . . . . . . . | | $60,000 | |
| Direct labor (20,000 × $\frac{3}{4}$ × $.50) . . . . . . . . . . . . . . . . . . . . . . | | 7,500 | |
| Factory overhead (20,000 × $\frac{3}{4}$ × $4.01) . . . . . . . . . . . . . . . . . | | 60,150 | 127,650 |
| Total costs to account for. . . . . . . . . . . . . . . . . . . . . . . . . . . . . | | | $352,500 |

by the individual fraction completed for each product cost and then by the individual CPEWU. When the cost of the ending inventory ($127,650) is added to the total cost of the 30,000 completed gallons ($224,850), the total is $352,500, which represents the total costs to account for and agrees with the total shown in column 5 of the production report in Exhibit 1.

Learning Objective **7**

Record the journal entries to account for the flow of production costs from one inventory account to another

## Journal Entries and T-Accounts for Processing Department 1

The journal entries for process costing are almost exactly the same as they are for job order costing. The only ones that will be different are the ones for factory overhead, where for the sake of simplicity we will assign the actual factory overhead costs to the product instead of the factory overhead applied using a predetermined rate.

If we assume that the raw materials used in August ($120,000) were also purchased in that month, the entry to record the purchase is:

| | | | |
|---|---|---|---|
| Aug. 31 | Raw Materials Inventory . . . . . . . . . . . . . . . . . . . . . . . . . | 120,000 | |
| | Accounts Payable (or Cash) . . . . . . . . . . . . . . . . . | | 120,000 |
| | To record purchase of raw materials. | | |

The journal entries to record the usage of direct materials and direct labor are:

| | | | |
|---|---|---|---|
| Aug. 31 | Work-in-Process Inventory 1 . . . . . . . . . . . . . . . . . . . . . | 120,000 | |
| | Raw Materials Inventory . . . . . . . . . . . . . . . . . . . . | | 120,000 |
| | To record direct materials used in production. | | |
| 31 | Work-in-Process Inventory 1 . . . . . . . . . . . . . . . . . . . . . | 21,500 | |
| | Salaries Payable . . . . . . . . . . . . . . . . . . . . . . . . . . | | 21,500 |
| | To record direct labor. | | |

The first entry to record factory overhead accumulates the numerous actual overhead costs during the month in the Factory Overhead Incurred account. The second entry transfers the total to Work-in-Process Inventory.

| | | | |
|---|---|---|---|
| Aug. 31 | Factory Overhead Incurred . . . . . . . . . . . . . . . . . . . . . . | 172,430 | |
| | Accounts Payable, Prepaid Rent, Accumulated | | |
| | Depreciation, etc. . . . . . . . . . . . . . . . . . . . . . . . . . . | | 172,430 |
| | To record the actual factory overhead costs for the month. | | |
| 31 | Work-in-Process Inventory 1 . . . . . . . . . . . . . . . . . . . . . | 172,430 | |
| | Factory Overhead Incurred . . . . . . . . . . . . . . . . . . | | 172,430 |
| | To transfer the overhead costs to work-in-process. | | |

After the production report and summary of costs report have been completed, an entry is made to record the transfer of the costs associated with the 30,000 completed gallons in processing department 1 to processing department 2:

| | | | |
|---|---|---|---|
| Aug. 31 | Work-in-Process Inventory 2 . . . . . . . . . . . . . . . . . . . . . | 224,850 | |
| | Work-in-Process Inventory 1 . . . . . . . . . . . . . . . . . | | 224,850 |
| | To record the transfer of costs related to completed | | |
| | gallons to Work-in-Process Inventory 2. | | |

**Exhibit 3** T-Account for Processing Department 1

### Work-in-Process Inventory 1

| | |
|---|---|
| Beginning inventory—10,000 units ($30,000 + $1,000 + $7,570) | 38,570 |
| *Plus* | |
| Costs incurred in August to complete beginning inventory and start 40,000 more ($120,000 + $21,500 + $172,430) | 313,930 |
| *Equals* | |
| Total costs to account for, associated with all 50,000 units | 352,500 |

*Less*

Cost of 30,000 units that were completed in department 1 ($38,570 + $36,080 + $150,200)      224,850

*The combination of these three costs—$224,850—is assigned to the 30,000 units that are transferred to processing department 2 in August. Processing department 2 will call these costs "transferred-in costs."*

*To Work-in-Process —processing department 2*

| | |
|---|---|
| *Equals* | |
| Ending inventory—20,000 units ($60,000 + $7,500 + $60,150) | $127,650 |

### Work-in-Process Inventory 2

| | |
|---|---|
| Beginning inventory − 5,000 units ($34,000 + $1,250 + $600 + $1,800) | 37,650 |
| *Plus* | |
| Costs incurred in August, including costs transferred in from processing department 1 | 224,850 |

After these entries are posted to the general ledger, the T-account for Work-in-Process Inventory 1 would appear as shown in Exhibit 3.

**ASK YOURSELF** ▶

1. What are the three basic accounting steps used in process costing?
2. How would you calculate the units completed and the units started and completed?
3. The production report determines three things: the equivalent whole units, the total costs to account for, and what else?
4. The total costs to account for are allocated between the completed units and the incomplete units in what process costing report?
5. What is the journal entry needed to record the transfer of the costs of completed units from one processing department to the next?

## THE ILLUSTRATION CONTINUED: PROCESSING DEPARTMENT 2

In the Tropical Blends example, the 30,000 gallons of pasteurized orange juice are transferred from processing department 1 to processing department 2, where the preservative is added. The costs of the 30,000 gallons of juice, $224,850, become a cost of processing department 2, where they are referred to as **transferred-in costs** and will be treated just like the costs of any other raw material that is added at the beginning of a process. The following example provides the information we need to know about processing department 2 in August.

## TROPICAL BLENDS — PROCESSING DEPARTMENT 2

In processing department 2 of Tropical Blends, a water solution containing preservatives and artificial sweeteners is added to the pasteurized juice evenly throughout the process, which takes several hours to complete. At the end of the process the Orangeade is pumped into large storage containers in the finished goods warehouse. On Aug. 1, there were 5,000 gallons in process, one-half complete (that is, one-half of the total processing time had elapsed). During August, all 30,000 gallons of pasteurized orange juice from processing department 1 had been added to processing department 2. Of the 35,000 gallons (5,000 + 30,000) worked on during August, 29,000 gallons were finished by Aug. 31, and the remaining gallons in the ending work-in-process were two-thirds complete.

The costs of the Aug. 1 beginning inventory of unfinished gallons and the costs incurred during August are determined from the accounting records to be as follows:

|  | Beginning Inventory Cost | Costs Incurred In August |
|---|---|---|
| Direct materials (water solution) .............. | $ 1,250 | $ 15,250 |
| Direct labor ................................ | 600 | 7,625 |
| Factory overhead ......................... | 1,800 | 22,875 |
| Transferred-in costs ....................... | 34,000 | 224,850 |
|  | $37,650 | $270,600 |

The conversion costs (direct labor and factory overhead) are incurred evenly throughout the process.

Note that the only costs in the list above that relate to the exhibits for processing department 1 are the transferred-in costs of $224,850 for 30,000 gallons of juice. These costs were determined in the summary of costs report for processing department 1 (Exhibit 2).

Learning Objective 4

Determine the number of units completed in a process and the numbers still incomplete at the end of the period

## Step 1 for Processing Department 2: Tracing the Physical Flow

Exhibit 4, the production report for processing department 2, shows that 29,000 gallons of Orangeade were completed during the month of August. The number of gallons that were not completed in processing department 2 at the end of August is determined as follows:

| | |
|---|---|
| Beginning inventory, work-in-process 2 ...... | 5,000 gal |
| Plus: Gallons started (transferred in from processing department 1 during August) ..... | 30,000 gal |
| Total to account for ..................... | 35,000 gal |
| Less: Gallons completed and transferred to finished goods ......................... | 29,000 gal |
| Ending inventory, work-in-process 2 ........ | 6,000 gal |

**Exhibit 4** Production Report for Processing Department 2

| Inventoriable Cost | (1a) Beginning Inventory Work-in-Process | (1b) Fraction Completed This Period | (1c) Started and Completed This Period | (2) Ending Inventory Work-in-Process | (3) Fraction Completed This Period | (4) Equivalent Whole Units | (5) Total Costs to Account for | (6) Cost per Equivalent Whole Unit |
|---|---|---|---|---|---|---|---|---|
| | | Units Completed (gal) | | | | | | |
| Transferred-in costs | 5,000 | 0 | 24,000 | 6,000 | 1 | 30,000 | $224,850 | $7.495 |
| Direct materials.... | 5,000 | $\frac{1}{2}$ | 24,000 | 6,000 | $\frac{2}{3}$ | 30,500 | 15,250 | .500 |
| Direct labor....... | 5,000 | $\frac{1}{2}$ | 24,000 | 6,000 | $\frac{2}{3}$ | 30,500 | 7,625 | .250 |
| Factory overhead | 5,000 | $\frac{1}{2}$ | 24,000 | 6,000 | $\frac{2}{3}$ | 30,500 | 22,875 | .750 |
| | | | | | | | $270,600 | $8.995 |

29,000
*Completed*

*Costs of beginning inventory* →

34,000
1,250
600
1,800

$308,250 *Costs incurred in current period*

## Step 2 for Processing Department 2: Preparing a Production Report

Exhibit 4, the production report for processing department 2, shows that four costs go into the finished product: the costs of processing the orange juice in the previous processing department (called transferred-in costs), the water solution (the direct materials), the direct labor, and the factory overhead.

### Units Completed

Columns 1a and 1c show that a total of 29,000 gallons were completed during August in processing department 2. Of this total, 5,000 (column 1a) were in process on Aug. 1; the remaining 29,000 − 5,000 = 24,000 gallons were started and completed in August.

Column 1b lists the fraction of the total production costs that were added during August to complete the *beginning* inventory. The costs of direct materials, direct labor, and factory overhead are assumed to be incurred evenly throughout the process. Since the beginning inventory was one-half complete on Aug. 1, one-half of the total materials, direct labor, and factory overhead must have been incurred in July. Thus, the last half—shown in column 1b—is added in August to complete the beginning inventory.

Remember that the transferred-in costs represent the costs that were assigned to units in processing department 1 and transferred to processing department 2. Normally we treat transferred-in costs just like the costs of raw materials that are transferred from a storeroom directly to the production process at the start of production. The only difference is in the name; instead of being called direct materials (such as orange juice or preservatives), they are called transferred-in costs to acknowledge that they originated not in a storeroom but in a previous department in the production process.

If the transferred-in costs are treated the same as direct materials added at the beginning of production, the fraction listed for transferred-in costs in column 1b of the production report is exactly the same as it would be for a direct material. Remember that the 5,000 gallons (as well as the transferred-in costs assigned to these gallons) in the beginning inventory on Aug. 1 would have been transferred from processing department 1 to processing department 2 during July. Therefore the work began on the 5,000 gallons in processing department 2 sometime during July. Any costs that are added at the beginning of production—such as direct materials or in this case the transferred-in costs—would have had to be completely added to the 5,000 gallons last month, because that is when those units were begun; so the fraction for the transferred-in costs needed to complete the 5,000 gallons is zero, just as it would be for a direct material that was added at the beginning of the process.

Column 1c, units started and completed this period, need not be accompanied by a separate "fraction completed" column, since 100% of all the inventoriable costs are incurred in the current period.

### Ending Inventory

Column 2 of Exhibit 4 shows the 6,000 gallons, two-thirds complete, that were still in process at the end of August, and column 3 indicates the fraction completed for each production cost. Since direct materials, direct labor, and factory overhead are all incurred evenly throughout the process, and since the ending inventory is two-thirds complete, the appropriate fraction completed for each of these costs is $\frac{2}{3}$.

As for transferred-in costs, don't forget that we treat them just like a direct material added at the beginning of the process. Since the processing of the 6,000 gallons has already begun—in fact, they are all two-thirds complete—the fraction for the transferred-in costs, given in column 3, is 1, just as it would be for a direct material added at the beginning of production. In other words, all of the ending inventory already incorporates transferred-in costs.

### Cost per Equivalent Whole Unit

Once again we can calculate the equivalent whole units for each inventoriable cost (column 4) by adding together the equivalent whole units for the following three parts:

1. Beginning inventory

   PLUS

2. Units started and completed

   PLUS

3. Units in ending inventory

| | (1a) (Beginning Inventory × | (1b) Fraction) + | (1c) Started and Completed + | (2) (Ending Inventory × | (3) Fraction) = | (4) Equivalent Whole units |
|---|---|---|---|---|---|---|
| Transferred-in costs ............... | (5,000 × | 0) + | 24,000 + | (6,000 × | 1) = | 30,000 |
| Direct Materials .................. | (5,000 × | $\frac{1}{2}$) + | 24,000 + | (6,000 × | $\frac{2}{3}$) = | 30,500 |
| Direct labor ..................... | (5,000 × | $\frac{1}{2}$) + | 24,000 + | (6,000 × | $\frac{2}{3}$) = | 30,500 |
| Factory overhead ................ | (5,000 × | $\frac{1}{2}$) + | 24,000 + | (6,000 × | $\frac{2}{3}$) = | 30,500 |

Column 5 in Exhibit 4, "Total Costs to Account For," includes the costs incurred in August plus the costs of the beginning inventory on Aug. 1. The costs

*These costs are transferred
to Finished Goods Inventory*

**Exhibit 5** Summary of Costs Report for Processing Department 2

| | | | |
|---|---|---:|---:|
| Cost of completed units (29,000 gal): | | | |
| Costs of beginning inventory (5,000 gal) . . . . . . . . . . . . . . . . . . . . . . . . . . . . . . . . . . . . | | $37,650 | |
| Costs to complete beginning inventory (5,000 gal): | | | |
| Transferred-in costs (5,000 × 0 × $7.495) . . . . . . . . . . . . . . . . . . . . . . . . . . | –0– | | |
| Direct materials (5,000 × ½ × $.50) . . . . . . . . . . . . . . . . . . . . . . . . . . . . . . . . . | $1,250 | | |
| Direct labor (5,000 × ½ × $.25) . . . . . . . . . . . . . . . . . . . . . . . . . . . . . . . . . . . . | 625 | | |
| Factory overhead (5,000 × ½ × $.75) . . . . . . . . . . . . . . . . . . . . . . . . . . . . . . . | 1,875 | 3,750 | |
| Total cost of 5,000 gal in beginning inventory. . . . . . . . . . . . . . . . . . . . . . . . . . . . . | | | $ 41,400 |
| Units started and completed (24,000 gal × $8.995) . . . . . . . . . . . . . . . . . . . . . . . . . . | | | 215,880 |
| Total cost of 29,000 gal completed . . . . . . . . . . . . . . . . . . . . . . . . . . . . . . . . . . . . | | | $257,280 |
| Cost of ending work-in-process (6,000 gal): | | | |
| Transferred-in costs (6,000 × 1 × $7.495) . . . . . . . . . . . . . . . . . . . . . . . . . . . . . | | $44,970 | |
| Direct materials (6,000 × ⅔ × $.50) . . . . . . . . . . . . . . . . . . . . . . . . . . . . . . . . . | | 2,000 | |
| Direct labor (6,000 × ⅔ × $.25). . . . . . . . . . . . . . . . . . . . . . . . . . . . . . . . . . . . . | | 1,000 | |
| Factory overhead (6,000 × ⅔ × $.75). . . . . . . . . . . . . . . . . . . . . . . . . . . . . . . . | | 3,000 | 50,970 |
| Total costs to account for . . . . . . . . . . . . . . . . . . . . . . . . . . . . . . . . . . . . . . . . . . . . | | | $308,250 |

*These costs remain
in Work-in-Process
Inventory for processing
department 2*

*These are the total
costs to account for*

incurred in August go in the top part of the column, where they can be divided by the equivalent whole units for August to get the CPEWUs. The beginning inventory costs go at the bottom of the column, where they can't enter into the CPEWU calculations.

The CPEWU for each inventoriable cost (column 6 in Exhibit 4) is determined as follows:

$$\text{CPEWU for transferred-in costs} = \frac{\$224,850}{30,000} = \$7.495$$

$$\text{CPEWU for direct materials} = \frac{\$15,250}{30,500} = .500$$

$$\text{CPEWU for direct labor} = \frac{\$\ 7,625}{30,500} = .250$$

$$\text{CPEWU for factory overhead} = \frac{\$22,875}{30,500} = \underline{.750}$$

(CPEWU for all four inventoriable costs combined) $\underline{\underline{\$8.995}}$

Learning
Objective 6

Allocate the production costs
between the complete and the
incomplete units in the summary of
costs report

## Step 3 for Processing Department 2: Preparing a Summary of Costs Report

The final step is to allocate the total costs to account for, shown in column 5, between the completed units and the ending inventory, as we did in processing department 1. This allocation is shown in the summary of costs report in Exhibit 5.

The costs assigned to the 29,000 completed gallons are made up of the following:

1. The cost of producing the 5,000 gallons in the beginning inventory. This cost is $41,400, the sum of: (a) the costs of the beginning inventory, which were incurred last period, $37,650, and (b) the costs incurred in the current period to complete the beginning inventory, $3,750.

   PLUS

2. The costs assigned to the gallons started and completed in August = 24,000 × $8.995 = $215,880.

The total, $257,280, is transferred to Finished Goods Inventory. The ending inventory in processing department 2, $50,970 ($44,970 + $2,000 + $1,000 + $3,000), represents the balance in Work-in-Process Inventory 2 on Aug. 31.

Learning<br>Objective 7 ## Journal Entries and T-Accounts for Processing Department 2

Record the journal entries to account for the flow of production costs from one inventory account to another

The journal entries for processing department 2 are almost exactly the same as those for processing department 1, except for the entry to record the transfer of completed gallons to Finished Goods Inventory instead of to another work-in-process account. The journal entries to record the usage of direct materials, direct labor, and factory overhead for August are:

| | | | | |
|---|---|---|---|---|
| Aug. 31 | Work-in-Process Inventory 2 . . . . . . . . . . . . . . . . . . . . . . . | 15,250 | |
| | Raw Materials Inventory . . . . . . . . . . . . . . . . . . . . . . . | | 15,250 |
| | To record raw materials used in production. | | |
| 31 | Work-in-Process Inventory 2 . . . . . . . . . . . . . . . . . . . . . . . | 7,625 | |
| | Salaries Payable . . . . . . . . . . . . . . . . . . . . . . . . . . . . | | 7,625 |
| | To record direct labor. | | |
| 31 | Factory Overhead Incurred . . . . . . . . . . . . . . . . . . . . . . . | 22,875 | |
| | Accounts Payable, Prepaid Rent, Accumulated Depreciation, etc . . . . . . . . . . . . . . . . . . . . . . . . . . . . . . . . . | | 22,875 |
| | To record the actual factory overhead costs for the month. | | |
| 31 | Work-in-Process Inventory 2 . . . . . . . . . . . . . . . . . . . . . . . | 22,875 | |
| | Factory Overhead Incurred. . . . . . . . . . . . . . . . . . . . . . | | 22,875 |
| | To transfer the overhead costs to work-in-process. | | |

The journal entry to record the transfer of 29,000 gallons from processing department 2 to finished goods is:

| | | | | |
|---|---|---|---|---|
| Aug. 31 | Finished Goods Inventory . . . . . . . . . . . . . . . . . . . . . . . | 257,280 | |
| | Work-in-Process Inventory 2 . . . . . . . . . . . . . . . . . | | 257,280 |
| | To record the transfer of completed units to finished goods. | | |

After these entries are posted to the general ledger, the T-account for Work-in-Process Inventory 2 would look like Exhibit 6.

**Exhibit 6** T-Account for Processing Department 2

### Work-in-Process Inventory 2

| | | | |
|---|---|---|---|
| Beginning inventory—5,000 units ($34,000 + $1,250 + $600 + $1,800) | 37,650 | | |
| *Plus* | | | |
| Costs incurred in August to complete beginning inventory and start 30,000 more ($224,850 + $15,250 + $7,625 + $22,875) | 270,600 | | *The combination of these three costs—$257,280—is assigned to the 29,000 units that are transferred to finished goods in August.* |
| *Equals* | | | |
| Total costs to account for, associated with all 35,000 units | 308,250 | | |
| | | *Less* | |
| | | Cost of 29,000 units that were completed in processing department 2 ($37,650 + $3,750 + $215,880) | 257,280 |
| | | | *To Finished Goods⟶ Inventory* |
| *Equals* | | | |
| Ending inventory—6,000 units ($44,970 + $2,000 + $1,000 + $3,000) | $ 50,970 | | |

## THE ILLUSTRATION CONCLUDED: SOME FINAL COMMENTS

### Combining Direct Labor and Factory Overhead

As a result of its declining role in many organizations, direct labor is sometimes combined with factory overhead and treated as one of many conversion costs, rather than being given individual attention. In addition, since direct labor and factory overhead are always assumed to occur evenly throughout the production process, the "fraction completed" columns in the production report will always be the same for both costs, resulting in equivalent whole units that will also be the same. For these reasons, in process costing accountants typically combine direct labor and factory overhead costs into their total—the *conversion costs*—and deal only with the combination. So, when you see conversion costs referred to, handle them as you would handle direct labor and factory overhead individually.

### Raw Materials Added at the End of Processing

Our examples showed how to handle the "fraction completed" columns for direct materials when the materials are either added at the beginning or added evenly throughout the process. However, a material, such as the packaging for a product, may also be added entirely at the end of processing. When this occurs, the "fraction completed" column of the production report (column 3) will always show a 0 for the ending inventory. Since the process is incomplete, it has not yet reached the stage at which the material is added.

When raw materials are added at the end of processing, the fraction completed for the beginning inventory (in column 1b of the production report) is always 1. Since the units were incomplete at the end of the previous month, the fraction completed for last month's ending inventory had to be 0. But last month's ending inventory becomes this month's beginning inventory, which will reach the end of processing during the current period. Since the raw materials have to be added during this period to complete the units in beginning inventory, the fraction completed must be 1.

### Sale of Goods

When the finished product is ultimately sold, the accounting for the sale and the related cost of goods sold is exactly the same under process costing as under job order costing. For example, assume that Tropical Blends sells for $550,000 finished goods having a cost of $230,000. Two journal entries are needed to record this transaction. The first entry records the revenue from the sale, and the second records the cost of the goods sold:

| | | | |
|---|---|---|---|
| Aug. 31 | Accounts Receivable (or Cash) . . . . . . . . . . . . . . . . . . . | 550,000 | |
| | Sales . . . . . . . . . . . . . . . . . . . . . . . . . . . . . . . . . | | 550,000 |
| | To record the revenue from the sale of goods. | | |
| 31 | Cost of Goods Sold . . . . . . . . . . . . . . . . . . . . . . . . . . | 230,000 | |
| | Finished Goods Inventory. . . . . . . . . . . . . . . . . . . . | | 230,000 |
| | To record the cost of goods sold during August. | | |

### The Flow of Costs from Beginning to End

The flow of costs through all the production accounts of Tropical Blends for August are now shown in the T-accounts in Exhibit 7. Notice that the accounting in T-account form for process costing is almost identical to that for job order costing. Remember, it's not the journal entries and T-accounts that differ for job order costing and process costing. What differs is the way we determine the cost of an individual unit or batch of units.

### AN OVERVIEW OF PROCESS COSTING

Now that you have read this chapter, you may find a complete overview of process costing useful. The chapter is condensed into its most basic elements in Exhibits 8 and 9. Exhibit 8 summarizes the items included in each of the three steps of process costing:

**STEP 1:** Tracing the physical flow
**STEP 2:** Preparing a production report
**STEP 3:** Preparing a summary of costs report

Exhibit 9 summarizes the "fraction completed" columns of the production report. It lists the appropriate fractions for the beginning and ending inventories of work-in-process, for direct materials, conversion costs (direct labor and factory overhead), and for transferred-in costs.

**Exhibit 7** T-Account Approach for Processing Departments 1 and 2

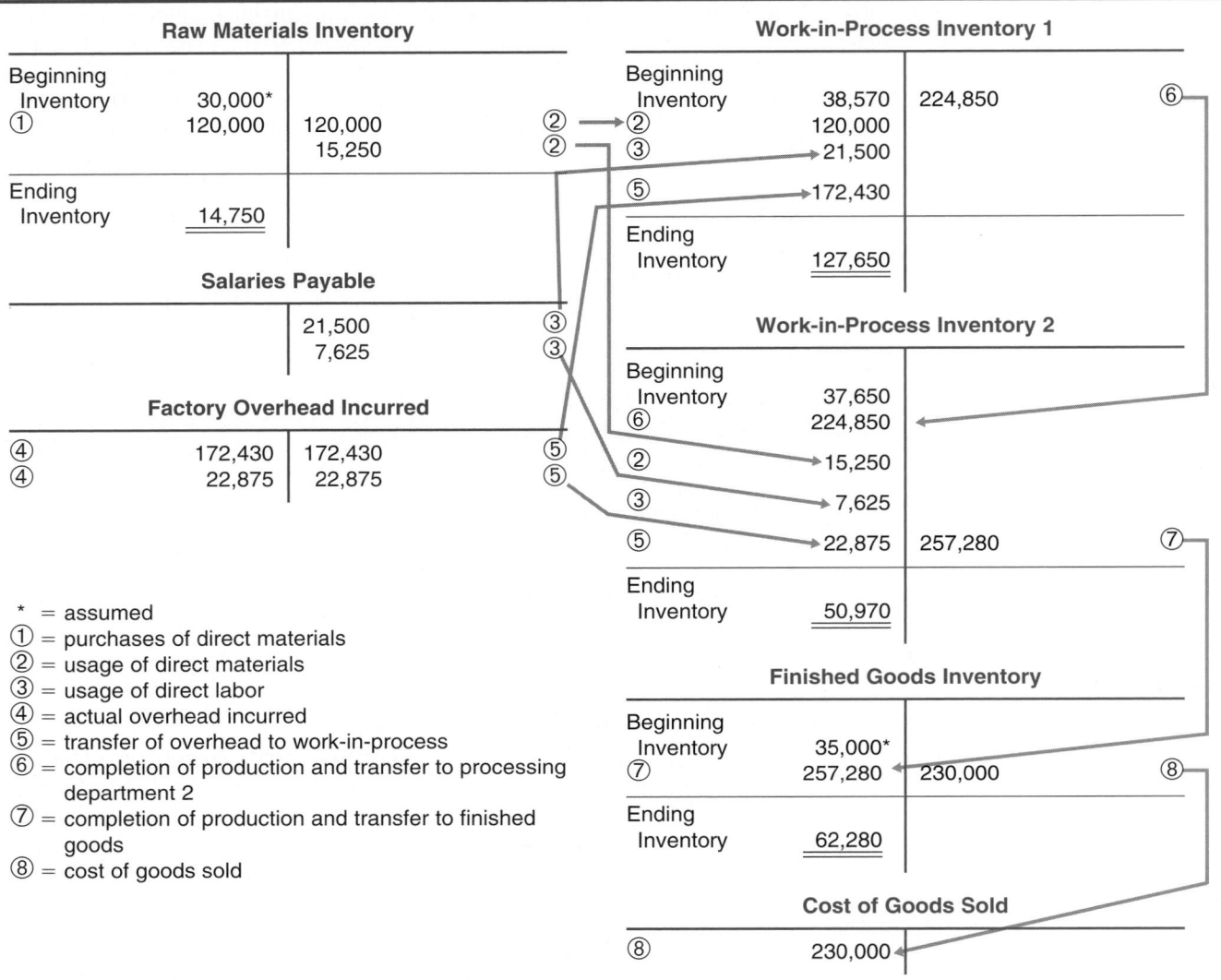

\* = assumed
① = purchases of direct materials
② = usage of direct materials
③ = usage of direct labor
④ = actual overhead incurred
⑤ = transfer of overhead to work-in-process
⑥ = completion of production and transfer to processing department 2
⑦ = completion of production and transfer to finished goods
⑧ = cost of goods sold

**Exhibit 8** Summary of the Three Steps in Process Costing

| Step 1 | Step 2 Prepare a Production Report | | | Step 3 Prepare a Summary of Costs Report | |
|---|---|---|---|---|---|
| Trace the Physical Flow | Equivalent Whole Units | Total Costs to Account for | Cost per Equivalent Whole Unit | Cost of Completed Units | Cost of Ending Inventory |
| Beginning inventory<br>+ Units started<br>= Total to account for<br>− Ending inventory<br>= Units completed<br>OR<br>− Units completed<br>= Ending Inventory | Beginning inventory × fraction completed in current period<br>+ Units started and completed in current period<br>+ Ending inventory × fraction completed in current period | Beginning inventory<br>+ Costs incurred in current period | Costs incurred in current period ÷ equivalent whole units | Cost of beginning inventory<br>+ Cost of completing beginning inventory<br>+ Cost of units started and completed | Ending inventory × fraction complete × individual cost per equivalent whole unit |

**Exhibit 9** Rules for "Fraction Completed" Columns of Production Reports

| Inventoriable Cost | Fraction for: | |
| --- | --- | --- |
| | Beginning Inventory | Ending Inventory |
| Direct material: | | |
| Added all at beginning of process | 0 | 1 |
| Added all at end of process | 1 | 0 |
| Added evenly throughout process | 1 minus the fraction representing how complete the WIP inventory is at the beginning of the period | The fraction representing how complete the WIP inventory is at the end of the period |
| Conversion costs—added evenly throughout the process | 1 minus the fraction representing how complete the WIP inventory is at the beginning of the period | The fraction representing how complete the WIP inventory is at the end of the period |
| Transferred-in costs— added at beginning of process | 0 | 1 |

ASK YOURSELF ▶

1. **What are transferred-in costs?**
2. **When raw materials are added evenly throughout a process, how do you determine the fraction completed in the production report for the beginning inventory of raw materials? For the ending inventory of raw materials?**

Learning Objective **8**

Explain how the just-in-time inventory philosophy can help an organization reduce its costs by preventing waste

## JUST-IN-TIME (JIT) PHILOSOPHY

The **just-in-time (JIT) philosophy** is a collection of concepts related to inventory control and aimed at the continuous reduction of an organization's costs. Most of the concepts of the JIT philosophy relate to production settings, especially those that involve continuous flows—which, as we have learned in this chapter, are characteristic of a process costing environment. However, many concepts are equally applicable to job order costing situations and to hybrid job order costing and process costing systems. Some JIT concepts can benefit service organizations as well as manufacturers.

The heart of the just-in-time philosophy is its emphasis on having inventory in position "just-in-time" for sale or use. The assurance of a final sale to a waiting customer is what triggers the start of production; and only when production is about to begin are raw materials purchased. Ideally, raw materials arrive just-in-time to be used in production, and production is completed just-in-time to meet the final customer's needs.

### "Just-in-Time" versus "Just-in-Case"

The JIT philosophy is also called the "demand pull approach" to inventories, meaning that nothing should ever be produced or purchased until it is needed, or demanded, by a customer. It is this *demand* from the end of the production line that pulls the inventory through the purchasing and production process.

This outlook is quite different from the traditional philosophy, still used by many manufacturers, called the "push" approach. It might also be called the "just-in-case" philosophy, because it contends that raw materials should be purchased, and finished units should be produced, in order to build up inventory levels "just-in-case" the materials or products will be needed for sale or use. The inventory is *pushed* through the production process to completion in order to create a desired "safety stock" that is not needed immediately, but serves as a safeguard against running out of stock and as a defense against disruption in production. The traditional philosophy also empha-sizes the production of inventories as a way of keeping all employees fully utilized, thereby using productive capacity efficiently and minimizing idle time.

Let's take a closer look at the three major concepts associated with the JIT philosophy.

### Major Concepts of the JIT Philosophy

#### Reduced Inventory Levels

Supporters of the JIT philosophy separate the activities associated with inventories into two groups: value-added activities and non-value-added activities. A **value-added** activity is anything an organization does that is perceived by a customer as adding value to the product by improving its quality, performance, reliability, or appearance. Although the costs of these activities can probably be reduced, they cannot be elimi-nated without affecting the customer's satisfaction with the product.

Conversely, a **non-value-added** activity is anything an organization does that is not perceived by a customer as adding value to the product. Most activities associated with inventory—such as negotiating prices, ordering, handling, inspecting, storing, moving, waiting, reworking, and counting—are considered to be non-value-added. Thus, maintaining a safety stock in inventory, just in case it may be needed, is considered to be an unnecessary evil that generates unneeded activities, which breed excessive costs. The JIT philosophy argues that non-value-added activities can and should be eliminated, because their elimination will not change the customer's will-ingness to purchase the product. The most obvious way to eliminate these activities is to reduce the inventory level to zero, which immediately reduces all related inventory costs to zero as well. With no accompanying reduction in revenues, and no sacrifice in quality, the profits for the firm will be improved.

Although the JIT philosophy does encourage organizations to maintain mini-mum inventory levels, it isn't realistic to expect many organizations to take the drastic action of reducing inventory levels to zero. In order to maintain zero inventories, significant accompanying changes would be needed in management attitudes, plant capacity, product design, setup times, plant layout, skills and training of employees, and relationships with suppliers and customers. Since few companies could make these changes immediately, emphasis is placed instead on continually reducing in-ventories, thereby reducing non-value-added activities and their related costs.

#### Total Quality Control

An integral part of the JIT philosophy is its emphasis on total quality control—on "doing it right the first time." Rather than allowing some defective units to be pro-duced and later reworked or discarded, JIT aims at zero defects—or at least as few defects as possible.

A production process that yields products with zero defects is likely to be expensive. If each and every unit is to meet all specifications of size, shape, appear-ance, and performance, direct materials have to be of the highest quality available; all the direct laborers and their supervisors need to be highly skilled, trained, motivated, and able to work well together; all machinery must be technologically advanced and constantly maintained in peak working order.

However, the costs of allowing defective units to be produced are also substantial. They can range anywhere from 10% to 30% of total production costs. They may relate to inspection, detection, rework, storage, or customer service. Less quantifiable but also significant are the costs of lost sales, lost customers, and lost reputation.

All things considered, supporters of JIT contend that striving for zero defects is much less costly, and more profitable to the firm in the long run, than even allowing a small percentage of products to be defective.

In a JIT environment, each worker is expected to be constantly alert for any problems and to correct them as quickly as possible. When problems surface, the production process must be immediately stopped, and repairs made by the production worker. Thus, workers must be trained not only to perform a specific production procedure but also to inspect their own work as well as others, and to make necessary repairs in an efficient and timely manner. This contrasts with the traditional approach in which defective units often go undetected until they reach an inspection point at the end of processing. Defective units are set aside to be reworked at a later time. If defects are detected during the production process, these units are also typically set aside until it is convenient for someone else to rework them. The accumulation of units awaiting rework represents a buildup of inventories, which means that non-value-added costs associated with maintaining an inventory are being incurred unnecessarily.

### Simplified Production and Reduced Production Time

In a JIT environment, continuous efforts are made to simplify the production process and to reduce production time. As long as they do not change the quality of the product in the minds of customers, these efforts lead to reduced costs and enhanced profits.

Production might be simplified by revising the product design in order to reduce the number of parts required in each product or to reduce the number of steps in the production process. Production time might be shortened by minimizing setup times for new production runs and revising plant layout in order to bring related activities closer together to save time in moving from the beginning to the end of processing. Such simplification often involves the identification of non-value-added activities that might be eliminated (such as inspecting, waiting, holding, reworking, and counting).

Another approach to saving production time involves replacing production workers with fully automated machinery or with robots that can perform many production functions and can move goods from one production stage to another.

**ASK YOURSELF** ▶

1. In the JIT philosophy, to what does the term "just-in-time" refer?
2. What are the three major concepts of the just-in-time philosophy?

### SUMMARY

• The **process costing method** is used by companies that have the following characteristics:

1. Units are produced continuously in large batches through one or more processing departments.
2. Units are all exactly the same. They have all been processed in the same manner, each taking the same amount of materials, time, and attention. Each unit is assigned exactly the same cost as any other unit.

- In process costing, the output is measured in **equivalent whole units,** which express the number of partially completed units in terms of an equivalent number of fully completed units. It is the sum of the completed units plus the incomplete units multiplied by the fraction completed during the current period.
- There are three basic steps in process costing:

1. Tracing the physical flow
2. Preparing a production report
3. Preparing a summary of costs report

- When we trace the physical flow, we determine the completed units, and the ending inventory of work-in-process, needed for the production report.
- A **production report** (1) determines the equivalent whole units for each different inventoriable cost, (2) accumulates the total costs to account for, and (3) computes the cost per equivalent whole unit.
- Within the production report, the completed units are divided into two parts: the units in the *beginning inventory,* which are assumed to be completed first; and the units that were *started and completed* in the current period.
- The number of units in the beginning inventory is multiplied by the fraction completed to determine the equivalent whole units. The fraction completed represents the fraction of the total materials, labor, and overhead that is added to the units in the current period to complete the beginning inventory.
- The fraction needed to complete the raw materials in the beginning inventory will be:

1. Zero if the raw materials are added at the beginning of processing
2. One if the raw materials are added at the end of processing
3. One minus the percentage representing how complete the inventory is at the beginning of the period, for raw materials added evenly throughout the process

- Since we assume that conversion costs (direct labor and factory overhead) are incurred evenly throughout the production process, the fraction to complete the beginning inventory will always be 1 minus the fraction representing how complete the inventory is at the beginning of the period.
- The units in ending inventory are multiplied by the fraction completed, as shown in the production report. The fraction used represents the fraction of the total materials, direct labor, and factory overhead added in the current period to the units that are still in process at the end of the period.
- The fraction multiplied by the ending inventory for raw materials will be:

1. One if the raw materials are added at the beginning of processing
2. Zero if the raw materials are added at the end of processing
3. The fraction representing how complete the inventory is at the end of the period, for raw materials added evenly throughout the process

- The fraction multiplied by the ending inventory for conversion costs will be the fraction representing how complete the inventory is at the end of the period.
- The number of equivalent whole units (EWU) for each different product cost is determined as follows:

$$\text{EWU} = \left[ \begin{array}{c} \text{beginning} \\ \text{inventory} \\ \text{of work-in-process} \end{array} \times \begin{array}{c} \text{fraction} \\ \text{completed} \\ \text{(in current period)} \end{array} \right]$$

$$+ \begin{array}{c} \text{started} \\ \text{and} \\ \text{completed} \end{array} + \left[ \begin{array}{c} \text{ending} \\ \text{inventory} \\ \text{of work-in-process} \end{array} \times \begin{array}{c} \text{fraction} \\ \text{completed} \\ \text{(in current period)} \end{array} \right]$$

- In the "total costs to account for" column of the production report, the costs of the beginning inventory are separated from the costs incurred in the current period. The costs incurred in the current period are placed at the top of the "total costs to account for" column, where they will be divided by the equivalent whole units to get the **cost per equivalent whole unit (CPEWU).** The costs of the beginning inventory are placed at the bottom of the "total costs to account for" column, where they do not enter into the CPEWU calculation.
- The third step in process costing is the preparation of a **summary of costs report.** The costs assigned to the completed units in a summary of costs report are composed of three parts: (1) the costs of the partially completed units in the beginning inventory (incurred in the previous period); (2) the costs to complete the beginning inventory (incurred in the current period); and (3) the costs to complete the units that were both started and completed in the current period.
- When units are transferred from one production department to another, the costs of the units transferred are referred to as **transferred-in costs** by the receiving department. In the production report of the receiving department, transferred-in costs are treated just like raw materials added at the beginning of production.
- The **just-in-time (JIT)** philosophy is a collection of concepts related to inventory control and aimed at the continuous reduction of an organization's costs by having inventory in position just in time for sale or use.
- The three major concepts of the just-in-time philosophy are: (1) reduced inventory levels; (2) total quality control; and (3) simplified production and reduced production time.

## 9   KEY TERMS

**Cost per equivalent whole unit (CPEWU)**

Costs incurred in the current period divided by the equivalent whole units.

**Equivalent whole units**

A measure of activity in process costing that expresses the number of partially completed units in terms of an equivalent number of fully completed units. It is the sum of (1) the incomplete units in beginning inventory multiplied by the fraction completed during the current period, plus (2) the units started and completed, plus (3) the incomplete units in ending inventory multiplied by the fraction completed during the current period. Also called simply *equivalent units.*

**Just-in-time (JIT) philosophy**

A collection of concepts related to inventory control and aimed at the continuous reduction of an organization's costs by having inventory in position just in time for sale or use. These concepts include reduced inventory levels, total quality control, simplified production, and reduced production time.

**Non-value-added activity**

Anything an organization does that is not perceived by a customer as adding value to a product.

**Process costing**

The method of accounting for the production of a large volume of indistinguishable units in a continuous process through multiple processing departments. An average cost, which is the same for all units, is determined by dividing the production costs incurred during the period by the equivalent whole units of production for the period.

**Production report**

A basic report in the process costing method, consisting of (1) the equivalent whole units, (2) the total costs to account for, and (3) the cost per equivalent whole unit.

**Summary of costs report**

The final step in the process costing method, in which the total costs to account for are allocated between the completed units and the ending work-in-process.

**Total costs to account for**

The total of the costs of the beginning inventory of work-in-process plus all the inventoriable costs incurred in the current period.

**Total units to account for**

Part of the first step in process costing, tracing the physical flow. The figure is found by adding together the beginning inventory (in units) of work-in-process plus the number of units started during the period. Ending inventory in work-in-process can then be subtracted to get the number of units completed, or the number of units completed can be subtracted to get the ending inventory.

**Transferred-in costs**   Costs incurred in one production stage that are transferred to the next production stage. Transferred-in costs are accounted for in the same way as the costs of direct materials added at the beginning of processing.

**Value-added activity**   Anything an organization does that is perceived by a customer as adding value to a product by improving its quality, performance, reliability, or appearance.

---

## DEMONSTRATION PROBLEM

The Esposito Rubber Company's hockey puck division supplies pucks to sporting goods stores. The pucks are produced in a two-stage process. At the beginning of stage 1, the ingredients (rubber, chemical agents, carbon black, and oils) are added all at once and then are blended for several hours. Then the blended mixture is transferred to stage 2, where it is rolled and flattened into long sheets of glob, cooled, molded, and packaged into boxes of 10 pucks. The boxes are added at the end of stage 2. The conversion costs are incurred evenly throughout both processes. Each pound of glob eventually makes three hockey pucks.

At the beginning of January 1997, Esposito Rubber had 1,000 pounds of glob in stage 1, one-fourth completed. During the month, 59,000 pounds were started, and at the end of January there were 3,000 pounds of glob in process, four-fifths completed.

The costs of the beginning inventory and the costs incurred during January for stage 1 were:

|  | Costs of Beginning Inventory | Costs Incurred during Month |
|---|---|---|
| Ingredients..................................... | $2,060 | $ 87,910 |
| Conversion costs.............................. | 125 | 29,575 |
|  | $2,185 | $117,485 |

On Jan. 1, stage 2 had 2,000 pounds of glob, two-fifths completed. During the month, 51,000 pounds (153,000 pucks) were boxed and sent to finished goods. The ending inventory in stage 2 was one-half completed.

The costs of the beginning inventory and the costs incurred during January for stage 2 were:

|  | Costs of Beginning Inventory | Costs Incurred during Month |
|---|---|---|
| Boxes....................................... | $   0 | $30,600 |
| Conversion costs.............................. | 300 | 21,680 |
| Transferred-in costs ......................... | 3,900 | * |
|  | $4,200 | $52,280 |

* See summary of costs report for stage 1 for January.

**Required:**

1. For stage 1:
   a. Determine the number of units that were completed in January.
   b. Prepare a production report.
   c. Prepare a summary of costs report.

2. For stage 2:
   a. Determine the number of units in process on Jan. 31.
   b. Prepare a production report.
   c. Prepare a summary of costs report.

## ■ Solution to Demonstration Problem

1. Stage 1
   a. Tracing the physical flow:

| | |
|---|---:|
| Beginning inventory | 1,000 lb |
| Units started | 59,000 lb |
| Total to account for | 60,000 lb |
| Ending inventory | 3,000 lb |
| Units completed | 57,000 lb |

   b. Production report:

| Inventoriable Cost | Beginning Inventory Work-in-Process | Fraction Completed | Started and Completed | Ending Inventory Work-in-Process | Fraction Completed | Equivalent Whole Units | Total Costs to Account for | Cost per Equivalent Whole Unit |
|---|---|---|---|---|---|---|---|---|
| | **Units Completed** | | | | | | | |
| Ingredients | 1,000 | –0– | 56,000 | 3,000 | 1 | 59,000 | $ 87,910 | $1.49 |
| Conversion Costs | 1,000 | $\frac{3}{4}$ | 56,000 | 3,000 | $\frac{4}{5}$ | 59,150 | 29,575 | .50 |
| | | | | | | *Costs of beginning inventory* | $117,485 | $1.99 |
| | | *57,000 Completed* | | | | | 2,060 | |
| | | | | | | | 125 | |
| | | | | | | | $119,670 | *Costs incurred in current period* |

   c. Summary of costs report:

| | | | |
|---|---|---:|---:|
| Cost of completed units: | | | |
|   Costs of beginning inventory | | $2,185 | |
|   Costs to complete beginning inventory: | | | |
|     Conversion costs (1,000 × $\frac{3}{4}$ × $.50) | 375 | $ 2,560 | |
|   Units started and completed (56,000 × $1.99) | | 111,440 | $114,000 |
| Cost of ending work-in-process: | | | |
|   Ingredients (3,000 × 1 × $1.49) | | 4,470 | |
|   Conversion costs (3,000 × $\frac{4}{5}$ × $.50) | | 1,200 | 5,670 |
| | | | $119,670 |

2. Stage 2

   a. Tracing the physical flow:

| | |
|---|---:|
| Beginning inventory | 2,000 lb |
| Units started | 57,000 lb |
| Total to account for | 59,000 lb |
| Units completed | 51,000 lb |
| Ending inventory | 8,000 lb |

   b. Production report:

| | Units Completed | | | | | | | |
|---|---|---|---|---|---|---|---|---|
| Inventoriable Cost | Beginning Inventory Work-in-Process | Fraction Completed | Started and Completed | Ending Inventory Work-in-Process | Fraction Completed | Equivalent Whole Units | Total Costs to Account for | Cost per Equivalent Whole Unit |
| Boxes | 2,000 | 1 | 49,000 | 8,000 | –0– | 51,000 | $ 30,600 | $ .60 |
| Conversion costs | 2,000 | $\frac{3}{5}$ | 49,000 | 8,000 | $\frac{1}{2}$ | 54,200 | 21,680 | .40 |
| Transferred-in costs | 2,000 | 0 | 49,000 | 8,000 | 1 | 57,000 | 114,000 | 2.00 |

51,000 Completed

Costs of beginning inventory: $166,280 ... 300 ... 3,900

$3.00

$170,480   *Costs incurred in current period*

   c. Summary of costs report:

| | | |
|---|---:|---:|
| Cost of completed units: | | |
|   Costs of beginning inventory | $ 4,200 | |
|   Costs to complete beginning inventory: | | |
|     Boxes (2,000 × 1 × $.60) | 1,200 | |
|     Conversion costs (2,000 × $\frac{3}{5}$ × $.40) | 480 | $ 5,880 |
|   Units started and completed (49,000 × $3.00) | | 147,000 |
| | | $152,880 |
| Cost of ending work-in-process: | | |
|   Conversion costs (8,000 × $\frac{1}{2}$ × $.40) | 1,600 | |
|   Transferred-in costs (8,000 × 1 × $2.00) | 16,000 | 17,600 |
| | | $170,480 |

## QUESTIONS FOR REVIEW AND FURTHER THOUGHT

### REVIEW QUESTIONS

1. Explain when process costing would be used instead of job order costing. Give several examples of industries in which process costing could be used.

2. Explain the differences between job order costing and process costing.

3. Explain the meaning of the term *equivalent whole units*. How is this figure determined?

4. What is the purpose of the first step, tracing the physical flow, in process costing?

5. How are total units to account for determined?

6. What are the three basic steps in the solution to any process costing problem?

7. What is the purpose of a production report?

8. What is meant by the term *total costs to account for?*

9. How does the summary of costs report relate to the production report?

10. Explain what is meant by the term *transferred-in costs.*

11. What is the just-in-time philosophy of inventory planning and control?

12. Explain what is meant by each of the following concepts related to the just-in-time philosophy:
    a. Zero inventory levels      b. Total quality control

13. Distinguish the "demand pull" from the "push" approach to planning for inventories.

## QUESTIONS FOR FURTHER THOUGHT

1. For each of the following products, indicate whether the job order costing method or the process costing method would be more appropriate:
   a. A CPA audit            h. Business cards
   b. Flour                  i. Tires
   c. Processed vegetables   j. Chemicals
   d. Stealth bombers        k. Custom home building
   e. Space shuttle          l. Advertising service
   f. Paper                  m. Grape juice
   g. Accounting textbooks   n. Nintendo games

2. When process costing involves several processing departments, the flow of the physical product is always sequential, from one department to another (from department 1 to department 2 to department 3, etc.). Do you agree? Explain your answer.

3. Must every production operation be accounted for strictly with either job order costing or process costing, or do you think that in some situations both job order and process costing could be used? If so, give an example. If not, explain why not.

4. Discuss why it is necessary to calculate equivalent whole units in process costing.

5. In order to trace the physical flow (the first step in process costing), it is necessary to know the stage of completion for the beginning and ending inventories. Do you agree? Explain.

6. How do you determine the appropriate fraction in the production report for the beginning inventory for:
   a. Direct materials      b. Conversion costs

7. A company has no units in process on Jan. 1, and starts 25,000 units during the month. At the end of January, there are 10,000 units, one-tenth completed. The total costs to account for are $50,000. Explain why the CPEWU should *not* be found by dividing the $50,000 by:
   a. The 25,000 units started      b. The 15,000 units completed

8. When we solve a process costing problem, we know our solution is correct if the total costs in the summary of costs report agree with the "total costs to account for" column in the production report. Do you agree with this statement? Why or why not?

## OBJECTIVE ASSIGNMENT

*True/False*   Indicate whether each statement below is *true* or *false* by placing a *T* or an *F* in the space provided.

_____ 1. A good example of a company that probably uses process costing is a custom boat builder.

_____ 2. In process costing, 4,000 units one-half completed is basically the equivalent of 2,000 units fully completed.

_____ 3. The number of equivalent whole units is simply the number of units completed when there are no beginning or ending inventories.

_____ 4. The cost per equivalent whole unit is found by dividing the total costs to account for by the equivalent whole units.

_____ 5. The costs of units transferred from one production process to another are called transferred-in costs.

*Multiple Choice*   Select the best choice to complete each statement or answer each question below. Write the letter corresponding to your choice in the space provided.

_____ 1. Which of the following is *not* a characteristic of a production process that uses process costing?
  a. All units are basically the same.
  b. All units are assigned the same amount of costs.
  c. The units are produced in one or more continuous processes.
  d. The units are made to customer specifications.

_____ 2. A process has 10,000 units (one-half completed) at the beginning of the month, and 4,000 units (three-fourths completed) at the end of the month. In addition, 40,000 units were started during the month. How many units were completed during the month?
  a. 40,000     c. 34,000
  b. 46,000     d. 54,000

_____ 3. A production process begins the month with an inventory of 10,000 units, and ends the month with only 5,000 units on hand. During the month, 40,000 units are completed. How many units were started during the month?
  a. 40,000     c. 35,000
  b. 45,000     d. 55,000

_____ 4. What are the total units to account for?
  a. The units started
  b. The units started and completed
  c. The units completed
  d. The units in beginning inventory plus the units started

_____ 5. The number of units completed is always:
  a. Equal to the number of units started and completed
  b. Greater than the number of units started and completed
  c. Either greater than or equal to the number of units started and completed
  d. Less than the number of units started and completed

_____ 6. Ten thousand units are in ending inventory, one-fourth complete. What fraction would be placed in the "fraction completed" column of the production report for conversion costs?
  a. $\frac{1}{4}$     c. 1
  b. $\frac{3}{4}$     d. 0

_____ 7. Seven thousand units are in beginning inventory, four-fifths complete. What fraction would be placed in the "fraction completed" column of the production report for a raw material that is added at the end of processing?
  a. $\frac{4}{5}$     c. 1
  b. $\frac{1}{5}$     d. 0

_____ 8. The journal entry to transfer units from processing department 1 to processing department 2 would be:
  a. Debit Work-in-Process Inventory 2 and credit Work-in-Process Inventory 1
  b. Debit Work-in-Process Inventory 1 and credit Work-in-Process Inventory 2
  c. Debit Finished Goods Inventory and credit Work-in-Process Inventory 1
  d. Debit Work-in-Process Inventory 2 and credit Raw Materials Inventory

_____ 9. Transferred-in costs represent:
   a. The costs incurred in one processing department that are transferred with the finished units to the next processing department.
   b. Raw materials incurred during the period.
   c. The cost of goods that are assigned to units sold during the period.
   d. The cost of raw materials that are transferred into raw materials inventory from an outside supplier.

_____ 10. The cost of units transferred to finished goods is determined in the summary of costs report. This cost consists of:
   a. The cost of units started
   b. The cost of units started and completed
   c. The cost of units started and completed plus the cost of the beginning inventory
   d. The cost of units started and completed plus the cost of the beginning inventory plus the cost of completing the beginning inventory.

## EXERCISES

1† **Exercise 1:** Tracing the Physical Flow with a Diagram

The High Flyer Corporation manufactures skateboards in a five-stage process. The board itself is cut and molded in stage 1. The wheels are produced in stage 2, and the shipping box is produced in stage 3. In stage 4 the skateboard is assembled, and in stage 5 the skateboards are inspected and boxed. Prepare a diagram that shows the flow of the physical product through these five stages of production.

6 **Exercise 2:** Preparing a Summary of Costs Report Based on a Production Report

A production report for the Montana Manufacturing Company is shown below.

| | | Units Completed | | | | | | |
|---|---|---|---|---|---|---|---|---|
| **Inventoriable Cost** | **Beginning Inventory Work-in-Process** | **Fraction Completed** | **Units Started and Completed** | **Ending Inventory Work-in-Process** | **Fraction Completed** | **Equivalent Whole Units** | **Total Costs to Account for** | **Costs per Equivalent Whole Unit** |
| Material . . . . . . . . . . . . . | 40,000 | –0– | 200,000 | 50,000 | 1 | 250,000 | $500,000 | $2.00 |
| Direct Labor . . . . . . . . . . | 40,000 | ¾ | 200,000 | 50,000 | ⅗ | 260,000 | 104,000 | .40 |
| Factory overhead . . . . . . | 40,000 | ¾ | 200,000 | 50,000 | ⅗ | 260,000 | 260,000 | 1.00 |
| | | | | | | | $864,000 | $3.40 |
| | | | | | | Costs of beginning inventory | 74,200 | |
| | | | | | | | 3,800 | |
| | | | | | | | 10,000 | |
| | | | | | | | $952,000 | |

a. Prepare the summary of costs report. _24-12 Exhibit 2_
b. Prepare the journal entry to record the transfer to finished goods.

▶ *(Check Figure: a. Cost of Work-in-Process, $142,000)*

7 **Exercise 3:** Making All Journal Entries for a Single Processing Department

The Supercaff Coffee Company has two processing departments. The costs associated with production during January for processing department 1 are given in the following T-account:

† The numbers in the margin refer to the Learning Objectives.

| Work-in-Process Inventory 1 | | | |
|---|---|---|---|
| Beginning inventory | 67,000 | Cost of completed goods | 280,000 |
| Direct materials | 100,000 | | |
| Direct labor | 150,000 | | |
| Factory overhead | 50,000 | | |
| Ending inventory | 87,000 | | |

Prepare all the journal entries affecting the Work-in-Process Inventory account for January. Assume that all overhead costs can be recorded in Accounts Payable.

4 5 6 7   **Exercise 4:** Answering Miscellaneous Questions

The High Energy Vitamin Company uses a process costing system to account for its two production processes. All materials are added at a constant rate in processing department 1. No additional materials are added in processing department 2. Conversion costs in both departments are added evenly. The work-in-process and finished goods T-accounts for the month are shown below.

| Work-in-Process Inventory 1 | | | |
|---|---|---|---|
| Beginning inventory | 201,000 | Cost of units transferred out | 840,000 |
| Direct materials | 300,000 | | |
| Conversion costs | 450,000 | | |
| Ending Inventory | 111,000 | | |

| Work-in-Process Inventory 2 | | | |
|---|---|---|---|
| Beginning inventory | 69,000 | Cost of goods transferred out | _____ |
| Transferred-in-Costs | 840,000 | | |
| Conversion costs | 165,000 | | |
| Ending inventory | 174,000 | | |

| Finished Goods Inventory | | | |
|---|---|---|---|
| Beginning inventory | 234,000 | Cost of goods sold | 873,000 |
| Cost of goods transferred in | _____ | | |
| Ending inventory | _____ | | |

a. If the average cost of the units transferred from processing department 1 to processing department 2 was $5, how many units were completed in processing department 1?

b. What costs were transferred from processing department 2 to finished goods?

c. If 50,000 units were completed in processing department 2, what was their average cost per unit?

d. What was the ending balance in Finished Goods Inventory?

▶ (Check Figure: a. 168,000 units; c. $18.00/unit)

5    **Exercise 5:** Determining the Fraction Completed for Ending
Work-in-Process

During December 1997, the Old Hickory Baked Beans Company completed 25,000 cans, and 5,000 cans were still in process on Dec. 31. Old Hickory uses the following four ingredients in its production process:

Material A: added at the beginning of production
Material B: added at the end of production
Material C: incurred evenly throughout production
Conversion costs: incurred evenly throughout production

Three different situations are listed below. Each represents a possible point in production reached by the 5,000 cans in inventory by month-end. For each situation, fill in the blanks for each inventoriable cost with the fraction completed in determining equivalent whole units (column 3 in the production report).

| Inventoriable Cost | Fraction Completed (column 3) | | |
|---|---|---|---|
| | $\frac{2}{5}$ Completed | $\frac{3}{5}$ Completed | $\frac{3}{4}$ Completed |
| Material A | _____ | _____ | _____ |
| Material B | _____ | _____ | _____ |
| Material C | _____ | _____ | _____ |
| Conversion costs | _____ | _____ | _____ |

5    **Exercise 6:** Determining the Fraction Completed for Beginning
Work-in-Process

Refer again to the facts given in Exercise 5. Now assume that on Dec. 1 there is a beginning inventory of 4,000 cans. Once again three situations are listed below, but this time they represent the beginning inventory rather than the ending inventory. Fill in the blanks with the fraction of work needed to complete the beginning inventory during December (column 1b in the production report).

| Inventoriable Cost | Fraction Completed (column 1b) | | |
|---|---|---|---|
| | $\frac{2}{5}$ Completed | $\frac{3}{5}$ Completed | $\frac{3}{4}$ Completed |
| Material A | _____ | _____ | _____ |
| Material B | _____ | _____ | _____ |
| Material C | _____ | _____ | _____ |
| Conversion costs | _____ | _____ | _____ |

4    **Exercise 7:** Tracing the Physical Flow

The first step in the process costing method is to trace the physical flow. The items listed below are needed to make this computation. Fill in the blanks with the missing quantities.

| | Situations | | |
|---|---|---|---|
| | 1 | 2 | 3 |
| Beginning inventory, work-in-process ................ | 4,000 | _____ | 22,000 |
| Units started .................................... | 16,000 | 9,000 | _____ |
| Total to account for................................ | _____ | 19,000 | 100,000 |
| Ending inventory, work-in-process................... | 8,000 | 5,000 | _____ |
| Units completed .................................. | _____ | _____ | 90,000 |

▶ *(Check Figure: Units completed, Situation 1, 12,000)*

5 **Exercise 8:** Completing a Production Report

Following is a partial production report for the Old Nellie Glue Factory. Fill in the blanks that will complete the report.

| Inventoriable Cost | Units Completed | | | Ending Inventory, Work-in-Process | Fraction Completed | Equivalent Whole Units | Total Costs to Account for | Cost per Equivalent Whole Unit |
|---|---|---|---|---|---|---|---|---|
| | Beginning Inventory, Work-in-Process | Fraction Completed | Units Started and Completed | | | | | |
| Material A . . . . . . | 2,000 | –0– | 6,000 | 1,000 | 1 | ___ | $ ___ | $2.50 |
| Material B . . . . . . | 2,000 | 1 | 6,000 | 1,000 | ___ | 8,000 | $ ___ | ___ |
| Conversion costs | 2,000 | $\frac{1}{5}$ | 6,000 | 1,000 | ___ | ___ | 28,600 | 4.00 |
| | | | | | | | $ ___ | $8.50 |
| | | | | | | | 4,800 | |
| | | | | | | | 0 | |
| | | | | | | | 6,240 | |
| | | | | | | | $ ___ | |

▶ *(Check Figure: Total of "Total costs to account for" column, $73,140)*

5 6 7 **Exercise 9:** Preparing a Production Report, Summary of Costs Report, and Related Journal Entry for a Nonsequential Flow

Clear Up is an acne medication. The ointment is manufactured in processing department 1 and the tube containers are manufactured in processing department 2. In processing department 3 the tubes are filled with the ointment. The tubes of ointment are then transferred to processing department 4, where they are boxed for shipment.

   Production in processing departments 1 and 2 for June was as follows:

```
Ounces of ointment completed and transferred
during the month (enough for 25,000 tubes
of Clear Up). . . . . . . . . . . . . . . . . . . . . . . . . . . . . . . .   100,000
Tubes completed and transferred . . . . . . . . . . . . .    25,000
```

The average costs of production were:

```
Cost per ounce . . . . . . . . . . . . . . . . . . . . . . . . . . . . . .   $.15
Cost per tube. . . . . . . . . . . . . . . . . . . . . . . . . . . . . . . .   $.10
```

There was no beginning inventory in processing department 3 on June 1. At the end of June, all the tubes had been filled and transferred to processing department 4 to be boxed. The costs incurred in processing department 3 during June were $6,250.

a. Prepare a production report for processing department 3 for June. (*Hint:* Use two different lines in the report for transferred-in costs.)
b. Prepare a summary of costs report for process 3 for June.
c. Prepare the journal entry needed to transfer the completed tubes from processing department 3 to processing department 4.

▶ *(Check Figure: b. Costs transferred to processing department 4, $23,750)*

## PROBLEMS: SET A

7† **Problem A1:** Recording Journal Entries for Two Processes

The Rawhide Company produces official footballs used by the International Football League. It has two production processes—cutting and sewing. Footballs go from cutting to sewing to

† The numbers in the margin refer to the Learning Objectives.

finished goods. During July, the month before the football season begins, Rawhide Company is extremely busy. The following facts relate to July:

| | Cutting | Sewing | Finished Goods |
|---|---|---|---|
| Purchases of raw materials . . . . . . . . . . . . . . . . . . . | $224,000 | $ 26,000 | — |
| Use of direct materials . . . . . . . . . . . . . . . . . . . . . . | 174,000 | 20,000 | — |
| Direct labor costs accrued . . . . . . . . . . . . . . . . . . . | 86,000 | 206,000 | — |
| Factory overhead: | | | |
|     Salaries accrued for supervisors . . . . . . . . . . . . | 66,000 | 90,000 | — |
|     Property taxes paid. . . . . . . . . . . . . . . . . . . . . . . | 4,000 | 4,000 | — |
|     Depreciation: machinery. . . . . . . . . . . . . . . . . . . | 16,000 | 10,000 | — |
| Cost of completed production . . . . . . . . . . . . . . . . | 488,000 | 354,000 | — |
| Cost of units sold . . . . . . . . . . . . . . . . . . . . . . . . . . . | — | — | $396,000 |

The balances in each inventory account on July 1 were as follows:

| | |
|---|---|
| Raw Materials. . . . . . . . . . . . . . . . . . . . . . . . . . . . . | $ 36,000 |
| Work-in-Process 1 . . . . . . . . . . . . . . . . . . . . . . . | 160,000 |
| Work-in-Process 2 . . . . . . . . . . . . . . . . . . . . . . . | 40,000 |
| Finished Goods. . . . . . . . . . . . . . . . . . . . . . . . . . | 222,000 |

Sales are made at a 100% markup over cost.

**Required:**

1. Prepare all the journal entries related to the transactions given above.
2. Determine the balances in each of the four inventory accounts on July 31.

▶ *(Check Figure: 2. Balance in Finished Goods Inventory, $180,000)*

4 5 6 7  **Problem A2:** Preparing a Production Report and Summary of Costs Report for a Single Process

The Yabbadoo Company produces a cereal called Stonerocks in a single process. All ingredients (artificial sweetener, syrup, nuts, flour, etc.) are added at the beginning of production, and a package is added at the very end. At the beginning of 1997, there were no units in process. During December, 1,200,000 units were begun, of which 500,000 were still in process (one-fifth complete) on Dec. 31.

    The costs incurred during December were as follows:

| | |
|---|---|
| Ingredients . . . . . . . . . . . . . . . . . . . . . . . . . . . . . . | $120,000 |
| Conversion costs . . . . . . . . . . . . . . . . . . . . . . . . | 100,000 |
| Package . . . . . . . . . . . . . . . . . . . . . . . . . . . . . . . | 14,000 |

**Required:**

1. Prepare a production report for December.
2. Prepare the summary of costs report for December.
3. Make the journal entry that would be needed to record the transfer to finished goods of completed cereal boxes.

▶ *(Check Figure: 1. Cost per equivalent whole unit for ingredients, $.10; 3. Debit to Finished Goods Inventory, $171,500)*

4 5 6 7  **Problem A3:** Preparing a Production Report, a Summary of Costs Report, and the Journal Entry to Transfer Completed Units

On Jan. 1, 1998, the Ny Ranger Sporting Company, which produces face masks for hockey players, had 8,000 unfinished masks in process. Each one was 25% complete. Its costs were:

| | |
|---|---|
| Direct materials. . . . . . . . . . . . . . . . . . . . . . . . . . | $11,800 |
| Direct labor . . . . . . . . . . . . . . . . . . . . . . . . . . . . . | 6,100 |
| Factory overhead . . . . . . . . . . . . . . . . . . . . . . . . | 1,900 |

During January, 20,000 masks were started; at the end of January, 1,000 masks remained in work-in-process, three-fifths completed. There were 27,000 masks finished in January and sent to finished goods. The costs incurred in January were $30,000 for direct materials, $77,250 for direct labor, and $25,750 for factory overhead. The direct materials are added at the beginning of the production process, and all conversion costs are incurred evenly over the entire production process.

**Required:**

1. Prepare a production report.
2. Prepare a summary of costs report.
3. Prepare the journal entry to record the transfer of completed units to finished goods.

▶ *(Check Figure: 1. Total of all costs per equivalent whole unit, $5.524; 2. Balance in Work-in-Process Inventory, $3,915)*

4 5 6 7   **Problem A4:** Preparing All Process Costing Reports for the Second of Two Departments

Sutton Supply manufacturers rugs for miniature golf courses in a two-process operation. During June, 240,000 square yards of rugs were transferred from department 1 to department 2 at a total cost of $360,000. On June 1, 30,000 square yards (two-thirds completed) of rugs were being processed in department 2. The cost of this inventory was as follows:

Direct materials . . . . . . . . . . . . . . . . . . . . . . . . . . . . .   −0−
Conversion costs  . . . . . . . . . . . . . . . . . . . . . . . . . .   $10,000
Transferred-in costs . . . . . . . . . . . . . . . . . . . . . . . .   90,000

The transferred-in costs were costs incurred in department 1 and assigned to units that were transferred from department 1 to department 2 in May, but not finished in department 2 at the end of May.

The direct materials are added at the end of department 2, and the conversion costs are incurred evenly.

During June, 260,000 square yards were completed in department 2 and sent to finished goods. The June 30 balance in work-in-process 2 is 10,000 square yards, one-fourth complete. The costs incurred in process 2 in June were $121,250 for conversion costs and $572,000 for direct materials.

**Required:**

1. Prepare a production report for department 2.
2. Determine the cost of the units transferred to finished goods during June.
3. Prepare a journal entry to record the transfer of completed units to Finished Goods Inventory.

▶ *(Check Figure: 1. Total of all costs per equivalent whole unit, $4.20; 2. $1,137,000)*

4 5 6   **Problem A5:** Preparing All Process Costing Reports for the Third of Three Departments (Nonsequential Order)

The Knockumout Company produces a decaffeinated sleep aid called No Snooze. The pills are produced in department 1 and are transferred to department 3, where they are buffered prior to being packaged in 100-pill jars at the end of the process. The jars are produced in department 2 and are transferred to department 3 in time for the pills to be packaged at the end of the buffering process.

During November, 10,000,000 No Snooze pills are transferred from department 1 to department 3. During the same month, 109,000 jars are produced in department 2, but only the number of jars needed to bottle the buffered pills is transferred to department 3.

In department 3 there were 1,000,000 partially buffered pills on Nov. 1, three-fourths completed. During November, 105,000 jars are transferred to finished goods. The ending inventory was four-fifths completed.

The costs of the beginning inventory and the costs incurred in November for department 3 are as follows:

| | Costs of Beginning Inventory | Costs Incurred |
|---|---|---|
| Conversion costs ...................................... | $2,200 | $30,450 |
| Transferred from Dept. 1 ............................. | 20,000 | 200,000 |
| Transferred from Dept. 2 ............................. | –0– | 10,900 |

**Required:**

1. Prepare a production report for department 3 for November. Calculate equivalent units in terms of the number of jars rather than the number of pills. Use two different lines in the production report for transferred-in costs.
2. Prepare a summary of costs report for department 3.

▶ *(Check Figure: 1. Total of all costs per equivalent whole unit, $2.40; 2. Cost of units completed and transferred to Finished Goods, $251,950)*

4 5 6  **Problem A6:** Preparing a Production Report and Summary of Costs Report for Two Departments

Freddy's Finer Furniture Company produces glass-topped coffee tables that go through an assembly department and a finishing department prior to completion. The wood is added at the beginning of assembly; the glass top is added at the 50% mark, and a package is added at the very end of finishing. These additional facts relate to production for Freddy's during October:

| | Assembly | Finishing |
|---|---|---|
| Beginning inventory, tables ........................ | 5,000 | 9,000 |
| | ($\frac{1}{2}$ completed) | ($\frac{2}{3}$ completed) |
| Tables started, or transferred-in .................... | 25,000 | ? |
| Completed tables.................................. | 16,000 | 21,000 |
| Ending inventory, tables .......................... | 14,000 | 4,000 |
| | ($\frac{6}{7}$ completed) | ($\frac{1}{4}$ completed) |
| Cost of beginning inventory: | | |
| Wood ...................................... | $ 85,000 | * |
| Transferred-in costs....................... | * | $217,000 |
| Glass....................................... | * | 107,250 |
| Package ..................................... | * | –0– |
| Conversion costs .......................... | 5,875 | 6,475 |
| Costs incurred in October: | | |
| Wood ...................................... | 512,500 | * |
| Glass....................................... | * | 150,000 |
| Package ..................................... | * | 10,500 |
| Conversion costs ............................. | 95,625 | 18,000 |

* Not applicable.

**Required:**

1. Prepare a production report and summary of costs report for the assembly department.
2. Prepare a production report and summary of costs report for the finishing department.

▶ *(Check Figure: 1. Total of all costs per equivalent whole unit, $24.25; Cost of ending Work-in-Process, $332,000. 2. Total of all costs per equivalent whole unit, $37.063; Cost of ending Work-in-Process, $92,877)*

## PROBLEMS: SET B

7 **Problem B1:** Recording Journal Entries for Two Processes

The Wild Turkey Bowling Ball Company produces bowling balls in a process involving two departments. Balls finished in department 1 are transferred to department 2; and balls finished in department 2 are transferred to finished goods. The following transactions relate to the month of July:

| | Department 1 | Department 2 | Finished Goods |
|---|---|---|---|
| Purchases of raw materials . . . . . . . . . . . . . . | $ 76,000 | — | — |
| Use of direct materials . . . . . . . . . . . . . . . . . | 66,000 | — | — |
| Direct labor costs paid . . . . . . . . . . . . . . . . . | 50,000 | $ 45,000 | — |
| Factory overhead: | | | |
|    Salaries paid. . . . . . . . . . . . . . . . . . . . . . . | 66,000 | 23,000 | — |
|    Insurance expired. . . . . . . . . . . . . . . . . . . | 9,000 | 6,000 | — |
|    Rent paid. . . . . . . . . . . . . . . . . . . . . . . . . | 15,000 | 12,000 | — |
| Cost of completed production . . . . . . . . . . . | 255,000 | 372,000 | — |
| Cost of units sold (@ a 50% markup) . . . . . . | — | — | $365,000 |

The balances in each inventory account on July 1 were as follows:

| | |
|---|---|
| Raw Materials . . . . . . . . . . . . . . . . . . . . . . . . . . . | $ 34,000 |
| Work-in-Process 1 . . . . . . . . . . . . . . . . . . . . . . . | 100,000 |
| Work-in-Process 2 . . . . . . . . . . . . . . . . . . . . . . . | 120,000 |
| Finished Goods. . . . . . . . . . . . . . . . . . . . . . . . . . | 99,000 |

**Required:**

1. Prepare all the journal entries related to the transactions given above.
2. Determine the balances in each of the four inventory accounts on July 31.

▶ *(Check Figure: 2. Balance in Finished Goods Inventory, $106,000)*

4 5 6 7 **Problem B2:** Preparing a Production Report and a Summary of Costs Report for a Single Process

The Courrier Shoe Company manufacturers tennis shoes in a continuous process. During the month of July, 40,000 pairs were started; at the end of the month, 2,000 were still in process, one-tenth complete. There were no pairs in process on July 1.

The only two inventoriable costs are for direct materials (which are added in their entirety at the beginning of production) and conversion costs (which are incurred uniformly throughout production). The costs incurred during July were $160,000 for direct materials and $114,600 for conversion costs.

**Required:**

1. Prepare a production report for July.
2. Prepare a summary of costs report for July.
3. Make the journal entry that would be needed to record the transfer of completed shoes.

▶ *(Check Figure: 1. Cost per equivalent whole unit for direct materials, $4.00; 3. Debit to Finished Goods Inventory, $266,000)*

4 5 6 7 **Problem B3:** Preparing a Production Report and a Summary of Costs Report, and the Journal Entry to Transfer Completed Units

The Selmon Corporation makes a citrus-flavored drink called Pick Me Up, which is being used at more and more colleges. It not only replaces the liquids lost through perspiration but also provides the daily requirements of all important nutrients needed by the human body. Pick Me Up allows coaches to practice straight through dinner, thereby saving the costs of one meal per day for the entire team.

During September 1997, the Selmon Corporation started 50,000 gallons of Pick Me Up and completed 45,000. The inventory on Sept. 30 was 7,500 gallons, one-half completed. The production costs incurred during September were as follows:

Direct materials . . . . . . . . . . . . . . . . . . . . . . . . . . . . . $50,000
Conversion costs . . . . . . . . . . . . . . . . . . . . . . . . .    95,625

The inventory on Sept. 1 was 2,500 gallons, three-fourths complete. The costs of this inventory were $2,500 for direct materials and $3,750 for conversion costs. Direct materials are added at the beginning of production.

**Required:**

1. Prepare a production report.
2. Prepare a summary of costs report.
3. Prepare the journal entry to record the transfer of completed units to finished goods inventory.

▶ *(Check Figure: 1. Total of all costs per equivalent whole unit, $3.04; 2. Balance in Work-in-Process Inventory, $15,150)*

4 5 6 7 **Problem B4:** Preparing All Process Costing Reports for the Second of Two Processing Departments

Valdes Corporation makes a product that goes through two production stages before it is sent to finished goods. During April, 15,000 units were transferred from processing department 1 to processing department 2. The costs assigned to these units (which include the cumulative production costs of processing department 1) were $105,000. During April, 23,000 units were completed in processing department 2 and sent to finished goods. The Apr. 1 balance in work-in-process for processing department 2 was 10,000 units, one-fourth complete, and the Apr. 30 balance was 2,000 units, one-fifth complete.

The costs incurred in processing department 2 in April were $21,945 for direct labor and $15,675 for factory overhead. No additional raw materials were added in processing department 2. The costs of the Apr. 1 inventory were:

Direct labor . . . . . . . . . . . . . . . . . . . . . . . . . . . . . . . $ 2,400
Factory overhead . . . . . . . . . . . . . . . . . . . . . . . . . .    1,800
Transferred-in costs . . . . . . . . . . . . . . . . . . . . . . . .   50,000

The transferred-in costs represent the costs assigned to units that were transferred from processing department 1 to processing department 2 in March, but were not finished in processing department 2 at the end of March. They are handled like raw materials added at the beginning of production.

**Required:**

1. Prepare a production report for processing department 2.
2. Determine the cost of the units transferred to finished goods during April.
3. Make the journal entries that affect the work-in-process account for processing department 2 in April.

▶ *(Check Figure: 1. Total of all costs per equivalent whole unit, $8.80; 2. 182,100)*

4 5 6 **Problem B5:** Preparing All Process Costing Reports for the Third of Three Departments (Nonsequential Order)

The Roadside Peanut Butter Factory produces a high-fat peanut butter, for people who like to live dangerously. The peanuts are shelled and cleaned in process 1 and then transferred to process 3, where they are roasted, ground, and packaged in 2-pound jars. The jars are produced in process 2 and are transferred to process 3 in time for the peanut butter to be packaged at the end of the roasting process.

During October, 60,000 pounds of shelled peanuts are transferred from process 1 to process 3. During the same month, 39,000 jars are produced in process 2, but only the ones needed to package the roasted peanuts are transferred to process 3.

In process 3 there were 16,000 pounds of partially roasted peanuts on Oct. 1, one-fourth completed. During November, 35,000 jars are transferred to finished goods. The ending inventory is one-third completed.

The costs of the beginning inventory and the costs incurred in October for process 3 are as follows:

| | Costs of Beginning Inventory | Costs Incurred |
|---|---|---|
| Conversion costs . . . . . . . . . . . . . . . . . . . . . . . . . . . . . . . . . . . | $550 | $34,000 |
| Transferred from process 1 . . . . . . . . . . . . . . . . . . . . . . . . . | 12,000 | 45,000 |
| Transferred from process 2 . . . . . . . . . . . . . . . . . . . . . . . . . | −0− | 7,000 |

**Required:**

1. Prepare a production report for process 3 for October. Calculate equivalent units in terms of the number of jars rather than the number of pounds. Use two different lines in the production report for transferred-in costs.
2. Prepare a summary of costs report for process 3.

▶ *(Check Figure: 1. Total of all costs per equivalent whole unit, $2.70; 2. Cost of units completed and transferred to Finished Goods, $93,050)*

4 5 6 **Problem B6:** Preparing a Production Report and a Summary of Costs Report for Two Processing Departments

The Spoilem Rotten Company makes sterling silver baby pacifiers in two production processes. In the first processing department the metal is finely molded. In the second processing department the pacifiers are polished and boxed (100 pacifiers to a box). The silver is added entirely at the beginning of processing department 1, and the pacifiers are boxed at the end of processing department 2.

| | Molding | Polishing |
|---|---|---|
| Beginning balance (Nov. 1), pacifiers . . . . . . . . . . . . . . . | 10,000 | 3,000 |
| Pacifiers started or transferred-in. . . . . . . . . . . . . . . . . . . | 50,000 | ? |
| Completed units: | | |
| Pacifiers. . . . . . . . . . . . . . . . . . . . . . . . . . . . . . . . . . . . . . | 55,000 | * |
| Boxes. . . . . . . . . . . . . . . . . . . . . . . . . . . . . . . . . . . . . . . . | * | 450 |
| Completion percentage: | | |
| Beginning inventory. . . . . . . . . . . . . . . . . . . . . . . . . . . . . | 75% | 50% |
| Ending inventory . . . . . . . . . . . . . . . . . . . . . . . . . . . . . . . | 25% | 75% |
| Costs of beginning inventory: | | |
| Metal . . . . . . . . . . . . . . . . . . . . . . . . . . . . . . . . . . . . . . . | $1,000,000 | $  * |
| Boxes. . . . . . . . . . . . . . . . . . . . . . . . . . . . . . . . . . . . . . . . | * | −0− |
| Conversion costs. . . . . . . . . . . . . . . . . . . . . . . . . . . . . . | 200,625 | 12,000 |
| Transferred-in costs . . . . . . . . . . . . . . . . . . . . . . . . . . . . | * | 375,000 |
| Costs incurred in November: | | |
| Metal . . . . . . . . . . . . . . . . . . . . . . . . . . . . . . . . . . . . . . . | 5,000,000 | * |
| Conversion costs. . . . . . . . . . . . . . . . . . . . . . . . . . . . . . | 1,486,875 | 426,000 |
| Boxes. . . . . . . . . . . . . . . . . . . . . . . . . . . . . . . . . . . . . . . . | * | 90,000 |

* Not applicable.

**Required:**

1. Prepare the production report and the summary of costs report for the molding department for November.
2. Prepare the production report and the summary of costs report for the polishing department for November.

▶ *(Check Figure: 1. Total of all costs per equivalent whole unit, $130.50; Cost of ending Work-in-Process, $538,125; 2. Total of all costs per equivalent whole unit, $139.99; Cost of ending Work-in-Process, $1,767,870)*

## DECISION PROBLEM

The Slumber Mattress Company's accountant resigned on Dec. 31, 1997, and the company has been looking for a replacement ever since. It was necessary for Slumber to have its treasurer prepare the production report and summary of costs report. Unfortunately, the treasurer never studied process costing and isn't comfortable with his results. His daughter has just studied process costing in her principles of accounting course, using this text. She looked at the following set of facts and wrote up a list of errors that she found. Look over the following list of basic facts and then see if you can find the same mistakes in the reports given below.

Materials: added at the beginning of production
Conversion costs: added uniformly
Units:
    Beginning inventory of work-in-process: 1,000 ($\frac{1}{4}$ completed)
    Started: 4,000
    Ending inventory: 1,500 ($\frac{4}{5}$ completed)

| Costs | Beginning Inventory | Incurred | Total |
|---|---|---|---|
| Direct materials ..................... | $51,000 | $200,000 | $251,000 |
| Conversion costs .................... | 6,250 | 106,800 | 113,050 |

Production report:

| Inventoriable Cost | Beginning Inventory Work-in-Process | Fraction Completed | Started and Completed | Ending Inventory Work-in-Process | Fraction Completed | Equivalent Whole Units | Total Costs to Account for | Cost per Equivalent Whole Unit |
|---|---|---|---|---|---|---|---|---|
| Direct material .. | 1,000 | 1 | 3,500 | 1,500 | 1 | 6,000 | $251,000 | $41,833 |
| Conversion costs | 1,000 | $\frac{1}{4}$ | 3,500 | 1,500 | $\frac{4}{5}$ | 4,950 | 113,050 | $22,838 |
| | | | | | | | $364,050 | $64,671 |

Summary of costs report:

| | | |
|---|---|---|
| Cost of completed units (4,500 × $64.671)..................... | | $291,020 |
| Cost of ending work-in-process: | | |
|   Direct material (1,500 × 1 × $41.833) .............. | $62,750 | |
|   Conversion costs (1,500 × $\frac{4}{5}$ × $22.838) ............. | 27,406 | 90,156 |
| | | $381,176 |

### Required:

1. Prepare a list of the mistakes that you found in the reports shown above.
2. Prepare a corrected production report and summary of costs report.

▶ *(Check Figure: 2. Total of all costs per equivalent whole unit, $74; Cost of units transferred to Finished Goods, $260,250)*

## ETHICS CASE

The Drexalt Drug Company manufactures a wide variety of drug products in continuous processes, but was closed down for several months due to civil unrest at one of its South American plants. It seems that the plant had been dumping hazardous waste into the river that supplies water to several surrounding communities. The citizens and employees then staged protests and vandalized company property, resulting in a complete immobilization of operations. Drexalt finally came to terms with the protesters and has been back in operation for several months.

Drexalt is the only manufacturer of a new drug that is very promising in reducing heart attacks. The demand for this drug in the United States is naturally significant, but Drexalt has been unable to accommodate it because of its recent problems. The plant is now running 7-day double shifts but is still falling far short of meeting the demand. One problem has been the extensive inspection process that is required for each shipment in order to verify the purity of the drug and the adherence to exact specifications. Drexalt has decided that, in order to speed up deliveries, it will inspect every other shipment rather than each shipment. It feels that since all past shipments have always been acceptable when inspected, there is very little probability that any will now be deficient. And if any shipment does fail the inspection, then the previous shipments that were not inspected will be recalled before they reach store shelves in the United States and will be redirected to customers in Third World markets.

One of the critical materials going into the drug is available from numerous suppliers. Drexalt has dealt primarily with one supplier because of its excellent reputation for quality. In fact, Drexalt investigated this supplier extensively (as it has always done with new suppliers) before it began to purchase any of its products. The other suppliers also have good reputations, but Drexalt has never investigated them directly to assure itself of the quality of their products.

Now that Drexalt has resumed operations following the plant closure, its supplier is not able to meet its needs completely, so Drexalt finds it necessary to purchase some of the critical material from another supplier without doing any background check. Drexalt's president feels that since no question about the quality of this supplier's product has arisen in the past, there is no reason to be concerned about it now, especially given the urgency of the production schedule. As it also turns out, the price for the new supplier's material is a little cheaper than what Drexalt has been typically paying.

When the end of the year came, no one remembered to determine the fraction of completion for the ending inventory, which was quite sizable at the time. In fact, no one seemed to notice when the last day of the year occurred, since all of Drexalt's managers were concentrating on running the shifts as productively and efficiently as possible. When the production report was later prepared, the controller suggested using the fraction three-fourths because that was the stage of completion at which the inventory had been at the beginning of the month.

Each month Drexalt's managers can get a bonus if either of two results can be achieved:

1. Production activity is increased above the level achieved in the previous month; or
2. The average cost per unit is reduced below the cost of the previous month.

At the end of December, the production manager received a generous bonus for achieving both objectives.

### Required:

Identify any actions taken by Drexalt that you consider to be questionable from an ethical perspective. Explain the possible consequences of these actions.

## ANSWERS TO OBJECTIVE ASSIGNMENT

### True/False

1. F    2. T    3. T    4. F    5. T

### Multiple Choice

1. d    2. b    3. c    4. d    5. c
6. a    7. c    8. a    9. a    10. d

# Variable Costs, Fixed Costs, and Mixed Costs

**LEARNING OBJECTIVES**

After studying this chapter, you should be able to do the following:

1 Differentiate cost drivers from activity

2 Distinguish how variable and fixed costs respond to changes in the cost driver (activity)

3 Define a mixed cost and explain why it is important to distinguish the variable and fixed components of a mixed cost

4 Determine the variable and fixed components of a mixed cost with the high-low method and the regression method

A business's success is measured by its profitability, and managers are evaluated on the basis of how much their activity center contributes to the overall profitability of the firm. Since profits are simply the excess of revenues over expired costs, controlling profits involves, among other things, understanding how an activity center's costs relate to its activity for the period. Some costs, such as rent and depreciation, remain the same no matter how much or how little is produced or sold. Other costs, such as direct materials, vary with the amount of activity. In addition, some costs are made of two parts—one part remaining the same regardless of the level of activity, and the other part varying with changes in activity.

In this chapter we will look at the behavior of costs, that is, how costs respond in total and on the average to changes in activity. We will be concerned with such questions as:

1. What is the relationship between cost drivers and activity?
2. What is the behavior of a particular cost—variable, fixed, or mixed?
3. Why is it important for a cost to be classified as variable, fixed, or mixed?
4. How can the behavior of a mixed cost be determined when it is not already known?

Learning Objective 1

Differentiate cost drivers from activity

## COST DRIVERS AND ACTIVITY

A **cost driver** is any factor that, when changed, causes a change in a center of activity's total costs. By changing the amount of a cost driver, total costs for a center of activity are "driven" to higher or lower amounts. There are many different types of cost drivers. One type of cost driver is the amount of **activity** during a period of time, such as the number of units produced or sold, the number of labor hours worked, the amount of machine time used, the number of requisitions processed, or the number of units inspected.

Other factors besides measures of activity can also be cost drivers. For example, the total costs of a center of activity might be influenced by the quality of raw materials, not just the quantity used; by the training and skill level of workers, not just the number of hours worked; by the number of parts in the finished product and the complexity of their design, not just the number of units produced; and by the condition of the machinery employed, rather than just the number of hours utilized.

Although we now understand that the level of activity is only a single (but very important) category of cost drivers, throughout this chapter we will continue to use (as we have done in previous chapters) the terms cost driver and activity interchangeably.

Learning Objective 2

Distinguish how variable and fixed costs respond to changes in the cost driver (activity)

## VARIABLE AND FIXED COSTS

Costs are classified as either variable or fixed depending on how they, in total, relate to changes in activity (the cost driver). **Variable costs** are costs that, in total, change in direct proportion to changes in activity. For example, as the number of units produced and sold increases, the total for a variable cost such as direct materials also increases. And conversely, as the number of units produced and sold decreases, the total variable costs decrease.

**Fixed costs** are those costs that, in total, are expected to remain the same, regardless of changes in activity. For example, depreciation on a machine is the same amount for the year no matter how many units are produced using that machine.

Let's assume that direct materials cost $4 per unit, and that depreciation on machinery is $10,000 per year. Notice in Exhibit 1 how the total costs of direct materials and depreciation respond to changes in activity.

**Exhibit 1** Relationship of Total Variable Costs and Total Fixed Costs to Activity

| Level of Activity (Units Produced and Sold) | Variable Cost: Total Cost of Direct Materials | Fixed Cost: Total Cost of Depreciation |
|---|---|---|
| 100 | 100 × $4 = $ 400 | $10,000 |
| 150 | 150 × $4 = 600 | 10,000 |
| 500 | 500 × $4 = 2,000 | 10,000 |
| 1,000 | 1,000 × $4 = 4,000 | 10,000 |
| 1,500 | 1,500 × $4 = 6,000 | 10,000 |

For direct materials—the variable cost—the total is found by multiplying $4 per unit times the number of units produced. As the number of units increases, the total goes up at a constant rate (we assume in this example that the variable cost per unit, or the *average variable cost,* remains the same—$4—no matter how many units are produced).

The total for depreciation—the fixed cost—is the same at all levels of activity. Annual depreciation is $10,000 when 100 units are produced, and it is $10,000 when 1,500 units are produced. Although *total fixed costs* remain the same at all levels of activity, *average fixed costs*—the fixed cost per unit—change with the level of activity. Remember, an average cost is found by simply dividing the total costs by the amount of activity. If only 100 units are produced, the average fixed cost for depreciation is $10,000/100 = $100 per unit. When 1,500 units are produced, average fixed costs are only $10,000/1,500 = $7 per unit. Thus, for any fixed cost, the higher the activity, the lower is the average cost; and conversely, the lower the activity, the higher is the average cost. This inverse relationship between average fixed costs and activity is shown for depreciation in Exhibit 2.

Other examples of variable and fixed costs that are found in many organizations are listed in Exhibit 3. The last three items in the variable cost column—utilities, payroll taxes, and janitorial services—are actually examples of **mixed costs,** or costs that are part variable and part fixed. For example, a manufacturer pays a basic fee for utilities such as electricity, even if the plant is shut down for the month; this is the fixed part of utilities cost. The customer also pays an amount based on the number of kilowatt hours used, which would fluctuate with the level of production; this is the variable part of utilities cost. Mixed costs will be discussed in great detail later in this chapter.

## Graphs for Variable and Fixed Costs

A graphic representation for variable costs is shown in Figure 1. The graph on the left is for *total* variable costs. The fact that the total variable cost curve is a straight line is the reason the definition for variable costs stated that the total "changes in *direct*

**Exhibit 2** Average Fixed Costs and Activity: An Inverse Relationship

| Total Fixed Costs: Depreciation | | Level of Activity (Units Produced and Sold) | | Average Fixed Costs |
|---|---|---|---|---|
| $10,000 | ÷ | 100 | = | $100 |
| 10,000 | ÷ | 150 | = | 67 |
| 10,000 | ÷ | 500 | = | 20 |
| 10,000 | ÷ | 1,000 | = | 10 |
| 10,000 | ÷ | 1,500 | = | 7 |

**Exhibit 3** Examples of Variable and Fixed Costs

| Variable Costs | Fixed Costs |
|---|---|
| Direct materials | Salaries |
| Direct labor | Insurance |
| Supplies | Property taxes |
| Commissions | Depreciation |
| Freight-in | Rent |
| Material handling costs | Promotions |
| Utilities | Advertising |
| Payroll taxes | Research |
| Janitorial services | Charitable contributions |

proportion to changes in activity." A total variable costs line behaves in this manner when the average variable cost per unit is the same at all levels of activity—which accountants almost always assume is the case. This unchanging *average* variable cost—the variable cost per unit—is shown as a horizontal line in the graph on the right side of Figure 1.

A graphic representation for fixed costs is shown in Figure 2. The graph on the left is for *total* fixed costs. The curve is a horizontal line, meaning that the total is the same at all levels of activity. The graph on the right is for *average* fixed costs—the fixed costs per unit. Average fixed costs start out high at low levels of activity but fall continuously as activity increases.

## Relevant Range of Activity

### Relevant Range and Fixed Costs

When we say that total fixed costs remain the same regardless of the level of activity, we need to define the *relevant range* of that activity.

Using our example of depreciation of $10,000 per year, let's assume that the most that can be produced each year—even if the machinery is running 100% of the time—is 5,000 units. Now suppose that the company is operating at full capacity but

**Figure 1** Total Variable Costs and Average Variable Cost per Unit

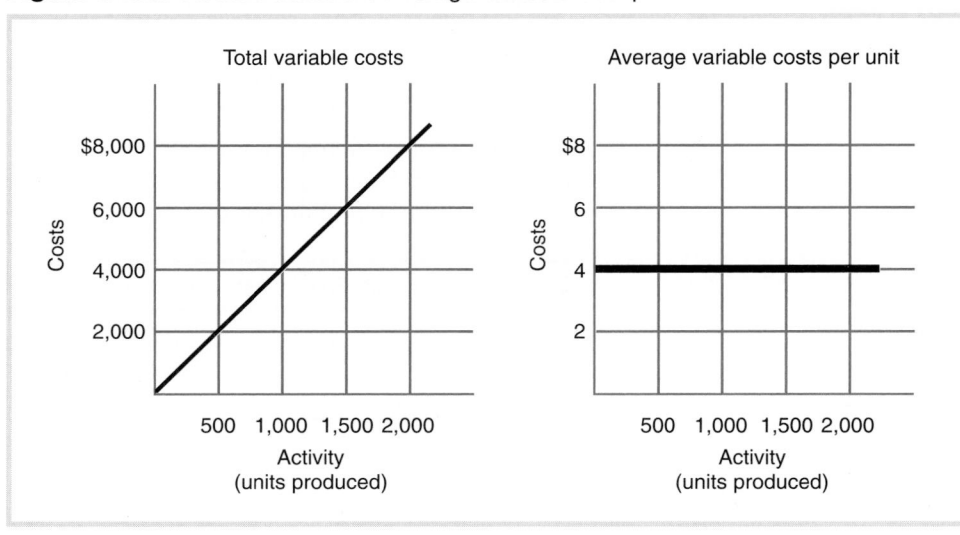

**Figure 2** Total Fixed Costs and Average Fixed Costs per Unit

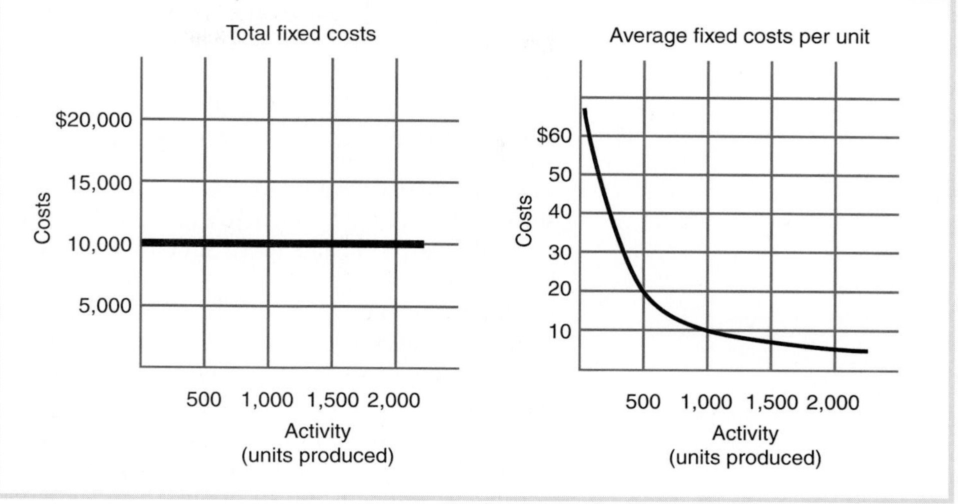

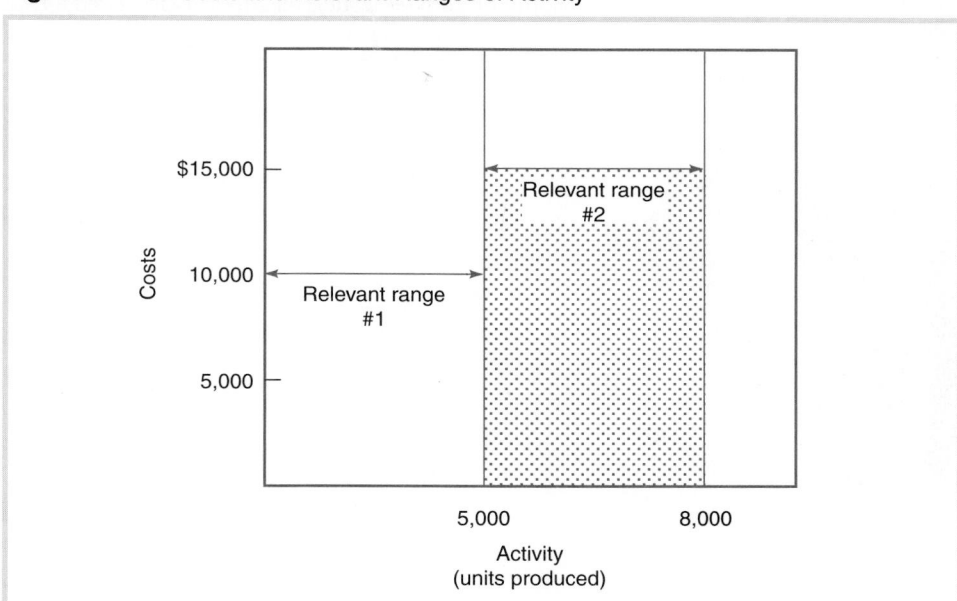

would like to increase production to 8,000 units per year. The only way to accomplish this is either to buy an additional machine or to replace the existing machine with one that has a higher capacity. When a major change like this is made, the depreciation will increase, as will other fixed costs such as wages for additional workers, insurance, and property taxes.

Assume that the additional machinery needed to increase the capacity to 8,000 units increases depreciation by $5,000—from $10,000 to $15,000. This means that if the company plans to produce in a range of 0 to 5,000 units, it can reasonably expect to do so with a fixed depreciation cost of only $10,000; but if it plans to produce in a range from 5,001 to 8,000 units, then the fixed costs can reasonably be expected to rise to $15,000. The range of production over which the behavior of fixed costs can reasonably be predicted is called the **relevant range of activity.** Costs are fixed only within that range. This situation is shown in Figure 3.

Even though total fixed costs usually do not change in response to changes in activity, this example shows that fixed costs can indeed increase if there is a large

**Figure 3** Fixed Costs and Relevant Ranges of Activity

enough increase in activity. In fact, fixed costs not only *can* increase, but are *expected* to increase if the firm goes from one relevant range of activity to another, higher one.

Thus, fixed costs can be defined more precisely as costs that in total are not expected to change in response to changes in activity, *within the relevant range of activity.*

### Relevant Range and Variable Costs

The concept of relevant range also relates to variable costs. The average variable costs sometimes change as the firm's activity shifts from one relevant range to another. For example, as more and more units are produced, the labor force may have to be increased, raising variable costs. As the work force becomes large enough to specialize, it may become more efficient and the average cost of production may fall. There comes a point, however, at which the size of the labor force may become awkward. When people begin to have trouble moving around without bumping into each other, they become less efficient and the average cost begins to rise again. When the average cost changes, the total variable cost curve is no longer straight—meaning that it no longer changes in direct proportion to changes in activity. The graphic representation of this possibility is shown in Figure 4.

Figure 4 also shows that the total variable cost curve may not be perfectly straight even within a single relevant range. From a practical standpoint, however, within a single relevant range a straight line is a close enough representation to be acceptable. Thus, we must be careful to say that total variable costs change in direct proportion to changes in activity, *within* the relevant range of activity.

Throughout this chapter we will assume, for simplicity, that all activity takes place within a single relevant range. Therefore our variable costs will always change in direct proportion to changes in activity.

Learning Objective 3

## MIXED COSTS

Define a mixed cost and explain why it is important to distinguish the variable and fixed components of a mixed cost

Some costs cannot be classified as either variable or fixed, but instead are *mixed costs,* a combination of the two. As we mentioned previously, a good example of such a cost is an electricity bill. The customer pays a basic fixed charge regardless of the level of activity, plus a variable charge based on the number of kilowatt hours used. The total of these two costs—the variable plus the fixed—is a mixed cost.

Another example of a mixed cost is a firm's total payment for wages and salaries. Some employees, such as supervisors, earn a salary that is the same amount regard-

**Figure 4** Variable Costs and Relevant Ranges of Activity

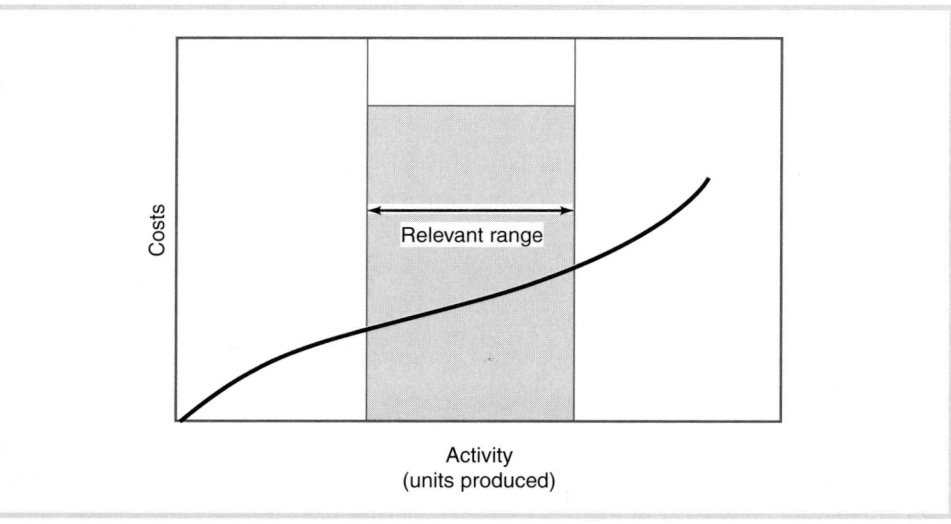

less of the firm's level of activity. Others, such as hourly workers, are hired and paid according to the level of activity. The total wages and salaries for the two categories of workers constitute a mixed cost.

The total costs for a department, or for an organization as a whole, usually include some costs that are strictly variable, some that are strictly fixed, and others that are mixed. Because the total costs of a department or an entire organization are the sum of these variable, fixed, and mixed costs, the grand total is considered to be a mixed cost.

Now assume for a moment that the $4 variable cost per unit for direct materials and the $10,000 of fixed costs for depreciation in Exhibit 1 represent the combination of all variable and fixed costs of a department. When we combine those variable and fixed costs, we get the mixed costs that are listed in Exhibit 4 and shown graphically in Figure 5. If we want to, we can easily determine the mixed costs at any level of activity besides the five levels that are listed — but only as long as we know the variable cost rate and the total fixed costs. Let's see why this is the case, and how these two components of mixed costs are determined.

### Determining the Variable Cost Rate and Total Fixed Costs for a Mixed Cost

A problem we sometimes face in dealing with mixed costs arises when we know the total mixed costs at different levels of activity, and we want to predict the mixed costs at a new and different level of activity, but we don't know the variable cost rate and the total fixed costs. Assume that all we know is the total mixed costs and the five different

**Exhibit 4** Mixed Costs at Various Levels of Activity

| Level of Activity (Units Produced and Sold) | Variable Costs | | Fixed Costs | | Total (Mixed Costs |
|---|---|---|---|---|---|
| 100 | $ 400 | + | $10,000 | = | $10,400 |
| 150 | 600 | + | 10,000 | = | 10,600 |
| 500 | 2,000 | + | 10,000 | = | 12,000 |
| 1,000 | 4,000 | + | 10,000 | = | 14,000 |
| 1,500 | 6,000 | + | 10,000 | = | 16,000 |

**Figure 5** Simplified Mixed Costs Graph

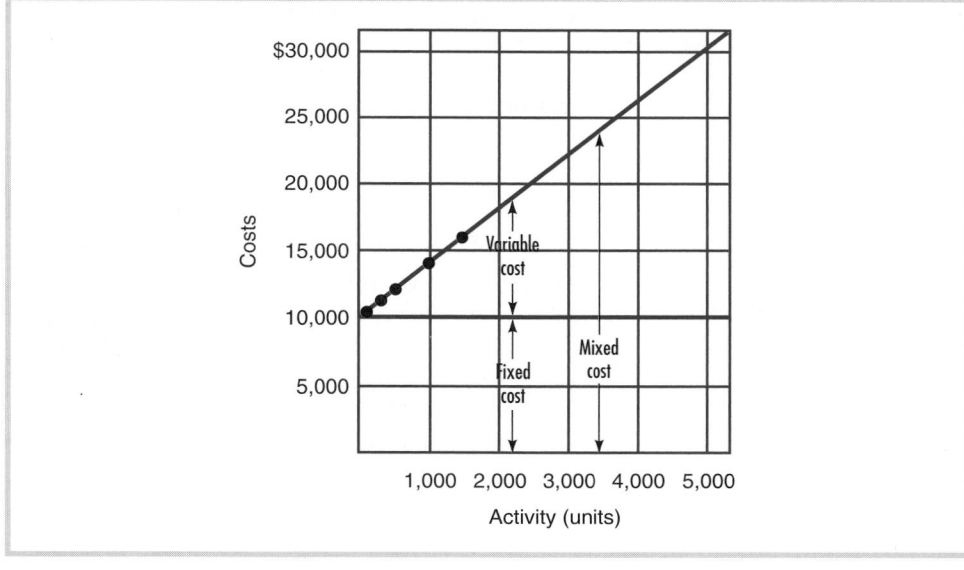

levels of activity shown in Exhibit 4; pretend that we do not know the variable cost rate and the total fixed costs. If we want to predict the total mixed costs at any other level of activity—say, for 2,500 units—we must first determine the variable cost per unit and the total fixed costs. Our starting point is to determine the variable cost rate.

Anytime we know the total mixed costs at two or more levels of activity, we can determine the variable cost rate with the following equation:

$$\text{Variable cost rate} = \frac{\text{change in total mixed costs}}{\text{change in activity}}$$

Using the mixed costs at 1,500 units and 100 units (our highest and lowest known levels of activity), we determine the variable cost rate to be $4 per unit, as follows:

$$\text{Variable cost per unit} = \frac{\$16,000 - \$10,400}{1,500 - 100}$$

$$= \frac{\$5,600}{1,400} = \$4 \text{ per unit}$$

Remember that each mixed cost is a combination of a total fixed cost plus a total variable cost, and that the total variable cost is the variable cost rate multiplied by the amount of activity.

**Total mixed costs = total fixed costs + total variable costs**

**Total mixed costs = total fixed costs + (variable cost rate × activity)**

Substituting into this equation (1) the total mixed costs, (2) the number of units, and (3) the variable cost per unit, from the variable cost rate calculation above, we determine the total fixed costs to be $10,000, as follows:

$$\$10,400 = \text{fixed costs} + \$4(100 \text{ units})$$

$$\$10,400 = \text{fixed costs} + \$400$$

$$\$10,000 = \text{fixed costs}$$

Now that we know the variable cost rate and the total fixed costs, we can determine the total mixed costs for 2,500 units with the following calculation:

$$\text{Total mixed costs} = \$10,000 + \$4(2,500)$$

$$\text{Total mixed costs} = \$10,000 + \$10,000 = \$20,000$$

The equation for total mixed costs is often shown more generally in mathematical form by substituting letters into the equation. The equation for total mixed costs is:

$$Y = a + bX \quad \text{(which you may remember from your high school algebra is also the equation for a straight line)}$$

**where** $Y$ = total mixed costs, also known as the **dependent variable**
$a$ = fixed costs, the point where a straight line crosses the vertical axis of the graph, also called the **Y-intercept** or **constant**
$b$ = variable cost rate, also called the **slope of the line** or **regression coefficient**
$X$ = activity or cost driver, also referred to as the **independent variable**

This general equation for total mixed costs now becomes:

$$Y = \$10,000 + \$4X$$

### Importance of Distinguishing Between Variable and Fixed Costs

Only through an understanding of the behavior of costs can the accountant assist management in a variety of ways, such as making intelligent predictions and rational decisions.

Notice first, in the example for Procrastination Company, how important it is that the accountant understand variable and fixed costs in order to make an intelligent prediction of utility costs.

# PROCRASTINATION COMPANY

The Procrastination Company is preparing a budget on Jan. 1, 1997, for the first 3 months of the year, but it is having difficulty with the estimate for utilities. The bill for December, a month in which 10,000 units were produced, was $800. The company is not sure whether to use a rate of $0.08 per unit ($800 ÷ 10,000) or not. The company controller called the utility company and learned that the December bill involved a $300 fixed charge plus a constant rate per kilowatt-hour. On the basis of an expected number of hours per unit, Procrastination converted the rate per hour to $0.05 per unit. With this knowledge of behavior, the utility costs for the Procrastination Company were predicted as follows:

| Month | Expected Activity (in Units) | Expected Utility Bill |
|---|---|---|
| January | 15,000 | $1,050 ($300 + $750) |
| February | 16,000 | $1,100 ($300 + $800) |
| March | 17,000 | $1,150 ($300 + $850) |

Had the Procrastination Company used the $0.08 rate, its predictions would have been $1,200, $1,280, and $1,360 instead.

Now look at the example for Doll Adoption Company. It shows how the rational decision is made only after the behavior of costs is determined.

# DOLL ADOPTION COMPANY

The Doll Adoption Company is considering dropping one of its 10 product lines, the Lettuce Patch doll, after examining the following condensed 1997 income statement:

| | |
|---|---|
| Sales of Lettuce Patch. . . . . . . . . . . . . . . . . . . . . . . . . . . . . . . . . . . . . | $10,000,000 |
| Total Costs for Lettuce Patch . . . . . . . . . . . . . . . . . . . . . . . . . . . . . . . | 12,000,000 |
| Net Income (Loss) for Lettuce Patch . . . . . . . . . . . . . . . . . . . . . . . . . | $ (2,000,000) |

The president wishes to drop Lettuce Patch, hoping to eliminate the $2 million loss. The controller, however, points out that only $7 million of the $12 million of costs were variable. The remaining costs were fixed and the company would incur them whether or not it dropped the Lettuce Patch line. The effect of dropping the product is shown below:

| | Do Not Drop Product | Drop Product | Effect on Profits |
|---|---|---|---|
| Sales......................... | $10,000,000 | –0– | $(10,000,000) |
| Total Costs: | | | |
| Variable...................... | $ 7,000,000 | –0– | $ 7,000,000 |
| Fixed ........................ | 5,000,000 | $ 5,000,000 | — |
| Total Costs .................... | $12,000,000 | $ 5,000,000 | $ 7,000,000 |
| Net Income .................... | $ (2,000,000) | $(5,000,000) | $ (3,000,000) |

Sales would be reduced by $10 million and total costs would be reduced by $7 million, resulting in a reduction of $3 million in net income, if the Lettuce Patch line is dropped. Instead of the $2 million loss being eliminated, as the president believes, the loss would be $3 million greater.

**ASK YOURSELF** ▶

1. What are variable costs? Fixed costs? Mixed costs?
2. What happens to average fixed costs as activity increases?
3. How does the relevant range of activity affect the behavior of variable costs? Of fixed costs?
4. How are the variable cost rate and total fixed costs for a mixed cost determined?

### A Problem of Oversimplification

When we calculated the $4 variable cost rate, we did so by using an approach called the **high-low method** of evaluating a mixed cost. Under this method—as the name implies—the mixed costs at the highest and lowest levels of activity are used to determine the variable cost rate. If we had used any other combination of costs and related activities from Exhibit 4, we would still have gotten the $4 variable cost per unit and the $10,000 of fixed costs. The reason it didn't matter which combination of data points we used is that the mixed costs from Exhibit 4, when plotted on the graph in Figure 5, all lie on a single, perfectly straight line. You see, the variable cost rate represents the slope—or slant—of the mixed costs line, and a straight line has only one slope. Therefore, as long as all mixed costs are on a single straight line, it doesn't matter which two points are chosen for the analysis. The slope of the line—the variable cost **rate**—will always be the same.

Unfortunately, when real firms analyze their actual mixed costs, the points representing total mixed costs and their related activity levels usually don't fall on a straight line. It is more likely that the actual mixed costs will be represented by a graph somewhat like the one shown in Figure 6. When this happens, every combination of two points, when substituted into the variable cost rate equation, probably leads to a different solution. In this situation, two questions should come to mind:

1. How do you determine the straight line that should be drawn to the widely dispersed group of points in Figure 6?

**Figure 6** More Realistic Mixed Costs Graph

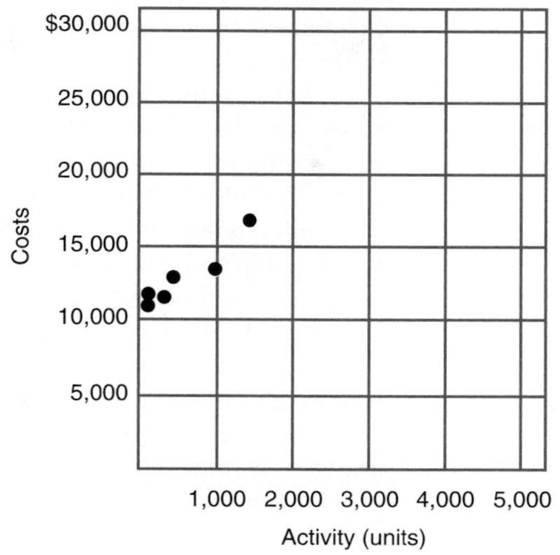

**2.** Which points do you use in the equation

$$\text{Variable cost rate} = \frac{\text{change in total cost}}{\text{change in activity}}$$

to determine the variable cost rate?

The answer to each of these questions depends upon which of the specific methods—high-low or regression analysis—is used, as we shall discuss in the remainder of this chapter.

First of all, let's look at an overview of the common steps that are involved to determine the variable cost rate and total fixed costs with each of the methods.

## An Overview

There are five steps in the evaluation of any mixed cost. They are:

**1.** Identify the dependent and independent variables that are to be evaluated—that is, the mixed cost and the related activity.
**2.** Take a sample of observations for the dependent and independent variables.
**3.** Plot the observations on a graph called a scatter diagram.
**4.** Use one of the two methods—high-low or regression analysis—to determine the variable cost rate and the total fixed costs.
**5.** Evaluate the results to determine their accuracy.

The first three steps are common to both methods of determining the variable and fixed cost components. The fifth step can be used only with regression analysis.

**STEP 1: The Dependent and Independent Variables**

The first step is to identify the dependent variable and the independent variable, which are the statistical terms we use to represent mixed costs and activity, respectively. We refer to the mixed costs as the **dependent variable,** since each mixed cost contains a variable portion which, in total, "depends" upon (thus the name *dependent variable*) the level of activity. As the level of activity changes, so too does the dependent variable—the mixed costs. We use the letter $Y$ to represent the dependent variable in the equation for mixed costs.

We refer to activity (the cost driver) as the **independent variable,** because the value of the independent variable does not depend upon any other variable. It is also referred to as the **explanatory variable,** since we need it to help "explain" the behavior of the mixed costs. We use the letter $X$ to represent the independent variable in the mixed cost equation.

Let's assume that we are trying to determine the variable and fixed costs for an inspection department of a manufacturer, which has as its purpose to ensure that each unit produced possesses the required standards of quality that are set by the company. The total costs of the inspection department would be the dependent variable, $Y$. The independent variable would need to be a measure of activity that has a close relationship with changes in the total costs of the inspection department—that factor which drives the costs up and down. Two possibilities would be the number of units inspected or the hours of inspection time.

### STEP 2: Taking a Sample

To analyze the component parts of a mixed cost, the analysis is usually based on a sample of results that have taken place in the past. A **sample** is a limited collection of observations that provide information about both the dependent variable and the independent variable. For example, each observation for our inspection department would indicate the number of units inspected (or the hours of inspection) for some period of time (such as weekly, monthly, or yearly) as well as the costs of the inspection department for that same period of time. A sample represents only a portion of the data that is available from a population of data. Our hope is that this small portion is representative of the population as a whole.

### STEP 3: The Scatter Diagram

The observations in the sample are now plotted on a graph called a **scatter diagram.** The vertical axis, or $Y$ axis, represents the mixed costs; the horizontal axis, or $X$ axis, represents activity. A scatter diagram provides a visual representation of the relationship between mixed costs and activity. It can be a useful aid in the analysis in several ways.

First of all, the scatter diagram can give us a good idea of whether or not mixed costs and activity are related. For example, in graph 1 of Figure 7 there is an upward trend of the costs in response to increases in activity, indicating that the costs are somewhat related to activity. On the other hand, graph 2 seems to show that activity has little, if any, effect on the costs. It would make little sense to spend any additional time doing steps 4 and 5, evaluating the situation presented in graph 2.

**Figure 7** Scatter Diagrams

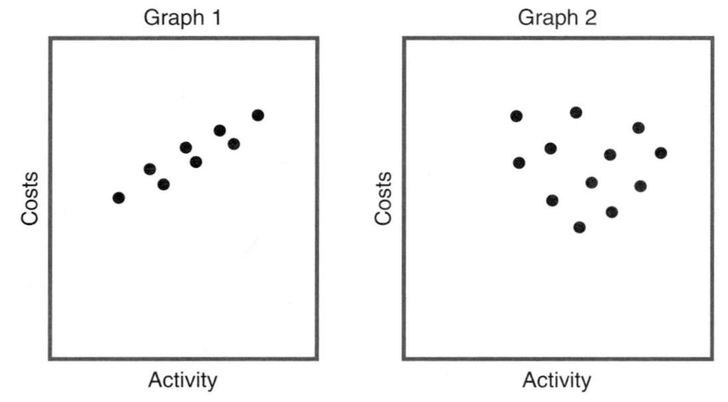

Second, the scatter diagram may also indicate that a curve rather than a straight line will provide a better fit to the observations. This would be the situation represented by the scatter diagram in Figure 8, where the trend of points is gradually but continually changing direction. In this situation it may be necessary to fit a curve to the distribution on points—a process that is more difficult than that of using a straight-line approximation. On the other hand, we may find out that the area of analysis actually includes several relevant ranges and that it is necessary to limit the analysis to a single relevant range where a straight-line approximation would be adequate.

Third, a scatter diagram shows those points that may not be typical—or representative—of the remaining cost data and therefore should be eliminated from the sample. For example, cost data recorded for a month in which the workers were on strike may not be typical of the cost data for other months in the sample. In Figure 9 you can see that one point is far different from the cluster and trend of the rest. If this point is left in the sample, it may cause a distortion of the results.

### STEP 4: Determining the Variable Cost Rate and the Total Fixed Costs

Once we have evaluated the scatter diagram, we are ready to use one or both of the methods (high-low or regression analysis) to determine the behavioral components (the variable cost rate and the total fixed costs) of the mixed costs. In each method we want to fit a line to the points in the scatter diagram that is representative of the trend and distribution of those points and to determine the equation for that line, $Y = a + bX$.

### STEP 5: Evaluating the Results

Once the equation for predicting mixed costs has been determined in Step 4, before we can use it to make predictions, we still need to know such things as: how accurate will the equation $Y = a + bX$ be in providing estimates of the mixed costs? Is there a statistically significant relationship between the dependent variable $Y$ and the independent variable $X$? Are the basic assumptions of our analysis valid?

The only method that supplies the answers to these important questions is regression analysis. The fact that high-low provides no objective way of evaluating these issues is a good justification for using regression analysis to evaluate mixed costs.

**Figure 8** Scatter Diagram Indicating That a Curve Is Preferable to a Straight Line

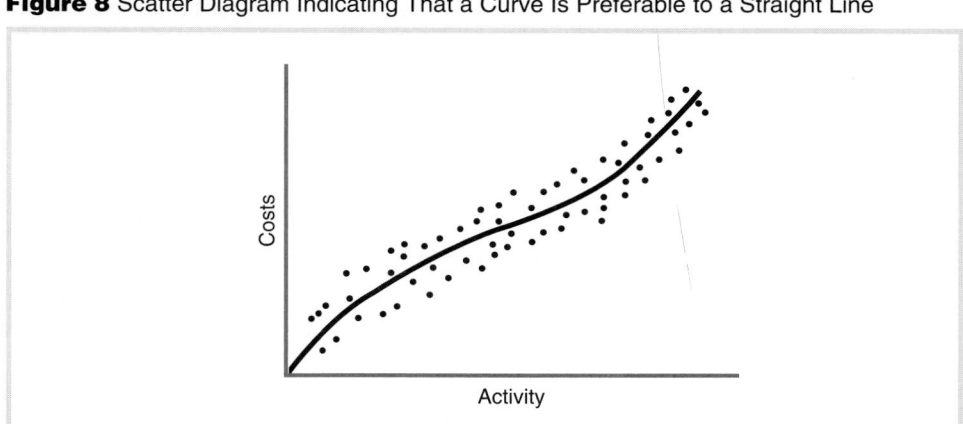

Activity

Costs

**Figure 9** Scatter Diagram—Nonrepresentative Observation

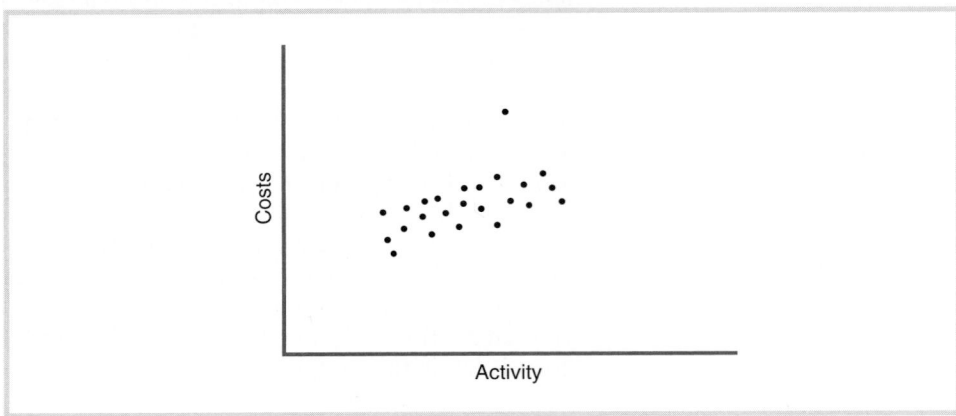

Learning Objective 4

## METHODS OF ANALYZING MIXED COSTS

Determine the variable and fixed components of a mixed cost with the high-low method and the regression method

The information provided for the Big Foot Company in the following example will be used to explain the high-low and regression methods.

# BIG FOOT COMPANY

The Big Foot Company wants to determine the behavior of the costs of its inspection department, which are incurred at the end of the production process. Big Foot wants to predict its costs of operation for the last 6 months of 1997 as part of a budget that management needs in order to apply for a bank loan. Big Foot has selected the number of units inspected as the best measure of activity and has collected the following historical cost data for the first 6 months of the year.

| Month | Inspection Department Costs ($Y$) | Units Inspected ($X$) | |
|---|---|---|---|
| January | $41,700 | 26,500 | *(Highest level of activity)* |
| February | 33,500 | 21,000 | *(lowest level of activity)* |
| March | 35,000 | 25,900 | |
| April | 37,800 | 26,000 | |
| May | 36,000 | 22,300 | |
| June | 40,000 | 23,500 | |

Having gathered these cost data, steps 1 and 2 of the mixed cost evaluation are completed. The third step for Big Foot is to prepare the scatter diagram shown in Figure 10.

The scatter diagram indicates that although there is no single straight line that can be drawn to connect the six points plotted, the points do indeed display an upward trend as activity increases. Therefore, a straight line can be drawn that, while not exact, presents a reasonable representative relationship between the costs of the inspection department and the number of units inspected.

**Figure 10** Scatter Diagram for the Big Foot Company

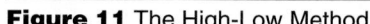

## High-Low Method

The **high-low method** is the easier of the two methods, consisting of the following steps, once the scatter diagram has been drawn:

**STEP 1:** A straight line is drawn through the points representing the highest and lowest levels of activity that are provided in the sample. For Big Foot, these would be for January (26,500 units) and February (21,000 units). This line is shown in Figure 11.

**STEP 2:** The variable cost rate is calculated by substituting into the equation the coordinates for the points having the highest and lowest amounts of activity:

$$\text{Variable cost rate} = \frac{\text{change in total cost at the highest and lowest levels of activity}}{\text{change in the highest and lowest levels of activity}}$$

**Figure 11** The High-Low Method

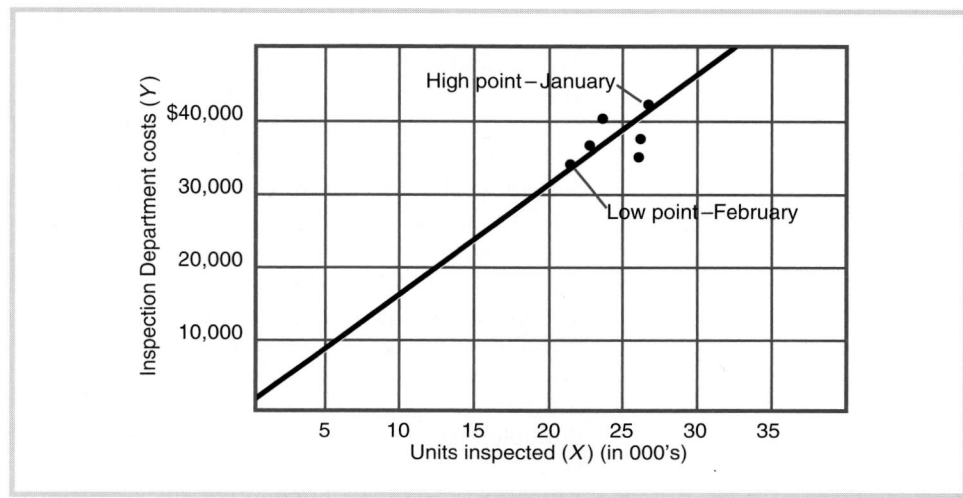

Using the data for January and February, we get:

$$\text{Variable cost per unit, } b = \frac{\$41,700 - \$33,500}{26,500 \text{ units} - 21,000 \text{ units}}$$

$$= \frac{\$8,200}{5,500 \text{ units}} = \$1.4909$$

**STEP 3:** The fixed costs, $a$, are determined at the high point by substituting the variable cost rate into the equation for total costs:

**Total mixed costs = fixed costs + (variable cost per unit × activity)**

$$\$41,700 = \text{fixed costs} + \$1.4909(26,500)$$

$$\text{Fixed costs} = \$41,700 - \$39,509 = \$2,191$$

We can also calculate the fixed costs by substituting $b$ into the equation for total mixed costs and using the low point:

$$\$33,500 = \text{fixed costs} + \$1.4909 \ (21,000)$$

$$\text{Fixed costs} = \$33,500 - \$31,409 = \$2,191$$

Using the high-low method, the resulting equation for the line is:

$$Y = \$2,191 + \$1.4909X$$

The high low method, while simple to calculate, is conceptually the weaker of the two methods. This is because no matter how many points are collected in a sample of observations, the only two that are considered in the high-low analysis are the highest and the lowest—no others. This assumes that the two points at the extreme ends are representative of the entire sample, an assumption that is probably incorrect.

A modification of the high-low method uses a "representative high" point and a "representative low" point. With this approach, one of the points at the high end of the sample and one of the points at the low end of the sample are chosen that appear to be the most representative points for the entire sample. These two points are then connected to draw the line, and their coordinates are substituted into the equations to determine the variable cost rate and fixed costs. Even with these modifications, however, the high-low method still ignores the information provided by all the other points in the sample.

### Regression Analysis with Least Squares

The second method, **regression analysis,** is a far more analytical approach to evaluating cost behavior than the high-low method. With the use of statistical formulas, regression analysis measures the average amount of change in the dependent variable that is related to—or influenced by—a change in one or more independent variables. The formula we use in regression analysis to determine the variable cost rate is a more sophisticated version of the formula (change in mixed costs ÷ change in activity) we used with the high-low method.

So far in our analysis of the Big Foot Company, we have used the high-low method to evaluate the relationship between one dependent and one independent variable. When we use regression analysis with such a two-variable model, we call it **simple regression.** Sometimes the behavior of the dependent variable may be influenced by changes in more than one independent variable, in which case we use a multiple-variable model. This means simply that there are two or more independent variables in the regression model and that the analysis is referred to as **multiple regression analysis.** For now we will be concerned only with simple regression; later we will explain in more detail multiple regression.

### Least Squares

There are several methods of regression analysis. The easiest to understand and the most commonly used is called the **least squares method.** Use of the least squares method provides the best equation for mixed costs, $Y = a + bX$, and the best graphical representation of that equation. The least squares method of regression analysis guarantees mathematically that the resulting line will have a better overall distribution (a tighter cluster) of points about it than will any other line. This line—which is called the **regression line**—will fit the points better than any other line possibly can. Let's see what this means.

### Minimizing the Sum of Squares of Error Terms

The least squares method results in the best possible line because it **minimizes the sum of squares of the error terms.** To understand what this means, we first need to understand what is meant by an "error term."

Look at Figue 12, which shows a line drawn through a group of points. Notice that the line is designated by the notation $Y'$ rather than $Y$. This is a way of distinguishing the $Y$ values that are part of the regression line from the $Y$ values that were actually observed and measured. As a rule, from now on whenever we have a line drawn through the trend of a group of points, any point that is a part of that line—the regression line—will be designated $Y'$. Any point that is an actual observation will be designated $Y$.

Also notice that for each actual observation, there is a line drawn vertically from the actual point $Y$ to a point $Y'$ on the regression line. This vertical distance, designated $(Y - Y')$, represents the amount of error that was incurred in using the regression line to predict $Y$ at level of activity $X$. For each observation there will be a unique $(Y - Y')$. Each $(Y - Y')$ is referred to as an **error term.** The least squares method says this: square each of these error terms, $(Y - Y')^2$, then sum all the squared error terms, $\Sigma(Y - Y')^2$, and the result is that the "sum of squares of the error terms" is less than it would be under any other method, resulting in any other line. It has been proven mathematically that the line that minimizes the sum of squares of the error terms represents the line that has the very best fit to the points in the sample.

### The Calculations for Least Squares

In the least squares method we substitute all the data from the sample into two equations—one for $b$ (the variable cost rate) and one for $a$ (the total fixed costs).

The equation for $b$ is:

$$b = \frac{\Sigma XY - (\Sigma X)\overline{Y}}{\Sigma X^2 - \dfrac{(\Sigma X)^2}{n}}$$

**Figure 12** Error Terms

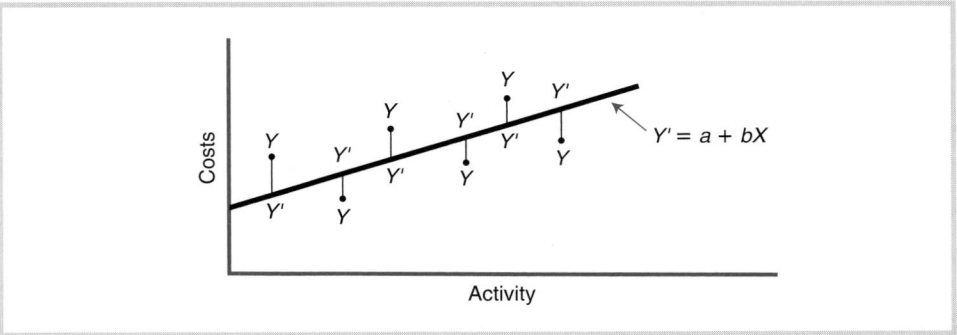

And the equation for $a$ is:

$$a = \overline{Y} - b\overline{X}$$

The data in Exhibit 5 are based on the sample for Big Foot. Zeroes have been dropped from all numbers so that the calculations won't be unnecessarily cumbersome.

Column 1 lists the values for the dependent variable $Y$, representing monthly inspection costs, the sum of which, ($\Sigma Y$), is 224. The average $Y$ value, or $\overline{Y}$—$\left(\overline{Y} = \dfrac{\Sigma Y}{n}\right)$—is 37.333.

Column 2 lists the values for the independent variable $X$, representing the number of units inspected each month. The sum of the $X$'s, ($\Sigma X$), is 145.2; and the average $X$ value, or $\overline{X}$—$\left(\overline{X} = \dfrac{\Sigma X}{n}\right)$—is 24.200.

Column 3 lists the values for $XY$, the multiple of each month's $X$ value times its $Y$ value. For example, for January $XY$ is 1,105.05 ($41.7 \times 26.5$). The sum of the values in column 3, $\Sigma XY$, is 5,440.65.

Column 4 lists the square of each $X$ value. For January $X^2$ is 702.25 ($26.5 \times 26.5$). The sum of all the $X^2$ values, $\Sigma(X^2)$, is 3,539.60.

If we substitute the values in Exhibit 5 into the equation for $b$, we get:

$$b = \frac{5{,}440.65 - 145.2(37.333)}{3{,}539.60 - \dfrac{(145.2)^2}{6}} = \frac{5{,}440.65 - 5{,}420.75}{3{,}539.60 - 3{,}513.84}$$

$$= \frac{19.90}{25.76} = .7725$$

$$= \$0.7725 \text{ per unit inspected}$$

And substituting $0.7725 into the equation for $a$, we get:

$$a = \$37.333 - \$0.7725(24.200) = \$37.333 - \$18.695 = \$18.638$$

If we now add the three dropped zeroes, the fixed costs are \$18,638.

---

**Exhibit 5** Values Needed for the Least Squares Formulas

| Month | (1) Inspection Costs: Dependent Variable $Y$ (in 000s) | (2) Units Inspected: Independent Variable $X$ (in 000s) | (3) $XY$ (in 000s) | (4) $X^2$ (in 000s) |
|---|---|---|---|---|
| January | 41.7 | 26.5 | 1,105.05 | 702.25 |
| February | 33.5 | 21.0 | 703.50 | 441.00 |
| March | 35.0 | 25.9 | 906.50 | 670.81 |
| April | 37.8 | 26.0 | 982.80 | 676.00 |
| May | 36.0 | 22.3 | 802.80 | 497.29 |
| June | 40.0 | 23.5 | 940.00 | 552.25 |
| | $\Sigma Y = 224.0$ | $\Sigma X = 145.2$ | $\Sigma XY = 5{,}440.65$ | $\Sigma(X^2) = 3{,}539.60$ |

$$\overline{Y} = \frac{\Sigma Y}{n} = \frac{224}{6} = 37.333 \qquad \overline{X} = \frac{\Sigma X}{n} = \frac{145.2}{6} = 24.200$$

Using the method of least squares, the resulting equation for the line is the following:

$$Y' = \$18{,}638 + \$0.7725X$$

The next thing we need to do is to draw the regression line in the scatter diagram that we saw in Figure 10. Using the high-low method we can draw a line before we ever make any calculation of the $a$ and $b$ values. But with least squares, only after we calculate the equation for $Y'$ can we draw the line.

There are three steps for drawing the regression line on the scatter diagram. They are as follows:

**STEP 1:** Find the fixed costs on the vertical axis—that will be where the total mixed cost line intercepts the $Y$ axis. This will be \$18,638 in Figure 13.

**STEP 2:** Substitute any possible value for $X$ into the equation

$$Y' = \$18{,}638 + \$0.7725X$$

and solve for $Y'$. Using an $X$ of 25,000 units the estimate of $Y$ is:

$$Y' = \$18{,}638 + \$0.7725(25{,}000 \text{ units})$$

$$= \$18{,}638 + \$19{,}313 = \$37{,}951$$

Find this point on the graph ($X = 25{,}000$ and $Y' = \$37{,}951$) in Figure 13.

**STEP 3:** With a straight line, connect the $Y$-intercept (\$18,638) with the point for $X = 25{,}000$ units and $Y' = \$37{,}951$. This is the regression line.

This line may not appear to be very different from the one we got using the high-low method (Figure 11). Sometimes we can have a line by high-low that will be pretty close to the regression line; sometimes it may be quite a bit different from the regression line. What you must realize is that the regression line found with the least squares method has been mathematically proven to be the best line possible. That is, there is no line that better fits the points or has a tighter distribution of points about the line.

### Evaluation of Results

Although the least squares method provides the regression line and the equation for the line that best fits the observed points, and thus produces the least error, this does not necessarily mean that the predictions are as accurate or as reliable as we might need them to be. You might say there's some bad news and some good news. The bad

**Figure 13** Least Squares Graph for Big Foot

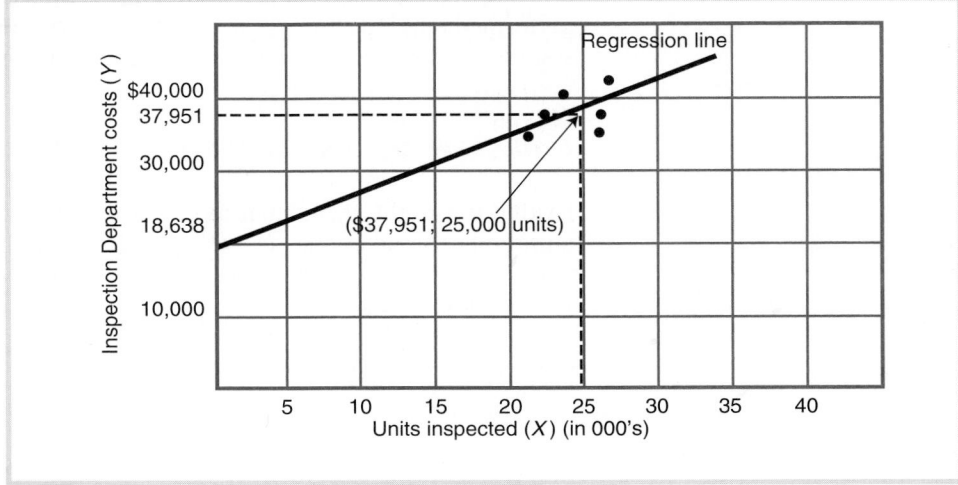

news is that it's quite possible for projections made with the regression equation to be way off the mark. Naturally, the user of the least squares method would like to have some warning about this possibility.

The good news is that when the results for the least squares method are obtained with most computer software packages, the user is usually provided with quite a few statistics—without even asking for them—that can help determine the accuracy of the predictions made with the regression equation. The most common statistic provided for the least squares method is the $R$-square ($R^2$), which is discussed in the appendix to this chapter.

### Multiple Regression Analysis

In the Big Foot Company example, we used one dependent variable and one independent variable. Sometimes, the behavior of the dependent variable can be more accurately described by changes in more than one independent variable. When we have this situation, the only method that can be used to evaluate the relationship between the dependent variable and the multiple independent variables is the least squares method of **multiple regression analysis.**

We cannot use the high-low method with multiple independent variables. Moreover, we cannot prepare a scatter diagram to assist in the multiple regression analysis. That's because most of us can depict only two dimensions on a graph, whereas multiple regression requires a multi-dimensional graph.

In some cases there are several independent variables that can each explain different things about the dependent variable. For example, assume that we are evaluating the costs of a shipping department. The costs would naturally be the dependent variable, but there are several independent variables that could each have a different influence on the costs of shipping. The number of units shipped would certainly affect the costs of the shipping department, but so too would the weight of the units shipped, as well as the distance they are shipped, and also the size of the units shipped. For this situation there would be four different independent variables, and the multiple regression equation for mixed costs would look like this:

$$Y' = a + b_1X_1 + b_2X_2 + b_3X_3 + b_4X_4$$

where $X_1, X_2, X_3$, and $X_4$ are the independent variables and $b_1, b_2, b_3$, and $b_4$ are the variable cost rates for the four independent variables.

With additional independent variables we hope to improve the accuracy of the predictions that will be made with this model. Logically, if the weight, size, and distance shipped have an influence on the costs of shipping the package—which is different from the influence of the number of units shipped alone—then the accuracy of the model that uses all four independent variables should be greater than the accuracy of a model that only includes the single independent variable.

Because the mechanics of multiple regression are so complicated and can be performed only with the use of a computer, we will not show you here exactly how a solution is derived, nor do we expect you to be able to do the mechanics by hand.

## A REVIEW OF THE DIFFERENT METHODS

Exhibit 6 lists the three methods of evaluating cost behavior and briefly describes numerous characteristics of each one. It should be helpful to you in reviewing the main elements of each method, without having to reread the entire chapter.

**Exhibit 6** Summary of Characteristics for Methods

| | Description | Preferability | Use of Scatter Diagrams | Number of Variables Used |
|---|---|---|---|---|
| High-low | Draws a line connecting points with high and low levels of activity. Uses the formula $b$ = change in mixed cost ÷ change in activity to get variable cost rate. Calculates fixed costs by substituting $X$ values for high or low point in the formula for mixed costs: $Y = a + bX$. | Objective, but not preferable since only two observations in the sample are considered. | Useful for all reasons described in the text. Line can be drawn before or after $a$ and $b$ values are determined. | 2 |
| Simple regression | Calculates $b$ and $a$ by substituting sample values into the following equations: $$b = \frac{\sum XY - (\sum X)\overline{Y}}{\sum X^2 - \frac{(\sum X)^2}{n}}$$ $$a = \overline{Y} - b\overline{X}$$ Regression line can only be drawn after the values for $a$ and $b$ are known. | With least squares method, ensures the very best line. The sum of squares of the error terms will be minimized. Can assess accuracy of predictions. | Useful for all reasons described in the text. Line can only be drawn after values for $a$ and $b$ are determined. | 2 |
| Multiple regression | Calculates $b$ and $a$ by substituting sample values into more complicated versions of the equations above for simple regression. For practical purposes can only be used with assistance of computer. The equation for mixed costs can never be shown graphically. | The same as simple regression, except that analysis can be performed with two or more independent variables. Major drawback is that the scatter diagram cannot be used in conjunction with this method. | Cannot be used with multiple regression. | 3 or more |

**ASK YOURSELF** ▶

1. What are the five steps in the evaluation of a mixed cost?
2. What points from a sample are used in the mixed cost formula when the high-low method is being used?
3. How is the regression line drawn to the sample of observations on the scatter diagram?
4. How does simple regression differ from multiple regression?

## CHAPTER SUMMARY

- Costs are variable or fixed, depending upon how their total responds to changes in activity (also called the cost driver).
- A **cost driver** is any factor, that, when changed, causes a change in the center of activity's total costs. Although cost drivers can be many things, activity (represented by the number of units, hours of direct labor, hours of machine time, etc.) is the most common type, and is the primary cost driver used in this chapter.
- **Variable costs** in total, change in direct proportion to changes in activity.
- **Average variable costs** remain unchanged at all levels of activity. That is, no matter how high or low the activity is, the average variable cost does not change.
- **Fixed costs,** in total, are not expected to change in response to changes in activity, within the relevant range of activity.
- **Average fixed costs** vary inversely with activity. That is, the lower the activity, the higher are the average fixed costs, and vice versa.
- The average variable costs and the total fixed costs are assumed to remain unchanged only within the **relevant range of activity.** The average variable costs and the total fixed costs may change as activity shifts from one relevant range to another.
- A **mixed cost** is a cost that is the sum of variable costs and fixed costs.
- When the variable and fixed components of a mixed cost are not known, the variable cost rate can be determined with the following equation:

$$\text{Variable cost rate} = \frac{\text{change in total costs}}{\text{change in activity}}$$

- Once the variable cost rate has been determined, the fixed component of a mixed cost is calculated as follows:

$$\text{Fixed costs} = \text{total mixed costs} - (\text{variable cost rate} \times \text{activity})$$

- This formula is an integral part of the **high-low method** which uses the mixed costs for the highest and lowest levels of activity.
- **Regression analysis** (with the **least squares method**) uses a much more complicated version of this formula to determine the variable and fixed elements of a mixed cost.
- Regression analysis that uses one independent variable is called **simple regression.** When two or more independent variables are used, the analysis is referred to as **multiple regression.**

## KEY TERMS

**Cost Driver**  Any factor that, when changed, causes a change in a center of activity's total costs. Although there can be many types of cost drivers, activity is the most common.

**Dependent Variable**  The total mixed costs to be evaluated when the variable and fixed components are not known. It is the $Y$ in the equation for total mixed costs, $Y = a + bX$. Its name comes from the fact that total costs are influenced by, or dependent upon, the level of activity.

**Fixed costs**  Costs that, in total, are expected to remain unchanged in response to changes in activity during a period of time and within a relevant range of activity.

**High-low method**  A method of determining the variable and fixed components of a mixed cost that uses the total mixed costs for the highest and lowest levels of activity.

**Independent Variable**  The level of activity (the cost driver) that the variable portion of a mixed cot is related to, or dependent upon. It is the $X$ in the equation for total mixed costs, $Y = a + bX$.

| Least Squares Method | The method used in regression analysis for determining the variable and fixed components of a mixed cost. The method ensures that the equation for total costs, $Y = a + bX$, resulting from its use is better than that provided by any other method. |
| --- | --- |
| Mixed costs | Total costs that are the sum of variable and fixed costs. |
| Multiple regression | Regression analysis that uses two or more independent variables. |
| Regression Analysis | A statistical approach to evaluating a mixed cost. The specific method usually employed in determining the variable and fixed components is the least squares method. |
| Relevant range of activity | The range of expected activity for a firm. Within this range the variable cost rate and the total fixed costs are expected to remain the same. |
| R-square | A statistic that measures the percentage of variability in the dependent variable that is explained by changes in the independent variables(s). |
| Scatter diagram | A graph that contains the plotted points from a sample. It is used in conjunction with both methods (high-low and regression analysis) of evaluating a mixed cost. |
| Simple regression | Regression analysis that uses one independent variable. |
| Variable costs | Costs that, in total, change in direct proportion to changes in activity. |

## DEMONSTRATION PROBLEM

The Auto Shop is responsible for monthly repairs and maintenance for the police squad cars in Pahoke, Florida. The city controller wants to predict the costs of running this department for January, 1998, based upon its experiences during the last four months of 1997. The following information is gathered for September through December of 1997.

| Month | Number of Arrests | Miles Driven by Squad Cars | Number of Police on Duty | Total Costs of Operating Auto Shop |
| --- | --- | --- | --- | --- |
| September | 100 | 20,000 | 20 | $23,000 |
| October | 120 | 22,000 | 21 | 23,300 |
| November | 85 | 25,000 | 22 | 23,750 |
| December | 90 | 23,000 | 23 | 23,450 |

**Required:**

1. What is the dependent variable?
2. What is the independent variable?
3. Plot the sample on a scatter diagram. What unique situation do you observe?
4. Use the high-low method to determine the equation for mixed costs, $Y = a + bX$.
5. Use the least squares method of regression analysis to determine the equation for mixed costs, $Y = a + bX$.

### ■ Solution to Demonstration Problem

1. The dependent variable is the mixed costs to be evaluated—the total operating costs of the auto shop.
2. The independent variable is the measure of activity that is most closely related to the total operating costs of the auto shop. It should be that factor which, when

changed, drives (no pun intended) the costs up and down in response to these changes. The costs of repairing and maintaining the squad cars would be related to the number of miles driven by the squad cars. The more miles that are driven by the squad cars, the greater the need for maintenance, and vice versa.

**3.**

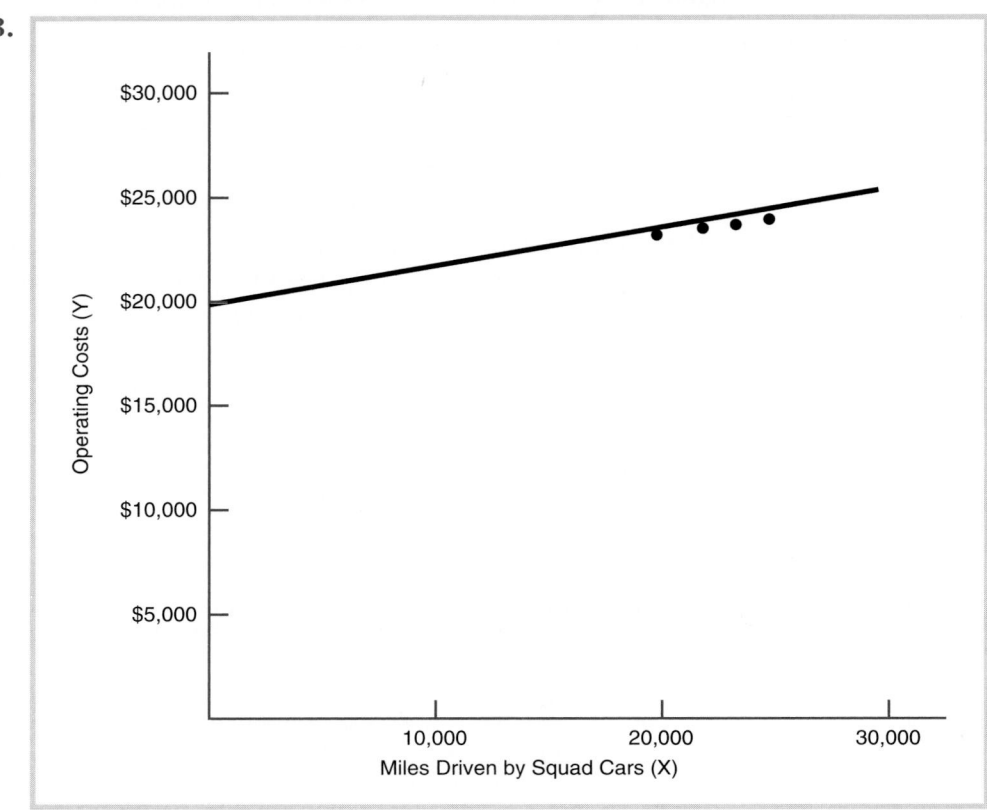

The unique feature of this scatter diagram is that all four points in the sample will fall perfectly on a single straight line. This means that the high-low method and the regression method will yield the same result.

**4. Variable cost rate** $= \dfrac{\textbf{change in total costs at the highest and lowest levels of activity}}{\textbf{change in the highest and lowest levels of activity}}$

Variable cost/mile $= \dfrac{\$23,750 - \$23,000}{25,000 - 20,000} = \dfrac{\$750}{5,000 \text{ miles}}$

$= \$.15/\text{mile}$

**Fixed costs = total mixed costs − (variable cost rate × activity)**

$= \$23,750 - \$.15(25,000)$

$= \$23,750 - \$3,750 = \$20,000$

$Y = a + bX = \$20,000 + \$.15/\text{mile} \times \text{miles driven}$

**5.**

| Month | Total Costs of Operating Auto Shop ($Y$) (in 000s) | Miles Driven ($X$) (in 000s) | $XY$ (in 000s) | $X^2$ (in 000s) |
|---|---|---|---|---|
| September | 230.00 | 200.00 | 46,000 | 40,000 |
| October | 233.00 | 220.00 | 51,260 | 48,400 |
| November | 237.50 | 250.00 | 59,375 | 62,500 |
| December | 234.50 | 230.00 | 53,935 | 52,900 |
| | 935.00 | 900.00 | 210,570 | 203,800 |

$$\overline{Y} = 935/4 = 233.75 \qquad \overline{X} = 900/4 = 225$$

$$b = \frac{210,570 - 900(233.75)}{203,800 - \dfrac{900^2}{4}} = \frac{210,570 - 210,375}{203,800 - 202,500} = \frac{195}{1,300}$$

$$b = \$.15/\text{mile}$$

$$a = \$233.75 - \$.15(225) = \$233.75 - 33.75 = \$200.00 \text{ (in 000s)}$$

$$a = \$20,000$$

$$Y = \$20,000 + \$.15/\text{mile} \times \text{miles driven}$$

## APPENDIX: MEASURE OF ACCURACY OF THE REGRESSION LINE

### R-Square ($R^2$)

We would like to think that by using the regression line equation we will be able to predict mixed costs that will be close approximations of the actual mixed costs we will observe in the future. One way to tell if the predictions will be close approximations or not is with the statistic referred to as $R^2$. But before we explain exactly what we mean by $R^2$, let's look first at the three diagrams shown in Figure 14. Assume that the three graphs represent three different possible samples that we might have taken to get our regression equation. Also assume that each sample resulted in the exact same regression line, having the same slope and the same $Y$-intercept. Naturally, this would mean that predictions of mixed costs for any given level of activity would be exactly the same, regardless of the sample (in graphs 1, 2, or 3 in Figure 14) from which the regression line was derived.

    If you could choose the sample that represented the distribution of points from which the regression line in Figure 14 had been taken, which sample would you prefer? Would it be the one with all the points on the line (graph 1)? The one with the points closely clustered about the line (graph 2)? Or the one in which the points are quite a distance from the line (graph 3)? Which one would give you the greatest confidence that predictions you make in the future with this line will be close to reality?

    If you chose graph 1, you're right. The observed points produced a regression line that precisely intersected each and every observed point in the sample. The fact that all the points are on the regression line means that the actual results in the past were described perfectly by the line. If the relationship between the dependent and independent variables continues to be the same in the future, then we could reasonably hope that any predictions we make in the future with the regression line will also describe perfectly the mixed costs. For example, assume that the slope and intercept for the regression line in graph 1 of Figure 14 were $5 per unit and $10,000, respectively. Since the actual observations in the past were all precisely on the regression line, we would then hope that the actual mixed costs in the future will also be on the regression line. If the units of activity were 10,000, then we'd expect the mixed costs to be exactly $60,000:

$$Y' = \$10,000 + (\$5 \times 10,000 \text{ units}) = \$60,000$$

Graphs 2 and 3 both show regression lines that are representative of the points in their respective samples. However, since the regression lines in these graphs do not provide exact predictions of the mixed costs in the past, there is no reason to expect the predictions in the future to be any better. Although predictions made with the line in graph 2 will be pretty close to the actual results, predictions resulting from the sample in graph 3 will be way off the mark.

When you first looked at Figure 14, it may have been obvious that graph 1 represented the best situation, because it indeed was the perfect situation. In most realistic situations, however, the actual observations are not going to fall exactly on the resulting regression line, and thus the line will not be a perfect reflection of reality. When the situation is not perfect, it is difficult to determine, visually and subjectively, when the line is going to make accurate predictions. So what we need is an objective measure of how closely the regression line will approximate actual results. Such a measure of the predictive accuracy of the regression line is **R-square,** or $R^2$ (the coefficient of determination).

To begin to understand what $R^2$ is all about, first consider graph 1 in Figure 14. There, $R^2$ is 100%, which means that 100% of the variation in the dependent variable is explained by the variation in the independent variable. In the Big Foot example, this would mean that 100% of the variation in the mixed costs of the inspection department can be completely explained by changes in the number of units inspected.

What we are trying to do when we analyze a mixed cost is to explain why it behaves, or varies, the way it does. In statistical terms, we want to evaluate how the dependent variable responds to changes in the independent variable. We would naturally like to have the independent variable explain perfectly the variability in the dependent variable so that, by merely knowing the level of activity, we would be able to predict exactly the mixed costs. Such is the situation depicted by graph 1 in Figure 14, where $R^2$ is 100%.

**Figure 14** Different Samples Given Different $R^2$'s

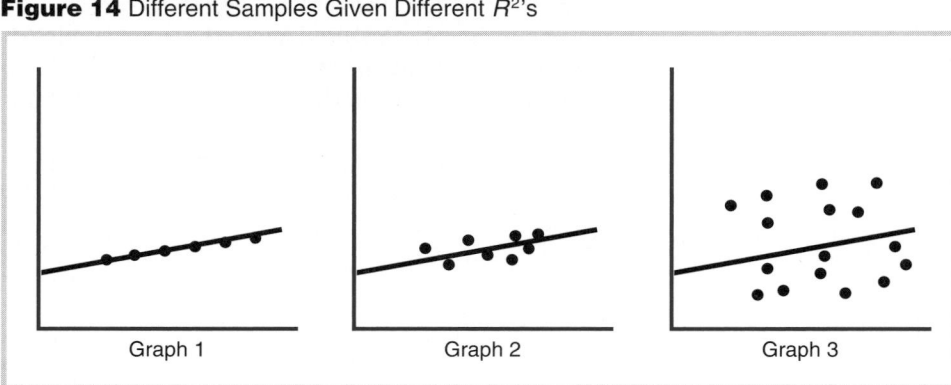

Graph 1          Graph 2          Graph 3

An $R^2$ of 100% occurs any time all the points in a sample fall perfectly on a nonhorizontal straight line. Since the points in graphs 2 and 3 do not all lie on the lines drawn in the graphs, the $R^2$ for each of them is less than 100%. Furthermore, we would expect the $R^2$ for graph 2 to be better than the $R^2$ for graph 3 because it has a tighter fit of points about the line. But the exact $R^2$ values for these two graphs cannot be determined without an elaborate formula.

The range of possible values for $R^2$ is 0 to 100%. We have already seen an example of an $R^2$ of 100%. But what will an $R^2$ of 0% look like? It can be shown in several different ways, all of which indicate that the independent variable explains none—0% —of the variability in the dependent variable. An $R^2$ of zero means that there are no variable costs—all costs are fixed. Both graphs in Figure 15 are examples of an $R^2$ of 0%.

Graph 1 shows a perfectly horizontal string of points, which is obviously a fixed cost; none of the variability in $Y$ is explained by $X$, because there is no variability in $Y$. Graph 2 shows a group of points that have been purposely drawn to be completely random. In this situation there is plenty of variability in $Y$, but none of it can be explained by $X$. The only line that can be drawn through this distribution of points is a horizontal line, with the value for $Y'$—all fixed costs—being the average $Y$ value for the sample.

All this has been leading up to the basic idea of what $R^2$ is all about. $R^2$ is a measure, expressed as a percent, of the variability of a dependent variable that can be explained by, or attributed to, changes in an independent variable.

Within this text we will not burden you with the mechanics of calculating $R^2$. You'll get enough of that in your statistics course. But we do want you to know what the $R^2$ is for the Big Foot Company. It is 50.02%, which means that only 50.02% of the variability in the mixed costs is explained by knowing the number of units inspected. This leaves another 49.98% of the variability in $Y$ that cannot be explained by $X$.

To what can we attribute this 49.98%? One possibility is that we might need a second independent variable. For example, the costs of inspecting units for Big Foot might also be affected by the nature of the units (size, weight, complexity, etc.) as well as by the number of units inspected. That is why we often use multiple regression instead of simple regression.

It's also possible, however, that the 49.98% could simply be a result of random, or chance, variation in $Y$ that cannot be explained by any other variable.

$R^2$ is just one of many statistics provided by most computer programs for the least squares method. All this information is quite important to the user in fully understanding how to properly use this sophisticated method. We have only discussed this one statistic in order to give you an appreciation of what is available to the informed user when he or she is evaluating cost behavior.

**Figure 15** Examples of $R^2 = 0\%$

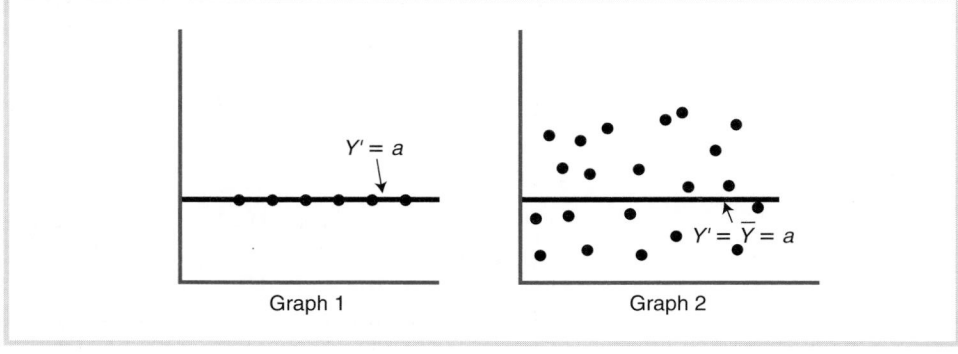

Graph 1

Graph 2

## QUESTIONS FOR REVIEW AND FURTHER THOUGHT

### REVIEW QUESTIONS

1. How do cost drivers and activity differ?

2. List and define the three types of costs classified by behavior.

3. Discuss the importance of *activity* to the definitions of variable and fixed costs.

4. Discuss the concept of *relevant range* and how it affects the definitions of variable and fixed costs.

5. The algebraic equation for total (mixed) costs is $Y = a + bX$. Define each element of the equation.

6. In determining the behavioral components of a mixed cost, what is the purpose of a scatter diagram?

7. Discuss what is meant by the *high-low method.*

8. Discuss the meaning of the statistic $R^2$.

9. What are the extreme values for $R^2$? Draw a scatter diagram that depicts each of these values.

### QUESTIONS FOR FURTHER THOUGHT

1. "A variable cost can be defined as one that changes." Comment.

2. "If a certain cost changes, it cannot be a fixed cost." Do you agree? Explain.

3. "The more activity increases, the lower the fixed cost per unit will be. Therefore, fixed costs can really be classified as variable costs." Explain why you agree or disagree with these statements.

4. Which of the inventoriable costs of a manufacturer would be classified as variable and which would be classified as fixed?

5. If you knew that a cost contained both variable and fixed components, but you did not know the variable rate or the amount that was fixed, how would you predict the total cost for some level of activity?

6. "The way to determine if a cost contains a variable portion is to first draw a scatter diagram. If all the points lie on a single, straight line, then the costs are variable." Do you agree? Explain.

7. Can the high-low and least squares methods ever have identical results? Explain.

8. The Jacobsen Company used regression analysis to evaluate the relationship between sales revenue $Y$ and advertising expenditures $X$. Its results were as follows:

Behavioral components:

| | |
|---|---|
| *a* value | 10,000 |
| *b* value | 1.50 |
| *R*-square | .18 |

How would you evaluate this model in terms of its ability to predict sales revenue?

## OBJECTIVE ASSIGNMENT

*True/False*   Indicate whether each statement below is true or false by placing a T or an F in the space provided.

_____ 1. Fixed costs are defined as costs that can never change.

_____ 2. A cost driver is any factor, a change in which will cause a change in the total costs of a center of activity.

_____ 3. A mixed cost is a cost that is made up of two parts: the variable part and the fixed part.

_____ 4. The high-low method and the least squares method of regression analysis can never result in the same answers.

_____ 5. Variable costs are always perfectly linear throughout all relevant ranges of activity.

*Multiple Choice*   Select the best choice to complete each statement or answer each question below. Write the letter corresponding to your choice in the space provided.

_____ 1. Mixed costs:
   a. Never change
   b. Change in direct proportion to changes in activity
   c. Can never be broken into their variable and fixed components
   d. Have an unchanging average mixed cost per unit

_____ 2. Which of the following is a type of cost driver?
   a. Number of units produced
   b. Number of hours of direct labor
   c. Quality of workers
   d. All of the above are types of cost drivers

_____ 3. What would probably be the best cost driver (measure of activity) for the shipping department of a manufacturer?
   a. The number of units shipped
   b. The number of units produced
   c. The number of direct labor hours used in production
   d. The number of machine hours used in production

_____ 4. What will average fixed costs do when activity increases?
   a. Increase
   b. Remain the same
   c. Decrease
   d. Display an erratic behavior

_____ 5. What might happen when a company goes from one relevant range of activity to a higher relevant range?
   a. Total fixed costs may increase
   b. Average variable costs may change
   c. Total mixed costs will increase
   d. All of the above may occur

_____ 6. Hall Company has total mixed costs of $70,000 when 10,000 units are produced and sold. If $20,000 of this total is fixed, what will the total mixed costs be if the units produced and sold double?
   a. $70,000        c. $120,000
   b. $140,000       d. $90,000

____ **7.** In the equation for a mixed cost, $Y = a = bX$, what name(s) is(are) used to describe $X$?

    **a.** Activity     **c.** Independent variable
    **b.** Cost driver     **d.** All of the above

____ **8.** Which of the following steps for evaluating a mixed cost would always be the first step?

    **a.** Evaluate the results
    **b.** Calculate the variable cost rate and total fixed costs
    **c.** Take a sample
    **d.** Identify the dependent and independent variables

____ **9.** The scatter diagram cannot be used with which of the following methods?

    **a.** Multiple regression
    **b.** Simple regression
    **c.** High-low
    **d.** High-low (using representative high and representative low points)

____ **10.** The Maggi Company had mixed costs of $180,000 and $300,000 in January and February when its production was 10,000 units and 25,000 units respectively. If production is expected to be 30,000 units in March, what should be Maggi's mixed costs?

    **a.** $540,000     **c.** $360,000
    **b.** $340,000     **d.** $400,000

## EXERCISES

4† **Exercise 1:** Determining *a* and *b* for a Mixed Cost

From the mixed costs below, determine the variable cost rate, total fixed costs, and resulting equation for mixed costs:

|  | Mixed Costs | Activity (in Units) |
| --- | --- | --- |
| Month 1 | $8,100 | 700 |
| Month 2 | 7,500 | 500 |

▶ *(Check Figure: Fixed costs = $6,000)*

2 **Exercise 2:** Predicting Total Mixed Costs

During December the McEnroe Company incurred $120,000 in one of its producing departments. The direct labor-hours for that month were 10,000 and the fixed costs were $30,000. Predict the costs for the first 3 months of the next year if the direct labor-hours are expected to be 8,000, 7,000, and 15,000 for January through March, respectively.

▶ *(Check figure: March = $165,000)*

† The numbers in the margin refer to the learning objectives.

2    **Exercise 3:** Classifying Costs by Behavior

Listed below are the costs of the assembly departments of the Stenerued Manufacturing Company. Classify each as a variable (V), fixed (F), or mixed (M) cost.

| | Variable, Fixed, or Mixed Cost |
|---|---|
| Direct materials | V |
| Direct labor | V |
| Indirect materials | V |
| Indirect labor | m |
| Utilities on factory | m |
| Property taxes on factory | f |
| Rent on salespeople's cars | f |
| Depreciation of equipment | f |
| Insurance on all company assets | f |
| Overtime premium | V |
| Payroll taxes on factory workers' salaries | m |
| Janitorial supplies | V |
| Bad debts | V |
| Advertising | f |
| Machine maintenance | m |
| Idle time | V |
| Freight-out | V |
| Entertainment costs (of salespeople) | f |
| Lubricants for machines | V |

2    **Exercise 4:** Drawing Graphs for Different Types of Costs

For each description below, draw the graph that best depicts the cost behavior being described. The horizontal axis is activity and the vertical axis is total cost.

a.  Direct materials costs.
b.  Straight-line depreciation.
c.  Payroll taxes based on wages and salaries of all workers in a production plant.
d.  A distribution of actual costs indicating that no relationship exists between costs and activity.
e.  A distribution of actual costs indicating that a positive relationship exists between costs and activity.
f.  A mixed cost that increases continuously up to the point in production at which the total costs reach a maximum.
g.  Property taxes—a fixed charge if the company operates under a certain level of productive activity. If the activity is above that level, no property taxes will be paid.
h.  Average fixed costs.
i.  Direct labor costs.
j.  Cost of lubricants, computed as follows:

| | | | |
|---|---|---|---|
| First 100,000 lb | $2.00/lb | Next 100,000 lb | $1.40/lb |
| Next 100,000 lb | $1.80/lb | etc. | etc. |
| Next 100,000 lb | $1.60/lb | | |

k.  Utilities—a fixed charge plus a variable portion based upon a constant rate per kilowatt-hour used.
l.  Rent—a fixed charge plus a variable portion only after a certain level of productive activity is reached.
m.  Salaries of supervisors—a supervisor can supervise only a limited number of employees. After that number has been reached, a new supervisor must be hired.
n.  Sum-of-the-years'-digits depreciation.

**2**   **Exercise 5:** Filling in the Blanks for an Income Statement

Fill in the blanks for the income statement of Rhett Butler Company for 1997 and 1998. Assume no beginning or ending inventories.

|  | Situation | | | |
|---|---|---|---|---|
|  | 1997 | | 1998 | |
| Sales ..................................... | $200,000 | | $400,000 | |
| Cost of Goods Sold: | | | | |
| Direct Materials ............. | $40,000 | | $ ? | |
| Direct Labor ................. | 60,000 | | ? | |
| Variable Overhead ........... | 20,000 | | ? | |
| Fixed Overhead ............. | ? | ? | ? | ? |
| Gross Profit ......................... | | $ 30,000 | | $ ? |
| Selling and Administrative: | | | | |
| Variable .................... | $ ? | | $ ? | |
| Fixed ...................... | 10,000 | ? | ? | ? |
| Net Income ......................... | | $10,000 | | $ ? |

▶ *(Check figure: Net income, 1998 = $80,000)*

**2**   **Exercise 6:** Determining Income Based on a Higher Level of Activity

The Packer Corporation sold 12,000 units in 1997 and had the following income statement:

| | | |
|---|---|---|
| Sales ......................................................... | | $132,000 |
| Variable Costs.......................................... | $ 96,000 | |
| Fixed Costs............................................. | 25,000 | 121,000 |
| Net Income............................................... | | $ 11,000 |

The fixed costs will be 50% higher for production in excess of 20,000 units, and the variable cost rate will be $0.50 per unit lower for all units when production is in excess of 20,000. If production and sales double in 1997, what will be Packer Corporation's net income?

▶ *(Check figure: Net income = $46,500)*

**4**   **Exercise 7:** Determining the *b* Value With Least Squares

The Bennett Company is attempting to predict its utility costs for December. The controller realizes that they are mixed in nature and that regression analysis is needed. The following sample has been taken:

| | Utility Costs | Machine-Hours |
|---|---|---|
| July | $420 | 8,000 |
| August | 388 | 7,200 |
| September | 460 | 9,000 |
| October | 480 | 9,500 |
| November | 500 | 10,000 |

a. What would be the equation for utility costs $(Y = a + bX)$ with the least squares method? Answer the question, however, without using the least square formulas.

   ▶ *(Check figure: b = $0.04)*

b. What would be the $R^2$ for the regression model? Explain what the $R^2$ indicates.

2 **Exercise 8:** Determining the Elements of a Mixed Cost Based on Averages

The operating costs for Krispy Dunk Donut Shoppe averaged $0.2875 per donut in 1997, but they fell to an average of $0.2750 per donut in 1998. The number of donuts sold in 1997 and 1998 were 700,000 and 800,000, respectively. Determine the total operating costs for 1999 if the sales increase to 900,000 donuts.

▶ *(Check figure: $238,750)*

2 **Exercise 9:** Determining the Effect of the Relevant Range on Cost Predictions

The variable and fixed costs for Merrill Corporation depend upon the relevant range of activity, as shown below:

| Range of Activity | Total Fixed Costs | Variable Cost per Unit |
|---|---|---|
| 0–20,000 | $15,000 | $2.00 |
| 20,001–40,000 | 25,000 | 2.20 |
| 40,001 and above | 30,000 | 2.30 |

You are to determine the total costs for Merrill Corporation for 20,000 units, 40,000 units, and 60,000 units.

4 **Exercise 10:** Using the High-Low and Least Square Methods

The Condo Company has collected the following sample in order to evaluate the behavior of a mixed cost:

| Observation | Mixed Cost | Activity (in Units) |
|---|---|---|
| 1 | $ 700 | 100 |
| 2 | 1,300 | 200 |
| 3 | 1,200 | 300 |

Determine the equation for the mixed costs ($Y = a + bX$) using the high-low, and least squares methods.

▶ *(Check figure: b, for least squares = $2.50)*

4 **Exercise 11:** Evaluating Results for $a$, $b$, and $R^2$

The shipping department of a large department store has recently finished using regression analysis to evaluate the relationship of shipping costs to the number of shipments made each week. A sample was selected from the results of the first 40 weeks of 1997. The results of the analysis are given below:

Intercept ................................. $70,000
Regression coefficient ..................... $1.75
R-square ................................. .85

a. Express these results in equation form ($Y = a + bX$).
b. On a graph, draw the line that represents the equation in part **a**. Make it as close to scale as possible.

4 **Exercise 12:** Comparing Methods When Results are Identical

The accountant for Watson's Beauty Supply outlet is preparing a budget for the first quarter of 1998, but he is unsure of the behavioral components of the costs of Watson's selling department. He has decided to gather a sample of observations from the last 3 months of 1997.

|  | Dollar Sales ($X$) | Total Costs ($Y$) |
|---|---|---|
| October | $50,000 | $22,500 |
| November | 70,000 | 23,500 |
| December | 95,000 | 24,750 |

a. Using the high-low method, determine the equation for the total costs of the selling department, $Y = a + bX$. First, do it for the months of October and November. Then do it again for the months of November and December.

b. Without making any calculations or plotting a scatter diagram, determine the equation for total costs, $Y = a + bX$, with the least squares method. Why is it that you can get the answers for these two methods without doing any additional work?

▶ *(Check figure: b = .05)*

c. What will the $R^2$ be for this sample?

4 **Exercise 13:** Evaluating Results of Regression Analysis

The following scatter diagram has been prepared for an operating department of Gung Ho Model Cars, Inc. Examine it carefully and then look at the results that supposedly relate to the sample depicted in the scatter diagram.

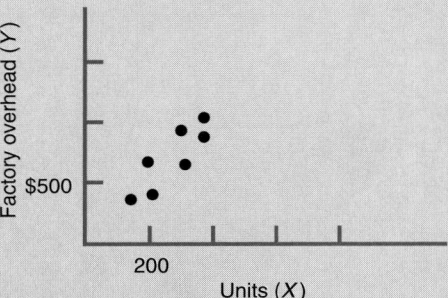

Results:
```
Intercept ...............................  $1,200
Regression coefficient ...................  -$3.50
R-square ................................    1.00
```

In what ways are the results inconsistent with the impression you get from the scatter diagram?

## PROBLEMS: SET A

2 4† **Problem A1:** Preparing Income Statements Having Mixed Costs

On January 1, 1997, the controller of Cheers Corporation, S. Maloney, prepared budgeted income statements for the first 2 months of 1997, when production and sales were expected to be 12,000 and 15,000 units, respectively. They are shown below:

| | January | | February | |
|---|---|---|---|---|
| Sales Revenue .................... | | $156,000 | | $195,000 |
| Cost of Goods Sold: | | | | |
| Direct Materials .......... | $36,000 | | $45,000 | |
| Direct Labor ............ | 48,000 | | 60,000 | |
| Factory Overhead ........ | 56,000 | 140,000 | 65,000 | 170,000 |
| Gross Profit ...................... | | $ 16,000 | | $ 25,000 |
| Selling and Administrative ........... | | 17,000 | | 20,000 |
| Net Income (Loss) ................. | | $ (1,000) | | $ 5,000 |

**Required:**

If the production and sales for March are expected to be 20,000 units, prepare a budgeted income statement for that month.

▶ *(Check figure: Net income = $15,000)*

2 **Problem A2:** Determining Losses From Fire

The Berns Safety Match Company is trying to determine the amount of inventory lost in a recent fire. It has gathered the following data concerning the inventories at the beginning of the year (when the last complete inventory was taken) and on the morning following the fire.

| | Beginning of Year, Jan. 1, 1997 | Undamaged Inventory Morning after Fire, Mar. 12, 1997 |
|---|---|---|
| Work-in-Process ..................... | $30,000 | $7,000 |
| Finished Goods ...................... | $44,000 | $12,000 |
| Additional information, 1/1/97–3/12/97: | | |
|   Sales ............................. | | $450,000 |
|   Gross Profit (%) .................... | | 60% |
|   Direct Materials Used ............... | | $50,000 |
| Direct Labor (percentage of prime costs)... | | $66\frac{2}{3}$% |
| Variable Overhead (percentage of variable | | |
|   conversion costs).................... | | $16\frac{2}{3}$% |
| Fixed Factory Overhead ............... | | $40,000 |
| Cost of Goods Completed.............. | | $205,000 |

**Required:**

Determine the amount of estimated loss for Work-in-Process and Finished Goods.

▶ *(Check figure: Loss of work-in-process = $28,000)*

† The numbers in the margin refer to the Learning Objectives.

**2    Problem A3:** Using Two Different Approaches to an Income Statement

The Annaheim Company produced and sold 10,000 units in October 1997, at $25 per unit. Its cost of goods sold averaged $15 per unit broken down as follows:

Direct Materials . . . . . . . . . . . . . . . . . . . . . . . . . . . . .     $ 4
Direct Labor . . . . . . . . . . . . . . . . . . . . . . . . . . . . . . . .       5
Factory Overhead ($\frac{2}{3}$ of which is variable). . . . . . . . . .       6

Total                                                              $15

Its selling and administrative costs averaged $4 ($\frac{1}{2}$ of which was variable). Annaheim expects to double production and sales in November.

**Required:**

1. If the cost-behavior assumptions are unchanged, prepare an income statement (in total dollars) for November, 1997.
2. Now prepare the income statement using a different format. For this part, first group all the variable costs together and subtract their total from sales, and then subtract the total for the fixed costs. This is referred to in the next chapter as the contribution margin format.

▶ *(Check figure: Gross profit = $220,000)*

**4    Problem A4:** Using Both Methods to Evaluate Mixed Costs

The Perriere Car Wash is trying to estimate its cost of operations for January, 1998. Its controller, Hal Culligan, points out that its operating costs are mixed and one of several approaches will have to be employed in order to determine the behavioral components. Hal proceeds to take a sample of eight observations from May to December, 1997. The sample is given below:

|           | Total Operating Cost ($Y$) | Number of Customers ($X$) |
|-----------|----------------------------|----------------------------|
| May       | $5,100                     | 3,000                      |
| June      | 6,200                      | 4,000                      |
| July      | 5,700                      | 2,500                      |
| August    | 5,800                      | 4,500                      |
| September | 6,700                      | 3,250                      |
| October   | 7,000                      | 5,000                      |
| November  | 5,200                      | 3,500                      |
| December  | 6,100                      | 4,200                      |

**Required:**

1. Prepare a scatter diagram.
2. Using the high-low method, determine the equation for total costs, $Y = a + bX$.
3. Using the least squares method, determine the equation for total costs.

▶ *(Check figure: 2.b = $0.52)*

**4    Problem A5:** Predicting Mixed Costs Based Upon the Results of the Least Squares Method

The R4-D4 Robot Company, which produces miniature robots for use in the home, attempts to control the quality of its product with an intensive inspection by the inspection department. The costs and units inspected during the last 6 weeks are given below:

| Week | Costs | Units |
|------|-------|-------|
| 1 | $4,100 | 12 |
| 2 | 3,850 | 14 |
| 3 | 4,500 | 17 |
| 4 | 4,000 | 20 |
| 5 | 3,200 | 9 |
| 6 | 3,700 | 10 |

The controller, L. Moonwalker, is trying to predict the costs for the inspection department in week 7 when 25 robots are scheduled to be produced.

**Required:**

Using the least squares method, project the total costs of the inspection department for week 7.

▶ (Check figure: b = 70.03)

**1 4 Problem A6:** Deciding on the Best Measure of Activity Based on a Scatter Diagram

The Bailey Company is trying to budget its indirect labor costs for January, 1997, but it is not sure of their behavioral nature. The controller collected a sample of observations for the last 6 months and asks your assistance in analyzing indirect labor.

| | | Measures of Activity | |
|-------------|------------------|------------------|------------------|
| Observation | Indirect Labor Costs | Units Produced | Labor-Hours |
| 1 | $20,000 | 1,400 | 4.200 |
| 2 | 32,000 | 2,400 | 8,400 |
| 3 | 24,900 | 1,800 | 5,760 |
| 4 | 30,000 | 3,000 | 8,250 |
| 5 | 52,500 | 3,400 | 12,920 |
| 6 | 23,000 | 2,000 | 5,200 |

**Required:**

1. Prepare two scatter diagrams. For the first one use units produced as the independent variable, and for the second one use labor-hours as the independent variable.
2. Which measure of activity would be the better independent variable—units produced or labor-hours? Explain.
3. Using the preferable measure of activity, determine the equation $Y = a + bX$ for indirect labor costs with the least squares method.
4. Repeat part 3, but exclude from your sample the fifth observation. Comment on the differences in your results in parts 3 and 4.

**4 Problem A7:** Using Least Squares When a Behavioral Assumption Has Changed

During the first 3 months of the year Hurts Truck Rental had exactly the same fixed costs in each month. During the next 3 month an expansion project resulted in an $8,000 increase in the fixed costs per month. The total costs for each month and their related activity levels are shown below:

| | Total Costs (Y) | Miles Driven (X) |
|---|---|---|
| January | $31,500 | 13,000 |
| February | 32,500 | 15,000 |
| March | 37,000 | 24,000 |
| April | 45,500 | 25,000 |
| May | 48,000 | 30,000 |
| June | 50,500 | 35,000 |

**Required:**

1. Using the least squares method, determine the equation $Y = a + bX$ for the total costs.
2. Prepare a scatter diagram, and place the line determined in part 1 on the diagram.
3. Now subtract the additional fixed costs of $8,000 from the total costs for April through June, and redo the analysis with the least squares method.
4. Prepare a new scatter diagram, this time using the total costs from part 3. Place the line that you determined in part 3 on the diagram.
5. Which results do you feel are more meaningful? Why?

▶ (Check figure: 1.a = $18,896)

## PROBLEMS: SET B

2  4† **Problem B1:** Preparing Income Statements That Have Mixed Costs

The Victorio Corporation has just completed operations for July 1997, and has prepared the following comparative income statements for June and July:

| | | June | | July |
|---|---|---|---|---|
| Sales | | $200,000 | | $240,000 |
| Cost of Goods Sold: | | | | |
| Direct Materials | $40,000 | | $48,000 | |
| Direct Labor | 50,000 | | 60,000 | |
| Factory Overhead | 45,000 | 135,000 | 51,000 | 159,000 |
| Gross Profit | | $ 65,000 | | $ 81,000 |
| Selling and Administrative | | 15,000 | | 18,000 |
| Net Income | | $ 50,000 | | $ 63,000 |

The selling price in each month was $10.

**Required:**

Victorio anticipates producing and selling 18,000 units during August. Prepare the income statement that Victorio would expect for that month.

▶ (Check figure: Net income = $43,500)

2 **Problem B2:** Determining Losses From Theft

The Precious Metals Manufacturing Company has been in operation just a short time and is concerned that it is having as much inventory stolen as it sells. The accounting department took a physical inventory last night and found the following balances in each inventory account:

| | |
|---|---|
| Raw Materials | $ –0– |
| Work-in-Process | 12,000 |
| Finished Goods | 4,000 |

† The numbers in the margin refer to the Learning Objectives.

There was no inventory of any kind when the company began business. Since beginning production, $40,000 of raw materials have been purchased. The following conversion costs were incurred during production:

Direct Labor ($\frac{1}{2}$ or prime costs and $\frac{2}{3}$ of variable
    conversion costs) ........................ $30,000
Fixed Factory Overhead..................... 8,000

Sales totaled $80,000 and cost of goods sold averaged 70% of sales. The cost of units completed was $71,000.

**Required:**

Calculate the amount of inventory stolen from raw materials, work-in-process, and finished goods.

▶ *(Check figure: Raw materials stolen = $10,000)*

**2** **Problem B3:** Using a New Format in Preparing an Income Statement

In March 1997, the Underhill Coffin Company manufactured and sold 14,000 coffins. Its controller, Ron Kelly, prepared the following income statement, given in total as well as on a per-unit basis:

| | | |
|---|---:|---:|
| Sales ..................................................... | $3,500,000 | $250/coffin |
| Cost of Goods Sold: | | |
|   Direct Materials ................................ | $1,400,000 | $100/coffin |
|   Direct Labor..................................... | 1,400,000 | 100/coffin |
|   Variable Overhead.............................. | 112,000 | 8/coffin |
|   Fixed Overhead................................. | 70,000 | 5/coffin |
|     Total ..................................... | $2,982,000 | $213/coffin |
| Gross Profit............................................ | $ 518,000 | $ 37/coffin |
| Selling and Administrative: | | |
|   Variable ..................................... | $ 126,000 | $ 9/coffin |
|   Fixed ........................................ | 14,000 | 1/coffin |
|     Total .................................... | $ 140,000 | $ 10/coffin |
| Net Income | $ 378,000 | $ 27/coffin |

**Required:**

Prepare an income statement (showing total dollars and dollars per coffin, as given above) for April if 16,000 coffins will be produced and sold.

▶ *(Check figure: Net income = $444,000)*

**4** **Problem B4:** Using Both Methods to Evaluate Mixed Costs

The controller, Beth Moon, of the Chattanooga Choo Choos Softball Team (one of the new teams in the women's professional softball league) has gathered a sample of six monthly observations for the team's operating costs. Beth wants to project operating costs for the upcoming months and feels that the variable component of its mixed costs fluctuates directly with the number of fans attending its games. The sample taken by Beth is given below:

| Week | Operating Costs ($Y$) | Number of Fans ($X$) |
|:---:|:---:|:---:|
| 1 | $36,000 | 1,920 |
| 2 | 40,500 | 3,300 |
| 3 | 37,500 | 1,550 |
| 4 | 34,500 | 2,700 |
| 5 | 32,100 | 1,200 |
| 6 | 42,600 | 2,550 |

**Required:**

1. Prepare a scatter diagram.
2. Using the high-low method, determine the equation for total mixed costs, $Y = a + bX$.
3. Using the method of least squares, determine the equation for total mixed costs, $Y = a + bX$.

▶ *(Check figure: 3.b = $3.052)*

4  **Problem B5:** Using the Least Squares Method to Evaluate Mixed Costs

P. Holder, controller of Kenny's Exports, is using the least squares method to evaluate the costs of its shipping department. A sample taken from the last 8 weeks of operations is given below:

| Week | Costs of Shipping Department | Number of Units Shipped |
|---|---|---|
| 1 | $6,250 | 1,500 |
| 2 | 7,600 | 2,400 |
| 3 | 5,800 | 1,200 |
| 4 | 5,200 | 800 |
| 5 | 4,900 | 600 |
| 6 | 6,400 | 1,600 |
| 7 | 6,700 | 1,800 |
| 8 | 7,150 | 2,100 |

**Required:**

Using the least squares method, determine the equation for the mixed costs, $Y = a + bX$.

▶ *(Check figure: b = $1.50)*

1 4  **Problem B6:** Deciding on the Best Measure of Activity Based on a Scatter Diagram

The Gearey Corporation is trying to budget the costs of its inspection department for 1997. The controller is sure that the total costs contain both variable and fixed components, but he is not sure of the correct breakdown between these two groups of costs. In addition, he is not sure of the best measure of activity to use for the independent variable. He has collected a sample of observations for the two possible measures of activity given below and asks your assistance in analyzing the costs of the inspection department.

| Observation | Inspection Department Costs | Measures of Activity | |
|---|---|---|---|
| | | Units Inspected | Labor-Hours |
| 1 | $25,000 | 1,750 | 5,250 |
| 2 | 40,000 | 3,000 | 10,500 |
| 3 | 31,120 | 2,250 | 7,200 |
| 4 | 37,500 | 3,750 | 10,310 |
| 5 | 65,620 | 4,250 | 16,150 |
| 6 | 28,750 | 2,500 | 6,500 |

**Required:**

1. Prepare two scatter diagrams. For the first one use units inspected as the independent variable, and for the second one use labor-hours as the independent variable.
2. Which measure of activity would be the better independent variable—units inspected or labor-hours? Explain.
3. Using the preferable measure of activity, determine the equation $Y = a + bX$ for inspection department costs with the least squares method.
4. Repeat part 3, but exclude from your sample the fifth observation. Comment on the differences in your results in parts 3 and 4.

▶ *(Check figure: 3.a = $4,071)*

4   **Problem B7:** Using Least Squares When a Behavior Assumption Has Changed

ABM Corporation is a small computer company that makes most of its sales through its outside sales force. The salespeople are reimbursed for their traveling expenses at a fixed amount per day plus a fixed amount per mile driven. In April, 1997, the company increased the mileage reimbursement by $0.05 per mile, and it paid this new rate for the next 3 months. The total travel reimbursements and related miles driven for the first 6 months of 1997 are given below:

|  | Total Costs ($Y$) | Miles Driven ($X$) |
|---|---|---|
| January | $36,500 | 100,000 |
| February | 39,500 | 115,000 |
| March | 40,500 | 120,000 |
| April | 44,000 | 110,000 |
| May | 49,000 | 130,000 |
| June | 39,000 | 90,000 |

**Required:**

1. Using the least squares method, determine the equation $Y = a + bX$ for the total costs.
2. Prepare a scatter diagram, and place the line determined in part 1 on the diagram.
3. Now subtract the additional variable costs at $0.05 per mile times the miles driven in April through June from the total costs for April through June. Then redo the analysis with the least squares method.
4. Prepare a new scatter diagram, this time using the total costs from part 3. Place the line that you determined in part 3 on the diagram.
5. Which results do you feel are more meaningful? Why?

▶ *(Check figure: 1.$b^2$, 2255; 3$b^2$, 20)*

**DECISION PROBLEM**

The Kayfred Precision Laser Company manufactures laser equipment for use in surveying and runs a repair shop for the equipment sold to its customers. It is attempting to determine a billing rate and wants to base it upon the variable costs of operating the repair shop. The problem is that the operating costs have not been separated into their variable and fixed components. A sample of the costs of this department has been collected for the last 27 months, and the resulting scatter diagram is shown below. The controller plans to use the least squares method of analysis, but first wants to evaluate the scatter diagram for any relevant information that may be helpful.

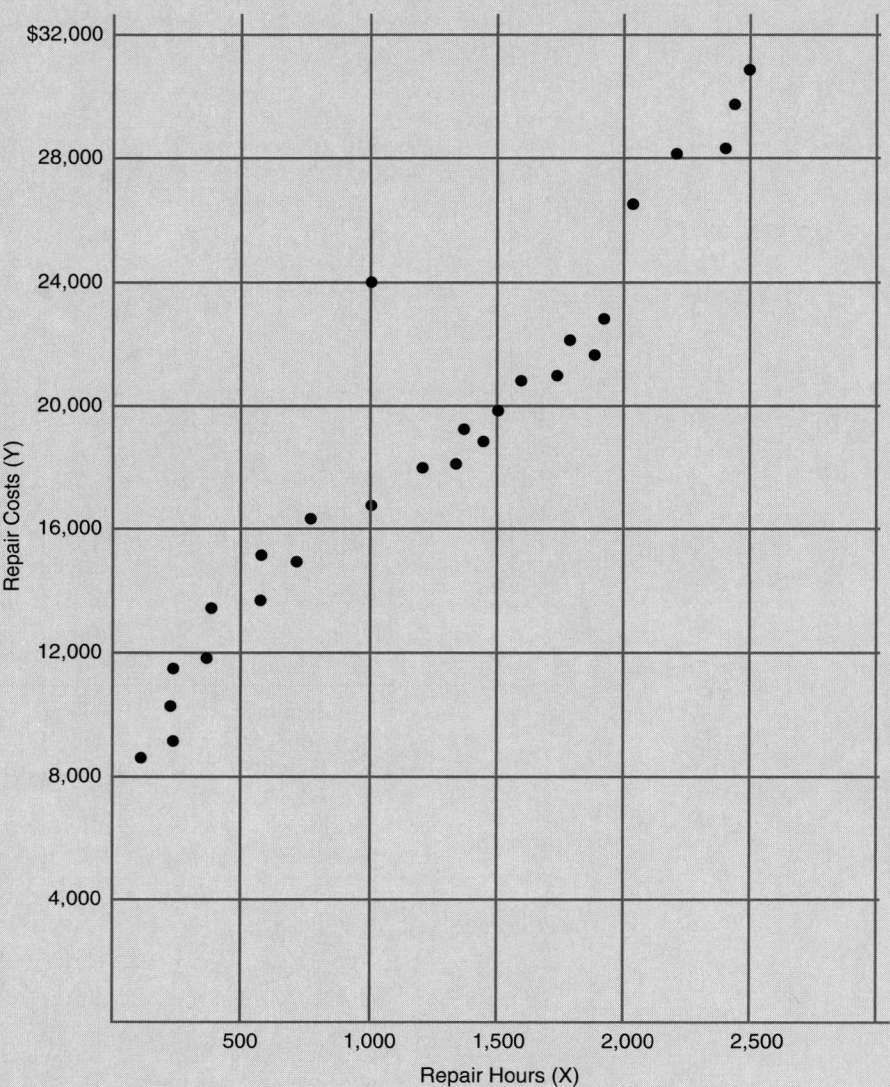

**Required:**

Entirely on the basis of the scatter diagram, specify as many different relevant bits of information as possible that you think may be helpful in evaluating the relationship between the dependent variable and the independent variable.

## OBJECTIVE ASSIGNMENT ANSWERS

**True/False**

1. F    2. T    3. T    4. F    5. F

**Multiple Choice**

1. b    2. d    3. a    4. c    5. d
6. c    7. d    8. d    9. a    10. b

# The Contribution Approach to Cost-Volume-Profit Analysis

**LEARNING OBJECTIVES**

After studying this chapter, you should be able to do the following:

1 Compute the breakeven point for a firm

2 Prepare the contribution margin income statement and explain how it differs from the traditional income statement

3 Calculate the variable cost per unit, the variable cost percentage, the contribution margin per unit and the contribution margin percentage

4 Use the income equation technique and the contribution margin technique to do cost-volume-profit analysis, with and without income taxes

5 Draw a graph that shows the many variables involved in cost-volume-profit analysis

6 Perform cost-volume-profit analysis for a multiproduct firm

7 Explain the simplifying assumptions of cost-volume-profit analysis

8 Distinguish direct costing from absorption costing

9 Define the key terms listed at the end of the chapter

**CHAPTER OUTLINE**

**INTRODUCTION TO THE TECHNIQUES OF COST-VOLUME-PROFIT ANALYSIS** • The Contribution Margin Format of the Income Statement • Additional Concepts Needed for Cost-Volume-Profit Analysis • **APPLYING THE TECHNIQUES OF COST-VOLUME-PROFIT ANALYSIS** • The Income Equation Technique • The Contribution Margin Technique • **THE MARGIN OF SAFETY** • **THE EFFECT OF INCOME TAXES** • **A GRAPHICAL APPROACH TO COST-VOLUME-PROFIT ANALYSIS** • **OVERVIEW OF COST-VOLUME-PROFIT RELATIONSHIPS** • **COST-VOLUME-PROFIT ANALYSIS FOR A MULTIPRODUCT FIRM** • Sales Mix • Sales Mix and C-V-P Analysis • **ASSUMPTIONS UNDERLYING COST-VOLUME-PROFIT ANALYSIS** • Direct Costing Versus Absorption Costing • The Difference Between Direct Costing and Absorption Costing

Learning Objective 1

Compute the breakeven point for a firm

## INTRODUCTION TO THE TECHNIQUES OF COST-VOLUME-PROFIT ANALYSIS

In the previous chapter we discussed the different ways that costs respond to changes in activity. You learned that variable costs change in direct proportion to changes in activity but that fixed costs are not expected to respond to changes in activity. In this chapter we are going to explain a tool used by accountants to help managers plan for the short run—a tool that can be used only if the accountant first knows which costs are variable and which costs are fixed. We refer to this tool as cost-volume-profit analysis.

**Cost-volume-profit analysis** enables accountants to evaluate the relationships among several interacting variables (such as the sale price, the variable and fixed costs, and the volume of production and sales) and the effect that changes in these variables have on an organization's profits. Cost-volume-profit analysis can be used to answer such questions as:

**1.** At different sales levels what will be the company's income or loss?
**2.** How many units must a company sell in order to have a certain amount of profit?
**3.** By how much can a company's sales decrease before it starts to lose money?

Let's start by looking at the facts given for the Undercover Book Company and then we'll introduce you to the techniques for using this helpful tool.

# UNDERCOVER BOOK COMPANY

The Undercover Book Company manufactures a full-color, hard-cover anthology of detective stories. The books will be sold through sales representatives at bookstores throughout the country. Undercover's management estimates that the initial costs of manufacturing and distributing the books will be as follows:

Variable costs:
| | |
|---|---|
| Direct materials...................... | $10 per unit |
| Direct labor ........................ | 15 per unit |
| Variable overhead.................... | 3 per unit |
| Variable selling and administrative........ | 2 per unit |
| Total variable costs..................... | $30 per unit |

Fixed costs:
| | |
|---|---|
| Fixed factory overhead................. | $40,000 |
| Fixed selling and administrative.......... | 25,000 |
| Total fixed costs ...................... | $65,000 |

The president of Undercover feels that the company can make an acceptable profit during its first year of operation if it sells each book for $50. At that price the company should be able to distribute a modest 8,000 books. And once more bookstores enter the program, there is every expectation that sales will double or triple in later years.

Shortly after operations commence, the president hires an accountant and asks her to determine how many books must be sold in order for the company's revenues to exactly cover all its costs in the first year, and how much profit is possible if the sales projection of 8,000 books is achieved.

A short while later the accountant returns to the president with the following information:

1. Undercover can cover all its costs by selling just 3,250 books.
2. If 8,000 books can be sold in the first year, the company will turn a profit of $95,000.

The 3,250 books that must be sold in order to cover all costs is called the breakeven point. At breakeven, a company has no profit and no loss. Thus, the **breakeven point** is the number of units sold (or dollars of sales) that will guarantee a zero profit for the firm. The accountant found this point—in units sold—by starting with the following general equation, called the *income equation:*

**Total sales − total costs = net income**

Keeping in mind that total costs are made up of variable costs and fixed costs, we modify the equation:

**Total sales − total variable costs − total fixed costs = net income**

And now, breaking down the equation's components a bit further, we get:

$$\left( \begin{array}{c} \textbf{Sales} \\ \textbf{price} \end{array} \times \begin{array}{c} \textbf{units} \\ \textbf{sold} \end{array} \right) - \left( \begin{array}{c} \textbf{variable cost} \\ \textbf{per unit} \end{array} \times \begin{array}{c} \textbf{units} \\ \textbf{sold} \end{array} \right) - \begin{array}{c} \textbf{total fixed} \\ \textbf{costs} \end{array} = \begin{array}{c} \textbf{net} \\ \textbf{income} \end{array}$$

Since the accountant did not know how many units would have to be sold to break even, she substituted the letter $X$ in the equation for units sold, let net income = 0, and solved the equation algebraically as follows:

$$\$50X - \$30X - \$65,000 = \$0$$

$$\$20X - \$65,000 = \$0$$

$$\$20X = \$65,000$$

$$X = \frac{\$65,000}{\$20} = 3,250 \text{ units}$$

The way the accountant for Undercover Book Company determined its breakeven point represents one of two techniques that can be used. She used what is called the income equation technique, but she could have employed a somewhat different approach called the contribution margin technique. Both of these techniques will be discussed in detail a little bit later, but before we examine them we need to find out what the contribution margin for a firm represents.

Learning Objective 2

Prepare the contribution margin income statement and explain how it differs from the traditional income statement

## The Contribution Margin Format of the Income Statement

If the breakeven point for Undercover is 3,250 units, this means that the bottom line on an income statement based on 3,250 units—the net income—must be zero. To demonstrate this point, we're going to introduce a new format for an income statement. So far in this book we have been using the **traditional format income statement.** This format, shown on the left at the top of the next page, is usually employed for statements issued to external users. The format on the right, called the **contribution margin format income statement,** is typically used internally, and is highly recommended for internal use. In the contribution margin format, the variable costs (production, selling, distribution, marketing, product design, administrative, etc.) are totaled and subtracted from sales. This difference between total sales and total variable costs represents the amount that sales contribute to the coverage of fixed costs. It is called the **total contribution margin (TCM).** Fixed costs (production, selling, distribution, marketing, product design, administrative, etc.) are then totaled and subtracted from the total contribution margin to get net income. We will use the contribution margin format in this and later chapters of this book.

| Traditional Format | Contribution Margin Format |
|---|---|
| Sales | Sales |
| Less: Cost of Goods Sold | Less: Total Variable Costs |
| Equals: Gross Profit | Equals: Total Contribution Margin |
| Less: Selling and Administrative Costs | Less: Total Fixed Costs |
| Equals: Net Income | Equals: Net Income |

The contribution margin income statement for Undercover Book Company at the breakeven point of 3,250 units is shown in Exhibit 1. In addition, the income statement for 8,000 units—the projected first-year sales for Undercover—is given in Exhibit 2.

The key item in the contribution margin statement is the *total contribution margin,* which is the dollar amount of sales remaining after the variable costs have been subtracted. In Exhibit 1 the total contribution margin is $65,000 ($162,500 sales revenue − $97,500 variable costs). If the total contribution margin is greater than the fixed costs, there is a profit. If the total contribution margin is less than the fixed costs, there is a loss. If the total contribution margin is exactly equal to the fixed costs, the firm is breaking even. Notice in Exhibit 1 that the total contribution margin is exactly equal to the fixed costs, confirming the accountant's calculation that 3,250 units is the breakeven point.

In Exhibit 2, on the basis of projected sales of 8,000 units, the total contribution margin increases to $160,000. This contribution margin exceeds the fixed costs of $65,000 by $95,000, which is the amount of profit, for sales of 8,000 units.

The income statement clearly shows that the key to generating a profit is to sell enough units so that the total contribution margin is greater than the total fixed costs.

**Exhibit 1** Contribution Margin Income Statement at the Breakeven Point of 3,250 Units

**UNDERCOVER BOOK COMPANY**
**Income Statement**
**Year Ended December 31, 1997**

| | | |
|---|---:|---:|
| Sales Revenue (3,250 books × $50) | | $162,500 |
| Total Variable Costs: | | |
| Direct Materials (3,250 books × $10) | $32,500 | |
| Direct Labor (3,250 books × $15) | 48,750 | |
| Variable Factory Overhead (3,250 books × $3) | 9,750 | |
| Variable Selling and Administrative (3,250 books × $2) | 6,500 | 97,500 |
| Total Contribution Margin | | $ 65,000 |
| Fixed Costs: | | |
| Fixed Factory Overhead | $40,000 | |
| Fixed Selling and Administrative | 25,000 | 65,000 |
| Net Income | | −0− |

---

**Exhibit 2** Contribution Margin Income Statement at Projected Sales of 8,000 Units

**UNDERCOVER BOOK COMPANY**
**Income Statement**
**Year Ended December 31, 1997**

| | | |
|---|---:|---:|
| Sales Revenue . . . . . . . . . . . . . . . . . . . . . . . . . . . . . . . . . . . . . . . . . . . . . | | $400,000 |
| Variable Costs: | | |
|    Direct Materials . . . . . . . . . . . . . . . . . . . . . . . . . . . . . . . . . | $ 80,000 | |
|    Direct Labor . . . . . . . . . . . . . . . . . . . . . . . . . . . . . . . . . . . . . | 120,000 | |
|    Variable Factory Overhead . . . . . . . . . . . . . . . . . . . . . . . . . . | 24,000 | |
|    Variable Selling and Administrative . . . . . . . . . . . . . . . . . . . . | 16,000 | |
|      Total Variable Costs . . . . . . . . . . . . . . . . . . . . . . . . . . . . . | | 240,000 |
| Total Contribution Margin . . . . . . . . . . . . . . . . . . . . . . . . . . . . . . . . . | | $160,000 |
| Fixed Costs: | | |
|    Fixed Factory Overhead . . . . . . . . . . . . . . . . . . . . . . . . . . . . | $ 40,000 | |
|    Fixed Selling and Administrative . . . . . . . . . . . . . . . . . . . . . . . | 25,000 | 65,000 |
| Net Income . . . . . . . . . . . . . . . . . . . . . . . . . . . . . . . . . . . . . . . . . . . . . . . | | $ 95,000 |

---

Learning
Objective  **3**

Calculate the variable cost per unit, the variable cost percentage, the contribution margin per unit, and the contribution margin percentage

## Additional Concepts Needed for Cost-Volume-Profit Analysis

Whichever cost-volume-profit technique is employed—the income equation technique or the contribution margin technique—it is often essential to know what the variable costs and contribution margin are (1) on a per-unit basis and (2) as a percentage of sales.

### Variable Cost per Unit

The variable cost per unit was given in our description of the Undercover Book Company; when it is unknown, however, it can be calculated, on the basis of totals from Exhibit 1 or 2. Exhibit 2 shows that Undercover incurs $240,000 of variable costs to produce and sell 8,000 units. The average **variable cost per unit (VCU)** can be calculated by dividing total variable costs by units sold:

$$\text{Variable cost per unit} = \frac{\text{total variable costs}}{\text{units sold}}$$

$$= \frac{\$240,000}{8,000 \text{ units}}$$

$$= \$30$$

### Variable Cost Percentage

The **variable cost percentage (VC%),** or **variable cost ratio,** represents the ratio of variable costs to sales dollars. To put it another way, the VC% represents the portion of total sales that is needed to cover the variable costs. The VC% for Undercover is 60%, which can be determined in several ways.

   1.  The first way uses total variable costs and total sales dollars:

$$\text{Variable cost percentage} = \frac{\text{total variable costs}}{\text{total sales dollars}}$$

$$= \frac{\$240,000}{\$400,000}$$

$$= .60 \text{ (or 60\%)}$$

For every sales dollar the company generates, the company has variable costs averaging 60% of that sales dollar. This means that the first 60% of the company's sales dollars is needed to cover its variable costs.

2. The second way to calculate the VC% uses the variable cost per unit and the sales price, as follows:

$$\text{Variable cost percentage} = \frac{\text{variable cost per unit}}{\text{sales price per unit}}$$

$$= \frac{\$30}{\$50}$$

$$= .60 \text{ (or 60\%)}$$

3. A third way to calculate the variable cost percentage involves the contribution margin. To use this approach, we need to understand the contribution margin per unit and the contribution margin percentage.

### Contribution Margin per Unit

In Exhibit 2 the Undercover Book Company is found to have a total contribution margin of $160,000. We can determine the amount that each unit sold contributes—the **contribution margin per unit (CMU)**—in two different ways.

1. In the first way we simply subtract the variable cost per unit from the sales price per unit:

$$\text{Contribution margin per unit} = \text{sales price per unit} - \text{variable cost per unit}$$

$$= \$50 - \$30$$

$$= \$20 \text{ per unit}$$

This means that each unit sold *contributes* $20 toward paying for the fixed costs. Furthermore, once the total fixed costs are covered, the $20 represents the amount that each unit contributes to net income; that is, every time a unit is sold, the profits increase by $20.

2. The second way to calculate the CMU is to divide the total contribution margin by the number of units sold:

$$\text{Contribution margin per unit} = \frac{\text{total contribution margin}}{\text{units sold}}$$

$$= \frac{\$160,000}{8,000 \text{ units}}$$

$$= \$20 \text{ per unit}$$

If 8,000 units contribute $160,000, then each unit must contribute $20.

### Contribution Margin Percentage

The **contribution margin percentage (CM%), or contribution margin ratio,** represents the portion of total sales that remains after the variable costs have been subtracted. It can be determined in three ways.

1. The first way is to divide the total contribution margin by total sales dollars. For the Undercover Book Company, it would be as follows:

$$\text{Contribution margin percentage} = \frac{\text{total contribution margin}}{\text{total sales dollars}}$$

$$= \frac{\$160,000}{\$400,000}$$

$$= .40 \text{ (or 40\%)}$$

A contribution margin percentage of 40% means that 40% of the sales dollars remain after the variable costs have been subtracted. In other words, 40% of the sales dollars are available to contribute to the coverage of fixed costs.

2. A second way to calculate the CM% involves the contribution margin per unit and the sales price per unit:

$$\text{Contribution margin percentage} = \frac{\text{contribution margin per unit}}{\text{sales price per unit}}$$

$$= \frac{\$20}{\$50}$$

$$= .40 \text{ (or 40\%)}$$

3. Finally, we can calculate the CM% by subtracting the variable cost percentage from 100%:

$$\textbf{CM\% = 100\% − VC\%}$$

$$= 100\% - 60\%$$

$$= 40\%$$

Using this relationship between the CM% and the VC%, we can determine the variable cost percentage in the following manner:

$$\textbf{VC\% = 100\% − CM\%}$$

$$= 100\% - 40\%$$

$$= 60\%$$

---

**Exhibit 3** Contribution Margin Income Statement, Showing Totals, Per Units, and Percentages

---

**UNDERCOVER BOOK COMPANY**
**Income Statement**
**Year Ended December 31, 1997**

| | Total Dollars | Units | Per Unit | % |
|---|---|---|---|---|
| Sales Revenue............................ | $400,000 | 8,000 | $50 | 100% |
| Variable Costs: | | | *SP* | |
| Direct Materials ................ | $ 80,000 | | | |
| Direct Labor.................... | 120,000 | | | |
| Variable Factory Overhead........ | 24,000 | | *VCU* | *VC%* |
| Variable Selling and Administrative.. | 16,000 | | | |
| Total Variable Costs .................... | 240,000 | 8,000 | 30 | 60% |
| Total Contribution Margin.................... | $160,000 | 8,000 | $20 | 40% |
| Fixed Costs: | | | | |
| Fixed Factory Overhead .......... | $ 40,000 | | *CMU* | |
| Fixed Selling and Administrative .... | 25,000 | 65,000 | | *CM%* |
| Net Income............................... | $ 95,000 | | | |

Naturally, this approach can be used only if the contribution margin percentage is already known.

Income statements prepared for internal use can easily be expanded to show unit and percentage breakdowns that provide figures for VCU, VC%, CMU, and CM%. The Undercover Book Company income statement for sales of 8,000 units is expanded in Exhibit 3 to show the revenue, variable costs, and contribution of each unit (in the per-unit column). The percent (%) column shows that the variable costs represent 60% of total sales ($30/$50) and that the contribution margin is 40% of total sales ($20/$50).

**ASK YOURSELF** ▶

1. **What is the breakeven point for a firm?**
2. **How does the contribution margin format differ from the traditional format?**
3. **Describe three ways that can be used to calculate the variable cost percentage.**

Learning 4
Objective

Use the income equation technique and the contribution margin technique to do cost-volume-profit analysis, with and without income taxes

## APPLYING THE TECHNIQUES OF COST-VOLUME-PROFIT ANALYSIS

Now that you are familiar with the basic concepts, you are ready to look at the income equation technique of C-V-P analysis in greater detail and to learn about the contribution margin technique as well. In the next few pages you will see how either C-V-P technique can be used to determine a firm's breakeven point and the level of sales a firm needs in order to generate any desired amount of profit. You will also learn how to employ these techniques to calculate answers in either unit sales or dollar sales, and how to do the analysis with or without income taxes.

### The Income Equation Technique

The **income equation technique** derives its name from its format for determining net income:

**Total sales − total variable costs − total fixed costs = net income**

OR

**(Sales price × units sold) − (VCU × units sold) − total fixed costs = net income**

Earlier, we used this equation to determine unit sales at the breakeven point for the Undercover Book Company to be 3,250. If Undercover wants to achieve a specific income, such as $95,000, then we merely substitute that desired income in the equation. For example, if Undercover is to have an income of $95,000, its sales must be 8,000 units:

$$\$50X - \$30X - \$65,000 = \$95,000$$
$$\$20X - \$65,000 = \$95,000$$
$$\$20X = \$160,000$$
$$X = \frac{\$160,000}{\$20} = 8,000 \text{ units}$$

The dollar sales at the breakeven point of 3,250 units and at the level of sales, 8,000 units, needed to generate a $95,000 profit can easily be determined by multiplying the unit sales by the sales price:

**Unit sales × sales price = dollar sales**

3,250 units × $50 = $162,500

and

$$8,000 \text{ units} \times \$50 = \$400,000$$

Or, we can let the unknown $S$ equal dollar sales, and use the income equation technique in the following manner:

$$S - VC\%(S) - \textbf{total fixed costs} = \textbf{net income}$$

The dollar sales at breakeven are $162,500:

$$S - .60S - \$65,000 = \$0$$

$$.40S - \$65,000 = \$0$$

$$.40S = \$65,000$$

$$S = \frac{\$65,000}{.40} = \$162,500$$

And the dollar sales needed to generate a profit of $95,000 are $400,000:

$$S - .60S - \$65,000 = \$95,000$$

$$.40S - \$65,000 = \$95,000$$

$$.40S = \$160,000$$

$$S = \frac{\$160,000}{.40} = \$400,000$$

### The Contribution Margin Technique

The **contribution margin technique,** the other approach to cost-volume-profit analysis, uses a formula for calculating the breakeven point directly. The only step in the contribution margin technique is actually the last step in the income equation technique.

If we designate $X$ to represent unit sales, then the solution will be in units, using the following formula:

$$X = \frac{\textbf{total fixed costs} + \textbf{net income}}{\textbf{CMU}}$$

By substituting zero for net income, once again we get a breakeven point of 3,250 units:

$$X = \frac{\$65,000 + \$0}{\$20} = 3,250 \text{ units}$$

If you look back at the income equation technique when we got this same answer, you'll see that in the last step there we also divided $65,000 by $20 per unit.

If Undercover desires a $95,000 profit, we replace zero in the numerator with $95,000 and find that the company must sell 8,000 units:

$$X = \frac{\$65,000 + \$95,000}{\$20} = \frac{\$160,000}{\$20} = 8,000 \text{ units}$$

If the analysis calls for dollar sales rather than unit sales, let $S$ represent the dollar sales in the following equation:

$$S = \frac{\textbf{total fixed costs} + \textbf{net income}}{\textbf{CM\%}}$$

In order to break even, Undercover must have dollar sales of $162,500:

$$S = \frac{\$65,000 + \$0}{.40} = \$162,500$$

And in order to show a profit of $95,000, the company will have to have dollar sales of $400,000:

$$S = \frac{\$65,000 + \$95,000}{.40} = \frac{\$160,000}{.40} = \$400,000$$

## THE MARGIN OF SAFETY

A firm is said to have a **margin of safety** when its actual or projected sales are in excess of breakeven. We calculate a margin of safety by subtracting the breakeven sales from the actual or budgeted sales for the period. The Undercover Book Company expected its sales to be 8,000 units ($400,000) during its first year of operation, and determined its breakeven point to be 3,250 units ($162,500). For Undercover the margin of safety (in units) is:

**Margin of safety = actual or budgeted sales − breakeven sales**
$$= 8,000 - 3,250 = 4,750 \text{ units}$$

We can also measure margin of safety in terms of sales dollars:

$$\text{Margin of safety} = \$400,000 - \$162,500 = \$237,500$$

The margin of safety represents the amount by which sales can decrease before a company experiences a loss. Undercover's sales can drop by as much as 4,750 units (or $237,500) from its budgeted level of 8,000 units ($400,000) before it has to worry about sustaining a loss for the year.

## THE EFFECT OF INCOME TAXES

In both the income equation technique and the contribution margin technique, an integral part of the calculation is the desired net income. For a company that has to pay income taxes—such as a corporation—the income is actually income before tax rather than net income. If the desired net income is given along with an income tax rate, the income before tax (IBT) must be determined as follows:

$$\text{Income before tax} = \frac{\text{net income}}{1 - \text{tax rate}}$$

Then this figure would be used in the cost-volume-profit analysis, like this:

$$X = \frac{\text{total fixed costs + IBT}}{\text{CMU}}$$

For example, if Undercover desires a net income of $28,000, and pays income taxes at a 30% tax rate, then the income before tax would be $40,000:

$$\text{IBT} = \frac{\$28,000}{1 - .30} = \frac{\$28,000}{.70} = \$40,000$$

And the number of units that must be sold to generate an income before tax of $40,000 would be 5,250, determined as follows:

$$X = \frac{\$65,000 + \$40,000}{\$20} = \frac{\$105,000}{\$20} = 5,250 \text{ units}$$

If a desired net income is given and there is no indication of income taxes, then the calculation of IBT is not necessary. Or, if income taxes are evident but income before tax is specified, then we would not have to make the calculation.

1. The margin of safety is another name for net income. Do you agree? Explain.
2. How do you determine income before tax when you are given the amount of net income?
3. What is the formula for the contribution margin technique of cost-volume-profit analysis?

Learning Objective **5**

Draw a graph that shows the many variables involved in cost-volume-profit analysis

## A GRAPHICAL APPROACH TO COST-VOLUME-PROFIT ANALYSIS

Until now we have used income statements and equations to analyze the relationships among revenues, costs, volume, and profit. Now we will analyze these interacting variables in a different way, by looking at them graphically.

Figures 1 and 2 present two similar, yet different approaches to the cost-volume-profit graph for Undercover Book Company. In both graphs the horizontal axis represents the number of units produced and sold and the vertical axis represents dollars of revenues, costs and profits.

In both cost-volume-profit graphs the sales line is drawn at a 45° angle extending from the origin upward and to the right. The total costs line begins on the vertical axis (the $65,000 of fixed costs for Undercover) and also extends upward and to the right—but with a lower slope than that of the sales line. The intersection of the sales line and the total costs line is the breakeven point, which we know is 3,250 units ($162,500) for Undercover.

At levels of activity above breakeven, the firm will experience a profit, as shown by the triangular area above the breakeven point. At levels of activity below breakeven, the firm will experience a loss, as shown by the triangular area below the breakeven point.

The only difference between Figures 1 and 2 is the manner in which the cost lines are drawn. In Figure 1, the fixed costs line ($65,000) is drawn first, and no line is drawn for the variable costs. Instead the total costs line is represented by the addition of the variable costs to the fixed costs. Thus we can say that the variable costs are graphed above the fixed costs.

In the cost-volume-profit graph in Figure 2, the variable costs line is drawn first. It begins at the origin and extends upward and to the right. Fixed costs are then added to the variable costs; the total costs line begins on the vertical axis at the amount of fixed costs at zero activity. The total costs line then runs parallel to the variable costs line. The space between these two lines (the dotted area) represents the fixed costs.

Does it make any difference which graph we use? Do both graphs show the same relevant information?

Look carefully at Figure 2 and see if you can find anything important that is missing from Figure 1—something that has been emphasized throughout this chapter.

Right—Figure 1 does not show the total contribution margin.

Remember, the total contribution margin is the difference between total sales and total variable costs. Since the variable costs line is drawn in Figure 2, it is easy to see the total contribution margin: It is the distance from the sales line to the variable costs line. By reading the dollars on the vertical axis, you can see in Figure 2 that the total contribution margin for 15,000 units is $300,000:

| | |
|---|---|
| Total sales. . . . . . . . . . . . . . . . . . . . . . . . . . . . . | $750,000 |
| Total variable costs. . . . . . . . . . . . . . . . . . . . . . . | 450,000 |
| Total contribution margin . . . . . . . . . . . . . . . . . . | $300,000 |

You can easily see in Figure 2 what the total contribution margin is for any level of activity from zero to 15,000 units—it is represented by the vertical distance from the sales line down to the variable costs line. As you can see, the total contribution margin is less than the fixed costs for any level of activity to the left of the breakeven

**Figure 1** Cost-Volume-Profit Graph: Variable Costs on Top of Fixed Costs

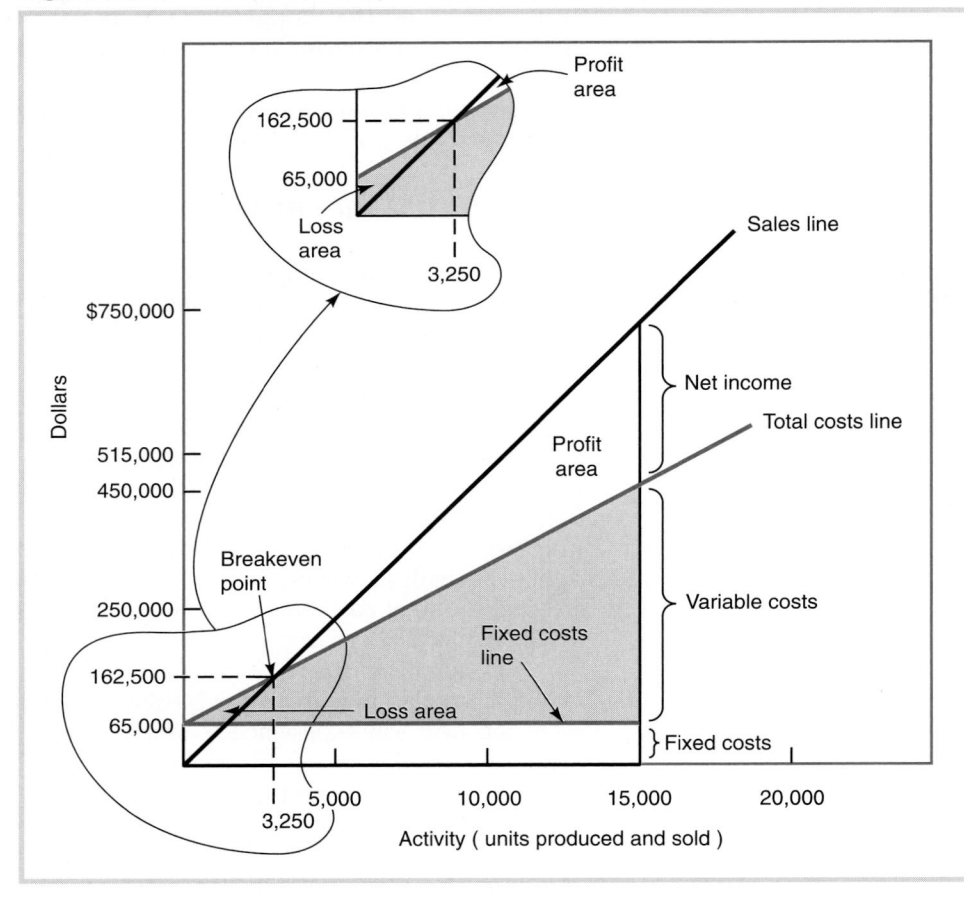

point; the result is a loss. At any level of activity above the breakeven point, the total contribution margin is greater than the total fixed costs; the result is a profit.

It is much more difficult to find the total contribution margin in Figure 1. At 15,000 units there is no vertical distance from one line to another representing total contribution margin, and there is no way to show total contribution margin in the range of activity from zero to 15,000 units.

## OVERVIEW OF COST-VOLUME-PROFIT RELATIONSHIPS

A summary of what you have just learned about cost-volume-profit analysis is presented in Exhibit 4. It reviews the numerous ways to calculate the variable cost

**Exhibit 4** Review of Cost-Volume-Profit Calculations

*Cost-volume-profit terminology:*

$$\text{Variable cost percentage} = \frac{\text{total variable costs}}{\text{total sales dollars}}$$

$$= \frac{\text{variable cost per unit}}{\text{sales price}}$$

$$= 100\% - \text{CM\%}$$

$$\text{Contribution margin per unit} = \frac{\text{total contribution margin}}{\text{units sold}}$$

$$= \text{sales price per unit} - \text{variable cost per unit}$$

*(Continued)*

**Figure 2** Cost-Volume-Profit Graph: Fixed Costs on Top of Variable Costs

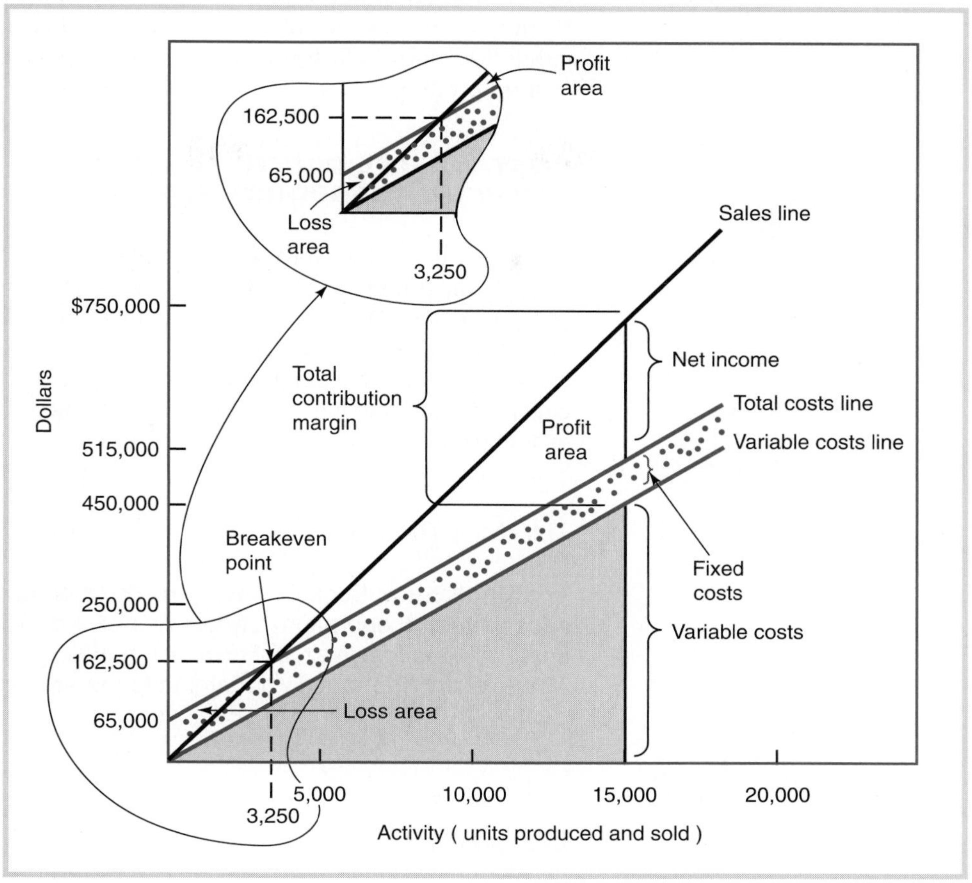

$$\text{Contribution margin percentage} = \frac{\text{total contribution margin}}{\text{total sales dollars}}$$

$$= \frac{\text{contribution margin per unit}}{\text{sales price per unit}}$$

$$= 100\% - \text{VC}\%$$

*Cost-volume-profit methods:*

Income equation technique:
  Solution in units (*X* = units sold):

$$\text{Sales price}(X) - \text{VCU}(X) - \text{total fixed costs} = \text{net income}$$

  Solution in dollars (*S* = dollar sales):

$$S - \text{VC}\%(S) - \text{total fixed costs} = \text{net income}$$

Contribution margin technique:
  Solution in units (*X* = units sold):

$$X = \frac{\text{total fixed costs} + \text{net income}}{\text{contribution margin per unit}}$$

  Solution in dollars (*S* = dollar sales):

$$S = \frac{\text{total fixed costs} + \text{net income}}{\text{contribution margin percentage}}$$

percentage, the contribution margin per unit, and the contribution margin percentage. It also shows how you can use the income equation and contribution margin techniques to solve problems in terms of either unit sales or dollar sales. Study this exhibit carefully before you go on to the discussion of how to apply these techniques to multiproduct firms.

Learning Objective 6

Perform cost-volume-profit analysis for a multiproduct firm

## COST-VOLUME-PROFIT ANALYSIS FOR A MULTIPRODUCT FIRM

Up until this point we have assumed that the Undercover Book Company planned to sell just one product, a detective anthology. However, most firms in the real world sell many products. We will now assume that Undercover decides also to publish a new anthology of mystery stories. The C-V-P analysis for a multiproduct firm is nearly the same as it is for a single-product firm, but there are some differences that are significant enough to warrant our attention. The facts concerning Undercover's products are as follows:

### THE MULTIPLE PRODUCTS OF UNDERCOVER BOOK COMPANY

The Undercover Book Company plans to produce and sell two anthologies in its second year of operation. Undercover expects to sell 8,000 copies of the detective stories during that year, but now also hopes to sell 2,000 copies of mystery stories. The relevant information pertaining to the anthologies is as follows:

|  | Anthology of Detective Stories | Anthology of Mystery Stories |
|---|---|---|
| Sales price | $50 | $55 |
| Variable cost per unit | 30 | 40 |
| Contribution margin per unit | $20 | $15 |

The two books will be produced in the same production facility, so the fixed costs will continue to be $65,000 no matter how many units of each book are produced.

An income statement based on the facts above is shown in Exhibit 5 for the organization as a whole. You can see that Undercover should be able to earn a total of $125,000 during its second year if it can sell 10,000 books. But how many must it sell to break even, or to have a profit of $95,000 or any other desired amount? The answers to these questions can be supplied by the same C-V-P formulas that we've been using all along—with just a few modifications.

**Exhibit 5** Product Line Income Statements

|  | Detective Stories 8,000 Units | Mystery Stories 2,000 Units | Total 10,000 Units |
|---|---|---|---|
| Sales Revenue | $400,000 | $110,000 | $510,000 |
| Total Variable Costs | 240,000 | 80,000 | 320,000 |
| Total Contribution Margin | $160,000 | $ 30,000 | $190,000 |
| Total Fixed Costs |  |  | 65,000 |
| Net Income |  |  | $125,000 |

## Sales Mix

First of all, because we are now dealing with more than one product, we must calculate the sales mix. The **sales mix** for a multiproduct firm represents the percentage of total sales that is distributed to each product line. Conversely, we might think of the sales mix as the percentage of each product line's sales to the combined sales for all product lines of the firm. The sales mix percentage for each product line for Undercover is computed as follows:

$$\text{Sales mix percentage} = \frac{\text{sales of individual product line}}{\text{sales of all product lines combined}}$$

The sales mix for a firm can be measured in terms of unit sales or dollar sales. For Undercover, we will be concerned only with the sales mix based on unit sales, which is calculated as follows:

| Product | Unit Sales | Sales Mix |
|---|---|---|
| Detective stories . . . . . . . . . . . . . . . . . . . . . . . . | 8,000 | 80% (8,000/10,000) |
| Mystery stories . . . . . . . . . . . . . . . . . . . . . . . . | 2,000 | 20% (2,000/10,000) |
| | 10,000 | 100% |

The anthology of detective stories represents 80% of total unit sales, and the anthology of mystery stories represents 20% of total unit sales.

## Sales Mix and C-V-P Analysis

There are four steps in doing C-V-P analysis for a multiproduct firm:

1. Determine the sales mix, as shown above.
2. Calculate the weighted average contribution margin per unit. This can be done in either of two ways. One way is to divide the total contribution margin for all the products combined by the total unit sales. For the Undercover Book Company, it is $19 per unit:

$$\text{Weighted average CMU} = \frac{\text{total CM (all products)}}{\text{total units (all products)}}$$

$$= \frac{\$190,000}{10,000} = \$19 \text{ per unit}$$

The other way to calculate the average CMU is to multiply each CMU by its respective sales mix percentage, and then add together the individual multiplications. We can do this for Undercover as follows:

| Product | Individual CMU | × Sales Mix % = | Average CMU |
|---|---|---|---|
| Detective stories . . . . . . . . . . . . . . . . . . . . . . . . | $20 | × 80% = | $16 |
| Mystery stories . . . . . . . . . . . . . . . . . . . . . . . . | $15 | × 20% = | 3 |
| | | | $19 |

Either way we get an average CMU of $19 per unit.

3. Use the traditional C-V-P formula, placing total fixed costs and desired net income in the numerator and the average CMU in the denominator. For Undercover, the

breakeven (in units) for both products combined is:

$$X = \frac{\$65,000 + \$0}{\$19 \text{ per unit}} = 3,421 \text{ units}$$

And the level of sales needed to generate a profit of $95,000 is:

$$X = \frac{\$65,000 + \$95,000}{\$19 \text{ per unit}} = 8,421 \text{ units}$$

4. Allocate the answer from step 3 among the different product lines, by multiplying each product's sales mix percentage by the total unit sales. For Undercover the allocation of the breakeven units of 3,421 is as follows:

| | Total Sales | × | Sales Mix % | = | Allocation to Products |
|---|---|---|---|---|---|
| Detective stories . . . . . . . . . . . . . . . . . . . . . . . . . | 3,421 | × | 80% | = | 2,737 |
| Mystery stories. . . . . . . . . . . . . . . . . . . . . . . . . . . | 3,421 | × | 20% | = | 684 |
| | | | | | 3,421 |

We would allocate the 8,421 units needed to generate a $95,000 profit in exactly the same manner, to determine the unit sales required of each product to provide this profit level.

Before we stop, it is important for you to know what assumption accountants make concerning the sales mix when doing C-V-P analysis. Unless told specifically otherwise, accountants assume that the sales mix remains the same. For the Undercover Book Company, this means we are assuming that the detective stories will be 80% and the mystery stories will be 20% of total sales, regardless of how many books are sold in all. The breakeven point of 3,421 units is correct only with the 80:20 sales mix. It would not be the breakeven point for any other sales mix. Likewise, the unit sales needed to generate a $95,000 profit are 8,421 units only with the 80:20 sales mix and will not be correct for any other sales mix.

In addition, we showed a profit in Exhibit 5 of $125,000, for combined sales of 10,000 units. This is the amount of profit for that level of sales only if the sales mix is 80:20. For any other sales mix, the profit for combined sales of 10,000 units will be a different amount.

You see, when the sales mix changes, so does the average CMU. And when the average CMU changes, so does every other computation in the C-V-P analysis.

---

**ASK YOURSELF ▶**

1. **What is the sales mix for a multiproduct firm? How does it affect the weighted average contribution margin per unit?**
2. **How is the breakeven point for a multiproduct firm determined?**

Learning Objective 7

Explain the simplifying assumptions of cost-volume-profit analysis

# ASSUMPTIONS UNDERLYING COST-VOLUME-PROFIT ANALYSIS

When we use cost-volume-profit analysis, our projections are reliable only if the assumptions we make are valid. The assumptions relate to the interacting variables in the analysis model, each of which is assumed to remain unchanged during the period that the model is used. We make six assumptions about the cost-volume-profit model:

1. Volume or activity (usually measured in units produced and sold) is the only cost driver—that is, the only variable that affects the behavior of costs.
2. Fixed and variable costs can be separated and accurately classified.
3. The variable cost per unit and the total fixed costs are expected to remain the same within the relevant range of cost-volume-profit analysis.
4. The sales price remains the same within the relevant range of cost-volume-profit analysis.
5. The analysis involves either a single product or a constant sales mix for a multi-product firm.
6. There is no significant difference in beginning and ending inventories of finished goods (that is, units produced are assumed to equal units sold).

When we originally used the cost-volume-profit model, we assumed that the Undercover Book Company sold a single product for $50 per unit, and that the variable and fixed costs were $30 per unit and $65,000 per year, respectively. We then calculated the breakeven point for Undercover:

$$X = \frac{\$65,000 + \$0}{\$50 - \$30} = \frac{\$65,000}{\$20} = 3,250 \text{ units}$$

The only way Undercover will actually break even when 3,250 units are sold is if the variables used in the model—the sales price, the variable cost per unit, and the total fixed costs—remain the same as they were predicted to be. If any of these variables change, then our projection for breakeven will be invalid.

When a variable in a model changes, we need to revise the model in order to accommodate the changes. For example, if:

1. The sales price is $55 instead of $50;
2. The variable costs per unit go from $30 to $32; and
3. The fixed costs decrease by $1,000 to $64,000,

then the model is revised to include these changes and the projected breakeven point becomes 2,783 units:

$$X = \frac{\$64,000 + \$0}{\$55 - \$32} = \frac{\$64,000}{\$23} = 2,783 \text{ units}$$

Learning
Objective     **8**     **Direct Costing versus Absorption Costing**

Distinguish direct costing from absorption costing

The sixth assumption underlying cost-volume-profit analysis—that there are no significant differences in the beginning and ending inventories of finished goods—needs further explanation.

Let's first look back to the beginning of the chapter at the two formats for income statements that we have used in this book. The format shown on the right is the one we've been using in this chapter. Recall that it is known as the *contribution margin format* (or the *behavioral format*) income statement. The one on the left is the one most often used in financial statements issued to the public. It is called the *traditional format* (or *functional format*) income statement.

The contribution margin format is used whenever a firm is employing the direct costing method of inventory costing. The traditional format is used whenever a firm is employing the absorption costing method of inventory costing.

## The Difference between Direct Costing and Absorption Costing

The difference between direct and absorption costing is simply that fixed factory overhead is an inventoriable cost under absorption costing but a period cost under direct costing.

Under the **absorption costing method,** the inventoriable costs are direct materials, direct labor, variable factory overhead, and fixed factory overhead. Remember that as inventoriable costs, these costs are assigned to inventory when units are produced, and become expenses (as part of cost of goods sold) only when the units to which they are assigned are sold. All costs that are assigned to the unsold units remain as an asset on the balance sheet. All other expenses (selling & administrative, distribution, customer service, etc.) are treated as period costs and are expensed when incurred.

Under the **direct costing method** the inventoriable costs include direct materials, direct labor, and variable factory overhead, which is consistent with their treatment under absorption costing. But the inventoriable costs do not include fixed factory overhead. We assign only the variable manufacturing costs to the units produced; only the variable manufacturing costs are expensed (as part of cost of goods sold) when the units are sold; and nothing but the variable manufacturing costs are assigned to the unsold units that remain on the balance sheet. Under direct costing, fixed factory overhead is considered a period cost instead of an inventoriable cost; this means that, like all the nonmanufacturing costs, it is expensed when incurred.

The income statements for Undercover, prepared under both methods, are shown in Exhibit 6. The key facts, originally given for Undercover as a single-product firm, are as follows:

| | | |
|---|---:|---:|
| Units produced and sold. . . . . . . . . . . . . . . . . . . . . . . . . . . . . . . . . . . . . . . . . . | | 8,000 |
| Sales price . . . . . . . . . . . . . . . . . . . . . . . . . . . . . . . . . . . . . . . . . . . . . . . . . . . . | | $50 per unit |
| Variable costs: | | |
|   Direct materials . . . . . . . . . . . . . . . . . . . . . . . . . . . . . . . . . | $10 per unit | |
|   Direct labor. . . . . . . . . . . . . . . . . . . . . . . . . . . . . . . . . . . . | 15 per unit | |
|   Variable factory overhead . . . . . . . . . . . . . . . . . . . . . . . . | 3 per unit | |
|   Variable selling and administrative . . . . . . . . . . . . . . . . | 2 per unit | |
|     Total variable costs . . . . . . . . . . . . . . . . . . . . . . . . . . . . . . . . . . . . . . . | | $30 per unit |
| Fixed costs: | | |
|   Fixed factory overhead . . . . . . . . . . . . . . . . . . . . . . . . . . | $40,000 | |
|   Fixed selling and administrative . . . . . . . . . . . . . . . . . . . | 25,000 | |
|     Total fixed costs. . . . . . . . . . . . . . . . . . . . . . . . . . . . . . . . . . . . . . . . . . . | | $65,000 |

The most important thing to notice in Exhibit 6 is the bottom line of the statement for each method: net income. The fact that net income under both direct costing and absorption costing is $95,000 helps explain the significance of our sixth assumption, that the number of units produced equals the number of units sold (the finished goods inventory is unchanged).

1. If that assumption is valid, then net income (and the breakeven point) under direct costing (which uses the contribution margin format) will be exactly the same as net income (and the breakeven point) under absorption costing (which uses the traditional format). This is because the amount of fixed factory overhead expensed under absorption costing as part of cost of goods sold is exactly the same as the amount of fixed factory overhead expensed under direct costing as a period cost. Notice in Exhibit 6 that the amount of fixed factory overhead expensed is $40,000 under both methods.

---

**Exhibit 6** Income Statements Prepared under Direct Costing and Absorption Costing
Production equals sales of 8,000 units

---

### Absorption Costing Method (Traditional Format)

| | | |
|---|---:|---:|
| Sales . . . . . . . . . . . . . . . . . . . . . . . . . . . . . . . . . . . . . . . . . . . . . . . . . . . . | | $400,000 |
| Cost of Goods Sold: | | |
|   Direct Materials . . . . . . . . . . . . . . . . . . . . . . . . . . . . . . . . . . | $ 80,000 | |
|   Direct Labor . . . . . . . . . . . . . . . . . . . . . . . . . . . . . . . . . . . . . | 120,000 | |
|   Variable Factory Overhead . . . . . . . . . . . . . . . . . . . . . . . . . | 24,000 | |
|   Fixed Factory Overhead . . . . . . . . . . . . . . . . . . . . . . . . . . . | 40,000 | |
|     Cost of Goods Sold . . . . . . . . . . . . . . . . . . . . . . . . . . . . . . | | 264,000 |
| Gross Profit . . . . . . . . . . . . . . . . . . . . . . . . . . . . . . . . . . . . . . . . . . . . | | $136,000 |
| Selling and Administrative Costs: | | |
|   Variable . . . . . . . . . . . . . . . . . . . . . . . . . . . . . . . . . . . . . . . | $ 16,000 | |
|   Fixed . . . . . . . . . . . . . . . . . . . . . . . . . . . . . . . . . . . . . . . . . | 25,000 | |
|     Total Selling and Administrative Costs . . . . . . . . . . . . . . . . . . | | 41,000 |
| Net Income . . . . . . . . . . . . . . . . . . . . . . . . . . . . . . . . . . . . . . . . . . | | $ 95,000 |

---

### Direct Costing Method (Contribution Margin Format)

| | | | |
|---|---:|---:|---:|
| Sales . . . . . . . . . . . . . . . . . . . . . . . . . . . . . . . . . . . . . . . . . . . . . . . . . | | | $400,000 |
| Variable Costs: | | | |
|   Variable Costs of Goods Sold: | | | |
|     Direct Materials . . . . . . . . . . . . . . . . . . . . . . . | $ 80,000 | | |
|     Direct Labor . . . . . . . . . . . . . . . . . . . . . . . . . . . | 120,000 | | |
|     Variable Factory Overhead . . . . . . . . . . . . . . . . | 24,000 | $224,000 | |
|     Variable Selling and Administrative . . . . . . . . . . . . . . . . . . . | | 16,000 | |
|     Total Variable Costs . . . . . . . . . . . . . . . . . . . . . . . . . . . . . . . | | | 240,000 |
| Total Contribution Margin . . . . . . . . . . . . . . . . . . . . . . . . . . . . . . . . | | | $160,000 |
| Fixed Costs: | | | |
|   Fixed Factory Overhead . . . . . . . . . . . . . . . . . . . . . . . . . . . . | $ 40,000 | | |
|   Fixed Selling and Administrative . . . . . . . . . . . . . . . . . . . . . . . | 25,000 | | |
|     Total Fixed Costs . . . . . . . . . . . . . . . . . . . . . . . . . . . . . . . | | | 65,000 |
| Net Income . . . . . . . . . . . . . . . . . . . . . . . . . . . . . . . . . . . . . . . . . . | | | $ 95,000 |

---

2. If the assumption is not valid—if the number of units produced is *not* equal to the number of units sold—then the net income (and the breakeven point) for direct costing will be different from the net income (and breakeven point) for absorption costing. This is because the fixed factory overhead expensed under absorption costing as part of cost of goods sold will no longer equal the amount of fixed factory overhead expensed under direct costing as a period cost.

An example of this situation occurs when the number of units produced exceeds the number sold, which is shown in Exhibit 7. In this situation production is still 8,000 units, but unit sales fall to 6,000, leaving an ending inventory in finished goods of 2,000 units. Now under absorption costing, some of the $40,000 of fixed factory overhead that is assigned to the units produced, will still be in finished goods inventory at the end of the period—some of the $40,000 of fixed factory overhead is not expensed in the current period. This is because some of the units produced were not sold. Although $40,000 of fixed factory overhead was assigned to the 8,000 units produced, averaging $5 per unit ($40,000 ÷ 8,000 units), $10,000 of the $40,000 remains in finished goods with the 2,000 unsold units ($5 × 2,000 units). This $10,000 is part of the $66,000 ending inventory shown in Exhibit 7. Therefore, of the $40,000 of fixed factory overhead incurred during the period, only $30,000 is expensed ($40,000 − $10,000) as part of the $198,000 in cost of goods sold.

Under direct costing, however, all of the $40,000 of fixed factory overhead is expensed, because as a period cost fixed factory overhead is entirely expensed when incurred. Since it is not an inventoriable cost, none of the $40,000 remains in the ending inventory with the 2,000 unsold units.

Since there is $10,000 more fixed factory overhead expensed under direct costing than absorption costing ($40,000 versus $30,000), the net income under direct costing will be $10,000 less than the net income under absorption costing. As you can see, this is the case in Exhibit 7 where the absorption costing net income is $65,000 and the net income for direct costing is $55,000.

3. If the number of units produced turns out to be less than the number sold (the finished goods inventory decreases), the results will be just the reverse. That is, net income under direct costing will be higher than net income under absorption costing. This is because the fixed factory overhead that is expensed with absorption costing will be greater than the $40,000 of fixed factory overhead that is still expensed under direct costing. The cost of goods sold for absorption costing not only includes all of the $40,000 of fixed factory overhead costs incurred in the current period, but also includes some additional fixed factory overhead costs incurred last period and included in the beginning inventory.

The three situations that we have just discussed are summarized in Exhibit 8.

---

**Exhibit 7** Income Statements—Prepared under Direct Costing and Absorption Costing
Production of 8,000 units; Sales of 6,000 units

### Absorption Costing (Traditional Format)

| | | | |
|---|---:|---:|---:|
| Sales . . . . . . . . . . . . . . . . . . . . . . . . . . . . . . . . . . . . . | | | $300,000 |
| Cost of Goods Sold | | | |
|     Direct Materials . . . . . . . . . . . . . . . . . . . . . . . . | $ 80,000 | | |
|     Direct Labor . . . . . . . . . . . . . . . . . . . . . . . . . . . | $120,000 | | |
|     Variable Factory Overhead . . . . . . . . . . . . . . . | 24,000 | | |
|     Fixed Factory Overhead . . . . . . . . . . . . . . . . . | 40,000 | | |
|     Total Production costs . . . . . . . . . . . . . . . . . . . . . | | $264,000 | |
|     Less: Ending Inv. Finished Goods . . . . . . . . . . . . . . . . . . . | | 66,000 | |
|       Cost of Goods Sold . . . . . . . . . . . . . . . . . . . . . . . . . | | | 198,000 |
| Gross Margin. . . . . . . . . . . . . . . . . . . . . . . . . . . . . . . . . | | | $102,000 |
| Selling and Administrative Costs | | | |
|     Variable . . . . . . . . . . . . . . . . . . . . . . . . . . . . . . | $ 12,000 | | |
|     Fixed. . . . . . . . . . . . . . . . . . . . . . . . . . . . . . . . . | 25,000 | | |
|       Total selling & admin. costs. . . . . . . . . . . . . . . . . . . . . . | | | 37,000 |
| Net Income . . . . . . . . . . . . . . . . . . . . . . . . . . . . . . . . . . . | | | $ 65,000 |

*$40,000 of fixed factory overhead is incurred and assigned to the 8,000 units produced ($5 per unit)*

*$10,000 (2,000 units × $5) of this ending inventory is fixed factory overhead. It is not expensed.*

*$30,000 of this total is fixed factory overhead. (6,000 units × $5)*

### Direct Costing Method (Contribution Margin Format)

| | | | |
|---|---:|---:|---:|
| Sales . . . . . . . . . . . . . . . . . . . . . . . . . . . . . . . . . . . . . | | | $300,000 |
| Variable Costs | | | |
|   Variable Costs Of Production | | | |
|     Direct Materials . . . . . . . . . . . . . . . . . . . . . . . . | $ 80,000 | | |
|     Direct Labor . . . . . . . . . . . . . . . . . . . . . . . . . . . | 120,000 | | |
|     Variable Fact. Overhead . . . . . . . . . . . . . . . . . . | 24,000 | $224,000 | |
|   Less: Ending Inv. of Finished Goods . . . . . . . . . . . . . . . . . . . . | | 56,000 | |
|   Variable Cost Of Goods Sold. . . . . . . . . . . . . . . . . . . . . | | $168,000 | |
|   Variable Selling & Administrative. . . . . . . . . . . . . . . . . . . . . . | | 12,000 | |
|     Total Variable costs . . . . . . . . . . . . . . . . . . . . . . . . . . . | | | 180,000 |
| Total Contribution Margin . . . . . . . . . . . . . . . . . . . . . . . . . | | | $120,000 |
| Fixed Costs | | | |
|   Fixed Factory Overhead . . . . . . . . . . . . . . . . . . . . . . . . | $ 40,000 | | |
|   Fixed Selling & Administrative . . . . . . . . . . . . . . . . . . . . . | 25,000 | | |
|     Total Fixed Costs. . . . . . . . . . . . . . . . . . . . . . . . . . | | | 65,000 |
| Net Income . . . . . . . . . . . . . . . . . . . . . . . . . . . . . . . . . . . | | | $ 55,000 |

*All $40,000 that is incurred is also expensed. None of it is in ending inventory.*

**Exhibit 8** Summary of relationships for $Q_s$ and $Q_p$

| Assumption Concerning Production and Sales | Finished Goods Inventory | Fixed Overhead Expensed | Net Income |
|---|---|---|---|
| Units produced exceed units sold $(Q_p > Q_s)$. | Ending inventory is higher than beginning inventory. | More expensed for direct costing | Higher for absorption costing |
| Units produced equal units sold $(Q_p = Q_s)$. | Beginning and ending inventories are the same. | Same for both methods | Same for both methods |
| Units sold exceed units produced $(Q_s > Q_p)$. | Ending inventory is lower than beginning inventory. | More expensed for absorption costing | Higher for direct costing |

**ASK YOURSELF ▶**

1. **What are the six assumptions accountants make when performing cost-volume-profit analysis?**
2. **In what main way does the direct costing method differ from the absorption costing method?**
3. **When a firm sells more units than it produces, which method yields the most income, direct costing or absorption costing?**

## SUMMARY

- **Variable costs,** in total, change in direct proportion to changes in activity.
- **Fixed costs,** in total, are not expected to change in response to changes in activity.
- **Cost-volume-profit analysis** is used by accountants to analyze and evaluate the relationships among interacting variables—prices, costs, and activity—and the effect that a change in any of these variables has on profits.
- Cost-volume-profit analysis can be used to determine a level of sales that will generate a desired amount of profit. One such level of sales is the breakeven point.
- The **breakeven point** for a firm is the level of sales (measured in terms of unit sales or dollar sales) where the total sales equals the total expenses (income is zero).
- The **contribution margin format income statement** separates the variable costs from the fixed costs. Within this statement the variable costs are grouped together and subtracted from sales; the difference is called the **total contribution margin.** Then the fixed costs are combined and subtracted from the total contribution margin, leaving net income.
- Although the **traditional format income statement** is usually employed in financial statements issued to external users, the contribution margin approach is considered superior for internal decision making.
- The **variable cost percentage** (or **variable cost ratio**) is the percentage of total sales needed to cover the variable costs.
- The **contribution margin per unit** is the amount that each unit contributes to the coverage of fixed costs and to the accumulation of profits. It is the sales price less the variable cost per unit.
- The **contribution margin percentage** is the percentage of total sales that remains after the total variable costs have been subtracted.
- Two techniques used in cost-volume-profit analysis are the income equation technique and the contribution margin technique.

- The **income equation technique** uses the following formula:

$$SP(X) - VCU(X) - \text{total fixed costs} = \text{income}$$

where $X$ = unit sales, or

$$S - VC\%(S) - \text{total fixed costs} = \text{income}$$

where $S$ = dollar sales.

- The contribution margin technique uses the following formula:

$$X = \frac{\text{total fixed costs} + \text{income}}{\text{CMU}}$$

where $X$ = unit sales, or

$$S = \frac{\text{total fixed costs} + \text{income}}{\text{CM\%}}$$

where $S$ = dollar sales

- If a company pays income tax and the desired income is "after tax," the income before tax (IBT) must first be determined in the following manner:

$$\text{IBT} = \frac{\text{net income}}{1 - \text{tax rate}}$$

The IBT is the income referred to in the C-V-P equations and formulas.

- The **margin of safety** is the excess of actual or budgeted sales above the break-even sales. It represents the amount by which sales can decrease before the firm incurs a loss.
- The **sales mix** for a multiproduct firm represents the percentage of total sales distributed to each product line.
- Different products usually have different contribution margins per unit. Therefore the weighted average contribution margin per unit (for all products) depends on the proportion that each product's sales are to total sales.
- Since cost-volume-profit formulas use a weighted average contribution margin per unit, the results of the analysis depend on the sales mix assumed.
- For the cost-volume-profit predictions to be correct, the sales mix that actually comes about must be the same as the sales mix assumed in the C-V-P model.
- An assumption underlying cost-volume-profit analysis is that the number of units produced equals the number of units sold. Only when this assumption is true will the net income for the direct costing method of inventory costing (which uses the contribution margin format income statement) be the same as the net income for the absorption costing method of inventory costing (which uses the traditional format income statement).
- The **direct costing method** defines inventoriable costs as direct materials, direct labor, and variable factory overhead. Fixed factory overhead, as well as all nonmanufacturing costs, are period costs under this method.
- The **absorption costing method** defines inventoriable costs as direct materials, direct labor, variable factory overhead, and fixed factory overhead. All nonmanufacturing costs are period costs under this method.

## 9   KEY TERMS

**Absorption costing method**   An inventory costing method that assigns both variable and fixed manufacturing costs to units being produced. The inventoriable costs include direct materials, direct labor, variable factory overhead, and fixed factory overhead. These costs are expensed, as part of cost of goods sold, only when the units to which they are assigned are sold.

**Breakeven point**   The level of sales (measured in units or dollars) for an organization at which net income is zero. At breakeven, total costs equal total sales dollars.

| | |
|---|---|
| **Contribution margin format income statement** | An income statement in which variable costs are separated from fixed costs. The variable costs are subtracted from sales to get total contribution margin. Fixed costs are subtracted next, resulting in net income. |
| **Contribution margin percentage (CM%)** | The percentage of total sales that remains after variable costs are subtracted. Also called **contribution margin ratio.** |
| **Contribution margin per unit (CMU)** | The sales price less the variable cost per unit. The CMU is the amount that each unit sold contributes to the coverage of fixed costs and the accumulation of profits. It is the amount that is added to net income every time an additional unit is sold. |
| **Contribution margin technique** | A method used in cost-volume-profit analysis. The level of sales that will generate a desired profit is determined by dividing the fixed costs plus net income by the contribution margin per unit (or contribution margin percentage). |
| **Cost-volume-profit (C-V-P) analysis** | A tool used by accountants to assist managers in the analysis and evaluation of the relationships among prices, costs, and activity, and the effect that a change in any of the variables has on profits. |
| **Direct costing method** | An inventory costing method that treats only the variable manufacturing costs as inventoriable costs. The inventoriable costs include direct materials, direct labor, and variable factory overhead. Fixed factory overhead is a period cost rather than an inventoriable cost and is expensed as incurred. |
| **Income equation technique** | A method used in cost-volume-profit analysis. The level of sales needed to generate a desired amount of profit is determined by substituting $X$ (for unit sales) or $S$ (for dollar sales) into the equation for net income (sales $-$ total variable costs $-$ total fixed costs = net income). |
| **Margin of safety** | The excess of actual or budgeted sales over breakeven sales. |
| **Sales mix** | For a multiproduct firm, the percentage of total sales that is distributed to each product line. |
| **Total contribution margin (TCM)** | Total sales less total variable costs. It is the amount contributed by sales to the coverage of fixed costs. If the total contribution margin is greater than total fixed costs, there is a profit; if the reverse is true, there is a loss. |
| **Traditional format income statement** | An income statement format that separates costs on the income statement according to their function—production, selling, and administration. The cost of goods sold is subtracted from sales to obtain gross profit; net income remains after selling and administrative expenses are subtracted from gross profit. |
| **Variable cost percentage (VC%)** | The percentage of total sales needed to cover the variable costs; the percentage that variable costs are to sales revenue. Also called **variable cost ratio.** |
| **Variable cost per unit (VCU)** | The amount by which total variable costs increase for each additional unit produced and sold. |

---

## DEMONSTRATION PROBLEM

Metal Edge Company manufactures portable CD players. Since Metal Edge is in its first year of operation, it is conducting a special promotion to spur its sales. With every CD player sold, the buyer receives a copy of the hot new platinum album entitled *Sync or Swim.* The costs of Metal Edge's operations for 1997, based on expected production and sales of 10,000 CD players, are as follows:

| Variable costs: | |
| --- | --- |
| Direct materials | $ 10 per unit |
| Direct labor | 8 per unit |
| Factory overhead | 7 per unit |
| Selling and administrative | 10 per unit |
| | $ 35 per unit |
| Fixed costs: | |
| Factory overhead | $ 70,000 |
| Selling and administrative | 37,000 |
| | $107,000 |

Metal Edge plans to sell the CDs for $100 a player. The expected tax rate for 1997 is 40%.

**Required:**

1. Determine the breakeven point (in units and in dollar sales) for Metal Edge for 1997.
2. How many CD players must Metal Edge sell in order to have an income before tax of $125,000?
3. How many CD players will Metal Edge need to sell in order to generate a net income of $36,000?
4. What should Metal Edge's margin of safety be in 1997?
5. Prepare an income statement for 1997, using the contribution margin format (show a subtotal for income before taxes).
6. Prepare an income statement for 1997, using the traditional format (show a subtotal for income before taxes).

### ■ Solution to Demonstration Problem

1. $X = \dfrac{\text{fixed costs + income}}{\text{CMU}} = \dfrac{\$107,000}{\$100 - \$35} = \dfrac{\$107,000}{\$65}$

   = 1,646 CD players to break even × $100 sales price

   $S = 1,646 \times \$100 = \$164,600$

2. $X = \dfrac{\text{fixed costs + income before tax}}{\text{CMU}} = \dfrac{\$107,000 + \$125,000}{\$65}$

   $= \dfrac{\$232,000}{\$65} = 3,569$ CD players to have an income before tax of $125,000

3. Income before tax $= \dfrac{\text{net income}}{1 - \text{tax rate}} = \dfrac{\$36,000}{1 - .40} = \dfrac{\$36,000}{.60}$

   $= \$60,000$

   $X = \dfrac{\$107,000 + \$60,000}{\$65} = \dfrac{\$167,000}{\$65}$

   = 2,569 CD players to have a net income of $36,000

4. Margin of safety = actual sales − breakeven sales

   = 10,000 − 1,646 = 8,354 CD players in excess of breakeven

   = $1,000,000 − $164,600 = $835,400 in excess of breakeven

5. Contribution margin format income statement:

### METAL EDGE COMPANY
### Income Statement
### Year Ended December 31, 1997

| | | |
|---|---:|---:|
| Sales | | $1,000,000 |
| Total Variable Costs: | | |
|   Direct Materials | $100,000 | |
|   Direct Labor | 80,000 | |
|   Factory Overhead | 70,000 | |
|   Selling and Administrative | 100,000 | 350,000 |
| Total Contribution Margin | | $ 650,000 |
| Total Fixed Costs: | | |
|   Factory Overhead | $ 70,000 | |
|   Selling and Administrative | 37,000 | 107,000 |
| Income before Taxes | | $ 543,000 |
| Income Tax (@ 40%) | | 217,200 |
| Net Income | | $ 325,800 |

6. Traditional format income statement:

### METAL EDGE COMPANY
### Income Statement
### Year Ended December 31, 1997

| | | |
|---|---:|---:|
| Sales | | $1,000,000 |
| Cost of Goods Sold: | | |
|   Direct Materials | $100,000 | |
|   Direct Labor | 80,000 | |
|   Variable Overhead | 70,000 | |
|   Fixed Overhead | 70,000 | 320,000 |
| Gross Profit | | $ 680,000 |
| Selling and Administrative Costs: | | |
|   Variable | $100,000 | |
|   Fixed | 37,000 | 137,000 |
| Income before Taxes | | $ 543,000 |
| Income Tax (@ 40%) | | 217,200 |
| Net Income | | $ 325,800 |

## QUESTIONS FOR REVIEW AND FURTHER THOUGHT

### REVIEW QUESTIONS

1. What is the contribution margin percentage? What are three different ways in which it can be determined?

2. Explain the difference between the contribution margin format and the traditional format for an income statement.

3. Define the term *margin of safety.* What does it measure for a firm?

4. Given the formula for the cost-volume-profit relationship:

$$X = \frac{\text{fixed costs + income}}{\text{CMU}}$$

Is the income before or after taxes?

5. Explain what is meant by the term *sales mix*.

6. List the six assumptions of cost-volume-profit analysis.

7. Define the terms *direct costing* and *absorption costing*.

## QUESTIONS FOR FURTHER THOUGHT

1. Are the terms *total contribution margin* and *gross margin* synonymous? Explain.

2. The increase in net income generated by an increase in activity is identical to the increase in total contribution margin, as long as which assumption underlying cost-volume-profit analysis is valid?

3. If a firm's sales are expected to increase by 50% in the upcoming period, what will happen to the breakeven point? Explain.

4. As long as a firm has a positive margin of safety, it will definitely also have a profit. Explain why this statement is correct or incorrect.

5. A firm sells two products, A and B. The contribution margins per unit are $10 and $4, respectively, and the total sales are expected to be distributed 50% to A and 50% to B during the first year of operation. Following the first year, it was determined that the sales mix was actually 75% for A and 25% for B. Discuss the effect of this change in the sales mix on the cost-volume-profit analysis for the firm.

6. Discuss the significance of the cost-volume-profit assumption that there are no changes in the sales mix.

7. Explain why the net income for absorption costing is higher than the net income for direct costing when the number of units produced is greater than the number of units sold.

8. Discuss the significance of the cost-volume-profit assumption that there are no significant differences in the number of units produced and the number of units sold.

## OBJECTIVE ASSIGNMENT

*True/False*   Indicate whether each statement below is *true* or *false* by placing a *T* or an *F* in the space provided.

_____ 1. When a company is at its breakeven point, there is no profit or loss.

_____ 2. The contribution margin per unit represents the amount that each unit sold contributes to the coverage of fixed costs.

_____ 3. Margin of safety is the same as net income.

_____ 4. The breakeven point for a firm can be found by dividing the total contribution margin by the contribution margin percentage.

_____ 5. Net income under direct costing is higher than net income under absorption costing whenever the number of units produced equals the number of units sold.

*Multiple Choice*   Select the best choice to complete each statement or answer each question below. Write the letter corresponding to your choice in the space provided.

_____ 1. A company will have a profit whenever which of the following is true?
  a. Total contribution margin exceeds total variable costs
  b. Total fixed costs are less than total contribution margin

    c. Total gross margin is positive

    d. Sales are greater than production

____ 2. If a company's sales price for its product is $40, its variable cost percentage is 30%, its sales are $200,000, and its fixed costs are $100,000, what will be its contribution margin percentage?

    a. $140,000    c. $28

    b. $40,000    d. 70%

____ 3. Which format for an income statement first subtracts variable costs from sales?

    a. Traditional format

    b. Sales format

    c. Contribution margin format

    d. Functional format

____ 4. During January, the Callie Company sold 25,000 units, resulting in a total contribution margin of $50,000. If Callie's sales price was $5 per unit, what was the variable cost per unit?

    a. $2    c. $7

    b. $5    d. $3

____ 5. Able Company sells a product for $50 per unit; its variable costs are $35 per unit and its total fixed costs are $45,000. What is Able's breakeven point?

    a. 3,000 units    c. 1,286 units

    b. 150,000 units    d. d. 64,286 units

____ 6. Extra Extra Newspaper Company had the following income statement in 1997.

| | |
|---|---:|
| Sales (5,000 units) | $100,000 |
| Variable Costs | 65,000 |
| | $ 35,000 |
| Fixed Costs | 20,000 |
| Income before Taxes | $ 15,000 |
| Income Taxes | 4,500 |
| Net Income | $ 10,500 |

What is Extra's contribution margin percentage?

    a. 65%    c. 30%

    b. 35%    d. 10.5%

____ 7. A firm that sells a product for $100 has variable costs of $60 per unit and total fixed costs of $80,000. If 3,500 units are sold during the year, what is the margin of safety, in dollars?

    a. $350,000    c. $60,000

    b. $140,000    d. $150,000

____ 8. During 1997, the income tax rate for corporations was 25%. Black Corporation's net income was $225,000 and its total contribution margin was $750,000. What was Black's income before taxes?

    a. $900,000    c. $562,500

    b. $300,000    d. $187,500

____ 9. The following information relates to two products made by Rounder Company:

| Product | Contribution Margin per Unit | Sales Mix |
|:---:|:---:|:---:|
| X | $60 | 20% |
| Y | $30 | 80% |

What is the weighted average contribution margin per unit?

    a. $36    c. $45

    b. $90    d. $100

____ 10. During 1997, the Robindob Company produced 10,000 units, of which 1,000 were still unsold at year-end. Which approach to determining net income would yield the higher net income?

    a. Direct costing    c. Neither

    b. Absorption costing    d. Cannot be answered without more information

## EXERCISES

3  **Exercise 1:** Determining Key Variables Used in C-V-P Analysis

During 1998, the Ramblin Reck Company sold 20,000 units. Its total variable costs were $60,000, its fixed costs were $15,000, and its net income was $22,000. What were its:

a. Total sales and sales price
b. Variable cost per unit and variable cost percentage
c. Total contribution margin
d. Contribution margin per unit and contribution margin percentage

▶ *(Check Figure: a. Sales price = $4.85; d. Contribution margin percentage = 38.14%)*

2  **Exercise 2:** Filling in the Blanks of an Income Statement

Fill in the missing amounts in the two income statements below.

|  | 1997 | 1998 |
|---|---|---|
| Sales. | $200,000 | $400,000 |
| Cost of Goods Sold: |  |  |
|    Direct Materials | $40,000 | $ |
|    Direct Labor | 60,000 |  |
|    Variable Overhead. | 20,000 |  |
|    Fixed Overhead |  |  |
| Gross Profit. | $ 30,000 | $ |
| Selling and Administrative: |  |  |
|    Variable | $ | $ |
|    Fixed. | 10,000 |  |
| Net Income | $ 10,000 | $ |

▶ *(Check Figure: Net income, 1998, = $80,000)*

2  **Exercise 3:** Preparing an Income Statement at the Breakeven Point

The following data relates to the Lame Duck Company's 1997 operations:

| | |
|---|---|
| Units sold | 450 units |
| Breakeven point | 260 units |
| Sales price | $600 |
| Variable costs per unit: | |
|    Manufacturing | $250 |
|    Selling and administrative | 150     $400 |
| Total fixed costs: | |
|    Manufacturing | $40,000 |
|    Selling and administrative | $12,000 |

Prepare two income statements: (a) one at the breakeven level of sales; and (b) the other for the units actually sold by Lame Duck in 1997. Use the contribution margin format. 26-5

▶ *(Check Figure: b. Net income = $38,000)*

**3** **Exercise 4:** Determining Key Variables Needed in C-V-P Analysis

For each independent situation below, fill in the missing items.

|  | A | B | C |
|---|---|---|---|
| Sales price . . . . . . . . . . . . . . . . . . . . . . . . . . . . . . . . . . . . . . . . | $150 | $ | $ |
| Variable cost per unit . . . . . . . . . . . . . . . . . . . . . . . . . . . . . . . . | $120 | $24 | $ |
| Contribution margin per unit. . . . . . . . . . . . . . . . . . . . . . . . . . | $ | $ | $60 |
| Variable cost percentage . . . . . . . . . . . . . . . . . . . . . . . . . . . . . | % | 20% | % |
| Contribution margin percentage . . . . . . . . . . . . . . . . . . . . . . . | % | % | 40% |

▶ *(Check Figure: Sales price, situation C, = $150)*

**1 2 4** **Exercise 5:** Doing a Simple C-V-P Analysis and Preparing an Income Statement

The Dream Land Doll Company sells dolls that speak for $100 per doll. Its variable costs average $60 per doll, and fixed costs are $1,600 per month.

a. How many dolls would need to be sold for Dream Land to break even each month?
b. How many dolls would have to be sold each month if a $14,400 profit is desired?
c. What would be the margin of safety (in units) for Dream Land if 45 dolls are sold each month?
d. Using a contribution margin format, prepare an income statement for a month in which 45 dolls are sold.

▶ *(Check Figure: b. 400 dolls; c. 5 dolls)*

**2 4** **Exercise 6:** Doing a C-V-P Analysis with Income Taxes and Preparing an Income Statement

The R&J Pharmaceutical Company produces and sells placebos for $25 per package. Its expected costs are as follows:

Variable manufacturing costs . . . . . . . . . . $14.00/package
Variable selling costs . . . . . . . . . . . . . . . . $ 6.00/package
Fixed manufacturing costs. . . . . . . . . . . . . . . . . $600,000
Fixed selling costs. . . . . . . . . . . . . . . . . . . . . . . $200,000
Tax rate. . . . . . . . . . . . . . . . . . . . . . . . . . . . . . . . 30%

a. Using a contribution margin format, prepare an income statement (after taxes) for the company if 200,000 packages are sold in 1997.
b. Determine how many packages the company must sell in order to generate an after-tax net income of $140,000.

▶ *(Check Figure: a. Net income = $140,000; b. 200,000 packages)*

**1 4** **Exercise 7:** Calculating the Margin of Safety

The Diana Leonard Skin Cream Company sells a 10-ounce bottle of skin cream called Soft-as-a-Baby for $50 a bottle. The variable and fixed costs of producing and selling each bottle are $8 and $65,000, respectively. If Diana sells 2,200 bottles of Soft-as-a-Baby in 1997, what will be her margin of safety in both units and dollars?

▶ *(Check Figure: $32,619)*

**1 2 4** **Exercise 8:** Analyzing the Effect of a Change on a Key Variable

For each situation described in the table below, determine the effect on the total contribution margin, the breakeven point, and the net income for the firm. Choose from the five following effects and place the appropriate letters in the spaces provided.

a. Doubles              c. Increases less than double     e. Decreases
b. Increases more than double    d. No change

| | Effect on: | | |
| --- | --- | --- | --- |
| | Contribution Margin | Breakeven Point | Net Income |
| 1. The number of units sold doubles | _____ | _____ | _____ |
| 2. The sales price doubles | _____ | _____ | _____ |
| 3. The variable cost per unit increases by 10% | _____ | _____ | _____ |
| 4. The sales price and the variable cost per unit both double | _____ | _____ | _____ |
| 5. Fixed costs double | _____ | _____ | _____ |
| 6. Fixed costs are cut in half | _____ | _____ | _____ |

4 **Exercise 9:** Doing Cost-Volume-Profit Analysis, with Income Expressed in Different Ways

The Tuff-Stuff Toy Company has a toy dump truck division that sells all of its dump trucks for $20 apiece. Its variable costs are $12 per truck and its total fixed costs are $100,000.

a. How many units would Tuff-Stuff have to sell to have a profit of 20% of its sales dollars?
b. What would the dollar sales have to be in order to have a profit of 30% of sales dollars?
c. How many trucks would need to be sold to generate a profit of $2 per unit?
d. What would the sales dollars have to be in order to have a profit of 20% of the total contribution margin?

▶ *(Check Figure: a. 25,000 trucks; b. $1,000,000)*

6 **Exercise 10:** C-V-P Analysis for a Multiproduct Firm

The Forest Hills Sports Company sells two tennis racket models—called the French and the British. The contribution margins per unit, respectively, are $40 and $20. The fixed costs for the company are $70,000. Sales are expected to be distributed to French and British in a 60:40 ratio.

a. Determine the number of units of each product that must be sold in order for Forest Hills to show a $100,000 profit, assuming the sales mix is exactly as expected.
b. If the sales mix changes from 60:40 to 50:50, how many units of each product would now be required to have a profit of $100,000?

▶ *(Check Figure: a. 3,187.5 French rackets; b. 2,833.5 French rackets)*

5 **Exercise 11:** Identifying Line Segments from a C-V-P Graph

Presented below is a cost-volume-profit graph. Identify the items described by placing the appropriate letters for the line segments in the spaces provided.

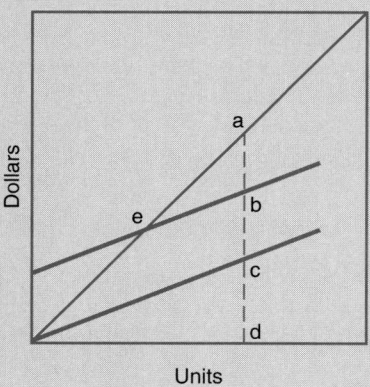

|  | Line Segment |
|---|---|
| **Example:** Sales revenue . . . . . . . . . . . . . . . . . . . . . . . . . . . . . . . . . . . | ad |
| **a.** Total variable costs. . . . . . . . . . . . . . . . . . . . . . . . . . . . . . . | _____ |
| **b.** Total fixed costs . . . . . . . . . . . . . . . . . . . . . . . . . . . . . . . . | _____ |
| **c.** Total contribution margin . . . . . . . . . . . . . . . . . . . . . . . . . . | _____ |
| **d.** Net income . . . . . . . . . . . . . . . . . . . . . . . . . . . . . . . . . . . | _____ |
| **e.** Total costs. . . . . . . . . . . . . . . . . . . . . . . . . . . . . . . . . . . | _____ |
| **f.** Breakeven point . . . . . . . . . . . . . . . . . . . . . . . . . . . . . . . . | _____ |

5    **Exercise 12:** Drawing a C-V-P graph

Draw a cost-volume-profit graph, on which the variable costs are graphed above the fixed costs. Assume that the vertical axis represents dollars and the horizontal axis represents the number of units produced and sold. Then identify the following items on your graph: (a) total sales; (b) total costs; (c) total contribution margin; and (d) net income. Ignore income taxes.

5    **Exercise 13:** Drawing a C-V-P graph

Draw a cost-volume-profit graph, on which the fixed costs are graphed above the variable costs. Assume that the vertical axis represents dollars and the horizontal axis represents the number of units produced and sold. Also assume that income taxes are paid at a constant percentage of income before tax. Then identify the following items on your graph: (a) total sales; (b) total costs; (c) total contribution margin; (d) income before taxes; and (e) net income.

8    **Exercise 14:** Determining Net Income Using Direct Costing and Absorption Costing

The Kirby Cleaner Company plans to produce and sell 10,000 units in 1997, and expects the following costs for the year:

| | |
|---|---|
| Direct materials. . . . . . . . . . . . . . . . . . . . . . . . | $10 per unit |
| Direct labor . . . . . . . . . . . . . . . . . . . . . . . . . . | $15 per unit |
| Variable overhead. . . . . . . . . . . . . . . . . . . . . . | $3 per unit |
| Variable selling . . . . . . . . . . . . . . . . . . . . . . . | $2 per unit |
| Variable administrative . . . . . . . . . . . . . . . . . . | $1 per unit |
| Fixed overhead. . . . . . . . . . . . . . . . . . . . . . . . | $100,000 |
| Fixed selling . . . . . . . . . . . . . . . . . . . . . . . . . | $60,000 |
| Fixed administrative . . . . . . . . . . . . . . . . . . . . | $30,000 |

The sales price is $50 per unit.

**a.** Compute the inventory cost per unit for the absorption costing method.
**b.** Compute the inventory cost per unit for the direct costing method.
**c.** Prepare an income statement for Kirby Cleaners
   **1.** Using the absorption costing method
   **2.** Using the direct costing method

▶ *[Check Figure: c. (1) Net income = $(0)]*

8    **Exercise 15:** Determining the Net Income for Direct and Absorption Costing When Production Exceeds Sales

Use the facts presented in Exercise 14 for Kirby Cleaners, but make a single change: Instead of assuming that 10,000 units were sold, assume that only 8,000 of the 10,000 units produced were sold. Now prepare an income statement for Kirby Cleaners:

**a.** Using the absorption costing method
**b.** Using the direct costing method

▶ *[Check Figure: a. Net income = $(18,000); b. Net income = $(38,000)]*

## PROBLEMS: SET A

2 4 **Problem A1:** Preparing an Income Statement and Doing a C-V-P Analysis

During 1997, the Carson Comedy Shorts Company produced and sold 20,000 videotapes at $100 per tape. At this level of activity the average costs were as follows:

|  | Per Kit |
|---|---|
| Variable manufacturing costs.................. | $30.00 |
| Variable selling............................. | 10.00 |
| Fixed manufacturing......................... | 20.00 |
| Fixed selling ................................ | 5.00 |
| Income taxes (at 40% of income before taxes).... | 14.00 |

**Required:**

1. Assume that 30,000 tapes are produced and sold in 1997 and prepare an income statement, using the contribution margin format.
2. If the company desires a profit in 1997 of $440,000 (before taxes), how many tapes need to be sold?

▶ *(Check Figure: 2. 15,667 units)*

4 **Problem A2:** Doing C-V-P Analysis with Income Taxes

The Bart Wimpson Company had the following income statement for 1998:

| | |
|---|---|
| Sales Revenue ............................................. | $360,000 |
| Variable Costs............................................. | 270,000 |
| Total Contribution Margin .................................. | $ 90,000 |
| Fixed Costs............................................... | 75,000 |
| Income before Taxes ....................................... | $ 15,000 |

Each unit sells for $40, and the income tax rate is 30%.

**Required:**

1. If Wimpson expects to have an income before taxes of $84,000 in 1999, how great must its sales revenue be?
2. If the company desires an after-tax net income of $42,000 in 1999, how many units must be sold?

▶ *(Check Figure: 1. $636,000; 2. 13,500 units)*

2 4 **Problem A3:** Doing C-V-P Analysis and Preparing Statements

The Moodi Milk Dairy Farm produced and sold 400,000 gallons of milk in 1997, incurring the following revenues, expenses, and income:

| | | |
|---|---:|---:|
| Sales . . . . . . . . . . . . . . . . . . . . . . . . . . . . . . . . . . . . . . . . . . . . . . . . . . . . . . . . . . . | | $800,000 |
| Cost of Sales: | | |
|   Direct Materials . . . . . . . . . . . . . . . . . . . . . . . . . . . . . . . . . . . . . . | $100,000 | |
|   Direct Labor . . . . . . . . . . . . . . . . . . . . . . . . . . . . . . . . . . . . . . . . . . | 50,000 | |
|   Variable Factory Overhead . . . . . . . . . . . . . . . . . . . . . . . . . . | 25,000 | |
|   Fixed Factory Overhead . . . . . . . . . . . . . . . . . . . . . . . . . . . . | 75,000 | 250,000 |
| Gross Profit . . . . . . . . . . . . . . . . . . . . . . . . . . . . . . . . . . . . . . . . . . . . . . . . | | $550,000 |
| Selling and Administrative Expenses* . . . . . . . . . . . . . . . . . . . . . . . . . . | | 60,000 |
| Net Income . . . . . . . . . . . . . . . . . . . . . . . . . . . . . . . . . . . . . . . . . . . . . . . | | $490,000 |

\* $30,000 of this total is fixed.

**Required:**

1. Reconstruct the 1997 income statement, using the contribution margin format.
2. Assume that the number of gallons produced and sold increases to 500,000 in 1997 as a result of an advertising expenditure of $20,000, and prepare a new income statement, using the contribution margin format.
3. How many gallons would have to be sold in 1997 (assuming the same advertising expenditure mentioned in requirement 2, above) in order to have an income of $200,000?

▶ *(Check Figure: 2. Net income = $618,750; 3. 218,487 gallons)*

1 4 **Problem A4:** Doing C-V-P Analysis with Changing Variables

During 1997, the *International Enquirer* (for those who want to keep up with the gossip while traveling abroad) sold 10,000,000 newspapers, and prepared the following income statement for the year:

| | | |
|---|---:|---:|
| Sales . . . . . . . . . . . . . . . . . . . . . . . . . . . . . . . . . . . . . . . . . . . . . . . . . . . . . | | $5,000,000 |
| Cost of Sales: | | |
|   Direct Materials . . . . . . . . . . . . . . . . . . . . . . . . . . . . . . . . . . . . . | $2,000,000 | |
|   Conversion Costs . . . . . . . . . . . . . . . . . . . . . . . . . . . . . . . . . . . | 1,000,000* | 3,000,000 |
| Gross Profit . . . . . . . . . . . . . . . . . . . . . . . . . . . . . . . . . . . . . . . . . . . . . . | | $2,000,000 |
| Operating Costs: | | |
|   Salaries . . . . . . . . . . . . . . . . . . . . . . . . . . . . . . . . . . . . . . . . . . . . | $ 400,000 | |
|   Shipping . . . . . . . . . . . . . . . . . . . . . . . . . . . . . . . . . . . . . . . . . . | 200,000 | |
|   Bribes . . . . . . . . . . . . . . . . . . . . . . . . . . . . . . . . . . . . . . . . . . . . | 400,000 | |
|   Royalties . . . . . . . . . . . . . . . . . . . . . . . . . . . . . . . . . . . . . . . . . | 400,000† | 1,400,000 |
| Net Income . . . . . . . . . . . . . . . . . . . . . . . . . . . . . . . . . . . . . . . . . . . . . . . | | $ 600,000 |

\* Of which $600,000 is variable.
† Of which $100,000 is fixed.

**Required:**

(Each requirement below is independent.)

1. How many newspapers must the company sell in order to break even?
2. If the current variable royalty is maintained for all newspapers sold up to the breakeven point, but is increased by $.05 for all newspapers sold in excess of the breakeven point, how many newspapers have to be sold in order to yield a net income of $300,000?
3. If the newspaper's contributors agree to accept an all-variable royalty of 10%, instead of a royalty that guarantees a fixed payment as a minimum, how many newspapers would have to be sold in 1998 in order to yield the same income as 1997?

▶ *[Check Figure: 1. 6,842,105 newspapers (rounded); 2. 8,984,962 newspapers (rounded); 3. 10,588,235 newspapers (rounded)]*

**1 2 6** **Problem A5:** Doing C-V-P Analysis for a Firm with Two Products

The Chief Osceola Gift Shop has recently opened a tax-free cigarette shop on a tribal reservation near Tampa. The shop purchases cigarettes from the tribe's North Carolina reservation each week. The income statement for last week is given below.

|  | Type of Cigarette | | |
|  | Low Tar | Low Nicotine | Total |
| --- | --- | --- | --- |
| Number of Packages. . . . . . . . . . . . . . . . . . . . . . . . . | 15,000 | 12,000 | 27,000 |
| Total Revenue. . . . . . . . . . . . . . . . . . . . . . . . . . . . . | $7,500 | $3,000 | $10,500 |
| Cost of Cigarettes . . . . . . . . . . . . . . . . . . . . . . . . . | 5,000 | 1,500 | 6,500 |
|  | $2,500 | $1,500 | $4,000 |
| Allocated Fixed Costs . . . . . . . . . . . . . . . . . . . . . . | 200 | 200 | 400 |
| Income for Week. . . . . . . . . . . . . . . . . . . . . . . . . . . | $2,300 | $1,300 | $ 3,600 |

**Required:**

1. Determine the sales mix based on the number of packages sold.
2. Assume that total sales for the week are 40,500 packages and that the sales mix remains the same. Prepare new income statements for the shop.
3. Determine the weighted average contribution margin per package.
4. Calculate the breakeven point in packages (in total and by product line).

▶ *(Check Figure: 2. Net income = $5,607; 4. 1,514 packages of Low Tar)*

**2 8** **Problem A6:** Preparing Income Statements for DC and AC when $Q_p \neq Q_s$

During 1997 the Billy Martin Company produced and sold 15,000 boxing punching bags and prepared the following income statement:

| | | |
| --- | --- | --- |
| Sales Revenue . . . . . . . . . . . . . . . . . . . . . . . . . . . . . . . . . . . . . . . . | | $600,000 |
| Cost of Goods Sold: | | |
|    Direct Materials . . . . . . . . . . . . . . . . . . . . . . . . . . . . . . | $ 80,000 | |
|    Direct Labor . . . . . . . . . . . . . . . . . . . . . . . . . . . . . . . . . | 100,000 | |
|    Variable Overhead. . . . . . . . . . . . . . . . . . . . . . . . . . . . . | 40,000 | |
|    Fixed Overhead . . . . . . . . . . . . . . . . . . . . . . . . . . . . . . | 60,000 | 280,000 |
| Gross Profit. . . . . . . . . . . . . . . . . . . . . . . . . . . . . . . . . . . . . . . . . . | | $320,000 |
| Selling and Administrative: | | |
|    Variable . . . . . . . . . . . . . . . . . . . . . . . . . . . . . . . . . . . | $130,000 | |
|    Fixed. . . . . . . . . . . . . . . . . . . . . . . . . . . . . . . . . . . . . . | 70,000 | 200,000 |
| Net Income . . . . . . . . . . . . . . . . . . . . . . . . . . . . . . . . . . . . . . . . . . | | $120,000 |

There were no beginning or ending inventories of finished goods.

**Required:**

1. Reconstruct the income statement using the contribution margin format.
2. Assume that 15,000 units were produced but that the unit sales were only 14,000. Prepare income statements for both direct costing and absorption costing.
3. Assume now that there were 2,000 units on hand in finished goods at the beginning of 1997. Billy Martin continued to produce 15,000 units, but 17,000 units were sold. The cost per unit in beginning inventory is the same as it is in 1977. Prepare income statements for direct and absorption costing.

▶ *(Check Figure: Absorption net income = $145,333)*

## PROBLEMS: SET B

2 4   **Problem B1:** Preparing an Income Statement and Doing C-V-P Analysis

During 1998, the Diamond Company produced and sold 10,000 baseball batting gloves. On the basis of this level of activity, the following cost per unit statement was prepared:

| | | |
|---|---:|---:|
| Sales Price . . . . . . . . . . . . . . . . . . . . . . . . . . . . . . . . . . . . . . . . . . . . . . . . . . . . . . | | $150/glove |
| Variable Manufacturing Cost . . . . . . . . . . . . . . . . . . . . . . . . . . . . . . . . . . . | $40 | |
| Fixed Manufacturing Cost . . . . . . . . . . . . . . . . . . . . . . . . . . . . . . . . . . . | 10 | 50/glove |
| Variable Selling Costs . . . . . . . . . . . . . . . . . . . . . . . . . . . . . . . . . . . . . . . | $20 | |
| Fixed Selling Costs. . . . . . . . . . . . . . . . . . . . . . . . . . . . . . . . . . . . . . . . . . . | 4 | 24/glove |
| Income before Taxes . . . . . . . . . . . . . . . . . . . . . . . . . . . . . . . . . . . . . . . . . . . | | $ 76/glove |
| Income Taxes. . . . . . . . . . . . . . . . . . . . . . . . . . . . . . . . . . . . . . . . . . . . . . . . . | | 38/glove |
| Net Income . . . . . . . . . . . . . . . . . . . . . . . . . . . . . . . . . . . . . . . . . . . . . . . . . . | | $ 38/glove |

**Required:**

1. Assume that 15,000 gloves were produced and sold during 1998, and prepare an income statement, using the contribution margin format.
2. If the company had an income before tax of $600,000 in 1998, how many gloves must have been sold?

▶ *(Check Figure: 2. 8,222 gloves)*

4   **Problem B2:** Doing C-V-P Analysis with Income Taxes

The Jimmy Moon Company had the following income statement for 1997:

| | |
|---|---:|
| Sales Revenue ($8 per unit). . . . . . . . . . . . . . . . . . . . . . . . . . . . . . . . . . . . . . | $320,000 |
| Variable Costs. . . . . . . . . . . . . . . . . . . . . . . . . . . . . . . . . . . . . . . . . . . . . . . . | 240,000 |
| Total Contribution Margin . . . . . . . . . . . . . . . . . . . . . . . . . . . . . . . . . . . . . | $ 80,000 |
| Fixed Costs. . . . . . . . . . . . . . . . . . . . . . . . . . . . . . . . . . . . . . . . . . . . . . . . . . | 54,000 |
| Income before Taxes . . . . . . . . . . . . . . . . . . . . . . . . . . . . . . . . . . . . . . . . . . | $ 26,000 |

The income tax rate is 40%.

**Required:**

1. If the company expects to have an income before taxes of $56,000 in 1997, how great must its sales revenue be?
2. If the company desires an after-tax net income of $40,000 in 1997, how many units must be sold?

▶ *(Check Figure: 1. $440,000; 2. 6,033.5 units)*

1 2 4   **Problem B3:** Doing C-V-P Analysis and Preparing Income Statements

During 1998, the Golden Gloves Company produced and sold 15,000 boxing punching bags and prepared the following income statement:

| | | |
|---|---:|---:|
| Sales Revenue . . . . . . . . . . . . . . . . . . . . . . . . . . . . . . . . . . . . . . . . . . . . . . . . | | $600,000 |
| Cost of Goods Sold: | | |
| Direct Materials . . . . . . . . . . . . . . . . . . . . . . . . . . . . . . . . . . . | $ 80,000 | |
| Direct Labor . . . . . . . . . . . . . . . . . . . . . . . . . . . . . . . . . . . . . . | 100,000 | |
| Variable Factory Overhead . . . . . . . . . . . . . . . . . . . . . . . . . | 40,000 | |
| Fixed Factory Overhead . . . . . . . . . . . . . . . . . . . . . . . . . . . . | 60,000 | 280,000 |
| Gross Profit. . . . . . . . . . . . . . . . . . . . . . . . . . . . . . . . . . . . . . . . . . . . . . . . . . | | $320,000 |
| Selling and Administrative Costs: | | |
| Variable . . . . . . . . . . . . . . . . . . . . . . . . . . . . . . . . . . . . . . . . | $130,000 | |
| Fixed. . . . . . . . . . . . . . . . . . . . . . . . . . . . . . . . . . . . . . . . . . | 70,000 | 200,000 |
| Net Income . . . . . . . . . . . . . . . . . . . . . . . . . . . . . . . . . . . . . . . . . . . . . . . . . | | $120,000 |

**Required:**

1. Reconstruct the income statement using the contribution margin format.
2. Assume that the number of units increases by 20% because of a 5% decrease in the sales price, and that the fixed overhead increases by $5,000. Prepare a new income statement, using the contribution margin format.
3. Calculate the breakeven point (in units) for the facts described in requirement 2, above.

▶ *(Check Figure: 2. Net income = $129,000; 3. 9,202.45 bags)*

1 4    **Problem B4:** Doing C-V-P Analysis with Changing Variables

During 1998, the Greenhouse Paperback Book Company manufactured and sold 500,000 books. Its income statement for the year was as follows:

| | | |
|---|---:|---:|
| Sales . . . . . . . . . . . . . . . . . . . . . . . . . . . . . . . . . . . . . . . . . . . . . . . . . . . . . . | | $1,250,000 |
| Cost of Sales: | | |
| Prime Costs. . . . . . . . . . . . . . . . . . . . . . . . . . . . . . . . . . . . . | $500,000 | |
| Factory Overhead . . . . . . . . . . . . . . . . . . . . . . . . . . . . . . . | 250,000* | 750,000 |
| Gross Profit . . . . . . . . . . . . . . . . . . . . . . . . . . . . . . . . . . . . . . . . . . . . . . . | | $ 500,000 |
| Operating Costs: | | |
| Salaries . . . . . . . . . . . . . . . . . . . . . . . . . . . . . . . . . . . . . . . | $100,000 | |
| Commissions. . . . . . . . . . . . . . . . . . . . . . . . . . . . . . . . . . . | 50,000 | |
| Advertising. . . . . . . . . . . . . . . . . . . . . . . . . . . . . . . . . . . . . | 100,000 | |
| Royalties . . . . . . . . . . . . . . . . . . . . . . . . . . . . . . . . . . . . . . | 100,000† | 350,000 |
| Net Income. . . . . . . . . . . . . . . . . . . . . . . . . . . . . . . . . . . . . . . . . . . . . . . | | $ 150,000 |

\* Of which $100,000 is fixed.
† The variable royalty is 6% of sales.

**Required:**

(Each requirement below is independent.)

1. How many books must the company sell in order to break even?
2. If the current variable royalty is maintained for all books sold up to the breakeven point, but is increased by $.05 for all books sold in excess of the breakeven point, how many books have to be sold in order to yield a net income of $150,000?
3. If the sales commissions in 1999 are discontinued in exchange for additional salaries of $60,000, how many books would have to be sold in order to yield the same amount of net income in 1999 as in 1998?

▶ *[Check Figure: 1. 342,105 books (rounded); 2. 508,772 books; 3. 509,524 books (rounded)]*

**1 2 6** **Problem B5:** C-V-P for a Company with Two Products

The Balltick Company has recently opened a ticket booth outside Yankee Stadium. The owner purchases his tickets from season ticket holders who cannot attend games and then resells them at an escalated price for any games that are sellouts. The income statement for the last game is given below.

| | General Admission | Reserved | Total |
|---|---|---|---|
| | **Type of Ticket** | | |
| | **General Admission** | **Reserved** | **Total** |
| Number of Tickets . . . . . . . . . . . . . . . . . . . . . . . . . | 600 | 200 | 800 |
| Total Revenue . . . . . . . . . . . . . . . . . . . . . . . . . . . | $6,000 | $3,000 | $9,000 |
| Cost of Tickets . . . . . . . . . . . . . . . . . . . . . . . . . . | 1,800 | 1,000 | 2,800 |
| | $4,200 | $2,000 | $6,200 |
| Allocated Fixed Costs . . . . . . . . . . . . . . . . . . . . | 400 | 400 | 800 |
| Income for Game . . . . . . . . . . . . . . . . . . . . . . . . | $3,800 | $1,600 | $5,400 |

**Required:**

1. Determine the sales mix based on the number of tickets sold.
2. Assume that total sales are 1,000 tickets and that the sales mix remains the same. Prepare new income statements for Balltick.
3. Determine the weighted average contribution margin per unit.
4. Calculate the breakeven point in tickets (in total and by product line).

▶ *(Check Figure: 2. Net income = $6,950; 4. 26 reserved tickets)*

**2 8** **Problem B6:** Preparing Income Statements for DC and AC when $Q_p \neq Q_s$

Charlie Moore Farms produced and sold 800,000 packages of eggs during 1997, incurring the following revenues, expenses, and income:

| | | |
|---|---|---|
| Sales . . . . . . . . . . . . . . . . . . . . . . . . . . . . . . . . . . . . . . . . . . . . . . . . . . . . . . | | $200,000 |
| Cost of Goods Sold: | | |
| Direct Materials . . . . . . . . . . . . . . . . . . . . . . . . . . . . . . . . . . . . . | $50,000 | |
| Direct Labor . . . . . . . . . . . . . . . . . . . . . . . . . . . . . . . . . . . . . . . . | 25,000 | |
| Variable Overhead . . . . . . . . . . . . . . . . . . . . . . . . . . . . . . . . . . . | 12,500 | |
| Fixed Overhead . . . . . . . . . . . . . . . . . . . . . . . . . . . . . . . . . . . . . | 37,500 | 125,000 |
| Gross Profit . . . . . . . . . . . . . . . . . . . . . . . . . . . . . . . . . . . . . . . . . . . . . . | | $ 75,000 |
| Selling and Administrative Expenses* . . . . . . . . . . . . . . . . . . . . . . . . . . . | | 30,000 |
| Net Income . . . . . . . . . . . . . . . . . . . . . . . . . . . . . . . . . . . . . . . . . . . . . . . | | $ 45,000 |

*$15,000 of this total is fixed.

At the beginning of 1998 Moore, the owner, estimates that he will produce 800,000 packages but will sell only 750,000.

**Required:**

1. Assume that in 1998 the results turned out as planned. Prepare new income statements for direct costing and absorption costing.
2. Assume now that 800,000 packages were produced in 1998 and that all of these were sold. In addition, however, another 100,000 packages were sold from the beginning inventory. Prepare income statements for direct and absorption costing. Assume there were only 100,000 units in beginning inventory.

## DECISION PROBLEM

 During 1997, the Petrograd Company sold 15,000 units at $40 apiece. Its variable and fixed costs were as follows:

| Variable Costs: | | Fixed Costs: | |
|---|---|---|---|
| Manufacturing | $10 per unit | Manufacturing | $125,000 |
| Selling | 5 per unit | Selling | 90,000 |
| | $15 per unit | | $215,000 |

Petrograd is considering reducing its variable production costs per unit by 20%, which will allow it to reduce its selling price by $2.50. In addition, a sales representative who is currently on commission (5% of total sales) would be switched to a fixed salary of $2,500 per month.

**Required:**

1. Determine the breakeven points for the original and revised set of facts.
2. Determine the incomes for sales of: (a) 12,000 units and (b) 24,000 units, using both the original and revised set of facts.
3. Determine the indifference point (that is, the level of sales for which the incomes for the original and revised sets of facts are equal).
4. Would Petrograd be better off with the original or the revised situation?

▶ *(Check Figure: 1. 9,245 units; 3. 20,000 units)*

---

## ETHICS CASE

Frantic Antics Novelties manufactures a wide variety of magic items, practical jokes, and costumes. Although it once was quite profitable, Frantic has suffered declining sales during the last 2 years, with accompanying falling profits. The president of Frantic, Willy Nilly, is frantic because his board of directors has given him the first 6 months of 1997 to turn things around. Unfortunately, it seems to be a lost cause, since sales apparently cannot be increased (even though production is at only 50% of capacity), and costs have already been cut to the bare bone.

One night during an intense nightmare, Willy comes up with an idea. He remembers that Frantic is using the absorption costing method to cost its inventories, and decides that he can probably improve the company's profit picture simply by increasing production. As soon as he gets to work, Willy orders production to be doubled, so that Frantic is now operating at full capacity. Willy continues this strategy during his entire 6-month probation. Amazingly, even though Frantic's sales do not improve—in fact, they actually continue to decline—the net income for the first 6 months of 1997 shows a significant increase and Willy is commended for saving the company. As a show of their appreciation, the board of directors even gives Willy a large cash bonus and a trip to the Bahamas.

**Required:**

1. Why did Frantic's income increase dramatically as a result of the actions taken by Willy Nilly?
2. What would be some extremely negative consequences for Frantic of the actions taken by Willy?
3. Do you consider Willy's actions to be ethical? Discuss.

---

## OBJECTIVE ASSIGNMENT ANSWERS

**True/False**

1. T    2. T    3. F    4. F    5. F

**Multiple Choice**

1. b    2. d    3. c    4. d    5. a
6. b    7. d    8. b    9. a    10. b

# The Master Budget

In almost every business setting, a number of different activities are going on at the same time—selling, producing, purchasing, distributing, and financing. All these activities are interrelated, and need to be coordinated to attain the organization's immediate and future goals. When managers set targets that they hope the organization will achieve and decide how they plan to achieve those goals, the accountant provides an extremely important service. It is the accountant's role to assist management in planning and control by translating management's objectives into financial terms. Accountants do this by preparing **budgets,** which are quantitative expressions of management's plans.

The mere existence of a budget provides no assurance that the goals will be achieved. That is entirely up to management, which must take specific actions in order to make their plans a reality. A budget is simply an expression of management's projections of future events.

Budgets can take many different forms; so as you read this chapter, keep the following points in mind:

- Budgets can be used for many different purposes. For example, budgets can predict revenues or expenses or the amount of profit at an anticipated level of sales. They can estimate the cash receipts and cash disbursements generated from operating activities. They can project the level of sales required to break even or to generate a desired amount of profit. They can forecast the long-run impact of a proposed capital investment on the value of the firm.

- No particular format must be used in preparing a budget. The accountant's main concern is simply to present the budget in a form that is understandable and useful to management.

- Although budgets are frequently expressed in terms of dollars and cents, they can also be expressed in nonfinancial terms. A production process, for example, might budget the number of direct labor hours worked, the number of defective units that need to be reworked, or the quantity of materials wasted or spoiled in production.

- A budget can be prepared for any period of time that is needed to satisfy management's needs. It might be for the upcoming week, month, year, or many years. In addition, budgets can be prepared before the period begins or after it has ended.

Learning Objective 1

## ADVANTAGES OF USING BUDGETS

Explain how all organizations can benefit from the use of budgets

People who don't understand why and how budgets are used often raise these objections:

"Budgets are too costly."

"My firm is small and uncomplicated. I can do all my planning in my head."

The employees don't respond well to the pressure imposed on them by budgets."

Although there may be some basis for these objections, budgets offer advantages and benefits that far outweigh the costs or disadvantages, regardless of the type and size of firm.

Budgets can benefit all firms because they provide: (1) direction for planning; (2) control of performance; (3) coordination of activities; and (4) positive motivation.

### Direction for Planning

When managers are aware that budgets have to be prepared—that goals and objectives have to be periodically converted into dollars and cents—they are forced to think about the organization's long- and short-run prospects. They must look ahead to the future and decide on the best course of action to take. In essence, the budgetary process forces management to set goals at all levels of the organization on a timely basis.

Once goals have been set, budgets indicate to management how profitable the firm is expected to be and what resources are expected to be generated or used during the forthcoming budget periods. When changes from normal operating activities are being considered, a budget can also inform managers of the consequences of alternative courses of action, thereby providing a basis for choosing among them.

Without a budget, managers can only hope that they are going in the best direction for the organization; they may have little idea of the results they can expect. With a budget, management has a better view of what it is likely to achieve during the budget period.

### Control of Performance

Many organizations develop control systems to evaluate the performance of employees. These evaluations are based on some predetermined measure of what a person doing a particular job is expected to accomplish. If the expectations in a budget are communicated to the affected personnel at the beginning of the budget period, then the budget provides the employees with definite objectives. They know exactly what is expected of them and on what basis they will be evaluated at the end of the period. The budget represents the goal against which actual performance can be compared. The performance report is prepared by the accountant after the budget period is over. A **performance report** compares an organization's or a department's actual results with its budget projections. Differences between budget and actual are referred to as *variances.* Management analyzes any significant variances so that they can determine the cause and appropriate remedy and thus try to shrink these variances during the next budget period.

### Coordination of Activities

The overall goals of the organization must be communicated to—and understood by—the managers of each department within the organization. The overall goals must be understood by the middle- and lower-level managers and accepted by them as consistent with their own unit's goals.

If the managers of different departments believe that by helping to attain the company's goals, they also accomplish their own goals, the chances are good that the efforts, activities, and goals of all managers will be coordinated toward achieving the goals of the organization. If each department is interested only in its own performance, the departments may become competitive rather than cooperative, and the organization as a whole may suffer.

Once the organization's overall goals have been communicated to each department, the manager of each department is responsible for his or her department's budget and for coordinating it with the budgets of the other departments. Each budget becomes an integral part of the *master budget,* which we'll describe soon.

### Positive Motivation

When employees' participation in the budgetary process is considered valuable and when the goals set by top management are considered fair and realistic, then employees are likely to accept the overall organization's goals as individual goals they want to achieve. In this situation, the budget should have a positive impact on employees' performance, motivating them to strive toward the goals that have been set for them.

In contrast, when budgets are used inappropriately as a device to pressure employees to achieve goals that they have not accepted as their own, budgets often have an extremely negative influence on the behavior of employees. Such pressure is likely to reduce morale and enthusiasm, resulting in a diminished effort by employees to achieve the goals set by top management.

It is important to realize that a budget is just an inanimate device that communicates management's plans throughout the organization. The budget itself should not be commended or condemned for the impact it has on human behavior. Whether or not the budget is a positive motivator depends on whether people at all levels are involved in the budgetary process, on the manner in which the budget is communicated to affected personnel, and on its perception as fair and reasonable.

**ASK YOURSELF ▶**

1. **What is a budget?**
2. **For what time periods can budgets be prepared?**
3. **Name four advantages of using budgets.**
4. **When is the performance report prepared, and how is it useful to management?**
5. **Budgets can only reduce the morale of employees. Do you agree with this statement?**

Learning 2
Objective

Distinguish among the different types of budgets that accountants use to assist management in the planning and control of operations in the short and long run

## TYPES OF BUDGETS

An organization may use many types of budgets in the planning and control of its activities. The types of budgets that we are going to look at in this and the next few chapters are the master budget, the flexible budget, and the capital budget.

The **master budget** is a primary planning tool in the short run. It is a comprehensive expression of the overall business plan for the entire organization for a period of 1 year or less. It illustrates how the activities of the organization's different departments are expected to interact.

The three main characteristics of the master budget are:

1. It is prepared before the period begins and is based on the most likely level of future activity.
2. It summarizes the budgets for the individual departments.
3. It combines the individual budgets into an integrated plan for the organization as a whole.

It is important to realize that the "most likely" level of activity — on which the master budget is based — is nothing more than an educated guess. The level of activity actually achieved might be anywhere above or below that level. For this reason budgets can be prepared that plan for many possible levels of future activity — each one of which would be what is called a **flexible budget.** Of the many flexible budgets that can be prepared at the beginning of the period, the one that is based on the most likely level of activity becomes the master budget, because it represents the very best guess.

After the period ends and the actual results are tabulated, the accountant assists management in the control of operations by preparing a performance report, which compares the actual and the budgeted results for the period. The budget presented in the performance report is also a flexible budget, but this time based on the level of activity actually achieved.

Budgets that help managers plan the long-run activities of the organization are called **capital budgets.** Organizations are often faced with the need to purchase additional property, plant, and equipment. Such investments usually require a substantial commitment of resources. The result of such investments is to significantly increase the organization's productive capacity. The goal, of course, is to improve long-term profits. Capital budgeting analysis offers several methods to assist management in making these decisions.

Learning Objective 3

Identify the typical participants in the budget process

## PARTICIPANTS IN THE BUDGET PROCESS

Managers at all levels in an organization must participate actively in preparing the master budget if it is to be a truly useful tool. The major sources of information in the master budget are the organization's various departments. Thus, sales managers, production supervisors, and purchasing agents are as involved in the budget process as the accounting department personnel and top-level executives.

Most large organizations have a **budget committee,** composed of top executives of the different divisions or departments of the company. A budget director and the budget committee provide guidance and coordination as the budget is prepared.

The **budget director**—who is typically an accountant serving on the controller's staff—is responsible primarily for the mechanical aspects of putting the budget package together. He or she provides the other budget committee members with any historical data that they may need to derive their estimates for the upcoming period. Then, using their estimates, the budget director develops the many schedules and statements needed for each department. Finally, the budget director combines the individual budgets for the numerous subunits of the organization into an integrated master budget for the organization as a whole.

**ASK YOURSELF** ▶

1. **What are the three main characteristics of a master budget?**
2. **What are the three types of budgets?**
3. **What groups and individuals are typically present on the budget committee of a large organization?**

## PREPARING THE MASTER BUDGET

The master budget consists of two groups of budgets: operating budgets and financial budgets.

Learning Objective 4

List and describe the different types of budgets that make up a master budget

### Components of the Master Budget

**Operating budgets** express the expected results of the firm's operations during the budget period through schedules and statements related to the estimated revenues, expenses, and resulting income. Operating budgets include, but are not limited to, the following:

* Sales forecast
* Budgeted schedule of cash collections
* Budgeted schedules of purchases and payments
* Budgeted schedule of selling and administrative expenses
* Budgeted income statement
* Budgeted retained earnings statement

**Financial budgets** project the sources, amounts, and uses of cash and other resources used in operations, as well as the ending balances in cash and other resources. This category is composed of the following budgeted statements:

* Budgeted statement of cash receipts and disbursements
* Budgeted balance sheet

## An Overview of the Budget Process

The preparation of a master budget is usually started several months before the budget period begins. The budget process involves a sequence of many steps, with each step building on the preceding ones. It begins as the budget director gathers the following:

- The company's budgeted balance sheet, which is for the day before the master budget period begins
- Predictions by top and middle management of activity for the forthcoming budget period
- Other relevant information describing some of the company's policies and expectations, such as sales terms, collection experience, desired ending inventories, and minimum cash balances

The process continues with the budget director's preparation of the numerous schedules that support the budgeted financial statements. These include:

1. Sales forecast
2. Budgeted schedule of cash collections
3. Budgeted schedule of purchases
4. Budgeted schedule of purchase payments
5. Budgeted schedule of selling and administrative expenses

The process concludes with the preparation of the budgeted statements themselves, namely:

6. Budgeted statement of cash receipts and disbursements
7. Budgeted income statement
8. Budgeted retained earnings statement
9. Budgeted balance sheet

Figure 1 shows the relationships among the schedules and statements that comprise the master budget and the sequence in which they are developed. Because these relationships are interdependent, we will make frequent references to Figure 1 as we later describe the steps in developing the master budget. Figure 1 will help you keep track of the relationships among these steps. Think of it as a road map or a flow chart to guide you through successive steps of development on the way to the master budget.

Learning Objective **5**

Prepare a master budget—from beginning to end

We will now examine the budget process in detail, using as our example the POTS (Plenty of Tears Security) Company.

# POTS COMPANY

Plenty of Tears Security (POTS) Company sells crime-prevention kits for home and automobile use. Each kit, selling for $25, includes two canisters of tear gas for home use, a key-chain tear-gas dispenser for trips outside the home, security warning stickers for home windows to scare off potential burglars, and CALL POLICE signs for car breakdowns.

During the last quarter of 1997, the controller of POTS Company, Al Waysredy, is working on the master budget for the first quarter of 1998. He begins with the budgeted balance sheet for Dec. 31, 1997, shown in Exhibit 1.

Next, Al obtains from the vice president for sales the predictions shown in Exhibit 2 for the last month of 1997 and the first 4 months of 1998.

**Figure 1** The Master Budget: The Sequence and Relationships of the Parts That Make up the Whole

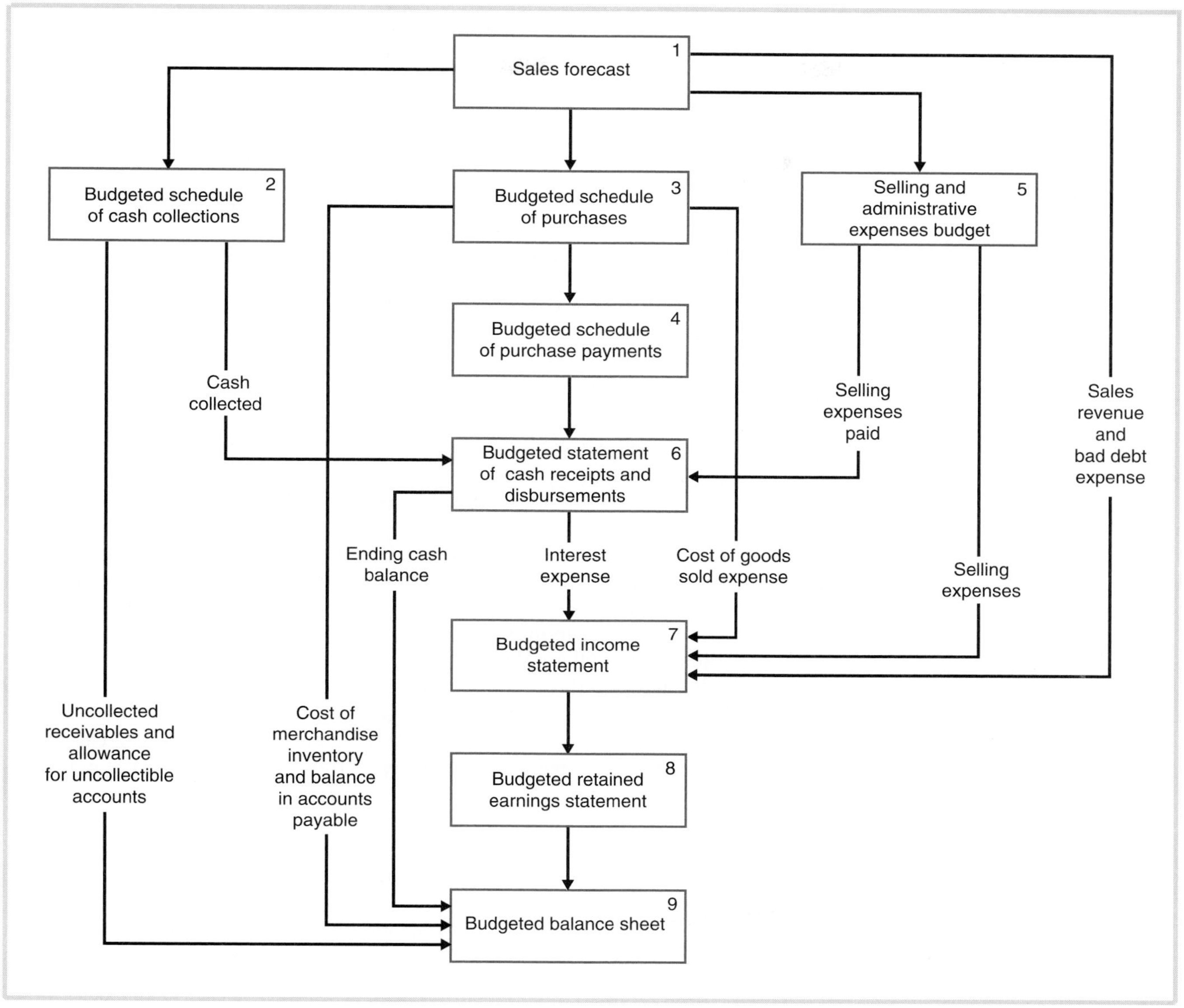

*Every step we take in preparing the master budget depends on the sales forecast (step 1), and leads toward the final product—the budgeted financial statements (steps 6–9).*

Collection experiences for the past few years (which Al expects to continue in 1998) indicate the following:

1. Cash sales typically average 25% of total sales.
2. About one-half of the remaining credit sales are collected in the month of sale, and the remainder is usually collected in the month following the month of sale.
3. POTS has never experienced any bad debts.
4. POTS offers no cash discounts for early payment of sales on account.

The purchasing agent, Justin Tyme, feels it is necessary to maintain at all times a minimum balance in merchandise inventory equal to at least 50% of the following month's projected unit sales. Merchandise costs 60% of its retail price, and all

**Exhibit 1** POTS Company Balance Sheet

**POTS COMPANY**
**Balance Sheet**
**December 31, 1997**

| Assets | | Liabilities | |
|---|---|---|---|
| Cash . . . . . . . . . . . . . . . . . . | $ 43,250 | Accounts Payable . . . . . . . . | $135,000 |
| Accounts Receivable . . . . . | 75,000 | Dividends Payable . . . . . . . . | 80,000 |
| Merchandise Inventory* . . . | 75,000 | Total Liabilities . . . . . . . . | $215,000 |
| Fixed Assets . . . . . . . . . . . | 420,000 | **Stockholders' Equity** | |
| Accumulated Depreciation . | (126,000) | | |
| | | Capital Stock . . . . . . . . . . . . | $200,000 |
| | | Retained Earnings . . . . . . . . | 72,250 |
| | | | $272,250 |
| | | Total Liabilities and | |
| Total Assets . . . . . . . . . . . | $ 487,250 | Stockholders' Equity . . . . . . | $487,250 |

* 5,000 units × $15 = $75,000.

purchases are made on account and will be paid in full in the month following purchase.

All selling and administrative expenses (except for depreciation of $1,500 per month) are completely paid for in the month incurred. The variable selling and administrative expenses are expected to be $2 per unit, and the fixed expenses are expected to be $8,000 per month.

Dividends of $80,000 are declared during the last month of each quarter, to be paid during the first month of the following quarter.

In January 1998, POTS plans to purchase new computers for the officers of the company, costing a total of $30,000. The $1,500 of depreciation mentioned above for the selling and administrative activities includes the depreciation for the new computers.

The treasurer, Joyce Tate, recommends that the company maintain at all times a minimum balance in cash of $50,000. Whenever the company anticipates falling below the minimum, a short-term loan will be arranged with a local bank. The loan will be taken out at the beginning of the month and repaid when the cash becomes available. Interest accrues at 14% of the unpaid balance in the loan, but is paid only when principal is repaid (and is based on the amount of principal repaid). All repayments take place at the end of the month.

**Exhibit 2** POTS Company Projected Sales

**POTS COMPANY**
**Projected Sales**
**December 1997–April 1998**

| | Unit Sales | Dollar Sales |
|---|---|---|
| December . . . . . . . . . . . . . . . . . . . . . . . . . . . . . . . . . . . . | 8,000 | $200,000 |
| January . . . . . . . . . . . . . . . . . . . . . . . . . . . . . . . . . . . . . | 10,000 | 250,000 |
| February . . . . . . . . . . . . . . . . . . . . . . . . . . . . . . . . . . . . | 20,000 | 500,000 |
| March . . . . . . . . . . . . . . . . . . . . . . . . . . . . . . . . . . . . . | 24,000 | 600,000 |
| April . . . . . . . . . . . . . . . . . . . . . . . . . . . . . . . . . . . . . . | 18,000 | 450,000 |

# The Cornerstone of All Budgeting May Be a Little Shaky

The sales forecast is considered the cornerstone—the starting point for all budgeting. As a result the entire master budget depends upon it. Unfortunately the cornerstone itself depends upon a future which is uncertain at best. Many feel that sales forecasts are the weakest feature of most business plans. A fortune teller with tea leaves and a copy of Lotus 1-2-3 could do better. Well maybe scratch the 1-2-3. Lotus Devel-

opment Corp. which makes 1-2-3, the software tool of choice among entrepreneurs working up their five-year forecasts, had perhaps the most wildly wrong forecast in modern business history. Mitchell D. Kapor, the founder, wrote in his initial plan that he expected first year sales of about $6 million. Ben Rosen, who invested in the Cambridge, Mass., company, expected the business would take in $3 million. Lotus went right ahead and ignored the plan, posting first-year sales of $53 million.

In 1982, Rosen and partner L. J. Sevin, a couple of lucky guys, invested in a company, then called Gateway Technology Inc. Gateway's plan said the company would make a portable computer compatible with IBM's personal computer and would sell 20,000 machines for $35 million in its first

year—"which we didn't believe for a moment." says Rosen. The sales projection for the second year was even more outrageous: $198 million. "Can you imagine seeing a business plan like this for a company going head-on against IBM, and projecting $198 million?" he asks. He and Sevin told the company to scale down its projections.

Gateway later changed its name to Compaq Computer Company. In its first year, sales were actually $111 million. And in its second year sales were a whopping $329 million. So much for sales forecasts.

*Source:* Adapted from "The Best-Laid Plans," by Erik Larson. Published in *Inc. Magazine,* February 1987 issue. Copyright © 1987 by Erik Larson. Reproduced by permission of Georges Borchardt, Inc. for the author.

## Steps in the Budget Process

### Step 1: The Sales Forecast

The first step in the budget process is the **sales forecast,** which is a prediction of expected sales throughout the budget period. The responsibility for developing the sales forecast is assigned to a top-level marketing officer. The sales forecast is considered the starting point in all budgeting (whether for a manufacturer or a nonmanufacturer) because all the other budgets—that is, all the other elements of the master budget—depend on it.

Look again at Figure 1. Notice that none of the steps shown in the figure can be determined until after the sales forecast (step 1) is developed. For example, until the sales are forecast, we cannot determine the amount of merchandise that has to be purchased (step 3). And only after we determine purchases can we determine the cash payments for merchandise inventory (step 4) and the ending balance in Accounts Payable.

The schedule of cash collections (step 2) depends on the sales forecast, and so does the selling and administrative expenses budget (step 5).

The four budgeted financial statements (steps 6 through 9) depend on the estimates in the preceding budgeted schedules (steps 2 through 5), which, of course, depend on the sales forecast. So everything in a master budget ultimately depends on the sales forecast.

It follows that the reliability of the schedules and statements that make up the master budget all depend on the accuracy of the sales forecast. All in all, the sales forecast is the most critical step in the budgetary process. It is also usually the most difficult, because it depends on such numerous and diverse factors as past sales, advertising, general economic conditions, position in the industry, and quality of the company's sales force. Not only are these factors often uncontrollable, but it is often difficult to determine which factors have an influence on sales and how much influence they have. The sales executive, with the help of others, is expected to consider all these factors and to derive, either subjectively or statistically, an accurate prediction of sales for each period. This is not an easy task.

**Exhibit 3** POTS's Sales Forecast:
Quarter 1, 1998

| Month of Sale | Sales Forecast | | |
| | Total | 25% Cash | 75% Credit |
| --- | --- | --- | --- |
| December | $ 200,000 | $ 50,000 | $ 150,000 |
| January | $ 250,000 | $ 62,500 | $ 187,500 |
| February | 500,000 | 125,000 | 375,000 |
| March | 600,000 | 150,000 | 450,000 |
| Totals | $1,350,000 | $337,500 | $1,012,500 |

This goes to budgeted income statement (Exhibit 10)

**Exhibit 4** Budgeted Schedule of Cash Collections:
Quarter 1, 1998

| Month of Collection | | Collections | | |
| | Cash Sales | 50% of Previous Month Credit Sales | 50% of Current Month Credit Sales | Total |
| --- | --- | --- | --- | --- |
| January | $ 62,500 | $ 75,000 | $ 93,750 | $ 231,250 |
| February | 125,000 | 93,750 | 187,500 | 406,250 |
| March | 150,000 | 187,500 | 225,000 | 562,500 |
| Totals | $337,500 | $356,250 | $506,250 | $1,200,000 |

These go to line 2 in budgeted statement of cash receipts and disbursements (Exhibit 9)

Legend:
— Cash sales collected in month of sale
- - - 50% of credit sales collected in month of sale
•••• 50% of credit sales collected in the following month

POTS's sales forecast for the first quarter of 1998 is shown in Exhibit 3 at left. The total sales are broken down into cash sales (25%) and credit sales (75%). In addition, Exhibit 3 includes the sales for the month of December. Because only one-half of the credit sales of that month will be collected in 1997, the other one-half will be collected in January 1998. We need to show where the cash collections (shown in Exhibit 4 at left) in January come from; some will come from January's sales and some will come from December's sales.

The total sales forecast for the quarter, $1,350,000, is recorded on the first line of the budgeted income statement, as you will see later, in Exhibit 10.

### Step 2: The Budgeted Schedule of Cash Collections

The colored arrows from the sales forecast (Exhibit 3) to the **budgeted schedule of cash collections** (Exhibit 4) point out the month in which each month's sales are expected to be collected. For example, in January the sales of $250,000 are $62,500 cash and $187,500 credit. The cash sales are obviously collected in the month of sale (shown by solid arrow). According to the facts given in our description of POTS's activities, 50% of the credit sales are to be collected in the month of sale, with the balance collected in the following month. Therefore, 50% of the credit sales in January, or $93,750, is collected in January (shown by a dashed arrow). The remaining $93,750 is collected in February (shown by a dotted arrow).

The cash collections for each month are composed of three parts. For January, they are:

1. The cash sales of the month, $62,500
2. The collections of 50% of January's credit sales, $93,750
3. The collection of 50% of December's credit sales, $75,000

The total of these three specific cash collections is $231,250 for January, $406,250 for February, and $562,500 for March. These totals, representing expected cash receipts each month during the first quarter, are transferred to the second line of the budgeted statement of cash receipts and disbursements, as you will see when we reach Exhibit 9. When the cash receipts are added to the beginning cash balance (for January), the sum of the two is the total cash available before current financing (line 3 in Exhibit 9). This total cash available should be large enough to cover the cash needs for the month. If not, financing will need to be arranged.

Of course, we must also account for the uncollected credit sales on Mar. 31, 1998. For POTS this balance is simply the 50% of March's credit sales that are expected to be collected in April. These uncollected credit sales of $225,000 appear as accounts receivable on the budgeted balance sheet for Mar. 31, 1998, as we will see in Exhibit 12. A useful general format for obtaining a budgeted balance in accounts receivable is shown in Exhibit 5.

In this simple example we have assumed that all credit sales would eventually be collected—no bad debts expense was expected. Realistically, however, some of the

**Exhibit 5** Expected Balance in Accounts Receivable: March 31, 1998

| Month | Total Sales | × | % Credit | = | Credit Sales | × | Percent of Credit Sales Uncollected by End of Quarter | = | Uncollected Amount at End of Quarter |
|-------|-------------|---|----------|---|--------------|---|------------------------------------------------------|---|--------------------------------------|
| March | $600,000 | × | .75 | = | $450,000 | × | .50 | = | $225,000 |

*The Accounts Receivable balance goes on the budgeted balance sheet (Exhibit 12)*

accounts are going to go bad. If POTS had expected some bad debts and had been using the estimation method for bad debts—such as percentage of sales—a few things would be different. First, there would be an Allowance for Uncollectibles account on the Dec. 31, 1997, balance sheet. Next, we would have some bad debts expense in the budgeted income statement (Exhibit 10). Finally, the Allowance for Uncollectibles account would have to be adjusted for the additional bad debts in the first quarter. When you go through the demonstration problem at the end of this chapter, you'll get a chance to see how bad debts complicate the schedules and statements.

### Step 3: The Budgeted Schedule of Purchases

The next step in building a master budget is to develop a budgeted schedule of purchases. The **budgeted schedule of purchases** tells planners how much inventory must be purchased (merchandise for a merchandising firm and raw materials for a manufacturer) during the upcoming period to satisfy the total needs for the period. **Total needs** are the inventory that must be on hand at some time during the budget period. They are made up of two parts. First, a merchandiser needs to have enough inventory to satisfy its sales projections. Second, most organizations feel the need to maintain some minimum level of merchandise on hand at all times—that is, a **desired ending inventory**—to avoid the possibility of losing sales should demand exceed the merchandise available for sale. Once the total needs are determined—by adding projected sales and the desired ending inventory—purchases are determined by subtracting the inventory that is on hand at the beginning of the budget period.

Inventory purchases can also be calculated by using the following formula:

**Desired ending inventory of merchandise**
**plus**
**Merchandise needed for current sales**
**equals**
**Total needs for the period**
**less**
**Beginning inventory of merchandise**
**equals**
**Units to be purchased**

The desired ending inventory for a period may be expressed in absolute or relative terms, as follows:

1. *In absolute terms,* the desired ending inventory would be the same amount each month regardless of the level of future inventory needs. For example, POTS may desire an ending inventory of 10,000 units, whether the following month's sales are expected to be 50,000 units or 1,000 units.
2. *In relative terms,* the desired ending inventory would be determined as a percentage of sales expected in future months. For example, POTS may prefer its ending inventory of merchandise to be at least 50% of the next month's expected sales.

Depending on the specific organization, the manager who determines desired inventory levels may be the vice president for manufacturing, the manager of inventory planning and control, or even the purchasing agent. This person must consider the likelihood of running out of inventory at different inventory levels and the trade-offs associated with holding too little and too much inventory. Holding too little inventory increases the odds of running out of stock when demand is high, resulting in lost sales and customers. Holding too much inventory leads to excessive costs (called *carrying costs*), such as insurance, interest, material handling, storage, and obsoles-

**Exhibit 6** Budgeted Schedule of Purchases: Quarter 1, 1998

|  | January | February | March |
|---|---|---|---|
| Desired ending inventory of merchandise* .... | 10,000 | 12,000 | 9,000 |
| Merchandise needed for current sales ....... | 10,000 | 20,000 | 24,000 |
| Total needs for the period ................. | 20,000 | 32,000 | 33,000 |
| Beginning inventory of merchandise ........ | 5,000 | 10,000 | 12,000 |
| Required purchases (in units) .............. | 15,000 | 22,000 | 21,000 |
| Cost per unit† ........................... | × $15 | × $15 | × $15 |
| Dollar purchases........................ | $225,000 | $330,000 | $315,000 |

*March's ending inventory × $15 unit cost ($135,000) goes on the budgeted balance sheet (Exhibit 12)*

*The purchases are needed to get purchase payments (Exhibit 7)*

\* 50% of sales (in units) for February, March, and April, respectively.
† Cost per unit = .60 × sales price = .60 × $25 = $15.

cence. Recently, more and more American companies have been following the lead of the Japanese and are attempting to reduce their inventories to a bare minimum, thus virtually eliminating most of these expensive carrying costs. Naturally, this approach requires a company to develop long-term relationships with reliable suppliers in order to ensure delivery of inventories just in time for sale or use.

The POTS Company, using the relative approach, has decided to maintain a balance in ending inventory equal to at least 50% of the unit sales of the following month. So, on Jan. 31, POTS will want its inventory to be at least 50% of February's sales of 20,000—which is 10,000 units. The required ending inventories for February and March are determined in a similar manner.

Starting with these figures for required ending inventory of merchandise each month, the number of units to be purchased is determined in Exhibit 6: 15,000 units in January, 22,000 units in February, and 21,000 units in March.

The beginning inventory for January was taken from the footnote to POTS's Dec. 31, 1997, balance sheet (Exhibit 1). The beginning inventory of merchandise for February is the ending inventory for January, and the beginning inventory for March is the ending inventory for February.

The dollar amount of purchases is found by multiplying the unit purchases by the cost per unit of $15 (.60 × the $25 sales price). The cost of the Mar. 31 merchandise inventory—shown as an asset on the budgeted balance sheet on Mar. 31 (Exhibit 12)—is the 9,000 units times the $15 cost per unit, or $135,000.

Cost of goods sold can also be determined from Exhibit 6. Simply add up the unit sales for the quarter in the exhibit (10,000 + 20,000 + 24,000 = 54,000) and multiply this sum times the cost per unit of $15:

$$54,000 \times \$15 = \$810,000$$

This amount, $810,000, goes on the budgeted income statement (Exhibit 10) as cost of goods sold.

A second way to determine budgeted cost of goods sold is to multiply the expected sales dollars in Exhibit 10 by the expected cost of goods sold percentage:

$$\$1,350,000 \times .60 = \$810,000$$

### Step 4: The Budgeted Schedule of Purchase Payments

The purchases shown in the budgeted schedule of purchases (Exhibit 6) are not paid for in the month of purchase. Instead, POTS typically pays for its purchases in the

**Exhibit 7** Budgeted Schedule of Purchase Payments: Quarter 1, 1998

| | | Quarter 1 | | | |
| | December | January | February | March | April |
|---|---|---|---|---|---|
| Purchases............... | $135,000 | $225,000 | $330,000 | $315,000* | |
| Payments—in month...... | | $135,000 | $225,000 | $330,000 | $315,000 |

*Trace these payments to line 4 of the budgeted statement of cash receipts and disbursements (Exhibit 9)*

\* On Mar. 31, the unpaid purchases represent the balance in Accounts Payable.

month following the month of purchase. The **budgeted schedule of purchase payments** (Exhibit 7) indicates what the cash payments will be in each month.

The payments in January, $135,000, are for the purchases of December. Since these purchases were not paid for before Dec. 31, 1997, they appeared as the balance in Accounts Payable on the Dec. 31, 1997, balance sheet (Exhibit 1). The cash payments in February and March are for the purchases in January and February. The purchases in March ($315,000) will not be paid for until April, so this $315,000 of unpaid bills represents the balance in Accounts Payable in the Mar. 31, 1998, budgeted balance sheet (Exhibit 12).

The cash payments from Exhibit 7 are listed on the fourth line in the budgeted statement of cash receipts and disbursements (Exhibit 9).

**Purchases for a Manufacturer** Determining purchases for a manufacturer requires more steps than it does for a wholesaler or retailer. First the number of units to be produced, based on the sales forecast, is calculated as follows:

**Desired minimum inventory of finished goods**
plus
**Unit sales expected in the forthcoming month**
equals
**Total inventory needs for the forthcoming period**
less
**Beginning inventory of finished goods**
equals
**Units to be produced**

Next, the budgeted number of units to be produced is used to determine the direct materials, direct labor, and factory overhead needed in production. Then, on the basis of the direct materials needed in production, the purchases of raw materials are calculated in the following manner:

**Desired ending inventory of raw materials**
plus
**Raw materials needed in production**
equals
**Total needed for the period**
less
**Beginning inventory of raw materials**
equals
**Required purchases**

### Step 5: The Budgeted Schedule of Selling and Administrative Expenses

The next step in building the master budget is to work out a **budgeted schedule of selling and administrative expenses.**

**Exhibit 8** Budgeted Schedule of Selling and Administrative Items—Expenses and Disbursements: Quarter 1, 1998

| | January | February | March | Total | |
|---|---|---|---|---|---|
| Variable* . . . . . . . . . . . . . . . . . . . . . | $20,000 | $40,000 | $48,000 | $108,000 | *The total expenses go to the budgeted income statement (Exhibit 10)* |
| Fixed . . . . . . . . . . . . . . . . . . . . . . . . | 8,000 | 8,000 | 8,000 | 24,000 | |
| Total expenses . . . . . . . . . . . . . . . . | $28,000 | $48,000 | $56,000 | $132,000 | |
| Total disbursements† . . . . . . . . . . . | $26,500 | $46,500 | $54,500 | $127,500 | *The disbursements are found in line 5 of Exhibit 9* |

\* $2 per unit sold × the number of units sold in each month.
† Total expenses less the $1,500 per month for depreciation—a noncash expense.

Selling expenses are the costs of promoting, selling, and shipping the product to the customers. These costs include a variety of items that can be divided into variable and fixed costs:

- *Variable selling costs,* such as commissions and shipping costs, can be estimated by taking a percentage of the total sales dollars or by multiplying a cost per unit by the number of units sold.
- *Fixed selling costs* include salaries, advertising, rent, and depreciation. They are budgeted at an unchanging amount per month.

Administrative costs include such activities as giving overall direction to the company and providing services for personnel. Although most administrative costs are fixed, some—such as supplies and telephone costs—are variable.

The selling and administrative expenses for POTS Company are estimated to be $2 per unit variable and $8,000 per month fixed. On the basis of the budgeted sales of 10,000, 20,000, and 24,000 units for the first 3 months of 1998 (Exhibit 2), a budget is prepared for the selling and administrative expenses, as shown in Exhibit 8. The total budgeted selling and administrative expenses for the quarter, $132,000, are transferred to the budgeted income statement (Exhibit 10).

Cash disbursements for selling and administrative items, with the exception of depreciation, are made when the expenses are incurred. Thus the total expenses for each month, less the $1,500 of depreciation, represent the selling and administrative cash disbursements for each month. These monthly disbursements are also listed as the fifth line in the budgeted statement of cash receipts and disbursements (Exhibit 9).

**ASK YOURSELF** ▶

1. What are the two different groups of budgets that make up the master budget? Name several types of each.
2. What is the first step in the budget process, and why does it come first?
3. In order to prepare a budgeted schedule of cash collections, what must be known about the projected sales for the budget period?
4. To which budgeted financial statement are the cash collections from the budgeted schedule of cash collections transferred? On which budgeted financial statement does the budgeted balance in accounts receivable go?
5. How are the budgeted purchases calculated for a merchandising firm? For a manufacturer?
6. Why would a company want to have an ending balance in inventory?
7. What are some examples of variable and fixed selling expenses? Of variable and fixed administrative expenses?

**Exhibit 9** Budgeted Statement of Cash Receipts and Disbursements: Quarter 1, 1998

|  | January | February | March |
|---|---|---|---|
| Beginning cash balance (Exhibit 1, for Jan.). | $ 43,250 | $ 50,000 | $136,653 |
| Cash receipts (Exhibit 4) | 231,250 | 406,250 | 562,500 |
| Total cash available before current financing | $274,500 | $456,250 | $699,153 |
| Total cash needs: | | | |
| Cash disbursements: | | | |
| Purchase payments (Exhibit 7) | $135,000 | $225,000 | $330,000 |
| Selling and Administrative (Exhibit 8) | 26,500 | 46,500 | 54,500 |
| Dividends paid (Exhibit 1) | 80,000 | –0– | –0– |
| Purchase of computers | 30,000 | –0– | –0– |
| Total cash disbursements | $271,500 | $271,500 | $384,500 |
| Minimum cash balance | 50,000 | 50,000 | 50,000 |
| Total cash needs | $321,500 | $321,500 | $434,500 |
| Excess (deficiency) of cash | $ (47,000) | $134,750 | $264,653 |
| Financing and repayments: | | | |
| Financing of deficiency | $ 47,000 | –0– | –0– |
| Repayment of excess: | | | |
| Principal | –0– | $ (47,000) | –0– |
| Interest | –0– | (1,097)* | –0– |
| Total effects of financing and repayments | $ 47,000 | $ (48,097) | –0– |
| Ending cash balance† | $ 50,000 | $136,653 | $314,653 |

*Goes to budgeted income statement (Exhibit 10)* — pointing to the Interest row.

*Goes to budgeted balance sheet (Exhibit 12)* — pointing to the $314,653 Ending cash balance.

* $47,000 × .14 = $6,580/year × $\frac{2}{12}$ = $1,097 for 2 months.

† Minimum cash balance + excess cash − total effects of repayments, or minimum cash balance − deficiency + total effects of financing.

### Step 6: The Budgeted Statement of Cash Receipts and Disbursements

As we saw at the beginning of our discussion of the master budget, the financial budgets are prepared by the budget director, and consist of the budgeted statement of cash receipts and disbursements and the budgeted balance sheet.

We have not yet completed the budgeted statement of cash receipts and disbursements, and until we do so we cannot complete the operating budgets. The budgeted income statement lacks one item and the budgeted retained earnings statement hasn't been started.

The item missing from the budgeted income statement is interest expense, which we cannot calculate until we know if any financing will be needed during the forthcoming quarter. We find out what financing is necessary in the budgeted statement of cash receipts and disbursements.

The purpose of the **budgeted statement of cash receipts and disbursements** is to show the amount and source of cash inflows and outflows expected throughout the budget period and the resulting anticipated cash balances at key times during the budget period. The budget indicates to management when the cash receipts will far exceed cash disbursements, resulting in large cash balances. In this situation management knows how long the excess cash will be available and must decide how it should be invested to earn maximum returns. The budgeted statement also points out when cash outflows are expected to be much larger than cash receipts, which could lead to seriously low cash balances. This information allows management to arrange financing in advance so that when the time comes to meet payrolls, distribute dividends, and pay creditors, the cash will be available.

The many items to be included in the budgeted statement of cash receipts and disbursements can be arranged in a variety of ways. We will use the following general format:

**Beginning cash balance**

**plus**

**Cash receipts**

**equals**

**Total cash available before current financing**

**less**

**Cash needs (cash disbursements plus minimum cash balance)**

**equals**

| **(If cash available exceeds cash needs)** | **OR** | **(If cash needs exceed cash available)** |
|---|---|---|
| **Excess of cash** | | **Deficiency of cash** |
| **less** | | **plus** |
| **Repayments from excess** | | **Financing of deficiency** |
| **less** | | **equals** |
| **Investment of excess** | | |
| **equals** | | |
| **Ending cash balance** | | **Ending cash balance** |

The budgeted statement of cash receipts and disbursements for the POTS Company is presented in Exhibit 9. It starts with the cash balance for Jan. 1, 1998, which was shown as the ending cash balance on the Dec. 31, 1997, balance sheet in Exhibit 1. The beginning cash balances for February and March will be the ending balances for January and February, respectively. The cash receipts (collections from customers), determined in Exhibit 4, are added to the beginning balance to get **total cash available before current financing.** From this amount will be deducted the many disbursements that follow.

The first two disbursements are for payments of merchandise purchases and for selling and administrative expenses, which we have already discussed. The cash disbursement for dividends paid in January follows from the December 1997 declaration. If you refer to the balance sheet for Dec. 31, 1997, in Exhibit 1, you'll see the $80,000 liability for dividends payable.

The $80,000 of dividends to be declared in March will be paid in April and therefore do not affect the cash receipts and disbursements during the first quarter. However, the dividends declared in March do reduce retained earnings (Exhibit 11) at that time, and the related liability for the April payment must be included on the Mar. 31, 1998, budgeted balance sheet (Exhibit 12).

The next line in Exhibit 9 shows the cash disbursement of $30,000 for the January cash purchase of computers. The depreciation of the computers is not included in this budgeted statement because it is a noncash item. It is included in the budgeted income statement, however, as a part of the selling and administrative expenses.

Notice in Exhibit 9 that the **total cash needs** are not represented entirely by cash disbursements. The minimum desired cash balance is also a cash need. To avoid running out of cash, businesses commonly set a minimum cash balance to be maintained throughout each month. If the combination of total cash disbursements plus minimum cash balance exceeds the total cash available before current financing, then a deficiency arises. In January, POTS's total cash needs are expected to be $321,500 ($271,500 + $50,000), and the total cash available before financing is expected to be $274,500. The difference of $47,000 is the anticipated deficiency, and financing needs to be arranged well in advance of the occurrence of the actual deficiency. If the minimum cash balance is ignored, and financing is arranged to cover merely the expected cash disbursements, then the cash balance at the end of the month will be zero.

If financing of exactly $47,000 is arranged, the actual cash balance at the end of the month should be equal to the minimum cash balance. If the financing is in excess of the deficiency, then the ending cash balance will be the minimum cash balance plus the amount of financing in excess of the deficiency. For example, if POTS borrows $48,000 instead of $47,000, then the cash balance will be the minimum cash balance of $50,000 plus the $1,000 of financing which is in excess of the deficiency ($48,000 − $47,000).

The expected ending cash balance for January of $50,000 becomes the beginning cash balance for February. During February, the cash available before financing is $456,250 ($50,000 + $406,250) and the total cash needs are $321,500 ($271,500 + $50,000); the difference represents excess cash of $134,750. Of the excess, $47,000 will be used to repay the entire principal of the loan made in January, and $1,097 will be used to repay the interest on the loan. The interest is for 2 months, since the principal was borrowed at the beginning of January and will not be repaid until the end of February. The Feb. 28 cash balance is $136,653. This ending cash balance is found by adding the excess cash that was not used to repay the loan and interest, to the minimum cash balance. Remember: When we have excess cash, it means that we have more than the minimum needed. Therefore, if we use only $48,097 of the excess to repay the loan, we will still have $86,653 ($134,750 − $48,097) of the excess remaining—$86,653 in excess of the $50,000 minimum, and a total ending cash balance of $136,653 ($50,000 minimum + $86,653 excess remaining).

In March the excess cash is expected to be $264,653. None of this is needed to repay a loan, so all the excess will be on hand at the end of the month in addition to the $50,000 minimum. Therefore the ending cash balance will be $314,653 ($264,653 + $50,000). It would be prudent in March to invest the excess cash in short-term securities, so that the firm would be using all its resources in the most profitable manner.

The Mar. 31 cash balance of $314,653 is transferred to the asset section of the Mar. 31, 1998, budgeted balance sheet (Exhibit 12).

### Steps 7 and 8: The Budgeted Statements of Income and Retained Earnings

Now that we have calculated interest expense, we can complete the **budgeted income statement,** shown in Exhibit 10. We see from Exhibit 9 that the interest

---

**Exhibit 10** Budgeted Income Statement: Quarter 1, 1998

| | |
|---|---:|
| Sales (Exhibit 3) | $1,350,000 |
| Cost of Goods Sold (60% × $1,350,000) | 810,000 |
| Gross Profit | $540,000 |
| Selling and Administrative Expenses (Exhibit 8) | 132,000 |
| Operating Income | $ 408,000 |
| Interest Expense (Exhibit 9) | 1,097 |
| Net Income | $ 406,903 |

*Goes to budgeted retained earnings statement (Exhibit 11)*

**Exhibit 11** Budgeted Retained Earnings Statement: Quarter 1, 1998

| | |
|---|---:|
| Retained Earnings, Jan. 1, 1998 (Exhibit 1) . . . . . . . . . . . . . . . . . . . . . . | $ 72,250 |
| Net Income (Exhibit 10) . . . . . . . . . . . . . . . . . . . . . . . . . . . . . . . . . . . . | 406,903 |
| | $479,153 |
| Dividends Declared . . . . . . . . . . . . . . . . . . . . . . . . . . . . . . . . . . . . . . . | 80,000 |
| Retained Earnings, Mar. 31, 1998. . . . . . . . . . . . . . . . . . . . . . . . . . . . | $399,153 |

*Goes to budgeted balance sheet (Exhibit 12)*

expense is $1,097. When we subtract this amount from the operating income in Exhibit 10, we get the net income: $406,903.

Since POTS is a corporation, one additional item should also be included in the income statement: income taxes. We did not integrate income taxes into the example for POTS Company because it could greatly complicate the analysis. If income taxes are considered, the bottom line of $406,903 would be the income before tax instead of net income. The income tax expense (called "provision for income taxes") would be calculated on the basis of the income before tax and then subtracted from income before tax to get net income. If the income tax is expected to be paid in the first quarter, the payment is included in the budgeted statement of cash receipts and disbursements. But if income taxes are not expected to be paid by the end of the quarter, then a liability for income taxes payable would appear on the Mar. 31, 1998, budgeted balance sheet.

From the Dec. 31, 1997, balance sheet (Exhibit 1), you can see that the Jan. 1, 1998, balance in Retained Earnings is $72,250. We add the budgeted net income for the quarter, $406,903, to this beginning balance for a total of $479,153, as shown in the **budgeted retained earnings statement** in Exhibit 11. From this amount we subtract the dividends of $80,000 that will be declared in March. The remainder of $399,153 is the Mar. 31 budgeted balance in Retained Earnings. It is transferred to the budgeted balance sheet (Exhibit 12), the only financial budget still to be completed.

### Step 9: The Budgeted Balance Sheet

The **budgeted balance sheet,** shown in Exhibit 12, represents the culmination of the budgeted schedules and statements that we have discussed in the previous sections. The budgeted balance sheet items that we have already identified are summarized in the schedule below.

| Balance Sheet Account | Source of Information | |
|---|---|---|
| Cash | Exhibit 9: | Budgeted Statement of Cash Receipts and Disbursements |
| Accounts Receivable | Exhibit 5: | Expected Balance in Accounts Receivable |
| Merchandise Inventory | Exhibit 6: | Budgeted Schedule of Purchases |
| Accounts Payable | Exhibit 7: | Budgeted Schedule of Purchase Payments |
| Dividends Payable | Discussion following Exhibit 9 | |
| Retained Earnings | Exhibit 11: | Budgeted Retained Earnings Statement |

**Exhibit 12** Budgeted Balance Sheet: March 31, 1998

| Assets | | Liabilities | |
|---|---|---|---|
| Cash . . . . . . . . . . . . . . . . . . . | $314,653 | Accounts Payable . . . . . . . . . . | $315,000 |
| Accounts Receivable . . . . . . . | 225,000 | Dividends Payable. . . . . . . . . . | 80,000 |
| Merchandise Inventory. . . . . . | 135,000 | Total Liabilities. . . . . . . . . . . . . | $395,000 |
| Fixed Assets. . . . . . . . . . . . . | 450,000 | **Stockholders' Equity** | |
| Accumulated Depreciation. . . | (130,500) | | |
| | | Capital Stock . . . . . . . . . . . . . | $200,000 |
| | | Retained Earnings. . . . . . . . . . | 399,153 |
| | | | $599,153 |
| | | Total Liabilities and | |
| Total Assets . . . . . . . . . . . . . | $994,153 | Stockholders' Equity . . . . . . . | $994,153 |

*This is what POTS expects its asset, liability, and stockholders' equity accounts to look like on Mar. 31, 1998.*

The only items that have not yet been explained are capital stock, fixed assets, and accumulated depreciation. Since no transactions affecting the Capital Stock account were expected for the first quarter, the budgeted balance of $200,000 on Mar. 31, shown in Exhibit 12, is exactly what it was on Dec. 31, 1997 (Exhibit 1).

The Dec. 31, 1997, balance in Fixed Assets (Exhibit 1) is $420,000. With the $30,000 purchase of computers during January, the balance on Mar. 31 should be $450,000. The balance in Accumulated Depreciation is $126,000 in the Dec. 31, 1997, balance sheet, and depreciation during the quarter was $4,500 (3 × $1,500) for selling and administrative assets. When we add the $4,500 of depreciation to the Dec. 31, 1997, balance in Accumulated Depreciation, we get $130,500—the amount shown in the budgeted balance sheet in Exhibit 12.

Notice in Exhibit 12 that the totals for the assets, liabilities, and stockholders' equity result in the proper balance of the accounting equation:

$$\text{Assets} = \text{Liabilities} + \text{Stockholders' Equity}$$

$$\$994,153 = \$395,000 + \$599,153$$

$$\$994,153 = \$994,153$$

The process of preparing the master budget started with the balance sheet on Dec. 31, 1997, continued with numerous budgeted schedules and statements, and finally ends with the preparation of the budgeted balance sheet for Mar. 31, 1998.

**ASK YOURSELF ▶**

1. What is the purpose of the budgeted statement of cash receipts and disbursements?
2. What are included in the "total cash needs" on the budgeted statement of cash receipts and disbursements?
3. How is the ending cash balance determined on the budgeted statement of cash receipts and disbursements? To what budgeted statement is this amount transferred?
4. Why does the budgeted statement of cash receipts and disbursements have to be completed before the budgeted income statement can be fully completed?
5. When the budgeted balance sheet is completed, the assets must be equal to what?

## SUMMARY

- A **budget** is a tool prepared by accountants as a quantitative expression of management's plans. Budgets offer advantages to all types and sizes of firms: (1) better direction for planning; (2) control of performance; (3) improved coordination of activities; and (4) positive motivation.
- Three major types of budgets are the master budget, the flexible budget, and the capital budget.
- The primary tool used by accountants to assist management in short-run planning is the **master budget,** which provides an overview of the short-term effects that a forecasted level of sales will have on operating results and financial position.
- The **flexible budget** is used primarily in the performance report to assist management in the control of short-run operations.
- The **capital budget** is used by accountants in long-run planning.
- All departments should participate actively in the budget process. Most large companies have a **budget committee,** which provides guidance and coordination in the preparation of the master budget. The **budget director,** who is typically a member of the controller's staff, is responsible for putting together the many schedules and statements that make up the master budget.
- The master budget is made up of operating budgets and financial budgets.
- **Operating budgets** express the expected results of the firm's operations during the budget period through schedules and statements associated with estimated revenues, expenses, and resulting income. **Financial budgets** report on sources, uses, and ending balances of cash and other resources used in operations.
- The starting point in the master budget process is the preparation of the **sales forecast.** All other elements of the master budget depend on the sales forecast.
- The **budgeted schedule of cash collections** points out the month in which each month's sales are expected to be collected. The uncollected sales at the end of each month represent the ending balance in Accounts Receivable.
- The amount of inventory to be purchased in each period of the master budget is determined in the **budgeted schedule of purchases.** For a retailer or wholesaler, the first step typically is to specify a desired monthly ending inventory and then use the following schedule:

**Desired ending inventory of merchandise**
plus
**Merchandise needed for current sales**
equals
**Total needs for the period**
less
**Beginning inventory of merchandise**
equals
**Required purchases of merchandise**

- For a manufacturer, in order to calculate purchases of raw materials, the units to be produced must first be determined. Then the direct materials needed for this production can be calculated. Finally, on the basis of the materials required, purchases of raw materials are determined in the following manner:

**Desired ending inventory of raw materials**
plus
**Raw materials needed in production**
equals
**Total needs for the period**
less
**Beginning inventory of raw materials**
equals
**Required purchases of raw materials**

- The **budgeted schedule of purchase payments** points out the month in which each month's purchases are expected to be paid. The unpaid credit purchases at the end of each month represent the ending balance in Accounts Payable.
- The **budgeted schedule of selling and administrative expenses** projects the selling and administrative expenses and their related disbursements for each month of the master budget period.
- The master budget is complete once the following four budgeted financial statements have been prepared:

1. The budgeted statement of cash receipts and disbursements
2. The budgeted income statement
3. The budgeted retained earnings statement
4. The budgeted balance sheet

- The **budgeted statement of cash receipts and disbursements** shows the amount and source of expected inflows and outflows of cash during the budget period, and the resulting anticipated cash balances at key times during the budget period.
- The **budgeted income statement** estimates the revenues, expenses, and resulting income for the budget period. This statement cannot be completed until the interest expense is determined from the budgeted statement of cash receipts and disbursements.
- The **budgeted retained earnings statement** shows the expected change in retained earnings during the budget period. The budgeted net income (or loss) is added to (or subtracted from) the beginning balance in retained earnings; then the budgeted dividends are subtracted to derive the budgeted ending balance in retained earnings.
- The budgeted balance sheet is the final step in the master budget process. It shows the budgeted assets, budgeted liabilities, and budgeted stockholders' equity at the end of the budget period.

## 6  KEY TERMS

| | |
|---|---|
| **Budget** | A formal quantitative tool used by accountants to assist management in planning to achieve its goals. |
| **Budget committee** | A committee composed of top-level executives from different departments within an organization and a budget director. The budget committee provides guidance and coordination in the preparation of the budget. |
| **Budget director** | The member of the budget committee (typically an accountant serving on the controller's staff) who is responsible for putting together the many schedules and statements that make up the master budget. |
| **Budgeted balance sheet** | A statement that depicts the estimated assets, liabilities, and stockholders' equity at the end of the budget period. |
| **Budgeted income statement** | A statement that predicts the estimated revenues, expenses, and resulting net income for a budget period. |
| **Budgeted retained earnings statement** | A statement that shows the estimated changes in the Retained Earnings balance during the budget period. |
| **Budgeted schedule of cash collections** | A schedule that lists the estimated collection of cash from cash and credit sales. |
| **Budgeted schedule of purchase payments** | A schedule that determines the amount of cash payments required each month to pay for the inventory that must be purchased. |

| | |
|---|---|
| **Budgeted schedule of purchases** | A schedule that determines the raw materials that must be purchased for manufacturing needs (for a manufacturer), or the merchandise that must be purchased to meet the sales demands (for a retailer or wholesaler). |
| **Budgeted schedule of selling and administrative expenses** | A schedule that projects the selling and administrative expenses and their related disbursements during a budget period. |
| **Budgeted statement of cash receipts and disbursements** | A statement that lists the different types of anticipated cash receipts and disbursements for a budget period, as well as the estimated ending cash balance. It helps management to be aware of when extra cash may be available, or when potential cash shortages may require additional short-term financing. |
| **Capital budget** | A budget used by accountants for long-range planning. |
| **Desired ending inventory** | A minimum balance in inventory desired at the end of a budget period. |
| **Financial budgets** | A category of the master budget that includes statements reporting on the projected sources, uses, and ending balances for cash and other resources used in company operations. |
| **Flexible budget** | A budget that can be prepared either before a period begins (in which case it is based on some possible levels of future activity) or after a period is over (in which case it is based on the level of activity actually achieved). |
| **Master budget** | A comprehensive budget that expresses the overall business plan for the organization for a period covering 1 year or less. |
| **Operating budgets** | A category of the master budget that includes schedules and statements related to estimated revenues, expenses, and resulting income. |
| **Performance report** | A comparison between an organization's or a department's actual results and its budget projections. |
| **Sales forecast** | The starting point for all budgeting: the projection of sales for the budget period. |
| **Total cash available before current financing** | The sum of the beginning cash balance plus the budgeted cash collections in the budgeted statement of cash receipts and disbursements. |
| **Total cash needs** | The sum of the total budgeted cash disbursements plus the minimum desired cash balance in the budgeted statement of cash receipts and disbursements. |
| **Total needs** | The total inventory that must be on hand at some time during the budget period — the sum of the desired ending inventory plus the projected sales for the period. |

## DEMONSTRATION PROBLEM

LeRoy's Replicars is a retailer of antique car kits that buyers can easily assemble into exact replicas of pre-1950 classic cars. LeRoy began its operations near the end of 1997, and prepared the following budgeted balance sheet for year-end.

**LEROY'S REPLICARS**
**Budgeted Balance Sheet**
**December 31, 1997**

| Assets | | | Liabilities | | |
|---|---|---|---|---|---|
| Cash | | $200,000 | Accounts Payable | | $640,000 |
| Accounts Receivable | $320,000 | | **Stockholders' Equity** | | |
| Less: Allowance for Uncollectible | | | | | |
| Accounts | (32,000) | 288,000 | Capital Stock | $200,000 | |
| Merchandise Inventory | | 400,000 | Retained Earnings | 48,000 | 248,000 |
| Total Assets | | $888,000 | Total Liabilities and Stockholders' Equity | | $888,000 |

LeRoy's sales projections for December 1997 and the first 3 months of 1998 are as follows:

| | |
|---|---|
| December | $400,000 |
| January | 600,000 |
| February | 800,000 |
| March | 900,000 |

LeRoy expects the total sales to be 80% credit and 20% cash. Of the credit sales, 90% are expected to be collected in the month following sale, and the remaining 10% are expected to be completely uncollectible. LeRoy uses the percentage-of-sales method to estimate bad debts; no accounts have yet been written off the books; and none are expected for the first few months of 1998.

The cost of the car kits averages 60% of their sales price to customers. LeRoy makes all its purchases on account, and plans to repay all its accounts during the month following purchase. The Accounts Payable account is used only to record purchases of merchandise. Starting in January, LeRoy plans to purchase enough car kits each month to cover the next month's sales.

LeRoy expects variable operating costs to average 10% of sales, and fixed operating costs to be $40,000 in January and $24,000 in February. Disbursements for operating expenses will be made entirely in the month incurred.

LeRoy likes to maintain a cash balance of at least $20,000. If the cash balance is ever expected to fall below the minimum, LeRoy plans to borrow money to meet the needs at the beginning of the month of the expected deficiency. Interest will be paid at 15% of the amount of principal repaid; all repayments will be made at the end of the month; and all borrowing and repayments will be made in multiples of $1,000.

LeRoy follows budget procedures very similar to those used by the POTS Company example in the text, with a few key differences. They are:

1. Purchases are calculated differently. Instead of maintaining some desired level of inventory, LeRoy's policy is simply to purchase enough inventory each month to cover the next month's sales.

2. LeRoy expects to have some bad accounts, which will be shown as Bad Debts Expense on the budgeted income statement and Allowance for Uncollectible Accounts on the budgeted balance sheet.

**3.** The amount to be borrowed, as shown on the budgeted statement of cash receipts and disbursements, is not fully repaid at the end of the budget period. Thus Notes Payable and Interest Payable will appear on the budgeted balance sheet. Also, more interest expense will appear on the budgeted income statement than appears in the budgeted statement of cash receipts and disbursements.

**Required:**

Prepare the master budget for LeRoy's Replicars for the first two months of 1998.

### ■ Solution to Demonstration Problem

Note that this solution has been annotated to help you review the flow of data.

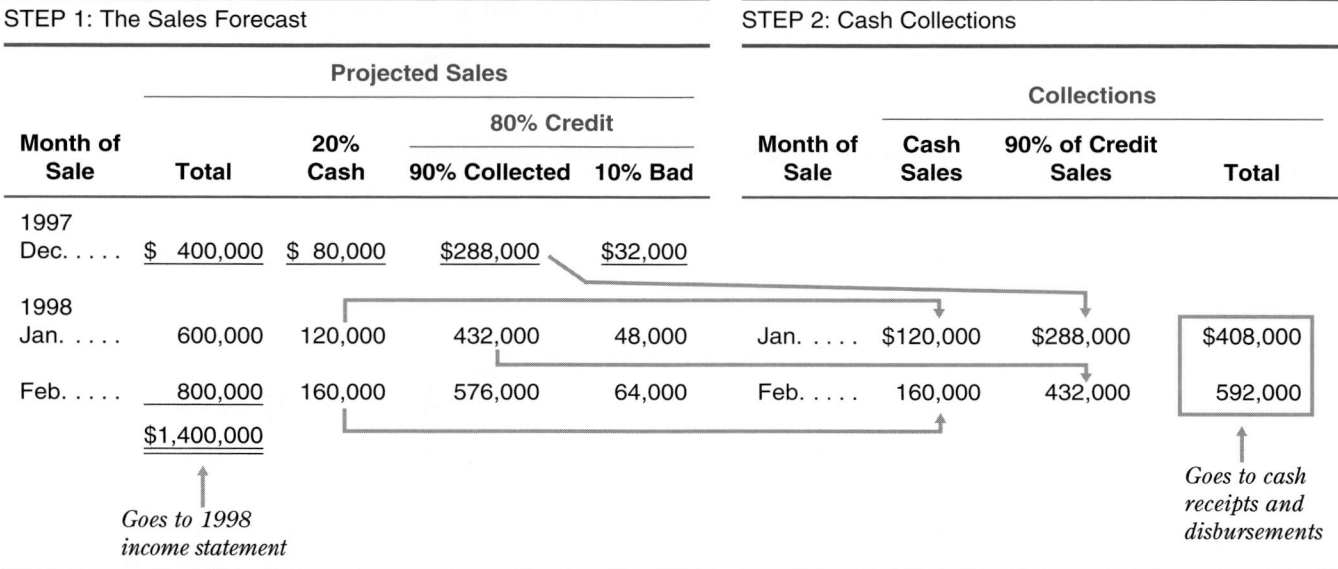

STEP 1: The Sales Forecast

| Month of Sale | Total | Projected Sales 20% Cash | 80% Credit 90% Collected | 80% Credit 10% Bad |
|---|---|---|---|---|
| 1997 Dec. . . . . | $ 400,000 | $ 80,000 | $288,000 | $32,000 |
| 1998 Jan. . . . . | 600,000 | 120,000 | 432,000 | 48,000 |
| Feb. . . . . | 800,000 | 160,000 | 576,000 | 64,000 |
| | $1,400,000 | | | |

*Goes to 1998 income statement*

STEP 2: Cash Collections

| Month of Sale | Cash Sales | Collections 90% of Credit Sales | Total |
|---|---|---|---|
| Jan. . . . . | $120,000 | $288,000 | $408,000 |
| Feb. . . . . | 160,000 | 432,000 | 592,000 |

*Goes to cash receipts and disbursements*

STEP 3: Uncollected Balance in Accounts Receivable, Bad Debts Expense, and Allowance for Uncollectible Accounts

| Month | Total Sales | × | Percent Credit | = | Credit Sales | × | Percent of Sales Uncollected by End of February | = | Uncollected Accounts at End of February | 10% Estimated Uncollectible |
|---|---|---|---|---|---|---|---|---|---|---|
| Dec. . . | $400,000 | × | .80 | = | $320,000 | × | .10 | = | $ 32,000 | $ 32,000 |
| Jan. . . | 600,000 | × | .80 | = | 480,000 | × | .10 | = | 48,000 | 48,000 |
| Feb. . . | 800,000 | × | .80 | = | 640,000 | × | 1.00 | = | 640,000 | 64,000 |
| | | | | | | | | | $720,000 | $144,000 |

*$112,000 goes to income statement— bad debts expense*

*Goes to balance sheet—accounts receivable*

*Goes to balance sheet— allowance for uncollectible accounts*

STEP 4: Schedule of Purchases and Payments, and Ending Balance in Inventory

| | Month of Sale | | |
| --- | --- | --- | --- |
| | January | February | March |
| Sales . . . . . . . . . . . . . . . . . . . . . . . . . . . . . . . . | $600,000 | $800,000 | $900,000 |
| Cost of sales (%). . . . . . . . . . . . . . . . . . . . . . . . | × .60 | × .60 | × .60 |
| Cost of goods sold. . . . . . . . . . . . . . . . . . . . . . | $360,000 | $480,000 | $540,000 |

| | December | January | February | March |
| --- | --- | --- | --- | --- |
| Purchases. . . . . . . . . . . . . . . . . . . | $640,000* | $480,000 | $540,000 ← *Accounts Payable, Feb. 29, 1998* | |
| Payment. . . . . . . . . . . . . . . . . . . . . . . . . . . . . | | $640,000 | $480,000 | $540,000 |

### February Balance in Merchandise Inventory

| | | |
| --- | --- | --- |
| Balance, Jan. 1 . . . . . . . . . . . . . . . . . . . . . . . . . . . . . . . . . . . . | | $ 400,000 |
| Purchases: | | |
| January. . . . . . . . . . . . . . . . . . . . . . . . . . . . . . . . . . . . . . . | $480,000 | |
| February . . . . . . . . . . . . . . . . . . . . . . . . . . . . . . . . . . . . . . | 540,000 | 1,020,000 |
| Total available . . . . . . . . . . . . . . . . . . . . . . . . . . . . . . . . . . . . | | $1,420,000 |
| Less: Cost of goods sold: | | |
| January. . . . . . . . . . . . . . . . . . . . . . . . . . . . . . . . . . . . . . . | $360,000 | |
| February . . . . . . . . . . . . . . . . . . . . . . . . . . . . . . . . . . . . . . | 480,000 | 840,000 |
| Ending Balance . . . . . . . . . . . . . . . . . . . . . . . . . . . . . . . . . . . . | | $ 580,000 |

*Goes to balance sheet*

* Shown as Dec. 31, 1997, balance in Accounts Payable.

STEP 5: Budgeted Schedule of Variable Operating Costs—Expenses and Disbursements

| | Month of Sale | | |
| --- | --- | --- | --- |
| | January | February | Total |
| Sales . . . . . . . . . . . . . . . . . . . . . . . . . | $600,000 | $800,000 | $1,400,000 |
| Variable cost (%) . . . . . . . . . . . . . . . . . . | × .10 | × .10 | × .10 |
| Variable operating costs . . . . . . . . . . . . | $ 60,000 | $ 80,000 | $ 140,000 |

*Goes to cash receipts and disbursements*

*Goes to income statement*

## STEP 6: Budgeted Statement of Cash Receipts and Disbursements

|  | January | February |  |
|---|---|---|---|
| Beginning cash balance. | $ 200,000 | $ 20,000 |  |
| Cash receipts | 408,000 | 592,000 |  |
| Total available before current financing | $ 608,000 | $612,000 |  |
| Total cash needs: |  |  |  |
| Cash disbursements: |  |  |  |
| Purchase payments | $ 640,000 | $480,000 |  |
| Variable operating expenses | 60,000 | 80,000 |  |
| Fixed operating expenses | 40,000 | 24,000 |  |
| Total cash disbursements | $ 740,000 | $584,000 |  |
| Minimum cash balance. | 20,000 | 20,000 |  |
| Total cash needs | $ 760,000 | $604,000 |  |
| Excess (deficiency) of cash | $(152,000) | $ 8,000 |  |
| Financing and repayments: |  |  |  |
| Financing of deficiency. | $ 152,000 | –0– | *Net of these two—* |
| Repayment of excess: |  |  | *$145,000—is in* |
| Principal | –0– | $ (7,000) | *Notes Payable* |
| Interest | –0– | (175)* | *Part of interest expense associated with $7,000 payment (additional amount associated with $145,000 note payable)* |
| Total effects of financing and repayments. | $ 152,000 | $ (7,175) |  |
| Ending cash balance | $ 20,000 | $ 20,825 |  |

*Goes to balance sheet*

\* 7,000 × .15 × $\frac{2}{12}$ = $175.

## STEP 7: Budgeted Income Statement

| Sales | | $1,400,000 |
|---|---|---|
| Cost of Goods Sold | | 840,000 |
| Gross Profit. | | $ 560,000 |
| Operating Costs: | | |
| Variable | $140,000 | |
| Fixed | 64,000 | |
| Bad Debts | 112,000 | 316,000 |
| Operating Income. | | $ 244,000 |
| Interest Expense. | | 3,800* |
| Net Income | | $ 240,200 |

\* See footnote to the balance sheet.

## STEP 8: Budgeted Balance Sheet

| Assets | | | Liabilities and Stockholders' Equity | | |
|---|---|---|---|---|---|
| Cash | | $20,825 | Accounts Payable. | $540,000 | |
| Accounts Receivable | $720,000 | | Notes Payable | 145,000 | |
| Less: Allowance for Uncollectible | | | Interest Payable | 3,625* | $ 688,625 |
| Accounts | (144,000) | 576,000 | Capital Stock | $200,000 | |
| Merchandise Inventory | | 580,000 | Retained Earnings | 288,200† | 488,200 |
| Total Assets. | | $1,176,825 | Total Liabilities and Stockholders' Equity | | $1,176,825 |

\* The $3,625 in interest that has accrued on the $145,000 note, at 15%, for 2 months. When added to the $175 of interest paid on the payment of $7,000 in principal, we get the total interest expense of $3,800, shown on the income statement.
† The beginning balance of $48,000 plus the budgeted net income of $240,200.

## QUESTIONS FOR REVIEW AND FURTHER THOUGHT

### REVIEW QUESTIONS

1. Why is the sales forecast often referred to as the starting point in all budgeting?

2. Discuss four of the advantages of budgeting.

3. Distinguish a master budget from a flexible budget.

4. When a master budget for 1998 is being prepared, is the balance sheet for Dec. 31, 1997, an actual balance sheet or a budgeted balance sheet? Explain.

5. The accountant bears sole responsibility for the preparation of all aspects of the master budget. Comment.

6. How do purchases of raw materials for a manufacturer relate to the sales forecast?

7. What would be the reasons for and against maintaining a minimum balance in merchandise inventory?

8. Discuss the purpose of preparing a budgeted statement of cash receipts and disbursements.

9. Total cash needs equal budgeted cash disbursements. Do you agree? Why?

10. Why is the budgeted income statement dependent on the budgeted statement of cash receipts and disbursements?

11. Why isn't depreciation expense included in the budgeted statement of cash receipts and disbursements?

### QUESTIONS FOR FURTHER THOUGHT

1. Budgets are always expressed in financial terms. Do you agree? Explain.

2. Why might preparing the sales forecast be a difficult step?

3. How can budgets have a negative impact on the motivation of employees?

4. The master budget includes all budgets prepared by accountants to assist in long-run and short-run planning. Do you agree? Explain.

5. If the sales forecast is considered the starting point in all budgeting, why is it that the sales forecast cannot be made until the budgeted schedule of selling and administrative expenses has been at least partially completed?

6. In order to avoid the consequences of running out of cash, a firm should maintain as much cash on hand as possible. Comment.

7. A company plans to purchase depreciable assets on account at the end of the next budget period. How would the purchase of these assets affect the different budgeted statements for the budget period?

8. When a firm expects high sales volume and significant profits for the period, this should guarantee the existence of an adequate inflow of cash. Comment.

9. Explain why dividends to be declared during a budget period might not be included in the budgeted statement of cash receipts and disbursements.

## OBJECTIVE ASSIGNMENT

*True/False*  Indicate whether each statement below is *true* or *false* by placing a *T* or an *F* in the space provided.

_____ 1. The sales forecast is the cornerstone for all budgeting.

_____ 2. The calculation of purchases is the same for retailers and manufacturers.

_____ 3. The master budget quantifies the overall business plan for a company for a year or less.

_____ 4. The two components of the master budget are the financial budget and the capital budget.

_____ 5. The income statement is one type of financial budget.

*Multiple Choice*  Select the best choice to complete each statement or answer each question below. Write the letter corresponding to your choice in the space provided.

_____ 1. Which of the following schedules or budgets associated with a master budget depends on the sales forecast?
  a. The purchases budget
  b. The budgeted schedule of cash collections
  c. The budgeted income statement
  d. All of the above

_____ 2. When is a master budget typically prepared?
  a. The day before the budget period begins
  b. As much as several months before the budget period begins
  c. During the budget period
  d. After the budget period is over

_____ 3. Which of the following budgets would probably be the last one prepared in the master budget process?
  a. The budgeted income statement
  b. The budgeted statement of cash receipts and disbursements
  c. The budgeted balance sheet
  d. The budgeted statement of retained earnings

_____ 4. The following facts relate to the month of January:

  Sales (@ $50 per unit)..................... $100,000
  Beginning inventory (@ $30 per unit) ......... $   6,000
  Desired ending inventory ................... 250 units

  How many units would have to be purchased in January?
  a. 1,920     c. 2,050
  b. 1,950     d. 2,080

_____ 5. The sales for January and February are $40,000 and $50,000, respectively. Of total sales, 25% are cash and the remainder are credit. Of the credit sales, 60% are collected in the month of sale and the remaining 40% are collected in the month following sale. What are the cash collections for February?
  a. $47,000     c. $34,500
  b. $12,500     d. $45,500

_____ 6. Which of the following items would not be found on the budgeted statement of cash receipts and disbursements?
  a. Depreciation     c. Payment of dividends
  b. Salaries paid     d. Minimum cash balance

_____ 7. In preparing a budgeted statement of cash receipts and disbursements, the following information is determined:

Cash balance, beginning of month . . . . . . . . . . . . $10,000
Minimum desired ending cash balance . . . . . . . . . . 12,000
Budgeted cash collections . . . . . . . . . . . . . . . . . . . . 60,000
Budgeted cash disbursements . . . . . . . . . . . . . . . 55,000

What is the amount of "total cash available" that would be shown on the budgeted statement of cash receipts and disbursements?
a. $72,000       c. $15,000
b. $70,000       d. $17,000

_____ 8. The Buegle Company has prepared a budgeted statement of cash receipts and disbursements for December. The following items have been taken from that budget:

Total cash available . . . . . . . . . . . . . . . . . . . . . . . . . $75,000
Cash disbursements . . . . . . . . . . . . . . . . . . . . . . . . . 77,000
Minimum desired cash balance . . . . . . . . . . . . . . . 10,700

Buegle borrows money in multiples of $500 when the budgeted statement of cash receipts and disbursements indicates a deficiency in cash for a month. How much financing will Buegle have to arrange for December?
a. $12,000       c. $13,000
b. $12,700       d. $ 2,000

_____ 9. Which of the following would never be on an income statement?
a. Depreciation       c. Rent
b. Salaries           d. Dividends

_____ 10. Which budget would be used in a performance report?
a. Sales forecast
b. Master budget
c. Capital budget
d. Flexible budget

## EXERCISES

4† **Exercise 1:** Specifying the Source of Items Found on Budgeted Statements

For each of the 13 items below, specify where the information would be found or how it would be determined. For example, payments for inventory purchases would be determined in the budgeted schedule of purchase payments.

a. Items on the budgeted income statement:
   1. Sales
   2. Interest expense
   3. Selling and administrative expenses
   4. Income tax expense
b. Items on the budgeted statement of cash receipts and disbursements:
   5. Cash receipts
   6. Payments for dividends declared in month prior to budget month
   7. Total cash needs
   8. Beginning cash balance (first month of budget period)
   9. Beginning cash balance (later months of budget period)
c. Items on the budgeted balance sheet:
   10. Accounts receivable
   11. Accumulated depreciation
   12. Interest payable
   13. Retained earnings

† The numbers in the margin refer to the Learning Objectives.

5  **Exercise 2:** Computing Cash Collection Amounts

Given below is the format for a sales forecast and a schedule of collections. Supply the missing amounts.

| Sales Forecast | | | | |
|---|---|---|---|---|
| | **December** | **January** | **February** | **March** |
| Cash sales ..................... | $5,000 | $ 7,500 | $ | $ |
| Credit Sales ................... | 3,000 | | | |
| Total sales..................... | $8,000 | $12,000 | $16,000 | $20,000 |

| Schedule of Collections | | | |
|---|---|---|---|
| | **January** | **February** | **March** |
| Cash sales................................ | $7,500 | $ | $ |
| Collection of credit sales: | | | |
| Current month ........................... | 900 | | |
| Previous month ......................... | 2,400 | 3,600 | |
| Total....................................... | $ | $14,800 | $ |

▶ *(Check Figure: Total cash collections in March = $18,800)*

5  **Exercise 3:** Determining Cash Collections and the Balance in Accounts Receivable

The Wiltom Company expects 10% of its sales to be cash sales and the remainder to be credit sales. Projected total sales for the next 4 months are as follows:

| | |
|---|---|
| March ..................................... | $10,000 |
| April...................................... | 24,000 |
| May ...................................... | 18,000 |
| June...................................... | 30,000 |

Wiltom expects the following collection experience of credit sales:

| | |
|---|---|
| Month of sale ............................... | 30% |
| Month following sale.......................... | 40% |
| Second month following sale ................... | 20% |
| Uncollectible ................................ | 10% |

a. Determine the expected cash collections for June.
b. If March was the first month of operation, determine the balance in the Accounts Receivable account on June 30. No accounts have been written off the books.
c. Assuming that Wiltom records estimated uncollectibles each month, but has not yet written any accounts off the books, determine the June 30 balance in the Allowance for Uncollectible Accounts account.

▶ *(Check Figure: a. $21,900; b. $26,820)*

5 **Exercise 4:** Using Different Ways to Determine Purchases

The projected sales and related cost-to-retail percentage are given below for Wynn Gasoline Supplier.

| Month | Projected Sales | Cost of Goods Sold Percentage |
|---|---|---|
| January | $100,000 | 55% |
| February | 140,000 | 60% |
| March | 190,000 | 65% |

During December, purchases totaled $80,000. All purchases are paid for in the month after they are made.

a. Wynn likes to maintain an ending inventory each month equal to 25% of the budgeted cost of sales of the following month. Determine the purchases and cash payments for January and February.

b. Assume instead that Wynn wants its purchases each month to be enough to cover the sales of the following month. Determine the purchases and cash payments for January and February.

▶ (Check Figure: a. Purchases for January = $62,250; b. Purchases for January = $84,000)

5 **Exercise 5:** Determining Purchases of Raw Materials

During the fourth quarter of 1997, the Armor Company plans to manufacture the following suits of armor:

| | |
|---|---|
| October | 300 suits |
| November | 500 suits |
| December | 700 suits |

Each suit requires 150 pounds of steel, which costs $2.50 per pound. On Oct. 1, 1997, there are 1,000 pounds of steel on hand. Armor wants to have a minimum of 1,500 pounds of steel on hand at the end of October and November, but 3,000 pounds at the end of December. Determine the cost of raw materials purchases in each month of the last quarter of 1997.

▶ (Check Figure: December, $266,250)

5 **Exercise 6:** Determining Units to Be Produced

At the beginning of 1998, the Ross Company plans to sell the following number of computers during the first quarter:

| | |
|---|---|
| January | 1,000 units |
| February | 1,100 units |
| March | 1,500 units |

Ross wants to have 10% of the following month's sales on hand at the end of each month. On Jan. 1, 1998, there are 100 computers in finished goods inventory. Determine the number of computers to be produced in January and February of 1998.

▶ (Check Figure: January, 1,010 computers)

5 **Exercise 7:** Determining Selling and Administrative Expenses and Cash Payments

The Prancer Company distributes chains of Christmas bells to retailers at $10 per chain. Its sales forecast for November and December of the current year project sales of $150,000 and $210,000, respectively. Prancer expects to incur the following selling expenses during these months:

Variable selling expenses:
Commissions . . . . . . . . . . . . . . . . . . . . . . 10% in November and 12% in December
Shipping . . . . . . . . . . . . . . . . . . . . . . . . . . . . . . . . . $.50 per chain of bells shipped
Fixed selling expenses (including $3,000 of depreciation) . . . . . . . . . . . . . . . $12,000

Of all cash payments related to the selling expenses, 50% will be made in the month incurred and 50% in the following month.

a. Determine the selling expenses that would appear on the budgeted income statement for December.
b. Determine the amount of payments for selling expenses that would appear on the budgeted statement of cash receipts and disbursements for December.

▶ *(Check Figure: a. $47,700)*

5   **Exercise 8:** Preparing a Budgeted Statement of Cash Receipts and Disbursements

During the last 2 months of 1997, the Munchies Candy Bar Company expects the following concerning its cash flows:

|  | **November** | **December** |
|---|---|---|
| Cash receipts. . . . . . . . . . . . . . . | $100,000 | $130,000 |
| Cash disbursements . . . . . . . . . | 112,000 | 125,000 |

The Nov. 1 cash balance was $18,000, and the company requires a minimum cash balance each month of $12,000. If a cash deficiency is expected during a month, a loan is arranged at the beginning of that month, at 12% interest. Any repayments of principal plus interest based on the principal repaid are made at the end of the month when cash becomes available. All borrowings and repayments of principal are made in multiples of $1,000.

Prepare a budgeted statement of cash receipts and disbursements for November and December.

▶ *(Check Figure: Budgeted cash balance on December 31 = $12,920)*

5   **Exercise 9:** Preparing a Budgeted Statement of Cash Receipts and Disbursements

The Sugarplum Dreamers Society, a nonprofit organization for hard-core insomniacs, is preparing a budgeted statement of cash receipts and disbursements for June and July of the year. Expected cash receipts are $28,000 and $35,000, and expected cash disbursements are $20,000 and $30,000 in June and July, respectively.

Sugarplum has a cash balance of $3,000 on June 1, which is also its minimum desired cash balance. At the end of each month in which excess cash is expected, Sugarplum has a policy of investing the excess at 8%, with interest being received at the end of the next month. All investments will be made in multiples of $500. The investments will be liquidated in any month that the company faces a deficiency of cash instead of an excess.

Prepare the budgeted statements of cash receipts and disbursements for June and July.

▶ *(Check Figure: Budgeted cash balance on July 31 = $3,053)*

5   **Exercise 10:** Preparing Budgeted Statements of Income and Retained Earnings

Rudolph's Supplies is a wholesaler of dog, cat, and reindeer food. During December 1997, Red Rudolph, the principal owner, expects to have sales of $534,000 (priced to sell at a 100% markup over cost), of which $356,000 will be collected by month-end. During December, Rudolph will purchase $300,000 of inventory, all of which will be paid in January of the new year.

The selling expenses are expected to be 5% of sales plus $30,000 per month. With the exception of depreciation, all of the selling expenses will be paid for in December. During December, Rudolph expects to purchase and pay $25,000 for new equipment. The depreciation of old and new equipment, starting in December, will be $2,000 per month.

Rudolph finds it necessary to finance its December operations by borrowing enough money from the bank in December to carry it through January 1998. The interest expense for December is expected to be $800, but all interest will be paid when the note is repaid to the bank on Jan. 31.

Income taxes average 30% of income before tax, but no payments will be made to the IRS until 1998.

Rudolph has a balance in Retained Earnings on Dec. 1 of $69,000, and plans to declare dividends of $50,000 in December, to be distributed in January.

a. Prepare the budgeted income statement for Rudolph's for December.
b. Prepare a budgeted statement of retained earnings for December.

▶ (Check Figure: a. Budgeted net income = $145,250)

## PROBLEMS: SET A

5† **Problem A1:** Preparing a Sales Forecast and Schedule of Cash Collections

Pools B' Clean is a distributor of pool-cleaning products in Tampa, Florida. One of its divisions is the distributor of three types of pool vacuums, ranging from manual to fully automatic. Sales projections for each vacuum for the third quarter of 1998 are supplied below:

|  | Product Line | | |
|---|---|---|---|
|  | Push n' Pull | Creeparound | Mr. Robot |
| Sales price ............................ | $75 | $200 | $300 |
| Projected unit sales: | | | |
| July ................................. | 50 | 100 | 40 |
| August ............................... | 60 | 110 | 45 |
| September............................. | 45 | 90 | 35 |

Cash sales are expected to be 30% of total sales, and credit sales are expected to be collected in the following manner:

40% in the month of sale
50% in the month following sale
10% uncollectible

On July 1, 1998, the Accounts Receivable balance is $15,000, of which $5,200 is expected to be uncollectible.

**Required:**

1. Prepare a sales forecast for the third quarter of 1998.
2. Prepare a budgeted schedule of cash collections for the third quarter of 1998.
3. Determine what the Sept. 30, 1998, balance in Accounts Receivable is expected to be, assuming that uncollectible accounts have not yet been written off by that time.

▶ (Check Figure: 2. Budgeted cash collections for July = $30,535; 3. $23,890)

5 **Problem A2:** Determining Units to Be Produced and Purchases
for a Manufacturer

The Gringo Company is a manufacturer of suede jackets. Each jacket requires 2 square yards of suede. During its first year of operation, the company expects to sell 4,000, 3,000, and 4,500 jackets in January, February, and March, respectively. The suede is purchased from an outside supplier for $25 a square yard, and all purchases are paid for 1 month after purchase.

† The numbers in the margin refer to the Learning Objectives.

Gringo hopes to maintain the following numbers in finished goods and raw materials at the end of each month:

Jackets . . . . . . . . . . . . . . . . . . . . . . . . 750 finished jackets
Suede . . . . . . . . . . . . . . . . . . . . . . . . . 2,000 square yards

At the beginning of its first year, Gringo obviously has no finished jackets, but does have 900 square yards of suede on hand, and an account payable for $22,500.

**Required:**

1. Determine the number of jackets to be produced in January, February, and March of the first year.
2. Determine the cost of the suede that needs to be purchased in each month.
3. Determine the payments for purchases in each of the first 3 months.

▶ *(Check Figure: 1. January, 4,750 jackets; 2. March, $225,000)*

---

5 **Problem A3:** Calculating Purchases for Multiple Products

The Fine Grind Coffee Company carries three different models of coffee-bean grinders. At the start of the fourth quarter, it had on hand 100 units of model XJ3, 225 units of model SR2, and 15 units of model Z100.

Fine Grind wants to maintain at least 70 units of model XJ3 on hand at all times, starting in October. Even though it was the most popular model, there weren't many sales in the fall of the year. For model SR2, Fine Grind maintains 10% of the following month's sales in ending inventory. Starting in October, the company is stocking only one display unit of the deluxe model, Z100, since customers are willing to wait for delivery.

Expected sales for each model in the fourth quarter are as follows:

| | Projected Sales (in Units) | | |
|---|---|---|---|
| Model No. | October | November | December |
| XJ3 | 300 | 240 | 70 |
| SR2 | 300 | 240 | 90 |
| Z100 | 80 | 70 | 25 |

**Required:**

Determine the required purchases for each grinder model for October and November.

▶ *(Check Figure: Budgeted purchases of model Z100 for November = 70)*

---

5 **Problem A4:** Preparing a Budgeted Statement of Cash Receipts and Disbursements

Carol Vance is a local CPA who had been working in a small partnership with another CPA, but decided to go out on her own. So on Oct. 1, 1997, she hung out her own shingle and began operations as a sole proprietorship. During the first month she realized how important her cash flow was going to be to her lavish lifestyle and that she had better prepare cash budgets for the next several months.

Carol had client billings of only $1,000 in October, but expected them to rise to $2,000 in November and $4,000 in December. Carol was unable to collect any of her October billings in that month and expected to collect only $200 of the October billings in November. The remainder related to a client who skipped town after Carol prepared a tax return for him that indicated a massive liability to the IRS. Starting in November, Carol expects to be able to collect a much larger portion of her billings, since she will no longer turn over her finished reports to her clients until they have paid the vast majority of Carol's fee. Carol now expects to collect 90% of her billings in the month of billing and the remainder in the following month.

Carol had or expects the following cash disbursements for October through December:

Salaries of $400 per month for a part-time college student and a part-time secretary.
Payment of $120 on Nov. 1, for her professional licenses for the year.
Purchase of office furniture costing $600 on Nov. 7. The useful life of the furniture is 6 years.
Utilities were billed to Carol and paid 1 month after they were incurred. Utilities for October, November, and December were expected to be $150, $175, and $200, respectively.
On Nov. 15, Carol signed a 3-year lease for office space and prepaid $1,200 for the first 3 months' rent. She could now move her office out of her apartment.

Carol had a $1,000 cash balance on Nov. 1, but hopes to maintain at least a $2,000 balance in cash starting in November. If the cash balance is expected to go below the minimum, Carol plans to finance the deficiency at the bank by borrowing (in multiples of $500) at 10%. All borrowings will be made at the beginning of the month, and all repayments of principal (in multiples of $500) will be repaid at the end of the month. Interest will be paid on the basis of the amount of principal repaid.

In any month where there is an anticipated excess of cash, any loans and interest outstanding will be repaid to the extent possible. When loans have been fully repaid, any remaining excess cash will be invested (in multiples of $500) in short-term marketable securities.

### Required:

Prepare budgeted statements of cash receipts and disbursements for the months of November and December.

▶ (Check Figure: Budgeted cash balance on December 31, $2,230)

---

5 **Problem A5:** Preparing Income Statements for 3 Months with Changing Assumptions

Antonio Chase has just been hired as the controller of Tomane Cream Donut Shoppes, replacing a controller who died. Tony is asked to prepare the master budget for the first quarter of 1998 and is provided with the master budget for December 1997. The budgeted income statement for December is as follows:

| | | |
|---|---:|---:|
| Sales | | $600,000 |
| Operating Expenses: | | |
| Cost of Donuts Sold | $270,000 | |
| Cost of Other Products Sold | 90,000 | |
| Salaries | 130,000 | |
| Advertising | 22,500 | |
| Rent | 62,500 | 575,000 |
| Operating Income | | $ 25,000 |

In addition, Tony learned the following about expectations for the next few months:

• Sales of 150,000 boxes of a dozen donuts each were projected for December at $2 per box. The remaining budgeted sales for December were for sandwiches. On Jan. 1, the price per box of donuts is expected to increase 4%, but the price of sandwiches will remain unchanged.

• Anticipated sales for the first quarter of 1998 are:

| Product | January | February | March |
|---|---:|---:|---:|
| Donuts (boxes of a dozen) | 175,000 | 200,000 | 225,000 |
| Other products | $325,000 | $350,000 | $387,500 |

- The cost of sandwiches will remain at the same percentage of sales.
- The salaries are expected to increase by 5%.
- Advertising is budgeted to increase by $5,000 each month above the amount of advertising in the previous month.
- The rental agreement is being revised so that, starting in January, rent will be 10% of total sales, but will never exceed $65,000.

**Required:**

Present the budgeted income statements for the first 3 months of 1998.

▶ *(Check Figure: Budgeted operating income for March = $95,250)*

5  **Problem A6:** Preparing a Complete Master Budget

Pain B' Gone Company sells an aspirin-free pain reliever in bottles that sell for $2.50 apiece. The company has been in operation for several years but never prepared a budget until the fourth quarter of 1997. Now the controller, Anna Sinn, is working on the master budget for the first quarter of 1998, and starts with the following budgeted balance sheet for Dec. 31, 1997.

---

**PAIN B' GONE COMPANY**
**Balance Sheet**
**December 31, 1997**

### Assets

| | |
|---|---|
| Cash. . . . . . . . . . . . . . . . . . . . . . . . . . . . . . . . . . . . . . . . . . . . | $ 22,000 |
| Accounts Receivable. . . . . . . . . . . . . . . . . . . . . . . . . . . . . . . . . . . . | 198,000 |
| Allowance for Uncollectible Accounts . . . . . . . . . . . . . . . . . . . . . . . . . . . | (36,000) |
| Merchandise Inventory . . . . . . . . . . . . . . . . . . . . . . . . . . . . . . . . . . | 160,000 |
| Prepaid Rent . . . . . . . . . . . . . . . . . . . . . . . . . . . . . . . . . . . . . . . | 18,000 |
| Total Assets . . . . . . . . . . . . . . . . . . . . . . . . . . . . . . . . . . . . . . . . | $362,000 |

### Liabilities and Stockholders' Equity

| | |
|---|---|
| Liabilities | |
| Accounts Payable . . . . . . . . . . . . . . . . . . . . . . . . . . . . . . . . . . . | $ 96,000 |
| Notes Payable . . . . . . . . . . . . . . . . . . . . . . . . . . . . . . . . . . . . . | 80,000 |
| Interest Payable . . . . . . . . . . . . . . . . . . . . . . . . . . . . . . . . . . . . | 1,334 |
| Total Liabilities . . . . . . . . . . . . . . . . . . . . . . . . . . . . . . . . | $177,334 |
| Stockholders' Equity | |
| Capital Stock . . . . . . . . . . . . . . . . . . . . . . . . . . . . . . . . . . . . . | $160,000 |
| Retained Earnings . . . . . . . . . . . . . . . . . . . . . . . . . . . . . . . . . . . | 24,666 |
| Total Stockholders' Equity . . . . . . . . . . . . . . . . . . . . . . . . . . . . | $184,666 |
| Total Liabilities and Stockholders' Equity . . . . . . . . . . . . . . . . . . . . . . . . | $362,000 |

---

Anna has also learned the following:

- The note was signed on Nov. 1, 1997, and is due to be repaid on Jan. 31, 1998, at 10% annual interest. If any future monthly cash balance is expected to fall below a minimum of $16,000, additional financing will have to be arranged at the beginning of that month.
- There are no cash sales. Collections on account are expected to be 50% in the month of sale, 30% in the first month after sale, 15% in the second month after sale, and 5% uncollectible (estimated and recorded at the end of each quarter.)
- No accounts considered as bad will be written off the books.
- The budgeted sales for the last quarter and the first 4 months of 1998 are as follows (assuming an unchanging $2.50 sales price):

| | |
|---|---|
| October 1997 ............................... | $200,000 |
| November 1997 ............................. | 240,000 |
| December 1997 ............................. | 280,000 |
| January 1998 ............................... | 320,000 |
| February 1998.............................. | 320,000 |
| March 1998................................. | 260,000 |
| April 1998 .................................. | 200,000 |

- Credit purchases are 60% of all purchases, and all of the credit purchases will be paid in the month after purchase.
- Pain B' Gone desires the following monthly ending inventories:

| | |
|---|---|
| November 1997 ..................... | 112,000 bottles |
| December 1997 ..................... | 128,000 bottles |
| January 1998 ....................... | 128,000 bottles |
| February 1998....................... | 96,000 bottles |
| March 1998.......................... | 70,400 bottles |

- The cost of the inventory is $1.25 per bottle. The only transactions recorded in Accounts Payable are for purchases of merchandise.
- The prepayment of rent was made on Oct. 1 for a 1-year lease.
- A $400,000 cash purchase of land is planned for March.
- Operating expenses are paid when incurred. They amount to $40,000 per month.

**Required:**

Prepare the following statements (with all supporting schedules) for the first quarter of 1998:

1. Budgeted income statement
2. Budgeted statement of retained earnings
3. Budgeted statement of cash receipts and disbursements (month by month)
4. Budgeted balance sheet

▶ *(Check Figure: 1. Budgeted net income = $277,007; 2. Budgeted retained earnings on March 31 = $301,673; 3. Budgeted cash balance on March 31 = $16,000; 4. Budgeted total assets = $681,000)*

## PROBLEMS: SET B

5† **Problem B1:** Preparing a Sales Forecast and Schedule of Cash Collections

Copy Cat Watch Company is a distributor of watches on Sunset Boulevard in Hollywood. One of its most popular divisions distributes imitation gold, silver, and platinum Rolex watches. Sales projections for the fourth quarter of 1997 are as follows:

| | Watch Model | | |
|---|---|---|---|
| | **Gold** | **Silver** | **Platinum** |
| Sales price..................................... | $ 30 | $ 20 | $ 40 |
| Projected unit sales: | | | |
| October ..................................... | 125 | 1,000 | 300 |
| November ................................... | 150 | 1,100 | 335 |
| December ................................... | 110 | 900 | 260 |

Cash sales are expected to be 80% of total sales, and credit sales are expected to be collected in the following manner:

80% in the month of sale
15% in the month following sale
5% uncollectible

† The numbers in the margin refer to the Learning Objectives.

On Oct. 1, 1997, the Accounts Receivable balance is $30,000, of which $10,400 is expected to be uncollectible.

**Required:**

1. Prepare a sales forecast for the fourth quarter of 1997.
2. Prepare a budgeted schedule of cash collections for the fourth quarter of 1997.
3. Determine what the Dec. 31, 1997, balance in Accounts Receivable is expected to be, assuming that uncollectible accounts have not yet been written off by that time.

▶ *(Check Figure: 2. Budgeted cash collections for October = $53,920; 3. $12,424.50)*

---

5   **Problem B2:** Determining Units to Be Produced and Purchases for a Manufacturer

The Congoll Company is a manufacturer of appliances. One of its products, a coffee grinder, is currently very popular. The company expects to sell 10,000, 12,000, and 15,000 units, respectively, during the first 3 months of 1998. One of its parts, the blade, is purchased from an outside supplier for $4.50 per blade. The supplier expects all purchases to be paid within 15 days of shipping. All orders are made at the beginning of each month, and a 1-week lead time is typical between date of order and date of receipt.

Congoll hopes to maintain the following month-end balances in finished goods and raw materials:

Coffee grinders. . . . . . . . . . . . . . . . . . . . . . . .   1,000 units
Blades. . . . . . . . . . . . . . . . . . . . . . . . . . . . . . .   1,500 units

In addition, Congoll has 800 coffee grinders and 1,300 blades on hand on Jan. 1, 1998.

**Required:**

1. Determine the number of coffee grinders to be produced in each of the first 3 months of 1998.
2. Determine the cost of the blades that need to be purchased in each of the first 3 months of 1998.
3. Determine the payments for purchases in each of the first 3 months of 1998.

▶ *(Check Figure: 1. January, 10,200 grinders; 2. March, $67,500)*

---

5   **Problem B3:** Calculating Purchases for Multiple Products

The Lott Rocksalt Company sells three different-size bags of salt for home water softeners. The balance on July 1 for each size is given below:

| Size of Bag | Number of Bags |
|---|---|
| 50 lb . . . . . . . . . . . . . . . . . . . . . . . . . . . . . | 1,000 |
| 80 lb . . . . . . . . . . . . . . . . . . . . . . . . . . . . . | 2,000 |
| 100 lb . . . . . . . . . . . . . . . . . . . . . . . . . . . . . | 2,500 |

Since the different-size bags have different lead times between their order and receipt, Lott has different policies concerning the desired ending balances of each size bag. They are:

| Size of Bag | Policy |
|---|---|
| 50 lb . . . . . . . . . . . | 800 bags at month-end |
| 80 lb . . . . . . . . . . . | 40% of the following month's sales |
| 100 lb . . . . . . . . . . . | 75% of the next month's sales |

Expected sales for each size bag for July, August, and September are as follows:

| Size of Bag | Projected Sales | | |
| --- | --- | --- | --- |
| | July | August | September |
| 50 lb | 15,000 | 18,000 | 17,000 |
| 80 lb | 25,000 | 27,000 | 26,000 |
| 100 lb | 32,000 | 40,000 | 36,000 |

**Required:**

Determine the required purchases for each size of bag for July and August.

▶ *(Check Figure: Budgeted purchases of 50 pound bags in August = 18,000)*

5   **Problem B4:** Preparing a Budgeted Statement of Cash Receipts and Disbursements

Julio Castro recently passed the bar exam and has decided to open his own law office. He realized how important it is to plan for and control his expenditures, especially in the early years, so he has decided to prepare cash budgets for the first several months of operations, starting with October. All client fees in September were billed on account, and by the end of the month $4,000 were still uncollected. One-half of this amount should be collected in October, but the remainder will never be collected because the client dropped dead upon hearing a guilty verdict.

During October and November, Julio expects his fees to be $8,000 and $10,000, respectively, 20% of which will be cash fees for wills and divorces. Half the credit fees are expected to be collected in each of the following 2 months. Julio expects the following cash disbursements during October and November:

- A $1,200 payment on Oct. 1, for the purchase of law books in September, which are expected to have a 10-year life
- Prepayment of $850 for 2 months of rent on Oct. 1
- Salaries of $1,600 per month for a full-time law clerk
- Birthday presents for the wives and children of judges, $200 per month
- Newspaper advertising of $500 in October and $1,500 in November

Julio had a $1,500 cash balance on Oct. 1, and hopes to maintain at least a $1,000 balance in cash starting in October. If the cash balance is expected to go below the minimum, Julio plans to finance the deficiency at the bank by borrowing (in multiples of $500) at 10%. All borrowings will be made at the beginning of the month, and all repayments of principal (in multiples of $500) will be repaid at the end of the month. Interest will be paid on the basis of the amount of principal repaid.

In any month where there is an anticipated excess of cash, any loans and interest outstanding will be repaid to the extent possible. When loans have been fully repaid, any remaining excess cash will be invested (in multiples of $500) in short-term marketable securities.

**Required:**

Prepare budgeted statements of cash receipts and disbursements for the months of October and November.

▶ *(Check Figure: Budgeted cash balance on November 30, $1,142)*

5   **Problem B5:** Preparing Income Statements for Different Levels of Sales and Changing Assumptions

Eric Wilde of the Corridor Greeting Card Company was preparing the master budget for the first quarter of 1998, and stopped to take a break after he finished the following budgeted income statement for January:

| Sales (100,000 boxes) | | $800,000 |
|---|---|---|
| Operating Costs: | | |
|     Cost of Goods Sold | $400,000 | |
|     Depreciation | 60,000 | |
|     Bad Debts | 30,000 | |
|     Salaries and Commissions | 240,000 | |
|     Royalties | 30,000 | |
|     Shipping | 25,000 | 785,000 |
| Operating Income | | $ 15,000 |
| Interest | | 12,000 |
| Net Income | | $ 3,000 |

It wasn't until a week later that Eric got back to the budget, and when he started to work on February and March he forgot how he had developed the numbers above. Luckily, Eric was able to find two pages of his scribbled notes. The first page said:

- Cost of sales is a constant cost per box, but will increase by $2 after January.
- To accompany the increase in the cost per box, the sales price will increase enough to maintain the previous markup percentage. The sales should increase by 10,000 boxes in February and another 10,000 boxes in March.
- Bad debts should drop $\frac{1}{2}$% as a percentage of sales starting in February.
- Salaries are fixed at $160,000, and commissions will remain at their current variable rate.
- Royalties and shipping are strictly variable and will remain at the same rate.
- The interest rate on debt will stay the same, but the amount of debt financing will increase by 20% in March.

The second piece of paper said:

- Do not lose the first piece of paper.

Eric laughed at his second note and sat down to complete the budgeted income statements for February and March.

### Required:

Present the budgeted income statements for February and March that Eric would have prepared for Corridor Greeting Card Company.

▶ *(Check Figure: Budgeted net income for March = $195,800)*

5    **Problem B6:** Preparing a Complete Master Budget

The Pinacina Company, which sells a hair dye called Natural, has just completed operations for 1997 and has prepared the following balance sheet:

**PINACINA COMPANY**
**Balance Sheet**
**December 31, 1997**

**Assets**

| | |
|---|---|
| Cash | $ 11,000 |
| Accounts Receivable | 94,000 |
| Merchandise Inventory | 80,000 |
| Building | 50,000 |
| Accumulated Depreciation | (2,400) |
| Prepaid Insurance | 9,000 |
| Total Assets | $241,600 |

*(Continued)*

### Liabilities and Stockholders' Equity

Liabilities
Accounts Payable . . . . . . . . . . . . . . . . . . . . . . . . . . . . . . . . . . . . . . . $  48,000
Notes Payable . . . . . . . . . . . . . . . . . . . . . . . . . . . . . . . . . . . . . . . . . . . . 40,000
Interest Payable . . . . . . . . . . . . . . . . . . . . . . . . . . . . . . . . . . . . . . . . . . . 667
 Total Liabilities . . . . . . . . . . . . . . . . . . . . . . . . . . . . . . . . . . . . . . . . $  88,667
Stockholders' Equity
Capital Stock . . . . . . . . . . . . . . . . . . . . . . . . . . . . . . . . . . . . . . . . . . . . $  80,000
Retained Earnings . . . . . . . . . . . . . . . . . . . . . . . . . . . . . . . . . . . . . . . . . . 72,933
 Total Stockholders' Equity . . . . . . . . . . . . . . . . . . . . . . . . . . . . . . . $152,933

Total Liabilities and Stockholders' Equity . . . . . . . . . . . . . . . . . . . . . . . . $241,600

These additional facts were also determined:

- The actual sales for November and December 1997 were $120,000 and $140,000, respectively. The projected sales for upcoming months are as follows:

  January 1998 . . . . . . . . . . . . . . . . . . . . . . . . . . . . $160,000
  February 1998 . . . . . . . . . . . . . . . . . . . . . . . . . . . . 160,000
  March 1998 . . . . . . . . . . . . . . . . . . . . . . . . . . . . . . 130,000
  April 1998 . . . . . . . . . . . . . . . . . . . . . . . . . . . . . . 100,000

  The sale price for all months is $10 per bottle.
- All sales are credit sales. Collections are expected to be made in the following manner:

    50% collected in the month of sale
    30% collected in the first month after sale
    20% collected in the second month after sale

- Sixty percent of the purchases are made on account, and all credit purchases are to be paid in the month following purchase. Pinacina Company desired to maintain the following ending inventories of Natural each month (at $5 per bottle):

  November 1997 . . . . . . . . . . . . . . . . . . . . . . 14,000 bottles
  December 1997 . . . . . . . . . . . . . . . . . . . . . . 16,000 bottles
  January 1998 . . . . . . . . . . . . . . . . . . . . . . . 16,000 bottles
  February 1998 . . . . . . . . . . . . . . . . . . . . . . . 12,000 bottles
  March 1998 . . . . . . . . . . . . . . . . . . . . . . . . . 8,800 bottles

  The only transactions recorded in Accounts Payable are for purchases of merchandise.
- The prepayment of insurance was made on Oct. 1, 1997, for a 1-year policy.
- The monthly cash operating expenses of $20,000 are paid when incurred.
- Depreciation expense is $200 per month.
- Pinacina plans to declare and pay dividends during March 1998 amounting to $50,000.
- A new building, costing $150,000, will be purchased at the end of March 1998 for cash.
- The note payable shown in the Dec. 31, 1997, balance sheet was signed on Nov. 1, 1997, and is due to be repaid plus 10% interest on Jan. 31, 1998. If any future monthly cash balance is expected to fall below a minimum of $10,000, additional financing will have to be arranged at 12% interest, at the beginning of that month.

#### Required:

Prepare the following statements (including all supporting schedules) for the first quarter of 1998:

1. Budgeted income statement
2. Budgeted retained earnings statement
3. Budgeted statement of cash receipts and disbursements
4. Budgeted balance sheet

▶ *(Check Figure: 1. Budgeted net income = $160,461; 2. Budgeted retained earnings on March 31 = $183,394; 3. Budgeted cash balance on March 31 = $10,000; 4. Budgeted total assets on March 31 = $354,000)*

## DECISION PROBLEMS

### Decision Problem 1

The Last Hurdle Supply Company has just finished preparing its master budget for the fourth quarter of 1997 and is disturbed by its poor cash position. The last 3 months of the year are usually its most profitable, and indeed the company does anticipate a profit for the fourth quarter. But its cash position seems to be getting worse and worse. The president of Last Hurdle hurries to a local banker to get a loan to tide the company over until the end of the year. The chief loan officer of the bank asks for a budgeted income statement and a cash budget for the last quarter of the year, which the president quickly provides.

     Assume that you are the loan officer, and have an hour to look over the budgets given below while the president goes to lunch. You promised the president to give the application a quick review and to estimate whether Last Hurdle's chances of securing a loan are good or poor. The president has provided you with the following information:

- All sales are credit sales, having 30-day terms. Some accounts are expected to go uncollected, and the direct write-off method is being used. No accounts have ever been written off.
- Purchases (all for cash) each month will be equal to the cost of the following month's sales.
- Salaries are typically paid in the month expensed, but commissions, advertising, and car rentals are paid in the month following the month expensed.
- Dividends are to be declared and paid in December.
- The note payable is due in 6 months.

| LAST HURDLE SUPPLY COMPANY<br>Budgeted Income Statements<br>Quarter 4 | | | |
|---|---|---|---|
| | **October** | **November** | **December** |
| Sales . . . . . . . . . . . . . . . . . . . . . . . . . . . . . . . . . . . | $500,000 | $450,000 | $400,000 |
| Cost of Goods Sold . . . . . . . . . . . . . . . . . . . . . . | 300,000 | 292,500 | 280,000 |
| Gross Profit . . . . . . . . . . . . . . . . . . . . . . . . . . . . | $200,000 | $157,500 | $120,000 |
| Commissions . . . . . . . . . . . . . . . . . . . . . . . . . . . | $ 50,000 | $ 45,000 | $ 40,000 |
| Advertising . . . . . . . . . . . . . . . . . . . . . . . . . . . . . | 22,000 | 25,000 | 30,000 |
| Depreciation . . . . . . . . . . . . . . . . . . . . . . . . . . . . | 15,000 | 15,000 | 15,000 |
| Car Rentals . . . . . . . . . . . . . . . . . . . . . . . . . . . . | –0– | –0– | 6,000 |
| Salaries/Bonuses . . . . . . . . . . . . . . . . . . . . . . . | 40,000 | 40,000 | 50,000 |
| | $127,000 | $125,000 | $141,000 |
| Net Income . . . . . . . . . . . . . . . . . . . . . . . . . . . . | $ 73,000 | $ 32,500 | $ (21,000) |

**LAST HURDLE SUPPLY COMPANY**
**Cash Budgets**
**Quarter 4**

|  | October | November | December |
|---|---|---|---|
| Beginning Cash Balance.................... | $ 5,000 | $ 86,500 | $ 96,500 |
| Cash Collections ........................... | 486,000 | 400,000 | 300,000 |
|  | $491,000 | $486,500 | $396,500 |
| Cash Disbursements: |  |  |  |
| Payments for Purchases ................. | $292,500 | $280,000 | $245,000 |
| Advertising ............................ | 22,000 | 20,000 | 25,000 |
| Salaries/Bonuses...................... | 40,000 | 40,000 | 50,000 |
| Commissions .......................... | 50,000 | 50,000 | 45,000 |
| Dividends ............................. | −0− | −0− | 50,000 |
|  | $404,500 | $390,000 | $415,000 |
| Ending Cash Balance ..................... | $ 86,500 | $ 96,500 | $ (18,500) |

**LAST HURDLE SUPPLY COMPANY**
**Budgeted Balance Sheet**
**December 31, 1997**

**Assets**

| | |
|---|---|
| Cash ................................................... | $ (18,500) |
| Accounts Receivable ......................................... | 410,000 |
| Inventory................................................. | 699,500 |
| Fixed Assets (Net) .......................................... | 175,500 |
| Total ................................................... | $1,266,500 |

**Liabilities and Stockholders' Equity**

| | |
|---|---|
| Accounts Payable* .......................................... | $ 76,000 |
| Note Payable .............................................. | 600,000 |
| Common Stock............................................. | 500,000 |
| Retained Earnings .......................................... | 90,500 |
| Total ................................................... | $1,266,500 |

* Includes car rentals, commissions, dividends, and advertising.

**Required:**

What concerns would you share with the president about whether the loan application would be approved?

### Decision Problem 2

During dinner one night, the president of Master Video Tape Sales, Sonny Croquet, decides to rent the vacant store next to his and double his inventory. He will go to the bank the very next day to arrange financing. Unfortunately, he knows that his banker will want to see some projections for the upcoming year, and his accountant is out of town on vacation. He then remembers that he had gotten a B in accounting principles in college and can probably handle the task by himself. After all, he thinks, what can be so hard? It's only a little number crunching.

The next day Sonny takes the following first-quarter projections to the bank:

| Income Statement for Quarter 1 | | |
|---|---:|---:|
| Sales | | $250,000 |
| Inventory Costs | | 125,000 |
| Income before Expenses | | $125,000 |
| Purchases of Shelves, Counters, etc. | $60,000 | |
| Salaries and Dividends | 55,000 | 115,000 |
| Income after Expenses | | $ 10,000 |

| Cash In and Out | | |
|---|---:|---:|
| Cash Collections | | $225,000 |
| Expenditures: | | |
| Depreciation | $ 25,000 | |
| Three Months' Rent Prepaid in December | 3,000 | |
| Cost of Sales | 65,000 | |
| Repayment of Note and Interest | 50,000 | |
| Salaries and Dividends | 55,000 | 198,000 |
| Difference | | $ 27,000 |

| Balance Sheet | | |
|---|---:|---:|
| **Debits** | | |
| Cash | | $ 12,000 |
| Other Assets | | 125,000 |
| Total | | $137,000 |
| **Credits** | | |
| Accounts, Notes, and Interest Payable | | $ 52,000 |
| Stock | | 25,000 |
| Income over Time | | 60,000 |
| Total | | $137,000 |

The banker takes a quick look at these estimates and tells Sonny it might be a good idea to wait until his accountant returns and have the budgets done a little more professionally. Sonny goes back to his office, calls his accountant in the Bahamas, and tells him to return immediately. When the accountant comes to work the next morning, Sonny tells him to get to work on a new set of projections, but first asks him what's wrong with his own.

**Required:**

As the accountant, what would you tell Sonny was wrong with the projections he had made?

## Decision Problem 3

At the end of 1997, Nick Claws is preparing a budgeted statement of cash receipts and disbursements for his company, Yule Tide, for the first quarter of 1998. He is unsure what the sales forecast should be for the first few months. His two sales managers have provided their best, and quite divergent, opinions:

| | Estimates of Sales Managers | |
| --- | --- | --- |
| | A. Blitzen | M. Dohner |
| Projected sales: | | |
| January | $225,000 | $225,000 |
| February | 200,000 | 300,000 |
| March | 180,000 | 400,000 |
| April | 180,000 | 400,000 |

Inventory costs average 60% of sales. Purchases each month are enough to cover the sales of the following month, and all purchases are paid for in the month of purchase.

Sales are all on account, and customers typically pay off their accounts in full 1 month after sale. Accounts receivable on Dec. 31 is $190,000.

Most of Yule Tide's operating expenses are fixed, at $45,000 per month; the remainder are variable, at 1% of sales. All operating expenses are paid in the month incurred.

Yule Tide has a cash balance on Jan. 1 of only $1,500 and wants it to be at least $20,000 at the end of every month starting in January. If cash is needed for any month, Nick hopes to be able to arrange financing with his bank well in advance.

## Required:

Assume that Nick prepares budgeted statements of cash receipts and disbursements for January–March 1998, based on the projections of both A. Blitzen and M. Dohner. How would the different sets of budgets affect the actions taken by Nick Claws at the end of 1997?

## ETHICS CASE

During the last months of 1997, the budget committee for High Road Manufacturing is working on the master budget for 1998. Each of the nonaccounting members of the committee (representatives from production, sales, purchasing, and finance) is expected to provide vital projections for the upcoming year to the controller in order for the controller to compile the many detailed budgeted schedules and statements that make up the master budget.

In order to try to motivate top-level executives to achieve superior performance, High Road's board of directors is implementing a firm-wide bonus plan for 1998 that will be based on a variety of performance measures relating to the achievement of sales, production, and income goals. Managers of each department can benefit substantially from performance that goes beyond goals set at the beginning of the year. At year-end, actual performance will be compared to the original projections in order to determine which departments and managers have met or exceeded their goals and deserve a year-end bonus.

**Required:**

1. If you were the vice presidents for sales and production, how could you try to use the budget process to increase your chances of receiving a year-end bonus?
2. In your opinion, would these actions be ethical?.

## OBJECTIVE ASSIGNMENT ANSWERS

**True/False**

**1.** T    **2.** F    **3.** T    **4.** F    **5.** F

**Multiple Choice**

**1.** d    **2.** b    **3.** c    **4.** c    **5.** a
**6.** a    **7.** b    **8.** c    **9.** d    **10.** d

# Controlling Costs with Flexible Budgets, Standard Costs, and Variances: Part One

**LEARNING OBJECTIVES**

After studying this chapter, you should be able to do the following:

1 Explain what a responsibility center is, and relate it to the concept of responsibility accounting

2 Prepare the performance report

3 Explain the concepts of effectiveness and efficiency, and why it is important to identify each in a performance report

4 Prepare a flexible budget

5 Describe how a flexible budget is used in a performance report to measure effectiveness and efficiency

6 Describe how standard costs can be used to assist management in planning, control, and inventory costing

7 Explain how standards are determined for each type of production cost

8 Calculate the price, quantity, and flexible budget variances for direct materials and direct labor

9 Define the key terms listed at the end of the chapter

**CHAPTER OUTLINE**  **RESPONSIBILITY CENTERS** • Responsibility Accounting • Controllability of Costs • **THE MASTER BUDGET REVISITED** • The Performance Report: Comparing the Master Budget to Actual Results • Effectiveness and Efficiency • **FLEXIBLE BUDGETS** • Flexible Budgets as a Planning Tool • Flexible Budgets as a Control Tool • **STANDARD COSTS** • The Uses of Standard Costs • Types of Standards and Variances • Standard Costs and Flexible Budgets: A Clarification • Direct Materials • Direct Labor • Using Standard Costs for Inventory Costing

The master budget is an important planning tool that predicts in quantitative terms what should happen during the upcoming period if sales occur as forecast. Now we are going to look back over a budget period that has just been completed, to compare what did happen to what should have happened, as a way of helping managers exert control over operations. We compare actual results to budgeted results, and highlight the differences, in a *performance report.*

When we make this comparison in the performance report, which budget do we use? Do we use the master budget, which is prepared before the period begins and is based upon the expected level of activity for the budget period? Or do we use a *flexible budget,* which is prepared after the period is over and is based on the level of activity actually achieved? Although the answer depends on the reasons for preparing the performance report, you will soon see that most of the time the master budget plays a relatively minor role in the performance report, whereas flexible budgets are used extensively.

In this chapter we will explain exactly what a flexible budget is, and why it is usually more appropriate than the master budget for use in the performance report. In addition, we will show you how to prepare the performance report, and explain how it is used by accountants to help management control current operations. We will also explain what *standard costs* are, and the role they play in flexible budgets and performance reports. Finally, we will discuss the different types of *variances,* which are the differences between the actual results and the flexible budget. We will limit the discussion of standard costs and variance analysis in this chapter to direct materials and direct labor. In the next chapter we will expand this discussion to include variable factory overhead and fixed factory overhead.

But first we will look at the control function of budgeting, to see how managers use performance reports and to learn what these managers are held responsible for.

## RESPONSIBILITY CENTERS

A **responsibility center** is an area of activity within an organization, managed by an individual who has been given both authority and responsibility for activities of that area. Within any organization there are many responsibility centers, big and small. For example, an entire company would be considered a responsibility center, with the president responsible for the activities of the organization as a whole. There also would be responsibility centers for the production, selling, product design, distribution, customer service, and administrative areas, for which vice presidents would be held accountable. Within each functional area—say, production—there would be responsibility centers for each department, with managers or superintendents as the accountable individuals. And within each department there could be several responsibility centers, with supervisors responsible for different groups of workers.

### Responsibility Accounting

Closely related to the concept of responsibility centers is the concept of responsibility accounting. **Responsibility accounting** is the process of:

1. Designating the responsibility centers within an organization
2. Delegating authority to the managers of the responsibility centers
3. Preparing budgets, accumulating results, and preparing performance reports for the responsibility centers
4. Holding managers responsible, or accountable, for their actions

Responsibility centers are the heart of a responsibility accounting system. Once we know what the responsibility centers are and who is in charge of them, we can formulate budgets and put them into action. Then the actual results can be accumu-

**Exhibit 1**

### ROBINJON COMPANY
### Budgeted Income Statement
### Master Budget Level of 15,000 Units for January 1997

|  | Per Unit | Total |
|---|---|---|
| Sales Revenue | $25 | | $375,000 |
| Total Variable Costs: | | | |
|   Direct Materials | $ 5 | $ 75,000 | |
|   Direct Labor | 6 | 90,000 | |
|   Variable Factory Overhead | 3 | 45,000 | |
| | $14 | $210,000 | |
|   Variable Selling and Administrative | 2 | 30,000 | |
| | $16 | | 240,000 |
| Total Contribution Margin | $ 9 | | $135,000 |
| Fixed Costs: | | | |
|   Fixed Factory Overhead | | $ 15,000 | |
|   Fixed Selling and Administrative | | 10,000 | |
| | | | 25,000 |
| Net Income | | | $110,000 |

lated, performance reports can be prepared, and a responsibility center's performance can be evaluated.

We will start our analysis of performance by looking at the company as a whole — the largest possible responsibility center — that has three departments, production, selling, and administration. Then we will look at a typical responsibility center within the production area. Although responsibility accounting concepts apply to all functional areas of an organization, as well as to all types of organizations, the most elaborate types of planning and control systems have been developed for the production area of a manufacturing organization, so this is where we will focus most of our attention.

### Controllability of Costs

Within each responsibility center, the manager is preferably held accountable only for the costs that he or she can control. **Controllable costs** are those costs within a responsibility center that can be significantly influenced by the manager of that center during a given period of time (usually the reporting period for the performance report). If a manager has no influence over a cost during a given period of time, then the cost is a **noncontrollable cost** (or **uncontrollable cost**). If the costs are noncontrollable, it normally doesn't make sense to hold a manager accountable for them.

### THE MASTER BUDGET REVISITED

Let's assume first that the budgeted income statement displayed in Exhibit 1 has been prepared at the beginning of 1997 for the Robinjon Company and is based on the projected production and sales of 15,000 units for January. It is part of the master budget package prepared by Robinjon at the beginning of the year.

For the sales revenue and each variable cost, the master budget amount is found by multiplying the budgeted amount per unit by the 15,000 units. Since total fixed costs are expected to be the same regardless of the level of activity, a per-unit cost is not given for either of the fixed costs. The budgeted fixed costs are $25,000 ($15,000 + $10,000), regardless of the level of activity expected.

Exhibit 1 tells us that if Robinjon does produce and sell the 15,000 units expected for January, its income is expected to be $110,000.

## The Performance Report: Comparing the Master Budget to Actual Results

At the end of January, the accountant for Robinjon gathers the following information for the month:

| | | |
|---|---:|---:|
| Units Produced and Sold.............................................. | | 12,500 |
| Actual Results: | | |
| Sales Revenue .......................................................... | | $312,500 |
| Total Variable Costs: | | |
|     Direct Materials................................................. | $ 65,000 | |
|     Direct Labor..................................................... | 78,000 | |
|     Variable Factory Overhead.................................... | 39,000 | |
| | $182,000 | |
|     Variable Selling and Administrative ..................... | 26,250 | 208,250 |
| Total Contribution Margin........................................... | | $104,250 |
| Fixed Costs: | | |
|     Fixed Factory Overhead........................................ | $ 14,900 | |
|     Fixed Selling and Administrative ......................... | $ 9,900 | 24,800 |
| Net Income............................................................... | | $ 79,450 |

**Learning Objective 2**

Prepare the performance report

These actual results are compared to the original budget figures in a **performance report,** which shows differences between actual and budget figures as variances. As you can see in Exhibit 2, the actual revenues, the actual costs, and the actual income are all less than Robinjon projected. Robinjon expected to produce and sell 15,000 units and to have an income of $110,000. It actually produced and sold 12,500 units, which resulted in only $79,450 of income for the month.

To properly assess the significance of having $30,550 less income than was expected at the beginning of January, we must first understand that there are two completely different reasons for the difference between the actual results and the original expectations. One reason has to do with effectiveness and the other has to do with efficiency.

**Learning Objective 3**

Explain the concepts of effectiveness and efficiency, and why it is important to identify each in a performance report

## Effectiveness and Efficiency

**Effectiveness** refers to the attainment of original goals. It is measured by comparing the actual output (the units produced and sold) to what was originally planned for. **Efficiency** refers to the relationship of the inputs to the outputs—that is, how well the company controls the use of its inputs (direct materials, direct labor, etc.) in producing and selling the outputs.

For example, let's assume you have a mouse in your kitchen, and you want to kill it. If you solve your problem by having an exterminator's tent put on your house at a cost of $450, your approach would be effective—you would kill the mouse. However, it wouldn't be efficient—$450 for one mouse. But if you borrow the neighbor's cat and she kills the mouse in exchange for a box of catnip treats costing $.99, you have been both effective—a dead mouse—and efficient—a cost of only $.99.

Looking back at Exhibit 2, we cannot tell how much of each variance has to do with ineffectiveness and how much has to do with inefficiency. Part of each variance results because Robinjon produced and sold 2,500 units fewer than projected. This is a measure of effectiveness because the original goals were not attained. Another part of

**Exhibit 2**

### ROBINJON COMPANY
### Performance Report for January
### Using the Master Budget

| | Actual Results (12,500) | Master Budget (15,000) | Variances |
|---|---|---|---|
| Sales Revenue . . . . . . . . . . . . . . . . . . . . . . . . . | $312,500 | $375,000 | $62,500 |
| Total Variable Costs: | | | |
|    Direct Materials . . . . . . . . . . . . . . . . . . . . . . | $ 65,000 | $ 75,000 | $10,000 |
|    Direct Labor . . . . . . . . . . . . . . . . . . . . . . . . | 78,000 | 90,000 | 12,000 |
|    Variable Factory Overhead . . . . . . . . . . . . . . | 39,000 | 45,000 | 6,000 |
| | $182,000 | $210,000 | $28,000 |
|    Variable Selling and Administrative . . . . . . . . | 26,250 | 30,000 | 3,750 |
| | $208,250 | $240,000 | $31,750 |
| Total Contribution Margin . . . . . . . . . . . . . . . . . | $104,250 | $135,000 | $30,750 |
| Fixed Costs: | | | |
|    Fixed Factory Overhead . . . . . . . . . . . . . . . . | $ 14,900 | $ 15,000 | $ 100 |
|    Fixed Selling and Administrative . . . . . . . . . . . | 9,900 | 10,000 | 100 |
| | $ 24,800 | $ 25,000 | $ 200 |
| Net Income . . . . . . . . . . . . . . . . . . . . . . . . . . . . | $ 79,450 | $110,000 | $30,550 |

each variance exists because the 12,500 units were produced and sold for more or less than they should have been—this is where efficiency comes in.

In order to distinguish effectiveness from efficiency in a performance report, we must use flexible budgets in addition to the master budget.

Learning Objective 4

## 4 FLEXIBLE BUDGETS

Prepare a flexible budget

**Flexible budgets** are predictions of costs, revenues, and income at various levels of activity. Flexible budgets can be prepared either before the period begins or after the period is completed. When prepared at the beginning of a period, flexible budgets simply predict the results at several possible levels of future activity. One of these flexible budgets—the one based on the most likely level of future activity—becomes the master budget. When flexible budgets are prepared at the beginning of the period, they are an integral part of the planning process.

### Flexible Budgets as a Planning Tool

For example, when we prepared the master budget for Robinjon Company based on the most likely level of activity of 15,000 units for the month, we might have also been interested in the possible results for 10,000 units and 20,000 units. Robinjon might have wanted to know the possible consequences of producing and selling at levels below and above the most likely level. These flexible budgets—one of which is the master budget—are shown in Exhibit 3.

For each possible level of activity (10,000, 15,000, and 20,000 units), the budgeted sales revenue is determined by multiplying the number of units sold times the sales price of $25. For each variable cost, the budgeted costs are determined by multiplying the three different levels of unit sales by the individual costs per unit ($5 for direct materials, $6 for direct labor, $3 for variable factory overhead, and $2 for variable selling and administrative costs). When the budgeted variable costs are

**Exhibit 3** Flexible Budgets for Several Future Levels of Activity

### ROBINJON COMPANY
### Budgeted Income Statements for January 1997
### Flexible Budgets for 10,000, 15,000, and 20,000 Units

*Notice that one of these flexible budgets is the master budget*

| | Per Unit | 10,000 Units | 15,000 Units | 20,000 Units |
|---|---|---|---|---|
| Sales Revenue. . . . . . . . . . . . . . . . . . . . . . . . . . . . . . | $25 | $250,000 | $375,000 | $500,000 |
| Total Variable Costs: | | | | |
| Direct Materials. . . . . . . . . . . . . . . . . . . . . . . . . . . | $ 5 | $ 50,000 | $ 75,000 | $100,000 |
| Direct Labor . . . . . . . . . . . . . . . . . . . . . . . . . . . . . | 6 | 60,000 | 90,000 | 120,000 |
| Variable Factory Overhead . . . . . . . . . . . . . . . . . | 3 | 30,000 | 45,000 | 60,000 |
| | $14 | $140,000 | $210,000 | $280,000 |
| Variable Selling and Administrative . . . . . . . . . . . . | 2 | 20,000 | 30,000 | 40,000 |
| | $16 | $160,000 | $240,000 | $320,000 |
| Total Contribution Margin. . . . . . . . . . . . . . . . . . . . | $ 9 | $ 90,000 | $135,000 | $180,000 |
| Fixed Costs: | | | | |
| Fixed Factory Overhead. . . . . . . . . . . . . . . . . . . . . | | $ 15,000 | $ 15,000 | $ 15,000 |
| Fixed Selling and Administrative . . . . . . . . . . . . . . | | 10,000 | 10,000 | 10,000 |
| | | $ 25,000 | $ 25,000 | $ 25,000 |
| Net Income. . . . . . . . . . . . . . . . . . . . . . . . . . . . . . . . | | $ 65,000 | $110,000 | $155,000 |

subtracted from the budgeted sales revenues, the differences are the budgeted contribution margins. Finally, when the budgeted fixed costs of $25,000 are subtracted from the budgeted contribution margins, we have the budgeted incomes for 10,000, 15,000, and 20,000 units.

Notice that the budgeted fixed costs of $25,000 are the same at all three levels of activity. They are not determined by multiplying a cost per unit times the number of units produced and sold, because total fixed costs are unaffected by changes in activity. They are, as the name implies, a fixed amount.

By preparing several flexible budgets at the beginning of the year, we know more than that our most likely result is an income of $110,000. We also know that the income might be as high as $155,000 or as low as $65,000.

## Flexible Budgets as a Control Tool

Flexible budgets can also be prepared after a period is completed and the actual activity is known; these flexible budgets show what the results were expected to be based on the actual level of activity. When flexible budgets are prepared after the fact, they are used as part of the control process.

During January, 12,500 units were actually produced. The flexible budget based on 12,500 units is represented by column 3 of the performance report shown in Exhibit 4. For the sales revenue and each variable cost, the budgeted totals are found by multiplying the per-unit amounts times the 12,500 units. The flexible budgets for the fixed costs are the same as they were in all previous budgets—an unchanging $25,000. The bottom line of column 3 indicates that we would expect the net income to be $87,500, based on the production and sale of 12,500 units in January.

The actual results are shown in column 1 of Exhibit 4. The differences between the actual results and the flexible budget are listed in column 2. Each of these differences is called a *flexible budget variance*. We will have more on the flexible budget variance in a later section, on measuring efficiency.

The master budget is now shown in column 5. When it is compared line by line to the flexible budget, the differences—called *sales volume variances*—are listed in

**Exhibit 4** A Performance Report That Measures Effectiveness and Efficiency

### ROBINJON COMPANY
#### Performance Report for January 1997
#### Using the Flexible Budget and Master Budget

| | (1) Actual Results (12,500 Units) | (2) Flexible Budget Variance | (3) Flexible Budget (12,500 Units) | (4) Sales Volume Variance | (5) Master Budget (15,000 Units) | |
|---|---|---|---|---|---|---|
| Sales Revenue . . . . . | $312,500 | –0– | $312,500 | $62,500 U | $375,000 | *The flexible budget variance (column 2) measures efficiency* |
| Total Variable Costs: | | | | | | |
| Direct Materials . . . | $ 65,000 | $2,500 U* | $ 62,500 | $12,500 F | $ 75,000 | |
| Direct Labor. . . . . . | 78,000 | 3,000 U | 75,000 | 15,000 F | 90,000 | |
| Variable Factory Overhead. . . . . . . | 39,000 | 1,500 U | 37,500 | 7,500 F | 45,000 | |
| | $182,000 | $7,000 U | $175,000 | $35,000 F | $210,000 | |
| Variable Selling and Administrative . . . | 26,250 | 1,250 U | 25,000 | 5,000 F | 30,000 | |
| | $208,250 | $8,250 U | $200,000 | $40,000 F | $240,000 | |
| Total Contribution Margin . . . . . . . . . . . | $104,250 | $8,250 U | $112,500 | $22,500 U | $135,000 | |
| Fixed Costs: | | | | | | |
| Fixed Factory Overhead. . . . . . . | $ 14,900 | $ 100 F | $ 15,000 | –0– | $ 15,000 | |
| Fixed Selling and Administrative . . . | 9,900 | 100 F | 10,000 | –0– | 10,000 | *The sales volume variance (column 4) measures effectiveness* |
| | $ 24,800 | $ 200 F | $ 25,000 | –0– | $ 25,000 | |
| Net Income . . . . . . . . | $ 79,450 | $8,050 U | $ 87,500 | $22,500 U | $110,000 | |

* U = unfavorable; F = favorable.

column 4. This type of variance is discussed in the next section, on measuring effectiveness.

With the addition of the flexible budget, based on 12,500 units produced and sold, to the performance report, we can now distinguish between the measures of effectiveness and efficiency.

Learning Objective 5

### Measuring Effectiveness

Describe how a flexible budget is used in a performance report to measure effectiveness and efficiency

The fact that Robinjon did not reach its original production and sales goal of 15,000 units means that Robinjon was not effective. The dollar measure of effectiveness is represented by the difference between the flexible budget income, based on the 12,500 actual units produced and sold (column 3), and the master budget income (column 5), based on the original expectation of 15,000 units. This difference is called the **sales volume variance** and is shown in column 4. The fact that 2,500 fewer units were produced and sold than expected means that the net income for the firm was $22,500 less than predicted. An easier way to determine the sales volume variance is simply to multiply the difference between the master budget units and the actual units produced and sold by the budgeted contribution margin per unit. For Robinjon, this is:

$$\text{Sales volume variance} = \begin{array}{c} \text{difference in units} \\ \text{budgeted and actual} \\ \text{units produced and sold} \end{array} \times \begin{array}{c} \text{contribution} \\ \text{margin} \\ \text{per unit} \end{array}$$

$$\text{SVV} = (15,000 - 12,500) \times \$9$$
$$= 2,500 \times \$9 = \$22,500 \text{ U}$$

Since Robinjon produced and sold fewer units than it planned to, the sales volume variance is classified as *unfavorable*—represented by the letter U. If Robinjon had produced and sold more than the master budget level, the income would have been more than expected, and the sales volume variance would be marked F for *favorable.*

### Measuring Efficiency

The measure of efficiency for Robinjon in January is represented by the *flexible budget variance* (column 2). For each item on the income statement, the flexible budget variance is the difference between the actual results (column 1) and the flexible budget for the units actually produced and sold (column 3). For example, in Exhibit 4, the actual sales revenue was identical to the flexible budget, meaning that the actual sales price must have been exactly as predicted—$25. But the actual costs for the direct materials to produce and sell 12,500 units, $65,000, was greater than the flexible budget of $62,500. The unfavorable difference, $2,500 U, means that Robinjon spent more than planned for direct materials to produce the 12,500 units.

For net income, the flexible budget variance was $8,050 U. This means that the net income was $8,050 less than expected for the 12,500 units that were produced and sold.

For all items combined, Robinjon was not as efficient as it could have been in January.

**ASK YOURSELF** ▶

1. **What is a responsibility center? What steps are involved in the process of responsibility accounting?**
2. **What is the distinction between controllable and noncontrollable costs?**
3. **What two elements are compared in a performance report?**
4. **Differentiate the concepts of effectiveness and efficiency.**
5. **What are flexible budgets? When are they prepared? What are they used for?**
6. **What variance measures effectiveness? How is it determined?**
7. **What does a flexible budget variance measure?**

## STANDARD COSTS

Learning Objective 6

Describe how standard costs can be used to assist management in planning, control, and inventory costing

In the performance report for Robinjon in Exhibit 4, we compared actual results to the flexible budget, and the flexible budget to the master budget. All the budgeted amounts for the variable costs were based on the budgeted cost per unit multiplied by units produced and sold.

Budgeted costs per unit can be either expected actual costs or standard costs. If the budgeted costs per unit in Exhibit 3 represent expected actual costs for the month, then the flexible budget and master budget in Exhibit 4 are simply estimates of what the total actual costs were expected to be for the 12,500 units and 15,000 units. But if the budgeted costs per unit are standard costs, then the flexible budget and master budget show what the costs *should have been* at those two levels of activity.

In this chapter, whenever we use a budgeted cost per unit, it will *always* be a standard cost per unit, rather than an expected actual cost per unit. **Standard costs** are carefully predetermined estimates of what costs should be (when we are looking into the future) or should have been (when we are looking back at the past) under continuing, efficient conditions. Standard costs are target costs to aim for rather than

---

**Exhibit 5** Flexible Budget Variances for Production Costs

---

**ROBINJON COMPANY**
**Production Department**
**Performance Report for January 1997**

| | (1)<br>Actual<br>Results<br>(12,500 Units) | (2)<br>Flexible<br>Budget<br>Variance | (3)<br>Flexible<br>Budget<br>(12,500 Units) |
|---|---|---|---|
| Direct Materials . . . . . . . . . . . . . . . . . . . | $ 65,000 | $2,500 U | $ 62,500 |
| Direct Labor . . . . . . . . . . . . . . . . . . . . . . | 78,000 | 3,000 U | 75,000 |
| Variable Factory Overhead . . . . . . . . . . . | 39,000 | 1,500 U | 37,500 |
| Fixed Factory Overhead . . . . . . . . . . . . . | 14,900 | 100 F | 15,000 |
| | $196,900 | $6,900 U | $190,000 |

---

anticipated actual costs. Standard costs are determined as precisely as possible, often with the assistance of statistical or engineering tools. They are not merely rough estimates or continuations of past trends.

### The Uses of Standard Costs

Standard costs can be used for planning, control, and/or inventory costing purposes. For *planning purposes,* standard costs per unit are used in the master budget, as shown in Exhibit 1, and in the flexible budgets in Exhibit 3, to estimate what the costs *should be*—not just what the results are expected to be—during an upcoming period of time.

For *control purposes,* standard costs are used to prepare the flexible budget in the performance report, which is needed to determine the flexible budget variance. If the per-unit amounts used to calculate column 3 of Exhibit 4 are standard costs, then the flexible budget represents what the costs *should have been* for the units produced and sold.

When standard costs are used for *inventory costing purposes,* this means that we assign the standard costs, rather than the actual costs, to the units produced. The cost of the units in inventory is the standard cost of producing them.

Although standard costs can be used for several purposes, and for many departments within a company, we will focus on their use in the control process, as well as for inventory costing, for the production department of Robinjon Company. We will begin with the condensed performance report for Robinjon shown in Exhibit 5 (taken from Exhibit 4). Notice that now we are interested only in the actual and flexible budget information (columns 1, 2, and 3) for Robinjon's four production costs. By introducing price and quantity standards, we will be able to evaluate the flexible budget variances further, by dividing them into their component parts—the price and quantity variances.

### Types of Standards and Variances

A standard cost per unit, for all *variable* production costs, is made up of two components: a price standard and a quantity standard. A **price standard** is the dollar cost that should be paid for each of the inputs going into the finished product—the output—such as a cost per pound, per gallon, or per hour.

A **quantity standard** represents the quantity of each input (pounds, gallons, hours) that should be used for each completed unit of output.

For example, for direct materials, the standard cost per unit is $5. Assume that each unit requires $\frac{1}{2}$ pound of direct material and that each pound should cost $10. The $10 per pound is the price standard, and the $\frac{1}{2}$ pound per unit is the quantity standard.

The price standard multiplied by the quantity standard gives the standard cost per unit:

$$\tfrac{1}{2} \text{ lb/unit} \times \$10/\text{lb} = \$5/\text{unit}$$

Variances occur whenever actual results are different from the standard. Because any standard cost per unit has two components, there are two corresponding variances: a price variance and a quantity variance. A **price variance** results whenever the actual price paid for a unit of input differs from the standard price that was allowed for that unit of input. A **quantity variance** occurs whenever the actual inputs differ from the standard quantity that was allowed for producing the units.

Adding together a price variance and a quantity variance gives a **flexible budget variance** (also called a **controllable variance**). For example, assume that the price variance for direct materials for Robinjon is $960 U and that the quantity variance is $1,540 U. The sum of the two ($960 U + $1,540 U) is $2,500 U, which is the flexible budget variance shown in column 2 of Exhibit 5 for direct materials. We'll show you how to calculate price and quantity variances in the next section.

There can be a price variance, a quantity variance, and a flexible budget variance for each variable production cost (direct materials, direct labor, and variable factory overhead). There can also be a flexible budget variance for variable selling and administrative costs, but this variance normally cannot be broken into price and quantity components.

For fixed factory overhead, there is a price variance but no quantity variance. In addition, fixed factory overhead has a distinctive type of variance, called the *production volume variance*.

In this chapter we will limit the analysis of price, quantity, and flexible budget variances to direct materials and direct labor, using the more elaborate illustration for Robinjon Company that follows. In the next chapter we will expand the illustration for Robinjon to include variable factory overhead and fixed factory overhead.

# ROBINJON COMPANY

Robinjon Company, a manufacturer of fountains, birdbaths, garden benches, and ornamental statuary, has recently developed a standard cost system for the control of its production operations. According to the controller, the following standards for direct materials and direct labor have been set for the production of each unit (a portable birdbath):

Direct materials: $\tfrac{1}{2}$ lb/unit at $10/lb = $5/unit

Direct labor: $1\tfrac{1}{2}$ hr/unit at $4/hr = $6/unit

At the beginning of January 1997, 15,000 units were budgeted for production. Only 12,500 units were actually produced during the month. The actual results for the month's production were as follows:

6,404 pounds purchased and used, costing $65,000 ($10.15 per pound, rounded)

20,000 hours worked; $78,000 of direct labor costs ($3.90/hr)

In the next few sections we will use these facts to calculate detailed variances for direct materials and direct labor for Robinjon Company. The standards given for the different production costs will be used to prepare the flexible budgets needed for the performance report. The standard costs per unit are the same as the budgeted costs per unit that were shown in Exhibit 1, and used in Exhibits 1 through 5.

Before we begin, however, we need to make one last clarification concerning standard costs and flexible budgets.

## Standard Costs and Flexible Budgets: A Clarification

Technically, the term *standard costs* refers to a cost per unit, a cost per pound, or a cost per hour, rather than total costs at some level of activity. Conversely, the flexible budget is technically a measure of total dollars, rather than dollars per unit or per hour. For example, if the standard cost for direct materials is $5 per unit, then the flexible budget for 12,500 units is $62,500. However, the conceptual difference between the two terms has tended to blur through indiscriminate usage. So, the $5 per unit standard cost can be referred to as the flexible budget per unit, and the $62,500 flexible budget can be called the total standard costs. This will be perfectly acceptable.[1]

**ASK YOURSELF** ▶

1. **What are standard costs and what are they used for?**
2. **How do standard costs differ from flexible budgets?**
3. **What are the two types of standards for any cost that is variable?**
4. **What is a price variance and a quantity variance? What variance do you have when you add these two variances together?**
5. **What variance do we have for fixed factory overhead that we do not have for any of the variable costs?**

Learning Objective 7

Explain how standards are determined for each type of production cost

## Direct Materials

The purchasing agent is usually responsible for determining the standard price for materials and for acquiring the proper quantity and quality of materials required for production. Determining the standard price can be a difficult task because it often is no more than a guess of what price the suppliers will be charging in the future rather than a carefully determined calculation of the price the company "ought" to be charged.

The purchasing agent shops around to find the best price for materials, being sure to take into consideration potential cash and quantity discounts. In addition, in determining the standard price, the purchasing agent must consider the different means and costs of transportation and the receiving and handling costs once the inventory reaches the company. Once the standard price is set, future purchases at any other price result in a price variance.

Quantity standards are set by the engineering department in companies that have one. Otherwise, the quantity standard will probably be determined by production superintendents and supervisors on the basis of their working knowledge of the materials needed for each unit, as well as the ability of laborers and the quality of the machinery to be used.

The quantity standard is converted into dollars by the accounting department. For example, Robinjon has a standard quantity for direct materials of $\frac{1}{2}$ pound per unit. In dollars this standard converts to $5 per unit ($\frac{1}{2}$ pound per unit × $10 per pound). And the flexible budget for the 12,500 units produced is $62,500 (12,500 units × $5 per unit).

Production supervisors are responsible for seeing that workers in their departments use the correct amount of materials. If the actual usage is different from the standard quantity allowed for the units produced, there will be a quantity variance.

[1] This is true only for variable production costs. For fixed factory overhead we will not calculate the flexible budget using a budgeted cost per unit.

*Calculating the Variances*

Calculate the price, quantity, and flexible budget variances for direct materials and direct labor

The purchasing agent has the responsibility to pay the established standard price for materials. If a purchase is made at a different price than the standard price, the resulting price variance should be based on the quantity purchased, even if some of the materials are not used until a later period. The price variance is not based on the quantity used (unless it is the same as the quantity purchased, as it currently is for Robinjon), because the event that causes the variance is the *purchase* of materials at a price different from standard—not the *usage* of materials. Furthermore, a price variance must be recognized at the time of purchase. If recognition is postponed, the explanation for paying the excessive price will no longer be useful information.

Whether we use the quantity purchased or the quantity used would be irrelevant—or at least immaterial—to those companies that apply the just-in-time (JIT) philosophy. An integral part of this philosophy is that maintaining too large an inventory represents waste to a company, bringing about excessive costs of handling, storage, insurance, and so on. It is considered preferable to maintain as little inventory as possible. Under JIT, the actual quantity of inventory purchased and used should be substantially the same, and the issue of whether to base the price variance on the quantity purchased or the quantity used becomes moot. It is an important issue only when the quantities purchased and the quantities used are significantly different.

The **materials price variance** for direct materials can be computed using the following formula:

$$\begin{array}{c} \text{Materials price} \\ \text{variance} \end{array} = \begin{array}{c} \text{actual quantity} \\ \text{purchased} \end{array} \times \begin{array}{c} \text{difference between the actual and the standard} \\ \text{cost per unit of input purchased} \end{array}$$

For Robinjon the price variance, where the materials price standard is $10.00 per pound, is:

$$\text{Materials price variance} = 6{,}404 \text{ lb} \times (\$10.15 - \$10.00)$$
$$= 6{,}404 \text{ lb} \times \$.15/\text{lb} = \$960 \text{ U}$$

The $960 materials price variance is unfavorable because the actual price paid for each pound purchased ($10.15) was higher than it should have been ($10.00).

The **materials quantity variance** for direct materials is based on the difference between the actual quantity used and the standard quantity allowed. The **standard quantity allowed** represents the quantity of direct materials that should have been used to make the units produced during the period. If this quantity is different from the actual quantity used, there is a quantity variance.

The dollar amount of the materials quantity variance can be calculated using the following formula:

$$\begin{array}{c} \text{Materials quantity} \\ \text{variance} \end{array} = \begin{array}{c} \text{difference between actual quantity} \\ \text{used and standard quantity allowed} \end{array} \times \begin{array}{c} \text{standard cost per unit} \\ \text{of input} \end{array}$$

The materials quantity variance for Robinjon, where the materials quantity standard is $\frac{1}{2}$ pound per unit, is:

$$\text{Materials quantity variance} = [6{,}404 \text{ lb} - (\tfrac{1}{2} \text{ lb})(12{,}500 \text{ units})] \times \$10.00/\text{lb}$$
$$= (6{,}404 \text{ lb} - 6{,}250 \text{ lb}) \times \$10.00/\text{lb}$$
$$= 154 \text{ lb} \times \$10.00/\text{lb} = \$1{,}540 \text{ U}$$

The materials quantity variance (also known as the **materials usage variance**) of $1,540 is unfavorable: Instead of using 6,250 pounds to produce 12,500 units, Robinjon used 6,404 pounds, or 154 pounds too many.

Notice that the standard cost per pound of $10.00, rather than the actual cost per pound of $10.15, is used to calculate the quantity variance. This is because the $.15 variance has already been recognized in the calculation of the price variance (6,404 lb × $.15/lb = $960 U). To use the actual cost per pound of $10.15 to calculate the quantity variance would be to double-count part of the price variance.

Another reason for using the standard cost per pound to calculate the quantity variance involves a basic tenet of responsibility accounting: Individuals should be held accountable only for those variances they can control. The production supervisor is responsible for the 154 pounds of quantity variance. But the purchasing agent is responsible for the actual price paid and the resulting $.15 price variance. Since the production supervisor is not responsible for the actual price paid, it should not be used to determine the quantity variance.

In a JIT environment we expect to have not only small price variances for materials, but small quantity variances as well. This is because an integral part of the JIT philosophy is the elimination of all waste. Heavy emphasis is placed on manufacturing a product that is the highest quality possible, or on having few if any defective units that need to be reworked. And excessive usage of materials is expected to be held to a bare minimum. Only in a production environment where the JIT philosophy is ignored would we expect to have large quantity variances for direct materials.

The flexible budget variance for direct materials is represented by the addition of the price variance and the quantity variance. For Robinjon the materials flexible budget variance is $2,500 unfavorable:

**Flexible budget variance = price variance + quantity variance**

$$= \$960 \text{ U} + \$1{,}540 \text{ U} = \$2{,}500 \text{ U}$$

### The Cause of Each Variance

Once the variances are calculated, the next step for a manager is to find out what caused them.

Was the quantity variance due to a change in the price? Buying in too small a quantity? Buying better-quality materials than were required?

Was the quantity variance due to improper standards? Machine breakdowns? Poor workmanship? Poor-quality materials?

Only after the causes have been determined can corrective action be taken. The standard may need to be revised; the laborers may need additional training; the purchasing agent may need to shop around for better deals. If the information revealed by the variances is not put to good use in making these kinds of corrections, then the costs of devising, implementing, and applying a standard cost system will be wasted.

### Alternative Approach to Variance Analysis

Another way to do variance analysis is to make use of an approach that is quite similar to a performance report. This approach, called a *three-column analysis,* is presented in Exhibit 6. Notice that in columns 2 and 3 of Exhibit 6 we are once again utilizing flexible budgets, this time to convert the standard costs per pound into total budgeted dollars. Since we are using standard costs, each flexible budget represents what the costs "should have been" for a specified level of activity. Column 2 (the flexible budget based on the actual quantity) indicates that we should have spent $10 per pound for each of the 6,404 pounds that were actually purchased and used to produce the 12,500 units. Column 3 (the flexible budget for the standard quantity allowed) indicates that we should have used 6,250 pounds at the standard price of $10 per pound to make the 12,500 units.

**Exhibit 6** Three-Column Analysis for Direct Materials
Quantity Purchased Equals Quantity Used
Based on actual production of 12,500 units

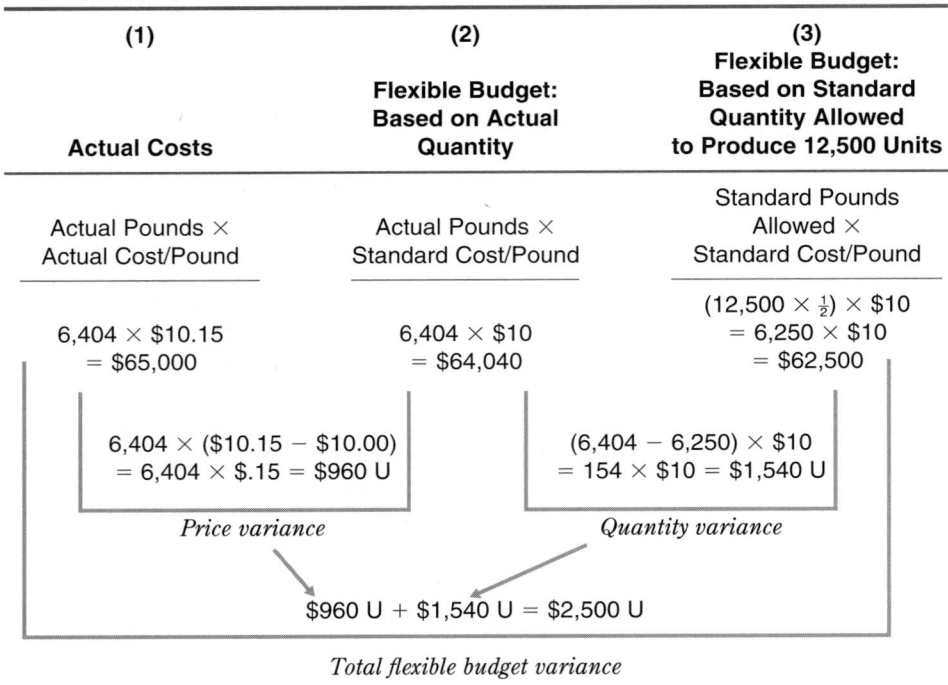

*Total flexible budget variance*

Column 1 shows that the actual costs incurred to purchase the 6,404 pounds at $10.15 a pound were $65,000. When we compare this to the flexible budget for the actual pounds purchased, which represents what we should have spent to purchase the 6,404 pounds ($64,040) — the difference is the price variance of $960, unfavorable. The exhibit also shows that the $960 is the result of multiplying the actual purchase of 6,404 pounds by the difference between the actual and standard price, $.15. This, of course, is exactly the same result produced by the formula for the materials quantity variance.

Column 3 indicates what we should have spent to produce 12,500 units: $62,500. We should have used 6,250 pounds — the standard quantity allowed — and we should have paid the standard price of $10 per pound. Column 2 indicates what we should have spent for the actual pounds we did use to produce the 12,500 units: 6,404 pounds × $10 per pound = $64,040. The difference between columns 2 and 3 represents the excessive costs that were incurred by using 154 pounds (6,404 − 6,250) too many to produce the 12,500 units. The difference of $1,540 (154 pounds × $10 per pound) is the quantity variance.

The addition of the price variance ($960) and the quantity variance ($1,540) is the flexible budget variance ($2,500).

### Variance Analysis for Direct Materials When Purchases and Usage are Different

The illustration for Robinjon specified that 6,404 pounds were both purchased and used. If the quantity purchased was different from the quantity used, the formula for the materials price variance does not change, that is:

**Materials price variance** = **actual quantity purchased** × **difference between the actual and the standard cost per unit of input purchased**

but the amount of the price variance does indeed change. For example, let's now assume that the quantity purchased is 6,500 pounds, instead of 6,404 pounds, at $10.15 per pound. Let's still assume that the quantity used is 6,404 pounds. First of all, the price variance is now $975 U, instead of $960.

$$\textbf{Materials price variance = 6,500 lb} \times \textbf{\$.15 = \$975 U}$$

The quantity variance is still $1,540 U (154 lb × $10), but the flexible budget variance is now $2,515 U ($975 U + $1,540 U).

The three column analysis, when purchases and usage are different, is shown in Exhibit 7. As you can see there are a couple minor adjustments. The middle column is now broken into two parts. On the left side of the middle column is the flexible budget for the 6,500 pounds purchased—6,500 lb × $10 = $65,000. On the right side of the middle column is the flexible budget for the 6,404 pounds that were actually used—6,404 lb × $10 = $64,040. The price variance of $975 is the difference between the actual costs ($65,975) and the flexible budget for the 6,500 pounds purchased ($65,000). The quantity variance of $1,540 is still the difference between the flexible budget for the 6,404 pounds used ($64,040) and the flexible budget for the 6,250 standard pounds allowed ($62,500).

One last point of importance. When the quantity purchased and used differ, notice in Exhibit 7 that the sum of the price and quantity variances are no longer the same as the difference between columns 1 and 3. When we subtract column 3 ($62,500) from column 1 ($65,975), we get $3,475—which is not the same as the correct amount of $2,515 ($975 + $1,540).

**Exhibit 7**  Three-Column Analysis for Direct Materials
Quantity Purchased Not Equal to Quantity Used
Based on actual production of 12,500 units

| (1) | (2) | | (3) |
|---|---|---|---|
| **Actual Costs** | **Flexible Budget:<br>Based on Actual<br>Quantity** | | **Flexible Budget:<br>Based on Standard<br>Quantity Allowed<br>to Produce 12,500 Units** |
| Actual Pounds<br>Purchased ×<br>Actual Cost per Pound | Actual Pounds ×<br>Standard Cost per Pound | | Standard Pounds<br>Allowed ×<br>Standard Cost per Pound |
| | Quantity<br>Purchased | Quantity<br>Used | |
| 6,500 × $10.15<br>= $65,975 | 6,500 × $10<br>= $65,000 | 6,404 × $10<br>= $64,040 | 6,250 × $10<br>= $62,500 |
| | 6,500 × ($10.15 − $10.00)<br>= 6,500 × $.15 = $975 U | (6,404 − 6,250) × $10<br>= 154 × $10 = $1,540 U | |
| | *Price variance* | *Quantity variance* | |

$975 U + $1,540 U = $2,515 U

*Total flexible budget variance*

Learning
Objective

Explain how standards are
determined for each type of
production cost

7 **Direct Labor**

The labor price (or rate) standard is not usually set by management. Instead, labor rates are typically determined either by labor contracts negotiated between management and labor or by local conditions of supply and demand for labor. The exact rates may also depend on conditions within the company, since different rates apply depending on a worker's position, seniority, and difficulty or skill of tasks performed. All these factors affect the direct labor price standard.

Labor quantity standards (also called labor efficiency standards) are often difficult to establish. Given a variety of workers, each with different skills and abilities, the idea behind a labor quantity standard is to determine what an average worker can accomplish under normal conditions. The method of making such a determination, called a **time-and-motion study,** is conducted by the engineering department. A time-and-motion study is a scientific analysis of an entire labor operation and its parts. It seeks to determine the best way to do each part, and what amount of time each step should take, so that the entire operation can be performed most efficiently.

Another way to set labor quantity standards is with test runs. Test runs of the labor operation are conducted for a short time under controlled conditions. The results are observed, documented, and analyzed, and then the labor quantity standards are based on this analysis.

Supervisors are usually held responsible for both the labor price (or rate) variance and the labor quantity (or efficiency) variance. Labor price variances should be quite small, since the rates are not usually subject to sudden change. However, they will probably not be zero, because a worker earning one rate might be substituted for another earning a different rate.

Learning
Objective

Calculate the price, quantity, and
flexible budget variances for direct
materials and direct labor

8 *Calculating the Variances*

As we saw in the preceding section, direct materials variances are calculated for two distinct events: the purchase of materials and the subsequent use of those materials. For direct labor, these two events occur simultaneously: The labor hours are purchased and used at the same time. Therefore, the labor price variance and labor quantity variance are both calculated on the basis of the actual hours used (or worked).

The **labor price variance** is calculated using the following formula:

$$\text{Labor price variance} = \text{actual hours worked} \times \begin{array}{l} \textbf{difference between the} \\ \textbf{actual wage rate and} \\ \textbf{standard wage rate} \end{array}$$

Compare this formula with the one for the direct materials price variance; note the similarities. Although labor deals with labor hours worked rather than quantity purchased, and the price for labor is a wage rate rather than a cost per pound, the formula for the price variance for materials and the one for labor have exactly the same form. Notice the words printed in teal in the formula for the labor price variance and compare these words to the words printed in teal in the formula for the materials price variance; then compare them to the formula for the variable overhead price variance that comes in the next chapter. All three price variances involve an actual quantity multiplied by the difference between actual and standard prices.

For the Robinjon Company, where the labor price standard is $4.00 per hour, the labor price variance is:

$$\text{Labor price variance} = 20,000 \text{ hr} \times (\$3.90 - \$4.00)$$

$$= 20,000 \text{ hr} \times \$.10/\text{hr} = \$2,000 \text{ F}$$

The labor price variance of $2,000 is favorable because the actual wage rate paid to workers ($3.90) was less than the standard rate ($4.00) set for the operation.

The **labor quantity variance** uses the following formula:

$$\text{Labor quantity variance} = \begin{array}{c} \text{difference between actual} \\ \text{hours worked and} \\ \text{standard hours allowed} \end{array} \times \text{standard rate per hour}$$

The term **standard hours allowed** represents the direct labor hours that should have been worked to produce the units completed during the period.

The formula for the direct labor quantity variance has the same form as the formulas for the direct materials quantity variance and the variable overhead quantity variance. Each quantity variance involves a difference between actual quantity used and standard quantity allowed, the difference multiplied by the standard price. Recognizing the similarities in variances for materials, labor, and variable overhead can be helpful in learning, understanding, and remembering them. It is easier to learn two basic variances—price variance and quantity variance—and to adapt them to the three production costs, than to learn six variances as if they were completely dissimilar.

The labor quantity variance for Robinjon Company, where the labor quantity standard is $1\frac{1}{2}$ hours per unit, is:

$$\text{Labor quantity variance} = [20,000 \text{ hr} - (1\tfrac{1}{2} \times 12,500 \text{ units})] \times \$4.00/\text{hr}$$

$$= (20,000 \text{ hr} - 18,750) \times \$4.00/\text{hr}$$

$$= 1,250 \text{ hr} \times \$4.00/\text{hr} = \$5,000 \text{ U}$$

The labor quantity variance is unfavorable, since 1,250 actual hours were used in excess of the standard allowed (20,000 − 18,750).

The flexible budget variance for direct labor is the sum of the labor price variance and the labor quantity variance:

$$\textbf{Flexible budget variance} = \textbf{price variance} + \textbf{quantity variance}$$

$$= \$2,000 \text{ F} + \$5,000 \text{ U} = \$3,000 \text{ U}$$

### The Cause of Each Variance

Once we have calculated the variances, we must determine their causes and take corrective action when warranted. A price variance can occur when different workers are used on the job rather than the ones we expected. For example, we may use a new worker with less seniority, and therefore pay a lower wage rate than we had planned on.

Labor quantity variances can occur for a variety of reasons. It could be that the new worker who is paid a lower rate because of inexperience (resulting in a favorable price variance) may take longer to finish the job than the usual, more experienced worker. The quantity variance could also be due to machine breakdowns, defective materials, poor workmanship, or inadequate supervision. In addition, it could be that since the quantity standard represents an average expectation for all workers, and since individual workers are not all exactly the same as the average, some of the workers are going to take a little longer to finish the job than the average and others a little less.

### An Alternative Approach for Direct Labor

The three-column approach to calculating the direct labor variances is shown in Exhibit 8. The price variance of $2,000 F is the difference between the actual costs

**Exhibit 8** Three-Column Analysis for Direct Labor
Based on actual production of 12,500 units

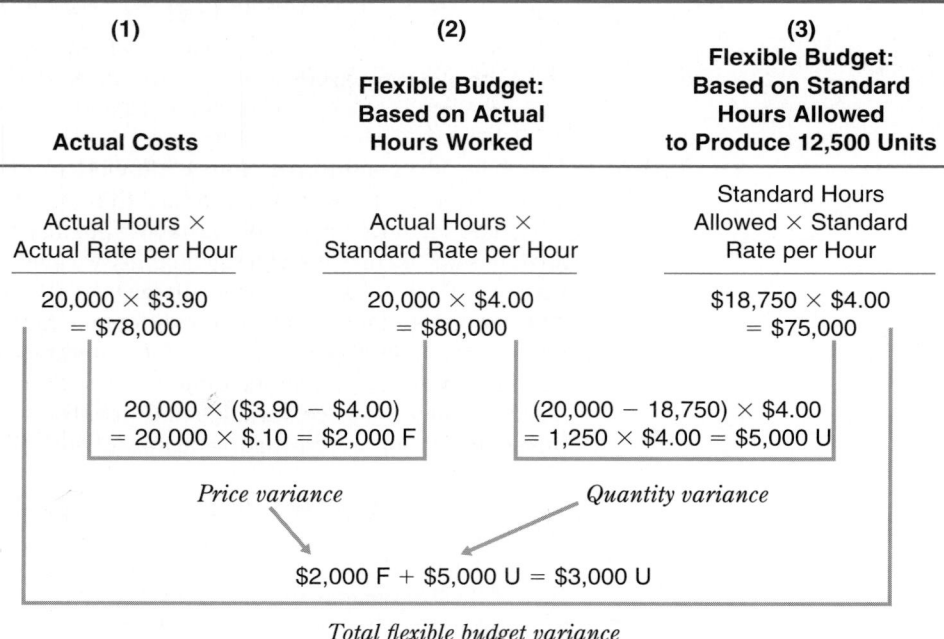

| (1) | (2) | (3) |
|---|---|---|
| | Flexible Budget: Based on Actual Hours Worked | Flexible Budget: Based on Standard Hours Allowed to Produce 12,500 Units |
| **Actual Costs** | | |

Actual Hours × Actual Rate per Hour | Actual Hours × Standard Rate per Hour | Standard Hours Allowed × Standard Rate per Hour

20,000 × $3.90 = $78,000 | 20,000 × $4.00 = $80,000 | $18,750 × $4.00 = $75,000

20,000 × ($3.90 − $4.00) = 20,000 × $.10 = $2,000 F

(20,000 − 18,750) × $4.00 = 1,250 × $4.00 = $5,000 U

*Price variance*          *Quantity variance*

$2,000 F + $5,000 U = $3,000 U

*Total flexible budget variance*

incurred ($78,000) for the 20,000 actual hours needed to produce the 12,500 units and the flexible budget based on the 20,000 actual hours ($80,000). The quantity variance of $5,000 U is the difference between the flexible budget based on the 20,000 actual hours worked ($80,000) and the flexible budget based on the standard hours allowed ($75,000). The flexible budget variance of $3,000 U is the sum of the individual variances.

### The Declining Role of Direct Labor

Many years ago, direct labor costs were a significant part of the total production costs for most manufacturers. In today's modern manufacturing environment, however, direct labor costs have greatly diminished for many companies. As long as direct labor was an important factor in the production process, it was appropriate to develop and carry out elaborate systems for controlling labor costs, even though these systems were usually costly to implement. The benefits to be derived from the time and attention directed to controlling direct labor were considered to be worth the costs involved. By finding ways to eliminate excessive hours of labor, manufacturers could reduce not only labor costs but also the ever-growing overhead costs that were always assumed to be closely related to direct labor.

As the manufacturing environment has become less labor-intensive and much more capital-intensive, direct labor has been substantially replaced by machine hours. In addition, the age-old assumption of a close relationship between direct labor and factory overhead costs has been seriously questioned. Many critics now contend that it is no longer necessary to have elaborate systems for controlling direct labor. Instead, attention is now being redirected toward improving the control systems for factory overhead costs, which are now quite substantial for many manufacturers. In fact, because direct labor in some companies is such a small component of costs, it is often combined with factory overhead and treated as just another conversion cost.

## Using Standard Costs for Inventory Costing

So far our primary emphasis in using standard costs has been their usefulness for control purposes. We compared standard costs to actual costs in order to determine if we spent too littlle or too much during the period, based on the production that took place. We calculated price and quantity variances for direct materials and direct labor.

We also mentioned earlier that we can use standard costs for inventory costing purposes. This means that the costs we assign to the units we produce are the standard costs of producing them. The standard costs we assign to the units, as their inventoriable costs, are called *the amount applied to production.* The amount applied to production is found by multiplying the standard quantity (or the number of units) times the standard rate. The amount applied is initially assigned to Work-in-Process Inventory, where it becomes the cost of the units being produced. When the units are completed, the amount applied to them is transferred to Finished Goods Inventory. Finally, when the units are sold, the amount applied to these units is transferred to Cost of Goods Sold.

For direct materials, direct labor, (this chapter) and variable factory overhead (next chapter), the amount applied is exactly the same as the flexible budget based on the standard quantity (or number of hours) allowed. Look back at Exhibits 6, 7, and 8 and note that in column 3 the flexible budgets based on the standard quantity (or number of hours) allowed are $62,500 for direct materials and $75,000 for direct labor. These amounts are also the amounts applied to production; that is, they are the costs assigned to the units produced for inventory costing purposes. So you see, for any cost that is variable, the standard quantity (or number of hours) times the standard rate is not only a flexible budget—a figure used for control purposes; it is also the standard costs applied—a figure needed for inventory costing purposes. In short, the same number serves two different cost accounting purposes.

**ASK YOURSELF** ▶

1. Why is the materials price variance based on the quantity purchased rather than the quantity used?
2. How do you calculate the price and quantity variances for direct materials and direct labor? How do they differ for direct materials and direct labor?
3. What are some possible reasons for price and quantity variances for direct materials? For direct labor?
4. In the three-column approach to analyzing variances, what does each of the three columns represent?
5. What has happened to the importance of direct labor in the modern manufacturing environment?
6. In a standard cost system, are the inventory costs the actual costs or the applied? Explain.

## SUMMARY

- Performance reports are prepared for different responsibility centers within an organization. A **responsibility center** is an area of activity managed by an individual who has been given authority to plan and control the activities, and has been assigned the responsibility for the activities.
- Accountants prepare performance reports to help managers control their operations. In a **performance report,** actual results are compared to budgeted results and the differences are spotlighted for investigation.
- A performance report can measure effectiveness or efficiency. **Effectiveness** measures the ability of an organization to reach its original goals. **Efficiency** mea-

sures the relationship of inputs to outputs. In order to measure either effectiveness or efficiency, flexible budgets must be prepared.

• **Flexible budgets** are predictions of costs, revenues, and income at various levels of activity, based on a knowledge of how these items behave in response to changes in activity. Flexible budgets can be prepared before the period begins or after the period is completed.

• Flexible budgets can be used to measure effectiveness by comparing the master budget income statement to the flexible budget income statement based on the number of units actually produced and sold. The difference in the incomes is called the sales volume variance.

• The **sales volume variance** specifies the amount of income lost or gained by producing and selling less or more than the master budget level of activity. It can be determined using the formula:

$$\text{Sales volume variance} = \begin{matrix} \text{difference in units} \\ \text{budgeted and actual} \\ \text{units produced and sold} \end{matrix} \times \begin{matrix} \text{contribution} \\ \text{margin} \\ \text{per unit} \end{matrix}$$

• **Standard costs** are carefully predetermined estimates of what costs should be under continuing, efficient operating conditions. Standard costs are typically considered to be a unit, rather than a total, concept. When standard unit costs are used in flexible budgets, the flexible budget represents what total costs should be or should have been at different levels of activity.

• There are two types of standards—**price standards** and **quantity standards**—for each variable production cost. When actual results differ from the standards, there is a **price variance** and a **quantity variance.** The sum of the price variance and the quantity variance is the **flexible budget variance.**

• The price variance is calculated for direct materials, direct labor (this chapter), and variable factory overhead (next chapter) as follows:

$$\text{Price variance} = \begin{matrix} \text{actual quantity} \\ \text{(or hours)} \end{matrix} \times \begin{matrix} \text{difference between actual} \\ \text{and standard costs per} \\ \text{unit of input} \end{matrix}$$

And the quantity variance is calculated as follows:

$$\text{Quantity variance} = \begin{matrix} \text{difference between actual} \\ \text{quantity (or hours) used and} \\ \text{standard quantity (or hours)} \\ \text{allowed} \end{matrix} \times \begin{matrix} \text{standard} \\ \text{cost per unit} \\ \text{of input} \end{matrix}$$

## 9  KEY TERMS

**Controllable cost**  A cost that can be significantly influenced by a manager of a responsibility center during a period of time.

**Controllable variance**  See **flexible budget variance.**

**Effectiveness**  A measure of whether or not objectives were attained; determined by comparing actual output to original goals.

**Efficiency**  A measure of how well a company controls the inputs used to generate outputs. Efficiency is measured by comparing actual inputs (direct materials, direct labor, and factory overhead) to what they were expected to be, based on the actual output (the finished units).

| | |
|---|---|
| **Flexible budget** | A prediction of costs, revenues, and/or profits at various levels of activity, based on a knowledge of how these items relate to changes in activity. Once we know what activity might be in the future or in the past, we can estimate these items at that level of activity. |
| **Flexible budget variance** | The price variance plus the quantity variance; also called the **controllable variance.** |
| **Labor price variance** | The actual hours worked multiplied by the difference between the actual wage rate paid and the standard wage rate. Also called the **labor rate variance.** |
| **Labor quantity variance** | The difference between the actual hours worked and the standard hours allowed multiplied by the standard wage rate. Also called the **labor efficiency variance.** |
| **Materials price variance** | For a particular direct material, the actual quantity purchased multiplied by the difference between the actual cost per unit of input and the standard cost per unit of input. |
| **Materials quantity variance** | For a particular direct material, the difference between the actual quantity used and the standard quantity allowed, multiplied by the standard cost per input used. Sometimes called the **materials usage variance.** |
| **Materials usage variance** | See **materials quantity variance.** |
| **Noncontrollable cost** | A cost that cannot be influenced over a given period of time by the manager of a responsibility center; also called **uncontrollable cost.** |
| **Performance report** | A report prepared by accountants to help managers control their operations. Performance reports compare actual results with budgeted results and highlight the differences, called variances. |
| **Price standard** | The dollar amount that should be paid for each of the inputs needed for production (such as a cost per pound or a cost per hour). |
| **Price variance** | A variance that results whenever the actual price paid differs from the standard price allowed for a unit of input. |
| **Quantity standard** | The amount of each input that should be used to produce a unit (such as the required number of pounds per unit or hours per unit). |
| **Quantity variance** | A variance that results when the actual quantity of inputs differs from the standard quantity allowed for the units actually produced. |
| **Responsibility accounting** | The process within an organization of: (1) designating the responsibility centers; (2) delegating authority to the managers of the responsibility centers; (3) preparing budgets, accumulating actual results, and preparing performance reports for responsibility centers; (4) holding the managers responsible for their actions. |
| **Responsibility center** | An area of activity managed by an individual who has been delegated the authority to plan and control the activities and has been assigned the responsibility for the activities and results. |
| **Sales volume variance** | The dollar measure of effectiveness, represented by the difference between the flexible budget income based on the actual units produced and the master budget income. |
| **Standard costs** | Carefully predetermined estimates of what costs should be or should have been. |
| **Standard hours allowed** | The labor hours that should have been worked to make the units that were produced during the period. |
| **Standard quantity allowed** | The quantity of direct materials that should have been used to make the units that were produced during the period. |
| **Time-and-motion study** | A method used by engineers to determine labor quantity standards. |
| **Uncontrollable cost** | See **noncontrollable cost.** |

## DEMONSTRATION PROBLEM

The controller of Wright's California Surfboard Company has recently developed the following standards for direct materials and direct labor related to the production of one of its most popular models:

Direct materials: 80 lb/surfboard at $.50/lb = $40.00/surfboard

Direct labor: 2 hr/surfboard at $8.00/hr = $16.00/surfboard

During January, 225 surfboards were budgeted for production, but only 200 were produced. The actual results related to this production were:

Direct materials: 19,000 lb purchased at $.52/lb
16,250 lb used

Direct labor: 425 hr at $8.15/hr

**Required:**

Compute the individual and flexible budget variances for direct materials and direct labor. Indicate whether each variance is favorable or unfavorable.

### ■ Solution to Demonstration Problem

Direct Materials
Based on actual production of 200 surfboards

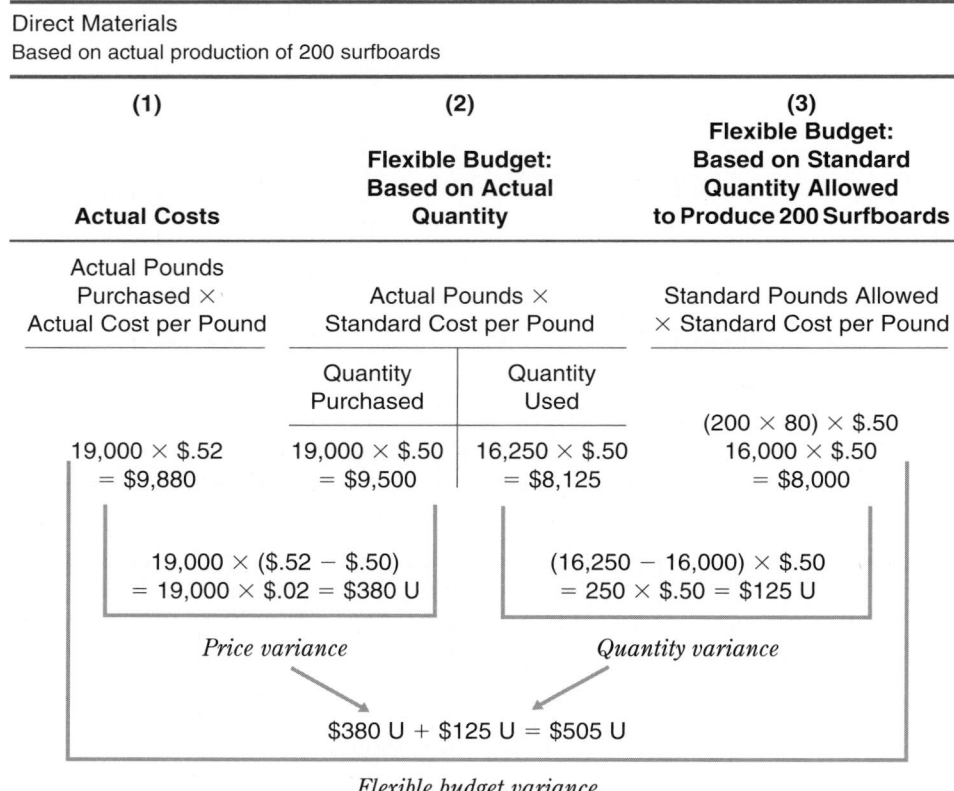

| (1) | (2) | (3) |
|-----|-----|-----|
| | **Flexible Budget: Based on Actual Quantity** | **Flexible Budget: Based on Standard Quantity Allowed to Produce 200 Surfboards** |
| **Actual Costs** | | |

Actual Pounds Purchased × Actual Cost per Pound

Actual Pounds × Standard Cost per Pound

Standard Pounds Allowed × Standard Cost per Pound

| | Quantity Purchased | Quantity Used | (200 × 80) × $.50 |

19,000 × $.52 = $9,880    19,000 × $.50 = $9,500    16,250 × $.50 = $8,125    16,000 × $.50 = $8,000

19,000 × ($.52 − $.50) = 19,000 × $.02 = $380 U

(16,250 − 16,000) × $.50 = 250 × $.50 = $125 U

*Price variance*    *Quantity variance*

$380 U + $125 U = $505 U

*Flexible budget variance*

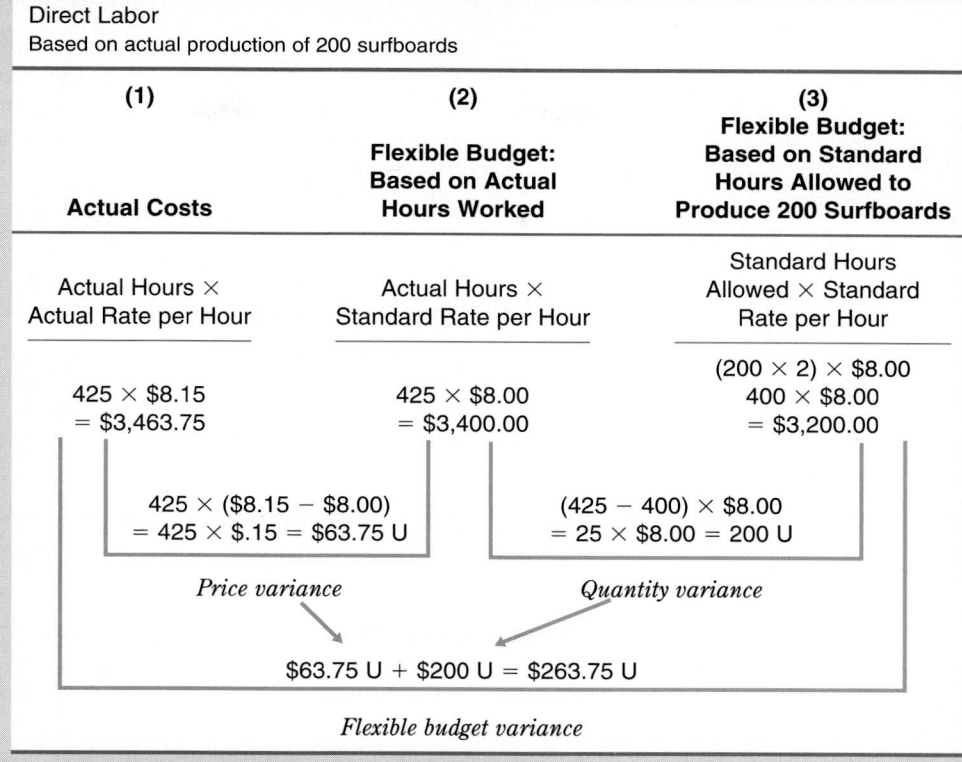

Direct Labor
Based on actual production of 200 surfboards

| (1) | (2) | (3) |
|---|---|---|
| | Flexible Budget: Based on Actual | Flexible Budget: Based on Standard Hours Allowed to |
| **Actual Costs** | **Hours Worked** | **Produce 200 Surfboards** |
| Actual Hours × Actual Rate per Hour | Actual Hours × Standard Rate per Hour | Standard Hours Allowed × Standard Rate per Hour |
| | | (200 × 2) × $8.00 |
| 425 × $8.15 | 425 × $8.00 | 400 × $8.00 |
| = $3,463.75 | = $3,400.00 | = $3,200.00 |

425 × ($8.15 − $8.00)
= 425 × $.15 = $63.75 U

(425 − 400) × $8.00
= 25 × $8.00 = 200 U

*Price variance*          *Quantity variance*

$63.75 U + $200 U = $263.75 U

*Flexible budget variance*

---

## QUESTIONS FOR REVIEW AND FURTHER THOUGHT

### REVIEW QUESTIONS

1. Discuss what a responsibility center is. Relate it to the definition of responsibility accounting.

2. What are flexible budgets? What are they used for? When are they prepared?

3. What is the difference between a master budget and a flexible budget?

4. Distinguish flexible budgets from standard costs.

5. How can you determine whether costs are controllable or noncontrollable?

6. What is the difference between effectiveness and efficiency?

7. Define the term *standard cost,* and list three uses for standard costs.

8. What is meant by a price variance? A quantity variance?

9. List some possible reasons for each of the following variances:
   a. Direct materials price variance
   b. Direct labor quantity variance

### QUESTIONS FOR FURTHER THOUGHT

1. Why shouldn't the master budget be compared to actual results in the performance report when the efficiency of a responsibility center is being evaluated?

2. Why would it be preferable to compare the actual results for the current period to standard costs, rather than to the actual costs of the previous period?

3. Explain how a department could be effective without being efficient, and efficient without being effective.

4. The purchasing agent should be blamed for all price variances. Do you agree with this statement? Explain.

5. Explain why a direct materials price variance should be based on the quantity purchased rather than the quantity used.

6. Who should be held responsible for extra production costs caused by a rush order? Explain.

7. The accountant is solely responsible for the development of standards used in a standard cost system. Discuss why you think this statement is correct or incorrect.

8. In the three-column approach to variance analysis, the flexible budget for direct materials for the units produced is exactly the same as the flexible budget based on the standard quantity allowed, which is exactly the same as the amount applied. Explain how these three elements can all be the same.

## OBJECTIVE ASSIGNMENT

*True/False*   Indicate whether each statement below is *true* or *false* by placing a *T* or an *F* in the space provided.

_____ 1. The master budget is prepared only before a budget period begins, but flexible budgets can be prepared either before the budget period begins or after the budget period is completed.

_____ 2. A firm can be effective or efficient but not both.

_____ 3. A standard cost represents what management thinks the firm will spend to produce a unit in an upcoming period.

_____ 4. The price variance for direct materials should be based on the quantity purchased rather than the quantity used, when the quantities purchased and used are different.

_____ 5. Standard costs can be used for planning, control, and inventory costing.

*Multiple Choice*   Select the best choice to complete each statement or answer each question below. Write the letter corresponding to your choice in the space provided.

_____ 1. Which of the following would probably be a responsibility center within a manufacturing organization?
   a. The assembly department
   b. The sales offices
   c. A storeroom
   d. All of the above

_____ 2. Which of the following variances would most likely be controllable by the purchasing agent?
   a. Direct materials price variance
   b. Direct materials quantity variance
   c. Direct labor price variance
   d. Direct labor quantity variance

_____ 3. Which of the following variances is an appropriate measure of effectiveness?
   a. Price variance
   b. Quantity variance
   c. Flexible budget variance
   d. Sales volume variance

_____ 4. During the month of December, Geronimo Company produced and sold 5,000 units, 300 more than expected. The costs of producing the units should have been $25,000 but were actually $25,760. Which of the following statements is true?
   a. Geronimo was effective but not efficient.
   b. Geronimo was efficient but not effective.
   c. Geronimo was both effective and efficient.
   d. Geronimo was neither effective nor efficient.

_____ 5. During January, Spencer Company produced 4,000 units, and used 23,000 gallons of direct materials to produce them. The standards for direct materials were $4 per gallon and 6 gallons per unit. The actual price paid per gallon was $4.25. What was the direct materials quantity variance?
   a. $4,000 F                                   c. $4,000 U
   b. $4,250 F                                   d. $250 U

_____ 6. The Seminole Company produces a product that requires 3 pounds of direct materials per unit, at a standard rate of $5 per pound. During July, Seminole produced 1,100 units, 100 more than expected for the month. The company used 3,500 pounds of materials, costing $16,000. What was the standard quantity of direct materials allowed for July?
   a. 3,000 pounds                               c. 3,300 pounds
   b. 3,200 pounds                               d. 3,500 pounds

_____ 7. During July, Appaloosa Company produced 400 units, which required 2,100 hours of direct labor ($10,600). The standard time to produce a unit is 5 hours and the standard rate is $5 per hour. What is the flexible budget for the standard hours allowed for July?
   a. $10,500                                    c. $10,000
   b. $10,600                                    d. $10,095

_____ 8. At the beginning of 1997, Pincher Co. budgeted 10,000 units, but only 9,000 units were produced during the year. Pincher expected its sales price to be $50, its variable costs to be $30 per unit, and its total fixed costs to be $125,000. It's actual income was $5,000 less than it had budgeted at the beginning of the year. What was Pincher's sales volume variance?
   a. $5,000 U                                   c. $55,000 F
   b. $15,000 F                                  d. $20,000 U

_____ 9. The standard time to make a unit is 4 hours and the standard price is $10 per hour. The actual hours needed to produce 5,000 units was 19,000, each hour costing $10.50. What is the direct labor price variance?
   a. $2,500 U                                   c. $10,000 U
   b. $9,500 F                                   d. $9,500 U

_____ 10. Based on the same facts presented in #9 above, what would be the direct labor quantity variance?
   a. $10,000 F                                  c. $10,500 U
   b. $10,000 U                                  d. $10,500 F

## EXERCISES

4† **Exercise 1:** Preparing Flexible Budgets Based on the Predictions Given in the Master Budget

The following master budget was prepared for a production department at the beginning of 1997. Prepare flexible budgets for 200,000 units and 300,000 units.

† The numbers in the margin refer to the Learning Objectives.

|  | Master Budget (Based on 240,000 Units) | |
|---|---|---|
| Supplies. | | $120,000 |
| Variable Utilities | | 24,000 |
| Fixed Utilities. | | 10,000 |
| Depreciation | | 23,000 |
| Property Taxes | | 35,000 |
| | | $212,000 |

▶ *(Check Figure: Budget for 200,000 units = $188,000)*

2 4 **Exercise 2:** Preparing a Performance Report for Production Costs

The Warrior Company uses flexible budgets to help managers plan and control its operations. It has the following rates per unit for its variable production costs:

| Direct materials | $5.00 per unit |
|---|---|
| Direct labor | $8.00 per unit |
| Variable factory overhead | $2.00 per unit |

Warrior budgets its fixed factory overhead costs at $40,000 per month.

During August 1997, Warrior Company produced 12,000 units and incurred the following actual costs:

| Direct materials | $ 66,000 |
|---|---|
| Direct labor | 100,000 |
| Variable factory overhead. | 22,000 |
| Fixed factory overhead. | 41,000 |
| | $229,000 |

a. Prepare flexible budgets for each production cost for 10,000 units, 15,000 units, and 20,000 units.

b. Prepare a three-column performance report for August. In the first column, enter the actual costs. In the third column, prepare the appropriate flexible budget. In the second column, determine the flexible budget variances.

▶ *(Check Figure: a. Budget for 20,000 units = $340,000)*

5 **Exercise 3:** Determining the Sales Volume Variance

The Jimhall Company prepared the following condensed master budget at the beginning of March, based upon 1,000 units.

| | Per Unit | Totals |
|---|---|---|
| Sales | $100 | $100,000 |
| Variable costs | 80 | 80,000 |
| Contribution margin. | $ 20 | $ 20,000 |
| Fixed costs | | 10,000 |
| Income. | | $ 10,000 |

If only 900 units are produced and sold in March, determine the sales volume variance.

▶ *(Check Figure: $2,000 U)*

8 **Exercise 4:** Calculating Variances for Direct Materials and Direct Labor

Patriot Company produces vitamins and uses standards to help control its operations. During January, the 10,000 cases budgeted for production were actually produced. Purchases of direct materials were 3,300,000 ounces at $.14 per ounce, of which 3,200,000 ounces were used in production. The direct labor incurred for January was 4,850 hours at $10.25 per hour. The standards per case are as follows:

Direct materials (300 oz @ $.15/oz) . . . . . . . . . . . . . .   $45
Direct labor ($\frac{1}{2}$ hr @ $10/hr) . . . . . . . . . . . . . . . . . . . . . .   5

Determine the price, quantity, and flexible budget variances for direct materials and direct labor. Indicate whether each variance is favorable (F) or unfavorable (U).

▶ (Check Figure: Materials price variance = $33,000 F)

### 8  **Exercise 5:** Analyzing Variances for Direct Labor

The Bureman Company makes a product expected to require 6 hours to produce, at an expected rate per hour of $7.50 for direct labor. During the month of January, 600 units were produced although 500 units had been budgeted. The actual labor costs were:

Direct labor (3,200 hr) . . . . . . . . . . . . . . . . . . . . . .   $24,160

Determine the price, quantity, and flexible budget variances for direct labor. Indicate with a U or an F whether each variance is unfavorable or favorable.

▶ (Check Figure: Quantity variance = $160 U)

### 5  **Exercise 6:** Distinguishing Effectiveness from Efficiency

The Osceola Company produces a beauty product called Coverup and uses a standard cost system. Osceola had budgeted 120 cases for June, but was able to produce and sell only 100 cases because of a strike during the last week of the month. The standards for direct labor were $\frac{1}{2}$ hour per case, at $7.00 per hour. The actual labor costs for June are $420, representing 56 hours at $7.50 per hour.

Osceola prices the product to its wholesalers to achieve a contribution margin of $5 per case.

Determine dollar measures of Osceola's (a) effectiveness and (b) efficiency for the month of June.

▶ (Check Figure: a. $100)

### 5  **Exercise 7:** Determining the Number of Budgeted Units
for an Ineffective Month

The Spear Company produced 5,000 boxes during the month, spending $151,000 of variable production costs. The sales price and standard variable costs per box were:

Sales price . . . . . . . . . . . . . . . . . . . . . . . . . . . . . . . . .   $60
Direct materials . . . . . . . . . . . . . . . . . . . . . . . . . . . . .   10
Direct labor . . . . . . . . . . . . . . . . . . . . . . . . . . . . . . . . .   12
Variable factory overhead . . . . . . . . . . . . . . . . . . . . . . .   8
Variable selling . . . . . . . . . . . . . . . . . . . . . . . . . . . . . .   4

Spear earned $5,200 less profit than originally predicted, because it produced and sold fewer units than budgeted. How many units were budgeted for the month?

▶ (Check Figure: 5,200 units)

### 2  8  **Exercise 8:** Determining Unknowns from a Performance Report
for Direct Materials

During August 1997, the Letitia Corporation produced 10,500 units, exactly the quantity that had been budgeted for the month. The standards used by Letitia to help control the purchase and usage of direct materials are as follows:

Direct materials: 2 lb/unit at $1.75/lb

During August, Letitia purchased and used the same quantity of raw materials. The performance report for August spotlighted the following variances:

| Direct materials: | |
|---|---|
| Price variance | $5,000 F |
| Quantity variance | 1,750 F |

Determine the following:

a. The actual pounds purchased and used
b. The actual price paid per pound

▶ *(Check Figure: b. $1.50)*

8  **Exercise 9:** Determining Unknowns on the Basis of Variances for Direct Labor

Bren Mar Corporation uses a standard cost system to control its labor costs. During the month of July, the direct labor costs were $120,000 (24,000 hours). Five thousand units were produced during this month. The direct labor price variance was $12,000 U, and the direct labor quantity variance was $4,500 U. Determine the following:

a. Standard rate per hour
b. Standard hours per unit

▶ *(Check Figure: a. $4.50)*

## PROBLEMS: SET A

2 4 5†  **Problem A1:** Preparing Flexible Budgets before Production and after Production Is Completed

The Westcott Company, a manufacturer of stopwatches, uses flexible budgets and standard costs to control its operations. Westcott expects its production and sales in January to be 20,000 units and selected production costs to be as follows:

| | |
|---|---|
| Direct labor | $60,000 |
| Direct materials | 4,800 |
| | $64,800 |

**Required:**

1. Prepare flexible budgets that might have been prepared at the beginning of the month for the following levels of production: 17,000 units, 21,000 units, and 25,000 units.
2. The actual units produced during January were 19,000; the actual hours worked were 117,000; and the actual materials purchased and used were 39,000 ounces. The standard time to produce one unit was 6 hours; and the standard quantity of materials was 2 ounces per unit. The actual costs incurred were as follows:

| | |
|---|---|
| Direct labor | $56,160 |
| Direct materials | 3,510 |
| | $59,670 |

Prepare a performance report for January that lists each of the production costs. The report should have six columns: (1) actual costs; (2) price variance; (3) flexible budget based on the actual hours worked, or pounds used; (4) quantity variance; (5) flexible budget based on the standard hours or pounds allowed; and (6) flexible budget variance.

▶ *(Check Figure: 2. Flexible budget based on actual hours worked = $63,180)*

† The numbers in the margin refer to the Learning Objectives.

**8**    **Problem A2:** Determining Price and Quantity Variances
for Direct Materials and Direct Labor

Snowbird Company, a manufacturer of ski jackets, uses standard costs to help control its
operations. The standard costs of producing one jacket are:

> Direct materials: 2 yd/jacket at $15/yd
> Direct labor: $1\frac{1}{2}$ hr/jacket at $10/hr

During March, 5,000 jackets were budgeted for production but only 4,000 jackets were
actually produced. The actual costs for March were as follows:

> Direct materials: 10,000 yd purchased ($152,000); 8,800 yd used
> Direct labor; 6,200 hr worked: $61,628

**Required:**

Compute the individual and flexible budget variances for each production cost. Indicate
whether each variance is favorable or unfavorable.

▶ *(Check Figure: Direct materials price variance = $2,000 U)*

**8**    **Problem A3:** Determining Unknown Values

The Sealed Gardner Company uses standard costs and flexible budgets to help in the control of
its operations. During July 1997, the company produced 20,000 units.

**Required:**

1. The standard quantity and rate for direct materials are 4 pounds and $5 per pound, respec-
   tively. The actual materials costs incurred during the month were $509,000. The price
   variance was $9,000 U and the quantity variance was $100,000 U. Assuming that all materials
   purchased were used, how many pounds of materials were actually purchased and used?
   What was the actual price paid per pound?
2. The standards for direct labor are 4 hours at $9 per hour. The actual wages paid were
   $787,500, and the quantity variance was $90,000 U. What is the standard cost of direct labor
   per unit? How many direct labor hours were used during the month? What was the labor
   price variance?

▶ *(Check Figure: 1. Materials purchased and used = 100,000; 2. Labor price variance = $22,500 F)*

**2 3 4 5**    **Problem A4:** Preparing Income Statements at the Actual and Budgeted Levels
of Activity

The Repass Company sells lightning surge protectors for television sets, at $18 per unit. Repass
expected to produce and sell only 3,000 units during August, but was able to produce and sell
4,000 units due to a substantial increase in lightning storms in several areas of the country. The
standard and actual results for the month were as follows:

|  | Standard | Actual |
|---|---|---|
| Variable manufacturing costs. . . . . . . . . . . . . . . . . . . . . . | $6/unit | $6.50/unit |
| Variable selling costs . . . . . . . . . . . . . . . . . . . . . . . . . . . . | $3/unit | $2.80/unit |
| Fixed manufacturing costs . . . . . . . . . . . . . . . . . . . . . . . . | $20,000/month | $20,600 |
| Fixed selling costs . . . . . . . . . . . . . . . . . . . . . . . . . . . . . . | $3,000/month | $3,500 |

Repass's actual revenues for August were $75,000.

**Required:**

1. Prepare income statements using the contribution margin format with the following five
   column headings:

| (1) | (2) | (3) | (4) | (5) |
|---|---|---|---|---|
|  |  | **Flexible Budget** |  | **Master** |
| **Actual Results** | **Difference** | **for Units Produced** | **Difference** | **Budget** |

2. Analyze the results for each of the difference columns (2 and 4).

▶ *(Check Figure: Sales volume variance = $9,000 F; Flexible budget variance for net income = $700 F)*

2 4 5 **Problem A5:** Finding the Unknowns in a Performance Report for the Entire Company

Skinny Dip Pools produces and sells above-ground pools for nighttime use. Each month a performance report is prepared that compares the actual results to both a flexible budget and the master budget for the entire company. The performance report prepared for 1997 is shown below:

| | Actual Results | Variance | Flexible Budget | Variance | Master Budget |
|---|---|---|---|---|---|
| Units—Pools | 300 | — | 300 | 100 | 400 |
| Sales | $650,000 | $50,000 | $600,000 | $200,000 | $800,000 |
| Variable Costs | 330,000 | 30,000 | 360,000 | 120,000 | 480,000 |
| Total Contribution Margin | $320,000 | $80,000 | $240,000 | $ 80,000 | $320,000 |
| Fixed Costs | 125,000 | 5,000 | 120,000 | –0– | 120,000 |
| Operating Income | $195,000 | $75,000 | $120,000 | $ 80,000 | $200,000 |

**Required:**
Answer each of the following questions related to Skinny Dip's performance report.

1. How many pools were budgeted for 1997?
2. What was the flexible budget variance for operating income?
3. How much operating income was budgeted for the pools that were built during 1997?
4. What was the best measure of effectiveness for the year?
5. Was the flexible budget variance for variable costs favorable or unfavorable? Why?
6. Was the sales volume variance favorable or unfavorable? Why?
7. What was the budgeted sales price for each pool? What was the actual sales price?
8. What was the budgeted contribution margin per pool?

▶ *(Check Figure: 4. $80,000)*

6 7 **Problem A6:** Analyzing Variances for Direct Materials and Direct Labor

The Domerjeff Company makes a product that requires 2 hours of direct labor and 15 square feet of direct materials for each unit produced. During November, 15,000 units were produced, 1,000 more than expected for the month. The actual square feet and labor hours used in production were 226,000 square feet and 27,000 hours respectively.
    The standard and actual prices for the inputs were as follows:

| | Standard | Actual |
|---|---|---|
| Direct materials | $3/square foot | $3.10/square foot |
| Direct labor | $8/hour | $8.20/hour |

In addition, the materials purchased during the month totaled 200,000 square feet.

**Required:**

1. Determine the price, quantity, and flexible budget variances for direct materials and direct labor.
2. Answer the following related questions:
    a. How much should Domerjeff have spent for the materials purchased during the month?
    b. How much should have been the cost of direct materials needed for November's production?
    c. What was the flexible budget for the units produced during the month, for direct labor?
    d. How much would be debited to Work-in-Process Inventory for direct labor costs in November?
    e. What is the amount of direct labor costs applied to November's production?

▶ *(Check Figure: 2a. $600,000)*

## PROBLEMS: SET B

2 4 5†   **Problem B1:** Preparing Flexible Budgets before Production and after Production Is Completed

Longmire Company manufactures after-ski boots and uses flexible budgets and standard costs to control its operations. Longmire expects its production and sales in July to be 60,000 units and its prime costs to be as follows:

| | |
|---|---|
| Direct labor | $120,000 |
| Direct materials | 600,000 |
| | $720,000 |

**Required:**

1. Prepare flexible budgets that might have been prepared at the beginning of the month for each of the following levels of production: 45,000 units, 54,000 units, and 66,000 units.
2. The actual units produced during July were 75,000; the actual hours worked were 156,000; and the actual pounds purchased and used were 40,000. The standard time to produce one unit was 2 hours, and the standard quantity of direct materials was $\frac{1}{2}$ pound per unit. The actual costs incurred were as follows:

| | |
|---|---|
| Direct labor | $147,000 |
| Direct materials | 840,000 |
| | $987,000 |

Prepare a performance report for July that lists each of the production costs. The report should have six columns: (1) actual costs; (2) price variance; (3) flexible budget based on the actual hours worked or pounds used; (4) quantity variance; (5) flexible budget based on the standard hours or pounds allowed; and (6) flexible budget variance.

▶ *(Check Figure: 2. Flexible budget based on standard hours or pounds allowed = $900,000)*

8   **Problem B2:** Determining Price and Quantity Variances for Direct Materials and Direct Labor

Altawasatch Company manufactures wall safes and uses standard costs to help control its operations. The standard costs of producing one wall safe are:

> Direct materials: 50 lb/safe at $10/lb
> Direct labor: 5 hr/safe at $20/hr

During April, 1,500 safes were budgeted for production, but 2,000 safes were actually produced. The actual costs for April were as follows:

> Direct materials: 110,000 lb purchased at $9.75/lb; 98,800 lb used
> Direct labor, 10,200 hr worked: $209,610

**Required:**
Compute the individual and flexible budget variances for each production cost. Indicate whether each variance is favorable or unfavorable.

▶ *(Check Figure: Direct materials price variance = $27,500 F)*

† The numbers in the margin refer to the Learning Objectives.

8 **Problem B3:** Determining Unknown Values

Brigton Pool Maintenance produces pool supplies and uses standard costs and flexible budgets to help control its operations. At the end of August, the chief cost accountant accumulated the following facts concerning production in August:

| | |
|---|---:|
| Units produced . . . . . . . . . . . . . . . . . . . . . . . . . . . . . . . . . . . . . . . . . . . . . . . . . | 100,000 |
| Direct materials: | |
|    Standards: 3 gal at $2.50/gal | |
|    Actual results: | |
|       Price variance . . . . . . . . . . . . . . . . . . . . . . . . . . . . . . . . . . . . . . . | $140,000 F |
|       Quantity variance. . . . . . . . . . . . . . . . . . . . . . . . . . . . . . . . . . . . . | 50,000 F |
| Direct labor: | |
|    Standards: 2 hr at $8.00/hr | |
|    Actual results: | |
|       Price variance . . . . . . . . . . . . . . . . . . . . . . . . . . . . . . . . . . . . . . . | $21,000 U |
|       Quantity variance. . . . . . . . . . . . . . . . . . . . . . . . . . . . . . . . . . . . . | 80,000 U |

**Required:**
Answer each of the following questions:

1. How many gallons were used, if the same amount of materials was purchased and used? What was the actual price paid per gallon?
2. What was the standard cost per unit for direct labor? How many direct labor hours were used? What was the actual wage rate?

▶ *(Check Figure: 1. Materials purchased and used = 280,000; 2. Actual wage rate = $8.10)*

2 3 4 5 **Problem B4:** Preparing a Performance Report That Displays Income Statements at the Actual and Budgeted Levels of Activity

The Diggumup Septic Tank Company budgeted 10,000 tanks to be produced in August 1998. Each tank is expected to be sold for $450. The controller expects the following costs for the month:

| | |
|---|---|
| Variable production costs . . . . . . . . . . . . . . . . . | $200/tank |
| Variable selling costs. . . . . . . . . . . . . . . . . . . . . . | $40/tank |
| Fixed production costs . . . . . . . . . . . . . . . | $300,000/month |
| Fixed selling costs. . . . . . . . . . . . . . . . . . . | $80,000/month |

The company managed to produce and sell only 8,000 tanks in August. Each tank was sold for $448. The actual costs for the month were as follows:

| | |
|---|---:|
| Variable production costs . . . . . . . . . . . . . . . . . | $1,580,000 |
| Variable selling costs. . . . . . . . . . . . . . . . . . . . . | 330,000 |
| Fixed production costs. . . . . . . . . . . . . . . . . . . | 310,000 |
| Fixed selling costs . . . . . . . . . . . . . . . . . . . . . . | 89,000 |

**Required:**

1. Prepare income statements using the contribution margin format with the following five column headings:

| (1) | (2) | (3) | (4) | (5) |
|---|---|---|---|---|
| | | Flexible Budget | | |
| Actual | | for Units | | Master |
| Results | Difference | Produced | Difference | Budget |

2. Explain what the difference columns (2 and 4) represent.

▶ *(Check Figure: 1. Sales volume variance = $420,000 U; Flexible budget variance for net income = $25,000 U)*

2 4 5    **Problem B5:** Finding the Unknowns in a Performance Report
for the Entire Company

Soni Lookalikes is a small manufacturer of television sets. The production process has been
fine-tuned to produce TVs that will break down just after the warranty expires. Each month a
performance report is prepared that compares the actual results to both a flexible budget and
the master budget for the entire company. The performance report prepared for September
1997 is shown below:

|  | Actual Results | Variance | Flexible Budget | Variance | Master Budget |
|---|---|---|---|---|---|
| Units (TVs) | 100 | — | 100 | 20 | 80 |
| Sales | $26,000 | $1,000 | $25,000 | $5,000 | $20,000 |
| Variable Costs | 10,500 | 500 | 10,000 | 2,000 | 8,000 |
| Total Contribution Margin | $15,500 | $ 500 | $15,000 | $3,000 | $12,000 |
| Fixed Costs | 11,900 | 100 | 12,000 | –0– | 12,000 |
| Operating Income | $ 3,600 | $ 600 | $ 3,000 | $3,000 | –0– |

**Required:**
Answer each of the following questions related to Soni Lookalikes' performance report.

1. How many TVs were budgeted for September?
2. What was the flexible budget variance for variable costs?
3. How much operating income was budgeted for the TVs that were expected to be built
during 1997?
4. What was the best measure of effectiveness for the year?
5. Was the flexible budget variance for operating income favorable or unfavorable? Why?
6. Was the sales volume variance favorable or unfavorable? Why?
7. What was the budgeted variable cost for each TV? What was the actual variable cost per TV?
8. What was the budgeted contribution margin per TV?

▶ *(Check Figure: 4. $3,000)*

7 8    **Problem B6:** Analyzing Variances for Direct Materials and Direct Labor

The Zodiac Company makes a product that requires 4 hours of direct labor and 10 pounds of
direct materials for each unit produced. During February, 6,000 units were produced, 500 less
than expected for the month. The actual pounds and labor hours used in production were
58,000 pounds and 24,500 hours respectively.
    The standard and actual prices for the inputs were as follows:

|  | Standard | Actual |
|---|---|---|
| Direct materials | $40/pound | $45/pound |
| Direct labor | $15/hour | $14/hour |

In addition, the materials purchased during the month totaled 65,000 pounds.

**Required:**

1. Determine the price, quantity, and flexible budget variances for direct materials and direct
labor.
2. Answer the following related questions:
   a. How much should Zodiac have spent for the materials purchased during the month?
   b. What was the flexible budget for the units produced during the month, for direct
   materials?
   c. How much would be debited to Work-in-Process Inventory for direct material costs in
   February?
   d. How much should have been the cost of direct labor needed for February's production?
   e. What is the amount of direct labor costs applied to February's production?

▶ *(Check Figure: 2c. $2,400,000)*

## ETHICS CASE

The plant manager for the Hang'em High Company has recently started an incentive program for production workers. Once the standards for the year have been set, the workers will receive a bonus based on the favorable variances they can generate during the year. Unfavorable variances will be netted against favorable variances in determining the bonus. If the net of all variances is unfavorable, the workers will not be expected to pay management for the difference.

The standards for the prime costs for 1997 were determined to be as follows:

Direct materials: 10 lb at $5/lb
Direct labor: 4 hr at $10/hr

During 1997, the purchasing agent, Rob Lynch, was able to get a great deal on the purchase of raw materials that were of much lower quality than specified by the standards. Rob got the entire order of 100,000 pounds of raw materials for only $3.50 per pound. The poorer-quality materials resulted in 22,000 pounds of waste and 7,000 excessive hours of labor. In addition, in an effort to minimize the waste, the production foreman shifted higher-paid workers to this operation to assist the less experienced workers.

The actual labor costs for the year for the 9,000 units produced were $516,000.

### Required:

1. Calculate the price and quantity variances for direct materials and direct labor. Classify each variance as either favorable (F) or unfavorable (U).
2. If you were the production foreman, what argument would you use against Rob Lynch's claim that the direct materials price variance was favorable?
3. If the production workers' bonus is 25% of the net favorable variance, what bonus should be paid to Rob Lynch from his point of view? What about from the production foreman's point of view?
4. Was Rob's decision to buy the "bargain" materials beneficial to the company?
5. Do you consider Rob's actions to be ethical? Explain your answer.

## OBJECTIVE ASSIGNMENT ANSWERS

### True/False

1. T    2. F    3. F    4. T    5. T

### Multiple Choice

1. d    2. a    3. d    4. a    5. a
6. c    7. c    8. d    9. d    10. a

# Controlling Costs With Flexible Budgets, Standard Costs, and Variances — Part Two

**LEARNING OBJECTIVES**

After studying this chapter, you should be able to do the following:

1 Discuss similarities in the variance analysis for direct materials, direct labor, and variable factory overhead

2 Explain how standards are determined for variable factory overhead costs

3 Calculate the price, quantity, and flexible budget variances for variable factory overhead

4 Calculate the price and flexible budget variances for fixed factory overhead

5 Calculate the predetermined fixed factory overhead rate, the fixed factory overhead applied, and the fixed factory overhead production volume variance

6 Define the key terms listed at the end of this chapter

In the previous chapter we demonstrated what flexible budgets are, showing you how they can be used by accountants in the preparation of performance reports to help management control current operations. We also explained what standard costs are, and the role they play in flexible budgets, performance reports, and variance analysis. We limited the discussion of standard costs and variance analysis to direct materials and direct labor. In this chapter we will expand this discussion to include variable and fixed factory overhead.

Learning Objective 1

Discuss similarities in the variance analysis for direct materials, direct labor, and variable factory overhead

## SIMILARITIES BETWEEN DIRECT MATERIALS, DIRECT LABOR AND VARIABLE FACTORY OVERHEAD

Remember from the previous chapter that for each type of variable production cost (direct materials, direct labor, and variable factory overhead) there are two types of standards—price standards and quantity standards. And for each type of standard there are two types of variances (summarized in Figure 1)—price variances and quantity variances. In addition, the sum of the price variance and quantity variance is the flexible budget variance for each of these variable production costs. In a few moments we will also see that the calculation of each of these variances is almost exactly the same for the variable factory overhead costs as it was for direct materials and direct labor.

**Figure 1** Types of Variances for Variable and Fixed Production Costs

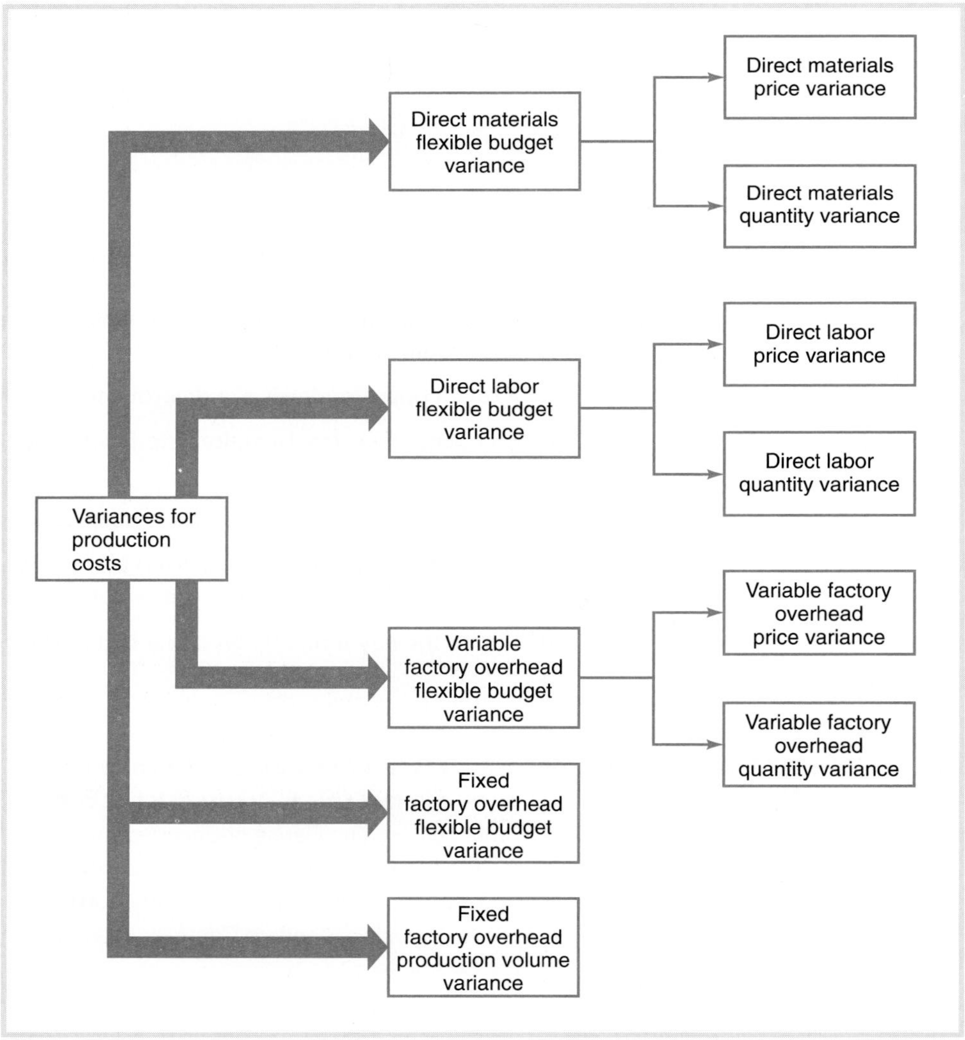

On the other hand, as Figure 1 shows, the analysis of fixed factory overhead is different from that of the variable production costs. Although there is a flexible budget variance, it is not composed of both a price variance and quantity variance. In addition, there is a completely new variance, called the production volume variance, that exists only for fixed factory overhead.

Let's look first at the analysis of variable factory overhead costs.

Learning<br>Objective **2 VARIABLE FACTORY OVERHEAD**

Explain how standards are determined for variable factory overhead costs

Direct materials and direct labor are direct costs because they are either physically related to or become an integral part of the units produced. It is possible to determine the exact amount of direct materials and direct labor that goes into each unit.

Variable overhead costs, in contrast, are indirectly related to production. Although such costs are necessary, they cannot normally be as closely associated with specific units of production as are direct materials and direct labor. For this reason, setting standards for variable overhead costs is usually different from setting standards for direct materials and direct labor. Rather than determining an exact amount of variable overhead that should be incurred every time a unit is completed, we calculate an average. The average represents how much overhead should be incurred per unit in a batch of units produced over an extended period of time.

For example, assume that the standard costs per unit for the production of tables with Formica tops includes $2.00 for Formica (a direct material) and $.50 for utilities (an indirect item of variable overhead). Each table would require one Formica table-top and thus $2.00 of materials cost, whether it was the first, tenth, or thousandth table produced. However, the $.50 per table for utilities has a different explanation. It would not be reasonable to expect the utility bill to increase by exactly $.50 every time a table was finished. But over a longer period of time—say, a month—we might expect the total utility bill to average $.50 per table.

To develop standards for variable overhead, we must deal with averages rather than exact costs per unit. We can determine these averages with the aid of statistical tools for evaluating the behavior of costs. These tools are covered in upper-level statistics and cost accounting courses. For our purposes now, we'll assume that the Robinjon Company (introduced in the previous chapter) has evaluated the behavior of its total overhead costs and has determined that the variable overhead costs should average $2.00 per hour. Since we already know (from the discussion of direct labor in the previous chapter) that the standard hours allowed per unit are $1\frac{1}{2}$, the standard variable overhead rate per unit is $3.00, determined as follows:

$$\begin{array}{c}\textbf{Variable overhead}\\ \textbf{cost per unit}\end{array} = \begin{array}{c}\textbf{standard hours}\\ \textbf{per unit}\end{array} \times \begin{array}{c}\textbf{variable overhead}\\ \textbf{cost per hour}\end{array}$$

$$= 1\tfrac{1}{2} \text{ hr/unit} \times \$2.00/\text{hr} = \$3.00/\text{unit}$$

Within the text and most of the homework problems, we assume that variable overhead costs are closely related to the number of direct labor hours—that direct labor hours is the most appropriate cost driver (measure of activity). In a little while we will discuss the potential weakness of this assumption and look at other possible cost drivers for the variable overhead costs.

Before going on to the variance calculations, look first at the expanded set of facts for Robinjon Company.

# Robinjon Company (Expanded Set of Facts)

Robinjon Company has the following standards for the production of each unit (a portable birdbath):

Direct materials: $\frac{1}{2}$ lb/unit at \$10/lb = \$5/unit

Direct labor: $1\frac{1}{2}$ hr/unit at \$4/hr = \$6/unit

Variable overhead: $1\frac{1}{2}$ hr/unit at \$2/hr = \$3/unit

Fixed overhead is budgeted at \$15,000 per month.

At the beginning of January 1997, 15,000 units were budgeted for production. Only 12,500 units were actually produced during the month. The actual results for the month's production were as follows:

6,404 pounds purchased and used, at a cost of \$10.15 per pound

20,000 hours worked; \$78,000 of direct labor costs (\$3.90/hr)

\$39,000 of variable overhead costs (\$1.95/hr)

\$14,900 of fixed overhead

Learning Objective 3

Calculate the price, quantity, and flexible budget variances for variable factory overhead

## Calculating the Variances

The calculation of price and quantity variances are nearly the same for variable overhead as for direct labor, as long as we can assume two things: (1) that factory overhead costs are closely related to direct labor hours; and (2) that the appropriate variable overhead rate is a rate per direct labor hour. Under these two assumptions, the **variable overhead price** (or **spending**) **variance** is calculated as follows:

$$\text{Variable overhead price variance} = \text{actual hours worked} \times \text{difference between actual cost per hour and standard cost per hour}$$

For Robinjon Company, it would be:

Variable overhead price variance = 20,000 hr × (\$1.95 − \$2.00)

= 20,000 hr × \$0.05/hr = \$1,000 F

The price variance is favorable because the average variable overhead cost incurred per hour (\$1.95) was \$.05 less than it was expected to be (\$2.00) for the 20,000 actual hours employed in production.

The formula for the **variable overhead quantity** (or **efficiency**) **variance** is:

$$\text{Variable overhead quantity variance} = \text{difference between actual hours worked and standard hours allowed} \times \text{standard cost per hour}$$

The quantity variance for Robinjon is:

Variable overhead quantity variance = (20,000 hr − 18,750 hr) × \$2.00/hr

= 1,250 hr × \$2.00/hr = \$2,500 U

The quantity variance for variable overhead is based on the difference in actual hours (20,000 hours) and standard hours (18,750 hours) of direct labor. Once these two quantities are determined, the dollar amount of quantity variance is derived by multiplying the quantity difference by the standard cost per hour.

The flexible budget variance for variable overhead is the sum of the price variance and the quantity variance:

**Flexible budget variance = price variance + quantity variance**

= \$1,000 F + \$2,500 U = \$1,500 U

The three-column approach for determining the price and quantity variances for variable factory overhead is shown in Exhibit 1. As you can see, the variances are calculated in almost exactly the same way that they were for direct labor. The only differences are the actual and standard rates per hour that were employed to calculate each variance.

### The Cause of Each Variance

If we assume that variable factory overhead is closely related to the number of direct labor hours used in production, anything that causes a quantity variance for direct labor also results in a quantity variance for variable overhead. So once we have determined the hours of variance for direct labor, and the causes of the variance, then we have also determined the hours of variance and the causes of the variance for variable overhead. The only difference between the variance for direct labor and variable overhead is the standard rate that is multiplied by the difference in the actual and standard hours.

The variable overhead price (or spending) variance represents the remainder of the flexible budget variance. It may arise for various reasons, the exact cause depending on the specific overhead cost being evaluated. It could be that the best measure of activity for some of the overhead costs may not be hours of labor, but for convenience the same measure of activity is being used for all overhead costs. As a result, the standard rate per hour may not result in as precise an estimate of costs in the flexible budget as we would like—resulting in a price variance. A price variance could also result from paying a higher average hourly rate than we should have for indirect laborers. Or it could even be due to an inefficient use of supplies that wasn't already explained by the quantity variance (i.e., wasn't due to the use of too many direct labor hours).

### More Detail for Variable Overhead

In practice, the variable overhead costs and variances would probably be broken down

---

**Exhibit 1** Three-Column Analysis for Variable Overhead
Based on actual production of 12,500 units

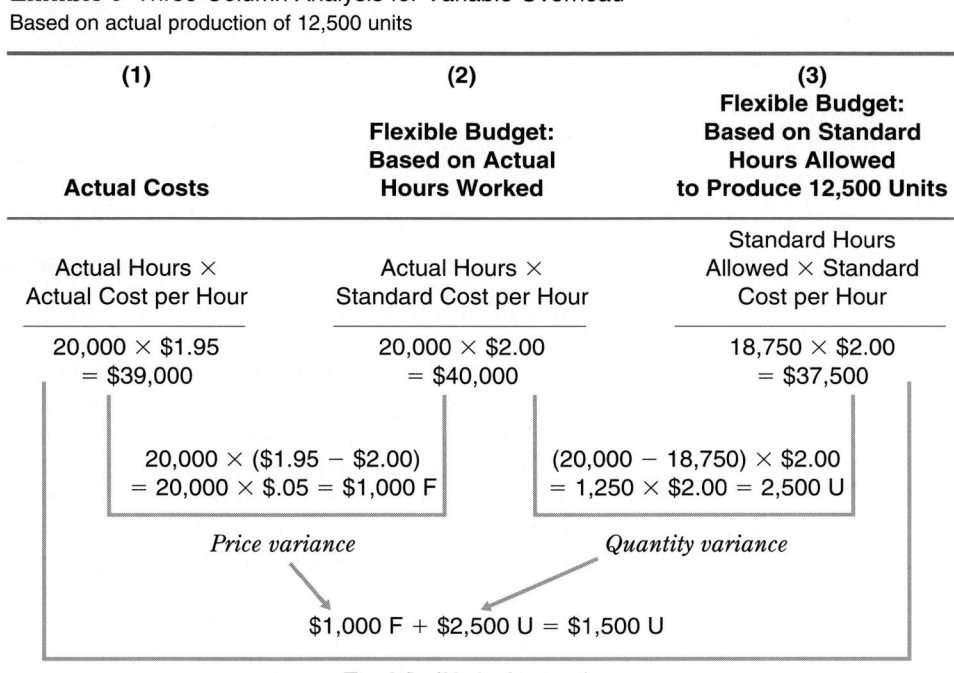

| (1) | (2) | (3) |
|---|---|---|
| Actual Costs | Flexible Budget: Based on Actual Hours Worked | Flexible Budget: Based on Standard Hours Allowed to Produce 12,500 Units |
| Actual Hours × Actual Cost per Hour | Actual Hours × Standard Cost per Hour | Standard Hours Allowed × Standard Cost per Hour |
| 20,000 × $1.95 = $39,000 | 20,000 × $2.00 = $40,000 | 18,750 × $2.00 = $37,500 |

20,000 × ($1.95 − $2.00) = 20,000 × $.05 = $1,000 F

(20,000 − 18,750) × $2.00 = 1,250 × $2.00 = 2,500 U

*Price variance*          *Quantity variance*

$1,000 F + $2,500 U = $1,500 U

*Total flexible budget variance*

into many specific variable overhead costs. An analysis of the variances would be performed for each cost item so that management would have the information needed to take corrective actions. For example, the $1,000 F price variance and the $2,500 U quantity variance might comprise the following items:

|  | Price Variance | Quantity Variance |
|---|---|---|
| Supplies ............................ | $1,800 U | $ 625 U |
| Utilities................................. | 600 U | 325 U |
| Indirect labor........................... | 3,400 F | 1,550 U |
|  | $1,000 F | $2,500 U |

Each variance must have its own cause, its own person responsible, and its own necessary corrective action.

If each of the variable overhead cost items must be treated individually rather than collectively, then separate variance calculations must be made for each item. But this should present no problem; the variance formulas will simply be used with specific items instead of for all variable overhead items combined. Take supplies, for example. If the individual standard cost per hour is $.50, and the actual rate averages $.59 per hour, the price variance is simply:

$$\text{Variable overhead price variance} = \text{actual hours worked} \times \begin{array}{c}\text{difference between actual}\\\text{cost per hour and standard}\\\text{cost per hour}\end{array}$$

$$= 20,000 \times (\$.59 - \$.50) = 20,000 \times \$0.09$$

$$= \$1,800 \text{ U}$$

And the variable overhead quantity variance for supplies would be:

$$\text{Variable overhead quantity variance} = \begin{array}{c}\text{difference between actual}\\\text{hours worked and standard}\\\text{hours allowed}\end{array} \times \begin{array}{c}\text{standard cost}\\\text{per hour}\end{array}$$

$$= (20,000 - 18,750) \times \$.50 = 1,250 \times \$.50$$

$$= \$625 \text{ U}$$

Naturally, we would calculate the variances for utilities and indirect labor in a similar manner.

## Alternative Measures of Activity (Cost Drivers)

In all of our exhibits we prepared flexible budgets for variable factory overhead based on a standard rate per direct labor hour. We assumed that each variable overhead item was closely related to direct labor: As the direct labor hours went up or down, the variable overhead costs should respond accordingly. As a result, the variance analysis for variable overhead was very similar to the analysis for direct labor.

The accuracy of the flexible budgets for variable overhead and of the resulting price and quantity variances depend on whether the variable overhead costs are more closely related to direct labor hours or to some alternative measures of activity. If variable overhead costs are more closely related to something other than direct labor, then the flexible budgets we prepared based on direct labor are probably inaccurate and the variances misleading. In the past, when factory overhead costs were quite small relative to other production costs, any inaccuracies that might have arisen from using direct labor were probably immaterial, and its use was considered to be "good enough." However, as factory overhead costs have increased dramatically and have become more important than direct labor in the modern manufacturing environment, "good enough" projections have become unacceptable. The need to budget overhead costs accurately is critical.

Critics of current cost accounting practices contend that using direct labor hours as a measure of activity is often a very poor way of analyzing overhead. For example, traditional overhead analysis assumes that the items listed at the left below vary with the number of direct labor hours. However, each cost is likely to be more closely related to some other measure of activity, such as the corresponding one listed at the right below.

| Overhead Cost | Alternative Measure of Activity (Cost Drivers) |
|---|---|
| Indirect labor | Direct labor dollars |
| Inspection costs | Hours of inspection time |
| Machine maintenance | Machine hours |
| Utilities | Kilowatt hours |
| Material handling | Number of units started |

If we continue to employ direct labor when more appropriate cost drivers are available, our projections will be inaccurate and therefore irrelevant for their intended use. Instead of blindly using direct labor, or any other single measure of activity, we need to look at each overhead item individually to determine the measure of activity that has the greatest influence on that item; and then to budget for that individual item using the appropriate measure of activity. The resulting flexible budgets and related variances in the performance report will probably be both more accurate and significantly different from what they would have been if direct labor had been employed.

**Exhibit 2** Summary of Variances for Variable Production Costs

| Variances: Terminology Employed in Text | Commonly Used Alternatives | Formula |
|---|---|---|
| Direct materials: | | |
| Price variance | None | Difference between actual price and standard price × actual quantity purchased |
| Quantity variance | Usage variance | Difference between actual quantity used and standard quantity allowed × standard price |
| Direct labor: | | |
| Price variance | Rate variance | Difference between actual rate and standard rate per hour × actual hours worked |
| Quantity variance | Efficiency, time, or usage variance | Difference between actual hours worked and standard hours allowed × standard rate per hour |
| Variable overhead: | | |
| Price variance | Spending variance | Difference between actual rate and standard rate per hour × actual hours worked |
| Quantity variance | Efficiency variance | Difference between actual hours worked and standard hours allowed × standard rate per hour |
| Flexible budget variance | Controllable variance | Price variance plus quantity variance |

In all our exhibits and most of our assignments, we will base the variable overhead analysis primarily on direct labor hours, for two reasons. First, many companies continue to use direct labor as their primary cost driver. Second, it is an easier way to demonstrate the budgeting process and the related variance analysis.

### A Choice in Terminology

Throughout our discussion of the variable production costs (direct materials, direct labor, and variable overhead), we have referred to price and quantity standards, and price and quantity variances.

We use only one set of terms in this text—*price* and *quantity*—to emphasize the similarity in form of each type of variance, regardless of whether we calculate it for direct materials, direct labor, or variable factory overhead. In actuality, different terms can be used.

Exhibit 2 lists commonly used terms for price and quantity variances and gives a summary of the formulas for calculating each variance.

**ASK YOURSELF** ▶

1. **How do you calculate the price, quantity, and flexible budget variances for variable factory overhead?**
2. **How do the price, quantity, and flexible budget variances for variable factory overhead compare to the same variances for direct labor?**
3. **When you are preparing flexible budgets for variable factory overhead, what cost drivers could you use besides direct labor hours?**

Learning Objective **4**

Calculate the price and flexible budget variances for fixed factory overhead

## FIXED FACTORY OVERHEAD

### Calculating the Price and Quantity Variances

The analysis of fixed factory overhead is somewhat different from the analysis for direct materials, direct labor, and variable factory overhead. For starters, even though there is a price variance for fixed factory overhead, it is determined much more easily than the price variances for the three variable production costs.

Second, there is never any quantity variance for fixed factory overhead, because fixed factory overhead is not affected by activity levels.

**Figure 2** Budgeted Fixed Factory Overhead

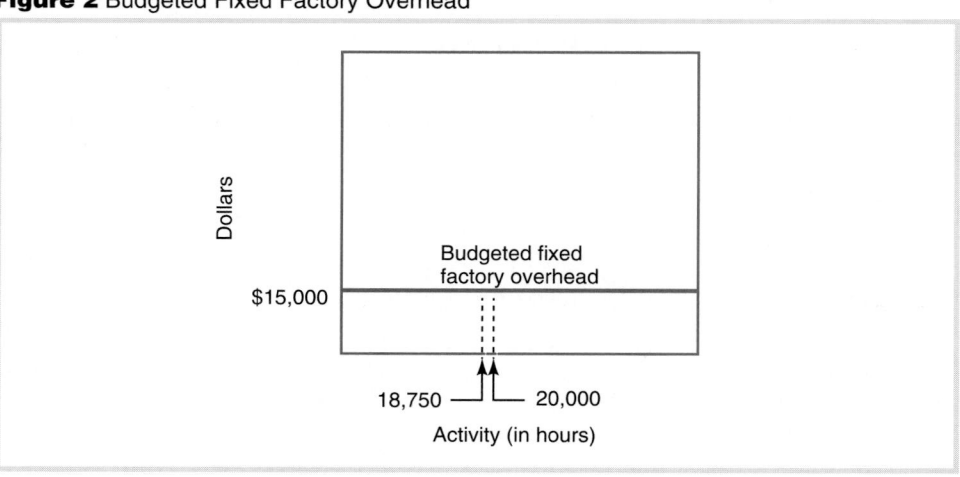

Third, there is a new variance to introduce—which exists only for fixed factory overhead. It is called the *production volume variance*. We will discuss this new variance after we have finished discussing the price and quantity variances.

The fixed factory overhead for Robinjon is expected to be $15,000 per month. Since total fixed costs are not expected to change in response to changes in activity, this $15,000 is the amount we budget, regardless of activity. Therefore the flexible budget based on the actual hours of 20,000 and the flexible budget based on the standard hours allowed of 18,750 are both the same amount: $15,000. You can see this in Figure 2, which diagrams Robinjon's budgeted fixed factory overhead. You can also see how this looks in columns 2 and 3 of the performance report in Exhibit 3.

If the hours in our performance report were 15,000 or 21,000 or 28,000 instead, the flexible budget for fixed factory overhead would still be $15,000. When we subtract the budgeted fixed factory overhead (column 2) in Exhibit 3 from the actual costs incurred (column 1), we get a favorable **fixed factory overhead price variance** (or **spending variance**) of $100:

$$\text{Fixed factory overhead price variance} = \text{actual fixed overhead costs incurred} - \text{budgeted fixed factory overhead costs}$$

$$= \$14,900 - \$15,000$$

$$= \$100 \text{ F}$$

This means that we actually spent $100 less in January than we expected to.

Notice that we did not calculate the fixed overhead price variance in the same way as we did the variable overhead price variance (difference in actual and standard rate per hour × actual hours worked). Not only didn't we do it this way in Exhibit 3, we will never do it this way—because the price variance for fixed factory overhead is not affected by the number of actual hours that we use.

Now look at columns 2 and 3 in Exhibit 3. Since the amount of fixed factory overhead that we budget for the actual hours and the standard hours are (and will always be) the same, there is never a quantity variance for fixed factory overhead. And

---

**Exhibit 3** Three-Column Analysis for Fixed Factory Overhead
Based on actual production of 12,500 units

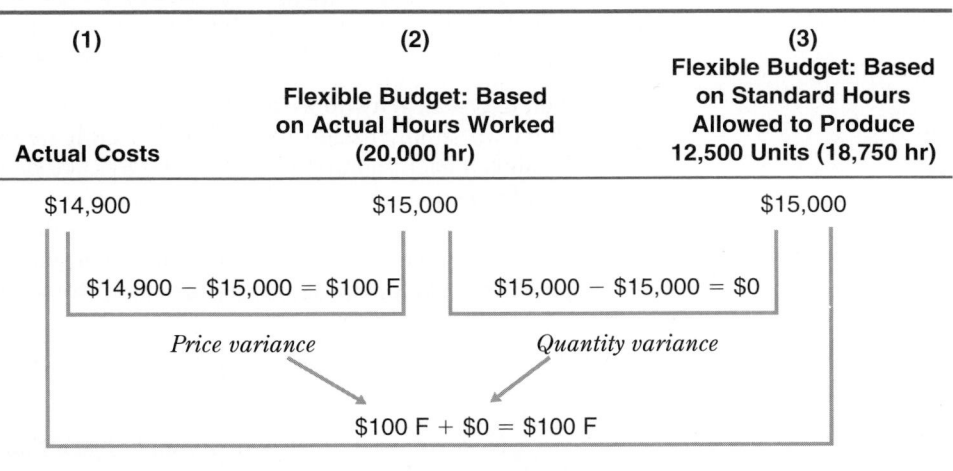

| (1) | (2) | (3) |
|---|---|---|
| | | **Flexible Budget: Based on Standard Hours Allowed to Produce** |
| | **Flexible Budget: Based on Actual Hours Worked** | |
| **Actual Costs** | **(20,000 hr)** | **12,500 Units (18,750 hr)** |
| $14,900 | $15,000 | $15,000 |

$14,900 − $15,000 = $100 F      $15,000 − $15,000 = $0

*Price variance*                    *Quantity variance*

$100 F + $0 = $100 F

*Total flexible budget variance*

since the quantity variance is always zero, the total **flexible budget variance** (or **controllable variance**) for fixed factory overhead will always equal its price variance:

$$\text{Total flexible budget variance for fixed factory overhead} = \text{Price variance} + \text{Quantity variance}$$

$$= \$100 \text{ F} + \$0$$

$$= \$100 \text{ F}$$

Learning Objective 5

## Using Standard Costs for Inventory Costing

Calculate the predetermined fixed factory overhead rate, the fixed factory overhead applied, and the fixed factory overhead production volume variance

We discussed in the previous chapter how the use of standard costs and flexible budgets to determine price and quantity variances is an integral part of the control purpose of cost accounting. We also pointed out that standard costs can be used for inventory costing—that the costs we assign to the units produced can be the standard costs of producing them. The standard costs we assign to the units, as their inventoriable costs, are called the *amount applied to production*. The amount applied to production is found by multiplying the standard quantity or hours allowed (or the number of units produced) times the standard rate.

For direct materials, direct labor and variable factory overhead, the amount applied is exactly the same as the flexible budget based on the standard quantity (or hours) allowed. Looking back at Exhibit 1 for variable factory overhead, we see in column 3 that the flexible budget based on the standard hours allowed is $37,500 for variable factory overhead. This amount is also the amount applied to production—that is, it is the costs assigned to the units produced for inventory costing purposes. This one amount, $37,500, therefore serves two different cost accounting purposes. Not only is it the flexible budget—a figure used for control purposes—it is also the standard costs applied—a figure needed for inventory costing purposes.

With fixed factory overhead, we do not use a standard rate for two different purposes. We do not multiply a standard rate per hour by the standard hours to get the flexible budget based on the standard hours allowed. As you can see in Exhibit 3, the fixed overhead budgeted is $15,000 regardless of the level of activity. We do need to use a standard rate for inventory costing purposes however, in order to apply fixed overhead costs to the units being produced.

### The Predetermined Fixed Factory Overhead Rate

You may ask, Why do we need a rate for fixed overhead when the total is fixed? Why don't we simply assign the $15,000 of budgeted fixed overhead costs to the units produced each month? Why can't the $15,000 be the inventoriable costs? These are good questions that deserve good answers.

For the moment, let's assume that we do assign the $15,000 to the units produced each month. That would mean that in January, the $15,000 would become the product costs for the 12,500 units, which would average $1.20 per unit:

$$\frac{\$15,000}{12,500 \text{ units}} = \$1.20/\text{unit}$$

Now suppose the production in February and March is 4,000 and 20,000 units, respectively; then the average costs per unit would be:

$$\frac{\$15,000}{4,000 \text{ units}} = \$3.75/\text{unit in February}$$

$$\frac{\$15,000}{20,000 \text{ units}} = \$.75/\text{unit in March}$$

Depending on the number of units produced, the fixed overhead cost per unit can fluctuate greatly from month to month. And when the overhead costs per unit fluctuate dramatically, we may end up with meaningless monthly income statements.

To avoid these wide swings from month to month, we calculate a predetermined fixed factory overhead rate at the beginning of the year, and we apply fixed overhead to the units produced in each month using this unchanging rate. We calculate this rate, and we apply this rate, for one purpose only: for inventory costing purposes. We never use this rate to determine a price variance or a quantity variance for fixed factory overhead.

The formula to determine the fixed factory overhead rate at the beginning of the year is:

$$\text{Predetermined fixed factory overhead rate} = \frac{\text{budgeted fixed factory overhead for the year}}{\text{estimated activity for the year}}$$

Or we can use the average monthly amounts, which are simply the yearly figures divided by 12:

$$\text{Predetermined fixed factory overhead rate} = \frac{\text{average monthly budgeted fixed factory overhead}}{\text{average monthly estimated activity}}$$

Assume that the monthly budgeted fixed factory overhead is $15,000, that estimated activity averages 15,000 units per month, and that the standard number of

---

**Exhibit 4** Four-Column Analysis for Fixed Factory Overhead
Based on actual production of 12,500 units

| (1) | (2) | (3) | (4) |
|---|---|---|---|
|  | **Flexible Budget: Based on Actual Hours Worked** | **Flexible Budget: Based on Standard Hours Allowed to Produce 12,500** | **Fixed Overhead Applied to 12,500 Units (std. hr ×** |
| **Actual Costs** | **(20,000 hr)** | **Units (18,750 hr)** | **std. rate)** |
| $14,900 | $15,000 | $15,000 | 18,750 × $.66⅔ = $12,500 |

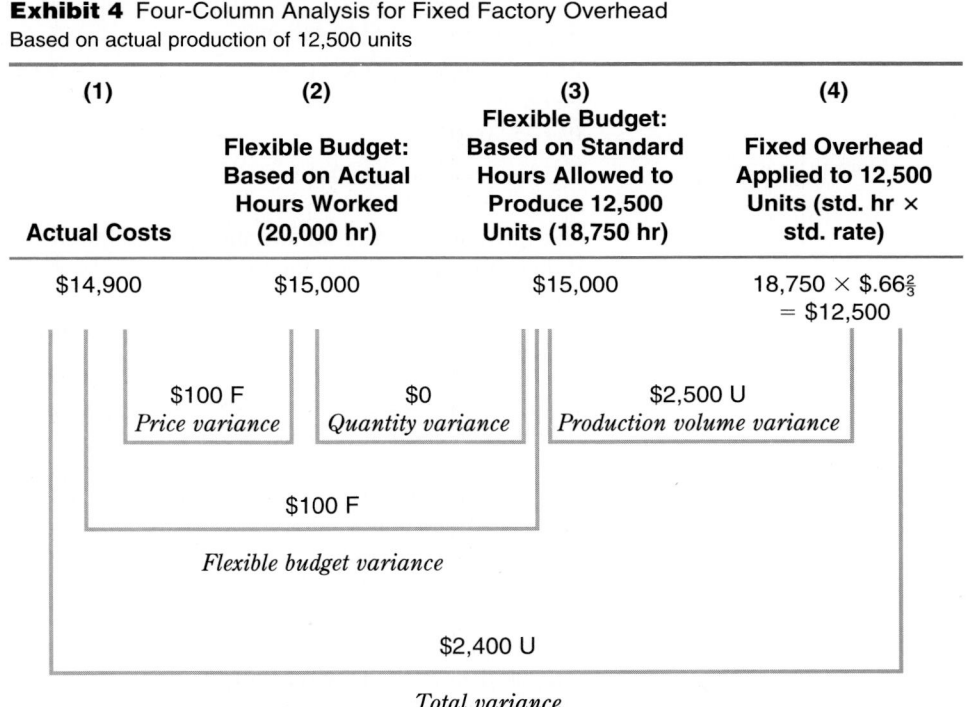

$100 F
*Price variance*

$0
*Quantity variance*

$2,500 U
*Production volume variance*

$100 F
*Flexible budget variance*

$2,400 U

*Total variance*

hours allowed is $1\frac{1}{2}$ hours per unit. The estimated activity for the year averages 22,500 hours per month:

$$1\tfrac{1}{2} \text{ hours/unit} \times 15,000 \text{ units} = 22,500 \text{ standard hours}$$

And the fixed overhead rate per standard hour is:

$$\text{Predetermined fixed factory overhead rate} = \frac{\$15,000}{22,500 \text{ standard hours of estimated activity}}$$

$$= \$.66\tfrac{2}{3} / \text{standard hour}$$

During January, the standard fixed overhead applied to production is:

$$\frac{18,750 \text{ standard}}{\text{hours allowed}} \times \$.66\tfrac{2}{3} / \text{standard hour} = \$12,500 \text{ fixed overhead applied}$$

In order to integrate the fixed overhead applied into the multicolumn analysis, we need to use four columns instead of the three that we have been using. Look at Exhibit 4 and notice that it is exactly the same as Exhibit 3, except that column 4—the fixed overhead applied—has been added.

### The Production Volume Variance

The **fixed overhead production volume variance,** or just **production volume variance,** is the difference between the fixed overhead budgeted (column 3 in Exhibit 4) and the fixed overhead applied. For Robinjon the production volume variance is $2,500, determined as follows:

| | |
|---|---|
| Fixed overhead budgeted................. | $15,000 |
| Fixed overhead applied (18,750 standard hr $\times$ $0.66$\tfrac{2}{3}$) ............................ | 12,500 |
| Production volume variance .............. | $ 2,500 U |

The production volume variance of $2,500 U means that we applied $2,500 fewer dollars to the units produced during the month than we budgeted to spend for the month.

Had we operated at 22,500 standard hours instead of 18,750, the applied would have been $15,000:

$$22,500 \text{ standard hours allowed} \times \$.66\tfrac{2}{3} \text{ per hour} = \$15,000$$

and there would have been no production volume variance:

| | |
|---|---|
| Fixed overhead budgeted.................... | $15,000 |
| Fixed overhead applied ..................... | 15,000 |
| Production volume variance................. | -0- |

When the standard hours allowed for current production are exactly the same as the expected level of activity, then we have fully utilized our capacity and there is no production volume variance.

The reason Robinjon had a production volume variance is that it produced less than expected for the month. It had some **idle capacity,** meaning that it underutilized its available capacity, which is unfavorable. The production volume variance represents the fixed costs associated with the capacity of the plant that was idle—that is, was not used productively.

If Robinjon's production had been greater than its original expectations, there would be a favorable production volume variance, because its capacity would have been used more productively than it had hoped for. When production exceeds expectations, we refer to this situation as being **over capacity.**

Since the production volume variance represents the fixed costs associated with the idle (or over) capacity, a second way to calculate the variance is to determine the amount of idle (or over) capacity, and then multiply this amount by the fixed overhead cost associated with each hour. For Robinjon, it would be:

$$\begin{array}{l}\textbf{Fixed overhead} \\ \textbf{production volume =} \\ \textbf{variance}\end{array} \quad \begin{array}{c}\textbf{idle (or over)} \\ \textbf{capacity}\end{array} \times \begin{array}{c}\textbf{fixed} \\ \textbf{overhead rate} \\ \textbf{per hour}\end{array}$$

$$= \begin{array}{c}\textbf{standard hours} \\ \textbf{allowed less estimated} \\ \textbf{hours of activity}\end{array} \times \begin{array}{c}\textbf{fixed} \\ \textbf{overhead rate} \\ \textbf{per hour}\end{array}$$

$$= (18{,}750 - 22{,}500) \times \$.66\tfrac{2}{3}$$

$$= 3{,}750 \times \$.66\tfrac{2}{3} = \$2{,}500\ U$$

The total variance for fixed factory overhead is the sum of the flexible budget variance and the production volume variance. For Robinjon, the total variance is:

$$\begin{array}{l}\textbf{Total variance} \\ \textbf{for fixed factory =} \\ \textbf{overhead}\end{array} \quad \begin{array}{c}\textbf{flexible} \\ \textbf{budget} \\ \textbf{variance}\end{array} + \begin{array}{c}\textbf{production} \\ \textbf{volume} \\ \textbf{variance}\end{array}$$

$$= \$100\ F + \$2{,}500\ U = \$2{,}400\ U$$

The total variance for fixed factory overhead is the sum of the flexible budget variance and the production volume variance. For Robinjon, the total variance is

$$\begin{array}{l}\textbf{Total variance} \\ \textbf{for fixed factory =} \\ \textbf{overhead}\end{array} \quad \begin{array}{c}\textbf{flexible} \\ \textbf{budget} \\ \textbf{variance}\end{array} + \begin{array}{c}\textbf{production} \\ \textbf{volume} \\ \textbf{variance}\end{array}$$

$$= \$100\ F + \$2{,}500\ U = \$2{,}400\ U$$

For the variable production costs (direct materials, direct labor, and variable factory overhead), the total variance equals the flexible budget variance. This is because there is never a production volume variance for any costs that are variable.

The total variance for fixed factory overhead is also referred to as the amount of underapplied (or overapplied) overhead. The total variance of $2,400 U is the difference between the actual costs of $14,900 (column 1) and the applied costs (column 4) of $12,500. In this case, since the applied is less than the actual, you would refer to the difference as **underapplied overhead,** which is unfavorable.

## Graphic Approach for Fixed Factory Overhead

The graph for fixed factory overhead displayed in Figure 3 shows separate lines for the fixed overhead budgeted and the fixed overhead applied. The budget line is the horizontal line representing an unchanging $15,000 at all levels of activity; the applied line starts at the origin and slopes upward and to the right. Each point on the applied line is determined by multiplying the fixed factory overhead rate of $.66 2/3 per hour times the standard hours allowed. For the current month the standard hours allowed were 18,750, so the amount applied for fixed factory overhead is $12,500 (18,750 hours × $.66 2/3 per hour). The vertical distance from this point on the applied line to the horizontal line is the production volume variance—$2,500 U ($15,000 − $12,500).

If the standard hours allowed had been 22,500 instead of 18,750, the fixed factory overhead applied would have been $15,000 (22,500 hours × $.66 2/3 per hour). In this case, the applied and the budgeted fixed factory overhead would both be $15,000 and there would be a zero production volume variance. There would be no vertical distance from the budget to the applied line.

Finally, if the standard hours allowed had been 30,000 instead of 18,750, the fixed factory overhead applied would have been $20,000 (30,000 hours × $.66 2/3 per hour). In this case, the production volume variance would be $5,000 F ($20,000 − $15,000) − represented by the vertical distance from the applied line ($20,000) to the horizontal line ($15,000).

The actual costs incurred for fixed factory overhead, $14,900, are represented by the point directly above the actual hours of 20,000. The vertical distance from this point to the horizontal line represents the fixed overhead price variance. In Figure 3 you can see it as $100 F ($14,900 − $15,000).

**Figure 3** Graphic Approach for Fixed Factory Overhead

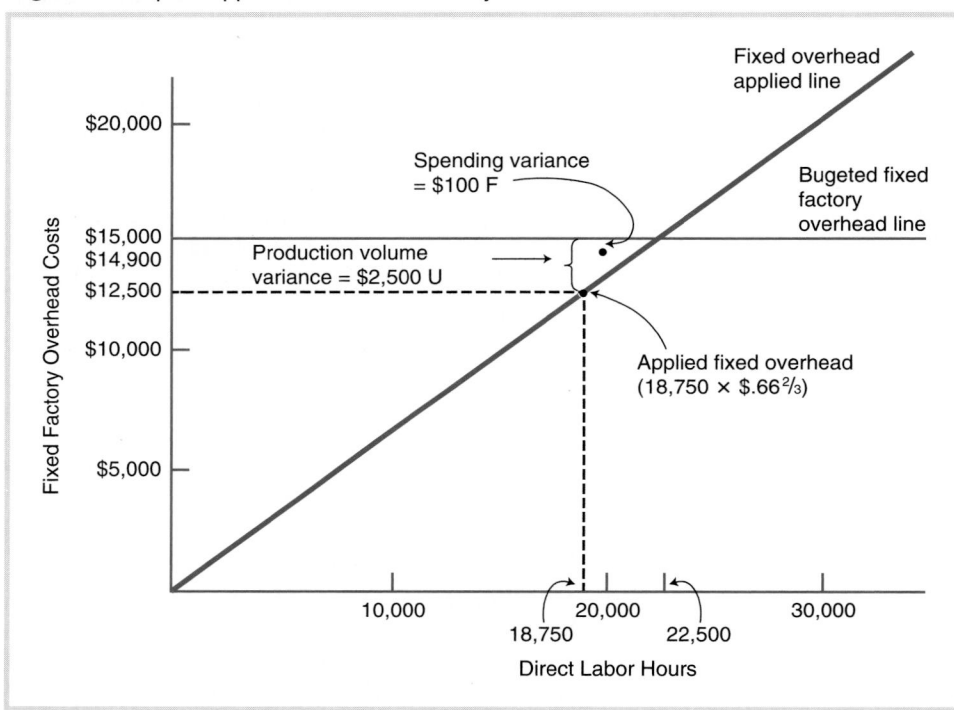

1. How do you determine the budgeted fixed factory overhead at different levels of activity?
2. The fixed overhead quantity variance is always what amount? Why?
3. How and when do you calculate the predetermined fixed factory overhead rate?
4. What is the fixed factory overhead production volume variance? How is it determined?

## SUMMARY

• There are two types of standards — **price standards** and **quantity standards** — for each variable production cost. When actual results differ from the standards, there is a **price variance** and a **quantity variance.** The sum of the price variance and the quantity variance is the **flexible budget variance.**

- The price variance is calculated for variable factory overhead as follows:

$$\text{Price variance} = \text{actual hours} \times \begin{array}{c}\textbf{difference between actual}\\ \textbf{and standard costs per}\\ \textbf{unit of input}\end{array}$$

And the quantity variance is calculated as follows:

$$\text{Quantity variance} = \begin{array}{c}\textbf{difference between actual}\\ \textbf{hours used and}\\ \textbf{standard hours allowed}\end{array} \times \begin{array}{c}\textbf{standard}\\ \textbf{cost per unit}\\ \textbf{of input}\end{array}$$

- The price variance for fixed factory overhead is simply the difference between the actual costs and the budgeted costs. There is never a quantity variance for fixed factory overhead.
- There will be a variance for fixed factory overhead that we do not have for any other cost; this is the **fixed overhead production volume variance**. This **production volume variance** is determined in the following manner:

$$\begin{array}{c}\textbf{Production}\\ \textbf{volume variance}\end{array} = \begin{array}{c}\textbf{budgeted fixed}\\ \textbf{factory overhead}\end{array} - \begin{array}{c}\textbf{applied fixed}\\ \textbf{factory overhead}\end{array}$$

The fixed factory overhead applied is found by multiplying the predetermined fixed overhead rate times the standard hours allowed. The predetermined rate is determined as follows:

$$\begin{array}{c}\textbf{Predetermined}\\ \textbf{fixed factory}\\ \textbf{overhead rate}\end{array} = \frac{\textbf{budgeted fixed factory overhead}}{\textbf{estimated activity}}$$

The production volume variance can also be determined as follows:

$$\begin{array}{c}\textbf{Production}\\ \textbf{volume}\\ \textbf{variance}\end{array} = \begin{array}{c}\textbf{standard hours allowed}\\ \textbf{less estimated hours of}\\ \textbf{activity}\end{array} \times \begin{array}{c}\textbf{fixed factory}\\ \textbf{overhead rate}\\ \textbf{per hour}\end{array}$$

## 6 KEY TERMS

**Fixed factory overhead price variance**
The difference between the actual fixed factory overhead costs and the budgeted fixed factory overhead costs. Also called the **controllable variance (flexible budget variance)** or the **spending variance.**

**Fixed overhead production volume variance**
The difference between the budgeted fixed factory overhead and the applied fixed factory overhead (where the applied is the standard hours allowed times the standard fixed factory overhead rate per hour). Also called simply **production volume variance.**

**Idle capacity**
Production capacity that is available but not utilized.

**Over capacity**
A situation in which production exceeds expectations.

**Production volume variance**
See **fixed overhead production volume variance.**

**Underapplied overhead**
A situation in which the overhead applied is less than the actual overhead costs incurred. When the overhead applied is greater than the actual overhead, the overhead is said to be overapplied.

**Variable overhead price variance**
The actual hours worked multiplied by the difference between the actual and standard variable overhead rates per hour. Also called the **variable overhead spending variance.**

**Variable overhead quantity variance**
The difference between the actual hours worked and the standard hours allowed multiplied by the standard variable overhead rate per hour. Also known as the **variable overhead efficiency variance.**

## DEMONSTRATION PROBLEM (EXPANDED FROM PREVIOUS CHAPTER)

The controller of Wright's California Surfboard Company has recently developed the following standards for the production of one of its most popular models:

Direct materials: 80 lb/surfboard at $.50/lb = $40.00/surfboard

Direct labor: 2 hr/surfboard at $8.00/hr = $16.00/surfboard

Variable factory overhead: 2 hr/surfboard at $2.00/hr = $4.00/surfboard

Fixed factory overhead: $4,500/month

During January, 225 surfboards were budgeted for production, but only 200 were produced. The average monthly activity (used to determine the fixed factory overhead rate) was the same number of units budgeted for this month: 225 surfboards. The actual results related to this production were:

Direct materials: 19,000 lb purchased at $.52/lb
16,250 lb used

Direct labor: 425 hr at $8.15/hr

Variable overhead: $765

Fixed overhead: $4,700

**Required:**

Compute the individual and flexible budget variances for variable and fixed factory overhead. Also, determine the production volume variance and total variance for fixed factory overhead. Indicate whether each variance is favorable or unfavorable.

### ■ Solution to Demonstration Problem

Variable Factory Overhead
Based on actual production of 200 surfboards

| (1) | (2) | (3) |
|---|---|---|
| | **Flexible Budget: Based on Actual** | **Flexible Budget: Based on Standard Hours Allowed to** |
| **Actual Costs** | **Hours Worked** | **Produce 200 Surfboards** |
| Actual Hours × Actual Rate per Hour | Actual Hours × Standard Rate per Hour | Standard Hours Allowed × Standard Rate per Hour |
| 425 × $1.80 = $765 | 425 × $2.00 = $850 | (200 × 2) × $2.00 400 × $2.00 = $800 |

425 × ($1.80 − $2.00)
= 425 × $.20 = $85 F

(425 − 400) × $2.00
= 25 × $2.00 = 50 U

*Price variance*          *Quantity variance*

$85 F + $50 U = $35 F

*Flexible budget variance*

CONTROLLING COSTS WITH FLEXIBLE BUDGETS, STANDARD COSTS, AND VARIANCES—PART TWO

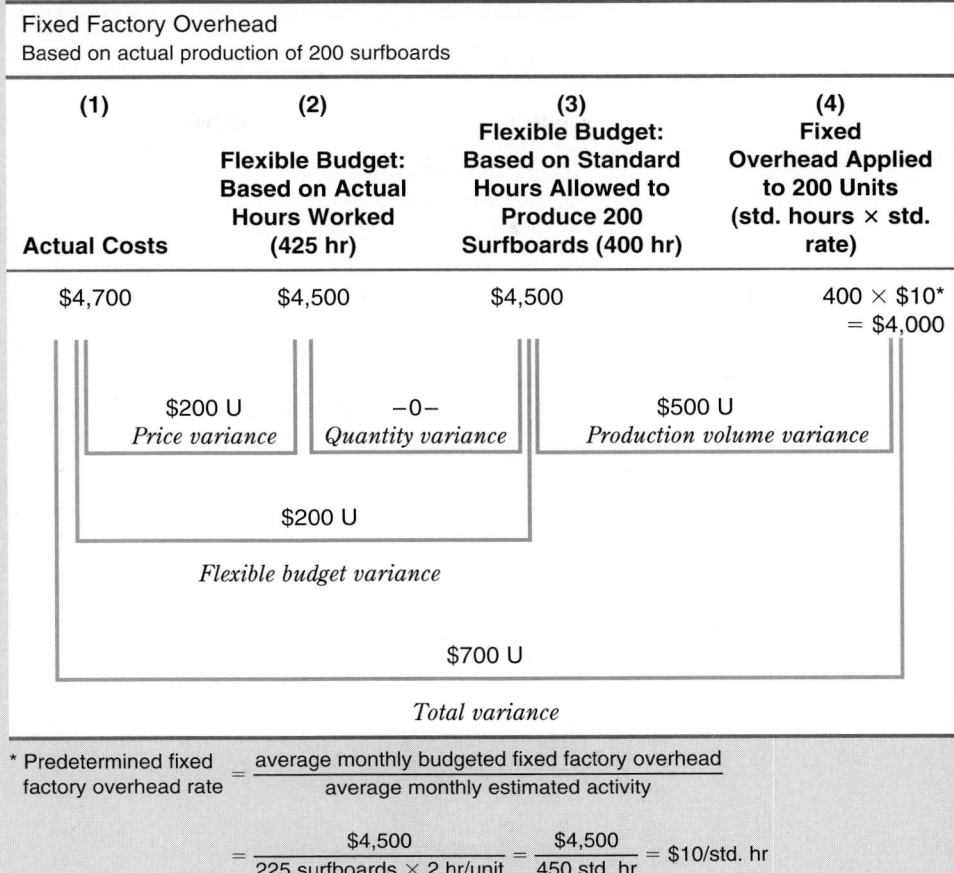

**Fixed Factory Overhead**
Based on actual production of 200 surfboards

| (1)<br><br><br><br><br>Actual Costs | (2)<br>Flexible Budget:<br>Based on Actual<br>Hours Worked<br>(425 hr) | (3)<br>Flexible Budget:<br>Based on Standard<br>Hours Allowed to<br>Produce 200<br>Surfboards (400 hr) | (4)<br>Fixed<br>Overhead Applied<br>to 200 Units<br>(std. hours × std.<br>rate) |
|---|---|---|---|
| $4,700 | $4,500 | $4,500 | 400 × $10*<br>= $4,000 |

$200 U
*Price variance*

−0−
*Quantity variance*

$500 U
*Production volume variance*

$200 U

*Flexible budget variance*

$700 U

*Total variance*

$$* \text{ Predetermined fixed} \atop \text{factory overhead rate} = \frac{\text{average monthly budgeted fixed factory overhead}}{\text{average monthly estimated activity}}$$

$$= \frac{\$4,500}{225 \text{ surfboards} \times 2 \text{ hr/unit}} = \frac{\$4,500}{450 \text{ std. hr}} = \$10/\text{std. hr}$$

## QUESTIONS FOR REVIEW AND FURTHER THOUGHT

### REVIEW QUESTIONS

1. How do the price and quantity variances for direct labor differ from those for variable overhead?

2. How is the fixed factory overhead applied determined for a period?

3. Explain why the production volume variance is unfavorable when the budgeted fixed factory overhead is greater than the fixed factory overhead applied.

4. List some possible reasons for each of the following variances:
   a. Variable overhead price variance
   b. Variable overhead quantity variance
   c. Fixed overhead production volume variance

5. Why is there never a quantity variance for fixed factory overhead?

6. What is the difference between fixed factory overhead budgeted and fixed factory overhead applied?

7. Explain why a department might have a fixed factory overhead production volume variance.

## QUESTIONS FOR FURTHER THOUGHT

1. When direct labor hours is the cost driver for all factory overhead costs, will the sign (favorable or unfavorable) of the direct labor quantity variance always be the same as the sign of the variable overhead quantity variance? Explain.

2. When direct labor hours is the cost driver for all factory overhead costs, will the sign (favorable or unfavorable) of the direct labor price variance always be the same as the sign of the variable overhead price variance? Explain.

3. The price variances for variable and fixed overhead are calculated in exactly the same way. Do you agree? Discuss.

4. Why is the price variance equal to the flexible budget variance for fixed factory overhead?

5. Why is the flexible budget variance equal to the total variance for variable factory overhead but not for fixed factory overhead?

6. In the three-column approach to variance analysis, the flexible budget for variable overhead for the units produced is exactly the same as the flexible budget based on the standard hours allowed, which is exactly the same as the amount applied. Explain how these three elements can all be the same.

7. For each of the following variable overhead costs, identify an alternative to direct labor hours as a possible measure of activity.
   a. Payroll taxes
   b. Material handling costs
   c. Costs of testing finished product for potential defects

8. Fixed overhead applied represents the amount of fixed overhead that should have been incurred during a period of time. Comment.

## OBJECTIVE ASSIGNMENT

*True/False*   Indicate whether each statement below is true or false by placing a T or an F in the space provided.

_____ 1. The mechanics of calculating the variable overhead quantity variance are nearly identical to those for direct labor.

_____ 2. As long as direct labor hours is the cost driver for variable overhead costs, whenever the quantity variance for direct labor is favorable the quantity variance for variable overhead will also be favorable.

_____ 3. The variable overhead applied will always be equal to the flexible budget for variable overhead based on the standard hours allowed.

_____ 4. There will never be a production volume variance for fixed factory overhead.

_____ 5. The fixed factory overhead quantity variance is always zero.

*Multiple-Choice*   Select the best choice to complete each statement or answer each question below. Write the letter corresponding to your choice in the space provided.

_____ 1. Which of the following could be a cost driver for variable overhead costs?
   a. Direct labor hours
   b. Machine hours
   c. Hours of inspection time
   d. All of the above

_____ 2. Which of the following variances below would least likely be controllable by a production superintendent?
   a. Direct materials price variance
   b. Variable overhead quantity variance
   c. Variable overhead price variance
   d. Fixed overhead price variance

____ 3. Which of the following variances would not be calculated using the same basic formula?
  a. Direct materials price variance
  b. Direct labor price variance
  c. Variable factory overhead price variance
  d. Fixed factory overhead price variance

____ 4. During January, Burkett Company produced 4,000 units, and used 23,000 hours to produce them. The standards for variable overhead were $4 per hour and 6 hours per unit. The actual cost per hour was $4.25. What was the variable overhead quantity variance?
  a. $4,000 F        c. $4,000 U
  b. $4,250 F        d. $250 U

____ 5. During June, Horsey Company produced 400 units, requiring 2,100 machine hours and $10,600 of variable overhead. The standard time to produce a unit is 5 machine hours and the standard rate is $5 per machine hour. What is the flexible budget for the standard hours allowed for June?
  a. $10,500        c. $10,000
  b. $10,600        d. $10,095

____ 6. Refer to the facts provided in #5 above. How much variable factory overhead would be applied to June's production?
  a. $10,500        c. $10,000
  b. $10,600        d. $10,095

____ 7. Which of the variances below is calculated only for fixed factory overhead?
  a. Price variance
  b. Quantity variance
  c. Flexible budget variance
  d. Production volume variance

____ 8. Which of the following variances is always zero?
  a. Direct materials price variance
  b. Direct labor quantity variance
  c. Variable factory overhead flexible budget variance
  d. Fixed factory overhead quantity variance

____ 9. The Gringo Company estimated its fixed factory overhead for the year to be $120,000 ($10,000 per month), and its direct labor hours to be 20,000. The standard time allowed to produce each unit was 2 hours. During January, 800 units were produced, which required 1,700 hours of direct labor. What amount of fixed factory overhead would be budgeted for January?
  a. $10,200        c. $10,600
  b. $10,000        d. $10,800

____ 10. Refer to the facts provided in #9 above. How much fixed factory overhead would be applied to January's production?
  a. $10,800        c. $10,600
  b. $9,600         d. $10,200

## EXERCISES

3† **Exercise 1:** Preparing a Performance Report for Factory Overhead Costs

The Savage Company uses flexible budgets and standard costs to help managers plan and control its operations. The standard for its variable overhead costs is $2.00 per unit. In addition, Savage budgets its fixed factory overhead costs at $40,000 per month.

† The numbers in the margin refer to the Learning Objectives.

During August 1997, Savage Company produced 12,000 units and incurred the following actual costs:

| | |
|---|---|
| Variable factory overhead.................... | 22,000 |
| Fixed factory overhead..................... | 41,000 |
| | $63,000 |

a. Prepare flexible budgets for each overhead cost for 10,000 units, 15,000 units, and 20,000 units.

b. Prepare a three-column performance report for August. In the first column, enter the actual costs. In the third column, prepare the appropriate flexible budget. In the second column, determine the flexible budget variances.

▶ *(Check Figure: a. Budget for 20,000 units = $81,000)*

## 2  Exercise 2: Analyzing Variances for Direct Labor and Variable Overhead

The Puritan Company makes a product expected to require 6 hours to produce, at expected rates per hour of $7.50 for direct labor and $3.75 for variable overhead. During the month of January, 600 units were produced although 700 units had been budgeted. The actual conversion costs were:

| | |
|---|---|
| Direct labor (3,200 hr)...................... | $24,160 |
| Variable overhead......................... | $11,904 |

Determine the price, quantity, and flexible budget variances for each of the conversion costs. Indicate with a U or an F whether each variance is unfavorable or favorable.

▶ *(Check Figure: Variable overhead quantity variance = $1,500 F)*

## 3  4  Exercise 3: Determining Variances for Variable and Fixed Overhead

The Dried Lettuce Company uses the following standards and budgets to control its overhead costs.

| | |
|---|---|
| Variable overhead .......... | 4 hours per unit @ $6/hour |
| Fixed overhead .................. | $25,000 per month |

During December, 1,000 units were produced, taking 3,700 hours. The actual overhead costs were $47,700, $25,500 of which were fixed.

Calculate the price, quantity, and flexible budget variances for variable overhead and for fixed overhead. Specify whether each variance is favorable or unfavorable.

▶ *(Check Figure: Fixed overhead price variance = $500 U)*

## 3  Exercise 4: Calculating Variance for Different Variable Overhead Costs

The standard time per unit for all variable overhead costs is 2 hours. The standard costs per unit for three different variable overhead costs is as follows:

| | |
|---|---|
| Supplies .................................... | $1.50/hr |
| Utilities .................................... | .75/hr |
| Maintenance............................... | 2.00/hr |

The actual costs of producing 10,000 units (taking 19,000 hours) during March were:

| | |
|---|---|
| Supplies .................................... | $32,500 |
| Utilities..................................... | 14,750 |
| Maintenance ................................ | 41,340 |

Calculate the price, quantity, and flexible budget variances for each variable overhead cost. Specify whether each variance is favorable or unfavorable.

▶ *(Check Figure: Price variance for supplies = $4,000 U)*

3   **Exercise 5:** Determining Unknowns from a Performance Report for Variable Overhead

During August 1997, the Shinpaugh Corporation produced 10,500 units, exactly the quantity that had been budgeted for the month. The standards used by Shinpaugh to help control variable overhead costs are as follows:

> Variable overhead: 2 hr/unit at $1.75/hr

The performance report for August spotlighted the following variances:

| | |
|---|---:|
| Variable overhead: | |
|    Price variance .......................................................... | $5,000 F |
|    Quantity variance........................................................ | 1,750 F |

Determine the following:

a. The actual hours
b. The actual cost per hour

▶ *(Check Figure: b. $1.50)*

3   **Exercise 6:** Determining Unknowns on the Basis of Variances

Parrott Corporation uses a standard cost system to control its variable overhead costs. During the month of July, the variable overhead costs were $120,000 (24,000 hours). Five thousand units were produced during this month. The variable overhead price variance was $12,000 U, and the variable overhead quantity variance was $4,500 U. Determine the following:

a. Standard rate per hour
b. Standard hours per unit

▶ *(Check Figure: a. $4.50)*

4   5   **Exercise 7:** Determining the Variances for Fixed Factory Overhead

Schleman Faucets, which produces washerless faucets, has determined that the standard time to produce a faucet is 30 minutes. During March, Schleman produced 80,000 faucets, which was 40,000 faucets below the average monthly estimated activity. Schleman budgeted its fixed costs to be $60,000 per month, but actually incurred $56,000 during March.

Determine the price variance, quantity variance, and production volume variance for fixed overhead.

▶ *(Check Figure: Production volume variance = $20,000 U)*

4   5   **Exercise 8:** Analyzing Fixed Overhead

During January 1998, the actual fixed costs for the assembly department of Swing Bicycle Company were $66,000. At the beginning of the year, Swing had budgeted its annual fixed costs to be $720,000 ($60,000 per month). In addition, Swing's standard cost system specified that 2 hours be used per unit. During January, 6,600 hours were employed to produce 3,000 units. The expected activity for Swing is 30,000 units per year. Calculate the following variances for Swing Bicycle Company:

a. Fixed overhead price variance
b. Fixed overhead quantity variance
c. Fixed overhead flexible budget variance
d. Fixed overhead production volume variance

▶ *(Check Figure: Production volume variance = $12,000 F)*

4  5  **Exercise 9:** Determining Unknowns for Fixed Factory Overhead

Posse Company applies fixed factory overhead to its products using a predetermined rate of $4 per direct labor hour. During November, Posse's performance report showed the following variances:

Fixed overhead price variance . . . . . . . . . . . . . . .  $4,000 U
Fixed overhead production volume variance . . . .    8,000 U

The actual fixed overhead costs incurred during the month were $44,000.

a. How much fixed factory overhead was budgeted for November?
b. How much fixed factory overhead was applied during November?
c. How many standard hours were allowed for the production in November?

▶ (Check Figure: b. $32,000)

## PROBLEMS: SET A

3  4†  **Problem A1:** Preparing Flexible Budgets before Production and after Production Is Completed

The Cawthon Company, a manufacturer of pencil sharpeners, uses flexible budgets and standard costs to control its operations. Cawthon expects its production and sales in January to be 20,000 units and selected production costs to be as follows:

Supplies . . . . . . . . . . . . . . . . . . . . . . . . . . . . . . . . .    4,800
Utilities. . . . . . . . . . . . . . . . . . . . . . . . . . . . . . . . . .    2,400
Rent. . . . . . . . . . . . . . . . . . . . . . . . . . . . . . . . . . . .    1,200
                                                                             $8,400

**Required:**

1. Prepare flexible budgets that might have been prepared at the beginning of the month for the following levels of production: 17,000 units, 21,000 units, and 25,000 units.
2. The actual units produced during January were 19,000, and the actual hours worked were 117,000. The standard time to produce one unit was 6 hours, and the actual costs incurred were as follows:

Supplies . . . . . . . . . . . . . . . . . . . . . . . . . . . . . . . . .    3,510
Utilities. . . . . . . . . . . . . . . . . . . . . . . . . . . . . . . . . .    2,457
Rent. . . . . . . . . . . . . . . . . . . . . . . . . . . . . . . . . . . .    1,400
                                                                             $7,367

Prepare a performance report for January that lists each of the three production costs. The report should have six columns: (1) actual costs; (2) price variance; (3) flexible budget based on the actual hours worked; (4) quantity variance; (5) flexible budget based on the standard hours allowed; and (6) flexible budget variance.

▶ (Check Figure: 2. Flexible budget based on actual hours worked = $8,220)

3  4  5  **Problem A2:** Determining Price and Quantity Variances for All Production Costs

Snowbird Company, a manufacturer of ski jackets, uses standard costs to help control its operations. The standard conversion costs of producing one jacket are:

Direct labor: $1\frac{1}{2}$ hr/jacket at $10/hr
Variable overhead: $1\frac{1}{2}$ hr/jacket at $15/hr
Fixed overhead: $10,000/month

† The numbers in the margin refer to the Learning Objectives.

During March, 5,000 jackets were budgeted for production (which was the level of activity used to determine the fixed overhead rate), but only 4,000 jackets were actually produced. The actual costs for March were as follows:

Direct labor; 6,200 hr worked: $61,628
Variable overhead: $96,720
Fixed overhead: $10,700

**Required:**

Compute the individual and flexible budget variances for each production cost. Indicate whether each variance is favorable or unfavorable. Also determine the fixed overhead production volume variance.

▶ *(Check Figure: Variable overhead quantity variance = $3,000 U*
*Fixed overhead production volume variance = $2,000 U)*

3 4 5 **Problem A3:** Determining Variances for All Production Costs

Standard costs for the Flying High Flagpole Company have recently been developed by the company controller with the help of a management consulting firm. The standards are the following:

Direct materials:
   (100 lb/flagpole @ $.05/lb) . . . . . . . .    $5 per flagpole
Direct labor:
   (1 hr/flagpole @ $2/hr) . . . . . . . . . .    2 per flagpole
Variable overhead:
   (1 hr/flagpole @ $1/hr) . . . . . . . . . .    1 per flagpole
Fixed overhead . . . . . . . . . . . . . . . . . .   12,000 per month

During December 1,200 flagpoles were budgeted for production (1,200 is also the level used for determining the fixed overhead rate) but only 1,000 were produced. The actual results related to this production were as follows:

Direct Materials. . . . . . . . .   104,000 pounds purchased @
                                         $.045 per pound
                                    110,000 pounds used
Direct labor . . . . . . . . . . . .   1,120 hours @ $2.075 per hour
Variable overhead. . . . . . .   $1,140
Fixed overhead . . . . . . . . .   $12,850

**Required:**

Compute the individual and flexible budget variances for each production cost. Indicate whether each variance is favorable for unfavorable. Also determine the production volume variance for fixed factory overhead.

▶ *(Check Figure: Direct materials price variance = $520 F)*

3 4 5 **Problem A4:** Doing Overhead Analysis With Mixed Costs

On the first day of January, Coby Stephens, the chief cost accountant with the Cincinnati Automotive Parts, gave a 1-month notice and said he'd be willing to train his replacement before he left. His boss, Margo Gunn, was so angry at Coby that she fired him on the spot. It took a month before Margo was able to hire a replacement, Bernie Dawg, to take Coby's place. One of the first things that Margo wanted from Bernie was a performance report for the overhead costs within the machining department for January. Bernie looked through the files that Coby had not thrown away and found the following flexible budgets, which Coby had prepared for January before he had left:

Possible levels of activity:

| | | |
|---|---|---|
| Units . . . . . . . . . . . . . . . . . . . . . . | 1,000 | 1,500 |
| Machine hours . . . . . . . . . . . . . . | 4,000 | 6,000 |

Overhead costs:

| | | |
|---|---|---|
| Salaries. . . . . . . . . . . . . . . . . . . . | $40,000 | $50,000 |
| Utilities . . . . . . . . . . . . . . . . . . . | 1,000 | 1,400 |
| Supplies . . . . . . . . . . . . . . . . . . . | 300 | 400 |
| Indirect materials . . . . . . . . . . . . | 4,000 | 6,000 |
| Depreciation. . . . . . . . . . . . . . . . . | 5,000 | 5,000 |
| Payroll taxes. . . . . . . . . . . . . . . . | 6,000 | 7,500 |
| | $56,300 | $70,300 |

Next, Bernie learned that 1,200 units were actually produced during the month and that the actual overhead costs totaled $64,000. In addition, he found out that there were 5,000 mchine hours used in January. The average estimated monthly level of activity is 1,250 units.

**Required:**

Prepare a condensed peformance report (not for each individual variance) for January that includes the following variances:
Price variance
Quantity variance
Flexible budget variance
Production volume variance
Total variance

▶ (Check Figure: Production volume variance = $1,132 U)

3  4  5   **Problem A5:** Determining Unknown Values

The Open Book Company uses standard costs and flexible budgets to help in the control of its operations. During October 1997, the company produced 20,000 units, taking 90,000 hours.

**Required:**

1. The standard variable overhead rate is $1 per hour; the average rate paid was $1.02; and the standard time to produce a unit is 4 hours. Determine the price variance, the quantity variance, and the flexible budget variance for variable overhead.

2. The fixed factory overhead flexible budget variance was $10,000 F. What were the actual fixed factory overhead costs for the month if the budgeted fixed factory overhead is $100,000? What where the applied, if the production volume variance is $20,000 U?

▶ (Check Figure: 2. Actual = $90,000)

3   **Problem A6:** Doing Variance Analysis with Alternative Activity Bases

The Callie Company uses standard costs and flexible budgets to assist in the control of its overhead costs. Prior to 1997, all variable overhead costs were assumed to vary in close relation to direct labor hours. Callie decided in 1997 that several overhead costs were more closely related to alternative activity bases and that direct labor was no longer appropriate for several costs. Starting in 1997, the standards for three variable overhead costs were as follows:

Indirect labor costs: 10% of standard direct labor costs
Machine maintenance costs: 2 hr of machine time/unit produced at $6/machine hr
Inspection costs: $\frac{1}{2}$ hour/unit inspected at $10/hour

In addition, the standard time for direct labor was 1 hour per unit, and the standard rate was $8 per hour. During January, Callie had the following actual results:

| | |
|---|---:|
| Units produced . . . . . . . . . . . . . . . . . . . . . . . . . . . . . . . . . . . . . . . . . . . . . . . . . . | 10,000 |
| Direct labor: | |
| Actual hours worked . . . . . . . . . . . . . . . . . . . . . . . . . . . . . . . . . . . . . . . . . . | 11,000 |
| Costs . . . . . . . . . . . . . . . . . . . . . . . . . . . . . . . . . . . . . . . . . . . . . . . . . . . . . | $87,000 |
| Inspection: | |
| Units. . . . . . . . . . . . . . . . . . . . . . . . . . . . . . . . . . . . . . . . . . . . . . . . . . . . . . | 9,000 |
| Hours. . . . . . . . . . . . . . . . . . . . . . . . . . . . . . . . . . . . . . . . . . . . . . . . . . . . . . | 4,600 |
| Costs . . . . . . . . . . . . . . . . . . . . . . . . . . . . . . . . . . . . . . . . . . . . . . . . . . . . . | $44,000 |
| Machine hours . . . . . . . . . . . . . . . . . . . . . . . . . . . . . . . . . . . . . . . . . . . . . . . | 20,100 |
| Machine maintenance costs. . . . . . . . . . . . . . . . . . . . . . . . . . . . . . . . . . . . . | $121,000 |
| Indirect labor costs . . . . . . . . . . . . . . . . . . . . . . . . . . . . . . . . . . . . . . . . . . . | $8,700 |

**Required:**

Calculate the price, quantity, and flexible budget variances for direct labor and for each of the three variable overhead costs.

▶ *(Check Figure: Price variance for inspection costs = $2,000 F; Quantity variance for machine maintenance costs = $600 U)*

## PROBLEMS: SET B

3† **Problem B1:** Preparing Flexible Budgets before Production and after Production Is Completed

Westcott Company manufactures vitamins and uses flexible budgets and standard costs to control its operations. Westcott expects its production and sales in July to be 60,000 units and selected production costs to be as follows (all the costs are variable):

| | |
|---|---:|
| Indirect labor. . . . . . . . . . . . . . . . . . . . . . . . . . . . . | $120,000 |
| Supplies . . . . . . . . . . . . . . . . . . . . . . . . . . . . . . . . | 6,000 |
| Utilities. . . . . . . . . . . . . . . . . . . . . . . . . . . . . . . . . | 3,000 |
| | $129,000 |

**Required:**

1. Prepare flexible budgets that might have been prepared at the beginning of the month for each of the following levels of production: 45,000 units, 54,000 units, and 66,000 units.
2. The actual units produced during July were 75,000 and the actual hours worked were 156,000. The standard time to produce one unit was 2 hours, and the actual costs incurred were as follows:

| | |
|---|---:|
| Indirect labor. . . . . . . . . . . . . . . . . . . . . . . . . . . . . | $147,000 |
| Supplies . . . . . . . . . . . . . . . . . . . . . . . . . . . . . . . . | 9,000 |
| Utilities. . . . . . . . . . . . . . . . . . . . . . . . . . . . . . . . . | 3,900 |
| | $159,900 |

Prepare a performance report for July that lists each of the three production costs. The report should have six columns: (1) actual costs; (2) price variance; (3) flexible budget based on the actual hours worked; (4) quantity variance; (5) flexible budget based on the standard hours allowed; and (6) flexible budget variance.

▶ *(Check Figure: 2. Flexible budget based on actual hours worked = $167,700)*

† The numbers in the margin refer to the Learning Objectives.

3 4 5 **Problem B2:** Determining Price and Quantity Variances
for Conversion Costs

Altawasatch Company manufactures wall safes and uses standard costs to help control its operations. The standard conversion costs of producing one wall safe are:

> Direct labor: 5 hr/safe at $20/hr
> Variable overhead: 5 hr/safe at $15/hr
> Fixed overhead: $18,000/month

During April, 1,500 safes were budgeted for production (which was the level of activity used to determine the fixed overhead rate), but 2,000 safes were actually produced. The actual costs for April were as follows:

> Direct labor, 10,200 hr worked: $209,610
> Variable overhead: $150,960
> Fixed overhead: $18,700

**Required:**

Compute the individual and flexible budget variances for each production cost. Indicate whether each variance is favorable or unfavorable. Also determine the fixed overhead production volume variance.

▶ *(Check Figure: Variable overhead quantity variance = $3,000 U;*
*Fixed overhead production volume variance = $6,000 F)*

3 4 5 **Problem B3:** Determining Variances for All Production Costs

The Sirrock Company manufactures leather belts and uses standard costs to assist in the control and inventory costing of its operations. The standard costs of producing a leather belt are:

Direct materials (3 lb/belt @ $2/lb) . . . . .   $6 per belt
Direct labor (2 hr/belt @ $5/hr) . . . . . . . .   10 per belt
Variable overhead (2 hr/belt @ $.50/hr) .   1 per belt
Fixed overhead . . . . . . . . . . . . . . . . . . . .   5,000 per month

During February 1,250 belts were budgeted for production (1,250 is also the level used for determining the fixed overhead rate) but only 1,000 were actually produced. The actual results for February were as follows:

Direct materials . . . . . . .   3,500 pounds purchased; $7,350
                                             3,300 pounds used
Direct labor . . . . . . . . . . .   1,900 hours worked; $9,405
Variable overhead . . . . .   $1,140
Fixed overhead. . . . . . . .   $5,200

**Required:**

Compute the individual and flexible budget variances for each production cost. Indicate whether each variance is favorable or unfavorable. Also determine the production volume variance for fixed factory overhead.

▶ *(Check Figure: Direct labor quantity variance = $500 F;*
*Production volume variance = $1,000 U)*

3 4 5 **Problem B4:** Doing Overhead Analysis With Mixed Costs

The Smillee Repair Shop uses standards and flexible budgets to help control its operations. It also determines the overhead cost of each job by applying overhead at a predetermined rate per machine hour. During the last 2 months Smillee had the following activities, budgeted total overhead (mixed costs) and applied total overhead.

|  | June | July |
|---|---|---|
| Repair jobs . . . . . . . . . . . . . . . . . . . . . . . . . . . . . . . . . . . . . . . . . | 23,000 | 27,000 |
| Machine hours |  |  |
|    Actual . . . . . . . . . . . . . . . . . . . . . . . . . . . . . . . . . . . . . . . . . . | 35,000 | 39,600 |
|    Standard . . . . . . . . . . . . . . . . . . . . . . . . . . . . . . . . . . . . . . . | 34,500 | 40,500 |
| Total budgeted overhead |  |  |
|    based on standard hours allowed . . . . . . . . . . . . . . . . . . . . | $87,750 | $ 96,750 |
| Total applied overhead. . . . . . . . . . . . . . . . . . . . . . . . . . . . . . | $86,250 | 101,250 |

In August 30,000 repairs were completed; the actual machine hours used in doing these repairs were 47,000; and the total overhead costs incurred with $108,900.

**Required:**

1. Calculate each of the following variances for August:
   Price variance
   Quantity variance
   Flexible budget variance
   Production volume variance
   Total variance
2. Determine the level of activity used to calculate the fixed factory overhead rate (in hours).

   ▶ *(Check Figure: 2. 36,000 hours)*

## 3 4 5   **Problem B5:** Determining Unknown Values

Solitude Company produces water softeners and uses standard costs and flexible budgets to help control its operations. At the end of September, the chief cost accountant accumulated the following facts concerning production in September:

| | |
|---|---|
| Units produced . . . . . . . . . . . . . . . . . . . . . . . . . . . . . . . . . . . . . . . | 100,000 |
| Direct labor: Actual hours worked. . . . . . . . . . . . . . . . . . . . . . . . | 210,000 |
| Variable factory overhead: | |
|    Standards: 2 hr at $6.00/hr | |
|    Actual results: Actual costs . . . . . . . . . . . . . . . . . . . . . . . . . . . | $1,281,000 |
| Fixed factory overhead: | |
|    Actual costs incurred. . . . . . . . . . . . . . . . . . . . . . . . . . . . . . . . . | $250,000 |
|    Price variance . . . . . . . . . . . . . . . . . . . . . . . . . . . . . . . . . . . . . . | 46,000 F |
|    Production volume variance . . . . . . . . . . . . . . . . . . . . . . . . . . . | 4,000 F |

**Required:**
Answer each of the following questions:

1. What was the price variance, the quantity variance, and the flexible budget variance for variable factory overhead?
2. How much fixed factory overhead was budgeted for the month? What was the fixed factory overhead flexible budget variance? How much fixed factory overhead was applied?

▶ *(Check Figure: 1. Quantity variance = $60,000 U)*

## 3   **Problem B6:** Doing Variance Analysis with Alternative Activity Bases

The Ever Changing Company uses standard costs and flexible budgets to assist in the control of its overhead costs. The controller decided in 1998 to base the budgets for several of its variable overhead costs on some activity other than direct labor hours. So in 1998 she began to budget utility costs on kilowatt hours, materials handling on hours of handling time, and inspection costs on hours of inspection time. The standards for these three variable overhead costs are as follows:

Utility costs: 0.2 kilowatt hours per unit produced at $.40 per kilowatt hour
Material handling costs: $\frac{1}{2}$ hour of material handling time per unit started at $5 per hour
Inspection costs: $\frac{1}{4}$ hour per unit inspected at $15 per hour

In addition, the standard time for direct labor is 2 hours per unit, and the standard rate is $12 per hour. During January, Ever Changing had the following actual results:

| | |
|---|---:|
| Units started . . . . . . . . . . . . . . . . . . . . . . . . . . . . . . . . . . . . . . . . . . . . . . . | 11,000 |
| Units produced (completed) . . . . . . . . . . . . . . . . . . . . . . . . . . . . . . . . . . . | 10,000 |
| Direct labor: | |
|   Actual hours worked . . . . . . . . . . . . . . . . . . . . . . . . . . . . . . . . . . . . . . | 20,500 |
|   Costs . . . . . . . . . . . . . . . . . . . . . . . . . . . . . . . . . . . . . . . . . . . . . . . . . . . | $245,000 |
| Inspection: | |
|   Units. . . . . . . . . . . . . . . . . . . . . . . . . . . . . . . . . . . . . . . . . . . . . . . . . . . . | 9,500 |
|   Hours. . . . . . . . . . . . . . . . . . . . . . . . . . . . . . . . . . . . . . . . . . . . . . . . . . . | 2,400 |
|   Costs . . . . . . . . . . . . . . . . . . . . . . . . . . . . . . . . . . . . . . . . . . . . . . . . . . . | $36,150 |
| Material handling hours . . . . . . . . . . . . . . . . . . . . . . . . . . . . . . . . . . . . . . | 5,600 |
| Material handling costs. . . . . . . . . . . . . . . . . . . . . . . . . . . . . . . . . . . . . . . | $27,450 |
| Utility costs . . . . . . . . . . . . . . . . . . . . . . . . . . . . . . . . . . . . . . . . . . . . . . . . | $825 |
| Kilowatt hours . . . . . . . . . . . . . . . . . . . . . . . . . . . . . . . . . . . . . . . . . . . . . . | 2,100 |

**Required:**
Calculate the price, quantity, and flexible budget variances for direct labor and for each of the three variable overhead costs.

▶ *(Check Figure: Price variance for utility costs = $15 F; Quantity variance for material handling costs = $500 U)*

## DECISION PROBLEM

Manpower Company uses a standard cost system to help plan for and control its factory overhead costs. It has been using direct labor as its activity base for two of its overhead costs, machine maintenance and inspection. Manpower produces two products, A and B, and its standards for direct labor and overhead are as follows:

| | Product A | Product B |
|---|:---:|:---:|
| Direct labor hours per unit . . . . . . . . . . . . . . . . . . . . . . . . . . | 3 | $\frac{1}{2}$ |
| Standard costs per hour: | | |
|   Direct labor . . . . . . . . . . . . . . . . . . . . . . . . . . . . . | $5.00/hr | |
|   Machine maintenance. . . . . . . . . . . . . . . . . . . . . | 3.00/hr | |
|   Inspection . . . . . . . . . . . . . . . . . . . . . . . . . . . . . . | .50/hr | |

**Required:**

1. Determine the standard cost per unit for products A and B for direct labor, machine maintenance, and inspection.

Assume that Manpower is now considering using alternative measures of activity for the two overhead items. Manpower thinks that machine maintenance costs are more closely related to machine hours worked than to direct labor hours; and that inspection costs are more closely related to hours of inspection time than to direct labor hours. On the basis of these measures of activity, Manpower comes up with the following standards for each product:

| | Product A | Product B |
|---|---|---|
| Machine maintenance: | | |
| Machine hours allowed per unit . . . . . . . . . . . . . . . . . . . . . . | 1 | 2 |
| Standard cost/machine hour . . . . . . . . . . . . . . . $ 2.40 | | |
| Inspection: | | |
| Hours of inspection time/unit . . . . . . . . . . . . . . . . . . . . . . | $\frac{1}{5}$ | –0– |
| Standard cost/hour of inspection . . . . . . . . . . . . $10.00 | | |

**Required:**

2. Determine the standard cost per unit for products A and B for direct labor, machine maintenance, and inspection. This time, base the calculations on the alternative measures of activity for maintenance costs and inspection costs.

3. Assume that 10,000 units of product A are produced and 20,000 units of product B are produced. Prepare flexible budgets for products A and B (and for their total) for each of the two overhead costs. (a) First do the calculations assuming that direct labor hours is the appropriate measure of activity for the two overhead costs. (b) Then do it a second time using the alternative measures of activity. (c) Compare your results in part (a) to those in part (b).

  Continue to assume that 10,000 units of product A and 20,000 units of product B were produced. Assume also that Manpower experienced the following actual results:

| | Product A | Product B | Totals |
|---|---|---|---|
| Direct labor hours. . . . . . . . . . . . . . . . . . . . . . . | 32,000 | 9,000 | 41,000 |
| Machine hours . . . . . . . . . . . . . . . . . . . . . . . . | 9,500 | 39,000 | 48,500 |
| Hours of inspection time . . . . . . . . . . . . . . . . . | 1,800 | –0– | 1,800 |
| Direct labor costs . . . . . . . . . . . . . . . . . . . . . . | | | $206,000 |
| Machine maintenance costs . . . . . . . . . . . . . . . | | | $122,000 |
| Inspection costs . . . . . . . . . . . . . . . . . . . . . . | | | $19,000 |

**Required:**

4. Determine the price, quantity, and flexible budget variances for direct labor for products A and B combined.

5. Determine the price, quantity, and flexible budget variances for each variable overhead cost for the two products combined. Assume that direct labor hours is the appropriate measure of activity.

6. Determine the price, quantity, and flexible budget variances for each variable overhead cost for the two products combined. Assume that the alternative activity bases are the appropriate measures of activity.

7. Which analysis of variance calculations (part 5 or part 6) do you believe is more meaningful? Discuss.

## OBJECTIVE ASSIGNMENT ANSWERS

**True/False**

1. T    2. T    3. T    4. F    5. T

**Multiple Choice**

1. d    2. a    3. d    4. a    5. c
6. c    7. d    8. d    9. b    10. b

# Evaluating the Performance of Cost Centers, Profit Centers, and Investment Centers

**LEARNING OBJECTIVES**

After studying this chapter, you should be able to do the following:

1 Describe the different types of cost centers for a manufacturer

2 Explain what service departments are, and allocate the costs of service departments to the operating departments for a manufacturer

3 Distinguish profit centers from cost centers

4 Evaluate the performance of profit centers and profit center managers with the contribution margin format of a segment income statement

5 Explain how an investment center differs from a profit center

6 Calculate the return on investment (ROI) for an investment center

7 Explain how the ROI is used to evaluate the performance of an investment center by separating the ROI into its component parts—asset turnover and return on sales

8 Define the key terms listed at the end of the chapter

In the previous two chapters, we saw how flexible budgets and standard costs are used to evaluate the performance of production departments for a manufacturer. We saw that each production department is a *responsibility center*—an area of activity managed by an individual who is responsible for its actions during some period of time. We also pointed out that there is an important distinction between controllable and noncontrollable costs.

A production department represents one type of responsibility center, called a *cost center*. Other types of responsibility centers are *profit centers* and *investment centers*. We will begin this chapter by looking at some aspects of cost centers that were not discussed previously, and then discuss profit centers and investment centers.

Learning
Objective 1

## COST CENTERS

Describe the different types of cost centers for a manufacturer

A **cost center** is a responsibility center whose manager can influence the costs incurred by the center, but cannot influence the revenues for the center or for the firm as a whole. In addition, the manager cannot influence the investment in fixed assets that generate revenues. Let us assume that the production supervisors have primary responsibility for controlling their departments' costs—direct materials, direct labor, variable factory overhead, and fixed factory overhead costs. (In fact, few production supervisors have much influence over fixed factory overhead costs.) A performance report for the production department of Robinjon Company is reproduced in Exhibit 1.

We could prepare a more detailed performance report for this cost center by separating the flexible budget variances for the variable costs into their component parts: the price variance and the quantity variance. We could also calculate and add up actual costs, budgeted costs, and the variance for the year to date, as well as for individual months. Or we could show what percentage of the budget each variance is, as a quick way to measure materiality of variances. In short, we have a great deal of flexibility in how we present a report that evaluates the performance of a cost center, a profit center, or an investment center. All the approaches we use in this chapter are definitely acceptable, but are not necessarily the only acceptable approaches that we could have employed.

### Multiple Cost Centers

We will now assume that Robinjon Company has three production departments: an assembly department, a machining department, and a finishing department. Each

**Exhibit 1** Robinjon Production Department Performance Report

**ROBINJON COMPANY**
**Production Department**
**Performance Report for January, 1997**

| | Col.1 Actual Costs (12,500 Units) | Col. 2 Flexible Budget Variance | Col. 3 Flexible Budget (12,500 Units) |
|---|---|---|---|
| Direct materials . . . . . . . . . . . . . . . . . . . | $ 65,000 | $2,500 U | $ 62,500 |
| Direct labor . . . . . . . . . . . . . . . . . . . . . . | 78,000 | 3,000 U | 75,000 |
| Variable factory overhead. . . . . . . . . . . . | 39,000 | 1,500 U | 37,500 |
| Fixed factory overhead . . . . . . . . . . . . . . | 14,900 | 100 F | 15,000 |
| | $196,900 | $6,900 U | $190,000 |

**Figure 1** Expanded Organization Chart for Robinjon Company

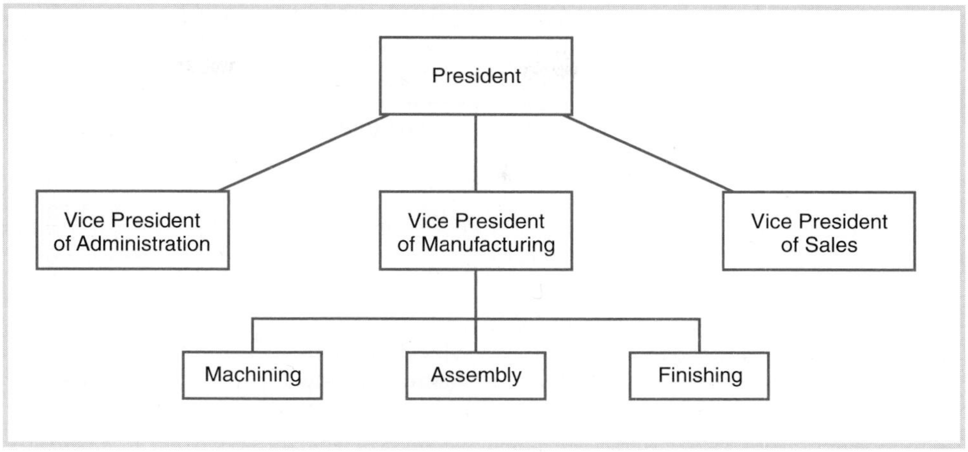

department represents a cost center whose manager reports to the vice president of manufacturing, as shown in Figure 1.

An expanded set of performance reports for Robinjon Company appears in Exhibit 2. At the bottom of the exhibit is the performance report for the assembly department. Notice how the summarized report (bottom-line totals) for the assembly department is combined with the summarized reports for the machining and finishing departments in the report to the vice president of manufacturing. The summarized report from the vice president of manufacturing is then combined with the summarized reports for sales and administration (and possibly product design, research and development, finance, customer service, etc) in the report to the president.

You also may have noticed in Exhibit 2 that fixed factory overhead appears in the assembly department report (and in other reports not shown), even though it is probably not controllable at the department manager level. Because it may be controllable at the vice president's level of responsibility, it is left in the analysis.

Learning
Objective    2

Explain what service departments are, and allocate the costs of service departments to the operating departments for a manufacturer

## Service Department Costs

So far in this text we have ignored an important group of cost centers for most manufacturers because these departments are not involved directly in the operating activities of the organization. They are, however, closely related to the producing departments and often to the selling and administrative areas as well. These are the **service departments.** The services they provide to the operating departments are often so valuable that the operating departments cannot operate efficiently without them. For example, a machine maintenance department is responsible for keeping the machinery functioning in all operating departments. This department is seldom involved directly in producing units, but without its services the producing department wouldn't be able to continue production for long.

Other typical service departments include the factory storeroom, the cafeteria, janitorial services, personnel (often called "human resources"), purchasing, quality control and inspection, factory administration, and a medical clinic.

Some service departments, such as machine maintenance, quality control, and factory administration, provide services primarily to production departments. These service departments are often housed in the manufacturing area of the company. Other service departments, such as the cafeteria, the personnel department, and the medical clinic, service all operating departments—both producing and nonproducing—and are therefore more likely to be centrally located.

Since service departments are needed to run operating departments efficiently, it seems reasonable to assign a portion of the costs of providing the services to each

**Exhibit 2** Progression of Performance Reports for Robinjon Company

| President | Actual Costs | Flexible Budget | Flexible Budget Variances |
|---|---|---|---|
| President's department | $ 18,000 | $ 18,200 | $ 200 F |
| Vice president, manufacturing | 557,400 | 560,750 | 3,350 F |
| Vice president, sales | 270,000 | 265,000 | 5,000 U |
| Vice president, administration | 65,000 | 64,000 | 1,000 U |
| Totals | $910,400 | $907,950 | $ 2,450 U |

*Company performance report (responsible manager: president)*

| Vice President Manufacturing | Actual Costs | Flexible Budget | Flexible Budget Variances |
|---|---|---|---|
| Vice president's department | $ 15,500 | $ 15,750 | $ 250 F |
| Machining department | 225,000 | 240,000 | 15,000 F |
| Assembly department | 196,900 | 190,000 | 6,900 U |
| Finishing department | 120,000 | 115,000 | 5,000 U |
| | $557,400 | $560,750 | $ 3,350 F |

*Manufacturing departments' performance reports (responsible manager: vice president of manufacturing)*

| Assembly Department | Actual Costs | Flexible Budget | Flexible Budget Variances |
|---|---|---|---|
| Direct materials | $ 65,000 | $ 62,500 | $ 2,500 U |
| Direct labor | 78,000 | 75,000 | 3,000 U |
| Variable factory overhead | 39,000 | 37,500 | 1,500 U |
| Fixed factory overhead | 14,900 | 15,000 | 100 F |
| | $196,900 | $190,000 | $ 6,900 U |

*Assembly department performance report (responsible manager: assembly supervisor)*

operating department that benefits from them. The accounting procedure used to do so is called **cost allocation.**

Once we have identified the departments that have received service, we allocate the service department costs to the recipients, using an appropriate allocation base. An **allocation base** is the link between the service department and the operating department. It is a way of measuring the amount of services provided to an operating department. Thus it provides the basis for determining the portion of costs to be allocated to each operating department.

For example, the number of hours the machine maintenance department spends working on an operating department's machinery would be an excellent allocation base for the service department. If 25% of the machine maintenance department's time is spent working on the machinery of the assembly department, then the assembly department will be allocated 25% of the costs. Possible allocation bases for the different types of service departments are shown in Exhibit 3.

### The Direct Method of Cost Allocation

In the following example, we will use Robinjon Company to illustrate the direct method to allocate service department costs. As its name implies, the **direct method** allocates service department costs to the operating departments in a single direct step.

**Exhibit 3** Allocation Bases for Different Types of Service Departments

| Service Department | Possible Allocation Base |
|---|---|
| Machine maintenance | Hours of maintenance time; hours of machine time worked in operating departments |
| Storeroom | Number of requisitions issued to each department |
| Cafeteria | Number of employees served |
| Janitorial | Square feet of space cleaned |
| Personnel (human resources) | Number of employees; direct labor hours; number of employees hired |
| Purchasing | Number of purchase orders processed |
| Inspection | Number of units inspected |
| Factory administration | Total labor hours |
| Medical clinic | Number of employees; number of patients |

With this method, the services that one service department provides to another are completely ignored; in other words, service department costs are not allocated to other service departments.

# ROBINJON COMPANY — DIRECT METHOD

Robinjon Company has three production departments—machining, assembly, and finishing; a selling and administrative department; and three service departments —cafeteria, human resources (personnel), and machine maintenance. The overhead costs budgeted for each department at the beginning of the year are as follows:

| | |
|---|---|
| Machining . . . . . . . . . . . . . . . . . . . . . . . . . . . . . . | $810,000 |
| Assembly. . . . . . . . . . . . . . . . . . . . . . . . . . . . . . . | 630,000 |
| Finishing . . . . . . . . . . . . . . . . . . . . . . . . . . . . . . . | 386,400 |
| Selling and administrative. . . . . . . . . . . . . . . . . . | 100,000 |
| Cafeteria . . . . . . . . . . . . . . . . . . . . . . . . . . . . . . . | 540,000 |
| Human resources . . . . . . . . . . . . . . . . . . . . . . . . | 264,000 |
| Machine maintenance. . . . . . . . . . . . . . . . . . . . . | 144,000 |

These costs represent the combined budgeted costs (only the overhead costs for the production departments) of each department for the entire year. The cafeteria and the human resources department service the employees of all seven departments, but machine maintenance services only the three production departments. The allocation base for the cafeteria is the expected total number of employees during the year; for human resources it is the number of employees expected to be hired during the year; and for machine maintenance it is the number of hours expected to be spent during the year repairing machines. Exhibit 4 summarizes the other budgeted data we need in order to use the direct method of allocation in this example.

The total costs of each service department are allocated as shown in Exhibit 5. Although the cafeteria and human resources departments service all the departments in the company, their costs are allocated only to the nonservice departments (production, selling and administrative). That's an integral part of the direct method. The machine maintenance department provides service only to the production depart-

**Exhibit 4** Budgeted Data Needed in the Direct Method of Service Department Allocations

| | Service Departments | | | | Selling and Admin. Dept. | Production Departments | | | | Total for All Depts. |
|---|---|---|---|---|---|---|---|---|---|---|
| Budgeted | Cafeteria | Human Resources | Machine Maint. | Total | | Machining | Assembly | Finishing | Total | |
| Number of repair hours | — | — | 9,120* | 9,120 | — | — | — | — | — | 9,120 |
| Number of employees | 10 | 15 | 5 | 30 | 10 | 65 | 175 | 150 | 390 | 430 |
| Number of employees hired | 2 | 1 | — | 3 | 1 | 4 | 11 | 9 | 24 | 28† |
| Direct labor hours | — | — | — | — | — | 144,000 | 312,000 | 264,000 | 720,000 | 720,000 |

* This total is expected to be used repairing machinery in the following manner:
   4,560 hours for machinery in the machining department
   2,280 hours for machinery in the assembly department
   2,280 hours for machinery in the finishing department
   0 hours for machinery in the selling and administrative department
† New employees are replacing retirees; total number of employees does not change during the year.

ments; therefore, none of its costs are allocated to the selling and administrative department.

The costs of operating the cafeteria, $540,000, are allocated on the basis of the expected number of employees during the year. Exhibit 4 shows that 430 workers are expected to be employed during the year by the entire company. Of this total, 400 (10 + 65 + 175 + 150 = 400) work in the production and the selling and administrative departments. Since the cafeteria costs are allocated only to these departments, the allocation base to use is the 400 workers in these four departments. Of these 400 employees, 10 work in selling and administrative departments, so 10/400, or 2.5%, of the cafeteria costs—$13,500—are allocated to the selling and administrative department. Since 65 of the 400 work in the machining department, 65/400, or 16.25%, of the cafeteria costs—$87,750—are allocated to machining. In a like manner, Exhibit 5 shows that $236,250 is allocated to assembly and $202,500 is allocated to finishing.

The total costs of the human resources department, $264,000, are allocated on the basis of expected number of replacement workers to be hired for each of the three producing departments and the selling and administrative department. As you can see in Exhibit 4, 24 new employees are expected to be hired for the production departments and 1 for the selling and administrative department. Thus the allocation base totals 25 new employees (replacing 25 who will be retiring during the year). Of this total, 1/25, or 4%, relates to selling and administration, so 4% of $264,000, or $10,560, is allocated to the selling and administrative department. The remainder of the $264,000 is allocated in a similar manner: $42,240 to machining, $116,160 to assembly, and $95,040 to finishing.

The total costs of the machine maintenance department, $144,000, are allocated on the basis of the number of hours spent maintaining the machinery of each production department. Exhibit 4 shows that the machine maintenance department will spend 9,120 hours providing maintenance. Of this total, 4,560 hours, or 50%, will be used for the machining department; 2,280 hours, or 25%, will be used for each of the other production departments. Therefore, as Exhibit 5 shows, 50% of the costs of the machine maintenance department, $72,000, are allocated to the machining department. In addition, 25% of the total costs—$36,000—are allocated to assembly, and 25% to finishing.

The total service department costs allocated to the selling and administrative department and the three production departments are shown in the next to last line of

**Exhibit 5** Direct Method of Service Department Cost Allocation

| | Service Departments | | | Selling and Admin. Depart. | Production Departments | | |
|---|---|---|---|---|---|---|---|
| | Cafeteria | Human Resources | Machine Maint. | | Machining | Assembly | Finishing |
| Overhead costs before allocation | $540,000 | $264,000 | $144,000 | $100,000 | $ 810,000 | $ 630,000 | $386,400 |
| Allocation of cafeteria to: | | | | | | | |
| Selling and Admin. $\frac{10}{400}$ = 2.50% | (13,500) | | | $ 13,500 | | | |
| Machining $\frac{65}{400}$ = 16.25% | (87,750) | | | | $ 87,750 | | |
| Assembly $\frac{175}{400}$ = 43.75% | (236,250) | | | | | $ 236,250 | |
| Finishing $\frac{150}{400}$ = 37.50% | (202,500) | | | | | | $202,500 |
| Remaining to be allocated | –0– | | | | | | |
| Allocation of human resources to: | | | | | | | |
| Selling and Admin. $\frac{1}{25}$ = 4% | | (10,560) | | 10,560 | | | |
| Machining $\frac{4}{25}$ = 16% | | (42,240) | | | 42,240 | | |
| Assembly $\frac{11}{25}$ = 44% | | (116,160) | | | | 116,160 | |
| Finishing $\frac{9}{25}$ = 36% | | (95,040) | | | | | 95,040 |
| Remaining to be allocated | | –0– | | | | | |
| Allocation of Machine Maintenance to: | | | | | | | |
| Selling and Admin. 0/9,120 = 0% | | | | (–0–) | –0– | | |
| Machining 4,560/9,120 = 50% | | | | (72,000) | 72,000 | | |
| Assembly 2,280/9,120 = 25% | | | | (36,000) | | 36,000 | |
| Finishing 2,280/9,120 = 25% | | | | (36,000) | | | 36,000 |
| Remaining to be allocated | | | | –0– | | | |
| Total allocated costs to each operating department | | | | $ 24,060 | $ 201,990 | $ 388,410 | $333,540 |
| Total overhead costs of operating departments | | | | $124,060 | $1,011,990 | $1,018,410 | $719,940 |

Exhibit 5. When they are added to the costs budgeted to be incurred in each department, the bottom line indicates the combined budgeted overhead costs—those budgeted for each department plus the allocated service department costs.

### How Operating Departments Use Allocated Service Department Costs

Once the service department costs have been allocated to the various operating departments, they are treated as part of those department's costs. For production departments they also become part of the cost of the products being produced in those departments. We add the allocated service department costs to the overhead costs incurred by each production department. This combined total for overhead is then assigned to the units produced in the department, as part of its predetermined overhead rate. It is important for us to know all the costs—including the service department costs—associated with the production of a product so that we can accurately determine the profitability of each product line and of the cost center that produces it. Only with accurate product costs do we have all the relevant information we need in order to make plans for the cost center before the period begins and to evaluate the performance of the cost center after the period is over.

**ASK YOURSELF** ▶

1. **What is a cost center?**
2. **Name several types of service departments.**
3. **Explain how the direct method is used to allocate service department costs to operating departments.**

**Figure 2** Profit Centers—Regions and Products

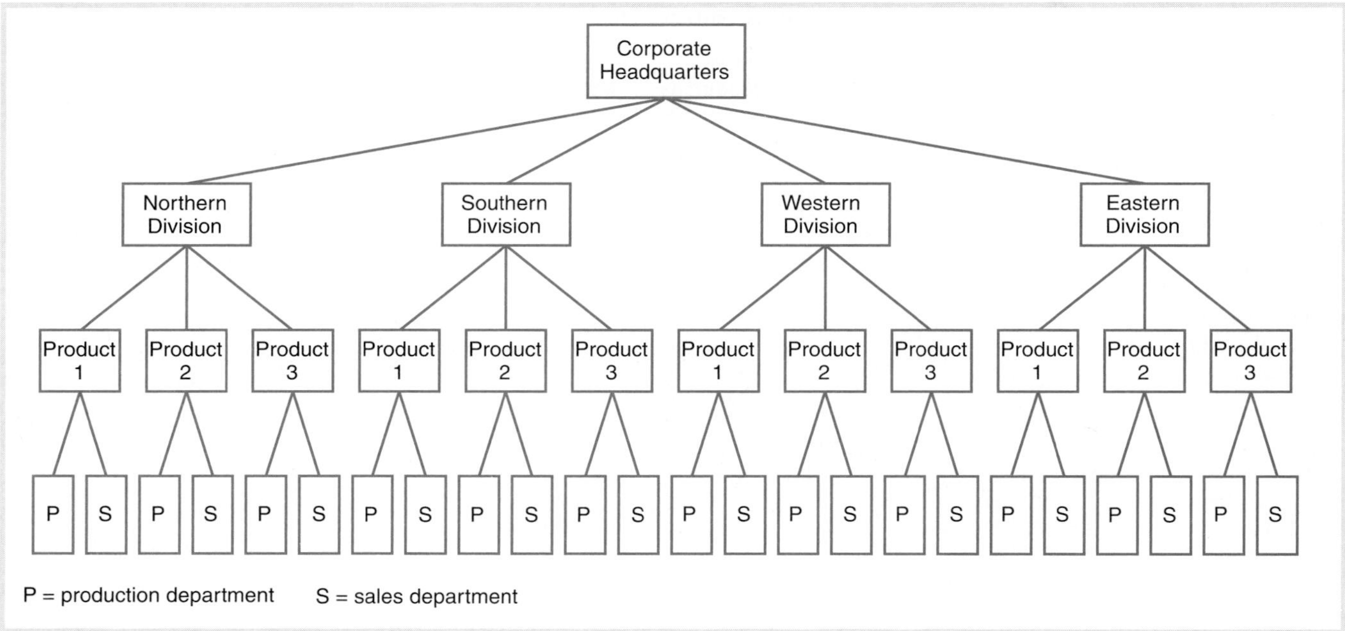

P = production department    S = sales department

Learning Objective 3

Distinguish profit centers from cost centers

## 3 PROFIT CENTERS

So far we have looked at only one type of responsibility center—the cost center. In a cost center, the manager is responsible for the costs incurred within the center, but has no responsibility for revenues. The second type of responsibility center is the **profit center,** in which the manager is given the responsibility not only for the costs but also for the revenues. This means that the manager is responsible for most aspects of profit (or loss).

A profit center may be a department, branch, division, or subsidiary within a company. But whatever the entity is called, a profit center's manager has the responsibility and the authority to generate a desirable profit for that center during a specific reporting period.

If, for example, the Robinjon Company is one division of a multidivision organization, and if each division president is responsible for generating an acceptable profit for the parent organization, then each of these divisions would be considered a profit center.

We have been assuming that Robinjon Company makes a single product, and now we will also assume that there are other divisions that also make a single product. This is a popular way to differentiate between profit centers: Each profit center handles a different major product line. For an organization that manufactures appliances, the different divisions might produce washing machines and dryers, refrigerators, stoves, and trash compactors.

Different profit centers may also be designated according to geographic location. For example, sections of the country, such as North, South, East, and West, might each represent a profit center responsible for the production and sale of many different product lines.

Some organizations are divided into geographic regions, with each region further differentiated by the types of products being produced and sold within that region. For example, the organization chart in Figure 2 shows four regions reporting to corporate headquarters. Within each region there are three product lines, and within each product line there are sales and production activities. Each of the four regional divisions would probably be a profit center, and each of the three product line divisions within the region would probably also be a profit center. The individual sales departments might also be profit centers, but the production departments would be cost centers because their managers would only be responsible for controlling costs within those departments.

Learning Objective 4

**Evaluate the performance of profit centers and profit center managers with the contribution margin format of a segment income statement**

## Evaluating the Performance of Profit Centers

The performance of a profit center (and of its manager) is evaluated on the basis of the information reported in **segment income statements.** A **segment** is simply any part of an organization for which both costs and revenues can be identified as relating to that part. For each segment, we can both identify and measure operating performance, usually on the basis of profitability. The segment income statements are simply the income statements we prepare for the various segments—which are the profit centers (or investment centers, as we'll see in the next section). And remember, the profit centers may be branches, departments, divisions, subsidiaries, product lines, or geographic locations.

The format recommended for segment income statements is the contribution margin approach:

> **Sales**
> **Less: Total variable costs**
> **Equals: Total contribution margin**
> **Less: Total fixed costs**
> **Equals: Net income**

Here the format will be more elaborate. It will distinguish variable costs from fixed costs, and it will also distinguish direct costs from indirect costs, and controllable costs from noncontrollable costs.

Remember, we are assuming that Robinjon Company is one division of a multi-division organization—which we will now call Multiseg, Inc.—and that the different divisions represent different product lines. (See Figure 3.) We will refer to the three divisions as Division A (Robinjon), Division B, and Division C. Since each division will be evaluated on the basis of the profit it generates, each division is a profit center, and the income statement for each division will be called a segment income statement. We

**Figure 3** Robinjon as a Product Line Division of Multiseg, Inc.

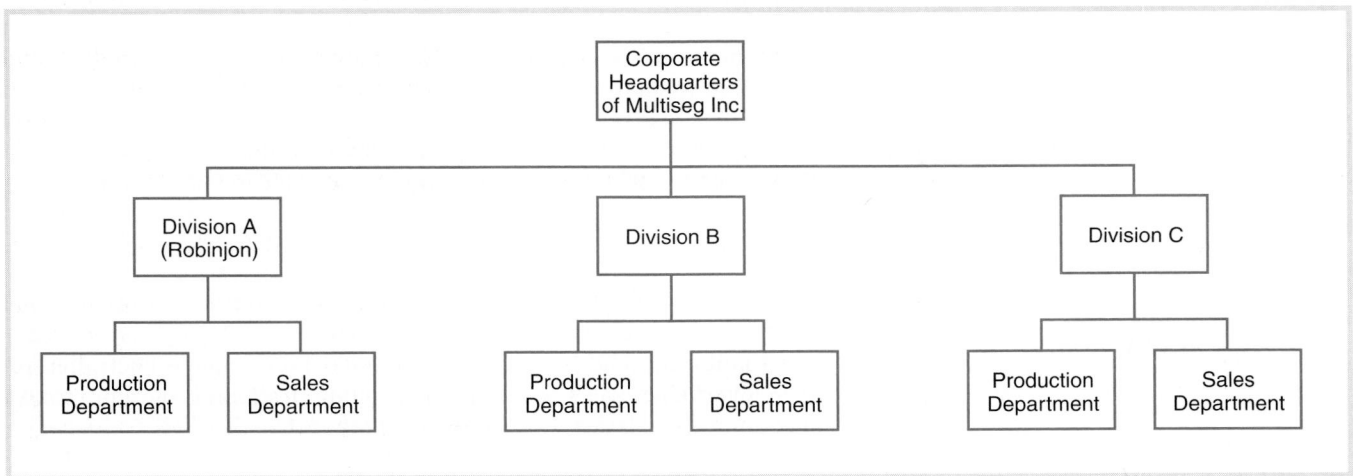

**Exhibit 6** A Segment Income Statement

MULTISEG, INC.
Segment Income Statement
For the Year 1997

| | Segments | | | Totals for all Segments |
| --- | --- | --- | --- | --- |
| | Division A (Robinjon) | Division B | Division C | |
| Sales ........................ | $1,252,000 | $500,000 | $435,000 | $2,187,000 |
| Less: Variable costs: | | | | |
| Variable manufacturing* ... | $1,034,000 | $345,000 | $240,000 | $1,619,000 |
| Variable selling and administration of segment .............. | 96,000 | 34,000 | 44,000 | 174,000 |
| | $1,130,000 | $379,000 | $284,000 | $1,793,000 |
| (1) Total contribution margin....... | $ 122,000 | $121,000 | $151,000 | $ 394,000 |
| Less: Direct fixed costs (controllable by segment manager)* ..... | 80,000 | 30,000 | 55,000 | 165,000 |
| (2) Contribution controllable by the segment manager ........ | $ 42,000 | $ 91,000 | $ 96,000 | $ 229,000 |
| Less: Fixed costs of segment not controllable by the segment manager*...... | 13,200 | 14,000 | 17,500 | 44,700 |
| (3) Contribution of the segment to common costs ............ | $ 28,800 | $ 77,000 | $ 78,500 | $ 184,300 |
| Common costs of all segments .. | 77,200 | 30,900 | 26,900 | 135,000 |
| (4) Net Income.................. | $ (48,400) | $ 46,100 | $ 51,600 | $ 49,300 |

* Including the allocated service department costs.

will also assume that all three division managers report directly to corporate head-quarters.

The segment income statements for Robinjon and the other two divisions of Multiseg are shown in Exhibit 6. (All numbers are assumed in this exhibit. Do not try to figure out where they came from by referring back to previous exhibits.)

### Total Contribution Margin

The first key line [identified by the number (1) in Exhibit 6] within the contribution margin section of the segment income statement is the *total contribution margin* for each division: total sales less total variable costs. This is the amount that each division contributes to the coverage of its own fixed costs. This amount is usually controllable by the division manager—who is also the segment manager in our example.

### Contribution Controllable by the Segment Manager

Direct fixed costs controllable by the segment manager are subtracted from the total contribution margin. The net is the *contribution controllable by the segment manager* [number (2) in Exhibit 6]. The fixed costs subtracted here include such division expenditures as advertising, sales promotion, recruiting, training programs, contributions, bonuses, and the salaries of key personnel other than the division manager.

However, many fixed costs of the division may be the responsibility of someone higher in the organization than the division manager. Those costs include the salary of the division manager, depreciation, property taxes, rent, insurance, research and development, and national advertising. All these costs may be the responsibility of someone at corporate headquarters, even though the costs are a part of the division to which they relate. If a division manager can control these costs, it is probably because the manager has been given the authority and responsibility to make the decisions that affect the productive capacity—the investment—of the division. We will discuss this alternative later in this chapter.

The contribution controllable by the segment manager usually represents the best measure of performance for the managers of profit centers, which in our example are the divisions. Any income figures that come later in this statement are less appropriate for this purpose, because the manager probably has little influence on the items that are subtracted in determining those figures.

### Contribution of the Segment to Common Costs

The next group of costs to be subtracted are the fixed costs over which the division manager has no control. We identified these fixed costs in the previous section. When these noncontrollable fixed costs are subtracted, the remainder is called the *contribution of the segment to common costs* [number (3) in Exhibit 6]. Basically, this amount is similar to the income that each division would earn on its own if it were an independent company.

The contribution of the segment to common costs is the best measure of profitability of the division, because all the costs relate directly to that division. However, this figure is not the key to evaluating the performance of the division manager. As we noted earlier, the manager is best evaluated by the *contribution controllable by the segment manager*.

### Net Income

Any costs that are incurred outside the division but are assigned to the division are indirect costs, or **common costs.** The common costs in our situation are the costs of the corporate headquarters. They are not incurred by any one division but are considered as being incurred for the benefit of all divisions, and thus indirectly related to each division.

How should we treat common costs when preparing the segment income statement? Should the common costs be fully allocated to the divisions, as we have done with the $135,000 in Exhibit 6? Or should no attempt be made to associate common costs with specific divisions? Many accountants feel that fully allocating common costs leads to the evaluation of divisions on the basis of the wrong performance measure—namely, net income instead of the segment's contribution to common costs. They believe that many of the allocated common costs, such as national advertising and administrative costs of corporate headquarters, would not be incurred if the segment were an independent company. Opponents of allocation prefer to delete the common costs from the individual segment statements and include them only in the total income column for the company as a whole.

Despite these objections, many companies do allocate their common costs to their divisions, just as we have done in Exhibit 6. These companies feel that each division has a responsibility to contribute enough to the company as a whole to cover all costs, including the common costs. It is not enough for each division merely to show a profit that would be considered acceptable to an independent company. Instead, the combined profit for all the divisions must cover the common costs and still leave a satisfactory profit for the company as a whole. Only by knowing its fair allocated share of common costs will each division fully realize its responsibility.

**Exhibit 7** A Segment Performance Report

### ROBINJON DIVISION
### Performance Report for Segment Income
### For the Year 1997

| | Col. 1 Actual Results | Col. 2 Col. 1–Col. 3 Flexible Budget Variance | Col. 3 Flexible Budget | Col. 4 Col. 3–Col. 5 Sales Volume Variance | Col. 5 Master Budget |
|---|---|---|---|---|---|
| Sales..................................... | $1,252,000 | $52,000 F | $1,200,000 | $300,000 U | $1,500,000 |
| Less: Variable costs: | | | | | |
| Variable manufacturing............. | $1,034,000 | $74,000 U | $ 960,000 | $240,000 F | $1,200,000 |
| Variable selling and administrative costs of segment................. | 96,000 | 6,000 U | 90,000 | 22,500 F | 112,500 |
| | $1,130,000 | $80,000 U | $1,050,000 | $262,500 F | $1,312,500 |
| (1) Total contribution margin ............... | $ 122,000 | $28,000 U | $ 150,000 | $ 37,500 U | $ 187,500 |
| Less: Direct fixed costs (controllable by segment manager) .............. | 80,000 | 2,000 F | 82,000 | –0– | 82,000 |
| (2) Contribution controllable by the segment manager ........................... | $ 42,000 | $26,000 U | $ 68,000 | $ 37,500 U | $ 105,500 |
| Less: Fixed costs of segment not controllable by the segment manager ...................... | 13,200 | 200 U | 13,000 | –0– | 13,000 |
| (3) Contribution of the segment to common costs .............................. | $ 28,800 | $26,200 U | $ 55,000 | $ 37,500 U | $ 92,500 |

## Assessment of Income Statements

Now that we have prepared segment income statements, just how do we use this information to evaluate the performance of each division manager and division? We can use the income called contribution controllable by the segment manager to evaluate the division manager, and use the income called contribution of the segment to common costs to evaluate the division. But how do we know from these numbers if the manager and the division were as profitable as they should have been?

One way to evaluate the profitability of the division manager and the division is to compare the actual income earned for the period to the income budgeted for the period in the master budget. We can also determine measures of efficiency and effectiveness by comparing the results to a flexible budget for income based on the level of activity actually achieved for the period. The general format of such a performance report would look like Exhibit 7 for Robinjon. The performance report ends with the segment's contribution to common costs, since this is the best measure of performance for the segment. (All numbers, with the exception of column 1, are assumed; the actual results in column 1 were given in Exhibit 6.)

We measure *efficiency* with the flexible budget variance (column 2) —the difference between the actual results (column 1) and the flexible budget (column 3), based on the actual units produced and sold. The flexible budget variance for sales is $52,000 F, which means that the units were sold at a higher average price than Robinjon expected. The unfavorable variance for the variable manufacturing costs and the selling and administrative costs—$74,000 and $6,000, respectively—indicate that higher than expected costs were incurred during Robinjon's production and sales for the period. In addition, the direct fixed costs were $2,000 less than budgeted for the period, and the fixed costs for the segment not controllable by the segment manager were $200 more than budgeted. The bottom line of column 2 shows that the income for the division was $26,200 less than it should have been, according to the production and sales actually achieved for the year.

If we have a standard cost system, we can also evaluate the individual components of the flexible budget variance, by calculating the price and quantity variances for each variable item in the statement.

*Effectiveness* is measured by the sales volume variance (column 4) — the difference between the flexible budget (column 3) and the master budget (column 5). It indicates the effect on income of falling below (or going beyond) the master budget level of activity. If Robinjon had been able to obtain sales of $1,500,000, its income could have been $92,500. Based on sales of $1,200,000, the income was budgeted to be $55,000, $37,500 less than Robinjon could have had if it had achieved the master budget level of activity.

Another way to evaluate the profitability of the division or the division manager would be to compare the results of one division with the results of other company divisions that have similar operations. The division or the division manager that contributes the most to profits is assessed as doing the best job. The division results can also be compared to the results of comparable entities outside the company.

It would be inappropriate to compare the profits of one division to another if they are not similar in size. For example, take two divisions that both show a profit of $100,000. With that information alone, would you consider them to be equally profitable? Would you feel the same way if you knew that one division had assets totaling $400,000 and the second division had assets totaling $4,000,000? Of course not. The one with more assets should certainly be able to generate more income. To compare divisions of dissimilar size, we need to consider the amount of investment as well as the amount of profit. The profitability measure that weighs profit against the amount of investment is called the *return on investment (ROI)*. We will now cover ROI as we talk about investment centers.

## ASK YOURSELF ▶

1. **What is the format for the contribution margin approach to the segment income statement?**
2. **How do common costs differ from costs that are associated directly with a profit center? Give some examples of each type of cost.**
3. **Once you have prepared a segment income statement for a profit center, how do you decide whether the profit is acceptable or not?**

Learning Objective 5

Explain how an investment center differs from a profit center

## INVESTMENT CENTERS

Closely related to profit centers is the third type of responsibility center: investment centers. Just about everything we have discussed about profit centers applies equally well to investment centers. An **investment center** merely takes the concept of profit centers one step further, by relating the profit to the investment that generated the profit.

In organizations that let division managers make all decisions that relate to their own destiny, the division managers control not only the revenues and costs but also the investment available to generate the profit. The division manager makes decisions that affect the amount of production, marketing, and administrative facilities to be invested in the division. As a result, the division manager will be able to control many of the division's fixed costs — if not in the short run, then at least in the long run.

If Robinjon had been an independent company prior to becoming a division of a larger company, it definitely would have been an investment center prior to being acquired. After its acquisition, it would still be considered an investment center if corporate management continued to let the division manager make most of the decisions related to sales, costs, and the investment in productive capacity. We will now assume that all three divisions of Multiseg shown in Exhibit 6 are investment centers and will be evaluated with the ratio called *return on investment.*

Learning
Objective 6   **Return on Investment (ROI)**

Calculate the return on investment
(ROI) for an investment center

The performance of an investment center is evaluated by its **return on investment, or ROI.** The ROI indicates the income of the investment center as a percentage of its investment. The investment is usually measured by the total assets of the investment center. The ROI for a division which is an investment center is calculated as follows:

$$\text{ROI} = \frac{\text{division income}}{\text{division assets}}$$

Since the best measure of profitability of a division is the income called contribution of the segment to common costs, this is the measure of income that we will use in the numerator of the ROI calculation.

To calculate the ROIs for the three divisions shown in Exhibit 6, we need to know how large the investment is for each division. So let's assume that the total assets of each division are as follows:

Robinjon (division A) . . . . . . . . . . . . . . . . . . . .   $2,000,000
Division B . . . . . . . . . . . . . . . . . . . . . . . . . . . .   550,000
Division C . . . . . . . . . . . . . . . . . . . . . . . . . . . .   314,000

We divide this investment into the contribution of the segment to common costs (found in Exhibit 6) to find the ROI for each division, as follows:

$$\text{ROI (Robinjon)} = \frac{\$28,800}{\$2,000,000} = 1.4\%$$

$$\text{ROI (Division B)} = \frac{\$77,000}{\$550,000} = 14.0\%$$

$$\text{ROI (Division C)} = \frac{\$78,500}{\$314,000} = 25.0\%$$

These ROIs enable us to see that the income for Robinjon was the smallest not only in dollar value but also as a percentage of investment. The income of $28,800 was only 1.4% of Robinjon's total assets, meaning that for every dollar of assets, the division was able to generate only an additional $.014 from operations—not very good any way you look at it. The 14% ROI for Division B is much better than Robinjon, but not nearly so good as Division C, which has a 25% ROI.

When you compare the results for Divisions B and C, you can see why it is important to use ROI, rather than merely dollar profits, to evaluate investment centers. Divisions B and C had almost exactly the same amount of profit, which gives an initial impression that they are equally profitable. But Division C earned roughly the same amount of profit as Division B on a much smaller investment in assets. Clearly, the manager of Division C did a much better job of using his or her investment than did the manager of Division B. Only with ROI can we properly assess the relative profitability of the three divisions.

Learning
Objective    **7**

Explain how the ROI is used to
evaluate the performance of an
investment center by separating the
ROI into its component parts—asset
turnover and return on sales

## Assessing Performance with ROI

Once we have the ROI percentages for each division, what do we do with this information? What do we compare it to? Obviously, we can compare the ROIs of the different divisions to see which is most profitable. The manager of the most profitable division will be a likely candidate for a promotion, raise, or year-end bonus.

Instead of comparing one division to another, it may be better to compare the division ROI to an ROI that was determined at the beginning of the period as a minimum needed for the division during the period. For example, different divisions may be involved in industries where the risk of failure is quite different; therefore an acceptable ROI for a division in one industry may be unacceptable for a division in another industry. In this case an acceptable ROI would be geared to the specific risk associated with each industry; high risk requires a greater return than does low risk. A firm has no reason to get involved in a business area with a high risk of failure, unless the ROI potential is much higher than it would be in other, "safer" areas.

Here is another situation where it might be better to compare the division ROI to a minimum ROI: A new manager is assigned to turn around a previously unsuccessful division. Will the new manager feel comfortable having his or her division compared to divisions that have a long history of success? Probably not. The new manager might reject the assignment, or accept it only if promised that rewards will be based on an improvement in the division's ROI.

It might also be informative to top management to compare current ROIs to ROIs in previous years, to ROIs of independent companies in the same industry, and to an industry average ROI. But it is unwise to assume that such comparisons provide good benchmarks for our division in the current year. The fact that we have done much better than last year, much better than a competitor, or much better than the average firm in our industry doesn't necessarily mean that we have done as well as we could have or should have.

### A Breakdown of ROI into Key Factors

To evaluate ROI properly for an investment center, it is a good idea to separate it into its component parts. It is easier to see how to improve ROI or to evaluate the reasons for a change in ROI if we realize that the ratio is actually made up of the *asset turnover* and *return on sales*.

$$\text{ROI} = \frac{\text{division income}}{\text{division assets}} = \text{asset turnover} \times \text{return on sales}$$

The **asset turnover** indicates the dollars of revenue that each dollar of assets is able to generate for the division. It is calculated as follows:

$$\text{Asset turnover} = \frac{\text{division sales}}{\text{division assets}}$$

The **return on sales** indicates the percentage of every sales dollar that remains after all costs have been covered. It is calculated with the following formula, using contribution to common costs as division income:

$$\text{Return on sales} = \frac{\text{division income}}{\text{division sales}}$$

The calculation of ROI, broken into its component parts, is now:

$$\text{ROI} = \frac{\text{division sales}}{\text{division assets}} \times \frac{\text{division income}}{\text{division sales}}$$

This is algebraically the same as dividing income by assets, since the sales shown in the numerator of asset turnover and the denominator of return on sales cancel each other out.

Using the facts from Exhibit 6 and the assets listed in the **Return on Investment (ROI)** section, we can see that the 1.4% ROI for Robinjon (Division A) is composed of the following two parts:

$$\text{ROI (Robinjon)} = \frac{\$1,252,000}{\$2,000,000} \times \frac{\$28,800}{\$1,252,000}$$

$$= .626 \times .023 = .014 = 1.4\%$$

The asset turnover indicates that Robinjon was able to generate only $.626 of sales for each dollar of assets. And the return on sales indicates that Robinjon was able to generate only $.023 of profit for each dollar of sales.

The breakdown of ROI for Divisions B and C would be done in the same manner. Division B's would be:

$$\text{ROI (Division B)} = \frac{\$500,000}{\$550,000} \times \frac{\$77,000}{\$500,000} = .9091 \times .154 = .14 = 14\%$$

And the component parts of Division C's ROI would be:

$$\text{ROI (Division C)} = \frac{\$435,000}{\$314,000} \times \frac{\$78,500}{\$435,000} = 1.3854 \times .1805 = .25 = 25\%$$

When the manager of Robinjon (Division A) sees the results for return on sales, asset turnover, and ROI, he or she will likely be disappointed, whether the results are being compared to Divisions B and C, other companies, industry averages, or minimum levels of performance. An ROI of 1.4% is pretty poor, especially when you realize that the value of the assets could instead be invested in risk-free government bonds and earn a higher rate. Improvements are needed, and this is where the two component parts of ROI come into play.

To improve ROI for Robinjon, or for any other investment center, management can do one of two things. It can increase the asset turnover without reducing the return on sales, or it can increase the return on sales without reducing the asset turnover. It can accomplish these goals by doing one of the following:

- Increase sales
- Reduce costs
- Reduce total assets

When sales are increased, the asset turnover improves (assuming that total assets don't also increase), but at the same time the return on sales is reduced (assuming no change in income). If nothing changes but sales dollars, then the offsetting effects on asset turnover and return on sales nullify each other. Ideally, however, an increase in sales will also increase income. An increase in income has a favorable impact on the return on sales, so whenever income increases, ROI will be improved.

A reduction in costs (without an equivalent reduction in sales) will increase the profits of the division, and therefore the return on sales. A larger return on sales, with no change in the asset turnover, will increase ROI.

Finally, a reduction in the asset base without a reduction in sales will also improve ROI. For one thing, the asset turnover will improve. For another, the return on sales may also improve if there is a reduction in the committed fixed costs that may be associated with the assets that have been reduced. For example, if we retire a productive asset that is still being depreciated, and the same work can be done with other assets that we currently own, then the sales remain the same, the depreciation expense goes down, the profit goes up, and the return on sales improves.

Let's see how Robinjon (Multiseg's Division A) plans to improve its ROI for next year.

## IMPROVING THE ROI FOR ROBINJON

The division manager for Robinjon feels that by slightly increasing its sales price, the division will increase total sales by 5% without increasing any of its variable costs. In addition, an old machine, which has served as a backup and is still being depreciated, will be retired at its book value. The book value of the machine is $200,000, and the annual depreciation has been $40,000. All other fixed costs will be unchanged.

The results of these changes will be as follows:

1. Total assets will decrease from $2,000,000 to $1,800,000.
2. Sales should increase to $1,314,600 ($1,252,000 × 1.05%), an increase of $62,600.
3. Costs will decrease by $40,000.
4. Income will increase by $102,600 ($62,600 + $40,000), to $131,400 ($28,800 + $102,600).

Robinjon's new ROI will be 7.3%:

$$\text{ROI} = \frac{\$1,314,600}{\$1,800,000} \times \frac{\$131,400}{\$1,314,600} = .73 \times .0999 = .073 = 7.3\%$$

By increasing the asset turnover from .626 to .73 and the return on sales from .023 to .0999, Robinjon will increase its ROI from 1.4% to 7.3%—still not outstanding, but much better than it was.

### Criticisms of Reliance on ROI

The use of ROI to determine which investment centers and investment center managers have done the best job and deserve to be rewarded has come under some harsh criticism. Its critics contend that ROI improperly motivates managers to focus their attention entirely on the short run and to make decisions that are detrimental to the firm in the long run. Remember, ROI is a short-run measure of success for an investment center; it measures profitability for a year or less. The success of the investment center manager usually depends on the performance of his or her division as measured by the reported ROI for the year. The higher the ROI, the bigger the bonus, the higher the raise, or the more likely the promotion. In addition, a high ROI makes it likely that more resources will be allocated to the investment center in the future, and the more resources the investment center manager has to work with, the greater the likelihood of continued success. It certainly is in the best interests of the division manager to do whatever it takes to maximize ROI.

When a manager attempts to improve ROI for his or her division without carefully considering the long-run impact, an improvement in ROI may actually have a negative impact on the long-run success of the division and of the firm as a whole. What may seem to be a good way to improve profits in the short run may impair the division's ability to operate profitably over the longer horizon. For example, each of the following popular approaches to improving ROI would have a negative long-run effect:

- Discretionary expenditures for items such as maintenance, inspection, training, research, and advertising might be postponed or eliminated. Each of these costs is likely to be vital to the long-run competitiveness and survival of the firm. However, it is often tempting to eliminate them in order to improve ROI for the year.

- Although current productive capacity may be old, inefficient, and unproductive, needed investments in new and modern plant and equipment are often delayed because such investments will have two negative effects on ROI. First, the asset base of the ROI calculation will increase, which decreases ROI. Second, depreciation expense will also increase. Since this reduces net income, it also results in a decreased ROI. On the positive side, the new investment is also expected to significantly increase the division's revenues and/or reduce other costs, either of which should improve ROI in the long run. These improvements may not materialize instantly, however, so they may be ignored because of their immediate negative effects on the asset base and depreciation expense.

- Any asset (such as investments in stocks and bonds, land, machinery, and equipment) having a book value less than its current market value might be sold in order to recognize the resulting gain on the current income statement. Despite the asset's usefulness in the long run and its potential contribution to future profits of the firm, the focus on short-run profits may overshadow long-run needs.

Everyone within the organization needs to realize that it is the long-run success of the firm that is of primary importance, and that extreme caution must be exercised in relying on ROI. Managers need to accept the fact that while it is certainly desirable to generate profits each and every year, the long-run horizon is more important, and decisions made solely to benefit the current year's ROI will not be tolerated. Top management needs to reinforce this policy by rewarding long-run as well as short-run achievements. Once division managers realize that contributions to the long-term success of the firm will be rewarded adequately and that their future in the organization will depend on this long-term success, they are likely to redirect their short-run focus.

**ASK YOURSELF** ▶

1. **What measure of performance is used to evaluate the profitability of an investment center? How is it calculated?**
2. **What are meant by asset turnover and return on sales?**
3. **Which of the following would increase the return on investment: an increase in sales, an increase in costs, or an increase in total assets?**
4. **Decisions that increase a division's ROI will always increase the firm's long-run profits as well. Do you agree?**

## SUMMARY

- There are three types of responsibility centers: cost centers, profit centers, and investment centers.
- In a **cost center** the responsible manager exerts influence over the costs incurred within that center, and is held accountable for keeping those costs within acceptable limits. The cost center manager has little if any influence over revenues or the investment in fixed assets that generates revenues.

- Many operating departments (production and selling and administrative departments) receive assistance from other departments that are not involved in operations, but are necessary for the efficient operation of the operating departments. These are **service departments.**
- Examples of service departments are machine maintenance, the storeroom, the cafeteria, personnel (human resources), purchasing, and factory administration. Since service departments are needed for operating departments to operate efficiently, their costs are assigned to the operating departments through a procedure called **cost allocation.**
- The service department costs allocated to production departments are treated as factory overhead costs of the production department.
- The **direct method** of cost allocation allocates the costs of each service department directly to the operating departments. With the direct method, the services that one service department provides to another are ignored; service department costs are not allocated to other service departments.
- The second type of responsibility center is the **profit center.** Within a profit center, the manager is responsible for both the costs and revenues generated by that center. The manager is held accountable for most aspects of profit. Examples of profit centers might include departments, branches, divisions, regions, and subsidiaries of a company.
- The performance of a profit center and the profit center manager are evaluated by the information reported in **segment income statements.** The segment income statement uses a contribution margin format; it distinguishes variable from fixed costs, direct from indirect costs, and controllable from uncontrollable costs.
- The profitability of a profit center manager is measured by the income called *contribution margin controllable by the segment manager.* The best measure of profitability for the entire profit center is the income called *contribution of the segment to common costs.*
- The third type of responsibility center is the **investment center.** An investment center's manager makes all decisions that relate to that center. The manager has control over the costs incurred and the revenues generated, as well as influence over the amount of investment available to generate the profit of that center.
- The performance of an investment center is evaluated by its **return on investment, or ROI.** ROI is calculated by dividing the investment center's income by its assets. The component parts that make up ROI are the asset turnover and return on sales:

$$\text{ROI} = \text{asset turnover} \times \text{return on sales}$$

$$\text{ROI} = \frac{\text{sales}}{\text{assets}} \times \frac{\text{income}}{\text{sales}} = \frac{\text{income}}{\text{assets}}$$

- The ROI for an investment center can be improved by either increasing the asset turnover without reducing the return on sales or increasing the return on sales without decreasing the asset turnover. This can be accomplished by increasing sales, reducing costs, or reducing total assets.
- Many critics contend that reliance on ROI may be inappropriate, because it often motivates managers to make decisions that improve short-run ROI at the expense of long-term profits. An investment center manager needs to be sure that any efforts to improve ROI for the current period do not have a negative impact on the firm's ability to compete and survive over the longer horizon.

## 8  KEY TERMS

| | |
|---|---|
| **Allocation base** | The link between a service department and the operating departments it services. The basis for determining the portion of service department costs to be allocated to each operating department. |
| **Asset turnover** | The dollars of revenue that each dollar of assets is able to generate, calculated as follows: Asset turnover = sales ÷ assets. |
| **Common costs** | Costs, such as the costs of running a corporate headquarters, that are related only indirectly to the different segments of the organization. |
| **Cost allocation** | The procedure used to assign the costs of service departments to operating departments. |
| **Cost center** | A responsibility center whose manager exerts influence over its costs, but not over the revenues that may be generated by the center or the investment that generates the revenues. |
| **Direct method** | The method of allocating service department costs, in a single direct step, to each of the operating departments serviced. |
| **Investment center** | A responsibility center whose manager makes all the decisions that relate to that center. The manager is given authority to control the costs and revenues, as well as the investment that generates the profit. |
| **Profit center** | A responsibility center whose manager is given the responsibility for controlling the costs and revenues of the center, but not for controlling the investment in assets that generates the costs and revenues. |
| **Return on investment (ROI)** | The measure of performance for an investment center. It is determined by dividing the investment center's assets into its income. |
| **Return on sales** | The percentage of every sales dollar that remains after all costs have been covered. Its calculation is: Return on sales = income ÷ sales. |
| **Segment** | Any part of an organization for which both costs and revenues can be identified as relating to that part. |
| **Segment income statement** | The evaluation tool for measuring the performance of profit centers and profit center managers. |
| **Service departments** | Departments that provide assistance, or service, to operating departments. They are not involved directly in the operations of the company but are needed to help the operating departments operate as efficiently as possible. |

## DEMONSTRATION PROBLEM

Keith Watson & Associates produces a variety of health and beauty supplies and operates in New Jersey, Utah, and Florida. Each of the three locations is set up as an independent division. Relevant information about these three divisions for 1998 is given below.

| | New Jersey | Utah | Florida |
|---|---|---|---|
| Sales. . . . . . . . . . . . . . . . . . . . . . . . . . . . . . . . . . . | $150,000 | $250,000 | $400,000 |
| Variable costs: | | | |
|   Manufacturing. . . . . . . . . . . . . . . . . . . . . . . . . . | 60,000 | 75,000 | 140,000 |
|   Selling and Administrative . . . . . . . . . . . . . . . . | 30,000 | 50,000 | 40,000 |
| Fixed costs of division: | | | |
|   Controllable by division manager. . . . . . . . . . . . | 38,000 | 57,000 | 95,000 |
|   Noncontrollable by division manager. . . . . . . . . | 16,000 | 17,000 | 32,000 |

The common costs of running the corporate headquarters ($66,000) are allocated equally among the three divisions.

**Required:**

1. Prepare a detailed segment income statement, with separate columns for each division and for the company as a whole.

2. Calculate the ROI, using the contribution of division to common costs as each division's income. The total assets of each division are as follows:

New Jersey . . . . . . . . . . . . . . . . . . . . . . . . . . $300,000
Utah. . . . . . . . . . . . . . . . . . . . . . . . . . . . . . . . . 400,000
Florida . . . . . . . . . . . . . . . . . . . . . . . . . . . . . . 350,000

Also determine the component parts (asset turnover and return on sales) that make up the ROI of each division.

3. Assume that sales for the Florida division are expected to increase to $600,000 in 1999 because of a $100,000 increase in the division's depreciable assets (10-year lives). The variable cost ratios will remain the same as they were in 1998. The fixed costs will change by the amount of additional depreciation. Calculate the ROI expected for the Florida division for 1999, showing each of the component parts.

■ **Solution to Demonstration Problem**

1.

### KEITH WATSON & ASSOCIATES
### Segment Income Statements
### For the Year 1998

| | New Jersey | Utah | Florida | Totals |
|---|---|---|---|---|
| Sales | $150,000 | $250,000 | $400,000 | $800,000 |
| Less: Variable costs: | | | | |
|     Variable manufacturing | $ 60,000 | $ 75,000 | $140,000 | $275,000 |
|     Variable selling and administrative of division | 30,000 | 50,000 | 40,000 | 120,000 |
| | $ 90,000 | $125,000 | $180,000 | $395,000 |
| Total contribution margin | $ 60,000 | $125,000 | $220,000 | $405,000 |
| Less: Fixed costs (controllable by division manager) | 38,000 | 57,000 | 95,000 | 190,000 |
| Contribution controllable by the division manager | $ 22,000 | $ 68,000 | $125,000 | $215,000 |
| Less: Fixed costs of division not controllable by the division manager | 16,000 | 17,000 | 32,000 | 65,000 |
| Contribution of the division to common costs | $  6,000 | $ 51,000 | $ 93,000 | $150,000 |
| Common costs of all divisions | 22,000 | 22,000 | 22,000 | 66,000 |
| Net Income | $ (16,000) | $ 29,000 | $ 71,000 | $ 84,000 |

2. New Jersey:

$$\text{ROI} = \text{asset turnover} \times \text{return on sales}$$

$$= \frac{\text{sales}}{\text{assets}} \times \frac{\text{income}}{\text{sales}} = \frac{\$150,000}{\$300,000} \times \frac{\$6,000}{\$150,000}$$

$$= .50 \times 4.00\% = 2.00\%$$

Utah:

$$\text{ROI} = \frac{\text{sales}}{\text{assets}} \times \frac{\text{income}}{\text{sales}} = \frac{\$250,000}{\$400,000} \times \frac{\$51,000}{\$250,000}$$

$$= .625 \times 20.40\% = 12.75\%$$

Florida:

$$\text{ROI} = \frac{\text{sales}}{\text{assets}} \times \frac{\text{income}}{\text{sales}} = \frac{\$400,000}{\$350,000} \times \frac{\$93,000}{\$400,000}$$

$$= 1.143 \times 23.25\% = 26.57\%$$

3.

$$\text{ROI} = \text{asset turnover} \times \text{return on sales}$$

$$= \frac{\$600,000}{\$450,000} \times \frac{\$193,000*}{\$600,000} = 1.3333 \times 32.166\% = 42.89\%$$

* $600,000 − .45($600,000) − ($95,000 + $32,000 + $10,000) = $193,000

## QUESTIONS FOR REVIEW AND FURTHER THOUGHT

### REVIEW QUESTIONS

1. What are the three types of responsibility centers? Explain each type.

2. Explain what a cost center is.

3. How can you evaluate the results of a cost center for a period of time?

4. What are service departments? Give several examples.

5. What is an allocation base? List the allocation bases that might be appropriate for several types of service departments.

6. Explain how service department costs are allocated with the direct method.

7. Explain what a profit center is. How does it differ from a cost center?

8. What is a segment income statement?

9. What are the three different ways of distinguishing costs within the segment income statement?

10. Within the segment income statement, there are three important subtotals: total contribution margin, contribution controllable by segment manager, and contribution of segment to common costs. Define each.

11. What is an investment center? How does it differ from a profit center?

12. How do we measure the performance of an investment center?

13. What is ROI? What are its component parts?

14. A manager can increase his or her division's ROI in one of three general ways. What are they?

### QUESTIONS FOR FURTHER THOUGHT

1. Why do we allocate the costs of service departments to the departments they service?

2. The costs of service departments for a manufacturer become a part of the cost of a manufactured good. Explain why this is so, since service department costs are not incurred within the producing departments.

3. When service department costs are allocated to production departments, are the allocated costs direct materials, direct labor, factory overhead, or all three? Explain your answer.

4. When a segment income statement is prepared, which measure of income should be used to evaluate the profit center? The profit center manager?

5. How would you evaluate the performance of a profit center manager once you have determined the contribution margin controllable by him or her?

6. What are common costs? Do you think they should be allocated to the different profit centers?

7. Why may it be inappropriate to base the size of bonuses or the timing of promotions for profit center managers on the amount of profit earned by each profit center?

8. How would each of the following changes affect a division's ROI for the year?
   a. An increase in total sales resulting from a reduction in the sales price
   b. Investment in depreciable assets, which has no impact on sales in the upcoming year
   c. Reduction in advertising expenditures, with no immediate impact on sales
   d. Termination of an incompetent employee
   e. Reduction in regular maintenance on machines from once a month to once a quarter
   f. An increase in the cost of raw materials
   g. Sale of an idle and fully depreciated asset at a loss

9. Each of the following actions has a positive impact on ROI in the short run. Discuss how each action might affect the firm's long-run profitability.
   a. Reducing labor costs by teaching workers how to be more efficient in performing their tasks
   b. Reducing the costs of inspection by inspecting every other unit instead of every single unit produced
   c. Disposal of productive assets at a gain
   d. Increasing sales by dumping defective goods in Third World markets
   e. Eliminating all routine maintenance costs on machinery used in production.

## OBJECTIVE ASSIGNMENT

*True/False*   Indicate whether each statement below is *true* or *false* by placing a *T* or an *F* in the space provided.

_____ 1. A production department is an example of a cost center.

_____ 2. The three types of responsibility centers are cost centers, profit centers, and contribution centers.

_____ 3. A manufacturer's service departments provide service only to its production departments.

_____ 4. ROI is a measure of performance for investment centers.

_____ 5. The contribution margin format is used with the segment income statement to evaluate the profitability of a profit center.

*Multiple Choice*   Select the best choice to complete each statement or answer each question below. Write the letter corresponding to your choice in the space provided.

_____ 1. Which of the following is *not* a type of responsibility center?
   a. Cost center      c. Segment center
   b. Profit center    d. Investment center

_____ 2. In a performance report for a cost center, the best measure of efficiency is:
   a. The quantity variance          c. The production volume variance
   b. The sales volume variance      d. The flexible budget variance

_____ 3. The allocation base that would probably be preferable for allocating the costs of a personnel department is:
   a. The number of direct labor hours      c. The amount of direct materials used
   b. The number of units produced          d. The number of employees

_____ 4. When service department costs are allocated to production departments, the production departments classify the allocated costs as:
   a. Direct materials costs
   b. Direct labor costs
   c. Factory overhead costs
   d. All of the above

_____ 5. The best measure of performance for a profit center manager is:
   a. Total contribution margin
   b. Contribution controllable by segment manager
   c. Contribution of segment to common costs
   d. Net income

_____ 6. The contribution margin format of a segment income statement distinguishes:
   a. Variable from fixed costs
   b. Direct from indirect costs
   c. Controllable from noncontrollable costs
   d. All of the above

_____ 7. When a manager has a significant influence over the revenues, the costs, and the investment in productive assets that generates a division's profits, this manager is most likely:
   a. A cost center manager
   b. A profit center manager
   c. An investment center manager
   d. None of the above

_____ 8. The ROI for an investment center is determined by the calculation:
   a. Income ÷ assets     c. Income ÷ sales
   b. Assets ÷ income     d. Income × sales

_____ 9. ROI is composed of two parts. They are:
   a. Asset turnover × return on sales
   b. Asset turnover ÷ return on sales
   c. Income × asset turnover
   d. Income × investment

_____ 10. The ROI for a profit center is reduced by:
   a. An increase in sales
   b. A decrease in costs
   c. An increase in assets
   d. All of the above

## EXERCISES

2† **Exercise 1:** Selecting an Allocation Base for Allocating Service Department Costs

For each type of service department listed in column A, select the best allocation base from column B and write the corresponding letter in the space provided.

**A. Service Department**

_____ 1. Machine maintenance
_____ 2. Medical clinic
_____ 3. Storeroom
_____ 4. Day care
_____ 5. Human Resources
_____ 6. Factory administration
_____ 7. Employees' lounge
_____ 8. Janitorial service
_____ 9. Computer services
_____ 10. Exercise room

**B. Allocation Base**

a. Number of units produced
b. Total labor hours worked
c. Number of employees serviced
d. Total employees
e. Machine hours used in production
f. Square feet of space
g. Number of requisitions
h. Hours of computer time

2 **Exercise 2:** Allocating Service Department Costs to Production and Nonproduction Departments

The Stickum Rubber Cement Company has two service departments, storeroom and cafeteria. These two departments provide service to two production departments, 1 and 2, as well as to the

† The numbers in the margin refer to the Learning Objectives.

selling department and the administrative offices. The costs of the service departments are allocated according to the following percentages:

| | Percentage Allocated to: | | | | |
| Service Dept. | Selling | Administrative | Dept. 1 | Dept. 2 | Total |
| --- | --- | --- | --- | --- | --- |
| Storeroom ............... | 10% | 5% | 50% | 35% | 100% |
| Cafeteria ................ | 20% | 20% | 30% | 30% | 100% |

The costs of operating the storeroom are $80,000, and the costs of operating the cafeteria are $150,000. Determine how each service department's costs are allocated to the two production departments, to the selling department, and to the administrative offices.

▶ *(Check Figure: Allocation of storeroom costs to department 2 = $28,000; to selling = $8,000)*

2 **Exercise 3:** Allocating Service Department Costs to Two Operating Departments

The Kitty Whiskers Cat Food Company has two service departments and two operating departments. The two service departments are factory administration and inspection—each one servicing only the two operating departments. The operating departments are cooking and canning. The costs of factory administration ($60,000) are allocated to the operating departments on the basis of the number of total labor hours worked in each of the two operating departments. The costs of inspection ($120,000) are allocated on the basis of the number of units inspected for each operating department. In addition, the following information relates to the two allocation bases:

| | Cooking | Canning |
| --- | --- | --- |
| Hours of labor time .................................... | 2,500 | 1,500 |
| Units inspected ....................................... | 5,000 | 15,000 |

Determine how the costs of each service department would be allocated to the cooking and canning departments.

▶ *(Check Figure: Allocation of inspection costs to canning = $90,000)*

4 **Exercise 4:** Identifying Key Items on a Segment Income Statement

Shown below is the format for a segment income statement. Identify which line of the statement is being described in the list that follows it by placing the number of the line in the space provided.

> (1) Sales
> (2) Less: Variable Costs:
>         Variable Manufacturing
>         Variable Selling and Administrative Costs of Segment
> (3) Total Contribution Margin
> (4) Less: Direct Fixed Costs Controllable by Segment Manager
> (5) Contribution Controllable by Segment Manager
> (6) Less: Fixed Costs of Segment Not Controllable by Segment Manager
> (7) Contribution of Segment to Common Costs
> (8) Common Costs for All Segments
> (9) Net Income

\_\_\_\_ **a.** The best measure of performance for the segment manager.
\_\_\_\_ **b.** The income the segment would have if it were an independent company.
\_\_\_\_ **c.** The sum of these for all segments represents net income for the entire firm.
\_\_\_\_ **d.** Advertising costs for the segment, determined by the segment manager.
\_\_\_\_ **e.** The amount by which the total income for the firm will decrease if the segment is eliminated.
\_\_\_\_ **f.** An example of this type of cost is depreciation on the building that houses the segment's operations.
\_\_\_\_ **g.** An example of this type of cost is national advertising for the firm as a whole.
\_\_\_\_ **h.** The most controllable measure of income in the short run.

▶ *(Check Figure: a. 5)*

4 **Exercise 5:** Preparing a Segment Income Statement

Florida Products is one division of a multidivisional conglomerate. Its results for 1997 are presented below.

| | |
|---|---:|
| Sales | $36,000,000 |
| Manufacturing Costs: | |
| Variable | 12,000,000 |
| Fixed—Controllable by Division Manager | 4,500,000 |
| —Noncontrollable by Division Manager | 3,000,000 |
| Selling and Administrative Costs of Division | |
| Variable | 3,000,000 |
| Fixed—Controllable by Division Manager | 1,500,000 |
| —Noncontrollable by Division Manager | 1,800,000 |
| Common Costs Allocated to Division | 2,250,000 |

Prepare a segment income statement using the format given in Exhibit 6.

▶ *(Check Figure: Net income = $7,950,000)*

6 7 **Exercise 6:** Evaluating ROI and Its Component Parts

The income statement below was prepared by the accounting department of the College Textbook Division of the Ervin Book Company:

| | | |
|---|---:|---:|
| Sales | | $52,000,000 |
| Less: Variable Costs: | | |
| Variable Manufacturing | $15,000,000 | |
| Variable Selling and Administration of Segment | 10,000,000 | 25,000,000 |
| Total Contribution Margin | | $27,000,000 |
| Less: Direct Fixed Costs Controllable by Segment Manager | | 10,000,000 |
| Contribution Controllable by Segment Manager | | $17,000,000 |
| Less: Fixed Costs of Segment not Controllable by Segment Manager | | 5,000,000 |
| Contribution of Segment to Common Costs | | $12,000,000 |
| Common Costs for All Segments | | 3,000,000 |
| Net Income | | $ 9,000,000 |

The total assets of the College Division are $30,000,000.

**a.** Calculate the ROI that would be the best measure of performance for the division manager. Also determine the component parts (asset turnover and return on sales) of the ROI.

**b.** Repeat part (a), but this time let the answer represent the best measure of performance for the division as a whole.

▶ *(Check Figure: b. Return on sales = 23.08%)*

**6 7 Exercise 7:** Calculating Asset Turnover, Return on Sales, and ROI

Return on investment (ROI) is used to evaluate the Southern Region of Whirley Helicopter Sales, Inc., as an investment center. During 1998, the operation had assets of $50,000,000 and earned an income of $2,500,000 from sales of $10,000,000. Determine the following performance measures:

a. Return on sales
b. Asset turnover
c. ROI

▶ *(Check Figure: ROI = 5%)*

**6 7 Exercise 8:** Calculating ROI Components

The Acrossamerica Company is a multidivision company that uses ROI to determine each division's profitability. Partial information concerning three of its divisions is shown below. Calculate all of the missing information to complete the analysis.

|  | Division A | Division B | Division C |
|---|---|---|---|
| Sales. . . . . . . . . . . . . . . . . . . . . . . . . . . . | $500,000 | $2,100,000 | $ _____ |
| Total assets . . . . . . . . . . . . . . . . . . . . . . . | 250,000 | | |
| Income . . . . . . . . . . . . . . . . . . . . . . . . . | 25,000 | | 30,000 |
| Return on sales . . . . . . . . . . . . . . . . . . . . | _____ | 15% | 1% |
| Asset turnover . . . . . . . . . . . . . . . . . . . . . | _____ | 3 | |
| ROI. . . . . . . . . . . . . . . . . . . . . . . . . . . . . | _____ | _____ | 4% |

▶ *(Check Figure: Division A ROI = 10%; Division B ROI = 45%)*

**6 7 Exercise 9:** Changing the ROI for a Profit Center

The Wholly Smoke Charcoal Division bases its ROI calculation for 1997 on the following results:

| | |
|---|---|
| Sales . . . . . . . . . . . . . . . . . . . . . . . . . . . . . . . . . . . . . . . . . . . . . . . . . . . . . . . . . | $1,000,000 |
| Variable Costs . . . . . . . . . . . . . . . . . . . . . . . . . . . . . . . . . . . . . . . . . . . . . . . . . . . | 600,000 |
| Total Contribution Margin . . . . . . . . . . . . . . . . . . . . . . . . . . . . . . . . . . . . . . . . . . | $ 400,000 |
| Fixed Costs . . . . . . . . . . . . . . . . . . . . . . . . . . . . . . . . . . . . . . . . . . . . . . . . . . . . . | 200,000 |
| Segment Income . . . . . . . . . . . . . . . . . . . . . . . . . . . . . . . . . . . . . . . . . . . . . . . . . | $ 200,000 |
| Total Assets of Division . . . . . . . . . . . . . . . . . . . . . . . . . . . . . . . . . . . . . . . . . . . | $2,000,000 |

a. Calculate ROI for 1997. Also determine the component parts of ROI (asset turnover and return on sales).

b. Assume that Wholly Smoke expects the following changes to take place in 1998:
   1. Sales will increase by 20% due to an increase in the division's productive assets.
   2. The investment in productive assets of $250,000 will increase annual depreciation expense by $25,000.
   Repeat the requirements in part (a), but this time calculate the expected ROI (and its component parts) for 1998.

c. Disregard part (b) and assume instead that Wholly Smoke expects to take the following actions in 1998:
   1. Reduce the advertising budget by $25,000.
   2. Dispose of productive assets having a cost of $100,000, which will result in a $20,000 gain on sale. The depreciation per year on this asset is $10,000.
   3. As a consequence of the two actions above, sales are expected to fall by $100,000.
   Repeat part (a) by calculating the expected ROI (and its component parts) for 1998.

▶ *(Check Figure: b. ROI = 11.33%; c. ROI = 11.32%)*

## PROBLEMS: SET A

2† **Problem A1:** Allocating Service Department Costs

Bitter Blue Company uses two production departments, A and B, to produce a combination chewing tobacco and garden fertilizer. In addition, there are a machine maintenance department and a storeroom. The costs of the machine maintenance department are allocated between departments A and B on the basis of the number of labor hours used by the maintenance department to keep the machines of each production department in good condition. The costs of the storeroom are allocated on the basis of the number of requisitions processed.

The costs of each production department (based on expected production of 100,000 cases of the product) were budgeted for 1998, as follows:

|  | Department A | Department B |
|---|---|---|
| Direct Materials. . . . . . . . . . . . . . . . . . . . . . . . . . . . . . | $ 800,000 | $ 300,000 |
| Direct Labor. . . . . . . . . . . . . . . . . . . . . . . . . . . . . . . . | 400,000 | 400,000 |
| Factory Overhead . . . . . . . . . . . . . . . . . . . . . . . . . . | 1,500,000 | 800,000 |
|  | $2,700,000 | $1,500,000 |

The budgeted costs for 1998 are $360,000 for the maintenance department and $120,000 for the storeroom. Bitter Blue expected the maintenance department to spend 8,000 hours during the year doing maintenance on the production machinery: 6,000 for department A and 2,000 for department B. Finally, the number of requisitions expected to be processed by the storeroom in 1998 are 8,000 for department A and 2,000 for department B.

**Required:**

1. Determine the amount of budgeted service department costs that would be assigned to each production department.
2. What are the total factory overhead costs budgeted for each production department?

▶ *(Check Figure: 2. Department A factory overhead = $1,866,000)*

4 6 **Problem A2:** Using ROI to Evaluate the Performance of Different Divisions

Weedbegone Company, a manufacturer of lawn products, has three divisions: grass seed, fertilizer, and weed killer. Relevant information about these three divisions for 1997 is given below:

|  | Grass Seed | Fertilizer | Weed Killer |
|---|---|---|---|
| Units Sold (bags) . . . . . . . . . . . . . . . . . . . . . . . . . . . | 10,000 | 15,000 | 28,000 |
| Sales Price . . . . . . . . . . . . . . . . . . . . . . . . . . . . . . . . | $45.00 | $12.50 | $6.00 |
| Variable Costs (per unit): |  |  |  |
|   Manufacturing . . . . . . . . . . . . . . . . . . . . . . . . . . . . | $15.00 | $4.00 | $1.80 |
|   Selling and Administrative . . . . . . . . . . . . . . . . . . | $ 4.50 | $1.00 | $0.50 |
| Fixed Costs of Division: |  |  |  |
|   Controllable by Division Manager. . . . . . . . . . . . . . | $70,000 | $45,000 | $20,000 |
|   Noncontrollable by Division Manager. . . . . . . . . . . | $70,000 | $70,000 | $30,000 |
| Allocated Common Costs. . . . . . . . . . . . . . . . . . . . . | $50,000 | $50,000 | $50,000 |

† The numbers in the margin refer to the Learning Objectives.

**Required:**

1. Prepare a detailed segment income statement. Use a separate column for each division and for the company as a whole.
2. Which income measure would be the best indicator of the performance of the division manager? Of the division?
3. Calculate ROI for each division if each division's total assets are as follows:

| | |
|---|---|
| Grass seed............................. | $300,000 |
| Fertilizer ................................ | 80,000 |
| Weed killer ............................. | 90,000 |

Assume that the income to be used in calculating ROI is the division's contribution to common costs.

▶ (Check Figure: 1. Net income for grass seed division = $65,000; 3. Weed killer division ROI = 59.56%)

**4   Problem A3:** Preparing Segment Income Statements for Divisions That Sell to Each Other

A leather division sells all the cut leather it produces to the baseball glove division of Sports Limited. The sales price of leather needed for one glove is $8, and the final sales price of a completed glove is $45. Other relevant data related to the production and sales of the two divisions is given below:

| | Leather Division | Baseball Glove Division |
|---|---|---|
| Unit Sales ......................................... | 200,000 | 200,000 |
| Sales Price ....................................... | $      8 | $      45 |
| Variable Cost per Unit: | | |
|   Manufacturing ...................................... | $      4 | $      22* |
|   Selling .......................................... | 1 | 5 |
| | $      5 | $      27 |
| Contribution Margin per Unit............................ | $      3 | $      18 |
| Total Fixed Costs: | | |
|   Manufacturing ...................................... | $240,000 | $400,000 |
|   Selling .......................................... | 110,000 | 75,000 |
| | $350,000 | $475,000 |

* Includes $8 for the cost of the leather.

**Required:**

1. Determine the operating incomes for the leather and baseball glove divisions. Also determine the combined incomes for the two divisions.
2. Repeat part (1), this time assuming that the sales price of the leather division is $10 instead of $8.
3. Comment on the results in parts (1) and (2). What effect does the price charged by the leather division have on the combined profits for Sports Limited?

▶ (Check Figure: 1. Combined incomes = $3,375,000; 2. Combined incomes = $3,375,000)

**4  6  7   Problem A4:** Calculating ROI, Asset Turnover, and Return on Sales for Different Situations

Wolves Dance Records is a division of Dunbar Enterprises. During 1998, the division turned a profit of $1,350,000.

| | |
|---|---|
| Sales (600,000 records) | $4,200,000 |
| Total Costs: | |
|   Total Variable Costs | ($1,800,000) |
|   Total Fixed Costs: | |
|     Directly Related to Wolves ...... $600,000 | |
|     Allocated Common Costs ...... 450,000 | (1,050,000) |
| Net Income | $1,350,000 |

During 1998, Wolves' total assets were $25,000,000.

**Required:**

1. Revise the income statement, using as a guide the format shown in Exhibit 6.
2. Calculate ROI for Wolves, using contribution of segment to common costs as the income measure. Also determine the component parts that make up ROI: asset turnover and return on sales.
3. Wolves is considering several changes to improve ROI. For each change given below, calculate the new asset turnover, return on sales, and ROI.
   a. Change no. 1: If the sales price is reduced by $1, unit sales should increase by 100,000 records.
   b. Change no. 2: A decrease of $.40 in the variable cost per unit and a reduction of $60,000 in the division's fixed costs are not expected to have any effect on the number of records sold.

▶ (Check Figure: 2. ROI = 7.2%; 3. Change no. 2, ROI = 8.4%)

**4   Problem A5:** Measuring Efficiency and Effectiveness of a Profit Center with a Segment Income Statement

The Come Alive Battery Charger Company uses standard costs and flexible budgets in the planning and control of its operations. The standards for the variable costs are as follows:

| | |
|---|---|
| Direct Materials | $ 6/unit |
| Direct Labor | 4/unit |
| Variable Overhead | 2/unit |
| Variable Selling | 1/unit |
| | $13/unit |

The budgeted fixed costs are the following:

| | |
|---|---|
| Factory Overhead | $500,000 |
| Selling | 200,000 |
| | $700,000 |

Come Alive expects to sell its battery chargers for $40 each. At the beginning of the year, Come Alive estimated that it would produce and sell 35,000 units, but when the year was over it had produced and sold 5,000 units fewer than that. The actual costs incurred for the year were as follows:

| | |
|---|---|
| Direct Materials | $196,000 |
| Direct Labor | 115,000 |
| Variable Overhead | 55,000 |
| Variable Selling | 29,400 |
| Fixed Factory Overhead | 510,000 |
| Fixed Selling | 199,000 |

The average selling price per unit for the year was $44.

**Required:**

1. Prepare a performance report for the entire income statement. Use the following format:

| | Actual Results | Flexible Budget Variance | Flexible Budget for 30,000 Units | Sales Volume Variance | Master Budget |
|---|---|---|---|---|---|
| Sales. . . . . . . . . . . . . . | | | | | |
| Variable Costs . . . . . . . | | | | | |
| • | | | | | |
| • | | | | | |
| • | | | | | |
| Net Income. . . . . . . . . | | | | | |

2. What does the sales volume variance represent?

▶ *(Check Figure: 1. Sales volume variance = $135,000 U)*

## PROBLEMS: SET B

2† **Problem B1:** Allocating Service Department Costs

The R. Jackson Company produces baseballs for university and college teams. There are two operating departments—cutting and sewing—and two service departments—stores and janitorial. At the beginning of 1997, the company controller determined the following budgeted amounts for the year.

| Operating Departments | Factory Overhead | Direct Labor Hours |
|---|---|---|
| Cutting . . . . . . . . . . . . . . . . . . . . . . . . . . . . . . . . . . . . | $480,000 | 20,000 |
| Sewing. . . . . . . . . . . . . . . . . . . . . . . . . . . . . . . . . . . . | 420,000 | 16,000 |

| Service Departments | Total Costs |
|---|---|
| Stores . . . . . . . . . . . . . . . . . . . . . . . . . . . . . . . . . . . . | $24,000 |
| Janitorial . . . . . . . . . . . . . . . . . . . . . . . . . . . . . . . . . . | 96,000 |

The budgeted costs of stores are allocated to the operating departments on the basis of the number of orders to be filled. The costs of the janitorial services are allocated on the basis of the number of square feet of space cleaned each night. At the beginning of the year the allocation bases were expected to be as follows:

| | Orders to Be Filled in 1997 | Square Feet to Be Cleaned in 1997 |
|---|---|---|
| Cutting Department. . . . . . . . . . . . . . . . . . . . . . . . | 3,600 | 1,000 |
| Sewing Department . . . . . . . . . . . . . . . . . . . . . . . | 1,200 | 3,000 |
| Stores Department . . . . . . . . . . . . . . . . . . . . . . . | n/a | 500 |
| Janitorial Department . . . . . . . . . . . . . . . . . . . . . . | n/a | 200 |

† The numbers in the margin refer to the Learning Objectives.

**Required:**

1. Determine the amount of budgeted service department costs that would be assigned to each operating department.
2. What are the total factory overhead costs budgeted for each operating department?

▶ *(Check Figure: 1. Stores costs allocated to cutting = $18,000; 2. Sewing = $498,000)*

4 6 **Problem B2:** Using ROI to Evaluate the Performance of Different Departments

Buffalo Chips Farm Supply has three departments: fertilizer, garden plants, and garden tools. Relevant information about these three departments for 1998 is given on the next page:

| | Fertilizer | Garden Plants | Garden Tools |
|---|---|---|---|
| Sales. . . . . . . . . . . . . . . . . . . . . . . . . . . . . . . . . . . | $60,000 | $40,000 | $50,000 |
| Variable Cost Percentages: | | | |
| Manufacturing . . . . . . . . . . . . . . . . . . . . . . . . . . . . | 40% | 30% | 35% |
| Selling and Administrative . . . . . . . . . . . . . . . . . . . . | 20% | 20% | 10% |
| Fixed Costs of Department: | | | |
| Controllable by Department Manager . . . . . . . . . . . | $ 8,000 | $ 7,000 | $15,000 |
| Noncontrollable by Department Manager . . . . . . . . | 6,000 | 7,000 | 10,000 |
| Allocated Common Costs. . . . . . . . . . . . . . . . . . . . . | 3,000 | 2,000 | 6,000 |

**Required:**

1. Prepare a detailed segment income statement. Use a separate column for each department and for the company as a whole.
2. Which income measure would be the best indicator of the performance of the department manager? Of the department?
3. Calculate ROI for each department if the total assets are as follows:

Fertilizer . . . . . . . . . . . . . . . . . . . . . . . . . . . . . . . . $300,000
Garden Plants . . . . . . . . . . . . . . . . . . . . . . . . . . . . 80,000
Garden Tools . . . . . . . . . . . . . . . . . . . . . . . . . . . . . 50,000

Assume that the income to be used in calculating ROI is the segment's contribution to common costs.

▶ *(Check Figure: 1. Net income for fertilizer department = $7,000; 3. ROI for tools department = 5%)*

4 **Problem B3:** Preparing Segment Income Statements for Divisions That Sell to Each Other

On Jan. 1, 1998, the Panasony Television Company acquired Sharp Image, a picture tube manufacturer. Starting immediately, Sharp Image must sell all the picture tubes it makes to Panasony.

Prior to 1998, Sharp had sold all its picture tubes to various American manufacturers for

$150 apiece, and Panasony purchased all its picture tubes from a company in Taiwan for $125 each. The income statements for both companies for 1997 are given below:

**PANASONY TELEVISION CO.**
**Income Statements**
**For the Year 1997**

|  | Sharp Image | Panasony Television |
|---|---|---|
| Unit Sales | 10,000 | 10,000 |
| Sales Revenue | $1,500,000 | $7,500,000 |
| Total Variable Costs: |  |  |
| Manufacturing | $ 600,000 | $4,000,000* |
| Selling | 150,000 | 750,000 |
|  | $ 750,000 | $4,750,000 |
| Total Contribution Margin | $ 750,000 | $2,750,000 |
| Total Fixed Costs: |  |  |
| Manufacturing | $ 500,000 | $1,000,000 |
| Selling | 150,000 | 200,000 |
|  | $ 650,000 | $1,200,000 |
| Operating Income | $ 100,000 | $1,550,000 |

* Includes $1,250,000 for the costs of picture tubes.

Sharp Image, which will operate as a division of Panasony, believes that the price for all shipments of picture tubes to Panasony should be the same as the price it received from American manufacturers in 1997, or $150 apiece. Panasony, however, thinks that the price should be the cost it paid the Taiwanese manufacturer, in 1997, or $125 apiece.

**Required:**

1. Determine the operating incomes for Sharp Image and Panasony individually, and for the two combined in 1998. Assume that Sharp Image continues to sell 10,000 picture tubes to Panasony, and that Panasony sells 10,000 televisions to the general public. Use the price of $150.
2. Repeat part (1), this time using the price of $125.
3. Comment on the results in parts (1) and (2). What effect does the price charged by Sharp Image have on the combined profits?

▶ *(Check Figure: 1. Combined incomes = $1,400,000; 2. Combined incomes = $1,400,000)*

4 6 7 **Problem B4:** Calculating ROI, Asset Turnover, and Return on Sales for Different Situations

Recap Tires is a wholly owned subsidiary of Zusuki Motors Corporation. Recap's condensed income statement for 1997 showed a net income of $2,000,000.

| | |
|---|---|
| Sales (300,000 tires) | $18,000,000 |
| Total Variable Costs | (9,000,000) |
| Total Fixed Costs: | |
| Directly Related to Recap Tires | (4,000,000) |
| Allocated Common Costs | (3,000,000) |
| Net Income | $ 2,000,000 |

The condensed balance sheet for Recap on Dec. 31, 1997, included the following items:

| | | | |
|---|---|---|---|
| Current Assets . . . . . . . . . . | $ 3,000,000 | Current Liabilities . . . . . . . . | $ 1,000,000 |
| Fixed Assets (net) . . . . . . . | 7,000,000 | Long-Term Liabilities . . . . . | 3,000,000 |
| | | Owners' Equity . . . . . . . . . | 6,000,000 |
| | $10,000,000 | | $10,000,000 |

**Required:**

1. Revise the income statement, using as a guide the format shown in Exhibit 6.
2. Calculate the ROI for Recap Tires, using contribution of segment to common costs as the income measure. Also determine the component parts that make up ROI: asset turnover and return on sales.
3. Recap is considering several changes to improve its ROI. For each change given below, calculate the new asset turnover, return on sales, and ROI.
   a. Change no. 1: If Recap's advertising is increased by $500,000, the unit sales should increase by 10%. There is no change in the sales price or variable cost per unit.
   b. Change no. 2: A decrease of 10% in the sales price (with no change in the variable cost per unit) is expected to increase unit sales by 100,000 tires.

▶ (Check Figure: 2. ROI = 50%; 3. Change no. 2, ROI = 56%)

4   **Problem B5:** Measuring Efficiency and Effectiveness of a Profit Center with a Segment Income Statement

At the beginning of the year, Masterdisk prepared the following budget for the upcoming 12 months (based on the expected production and sales of 10,000 boxes of floppy disks).

| | | | |
|---|---|---|---|
| Sales . . . . . . . . . . . . . . . . . . . . . . . . . . . . . . . . . . . . . . . . . . . . . . . . . . . . | | | $200,000 |
| Total Variable Costs: | | | |
| Direct Materials . . . . . . . . . . . . . . . . . . . . . . . . . . . . . . . . . . . . . | | $30,000 | |
| Direct Labor . . . . . . . . . . . . . . . . . . . . . . . . . . . . . . . . . . . . . . . | | 40,000 | |
| Variable Overhead . . . . . . . . . . . . . . . . . . . . . . . . . . . . . . . . . . | | 10,000 | |
| | | $80,000 | |
| Variable Selling . . . . . . . . . . . . . . . . . . . . . . . . . . . . . . . . . . . . . | | 20,000 | 100,000 |
| Total Contribution Margin . . . . . . . . . . . . . . . . . . . . . . . . . . . . . . . . | | | $100,000 |
| Total Fixed Costs: | | | |
| Manufacturing . . . . . . . . . . . . . . . . . . . . . . . . . . . . . . . . . . . . . . | | $60,000 | |
| Selling . . . . . . . . . . . . . . . . . . . . . . . . . . . . . . . . . . . . . . . . . . . | | 30,000 | 90,000 |
| Net Income . . . . . . . . . . . . . . . . . . . . . . . . . . . . . . . . . . . . . . . . . | | | $ 10,000 |

Masterdisk uses a standard cost system to assist in the planning and control of operations. The standards for the variable costs are:

| | |
|---|---|
| Direct Materials . . . . . . . . . . . . . . . . . . . . . . . . . | $3.00/box |
| Direct Labor . . . . . . . . . . . . . . . . . . . . . . . . . . . | $4.00/box |
| Variable Overhead . . . . . . . . . . . . . . . . . . . . . . . | $1.00/box |
| Variable Selling . . . . . . . . . . . . . . . . . . . . . . . . | $2.00/box |

During the year, Masterdisk produced and sold 8,000 boxes, and the actual costs incurred were as follows:

| | |
|---|---|
| Direct Materials . . . . . . . . . . . . . . . . . . . . . . . . . . . | $28,000 |
| Direct Labor . . . . . . . . . . . . . . . . . . . . . . . . . . . . | 31,005 |
| Variable Overhead . . . . . . . . . . . . . . . . . . . . . . . . | 8,500 |
| Variable Selling . . . . . . . . . . . . . . . . . . . . . . . . . | 15,200 |
| Fixed Factory Overhead . . . . . . . . . . . . . . . . . . . . | 62,000 |
| Fixed Selling . . . . . . . . . . . . . . . . . . . . . . . . . . . | 31,000 |

The average selling price per unit for the year was $1 less than expected.

**Required:**

1. Prepare a performance report for the entire income statement. Use the following format:

| | Actual Results | Flexible Budget Variance | Flexible Budget for 8,000 Units | Sales Volume Variance | Master Budget |
|---|---|---|---|---|---|
| Sales . . . . . . . . . . . . . . . . | | | | | |
| Variable Costs . . . . . . . . . . | | | | | |
|     &bull; | | | | | |
|     &bull; | | | | | |
|     &bull; | | | | | |
| Net Income. . . . . . . . . . . . | | | | | |

2. What does the sales volume variance represent?

▶ *(Check Figure: 1. Sales volume variance = $20,000 U)*

## DECISION PROBLEM

Given below is information related to the three territories in which J. R. Dallas Oil Company operates.

| | United States | Canada | Middle East |
|---|---|---|---|
| Sales . . . . . . . . . . . . . . . . . . . . . . . . . . | $87,000,000 | $42,000,000 | $96,000,000 |
| Total Contribution Margin . . . . . . . . . . . . | $23,000,000 | $10,000,000 | $58,000,000 |
| Contribution Controllable by Segment Manager . . . . . . . . . . . . . . . . . . . . . . . . | $15,000,000 | $ 4,000,000 | $28,000,000 |
| Contribution of Segment to Common Costs . . . . . . . . . . . . . . . . . . . . . . . . . | $10,000,000 | $ 1,500,000 | $16,800,000 |
| Net Income. . . . . . . . . . . . . . . . . . . . . . | $ 7,000,000 | $ (700,000) | $12,000,000 |

The total assets for each territory are $50,000,000 for the United States, $30,000,000 for Canada, and $60,000,000 for the Middle East.

Each territory is expected to earn a minimum ROI that is closely related to the level of risk involved, the industry in which it operates, and its past performance. The United States division is expected to earn at least the average ROI for the industry, which is 16%. The Canadian division has been extremely unprofitable during the last 10 years, so not much is expected of it. The company will be satisfied if the new division manager is able to show any profit at all in the current year. Finally, all investments in the Middle East territory are considered extremely risky, so that division is expected to generate an ROI of at least 30% to compensate for the high risk of investments.

**Required:**

1. Calculate the appropriate ROI for evaluating the performance of each division.
2. If all divisions experienced equal risk, and if you ignore the industry in which the division operates and past performances, how would you rank the divisions, from most to least profitable?
3. Comparing the actual ROI and the minimum expected ROI for each division, once again rank the divisions from best to worst. This time, base the profitability ranking on how far the actual ROI exceeds the minimum ROI.

4. J. R. Dallas has an opportunity to do business in the Far East, but needs to withdraw from one of its current investments in order to finance the new venture. From which of the three existing divisions should it withdraw? Explain.

▶ *(Check Figure: 1. ROI for United States = 20%)*

---

## ETHICS CASE

Salty Pellet is the division manager of the water softener division of Perryaire Water Products, Inc. During his year-end performance evaluation for 1997, he was told by the corporate office that he would be given one more year to turn his division around or his position would be in jeopardy. Salty was quite perturbed, for when he was hired in 1996 he had been promised that he would be given 5 full years to get his division's ROI up to the 10% minimum expected for all divisions, as long as there appeared to be substantial progress in each year. Salty pointed to the results below for his first 2 years as division manager, arguing that they were significantly better than the $200,000 loss (and ROI of minus 5.00%) in 1995, the year before he was hired.

|  | 1996 | 1997 |
|---|---|---|
| Sales . . . . . . . . . . . . . . . . . . | $1,000,000 | $1,500,000 |
| Variable Expenses. . . . . . . . | 780,000 | 1,000,000 |
| Total Contribution Margin . . . | $ 220,000 | $ 500,000 |
| Fixed Costs of Division . . . . . | 240,000 | 200,000 |
| Contribution Controllable by Division Manager . . . . . . | $ (20,000) | $ 300,000 |
| ROI. . . . . . . . . . . . . . . . . . . . | (.33%) | 5.00% |

Salty was told that times had changed and that top management was getting impatient for better results from his division.

At home that night, Salty remembered that he had also been told when he was hired that if he could get the ROI up to 15%, he would receive an especially large bonus. Perhaps management did not want to pay the bonus, now that they realized that Salty was easily on target to reach the goal that had once seemed unattainable. Salty realized that both his job and his bonus depended on his division's having a great year in 1998.

Salty thought about what he could do to make sure the 15% ROI would be reached in 1998, so that he could be assured of the bonus. He was a little concerned because the prospects for 1998 weren't all that good: it looked like there was going to be another downturn in the economy for the next year or two. He figured that he could expect sales to be no more than $2,000,000. Grasping at straws, Salty came up with the following ideas:

1. Reduce the number of foremen from three to two, thereby reducing salaries expense by $30,000. The remaining foremen would be expected to take up the slack.
2. Sell a piece of land—which had been purchased for $1,000,000 as a future plant site—at no gain. Property taxes would thereby be reduced by $20,000.
3. Improve the contribution margin percentage to 45% by (a) purchasing lower-quality materials at a substantially reduced price and (b) firing laborers who were being paid a relatively high wage and replacing them with inexperienced workers at a much lower wage.

**Required:**

1. Calculate the division's ROI for 1998 if all things turn out as Salty predicted, and if he makes the changes needed to attain his 15% goal.
2. Do you think that the actions planned by Salty to improve the division's ROI are unethical, or are they simply good business decisions?

▶ *(Check Figure: ROI = 15%)*

---

## OBJECTIVE ASSIGNMENT ANSWERS

### True/False

1. T   2. F   3. F   4. T   5. T

### Multiple Choice

1. c   2. d   3. d   4. c   5. b
6. d   7. c   8. a   9. a   10. c

# Relevant Information for Planning Short-Run Decisions

The decisions made by management determine an organization's profitability. The profits that a firm reports on its income statement reflect the results of decisions made in that year and many preceding years. And the decisions that managers make today affect not only this year's profits, but perhaps the profits for many years to come. Management must resolve such questions as whether to accept a special order at a cut-rate price, whether to drop an apparently unprofitable product line, and whether to invest in new equipment—to name just a few. All these decision-making situations force management to choose between two or more alternative courses of action. In each case management is expected to select the alternative that will be most profitable for the firm in both the immediate and the distant future.

This is where the accountant comes in. Management depends on accountants to provide complete, accurate, and timely information concerning each alternative. In addition, the information that accountants provide to managers must have another, special quality: relevance.

Within this chapter we first explain what relevance means and why it is important to the decision making process. Then we look at the application of this concept to decisions that impact primarily the immediate future of an organization, and/or those that are not normally analyzed with present value and other capital budgeting techniques. In the next chapter we turn our attention to those decisions that affect the distant future and normally require the use of capital budgeting methodology.

Learning Objective 1

List the two criteria that make information relevant to a decision that involves choosing between two or more alternative courses of action.

## THE CONCEPT OF RELEVANCE

**Relevant information** about costs and revenues must meet two criteria:

**1.** It must relate to the future.
**2.** It must be different for each of the alternatives being considered.

Information that fails to meet either or both of these two criteria is considered to be irrelevant.

The information must relate to the future because the decisions relate to the future. Each decision considers at least two alternative courses of action that might be taken in the future—not the past. Managers are concerned with what they are going to do today and tomorrow; it's too late to be concerned with what they could have done yesterday or last year. Since management's choices involve future courses of action, the information gathered by accountants must relate to the same time frame.

Although this means that information about the past is always irrelevant to a decision, this in no way implies that information about the past is useless in coming to a decision about the future. Past results may be extremely useful in making estimates about the future. For example, if past labor rates were $12 an hour, and a union contract guarantees a 20% raise next year, then the $12 past rate is irrelevant, but it is quite useful in determining the $14.40 ($12 × 120%) rate expected in the future.

Is the $14.40 rate relevant? That depends on whether or not the second criterion for relevance is met: The information must also be different for each of the alternatives being considered. Otherwise there is no quantitative basis for a decision. If all the choices add up to the same thing, how can we decide that one course of action is better than any other? If we are considering the replacement of laborers with robots, then the direct labor costs, at $14.40 per hour, will be relevant to the decision, because the total labor costs will most likely be different if the product is assembled by robots rather than by humans.

Assume now that you are trying to decide where you want to go to dinner, and are considering only two possibilities—McDonalds and Wendys—both of which are located one mile from your apartment. The last time you went to McDonalds, a hamburger, fries, and a cola cost you $3.29; the same dinner cost you only $2.99 at

Wendy's. You've heard however, that the same dinner now costs $2.75 at McDonald's and $2.49 at Wendy's. You figure that it will cost $.30 for gas no matter where you go to eat. Assuming that you like the meals as much at McDonald's as you do those at Wendy's, where would you go for dinner in order to keep your costs as low as possible?

The key to any decision—whether it's as simple as where to go to dinner or extremely complex—is to first decide what information is relevant to the decision and what information is irrelevant. For the situation above, the only information that is relevant is the cost that you will pay for dinner—$2.75 at McDonald's and $2.49 at Wendy's. These are the only two items that both relate to the future and are different for the two alternatives. The amounts you paid in the past are irrelevant because they do not relate to the future. The cost of gasoline is irrelevant because it is the same wherever you go to eat. So, if you want to minimize your costs, go to Wendy's and save $.26.

Naturally, the decision situations that we will discuss in this and the next chapter are more involved than your dinner decision. But the concept of relevance never changes. The two criteria for relevance can—and must—be applied to any decision situation.

## QUANTITATIVE VERSUS QUALITATIVE FACTORS IN DECISION MAKING

When a manager makes a decision, he or she needs to consider both the quantitative and qualitative factors involved in the decision. **Quantitative factors** are those that can be measured in financial terms—that is, in dollars and cents. When a product line is dropped, the elimination of a supervisor's salary of $20,000 is a quantitative factor.

**Qualitative factors** are those that cannot be expressed—at least not with a reasonable degree of accuracy—in dollars and cents, yet that may still have a significant influence on a manager's decision. For example, if a firm is considering moving its manufacturing operations from Delaware to Mexico, a qualitative factor might be the impact on morale of the employees who would be forced to relocate. Another might be the negative publicity generated by the highly publicized firing of employees or the impact of lost jobs on the local economy.

It's not that qualitative factors have no financial effect on a decision; they do, but it cannot yet be measured. Obviously, if a move to Mexico does cause the employees who relocate to become demoralized and less productive, then operating profits will be lower than they would have been otherwise. However, if no one knows for sure whether the move will affect morale, nor how much low morale will reduce the profits, then there is no objective way to integrate these factors—in dollars and cents—into the analysis.

It is up to the individual manager to assess subjectively the importance of a qualitative factor in a decision situation. Qualitative factors may be given very little weight in some situations but may be the determining factor in others.

Since accountants are involved primarily with the quantitative factors in a decision, we'll emphasize those factors in this chapter. Bear in mind, though, that if we as accountants are to be of real assistance to managers, then we need to quantify as many qualitative factors as possible so as to reduce the degree of subjectivity reflected in a manager's decision.

## TYPES OF DECISION SITUATIONS

In this chapter we will concentrate on five types of decision situations, each of which involves alternatives that primarily affect profits in the short run (although each can also have an impact on longer-run profits). They are:

1. Accepting special orders
2. Dropping a product line
3. Maximizing profits with sales mix analysis
4. Making or buying raw materials
5. Selling a joint product at split-off or processing it further

A common element of each of these short-run decision situations is that it utilizes current productive capacity; there is no need to purchase or build additional fixed assets in order to implement the decision. The accountant's role is to help managers determine the most profitable way to use that productive capacity.

Because each of these decisions primarily affects short-run income, the preferable alternative in each decision is naturally the one that provides the most income to the firm during a year or less. The approach we typically take to determine the best alternative is to prepare budgeted income statements for each alternative and select the one that provides the most income.

By now, you should be familiar with the two formats for an income statement—the *contribution margin format* and the *traditional format*. Theoretically, it shouldn't matter which format we use: Both formats should yield the same decision. Practically speaking, however, the contribution margin format seems better suited to getting correct answers while avoiding mistakes.

**ASK YOURSELF** ▶

1. **What criteria must information meet in order to be considered relevant?**
2. **What is the difference between qualitative factors and quantitative factors involved in a decision?**
3. **Name four types of short-run decision situations.**

Learning Objective 2

Analyze comparative profits to determine when an organization should accept a special order

## Accepting Special Orders

When a firm is operating below full capacity, it may have an opportunity to accept additional business—a **special order**—at a special price. If the proposed price is the normal selling price, or even higher, the firm would probably accept the order in a flash, because the order would obviously increase the firm's profits. But when the proposed selling price is lower than the normal selling price, the decision may be difficult, especially if the opportunity involves a new customer in the same market as the regular customers of the firm.

At a price lower than the regular price, short-run profits for the firm may actually fall if the order is accepted. And if the order is from a customer in the same market as the firm's regular customers, long-run profits may be severely damaged. If the firm's regular customers find out that it sold the same product to a one-time customer at a lower price than they paid, the company may lose their business or be forced to reduce the price for them, too.

The firm certainly wants to increase its profits in the short run, but not if the consequence is a reduction of profits in the long run. Keep that in mind as you consider any decision situation.

Now we'll use the facts in the example below to analyze a special-order decision.

# SAFETY BREW COMPANY

Safety Brew Company specializes in the production and distribution of nonalcoholic products that taste just like the alcoholic version. They have become quite popular in the southeastern United States. One particularly popular product is its nonalcoholic brand of tequila, called Tequila Mockingbird. Salina, a Mexican salt products company, has just begun to diversify, and needs to supplement its own production of nonalcoholic tequila during the first several months of operation. It would like to purchase 10,000 cases from Safety Brew and sell Safety Brew's product under its own label until it can get production up to the level needed to satisy demand. Salina wishes to purchase the one-time order at $50 a case. This is not only below Safety Brew's normal selling price of $125 per case but also much lower than Safety Brew's cost of production. That cost is $80, as shown in its budgeted income statement, which is based on the expected sales without the special order:

|  | Totals | Per Case |
|---|---|---|
| Sales (50,000 cases) | $6,250,000 | $125 |
| Cost of Goods Sold | 4,000,000 | 80 |
| Gross Profit | $2,250,000 | $ 45 |
| Selling and Administrative Expenses | 1,100,000 | 22 |
| Operating Income | $1,150,000 | $ 23 |

Included in the cost of goods sold and selling and administrative expenses are fixed costs of $2,000,000 and $600,000, respectively. The remaining costs are variable. The variable selling and administrative expenses are entirely for delivery costs. For this deal, however, Salina will pick up its order at the factory door. Although Safety Brew does not normally pay commissions to its salespersons, a $50,000 payment will be made to the sales vice president for arranging the deal.

Safety Brew's production capacity is 70,000 cases; if its excess capacity is not used for the special order, it will not be used for any other purpose. Since none of Safety Brew's regular customers are in Mexico, there is little chance that any of them will learn of this deal and demand a comparable price. And since Safety Brew doesn't expect to develop a continuing relationship with Salina, the low price for this deal is not expected to set any precedent for future deals.

Should Safety Brew accept the special order?

### Faulty Reasoning

Note that the format used in the budgeted income statement above is the traditional format. This approach leads us to reason that the order should be rejected, because the $50 price is less than the average cost of producing each case:

$$\text{Cost of goods sold per case} = \frac{\$4,000,000}{50,000 \text{ cases}} = \$80 \text{ per case}$$

The gross profit is a negative $30/case ($50 − $80). If a 10,000-case order is accepted, then won't the gross profit be a negative $300,000? And since the gross profit is negative, won't net income also be negative?

We hope you weren't misled by this line of reasoning. In fact, Safety Brew should accept the order, because it can substantially improve the profits for the firm. How can this be true, since the cost of goods sold per unit is greater than the sales price?

The problem is that the Safety Brew example shows a traditional income statement, which can be very misleading. Included within the cost of goods sold for Safety Brew is $2,000,000 of fixed factory overhead. When we calculated the cost per case of $80, we concluded that each additional case would cost an additional $80 to produce.

This is not true, however, because the total fixed overhead should not increase with additional production. Therefore the cost of goods sold will increase not by $800,000 (10,000 cases × $80), but by only $400,000—which is just the variable portion of cost of goods sold.

| | |
|---|---|
| Additional variable manufacturing costs (10,000 cases × $40) . . . . . . . . . . | $400,000 |
| Additional fixed manufacturing costs. . . . . . . . . . . . . . . . . . . . . . . . . . . . . . . | −0− |
| Additional cost of goods sold . . . . . . . . . . . . . . . . . . . . . . . . . . . . . . . . . . . . | $400,000 |

So you see, the additional, or *differential,* sales of $500,000 will be greater—not less—than the additional (or differential) cost of goods sold of $400,000. The difference is $100,000, or $10 per case ($50 − $40).

This type of reasoning error can be a problem any time the traditional format is used. Since the cost of goods sold is often mentioned on a per-unit basis, it is easy to forget that the additional cost of goods sold cannot be calculated by simply multiplying the average cost per unit by the number of units sold. The variable and fixed portions must be calculated separately.

This doesn't mean that we can't make correct decisions with the traditional approach. It simply means that the contribution margin approach is safer, because it requires that variable and fixed costs be evaluated separately.

### The Better Approach

The first thing we should do is revise the budgeted income statement for Safety Brew, this time using the contribution margin format.

**SAFETY BREW**
**Revised Income Statement**
**Contribution Margin Format**

| | | |
|---|---|---|
| Sales (50,000 cases × $125 per case) . . . . . . . . . . . . . . . . . . . . . . . . . . . . | | $6,250,000 |
| Variable Costs: | | |
| Manufacturing ($40 per case) . . . . . . . . . . . . . . . . . . . . . . . | $2,000,000 | |
| Selling and Administrative ($10 per case). . . . . . . . . . . . . . | 500,000 | 2,500,000 |
| Total Contribution Margin . . . . . . . . . . . . . . . . . . . . . . . . . . . . . . . . . . . . | | $3,750,000 |
| Total Fixed Costs: | | |
| Manufacturing. . . . . . . . . . . . . . . . . . . . . . . . . . . . . . . . . . . . . | $2,000,000 | |
| Selling and Administrative . . . . . . . . . . . . . . . . . . . . . . . . . . | 600,000 | 2,600,000 |
| Operating Income . . . . . . . . . . . . . . . . . . . . . . . . . . . . . . . . . . . . . . . . . . | | $1,150,000 |

Next we will present the information about the special order in a three-column format. In Exhibit 1, column 1 shows Safety Brew's expected operating income ($1,150,000) if it rejects the order. Column 2 shows Safety Brew's expected income if it accepts the order. And column 3 reports the differences between columns 1 and 2—the differences in revenues, costs, and income. Only relevant items appear in the differences column.

**Exhibit 1** Contribution Margin Format to Solution

| | (1)<br>Reject<br>Order | (2)<br>Accept<br>Order | (3)<br>Differences |
|---|---|---|---|
| Sales | $6,250,000 | $6,750,000 | $500,000 |
| Variable Costs: | | | |
|   Manufacturing | $2,000,000 | $2,400,000 | ($400,000) |
|   Selling and Administrative Costs | 500,000 | 500,000 | –0– |
|     Total Variable Costs | $2,500,000 | $2,900,000 | ($400,000) |
| Total Contribution Margin | $3,750,000 | $3,850,000 | $100,000 |
| Fixed Costs: | | | |
|   Manufacturing | $2,000,000 | $2,000,000 | –0– |
|   Selling and Administrative Costs | 600,000 | 650,000 | (50,000) |
|     Total Fixed Costs | $2,600,000 | $2,650,000 | $(50,000) |
| Operating Income | $1,150,000 | $1,200,000 | $ 50,000 |

If Safety Brew accepts the special order, sales will increase by $500,000, more than enough to offset the additional variable costs of $400,000. There are no additional variable selling and administrative costs (in the form of delivery costs), because Salina will pick up the order at the factory door. Therefore the variable selling and administrative costs are irrelevant. The additional contribution margin of $100,000 exceeds the additional fixed selling costs (the $50,000 payment to the vice president) by $50,000—which is the increase in operating income from accepting the order. The fixed manufacturing costs are irrelevant because they are expected to be $2,000,000 with or without the special order.

If Safety Brew's management is willing to accept any one-time order that adds to the profits of the firm, then it should accept this one, because it promises to increase income by $50,000.

### Exclusion of Irrelevant Items

Notice in Exhibit 1 that the variable selling and administrative costs and the fixed factory overhead costs were included in the solution even though they were irrelevant to the decision. Including irrelevant items in any decision analysis is usually acceptable, but only if the amounts for each irrelevant item are the same for both alternatives, as they were in Exhibit 1.

In most situations, if you prefer to delete the irrelevant items from the analysis, and there is nothing specified in the problem to the contrary, then it is acceptable to do so. Sometimes, however, you don't have a choice. For example, if the requirements of a problem specify that complete income statements are required, then as long as an item is a component of income, whether it is relevant or not, it must be included in the analysis.

Learning<br>Objective  **3**

### Dropping a Product Line

Identify those product lines that should be dropped by a multiproduct firm

Because most companies sell many different product lines, they are called **multiproduct firms.** Many of these companies prepare individual product income statements periodically, in order to find out which products are still contributing satisfactorily to the firm's profits and which ones are not. If a product is not carrying its own weight, it may need to be dropped. It is important to be able to look at product line income statements and determine when product lines are in trouble.

Let's look at the situation for Snapping Mower Company and see if any changes are advisable for its product lines.

# SNAPPING MOWER COMPANY

The Snapping Mower Company manufactures and distributes three different models of its Lawn Pro mower line. Its commercial product is the 6-horsepower model (6HP), and its residential products are the 4-horsepower (4HP) and 2-horsepower (2HP) models. Its budgeted income statement for 1997 showed an expected overall profit for the firm, with two of the three products (6HP and 4HP) appearing to be profitable and one product line (2HP) showing an expected loss.

**SNAPPING MOWER COMPANY**
**Budgeted Income Statement**
**For the Year 1997**

| | Model | | | |
| | 6HP | 4HP | 2HP | Totals |
|---|---|---|---|---|
| Sales......... | $800,000 | $960,000 | $800,000 | $2,560,000 |
| Variable Expenses (and % of total sales).... | 480,000 (60%) | 720,000 (75%) | 560,000 (70%) | 1,760,000 |
| Total Contribution Margin (and % of total sales)........ | $320,000 (40%) | $240,000 (25%) | $240,000 (30%) | $ 800,000 |
| Fixed Expenses | 240,000 | 200,000 | 250,000* | 690,000 |
| Operating Income ........ | $ 80,000 | $ 40,000 | $(10,000) | $ 110,000 |
| Unit Sales ..... | 1,250 | 2,400 | 3,200 | 6,850 |

\* $60,000 is for the salary of a product-line supervisor who will be retired if the product line is dropped.

The controller, Brigg Strattin, thinks that the 2HP model should be dropped, since it is the only product showing a loss. Obviously the productive capacity could be used more profitably by manufacturing and distributing more units of the two profitable lines. Brigg says, "Even if we don't make any additional units of the 6HP and 4HP models, we can increase our profits by $10,000 if we eliminate the 2HP model, because we'll no longer have the $10,000 loss."

Brigg's assessment of the situation is both right and wrong. He is right in saying that the 2HP model is showing a loss, but he is wrong in thinking that simply eliminating the 2HP model will improve the profits for the firm. Income will not increase by $10,000. Instead it will actually fall by $180,000, as shown at the bottom of the differences column in Exhibit 2. Let's see why.

**Exhibit 2** Comparative Analysis: Dropping a Product Line

| | (1) Keep 2HP | (2) Drop 2HP | (3) Difference |
|---|---|---|---|
| Sales..................... | $2,560,000 | $1,760,000 | $(800,000) |
| Variable Expenses ................. | 1,760,000 | 1,200,000 | 560,000 |
| Total Contribution Margin............. | $ 800,000 | $ 560,000 | $(240,000) |
| Fixed Expenses ................. | 690,000 | 630,000 | 60,000 |
| Operating Income................. | $ 110,000 | $ (70,000) | $(180,000) |

If model 2HP is dropped, both the sales ($800,000) and the variable costs ($560,000) for that model will be eliminated. The net result is to reduce the total contribution margin by $240,000 ($800,000 − $560,000).

Notice in Exhibit 2 that the fixed costs were not reduced by the full $250,000 associated with model 2HP. When there is no change in the productive capacity of the firm, you should assume—unless you are specifically told otherwise—that the fixed costs associated with that unchanging capacity will remain the same. The footnote in Snapping Mower's income statement says that a supervisor will be retired if model 2HP is dropped. The supervisor's $60,000 salary is the only change in the fixed costs shown in the differences column.

Since the reduction in total contribution margin of $240,000 is $180,000 greater than the reduction of $60,000 in fixed costs, the income will be reduced by $180,000 if model 2HP is dropped. This reduction in income indicates that model 2HP should not be dropped—unless the excess capacity could then be used in some other profitable manner.

### Additional Considerations

There are several variations on the analysis of dropping a product line. One involves using the newly available productive capacity to make additional units of an existing or new product line. In this case, the analysis would look a lot like it does in Exhibit 2, except that there would be both a reduction and an addition for most of the items on the income statement. Dropping model 2HP, for example, would reduce sales, variable costs, and possibly fixed costs; while adding to another product line would most likely increase those same items. The net of all the changes would determine the amount of increase or decrease in the income for the firm.

Assume that the productive capacity that had been used to manufacture the 2HP model can now be used to produce additional units of the 6HP model, increasing the sales of 6HP by $500,000. Assume also that the variable cost percentage for 6HP will continue to be 60% and that the $60,000 supervisor's salary for 2HP will still be eliminated if that line is dropped. The solution to the revised example for Snapping Mower Company is shown in Exhibit 3.

The total sales will now be $2,260,000 if 2HP is dropped and 6HP is expanded—a reduction of $300,000. The variable expenses will also be lower—by $260,000, resulting in a reduction of $40,000 in the contribution margin for Snapping Mower. Since the product line supervisor will be terminated, the $60,000 savings in fixed costs is now great enough to offset the reduced contribution margin. The net effect is to increase net income by $20,000. In this scenario, the 2HP model should be dropped.

A second variation in the analysis of product profitability involves changing the sales mix of the different product lines. Although this could also involve dropping a

---

**Exhibit 3** Comparative Analysis: Dropping and Adding to Product Lines

|  | (1)<br>Keep<br>2HP | (2)<br>Drop 2HP<br>Add to 6HP | (3)<br>Difference |
|---|---|---|---|
| Sales | $2,560,000 | $2,260,000* | $(300,000) |
| Variable Expenses | 1,760,000 | 1,500,000** | 260,000 |
| Total Contribution Margin | $ 800,000 | $ 760,000 | $( 40,000) |
| Fixed Expenses | 690,000 | 630,000 | 60,000 |
| Operating Income | $ 110,000 | $ 130,000 | $ 20,000 |

\* $2,560,000 − 800,000 + 500,000 = $2,260,000
\*\* $1,760,000 − 560,000 + 500,000(.60) = $1,500,000

product, it might simply require subtle changes in the sales mix of the existing products. This topic is covered in the next section.

A final variation is to adapt the product line analysis to a larger scale—say, for a company that has multiple departments, branches, or divisions. The analysis could just as easily be used to determine whether a department, branch, or division of the company is less profitable than desired and should be discontinued.

Learning Objective 4

## Maximizing Profits with Sales Mix Analysis

Calculate the unique sales mix that maximizes profits for a multiproduct firm

When we discussed multi-product firms in the Cost-Volume-Profit Analysis chapter, we defined the term **sales mix** as the proportion of total sales that is distributed to each product line. We also discussed how the sales mix for a firm has a big impact on profits. For any given level of total sales, each sales mix results in a different profit.

In the Snapping Mower Company example, the original sales mix for each product line (based on unit sales) was as follows:

| Model | Sales Units | Sales Mix |
|-------|-------------|-----------|
| 6HP | 1,250 | 1,250 ÷ 6,850 = 18.3% |
| 4HP | 2,400 | 2,400 ÷ 6,850 = 35.0% |
| 2HP | 3,200 | 3,200 ÷ 6,850 = 46.7% |
| | 6,850 | 100.0% |

At this sales mix, the combined income for the firm is $110,000. For any other sales mix the income would be a different amount.

Dropping model 2HP represents one possible change in the sales mix for Snapping Mower. Many other changes in the sales mix could be considered as well: dropping both the 2HP and 4HP models, dropping model 2HP and increasing the production and sales of model 6HP, replacing model 2HP with a new model, or just slightly changing the current sales mix.

For every firm, there is one best sales mix at which the firm is most profitable, at least in the short run. That is, there is one way of distributing total sales to the various product lines so that the income for the firm is maximized. The problem is to find that sales mix quickly, without having to consider an endless number of possibilities.

The starting point is to determine the *contribution margin per unit* (CMU) for each product, as follows:

| | 6HP | 4HP | 2HP |
|---|---|---|---|
| Total contribution margin . . . . . . . . . . . . . . . . . . . . | $320,000 | $240,000 | $240,000 |
| Units sold . . . . . . . . . . . . . . . . . . . . . . . . . . . . . . . | ÷ 1,250 | ÷ 2,400 | ÷ 3,200 |
| Contribution margin per unit. . . . . . . . . . . . . . . . . | $ 256 | $ 100 | $ 75 |

At first glance, 6HP again seems to be the most profitable and 2HP the least profitable model. In these situations, however, looks can be deceiving. For example, assume that the total hours of machine time available to produce all three products is 32,500; that Snapping Mower plans to operate at full capacity; and that different amounts of time are required to produce one unit of the different products.

| Model | 6HP | 4HP | 2HP |
|-------|-----|-----|-----|
| Hours required per unit. . . . . . . . . . . . . . . . . . . . . . . . . . . . . . . . . . | 10 | 5 | 2.5 |

The number of units of each product that can be produced is significantly different.

| Model | 6HP | 4HP | 2HP |
|---|---|---|---|
| Total hours available. . . . . . . . . . . . . . . . . . . . . . . . . . . . . . . | 32,500 | 32,500 | 32,500 |
| Hours required per unit. . . . . . . . . . . . . . . . . . . . . . . . . . . . | ÷ 10 | ÷ 5 | ÷ 2.5 |
| Total units that can be produced . . . . . . . . . . . . . . . . . . . | 3,250 | 6,500 | 13,000 |

Model 6HP may indeed have the most contribution margin every time a unit is sold, but since it takes so long to make one, not many can be produced. And if only a few of the 6HP models can be produced and sold, the total contribution margin can't be very great no matter how good it is on a per-unit basis.

Even though model 2HP provides relatively little contribution margin per unit, a large number can be produced and sold because it takes so little time to produce. Therefore, model 2HP can generate a large total contribution margin.

Based on the total units that can be produced, and assuming they can all be sold, the following table shows the income for each product if only that product is produced and sold.

| | 6HP | 4HP | 2HP |
|---|---|---|---|
| Total Units That Can Be Produced and Sold . . . . . | 3,250 | 6,500 | 13,000 |
| Contribution Margin per Unit. . . . . . . . . . . . . . . . . | × $256 | × $100 | × $75 |
| Total Contribution Margin . . . . . . . . . . . . . . . . . . . | $832,000 | $650,000 | $975,000 |
| Total Fixed Costs*. . . . . . . . . . . . . . . . . . . . . . . . . | 690,000 | 690,000 | 690,000 |
| Income. . . . . . . . . . . . . . . . . . . . . . . . . . . . . . . . . . | $142,000 | $ (40,000) | $285,000 |

* Assuming that the product-line supervisor's position will not be eliminated.

The product that we were about to drop, model 2HP, turns out to be the most profitable. For this situation, we should produce and sell 13,000 2HP mowers (100% of productive capacity) and drop the 6HP and 4HP models.

This unique sales mix assumes that Snapping can sell all the 2HP mowers that it produces. Realistically, however, that may not be the case. In that event, Snapping would produce as many 2HP mowers as it could sell, and then would use the excess productive capacity to produce one or both of the other product lines.

When there are limits on what we can produce and sell, things can get a lot more complicated than we've shown in our example for Snapping. Such situations require that we use a quantitative tool called *linear programming,* which can solve complex problems using readily available computer software programs. Linear programming is covered in operations research courses.

## Making or Buying Raw Materials

Learning Objective 5

Determine whether to produce a raw material needed in a finished product or to purchase it from an outside supplier

A manufacturer is often faced with an interesting option: It can buy the raw material that goes into the finished product, or it can produce its own raw material. Sometimes it is more economical to produce the raw material internally. Also, the manufacturer can maintain better control over the quality and availability of a raw material if it is made internally. The main problem with producing one's own raw material is that it may take some of the firm's productive capacity away from the production of the finished product. As a result, the firm may not be able to make and sell enough of the main product to be profitable.

The analysis of a make-or-buy decision simply determines the relevant costs of making the raw material and compares them to the relevant costs of buying them from an outsider. Let's consider a typical make-or-buy situation for Zealot Fan Company.

# ZEALOT FAN COMPANY

The Zealot Fan Company manufactures many types and sizes of window and ceiling fans and is currently also producing the blades that go into all models of their fans. Zealot is considering purchasing the blades for its ceiling fans from another manufacturer instead. The total costs associated with the production of 60,000 blades is $72,000, itemized as follows:

| | | |
|---|---:|---|
| Direct Materials | $48,000 | $ .80/blade |
| Direct Labor | 12,000 | .20/blade |
| Variable Overhead | 6,000 | .10/blade |
| Fixed Factory Overhead | 6,000 | .10/blade |
| | $72,000 | $1.20/blade |

Zealot is considering purchasing the 60,000 blades from Casanegro Fan Company for $1.18 per blade plus a fixed charge of $3,000 for shipping and handling.

The best decision for Zealot is illustrated in Exhibit 4. The first column shows the total costs to make the blades, the second column shows the total costs of purchasing the blades from Casanegro, and the third column shows the difference in costs between making and buying the blades.

For the variable items, the costs of buying are $4,800 more than the costs of making ($70,800 − $66,000). The fixed overhead is irrelevant; it is $6,000 regardless of Zealot's decision. Remember, for all the decision situations we evaluate, unless you are told otherwise, the total fixed costs in the short run are assumed to remain the same regardless of activity. In a situation such as this one, the fixed overhead costs might actually change; buying the blades might reduce the number of supervisors needed, for instance. However, we are not assuming a change of that sort for Zealot.

The last item, for $3,000, is the difference in shipping and handling costs incurred if the blades are purchased from Casanegro. Adding this $3,000 difference to the $4,800 difference gives us a sum of all differences of $7,800, in favor of making the fan blades. That is, if Zealot buys the blades from Casanegro instead of making them

---

**Exhibit 4** Make-or-Buy Comparison for Fan Blades

| | Alternatives | | |
|---|---|---|---|
| | **(1)** **Make** **Blades** | **(2)** **Buy** **Blades** | **(3)** **Differences** |
| Variable Costs: | | | |
| Direct Materials | $48,000 | −0− | $ 48,000 |
| Direct Labor | 12,000 | −0− | 12,000 |
| Variable Factory Overhead | 6,000 | −0− | 6,000 |
| Purchase of 60,000 Blades | −0− | $70,800 | (70,800) |
| | $66,000 | $70,800 | $ (4,800) |
| Fixed Costs: | | | |
| Fixed Factory Overhead | $ 6,000 | $ 6,000 | −0− |
| Shipping and Handling | −0− | 3,000 | $ (3,000) |
| | $ 6,000 | $ 9,000 | $ (3,000) |
| Total Costs | $72,000 | $79,800 | $ (7,800) |

itself, its costs of production will increase by $7,800, and the firm's profits will decrease by the same amount. Zealot should probably continue to produce the blades internally.

An important additional factor should be considered. If Zealot stops making its own blades, excess capacity will become available, which Zealot can probably use in some other profitable manner. Perhaps it could increase production of another product line, thereby increasing the contribution margin for that product. Or Zealot could lease the excess capacity to another manufacturer. Either way, the firm would forgo a profit—called an **opportunity cost**—if it continues to produce the blades internally. If opportunities such as the ones we've mentioned do exist, they could indeed be relevant to the decision and would have to be integrated into the analysis.

There are numerous applications of the make or buy type of decision outside of the production function for an organization. For example, any type of organization, whether it be a manufacturer, a merchant, a service entity or a governmental unit, might employ its own attorneys to handle its lawsuits and other legal matters, or it may instead hire an outside law firm. The same organization may also consider (among other things) doing its own accounting work, computer processing, advertising campaigns, personnel investigations or garbage pickup. It may instead hire a CPA firm, a computer processing company, an advertising agency, a private investigator, or a waste management company. Each of these considerations compares the relevant costs of performing a function inside the company versus paying to have it done externally—just like we did above for the make versus buy decision.

Learning 6
Objective

Decide when to sell a joint product at the split-off point and when to process it further.

## Joint Products: To Sell or Process Further

Many production processes begin with a single raw material and end up with two or more final products. A prime example involves the many final products that come from a single steer—hides, hamburger, steaks, pet food, etc. Another is a barrel of crude oil that ends up being kerosene, regular and unleaded gasoline, and other petroleum products. Other examples can be found in the lumber and chemicals industries.

The raw material is treated as a single product up until a point in production called the **split-off point.** At this point, the single product divides into two or more products, called **joint products.** The joint products are not individually identifiable until after the split-off point.

The costs of producing the single product up to the split-off point are the **joint product costs.** These costs are common to all the units produced and cannot be associated directly with the units once they split into the individual products. Take, for example, the costs of raising a herd of cattle. The costs of buying, feeding, caring for, and transporting each cow to market are the joint product costs. When the cows are slaughtered—the split-off point—there really is no way to tell how much of the joint costs were costs of the hide, the hamburger, or the steaks.

This processing of cattle is depicted in the simplified diagram at the top of the next page.

Sometimes we can sell a joint product immediately after the split-off point. In other situations we may have to process the joint products beyond the split-off before it can be sold. We may even have the option of selling at split-off or processing further.

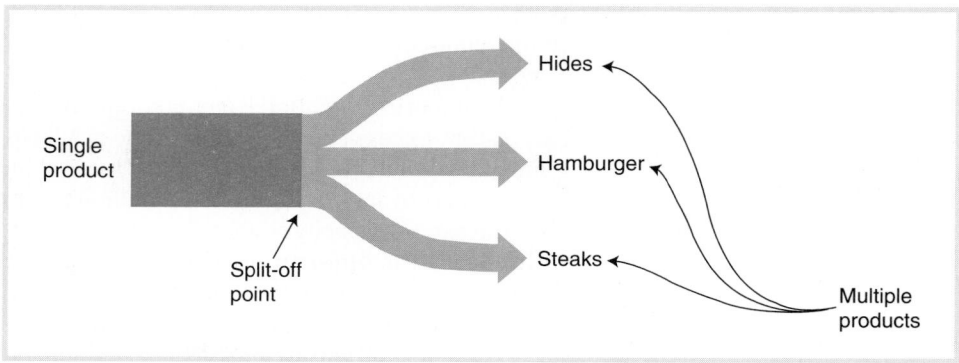

A more elaborate diagram for joint products is given below. It shows both the sales at split-off and any additional processing that may be needed for two joint products, product A and product B.

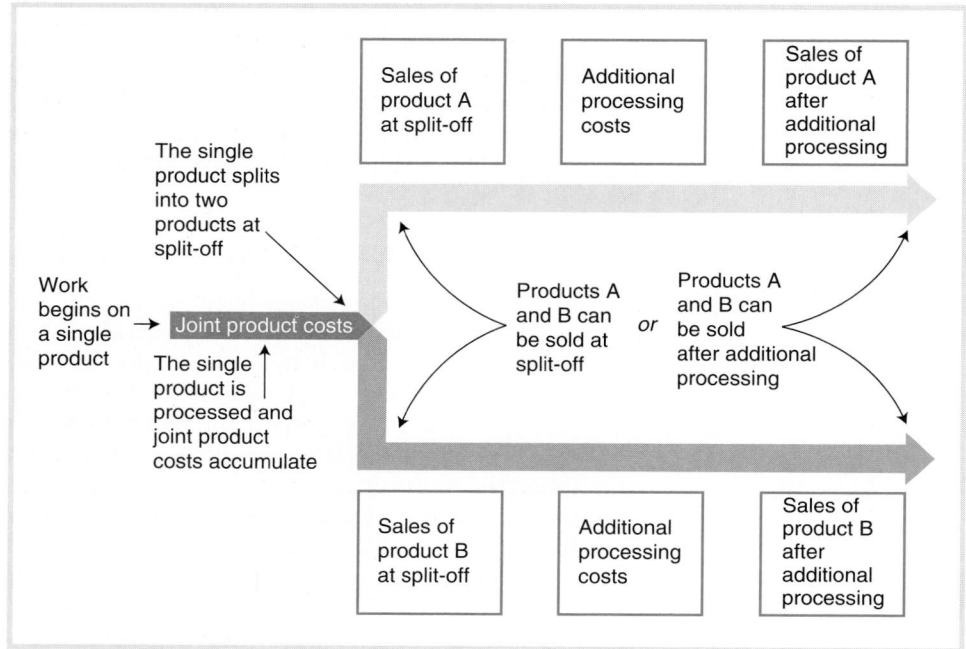

This type of diagram can be very useful when you do your homework. If you place the key facts from a problem into the appropriate positions in the diagram, you can get a complete overview of what you are about to evaluate.

### Sell at Split-Off or Process Further

When a firm has the option of selling a joint product at the split-off point or processing it further, it will naturally select the option with the more favorable effect on profits. The key to making the correct decision is knowing which information is relevant and which information is irrelevant.

Let's look at such a situation for Jimmy Joe's Peanut Farm.

# JIMMY JOE'S PEANUT FARM

Jimmy Joe James has recently purchased substantial farmland in Georgia and is currently growing peanuts. At harvest time the crop is divided into nuts and shells. The nuts can be sold immediately to a grocery store chain or processed into vegetable oil. The shells can be burned or ground into a powder. The powder can be sold to a drug company, which uses it in a new medicine for acne.

The costs of growing the crop, harvesting it, and separating it into the two products are $400,000. At harvest the following information pertains to Jimmy Joe's choices:

|  | Sales at Harvest Time (Split-Off) | Additional Processing Costs | Sales after Additional Processing |
|---|---|---|---|
| Nuts. . . . . . . . . . . . . . . . . . . . . . . . . | $750,000 | $500,000 | $1,200,000 |
| Shells . . . . . . . . . . . . . . . . . . . . . . . | −0− | 50,000 | 100,000 |

What actions should Jimmy Joe take to maximize profits?

Before evaluating Jimmy Joe's alternatives, an overview of the situation is provided in the diagram below.

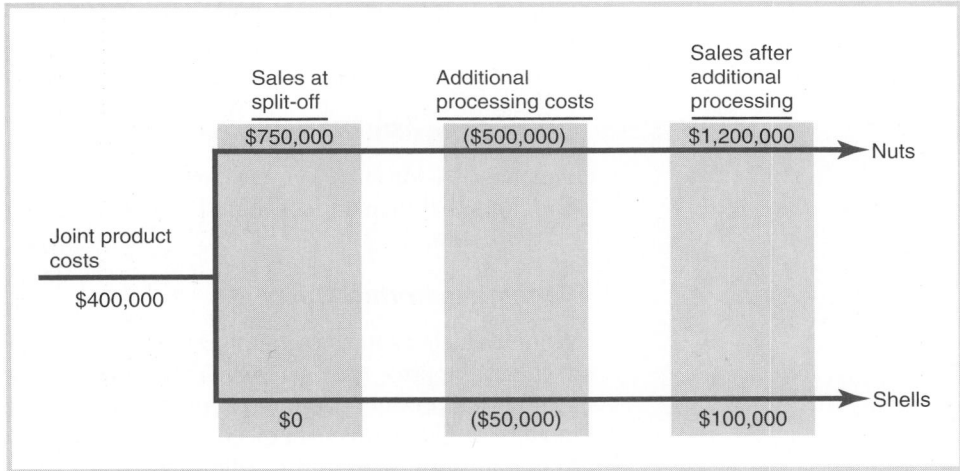

Notice in this diagram that the only way Jimmy can produce nuts and shells is to spend $400,000 developing the crop up to the split-off point. No matter what you decide he should do with the nuts and shells—that is, sell at split-off or process further—he first has to spend the $400,000. Since the joint product costs are not affected by the decision you make, they must be irrelevant to the decision.

The items that are relevant to the decision of selling at split-off or processing further are those that come after the single product splits into two or more joint products. Let's look now at the relevant items, first for the nuts and then for the shells.

For the nut crop, you can see in the diagram that there are two choices. Jimmy can sell it at split-off for $750,000 or he can process it further. If he spends $500,000 to process the nut crop further, he can then sell it for $1,200,000, a net of $700,000 ($1,200,000 − $500,000). If you were Jimmy Joe, would you rather have the $750,000 or the $700,000? Assuming that you'd like to make as big a profit as possible, we feel sure that you would rather have the $750,000—you would sell the nuts at the split-off point.

**Exhibit 5** Sell at Split-Off or Process Further—An Incremental Approach

| | | Process Further | | | | |
| | Sales at Split-off | Sales after Processing | — Additional Processing Costs | = Net | Best Decision |
|---|---|---|---|---|---|
| Nuts | $750,000 | $1,200,000 | — $500,000 | = $700,000 | $750,000 Sell at split-off |
| Shells | –0– | $ 100,000 | — $ 50,000 | = $ 50,000 | 50,000 Sell after processing |

| | |
|---|---|
| Maximum profits before joint product costs . . . . . . . . . . . . . . . . . | $800,000 |
| Joint product costs . . . . . . . . . . . . . . . . . . . . . . . . . . . . . . . . . . . | 400,000 |
| Maximum profits . . . . . . . . . . . . . . . . . . . . . . . . . . . . . . . . . . . . . | $400,000 |

Although technically you have two choices for the shells, telling Jimmy to dispose of them at split-off would probably be the last resort. By processing them further, Jimmy can increase his profits by $50,000 ($100,000 − $50,000). Since this is obviously preferable to receiving zero at the split-off, the shells should be processed further.

The format that accommodates this evaluation of nuts and shells is presented in Exhibit 5. It shows that the maximum profit before subtracting the joint costs is $800,000—if the nuts are sold at split-off and the shells are processed further. After the joint costs are deducted, the maximum profit for Jimmy Joe's farm is $400,000.

## Other Short-Run Decisions

The five decision situations we have just discussed are hardly an all-inclusive list of the decisions that managers face in the short run. Several other examples are described briefly below.

### Setting the Normal Price

When managers have some discretion in setting the price for regular sales of their product, the price they set is typically based on the expected costs of producing and selling that product. Revenues generated by the firm, based on the price that is set, must be sufficient to cover all costs and provide a reasonable return for the company. Many companies base the selling price of their product on the absorption cost of goods sold (direct materials, direct labor, variable factory overhead, and fixed factory overhead). They get the sales price per unit by first combining the absorption costs per unit, then adding a desired markup—the gross profit—to these costs. A variation of this traditional approach is called the *full costing approach:* The cost per unit that is used to set the price includes not only the cost of goods sold but also nonproduction costs.

Some companies use a pricing method based on the variable costs. This method is called the *contribution margin approach.* First the combined variable costs per unit are determined (direct materials, direct labor, variable factory overhead, variable selling, and variable administrative costs). Then a desired contribution margin per unit is added to the variable costs to get the sales price per unit.

### Obsolete Inventory

When inventory goes unsold for a long time, there is a good chance that it will never be sold for its original price because it has become obsolete. Management often has the option of either selling obsolete inventory as is, for a minimal price, or spending some money to put it into a more salable form so that it can be sold for a price much closer to the original price. To make this decision, the potential sales revenue for the obsolete inventory in its present form has to be compared to the anticipated net sales (sales after additional work less costs of additional work).

### Defective Units

The popular philosophy in the modern manufacturing environment is that each and every unit produced needs to be done correctly the very first time. Unless all units meet all size, shape, and quality standards, the company has wasted its resources. Some manufacturers, however, are still willing to accept a small number of defective units as a normal part of continuing, efficient operations, given the current quality of materials, labor, machinery, and supervision. Knowing that some defective units may occur in the short run, what should a firm decide to do with them? Should it sell them as is, for a minimal price, or correct their deficiencies and sell them at a price that is closer to the regular price? These options—sell as is or do some additional work—are similar to those for obsolete inventory.

**ASK YOURSELF ▶**

1. **What are several important factors to consider before accepting a special order?**
2. **"Any product line that is experiencing a loss should be dropped." Do you agree with this statement? Why or why not?**
3. **"In order to maximize profits in a multiproduct firm, the product having the largest contribution margin per unit should always be emphasized." What is wrong with this generalization?**
4. **When considering whether to make a part internally or to buy it from an outside supplier, "beware of fixed factory overhead." Why is this an important warning?**
5. **What are joint products?**

# The "Cost Plus the Kitchen Sink" Method of Pricing

In case you've wondered how the costs of so many products purchased by so many agencies and departments of the federal government cost so doggone much money, this example is for a $436 hammer that was manufactured for the U.S. Navy by Gould Electronics. Notice that the materials were only $7; the mechanical subassembly took only .3 hour and cost approximately $3.58 (.3 hr/7.8 hr × $93); and that a wide assortment of other non-direct items cost the remaining $425.42.

    This is an example of the "cost plus the kitchen sink" method of pricing. And to think that the Navy could have bought one from Sears for less than $20.

*Source:* Proceedings & Debate of the 98th Congress, Second Session, *Congressional Record,* Vol. 130, No. 63, p. H3923, March 15, 1984.

| | | |
|---|---|---:|
| Direct material | | $7.00 |
| Material packaging | | 1.00 |
| Material handling overhead (19.8%) | | 2.00 |
| Engineering support: | | |
|   Spares/repair department | 1.0 hr | |
|   Program support/administration | 0.4 | |
|   Program management | 1.0 | |
|   Secretarial | 0.2 | |
| | 2.6 hr | 37.00 |
| Engineering overhead (110%) | | 41.00 |
| Manufacturing support: | | |
|   Mechanical subassembly | 0.3 hr | |
|   Quality control | 0.9 | |
|   Operations program management | 1.5 | |
|   Program planning | 4.0 | |
|   Manufacturing project engineering | 1.0 | |
|   Quality assurance | 0.1 | |
| | 7.8 hr | 93.00 |
| Manufacturing overhead (110%) | | 102.00 |
| | | 283.00 |
| General and administrative expenses (31.8%) | | 90.00 |
| Negotiation fee | | 56.00 |
| Interest charge | | 7.00 |
| Total Price | | $436.00 |

## SUMMARY

- Managers face a variety of decisions that affect both short-run and long-run profits. Accountants have the responsibility to assist management in the decision-making process by providing them with information that is relevant to the decision at hand. In order for information to be *relevant,* it must meet two criteria. First, it must relate to the future. Second, it must be different for each alternative being considered.
- The income statement format best suited for helping management in the decision-making process is the *contribution margin format.* On the contribution margin income statement, sales less total variable costs equals total contribution margin. And, the total contribution margin less total fixed costs equals net income.
- When an organization has excess productive capacity, it is often willing to accept a **special order** at a reduced price from a customer in a different market. The order should be accepted if the additional contribution margin is greater than the additional fixed costs from the order, and if the order does not reduce sales to regular customers.
- A firm that sells more than one product is called a **multiproduct firm.** When the profits for one or more of the product lines are unacceptable, management must decide whether to drop the product(s). Generally, the product should not be dropped as long as (1) it is making a positive contribution to fixed costs, and (2) the reduced contribution margin from dropping the product line is greater than the reduction in fixed costs.
- There is one **sales mix** for a multiproduct firm that maximizes the profits for the firm. The optimum sales mix depends upon two key variables: (1) the contribution margin per unit for each product, and (2) the restrictions upon the production and sales of each product line.
- Many organizations produce raw materials needed for a finished product as well as the finished good itself. They may find it more economical to purchase the raw material from an outside supplier. The decision to *make or buy* is determined by comparing the relevant costs of producing the raw materials internally to the relevant costs of purchasing them from an outside supplier.
- **Joint products** come about when a single product divides into two or more products at a **split-off point.** An important decision for a firm with joint products is whether to sell them at split-off or process them further. The joint product should be processed further if the incremental revenue (sales after processing less additional processing costs) exceeds the sales at split-off. **Joint product costs** are always irrelevant to the decision.
- Other short-run decisions that require relevant information include setting a normal price for regular sales during the year, and determining whether to sell obsolete or defective units as is, or to do additional work so they can be sold at a price closer to the regular price.

## 7 KEY TERMS

**Joint product costs**  The costs associated with a single product up until the split-off point in a joint product situation.

**Joint products**  Multiple products that result from the division of a single product at the split-off point in production.

**Multiproduct firm**  A firm that makes and/or sells more than one product line.

**Opportunity cost**  Potential profit forgone by rejecting one alternative in favor of another.

**Qualitative factors**  Factors to be considered in a decision situation that cannot be expressed in dollars and cents, yet may have a significant influence on a manager's decision.

| | |
|---|---|
| **Quantitative factors** | Factors to be considered in a decision situation that can be expressed in financial terms—that is, in dollars and cents. |
| **Relevant information** | Information that (1) relates to the future, and (2) is different for each alternative being considered. |
| **Sales mix** | For a multiproduct firm, the percentage of total sales distributed to each product line. |
| **Special order** | An order received from a customer in a different market at a price typically lower than the regular sales price. |
| **Split-off point** | A point in production at which a single product divides into two or more joint products. |

## DEMONSTRATION PROBLEM

The Longex Watch Company produced and sold a total of 72,000 digital watches in 1997. The total is broken down by product line in the 1997 income statement.

**LONGEX WATCH COMPANY**
**Income Statement**
**Year Ended Dec. 31, 1997**

| | Product Line | | |
|---|---|---|---|
| | **Luxury** | **Diver** | **Sports** |
| Unit Sales . . . . . . . . . . . . . . . . . . . . . . . . | 20,000 | 2,000 | 50,000 |
| Sales Revenue . . . . . . . . . . . . . . . . . . . . | $ 5,000,000 | $2,000,000 | $8,000,000 |
| Cost of Goods Sold: | | | |
| Variable . . . . . . . . . . . . . . . . . . . . . . . . | $ 4,000,000 | $1,500,000 | $3,500,000 |
| Fixed . . . . . . . . . . . . . . . . . . . . . . . . . . | 800,000 | 600,000 | 1,000,000 |
| | $ 4,800,000 | $2,100,000 | $4,500,000 |
| Gross Profit . . . . . . . . . . . . . . . . . . . . . . | $ 200,000 | $ (100,000) | $3,500,000 |
| Operating Costs: | | | |
| Variable . . . . . . . . . . . . . . . . . . . . . . . . | $ 1,100,000 | $ 300,000 | $ 500,000 |
| Fixed . . . . . . . . . . . . . . . . . . . . . . . . . . | 500,000 | 100,000 | 500,000 |
| | $ 1,600,000 | $ 400,000 | $1,000,000 |
| Net Income . . . . . . . . . . . . . . . . . . . . . . | $(1,400,000) | $ (500,000) | $2,500,000 |

**Required:**

Answer the questions below. Each question is completely independent of all the others.

1. Which product(s), if any, should be dropped? Support your answer with organized calculations.

2. Assume now that Longex is considering a special order from the Russian sports federation for 5,000 Sports watches, at a price of $90 per watch. Longex sales people usually work on a fixed salary, but if this order is accepted, the salesperson who arranged the deal will receive a $2,000 bonus. Since production of Diver watches is slow, one of the supervisors for this product line (who is paid $25,000 per year) will supervise production of the special order during regular hours. Longex figures that it can reduce the variable production costs by 20% per unit, by substituting cheaper materials for what is usually used. By what amount will Longex's income change if the special order is accepted?

3. Assume finally that the following times are required to produce each unit:

| | Hours to Produce per Unit |
|---|---|
| Luxury.................................. | 4 |
| Diver.................................... | 2 |
| Sports.................................. | 1 |

In addition, the total hours of machine capacity are 134,000. How many units of each product should be sold in order to maximize profits? What are the maximum profits possible for Longex?

## ■ Solution to Demonstration Problem

1. The income statement using a contribution margin format is as follows:

| | Product Line | | |
|---|---|---|---|
| | **Luxury** | **Diver** | **Sports** |
| Unit Sales .......................... | 20,000 | 2,000 | 50,000 |
| Sales Revenue ..................... | $ 5,000,000 | $2,000,000 | $8,000,000 |
| Variable Costs: | | | |
| Production....................... | $ 4,000,000 | $1,500,000 | $3,500,000 |
| Operating........................ | 1,100,000 | 300,000 | 500,000 |
| | $ 5,100,000 | $1,800,000 | $4,000,000 |
| Total Contribution Margin............. | $ (100,000) | $ 200,000 | $4,000,000 |
| Fixed Costs: | | | |
| Production....................... | $ 800,000 | $ 600,000 | $1,000,000 |
| Operating........................ | 500,000 | 100,000 | 500,000 |
| | $ 1,300,000 | $ 700,000 | $1,500,000 |
| Net Income ........................ | $(1,400,000) | $ (500,000) | $2,500,000 |

Even though both the Luxury and Diver models showed losses, only Luxury has a negative contribution margin. The only way the profit picture for Longex can be improved is by dropping Luxury—as is shown by the calculations below. Income will increase by $100,000, from $600,000 to $700,000.

| | Combined Net Income If: | | | |
|---|---|---|---|---|
| | **No Products Are Dropped** | **Luxury Is Dropped** | **Diver Is Dropped** | **Sports Is Dropped** |
| Sales Revenue .......... | $15,000,000 | $10,000,000 | $13,000,000 | $ 7,000,000 |
| Variable Costs: | | | | |
| Production............ | $ 9,000,000 | $ 5,000,000 | $ 7,500,000 | $ 5,500,000 |
| Operating ............ | 1,900,000 | 800,000 | 1,600,000 | 1,400,000 |
| | $10,900,000 | $ 5,800,000 | $ 9,100,000 | $ 6,900,000 |
| Total Contribution Margin.. | $ 4,100,000 | $ 4,200,000 | $ 3,900,000 | $ 100,000 |
| Fixed Costs: | | | | |
| Production............ | $ 2,400,000 | $ 2,400,000 | $ 2,400,000 | $ 2,400,000 |
| Operating ............ | 1,100,000 | 1,100,000 | 1,100,000 | 1,100,000 |
| | $ 3,500,000 | $ 3,500,000 | $ 3,500,000 | $ 3,500,000 |
| Net Income ............ | $ 600,000 | $ 700,000 | $ 400,000 | $(3,400,000) |

**2.**

|  | Reject Order | Accept Order | Difference |
|---|---|---|---|
| Sales Revenue | $15,000,000 | $15,450,000 | $450,000 |
| Variable Costs: |  |  |  |
| Production | $ 9,000,000 | $ 9,280,000* | $280,000 |
| Operating | 1,900,000 | 1,900,000 | –0– |
|  | $10,900,000 | $11,180,000 | $280,000 |
| Total Contribution Margin | $ 4,100,000 | $ 4,270,000 | $170,000 |
| Fixed Costs: |  |  |  |
| Production | $ 2,400,000 | $ 2,400,000 | –0– |
| Operating | 1,100,000 | 1,102,000 | $ 2,000 |
|  | $ 3,500,000 | $ 3,502,000 | $ 2,000 |
| Net Income | $ 600,000 | $ 768,000 | $168,000 |

\* Variable production (Sports) $= \dfrac{\$3,500,000}{50,000} = \$70 \times .80$ .............................. $56

$\times 5,000$

Additional variable production costs ......................................... $ 280,000

Variable production costs if order is rejected ................................. 9,000,000

Variable production costs if order is accepted ................................. $9,280,000

**3.** The contribution margin per unit for each product line is first determined as follows, based on the original set of facts:

|  | Luxury | Diver | Sports |
|---|---|---|---|
| Total Contribution Margin | $(100,000) | $200,000 | $4,000,000 |
| Units Sold | ÷ 20,000 | ÷ 2,000 | ÷ 50,000 |
| Contribution Margin per Unit | $ (5) | $ 100 | $ 80 |

Next, the contribution margin per hour can be determined.

|  | Luxury | Diver | Sports |
|---|---|---|---|
| Contribution Margin per Unit | $ (5) | $100 | $80 |
| Hours per Unit | ÷ 4 | ÷ 2 | ÷ 1 |
| Contribution Margin per Hour | $(1.25) | $ 50 | $80 |

The most profitable line—considering the hourly constraint—is Sports, followed by Diver. So, as long as Sports sells, it should be produced. Since no sales constraint is given, meaning that all the units that are produced can be sold, then the most profitable combination of product lines is to use all the productive capacity to produce the Sports model. The maximum profits for Longex will be $7,220,000, determined as follows:

|  | Luxury | Diver | Sports |
|---|---|---|---|
| Total Hours Available | 134,000 | 134,000 | 134,000 |
| Hours per Unit | ÷ 4 | ÷ 2 | ÷ 1 |
| Total Units Produced and Sold | 33,500 | 67,000 | 134,000 |
| Contribution Margin per Unit | $ (5) | $ 100 | $ 80 |
| Total Contribution Margin | $ (167,500) | $6,700,000 | $10,720,000 |
| Total Fixed Costs | 3,500,000 | 3,500,000 | 3,500,000 |
| Maximum Profits | $(3,667,500) | $3,200,000 | $ 7,220,000 |

## QUESTIONS FOR REVIEW AND FURTHER THOUGHT

### REVIEW QUESTIONS

1. Explain what is meant by the term *relevant information*.

2. Information must be accurate in order to be relevant. Comment.

3. Since fixed costs are not expected to change, can they be relevant to a decision? Explain.

4. What are qualitative factors? Is it possible for them to influence a decision? Explain.

5. How does the contribution margin format to an income statement differ from the traditional format?

6. Give several reasons that a firm would make a raw material needed in production rather than buy it from an outside supplier.

7. What is an opportunity cost?

8. Give several examples of a make or buy type of decision that do not involve parts or raw materials in a production department of a manufacturer.

9. Define joint product costs.

### QUESTIONS FOR FURTHER THOUGHT

1. All differential costs relate to relevant items. Why?

2. Since past costs are irrelevant, is it possible for them to be useful to the decision maker? Explain.

3. A special order should be accepted only if the gross profit for the special order is positive. Comment on this statement.

4. In a multiproduct firm, the firm can maximize profits by producing and selling only that product with the highest contribution margin per unit. Comment.

5. Discuss whether and why the following statements are true or false.
   a. A product should always be dropped by a firm when the product line income is negative.
   b. As long as a product line is showing a profit, it should never be dropped.
   c. It's not very important whether a product line has a positive or negative contribution margin. What's important is whether or not it has a favorable amount of net income.

6. "Opportunity costs are always relevant." Do you agree? Explain.

7. Why are joint product costs irrelevant to the decision of whether to sell at split-off or process further?

### OBJECTIVE ASSIGNMENT

*True/False*   Indicate whether each statement below is *true* or *false* by placing a *T* or an *F* in the space provided.

_____ 1. Information is relevant to a decision if it relates to the future and is different for the alternatives being considered.

_____ 2. All fixed costs are irrelevant.

_____ 3. Only quantitative factors should be considered by a manager in making a decision.

_____ 4. A product line should never be dropped when it has a positive contribution margin.

_____ 5. Joint product costs are always irrelevant to a decision of whether to sell at split-off or process further.

*Multiple Choice*   Select the best choice to complete each statement or answer each question below. Write the letter corresponding to your choice in the space provided.

_____ 1. The Nassa Space Parts Company is considering a special order to sell to Kwaitin Company 5,000 units of a missile part for $1,500 per unit—which is $500 less than its regular price. The costs associated with the regular production and sale of this part are as follows:

Variable manufacturing costs. . . . . . . . . . . . . . .    $800/unit
Fixed manufacturing costs. . . . . . . . . . . . . . . . .     400/unit
Variable selling costs . . . . . . . . . . . . . . . . . . . . .    100/unit
Fixed selling costs . . . . . . . . . . . . . . . . . . . . . . .     50/unit

Sales commissions—representing all the variable selling costs—will not have to be paid on the special order. By what amount will the net income for Nassa increase if the special order is accepted?
a. $3,500,000       c. $75,000
b. $3,000,000       d. $150,000

_____ 2. The End of the Line Company has a product that is expected to show a loss in 1998 of $15,000, based on sales of 10,000 units. Its expected contribution margin is $2 per unit. If the product line is dropped, what will happen to End of the Line's income for 1998?
a. Decrease by $15,000       c. Increase by $15,000
b. Decrease by $20,000       d. Increase by $20,000

_____ 3. Presto Magic Manufacturers produces and sells three different magic kits for new magicians. The relevant information related to each kit is given below:

| Product Line | Contribution Margin/Unit | Hours/Unit to Produce |
|---|---|---|
| Starter Kit. . . . . . . . . . . . . . . . . . . . . . . . . . . . . | $25 | 5 |
| Handy Kit . . . . . . . . . . . . . . . . . . . . . . . . . . . . . | 15 | 2 |
| All-in-One Kit . . . . . . . . . . . . . . . . . . . . . . . . . . | 10 | 1 |

Presto has 20,000 hours of capacity available and can sell all the magic kits it can produce. If its fixed costs are $100,000, what is the maximum profit possible for Presto?
a. $100,000       c. $200,000
b. $150,000       d. $350,000

_____ 4. The costs per unit of manufacturing a raw material used in production of a finished product are as follows:

Direct materials . . . . . . . . . . . . . . . . . . . . . . . . . . . . .    $25
Direct labor . . . . . . . . . . . . . . . . . . . . . . . . . . . . . . . . .      5
Variable factory overhead. . . . . . . . . . . . . . . . . . . . . . .     10
Fixed factory overhead . . . . . . . . . . . . . . . . . . . . . . . .      4

If 10,000 units of the raw materials are purchased for $43 per unit from an outside supplier instead of being produced internally, by what amount will the income increase or decrease?
a. $10,000 increase       c. $30,000 decrease
b. $10,000 decrease       d. $430,000 increase

_____ 5. Which of the following is (are) not a necessary criteria in order for information to be relevant.
   a. It must relate to the future.
   b. It must be different for the alternatives being considered.
   c. It must be accurate.
   d. None of the above are appropriate criteria.

_____ 6. In a decision to sell a joint product at the split-off point or process it further, which of the items below would always be irrelevant?
   a. The sales at the split-off point
   b. The sales after additional processing
   c. The additional processing costs
   d. The joint product costs

_____ 7. Cromatim Company incurs $10,000 of joint product costs to produce a product that splits into Product A and Product B at a split-off point. At that point Product A can be sold for $50,000 and B can be sold for $100,000. Instead, Product A can be sold after additional processing costs of $25,000 for $70,000. Product B can be sold after additional processing costs of $40,000 for $150,000. In order to maximize profits where should each product be sold?
   a. Product A at split-off and Product B after processing
   b. Product B at split-off and Product A after processing
   c. Both Product A and Product B at split-off
   d. Both Product A and Product B after processing

_____ 8. Products A and B have contribution margins per unit of $20 and $10 respectively. Product A takes 5 hours to produce and Product B takes 2 hours. If the company can sell all of any products it manufactures, which product is more profitable for the company?
   a. Product A
   b. Product B
   c. They are equally profitable
   d. Cannot be determined without more information

_____ 9. The fixed costs of producing and selling 18,000 units of Product X (having a $5 contribution margin per unit) are $100,000. The company is considering dropping this product line and replacing it with 7,000 units of Product Y, each having a contribution margin per unit of $12. If X is dropped and Y is added, by what amount will the company's income increase or decrease?
   a. $94,000 increase
   b. $84,000 increase
   c. $6,000 decrease
   d. $104,000 decrease

_____ 10. Which of the following costs would likely be relevant in a make or buy decision?
   a. The costs of buying the part from an outside supplier
   b. The variable costs of manufacturing the part internally
   c. The fixed costs that can be eliminated if the part is no longer produced internally
   d. All of the above

## EXERCISES

2† **Exercise 1:** Deciding Whether to Accept or Reject a Special Order

The Universal Electric Corporation sells tape recorders for $100 each. The average cost to produce and sell a tape recorder (based on production and sales of 20,000 per year) is shown on top of the next page.

† The numbers in the margin refer to the Learning Objectives.

Cost of Goods Sold:
    Variable. . . . . . . . . . . . . . . . . . . . . . . . . . . . . . . . . . . . . . . . . $40
    Fixed. . . . . . . . . . . . . . . . . . . . . . . . . . . . . . . . . . . . . . . . . . 20
Selling Costs:
    Variable (shipping) . . . . . . . . . . . . . . . . . . . . . . . . . . . . . 20
    Fixed. . . . . . . . . . . . . . . . . . . . . . . . . . . . . . . . . . . . . . . . . . 10

The company is considering a special order of 3,000 tape recorders, for $56 each. The buyer will pick up the order at the door.

Should the special order be accepted? How much more (or less) income will Universal Electric have if it accepts the order?

▶ *(Check Figure: Additional income = $48,000)*

3   **Exercise 2:** Determining Whether an Unprofitable Product Should Be Dropped

The Star Wars Robot Company sells three lines of robots. Its president is dissatisfied with the product-line income statements shown below, and is considering dropping at least one of the unprofitable lines.

| | Robot Line | | |
| --- | --- | --- | --- |
| | **R1D1** | **R3D3** | **R4D4** |
| Sales | $600,000 | $360,000 | $ 330,000 |
| Variable Costs | 330,000 | 300,000 | 360,000 |
| | $270,000 | $ 60,000 | $ (30,000) |
| Fixed Costs | 90,000 | 90,000 | 90,000 |
| Net Income | $180,000 | $ (30,000) | $(120,000) |

The total fixed costs will not be affected by the number of product lines being manufactured.

a. Should the R3D3 be dropped? Why? Prepare an income statement assuming that this product line is the only one dropped.

b. Should the R4D4 be dropped? Why? Prepare an income statement assuming that this product line is the only one dropped.

c. Prepare income statements for each product if the $270,000 of fixed costs is distributed to R1D1, R3D3, and R4D4 in a 60% : 20% : 20% ratio, rather than the equal distribution shown in the income statements above. Compare the total income to what it is in the original situation. Should any product be dropped now?

▶ *(Check Figure: a. Net loss = $30,000)*

4   **Exercise 3:** Maximizing Profits for a Multiproduct Firm

The Ivey Company sells two products, X and Y, that have contribution margins per unit of $12 and $8, respectively. Product X takes 3 hours to produce and product Y requires 1 hour. There are 30,000 hours of productive capacity available. The company can sell all it produces, and the fixed costs are $34,000.

a. If all the productive capacity is used to produce product X, how many units will be produced and sold? What would be the net income for Ivey?

b. If all the productive capacity is used to produce product Y, how many units will be produced and sold? What would be the net income for Ivey?

c. Which product should be produced? Why?

d. What difference would it make if Ivey couldn't sell all the product that it produces?

▶ *(Check Figure: a. Net income = $86,000)*

---

5 **Exercise 4:** Deciding Whether to Purchase a Part or Produce It Internally

The costs for Harris Company of producing 10,000 parts that go into the production of a main product line are the following:

| | |
|---|---|
| Direct materials. . . . . . . . . . . . . . . . . . . . . . . . . . . . . . | $1.50 |
| Direct labor . . . . . . . . . . . . . . . . . . . . . . . . . . . . . . . . | .75 |
| Variable overhead. . . . . . . . . . . . . . . . . . . . . . . . . . . . | .75 |
| Fixed overhead . . . . . . . . . . . . . . . . . . . . . . . . . . . . . . | .50 |
| | $3.50 |

     The vice president for production is considering buying the part from a supplier for $3.15 per unit, and discontinuing internal production.

a. Assume that none of the fixed factory overhead will be eliminated if production of the part is ceased. Determine whether the part should be purchased or produced internally. Provide computations to support your answer.

b. Now assume that four-fifths of the fixed overhead will exist regardless of the decision. The remainder will occur only if the part is produced. Determine whether the part should be purchased or produced internally. Provide computations to support your answer.

▶ *(Check Figure: b. Continuing to produce internally will save $.05 per part)*

---

5 **Exercise 5:** Adapting the Make or Buy Analysis to a Nonproduction Setting

The Tort Tort Bakery uses a local law firm, called Ambulance Chasers, Inc., for all its legal work. Tort Tort pays Ambulance Chasers a $30,000 annual retainer in order to have immediate access to the managing partner of the law firm in the case of an emergency. In addition, Tort Tort pays the firm $100 an hour for the actual legal services rendered. During 1997, Ambulance Chasers provided 300 hours of legal assistance, and Tort Tort expects that number to double in 1998.

     Tort Tort is considering hiring its own attorney to replace Ambulance Chasers at an annual salary of $50,000. In addition, Tort Tort would have to add a small support staff costing $20,000 for the year. In case of emergencies that cannot be handled internally, Tort Tort will still keep Ambulance Chasers on a smaller $5,000 retainer.

     Should Tort Tort hire its own attorney? Support your answer will calculations.

▶ *(Check figure: Difference = $15,000)*

---

6 **Exercise 6:** Deciding Whether it's Better to Sell a Joint Product at Split-Off or to Process Further

The Banana Split Fruit Company makes a product that breaks into three products at a split-off point. Information concerning the three products is as follows:

1. Product X can be sold at the split-off point for $90,000 or processed further (additional processing costs are $35,000) and sold for $115,000.

2. Product Y can be sold only after further processing (additional processing costs are $40,000) for $70,000.

3. Product Z can be sold only at the split-off point for $60,000.

The joint product costs are $135,000.

     Determine whether each product should be sold at the split-off point or after additional processing. What are the maximum profits possible for Banana Split?

▶ *(Check figure: Maximum profits = $45,000)*

6  **Exercise 7:** Maximizing Profits in a Joint Product Situation

In 1997 the Energetics Company produced two chemicals, Oxydol and Pectic, from a single compound. The following income statement relates to that year:

|  | Oxydol | Pectic | Total |
|---|---|---|---|
| Sales. . . . . . . . . . . . . . . . . . . . . . . . . . . . . . . . | $150,000 | $220,000 | $370,000 |
| Additional Processing Costs . . . . . . . . . . . . . . | $ 60,000 | $180,000 | $240,000 |
| Allocated Joint Product Costs . . . . . . . . . . . . . | 45,000 | 50,000 | 95,000 |
|  | $105,000 | $230,000 | $335,000 |
| Net Income | $ 45,000 | $(10,000) | $ 35,000 |

a. Energetics is considering dropping Pectic (because of its reported loss and the fact that it cannot be sold at split off). Prepare a new income statement to reflect this action. Is it a good idea to drop the product?

b. Assume instead that Energetics can sell Oxydol and Pectic at the split-off point for $100,000 and $35,000, respectively. When should each product now be sold in order to maximize profits? What are the maximum profits possible?

▶ *(Check figure: b. Maximum profits = $45,000)*

## PROBLEMS: SET A

2†  **Problem A1:** Deciding Whether to Accept or Reject a Special Order

Wake-the-Dead Corporation produces super-loud alarm clocks. They are priced to sell at $75 per clock. In 1998, when 12,000 clocks were produced and sold, well below full capacity, the income statement for Wake-the-Dead was as follows:

| | | |
|---|---|---|
| Sales . . . . . . . . . . . . . . . . . . . . . . . . . . . . . . . . . . . . . . . . . . . . . . . . . . . . . . . |  | $900,000 |
| Cost of Goods Sold: |  |  |
|     Direct Materials. . . . . . . . . . . . . . . . . . . . . . . . . . . . . . . . . . . . . . . | $180,000 |  |
|     Direct Labor. . . . . . . . . . . . . . . . . . . . . . . . . . . . . . . . . . . . . . . . . . | 240,000 |  |
|     Variable Overhead . . . . . . . . . . . . . . . . . . . . . . . . . . . . . . . . . . . | 72,000 |  |
|     Fixed Overhead. . . . . . . . . . . . . . . . . . . . . . . . . . . . . . . . . . . . . . . | 28,000 | 520,000 |
| Gross Profit . . . . . . . . . . . . . . . . . . . . . . . . . . . . . . . . . . . . . . . . . . . . . . . . |  | $380,000 |
| Operating Expenses: |  |  |
|     Variable Selling. . . . . . . . . . . . . . . . . . . . . . . . . . . . . . . . . . . . . . | $108,000 |  |
|     Fixed Selling . . . . . . . . . . . . . . . . . . . . . . . . . . . . . . . . . . . . . . . . | 52,000 | 160,000 |
| Net Income. . . . . . . . . . . . . . . . . . . . . . . . . . . . . . . . . . . . . . . . . . . . . . . . . . |  | $220,000 |

Wake-the-Dead is considering a special order for 2,400 clocks from a Swiss company, at only $50 per clock. If the order is accepted, the materials used will be of an inferior quality, costing $2.50 less per clock. Direct labor will require 10% fewer hours, and variable overhead fluctuates with direct labor hours. In addition, if the deal goes through, the sales representative will receive a bonus of $2,000.

**Required:**

Determine whether or not the special order should be accepted. What will be Wake-the-Dead's net income if the order is accepted?

▶ *(Check Figure: Net income = $230,240)*

† The numbers in the margin refer to the Learning Objectives.

3   **Problem A2:** Increasing Income by Dropping Product Lines

The Robles Company sells three sizes of fishing boats, and has prepared the following income statements for 1997:

| | Product | | | |
| --- | --- | --- | --- | --- |
| | **12 ft** | **15 ft** | **18 ft** | **Total** |
| Sales...................... | $800,000 | $ 640,000 | $1,200,000 | $2,640,000 |
| Cost of Goods Sold .......... | 520,000 | 600,000 | 560,000 | 1,680,000 |
| Gross Margin ............... | $280,000 | $ 40,000 | $ 640,000 | $ 960,000 |
| Operating Expenses.......... | 320,000 | 280,000 | 280,000 | 880,000 |
| Net Income ................. | $(40,000) | $(240,000) | $ 360,000 | $ 80,000 |

The fixed costs included in cost of goods sold and operating expenses are as follows:

| | Fixed Costs Included in: | |
| --- | --- | --- |
| **Product** | **Cost of Goods Sold** | **Operating Expenses** |
| 12 ft | $200,000 | $160,000 |
| 15 ft | 120,000 | 80,000 |
| 18 ft | 160,000 | 200,000 |
| | $480,000 | $440,000 |

**Required:**

1. Reconstruct the income statement in the contribution margin format.
2. Assuming that the total fixed costs will not be affected by the decision, should any of the product lines be dropped? Why? By what amount will income change?
3. Assume only in this part that the 15-ft and 18-ft boats are dropped, and that the fixed overhead costs that could be reduced by dropping each line are $80,000 and $64,000, respectively. By how much would the profits for the firm be reduced or increased?

▶ *(Check Figure: 3. Reduced by $536,000)*

4   **Problem A3:** Maximizing Profits for a Two-Product Firm

Ace Corporation produces two product lines that share the facilities of a single plant. Per-package costs of production are given below.

| | Hammers (200,000 Packages) | Drills (400,000 Packages) |
| --- | --- | --- |
| Sales Price ...................................... | $10.00 | $20.00 |
| Cost of Goods Sold: | | |
|   Variable ...................................... | $ 2.00 | $ 8.00 |
|   Fixed ...................................... | 3.00 | 3.50 |
| | $ 5.00 | $11.50 |
| Gross Profit...................................... | $ 5.00 | $ 8.50 |
| Operating (all Variable)........................... | 1.00 | 2.00 |
| Income........................................... | $ 4.00 | $ 6.50 |

In addition, it takes 30 minutes to make one package of hammers and 60 minutes to make one package of drills. The total productive capacity is 200,000 hours, and Ace can sell all the units it produces.

**Required:**

1. Determine the number of packages of each product that must be produced and sold in order to maximize profits.
2. What are the maximum possible profits for Ace?
3. Would the answers in parts (1) and (2) be the same if Ace could sell only 320,000 packages of hammers and 168,000 packages of drills? Explain.

▶ *(Check Figure: 2. $800,000)*

5 **Problem A4:** Deciding Whether to Make or Buy a Part

Holstrum Company makes its own engines, which are used in the production of jet skis. One engine, #120, was used in 1,000 jet skis last year. The costs of producing #120 were as follows:

| | |
|---|---:|
| Direct materials | $ 80,000 |
| Direct labor | 120,000 |
| Variable overhead | 40,000 |
| Fixed overhead | 160,000 |
| | $400,000 |

Holstrum is considering purchasing the 1,000 engines from Sandbar, Inc., for $270 per engine (plus shipping costs of $10 per engine).

Three-fourths of the fixed overhead costs represent the salary of supervisors who will retire if the engines are purchased from an outside supplier. The remaining fixed overhead will continue to be incurred even if the production of #120 is ceased.

**Required:**

Determine whether the engines should be purchased or produced internally.

▶ *(Check Figure: Difference between make or buy = $80,000)*

6 **Problem A5:** Preparing Income Statements and Maximizing Profits for Joint Products

The Generic Component Company produces a liquid in a heating process which, at 525 degrees, splits into two products that can be sold to drug manufacturing companies. The first product, TR3, can be sold at the split-off point for $2,400,000, or processed further. The product's additional processing will cost $450,000 but will increase sales to $3,600,000.

The second product, SX100, can also be sold at split-off or processed further. Sales at split-off would be $1,800,000; after additional processing, $2,250,000. The additional processing costs will be $600,000. The joint product costs are $3,000,000.

**Required:**

1. Draw a diagram depicting the situation described above.
2. Assume that the joint costs are allocated $1,050,000 to TR3 and $1,950,000 to SX100. If both products are sold at split-off, what would be the income for the firm as a whole as well as for each product?
3. Answer part 2 again but assume that both products are sold after additional processing.
4. In order to maximize profits for the firm, should each product be sold at split-off or processed further?
5. Using the answer to part 4 and assuming the same cost allocation as in part 2, determine the income for the firm as a whole as well as for each product line.

▶ *(Check figure: 5. Net income = $1,950,000)*

**4** **Problem A6:** Maximizing Profits in a Two-Product Firm With Constraints

The Toysuki Company produces two models of television sets. The following information relates to the production and sale of each model:

|  | Portable | Console |
|---|---|---|
| Sales price | $400 | $500 |
| Variable cost per unit | $320 | $300 |
| Allocated fixed costs | $1,620,000 | $3,580,000 |
| Hours needed to produce | 2 | 10 |
| Maximum unit sales | 100,000 | 20,000 |

The total hours of productive capacity are 250,000. The controller is trying to decide how to distribute the productive capacity to the two products in order to maximize profits, and she asks for your advice.

**Required:**

Determine the number of units of each product that should be produced and sold in order to maximize profits. What are the maximum possible profits for Toysuki?

▶ *(Check figure: Maximum profits = $3,800,000)*

**2 3 4** **Problem A7:** Making Decisions Concerning Multiple Products

The controller of Sonymax Electronics has prepared the following product-line income statements for 1997, and the president is extremely dissatisfied with the profits from his SR25 and SR100 lines.

|  | SR25 | SR50 | SR100 |
|---|---|---|---|
| Units Produced and Sold | 12,500 | 15,000 | 8,000 |
| Sales | $500,000 | $300,000 | $250,000 |
| Variable Costs: |  |  |  |
| Production | $300,000 | $105,000 | $110,000 |
| Selling | 100,000 | 45,000 | 40,000 |
|  | $400,000 | $150,000 | $150,000 |
| Fixed Costs (allocated by set ratio): |  |  |  |
| Production | $ 75,000 | $ 60,000 | $ 70,000 |
| Selling | 50,000 | 40,000 | 50,000 |
|  | $125,000 | $100,000 | $120,000 |
| Income | $ (25,000) | $ 50,000 | $ (20,000) |

**Required:**

Answer each *independent* question below:

1. What will be Sonymax's profits if SR25 or SR100 is dropped? Would you recommend that either one be dropped?
2. Assume that Sonymax is considering a special order of 2,000 SR50 units at $14 per unit. It will not be necessary to incur any additional shipping costs (shipping costs are two-thirds of the variable selling costs). If Sonymax accepts the special order, the variable production costs will be $3 higher per unit because higher labor rates must be paid for overtime work. Should the order be accepted? Show all work.
3. Sonymax is hoping to shift some of the production and sales from SR25 to SR100. It wants to have a sales mix of 20:40:40 for SR25, SR50, and SR100, respectively. How many units would the firm have to sell to generate a profit of $75,000 if the desired sales mix can be attained?

4. Assume that it takes 1 hour to produce SR25, 2 hours for SR50, and 4 hours for SR100 and that the total hours of machine time available are 74,500 per year. In addition, the maximum demand for each product is estimated to be the following:

| Maximum Sales | |
|---|---|
| SR25 | 25,000 |
| SR50 | 30,000 |
| SR100 | 19,000 |

How many units of each product line should be sold in order to maximize profits? What are the maximum profits possible for Sonymax?

▶ *(Check figure: 3. 39,623)*

## PROBLEMS: SET B

2† **Problem B1:** Deciding Whether to Accept or Reject a Special Order

The Justincase Shutter Company produces and sells hurricane shutters in Texas border towns. During 1997, Justincase had the following operating results:

| | | | |
|---|---|---|---|
| Sales ($45 per shutter) | | | $225,000 |
| Cost of Goods Sold: | | | |
| Direct Materials | $25,000 | | |
| Direct Labor | 30,000 | | |
| Variable Overhead | 20,000 | $75,000 | |
| Fixed Overhead | | 15,000 | 90,000 |
| Gross Profit | | | $135,000 |
| Selling and Administrative: | | | |
| Variable: | | | |
| Commissions | $ 6,000 | | |
| Shipping | 9,000 | $15,000 | |
| Fixed | | 3,000 | 18,000 |
| Net Income | | | $117,000 |

Justincase is considering a special order from Gulf Motel during a slow month, for 1,000 shutters at $30 per shutter. If the order is accepted, there will be no sales commissions on the transaction. Since the order is a one-time deal, Justincase figures it can cut its direct materials costs by 20% per shutter by using cheaper materials.

**Required:**

Determine whether or not Justincase should accept the special order. What will be the effect on profits of the firm if the order is accepted?

▶ *(Check Figure: Profits will increase by $14,200)*

3 **Problem B2:** Determining Whether a Product Line Should Be Dropped

The Famous Faces Mask Company sells three different versions of rubber masks, called the George, the Colin, and the Norman. Its income statement for 1998 indicates two apparently unprofitable product lines, both of which may be dropped by the president of Famous Faces.

† The numbers in the margin refer to the Learning Objectives.

| | Product | | | |
| --- | --- | --- | --- | --- |
| | George | Colin | Norman | Total |
| Sales .......................... | $90,000 | $75,000 | $250,000 | $415,000 |
| Cost of Goods Sold: | | | | |
| Variable ...................... | $40,000 | $45,000 | $150,000 | $235,000 |
| Fixed ......................... | 9,000 | 10,000 | 25,000 | 44,000 |
| | $49,000 | $55,000 | $175,000 | $279,000 |
| Gross Profit..................... | $41,000 | $20,000 | $ 75,000 | $136,000 |
| Selling and Administrative: | | | | |
| Variable ...................... | $10,000 | $15,000 | $105,000 | $130,000 |
| Fixed ......................... | 6,000 | 7,500 | 20,000 | 33,500 |
| | $16,000 | $22,500 | $125,000 | $163,500 |
| Net Income ..................... | $25,000 | $(2,500) | $(50,000) | $(27,500) |

**Required:**

1. Reconstruct the income statement in the contribution margin format.
2. Assuming that the total fixed costs will not be affected by the decision, should any product lines be dropped? Why? By what amount will income change?
3. Assume, for this part only, that Colin and Norman are being dropped and that the fixed overhead costs that are reduced by dropping each line are $7,500 and $12,500, respectively. By how much will the deletion of these products increase or decrease the net income for the firm?

▶ *(Check Figure: 3. Net income will increase by $10,000)*

4  **Problem B3:** Maximizing Products for a Two-Product Firm

The Igo Car Company produces two models of automobiles. The following information relates to the production and sale of each model:

| | Sedan | Coupe |
| --- | --- | --- |
| Sales price ..................................... | $4,000 | $5,000 |
| Variable cost per unit ........................... | $3,200 | $3,000 |
| Allocated fixed costs............................ | $16,200,000 | $35,800,000 |
| Hours needed to produce......................... | 20 | 100 |
| Maximum unit sales ............................. | Unlimited | Unlimited |

The total hours of productive capacity are 2,500,000.

The controller is trying to decide how to distribute the productive capacity to the two products in order to maximize profits, and asks for your advice.

**Required:**

1. Determine the number of units of each product to be produced and sold in order to maximize profits.
2. What are the maximum possible profits for Igo?

3. Would the answers in parts (1) and (2) be the same if Igo could sell only 100,000 of the Sedan and 20,000 of the Coupe? Explain.

▶ *(Check Figure: 2. $48,000,000)*

5    **Problem B4:** Determining Whether Profits Will Be Increased by Making Instead of Buying a Raw Material

The Cures Bottling Company produces and sells a fruit cola drink. One of the ingredients, fruit juice flavoring, was purchased from a supplier, but Cures is now considering producing it internally. During 1997, 10,000 gallons of fruit juice flavoring will be required for production, which if purchased externally would cost $1.00 per gallon. The costs of receiving and handling these purchases average $0.12 per gallon.

The costs of producing fruit juice flavoring internally are as follows:

| | |
|---|---|
| Direct materials ...................... | $ .20/gallon |
| Direct labor ...................... | .80/gallon |
| Variable overhead...................... | .10/gallon |
| Fixed overhead ...................... | .15/gallon |
| | $1.25/gallon |

The fixed overhead for the company in total will not change. Some of the total is assigned to the production of fruit juice flavoring, since it does utilize some of the productive capacity.

**Required:**

Determine whether Cures should produce the fruit juice flavoring internally or purchase it from an outside supplier.

▶ *(Check Figure: Savings = $200)*

6    **Problem B5:** Preparing Income Statements and Maximizing Profits for Joint Products

The Stockstill Lumber Company incurs costs of $200,000 in cutting and transporting trees to the sawmills, at which time the trees are split into three products: wood, pulp, and sawdust. Wood can be sold immediately for $170,000 or processed further in order to be sold for $185,000. Pulp can be sold at split-off for $120,000 or after processing for $130,000. Sawdust can be sold only at split-off for $40,000. The additional processing costs are $10,000 for wood and $20,000 for pulp.

**Required:**

1. Draw a diagram depicting the situation described above.
2. Assume that the joint costs are allocated as follows: $80,000 to wood, $70,000 to pulp, and $50,000 to sawdust. If all products are sold at split-off, what would be the income for each product and for the firm as a whole?
3. Answer part 2, but assume that wood and pulp are sold after additional processing.
4. Should each product be sold at split-off or processed further? Determine the maximum profits for the firm.

▶ *(Check figure: 4. $135,000)*

**4**  **Problem B6:** Maximizing Profits in a Multi-Product Firm

The Cuomo Corporation is about to introduce two new product lines that will share the facilities of a single plant. Estimates concerning the potential per-unit revenues and costs are given below:

|  | Product X | Product Y |
|---|---|---|
| Sales Price. . . . . . . . . . . . . . . . . . . . . . . . . . . . . . . . . . . . | $100 | $200 |
| Cost of Goods Sold: | | |
|    Variable. . . . . . . . . . . . . . . . . . . . . . . . . . . . . . . . . . . | $ 20 | $ 80 |
|    Fixed . . . . . . . . . . . . . . . . . . . . . . . . . . . . . . . . . . . . . | 10 | 15 |
| | $ 30 | $ 95 |
| Gross Profit . . . . . . . . . . . . . . . . . . . . . . . . . . . . . . . . . | $ 70 | $105 |
| Operating (all variable). . . . . . . . . . . . . . . . . . . . . . . . . | 10 | 20 |
| Income . . . . . . . . . . . . . . . . . . . . . . . . . . . . . . . . . . . . . | **$ 60** | **$ 85** |

In addition, it will take 2 hours to make one unit of product X and 4 hours to make one unit of product Y. The total productive capacity is 100,000 hours, and Cuomo can sell all the units it produces.

**Required:**

1. How many units of each product need to be produced and sold in order to maximize profits for Cuomo?
2. Assume now that the maximum demand for X and Y is 15,000 and 20,000 units, respectively. How many units of each product should be produced and sold in order to maximize profits? What is the maximum total contribution margin for Cuomo?

▶ *(Check figure: 2. Product Y = 17,500 units)*

**2 3 4**  **Problem B7:** Making Decisions Concerning Multiple Products

The Beep Em Company produces and sells cellular phones and beepers. The 1997 income statement is shown below.

**BEEP EM COMPANY**
**Income Statement**
**Year Ended Dec. 31, 1997**

| | Phones | | |
|---|---|---|---|
| | Standard | Deluxe | Beepers |
| Unit sales . . . . . . . . . . . . . . . . . . . . . . . | 10,000 | 2,000 | 100,000 |
| Sales revenue . . . . . . . . . . . . . . . . . . . | $2,500,000 | $1,000,000 | $16,000,000 |
| Cost of goods sold: | | | |
|    Variable. . . . . . . . . . . . . . . . . . . . . . | $2,000,000 | $ 800,000 | $ 7,000,000 |
|    Fixed . . . . . . . . . . . . . . . . . . . . . . . . | 400,000 | 300,000 | 2,000,000 |
| | $2,400,000 | $1,100,000 | $9,000,000 |
| Gross profit. . . . . . . . . . . . . . . . . . . . . | $ 100,000 | $ (100,000) | $7,000,000 |
| Operating Costs: | | | |
|    Variable. . . . . . . . . . . . . . . . . . . . . . | $ 550,000 | $ 100,000 | $1,000,000 |
|    Fixed . . . . . . . . . . . . . . . . . . . . . . . . | 250,000 | 100,000 | 1,000,000 |
| | $ 800,000 | $ 200,000 | $2,000,000 |
| Net income. . . . . . . . . . . . . . . . . . . . . . | $( 700,00) | $ (300,000) | $5,000,000 |

**Required:**

Answer the question below. Each question is completely independent of all the others.

1. Beep Em is considering a special order from a customer in an unrelated market for 10,000 Beepers, at a price of $100 per beeper. Beep Em's sales force will receive a 2% sales commission if this order is accepted. There will be no other additional variable operation costs on the special order. One of the supervisors for the Beeper product line (who is paid $30,000 per year) will supervise production of the special order during weekends at a cost of $1,000. Beep Em also decides it can reduce the variable production costs by 10% per unit, by substituting less experienced workers than are usually used. By what amount will Beep Em's income change if the special order is accepted?

2. Which product(s), if any, should be dropped? Support your answer with organized calculations.

3. Assume now that Beep Em has 130,000 hours of machine capacity and that it takes the following times to produce each unit:

|  | Hours to Produce Per Unit |
|---|---|
| Standard | 2 |
| Deluxe | 4 |
| Beeper | 1 |

How many units of each product should be sold in order to maximize profits? What are the maximum profits possible for Beep Em?

▶ (Check Figure: 3. $6,350,000)

## DECISION PROBLEM

The Sugar and Spice Sweets Company produces three different lines of candy products. The condensed results for the company for the previous year are presented below.

|  | Chewing Gum | Jelly Beans | Mint Chocolates |
|---|---|---|---|
| Sales | $225,000 | $130,000 | $215,000 |
| Cost of Goods Sold | 200,000 | 135,000 | 155,000 |
| Gross Profit | $ 25,000 | $( 5,000) | $ 60,000 |
| Operating Expenses | 30,000 | 15,000 | 20,000 |
| Net Income | $( 5,000) | $(20,000) | $ 40,000 |

At first glance, it appears obvious to the president of Sugar and Spice that the production and sale of gum and jelly beans should be stopped. Before making a final decision, he asks the company controller to provide a more detailed breakdown of costs in the cost of goods sold and operating sections of the income statement. The controller goes back to her spreadsheet and comes up with the following supporting details concerning these costs:

|  | Chewing Gum | Jelly Beans | Mint Chocolates |
|---|---|---|---|
| Cost of Sales: |  |  |  |
|   Variable Manufacturing Costs | $120,000 | $90,000 | $120,000 |
|   Fixed Manufacturing Costs | 80,000 | 45,000 | 35,000 |
| Operating Costs: |  |  |  |
|   Variable | 20,000 | 10,000 | 12,000 |
|   Fixed | 10,000 | 5,000 | 8,000 |

The president carefully studies all this information overnight, and returns the next morning, confident that the best decision is to drop the two unprofitable product lines.

**Required:**

1. Entirely on the basis of the information above, what must have been the president's logic for deciding to drop these two product lines?
2. Entirely on the basis of this information, do you agree with the president's logic? What additional information might you want to have before you make a final decision?
3. Assume that the president wishes to fully utilize the firm's productive capacity and wants to maximize the firm's short-run profits. Also assume that the total fixed costs will not be affected by the mix of products produced and sold. What additional information would you need in order to make this decision? How would this information affect the decision?

## ETHICS CASE

Penn Steel is a medium-sized steel company that has been operating in Ore City, Pennsylvania, for 65 years. Most of the workers, as well as their parents and grandparents, have been employed by Penn Steel for most of their lives. The economy of Ore City is completely dependent on Penn Steel.

Penn Steel has been losing money for many years and is desperate for a change. Its machinery is outdated, inefficient, and constantly in need of repair. Its labor force is paid relatively high wages due to the recent emergence of an extremely strong union. In addition, its taxes, both property and income (when it makes a profit), are extremely high.

Penn Steel has been approached by a small parish in Louisiana that has been economically depressed for many years. The parish commissioners have offered Penn Steel the following incentives to move its operation from Pennsylvania to Louisiana:

1. A 10-acre tract of land at no cost, with no property taxes for the first 10 years.
2. A work force that has an average wage scale 40% lower than that of the company's employees in Pennsylvania. Not only are wages typically lower in the South, but no union is expected to form for many years.

3. In exchange, Penn Steel must agree to employ residents of the surrounding parishes and to close down its operations in Pennsylvania.

Penn management realizes that this move would be its opportunity to modernize the firm's production operation and make it much more competitive, especially in foreign markets. New labor-saving devices would replace the old labor-intensive equipment, thereby saving labor costs. With the lower wages for the new workers and greatly reduced taxes, Penn managers believe that the firm would soon be profitable again and that its prospects for long-run survival would be greatly enhanced.

**Required:**

1. List as many factors as you can, both quantitative and qualitative, that should have a bearing on this decision.
2. Does the move appear to be a good business decision for Penn Steel?
3. Do you feel that there are ethical factors that Penn management needs to consider? What are they?
4. Which are the more important factors in this situation—good business or good ethics?

## OBJECTIVE ASSIGNMENT ANSWERS

### True/False

1. T    2. F    3. F    4. F    5. T

### Multiple Choice

1. a    2. b    3. a    4. c    5. c
6. d    7. a    8. b    9. c    10. d

# Capital Budgeting: An Introduction to the Discounted and Nondiscounted Cash-Flow Methods

In the previous chapter we discussed numerous decisions that managers make in running their day-to-day operations. A common element of each was the use of current productive capacity; that is, it was not necessary to purchase or build additional fixed assets in order to implement the decision. In our role as accountants we tried to help managers determine the most profitable way to use that productive capacity. Each decision affected primarily short-run profits—one year or less.

Once a firm makes changes in its productive capacity, the impact of these decisions on the cash flows and profitability of the firm will be felt for many years. Whether a firm is considering increasing the size of its factory, adding to the number of machines being used, replacing old equipment with new equipment, or reducing the number of laborers with laborsaving equipment, there are common elements in all these decisions:

1. A significant, immediate outlay of resources must be made by the firm.
2. The firm must commit itself to the project for an extended period of time.

Since changes in productive capacity can have such a significant effect on the long-run prospects of an organization, accountants must be able to help managers make the best decisions. Accountants need to have reliable evaluation methods at their disposal that properly consider the relevant information associated with each alternative.

There are, in fact, quite a few evaluation methods that are available to accountants—called capital budgeting methods—and some of them are more reliable than others.

## PLANNING LONG-RUN DECISIONS: CAPITAL BUDGETING'S ROLE

*Learning Objective 1*

Explain how capital budgeting is used to assist management in planning for long-run investment decisions

Capital budgeting is the process by which accountants help managers plan for the acquisition and financing of long-term investments. These investments may involve the types of changes in productive capacity that we mentioned above, but they may also involve other types of proposals as well. For example, each of the following investment proposals might utilize the capital budgeting process to evaluate its impact on the firm's long-run profitability.

1. Should the plant layout be rearranged in order to provide a more efficient flow of materials through the different stages of production?
2. Would the advantages of reduced competition offset the cost of purchasing a patent to a new process?
3. Should we undertake a substantial advertising campaign that holds the promise of significantly increasing our sales for many years?
4. Should we develop an in-house training facility to minimize the amount of on-the-job training required of new employees?

Accountants use numerous analytical tools to evaluate these and other investment proposals. The four we will discuss are classified as either discounted cash-flow methods or nondiscounted cash-flow methods. They are:

Discounted cash-flow (DCF) methods
1. Net present value (NPV)
2. Internal rate of return (IRR)
Nondiscounted cash-flow (NDCF) methods
1. Payback period (PP)
2. Accountant's rate of return (ARR)

Each of these methods begins with the same step. The information that is relevant to a decision (that is, relates to the future and is different for the alternatives being considered) is placed in one of two categories: (1) the incremental investment and (2) the incremental cash flows. The **incremental investment** represents what the firm spends at the beginning of the project to acquire the new asset and prepare it for use. The **incremental cash flows** represent the additional cash the project generates for the firm in each year of its life, due to the incremental investment made at the beginning of the project.

Learning Objective **2**

Calculate the discounted cash-flow (DCF) methods of capital budgeting —net present value and internal rate of return.

## DISCOUNTED CASH-FLOW (DCF) METHODS

The main characteristic of the **discounted cash-flow methods** is that they consider the time value of money through the application of present value analysis. In this chapter you will learn how to use present value in capital budgeting. First, let's review some present value concepts.

### Concepts of Present Value

Present value analysis recognizes the present value of money; that is, cash invested today will accumulate to greater amounts in future periods, due to the compounding of interest. For example, if $1 is invested today (referred to as time period zero), at 10%, cash will accumulate in the following manner:

| | |
|---|---|
| Investment today . . . . . . . . . . . . . . . . . . . . . . . . . . . . . . . . . . . . . . . | $1.000 |
| Interest in year 1 at 10% . . . . . . . . . . . . . . . . . . . . . . . . . . . . . . . . | .100 ($1.000 × .10) |
| Investment at end of year 1. . . . . . . . . . . . . . . . . . . . . . . . . . . . . . | $1.100 |
| Interest in year 2 . . . . . . . . . . . . . . . . . . . . . . . . . . . . . . . . . . . . . . . | .110 ($1.100 × .10) |
| Investment at end of year 2. . . . . . . . . . . . . . . . . . . . . . . . . . . . . . | $1.210 |
| Interest in year 3 . . . . . . . . . . . . . . . . . . . . . . . . . . . . . . . . . . . . . . . | .121 ($1.210 × .10) |
| Investment at end of year 3. . . . . . . . . . . . . . . . . . . . . . . . . . . . . . | $1.331 |

By the end of 3 years, interest of $0.331 ($.100 + $.110 + $.121) will have been added to the $1 investment, totaling $1.331.

This accumulation of cash can also be shown by the following diagram:

| | Amount Accumulated by End of Year | | |
|---|---|---|---|
| **Amount Invested in Year 0*** | **1** | **2** | **3** |
| | | | $1.331 |
| | | $1.210 | |
| | $1.100 | | |
| $1.000 | | | |

* The beginning of year 1 is treated as year 0 in capital budgeting.

Let's assume now that you want to invest $10,000. What amount would $10,000 accumulate to in 3 years? One way to find out is to multiply the amount to which $1.00 accumulates in 3 years, $1.331, by the $10,000 investment:

$$\$1.331 \times \$10,000 = \$13,310$$

Another way to show this accumulation of cash is with the following diagram:

| Amount Invested in Year 0* | Amount Accumulated by End of Year | | |
|---|---|---|---|
| | 1 | 2 | 3 |
| | | | $13,310 |
| | | $12,100 | |
| | $11,000 | | |
| $10,000 | | | |

* The beginning of year 1 is treated as year 0 in capital budgeting.

You would have $13,310 in your account in 3 years.

Now let's turn things around a bit. Assume that you want to have $13,310 in your bank account in 3 years but are wondering how much you have to invest today at 10% to accumulate to $13,310. We know from the above that the amount is $10,000. But we could determine it by doing the reverse of the computation above. That is:

$$\$13,310 \div 1.331 = \$10,000$$

An alternative way to show this calculation is:

$$\$13,310 \times \frac{1}{1.331} = \$10,000$$

A third way is as follows:

$$\$13,310 \times .7513 = \$10,000$$

The number .7513 is merely the decimal form for the fraction 1/1.331. This number, .7513, is called the present value of $1 in 3 years at 10%. What it means is that $0.7513 invested today at 10% will accumulate to $1 in 3 years:

| | |
|---|---|
| Investment today . . . . . . . . . . . . . . . . . . . . . . . . . . . . . . . . . . . . . . | $.7513 |
| Interest in year 1 at 10% . . . . . . . . . . . . . . . . . . . . . . . . . . . . . | .0751 |
| Investment at end of year 1 . . . . . . . . . . . . . . . . . . . . . . . . . . . | $.8264 |
| Interest in year 2. . . . . . . . . . . . . . . . . . . . . . . . . . . . . . . . . . . . . | .0826 |
| Investment at end of year 2 . . . . . . . . . . . . . . . . . . . . . . . . . . . | $.9090 |
| Interest in year 3. . . . . . . . . . . . . . . . . . . . . . . . . . . . . . . . . . . . . | .0909 |
| Accumulation at end of year 3 . . . . . . . . . . . . . . . . . . . . . . . . . | $.9999 = $1.0000 |
| | (rounded) |

When we multiply .7513 by $13,310, the $10,000 result represents the present value of $13,310 in 3 years at 10%—meaning that $10,000 invested today at 10% will accumulate to $13,310 in 3 years.

The number .7513 is found in the present value of $1 table (Table 1) at the intersection of the 10% column and the 3-year row. The present value of $1 for other combinations of years and interest rates can also be found in Table 1. Therefore, any time you need to determine the present value of some lump-sum amount of cash in the future, you merely find the appropriate number (called a present value factor) in Table 1 and multiply by the future lump sum.

**Table 1** Present Value of $1

$$p_{\overline{n}1} = \frac{1}{(1 + i)^n}$$

| n \ i | 1% | 2% | 3% | 4% | 5% | 6% | 7% | 8% | 9% | 10% | 12% | 14% | 15% |
|---|---|---|---|---|---|---|---|---|---|---|---|---|---|
| 1 | 0.990 | 0.980 | 0.970 | 0.961 | 0.952 | 0.943 | 0.934 | 0.925 | 0.917 | 0.909 | 0.892 | 0.877 | 0.869 |
| 2 | 0.980 | 0.961 | 0.942 | 0.924 | 0.907 | 0.889 | 0.873 | 0.857 | 0.841 | 0.826 | 0.797 | 0.769 | 0.756 |
| 3 | 0.970 | 0.942 | 0.915 | 0.888 | 0.863 | 0.839 | 0.816 | 0.793 | 0.772 | 0.751 | 0.711 | 0.675 | 0.657 |
| 4 | 0.960 | 0.923 | 0.888 | 0.854 | 0.822 | 0.792 | 0.762 | 0.735 | 0.708 | 0.683 | 0.635 | 0.592 | 0.571 |
| 5 | 0.951 | 0.905 | 0.862 | 0.821 | 0.783 | 0.747 | 0.712 | 0.680 | 0.649 | 0.620 | 0.567 | 0.519 | 0.497 |
| 6 | 0.942 | 0.887 | 0.837 | 0.790 | 0.746 | 0.704 | 0.666 | 0.630 | 0.596 | 0.564 | 0.506 | 0.455 | 0.432 |
| 7 | 0.932 | 0.870 | 0.813 | 0.759 | 0.710 | 0.665 | 0.622 | 0.583 | 0.547 | 0.513 | 0.452 | 0.399 | 0.375 |
| 8 | 0.923 | 0.853 | 0.789 | 0.730 | 0.676 | 0.627 | 0.582 | 0.540 | 0.501 | 0.466 | 0.403 | 0.350 | 0.326 |
| 9 | 0.914 | 0.836 | 0.766 | 0.702 | 0.644 | 0.591 | 0.543 | 0.500 | 0.460 | 0.424 | 0.360 | 0.307 | 0.284 |
| 10 | 0.905 | 0.820 | 0.744 | 0.675 | 0.613 | 0.558 | 0.508 | 0.463 | 0.422 | 0.385 | 0.321 | 0.269 | 0.247 |
| 11 | 0.896 | 0.804 | 0.722 | 0.649 | 0.584 | 0.526 | 0.475 | 0.428 | 0.387 | 0.350 | 0.287 | 0.236 | 0.214 |
| 12 | 0.887 | 0.788 | 0.701 | 0.624 | 0.556 | 0.496 | 0.444 | 0.397 | 0.355 | 0.318 | 0.256 | 0.207 | 0.186 |
| 13 | 0.878 | 0.773 | 0.680 | 0.600 | 0.530 | 0.468 | 0.414 | 0.367 | 0.326 | 0.289 | 0.229 | 0.182 | 0.162 |
| 14 | 0.869 | 0.757 | 0.661 | 0.577 | 0.505 | 0.442 | 0.387 | 0.340 | 0.299 | 0.263 | 0.204 | 0.159 | 0.141 |
| 15 | 0.861 | 0.743 | 0.641 | 0.555 | 0.481 | 0.417 | 0.362 | 0.315 | 0.274 | 0.239 | 0.182 | 0.140 | 0.122 |
| 16 | 0.852 | 0.728 | 0.623 | 0.533 | 0.458 | 0.393 | 0.338 | 0.291 | 0.251 | 0.217 | 0.163 | 0.122 | 0.106 |
| 17 | 0.844 | 0.714 | 0.605 | 0.513 | 0.436 | 0.371 | 0.316 | 0.270 | 0.231 | 0.197 | 0.145 | 0.107 | 0.092 |
| 18 | 0.836 | 0.700 | 0.587 | 0.493 | 0.415 | 0.350 | 0.295 | 0.250 | 0.211 | 0.179 | 0.130 | 0.094 | 0.080 |
| 19 | 0.827 | 0.686 | 0.570 | 0.474 | 0.395 | 0.330 | 0.276 | 0.231 | 0.194 | 0.163 | 0.116 | 0.082 | 0.070 |
| 20 | 0.819 | 0.672 | 0.553 | 0.456 | 0.376 | 0.311 | 0.258 | 0.214 | 0.178 | 0.148 | 0.103 | 0.072 | 0.061 |
| 21 | 0.811 | 0.659 | 0.537 | 0.438 | 0.358 | 0.294 | 0.241 | 0.198 | 0.163 | 0.135 | 0.092 | 0.063 | 0.053 |
| 22 | 0.803 | 0.646 | 0.521 | 0.421 | 0.341 | 0.277 | 0.225 | 0.183 | 0.150 | 0.122 | 0.082 | 0.055 | 0.046 |
| 23 | 0.795 | 0.634 | 0.506 | 0.405 | 0.325 | 0.261 | 0.210 | 0.170 | 0.137 | 0.111 | 0.073 | 0.049 | 0.040 |
| 24 | 0.787 | 0.621 | 0.491 | 0.390 | 0.310 | 0.246 | 0.197 | 0.157 | 0.126 | 0.101 | 0.065 | 0.043 | 0.034 |
| 25 | 0.779 | 0.609 | 0.477 | 0.375 | 0.295 | 0.232 | 0.184 | 0.146 | 0.115 | 0.092 | 0.058 | 0.037 | 0.030 |
| 26 | 0.772 | 0.597 | 0.463 | 0.360 | 0.281 | 0.219 | 0.172 | 0.135 | 0.106 | 0.083 | 0.052 | 0.033 | 0.026 |
| 27 | 0.764 | 0.585 | 0.450 | 0.346 | 0.267 | 0.207 | 0.160 | 0.125 | 0.097 | 0.076 | 0.046 | 0.029 | 0.022 |
| 28 | 0.756 | 0.574 | 0.437 | 0.333 | 0.255 | 0.195 | 0.150 | 0.115 | 0.089 | 0.069 | 0.041 | 0.025 | 0.019 |
| 29 | 0.749 | 0.563 | 0.424 | 0.320 | 0.242 | 0.184 | 0.140 | 0.107 | 0.082 | 0.063 | 0.037 | 0.022 | 0.017 |
| 30 | 0.741 | 0.552 | 0.411 | 0.308 | 0.231 | 0.174 | 0.131 | 0.099 | 0.075 | 0.057 | 0.033 | 0.019 | 0.015 |
| 31 | 0.734 | 0.541 | 0.399 | 0.296 | 0.220 | 0.164 | 0.122 | 0.092 | 0.069 | 0.052 | 0.029 | 0.017 | 0.013 |
| 32 | 0.727 | 0.530 | 0.388 | 0.285 | 0.209 | 0.154 | 0.114 | 0.085 | 0.063 | 0.047 | 0.026 | 0.015 | 0.011 |
| 33 | 0.720 | 0.520 | 0.377 | 0.274 | 0.199 | 0.146 | 0.107 | 0.078 | 0.058 | 0.043 | 0.023 | 0.013 | 0.009 |
| 34 | 0.712 | 0.510 | 0.366 | 0.263 | 0.190 | 0.137 | 0.100 | 0.073 | 0.053 | 0.039 | 0.021 | 0.011 | 0.008 |
| 35 | 0.705 | 0.500 | 0.355 | 0.253 | 0.181 | 0.130 | 0.093 | 0.067 | 0.048 | 0.035 | 0.018 | 0.010 | 0.007 |
| 36 | 0.698 | 0.490 | 0.345 | 0.243 | 0.172 | 0.122 | 0.087 | 0.062 | 0.044 | 0.032 | 0.016 | 0.008 | 0.006 |
| 37 | 0.692 | 0.480 | 0.334 | 0.234 | 0.164 | 0.115 | 0.081 | 0.057 | 0.041 | 0.029 | 0.015 | 0.007 | 0.005 |
| 38 | 0.685 | 0.471 | 0.325 | 0.225 | 0.156 | 0.109 | 0.076 | 0.053 | 0.037 | 0.026 | 0.013 | 0.006 | 0.004 |
| 39 | 0.678 | 0.461 | 0.315 | 0.216 | 0.149 | 0.103 | 0.071 | 0.049 | 0.034 | 0.024 | 0.012 | 0.006 | 0.004 |
| 40 | 0.671 | 0.452 | 0.306 | 0.208 | 0.142 | 0.097 | 0.066 | 0.046 | 0.031 | 0.022 | 0.010 | 0.005 | 0.003 |
| 41 | 0.665 | 0.444 | 0.297 | 0.200 | 0.135 | 0.091 | 0.062 | 0.042 | 0.029 | 0.020 | 0.009 | 0.004 | 0.003 |
| 42 | 0.658 | 0.435 | 0.288 | 0.192 | 0.128 | 0.086 | 0.058 | 0.039 | 0.026 | 0.018 | 0.008 | 0.004 | 0.002 |
| 43 | 0.651 | 0.426 | 0.280 | 0.185 | 0.122 | 0.081 | 0.054 | 0.036 | 0.024 | 0.016 | 0.007 | 0.003 | 0.002 |
| 44 | 0.645 | 0.418 | 0.272 | 0.178 | 0.116 | 0.077 | 0.050 | 0.033 | 0.022 | 0.015 | 0.006 | 0.003 | 0.002 |
| 45 | 0.639 | 0.410 | 0.264 | 0.171 | 0.111 | 0.072 | 0.047 | 0.031 | 0.020 | 0.013 | 0.006 | 0.002 | 0.001 |
| 46 | 0.632 | 0.402 | 0.256 | 0.164 | 0.105 | 0.068 | 0.044 | 0.029 | 0.018 | 0.012 | 0.005 | 0.002 | 0.001 |
| 47 | 0.626 | 0.394 | 0.249 | 0.158 | 0.100 | 0.064 | 0.041 | 0.026 | 0.017 | 0.011 | 0.004 | 0.002 | 0.001 |
| 48 | 0.620 | 0.386 | 0.241 | 0.152 | 0.096 | 0.060 | 0.038 | 0.024 | 0.015 | 0.010 | 0.004 | 0.001 | 0.001 |
| 49 | 0.614 | 0.378 | 0.234 | 0.146 | 0.091 | 0.057 | 0.036 | 0.023 | 0.014 | 0.009 | 0.003 | 0.001 | 0.001 |
| 50 | 0.608 | 0.371 | 0.228 | 0.140 | 0.087 | 0.054 | 0.033 | 0.021 | 0.013 | 0.008 | 0.003 | 0.001 | 0.000 |

## Table 2 Present Value of an Ordinary Annuity of $1

$$P_{\overline{n}|i} = \frac{1 - \dfrac{1}{(1 + i)n}}{i}$$

| n | 1% | 2% | 3% | 4% | 5% | 6% | 7% | 8% | 9% | 10% | 12% | 14% | 15% |
|---|----|----|----|----|----|----|----|----|----|-----|-----|-----|-----|
| 1 | 0.990 | 0.980 | 0.970 | 0.961 | 0.952 | 0.943 | 0.934 | 0.925 | 0.917 | 0.909 | 0.892 | 0.877 | 0.869 |
| 2 | 1.970 | 1.941 | 1.913 | 1.886 | 1.850 | 1.833 | 1.808 | 1.783 | 1.759 | 1.735 | 1.690 | 1.646 | 1.625 |
| 3 | 2.940 | 2.883 | 2.828 | 2.775 | 2.723 | 2.673 | 2.624 | 2.577 | 2.531 | 2.486 | 2.401 | 2.321 | 2.283 |
| 4 | 3.901 | 3.807 | 3.717 | 3.629 | 3.545 | 3.465 | 3.387 | 3.312 | 3.239 | 3.169 | 3.037 | 2.913 | 2.834 |
| 5 | 4.853 | 4.713 | 4.579 | 4.451 | 4.329 | 4.212 | 4.100 | 3.992 | 3.889 | 3.790 | 3.604 | 3.433 | 3.352 |
| 6 | 5.795 | 5.601 | 5.417 | 5.242 | 5.075 | 4.917 | 4.766 | 4.622 | 4.485 | 4.355 | 4.111 | 3.888 | 3.784 |
| 7 | 6.728 | 6.471 | 6.230 | 6.002 | 5.786 | 5.582 | 5.389 | 5.206 | 5.032 | 4.868 | 4.563 | 4.288 | 4.160 |
| 8 | 7.651 | 7.325 | 7.019 | 6.732 | 6.463 | 6.209 | 5.971 | 5.746 | 5.534 | 5.334 | 4.967 | 4.638 | 4.487 |
| 9 | 8.566 | 8.162 | 7.786 | 7.435 | 7.107 | 6.801 | 6.515 | 6.246 | 5.995 | 5.759 | 5.328 | 4.946 | 4.771 |
| 10 | 9.471 | 8.982 | 8.530 | 8.110 | 7.721 | 7.360 | 7.023 | 6.710 | 6.417 | 6.144 | 5.650 | 5.216 | 5.018 |
| 11 | 10.367 | 9.786 | 9.252 | 8.760 | 8.306 | 7.886 | 7.498 | 7.138 | 6.805 | 6.495 | 5.937 | 5.452 | 5.233 |
| 12 | 11.255 | 10.575 | 9.954 | 9.385 | 8.863 | 8.383 | 7.942 | 7.536 | 7.160 | 6.813 | 6.194 | 5.660 | 5.420 |
| 13 | 12.133 | 11.348 | 10.634 | 9.985 | 9.393 | 8.852 | 8.357 | 7.903 | 7.486 | 7.103 | 6.423 | 5.842 | 5.583 |
| 14 | 13.003 | 12.106 | 11.296 | 10.563 | 9.898 | 9.294 | 8.745 | 8.244 | 7.786 | 7.366 | 6.628 | 6.002 | 5.724 |
| 15 | 13.865 | 12.849 | 11.937 | 11.118 | 10.379 | 9.712 | 9.107 | 8.559 | 8.060 | 7.606 | 6.810 | 6.142 | 5.847 |
| 16 | 14.717 | 13.577 | 12.561 | 11.652 | 10.837 | 10.105 | 9.446 | 8.851 | 8.312 | 7.823 | 6.973 | 6.265 | 5.954 |
| 17 | 15.562 | 14.291 | 13.166 | 12.165 | 11.274 | 10.477 | 9.763 | 9.121 | 8.543 | 8.021 | 7.119 | 6.372 | 6.047 |
| 18 | 16.398 | 14.992 | 13.753 | 12.659 | 11.689 | 10.827 | 10.059 | 9.371 | 8.755 | 8.201 | 7.249 | 6.467 | 6.127 |
| 19 | 17.226 | 15.678 | 14.323 | 13.133 | 12.058 | 11.158 | 10.335 | 9.603 | 8.950 | 8.364 | 7.365 | 6.530 | 6.198 |
| 20 | 18.045 | 16.351 | 14.877 | 13.590 | 12.462 | 11.469 | 10.594 | 9.818 | 9.128 | 8.513 | 7.469 | 6.623 | 6.259 |
| 21 | 18.856 | 17.011 | 15.415 | 14.029 | 12.821 | 11.764 | 10.835 | 10.016 | 9.292 | 8.648 | 7.562 | 6.686 | 6.312 |
| 22 | 19.660 | 17.658 | 15.936 | 14.451 | 13.163 | 12.041 | 11.061 | 10.200 | 9.442 | 8.771 | 7.644 | 6.742 | 6.358 |
| 23 | 20.455 | 18.292 | 16.443 | 14.856 | 13.488 | 12.303 | 11.272 | 10.371 | 9.580 | 8.883 | 7.718 | 6.749 | 6.398 |
| 24 | 21.243 | 18.913 | 16.935 | 15.246 | 13.798 | 12.550 | 11.469 | 10.528 | 9.706 | 8.984 | 7.784 | 6.835 | 6.433 |
| 25 | 22.023 | 19.523 | 17.413 | 15.622 | 14.093 | 12.783 | 11.653 | 10.674 | 9.822 | 9.077 | 7.843 | 6.872 | 6.464 |
| 26 | 22.795 | 20.121 | 17.876 | 15.982 | 14.375 | 13.003 | 11.825 | 10.809 | 9.928 | 9.160 | 7.895 | 6.906 | 6.490 |
| 27 | 23.559 | 20.706 | 18.327 | 16.329 | 14.643 | 13.210 | 11.986 | 10.935 | 10.026 | 9.237 | 7.942 | 6.935 | 6.513 |
| 28 | 24.316 | 21.281 | 18.764 | 16.663 | 14.898 | 13.406 | 12.137 | 11.051 | 10.116 | 9.306 | 7.984 | 6.960 | 6.533 |
| 29 | 25.065 | 21.844 | 19.188 | 16.983 | 15.141 | 13.590 | 12.277 | 11.158 | 10.198 | 9.369 | 8.021 | 6.983 | 6.550 |
| 30 | 25.807 | 22.396 | 19.600 | 17.292 | 15.372 | 13.764 | 12.409 | 11.257 | 10.273 | 9.426 | 8.055 | 7.002 | 6.563 |
| 31 | 26.542 | 22.937 | 20.000 | 17.589 | 15.592 | 13.929 | 12.531 | 11.349 | 10.342 | 9.479 | 8.084 | 7.019 | 6.579 |
| 32 | 27.269 | 23.468 | 20.388 | 17.873 | 15.802 | 14.084 | 12.646 | 11.434 | 10.406 | 9.526 | 8.111 | 7.034 | 6.590 |
| 33 | 27.989 | 23.988 | 20.765 | 18.147 | 16.002 | 14.230 | 12.753 | 11.513 | 10.464 | 9.569 | 8.135 | 7.048 | 6.600 |
| 34 | 28.702 | 24.498 | 21.131 | 18.411 | 16.192 | 14.368 | 12.854 | 11.586 | 10.517 | 9.608 | 8.156 | 7.059 | 6.609 |
| 35 | 29.408 | 24.998 | 21.487 | 18.664 | 16.374 | 14.498 | 12.947 | 11.654 | 10.566 | 9.644 | 8.175 | 7.070 | 6.616 |
| 36 | 30.107 | 25.488 | 21.832 | 18.908 | 16.546 | 14.620 | 13.035 | 11.717 | 10.611 | 9.676 | 8.192 | 7.078 | 6.623 |
| 37 | 30.799 | 25.969 | 22.167 | 19.142 | 16.711 | 14.736 | 13.117 | 11.775 | 10.652 | 9.705 | 8.207 | 7.086 | 6.628 |
| 38 | 31.484 | 26.440 | 22.492 | 19.367 | 16.867 | 14.846 | 13.193 | 11.828 | 10.690 | 9.732 | 8.220 | 7.093 | 6.633 |
| 39 | 32.163 | 26.902 | 22.808 | 19.584 | 17.071 | 14.949 | 13.264 | 11.878 | 10.725 | 9.756 | 8.233 | 7.099 | 6.638 |
| 40 | 32.834 | 27.355 | 23.114 | 19.792 | 17.159 | 15.046 | 13.331 | 11.924 | 10.757 | 9.779 | 8.243 | 7.105 | 6.641 |
| 41 | 33.499 | 27.799 | 23.412 | 19.993 | 17.294 | 15.138 | 13.394 | 11.967 | 10.786 | 9.799 | 8.253 | 7.109 | 6.645 |
| 42 | 34.158 | 28.234 | 23.701 | 20.185 | 17.423 | 15.224 | 13.452 | 12.006 | 10.813 | 9.817 | 8.261 | 7.113 | 6.647 |
| 43 | 34.810 | 28.661 | 23.981 | 20.370 | 17.545 | 15.306 | 13.506 | 12.043 | 10.837 | 9.833 | 8.269 | 7.117 | 6.650 |
| 44 | 35.455 | 29.079 | 24.254 | 20.548 | 17.662 | 15.383 | 13.557 | 12.077 | 10.860 | 9.849 | 8.276 | 7.120 | 6.652 |
| 45 | 36.094 | 29.490 | 24.518 | 20.720 | 17.774 | 15.455 | 13.605 | 12.108 | 10.881 | 9.862 | 8.282 | 7.123 | 6.654 |
| 46 | 36.727 | 29.892 | 24.775 | 20.884 | 17.880 | 15.524 | 13.650 | 12.137 | 10.900 | 9.875 | 8.287 | 7.125 | 6.655 |
| 47 | 37.353 | 30.286 | 25.024 | 21.042 | 17.981 | 15.589 | 13.691 | 12.164 | 10.917 | 9.886 | 8.292 | 7.127 | 6.657 |
| 48 | 37.973 | 30.673 | 25.266 | 21.195 | 18.077 | 15.650 | 13.730 | 12.189 | 10.933 | 9.896 | 8.297 | 7.129 | 6.658 |
| 49 | 38.588 | 31.052 | 25.601 | 21.341 | 18.168 | 15.707 | 13.766 | 12.212 | 10.948 | 9.906 | 8.301 | 7.131 | 6.659 |
| 50 | 39.196 | 31.423 | 25.729 | 21.482 | 18.255 | 15.761 | 13.800 | 12.233 | 10.961 | 9.914 | 8.304 | 7.132 | 6.660 |

Let's look at the facts in the following example to see how these present value concepts apply to investment decisions.

### Net Present Value

# COBB CONTRACTING COMPANY

Laurie Cobb, the owner of a local road-building company, is considering an investment of $10,520 in lane-painting equipment. The equipment is expected to have a useful life of 8 years, and the incremental cash flows are expected to be $2,000 per year for the firm. The interest rate used to determine the present value of cash flows, called the **cost of capital,** is 10%. The cost of capital is the cost of raising funds to finance the project.

### *Determining Net Present Value*

With the net present value method, we first calculate the total present value of all future cash flows and then compare this amount to the initial cost of the project—the incremental investment. If the total present value of all the future cash flows exceeds the investment, then the project has a positive **net present value (NPV),** and is considered acceptable. If the total present value is less than the investment, resulting in a negative net present value, then the project is rejected. We accept only projects with positive NPVs because a positive NPV means that the value of what we get back from the investment is greater than what it costs us to invest in the project. And only when we invest in a project with a positive NPV will the value of the firm as a whole be increased. The three steps we take to determine NPV are as follows:

**STEP 1:** Determine the total present value (TPV) of the future cash flows using the interest rate called the cost of capital.

When the cash flows are the same amount per year—called an *annuity*—we can determine the total present value in one of two ways. We can find the present value of each separate $2,000 receipt for years 1 through 8 (the useful life) using the present value of $1 table (Table 1). Or we can simply use the present value of an ordinary annuity of $1 table (Table 2). For example, at 10%, the first eight factors from the present value of $1 table are as follows:

| | | |
|---|---|---|
| PV of $1 at 10% in 1 year | $(p_{\overline{1}|10\%})$ = | .909 |
| PV of $1 at 10% in 2 years | $(p_{\overline{2}|10\%})$ = | .826 |
| PV of $1 at 10% in 3 years | $(p_{\overline{3}|10\%})$ = | .751 |
| PV of $1 at 10% in 4 years | $(p_{\overline{4}|10\%})$ = | .683 |
| PV of $1 at 10% in 5 years | $(p_{\overline{5}|10\%})$ = | .620 |
| PV of $1 at 10% in 6 years | $(p_{\overline{6}|10\%})$ = | .564 |
| PV of $1 at 10% in 7 years | $(p_{\overline{7}|10\%})$ = | .513 |
| PV of $1 at 10% in 8 years | $(p_{\overline{8}|10\%})$ = | .466 |
| Summation of PV of $1 factors, at 10%, for years 1–8 | | = 5.332 |

The sum of these present value factors for 8 years at 10% equals 5.332. If you look at the present value of an ordinary annuity table (Table 2) for 8 years at 10%, you will see the same number, 5.334. (The difference between the 5.332 above and the 5.334 is due to rounding in the calculations of individual present value factors.)

Using this annuity factor of 5.334, represented by the symbol ($P_{\overline{8}|10\%}$), we can compute the total present value as follows:

$$TPV = PV \text{ of } \$2,000 \text{ at } 10\% \text{ for } 8 \text{ years}$$

$$= P_{\overline{8}|10\%} \times \$2,000$$

$$= 5.334 \times \$2,000 = \$10,668$$

**STEP 2:** Subtract the incremental investment from the TPV. This difference is the net present value (NPV).

**NPV = TPV − incremental investment**

$$= \$10,668 - \$10,520 = \$148$$

**STEP 3:** If the NPV is greater than $0 (or positive), the project is acceptable. If the NPV is less than $0 (or negative), it is rejected. If it is zero, the decision maker is indifferent to accepting or rejecting.

Since the NPV of $148 is greater than zero, or positive, the project is acceptable to Cobb. And as long as no projects with better NPVs are competing for the firm's limited funds, the firm will probably purchase the lane-painting equipment.

### NPV for Projects with Uneven Cash Flows

We determined the total present value for the equipment in the Cobb Contracting Company example by using the present value of an ordinary annuity of $1 table (Table 2). We could do it this way because the cash flows were the same each year, $2,000—an annuity.

When the cash flows are not the same each year, we no longer have an annuity, so we cannot use the present value of an annuity table to get TPV. We must use the present value of $1 table (Table 1) instead.

Let's look now at the effect of a change in cash flows for Cobb Contracting Company.

# COBB CONTRACTING COMPANY—UNEVEN CASH FLOWS

Assume that all the facts are unchanged, except that the cash flows are now the following amounts per year:

| | | | |
|---|---|---|---|
| **1.** $4,000 | **3.** $3,000 | **5.** $1,000 | **7.** $1,000 |
| **2.** $3,000 | **4.** $2,000 | **6.** $1,000 | **8.** $1,000 |

Using the present value of $1 table, the TPV would be $11,896:

| | |
|---|---|
| PV of $4,000 at 10% in year 1 = $4,000 × .909 = | $ 3,636 |
| PV of $3,000 at 10% in year 2 = $3,000 × .826 = | 2,478 |
| PV of $3,000 at 10% in year 3 = $3,000 × .751 = | 2,253 |
| PV of $2,000 at 10% in year 4 = $2,000 × .683 = | 1,366 |
| PV of $1,000 at 10% in year 5 = $1,000 × .620 = | 620 |
| PV of $1,000 at 10% in year 6 = $1,000 × .564 = | 564 |
| PV of $1,000 at 10% in year 7 = $1,000 × .513 = | 513 |
| PV of $1,000 at 10% in year 8 = $1,000 × .466 = | 466 |
| TPV = | $11,896 |

The NPV would be a positive $1,376:

$$NPV = \$11,896 - \$10,520 = \$1,376$$

### An Adaptable Format for NPV

The calculations for project B were a little more cumbersome than they were for project A because of the uneven stream of cash inflows for project B. Even so, they were still rather simple and straightforward, when compared to what they can be in some capital budgeting problems. So let's now make project B somewhat more complicated so that we can show you a useful format for calculating NPV which is really needed only when the problems get a little more difficult.

# ADDITIONAL FACTS FOR COBB CONTRACTING COMPANY

Assume that in the previous example for Cobb Contracting the machine required for project B also necessitates an investment in current assets of $1,000 at the beginning of the project, all of which will be recovered at the end of the useful life of the project. Also, a major overhaul will be needed at the beginning of year 6. In addition, the acceptance of project B will involve the use of building space that is currently being leased to the Apex Company for $200 per year. Finally, the machine can be sold for $2,500 at the end of the project's useful life.

In addition to the cash receipts from operations, we must now consider an investment in current assets, a major overhaul, a disposal, and some lost rentals.

The new solution for project B is presented in Exhibit 1. What we want to emphasize in this solution is the format that we are using to compute the NPV—a format that can be easily adapted to any NPV situation, no matter how simple or detailed the situation may be.

The key to the format is in the headings that run from left to right across the top of the page:

| | | | Yearly Sketch of Cash Flows | | | | | | | | |
|---|---|---|---|---|---|---|---|---|---|---|---|
| Description | PV Factor | Present Value | 0 | 1 | 2 | 3 | 4 | 5 | 6 | 7 | 8 |

The first item in Exhibit 1 comes from the original facts for Cobb Contracting. The initial outlay of $10,000 goes in year 0 (the beginning of year 1), and its present value is $(10,000)—shown in parentheses to represent an outflow. The cash receipts from operations are shown in the sketch of cash flows for years 1 through 8, and eight different present value computations are made.

The remaining items come from the additional complications introduced above. They are discussed below.

**The Investment in Nondepreciable Assets**   Sometimes an incremental investment in depreciable assets is accompanied by an investment in nondepreciable assets. For example, it's quite possible that an increased demand for a product may make it necessary to maintain a larger balance in inventory over the life of the project. In addition, more credit may be extended to customers, causing the average balance in accounts receivable to increase. And the average balance in cash may need to be increased in order to handle the greater volume of business. Each of these increases in current assets—the inventory, the accounts receivable, and the cash—represents an investment in nondepreciable assets.

Investments in nondepreciable assets usually take place at the beginning of a project and are treated in much the same way as the initial outlay for depreciable assets. For Cobb, the initial investment of $1,000 in nondepreciable assets is shown in Exhibit 1 as an outlay in year 0. At the end of the project's useful life, the current assets

**Exhibit 1** Solution to Expanded Example for Cobb Contraction—Projects B

| Description | 10% PV Factor | 10% Present Value | Yearly Sketch of Cash Flows | | | | | | | | |
|---|---|---|---|---|---|---|---|---|---|---|---|
| | | | 0 | 1 | 2 | 3 | 4 | 5 | 6 | 7 | 8 |
| Net incremental investment— depreciable ......... | 1.000 | (10,000) | (10,000) | | | | | | | | |
| Investment in nondepreciable assets ..... | 1.000 | ( 1,000) | ( 1,000) | | | | | | | | |
| Recovery of nondepreciable assets ........ | .466 | 466 | | | | | | | | | 1,000 |
| Cash receipts from operations: | | | | | | | | | | | |
| Year 1 ............ | .909 | 3,636 | | 4,000 | | | | | | | |
| Year 2 ............ | .826 | 2,478 | | | 3,000 | | | | | | |
| Year 3 ............ | .751 | 2,253 | | | | 3,000 | | | | | |
| Year 4 ............ | .683 | 1,366 | | | | | 2,000 | | | | |
| Year 5 ............ | .620 | 620 | | | | | | 1,000 | | | |
| Year 6 ............ | .564 | 564 | | | | | | | 1,000 | | |
| Year 7 ............ | .513 | 513 | | | | | | | | 1,000 | |
| Year 8 ............ | .466 | 466 | | | | | | | | | 1,000 |
| Major overhaul ....... | .620 | ( 310) | | | | | | (500) | | | |
| Opportunity cost: lost rentals.......... | 5.334 | ( 1,067) | | (200) | (200) | (200) | (200) | (200) | (200) | (200) | (200) |
| Disposal of machine ... | .466 | 1,165 | | | | | | | | | 2,500 |
| Net present value ..... | | 1,150 | (11,000) | 3,800 | 2,800 | 2,800 | 1,800 | 300 | 800 | 800 | 4,300 |

are fully recovered. Therefore, the $1,000 is shown as a cash inflow in year 8. The difference in the present values of the $1,000 outlay in year 0 ($1,000) and the $1,000 inflow in year 8 ($466) represents the interest that was lost on the $1,000 because it was tied up in non-interest-bearing current assets.

**The Major Overhaul** Cobb expects that machine B will need a major overhaul at the beginning of year 6. Since this is not a recurring item, it is not included in the cash receipts from operations. For this reason it's shown separately in Exhibit 1 as an outflow. We place it in year 5 rather than year 6 because it comes at the beginning of the year, which is treated the same as the last day of the previous year. The present value of the overhaul is $(310).

**The Lost Rentals** The $200 of lost rentals represents an opportunity cost to the firm. Even though the lost rentals are not actually cash outflows, they will still have a negative impact on the firm's cash position. If the space is rented, the cash receipts will be $200 per year. But if the space is not rented, then the cash receipts will be reduced by the $200—the opportunity foregone. The present value of the annuity of reduced rentals is $(1,067).

**Disposal Value** The value of most productive assets declines substantially through use, over the assets' useful lives. Cobb feels that machine B will be worth only $2,500 at the end of 8 years, when he expects to dispose of it. In Exhibit 1 the $2,500 is treated as a cash inflow in year 8, and its present value is $1,165.

The NPV for project B—with all the added complications—is now $1,150.

As long as the facts within a problem are no more complicated than they were originally, there really is no reason for you to use the format we've just shown you. However, for the more complicated situations we recommend that you use the format shown in Exhibit 1, because all the facts in the solution can be easily seen and followed by you or anyone reviewing your work.

### Internal Rate of Return

The **internal rate of return (IRR)** is the actual, effective, or true rate of return that we are earning on a project. It can be defined as the interest rate at which the TPV of the project's cash inflows is exactly equal to the incremental investment—the interest rate that results in an NPV of zero.

Once the IRR is determined, we compare it to the cost of capital, $r$, in order to decide whether or not the project is acceptable. If the project is earning a rate of return greater than the cost to finance it (IRR $> r$), it is acceptable; if the reverse is true (IRR $< r$), then the project is rejected; and if the rate of return equals the cost of capital (IRR $= r$), then we are indifferent to accepting or rejecting the project.

#### Determining the IRR for Projects with Even Cash Flows

The original example for Cobb Contracting assumed that the cash flows would be $2,000 per year during the equipment's 8-year useful life. In determining IRR, we are trying to find the unique interest rate that yields a total present value of this $2,000 annuity of exactly $10,520—the amount of the incremental investment. Since the cash receipts are the same amount each year—an annuity—we look for that interest rate in the present value of an annuity table (Table 2). We need to find an interest rate that has a factor which, when multiplied by $2,000, will give us a total present value of $10,520. The only factor that can do this, of course, is 5.260:

$$5.260 = \$10,520 \div \$2,000$$

Now find this factor in the 8-year row of Table 2. The interest rate at the top of the column is the IRR. Although you may not find the exact factor you want, you can get very close to it. As you can see, the factor 5.260 falls between the factors 5.334 for 10% and 4.967 for 12%. Therefore the IRR falls somewhere between 10% and 12%. If we want to find the exact value for IRR, we can determine it with **interpolation,** which is a procedure used to find an exact answer when you know it lies between two other numbers.

This process of finding the IRR for a project that has even cash flows is converted into the following mechanical steps:

**STEP 1:** Divide the incremental investment by the cash flow per year (annuity). This results in a present value of an annuity factor ($P_{\overline{n}|i}$):

$$\text{Factor} = \frac{\text{incremental investment}}{\text{cash flow per year}}$$

$$= \frac{\$10,520}{\$2,000} = 5.260$$

**STEP 2:** Turn to the present value of an ordinary annuity of $1 table (Table 2) and find the row representing the life of the project. Scan across this row looking for the factor determined in step 1. It will probably lie between the factors for two other interest rates.

Present Value of an Ordinary Annuity of $1
(Table 2)

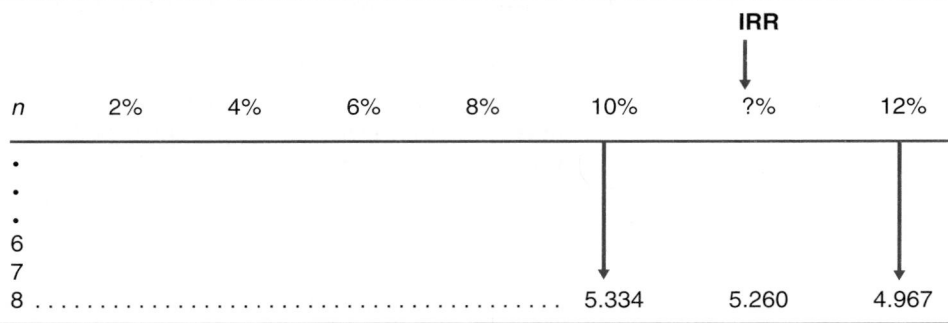

| n | 2% | 4% | 6% | 8% | 10% | ?% | 12% |
|---|----|----|----|----|-----|-----|-----|
| . | | | | | | | |
| . | | | | | | | |
| . | | | | | | | |
| 6 | | | | | | | |
| 7 | | | | | | | |
| 8 | | | | | | 5.334 | 5.260 | 4.967 |

**STEP 3:** Find the exact IRR by the process of interpolation. This involves, first of all, finding the distance between the two factors that are closest to the one for the IRR—the distance from 5.334 to 4.967. Then you need to determine the distance from the factor for the lower interest rate to the factor for the IRR—from 5.334 to 5.260. These distances are:

| | Factors | |
|---|---|---|
| 10% | 5.334 | 5.334 |
| IRR | | 5.260 |
| 12% | 4.967 | |
| Differences | .367 | .074 |

Next, divide .074 by .367 to determine the percentage of the distance that 5.260 lies between 5.334 and 4.967:

$$\frac{.074}{.367} = 20\%$$

Since the factor 5.260 lies 20% of the distance from 5.334 to 4.967, IRR is 20% of the way from 10% to 12%:

$$20\% \times (12\% - 10\%) = .40\%$$

When added to 10%, the IRR becomes 10.40%:

$$\text{IRR} = 10\% + .40\% = 10.40\%$$

Since the IRR exceeds the 10% cost of capital, you can consider it to be acceptable, since this means that the actual return being earned on the project is greater than the cost of funds being used to finance the project. And since these funds can earn more than it costs to raise them, the value of the firm will increase by investing in the project—unless, that is, another competing project promises to earn a higher return than 10.40%.

### Determining the IRR for Projects with Uneven Cash Flows

We cannot calculate the IRR for projects with uneven cash flows the same way as we do for projects with an even stream of cash per year. Since the cash is different every year, we no longer have an annuity and cannot use the present value of an annuity table. Instead we have to employ an alternative approach called **trial and error,** which uses the present value of $1 table (Table 1).

Let's first of all remember what the IRR represents. It is an interest rate for which the total present value of the cash flows—even or uneven—equals the incremental investment, resulting in an NPV of zero. Look back now at the earlier calculation of TPV for Cobb Contracting, which used a cost of capital ($r$) of 10%. The TPV was $11,896, and the NPV was $1,376. Since the TPV was not equal to $10,520 and the NPV was not zero, there is no way that 10% can be the IRR. Since the NPV is positive at 10%, only an interest rate higher than 10% can reduce the NPV to zero. Let's try 12%, 14%, and 15% and see what happens:

| Year | Cash Flow | 10% Present Value | 12% Present Value | 14% Present Value | 15% Present Value |
|---|---|---|---|---|---|
| 1 | $4,000 | $ 3,636 | $ 3,568 | 3,508 | $3,476 |
| 2 | 3,000 | 2,478 | 2,391 | 2,307 | 2,268 |
| 3 | 3,000 | 2,253 | 2,133 | 2,025 | 1,971 |
| 4 | 2,000 | 1,366 | 1,270 | 1,184 | 1,142 |
| 5 | 1,000 | 620 | 567 | 519 | 497 |
| 6 | 1,000 | 564 | 506 | 455 | 432 |
| 7 | 1,000 | 513 | 452 | 399 | 375 |
| 8 | 1,000 | 466 | 403 | 350 | 326 |
| TPV | | $11,896 | $11,290 | $10,747 | $10,487 |
| Incremental investment | | 10,520 | 10,520 | 10,520 | 10,520 |
| NPV | | $ 1,376 | $ 770 | $ 227 | $ (33) |

Note that as the interest rate gets higher, the NPV gets closer to zero, becoming negative at 15%. Since the NPV is positive at 14% and negative at 15%, the IRR—the rate at which the NPV is zero—must be between 14% and 15%. The exact rate is determined with interpolation, something like this:

| | TPV | TPV |
|---|---|---|
| 14% | $10,747 | $10,747 |
| IRR | | 10,520 |
| 15% | 10,487 | |
| | $ 260 | $ 227 |

$$\frac{\$227}{\$260} = 87\% \times (15\% - 14\%) = .87\%$$

$$14.00\%$$

$$\text{IRR} = \underline{14.87\%}$$

The steps we have just described for determining IRR with the trial-and-error method, for any situation that involves uneven cash flows, can be summarized as follows:

**STEP 1:** Select any interest rate and calculate the NPV of the cash flows, using the present value of $1 table.

**STEP 2:** If the NPV is not zero, repeat step 1, using a higher rate if the NPV is > 0 and a lower rate if the NPV is < 0.

**STEP 3:** Continue repeating step 2 until you have one NPV > 0 and another NPV < 0.

**STEP 4:** Interpolate to determine the exact IRR.

## NONDISCOUNTED CASH FLOW (NDCF) METHODS

Learning
Objective **3**

Calculate the nondiscounted cash-flow (NDCF) methods of capital budgeting—payback period and accountant's rate of return

As the name implies, the distinguishing characteristic of the **nondiscounted cash-flow methods** of analyzing long-term investments is that they do not require the use of present value techniques. The two most popular nondiscounted cash-flow methods are the payback period and the accountant's rate of return.

### Payback Period

The **payback period** (PP) is the number of years it takes a project to accumulate enough cash to pay for the initial incremental investment.

#### Determining the Payback Period

When the cash flows are the same amount each year—as they were in the first Cobb Contracting Company example—we determine the payback period by dividing the incremental investment by the cash flows per year, as follows:

$$\text{Payback period (PP)} = \frac{\text{incremental investment}}{\text{cash flows per year}}$$

$$= \frac{\$10,520}{\$2,000} = 5.26 \text{ years}$$

This solution indicates that it takes 5.26 years for the accumulation of cash inflows at $2,000 per year to pay for the $10,520 investment.

The shorter the payback period, the more desirable the investment is to the firm, since the invested funds will be available for other purposes in a shorter period of time. Using this method, you would decide whether or not this is a good investment by comparing it with other available alternatives and with a minimum acceptable payback period, as determined by management.

When cash inflows are not the same amount each year—as is the case in the second example for Cobb Contracting Company—we must accumulate the cash flows, year by year, until the accumulated total equals the incremental investment. Using the cash flows for Cobb, we get a payback period of 3.26 years in the following manner:

| Year | Cash Flow per Year | Cumulative Cash Flow |
|---|---|---|
| 1 | $4,000 | $ 4,000 |
| 2 | 3,000 | 7,000 |
| 3 | 3,000 | 10,000 |
| Payback period | | 10,520 |
| 4 | 2,000 | 12,000 |

At some point during the fourth year, the investment of $10,520 will be fully paid for. If the cash flows are generated evenly throughout the year, the exact answer can be determined by interpolation. This is how it works:

| | | Cumulative Cash Flows |
|---|---|---|
| End of year 3. . . . . . . . . . . . . . . . . . . . . . . . . . . . . . . . . . | $10,000 | $10,000 |
| Needed to pay for investment. . . . . . . . . . . . . . . . . . . . . . | 10,520 | |
| End of year 4. . . . . . . . . . . . . . . . . . . . . . . . . . . . . . . . . . | | 12,000 |
| Differences . . . . . . . . . . . . . . . . . . . . . . . . . . . . . . . . . . | $ 520 | $ 2,000 |

$$\text{Fraction of year} = \frac{\text{cash flow needed during year to pay for investment}}{\text{cash flow for full year}}$$

$$= \frac{\$520}{\$2,000} = .26 \text{ year}$$

Payback period $= 3$ years $+ .26$ year $= 3.26$ years

Now the payback period is 3.26 years, which places it at the end of March in year 4.

### Decision Criteria and Resulting Weaknesses of Payback

If we accept or reject projects entirely on the basis of the projects' payback periods, we would naturally select those projects with the shortest payback periods. There are two problems with using payback for this purpose. First, the payback period ignores the time value of money. Second, payback ignores the useful life of the project. It is possible that a project with an extremely short payback period could also have a poor NPV. And it's also possible that a project with a long payback period could have a terrific NPV.

For example, assume that two competing projects, A and B, each cost $5,000. The cash flows for project A are $1,000 per year and the cash flows for project B are $1,250 per year. Project A has a payback of 5 years and project B has a payback of 4 years. On the basis of the payback period alone, project B should be selected. Now add to this information the fact that the life of project B is only 4 years, the same as its payback period, while project A has a useful life of 20 years. At a 10% cost of capital, the NPV for project A is a positive $3,513 (8.513 × $1,000 − $5,000), while the NPV for project B is a negative $1,039 (3.169 × $1,250 − $5,000). There is no doubt that project A is better for the firm.

As you can see, the use of the payback period by itself can lead to decisions that reduce rather than improve the value of a firm.

## Accountant's Rate of Return

The final capital budgeting method we will look at is the **accountant's rate of return (ARR),** which is also known as the *accounting rate of return,* the *book rate of return,* and the *unadjusted rate of return.* The ARR represents the percentage that the expected average annual income will be of the investment required to generate this income. The ARR is determined with the following formula:

$$\text{ARR} = \frac{\text{average net income}}{\text{incremental investment}}$$

The ARR is an *average* rate of return for the entire life of the project. Since it is an average, it makes no difference if the cash flows are even or uneven. We merely divide the total cash flows by the number of years. Whether the total cash all comes at the beginning of a project or at the end of a project, or is distributed evenly over the life of a project, is not considered in calculating the average. The fact that the timing of the project's cash flows has no effect on the results for ARR is, in fact, a serious weakness of the ARR method.

Did you notice that we've been going on about the cash flows for a project—the total and the average—but the formula for ARR does not mention cash flows? The numerator is average net income, not average cash flows. However, net income and cash flows are closely related, so we can easily convert the ARR formula into a form that will better accommodate the facts we have been given. The main difference between cash flows for an organization and its net income is depreciation.[1] Therefore, the relationship of cash flows to net income is as follows:

**Cash flows − depreciation = net income**

[1] Net income and cash flows also differ due to the amortization of intangibles and any other write-off of long-term fixed assets. Here, however, we are concerned only with depreciation.

Now, we can substitute the term *average cash flows − depreciation* for average net income in the numerator of ARR, and we get:

$$\text{ARR} = \frac{\text{average cash flows (from operations)} - \text{depreciation}}{\text{incremental investment}}$$

The average cash flows (ACF) for any project can easily be determined with the following formula:

$$\text{ACF} = \frac{\text{total cash flows (from operations) for entire useful life}}{\text{useful life}}$$

In the first Cobb Contracting Company example, the cash flows are $2,000 per year for 8 years, and the average is also $2,000, as shown below:

$$\text{ACF} = \frac{\$2,000 + \$2,000 + \$2,000 + \$2,000 + \$2,000 + \$2,000 + \$2,000 + \$2,000}{8 \text{ years}}$$

$$= \frac{\$16,000}{8} = \$2,000$$

Obviously, this average didn't have to be calculated. Since the cash flow in each year was $2,000, it was apparent that the average would also have to be $2,000.

In the second Cobb Contracting Company example, the average isn't so obvious. But once we substitute the annual cash flows into the formula, you can see that the average is $2,000 in this situation too:

$$\text{ACF} = \frac{\$4,000 + \$3,000 + \$3,000 + \$2,000 + \$1,000 + \$1,000 + \$1,000 + \$1,000}{8 \text{ years}}$$

$$= \frac{\$16,000}{8} = \$2,000$$

The reason the average cash flows for both Cobb examples are the same is that the total cash flow for both projects is the same—$16,000—and the life for both projects is the same—8 years.

Depreciation (D) is determined by:

$$\text{D} = \frac{\text{incremental investment} - \text{salvage value}}{\text{useful life}}$$

$$= \frac{\$10,520 - \$0}{8 \text{ years}} = \$1,315$$

Since no salvage value was given in either Cobb example, it is assumed to be zero. If a salvage value had been given, it would have been included in the numerator of the depreciation calculation. However, it would not be included in the average cash flow from operations (ACF) calculation, since the salvage value is generated by selling the asset, not by operating it. Any salvage value would also have to be considered in the NPV, IRR, and payback calculations. For NPV and IRR calculations, the present value of the cash flow from the salvage would be determined in the last year of the useful life of the project. And for the payback calculation, the salvage value would be treated just like any other cash flow in the last year of the useful life.

Finally, we are ready to calculate the ARR. For either set of facts given in the two examples for Cobb Contracting Company, it is:

$$\text{ARR} = \frac{\$2,000 - \$1,315}{\$10,520} = \frac{\$685}{\$10,520} = 6.51\%$$

And here's what an ARR of 6.51% means. For an investment of $10,520, the average income earned from the investment, $685 per year, is expected to average 6.51% of the initial cost of the investment over the 8-year life. As you might expect, the higher the ARR, the better the project. And in order for a project to be acceptable, the ARR must be higher than the cost of capital—the cost of financing the investment. If the firm must finance the investment with capital costing 10%, an ARR of 6.51% would mean that the project should be rejected.

## Overview of Capital Budgeting Methods

Exhibit 2 reviews each of the four capital budgeting methods we have just discussed; NPV, IRR, PP, and ARR. It provides a definition for each method, the calculation needed to determine each method, and the criterion for determining whether the project is acceptable when that method is used.

**Exhibit 2** Comparative Overview of Capital Budgeting Methods

| Method | Definition | Calculation | Criterion for Acceptance: Project Is Acceptable if: |
|---|---|---|---|
| Net present value (NPV) | Difference in total present value of future cash inflows and the incremental investment | NPV = PV of cash inflows at $r$, less incremental investment (for both even and uneven cash flows) | NPV > 0 |
| Internal rate of return (IRR) | The interest rate being earned by a project. At this rate the TPV of future cash inflows equals the incremental investment, resulting in a NPV of zero. | 1. Even cash flows: $$\text{Factor} = \frac{\text{incremental investment}}{\text{cash flow/year}}$$ Look up factor in PV of annuity table, trying to find an interest rate having that factor. The factor will typically fall between factors for two other interest rates. Determine exact answer by interpolating between these two interest rates. <br> 2. Uneven cash flows: Use trial and error to find one interest rate that results in a small positive NPV and one that results in a small negative NPV. Find exact answer by interpolating between these two interest rates. | IRR > $r$ (cost of capital) |
| Payback period (PP) | Number of years needed to recoup the original investment | 1. Even cash flows: $$PP = \frac{\text{incremental investment}}{\text{cash flow/year}}$$ 2. Uneven cash flows: Accumulate cash flows until cumulative amount equals incremental investment. | Short number of years |
| Accountant's rate of return (ARR) | Average net income per dollar of investment | $$ARR = \frac{\text{average cash flows} - \text{average depreciation}}{\text{incremental investment}}$$ (for both even and uneven cash flows) | ARR > $r$ (cost of capital) |

ASK YOURSELF ▶

1. What is the net present value for a project?
2. How would you use the internal rate of return method to determine whether to accept or reject a project?
3. How would you determine the payback period for a project when the cash flows are uneven?
4. What is the formula for the accountant's rate of return?

Learning Objective 4

Integrate tax considerations into the discounted and nondiscounted cash-flow methods of capital budgeting

## INCOME TAX CONSIDERATIONS WITH CAPITAL BUDGETING

So far, we have ignored the effects of income taxes in capital budgeting analysis because we wanted to keep our discussion simple as you began to gain an understanding of these useful tools. Now we will expand our analysis to include some income tax considerations that affect all capital budgeting decisions.

Although the consideration of income taxes does complicate the analysis somewhat, the mechanics of each capital budgeting method—NPV, IRR, PP, and ARR—are the same as the procedures you learned earlier in this chapter. The only difference is that now we must use *aftertax cash flows* rather than *pretax cash flows* to calculate each method. Everything you have learned so far applies to this discussion, except that now you have to determine the aftertax cash flows before you can begin.

Let's go back to the original set of facts for Cobb Contracting, with a few additional details.

## COBB CONTRACTING COMPANY—REVISITED

### ORIGINAL FACTS

| | |
|---|---|
| Cost of lane painting equipment. . . . . . . . . . . . . . | $10,520 |
| Cash flows per year . . . . . . . . . . . . . . . . . . . . . . | $ 2,000 |
| Estimated useful life . . . . . . . . . . . . . . . . . . . . . | 8 years |
| Cost of capital . . . . . . . . . . . . . . . . . . . . . . . . . . | .10 |

### ADDITIONAL FACTS

| | |
|---|---|
| Depreciation method . . . . . . . . . . . . . . . . . . . . | Straight-line |
| Tax rate . . . . . . . . . . . . . . . . . . . . . . . . . . . . . . | .40 |

### Determining Aftertax Cash Flows

The critical factor in doing the analysis is to determine the aftertax cash flows. In order to do this, we need separately to calculate:

1. The net-of-tax cash flow from operations
2. The tax savings from depreciation

Once we have these two figures, we sum them to determine the aftertax cash flows for the proposed project.

### Net-of-Tax Cash Flow from Operations

The cash flow from operations for Cobb Contracting is $2,000 per year. Based on a 40% tax rate, the income tax Cobb would have to pay on $2,000 of taxable income is $800, and the **net-of-tax cash flow from operations** is $1,200.

| | |
|---|---|
| Cash Flow from Operations . . . . . . . . . . . . . . . . . . . . . . . . . . . . . . . . . . . . . . . . . . | $2,000 |
| Tax Effect (40% × $2,000). . . . . . . . . . . . . . . . . . . . . . . . . . . . . . . . . . . . . . . . . . | 800 |
| Net-of-Tax Cash Flow from Operations . . . . . . . . . . . . . . . . . . . . . . . . . . . . . . . . | $1,200 |

### Tax Savings from Depreciation

When taxable income for the firm is determined, depreciation is an allowable deduction on the tax return. Although depreciation itself is not a cash item—that is, it does not involve a cash inflow or outflow—it does have a very favorable effect on cash flows. Since depreciation is a deduction on the tax return, it shields, or protects, income from being taxed. That's why depreciation is often referred to as a **tax shield.** The company reduces its taxes because of depreciation, and reduced taxes mean more cash. The reduction in taxes due to the depreciation tax shield is referred to as the **tax savings from depreciation.**

Cobb Contracting has $1,315 of depreciation per year, using the straight-line method.

$$\text{Depreciation} = \frac{\$10,520 - \$0}{8 \text{ years}} = \$1,315 \text{ per year}$$

This $1,315 of depreciation shields $1,315 of income from being taxed. This means that the $526 of taxes (at 40% of taxable income) that would otherwise have to be paid on this income does not have to be paid:

$$\text{Tax savings from depreciation} = \text{depreciation} \times \text{tax rate}$$
$$= \$1,315 \times .40 = \$526$$

### Aftertax Cash Flow for Project

The aftertax cash flow for the proposed project is the sum of the two parts, or $1,726:

| | |
|---|---|
| Net-of-Tax Cash Flow from Operations . . . . . . . . . . . . . . . . . . . . . . . . . . . . . . . . | $1,200 |
| Tax Savings from Depreciation . . . . . . . . . . . . . . . . . . . . . . . . . . . . . . . . . . . . . . | 526 |
| Aftertax Cash Flow for Project . . . . . . . . . . . . . . . . . . . . . . . . . . . . . . . . . . . . . . | $1,726 |

## Capital Budgeting Methods Using Aftertax Cash Flows

Now that we have the aftertax cash flow of $1,726 for the proposed project, we use the $1,726 instead of the pretax $2,000 to apply each of the four capital budgeting methods.

The aftertax NPV is $(1,314), determined as follows:

$$\text{TPV} = 5.334 \times \$1,726 = \$9,206$$

$$\text{NPV} = \$9,206 - \$10,520 = \$(1,314)$$

The present value of annuity factor needed to determine IRR is 6.095:

$$\text{Factor} = \frac{\$10,520}{\$1,726} = 6.095$$

Looking for this factor on the 8-year row of the present value of annuity table, we find it between the factors for 6% and 7%. Using interpolation to find the exact answer, we get an IRR of 6.479%.

The payback period (PP) is now 6.095 years:

$$\text{Payback} = \frac{\$10,520}{\$1,726} = 6.095 \text{ years}$$

And the accountant's rate of return (ARR) is 3.91%:

$$\text{ARR} = \frac{\$1,726 - \$1,315}{\$10,520} = \frac{\$411}{\$10,520} = 3.91\%$$

As you can see, the calculations for each method are exactly the same as for the earlier ones, except that the cash flow used in each method is the aftertax amount of $1,726, instead of the pretax amount of $2,000.

We only showed you how to consider taxes when the cash flows are expected to be the same in each year of the project's life. We also simplified the depreciation calculations that would be required under the current tax laws. Both of these complications are covered in finance and cost accounting courses.

ASK YOURSELF ▶

1. **What effect does depreciation have on the cash flows for a project?**
2. **What is a tax shield? What are tax savings from depreciation?**

## SUMMARY

- **Capital budgeting** is the planning for the acquisition and financing of long-term investments—primarily in fixed assets. Four methods used to evaluate investment proposals are net present value, internal rate of return, payback period, and accountant's rate of return.
- The **net present value (NPV)** method finds the present value of all future cash inflows and from this amount subtracts the **incremental investment** for the proposed project. If the excess (the NPV) is positive, the project is acceptable; if the NPV is negative, the project should be rejected, and if NPV equals 0, the firm will be indifferent to accepting or rejecting.
- The present value of cash flows is found by multiplying the present value factor (for the appropriate cost of capital and time period) from either the present value of an ordinary annuity of $1 table (for even cash flows) or the present value of $1 table (for uneven cash flows) times the cash flows from the project.
- The **internal rate of return (IRR)** is the exact return to be earned on a proposed project. At that rate the total present value (TPV) of the cash inflows is equal to the incremental investment, resulting in an NPV of zero. If the IRR is greater than the cost of capital ($r$), the proposed project is acceptable; if IRR is less than $r$, the project should be rejected; and if IRR equals $r$, the firm will be indifferent to accepting or rejecting.
- The **payback period (PP)** is the number of years needed for a project to accumulate enough cash flows to pay for the incremental investment. For a project with even cash flows, the incremental investment is divided by the cash flow. For uneven cash flows, the cash flow is accumulated each year until the cumulative total reaches the incremental investment.

- **The accountant's rate of return (ARR)** is the percentage that the expected annual net income is to the investment required to generate this income. It is determined as follows:

$$\text{ARR} = \frac{\text{average cash flows (from operations)} - \text{depreciation}}{\text{incremental investment}}$$

The accountant's rate of return is the only method in which averages are employed. In all other methods, the use of an average would distort the answer.

- When income taxes are considered, each of the capital budgeting methods is calculated with aftertax cash flows instead of with pretax cash flows. The aftertax cash flows for a project are the sum of these two parts: (1) the net-of-tax cash flow from operations and (2) the tax savings from depreciation.

- The **net-of-tax cash flow from operations** is determined as follows:

> **Cash flow from operations**
>
> **Less: Income tax (cash flow from operations × income tax rate)**
>
> **Equals: Net-of-tax cash flow from operations**

- **Tax savings from depreciation** represent the income taxes that do not have to be paid on income as a result of the deductibility of depreciation on the tax return. Depreciation that protects income from being taxed is called a **tax shield.**

## 5    KEY TERMS

| | |
|---|---|
| **Accountant's rate of return (ARR)** | The ratio of average annual net income to the investment required to generate the income (average net income divided by incremental investment). |
| **Capital budgeting** | The planning process for acquiring and financing long-term investments. |
| **Cost of capital** | The interest rate used to determine the present value of cash flows in a capital budgeting problem. |
| **Discounted cash-flow methods** | The category of capital budgeting methods that employs present value analysis. The two discounted cash-flow methods are net present value (NPV) and internal rate of return (IRR). |
| **Incremental cash flows** | The cash generated by the incremental investment in capital budgeting. |
| **Incremental investment** | The required outlay of resources to obtain a fixed asset and prepare it for productive use. |
| **Internal rate of return (IRR)** | The interest rate at which the total present value for a project equals the incremental investment; the NPV is zero. It is the exact rate of return to be earned on a project. |
| **Interpolation** | The process of finding an exact answer that falls between two other answers. |
| **Net-of-tax cash flow from operations** | The cash flows from operations for a project less the applicable income tax (cash flow from operations × income tax rate). |
| **Net present value (NPV)** | The difference between the total present value of the future cash flows and the incremental investment of the project. |
| **Nondiscounted cash-flow methods** | The category of capital budgeting methods that does not use present value analysis. The two nondiscounted cash-flow methods are payback period and accountant's rate of return. |
| **Payback period (PP)** | The number of years needed for a project to accumulate enough cash flows to pay for the initial cost of the investment. |
| **Tax savings from depreciation** | Income taxes that do not have to be paid because depreciation (a tax shield) can be deducted on the tax return, thereby reducing the amount of income that is subject to taxation. |

| | |
|---|---|
| **Tax shield** | Any deduction on a tax return, such as depreciation, that shields, or protects, income from being taxed. |
| **Trial and error** | The manner of determining the internal rate of return when the cash flows for a project are not the same amount in each year of the project's life. |

## DEMONSTRATION PROBLEM

The Fax of Life Company is considering the purchase of 100 FAX machines which will be leased to a convenience store chain. Individual convenience stores will then charge a small fee for the copies that are faxed by its customers. The FAX machines will cost $70,000 and should have a $16,000 salvage value at the end of their 4 year lives. The annual cash inflow from the leasing of the machines is expected to be $20,000; the tax rate is 25%; and the cost of capital is 12%.

### Required:

Calculate the answer for each of the following capital budgeting methods.

1. Net Present Value
2. Internal Rate of Return
3. Payback Period
4. Accountant's Rate of Return

### ■ Solution to Demonstration Problem

| | |
|---|---:|
| Cash Flow from Operations | $20,000 |
| Tax Effect (25% × $20,000) | 5,000 |
| Net-of-Tax Cash Flow from Operations | $15,000 |

$$\text{Depreciation} = (\$70,000 - \$16,000) \div 4 = \$13,500/\text{year}$$

$$\text{Tax savings from depreciation} = \text{depreciation} \times \text{tax rate}$$

$$= \$13,500 \times .25 = \$3,375$$

| | |
|---|---:|
| Net-of-Tax Cash Flows from Operations | $15,000 |
| Tax Savings from Depreciation | 3,375 |
| Aftertax Cash Flow for Project | $18,375 |

1. Net Present Value

$$\text{TPV} = \text{PV of \$18,375 at 12\% for 4 years plus PV of \$16,000 at 12\% in year 4}$$

$$= (3.037 \times \$18,375) + (.635 \times \$16,000)$$

$$= \$55,805 + \$10,160 = \$65,965$$

**NPV = TPV − incremental investment**

$$= \$65,965 - \$70,000 = \$(4,035)$$

**2.** Internal Rate of Return

| Year | Cash Flow | Net Present Value 9% | Net Present Value 10% | Net Present Value 12% |
|------|-----------|-----------|-----------|-----------|
| 1–4 | $18,375 | $59,517 | $58,230 | $55,805 |
| 4 | 16,000 | 11,328 | 10,928 | 10,160 |
| | TPV | $70,845 | $69,158 | $65,965 |
| | Investment | 70,000 | 70,000 | 70,000 |
| | NPV | $    845 | $(    842) | $( 4,035) |

| | TPV | TPV |
|------|------|------|
| 9% | $70,845 | $70,845 |
| IRR | | 70,000 |
| 10% | 69,158 | |
| | $ 1,687 | $    845 |

$$\frac{\$\ 845}{\$1,687} = 50\% \times (10\% - 9\%) =\ \ .50\%$$

$$9.00\%$$

$$IRR = \underline{9.50\%}$$

**3.** Payback Period

$$\text{Payback period (PP)} = \frac{\text{incremental investment}}{\text{cash flows per year}}$$

$$= \frac{\$70,000}{\$18,375} = 3.81 \text{ years}$$

**4.** Accountant's Rate of Return

$$ARR = \frac{\text{average cash flows (from operations)} - \text{depreciation}}{\text{incremental investment}}$$

$$ARR = \frac{\$18,375 - \$13,500}{\$70,000} = \frac{\$\ 4,875}{\$70,000} = \underline{6.96\%}$$

# QUESTIONS FOR REVIEW AND FURTHER THOUGHT

## REVIEW QUESTIONS

1. Define capital budgeting. How is it used to help management in the planning process?

2. Give several decision situations in which the capital budgeting planning models discussed in this chapter would be applicable.

3. Explain why an understanding of the time value of money is important in capital budgeting analysis.

4. What is the internal rate of return for a project? When using IRR, how do you decide whether the project is acceptable or not?

5. Explain how trial and error is used to determine the internal rate of return for a project.

6. What are the criteria for acceptance or rejection of a project when the internal rate of return method is used?

7. What is the main difference between the capital budgeting methods that are classified as discounted cash-flow methods and those that are called nondiscounted cash-flow methods?

8. What is the payback period for a project? What are some deficiencies in using this method to decide which projects to choose?

9. Why is depreciation referred to as a *tax shield?*

10. What are tax savings from depreciation?

## QUESTIONS FOR FURTHER THOUGHT

1. What are the two most important factors to be considered in the use of all the capital budgeting methods? Name three other factors that are common to the use of most capital budgeting methods.

2. Is it the amount or the timing of cash flows that affects the present value of a project?

3. Net present value can be positive or negative, but never exactly zero. Do you agree? Explain.

4. "The higher the cost of capital, the lower the net present value." Do you agree? Explain.

5. "The higher the cost of capital, the lower the internal rate of return." Do you agree? Explain.

6. "As long as the present value of a project is greater than zero, the project should always be accepted by the firm." Comment.

7. Explain how a discounted cash-flow method and a nondiscounted cash-flow method might be used together to evaluate a capital project.

8. A project having a short payback period should always be invested in before a project that has a longer payback period. Do you agree?

9. When two projects are being compared, the one with the greater cash flows in the early years of life will always have the greater NPV. Do you agree or disagree with this statement, and why?

10. The accountant's rate of return will be higher if the cash flows from a project are heavier in the earlier years of life rather than in later years. Do you agree? Explain.

11. If depreciation is not a cash flow, explain how it can affect the cash flows for a project.

12. The selection of a depreciation method will not affect the accountant's rate of return. Why?

13. "Financial accounting and capital budgeting relate to different periods and to different segments within the organization." Explain what is meant by this observation.

## OBJECTIVE ASSIGNMENT

*True/False*   Indicate whether each statement below is *true* or *false* by placing a *T* or an *F* in the space provided.

_____ 1. The capital budgeting methods can only be used to evaluate the investment in fixed assets.

_____ 2. All capital budgeting methods use the present value tables.

_____ 3. The higher the cost of capital the lower the internal rate of return.

_____ 4. The payback period method ignores the useful life of the project being considered.

_____ 5. The internal rate of return is the same as the cost of capital.

*Multiple Choice*  Select the best choice to complete each statement or answer each question below. Write the letter corresponding to your choice in the space provided.

_____ 1. Which of the following is a type of nondiscounted cash-flow method?
a. Accountant's rate of return
b. Internal rate of return
c. Net present value
d. Cost of capital

_____ 2. If a project is accepted when the firm's cost of capital is 10%, which of the following must be correct?
a. The NPV = $0
b. The NPV is less than zero
c. The IRR is less than the cost of capital
d. The IRR is greater than zero

_____ 3. Which of the following is the only capital budgeting method that employs averages?
a. Payback period
b. Accountant's rate of return
c. Net present value
d. Internal rate of return

_____ 4. How is the internal rate of return determined when the cash flows are different amounts each year?
a. Interpolation
b. Averaging
c. Trial and error
d. Smoothing

_____ 5. A new machine, costing $100,000, is expected to generate the following cash flow over its 3-year useful life:

| Year | Cash Flow |
|------|-----------|
| 1 ............ | $50,000 |
| 2 ............ | 40,000 |
| 3 ............ | 30,000 |

The present value factors for the firm's cost of capital are presented below. Determine the net present value for the machine.

| Year | Present Value of $1 | Present Value of Annuity of $1 |
|------|---------------------|-------------------------------|
| 1 ............ | .909 | .909 |
| 2 ............ | .826 | 1.735 |
| 3 ............ | .751 | 2.486 |

a. $(560)     c. $24,300
b. $1,020     d. $101,020

_____ 6. A proposed investment of $20,000 in a new delivery truck is expected to generate $5,000 per year for 5 years. Using the partial present value tables below, determine the internal rate of return.

| Interest Rate | Present Value of $1 for 5 Years | Present Value of Annuity of $1 for 5 Years |
|---|---|---|
| 3% | .862 | 4.579 |
| 6% | .747 | 4.212 |
| 9% | .649 | 3.889 |
| 12% | .567 | 3.604 |
| 15% | .497 | 3.352 |

a. 1.969%  c. 7.031%
b. 6.656%  d. 7.969%

_____ 7. Bangor Corporation is considering an investment in a new printing press, costing $200,000, which will substantially increase the sales of its publications. If the press is purchased, its life will be 4 years and the increased cash flows will be the following amount in each year:

| Year | Cash Flow |
|---|---|
| 1 | $ 50,000 |
| 2 | 100,000 |
| 3 | 200,000 |
| 4 | 300,000 |
| | $650,000 |

What is the payback period for this project?
a. 1.231 years  c. 3.000 years
b. 2.250 years  d. 4.000 years

_____ 8. A company is considering the purchase of a new machine costing $35,000. The machine is expected to have a 4-year life and cash flows per year of $10,000. What is the accountant's rate of return for this machine?
a. 28.57%  c. 10.00%
b. 25.00%  d. 3.57%

_____ 9. Assume the same facts as in question 8, except that the company must pay income taxes at a rate of 40%. If the machine is depreciated with the straight-line method, determine the annual aftertax cash flows for the project.
a. $7,500  c. $9,250
b. $9,500  d. $11,250

_____ 10. What is the aftertax payback period for the machine referred to in questions 8 and 9?
a. 2.211 years  c. 3.684 years
b. 3.500 years  d. 4.000 years

## EXERCISES

2 3 **Exercise 1:** Computing NPV, IRR, PP, and ARR for Even Cash Flows

The McElroy Company is considering the purchase of a new machine that will cost $50,000 and generate cash flows per year of $10,000. The useful life of the machine is 8 years, and the cost of capital is 10%.

a. Determine the net present value for the project.
b. Determine the internal rate of return.
c. Calculate the payback period.
d. Assume, for this part only, that the machine is expected to have a $2,000 salvage value at the end of year 8. Determine the accountant's rate of return.

▶ (Check Figure: b. IRR = 11.82%)

**3**    **Exercise 2:** Determining Payback with Uneven Cash Flows

The Low-Cal Yogurt Company has just purchased new yogurt dispensers for $45,000. The expected life of the dispensers is 4 years, and the expected cash flows from their use over the 4 years are as follows:

| Year | Cash Flows |
|------|------------|
| 1 .................................... | $24,000 |
| 2 .................................... | 18,000 |
| 3 .................................... | 15,000 |
| 4 .................................... | 9,000 |

Determine the payback period for the new yogurt dispensers.

▶ *(Check Figure: PP = 2.2 years)*

**2  3**    **Exercise 3:** Evaluating an Acquisition Using Each of the Capital Budgeting Methods

The following facts relate to a proposed acquisition of production machinery for Wilde Company:

| | |
|---|---|
| Cost of machinery.......................... | $55,000 |
| Estimated life............................. | 5 years |
| Salvage value............................. | $ –0– |
| Cost of capital............................ | 12% |
| Cash flows: Year 1........................ | $ 4,000 |
| 2........................ | 14,000 |
| 3........................ | 20,000 |
| 4........................ | 30,000 |
| 5........................ | 15,000 |

Calculate each of the following:

a. Payback period
b. Accountant's rate of return
c. Net present value
d. Internal rate of return

▶ *(Check Figure: b. ARR = 10.18%; d. IRR = 12.94%)*

**2  3**    **Exercise 4:** Miscellaneous Present Value Questions

Answer each of the miscellaneous present value questions, using Tables 1 and 2.

a. What is the factor for the present value of $1 in 5 years at 10%?
b. What is the factor for $P_{\overline{10}|8\%}$?
c. How much must be invested today to accumulate to $1 in 5 years at 10%?
d. How much must be invested today at 4% in order to receive $1 per year for 4 years?
e. What is the maximum amount that you would invest today at 12% in exchange for annual receipts of $10,000 for 8 years?
f. If you invest $321 today, which will accumulate to $1,000 in 10 years, at what interest rate is the money invested?
g. If an investment of $6,144 at 10% promises a return of $1,000 per year, for how many years will the $1,000 be expected?
h. What is the present value of $2,500 per year for 20 years if the interest rate is 8%?
i. If the payback period for a 5-year machine is 3.604 years, what is the internal rate of return?
j. If the NPV for a project is zero using a cost of capital of 11%, what is the internal rate of return?

▶ *(Check Figure: e. $49,670; g. 10 years)*

2 3 **Exercise 5:** Determining the Characteristics of Different Capital Budgeting Methods

For each description given below, place an X in the column(s) representing the method(s) to which the description applies:

| | PP | ARR | NPV | IRR |
|---|---|---|---|---|
| a. **Example:** The answer is stated in number of years | X | | | |
| b. The answer is given in dollars | ____ | ____ | ____ | ____ |
| c. The answer is stated as a percentage | ____ | ____ | ____ | ____ |
| d. Acceptable whenever the answer is positive | ____ | ____ | ____ | ____ |
| e. Disregards the time value of money | ____ | ____ | ____ | ____ |
| f. Disregards the timing of cash flows | ____ | ____ | ____ | ____ |
| g. Is dependent on the value for $r$ | ____ | ____ | ____ | ____ |
| h. Is always positive when the IRR $> r$ | ____ | ____ | ____ | ____ |
| i. Equals $r$ whenever NPV $= 0$ | ____ | ____ | ____ | ____ |

2 3 4 **Exercise 6:** Doing Capital Methods with Aftertax Cash Flows

The Dr. Air Jardin Basketball Shoe Company is considering an investment in a machine that costs $21,000 and has a 7-year life. The cash receipts per year are expected to be $6,000; the tax rate is 40%; and the cost of capital is 10%. Depreciation will be $3,000 per year.

a. Determine the annual net-of-tax cash flow from operations.
b. Determine the tax savings from depreciation per year.
c. Determine the aftertax cash flows for the proposed investment [sum of parts (a) and (b)].
d. Using the aftertax cash flows, determine each of the following for the project:
   1. Net present value
   2. Internal rate of return
   3. Payback period
   4. Accountant's rate of return

▶ *(Check Figure: c. $4,800; d. (1.) $2,366)*

## PROBLEMS: SET A

2 3† **Problem A1:** Calculating PP, ARR, NPV, and IRR with Uneven Cash Flows

Joe Friday's Shipping Service is considering the purchase of a FAX machine to help diversify his services to customers and substantially increase his cash receipts. The machine will cost $1,700 and is expected to last 4 years. During that time, the increased cash receipts are predicted to be as follows:

| Year | Increased Cash Receipts |
|---|---|
| 1 | $300 |
| 2 | 450 |
| 3 | 800 |
| 4 | 800 |

At the end of 4 years, Joe expects to sell the machine for $100. The shipping service's cost of capital is 10%.

**Required:**

1. Determine the payback period.
2. Determine the accountant's rate of return.
3. Calculate the net present value.
4. Calculate the internal rate of return.

▶ *(Check Figure: 2. ARR = 11.03%; 4. IRR = 13.59%)*

† The numbers in the margin refer to the Learning Objectives.

2    **Problem A2:** Calculating NPV for an Equipment Purchase

Andre Chang, a tennis star since he was 12, has just retired at the age of 21 and opened a tennis complex. Andre would like to purchase ball machines, which automatically serve balls to players every few seconds, at a variety of speeds, spins, and trajectories. The ball machines cost $7,200 each and are expected to last for 5 years. At the end of their useful life, they should have a disposal value of $2,000 each.

      The machines are expected to generate additional cash receipts for the complex of $20,000 per year. They will require the addition of one employee for an annual salary of $16,000. Finally, an overhaul will probably be required at the end of year 3, costing $1,600.

**Required:**

Using the net present value method (assuming a 12% cost of capital), determine whether or not the ball machines should be purchased.

▶ *(Check Figure: NPV = $7,212.40)*

2    **Problem A3:** Deciding Whether or Not to Buy a Patent

The administrator of City Hospital has been approached by an inventor, Denise Jossi, who is trying to sell a new patent. If purchased, the patent would enable City Hospital to convert its semiautomatic x-ray machinery to automatic. Such a change would reduce the hospital's variable labor costs of operation. The patent would cost $175,000, and it would be necessary to spend an additional $50,000 to make the machinery conversions. The variable cost per x-ray with the semiautomatic machinery is $9 and the expected cost with the automatic machinery is $7 per x-ray.

      Patients are billed $25 apiece for x-rays. If the machinery is converted to automatic, 12,000 x-rays can be processed, 3,000 more than the semiautomatic machinery can handle.

      The machinery has a remaining 5-year life and will have a $2,000 higher salvage in 5 years if it is fully automated. The patent is expected to be sold for $5,000 in 5 years.

      The cost of capital is 12%.

**Required:**

Using the net present value method, decide whether City Hospital should purchase the patent from Jossi.

▶ *(Check figure: PV for automatic = $557,433)*

2 3    **Problem A4:** Expanding the Analysis of Problem A3

**Required:**

Refer to the facts given in Problem A3. Calculate each of the following:

1. The internal rate of return
2. The payback period
3. The accountant's rate of return

▶ *(Check figure: 1, 18.781%)*

2    **Problem A5:** Calculating the NPV for Rearranging a Plant

The president of the Instant Charge Battery Corporation has asked the management advisory department of its CPA firm to help it decide whether production efficiency can be improved by rearranging the plant layout. The consultant recommended that rearrangements should be undertaken and estimated that the costs of rearrangement would be $300,000. The consultant also estimated that such a change would substantially reduce direct labor during the next 5 years. In the first year, direct labor should decrease by $1.50 per unit produced. For years 2 to 5 the reduction should increase to $3 per unit. In addition, one less supervisor will be needed in each of the 5 years, a savings of $17,000 per year. The units to be produced in each year are expected to be 20,000 in year 1, 22,000 in year 2, and 30,000 per year for years 3 to 5.

**Required**

Using the net present value method, determining whether or not the plant layout should be rearranged. The firm's cost of capital is 12%.

▶ *(Check figure: NPV = $12,800)*

**2 3 4    Problem A6:** Doing Capital Budgeting Methods with Aftertax Cash Flows

The Bay Area Pool Company services swimming pools and spas in the Tampa Bay area. It is considering purchasing some new equipment that will drastically cut down on the labor costs associated with each service call. The new machine evaluates the chemical level of a pool or spa and then automatically dispenses the proper amount of chlorine and other chemicals. The new equipment will cost $36,000 and is expected to reduce operating costs by $9,500 per year over its 6-year useful life. It will have no salvage value at the end of its useful life.

Bay Area's cost of capital is 12% and its expected tax rate is 30%. Bay Area will use the straight-line depreciation method.

**Required:**

Using the aftertax cash flows, determine each of the following for the new equipment:

1. Net present value
2. Internal rate of return
3. Payback period
4. Accountant's rate of return

▶ *(Check Figure: 1. NPV = $(1,262); 2. IRR = 10.78%)*

## PROBLEMS: SET B

**2 3†    Problem B1:** Calculating the PP, ARR, NPV, and IRR for Uneven Cash Flows

Brenda's Isometric Gym is considering the purchase of an exercise machine for $2,300, which is expected to reduce operating costs over the next 4 years. The operating costs should be reduced by the following amounts:

| Year | Reduced Labor Costs |
|------|---------------------|
| 1 ............ | $700 |
| 2 ............ | 800 |
| 3 ............ | 900 |
| 4 ............ | 300 |

At the end of 4 years, Brenda should be able to sell the exercise machine for $400. The gym's cost of capital is 10%.

**Required:**

1. Determine the payback period.
2. Determine the accountant's rate of return.
3. Determine the net present value for the project.
4. Determine the internal rate of return.

▶ *(Check Figure: 2. ARR = 8.70%; 4. IRR = 13.02%)*

**2    Problem B2:** Finding the NPV for a New Spa

T. P. Petty is the director of the Southwest Boys Club and is considering the purchase of a new spa. Club members will pay a small fee each time they use the spa. T. P. feels that the spa could substantially increase revenues for the club.

† The numbers in the margin refer to the Learning Objectives.

The spa costs $2,500 and should last for 10 years. At the end of its useful life, the spa is expected to have a disposal value of $400. The additional revenues are expected to increase cash receipts by $6,000 per year but will necessitate hiring an attendant for $4,000 per year.

At the end of each year, it is expected that the spa will need to undergo $500 of maintenance in order to last the full 10 years.

**Required:**

Using the net present value method, determine if the spa should or should not be purchased. Assume a 12% cost of capital.

▶ *(Check Figure: NPV = $6,103.40)*

## 2    **Problem B3:** Computing the NPV of a Patent

The president of the Trim Lines Jeans Company is approached by an inventor, Mark Carnac, concerning a new patent. The patent would enable Trim Lines to convert its manual machinery to semiautomatic, thereby reducing the labor costs of production. The patent would cost $900,000, and an additional $300,000 would be required to make the machinery conversions. The variable costs per unit using the manual and semiautomatic machinery are $10 and $8, respectively.

If Trim Lines decides to acquire the patent, it will produce and sell 100,000 units per year for the next 5 years. If Trim Lines continues to use the manual equipment, production and sales will be only 70,000 units per year. The sales price will be $16 per unit, regardless of the decision made.

The patent will be worthless in 5 years, but the disposal value of the semiautomatic machinery will be $15,000 higher than that of the manual machinery.

If the patent is acquired, Trim Lines will have to increase its investment in inventory by $25,000 at the beginning of the patent's life—all of which will be recovered at the end of 5 years.

The cost of capital for Trim Lines is 10%.

**Required:**

Using the net present value method, decide whether Trim Lines should purchase the patent from Carnac.

▶ *(Check figure: NPV = $240,000)*

## 2  3    **Problem B4:** Expanding the Analysis of Problem B3

Using the information presented for Trim Lines Jeans Company in Problem B3:

**Required:**

1. Determine the internal rate of return for the incremental investment.
2. Determine the payback period for the incremental investment.
3. Determine the accountant's rate of return for the incremental investment.

▶ *(Check figure: 3, 11.673%)*

## 2    **Problem B5:** Deciding Whether a Plant Layout Should Be Rearranged

A foreman on the assembly line at Mitsui Motorscooters took advantage of the company's suggestion box by recommending that the arrangement of machinery within the factory be changed. He felt that the efficiency of the production operation could be vastly improved by arranging machinery so that the flow of goods from one worker to another would be more orderly and less time consuming.

The president of Mitsui hired a team of consultants to determine whether the foreman was correct. The final report of the consultants not only supported the foreman's claim but made suggestions on how the rearrangement should be done. The consulting team estimated that it would cost $375,000 to make the rearrangements, which would result in substantial reductions in the costs of production over the next 5 years. The direct labor costs would be reduced by $1 per unit in year 1. In years 2 through 5, after the laborers have become more familiar with the revised flow of production, the direct labor costs should be reduced by $2 per unit. In addition, one less foreman will be needed in years 2 through 5, a savings of $10,000 per year. The units to be produced during the next 5 years are predicted to be:

| Year | Production |
| --- | --- |
| 1 | 50,000 |
| 2 | 60,000 |
| 3 | 75,000 |
| 4 | 75,000 |
| 5 | 75,000 |

The consultants charged the company $15,000 for the analysis and final report, and the foreman received $500 for his suggestion.

**Required:**

Using the net present value method, determine whether or not the plant layout should be rearranged. The cost of capital is 15%.

▶ *(Check figure: NPV = $42,730)*

2 3 4 **Problem B6:** Using Capital Budgeting Methods with Aftertax Cash Flows

Once is Enough Book Publishers is considering an investment in a new process for producing textbooks. A special ink is used that will automatically activate when the owner closes the book after reading the last page. The ink runs over the pages and ruins the book, so it cannot be resold. Once Is Enough will obviously benefit because of the additional sales of new books during each year of the books' life cycle.

The process will cost $100,000 and will have a useful life of 10 years. During that time, Once Is Enough expects to increase its cash flow by $22,000 per year. The process will have no salvage value at the end of its useful life.

Once Is Enough will use the straight-line depreciation method; its cost of capital is 15%; and the tax rate is 30%.

**Required:**

Using the aftertax cash flows, determine each of the following for the new process:

1. Net present value
2. Internal rate of return
3. Payback period
4. Accountant's rate of return

▶ *(Check Figure: 1. NPV = $(7,669); 2. IRR = 12.99%)*

## DECISION PROBLEM

 The controller of Ajax Manufacturing is considering two competing projects, A and B, only one of which will be purchased by the company. The relevant facts relating to these projects are:

|  | Project A | Project B |
|---|---|---|
| Size of investment | $10,000 | $25,000 |
| Life | 3 years | 10 years |
| Payback period | 2 years | 6 years |
| Internal rate of return | 9.5% | 15.0% |

In addition, the firm's cost of capital is 10%.

**Required:**

1. As the controller making a report to management, which of the two projects would you recommend?
2. What problems might be associated with comparing these two extremely different projects?

## OBJECTIVE ASSIGNMENT ANSWERS

**True/False**

**1.** F    **2.** F    **3.** F    **4.** T    **5.** F

**Multiple Choice**

**1.** a    **2.** d    **3.** b    **4.** c    **5.** b
**6.** d    **7.** b    **8.** d    **9.** b    **10.** c

# Index